This Bible Was Presented To

Name

ON

Date

BY

BIRTH RECORD

____
Name

WAS BORN TO

____
Parents Names

ON ______________________ AT ______________
Date Time

IN ____
Place

DOCTORS ______________________

____

NURSES ______________________

____

WEIGHT____POUNDS____OUNCES

LENGTH ______________ INCHES

BIRTHMARKS:

FOOTPRINT

I will praise thee; for I am fearfully and wonderfully made...Psalm 139:14

FAMILY RECORD

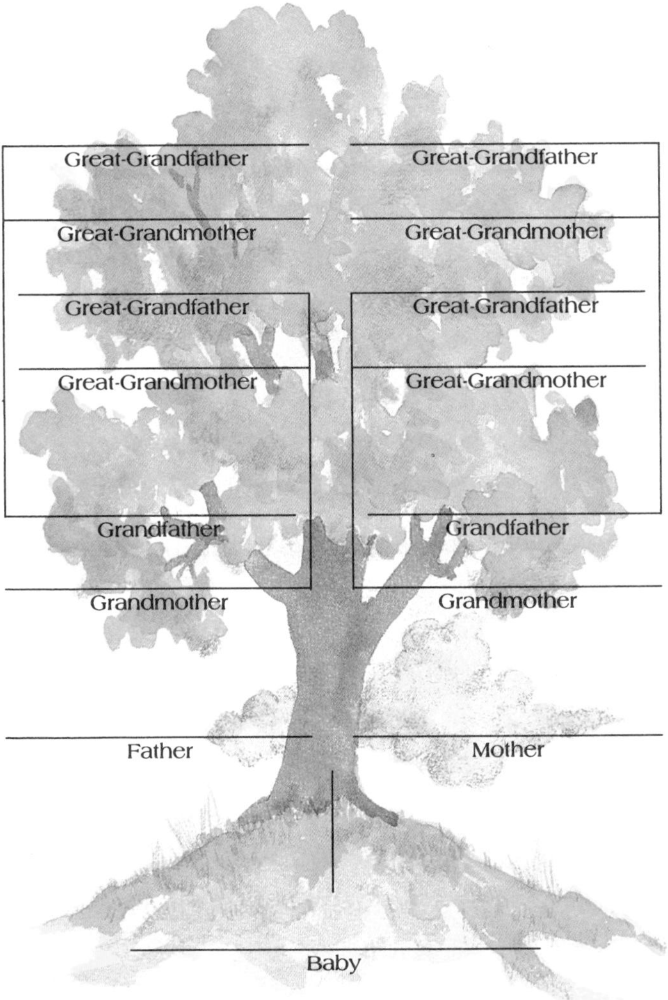

SPECIAL OCCASION

ON ______________________ WE BROUGHT ______________________
Date Baby's Name

TO ____
Church

WHERE ____
Minister's Name

PERFORMED A CEREMONY OF ______________________

GODPARENTS, SPONSORS, WITNESSES:

Train up a child in the way he should go; and when he is old, he will not depart from it. Proverbs 22:6

Prayers and Wishes On This Blessed Event

CHURCH FIRSTS

FIRST CHURCH ATTENDED ______________________________

FIRST DATE ATTENDED ______________________________

FIRST NURSERY
ATTENDANT ______________________________
Name

FIRST CHURCH SCHOOL
TEACHER ______________________________
Name

FIRST MINISTER ______________________________
Name

FIRST RECITATION OR PART
IN A CHURCH PLAY OR MUSICAL ______________________________

FIRST VACATION
BIBLE SCHOOL ATTENDED __________

____

OTHER CHURCH FIRSTS:

First Questions and Observations About God

Firsts For Our Baby

	Age
TURNS OVER	__________
SLEEPS THROUGH THE NIGHT	__________
BEGINS TO FOLLOW OBJECTS WITH EYES	__________
HOLDS HEAD UP	__________
SMILES	__________
LAUGHS	__________
COOS, MAKES NOISES	__________
EATS SOLID FOOD	__________
HOLDS SPOON	__________
DRINKS FROM CUP	__________
SITS UNASSISTED	__________
CRAWLS	__________
TRIES TO STAND	__________
TAKES FIRST STEP	__________
SAYS FIRST WORDS	__________

OTHER FIRSTS:

THE
HOLY BIBLE

CONTAINING

THE OLD AND NEW TESTAMENTS

TRANSLATED OUT OF THE ORIGINAL TONGUES
AND WITH THE FORMER TRANSLATIONS
DILIGENTLY COMPARED AND REVISED

Authorized King James Version

THOMAS NELSON®
Since 1798

www.ThomasNelson.com

The Greatest Story Book Ever!

Let's pretend for a minute that something terrific has just happened. You've just found the greatest story book ever!

It is a wonderful book filled with the greatest stories of all time. It includes dozens of stories, something for everyone. There are breathtaking adventure stories about daring rescue missions and brave soldiers fighting against evil empires. There are touching romantic stories about men and women falling in love.

There are stories about history that let you meet people, see places and relive events from long, long ago. There are stories that make you happy, stories that make you laugh and stories that make you sad. Every kind of story you could ever imagine is right there in that one book.

Sound unbelievable? It isn't. In fact you really have just found the greatest book of stories ever. You're holding it in your hands right now. The most amazing thing is that the stories tell about people who really lived and events that really happened. The stories are true! It's the greatest book of stories because it's the Bible, God's Word.

What Kinds of Stories Are in the Bible?

The Bible is full of stories about hundreds of different people, the way they lived and the things they did. No matter what kind of stories you like, you'll find them in the Bible.

You probably know some of the stories in the Bible: Adam and Eve, Noah's ark, and the first Christmas, for example. But you may not realize that these are only a few of the dozens of great stories that come to life in the pages of the Bible. You may not know about some of these others that are just as fascinating to read:

Abraham and 300 men conduct a midnight raid to rescue a family that has been taken captive by a huge army.

Jacob and Rachel: He loves her so much that he works for fourteen years to earn the right to marry her.

Deborah and Jael: Two women lead an army to victory.

Gideon sends almost all of his army home right before the battle and easily defeats the enemy, using trumpets and torches instead of weapons.

Samuel, the story of a little boy who hears a mysterious voice in the night.

Solomon, the wisest and richest man who ever lived.

Esther: A young woman wins a beauty contest to become queen of Persia and risks her life to save her people.

The Jail Keeper's Surprise: A Philippian jailer is amazed when an earthquake frees his prisoners, and they decide to stay in jail.

What Is the Bible?

To most people, the Bible is a book. Really, it's more than that. With 66 books, it's a whole library! In includes books on a lot of different subjects: history, poetry, law, advice and even predictions of the future.

The First Book: The Story of the Beginning of the World. The first book in the Bible is named "Genesis," which means "beginnings." It tells the story of the creation, or beginning, of the world. It tells us about some bad people who let sin come between them and God. And it also shows us some good people, like Abraham, who listened to God and obeyed Him. The book ends as Abraham's great-grandchildren and their families (called Israelites) are enslaved by a wicked Pharaoh in Egypt.

The Miraculous Escape. The books of Exodus, Leviticus, Numbers and Deuteronomy tell of the Israelites' miraculous escape from Egypt and their 40-year journey to the land that God had promised them.

Capturing the Promised Land. After the Book of Deuteronomy comes the exciting Book of Joshua and its thrilling adventure stories of the Israelites' conquest of the Promised Land. The story changes in the Book of Judges. God's people forgot about all the things He had done for them, and He allowed enemy armies to beat them down until they changed their ways.

Famous Kings, Exciting Stories. The history of Israel continues in the books of Samuel, Kings, Chronicles and Ezra. Here we meet famous kings like Saul, David and Solomon. These books include some of the Bible's most exciting stories. You'll get to see David turn a gang of unhappy rebellious men into a strong, skillful band of warriors. You can admire David's skill at staying one step ahead of Saul, who is chasing him with 3,000 of the best soldiers in the kingdom.

Real Heroes. The books of Ruth, Nehemiah and Esther tell the stories of three real heroes who believed in God during the most difficult of times. The Book of Job is another story of faith. Satan does everything he can to force Job to turn away from God. He kills Job's family, takes away everything he owns and makes him very sick. But Job never loses his trust in God, and God restores Job.

Poetry and Wisdom. Job is followed by four books of poetry and wisdom. The Book of Psalms is a collection of 150 songs, prayers and poems which have been used by Jews and Christians for centuries to worship and praise God. Proverbs is a collection of wise sayings that are just as true today as they were 3,000 years ago. Ecclesiastes explains that it is far more important to obey God than to try to become rich. The Song of Solomon is a love poem with special spiritual meanings.

Foretelling the Future. The final 17 books of the Old Testament are books of prophecy. The accounts here are about God's messengers, the prophets. "You people are special to God," the prophets say to the people of Israel. "God wants you to obey Him, be kind to each other, and be just in all you do!" When the people didn't listen to the prophets, bad things happened. But these books also look to the future and promise that God will send a Messiah, a Savior, into the world.

The Story of Jesus. The New Testament begins about 400 years after the end of the Old Testament. It is the story of how the Old Testament promises came true. It is the story of how Jesus came, His life here on earth, His teachings and the early years of His church.

The Best News the World Ever Heard. The coming of Jesus and His message of God's love was the best news the world had ever heard. So the four books about Jesus' life are called "Gospels," which means "good news." Each of the writers of the four Gospels tells the story from a different point of view.

Matthew was impressed by the Old Testament promises and how Jesus had made them come true. He quotes the books of prophecy every chance he gets.

Mark was probably a young boy when Jesus lived on earth. His story shows Jesus as a hard-working, fast-moving teacher and healer.

Luke probably never met or saw Jesus. He probably talked to lots of people who knew Jesus, maybe even Jesus' family. He records several important events in Jesus' life that the other Gospels do not.

John's Gospel is very different from the others. It was probably one of the last books of the Bible to be written. It shows Jesus as the Son of God and the light of the world.

They Refused to Stop Preaching. The Book of Acts is an exciting history of the first 30 years of Jesus' church. It was written by Luke and shows how quickly faith in Jesus spread after He died and was raised to live again. It also shows the strong faith of the early Christians. They refused to stop preaching about Jesus even though they were thrown in jail, beaten and threatened with death.

Letters to Friends. The letters of Paul, Peter, James, John and Jude talk about many things. Some were written as thank you notes. One was written to get a runaway slave out of trouble. In another, Paul asks Timothy to return some valuables he had left behind. But the letters are much more than that. Their real purpose was to give advice to Christians. Reading these letters is almost like listening to early church leaders talk about Jesus.

The Strangest Book You Ever Read. Revelation, the last book of the New Testament, seems at times like science fiction. It is a book of prophecy written by the apostle John. It predicts a great war between the forces of good and the forces of evil. History will end with a victory for God's people.

Who Wrote the Bible?

The Bible was written over a period of thousands of years by more than 30 different men. Some of them were:

Moses, one of the best-educated men of his time.
Ezra, a religious scholar.
David, a shepherd boy who grew up to be king.
Solomon, David's son, was given special gifts of riches and wisdom by God.
Jeremiah, a shy young man who thought he was too young to be God's spokesman.
Matthew, a tax collector who was hated by his fellow men.
Luke, a doctor.
Peter, James and John, three fishermen.
The apostle Paul, as well-educated in his time as Moses had been hundreds of years earlier.

The other men who helped write the Bible came from backgrounds just as varied as these. The one thing they all had in common was that they were guided by God through the Holy Spirit.

How Did the Bible Come to Be?

One of the most exciting stories of all times is the story of how the Bible came to be. It is a miracle that all of the books of the Bible have been preserved for us to read today. After all, the first book of the Bible was written over 3,000 years ago, and the last one was finished nearly 2,000 years ago. Since there were no printing presses until just the last few hundred years, there was no way to make copies of the Bible except to write them by hand. You can imagine how long that would take.

The 66 books that make up the Bible were first collected together about 300 years after the last book was completed. Jews had used the Old Testament for years (and still use it today). Christians had been sharing the New Testament books with each other all along. But the entire Bible was not available until about A.D. 400.

Courageous Jews and Christians. If it hadn't been for the courage of many Jews and Christians over the last 3,000 years, we would not have the Bible at all today. In the years before Jesus was born, several nations invaded Israel, and every one of them tried to destroy the Bible. One evil ruler, Antiochus, even passed a law in 168 B.C. saying that anyone found with a copy of the Scriptures would be put to death.

The power of the Bible. But these enemies didn't count on one thing. They didn't count on the power of God and the faith and courage He gave to people who read the Bible. Every time the enemy tried to destroy the Bible, brave men and women hid it away and saved it.

A language people couldn't understand. Even as late as 500 years ago, some kings and powerful church leaders tried to keep people from knowing what was in the Bible. They didn't want people thinking for themselves about God. In those days it was easy to keep people from reading the Bible. Printing had not been invented, so the Bible had to be copied by hand. Besides, the Bible was only available in Latin, a language that few people could understand.

Sentenced to death for smuggling Bibles. William Tyndale was one of the first people to try to make the Bible available to people in English. His story is like an exciting spy thriller. In England it was against the law to translate the Bible into English, so he went to Germany. There, he translated the New Testament into English and began smuggling copies of it into England. He was arrested in Belgium, thrown into prison and, finally, sentenced to death.

At last! Bibles people can read. A little over 400 years ago, the rulers finally allowed the Bible to be translated into English. Several men wrote several different English versions of the Bible. One of these, the King James Version, came to be used by Christians all over the world. Even non-Christians are impressed by its beautiful language.

Since that time, many other English versions of the Bible have been published. In fact, Bibles are so plentiful today that it is hard to imagine that there was ever a time when people couldn't read the Bible in English for themselves.

How Do I Read the Bible?

The Bible is such a big book that it scares a lot of people. They think they don't know how to read it, where to start reading or when to read. The amazing thing about the Bible is that it really doesn't matter how you read it, when you read it or where you start reading.

Anywhere, anytime. You can read it anytime, anywhere, for any reason. You can start in the Old Testament, or you can start in the New Testament. And you can read the same Bible stories again and again. How you read does not matter. The important thing is that you get started right away and that you read from God's Word often.

Start with the great Bible stories. Many people like to start by reading the great Bible stories. After all, the Bible is the greatest book of true stories ever written. The following pages offer a list of some of the super stories you'll find in the Bible.

The Great Bible Stories

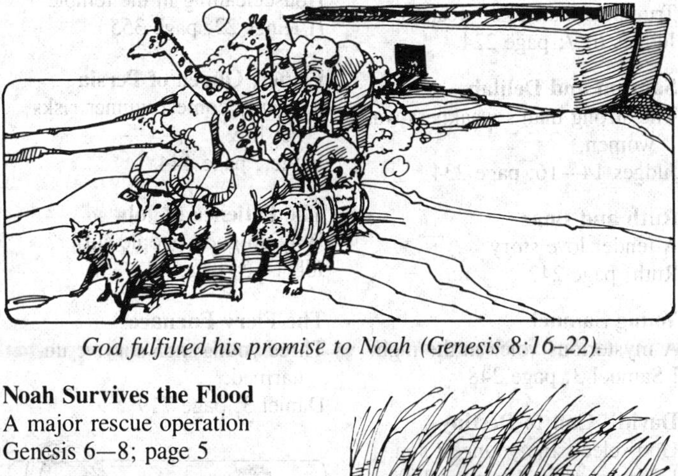

God fulfilled his promise to Noah (Genesis 8:16–22).

Baby Moses floated along a riverbank until rescued by royalty (Exodus 2:1–9).

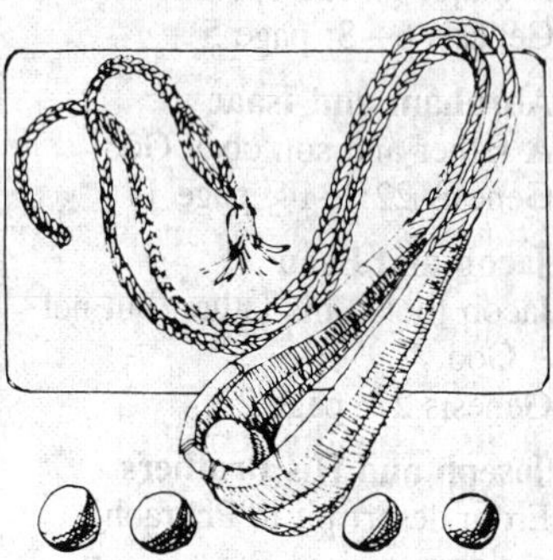

Boy David used a sling and a stone to slay a giant (I Samuel 17:49, 50).

Special Stories About Jesus

Feeding the Five Thousand
A little boy's lunch goes a long way.
John 6:1–14; page 89

The Children and the Blessing
Jesus does something special for children.
Luke 18:15–17; page 75

"The good shepherd giveth his life for the sheep," Jesus taught (John 10:11).

The Good Shepherd
He loved his sheep.
John 10:1–21; page 95

Raising Lazarus from the Dead
Jesus brings back a friend.
John 11:1–45; page 96

A Triumphal Entry
Palm branches in the street
Matthew 21:1–11; Mark 11:1–11; pages 20 and 44

The Last Supper
Jesus' parting words to his apostles
Matthew 19:28; 20:25–28; Mark 10:42–45; Luke 22:21–38; John 13—17; pages 19, 20, 43, 80, and 99

Betrayed by a Kiss
Jesus is arrested and taken to trial.
Matthew 26; Mark 14; Luke 22; John 18; pages 27, 47, 79, and 104

Jesus was crucified on a cross, on a hill where two thieves were also put to death (Mark 15:27, 28).

Crucifixion
Jesus hangs between two thieves.
Matthew 27; Mark 15; Luke 23; John 19; pages 29, 49, 81, and 105

Resurrection
His friends find an empty tomb.
Matthew 28; Mark 16; Luke 24; John 20; pages 31, 50, 82, and 106

Jesus, His Life, His Friends, His Enemies

"We've found him! We've found the Messiah, the Christ!"

With shouts of joy and wonderment men spread the news about Jesus of Nazareth hundreds of years ago in Palestine. A fisherman named Andrew rushed off to find his brother, Peter. A man named Philip, breathless with excitement, told his friend Nathanael.

Nathanael found the news hard to believe. Like other God-fearing men of his day, he had hoped the Messiah would come in his lifetime—but from Nazareth! That no-account town in the back hills of Galilee! "Can anything good come out of Nazareth?" he asked.

"Come and see," said Philip.

Many came and saw Jesus of Nazareth, to find out for themselves if he was truly the Messiah. What they saw and what happened is told in the four stories about Jesus in the New Testament. The four men who wrote them, Matthew, Mark, Luke, and John, each set down in his Gospel what he remembered best and what seemed to him most important about Jesus' appearance on earth. John said he wrote his Gospel so that his readers could discover what he had discovered: "that Jesus is the Christ, the Son of God."

At the time John lived, the dream of a Messiah, or Savior, was already centuries old, going all the way back to the Old Testament prophets. The promise, clearly sounded in Isaiah, Micah, and other prophets, foretold the coming of one who would be called "The Prince of Peace" and "Immanuel." "Immanuel" means "God with us."

To those who saw that Jesus was the Messiah, that he was the "God with us" promised in the Scriptures, his coming was world-shaking good news. That, of course, is why the four New Testament stories about Jesus are called "Gospels," which means "good news." All four Gospel writers tell about some things, like feeding the 5,000 and the week of the crucifixion. Other happenings appear in only one or two of the Gospels. By piecing together the different stories we can form a good picture of Jesus' life.

Luke tells of that awesome day when an angel suddenly appeared to a young Jewish girl named Mary. She was startled, but the angel calmed her, saying "thou hast found favour with God." And he told her that she would be the mother of a child who "shall be called the Son of God." According to Matthew, an angel of God appeared to Mary's husband-to-be, Joseph, in a dream, telling him about the child and instructing him to name the boy "Jesus."

Luke also describes the wondrous night when Jesus was born: Shepherds drowsily guarding their flocks on a hillside near Bethlehem were jolted wide awake by a great light flooding the sky. And an angel of the Lord appeared, announcing the birth of "a Saviour, which is Christ the Lord." And he told them they would find the baby wrapped in swaddling clothes, lying in a manger. The shepherds, abandoning their sheep, hastened to find the child. When they saw the baby Jesus they were filled with wonder. And they hurried away to tell others what they had seen.

When Jesus was twelve years old, he went with his family to Jerusalem to celebrate the Passover, the anniversary of the Israelites' escape from slavery in Egypt. During that visit Jesus listened and watched and questioned the teachers in the Temple. Luke says that he amazed everyone with "his understanding and answers."

Of the next eighteen years of Jesus' life we find nothing in the New Testament. Probably he worked with Joseph in Nazareth as a carpenter. Some think Joseph may have died fairly early and that Jesus worked as a carpenter to help support the family. He always had the strongest sympathy for the poor and humble, the kind of sympathy that comes from firsthand experience.

It was not until his thirtieth year, more or less, that Jesus left home. He journeyed to the Jordan River to seek out John the Baptist, a fiery reformer who was preaching to the people and telling them about the coming of the Messiah. Believing himself unworthy, John at first didn't want to baptize Jesus. But Jesus said "Suffer it to be so now" and was baptized. And then the Holy Spirit descended upon Jesus, filling him with strength for his mission.

To prepare himself for his work Jesus spent forty days in the wilderness praying and fasting. While he was there the devil came and tried, with the slyest tricks he could invent, to tempt Jesus. But Jesus resisted every temptation, outwitting the devil at every turn.

John tells us about Jesus' going to Jerusalem at Passover where, boiling with holy anger, he drove the greedy merchants and money-changers from the temple area. While in Jerusalem he had an important talk with a Jewish ruler, Nicodemus. Here we find one of the best-known verses in the Bible: "For God so loved the world, that he gave his only begotten Son, that whosoever believeth in him should not perish, but have everlasting life."

A few months later Jesus returned to Galilee. Jerusalem, especially its leaders, had not accepted John the Baptist's teachings nor answered Jesus' call to God. So Jesus settled in the town of Capernaum on the Sea of Galilee.

About midway through his second year of teaching Jesus chose twelve men to be his disciples: Peter, aggressive and quick-acting, and his brother Andrew, both fishermen. The brothers James and John, who were also fishermen. Simon and Judas Iscariot. Matthew, the tax collector. Philip, Bartholomew, and Thomas, the doubting one, Judas and James. None seemed the kind of person who would change the world.

As Jesus went about talking to people, he talked about things they could understand. He talked about fig trees that didn't produce good fruit, about wild wheat growing among the good wheat, about birds being fed by the heavenly Father, about a shepherd searching long and hard for one lost sheep. He used everyday things from their own experience to explain about life and God.

He used stories or parables to show what God was like and how he wanted people to live. In the Sermon on the Mount he taught people to love their enemies. To those who were beaten down with life's problems and discouraged with their efforts to please God, Jesus extended this generous call: "Come unto me, all ye that labour and are heavy laden, and I will give you rest."

Sometimes it seemed that Jesus could see right through good men and bad men alike. A lawyer, who knew perfectly well that he couldn't have eternal life without loving his neighbor, tried to wiggle out by putting this question to Jesus: "And who is my neighbour?" Instead of replying directly, Jesus told the story of the Good Samaritan. When he had finished, the embarrassed lawyer could answer his own question: All people were his neighbors.

Because he kept putting his finger on the sore spots in men's consciences, Jesus soon made enemies. And it was the religious leaders of the day, the scribes, the Pharisees, and the Sadducees, who got the angriest. They became more and more enraged as he exposed their falseness and broke down their authority with the common people.

Jesus occasionally grew weary from the crowds that constantly surrounded him to hear him preach, the sick and the lame that came to be healed. He often went into the wilderness to pray and gather strength. One day he and his disciples got into a boat and crossed the Sea of Galilee to get some rest. But someone saw them leave and the crowds followed. Jesus knew that these people were so eager to hear about the things of God that they had left their shops and fields to follow him. So he taught them and healed the sick.

Suppertime came and there was no food for the multitude that had gathered around Jesus. But a young boy among them had with him five loaves of barley bread and two fish. When he gave these to Jesus, Jesus blessed them, broke them into pieces, and fed the whole multitude. There was even some left over. John helps us see what this meant to Jesus for he tells us what Jesus said about it the next day:

"I am the bread of life: he that cometh to me shall never hunger and he that believeth in me shall never thirst . . . And the bread that I will give is my flesh, which I will give for the life of the world . . ."

When Jesus spoke this way people didn't understand him and many of his followers left him. His original twelve disciples said they would stay with him, but they too must have been puzzled by his words.

They didn't have long to wonder about what Jesus meant. Now he began to speak quite openly about his coming death, telling them that the time had come for him to give up his life for mankind. He headed once more for Jerusalem, going in and out of the city for special religious occasions, when there were many people gathered in the town, to make his last appeal. But the religious leaders wouldn't listen. They only tried to trap him with trick questions, hoping to catch him in a slip-up, perhaps to find an excuse for arresting him.

Jesus had performed many miracles, making the blind see, the deaf hear, the crippled walk. He had cast out demons, made the sick well, and even brought some who were dead back to life again. Popular excitement was raised to a new pitch when word got around that Jesus had raised his friend Lazarus from the dead. So when Jesus entered Jerusalem the week before his last Passover, the road was lined with crowds of children and common people spreading branches before him and shouting "Hosanna: Blessed is the King of Israel that cometh in the name of the Lord."

Jesus knew that most of the people didn't have an inkling of what he had really come to do on earth. And he foresaw that Jerusalem would come under the judgment of God for rejecting his message. As he looked out over the city and thought about these things, he wept.

When the Passover evening arrived, Jesus and his twelve disciples gathered to eat what was to be their last meal together. No servants were present to perform the usual footwashing and none of the disciples offered to do it for the others. So Jesus rose, took a basin of water and a towel, and proceeded to wash his disciples' feet. "Whosoever would be great among you," he had often told them, "must be your servant."

Then Jesus took bread, broke it, and gave it to his disciples, saying, "Take, eat, this is my body." Then he took a cup of wine, gave thanks, and passed it to them, saying, "Drink of it, all of you . . . This is my blood, shed for you."

That night, John tells us, Jesus also talked about the future. He spoke of going to his Father to prepare a place for all who believed in him. He promised that though he was soon to leave them, the Holy Spirit of God would come and live within them, so that it would be like Jesus himself going with them wherever they went. And he said that just as God had sent him into the world, he was sending them out into the world with his message. Finally, he promised to return again.

Afterwards Jesus went to the Garden of Gethsemane to pray. At first he asked God if it was possible to be spared from the death he knew awaited him. But he ended his prayer with "nevertheless not my will, but thine, be done."

The traitor Judas, followed by a band of soldiers, came into the Garden and identified Jesus with a kiss. The disciples fled in panic while Jesus underwent an illegal trial in the small hours of the morning. The enemies of Jesus urged Pilate, the Roman governor, to put Jesus to death because he claimed to be a king. But Pilate, who viewed this so-called kingdom of God as a harmless daydream, could see that Jesus had not done anything to deserve death.

Then he had an idea. Knowing that the Jewish people had a custom of releasing a prisoner to celebrate the joy of the Passover season, Pilate suggested that Jesus be the one released. But the crowd was so stirred up against Jesus that they shouted "Away with this man, and release unto us Barabbas."

Pilate knew that the rulers of the temple were leading the people to make this demand, but he felt powerless to stop them.

"What will ye then that I shall do unto him whom ye call the King of the Jews?" he asked.

And the crowd cried out, "Crucify him!"

So at last Pilate gave the order, and the crucifixion was carried out by Roman soldiers. People passing by jeered, "He saved others; himself he cannot save." Jesus, hanging on the cross, asked God to forgive those who had put him there and he comforted a thief dying on the cross beside him. He asked John to care for his mother.

And now a great darkness came over the land and lasted from the sixth hour to the ninth hour. All that the Scriptures had said about the coming of the Savior had now been fulfilled, and Jesus gave up his spirit with a cry, "It is finished!" The ground shook with a great earthquake and rocks split open. "Truly this was the Son of God," said a Roman soldier standing nearby.

But this was not the end.

Friends of Jesus took his body from the cross and laid it in a tomb. Early in the morning on the first day of the week, Mark tells us, Mary Magdalene, Mary the mother of James, and Salome brought sweet spices to the tomb to anoint Jesus' body. They found the stone rolled away from the door of the tomb and Jesus gone. A young man in a shining garment sat inside and they were afraid. "He is risen," the young man said. And he told them to tell the disciples what had happened.

That very day Jesus himself appeared to two of the disciples who were walking to the town of Emmaus. During the next forty days he appeared to other disciples again and again to convince them that he was really alive and that all had happened as he had said it would. Evil had not won at all. The Messiah had suffered according to prophecy and had triumphed over both death and evil. In his last meeting with the disciples on a mountain, as reported by Matthew, he sent them out to teach all nations, telling them "I am with you alway, even unto the end of the world."

There is much more about Jesus, about what he said and did that so stirred up the world, in the Gospels of Matthew, Mark, Luke, and John. You will find it easy to select the stories that interest you most from the reading guide that follows this. When the same story appears in different Gospels the guide tells you where to find it in each, so that you can compare the way the different writers tell it.

But this is just the beginning. The only way to get the whole great story of Jesus is to read all four Gospels through. You can learn for yourself why millions of people follow him as the Messiah.

Stories About Jesus

The Birth of Jesus *Familiar stories of shepherds and wise men*	Matthew 1, 2; Luke 1, 2
A Visit to the Temple *Amazing the religious leaders*	Luke 2:41–52
Baptism and Temptation *A voice from heaven*	Matthew 3; 4; Mark 1:9–13; Luke 3:21, 22; 4:1–13
Nicodemus in the Night *A most unusual interview*	John 3
Early Miracles in Galilee *Christ's power is displayed*	Mark 1:14—2:28
Trouble in His Hometown *A prophet without honor*	Luke 4:16–30
Choosing the Twelve Apostles *An interesting group of men*	Mark 3:13–19
Sermon on the Mount *The longest teaching of Jesus*	Matthew 5—7; Luke 6:20–49
The Lord's Prayer *"After this manner pray"*	Matthew 6:9–13; Luke 11:1–4
Invitation to Rest *Rest for the soul*	Matthew 11:28–30
Parables of the Kingdom *Some did not understand*	Matthew 13; Mark 4:1–33; Luke 8:4–18; 10:25–37; 13:18–21
The Good Samaritan *A lesson in neighborliness*	Luke 10:25–37
Lost Sheep, Lost Coin, Lost Son *Rejoice when the lost is found*	Matthew 18:12–14; Luke 15:3–32
Feeding the Five Thousand *A boy's lunch is multiplied*	John 6:1–14

The Good Shepherd *He loved his sheep*	John 10:1–21
Foretelling His Death *A ransom for many*	Matthew 16:21–27; 20:17–19; Luke 18:31–34; John 3:14–16
Judging the Religious Leaders *Harsh words from Jesus*	Matthew 23; Luke 11:39–54
Raising of Lazarus *The resurrection and the life*	John 11:1–45
Triumphal Entry *Palm branches in the street*	Matthew 21:1–11; Mark 11:1–11
Prediction of the Future *Wars and rumors of wars*	Matthew 24; 25
The Last Supper *Parting words to his apostles*	Matthew 19:28; 20:25–28; Mark 10:42–45; Luke 22:21–38; John 13—17
Betrayal and Trial *Betrayed by a kiss*	Matthew 26; Mark 14; Luke 22; John 18
Crucifixion *Between two thieves*	Matthew 27; Mark 15; Luke 23; John 19
Resurrection *The empty tomb*	Matthew 28; Mark 16; Luke 24; John 20

Your Life in Bible Times

What would you like to do?

Tent under the Near Eastern stars with Jacob? Go hunting in the mountains with David? Stand before the walls of Jericho with the army of Joshua? Rough it with John the Baptist on the barren plateaus of Jordan? Hear Jesus talking to the multitudes by the sea? Sail the Mediterranean with Paul?

You might have done any of these things if you had lived in Bible times. But which one of them you did would depend on when you lived, for Bible times stretch over some thousands of years. You could be sure of one thing, though: Whether you lived in the ancient days of Abraham or in the time of Jesus, there would be excitement in your life. In fact, just being a Christian could be dangerous in the days when the apostles of Jesus were trying to start the church.

Biblical Palestine was a wild land. Outside the tiny villages, gangs of robbers prowled in search of plunder. Wild animals threatened the livestock in the pastures. There were big wars between nations and little wars between tribes. Enemy soldiers frequently seized crops and animals and sometimes carried away people. Israel suffered greatly from frequent wars in the troubled times told about in Judges—and again after the reigns of King David and King Solomon, when Israel and Judah were fighting each other.

Even the climate sometimes made life uncertain. Much of Palestine is very hot, although it gets quite cold in the northern mountains. In the Jordan Valley the temperature goes over 100°. Here you need a cloth over your head to protect it from the hot sun and a loose robe to protect your body against the hot winds—loose so that air could flow inside to help keep your body cool.

The Jordan River cannot be used to water the land because it lies too far below sea level. To raise the crops needed for your family and to water the pasture for your livestock you would have to depend on the rainfall. The rainy season is from November to April, with the most rain at the beginning and the end of this time. The Bible often speaks of these "former" and "latter" rains. You might dig a wide hole in the ground and make a cistern to catch and hold water for use between rains.

You would plow the ground after the "former" rain and plant the seed so that it would be watered by the "latter" rain. Barley and wheat would be your main crops, harvested between April and June. You could grow grapevines and olive trees on the hillsides. These would be harvested in late summer. If the rains failed, as they did in Elijah's day, you would be facing hunger, even starvation.

Big things happened in biblical Palestine. This is where the children of Israel came seeking the "Promised Land" God had offered them. This is where such Old Testament heroes as David, Samson, Daniel, and Gideon rose to fame. This is where King Solomon built a splendid empire and also where he built the most magnificent temple in all Israel to glorify God. And this is where the greatest happening of all took place: The coming of Jesus Christ.

All this—and much more—occurred in a tiny land about 150 miles long and 30 to 50 miles wide, smaller than the state of Vermont. It was called Canaan at the time Joshua's armies stormed through it. Today its general name is Palestine. Some of the old Bible lands are now part of Syria and that part of Jordan formerly called Transjordan. The powerful kingdoms of David and Solomon extended from Syria in the north to Egypt in the south, from the Mediterranean Sea in the west to the Arabian desert in the east. By the time of Jesus, however, Palestine had been broken into tiny provinces by its several conquerors.

Trouble often came to Palestine from outside. The only main road between Egypt and Syria, and to the lands beyond Syria, ran right through it. This was fine for Israel in peacetime, when money could be made on trade between the north and the south. Solomon enriched the country by buying and selling horses in the trading between Egypt and Cilicia. But disaster traveled the road, too. When there was war between the big powers, Israel was caught in the middle. King Josiah was killed when he tried to intercept an Egyptian force enroute to fight the Babylonians.

How you lived and what you did in Bible times would depend not only on when you lived, but also on where you lived. Palestine divides into four belts running north and south, each very different from the others. If you lived in the western belt along the shores of the Mediterranean Sea, you might have been a fisherman, but not a sailor on a freight-carrying ship, for there were no big natural harbors on the coast. Herod built the port of Caesarea in New Testament times and you might have traveled there with the apostle Paul.

The hill country in the stories of Gideon, Samson, David, and Elijah is in the next belt to the east, which contains a high tableland. You would have traveled this country if you had been following Jesus and the disciples between Galilee and Jerusalem.

If you were marching with the armies of Joshua or, hundreds of years later, tramping through Jordan with John the Baptist, you would be in the next belt to the east. Here in the Jordan Valley is the lowest point on earth, 1,275 feet below sea level at the Dead Sea. In Old Testament times it was called the "jungle of the Jordan" and lions roamed through it.

Between the valley and the eastern desert is the fourth belt, a high tableland once called Transjordan. Here were the kingdoms of Bashan, Heshbon, Ammon, Moab, and Edom that were conquered by the children of Israel coming through from Egypt on their way to the land of Canaan. If you had been with the children of Israel then you would have been part of their great quest for the Promised Land.

Solomon was the last king to keep Israel together as a nation. After he died a civil war tore it in two, a northern kingdom called Israel or Samaria and a southern kingdom called Judah. Your life in Israel then would have been one war after another, first with Syria and then with Assyria, the nation that finally conquered Israel.

At this time you would have found more peace in Judah, in the more isolated hill country around Jerusalem. When you think about what happened to Israel you can understand why the prophets insisted that Judah's safety lay in avoiding dealings with other nations. And the prophets were right. Judah survived another 150 years after Israel fell.

You wonder how people could have families and homes in a land so torn by strife and, in many ways, difficult to live in. The fact is, family ties were undoubtedly stronger in Bible times than they are today. Life was centered in the family, in work, and in religion. And the family wasn't just mother and father and children. Your household might also include uncles, aunts, cousins, and grandparents. When Jacob and his family moved to Egypt, his family included 66 people—almost a tribe in itself.

The father's word would be law. He would have the power of life and death over children, grandchildren, servants. In this ancient world women were not considered the equals of men. In early Old Testament times a wife was almost like a piece of property. The husband could divorce her by simply saying "I divorce you," but the woman could not divorce her husband. Moses made this a little better for the women by requiring the husband to give his divorced wife a certificate of divorcement. Later, Jesus limited divorce and further increased the rights of women.

Most people in Old Testament times were simple farmers. There were not many jobs for the ordinary person. There were no factories because Israel didn't have materials with which to make things. Boys learned to farm, to raise animals, and to live in the outdoors. Girls learned to cook, sew, weave cloth, and help in the fields. You would rarely go far from home because the only way to get any place was to walk, except for an occasional donkey ride.

In early Bible times especially you would probably have lived in a tent, the best kind of home for those traveling with their flocks. The material for the tents was woven from animal hair. When the rain wet it, the material shrank, drawing the fibers closer together, so that it was almost waterproof. Some tents had curtains to separate the women's quarters from the men's. As the family grew, the mother simply wove some more material to make the tent larger.

Later on, with the coming of the Greeks and Romans, life became somewhat more comfortable in the villages. Houses of mud or clay were built around an open space we might call a courtyard. The houses were usually two stories high with a flat roof. The wealthy sometimes built a room on the roof or made a covering of thatch to shade part of it. You read about this kind of building in the story of Jesus' healing a crippled man who was lowered by his friends through the roof of a crowded house.

Even people who were lucky enough to have houses usually had little furniture—a mat or cot and a few chairs. And you would also have to use the house as a place to store tools and winter food. During wartime as well as during the winter the house, or at least the courtyard, had to be shared with the family's livestock. Olive oil lamps (like those in the parable of the wise and foolish virgins) were used for light. Those who could afford it had lampstands that held several lamps. One lamp was kept burning at night.

Your clothing would be simple. In fact, you might make it yourself out of animal skins. (In New Testament times, however, John the Baptist's "raiment of camel's hair" was considered odd.) Women wove cloth for clothing as they did material for tents. Dyes to color the cloth were difficult to make, so clothing was often made in the natural cloth color. Purple dye, which was made from a kind of shellfish, was so rare and expensive that it became the color often worn by kings.

Generally both men and women wore a close-fitting tunic that reached to the knees. A loose robe fastened over the shoulders was worn as an outer garment. The woman's robe would be longer than the man's and probably be decorated with embroidery. The poor man would take off his outer robe when working in hot weather, but the wealthy man would not be seen in public without it.

You would wear a wide belt called a girdle, a kind of carry-all for your farm tools, your valuables, or even your lunch. If your robe got in your way when you were working, you would gird yourself: that is, you would tuck the loose ends of the robe under your girdle.

Women in Bible times didn't wear much make-up to beautify themselves. Some put paint around their eyes for decoration. They also put it around their children's eyes, believing that paint strengthened the eyes. Most women had combs, but only a few owned mirrors, which were made from polished bronze. There was no glass.

Your meals would be as simple as your clothing. Having meat to eat was a special treat. The usual foods were bread, fruit, honey, milk, butter, and cheese. Eggs and fish were not well liked, but locusts were. John the Baptist was not the only person who ate them. You could get milk from goats, sheep, and camels, but it spoiled quickly because there were no refrigerators. When the milk soured, the thick part would be eaten as cheese. You could make butter by pouring cream into a goatskin bag and rocking it against your knee until butter formed.

Food did not come easily. A housewife had to work hard to provide such a common food as bread. After cleaning and washing the threshed grain, she had to pound and grind it into flour a handful at a time. She mixed the dough, sometimes putting in yeast, then baked the bread in flat loaves on hot rocks. In Bible times you would not slice the bread, but break it from the loaf with your hands. Because bread was such an important food, it came to mean life itself. If you cut the bread your neighbors would think you didn't value life.

Your family would eat twice a day, once in the morning and again in the cool of the evening. The meal would be put in a single bowl and all the family would eat from it with their fingers. You would have your own cup and the usual mealtime drink was wine mixed with water. Dishes and cooking utensils were scarce: a few clay or copper cooking pots, leather bottles, and the cups.

Your life in Bible times would be planned around the religious holidays and the farming season. The religious calendar of the Jews began in March or April, according to the moon. The regular calendar began in September or October, the beginning of seeding time. Isaiah, Jeremiah, Ezekiel, and the other prophets used the religious calendar.

The religious holidays were, of course, timed by the religious calendar. Passover, celebrating the deliverance of the children of Israel from slavery in Egypt, began on the fourteenth day of the first month. In the third month came the Feast of Weeks, marked by the firstfruits of the wheat harvest. The seventh month brought the Feast of Trumpets, the Day of Atonement (when the priests offered sacrifices for the sins of the people), and the Feast of Tabernacles.

All of these festivals were set up by Moses and continued right on through to the present day. Jesus timed his appearances in Jerusalem with the feast days, when Jews would be there not only from Palestine, but also from the surrounding country.

Devout families worshipped and sacrificed regularly according to the Old Testament rules. For example, Mary and Joseph made an offering of a pair of doves or two young pigeons when they brought the baby Jesus to the temple. Strict rules told what foods to eat, how to cook them, and even how to wash the dishes.

In the early days there were no churches, no special buildings for worship and sacrifice, except for tents called "tabernacles." Altars for worship were built in the countryside up to the time of King David. When Solomon built the magnificent temple in Jerusalem, it was a lasting sign of God's presence among his people.

Jewish churches, called "synagogues," were common by New Testament times as places for Jews to worship on the Sabbath. Jesus worshipped regularly according to the customs of the Jews. After he rose from the dead, Christians gathered on Sundays for a celebration of Jesus' resurrection and continuing life among them.

Families celebrated together every chance they got: at harvest time, weddings, homecomings of some member of the family, victory in battle, at the coronation of a king. After the celebration, which would include eating, dancing, and singing, there would be storytelling and riddles. Everyone liked to stump his friends with a riddle—Samson loved to ask riddles.

You would have great fun at a wedding celebration. The wedding itself was simple, but there would be a big celebration afterward. The husband-to-be would dress up in his best clothing and, with some friends, go to the bride's home. She would have done everything she could to make herself attractive, even borrowing some jewels to weave into her braided hair. The bride and her friends would join the husband and his friends to form a kind of parade going through the streets back to the husband-to-be's home, which is where they will live. Then begins the fun—a wedding feast that may last a week, with all of the wedding guests staying at the house.

You would work hard and long, but there would be time for play. Lifting weights, like barbells, and wrestling were popular for men and boys. Shooting a bow and arrow was necessary for hunting and warfare, but it was also a sport in which one tried to outdo another. "Fifty-five Holes" was a popular game played with ivory or wooden pegs moved from hole to hole according to the roll of the dice.

The children copied Egyptian games, playing tug-of-war, catch, and tag. Girls played with leather balls. Scientists have not found any dolls buried with the ruins of houses built in biblical times, but they have found rattles, toy chariots, animals, and make-believe toys used for playing "house." A big favorite among the boys was the sling, which was also a useful weapon for protecting the flocks from wild animals. This is probably how David developed the skill that enabled him to overcome Goliath with only a sling for a weapon.

Many evenings at home would be spent with family talk and storytelling. This is how you would learn about the Bible, since hardly anyone could read or write in those days. Bible stories were great favorites, just as exciting to people then as they are today. Along with the Bible stories, parents taught their children about religion. Religion was an everyday matter then, not just for the Sabbath, and the laws of Moses were followed through all of daily life. But by the time of Jesus and Paul the religious rules and rites had become so complicated that they had become a burden instead of a way of finding joyful release in knowing God.

The religious family would extend welcome to a stranger as one sent by God. If you were traveling, you would find that inns were rare and, anyhow, used mainly by the rich. So it would be best to find a family to take you in for the night. As you entered the home, the host would bow to the ground and greet you with a kiss. Take off your sandals and he will wash the travel dust from your feet. He will give you oil to anoint your head—if he doesn't do this you haven't been truly welcomed. A meal taken with the family becomes a bond of friendship between you.

Gradually, in the years between the Old and New Testaments, things changed. The Greek and Roman conquerors brought with them new ways of life. There were more possibilities for travel, study, and learning a trade or a profession. Paul was a tentmaker and Luke was a doctor. There were roads, courts with judges, sports, and entertainment, and there was trade with other countries. The people of Palestine were more in touch with the outside world. Life was more comfortable in the cities and towns. Roman rulers and wealthy Palestinians could afford splendid palaces, summer homes, and foods brought in from other countries.

This was the world into which Jesus was born. The towns and cities he, Peter, James, and Paul visited were highly civilized, although life in the country was not far different from life in Old Testament times. But Jesus brought another kind of change, a much more important change, to all who believed in him.

The reading guide that follows this article makes it easy for you to read more about the people of Bible times and how they lived.

Readings About Life in Bible Times

Abraham and Lot
Family quarrel over grazing land Genesis 13

The Twelve Spies
A first glimpse of the Promised Land Numbers 13; 14

Three Solemn Feasts
The heart of Jewish religious life Deuteronomy 16

Be Kind to Animals
The importance of animals is seen Exodus 23:1–12

Samson's Riddle
Fun at a wedding Judges 14

Ruth the Gleaner
Harvesting the grain Ruth 2

Battling the Philistines
Notice how the battle was fought I Samuel 4

David the Musician
Music at the king's court I Samuel 16:14–23; 18:6, 7

Solomon's Riches *Even other rulers were amazed*	I Kings 4:21; 5:18; 10
Elijah Predicts a Famine *Drought a constant threat*	I Kings 17
How a Wall Was Built *Inside story on a construction job*	Nehemiah 4—6
Psalm of Wandering *Notice the references to nature*	Psalm 78
A Life of Luxury *The king's enjoyment of pleasure*	Ecclesiastes 2:1–8
A Time for Everything *Notice what there was time for*	Ecclesiastes 3:1–9
The Potter's Wheel *A skilled craftsman worth watching*	Jeremiah 18:1–6
Farming with Problems *Drought, disease, insects*	Joel 1
Weeds in the Field *The farmer's dilemma*	Matthew 13:24–30
Weather Prediction *Signs in the sky*	Matthew 16:1–3
Parable of the Talents *Lesson in investing money*	Matthew 25:14–30
Paralytic Carried by Four Friends *Through the roof for healing*	Mark 2:1–12
Render to Caesar *Question about taxes*	Mark 12:13–17
Storm on the Sea of Galilee *Jesus commands the winds*	Luke 8:22–25
The Good Samaritan *Crime on the Road to Jericho*	Luke 10:25–37
Parable of the Fig Tree *How to grow figs*	Luke 13:6–9
Riot in Jerusalem *The importance of citizenship*	Acts 22:22–29
Shipwreck in the Mediterranean *A story for sailors*	Acts 27
Paul's Persecutions *Difficulties for early Christians*	II Corinthians 11:24–27

Bible Time Chart

The Bible takes us all the way back to the beginning of time, when God created the world. It does not tell us when this was. In the early seventeenth century, Bishop James Ussher, an Irish biblical scholar, set the date of the creation of the world at 4004 years before the birth of Christ. Some modern scientists believe the world must have been created more than ten billion years ago. Other attempts to fix the date of creation give us times between these two.

Similarly, many people have tried to work out dates for such early Bible stories as Adam and Eve and Noah and the Flood. But these happened so long ago that not enough clues have been found to show when they happened.

The first important biblical happening for which a probable date can be set is Abraham's journey from Ur in Chaldea to Canaan. This and the other dates in the Time Chart are those generally agreed upon by most modern scholars. Other scholars favor a different set of dates. Some would, for example, set 1300 B.C. instead of 1450 B.C. as the date when Moses led the Israelites out of Egypt. Although the dates used in the Time Chart are believed to be the most reliable, some of them are uncertain and these are followed by a question mark. Dates given apply to the first of the events listed after them.

B.C. Beginnings

Creation, Adam and Eve. Chapters 1 to 5 of Genesis cover a long period of time, including the creation of the world and the beginnings of mankind. God creates the world and everything in it for the benefit of man and entrusts man to rule over it. Man's first disobedience of God brought the problems of sin and death to mankind.

B.C. End and a New Beginning

The Flood, Noah. Chapters 6 to 9 of Genesis cover the great flood that destroyed all mankind except Noah and his family. The story shows the importance of doing right and the certainty of God's judgment when men fall into unrighteousness. Chapters 10 and 11 tell of a new start for mankind.

2100? B.C. Abraham Finds a Home

Abraham is led from Ur of the Chaldeans to settle in the land of Canaan. God promises to bless Abraham and his descendants, thus making a solemn agreement or covenant, with man (Genesis 11:31—13:18).

1900? B.C. Joseph Succeeds

Abraham's great-grandson, Joseph, becomes "prime minister" in Egypt. Joseph's brothers and their families settle in Egypt (Genesis 41—47).

1450? B.C. Captivity and Escape

The unfriendly Egyptian Pharaoh enslaves the people of Israel, so-called because they are all descended from Abraham's grandson, Jacob, who was renamed Israel. With God's help Moses leads the people out of Egypt and through the wilderness to Canaan, the "Promised Land." Under Joshua the Israelites conquer most of the frontier fortresses and settle themselves in the hill country of Palestine (Exodus 1—14; Joshua 1—16).

1000? B.C. The Great Kings

Kings Saul, David, and Solomon. Under these rulers Israel gradually completes the conquest of Palestine from Syria in the north to Egypt in the south. Solomon builds the great Temple in Jerusalem. But he takes women from other nations as wives and they turn him toward other gods. As a result Solomon leads Israel away from God (I Samuel 9 to end; II Samuel; I Kings 1—12).

925 B.C. The Nation Divides

Civil war divides Israel into two nations, the northern kingdom of Israel and the southern kingdom of Judah. Israel drifts farther and farther away from the law of Moses and the true worship of God (I Kings 12 and following).

722 B.C. Israel Falls

After many warnings by prophets such as Elijah and Elisha, Israel falls to Assyria and many of the Israelites are taken away into captivity (II Kings 17).

587 B.C. Judah Falls

The kingdom of Judah has gradually followed the bad example of Israel, turning away from God. Finally, Jerusalem falls to Nebuchadnezzar, king of Babylon and conqueror of Assyria. The prophet Ezekiel goes into exile with his people (II Kings 20—25).

538 B.C. Return to Jerusalem

Some Jews—we stop calling them Israelites after the fall of Israel—are permitted to return to Jerusalem by Cyrus, king of Persia and conqueror of Babylon. Ezra and Nehemiah eventually join their fellow Jews in rebuilding the walls of Jerusalem and helping the Jews make a new life (Ezra; Nehemiah).

333 B.C. Alexander Takes Palestine

Alexander the Great, founder of the Macedonian Empire and conqueror of the Persian Empire, starts a war that adds Palestine, along with Syria and Egypt, to his empire. After Alexander's death, his generals divide the empire among themselves, and Palestine suffers occupation and mistreatment at the hands of rival powers.

167 B.C. Freedom for the Jews

The Jews gain their freedom under the leadership of the Maccabees, a family of Jewish patriots. They manage to keep their freedom for about a hundred years.

63 B.C. Rome Takes Palestine

The Roman general Pompey takes control of Palestine. In 46 B.C. Julius Caesar was appointed dictator in Rome for ten years, but was assassinated two years later.

5? B.C. The Savior Comes

Jesus Christ is born. When the Christian calendar was set up it was intended that the year of Christ's birth should be A.D. 1—"A.D." the Latin for "Anno Domini," "year of the Lord." But a mistake was made in the date assigned to Herod's death, which came shortly after Christ was born and was used to calculate the time of Christ's birth, and this led to a mistake in setting up the calendar. To correct this error, Christ's birth date must be now given as 4 B.C. or, if it is assumed that he was born in December, 5 B.C. (Luke 2:8–20).

A.D. 30? Christ Wins over Death

Crucifixion and resurrection of Christ. The Gospels tell us little of Christ's boyhood. Chapter 2 of Luke tells us about Mary and Joseph taking Christ as an infant to the Temple to be presented to the Lord and of the young Jesus talking with the teachers in the Temple when he was about 12. His ministry, which began after he was baptized by John the Baptist, was about three years (Matthew 27:15—28:16; other Gospels).

A.D. 33? Paul's Work Begins

Conversion of Paul and the beginning of Paul's great missionary journeys, which spread Christianity to the Roman provinces in Asia Minor (modern Turkey) and Europe (the Book of Acts).

A.D. 70 The Fall of Jerusalem

After a siege of four years, Jerusalem fell to the Roman army, and the Temple was destroyed. But the apostles and other followers of Christ had laid the foundation for the Christian church, and the good news of Christ and the redemption of man was to sweep through all of the western world.

(Dates compiled by the Bible staff of Thomas Nelson Inc.)

THE HOLY BIBLE

CONTAINING

THE OLD AND NEW TESTAMENTS

TRANSLATED OUT OF THE ORIGINAL TONGUES

AND WITH THE FORMER TRANSLATIONS

DILIGENTLY COMPARED AND REVISED

Authorized King James Version

THOMAS NELSON

Since 1798

www.ThomasNelson.com

The KJV Classic Children's Bible, Seaside Edition

Published in Nashville, TN, by Thomas Nelson. Thomas Nelson is a registered trademark of HarperCollins Christian Publishing, Inc.

The Holy Bible, King James Version

This Bible was set in the Thomas Nelson KJV Font,
created at the 2K/DENMARK type foundry.

Printed in China

23 24 25 26 27 28 29 30 /DSC/ 85 84 83 82 81 80 79 78

THE OLD TESTAMENT

THE NEW TESTAMENT

BOOKS OF THE BIBLE
LISTED ALPHABETICALLY

(OT—Old Testament page NT—New Testament page)

GUIDE TO PRONUNCIATION

ā	as in fame	ĭ	as in sit, dim
ă	as in cat	ō	as in bone, boat
â	as in share, dare	ŏ	as in bottle, gone
ä	as in farm, father	ô	as in shore, born
āi	as in pail	o͞o	as in pool
aī	as in aisle	ū	as in cute, tune
ē	as in beat, street	ŭ	as in fuss
ĕ	as in jet, met	û	as in crude
ī	as in kite, shine	u	as in burner

In proper names ch is generally pronounced as k, ph as f

THE FIRST BOOK OF MOSES
CALLED

GENESIS

CHAPTER 1

IN the beginning God created the
heaven and the earth.
2 And the earth was without form,
and void; and darkness *was* upon the
face of the deep. And the Spirit of God
moved upon the face of the waters.
3 ¶And God said, Let there be light:
and there was light.
4 And God saw the light, that *it was*
good: and God divided the light from
the darkness.
5 And God called the light Day, and
the darkness he called Night. And the
evening and the morning were the first
day.
6 ¶And God said, Let there be a fir-
mament in the midst of the waters, and
let it divide the waters from the waters.
7 And God made the firmament, and
divided the waters which *were* under
the firmament from the waters which
were above the firmament: and it was
so.
8 And God called the firmament
Heaven. And the evening and the morn-
ing were the second day.
9 ¶And God said, Let the waters un-
der the heaven be gathered together
unto one place, and let the dry *land* ap-
pear: and it was so.
10 And God called the dry *land* Earth;
and the gathering together of the
waters called he Seas: and God saw
that *it was* good.
11 And God said, Let the earth bring
forth grass, the herb yielding seed, *and*
the fruit tree yielding fruit after his
kind, whose seed *is* in itself, upon the
earth: and it was so.
12 And the earth brought forth grass,
and herb yielding seed after his kind,
and the tree yielding fruit, whose seed
was in itself, after his kind: and God
saw that *it was* good.
13 And the evening and the morning
were the third day.
14 ¶And God said, Let there be lights
in the firmament of the heaven to di-
vide the day from the night; and let
them be for signs, and for seasons, and
for days, and years:
15 And let them be for lights in the
firmament of the heaven to give light
upon the earth: and it was so.
16 And God made two great lights;
the greater light to rule the day, and the
lesser light to rule the night: *he made*
the stars also.
17 And God set them in the firma-
ment of the heaven to give light upon
the earth,
18 And to rule over the day and over
the night, and to divide the light from
the darkness: and God saw that *it was*
good.
19 And the evening and the morning
were the fourth day.
20 ¶And God said, Let the waters
bring forth abundantly the moving
creature that hath life, and fowl *that*
may fly above the earth in the open fir-
mament of heaven.
21 And God created great whales,
and every living creature that moveth,
which the waters brought forth abun-
dantly, after their kind, and every
winged fowl after his kind: and God
saw that *it was* good.
22 And God blessed them, saying, Be
fruitful, and multiply, and fill the waters
in the seas, and let fowl multiply in
the earth.
23 And the evening and the morning
were the fifth day.
24 ¶And God said, Let the earth bring
forth the living creature after his kind,
cattle, and creeping thing, and beast of
the earth after his kind: and it was so.
25 And God made the beast of the
earth after his kind, and cattle after
their kind, and every thing that creep-
eth upon the earth after his kind: and
God saw that *it was* good.
26 ¶And God said, Let us make man
in our image, after our likeness: and let
them have dominion over the fish of
the sea, and over the fowl of the air, and
over the cattle, and over all the earth,
and over every creeping thing that
creepeth upon the earth.
27 So God created man in his *own*
image, in the image of God created he
him; male and female created he them.
28 And God blessed them, and God
said unto them, Be fruitful, and mul-
tiply, and replenish the earth, and sub-
due it: and have dominion over the
fish of the sea, and over the fowl of the
air, and over every living thing that
moveth upon the earth.
29 ¶And God said, Behold, I have giv-
en you every herb bearing seed, which
is upon the face of all the earth, and
every tree, in the which *is* the fruit of a
tree yielding seed; to you it shall be for
meat.
30 And to every beast of the earth,
and to every fowl of the air, and to

every thing that creepeth upon the
earth, wherein *there is* life, *I have given*
every green herb for meat: and it was
so.
31 And God saw every thing that he
had made, and, behold, *it was* very
good. And the evening and the morning
were the sixth day.

CHAPTER 2

THUS the heavens and the earth were
finished, and all the host of them.
2 And on the seventh day God ended
his work which he had made; and he
rested on the seventh day from all his
work which he had made.
3 And God blessed the seventh day,
and sanctified it: because that in it he
had rested from all his work which God
created and made.
4 ¶These *are* the generations of the
heavens and of the earth when they
were created, in the day that the LORD
God made the earth and the heavens,
5 And every plant of the field before
it was in the earth, and every herb of
the field before it grew: for the LORD
God had not caused it to rain upon the
earth, and *there was* not a man to till
the ground.
6 But there went up a mist from the
earth, and watered the whole face of
the ground.
7 And the LORD God formed man *of*
the dust of the ground, and breathed
into his nostrils the breath of life; and
man became a living soul.
8 ¶And the LORD God planted a gar-
den eastward in Eden; and there he put
the man whom he had formed.
9 And out of the ground made the
LORD God to grow every tree that is
pleasant to the sight, and good for food;
the tree of life also in the midst of the
garden, and the tree of knowledge of
good and evil.
10 And a river went out of Eden to
water the garden; and from thence it
was parted, and became into four
heads.
11 The name of the first *is* Pī'sŏn: that
is it which compasseth the whole land
of Hăv'i-lah, where *there is* gold;
12 And the gold of that land *is* good:
there *is* bdellium and the onyx stone.
13 And the name of the second river
is Gī'hŏn: the same *is* it that compass-
eth the whole land of Ē-thĭ-ō'pĭ-a.
14 And the name of the third river *is*
Hĭd'de-kĕl: that *is* it which goeth to-
ward the east of Assyria. And the
fourth river *is* Eū-phrā'tēs.
15 And the LORD God took the man,
and put him into the garden of Eden to
dress it and to keep it.
16 And the LORD God commanded
the man, saying, Of every tree of the
garden thou mayest freely eat:
17 But of the tree of the knowledge of
good and evil, thou shalt not eat of it:
for in the day that thou eatest thereof
thou shalt surely die.
18 ¶And the LORD God said, *It is* not
good that the man should be alone; I
will make him an help meet for him.
19 And out of the ground the LORD
God formed every beast of the field,
and every fowl of the air; and brought
them unto Adam to see what he would
call them: and whatsoever Adam
called every living creature, that *was*
the name thereof.
20 And Adam gave names to all
cattle, and to the fowl of the air, and to
every beast of the field; but for Adam
there was not found an help meet for
him.
21 And the LORD God caused a deep
sleep to fall upon Adam, and he slept:
and he took one of his ribs, and closed
up the flesh instead thereof;
22 And the rib, which the LORD God
had taken from man, made he a wom-
an, and brought her unto the man.
23 And Adam said, This *is* now bone
of my bones, and flesh of my flesh: she
shall be called Woman, because she
was taken out of Man.
24 Therefore shall a man leave his
father and his mother, and shall cleave
unto his wife: and they shall be one
flesh.
25 And they were both naked, the
man and his wife, and were not
ashamed.

CHAPTER 3

NOW the serpent was more subtil than
any beast of the field which the LORD
God had made. And he said unto the
woman, Yea, hath God said, Ye shall
not eat of every tree of the garden?
2 And the woman said unto the ser-
pent, We may eat of the fruit of the
trees of the garden:
3 But of the fruit of the tree which *is*
in the midst of the garden, God hath
said, Ye shall not eat of it, neither shall
ye touch it, lest ye die.
4 And the serpent said unto the wom-
an, Ye shall not surely die:
5 For God doth know that in the day
ye eat thereof, then your eyes shall be
opened, and ye shall be as gods, know-
ing good and evil.
6 And when the woman saw that the
tree *was* good for food, and that it *was*
pleasant to the eyes, and a tree to be
desired to make *one* wise, she took of
the fruit thereof, and did eat, and gave

also unto her husband with her; and he did eat.

7 And the eyes of them both were opened, and they knew that they *were* naked; and they sewed fig leaves together, and made themselves aprons.

8 And they heard the voice of the LORD God walking in the garden in the cool of the day: and Adam and his wife hid themselves from the presence of the LORD God amongst the trees of the garden.

9 And the LORD God called unto Adam, and said unto him, Where *art* thou?

10 And he said, I heard thy voice in the garden, and I was afraid, because I *was* naked; and I hid myself.

11 And he said, Who told thee that thou *wast* naked? Hast thou eaten of the tree, whereof I commanded thee that thou shouldest not eat?

12 And the man said, The woman whom thou gavest *to be* with me, she gave me of the tree, and I did eat.

13 And the LORD God said unto the woman, What *is* this *that* thou hast done? And the woman said, The serpent beguiled me, and I did eat.

14 And the LORD God said unto the serpent, Because thou hast done this, thou *art* cursed above all cattle, and above every beast of the field; upon thy belly shalt thou go, and dust shalt thou eat all the days of thy life:

15 And I will put enmity between thee and the woman, and between thy seed and her seed; it shall bruise thy head, and thou shalt bruise his heel.

16 Unto the woman he said, I will greatly multiply thy sorrow and thy conception; in sorrow thou shalt bring forth children; and thy desire *shall be* to thy husband, and he shall rule over thee.

17 And unto Adam he said, Because thou hast hearkened unto the voice of thy wife, and hast eaten of the tree, of which I commanded thee, saying, Thou shalt not eat of it: cursed *is* the ground for thy sake; in sorrow shalt thou eat *of* it all the days of thy life;

18 Thorns also and thistles shall it bring forth to thee; and thou shalt eat the herb of the field;

19 In the sweat of thy face shalt thou eat bread, till thou return unto the ground; for out of it wast thou taken: for dust thou *art*, and unto dust shalt thou return.

20 And Adam called his wife's name Eve; because she was the mother of all living.

21 Unto Adam also and to his wife did the LORD God make coats of skins, and clothed them.

22 ¶And the LORD God said, Behold, the man is become as one of us, to know good and evil: and now, lest he put forth his hand, and take also of the tree of life, and eat, and live for ever:

23 Therefore the LORD God sent him forth from the garden of Eden, to till the ground from whence he was taken.

24 So he drove out the man; and he placed at the east of the garden of Eden Chĕr′u-bĭms, and a flaming sword which turned every way, to keep the way of the tree of life.

CHAPTER 4

AND Adam knew Eve his wife; and she conceived, and bare Cain, and said, I have gotten a man from the LORD.

2 And she again bare his brother Abel. And Abel was a keeper of sheep, but Cain was a tiller of the ground.

3 And in process of time it came to pass, that Cain brought of the fruit of the ground an offering unto the LORD.

4 And Abel, he also brought of the firstlings of his flock and of the fat thereof. And the LORD had respect unto Abel and to his offering:

5 But unto Cain and to his offering he had not respect. And Cain was very wroth, and his countenance fell.

6 And the LORD said unto Cain, Why art thou wroth? and why is thy countenance fallen?

7 If thou doest well, shalt thou not be accepted? and if thou doest not well, sin lieth at the door. And unto thee *shall be* his desire, and thou shalt rule over him.

8 And Cain talked with Abel his brother: and it came to pass, when they were in the field, that Cain rose up against Abel his brother, and slew him.

9 And the LORD said unto Cain, Where *is* Abel thy brother? And he said, I know not: *Am* I my brother's keeper?

10 And he said, What hast thou done? the voice of thy brother's blood crieth unto me from the ground.

11 And now *art* thou cursed from the earth, which hath opened her mouth to receive thy brother's blood from thy hand;

12 When thou tillest the ground, it shall not henceforth yield unto thee her strength; a fugitive and a vagabond shalt thou be in the earth.

13 And Cain said unto the LORD, My punishment *is* greater than I can bear.

14 Behold, thou hast driven me out this day from the face of the earth; and from thy face shall I be hid; and I shall

be a fugitive and a vagabond in the earth; and it shall come to pass, *that* every one that findeth me shall slay me.

15 And the LORD said unto him, Therefore whosoever slayeth Cain, vengeance shall be taken on him sevenfold. And the LORD set a mark upon Cain, lest any finding him should kill him.

16 ¶And Cain went out from the presence of the LORD, and dwelt in the land of Nod, on the east of Eden.

17 And Cain knew his wife; and she conceived, and bare Ē′noch: and he builded a city, and called the name of the city, after the name of his son, Ē′noch.

18 And unto Ē′noch was born Ī′răd: and Ī′răd begat Me-hū′ja-el: and Me-hū′ja-el begat Me-thū′sa-el: and Me-thū′sa-el begat Lā′mech.

19 ¶And Lā′mech took unto him two wives: the name of the one *was* Adah, and the name of the other Zĭl′lah.

20 And Adah bare Jā′bal: he was the father of such as dwell in tents, and *of such as have* cattle.

21 And his brother's name *was* Jū′bal: he was the father of all such as handle the harp and organ.

22 And Zĭl′lah, she also bare Tū′bal–cāin, an instructer of every artificer in brass and iron: and the sister of Tū′bal–cāin *was* Nā′a-mah.

23 And Lā′mech said unto his wives, Adah and Zĭl′lah, Hear my voice; ye wives of Lā′mech, hearken unto my speech: for I have slain a man to my wounding, and a young man to my hurt.

24 If Cain shall be avenged sevenfold, truly Lā′mech seventy and sevenfold.

25 ¶And Adam knew his wife again; and she bare a son, and called his name Seth: For God, *said she,* hath appointed me another seed instead of Abel, whom Cain slew.

26 And to Seth, to him also there was born a son; and he called his name Enos: then began men to call upon the name of the LORD.

CHAPTER 5

THIS *is* the book of the generations of Adam. In the day that God created man, in the likeness of God made he him;

2 Male and female created he them; and blessed them, and called their name Adam, in the day when they were created.

3 ¶And Adam lived an hundred and thirty years, and begat *a son* in his own likeness, after his image; and called his name Seth:

4 And the days of Adam after he had begotten Seth were eight hundred years: and he begat sons and daughters:

5 And all the days that Adam lived were nine hundred and thirty years: and he died.

6 ¶And Seth lived an hundred and five years, and begat Enos:

7 And Seth lived after he begat Enos eight hundred and seven years, and begat sons and daughters:

8 And all the days of Seth were nine hundred and twelve years: and he died.

9 ¶And Enos lived ninety years, and begat Cā-i′nan:

10 And Enos lived after he begat Cā-i′nan eight hundred and fifteen years, and begat sons and daughters:

11 And all the days of Enos were nine hundred and five years: and he died.

12 ¶And Cā-i′nan lived seventy years, and begat Ma-hă′la-le-el:

13 And Cā-i′nan lived after he begat Ma-hă′la-le-el eight hundred and forty years, and begat sons and daughters:

14 And all the days of Cā-i′nan were nine hundred and ten years: and he died.

15 ¶And Ma-hă′la-le-el lived sixty and five years, and begat Jâ′red:

16 And Ma-hă′la-le-el lived after he begat Jâ′red eight hundred and thirty years, and begat sons and daughters:

17 And all the days of Ma-hă′la-le-el were eight hundred ninety and five years: and he died.

18 ¶And Jâ′red lived an hundred sixty and two years, and he begat Ē′noch:

19 And Jâ′red lived after he begat Ē′noch eight hundred years, and begat sons and daughters:

20 And all the days of Jâ′red were nine hundred sixty and two years: and he died.

21 ¶And Ē′noch lived sixty and five years, and begat Me-thū′se-lah:

22 And Ē′noch walked with God after he begat Me-thū′se-lah three hundred years, and begat sons and daughters:

23 And all the days of Ē′noch were three hundred sixty and five years:

24 And Ē′noch walked with God: and he *was* not; for God took him.

25 ¶And Me-thū′se-lah lived an hundred eighty and seven years, and begat Lā′mech:

26 And Me-thū′se-lah lived after he begat Lā′mech seven hundred eighty and two years, and begat sons and daughters:

27 And all the days of Me-thū′se-lah were nine hundred sixty and nine years: and he died.

28 ¶And Lā′mech lived an hundred eighty and two years, and begat a son:

29 And he called his name Noah, saying, This *same* shall comfort us concerning our work and toil of our hands, because of the ground which the LORD hath cursed.

30 And Lā′mech lived after he begat Noah five hundred ninety and five years, and begat sons and daughters:

31 And all the days of Lā′mech were seven hundred seventy and seven years: and he died.

32 ¶And Noah was five hundred years old: and Noah begat Shem, Ham, and Jā′pheth.

CHAPTER 6

AND it came to pass, when men began to multiply on the face of the earth, and daughters were born unto them,

2 That the sons of God saw the daughters of men that they *were* fair; and they took them wives of all which they chose.

3 And the LORD said, My spirit shall not always strive with man, for that he also *is* flesh: yet his days shall be an hundred and twenty years.

4 There were giants in the earth in those days; and also after that, when the sons of God came in unto the daughters of men, and they bare *children* to them, the same *became* mighty men which *were* of old, men of renown.

5 ¶And God saw that the wickedness of man *was* great in the earth, and *that* every imagination of the thoughts of his heart *was* only evil continually.

6 And it repented the LORD that he had made man on the earth, and it grieved him at his heart.

7 And the LORD said, I will destroy man whom I have created from the face of the earth; both man, and beast, and the creeping thing, and the fowls of the air; for it repenteth me that I have made them.

8 But Noah found grace in the eyes of the LORD.

9 ¶These *are* the generations of Noah: Noah was a just man *and* perfect in his generations, *and* Noah walked with God.

10 And Noah begat three sons, Shem, Ham, and Jā′pheth.

11 The earth also was corrupt before God, and the earth was filled with violence.

12 And God looked upon the earth, and, behold, it was corrupt; for all flesh had corrupted his way upon the earth.

13 And God said unto Noah, The end of all flesh is come before me; for the earth is filled with violence through them; and, behold, I will destroy them with the earth.

14 Make thee an ark of gopher wood; rooms shalt thou make in the ark, and shalt pitch it within and without with pitch.

15 And this *is the fashion* which thou shalt make it *of*: The length of the ark *shall be* three hundred cubits, the breadth of it fifty cubits, and the height of it thirty cubits.

16 A window shalt thou make to the ark, and in a cubit shalt thou finish it above; and the door of the ark shalt thou set in the side thereof; *with* lower, second, and third *stories* shalt thou make it.

17 And, behold, I, even I, do bring a flood of waters upon the earth, to destroy all flesh, wherein *is* the breath of life, from under heaven; *and* every thing that *is* in the earth shall die.

18 But with thee will I establish my covenant; and thou shalt come into the ark, thou, and thy sons, and thy wife, and thy sons' wives with thee.

19 And of every living thing of all flesh, two of every *sort* shalt thou bring into the ark, to keep *them* alive with thee; they shall be male and female.

20 Of fowls after their kind, and of cattle after their kind, of every creeping thing of the earth after his kind, two of every *sort* shall come unto thee, to keep *them* alive.

21 And take thou unto thee of all food that is eaten, and thou shalt gather *it* to thee; and it shall be for food for thee, and for them.

22 Thus did Noah; according to all that God commanded him, so did he.

CHAPTER 7

AND the LORD said unto Noah, Come thou and all thy house into the ark; for thee have I seen righteous before me in this generation.

2 Of every clean beast thou shalt take to thee by sevens, the male and his female: and of beasts that *are* not clean by two, the male and his female.

3 Of fowls also of the air by sevens, the male and the female; to keep seed alive upon the face of all the earth.

4 For yet seven days, and I will cause it to rain upon the earth forty days and forty nights; and every living substance that I have made will I destroy from off the face of the earth.

5 And Noah did according unto all that the LORD commanded him.

6 And Noah *was* six hundred years old when the flood of waters was upon the earth.

7 And Noah went in, and his sons,

and his wife, and his sons' wives with him, into the ark, because of the waters of the flood.

8 Of clean beasts, and of beasts that *are* not clean, and of fowls, and of every thing that creepeth upon the earth,

9 There went in two and two unto Noah into the ark, the male and the female, as God had commanded Noah.

10 And it came to pass after seven days, that the waters of the flood were upon the earth.

11 In the six hundredth year of Noah's life, in the second month, the seventeenth day of the month, the same day were all the fountains of the great deep broken up, and the windows of heaven were opened.

12 And the rain was upon the earth forty days and forty nights.

13 In the selfsame day entered Noah, and Shem, and Ham, and Jā'pheth, the sons of Noah, and Noah's wife, and the three wives of his sons with them, into the ark;

14 They, and every beast after his kind, and all the cattle after their kind, and every creeping thing that creepeth upon the earth after his kind, and every fowl after his kind, every bird of every sort.

15 And they went in unto Noah into the ark, two and two of all flesh, wherein *is* the breath of life.

16 And they that went in, went in male and female of all flesh, as God had commanded him: and the LORD shut him in.

17 And the flood was forty days upon the earth; and the waters increased, and bare up the ark, and it was lift up above the earth.

18 And the waters prevailed, and were increased greatly upon the earth; and the ark went upon the face of the waters.

19 And the waters prevailed exceedingly upon the earth; and all the high hills, that *were* under the whole heaven, were covered.

20 Fifteen cubits upward did the waters prevail; and the mountains were covered.

21 And all flesh died that moved upon the earth, both of fowl, and of cattle, and of beast, and of every creeping thing that creepeth upon the earth, and every man:

22 All in whose nostrils *was* the breath of life, of all that *was* in the dry *land*, died.

23 And every living substance was destroyed which was upon the face of the ground, both man, and cattle, and the creeping things, and the fowl of the heaven; and they were destroyed from the earth: and Noah only remained *alive*, and they that *were* with him in the ark.

24 And the waters prevailed upon the earth an hundred and fifty days.

CHAPTER 8

AND God remembered Noah, and every living thing, and all the cattle that *was* with him in the ark: and God made a wind to pass over the earth, and the waters asswaged;

2 The fountains also of the deep and the windows of heaven were stopped, and the rain from heaven was restrained;

3 And the waters returned from off the earth continually: and after the end of the hundred and fifty days the waters were abated.

4 And the ark rested in the seventh month, on the seventeenth day of the month, upon the mountains of Ăr'a-răt.

5 And the waters decreased continually until the tenth month: in the tenth *month*, on the first *day* of the month, were the tops of the mountains seen.

6 ¶And it came to pass at the end of forty days, that Noah opened the window of the ark which he had made:

7 And he sent forth a raven, which went forth to and fro, until the waters were dried up from off the earth.

8 Also he sent forth a dove from him, to see if the waters were abated from off the face of the ground;

9 But the dove found no rest for the sole of her foot, and she returned unto him into the ark, for the waters *were* on the face of the whole earth: then he put forth his hand, and took her, and pulled her in unto him into the ark.

10 And he stayed yet other seven days; and again he sent forth the dove out of the ark;

11 And the dove came in to him in the evening; and, lo, in her mouth *was* an olive leaf pluckt off: so Noah knew that the waters were abated from off the earth.

12 And he stayed yet other seven days; and sent forth the dove; which returned not again unto him any more.

13 ¶And it came to pass in the six hundredth and first year, in the first *month*, the first *day* of the month, the waters were dried up from off the earth: and Noah removed the covering of the ark, and looked, and, behold, the face of the ground was dry.

14 And in the second month, on the seven and twentieth day of the month, was the earth dried.

15 ¶And God spake unto Noah,
saying,
16 Go forth of the ark, thou, and thy
wife, and thy sons, and thy sons' wives
with thee.
17 Bring forth with thee every living
thing that *is* with thee, of all flesh, *both*
of fowl, and of cattle, and of every
creeping thing that creepeth upon the
earth; that they may breed abundantly
in the earth, and be fruitful, and mul-
tiply upon the earth.
18 And Noah went forth, and his
sons, and his wife, and his sons' wives
with him:
19 Every beast, every creeping thing,
and every fowl, *and* whatsoever creep-
eth upon the earth, after their kinds,
went forth out of the ark.
20 ¶And Noah builded an altar unto
the LORD; and took of every clean beast,
and of every clean fowl, and offered
burnt offerings on the altar.
21 And the LORD smelled a sweet sa-
vour; and the LORD said in his heart, I
will not again curse the ground any
more for man's sake; for the imagina-
tion of man's heart *is* evil from his
youth; neither will I again smite any
more every thing living, as I have done.
22 While the earth remaineth, seed-
time and harvest, and cold and heat,
and summer and winter, and day and
night shall not cease.

CHAPTER 9

AND God blessed Noah and his sons,
and said unto them, Be fruitful, and
multiply, and replenish the earth.
2 And the fear of you and the dread of
you shall be upon every beast of the
earth, and upon every fowl of the air,
upon all that moveth *upon* the earth,
and upon all the fishes of the sea; into
your hand are they delivered.
3 Every moving thing that liveth shall
be meat for you; even as the green herb
have I given you all things.
4 But flesh with the life thereof,
which is the blood thereof, shall ye not
eat.
5 And surely your blood of your lives
will I require; at the hand of every beast
will I require it, and at the hand of man;
at the hand of every man's brother will
I require the life of man.
6 Whoso sheddeth man's blood, by
man shall his blood be shed: for in the
image of God made he man.
7 And you, be ye fruitful, and mul-
tiply; bring forth abundantly in the
earth, and multiply therein.
8 ¶And God spake unto Noah, and to
his sons with him, saying,
9 And I, behold, I establish my cov-
enant with you, and with your seed after
you;
10 And with every living creature
that *is* with you, of the fowl, of the
cattle, and of every beast of the earth
with you; from all that go out of the ark,
to every beast of the earth.
11 And I will establish my covenant
with you; neither shall all flesh be cut
off any more by the waters of a flood;
neither shall there any more be a flood
to destroy the earth.
12 And God said, This *is* the token of
the covenant which I make between
me and you and every living creature
that *is* with you, for perpetual genera-
tions:
13 I do set my bow in the cloud, and it
shall be for a token of a covenant be-
tween me and the earth.
14 And it shall come to pass, when I
bring a cloud over the earth, that the
bow shall be seen in the cloud:
15 And I will remember my covenant,
which *is* between me and you and
every living creature of all flesh; and
the waters shall no more become a
flood to destroy all flesh.
16 And the bow shall be in the cloud;
and I will look upon it, that I may
remember the everlasting covenant
between God and every living creature
of all flesh that *is* upon the earth.
17 And God said unto Noah, This *is*
the token of the covenant, which I have
established between me and all flesh
that *is* upon the earth.
18 ¶And the sons of Noah, that went
forth of the ark, were Shem, and Ham,
and Jā'pheth: and Ham *is* the father of
Canaan.
19 These *are* the three sons of Noah:
and of them was the whole earth over-
spread.
20 ¶And Noah began *to be* an husband-
man, and he planted a vineyard:
21 And he drank of the wine, and was
drunken; and he was uncovered within
his tent.
22 And Ham, the father of Canaan,
saw the nakedness of his father, and
told his two brethren without.
23 And Shem and Jā'pheth took a
garment, and laid *it* upon both their
shoulders, and went backward, and
covered the nakedness of their father;
and their faces *were* backward, and
they saw not their father's nakedness.
24 And Noah awoke from his wine,
and knew what his younger son had
done unto him.
25 And he said, Cursed *be* Canaan; a
servant of servants shall he be unto his
brethren.
26 And he said, Blessed *be* the LORD

God of Shem; and Canaan shall be his servant.

27 God shall enlarge Jā'pheth, and he shall dwell in the tents of Shem; and Canaan shall be his servant.

28 And Noah lived after the flood three hundred and fifty years.

29 And all the days of Noah were nine hundred and fifty years: and he died.

CHAPTER 10

NOW these *are* the generations of the sons of Noah, Shem, Ham, and Jā'pheth: and unto them were sons born after the flood.

2 The sons of Jā'pheth; Gō'mer, and Mā'gŏg, and Mād'a-ī, and Jā'van, and Tū'bal, and Mē'shĕch, and Tī'ras.

3 And the sons of Gō'mer; Ăsh'ke-năz, and Rī'phăth, and Tō-gär'mah.

4 And the sons of Jā'van; E-lī'shah, and Tarshish, Kittim, and Dō'da-nĭm.

5 By these were the isles of the Gentiles divided in their lands; every one after his tongue, after their families, in their nations.

6 ¶And the sons of Ham; Cush, and Mĭz'ra-im, and Phut, and Canaan.

7 And the sons of Cush; Sē'ba, and Hăv'i-lah, and Săb'tah, and Rā'a-mah, and Săb'te-chah:and the sons of Rā'a-mah; Shē'ba, and Dē'dan.

8 And Cush begat Nimrod: he began to be a mighty one in the earth.

9 He was a mighty hunter before the LORD: wherefore it is said, Even as Nimrod the mighty hunter before the LORD.

10 And the beginning of his kingdom was Babel, and E'rĕch, and Ăc'căd, and Căl'nĕh, in the land of Shī'när.

11 Out of that land went forth Asshur, and builded Nĭn'e-veh, and the city Re-hō'bŏth, and Cā'lah,

12 And Rē'sen between Nĭn'e-veh and Cā'lah: the same *is* a great city.

13 And Mĭz'ra-im begat Lū'dim, and Ăn'a-mĭm, and Le'hā-bĭm, and Năph'tu-hĭm,

14 And Path-rū'sĭm, and Căs'lu-hĭm, (out of whom came Phĭ-lĭs'tĭm,) and Căph'to-rĭm.

15 ¶And Canaan begat Sī'don his firstborn, and Heth,

16 And the Jēb'u-sīte, and the Ăm'or-īte, and the Gir'ga-sīte,

17 And the Hī'vīte, and the Ärk'īte, and the Sĭn'īte,

18 And the Är'vad-īte, and the Zĕm'a-rīte, and the Hā'math-īte: and afterward were the families of the Canaanites spread abroad.

19 And the border of the Canaanites was from Sī'don, as thou comest to Ge'rär, unto Gā'za; as thou goest, unto Sodom, and Go-mor'rah, and Ăd'mah, and Ze-bō'im, even unto Lā'sha.

20 These *are* the sons of Ham, after their families, after their tongues, in their countries, *and* in their nations.

21 ¶Unto Shem also, the father of all the children of Ē'ber, the brother of Jā'pheth the elder, even to him were *children* born.

22 The children of Shem; Ē'lam, and Asshur, and Är-phăx'ăd, and Lud, and Â'ram.

23 And the children of Â'ram; Uz, and Hul, and Gē'ther, and Mash.

24 And Är-phăx'ăd begat Sā'lah; and Sā'lah begat Ē'ber.

25 And unto Ē'ber were born two sons: the name of one *was* Pē'lĕg; for in his days was the earth divided; and his brother's name *was* Jŏk'tăn.

26 And Jŏk'tăn begat Ăl-mō'dăd, and Shē'leph, and Hā-zar-mā'veth, and Je'rah,

27 And Ha-dō'ram, and Ū'zal, and Dĭk'lah,

28 And Ō'bal, and A-bĭm'a-el, and Shē'ba,

29 And Ō'phir, and Hăv'i-lah, and Jō'băb: all these *were* the sons of Jŏk'tăn.

30 And their dwelling was from Mē'sha, as thou goest unto Sĕ'phar a mount of the east.

31 These *are* the sons of Shem, after their families, after their tongues, in their lands, after their nations.

32 These *are* the families of the sons of Noah, after their generations, in their nations: and by these were the nations divided in the earth after the flood.

CHAPTER 11

AND the whole earth was of one language, and of one speech.

2 And it came to pass, as they journeyed from the east, that they found a plain in the land of Shī'när; and they dwelt there.

3 And they said one to another, Go to, let us make brick, and burn them throughly. And they had brick for stone, and slime had they for morter.

4 And they said, Go to, let us build us a city and a tower, whose top *may reach* unto heaven; and let us make us a name, lest we be scattered abroad upon the face of the whole earth.

5 And the LORD came down to see the city and the tower, which the children of men builded.

6 And the LORD said, Behold, the people *is* one, and they have all one language; and this they begin to do: and now nothing will be restrained from them, which they have imagined to do.

7 Go to, let us go down, and there confound their language, that they may not understand one another's speech.

8 So the LORD scattered them abroad from thence upon the face of all the earth: and they left off to build the city.

9 Therefore is the name of it called Babel; because the LORD did there confound the language of all the earth: and from thence did the LORD scatter them abroad upon the face of all the earth.

10 ¶These *are* the generations of Shem: Shem *was* an hundred years old, and begat Är-phăx'ăd two years after the flood:

11 And Shem lived after he begat Är-phăx'ăd five hundred years, and begat sons and daughters.

12 And Är-phăx'ăd lived five and thirty years, and begat Sā'lah:

13 And Är-phăx'ăd lived after he begat Sā'lah four hundred and three years, and begat sons and daughters.

14 And Sā'lah lived thirty years, and begat Ē'ber:

15 And Sā'lah lived after he begat Ē'ber four hundred and three years, and begat sons and daughters.

16 And Ē'ber lived four and thirty years, and begat Pē'lĕg:

17 And Ē'ber lived after he begat Pē'lĕg four hundred and thirty years, and begat sons and daughters.

18 And Pē'lĕg lived thirty years, and begat Rē'ū:

19 And Pē'lĕg lived after he begat Rē'ū two hundred and nine years, and begat sons and daughters.

20 And Rē'ū lived two and thirty years, and begat Se'rŭg:

21 And Rē'ū lived after he begat Se'rŭg two hundred and seven years, and begat sons and daughters.

22 And Se'rŭg lived thirty years, and begat Nahor:

23 And Se'rŭg lived after he begat Nahor two hundred years, and begat sons and daughters.

24 And Nahor lived nine and twenty years, and begat Te'rah:

25 And Nahor lived after he begat Te'rah an hundred and nineteen years, and begat sons and daughters.

26 And Te'rah lived seventy years, and begat Abram, Nahor, and Hâ'ran.

27 ¶Now these *are* the generations of Te'rah: Te'rah begat Abram, Nahor, and Hâ'ran; and Hâ'ran begat Lot.

28 And Hâ'ran died before his father Te'rah in the land of his nativity, in Ur of the Chăl'deeṡ.

29 And Abram and Nahor took them wives: the name of Abram's wife *was* Sâ'raī; and the name of Nahor's wife, Mĭl'cah, the daughter of Hâ'ran, the father of Mĭl'cah, and the father of Ĭs'cah.

30 But Sâ'raī was barren; she *had* no child.

31 And Te'rah took Abram his son, and Lot the son of Hâ'ran his son's son, and Sâ'raī his daughter in law, his son Abram's wife; and they went forth with them from Ur of the Chăl'deeṡ, to go into the land of Canaan; and they came unto Hâ'ran, and dwelt there.

32 And the days of Te'rah were two hundred and five years: and Te'rah died in Hâ'ran.

CHAPTER 12

NOW the LORD had said unto Abram, Get thee out of thy country, and from thy kindred, and from thy father's house, unto a land that I will shew thee:

2 And I will make of thee a great nation, and I will bless thee, and make thy name great; and thou shalt be a blessing:

3 And I will bless them that bless thee, and curse him that curseth thee: and in thee shall all families of the earth be blessed.

4 So Abram departed, as the LORD had spoken unto him; and Lot went with him: and Abram *was* seventy and five years old when he departed out of Hâ'ran.

5 And Abram took Sâ'raī his wife, and Lot his brother's son, and all their substance that they had gathered, and the souls that they had gotten in Hâ'ran; and they went forth to go into the land of Canaan; and into the land of Canaan they came.

6 ¶And Abram passed through the land unto the place of Sī'chem, unto the plain of Mô'reh. And the Canaanite *was* then in the land.

7 And the LORD appeared unto Abram, and said, Unto thy seed will I give this land: and there builded he an altar unto the LORD, who appeared unto him.

8 And he removed from thence unto a mountain on the east of Bĕth-el, and pitched his tent, *having* Bĕth-el on the west, and Hā'ī on the east: and there he builded an altar unto the LORD, and called upon the name of the LORD.

9 And Abram journeyed, going on still toward the south.

10 ¶And there was a famine in the land: and Abram went down into Egypt to sojourn there; for the famine *was* grievous in the land.

11 And it came to pass, when he was come near to enter into Egypt, that he said unto Sâ'raī his wife, Behold now, I

know that thou *art* a fair woman to look upon:

12 Therefore it shall come to pass, when the Egyptians shall see thee, that they shall say, This *is* his wife: and they will kill me, but they will save thee alive.

13 Say, I pray thee, thou *art* my sister: that it may be well with me for thy sake; and my soul shall live because of thee.

14 ¶And it came to pass, that, when Abram was come into Egypt, the Egyptians beheld the woman that she *was* very fair.

15 The princes also of Pharaoh saw her, and commended her before Pharaoh: and the woman was taken into Pharaoh's house.

16 And he entreated Abram well for her sake: and he had sheep, and oxen, and he asses, and menservants, and maidservants, and she asses, and camels.

17 And the LORD plagued Pharaoh and his house with great plagues because of Sâ'raī Abram's wife.

18 And Pharaoh called Abram, and said, What *is* this *that* thou hast done unto me? why didst thou not tell me that she *was* thy wife?

19 Why saidst thou, She *is* my sister? so I might have taken her to me to wife: now therefore behold thy wife, take *her*, and go thy way.

20 And Pharaoh commanded *his* men concerning him: and they sent him away, and his wife, and all that he had.

CHAPTER 13

AND Abram went up out of Egypt, he, and his wife, and all that he had, and Lot with him, into the south.

2 And Abram *was* very rich in cattle, in silver, and in gold.

3 And he went on his journeys from the south even to Bĕth-el, unto the place where his tent had been at the beginning, between Bĕth-el and Hā'ī;

4 Unto the place of the altar, which he had made there at the first: and there Abram called on the name of the LORD.

5 ¶And Lot also, which went with Abram, had flocks, and herds, and tents.

6 And the land was not able to bear them, that they might dwell together: for their substance was great, so that they could not dwell together.

7 And there was a strife between the herdmen of Abram's cattle and the herdmen of Lot's cattle: and the Canaanite and the Pĕr'izz-īte dwelled then in the land.

8 And Abram said unto Lot, Let there be no strife, I pray thee, between me and thee, and between my herdmen and thy herdmen; for we *be* brethren.

9 *Is* not the whole land before thee? separate thyself, I pray thee, from me: if *thou wilt take* the left hand, then I will go to the right; or if *thou depart* to the right hand, then I will go to the left.

10 And Lot lifted up his eyes, and beheld all the plain of Jordan, that it *was* well watered every where, before the LORD destroyed Sodom and Go-mŏr'rah, *even* as the garden of the LORD, like the land of Egypt, as thou comest unto Zō'ar.

11 Then Lot chose him all the plain of Jordan; and Lot journeyed east: and they separated themselves the one from the other.

12 Abram dwelled in the land of Canaan, and Lot dwelled in the cities of the plain, and pitched *his* tent toward Sodom.

13 But the men of Sodom *were* wicked and sinners before the LORD exceedingly.

14 ¶And the LORD said unto Abram, after that Lot was separated from him, Lift up now thine eyes, and look from the place where thou art northward, and southward, and eastward, and westward:

15 For all the land which thou seest, to thee will I give it, and to thy seed for ever.

16 And I will make thy seed as the dust of the earth: so that if a man can number the dust of the earth, *then* shall thy seed also be numbered.

17 Arise, walk through the land in the length of it and in the breadth of it; for I will give it unto thee.

18 Then Abram removed *his* tent, and came and dwelt in the plain of Măm're, which *is* in Hē'bron, and built there an altar unto the LORD.

CHAPTER 14

AND it came to pass in the days of Ăm'ra-phĕl king of Shī'năr, Â'rī-ŏch king of Ĕl'la-săr, Chĕd-or-lā'ō-mer king of Ē'lam, and Tī'dal king of nations;

2 *That these* made war with Be'ra king of Sodom, and with Bir'sha king of Go-mŏr'rah, Shī'-năb king of Ăd'mah, and Shĕm-ē'ber king of Ze-boi'im, and the king of Bē'la, which is Zō'ar.

3 All these were joined together in the vale of Sĭd'dĭm, which is the salt sea.

4 Twelve years they served Chĕd-or-lā'ō-mer, and in the thirteenth year they rebelled.

5 And in the fourteenth year came Chĕd-or-lā'ō-mer, and the kings that

were with him, and smote the Rĕph′a-
imṡ in Ăsh′te-rŏth Kär-nā′im, and the
Zū′zĭmṡ in Ham, and the Ē′mĭmṡ in
Shā′veh Kĭr-ĭ-a-thā′im,
6 And the Hô′rītes in their mount
Sē′ir, unto Ēl-pâ′ran, which *is* by the
wilderness.
7 And they returned, and came to Ĕn-
mĭsh′păt, which *is* Kā′desh, and smote
all the country of the Am′ă-lek-ītes,
and also the Ămorītes, that dwelt in
Hăz′e-zŏn-tā′mar.
8 And there went out the king of Sod-
om, and the king of Go-mŏr′rah, and
the king of Ăd′mah, and the king of Ze-
boi′im, and the king of Bē′la (the same
is Zō′ar;) and they joined battle with
them in the vale of Sĭd′dĭm;
9 With Chĕd-or-lā′ō-mer the king of
Ē′lam, and with Tī′dal king of nations,
and Ăm′ra-phĕl king of Shī′när, and Â′-
rĭ-ŏch king of Ĕl′la-sär; four kings with
five.
10 And the vale of Sĭd′dĭm *was full of*
slimepits; and the kings of Sodom and
Go-mŏr′rah fled, and fell there; and
they that remained fled to the moun-
tain.
11 And they took all the goods of Sod-
om and Go-mŏr′rah, and all their vic-
tuals, and went their way.
12 And they took Lot, Abram's broth-
er's son, who dwelt in Sodom, and his
goods, and departed.
13 ¶And there came one that had es-
caped, and told Abram the Hebrew; for
he dwelt in the plain of Măm′re the
Ămorīte, brother of Ĕsh′cōl, and
brother of Aner: and these *were* con-
federate with Abram.
14 And when Abram heard that his
brother was taken captive, he armed
his trained *servants*, born in his own
house, three hundred and eighteen, and
pursued *them* unto Dan.
15 And he divided himself against
them, he and his servants, by night, and
smote them, and pursued them unto
Hō′bah, which *is* on the left hand of Da-
mascus.
16 And he brought back all the goods,
and also brought again his brother Lot,
and his goods, and the women also, and
the people.
17 ¶And the king of Sodom went out
to meet him after his return from the
slaughter of Chĕd-or-lā′ō-mer, and of
the kings that *were* with him, at the val-
ley of Shā′veh, which *is* the king's dale.
18 And Mĕl-chĭz′e-dĕk king of Salem
brought forth bread and wine: and he
was the priest of the most high God.
19 And he blessed him, and said,
Blessed *be* Abram of the most high
God, possessor of heaven and earth:
20 And blessed be the most high God,
which hath delivered thine enemies
into thy hand. And he gave him tithes
of all.
21 And the king of Sodom said unto
Abram, Give me the persons, and take
the goods to thyself.
22 And Abram said to the king of Sod-
om, I have lift up mine hand unto the
LORD, the most high God, the possessor
of heaven and earth,
23 That I will not *take* from a thread
even to a shoelatchet, and that I will not
take any thing that *is* thine, lest thou
shouldest say, I have made Abram rich:
24 Save only that which the young
men have eaten, and the portion of the
men which went with me, Aner, Ĕsh′-
cōl, and Măm′re; let them take their
portion.

CHAPTER 15

AFTER these things the word of the
LORD came unto Abram in a vision,
saying, Fear not, Abram: I *am* thy
shield, *and* thy exceeding great reward.
2 And Abram said, Lord GOD, what
wilt thou give me, seeing I go childless,
and the steward of my house *is* this Ĕ-lĭ-
ē′zer of Damascus?
3 And Abram said, Behold, to me
thou hast given no seed: and, lo, one
born in my house is mine heir.
4 And, behold, the word of the LORD
came unto him, saying, This shall not
be thine heir; but he that shall come
forth out of thine own bowels shall be
thine heir.
5 And he brought him forth abroad,
and said, Look now toward heaven,
and tell the stars, if thou be able to
number them: and he said unto him, So
shall thy seed be.
6 And he believed in the LORD; and he
counted it to him for righteousness.
7 And he said unto him, I *am* the LORD
that brought thee out of Ur of the Chăl′-
deeṡ, to give thee this land to inherit it.
8 And he said, Lord GOD, whereby
shall I know that I shall inherit it?
9 And he said unto him, Take me an
heifer of three years old, and a she goat
of three years old, and a ram of three
years old, and a turtledove, and a
young pigeon.
10 And he took unto him all these,
and divided them in the midst, and laid
each piece one against another: but the
birds divided he not.
11 And when the fowls came down
upon the carcases, Abram drove them
away.
12 And when the sun was going
down, a deep sleep fell upon Abram;

and, lo, an horror of great darkness fell
upon him.
13 And he said unto Abram, Know of
a surety that thy seed shall be a stranger
in a land *that is* not theirs, and shall
serve them; and they shall afflict them
four hundred years;
14 And also that nation, whom they
shall serve, will I judge: and afterward
shall they come out with great sub-
stance.
15 And thou shalt go to thy fathers in
peace; thou shalt be buried in a good
old age.
16 But in the fourth generation they
shall come hither again: for the iniquity
of the Ămorītes *is* not yet full.
17 And it came to pass, that, when
the sun went down, and it was dark, be-
hold a smoking furnace, and a burning
lamp that passed between those pieces.
18 In the same day the LORD made a
covenant with Abram, saying, Unto thy
seed have I given this land, from the
river of Egypt unto the great river, the
river Eū-phrā'tēṡ:
19 The Kēn'ītes, and the Kĕn'iz-zītes,
and the Kăd'mon-ītes,
20 And the Hittites, and the Pĕr'iz-
zītes, and the Rĕph'a-imṡ,
21 And the Ămorītes, and the Canaan-
ites, and the Gir'ga-shītes, and the
Jēb'u-sītes.

CHAPTER 16

NOW Sâ'raī Abram's wife bare him no
children: and she had an handmaid, an
Egyptian, whose name *was* Hā'gär.
2 And Sâ'raī said unto Abram, Be-
hold now, the LORD hath restrained me
from bearing: I pray thee, go in unto my
maid; it may be that I may obtain chil-
dren by her. And Abram hearkened to
the voice of Sâ'raī.
3 And Sâ'raī Abram's wife took Hā'-
gär her maid the Egyptian, after Abram
had dwelt ten years in the land of Ca-
naan, and gave her to her husband
Abram to be his wife.
4 And he went in unto Hā'gär, and
she conceived: and when she saw that
she had conceived, her mistress was
despised in her eyes.
5 And Sâ'raī said unto Abram, My
wrong *be* upon thee: I have given my
maid into thy bosom; and when she
saw that she had conceived, I was de-
spised in her eyes: the LORD judge be-
tween me and thee.
6 But Abram said unto Sâ'raī, Behold,
thy maid *is* in thy hand; do to her as it
pleaseth thee. And when Sâ'raī dealt
hardly with her, she fled from her face.
7 ¶And the angel of the LORD found
her by a fountain of water in the wilder-
ness, by the fountain in the way to
Shur.
8 And he said, Hā'gär, Sâ'raī's maid,
whence camest thou? and whither wilt
thou go? And she said, I flee from the
face of my mistress Sâ'raī.
9 And the angel of the LORD said unto
her, Return to thy mistress, and submit
thyself under her hands.
10 And the angel of the LORD said
unto her, I will multiply thy seed ex-
ceedingly, that it shall not be numbered
for multitude.
11 And the angel of the LORD said
unto her, Behold, thou *art* with child,
and shalt bear a son, and shalt call his
name Īsh'ma-el; because the LORD hath
heard thy affliction.
12 And he will be a wild man; his
hand *will be* against every man, and
every man's hand against him; and he
shall dwell in the presence of all his
brethren.
13 And she called the name of the
LORD that spake unto her, Thou God
seest me: for she said, Have I also here
looked after him that seeth me?
14 Wherefore the well was called
Be'er-la-haī'-roi; behold, *it is* between
Kā'desh and Be'rĕd.
15 And Hā'gär bare Abram a son: and
Abram called his son's name, which
Hā'gär bare, Īsh'ma-el.
16 And Abram *was* fourscore and six
years old, when Hā'gär bare Īsh'ma-el
to Abram.

CHAPTER 17

AND when Abram was ninety years
old and nine, the LORD appeared to
Abram, and said unto him, I *am* the Al-
mighty God; walk before me, and be
thou perfect.
2 And I will make my covenant be-
tween me and thee, and will multiply
thee exceedingly.
3 And Abram fell on his face: and
God talked with him, saying,
4 As for me, behold, my covenant *is*
with thee, and thou shalt be a father of
many nations.
5 Neither shall thy name any more be
called Abram, but thy name shall be
Abraham; for a father of many nations
have I made thee.
6 And I will make thee exceeding
fruitful, and I will make nations of thee,
and kings shall come out of thee.
7 And I will establish my covenant
between me and thee and thy seed after
thee in their generations for an ever-
lasting covenant, to be a God unto thee,
and to thy seed after thee.
8 And I will give unto thee, and to thy
seed after thee, the land wherein thou

art a stranger, all the land of Canaan,
for an everlasting possession; and I will
be their God.
9 ¶And God said unto Abraham,
Thou shalt keep my covenant there-
fore, thou, and thy seed after thee in
their generations.
10 This *is* my covenant, which ye
shall keep, between me and you and
thy seed after thee; Every man child
among you shall be circumcised.
11 And ye shall circumcise the flesh
of your foreskin; and it shall be a token
of the covenant betwixt me and you.
12 And he that is eight days old shall
be circumcised among you, every man
child in your generations, he that is
born in the house, or bought with mon-
ey of any stranger, which *is* not of thy
seed.
13 He that is born in thy house, and
he that is bought with thy money, must
needs be circumcised: and my covenant
shall be in your flesh for an everlasting
covenant.
14 And the uncircumcised man child
whose flesh of his foreskin is not cir-
cumcised, that soul shall be cut off
from his people; he hath broken my
covenant.
15 ¶And God said unto Abraham, As
for Sâ′raī thy wife, thou shalt not call
her name Sâ′raī, but Sarah *shall* her
name *be*.
16 And I will bless her, and give thee
a son also of her: yea, I will bless her,
and she shall be *a mother* of nations;
kings of people shall be of her.
17 Then Abraham fell upon his face,
and laughed, and said in his heart, Shall
a child be born unto him that is an
hundred years old? and shall Sarah,
that is ninety years old, bear?
18 And Abraham said unto God, O
that Īsh′ma-el might live before thee!
19 And God said, Sarah thy wife shall
bear thee a son indeed; and thou shalt
call his name Isaac: and I will establish
my covenant with him for an everlasting
covenant, *and* with his seed after
him.
20 And as for Īsh′ma-el, I have heard
thee: Behold, I have blessed him, and
will make him fruitful, and will mul-
tiply him exceedingly; twelve princes
shall he beget, and I will make him a
great nation.
21 But my covenant will I establish
with Isaac, which Sarah shall bear unto
thee at this set time in the next year.
22 And he left off talking with him,
and God went up from Abraham.
23 ¶And Abraham took Īsh′ma-el his
son, and all that were born in his house,
and all that were bought with his mon-
ey, every male among the men of
Abraham's house; and circumcised the
flesh of their foreskin in the selfsame
day, as God had said unto him.
24 And Abraham *was* ninety years
old and nine, when he was circumcised
in the flesh of his foreskin.
25 And Īsh′ma-el his son *was* thirteen
years old, when he was circumcised in
the flesh of his foreskin.
26 In the selfsame day was Abraham
circumcised, and Īsh′ma-el his son.
27 And all the men of his house, born
in the house, and bought with money of
the stranger, were circumcised with
him.

CHAPTER 18

AND the LORD appeared unto him in
the plains of Măm′re: and he sat in the
tent door in the heat of the day;
2 And he lift up his eyes and looked,
and, lo, three men stood by him: and
when he saw *them*, he ran to meet them
from the tent door, and bowed himself
toward the ground,
3 And said, My Lord, if now I have
found favour in thy sight, pass not
away, I pray thee, from thy servant:
4 Let a little water, I pray you, be
fetched, and wash your feet, and rest
yourselves under the tree:
5 And I will fetch a morsel of bread,
and comfort ye your hearts; after that
ye shall pass on: for therefore are ye
come to your servant. And they said,
So do, as thou hast said.
6 And Abraham hastened into the
tent unto Sarah, and said, Make ready
quickly three measures of fine meal,
knead *it*, and make cakes upon the
hearth.
7 And Abraham ran unto the herd,
and fetcht a calf tender and good, and
gave *it* unto a young man; and he
hasted to dress it.
8 And he took butter, and milk, and
the calf which he had dressed, and set *it*
before them; and he stood by them un-
der the tree, and they did eat.
9 ¶And they said unto him, Where *is*
Sarah thy wife? And he said, Behold, in
the tent.
10 And he said, I will certainly return
unto thee according to the time of life;
and, lo, Sarah thy wife shall have a son.
And Sarah heard *it* in the tent door,
which *was* behind him.
11 Now Abraham and Sarah *were* old
and well stricken in age; *and* it ceased
to be with Sarah after the manner of
women.
12 Therefore Sarah laughed within
herself, saying, After I am waxed old

shall I have pleasure, my lord being old
also?
13 And the LORD said unto Abraham,
Wherefore did Sarah laugh, saying,
Shall I of a surety bear a child, which
am old?
14 Is any thing too hard for the LORD?
At the time appointed I will return unto
thee, according to the time of life, and
Sarah shall have a son.
15 Then Sarah denied, saying, I
laughed not; for she was afraid. And he
said, Nay; but thou didst laugh.
16 ¶And the men rose up from
thence, and looked toward Sodom: and
Abraham went with them to bring
them on the way.
17 And the LORD said, Shall I hide
from Abraham that thing which I do;
18 Seeing that Abraham shall surely
become a great and mighty nation, and
all the nations of the earth shall be
blessed in him?
19 For I know him, that he will com-
mand his children and his household
after him, and they shall keep the way
of the LORD, to do justice and judg-
ment; that the LORD may bring upon
Abraham that which he hath spoken of
him.
20 And the LORD said, Because the
cry of Sodom and Go-mŏr′rah is great,
and because their sin is very grievous;
21 I will go down now, and see
whether they have done altogether ac-
cording to the cry of it, which is come
unto me; and if not, I will know.
22 And the men turned their faces
from thence, and went toward Sodom:
but Abraham stood yet before the
LORD.
23 ¶And Abraham drew near, and
said, Wilt thou also destroy the
righteous with the wicked?
24 Peradventure there be fifty
righteous within the city: wilt thou also
destroy and not spare the place for the
fifty righteous that *are* therein?
25 That be far from thee to do after
this manner, to slay the righteous with
the wicked: and that the righteous
should be as the wicked, that be far
from thee: Shall not the Judge of all the
earth do right?
26 And the LORD said, If I find in Sod-
om fifty righteous within the city,
then I will spare all the place for their
sakes.
27 And Abraham answered and said,
Behold now, I have taken upon me to
speak unto the Lord, which *am but* dust
and ashes:
28 Peradventure there shall lack five
of the fifty righteous: wilt thou destroy
all the city for *lack of* five? And he said,
If I find there forty and five, I will not
destroy *it*.
29 And he spake unto him yet again,
and said, Peradventure there shall be
forty found there. And he said, I will
not do *it* for forty's sake.
30 And he said *unto him*, Oh let not
the Lord be angry, and I will speak:
Peradventure there shall thirty be
found there. And he said, I will not do
it, if I find thirty there.
31 And he said, Behold now, I have
taken upon me to speak unto the Lord:
Peradventure there shall be twenty
found there. And he said, I will not
destroy *it* for twenty's sake.
32 And he said, Oh let not the Lord be
angry, and I will speak yet but this
once: Peradventure ten shall be found
there. And he said, I will not destroy *it*
for ten's sake.
33 And the LORD went his way, as
soon as he had left communing with
Abraham: and Abraham returned unto
his place.

CHAPTER 19

AND there came two angels to Sodom
at even; and Lot sat in the gate of Sod-
om: and Lot seeing *them* rose up to
meet them; and he bowed himself with
his face toward the ground;
2 And he said, Behold now, my lords,
turn in, I pray you, into your servant's
house, and tarry all night, and wash
your feet, and ye shall rise up early, and
go on your ways. And they said, Nay;
but we will abide in the street all night.
3 And he pressed upon them greatly;
and they turned in unto him, and en-
tered into his house; and he made them
a feast, and did bake unleavened bread,
and they did eat.
4 ¶But before they lay down, the men
of the city, *even* the men of Sodom,
compassed the house round, both old
and young, all the people from every
quarter:
5 And they called unto Lot, and said
unto him, Where *are* the men which
came in to thee this night? bring them
out unto us, that we may know them.
6 And Lot went out at the door unto
them, and shut the door after him,
7 And said, I pray you, brethren, do
not so wickedly.
8 Behold now, I have two daughters
which have not known man; let me, I
pray you, bring them out unto you, and
do ye to them as *is* good in your eyes:
only unto these men do nothing; for
therefore came they under the shadow
of my roof.
9 And they said, Stand back. And
they said *again*, This one *fellow* came in

to sojourn, and he will needs be a
judge: now will we deal worse with
thee, than with them. And they pressed
sore upon the man, *even* Lot, and came
near to break the door.
10 But the men put forth their hand,
and pulled Lot into the house to them,
and shut to the door.
11 And they smote the men that *were*
at the door of the house with blindness,
both small and great: so that they
wearied themselves to find the door.
12 ¶And the men said unto Lot, Hast
thou here any besides? son in law, and
thy sons, and thy daughters, and what-
soever thou hast in the city, bring *them*
out of this place:
13 For we will destroy this place, be-
cause the cry of them is waxen great
before the face of the LORD; and the
LORD hath sent us to destroy it.
14 And Lot went out, and spake unto
his sons in law, which married his
daughters, and said, Up, get you out of
this place; for the LORD will destroy this
city. But he seemed as one that mocked
unto his sons in law.
15 ¶And when the morning arose,
then the angels hastened Lot, saying,
Arise, take thy wife, and thy two
daughters, which are here; lest thou be
consumed in the iniquity of the city.
16 And while he lingered, the men
laid hold upon his hand, and upon the
hand of his wife, and upon the hand of
his two daughters; the LORD being merci-
ful unto him: and they brought him
forth, and set him without the city.
17 And it came to pass, when they
had brought them forth abroad, that he
said, Escape for thy life; look not be-
hind thee, neither stay thou in all the
plain; escape to the mountain, lest thou
be consumed.
18 And Lot said unto them, Oh, not
so, my Lord:
19 Behold now, thy servant hath
found grace in thy sight, and thou hast
magnified thy mercy, which thou hast
shewed unto me in saving my life; and I
cannot escape to the mountain, lest
some evil take me, and I die:
20 Behold now, this city *is* near to flee
unto, and it *is* a little one: Oh, let me
escape thither, (*is* it not a little one?)
and my soul shall live.
21 And he said unto him, See, I have
accepted thee concerning this thing
also, that I will not overthrow this city,
for the which thou hast spoken.
22 Haste thee, escape thither; for I
cannot do any thing till thou be come
thither. Therefore the name of the city
was called Zō'ar.
23 The sun was risen upon the earth
when Lot entered into Zō'ar.
24 Then the LORD rained upon Sodom
and upon Go-mŏr'rah brimstone and
fire from the LORD out of heaven;
25 And he overthrew those cities, and
all the plain, and all the inhabitants of
the cities, and that which grew upon
the ground.
26 But his wife looked back from be-
hind him, and she became a pillar of
salt.
27 And Abraham gat up early in the
morning to the place where he stood
before the LORD:
28 And he looked toward Sodom and
Go-mŏr'rah, and toward all the land of
the plain, and beheld, and, lo, the
smoke of the country went up as the
smoke of a furnace.
29 ¶And it came to pass, when God
destroyed the cities of the plain, that
God remembered Abraham, and sent
Lot out of the midst of the overthrow,
when he overthrew the cities in the
which Lot dwelt.
30 ¶And Lot went up out of Zō'ar, and
dwelt in the mountain, and his two
daughters with him; for he feared to
dwell in Zō'ar: and he dwelt in a cave,
he and his two daughters.
31 And the firstborn said unto the
younger, Our father *is* old, and *there is*
not a man in the earth to come in unto
us after the manner of all the earth:
32 Come, let us make our father drink
wine, and we will lie with him, that we
may preserve seed of our father.
33 And they made their father drink
wine that night: and the firstborn went
in, and lay with her father; and he per-
ceived not when she lay down, nor
when she arose.
34 And it came to pass on the
morrow, that the firstborn said unto
the younger, Behold, I lay yesternight
with my father: let us make him drink
wine this night also; and go thou in, *and*
lie with him, that we may preserve seed
of our father.
35 And they made their father drink
wine that night also: and the younger
arose, and lay with him; and he per-
ceived not when she lay down, nor
when she arose.
36 Thus were both the daughters of
Lot with child by their father.
37 And the firstborn bare a son, and
called his name Moab: the same *is* the
father of the Moabites unto this day.
38 And the younger, she also bare a
son, and called his name Bĕn-ăm'mi:
the same *is* the father of the children of
Ammon unto this day.

CHAPTER 20

AND Abraham journeyed from thence toward the south country, and dwelled between Kā'desh and Shur, and sojourned in Ge'rär.

2 And Abraham said of Sarah his wife, She *is* my sister: and A-bĭm'e-lĕch king of Ge'rär sent, and took Sarah.

3 But God came to A-bĭm'e-lĕch in a dream by night, and said to him, Behold, thou *art but* a dead man, for the woman which thou hast taken; for she *is* a man's wife.

4 But A-bĭm'e-lĕch had not come near her: and he said, Lord, wilt thou slay also a righteous nation?

5 Said he not unto me, She *is* my sister? and she, even she herself said, He *is* my brother: in the integrity of my heart and innocency of my hands have I done this.

6 And God said unto him in a dream, Yea, I know that thou didst this in the integrity of thy heart; for I also withheld thee from sinning against me: therefore suffered I thee not to touch her.

7 Now therefore restore the man *his* wife; for he *is* a prophet, and he shall pray for thee, and thou shalt live: and if thou restore *her* not, know thou that thou shalt surely die, thou, and all that *are* thine.

8 Therefore A-bĭm'e-lĕch rose early in the morning, and called all his servants, and told all these things in their ears: and the men were sore afraid.

9 Then A-bĭm'e-lĕch called Abraham, and said unto him, What hast thou done unto us? and what have I offended thee, that thou hast brought on me and on my kingdom a great sin? thou hast done deeds unto me that ought not to be done.

10 And A-bĭm'e-lĕch said unto Abraham, What sawest thou, that thou hast done this thing?

11 And Abraham said, Because I thought, Surely the fear of God *is* not in this place; and they will slay me for my wife's sake.

12 And yet indeed *she is* my sister; she *is* the daughter of my father, but not the daughter of my mother; and she became my wife.

13 And it came to pass, when God caused me to wander from my father's house, that I said unto her, This *is* thy kindness which thou shalt shew unto me; at every place whither we shall come, say of me, He *is* my brother.

14 And A-bĭm'e-lĕch took sheep, and oxen, and menservants, and womenservants, and gave *them* unto Abraham, and restored him Sarah his wife.

15 And A-bĭm'e-lĕch said, Behold, my land *is* before thee: dwell where it pleaseth thee.

16 And unto Sarah he said, Behold, I have given thy brother a thousand *pieces* of silver: behold, he *is* to thee a covering of the eyes, unto all that *are* with thee, and with all *other*: thus she was reproved.

17 So Abraham prayed unto God: and God healed A-bĭm'e-lĕch, and his wife, and his maidservants; and they bare *children*.

18 For the LORD had fast closed up all the wombs of the house of A-bĭm'e-lĕch, because of Sarah Abraham's wife.

CHAPTER 21

AND the LORD visited Sarah as he had said, and the LORD did unto Sarah as he had spoken.

2 For Sarah conceived, and bare Abraham a son in his old age, at the set time of which God had spoken to him.

3 And Abraham called the name of his son that was born unto him, whom Sarah bare to him, Isaac.

4 And Abraham circumcised his son Isaac being eight days old, as God had commanded him.

5 And Abraham was an hundred years old, when his son Isaac was born unto him.

6 And Sarah said, God hath made me to laugh, *so that* all that hear will laugh with me.

7 And she said, Who would have said unto Abraham, that Sarah should have given children suck? for I have born *him* a son in his old age.

8 And the child grew, and was weaned: and Abraham made a great feast the *same* day that Isaac was weaned.

9 ¶And Sarah saw the son of Hā'gär the Egyptian, which she had born unto Abraham, mocking.

10 Wherefore she said unto Abraham, Cast out this bondwoman and her son: for the son of this bondwoman shall not be heir with my son, *even* with Isaac.

11 And the thing was very grievous in Abraham's sight because of his son.

12 And God said unto Abraham, Let it not be grievous in thy sight because of the lad, and because of thy bondwoman; in all that Sarah hath said unto thee, hearken unto her voice; for in Isaac shall thy seed be called.

13 And also of the son of the bondwoman will I make a nation, because he *is* thy seed.

14 And Abraham rose up early in the morning, and took bread, and a bottle of water, and gave *it* unto Hā'gär, putting *it* on her shoulder, and the child, and sent her away: and she departed, and wandered in the wilderness of Be'er-shē'ba.

15 And the water was spent in the bottle, and she cast the child under one of the shrubs.

16 And she went, and sat her down over against *him* a good way off, as it were a bowshot: for she said, Let me not see the death of the child. And she sat over against *him*, and lift up her voice, and wept.

17 And God heard the voice of the lad; and the angel of God called to Hā'gär out of heaven, and said unto her, What aileth thee, Hā'gär? fear not; for God hath heard the voice of the lad where he *is*.

18 Arise, lift up the lad, and hold him in thine hand; for I will make him a great nation.

19 And God opened her eyes, and she saw a well of water; and she went, and filled the bottle with water, and gave the lad drink.

20 And God was with the lad; and he grew, and dwelt in the wilderness, and became an archer.

21 And he dwelt in the wilderness of Paran: and his mother took him a wife out of the land of Egypt.

22 ¶And it came to pass at that time, that A-bĭm'e-lĕch and Phī'chŏl the chief captain of his host spake unto Abraham, saying, God *is* with thee in all that thou doest:

23 Now therefore swear unto me here by God that thou wilt not deal falsely with me, nor with my son, nor with my son's son: *but* according to the kindness that I have done unto thee, thou shalt do unto me, and to the land wherein thou hast sojourned.

24 And Abraham said, I will swear.

25 And Abraham reproved A-bĭm'e-lĕch because of a well of water, which A-bĭm'e-lĕch's servants had violently taken away.

26 And A-bĭm'e-lĕch said, I wot not who hath done this thing: neither didst thou tell me, neither yet heard I *of it*, but to day.

27 And Abraham took sheep and oxen, and gave them unto A-bĭm'e-lĕch; and both of them made a covenant.

28 And Abraham set seven ewe lambs of the flock by themselves.

29 And A-bĭm'e-lĕch said unto Abraham, What *mean* these seven ewe lambs which thou hast set by themselves?

30 And he said, For *these* seven ewe lambs shalt thou take of my hand, that they may be a witness unto me, that I have digged this well.

31 Wherefore he called that place Be'er-shē'ba; because there they sware both of them.

32 Thus they made a covenant at Be'er-shē'ba: then A-bĭm'e-lĕch rose up, and Phī'chŏl the chief captain of his host, and they returned into the land of the Philistines.

33 ¶And *Abraham* planted a grove in Be'er-shē'ba, and called there on the name of the LORD, the everlasting God.

34 And Abraham sojourned in the Philistines' land many days.

CHAPTER 22

AND it came to pass after these things, that God did tempt Abraham, and said unto him, Abraham: and he said, Behold, *here* I *am*.

2 And he said, Take now thy son, thine only *son* Isaac, whom thou lovest, and get thee into the land of Mō-rī'ah; and offer him there for a burnt offering upon one of the mountains which I will tell thee of.

3 And Abraham rose up early in the morning, and saddled his ass, and took two of his young men with him, and Isaac his son, and clave the wood for the burnt offering, and rose up, and went unto the place of which God had told him.

4 Then on the third day Abraham lifted up his eyes, and saw the place afar off.

5 And Abraham said unto his young men, Abide ye here with the ass; and I and the lad will go yonder and worship, and come again to you.

6 And Abraham took the wood of the burnt offering, and laid *it* upon Isaac his son; and he took the fire in his hand, and a knife; and they went both of them together.

7 And Isaac spake unto Abraham his father, and said, My father: and he said, Here *am* I, my son. And he said, Behold the fire and the wood: but where *is* the lamb for a burnt offering?

8 And Abraham said, My son, God will provide himself a lamb for a burnt offering: so they went both of them together.

9 And they came to the place which God had told him of; and Abraham built an altar there, and laid the wood in order, and bound Isaac his son, and laid him on the altar upon the wood.

10 And Abraham stretched forth his
hand, and took the knife to slay his son.
11 And the angel of the LORD called
unto him out of heaven, and said, Abra-
ham, Abraham: and he said, Here *am* I.
12 And he said, Lay not thine hand
upon the lad, neither do thou any thing
unto him: for now I know that thou
fearest God, seeing thou hast not
withheld thy son, thine only *son* from
me.
13 And Abraham lifted up his eyes,
and looked, and behold behind *him* a
ram caught in a thicket by his horns:
and Abraham went and took the ram,
and offered him up for a burnt offering
in the stead of his son.
14 And Abraham called the name of
that place Je-hō′vah–jī′reh: as it is said
to this day, In the mount of the LORD it
shall be seen.
15 ¶And the angel of the LORD called
unto Abraham out of heaven the sec-
ond time,
16 And said, By myself have I sworn,
saith the LORD, for because thou hast
done this thing, and hast not withheld
thy son, thine only *son:*
17 That in blessing I will bless thee,
and in multiplying I will multiply thy
seed as the stars of the heaven, and as
the sand which *is* upon the sea shore;
and thy seed shall possess the gate of
his enemies;
18 And in thy seed shall all the na-
tions of the earth be blessed; because
thou hast obeyed my voice.
19 So Abraham returned unto his
young men, and they rose up and went
together to Be′er–shē′ba; and Abraham
dwelt at Be′er–shē′ba.
20 ¶And it came to pass after these
things, that it was told Abraham,
saying, Behold, Mĭl′cah, she hath also
born children unto thy brother Nahor;
21 Huz his firstborn, and Buz his
brother, and Kĕ-mū′el the father of
Ā′ram,
22 And Chē′sĕd, and Hā′zō, and
Pĭl′dăsh, and Jĭd′lăph, and Beth-ū′el.
23 And Beth-ū′el begat Rebekah:
these eight Mĭl′cah did bear to Nahor,
Abraham's brother.
24 And his concubine, whose name
was Reū′mah, she bare also Tē′bah,
and Gā′hăm, and Thā′hăsh, and Mā′a-
chah.

CHAPTER 23

AND Sarah was an hundred and seven
and twenty years old: *these were* the
years of the life of Sarah.
2 And Sarah died in Kir′jath–är′ba; the
same *is* Hēbron in the land of Canaan:
and Abraham came to mourn for
Sarah, and to weep for her.
3 ¶And Abraham stood up from be-
fore his dead, and spake unto the sons
of Heth, saying,
4 I *am* a stranger and a sojourner
with you: give me a possession of a bury-
ingplace with you, that I may bury my
dead out of my sight.
5 And the children of Heth answered
Abraham, saying unto him,
6 Hear us, my lord: thou *art* a mighty
prince among us: in the choice of our
sepulchres bury thy dead; none of us
shall withhold from thee his sepulchre,
but that thou mayest bury thy dead.
7 And Abraham stood up, and bowed
himself to the people of the land, *even*
to the children of Heth.
8 And he communed with them,
saying, If it be your mind that I should
bury my dead out of my sight; hear me,
and intreat for me to Ē′phrŏn the son of
Zō′här,
9 That he may give me the cave of
Măch-pē′läh, which he hath, which *is* in
the end of his field; for as much money
as it is worth he shall give it me for a
possession of a buryingplace amongst
you.
10 And Ē′phrŏn dwelt among the
children of Heth: and Ē′phrŏn the Hit-
tite answered Abraham in the audience
of the children of Heth, *even* of all that
went in at the gate of his city, saying,
11 Nay, my lord, hear me: the field
give I thee, and the cave that *is* therein,
I give it thee; in the presence of the sons
of my people give I it thee: bury thy
dead.
12 And Abraham bowed down him-
self before the people of the land.
13 And he spake unto Ē′phrŏn in the
audience of the people of the land,
saying, But if thou *wilt give it,* I pray
thee, hear me: I will give thee money
for the field; take *it* of me, and I will
bury my dead there.
14 And Ē′phrŏn answered Abraham,
saying unto him,
15 My lord, hearken unto me: the
land *is worth* four hundred shekels of
silver; what *is* that betwixt me and
thee? bury therefore thy dead.
16 And Abraham hearkened unto
Ē′phrŏn; and Abraham weighed to
Ē′phrŏn the silver, which he had named
in the audience of the sons of Heth, four
hundred shekels of silver, current *mon-
ey* with the merchant.
17 And the field of Ē′phrŏn, which
was in Măch-pē′läh, which *was* before
Măm′re, the field, and the cave which
was therein, and all the trees that *were*

in the field, that *were* in all the borders
round about, were made sure
18 Unto Abraham for a possession in
the presence of the children of Heth,
before all that went in at the gate of his
city.
19 And after this, Abraham buried
Sarah his wife in the cave of the field of
Măch-pē'lăh before Măm're: the same
is Hebron in the land of Canaan.
20 And the field, and the cave that *is*
therein, were made sure unto Abraham
for a possession of a buryingplace by
the sons of Heth.

CHAPTER 24

AND Abraham was old, *and* well strick-
en in age: and the LORD had blessed
Abraham in all things.
2 And Abraham said unto his eldest
servant of his house, that ruled over all
that he had, Put, I pray thee, thy hand
under my thigh:
3 And I will make thee swear by the
LORD, the God of heaven, and the God
of the earth, that thou shalt not take a
wife unto my son of the daughters of
the Canaanites, among whom I dwell:
4 But thou shalt go unto my country,
and to my kindred, and take a wife unto
my son Isaac.
5 And the servant said unto him,
Peradventure the woman will not be
willing to follow me unto this land:
must I needs bring thy son again unto
the land from whence thou camest?
6 And Abraham said unto him, Be-
ware thou that thou bring not my son
thither again.
7 The LORD God of heaven, which
took me from my father's house, and
from the land of my kindred, and which
spake unto me, and that sware unto
me, saying, Unto thy seed will I give
this land; he shall send his angel before
thee, and thou shalt take a wife unto
my son from thence.
8 And if the woman will not be will-
ing to follow thee, then thou shalt be
clear from this my oath: only bring not
my son thither again.
9 And the servant put his hand under
the thigh of Abraham his master, and
sware to him concerning that matter.
10 ¶And the servant took ten camels
of the camels of his master, and de-
parted; for all the goods of his master
were in his hand: and he arose, and
went to Měs-o-po-tā'mĭ-a, unto the city
of Nahor.
11 And he made his camels to kneel
down without the city by a well of wa-
ter at the time of the evening, *even* the
time that women go out to draw *water*.
12 And he said, O LORD God of my
master Abraham, I pray thee, send me
good speed this day, and shew kind-
ness unto my master Abraham.
13 Behold, I stand *here* by the well of
water; and the daughters of the men of
the city come out to draw water:
14 And let it come to pass, that the
damsel to whom I shall say, Let down
thy pitcher, I pray thee, that I may
drink; and she shall say, Drink, and I
will give thy camels drink also: *let the
same be* she *that* thou hast appointed
for thy servant Isaac; and thereby shall
I know that thou hast shewed kindness
unto my master.
15 ¶And it came to pass, before he
had done speaking, that, behold, Rebek-
ah came out, who was born to Beth-
ū'el, son of Mĭl'cah, the wife of Nahor,
Abraham's brother, with her pitcher
upon her shoulder.
16 And the damsel *was* very fair to
look upon, a virgin, neither had any
man known her: and she went down to
the well, and filled her pitcher, and
came up.
17 And the servant ran to meet her,
and said, Let me, I pray thee, drink a
little water of thy pitcher.
18 And she said, Drink, my lord: and
she hasted, and let down her pitcher
upon her hand, and gave him drink.
19 And when she had done giving
him drink, she said, I will draw *water*
for thy camels also, until they have
done drinking.
20 And she hasted, and emptied her
pitcher into the trough, and ran again
unto the well to draw *water*, and drew
for all his camels.
21 And the man wondering at her
held his peace, to wit whether the LORD
had made his journey prosperous or
not.
22 And it came to pass, as the camels
had done drinking, that the man took a
golden earring of half a shekel weight,
and two bracelets for her hands of ten
shekels weight of gold;
23 And said, Whose daughter *art*
thou? tell me, I pray thee: is there room
in thy father's house for us to lodge in?
24 And she said unto him, I *am* the
daughter of Beth-ū'el the son of Mĭl'-
cah, which she bare unto Nahor.
25 She said moreover unto him, We
have both straw and provender
enough, and room to lodge in.
26 And the man bowed down his
head, and worshipped the LORD.
27 And he said, Blessed *be* the LORD
God of my master Abraham, who hath
not left destitute my master of his
mercy and his truth: I *being* in the way,

the LORD led me to the house of my master's brethren.

28 And the damsel ran, and told *them of* her mother's house these things.

29 ¶And Rebekah had a brother, and his name *was* Lāban: and Lāban ran out unto the man, unto the well.

30 And it came to pass, when he saw the earring and bracelets upon his sister's hands, and when he heard the words of Rebekah his sister, saying, Thus spake the man unto me; that he came unto the man; and, behold, he stood by the camels at the well.

31 And he said, Come in, thou blessed of the LORD; wherefore standest thou without? for I have prepared the house, and room for the camels.

32 And the man came into the house: and he ungirded his camels, and gave straw and provender for the camels, and water to wash his feet, and the men's feet that *were* with him.

33 And there was set *meat* before him to eat: but he said, I will not eat, until I have told mine errand. And he said, Speak on.

34 And he said, I *am* Abraham's servant.

35 And the LORD hath blessed my master greatly; and he is become great: and he hath given him flocks, and herds, and silver, and gold, and menservants, and maidservants, and camels, and asses.

36 And Sarah my master's wife bare a son to my master when she was old: and unto him hath he given all that he hath.

37 And my master made me swear, saying, Thou shalt not take a wife to my son of the daughters of the Canaanites, in whose land I dwell:

38 But thou shalt go unto my father's house, and to my kindred, and take a wife unto my son.

39 And I said unto my master, Peradventure the woman will not follow me.

40 And he said unto me, The LORD, before whom I walk, will send his angel with thee, and prosper thy way; and thou shalt take a wife for my son of my kindred, and of my father's house:

41 Then shalt thou be clear from *this* my oath, when thou comest to my kindred; and if they give not thee *one*, thou shalt be clear from my oath.

42 And I came this day unto the well, and said, O LORD God of my master Abraham, if now thou do prosper my way which I go:

43 Behold, I stand by the well of water; and it shall come to pass, that when the virgin cometh forth to draw *water*, and I say to her, Give me, I pray thee, a little water of thy pitcher to drink;

44 And she say to me, Both drink thou, and I will also draw for thy camels: *let* the same *be* the woman whom the LORD hath appointed out for my master's son.

45 And before I had done speaking in mine heart, behold, Rebekah came forth with her pitcher on her shoulder; and she went down unto the well, and drew *water*: and I said unto her, Let me drink, I pray thee.

46 And she made haste, and let down her pitcher from her *shoulder*, and said, Drink, and I will give thy camels drink also: so I drank, and she made the camels drink also.

47 And I asked her, and said, Whose daughter *art* thou? And she said, The daughter of Beth-ū'el, Nahor's son, whom Mĭl'cah bare unto him: and I put the earring upon her face, and the bracelets upon her hands.

48 And I bowed down my head, and worshipped the LORD, and blessed the LORD God of my master Abraham, which had led me in the right way to take my master's brother's daughter unto his son.

49 And now if ye will deal kindly and truly with my master, tell me: and if not, tell me; that I may turn to the right hand, or to the left.

50 Then Lāban and Beth-ū'el answered and said, The thing proceedeth from the LORD: we cannot speak unto thee bad or good.

51 Behold, Rebekah *is* before thee, take *her*, and go, and let her be thy master's son's wife, as the LORD hath spoken.

52 And it came to pass, that, when Abraham's servant heard their words, he worshipped the LORD, *bowing himself* to the earth.

53 And the servant brought forth jewels of silver, and jewels of gold, and raiment, and gave *them* to Rebekah: he gave also to her brother and to her mother precious things.

54 And they did eat and drink, he and the men that *were* with him, and tarried all night; and they rose up in the morning, and he said, Send me away unto my master.

55 And her brother and her mother said, Let the damsel abide with us *a few* days, at the least ten; after that she shall go.

56 And he said unto them, Hinder me not, seeing the LORD hath prospered my way; send me away that I may go to my master.

57 And they said, We will call the damsel, and enquire at her mouth.

58 And they called Rebekah, and said unto her, Wilt thou go with this man? And she said, I will go.

59 And they sent away Rebekah their sister, and her nurse, and Abraham's servant, and his men.

60 And they blessed Rebekah, and said unto her, Thou *art* our sister, be thou *the mother* of thousands of millions, and let thy seed possess the gate of those which hate them.

61 ¶And Rebekah arose, and her damsels, and they rode upon the camels, and followed the man: and the servant took Rebekah, and went his way.

62 And Isaac came from the way of the well La-haī′roi; for he dwelt in the south country.

63 And Isaac went out to meditate in the field at the eventide: and he lifted up his eyes, and saw, and, behold, the camels *were* coming.

64 And Rebekah lifted up her eyes, and when she saw Isaac, she lighted off the camel.

65 For she *had* said unto the servant, What man *is* this that walketh in the field to meet us? And the servant *had* said, It *is* my master: therefore she took a vail, and covered herself.

66 And the servant told Isaac all things that he had done.

67 And Isaac brought her into his mother Sarah's tent, and took Rebekah, and she became his wife; and he loved her: and Isaac was comforted after his mother's *death.*

CHAPTER 25

THEN again Abraham took a wife, and her name *was* Ke-tū′rah.

2 And she bare him Zĭmrăn, and Jŏk′shăn, and Mē′dăn, and Mĭd′ĭ-an, and Ĭsh-băk, and Shū′ah.

3 And Jŏk′shăn begat Shē′ba, and Dē′dan. And the sons of Dē′dan were As-shu′rim, and Le-tū′shim, and Lē-ŭm′mĭm.

4 And the sons of Mĭd′ĭ-an; Ē′phah, and Ē′pher, and Hā′nŏch, and A-bī′-dah, and Ĕl′dā-ah. All these *were* the children of Ke-tū′rah.

5 And Abraham gave all that he had unto Isaac.

6 But unto the sons of the concubines, which Abraham had, Abraham gave gifts, and sent them away from Isaac his son, while he yet lived, eastward, unto the east country.

7 And these *are* the days of the years of Abraham's life which he lived, an hundred threescore and fifteen years.

8 Then Abraham gave up the ghost, and died in a good old age, an old man, and full *of years;* and was gathered to his people.

9 And his sons Isaac and Ĭsh′ma-el buried him in the cave of Măch-pē′-läh, in the field of Ē′phrŏn the son of Zō′här the Hittite, which *is* before Măm′re;

10 The field which Abraham purchased of the sons of Heth: there was Abraham buried, and Sarah his wife.

11 And it came to pass after the death of Abraham, that God blessed his son Isaac; and Isaac dwelt by the well La-haī′roi.

12 ¶Now these *are* the generations of Ĭsh′ma-el, Abraham's son, whom Hā′-gär the Egyptian, Sarah's handmaid, bare unto Abraham:

13 And these *are* the names of the sons of Ĭsh′ma-el, by their names, according to their generations: the firstborn of Ĭsh′ma-el, Ne-bā′jŏth; and Kē′-dar, and Ad′be-el, and Mĭb′săm,

14 And Mĭsh′ma, and Dū′mah, and Măs′sa,

15 Hā′där, and Tē′ma, Jē′tur, Nā′-phĭsh, and Kĕd′e-mah:

16 These *are* the sons of Ĭsh′ma-el, and these *are* their names, by their towns, and by their castles; twelve princes according to their nations.

17 And these *are* the years of the life of Ĭsh′ma-el, an hundred and thirty and seven years: and he gave up the ghost and died; and was gathered unto his people.

18 And they dwelt from Hăv′i-lah unto Shur, that *is* before Egypt, as thou goest toward Assyria: *and* he died in the presence of all his brethren.

19 ¶And these *are* the generations of Isaac, Abraham's son: Abraham begat Isaac:

20 And Isaac was forty years old when he took Rebekah to wife, the daughter of Beth-ū′el the Syrian of Pă′dan-â′ram, the sister to Lāban the Syrian.

21 And Isaac intreated the LORD for his wife, because she *was* barren: and the LORD was intreated of him, and Rebekah his wife conceived.

22 And the children struggled together within her; and she said, If *it be* so, why *am* I thus? And she went to enquire of the LORD.

23 And the LORD said unto her, Two nations *are* in thy womb, and two manner of people shall be separated from thy bowels; and *the one* people shall be stronger than *the other* people; and the elder shall serve the younger.

24 And when her days to be delivered

were fulfilled, behold, *there were* twins in her womb.

25 And the first came out red, all over like an hairy garment; and they called his name Esau.

26 And after that came his brother out, and his hand took hold on Esau's heel; and his name was called Jacob: and Isaac *was* threescore years old when she bare them.

27 And the boys grew: and Esau was a cunning hunter, a man of the field; and Jacob *was* a plain man, dwelling in tents.

28 And Isaac loved Esau, because he did eat of *his* venison: but Rebekah loved Jacob.

29 And Jacob sod pottage: and Esau came from the field, and he *was* faint:

30 And Esau said to Jacob, Feed me, I pray thee, with that same red *pottage;* for I *am* faint: therefore was his name called Edom.

31 And Jacob said, Sell me this day thy birthright.

32 And Esau said, Behold, I *am* at the point to die: and what profit shall this birthright do to me?

33 And Jacob said, Swear to me this day; and he sware unto him: and he sold his birthright unto Jacob.

34 Then Jacob gave Esau bread and pottage of lentiles; and he did eat and drink, and rose up, and went his way: thus Esau despised *his* birthright.

CHAPTER 26

AND there was a famine in the land, beside the first famine that was in the days of Abraham. And Isaac went unto A-bĭm'e-lĕch king of the Philistines unto Ge'rär.

2 And the Lord appeared unto him, and said, Go not down into Egypt; dwell in the land which I shall tell thee of:

3 Sojourn in this land, and I will be with thee, and will bless thee; for unto thee, and unto thy seed, I will give all these countries, and I will perform the oath which I sware unto Abraham thy father;

4 And I will make thy seed to multiply as the stars of heaven, and will give unto thy seed all these countries; and in thy seed shall all the nations of the earth be blessed;

5 Because that Abraham obeyed my voice, and kept my charge, my commandments, my statutes, and my laws.

6 ¶And Isaac dwelt in Ge'rär:

7 And the men of the place asked *him* of his wife; and he said, She *is* my sister: for he feared to say, *She is* my wife; lest, *said he,* the men of the place should kill me for Rebekah; because she *was* fair to look upon.

8 And it came to pass, when he had been there a long time, that A-bĭm'e-lĕch king of the Philistines looked out at a window, and saw, and, behold, Isaac *was* sporting with Rebekah his wife.

9 And A-bĭm'e-lĕch called Isaac, and said, Behold, of a surety she *is* thy wife: and how saidst thou, She *is* my sister? And Isaac said unto him, Because I said, Lest I die for her.

10 And A-bĭm'e-lĕch said, What *is* this thou hast done unto us? one of the people might lightly have lien with thy wife, and thou shouldest have brought guiltiness upon us.

11 And A-bĭm'e-lĕch charged all *his* people, saying, He that toucheth this man or his wife shall surely be put to death.

12 Then Isaac sowed in that land, and received in the same year an hundredfold: and the Lord blessed him.

13 And the man waxed great, and went forward, and grew until he became very great:

14 For he had possession of flocks, and possession of herds, and great store of servants: and the Philistines envied him.

15 For all the wells which his father's servants had digged in the days of Abraham his father, the Philistines had stopped them, and filled them with earth.

16 And A-bĭm'e-lĕch said unto Isaac, Go from us; for thou art much mightier than we.

17 ¶And Isaac departed thence, and pitched his tent in the valley of Ge'rär, and dwelt there.

18 And Isaac digged again the wells of water, which they had digged in the days of Abraham his father; for the Philistines had stopped them after the death of Abraham: and he called their names after the names by which his father had called them.

19 And Isaac's servants digged in the valley, and found there a well of springing water.

20 And the herdmen of Ge'rär did strive with Isaac's herdmen, saying, The water *is* ours: and he called the name of the well Ē'sĕk; because they strove with him.

21 And they digged another well, and strove for that also: and he called the name of it Sĭt'nah.

22 And he removed from thence, and digged another well; and for that they strove not: and he called the name of it Re-hō'bŏth; and he said, For now the

LORD hath made room for us, and we shall be fruitful in the land.

23 And he went up from thence to Be'er-shē'ba.

24 And the LORD appeared unto him the same night, and said, I *am* the God of Abraham thy father: fear not, for I *am* with thee, and will bless thee, and multiply thy seed for my servant Abraham's sake.

25 And he builded an altar there, and called upon the name of the LORD, and pitched his tent there: and there Isaac's servants digged a well.

26 ¶Then A-bĭm'e-lĕch went to him from Ge'rär, and A-hŭz'zăth one of his friends, and Phī'chŏl the chief captain of his army.

27 And Isaac said unto them, Wherefore come ye to me, seeing ye hate me, and have sent me away from you?

28 And they said, We saw certainly that the LORD was with thee: and we said, Let there be now an oath betwixt us, *even* betwixt us and thee, and let us make a covenant with thee;

29 That thou wilt do us no hurt, as we have not touched thee, and as we have done unto thee nothing but good, and have sent thee away in peace: thou *art* now the blessed of the LORD.

30 And he made them a feast, and they did eat and drink.

31 And they rose up betimes in the morning, and sware one to another: and Isaac sent them away, and they departed from him in peace.

32 And it came to pass the same day, that Isaac's servants came, and told him concerning the well which they had digged, and said unto him, We have found water.

33 And he called it Shē'bah: therefore the name of the city *is* Be'er-shē'ba unto this day.

34 ¶And Esau was forty years old when he took to wife Judith the daughter of Bē-e'rī the Hittite, and Băsh'e-măth the daughter of Ē'lŏn the Hittite:

35 Which were a grief of mind unto Isaac and to Rebekah.

CHAPTER 27

AND it came to pass, that when Isaac was old, and his eyes were dim, so that he could not see, he called Esau his eldest son, and said unto him, My son: and he said unto him, Behold, *here am* I.

2 And he said, Behold now, I am old, I know not the day of my death:

3 Now therefore take, I pray thee, thy weapons, thy quiver and thy bow, and go out to the field, and take me *some* venison;

4 And make me savoury meat, such as I love, and bring *it* to me, that I may eat; that my soul may bless thee before I die.

5 And Rebekah heard when Isaac spake to Esau his son. And Esau went to the field to hunt *for* venison, *and* to bring *it*.

6 ¶And Rebekah spake unto Jacob her son, saying, Behold, I heard thy father speak unto Esau thy brother, saying,

7 Bring me venison, and make me savoury meat, that I may eat, and bless thee before the LORD before my death.

8 Now therefore, my son, obey my voice according to that which I command thee.

9 Go now to the flock, and fetch me from thence two good kids of the goats; and I will make them savoury meat for thy father, such as he loveth:

10 And thou shalt bring *it* to thy father, that he may eat, and that he may bless thee before his death.

11 And Jacob said to Rebekah his mother, Behold, Esau my brother *is* a hairy man, and I *am* a smooth man:

12 My father peradventure will feel me, and I shall seem to him as a deceiver; and I shall bring a curse upon me, and not a blessing.

13 And his mother said unto him, Upon me *be* thy curse, my son: only obey my voice, and go fetch me *them*.

14 And he went, and fetched, and brought *them* to his mother: and his mother made savoury meat, such as his father loved.

15 And Rebekah took goodly raiment of her eldest son Esau, which *were* with her in the house, and put them upon Jacob her younger son:

16 And she put the skins of the kids of the goats upon his hands, and upon the smooth of his neck:

17 And she gave the savoury meat and the bread, which she had prepared, into the hand of her son Jacob.

18 ¶And he came unto his father, and said, My father: and he said, Here *am* I; who *art* thou, my son?

19 And Jacob said unto his father, I *am* Esau thy firstborn; I have done according as thou badest me: arise, I pray thee, sit and eat of my venison, that thy soul may bless me.

20 And Isaac said unto his son, How *is it* that thou hast found *it* so quickly, my son? And he said, Because the LORD thy God brought *it* to me.

21 And Isaac said unto Jacob, Come near, I pray thee, that I may feel thee,

my son, whether thou *be* my very son Esau or not.

22 And Jacob went near unto Isaac his father; and he felt him, and said, The voice *is* Jacob's voice, but the hands *are* the hands of Esau.

23 And he discerned him not, because his hands were hairy, as his brother Esau's hands: so he blessed him.

24 And he said, *Art* thou my very son Esau? And he said, I *am*.

25 And he said, Bring *it* near to me, and I will eat of my son's venison, that my soul may bless thee. And he brought *it* near to him, and he did eat: and he brought him wine, and he drank.

26 And his father Isaac said unto him, Come near now, and kiss me, my son.

27 And he came near, and kissed him: and he smelled the smell of his raiment, and blessed him, and said, See, the smell of my son *is* as the smell of a field which the LORD hath blessed:

28 Therefore God give thee of the dew of heaven, and the fatness of the earth, and plenty of corn and wine:

29 Let people serve thee, and nations bow down to thee: be lord over thy brethren, and let thy mother's sons bow down to thee: cursed *be* every one that curseth thee, and blessed *be* he that blesseth thee.

30 ¶And it came to pass, as soon as Isaac had made an end of blessing Jacob, and Jacob was yet scarce gone out from the presence of Isaac his father, that Esau his brother came in from his hunting.

31 And he also had made savoury meat, and brought it unto his father, and said unto his father, Let my father arise, and eat of his son's venison, that thy soul may bless me.

32 And Isaac his father said unto him, Who *art* thou? And he said, I *am* thy son, thy firstborn Esau.

33 And Isaac trembled very exceedingly, and said, Who? where *is* he that hath taken venison, and brought *it* me, and I have eaten of all before thou camest, and have blessed him? yea, *and* he shall be blessed.

34 And when Esau heard the words of his father, he cried with a great and exceeding bitter cry, and said unto his father, Bless me, *even* me also, O my father.

35 And he said, Thy brother came with subtilty, and hath taken away thy blessing.

36 And he said, Is not he rightly named Jacob? for he hath supplanted me these two times: he took away my birthright; and, behold, now he hath taken away my blessing. And he said, Hast thou not reserved a blessing for me?

37 And Isaac answered and said unto Esau, Behold, I have made him thy lord, and all his brethren have I given to him for servants; and with corn and wine have I sustained him: and what shall I do now unto thee, my son?

38 And Esau said unto his father, Hast thou but one blessing, my father? bless me, *even* me also, O my father. And Esau lifted up his voice, and wept.

39 And Isaac his father answered and said unto him, Behold, thy dwelling shall be the fatness of the earth, and of the dew of heaven from above;

40 And by thy sword shalt thou live, and shalt serve thy brother; and it shall come to pass when thou shalt have the dominion, that thou shalt break his yoke from off thy neck.

41 ¶And Esau hated Jacob because of the blessing wherewith his father blessed him: and Esau said in his heart, The days of mourning for my father are at hand; then will I slay my brother Jacob.

42 And these words of Esau her elder son were told to Rebekah: and she sent and called Jacob her younger son, and said unto him, Behold, thy brother Esau, as touching thee, doth comfort himself, *purposing* to kill thee.

43 Now therefore, my son, obey my voice; and arise, flee thou to Lāban my brother to Hâ'ran;

44 And tarry with him a few days, until thy brother's fury turn away;

45 Until thy brother's anger turn away from thee, and he forget *that* which thou hast done to him: then I will send, and fetch thee from thence: why should I be deprived also of you both in one day?

46 And Rebekah said to Isaac, I am weary of my life because of the daughters of Heth: if Jacob take a wife of the daughters of Heth, such as these *which are* of the daughters of the land, what good shall my life do me?

CHAPTER 28

AND Isaac called Jacob, and blessed him, and charged him, and said unto him, Thou shalt not take a wife of the daughters of Canaan.

2 Arise, go to Pă'dan–â'ram, to the house of Beth-ū'el thy mother's father; and take thee a wife from thence of the daughters of Lāban thy mother's brother.

3 And God Almighty bless thee, and make thee fruitful, and multiply thee,

that thou mayest be a multitude of
people;
4 And give thee the blessing of Abra-
ham, to thee, and to thy seed with thee;
that thou mayest inherit the land where-
in thou art a stranger, which God
gave unto Abraham.
5 And Isaac sent away Jacob: and he
went to Pă′dan-â′ram unto Lāban, son
of Beth-ū′el the Syrian, the brother of
Rebekah, Jacob's and Esau's mother.
6 ¶When Esau saw that Isaac had
blessed Jacob, and sent him away to
Pă′dan-â′ram, to take him a wife from
thence; and that as he blessed him he
gave him a charge, saying, Thou shalt
not take a wife of the daughters of Ca-
naan;
7 And that Jacob obeyed his father
and his mother, and was gone to
Pă′dan-â′ram;
8 And Esau seeing that the daughters
of Canaan pleased not Isaac his father;
9 Then went Esau unto Ĭsh′ma-el, and
took unto the wives which he had
Mā′ha-lăth the daughter of Ĭsh′ma-el
Abraham's son, the sister of Ne-bā′-
jŏth, to be his wife.
10 ¶And Jacob went out from
Be′er-shē′ba, and went toward Hâ′ran.
11 And he lighted upon a certain
place, and tarried there all night, be-
cause the sun was set; and he took of
the stones of that place, and put *them*
for his pillows, and lay down in that
place to sleep.
12 And he dreamed, and behold a lad-
der set up on the earth, and the top of it
reached to heaven: and behold the an-
gels of God ascending and descending
on it.
13 And, behold, the LORD stood above
it, and said, I *am* the LORD God of Abra-
ham thy father, and the God of Isaac:
the land whereon thou liest, to thee will
I give it, and to thy seed;
14 And thy seed shall be as the dust of
the earth, and thou shalt spread abroad
to the west, and to the east, and to the
north, and to the south: and in thee and
in thy seed shall all the families of the
earth be blessed.
15 And, behold, I *am* with thee, and
will keep thee in all *places* whither thou
goest, and will bring thee again into
this land; for I will not leave thee, until I
have done *that* which I have spoken to
thee of.
16 ¶And Jacob awaked out of his
sleep, and he said, Surely the LORD is in
this place; and I knew *it* not.
17 And he was afraid, and said, How
dreadful *is* this place! this *is* none other
but the house of God, and this *is* the
gate of heaven.
18 And Jacob rose up early in the
morning, and took the stone that he
had put *for* his pillows, and set it up *for*
a pillar, and poured oil upon the top of
it.
19 And he called the name of that
place Bĕth-el: but the name of that city
was called Luz at the first.
20 And Jacob vowed a vow, saying, If
God will be with me, and will keep me
in this way that I go, and will give me
bread to eat, and raiment to put on,
21 So that I come again to my father's
house in peace; then shall the LORD be
my God:
22 And this stone, which I have set
for a pillar, shall be God's house: and of
all that thou shalt give me I will surely
give the tenth unto thee.

CHAPTER 29

THEN Jacob went on his journey, and
came into the land of the people of the
east.
2 And he looked, and behold a well in
the field, and, lo, there *were* three
flocks of sheep lying by it; for out of
that well they watered the flocks: and a
great stone *was* upon the well's mouth.
3 And thither were all the flocks gath-
ered: and they rolled the stone from
the well's mouth, and watered the
sheep, and put the stone again upon the
well's mouth in his place.
4 And Jacob said unto them, My
brethren, whence *be* ye? And they said,
Of Hâ′ran *are* we.
5 And he said unto them, Know ye
Lā′ban the son of Nahor? And they
said, We know *him*.
6 And he said unto them, *Is* he well?
And they said, *He is* well: and, behold,
Rāchel his daughter cometh with the
sheep.
7 And he said, Lo, *it is* yet high day,
neither *is it* time that the cattle should
be gathered together: water ye the
sheep, and go *and* feed *them*.
8 And they said, We cannot, until all
the flocks be gathered together, and *till*
they roll the stone from the well's
mouth; then we water the sheep.
9 ¶And while he yet spake with them,
Rāchel came with her father's sheep:
for she kept them.
10 And it came to pass, when Jacob
saw Rāchel the daughter of Lāban his
mother's brother, and the sheep of Lā-
ban his mother's brother, that Jacob
went near, and rolled the stone from
the well's mouth, and watered the flock
of Lāban his mother's brother.
11 And Jacob kissed Rāchel, and
lifted up his voice, and wept.
12 And Jacob told Rāchel that he *was*

her father's brother, and that he *was*
Rebekah's son: and she ran and told her
father.
13 And it came to pass, when Lāban
heard the tidings of Jacob his sister's
son, that he ran to meet him, and em-
braced him, and kissed him, and
brought him to his house. And he told
Lāban all these things.
14 And Lāban said to him, Surely
thou *art* my bone and my flesh. And he
abode with him the space of a month.
15 ¶And Lāban said unto Jacob, Be-
cause thou *art* my brother, shouldest
thou therefore serve me for nought?
tell me, what *shall* thy wages *be?*
16 And Lāban had two daughters: the
name of the elder *was* Leah, and the
name of the younger *was* Rāchel.
17 Leah *was* tender eyed; but Rāchel
was beautiful and well favoured.
18 And Jacob loved Rāchel; and said,
I will serve thee seven years for Rāchel
thy younger daughter.
19 And Lāban said, *It is* better that I
give her to thee, than that I should give
her to another man: abide with me.
20 And Jacob served seven years for
Rāchel; and they seemed unto him *but*
a few days, for the love he had to her.
21 ¶And Jacob said unto Lāban, Give
me my wife, for my days are fulfilled,
that I may go in unto her.
22 And Lāban gathered together all
the men of the place, and made a feast.
23 And it came to pass in the evening,
that he took Leah his daughter, and
brought her to him; and he went in unto
her.
24 And Lāban gave unto his daughter
Leah Zĭlpah his maid *for* an handmaid.
25 And it came to pass, that in the
morning, behold, it *was* Leah: and he
said to Lāban, What *is* this thou hast
done unto me? did not I serve with thee
for Rāchel? wherefore then hast thou
beguiled me?
26 And Lāban said, It must not be so
done in our country, to give the youn-
ger before the firstborn.
27 Fulfil her week, and we will give
thee this also for the service which thou
shalt serve with me yet seven other
years.
28 And Jacob did so, and fulfilled her
week: and he gave him Rāchel his
daughter to wife also.
29 And Lāban gave to Rāchel his
daughter Bĭl'hah his handmaid to be
her maid.
30 And he went in also unto Rāchel,
and he loved also Rāchel more than
Leah, and served with him yet seven
other years.
31 ¶And when the LORD saw that
Leah *was* hated, he opened her womb:
but Rāchel *was* barren.
32 And Leah conceived, and bare a
son, and she called his name Reuben:
for she said, Surely the LORD hath
looked upon my affliction; now there-
fore my husband will love me.
33 And she conceived again, and bare
a son; and said, Because the LORD hath
heard that I *was* hated, he hath there-
fore given me this *son* also: and she
called his name Simeon.
34 And she conceived again, and bare
a son; and said, Now this time will my
husband be joined unto me, because I
have born him three sons: therefore
was his name called Levi.
35 And she conceived again, and bare
a son: and she said, Now will I praise
the LORD: therefore she called his name
Jūdah; and left bearing.

CHAPTER 30

AND when Rāchel saw that she bare
Jacob no children, Rāchel envied her
sister; and said unto Jacob, Give me
children, or else I die.
2 And Jacob's anger was kindled
against Rāchel: and he said, *Am* I in
God's stead, who hath withheld from
thee the fruit of the womb?
3 And she said, Behold my maid Bĭl'-
hah, go in unto her; and she shall bear
upon my knees, that I may also have
children by her.
4 And she gave him Bĭl'hah her hand-
maid to wife: and Jacob went in unto
her.
5 And Bĭl'hah conceived, and bare Ja-
cob a son.
6 And Rāchel said, God hath judged
me, and hath also heard my voice, and
hath given me a son: therefore called
she his name Dan.
7 And Bĭl'hah Rāchel's maid con-
ceived again, and bare Jacob a second
son.
8 And Rāchel said, With great wres-
tlings have I wrestled with my sister, and
I have prevailed: and she called his
name Năph'ta-lī.
9 When Leah saw that she had left
bearing, she took Zilpah her maid, and
gave her Jacob to wife.
10 And Zĭlpah Leah's maid bare Ja-
cob a son.
11 And Leah said, A troop cometh:
and she called his name Gad.
12 And Zĭlpah Leah's maid bare Ja-
cob a second son.
13 And Leah said, Happy am I, for the
daughters will call me blessed: and she
called his name Asher.

14 ¶And Reuben went in the days of wheat harvest, and found mandrakes in the field, and brought them unto his mother Leah. Then Rāchel said to Leah, Give me, I pray thee, of thy son's mandrakes.

15 And she said unto her, *Is it* a small matter that thou hast taken my husband? and wouldest thou take away my son's mandrakes also? And Rāchel said, Therefore he shall lie with thee to night for thy son's mandrakes.

16 And Jacob came out of the field in the evening, and Leah went out to meet him, and said, Thou must come in unto me; for surely I have hired thee with my son's mandrakes. And he lay with her that night.

17 And God hearkened unto Leah, and she conceived, and bare Jacob the fifth son.

18 And Leah said, God hath given me my hire, because I have given my maiden to my husband: and she called his name Īs'sa-char.

19 And Leah conceived again, and bare Jacob the sixth son.

20 And Leah said, God hath endued me *with* a good dowry; now will my husband dwell with me, because I have born him six sons: and she called his name Zĕb'u-lun.

21 And afterwards she bare a daughter, and called her name Dinah.

22 ¶And God remembered Rāchel, and God hearkened to her, and opened her wŏmb.

23 And she conceived, and bare a son; and said, God hath taken away my reproach:

24 And she called his name Joseph; and said, The LORD shall add to me another son.

25 ¶And it came to pass, when Rāchel had born Joseph, that Jacob said unto Lāban, Send me away, that I may go unto mine own place, and to my country.

26 Give *me* my wives and my children, for whom I have served thee, and let me go: for thou knowest my service which I have done thee.

27 And Lāban said unto him, I pray thee, if I have found favour in thine eyes, *tarry: for* I have learned by experience that the LORD hath blessed me for thy sake.

28 And he said, Appoint me thy wages, and I will give *it*.

29 And he said unto him, Thou knowest how I have served thee, and how thy cattle was with me.

30 For *it was* little which thou hadst before I *came*, and it is *now* increased unto a multitude; and the LORD hath blessed thee since my coming: and now when shall I provide for mine own house also?

31 And he said, What shall I give thee? And Jacob said, Thou shalt not give me any thing: if thou wilt do this thing for me, I will again feed *and* keep thy flock.

32 I will pass through all thy flock to day, removing from thence all the speckled and spotted cattle, and all the brown cattle among the sheep, and the spotted and speckled among the goats: and *of such* shall be my hire.

33 So shall my righteousness answer for me in time to come, when it shall come for my hire before thy face: every one that *is* not speckled and spotted among the goats, and brown among the sheep, that shall be counted stolen with me.

34 And Lāban said, Behold, I would it might be according to thy word.

35 And he removed that day the he goats that were ringstraked and spotted, and all the she goats that were speckled and spotted, *and* every one that had *some* white in it, and all the brown among the sheep, and gave *them* into the hand of his sons.

36 And he set three days' journey betwixt himself and Jacob: and Jacob fed the rest of Lāban's flocks.

37 ¶And Jacob took him rods of green poplar, and of the hazel and chesnut tree; and pilled white strakes in them, and made the white appear which *was* in the rods.

38 And he set the rods which he had pilled before the flocks in the gutters in the watering troughs when the flocks came to drink, that they should conceive when they came to drink.

39 And the flocks conceived before the rods, and brought forth cattle ringstraked, speckled, and spotted.

40 And Jacob did separate the lambs, and set the faces of the flocks toward the ringstraked, and all the brown in the flock of Lāban; and he put his own flocks by themselves, and put them not unto Lāban's cattle.

41 And it came to pass, whensoever the stronger cattle did conceive, that Jacob laid the rods before the eyes of the cattle in the gutters, that they might conceive among the rods.

42 But when the cattle were feeble, he put *them* not in: so the feebler were Lāban's, and the stronger Jacob's.

43 And the man increased exceedingly, and had much cattle, and maidservants, and menservants, and camels, and asses.

CHAPTER 31

AND he heard the words of Lāban's sons, saying, Jacob hath taken away all that *was* our father's; and of *that* which *was* our father's hath he gotten all this glory.

2 And Jacob beheld the countenance of Lāban, and, behold, it *was* not toward him as before.

3 And the LORD said unto Jacob, Return unto the land of thy fathers, and to thy kindred; and I will be with thee.

4 And Jacob sent and called Rāchel and Leah to the field unto his flock,

5 And said unto them, I see your father's countenance, that it *is* not toward me as before; but the God of my father hath been with me.

6 And ye know that with all my power I have served your father.

7 And your father hath deceived me, and changed my wages ten times; but God suffered him not to hurt me.

8 If he said thus, The speckled shall be thy wages; then all the cattle bare speckled: and if he said thus, The ringstraked shall be thy hire; then bare all the cattle ringstraked.

9 Thus God hath taken away the cattle of your father, and given *them* to me.

10 And it came to pass at the time that the cattle conceived, that I lifted up mine eyes, and saw in a dream, and, behold, the rams which leaped upon the cattle *were* ringstraked, speckled, and grisled.

11 And the angel of God spake unto me in a dream, *saying*, Jacob: and I said, Here *am* I.

12 And he said, Lift up now thine eyes, and see, all the rams which leap upon the cattle *are* ringstraked, speckled, and grisled: for I have seen all that Lāban doeth unto thee.

13 I *am* the God of Bĕth-el, where thou anointedst the pillar, *and* where thou vowedst a vow unto me: now arise, get thee out from this land, and return unto the land of thy kindred.

14 And Rāchel and Leah answered and said unto him, *Is there* yet any portion or inheritance for us in our father's house?

15 Are we not counted of him strangers? for he hath sold us, and hath quite devoured also our money.

16 For all the riches which God hath taken from our father, that *is* ours, and our children's: now then, whatsoever God hath said unto thee, do.

17 ¶Then Jacob rose up, and set his sons and his wives upon camels;

18 And he carried away all his cattle, and all his goods which he had gotten, the cattle of his getting, which he had gotten in Pă'dan-ā'ram, for to go to Isaac his father in the land of Canaan.

19 And Lāban went to shear his sheep: and Rāchel had stolen the images that *were* her father's.

20 And Jacob stole away unawares to Lāban the Syrian, in that he told him not that he fled.

21 So he fled with all that he had; and he rose up, and passed over the river, and set his face *toward* the mount Gilead.

22 And it was told Lāban on the third day that Jacob was fled.

23 And he took his brethren with him, and pursued after him seven days' journey; and they overtook him in the mount Gilead.

24 And God came to Lāban the Syrian in a dream by night, and said unto him, Take heed that thou speak not to Jacob either good or bad.

25 ¶Then Lāban overtook Jacob. Now Jacob had pitched his tent in the mount: and Lāban with his brethren pitched in the mount of Gilead.

26 And Lāban said to Jacob, What hast thou done, that thou hast stolen away unawares to me, and carried away my daughters, as captives *taken* with the sword?

27 Wherefore didst thou flee away secretly, and steal away from me; and didst not tell me, that I might have sent thee away with mirth, and with songs, with tabret, and with harp?

28 And hast not suffered me to kiss my sons and my daughters? thou hast now done foolishly in *so* doing.

29 It is in the power of my hand to do you hurt: but the God of your father spake unto me yesternight, saying, Take thou heed that thou speak not to Jacob either good or bad.

30 And now, *though* thou wouldest needs be gone, because thou sore longedst after thy father's house, *yet* wherefore hast thou stolen my gods?

31 And Jacob answered and said to Lāban, Because I was afraid: for I said, Peradventure thou wouldest take by force thy daughters from me.

32 With whomsoever thou findest thy gods, let him not live: before our brethren discern thou what *is* thine with me, and take *it* to thee. For Jacob knew not that Rāchel had stolen them.

33 And Laban went into Jacob's tent, and into Leah's tent, and into the two maidservants' tents; but he found *them* not. Then went he out of Leah's tent, and entered into Rāchel's tent.

34 Now Rāchel had taken the images,

and put them in the camel's furniture, and sat upon them. And Laban searched all the tent, but found *them* not.
35 And she said to her father, Let it not displease my lord that I cannot rise up before thee; for the custom of women *is* upon me. And he searched, but found not the images.
36 ¶And Jacob was wroth, and chode with Lāban: and Jacob answered and said to Lāban, What *is* my trespass? what *is* my sin, that thou hast so hotly pursued after me?
37 Whereas thou hast searched all my stuff, what hast thou found of all thy household stuff? set *it* here before my brethren and thy brethren, that they may judge betwixt us both.
38 This twenty years *have* I *been* with thee; thy ewes and thy she goats have not cast their young, and the rams of thy flock have I not eaten.
39 That which was torn *of beasts* I brought not unto thee; I bare the loss of it; of my hand didst thou require it, *whether* stolen by day, or stolen by night.
40 *Thus* I was; in the day the drought consumed me, and the frost by night; and my sleep departed from mine eyes.
41 Thus have I been twenty years in thy house; I served thee fourteen years for thy two daughters, and six years for thy cattle: and thou hast changed my wages ten times.
42 Except the God of my father, the God of Abraham, and the fear of Isaac, had been with me, surely thou hadst sent me away now empty. God hath seen mine affliction and the labour of my hands, and rebuked *thee* yesternight.
43 ¶And Lāban answered and said unto Jacob, *These* daughters *are* my daughters, and *these* children *are* my children, and *these* cattle *are* my cattle, and all that thou seest *is* mine: and what can I do this day unto these my daughters, or unto their children which they have born?
44 Now therefore come thou, let us make a covenant, I and thou; and let it be for a witness between me and thee.
45 And Jacob took a stone, and set it up *for* a pillar.
46 And Jacob said unto his brethren, Gather stones; and they took stones, and made an heap: and they did eat there upon the heap.
47 And Lāban called it Jē′gar-sā-ha-dū′tha: but Jacob called it Găl′e-ed.
48 And Lāban said, This heap *is* a witness between me and thee this day. Therefore was the name of it called Găl′e-ed;
49 And Mizpah; for he said, The LORD watch between me and thee, when we are absent one from another.
50 If thou shalt afflict my daughters, or if thou shalt take *other* wives beside my daughters, no man *is* with us; see, God *is* witness betwixt me and thee.
51 And Lāban said to Jacob, Behold this heap, and behold *this* pillar, which I have cast betwixt me and thee;
52 This heap *be* witness, and *this* pillar *be* witness, that I will not pass over this heap to thee, and that thou shalt not pass over this heap and this pillar unto me, for harm.
53 The God of Abraham, and the God of Nahor, the God of their father, judge betwixt us. And Jacob sware by the fear of his father Isaac.
54 Then Jacob offered sacrifice upon the mount, and called his brethren to eat bread: and they did eat bread, and tarried all night in the mount.
55 And early in the morning Lāban rose up, and kissed his sons and his daughters, and blessed them: and Lāban departed, and returned unto his place.

CHAPTER 32

AND Jacob went on his way, and the angels of God met him.
2 And when Jacob saw them, he said, This *is* God's host: and he called the name of that place Mā-ha-nā′im.
3 And Jacob sent messengers before him to Esau his brother unto the land of Sē′ir, the country of Edom.
4 And he commanded them, saying, Thus shall ye speak unto my lord Esau; Thy servant Jacob saith thus, I have sojourned with Lāban, and stayed there until now:
5 And I have oxen, and asses, flocks, and menservants, and womenservants: and I have sent to tell my lord, that I may find grace in thy sight.
6 ¶And the messengers returned to Jacob, saying, We came to thy brother Esau, and also he cometh to meet thee, and four hundred men with him.
7 Then Jacob was greatly afraid and distressed: and he divided the people that *was* with him, and the flocks, and herds, and the camels, into two bands;
8 And said, If Esau come to the one company, and smite it, then the other company which is left shall escape.
9 ¶And Jacob said, O God of my father Abraham, and God of my father Isaac, the LORD which saidst unto me, Return unto thy country, and to thy kindred, and I will deal well with thee:

10 I am not worthy of the least of all the mercies, and of all the truth, which thou hast shewed unto thy servant; for with my staff I passed over this Jordan; and now I am become two bands.

11 Deliver me, I pray thee, from the hand of my brother, from the hand of Esau: for I fear him, lest he will come and smite me, *and* the mother with the children.

12 And thou saidst, I will surely do thee good, and make thy seed as the sand of the sea, which cannot be numbered for multitude.

13 ¶And he lodged there that same night; and took of that which came to his hand a present for Esau his brother;

14 Two hundred she goats, and twenty he goats, two hundred ewes, and twenty rams,

15 Thirty milch camels with their colts, forty kine, and ten bulls, twenty she asses, and ten foals.

16 And he delivered *them* into the hand of his servants, every drove by themselves; and said unto his servants, Pass over before me, and put a space betwixt drove and drove.

17 And he commanded the foremost, saying, When Esau my brother meeteth thee, and asketh thee, saying, Whose *art* thou? and whither goest thou? and whose *are* these before thee?

18 Then thou shalt say, *They be* thy servant Jacob's; it *is* a present sent unto my lord Esau: and, behold, also he *is* behind us.

19 And so commanded he the second, and the third, and all that followed the droves, saying, On this manner shall ye speak unto Esau, when ye find him.

20 And say ye moreover, Behold, thy servant Jacob *is* behind us. For he said, I will appease him with the present that goeth before me, and afterward I will see his face; peradventure he will accept of me.

21 So went the present over before him: and himself lodged that night in the company.

22 And he rose up that night, and took his two wives, and his two womenservants, and his eleven sons, and passed over the ford Jabbok.

23 And he took them, and sent them over the brook, and sent over that he had.

24 ¶And Jacob was left alone; and there wrestled a man with him until the breaking of the day.

25 And when he saw that he prevailed not against him, he touched the hollow of his thigh; and the hollow of Jacob's thigh was out of joint, as he wrestled with him.

26 And he said, Let me go, for the day breaketh. And he said, I will not let thee go, except thou bless me.

27 And he said unto him, What *is* thy name? And he said, Jacob.

28 And he said, Thy name shall be called no more Jacob, but Israel: for as a prince hast thou power with God and with men, and hast prevailed.

29 And Jacob asked *him,* and said, Tell *me,* I pray thee, thy name. And he said, Wherefore *is* it *that* thou dost ask after my name? And he blessed him there.

30 And Jacob called the name of the place Pe-nī'el: for I have seen God face to face, and my life is preserved.

31 And as he passed over Pe-nū'el the sun rose upon him, and he halted upon his thigh.

32 Therefore the children of Israel eat not *of* the sinew which shrank, which *is* upon the hollow of the thigh, unto this day: because he touched the hollow of Jacob's thigh in the sinew that shrank.

CHAPTER 33

AND Jacob lifted up his eyes and looked, and, behold, Esau came, and with him four hundred men. And he divided the children unto Leah, and unto Rāchel, and unto the two handmaids.

2 And he put the handmaids and their children foremost, and Leah and her children after, and Rāchel and Joseph hindermost.

3 And he passed over before them, and bowed himself to the ground seven times, until he came near to his brother.

4 And Esau ran to meet him, and embraced him, and fell on his neck, and kissed him: and they wept.

5 And he lifted up his eyes, and saw the women and the children; and said, Who *are* those with thee? And he said, The children which God hath graciously given thy servant.

6 Then the handmaidens came near, they and their children, and they bowed themselves.

7 And Leah also with her children came near, and bowed themselves: and after came Joseph near and Rāchel, and they bowed themselves.

8 And he said, What *meanest* thou by all this drove which I met? And he said, *These are* to find grace in the sight of my lord.

9 And Esau said, I have enough, my brother; keep that thou hast unto thyself.

10 And Jacob said, Nay, I pray thee, if now I have found grace in thy sight, then receive my present at my hand: for therefore I have seen thy face, as

though I had seen the face of God, and
thou wast pleased with me.
11 Take, I pray thee, my blessing that
is brought to thee; because God hath
dealt graciously with me, and because I
have enough. And he urged him, and he
took *it*.
12 And he said, Let us take our jour-
ney, and let us go, and I will go before
thee.
13 And he said unto him, My lord
knoweth that the children *are* tender,
and the flocks and herds with young
are with me: and if men should over-
drive them one day, all the flock will
die.
14 Let my lord, I pray thee, pass over
before his servant: and I will lead on
softly, according as the cattle that
goeth before me and the children be
able to endure, until I come unto my
lord unto Sē'ir.
15 And Esau said, Let me now leave
with thee *some* of the folk that *are* with
me. And he said, What needeth it? let
me find grace in the sight of my lord.
16 ¶So Esau returned that day on his
way unto Sē'ir.
17 And Jacob journeyed to Sŭc'coth,
and built him an house, and made
booths for his cattle: therefore the
name of the place is called Sŭc'coth.
18 ¶And Jacob came to Shā'lem, a
city of Shĕ'chem, which *is* in the land of
Canaan, when he came from Pă'dan-
â'ram; and pitched his tent before
the city.
19 And he bought a parcel of a field,
where he had spread his tent, at the
hand of the children of Hā'môr, Shĕ'-
chem's father, for an hundred pieces of
money.
20 And he erected there an altar, and
called it Ĕl-e-lō'hē-Ĭsraēl.

CHAPTER 34

AND Dinah the daughter of Leah,
which she bare unto Jacob, went out to
see the daughters of the land.
2 And when Shĕ'chem the son of Hā'-
môr the Hī'vīte, prince of the country,
saw her, he took her, and lay with her,
and defiled her.
3 And his soul clave unto Dinah the
daughter of Jacob, and he loved the
damsel, and spake kindly unto the
damsel.
4 And Shĕ'chem spake unto his
father Hā'môr, saying, Get me this
damsel to wife.
5 And Jacob heard that he had defiled
Dinah his daughter: now his sons were
with his cattle in the field: and Jacob
held his peace until they were come.
6 ¶And Hā'môr the father of Shĕ'-
chem went out unto Jacob to commune
with him.
7 And the sons of Jacob came out of
the field when they heard *it*: and the
men were grieved, and they were very
wroth, because he had wrought folly in
Israel in lying with Jacob's daughter;
which thing ought not to be done.
8 And Hā'môr communed with them,
saying, The soul of my son Shĕ'chem
longeth for your daughter: I pray you
give her him to wife.
9 And make ye marriages with us,
and give your daughters unto us, and
take our daughters unto you.
10 And ye shall dwell with us: and the
land shall be before you; dwell and
trade ye therein, and get you posses-
sions therein.
11 And Shĕ'chem said unto her father
and unto her brethren, Let me find
grace in your eyes, and what ye shall
say unto me I will give.
12 Ask me never so much dowry and
gift, and I will give according as ye
shall say unto me: but give me the dam-
sel to wife.
13 And the sons of Jacob answered
Shĕ'chem and Hā'môr his father de-
ceitfully, and said, because he had de-
filed Dinah their sister:
14 And they said unto them, We can-
not do this thing, to give our sister to
one that is uncircumcised; for that
were a reproach unto us:
15 But in this will we consent unto
you: If ye will be as we *be*, that every
male of you be circumcised;
16 Then will we give our daughters
unto you, and we will take your daugh-
ters to us, and we will dwell with you,
and we will become one people.
17 But if ye will not hearken unto us,
to be circumcised; then will we take
our daughter, and we will be gone.
18 And their words pleased Hā'môr,
and Shĕ'chem Hā'môr's son.
19 And the young man deferred not
to do the thing, because he had delight
in Jacob's daughter: and he *was* more
honourable than all the house of his
father.
20 And Hā'môr and Shĕ'chem his son
came unto the gate of their city, and
communed with the men of their city,
saying,
21 These men *are* peaceable with us;
therefore let them dwell in the land,
and trade therein; for the land, behold,
it is large enough for them; let us take
their daughters to us for wives, and let
us give them our daughters.
22 Only herein will the men consent
unto us for to dwell with us, to be one

people, if every male among us be circumcised, as they *are* circumcised.

23 *Shall* not their cattle and their substance and every beast of theirs *be* ours? only let us consent unto them, and they will dwell with us.

24 And unto Hā'môr and unto Shĕ'chem his son hearkened all that went out of the gate of his city; and every male was circumcised, all that went out of the gate of his city.

25 ¶And it came to pass on the third day, when they were sore, that two of the sons of Jacob, Simeon and Levi, Dinah's brethren, took each man his sword, and came upon the city boldly, and slew all the males.

26 And they slew Hā'môr and Shĕ'chem his son with the edge of the sword, and took Dinah out of Shĕ'chem's house, and went out.

27 The sons of Jacob came upon the slain, and spoiled the city, because they had defiled their sister.

28 They took their sheep, and their oxen, and their asses, and that which *was* in the city, and that which *was* in the field,

29 And all their wealth, and all their little ones, and their wives took they captive, and spoiled even all that *was* in the house.

30 And Jacob said to Simeon and Levi, Ye have troubled me to make me to stink among the inhabitants of the land, among the Canaanites and the Pĕr'iz-zītes: and I *being* few in number, they shall gather themselves together against me, and slay me; and I shall be destroyed, I and my house.

31 And they said, Should he deal with our sister as with an harlot?

CHAPTER 35

AND God said unto Jacob, Arise, go up to Beth-el, and dwell there: and make there an altar unto God, that appeared unto thee when thou fleddest from the face of Esau thy brother.

2 Then Jacob said unto his household, and to all that *were* with him, Put away the strange gods that *are* among you, and be clean, and change your garments:

3 And let us arise, and go up to Bĕth-el; and I will make there an altar unto God, who answered me in the day of my distress, and was with me in the way which I went.

4 And they gave unto Jacob all the strange gods which *were* in their hand, and *all their* earrings which *were* in their ears; and Jacob hid them under the oak which *was* by Shĕ'chem.

5 And they journeyed: and the terror of God was upon the cities that *were* round about them, and they did not pursue after the sons of Jacob.

6 ¶So Jacob came to Luz, which *is* in the land of Canaan, that *is*, Bĕth-el, he and all the people that *were* with him.

7 And he built there an altar, and called the place Ĕl-bĕth-el: because there God appeared unto him, when he fled from the face of his brother.

8 But Dĕborah Rebekah's nurse died, and she was buried beneath Bĕth-el under an oak: and the name of it was called Ăl'lon-băch'uth.

9 ¶And God appeared unto Jacob again, when he came out of Pă'dan-â'ram, and blessed him.

10 And God said unto him, Thy name *is* Jacob: thy name shall not be called any more Jacob, but Israel shall be thy name: and he called his name Israel.

11 And God said unto him, I *am* God Almighty: be fruitful and multiply; a nation and a company of nations shall be of thee, and kings shall come out of thy loins;

12 And the land which I gave Abraham and Isaac, to thee I will give it, and to thy seed after thee will I give the land.

13 And God went up from him in the place where he talked with him.

14 And Jacob set up a pillar in the place where he talked with him, *even* a pillar of stone: and he poured a drink offering thereon, and he poured oil thereon.

15 And Jacob called the name of the place where God spake with him, Bĕth-el.

16 ¶And they journeyed from Bĕth-el; and there was but a little way to come to Ĕph'rath: and Rāchel travailed, and she had hard labour.

17 And it came to pass, when she was in hard labour, that the midwife said unto her, Fear not; thou shalt have this son also.

18 And it came to pass, as her soul was in departing, (for she died) that she called his name Bĕn-ō'nī: but his father called him Benjamin.

19 And Rāchel died, and was buried in the way to Ĕph'rath, which *is* Bĕth-lehĕm.

20 And Jacob set a pillar upon her grave: that *is* the pillar of Rāchel's grave unto this day.

21 ¶And Israel journeyed, and spread his tent beyond the tower of Ē'dar.

22 And it came to pass, when Israel dwelt in that land, that Reuben went and lay with Bĭl'hah his father's concubine: and Israel heard *it*. Now the sons of Jacob were twelve:

23 The sons of Leah; Reuben, Jacob's
firstborn, and Simeon, and Levi, and
Jūdah, and Ĭs'sa-char, and Zĕb'u-lun:
24 The sons of Rāchel; Joseph, and
Benjamin:
25 And the sons of Bĭl'hah, Rāchel's
handmaid; Dan, and Năph'ta-lī:
26 And the sons of Zĭlpah, Leah's
handmaid; Gad, and Asher: these *are*
the sons of Jacob, which were born to
him in Pă'dan–â'ram.
27 ¶And Jacob came unto Isaac his
father unto Măm're, unto the city of
Är'bah, which *is* Hēbron, where Abra-
ham and Isaac sojourned.
28 And the days of Isaac were an
hundred and fourscore years.
29 And Isaac gave up the ghost, and
died, and was gathered unto his people,
being old and full of days: and his sons
Esau and Jacob buried him.

CHAPTER 36

NOW these *are* the generations of
Esau, who *is* Edom.
2 Esau took his wives of the daughters
of Canaan; Adah the daughter of Ē'lŏn
the Hittite, and A-hŏl-ĭ-bă'mah the
daughter of Ā'nah the daughter of
Zĭb'e-on the Hī'vīte;
3 And Băsh'e-măth Ĭsh'ma-el's
daughter, sister of Ne-bā'jŏth.
4 And Adah bare to Esau Ĕl'i-phăz;
and Băsh'e-măth bare Reū'el;
5 And A-hŏl-ĭ-bă'mah bare Jē'ŭsh,
and Jā-a'lam, and Korah: these *are* the
sons of Esau, which were born unto
him in the land of Canaan.
6 And Esau took his wives, and his
sons, and his daughters, and all the per-
sons of his house, and his cattle, and all
his beasts, and all his substance, which
he had got in the land of Canaan; and
went into the country from the face of
his brother Jacob.
7 For their riches were more than
that they might dwell together; and the
land wherein they were strangers
could not bear them because of their
cattle.
8 Thus dwelt Esau in mount Sē'ir:
Esau *is* Edom.
9 ¶And these *are* the generations of
Esau the father of the Edomites in
mount Sē'ir:
10 These *are* the names of Esau's
sons; Ĕl'i-phăz the son of Adah the wife
of Esau, Reū'el the son of Băsh'e-măth
the wife of Esau.
11 And the sons of Ĕl'i-phăz were Tē'-
man, Omar, Zē'phō, and Gă'tam, and
Kē'năz.
12 And Tĭm'na was concubine to Ĕl'i-
phăz Esau's son; and she bare to Ĕl'i-
phăz Ăm'a-lĕk: these *were* the sons of
Adah Esau's wife.
13 And these *are* the sons of Reū'el;
Nā'hăth, and Ze'rah, Shăm'mah, and
Mĭz'zah: these were the sons of Băsh'e-
măth Esau's wife.
14 And these were the sons of A-hŏl-
ĭ-bă'mah, the daughter of Ā'nah the
daughter of Zĭb'e-on, Esau's wife: and
she bare to Esau Jē'ŭsh, and Jā-a'lam,
and Kôrah.
15 ¶These *were* dukes of the sons of
Esau: the sons of Ĕl'i-phăz the firstborn
son of Esau; duke Tē'man, duke Omar,
duke Zē'phō, duke Kē'năz,
16 Duke Kôrah, duke Gă'tam, *and*
duke Ăm'a-lĕk: these *are* the dukes *that*
came of Ĕl'i-phăz in the land of Edom;
these *were* the sons of Adah.
17 And these *are* the sons of Reū'el
Esau's son; duke Na'hăth, duke Ze'rah,
duke Shăm'mah, duke Mĭz'zah: these
are the dukes *that came* of Reū'el in the
land of Edom; these *are* the sons of
Băsh'e-măth Esau's wife.
18 And these *are* the sons of A-hŏl-ĭ-
bă'mah Esau's wife; duke Jē'ŭsh, duke
Jā-a'lam, duke Kôrah: these *were* the
dukes *that came* of A-hŏl-ĭ-bă'mah the
daughter of Ā'nah, Esau's wife.
19 These *are* the sons of Esau, who *is*
Edom, and these *are* their dukes.
20 ¶These *are* the sons of Sē'ir the
Hô'rīte, who inhabited the land; Lō'tăn,
and Shō'bal, and Zĭb'e-on, and Ā'nah,
21 And Dī'shŏn, and Ē'zer, and Dī'-
shăn: these *are* the dukes of the Hô'-
rītes, the children of Sē'ir in the land of
Edom.
22 And the children of Lō'tăn were
Hô'rī and Hē'mam; and Lō'tăn's sister
was Tĭm'na.
23 And the children of Shō'bal *were*
these; Ăl'van, and Măn'a-hăth, and
Ebal, Shē'phō, and Ō'nam.
24 And these *are* the children of
Zĭb'e-on; both Ā'jah, and Ā'nah: this
was that Ā'nah that found the mules in
the wilderness, as he fed the asses of
Zĭb'e-on his father.
25 And the children of Ā'nah *were*
these; Dī'shŏn, and A-hŏl-ĭ-bă'mah the
daughter of Ā'nah.
26 And these *are* the children of
Dī'shŏn; Hĕm'dăn, and Ĕsh'băn, and
Ĭth'răn, and Chĕ'ran.
27 The children of Ē'zer *are* these;
Bĭl'hăn, and Zā'a-văn, and Ā'kăn.
28 The children of Dī'shăn *are* these;
Uz, and Â'răn.
29 These *are* the dukes *that came* of
the Hô'rītes; duke Lō'tăn, duke Shō'-
bal, duke Zĭb'e-on, duke Ā'nah,
30 Duke Dī'shŏn, duke Ē'zer, duke
Dī'shăn: these *are* the dukes *that came*

of Hô'rī, among their dukes in the land of Sē'ir.
31 ¶And these *are* the kings that reigned in the land of Edom, before there reigned any king over the children of Israel.
32 And Bē'la the son of Bē'ôr reigned in Edom: and the name of his city *was* Dĭn'ha-bah.
33 And Bē'la died, and Jō'băb the son of Ze'rah of Bŏz'rah reigned in his stead.
34 And Jō'băb died, and Hu'sham of the land of Tĕm'a-nī reigned in his stead.
35 And Hu'sham died, and Hā'dăd the son of Bē'dăd, who smote Mĭd'ĭ-an in the field of Moab, reigned in his stead: and the name of his city *was* Ā'vĭth.
36 And Hā'dăd died, and Săm'lah of Măs're-kah reigned in his stead.
37 And Săm'lah died, and Saul of Re-hō'bŏth *by* the river reigned in his stead.
38 And Saul died, and Bā'al-hā'nan the son of Ăch'bôr reigned in his stead.
39 And Bā'al-hā'nan the son of Ăch'-bôr died, and Hā'där reigned in his stead: and the name of his city *was* Pā'ū; and his wife's name *was* Me-hĕt'a-bĕl, the daughter of Mā'tred, the daughter of Mĕz'a-hăb.
40 ¶And these *are* the names of the dukes *that came* of Esau, according to their families, after their places, by their names; duke Tĭm'nah, duke Ăl'vah, duke Jē'thĕth,
41 Duke A-hŏl-ĭ-bā'mah, duke Ē'lah, duke Pī'nŏn,
42 Duke Kē'năz, duke Tē'man, duke Mĭb'zär,
43 Duke Măg'dĭ-el, duke Ī'răm: these *be* the dukes of Edom, according to their habitations in the land of their possession: he *is* Esau the father of the Edomites.

CHAPTER 37

AND Jacob dwelt in the land wherein his father was a stranger, in the land of Canaan.
2 These *are* the generations of Jacob. Joseph, *being* seventeen years old, was feeding the flock with his brethren; and the lad *was* with the sons of Bĭl'hah, and with the sons of Zĭl'pah, his father's wives: and Joseph brought unto his father their evil report.
3 Now Israel loved Joseph more than all his children, because he *was* the son of his old age: and he made him a coat of *many* colours.
4 And when his brethren saw that their father loved him more than all his brethren, they hated him, and could not speak peaceably unto him.
5 ¶And Joseph dreamed a dream, and he told *it* his brethren: and they hated him yet the more.
6 And he said unto them, Hear, I pray you, this dream which I have dreamed:
7 For, behold, we *were* binding sheaves in the field, and, lo, my sheaf arose, and also stood upright; and, behold, your sheaves stood round about, and made obeisance to my sheaf.
8 And his brethren said to him, Shalt thou indeed reign over us? or shalt thou indeed have dominion over us? And they hated him yet the more for his dreams, and for his words.
9 And he dreamed yet another dream, and told it his brethren, and said, Behold, I have dreamed a dream more; and, behold, the sun and the moon and the eleven stars made obeisance to me.
10 And he told *it* to his father, and to his brethren: and his father rebuked him, and said unto him, What *is* this dream that thou hast dreamed? Shall I and thy mother and thy brethren indeed come to bow down ourselves to thee to the earth?
11 And his brethren envied him; but his father observed the saying.
12 ¶And his brethren went to feed their father's flock in Shĕ'chem.
13 And Israel said unto Joseph, Do not thy brethren feed *the flock* in Shĕ'-chem? come, and I will send thee unto them. And he said to him, Here *am I*.
14 And he said to him, Go, I pray thee, see whether it be well with thy brethren, and well with the flocks; and bring me word again. So he sent him out of the vale of Hē'bron, and he came to Shĕ'chem.
15 And a certain man found him, and, behold, *he was* wandering in the field: and the man asked him, saying, What seekest thou?
16 And he said, I seek my brethren: tell me, I pray thee, where they feed *their flocks*.
17 And the man said, They are departed hence; for I heard them say, Let us go to Dō'than. And Joseph went after his brethren, and found them in Dō'than.
18 ¶And when they saw him afar off, even before he came near unto them, they conspired against him to slay him.
19 And they said one to another, Behold, this dreamer cometh.
20 Come now therefore, and let us slay him, and cast him into some pit, and we will say, Some evil beast hath

devoured him: and we shall see what
will become of his dreams.
21 And Reuben heard *it*, and he deliv-
ered him out of their hands; and said,
Let us not kill him.
22 And Reuben said unto them, Shed
no blood, *but* cast him into this pit that
is in the wilderness, and lay no hand
upon him; that he might rid him out of
their hands, to deliver him to his father
again.
23 ¶And it came to pass, when Joseph
was come unto his brethren, that they
stript Joseph out of his coat, *his* coat of
many colours that *was* on him;
24 And they took him, and cast him
into a pit: and the pit *was* empty, *there*
was no water in it.
25 And they sat down to eat bread:
and they lifted up their eyes and
looked, and, behold, a company of
Ish'me-el-ītes came from Gilead with
their camels bearing spicery and balm
and myrrh, going to carry *it* down to
Egypt.
26 And Jūdah said unto his brethren,
What profit *is it* if we slay our brother,
and conceal his blood?
27 Come, and let us sell him to the
Ish'me-el-ītes, and let not our hand be
upon him; for he *is* our brother *and* our
flesh. And his brethren were content.
28 Then there passed by Mĭd'ĭ-an-
ītes merchantmen; and they drew and
lifted up Joseph out of the pit, and sold
Joseph to the Ĭsh'me-el-ītes for twenty
pieces of silver: and they brought Jo-
seph into Egypt.
29 ¶And Reuben returned unto the
pit; and, behold, Joseph *was* not in the
pit; and he rent his clothes.
30 And he returned unto his brethren,
and said, The child *is* not; and I, whither
shall I go?
31 ¶And they took Joseph's coat, and
killed a kid of the goats and dipped
the coat in the blood;
32 And they sent the coat of *many* col-
ours, and they brought *it* to their
father; and said, This have we found:
know now whether it *be* thy son's coat
or no.
33 And he knew it, and said, *It is* my
son's coat; an evil beast hath devoured
him; Joseph is without doubt rent in
pieces.
34 And Jacob rent his clothes, and
put sackcloth upon his loins, and
mourned for his son many days.
35 And all his sons and all his daugh-
ters rose up to comfort him; but he re-
fused to be comforted; and he said, For
I will go down into the grave unto my
son mourning. Thus his father wept for
him.
36 And the Mĭd'ĭ-an-ītes sold him into
Egypt unto Pŏt'i-phar, an officer of
Pharaoh's, *and* captain of the guard.

CHAPTER 38

AND it came to pass at that time, that
Jūdah went down from his brethren,
and turned in to a certain A-dŭl'lam-īte,
whose name *was* Hī'rah.
2 And Jūdah saw there a daughter of
a certain Canaanite, whose name *was*
Shū'ah; and he took her, and went in
unto her.
3 And she conceived, and bare a son;
and he called his name Er.
4 And she conceived again, and bare
a son; and she called his name Ō'nan.
5 And she yet again conceived, and
bare a son; and called his name She'lah:
and he was at Chē'zĭb, when she bare
him.
6 And Jūdah took a wife for Er his
firstborn, whose name *was* Tā'mar.
7 And Er, Jūdah's firstborn, was
wicked in the sight of the LORD; and the
LORD slew him.
8 And Jūdah said unto Ō'nan, Go in
unto thy brother's wife, and marry her,
and raise up seed to thy brother.
9 And Ō'nan knew that the seed
should not be his; and it came to pass,
when he went in unto his brother's
wife, that he spilled *it* on the ground,
lest that he should give seed to his
brother.
10 And the thing which he did dis-
pleased the LORD: wherefore he slew
him also.
11 Then said Judah to Tā'mar his
daughter in law, Remain a widow at
thy father's house, till Shē'lah my son
be grown: for he said, Lest peradven-
ture he die also, as his brethren *did*.
And Tā'mar went and dwelt in her fa-
ther's house.
12 ¶And in process of time the
daughter of Shū'ah Jūdah's wife died;
and Jūdah was comforted, and went up
unto his sheepshearers to Tĭm'năth, he
and his friend Hī'rah the A-dŭl'lam-īte.
13 And it was told Tā'mar, saying,
Behold thy father in law goeth up to
Tĭm'năth to shear his sheep.
14 And she put her widow's gar-
ments off from her, and covered her
with a vail, and wrapped herself, and
sat in an open place, which *is* by the
way to Tĭm'năth; for she saw that Shē'-
lah was grown, and she was not given
unto him to wife.
15 When Jūdah saw her, he thought
her *to be* an harlot; because she had
covered her face.
16 And he turned unto her by the
way, and said, Go to, I pray thee, let me

come in unto thee; (for he knew not that she *was* his daughter in law.) And she said, What wilt thou give me, that thou mayest come in unto me?
17 And he said, I will send *thee* a kid from the flock. And she said, Wilt thou give *me* a pledge, till thou send *it?*
18 And he said, What pledge shall I give thee? And she said, Thy signet, and thy bracelets, and thy staff that *is* in thine hand. And he gave *it* her, and came in unto her, and she conceived by him.
19 And she arose, and went away, and laid by her vail from her, and put on the garments of her widowhood.
20 And Jūdah sent the kid by the hand of his friend the A-dŭl′lam-īte, to receive *his* pledge from the woman's hand: but he found her not.
21 Then he asked the men of that place, saying, Where *is* the harlot, that *was* openly by the way side? And they said, There was no harlot in this *place.*
22 And he returned to Jūdah, and said, I cannot find her; and also the men of the place said, *that* there was no harlot in this *place.*
23 And Jūdah said, Let her take *it* to her, lest we be shamed: behold, I sent this kid, and thou hast not found her.
24 ¶And it came to pass about three months after, that it was told Jūdah, saying, Tā′mar thy daughter in law hath played the harlot; and also, behold, she *is* with child by whoredom. And Jūdah said, Bring her forth, and let her be burnt.
25 When she *was* brought forth, she sent to her father in law, saying, By the man, whose these *are, am* I with child: and she said, Discern, I pray thee, whose *are* these, the signet, and bracelets, and staff.
26 And Jūdah acknowledged *them,* and said, She hath been more righteous than I; because that I gave her not to Shē′lah my son. And he knew her again no more.
27 ¶And it came to pass in the time of her travail, that, behold, twins *were* in her womb.
28 And it came to pass, when she travailed, that *the one* put out *his* hand: and the midwife took and bound upon his hand a scarlet thread, saying, This came out first.
29 And it came to pass, as he drew back his hand, that, behold, his brother came out: and she said, How hast thou broken forth? *this* breach *be* upon thee: therefore his name was called Phâ′rĕz.
30 And afterward came out his brother, that had the scarlet thread upon his hand: and his name was called Zâ′rah.

CHAPTER 39

AND Joseph was brought down to Egypt; and Pŏt′i-phar, an officer of Pharaoh, captain of the guard, an Egyptian, bought him of the hands of the Ĭsh′me-el-ītes, which had brought him down thither.
2 And the LORD was with Joseph, and he was a prosperous man; and he was in the house of his master the Egyptian.
3 And his master saw that the LORD *was* with him, and that the LORD made all that he did to prosper in his hand.
4 And Joseph found grace in his sight, and he served him: and he made him overseer over his house, and all *that* he had he put into his hand.
5 And it came to pass from the time *that* he had made him overseer in his house, and over all that he had, that the LORD blessed the Egyptian's house for Joseph's sake; and the blessing of the LORD was upon all that he had in the house, and in the field.
6 And he left all that he had in Joseph's hand; and he knew not ought he had, save the bread which he did eat. And Joseph was *a* goodly *person,* and well favoured.
7 ¶And it came to pass after these things, that his master's wife cast her eyes upon Joseph; and she said, Lie with me.
8 But he refused, and said unto his master's wife, Behold, my master wotteth not what *is* with me in the house, and he hath committed all that he hath to my hand;
9 *There is* none greater in this house than I; neither hath he kept back any thing from me but thee, because thou *art* his wife: how then can I do this great wickedness, and sin against God?
10 And it came to pass, as she spake to Joseph day by day, that he hearkened not unto her, to lie by her, *or* to be with her.
11 And it came to pass about this time, that *Joseph* went into the house to do his business; and *there was* none of the men of the house there within.
12 And she caught him by his garment, saying, Lie with me: and he left his garment in her hand, and fled, and got him out.
13 And it came to pass, when she saw that he had left his garment in her hand, and was fled forth,
14 That she called unto the men of her house, and spake unto them, saying, See, he hath brought in an Hebrew unto us to mock us; he came in

unto me to lie with me, and I cried with a loud voice:

15 And it came to pass, when he heard that I lifted up my voice and cried, that he left his garment with me, and fled, and got him out.

16 And she laid up his garment by her, until his lord came home.

17 And she spake unto him according to these words, saying, The Hebrew servant, which thou hast brought unto us, came in unto me to mock me:

18 And it came to pass, as I lifted up my voice and cried, that he left his garment with me, and fled out.

19 And it came to pass, when his master heard the words of his wife, which she spake unto him, saying, After this manner did thy servant to me; that his wrath was kindled.

20 And Joseph's master took him, and put him into the prison, a place where the king's prisoners *were* bound: and he was there in the prison.

21 But the LORD was with Joseph, and shewed him mercy, and gave him favour in the sight of the keeper of the prison.

22 And the keeper of the prison committed to Joseph's hand all the prisoners that *were* in the prison; and whatsoever they did there, he was the doer *of it*.

23 The keeper of the prison looked not to any thing *that was* under his hand; because the LORD was with him, and *that* which he did, the LORD made *it* to prosper.

CHAPTER 40

AND it came to pass after these things, *that* the butler of the king of Egypt and *his* baker had offended their lord the king of Egypt.

2 And Pharaoh was wroth against two *of* his officers, against the chief of the butlers, and against the chief of the bakers.

3 And he put them in ward in the house of the captain of the guard, into the prison, the place where Joseph *was* bound.

4 And the captain of the guard charged Joseph with them, and he served them: and they continued a season in ward.

5 ¶And they dreamed a dream both of them, each man his dream in one night, each man according to the interpretation of his dream, the butler and the baker of the king of Egypt, which *were* bound in the prison.

6 And Joseph came in unto them in the morning, and looked upon them, and, behold, they *were* sad.

7 And he asked Pharaoh's officers that *were* with him in the ward of his lord's house, saying, Wherefore look ye *so* sadly to day?

8 And they said unto him, We have dreamed a dream, and *there is* no interpreter of it. And Joseph said unto them, *Do* not interpretations *belong* to God? tell me *them*, I pray you.

9 And the chief butler told his dream to Joseph, and said to him, In my dream, behold, a vine *was* before me;

10 And in the vine *were* three branches: and it *was* as though it budded, *and* her blossoms shot forth; and the clusters thereof brought forth ripe grapes:

11 And Pharaoh's cup *was* in my hand: and I took the grapes, and pressed them into Pharaoh's cup, and I gave the cup into Pharaoh's hand.

12 And Joseph said unto him, This *is* the interpretation of it: The three branches *are* three days:

13 Yet within three days shall Pharaoh lift up thine head, and restore thee unto thy place: and thou shalt deliver Pharaoh's cup into his hand, after the former manner when thou wast his butler.

14 But think on me when it shall be well with thee, and shew kindness, I pray thee, unto me, and make mention of me unto Pharaoh, and bring me out of this house:

15 For indeed I was stolen away out of the land of the Hebrews: and here also have I done nothing that they should put me into the dungeon.

16 When the chief baker saw that the interpretation was good, he said unto Joseph, I also *was* in my dream, and, behold, *I had* three white baskets on my head:

17 And in the uppermost basket *there was* of all manner of bakemeats for Pharaoh; and the birds did eat them out of the basket upon my head.

18 And Joseph answered and said, This *is* the interpretation thereof: The three baskets *are* three days:

19 Yet within three days shall Pharaoh lift up thy head from off thee, and shall hang thee on a tree; and the birds shall eat thy flesh from off thee.

20 ¶And it came to pass the third day, *which was* Pharaoh's birthday, that he made a feast unto all his servants: and he lifted up the head of the chief butler and of the chief baker among his servants.

21 And he restored the chief butler unto his butlership again; and he gave the cup into Pharaoh's hand:

22 But he hanged the chief baker: as Joseph had interpreted to them.
23 Yet did not the chief butler remember Joseph, but forgat him.

CHAPTER 41

AND it came to pass at the end of two full years, that Pharaoh dreamed: and, behold, he stood by the river.
2 And, behold, there came up out of the river seven well favoured kine and fatfleshed; and they fed in a meadow.
3 And, behold, seven other kine came up after them out of the river, ill favoured and leanfleshed; and stood by the *other* kine upon the brink of the river.
4 And the ill favoured and leanfleshed kine did eat up the seven well favoured and fat kine. So Pharaoh awoke.
5 And he slept and dreamed the second time: and, behold, seven ears of corn came up upon one stalk, rank and good.
6 And, behold, seven thin ears and blasted with the east wind sprung up after them.
7 And the seven thin ears devoured the seven rank and full ears. And Pharaoh awoke, and, behold, *it was* a dream.
8 And it came to pass in the morning that his spirit was troubled; and he sent and called for all the magicians of Egypt, and all the wise men thereof: and Pharaoh told them his dream; but *there was* none that could interpret them unto Pharaoh.
9 ¶Then spake the chief butler unto Pharaoh, saying, I do remember my faults this day:
10 Pharaoh was wroth with his servants, and put me in ward in the captain of the guard's house, *both* me and the chief baker:
11 And we dreamed a dream in one night, I and he; we dreamed each man according to the interpretation of his dream.
12 And *there was* there with us a young man, an Hebrew, servant to the captain of the guard; and we told him, and he interpreted to us our dreams; to each man according to his dream he did interpret.
13 And it came to pass, as he interpreted to us, so it was; me he restored unto mine office, and him he hanged.
14 ¶Then Pharaoh sent and called Joseph, and they brought him hastily out of the dungeon: and he shaved *himself*, and changed his raiment, and came in unto Pharaoh.
15 And Pharaoh said unto Joseph, I have dreamed a dream, and *there is* none that can interpret it: and I have heard say of thee, *that* thou canst understand a dream to interpret it.
16 And Joseph answered Pharaoh, saying, *It is* not in me: God shall give Pharaoh an answer of peace.
17 And Pharaoh said unto Joseph, In my dream, behold, I stood upon the bank of the river:
18 And, behold, there came up out of the river seven kine, fatfleshed and well favoured; and they fed in a meadow:
19 And, behold, seven other kine came up after them, poor and very ill favoured and leanfleshed, such as I never saw in all the land of Egypt for badness:
20 And the lean and the ill favoured kine did eat up the first seven fat kine:
21 And when they had eaten them up, it could not be known that they had eaten them; but they *were* still ill favoured, as at the beginning. So I awoke.
22 And I saw in my dream, and, behold, seven ears came up in one stalk, full and good:
23 And, behold, seven ears, withered, thin, *and* blasted with the east wind, sprung up after them:
24 And the thin ears devoured the seven good ears: and I told *this* unto the magicians; but *there was* none that could declare *it* to me.
25 ¶And Joseph said unto Pharaoh, The dream of Pharaoh *is* one: God hath shewed Pharaoh what he *is* about to do.
26 The seven good kine *are* seven years; and the seven good ears *are* seven years: the dream *is* one.
27 And the seven thin and ill favoured kine that came up after them *are* seven years; and the seven empty ears blasted with the east wind shall be seven years of famine.
28 This *is* the thing which I have spoken unto Pharaoh: What God *is* about to do he sheweth unto Pharaoh.
29 Behold, there come seven years of great plenty throughout all the land of Egypt:
30 And there shall arise after them seven years of famine; and all the plenty shall be forgotten in the land of Egypt; and the famine shall consume the land;
31 And the plenty shall not be known in the land by reason of that famine following; for it *shall be* very grievous.
32 And for that the dream was doubled unto Pharaoh twice; *it is* because the thing *is* established by God, and God will shortly bring it to pass.

33 Now therefore let Pharaoh look out a man discreet and wise, and set him over the land of Egypt.
34 Let Pharaoh do *this,* and let him appoint officers over the land, and take up the fifth part of the land of Egypt in the seven plenteous years.
35 And let them gather all the food of those good years that come, and lay up corn under the hand of Pharaoh, and let them keep food in the cities.
36 And that food shall be for store to the land against the seven years of famine, which shall be in the land of Egypt; that the land perish not through the famine.
37 ¶And the thing was good in the eyes of Pharaoh, and in the eyes of all his servants.
38 And Pharaoh said unto his servants, Can we find *such a one* as this *is,* a man in whom the Spirit of God *is?*
39 And Pharaoh said unto Joseph, Forasmuch as God hath shewed thee all this, *there is* none so discreet and wise as thou *art:*
40 Thou shalt be over my house, and according unto thy word shall all my people be ruled: only in the throne will I be greater than thou.
41 And Pharaoh said unto Joseph, See, I have set thee over all the land of Egypt.
42 And Pharaoh took off his ring from his hand, and put it upon Joseph's hand, and arrayed him in vestures of fine linen, and put a gold chain about his neck;
43 And he made him to ride in the second chariot which he had; and they cried before him, Bow the knee: and he made him *ruler* over all the land of Egypt.
44 And Pharaoh said unto Joseph, I *am* Pharaoh, and without thee shall no man lift up his hand or foot in all the land of Egypt.
45 And Pharaoh called Joseph's name Zăph'năth–pā-a-nē'ah; and he gave him to wife Ăs'e-năth the daughter of Po-tĭph'e-rah priest of On. And Joseph went out over *all* the land of Egypt.
46 And Joseph *was* thirty years old when he stood before Pharaoh king of Egypt. And Joseph went out from the presence of Pharaoh, and went throughout all the land of Egypt.
47 And in the seven plenteous years the earth brought forth by handfuls.
48 And he gathered up all the food of the seven years, which were in the land of Egypt, and laid up the food in the cities: the food of the field, which *was* round about every city, laid he up in the same.
49 And Joseph gathered corn as the sand of the sea, very much, until he left numbering; for *it was* without number.
50 And unto Joseph were born two sons before the years of famine came, which Ăs'e-năth the daughter of Po-tĭph'e-rah priest of On bare unto him.
51 And Joseph called the name of the firstborn Ma-năs'seh: For God, *said he,* hath made me forget all my toil, and all my father's house.
52 And the name of the second called he Ē'phra-im: For God hath caused me to be fruitful in the land of my affliction.
53 ¶And the seven years of plenteousness, that was in the land of Egypt, were ended.
54 And the seven years of dearth began to come, according as Joseph had said: and the dearth was in all lands; but in all the land of Egypt there was bread.
55 And when all the land of Egypt was famished, the people cried to Pharaoh for bread: and Pharaoh said unto all the Egyptians, Go unto Joseph; what he saith to you, do.
56 And the famine was over all the face of the earth: And Joseph opened all the storehouses, and sold unto the Egyptians; and the famine waxed sore in the land of Egypt.
57 And all countries came into Egypt to Joseph for to buy *corn;* because that the famine was *so* sore in all lands.

CHAPTER 42

NOW when Jacob saw that there was corn in Egypt, Jacob said unto his sons, Why do ye look one upon another?
2 And he said, Behold, I have heard that there is corn in Egypt: get you down thither, and buy for us from thence; that we may live, and not die.
3 ¶And Joseph's ten brethren went down to buy corn in Egypt.
4 But Benjamin, Joseph's brother, Jacob sent not with his brethren; for he said, Lest peradventure mischief befall him.
5 And the sons of Israel came to buy *corn* among those that came: for the famine was in the land of Canaan.
6 And Joseph *was* the governor over the land, *and* he *it was* that sold to all the people of the land: and Joseph's brethren came, and bowed down themselves before him *with* their faces to the earth.
7 And Joseph saw his brethren, and he knew them, but made himself strange unto them, and spake roughly

unto them; and he said unto them, Whence come ye? And they said, From the land of Canaan to buy food.

8 And Joseph knew his brethren, but they knew not him.

9 And Joseph remembered the dreams which he dreamed of them, and said unto them, Ye *are* spies; to see the nakedness of the land ye are come.

10 And they said unto him, Nay, my lord, but to buy food are thy servants come.

11 We *are* all one man's sons; we *are* true *men*, thy servants are no spies.

12 And he said unto them, Nay, but to see the nakedness of the land ye are come.

13 And they said, Thy servants *are* twelve brethren, the sons of one man in the land of Canaan; and, behold, the youngest *is* this day with our father, and one *is* not.

14 And Joseph said unto them, That *is it* that I spake unto you, saying, Ye *are* spies:

15 Hereby ye shall be proved: By the life of Pharaoh ye shall not go forth hence, except your youngest brother come hither.

16 Send one of you, and let him fetch your brother, and ye shall be kept in prison, that your words may be proved, whether *there be any* truth in you: or else by the life of Pharaoh surely ye *are* spies.

17 And he put them all together into ward three days.

18 And Joseph said unto them the third day, This do, and live; *for* I fear God:

19 If ye *be* true *men*, let one of your brethren be bound in the house of your prison: go ye, carry corn for the famine of your houses:

20 But bring your youngest brother unto me; so shall your words be verified, and ye shall not die. And they did so.

21 ¶And they said one to another, We *are* verily guilty concerning our brother, in that we saw the anguish of his soul, when he besought us, and we would not hear; therefore is this distress come upon us.

22 And Reuben answered them, saying, Spake I not unto you, saying, Do not sin against the child; and ye would not hear? therefore, behold, also his blood is required.

23 And they knew not that Joseph understood *them*; for he spake unto them by an interpreter.

24 And he turned himself about from them, and wept; and returned to them again, and communed with them, and took from them Simeon, and bound him before their eyes.

25 ¶Then Joseph commanded to fill their sacks with corn, and to restore every man's money into his sack, and to give them provision for the way: and thus did he unto them.

26 And they laded their asses with the corn, and departed thence.

27 And as one of them opened his sack to give his ass provender in the inn, he espied his money; for, behold, it *was* in his sack's mouth.

28 And he said unto his brethren, My money is restored; and, lo, *it is* even in my sack: and their heart failed *them*, and they were afraid, saying one to another, What *is* this *that* God hath done unto us?

29 ¶And they came unto Jacob their father unto the land of Canaan, and told him all that befell unto them; saying,

30 The man, *who is* the lord of the land, spake roughly to us, and took us for spies of the country.

31 And we said unto him, We *are* true *men*; we are no spies:

32 We *be* twelve brethren, sons of our father; one *is* not, and the youngest *is* this day with our father in the land of Canaan.

33 And the man, the lord of the country, said unto us, Hereby shall I know that ye *are* true *men*; leave one of your brethren *here* with me, and take *food for* the famine of your households, and be gone:

34 And bring your youngest brother unto me: then shall I know that ye *are* no spies, but *that* ye *are* true *men*: *so* will I deliver you your brother, and ye shall traffick in the land.

35 And it came to pass as they emptied their sacks, that, behold, every man's bundle of money *was* in his sack: and when *both* they and their father saw the bundles of money, they were afraid.

36 And Jacob their father said unto them, Me have ye bereaved *of my children*: Joseph *is* not, and Simeon *is* not, and ye will take Benjamin *away*: all these things are against me.

37 And Reuben spake unto his father, saying, Slay my two sons, if I bring him not to thee: deliver him into my hand, and I will bring him to thee again.

38 And he said, My son shall not go down with you; for his brother is dead, and he is left alone: if mischief befall him by the way in the which ye go, then shall ye bring down my gray hairs with sorrow to the grave.

CHAPTER 43

AND the famine *was* sore in the land.
2 And it came to pass, when they had
eaten up the corn which they had
brought out of Egypt, their father said
unto them, Go again, buy us a little
food.
3 And Judah spake unto him, saying,
The man did solemnly protest unto us,
saying, Ye shall not see my face, except
your brother *be* with you.
4 If thou wilt send our brother with
us, we will go down and buy thee food:
5 But if thou wilt not send *him*, we
will not go down: for the man said unto
us, Ye shall not see my face, except
your brother *be* with you.
6 And Israel said, Wherefore dealt ye
so ill with me, *as* to tell the man
whether ye had yet a brother?
7 And they said, The man asked us
straitly of our state, and of our kindred,
saying, *Is* your father yet alive? have ye
another brother? and we told him ac-
cording to the tenor of these words:
could we certainly know that he would
say, Bring your brother down?
8 And Judah said unto Israel his
father, Send the lad with me, and we
will arise and go; that we may live, and
not die, both we, and thou, *and* also our
little ones.
9 I will be surety for him; of my hand
shalt thou require him: if I bring him
not unto thee, and set him before thee,
then let me bear the blame for ever:
10 For except we had lingered, surely
now we had returned this second time.
11 And their father Israel said unto
them, If *it must be* so now, do this; take
of the best fruits in the land in your ves-
sels, and carry down the man a present,
a little balm, and a little honey, spices,
and myrrh, nuts, and almonds:
12 And take double money in your
hand; and the money that was brought
again in the mouth of your sacks, carry
it again in your hand; peradventure it
was an oversight:
13 Take also your brother, and arise,
go again unto the man:
14 And God Almighty give you
mercy before the man, that he may
send away your other brother, and
Benjamin. If I be bereaved *of my chil-
dren*, I am bereaved.
15 ¶And the men took that present,
and they took double money in their
hand, and Benjamin; and rose up, and
went down to Egypt, and stood before
Joseph.
16 And when Joseph saw Benjamin
with them, he said to the ruler of his
house, Bring *these* men home, and slay,
and make ready; for *these* men shall
dine with me at noon.
17 And the man did as Joseph bade;
and the man brought the men into Jo-
seph's house.
18 And the men were afraid, because
they were brought into Joseph's house;
and they said, Because of the money
that was returned in our sacks at the
first time are we brought in; that he
may seek occasion against us, and fall
upon us, and take us for bondmen, and
our asses.
19 And they came near to the stew-
ard of Joseph's house, and they com-
muned with him at the door of the
house,
20 And said, O sir, we came indeed
down at the first time to buy food:
21 And it came to pass, when we
came to the inn, that we opened our
sacks, and, behold, *every* man's money
was in the mouth of his sack, our mon-
ey in full weight: and we have brought
it again in our hand.
22 And other money have we brought
down in our hands to buy food: we can-
not tell who put our money in our
sacks.
23 And he said, Peace *be* to you, fear
not: your God, and the God of your
father, hath given you treasure in your
sacks: I had your money. And he
brought Simeon out unto them.
24 And the man brought the men into
Joseph's house, and gave *them* water,
and they washed their feet; and he gave
their asses provender.
25 And they made ready the present
against Joseph came at noon: for they
heard that they should eat bread there.
26 And when Joseph came home,
they brought him the present which
was in their hand into the house, and
bowed themselves to him to the earth.
27 And he asked them of *their* wel-
fare, and said, *Is* your father well, the
old man of whom ye spake? *Is* he yet
alive?
28 And they answered, Thy servant
our father *is* in good health, he *is* yet
alive. And they bowed down their
heads, and made obeisance.
29 And he lifted up his eyes, and saw
his brother Benjamin, his mother's son,
and said, *Is* this your younger brother,
of whom ye spake unto me? And he
said, God be gracious unto thee, my
son.
30 And Joseph made haste; for his
bowels did yearn upon his brother: and
he sought *where* to weep; and he en-
tered into *his* chamber, and wept there.
31 And he washed his face, and went

out, and refrained himself, and said,
Set on bread.
32 And they set on for him by him-
self, and for them by themselves, and
for the Egyptians, which did eat with
him, by themselves: because the Egyp-
tians might not eat bread with the
Hebrews; for that *is* an abomination
unto the Egyptians.
33 And they sat before him, the first-
born according to his birthright, and
the youngest according to his youth:
and the men marvelled one at another.
34 And he took *and sent* messes unto
them from before him: but Benjamin's
mess was five times so much as any of
theirs. And they drank, and were merry
with him.

CHAPTER 44

AND he commanded the steward of his
house, saying, Fill the men's sacks *with*
food, as much as they can carry, and
put every man's money in his sack's
mouth.
2 And put my cup, the silver cup, in
the sack's mouth of the youngest, and
his corn money. And he did according
to the word that Joseph had spoken.
3 As soon as the morning was light,
the men were sent away, they and their
asses.
4 *And* when they were gone out of the
city, *and* not *yet* far off, Joseph said
unto his steward, Up, follow after the
men; and when thou dost overtake
them, say unto them, Wherefore have
ye rewarded evil for good?
5 *Is* not this *it* in which my lord drink-
eth, and whereby indeed he divineth?
ye have done evil in so doing.
6 And he overtook them, and he
spake unto them these same words.
7 And they said unto him, Wherefore
saith my lord these words? God forbid
that thy servants should do according
to this thing:
8 Behold, the money, which we found
in our sacks' mouths, we brought again
unto thee out of the land of Canaan:
how then should we steal out of thy
lord's house silver or gold?
9 With whomsoever of thy servants it
be found, both let him die, and we also
will be my lord's bondmen.
10 And he said, Now also *let* it *be* ac-
cording unto your words: he with
whom it is found shall be my servant;
and ye shall be blameless.
11 Then they speedily took down
every man his sack to the ground, and
opened every man his sack.
12 And he searched, *and* began at the
eldest, and left at the youngest: and the
cup was found in Benjamin's sack.
13 Then they rent their clothes, and
laded every man his ass, and returned
to the city.
14 And Jūdah and his brethren came
to Joseph's house; for he *was* yet there:
and they fell before him on the ground.
15 And Joseph said unto them, What
deed *is* this that ye have done? wot ye
not that such a man as I can certainly
divine?
16 And Jūdah said, What shall we say
unto my lord? what shall we speak? or
how shall we clear ourselves? God hath
found out the iniquity of thy servants:
behold, we *are* my lord's servants, both
we, and *he* also with whom the cup is
found.
17 And he said, God forbid that I
should do so: *but* the man in whose
hand the cup is found, he shall be my
servant; and as for you, get you up in
peace unto your father.
18 ¶Then Jūdah came near unto him,
and said, Oh my lord, let thy servant, I
pray thee, speak a word in my lord's
ears, and let not thine anger burn
against thy servant: for thou *art* even as
Pharaoh.
19 My lord asked his servants,
saying, Have ye a father, or a brother?
20 And we said unto my lord, We
have a father, an old man, and a child of
his old age, a little one; and his brother
is dead, and he alone is left of his
mother, and his father loveth him.
21 And thou saidst unto thy servants,
Bring him down unto me, that I may set
mine eyes upon him.
22 And we said unto my lord, The lad
cannot leave his father: for *if* he should
leave his father, *his father* would die.
23 And thou saidst unto thy servants,
Except your youngest brother come
down with you, ye shall see my face no
more.
24 And it came to pass when we came
up unto thy servant my father, we told
him the words of my lord.
25 And our father said, Go again, *and*
buy us a little food.
26 And we said, We cannot go down:
if our youngest brother be with us, then
will we go down: for we may not see the
man's face, except our youngest
brother *be* with us.
27 And thy servant my father said
unto us, Ye know that my wife bare me
two *sons:*
28 And the one went out from me,
and I said, Surely he is torn in pieces;
and I saw him not since:
29 And if ye take this also from me,
and mischief befall him, ye shall bring
down my gray hairs with sorrow to the
grave.

30 Now therefore when I come to thy
servant my father, and the lad *be* not
with us; seeing that his life is bound up
in the lad's life;
31 It shall come to pass, when he
seeth that the lad *is* not *with us*, that he
will die: and thy servants shall bring
down the gray hairs of thy servant our
father with sorrow to the grave.
32 For thy servant became surety for
the lad unto my father, saying, If I bring
him not unto thee, then I shall bear the
blame to my father for ever.
33 Now therefore, I pray thee, let thy
servant abide instead of the lad a bond-
man to my lord; and let the lad go up
with his brethren.
34 For how shall I go up to my father,
and the lad *be* not with me? lest per-
adventure I see the evil that shall come
on my father.

CHAPTER 45

THEN Joseph could not refrain himself
before all them that stood by him; and
he cried, Cause every man to go out
from me. And there stood no man with
him, while Joseph made himself known
unto his brethren.
2 And he wept aloud: and the Egyp-
tians and the house of Pharaoh heard.
3 And Joseph said unto his brethren, I
am Joseph; doth my father yet live?
And his brethren could not answer
him; for they were troubled at his pres-
ence.
4 And Joseph said unto his brethren,
Come near to me, I pray you. And they
came near. And he said, I *am* Joseph
your brother, whom ye sold into Egypt.
5 Now therefore be not grieved, nor
angry with yourselves, that ye sold me
hither: for God did send me before you
to preserve life.
6 For these two years *hath* the famine
been in the land: and yet *there are* five
years, in the which *there shall* neither
be earing nor harvest.
7 And God sent me before you to pre-
serve you a posterity in the earth, and
to save your lives by a great deliver-
ance.
8 So now *it was* not you *that* sent me
hither, but God: and he hath made me a
father to Pharaoh, and lord of all his
house, and a ruler throughout all the
land of Egypt.
9 Haste ye, and go up to my father,
and say unto him, Thus saith thy son
Joseph, God hath made me lord of all
Egypt: come down unto me, tarry not:
10 And thou shalt dwell in the land of
Goshen, and thou shalt be near unto
me, thou, and thy children, and thy
children's children, and thy flocks, and
thy herds, and all that thou hast:
11 And there will I nourish thee; for
yet *there are* five years of famine; lest
thou, and thy household, and all that
thou hast, come to poverty.
12 And, behold, your eyes see, and
the eyes of my brother Benjamin, that
it is my mouth that speaketh unto you.
13 And ye shall tell my father of all
my glory in Egypt, and of all that ye
have seen; and ye shall haste and bring
down my father hither.
14 And he fell upon his brother Ben-
jamin's neck, and wept; and Benjamin
wept upon his neck.
15 Moreover he kissed all his breth-
ren, and wept upon them: and after
that his brethren talked with him.
16 ¶And the fame thereof was heard
in Pharaoh's house, saying, Joseph's
brethren are come: and it pleased
Pharaoh well, and his servants.
17 And Pharaoh said unto Joseph,
Say unto thy brethren, This do ye; lade
your beasts, and go, get you unto the
land of Canaan;
18 And take your father and your
households, and come unto me: and I
will give you the good of the land of
Egypt, and ye shall eat the fat of the
land.
19 Now thou art commanded, this do
ye; take you wagons out of the land of
Egypt for your little ones, and for your
wives, and bring your father, and
come.
20 Also regard not your stuff; for the
good of all the land of Egypt *is* yours.
21 And the children of Israel did so:
and Joseph gave them wagons, accord-
ing to the commandment of Pharaoh,
and gave them provision for the way.
22 To all of them he gave each man
changes of raiment; but to Benjamin he
gave three hundred *pieces* of silver,
and five changes of raiment.
23 And to his father he sent after this
manner; ten asses laden with the good
things of Egypt, and ten she asses laden
with corn and bread and meat for his
father by the way.
24 So he sent his brethren away, and
they departed: and he said unto them,
See that ye fall not out by the way.
25 And they went up out of Egypt,
and came into the land of Canaan unto
Jacob their father,
26 And told him, saying, Joseph *is* yet
alive, and he *is* governor over all the
land of Egypt. And Jacob's heart
fainted, for he believed them not.
27 And they told him all the words of
Joseph, which he had said unto them:
and when he saw the wagons which Jo-

seph had sent to carry him, the spirit of Jacob their father revived:
28 And Israel said, *It is* enough; Joseph my son *is* yet alive: I will go and see him before I die.

CHAPTER 46

AND Israel took his journey with all that he had, and came to Be'er–shē'ba, and offered sacrifices unto the God of his father Isaac.
2 And God spake unto Israel in the visions of the night, and said, Jacob, Jacob. And he said, Here *am* I.
3 And he said, I *am* God, the God of thy father: fear not to go down into Egypt; for I will there make of thee a great nation:
4 I will go down with thee into Egypt; and I will also surely bring thee up *again*: and Joseph shall put his hand upon thine eyes.
5 And Jacob rose up from Be'er–shē'ba: and the sons of Israel carried Jacob their father, and their little ones, and their wives, in the wagons which Pharaoh had sent to carry him.
6 And they took their cattle, and their goods, which they had gotten in the land of Canaan, and came into Egypt, Jacob, and all his seed with him:
7 His sons, and his sons' sons with him, his daughters, and his sons' daughters, and all his seed brought he with him into Egypt.
8 ¶And these *are* the names of the children of Israel, which came into Egypt, Jacob and his sons: Reuben, Jacob's firstborn.
9 And the sons of Reuben; Hā'nŏch, and Phăl'lū, and Hĕz'ron, and Cär'mī.
10 And the sons of Simeon; Jĕ-mu'el, and Jā'mĭn, and Ō'hăd, and Jā'chin, and Zō'här, and Shā'ul the son of a Canaanitish woman.
11 And the sons of Levi; Ger'shon, Kō'hăth, and Me-râ'rī.
12 And the sons of Judah; Er, and Ō'nan, and Shē'lah, and Phâ'rĕz, and Zâ'rah: but Er and Ō'nan died in the land of Canaan. And the sons of Phâ'rĕz were Hĕz'ron and Hā'mul.
13 And the sons of Ĭs'sa-char; Tō'la, and Phū'vah, and Job, and Shĭm'rŏn.
14 And the sons of Zĕb'u-lun; Se'rĕd, and Ē'lŏn, and Jäh'le-el.
15 These *be* the sons of Leah, which she bare unto Jacob in Pă'dan–â'ram, with his daughter Dinah: all the souls of his sons and his daughters *were* thirty and three.
16 And the sons of Gad; Zĭph'ī-on, and Hăg'gī, Shū'nī, and Ĕz'bŏn, E'rī, and Âr'o-dī, and A-rē'lī.
17 And the sons of Asher; Jĭm'nah, and Ĭsh'ū-ah, and Ĭs'ū-ī, and Be-rī'ah, and Se'rah their sister: and the sons of Be-rī'ah; Hē'ber, and Măl'chī-el.
18 These *are* the sons of Zĭl'pah, whom Lāban gave to Leah his daughter, and these she bare unto Jacob, *even* sixteen souls.
19 The sons of Rāchel Jacob's wife; Joseph, and Benjamin.
20 And unto Joseph in the land of Egypt were born Ma-năs'seh and Ē'phra-im, which Ăs'e-năth the daughter of Po-tĭph'e-rah priest of On bare unto him.
21 And the sons of Benjamin *were* Bē'lah, and Bē'cher, and Ăsh'bĕl, Ge'ra, and Nā'a-man, Ē'hī, and Rosh, Mŭp'-pĭm, and Hŭp'pĭm, and Ard.
22 These *are* the sons of Rāchel, which were born to Jacob: all the souls *were* fourteen.
23 And the sons of Dan; Hu'shĭm.
24 And the sons of Năph'ta-lī; Jäh'ze-el, and Gū'nī, and Jē'zer, and Shĭl'lem.
25 These *are* the sons of Bĭl'hah, which Lāban gave unto Rāchel his daughter, and she bare these unto Jacob: all the souls *were* seven.
26 All the souls that came with Jacob into Egypt, which came out of his loins, besides Jacob's sons' wives, all the souls *were* threescore and six;
27 And the sons of Joseph, which were born him in Egypt, *were* two souls: all the souls of the house of Jacob, which came into Egypt, *were* threescore and ten.
28 ¶And he sent Judah before him unto Joseph, to direct his face unto Goshen; and they came into the land of Goshen.
29 And Joseph made ready his chariot, and went up to meet Israel his father, to Goshen, and presented himself unto him; and he fell on his neck, and wept on his neck a good while.
30 And Israel said unto Joseph, Now let me die, since I have seen thy face, because thou *art* yet alive.
31 And Joseph said unto his brethren, and unto his father's house, I will go up, and shew Pharaoh, and say unto him, My brethren, and my father's house, which *were* in the land of Canaan, are come unto me;
32 And the men *are* shepherds, for their trade hath been to feed cattle; and they have brought their flocks, and their herds, and all that they have.
33 And it shall come to pass, when Pharaoh shall call you, and shall say, What *is* your occupation?
34 That ye shall say, Thy servants' trade hath been about cattle from our

youth even until now, both we, *and* also our fathers: that ye may dwell in the land of Goshen; for every shepherd *is* an abomination unto the Egyptians.

CHAPTER 47

THEN Joseph came and told Pharaoh, and said, My father and my brethren, and their flocks, and their herds, and all that they have, are come out of the land of Canaan; and, behold, they *are* in the land of Goshen.

2 And he took some of his brethren, *even* five men, and presented them unto Pharaoh.

3 And Pharaoh said unto his brethren, What *is* your occupation? And they said unto Pharaoh, Thy servants *are* shepherds, both we, *and* also our fathers.

4 They said moreover unto Pharaoh, For to sojourn in the land are we come; for thy servants have no pasture for their flocks; for the famine *is* sore in the land of Canaan: now therefore, we pray thee, let thy servants dwell in the land of Goshen.

5 And Pharaoh spake unto Joseph, saying, Thy father and thy brethren are come unto thee:

6 The land of Egypt *is* before thee; in the best of the land make thy father and brethren to dwell; in the land of Goshen let them dwell: and if thou knowest *any* men of activity among them, then make them rulers over my cattle.

7 And Joseph brought in Jacob his father, and set him before Pharaoh: and Jacob blessed Pharaoh.

8 And Pharaoh said unto Jacob, How old *art* thou?

9 And Jacob said unto Pharaoh, The days of the years of my pilgrimage *are* an hundred and thirty years: few and evil have the days of the years of my life been, and have not attained unto the days of the years of the life of my fathers in the days of their pilgrimage.

10 And Jacob blessed Pharaoh, and went out from before Pharaoh.

11 ¶And Joseph placed his father and his brethren, and gave them a possession in the land of Egypt, in the best of the land, in the land of Răm′e-sēs, as Pharaoh had commanded.

12 And Joseph nourished his father, and his brethren, and all his father's household, with bread, according to *their* families.

13 ¶And *there was* no bread in all the land; for the famine *was* very sore, so that the land of Egypt and *all* the land of Canaan fainted by reason of the famine.

14 And Joseph gathered up all the money that was found in the land of Egypt, and in the land of Canaan, for the corn which they bought: and Joseph brought the money into Pharaoh's house.

15 And when money failed in the land of Egypt, and in the land of Canaan, all the Egyptians came unto Joseph, and said, Give us bread: for why should we die in thy presence? for the money faileth.

16 And Joseph said, Give your cattle; and I will give you for your cattle, if money fail.

17 And they brought their cattle unto Joseph: and Joseph gave them bread *in exchange* for horses, and for the flocks, and for the cattle of the herds, and for the asses: and he fed them with bread for all their cattle for that year.

18 When that year was ended, they came unto him the second year, and said unto him, We will not hide *it* from my lord, how that our money is spent; my lord also hath our herds of cattle; there is not ought left in the sight of my lord, but our bodies, and our lands:

19 Wherefore shall we die before thine eyes, both we and our land? buy us and our land for bread, and we and our land will be servants unto Pharaoh: and give *us* seed, that we may live, and not die, that the land be not desolate.

20 And Joseph bought all the land of Egypt for Pharaoh; for the Egyptians sold every man his field, because the famine prevailed over them: so the land became Pharaoh's.

21 And as for the people, he removed them to cities from *one* end of the borders of Egypt even to the *other* end thereof.

22 Only the land of the priests bought he not; for the priests had a portion *assigned them* of Pharaoh, and did eat their portion which Pharaoh gave them: wherefore they sold not their lands.

23 Then Joseph said unto the people, Behold, I have bought you this day and your land for Pharaoh: lo, *here is* seed for you, and ye shall sow the land.

24 And it shall come to pass in the increase, that ye shall give the fifth *part* unto Pharaoh, and four parts shall be your own, for seed of the field, and for your food, and for them of your households, and for food for your little ones.

25 And they said, Thou hast saved our lives: let us find grace in the sight of my lord, and we will be Pharaoh's servants.

26 And Joseph made it a law over the land of Egypt unto this day, *that* Pharaoh should have the fifth *part;* ex-

cept the land of the priests only, *which* became not Pharaoh's.

27 ¶And Israel dwelt in the land of Egypt, in the country of Goshen; and they had possessions therein, and grew, and multiplied exceedingly.

28 And Jacob lived in the land of Egypt seventeen years: so the whole age of Jacob was an hundred forty and seven years.

29 And the time drew nigh that Israel must die: and he called his son Joseph, and said unto him, If now I have found grace in thy sight, put, I pray thee, thy hand under my thigh, and deal kindly and truly with me; bury me not, I pray thee, in Egypt:

30 But I will lie with my fathers, and thou shalt carry me out of Egypt, and bury me in their buryingplace. And he said, I will do as thou hast said.

31 And he said, Swear unto me. And he sware unto him. And Israel bowed himself upon the bed's head.

CHAPTER 48

AND it came to pass after these things, that *one* told Joseph, Behold, thy father *is* sick: and he took with him his two sons, Ma-năs'seh and Ē'phra-im.

2 And *one* told Jacob, and said, Behold, thy son Joseph cometh unto thee: and Israel strengthened himself, and sat upon the bed.

3 And Jacob said unto Joseph, God Almighty appeared unto me at Luz in the land of Canaan, and blessed me,

4 And said unto me, Behold, I will make thee fruitful, and multiply thee, and I will make of thee a multitude of people; and will give this land to thy seed after thee *for* an everlasting possession.

5 And now thy two sons, Ē'phra-im and Ma-năs'seh, which were born unto thee in the land of Egypt before I came unto thee into Egypt, *are* mine; as Reuben and Simeon, they shall be mine.

6 And thy issue, which thou begettest after them, shall be thine, *and* shall be called after the name of their brethren in their inheritance.

7 And as for me, when I came from Pă'dan, Rāchel died by me in the land of Canaan in the way, when yet *there was* but a little way to come unto Ĕph'rath: and I buried her there in the way of Ĕph'rath; the same *is* Bĕth–lehĕm.

8 And Israel beheld Joseph's sons, and said, Who *are* these?

9 And Joseph said unto his father, They *are* my sons, whom God hath given me in this *place*. And he said, Bring them, I pray thee, unto me, and I will bless them.

10 Now the eyes of Israel were dim for age, *so that* he could not see. And he brought them near unto him; and he kissed them, and embraced them.

11 And Israel said unto Joseph, I had not thought to see thy face: and, lo, God hath shewed me also thy seed.

12 And Joseph brought them out from between his knees, and he bowed himself with his face to the earth.

13 And Joseph took them both, Ē'phra-im in his right hand toward Israel's left hand, and Ma-năs'seh in his left hand toward Israel's right hand, and brought *them* near unto him.

14 And Israel stretched out his right hand, and laid *it* upon Ē'phra-im's head, who *was* the younger, and his left hand upon Ma-năs'seh's head, guiding his hands wittingly; for Ma-năs'seh *was* the firstborn.

15 ¶And he blessed Joseph, and said, God, before whom my fathers Abraham and Isaac did walk, the God which fed me all my life long unto this day,

16 The Angel which redeemed me from all evil, bless the lads; and let my name be named on them, and the name of my fathers Abraham and Isaac; and let them grow into a multitude in the midst of the earth.

17 And when Joseph saw that his father laid his right hand upon the head of Ē'phra-im, it displeased him: and he held up his father's hand, to remove it from Ē'phra-im's head unto Ma-năs'seh's head.

18 And Joseph said unto his father, Not so, my father: for this *is* the firstborn; put thy right hand upon his head.

19 And his father refused, and said, I know *it*, my son, I know *it;* he also shall become a people, and he also shall be great: but truly his younger brother shall be greater than he, and his seed shall become a multitude of nations.

20 And he blessed them that day, saying, In thee shall Israel bless, saying, God make thee as Ē'phra-im and as Ma-năs'seh: and he set Ē'phraim before Ma-năs'seh.

21 And Israel said unto Joseph, Behold, I die: but God shall be with you, and bring you again unto the land of your fathers.

22 Moreover I have given to thee one portion above thy brethren, which I took out of the hand of the Ămorīte with my sword and with my bow.

CHAPTER 49

AND Jacob called unto his sons, and said, Gather yourselves together, that I

may tell you *that* which shall befall you
in the last days.
2 Gather yourselves together, and
hear, ye sons of Jacob; and hearken
unto Israel your father.
3 ¶Reuben, thou *art* my firstborn, my
might, and the beginning of my
strength, the excellency of dignity, and
the excellency of power:
4 Unstable as water, thou shalt not
excel; because thou wentest up to thy
father's bed; then defiledst thou *it*: he
went up to my couch.
5 ¶Simeon and Levi *are* brethren;
instruments of cruelty *are in* their habi-
tations.
6 O my soul, come not thou into their
secret; unto their assembly, mine hon-
our, be not thou united: for in their an-
ger they slew a man, and in their self-
will they digged down a wall.
7 Cursed *be* their anger, for *it was*
fierce; and their wrath, for it was cruel:
I will divide them in Jacob, and scatter
them in Israel.
8 ¶Judah, thou *art he* whom thy
brethren shall praise: thy hand *shall be*
in the neck of thine enemies; thy father's
children shall bow down before
thee.
9 Jūdah *is* a lion's whelp: from the
prey, my son, thou art gone up: he
stooped down, he couched as a lion, and
as an old lion; who shall rouse him up?
10 The sceptre shall not depart from
Jūdah, nor a lawgiver from between his
feet, until Shīlōh come; and unto him
shall the gathering of the people *be*.
11 Binding his foal unto the vine, and
his ass's colt unto the choice vine; he
washed his garments in wine, and his
clothes in the blood of grapes:
12 His eyes *shall be* red with wine,
and his teeth white with milk.
13 ¶Zĕb'u-lun shall dwell at the
haven of the sea; and he *shall be* for an
haven of ships; and his border *shall be*
unto Zī'don.
14 ¶Is'sa-char *is* a strong ass couch-
ing down between two burdens:
15 And he saw that rest *was* good,
and the land that *it was* pleasant; and
bowed his shoulder to bear, and be-
came a servant unto tribute.
16 ¶Dan shall judge his people, as one
of the tribes of Israel.
17 Dan shall be a serpent by the way,
an adder in the path, that biteth the
horse heels, so that his rider shall fall
backward.
18 I have waited for thy salvation, O
LORD.
19 ¶Gad, a troop shall overcome him:
but he shall overcome at the last.
20 ¶Out of Asher his bread *shall be*
fat, and he shall yield royal dainties.
21 ¶Năph'ta-lī *is* a hind let loose: he
giveth goodly words.
22 ¶Joseph *is* a fruitful bough, *even* a
fruitful bough by a well; *whose*
branches run over the wall:
23 The archers have sorely grieved
him, and shot *at him*, and hated him:
24 But his bow abode in strength, and
the arms of his hands were made
strong by the hands of the mighty *God*
of Jacob; (from thence *is* the shepherd,
the stone of Israel:)
25 *Even* by the God of thy father, who
shall help thee; and by the Almighty,
who shall bless thee with blessings of
heaven above, blessings of the deep
that lieth under, blessings of the
breasts, and of the womb:
26 The blessings of thy father have
prevailed above the blessings of my
progenitors unto the utmost bound of
the everlasting hills: they shall be on
the head of Joseph, and on the crown of
the head of him that was separate from
his brethren.
27 ¶Benjamin shall ravin *as* a wolf: in
the morning he shall devour the prey,
and at night he shall divide the spoil.
28 ¶All these *are* the twelve tribes of
Israel: and this *is it* that their father
spake unto them, and blessed them;
every one according to his blessing he
blessed them.
29 And he charged them, and said
unto them, I am to be gathered unto my
people: bury me with my fathers in the
cave that *is* in the field of Ē'phrŏn the
Hittite,
30 In the cave that *is* in the field of
Măch-pē'läh, which *is* before Măm're,
in the land of Canaan, which Abraham
bought with the field of Ē'phrŏn the
Hittite for a possession of a burying-
place.
31 There they buried Abraham and
Sarah his wife; there they buried Isaac
and Rebekah his wife; and there I
buried Leah.
32 The purchase of the field and of
the cave that *is* therein *was* from the
children of Heth.
33 And when Jacob had made an end
of commanding his sons, he gathered
up his feet into the bed, and yielded up
the ghost, and was gathered unto his
people.

CHAPTER 50

AND Joseph fell upon his father's face,
and wept upon him, and kissed him.
2 And Joseph commanded his ser-
vants the physicians to embalm his
father: and the physicians embalmed
Israel.

3 And forty days were fulfilled for
him; for so are fulfilled the days of
those which are embalmed: and the
Egyptians mourned for him threescore
and ten days.
4 And when the days of his mourning
were past, Joseph spake unto the house
of Pharaoh, saying, If now I have found
grace in your eyes, speak, I pray you, in
the ears of Pharaoh, saying,
5 My father made me swear, saying,
Lo, I die: in my grave which I have
digged for me in the land of Canaan,
there shalt thou bury me. Now there-
fore let me go up, I pray thee, and bury
my father, and I will come again.
6 And Pharaoh said, Go up, and bury
thy father, according as he made thee
swear.
7 ¶And Joseph went up to bury his
father: and with him went up all the
servants of Pharaoh, the elders of his
house, and all the elders of the land of
Egypt,
8 And all the house of Joseph, and his
brethren, and his father's house: only
their little ones, and their flocks, and
their herds, they left in the land of
Goshen.
9 And there went up with him both
chariots and horsemen: and it was a
very great company.
10 And they came to the threshing-
floor of Ā'tăd, which *is* beyond Jordan,
and there they mourned with a great
and very sore lamentation: and he
made a mourning for his father seven
days.
11 And when the inhabitants of the
land, the Canaanites, saw the mourn-
ing in the floor of Ā'tăd, they said, This
is a grievous mourning to the Egyp-
tians: wherefore the name of it was
called Ā'bel-mĭz'rā-im, which *is* beyond
Jordan.
12 And his sons did unto him accord-
ing as he commanded them:
13 For his sons carried him into the
land of Canaan, and buried him in the
cave of the field of Măch-pē'läh, which
Abraham bought with the field for a
possession of a burying place of
Ē'phrŏn the Hittite, before Măm're.
14 And Joseph returned into Egypt,
he, and his brethren, and all that went
up with him to bury his father, after he
had buried his father.
15 ¶And when Joseph's brethren saw
that their father was dead, they said,
Joseph will peradventure hate us, and
will certainly requite us all the evil
which we did unto him.
16 And they sent a messenger unto
Joseph, saying, Thy father did com-
mand before he died, saying,
17 So shall ye say unto Joseph, For-
give, I pray thee now, the trespass of
thy brethren, and their sin; for they did
unto thee evil: and now, we pray thee,
forgive the trespass of the servants of
the God of thy father. And Joseph wept
when they spake unto him.
18 And his brethren also went and
fell down before his face; and they said,
Behold, we *be* thy servants.
19 And Joseph said unto them, Fear
not: for *am* I in the place of God?
20 But as for you, ye thought evil
against me; *but* God meant it unto
good, to bring to pass, as *it is* this day,
to save much people alive.
21 Now therefore fear ye not: I will
nourish you, and your little ones. And
he comforted them, and spake kindly
unto them.
22 ¶And Joseph dwelt in Egypt, he,
and his father's house: and Joseph
lived an hundred and ten years.
23 And Joseph saw Ē'phra-im's chil-
dren of the third *generation:* the chil-
dren also of Mā'chĭr the son of Ma-năs'-
seh were brought up upon Joseph's
knees.
24 And Joseph said unto his brethren,
I die: and God will surely visit you, and
bring you out of this land unto the land
which he sware to Abraham, to Isaac,
and to Jacob.
25 And Joseph took an oath of the
children of Israel, saying, God will sure-
ly visit you, and ye shall carry up my
bones from hence.
26 So Joseph died, *being* an hundred
and ten years old: and they embalmed
him, and he was put in a coffin in
Egypt.

THE SECOND BOOK OF MOSES
CALLED

EXODUS

CHAPTER 1

NOW these *are* the names of the chil-
dren of Israel, which came into Egypt;
every man and his household came
with Jacob.
2 Reuben, Simeon, Levi, and Jūdah,
3 Ĭs'sa-char, Zĕb'u-lun, and Ben-
jamin,
4 Dan, and Năph'ta-lī, Gad, and
Asher.

5 And all the souls that came out of the loins of Jacob were seventy souls: for Joseph was in Egypt *already*.

6 And Joseph died, and all his brethren, and all that generation.

7 And the children of Israel were fruitful, and increased abundantly, and multiplied, and waxed exceeding mighty; and the land was filled with them.

8 ¶Now there arose up a new king over Egypt, which knew not Joseph.

9 And he said unto his people, Behold, the people of the children of Israel *are* more and mightier than we:

10 Come on, let us deal wisely with them; lest they multiply, and it come to pass, that, when there falleth out any war, they join also unto our enemies, and fight against us, and *so* get them up out of the land.

11 Therefore they did set over them taskmasters to afflict them with their burdens. And they built for Pharaoh treasure cities, Pī′thom and Rā-ăm′sēs.

12 But the more they afflicted them, the more they multiplied and grew. And they were grieved because of the children of Israel.

13 And the Egyptians made the children of Israel to serve with rigour:

14 And they made their lives bitter with hard bondage, in morter, and in brick, and in all manner of service in the field: all their service, wherein they made them serve, *was* with rigour.

15 ¶And the king of Egypt spake to the Hebrew midwives, of which the name of the one *was* Shĭph′rah, and the name of the other Pū′ah:

16 And he said, When ye do the office of a midwife to the Hebrew women, and see *them* upon the stools; if it *be* a son, then ye shall kill him: but if it *be* a daughter, then she shall live.

17 But the midwives feared God, and did not as the king of Egypt commanded them, but saved the men children alive.

18 And the king of Egypt called for the midwives, and said unto them, Why have ye done this thing, and have saved the men children alive?

19 And the midwives said unto Pharaoh, Because the Hebrew women *are* not as the Egyptian women; for they *are* lively, and are delivered ere the midwives come in unto them.

20 Therefore God dealt well with the midwives: and the people multiplied, and waxed very mighty.

21 And it came to pass, because the midwives feared God, that he made them houses.

22 And Pharaoh charged all his people, saying, Every son that is born ye shall cast into the river, and every daughter ye shall save alive.

CHAPTER 2

AND there went a man of the house of Levi, and took *to wife* a daughter of Levi.

2 And the woman conceived, and bare a son: and when she saw him that he *was a* goodly *child*, she hid him three months.

3 And when she could not longer hide him, she took for him an ark of bulrushes, and daubed it with slime and with pitch, and put the child therein; and she laid *it* in the flags by the river's brink.

4 And his sister stood afar off, to wit what would be done to him.

5 ¶And the daughter of Pharaoh came down to wash *herself* at the river; and her maidens walked along by the river's side; and when she saw the ark among the flags, she sent her maid to fetch it.

6 And when she had opened *it*, she saw the child: and, behold, the babe wept. And she had compassion on him, and said, This *is one* of the Hebrews' children.

7 Then said his sister to Pharaoh's daughter, Shall I go and call to thee a nurse of the Hebrew women, that she may nurse the child for thee?

8 And Pharaoh's daughter said to her, Go. And the maid went and called the child's mother.

9 And Pharaoh's daughter said unto her, Take this child away, and nurse it for me, and I will give *thee* thy wages. And the woman took the child, and nursed it.

10 And the child grew, and she brought him unto Pharaoh's daughter, and he became her son. And she called his name Moses: and she said, Because I drew him out of the water.

11 ¶And it came to pass in those days, when Moses was grown, that he went out unto his brethren, and looked on their burdens: and he spied an Egyptian smiting an Hebrew, one of his brethren.

12 And he looked this way and that way, and when he saw that *there was* no man, he slew the Egyptian, and hid him in the sand.

13 And when he went out the second day, behold, two men of the Hebrews strove together: and he said to him that did the wrong, Wherefore smitest thou thy fellow?

14 And he said, Who made thee a prince and a judge over us? intendest thou to kill me, as thou killedst the Egyptian? And Moses feared, and said, Surely this thing is known.
15 Now when Pharaoh heard this thing, he sought to slay Moses. But Moses fled from the face of Pharaoh, and dwelt in the land of Mĭd'ĭ-an: and he sat down by a well.
16 Now the priest of Mĭd'ĭ-an had seven daughters: and they came and drew *water*, and filled the troughs to water their father's flock.
17 And the shepherds came and drove them away: but Moses stood up and helped them, and watered their flock.
18 And when they came to Reū'el their father, he said, How *is it that* ye are come so soon to day?
19 And they said, An Egyptian delivered us out of the hand of the shepherds, and also drew *water* enough for us, and watered the flock.
20 And he said unto his daughters, And where *is* he? why *is* it *that* ye have left the man? call him, that he may eat bread.
21 And Moses was content to dwell with the man: and he gave Moses Zĭp-po'rah his daughter.
22 And she bare *him* a son, and he called his name Ger'shom: for he said, I have been a stranger in a strange land.
23 ¶And it came to pass in process of time, that the king of Egypt died: and the children of Israel sighed by reason of the bondage, and they cried, and their cry came up unto God by reason of the bondage.
24 And God heard their groaning, and God remembered his covenant with Abraham, with Isaac, and with Jacob.
25 And God looked upon the children of Israel, and God had respect unto *them*.

CHAPTER 3

NOW Moses kept the flock of Jĕth'rō his father in law, the priest of Mĭd'ĭ-an: and he led the flock to the backside of the desert, and came to the mountain of God, *even* to Hō'rĕb.
2 And the angel of the LORD appeared unto him in a flame of fire out of the midst of a bush: and he looked, and, behold, the bush burned with fire, and the bush *was* not consumed.
3 And Moses said, I will now turn aside, and see this great sight, why the bush is not burnt.
4 And when the LORD saw that he turned aside to see, God called unto him out of the midst of the bush, and said, Moses, Moses. And he said, Here *am* I.
5 And he said, Draw not nigh hither: put off thy shoes from off thy feet, for the place whereon thou standest *is* holy ground.
6 Moreover he said, I *am* the God of thy father, the God of Abraham, the God of Isaac, and the God of Jacob. And Moses hid his face; for he was afraid to look upon God.
7 ¶And the LORD said, I have surely seen the affliction of my people which *are* in Egypt, and have heard their cry by reason of their taskmasters; for I know their sorrows;
8 And I am come down to deliver them out of the hand of the Egyptians, and to bring them up out of that land unto a good land and a large, unto a land flowing with milk and honey; unto the place of the Canaanites, and the Hittites, and the Ămorītes, and the Pĕr'-iz-zītes, and the Hī'vītes, and the Jēb'u-sītes.
9 Now therefore, behold, the cry of the children of Israel is come unto me: and I have also seen the oppression wherewith the Egyptians oppress them.
10 Come now therefore, and I will send thee unto Pharaoh, that thou mayest bring forth my people the children of Israel out of Egypt.
11 ¶And Moses said unto God, Who *am* I, that I should go unto Pharaoh, and that I should bring forth the children of Israel out of Egypt?
12 And he said, Certainly I will be with thee; and this *shall be* a token unto thee, that I have sent thee: When thou hast brought forth the people out of Egypt, ye shall serve God upon this mountain.
13 And Moses said unto God, Behold, *when* I come unto the children of Israel, and shall say unto them, The God of your fathers hath sent me unto you; and they shall say to me, What *is* his name? what shall I say unto them?
14 And God said unto Moses, I AM THAT I AM: and he said, Thus shalt thou say unto the children of Israel, I AM hath sent me unto you.
15 And God said moreover unto Moses, Thus shalt thou say unto the children of Israel, the LORD God of your fathers, the God of Abraham, the God of Isaac, and the God of Jacob, hath sent me unto you: this *is* my name for ever, and this *is* my memorial unto all generations.

16 Go, and gather the elders of Israel
together, and say unto them, The LORD
God of your fathers, the God of Abra-
ham, of Isaac, and of Jacob, appeared
unto me, saying, I have surely visited
you, and *seen* that which is done to you
in Egypt:
17 And I have said, I will bring you up
out of the affliction of Egypt unto the
land of the Canaanites, and the Hit-
tites, and the Ămorītes, and the Pĕr′iz-
zītes, and the Hī′vītes, and the Jeb′u-
sītes, unto a land flowing with milk and
honey.
18 And they shall hearken to thy
voice: and thou shalt come, thou and
the elders of Israel, unto the king of
Egypt, and ye shall say unto him, The
LORD God of the Hebrews hath met
with us: and now let us go, we beseech
thee, three days' journey into the wil-
derness, that we may sacrifice to the
LORD our God.
19 And I am sure that the king of
Egypt will not let you go, no, not by a
mighty hand.
20 And I will stretch out my hand,
and smite Egypt with all my wonders
which I will do in the midst thereof: and
after that he will let you go.
21 And I will give this people favour
in the sight of the Egyptians: and it
shall come to pass, that, when ye go, ye
shall not go empty:
22 But every woman shall borrow of
her neighbour, and of her that sojourn-
eth in her house, jewels of silver, and
jewels of gold, and raiment: and ye
shall put *them* upon your sons, and
upon your daughters; and ye shall spoil
the Egyptians.

CHAPTER 4

AND Moses answered and said, But,
behold, they will not believe me, nor
hearken unto my voice: for they will
say, The LORD hath not appeared unto
thee.
2 And the LORD said unto him, What
is that in thine hand? And he said, A
rod.
3 And he said, Cast it on the ground.
And he cast it on the ground, and it be-
came a serpent; and Moses fled from
before it.
4 And the LORD said unto Moses, Put
forth thine hand, and take it by the tail.
And he put forth his hand, and caught
it, and it became a rod in his hand:
5 That they may believe that the LORD
God of their fathers, the God of Abra-
ham, the God of Isaac, and the God of
Jacob, hath appeared unto thee.
6 ¶And the LORD said furthermore
unto him, Put now thine hand into thy
bosom. And he put his hand into his bo-
som: and when he took it out, behold,
his hand *was* leprous as snow.
7 And he said, Put thine hand into thy
bosom again. And he put his hand into
his bosom again; and plucked it out of
his bosom, and, behold, it was turned
again as his *other* flesh.
8 And it shall come to pass, if they
will not believe thee, neither hearken to
the voice of the first sign, that they will
believe the voice of the latter sign.
9 And it shall come to pass, if they
will not believe also these two signs,
neither hearken unto thy voice, that
thou shalt take of the water of the river,
and pour *it* upon the dry *land:* and the
water which thou takest out of the river
shall become blood upon the dry *land.*
10 ¶And Moses said unto the LORD, O
my Lord, I *am* not eloquent, neither
heretofore, nor since thou hast spoken
unto thy servant: but I *am* slow of
speech, and of a slow tongue.
11 And the LORD said unto him, Who
hath made man's mouth? or who
maketh the dumb, or deaf, or the
seeing, or the blind? have not I the
LORD?
12 Now therefore go, and I will be
with thy mouth, and teach thee what
thou shalt say.
13 And he said, O my Lord, send, I
pray thee, by the hand *of him whom*
thou wilt send.
14 And the anger of the LORD was
kindled against Moses, and he said, *Is*
not Aaron the Levite thy brother? I
know that he can speak well. And also,
behold, he cometh forth to meet thee:
and when he seeth thee, he will be glad
in his heart.
15 And thou shalt speak unto him,
and put words in his mouth: and I will
be with thy mouth, and with his mouth,
and will teach you what ye shall do.
16 And he shall be thy spokesman
unto the people: and he shall be, *even*
he shall be to thee instead of a mouth,
and thou shalt be to him instead of God.
17 And thou shalt take this rod in
thine hand, wherewith thou shalt do
signs.
18 ¶And Moses went and returned to
Jĕth′rō his father in law, and said unto
him, Let me go, I pray thee, and return
unto my brethren which *are* in Egypt,
and see whether they be yet alive. And
Jĕth′rō said to Moses, Go in peace.
19 And the LORD said unto Moses in
Mĭd′ĭ-an, Go, return into Egypt: for all
the men are dead which sought thy life.
20 And Moses took his wife and his
sons, and set them upon an ass, and he

returned to the land of Egypt: and Moses took the rod of God in his hand.

21 And the LORD said unto Moses, When thou goest to return into Egypt, see that thou do all those wonders before Pharaoh, which I have put in thine hand: but I will harden his heart, that he shall not let the people go.

22 And thou shalt say unto Pharaoh, Thus saith the LORD, Israel *is* my son, *even* my firstborn:

23 And I say unto thee, Let my son go, that he may serve me: and if thou refuse to let him go, behold, I will slay thy son, *even* thy firstborn.

24 ¶And it came to pass by the way in the inn, that the LORD met him, and sought to kill him.

25 Then Zĭp-po′rah took a sharp stone, and cut off the foreskin of her son, and cast *it* at his feet, and said, Surely a bloody husband *art* thou to me.

26 So he let him go: then she said, A bloody husband *thou art*, because of the circumcision.

27 ¶And the LORD said to Aaron, Go into the wilderness to meet Moses. And he went, and met him in the mount of God, and kissed him.

28 And Moses told Aaron all the words of the LORD who had sent him, and all the signs which he had commanded him.

29 ¶And Moses and Aaron went and gathered together all the elders of the children of Israel:

30 And Aaron spake all the words which the LORD had spoken unto Moses, and did the signs in the sight of the people.

31 And the people believed: and when they heard that the LORD had visited the children of Israel, and that he had looked upon their affliction, then they bowed their heads and worshipped.

CHAPTER 5

AND afterward Moses and Aaron went in, and told Pharaoh, Thus saith the LORD God of Israel, Let my people go, that they may hold a feast unto me in the wilderness.

2 And Pharaoh said, Who *is* the LORD, that I should obey his voice to let Israel go? I know not the LORD, neither will I let Israel go.

3 And they said, The God of the Hebrews hath met with us: let us go, we pray thee, three days' journey into the desert, and sacrifice unto the LORD our God; lest he fall upon us with pestilence, or with the sword.

4 And the king of Egypt said unto them, Wherefore do ye, Moses and Aaron, let the people from their works? get you unto your burdens.

5 And Pharaoh said, Behold, the people of the land now *are* many, and ye make them rest from their burdens.

6 And Pharaoh commanded the same day the taskmasters of the people, and their officers, saying,

7 Ye shall no more give the people straw to make brick, as heretofore: let them go and gather straw for themselves.

8 And the tale of the bricks, which they did make heretofore, ye shall lay upon them; ye shall not diminish *ought* thereof: for they *be* idle; therefore they cry, saying, Let us go *and* sacrifice to our God.

9 Let there more work be laid upon the men, that they may labour therein; and let them not regard vain words.

10 ¶And the taskmasters of the people went out, and their officers, and they spake to the people, saying, Thus saith Pharaoh, I will not give you straw.

11 Go ye, get you straw where ye can find it: yet not ought of your work shall be diminished.

12 So the people were scattered abroad throughout all the land of Egypt to gather stubble instead of straw.

13 And the taskmasters hasted *them*, saying, Fulfil your works, *your* daily tasks, as when there was straw.

14 And the officers of the children of Israel, which Pharaoh's taskmasters had set over them, were beaten, *and* demanded, Wherefore have ye not fulfilled your task in making brick both yesterday and to day, as heretofore?

15 ¶Then the officers of the children of Israel came and cried unto Pharaoh, saying, Wherefore dealest thou thus with thy servants?

16 There is no straw given unto thy servants, and they say to us, Make brick: and, behold, thy servants *are* beaten; but the fault *is* in thine own people.

17 But he said, Ye *are* idle, *ye are* idle: therefore ye say, Let us go *and* do sacrifice to the LORD.

18 Go therefore now, *and* work; for there shall no straw be given you, yet shall ye deliver the tale of bricks.

19 And the officers of the children of Israel did see *that* they *were* in evil *case*, after it was said, Ye shall not minish *ought* from your bricks of your daily task.

20 ¶And they met Moses and Aaron, who stood in the way, as they came forth from Pharaoh:

21 And they said unto them, The

LORD look upon you, and judge; because ye have made our savour to be abhorred in the eyes of Pharaoh, and in the eyes of his servants, to put a sword in their hand to slay us.
22 And Moses returned unto the LORD, and said, Lord, wherefore hast thou *so* evil entreated this people? why *is* it *that* thou hast sent me?
23 For since I came to Pharaoh to speak in thy name, he hath done evil to this people; neither hast thou delivered thy people at all.

CHAPTER 6

THEN the LORD said unto Moses, Now shalt thou see what I will do to Pharaoh: for with a strong hand shall he let them go, and with a strong hand shall he drive them out of his land.
2 And God spake unto Moses, and said unto him, I *am* the LORD:
3 And I appeared unto Abraham, unto Isaac, and unto Jacob, by *the name of* God Almighty, but by my name JEHOVAH was I not known to them.
4 And I have also established my covenant with them, to give them the land of Canaan, the land of their pilgrimage, wherein they were strangers.
5 And I have also heard the groaning of the children of Israel, whom the Egyptians keep in bondage; and I have remembered my covenant.
6 Wherefore say unto the children of Israel, I *am* the LORD, and I will bring you out from under the burdens of the Egyptians, and I will rid you out of their bondage, and I will redeem you with a stretched out arm, and with great judgments:
7 And I will take you to me for a people, and I will be to you a God: and ye shall know that I *am* the LORD your God, which bringeth you out from under the burdens of the Egyptians.
8 And I will bring you in unto the land, concerning the which I did swear to give it to Abraham, to Isaac, and to Jacob; and I will give it you for an heritage: I *am* the LORD.
9 ¶And Moses spake so unto the children of Israel: but they hearkened not unto Moses for anguish of spirit, and for cruel bondage.
10 And the LORD spake unto Moses, saying,
11 Go in, speak unto Pharaoh king of Egypt, that he let the children of Israel go out of his land.
12 And Moses spake before the LORD, saying, Behold, the children of Israel have not hearkened unto me; how then shall Pharaoh hear me, who *am* of uncircumcised lips?
13 And the LORD spake unto Moses and unto Aaron, and gave them a charge unto the children of Israel, and unto Pharaoh king of Egypt, to bring the children of Israel out of the land of Egypt.
14 ¶These *be* the heads of their fathers' houses: The sons of Reuben the firstborn of Israel; Hā'nŏch, and Păl'lū, Hĕz'ron, and Căr'mī: these *be* the families of Reuben.
15 And the sons of Simeon; Jĕ-mu'el, and Jā'mĭn, and Ō'hăd, and Jā'chin, and Zō'här, and Shā'ul the son of a Canaanitish woman: these *are* the families of Simeon.
16 And these *are* the names of the sons of Levi according to their generations; Ger'shon, and Kō'hăth, and Me-râ'rī: and the years of the life of Levi *were* an hundred thirty and seven years.
17 The sons of Ger'shon; Lĭb'nī, and Shĭ'mī, according to their families.
18 And the sons of Kō'hăth; Ăm'răm, and Ĭz'här, and Hē-bron, and Ŭz'zī-el: and the years of the life of Kō'hăth *were* an hundred thirty and three years.
19 And the sons of Me-râ'rī; Mă'ha-lī and Mū'shī: these *are* the families of Levi according to their generations.
20 And Ăm'răm took him Jŏch'e-bĕd his father's sister to wife; and she bare him Aaron and Moses: and the years of the life of Ăm'răm *were* an hundred and thirty and seven years.
21 And the sons of Ĭz'här; Kô'rah, and Nē'phĕg, and Zĭch'rī.
22 And the sons of Ŭz'zī-el; Mĭsh'a-el, and Ĕl'zā-phăn, and Zĭth'rī.
23 And Aaron took him E-lĭsh'e-ba, daughter of Am-mĭn'a-dăb, sister of Nā-ăsh'on, to wife; and she bare him Nādăb, and A-bī'hū, Ĕ-le-ā'zar, and Ĭth'a-mär.
24 And the sons of Kô'rah; Ăs'sir, and Ĕl'kā-nah, and Ă-bī'a-săph: these *are* the families of the Kōr'hītes.
25 And Ĕ-le-ā'zar Aaron's son took him *one* of the daughters of Pū'tī-el to wife; and she bare him Phĭn'e-has: these *are* the heads of the fathers of the Lēvītes according to their families.
26 These *are* that Aaron and Moses, to whom the LORD said, Bring out the children of Israel from the land of Egypt according to their armies.
27 These *are* they which spake to Pharaoh king of Egypt, to bring out the children of Israel from Egypt: these *are* that Moses and Aaron.
28 ¶And it came to pass on the day

when the LORD spake unto Moses in the land of Egypt,

29 That the LORD spake unto Moses, saying, I *am* the LORD: speak thou unto Pharaoh king of Egypt all that I say unto thee.

30 And Moses said before the LORD, Behold, I *am* of uncircumcised lips, and how shall Pharaoh hearken unto me?

CHAPTER 7

AND the LORD said unto Moses, See, I have made thee a god to Pharaoh: and Aaron thy brother shall be thy prophet.

2 Thou shalt speak all that I command thee: and Aaron thy brother shall speak unto Pharaoh, that he send the children of Israel out of his land.

3 And I will harden Pharaoh's heart, and multiply my signs and my wonders in the land of Egypt.

4 But Pharaoh shall not hearken unto you, that I may lay my hand upon Egypt, and bring forth mine armies, *and* my people the children of Israel, out of the land of Egypt by great judgments.

5 And the Egyptians shall know that I *am* the LORD, when I stretch forth mine hand upon Egypt, and bring out the children of Israel from among them.

6 And Moses and Aaron did as the LORD commanded them, so did they.

7 And Moses *was* fourscore years old, and Aaron fourscore and three years old, when they spake unto Pharaoh.

8 ¶And the LORD spake unto Moses and unto Aaron, saying,

9 When Pharaoh shall speak unto you, saying, Shew a miracle for you: then thou shalt say unto Aaron, Take thy rod, and cast *it* before Pharaoh, *and* it shall become a serpent.

10 ¶And Moses and Aaron went in unto Pharaoh, and they did so as the LORD had commanded: and Aaron cast down his rod before Pharaoh, and before his servants, and it became a serpent.

11 Then Pharaoh also called the wise men and the sorcerers: now the magicians of Egypt, they also did in like manner with their enchantments.

12 For they cast down every man his rod, and they became serpents: but Aaron's rod swallowed up their rods.

13 And he hardened Pharaoh's heart, that he hearkened not unto them; as the LORD had said.

14 ¶And the LORD said unto Moses, Pharaoh's heart *is* hardened, he refuseth to let the people go.

15 Get thee unto Pharaoh in the morning; lo, he goeth out unto the water; and thou shalt stand by the river's brink against he come; and the rod which was turned to a serpent shalt thou take in thine hand.

16 And thou shalt say unto him, The LORD God of the Hebrews hath sent me unto thee, saying, Let my people go, that they may serve me in the wilderness: and, behold, hitherto thou wouldest not hear.

17 Thus saith the LORD, In this thou shalt know that I *am* the LORD: behold, I will smite with the rod that *is* in mine hand upon the waters which *are* in the river, and they shall be turned to blood.

18 And the fish that *is* in the river shall die, and the river shall stink; and the Egyptians shall lothe to drink of the water of the river.

19 ¶And the LORD spake unto Moses, Say unto Aaron, Take thy rod, and stretch out thine hand upon the waters of Egypt, upon their streams, upon their rivers, and upon their ponds, and upon all their pools of water, that they may become blood; and *that* there may be blood throughout all the land of Egypt, both in *vessels of* wood, and in *vessels of* stone.

20 And Moses and Aaron did so, as the LORD commanded; and he lifted up the rod, and smote the waters that *were* in the river, in the sight of Pharaoh, and in the sight of his servants; and all the waters that *were* in the river were turned to blood.

21 And the fish that *was* in the river died; and the river stank, and the Egyptians could not drink of the water of the river; and there was blood throughout all the land of Egypt.

22 And the magicians of Egypt did so with their enchantments: and Pharaoh's heart was hardened, neither did he hearken unto them; as the LORD had said.

23 And Pharaoh turned and went into his house, neither did he set his heart to this also.

24 And all the Egyptians digged round about the river for water to drink; for they could not drink of the water of the river.

25 And seven days were fulfilled, after that the LORD had smitten the river.

CHAPTER 8

AND the LORD spake unto Moses, Go unto Pharaoh, and say unto him, Thus saith the LORD, Let my people go, that they may serve me.

2 And if thou refuse to let *them* go, behold, I will smite all thy borders with frogs:

3 And the river shall bring forth frogs

abundantly, which shall go up and come into thine house, and into thy bedchamber, and upon thy bed, and into the house of thy servants, and upon thy people, and into thine ovens, and into thy kneadingtroughs:

4 And the frogs shall come up both on thee, and upon thy people, and upon all thy servants.

5 ¶And the LORD spake unto Moses, Say unto Aaron, Stretch forth thine hand with thy rod over the streams, over the rivers, and over the ponds, and cause frogs to come up upon the land of Egypt.

6 And Aaron stretched out his hand over the waters of Egypt; and the frogs came up, and covered the land of Egypt.

7 And the magicians did so with their enchantments, and brought up frogs upon the land of Egypt.

8 ¶Then Pharaoh called for Moses and Aaron, and said, Intreat the LORD, that he may take away the frogs from me, and from my people; and I will let the people go, that they may do sacrifice unto the LORD.

9 And Moses said unto Pharaoh, Glory over me: when shall I intreat for thee, and for thy servants, and for thy people, to destroy the frogs from thee and thy houses, *that* they may remain in the river only?

10 And he said, To morrow. And he said, *Be it* according to thy word: that thou mayest know that *there is* none like unto the LORD our God.

11 And the frogs shall depart from thee, and from thy houses, and from thy servants, and from thy people; they shall remain in the river only.

12 And Moses and Aaron went out from Pharaoh: and Moses cried unto the LORD because of the frogs which he had brought against Pharaoh.

13 And the LORD did according to the word of Moses; and the frogs died out of the houses, out of the villages, and out of the fields.

14 And they gathered them together upon heaps: and the land stank.

15 But when Pharaoh saw that there was respite, he hardened his heart, and hearkened not unto them; as the LORD had said.

16 ¶And the LORD said unto Moses, Say unto Aaron, Stretch out thy rod, and smite the dust of the land, that it may become lice throughout all the land of Egypt.

17 And they did so; for Aaron stretched out his hand with his rod, and smote the dust of the earth, and it became lice in man, and in beast; all the dust of the land became lice throughout all the land of Egypt.

18 And the magicians did so with their enchantments to bring forth lice, but they could not: so there were lice upon man, and upon beast.

19 Then the magicians said unto Pharaoh, This *is* the finger of God: and Pharaoh's heart was hardened, and he hearkened not unto them; as the LORD had said.

20 ¶And the LORD said unto Moses, Rise up early in the morning, and stand before Pharaoh; lo, he cometh forth to the water; and say unto him, Thus saith the LORD, Let my people go, that they may serve me.

21 Else, if thou wilt not let my people go, behold, I will send swarms *of flies* upon thee, and upon thy servants, and upon thy people, and into thy houses: and the houses of the Egyptians shall be full of swarms *of flies*, and also the ground whereon they *are*.

22 And I will sever in that day the land of Goshen, in which my people dwell, that no swarms *of flies* shall be there; to the end thou mayest know that I *am* the LORD in the midst of the earth.

23 And I will put a division between my people and thy people: to morrow shall this sign be.

24 And the LORD did so; and there came a grievous swarm *of flies* into the house of Pharaoh, and *into* his servants' houses, and into all the land of Egypt: the land was corrupted by reason of the swarm *of flies*.

25 ¶And Pharaoh called for Moses and for Aaron, and said, Go ye, sacrifice to your God in the land.

26 And Moses said, It is not meet so to do; for we shall sacrifice the abomination of the Egyptians to the LORD our God: lo, shall we sacrifice the abomination of the Egyptians before their eyes, and will they not stone us?

27 We will go three days' journey into the wilderness, and sacrifice to the LORD our God, as he shall command us.

28 And Pharaoh said, I will let you go, that ye may sacrifice to the LORD your God in the wilderness; only ye shall not go very far away: intreat for me.

29 And Moses said, Behold, I go out from thee, and I will intreat the LORD that the swarms *of flies* may depart from Pharaoh, from his servants, and from his people, to morrow: but let not Pharaoh deal deceitfully any more in not letting the people go to sacrifice to the LORD.

30 And Moses went out from Pharaoh, and intreated the LORD.

31 And the LORD did according to the
word of Moses; and he removed the
swarms *of flies* from Pharaoh, from his
servants, and from his people; there remained not one.
32 And Pharaoh hardened his heart
at this time also, neither would he let
the people go.

CHAPTER 9

THEN the LORD said unto Moses, Go in
unto Pharaoh, and tell him, Thus saith
the LORD God of the Hebrews, Let my
people go, that they may serve me.
2 For if thou refuse to let *them* go,
and wilt hold them still,
3 Behold, the hand of the LORD is
upon thy cattle which *is* in the field,
upon the horses, upon the asses, upon
the camels, upon the oxen, and upon
the sheep: *there shall be* a very grievous murrain.
4 And the LORD shall sever between
the cattle of Israel and the cattle of
Egypt: and there shall nothing die of all
that is the children's of Israel.
5 And the LORD appointed a set time,
saying, To morrow the LORD shall do
this thing in the land.
6 And the LORD did that thing on the
morrow, and all the cattle of Egypt
died: but of the cattle of the children of
Israel died not one.
7 And Pharaoh sent, and, behold,
there was not one of the cattle of the
Israelites dead. And the heart of
Pharaoh was hardened, and he did not
let the people go.
8 ¶And the LORD said unto Moses and
unto Aaron, Take to you handfuls of
ashes of the furnace, and let Moses
sprinkle it toward the heaven in the
sight of Pharaoh.
9 And it shall become small dust in all
the land of Egypt, and shall be a boil
breaking forth *with* blains upon man,
and upon beast, throughout all the land
of Egypt.
10 And they took ashes of the furnace, and stood before Pharaoh; and
Moses sprinkled it up toward heaven;
and it became a boil breaking forth
with blains upon man, and upon beast.
11 And the magicians could not stand
before Moses because of the boils; for
the boil was upon the magicians, and
upon all the Egyptians.
12 And the LORD hardened the heart
of Pharaoh, and he hearkened not unto
them; as the LORD had spoken unto
Moses.
13 ¶And the LORD said unto Moses,
Rise up early in the morning, and stand
before Pharaoh, and say unto him,
Thus saith the LORD God of the
Hebrews, Let my people go, that they
may serve me.
14 For I will at this time send all my
plagues upon thine heart, and upon thy
servants, and upon thy people; that
thou mayest know that *there is* none
like me in all the earth.
15 For now I will stretch out my
hand, that I may smite thee and thy
people with pestilence; and thou shalt
be cut off from the earth.
16 And in very deed for this *cause*
have I raised thee up, for to shew *in*
thee my power; and that my name may
be declared throughout all the earth.
17 As yet exaltest thou thyself
against my people, that thou wilt not
let them go?
18 Behold, to morrow about this time
I will cause it to rain a very grievous
hail, such as hath not been in Egypt
since the foundation thereof even until
now.
19 Send therefore now, *and* gather
thy cattle, and all that thou hast in the
field; *for upon* every man and beast
which shall be found in the field, and
shall not be brought home, the hail
shall come down upon them, and they
shall die.
20 He that feared the word of the
LORD among the servants of Pharaoh
made his servants and his cattle flee
into the houses:
21 And he that regarded not the word
of the LORD left his servants and his
cattle in the field.
22 ¶And the LORD said unto Moses,
Stretch forth thine hand toward
heaven, that there may be hail in all the
land of Egypt, upon man, and upon
beast, and upon every herb of the field,
throughout the land of Egypt.
23 And Moses stretched forth his rod
toward heaven: and the LORD sent
thunder and hail, and the fire ran along
upon the ground; and the LORD rained
hail upon the land of Egypt.
24 So there was hail, and fire mingled
with the hail, very grievous, such as
there was none like it in all the land of
Egypt since it became a nation.
25 And the hail smote throughout all
the land of Egypt all that *was* in the
field, both man and beast; and the hail
smote every herb of the field, and brake
every tree of the field.
26 Only in the land of Goshen, where
the children of Israel *were*, was there
no hail.
27 ¶And Pharaoh sent, and called for
Moses and Aaron, and said unto them, I
have sinned this time: the LORD *is*
righteous, and I and my people *are*
wicked.

28 Intreat the LORD (for *it is* enough)
that there be no *more* mighty thunder-
ings and hail; and I will let you go, and
ye shall stay no longer.
29 And Moses said unto him, As soon
as I am gone out of the city, I will
spread abroad my hands unto the
LORD; *and* the thunder shall cease,
neither shall there be any more hail;
that thou mayest know how that the
earth *is* the LORD'S.
30 But as for thee and thy servants, I
know that ye will not yet fear the LORD
God.
31 And the flax and the barley was
smitten: for the barley *was* in the ear,
and the flax *was* bolled.
32 But the wheat and the rie were not
smitten: for they *were* not grown up.
33 And Moses went out of the city
from Pharaoh, and spread abroad his
hands unto the LORD: and the thunders
and hail ceased, and the rain was not
poured upon the earth.
34 And when Pharaoh saw that the
rain and the hail and the thunders were
ceased, he sinned yet more, and har-
dened his heart, he and his servants.
35 And the heart of Pharaoh was har-
dened, neither would he let the children
of Israel go; as the LORD had spoken by
Moses.

CHAPTER 10

AND the LORD said unto Moses, Go in
unto Pharaoh: for I have hardened his
heart, and the heart of his servants,
that I might shew these my signs be-
fore him:
2 And that thou mayest tell in the
ears of thy son, and of thy son's son,
what things I have wrought in Egypt,
and my signs which I have done among
them; that ye may know how that I *am*
the LORD.
3 And Moses and Aaron came in unto
Pharaoh, and said unto him, Thus saith
the LORD God of the Hebrews, How
long wilt thou refuse to humble thyself
before me? let my people go, that they
may serve me.
4 Else, if thou refuse to let my people
go, behold, to morrow will I bring the
locusts into thy coast:
5 And they shall cover the face of the
earth, that one cannot be able to see the
earth: and they shall eat the residue of
that which is escaped, which re-
maineth unto you from the hail, and
shall eat every tree which groweth for
you out of the field:
6 And they shall fill thy houses, and
the houses of all thy servants, and the
houses of all the Egyptians; which
neither thy fathers, nor thy fathers'
fathers have seen, since the day that
they were upon the earth unto this day.
And he turned himself, and went out
from Pharaoh.
7 And Pharaoh's servants said unto
him, How long shall this man be a snare
unto us? let the men go, that they may
serve the LORD their God: knowest thou
not yet that Egypt is destroyed?
8 And Moses and Aaron were
brought again unto Pharaoh: and he
said unto them, Go, serve the LORD
your God: *but* who *are* they that shall
go?
9 And Moses said, We will go with
our young and with our old, with our
sons and with our daughters, with our
flocks and with our herds will we go;
for we *must hold* a feast unto the LORD.
10 And he said unto them, Let the
LORD be so with you, as I will let you go,
and your little ones: look *to it;* for evil *is*
before you.
11 Not so: go now ye *that are* men,
and serve the LORD; for that ye did de-
sire. And they were driven out from
Pharaoh's presence.
12 ¶And the LORD said unto Moses,
Stretch out thine hand over the land of
Egypt for the locusts, that they may
come up upon the land of Egypt, and
eat every herb of the land, *even* all that
the hail hath left.
13 And Moses stretched forth his rod
over the land of Egypt, and the LORD
brought an east wind upon the land all
that day, and all *that* night; *and* when it
was morning, the east wind brought
the locusts.
14 And the locusts went up over all
the land of Egypt, and rested in all the
coasts of Egypt: very grievous *were
they;* before them there were no such
locusts as they, neither after them shall
be such.
15 For they covered the face of the
whole earth, so that the land was dark-
ened; and they did eat every herb of the
land, and all the fruit of the trees which
the hail had left: and there remained
not any green thing in the trees, or in
the herbs of the field, through all the
land of Egypt.
16 ¶Then Pharaoh called for Moses
and Aaron in haste; and he said, I have
sinned against the LORD your God, and
against you.
17 Now therefore forgive, I pray thee,
my sin only this once, and intreat the
LORD your God, that he may take away
from me this death only.
18 And he went out from Pharaoh,
and intreated the LORD.
19 And the LORD turned a mighty
strong west wind, which took away the

locusts, and cast them into the Red sea; there remained not one locust in all the coasts of Egypt.

20 But the LORD hardened Pharaoh's heart, so that he would not let the children of Israel go.

21 ¶And the LORD said unto Moses, Stretch out thine hand toward heaven, that there may be darkness over the land of Egypt, even darkness *which* may be felt.

22 And Moses stretched forth his hand toward heaven; and there was a thick darkness in all the land of Egypt three days:

23 They saw not one another, neither rose any from his place for three days: but all the children of Israel had light in their dwellings.

24 ¶And Pharaoh called unto Moses, and said, Go ye, serve the LORD; only let your flocks and your herds be stayed: let your little ones also go with you.

25 And Moses said, Thou must give us also sacrifices and burnt offerings, that we may sacrifice unto the LORD our God.

26 Our cattle also shall go with us; there shall not an hoof be left behind; for thereof must we take to serve the LORD our God; and we know not with what we must serve the LORD, until we come thither.

27 ¶But the LORD hardened Pharaoh's heart, and he would not let them go.

28 And Pharaoh said unto him, Get thee from me, take heed to thyself, see my face no more; for in *that* day thou seest my face thou shalt die.

29 And Moses said, Thou hast spoken well, I will see thy face again no more.

CHAPTER 11

AND the LORD said unto Moses, Yet will I bring one plague *more* upon Pharaoh, and upon Egypt; afterwards he will let you go hence: when he shall let *you* go, he shall surely thrust you out hence altogether.

2 Speak now in the ears of the people, and let every man borrow of his neighbour, and every woman of her neighbour, jewels of silver, and jewels of gold.

3 And the LORD gave the people favour in the sight of the Egyptians. Moreover the man Moses *was* very great in the land of Egypt, in the sight of Pharaoh's servants, and in the sight of the people.

4 ¶And Moses said, Thus saith the LORD, About midnight will I go out into the midst of Egypt:

5 And all the firstborn in the land of Egypt shall die, from the firstborn of Pharaoh that sitteth upon his throne, even unto the firstborn of the maidservant that *is* behind the mill; and all the firstborn of beasts.

6 And there shall be a great cry throughout all the land of Egypt, such as there was none like it, nor shall be like it any more.

7 But against any of the children of Israel shall not a dog move his tongue, against man or beast: that ye may know how that the LORD doth put a difference between the Egyptians and Israel.

8 And all these thy servants shall come down unto me, and bow down themselves unto me, saying, Get thee out, and all the people that follow thee: and after that I will go out. And he went out from Pharaoh in a great anger.

9 And the LORD said unto Moses, Pharaoh shall not hearken unto you; that my wonders may be multiplied in the land of Egypt.

10 And Moses and Aaron did all these wonders before Pharaoh: and the LORD hardened Pharaoh's heart, so that he would not let the children of Israel go out of his land.

CHAPTER 12

AND the LORD spake unto Moses and Aaron in the land of Egypt, saying,

2 This month *shall be* unto you the beginning of months: it *shall be* the first month of the year to you.

3 ¶Speak ye unto all the congregation of Israel, saying, In the tenth *day* of this month they shall take to them every man a lamb, according to the house of *their* fathers, a lamb for an house:

4 And if the household be too little for the lamb, let him and his neighbour next unto his house take *it* according to the number of the souls; every man according to his eating shall make your count for the lamb.

5 Your lamb shall be without blemish, a male of the first year: ye shall take *it* out from the sheep, or from the goats:

6 And ye shall keep it up until the fourteenth day of the same month: and the whole assembly of the congregation of Israel shall kill it in the evening.

7 And they shall take of the blood, and strike *it* on the two side posts and on the upper door post of the houses, wherein they shall eat it.

8 And they shall eat the flesh in that night, roast with fire, and unleavened bread; *and* with bitter *herbs* they shall eat it.

9 Eat not of it raw, nor sodden at all with water, but roast *with* fire; his head

with his legs, and with the purtenance thereof.

10 And ye shall let nothing of it remain until the morning; and that which remaineth of it until the morning ye shall burn with fire.

11 And thus shall ye eat it; *with* your loins girded, your shoes on your feet, and your staff in your hand; and ye shall eat it in haste: it *is* the LORD's passover.

12 For I will pass through the land of Egypt this night, and will smite all the firstborn in the land of Egypt, both man and beast; and against all the gods of Egypt I will execute judgment: I *am* the LORD.

13 And the blood shall be to you for a token upon the houses where ye *are:* and when I see the blood, I will pass over you, and the plague shall not be upon you to destroy *you,* when I smite the land of Egypt.

14 And this day shall be unto you for a memorial; and ye shall keep it a feast to the LORD throughout your generations; ye shall keep it a feast by an ordinance for ever.

15 ¶Seven days shall ye eat unleavened bread; even the first day ye shall put away leaven out of your houses: for whosoever eateth leavened bread from the first day until the seventh day, that soul shall be cut off from Israel.

16 And in the first day *there shall be* an holy convocation, and in the seventh day there shall be an holy convocation to you; no manner of work shall be done in them, save *that* which every man must eat, that only may be done of you.

17 And ye shall observe *the feast of* unleavened bread; for in this selfsame day have I brought your armies out of the land of Egypt: therefore shall ye observe this day in your generations by an ordinance for ever.

18 In the first *month,* on the fourteenth day of the month at even, ye shall eat unleavened bread, until the one and twentieth day of the month at even.

19 Seven days shall there be no leaven found in your houses: for whosoever eateth that which is leavened, even that soul shall be cut off from the congregation of Israel, whether he be a stranger, or born in the land.

20 Ye shall eat nothing leavened; in all your habitations shall ye eat unleavened bread.

21 ¶Then Moses called for all the elders of Israel, and said unto them, Draw out and take you a lamb according to your families, and kill the passover.

22 And ye shall take a bunch of hyssop, and dip *it* in the blood that *is* in the bason, and strike the lintel and the two side posts with the blood that *is* in the bason: and none of you shall go out at the door of his house until the morning.

23 For the LORD will pass through to smite the Egyptians; and when he seeth the blood upon the lintel, and on the two side posts, the LORD will pass over the door, and will not suffer the destroyer to come in unto your houses to smite *you.*

24 And ye shall observe this thing for an ordinance to thee and to thy sons for ever.

25 And it shall come to pass, when ye be come to the land which the LORD will give you, according as he hath promised, that ye shall keep this service.

26 And it shall come to pass, when your children shall say unto you, What mean ye by this service?

27 That ye shall say, It *is* the sacrifice of the LORD's passover, who passed over the houses of the children of Israel in Egypt, when he smote the Egyptians, and delivered our houses. And the people bowed the head and worshipped.

28 And the children of Israel went away, and did as the LORD had commanded Moses and Aaron, so did they.

29 ¶And it came to pass, that at midnight the LORD smote all the firstborn in the land of Egypt, from the firstborn of Pharaoh that sat on his throne unto the firstborn of the captive that *was* in the dungeon; and all the firstborn of cattle.

30 And Pharaoh rose up in the night, he, and all his servants, and all the Egyptians; and there was a great cry in Egypt; for *there was* not a house where *there was* not one dead.

31 ¶And he called for Moses and Aaron by night, and said, Rise up, *and* get you forth from among my people, both ye and the children of Israel; and go, serve the LORD, as ye have said.

32 Also take your flocks and your herds, as ye have said, and be gone; and bless me also.

33 And the Egyptians were urgent upon the people, that they might send them out of the land in haste; for they said, We *be* all dead *men.*

34 And the people took their dough before it was leavened, their kneadingtroughs being bound up in their clothes upon their shoulders.

35 And the children of Israel did according to the word of Moses; and they

borrowed of the Egyptians jewels of silver, and jewels of gold, and raiment:

36 And the LORD gave the people favour in the sight of the Egyptians, so that they lent unto them *such things as they required.* And they spoiled the Egyptians.

37 ¶And the children of Israel journeyed from Răm'e-sēṡ to Sŭc'coth, about six hundred thousand on foot *that were* men, beside children.

38 And a mixed multitude went up also with them; and flocks, and herds, *even* very much cattle.

39 And they baked unleavened cakes of the dough which they brought forth out of Egypt, for it was not leavened; because they were thrust out of Egypt, and could not tarry, neither had they prepared for themselves any victual.

40 ¶Now the sojourning of the children of Israel, who dwelt in Egypt, *was* four hundred and thirty years.

41 And it came to pass at the end of the four hundred and thirty years, even the selfsame day it came to pass, that all the hosts of the LORD went out from the land of Egypt.

42 It *is* a night to be much observed unto the LORD for bringing them out from the land of Egypt: this *is* that night of the LORD to be observed of all the children of Israel in their generations.

43 ¶And the LORD said unto Moses and Aaron, This *is* the ordinance of the passover: There shall no stranger eat thereof:

44 But every man's servant that is bought for money, when thou hast circumcised him, then shall he eat thereof.

45 A foreigner and an hired servant shall not eat thereof.

46 In one house shall it be eaten; thou shalt not carry forth ought of the flesh abroad out of the house; neither shall ye break a bone thereof.

47 All the congregation of Israel shall keep it.

48 And when a stranger shall sojourn with thee, and will keep the passover to the LORD, let all his males be circumcised, and then let him come near and keep it; and he shall be as one that is born in the land: for no uncircumcised person shall eat thereof.

49 One law shall be to him that is homeborn, and unto the stranger that sojourneth among you.

50 Thus did all the children of Israel; as the LORD commanded Moses and Aaron, so did they.

51 And it came to pass the selfsame day, *that* the LORD did bring the children of Israel out of the land of Egypt by their armies.

CHAPTER 13

AND the LORD spake unto Moses, saying,

2 Sanctify unto me all the firstborn, whatsoever openeth the womb among the children of Israel, *both* of man and of beast: it *is* mine.

3 ¶And Moses said unto the people, Remember this day, in which ye came out from Egypt, out of the house of bondage; for by strength of hand the LORD brought you out from this *place:* there shall no leavened bread be eaten.

4 This day came ye out in the month Ābĭb.

5 And it shall be when the LORD shall bring thee into the land of the Canaanites, and the Hittites, and the Ămorītes, and the Hī'vītes, and the Jeb'u-sītes, which he sware unto thy fathers to give thee, a land flowing with milk and honey, that thou shalt keep this service in this month.

6 Seven days thou shalt eat unleavened bread, and in the seventh day *shall be* a feast to the LORD.

7 Unleavened bread shall be eaten seven days; and there shall no leavened bread be seen with thee, neither shall there be leaven seen with thee in all thy quarters.

8 And thou shalt shew thy son in that day, saying, *This is done* because of that *which* the LORD did unto me when I came forth out of Egypt.

9 And it shall be for a sign unto thee upon thine hand, and for a memorial between thine eyes, that the LORD's law may be in thy mouth: for with a strong hand hath the LORD brought thee out of Egypt.

10 Thou shalt therefore keep this ordinance in his season from year to year.

11 ¶And it shall be when the LORD shall bring thee into the land of the Canaanites, as he sware unto thee and to thy fathers, and shall give it thee,

12 That thou shalt set apart unto the LORD all that openeth the matrix, and every firstling that cometh of a beast which thou hast; the males *shall be* the LORD's.

13 And every firstling of an ass thou shalt redeem with a lamb; and if thou wilt not redeem it, then thou shalt break his neck: and all the firstborn of man among thy children shalt thou redeem.

14 ¶And it shall be when thy son asketh thee in time to come, saying, What *is* this? that thou shalt say unto him, By strength of hand the LORD

Adam Names the Animals (Gen 2)

Noah and the Ark (Gen 7)

brought us out from Egypt, from the house of bondage:

15 And it came to pass, when Pharaoh would hardly let us go, that the LORD slew all the firstborn in the land of Egypt, both the firstborn of man, and the firstborn of beast: therefore I sacrifice to the LORD all that openeth the matrix, being males; but all the firstborn of my children I redeem.

16 And it shall be for a token upon thine hand, and for frontlets between thine eyes: for by strength of hand the LORD brought us forth out of Egypt.

17 ¶And it came to pass, when Pharaoh had let the people go, that God led them not *through* the way of the land of the Philistines, although that *was* near; for God said, Lest peradventure the people repent when they see war, and they return to Egypt:

18 But God led the people about, *through* the way of the wilderness of the Red sea: and the children of Israel went up harnessed out of the land of Egypt.

19 And Moses took the bones of Joseph with him: for he had straitly sworn the children of Israel, saying, God will surely visit you; and ye shall carry up my bones away hence with you.

20 ¶And they took their journey from Sŭc'coth, and encamped in Ē'tham, in the edge of the wilderness.

21 And the LORD went before them by day in a pillar of a cloud, to lead them the way; and by night in a pillar of fire, to give them light; to go by day and night:

22 He took not away the pillar of the cloud by day, nor the pillar of fire by night, *from* before the people.

CHAPTER 14

AND the LORD spake unto Moses, saying,

2 Speak unto the children of Israel, that they turn and encamp before Pī'-ha-hī'rŏth, between Mĭg'dŏl and the sea, over against Bā'al-zē'phŏn: before it shall ye encamp by the sea.

3 For Pharaoh will say of the children of Israel, They *are* entangled in the land, the wilderness hath shut them in.

4 And I will harden Pharaoh's heart, that he shall follow after them; and I will be honoured upon Pharaoh, and upon all his host; that the Egyptians may know that I *am* the LORD. And they did so.

5 ¶And it was told the king of Egypt that the people fled: and the heart of Pharaoh and of his servants was turned against the people, and they said, Why have we done this, that we have let Israel go from serving us?

6 And he made ready his chariot, and took his people with him:

7 And he took six hundred chosen chariots, and all the chariots of Egypt, and captains over every one of them.

8 And the LORD hardened the heart of Pharaoh king of Egypt, and he pursued after the children of Israel: and the children of Israel went out with an high hand.

9 But the Egyptians pursued after them, all the horses *and* chariots of Pharaoh, and his horsemen, and his army, and overtook them encamping by the sea, beside Pī'-ha-hī'rŏth, before Bā'al-zē'phŏn.

10 ¶And when Pharaoh drew nigh, the children of Israel lifted up their eyes, and, behold, the Egyptians marched after them; and they were sore afraid: and the children of Israel cried out unto the LORD.

11 And they said unto Moses, Because *there were* no graves in Egypt, hast thou taken us away to die in the wilderness? wherefore hast thou dealt thus with us, to carry us forth out of Egypt?

12 *Is* not this the word that we did tell thee in Egypt, saying, Let us alone, that we may serve the Egyptians? For *it had been* better for us to serve the Egyptians, than that we should die in the wilderness.

13 ¶And Moses said unto the people, Fear ye not, stand still, and see the salvation of the LORD, which he will shew to you to day: for the Egyptians whom ye have seen to day, ye shall see them again no more for ever.

14 The LORD shall fight for you, and ye shall hold your peace.

15 ¶And the LORD said unto Moses, Wherefore criest thou unto me? speak unto the children of Israel, that they go forward:

16 But lift thou up thy rod, and stretch out thine hand over the sea, and divide it: and the children of Israel shall go on dry *ground* through the midst of the sea.

17 And I, behold, I will harden the hearts of the Egyptians, and they shall follow them: and I will get me honour upon Pharaoh, and upon all his host, upon his chariots, and upon his horsemen.

18 And the Egyptians shall know that I *am* the LORD, when I have gotten me honour upon Pharaoh, upon his chariots, and upon his horsemen.

19 ¶And the angel of God, which went before the camp of Israel, removed and went behind them; and the pillar of the cloud went from before their face, and stood behind them:

20 And it came between the camp of the Egyptians and the camp of Israel; and it was a cloud and darkness *to them,* but it gave light by night *to these:* so that the one came not near the other all the night.

21 And Moses stretched out his hand over the sea; and the LORD caused the sea to go *back* by a strong east wind all that night, and made the sea dry *land,* and the waters were divided.

22 And the children of Israel went into the midst of the sea upon the dry *ground:* and the waters *were* a wall unto them on their right hand, and on their left.

23 ¶And the Egyptians pursued, and went in after them to the midst of the sea, *even* all Pharaoh's horses, his chariots, and his horsemen.

24 And it came to pass, that in the morning watch the LORD looked unto the host of the Egyptians through the pillar of fire and of the cloud, and troubled the host of the Egyptians,

25 And took off their chariot wheels, that they drave them heavily: so that the Egyptians said, Let us flee from the face of Israel; for the LORD fighteth for them against the Egyptians.

26 And the LORD said unto Moses, Stretch out thine hand over the sea, that the waters may come again upon the Egyptians, upon their chariots, and upon their horsemen.

27 And Moses stretched forth his hand over the sea, and the sea returned to his strength when the morning appeared; and the Egyptians fled against it; and the LORD overthrew the Egyptians in the midst of the sea.

28 And the waters returned, and covered the chariots, and the horsemen, *and* all the host of Pharaoh that came into the sea after them; there remained not so much as one of them.

29 But the children of Israel walked upon dry *land* in the midst of the sea; and the waters *were* a wall unto them on their right hand, and on their left.

30 Thus the LORD saved Israel that day out of the hand of the Egyptians; and Israel saw the Egyptians dead upon the sea shore.

31 And Israel saw that great work which the LORD did upon the Egyptians: and the people feared the LORD, and believed the LORD, and his servant Moses.

CHAPTER 15

THEN sang Moses and the children of Israel this song unto the LORD, and spake, saying, I will sing unto the LORD, for he hath triumphed gloriously: the horse and his rider hath he thrown into the sea.

2 The LORD *is* my strength and song, and he is become my salvation: he *is* my God, and I will prepare him an habitation; my father's God, and I will exalt him.

3 The LORD *is* a man of war: the LORD *is* his name.

4 Pharaoh's chariots and his host hath he cast into the sea: his chosen captains also are drowned in the Red sea.

5 The depths have covered them: they sank into the bottom as a stone.

6 Thy right hand, O LORD, is become glorious in power: thy right hand, O LORD, hath dashed in pieces the enemy.

7 And in the greatness of thine excellency thou hast overthrown them that rose up against thee: thou sentest forth thy wrath, *which* consumed them as stubble.

8 And with the blast of thy nostrils the waters were gathered together, the floods stood upright as an heap, *and* the depths were congealed in the heart of the sea.

9 The enemy said, I will pursue, I will overtake, I will divide the spoil; my lust shall be satisfied upon them; I will draw my sword, my hand shall destroy them.

10 Thou didst blow with thy wind, the sea covered them: they sank as lead in the mighty waters.

11 Who *is* like unto thee, O LORD, among the gods? who *is* like thee, glorious in holiness, fearful *in* praises, doing wonders?

12 Thou stretchedst out thy right hand, the earth swallowed them.

13 Thou in thy mercy hast led forth the people *which* thou hast redeemed: thou hast guided *them* in thy strength unto thy holy habitation.

14 The people shall hear, *and* be afraid: sorrow shall take hold on the inhabitants of Palestina.

15 Then the dukes of Ēdom shall be amazed; the mighty men of Moab, trembling shall take hold upon them; all the inhabitants of Canaan shall melt away.

16 Fear and dread shall fall upon them; by the greatness of thine arm they shall be *as* still as a stone; till thy people pass over, O LORD, till the people pass over, *which* thou hast purchased.

17 Thou shalt bring them in, and plant them in the mountain of thine inheritance, *in* the place, O LORD, *which* thou hast made for thee to dwell in, *in* the Sanctuary, O Lord *which* thy hands have established.
18 The LORD shall reign for ever and ever.
19 For the horse of Pharaoh went in with his chariots and with his horsemen into the sea, and the LORD brought again the waters of the sea upon them; but the children of Israel went on dry *land* in the midst of the sea.
20 ¶And Miriam the prophetess, the sister of Aaron, took a timbrel in her hand; and all the women went out after her with timbrels and with dances.
21 And Miriam answered them, Sing ye to the LORD, for he hath triumphed gloriously; the horse and his rider hath he thrown into the sea.
22 ¶So Moses brought Israel from the Red sea, and they went out into the wilderness of Shur; and they went three days in the wilderness, and found no water.
23 ¶And when they came to Mâ'rah, they could not drink of the waters of Mâ'rah, for they *were* bitter: therefore the name of it was called Mâ'rah.
24 And the people murmured against Moses, saying, What shall we drink?
25 And he cried unto the LORD; and the LORD shewed him a tree, *which* when he had cast into the waters, the waters were made sweet: there he made for them a statute and an ordinance, and there he proved them,
26 And said, If thou wilt diligently hearken to the voice of the LORD thy God, and wilt do that which is right in his sight, and wilt give ear to his commandments, and keep all his statutes, I will put none of these diseases upon thee, which I have brought upon the Egyptians: for I *am* the LORD that healeth thee.
27 ¶And they came to Elim, where *were* twelve wells of water, and threescore and ten palm trees: and they encamped there by the waters.

CHAPTER 16

AND they took their journey from Elim, and all the congregation of the children of Israel came unto the wilderness of Sin, which *is* between Elim and Sī'naī, on the fifteenth day of the second month after their departing out of the land of Egypt.
2 And the whole congregation of the children of Israel murmured against Moses and Aaron in the wilderness:
3 And the children of Israel said unto them, Would to God we had died by the hand of the LORD in the land of Egypt, when we sat by the flesh pots, *and* when we did eat bread to the full; for ye have brought us forth into this wilderness, to kill this whole assembly with hunger.
4 ¶Then said the LORD unto Moses, Behold, I will rain bread from heaven for you; and the people shall go out and gather a certain rate every day, that I may prove them, whether they will walk in my law, or no.
5 And it shall come to pass, that on the sixth day they shall prepare *that* which they bring in; and it shall be twice as much as they gather daily.
6 And Moses and Aaron said unto all the children of Israel, At even, then ye shall know that the LORD hath brought you out from the land of Egypt:
7 And in the morning, then ye shall see the glory of the LORD; for that he heareth your murmurings against the LORD: and what *are* we, that ye murmur against us?
8 And Moses said, *This shall be,* when the LORD shall give you in the evening flesh to eat, and in the morning bread to the full; for that the LORD heareth your murmurings which ye murmur against him: and what *are* we? your murmurings *are* not against us, but against the LORD.
9 And Moses spake unto Aaron, Say unto all the congregation of the children of Israel, Come near before the LORD: for he hath heard your murmurings.
10 ¶And it came to pass, as Aaron spake unto the whole congregation of the children of Israel, that they looked toward the wilderness, and, behold, the glory of the LORD appeared in the cloud.
11 And the LORD spake unto Moses, saying,
12 I have heard the murmurings of the children of Israel: speak unto them, saying, At even ye shall eat flesh, and in the morning ye shall be filled with bread; and ye shall know that I *am* the LORD your God.
13 And it came to pass, that at even the quails came up, and covered the camp: and in the morning the dew lay round about the host.
14 And when the dew that lay was gone up, behold, upon the face of the wilderness *there lay* a small round thing, *as* small as the hoar frost on the ground.
15 And when the children of Israel

saw *it,* they said one to another, It *is* manna: for they wist not what it *was.* And Moses said unto them, This *is* the bread which the LORD hath given you to eat.

16 This *is* the thing which the LORD hath commanded, Gather of it every man according to his eating, an omer for every man, *according to* the number of your persons; take ye every man for *them* which *are* in his tents.

17 And the children of Israel did so, and gathered, some more, some less.

18 And when they did mete *it* with an omer, he that gathered much had nothing over, and he that gathered little had no lack; they gathered every man according to his eating.

19 And Moses said, Let no man leave of it till the morning.

20 Notwithstanding they hearkened not unto Moses; but some of them left of it until the morning, and it bred worms, and stank: and Moses was wroth with them.

21 And they gathered it every morning, every man according to his eating: and when the sun waxed hot, it melted.

22 ¶And it came to pass, *that* on the sixth day they gathered twice as much bread, two omers for one *man:* and all the rulers of the congregation came and told Moses.

23 And he said unto them, This *is that* which the LORD hath said, To morrow *is* the rest of the holy sabbath unto the LORD: bake *that* which ye will bake *to day,* and seethe that ye will seethe; and that which remaineth over lay up for you to be kept until the morning.

24 And they laid it up till the morning, as Moses bade: and it did not stink, neither was there any worm therein.

25 And Moses said, Eat that to day; for to day *is* a sabbath unto the LORD: to day ye shall not find it in the field.

26 Six days ye shall gather it; but on the seventh day, *which is* the sabbath, in it there shall be none.

27 ¶And it came to pass, *that* there went out *some* of the people on the seventh day for to gather, and they found none.

28 And the LORD said unto Moses, How long refuse ye to keep my commandments and my laws?

29 See, for that the LORD hath given you the sabbath, therefore he giveth you on the sixth day the bread of two days; abide ye every man in his place, let no man go out of his place on the seventh day.

30 So the people rested on the seventh day.

31 And the house of Israel called the name thereof Manna: and it *was* like coriander seed, white; and the taste of it *was* like wafers *made* with honey.

32 ¶And Moses said, This *is* the thing which the LORD commandeth, Fill an omer of it to be kept for your generations; that they may see the bread wherewith I have fed you in the wilderness, when I brought you forth from the land of Egypt.

33 And Moses said unto Aaron, Take a pot, and put an omer full of manna therein, and lay it up before the LORD, to be kept for your generations.

34 As the LORD commanded Moses, so Aaron laid it up before the Testimony, to be kept.

35 And the children of Israel did eat manna forty years, until they came to a land inhabited; they did eat manna, until they came unto the borders of the land of Canaan.

36 Now an omer *is* the tenth *part* of an ēphah.

CHAPTER 17

AND all the congregation of the children of Israel journeyed from the wilderness of Sin, after their journeys, according to the commandment of the LORD, and pitched in Rĕph′i-dĭm: and *there was* no water for the people to drink.

2 Wherefore the people did chide with Moses, and said, Give us water that we may drink. And Moses said unto them, Why chide ye with me? wherefore do ye tempt the LORD?

3 And the people thirsted there for water; and the people murmured against Moses, and said, Wherefore *is* this *that* thou hast brought us up out of Egypt, to kill us and our children and our cattle with thirst?

4 And Moses cried unto the LORD, saying, What shall I do unto this people? they be almost ready to stone me.

5 And the LORD said unto Moses, Go on before the people, and take with thee of the elders of Israel; and thy rod, wherewith thou smotest the river, take in thine hand, and go.

6 Behold, I will stand before thee there upon the rock in Hô′rĕb; and thou shalt smite the rock, and there shall come water out of it, that the people may drink. And Moses did so in the sight of the elders of Israel.

7 And he called the name of the place Măs′sah, and Mĕr′i-bah, because of the chiding of the children of Israel, and because they tempted the LORD, saying, Is the LORD among us, or not?

8 ¶Then came Ăm'a-lĕk, and fought
with Israel in Rĕph'i-dĭm.
9 And Moses said unto Joshua,
Choose us out men, and go out, fight
with Ăm'a-lĕk: to morrow I will stand
on the top of the hill with the rod of God
in mine hand.
10 So Joshua did as Moses had said to
him, and fought with Ăm'a-lĕk: and
Moses, Aaron, and Hur went up to the
top of the hill.
11 And it came to pass, when Moses
held up his hand, that Israel prevailed:
and when he let down his hand, Ăm'a-
lĕk prevailed.
12 But Moses' hands *were* heavy; and
they took a stone, and put *it* under him,
and he sat thereon; and Aaron and Hur
stayed up his hands, the one on the one
side, and the other on the other side;
and his hands were steady until the
going down of the sun.
13 And Joshua discomfited Ăm'a-lĕk
and his people with the edge of the
sword.
14 And the LORD said unto Moses,
Write this *for* a memorial in a book, and
rehearse *it* in the ears of Joshua: for I
will utterly put out the remembrance of
Ăm'a-lĕk from under heaven.
15 And Moses built an altar, and
called the name of it Je-hō'vah-nĭs'sī:
16 For he said, Because the LORD hath
sworn *that* the LORD *will have* war with
Ăm'a-lĕk from generation to genera-
tion.

CHAPTER 18

WHEN Jĕth'rō, the priest of Mĭd'ĭ-an,
Moses' father in law, heard of all that
God had done for Moses, and for Israel
his people, *and* that the LORD had
brought Israel out of Egypt;
2 Then Jĕth'rō, Moses' father in law,
took Zĭp-po'rah, Moses' wife, after he
had sent her back,
3 And her two sons; of which the
name of the one *was* Ger'shom; for he
said, I have been an alien in a strange
land:
4 And the name of the other *was* Ĕ-lĭ-
ē'zer; for the God of my father, *said he,*
was mine help, and delivered me from
the sword of Pharaoh:
5 And Jĕth'rō, Moses' father in law,
came with his sons and his wife unto
Moses into the wilderness, where he
encamped at the mount of God:
6 And he said unto Moses, I thy father
in law Jĕth'rō am come unto thee, and
thy wife, and her two sons with her.
7 And Moses went out to meet his
father in law, and did obeisance, and
kissed him; and they asked each other
of *their* welfare; and they came into the
tent.
8 And Moses told his father in law all
that the LORD had done unto Pharaoh
and to the Egyptians for Israel's sake,
and all the travail that had come upon
them by the way, and *how* the LORD de-
livered them.
9 And Jĕth'rō rejoiced for all the
goodness which the LORD had done to
Israel, whom he had delivered out of
the hand of the Egyptians.
10 And Jĕth'rō said, Blessed *be* the
LORD, who hath delivered you out of the
hand of the Egyptians, and out of the
hand of Pharaoh, who hath delivered
the people from under the hand of the
Egyptians.
11 Now I know that the LORD *is* great-
er than all gods: for in the thing where-
in they dealt proudly *he was* above
them.
12 And Jĕth'rō, Moses' father in law,
took a burnt offering and sacrifices for
God: and Aaron came, and all the elders
of Israel, to eat bread with Moses'
father in law before God.
13 ¶And it came to pass on the
morrow, that Moses sat to judge the
people: and the people stood by Moses
from the morning unto the evening.
14 And when Moses' father in law
saw all that he did to the people, he
said, What *is* this thing that thou doest
to the people? why sittest thou thyself
alone, and all the people stand by thee
from morning unto even?
15 And Moses said unto his father in
law, Because the people come unto me
to enquire of God:
16 When they have a matter, they
come unto me; and I judge between one
and another, and I do make *them* know
the statutes of God, and his laws.
17 And Moses' father in law said unto
him, The thing that thou doest *is* not
good.
18 Thou wilt surely wear away, both
thou, and this people that *is* with thee:
for this thing *is* too heavy for thee; thou
art not able to perform it thyself alone.
19 Hearken now unto my voice, I will
give thee counsel, and God shall be
with thee: Be thou for the people to
God-ward, that thou mayest bring the
causes unto God:
20 And thou shalt teach them ordi-
nances and laws, and shalt shew them
the way wherein they must walk, and
the work that they must do.
21 Moreover thou shalt provide out
of all the people able men, such as fear
God, men of truth, hating covetous-
ness; and place *such* over them, *to be*
rulers of thousands, *and* rulers of hun-

dreds, rulers of fifties, and rulers of
tens:
22 And let them judge the people at
all seasons: and it shall be, *that* every
great matter they shall bring unto thee,
but every small matter they shall
judge: so shall it be easier for thyself,
and they shall bear *the burden* with
thee.
23 If thou shalt do this thing, and God
command thee *so,* then thou shalt be
able to endure, and all this people shall
also go to their place in peace.
24 So Moses hearkened to the voice
of his father in law, and did all that he
had said.
25 And Moses chose able men out of
all Israel, and made them heads over
the people, rulers of thousands, rulers
of hundreds, rulers of fifties, and rulers
of tens.
26 And they judged the people at all
seasons: the hard causes they brought
unto Moses, but every small matter
they judged themselves.
27 ¶And Moses let his father in law
depart; and he went his way into his
own land.

CHAPTER 19

IN the third month, when the children
of Israel were gone forth out of the land
of Egypt, the same day came they *into*
the wilderness of Sī'naī.
2 For they were departed from
Rĕph'i-dĭm, and were come *to* the des-
ert of Sī'naī, and had pitched in the
wilderness; and there Israel camped
before the mount.
3 And Moses went up unto God, and
the LORD called unto him out of the
mountain, saying, Thus shalt thou say
to the house of Jacob, and tell the chil-
dren of Israel;
4 Ye have seen what I did unto the
Egyptians, and *how* I bare you on
eagles' wings, and brought you unto
myself.
5 Now therefore, if ye will obey my
voice indeed, and keep my covenant,
then ye shall be a peculiar treasure
unto me above all people: for all the
earth *is* mine:
6 And ye shall be unto me a kingdom
of priests, and an holy nation. These *are*
the words which thou shalt speak unto
the children of Israel.
7 ¶And Moses came and called for
the elders of the people, and laid before
their faces all these words which the
LORD commanded him.
8 And all the people answered togeth-
er, and said, All that the LORD hath
spoken we will do. And Moses returned
the words of the people unto the LORD.
9 And the LORD said unto Moses, Lo, I
come unto thee in a thick cloud, that
the people may hear when I speak with
thee, and believe thee for ever. And
Moses told the words of the people
unto the LORD.
10 ¶And the LORD said unto Moses,
Go unto the people, and sanctify them
to day and to morrow, and let them
wash their clothes,
11 And be ready against the third
day: for the third day the LORD will
come down in the sight of all the people
upon mount Sī'naī.
12 And thou shalt set bounds unto
the people round about, saying, Take
heed to yourselves, *that ye* go *not* up
into the mount, or touch the border of
it: whosoever toucheth the mount shall
be surely put to death:
13 There shall not an hand touch it,
but he shall surely be stoned, or shot
through; whether *it be* beast or man, it
shall not live: when the trumpet sound-
eth long, they shall come up to the
mount.
14 ¶And Moses went down from the
mount unto the people, and sanctified
the people; and they washed their
clothes.
15 And he said unto the people, Be
ready against the third day: come not
at *your* wives.
16 ¶And it came to pass on the third
day in the morning, that there were
thunders and lightnings, and a thick
cloud upon the mount, and the voice of
the trumpet exceeding loud; so that all
the people that *was* in the camp
trembled.
17 And Moses brought forth the
people out of the camp to meet with
God; and they stood at the nether part
of the mount.
18 And mount Sī'naī was altogether
on a smoke, because the LORD de-
scended upon it in fire: and the smoke
thereof ascended as the smoke of a fur-
nace, and the whole mount quaked
greatly.
19 And when the voice of the trumpet
sounded long, and waxed louder and
louder, Moses spake, and God an-
swered him by a voice.
20 And the LORD came down upon
mount Sī'naī, on the top of the mount:
and the LORD called Moses *up* to the top
of the mount; and Moses went up.
21 And the LORD said unto Moses, Go
down, charge the people, lest they
break through unto the LORD to gaze,
and many of them perish.
22 And let the priests also, which
come near to the LORD, sanctify them-

selves, lest the LORD break forth upon them.

23 And Moses said unto the LORD, The people cannot come up to mount Sī'naī: for thou chargedst us, saying, Set bounds about the mount, and sanctify it.

24 And the LORD said unto him, Away, get thee down, and thou shalt come up, thou, and Aaron with thee: but let not the priests and the people break through to come up unto the LORD, lest he break forth upon them.

25 So Moses went down unto the people, and spake unto them.

CHAPTER 20

AND God spake all these words, saying,

2 I *am* the LORD thy God, which have brought thee out of the land of Egypt, out of the house of bondage.

3 Thou shalt have no other gods before me.

4 Thou shalt not make unto thee any graven image, or any likeness *of any thing* that *is* in heaven above, or that *is* in the earth beneath, or that *is* in the water under the earth:

5 Thou shalt not bow down thyself to them, nor serve them: for I the LORD thy God *am* a jealous God, visiting the iniquity of the fathers upon the children unto the third and fourth *generation* of them that hate me;

6 And shewing mercy unto thousands of them that love me, and keep my commandments.

7 Thou shalt not take the name of the LORD thy God in vain; for the LORD will not hold him guiltless that taketh his name in vain.

8 Remember the sabbath day, to keep it holy.

9 Six days shalt thou labour, and do all thy work:

10 But the seventh day *is* the sabbath of the LORD thy God: *in it* thou shalt not do any work, thou, nor thy son, nor thy daughter, thy manservant, nor thy maidservant, nor thy cattle, nor thy stranger that *is* within thy gates:

11 For *in* six days the LORD made heaven and earth, the sea, and all that in them *is*, and rested the seventh day: wherefore the LORD blessed the sabbath day, and hallowed it.

12 ¶Honour thy father and thy mother: that thy days may be long upon the land which the LORD thy God giveth thee.

13 Thou shalt not kill.

14 Thou shalt not commit adultery.

15 Thou shalt not steal.

16 Thou shalt not bear false witness against thy neighbour.

17 Thou shalt not covet thy neighbour's house, thou shalt not covet thy neighbour's wife, nor his manservant, nor his maidservant, nor his ox, nor his ass, nor any thing that *is* thy neighbour's.

18 ¶And all the people saw the thunderings, and the lightnings, and the noise of the trumpet, and the mountain smoking: and when the people saw *it*, they removed, and stood afar off.

19 And they said unto Moses, Speak thou with us, and we will hear: but let not God speak with us, lest we die.

20 And Moses said unto the people, Fear not: for God is come to prove you, and that his fear may be before your faces, that ye sin not.

21 And the people stood afar off, and Moses drew near unto the thick darkness where God *was*.

22 ¶And the LORD said unto Moses, Thus thou shalt say unto the children of Israel, Ye have seen that I have talked with you from heaven.

23 Ye shall not make with me gods of silver, neither shall ye make unto you gods of gold.

24 An altar of earth thou shalt make unto me, and shalt sacrifice thereon thy burnt offerings, and thy peace offerings, thy sheep, and thine oxen: in all places where I record my name I will come unto thee, and I will bless thee.

25 And if thou wilt make me an altar of stone, thou shalt not build it of hewn stone: for if thou lift up thy tool upon it, thou hast polluted it.

26 Neither shalt thou go up by steps unto mine altar, that thy nakedness be not discovered thereon.

CHAPTER 21

NOW these *are* the judgments which thou shalt set before them.

2 If thou buy an Hebrew servant, six years he shall serve: and in the seventh he shall go out free for nothing.

3 If he came in by himself, he shall go out bv himself: if he were married, then his wife shall go out with him.

4 If his master have given him a wife, and she have born him sons or daughters; the wife and her children shall be her master's, and he shall go out by himself.

5 And if the servant shall plainly say, I love my master, my wife, and my children; I will not go out free:

6 Then his master shall bring him unto the judges; he shall also bring him to the door, or unto the door post; and his master shall bore his ear through

with an aul; and he shall serve him for ever.

7 ¶And if a man sell his daughter to be a maidservant, she shall not go out as the menservants do.

8 If she please not her master, who hath betrothed her to himself, then shall he let her be redeemed: to sell her unto a strange nation he shall have no power, seeing he hath dealt deceitfully with her.

9 And if he have betrothed her unto his son, he shall deal with her after the manner of daughters.

10 If he take him another *wife;* her food, her raiment, and her duty of marriage, shall he not diminish.

11 And if he do not these three unto her, then shall she go out free without money.

12 ¶He that smiteth a man, so that he die, shall be surely put to death.

13 And if a man lie not in wait, but God deliver *him* into his hand; then I will appoint thee a place whither he shall flee.

14 But if a man come presumptuously upon his neighbour, to slay him with guile; thou shalt take him from mine altar, that he may die.

15 And he that smiteth his father, or his mother, shall be surely put to death.

16 ¶And he that stealeth a man, and selleth him, or if he be found in his hand, he shall surely be put to death.

17 ¶And he that curseth his father, or his mother, shall surely be put to death.

18 ¶And if men strive together, and one smite another with a stone, or with *his* fist, and he die not, but keepeth *his* bed:

19 If he rise again, and walk abroad upon his staff, then shall he that smote *him* be quit: only he shall pay *for* the loss of his time, and shall cause *him* to be thoroughly healed.

20 ¶And if a man smite his servant, or his maid, with a rod, and he die under his hand; he shall be surely punished.

21 Notwithstanding, if he continue a day or two, he shall not be punished: for he *is* his money.

22 ¶If men strive, and hurt a woman with child, so that her fruit depart *from her,* and yet no mischief follow: he shall be surely punished, according as the woman's husband will lay upon him; and he shall pay as the judges *determine.*

23 And if *any* mischief follow, then thou shalt give life for life,

24 Eye for eye, tooth for tooth, hand for hand, foot for foot,

25 Burning for burning, wound for wound, stripe for stripe.

26 ¶And if a man smite the eye of his servant, or the eye of his maid, that it perish; he shall let him go free for his eye's sake.

27 And if he smite out his manservant's tooth, or his maidservant's tooth; he shall let him go free for his tooth's sake.

28 ¶If an ox gore a man or a woman, that they die: then the ox shall be surely stoned, and his flesh shall not be eaten; but the owner of the ox *shall be* quit.

29 But if the ox were wont to push with his horn in time past, and it hath been testified to his owner, and he hath not kept him in, but that he hath killed a man or a woman; the ox shall be stoned, and his owner also shall be put to death.

30 If there be laid on him a sum of money, then he shall give for the ransom of his life whatsoever is laid upon him.

31 Whether he have gored a son, or have gored a daughter, according to this judgment shall it be done unto him.

32 If the ox shall push a manservant or a maidservant; he shall give unto their master thirty shekels of silver, and the ox shall be stoned.

33 ¶And if a man shall open a pit, or if a man shall dig a pit, and not cover it, and an ox or an ass fall therein;

34 The owner of the pit shall make *it* good, *and* give money unto the owner of them; and the dead *beast* shall be his.

35 ¶And if one man's ox hurt another's, that he die; then they shall sell the live ox, and divide the money of it; and the dead *ox* also they shall divide.

36 Or if it be known that the ox hath used to push in time past, and his owner hath not kept him in; he shall surely pay ox for ox; and the dead shall be his own.

CHAPTER 22

IF a man shall steal an ox, or a sheep, and kill it, or sell it; he shall restore five oxen for an ox, and four sheep for a sheep.

2 If a thief be found breaking up, and be smitten that he die, *there shall* no blood *be shed* for him.

3 If the sun be risen upon him, *there shall be* blood *shed* for him; *for* he should make full restitution; if he have nothing, then he shall be sold for his theft.

4 If the theft be certainly found in his hand alive, whether it be ox, or ass, or sheep; he shall restore double.

5 ¶If a man shall cause a field or vineyard to be eaten, and shall put in his beast, and shall feed in another man's

field; of the best of his own field, and of the best of his own vineyard, shall he make restitution.

6 ¶If fire break out, and catch in thorns, so that the stacks of corn, or the standing corn, or the field, be consumed *therewith;* he that kindled the fire shall surely make restitution.

7 ¶If a man shall deliver unto his neighbour money or stuff to keep, and it be stolen out of the man's house; if the thief be found, let him pay double.

8 If the thief be not found, then the master of the house shall be brought unto the judges, *to see* whether he have put his hand unto his neighbour's goods.

9 For all manner of trespass, *whether it be* for ox, for ass, for sheep, for raiment, *or* for any manner of lost thing, which *another* challengeth to be his, the cause of both parties shall come before the judges; *and* whom the judges shall condemn, he shall pay double unto his neighbour.

10 If a man deliver unto his neighbour an ass, or an ox, or a sheep, or any beast, to keep; and it die, or be hurt, or driven away, no man seeing *it:*

11 *Then* shall an oath of the LORD be between them both, that he hath not put his hand unto his neighbour's goods; and the owner of it shall accept *thereof,* and he shall not make *it* good.

12 And if it be stolen from him, he shall make restitution unto the owner thereof.

13 If it be torn in pieces, *then* let him bring it *for* witness, *and* he shall not make good that which was torn.

14 ¶And if a man borrow *ought* of his neighbour, and it be hurt, or die, the owner thereof *being* not with it, he shall surely make *it* good.

15 *But* if the owner thereof *be* with it, he shall not make *it* good: if it *be* an hired *thing,* it came for his hire.

16 ¶And if a man entice a maid that is not betrothed, and lie with her, he shall surely endow her to be his wife.

17 If her father utterly refuse to give her unto him, he shall pay money according to the dowry of virgins.

18 ¶Thou shalt not suffer a witch to live.

19 ¶Whosoever lieth with a beast shall surely be put to death.

20 ¶He that sacrificeth unto *any* god, save unto the LORD only, he shall be utterly destroyed.

21 ¶Thou shalt neither vex a stranger, nor oppress him: for ye were strangers in the land of Egypt.

22 Ye shall not afflict any widow, or fatherless child.

23 If thou afflict them in any wise, and they cry at all unto me, I will surely hear their cry;

24 And my wrath shall wax hot, and I will kill you with the sword; and your wives shall be widows, and your children fatherless.

25 ¶If thou lend money to *any of* my people *that is* poor by thee, thou shalt not be to him as an usurer, neither shalt thou lay upon him usury.

26 If thou at all take thy neighbour's raiment to pledge, thou shalt deliver it unto him by that the sun goeth down:

27 For that *is* his covering only, it *is* his raiment for his skin: wherein shall he sleep? and it shall come to pass, when he crieth unto me, that I will hear; for I *am* gracious.

28 ¶Thou shalt not revile the gods, nor curse the ruler of thy people.

29 ¶Thou shalt not delay *to offer* the first of thy ripe fruits, and of thy liquors: the firstborn of thy sons shalt thou give unto me.

30 Likewise shalt thou do with thine oxen, *and* with thy sheep: seven days it shall be with his dam; on the eighth day thou shalt give it me.

31 ¶And ye shall be holy men unto me: neither shall ye eat *any* flesh *that is* torn of beasts in the field; ye shall cast it to the dogs.

CHAPTER 23

THOU shalt not raise a false report: put not thine hand with the wicked to be an unrighteous witness.

2 Thou shalt not follow a multitude to *do* evil; neither shalt thou speak in a cause to decline after many to wrest *judgment:*

3 Neither shalt thou countenance a poor man in his cause.

4 ¶If thou meet thine enemy's ox or his ass going astray, thou shalt surely bring it back to him again.

5 If thou see the ass of him that hateth thee lying under his burden, and wouldest forbear to help him, thou shalt surely help with him.

6 ¶Thou shalt not wrest the judgment of thy poor in his cause.

7 Keep thee far from a false matter; and the innocent and righteous slay thou not: for I will not justify the wicked.

8 ¶And thou shalt take no gift: for the gift blindeth the wise, and perverteth the words of the righteous.

9 ¶Also thou shalt not oppress a stranger: for ye know the heart of a stranger, seeing ye were strangers in the land of Egypt.

10 And six years thou shalt sow thy

land, and shalt gather in the fruits thereof:
11 But the seventh *year* thou shalt let it rest and lie still; that the poor of thy people may eat: and what they leave the beasts of the field shall eat. In like manner thou shalt deal with thy vineyard, *and* with thy oliveyard.
12 Six days thou shalt do thy work, and on the seventh day thou shalt rest: that thine ox and thine ass may rest, and the son of thy handmaid, and the stranger, may be refreshed.
13 And in all *things* that I have said unto you be circumspect: and make no mention of the name of other gods, neither let it be heard out of thy mouth.
14 ¶Three times thou shalt keep a feast unto me in the year.
15 Thou shalt keep the feast of unleavened bread: (thou shalt eat unleavened bread seven days, as I commanded thee, in the time appointed of the month Ā'bĭb; for in it thou camest out from Egypt: and none shall appear before me empty:)
16 And the feast of harvest, the firstfruits of thy labours, which thou hast sown in the field: and the feast of ingathering, *which is* in the end of the year, when thou hast gathered in thy labours out of the field.
17 Three times in the year all thy males shall appear before the Lord GOD.
18 Thou shalt not offer the blood of my sacrifice with leavened bread; neither shall the fat of my sacrifice remain until the morning.
19 The first of the firstfruits of thy land thou shalt bring into the house of the LORD thy God. Thou shalt not seethe a kid in his mother's milk.
20 ¶Behold, I send an Angel before thee, to keep thee in the way, and to bring thee into the place which I have prepared.
21 Beware of him, and obey his voice, provoke him not; for he will not pardon your transgressions: for my name *is* in him.
22 But if thou shalt indeed obey his voice, and do all that I speak; then I will be an enemy unto thine enemies, and an adversary unto thine adversaries.
23 For mine Angel shall go before thee, and bring thee in unto the Amorites, and the Hittites, and the Pĕr'iz-zītes, and the Canaanites, the Hī'vītes, and the Jĕb'u-sītes: and I will cut them off.
24 Thou shalt not bow down to their gods, nor serve them, nor do after their works: but thou shalt utterly overthrow them, and quite break down their images.
25 And ye shall serve the LORD your God, and he shall bless thy bread, and thy water; and I will take sickness away from the midst of thee.
26 ¶There shall nothing cast their young, nor be barren, in thy land: the number of thy days I will fulfil.
27 I will send my fear before thee, and will destroy all the people to whom thou shalt come, and I will make all thine enemies turn their backs unto thee.
28 And I will send hornets before thee, which shall drive out the Hī'vīte, the Canaanite, and the Hittite, from before thee.
29 I will not drive them out from before thee in one year; lest the land become desolate, and the beast of the field multiply against thee.
30 By little and little I will drive them out from before thee, until thou be increased, and inherit the land.
31 And I will set thy bounds from the Red sea even unto the sea of the Philistines, and from the desert unto the river: for I will deliver the inhabitants of the land into your hand; and thou shalt drive them out before thee.
32 Thou shalt make no covenant with them, nor with their gods.
33 They shall not dwell in thy land, lest they make thee sin against me: for if thou serve their gods, it will surely be a snare unto thee.

CHAPTER 24

AND he said unto Moses, Come up unto the LORD, thou, and Aaron, Nā'-dăb, and A-bī'hū, and seventy of the elders of Israel; and worship ye afar off.
2 And Moses alone shall come near the LORD: but they shall not come nigh; neither shall the people go up with him.
3 ¶And Moses came and told the people all the words of the LORD, and all the judgments: and all the people answered with one voice, and said, All the words which the LORD hath said will we do.
4 And Moses wrote all the words of the LORD, and rose up early in the morning, and builded an altar under the hill, and twelve pillars, according to the twelve tribes of Israel.
5 And he sent young men of the children of Israel, which offered burnt offerings, and sacrificed peace offerings of oxen unto the LORD.
6 And Moses took half of the blood, and put *it* in basons; and half of the blood he sprinkled on the altar.
7 And he took the book of the cov-

enant, and read in the audience of the people: and they said, All that the LORD hath said will we do, and be obedient.

8 And Moses took the blood, and sprinkled *it* on the people, and said, Behold the blood of the covenant, which the LORD hath made with you concerning all these words.

9 ¶Then went up Moses, and Aaron, Na'dăb, and A-bī'hū, and seventy of the elders of Israel:

10 And they saw the God of Israel: and *there was* under his feet as it were a paved work of a sapphire stone, and as it were the body of heaven in *his* clearness.

11 And upon the nobles of the children of Israel he laid not his hand: also they saw God, and did eat and drink.

12 ¶And the LORD said unto Moses, Come up to me into the mount, and be there: and I will give thee tables of stone, and a law, and commandments which I have written; that thou mayest teach them.

13 And Moses rose up, and his minister Joshua: and Moses went up into the mount of God.

14 And he said unto the elders, Tarry ye here for us, until we come again unto you: and, behold, Aaron and Hur *are* with you: if any man have any matters to do, let him come unto them.

15 ¶And Moses went up into the mount, and a cloud covered the mount.

16 And the glory of the LORD abode upon mount Sī'naī, and the cloud covered it six days: and the seventh day he called unto Moses out of the midst of the cloud.

17 And the sight of the glory of the LORD *was* like devouring fire on the top of the mount in the eyes of the children of Israel.

18 And Moses went into the midst of the cloud, and gat him up into the mount: and Moses was in the mount forty days and forty nights.

CHAPTER 25

AND the LORD spake unto Moses, saying,

2 Speak unto the children of Israel, that they bring me an offering: of every man that giveth it willingly with his heart ye shall take my offering.

3 And this *is* the offering which ye shall take of them; gold, and silver, and brass,

4 And blue, and purple, and scarlet, and fine linen, and goats' *hair*,

5 And rams' skins dyed red, and badgers' skins, and shittim wood,

6 Oil for the light, spices for anointing oil, and for sweet incense,

7 Onyx stones, and stones to be set in the ephod, and in the breastplate.

8 And let them make me a sanctuary; that I may dwell among them.

9 According to all that I shew thee, *after* the pattern of the tabernacle, and the pattern of all the instruments thereof, even so shall ye make *it*.

10 ¶And they shall make an ark *of* shittim wood: two cubits and a half *shall be* the length thereof, and a cubit and a half the breadth thereof, and a cubit and a half the height thereof.

11 And thou shalt overlay it with pure gold, within and without shalt thou overlay it, and shalt make upon it a crown of gold round about.

12 And thou shalt cast four rings of gold for it, and put *them* in the four corners thereof; and two rings *shall be* in the one side of it, and two rings in the other side of it.

13 And thou shalt make staves *of* shittim wood, and overlay them with gold.

14 And thou shalt put the staves into the rings by the sides of the ark, that the ark may be borne with them.

15 The staves shall be in the rings of the ark: they shall not be taken from it.

16 And thou shalt put into the ark the testimony which I shall give thee.

17 ¶And thou shalt make a mercy seat *of* pure gold: two cubits and a half *shall be* the length thereof, and a cubit and a half the breadth thereof.

18 And thou shalt make two cherubims *of* gold, *of* beaten work shalt thou make them, in the two ends of the mercy seat.

19 And make one cherub on the one end, and the other cherub on the other end: *even* of the mercy seat shall ye make the cherubims on the two ends thereof.

20 And the cherubims shall stretch forth *their* wings on high, covering the mercy seat with their wings, and their faces *shall look* one to another; toward the mercy seat shall the faces of the cherubims be.

21 And thou shalt put the mercy seat above upon the ark; and in the ark thou shalt put the testimony that I shall give thee.

22 And there I will meet with thee, and I will commune with thee from above the mercy seat, from between the two cherubims which *are* upon the ark of the testimony, of all *things* which I will give thee in commandment unto the children of Israel.

23 ¶Thou shalt also make a table *of* shittim wood: two cubits *shall be* the length thereof, and a cubit the breadth

thereof, and a cubit and a half the height thereof.
24 And thou shalt overlay it with pure gold, and make thereto a crown of gold round about.
25 And thou shalt make unto it a border of an hand breadth round about, and thou shalt make a golden crown to the border thereof round about.
26 And thou shalt make for it four rings of gold, and put the rings in the four corners that *are* on the four feet thereof.
27 Over against the border shall the rings be for places of the staves to bear the table.
28 And thou shalt make the staves *of* shittim wood, and overlay them with gold, that the table may be borne with them.
29 And thou shalt make the dishes thereof, and spoons thereof, and covers thereof, and bowls thereof, to cover withal: *of* pure gold shalt thou make them.
30 And thou shalt set upon the table shewbread before me alway.
31 ¶And thou shalt make a candlestick *of* pure gold: *of* beaten work shall the candlestick be made: his shaft, and his branches, his bowls, his knops, and his flowers, shall be of the same.
32 And six branches shall come out of the sides of it; three branches of the candlestick out of the one side, and three branches of the candlestick out of the other side:
33 Three bowls made like unto almonds, *with* a knop and a flower in one branch; and three bowls made like almonds in the other branch, *with* a knop and a flower: so in the six branches that come out of the candlestick.
34 And in the candlestick *shall be* four bowls made like unto almonds, *with* their knops and their flowers.
35 And *there shall be* a knop under two branches of the same, and a knop under two branches of the same, and a knop under two branches of the same, according to the six branches that proceed out of the candlestick.
36 Their knops and their branches shall be of the same: all it *shall be* one beaten work *of* pure gold.
37 And thou shalt make the seven lamps thereof: and they shall light the lamps thereof, that they may give light over against it.
38 And the tongs thereof, and the snuffdishes thereof, *shall be of* pure gold.
39 *Of* a talent of pure gold shall he make it, with all these vessels.
40 And look that thou make *them* after their pattern, which was shewed thee in the mount.

CHAPTER 26

MOREOVER thou shalt make the tabernacle *with* ten curtains *of* fine twined linen, and blue, and purple, and scarlet: *with* cherubims of cunning work shalt thou make them.
2 The length of one curtain *shall be* eight and twenty cubits, and the breadth of one curtain four cubits: and every one of the curtains shall have one measure.
3 The five curtains shall be coupled together one to another; and *other* five curtains *shall be* coupled one to another.
4 And thou shalt make loops of blue upon the edge of the one curtain from the selvedge in the coupling; and likewise shalt thou make in the uttermost edge of *another* curtain, in the coupling of the second.
5 Fifty loops shalt thou make in the one curtain, and fifty loops shalt thou make in the edge of the curtain that *is* in the coupling of the second; that the loops may take hold one of another.
6 And thou shalt make fifty taches of gold, and couple the curtains together with the taches: and it shall be one tabernacle.
7 ¶And thou shalt make curtains *of* goats' *hair* to be a covering upon the tabernacle: eleven curtains shalt thou make.
8 The length of one curtain *shall be* thirty cubits, and the breadth of one curtain four cubits: and the eleven curtains *shall be all* of one measure.
9 And thou shalt couple five curtains by themselves, and six curtains by themselves, and shalt double the sixth curtain in the forefront of the tabernacle.
10 And thou shalt make fifty loops on the edge of the one curtain *that is* outmost in the coupling, and fifty loops in the edge of the curtain which coupleth the second.
11 And thou shalt make fifty taches of brass, and put the taches into the loops, and couple the tent together, that it may be one.
12 And the remnant that remaineth of the curtains of the tent, the half curtain that remaineth, shall hang over the backside of the tabernacle.
13 And a cubit on the one side, and a cubit on the other side of that which remaineth in the length of the curtains of the tent, it shall hang over the sides of the tabernacle on this side and on that side, to cover it.

14 And thou shalt make a covering
for the tent *of* rams' skins dyed red, and
a covering above *of* badgers' skins.
15 ¶And thou shalt make boards for
the tabernacle *of* shittim wood stand-
ing up.
16 Ten cubits *shall be* the length of a
board, and a cubit and a half *shall be*
the breadth of one board.
17 Two tenons *shall there be* in one
board, set in order one against another:
thus shalt thou make for all the boards
of the tabernacle.
18 And thou shalt make the boards
for the tabernacle, twenty boards on
the south side southward.
19 And thou shalt make forty sockets
of silver under the twenty boards; two
sockets under one board for his two ten-
ons, and two sockets under another
board for his two tenons.
20 And for the second side of the taber-
nacle on the north side *there shall
be* twenty boards:
21 And their forty sockets *of* silver;
two sockets under one board, and two
sockets under another board.
22 And for the sides of the tabernacle
westward thou shalt make six boards.
23 And two boards shalt thou make
for the corners of the tabernacle in the
two sides.
24 And they shall be coupled togeth-
er beneath, and they shall be coupled
together above the head of it unto one
ring: thus shall it be for them both; they
shall be for the two corners.
25 And they shall be eight boards,
and their sockets *of* silver, sixteen
sockets; two sockets under one board,
and two sockets under another board.
26 ¶And thou shalt make bars *of* shit-
tim wood; five for the boards of the one
side of the tabernacle,
27 And five bars for the boards of the
other side of the tabernacle, and five
bars for the boards of the side of the
tabernacle, for the two sides westward.
28 And the middle bar in the midst of
the boards shall reach from end to end.
29 And thou shalt overlay the boards
with gold, and make their rings *of* gold
for places for the bars: and thou shalt
overlay the bars with gold.
30 And thou shalt rear up the taber-
nacle according to the fashion thereof
which was shewed thee in the mount.
31 ¶And thou shalt make a vail *of*
blue, and purple, and scarlet, and fine
twined linen of cunning work: with
cherubims shall it be made:
32 And thou shalt hang it upon four
pillars of shittim *wood* overlaid with
gold: their hooks *shall be of* gold, upon
the four sockets of silver.
33 And thou shalt hang up the vail
under the taches, that thou mayest
bring in thither within the vail the ark
of the testimony: and the vail shall di-
vide unto you between the holy *place*
and the most holy.
34 And thou shalt put the mercy seat
upon the ark of the testimony in the
most holy *place*.
35 And thou shalt set the table
without the vail, and the candlestick
over against the table on the side of the
tabernacle toward the south: and thou
shalt put the table on the north side.
36 ¶And thou shalt make an hanging
for the door of the tent, *of* blue, and
purple, and scarlet, and fine twined lin-
en, wrought with needlework.
37 And thou shalt make for the hang-
ing five pillars *of* shittim *wood*, and
overlay them with gold, *and* their
hooks *shall be of* gold: and thou shalt
cast five sockets of brass for them.

CHAPTER 27

AND thou shalt make an altar *of* shit-
tim wood, five cubits long, and five cu-
bits broad; the altar shall be four-
square: and the height thereof *shall be*
three cubits.
2 And thou shalt make the horns of it
upon the four corners thereof: his
horns shall be of the same: and thou
shalt overlay it with brass.
3 And thou shalt make his pans to re-
ceive his ashes, and his shovels, and his
basons, and his fleshhooks, and his
firepans: all the vessels thereof thou
shalt make *of* brass.
4 And thou shalt make for it a grate of
network *of* brass; and upon the net
shalt thou make four brasen rings in
the four corners thereof.
5 And thou shalt put it under the
compass of the altar beneath, that the
net may be even to the midst of the al-
tar.
6 And thou shalt make staves for the
altar, staves *of* shittim wood, and over-
lay them with brass.
7 And the staves shall be put into the
rings, and the staves shall be upon the
two sides of the altar, to bear it.
8 Hollow with boards shalt thou
make it: as it was shewed thee in the
mount, so shall they make *it*.
9 ¶And thou shalt make the court of
the tabernacle: for the south side
southward *there shall be* hangings for
the court *of* fine twined linen of an
hundred cubits long for one side:
10 And the twenty pillars thereof and
their twenty sockets *shall be of* brass;
the hooks of the pillars and their fillets
shall be of silver.

11 And likewise for the north side in length *there shall be* hangings of an hundred *cubits* long, and his twenty pillars and their twenty sockets *of* brass; the hooks of the pillars and their fillets *of* silver.

12 And *for* the breadth of the court on the west side *shall be* hangings of fifty cubits: their pillars ten, and their sockets ten.

13 And the breadth of the court on the east side eastward *shall be* fifty cubits.

14 The hangings of one side *of the gate shall be* fifteen cubits: their pillars three, and their sockets three.

15 And on the other side *shall be* hangings fifteen *cubits:* their pillars three, and their sockets three.

16 And for the gate of the court *shall be* an hanging of twenty cubits, *of* blue, and purple, and scarlet, and fine twined linen, wrought with needlework: *and* their pillars *shall be* four, and their sockets four.

17 All the pillars round about the court *shall be* filleted with silver; their hooks *shall be of* silver, and their sockets *of* brass.

18 The length of the court *shall be* an hundred cubits, and the breadth fifty every where, and the height five cubits *of* fine twined linen, and their sockets *of* brass.

19 All the vessels of the tabernacle in all the service thereof, and all the pins thereof, and all the pins of the court, *shall be of* brass.

20 ¶And thou shalt command the children of Israel, that they bring thee pure oil olive beaten for the light, to cause the lamp to burn always.

21 In the tabernacle of the congregation without the vail, which *is* before the testimony, Aaron and his sons shall order it from evening to morning before the LORD: *it shall be* a statute for ever unto their generations on the behalf of the children of Israel.

CHAPTER 28

AND take thou unto thee Aaron thy brother, and his sons with him, from among the children of Israel, that he may minister unto me in the priest's office, *even* Aaron, Nā′dăb and A-bī′hū, Ĕ-le-ā′zar and Ĭth′a-mär, Aaron's sons.

2 And thou shalt make holy garments for Aaron thy brother for glory and for beauty.

3 And thou shalt speak unto all *that are* wise hearted, whom I have filled with the spirit of wisdom, that they may make Aaron's garments to consecrate him, that he may minister unto me in the priest's office.

4 And these *are* the garments which they shall make; a breastplate, and an ephod, and a robe, and a broidered coat, a mitre, and a girdle: and they shall make holy garments for Aaron thy brother, and his sons, that he may minister unto me in the priest's office.

5 And they shall take gold, and blue, and purple, and scarlet, and fine linen.

6 ¶And they shall make the ephod *of* gold, *of* blue, and *of* purple, *of* scarlet, and fine twined linen, with cunning work.

7 It shall have the two shoulderpieces thereof joined at the two edges thereof; and *so* it shall be joined together.

8 And the curious girdle of the ephod, which *is* upon it, shall be of the same, according to the work thereof; *even of* gold, *of* blue, and purple, and scarlet, and fine twined linen.

9 And thou shalt take two onyx stones, and grave on them the names of the children of Israel:

10 Six of their names on one stone, and *the other* six names of the rest on the other stone, according to their birth.

11 With the work of an engraver in stone, *like* the engravings of a signet, shalt thou engrave the two stones with the names of the children of Israel: thou shalt make them to be set in ouches of gold.

12 And thou shalt put the two stones upon the shoulders of the ephod *for* stones of memorial unto the children of Israel: and Aaron shall bear their names before the LORD upon his two shoulders for a memorial.

13 And thou shalt make ouches *of* gold;

14 And two chains *of* pure gold at the ends; *of* wreathen work shalt thou make them, and fasten the wreathen chains to the ouches.

15 ¶And thou shalt make the breastplate of judgment with cunning work; after the work of the ephod thou shalt make it; *of* gold, *of* blue, and *of* purple, and *of* scarlet, and *of* fine twined linen, shalt thou make it.

16 Foursquare it shall be *being* doubled; a span *shall be* the length thereof, and a span *shall be* the breadth thereof.

17 And thou shalt set in it settings of stones, *even* four rows of stones: *the first* row *shall be* a sardius, a topaz, and a carbuncle: *this shall be* the first row.

18 And the second row *shall be* an emerald, a sapphire, and a diamond.

19 And the third row a ligure, an agate, and an amethyst.

20 And the fourth row a beryl, and an onyx, and a jasper: they shall be set in gold in their inclosings.

21 And the stones shall be with the names of the children of Israel, twelve, according to their names, *like* the engravings of a signet; every one with his name shall they be according to the twelve tribes.

22 And thou shalt make upon the breastplate chains at the ends *of* wreathen work *of* pure gold.

23 And thou shalt make upon the breastplate two rings of gold, and shalt put the two rings on the two ends of the breastplate.

24 And thou shalt put the two wreathen *chains* of gold in the two rings *which are* on the ends of the breastplate.

25 And *the other* two ends of the two wreathen *chains* thou shalt fasten in the two ouches, and put *them* on the shoulderpieces of the ephod before it.

26 And thou shalt make two rings of gold, and thou shalt put them upon the two ends of the breastplate in the border thereof, which *is* in the side of the ephod inward.

27 And two *other* rings of gold thou shalt make, and shalt put them on the two sides of the ephod underneath, toward the forepart thereof, over against the *other* coupling thereof, above the curious girdle of the ephod.

28 And they shall bind the breastplate by the rings thereof unto the rings of the ephod with a lace of blue, that *it* may be above the curious girdle of the ephod, and that the breastplate be not loosed from the ephod.

29 And Aaron shall bear the names of the children of Israel in the breastplate of judgment upon his heart, when he goeth in unto the holy *place*, for a memorial before the LORD continually.

30 ¶And thou shalt put in the breastplate of judgment the Ū'rĭm and the Thŭm'mĭm; and they shall be upon Aaron's heart, when he goeth in before the LORD: and Aaron shall bear the judgment of the children of Israel upon his heart before the LORD continually.

31 ¶And thou shalt make the robe of the ephod all *of* blue.

32 And there shall be an hole in the top of it, in the midst thereof: it shall have a binding of woven work round about the hole of it, as it were the hole of an habergeon, that it be not rent.

33 And *beneath* upon the hem of it thou shalt make pomegranates *of* blue, and *of* purple, and *of* scarlet, round about the hem thereof; and bells of gold between them round about:

34 A golden bell and a pomegranate, a golden bell and a pomegranate, upon the hem of the robe round about.

35 And it shall be upon Aaron to minister: and his sound shall be heard when he goeth in unto the holy *place* before the LORD, and when he cometh out, that he die not.

36 ¶And thou shalt make a plate *of* pure gold, and grave upon it, *like* the engravings of a signet, HOLINESS TO THE LORD.

37 And thou shalt put it on a blue lace, that it may be upon the mitre; upon the forefront of the mitre it shall be.

38 And it shall be upon Aaron's forehead, that Aaron may bear the iniquity of the holy things, which the children of Israel shall hallow in all their holy gifts; and it shall be always upon his forehead, that they may be accepted before the LORD.

39 ¶And thou shalt embroider the coat of fine linen, and thou shalt make the mitre *of* fine linen, and thou shalt make the girdle *of* needlework.

40 ¶And for Aaron's sons thou shalt make coats, and thou shalt make for them girdles, and bonnets shalt thou make for them, for glory and for beauty.

41 And thou shalt put them upon Aaron thy brother, and his sons with him; and shalt anoint them, and consecrate them, and sanctify them, that they may minister unto me in the priest's office.

42 And thou shalt make them linen breeches to cover their nakedness; from the loins even unto the thighs they shall reach.

43 And they shall be upon Aaron, and upon his sons, when they come in unto the tabernacle of the congregation, or when they come near unto the altar to minister in the holy *place;* that they bear not iniquity, and die: *it shall be* a statute for ever unto him and his seed after him.

CHAPTER 29

AND this *is* the thing that thou shalt do unto them to hallow them, to minister unto me in the priest's office: Take one young bullock, and two rams without blemish,

2 And unleavened bread, and cakes unleavened tempered with oil, and wafers unleavened anointed with oil: *of* wheaten flour shalt thou make them.

3 And thou shalt put them into one

basket, and bring them in the basket, with the bullock and the two rams.
4 And Aaron and his sons thou shalt bring unto the door of the tabernacle of the congregation, and shalt wash them with water.
5 And thou shalt take the garments, and put upon Aaron the coat, and the robe of the ephod, and the ephod, and the breastplate, and gird him with the curious girdle of the ephod:
6 And thou shalt put the mitre upon his head, and put the holy crown upon the mitre.
7 Then shalt thou take the anointing oil, and pour *it* upon his head, and anoint him.
8 And thou shalt bring his sons, and put coats upon them.
9 And thou shalt gird them with girdles, Aaron and his sons, and put the bonnets on them: and the priest's office shall be theirs for a perpetual statute: and thou shalt consecrate Aaron and his sons.
10 And thou shalt cause a bullock to be brought before the tabernacle of the congregation: and Aaron and his sons shall put their hands upon the head of the bullock.
11 And thou shalt kill the bullock before the LORD, *by* the door of the tabernacle of the congregation.
12 And thou shalt take of the blood of the bullock, and put *it* upon the horns of the altar with thy finger, and pour all the blood beside the bottom of the altar.
13 And thou shalt take all the fat that covereth the inwards, and the caul *that is* above the liver, and the two kidneys, and the fat that *is* upon them, and burn *them* upon the altar.
14 But the flesh of the bullock, and his skin, and his dung, shalt thou burn with fire without the camp: it *is* a sin offering.
15 ¶Thou shalt also take one ram; and Aaron and his sons shall put their hands upon the head of the ram.
16 And thou shalt slay the ram, and thou shalt take his blood, and sprinkle *it* round about upon the altar.
17 And thou shalt cut the ram in pieces, and wash the inwards of him, and his legs, and put *them* unto his pieces, and unto his head.
18 And thou shalt burn the whole ram upon the altar: it *is* a burnt offering unto the LORD: it *is* a sweet savour, an offering made by fire unto the LORD.
19 And thou shalt take the other ram; and Aaron and his sons shall put their hands upon the head of the ram.
20 Then shalt thou kill the ram, and take of his blood, and put *it* upon the tip of the right ear of Aaron, and upon the tip of the right ear of his sons, and upon the thumb of their right hand, and upon the great toe of their right foot, and sprinkle the blood upon the altar round about.
21 And thou shalt take of the blood that *is* upon the altar, and of the anointing oil, and sprinkle *it* upon Aaron, and upon his garments, and upon his sons, and upon the garments of his sons with him: and he shall be hallowed, and his garments, and his sons, and his sons' garments with him.
22 Also thou shalt take of the ram the fat and the rump, and the fat that covereth the inwards, and the caul *above* the liver, and the two kidneys, and the fat that *is* upon them, and the right shoulder; for it *is* a ram of consecration:
23 And one loaf of bread, and one cake of oiled bread, and one wafer out of the basket of the unleavened bread that *is* before the LORD:
24 And thou shalt put all in the hands of Aaron, and in the hands of his sons; and shalt wave them *for* a wave offering before the LORD.
25 And thou shalt receive them of their hands, and burn *them* upon the altar for a burnt offering, for a sweet savour before the LORD: it *is* an offering made by fire unto the LORD.
26 And thou shalt take the breast of the ram of Aaron's consecration, and wave it *for* a wave offering before the LORD: and it shall be thy part.
27 And thou shalt sanctify the breast of the wave offering, and the shoulder of the heave offering, which is waved, and which is heaved up, of the ram of the consecration, *even* of *that* which *is* for Aaron, and of *that* which is for his sons:
28 And it shall be Aaron's and his sons' by a statute for ever from the children of Israel: for it *is* an heave offering: and it shall be an heave offering from the children of Israel of the sacrifice of their peace offerings, *even* their heave offering unto the LORD.
29 ¶And the holy garments of Aaron shall be his sons' after him, to be anointed therein, and to be consecrated in them.
30 *And* that son that is priest in his stead shall put them on seven days, when he cometh into the tabernacle of the congregation to minister in the holy *place*.
31 ¶And thou shalt take the ram of

the consecration, and seethe his flesh in the holy place.

32 And Aaron and his sons shall eat the flesh of the ram, and the bread that *is* in the basket, *by* the door of the tabernacle of the congregation.

33 And they shall eat those things wherewith the atonement was made, to consecrate *and* to sanctify them: but a stranger shall not eat *thereof*, because they *are* holy.

34 And if ought of the flesh of the consecrations, or of the bread, remain unto the morning, then thou shalt burn the remainder with fire: it shall not be eaten, because it *is* holy.

35 And thus shalt thou do unto Aaron, and to his sons, according to all *things* which I have commanded thee: seven days shalt thou consecrate them.

36 And thou shalt offer every day a bullock *for* a sin offering for atonement: and thou shalt cleanse the altar, when thou hast made an atonement for it, and thou shalt anoint it, to sanctify it.

37 Seven days thou shalt make an atonement for the altar, and sanctify it; and it shall be an altar most holy: whatsoever toucheth the altar shall be holy.

38 ¶Now this *is that* which thou shalt offer upon the altar; two lambs of the first year day by day continually.

39 The one lamb thou shalt offer in the morning; and the other lamb thou shalt offer at even:

40 And with the one lamb a tenth deal of flour mingled with the fourth part of an hin of beaten oil; and the fourth part of an hin of wine *for* a drink offering.

41 And the other lamb thou shalt offer at even, and shalt do thereto according to the meat offering of the morning, and according to the drink offering thereof, for a sweet savour, an offering made by fire unto the LORD.

42 *This shall be* a continual burnt offering throughout your generations *at* the door of the tabernacle of the congregation before the LORD: where I will meet you, to speak there unto thee.

43 And there I will meet with the children of Israel, and *the tabernacle* shall be sanctified by my glory.

44 And I will sanctify the tabernacle of the congregation, and the altar: I will sanctify also both Aaron and his sons, to minister to me in the priest's office.

45 And I will dwell among the children of Israel, and will be their God.

46 And they shall know that I *am* the LORD their God, that brought them forth out of the land of Egypt, that I may dwell among them: I *am* the LORD their God.

CHAPTER 30

AND thou shalt make an altar to burn incense upon: *of* shittim wood shalt thou make it.

2 A cubit *shall be* the length thereof, and a cubit the breadth thereof; foursquare shall it be: and two cubits *shall be* the height thereof: the horns thereof *shall be* of the same.

3 And thou shalt overlay it with pure gold, the top thereof, and the sides thereof round about, and the horns thereof; and thou shalt make unto it a crown of gold round about.

4 And two golden rings shalt thou make to it under the crown of it, by the two corners thereof, upon the two sides of it shalt thou make *it;* and they shall be for places for the staves to bear it withal.

5 And thou shalt make the staves *of* shittim wood, and overlay them with gold.

6 And thou shalt put it before the vail that *is* by the ark of the testimony, before the mercy seat that *is* over the testimony, where I will meet with thee.

7 And Aaron shall burn thereon sweet incense every morning: when he dresseth the lamps, he shall burn incense upon it.

8 And when Aaron lighteth the lamps at even, he shall burn incense upon it, a perpetual incense before the LORD throughout your generations.

9 Ye shall offer no strange incense thereon, nor burnt sacrifice, nor meat offering; neither shall ye pour drink offering thereon.

10 And Aaron shall make an atonement upon the horns of it once in a year with the blood of the sin offering of atonements: once in the year shall he make atonement upon it throughout your generations: it *is* most holy unto the LORD.

11 ¶And the LORD spake unto Moses, saying,

12 When thou takest the sum of the children of Israel after their number, then shall they give every man a ransom for his soul unto the LORD, when thou numberest them; that there be no plague among them, when *thou* numberest them.

13 This they shall give, every one that passeth among them that are numbered, half a shekel after the shekel of the sanctuary: (a shekel *is* twenty gerahs:) an half shekel *shall be* the offering of the LORD.

14 Every one that passeth among them that are numbered, from twenty years old and above, shall give an offering unto the LORD.

15 The rich shall not give more, and the poor shall not give less than half a shekel, when *they* give an offering unto the LORD, to make an atonement for your souls.

16 And thou shalt take the atonement money of the children of Israel, and shalt appoint it for the service of the tabernacle of the congregation; that it may be a memorial unto the children of Israel before the LORD, to make an atonement for your souls.

17 ¶And the LORD spake unto Moses, saying,

18 Thou shalt also make a laver *of* brass, and his foot *also of* brass, to wash *withal:* and thou shalt put it between the tabernacle of the congregation and the altar, and thou shalt put water therein.

19 For Aaron and his sons shall wash their hands and their feet thereat:

20 When they go into the tabernacle of the congregation, they shall wash with water, that they die not; or when they come near to the altar to minister, to burn offering made by fire unto the LORD:

21 So they shall wash their hands and their feet, that they die not: and it shall be a statute for ever to them, *even* to him and to his seed throughout their generations.

22 ¶Moreover the LORD spake unto Moses, saying,

23 Take thou also unto thee principal spices, of pure myrrh five hundred *shekels*, and of sweet cinnamon half so much, *even* two hundred and fifty *shekels*, and of sweet calamus two hundred and fifty *shekels*,

24 And of cassia five hundred *shekels*, after the shekel of the sanctuary, and of oil olive an hin:

25 And thou shalt make it an oil of holy ointment, an ointment compound after the art of the apothecary: it shall be an holy anointing oil.

26 And thou shalt anoint the tabernacle of the congregation therewith, and the ark of the testimony,

27 And the table and all his vessels, and the candlestick and his vessels, and the altar of incense,

28 And the altar of burnt offering with all his vessels, and the laver and his foot.

29 And thou shalt sanctify them, that they may be most holy: whatsoever toucheth them shall be holy.

30 And thou shalt anoint Aaron and his sons, and consecrate them, that *they* may minister unto me in the priest's office.

31 And thou shalt speak unto the children of Israel, saying, This shall be an holy anointing oil unto me throughout your generations.

32 Upon man's flesh shall it not be poured, neither shall ye make *any other* like it, after the composition of it: it *is* holy, *and* it shall be holy unto you.

33 Whosoever compoundeth *any* like it, or whosoever putteth *any* of it upon a stranger, shall even be cut off from his people.

34 ¶And the LORD said unto Moses, Take unto thee sweet spices, stacte, and onycha, and galbanum; *these* sweet spices with pure frankincense: of each shall there be a like *weight:*

35 And thou shalt make it a perfume, a confection after the art of the apothecary, tempered together, pure *and* holy:

36 And thou shalt beat *some* of it very small, and put of it before the testimony in the tabernacle of the congregation, where I will meet with thee: it shall be unto you most holy.

37 And *as for* the perfume which thou shalt make, ye shall not make to yourselves according to the composition thereof: it shall be unto thee holy for the LORD.

38 Whosoever shall make like unto that, to smell thereto, shall even be cut off from his people.

CHAPTER 31

AND the LORD spake unto Moses, saying,

2 See, I have called by name Be-zăl'e-el the son of Ū'rī, the son of Hur, of the tribe of Jūdah:

3 And I have filled him with the spirit of God, in wisdom, and in understanding, and in knowledge, and in all manner of workmanship,

4 To devise cunning works, to work in gold, and in silver, and in brass,

5 And in cutting of stones, to set *them*, and in carving of timber, to work in all manner of workmanship.

6 And I, behold, I have given with him A-hō'lĭ-ăb, the son of A-hĭs'a-măch, of the tribe of Dan: and in the hearts of all that are wise hearted I have put wisdom, that they may make all that I have commanded thee;

7 The tabernacle of the congregation, and the ark of the testimony, and the mercy seat that *is* thereupon, and all the furniture of the tabernacle,

8 And the table and his furniture, and the pure candlestick with all his furniture, and the altar of incense,

9 And the altar of burnt offering with
all his furniture, and the laver and his
foot,
10 And the cloths of service, and the
holy garments for Aaron the priest, and
the garments of his sons, to minister in
the priest's office,
11 And the anointing oil, and sweet
incense for the holy *place:* according to
all that I have commanded thee shall
they do.
12 ¶And the LORD spake unto Moses,
saying,
13 Speak thou also unto the children
of Israel, saying, Verily my sabbaths ye
shall keep: for it *is* a sign between me
and you throughout your generations;
that *ye* may know that I *am* the LORD
that doth sanctify you.
14 Ye shall keep the sabbath there-
fore; for it *is* holy unto you: every one
that defileth it shall surely be put to
death: for whosoever doeth *any* work
therein, that soul shall be cut off from
among his people.
15 Six days may work be done; but in
the seventh *is* the sabbath of rest, holy
to the LORD: whosoever doeth *any*
work in the sabbath day, he shall surely
be put to death.
16 Wherefore the children of Israel
shall keep the sabbath, to observe the
sabbath throughout their generations,
for a perpetual covenant.
17 It *is* a sign between me and the
children of Israel for ever: for *in* six
days the LORD made heaven and earth,
and on the seventh day he rested, and
was refreshed.
18 ¶And he gave unto Moses, when
he had made an end of communing
with him upon mount Sī'naī, two tables
of testimony, tables of stone, written
with the finger of God.

CHAPTER 32

AND when the people saw that Moses
delayed to come down out of the
mount, the people gathered themselves
together unto Aaron, and said unto
him, Up, make us gods, which shall go
before us; for *as for* this Moses, the
man that brought us up out of the land
of Egypt, we wot not what is become of
him.
2 And Aaron said unto them, Break
off the golden earrings, which *are* in the
ears of your wives, of your sons, and of
your daughters, and bring *them* unto
me.
3 And all the people brake off the gold-
en earrings which *were* in their ears,
and brought *them* unto Aaron.
4 And he received *them* at their hand,
and fashioned it with a graving tool, af-
ter he had made it a molten calf: and
they said, These *be* thy gods, O Israel,
which brought thee up out of the land
of Egypt.
5 And when Aaron saw *it*, he built an
altar before it; and Aaron made procla-
mation, and said, To morrow *is* a feast
to the LORD.
6 And they rose up early on the
morrow, and offered burnt offerings,
and brought peace offerings; and the
people sat down to eat and to drink,
and rose up to play.
7 ¶And the LORD said unto Moses, Go,
get thee down; for thy people, which
thou broughtest out of the land of
Egypt, have corrupted *themselves:*
8 They have turned aside quickly out
of the way which I commanded them:
they have made them a molten calf,
and have worshipped it, and have sac-
rificed thereunto, and said, These *be*
thy gods, O Israel, which have brought
thee up out of the land of Egypt.
9 And the LORD said unto Moses, I
have seen this people, and, behold, it *is*
a stiffnecked people:
10 Now therefore let me alone, that
my wrath may wax hot against them,
and that I may consume them: and I
will make of thee a great nation.
11 And Moses besought the LORD his
God, and said, LORD, why doth thy
wrath wax hot against thy people,
which thou hast brought forth out of
the land of Egypt with great power, and
with a mighty hand?
12 Wherefore should the Egyptians
speak, and say, For mischief did he
bring them out, to slay them in the
mountains, and to consume them from
the face of the earth? Turn from thy
fierce wrath, and repent of this evil
against thy people.
13 Remember Abraham, Isaac, and
Israel, thy servants, to whom thou
swarest by thine own self, and saidst
unto them, I will multiply your seed as
the stars of heaven, and all this land
that I have spoken of will I give unto
your seed, and they shall inherit *it* for
ever.
14 And the LORD repented of the evil
which he thought to do unto his people.
15 ¶And Moses turned, and went
down from the mount, and the two
tables of the testimony *were* in his
hand: the tables *were* written on both
their sides; on the one side and on the
other *were* they written.
16 And the tables *were* the work of
God, and the writing *was* the writing of
God, graven upon the tables.
17 And when Joshua heard the noise
of the people as they shouted, he said

unto Moses, *There is* a noise of war in
the camp.
18 And he said, *It is* not the voice of
them that shout for mastery, neither *is*
it the voice of *them that* cry for being
overcome: *but* the noise of *them that*
sing do I hear.
19 ¶And it came to pass, as soon as he
came nigh unto the camp, that he saw
the calf, and the dancing: and Moses'
anger waxed hot, and he cast the tables
out of his hands, and brake them be-
neath the mount.
20 And he took the calf which they
had made, and burnt *it* in the fire, and
ground *it* to powder, and strawed *it*
upon the water, and made the children
of Israel drink *of it*.
21 And Moses said unto Aaron, What
did this people unto thee, that thou hast
brought so great a sin upon them?
22 And Aaron said, Let not the anger
of my lord wax hot: thou knowest the
people, that they *are set* on mischief.
23 For they said unto me, Make us
gods, which shall go before us: for *as*
for this Moses, the man that brought us
up out of the land of Egypt, we wot not
what is become of him.
24 And I said unto them, Whosoever
hath any gold, let them break *it* off. So
they gave *it* me: then I cast it into the
fire, and there came out this calf.
25 ¶And when Moses saw that the
people *were* naked; (for Aaron had
made them naked unto *their* shame
among their enemies:)
26 Then Moses stood in the gate of
the camp, and said, Who *is* on the
LORD's side? *let him come* unto me. And
all the sons of Levi gathered them-
selves together unto him.
27 And he said unto them, Thus saith
the LORD God of Israel, Put every man
his sword by his side, *and* go in and out
from gate to gate throughout the camp,
and slay every man his brother, and
every man his companion, and every
man his neighbour.
28 And the children of Levi did accord-
ing to the word of Moses: and there
fell of the people that day about three
thousand men.
29 For Moses had said, Consecrate
yourselves to day to the LORD, even
every man upon his son, and upon his
brother; that he may bestow upon you
a blessing this day.
30 ¶And it came to pass on the
morrow, that Moses said unto the
people, Ye have sinned a great sin: and
now I will go up unto the LORD; per-
adventure I shall make an atonement
for your sin.
31 And Moses returned unto the
LORD, and said, Oh, this people have
sinned a great sin, and have made them
gods of gold.
32 Yet now, if thou wilt forgive their
sin—; and if not, blot me, I pray thee,
out of thy book which thou hast writ-
ten.
33 And the LORD said unto Moses,
Whosoever hath sinned against me,
him will I blot out of my book.
34 Therefore now go, lead the people
unto *the place* of which I have spoken
unto thee: behold, mine Angel shall go
before thee: nevertheless in the day
when I visit I will visit their sin upon
them.
35 And the LORD plagued the people,
because they made the calf, which
Aaron made.

CHAPTER 33

AND the LORD said unto Moses, De-
part, *and* go up hence, thou and the
people which thou hast brought up out
of the land of Egypt, unto the land
which I sware unto Abraham, to Isaac,
and to Jacob, saying, Unto thy seed will
I give it:
2 And I will send an angel before
thee; and I will drive out the Canaanite,
the Ămorīte, and the Hittite, and the
Pĕr′iz-zīte, the Hī′vīte, and the Jĕb′u-
sīte:
3 Unto a land flowing with milk and
honey: for I will not go up in the midst
of thee; for thou *art* a stiffnecked peo-
ple: lest I consume thee in the way.
4 ¶And when the people heard these
evil tidings, they mourned: and no man
did put on him his ornaments.
5 For the LORD had said unto Moses,
Say unto the children of Israel, Ye *are* a
stiffnecked people: I will come up into
the midst of thee in a moment, and con-
sume thee: therefore now put off thy
ornaments from thee, that I may know
what to do unto thee.
6 And the children of Israel stripped
themselves of their ornaments by the
mount Hô′rĕb.
7 And Moses took the tabernacle,
and pitched it without the camp, afar
off from the camp, and called it the
Tabernacle of the congregation. And it
came to pass, *that* every one which
sought the LORD went out unto the taber-
nacle of the congregation, which
was without the camp.
8 And it came to pass, when Moses
went out unto the tabernacle, *that* all
the people rose up, and stood every
man *at* his tent door, and looked after
Moses, until he was gone into the taber-
nacle.
9 And it came to pass, as Moses en-

tered into the tabernacle, the cloudy
pillar descended, and stood *at* the door
of the tabernacle, and *the* LORD talked
with Moses.
10 And all the people saw the cloudy
pillar stand *at* the tabernacle door: and
all the people rose up and worshipped,
every man *in* his tent door.
11 And the LORD spake unto Moses
face to face, as a man speaketh unto his
friend. And he turned again into the
camp: but his servant Joshua, the son
of Nun, a young man, departed not out
of the tabernacle.
12 ¶And Moses said unto the LORD,
See, thou sayest unto me, Bring up this
people: and thou hast not let me know
whom thou wilt send with me. Yet thou
hast said, I know thee by name, and
thou hast also found grace in my sight.
13 Now therefore, I pray thee, if I
have found grace in thy sight, shew me
now thy way, that I may know thee,
that I may find grace in thy sight: and
consider that this nation *is* thy people.
14 And he said, My presence shall go
with thee, and I will give thee rest.
15 And he said unto him, If thy pres-
ence go not *with me,* carry us not up
hence.
16 For wherein shall it be known here
that I and thy people have found grace
in thy sight? *is it* not in that thou goest
with us? so shall we be separated, I and
thy people, from all the people that *are*
upon the face of the earth.
17 And the LORD said unto Moses, I
will do this thing also that thou hast
spoken: for thou hast found grace in
my sight, and I know thee by name.
18 And he said, I beseech thee, shew
me thy glory.
19 And he said, I will make all my
goodness pass before thee, and I will
proclaim the name of the LORD before
thee; and will be gracious to whom I
will be gracious, and will shew mercy
on whom I will shew mercy.
20 And he said, Thou canst not see
my face: for there shall no man see me,
and live.
21 And the LORD said, Behold, *there is*
a place by me, and thou shalt stand
upon a rock:
22 And it shall come to pass, while
my glory passeth by, that I will put thee
in a clift of the rock, and will cover thee
with my hand while I pass by:
23 And I will take away mine hand,
and thou shalt see my back parts: but
my face shall not be seen.

CHAPTER 34

AND the LORD said unto Moses, Hew
thee two tables of stone like unto the
first: and I will write upon *these* tables
the words that were in the first tables,
which thou brakest.
2 And be ready in the morning, and
come up in the morning unto mount Sī'-
naī, and present thyself there to me in
the top of the mount.
3 And no man shall come up with
thee, neither let any man be seen
throughout all the mount; neither let
the flocks nor herds feed before that
mount.
4 ¶And he hewed two tables of stone
like unto the first; and Moses rose up
early in the morning, and went up unto
mount Sī'naī, as the LORD had com-
manded him, and took in his hand the
two tables of stone.
5 And the LORD descended in the
cloud, and stood with him there, and
proclaimed the name of the LORD.
6 And the LORD passed by before him,
and proclaimed, The LORD, The LORD
God, merciful and gracious, longsuffer-
ing, and abundant in goodness and
truth,
7 Keeping mercy for thousands, for-
giving iniquity and transgression and
sin, and that will by no means clear *the*
guilty; visiting the iniquity of the fathers
upon the children, and upon the
children's children, unto the third and
to the fourth *generation.*
8 And Moses made haste, and bowed
his head toward the earth, and wor-
shipped.
9 And he said, If now I have found
grace in thy sight, O Lord, let my Lord, I
pray thee, go among us; for it *is* a stiff-
necked people; and pardon our iniquity
and our sin, and take us for thine inheri-
tance.
10 ¶And he said, Behold, I make a
covenant: before all thy people I will do
marvels, such as have not been done in
all the earth, nor in any nation: and all
the people among which thou *art* shall
see the work of the LORD: for it *is* a ter-
rible thing that I will do with thee.
11 Observe thou that which I com-
mand thee this day: behold, I drive out
before thee the Amorite, and the Ca-
naanite, and the Hittite, and the Pĕr'iz-
zīte, and the Hī'vīte, and the Jēb'u-sīte.
12 Take heed to thyself, lest thou
make a covenant with the inhabitants
of the land whither thou goest, lest it be
for a snare in the midst of thee:
13 But ye shall destroy their altars,
break their images, and cut down their
groves:
14 For thou shalt worship no other
god: for the LORD, whose name *is*
Jealous, *is* a jealous God:
15 Lest thou make a covenant with

the inhabitants of the land, and they go a whoring after their gods, and do sacrifice unto their gods, and *one* call thee, and thou eat of his sacrifice;
16 And thou take of their daughters unto thy sons, and their daughters go a whoring after their gods, and make thy sons go a whoring after their gods.
17 Thou shalt make thee no molten gods.
18 ¶The feast of unleavened bread shalt thou keep. Seven days thou shalt eat unleavened bread, as I commanded thee, in the time of the month Ā'bīb: for in the month Ā'bīb thou camest out from Egypt.
19 All that openeth the matrix *is* mine; and every firstling among thy cattle, *whether* ox or sheep, *that is male*.
20 But the firstling of an ass thou shalt redeem with a lamb: and if thou redeem *him* not, then shalt thou break his neck. All the firstborn of thy sons thou shalt redeem. And none shall appear before me empty.
21 ¶Six days thou shalt work, but on the seventh day thou shalt rest: in earing time and in harvest thou shalt rest.
22 ¶And thou shalt observe the feast of weeks, of the firstfruits of wheat harvest, and the feast of ingathering at the year's end.
23 ¶Thrice in the year shall all your menchildren appear before the Lord GOD, the God of Israel.
24 For I will cast out the nations before thee, and enlarge thy borders: neither shall any man desire thy land, when thou shalt go up to appear before the LORD thy God thrice in the year.
25 Thou shalt not offer the blood of my sacrifice with leaven; neither shall the sacrifice of the feast of the passover be left unto the morning.
26 The first of the firstfruits of thy land thou shalt bring unto the house of the LORD thy God. Thou shalt not seethe a kid in his mother's milk.
27 And the LORD said unto Moses, Write thou these words: for after the tenor of these words I have made a covenant with thee and with Israel.
28 And he was there with the LORD forty days and forty nights; he did neither eat bread, nor drink water. And he wrote upon the tables the words of the covenant, the ten commandments.
29 ¶And it came to pass, when Moses came down from mount Sī'naī with the two tables of testimony in Moses' hand, when he came down from the mount, that Moses wist not that the skin of his face shone while he talked with him.
30 And when Aaron and all the children of Israel saw Moses, behold, the skin of his face shone; and they were afraid to come nigh him.
31 And Moses called unto them; and Aaron and all the rulers of the congregation returned unto him: and Moses talked with them.
32 And afterward all the children of Israel came nigh: and he gave them in commandment all that the LORD had spoken with him in mount Sī'naī.
33 And *till* Moses had done speaking with them, he put a vail on his face.
34 But when Moses went in before the LORD to speak with him, he took the vail off, until he came out. And he came out, and spake unto the children of Israel *that* which he was commanded.
35 And the children of Israel saw the face of Moses, that the skin of Moses' face shone: and Moses put the vail upon his face again, until he went in to speak with him.

CHAPTER 35

AND Moses gathered all the congregation of the children of Israel together, and said unto them, These *are* the words which the LORD hath commanded, that *ye* should do them.
2 Six days shall work be done, but on the seventh day there shall be to you an holy day, a sabbath of rest to the LORD: whosoever doeth work therein shall be put to death.
3 Ye shall kindle no fire throughout your habitations upon the sabbath day.
4 ¶And Moses spake unto all the congregation of the children of Israel, saying, This *is* the thing which the LORD commanded, saying,
5 Take ye from among you an offering unto the LORD: whosoever *is* of a willing heart, let him bring it, an offering of the LORD; gold, and silver, and brass,
6 And blue, and purple, and scarlet, and fine linen, and goats' *hair*,
7 And rams' skins dyed red, and badgers' skins, and shittim wood,
8 And oil for the light, and spices for anointing oil, and for the sweet incense,
9 And onyx stones, and stones to be set for the ephod, and for the breastplate.
10 And every wise hearted among you shall come, and make all that the LORD hath commanded;
11 The tabernacle, his tent, and his covering, his taches, and his boards, his bars, his pillars, and his sockets,
12 The ark, and the staves thereof,

with the mercy seat, and the vail of the
covering,
13 The table, and his staves, and all
his vessels, and the shewbread,
14 The candlestick also for the light,
and his furniture, and his lamps, with
the oil for the light,
15 And the incense altar, and his
staves, and the anointing oil, and the
sweet incense, and the hanging for the
door at the entering in of the taber-
nacle,
16 The altar of burnt offering, with
his brasen grate, his staves, and all his
vessels, the laver and his foot,
17 The hangings of the court, his pil-
lars, and their sockets, and the hanging
for the door of the court,
18 The pins of the tabernacle, and the
pins of the court, and their cords,
19 The cloths of service, to do service
in the holy *place*, the holy garments for
Aaron the priest, and the garments of
his sons, to minister in the priest's of-
fice.
20 ¶And all the congregation of the
children of Israel departed from the
presence of Moses.
21 And they came, every one whose
heart stirred him up, and every one
whom his spirit made willing, *and* they
brought the LORD's offering to the work
of the tabernacle of the congregation,
and for all his service, and for the holy
garments.
22 And they came, both men and wom-
en, as many as were willing hearted,
and brought bracelets, and earrings,
and rings, and tablets, all jewels of
gold: and every man that offered *of-
fered* an offering of gold unto the LORD.
23 And every man, with whom was
found blue, and purple, and scarlet, and
fine linen, and goats' *hair*, and red skins
of rams, and badgers' skins, brought
them.
24 Every one that did offer an offer-
ing of silver and brass brought the
LORD's offering: and every man, with
whom was found shittim wood for any
work of the service, brought *it*.
25 And all the women that were wise
hearted did spin with their hands, and
brought that which they had spun, *both*
of blue, and of purple, *and* of scarlet,
and of fine linen.
26 And all the women whose heart
stirred them up in wisdom spun goats'
hair.
27 And the rulers brought onyx
stones, and stones to be set, for the
ephod, and for the breastplate;
28 And spice, and oil for the light, and
for the anointing oil, and for the sweet
incense.
29 The children of Israel brought a
willing offering unto the LORD, every
man and woman, whose heart made
them willing to bring for all manner of
work, which the LORD had commanded
to be made by the hand of Moses.
30 ¶And Moses said unto the children
of Israel, See, the LORD hath called by
name Be-zăl'e-el the son of Ū'rī, the son
of Hur, of the tribe of Jūdah;
31 And he hath filled him with the
spirit of God, in wisdom, in understand-
ing, and in knowledge, and in all
manner of workmanship;
32 And to devise curious works, to
work in gold, and in silver, and in brass,
33 And in the cutting of stones, to set
them, and in carving of wood, to make
any manner of cunning work.
34 And he hath put in his heart that
he may teach, *both* he, and A-hō'lī-ăb,
the son of A-hĭs'a-măch, of the tribe of
Dan.
35 Them hath he filled with wisdom
of heart, to work all manner of work, of
the engraver, and of the cunning work-
man, and of the embroiderer, in blue,
and in purple, in scarlet, and in fine lin-
en, and of the weaver, *even* of them
that do any work, and of those that de-
vise cunning work.

CHAPTER 36

THEN wrought Be-zăl'e-el and A-hō'lī-
ăb, and every wise hearted man, in
whom the LORD put wisdom and under-
standing to know how to work all man-
ner of work for the service of the sanc-
tuary, according to all that the LORD
had commanded.
2 And Moses called Be-zăl'e-el and A-
hō'lī-ăb, and every wise hearted man,
in whose heart the LORD had put wis-
dom, *even* every one whose heart
stirred him up to come unto the work to
do it:
3 And they received of Moses all the
offering, which the children of Israel
had brought for the work of the service
of the sanctuary, to make it *withal*. And
they brought yet unto him free offer-
ings every morning.
4 ¶And all the wise men, that
wrought all the work of the sanctuary,
came every man from his work which
they made;
5 And they spake unto Moses, saying,
The people bring much more than
enough for the service of the work,
which the LORD commanded to make.
6 And Moses gave commandment,
and they caused it to be proclaimed
throughout the camp, saying, Let
neither man nor woman make any
more work for the offering of the sanc-

tuary. So the people were restrained
from bringing.
7 For the stuff they had was suffi-
cient for all the work to make it, and too
much.
8 ¶And every wise hearted man
among them that wrought the work of
the tabernacle made ten curtains *of*
fine twined linen, and blue, and purple,
and scarlet: *with* cherubims of cunning
work made he them.
9 The length of one curtain *was*
twenty and eight cubits, and the
breadth of one curtain four cubits: the
curtains *were* all of one size.
10 And he coupled the five curtains
one unto another: and *the other* five
curtains he coupled one unto another.
11 And he made loops of blue on the
edge of one curtain from the selvedge
in the coupling: likewise he made in the
uttermost side of *another* curtain, in
the coupling of the second.
12 Fifty loops made he in one curtain,
and fifty loops made he in the edge of
the curtain which *was* in the coupling
of the second: the loops held one *cur-*
tain to another.
13 And he made fifty taches of gold,
and coupled the curtains one unto an-
other with the taches: so it became one
tabernacle.
14 ¶And he made curtains *of* goats'
hair for the tent over the tabernacle:
eleven curtains he made them.
15 The length of one curtain *was*
thirty cubits, and four cubits *was* the
breadth of one curtain: the eleven cur-
tains *were* of one size.
16 And he coupled five curtains by
themselves, and six curtains by them-
selves.
17 And he made fifty loops upon the
uttermost edge of the curtain in the
coupling, and fifty loops made he upon
the edge of the curtain which coupleth
the second.
18 And he made fifty taches *of* brass
to couple the tent together, that it
might be one.
19 ¶And he made a covering for the
tent *of* rams' skins dyed red, and a
covering *of* badgers' skins above *that*.
20 ¶And he made boards for the taber-
nacle *of* shĭttĭm wood, standing up.
21 The length of a board *was* ten
cubits, and the breadth of a board one
cubit and a half.
22 One board had two tenons,
equally distant one from another: thus
did he make for all the boards of the
tabernacle.
23 And he made boards for the taber-
nacle; twenty boards for the south side
southward:
24 And forty sockets of silver he
made under the twenty boards; two
sockets under one board for his two ten-
ons, and two sockets under another
board for his two tenons.
25 And for the other side of the taber-
nacle, *which is* toward the north cor-
ner, he made twenty boards,
26 And their forty sockets of silver;
two sockets under one board, and two
sockets under another board.
27 And for the sides of the tabernacle
westward he made six boards.
28 And two boards made he for the
corners of the tabernacle in the two
sides.
29 And they were coupled beneath,
and coupled together at the head there-
of, to one ring: thus he did to both of
them in both the corners.
30 And there were eight boards; and
their sockets *were* sixteen sockets of
silver, under every board two sockets.
31 ¶And he made bars of shĭttĭm
wood; five for the boards of the one
side of the tabernacle,
32 And five bars for the boards of the
other side of the tabernacle, and five
bars for the boards of the tabernacle
for the sides westward.
33 And he made the middle bar to
shoot through the boards from the one
end to the other.
34 And he overlaid the boards with
gold, and made their rings *of* gold *to be*
places for the bars, and overlaid the
bars with gold.
35 ¶And he made a vail *of* blue, and
purple, and scarlet, and fine twined lin-
en: *with* cherubims made he it of cun-
ning work.
36 And he made thereunto four pil-
lars *of* shĭttĭm *wood*, and overlaid them
with gold: their hooks *were of* gold; and
he cast for them four sockets of silver.
37 ¶And he made an hanging for the
tabernacle door *of* blue, and purple,
and scarlet, and fine twined linen, of
needlework;
38 And the five pillars of it with their
hooks: and he overlaid their chapiters
and their fillets with gold: but their five
sockets *were of* brass.

CHAPTER 37

AND Be-zăl′e-el made the ark *of* shĭt-
tĭm wood: two cubits and a half *was*
the length of it, and a cubit and a half
the breadth of it, and a cubit and a half
the height of it:
2 And he overlaid it with pure gold
within and without, and made a crown
of gold to it round about.
3 And he cast for it four rings of gold,
to be set by the four corners of it; even

two rings upon the one side of it, and
two rings upon the other side of it.
4 And he made staves *of* shĭttĭm
wood, and overlaid them with gold.
5 And he put the staves into the rings
by the sides of the ark, to bear the ark.
6 ¶And he made the mercy seat *of*
pure gold: two cubits and a half *was* the
length thereof, and one cubit and a half
the breadth thereof.
7 And he made two cherubims *of*
gold, beaten out of one piece made he
them, on the two ends of the mercy
seat;
8 One cherub on the end on this side,
and another cherub on the *other* end on
that side: out of the mercy seat made he
the cherubims on the two ends thereof.
9 And the cherubims spread out *their*
wings on high, *and* covered with their
wings over the mercy seat, with their
faces one to another; *even* to the mercy
seatward were the faces of the cheru-
bims.
10 ¶And he made the table *of* shĭttĭm
wood: two cubits *was* the length there-
of, and a cubit the breadth thereof,
and a cubit and a half the height there-
of:
11 And he overlaid it with pure gold,
and made thereunto a crown of gold
round about.
12 Also he made thereunto a border
of an handbreadth round about; and
made a crown of gold for the border
thereof round about.
13 And he cast for it four rings of
gold, and put the rings upon the four
corners that *were* in the four feet there-
of.
14 Over against the border were the
rings, the places for the staves to bear
the table.
15 And he made the staves *of* shĭttĭm
wood, and overlaid them with gold, to
bear the table.
16 And he made the vessels which
were upon the table, his dishes, and his
spoons, and his bowls, and his covers
to cover withal, *of* pure gold.
17 ¶And he made the candlestick *of*
pure gold: *of* beaten work made he the
candlestick; his shaft, and his branch,
his bowls, his knops, and his flowers,
were of the same:
18 And six branches going out of the
sides thereof; three branches of the
candlestick out of the one side thereof,
and three branches of the candlestick
out of the other side thereof:
19 Three bowls made after the
fashion of almonds in one branch, a
knop and a flower; and three bowls
made like almonds in another branch, a
knop and a flower: so throughout the
six branches going out of the candle-
stick.
20 And in the candlestick *were* four
bowls made like almonds, his knops,
and his flowers:
21 And a knop under two branches of
the same, and a knop under two
branches of the same, and a knop under
two branches of the same, according to
the six branches going out of it.
22 Their knops and their branches
were of the same: all of it *was* one beat-
en work *of* pure gold.
23 And he made his seven lamps, and
his snuffers, and his snuffdishes, *of*
pure gold.
24 *Of* a talent of pure gold made he it,
and all the vessels thereof.
25 ¶And he made the incense altar *of*
shĭttĭm wood: the length of it *was* a cu-
bit, and the breadth of it a cubit; *it was*
foursquare; and two cubits *was* the
height of it; the horns thereof were of
the same.
26 And he overlaid it with pure gold,
both the top of it, and the sides thereof
round about, and the horns of it: also he
made unto it a crown of gold round
about.
27 And he made two rings of gold for
it under the crown thereof, by the two
corners of it, upon the two sides there-
of, to be places for the staves to bear
it withal.
28 And he made the staves *of* shĭttĭm
wood, and overlaid them with gold.
29 ¶And he made the holy anointing
oil, and the pure incense of sweet
spices, according to the work of the
apothecary.

CHAPTER 38

AND he made the altar of burnt offer-
ing *of* shĭttĭm wood: five cubits *was* the
length thereof, and five cubits the
breadth thereof; *it was* foursquare; and
three cubits the height thereof.
2 And he made the horns thereof on
the four corners of it; the horns thereof
were of the same: and he overlaid it
with brass.
3 And he made all the vessels of the
altar, the pots, and the shovels, and the
basons, *and* the fleshhooks, and the
firepans: all the vessels thereof made
he *of* brass.
4 And he made for the altar a brasen
grate of network under the compass
thereof beneath unto the midst of it.
5 And he cast four rings for the four
ends of the grate of brass, *to be* places
for the staves.
6 And he made the staves *of* shĭttĭm
wood, and overlaid them with brass.
7 And he put the staves into the rings

on the sides of the altar, to bear it withal; he made the altar hollow with boards.

8 ¶And he made the laver *of* brass, and the foot of it *of* brass, of the lookingglasses of *the women* assembling, which assembled *at* the door of the tabernacle of the congregation.

9 ¶And he made the court: on the south side southward the hangings of the court *were of* fine twined linen, an hundred cubits:

10 Their pillars *were* twenty, and their brasen sockets twenty; the hooks of the pillars and their fillets *were of* silver.

11 And for the north side *the hangings were* an hundred cubits, their pillars *were* twenty, and their sockets of brass twenty; the hooks of the pillars and their fillets *of* silver.

12 And for the west side *were* hangings of fifty cubits, their pillars ten, and their sockets ten; the hooks of the pillars and their fillets *of* silver.

13 And for the east side eastward fifty cubits.

14 The hangings of the one side *of the gate were* fifteen cubits; their pillars three, and their sockets three.

15 And for the other side of the court gate, on this hand and that hand, *were* hangings of fifteen cubits; their pillars three, and their sockets three.

16 All the hangings of the court round about *were* of fine twined linen.

17 And the sockets for the pillars *were of* brass; the hooks of the pillars and their fillets *of* silver; and the overlaying of their chapiters *of* silver; and all the pillars of the court *were* filleted with silver.

18 And the hanging for the gate of the court *was* needlework, *of* blue, and purple, and scarlet, and fine twined linen: and twenty cubits *was* the length, and the height in the breadth *was* five cubits, answerable to the hangings of the court.

19 And their pillars *were* four, and their sockets *of* brass four; their hooks *of* silver, and the overlaying of their chapiters and their fillets *of* silver.

20 And all the pins of the tabernacle, and of the court round about, *were of* brass.

21 ¶This is the sum of the tabernacle, *even* of the tabernacle of testimony, as it was counted, according to the commandment of Moses, *for* the service of the Lēvītes, by the hand of Ĭth'a-mär, son to Aaron the priest.

22 And Be-zăl'e-el the son of Ū'rī, the son of Hur, of the tribe of Jūdah, made all that the LORD commanded Moses.

23 And with him *was* A-hō'lĭ-ăb, son of A-hĭs'a-măch, of the tribe of Dan, an engraver, and a cunning workman, and an embroiderer in blue, and in purple, and in scarlet, and fine linen.

24 All the gold that was occupied for the work in all the work of the holy *place*, even the gold of the offering, was twenty and nine talents, and seven hundred and thirty shekels, after the shekel of the sanctuary.

25 And the silver of them that were numbered of the congregation *was* an hundred talents, and a thousand seven hundred and threescore and fifteen shekels, after the shekel of the sanctuary:

26 A bekah for every man, *that is*, half a shekel, after the shekel of the sanctuary, for every one that went to be numbered, from twenty years old and upward, for six hundred thousand and three thousand and five hundred and fifty *men*.

27 And of the hundred talents of silver were cast the sockets of the sanctuary, and the sockets of the vail; an hundred sockets of the hundred talents, a talent for a socket.

28 And of the thousand seven hundred seventy and five *shekels* he made hooks for the pillars, and overlaid their chapiters, and filleted them.

29 And the brass of the offering *was* seventy talents, and two thousand and four hundred shekels.

30 And therewith he made the sockets to the door of the tabernacle of the congregation, and the brasen altar, and the brasen grate for it, and all the vessels of the altar,

31 And the sockets of the court round about, and the sockets of the court gate, and all the pins of the tabernacle, and all the pins of the court round about.

CHAPTER 39

AND of the blue, and purple, and scarlet, they made cloths of service, to do service in the holy *place*, and made the holy garments for Aaron; as the LORD commanded Moses.

2 And he made the ephod *of* gold, blue, and purple, and scarlet, and fine twined linen.

3 And they did beat the gold into thin plates, and cut *it into* wires, to work *it* in the blue, and in the purple, and in the scarlet, and in the fine linen, *with* cunning work.

4 They made shoulderpieces for it, to couple *it* together: by the two edges was it coupled together.

5 And the curious girdle of his ephod,

that *was* upon it, *was* of the same, according to the work thereof; *of* gold, blue, and purple, and scarlet, and fine twined linen; as the LORD commanded Moses.

6 ¶And they wrought onyx stones inclosed in ouches of gold, graven, as signets are graven, with the names of the children of Israel.

7 And he put them on the shoulders of the ephod, *that they should be* stones for a memorial to the children of Israel; as the LORD commanded Moses.

8 ¶And he made the breastplate *of* cunning work, like the work of the ephod; *of* gold, blue, and purple, and scarlet, and fine twined linen.

9 It was foursquare; they made the breastplate double: a span *was* the length thereof, and a span the breadth thereof, *being* doubled.

10 And they set in it four rows of stones: *the first* row *was* a sardius, a topaz, and a carbuncle: this *was* the first row.

11 And the second row, an emerald, a sapphire, and a diamond.

12 And the third row, a ligure, an agate, and an amethyst.

13 And the fourth row, a beryl, an onyx, and a jasper: *they were* inclosed in ouches of gold in their inclosings.

14 And the stones *were* according to the names of the children of Israel, twelve, according to their names, *like* the engravings of a signet, every one with his name, according to the twelve tribes.

15 And they made upon the breastplate chains at the ends, *of* wreathen work *of* pure gold.

16 And they made two ouches *of* gold, and two gold rings; and put the two rings in the two ends of the breastplate.

17 And they put the two wreathen chains of gold in the two rings on the ends of the breastplate.

18 And the two ends of the two wreathen chains they fastened in the two ouches, and put them on the shoulderpieces of the ephod, before it.

19 And they made two rings of gold, and put *them* on the two ends of the breastplate, upon the border of it, which *was* on the side of the ephod inward.

20 And they made two *other* golden rings, and put them on the two sides of the ephod underneath, toward the forepart of it, over against the *other* coupling thereof, above the curious girdle of the ephod.

21 And they did bind the breastplate by his rings unto the rings of the ephod with a lace of blue, that it might be above the curious girdle of the ephod, and that the breastplate might not be loosed from the ephod; as the LORD commanded Moses.

22 ¶And he made the robe of the ephod *of* woven work, all *of* blue.

23 And *there was* an hole in the midst of the robe, as the hole of an habergeon, *with* a band round about the hole, that it should not rend.

24 And they made upon the hems of the robe pomegranates *of* blue, and purple, and scarlet, *and* twined *linen*.

25 And they made bells *of* pure gold, and put the bells between the pomegranates upon the hem of the robe, round about between the pomegranates;

26 A bell and a pomegranate, a bell and a pomegranate, round about the hem of the robe to minister *in*; as the LORD commanded Moses.

27 ¶And they made coats *of* fine linen *of* woven work for Aaron, and for his sons,

28 And a mitre *of* fine linen, and goodly bonnets *of* fine linen, and linen breeches *of* fine twined linen,

29 And a girdle *of* fine twined linen, and blue, and purple, and scarlet, *of* needlework; as the LORD commanded Moses.

30 ¶And they made the plate of the holy crown *of* pure gold, and wrote upon it a writing, *like to* the engravings of a signet, HOLINESS TO THE LORD.

31 And they tied unto it a lace of blue, to fasten *it* on high upon the mitre; as the LORD commanded Moses.

32 Thus was all the work of the tabernacle of the tent of the congregation finished: and the children of Israel did according to all that the LORD commanded Moses, so did they.

33 ¶And they brought the tabernacle unto Moses, the tent, and all his furniture, his taches, his boards, his bars, and his pillars, and his sockets,

34 And the covering of rams' skins dyed red, and the covering of badgers' skins, and the vail of the covering,

35 The ark of the testimony, and the staves thereof, and the mercy seat,

36 The table, *and* all the vessels thereof, and the shewbread,

37 The pure candlestick, *with* the lamps thereof, *even with* the lamps to be set in order, and all the vessels thereof, and the oil for light,

38 And the golden altar, and the anointing oil, and the sweet incense, and the hanging for the tabernacle door,

39 The brasen altar, and his grate of

brass, his staves, and all his vessels, the laver and his foot,

40 The hangings of the court, his pillars, and his sockets, and the hanging for the court gate, his cords, and his pins, and all the vessels of the service of the tabernacle, for the tent of the congregation,

41 The cloths of service to do service in the holy *place*, and the holy garments for Aaron the priest, and his sons' garments, to minister in the priest's office.

42 According to all that the LORD commanded Moses, so the children of Israel made all the work.

43 And Moses did look upon all the work, and, behold, they had done it as the LORD had commanded, even so had they done it: and Moses blessed them.

CHAPTER 40

AND the LORD spake unto Moses, saying,

2 On the first day of the first month shalt thou set up the tabernacle of the tent of the congregation.

3 And thou shalt put therein the ark of the testimony, and cover the ark with the vail.

4 And thou shalt bring in the table, and set in order the things that are to be set in order upon it; and thou shalt bring in the candlestick, and light the lamps thereof.

5 And thou shalt set the altar of gold for the incense before the ark of the testimony, and put the hanging of the door to the tabernacle.

6 And thou shalt set the altar of the burnt offering before the door of the tabernacle of the tent of the congregation.

7 And thou shalt set the laver between the tent of the congregation and the altar, and shalt put water therein.

8 And thou shalt set up the court round about, and hang up the hanging at the court gate.

9 And thou shalt take the anointing oil, and anoint the tabernacle, and all that *is* therein, and shalt hallow it, and all the vessels thereof: and it shall be holy.

10 And thou shalt anoint the altar of the burnt offering, and all his vessels, and sanctify the altar: and it shall be an altar most holy.

11 And thou shalt anoint the laver and his foot, and sanctify it.

12 And thou shalt bring Aaron and his sons unto the door of the tabernacle of the congregation, and wash them with water.

13 And thou shalt put upon Aaron the holy garments, and anoint him, and sanctify him; that he may minister unto me in the priest's office.

14 And thou shalt bring his sons, and clothe them with coats:

15 And thou shalt anoint them, as thou didst anoint their father, that they may minister unto me in the priest's office: for their anointing shall surely be an everlasting priesthood throughout their generations.

16 Thus did Moses: according to all that the LORD commanded him, so did he.

17 ¶And it came to pass in the first month in the second year, on the first *day* of the month, *that* the tabernacle was reared up.

18 And Moses reared up the tabernacle, and fastened his sockets, and set up the boards thereof, and put in the bars thereof, and reared up his pillars.

19 And he spread abroad the tent over the tabernacle, and put the covering of the tent above upon it; as the LORD commanded Moses.

20 ¶And he took and put the testimony into the ark, and set the staves on the ark, and put the mercy seat above upon the ark:

21 And he brought the ark into the tabernacle, and set up the vail of the covering, and covered the ark of the testimony; as the LORD commanded Moses.

22 ¶And he put the table in the tent of the congregation, upon the side of the tabernacle northward, without the vail.

23 And he set the bread in order upon it before the LORD; as the LORD had commanded Moses.

24 ¶And he put the candlestick in the tent of the congregation, over against the table, on the side of the tabernacle southward.

25 And he lighted the lamps before the LORD; as the LORD commanded Moses.

26 ¶And he put the golden altar in the tent of the congregation before the vail:

27 And he burnt sweet incense thereon; as the LORD commanded Moses.

28 ¶And he set up the hanging *at* the door of the tabernacle.

29 And he put the altar of burnt offering *by* the door of the tabernacle of the tent of the congregation, and offered upon it the burnt offering and the meat offering; as the LORD commanded Moses.

30 ¶And he set the laver between the tent of the congregation and the altar, and put water there, to wash *withal*.

31 And Moses and Aaron and his sons washed their hands and their feet thereat:

32 When they went into the tent of the congregation, and when they came near unto the altar, they washed; as the LORD commanded Moses.

33 And he reared up the court round about the tabernacle and the altar, and set up the hanging of the court gate. So Moses finished the work.

34 ¶Then a cloud covered the tent of the congregation, and the glory of the LORD filled the tabernacle.

35 And Moses was not able to enter into the tent of the congregation, because the cloud abode thereon, and the glory of the LORD filled the tabernacle.

36 And when the cloud was taken up from over the tabernacle, the children of Israel went onward in all their journeys:

37 But if the cloud were not taken up, then they journeyed not till the day that it was taken up.

38 For the cloud of the LORD *was* upon the tabernacle by day, and fire was on it by night, in the sight of all the house of Israel, throughout all their journeys.

THE THIRD BOOK OF MOSES
CALLED

LEVITICUS

CHAPTER 1

AND the LORD called unto Moses, and spake unto him out of the tabernacle of the congregation, saying,

2 Speak unto the children of Israel, and say unto them, If any man of you bring an offering unto the LORD, ye shall bring your offering of the cattle, *even* of the herd, and of the flock.

3 If his offering *be* a burnt sacrifice of the herd, let him offer a male without blemish: he shall offer it of his own voluntary will at the door of the tabernacle of the congregation before the LORD.

4 And he shall put his hand upon the head of the burnt offering; and it shall be accepted for him to make atonement for him.

5 And he shall kill the bullock before the LORD: and the priests, Aaron's sons, shall bring the blood, and sprinkle the blood round about upon the altar that *is by* the door of the tabernacle of the congregation.

6 And he shall flay the burnt offering, and cut it into his pieces.

7 And the sons of Aaron the priest shall put fire upon the altar, and lay the wood in order upon the fire:

8 And the priests, Aaron's sons, shall lay the parts, the head, and the fat, in order upon the wood that *is* on the fire which *is* upon the altar:

9 But his inwards and his legs shall he wash in water: and the priest shall burn all on the altar, *to be* a burnt sacrifice, an offering made by fire, of a sweet savour unto the LORD.

10 ¶And if his offering *be* of the flocks, *namely*, of the sheep, or of the goats, for a burnt sacrifice; he shall bring it a male without blemish.

11 And he shall kill it on the side of the altar northward before the LORD: and the priests, Aaron's sons, shall sprinkle his blood round about upon the altar.

12 And he shall cut it into his pieces, with his head and his fat: and the priest shall lay them in order on the wood that *is* on the fire which *is* upon the altar:

13 But he shall wash the inwards and the legs with water: and the priest shall bring *it* all, and burn *it* upon the altar: it *is* a burnt sacrifice, an offering made by fire, of a sweet savour unto the LORD.

14 ¶And if the burnt sacrifice for his offering to the LORD *be* of fowls, then he shall bring his offering of turtledoves, or of young pigeons.

15 And the priest shall bring it unto the altar, and wring off his head, and burn *it* on the altar; and the blood thereof shall be wrung out at the side of the altar:

16 And he shall pluck away his crop with his feathers, and cast it beside the altar on the east part, by the place of the ashes:

17 And he shall cleave it with the wings thereof, *but* shall not divide *it* asunder: and the priest shall burn it upon the altar, upon the wood that *is* upon the fire: it *is* a burnt sacrifice, an offering made by fire, of a sweet savour unto the LORD.

CHAPTER 2

AND when any will offer a meat offering unto the LORD, his offering shall be *of* fine flour; and he shall pour oil upon it, and put frankincense thereon:

2 And he shall bring it to Aaron's sons the priests: and he shall take thereout his handful of the flour thereof, and of the oil thereof, with all the

frankincense thereof; and the priest shall burn the memorial of it upon the altar, *to be* an offering made by fire, of a sweet savour unto the LORD:

3 And the remnant of the meat offering *shall be* Aaron's and his sons': *it is* a thing most holy of the offerings of the LORD made by fire.

4 ¶And if thou bring an oblation of a meat offering baken in the oven, *it shall be* unleavened cakes of fine flour mingled with oil, or unleavened wafers anointed with oil.

5 ¶And if thy oblation *be* a meat offering *baken* in a pan, it shall be *of* fine flour unleavened, mingled with oil.

6 Thou shalt part it in pieces, and pour oil thereon: it *is* a meat offering.

7 ¶And if thy oblation *be* a meat offering *baken* in the fryingpan, it shall be made *of* fine flour with oil.

8 And thou shalt bring the meat offering that is made of these things unto the LORD: and when it is presented unto the priest, he shall bring it unto the altar.

9 And the priest shall take from the meat offering a memorial thereof, and shall burn *it* upon the altar: *it is* an offering made by fire, of a sweet savour unto the LORD.

10 And that which is left of the meat offering *shall be* Aaron's and his sons': *it is* a thing most holy of the offerings of the LORD made by fire.

11 No meat offering, which ye shall bring unto the LORD, shall be made with leaven: for ye shall burn no leaven, nor any honey, in any offering of the LORD made by fire.

12 ¶As for the oblation of the firstfruits, ye shall offer them unto the LORD: but they shall not be burnt on the altar for a sweet savour.

13 And every oblation of thy meat offering shalt thou season with salt; neither shalt thou suffer the salt of the covenant of thy God to be lacking from thy meat offering: with all thine offerings thou shalt offer salt.

14 And if thou offer a meat offering of thy firstfruits unto the LORD, thou shalt offer for the meat offering of thy firstfruits green ears of corn dried by the fire, *even* corn beaten out of full ears.

15 And thou shalt put oil upon it, and lay frankincense thereon: it *is* a meat offering.

16 And the priest shall burn the memorial of it, *part* of the beaten corn thereof, and *part* of the oil thereof, with all the frankincense thereof: *it is* an offering made by fire unto the LORD.

CHAPTER 3

AND if his oblation *be* a sacrifice of peace offering, if he offer *it* of the herd; whether *it be* a male or female, he shall offer it without blemish before the LORD.

2 And he shall lay his hand upon the head of his offering, and kill it *at* the door of the tabernacle of the congregation: and Aaron's sons the priests shall sprinkle the blood upon the altar round about.

3 And he shall offer of the sacrifice of the peace offering an offering made by fire unto the LORD; the fat that covereth the inwards, and all the fat that *is* upon the inwards,

4 And the two kidneys, and the fat that *is* on them, which *is* by the flanks, and the caul above the liver, with the kidneys, it shall he take away.

5 And Aaron's sons shall burn it on the altar upon the burnt sacrifice, which *is* upon the wood that *is* on the fire: *it is* an offering made by fire, of a sweet savour unto the LORD.

6 ¶And if his offering for a sacrifice of peace offering unto the LORD *be* of the flock; male or female, he shall offer it without blemish.

7 If he offer a lamb for his offering, then shall he offer it before the LORD.

8 And he shall lay his hand upon the head of his offering, and kill it before the tabernacle of the congregation: and Aaron's sons shall sprinkle the blood thereof round about upon the altar.

9 And he shall offer of the sacrifice of the peace offering an offering made by fire unto the LORD; the fat thereof, *and* the whole rump, it shall he take off hard by the backbone; and the fat that covereth the inwards, and all the fat that *is* upon the inwards,

10 And the two kidneys, and the fat that *is* upon them, which *is* by the flanks, and the caul above the liver, with the kidneys, it shall he take away.

11 And the priest shall burn it upon the altar: *it is* the food of the offering made by fire unto the LORD.

12 ¶And if his offering *be* a goat, then he shall offer it before the LORD.

13 And he shall lay his hand upon the head of it, and kill it before the tabernacle of the congregation: and the sons of Aaron shall sprinkle the blood thereof upon the altar round about.

14 And he shall offer thereof his offering, *even* an offering made by fire unto the LORD; the fat that covereth the inwards, and all the fat that *is* upon the inwards,

15 And the two kidneys, and the fat

that *is* upon them, which *is* by the flanks, and the caul above the liver, with the kidneys, it shall he take away.

16 And the priest shall burn them upon the altar: *it is* the food of the offering made by fire for a sweet savour: all the fat *is* the LORD's.

17 *It shall be* a perpetual statute for your generations throughout all your dwellings, that ye eat neither fat nor blood.

CHAPTER 4

AND the LORD spake unto Moses, saying,

2 Speak unto the children of Israel, saying, If a soul shall sin through ignorance against any of the commandments of the LORD *concerning things* which ought not to be done, and shall do against any of them:

3 If the priest that is anointed do sin according to the sin of the people; then let him bring for his sin, which he hath sinned, a young bullock without blemish unto the LORD for a sin offering.

4 And he shall bring the bullock unto the door of the tabernacle of the congregation before the LORD; and shall lay his hand upon the bullock's head, and kill the bullock before the LORD.

5 And the priest that is anointed shall take of the bullock's blood, and bring it to the tabernacle of the congregation:

6 And the priest shall dip his finger in the blood, and sprinkle of the blood seven times before the LORD, before the vail of the sanctuary.

7 And the priest shall put *some* of the blood upon the horns of the altar of sweet incense before the LORD, which *is* in the tabernacle of the congregation; and shall pour all the blood of the bullock at the bottom of the altar of the burnt offering, which *is at* the door of the tabernacle of the congregation.

8 And he shall take off from it all the fat of the bullock for the sin offering; the fat that covereth the inwards, and all the fat that *is* upon the inwards,

9 And the two kidneys, and the fat that *is* upon them, which *is* by the flanks, and the caul above the liver, with the kidneys, it shall he take away,

10 As it was taken off from the bullock of the sacrifice of peace offerings: and the priest shall burn them upon the altar of the burnt offering.

11 And the skin of the bullock, and all his flesh, with his head, and with his legs, and his inwards, and his dung,

12 Even the whole bullock shall he carry forth without the camp unto a clean place, where the ashes are poured out, and burn him on the wood with fire: where the ashes are poured out shall he be burnt.

13 ¶And if the whole congregation of Israel sin through ignorance, and the thing be hid from the eyes of the assembly, and they have done *somewhat against* any of the commandments of the LORD *concerning things* which should not be done, and are guilty;

14 When the sin, which they have sinned against it, is known, then the congregation shall offer a young bullock for the sin, and bring him before the tabernacle of the congregation.

15 And the elders of the congregation shall lay their hands upon the head of the bullock before the LORD: and the bullock shall be killed before the LORD.

16 And the priest that is anointed shall bring of the bullock's blood to the tabernacle of the congregation:

17 And the priest shall dip his finger *in some* of the blood, and sprinkle *it* seven times before the LORD, *even* before the vail.

18 And he shall put *some* of the blood upon the horns of the altar which *is* before the LORD, that *is* in the tabernacle of the congregation, and shall pour out all the blood at the bottom of the altar of the burnt offering, which *is at* the door of the tabernacle of the congregation.

19 And he shall take all his fat from him, and burn *it* upon the altar.

20 And he shall do with the bullock as he did with the bullock for a sin offering, so shall he do with this: and the priest shall make an atonement for them, and it shall be forgiven them.

21 And he shall carry forth the bullock without the camp, and burn him as he burned the first bullock: it *is* a sin offering for the congregation.

22 ¶When a ruler hath sinned, and done *somewhat* through ignorance *against* any of the commandments of the LORD his God *concerning things* which should not be done, and is guilty;

23 Or if his sin, wherein he hath sinned, come to his knowledge; he shall bring his offering, a kid of the goats, a male without blemish:

24 And he shall lay his hand upon the head of the goat, and kill it in the place where they kill the burnt offering before the LORD: it *is* a sin offering.

25 And the priest shall take of the blood of the sin offering with his finger, and put *it* upon the horns of the altar of burnt offering, and shall pour out his blood at the bottom of the altar of burnt offering.

26 And he shall burn all his fat upon

the altar, as the fat of the sacrifice of peace offerings: and the priest shall make an atonement for him as concerning his sin, and it shall be forgiven him.

27 ¶And if any one of the common people sin through ignorance, while he doeth *somewhat against* any of the commandments of the LORD *concerning things* which ought not to be done, and be guilty;

28 Or if his sin, which he hath sinned, come to his knowledge: then he shall bring his offering, a kid of the goats, a female without blemish, for his sin which he hath sinned.

29 And he shall lay his hand upon the head of the sin offering, and slay the sin offering in the place of the burnt offering.

30 And the priest shall take of the blood thereof with his finger, and put *it* upon the horns of the altar of burnt offering, and shall pour out all the blood thereof at the bottom of the altar.

31 And he shall take away all the fat thereof, as the fat is taken away from off the sacrifice of peace offerings; and the priest shall burn *it* upon the altar for a sweet savour unto the LORD; and the priest shall make an atonement for him, and it shall be forgiven him.

32 And if he bring a lamb for a sin offering, he shall bring it a female without blemish.

33 And he shall lay his hand upon the head of the sin offering, and slay it for a sin offering in the place where they kill the burnt offering.

34 And the priest shall take of the blood of the sin offering with his finger, and put *it* upon the horns of the altar of burnt offering, and shall pour out all the blood thereof at the bottom of the altar:

35 And he shall take away all the fat thereof, as the fat of the lamb is taken away from the sacrifice of the peace offerings; and the priest shall burn them upon the altar, according to the offerings made by fire unto the LORD: and the priest shall make an atonement for his sin that he hath committed, and it shall be forgiven him.

CHAPTER 5

AND if a soul sin, and hear the voice of swearing, and *is* a witness, whether he hath seen or known *of it;* if he do not utter *it*, then he shall bear his iniquity.

2 Or if a soul touch any unclean thing, whether *it be* a carcase of an unclean beast, or a carcase of unclean cattle, or the carcase of unclean creeping things, and *if* it be hidden from him; he also shall be unclean, and guilty.

3 Or if he touch the uncleanness of man, whatsoever uncleanness *it be* that a man shall be defiled withal, and it be hid from him; when he knoweth *of it*, then he shall be guilty.

4 Or if a soul swear, pronouncing with *his* lips to do evil, or to do good, whatsoever *it be* that a man shall pronounce with an oath, and it be hid from him; when he knoweth *of it*, then he shall be guilty in one of these.

5 And it shall be, when he shall be guilty in one of these *things*, that he shall confess that he hath sinned in that *thing:*

6 And he shall bring his trespass offering unto the LORD for his sin which he hath sinned, a female from the flock, a lamb or a kid of the goats, for a sin offering; and the priest shall make an atonement for him concerning his sin.

7 And if he be not able to bring a lamb, then he shall bring for his trespass, which he hath committed, two turtledoves, or two young pigeons, unto the LORD; one for a sin offering, and the other for a burnt offering.

8 And he shall bring them unto the priest, who shall offer *that* which *is* for the sin offering first, and wring off his head from his neck, but shall not divide *it* asunder:

9 And he shall sprinkle of the blood of the sin offering upon the side of the altar; and the rest of the blood shall be wrung out at the bottom of the altar: it *is* a sin offering.

10 And he shall offer the second *for* a burnt offering, according to the manner: and the priest shall make an atonement for him for his sin which he hath sinned, and it shall be forgiven him.

11 But if he be not able to bring two turtledoves, or two young pigeons, then he that sinned shall bring for his offering the tenth part of an ephah of fine flour for a sin offering; he shall put no oil upon it, neither shall he put *any* frankincense thereon: for it *is* a sin offering.

12 Then shall he bring it to the priest, and the priest shall take his handful of it, *even* a memorial thereof, and burn *it* on the altar, according to the offerings made by fire unto the LORD: it *is* a sin offering.

13 And the priest shall make an atonement for him as touching his sin that he hath sinned in one of these, and it shall be forgiven him: and *the remnant* shall be the priest's, as a meat offering.

14 ¶And the LORD spake unto Moses, saying,

15 If a soul commit a trespass, and sin through ignorance, in the holy things of the LORD; then he shall bring for his trespass unto the LORD a ram without blemish out of the flocks, with thy estimation by shekels of silver, after the shekel of the sanctuary, for a trespass offering:

16 And he shall make amends for the harm that he hath done in the holy thing, and shall add the fifth part thereto, and give it unto the priest: and the priest shall make an atonement for him with the ram of the trespass offering, and it shall be forgiven him.

17 ¶And if a soul sin, and commit any of these things which are forbidden to be done by the commandments of the LORD; though he wist *it* not, yet is he guilty, and shall bear his iniquity.

18 And he shall bring a ram without blemish out of the flock, with thy estimation, for a trespass offering, unto the priest: and the priest shall make an atonement for him concerning his ignorance wherein he erred and wist *it* not, and it shall be forgiven him.

19 It *is* a trespass offering: he hath certainly trespassed against the LORD.

CHAPTER 6

AND the LORD spake unto Moses, saying,

2 If a soul sin, and commit a trespass against the LORD, and lie unto his neighbour in that which was delivered him to keep, or in fellowship, or in a thing taken away by violence, or hath deceived his neighbour;

3 Or have found that which was lost, and lieth concerning it, and sweareth falsely; in any of all these that a man doeth, sinning therein:

4 Then it shall be, because he hath sinned, and is guilty, that he shall restore that which he took violently away, or the thing which he hath deceitfully gotten, or that which was delivered him to keep, or the lost thing which he found,

5 Or all that about which he hath sworn falsely; he shall even restore it in the principal, and shall add the fifth part more thereto, *and* give it unto him to whom it appertaineth, in the day of his trespass offering.

6 And he shall bring his trespass offering unto the LORD, a ram without blemish out of the flock, with thy estimation, for a trespass offering, unto the priest:

7 And the priest shall make an atonement for him before the LORD: and it shall be forgiven him for any thing of all that he hath done in trespassing therein.

8 ¶And the LORD spake unto Moses, saying,

9 Command Aaron and his sons, saying, This *is* the law of the burnt offering: It *is* the burnt offering, because of the burning upon the altar all night unto the morning, and the fire of the altar shall be burning in it.

10 And the priest shall put on his linen garment, and his linen breeches shall he put upon his flesh, and take up the ashes which the fire hath consumed with the burnt offering on the altar, and he shall put them beside the altar.

11 And he shall put off his garments, and put on other garments, and carry forth the ashes without the camp unto a clean place.

12 And the fire upon the altar shall be burning in it; it shall not be put out: and the priest shall burn wood on it every morning, and lay the burnt offering in order upon it; and he shall burn thereon the fat of the peace offerings.

13 The fire shall ever be burning upon the altar; it shall never go out.

14 ¶And this *is* the law of the meat offering: the sons of Aaron shall offer it before the LORD, before the altar.

15 And he shall take of it his handful, of the flour of the meat offering, and of the oil thereof, and all the frankincense which *is* upon the meat offering, and shall burn *it* upon the altar *for* a sweet savour, *even* the memorial of it, unto the LORD.

16 And the remainder thereof shall Aaron and his sons eat: with unleavened bread shall it be eaten in the holy place; in the court of the tabernacle of the congregation they shall eat it.

17 It shall not be baken with leaven. I have given it *unto them for* their portion of my offerings made by fire; it *is* most holy, as *is* the sin offering, and as the trespass offering.

18 All the males among the children of Aaron shall eat of it. *It shall be* a statute for ever in your generations concerning the offerings of the LORD made by fire: every one that toucheth them shall be holy.

19 ¶And the LORD spake unto Moses, saying,

20 This *is* the offering of Aaron and of his sons, which they shall offer unto the LORD in the day when he is anointed; the tenth part of an ephah of fine flour for a meat offering perpetual, half of it in the morning, and half thereof at night.

21 In a pan it shall be made with oil; *and when it is* baken, thou shalt bring it in: *and* the baken pieces of the meat offering shalt thou offer *for* a sweet savour unto the LORD.

22 And the priest of his sons that is anointed in his stead shall offer it: *it is* a statute for ever unto the LORD; it shall be wholly burnt.

23 For every meat offering for the priest shall be wholly burnt: it shall not be eaten.

24 ¶And the LORD spake unto Moses, saying,

25 Speak unto Aaron and to his sons, saying, This *is* the law of the sin offering: In the place where the burnt offering is killed shall the sin offering be killed before the LORD: it *is* most holy.

26 The priest that offereth it for sin shall eat it: in the holy place shall it be eaten, in the court of the tabernacle of the congregation.

27 Whatsoever shall touch the flesh thereof shall be holy: and when there is sprinkled of the blood thereof upon any garment, thou shalt wash that whereon it was sprinkled in the holy place.

28 But the earthen vessel wherein it is sodden shall be broken: and if it be sodden in a brasen pot, it shall be both scoured, and rinsed in water.

29 All the males among the priests shall eat thereof: it *is* most holy.

30 And no sin offering, whereof *any* of the blood is brought into the tabernacle of the congregation to reconcile *withal* in the holy *place*, shall be eaten: it shall be burnt in the fire.

CHAPTER 7

LIKEWISE this *is* the law of the trespass offering: it *is* most holy.

2 In the place where they kill the burnt offering shall they kill the trespass offering: and the blood thereof shall he sprinkle round about upon the altar.

3 And he shall offer of it all the fat thereof; the rump, and the fat that covereth the inwards,

4 And the two kidneys, and the fat that *is* on them, which *is* by the flanks, and the caul *that is* above the liver, with the kidneys, it shall he take away:

5 And the priest shall burn them upon the altar *for* an offering made by fire unto the LORD: it *is* a trespass offering.

6 Every male among the priests shall eat thereof: it shall be eaten in the holy place: it *is* most holy.

7 As the sin offering *is*, so *is* the trespass offering: *there is* one law for them: the priest that maketh atonement therewith shall have *it*.

8 And the priest that offereth any man's burnt offering, *even* the priest shall have to himself the skin of the burnt offering which he hath offered.

9 And all the meat offering that is baken in the oven, and all that is dressed in the fryingpan, and in the pan, shall be the priest's that offereth it.

10 And every meat offering, mingled with oil, and dry, shall all the sons of Aaron have, one *as much* as another.

11 ¶And this *is* the law of the sacrifice of peace offerings, which he shall offer unto the LORD.

12 If he offer it for a thanksgiving, then he shall offer with the sacrifice of thanksgiving unleavened cakes mingled with oil, and unleavened wafers anointed with oil, and cakes mingled with oil, of fine flour, fried.

13 Besides the cakes, he shall offer *for* his offering leavened bread with the sacrifice of thanksgiving of his peace offerings.

14 And of it he shall offer one out of the whole oblation *for* an heave offering unto the LORD, *and* it shall be the priest's that sprinkleth the blood of the peace offerings.

15 And the flesh of the sacrifice of his peace offerings for thanksgiving shall be eaten the same day that it is offered; he shall not leave any of it until the morning.

16 But if the sacrifice of his offering *be* a vow, or a voluntary offering, it shall be eaten the same day that he offereth his sacrifice: and on the morrow also the remainder of it shall be eaten:

17 But the remainder of the flesh of the sacrifice on the third day shall be burnt with fire.

18 And if *any* of the flesh of the sacrifice of his peace offerings be eaten at all on the third day, it shall not be accepted, neither shall it be imputed unto him that offereth it: it shall be an abomination, and the soul that eateth of it shall bear his iniquity.

19 And the flesh that toucheth any unclean *thing* shall not be eaten; it shall be burnt with fire: and as for the flesh, all that be clean shall eat thereof.

20 But the soul that eateth *of* the flesh of the sacrifice of peace offerings, that *pertain* unto the LORD, having his uncleanness upon him, even that soul shall be cut off from his people.

21 Moreover the soul that shall touch any unclean *thing*, *as* the uncleanness of man, or *any* unclean beast, or any abominable unclean *thing*, and eat of the flesh of the sacrifice of peace offerings, which *pertain* unto the LORD, even

that soul shall be cut off from his people.

22 ¶And the LORD spake unto Moses, saying,

23 Speak unto the children of Israel, saying, Ye shall eat no manner of fat, of ox, or of sheep, or of goat.

24 And the fat of the beast that dieth of itself, and the fat of that which is torn with beasts, may be used in any other use: but ye shall in no wise eat of it.

25 For whosoever eateth the fat of the beast, of which men offer an offering made by fire unto the LORD, even the soul that eateth *it* shall be cut off from his people.

26 Moreover ye shall eat no manner of blood, *whether it be* of fowl or of beast, in any of your dwellings.

27 Whatsoever soul *it be* that eateth any manner of blood, even that soul shall be cut off from his people.

28 ¶And the LORD spake unto Moses, saying,

29 Speak unto the children of Israel, saying, He that offereth the sacrifice of his peace offerings unto the LORD shall bring his oblation unto the LORD of the sacrifice of his peace offerings.

30 His own hands shall bring the offerings of the LORD made by fire, the fat with the breast, it shall he bring, that the breast may be waved *for* a wave offering before the LORD.

31 And the priest shall burn the fat upon the altar: but the breast shall be Aaron's and his sons'.

32 And the right shoulder shall ye give unto the priest *for* an heave offering of the sacrifices of your peace offerings.

33 He among the sons of Aaron, that offereth the blood of the peace offerings, and the fat, shall have the right shoulder for *his* part.

34 For the wave breast and the heave shoulder have I taken of the children of Israel from off the sacrifices of their peace offerings, and have given them unto Aaron the priest and unto his sons by a statute for ever from among the children of Israel.

35 ¶This *is the portion* of the anointing of Aaron, and of the anointing of his sons, out of the offerings of the LORD made by fire, in the day *when* he presented them to minister unto the LORD in the priest's office;

36 Which the LORD commanded to be given them of the children of Israel, in the day that he anointed them, *by* a statute for ever throughout their generations.

37 This *is* the law of the burnt offering, of the meat offering, and of the sin offering, and of the trespass offering, and of the consecrations, and of the sacrifice of the peace offerings;

38 Which the LORD commanded Moses in mount Sī′naī, in the day that he commanded the children of Israel to offer their oblations unto the LORD, in the wilderness of Sī′naī.

CHAPTER 8

AND the LORD spake unto Moses, saying,

2 Take Aaron and his sons with him, and the garments, and the anointing oil, and a bullock for the sin offering, and two rams, and a basket of unleavened bread;

3 And gather thou all the congregation together unto the door of the tabernacle of the congregation.

4 And Moses did as the LORD commanded him; and the assembly was gathered together unto the door of the tabernacle of the congregation.

5 And Moses said unto the congregation, This *is* the thing which the LORD commanded to be done.

6 And Moses brought Aaron and his sons, and washed them with water.

7 And he put upon him the coat, and girded him with the girdle, and clothed him with the robe, and put the ephod upon him, and he girded him with the curious girdle of the ephod, and bound *it* unto him therewith.

8 And he put the breastplate upon him: also he put in the breastplate the Ū′rĭm and the Thŭm′mĭm.

9 And he put the mitre upon his head; also upon the mitre, *even* upon his forefront, did he put the golden plate, the holy crown; as the LORD commanded Moses.

10 And Moses took the anointing oil, and anointed the tabernacle and all that *was* therein, and sanctified them.

11 And he sprinkled thereof upon the altar seven times, and anointed the altar and all his vessels, both the laver and his foot, to sanctify them.

12 And he poured of the anointing oil upon Aaron's head, and anointed him, to sanctify him.

13 And Moses brought Aaron's sons, and put coats upon them, and girded them with girdles, and put bonnets upon them; as the LORD commanded Moses.

14 ¶And he brought the bullock for the sin offering: and Aaron and his sons laid their hands upon the head of the bullock for the sin offering.

15 And he slew *it;* and Moses took the blood, and put *it* upon the horns of the

altar round about with his finger, and purified the altar, and poured the blood at the bottom of the altar, and sanctified it, to make reconciliation upon it.

16 And he took all the fat that *was* upon the inwards, and the caul *above* the liver, and the two kidneys, and their fat, and Moses burned *it* upon the altar.

17 But the bullock, and his hide, his flesh, and his dung, he burnt with fire without the camp as the LORD commanded Moses.

18 ¶And he brought the ram for the burnt offering: and Aaron and his sons laid their hands upon the head of the ram.

19 And he killed *it;* and Moses sprinkled the blood upon the altar round about.

20 And he cut the ram into pieces; and Moses burnt the head, and the pieces, and the fat.

21 And he washed the inwards and the legs in water; and Moses burnt the whole ram upon the altar: it *was* a burnt sacrifice for a sweet savour, *and* an offering made by fire unto the LORD; as the LORD commanded Moses.

22 ¶And he brought the other ram, the ram of consecration: and Aaron and his sons laid their hands upon the head of the ram.

23 And he slew *it;* and Moses took of the blood of it, and put *it* upon the tip of Aaron's right ear, and upon the thumb of his right hand, and upon the great toe of his right foot.

24 And he brought Aaron's sons, and Moses put of the blood upon the tip of their right ear, and upon the thumbs of their right hands, and upon the great toes of their right feet: and Moses sprinkled the blood upon the altar round about.

25 And he took the fat, and the rump, and all the fat that *was* upon the inwards, and the caul *above* the liver, and the two kidneys, and their fat, and the right shoulder:

26 And out of the basket of unleavened bread, that *was* before the LORD, he took one unleavened cake, and a cake of oiled bread, and one wafer, and put *them* on the fat, and upon the right shoulder:

27 And he put all upon Aaron's hands, and upon his sons' hands, and waved them *for* a wave offering before the LORD.

28 And Moses took them from off their hands, and burnt *them* on the altar upon the burnt offering: they *were* consecrations for a sweet savour: it *is* an offering made by fire unto the LORD.

29 And Moses took the breast, and waved it *for* a wave offering before the LORD: *for* of the ram of consecration it was Moses' part; as the LORD commanded Moses.

30 And Moses took of the anointing oil, and of the blood which *was* upon the altar, and sprinkled *it* upon Aaron, *and* upon his garments, and upon his sons, and upon his sons' garments with him; and sanctified Aaron, *and* his garments, and his sons, and his sons' garments with him.

31 ¶And Moses said unto Aaron and to his sons, Boil the flesh *at* the door of the tabernacle of the congregation: and there eat it with the bread that *is* in the basket of consecrations, as I commanded, saying, Aaron and his sons shall eat it.

32 And that which remaineth of the flesh and of the bread shall ye burn with fire.

33 And ye shall not go out of the door of the tabernacle of the congregation *in* seven days, until the days of your consecration be at an end: for seven days shall he consecrate you.

34 As he hath done this day, *so* the LORD hath commanded to do, to make an atonement for you.

35 Therefore shall ye abide *at* the door of the tabernacle of the congregation day and night seven days, and keep the charge of the LORD, that ye die not: for so I am commanded.

36 So Aaron and his sons did all things which the LORD commanded by the hand of Moses.

CHAPTER 9

AND it came to pass on the eighth day, *that* Moses called Aaron and his sons, and the elders of Israel;

2 And he said unto Aaron, Take thee a young calf for a sin offering, and a ram for a burnt offering, without blemish, and offer *them* before the LORD.

3 And unto the children of Israel thou shalt speak, saying, Take ye a kid of the goats for a sin offering; and a calf and a lamb, *both* of the first year, without blemish, for a burnt offering;

4 Also a bullock and a ram for peace offerings, to sacrifice before the LORD; and a meat offering mingled with oil: for to day the LORD will appear unto you.

5 ¶And they brought *that* which Moses commanded before the tabernacle of the congregation: and all the congregation drew near and stood before the LORD.

6 And Moses said, This *is* the thing which the LORD commanded that ye

should do: and the glory of the LORD
shall appear unto you.
7 And Moses said unto Aaron, Go
unto the altar, and offer thy sin offering,
and thy burnt offering, and make
an atonement for thyself, and for the
people: and offer the offering of the
people, and make an atonement for
them; as the LORD commanded.
8 ¶Aaron therefore went unto the altar,
and slew the calf of the sin offering,
which *was* for himself.
9 And the sons of Aaron brought the
blood unto him: and he dipped his finger
in the blood, and put *it* upon the
horns of the altar, and poured out the
blood at the bottom of the altar:
10 But the fat, and the kidneys, and
the caul above the liver of the sin offering,
he burnt upon the altar; as the
LORD commanded Moses.
11 And the flesh and the hide he
burnt with fire without the camp.
12 And he slew the burnt offering;
and Aaron's sons presented unto him
the blood, which he sprinkled round
about upon the altar.
13 And they presented the burnt offering
unto him, with the pieces thereof,
and the head: and he burnt *them*
upon the altar.
14 And he did wash the inwards and
the legs, and burnt *them* upon the burnt
offering on the altar.
15 ¶And he brought the people's offering,
and took the goat, which *was*
the sin offering for the people, and slew
it, and offered it for sin, as the first.
16 And he brought the burnt offering,
and offered it according to the manner.
17 And he brought the meat offering,
and took an handful thereof, and burnt
it upon the altar, beside the burnt sacrifice
of the morning.
18 He slew also the bullock and the
ram *for* a sacrifice of peace offerings,
which *was* for the people: and Aaron's
sons presented unto him the blood,
which he sprinkled upon the altar
round about,
19 And the fat of the bullock and of
the ram, the rump, and that which covereth
the inwards, and the kidneys, and
the caul *above* the liver:
20 And they put the fat upon the
breasts, and he burnt the fat upon the
altar:
21 And the breasts and the right
shoulder Aaron waved *for* a wave offering
before the LORD; as Moses commanded.
22 And Aaron lifted up his hand toward
the people, and blessed them, and
came down from offering of the sin offering,
and the burnt offering, and
peace offerings.
23 And Moses and Aaron went into
the tabernacle of the congregation, and
came out, and blessed the people: and
the glory of the LORD appeared unto all
the people.
24 And there came a fire out from before
the LORD, and consumed upon the
altar the burnt offering and the fat:
which when all the people saw, they
shouted, and fell on their faces.

CHAPTER 10

AND Nādăb and A-bī'hū, the sons of
Aaron, took either of them his censer,
and put fire therein, and put incense
thereon, and offered strange fire before
the LORD, which he commanded them
not.
2 And there went out fire from the
LORD, and devoured them, and they
died before the LORD.
3 Then Moses said unto Aaron, This
is it that the LORD spake, saying, I will
be sanctified in them that come nigh
me, and before all the people I will be
glorified. And Aaron held his peace.
4 And Moses called Mĭsh'a-el and
Ĕl'zā-phăn, the sons of Ŭz'zĭ-el the uncle
of Aaron, and said unto them, Come
near, carry your brethren from before
the sanctuary out of the camp.
5 So they went near, and carried
them in their coats out of the camp; as
Moses had said.
6 And Moses said unto Aaron, and
unto Ĕ-le-ā'zar and unto Ĭth'a-mär, his
sons, Uncover not your heads, neither
rend your clothes; lest ye die, and lest
wrath come upon all the people: but let
your brethren, the whole house of
Israel, bewail the burning which the
LORD hath kindled.
7 And ye shall not go out from the
door of the tabernacle of the congregation,
lest ye die: for the anointing oil of
the LORD *is* upon you. And they did according
to the word of Moses.
8 ¶And the LORD spake unto Aaron,
saying,
9 Do not drink wine nor strong drink,
thou, nor thy sons with thee, when ye
go into the tabernacle of the congregation,
lest ye die: *it shall be* a statute for
ever throughout your generations:
10 And that ye may put difference
between holy and unholy, and between
unclean and clean;
11 And that ye may teach the children
of Israel all the statutes which the
LORD hath spoken unto them by the
hand of Moses.
12 ¶And Moses spake unto Aaron,
and unto Ĕ-le-ā'zar and unto Ĭth'a-mär,

his sons that were left, Take the meat offering that remaineth of the offerings of the LORD made by fire, and eat it without leaven beside the altar: for it *is* most holy:

13 And ye shall eat it in the holy place, because it *is* thy due, and thy sons' due, of the sacrifices of the LORD made by fire: for so I am commanded.

14 And the wave breast and heave shoulder shall ye eat in a clean place; thou, and thy sons, and thy daughters with thee: for *they be* thy due, and thy sons' due, *which* are given out of the sacrifices of peace offerings of the children of Israel.

15 The heave shoulder and the wave breast shall they bring with the offerings made by fire of the fat, to wave *it for* a wave offering before the LORD; and it shall be thine, and thy sons' with thee, by a statute for ever; as the LORD hath commanded.

16 ¶And Moses diligently sought the goat of the sin offering, and, behold, it was burnt: and he was angry with Ĕ-le-ā'zar and Ĭth'a-mär, the sons of Aaron *which were* left *alive*, saying,

17 Wherefore have ye not eaten the sin offering in the holy place, seeing it *is* most holy, and *God* hath given it you to bear the iniquity of the congregation, to make atonement for them before the LORD?

18 Behold, the blood of it was not brought in within the holy *place*: ye should indeed have eaten it in the holy *place*, as I commanded.

19 And Aaron said unto Moses, Behold, this day have they offered their sin offering and their burnt offering before the LORD; and such things have befallen me: and *if* I had eaten the sin offering to day, should it have been accepted in the sight of the LORD?

20 And when Moses heard *that*, he was content.

CHAPTER 11

AND the LORD spake unto Moses and to Aaron, saying unto them,

2 Speak unto the children of Israel, saying, These *are* the beasts which ye shall eat among all the beasts that *are* on the earth.

3 Whatsoever parteth the hoof, and is clovenfooted, *and* cheweth the cud, among the beasts, that shall ye eat.

4 Nevertheless these shall ye not eat of them that chew the cud, or of them that divide the hoof: *as* the camel, because he cheweth the cud, but divideth not the hoof; he *is* unclean unto you.

5 And the coney, because he cheweth the cud, but divideth not the hoof; he *is* unclean unto you.

6 And the hare, because he cheweth the cud, but divideth not the hoof; he *is* unclean unto you.

7 And the swine, though he divide the hoof, and be clovenfooted, yet he cheweth not the cud; he *is* unclean to you.

8 Of their flesh shall ye not eat, and their carcase shall ye not touch; they *are* unclean to you.

9 ¶These shall ye eat of all that *are* in the waters: whatsoever hath fins and scales in the waters, in the seas, and in the rivers, them shall ye eat.

10 And all that have not fins and scales in the seas, and in the rivers, of all that move in the waters, and of any living thing which *is* in the waters, they *shall be* an abomination unto you:

11 They shall be even an abomination unto you; ye shall not eat of their flesh, but ye shall have their carcases in abomination.

12 Whatsoever hath no fins nor scales in the waters, that *shall be* an abomination unto you.

13 ¶And these *are they which* ye shall have in abomination among the fowls; they shall not be eaten, they *are* an abomination: the eagle, and the ossifrage, and the ospray,

14 And the vulture, and the kite after his kind;

15 Every raven after his kind;

16 And the owl, and the night hawk, and the cuckow, and the hawk after his kind,

17 And the little owl, and the cormorant, and the great owl,

18 And the swan, and the pelican, and the gier eagle,

19 And the stork, the heron after her kind, and the lapwing, and the bat.

20 All fowls that creep, going upon *all* four, *shall be* an abomination unto you.

21 Yet these may ye eat of every flying creeping thing that goeth upon *all* four, which have legs above their feet, to leap withal upon the earth;

22 *Even* these of them ye may eat; the locust after his kind, and the bald locust after his kind, and the beetle after his kind, and the grasshopper after his kind.

23 But all *other* flying creeping things, which have four feet, *shall be* an abomination unto you.

24 And for these ye shall be unclean: whosoever toucheth the carcase of them shall be unclean until the even.

25 And whosoever beareth *ought* of the carcase of them shall wash his clothes, and be unclean until the even.

26 *The carcases* of every beast which divideth the hoof, and *is* not clovenfooted, nor cheweth the cud, *are* unclean unto you: every one that toucheth them shall be unclean.
27 And whatsoever goeth upon his paws, among all manner of beasts that go on *all* four, those *are* unclean unto you: whoso toucheth their carcase shall be unclean until the even.
28 And he that beareth the carcase of them shall wash his clothes, and be unclean until the even: they *are* unclean unto you.
29 ¶These also *shall be* unclean unto you among the creeping things that creep upon the earth; the weasel, and the mouse, and the tortoise after his kind,
30 And the ferret, and the chameleon, and the lizard, and the snail, and the mole.
31 These *are* unclean to you among all that creep: whosoever doth touch them, when they be dead, shall be unclean until the even.
32 And upon whatsoever *any* of them, when they are dead, doth fall, it shall be unclean; whether *it be* any vessel of wood, or raiment, or skin, or sack, whatsoever vessel *it be*, wherein *any* work is done, it must be put into water, and it shall be unclean until the even; so it shall be cleansed.
33 And every earthen vessel, whereinto *any* of them falleth, whatsoever *is* in it shall be unclean; and ye shall break it.
34 Of all meat which may be eaten, *that* on which *such* water cometh shall be unclean: and all drink that may be drunk in every *such* vessel shall be unclean.
35 And every *thing* whereupon *any part* of their carcase falleth shall be unclean; *whether it be* oven, or ranges for pots, they shall be broken down: *for* they *are* unclean, and shall be unclean unto you.
36 Nevertheless a fountain or pit, *wherein there is* plenty of water, shall be clean: but that which toucheth their carcase shall be unclean.
37 And if *any part* of their carcase fall upon any sowing seed which is to be sown, it *shall be* clean.
38 But if *any* water be put upon the seed, and *any part* of their carcase fall thereon, it *shall be* unclean unto you.
39 And if any beast, of which ye may eat, die; he that toucheth the carcase thereof shall be unclean until the even.
40 And he that eateth of the carcase of it shall wash his clothes, and be unclean until the even: he also that beareth the carcase of it shall wash his clothes, and be unclean until the even.
41 And every creeping thing that creepeth upon the earth *shall be* an abomination; it shall not be eaten.
42 Whatsoever goeth upon the belly, and whatsoever goeth upon *all* four, or whatsoever hath more feet among all creeping things that creep upon the earth, them ye shall not eat; for they *are* an abomination.
43 Ye shall not make yourselves abominable with any creeping thing that creepeth, neither shall ye make yourselves unclean with them, that ye should be defiled thereby.
44 For I *am* the LORD your God: ye shall therefore sanctify yourselves, and ye shall be holy; for I *am* holy: neither shall ye defile yourselves with any manner of creeping thing that creepeth upon the earth.
45 For I *am* the LORD that bringeth you up out of the land of Egypt, to be your God: ye shall therefore be holy, for I *am* holy.
46 This *is* the law of the beasts, and of the fowl, and of every living creature that moveth in the waters, and of every creature that creepeth upon the earth:
47 To make a difference between the unclean and the clean, and between the beast that may be eaten and the beast that may not be eaten.

CHAPTER 12

AND the LORD spake unto Moses, saying,
2 Speak unto the children of Israel, saying, If a woman have conceived seed, and born a man child: then she shall be unclean seven days; according to the days of the separation for her infirmity shall she be unclean.
3 And in the eighth day the flesh of his foreskin shall be circumcised.
4 And she shall then continue in the blood of her purifying three and thirty days; she shall touch no hallowed thing, nor come into the sanctuary, until the days of her purifying be fulfilled.
5 But if she bear a maid child, then she shall be unclean two weeks, as in her separation: and she shall continue in the blood of her purifying threescore and six days.
6 And when the days of her purifying are fulfilled, for a son, or for a daughter, she shall bring a lamb of the first year for a burnt offering, and a young pigeon, or a turtledove, for a sin offering, unto the door of the tabernacle of the congregation, unto the priest:
7 Who shall offer it before the LORD, and make an atonement for her; and

she shall be cleansed from the issue of
her blood. This *is* the law for her that
hath born a male or a female.
8 And if she be not able to bring a
lamb, then she shall bring two turtles,
or two young pigeons; the one for the
burnt offering, and the other for a sin
offering: and the priest shall make an
atonement for her, and she shall be
clean.

CHAPTER 13

AND the LORD spake unto Moses and
Aaron, saying,
2 When a man shall have in the skin
of his flesh a rising, a scab, or bright
spot, and it be in the skin of his flesh
like the plague of leprosy; then he shall
be brought unto Aaron the priest, or
unto one of his sons the priests:
3 And the priest shall look on the
plague in the skin of the flesh: and
when the hair in the plague is turned
white, and the plague in sight *be* deeper
than the skin of his flesh, it *is* a plague
of leprosy: and the priest shall look on
him, and pronounce him unclean.
4 If the bright spot *be* white in the
skin of his flesh, and in sight *be* not deep-
er than the skin, and the hair thereof
be not turned white; then the priest
shall shut up *him that hath* the plague
seven days:
5 And the priest shall look on him the
seventh day: and, behold, *if* the plague
in his sight be at a stay, *and* the plague
spread not in the skin; then the priest
shall shut him up seven days more:
6 And the priest shall look on him
again the seventh day: and, behold, *if*
the plague *be* somewhat dark, *and* the
plague spread not in the skin, the priest
shall pronounce him clean: it *is but* a
scab: and he shall wash his clothes, and
be clean.
7 But if the scab spread much abroad
in the skin, after that he hath been seen
of the priest for his cleansing, he shall
be seen of the priest again:
8 And *if* the priest see that, behold,
the scab spreadeth in the skin, then the
priest shall pronounce him unclean: it
is a leprosy.
9 ¶When the plague of leprosy is in a
man, then he shall be brought unto the
priest;
10 And the priest shall see *him*: and,
behold, *if* the rising *be* white in the skin,
and it have turned the hair white, and
there be quick raw flesh in the rising;
11 It *is* an old leprosy in the skin of his
flesh, and the priest shall pronounce
him unclean, and shall not shut him up:
for he *is* unclean.
12 And if a leprosy break out abroad
in the skin, and the leprosy cover all the
skin of *him that hath* the plague from
his head even to his foot, wheresoever
the priest looketh;
13 Then the priest shall consider:
and, behold, *if* the leprosy have
covered all his flesh, he shall pro-
nounce *him* clean *that hath* the plague:
it is all turned white: he *is* clean.
14 But when raw flesh appeareth in
him, he shall be unclean.
15 And the priest shall see the raw
flesh, and pronounce him to be un-
clean: *for* the raw flesh *is* unclean: it *is* a
leprosy.
16 Or if the raw flesh turn again, and
be changed unto white, he shall come
unto the priest;
17 And the priest shall see him: and,
behold, *if* the plague be turned into
white; then the priest shall pronounce
him clean *that hath* the plague: he *is*
clean.
18 ¶The flesh also, in which, *even* in
the skin thereof, was a boil, and is
healed,
19 And in the place of the boil there
be a white rising, or a bright spot,
white, and somewhat reddish, and it be
shewed to the priest;
20 And if, when the priest seeth it, be-
hold, it *be* in sight lower than the skin,
and the hair thereof be turned white;
the priest shall pronounce him unclean:
it *is* a plague of leprosy broken out of
the boil.
21 But if the priest look on it, and, be-
hold, *there be* no white hairs therein,
and *if* it *be* not lower than the skin, but
be somewhat dark; then the priest shall
shut him up seven days:
22 And if it spread much abroad in
the skin, then the priest shall pro-
nounce him unclean: it *is* a plague.
23 But if the bright spot stay in his
place, *and* spread not, it *is* a burning
boil; and the priest shall pronounce him
clean.
24 ¶Or if there be *any* flesh, in the
skin whereof *there is* a hot burning, and
the quick *flesh* that burneth have a
white bright spot, somewhat reddish,
or white;
25 Then the priest shall look upon it:
and, behold, *if* the hair in the bright
spot be turned white, and it *be in* sight
deeper than the skin; it *is* a leprosy
broken out of the burning: wherefore
the priest shall pronounce him unclean:
it *is* the plague of leprosy.
26 But if the priest look on it, and, be-
hold, *there be* no white hair in the
bright spot, and it *be* no lower than the
other skin, but *be* somewhat dark; then
the priest shall shut him up seven days:

27 And the priest shall look upon him the seventh day: *and* if it be spread much abroad in the skin, then the priest shall pronounce him unclean: it *is* the plague of leprosy.
28 And if the bright spot stay in his place, *and* spread not in the skin, but it *be* somewhat dark; it *is* a rising of the burning, and the priest shall pronounce him clean: for it *is* an inflammation of the burning.
29 ¶If a man or woman have a plague upon the head or the beard;
30 Then the priest shall see the plague: and, behold, if it *be* in sight deeper than the skin; *and there be* in it a yellow thin hair; then the priest shall pronounce him unclean: it *is* a dry scall, *even* a leprosy upon the head or beard.
31 And if the priest look on the plague of the scall, and, behold, it *be* not in sight deeper than the skin, and *that there is* no black hair in it; then the priest shall shut up *him that hath* the plague of the scall seven days:
32 And in the seventh day the priest shall look on the plague: and, behold, *if* the scall spread not, and there be in it no yellow hair, and the scall *be* not in sight deeper than the skin;
33 He shall be shaven, but the scall shall he not shave; and the priest shall shut up *him that hath* the scall seven days more:
34 And in the seventh day the priest shall look on the scall: and, behold, *if* the scall be not spread in the skin, nor *be* in sight deeper than the skin; then the priest shall pronounce him clean: and he shall wash his clothes, and be clean.
35 But if the scall spread much in the skin after his cleansing;
36 Then the priest shall look on him: and, behold, if the scall be spread in the skin, the priest shall not seek for yellow hair; he *is* unclean.
37 But if the scall be in his sight at a stay, and *that* there is black hair grown up therein; the scall is healed, he *is* clean: and the priest shall pronounce him clean.
38 ¶If a man also or a woman have in the skin of their flesh bright spots, *even* white bright spots;
39 Then the priest shall look: and, behold, *if* the bright spots in the skin of their flesh *be* darkish white; it *is* a freckled spot *that* groweth in the skin; he *is* clean.
40 And the man whose hair is fallen off his head, he *is* bald; *yet is* he clean.
41 And he that hath his hair fallen off from the part of his head toward his face, he *is* forehead bald: *yet is* he clean.
42 And if there be in the bald head, or bald forehead, a white reddish sore; it *is* a leprosy sprung up in his bald head, or his bald forehead.
43 Then the priest shall look upon it: and, behold, *if* the rising of the sore *be* white reddish in his bald head, or in his bald forehead, as the leprosy appeareth in the skin of the flesh;
44 He is a leprous man, he *is* unclean: the priest shall pronounce him utterly unclean; his plague *is* in his head.
45 And the leper in whom the plague *is*, his clothes shall be rent, and his head bare, and he shall put a covering upon his upper lip, and shall cry, Unclean, unclean.
46 All the days wherein the plague *shall be* in him he shall be defiled; he *is* unclean: he shall dwell alone; without the camp *shall* his habitation *be*.
47 ¶The garment also that the plague of leprosy is in, *whether it be* a woollen garment, or a linen garment;
48 Whether *it be* in the warp, or woof; of linen, or of woollen; whether in a skin, or in any thing made of skin;
49 And if the plague be greenish or reddish in the garment, or in the skin, either in the warp, or in the woof, or in any thing of skin; it *is* a plague of leprosy, and shall be shewed unto the priest:
50 And the priest shall look upon the plague, and shut up *it that hath* the plague seven days:
51 And he shall look on the plague on the seventh day: if the plague be spread in the garment, either in the warp, or in the woof, or in a skin, *or* in any work that is made of skin; the plague *is* a fretting leprosy; it *is* unclean.
52 He shall therefore burn that garment, whether warp or woof, in woollen or in linen, or any thing of skin, wherein the plague is: for it *is* a fretting leprosy; it shall be burnt in the fire.
53 And if the priest shall look, and, behold, the plague be not spread in the garment, either in the warp, or in the woof, or in any thing of skin;
54 Then the priest shall command that they wash *the thing* wherein the plague *is*, and he shall shut it up seven days more:
55 And the priest shall look on the plague, after that it is washed: and, behold, *if* the plague have not changed his colour, and the plague be not spread; it *is* unclean; thou shalt burn it in the fire; it *is* fret inward, *whether* it *be* bare within or without.
56 And if the priest look, and, behold,

the plague *be* somewhat dark after the washing of it; then he shall rend it out of the garment, or out of the skin, or out of the warp, or out of the woof:

57 And if it appear still in the garment, either in the warp, or in the woof, or in any thing of skin; it *is* a spreading *plague:* thou shalt burn that wherein the plague *is* with fire.

58 And the garment, either warp, or woof, or whatsoever thing of skin *it be,* which thou shalt wash, if the plague be departed from them, then it shall be washed the second time, and shall be clean.

59 This *is* the law of the plague of leprosy in a garment of woollen or linen, either in the warp, or woof, or any thing of skins, to pronounce it clean, or to pronounce it unclean.

CHAPTER 14

AND the LORD spake unto Moses, saying,

2 This shall be the law of the leper in the day of his cleansing: He shall be brought unto the priest:

3 And the priest shall go forth out of the camp; and the priest shall look, and, behold, *if* the plague of leprosy be healed in the leper;

4 Then shall the priest command to take for him that is to be cleansed two birds alive *and* clean, and cedar wood, and scarlet, and hyssop:

5 And the priest shall command that one of the birds be killed in an earthen vessel over running water:

6 As for the living bird, he shall take it, and the cedar wood, and the scarlet, and the hyssop, and shall dip them and the living bird in the blood of the bird *that was* killed over the running water:

7 And he shall sprinkle upon him that is to be cleansed from the leprosy seven times, and shall pronounce him clean, and shall let the living bird loose into the open field.

8 And he that is to be cleansed shall wash his clothes, and shave off all his hair, and wash himself in water, that he may be clean: and after that he shall come into the camp, and shall tarry abroad out of his tent seven days.

9 But it shall be on the seventh day, that he shall shave all his hair off his head and his beard and his eyebrows, even all his hair he shall shave off: and he shall wash his clothes, also he shall wash his flesh in water, and he shall be clean.

10 And on the eighth day he shall take two he lambs without blemish, and one ewe lamb of the first year without blemish, and three tenth deals of fine flour *for* a meat offering, mingled with oil, and one log of oil.

11 And the priest that maketh *him* clean shall present the man that is to be made clean, and those things, before the LORD, *at* the door of the tabernacle of the congregation:

12 And the priest shall take one he lamb, and offer him for a trespass offering, and the log of oil, and wave them *for* a wave offering before the LORD:

13 And he shall slay the lamb in the place where he shall kill the sin offering and the burnt offering, in the holy place: for as the sin offering *is* the priest's, *so is* the trespass offering: it *is* most holy:

14 And the priest shall take *some* of the blood of the trespass offering, and the priest shall put *it* upon the tip of the right ear of him that is to be cleansed, and upon the thumb of his right hand, and upon the great toe of his right foot:

15 And the priest shall take *some* of the log of oil, and pour *it* into the palm of his own left hand:

16 And the priest shall dip his right finger in the oil that *is* in his left hand, and shall sprinkle of the oil with his finger seven times before the LORD:

17 And of the rest of the oil that *is* in his hand shall the priest put upon the tip of the right ear of him that is to be cleansed, and upon the thumb of his right hand, and upon the great toe of his right foot, upon the blood of the trespass offering:

18 And the remnant of the oil that *is* in the priest's hand he shall pour upon the head of him that is to be cleansed: and the priest shall make an atonement for him before the LORD.

19 And the priest shall offer the sin offering, and make an atonement for him that is to be cleansed from his uncleanness; and afterward he shall kill the burnt offering:

20 And the priest shall offer the burnt offering and the meat offering upon the altar: and the priest shall make an atonement for him, and he shall be clean.

21 And if he *be* poor, and cannot get so much; then he shall take one lamb *for* a trespass offering to be waved, to make an atonement for him, and one tenth deal of fine flour mingled with oil for a meat offering, and a log of oil;

22 And two turtledoves, or two young pigeons, such as he is able to get; and the one shall be a sin offering, and the other a burnt offering.

23 And he shall bring them on the eighth day for his cleansing unto the

priest, unto the door of the tabernacle
of the congregation, before the LORD.
24 And the priest shall take the lamb
of the trespass offering, and the log of
oil, and the priest shall wave them *for* a
wave offering before the LORD:
25 And he shall kill the lamb of the
trespass offering, and the priest shall
take *some* of the blood of the trespass
offering, and put *it* upon the tip of the
right ear of him that is to be cleansed,
and upon the thumb of his right hand,
and upon the great toe of his right foot:
26 And the priest shall pour of the oil
into the palm of his own left hand:
27 And the priest shall sprinkle with
his right finger *some* of the oil that *is* in
his left hand seven times before the
LORD:
28 And the priest shall put of the oil
that *is* in his hand upon the tip of the
right ear of him that is to be cleansed,
and upon the thumb of his right hand,
and upon the great toe of his right foot,
upon the place of the blood of the tres-
pass offering:
29 And the rest of the oil that *is* in the
priest's hand he shall put upon the head
of him that is to be cleansed, to make
an atonement for him before the LORD.
30 And he shall offer the one of the
turtledoves, or of the young pigeons,
such as he can get;
31 *Even* such as he is able to get, the
one *for* a sin offering, and the other *for*
a burnt offering, with the meat offer-
ing: and the priest shall make an atone-
ment for him that is to be cleansed be-
fore the LORD.
32 This *is* the law *of him* in whom *is*
the plague of leprosy, whose hand is
not able to get *that which pertaineth* to
his cleansing.
33 ¶And the LORD spake unto Moses
and unto Aaron, saying,
34 When ye be come into the land of
Canaan, which I give to you for a pos-
session, and I put the plague of leprosy
in a house of the land of your posses-
sion;
35 And he that owneth the house
shall come and tell the priest, saying, It
seemeth to me *there is* as it were a
plague in the house:
36 Then the priest shall command
that they empty the house, before the
priest go *into it* to see the plague, that
all that *is* in the house be not made un-
clean: and afterward the priest shall go
in to see the house:
37 And he shall look on the plague,
and, behold, *if* the plague *be* in the
walls of the house with hollow strakes,
greenish or reddish, which in sight *are*
lower than the wall;
38 Then the priest shall go out of the
house to the door of the house, and shut
up the house seven days:
39 And the priest shall come again
the seventh day, and shall look: and,
behold, *if* the plague be spread in the
walls of the house;
40 Then the priest shall command
that they take away the stones in which
the plague *is*, and they shall cast them
into an unclean place without the city:
41 And he shall cause the house to be
scraped within round about, and they
shall pour out the dust that they scrape
off without the city into an unclean
place:
42 And they shall take other stones,
and put *them* in the place of those
stones; and he shall take other morter,
and shall plaister the house.
43 And if the plague come again, and
break out in the house, after that he
hath taken away the stones, and after
he hath scraped the house, and after it
is plaistered;
44 Then the priest shall come and
look, and, behold, *if* the plague be
spread in the house, it *is* a fretting
leprosy in the house: it *is* unclean.
45 And he shall break down the
house, the stones of it, and the timber
thereof, and all the morter of the house;
and he shall carry *them* forth out of the
city into an unclean place.
46 Moreover he that goeth into the
house all the while that it is shut up
shall be unclean until the even.
47 And he that lieth in the house shall
wash his clothes; and he that eateth in
the house shall wash his clothes.
48 And if the priest shall come in, and
look *upon it*, and, behold, the plague
hath not spread in the house, after the
house was plaistered: then the priest
shall pronounce the house clean, be-
cause the plague is healed.
49 And he shall take to cleanse the
house two birds, and cedar wood, and
scarlet, and hyssop:
50 And he shall kill the one of the
birds in an earthen vessel over running
water:
51 And he shall take the cedar wood,
and the hyssop, and the scarlet, and the
living bird, and dip them in the blood of
the slain bird, and in the running water,
and sprinkle the house seven times:
52 And he shall cleanse the house
with the blood of the bird, and with the
running water, and with the living bird,
and with the cedar wood, and with the
hyssop, and with the scarlet:
53 But he shall let go the living bird
out of the city into the open fields, and

make an atonement for the house: and
it shall be clean.
54 This *is* the law for all manner of
plague of leprosy, and scall,
55 And for the leprosy of a garment,
and of a house,
56 And for a rising, and for a scab,
and for a bright spot:
57 To teach when *it is* unclean, and
when *it is* clean: this *is* the law of
leprosy.

CHAPTER 15

AND the LORD spake unto Moses and
to Aaron, saying,
2 Speak unto the children of Israel,
and say unto them, When any man
hath a running issue out of his flesh, *be-*
cause of his issue he *is* unclean.
3 And this shall be his uncleanness in
his issue: whether his flesh run with his
issue, or his flesh be stopped from his
issue, it *is* his uncleanness.
4 Every bed, whereon he lieth that
hath the issue, is unclean: and every
thing, whereon he sitteth, shall be un-
clean.
5 And whosoever toucheth his bed
shall wash his clothes, and bathe *him-*
self in water, and be unclean until the
even.
6 And he that sitteth on *any* thing
whereon he sat that hath the issue shall
wash his clothes, and bathe *himself* in
water, and be unclean until the even.
7 And he that toucheth the flesh of
him that hath the issue shall wash his
clothes, and bathe *himself* in water,
and be unclean until the even.
8 And if he that hath the issue spit
upon him that is clean; then he shall
wash his clothes, and bathe *himself* in
water, and be unclean until the even.
9 And what saddle soever he rideth
upon that hath the issue shall be un-
clean.
10 And whosoever toucheth any
thing that was under him shall be un-
clean until the even: and he that bear-
eth *any of* those things shall wash his
clothes, and bathe *himself* in water,
and be unclean until the even.
11 And whomsoever he toucheth that
hath the issue, and hath not rinsed his
hands in water, he shall wash his
clothes, and bathe *himself* in water,
and be unclean until the even.
12 And the vessel of earth, that he
toucheth which hath the issue, shall be
broken: and every vessel of wood shall
be rinsed in water.
13 And when he that hath an issue is
cleansed of his issue; then he shall
number to himself seven days for his
cleansing, and wash his clothes, and
bathe his flesh in running water, and
shall be clean.
14 And on the eighth day he shall
take to him two turtledoves, or two
young pigeons, and come before the
LORD unto the door of the tabernacle of
the congregation, and give them unto
the priest:
15 And the priest shall offer them, the
one *for* a sin offering, and the other *for*
a burnt offering; and the priest shall
make an atonement for him before the
LORD for his issue.
16 And if any man's seed of copula-
tion go out from him, then he shall
wash all his flesh in water, and be un-
clean until the even.
17 And every garment, and every
skin, whereon is the seed of copulation,
shall be washed with water, and be
unclean until the even.
18 The woman also with whom man
shall lie *with* seed of copulation, they
shall *both* bathe *themselves* in water,
and be unclean until the even.
19 ¶And if a woman have an issue,
and her issue in her flesh be blood, she
shall be put apart seven days: and
whosoever toucheth her shall be un-
clean until the even.
20 And every thing that she lieth
upon in her separation shall be un-
clean: every thing also that she sitteth
upon shall be unclean.
21 And whosoever toucheth her bed
shall wash his clothes, and bathe *him-*
self in water, and be unclean until the
even.
22 And whosoever toucheth any
thing that she sat upon shall wash his
clothes, and bathe *himself* in water,
and be unclean until the even.
23 And if it *be* on *her* bed, or on any
thing whereon she sitteth, when he
toucheth it, he shall be unclean until
the even.
24 And if any man lie with her at all,
and her flowers be upon him, he shall
be unclean seven days; and all the bed
whereon he lieth shall be unclean.
25 And if a woman have an issue of
her blood many days out of the time of
her separation, or if it run beyond the
time of her separation; all the days of
the issue of her uncleanness shall be as
the days of her separation: she *shall be*
unclean.
26 Every bed whereon she lieth all
the days of her issue shall be unto her
as the bed of her separation: and what-
soever she sitteth upon shall be un-
clean, as the uncleanness of her separa-
tion.
27 And whosoever toucheth those
things shall be unclean, and shall wash

his clothes, and bathe *himself* in water, and be unclean until the even.

28 But if she be cleansed of her issue, then she shall number to herself seven days, and after that she shall be clean.

29 And on the eighth day she shall take unto her two turtles, or two young pigeons, and bring them unto the priest, to the door of the tabernacle of the congregation.

30 And the priest shall offer the one *for* a sin offering, and the other *for* a burnt offering; and the priest shall make an atonement for her before the LORD for the issue of her uncleanness.

31 Thus shall ye separate the children of Israel from their uncleanness; that they die not in their uncleanness, when they defile my tabernacle that *is* among them.

32 This *is* the law of him that hath an issue, and *of him* whose seed goeth from him, and is defiled therewith;

33 And of her that is sick of her flowers, and of him that hath an issue, of the man, and of the woman, and of him that lieth with her that is unclean.

CHAPTER 16

AND the LORD spake unto Moses after the death of the two sons of Aaron, when they offered before the LORD, and died;

2 And the LORD said unto Moses, Speak unto Aaron thy brother, that he come not at all times into the holy *place* within the vail before the mercy seat, which *is* upon the ark; that he die not: for I will appear in the cloud upon the mercy seat.

3 Thus shall Aaron come into the holy *place:* with a young bullock for a sin offering, and a ram for a burnt offering.

4 He shall put on the holy linen coat, and he shall have the linen breeches upon his flesh, and shall be girded with a linen girdle, and with the linen mitre shall he be attired: these *are* holy garments; therefore shall he wash his flesh in water, and *so* put them on.

5 And he shall take of the congregation of the children of Israel two kids of the goats for a sin offering, and one ram for a burnt offering.

6 And Aaron shall offer his bullock of the sin offering, which *is* for himself, and make an atonement for himself, and for his house.

7 And he shall take the two goats, and present them before the LORD *at* the door of the tabernacle of the congregation.

8 And Aaron shall cast lots upon the two goats; one lot for the LORD, and the other lot for the scapegoat.

9 And Aaron shall bring the goat upon which the LORD's lot fell, and offer him *for* a sin offering.

10 But the goat, on which the lot fell to be the scapegoat, shall be presented alive before the LORD, to make an atonement with him, *and* to let him go for a scapegoat into the wilderness.

11 And Aaron shall bring the bullock of the sin offering, which *is* for himself, and shall make an atonement for himself, and for his house, and shall kill the bullock of the sin offering which *is* for himself:

12 And he shall take a censer full of burning coals of fire from off the altar before the LORD, and his hands full of sweet incense beaten small, and bring *it* within the vail:

13 And he shall put the incense upon the fire before the LORD, that the cloud of the incense may cover the mercy seat that *is* upon the testimony, that he die not:

14 And he shall take of the blood of the bullock, and sprinkle *it* with his finger upon the mercy seat eastward; and before the mercy seat shall he sprinkle of the blood with his finger seven times.

15 Then shall he kill the goat of the sin offering, that *is* for the people, and bring his blood within the vail, and do with that blood as he did with the blood of the bullock, and sprinkle it upon the mercy seat, and before the mercy seat:

16 And he shall make an atonement for the holy *place,* because of the uncleanness of the children of Israel, and because of their transgressions in all their sins: and so shall he do for the tabernacle of the congregation, that remaineth among them in the midst of their uncleanness.

17 And there shall be no man in the tabernacle of the congregation when he goeth in to make an atonement in the holy *place,* until he come out, and have made an atonement for himself, and for his household, and for all the congregation of Israel.

18 And he shall go out unto the altar that *is* before the LORD, and make an atonement for it; and shall take of the blood of the bullock, and of the blood of the goat, and put *it* upon the horns of the altar round about.

19 And he shall sprinkle of the blood upon it with his finger seven times, and cleanse it, and hallow it from the uncleanness of the children of Israel.

20 ¶And when he hath made an end of reconciling the holy *place,* and the tabernacle of the congregation, and the altar, he shall bring the live goat:

21 And Aaron shall lay both his hands upon the head of the live goat, and confess over him all the iniquities of the children of Israel, and all their transgressions in all their sins, putting them upon the head of the goat, and shall send *him* away by the hand of a fit man into the wilderness:

22 And the goat shall bear upon him all their iniquities unto a land not inhabited: and he shall let go the goat in the wilderness.

23 And Aaron shall come into the tabernacle of the congregation, and shall put off the linen garments, which he put on when he went into the holy *place*, and shall leave them there:

24 And he shall wash his flesh with water in the holy place, and put on his garments, and come forth, and offer his burnt offering, and the burnt offering of the people, and make an atonement for himself, and for the people.

25 And the fat of the sin offering shall he burn upon the altar.

26 And he that let go the goat for the scapegoat shall wash his clothes, and bathe his flesh in water, and afterward come into the camp.

27 And the bullock *for* the sin offering, and the goat *for* the sin offering, whose blood was brought in to make atonement in the holy *place*, shall *one* carry forth without the camp; and they shall burn in the fire their skins, and their flesh, and their dung.

28 And he that burneth them shall wash his clothes, and bathe his flesh in water, and afterward he shall come into the camp.

29 ¶And *this* shall be a statute for ever unto you: *that* in the seventh month, on the tenth *day* of the month, ye shall afflict your souls, and do no work at all, *whether it be* one of your own country, or a stranger that sojourneth among you:

30 For on that day shall *the priest* make an atonement for you, to cleanse you, *that* ye may be clean from all your sins before the LORD.

31 It *shall be* a sabbath of rest unto you, and ye shall afflict your souls, by a statute for ever.

32 And the priest, whom he shall anoint, and whom he shall consecrate to minister in the priest's office in his father's stead, shall make the atonement, and shall put on the linen clothes, *even* the holy garments:

33 And he shall make an atonement for the holy sanctuary, and he shall make an atonement for the tabernacle of the congregation, and for the altar, and he shall make an atonement for the priests, and for all the people of the congregation.

34 And this shall be an everlasting statute unto you, to make an atonement for the children of Israel for all their sins once a year. And he did as the LORD commanded Moses.

CHAPTER 17

AND the LORD spake unto Moses, saying,

2 Speak unto Aaron, and unto his sons, and unto all the children of Israel, and say unto them; This *is* the thing which the LORD hath commanded, saying,

3 What man soever *there be* of the house of Israel, that killeth an ox, or lamb, or goat, in the camp, or that killeth *it* out of the camp,

4 And bringeth it not unto the door of the tabernacle of the congregation, to offer an offering unto the LORD before the tabernacle of the LORD; blood shall be imputed unto that man; he hath shed blood; and that man shall be cut off from among his people:

5 To the end that the children of Israel may bring their sacrifices, which they offer in the open field, even that they may bring them unto the LORD, unto the door of the tabernacle of the congregation, unto the priest, and offer them *for* peace offerings unto the LORD.

6 And the priest shall sprinkle the blood upon the altar of the LORD *at* the door of the tabernacle of the congregation, and burn the fat for a sweet savour unto the LORD.

7 And they shall no more offer their sacrifices unto devils, after whom they have gone a whoring. This shall be a statute for ever unto them throughout their generations.

8 And thou shalt say unto them, Whatsoever man *there be* of the house of Israel, or of the strangers which sojourn among you, that offereth a burnt offering or sacrifice,

9 And bringeth it not unto the door of the tabernacle of the congregation, to offer it unto the LORD; even that man shall be cut off from among his people.

10 ¶And whatsoever man *there be* of the house of Israel, or of the strangers that sojourn among you, that eateth any manner of blood; I will even set my face against that soul that eateth blood, and will cut him off from among his people.

11 For the life of the flesh *is* in the blood: and I have given it to you upon the altar to make an atonement for your souls: for it *is* the blood *that* maketh an atonement for the soul.

12 Therefore I said unto the children of Israel, No soul of you shall eat blood, neither shall any stranger that sojourneth among you eat blood.

13 And whatsoever man *there be* of the children of Israel, or of the strangers that sojourn among you, which hunteth and catcheth any beast or fowl that may be eaten; he shall even pour out the blood thereof, and cover it with dust.

14 For *it is* the life of all flesh; the blood of it *is* for the life thereof: therefore I said unto the children of Israel, Ye shall eat the blood of no manner of flesh: for the life of all flesh *is* the blood thereof: whosoever eateth it shall be cut off.

15 And every soul that eateth that which died *of itself,* or that which was torn *with beasts, whether it be* one of your own country, or a stranger, he shall both wash his clothes, and bathe *himself* in water, and be unclean until the even: then shall he be clean.

16 But if he wash *them* not, nor bathe his flesh; then he shall bear his iniquity.

CHAPTER 18

AND the LORD spake unto Moses, saying,

2 Speak unto the children of Israel, and say unto them, I am the LORD your God.

3 After the doings of the land of Egypt, wherein ye dwelt, shall ye not do: and after the doings of the land of Canaan, whither I bring you, shall ye not do: neither shall ye walk in their ordinances.

4 Ye shall do my judgments, and keep mine ordinances, to walk therein; I *am* the LORD your God.

5 Ye shall therefore keep my statutes, and my judgments: which if a man do, he shall live in them: I *am* the LORD.

6 ¶None of you shall approach to any that is near of kin to him, to uncover *their* nakedness: I *am* the LORD.

7 The nakedness of thy father, or the nakedness of thy mother, shalt thou not uncover: she *is* thy mother; thou shalt not uncover her nakedness.

8 The nakedness of thy father's wife shalt thou not uncover: it *is* thy father's nakedness.

9 The nakedness of thy sister, the daughter of thy father, or daughter of thy mother, *whether she be* born at home, or born abroad, *even* their nakedness thou shalt not uncover.

10 The nakedness of thy son's daughter, or of thy daughter's daughter, *even* their nakedness thou shalt not uncover: for theirs *is* thine own nakedness.

11 The nakedness of thy father's wife's daughter, begotten of thy father, she *is* thy sister, thou shalt not uncover her nakedness.

12 Thou shalt not uncover the nakedness of thy father's sister: she *is* thy father's near kinswoman.

13 Thou shalt not uncover the nakedness of thy mother's sister: for she *is* thy mother's near kinswoman.

14 Thou shalt not uncover the nakedness of thy father's brother, thou shalt not approach to his wife: she *is* thine aunt.

15 Thou shalt not uncover the nakedness of thy daughter in law: she *is* thy son's wife; thou shalt not uncover her nakedness.

16 Thou shalt not uncover the nakedness of thy brother's wife: it *is* thy brother's nakedness.

17 Thou shalt not uncover the nakedness of a woman and her daughter, neither shalt thou take her son's daughter, or her daughter's daughter, to uncover her nakedness; *for* they *are* her near kinswomen: it *is* wickedness.

18 Neither shalt thou take a wife to her sister, to vex *her,* to uncover her nakedness, beside the other in her life *time.*

19 Also thou shalt not approach unto a woman to uncover her nakedness, as long as she is put apart for her uncleanness.

20 Moreover thou shalt not lie carnally with thy neighbour's wife, to defile thyself with her.

21 And thou shalt not let any of thy seed pass through *the fire* to Mō̆lĕch, neither shalt thou profane the name of thy God: I *am* the LORD.

22 Thou shalt not lie with mankind, as with womankind: it *is* abomination.

23 Neither shalt thou lie with any beast to defile thyself therewith: neither shall any woman stand before a beast to lie down thereto: it *is* confusion.

24 Defile not ye yourselves in any of these things: for in all these the nations are defiled which I cast out before you:

25 And the land is defiled: therefore I do visit the iniquity thereof upon it, and the land itself vomiteth out her inhabitants.

26 Ye shall therefore keep my statutes and my judgments, and shall not commit *any* of these abominations; *neither* any of your own nation, nor any stranger that sojourneth among you:

27 (For all these abominations have

the men of the land done, which *were* before you, and the land is defiled;)

28 That the land spue not you out also, when ye defile it, as it spued out the nations that *were* before you.

29 For whosoever shall commit any of these abominations, even the souls that commit *them* shall be cut off from among their people.

30 Therefore shall ye keep mine ordinance, that *ye* commit not *any one* of these abominable customs, which were committed before you, and that ye defile not yourselves therein: I *am* the LORD your God.

CHAPTER 19

AND the LORD spake unto Moses, saying,

2 Speak unto all the congregation of the children of Israel, and say unto them, Ye shall be holy: for I the LORD your God *am* holy.

3 ¶Ye shall fear every man his mother, and his father, and keep my sabbaths: I *am* the LORD your God.

4 ¶Turn ye not unto idols, nor make to yourselves molten gods: I *am* the LORD your God.

5 ¶And if ye offer a sacrifice of peace offerings unto the LORD, ye shall offer it at your own will.

6 It shall be eaten the same day ye offer it, and on the morrow: and if ought remain until the third day, it shall be burnt in the fire.

7 And if it be eaten at all on the third day, it *is* abominable; it shall not be accepted.

8 Therefore *every one* that eateth it shall bear his iniquity, because he hath profaned the hallowed thing of the LORD: and that soul shall be cut off from among his people.

9 ¶And when ye reap the harvest of your land, thou shalt not wholly reap the corners of thy field, neither shalt thou gather the gleanings of thy harvest.

10 And thou shalt not glean thy vineyard, neither shalt thou gather *every* grape of thy vineyard; thou shalt leave them for the poor and stranger: I *am* the LORD your God.

11 ¶Ye shall not steal, neither deal falsely, neither lie one to another.

12 ¶And ye shall not swear by my name falsely, neither shalt thou profane the name of thy God: I *am* the LORD.

13 ¶Thou shalt not defraud thy neighbour, neither rob *him:* the wages of him that is hired shall not abide with thee all night until the morning.

14 ¶Thou shalt not curse the deaf, nor put a stumbling block before the blind, but shalt fear thy God: I *am* the LORD.

15 ¶Ye shall do no unrighteousness in judgment: thou shalt not respect the person of the poor, nor honour the person of the mighty: *but* in righteousness shalt thou judge thy neighbour.

16 ¶Thou shalt not go up and down *as* a talebearer among thy people: neither shalt thou stand against the blood of thy neighbour: I *am* the LORD.

17 ¶Thou shalt not hate thy brother in thine heart: thou shalt in any wise rebuke thy neighbour, and not suffer sin upon him.

18 ¶Thou shalt not avenge, nor bear any grudge against the children of thy people, but thou shalt love thy neighbour as thyself: I *am* the LORD.

19 ¶Ye shall keep my statutes. Thou shalt not let thy cattle gender with a diverse kind: thou shalt not sow thy field with mingled seed: neither shall a garment mingled of linen and woollen come upon thee.

20 ¶And whosoever lieth carnally with a woman, that *is* a bondmaid, betrothed to an husband, and not at all redeemed, nor freedom given her; she shall be scourged; they shall not be put to death, because she was not free.

21 And he shall bring his trespass offering unto the LORD, unto the door of the tabernacle of the congregation, *even* a ram for a trespass offering.

22 And the priest shall make an atonement for him with the ram of the trespass offering before the LORD for his sin which he hath done: and the sin which he hath done shall be forgiven him.

23 ¶And when ye shall come into the land, and shall have planted all manner of trees for food, then ye shall count the fruit thereof as uncircumcised: three years shall it be as uncircumcised unto you: it shall not be eaten of.

24 But in the fourth year all the fruit thereof shall be holy to praise the LORD *withal.*

25 And in the fifth year shall ye eat of the fruit thereof, that it may yield unto you the increase thereof: I *am* the LORD your God.

26 ¶Ye shall not eat *any thing* with the blood: neither shall ye use enchantment, nor observe times.

27 Ye shall not round the corners of your heads, neither shalt thou mar the corners of thy beard.

28 Ye shall not make any cuttings in your flesh for the dead, nor print any marks upon you: I *am* the LORD.

29 ¶Do not prostitute thy daughter,

to cause her to be a whore; lest the land fall to whoredom, and the land become full of wickedness.

30 ¶Ye shall keep my sabbaths, and reverence my sanctuary: I *am* the LORD.

31 ¶Regard not them that have familiar spirits, neither seek after wizards, to be defiled by them: I *am* the LORD your God.

32 ¶Thou shalt rise up before the hoary head, and honour the face of the old man, and fear thy God: I *am* the LORD.

33 ¶And if a stranger sojourn with thee in your land, ye shall not vex him.

34 *But* the stranger that dwelleth with you shall be unto you as one born among you, and thou shalt love him as thyself; for ye were strangers in the land of Egypt: I *am* the LORD your God.

35 ¶Ye shall do no unrighteousness in judgment, in meteyard, in weight, or in measure.

36 Just balances, just weights, a just ephah, and a just hin, shall ye have: I *am* the LORD your God, which brought you out of the land of Egypt.

37 Therefore shall ye observe all my statutes, and all my judgments, and do them: I *am* the LORD.

CHAPTER 20

AND the LORD spake unto Moses, saying,

2 Again, thou shalt say to the children of Israel, Whosoever *he be* of the children of Israel, or of the strangers that sojourn in Israel, that giveth *any* of his seed unto Mōlĕch; he shall surely be put to death: the people of the land shall stone him with stones.

3 And I will set my face against that man, and will cut him off from among his people; because he hath given of his seed unto Mōlĕch, to defile my sanctuary, and to profane my holy name.

4 And if the people of the land do any ways hide their eyes from the man, when he giveth of his seed unto Mōlĕch, and kill him not:

5 Then I will set my face against that man, and against his family, and will cut him off, and all that go a whoring after him, to commit whoredom with Mōlĕch, from among their people.

6 ¶And the soul that turneth after such as have familiar spirits, and after wizards, to go a whoring after them, I will even set my face against that soul, and will cut him off from among his people.

7 Sanctify yourselves therefore, and be ye holy: for I *am* the LORD your God.

8 And ye shall keep my statutes, and do them: I *am* the LORD which sanctify you.

9 ¶For every one that curseth his father or his mother shall be surely put to death: he hath cursed his father or his mother; his blood *shall be* upon him.

10 ¶And the man that committeth adultery with *another* man's wife, *even he* that committeth adultery with his neighbour's wife, the adulterer and the adulteress shall surely be put to death.

11 And the man that lieth with his father's wife hath uncovered his father's nakedness: both of them shall surely be put to death; their blood *shall be* upon them.

12 And if a man lie with his daughter in law, both of them shall surely be put to death: they have wrought confusion; their blood *shall be* upon them.

13 ¶If a man also lie with mankind, as he lieth with a woman, both of them have committed an abomination: they shall surely be put to death; their blood *shall be* upon them.

14 And if a man take a wife and her mother, it *is* wickedness: they shall be burnt with fire, both he and they; that there be no wickedness among you.

15 And if a man lie with a beast, he shall surely be put to death: and ye shall slay the beast.

16 And if a woman approach unto any beast, and lie down thereto, thou shalt kill the woman, and the beast: they shall surely be put to death; their blood *shall be* upon them.

17 And if a man shall take his sister, his father's daughter, or his mother's daughter, and see her nakedness, and she see his nakedness; it *is* a wicked thing; and they shall be cut off in the sight of their people: he hath uncovered his sister's nakedness; he shall bear his iniquity.

18 And if a man shall lie with a woman having her sickness, and shall uncover her nakedness; he hath discovered her fountain, and she hath uncovered the fountain of her blood: and both of them shall be cut off from among their people.

19 And thou shalt not uncover the nakedness of thy mother's sister, nor of thy father's sister: for he uncovereth his near kin: they shall bear their iniquity.

20 And if a man shall lie with his uncle's wife, he hath uncovered his uncle's nakedness: they shall bear their sin; they shall die childless.

21 And if a man shall take his brother's wife, it *is* an unclean thing: he hath

uncovered his brother's nakedness; they shall be childless.

22 ¶Ye shall therefore keep all my statutes, and all my judgments, and do them: that the land, whither I bring you to dwell therein, spue you not out.

23 And ye shall not walk in the manners of the nation, which I cast out before you: for they committed all these things, and therefore I abhorred them.

24 But I have said unto you, Ye shall inherit their land, and I will give it unto you to possess it, a land that floweth with milk and honey: I *am* the LORD your God, which have separated you from *other* people.

25 Ye shall therefore put difference between clean beasts and unclean, and between unclean fowls and clean: and ye shall not make your souls abominable by beast, or by fowl, or by any manner of living thing that creepeth on the ground, which I have separated from you as unclean.

26 And ye shall be holy unto me: for I the LORD *am* holy, and have severed you from *other* people, that ye should be mine.

27 ¶A man also or woman that hath a familiar spirit, or that is a wizard, shall surely be put to death: they shall stone them with stones: their blood *shall be* upon them.

CHAPTER 21

AND the LORD said unto Moses, Speak unto the priests the sons of Aaron, and say unto them, There shall none be defiled for the dead among his people:

2 But for his kin, that is near unto him, *that is,* for his mother, and for his father, and for his son, and for his daughter, and for his brother,

3 And for his sister a virgin, that is nigh unto him, which hath had no husband; for her may he be defiled.

4 *But* he shall not defile himself, *being* a chief man among his people, to profane himself.

5 They shall not make baldness upon their head, neither shall they shave off the corner of their beard, nor make any cuttings in their flesh.

6 They shall be holy unto their God, and not profane the name of their God: for the offerings of the LORD made by fire, *and* the bread of their God, they do offer: therefore they shall be holy.

7 They shall not take a wife *that is* a whore, or profane; neither shall they take a woman put away from her husband: for he *is* holy unto his God.

8 Thou shalt sanctify him therefore; for he offereth the bread of thy God: he shall be holy unto thee: for I the LORD, which sanctify you, *am* holy.

9 And the daughter of any priest, if she profane herself by playing the whore, she profaneth her father: she shall be burnt with fire.

10 ¶And *he that is* the high priest among his brethren, upon whose head the anointing oil was poured, and that is consecrated to put on the garments, shall not uncover his head, nor rend his clothes;

11 Neither shall he go in to any dead body, nor defile himself for his father, or for his mother;

12 Neither shall he go out of the sanctuary, nor profane the sanctuary of his God; for the crown of the anointing oil of his God *is* upon him: I *am* the LORD.

13 And he shall take a wife in her virginity.

14 A widow, or a divorced woman, or profane, *or* an harlot, these shall he not take: but he shall take a virgin of his own people to wife.

15 Neither shall he profane his seed among his people: for I the LORD do sanctify him.

16 ¶And the LORD spake unto Moses, saying,

17 Speak unto Aaron, saying, Whosoever *he be* of thy seed in their generations that hath *any* blemish, let him not approach to offer the bread of his God.

18 For whatsoever man *he be* that hath a blemish, he shall not approach: a blind man, or a lame, or he that hath a flat nose, or any thing superfluous,

19 Or a man that is brokenfooted, or brokenhanded,

20 Or crookbackt, or a dwarf, or that hath a blemish in his eye, or be scurvy, or scabbed, or hath his stones broken;

21 No man that hath a blemish of the seed of Aaron the priest shall come nigh to offer the offerings of the LORD made by fire: he hath a blemish; he shall not come nigh to offer the bread of his God.

22 He shall eat the bread of his God, *both* of the most holy, and of the holy.

23 Only he shall not go in unto the vail, nor come nigh unto the altar, because he hath a blemish; that he profane not my sanctuaries: for I the LORD do sanctify them.

24 And Moses told *it* unto Aaron, and to his sons, and unto all the children of Israel.

CHAPTER 22

AND the LORD spake unto Moses, saying,

2 Speak unto Aaron and to his sons,

that they separate themselves from the
holy things of the children of Israel, and
that they profane not my holy name *in*
those things which they hallow unto
me: I *am* the LORD.
3 Say unto them, Whosoever *he be* of
all your seed among your generations,
that goeth unto the holy things, which
the children of Israel hallow unto the
LORD, having his uncleanness upon
him, that soul shall be cut off from my
presence: I *am* the LORD.
4 What man soever of the seed of
Aaron *is* a leper, or hath a running
issue; he shall not eat of the holy things,
until he be clean. And whoso toucheth
any thing *that is* unclean *by* the dead,
or a man whose seed goeth from him;
5 Or whosoever toucheth any
creeping thing, whereby he may be
made unclean, or a man of whom he
may take uncleanness, whatsoever
uncleanness he hath;
6 The soul which hath touched any
such shall be unclean until even, and
shall not eat of the holy things, unless
he wash his flesh with water.
7 And when the sun is down, he shall
be clean, and shall afterward eat of the
holy things; because it *is* his food.
8 That which dieth of itself, or is torn
with beasts, he shall not eat to defile
himself therewith: I *am* the LORD.
9 They shall therefore keep mine or-
dinance, lest they bear sin for it, and die
therefore, if they profane it: I the LORD
do sanctify them.
10 There shall no stranger eat *of* the
holy thing: a sojourner of the priest, or
an hired servant, shall not eat *of* the
holy thing.
11 But if the priest buy *any* soul with
his money, he shall eat of it, and he that
is born in his house: they shall eat of his
meat.
12 If the priest's daughter also be
married unto a stranger, she may not
eat of an offering of the holy things.
13 But if the priest's daughter be a wid-
ow, or divorced, and have no child,
and is returned unto her father's house,
as in her youth, she shall eat of her fa-
ther's meat: but there shall no stranger
eat thereof.
14 And if a man eat *of* the holy thing
unwittingly, then he shall put the fifth
part thereof unto it, and shall give *it*
unto the priest with the holy thing.
15 And they shall not profane the
holy things of the children of Israel,
which they offer unto the LORD;
16 Or suffer them to bear the iniquity
of trespass, when they eat their holy
things: for I the LORD do sanctify them.
17 ¶And the LORD spake unto Moses,
saying,
18 Speak unto Aaron, and to his sons,
and unto all the children of Israel, and
say unto them, Whatsoever *he be* of the
house of Israel, or of the strangers in
Israel, that will offer his oblation for all
his vows, and for all his freewill offer-
ings, which they will offer unto the
LORD for a burnt offering;
19 *Ye shall offer* at your own will a
male without blemish, of the beeves, of
the sheep, or of the goats.
20 *But* whatsoever hath a blemish,
that shall ye not offer: for it shall not be
acceptable for you.
21 And whosoever offereth a sacri-
fice of peace offerings unto the LORD to
accomplish *his* vow, or a freewill offer-
ing in beeves or sheep, it shall be per-
fect to be accepted; there shall be no
blemish therein.
22 Blind, or broken, or maimed, or
having a wen, or scurvy, or scabbed, ye
shall not offer these unto the LORD, nor
make an offering by fire of them upon
the altar unto the LORD.
23 Either a bullock or a lamb that
hath any thing superfluous or lacking
in his parts, that mayest thou offer *for* a
freewill offering; but for a vow it shall
not be accepted.
24 Ye shall not offer unto the LORD
that which is bruised, or crushed, or
broken, or cut; neither shall ye make
any offering thereof in your land.
25 Neither from a stranger's hand
shall ye offer the bread of your God of
any of these; because their corruption
is in them, *and* blemishes *be* in them:
they shall not be accepted for you.
26 ¶And the LORD spake unto Moses,
saying,
27 When a bullock, or a sheep, or a
goat, is brought forth, then it shall be
seven days under the dam; and from
the eighth day and thenceforth it shall
be accepted for an offering made by
fire unto the LORD.
28 And *whether it be* cow or ewe, ye
shall not kill it and her young both in
one day.
29 ¶And when ye will offer a sacrifice
of thanksgiving unto the LORD, offer *it*
at your own will.
30 On the same day it shall be eaten
up; ye shall leave none of it until the
morrow: I *am* the LORD.
31 Therefore shall ye keep my com-
mandments, and do them: I *am* the
LORD.
32 Neither shall ye profane my holy
name; but I will be hallowed among the
children of Israel: I *am* the LORD which
hallow you,

33 That brought you out of the land of Egypt, to be your God: I *am* the LORD.

CHAPTER 23

AND the LORD spake unto Moses, saying,

2 Speak unto the children of Israel, and say unto them, *Concerning* the feasts of the LORD, which ye shall proclaim *to be* holy convocations, *even* these *are* my feasts.

3 Six days shall work be done: but the seventh day *is* the sabbath of rest, an holy convocation; ye shall do no work *therein*: it *is* the sabbath of the LORD in all your dwellings.

4 ¶These *are* the feasts of the LORD, *even* holy convocations, which ye shall proclaim in their seasons.

5 In the fourteenth *day* of the first month at even *is* the LORD's passover.

6 And on the fifteenth day of the same month *is* the feast of unleavened bread unto the LORD: seven days ye must eat unleavened bread.

7 In the first day ye shall have an holy convocation: ye shall do no servile work therein.

8 But ye shall offer an offering made by fire unto the LORD seven days: in the seventh day *is* an holy convocation: ye shall do no servile work *therein*.

9 ¶And the LORD spake unto Moses, saying,

10 Speak unto the children of Israel, and say unto them, When ye be come into the land which I give unto you, and shall reap the harvest thereof, then ye shall bring a sheaf of the firstfruits of your harvest unto the priest:

11 And he shall wave the sheaf before the LORD, to be accepted for you: on the morrow after the sabbath the priest shall wave it.

12 And ye shall offer that day when ye wave the sheaf an he lamb without blemish of the first year for a burnt offering unto the LORD.

13 And the meat offering thereof *shall be* two tenth deals of fine flour mingled with oil, an offering made by fire unto the LORD *for* a sweet savour: and the drink offering thereof *shall be* of wine, the fourth *part* of an hin.

14 And ye shall eat neither bread, nor parched corn, nor green ears, until the selfsame day that ye have brought an offering unto your God: *it shall be* a statute for ever throughout your generations in all your dwellings.

15 ¶And ye shall count unto you from the morrow after the sabbath, from the day that ye brought the sheaf of the wave offering; seven sabbaths shall be complete:

16 Even unto the morrow after the seventh sabbath shall ye number fifty days; and ye shall offer a new meat offering unto the LORD.

17 Ye shall bring out of your habitations two wave loaves of two tenth deals: they shall be of fine flour; they shall be baken with leaven; *they are* the firstfruits unto the LORD.

18 And ye shall offer with the bread seven lambs without blemish of the first year, and one young bullock, and two rams: they shall be *for* a burnt offering unto the LORD, with their meat offering, and their drink offerings, *even* an offering made by fire, of sweet savour unto the LORD.

19 Then ye shall sacrifice one kid of the goats for a sin offering, and two lambs of the first year for a sacrifice of peace offerings.

20 And the priest shall wave them with the bread of the firstfruits *for* a wave offering before the LORD, with the two lambs: they shall be holy to the LORD for the priest.

21 And ye shall proclaim on the selfsame day, *that* it may be an holy convocation unto you: ye shall do no servile work *therein: it shall be* a statute for ever in all your dwellings throughout your generations.

22 ¶And when ye reap the harvest of your land, thou shalt not make clean riddance of the corners of thy field when thou reapest, neither shalt thou gather any gleaning of thy harvest: thou shalt leave them unto the poor, and to the stranger: I *am* the LORD your God.

23 ¶And the LORD spake unto Moses, saying,

24 Speak unto the children of Israel, saying, In the seventh month, in the first *day* of the month, shall ye have a sabbath, a memorial of blowing of trumpets, an holy convocation.

25 Ye shall do no servile work *therein*: but ye shall offer an offering made by fire unto the LORD.

26 ¶And the LORD spake unto Moses, saying,

27 Also on the tenth *day* of this seventh month *there shall be* a day of atonement: it shall be an holy convocation unto you; and ye shall afflict your souls, and offer an offering made by fire unto the LORD.

28 And ye shall do no work in that same day: for it *is* a day of atonement, to make an atonement for you before the LORD your God.

29 For whatsoever soul *it be* that shall not be afflicted in that same day,

he shall be cut off from among his
people.
30 And whatsoever soul *it be* that
doeth any work in that same day, the
same soul will I destroy from among
his people.
31 Ye shall do no manner of work: *it*
shall be a statute for ever throughout
your generations in all your dwellings.
32 It *shall be* unto you a sabbath of
rest, and ye shall afflict your souls: in
the ninth *day* of the month at even,
from even unto even, shall ye celebrate
your sabbath.
33 ¶And the LORD spake unto Moses,
saying,
34 Speak unto the children of Israel,
saying, The fifteenth day of this
seventh month *shall be* the feast of tab-
ernacles *for* seven days unto the
LORD.
35 On the first day *shall be* an holy
convocation: ye shall do no servile
work *therein*.
36 Seven days ye shall offer an offer-
ing made by fire unto the LORD: on the
eighth day shall be an holy convocation
unto you; and ye shall offer an offering
made by fire unto the LORD: it *is* a sol-
emn assembly; *and* ye shall do no ser-
vile work *therein*.
37 These *are* the feasts of the LORD,
which ye shall proclaim *to be* holy con-
vocations, to offer an offering made by
fire unto the LORD, a burnt offering, and
a meat offering, a sacrifice, and drink
offerings, every thing upon his day:
38 Beside the sabbaths of the LORD,
and beside your gifts, and beside all
your vows, and beside all your freewill
offerings, which ye give unto the LORD.
39 Also in the fifteenth day of the
seventh month, when ye have gathered
in the fruit of the land, ye shall keep a
feast unto the LORD seven days: on the
first day *shall be* a sabbath, and on the
eighth day *shall be* a sabbath.
40 And ye shall take you on the first
day the boughs of goodly trees,
branches of palm trees, and the boughs
of thick trees, and willows of the brook;
and ye shall rejoice before the LORD
your God seven days.
41 And ye shall keep it a feast unto
the LORD seven days in the year. *It shall*
be a statute for ever in your genera-
tions: ye shall celebrate it in the
seventh month.
42 Ye shall dwell in booths seven
days; all that are Israelites born shall
dwell in booths:
43 That your generations may know
that I made the children of Israel to
dwell in booths, when I brought them
out of the land of Egypt: I *am* the LORD
your God.
44 And Moses declared unto the
children of Israel the feasts of the LORD.

CHAPTER 24

AND the LORD spake unto Moses,
saying,
2 Command the children of Israel,
that they bring unto thee pure oil olive
beaten for the light, to cause the lamps
to burn continually.
3 Without the vail of the testimony,
in the tabernacle of the congregation,
shall Aaron order it from the evening
unto the morning before the LORD con-
tinually: *it shall be* a statute for ever in
your generations.
4 He shall order the lamps upon the
pure candlestick before the LORD con-
tinually.
5 ¶And thou shalt take fine flour, and
bake twelve cakes thereof: two tenth
deals shall be in one cake.
6 And thou shalt set them in two
rows, six on a row, upon the pure table
before the LORD.
7 And thou shalt put pure frankin-
cense upon *each* row, that it may be on
the bread for a memorial, *even* an offer-
ing made by fire unto the LORD.
8 Every sabbath he shall set it in or-
der before the LORD continually, *being*
taken from the children of Israel by an
everlasting covenant.
9 And it shall be Aaron's and his
sons'; and they shall eat it in the holy
place: for it *is* most holy unto him of the
offerings of the LORD made by fire by a
perpetual statute.
10 ¶And the son of an Israelitish wom-
an, whose father *was* an Egyptian,
went out among the children of Israel:
and this son of the Israelitish *woman*
and a man of Israel strove together in
the camp;
11 And the Israelitish woman's son
blasphemed the name *of the LORD*, and
cursed. And they brought him unto
Moses: (and his mother's name *was*
Shel'ō-mĭth, the daughter of Dĭb'rī, of
the tribe of Dan:)
12 And they put him in ward, that the
mind of the LORD might be shewed
them.
13 And the LORD spake unto Moses,
saying,
14 Bring forth him that hath cursed
without the camp; and let all that heard
him lay their hands upon his head, and
let all the congregation stone him.
15 And thou shalt speak unto the
children of Israel, saying, Whosoever
curseth his God shall bear his sin.
16 And he that blasphemeth the

name of the LORD, he shall surely be put to death, *and* all the congregation shall certainly stone him: as well the stranger, as he that is born in the land, when he blasphemeth the name *of the LORD*, shall be put to death.

17 And he that killeth any man shall surely be put to death.

18 And he that killeth a beast shall make it good; beast for beast.

19 And if a man cause a blemish in his neighbour; as he hath done, so shall it be done to him;

20 Breach for breach, eye for eye, tooth for tooth: as he hath caused a blemish in a man, so shall it be done to him *again*.

21 And he that killeth a beast, he shall restore it: and he that killeth a man, he shall be put to death.

22 Ye shall have one manner of law, as well for the stranger, as for one of your own country: for I *am* the LORD your God.

23 ¶And Moses spake to the children of Israel, that they should bring forth him that had cursed out of the camp, and stone him with stones. And the children of Israel did as the LORD commanded Moses.

CHAPTER 25

AND the LORD spake unto Moses in mount Sī′naī, saying,

2 Speak unto the children of Israel, and say unto them, When ye come into the land which I give you, then shall the land keep a sabbath unto the LORD.

3 Six years thou shalt sow thy field, and six years thou shalt prune thy vineyard, and gather in the fruit thereof;

4 But in the seventh year shall be a sabbath of rest unto the land, a sabbath for the LORD: thou shalt neither sow thy field, nor prune thy vineyard.

5 That which groweth of its own accord of thy harvest thou shalt not reap, neither gather the grapes of thy vine undressed: *for* it is a year of rest unto the land.

6 And the sabbath of the land shall be meat for you; for thee, and for thy servant, and for thy maid, and for thy hired servant, and for thy stranger that sojourneth with thee,

7 And for thy cattle, and for the beast that *are* in thy land, shall all the increase thereof be meat.

8 ¶And thou shalt number seven sabbaths of years unto thee, seven times seven years; and the space of the seven sabbaths of years shall be unto thee forty and nine years.

9 Then shalt thou cause the trumpet of the jubile to sound on the tenth *day* of the seventh month, in the day of atonement shall ye make the trumpet sound throughout all your land.

10 And ye shall hallow the fiftieth year, and proclaim liberty throughout *all* the land unto all the inhabitants thereof: it shall be a jubile unto you; and ye shall return every man unto his possession, and ye shall return every man unto his family.

11 A jubile shall that fiftieth year be unto you: ye shall not sow, neither reap that which groweth of itself in it, nor gather *the grapes* in it of thy vine undressed.

12 For it *is* the jubile; it shall be holy unto you: ye shall eat the increase thereof out of the field.

13 In the year of this jubile ye shall return every man unto his possession.

14 And if thou sell ought unto thy neighbour, or buyest *ought* of thy neighbour's hand, ye shall not oppress one another:

15 According to the number of years after the jubile thou shalt buy of thy neighbour, *and* according unto the number of years of the fruits he shall sell unto thee:

16 According to the multitude of years thou shalt increase the price thereof, and according to the fewness of years thou shalt diminish the price of it: for *according* to the number *of the years* of the fruits doth he sell unto thee.

17 Ye shall not therefore oppress one another; but thou shalt fear thy God: for I *am* the LORD your God.

18 ¶Wherefore ye shall do my statutes, and keep my judgments, and do them; and ye shall dwell in the land in safety.

19 And the land shall yield her fruit, and ye shall eat your fill, and dwell therein in safety.

20 And if ye shall say, What shall we eat the seventh year? behold, we shall not sow, nor gather in our increase:

21 Then I will command my blessing upon you in the sixth year, and it shall bring forth fruit for three years.

22 And ye shall sow the eighth year, and eat *yet* of old fruit until the ninth year; until her fruits come in ye shall eat *of* the old *store*.

23 ¶The land shall not be sold for ever: for the land *is* mine; for ye *are* strangers and sojourners with me.

24 And in all the land of your possession ye shall grant a redemption for the land.

25 ¶If thy brother be waxen poor, and hath sold away *some* of his possession, and if any of his kin come to redeem it,

then shall he redeem that which his brother sold.

26 And if the man have none to redeem it, and himself be able to redeem it;

27 Then let him count the years of the sale thereof, and restore the overplus unto the man to whom he sold it; that he may return unto his possession.

28 But if he be not able to restore *it* to him, then that which is sold shall remain in the hand of him that hath bought it until the year of jubile: and in the jubile it shall go out, and he shall return unto his possession.

29 And if a man sell a dwelling house in a walled city, then he may redeem it within a whole year after it is sold; *within* a full year may he redeem it.

30 And if it be not redeemed within the space of a full year, then the house that *is* in the walled city shall be established for ever to him that bought it throughout his generations: it shall not go out in the jubile.

31 But the houses of the villages which have no wall round about them shall be counted as the fields of the country: they may be redeemed, and they shall go out in the jubile.

32 Notwithstanding the cities of the Lēvītes, *and* the houses of the cities of their possession, may the Lēvītes redeem at any time.

33 And if a man purchase of the Lēvītes, then the house that was sold, and the city of his possession, shall go out in *the year of* jubile: for the houses of the cities of the Lēvītes *are* their possession among the children of Israel.

34 But the field of the suburbs of their cities may not be sold; for it *is* their perpetual possession.

35 ¶And if thy brother be waxen poor, and fallen in decay with thee; then thou shalt relieve him: *yea, though he be* a stranger, or a sojourner; that he may live with thee.

36 Take thou no usury of him, or increase: but fear thy God; that thy brother may live with thee.

37 Thou shalt not give him thy money upon usury, nor lend him thy victuals for increase.

38 I *am* the Lord your God, which brought you forth out of the land of Egypt, to give you the land of Canaan, *and* to be your God.

39 ¶And if thy brother *that dwelleth* by thee be waxen poor, and be sold unto thee; thou shalt not compel him to serve as a bondservant:

40 *But* as an hired servant, *and* as a sojourner, he shall be with thee, *and* shall serve thee unto the year of jubile:

41 And *then* shall he depart from thee, *both* he and his children with him, and shall return unto his own family, and unto the possession of his fathers shall he return.

42 For they *are* my servants, which I brought forth out of the land of Egypt: they shall not be sold as bondmen.

43 Thou shalt not rule over him with rigour; but shalt fear thy God.

44 Both thy bondmen, and thy bondmaids, which thou shalt have, *shall be* of the heathen that are round about you; of them shall ye buy bondmen and bondmaids.

45 Moreover of the children of the strangers that do sojourn among you, of them shall ye buy, and of their families that *are* with you, which they begat in your land: and they shall be your possession.

46 And ye shall take them as an inheritance for your children after you, to inherit *them for* a possession; they shall be your bondmen for ever: but over your brethren the children of Israel, ye shall not rule one over another with rigour.

47 ¶And if a sojourner or stranger wax rich by thee, and thy brother *that dwelleth* by him wax poor, and sell himself unto the stranger *or* sojourner by thee, or to the stock of the stranger's family:

48 After that he is sold he may be redeemed again; one of his brethren may redeem him:

49 Either his uncle, or his uncle's son, may redeem him, or *any* that is nigh of kin unto him of his family may redeem him; or if he be able, he may redeem himself.

50 And he shall reckon with him that bought him from the year that he was sold to him unto the year of jubile: and the price of his sale shall be according unto the number of years, according to the time of an hired servant shall it be with him.

51 If *there be* yet many years *behind,* according unto them he shall give again the price of his redemption out of the money that he was bought for.

52 And if there remain but few years unto the year of jubile, then he shall count with him, *and* according unto his years shall he give him again the price of his redemption.

53 *And* as a yearly hired servant shall he be with him: *and the other* shall not rule with rigour over him in thy sight.

54 And if he be not redeemed in these *years,* then he shall go out in the year of jubile, *both* he, and his children with him.

55 For unto me the children of Israel *are* servants; they *are* my servants whom I brought forth out of the land of Egypt: I *am* the LORD your God.

CHAPTER 26

YE shall make you no idols nor graven image, neither rear you up a standing image, neither shall ye set up *any* image of stone in your land, to bow down unto it: for I *am* the LORD your God.

2 Ye shall keep my sabbaths, and reverence my sanctuary: I *am* the LORD.

3 ¶If ye walk in my statutes, and keep my commandments, and do them;

4 Then I will give you rain in due season, and the land shall yield her increase, and the trees of the field shall yield their fruit.

5 And your threshing shall reach unto the vintage, and the vintage shall reach unto the sowing time: and ye shall eat your bread to the full, and dwell in your land safely.

6 And I will give peace in the land, and ye shall lie down, and none shall make *you* afraid: and I will rid evil beasts out of the land, neither shall the sword go through your land.

7 And ye shall chase your enemies, and they shall fall before you by the sword.

8 And five of you shall chase an hundred, and an hundred of you shall put ten thousand to flight: and your enemies shall fall before you by the sword.

9 For I will have respect unto you, and make you fruitful, and multiply you, and establish my covenant with you.

10 And ye shall eat old store, and bring forth the old because of the new.

11 And I will set my tabernacle among you: and my soul shall not abhor you.

12 And I will walk among you, and will be your God, and ye shall be my people.

13 I *am* the LORD your God, which brought you forth out of the land of Egypt, that ye should not be their bondmen; and I have broken the bands of your yoke, and made you go upright.

14 ¶But if ye will not hearken unto me, and will not do all these commandments;

15 And if ye shall despise my statutes, or if your soul abhor my judgments, so that ye will not do all my commandments, *but* that ye break my covenant:

16 I also will do this unto you; I will even appoint over you terror, consumption, and the burning ague, that shall consume the eyes, and cause sorrow of heart: and ye shall sow your seed in vain, for your enemies shall eat it.

17 And I will set my face against you, and ye shall be slain before your enemies: they that hate you shall reign over you; and ye shall flee when none pursueth you.

18 And if ye will not yet for all this hearken unto me, then I will punish you seven times more for your sins.

19 And I will break the pride of your power; and I will make your heaven as iron, and your earth as brass:

20 And your strength shall be spent in vain: for your land shall not yield her increase, neither shall the trees of the land yield their fruits.

21 And if ye walk contrary unto me, and will not hearken unto me; I will bring seven times more plagues upon you according to your sins.

22 I will also send wild beasts among you, which shall rob you of your children, and destroy your cattle, and make you few in number; and your *high* ways shall be desolate.

23 And if ye will not be reformed by me by these things, but will walk contrary unto me;

24 Then will I also walk contrary unto you, and will punish you yet seven times for your sins.

25 And I will bring a sword upon you, that shall avenge the quarrel of *my* covenant: and when ye are gathered together within your cities, I will send the pestilence among you; and ye shall be delivered into the hand of the enemy.

26 *And* when I have broken the staff of your bread, ten women shall bake your bread in one oven, and they shall deliver *you* your bread again by weight: and ye shall eat, and not be satisfied.

27 And if ye will not for all this hearken unto me, but walk contrary unto me;

28 Then I will walk contrary unto you also in fury; and I, even I, will chastise you seven times for your sins.

29 And ye shall eat the flesh of your sons, and the flesh of your daughters shall ye eat.

30 And I will destroy your high places, and cut down your images, and cast your carcases upon the carcases of your idols, and my soul shall abhor you.

31 And I will make your cities waste, and bring your sanctuaries unto desolation, and I will not smell the savour of your sweet odours.

32 And I will bring the land into deso-

lation: and your enemies which dwell therein shall be astonished at it.

33 And I will scatter you among the heathen, and will draw out a sword after you: and your land shall be desolate, and your cities waste.

34 Then shall the land enjoy her sabbaths, as long as it lieth desolate, and ye *be* in your enemies' land; *even* then shall the land rest, and enjoy her sabbaths.

35 As long as it lieth desolate it shall rest; because it did not rest in your sabbaths, when ye dwelt upon it.

36 And upon them that are left *alive* of you I will send a faintness into their hearts in the lands of their enemies; and the sound of a shaken leaf shall chase them; and they shall flee, as fleeing from a sword; and they shall fall when none pursueth.

37 And they shall fall one upon another, as it were before a sword, when none pursueth: and ye shall have no power to stand before your enemies.

38 And ye shall perish among the heathen, and the land of your enemies shall eat you up.

39 And they that are left of you shall pine away in their iniquity in your enemies' lands; and also in the iniquities of their fathers shall they pine away with them.

40 If they shall confess their iniquity, and the iniquity of their fathers, with their trespass which they trespassed against me, and that also they have walked contrary unto me;

41 And *that* I also have walked contrary unto them, and have brought them into the land of their enemies; if then their uncircumcised hearts be humbled, and they then accept of the punishment of their iniquity:

42 Then will I remember my covenant with Jacob, and also my covenant with Isaac, and also my covenant with Abraham will I remember; and I will remember the land.

43 The land also shall be left of them, and shall enjoy her sabbaths, while she lieth desolate without them: and they shall accept of the punishment of their iniquity: because, even because they despised my judgments, and because their soul abhorred my statutes.

44 And yet for all that, when they be in the land of their enemies, I will not cast them away, neither will I abhor them, to destroy them utterly, and to break my covenant with them: for I *am* the LORD their God.

45 But I will for their sakes remember the covenant of their ancestors, whom I brought forth out of the land of Egypt in the sight of the heathen, that I might be their God: I *am* the LORD.

46 These *are* the statutes and judgments and laws, which the LORD made between him and the children of Israel in mount Sī'naī by the hand of Moses.

CHAPTER 27

AND the LORD spake unto Moses, saying,

2 Speak unto the children of Israel, and say unto them, When a man shall make a singular vow, the persons *shall be* for the LORD by thy estimation.

3 And thy estimation shall be of the male from twenty years old even unto sixty years old, even thy estimation shall be fifty shekels of silver, after the shekel of the sanctuary.

4 And if it *be* a female, then thy estimation shall be thirty shekels.

5 And if *it be* from five years old even unto twenty years old, then thy estimation shall be of the male twenty shekels, and for the female ten shekels.

6 And if *it be* from a month old even unto five years old, then thy estimation shall be of the male five shekels of silver, and for the female thy estimation *shall be* three shekels of silver.

7 And if *it be* from sixty years old and above; if *it be* a male, then thy estimation shall be fifteen shekels, and for the female ten shekels.

8 But if he be poorer than thy estimation, then he shall present himself before the priest, and the priest shall value him; according to his ability that vowed shall the priest value him.

9 And if *it be* a beast, whereof men bring an offering unto the LORD, all that *any man* giveth of such unto the LORD shall be holy.

10 He shall not alter it, nor change it, a good for a bad, or a bad for a good: and if he shall at all change beast for beast, then it and the exchange thereof shall be holy.

11 And if *it be* any unclean beast, of which they do not offer a sacrifce unto the LORD, then he shall present the beast before the priest:

12 And the priest shall value it, whether it be good or bad; as thou valuest it, *who art* the priest, so shall it be.

13 But if he will at all redeem it, then he shall add a fifth *part* thereof unto thy estimation.

14 ¶And when a man shall sanctify his house *to be* holy unto the LORD, then the priest shall estimate it, whether it be good or bad: as the priest shall estimate it, so shall it stand.

15 And if he that sanctified it will redeem his house, then he shall add the

fifth *part* of the money of thy estimation unto it, and it shall be his.
16 And if a man shall sanctify unto the LORD *some part* of a field of his possession, then thy estimation shall be according to the seed thereof: an homer of barley seed *shall be valued* at fifty shekels of silver.
17 If he sanctify his field from the year of jubile, according to thy estimation it shall stand.
18 But if he sanctify his field after the jubile, then the priest shall reckon unto him the money according to the years that remain, even unto the year of the jubile, and it shall be abated from thy estimation.
19 And if he that sanctified the field will in any wise redeem it, then he shall add the fifth *part* of the money of thy estimation unto it, and it shall be assured to him.
20 And if he will not redeem the field, or if he have sold the field to another man, it shall not be redeemed any more.
21 But the field, when it goeth out in the jubile, shall be holy unto the LORD, as a field devoted; the possession thereof shall be the priest's.
22 And if *a man* sanctify unto the LORD a field which he hath bought, which *is* not of the fields of his possession;
23 Then the priest shall reckon unto him the worth of thy estimation, *even* unto the year of the jubile: and he shall give thine estimation in that day, *as* a holy thing unto the LORD.
24 In the year of the jubile the field shall return unto him of whom it was bought, *even* to him to whom the possession of the land *did belong*.
25 And all thy estimations shall be according to the shekel of the sanctuary: twenty gerahs shall be the shekel.
26 ¶Only the firstling of the beasts, which should be the LORD's firstling, no man shall sanctify it; whether *it be* ox, or sheep: it *is* the LORD's.
27 And if *it be* of an unclean beast, then he shall redeem *it* according to thine estimation, and shall add a fifth *part* of it thereto: or if it be not redeemed, then it shall be sold according to thy estimation.
28 Notwithstanding no devoted thing, that a man shall devote unto the LORD of all that he hath, *both* of man and beast, and of the field of his possession, shall be sold or redeemed: every devoted thing *is* most holy unto the LORD.
29 None devoted, which shall be devoted of men, shall be redeemed; *but* shall surely be put to death.
30 And all the tithe of the land, *whether* of the seed of the land, *or* of the fruit of the tree, *is* the LORD's: *it is* holy unto the LORD.
31 And if a man will at all redeem *ought* of his tithes, he shall add thereto the fifth *part* thereof.
32 And concerning the tithe of the herd, or of the flock, *even* of whatsoever passeth under the rod, the tenth shall be holy unto the LORD.
33 He shall not search whether it be good or bad, neither shall he change it: and if he change it at all, then both it and the change thereof shall be holy; it shall not be redeemed.
34 These *are* the commandments, which the LORD commanded Moses for the children of Israel in mount Sī′naī.

THE FOURTH BOOK OF MOSES
CALLED

NUMBERS

CHAPTER 1

AND the LORD spake unto Moses in the wilderness of Sī′naī, in the tabernacle of the congregation, on the first *day* of the second month, in the second year after they were come out of the land of Egypt, saying,
2 Take ye the sum of all the congregation of the children of Israel, after their families, by the house of their fathers, with the number of *their* names, every male by their polls;
3 From twenty years old and upward, all that are able to go forth to war in Israel: thou and Aaron shall number them by their armies.
4 And with you there shall be a man of every tribe; every one head of the house of his fathers.
5 ¶And these *are* the names of the men that shall stand with you: of *the tribe of* Reuben; E-lī′zur the son of Shĕd′e-ur.
6 Of Simeon; She-lū′mī-el the son of Zū-rĭ-shăd′da-ī.
7 Of Jūdah; Näh′shŏn the son of Am-mĭn′a-dăb.
8 Of Ĭs′sa-char; Ne-thăn′e-el the son of Zū′ar.

9 Of Zĕb′u-lun; E-lī′ab the son of Hē′-lŏn.

10 Of the children of Joseph: of Ē′phra-im; E-lĭsh′a-ma the son of Ăm-mī′hŭd: of Ma-năs′seh; Ga-mā′lī-el the son of Pe-dăh′zur.

11 Of Benjamin; Ab′ī-dan the son of Gĭd-e-ō′nī.

12 Of Dan; Ā-hī-ē′zer the son of Ăm-mĭ-shăd′da-ī.

13 Of Asher; Pā′gĭ-el the son of Ŏc′ran.

14 Of Gad; E-lī′a-săph the son of Deū′el.

15 Of Năph′ta-lī; A-hī′ra the son of Ē′nan.

16 These *were* the renowned of the congregation, princes of the tribes of their fathers, heads of thousands in Israel.

17 ¶And Moses and Aaron took these men which are expressed by *their* names:

18 And they assembled all the congregation together on the first *day* of the second month, and they declared their pedigrees after their families, by the house of their fathers, according to the number of the names, from twenty years old and upward, by their polls.

19 As the LORD commanded Moses, so he numbered them in the wilderness of Sī′naī.

20 ¶And the children of Reuben, Israel's eldest son, by their generations, after their families, by the house of their fathers, according to the number of the names, by their polls, every male from twenty years old and upward, all that were able to go forth to war;

21 Those that were numbered of them, *even* of the tribe of Reuben, *were* forty and six thousand and five hundred.

22 ¶Of the children of Simeon, by their generations, after their families, by the house of their fathers, those that were numbered of them, according to the number of the names, by their polls, every male from twenty years old and upward, all that were able to go forth to war;

23 Those that were numbered of them, *even* of the tribe of Simeon, *were* fifty and nine thousand and three hundred.

24 ¶Of the children of Gad, by their generations, after their families, by the house of their fathers, according to the number of the names, from twenty years old and upward, all that were able to go forth to war;

25 Those that were numbered of them, *even* of the tribe of Gad, *were* forty and five thousand six hundred and fifty.

26 ¶Of the children of Jūdah, by their generations, after their families, by the house of their fathers, according to the number of the names, from twenty years old and upward, all that were able to go forth to war;

27 Those that were numbered of them, *even* of the tribe of Jūdah, *were* threescore and fourteen thousand and six hundred.

28 ¶Of the children of Īs′sa-char, by their generations, after their families, by the house of their fathers, according to the number of the names, from twenty years old and upward, all that were able to go forth to war;

29 Those that were numbered of them, *even* of the tribe of Īs′sa-char, *were* fifty and four thousand and four hundred.

30 ¶Of the children of Zĕb′u-lun, by their generations, after their families, by the house of their fathers, according to the number of the names, from twenty years old and upward, all that were able to go forth to war;

31 Those that were numbered of them, *even* of the tribe of Zĕb′u-lun, *were* fifty and seven thousand and four hundred.

32 ¶Of the children of Joseph, *namely*, of the children of Ē′phra-im, by their generations, after their families, by the house of their fathers, according to the number of the names, from twenty years old and upward, all that were able to go forth to war;

33 Those that were numbered of them, *even* of the tribe of Ē′phra-im, *were* forty thousand and five hundred.

34 ¶Of the children of Ma-năs′seh, by their generations, after their families, by the house of their fathers, according to the number of the names, from twenty years old and upward, all that were able to go forth to war;

35 Those that were numbered of them, *even* of the tribe of Ma-năs′seh, *were* thirty and two thousand and two hundred.

36 ¶Of the children of Benjamin, by their generations, after their families, by the house of their fathers, according to the number of the names, from twenty years old and upward, all that were able to go forth to war;

37 Those that were numbered of them, *even* of the tribe of Benjamin, *were* thirty and five thousand and four hundred.

38 ¶Of the children of Dan, by their generations, after their families, by the house of their fathers, according to the

number of the names, from twenty years old and upward, all that were able to go forth to war;

39 Those that were numbered of them, *even* of the tribe of Dan, *were* threescore and two thousand and seven hundred.

40 ¶Of the children of Asher, by their generations, after their families, by the house of their fathers, according to the number of the names, from twenty years old and upward, all that were able to go forth to war;

41 Those that were numbered of them, *even* of the tribe of Asher, *were* forty and one thousand and five hundred.

42 ¶Of the children of Năph'ta-lī, throughout their generations, after their families, by the house of their fathers, according to the number of the names, from twenty years old and upward, all that were able to go forth to war;

43 Those that were numbered of them, *even* of the tribe of Năph'ta-lī, *were* fifty and three thousand and four hundred.

44 ¶These *are* those that were numbered, which Moses and Aaron numbered, and the princes of Israel, *being* twelve men: each one was for the house of his fathers.

45 So were all those that were numbered of the children of Israel, by the house of their fathers, from twenty years old and upward, all that were able to go forth to war in Israel;

46 Even all they that were numbered were six hundred thousand and three thousand and five hundred and fifty.

47 ¶But the Lēvītes after the tribe of their fathers were not numbered among them.

48 For the LORD had spoken unto Moses, saying,

49 Only thou shalt not number the tribe of Levi, neither take the sum of them among the children of Israel:

50 But thou shalt appoint the Lēvītes over the tabernacle of testimony, and over all the vessels thereof, and over all things that *belong* to it: they shall bear the tabernacle, and all the vessels thereof; and they shall minister unto it, and shall encamp round about the tabernacle.

51 And when the tabernacle setteth forward, the Lēvītes shall take it down: and when the tabernacle is to be pitched, the Levites shall set it up: and the stranger that cometh nigh shall be put to death.

52 And the children of Israel shall pitch their tents, every man by his own camp, and every man by his own standard, throughout their hosts.

53 But the Lēvītes shall pitch round about the tabernacle of testimony, that there be no wrath upon the congregation of the children of Israel: and the Lēvītes shall keep the charge of the tabernacle of testimony.

54 And the children of Israel did according to all that the LORD commanded Moses, so did they.

CHAPTER 2

AND the LORD spake unto Moses and unto Aaron, saying,

2 Every man of the children of Israel shall pitch by his own standard, with the ensign of their father's house: far off about the tabernacle of the congregation shall they pitch.

3 ¶And on the east side toward the rising of the sun shall they of the standard of the camp of Jūdah pitch throughout their armies: and Näh'shŏn the son of Am-mĭn'a-dăb *shall be* captain of the children of Jūdah.

4 And his host, and those that were numbered of them, *were* threescore and fourteen thousand and six hundred.

5 And those that do pitch next unto him *shall be* the tribe of Ĭs'sa-char: and Ne-thăn'e-el the son of Zū'ar *shall be* captain of the children of Ĭs'sa-char.

6 And his host, and those that were numbered thereof, *were* fifty and four thousand and four hundred.

7 *Then* the tribe of Zĕb'u-lun: and E-lī'ab the son of Hē'lŏn *shall be* captain of the children of Zĕb'u-lun.

8 And his host, and those that were numbered thereof, *were* fifty and seven thousand and four hundred.

9 All that were numbered in the camp of Jūdah *were* an hundred thousand and fourscore thousand and six thousand and four hundred, throughout their armies. These shall first set forth.

10 ¶On the south side *shall be* the standard of the camp of Reuben according to their armies: and the captain of the children of Reuben *shall be* E-lī'zur the son of Shĕd'e-ur.

11 And his host, and those that were numbered thereof, *were* forty and six thousand and five hundred.

12 And those which pitch by him *shall be* the tribe of Simeon: and the captain of the children of Simeon *shall be* She-lū'mī-el the son of Zū-rī-shăd'-da-ī.

13 And his host, and those that were numbered of them, *were* fifty and nine thousand and three hundred.

14 Then the tribe of Gad: and the cap-

tain of the sons of Gad *shall be* E-lī'a-
săph the son of Reū'el.
15 And his host, and those that were
numbered of them, *were* forty and five
thousand and six hundred and fifty.
16 All that were numbered in the
camp of Reuben *were* an hundred thou-
sand and fifty and one thousand and
four hundred and fifty, throughout
their armies. And they shall set forth in
the second rank.
17 ¶Then the tabernacle of the con-
gregation shall set forward with the
camp of the Lēvītes in the midst of the
camp: as they encamp, so shall they set
forward, every man in his place by
their standards.
18 ¶On the west side *shall be* the
standard of the camp of Ē'phra-im ac-
cording to their armies: and the captain
of the sons of Ē'phra-im *shall be*
E-lĭsh'a-ma the son of Ăm-mī'hŭd.
19 And his host, and those that were
numbered of them, *were* forty thou-
sand and five hundred.
20 And by him *shall be* the tribe of
Ma-năs'seh: and the captain of the
children of Ma-năs'seh *shall be* Ga-
mā'lī-el the son of Pe-dāh'zur.
21 And his host, and those that were
numbered of them, *were* thirty and two
thousand and two hundred.
22 Then the tribe of Benjamin: and
the captain of the sons of Benjamin
shall be Ab'ī-dan the son of Gĭd-e-ō'nī.
23 And his host, and those that were
numbered of them, *were* thirty and five
thousand and four hundred.
24 All that were numbered of the
camp of Ē'phra-im *were* an hundred
thousand and eight thousand and an
hundred, throughout their armies. And
they shall go forward in the third rank.
25 ¶The standard of the camp of Dan
shall be on the north side by their
armies: and the captain of the children
of Dan *shall be* Ā-hī-ē'zer the son of
Ăm-mī-shăd'da-ī.
26 And his host, and those that were
numbered of them, *were* threescore
and two thousand and seven hundred.
27 And those that encamp by him
shall be the tribe of Asher: and the cap-
tain of the children of Asher *shall be*
Pā'gī-el the son of Ŏc'ran.
28 And his host, and those that were
numbered of them, *were* forty and one
thousand and five hundred.
29 ¶Then the tribe of Năph'ta-lī: and
the captain of the children of Năph'ta-lī
shall be A-hī'ra the son of Ē'nan.
30 And his host, and those that were
numbered of them, *were* fifty and three
thousand and four hundred.
31 All they that were numbered in the
camp of Dan *were* an hundred thou-
sand and fifty and seven thousand and
six hundred. They shall go hindmost
with their standards.
32 ¶These *are* those which were
numbered of the children of Israel by
the house of their fathers: all those
that were numbered of the camps
throughout their hosts *were* six hun-
dred thousand and three thousand and
five hundred and fifty.
33 But the Lēvītes were not num-
bered among the children of Israel; as
the LORD commanded Moses.
34 And the children of Israel did ac-
cording to all that the LORD com-
manded Moses: so they pitched by
their standards, and so they set for-
ward, every one after their families, ac-
cording to the house of their fathers.

CHAPTER 3

THESE also *are* the generations of
Aaron and Moses in the day *that* the
LORD spake with Moses in mount Sī'-
naī.
2 And these *are* the names of the sons
of Aaron; Nādăb the firstborn, and A-
bī'hū, Ē-le-ā'zar, and Ĭth'a-mär.
3 These *are* the names of the sons of
Aaron, the priests which were
anointed, whom he consecrated to min-
ister in the priest's office.
4 And Nādăb and A-bī'hū died before
the LORD, when they offered strange
fire before the LORD, in the wilderness
of Sī'naī, and they had no children: and
Ē-le-ā'zar and Ĭth'a-mär ministered in
the priest's office in the sight of Aaron
their father.
5 ¶And the LORD spake unto Moses,
saying,
6 Bring the tribe of Levi near, and
present them before Aaron the priest,
that they may minister unto him.
7 And they shall keep his charge, and
the charge of the whole congregation
before the tabernacle of the congrega-
tion, to do the service of the tabernacle.
8 And they shall keep all the instru-
ments of the tabernacle of the congre-
gation, and the charge of the children
of Israel, to do the service of the taber-
nacle.
9 And thou shalt give the Lēvītes
unto Aaron and to his sons: they *are*
wholly given unto him out of the chil-
dren of Israel.
10 And thou shalt appoint Aaron and
his sons, and they shall wait on their
priest's office: and the stranger that
cometh nigh shall be put to death.
11 ¶And the LORD spake unto Moses,
saying,
12 And I, behold, I have taken the Lē-

vītes from among the children of Israel instead of all the firstborn that openeth the matrix among the children of Israel: therefore the Lēvītes shall be mine;

13 Because all the firstborn *are* mine; *for* on the day that I smote all the firstborn in the land of Egypt I hallowed unto me all the firstborn in Israel, both man and beast: mine shall they be: I *am* the LORD.

14 ¶And the LORD spake unto Moses in the wilderness of Sī′naī, saying,

15 Number the children of Levi after the house of their fathers, by their families: every male from a month old and upward shalt thou number them.

16 And Moses numbered them according to the word of the LORD, as he was commanded.

17 And these were the sons of Levi by their names; Ger′shon, and Kō′hăth, and Me-râ′rī.

18 And these *are* the names of the sons of Ger′shon by their families; Lĭb′-nī, and Shĭm′e-ī.

19 And the sons of Kō′hăth by their families; Ămrăm, and Ĭz′e-här, Hēbron, and Ŭz′zī-el.

20 And the sons of Me-râ′rī by their families; Mäh′lī, and Mū′shī. These *are* the families of the Lēvītes according to the house of their fathers.

21 ¶Of Ger′shon *was* the family of the Lĭb′nītes, and the family of the Shĭm′-ītes: these *are* the families of the Ger′shon-ītes.

22 Those that were numbered of them, according to the number of all the males, from a month old and upward, *even* those that were numbered of them *were* seven thousand and five hundred.

23 The families of the Ger′shon-ītes shall pitch behind the tabernacle westward.

24 And the chief of the house of the father of the Ger′shon-ītes *shall be* E-lī′a-săph the son of Lā′el.

25 And the charge of the sons of Ger′shon in the tabernacle of the congregation *shall be* the tabernacle, and the tent, the covering thereof, and the hanging for the door of the tabernacle of the congregation,

26 And the hangings of the court, and the curtain for the door of the court, which *is* by the tabernacle, and by the altar round about, and the cords of it for all the service thereof.

27 ¶And of Kō′hăth *was* the family of the Am′ra-mītes, and the family of the Iz′e-här-ītes, and the family of the Hē′-bro-nītes, and the family of the Ŭz′zī-el-ītes: these *are* the families of the Kō′hăth-ītes.

28 In the number of all the males, from a month old and upward, *were* eight thousand and six hundred, keeping the charge of the sanctuary.

29 The families of the sons of Kō′hăth shall pitch on the side of the tabernacle southward.

30 And the chief of the house of the father of the families of the Kō′hăth-ītes *shall be* Ĕ-liz′ā-phăn the son of Ŭz′zī-el.

31 And their charge *shall be* the ark, and the table, and the candlestick, and the altars, and the vessels of the sanctuary wherewith they minister, and the hanging, and all the service thereof.

32 And Ĕ-le-ā′zar the son of Aaron the priest *shall be* chief over the chief of the Lēvītes, *and have* the oversight of them that keep the charge of the sanctuary.

33 ¶Of Me-râ′rī *was* the family of the Mäh′lītes, and the family of the Mū′-shītes: these *are* the families of Me-râ′-rī.

34 And those that were numbered of them, according to the number of all the males, from a month old and upward, *were* six thousand and two hundred.

35 And the chief of the house of the father of the families of Me-râ′rī *was* Zū′rī-el the son of Ăb-i-hā′il: *these* shall pitch on the side of the tabernacle northward.

36 And *under* the custody and charge of the sons of Me-râ′rī *shall be* the boards of the tabernacle, and the bars thereof, and the pillars thereof, and the sockets thereof, and all the vessels thereof, and all that serveth thereto,

37 And the pillars of the court round about, and their sockets, and their pins, and their cords.

38 ¶But those that encamp before the tabernacle toward the east, *even* before the tabernacle of the congregation eastward, *shall be* Moses, and Aaron and his sons, keeping the charge of the sanctuary for the charge of the children of Israel; and the stranger that cometh nigh shall be put to death.

39 All that were numbered of the Lē-vītes, which Moses and Aaron numbered at the commandment of the LORD, throughout their families, all the males from a month old and upward, *were* twenty and two thousand.

40 ¶And the LORD said unto Moses, Number all the firstborn of the males of the children of Israel from a month old and upward, and take the number of their names.

41 And thou shalt take the Lēvītes for me (I *am* the LORD) instead of all the firstborn among the children of Israel; and the cattle of the Lēvītes instead of all the firstlings among the cattle of the children of Israel.

42 And Moses numbered, as the LORD commanded him, all the firstborn among the children of Israel.

43 And all the firstborn males by the number of names, from a month old and upward, of those that were numbered of them, were twenty and two thousand two hundred and threescore and thirteen.

44 ¶And the LORD spake unto Moses, saying,

45 Take the Lēvītes instead of all the firstborn among the children of Israel, and the cattle of the Lēvītes instead of their cattle; and the Lēvītes shall be mine: I *am* the LORD.

46 And for those that are to be redeemed of the two hundred and threescore and thirteen of the firstborn of the children of Israel, which are more than the Lēvītes;

47 Thou shalt even take five shekels apiece by the poll, after the shekel of the sanctuary shalt thou take *them:* (the shekel *is* twenty gerahs:)

48 And thou shalt give the money, wherewith the odd number of them is to be redeemed, unto Aaron and to his sons.

49 And Moses took the redemption money of them that were over and above them that were redeemed by the Lēvītes:

50 Of the firstborn of the children of Israel took he the money; a thousand three hundred and threescore and five *shekels,* after the shekel of the sanctuary:

51 And Moses gave the money of them that were redeemed unto Aaron and to his sons, according to the word of the LORD, as the LORD commanded Moses.

CHAPTER 4

AND the LORD spake unto Moses and unto Aaron, saying,

2 Take the sum of the sons of Kō'hăth from among the sons of Levi, after their families, by the house of their fathers,

3 From thirty years old and upward even until fifty years old, all that enter into the host, to do the work in the tabernacle of the congregation.

4 ¶This *shall be* the service of the sons of Kō'hăth in the tabernacle of the congregation, *about* the most holy things:

5 And when the camp setteth forward, Aaron shall come, and his sons, and they shall take down the covering vail, and cover the ark of testimony with it:

6 And shall put thereon the covering of badgers' skins, and shall spread over *it* a cloth wholly of blue, and shall put in the staves thereof.

7 And upon the table of shewbread they shall spread a cloth of blue, and put thereon the dishes, and the spoons, and the bowls, and covers to cover withal: and the continual bread shall be thereon:

8 And they shall spread upon them a cloth of scarlet, and cover the same with a covering of badgers' skins, and shall put in the staves thereof.

9 And they shall take a cloth of blue, and cover the candlestick of the light, and his lamps, and his tongs, and his snuffdishes, and all the oil vessels thereof, wherewith they minister unto it:

10 And they shall put it and all the vessels thereof within a covering of badgers' skins, and shall put *it* upon a bar.

11 And upon the golden altar they shall spread a cloth of blue, and cover it with a covering of badgers' skins, and shall put to the staves thereof:

12 And they shall take all the instruments of ministry, wherewith they minister in the sanctuary, and put *them* in a cloth of blue, and cover them with a covering of badgers' skins, and shall put *them* on a bar:

13 And they shall take away the ashes from the altar, and spread a purple cloth thereon:

14 And they shall put upon it all the vessels thereof, wherewith they minister about it, *even* the censers, the fleshhooks, and the shovels, and the basons, all the vessels of the altar; and they shall spread upon it a covering of badgers' skins, and put to the staves of it.

15 And when Aaron and his sons have made an end of covering the sanctuary, and all the vessels of the sanctuary, as the camp is to set forward; after that, the sons of Kō'hăth shall come to bear *it:* but they shall not touch *any* holy thing, lest they die. These *things are* the burden of the sons of Kō'hăth in the tabernacle of the congregation.

16 ¶And to the office of Ē-le-ā'zar the son of Aaron the priest *pertaineth* the oil for the light, and the sweet incense, and the daily meat offering, and the anointing oil, *and* the oversight of all the tabernacle, and of all that therein *is,* in the sanctuary, and in the vessels thereof.

17 ¶And the LORD spake unto Moses
and unto Aaron, saying,
18 Cut ye not off the tribe of the fam-
ilies of the Kō′hăth-ītes from among
the Lēvītes:
19 But thus do unto them, that they
may live, and not die, when they ap-
proach unto the most holy things:
Aaron and his sons shall go in, and ap-
point them every one to his service and
to his burden:
20 But they shall not go in to see
when the holy things are covered, lest
they die.
21 ¶And the LORD spake unto Moses,
saying,
22 Take also the sum of the sons of
Ger′shon, throughout the houses of
their fathers, by their families;
23 From thirty years old and upward
until fifty years old shalt thou number
them; all that enter in to perform the
service, to do the work in the taber-
nacle of the congregation.
24 This *is* the service of the families
of the Ger′shon-ītes, to serve, and for
burdens:
25 And they shall bear the curtains of
the tabernacle, and the tabernacle of
the congregation, his covering, and the
covering of the badgers' skins that *is*
above upon it, and the hanging for the
door of the tabernacle of the congrega-
tion,
26 And the hangings of the court, and
the hanging for the door of the gate of
the court, which *is* by the tabernacle
and by the altar round about, and their
cords, and all the instruments of their
service, and all that is made for them:
so shall they serve.
27 At the appointment of Aaron and
his sons shall be all the service of the
sons of the Ger′shon-ītes, in all their
burdens, and in all their service: and ye
shall appoint unto them in charge all
their burdens.
28 This *is* the service of the families
of the sons of Ger′shon in the taber-
nacle of the congregation: and their
charge *shall be* under the hand of Ĭth′a-
mär the son of Aaron the priest.
29 ¶As for the sons of Me-râ′rī, thou
shalt number them after their families,
by the house of their fathers;
30 From thirty years old and upward
even unto fifty years old shalt thou
number them, every one that entereth
into the service, to do the work of the
tabernacle of the congregation.
31 And this *is* the charge of their bur-
den, according to all their service in the
tabernacle of the congregation; the
boards of the tabernacle, and the bars
thereof, and the pillars thereof, and
sockets thereof,
32 And the pillars of the court round
about, and their sockets, and their pins,
and their cords, with all their instru-
ments, and with all their service: and
by name ye shall reckon the instru-
ments of the charge of their burden.
33 This *is* the service of the families
of the sons of Me-râ′rī, according to all
their service, in the tabernacle of the
congregation, under the hand of Ĭth′a-
mär the son of Aaron the priest.
34 ¶And Moses and Aaron and the
chief of the congregation numbered the
sons of the Kō′hăth-ītes after their fam-
ilies, and after the house of their fa-
thers,
35 From thirty years old and upward
even unto fifty years old, every one that
entereth into the service, for the work
in the tabernacle of the congregation:
36 And those that were numbered of
them by their families were two thou-
sand seven hundred and fifty.
37 These *were* they that were num-
bered of the families of the Kō′hăth-
ītes, all that might do service in the
tabernacle of the congregation, which
Moses and Aaron did number accord-
ing to the commandment of the LORD
by the hand of Moses.
38 ¶And those that were numbered of
the sons of Ger′shon, throughout their
families, and by the house of their fa-
thers,
39 From thirty years old and upward
even unto fifty years old, every one that
entereth into the service, for the work
in the tabernacle of the congregation,
40 Even those that were numbered of
them, throughout their families, by the
house of their fathers, were two thou-
sand and six hundred and thirty.
41 These *are* they that were num-
bered of the families of the sons of
Ger′shon, of all that might do service in
the tabernacle of the congregation,
whom Moses and Aaron did number
according to the commandment of the
LORD.
42 ¶And those that were numbered of
the families of the sons of Me-râ′rī,
throughout their families, by the house
of their fathers,
43 From thirty years old and upward
even unto fifty years old, every one that
entereth into the service, for the work
in the tabernacle of the congregation,
44 Even those that were numbered of
them after their families, were three
thousand and two hundred.
45 These *be* those that were num-
bered of the families of the sons of Me-
râ′rī, whom Moses and Aaron num-

Joseph Reveals Himself to His Brothers (Gen 45)

The Wall of Jericho Falls Down (Josh 6)

bered according to the word of the LORD by the hand of Moses.

46 All those that were numbered of the Lēvītes, whom Moses and Aaron and the chief of Israel numbered, after their families, and after the house of their fathers,

47 From thirty years old and upward even unto fifty years old, every one that came to do the service of the ministry, and the service of the burden in the tabernacle of the congregation.

48 Even those that were numbered of them, were eight thousand and five hundred and fourscore.

49 According to the commandment of the LORD they were numbered by the hand of Moses, every one according to his service, and according to his burden: thus were they numbered of him, as the LORD commanded Moses.

CHAPTER 5

AND the LORD spake unto Moses, saying,

2 Command the children of Israel, that they put out of the camp every leper, and every one that hath an issue, and whosoever is defiled by the dead:

3 Both male and female shall ye put out, without the camp shall ye put them; that they defile not their camps, in the midst whereof I dwell.

4 And the children of Israel did so, and put them out without the camp: as the LORD spake unto Moses, so did the children of Israel.

5 ¶And the LORD spake unto Moses, saying,

6 Speak unto the children of Israel, When a man or woman shall commit any sin that men commit, to do a trespass against the LORD, and that person be guilty;

7 Then they shall confess their sin which they have done: and he shall recompense his trespass with the principal thereof, and add unto it the fifth *part* thereof, and give *it* unto *him* against whom he hath trespassed.

8 But if the man have no kinsman to recompense the trespass unto, let the trespass be recompensed unto the LORD, *even* to the priest; beside the ram of the atonement, whereby an atonement shall be made for him.

9 And every offering of all the holy things of the children of Israel, which they bring unto the priest, shall be his.

10 And every man's hallowed things shall be his: whatsoever any man giveth the priest, it shall be his.

11 ¶And the LORD spake unto Moses, saying,

12 Speak unto the children of Israel, and say unto them, If any man's wife go aside, and commit a trespass against him,

13 And a man lie with her carnally, and it be hid from the eyes of her husband, and be kept close, and she be defiled, and *there be* no witness against her, neither she be taken *with the manner;*

14 And the spirit of jealousy come upon him, and he be jealous of his wife, and she be defiled: or if the spirit of jealousy come upon him, and he be jealous of his wife, and she be not defiled:

15 Then shall the man bring his wife unto the priest, and he shall bring her offering for her, the tenth *part* of an ephah of barley meal; he shall pour no oil upon it, nor put frankincense thereon; for it *is* an offering of jealousy, an offering of memorial, bringing iniquity to remembrance.

16 And the priest shall bring her near, and set her before the LORD:

17 And the priest shall take holy water in an earthen vessel; and of the dust that is in the floor of the tabernacle the priest shall take, and put *it* into the water:

18 And the priest shall set the woman before the LORD, and uncover the woman's head, and put the offering of memorial in her hands, which *is* the jealousy offering: and the priest shall have in his hand the bitter water that causeth the curse:

19 And the priest shall charge her by an oath, and say unto the woman, If no man have lain with thee, and if thou hast not gone aside to uncleanness *with another* instead of thy husband, be thou free from this bitter water that causeth the curse:

20 But if thou hast gone aside *to another* instead of thy husband, and if thou be defiled, and some man have lain with thee beside thine husband:

21 Then the priest shall charge the woman with an oath of cursing, and the priest shall say unto the woman, The LORD make thee a curse and an oath among thy people, when the LORD doth make thy thigh to rot, and thy belly to swell;

22 And this water that causeth the curse shall go into thy bowels, to make *thy* belly to swell, and *thy* thigh to rot: And the woman shall say, Amen, amen.

23 And the priest shall write these curses in a book, and he shall blot *them* out with the bitter water:

24 And he shall cause the woman to drink the bitter water that causeth the curse: and the water that causeth the

curse shall enter into her, *and become* bitter.

25 Then the priest shall take the jealousy offering out of the woman's hand, and shall wave the offering before the LORD, and offer it upon the altar:

26 And the priest shall take an handful of the offering, *even* the memorial thereof, and burn *it* upon the altar, and afterward shall cause the woman to drink the water.

27 And when he hath made her to drink the water, then it shall come to pass, *that*, if she be defiled, and have done trespass against her husband, that the water that causeth the curse shall enter into her, *and become* bitter, and her belly shall swell, and her thigh shall rot: and the woman shall be a curse among her people.

28 And if the woman be not defiled, but be clean; then she shall be free, and shall conceive seed.

29 This *is* the law of jealousies, when a wife goeth aside *to another* instead of her husband, and is defiled;

30 Or when the spirit of jealousy cometh upon him, and he be jealous over his wife, and shall set the woman before the LORD, and the priest shall execute upon her all this law.

31 Then shall the man be guiltless from iniquity, and this woman shall bear her iniquity.

CHAPTER 6

AND the LORD spake unto Moses, saying,

2 Speak unto the children of Israel, and say unto them, When either man or woman shall separate *themselves* to vow a vow of a Nazarite, to separate *themselves* unto the LORD:

3 He shall separate *himself* from wine and strong drink, and shall drink no vinegar of wine, or vinegar of strong drink, neither shall he drink any liquor of grapes, nor eat moist grapes, or dried.

4 All the days of his separation shall he eat nothing that is made of the vine tree, from the kernels even to the husk.

5 All the days of the vow of his separation there shall no razor come upon his head: until the days be fulfilled, in the which he separateth *himself* unto the LORD, he shall be holy, *and* shall let the locks of the hair of his head grow.

6 All the days that he separateth *himself* unto the LORD he shall come at no dead body.

7 He shall not make himself unclean for his father, or for his mother, for his brother, or for his sister, when they die: because the consecration of his God *is* upon his head.

8 All the days of his separation he *is* holy unto the LORD.

9 And if any man die very suddenly by him, and he hath defiled the head of his consecration; then he shall shave his head in the day of his cleansing, on the seventh day shall he shave it.

10 And on the eighth day he shall bring two turtles, or two young pigeons, to the priest, to the door of the tabernacle of the congregation:

11 And the priest shall offer the one for a sin offering, and the other for a burnt offering, and make an atonement for him, for that he sinned by the dead, and shall hallow his head that same day.

12 And he shall consecrate unto the LORD the days of his separation, and shall bring a lamb of the first year for a trespass offering: but the days that were before shall be lost, because his separation was defiled.

13 ¶And this *is* the law of the Nazarite, when the days of his separation are fulfilled: he shall be brought unto the door of the tabernacle of the congregation:

14 And he shall offer his offering unto the LORD, one he lamb of the first year without blemish for a burnt offering, and one ewe lamb of the first year without blemish for a sin offering, and one ram without blemish for peace offerings,

15 And a basket of unleavened bread, cakes of fine flour mingled with oil, and wafers of unleavened bread anointed with oil, and their meat offering, and their drink offerings.

16 And the priest shall bring *them* before the LORD, and shall offer his sin offering, and his burnt offering:

17 And he shall offer the ram *for* a sacrifice of peace offerings unto the LORD, with the basket of unleavened bread: the priest shall offer also his meat offering, and his drink offering.

18 And the Nazarite shall shave the head of his separation *at* the door of the tabernacle of the congregation, and shall take the hair of the head of his separation, and put *it* in the fire which *is* under the sacrifice of the peace offerings.

19 And the priest shall take the sodden shoulder of the ram, and one unleavened cake out of the basket, and one unleavened wafer, and shall put *them* upon the hands of the Nazarite, after *the hair of* his separation is shaven:

20 And the priest shall wave them *for*

a wave offering before the LORD: this *is*
holy for the priest, with the wave
breast and heave shoulder: and after
that the Nazarite may drink wine.
21 This *is* the law of the Nazarite who
hath vowed, *and of* his offering unto
the LORD for his separation, beside *that*
that his hand shall get: according to the
vow which he vowed, so he must do after the law of his separation.
22 ¶And the LORD spake unto Moses,
saying,
23 Speak unto Aaron and unto his
sons, saying, On this wise ye shall bless
the children of Israel, saying unto
them,
24 The LORD bless thee, and keep
thee:
25 The LORD make his face shine
upon thee, and be gracious unto thee:
26 The LORD lift up his countenance
upon thee, and give thee peace.
27 And they shall put my name upon
the children of Israel; and I will bless
them.

CHAPTER 7

AND it came to pass on the day that
Moses had fully set up the tabernacle,
and had anointed it, and sanctified it,
and all the instruments thereof, both
the altar and all the vessels thereof, and
had anointed them, and sanctified
them;
2 That the princes of Israel, heads of
the house of their fathers, who *were* the
princes of the tribes, and were over
them that were numbered, offered:
3 And they brought their offering before the LORD, six covered wagons, and
twelve oxen; a wagon for two of the
princes, and for each one an ox: and
they brought them before the tabernacle.
4 And the LORD spake unto Moses,
saying,
5 Take *it* of them, that they may be to
do the service of the tabernacle of the
congregation; and thou shalt give them
unto the Lēvītes, to every man according to his service.
6 And Moses took the wagons and
the oxen, and gave them unto the Lēvītes.
7 Two wagons and four oxen he gave
unto the sons of Ger'shon, according to
their service:
8 And four wagons and eight oxen he
gave unto the sons of Me-râ'rī, according unto their service, under the hand
of Ĭth'a-mär the son of Aaron the priest.
9 But unto the sons of Kō'hăth he
gave none: because the service of the
sanctuary belonging unto them *was*
that they should bear upon their shoulders.
10 ¶And the princes offered for dedicating of the altar in the day that it was
anointed, even the princes offered their
offering before the altar.
11 And the LORD said unto Moses,
They shall offer their offering, each
prince on his day, for the dedicating of
the altar.
12 ¶And he that offered his offering
the first day was Näh'shŏn the son of
Am-mĭn'a-dăb, of the tribe of Jūdah:
13 And his offering *was* one silver
charger, the weight thereof *was* an
hundred and thirty *shekels*, one silver
bowl of seventy shekels, after the
shekel of the sanctuary; both of them
were full of fine flour mingled with oil
for a meat offering:
14 One spoon of ten *shekels* of gold,
full of incense:
15 One young bullock, one ram, one
lamb of the first year, for a burnt offering:
16 One kid of the goats for a sin offering:
17 And for a sacrifice of peace offerings, two oxen, five rams, five he goats,
five lambs of the first year: this *was* the
offering of Näh'shŏn the son of Am-mĭn'a-dăb.
18 ¶On the second day Ne-thăn'e-el
the son of Zū'ar, prince of Ĭs'sa-char,
did offer:
19 He offered *for* his offering one silver charger, the weight whereof *was* an
hundred and thirty *shekels*, one silver
bowl of seventy shekels, after the
shekel of the sanctuary; both of them
full of fine flour mingled with oil for a
meat offering:
20 One spoon of gold of ten *shekels*,
full of incense:
21 One young bullock, one ram, one
lamb of the first year, for a burnt offering:
22 One kid of the goats for a sin offering:
23 And for a sacrifice of peace offerings, two oxen, five rams, five he goats,
five lambs of the first year: this *was* the
offering of Ne-thăn'e-el the son of
Zū'ar.
24 ¶On the third day E-lī'ab the son of
Hē'lŏn, prince of the children of Zĕb'u-lun, *did offer*:
25 His offering *was* one silver charger, the weight whereof *was* an
hundred and thirty *shekels*, one silver
bowl of seventy shekels, after the
shekel of the sanctuary; both of them
full of fine flour mingled with oil for a
meat offering:

26 One golden spoon of ten *shekels,* full of incense:

27 One young bullock, one ram, one lamb of the first year, for a burnt offering:

28 One kid of the goats for a sin offering:

29 And for a sacrifice of peace offerings, two oxen, five rams, five he goats, five lambs of the first year: this *was* the offering of E-lī'ab the son of Hē'lŏn.

30 ¶On the fourth day E-lī'zur the son of Shĕd'e-ur, prince of the children of Reuben, *did offer:*

31 His offering *was* one silver charger of the weight of an hundred and thirty *shekels,* one silver bowl of seventy shekels, after the shekel of the sanctuary; both of them full of fine flour mingled with oil for a meat offering:

32 One golden spoon of ten *shekels,* full of incense:

33 One young bullock, one ram, one lamb of the first year, for a burnt offering:

34 One kid of the goats for a sin offering:

35 And for a sacrifice of peace offerings, two oxen, five rams, five he goats, five lambs of the first year: this *was* the offering of E-lī'zur the son of Shĕd'e-ur.

36 ¶On the fifth day She-lū'mī-el the son of Zū-rī-shăd'da-ī, prince of the children of Simeon, *did offer:*

37 His offering *was* one silver charger, the weight whereof *was* an hundred and thirty *shekels,* one silver bowl of seventy shekels, after the shekel of the sanctuary; both of them full of fine flour mingled with oil for a meat offering:

38 One golden spoon of ten *shekels,* full of incense:

39 One young bullock, one ram, one lamb of the first year, for a burnt offering:

40 One kid of the goats for a sin offering:

41 And for a sacrifice of peace offerings, two oxen, five rams, five he goats, five lambs of the first year: this *was* the offering of She-lū'mī-el the son of Zū-rī-shăd'da-ī.

42 ¶On the sixth day E-lī'a-săph the son of Deū'el, prince of the children of Gad, *offered:*

43 His offering *was* one silver charger of the weight of an hundred and thirty *shekels,* a silver bowl of seventy shekels, after the shekel of the sanctuary; both of them full of fine flour mingled with oil for a meat offering:

44 One golden spoon of ten *shekels,* full of incense:

45 One young bullock, one ram, one lamb of the first year, for a burnt offering:

46 One kid of the goats for a sin offering:

47 And for a sacrifice of peace offerings, two oxen, five rams, five he goats, five lambs of the first year: this *was* the offering of E-lī'a-săph the son of Deū'el.

48 ¶On the seventh day E-lĭsh'a-ma the son of Ăm-mī'hŭd, prince of the children of Ē'phra-im, *offered:*

49 His offering *was* one silver charger, the weight whereof *was* an hundred and thirty *shekels,* one silver bowl of seventy shekels, after the shekel of the sanctuary; both of them full of fine flour mingled with oil for a meat offering:

50 One golden spoon of ten *shekels,* full of incense:

51 One young bullock, one ram, one lamb of the first year, for a burnt offering:

52 One kid of the goats for a sin offering:

53 And for a sacrifice of peace offerings, two oxen, five rams, five he goats, five lambs of the first year: this *was* the offering of E-lĭsh'a-ma the son of Ăm-mī'hŭd.

54 ¶On the eighth day *offered* Ga-mā'lī-el the son of Pe-dāh'zur, prince of the children of Ma-năs'seh:

55 His offering *was* one silver charger of the weight of an hundred and thirty *shekels,* one silver bowl of seventy shekels, after the shekel of the sanctuary; both of them full of fine flour mingled with oil for a meat offering:

56 One golden spoon of ten *shekels,* full of incense:

57 One young bullock, one ram, one lamb of the first year, for a burnt offering:

58 One kid of the goats for a sin offering:

59 And for a sacrifice of peace offerings, two oxen, five rams, five he goats, five lambs of the first year: this *was* the offering of Ga-mā'lī-el the son of Pe-dāh'zur.

60 ¶On the ninth day Ab'ī-dan the son of Gĭd-e-ō'nī, prince of the children of Benjamin, *offered:*

61 His offering *was* one silver charger, the weight whereof *was* an hundred and thirty *shekels,* one silver bowl of seventy shekels, after the shekel of the sanctuary; both of them full of fine flour mingled with oil for a meat offering:

62 One golden spoon of ten *shekels,* full of incense:

63 One young bullock, one ram, one lamb of the first year, for a burnt offering:
64 One kid of the goats for a sin offering:
65 And for a sacrifice of peace offerings, two oxen, five rams, five he goats, five lambs of the first year: this *was* the offering of Ab'ĭ-dan the son of Gĭd-e-ō'nī.
66 ¶On the tenth day Ā-hī-ē'zer the son of Ăm-mī-shăd'da-ī, prince of the children of Dan, *offered:*
67 His offering *was* one silver charger, the weight whereof *was* an hundred and thirty *shekels,* one silver bowl of seventy shekels, after the shekel of the sanctuary; both of them full of fine flour mingled with oil for a meat offering:
68 One golden spoon of ten *shekels,* full of incense:
69 One young bullock, one ram, one lamb of the first year, for a burnt offering:
70 One kid of the goats for a sin offering:
71 And for a sacrifice of peace offerings, two oxen, five rams, five he goats, five lambs of the first year: this *was* the offering of Ā-hī-ē'zer the son of Ăm-mī-shăd'da-ī.
72 ¶On the eleventh day Pā'gī-el the son of Ōc'ran, prince of the children of Asher, *offered:*
73 His offering *was* one silver charger, the weight whereof *was* an hundred and thirty *shekels,* one silver bowl of seventy shekels, after the shekel of the sanctuary; both of them full of fine flour mingled with oil for a meat offering:
74 One golden spoon of ten *shekels,* full of incense:
75 One young bullock, one ram, one lamb of the first year, for a burnt offering:
76 One kid of the goats for a sin offering:
77 And for a sacrifice of peace offerings, two oxen, five rams, five he goats, five lambs of the first year: this *was* the offering of Pā'gī-el the son of Ōc'ran.
78 ¶On the twelfth day A-hī'ra the son of Ē'nan, prince of the children of Năph'ta-lī, *offered:*
79 His offering *was* one silver charger, the weight whereof *was* an hundred and thirty *shekels,* one silver bowl of seventy shekels, after the shekel of the sanctuary; both of them full of fine flour mingled with oil for a meat offering:
80 One golden spoon of ten *shekels,* full of incense:
81 One young bullock, one ram, one lamb of the first year, for a burnt offering:
82 One kid of the goats for a sin offering:
83 And for a sacrifice of peace offerings, two oxen, five rams, five he goats, five lambs of the first year: this *was* the offering of A-hī'ra the son of Ē'nan.
84 This *was* the dedication of the altar, in the day when it was anointed, by the princes of Israel: twelve chargers of silver, twelve silver bowls, twelve spoons of gold:
85 Each charger of silver *weighing* an hundred and thirty *shekels,* each bowl seventy: all the silver vessels *weighed* two thousand and four hundred *shekels,* after the shekel of the sanctuary:
86 The golden spoons *were* twelve, full of incense, *weighing* ten *shekels* apiece, after the shekel of the sanctuary: all the gold of the spoons *was* an hundred and twenty *shekels.*
87 All the oxen for the burnt offering *were* twelve bullocks, the rams twelve, the lambs of the first year twelve, with their meat offering: and the kids of the goats for sin offering twelve.
88 And all the oxen for the sacrifice of the peace offerings *were* twenty and four bullocks, the rams sixty, the he goats sixty, the lambs of the first year sixty. This *was* the dedication of the altar, after that it was anointed.
89 And when Moses was gone into the tabernacle of the congregation to speak with him, then he heard the voice of one speaking unto him from off the mercy seat that *was* upon the ark of testimony, from between the two cherubims: and he spake unto him.

CHAPTER 8

AND the LORD spake unto Moses, saying,
2 Speak unto Aaron, and say unto him, When thou lightest the lamps, the seven lamps shall give light over against the candlestick.
3 And Aaron did so; he lighted the lamps thereof over against the candlestick, as the LORD commanded Moses.
4 And this work of the candlestick *was of* beaten gold, unto the shaft thereof, unto the flowers thereof, *was* beaten work: according unto the pattern which the LORD had shewed Moses, so he made the candlestick.
5 ¶And the LORD spake unto Moses, saying,
6 Take the Lēvītes from among the children of Israel, and cleanse them.
7 And thus shalt thou do unto them,

to cleanse them: Sprinkle water of purifying upon them, and let them shave all their flesh, and let them wash their clothes, and *so* make themselves clean.

8 Then let them take a young bullock with his meat offering, *even* fine flour mingled with oil, and another young bullock shalt thou take for a sin offering.

9 And thou shalt bring the Lēvītes before the tabernacle of the congregation: and thou shalt gather the whole assembly of the children of Israel together:

10 And thou shalt bring the Lēvītes before the LORD: and the children of Israel shall put their hands upon the Lēvītes:

11 And Aaron shall offer the Lēvītes before the LORD *for* an offering of the children of Israel, that they may execute the service of the LORD.

12 And the Lēvītes shall lay their hands upon the heads of the bullocks: and thou shalt offer the one *for* a sin offering, and the other *for* a burnt offering, unto the LORD, to make an atonement for the Lēvītes.

13 And thou shalt set the Lēvītes before Aaron, and before his sons, and offer them *for* an offering unto the LORD.

14 Thus shalt thou separate the Lēvītes from among the children of Israel: and the Lēvītes shall be mine.

15 And after that shall the Lēvītes go in to do the service of the tabernacle of the congregation: and thou shalt cleanse them, and offer them *for* an offering.

16 For they *are* wholly given unto me from among the children of Israel; instead of such as open every womb, *even instead of* the firstborn of all the children of Israel, have I taken them unto me.

17 For all the firstborn of the children of Israel *are* mine, *both* man and beast: on the day that I smote every firstborn in the land of Egypt I sanctified them for myself.

18 And I have taken the Lēvītes for all the firstborn of the children of Israel.

19 And I have given the Lēvītes *as* a gift to Aaron and to his sons from among the children of Israel, to do the service of the children of Israel in the tabernacle of the congregation, and to make an atonement for the children of Israel: that there be no plague among the children of Israel, when the children of Israel come nigh unto the sanctuary.

20 And Moses, and Aaron, and all the congregation of the children of Israel, did to the Lēvītes according unto all that the LORD commanded Moses concerning the Lēvītes, so did the children of Israel unto them.

21 And the Lēvītes were purified, and they washed their clothes; and Aaron offered them *as* an offering before the LORD; and Aaron made an atonement for them to cleanse them.

22 And after that went the Lēvītes in to do their service in the tabernacle of the congregation before Aaron, and before his sons: as the LORD had commanded Moses concerning the Lēvītes, so did they unto them.

23 ¶And the LORD spake unto Moses, saying,

24 This *is it* that *belongeth* unto the Lēvītes: from twenty and five years old and upward they shall go in to wait upon the service of the tabernacle of the congregation:

25 And from the age of fifty years they shall cease waiting upon the service *thereof*, and shall serve no more:

26 But shall minister with their brethren in the tabernacle of the congregation, to keep the charge, and shall do no service. Thus shalt thou do unto the Lēvītes touching their charge.

CHAPTER 9

AND the LORD spake unto Moses in the wilderness of Sī'naī, in the first month of the second year after they were come out of the land of Egypt, saying,

2 Let the children of Israel also keep the passover at his appointed season.

3 In the fourteenth day of this month, at even, ye shall keep it in his appointed season: according to all the rites of it, and according to all the ceremonies thereof, shall ye keep it.

4 And Moses spake unto the children of Israel, that they should keep the passover.

5 And they kept the passover on the fourteenth day of the first month at even in the wilderness of Sī'naī: according to all that the LORD commanded Moses, so did the children of Israel.

6 ¶And there were certain men, who were defiled by the dead body of a man, that they could not keep the passover on that day: and they came before Moses and before Aaron on that day:

7 And those men said unto him, We *are* defiled by the dead body of a man: wherefore are we kept back, that we may not offer an offering of the LORD in his appointed season among the children of Israel?

8 And Moses said unto them, Stand still, and I will hear what the LORD will command concerning you.

9 ¶And the LORD spake unto Moses, saying,

10 Speak unto the children of Israel, saying, If any man of you or of your posterity shall be unclean by reason of a dead body, or *be* in a journey afar off, yet he shall keep the passover unto the LORD.

11 The fourteenth day of the second month at even they shall keep it, *and* eat it with unleavened bread and bitter *herbs*.

12 They shall leave none of it unto the morning, nor break any bone of it: according to all the ordinances of the passover they shall keep it.

13 But the man that *is* clean, and is not in a journey, and forbeareth to keep the passover, even the same soul shall be cut off from among his people: because he brought not the offering of the LORD in his appointed season, that man shall bear his sin.

14 And if a stranger shall sojourn among you, and will keep the passover unto the LORD; according to the ordinance of the passover, and according to the manner thereof, so shall he do: ye shall have one ordinance, both for the stranger, and for him that was born in the land.

15 ¶And on the day that the tabernacle was reared up the cloud covered the tabernacle, *namely*, the tent of the testimony: and at even there was upon the tabernacle as it were the appearance of fire, until the morning.

16 So it was alway: the cloud covered it *by day*, and the appearance of fire by night.

17 And when the cloud was taken up from the tabernacle, then after that the children of Israel journeyed: and in the place where the cloud abode, there the children of Israel pitched their tents.

18 At the commandment of the LORD the children of Israel journeyed, and at the commandment of the LORD they pitched: as long as the cloud abode upon the tabernacle they rested in their tents.

19 And when the cloud tarried long upon the tabernacle many days, then the children of Israel kept the charge of the LORD, and journeyed not.

20 And *so* it was, when the cloud was a few days upon the tabernacle; according to the commandment of the LORD they abode in their tents, and according to the commandment of the LORD they journeyed.

21 And *so* it was, when the cloud abode from even unto the morning, and *that* the cloud was taken up in the morning, then they journeyed: whether *it was* by day or by night that the cloud was taken up, they journeyed.

22 Or *whether it were* two days, or a month, or a year, that the cloud tarried upon the tabernacle, remaining thereon, the children of Israel abode in their tents, and journeyed not: but when it was taken up, they journeyed.

23 At the commandment of the LORD they rested in the tents, and at the commandment of the LORD they journeyed: they kept the charge of the LORD, at the commandment of the LORD by the hand of Moses.

CHAPTER 10

AND the LORD spake unto Moses, saying,

2 Make thee two trumpets of silver; of a whole piece shalt thou make them: that thou mayest use them for the calling of the assembly, and for the journeying of the camps.

3 And when they shall blow with them, all the assembly shall assemble themselves to thee at the door of the tabernacle of the congregation.

4 And if they blow *but* with one *trumpet*, then the princes, *which are* heads of the thousands of Israel, shall gather themselves unto thee.

5 When ye blow an alarm, then the camps that lie on the east parts shall go forward.

6 When ye blow an alarm the second time, then the camps that lie on the south side shall take their journey: they shall blow an alarm for their journeys.

7 But when the congregation is to be gathered together, ye shall blow, but ye shall not sound an alarm.

8 And the sons of Aaron, the priests, shall blow with the trumpets; and they shall be to you for an ordinance for ever throughout your generations.

9 And if ye go to war in your land against the enemy that oppresseth you, then ye shall blow an alarm with the trumpets; and ye shall be remembered before the LORD your God, and ye shall be saved from your enemies.

10 Also in the day of your gladness, and in your solemn days, and in the beginnings of your months, ye shall blow with the trumpets over your burnt offerings, and over the sacrifices of your peace offerings; that they may be to you for a memorial before your God: I *am* the LORD your God.

11 ¶And it came to pass on the twentieth *day* of the second month, in the second year, that the cloud was taken up from off the tabernacle of the testimony.

12 And the children of Israel took

their journeys out of the wilderness of Sī′naī: and the cloud rested in the wilderness of Paran.

13 And they first took their journey according to the commandment of the LORD by the hand of Moses.

14 ¶In the first *place* went the standard of the camp of the children of Jū-dah according to their armies: and over his host *was* Näh′shŏn the son of Am-mĭn′a-dăb.

15 And over the host of the tribe of the children of Ĭs′sa-char *was* Ne-thăn′e-el the son of Zū′ar.

16 And over the host of the tribe of the children of Zĕb′u-lun *was* E-lī′ab the son of Hē′lŏn.

17 And the tabernacle was taken down; and the sons of Ger′shon and the sons of Me-râ′rī set forward, bearing the tabernacle.

18 And the standard of the camp of Reuben set forward according to their armies: and over his host *was* E-lī′zur the son of Shĕd′e-ur.

19 And over the host of the tribe of the children of Simeon *was* She-lū′mī-el the son of Zū-rī-shăd′da-ī.

20 And over the host of the tribe of the children of Gad *was* E-lī′a-săph the son of Deū′el.

21 And the Kō′hăth-ītes set forward, bearing the sanctuary: and *the other* did set up the tabernacle against they came.

22 And the standard of the camp of the children of Ē′phra-im set forward according to their armies: and over his host *was* E′lĭsh′a-ma the son of Ăm-mī′hŭd.

23 And over the host of the tribe of the children of Ma-năs′seh *was* Ga-mā′lī-el the son of Pe-däh′zur.

24 And over the host of the tribe of the children of Benjamin *was* Ab′ĭ-dan the son of Gĭd-e-ō′nī.

25 And the standard of the camp of the children of Dan set forward, *which was* the rereward of all the camps throughout their hosts: and over his host *was* Ā-hī-ē′zer the son of Ăm-mĭ-shăd′da-ī.

26 And over the host of the tribe of the children of Asher *was* Pā′gĭ-el the son of Ŏc′ran.

27 And over the host of the tribe of the children of Năph′ta-lī *was* A-hī′ra the son of Ē′nan.

28 Thus *were* the journeyings of the children of Israel according to their armies, when they set forward.

29 ¶And Moses said unto Hō′băb, the son of Ră-gū′el the Mĭd′ĭ-an-īte, Moses' father in law, We are journeying unto the place of which the LORD said, I will give it you: come thou with us, and we will do thee good: for the LORD hath spoken good concerning Israel.

30 And he said unto him, I will not go; but I will depart to mine own land, and to my kindred.

31 And he said, Leave us not, I pray thee; forasmuch as thou knowest how we are to encamp in the wilderness, and thou mayest be to us instead of eyes.

32 And it shall be, if thou go with us, yea, it shall be, that what goodness the LORD shall do unto us, the same will we do unto thee.

33 ¶And they departed from the mount of the LORD three days' journey: and the ark of the covenant of the LORD went before them in the three days' journey, to search out a resting place for them.

34 And the cloud of the LORD *was* upon them by day, when they went out of the camp.

35 And it came to pass, when the ark set forward, that Moses said, Rise up, LORD, and let thine enemies be scattered; and let them that hate thee flee before thee.

36 And when it rested, he said, Return, O LORD, unto the many thousands of Israel.

CHAPTER 11

AND *when* the people complained, it displeased the LORD: and the LORD heard *it;* and his anger was kindled; and the fire of the LORD burnt among them, and consumed *them that were* in the uttermost parts of the camp.

2 And the people cried unto Moses; and when Moses prayed unto the LORD, the fire was quenched.

3 And he called the name of the place Tăb′e-rah: because the fire of the LORD burnt among them.

4 ¶And the mixt multitude that *was* among them fell a lusting: and the children of Israel also wept again, and said, Who shall give us flesh to eat?

5 We remember the fish, which we did eat in Egypt freely; the cucumbers, and the melons, and the leeks, and the onions, and the garlick:

6 But now our soul *is* dried away: *there is* nothing at all, beside this manna, *before* our eyes.

7 And the manna *was* as coriander seed, and the colour thereof as the colour of bdellium.

8 *And* the people went about, and gathered *it,* and ground *it* in mills, or beat *it* in a mortar, and baked *it* in pans, and made cakes of it: and the taste of it was as the taste of fresh oil.

9 And when the dew fell upon the camp in the night, the manna fell upon it.

10 ¶Then Moses heard the people weep throughout their families, every man in the door of his tent: and the anger of the LORD was kindled greatly; Moses also was displeased.

11 And Moses said unto the LORD, Wherefore hast thou afflicted thy servant? and wherefore have I not found favour in thy sight, that thou layest the burden of all this people upon me?

12 Have I conceived all this people? have I begotten them, that thou shouldest say unto me, Carry them in thy bosom, as a nursing father beareth the sucking child, unto the land which thou swarest unto their fathers?

13 Whence should I have flesh to give unto all this people? for they weep unto me, saying, Give us flesh, that we may eat.

14 I am not able to bear all this people alone, because *it is* too heavy for me.

15 And if thou deal thus with me, kill me, I pray thee, out of hand, if I have found favour in thy sight; and let me not see my wretchedness.

16 ¶And the LORD said unto Moses, Gather unto me seventy men of the elders of Israel, whom thou knowest to be the elders of the people, and officers over them; and bring them unto the tabernacle of the congregation, that they may stand there with thee.

17 And I will come down and talk with thee there: and I will take of the spirit which *is* upon thee, and will put *it* upon them; and they shall bear the burden of the people with thee, that thou bear *it* not thyself alone.

18 And say thou unto the people, Sanctify yourselves against to morrow, and ye shall eat flesh: for ye have wept in the ears of the LORD, saying, Who shall give us flesh to eat? for *it was* well with us in Egypt: therefore the LORD will give you flesh, and ye shall eat.

19 Ye shall not eat one day, nor two days, nor five days, neither ten days, nor twenty days;

20 *But* even a whole month, until it come out at your nostrils, and it be loathsome unto you: because that ye have despised the LORD which *is* among you, and have wept before him, saying, Why came we forth out of Egypt?

21 And Moses said, The people, among whom I *am, are* six hundred thousand footmen; and thou hast said, I will give them flesh, that they may eat a whole month.

22 Shall the flocks and the herds be slain for them, to suffice them? or shall all the fish of the sea be gathered together for them, to suffice them?

23 And the LORD said unto Moses, Is the LORD's hand waxed short? thou shalt see now whether my word shall come to pass unto thee or not.

24 ¶And Moses went out, and told the people the words of the LORD, and gathered the seventy men of the elders of the people, and set them round about the tabernacle.

25 And the LORD came down in a cloud, and spake unto him, and took of the spirit that *was* upon him, and gave *it* unto the seventy elders: and it came to pass, *that,* when the spirit rested upon them, they prophesied, and did not cease.

26 But there remained two *of the* men in the camp, the name of the one *was* Ĕl′dăd, and the name of the other Mē′dăd: and the spirit rested upon them; and they *were* of them that were written, but went not out unto the tabernacle: and they prophesied in the camp.

27 And there ran a young man, and told Moses, and said, Ĕl′dăd and Mē′dăd do prophesy in the camp.

28 And Joshua the son of Nun, the servant of Moses, *one* of his young men, answered and said, My lord Moses, forbid them.

29 And Moses said unto him, Enviest thou for my sake? would God that all the LORD's people were prophets, *and* that the LORD would put his spirit upon them!

30 And Moses gat him into the camp, he and the elders of Israel.

31 ¶And there went forth a wind from the LORD, and brought quails from the sea, and let *them* fall by the camp, as it were a day's journey on this side, and as it were a day's journey on the other side, round about the camp, and as it were two cubits *high* upon the face of the earth.

32 And the people stood up all that day, and all *that* night, and all the next day, and they gathered the quails: he that gathered least gathered ten homers: and they spread *them* all abroad for themselves round about the camp.

33 And while the flesh *was* yet between their teeth, ere it was chewed, the wrath of the LORD was kindled against the people, and the LORD smote the people with a very great plague.

34 And he called the name of that place Kĭb′rŏth-hat-tā′a-vah: because there they buried the people that lusted.

35 *And* the people journeyed from Kĭb'rŏth-hat-tā'a-vah unto Ha-ze'rŏth; and abode at Ha-ze'rŏth.

CHAPTER 12

AND Miriam and Aaron spake against Moses because of the Ē-thĭ-ō'pĭ-an woman whom he had married: for he had married an Ē-thĭ-ō'pĭ-an woman.
2 And they said, Hath the LORD indeed spoken only by Moses? hath he not spoken also by us? And the LORD heard *it*.
3 (Now the man Moses *was* very meek, above all the men which *were* upon the face of the earth.)
4 And the LORD spake suddenly unto Moses, and unto Aaron, and unto Miriam, Come out ye three unto the tabernacle of the congregation. And they three came out.
5 And the LORD came down in the pillar of the cloud, and stood *in* the door of the tabernacle, and called Aaron and Miriam: and they both came forth.
6 And he said, Hear now my words: If there be a prophet among you, *I* the LORD will make myself known unto him in a vision, *and* will speak unto him in a dream.
7 My servant Moses *is* not so, who *is* faithful in all mine house.
8 With him will I speak mouth to mouth, even apparently, and not in dark speeches; and the similitude of the LORD shall he behold: wherefore then were ye not afraid to speak against my servant Moses?
9 And the anger of the LORD was kindled against them; and he departed.
10 And the cloud departed from off the tabernacle; and, behold, Miriam *became* leprous, *white* as snow: and Aaron looked upon Miriam, and, behold, *she was* leprous.
11 And Aaron said unto Moses, Alas, my lord, I beseech thee, lay not the sin upon us, wherein we have done foolishly, and wherein we have sinned.
12 Let her not be as one dead, of whom the flesh is half consumed when he cometh out of his mother's womb.
13 And Moses cried unto the LORD, saying, Heal her now, O God, I beseech thee.
14 ¶And the LORD said unto Moses, If her father had but spit in her face, should she not be ashamed seven days? let her be shut out from the camp seven days, and after that let her be received in *again*.
15 And Miriam was shut out from the camp seven days: and the people journeyed not till Miriam was brought in *again*.
16 And afterward the people removed from Ha-ze'rŏth, and pitched in the wilderness of Paran.

CHAPTER 13

AND the LORD spake unto Moses, saying,
2 Send thou men, that they may search the land of Canaan, which I give unto the children of Israel: of every tribe of their fathers shall ye send a man, every one a ruler among them.
3 And Moses by the commandment of the LORD sent them from the wilderness of Paran: all those men *were* heads of the children of Israel.
4 And these *were* their names: of the tribe of Reuben, Shăm-mū'a the son of Zăc'cur.
5 Of the tribe of Simeon, Shā'phat the son of Hō'rī.
6 Of the tribe of Jūdah, Caleb the son of Je-phŭn'neh.
7 Of the tribe of Ĭs'sa-char, Ī'găl the son of Joseph.
8 Of the tribe of Ē'phra-im, Ō-shē'a the son of Nun.
9 Of the tribe of Benjamin, Păl'tī the son of Rā'phū.
10 Of the tribe of Zĕb'u-lun, Găd'dī-el the son of Sō'dī.
11 Of the tribe of Joseph, *namely*, of the tribe of Ma-năs'seh, Găd'dī the son of Sū'sī.
12 Of the tribe of Dan, Ăm'mī-el the son of Ge-măl'lī.
13 Of the tribe of Asher, Sē'thur the son of Michael.
14 Of the tribe of Năph'ta-lī, Näh'bī the son of Vŏph'sī.
15 Of the tribe of Gad, Ge-ū'el the son of Mā'chī.
16 These *are* the names of the men which Moses sent to spy out the land. And Moses called Ō-shē'a the son of Nun Je-hŏsh'u-a.
17 ¶And Moses sent them to spy out the land of Canaan, and said unto them, Get you up this *way* southward, and go up into the mountain:
18 And see the land, what it *is;* and the people that dwelleth therein, whether they *be* strong or weak, few or many;
19 And what the land *is* that they dwell in, whether it *be* good or bad; and what cities *they be* that they dwell in, whether in tents, or in strong holds;
20 And what the land *is,* whether it *be* fat or lean, whether there be wood therein, or not. And be ye of good courage, and bring of the fruit of the

land. Now the time *was* the time of the
firstripe grapes.
21 So they went up, and searched the
land from the wilderness of Zin unto
Rē'hŏb, as men come to Hā'măth.
22 And they ascended by the south,
and came unto Hēbron; where A-hī'-
man, Shē'shaī, and Tăl'maī, the chil-
dren of Anak, *were.* (Now Hēbron was
built seven years before Zō'an in
Egypt.)
23 And they came unto the brook of
Ĕsh'cōl, and cut down from thence a
branch with one cluster of grapes, and
they bare it between two upon a staff;
and *they brought* of the pomegranates,
and of the figs.
24 The place was called the brook
Ĕsh'cōl, because of the cluster of
grapes which the children of Israel cut
down from thence.
25 And they returned from searching
of the land after forty days.
26 ¶And they went and came to
Moses, and to Aaron, and to all the
congregation of the children of Israel,
unto the wilderness of Paran, to Kā'-
desh; and brought back word unto
them, and unto all the congregation,
and shewed them the fruit of the land.
27 And they told him, and said, We
came unto the land whither thou sent-
est us, and surely it floweth with milk
and honey; and this *is* the fruit of it.
28 Nevertheless the people *be* strong
that dwell in the land, and the cities *are*
walled, *and* very great: and moreover
we saw the children of Anak there.
29 The Am'ă-lek-ītes dwell in the
land of the south: and the Hittites, and
the Jēb'u-sītes, and the Ămorītes, dwell
in the mountains: and the Canaanites
dwell by the sea, and by the coast of
Jordan.
30 And Caleb stilled the people be-
fore Moses, and said, Let us go up at
once, and possess it; for we are well
able to overcome it.
31 But the men that went up with him
said, We be not able to go up against
the people; for they *are* stronger than
we.
32 And they brought up an evil report
of the land which they had searched
unto the children of Israel, saying, The
land, through which we have gone to
search it, *is* a land that eateth up the
inhabitants thereof; and all the people
that we saw in it *are* men of a great stat-
ure.
33 And there we saw the giants, the
sons of Anak, *which come* of the
giants: and we were in our own sight as
grasshoppers, and so we were in their
sight.

CHAPTER 14

AND all the congregation lifted up
their voice, and cried; and the people
wept that night.
2 And all the children of Israel mur-
mured against Moses and against
Aaron: and the whole congregation
said unto them, Would God that we
had died in the land of Egypt! or would
God we had died in this wilderness!
3 And wherefore hath the LORD
brought us unto this land, to fall by the
sword, that our wives and our children
should be a prey? were it not better for
us to return into Egypt?
4 And they said one to another, Let us
make a captain, and let us return into
Egypt.
5 Then Moses and Aaron fell on their
faces before all the assembly of the
congregation of the children of Israel.
6 And Joshua the son of Nun, and
Caleb the son of Je-phŭn'neh, *which
were* of them that searched the land,
rent their clothes:
7 And they spake unto all the com-
pany of the children of Israel, saying,
The land, which we passed through to
search it, *is* an exceeding good land.
8 If the LORD delight in us, then he
will bring us into this land, and give it
us; a land which floweth with milk and
honey.
9 Only rebel not ye against the LORD,
neither fear ye the people of the land;
for they *are* bread for us: their defence
is departed from them, and the LORD *is*
with us: fear them not.
10 But all the congregation bade
stone them with stones. And the glory
of the LORD appeared in the tabernacle
of the congregation before all the chil-
dren of Israel.
11 ¶And the LORD said unto Moses,
How long will this people provoke me?
and how long will it be ere they believe
me, for all the signs which I have
shewed among them?
12 I will smite them with the pesti-
lence, and disinherit them, and will
make of thee a greater nation and
mightier than they.
13 And Moses said unto the LORD,
Then the Egyptians shall hear *it,* (for
thou broughtest up this people in thy
might from among them;)
14 And they will tell *it* to the inhabi-
tants of this land: *for* they have heard
that thou LORD *art* among this people,
that thou LORD art seen face to face,
and *that* thy cloud standeth over them,
and *that* thou goest before them, by
day time in a pillar of a cloud, and in a
pillar of fire by night.
15 Now *if* thou shalt kill *all* this peo-

ple as one man, then the nations which have heard the fame of thee will speak, saying,

16 Because the Lord was not able to bring this people into the land which he sware unto them, therefore he hath slain them in the wilderness.

17 And now, I beseech thee, let the power of my Lord be great, according as thou hast spoken, saying,

18 The Lord *is* longsuffering, and of great mercy, forgiving iniquity and transgression, and by no means clearing *the guilty,* visiting the iniquity of the fathers upon the children unto the third and fourth *generation.*

19 Pardon, I beseech thee, the iniquity of this people according unto the greatness of thy mercy, and as thou hast forgiven this people, from Egypt even until now.

20 And the Lord said, I have pardoned according to thy word:

21 But *as* truly *as* I live, all the earth shall be filled with the glory of the Lord.

22 Because all those men which have seen my glory, and my miracles, which I did in Egypt and in the wilderness, and have tempted me now these ten times, and have not hearkened to my voice;

23 Surely they shall not see the land which I sware unto their fathers, neither shall any of them that provoked me see it:

24 But my servant Caleb, because he had another spirit with him, and hath followed me fully, him will I bring into the land whereinto he went; and his seed shall possess it.

25 (Now the Am'ă-lek-ītes and the Canaanites dwelt in the valley.) To-morrow turn you, and get you into the wilderness by the way of the Red sea.

26 ¶And the Lord spake unto Moses and unto Aaron, saying,

27 How long *shall I bear with* this evil congregation, which murmur against me? I have heard the murmurings of the children of Israel, which they murmur against me.

28 Say unto them, *As truly as* I live, saith the Lord, as ye have spoken in mine ears, so will I do to you:

29 Your carcases shall fall in this wilderness; and all that were numbered of you, according to your whole number, from twenty years old and upward, which have murmured against me,

30 Doubtless ye shall not come into the land, *concerning* which I sware to make you dwell therein, save Caleb the son of Je-phŭn'neh, and Joshua the son of Nun.

31 But your little ones, which ye said should be a prey, them will I bring in, and they shall know the land which ye have despised.

32 But *as for* you, your carcases, they shall fall in this wilderness.

33 And your children shall wander in the wilderness forty years, and bear your whoredoms, until your carcases be wasted in the wilderness.

34 After the number of the days in which ye searched the land, *even* forty days, each day for a year, shall ye bear your iniquities, *even* forty years, and ye shall know my breach of promise.

35 I the Lord have said, I will surely do it unto all this evil congregation, that are gathered together against me: in this wilderness they shall be consumed, and there they shall die.

36 And the men, which Moses sent to search the land, who returned, and made all the congregation to murmur against him, by bringing up a slander upon the land,

37 Even those men that did bring up the evil report upon the land, died by the plague before the Lord.

38 But Joshua the son of Nun, and Caleb the son of Je-phŭn'neh, *which were* of the men that went to search the land, lived *still.*

39 And Moses told these sayings unto all the children of Israel: and the people mourned greatly.

40 And they rose up early in the morning, and gat them up into the top of the mountain, saying, Lo, we *be here,* and will go up unto the place which the Lord hath promised: for we have sinned.

41 And Moses said, Wherefore now do ye transgress the commandment of the Lord? but it shall not prosper.

42 Go not up, for the Lord *is* not among you; that ye be not smitten before your enemies.

43 For the Am'ă-lek-ītes and the Canaanites *are* there before you, and ye shall fall by the sword: because ye are turned away from the Lord, therefore the Lord will not be with you.

44 But they presumed to go up unto the hill top: nevertheless the ark of the covenant of the Lord, and Moses, departed not out of the camp.

45 Then the Am'ă-lek-ītes came down, and the Canaanites which dwelt in that hill, and smote them, and discomfited them, *even* unto Hôr'mah.

CHAPTER 15

AND the Lord spake unto Moses, saying,

2 Speak unto the children of Israel, and say unto them, When ye be come into the land of your habitations, which I give unto you,

3 And will make an offering by fire unto the LORD, a burnt offering, or a sacrifice in performing a vow, or in a freewill offering, or in your solemn feasts, to make a sweet savour unto the LORD, of the herd, or of the flock:

4 Then shall he that offereth his offering unto the LORD bring a meat offering of a tenth deal of flour mingled with the fourth *part* of an hin of oil.

5 And the fourth *part* of an hin of wine for a drink offering shalt thou prepare with the burnt offering or sacrifice, for one lamb.

6 Or for a ram, thou shalt prepare *for* a meat offering two tenth deals of flour mingled with the third *part* of an hin of oil.

7 And for a drink offering thou shalt offer the third *part* of an hin of wine, *for* a sweet savour unto the LORD.

8 And when thou preparest a bullock *for* a burnt offering, or *for* a sacrifice in performing a vow, or peace offerings unto the LORD:

9 Then shall he bring with a bullock a meat offering of three tenth deals of flour mingled with half an hin of oil.

10 And thou shalt bring for a drink offering half an hin of wine, *for* an offering made by fire, of a sweet savour unto the LORD.

11 Thus shall it be done for one bullock, or for one ram, or for a lamb, or a kid.

12 According to the number that ye shall prepare, so shall ye do to every one according to their number.

13 All that are born of the country shall do these things after this manner, in offering an offering made by fire, of a sweet savour unto the LORD.

14 And if a stranger sojourn with you, or whosoever *be* among you in your generations, and will offer an offering made by fire, of a sweet savour unto the LORD; as ye do, so he shall do.

15 One ordinance *shall be both* for you of the congregation, and also for the stranger that sojourneth *with you*, an ordinance for ever in your generations: as ye *are*, so shall the stranger be before the LORD.

16 One law and one manner shall be for you, and for the stranger that sojourneth with you.

17 ¶And the LORD spake unto Moses, saying,

18 Speak unto the children of Israel, and say unto them, When ye come into the land whither I bring you,

19 Then it shall be, that, when ye eat of the bread of the land, ye shall offer up an heave offering unto the LORD.

20 Ye shall offer up a cake of the first of your dough *for* an heave offering: as *ye do* the heave offering of the threshingfloor, so shall ye heave it.

21 Of the first of your dough ye shall give unto the LORD an heave offering in your generations.

22 ¶And if ye have erred, and not observed all these commandments, which the LORD hath spoken unto Moses,

23 *Even* all that the LORD hath commanded you by the hand of Moses, from the day that the LORD commanded *Moses*, and henceforward among your generations;

24 Then it shall be, if *ought* be committed by ignorance without the knowledge of the congregation, that all the congregation shall offer one young bullock for a burnt offering, for a sweet savour unto the LORD, with his meat offering, and his drink offering, according to the manner, and one kid of the goats for a sin offering.

25 And the priest shall make an atonement for all the congregation of the children of Israel, and it shall be forgiven them; for it *is* ignorance: and they shall bring their offering, a sacrifice made by fire unto the LORD, and their sin offering before the LORD, for their ignorance:

26 And it shall be forgiven all the congregation of the children of Israel, and the stranger that sojourneth among them; seeing all the people *were* in ignorance.

27 ¶And if any soul sin through ignorance, then he shall bring a she goat of the first year for a sin offering.

28 And the priest shall make an atonement for the soul that sinneth ignorantly, when he sinneth by ignorance before the LORD, to make an atonement for him; and it shall be forgiven him.

29 Ye shall have one law for him that sinneth through ignorance, *both for* him that is born among the children of Israel, and for the stranger that sojourneth among them.

30 ¶But the soul that doeth *ought* presumptuously, *whether he be* born in the land, or a stranger, the same reproacheth the LORD; and that soul shall be cut off from among his people.

31 Because he hath despised the word of the LORD, and hath broken his commandment, that soul shall utterly be cut off; his iniquity *shall be* upon him.

32 ¶And while the children of Israel were in the wilderness, they found a man that gathered sticks upon the sabbath day.

33 And they that found him gathering sticks brought him unto Moses and Aaron, and unto all the congregation.

34 And they put him in ward, because it was not declared what should be done to him.

35 And the LORD said unto Moses, The man shall be surely put to death: all the congregation shall stone him with stones without the camp.

36 And all the congregation brought him without the camp, and stoned him with stones, and he died; as the LORD commanded Moses.

37 ¶And the LORD spake unto Moses, saying,

38 Speak unto the children of Israel, and bid them that they make them fringes in the borders of their garments throughout their generations, and that they put upon the fringe of the borders a ribband of blue:

39 And it shall be unto you for a fringe, that ye may look upon it, and remember all the commandments of the LORD, and do them; and that ye seek not after your own heart and your own eyes, after which ye use to go a whoring:

40 That ye may remember, and do all my commandments, and be holy unto your God.

41 I *am* the LORD your God, which brought you out of the land of Egypt, to be your God: I *am* the LORD your God.

CHAPTER 16

NOW Kôrah, the son of Ĭz'här, the son of Kō'hăth, the son of Levi, and Dā'than and A-bī'ram, the sons of E-lī'ab, and On, the son of Pē'lĕth, sons of Reuben, took *men:*

2 And they rose up before Moses, with certain of the children of Israel, two hundred and fifty princes of the assembly, famous in the congregation, men of renown:

3 And they gathered themselves together against Moses and against Aaron, and said unto them, *Ye take* too much upon you, seeing all the congregation *are* holy, every one of them, and the LORD *is* among them: wherefore then lift ye up yourselves above the congregation of the LORD?

4 And when Moses heard *it* he fell upon his face:

5 And he spake unto Kôrah and unto all his company, saying, Even to morrow the LORD will shew who *are* his, and *who is* holy; and will cause *him* to come near unto him: even *him* whom he hath chosen will he cause to come near unto him.

6 This do; Take you censers, Kôrah, and all his company;

7 And put fire therein, and put incense in them before the LORD to morrow: and it shall be *that* the man whom the LORD doth choose, he *shall be* holy: *ye take* too much upon you, ye sons of Levi.

8 And Moses said unto Kôrah, Hear, I pray you, ye sons of Levi:

9 *Seemeth it but* a small thing unto you, that the God of Israel hath separated you from the congregation of Israel, to bring you near to himself to do the service of the tabernacle of the LORD, and to stand before the congregation to minister unto them?

10 And he hath brought thee near *to him*, and all thy brethren the sons of Levi with thee: and seek ye the priesthood also?

11 For which cause *both* thou and all thy company *are* gathered together against the LORD: and what *is* Aaron, that ye murmur against him?

12 ¶And Moses sent to call Dā'than and A-bī'ram, the sons of E-lī'ab: which said, We will not come up:

13 *Is it* a small thing that thou hast brought us up out of a land that floweth with milk and honey, to kill us in the wilderness, except thou make thyself altogether a prince over us?

14 Moreover thou hast not brought us into a land that floweth with milk and honey, or given us inheritance of fields and vineyards: wilt thou put out the eyes of these men? we will not come up.

15 And Moses was very wroth, and said unto the LORD, Respect not thou their offering: I have not taken one ass from them, neither have I hurt one of them.

16 And Moses said unto Kôrah, Be thou and all thy company before the LORD, thou, and they, and Aaron, to morrow:

17 And take every man his censer, and put incense in them, and bring ye before the LORD every man his censer, two hundred and fifty censers; thou also, and Aaron, each *of you* his censer.

18 And they took every man his censer, and put fire in them, and laid incense thereon, and stood in the door of the tabernacle of the congregation with Moses and Aaron.

19 And Kôrah gathered all the con-

gregation against them unto the door
of the tabernacle of the congregation:
and the glory of the LORD appeared
unto all the congregation.
20 And the LORD spake unto Moses
and unto Aaron, saying,
21 Separate yourselves from among
this congregation, that I may consume
them in a moment.
22 And they fell upon their faces, and
said, O God, the God of the spirits of all
flesh, shall one man sin, and wilt thou
be wroth with all the congregation?
23 ¶And the LORD spake unto Moses,
saying,
24 Speak unto the congregation, say-
ing, Get you up from about the taber-
nacle of Kôrah, Dā'than, and A-
bī'ram.
25 And Moses rose up and went unto
Dā'than and A-bī'ram; and the elders of
Israel followed him.
26 And he spake unto the congrega-
tion, saying, Depart, I pray you, from
the tents of these wicked men, and
touch nothing of theirs, lest ye be con-
sumed in all their sins.
27 So they gat up from the tabernacle
of Kôrah, Dā'than, and A-bī'ram, on
every side: and Dā'than and A-bī'ram
came out, and stood in the door of their
tents, and their wives, and their sons,
and their little children.
28 And Moses said, Hereby ye shall
know that the LORD hath sent me to do
all these works; for *I have* not *done
them* of mine own mind.
29 If these men die the common
death of all men, or if they be visited
after the visitation of all men; *then* the
LORD hath not sent me.
30 But if the LORD make a new thing,
and the earth open her mouth, and
swallow them up, with all that *apper-
tain* unto them, and they go down quick
into the pit; then ye shall understand
that these men have provoked the
LORD.
31 ¶And it came to pass, as he had
made an end of speaking all these
words, that the ground clave asunder
that *was* under them.
32 And the earth opened her mouth,
and swallowed them up, and their
houses, and all the men that *apper-
tained* unto Kôrah, and all *their* goods.
33 They, and all that *appertained* to
them, went down alive into the pit, and
the earth closed upon them: and they
perished from among the congrega-
tion.
34 And all Israel that *were* round
about them fled at the cry of them: for
they said, Lest the earth swallow us up
also.
35 And there came out a fire from the
LORD, and consumed the two hundred
and fifty men that offered incense.
36 ¶And the LORD spake unto Moses,
saying,
37 Speak unto Ĕ-le-ā'zar the son of
Aaron the priest, that he take up the
censers out of the burning, and scatter
thou the fire yonder; for they are hal-
lowed.
38 The censers of these sinners
against their own souls, let them make
them broad plates *for* a covering of the
altar: for they offered them before the
LORD, therefore they are hallowed: and
they shall be a sign unto the children of
Israel.
39 And Ĕ-le-ā'zar the priest took the
brasen censers, wherewith they that
were burnt had offered; and they were
made broad *plates for* a covering of the
altar:
40 *To be* a memorial unto the chil-
dren of Israel, that no stranger, which
is not of the seed of Aaron, come near
to offer incense before the LORD; that
he be not as Kôrah, and as his com-
pany: as the LORD said to him by the
hand of Moses.
41 ¶But on the morrow all the congre-
gation of the children of Israel mur-
mured against Moses and against
Aaron, saying, Ye have killed the peo-
ple of the LORD.
42 And it came to pass, when the
congregation was gathered against
Moses and against Aaron, that they
looked toward the tabernacle of the
congregation: and, behold, the cloud
covered it, and the glory of the LORD
appeared.
43 And Moses and Aaron came be-
fore the tabernacle of the congrega-
tion.
44 And the LORD spake unto Moses,
saying,
45 Get you up from among this con-
gregation, that I may consume them as
in a moment. And they fell upon their
faces.
46 And Moses said unto Aaron, Take
a censer, and put fire therein from off
the altar, and put on incense, and go
quickly unto the congregation, and
make an atonement for them: for there
is wrath gone out from the LORD; the
plague is begun.
47 And Aaron took as Moses com-
manded, and ran into the midst of the
congregation; and, behold, the plague
was begun among the people: and he
put on incense, and made an atone-
ment for the people.
48 And he stood between the dead

and the living; and the plague was stayed.

49 Now they that died in the plague were fourteen thousand and seven hundred, beside them that died about the matter of Kôrah.

50 And Aaron returned unto Moses unto the door of the tabernacle of the congregation: and the plague was stayed.

CHAPTER 17

AND the LORD spake unto Moses, saying,

2 Speak unto the children of Israel, and take of every one of them a rod according to the house of *their* fathers, of all their princes according to the house of their fathers twelve rods: write thou every man's name upon his rod.

3 And thou shalt write Aaron's name upon the rod of Levi: for one rod *shall be* for the head of the house of their fathers.

4 And thou shalt lay them up in the tabernacle of the congregation before the testimony, where I will meet with you.

5 And it shall come to pass, *that* the man's rod, whom I shall choose, shall blossom: and I will make to cease from me the murmurings of the children of Israel, whereby they murmur against you.

6 ¶And Moses spake unto the children of Israel, and every one of their princes gave him a rod apiece, for each prince one, according to their fathers' houses, *even* twelve rods: and the rod of Aaron *was* among their rods.

7 And Moses laid up the rods before the LORD in the tabernacle of witness.

8 And it came to pass, that on the morrow Moses went into the tabernacle of witness; and, behold, the rod of Aaron for the house of Levi was budded, and brought forth buds, and bloomed blossoms, and yielded almonds.

9 And Moses brought out all the rods from before the LORD unto all the children of Israel: and they looked, and took every man his rod.

10 ¶And the LORD said unto Moses, Bring Aaron's rod again before the testimony, to be kept for a token against the rebels; and thou shalt quite take away their murmurings from me, that they die not.

11 And Moses did *so:* as the LORD commanded him, so did he.

12 And the children of Israel spake unto Moses, saying, Behold, we die, we perish, we all perish.

13 Whosoever cometh any thing near unto the tabernacle of the LORD shall die: shall we be consumed with dying?

CHAPTER 18

AND the LORD said unto Aaron, Thou and thy sons and thy father's house with thee shall bear the iniquity of the sanctuary: and thou and thy sons with thee shall bear the iniquity of your priesthood.

2 And thy brethren also of the tribe of Levi, the tribe of thy father, bring thou with thee, that they may be joined unto thee, and minister unto thee: but thou and thy sons with thee *shall minister* before the tabernacle of witness.

3 And they shall keep thy charge, and the charge of all the tabernacle: only they shall not come nigh the vessels of the sanctuary and the altar, that neither they, nor ye also, die.

4 And they shall be joined unto thee, and keep the charge of the tabernacle of the congregation, for all the service of the tabernacle: and a stranger shall not come nigh unto you.

5 And ye shall keep the charge of the sanctuary, and the charge of the altar: that there be no wrath any more upon the children of Israel.

6 And I, behold, I have taken your brethren the Lēvītes from among the children of Israel: to you *they are* given *as* a gift for the LORD, to do the service of the tabernacle of the congregation.

7 Therefore thou and thy sons with thee shall keep your priest's office for every thing of the altar, and within the vail; and ye shall serve: I have given your priest's office *unto you as* a service of gift: and the stranger that cometh nigh shall be put to death.

8 ¶And the LORD spake unto Aaron, Behold, I also have given thee the charge of mine heave offerings of all the hallowed things of the children of Israel; unto thee have I given them by reason of the anointing, and to thy sons, by an ordinance for ever.

9 This shall be thine of the most holy things, *reserved* from the fire: every oblation of theirs, every meat offering of theirs, and every sin offering of theirs, and every trespass offering of theirs which they shall render unto me, *shall be* most holy for thee and for thy sons.

10 In the most holy *place* shalt thou eat it; every male shall eat it: it shall be holy unto thee.

11 And this *is* thine; the heave offering of their gift, with all the wave offer-

ings of the children of Israel: I have given them unto thee, and to thy sons and to thy daughters with thee, by a statute for ever: every one that is clean in thy house shall eat of it.
12 All the best of the oil, and all the best of the wine, and of the wheat, the firstfruits of them which they shall offer unto the LORD, them have I given thee.
13 *And* whatsoever is first ripe in the land, which they shall bring unto the LORD, shall be thine; every one that is clean in thine house shall eat *of* it.
14 Every thing devoted in Israel shall be thine.
15 Every thing that openeth the matrix in all flesh, which they bring unto the LORD, *whether it be* of men or beasts, shall be thine: nevertheless the firstborn of man shalt thou surely redeem, and the firstling of unclean beasts shalt thou redeem.
16 And those that are to be redeemed from a month old shalt thou redeem, according to thine estimation, for the money of five shekels, after the shekel of the sanctuary, which *is* twenty gerahs.
17 But the firstling of a cow, or the firstling of a sheep, or the firstling of a goat, thou shalt not redeem; they *are* holy: thou shalt sprinkle their blood upon the altar, and shalt burn their fat *for* an offering made by fire, for a sweet savour unto the LORD.
18 And the flesh of them shall be thine, as the wave breast and as the right shoulder are thine.
19 All the heave offerings of the holy things, which the children of Israel offer unto the LORD, have I given thee, and thy sons and thy daughters with thee, by a statute for ever: it *is* a covenant of salt for ever before the LORD unto thee and to thy seed with thee.
20 ¶And the LORD spake unto Aaron, Thou shalt have no inheritance in their land, neither shalt thou have any part among them: I *am* thy part and thine inheritance among the children of Israel.
21 And, behold, I have given the children of Levi all the tenth in Israel for an inheritance, for their service which they serve, *even* the service of the tabernacle of the congregation.
22 Neither must the children of Israel henceforth come nigh the tabernacle of the congregation, lest they bear sin, and die.
23 But the Lēvītes shall do the service of the tabernacle of the congregation, and they shall bear their iniquity: *it shall be* a statute for ever throughout your generations, that among the children of Israel they have no inheritance.
24 But the tithes of the children of Israel, which they offer *as* an heave offering unto the LORD, I have given to the Lēvītes to inherit: therefore I have said unto them, Among the children of Israel they shall have no inheritance.
25 ¶And the LORD spake unto Moses, saying,
26 Thus speak unto the Lēvītes, and say unto them, When ye take of the children of Israel the tithes which I have given you from them for your inheritance, then ye shall offer up an heave offering of it for the LORD, *even* a tenth *part* of the tithe.
27 And *this* your heave offering shall be reckoned unto you, as though *it were* the corn of the threshingfloor, and as the fulness of the winepress.
28 Thus ye also shall offer an heave offering unto the LORD of all your tithes, which ye receive of the children of Israel; and ye shall give thereof the LORD's heave offering to Aaron the priest.
29 Out of all your gifts ye shall offer every heave offering of the LORD, of all the best thereof, *even* the hallowed part thereof out of it.
30 Therefore thou shalt say unto them, When ye have heaved the best thereof from it, then it shall be counted unto the Lēvītes as the increase of the threshingfloor, and as the increase of the winepress.
31 And ye shall eat it in every place, ye and your households: for it *is* your reward for your service in the tabernacle of the congregation.
32 And ye shall bear no sin by reason of it, when ye have heaved from it the best of it: neither shall ye pollute the holy things of the children of Israel, lest ye die.

CHAPTER 19

AND the LORD spake unto Moses and unto Aaron, saying,
2 This *is* the ordinance of the law which the LORD hath commanded, saying, Speak unto the children of Israel, that they bring thee a red heifer without spot, wherein *is* no blemish, *and* upon which never came yoke:
3 And ye shall give her unto Ĕ-le-ā′zar the priest, that he may bring her forth without the camp, and *one* shall slay her before his face:
4 And Ĕ-le-ā′zar the priest shall take of her blood with his finger, and sprinkle of her blood directly before the tabernacle of the congregation seven times:

5 And *one* shall burn the heifer in his sight; her skin, and her flesh, and her blood, with her dung, shall he burn:

6 And the priest shall take cedar wood, and hyssop, and scarlet, and cast *it* into the midst of the burning of the heifer.

7 Then the priest shall wash his clothes, and he shall bathe his flesh in water, and afterward he shall come into the camp, and the priest shall be unclean until the even.

8 And he that burneth her shall wash his clothes in water, and bathe his flesh in water, and shall be unclean until the even.

9 And a man *that is* clean shall gather up the ashes of the heifer, and lay *them* up without the camp in a clean place, and it shall be kept for the congregation of the children of Israel for a water of separation: it *is* a purification for sin.

10 And he that gathereth the ashes of the heifer shall wash his clothes, and be unclean until the even: and it shall be unto the children of Israel, and unto the stranger that sojourneth among them, for a statute for ever.

11 ¶He that toucheth the dead body of any man shall be unclean seven days.

12 He shall purify himself with it on the third day, and on the seventh day he shall be clean: but if he purify not himself the third day, then the seventh day he shall not be clean.

13 Whosoever toucheth the dead body of any man that is dead, and purifieth not himself, defileth the tabernacle of the LORD; and that soul shall be cut off from Israel: because the water of separation was not sprinkled upon him, he shall be unclean; his uncleanness *is* yet upon him.

14 This *is* the law, when a man dieth in a tent: all that come into the tent, and all that *is* in the tent, shall be unclean seven days.

15 And every open vessel, which hath no covering bound upon it, *is* unclean.

16 And whosoever toucheth one that is slain with a sword in the open fields, or a dead body, or a bone of a man, or a grave, shall be unclean seven days.

17 And for an unclean *person* they shall take of the ashes of the burnt heifer of purification for sin, and running water shall be put thereto in a vessel:

18 And a clean person shall take hyssop, and dip *it* in the water, and sprinkle *it* upon the tent, and upon all the vessels, and upon the persons that were there, and upon him that touched a bone, or one slain, or one dead, or a grave:

19 And the clean *person* shall sprinkle upon the unclean on the third day, and on the seventh day: and on the seventh day he shall purify himself, and wash his clothes, and bathe himself in water, and shall be clean at even.

20 But the man that shall be unclean, and shall not purify himself, that soul shall be cut off from among the congregation, because he hath defiled the sanctuary of the LORD: the water of separation hath not been sprinkled upon him; he *is* unclean.

21 And it shall be a perpetual statute unto them, that he that sprinkleth the water of separation shall wash his clothes; and he that toucheth the water of separation shall be unclean until even.

22 And whatsoever the unclean *person* toucheth shall be unclean; and the soul that toucheth *it* shall be unclean until even.

CHAPTER 20

THEN came the children of Israel, *even* the whole congregation, into the desert of Zin in the first month: and the people abode in Kā'desh; and Miriam died there, and was buried there.

2 And there was no water for the congregation: and they gathered themselves together against Moses and against Aaron.

3 And the people chode with Moses, and spake, saying, Would God that we had died when our brethren died before the LORD!

4 And why have ye brought up the congregation of the LORD into this wilderness, that we and our cattle should die there?

5 And wherefore have ye made us to come up out of Egypt, to bring us in unto this evil place? it *is* no place of seed, or of figs, or of vines, or of pomegranates; neither *is* there any water to drink.

6 And Moses and Aaron went from the presence of the assembly unto the door of the tabernacle of the congregation, and they fell upon their faces: and the glory of the LORD appeared unto them.

7 ¶And the LORD spake unto Moses, saying,

8 Take the rod, and gather thou the assembly together, thou, and Aaron thy brother, and speak ye unto the rock before their eyes; and it shall give forth his water, and thou shalt bring forth to them water out of the rock: so thou

shalt give the congregation and their beasts drink.

9 And Moses took the rod from before the LORD, as he commanded him.

10 And Moses and Aaron gathered the congregation together before the rock, and he said unto them, Hear now, ye rebels; must we fetch you water out of this rock?

11 And Moses lifted up his hand, and with his rod he smote the rock twice: and the water came out abundantly, and the congregation drank, and their beasts *also*.

12 ¶And the LORD spake unto Moses and Aaron, Because ye believed me not, to sanctify me in the eyes of the children of Israel, therefore ye shall not bring this congregation into the land which I have given them.

13 This *is* the water of Mĕr′i-bah; because the children of Israel strove with the LORD, and he was sanctified in them.

14 ¶And Moses sent messengers from Kā′desh unto the king of Ē̄dom, Thus saith thy brother Israel, Thou knowest all the travail that hath befallen us:

15 How our fathers went down into Egypt, and we have dwelt in Egypt a long time; and the Egyptians vexed us, and our fathers:

16 And when we cried unto the LORD, he heard our voice, and sent an angel, and hath brought us forth out of Egypt: and, behold, we *are* in Kā′desh, a city in the uttermost of thy border:

17 Let us pass, I pray thee, through thy country: we will not pass through the fields, or through the vineyards, neither will we drink *of* the water of the wells: we will go by the king's *high* way, we will not turn to the right hand nor to the left, until we have passed thy borders.

18 And Ēdom said unto him, Thou shalt not pass by me, lest I come out against thee with the sword.

19 And the children of Israel said unto him, We will go by the high way: and if I and my cattle drink of thy water, then I will pay for it: I will only, without *doing* anything *else*, go through on my feet.

20 And he said, Thou shalt not go through. And Ēdom came out against him with much people, and with a strong hand.

21 Thus Ēdom refused to give Israel passage through his border: wherefore Israel turned away from him.

22 ¶And the children of Israel, *even* the whole congregation, journeyed from Kā′desh, and came unto mount Hor.

23 And the LORD spake unto Moses and Aaron in mount Hor, by the coast of the land of Ēdom, saying,

24 Aaron shall be gathered unto his people: for he shall not enter into the land which I have given unto the children of Israel, because ye rebelled against my word at the water of Mĕr′i-bah.

25 Take Aaron and Ĕ-le-ā′zar his son, and bring them up unto mount Hor:

26 And strip Aaron of his garments, and put them upon Ĕ-le-ā′zar his son: and Aaron shall be gathered *unto his people*, and shall die there.

27 And Moses did as the LORD commanded: and they went up into mount Hor in the sight of all the congregation.

28 And Moses stripped Aaron of his garments, and put them upon Ĕ-le-ā′zar his son; and Aaron died there in the top of the mount: and Moses and Ĕ-le-ā′zar came down from the mount.

29 And when all the congregation saw that Aaron was dead, they mourned for Aaron thirty days, *even* all the house of Israel.

CHAPTER 21

AND *when* king Â′răd the Canaanite, which dwelt in the south, heard tell that Israel came by the way of the spies; then he fought against Israel, and took *some* of them prisoners.

2 And Israel vowed a vow unto the LORD, and said, If thou wilt indeed deliver this people into my hand, then I will utterly destroy their cities.

3 And the LORD hearkened to the voice of Israel, and delivered up the Canaanites; and they utterly destroyed them and their cities: and he called the name of the place Hôr′mah.

4 ¶And they journeyed from mount Hor by the way of the Red sea, to compass the land of Ēdom: and the soul of the people was much discouraged because of the way.

5 And the people spake against God, and against Moses, Wherefore have ye brought us up out of Egypt to die in the wilderness? for *there is* no bread, neither *is there any* water; and our soul loatheth this light bread.

6 And the LORD sent fiery serpents among the people, and they bit the people; and much people of Israel died.

7 Therefore the people came to Moses, and said, We have sinned, for we have spoken against the LORD, and against thee; pray unto the LORD, that he take away the serpents from us. And Moses prayed for the people.

8 And the LORD said unto Moses, Make thee a fiery serpent, and set it upon a pole: and it shall come to pass, that every one that is bitten, when he looketh upon it, shall live.

9 And Moses made a serpent of brass, and put it upon a pole, and it came to pass, that if a serpent had bitten any man, when he beheld the serpent of brass, he lived.

10 ¶And the children of Israel set forward, and pitched in Ō'bŏth.

11 And they journeyed from Ō'bŏth, and pitched at Ī'j'e-ăb'a-rīm, in the wilderness which *is* before Moab, toward the sunrising.

12 ¶From thence they removed, and pitched in the valley of Za'red.

13 From thence they removed, and pitched on the other side of Arnon, which *is* in the wilderness that cometh out of the coasts of the Ămorītes: for Arnon *is* the border of Moab, between Moab and the Ămorītes.

14 Wherefore it is said in the book of the wars of the LORD, What he did in the Red sea, and in the brooks of Arnon,

15 And at the stream of the brooks that goeth down to the dwelling of Ar, and lieth upon the border of Moab.

16 ¶And from thence *they went* to Beer: that *is* the well whereof the LORD spake unto Moses, Gather the people together, and I will give them water.

17 Then Israel sang this song, Spring up, O well; sing ye unto it:

18 The princes digged the well, the nobles of the people digged it, by *the direction of* the lawgiver, with their staves. And from the wilderness *they went* to Măt'ta-nah:

19 And from Măt'ta-nah to Na-hā'lĭ-el: and from Na-hā'lĭ-el to Bā'mŏth:

20 And from Bā'mŏth *in* the valley, that *is* in the country of Moab, to the top of Pĭs'gah, which looketh toward Jesh'ī-mon.

21 ¶And Israel sent messengers unto Sihon king of the Ămorītes, saying,

22 Let me pass through thy land: we will not turn into the fields, or into the vineyards; we will not drink *of* the waters of the well: *but* we will go along by the king's *high* way, until we be past thy borders.

23 And Sihon would not suffer Israel to pass through his border: but Sihon gathered all his people together, and went out against Israel into the wilderness: and he came to Jā'hăz, and fought against Israel.

24 And Israel smote him with the edge of the sword, and possessed his land from Arnon unto Jabbok, even unto the children of Ammon: for the border of the children of Ammon *was* strong.

25 And Israel took all these cities: and Israel dwelt in all the cities of the Ămorītes, in Hĕsh'bŏn, and in all the villages thereof.

26 For Hĕsh'bŏn *was* the city of Sihon the king of the Ămorītes, who had fought against the former king of Moab, and taken all his land out of his hand, even unto Arnon.

27 Wherefore they that speak in proverbs say, Come into Hĕsh'bŏn, let the city of Sihon be built and prepared:

28 For there is a fire gone out of Hĕsh'bŏn, a flame from the city of Sihon: it hath consumed Ar of Moab, *and* the lords of the high places of Arnon.

29 Woe to thee, Moab! thou art undone, O people of Chē'mŏsh: he hath given his sons that escaped, and his daughters, into captivity unto Sihon king of the Ămorītes.

30 We have shot at them; Hĕsh'bŏn is perished even unto Dī'bŏn, and we have laid them waste even unto Nō'phah, which *reacheth* unto Mĕd'e-ba.

31 ¶Thus Israel dwelt in the land of the Ămorītes.

32 And Moses sent to spy out Jā-ā'zer, and they took the villages thereof, and drove out the Ămorītes that *were* there.

33 ¶And they turned and went up by the way of Bā'shan: and Og the king of Bā'shan went out against them, he, and all his people, to the battle at Ĕd're-ī.

34 And the LORD said unto Moses, Fear him not: for I have delivered him into thy hand, and all his people, and his land; and thou shalt do to him as thou didst unto Sihon king of the Ămorītes, which dwelt at Hĕsh'bŏn.

35 So they smote him, and his sons, and all his people, until there was none left him alive: and they possessed his land.

CHAPTER 22

AND the children of Israel set forward, and pitched in the plains of Moab on this side Jordan *by* Jericho.

2 ¶And Bā'lăk the son of Zippor saw all that Israel had done to the Amorites.

3 And Moab was sore afraid of the people, because they *were* many: and Moab was distressed because of the children of Israel.

4 And Moab said unto the elders of Mĭd'ī-an, Now shall this company lick up all *that are* round about us, as the ox licketh up the grass of the field. And Bā'lăk the son of Zippor *was* king of the Moabites at that time.

5 He sent messengers therefore unto

Bā'laam the son of Bē'ôr to Pē'thôr,
which *is* by the river of the land of the
children of his people, to call him,
saying, Behold, there is a people come
out from Egypt: behold, they cover the
face of the earth, and they abide over
against me:
6 Come now therefore, I pray thee,
curse me this people; for they *are* too
mighty for me: peradventure I shall
prevail, *that* we may smite them, and
that I may drive them out of the land:
for I wot that he whom thou blessest *is*
blessed, and he whom thou cursest is
cursed.
7 And the elders of Moab and the el-
ders of Mĭd'ĭ-an departed with the re-
wards of divination in their hand; and
they came unto Bā'laam, and spake
unto him the words of Bālăk.
8 And he said unto them, Lodge here
this night, and I will bring you word
again, as the LORD shall speak unto me:
and the princes of Moab abode with
Bā'laam.
9 And God came unto Bā'laam, and
said, What men *are* these with thee?
10 And Bā'laam said unto God, Bālăk
the son of Zippor, king of Moab, hath
sent unto me, *saying*,
11 Behold, *there is* a people come out
of Egypt, which covereth the face of
the earth: come now, curse me them;
peradventure I shall be able to over-
come them, and drive them out.
12 And God said unto Bā'laam, Thou
shalt not go with them; thou shalt not
curse the people: for they *are* blessed.
13 And Bā'laam rose up in the morn-
ing, and said unto the princes of Bālăk,
Get you into your land: for the LORD re-
fuseth to give me leave to go with you.
14 And the princes of Moab rose up,
and they went unto Bālăk, and said,
Bā'laam refuseth to come with us.
15 ¶And Bālăk sent yet again princes,
more, and more honourable than they.
16 And they came to Bā'laam, and
said to him, Thus saith Bālăk the son of
Zippor, Let nothing, I pray thee, hinder
thee from coming unto me:
17 For I will promote thee unto very
great honour, and I will do whatsoever
thou sayest unto me: come therefore, I
pray thee, curse me this people.
18 And Bā'laam answered and said
unto the servants of Bālăk, If Bālăk
would give me his house full of silver
and gold, I cannot go beyond the word
of the LORD my God, to do less or more.
19 Now therefore, I pray you, tarry ye
also here this night, that I may know
what the LORD will say unto me more.
20 And God came unto Bā'laam at
night, and said unto him, If the men
come to call thee, rise up, *and* go with
them; but yet the word which I shall
say unto thee, that shalt thou do.
21 And Bā'laam rose up in the morn-
ing, and saddled his ass, and went with
the princes of Moab.
22 ¶And God's anger was kindled be-
cause he went: and the angel of the
LORD stood in the way for an adversary
against him. Now he was riding upon
his ass, and his two servants *were* with
him.
23 And the ass saw the angel of the
LORD standing in the way, and his
sword drawn in his hand: and the ass
turned aside out of the way, and went
into the field: and Bā'laam smote the
ass, to turn her into the way.
24 But the angel of the LORD stood in
a path of the vineyards, a wall *being* on
this side, and a wall on that side.
25 And when the ass saw the angel of
the LORD, she thrust herself unto the
wall, and crushed Bā'laam's foot
against the wall: and he smote her
again.
26 And the angel of the LORD went
further, and stood in a narrow place,
where *was* no way to turn either to the
right hand or to the left.
27 And when the ass saw the angel of
the LORD, she fell down under Bā'laam:
and Bā'laam's anger was kindled, and
he smote the ass with a staff.
28 And the LORD opened the mouth of
the ass, and she said unto Bā'laam,
What have I done unto thee, that thou
hast smitten me these three times?
29 And Bā'laam said unto the ass, Be-
cause thou hast mocked me: I would
there were a sword in mine hand, for
now would I kill thee.
30 And the ass said unto Bā'laam, *Am*
not I thine ass, upon which thou hast
ridden ever since *I was* thine unto this
day? was I ever wont to do so unto
thee? And he said, Nay.
31 Then the LORD opened the eyes of
Bā'laam, and he saw the angel of the
LORD standing in the way, and his
sword drawn in his hand: and he bowed
down his head, and fell flat on his face.
32 And the angel of the LORD said
unto him, Wherefore hast thou smitten
thine ass these three times? behold, I
went out to withstand thee, because
thy way is perverse before me:
33 And the ass saw me, and turned
from me these three times: unless she
had turned from me, surely now also I
had slain thee, and saved her alive.
34 And Bā'laam said unto the angel of
the LORD, I have sinned; for I knew not
that thou stoodest in the way against

me: now therefore, if it displease thee, I will get me back again.

35 And the angel of the LORD said unto Bā'laam, Go with the men: but only the word that I shall speak unto thee, that thou shalt speak. So Bā'laam went with the princes of Bālăk.

36 ¶And when Bālăk heard that Bā'laam was come, he went out to meet him unto a city of Moab, which *is* in the border of Arnon, which *is* in the utmost coast.

37 And Bālăk said unto Bā'laam, Did I not earnestly send unto thee to call thee? wherefore camest thou not unto me? am I not able indeed to promote thee to honour?

38 And Bā'laam said unto Bālăk, Lo, I am come unto thee: have I now any power at all to say any thing? the word that God putteth in my mouth, that shall I speak.

39 And Bā'laam went with Bālăk, and they came unto Kir'jath-hŭ'zŏth.

40 And Bālăk offered oxen and sheep, and sent to Bā'laam, and to the princes that *were* with him.

41 And it came to pass on the morrow, that Bālăk took Bā'laam, and brought him up into the high places of Bā'al, that thence he might see the utmost *part* of the people.

CHAPTER 23

AND Bā'laam said unto Bālăk, Build me here seven altars, and prepare me here seven oxen and seven rams.

2 And Bālăk did as Bā'laam had spoken: and Bālăk and Bā'laam offered on *every* altar a bullock and a ram.

3 And Bā'laam said unto Bālăk, Stand by thy burnt offering, and I will go: peradventure the LORD will come to meet me: and whatsoever he sheweth me I will tell thee. And he went to an high place.

4 And God met Bā'laam: and he said unto him, I have prepared seven altars, and I have offered upon *every* altar a bullock and a ram.

5 And the LORD put a word in Bā'laam's mouth, and said, Return unto Bālăk, and thus thou shalt speak.

6 And he returned unto him, and, lo, he stood by his burnt sacrifice, he, and all the princes of Moab.

7 And he took up his parable, and said, Bālăk the king of Moab hath brought me from Â'ram, out of the mountains of the east, *saying*, Come, curse me Jacob, and come, defy Israel.

8 How shall I curse, whom God hath not cursed? or how shall I defy, *whom* the LORD hath not defied?

9 For from the top of the rocks I see him, and from the hills I behold him: lo, the people shall dwell alone, and shall not be reckoned among the nations.

10 Who can count the dust of Jacob, and the number of the fourth *part* of Israel? Let me die the death of the righteous, and let my last end be like his!

11 And Bālăk said unto Bā'laam, What hast thou done unto me? I took thee to curse mine enemies, and, behold, thou hast blessed *them* altogether.

12 And he answered and said, Must I not take heed to speak that which the LORD hath put in my mouth?

13 And Bālăk said unto him, Come, I pray thee, with me unto another place, from whence thou mayest see them: thou shalt see but the utmost part of them, and shalt not see them all: and curse me them from thence.

14 ¶And he brought him into the field of Zō'phĭm, to the top of Pĭs'gah, and built seven altars, and offered a bullock and a ram on *every* altar.

15 And he said unto Bālăk, Stand here by thy burnt offering, while I meet *the* LORD yonder.

16 And the LORD met Bā'laam, and put a word in his mouth, and said, Go again unto Bālăk, and say thus.

17 And when he came to him, behold, he stood by his burnt offering, and the princes of Moab with him. And Bālăk said unto him, What hath the LORD spoken?

18 And he took up his parable, and said, Rise up, Bālăk, and hear; hearken unto me, thou son of Zippor:

19 God *is* not a man, that he should lie; neither the son of man, that he should repent: hath he said, and shall he not do *it?* or hath he spoken, and shall he not make it good?

20 Behold, I have received *commandment* to bless: and he hath blessed; and I cannot reverse it.

21 He hath not beheld iniquity in Jacob, neither hath he seen perverseness in Israel: the LORD his God *is* with him, and the shout of a king *is* among them.

22 God brought them out of Egypt; he hath as it were the strength of an unicorn.

23 Surely *there is* no enchantment against Jacob, neither *is there* any divination against Israel: according to this time it shall be said of Jacob and of Israel, What hath God wrought!

24 Behold, the people shall rise up as a great lion, and lift up himself as a young lion: he shall not lie down until he eat *of* the prey, and drink the blood of the slain.

25 ¶And Bālăk said unto Bā'laam, Neither curse them at all, nor bless them at all.

26 But Bā'laam answered and said unto Bālăk, Told not I thee, saying, All that the LORD speaketh, that I must do?

27 ¶And Bālăk said unto Bā'laam, Come, I pray thee, I will bring thee unto another place; peradventure it will please God that thou mayest curse me them from thence.

28 And Bālăk brought Bā'laam unto the top of Pē'or, that looketh toward Jesh'ī-mon.

29 And Bā'laam said unto Bālăk, Build me here seven altars, and prepare me here seven bullocks and seven rams.

30 And Bālăk did as Bā'laam had said, and offered a bullock and a ram on *every* altar.

CHAPTER 24

AND when Bā'laam saw that it pleased the LORD to bless Israel, he went not, as at other times, to seek for enchantments, but he set his face toward the wilderness.

2 And Bā'laam lifted up his eyes, and he saw Israel abiding *in his tents* according to their tribes; and the spirit of God came upon him.

3 And he took up his parable, and said, Bā'laam the son of Bē'ôr hath said, and the man whose eyes are open hath said:

4 He hath said, which heard the words of God, which saw the vision of the Almighty, falling *into a trance*, but having his eyes open:

5 How goodly are thy tents, O Jacob, *and* thy tabernacles, O Israel!

6 As the valleys are they spread forth, as gardens by the river's side, as the trees of lign aloes which the LORD hath planted, *and* as cedar trees beside the waters.

7 He shall pour the water out of his buckets, and his seed *shall be* in many waters, and his king shall be higher than Āgăg, and his kingdom shall be exalted.

8 God brought him forth out of Egypt; he hath as it were the strength of an unicorn: he shall eat up the nations his enemies, and shall break their bones, and pierce *them* through with his arrows.

9 He couched, he lay down as a lion, and as a great lion: who shall stir him up? Blessed *is* he that blesseth thee, and cursed *is* he that curseth thee.

10 ¶And Bālăk's anger was kindled against Bā'laam, and he smote his hands together: and Bālăk said unto Bā'laam, I called thee to curse mine enemies, and, behold, thou hast altogether blessed *them* these three times.

11 Therefore now flee thou to thy place: I thought to promote thee unto great honour; but, lo, the LORD hath kept thee back from honour.

12 And Bā'laam said unto Bālăk, Spake I not also to thy messengers which thou sentest unto me, saying,

13 If Bālăk would give me his house full of silver and gold, I cannot go beyond the commandment of the LORD, to do *either* good or bad of mine own mind; *but* what the LORD saith, that will I speak?

14 And now, behold, I go unto my people: come *therefore, and* I will advertise thee what this people shall do to thy people in the latter days.

15 And he took up his parable, and said, Bā'laam the son of Bē'ôr hath said, and the man whose eyes are open hath said:

16 He hath said, which heard the words of God, and knew the knowledge of the most High, *which* saw the vision of the Almighty, falling *into a trance*, but having his eyes open:

17 I shall see him, but not now: I shall behold him, but not nigh: there shall come a Star out of Jacob, and a Sceptre shall rise out of Israel, and shall smite the corners of Moab, and destroy all the children of Sheth.

18 And Ēdom shall be a possession, Sē'ir also shall be a possession for his enemies; and Israel shall do valiantly.

19 Out of Jacob shall come he that shall have dominion, and shall destroy him that remaineth of the city.

20 And when he looked on Ăm'a-lĕk, he took up his parable, and said, Ăm'a-lĕk *was* the first of the nations; but his latter end *shall be* that he perish for ever.

21 And he looked on the Kēn'ītes, and took up his parable, and said, Strong is thy dwellingplace, and thou puttest thy nest in a rock.

22 Nevertheless the Kēn'īte shall be wasted, until Asshur shall carry thee away captive.

23 And he took up his parable, and said, Alas, who shall live when God doeth this!

24 And ships *shall come* from the coast of Chittim, and shall afflict Asshur, and shall afflict Ē'ber, and he also shall perish for ever.

25 And Bā'laam rose up, and went and returned to his place: and Bālăk also went his way.

CHAPTER 25

AND Israel abode in Shĭt'tĭm, and the people began to commit whoredom with the daughters of Moab.

2 And they called the people unto the sacrifices of their gods: and the people did eat, and bowed down to their gods.

3 And Israel joined himself unto Bā'al-pē'ôr: and the anger of the Lord was kindled against Israel.

4 And the Lord said unto Moses, Take all the heads of the people, and hang them up before the Lord against the sun, that the fierce anger of the Lord may be turned away from Israel.

5 And Moses said unto the judges of Israel, Slay ye every one his men that were joined unto Bā'al-pē'ôr.

6 ¶And, behold, one of the children of Israel came and brought unto his brethren a Mĭd'ĭ-an-ĭt-ĭsh woman in the sight of Moses, and in the sight of all the congregation of the children of Israel, who *were* weeping *before* the door of the tabernacle of the congregation.

7 And when Phĭn'e-has, the son of Ĕ-le-ā'zar, the son of Aaron the priest, saw *it*, he rose up from among the congregation, and took a javelin in his hand;

8 And he went after the man of Israel into the tent, and thrust both of them through, the man of Israel, and the woman through her belly. So the plague was stayed from the children of Israel.

9 And those that died in the plague were twenty and four thousand.

10 ¶And the Lord spake unto Moses, saying,

11 Phĭn'e-has, the son of Ĕ-le-ā'zar, the son of Aaron the priest, hath turned my wrath away from the children of Israel, while he was zealous for my sake among them, that I consumed not the children of Israel in my jealousy.

12 Wherefore say, Behold, I give unto him my covenant of peace:

13 And he shall have it, and his seed after him, *even* the covenant of an everlasting priesthood; because he was zealous for his God, and made an atonement for the children of Israel.

14 Now the name of the Israelite that was slain, *even* that was slain with the Mĭd'ĭ-an-ĭt-ĭsh woman, *was* Zimri, the son of Sā'lū, a prince of a chief house among the Simeonites.

15 And the name of the Mĭd'ĭ-an-ĭt-ĭsh woman that was slain *was* Cŏz'bĭ, the daughter of Zur; he *was* head over a people, *and* of a chief house in Mĭd'ĭ-an.

16 ¶And the Lord spake unto Moses, saying,

17 Vex the Mĭd'ĭan-ītes, and smite them:

18 For they vex you with their wiles, wherewith they have beguiled you in the matter of Pē'or, and in the matter of Cŏz'bĭ, the daughter of a prince of Mĭd'ĭ-an, their sister, which was slain in the day of the plague for Pē'or's sake.

CHAPTER 26

AND it came to pass after the plague, that the Lord spake unto Moses and unto Ĕ-le-ā'zar the son of Aaron the priest, saying,

2 Take the sum of all the congregation of the children of Israel, from twenty years old and upward, throughout their fathers' house, all that are able to go to war in Israel.

3 And Moses and Ĕ-le-ā'zar the priest spake with them in the plains of Moab by Jordan *near* Jericho, saying,

4 *Take the sum of the people*, from twenty years old and upward; as the Lord commanded Moses and the children of Israel, which went forth out of the land of Egypt.

5 ¶Reuben, the eldest son of Israel: the children of Reuben; Hā'nŏch, *of whom cometh* the family of the Hā'noch-ītes: of Păl'lū, the family of the Păl'lū-ītes:

6 Of Hĕz'ron, the family of the Hez'ron-ītes: of Cär'mī, the family of the Cär'mītes.

7 These *are* the families of the Reubenites: and they that were numbered of them were forty and three thousand and seven hundred and thirty.

8 And the sons of Păl'lū; E-lī'ab.

9 And the sons of E-lī'ab; Nĕ-mū'el, and Dā'than, and A-bī'ram. This *is that* Dā'than and A-bī'ram, *which were* famous in the congregation, who strove against Moses and against Aaron in the company of Kôrah, when they strove against the Lord:

10 And the earth opened her mouth, and swallowed them up together with Kôrah, when that company died, what time the fire devoured two hundred and fifty men: and they became a sign.

11 Notwithstanding the children of Kôrah died not.

12 ¶The sons of Simeon after their families: of Nĕ-mū'el, the family of the Nĕ-mū'el-ītes: of Jā'mĭn, the family of the Jā'min-ītes: of Jā'chin, the family of the Jā'chin-ītes:

13 Of Ze'rah, the family of the Zär'hītes: of Shā'ul, the family of the Shā'ul-ītes.

14 These *are* the families of the Simeonites, twenty and two thousand and two hundred.

15 ¶The children of Gad after their families: of Zē'phŏn, the family of the Zĕ'phon-ītes: of Hăg'gī, the family of the Hăg'gītes: of Shū'nī, the family of the Shū'nītes:

16 Of Ŏz'nī, the family of the Ŏz'nītes: of E'rī, the family of the E'rītes:

17 Of Ā'rŏd, the family of the Ā'rodītes: of A-rē'lī, the family of the A-rē'lītes.

18 These *are* the families of the children of Gad according to those that were numbered of them, forty thousand and five hundred.

19 ¶The sons of Jūdah *were* Er and Ō'nan: and Er and Ō'nan died in the land of Canaan.

20 And the sons of Jūdah after their families were; of Shē'lah, the family of the Shē'lan-ītes: of Phâ'rĕz, the family of the Phär'zītes: of Ze'rah, the family of the Zär'hītes.

21 And the sons of Phâ'rĕz were; of Hĕz'ron, the family of the Hez'ron-ītes: of Hā'mul, the family of the Hā'mulītes.

22 These *are* the families of Jūdah according to those that were numbered of them, threescore and sixteen thousand and five hundred.

23 ¶*Of* the sons of Ĭs'sa-char after their families: *of* Tō'la, the family of the Tō'la-ītes: of Pū'a, the family of the Pū'nītes:

24 Of Jāsh'ub, the family of the Jāsh'ub-ītes: of Shĭm'rŏn, the family of the Shĭm'ron-ītes.

25 These *are* the families of Ĭs'sa-char according to those that were numbered of them, threescore and four thousand and three hundred.

26 ¶*Of* the sons of Zĕb'u-lun after their families: of Se'rĕd, the family of the Sär'dītes: of Ē'lŏn, the family of the Ē'lon-ītes: of Jäh'le-el, the family of the Jäh'le-el-ītes.

27 These *are* the families of the Zĕb'u-lun-ītes according to those that were numbered of them, threescore thousand and five hundred.

28 ¶The sons of Joseph after their families *were* Ma-năs'seh and Ē'phra-im.

29 Of the sons of Ma-năs'seh: of Mā'chĭr, the family of the Mā'chir-ītes: and Mā'chĭr begat Gilead: of Gilead *come* the family of the Gĭleadītes.

30 These *are* the sons of Gilead: *of* Je-ē'zer, the family of the Je-ē'zer-ītes: of Hē'lĕk, the family of the Hē'lek-ītes:

31 And *of* Ăs'rĭ-el, the family of the Ăs'rĭ-el-ītes: and *of* Shĕ'chem, the family of the Shĕ'chem-ītes:

32 And *of* She-mī'da, the family of the She-mī'da-ītes: and *of* Hē'pher, the family of the Hē'pher-ītes.

33 And Ze-lō'phe-hăd the son of Hē'pher had no sons, but daughters: and the names of the daughters of Ze-lō'phe-hăd *were* Mäh'lah, and Noah, Hŏg'lah, Mĭl'cah, and Tir'zah.

34 These *are* the families of Ma-năs'seh, and those that were numbered of them, fifty and two thousand and seven hundred.

35 ¶These *are* the sons of Ē'phra-im after their families: of Shū'the-lah, the family of the Shū'thal-hītes: of Bē'cher, the family of the Băch'rītes: of Tā'hăn, the family of the Tā'han-ītes.

36 And these *are* the sons of Shū'the-lah: of E'răn, the family of the E'rănītes.

37 These *are* the families of the sons of Ē'phra-im according to those that were numbered of them, thirty and two thousand and five hundred. These *are* the sons of Joseph after their families.

38 ¶The sons of Benjamin after their families: of Bē'la, the family of the Bē'la-ītes: of Ăsh'bĕl, the family of the Ăsh'bel-ītes; of A-hī'ram, the family of the A-hī'ram-ītes:

39 Of Shū'pham, the family of the Shū'pham-ītes: of Hū'pham, the family of the Hū'pham-ītes.

40 And the sons of Bē'la were Ard and Nā'a-man: *of Ard*, the family of the Ärd'ītes: *and* of Nā'a-man, the family of the Nā'a-mītes.

41 These *are* the sons of Benjamin after their families: and they that were numbered of them *were* forty and five thousand and six hundred.

42 ¶These *are* the sons of Dan after their families: of Shū'hăm, the family of the Shū'ham-ītes. These *are* the families of Dan after their families.

43 All the families of the Shū'hamītes, according to those that were numbered of them, *were* threescore and four thousand and four hundred.

44 ¶*Of* the children of Asher after their families: of Jĭm'na, the family of the Jĭm'nītes: of Jĕs'ū-ī, the family of the Jĕs'ū-ītes: of Be-rī'ah, the family of the Be-rī'ītes.

45 Of the sons of Be-rī'ah: of Hē'ber, the family of the Hē'ber-ītes: of Măl'chĭ-el, the family of the Măl'chĭ-el-ītes.

46 And the name of the daughter of Asher *was* Sarah.

47 These *are* the families of the sons of Asher according to those that were numbered of them; *who were* fifty and three thousand and four hundred.

48 ¶*Of* the sons of Năph'ta-lī after their families: of Jäh'ze-el, the family of the Jäh'ze-el-ītes: of Gū'nī, the family of the Gū'nītes:

49 Of Jē'zer, the family of the Jē'zer-

ītes: of Shĭl′lem, the family of the Shĭl′-lem-ītes.

50 These *are* the families of Năph′ta-lī according to their families: and they that were numbered of them *were* forty and five thousand and four hundred.

51 These *were* the numbered of the children of Israel, six hundred thousand and a thousand seven hundred and thirty.

52 ¶And the LORD spake unto Moses, saying,

53 Unto these the land shall be divided for an inheritance according to the number of names.

54 To many thou shalt give the more inheritance, and to few thou shalt give the less inheritance: to every one shall his inheritance be given according to those that were numbered of him.

55 Notwithstanding the land shall be divided by lot: according to the names of the tribes of their fathers they shall inherit.

56 According to the lot shall the possession thereof be divided between many and few.

57 ¶And these *are* they that were numbered of the Levites after their families: of Ger′shon, the family of the Ger′shon-ītes: of Kō′hăth, the family of the Kō′hăth-ītes: of Me-râ′rī, the family of the Me-râ′rītes.

58 These *are* the families of the Levites: the family of the Lĭb′nītes, the family of the Hē′bro-nītes, the family of the Măh′lītes, the family of the Mū′-shītes, the family of the Kō′rath-ītes. And Kō′hăth begat Ămrăm.

59 And the name of Ămrăm's wife *was* Jŏch′e-bĕd, the daughter of Levi, whom *her mother* bare to Levi in Egypt: and she bare unto Ămrăm Aaron and Moses, and Miriam their sister.

60 And unto Aaron was born Nādăb, and A-bī′hū, Ĕ-le-ā′zar, and Ĭth′a-mär.

61 And Nādăb and A-bī′hū died, when they offered strange fire before the LORD.

62 And those that were numbered of them were twenty and three thousand, all males from a month old and upward: for they were not numbered among the children of Israel, because there was no inheritance given them among the children of Israel.

63 ¶These *are* they that were numbered by Moses and Ĕ-le-ā′zar the priest, who numbered the children of Israel in the plains of Moab by Jordan *near* Jericho.

64 But among these there was not a man of them whom Moses and Aaron the priest numbered, when they numbered the children of Israel in the wilderness of Sī′naī.

65 For the LORD had said of them, They shall surely die in the wilderness. And there was not left a man of them, save Caleb the son of Je-phŭn′neh, and Joshua the son of Nun.

CHAPTER 27

THEN came the daughters of Ze-lō′phe-hăd, the son of Hē′pher, the son of Gilead, the son of Mā′chĭr, the son of Ma-năs′seh, of the families of Ma-năs′-seh the son of Joseph: and these *are* the names of his daughters; Măh′lah, Noah, and Hŏg′lah, and Mĭl′cah, and Tir′zah.

2 And they stood before Moses, and before Ĕ-le-ā′zar the priest, and before the princes and all the congregation, *by* the door of the tabernacle of the congregation, saying,

3 Our father died in the wilderness, and he was not in the company of them that gathered themselves together against the LORD in the company of Kô-rah; but died in his own sin, and had no sons.

4 Why should the name of our father be done away from among his family, because he hath no son? Give unto us *therefore* a possession among the brethren of our father.

5 And Moses brought their cause before the LORD.

6 ¶And the LORD spake unto Moses, saying,

7 The daughters of Ze-lō′phe-hăd speak right: thou shalt surely give them a possession of an inheritance among their father's brethren; and thou shalt cause the inheritance of their father to pass unto them.

8 And thou shalt speak unto the children of Israel, saying, If a man die, and have no son, then ye shall cause his inheritance to pass unto his daughter.

9 And if he have no daughter, then ye shall give his inheritance unto his brethren.

10 And if he have no brethren, then ye shall give his inheritance unto his father's brethren.

11 And if his father have no brethren, then ye shall give his inheritance unto his kinsman that is next to him of his family, and he shall possess it: and it shall be unto the children of Israel a statute of judgment, as the LORD commanded Moses.

12 ¶And the LORD said unto Moses, Get thee up into this mount Ăb′a-rĭm, and see the land which I have given unto the children of Israel.

13 And when thou hast seen it, thou

also shalt be gathered unto thy people, as Aaron thy brother was gathered.

14 For ye rebelled against my commandment in the desert of Zin, in the strife of the congregation, to sanctify me at the water before their eyes: that *is* the water of Mĕr'i-bah in Kā'desh in the wilderness of Zin.

15 ¶And Moses spake unto the LORD, saying,

16 Let the LORD, the God of the spirits of all flesh, set a man over the congregation,

17 Which may go out before them, and which may go in before them, and which may lead them out, and which may bring them in; that the congregation of the LORD be not as sheep which have no shepherd.

18 ¶And the LORD said unto Moses, Take thee Joshua the son of Nun, a man in whom *is* the spirit, and lay thine hand upon him;

19 And set him before Ĕ-le-ā'zar the priest, and before all the congregation; and give him a charge in their sight.

20 And thou shalt put *some* of thine honour upon him, that all the congregation of the children of Israel may be obedient.

21 And he shall stand before Ĕ-le-ā'zar the priest, who shall ask *counsel* for him after the judgment of Ū'rĭm before the LORD: at his word shall they go out, and at his word they shall come in, *both* he, and all the children of Israel with him, even all the congregation.

22 And Moses did as the LORD commanded him: and he took Joshua, and set him before Ĕ-le-ā'zar the priest, and before all the congregation:

23 And he laid his hands upon him, and gave him a charge, as the LORD commanded by the hand of Moses.

CHAPTER 28

AND the LORD spake unto Moses, saying,

2 Command the children of Israel, and say unto them, My offering, *and* my bread for my sacrifices made by fire, *for* a sweet savour unto me, shall ye observe to offer unto me in their due season.

3 And thou shalt say unto them, This *is* the offering made by fire which ye shall offer unto the LORD; two lambs of the first year without spot day by day, *for* a continual burnt offering.

4 The one lamb shalt thou offer in the morning, and the other lamb shalt thou offer at even;

5 And a tenth *part* of an ephah of flour for a meat offering, mingled with the fourth *part* of an hin of beaten oil.

6 *It is* a continual burnt offering, which was ordained in mount Sī'naī for a sweet savour, a sacrifice made by fire unto the LORD.

7 And the drink offering thereof *shall be* the fourth *part* of an hin for the one lamb: in the holy *place* shalt thou cause the strong wine to be poured unto the LORD *for* a drink offering.

8 And the other lamb shalt thou offer at even: as the meat offering of the morning, and as the drink offering thereof, thou shalt offer *it*, a sacrifice made by fire, of a sweet savour unto the LORD.

9 ¶And on the sabbath day two lambs of the first year without spot, and two tenth deals of flour *for* a meat offering, mingled with oil, and the drink offering thereof:

10 *This is* the burnt offering of every sabbath, beside the continual burnt offering, and his drink offering.

11 ¶And in the beginnings of your months ye shall offer a burnt offering unto the LORD; two young bullocks, and one ram, seven lambs of the first year without spot;

12 And three tenth deals of flour *for* a meat offering, mingled with oil, for one bullock; and two tenth deals of flour *for* a meat offering, mingled with oil, for one ram;

13 And a several tenth deal of flour mingled with oil *for* a meat offering unto one lamb; *for* a burnt offering of a sweet savour, a sacrifice made by fire unto the LORD.

14 And their drink offerings shall be half an hin of wine unto a bullock, and the third *part* of an hin unto a ram, and a fourth *part* of an hin unto a lamb: this *is* the burnt offering of every month throughout the months of the year.

15 And one kid of the goats for a sin offering unto the LORD shall be offered, beside the continual burnt offering, and his drink offering.

16 ¶And in the fourteenth day of the first month *is* the passover of the LORD.

17 And in the fifteenth day of this month *is* the feast: seven days shall unleavened bread be eaten.

18 In the first day *shall be* an holy convocation; ye shall do no manner of servile work *therein*:

19 But ye shall offer a sacrifice made by fire *for* a burnt offering unto the LORD; two young bullocks, and one ram, and seven lambs of the first year: they shall be unto you without blemish:

20 And their meat offering *shall be of* flour mingled with oil: three tenth deals shall ye offer for a bullock, and two tenth deals for a ram;

21 A several tenth deal shalt thou offer for every lamb, throughout the seven lambs:

22 And one goat *for* a sin offering, to make an atonement for you.

23 Ye shall offer these beside the burnt offering in the morning, which *is* for a continual burnt offering.

24 After this manner ye shall offer daily, throughout the seven days, the meat of the sacrifice made by fire, of a sweet savour unto the LORD: it shall be offered beside the continual burnt offering, and his drink offering.

25 And on the seventh day ye shall have an holy convocation; ye shall do no servile work.

26 ¶Also in the day of the firstfruits, when ye bring a new meat offering unto the LORD, after your weeks *be out*, ye shall have an holy convocation; ye shall do no servile work:

27 But ye shall offer the burnt offering for a sweet savour unto the LORD; two young bullocks, one ram, seven lambs of the first year;

28 And their meat offering of flour mingled with oil, three tenth deals unto one bullock, two tenth deals unto one ram,

29 A several tenth deal unto one lamb, throughout the seven lambs;

30 *And* one kid of the goats, to make an atonement for you.

31 Ye shall offer *them* beside the continual burnt offering, and his meat offering, (they shall be unto you without blemish) and their drink offerings.

CHAPTER 29

AND in the seventh month, on the first *day* of the month, ye shall have an holy convocation; ye shall do no servile work: it is a day of blowing the trumpets unto you.

2 And ye shall offer a burnt offering for a sweet savour unto the LORD; one young bullock, one ram, *and* seven lambs of the first year without blemish:

3 And their meat offering *shall be of* flour mingled with oil, three tenth deals for a bullock, *and* two tenth deals for a ram,

4 And one tenth deal for one lamb, throughout the seven lambs:

5 And one kid of the goats *for* a sin offering, to make an atonement for you:

6 Beside the burnt offering of the month, and his meat offering, and the daily burnt offering, and his meat offering, and their drink offerings, according unto their manner, for a sweet savour, a sacrifice made by fire unto the LORD.

7 ¶And ye shall have on the tenth *day* of this seventh month an holy convocation; and ye shall afflict your souls: ye shall not do any work *therein:*

8 But ye shall offer a burnt offering unto the LORD *for* a sweet savour; one young bullock, one ram, *and* seven lambs of the first year; they shall be unto you without blemish:

9 And their meat offering *shall be of* flour mingled with oil, three tenth deals to a bullock, *and* two tenth deals to one ram,

10 A several tenth deal for one lamb, throughout the seven lambs:

11 One kid of the goats *for* a sin offering; beside the sin offering of atonement, and the continual burnt offering, and the meat offering of it, and their drink offerings.

12 ¶And on the fifteenth day of the seventh month ye shall have an holy convocation; ye shall do no servile work, and ye shall keep a feast unto the LORD seven days:

13 And ye shall offer a burnt offering, a sacrifice made by fire, of a sweet savour unto the LORD; thirteen young bullocks, two rams, *and* fourteen lambs of the first year; they shall be without blemish:

14 And their meat offering *shall be of* flour mingled with oil, three tenth deals unto every bullock of the thirteen bullocks, two tenth deals to each ram of the two rams,

15 And a several tenth deal to each lamb of the fourteen lambs:

16 And one kid of the goats *for* a sin offering; beside the continual burnt offering, his meat offering, and his drink offering.

17 ¶And on the second day *ye shall offer* twelve young bullocks, two rams, fourteen lambs of the first year without spot:

18 And their meat offering and their drink offerings for the bullocks, for the rams, and for the lambs, *shall be* according to their number, after the manner:

19 And one kid of the goats *for* a sin offering; beside the continual burnt offering, and the meat offering thereof, and their drink offerings.

20 ¶And on the third day eleven bullocks, two rams, fourteen lambs of the first year without blemish;

21 And their meat offering and their drink offerings for the bullocks, for the rams, and for the lambs, *shall be* according to their number, after the manner:

22 And one goat *for* a sin offering; beside the continual burnt offering, and his meat offering, and his drink offering.

23 ¶And on the fourth day ten bullocks, two rams, *and* fourteen lambs of the first year without blemish:
24 Their meat offering and their drink offerings for the bullocks, for the rams, and for the lambs, *shall be* according to their number, after the manner:
25 And one kid of the goats *for* a sin offering; beside the continual burnt offering, his meat offering, and his drink offering.
26 ¶And on the fifth day nine bullocks, two rams, *and* fourteen lambs of the first year without spot:
27 And their meat offering and their drink offerings for the bullocks, for the rams, and for the lambs, *shall be* according to their number, after the manner:
28 And one goat *for* a sin offering; beside the continual burnt offering, and his meat offering, and his drink offering.
29 ¶And on the sixth day eight bullocks, two rams, *and* fourteen lambs of the first year without blemish:
30 And their meat offering and their drink offerings for the bullocks, for the rams, and for the lambs, *shall be* according to their number, after the manner:
31 And one goat *for* a sin offering; beside the continual burnt offering, his meat offering, and his drink offering.
32 ¶And on the seventh day seven bullocks, two rams, *and* fourteen lambs of the first year without blemish:
33 And their meat offering and their drink offerings for the bullocks, for the rams, and for the lambs, *shall be* according to their number, after the manner:
34 And one goat *for* a sin offering; beside the continual burnt offering, his meat offering, and his drink offering.
35 ¶On the eighth day ye shall have a solemn assembly: ye shall do no servile work *therein:*
36 But ye shall offer a burnt offering, a sacrifice made by fire, of a sweet savour unto the LORD: one bullock, one ram, seven lambs of the first year without blemish:
37 Their meat offering and their drink offerings for the bullock, for the ram, and for the lambs, *shall be* according to their number, after the manner:
38 And one goat *for* a sin offering; beside the continual burnt offering, and his meat offering, and his drink offering.
39 These *things* ye shall do unto the LORD in your set feasts, beside your vows, and your freewill offerings, for your burnt offerings, and for your meat offerings, and for your drink offerings, and for your peace offerings.
40 And Moses told the children of Israel according to all that the LORD commanded Moses.

CHAPTER 30

AND Moses spake unto the heads of the tribes concerning the children of Israel, saying, This *is* the thing which the LORD hath commanded.
2 If a man vow a vow unto the LORD, or swear an oath to bind his soul with a bond; he shall not break his word, he shall do according to all that proceedeth out of his mouth.
3 If a woman also vow a vow unto the LORD, and bind *herself* by a bond, *being* in her father's house in her youth;
4 And her father hear her vow, and her bond wherewith she hath bound her soul, and her father shall hold his peace at her: then all her vows shall stand, and every bond wherewith she hath bound her soul shall stand.
5 But if her father disallow her in the day that he heareth; not any of her vows, or of her bonds wherewith she hath bound her soul, shall stand: and the LORD shall forgive her, because her father disallowed her.
6 And if she had at all an husband, when she vowed, or uttered ought out of her lips, wherewith she bound her soul;
7 And her husband heard *it,* and held his peace at her in the day that he heard *it:* then her vows shall stand, and her bonds wherewith she bound her soul shall stand.
8 But if her husband disallowed her on the day that he heard *it;* then he shall make her vow which she vowed, and that which she uttered with her lips, wherewith she bound her soul, of none effect: and the LORD shall forgive her.
9 But every vow of a widow, and of her that is divorced, wherewith they have bound their souls, shall stand against her.
10 And if she vowed in her husband's house, or bound her soul by a bond with an oath;
11 And her husband heard *it,* and held his peace at her, *and* disallowed her not: then all her vows shall stand, and every bond wherewith she bound her soul shall stand.
12 But if her husband hath utterly made them void on the day he heard *them; then* whatsoever proceeded out of her lips concerning her vows, or concerning the bond of her soul, shall not stand: her husband hath made them void; and the LORD shall forgive her.
13 Every vow, and every binding oath to afflict the soul, her husband

may establish it, or her husband may make it void.

14 But if her husband altogether hold his peace at her from day to day; then he establisheth all her vows, or all her bonds, which *are* upon her: he confirmeth them, because he held his peace at her in the day that he heard *them*.

15 But if he shall any ways make them void after that he hath heard *them*; then he shall bear her iniquity.

16 These *are* the statutes, which the LORD commanded Moses, between a man and his wife, between the father and his daughter, *being yet* in her youth in her father's house.

CHAPTER 31

AND the LORD spake unto Moses, saying,

2 Avenge the children of Israel of the Mĭd′ĭ-an-ītes: afterward shalt thou be gathered unto thy people.

3 And Moses spake unto the people, saying, Arm some of yourselves unto the war, and let them go against the Mĭd′ĭ-an-ītes, and avenge the LORD of Mĭd′ĭ-an.

4 Of every tribe a thousand, throughout all the tribes of Israel, shall ye send to the war.

5 So there were delivered out of the thousands of Israel, a thousand of *every* tribe, twelve thousand armed for war.

6 And Moses sent them to the war, a thousand of *every* tribe, them and Phĭn′e-has the son of Ĕ-le-ā′zar the priest, to the war, with the holy instruments, and the trumpets to blow in his hand.

7 And they warred against the Mĭd′ĭ-an-ītes, as the LORD commanded Moses; and they slew all the males.

8 And they slew the kings of Mĭd′ĭ-an, beside the rest of them that were slain; *namely*, Ē′vī, and Rē′kem, and Zur, and Hur, and Rē′ba, five kings of Mĭd′ĭ-an: Bā′laam also the son of Bē′ôr they slew with the sword.

9 And the children of Israel took *all* the women of Mĭd′ĭ-an captives, and their little ones, and took the spoil of all their cattle, and all their flocks, and all their goods.

10 And they burnt all their cities wherein they dwelt, and all their goodly castles, with fire.

11 And they took all the spoil, and all the prey, *both* of men and of beasts.

12 And they brought the captives, and the prey, and the spoil, unto Moses, and Ĕ-le-ā′zar the priest, and unto the congregation of the children of Israel, unto the camp at the plains of Moab, which *are* by Jordan *near* Jericho.

13 ¶And Moses, and Ĕ-le-ā′zar the priest, and all the princes of the congregation, went forth to meet them without the camp.

14 And Moses was wroth with the officers of the host, *with* the captains over thousands, and captains over hundreds, which came from the battle.

15 And Moses said unto them, Have ye saved all the women alive?

16 Behold, these caused the children of Israel, through the counsel of Bā′laam, to commit trespass against the LORD in the matter of Pē′or, and there was a plague among the congregation of the LORD.

17 Now therefore kill every male among the little ones, and kill every woman that hath known man by lying with him.

18 But all the women children, that have not known a man by lying with him, keep alive for yourselves.

19 And do ye abide without the camp seven days: whosoever hath killed any person, and whosoever hath touched any slain, purify *both* yourselves and your captives on the third day, and on the seventh day.

20 And purify all *your* raiment, and all that is made of skins, and all work of goats' *hair*, and all things made of wood.

21 ¶And Ĕ-le-ā′zar the priest said unto the men of war which went to the battle, This *is* the ordinance of the law which the LORD commanded Moses;

22 Only the gold, and the silver, the brass, the iron, the tin, and the lead,

23 Every thing that may abide the fire, ye shall make *it* go through the fire, and it shall be clean: nevertheless it shall be purified with the water of separation: and all that abideth not the fire ye shall make go through the water.

24 And ye shall wash your clothes on the seventh day, and ye shall be clean, and afterward ye shall come into the camp.

25 ¶And the LORD spake unto Moses, saying,

26 Take the sum of the prey that was taken, *both* of man and of beast, thou, and Ĕ-le-ā′zar the priest, and the chief fathers of the congregation:

27 And divide the prey into two parts; between them that took the war upon them, who went out to battle, and between all the congregation:

28 And levy a tribute unto the LORD of the men of war which went out to battle: one soul of five hundred, *both* of

the persons, and of the beeves, and of the asses, and of the sheep:

29 Take *it* of their half, and give *it* unto Ĕ-le-ā'zar the priest, *for* an heave offering of the LORD.

30 And of the children of Israel's half, thou shalt take one portion of fifty, of the persons, of the beeves, of the asses, and of the flocks, of all manner of beasts, and give them unto the Lē'vītes, which keep the charge of the tabernacle of the LORD.

31 And Moses and Ĕ-le-ā'zar the priest did as the LORD commanded Moses.

32 And the booty, *being* the rest of the prey which the men of war had caught, was six hundred thousand and seventy thousand and five thousand sheep,

33 And threescore and twelve thousand beeves,

34 And threescore and one thousand asses,

35 And thirty and two thousand persons in all, of women that had not known man by lying with him.

36 And the half, *which was* the portion of them that went out to war, was in number three hundred thousand and seven and thirty thousand and five hundred sheep:

37 And the LORD's tribute of the sheep was six hundred and threescore and fifteen.

38 And the beeves *were* thirty and six thousand; of which the LORD's tribute *was* threescore and twelve.

39 And the asses *were* thirty thousand and five hundred; of which the LORD's tribute *was* threescore and one.

40 And the persons *were* sixteen thousand; of which the LORD's tribute *was* thirty and two persons.

41 And Moses gave the tribute, *which was* the LORD's heave offering, unto Ĕ-le-ā'zar the priest, as the LORD commanded Moses.

42 And of the children of Israel's half, which Moses divided from the men that warred,

43 (Now the half *that pertained unto* the congregation was three hundred thousand and thirty thousand *and* seven thousand and five hundred sheep,

44 And thirty and six thousand beeves,

45 And thirty thousand asses and five hundred,

46 And sixteen thousand persons;)

47 Even of the children of Israel's half, Moses took one portion of fifty, *both* of man and of beast, and gave them unto the Lē'vītes, which kept the charge of the tabernacle of the LORD; as the LORD commanded Moses.

48 ¶And the officers which *were* over thousands of the host, the captains of thousands, and captains of hundreds, came near unto Moses:

49 And they said unto Moses, Thy servants have taken the sum of the men of war which *are* under our charge, and there lacketh not one man of us.

50 We have therefore brought an oblation for the LORD, what every man hath gotten, of jewels of gold, chains, and bracelets, rings, earrings, and tablets, to make an atonement for our souls before the LORD.

51 And Moses and Ĕ-le-ā'zar the priest took the gold of them, *even* all wrought jewels.

52 And all the gold of the offering that they offered up to the LORD, of the captains of thousands, and of the captains of hundreds, was sixteen thousand seven hundred and fifty shekels.

53 (*For* the men of war had taken spoil, every man for himself.)

54 And Moses and Ĕ-le-ā'zar the priest took the gold of the captains of thousands and of hundreds, and brought it into the tabernacle of the congregation, *for* a memorial for the children of Israel before the LORD.

CHAPTER 32

NOW the children of Reuben and the children of Gad had a very great multitude of cattle: and when they saw the land of Jā'zer, and the land of Gilead, that, behold, the place *was* a place for cattle;

2 The children of Gad and the children of Reuben came and spake unto Moses, and to Ĕ-le-ā'zar the priest, and unto the princes of the congregation, saying,

3 Ăt'a-rŏth, and Dī'bŏn, and Jā'zer, and Nĭm'rah, and Hĕsh'bŏn, and Ĕ-le-ā'leh, and Shē'băm, and Nebo, and Bē'-ŏn,

4 *Even* the country which the LORD smote before the congregation of Israel, *is* a land for cattle, and thy servants have cattle:

5 Wherefore, said they, if we have found grace in thy sight, let this land be given unto thy servants for a possession, *and* bring us not over Jordan.

6 ¶And Moses said unto the children of Gad and to the children of Reuben, Shall your brethren go to war, and shall ye sit here?

7 And wherefore discourage ye the heart of the children of Israel from going over into the land which the LORD hath given them?

8 Thus did your fathers, when I sent them from Kā′desh-bär′ne-a to see the land.
9 For when they went up unto the valley of Ĕsh′cōl, and saw the land, they discouraged the heart of the children of Israel, that they should not go into the land which the LORD had given them.
10 And the LORD's anger was kindled the same time, and he sware, saying,
11 Surely none of the men that came up out of Egypt, from twenty years old and upward, shall see the land which I sware unto Abraham, unto Isaac, and unto Jacob; because they have not wholly followed me:
12 Save Caleb the son of Je-phŭn′neh the Kĕn′ez-īte, and Joshua the son of Nun: for they have wholly followed the LORD.
13 And the LORD's anger was kindled against Israel, and he made them wander in the wilderness forty years, until all the generation, that had done evil in the sight of the LORD, was consumed.
14 And, behold, ye are risen up in your fathers' stead, an increase of sinful men, to augment yet the fierce anger of the LORD toward Israel.
15 For if ye turn away from after him, he will yet again leave them in the wilderness; and ye shall destroy all this people.
16 ¶And they came near unto him, and said, We will build sheepfolds here for our cattle, and cities for our little ones:
17 But we ourselves will go ready armed before the children of Israel, until we have brought them unto their place: and our little ones shall dwell in the fenced cities because of the inhabitants of the land.
18 We will not return unto our houses, until the children of Israel have inherited every man his inheritance.
19 For we will not inherit with them on yonder side Jordan, or forward; because our inheritance is fallen to us on this side Jordan eastward.
20 ¶And Moses said unto them, If ye will do this thing, if ye will go armed before the LORD to war,
21 And will go all of you armed over Jordan before the LORD, until he hath driven out his enemies from before him,
22 And the land be subdued before the LORD: then afterward ye shall return, and be guiltless before the LORD, and before Israel; and this land shall be your possession before the LORD.
23 But if ye will not do so, behold, ye have sinned against the LORD: and be sure your sin will find you out.
24 Build you cities for your little ones, and folds for your sheep; and do that which hath proceeded out of your mouth.
25 And the children of Gad and the children of Reuben spake unto Moses, saying, Thy servants will do as my lord commandeth.
26 Our little ones, our wives, our flocks, and all our cattle, shall be there in the cities of Gilead:
27 But thy servants will pass over, every man armed for war, before the LORD to battle, as my lord saith.
28 So concerning them Moses commanded Ĕ-le-ā′zar the priest, and Joshua the son of Nun, and the chief fathers of the tribes of the children of Israel:
29 And Moses said unto them, If the children of Gad and the children of Reuben will pass with you over Jordan, every man armed to battle, before the LORD, and the land shall be subdued before you; then ye shall give them the land of Gilead for a possession:
30 But if they will not pass over with you armed, they shall have possessions among you in the land of Canaan.
31 And the children of Gad and the children of Reuben answered, saying, As the LORD hath said unto thy servants, so will we do.
32 We will pass over armed before the LORD into the land of Canaan, that the possession of our inheritance on this side Jordan *may be* ours.
33 And Moses gave unto them, *even* to the children of Gad, and to the children of Reuben, and unto half the tribe of Ma-năs′seh the son of Joseph, the kingdom of Sihon king of the Ăm′o-rītes, and the kingdom of Og king of Bā′shan, the land, with the cities thereof in the coasts, *even* the cities of the country round about.
34 ¶And the children of Gad built Dī′bŏn, and Ăt′a-rŏth, and Ar′ō-er,
35 And Ăt′rŏth, Shō′phăn, and Jā-ā′zer, and Jŏg′be-hah,
36 And Bĕth-nĭm′rah, and Bĕth-hā′ran, fenced cities: and folds for sheep.
37 And the children of Reuben built Hĕsh′bŏn, and Ĕ-le-ā′leh, and Kĭr-jath-ā′ĭm,
38 And Nebo, and Bā′al-mē′ŏn, (their names being changed,) and Shĭb′mah: and gave other names unto the cities which they builded.
39 And the children of Mā′chĭr the son of Ma-năs′seh went to Gilead, and took it, and dispossessed the Amorite which *was* in it.
40 And Moses gave Gilead unto

Mā'chīr the son of Ma-năs'seh; and he dwelt therein.
41 And Jā'ir the son of Ma-năs'seh went and took the small towns thereof, and called them Hă'vŏth-jā'ir.
42 And Nō'bah went and took Kē'-năth, and the villages thereof, and called it Nō'bah, after his own name.

CHAPTER 33

THESE *are* the journeys of the children of Israel, which went forth out of the land of Egypt with their armies under the hand of Moses and Aaron.
2 And Moses wrote their goings out according to their journeys by the commandment of the LORD: and these *are* their journeys according to their goings out.
3 And they departed from Răm'e-sēs in the first month, on the fifteenth day of the first month; on the morrow after the passover the children of Israel went out with an high hand in the sight of all the Egyptians.
4 For the Egyptians buried all *their* firstborn, which the LORD had smitten among them: upon their gods also the LORD executed judgments.
5 And the children of Israel removed from Răm'e-sēs, and pitched in Sŭc'-coth.
6 And they departed from Sŭc'coth, and pitched in Ē'tham, which *is* in the edge of the wilderness.
7 And they removed from Ē'tham, and turned again unto Pī'-ha-hī'rŏth, which *is* before Bā'al-zē'phŏn: and they pitched before Mĭg'dŏl.
8 And they departed from before Pī'-ha-hī'rŏth, and passed through the midst of the sea into the wilderness, and went three days' journey in the wilderness of Ē'tham, and pitched in Mâ'rah.
9 And they removed from Mâ'rah, and came unto Elim: and in Elim *were* twelve fountains of water, and threescore and ten palm trees; and they pitched there.
10 And they removed from Elim, and encamped by the Red sea.
11 And they removed from the Red sea, and encamped in the wilderness of Sin.
12 And they took their journey out of the wilderness of Sin, and encamped in Dŏph'kah.
13 And they departed from Dŏph'-kah, and encamped in Ā'lŭsh.
14 And they removed from Ā'lŭsh, and encamped at Rĕph'i-dĭm, where was no water for the people to drink.
15 And they departed from Rĕph'i-dĭm, and pitched in the wilderness of Sī'naī.
16 And they removed from the desert of Sī'naī, and pitched at Kĭb'rŏth-hat-tā'a-vah.
17 And they departed from Kĭb'rŏth-hat-tā'a-vah, and encamped at Ha-ze'-rŏth.
18 And they departed from Ha-ze'-rŏth, and pitched in Rĭth'mah.
19 And they departed from Rĭth'mah, and pitched at Rĭm'mon-pâ'rez.
20 And they departed from Rĭm'mon-pâ'rez, and pitched in Lĭb'nah.
21 And they removed from Lĭb'nah, and pitched at Rĭs'sah.
22 And they journeyed from Rĭs'sah and pitched in Kē-hel'ā-thah.
23 And they went from Kē-hel'ā-thah, and pitched in mount Shā'pher.
24 And they removed from mount Shā'pher, and encamped in Har'ā-dah.
25 And they removed from Har'ā-dah, and pitched in Măk-hē'lŏth.
26 And they removed from Măk-hē'-lŏth, and encamped at Tā'hăth.
27 And they departed from Tā'hăth, and pitched at Tâ'rah.
28 And they removed from Tâ'rah, and pitched in Mĭth'cah.
29 And they went from Mĭth'cah, and pitched in Hăsh-mō'nah.
30 And they departed from Hăsh-mō'nah, and encamped at Mō-sē'rŏth.
31 And they departed from Mō-sē'-rŏth, and pitched in Bĕn-e-jā'a-kan.
32 And they removed from Bĕn-e-jā'a-kan, and encamped at Hôr'-ha-gĭd'găd.
33 And they went from Hôr'-ha-gĭd'-găd, and pitched in Jŏt'ba-thah.
34 And they removed from Jŏt'ba-thah, and encamped at E-brō'nah.
35 And they departed from E-brō'-nah, and encamped at Ĕ'zī-on-gā'ber.
36 And they removed from Ĕ'zī-on-gā'ber, and pitched in the wilderness of Zin, which *is* Kā'desh.
37 And they removed from Kā'desh, and pitched in mount Hor, in the edge of the land of Ē'dom.
38 And Aaron the priest went up into mount Hor at the commandment of the LORD, and died there, in the fortieth year after the children of Israel were come out of the land of Egypt, in the first *day* of the fifth month.
39 And Aaron *was* an hundred and twenty and three years old when he died in mount Hor.
40 And king Â'răd the Canaanite, which dwelt in the south in the land of Canaan, heard of the coming of the children of Israel.

41 And they departed from mount Hor, and pitched in Zăl-mō'nah.
42 And they departed from Zăl-mō'nah, and pitched in Pū'nŏn.
43 And they departed from Pū'nŏn, and pitched in Ō'bŏth.
44 And they departed from Ō'bŏth, and pitched in Ī'je-ăb'a-rĭm, in the border of Moab.
45 And they departed from Ī'im, and pitched in Dī'bŏn-găd.
46 And they removed from Dī'bŏn-găd, and encamped in Ăl'mon-dĭb-la-thā'im.
47 And they removed from Ăl'mon-dĭb-la-thā'im, and pitched in the mountains of Ăb'a-rĭm, before Nebo.
48 And they departed from the mountains of Ăb'a-rĭm, and pitched in the plains of Moab by Jordan *near* Jericho.
49 And they pitched by Jordan, from Bĕth-jĕs'i-mŏth *even* unto Ā'bel-shĭt'-tĭm in the plains of Moab.
50 ¶And the LORD spake unto Moses in the plains of Moab by Jordan *near* Jericho, saying,
51 Speak unto the children of Israel, and say unto them, When ye are passed over Jordan into the land of Canaan;
52 Then ye shall drive out all the inhabitants of the land from before you, and destroy all their pictures, and destroy all their molten images, and quite pluck down all their high places:
53 And ye shall dispossess *the inhabitants of* the land, and dwell therein: for I have given you the land to possess it.
54 And ye shall divide the land by lot for an inheritance among your families: *and* to the more ye shall give the more inheritance, and to the fewer ye shall give the less inheritance: every man's *inheritance* shall be in the place where his lot falleth; according to the tribes of your fathers ye shall inherit.
55 But if ye will not drive out the inhabitants of the land from before you; then it shall come to pass, that those which ye let remain of them *shall be* pricks in your eyes, and thorns in your sides, and shall vex you in the land wherein ye dwell.
56 Moreover it shall come to pass, *that* I shall do unto you, as I thought to do unto them.

CHAPTER 34

AND the LORD spake unto Moses, saying,
2 Command the children of Israel, and say unto them, When ye come into the land of Canaan; (this *is* the land that shall fall unto you for an inheritance, *even* the land of Canaan with the coasts thereof:)
3 Then your south quarter shall be from the wilderness of Zin along by the coast of Ĕdom, and your south border shall be the outmost coast of the salt sea eastward:
4 And your border shall turn from the south to the ascent of Ă-krăb'bĭm, and pass on to Zin: and the going forth thereof shall be from the south to Kā'-desh-bär'ne-a, and shall go on to Hā'-zar-ăd'dar, and pass on to Ăz'mon:
5 And the border shall fetch a compass from Ăz'mon unto the river of Egypt, and the goings out of it shall be at the sea.
6 And *as for* the western border, ye shall even have the great sea for a border: this shall be your west border.
7 And this shall be your north border: from the great sea ye shall point out for you mount Hor:
8 From mount Hor ye shall point out *your border* unto the entrance of Hā'-măth; and the goings forth of the border shall be to Zē'dăd:
9 And the border shall go on to Zĭph'-rŏn, and the goings out of it shall be at Hā'zar-ē'nan: this shall be your north border.
10 And ye shall point out your east border from Hā'zar-ē'nan to Shē'pham:
11 And the coast shall go down from Shē'pham to Rĭb'lah, on the east side of Ā'ĭn; and the border shall descend, and shall reach unto the side of the sea of Chĭn'ne-rĕth eastward:
12 And the border shall go down to Jordan, and the goings out of it shall be at the salt sea: this shall be your land with the coasts thereof round about.
13 And Moses commanded the children of Israel, saying, This *is* the land which ye shall inherit by lot, which the LORD commanded to give unto the nine tribes, and to the half tribe:
14 For the tribe of the children of Reuben according to the house of their fathers, and the tribe of the children of Gad according to the house of their fathers, have received *their inheritance*; and half the tribe of Ma-năs'seh have received their inheritance:
15 The two tribes and the half tribe have received their inheritance on this side Jordan *near* Jericho eastward, toward the sunrising.
16 ¶And the LORD spake unto Moses, saying,
17 These *are* the names of the men which shall divide the land unto you: Ĕ-le-ā'zar the priest, and Joshua the son of Nun.
18 And ye shall take one prince of

every tribe, to divide the land by inheri-
tance.
19 And the names of the men *are*
these: Of the tribe of Jūdah, Caleb the
son of Je-phŭn'neh.
20 And of the tribe of the children of
Simeon, Shĕ-mū'el the son of Ăm-
mī'hŭd.
21 Of the tribe of Benjamin, E-lī'dăd
the son of Chĭs'lŏn.
22 And the prince of the tribe of the
children of Dan, Bŭk'kī the son of Jŏg'-
lī.
23 The prince of the children of Jo-
seph, for the tribe of the children of Ma-
năs'seh, Hăn'nī-el the son of Ephod.
24 And the prince of the tribe of the
children of Ē'phra-im, Kĕ-mū'el the son
of Shĭph'tăn.
25 And the prince of the tribe of the
children of Zĕb'u-lun, Ē-liz'ā-phăn the
son of Pär'năch.
26 And the prince of the tribe of the
children of Ĭs'sa-char, Păl'tī-el the son
of Ăz'zan.
27 And the prince of the tribe of the
children of Asher, A-hī'hŭd the son of
Shel'ō-mī.
28 And the prince of the tribe of the
children of Năph'ta-lī, Pĕd'a-hĕl the
son of Ăm-mī'hŭd.
29 These *are they* whom the LORD
commanded to divide the inheritance
unto the children of Israel in the land of
Canaan.

CHAPTER 35

AND the LORD spake unto Moses in the
plains of Moab by Jordan *near* Jericho,
saying,
2 Command the children of Israel,
that they give unto the Lē'vītes of the
inheritance of their possession cities to
dwell in; and ye shall give *also* unto the
Lē'vītes suburbs for the cities round
about them.
3 And the cities shall they have to
dwell in; and the suburbs of them shall
be for their cattle, and for their goods,
and for all their beasts.
4 And the suburbs of the cities, which
ye shall give unto the Lē'vītes, *shall
reach* from the wall of the city and out-
ward a thousand cubits round about.
5 And ye shall measure from without
the city on the east side two thousand
cubits, and on the south side two thou-
sand cubits, and on the west side two
thousand cubits, and on the north side
two thousand cubits; and the city *shall
be* in the midst: this shall be to them the
suburbs of the cities.
6 And among the cities which ye shall
give unto the Lē'vītes *there shall be* six
cities for refuge, which ye shall appoint
for the manslayer, that he may flee
thither: and to them ye shall add forty
and two cities.
7 *So* all the cities which ye shall give
to the Lē'vītes *shall be* forty and eight
cities: them *shall ye give* with their sub-
urbs.
8 And the cities which ye shall give
shall be of the possession of the chil-
dren of Israel: from *them that have*
many ye shall give many; but from
them that have few ye shall give few:
every one shall give of his cities unto
the Lē'vītes according to his inheri-
tance which he inheriteth.
9 ¶And the LORD spake unto Moses,
saying,
10 Speak unto the children of Israel,
and say unto them, When ye be come
over Jordan into the land of Canaan;
11 Then ye shall appoint you cities to
be cities of refuge for you; that the
slayer may flee thither, which killeth
any person at unawares.
12 And they shall be unto you cities
for refuge from the avenger; that the
manslayer die not, until he stand before
the congregation in judgment.
13 And of these cities which ye shall
give six cities shall ye have for refuge.
14 Ye shall give three cities on this
side Jordan, and three cities shall ye
give in the land of Canaan, *which* shall
be cities of refuge.
15 These six cities shall be a refuge,
both for the children of Israel, and for
the stranger, and for the sojourner
among them; that every one that killeth
any person unawares may flee thither.
16 And if he smite him with an instru-
ment of iron, so that he die, he *is* a mur-
derer: the murderer shall surely be put
to death.
17 And if he smite him with throwing
a stone, wherewith he may die, and he
die, he *is* a murderer: the murderer
shall surely be put to death.
18 Or *if* he smite him with an hand
weapon of wood, wherewith he may
die, and he die, he *is* a murderer: the
murderer shall surely be put to death.
19 The revenger of blood himself
shall slay the murderer: when he meet-
eth him, he shall slay him.
20 But if he thrust him of hatred, or
hurl at him by laying of wait, that he
die;
21 Or in enmity smite him with his
hand, that he die: he that smote *him*
shall surely be put to death; *for* he *is* a
murderer: the revenger of blood shall
slay the murderer, when he meeteth
him.
22 But if he thrust him suddenly

without enmity, or have cast upon him any thing without laying of wait,

23 Or with any stone, wherewith a man may die, seeing *him* not, and cast *it* upon him, that he die, and *was* not his enemy, neither sought his harm:

24 Then the congregation shall judge between the slayer and the revenger of blood according to these judgments:

25 And the congregation shall deliver the slayer out of the hand of the revenger of blood, and the congregation shall restore him to the city of his refuge, whither he was fled: and he shall abide in it unto the death of the high priest, which was anointed with the holy oil.

26 But if the slayer shall at any time come without the border of the city of his refuge, whither he was fled;

27 And the revenger of blood find him without the borders of the city of his refuge, and the revenger of blood kill the slayer; he shall not be guilty of blood:

28 Because he should have remained in the city of his refuge until the death of the high priest: but after the death of the high priest the slayer shall return into the land of his possession.

29 So these *things* shall be for a statute of judgment unto you throughout your generations in all your dwellings.

30 Whoso killeth any person, the murderer shall be put to death by the mouth of witnesses: but one witness shall not testify against any person *to cause him* to die.

31 Moreover ye shall take no satisfaction for the life of a murderer, which *is* guilty of death: but he shall be surely put to death.

32 And ye shall take no satisfaction for him that is fled to the city of his refuge, that he should come again to dwell in the land, until the death of the priest.

33 So ye shall not pollute the land wherein ye *are*: for blood it defileth the land: and the land cannot be cleansed of the blood that is shed therein, but by the blood of him that shed it.

34 Defile not therefore the land which ye shall inhabit, wherein I dwell: for I the LORD dwell among the children of Israel.

CHAPTER 36

AND the chief fathers of the families of the children of Gilead, the son of Mā'chĭr, the son of Ma-năs'seh, of the families of the sons of Joseph, came near, and spake before Moses, and before the princes, the chief fathers of the children of Israel:

2 And they said, The LORD commanded my lord to give the land for an inheritance by lot to the children of Israel: and my lord was commanded by the LORD to give the inheritance of Ze-lō'phe-hăd our brother unto his daughters.

3 And if they be married to any of the sons of the *other* tribes of the children of Israel, then shall their inheritance be taken from the inheritance of our fathers, and shall be put to the inheritance of the tribe whereunto they are received: so shall it be taken from the lot of our inheritance.

4 And when the jubile of the children of Israel shall be, then shall their inheritance be put unto the inheritance of the tribe whereunto they are received: so shall their inheritance be taken away from the inheritance of the tribe of our fathers.

5 And Moses commanded the children of Israel according to the word of the LORD, saying, The tribe of the sons of Joseph hath said well.

6 This *is* the thing which the LORD doth command concerning the daughters of Ze-lō'phe-hăd, saying, Let them marry to whom they think best; only to the family of the tribe of their father shall they marry.

7 So shall not the inheritance of the children of Israel remove from tribe to tribe: for every one of the children of Israel shall keep himself to the inheritance of the tribe of his fathers.

8 And every daughter, that possesseth an inheritance in any tribe of the children of Israel, shall be wife unto one of the family of the tribe of her father, that the children of Israel may enjoy every man the inheritance of his fathers.

9 Neither shall the inheritance remove from *one* tribe to another tribe; but every one of the tribes of the children of Israel shall keep himself to his own inheritance.

10 Even as the LORD commanded Moses, so did the daughters of Ze-lō'phe-hăd:

11 For Māh'lah, Tir'zah, and Hŏg'lah, and Mĭl'cah, and Noah, the daughters of Ze-lō'phe-hăd, were married unto their father's brothers' sons:

12 *And* they were married into the families of the sons of Ma-năs'seh the son of Joseph, and their inheritance remained in the tribe of the family of their father.

13 These *are* the commandements and the judgments, which the LORD commanded by the hand of Moses unto the children of Israel in the plains of Moab by Jordan *near* Jericho.

THE FIFTH BOOK OF MOSES
CALLED

DEUTERONOMY

CHAPTER 1

THESE *be* the words which Moses spake unto all Israel on this side Jordan in the wilderness, in the plain over against the Red *sea*, between Paran, and Tō′phel, and Lā′ban, and Ha-ze′-rŏth, and Dĭz′a-hăb.

2 (*There are* eleven days' *journey* from Hô′rĕb by the way of mount Sē′ir unto Kā′desh-bär′ne-a.)

3 And it came to pass in the fortieth year, in the eleventh month, on the first *day* of the month, *that* Moses spake unto the children of Israel, according unto all that the LORD had given him in commandment unto them;

4 After he had slain Sihon the king of the Ăm′o-rītes, which dwelt in Hĕsh′-bŏn, and Og the king of Bā′shan, which dwelt at Ăs′ta-rŏth in Ĕd′re-ī:

5 On this side Jordan, in the land of Moab, began Moses to declare this law, saying,

6 The LORD our God spake unto us in Hô′rĕb, saying, Ye have dwelt long enough in this mount:

7 Turn you, and take your journey, and go to the mount of the Ăm′o-rītes, and unto all *the places* nigh thereunto, in the plain, in the hills, and in the vale, and in the south, and by the sea side, to the land of the Canaanites, and unto Lebanon, unto the great river, the river Eū-phrā′tēs.

8 Behold, I have set the land before you: go in and possess the land which the LORD sware unto your fathers, Abraham, Isaac, and Jacob, to give unto them and to their seed after them.

9 ¶And I spake unto you at that time, saying, I am not able to bear you myself alone:

10 The LORD your God hath multiplied you, and, behold, ye *are* this day as the stars of heaven for multitude.

11 (The LORD God of your fathers make you a thousand times so many more as ye *are*, and bless you, as he hath promised you!)

12 How can I myself alone bear your cumbrance, and your burden, and your strife?

13 Take you wise men, and understanding, and known among your tribes, and I will make them rulers over you.

14 And ye answered me, and said, The thing which thou hast spoken *is* good *for us* to do.

15 So I took the chief of your tribes, wise men, and known, and made them heads over you, captains over thousands, and captains over hundreds, and captains over fifties, and captains over tens, and officers among your tribes.

16 And I charged your judges at that time, saying, Hear *the causes* between your brethren, and judge righteously between *every* man and his brother, and the stranger *that is* with him.

17 Ye shall not respect persons in judgment; *but* ye shall hear the small as well as the great; ye shall not be afraid of the face of man; for the judgment *is* God's: and the cause that is too hard for you, bring *it* unto me, and I will hear it.

18 And I commanded you at that time all the things which ye should do.

19 ¶And when we departed from Hô′-rĕb, we went through all that great and terrible wilderness, which ye saw by the way of the mountain of the Ăm′o-rītes, as the LORD our God commanded us; and we came to Kā′desh-bär′ne-a.

20 And I said unto you, Ye are come unto the mountain of the Ăm′o-rītes, which the LORD our God doth give unto us.

21 Behold, the LORD thy God hath set the land before thee: go up *and* possess *it*, as the LORD God of thy fathers hath said unto thee; fear not, neither be discouraged.

22 ¶And ye came near unto me every one of you, and said, We will send men before us, and they shall search us out the land, and bring us word again by what way we must go up, and into what cities we shall come.

23 And the saying pleased me well: and I took twelve men of you, one of a tribe:

24 And they turned and went up into the mountain, and came unto the valley of Ĕsh′cōl, and searched it out.

25 And they took of the fruit of the land in their hands, and brought *it* down unto us, and brought us word again, and said, *It is* a good land which the LORD our God doth give us.

26 Notwithstanding ye would not go up, but rebelled against the commandment of the LORD your God:

27 And ye murmured in your tents, and said, Because the LORD hated us, he hath brought us forth out of the land of Egypt, to deliver us into the hand of the Ăm′o-rītes, to destroy us.

28 Whither shall we go up? our brethren have discouraged our heart,

saying, The people *is* greater and taller
than we; the cities *are* great and walled
up to heaven; and moreover we have
seen the sons of the Anakims there.
29 Then I said unto you, Dread not,
neither be afraid of them.
30 The LORD your God which goeth
before you, he shall fight for you, ac-
cording to all that he did for you in
Egypt before your eyes;
31 And in the wilderness, where thou
hast seen how that the LORD thy God
bare thee, as a man doth bear his son, in
all the way that ye went, until ye came
into this place.
32 Yet in this thing ye did not believe
the LORD your God,
33 Who went in the way before you,
to search you out a place to pitch your
tents *in*, in fire by night, to shew you by
what way ye should go, and in a cloud
by day.
34 And the LORD heard the voice of
your words, and was wroth, and sware,
saying,
35 Surely there shall not one of these
men of this evil generation see that
good land, which I sware to give unto
your fathers,
36 Save Caleb the son of Je-phŭn′-
neh; he shall see it, and to him will I
give the land that he hath trodden
upon, and to his children, because he
hath wholly followed the LORD.
37 Also the LORD was angry with me
for your sakes, saying, Thou also shalt
not go in thither.
38 *But* Joshua the son of Nun, which
standeth before thee, he shall go in
thither: encourage him: for he shall
cause Israel to inherit it.
39 Moreover your little ones, which
ye said should be a prey, and your
children, which in that day had no
knowledge between good and evil, they
shall go in thither, and unto them will I
give it, and they shall possess it.
40 But *as for* you, turn you, and take
your journey into the wilderness by the
way of the Red sea.
41 Then ye answered and said unto
me, We have sinned against the LORD,
we will go up and fight, according to all
that the LORD our God commanded us.
And when ye had girded on every man
his weapons of war, ye were ready to
go up into the hill.
42 And the LORD said unto me, Say
unto them, Go not up, neither fight; for
I *am* not among you; lest ye be smitten
before your enemies.
43 So I spake unto you; and ye would
not hear, but rebelled against the com-
mandment of the LORD, and went pre-
sumptuously up into the hill.
44 And the Ăm′o-rītes, which dwelt
in that mountain, came out against
you, and chased you, as bees do, and
destroyed you in Sē′ir, *even* unto Hôr′-
mah.
45 And ye returned and wept before
the LORD; but the LORD would not hear-
ken to your voice, nor give ear unto
you.
46 So ye abode in Kā′desh many
days, according unto the days that ye
abode *there*.

CHAPTER 2

THEN we turned, and took our journey
into the wilderness by the way of the
Red sea, as the LORD spake unto me:
and we compassed mount Sē′ir many
days.
2 And the LORD spake unto me,
saying,
3 Ye have compassed this mountain
long enough: turn you northward.
4 And command thou the people,
saying, Ye *are* to pass through the
coast of your brethren the children of
Esau, which dwell in Sē′ir; and they
shall be afraid of you: take ye good
heed unto yourselves therefore:
5 Meddle not with them; for I will not
give you of their land, no, not so much
as a foot breadth; because I have given
mount Sē′ir unto Esau *for* a possession.
6 Ye shall buy meat of them for mon-
ey, that ye may eat; and ye shall also
buy water of them for money, that ye
may drink.
7 For the LORD thy God hath blessed
thee in all the works of thy hand: he
knoweth thy walking through this
great wilderness: these forty years the
LORD thy God *hath been* with thee; thou
hast lacked nothing.
8 And when we passed by from our
brethren the children of Esau, which
dwelt in Sē′ir, through the way of the
plain from Ē′lăth, and from Ĕ′zĭ-on-
gā′ber, we turned and passed by the way
of the wilderness of Moab.
9 And the LORD said unto me, Dis-
tress not the Moabites, neither contend
with them in battle: for I will not give
thee of their land *for* a possession; be-
cause I have given Ar unto the children
of Lot *for* a possession.
10 The Ē′mĭms dwelt therein in times
past, a people great, and many, and tall,
as the Anakims;
11 Which also were accounted
giants, as the Anakims; but the Moab-
ites call them Ē′mĭms.
12 The Hô′rĭms also dwelt in Sē′ir
beforetime; but the children of Esau suc-
ceeded them, when they had destroyed
them from before them, and dwelt in

their stead; as Israel did unto the land of his possession, which the LORD gave unto them.

13 Now rise up, *said I*, and get you over the brook Ze′red. And we went over the brook Ze′red.

14 And the space in which we came from Kā′desh–bär′ne-a, until we were come over the brook Ze′red, *was* thirty and eight years; until all the generation of the men of war were wasted out from among the host, as the LORD sware unto them.

15 For indeed the hand of the LORD was against them, to destroy them from among the host, until they were consumed.

16 ¶So it came to pass, when all the men of war were consumed and dead from among the people,

17 That the LORD spake unto me, saying,

18 Thou art to pass over through Ar, the coast of Moab, this day:

19 And *when* thou comest nigh over against the children of Ammon, distress them not, nor meddle with them: for I will not give thee of the land of the children of Ammon *any* possession; because I have given it unto the children of Lot *for* a possession.

20 (That also was accounted a land of giants: giants dwelt therein in old time; and the Ammonites call them Zăm-zŭm′mĭms;

21 A people great, and many, and tall, as the Anakims; but the LORD destroyed them before them; and they succeeded them, and dwelt in their stead:

22 As he did to the children of Esau, which dwelt in Sē′ir, when he destroyed the Hô′rĭms from before them; and they succeeded them, and dwelt in their stead even unto this day:

23 And the Ā′vĭms which dwelt in Ha-ze′rĭm, *even* unto Ăz′zah, the Căph′to-rĭms, which came forth out of Căph′tôr, destroyed them, and dwelt in their stead.)

24 ¶Rise ye up, take your journey, and pass over the river Arnon: behold, I have given into thine hand Sihon the Ăm′o-rīte, king of Hĕsh′bŏn, and his land: begin to possess *it*, and contend with him in battle.

25 This day will I begin to put the dread of thee and the fear of thee upon the nations *that are* under the whole heaven, who shall hear report of thee, and shall tremble, and be in anguish because of thee.

26 ¶And I sent messengers out of the wilderness of Kĕd′e-mŏth unto Sihon king of Hĕsh′bŏn with words of peace, saying,

27 Let me pass through thy land: I will go along by the high way, I will neither turn unto the right hand nor to the left.

28 Thou shalt sell me meat for money, that I may eat; and give me water for money, that I may drink: only I will pass through on my feet;

29 (As the children of Esau which dwell in Sē′ir, and the Moabites which dwell in Ar, did unto me;) until I shall pass over Jordan into the land which the LORD our God giveth us.

30 But Sihon king of Hĕsh′bŏn would not let us pass by him: for the LORD thy God hardened his spirit, and made his heart obstinate, that he might deliver him into thy hand, as *appeareth* this day.

31 And the LORD said unto me, Behold, I have begun to give Sihon and his land before thee: begin to possess, that thou mayest inherit his land.

32 Then Sihon came out against us, he and all his people, to fight at Jā′hăz.

33 And the LORD our God delivered him before us; and we smote him, and his sons, and all his people.

34 And we took all his cities at that time, and utterly destroyed the men, and the women, and the little ones, of every city, we left none to remain:

35 Only the cattle we took for a prey unto ourselves, and the spoil of the cities which we took.

36 From Ar′ō-er, which *is* by the brink of the river of Arnon, and *from* the city that *is* by the river, even unto Gilead, there was not one city too strong for us: the LORD our God delivered all unto us:

37 Only unto the land of the children of Ammon thou camest not, *nor* unto any place of the river Jabbok, nor unto the cities in the mountains, nor unto whatsoever the LORD our God forbad us.

CHAPTER 3

THEN we turned, and went up the way to Bā′shan: and Og the king of Bā′shan came out against us, he and all his people, to battle at Ĕd′re-ī.

2 And the LORD said unto me, Fear him not: for I will deliver him, and all his people, and his land, into thy hand; and thou shalt do unto him as thou didst unto Sihon king of the Ăm′o-rītes, which dwelt at Hĕsh′bŏn.

3 So the LORD our God delivered into our hands Og also, the king of Bā′shan, and all his people: and we smote him until none was left to him remaining.

4 And we took all his cities at that time, there was not a city which we

took not from them, threescore cities,
all the region of Är′gŏb, the kingdom of
Og in Bā′shan.
5 All these cities *were* fenced with
high walls, gates, and bars; beside un-
walled towns a great many.
6 And we utterly destroyed them, as
we did unto Sihon king of Hĕsh′bŏn, ut-
terly destroying the men, women, and
children, of every city.
7 But all the cattle, and the spoil of
the cities, we took for a prey to our-
selves.
8 And we took at that time out of the
hand of the two kings of the Ăm′o-rītes
the land that *was* on this side Jordan,
from the river of Arnon unto mount
Hermon;
9 (*Which* Hermon the Si-dō′ni-anṡ
call Sĭr′i-on; and the Ăm′o-rītes call it
She′nir;)
10 All the cities of the plain, and all
Gilead, and all Bā′shan, unto Săl′chah
and Ĕd′re-ī, cities of the kingdom of Og
in Bā′shan.
11 For only Og king of Bā′shan re-
mained of the remnant of giants; be-
hold, his bedstead *was* a bedstead of
iron; *is* it not in Răb′bath of the children
of Ammon? nine cubits *was* the length
thereof, and four cubits the breadth of
it, after the cubit of a man.
12 And this land, *which* we possessed
at that time, from Ar′ō-er, which *is* by
the river Arnon, and half mount Gilead,
and the cities thereof, gave I unto the
Reubenites and to the Găd′ītes.
13 And the rest of Gilead, and all
Bā′shan, *being* the kingdom of Og, gave
I unto the half tribe of Ma-năs′seh; all
the region of Är′gŏb, with all Bā′shan,
which was called the land of giants.
14 Jā′ir the son of Ma-năs′seh took all
the country of Är′gŏb unto the coasts of
Gĕsh′u-rī and Mā-ăch′a-thī; and called
them after his own name, Bā′shan–hā′-
vŏth–jāir, unto this day.
15 And I gave Gilead unto Mā′chĭr.
16 And unto the Reubenites and unto
the Găd′ītes I gave from Gilead even
unto the river Arnon half the valley,
and the border even unto the river Jab-
bok, *which is* the border of the children
of Ammon;
17 The plain also, and Jordan, and the
coast *thereof*, from Chĭn′ne-rĕth even
unto the sea of the plain, *even* the salt
sea, under Ăsh′dŏth–pĭs′gah eastward.
18 ¶And I commanded you at that
time, saying, The LORD your God hath
given you this land to possess it: ye
shall pass over armed before your
brethren the children of Israel, all *that*
are meet for the war.
19 But your wives, and your little
ones, and your cattle, (*for* I know that
ye have much cattle,) shall abide in
your cities which I have given you;
20 Until the LORD have given rest
unto your brethren, as well as unto you,
and *until* they also possess the land
which the LORD your God hath given
them beyond Jordan: and *then* shall ye
return every man unto his possession,
which I have given you.
21 ¶And I commanded Joshua at that
time, saying, Thine eyes have seen all
that the LORD your God hath done unto
these two kings: so shall the LORD do
unto all the kingdoms whither thou
passest.
22 Ye shall not fear them: for the
LORD your God he shall fight for you.
23 ¶And I besought the LORD at that
time, saying,
24 O Lord GOD, thou hast begun to
shew thy servant thy greatness, and
thy mighty hand: for what God *is there*
in heaven or in earth, that can do ac-
cording to thy works, and according to
thy might?
25 I pray thee, let me go over, and see
the good land that *is* beyond Jordan,
that goodly mountain, and Lebanon.
26 But the LORD was wroth with me
for your sakes, and would not hear me:
and the LORD said unto me, Let it suf-
fice thee; speak no more unto me of this
matter.
27 Get thee up into the top of Pĭṡ′gah,
and lift up thine eyes westward, and
northward, and southward, and east-
ward, and behold *it* with thine eyes: for
thou shalt not go over this Jordan.
28 But charge Joshua, and encourage
him, and strengthen him: for he shall go
over before this people, and he shall
cause them to inherit the land which
thou shalt see.
29 So we abode in the valley over
against Bĕth–pē′ôr.

CHAPTER 4

NOW therefore hearken, O Israel, unto
the statutes and unto the judgments,
which I teach you, for to do *them*, that
ye may live, and go in and possess the
land which the LORD God of your fathers
giveth you.
2 Ye shall not add unto the word
which I command you, neither shall ye
diminish *ought* from it, that ye may
keep the commandments of the LORD
your God which I command you.
3 Your eyes have seen what the LORD
did because of Bā′al–pē′ôr: for all the
men that followed Bā′al–pē′ôr, the LORD
thy God hath destroyed them from
among you.
4 But ye that did cleave unto the LORD

your God *are* alive every one of you this
day.
5 Behold, I have taught you statutes
and judgments, even as the LORD my
God commanded me, that ye should do
so in the land whither ye go to possess
it.
6 Keep therefore and do *them*; for
this *is* your wisdom and your under-
standing in the sight of the nations,
which shall hear all these statutes, and
say, Surely this great nation *is* a wise
and understanding people.
7 For what nation *is there so* great,
who *hath* God *so* nigh unto them, as the
LORD our God *is* in all *things that* we
call upon him *for*?
8 And what nation *is there so* great,
that hath statutes and judgments *so*
righteous as all this law, which I set be-
fore you this day?
9 Only take heed to thyself, and keep
thy soul diligently, lest thou forget the
things which thine eyes have seen, and
lest they depart from thy heart all the
days of thy life: but teach them thy
sons, and thy sons' sons;
10 *Specially* the day that thou stood-
est before the LORD thy God in Hô'rĕb,
when the LORD said unto me, Gather
me the people together, and I will make
them hear my words, that they may
learn to fear me all the days that they
shall live upon the earth, and *that* they
may teach their children.
11 And ye came near and stood under
the mountain; and the mountain
burned with fire unto the midst of
heaven, with darkness, clouds, and
thick darkness.
12 And the LORD spake unto you out
of the midst of the fire: ye heard the
voice of the words, but saw no simili-
tude; only *ye heard* a voice.
13 And he declared unto you his
covenant, which he commanded you to
perform, *even* ten commandments;
and he wrote them upon two tables of
stone.
14 ¶And the LORD commanded me at
that time to teach you statutes and
judgments, that ye might do them in
the land whither ye go over to possess
it.
15 Take ye therefore good heed unto
yourselves; for ye saw no manner of si-
militude on the day *that* the LORD spake
unto you in Hô'rĕb out of the midst of
the fire:
16 Lest ye corrupt *yourselves*, and
make you a graven image, the simili-
tude of any figure, the likeness of male
or female,
17 The likeness of any beast that *is* on
the earth, the likeness of any winged
fowl that flieth in the air,
18 The likeness of any thing that
creepeth on the ground, the likeness of
any fish that *is* in the waters beneath
the earth:
19 And lest thou lift up thine eyes
unto heaven, and when thou seest the
sun, and the moon, and the stars, *even*
all the host of heaven, shouldest be driv-
en to worship them, and serve them,
which the LORD thy God hath divided
unto all nations under the whole
heaven.
20 But the LORD hath taken you, and
brought you forth out of the iron fur-
nace, *even* out of Egypt, to be unto him
a people of inheritance, as *ye are* this
day.
21 Furthermore the LORD was angry
with me for your sakes, and sware that
I should not go over Jordan, and that I
should not go in unto that good land,
which the LORD thy God giveth thee *for*
an inheritance:
22 But I must die in this land, I must
not go over Jordan: but ye shall go
over, and possess that good land.
23 Take heed unto yourselves, lest ye
forget the covenant of the LORD your
God, which he made with you, and
make you a graven image, *or* the like-
ness of any *thing*, which the LORD thy
God hath forbidden thee.
24 For the LORD thy God *is* a consum-
ing fire, *even* a jealous God.
25 ¶When thou shalt beget children,
and children's children, and ye shall
have remained long in the land, and
shall corrupt *yourselves*, and make a
graven image, *or* the likeness of any
thing, and shall do evil in the sight of
the LORD thy God, to provoke him to
anger:
26 I call heaven and earth to witness
against you this day, that ye shall soon
utterly perish from off the land where-
unto ye go over Jordan to possess it;
ye shall not prolong *your* days upon it,
but shall utterly be destroyed.
27 And the LORD shall scatter you
among the nations, and ye shall be left
few in number among the heathen,
whither the LORD shall lead you.
28 And there ye shall serve gods, the
work of men's hands, wood and stone,
which neither see, nor hear, nor eat, nor
smell.
29 But if from thence thou shalt seek
the LORD thy God, thou shalt find *him*,
if thou seek him with all thy heart and
with all thy soul.
30 When thou art in tribulation, and
all these things are come upon thee,
even in the latter days, if thou turn to

the LORD thy God, and shalt be obedi-
ent unto his voice;
31 (For the LORD thy God *is* a merci-
ful God;) he will not forsake thee,
neither destroy thee, nor forget the
covenant of thy fathers which he sware
unto them.
32 For ask now of the days that are
past, which were before thee, since the
day that God created man upon the
earth, and *ask* from the one side of
heaven unto the other, whether there
hath been *any such thing* as this great
thing *is*, or hath been heard like it?
33 Did *ever* people hear the voice of
God speaking out of the midst of the
fire, as thou hast heard, and live?
34 Or hath God assayed to go *and*
take him a nation from the midst of *an-
other* nation, by temptations, by signs,
and by wonders, and by war, and by a
mighty hand, and by a stretched out
arm, and by great terrors, according to
all that the LORD your God did for you
in Egypt before your eyes?
35 Unto thee it was shewed, that thou
mightest know that the LORD he *is* God;
there is none else beside him.
36 Out of heaven he made thee to
hear his voice, that he might instruct
thee: and upon earth he shewed thee
his great fire; and thou heardest his
words out of the midst of the fire.
37 And because he loved thy fathers,
therefore he chose their seed after
them, and brought thee out in his sight
with his mighty power out of Egypt;
38 To drive out nations from before
thee greater and mightier than thou *art*,
to bring thee in, to give thee their land
for an inheritance, as *it is* this day.
39 Know therefore this day, and con-
sider *it* in thine heart, that the LORD he
is God in heaven above, and upon the
earth beneath: *there is* none else.
40 Thou shalt keep therefore his stat-
utes, and his commandments, which I
command thee this day, that it may go
well with thee, and with thy children
after thee, and that thou mayest pro-
long *thy* days upon the earth, which the
LORD thy God giveth thee, for ever.
41 ¶Then Moses severed three cities
on this side Jordan toward the sunris-
ing;
42 That the slayer might flee thither,
which should kill his neighbour un-
awares, and hated him not in times past;
and that fleeing unto one of these cities
he might live:
43 *Namely*, Bē′zer in the wilderness,
in the plain country, of the Reubenites;
and Rā′mŏth in Gilead, of the Găd′ītes;
and Gō′lan in Bā′shan, of the Ma-năs′-
sītes.
44 ¶And this *is* the law which Moses
set before the children of Israel:
45 These *are* the testimonies, and the
statutes, and the judgments, which
Moses spake unto the children of
Israel, after they came forth out of
Egypt,
46 On this side Jordan, in the valley
over against Bĕth-pē′ôr, in the land of
Sihon king of the Ăm′o-rītes, who
dwelt at Hĕsh′bŏn, whom Moses and
the children of Israel smote, after they
were come forth out of Egypt:
47 And they possessed his land, and
the land of Og king of Bā′shan, two
kings of the Ăm′o-rītes, which *were* on
this side Jordan toward the sunrising;
48 From Ar′ō-er, which *is* by the bank
of the river Arnon, even unto mount
Sion, which *is* Hermon,
49 And all the plain on this side Jor-
dan eastward, even unto the sea of the
plain, under the springs of Pĭs′gah.

CHAPTER 5

AND Moses called all Israel, and said
unto them, Hear, O Israel, the statutes
and judgments which I speak in your
ears this day, that ye may learn them,
and keep, and do them.
2 The LORD our God made a covenant
with us in Hô′rĕb.
3 The LORD made not this covenant
with our fathers, but with us, *even* us,
who *are* all of us here alive this day.
4 The LORD talked with you face to
face in the mount out of the midst of the
fire,
5 (I stood between the LORD and you
at that time, to shew you the word of
the LORD: for ye were afraid by reason
of the fire, and went not up into the
mount;) saying,
6 ¶I *am* the LORD thy God, which
brought thee out of the land of Egypt,
from the house of bondage.
7 Thou shalt have none other gods
before me.
8 Thou shalt not make thee *any* grav-
en image, *or* any likeness *of any thing*
that *is* in heaven above, or that *is* in the
earth beneath, or that *is* in the waters
beneath the earth:
9 Thou shalt not bow down thyself
unto them, nor serve them: for I the
LORD thy God *am* a jealous God, visit-
ing the iniquity of the fathers upon the
children unto the third and fourth *gen-
eration* of them that hate me,
10 And shewing mercy unto thou-
sands of them that love me and keep
my commandments.
11 Thou shalt not take the name of
the LORD thy God in vain: for the LORD

will not hold *him* guiltless that taketh his name in vain.

12 Keep the sabbath day to sanctify it, as the LORD thy God hath commanded thee.

13 Six days thou shalt labour, and do all thy work:

14 But the seventh day is the sabbath of the LORD thy God: *in it* thou shalt not do any work, thou, nor thy son, nor thy daughter, nor thy manservant, nor thy maidservant, nor thine ox, nor thine ass, nor any of thy cattle, nor thy stranger that *is* within thy gates; that thy manservant and thy maidservant may rest as well as thou.

15 And remember that thou wast a servant in the land of Egypt, and *that* the LORD thy God brought thee out thence through a mighty hand and by a stretched out arm: therefore the LORD thy God commanded thee to keep the sabbath day.

16 ¶Honour thy father and thy mother, as the LORD thy God hath commanded thee; that thy days may be prolonged, and that it may go well with thee, in the land which the LORD thy God giveth thee.

17 Thou shalt not kill.

18 Neither shalt thou commit adultery.

19 Neither shalt thou steal.

20 Neither shalt thou bear false witness against thy neighbour.

21 Neither shalt thou desire thy neighbour's wife, neither shalt thou covet thy neighbour's house, his field, or his manservant, or his maidservant, his ox, or his ass, or any *thing* that *is* thy neighbour's.

22 ¶These words the LORD spake unto all your assembly in the mount out of the midst of the fire, of the cloud, and of the thick darkness, with a great voice: and he added no more. And he wrote them in two tables of stone, and delivered them unto me.

23 And it came to pass, when ye heard the voice out of the midst of the darkness, (for the mountain did burn with fire,) that ye came near unto me, *even* all the heads of your tribes, and your elders;

24 And ye said, Behold, the LORD our God hath shewed us his glory and his greatness, and we have heard his voice out of the midst of the fire: we have seen this day that God doth talk with man, and he liveth.

25 Now therefore why should we die? for this great fire will consume us: if we hear the voice of the LORD our God any more, then we shall die.

26 For who *is there of* all flesh, that hath heard the voice of the living God speaking out of the midst of the fire, as we *have*, and lived?

27 Go thou near, and hear all that the LORD our God shall say: and speak thou unto us all that the LORD our God shall speak unto thee; and we will hear *it*, and do *it*.

28 And the LORD heard the voice of your words, when ye spake unto me; and the LORD said unto me, I have heard the voice of the words of this people, which they have spoken unto thee: they have well said all that they have spoken.

29 O that there were such an heart in them, that they would fear me, and keep all my commandments always, that it might be well with them, and with their children for ever!

30 Go say to them, Get you into your tents again.

31 But as for thee, stand thou here by me, and I will speak unto thee all the commandments, and the statutes, and the judgments, which thou shalt teach them, that they may do *them* in the land which I give them to possess it.

32 Ye shall observe to do therefore as the LORD your God hath commanded you: ye shall not turn aside to the right hand or to the left.

33 Ye shall walk in all the ways which the LORD your God hath commanded you, that ye may live, and *that it may be* well with you, and *that* ye may prolong *your* days in the land which ye shall possess.

CHAPTER 6

NOW these *are* the commandments, the statutes, and the judgments, which the LORD your God commanded to teach you, that ye might do *them* in the land whither ye go to possess it:

2 That thou mightest fear the LORD thy God, to keep all his statutes and his commandments, which I command thee, thou, and thy son, and thy son's son, all the days of thy life; and that thy days may be prolonged.

3 ¶Hear therefore, O Israel, and observe to do *it*; that it may be well with thee, and that ye may increase mightily, as the LORD God of thy fathers hath promised thee, in the land that floweth with milk and honey.

4 Hear, O Israel: The LORD our God *is* one LORD:

5 And thou shalt love the LORD thy God with all thine heart, and with all thy soul, and with all thy might.

6 And these words, which I command thee this day, shall be in thine heart:

7 And thou shalt teach them diligently unto thy children, and shalt talk of them when thou sittest in thine house, and when thou walkest by the way, and when thou liest down, and when thou risest up.

8 And thou shalt bind them for a sign upon thine hand, and they shall be as frontlets between thine eyes.

9 And thou shalt write them upon the posts of thy house, and on thy gates.

10 And it shall be, when the LORD thy God shall have brought thee into the land which he sware unto thy fathers, to Abraham, to Isaac, and to Jacob, to give thee great and goodly cities, which thou buildedst not,

11 And houses full of all good *things*, which thou filledst not, and wells digged, which thou diggedst not, vineyards and olive trees, which thou plantedst not; when thou shalt have eaten and be full;

12 *Then* beware lest thou forget the LORD, which brought thee forth out of the land of Egypt, from the house of bondage.

13 Thou shalt fear the LORD thy God, and serve him, and shalt swear by his name.

14 Ye shall not go after other gods, of the gods of the people which *are* round about you;

15 (For the LORD thy God *is* a jealous God among you) lest the anger of the LORD thy God be kindled against thee, and destroy thee from off the face of the earth.

16 ¶Ye shall not tempt the LORD your God, as ye tempted *him* in Măs′sah.

17 Ye shall diligently keep the commandments of the LORD your God, and his testimonies, and his statutes, which he hath commanded thee.

18 And thou shalt do *that which is* right and good in the sight of the LORD: that it may be well with thee, and that thou mayest go in and possess the good land which the LORD sware unto thy fathers,

19 To cast out all thine enemies from before thee, as the LORD hath spoken.

20 ¶*And* when thy son asketh thee in time to come, saying, What *mean* the testimonies, and the statutes, and the judgments, which the LORD our God hath commanded you?

21 Then thou shalt say unto thy son, We were Pharaoh's bondmen in Egypt; and the LORD brought us out of Egypt with a mighty hand:

22 And the LORD shewed signs and wonders, great and sore, upon Egypt, upon Pharaoh, and upon all his household, before our eyes:

23 And he brought us out from thence, that he might bring us in, to give us the land which he sware unto our fathers.

24 And the LORD commanded us to do all these statutes, to fear the LORD our God, for our good always, that he might preserve us alive, as *it is* at this day.

25 And it shall be our righteousness, if we observe to do all these commandments before the LORD our God, as he hath commanded us.

CHAPTER 7

WHEN the LORD thy God shall bring thee into the land whither thou goest to possess it, and hath cast out many nations before thee, the Hittites, and the Gir′ga-shītes, and the Ăm′o-rītes, and the Canaanites, and the Pĕr′iz-zītes, and the Hī′vītes, and the Jēb′u-sītes, seven nations greater and mightier than thou;

2 And when the LORD thy God shall deliver them before thee; thou shalt smite them, *and* utterly destroy them; thou shalt make no covenant with them, nor shew mercy unto them:

3 Neither shalt thou make marriages with them; thy daughter thou shalt not give unto his son, nor his daughter shalt thou take unto thy son.

4 For they will turn away thy son from following me, that they may serve other gods: so will the anger of the LORD be kindled against you, and destroy thee suddenly.

5 But thus shall ye deal with them; ye shall destroy their altars, and break down their images, and cut down their groves, and burn their graven images with fire.

6 For thou *art* an holy people unto the LORD thy God: the LORD thy God hath chosen thee to be a special people unto himself, above all people that *are* upon the face of the earth.

7 The LORD did not set his love upon you, nor choose you, because ye were more in number than any people; for ye *were* the fewest of all people:

8 But because the LORD loved you, and because he would keep the oath which he had sworn unto your fathers, hath the LORD brought you out with a mighty hand, and redeemed you out of the house of bondmen, from the hand of Pharaoh king of Egypt.

9 Know therefore that the LORD thy God, he *is* God, the faithful God, which keepeth covenant and mercy with them that love him and keep his commandments to a thousand generations;

10 And repayeth them that hate him

to their face, to destroy them: he will
not be slack to him that hateth him, he
will repay him to his face.
11 Thou shalt therefore keep the
commandments, and the statutes, and
the judgments, which I command thee
this day, to do them.
12 Wherefore it shall come to pass, if
ye hearken to these judgments, and
keep, and do them, that the LORD thy
God shall keep unto thee the covenant
and the mercy which he sware unto thy
fathers:
13 And he will love thee, and bless
thee, and multiply thee: he will also
bless the fruit of thy womb, and the
fruit of thy land, thy corn, and thy wine,
and thine oil, the increase of thy kine,
and the flocks of thy sheep, in the land
which he sware unto thy fathers to give
thee.
14 Thou shalt be blessed above all
people: there shall not be male or fe-
male barren among you, or among your
cattle.
15 And the LORD will take away from
thee all sickness, and will put none of
the evil diseases of Egypt, which thou
knowest, upon thee; but will lay them
upon all *them* that hate thee.
16 And thou shalt consume all the
people which the LORD thy God shall
deliver thee; thine eye shall have no
pity upon them: neither shalt thou
serve their gods; for that *will be* a snare
unto thee.
17 If thou shalt say in thine heart,
These nations *are* more than I; how can
I dispossess them?
18 Thou shalt not be afraid of them:
but shalt well remember what the LORD
thy God did unto Pharaoh, and unto all
Egypt;
19 The great temptations which thine
eyes saw, and the signs, and the won-
ders, and the mighty hand, and the
stretched out arm, whereby the LORD
thy God brought thee out: so shall the
LORD thy God do unto all the people of
whom thou art afraid.
20 Moreover the LORD thy God will
send the hornet among them, until they
that are left, and hide themselves from
thee, be destroyed.
21 Thou shalt not be affrighted at
them: for the LORD thy God *is* among
you, a mighty God and terrible.
22 And the LORD thy God will put out
those nations before thee by little and
little: thou mayest not consume them
at once, lest the beasts of the field in-
crease upon thee.
23 But the LORD thy God shall deliver
them unto thee, and shall destroy them
with a mighty destruction, until they be
destroyed.
24 And he shall deliver their kings
into thine hand, and thou shalt destroy
their name from under heaven: there
shall no man be able to stand before
thee, until thou have destroyed them.
25 The graven images of their gods
shall ye burn with fire: thou shalt not
desire the silver or gold *that is* on them,
nor take *it* unto thee, lest thou be
snared therin: for it *is* an abomination
to the LORD thy God.
26 Neither shalt thou bring an abomi-
nation into thine house, lest thou be a
cursed thing like it: *but* thou shalt ut-
terly detest it, and thou shalt utterly
abhor it; for it *is* a cursed thing.

CHAPTER 8

ALL the commandments which I com-
mand thee this day shall ye observe to
do, that ye may live, and mulitply, and
go in and possess the land which the
LORD sware unto your fathers.
2 And thou shalt remember all the
way which the LORD thy God led thee
these forty years in the wilderness, to
humble thee, *and* to prove thee, to
know what *was* in thine heart, whether
thou wouldest keep his command-
ments, or no.
3 And he humbled thee, and suffered
thee to hunger, and fed thee with
manna, which thou knewest not,
neither did thy fathers know; that he
might make thee know that man doth
not live by bread only, but by every
word that proceedeth out of the mouth
of the LORD doth man live.
4 Thy raiment waxed not old upon
thee, neither did thy foot swell, these
forty years.
5 Thou shalt also consider in thine
heart, that, as a man chasteneth his
son, *so* the LORD thy God chasteneth
thee.
6 Therefore thou shalt keep the com-
mandments of the LORD thy God, to
walk in his ways, and to fear him.
7 For the LORD thy God bringeth thee
into a good land, a land of brooks of
water, of fountains and depths that
spring out of valleys and hills;
8 A land of wheat, and barley, and
vines, and fig trees, and pomegranates;
a land of oil olive, and honey;
9 A land wherein thou shalt eat bread
without scarceness, thou shalt not lack
any *thing* in it; a land whose stones *are*
iron, and out of whose hills thou
mayest dig brass.
10 When thou hast eaten and art full,
then thou shalt bless the LORD thy God

for the good land which he hath given
thee.
11 Beware that thou forget not the
LORD thy God, in not keeping his com-
mandments, and his judgments, and
his statutes, which I command thee
this day:
12 Lest *when* thou hast eaten and art
full, and hast built goodly houses, and
dwelt *therein*;
13 And *when* thy herds and thy flocks
multiply, and thy silver and thy gold is
multiplied, and all that thou hast is
multiplied;
14 Then thine heart be lifted up, and
thou forget the LORD thy God, which
brought thee forth out of the land of
Egypt, from the house of bondage;
15 Who led thee through that great
and terrible wilderness, *wherein were*
fiery serpents, and scorpions, and
drought, where *there was* no water;
who brought thee forth water out of the
rock of flint;
16 Who fed thee in the wilderness
with manna, which thy fathers knew
not, that he might humble thee, and
that he might prove thee, to do thee
good at thy latter end;
17 And thou say in thine heart, My
power and the might of *mine* hand hath
gotten me this wealth.
18 But thou shalt remember the LORD
thy God: for *it is* he that giveth thee
power to get wealth, that he may estab-
lish his covenant which he sware unto
thy fathers, as *it is* this day.
19 And it shall be, if thou do at all for-
get the LORD thy God, and walk after
other gods, and serve them, and wor-
ship them, I testify against you this day
that ye shall surely perish.
20 As the nations which the LORD
destroyeth before your face, so shall ye
perish; because ye would not be obedi-
ent unto the voice of the LORD your
God.

CHAPTER 9

HEAR, O Israel: Thou *art* to pass over
Jordan this day, to go in to possess na-
tions greater and mightier than thyself,
cities great and fenced up to heaven,
2 A people great and tall, the children
of the Anakims, whom thou knowest,
and *of whom* thou hast heard *say*, Who
can stand before the children of Anak!
3 Understand therefore this day, that
the LORD thy God *is* he which goeth
over before thee; *as* a consuming fire
he shall destroy them, and he shall
bring them down before thy face: so
shalt thou drive them out, and destroy
them quickly, as the LORD hath said
unto thee.
4 Speak not thou in thine heart, after
that the LORD thy God hath cast them
out from before thee, saying, For my
righteousness the LORD hath brought
me in to possess this land: but for the
wickedness of these nations the LORD
doth drive them out from before thee.
5 Not for thy righteousness, or for the
uprightness of thine heart, dost thou go
to possess their land: but for the
wickedness of these nations the LORD
thy God doth drive them out from be-
fore thee, and that he may perform the
word which the LORD sware unto thy
fathers, Abraham, Isaac, and Jacob.
6 Understand therefore, that the
LORD thy God giveth thee not this good
land to possess it for thy righteousness;
for thou *art* a stiffnecked people.
7 ¶Remember, *and* forget not, how
thou provokedst the LORD thy God to
wrath in the wilderness: from the day
that thou didst depart out of the land of
Egypt, until ye came unto this place, ye
have been rebellious against the LORD.
8 Also in Hô'rĕb ye provoked the
LORD to wrath, so that the LORD was
angry with you to have destroyed you.
9 When I was gone up into the mount
to receive the tables of stone, *even* the
tables of the covenant which the LORD
made with you, then I abode in the
mount forty days and forty nights, I
neither did eat bread nor drink water.
10 And the LORD delivered unto me
two tables of stone written with the fin-
ger of God; and on them *was written*
according to all the words, which the
LORD spake with you in the mount out
of the midst of the fire in the day of the
assembly.
11 And it came to pass at the end of
forty days and forty nights, *that* the
LORD gave me the two tables of stone,
even the tables of the covenant.
12 And the LORD said unto me, Arise,
get thee down quickly from hence; for
thy people which thou hast brought
forth out of Egypt have corrupted
themselves; they are quickly turned
aside out of the way which I com-
manded them; they have made them a
molten image.
13 Furthermore the LORD spake unto
me, saying, I have seen this people,
and, behold, it *is* a stiffnecked people:
14 Let me alone, that I may destroy
them, and blot out their name from un-
der heaven: and I will make of thee a
nation mightier and greater than they.
15 So I turned and came down from
the mount, and the mount burned with
fire: and the two tables of the covenant
were in my two hands.
16 And I looked, and, behold, ye had

sinned against the LORD your God, *and*
had made you a molten calf: ye had
turned aside quickly out of the way
which the LORD had commanded you.
17 And I took the two tables, and cast
them out of my two hands, and brake
them before your eyes.
18 And I fell down before the LORD, as
at the first, forty days and forty nights:
I did neither eat bread, nor drink water,
because of all your sins which ye
sinned, in doing wickedly in the sight of
the LORD, to provoke him to anger.
19 For I was afraid of the anger and
hot displeasure, wherewith the LORD
was wroth against you to destroy you.
But the LORD hearkened unto me at that
time also.
20 And the LORD was very angry with
Aaron to have destroyed him: and I
prayed for Aaron also the same time.
21 And I took your sin, the calf which
ye had made, and burnt it with fire, and
stamped it, *and* ground *it* very small,
even until it was as small as dust: and I
cast the dust thereof into the brook
that descended out of the mount.
22 And at Tăb'e-rah, and at Măs'sah,
and at Kĭb'rŏth-hat-tā'a-vah, ye pro-
voked the LORD to wrath.
23 Likewise when the LORD sent you
from Kā'desh-bär'ne-a, saying, Go up
and possess the land which I have giv-
en you; then ye rebelled against the
commandment of the LORD your God,
and ye believed him not, nor hearkened
to his voice.
24 Ye have been rebellious against
the LORD from the day that I knew you.
25 Thus I fell down before the LORD
forty days and forty nights, as I fell
down *at the first*; because the LORD had
said he would destroy you.
26 I prayed therefore unto the LORD,
and said, O Lord GOD, destroy not thy
people and thine inheritance, which
thou hast redeemed through thy great-
ness, which thou hast brought forth out
of Egypt with a mighty hand.
27 Remember thy servants, Abra-
ham, Isaac, and Jacob; look not unto
the stubbornness of this people, nor to
their wickedness, nor to their sin:
28 Lest the land whence thou
broughtest us out say, Because the
LORD was not able to bring them into
the land which he promised them, and
because he hated them, he hath
brought them out to slay them in the
wilderness.
29 Yet they *are* thy people and thine
inheritance, which thou broughtest out
by thy mighty power and by thy
stretched out arm.

CHAPTER 10

AT that time the LORD said unto me,
Hew thee two tables of stone like unto
the first, and come up unto me into the
mount, and make thee an ark of wood.
2 And I will write on the tables the
words that were in the first tables
which thou brakest, and thou shalt put
them in the ark.
3 And I made an ark *of* shittim wood,
and hewed two tables of stone like unto
the first, and went up into the mount,
having the two tables in mine hand.
4 And he wrote on the tables, accord-
ing to the first writing, the ten com-
mandments, which the LORD spake
unto you in the mount out of the midst
of the fire in the day of the assembly:
and the LORD gave them unto me.
5 And I turned myself and came
down from the mount, and put the
tables in the ark which I had made; and
there they be, as the LORD commanded
me.
6 ¶And the children of Israel took
their journey from Bē-ĕ'rŏth of the
children of Jā'a-kăn to Mō-sē'ra: there
Aaron died, and there he was buried;
and Ĕ-le-ā'zar his son ministered in the
priest's office in his stead.
7 From thence they journeyed unto
Gŭd'gō-dah; and from Gŭd'gō-dah to
Jŏt'băth, a land of rivers of waters.
8 ¶At that time the LORD separated
the tribe of Levi, to bear the ark of the
covenant of the LORD, to stand before
the LORD to minister unto him, and to
bless in his name, unto this day.
9 Wherefore Levi hath no part nor in-
heritance with his brethren; the LORD *is*
his inheritance, according as the LORD
thy God promised him.
10 ¶And I stayed in the mount, accord-
ing to the first time, forty days and
forty nights; and the LORD hearkened
unto me at that time also, *and* the LORD
would not destroy thee.
11 And the LORD said unto me, Arise,
take *thy* journey before the people, that
they may go in and possess the land,
which I sware unto their fathers to give
unto them.
12 ¶And now, Israel, what doth the
LORD thy God require of thee, but to
fear the LORD thy God, to walk in all his
ways, and to love him, and to serve the
LORD thy God with all thy heart and
with all thy soul,
13 To keep the commandments of the
LORD, and his statutes, which I com-
mand thee this day for thy good?
14 Behold, the heaven and the heaven
of heavens *is* the LORD's thy God, the
earth *also*, with all that therein *is*.

15 Only the LORD had a delight in thy
fathers to love them, and he chose their
seed after them, *even* you above all
people, as *it is* this day.
16 Circumcise therefore the foreskin
of your heart, and be no more stiff-
necked.
17 For the LORD your God *is* God of
gods, and Lord of lords, a great God, a
mighty, and a terrible, which regardeth
not persons, nor taketh reward:
18 He doth execute the judgment of
the fatherless and widow, and loveth
the stranger, in giving him food and rai-
ment.
19 Love ye therefore the stranger: for
ye were strangers in the land of Egypt.
20 Thou shalt fear the LORD thy God;
him shalt thou serve, and to him shalt
thou cleave, and swear by his name.
21 He *is* thy praise, and he *is* thy God,
that hath done for thee these great and
terrible things, which thine eyes have
seen.
22 Thy fathers went down into Egypt
with threescore and ten persons; and
now the LORD thy God hath made thee
as the stars of heaven for multitude.

CHAPTER 11

THEREFORE thou shalt love the LORD
thy God, and keep his charge, and his
statutes, and his judgments, and his
commandments, alway.
2 And know ye this day: for *I speak*
not with your children which have not
known, and which have not seen the
chastisement of the LORD your God, his
greatness, his mighty hand, and his
stretched out arm,
3 And his miracles, and his acts,
which he did in the midst of Egypt unto
Pharaoh the king of Egypt, and unto all
his land;
4 And what he did unto the army of
Egypt, unto their horses, and to their
chariots; how he made the water of the
Red sea to overflow them as they
pursued after you, and *how* the LORD
hath destroyed them unto this day;
5 And what he did unto you in the wil-
derness, until ye came into this place;
6 And what he did unto Dā'than and
A-bī'ram, the sons of E-lī'ab, the son of
Reuben: how the earth opened her
mouth, and swallowed them up, and
their households, and their tents, and
all the substance that *was* in their pos-
session, in the midst of all Israel:
7 But your eyes have seen all the
great acts of the LORD which he did.
8 Therefore shall ye keep all the com-
mandments which I command you this
day, that ye may be strong, and go in
and possess the land, whither ye go to
possess it;
9 And that ye may prolong *your* days
in the land, which the LORD sware unto
your fathers to give unto them and to
their seed, a land that floweth with
milk and honey.
10 ¶For the land, whither thou goest
in to possess it, *is* not as the land of
Egypt, from whence ye came out,
where thou sowedst thy seed, and
wateredst *it* with thy foot, as a garden
of herbs:
11 But the land, whither ye go to pos-
sess it, *is* a land of hills and valleys, *and*
drinketh water of the rain of heaven:
12 A land which the LORD thy God
careth for: the eyes of the LORD thy God
are always upon it, from the beginning
of the year even unto the end of the
year.
13 ¶And it shall come to pass, if ye
shall hearken diligently unto my com-
mandments which I command you this
day, to love the LORD your God, and to
serve him with all your heart and with
all your soul,
14 That I will give *you* the rain of your
land in his due season, the first rain and
the latter rain, that thou mayest gather
in thy corn, and thy wine, and thine oil.
15 And I will send grass in thy fields
for thy cattle, that thou mayest eat and
be full.
16 Take heed to yourselves, that your
heart be not deceived, and ye turn
aside, and serve other gods, and wor-
ship them;
17 And *then* the LORD's wrath be
kindled against you, and he shut up the
heaven, that there be no rain, and that
the land yield not her fruit; and *lest* ye
perish quickly from off the good land
which the LORD giveth you.
18 ¶Therefore shall ye lay up these
my words in your heart and in your
soul, and bind them for a sign upon
your hand, that they may be as
frontlets between your eyes.
19 And ye shall teach them your
children, speaking of them when thou
sittest in thine house, and when thou
walkest by the way, when thou liest
down, and when thou risest up.
20 And thou shalt write them upon
the door posts of thine house, and upon
thy gates:
21 That your days may be multiplied,
and the days of your children, in the
land which the LORD sware unto your
fathers to give them, as the days of
heaven upon the earth.
22 ¶For if ye shall diligently keep all
these commandments which I com-
mand you, to do them, to love the LORD

your God, to walk in all his ways, and to cleave unto him;

23 Then will the LORD drive out all these nations from before you, and ye shall possess greater nations and mightier than yourselves.

24 Every place whereon the soles of your feet shall tread shall be yours: from the wilderness and Lebanon, from the river, the river Eū-phrā'tēs, even unto the uttermost sea shall your coast be.

25 There shall no man be able to stand before you: *for* the LORD your God shall lay the fear of you and the dread of you upon all the land that ye shall tread upon, as he hath said unto you.

26 ¶Behold, I set before you this day a blessing and a curse;

27 A blessing, if ye obey the commandments of the LORD your God, which I command you this day:

28 And a curse, if ye will not obey the commandments of the LORD your God, but turn aside out of the way which I command you this day, to go after other gods, which ye have not known.

29 And it shall come to pass, when the LORD thy God hath brought thee in unto the land whither thou goest to possess it, that thou shalt put the blessing upon mount Gĕr'i-zĭm, and the curse upon mount Ebal.

30 *Are* they not on the other side Jordan, by the way where the sun goeth down, in the land of the Canaanites, which dwell in the champaign over against Gilgal, beside the plains of Mô'reh?

31 For ye shall pass over Jordan to go in to possess the land which the LORD your God giveth you, and ye shall possess it, and dwell therein.

32 And ye shall observe to do all the statutes and judgments which I set before you this day.

CHAPTER 12

THESE *are* the statutes and judgments, which ye shall observe to do in the land, which the LORD God of thy fathers giveth thee to possess it, all the days that ye live upon the earth.

2 Ye shall utterly destroy all the places, wherein the nations which ye shall possess served their gods, upon the high mountains, and upon the hills, and under every green tree:

3 And ye shall overthrow their altars, and break their pillars, and burn their groves with fire; and ye shall hew down the graven images of their gods, and destroy the names of them out of that place.

4 Ye shall not do so unto the LORD your God.

5 But unto the place which the LORD your God shall choose out of all your tribes to put his name there, *even* unto his habitation shall ye seek, and thither thou shalt come:

6 And thither ye shall bring your burnt offerings, and your sacrifices, and your tithes, and heave offerings of your hand, and your vows, and your freewill offerings, and the firstlings of your herds and of your flocks:

7 And there ye shall eat before the LORD your God, and ye shall rejoice in all that ye put your hand unto, ye and your households, wherein the LORD thy God hath blessed thee.

8 Ye shall not do after all *the things* that we do here this day, every man whatsoever *is* right in his own eyes.

9 For ye are not as yet come to the rest and to the inheritance, which the LORD your God giveth you.

10 But *when* ye go over Jordan, and dwell in the land which the LORD your God giveth you to inherit, and *when* he giveth you rest from all your enemies round about, so that ye dwell in safety;

11 Then there shall be a place which the LORD your God shall choose to cause his name to dwell there; thither shall ye bring all that I command you; your burnt offerings, and your sacrifices, your tithes, and the heave offering of your hand, and all your choice vows which ye vow unto the LORD:

12 And ye shall rejoice before the LORD your God, ye, and your sons, and your daughters, and your menservants, and your maidservants, and the Levite that *is* within your gates; forasmuch as he hath no part nor inheritance with you.

13 Take heed to thyself that thou offer not thy burnt offerings in every place that thou seest:

14 But in the place which the LORD shall choose in one of thy tribes, there thou shalt offer thy burnt offerings, and there thou shalt do all that I command thee.

15 Notwithstanding thou mayest kill and eat flesh in all thy gates, whatsoever thy soul lusteth after, according to the blessing of the LORD thy God which he hath given thee: the unclean and the clean may eat thereof, as of the roebuck, and as of the hart.

16 Only ye shall not eat the blood; ye shall pour it upon the earth as water.

17 ¶Thou mayest not eat within thy gates the tithe of thy corn, or of thy wine, or of thy oil, or the firstlings of thy herds or of thy flock, nor any of thy

vows which thou vowest, nor thy free-
will offerings, or heave offering of
thine hand:
18 But thou must eat them before the
LORD thy God in the place which the
LORD thy God shall choose, thou, and
thy son, and thy daughter, and thy
manservant, and thy maidservant, and
the Levite that *is* within thy gates: and
thou shalt rejoice before the LORD thy
God in all that thou puttest thine hands
unto.
19 Take heed to thyself that thou for-
sake not the Levite as long as thou liv-
est upon the earth.
20 ¶When the LORD thy God shall en-
large thy border, as he hath promised
thee, and thou shalt say, I will eat flesh,
because thy soul longeth to eat flesh;
thou mayest eat flesh, whatsoever thy
soul lusteth after.
21 If the place which the LORD thy
God hath chosen to put his name there
be too far from thee, then thou shalt kill
of thy herd and of thy flock, which the
LORD hath given thee, as I have com-
manded thee, and thou shalt eat in thy
gates whatsoever thy soul lusteth after.
22 Even as the roebuck and the hart is
eaten, so thou shalt eat them: the un-
clean and the clean shall eat *of* them
alike.
23 Only be sure that thou eat not the
blood: for the blood *is* the life; and thou
mayest not eat the life with the flesh.
24 Thou shalt not eat it; thou shalt
pour it upon the earth as water.
25 Thou shalt not eat it; that it may go
well with thee, and with thy children
after thee, when thou shalt do *that
which is* right in the sight of the LORD.
26 Only thy holy things which thou
hast, and thy vows, thou shalt take, and
go unto the place which the LORD shall
choose:
27 And thou shalt offer thy burnt of-
ferings, the flesh and the blood, upon
the altar of the LORD thy God: and the
blood of thy sacrifices shall be poured
out upon the altar of the LORD thy God,
and thou shalt eat the flesh.
28 Observe and hear all these words
which I command thee, that it may go
well with thee, and with thy children
after thee for ever, when thou doest
that which is good and right in the sight
of the LORD thy God.
29 ¶When the LORD thy God shall cut
off the nations from before thee,
whither thou goest to possess them,
and thou succeedest them, and dwell-
est in their land;
30 Take heed to thyself that thou be
not snared by following them, after
that they be destroyed from before
thee; and that thou enquire not after
their gods, saying, How did these na-
tions serve their gods? even so will I do
likewise.
31 Thou shalt not do so unto the LORD
thy God: for every abomination to the
LORD, which he hateth, have they done
unto their gods; for even their sons and
their daughters they have burnt in the
fire to their gods.
32 What thing soever I command
you, observe to do it: thou shalt not add
thereto, nor diminish from it.

CHAPTER 13

IF there arise among you a prophet, or
a dreamer of dreams, and giveth thee a
sign or a wonder,
2 And the sign or the wonder come to
pass, whereof he spake unto thee,
saying, Let us go after other gods,
which thou hast not known, and let us
serve them;
3 Thou shalt not hearken unto the
words of that prophet, or that dreamer
of dreams: for the LORD your God prov-
eth you, to know whether ye love the
LORD your God with all your heart and
with all your soul.
4 Ye shall walk after the LORD your
God, and fear him, and keep his com-
mandments, and obey his voice, and ye
shall serve him, and cleave unto him.
5 And that prophet, or that dreamer
of dreams, shall be put to death; be-
cause he hath spoken to turn *you* away
from the LORD your God, which
brought you out of the land of Egypt,
and redeemed you out of the house of
bondage, to thrust thee out of the way
which the LORD thy God commanded
thee to walk in. So shalt thou put the
evil away from the midst of thee.
6 ¶If thy brother, the son of thy
mother, or thy son, or thy daughter, or
the wife of thy bosom, or thy friend,
which *is* as thine own soul, entice thee
secretly, saying, Let us go and serve
other gods, which thou hast not known,
thou, nor thy fathers;
7 *Namely*, of the gods of the people
which *are* round about you, nigh unto
thee, or far off from thee, from the *one*
end of the earth even unto the *other* end
of the earth;
8 Thou shalt not consent unto him,
nor hearken unto him; neither shall
thine eye pity him, neither shalt thou
spare, neither shalt thou conceal him:
9 But thou shalt surely kill him; thine
hand shall be first upon him to put him
to death, and afterwards the hand of all
the people.
10 And thou shalt stone him with
stones, that he die; because he hath

sought to thrust thee away from the
LORD thy God, which brought thee out
of the land of Egypt, from the house of
bondage.
11 And all Israel shall hear, and fear,
and shall do no more any such wicked-
ness as this is among you.
12 ¶If thou shalt hear *say* in one of
thy cities, which the LORD thy God hath
given thee to dwell there, saying,
13 *Certain* men, the children of Bē′lī-
al, are gone out from among you, and
have withdrawn the inhabitants of
their city, saying, Let us go and serve
other gods, which ye have not known;
14 Then shalt thou enquire, and make
search, and ask diligently, and, behold,
if it be truth, *and* the thing certain, *that*
such abomination is wrought among
you;
15 Thou shalt surely smite the inhabi-
tants of that city with the edge of the
sword, destroying it utterly, and all
that *is* therein, and the cattle thereof,
with the edge of the sword.
16 And thou shalt gather all the spoil
of it into the midst of the street thereof,
and shalt burn with fire the city, and all
the spoil thereof every whit, for the
LORD thy God: and it shall be an heap
for ever; it shall not be built again.
17 And there shall cleave nought of
the cursed thing to thine hand: that the
LORD may turn from the fierceness of
his anger, and shew thee mercy, and
have compassion upon thee, and mul-
tiply thee, as he hath sworn unto thy
fathers;
18 When thou shalt hearken to the
voice of the LORD thy God, to keep all
his commandments which I command
thee this day, to do *that which is* right
in the eyes of the LORD thy God.

CHAPTER 14

YE *are* the children of the LORD your
God: ye shall not cut yourselves, nor
make any baldness between your eyes
for the dead.
2 For thou *art* an holy people unto the
LORD thy God, and the LORD hath cho-
sen thee to be a peculiar people unto
himself, above all the nations that *are*
upon the earth.
3 ¶Thou shalt not eat any abominable
thing.
4 These *are* the beasts which ye shall
eat: the ox, the sheep, and the goat,
5 The hart, and the roebuck, and the
fallow deer, and the wild goat, and the
pygarg, and the wild ox, and the cham-
ois.
6 And every beast that parteth the
hoof, and cleaveth the cleft into two
claws, *and* cheweth the cud among the
beasts, that ye shall eat.
7 Nevertheless these ye shall not eat
of them that chew the cud, or of them
that divide the cloven hoof; *as* the
camel, and the hare, and the coney: for
they chew the cud, but divide not the
hoof; *therefore* they *are* unclean unto
you.
8 And the swine, because it divideth
the hoof, yet cheweth not the cud, it *is*
unclean unto you: ye shall not eat of
their flesh, nor touch their dead car-
case.
9 ¶These ye shall eat of all that *are* in
the waters: all that have fins and scales
shall ye eat:
10 And whatsoever hath not fins and
scales ye may not eat; it *is* unclean unto
you.
11 ¶*Of* all clean birds ye shall eat.
12 But these *are they* of which ye
shall not eat: the eagle, and the ossi-
frage, and the ospray,
13 And the glede, and the kite, and
the vulture after his kind,
14 And every raven after his kind,
15 And the owl, and the night hawk,
and the cuckow, and the hawk after his
kind,
16 The little owl, and the great owl,
and the swan,
17 And the pelican, and the gier
eagle, and the cormorant,
18 And the stork, and the heron after
her kind, and the lapwing, and the bat.
19 And every creeping thing that
flieth *is* unclean unto you: they shall
not be eaten.
20 *But of* all clean fowls ye may eat.
21 ¶Ye shall not eat *of* any thing that
dieth of itself: thou shalt give it unto the
stranger that *is* in thy gates, that he
may eat it; or thou mayest sell it unto
an alien: for thou *art* an holy people
unto the LORD thy God. Thou shalt not
seethe a kid in his mother's milk.
22 Thou shalt truly tithe all the in-
crease of thy seed, that the field bring-
eth forth year by year.
23 And thou shalt eat before the LORD
thy God, in the place which he shall
choose to place his name there, the
tithe of thy corn, of thy wine, and of
thine oil, and the firstlings of thy herds
and of thy flocks; that thou mayest
learn to fear the LORD thy God always.
24 And if the way be too long for thee,
so that thou art not able to carry it; *or* if
the place be too far from thee, which
the LORD thy God shall choose to set his
name there, when the LORD thy God
hath blessed thee:
25 Then shalt thou turn *it* into money,
and bind up the money in thine hand,

and shalt go unto the place which the LORD thy God shall choose:

26 And thou shalt bestow that money for whatsoever thy soul lusteth after, for oxen, or for sheep, or for wine, or for strong drink, or for whatsoever thy soul desireth: and thou shalt eat there before the LORD thy God, and thou shalt rejoice, thou, and thine household,

27 And the Levite that *is* within thy gates; thou shalt not forsake him; for he hath no part nor inheritance with thee.

28 ¶At the end of three years thou shalt bring forth all the tithe of thine increase the same year, and shalt lay *it* up within thy gates:

29 And the Levite, (because he hath no part nor inheritance with thee,) and the stranger, and the fatherless, and the widow, which *are* within thy gates, shall come, and shall eat and be satisfied; that the LORD thy God may bless thee in all the work of thine hand which thou doest.

CHAPTER 15

AT the end of *every* seven years thou shalt make a release.

2 And this *is* the manner of the release: Every creditor that lendeth *ought* unto his neighbour shall release *it;* he shall not exact *it* of his neighbour, or of his brother; because it is called the LORD's release.

3 Of a foreigner thou mayest exact *it again:* but *that* which is thine with thy brother thine hand shall release;

4 Save when there shall be no poor among you; for the LORD shall greatly bless thee in the land which the LORD thy God giveth thee *for* an inheritance to possess it:

5 Only if thou carefully hearken unto the voice of the LORD thy God, to observe to do all these commandments which I command thee this day.

6 For the LORD thy God blesseth thee, as he promised thee: and thou shalt lend unto many nations, but thou shalt not borrow; and thou shalt reign over many nations, but they shall not reign over thee.

7 ¶If there be among you a poor man of one of thy brethren within any of thy gates in thy land which the LORD thy God giveth thee, thou shalt not harden thine heart, nor shut thine hand from thy poor brother:

8 But thou shalt open thine hand wide unto him, and shalt surely lend him sufficient for his need, *in that* which he wanteth.

9 Beware that there be not a thought in thy wicked heart, saying, The seventh year, the year of release, is at hand; and thine eye be evil against thy poor brother, and thou givest him nought; and he cry unto the LORD against thee, and it be sin unto thee.

10 Thou shalt surely give him, and thine heart shall not be grieved when thou givest unto him: because that for this thing the LORD thy God shall bless thee in all thy works, and in all that thou puttest thine hand unto.

11 For the poor shall never cease out of the land: therefore I command thee, saying, Thou shalt open thine hand wide unto thy brother, to thy poor, and to thy needy, in thy land.

12 ¶*And* if thy brother, an Hebrew man, or an Hebrew woman, be sold unto thee, and serve thee six years; then in the seventh year thou shalt let him go free from thee.

13 And when thou sendest him out free from thee, thou shalt not let him go away empty:

14 Thou shalt furnish him liberally out of thy flock, and out of thy floor, and out of thy winepress: *of that* wherewith the LORD thy God hath blessed thee thou shalt give unto him.

15 And thou shalt remember that thou wast a bondman in the land of Egypt, and the LORD thy God redeemed thee: therefore I command thee this thing to day.

16 And it shall be, if he say unto thee, I will not go away from thee; because he loveth thee and thine house, because he is well with thee;

17 Then thou shalt take an aul, and thrust *it* through his ear unto the door, and he shall be thy servant for ever. And also unto thy maidservant thou shalt do likewise.

18 It shall not seem hard unto thee, when thou sendest him away free from thee; for he hath been worth a double hired servant *to thee,* in serving thee six years: and the LORD thy God shall bless thee in all that thou doest.

19 ¶All the firstling males that come of thy herd and of thy flock thou shalt sanctify unto the LORD thy God: thou shalt do no work with the firstling of thy bullock, nor shear the firstling of thy sheep.

20 Thou shalt eat *it* before the LORD thy God year by year in the place which the LORD shall choose, thou and thy household.

21 And if there be *any* blemish therein, *as if it be* lame, or blind, *or have* any ill blemish, thou shalt not sacrifice it unto the LORD thy God.

22 Thou shalt eat it within thy gates: the unclean and the clean *person shall*

eat it alike, as the roebuck, and as the hart.

23 Only thou shalt not eat the blood thereof; thou shalt pour it upon the ground as water.

CHAPTER 16

OBSERVE the month of A'bīb, and keep the passover unto the LORD thy God: for in the month of A'bīb the LORD thy God brought thee forth out of Egypt by night.

2 Thou shalt therefore sacrifice the passover unto the LORD thy God, of the flock and the herd, in the place which the LORD shall choose to place his name there.

3 Thou shalt eat no leavened bread with it; seven days shalt thou eat unleavened bread therewith, *even* the bread of affliction; for thou camest forth out of the land of Egypt in haste: that thou mayest remember the day when thou camest forth out of the land of Egypt all the days of thy life.

4 And there shall be no leavened bread seen with thee in all thy coast seven days; neither shall there *any thing* of the flesh, which thou sacrificedst the first day at even, remain all night until the morning.

5 Thou mayest not sacrifice the passover within any of thy gates, which the LORD thy God giveth thee:

6 But at the place which the LORD thy God shall choose to place his name in, there thou shalt sacrifice the passover at even, at the going down of the sun, at the season that thou camest forth out of Egypt.

7 And thou shalt roast and eat *it* in the place which the LORD thy God shall choose: and thou shalt turn in the morning, and go unto thy tents.

8 Six days thou shalt eat unleavened bread: and on the seventh day *shall be* a solemn assembly to the LORD thy God: thou shalt do no work *therein*.

9 ¶Seven weeks shalt thou number unto thee: begin to number the seven weeks from *such time as* thou beginnest *to put* the sickle to the corn.

10 And thou shalt keep the feast of weeks unto the LORD thy God with a tribute of a freewill offering of thine hand, which thou shalt give *unto the* LORD *thy God*, according as the LORD thy God hath blessed thee:

11 And thou shalt rejoice before the LORD thy God, thou, and thy son, and thy daughter, and thy manservant, and thy maidservant, and the Levite that *is* within thy gates, and the stranger, and the fatherless, and the widow, that *are* among you, in the place which the LORD thy God hath chosen to place his name there.

12 And thou shalt remember that thou wast a bondman in Egypt: and thou shalt observe and do these statutes.

13 ¶Thou shalt observe the feast of tabernacles seven days, after that thou hast gathered in thy corn and thy wine:

14 And thou shalt rejoice in thy feast, thou, and thy son, and thy daughter, and thy manservant, and thy maidservant, and the Levite, the stranger, and the fatherless, and the widow, that *are* within thy gates.

15 Seven days shalt thou keep a solemn feast unto the LORD thy God in the place which the LORD shall choose: because the LORD thy God shall bless thee in all thine increase, and in all the works of thine hands, therefore thou shalt surely rejoice.

16 ¶Three times in a year shall all thy males appear before the LORD thy God in the place which he shall choose; in the feast of unleavened bread, and in the feast of weeks, and in the feast of tabernacles: and they shall not appear before the LORD empty:

17 Every man *shall give* as he is able, according to the blessing of the LORD thy God which he hath given thee.

18 ¶Judges and officers shalt thou make thee in all thy gates, which the LORD thy God giveth thee, throughout thy tribes: and they shall judge the people with just judgment.

19 Thou shalt not wrest judgment; thou shalt not respect persons, neither take a gift: for a gift doth blind the eyes of the wise, and pervert the words of the righteous.

20 That which is altogether just shalt thou follow, that thou mayest live, and inherit the land which the LORD thy God giveth thee.

21 Thou shalt not plant thee a grove of any trees near unto the altar of the LORD thy God, which thou shalt make thee.

22 Neither shalt thou set thee up *any* image; which the LORD thy God hateth.

CHAPTER 17

THOU shalt not sacrifice unto the LORD thy God *any* bullock, or sheep, wherein is blemish, *or* any evilfavouredness: for that *is* an abomination unto the LORD thy God.

2 ¶If there be found among you, within any of thy gates which the LORD thy God giveth thee, man or woman, that hath wrought wickedness in the sight of the LORD thy God, in transgressing his covenant,

3 And hath gone and served other gods, and worshipped them, either the sun, or moon, or any of the host of heaven, which I have not commanded;

4 And it be told thee, and thou hast heard *of it*, and enquired diligently, and, behold, *it be* true, *and* the thing certain, *that* such abomination is wrought in Israel:

5 Then shalt thou bring forth that man or that woman, which have committed that wicked thing, unto thy gates, *even* that man or that woman, and shalt stone them with stones, till they die.

6 At the mouth of two witnesses, or three witnesses, shall he that is worthy of death be put to death; *but* at the mouth of one witness he shall not be put to death.

7 The hands of the witnesses shall be first upon him to put him to death, and afterward the hands of all the people. So thou shalt put the evil away from among you.

8 ¶If there arise a matter too hard for thee in judgment, between blood and blood, between plea and plea, and between stroke and stroke, *being* matters of controversy within thy gates: then shalt thou arise, and get thee up into the place which the LORD thy God shall choose;

9 And thou shalt come unto the priests the Lēvītes, and unto the judge that shall be in those days, and enquire; and they shall shew thee the sentence of judgment:

10 And thou shalt do according to the sentence, which they of that place which the LORD shall choose shall shew thee; and thou shalt observe to do according to all that they inform thee:

11 According to the sentence of the law which they shall teach thee, and according to the judgment which they shall tell thee, thou shalt do: thou shalt not decline from the sentence which they shall shew thee, *to* the right hand, nor *to* the left.

12 And the man that will do presumptuously, and will not hearken unto the priest that standeth to minister there before the LORD thy God, or unto the judge, even that man shall die: and thou shalt put away the evil from Israel.

13 And all the people shall hear, and fear, and do no more presumptuously.

14 ¶When thou art come unto the land which the LORD thy God giveth thee, and shalt possess it, and shalt dwell therein, and shalt say, I will set a king over me, like as all the nations that *are* about me;

15 Thou shalt in any wise set *him* king over thee, whom the LORD thy God shall choose: *one* from among thy brethren shalt thou set king over thee: thou mayest not set a stranger over thee, which *is* not thy brother.

16 But he shall not multiply horses to himself, nor cause the people to return to Egypt, to the end that he should multiply horses: forasmuch as the LORD hath said unto you, Ye shall henceforth return no more that way.

17 Neither shall he multiply wives to himself, that his heart turn not away: neither shall he greatly multiply to himself silver and gold.

18 And it shall be, when he sitteth upon the throne of his kingdom, that he shall write him a copy of this law in a book out of *that which is* before the priests the Lēvītes:

19 And it shall be with him, and he shall read therein all the days of his life: that he may learn to fear the LORD his God, to keep all the words of this law and these statutes, to do them:

20 That his heart be not lifted up above his brethren, and that he turn not aside from the commandment, *to* the right hand, or *to* the left: to the end that he may prolong *his* days in his kingdom, he, and his children, in the midst of Israel.

CHAPTER 18

THE priests the Lēvītes, *and* all the tribe of Levi, shall have no part nor inheritance with Israel: they shall eat the offerings of the LORD made by fire, and his inheritance.

2 Therefore shall they have no inheritance among their brethren: the LORD *is* their inheritance, as he hath said unto them.

3 ¶And this shall be the priest's due from the people, from them that offer a sacrifice, whether *it be* ox or sheep; and they shall give unto the priest the shoulder, and the two cheeks, and the maw.

4 The firstfruit *also* of thy corn, of thy wine, and of thine oil, and the first of the fleece of thy sheep, shalt thou give him.

5 For the LORD thy God hath chosen him out of all thy tribes, to stand to minister in the name of the LORD, him and his sons for ever.

6 ¶And if a Levite come from any of thy gates out of all Israel, where he sojourned, and come with all the desire of his mind unto the place which the LORD shall choose;

7 Then he shall minister in the name of the LORD his God, as all his brethren

the Lēvītes *do*, which stand there before the LORD.

8 They shall have like portions to eat, beside that which cometh of the sale of his patrimony.

9 ¶When thou art come into the land which the LORD thy God giveth thee, thou shalt not learn to do after the abominations of those nations.

10 There shall not be found among you *any one* that maketh his son or his daughter to pass through the fire, *or* that useth divination, *or* an observer of times, or an enchanter, or a witch,

11 Or a charmer, or a consulter with familiar spirits, or a wizard, or a necromancer.

12 For all that do these things *are* an abomination unto the LORD: and because of these abominations the LORD thy God doth drive them out from before thee.

13 Thou shalt be perfect with the LORD thy God.

14 For these nations, which thou shalt possess, hearkened unto observers of times, and unto diviners: but as for thee, the LORD thy God hath not suffered thee so *to do*.

15 ¶The LORD thy God will raise up unto thee a Prophet from the midst of thee, of thy brethren, like unto me; unto him ye shall hearken;

16 According to all that thou desiredst of the LORD thy God in Hô'rĕb in the day of the assembly, saying, Let me not hear again the voice of the LORD my God, neither let me see this great fire any more, that I die not.

17 And the LORD said unto me, They have well *spoken that* which they have spoken.

18 I will raise them up a Prophet from among their brethren, like unto thee, and will put my words in his mouth; and he shall speak unto them all that I shall command him.

19 And it shall come to pass, *that* whosoever will not hearken unto my words which he shall speak in my name, I will require *it* of him.

20 But the prophet, which shall presume to speak a word in my name, which I have not commanded him to speak, or that shall speak in the name of other gods, even that prophet shall die.

21 And if thou say in thine heart, How shall we know the word which the LORD hath not spoken?

22 When a prophet speaketh in the name of the LORD, if the thing follow not, nor come to pass, that *is* the thing which the LORD hath not spoken, *but* the prophet hath spoken it presumptuously: thou shalt not be afraid of him.

CHAPTER 19

WHEN the LORD thy God hath cut off the nations, whose land the LORD thy God giveth thee, and thou succeedest them, and dwellest in their cities, and in their houses;

2 Thou shalt separate three cities for thee in the midst of thy land, which the LORD thy God giveth thee to possess it.

3 Thou shalt prepare thee a way, and divide the coasts of thy land, which the LORD thy God giveth thee to inherit, into three parts, that every slayer may flee thither.

4 ¶And this *is* the case of the slayer, which shall flee thither, that he may live: Whoso killeth his neighbour ignorantly, whom he hated not in time past;

5 As when a man goeth into the wood with his neighbour to hew wood, and his hand fetcheth a stroke with the axe to cut down the tree, and the head slippeth from the helve, and lighteth upon his neighbour, that he die; he shall flee unto one of those cities, and live:

6 Lest the avenger of the blood pursue the slayer, while his heart is hot, and overtake him, because the way is long, and slay him; whereas he *was* not worthy of death, inasmuch as he hated him not in time past.

7 Wherefore I command thee, saying, Thou shalt separate three cities for thee.

8 And if the LORD thy God enlarge thy coast, as he hath sworn unto thy fathers, and give thee all the land which he promised to give unto thy fathers;

9 If thou shalt keep all these commandments to do them, which I command thee this day, to love the LORD thy God, and to walk ever in his ways; then shalt thou add three cities more for thee, beside these three:

10 That innocent blood be not shed in thy land, which the LORD thy God giveth thee *for* an inheritance, and *so* blood be upon thee.

11 ¶But if any man hate his neighbour, and lie in wait for him, and rise up against him, and smite him mortally that he die, and fleeth into one of these cities:

12 Then the elders of his city shall send and fetch him thence, and deliver him into the hand of the avenger of blood, that he may die.

13 Thine eye shall not pity him, but thou shalt put away *the guilt of* innocent blood from Israel, that it may go well with thee.

14 ¶Thou shalt not remove thy neigh-

bour's landmark, which they of old time have set in thine inheritance, which thou shalt inherit in the land that the LORD thy God giveth thee to possess it.

15 ¶One witness shall not rise up against a man for any iniquity, or for any sin, in any sin that he sinneth: at the mouth of two witnesses, or at the mouth of three witnesses, shall the matter be established.

16 If a false witness rise up against any man to testify against him *that which is* wrong;

17 Then both the men, between whom the controversy *is*, shall stand before the LORD, before the priests and the judges, which shall be in those days;

18 And the judges shall make diligent inquisition: and, behold, *if* the witness *be* a false witness, *and* hath testified falsely against his brother;

19 Then shall ye do unto him, as he had thought to have done unto his brother: so shalt thou put the evil away from among you.

20 And those which remain shall hear, and fear, and shall henceforth commit no more any such evil among you.

21 And thine eye shall not pity; *but* life *shall go* for life, eye for eye, tooth for tooth, hand for hand, foot for foot.

CHAPTER 20

WHEN thou goest out to battle against thine enemies, and seest horses, and chariots, *and* a people more than thou, be not afraid of them: for the LORD thy God *is* with thee, which brought thee up out of the land of Egypt.

2 And it shall be, when ye are come nigh unto the battle, that the priest shall approach and speak unto the people,

3 And shall say unto them, Hear, O Israel, ye approach this day unto battle against your enemies: let not your hearts faint, fear not, and do not tremble, neither be ye terrified because of them;

4 For the LORD your God *is* he that goeth with you, to fight for you against your enemies, to save you.

5 ¶And the officers shall speak unto the people, saying, What man *is there* that hath built a new house, and hath not dedicated it? let him go and return to his house, lest he die in the battle, and another man dedicate it.

6 And what man *is he* that hath planted a vineyard, and hath not *yet* eaten of it? let him *also* go and return unto his house, lest he die in the battle, and another man eat of it.

7 And what man *is there* that hath betrothed a wife, and hath not taken her? let him go and return unto his house, lest he die in the battle, and another man take her.

8 And the officers shall speak further unto the people, and they shall say, What man *is there that is* fearful and fainthearted? let him go and return unto his house, lest his brethren's heart faint as well as his heart.

9 And it shall be, when the officers have made an end of speaking unto the people, that they shall make captains of the armies to lead the people.

10 ¶When thou comest nigh unto a city to fight against it, then proclaim peace unto it.

11 And it shall be, if it make thee answer of peace, and open unto thee, then it shall be, *that* all the people *that is* found therein shall be tributaries unto thee, and they shall serve thee.

12 And if it will make no peace with thee, but will make war against thee, then thou shalt besiege it:

13 And when the LORD thy God hath delivered it into thine hands, thou shalt smite every male thereof with the edge of the sword:

14 But the women, and the little ones, and the cattle, and all that is in the city, *even* all the spoil thereof, shalt thou take unto thyself; and thou shalt eat the spoil of thine enemies, which the LORD thy God hath given thee.

15 Thus shalt thou do unto all the cities *which are* very far off from thee, which *are* not of the cities of these nations.

16 But of the cities of these people, which the LORD thy God doth give thee *for* an inheritance, thou shalt save alive nothing that breatheth:

17 But thou shalt utterly destroy them; *namely*, the Hittites, and the Ăm'o-rītes, the Canaanites, and the Pĕr'iz-zītes, the Hī'vītes, and the Jĕb'u-sītes; as the LORD thy God hath commanded thee:

18 That they teach you not to do after all their abominations, which they have done unto their gods; so should ye sin against the LORD your God.

19 ¶When thou shalt besiege a city a long time, in making war against it to take it, thou shalt not destroy the trees thereof by forcing an axe against them: for thou mayest eat of them, and thou shalt not cut them down (for the tree of the field *is* man's *life*) to employ *them* in the siege:

20 Only the trees which thou know-

est that they *be* not trees for meat,
thou shalt destroy and cut them down;
and thou shalt build bulwarks against
the city that maketh war with thee, un-
til it be subdued.

CHAPTER 21

IF *one* be found slain in the land which
the LORD thy God giveth thee to possess
it, lying in the field, *and* it be not known
who hath slain him:
2 Then thy elders and thy judges shall
come forth, and they shall measure
unto the cities which *are* round about
him that is slain:
3 And it shall be, *that* the city *which*
is next unto the slain man, even the el-
ders of that city shall take an heifer,
which hath not been wrought with, *and*
which hath not drawn in the yoke;
4 And the elders of that city shall
bring down the heifer unto a rough val-
ley, which is neither eared nor sown,
and shall strike off the heifer's neck
there in the valley:
5 And the priests the sons of Levi
shall come near; for them the LORD thy
God hath chosen to minister unto him,
and to bless in the name of the LORD;
and by their word shall every contro-
versy and every stroke be *tried:*
6 And all the elders of that city, *that*
are next unto the slain *man*, shall wash
their hands over the heifer that is be-
headed in the valley:
7 And they shall answer and say, Our
hands have not shed this blood, neither
have our eyes seen *it.*
8 Be merciful, O LORD, unto thy peo-
ple Israel, whom thou hast redeemed,
and lay not innocent blood unto thy
people of Israel's charge. And the blood
shall be forgiven them.
9 So shalt thou put away the *guilt of*
innocent blood from among you, when
thou shalt do *that which is* right in the
sight of the LORD.
10 ¶When thou goest forth to war
against thine enemies, and the LORD
thy God hath delivered them into thine
hands, and thou hast taken them cap-
tive,
11 And seest among the captives a
beautiful woman, and hast a desire
unto her, that thou wouldest have her
to thy wife;
12 Then thou shalt bring her home to
thine house; and she shall shave her
head, and pare her nails;
13 And she shall put the raiment of
her captivity from off her, and shall re-
main in thine house, and bewail her
father and her mother a full month: and
after that thou shalt go in unto her, and
be her husband, and she shall be thy
wife.
14 And it shall be, if thou have no de-
light in her, then thou shalt let her go
whither she will; but thou shalt not sell
her at all for money, thou shalt not
make merchandise of her, because
thou hast humbled her.
15 ¶If a man have two wives, one be-
loved, and another hated, and they
have born him children, *both* the be-
loved and the hated; and *if* the firstborn
son be hers that was hated:
16 Then it shall be, when he maketh
his sons to inherit *that* which he hath,
that he may not make the son of the
beloved firstborn before the son of the
hated, *which is indeed* the firstborn:
17 But he shall acknowledge the son
of the hated *for* the firstborn, by giving
him a double portion of all that he hath:
for he *is* the beginning of his strength;
the right of the firstborn *is* his.
18 ¶If a man have a stubborn and re-
bellious son, which will not obey the
voice of his father, or the voice of his
mother, and *that*, when they have chas-
tened him, will not hearken unto them:
19 Then shall his father and his
mother lay hold on him, and bring him
out unto the elders of his city, and unto
the gate of his place;
20 And they shall say unto the elders
of his city, This our son *is* stubborn and
rebellious, he will not obey our voice;
he is a glutton, and a drunkard.
21 And all the men of his city shall
stone him with stones, that he die: so
shalt thou put evil away from among
you; and all Israel shall hear, and fear.
22 ¶And if a man have committed a
sin worthy of death, and he be to be put
to death, and thou hang him on a tree:
23 His body shall not remain all night
upon the tree, but thou shalt in any
wise bury him that day; (for he that is
hanged *is* accursed of God;) that thy
land be not defiled, which the LORD thy
God giveth thee *for* an inheritance.

CHAPTER 22

THOU shalt not see thy brother's ox or
his sheep go astray, and hide thyself
from them: thou shalt in any case bring
them again unto thy brother.
2 And if thy brother *be* not nigh unto
thee, or if thou know him not, then thou
shalt bring it unto thine own house, and
it shall be with thee until thy brother
seek after it, and thou shalt restore it to
him again.
3 In like manner shalt thou do with
his ass; and so shalt thou do with his
raiment; and with all lost things of thy
brother's, which he hath lost, and thou

hast found, shalt thou do likewise: thou mayest not hide thyself.

4 ¶Thou shalt not see thy brother's ass or his ox fall down by the way, and hide thyself from them: thou shalt surely help him to lift *them* up again.

5 ¶The woman shall not wear that which pertaineth unto a man, neither shall a man put on a woman's garment: for all that do so *are* abomination unto the LORD thy God.

6 ¶If a bird's nest chance to be before thee in the way in any tree, or on the ground, *whether they be* young ones, or eggs, and the dam sitting upon the young, or upon the eggs, thou shalt not take the dam with the young:

7 *But* thou shalt in any wise let the dam go, and take the young to thee; that it may be well with thee, and *that* thou mayest prolong *thy* days.

8 ¶When thou buildest a new house, then thou shalt make a battlement for thy roof, that thou bring not blood upon thine house, if any man fall from thence.

9 ¶Thou shalt not sow thy vineyard with divers seeds: lest the fruit of thy seed which thou hast sown, and the fruit of thy vineyard, be defiled.

10 ¶Thou shalt not plow with an ox and an ass together.

11 ¶Thou shalt not wear a garment of divers sorts, *as* of woollen and linen together.

12 ¶Thou shalt make thee fringes upon the four quarters of thy vesture, wherewith thou coverest *thyself*.

13 ¶If any man take a wife, and go in unto her, and hate her,

14 And give occasions of speech against her, and bring up an evil name upon her, and say, I took this woman, and when I came to her, I found her not a maid:

15 Then shall the father of the damsel, and her mother, take and bring forth *the tokens of* the damsel's virginity unto the elders of the city in the gate:

16 And the damsel's father shall say unto the elders, I gave my daughter unto this man to wife, and he hateth her;

17 And, lo, he hath given occasions of speech *against her*, saying, I found not thy daughter a maid; and yet these *are the tokens of* my daughter's virginity. And they shall spread the cloth before the elders of the city.

18 And the elders of that city shall take that man and chastise him;

19 And they shall amerce him in an hundred *shekels* of silver, and give *them* unto the father of the damsel, because he hath brought up an evil name upon a virgin of Israel: and she shall be his wife; he may not put her away all his days.

20 But if this thing be true, *and the tokens of* virginity be not found for the damsel:

21 Then they shall bring out the damsel to the door of her father's house, and the men of her city shall stone her with stones that she die: because she hath wrought folly in Israel, to play the whore in her father's house: so shalt thou put evil away from among you.

22 ¶If a man be found lying with a woman married to an husband, then they shall both of them die, *both* the man that lay with the woman, and the woman: so shalt thou put away evil from Israel.

23 If a damsel *that is* a virgin be betrothed unto an husband, and a man find her in the city, and lie with her;

24 Then ye shall bring them both out unto the gate of that city, and ye shall stone them with stones that they die; the damsel, because she cried not, *being* in the city; and the man, because he hath humbled his neighbour's wife: so thou shalt put away evil from among you.

25 ¶But if a man find a betrothed damsel in the field, and the man force her, and lie with her: then the man only that lay with her shall die:

26 But unto the damsel thou shalt do nothing; *there is* in the damsel no sin *worthy* of death: for as when a man riseth against his neighbour, and slayeth him, even so *is* this matter:

27 For he found her in the field, *and* the betrothed damsel cried, and *there was* none to save her.

28 ¶If a man find a damsel *that is* a virgin, which is not betrothed, and lay hold on her, and lie with her, and they be found;

29 Then the man that lay with her shall give unto the damsel's father fifty *shekels* of silver, and she shall be his wife; because he hath humbled her, he may not put her away all his days.

30 ¶A man shall not take his father's wife, nor discover his father's skirt.

CHAPTER 23

HE that is wounded in the stones, or hath his privy member cut off, shall not enter into the congregation of the LORD.

2 A bastard shall not enter into the congregation of the LORD; even to his tenth generation shall he not enter into the congregation of the LORD.

3 An Ammonite or Moabite shall not

enter into the congregation of the LORD; even to their tenth generation shall they not enter into the congregation of the LORD for ever:

4 Because they met you not with bread and with water in the way, when ye came forth out of Egypt; and because they hired against thee Bā'laam the son of Bē'ôr of Pē'thôr of Mĕs-o-po-tā'mĭ-a, to curse thee.

5 Nevertheless the LORD thy God would not hearken unto Bā'laam; but the LORD thy God turned the curse into a blessing unto thee, because the LORD thy God loved thee.

6 Thou shalt not seek their peace nor their prosperity all thy days for ever.

7 Thou shalt not abhor an Edomite; for he *is* thy brother: thou shalt not abhor an Egyptian; because thou wast a stranger in his land.

8 The children that are begotten of them shall enter into the congregation of the LORD in their third generation.

9 ¶When the host goeth forth against thine enemies, then keep thee from every wicked thing.

10 If there be among you any man, that is not clean by reason of uncleanness that chanceth him by night, then shall he go abroad out of the camp, he shall not come within the camp:

11 But it shall be, when evening cometh on, he shall wash *himself* with water: and when the sun is down, he shall come into the camp *again.*

12 Thou shalt have a place also without the camp, whither thou shalt go forth abroad:

13 And thou shalt have a paddle upon thy weapon; and it shall be, when thou wilt ease thyself abroad, thou shalt dig therewith, and shalt turn back and cover that which cometh from thee:

14 For the LORD thy God walketh in the midst of thy camp, to deliver thee, and to give up thine enemies before thee; therefore shall thy camp be holy: that he see no unclean thing in thee, and turn away from thee.

15 ¶Thou shalt not deliver unto his master the servant which is escaped from his master unto thee:

16 He shall dwell with thee, *even* among you, in that place which he shall choose in one of thy gates, where it liketh him best: thou shalt not oppress him.

17 ¶There shall be no whore of the daughters of Israel, nor a sodomite of the sons of Israel.

18 Thou shalt not bring the hire of a whore, or the price of a dog, into the house of the LORD thy God for any vow: for even both these *are* abomination unto the LORD thy God.

19 ¶Thou shalt not lend upon usury to thy brother; usury of money, usury of victuals, usury of any thing that is lent upon usury:

20 Unto a stranger thou mayest lend upon usury; but unto thy brother thou shalt not lend upon usury: that the LORD thy God may bless thee in all that thou settest thine hand to in the land whither thou goest to possess it.

21 ¶When thou shalt vow a vow unto the LORD thy God, thou shalt not slack to pay it: for the LORD thy God will surely require it of thee; and it would be sin in thee.

22 But if thou shalt forbear to vow, it shall be no sin in thee.

23 That which is gone out of thy lips thou shalt keep and perform; *even* a freewill offering, according as thou hast vowed unto the LORD thy God, which thou hast promised with thy mouth.

24 ¶When thou comest into thy neighbour's vineyard, then thou mayest eat grapes thy fill at thine own pleasure; but thou shalt not put *any* in thy vessel.

25 When thou comest into the standing corn of thy neighbour, then thou mayest pluck the ears with thine hand; but thou shalt not move a sickle unto thy neighbour's standing corn.

CHAPTER 24

WHEN a man hath taken a wife, and married her, and it come to pass that she find no favour in his eyes, because he hath found some uncleanness in her: then let him write her a bill of divorcement, and give *it* in her hand, and send her out of his house.

2 And when she is departed out of his house, she may go and be another man's *wife.*

3 And *if* the latter husband hate her, and write her a bill of divorcement, and giveth *it* in her hand, and sendeth her out of his house; or if the latter husband die, which took her *to be* his wife;

4 Her former husband, which sent her away, may not take her again to be his wife, after that she is defiled; for that *is* abomination before the LORD: and thou shalt not cause the land to sin, which the LORD thy God giveth thee *for* an inheritance.

5 ¶When a man hath taken a new wife, he shall not go out to war, neither shall he be charged with any business: *but* he shall be free at home one year, and shall cheer up his wife which he hath taken.

6 ¶No man shall take the nether or the upper millstone to pledge: for he taketh *a man's* life to pledge.

7 ¶If a man be found stealing any of his brethren of the children of Israel, and maketh merchandise of him, or selleth him; then that thief shall die; and thou shalt put evil away from among you.

8 ¶Take heed in the plague of leprosy, that thou observe diligently, and do according to all that the priests the Lē-vītes shall teach you: as I commanded them, *so* ye shall observe to do.

9 Remember what the LORD thy God did unto Miriam by the way, after that ye were come forth out of Egypt.

10 ¶When thou dost lend thy brother any thing, thou shalt not go into his house to fetch his pledge.

11 Thou shalt stand abroad, and the man to whom thou dost lend shall bring out the pledge abroad unto thee.

12 And if the man *be* poor, thou shalt not sleep with his pledge:

13 In any case thou shalt deliver him the pledge again when the sun goeth down, that he may sleep in his own raiment, and bless thee: and it shall be righteousness unto thee before the LORD thy God.

14 ¶Thou shalt not oppress an hired servant *that is* poor and needy, *whether he be* of thy brethren, or of thy strangers that *are* in thy land within thy gates:

15 At his day thou shalt give *him* his hire, neither shall the sun go down upon it; for he *is* poor, and setteth his heart upon it: lest he cry against thee unto the LORD: and it be sin unto thee.

16 ¶The fathers shall not be put to death for the children, neither shall the children be put to death for the fathers: every man shall be put to death for his own sin.

17 ¶Thou shalt not pervert the judgment of the stranger, *nor* of the fatherless; nor take a widow's raiment to pledge:

18 But thou shalt remember that thou wast a bondman in Egypt, and the LORD thy God redeemed thee thence: therefore I command thee to do this thing.

19 ¶When thou cuttest down thine harvest in thy field, and hast forgot a sheaf in the field, thou shalt not go again to fetch it: it shall be for the stranger, for the fatherless, and for the widow: that the LORD thy God may bless thee in all the work of thine hands.

20 When thou beatest thine olive tree, thou shalt not go over the boughs again: it shall be for the stranger, for the fatherless, and for the widow.

21 When thou gatherest the grapes of thy vineyard, thou shalt not glean *it* afterward: it shall be for the stranger, for the fatherless, and for the widow.

22 And thou shalt remember that thou wast a bondman in the land of Egypt: therefore I command thee to do this thing.

CHAPTER 25

IF there be a controversy between men, and they come unto judgment, that *the judges* may judge them; then they shall justify the righteous, and condemn the wicked.

2 And it shall be, if the wicked man *be* worthy to be beaten, that the judge shall cause him to lie down, and to be beaten before his face, according to his fault, by a certain number.

3 Forty stripes he may give him, *and* not exceed: lest, *if* he should exceed, and beat him above these with many stripes, then thy brother should seem vile unto thee.

4 ¶Thou shalt not muzzle the ox when he treadeth out *the corn*.

5 ¶If brethren dwell together, and one of them die, and have no child, the wife of the dead shall not marry without unto a stranger: her husband's brother shall go in unto her, and take her to him to wife, and perform the duty of an husband's brother unto her.

6 And it shall be, *that* the firstborn which she beareth shall succeed in the name of his brother *which is* dead, that his name be not put out of Israel.

7 And if the man like not to take his brother's wife, then let his brother's wife go up to the gate unto the elders, and say, My husband's brother refuseth to raise up unto his brother a name in Israel, he will not perform the duty of my husband's brother.

8 Then the elders of his city shall call him, and speak unto him: and *if* he stand *to it*, and say, I like not to take her;

9 Then shall his brother's wife come unto him in the presence of the elders, and loose his shoe from off his foot, and spit in his face, and shall answer and say, So shall it be done unto that man that will not build up his brother's house.

10 And his name shall be called in Israel, The house of him that hath his shoe loosed.

11 ¶When men strive together one with another, and the wife of the one draweth near for to deliver her husband out of the hand of him that smiteth him, and putteth forth her hand, and taketh him by the secrets:

12 Then thou shalt cut off her hand, thine eye shall not pity *her*.

13 ¶Thou shalt not have in thy bag divers weights, a great and a small.

14 Thou shalt not have in thine house divers measures, a great and a small.

15 *But* thou shalt have a perfect and just weight, a perfect and just measure shalt thou have: that thy days may be lengthened in the land which the LORD thy God giveth thee.

16 For all that do such things, *and* all that do unrighteously, *are* an abomination unto the LORD thy God.

17 ¶Remember what Ăm′a-lĕk did unto thee by the way, when ye were come forth out of Egypt;

18 How he met thee by the way, and smote the hindmost of thee, *even* all *that were* feeble behind thee, when thou *wast* faint and weary; and he feared not God.

19 Therefore it shall be, when the LORD thy God hath given thee rest from all thine enemies round about, in the land which the LORD thy God giveth thee *for* an inheritance to possess it, *that* thou shalt blot out the remembrance of Ăm′a-lĕk from under heaven; thou shalt not forget *it*.

CHAPTER 26

AND it shall be, when thou *art* come in unto the land which the LORD thy God giveth thee *for* an inheritance, and possessest it, and dwellest therein;

2 That thou shalt take of the first of all the fruit of the earth, which thou shalt bring of thy land that the LORD thy God giveth thee, and shalt put *it* in a basket, and shalt go unto the place which the LORD thy God shall choose to place his name there.

3 And thou shalt go unto the priest that shall be in those days, and say unto him, I profess this day unto the LORD thy God, that I am come unto the country which the LORD sware unto our fathers for to give us.

4 And the priest shall take the basket out of thine hand, and set it down before the altar of the LORD thy God.

5 And thou shalt speak and say before the LORD thy God, A Syrian ready to perish *was* my father, and he went down into Egypt, and sojourned there with a few, and became there a nation, great, mighty, and populous:

6 And the Egyptians evil entreated us, and afflicted us, and laid upon us hard bondage:

7 And when we cried unto the LORD God of our fathers, the LORD heard our voice, and looked on our affliction, and our labour, and our oppression:

8 And the LORD brought us forth out of Egypt with a mighty hand, and with an outstretched arm, and with great terribleness, and with signs, and with wonders:

9 And he hath brought us into this place, and hath given us this land, *even* a land that floweth with milk and honey.

10 And now, behold, I have brought the firstfruits of the land, which thou, O LORD, hast given me. And thou shalt set it before the LORD thy God, and worship before the LORD thy God:

11 And thou shalt rejoice in every good *thing* which the LORD thy God hath given unto thee, and unto thine house, thou, and the Levite, and the stranger that *is* among you.

12 ¶When thou hast made an end of tithing all the tithes of thine increase the third year, *which is* the year of tithing, and hast given *it* unto the Levite, the stranger, the fatherless, and the widow, that they may eat within thy gates, and be filled;

13 Then thou shalt say before the LORD thy God, I have brought away the hallowed things out of *mine* house, and also have given them unto the Levite, and unto the stranger, to the fatherless, and to the widow, according to all thy commandments which thou hast commanded me: I have not transgressed thy commandments, neither have I forgotten *them*:

14 I have not eaten thereof in my mourning, neither have I taken away *ought* thereof for *any* unclean *use*, nor given *ought* thereof for the dead: *but* I have hearkened to the voice of the LORD my God, *and* have done according to all that thou hast commanded me.

15 Look down from thy holy habitation, from heaven, and bless thy people Israel, and the land which thou hast given us, as thou swarest unto our fathers, a land that floweth with milk and honey.

16 ¶This day the LORD thy God hath commanded thee to do these statutes and judgments: thou shalt therefore keep and do them with all thine heart, and with all thy soul.

17 Thou hast avouched the LORD this day to be thy God, and to walk in his ways, and to keep his statutes, and his commandments, and his judgments, and to hearken unto his voice:

18 And the LORD hath avouched thee this day to be his peculiar people, as he hath promised thee, and that *thou* shouldest keep all his commandments;

19 And to make thee high above all nations which he hath made, in praise,

and in name, and in honour; and that thou mayest be an holy people unto the LORD thy God, as he hath spoken.

CHAPTER 27

AND Moses with the elders of Israel commanded the people, saying, Keep all the commandments which I command you this day.

2 And it shall be on the day when ye shall pass over Jordan unto the land which the LORD thy God giveth thee, that thou shalt set thee up great stones, and plaister them with plaister:

3 And thou shalt write upon them all the words of this law, when thou art passed over, that thou mayest go in unto the land which the LORD thy God giveth thee, a land that floweth with milk and honey; as the LORD God of thy fathers hath promised thee.

4 Therefore it shall be when ye be gone over Jordan, *that* ye shall set up these stones, which I command you this day, in mount Ebal, and thou shalt plaister them with plaister.

5 And there shalt thou build an altar unto the LORD thy God, an altar of stones: thou shalt not lift up *any* iron *tool* upon them.

6 Thou shalt build the altar of the LORD thy God of whole stones: and thou shalt offer burnt offerings thereon unto the LORD thy God:

7 And thou shalt offer peace offerings, and shalt eat there, and rejoice before the LORD thy God.

8 And thou shalt write upon the stones all the words of this law very plainly.

9 ¶And Moses and the priests the Lē-vītes spake unto all Israel, saying, Take heed, and hearken, O Israel; this day thou art become the people of the LORD thy God.

10 Thou shalt therefore obey the voice of the LORD thy God, and do his commandments and his statutes, which I command thee this day.

11 ¶And Moses charged the people the same day, saying,

12 These shall stand upon mount Gĕr'i-zĭm to bless the people, when ye are come over Jordan; Simeon, and Levi, and Judah, and Ĭs'sa-char, and Joseph, and Benjamin:

13 And these shall stand upon mount Ebal to curse; Reuben, Gad, and Asher, and Zĕb'u-lun, Dan, and Năph'ta-lī.

14 ¶And the Lēvītes shall speak, and say unto all the men of Israel with a loud voice,

15 Cursed *be* the man that maketh *any* graven or molten image, an abomination unto the LORD, the work of the hands of the craftsman, and putteth *it* in *a* secret *place*. And all the people shall answer and say, Amen.

16 Cursed *be* he that setteth light by his father or his mother. And all the people shall say, Amen.

17 Cursed *be* he that removeth his neighbour's landmark. And all the people shall say, Amen.

18 Cursed *be* he that maketh the blind to wander out of the way. And all the people shall say, Amen.

19 Cursed *be* he that perverteth the judgment of the stranger, fatherless, and widow. And all the people shall say, Amen.

20 Cursed *be* he that lieth with his father's wife; because he uncovereth his father's skirt. And all the people shall say, Amen.

21 Cursed *be* he that lieth with any manner of beast. And all the people shall say, Amen.

22 Cursed *be* he that lieth with his sister, the daughter of his father, or the daughter of his mother. And all the people shall say, Amen.

23 Cursed *be* he that lieth with his mother in law. And all the people shall say, Amen.

24 Cursed *be* he that smiteth his neighbour secretly. And all the people shall say, Amen.

25 Cursed *be* he that taketh reward to slay an innocent person. And all the people shall say, Amen.

26 Cursed *be* he that confirmeth not *all* the words of this law to do them. And all the people shall say, Amen.

CHAPTER 28

AND it shall come to pass, if thou shalt hearken diligently unto the voice of the LORD thy God, to observe *and* to do all his commandments which I command thee this day, that the LORD thy God will set thee on high above all nations of the earth:

2 And all these blessings shall come on thee, and overtake thee, if thou shalt hearken unto the voice of the LORD thy God.

3 Blessed *shalt* thou *be* in the city, and blessed *shalt* thou *be* in the field.

4 Blessed *shall be* the fruit of thy body, and the fruit of thy ground, and the fruit of thy cattle, the increase of thy kine, and the flocks of thy sheep.

5 Blessed *shall be* thy basket and thy store.

6 Blessed *shalt* thou *be* when thou comest in, and blessed *shalt* thou *be* when thou goest out.

7 The LORD shall cause thine enemies that rise up against thee to be smitten

before thy face: they shall come out against thee one way, and flee before thee seven ways.

8 The LORD shall command the blessing upon thee in thy storehouses, and in all that thou settest thine hand unto; and he shall bless thee in the land which the LORD thy God giveth thee.

9 The LORD shall establish thee an holy people unto himself, as he hath sworn unto thee, if thou shalt keep the commandments of the LORD thy God, and walk in his ways.

10 And all people of the earth shall see that thou art called by the name of the LORD; and they shall be afraid of thee.

11 And the LORD shall make thee plenteous in goods, in the fruit of thy body, and in the fruit of thy cattle, and in the fruit of thy ground, in the land which the LORD sware unto thy fathers to give thee.

12 The LORD shall open unto thee his good treasure, the heaven to give the rain unto thy land in his season, and to bless all the work of thine hand: and thou shalt lend unto many nations, and thou shalt not borrow.

13 And the LORD shall make thee the head, and not the tail; and thou shalt be above only, and thou shalt not be beneath; if that thou hearken unto the commandments of the LORD thy God, which I command thee this day, to observe and to do *them*:

14 And thou shalt not go aside from any of the words which I command thee this day, *to* the right hand, or *to* the left, to go after other gods to serve them.

15 ¶But it shall come to pass, if thou wilt not hearken unto the voice of the LORD thy God, to observe to do all his commandments and his statutes which I command thee this day; that all these curses shall come upon thee, and overtake thee:

16 Cursed *shalt* thou *be* in the city, and cursed *shalt* thou *be* in the field.

17 Cursed *shall be* thy basket and thy store.

18 Cursed *shall be* the fruit of thy body, and the fruit of thy land, the increase of thy kine, and the flocks of thy sheep.

19 Cursed *shalt* thou *be* when thou comest in, and cursed *shalt* thou *be* when thou goest out.

20 The LORD shall send upon thee cursing, vexation, and rebuke, in all that thou settest thine hand unto for to do, until thou be destroyed, and until thou perish quickly; because of the wickedness of thy doings, whereby thou hast forsaken me.

21 The LORD shall make the pestilence cleave unto thee, until he have consumed thee from off the land, whither thou goest to possess it.

22 The LORD shall smite thee with a consumption, and with a fever, and with an inflammation, and with an extreme burning, and with the sword, and with blasting, and with mildew; and they shall pursue thee until thou perish.

23 And thy heaven that *is* over thy head shall be brass, and the earth that *is* under thee *shall be* iron.

24 The LORD shall make the rain of thy land powder and dust: from heaven shall it come down upon thee, until thou be destroyed.

25 The LORD shall cause thee to be smitten before thine enemies: thou shalt go out one way against them, and flee seven ways before them: and shalt be removed into all the kingdoms of the earth.

26 And thy carcase shall be meat unto all fowls of the air, and unto the beasts of the earth, and no man shall fray *them* away.

27 The LORD will smite thee with the botch of Egypt, and with the emerods, and with the scab, and with the itch, whereof thou canst not be healed.

28 The LORD shall smite thee with madness, and blindness, and astonishment of heart:

29 And thou shalt grope at noonday, as the blind gropeth in darkness, and thou shalt not prosper in thy ways: and thou shalt be only oppressed and spoiled evermore, and no man shall save *thee*.

30 Thou shalt betroth a wife, and another man shall lie with her: thou shalt build an house, and thou shalt not dwell therein: thou shalt plant a vineyard, and shalt not gather the grapes thereof.

31 Thine ox *shall be* slain before thine eyes, and thou shalt not eat thereof: thine ass *shall be* violently taken away from before thy face, and shall not be restored to thee: thy sheep *shall be* given unto thine enemies, and thou shalt have none to rescue *them*.

32 Thy sons and thy daughters *shall be* given unto another people, and thine eyes shall look, and fail *with longing* for them all the day long: and *there shall be* no might in thine hand.

33 The fruit of thy land, and all thy labours, shall a nation which thou knowest not eat up; and thou shalt be only oppressed and crushed alway:

34 So that thou shalt be mad for the sight of thine eyes which thou shalt see.

35 The LORD shall smite thee in the knees, and in the legs, with a sore botch that cannot be healed, from the sole of thy foot unto the top of thy head.

36 The LORD shall bring thee, and thy king which thou shalt set over thee, unto a nation which neither thou nor thy fathers have known; and there shalt thou serve other gods, wood and stone.

37 And thou shalt become an astonishment, a proverb, and a byword, among all nations whither the LORD shall lead thee.

38 Thou shalt carry much seed out into the field, and shalt gather *but* little in; for the locust shall consume it.

39 Thou shalt plant vineyards, and dress *them*, but shalt neither drink *of* the wine, nor gather *the grapes;* for the worms shall eat them.

40 Thou shalt have olive trees throughout all thy coasts, but thou shalt not anoint *thyself* with the oil; for thine olive shall cast *his fruit*.

41 Thou shall beget sons and daughters, but thou shalt not enjoy them; for they shall go into captivity.

42 All thy trees and fruit of thy land shall the locust consume.

43 The stranger that *is* within thee shall get up above thee very high; and thou shalt come down very low.

44 He shall lend to thee, and thou shalt not lend to him: he shall be the head, and thou shalt be the tail.

45 Moreover all these curses shall come upon thee, and shall pursue thee, and overtake thee, till thou be destroyed; because thou hearkenedst not unto the voice of the LORD thy God, to keep his commandments and his statutes which he commanded thee:

46 And they shall be upon thee for a sign and for a wonder, and upon thy seed for ever.

47 Because thou servedst not the LORD thy God with joyfulness, and with gladness of heart, for the abundance of all *things*;

48 Therefore shalt thou serve thine enemies which the LORD shall send against thee, in hunger, and in thirst, and in nakedness, and in want of all *things*: and he shall put a yoke of iron upon thy neck, until he have destroyed thee.

49 The LORD shall bring a nation against thee from far, from the end of the earth, *as swift* as the eagle flieth; a nation whose tongue thou shalt not understand;

50 A nation of fierce countenance, which shall not regard the person of the old, nor shew favour to the young:

51 And he shall eat the fruit of thy cattle, and the fruit of thy land, until thou be destroyed: which *also* shall not leave thee *either* corn, wine, or oil, *or* the increase of thy kine, or flocks of thy sheep, until he have destroyed thee.

52 And he shall besiege thee in all thy gates, until thy high and fenced walls come down, wherein thou trustedst, throughout all thy land: and he shall besiege thee in all thy gates throughout all thy land, which the LORD thy God hath given thee.

53 And thou shalt eat the fruit of thine own body, the flesh of thy sons and of thy daughters, which the LORD thy God hath given thee, in the siege, and in the straitness, wherewith thine enemies shall distress thee:

54 *So that* the man *that is* tender among you, and very delicate, his eye shall be evil toward his brother, and toward the wife of his bosom, and toward the remnant of his children which he shall leave:

55 So that he will not give to any of them of the flesh of his children whom he shall eat: because he hath nothing left him in the siege, and in the straitness, wherewith thine enemies shall distress thee in all thy gates.

56 The tender and delicate woman among you, which would not adventure to set the sole of her foot upon the ground for delicateness and tenderness, her eye shall be evil toward the husband of her bosom, and toward her son, and toward her daughter,

57 And toward her young one that cometh out from between her feet, and toward her children which she shall bear: for she shall eat them for want of all *things* secretly in the siege and straitness, wherewith thine enemy shall distress thee in thy gates.

58 If thou wilt not observe to do all the words of this law that are written in this book, that thou mayest fear this glorious and fearful name, THE LORD THY GOD;

59 Then the LORD will make thy plagues wonderful, and the plagues of thy seed, *even* great plagues, and of long continuance, and sore sicknesses, and of long continuance.

60 Moreover he will bring upon thee all the diseases of Egypt, which thou wast afraid of; and they shall cleave unto thee.

61 Also every sickness, and every plague, which *is* not written in the book of this law, them will the LORD bring upon thee, until thou be destroyed.

62 And ye shall be left few in number, whereas ye were as the stars of heaven

Samson Destroys an Idol's Temple (Judg 16)

Ruth in the Field of Boaz (Ruth 2)

for multitude; because thou wouldest
not obey the voice of the LORD thy God.
63 And it shall come to pass, *that* as
the LORD rejoiced over you to do you
good, and to multiply you; so the LORD
will rejoice over you to destroy you,
and to bring you to nought; and ye shall
be plucked from off the land whither
thou goest to possess it.
64 And the LORD shall scatter thee
among all people, from the one end of
the earth even unto the other; and there
thou shalt serve other gods, which
neither thou nor thy fathers have
known, *even* wood and stone.
65 And among these nations shalt
thou find no ease, neither shall the sole
of thy foot have rest: but the LORD shall
give thee there a trembling heart, and
failing of eyes, and sorrow of mind:
66 And thy life shall hang in doubt be-
fore thee; and thou shalt fear day and
night, and shalt have none assurance of
thy life:
67 In the morning thou shalt say,
Would God it were even! and at even
thou shalt say, Would God it were morn-
ing! for the fear of thine heart where-
with thou shalt fear, and for the
sight of thine eyes which thou shalt see.
68 And the LORD shall bring thee into
Egypt again with ships, by the way
whereof I spake unto thee, Thou shalt
see it no more again: and there ye shall
be sold unto your enemies for bondmen
and bondwomen, and no man shall buy
you.

CHAPTER 29

THESE *are* the words of the covenant,
which the LORD commanded Moses to
make with the children of Israel in the
land of Moab, beside the covenant
which he made with them in Hō'rĕb.
2 ¶And Moses called unto all Israel,
and said unto them, Ye have seen all
that the LORD did before your eyes in
the land of Egypt unto Pharaoh, and
unto all his servants, and unto all his
land;
3 The great temptations which thine
eyes have seen, the signs, and those
great miracles:
4 Yet the LORD hath not given you an
heart to perceive, and eyes to see, and
ears to hear, unto this day.
5 And I have led you forty years in the
wilderness: your clothes are not waxen
old upon you, and thy shoe is not
waxen old upon thy foot.
6 Ye have not eaten bread, neither
have ye drunk wine or strong drink:
that ye might know that I *am* the LORD
your God.
7 And when ye came unto this place,
Sihon the king of Hĕsh'bŏn, and Og the
king of Bā'shan, came out against us
unto battle, and we smote them:
8 And we took their land, and gave it
for an inheritance unto the Reubenites,
and to the Gadites, and to the half tribe
of Ma-năs'seh.
9 Keep therefore the words of this
covenant, and do them, that ye may
prosper in all that ye do.
10 ¶Ye stand this day all of you be-
fore the LORD your God; your captains
of your tribes, your elders, and your of-
ficers, *with* all the men of Israel,
11 Your little ones, your wives, and
thy stranger that *is* in thy camp, from
the hewer of thy wood unto the drawer
of thy water:
12 That thou shouldest enter into
covenant with the LORD thy God, and
into his oath, which the LORD thy God
maketh with thee this day:
13 That he may establish thee to day
for a people unto himself, and *that* he
may be unto thee a God, as he hath said
unto thee, and as he hath sworn unto
thy fathers, to Abraham, to Isaac, and
to Jacob.
14 Neither with you only do I make
this covenant and this oath;
15 But with *him* that standeth here
with us this day before the LORD our
God, and also with *him* that *is* not here
with us this day:
16 (For ye know how we have dwelt
in the land of Egypt; and how we came
through the nations which ye passed
by;
17 And ye have seen their abomina-
tions, and their idols, wood and stone,
silver and gold, which *were* among
them:)
18 Lest there should be among you
man, or woman, or family, or tribe,
whose heart turneth away this day
from the LORD our God, to go *and* serve
the gods of these nations; lest there
should be among you a root that bear-
eth gall and wormwood;
19 And it come to pass, when he hear-
eth the words of this curse, that he
bless himself in his heart, saying, I shall
have peace, though I walk in the imagi-
nation of mine heart, to add drunken-
ness to thirst:
20 The LORD will not spare him, but
then the anger of the LORD and his
jealousy shall smoke against that man,
and all the curses that are written in
this book shall lie upon him, and the
LORD shall blot out his name from un-
der heaven.
21 And the LORD shall separate him
unto evil out of all the tribes of Israel,
according to all the curses of the cov-

enant that are written in this book of the law:

22 So that the generation to come of your children that shall rise up after you, and the stranger that shall come from a far land, shall say, when they see the plagues of that land, and the sicknesses which the LORD hath laid upon it;

23 *And that* the whole land thereof *is* brimstone, and salt, *and* burning, *that* it is not sown, nor beareth, nor any grass groweth therein, like the overthrow of Sodom, and Go-mŏr'rah, Ăd'mah, and Ze-bō'im, which the LORD overthrew in his anger, and in his wrath:

24 Even all nations shall say, Wherefore hath the LORD done thus unto this land? what *meaneth* the heat of this great anger?

25 Then men shall say, Because they have forsaken the covenant of the LORD God of their fathers, which he made with them when he brought them forth out of the land of Egypt:

26 For they went and served other gods, and worshipped them, gods whom they knew not, and *whom* he had not given unto them:

27 And the anger of the LORD was kindled against this land, to bring upon it all the curses that are written in this book:

28 And the LORD rooted them out of their land in anger, and in wrath, and in great indignation, and cast them into another land, as *it is* this day.

29 The secret *things belong* unto the LORD our God: but those *things which are* revealed *belong* unto us and to our children for ever, that *we* may do all the words of this law.

CHAPTER 30

AND it shall come to pass, when all these things are come upon thee, the blessing and the curse, which I have set before thee, and thou shalt call *them* to mind among all the nations, whither the LORD thy God hath driven thee,

2 And shalt return unto the LORD thy God, and shalt obey his voice according to all that I command thee this day, thou and thy children, with all thine heart, and with all thy soul;

3 That then the LORD thy God will turn thy captivity, and have compassion upon thee, and will return and gather thee from all the nations, whither the LORD thy God hath scattered thee.

4 If *any* of thine be driven out unto the outmost *parts* of heaven, from thence will the LORD thy God gather thee, and from thence will he fetch thee:

5 And the LORD thy God will bring thee into the land which thy fathers possessed, and thou shalt possess it; and he will do thee good, and multiply thee above thy fathers.

6 And the LORD thy God will circumcise thine heart, and the heart of thy seed, to love the LORD thy God with all thine heart, and with all thy soul, that thou mayest live.

7 And the LORD thy God will put all these curses upon thine enemies, and on them that hate thee, which persecuted thee.

8 And thou shalt return and obey the voice of the LORD, and do all his commandments which I command thee this day.

9 And the LORD thy God will make thee plenteous in every work of thine hand, in the fruit of thy body, and in the fruit of thy cattle, and in the fruit of thy land, for good: for the LORD will again rejoice over thee for good, as he rejoiced over thy fathers:

10 If thou shalt hearken unto the voice of the LORD thy God, to keep his commandments and his statutes which are written in this book of the law, *and* if thou turn unto the LORD thy God with all thine heart, and with all thy soul.

11 ¶For this commandment which I command thee this day, it *is* not hidden from thee, neither *is* it far off.

12 It *is* not in heaven, that thou shouldest say, Who shall go up for us to heaven, and bring it unto us, that we may hear it, and do it?

13 Neither *is* it beyond the sea, that thou shouldest say, Who shall go over the sea for us, and bring it unto us, that we may hear it, and do it?

14 But the word *is* very nigh unto thee, in thy mouth, and in thy heart, that thou mayest do it.

15 ¶See, I have set before thee this day life and good, and death and evil;

16 In that I command thee this day to love the LORD thy God, to walk in his ways, and to keep his commandments and his statutes and his judgments, that thou mayest live and multiply: and the LORD thy God shall bless thee in the land whither thou goest to possess it.

17 But if thine heart turn away, so that thou wilt not hear, but shalt be drawn away, and worship other gods, and serve them;

18 I denounce unto you this day, that ye shall surely perish, *and that* ye shall not prolong *your* days upon the land, whither thou passest over Jordan to go to possess it.

19 I call heaven and earth to record this day against you, *that* I have set be-

fore you life and death, blessing and
cursing: therefore choose life, that both
thou and thy seed may live:
20 That thou mayest love the LORD
thy God, *and* that thou mayest obey his
voice, and that thou mayest cleave
unto him: for he *is* thy life, and the
length of thy days: that thou mayest
dwell in the land which the LORD sware
unto thy fathers, to Abraham, to Isaac,
and to Jacob, to give them.

CHAPTER 31

AND Moses went and spake these
words unto all Israel.
2 And he said unto them, I *am* an
hundred and twenty years old this day;
I can no more go out and come in: also
the LORD hath said unto me, Thou shalt
not go over this Jordan.
3 The LORD thy God, he will go over
before thee, *and* he will destroy these
nations from before thee, and thou
shalt possess them: *and* Joshua, he
shall go over before thee, as the LORD
hath said.
4 And the LORD shall do unto them as
he did to Sihon and to Og, kings of the
Amorites, and unto the land of them,
whom he destroyed.
5 And the LORD shall give them up be-
fore your face, that ye may do unto
them according unto all the command-
ments which I have commanded you.
6 Be strong and of a good courage,
fear not, nor be afraid of them: for the
LORD thy God, he *it is* that doth go with
thee; he will not fail thee, nor forsake
thee.
7 ¶And Moses called unto Joshua,
and said unto him in the sight of all
Israel, Be strong and of a good courage:
for thou must go with this people unto
the land which the LORD hath sworn
unto their fathers to give them; and
thou shalt cause them to inherit it.
8 And the LORD, he *it is* that doth go
before thee; he will be with thee, he will
not fail thee, neither forsake thee: fear
not, neither be dismayed.
9 ¶And Moses wrote this law, and de-
livered it unto the priests the sons of
Levi, which bare the ark of the covenant
of the LORD, and unto all the elders
of Israel.
10 And Moses commanded them,
saying, At the end of *every* seven years,
in the solemnity of the year of release,
in the feast of tabernacles,
11 When all Israel is come to appear
before the LORD thy God in the place
which he shall choose, thou shalt read
this law before all Israel in their hear-
ing.
12 Gather the people together, men,
and women, and children, and thy
stranger that *is* within thy gates, that
they may hear, and that they may
learn, and fear the LORD your God, and
observe to do all the words of this law:
13 And *that* their children, which
have not known *any thing*, may hear,
and learn to fear the LORD your God, as
long as ye live in the land whither ye go
over Jordan to possess it.
14 ¶And the LORD said unto Moses,
Behold, thy days approach that thou
must die: call Joshua, and present
yourselves in the tabernacle of the
congregation, that I may give him a
charge. And Moses and Joshua went,
and presented themselves in the taber-
nacle of the congregation.
15 And the LORD appeared in the
tabernacle in a pillar of a cloud: and the
pillar of the cloud stood over the door
of the tabernacle.
16 ¶And the LORD said unto Moses,
Behold, thou shalt sleep with thy
fathers; and this people will rise up,
and go a whoring after the gods of the
strangers of the land, whither they go
to be among them, and will forsake me,
and break my covenant which I have
made with them.
17 Then my anger shall be kindled
against them in that day, and I will for-
sake them, and I will hide my face from
them, and they shall be devoured, and
many evils and troubles shall befall
them; so that they will say in that day,
Are not these evils come upon us, be-
cause our God *is* not among us?
18 And I will surely hide my face in
that day for all the evils which they
shall have wrought, in that they are
turned unto other gods.
19 Now therefore write ye this song
for you, and teach it the children of
Israel: put it in their mouths, that this
song may be a witness for me against
the children of Israel.
20 For when I shall have brought
them into the land which I sware unto
their fathers, that floweth with milk
and honey; and they shall have eaten
and filled themselves, and waxen fat;
then will they turn unto other gods, and
serve them, and provoke me, and break
my covenant.
21 And it shall come to pass, when
many evils and troubles are befallen
them, that this song shall testify
against them as a witness; for it shall
not be forgotten out of the mouths of
their seed: for I know their imagination
which they go about, even now, before
I have brought them into the land
which I sware.
22 Moses therefore wrote this song

the same day, and taught it the children
of Israel.
23 And he gave Joshua the son of
Nun a charge, and said, Be strong and
of a good courage: for thou shalt bring
the children of Israel into the land
which I sware unto them: and I will be
with thee.
24 ¶And it came to pass, when Moses
had made an end of writing the words
of this law in a book, until they were
finished,
25 That Moses commanded the Lē-
vītes, which bare the ark of the covenant
of the LORD, saying,
26 Take this book of the law, and put
it in the side of the ark of the covenant
of the LORD your God, that it may be
there for a witness against thee.
27 For I know thy rebellion, and thy
stiff neck: behold, while I am yet alive
with you this day, ye have been rebel-
lious against the LORD; and how much
more after my death?
28 Gather unto me all the elders of
your tribes, and your officers, that I
may speak these words in their ears,
and call heaven and earth to record
against them.
29 For I know that after my death ye
will utterly corrupt *yourselves,* and
turn aside from the way which I have
commanded you; and evil will befall
you in the latter days; because ye will
do evil in the sight of the LORD, to pro-
voke him to anger through the work of
your hands.
30 And Moses spake in the ears of all
the congregation of Israel the words of
this song, until they were ended.

CHAPTER 32

GIVE ear, O ye heavens, and I will
speak; and hear, O earth, the words of
my mouth.
2 My doctrine shall drop as the rain,
my speech shall distil as the dew, as the
small rain upon the tender herb, and as
the showers upon the grass:
3 Because I will publish the name of
the LORD: ascribe ye greatness unto our
God.
4 *He is* the Rock, his work *is* perfect:
for all his ways *are* judgment: a God of
truth and without iniquity, just and
right *is* he.
5 They have corrupted themselves,
their spot *is* not *the spot* of his children:
they are a perverse and crooked gen-
eration.
6 Do ye thus requite the LORD, O
foolish people and unwise? *is* not he thy
father *that* hath bought thee? hath he
not made thee, and established thee?
7 Remember the days of old, consider
the years of many generations: ask thy
father, and he will shew thee; thy elders,
and they will tell thee.
8 When the Most High divided to the
nations their inheritance, when he sepa-
rated the sons of Adam, he set the
bounds of the people according to the
number of the children of Israel.
9 For the LORD's portion *is* his people;
Jacob *is* the lot of his inheritance.
10 He found him in a desert land, and
in the waste howling wilderness; he led
him about, he instructed him, he kept
him as the apple of his eye.
11 As an eagle stirreth up her nest,
fluttereth over her young, spreadeth
abroad her wings, taketh them, beareth
them on her wings:
12 *So* the LORD alone did lead him,
and *there was* no strange god with him.
13 He made him ride on the high
places of the earth, that he might eat
the increase of the fields; and he made
him to suck honey out of the rock, and
oil out of the flinty rock;
14 Butter of kine, and milk of sheep,
with fat of lambs, and rams of the breed
of Bā'shan, and goats, with the fat of
kidneys of wheat; and thou didst drink
the pure blood of the grape.
15 But Jĕsh'u-run waxed fat, and
kicked: thou art waxen fat, thou art
grown thick, thou art covered *with fat-
ness;* then he forsook God *which* made
him, and lightly esteemed the Rock of
his salvation.
16 They provoked him to jealousy
with strange *gods,* with abominations
provoked they him to anger.
17 They sacrificed unto devils, not to
God; to gods whom they knew not, to
new *gods that* came newly up, whom
your fathers feared not.
18 Of the Rock *that* begat thee thou
art unmindful, and hast forgotten God
that formed thee.
19 And when the LORD saw *it,* he
abhorred *them,* because of the provok-
ing of his sons, and of his daughters.
20 And he said, I will hide my face
from them, I will see what their end
shall be: for they *are* a very froward gen-
eration, children in whom *is* no faith.
21 They have moved me to jealousy
with *that which is* not God; they have
provoked me to anger with their vani-
ties: and I will move them to jealousy
with *those which are* not a people; I will
provoke them to anger with a foolish
nation.
22 For a fire is kindled in mine anger,
and shall burn unto the lowest hell, and
shall consume the earth with her in-
crease, and set on fire the foundations
of the mountains.

23 I will heap mischiefs upon them; I will spend mine arrows upon them.

24 *They shall be* burnt with hunger, and devoured with burning heat, and with bitter destruction: I will also send the teeth of beasts upon them, with the poison of serpents of the dust.

25 The sword without, and terror within, shall destroy both the young man and the virgin, the suckling *also* with the man of gray hairs.

26 I said, I would scatter them into corners, I would make the remembrance of them to cease from among men:

27 Were it not that I feared the wrath of the enemy, lest their adversaries should behave themselves strangely, *and* lest they should say, Our hand *is* high, and the LORD hath not done all this.

28 For they *are* a nation void of counsel, neither *is there any* understanding in them.

29 O that they were wise, *that* they understood this, *that* they would consider their latter end!

30 How should one chase a thousand, and two put ten thousand to flight, except their Rock had sold them, and the LORD had shut them up?

31 For their rock *is* not as our Rock, even our enemies themselves *being* judges.

32 For their vine *is* of the vine of Sodom, and of the fields of Gō-mŏr'rah: their grapes *are* grapes of gall, their clusters *are* bitter:

33 Their wine *is* the poison of dragons, and the cruel venom of asps.

34 *Is* not this laid up in store with me, *and* sealed up among my treasures?

35 To me *belongeth* vengeance, and recompence; their foot shall slide in *due* time: for the day of their calamity *is* at hand, and the things that shall come upon them make haste.

36 For the LORD shall judge his people, and repent himself for his servants, when he seeth that *their* power is gone, and *there is* none shut up, or left.

37 And he shall say, Where *are* their gods, *their* rock in whom they trusted,

38 Which did eat the fat of their sacrifices, *and* drank the wine of their drink offerings? let them rise up and help you, *and* be your protection.

39 See now that I, *even* I, *am* he, and *there is* no god with me: I kill, and I make alive; I wound, and I heal: neither *is there any* that can deliver out of my hand.

40 For I lift up my hand to heaven, and say, I live for ever.

41 If I whet my glittering sword, and mine hand take hold on judgment; I will render vengeance to mine enemies, and will reward them that hate me.

42 I will make mine arrows drunk with blood, and my sword shall devour flesh; *and that* with the blood of the slain and of the captives, from the beginning of revenges upon the enemy.

43 Rejoice, O ye nations, *with* his people: for he will avenge the blood of his servants, and will render vengeance to his adversaries, and will be merciful unto his land, *and* to his people.

44 ¶And Moses came and spake all the words of this song in the ears of the people, he, and Hō-shē'a the son of Nun.

45 And Moses made an end of speaking all these words to all Israel:

46 And he said unto them, Set your hearts unto all the words which I testify among you this day, which ye shall command your children to observe to do, all the words of this law.

47 For it *is* not a vain thing for you; because it *is* your life: and through this thing ye shall prolong *your* days in the land, whither ye go over Jordan to possess it.

48 ¶And the LORD spake unto Moses that selfsame day, saying,

49 Get thee up into this mountain Ăb'a-rĭm, *unto* mount Nebo, which *is* in the land of Moab, that *is* over against Jericho; and behold the land of Canaan, which I give unto the children of Israel for a possession:

50 And die in the mount whither thou goest up, and be gathered unto thy people; as Aaron thy brother died in mount Hor, and was gathered unto his people:

51 Because ye trespassed against me among the children of Israel at the waters of Mĕr'ibah-Kā'desh, in the wilderness of Zin; because ye sanctified me not in the midst of the children of Israel.

52 Yet thou shalt see the land before *thee;* but thou shalt not go thither unto the land which I give the children of Israel.

CHAPTER 33

AND this *is* the blessing, wherewith Moses the man of God blessed the children of Israel before his death.

2 And he said, The LORD came from Sī'naī, and rose up from Sē'ir unto them; he shined forth from mount Paran, and he came with ten thousands of saints: from his right hand *went* a fiery law for them.

3 Yea, he loved the people; all his

saints *are* in thy hand: and they sat down at thy feet; *every one* shall receive of thy words.

4 Moses commanded us a law, *even* the inheritance of the congregation of Jacob.

5 And he was king in Jĕsh'u-run, when the heads of the people *and* the tribes of Israel were gathered together.

6 ¶Let Reuben live, and not die; and let *not* his men be few.

7 ¶And this *is the blessing* of Judah: and he said, Hear, LORD, the voice of Judah, and bring him unto his people: let his hands be sufficient for him; and be thou an help *to him* from his enemies.

8 ¶And of Levi he said, *Let* thy Thŭm'mĭm and thy Û'rĭm *be* with thy holy one, whom thou didst prove at Măs'sah, *and with* whom thou didst strive at the waters of Mĕr'i-bah;

9 Who said unto his father and to his mother, I have not seen him; neither did he acknowledge his brethren, nor knew his own children: for they have observed thy word, and kept thy covenant.

10 They shall teach Jacob thy judgments, and Israel thy law: they shall put incense before thee, and whole burnt sacrifice upon thine altar.

11 Bless, LORD, his substance, and accept the work of his hands: smite through the loins of them that rise against him, and of them that hate him, that they rise not again.

12 ¶*And* of Benjamin he said, The beloved of the LORD shall dwell in safety by him; *and the LORD* shall cover him all the day long, and he shall dwell between his shoulders.

13 ¶And of Joseph he said, Blessed of the LORD *be* his land, for the precious things of heaven, for the dew, and for the deep that coucheth beneath,

14 And for the precious fruits *brought forth* by the sun, and for the precious things put forth by the moon,

15 And for the chief things of the ancient mountains, and for the precious things of the lasting hills,

16 And for the precious things of the earth and fulness thereof, and *for* the good will of him that dwelt in the bush: let *the blessing* come upon the head of Joseph, and upon the top of the head of him *that was* separated from his brethren.

17 His glory *is like* the firstling of his bullock, and his horns *are like* the horns of unicorns: with them he shall push the people together to the ends of the earth: and they *are* the ten thousands of Ē'phra-im, and they *are* the thousands of Ma-năs'seh.

18 ¶And of Zĕb'u-lun he said, Rejoice, Zĕb'u-lun, in thy going out; and, Ĭs'sa-char, in thy tents.

19 They shall call the people unto the mountain; there they shall offer sacrifices of righteousness: for they shall suck *of* the abundance of the seas, and *of* treasures hid in the sand.

20 ¶And of Gad he said, Blessed *be* he that enlargeth Gad: he dwelleth as a lion, and teareth the arm with the crown of the head.

21 And he provided the first part for himself, because there, *in* a portion of the lawgiver, *was he* seated; and he came with the heads of the people, he executed the justice of the LORD, and his judgments with Israel.

22 ¶And of Dan he said, Dan *is* a lion's whelp: he shall leap from Bā'shan.

23 ¶And of Năph'ta-lī he said, O Năph'ta-lī, satisfied with favour, and full with the blessing of the LORD: possess thou the west and the south.

24 ¶And of Asher he said, *Let* Asher *be* blessed with children; let him be acceptable to his brethren, and let him dip his foot in oil.

25 Thy shoes *shall be* iron and brass; and as thy days, *so shall* thy strength *be*.

26 ¶*There is* none like unto the God of Jĕsh'u-run, *who* rideth upon the heaven in thy help, and in his excellency on the sky.

27 The eternal God *is thy* refuge, and underneath *are* the everlasting arms: and he shall thrust out the enemy from before thee; and shall say, Destroy *them*.

28 Israel then shall dwell in safety alone: the fountain of Jacob *shall be* upon a land of corn and wine; also his heavens shall drop down dew.

29 Happy *art* thou, O Israel: who *is* like unto thee, O people saved by the LORD, the shield of thy help, and who *is* the sword of thy excellency! and thine enemies shall be found liars unto thee; and thou shalt tread upon their high places.

CHAPTER 34

AND Moses went up from the plains of Moab unto the mountain of Nebo, to the top of Pĭs'gah, that *is* over against Jericho. And the LORD shewed him all the land of Gilead, unto Dan,

2 And all Năph'ta-lī, and the land of Ē'phra-im, and Ma-năs'seh, and all the land of Judah, unto the utmost sea,

3 And the south, and the plain of the valley of Jericho, the city of palm trees, unto Zō'ar.

4 And the LORD said unto him, This *is* the land which I sware unto Abraham, unto Isaac, and unto Jacob, saying, I will give it unto thy seed: I have caused thee to see *it* with thine eyes, but thou shalt not go over thither.

5 ¶So Moses the servant of the LORD died there in the land of Moab, according to the word of the LORD.

6 And he buried him in a valley in the land of Moab, over against Bĕth-pē'ôr: but no man knoweth of his sepulchre unto this day.

7 ¶And Moses *was* an hundred and twenty years old when he died: his eye was not dim, nor his natural force abated.

8 ¶And the children of Israel wept for Moses in the plains of Moab thirty days: so the days of weeping *and* mourning for Moses were ended.

9 ¶And Joshua the son of Nun was full of the spirit of wisdom; for Moses had laid his hands upon him: and the children of Israel hearkened unto him, and did as the LORD commanded Moses.

10 ¶And there arose not a prophet since in Israel like unto Moses, whom the LORD knew face to face,

11 In all the signs and the wonders, which the LORD sent him to do in the land of Egypt to Pharaoh, and to all his servants, and to all his land,

12 And in all that mighty hand, and in all the great terror which Moses shewed in the sight of all Israel.

THE BOOK OF JOSHUA

CHAPTER 1

NOW after the death of Moses the servant of the LORD it came to pass, that the LORD spake unto Joshua the son of Nun, Moses' minister, saying,

2 Moses my servant is dead; now therefore arise, go over this Jordan, thou, and all this people, unto the land which I do give to them, *even* to the children of Israel.

3 Every place that the sole of your foot shall tread upon, that have I given unto you, as I said unto Moses.

4 From the wilderness and this Lebanon even unto the great river, the river Eū-phrā'tēṡ, all the land of the Hittites, and unto the great sea toward the going down of the sun, shall be your coast.

5 There shall not any man be able to stand before thee all the days of thy life: as I was with Moses, *so* I will be with thee: I will not fail thee, nor forsake thee.

6 Be strong and of a good courage: for unto this people shalt thou divide for an inheritance the land, which I sware unto their fathers to give them.

7 Only be thou strong and very courageous, that thou mayest observe to do according to all the law, which Moses my servant commanded thee: turn not from it *to* the right hand or *to* the left, that thou mayest prosper withersoever thou goest.

8 This book of the law shall not depart out of thy mouth; but thou shalt meditate therein day and night, that thou mayest observe to do according to all that is written therein: for then thou shalt make thy way prosperous, and then thou shalt have good success.

9 Have not I commanded thee? Be strong and of a good courage; be not afraid, neither be thou dismayed: for the LORD thy God *is* with thee whithersoever thou goest.

10 ¶Then Joshua commanded the officers of the people, saying,

11 Pass through the host, and command the people, saying, Prepare you victuals; for within three days ye shall pass over this Jordan, to go in to possess the land, which the LORD your God giveth you to possess it.

12 ¶And to the Reubenites, and to the Gadites, and to half the tribe of Manăs'seh, spake Joshua, saying,

13 Remember the word which Moses the servant of the LORD commanded you, saying, The LORD your God hath given you rest, and hath given you this land.

14 Your wives, your little ones, and your cattle, shall remain in the land which Moses gave you on this side Jordan; but ye shall pass before your brethren armed, all the mighty men of valour, and help them;

15 Until the LORD have given your brethren rest, as *he hath given* you, and they also have possessed the land which the LORD your God giveth them: then ye shall return unto the land of your possession, and enjoy it, which Moses the LORD's servant gave you on this side Jordan toward the sunrising.

16 ¶And they answered Joshua, saying, All that thou commandest us we will do, and whithersoever thou sendest us, we will go.

17 According as we hearkened unto Moses in all things, so will we hearken unto thee: only the LORD thy God be with thee, as he was with Moses.
18 Whosoever *he be* that doth rebel against thy commandment, and will not hearken unto thy words in all that thou commandest him, he shall be put to death: only be strong and of a good courage.

CHAPTER 2

AND Joshua the son of Nun sent out of Shĭt'tĭm two men to spy secretly, saying, Go view the land, even Jericho. And they went, and came into an harlot's house, named Rahab, and lodged there.
2 And it was told the king of Jericho, saying, Behold, there came men in hither to night of the children of Israel to search out the country.
3 And the king of Jericho sent unto Rahab, saying, Bring forth the men that are come to thee, which are entered into thine house: for they be come to search out all the country.
4 And the woman took the two men, and hid them, and said thus, There came men unto me, but I wist not whence they *were:*
5 And it came to pass *about the time* of shutting of the gate, when it was dark, that the men went out: whither the men went I wot not: pursue after them quickly; for ye shall overtake them.
6 But she had brought them up to the roof of the house, and hid them with the stalks of flax, which she had laid in order upon the roof.
7 And the men pursued after them the way to Jordan unto the fords: and as soon as they which pursued after them were gone out, they shut the gate.
8 ¶And before they were laid down, she came up unto them upon the roof;
9 And she said unto the men, I know that the LORD hath given you the land, and that your terror is fallen upon us, and that all the inhabitants of the land faint because of you.
10 For we have heard how the LORD dried up the water of the Red sea for you, when ye came out of Egypt; and what ye did unto the two kings of the Amorites, that *were* on the other side Jordan, Sihon and Og, whom ye utterly destroyed.
11 And as soon as we had heard *these things*, our hearts did melt, neither did there remain any more courage in any man, because of you: for the LORD your God, he *is* God in heaven above, and in earth beneath.
12 Now therefore, I pray you, swear unto me by the LORD, since I have shewed you kindness, that ye will also shew kindness unto my father's house, and give me a true token:
13 And *that* ye will save alive my father, and my mother, and my brethren, and my sisters, and all that they have, and deliver our lives from death.
14 And the men answered her, Our life for yours, if ye utter not this our business. And it shall be, when the LORD hath given us the land, that we will deal kindly and truly with thee.
15 Then she let them down by a cord through the window: for her house *was* upon the town wall, and she dwelt upon the wall.
16 And she said unto them, Get you to the mountain, lest the pursuers meet you; and hide yourselves there three days, until the pursuers be returned: and afterward may ye go your way.
17 And the men said unto her, We *will be* blameless of this thine oath which thou hast made us swear.
18 Behold, *when* we come into the land, thou shalt bind this line of scarlet thread in the window which thou didst let us down by: and thou shalt bring thy father, and thy mother, and thy brethren, and all thy father's household, home unto thee.
19 And it shall be, *that* whosoever shall go out of the doors of thy house into the street, his blood *shall be* upon his head, and we *will be* guiltless: and whosoever shall be with thee in the house, his blood *shall be* on our head, if *any* hand be upon him.
20 And if thou utter this our business, then we will be quit of thine oath which thou hast made us to swear.
21 And she said, According unto your words, so *be* it. And she sent them away, and they departed: and she bound the scarlet line in the window.
22 And they went, and came unto the mountain, and abode there three days, until the pursuers were returned: and the pursuers sought *them* throughout all the way, but found *them* not.
23 So the two men returned, and descended from the mountain, and passed over, and came to Joshua the son of Nun, and told him all *things* that befell them:
24 And they said unto Joshua, Truly the LORD hath delivered into our hands all the land; for even all the inhabitants of the country do faint because of us.

CHAPTER 3

AND Joshua rose early in the morning; and they removed from Shĭt'tĭm, and came to Jordan, he and all the children of Israel, and lodged there before they passed over.

2 And it came to pass after three days, that the officers went through the host;

3 And they commanded the people, saying, When ye see the ark of the covenant of the LORD your God, and the priests the Lēvītes bearing it, then ye shall remove from your place, and go after it.

4 Yet there shall be a space between you and it, about two thousand cubits by measure: come not near unto it, that ye may know the way by which ye must go: for ye have not passed *this* way heretofore.

5 And Joshua said unto the people, Sanctify yourselves: for to morrow the LORD will do wonders among you.

6 And Joshua spake unto the priests, saying, Take up the ark of the covenant, and pass over before the people. And they took up the ark of the covenant, and went before the people.

7 ¶And the LORD said unto Joshua, This day will I begin to magnify thee in the sight of all Israel, that they may know that, as I was with Moses, *so* I will be with thee.

8 And thou shalt command the priests that bear the ark of the covenant, saying, When ye are come to the brink of the water of Jordan, ye shall stand still in Jordan.

9 ¶And Joshua said unto the children of Israel, Come hither, and hear the words of the LORD your God.

10 And Joshua said, Hereby ye shall know that the living God *is* among you, and *that* he will without fail drive out from before you the Canaanites, and the Hittites, and the Hī'vītes, and the Pĕr'iz-zītes, and the Gir'ga-shītes, and the Ămorītes, and the Jēb'u-sītes.

11 Behold, the ark of the covenant of the Lord of all the earth passeth over before you into Jordan.

12 Now therefore take you twelve men out of the tribes of Israel, out of every tribe a man.

13 And it shall come to pass, as soon as the soles of the feet of the priests that bear the ark of the LORD, the Lord of all the earth, shall rest in the waters of Jordan, *that* the waters of Jordan shall be cut off *from* the waters that come down from above; and they shall stand upon an heap.

14 ¶And it came to pass, when the people removed from their tents, to pass over Jordan, and the priests bearing the ark of the covenant before the people;

15 And as they that bare the ark were come unto Jordan, and the feet of the priests that bare the ark were dipped in the brim of the water, (for Jordan overfloweth all his banks all the time of harvest,)

16 That the waters which came down from above stood *and* rose up upon an heap very far from the city Adam, that *is* beside Zăr'e-tăn: and those that came down toward the sea of the plain, *even* the salt sea, failed, *and* were cut off: and the people passed over right against Jericho.

17 And the priests that bare the ark of the covenant of the LORD stood firm on dry ground in the midst of Jordan, and all the Israelites passed over on dry ground, until all the people were passed clean over Jordan.

CHAPTER 4

AND it came to pass, when all the people were clean passed over Jordan, that the LORD spake unto Joshua, saying,

2 Take you twelve men out of the people, out of every tribe a man,

3 And command ye them, saying, Take you hence out of the midst of Jordan, out of the place where the priests' feet stood firm, twelve stones, and ye shall carry them over with you, and leave them in the lodging place, where ye shall lodge this night.

4 Then Joshua called the twelve men, whom he had prepared of the children of Israel, out of every tribe a man:

5 And Joshua said unto them, Pass over before the ark of the LORD your God into the midst of Jordan, and take you up every man of you a stone upon his shoulder, according unto the number of the tribes of the children of Israel:

6 That this may be a sign among you, *that* when your children ask *their fathers* in time to come, saying, What *mean* ye by these stones?

7 Then ye shall answer them, That the waters of Jordan were cut off before the ark of the covenant of the LORD; when it passed over Jordan, the waters of Jordan were cut off: and these stones shall be for a memorial unto the children of Israel for ever.

8 And the children of Israel did so as Joshua commanded, and took up twelve stones out of the midst of Jordan, as the LORD spake unto Joshua, according to the number of the tribes of the children of Israel, and carried them over with them unto the place where they lodged, and laid them down there.

9 And Joshua set up twelve stones in

the midst of Jordan, in the place where the feet of the priests which bare the ark of the covenant stood: and they are there unto this day.

10 ¶For the priests which bare the ark stood in the midst of Jordan, until everything was finished that the LORD commanded Joshua to speak unto the people, according to all that Moses commanded Joshua: and the people hasted and passed over.

11 And it came to pass, when all the people were clean passed over, that the ark of the LORD passed over, and the priests, in the presence of the people.

12 And the children of Reuben, and the children of Gad, and half the tribe of Ma-năs′seh, passed over armed before the children of Israel, as Moses spake unto them:

13 About forty thousand prepared for war passed over before the LORD unto battle, to the plains of Jericho.

14 ¶On that day the LORD magnified Joshua in the sight of all Israel; and they feared him, as they feared Moses, all the days of his life.

15 ¶And the LORD spake unto Joshua, saying,

16 Command the priests that bear the ark of the testimony, that they come up out of Jordan.

17 Joshua therefore commanded the priests, saying, Come ye up out of Jordan.

18 And it came to pass, when the priests that bare the ark of the covenant of the LORD were come up out of the midst of Jordan, *and* the soles of the priests' feet were lifted up unto the dry land, that the waters of Jordan returned unto their place, and flowed over all his banks, as *they did* before.

19 ¶And the people came up out of Jordan on the tenth *day* of the first month, and encamped in Gilgal, in the east border of Jericho.

20 And those twelve stones, which they took out of Jordan, did Joshua pitch in Gilgal.

21 And he spake unto the children of Israel, saying, When your children shall ask their fathers in time to come, saying, What *mean* these stones?

22 Then ye shall let your children know, saying, Israel came over this Jordan on dry land.

23 For the LORD your God dried up the waters of Jordan from before you, until ye were passed over, as the LORD your God did to the Red sea, which he dried up from before us, until we were gone over:

24 That all the people of the earth might know the hand of the LORD, that it *is* mighty: that ye might fear the LORD your God for ever.

CHAPTER 5

AND it came to pass, when all the kings of the Ămorītes, which *were* on the side of Jordan westward, and all the kings of the Canaanites, which *were* by the sea, heard that the LORD had dried up the waters of Jordan from before the children of Israel, until we were passed over, that their heart melted, neither was there spirit in them any more, because of the children of Israel.

2 ¶At that time the LORD said unto Joshua, Make thee sharp knives, and circumcise again the children of Israel the second time.

3 And Joshua made him sharp knives, and circumcised the children of Israel at the hill of the foreskins.

4 And this *is* the cause why Joshua did circumcise: All the people that came out of Egypt, *that were* males, *even* all the men of war, died in the wilderness by the way, after they came out of Egypt.

5 Now all the people that came out were circumcised: but all the people *that were* born in the wilderness by the way as they came forth out of Egypt, *them* they had not circumcised.

6 For the children of Israel walked forty years in the wilderness, till all the people *that were* men of war, which came out of Egypt, were consumed, because they obeyed not the voice of the LORD: unto whom the LORD sware that he would not shew them the land, which the LORD sware unto their fathers that he would give us, a land that floweth with milk and honey.

7 And their children, *whom* he raised up in their stead, them Joshua circumcised: for they were uncircumcised, because they had not circumcised them by the way.

8 And it came to pass, when they had done circumcising all the people, that they abode in their places in the camp, till they were whole.

9 And the LORD said unto Joshua, This day have I rolled away the reproach of Egypt from off you. Wherefore the name of the place is called Gilgal unto this day.

10 ¶And the children of Israel encamped in Gilgal, and kept the passover on the fourteenth day of the month at even in the plains of Jericho.

11 And they did eat of the old corn of the land on the morrow after the passover, unleavened cakes, and parched *corn* in the selfsame day.

12 ¶And the manna ceased on the

morrow after they had eaten of the old corn of the land; neither had the children of Israel manna any more; but they did eat of the fruit of the land of Canaan that year.

13 ¶And it came to pass, when Joshua was by Jericho, that he lifted up his eyes and looked, and, behold, there stood a man over against him with his sword drawn in his hand: and Joshua went unto him, and said unto him, *Art* thou for us, or for our adversaries?

14 And he said, Nay; but *as* captain of the host of the LORD am I now come. And Joshua fell on his face to the earth, and did worship, and said unto him, What saith my lord unto his servant?

15 And the captain of the LORD's host said unto Joshua, Loose thy shoe from off thy foot; for the place whereon thou standest *is* holy. And Joshua did so.

CHAPTER 6

NOW Jericho was straitly shut up because of the children of Israel: none went out, and none came in.

2 And the LORD said unto Joshua, See, I have given into thine hand Jericho, and the king thereof, *and* the mighty men of valour.

3 And ye shall compass the city, all *ye* men of war, *and* go round about the city once. Thus shalt thou do six days.

4 And seven priests shall bear before the ark seven trumpets of rams' horns: and the seventh day ye shall compass the city seven times, and the priests shall blow with the trumpets.

5 And it shall come to pass, that when they make a long *blast* with the ram's horn, *and* when ye hear the sound of the trumpet, all the people shall shout with a great shout; and the wall of the city shall fall down flat, and the people shall ascend up every man straight before him.

6 ¶And Joshua the son of Nun called the priests, and said unto them, Take up the ark of the covenant, and let seven priests bear seven trumpets of rams' horns before the ark of the LORD.

7 And he said unto the people, Pass on, and compass the city, and let him that is armed pass on before the ark of the LORD.

8 ¶And it came to pass, when Joshua had spoken unto the people, that the seven priests bearing the seven trumpets of rams' horns passed on before the LORD, and blew with the trumpets: and the ark of the covenant of the LORD followed them.

9 And the armed men went before the priests that blew with the trumpets, and the rereward came after the ark, *the priests* going on, and blowing with the trumpets.

10 And Joshua had commanded the people, saying, Ye shall not shout, nor make any noise with your voice, neither shall *any* word proceed out of your mouth, until the day I bid you shout; then shall ye shout.

11 So the ark of the LORD compassed the city, going about *it* once: and they came into the camp, and lodged in the camp.

12 ¶And Joshua rose early in the morning, and the priests took up the ark of the LORD.

13 And seven priests bearing seven trumpets of rams' horns before the ark of the LORD went on continually, and blew with the trumpets: and the armed men went before them; but the rereward came after the ark of the LORD, *the priests* going on, and blowing with the trumpets.

14 And the second day they compassed the city once, and returned into the camp: so they did six days.

15 And it came to pass on the seventh day, that they rose early about the dawning of the day, and compassed the city after the same manner seven times: only on that day they compassed the city seven times.

16 And it came to pass at the seventh time, when the priests blew with the trumpets, Joshua said unto the people, Shout; for the LORD hath given you the city.

17 And the city shall be accursed, *even* it, and all that *are* therein, to the LORD: only Rahab the harlot shall live, she and all that *are* with her in the house, because she hid the messengers that we sent.

18 And ye, in any wise keep *yourselves* from the accursed thing, lest ye make *yourselves* accursed, when ye take of the accursed thing, and make the camp of Israel a curse, and trouble it.

19 But all the silver, and gold, and vessels of brass and iron, *are* consecrated unto the LORD: they shall come into the treasury of the LORD.

20 So the people shouted when *the priests* blew with the trumpets: and it came to pass, when the people heard the sound of the trumpet, and the people shouted with a great shout, that the wall fell down flat, so that the people went up into the city, every man straight before him, and they took the city.

21 And they utterly destroyed all that *was* in the city, both man and woman,

young and old, and ox, and sheep, and ass, with the edge of the sword.

22 But Joshua had said unto the two men that had spied out the country, Go into the harlot's house, and bring out thence the woman, and all that she hath, as ye sware unto her.

23 And the young men that were spies went in, and brought out Rahab, and her father, and her mother, and her brethren, and all that she had; and they brought out all her kindred, and left them without the camp of Israel.

24 And they burnt the city with fire, and all that *was* therein: only the silver, and the gold, and the vessels of brass and of iron, they put into the treasury of the house of the LORD.

25 And Joshua saved Rahab the harlot alive, and her father's household, and all that she had; and she dwelleth in Israel *even* unto this day; because she hid the messengers, which Joshua sent to spy out Jericho.

26 ¶And Joshua adjured *them* at that time, saying, Cursed *be* the man before the LORD, that riseth up and buildeth this city Jericho: he shall lay the foundation thereof in his firstborn, and in his youngest *son* shall he set up the gates of it.

27 So the LORD was with Joshua; and his fame was *noised* throughout all the country.

CHAPTER 7

BUT the children of Israel committed a trespass in the accursed thing: for Ā'chăn, the son of Căr'mī, the son of Zăb'dī, the son of Ze'rah, of the tribe of Judah, took of the accursed thing: and the anger of the LORD was kindled against the children of Israel.

2 And Joshua sent men from Jericho to Ā'ī, which *is* beside Bĕth-ā'ven, on the east side of Bĕth-el, and spake unto them, saying, Go up and view the country. And the men went up and viewed Ā'ī.

3 And they returned to Joshua, and said unto him, Let not all the people go up; but let about two or three thousand men go up and smite Ā'ī; *and* make not all the people to labour thither; for they *are but* few.

4 So there went up thither of the people about three thousand men: and they fled before the men of Ā'ī.

5 And the men of Ā'ī smote of them about thirty and six men: for they chased them *from* before the gate *even* unto Shĕb'a-rīm, and smote them in the going down: wherefore the hearts of the people melted, and became as water.

6 ¶And Joshua rent his clothes, and fell to the earth upon his face before the ark of the LORD until the eventide, he and the elders of Israel, and put dust upon their heads.

7 And Joshua said, Alas, O Lord GOD, wherefore hast thou at all brought this people over Jordan, to deliver us into the hand of the Amorites, to destroy us? would to God we had been content, and dwelt on the other side Jordan!

8 O Lord, what shall I say, when Israel turneth their backs before their enemies!

9 For the Canaanites and all the inhabitants of the land shall hear *of it*, and shall environ us round, and cut off our name from the earth: and what wilt thou do unto thy great name?

10 ¶And the LORD said unto Joshua, Get thee up; wherefore liest thou thus upon thy face?

11 Israel hath sinned, and they have also transgressed my covenant which I commanded them: for they have even taken of the accursed thing, and have also stolen, and dissembled also, and they have put *it* even among their own stuff.

12 Therefore the children of Israel could not stand before their enemies, *but* turned *their* backs before their enemies, because they were accursed: neither will I be with you any more, except ye destroy the accursed from among you.

13 Up, sanctify the people, and say, Sanctify yourselves against to morrow: for thus saith the LORD God of Israel, *There is* an accursed thing in the midst of thee, O Israel: thou canst not stand before thine enemies, until ye take away the accursed thing from among you.

14 In the morning therefore ye shall be brought according to your tribes: and it shall be, *that* the tribe which the LORD taketh shall come according to the families *thereof*; and the family which the LORD shall take shall come by households; and the household which the LORD shall take shall come man by man.

15 And it shall be, *that* he that is taken with the accursed thing shall be burnt with fire, he and all that he hath: because he hath transgressed the covenant of the LORD, and because he hath wrought folly in Israel.

16 ¶So Joshua rose up early in the morning, and brought Israel by their tribes; and the tribe of Judah was taken:

17 And he brought the family of Judah; and he took the family of the

Zär′hītes: and he brought the family of
the Zär′hītes man by man; and Zăb′dī
was taken:
18 And he brought his household
man by man; and Ā′chăn, the son of
Cär′mī, the son of Zăb′dī, the son of
Ze′rah, of the tribe of Jūdah, was taken.
19 And Joshua said unto Ā′chăn, My
son, give, I pray thee, glory to the LORD
God of Israel, and make confession
unto him; and tell me now what thou
hast done; hide *it* not from me.
20 And Ā′chăn answered Joshua, and
said, Indeed I have sinned against the
LORD God of Israel, and thus and thus
have I done:
21 When I saw among the spoils a
goodly Babylonish garment, and two
hundred shekels of silver, and a wedge
of gold of fifty shekels weight, then I
coveted them, and took them; and, be-
hold, they *are* hid in the earth in the
midst of my tent, and the silver under
it.
22 So Joshua sent messengers, and
they ran unto the tent; and, behold, *it
was* hid in his tent, and the silver under
it.
23 And they took them out of the
midst of the tent, and brought them
unto Joshua, and unto all the children
of Israel, and laid them out before the
LORD.
24 And Joshua, and all Israel with
him, took Ā′chăn the son of Ze′rah, and
the silver, and the garment, and the
wedge of gold, and his sons, and his
daughters, and his oxen, and his asses,
and his sheep, and his tent, and all that
he had: and they brought them unto the
valley of Ā′chôr.
25 And Joshua said, Why hast thou
troubled us? the LORD shall trouble thee
this day. And all Israel stoned him with
stones, and burned them with fire, after
they had stoned them with stones.
26 And they raised over him a great
heap of stones unto this day. So the
LORD turned from the fierceness of his
anger. Wherefore the name of that
place was called, The valley of Ā′chôr,
unto this day.

CHAPTER 8

AND the LORD said unto Joshua, Fear
not, neither be thou dismayed: take all
the people of war with thee, and arise,
go up to Ā′ī: see, I have given into thy
hand the king of Ā′ī, and his people, and
his city, and his land:
2 And thou shalt do to Ā′ī and her
king as thou didst unto Jericho and her
king: only the spoil thereof, and the
cattle thereof, shall ye take for a prey
unto yourselves: lay thee an ambush
for the city behind it.
3 ¶So Joshua arose, and all the people
of war, to go up against Ā′ī: and Joshua
chose out thirty thousand mighty men
of valour, and sent them away by night.
4 And he commanded them, saying,
Behold, ye shall lie in wait against the
city, *even* behind the city: go not very
far from the city, but be ye all ready:
5 And I, and all the people that *are*
with me, will approach unto the city:
and it shall come to pass, when they
come out against us, as at the first, that
we will flee before them,
6 (For they will come out after us) till
we have drawn them from the city; for
they will say, They flee before us, as at
the first: therefore we will flee before
them.
7 Then ye shall rise up from the am-
bush, and seize upon the city: for the
LORD your God will deliver it into your
hand.
8 And it shall be, when ye have taken
the city, *that* ye shall set the city on fire:
according to the commandment of the
LORD shall ye do. See, I have com-
manded you.
9 Joshua therefore sent them forth:
and they went to lie in ambush, and
abode between Bĕth-el and Ā′ī, on the
west side of Ā′ī: but Joshua lodged that
night among the people.
10 And Joshua rose up early in the
morning, and numbered the people,
and went up, he and the elders of Israel,
before the people to Ā′ī.
11 And all the people, *even the people*
of war that *were* with him, went up,
and drew nigh, and came before the
city, and pitched on the north side of
Ā′ī: now *there was* a valley between
them and Ā′ī.
12 And he took about five thousand
men, and set them to lie in ambush be-
tween Bĕth-el and Ā′ī, on the west side
of the city.
13 And when they had set the people,
even all the host that *was* on the north
of the city, and their liers in wait on the
west of the city, Joshua went that night
into the midst of the valley.
14 And it came to pass, when the king
of Ā′ī saw *it*, that they hasted and rose
up early, and the men of the city went
out against Israel to battle, he and all
his people, at a time appointed, before
the plain; but he wist not that *there
were* liers in ambush against him be-
hind the city.
15 And Joshua and all Israel made as
if they were beaten before them, and
fled by the way of the wilderness.
16 And all the people that *were* in Ā′ī

were called together to pursue after them: and they pursued after Joshua, and were drawn away from the city.

17 And there was not a man left in Ā′ī or Bĕth-el, that went not out after Israel: and they left the city open, and pursued after Israel.

18 And the LORD said unto Joshua, Stretch out the spear that *is* in thy hand toward Ā′ī; for I will give it into thine hand. And Joshua stretched out the spear that *he had* in his hand toward the city.

19 And the ambush arose quickly out of their place, and they ran as soon as he had stretched out his hand: and they entered into the city, and took it, and hasted and set the city on fire.

20 And when the men of Ā′ī looked behind them, they saw, and, behold, the smoke of the city ascended up to heaven, and they had no power to flee this way or that way: and the people that fled to the wilderness turned back upon the pursuers.

21 And when Joshua and all Israel saw that the ambush had taken the city, and that the smoke of the city ascended, then they turned again, and slew the men of Ā′ī.

22 And the other issued out of the city against them; so they were in the midst of Israel, some on this side, and some on that side: and they smote them, so that they let none of them remain or escape.

23 And the king of Ā′ī they took alive, and brought him to Joshua.

24 And it came to pass, when Israel had made an end of slaying all the inhabitants of Ā′ī in the field, in the wilderness wherein they chased them, and when they were all fallen on the edge of the sword, until they were consumed, that all the Israelites returned unto Ā′ī, and smote it with the edge of the sword.

25 And *so* it was, *that* all that fell that day, both of men and women, *were* twelve thousand, *even* all the men of Ā′ī.

26 For Joshua drew not his hand back, wherewith he stretched out the spear, until he had utterly destroyed all the inhabitants of Ā′ī.

27 Only the cattle and the spoil of that city Israel took for a prey unto themselves, according unto the word of the LORD which he commanded Joshua.

28 And Joshua burnt Ā′ī, and made it an heap for ever, *even* a desolation unto this day.

29 And the king of Ā′ī he hanged on a tree until eventide: and as soon as the sun was down, Joshua commanded that they should take his carcase down from the tree, and cast it at the entering of the gate of the city, and raise thereon a great heap of stones, *that remaineth* unto this day.

30 ¶Then Joshua built an altar unto the LORD God of Israel in mount Ebal,

31 As Moses the servant of the LORD commanded the children of Israel, as it is written in the book of the law of Moses, an altar of whole stones, over which no man hath lift up *any* iron: and they offered thereon burnt offerings unto the LORD, and sacrificed peace offerings.

32 And he wrote there upon the stones a copy of the law of Moses, which he wrote in the presence of the children of Israel.

33 And all Israel, and their elders, and officers, and their judges, stood on this side the ark and on that side before the priests the Levites, which bare the ark of the covenant of the LORD, as well the stranger, as he that was born among them; half of them over against mount Gĕr′i-zīm, and half of them over against mount Ebal; as Moses the servant of the LORD had commanded before, that they should bless the people of Israel.

34 And afterward he read all the words of the law, the blessings and cursings, according to all that is written in the book of the law.

35 There was not a word of all that Moses commanded, which Joshua read not before all the congregation of Israel, with the women, and the little ones, and the strangers that were conversant among them.

CHAPTER 9

AND it came to pass, when all the kings which *were* on this side Jordan, in the hills, and in the valleys, and in all the coasts of the great sea over against Lebanon, the Hittite, and the Ămorīte, the Canaanite, the Pĕr′iz-zīte, the Hī′vīte, and the Jēb′u-sīte, heard *thereof;*

2 That they gathered themselves together, to fight with Joshua and with Israel, with one accord.

3 ¶And when the inhabitants of Gĭb′eon heard what Joshua had done unto Jericho and to Ā′ī,

4 They did work wilily, and went and made as if they had been ambassadors, and took old sacks upon their asses, and wine bottles, old, and rent, and bound up;

5 And old shoes and clouted upon their feet, and old garments upon them;

and all the bread of their provision was
dry *and* mouldy.
6 And they went to Joshua unto the
camp at Gilgal, and said unto him, and
to the men of Israel, We be come from a
far country: now therefore make ye a
league with us.
7 And the men of Israel said unto the
Hī'vītes, Peradventure ye dwell among
us; and how shall we make a league
with you?
8 And they said unto Joshua, We *are*
thy servants. And Joshua said unto
them, Who *are* ye? and from whence
come ye?
9 And they said unto him, From a
very far country thy servants are come
because of the name of the LORD thy
God: for we have heard the fame of
him, and all that he did in Egypt,
10 And all that he did to the two kings
of the Ămorītes, that *were* beyond Jor-
dan, to Sihon king of Hĕsh'bŏn, and to
Og king of Bā'shan, which *was* at
Ăsh'ta-rŏth.
11 Wherefore our elders and all the
inhabitants of our country spake to us,
saying, Take victuals with you for the
journey, and go to meet them, and say
unto them, We *are* your servants: there-
fore now make ye a league with us.
12 This our bread we took hot *for* our
provision out of our houses on the day
we came forth to go unto you; but now,
behold, it is dry, and it is mouldy:
13 And these bottles of wine, which
we filled, *were* new; and, behold, they
be rent: and these our garments and
our shoes are become old by reason of
the very long journey.
14 And the men took of their victuals,
and asked not *counsel* at the mouth of
the LORD.
15 And Joshua made peace with
them, and made a league with them, to
let them live: and the princes of the
congregation sware unto them.
16 ¶And it came to pass at the end of
three days after they had made a
league with them, that they heard that
they *were* their neighbours, and *that*
they dwelt among them.
17 And the children of Israel jour-
neyed, and came unto their cities on the
third day. Now their cities *were* Gĭb-
eon, and Che-phī'rah, and Bē-ē'rŏth,
and Kir'jath-jē'a-rĭm.
18 And the children of Israel smote
them not, because the princes of the
congregation had sworn unto them by
the LORD God of Israel. And all the
congregation murmured against the
princes.
19 But all the princes said unto all the
congregation, We have sworn unto
them by the LORD God of Israel: now
therefore we may not touch them.
20 This we will do to them; we will
even let them live, lest wrath be upon
us, because of the oath which we sware
unto them.
21 And the princes said unto them,
Let them live; but let them be hewers of
wood and drawers of water unto all the
congregation; as the princes had prom-
ised them.
22 ¶And Joshua called for them, and
he spake unto them, saying, Wherefore
have ye beguiled us, saying, We *are*
very far from you; when ye dwell
among us?
23 Now therefore ye *are* cursed, and
there shall none of you be freed from
being bondmen, and hewers of wood
and drawers of water for the house of
my God.
24 And they answered Joshua, and
said, Because it was certainly told thy
servants, how that the LORD thy God
commanded his servant Moses to give
you all the land, and to destroy all the
inhabitants of the land from before
you, therefore we were sore afraid of
our lives because of you, and have done
this thing.
25 And now, behold, we *are* in thine
hand: as it seemeth good and right unto
thee to do unto us, do.
26 And so did he unto them, and de-
livered them out of the hand of the
children of Israel, that they slew them
not.
27 And Joshua made them that day
hewers of wood and drawers of water
for the congregation, and for the altar
of the LORD, even unto this day, in the
place which he should choose.

CHAPTER 10

NOW it came to pass, when A-dō'nī-
zē'dĕc king of Jerusalem had heard
how Joshua had taken Ā'ī, and had ut-
terly destroyed it; as he had done to
Jericho and her king, so he had done to
Ā'ī and her king; and how the inhabi-
tants of Gĭbeon had made peace with
Israel, and were among them;
2 That they feared greatly, because
Gibeon *was* a great city, as one of the
royal cities, and because it *was* greater
than Ā'ī, and all the men thereof *were*
mighty.
3 Wherefore A-dō'nī-zē'dĕc king of
Jerusalem sent unto Hō-hăm king of
Hĕbron, and unto Pī'ram king of Jär'-
mŭth, and unto Ja-phī'a king of Lā'-
chĭsh, and unto Dē'bir king of Ĕg'-
lŏn, saying,
4 Come up unto me, and help me, that
we may smite Gĭbeon: for it hath made

peace with Joshua and with the children of Israel.

5 Therefore the five kings of the Ămorītes, the king of Jerusalem, the king of Hēbron, the king of Jär'mŭth, the king of Lā'chĭsh, the king of Ĕg'lŏn, gathered themselves together, and went up, they and all their hosts, and encamped before Gĭbeon, and made war against it.

6 ¶And the men of Gĭbeon sent unto Joshua to the camp to Gilgal, saying, Slack not thy hand from thy servants; come up to us quickly, and save us, and help us: for all the kings of the Ămorītes that dwell in the mountains are gathered together against us.

7 So Joshua ascended from Gilgal, he, and all the people of war with him, and all the mighty men of valour.

8 ¶And the LORD said unto Joshua, Fear them not: for I have delivered them into thine hand; there shall not a man of them stand before thee.

9 Joshua therefore came unto them suddenly, *and* went up from Gilgal all night.

10 And the LORD discomfited them before Israel, and slew them with a great slaughter at Gĭbeon, and chased them along the way that goeth up to Bĕth-hô'ron, and smote them to A-zē'kah, and unto Mak-kē'dah.

11 And it came to pass, as they fled from before Israel, *and* were in the going down to Bĕth-hô'ron, that the LORD cast down great stones from heaven upon them unto A-zē'kah, and they died: *they were* more which died with hailstones than *they* whom the children of Israel slew with the sword.

12 ¶Then spake Joshua to the LORD in the day when the LORD delivered up the Amorites before the children of Israel, and he said in the sight of Israel, Sun, stand thou still upon Gĭbeon; and thou, Moon, in the valley of Ăj'a-lŏn.

13 And the sun stood still, and the moon stayed, until the people had avenged themselves upon their enemies. *Is* not this written in the book of Jā'sher? So the sun stood still in the midst of heaven, and hasted not to go down about a whole day.

14 And there was no day like that before it or after it, that the LORD hearkened unto the voice of a man: for the LORD fought for Israel.

15 ¶And Joshua returned, and all Israel with him, unto the camp to Gilgal.

16 But these five kings fled, and hid themselves in a cave at Mak-kē'dah.

17 And it was told Joshua, saying, The five kings are found hid in a cave at Mak-kē'dah.

18 And Joshua said, Roll great stones upon the mouth of the cave, and set men by it for to keep them:

19 And stay ye not, *but* pursue after your enemies, and smite the hindmost of them; suffer them not to enter into their cities: for the LORD your God hath delivered them into your hand.

20 And it came to pass, when Joshua and the children of Israel had made an end of slaying them with a very great slaughter, till they were consumed, that the rest *which* remained of them entered into fenced cities.

21 And all the people returned to the camp to Joshua at Mak-kē'dah in peace: none moved his tongue against any of the children of Israel.

22 Then said Joshua, Open the mouth of the cave, and bring out those five kings unto me out of the cave.

23 And they did so, and brought forth those five kings unto him out of the cave, the king of Jerusalem, the king of Hēbron, the king of Jär'mŭth, the king of Lā'chĭsh, *and* the king of Ĕg'lŏn.

24 And it came to pass, when they brought out those kings unto Joshua, that Joshua called for all the men of Israel, and said unto the captains of the men of war which went with him, Come near, put your feet upon the necks of these kings. And they came near, and put their feet upon the necks of them.

25 And Joshua said unto them, Fear not, nor be dismayed, be strong and of good courage: for thus shall the LORD do to all your enemies against whom ye fight.

26 And afterward Joshua smote them, and slew them, and hanged them on five trees: and they were hanging upon the trees until the evening.

27 And it came to pass at the time of the going down of the sun, *that* Joshua commanded, and they took them down off the trees, and cast them into the cave wherein they had been hid, and laid great stones in the cave's mouth, *which remain* until this very day.

28 ¶And that day Joshua took Mak-kē'dah, and smote it with the edge of the sword, and the king thereof he utterly destroyed, them, and all the souls that *were* therein; he let none remain: and he did to the king of Mak-kē'dah as he did unto the king of Jericho.

29 Then Joshua passed from Mak-kē'dah, and all Israel with him, unto Lĭb'nah, and fought against Lĭb'nah:

30 And the LORD delivered it also, and the king thereof, into the hand of Israel;

and he smote it with the edge of the sword, and all the souls that *were* therein; he let none remain in it; but did unto the king thereof as he did unto the king of Jericho.
31 ¶And Joshua passed from Lĭb'nah, and all Israel with him, unto Lā'chĭsh, and encamped against it, and fought against it:
32 And the LORD delivered Lā'chĭsh into the hand of Israel, which took it on the second day, and smote it with the edge of the sword, and all the souls that *were* therein, according to all that he had done to Lĭb'nah.
33 ¶Then Hô'răm king of Gē'zer came up to help Lā'chĭsh; and Joshua smote him and his people, until he had left him none remaining.
34 ¶And from Lā'chĭsh Joshua passed unto Ĕg'lŏn, and all Israel with him; and they encamped against it, and fought against it:
35 And they took it on that day, and smote it with the edge of the sword, and all the souls that *were* therein he utterly destroyed that day, according to all that he had done to Lā'chĭsh.
36 And Joshua went up from Ĕg'lŏn, and all Israel with him, unto Hēbron; and they fought against it:
37 And they took it, and smote it with the edge of the sword, and the king thereof, and all the cities thereof, and all the souls that *were* therein; he left none remaining, according to all that he had done to Ĕg'lŏn; but destroyed it utterly, and all the souls that *were* therein.
38 ¶And Joshua returned, and all Israel with him, to Dē'bir; and fought against it:
39 And he took it, and the king thereof, and all the cities thereof; and they smote them with the edge of the sword, and utterly destroyed all the souls that *were* therein; he left none remaining: as he had done to Hēbron, so he did to Dē'bir, and to the king thereof; as he had done also to Lĭb'nah, and to her king.
40 ¶So Joshua smote all the country of the hills, and of the south, and of the vale, and of the springs, and all their kings: he left none remaining, but utterly destroyed all that breathed, as the LORD God of Israel commanded.
41 And Joshua smote them from Kā'desh-bär'ne-a even unto Gā'za, and all the country of Goshen, even unto Gĭbeon.
42 And all these kings and their land did Joshua take at one time, because the LORD God of Israel fought for Israel.
43 And Joshua returned, and all Israel with him, unto the camp to Gilgal.

CHAPTER 11

AND it came to pass, when Jā'bin king of Hā'zôr had heard *those things*, that he sent to Jō'băb king of Mā'dŏn, and to the king of Shĭm'rŏn, and to the king of Ăch'shăph,
2 And to the kings that *were* on the north of the mountains, and of the plains south of Chĭn'ne-rŏth, and in the valley, and in the borders of Dor on the west,
3 *And to* the Canaanite on the east and on the west, and *to* the Ămorīte, and the Hittite, and the Pĕr'iz-zīte, and the Jēb'u-sīte in the mountains, and *to* the Hī'vīte under Hermon in the land of Mĭz'peh.
4 And they went out, they and all their hosts with them, much people, even as the sand that *is* upon the sea shore in multitude, with horses and chariots very many.
5 And when all these kings were met together, they came and pitched together at the waters of Me'rom, to fight against Israel.
6 ¶And the LORD said unto Joshua, Be not afraid because of them: for to morrow about this time will I deliver them up all slain before Israel: thou shalt hough their horses, and burn their chariots with fire.
7 So Joshua came, and all the people of war with him, against them by the waters of Me'rom suddenly; and they fell upon them.
8 And the LORD delivered them into the hand of Israel, who smote them, and chased them unto great Zī'don, and unto Mĭs're-phŏth-mā'im, and unto the valley of Mĭz'peh eastward; and they smote them, until they left them none remaining.
9 And Joshua did unto them as the LORD bade him: he houghed their horses, and burnt their chariots with fire.
10 ¶And Joshua at that time turned back, and took Hā'zôr, and smote the king thereof with the sword: for Hā'zôr beforetime was the head of all those kingdoms.
11 And they smote all the souls that *were* therein with the edge of the sword, utterly destroying *them:* there was not any left to breathe: and he burnt Hā'zôr with fire.
12 And all the cities of those kings, and all the kings of them, did Joshua take, and smote them with the edge of the sword, *and* he utterly destroyed

them, as Moses the servant of the LORD commanded.

13 But *as for* the cities that stood still in their strength, Israel burned none of them, save Hā'zôr only; *that* did Joshua burn.

14 And all the spoil of these cities, and the cattle the children of Israel took for a prey unto themselves; but every man they smote with the edge of the sword, until they had destroyed them, neither left they any to breathe.

15 As the LORD commanded Moses his servant, so did Moses command Joshua, and so did Joshua; he left nothing undone of all that the LORD commanded Moses.

16 So Joshua took all that land, the hills, and all the south country, and all the land of Goshen, and the valley, and the plain, and the mountain of Israel, and the valley of the same;

17 *Even* from the mount Hā'lăk, that goeth up to Sē'ir, even unto Bā'al-găd in the valley of Lebanon under mount Hermon: and all their kings he took, and smote them, and slew them.

18 Joshua made war a long time with all those kings.

19 There was not a city that made peace with the children of Israel, save the Hī'vītes the inhabitants of Gĭbeon: all *other* they took in battle.

20 For it was of the LORD to harden their hearts, that they should come against Israel in battle, that he might destroy them utterly, *and* that they might have no favour, but that he might destroy them, as the LORD commanded Moses.

21 ¶And at that time came Joshua, and cut off the Anakims from the mountains, from Hēbron, from Dē'bir, from Anăb, and from all the mountains of Judah, and from all the mountains of Israel: Joshua destroyed them utterly with their cities.

22 There was none of the Anakims left in the land of the children of Israel: only in Gā'za, in Gath, and in Ăsh'dŏd, there remained.

23 So Joshua took the whole land, according to all that the LORD said unto Moses; and Joshua gave it for an inheritance unto Israel according to their divisions by their tribes. And the land rested from war.

CHAPTER 12

NOW these *are* the kings of the land, which the children of Israel smote, and possessed their land on the other side Jordan toward the rising of the sun, from the river Arnon unto mount Hermon, and all the plain on the east:

2 Sihon king of the Ămorītes, who dwelt in Hĕsh'bŏn, *and* ruled from Ar'ō-er, which *is* upon the bank of the river Arnon, and from the middle of the river, and from half Gilead, even unto the river Jabbok, *which is* the border of the children of Ammon;

3 And from the plain to the sea of Chĭn'ne-rŏth on the east, and unto the sea of the plain, *even* the salt sea on the east, the way to Bĕth-jĕsh'i-mŏth; and from the south, under Ăsh'dŏth-pĭs'gah:

4 And the coast of Og king of Bā'shan, *which was* of the remnant of the giants, that dwelt at Ăsh'ta-rŏth and at Ĕd're-ī,

5 And reigned in mount Hermon, and in Săl'cah, and in all Bā'shan, unto the border of the Gĕsh'u-rītes, and the Mā-ăch'a-thītes, and half Gilead, the border of Sihon king of Hĕsh'bŏn.

6 Them did Moses the servant of the LORD and the children of Israel smite: and Moses the servant of the LORD gave it *for* a possession unto the Reubenites, and the Gădītes, and the half tribe of Ma-năs'seh.

7 ¶And these *are* the kings of the country which Joshua and the children of Israel smote on this side Jordan on the west, from Bā'al-găd in the valley of Lebanon even unto the mount Hā'lăk, that goeth up to Sē'ir; which Joshua gave unto the tribes of Israel *for* a possession according to their divisions;

8 In the mountains, and in the valleys, and in the plains, and in the springs, and in the wilderness, and in the south country; the Hittites, the Ămorītes, and the Canaanites, the Pĕr'izzītes, the Hī'vītes, and the Jēb'u-sītes:

9 The king of Jericho, one; the king of Ā'ī, which *is* beside Bĕth-el, one;

10 The king of Jerusalem, one; the king of Hēbron, one;

11 The king of Jär'mŭth, one; the king of Lā'chĭsh, one;

12 The king of Ĕg'lŏn, one; the king of Gē'zer, one;

13 The king of Dē'bir, one; the king of Gē'der, one;

14 The king of Hôr'mah, one; the king of Ā'răd, one;

15 The king of Lĭb'nah, one; the king of Adŭllam, one;

16 The king of Mak-kē'dah, one; the king of Bĕth-el, one;

17 The king of Tăp'pū-ah, one; the king of Hē'pher, one;

18 The king of Ā'phĕk, one; the king of Lă-shâr'on, one;

19 The king of Mā'dŏn, one; the king of Hā'zôr, one;

20 The king of Shĭm'rŏn-me'rŏn, one; the king of Ăch'shăph, one;

21 The king of Tā'a-năch, one; the
king of Me-gĭd'dō, one;
22 The king of Kē'dĕsh, one; the king
of Jŏk'ne-am of Carmel, one;
23 The king of Dor in the coast of Dor,
one; the king of the nations of Gilgal,
one;
24 The king of Tir'zah, one: all the
kings thirty and one.

CHAPTER 13

NOW Joshua was old *and* stricken in
years; and the LORD said unto him,
Thou art old *and* stricken in years, and
there remaineth yet very much land to
be possessed.
2 This *is* the land that yet remaineth:
all the borders of the Philistines, and all
Gĕsh'u-rī,
3 From Sī'hôr, which *is* before Egypt,
even unto the borders of Ēkron north-
ward, *which* is counted to the Canaan-
ite: five lords of the Philistines; the
Gā'zath-ītes, and the Ăsh'dŏth-ītes, the
Ĕsh'ka-lon-ītes, the Gĭt'tītes, and the
Ĕkronītes; also the Ā'vītes:
4 From the south, all the land of the
Canaanites, and Mē-â'rah that *is* beside
the Si-dō'ni-ans, unto Ā'phĕk, to the
borders of the Ămorītes:
5 And the land of the Gĭb'lītes, and all
Lebanon, toward the sunrising, from
Bā'al-găd under mount Hermon unto
the entering into Hā'măth.
6 All the inhabitants of the hill coun-
try from Lebanon unto Mĭs're-
phŏth-mā'im, *and* all the Si-dō'ni-ans,
them will I drive out from before the
children of Israel: only divide thou it by
lot unto the Israelites for an inheri-
tance, as I have commanded thee.
7 Now therefore divide this land for
an inheritance unto the nine tribes, and
the half tribe of Ma-năs'seh,
8 With whom the Reubenites and the
Gădītes have received their inheri-
tance, which Moses gave them, beyond
Jordan eastward, *even* as Moses the
servant of the LORD gave them;
9 From Ar'ō-er, that *is* upon the bank
of the river Arnon, and the city that *is* in
the midst of the river, and all the plain
of Mĕd'e-ba unto Dī'bŏn;
10 And all the cities of Sihon king of
the Ămorītes, which reigned in Hĕsh'-
bŏn, unto the border of the children of
Ammon;
11 And Gilead, and the border of the
Gĕsh'u-rītes and Mā-ăch'a-thītes, and
all mount Hermon, and all Bā'shan
unto Săl'cah;
12 All the kingdom of Og in Bā'shan,
which reigned in Ăsh'ta-rŏth and in
Ĕd're-ī, who remained of the remnant
of the giants: for these did Moses smite,
and cast them out.
13 Nevertheless the children of Israel
expelled not the Gĕsh'u-rītes, nor the
Mā-ăch'a-thītes: but the Gĕsh'u-rītes
and the Mā-ăch'a-thītes dwell among
the Israelites until this day.
14 Only unto the tribe of Levi he gave
none inheritance; the sacrifices of the
LORD God of Israel made by fire *are*
their inheritance, as he said unto them.
15 ¶And Moses gave unto the tribe of
the children of Reuben *inheritance* ac-
cording to their families.
16 And their coast was from Ar'ō-er,
that *is* on the bank of the river Arnon,
and the city that *is* in the midst of the
river, and all the plain by Mĕd'e-ba;
17 Hĕsh'bŏn, and all her cities that
are in the plain; Dī'bŏn, and Bā'-
mŏth-bā'al, and Bĕth-bā'al-mē'ŏn,
18 And Ja-hā'za, and Kĕd'e-mŏth,
and Mĕph'a-ăth,
19 And Kĭr-jath-ā'ĭm, and Sĭb'mah,
and Zā'reth-shā'här in the mount of the
valley,
20 And Bĕth-pē'ôr, and Ăsh'-
dŏth-pĭs'gah, and Bĕth-jĕsh'i-mŏth,
21 And all the cities of the plain, and
all the kingdom of Sihon king of the
Amorites, which reigned in Hĕsh'bŏn,
whom Moses smote with the princes of
Mĭd'ī-an, Ē'vī, and Rē'kem, and Zur,
and Hur, and Rē'ba, *which were* dukes
of Sihon, dwelling in the country.
22 ¶Bā'laam also the son of Bē'ôr, the
soothsayer, did the children of Israel
slay with the sword among them that
were slain by them.
23 And the border of the children of
Reuben was Jordan, and the border
thereof. This *was* the inheritance of the
children of Reuben after their families,
the cities and the villages thereof.
24 ¶And Moses gave *inheritance* unto
the tribe of Gad, *even* unto the children
of Gad according to their families.
25 And their coast was Jā'zer, and all
the cities of Gilead, and half the land of
the children of Ammon, unto Ar'ō-er
that *is* before Răb'bah;
26 And from Hĕsh'bŏn unto Rā-
math-mĭz'peh, and Bĕt'o-nĭm; and from
Mā-ha-nā'im unto the border of Dē'bir;
27 And in the valley, Bĕth-a'râm, and
Bĕth-nĭm'rah, and Sŭc'coth, and
Zā'phŏn, the rest of the kingdom of Si-
hon king of Hĕsh'bŏn, Jordan and *his*
border, *even* unto the edge of the sea of
Chĭn'ne-rĕth on the other side Jordan
eastward.
28 This *is* the inheritance of the chil-
dren of Gad after their families, the
cities, and their villages.
29 ¶And Moses gave *inheritance* unto

the half tribe of Ma-năs'seh: and *this* was *the possession* of the half tribe of the children of Ma-năs'seh by their families.

30 And their coast was from Mā-ha-nā'im, all Bā'shan, all the kingdom of Og king of Bā'shan, and all the towns of Jā'ir, which *are* in Bā'shan, threescore cities:

31 And half Gilead, and Ăsh'ta-rŏth, and Ĕd're-ī, cities of the kingdom of Og in Bā'shan, *were pertaining* unto the children of Mā'chīr the son of Ma'năs'-seh, *even* to the one half of the children of Mā'chīr by their families.

32 These *are the countries* which Moses did distribute for inheritance in the plains of Moab, on the other side Jordan, by Jericho, eastward.

33 But unto the tribe of Levi Moses gave not *any* inheritance: the LORD God of Israel *was* their inheritance, as he said unto them.

CHAPTER 14

AND these *are the countries* which the children of Israel inherited in the land of Canaan, which Ĕ-le-ā'zar the priest, and Joshua the son of Nun, and the heads of the fathers of the tribes of the children of Israel, distributed for inheritance to them.

2 By lot *was* their inheritance, as the LORD commanded by the hand of Moses, for the nine tribes, and *for* the half tribe.

3 For Moses had given the inheritance of two tribes and an half tribe on the other side Jordan: but unto the Lē'vītes he gave none inheritance among them.

4 For the children of Joseph were two tribes, Ma-năs'seh and Ē'phra-im: therefore they gave no part unto the Lē-vītes in the land, save cities to dwell *in*, with their suburbs for their cattle and for their substance.

5 As the LORD commanded Moses, so the children of Israel did, and they divided the land.

6 ¶Then the children of Jūdah came unto Joshua in Gilgal: and Caleb the son of Je-phŭn'neh the Kĕn'ez-īte said unto him, Thou knowest the thing that the LORD said unto Moses the man of God concerning me and thee in Kā'-desh–bär'ne-a.

7 Forty years old *was* I when Moses the servant of the LORD sent me from Kā'desh–bär'ne-a to espy out the land; and I brought him word again as *it was* in mine heart.

8 Nevertheless my brethren that went up with me made the heart of the people melt: but I wholly followed the LORD my God.

9 And Moses sware on that day, saying, Surely the land whereon thy feet have trodden shall be thine inheritance, and thy children's for ever, because thou hast wholly followed the LORD my God.

10 And now, behold, the LORD hath kept me alive, as he said, these forty and five years, even since the LORD spake this word unto Moses, while *the children of* Israel wandered in the wilderness: and now, lo, I *am* this day fourscore and five years old.

11 As yet I *am as* strong this day as *I was* in the day that Moses sent me: as my strength *was* then, even so *is* my strength now, for war, both to go out, and to come in.

12 Now therefore give me this mountain, whereof the LORD spake in that day; for thou heardest in that day how the Anakims *were* there, and *that* the cities *were* great *and* fenced: if so be the LORD *will be* with me, then I shall be able to drive them out, as the LORD said.

13 And Joshua blessed him, and gave unto Caleb the son of Je-phŭn'neh Hē-bron for an inheritance.

14 Hēbron therefore became the inheritance of Caleb the son of Je-phŭn'-neh the Kĕn'ez-īte unto this day, because that he wholly followed the LORD God of Israel.

15 And the name of Hēbron before *was* Kir'jath–är'ba; *which Ar'ba was* a great man among the Anakims. And the land had rest from war.

CHAPTER 15

THIS then was the lot of the tribe of the children of Jūdah by their families; *even* to the border of Ēdom the wilderness of Zin southward *was* the uttermost part of the south coast.

2 And their south border was from the shore of the salt sea, from the bay that looketh southward:

3 And it went out to the south side to Mā-al'eh–ă-crăb'bĭm, and passed along to Zin, and ascended up on the south side unto Kā'desh–bär'ne-a, and passed along to Hĕz'ron, and went up to Ā'där, and fetched a compass to Kär'ka-a:

4 *From thence* it passed toward Ăz'mon, and went out unto the river of Egypt; and the goings out of that coast were at the sea: this shall be your south coast.

5 And the east border *was* the salt sea, *even* unto the end of Jordan. And *their* border in the north quarter *was* from the bay of the sea at the uttermost part of Jordan:

6 And the border went up to
Bĕth–hŏg'la, and passed along by the
north of Bĕth–ăr'a-bah; and the border
went up to the stone of Bō'hăn the son
of Reuben:
7 And the border went up toward
Dē'bir from the valley of Ā'chôr, and so
northward, looking toward Gilgal, that
is before the going up to A-dŭm'mĭm,
which *is* on the south side of the river:
and the border passed toward the wa-
ters of Ĕn–shĕ'-mesh, and the goings
out thereof were at Ĕn–rō'gel:
8 And the border went up by the val-
ley of the son of Hĭn'nom unto the
south side of the Jēb'u-sīte; the same *is*
Jerusalem: and the border went up to
the top of the mountain that *lieth* be-
fore the valley of Hĭn'nom westward,
which *is* at the end of the valley of the
giants northward:
9 And the border was drawn from the
top of the hill unto the fountain of the
water of Nĕph'tō-ah, and went out to
the cities of mount Ē'phrŏn; and the
border was drawn to Bā'al-ah, which *is*
Kir'jath–jē'a-rĭm:
10 And the border compassed from
Bā'al-ah westward unto mount Sē'ir,
and passed along unto the side of
mount Jē'a-rĭm, which *is* Chĕs'a-lŏn, on
the north side, and went down to
Bĕth–shĕ'mesh, and passed on to Tĭm'-
nah:
11 And the border went out unto the
side of Ekron northward: and the bor-
der was drawn to Shĭ'crŏn, and passed
along to mount Bā'al-ah, and went out
unto Jăb'ne-el; and the goings out of
the border were at the sea.
12 And the west border *was* to the
great sea, and the coast *thereof*. This *is*
the coast of the children of Jūdah round
about according to their families.
13 ¶And unto Caleb the son of Je-
phŭn'neh he gave a part among the
children of Jūdah, according to the
commandment of the LORD to Joshua,
even the city of Ärba the father of
Anak, which *city is* Hēbron.
14 And Caleb drove thence the three
sons of Anak, Shē'shaī, and A-hī'man,
and Tăl'maī, the children of Anak.
15 And he went up thence to the
inhabitants of Dē'bir: and the name of
Dē'bir before *was* Kir'jath–sē'pher.
16 And Caleb said, He that smiteth
Kir'jath–sē'pher, and taketh it, to him
will I give Ăch'sah my daughter to wife.
17 And Ŏth'nī-el the son of Kē'năz,
the brother of Caleb, took it: and he
gave him Ăch'sah his daughter to wife.
18 And it came to pass, as she came
unto him, that she moved him to ask of
her father a field: and she lighted off
her ass; and Caleb said unto her, What
wouldest thou?
19 Who answered, Give me a bless-
ing; for thou hast given me a south
land; give me also springs of water.
And he gave her the upper springs, and
the nether springs.
20 This *is* the inheritance of the tribe
of the children of Jūdah according to
their families.
21 ¶And the uttermost cities of the
tribe of the children of Jūdah toward
the coast of Ēdom southward were
Kăb'ze-el, and Ē'der, and Jā'gur,
22 And Kī'nah, and Dī-mō'nah, and
Ăd'a-dah,
23 And Kē'dĕsh, and Hā'zôr, and Ĭth'-
năn,
24 Ziph, and Tē'lĕm, and Bē'a-lŏth,
25 And Hā'zôr, Ha-dăt'tah, and Kĕ'rĭ-
ŏth, *and* Hĕz'ron, which *is* Hā'zôr,
26 Ā'măm, and Shē'ma, and Mŏl'a-
dah,
27 And Hā'zar–găd'dah, and Hĕsh'-
mŏn, and Bĕth–pā'let,
28 And Hā'zar–shū'al, and Be'er-
shē'ba, and Bĭz-jōth'jah,
29 Bā'al-ah, and Ī'im, and Ā'zem,
30 And Ĕl'tō-lăd, and Chē'sil, and
Hôr'mah,
31 And Ziklag, and Măd-măn'nah,
and Săn-săn'nah,
32 And Leb'ā-ŏth, and Shĭl'hĭm, and
Ā'ĭn, and Rimmon: all the cities *are*
twenty and nine, with their villages:
33 *And* in the valley, Ĕsh'ta-ol, and
Zō'rē-ah, and Ăsh'nah,
34 And Za'nō'ah, and Ĕn–găn'nĭm,
Tăp'pū-ah, and Ē'nam,
35 Jär'mŭth, and Adŭllam, Sō'cōh,
and A-zē'kah,
36 And Sha-rā'im, and Ăd-i-thā'im,
and Ge-de'rah, and Ged-e-roth-ā'ĭm;
fourteen cities with their villages:
37 Zē'nan, and Had'ă-shah, and Mĭg'-
dal–găd,
38 And Dĭl'e-an, and Mĭz'peh, and
Jŏk'the-el,
39 Lā'chĭsh, and Bŏz'kăth, and Ĕg'-
lŏn,
40 And Căb'bon, and Läh'măm, and
Kĭth'lĭsh,
41 And Ge-de'rŏth, Bĕth–dā'gon, and
Nā'a-mah, and Mak-kē'dah; sixteen
cities with their villages:
42 Lĭb'nah, and Ē'ther, and Ā'shan,
43 And Jĭph'tah, and Ăsh'nah, and
Nē'zĭb,
44 And Keī'lah, and Ăch'zĭb, and Ma-
rē'shah; nine cities with their villages:
45 Ĕkron, with her towns and her vil-
lages:
46 From Ĕkron even unto the sea, all
that *lay* near Ăsh'dŏd, with their vil-
lages:

47 Ăsh′dŏd with her towns and her
villages, Gā′za with her towns and her
villages, unto the river of Egypt, and
the great sea, and the border *thereof*:
48 And in the mountains, Shā′mir,
and Jăt′tir, and Sō′cōh,
49 And Dăn′nah, and Kir′jath–
săn′nah, which *is* Dē′bir,
50 And Anăb, and Ĕsh′te-mōh, and
Ā′nĭm,
51 And Goshen, and Hō′lŏn, and Gī′-
lōh; eleven cities with their villages:
52 Arab, and Dū′mah, and Ē′she-an,
53 And Jānum, and Bĕth–tăp′pū-ah,
and A-phē′kah,
54 And Hŭm′tah, and Kir′jath–är′ba,
which *is* Hēbron, and Zī′ôr; nine cities
with their villages:
55 Mā′on, Carmel, and Ziph, and
Jŭt′tah,
56 And Jĕz′re-el, and Jŏk′de-am, and
Za-nō′ah,
57 Cain, Gĭb′e-ah, and Tĭm′nah; ten
cities with their villages:
58 Hăl′hŭl, Bĕth′–zûr, and Gē′dôr,
59 And Mā′a-răth, and Bĕth–ā′nŏth,
and Ĕl′te-kŏn; six cities with their vil-
lages:
60 Kir′jath–bā′al, which *is* Kir′jath–
jē′a-rĭm, and Răb′bah; two cities with
their villages:
61 In the wilderness, Bĕth–ăr′a-bah,
Mĭd′din, and Sec′ā-cah,
62 And Nĭb′shăn, and the city of Salt,
and Ĕn–gĕ′dī; six cities with their vil-
lages.
63 ¶As for the Jēb′u-sītes the inhabi-
tants of Jerusalem, the children of Jū-
dah could not drive them out: but the
Jēb′u-sītes dwell with the children of
Jūdah at Jerusalem unto this day.

CHAPTER 16

AND the lot of the children of Joseph
fell from Jordan by Jericho, unto the
water of Jericho on the east, to the wil-
derness that goeth up from Jericho
throughout mount Bĕth–el,
2 And goeth out from Bĕth–el to Luz,
and passeth along unto the borders of
Är′chī to Ăt′a-rŏth,
3 And goeth down westward to the
coast of Jăph-le′tī, unto the coast of
Bĕth–hô′ron the nether, and to Gē′zer;
and the goings out thereof are at the
sea.
4 So the children of Joseph, Ma-năs′-
seh and Ē′phra-im, took their inheri-
tance.
5 ¶And the border of the children of
Ē′phra-im according to their families
was *thus*: even the border of their in-
heritance on the east side was Ăt′-a-
rŏth–ăd′dar, unto Bĕth–hô′ron the
upper;
6 And the border went out toward the
sea to Mĭch′me-thah on the north side;
and the border went about eastward
unto Tā′a-năth–shī′lōh, and passed by it
on the east to Ja-nō′hah;
7 And it went down from Ja-nō′hah
to Ăt′a-rŏth, and to Nā′a-răth, and
came to Jericho, and went out at Jor-
dan.
8 The border went out from Tăp′pū-
ah westward unto the river Kā′nah; and
the goings out thereof were at the sea.
This *is* the inheritance of the tribe of the
children of Ē′phra-im by their families.
9 And the separate cities for the
children of Ē′phra-im *were* among the
inheritance of the children of Ma-năs′-
seh, all the cities with their villages.
10 And they drave not out the Canaan-
ites that dwelt in Gē′zer: but the Ca-
naanites dwell among the Ē′phra-im-
ītes unto this day, and serve under
tribute.

CHAPTER 17

THERE was also a lot for the tribe of
Ma-năs′seh; for he *was* the firstborn of
Joseph; *to wit*, for Mā′chĭr the firstborn
of Ma-năs′seh, the father of Gilead: be-
cause he was a man of war, therefore
he had Gilead and Bā′shan.
2 There was also *a lot* for the rest of
the children of Ma-năs′seh by their fam-
ilies; for the children of Ā-bī-ē′zer,
and for the children of Hē′lĕk, and for
the children of Ăs′rĭ-el, and for the
children of Shĕ′chem, and for the chil-
dren of Hē′pher, and for the children of
She-mi′da: these *were* the male chil-
dren of Ma-năs′seh the son of Joseph
by their families.
3 ¶But Ze-lō′phe-hăd, the son of
Hē′pher, the son of Gilead, the son of
Mā′chĭr, the son of Ma-năs′seh, had no
sons, but daughters: and these *are* the
names of his daughters, Māh′lah, and
Noah, Hŏg′lah, Mĭl′cah, and Tir′zah.
4 And they came near before Ē-le-ā′-
zar the priest, and before Joshua the
son of Nun, and before the princes,
saying, The LORD commanded Moses
to give us an inheritance among our
brethren. Therefore according to the
commandment of the LORD he gave
them an inheritance among the breth-
ren of their father.
5 And there fell ten portions to Ma-
năs′seh, beside the land of Gilead and
Bā′shan, which *were* on the other side
Jordan;
6 Because the daughters of Ma-năs′-
seh had an inheritance among his
sons: and the rest of Ma-năs′seh's sons
had the land of Gilead.
7 ¶And the coast of Ma-năs′seh was
from Asher to Mĭch′me-thah, that *lieth*

before Shĕ'chem; and the border went
along on the right hand unto the inhabi-
tants of Ĕn-tăp'pû-ah.
8 *Now* Ma-năs'seh had the land of
Tăp'pū-ah: but Tăp'pū-ah on the border
of Ma-năs'seh *belonged* to the children
of Ē'phra-im;
9 And the coast descended unto the
river Kā'nah, southward of the river:
these cities of Ē'phra-im *are* among the
cities of Ma-năs'seh: the coast of Ma-
năs'seh also *was* on the north side of
the river, and the outgoings of it were
at the sea:
10 Southward *it was* Ē'phra-im's, and
northward *it was* Ma-năs'seh's, and the
sea is his border; and they met together
in Asher on the north, and in Ĭs'sa-char
on the east.
11 And Ma-năs'seh had in Ĭs'sa-char
and in Asher Bĕth-shē'an and her
towns, and Ĭb'le-am and her towns, and
the inhabitants of Dor and her towns,
and the inhabitants of Ĕn-dôr and her
towns, and the inhabitants of Tā'a-
năch and her towns, and the inhabi-
tants of Me-gĭd'dō and her towns, *even*
three countries.
12 Yet the children of Ma-năs'seh
could not drive out *the inhabitants of*
those cities; but the Canaanites would
dwell in that land.
13 Yet it came to pass, when the
children of Israel were waxen strong,
that they put the Canaanites to tribute,
but did not utterly drive them out.
14 ¶And the children of Joseph spake
unto Joshua, saying, Why hast thou giv-
en me *but* one lot and one portion to
inherit, seeing I *am* a great people, for-
asmuch as the LORD hath blessed me
hitherto?
15 And Joshua answered them, If
thou *be* a great people, *then* get thee up
to the wood *country*, and cut down for
thyself there in the land of the Pĕr'iz-
zītes and of the giants, if mount Ē'phra-
im be too narrow for thee.
16 And the children of Joseph said,
The hill is not enough for us: and all the
Canaanites that dwell in the land of the
valley have chariots of iron, *both they*
who *are* of Bĕth-shē'an and her towns,
and *they* who *are* of the valley of Jĕz're-
el.
17 And Joshua spake unto the house
of Joseph, *even* to Ē'phra-im and to Ma-
năs'seh, saying, Thou *art* a great peo-
ple, and hast great power: thou shalt
not have one lot *only*:
18 But the mountain shall be thine;
for it *is* a wood, and thou shalt cut it
down: and the outgoings of it shall be
thine: for thou shalt drive out the Ca-
naanites, though they have iron chariots,
and though they *be* strong.

CHAPTER 18

AND the whole congregation of the
children of Israel assembled together
at Shī'lōh, and set up the tabernacle of
the congregation there. And the land
was subdued before them.
2 And there remained among the
children of Israel seven tribes, which
had not yet received their inheritance.
3 And Joshua said unto the children
of Israel, How long *are* ye slack to go to
possess the land, which the LORD God
of your fathers hath given you?
4 Give out from among you three
men for *each* tribe: and I will send
them, and they shall rise, and go
through the land, and describe it accord-
ing to the inheritance of them; and
they shall come *again* to me.
5 And they shall divide it into seven
parts: Jūdah shall abide in their coast
on the south, and the house of Joseph
shall abide in their coasts on the north.
6 Ye shall therefore describe the land
into seven parts, and bring *the descrip-
tion* hither to me, that I may cast lots
for you here before the LORD our God.
7 But the Lēvītes have no part among
you; for the priesthood of the LORD *is*
their inheritance: and Gad, and Reu-
ben, and half the tribe of Ma-năs'seh,
have received their inheritance beyond
Jordan on the east, which Moses the
servant of the LORD gave them.
8 ¶And the men arose, and went
away: and Joshua charged them that
went to describe the land, saying, Go
and walk through the land, and describe
it, and come again to me, that I
may here cast lots for you before the
LORD in Shī'lōh.
9 And the men went and passed
through the land, and described it by
cities into seven parts in a book, and
came *again* to Joshua to the host at
Shī'lōh.
10 And Joshua cast lots for them in
Shī'lōh before the LORD: and there
Joshua divided the land unto the chil-
dren of Israel according to their divi-
sions.
11 ¶And the lot of the tribe of the
children of Benjamin came up accord-
ing to their families: and the coast of
their lot came forth between the chil-
dren of Jūdah and the children of Jo-
seph.
12 And their border on the north side
was from Jordan; and the border went
up to the side of Jericho on the north
side, and went up through the moun-
tains westward; and the goings out

thereof were at the wilderness of Bĕth–ā'ven.

13 And the border went over from thence toward Luz, to the side of Luz, which *is* Bĕth–el, southward; and the border descended to Ăt'a-rŏth–ă'dar, near the hill that *lieth* on the south side of the nether Bĕth–hô'ron.

14 And the border was drawn *thence*, and compassed the corner of the sea southward, from the hill that *lieth* before Bĕth–hô'ron southward; and the goings out thereof were at Kir'-jath–bā'al, which *is* Kir'jath–jē'a-rĭm, a city of the children of Judah: this *was* the west quarter.

15 And the south quarter *was* from the end of Kir'jath–jē'a-rĭm, and the border went out on the west, and went out to the well of waters of Nĕph'tō-ah:

16 And the border came down to the end of the mountain that *lieth* before the valley of the son of Hĭn'nom, *and* which *is* in the valley of the giants on the north, and descended to the valley of Hĭn'nom, to the side of Jē-bu'sī on the south, and descended to Ēn-rō'gel,

17 And was drawn from the north, and went forth to Ēn–shĕ'mesh, and went forth toward Gel'ī-lŏth, which *is* over against the going up of A-dŭm'mĭm, and descended to the stone of Bō'hăn the son of Reuben,

18 And passed along toward the side over against Ăr'a-bah northward, and went down unto Ăr'a-bah:

19 And the border passed along to the side of Bĕth–hŏg'lah northward: and the outgoings of the border were at the north bay of the salt sea at the south end of Jordan: this *was* the south coast.

20 And Jordan was the border of it on the east side. This *was* the inheritance of the children of Benjamin, by the coasts thereof round about, according to their families.

21 Now the cities of the tribe of the children of Benjamin according to their families were Jericho, and Bĕth–hŏg'lah, and the valley of Kē'zĭz,

22 And Bĕth–ăr'a-bah, and Zĕm-a-rā'im, and Bĕth–el,

23 And Ā'vĭm, and Pâ'rah, and Ŏph'rah,

24 And Chē'phar–hă-ăm'mo-naī, and Ŏph'nī, and Gā'ba; twelve cities with their villages:

25 Gĭbeon, and Rā'mah, and Bē-ĕ'rŏth,

26 And Mĭz'peh, and Che-phī'rah, and Mō'zah,

27 And Rē'kem, and Ĭr'pe-el, and Tăr'a-lah,

28 And Zē'lah, Ē'lĕph, and Jē-bu'sī, which *is* Jerusalem, Gĭb'e-ath, *and* Kĭr'-jăth; fourteen cities with their villages. This *is* the inheritance of the children of Benjamin according to their families.

CHAPTER 19

AND the second lot came forth to Simeon, *even* for the tribe of the children of Simeon according to their families: and their inheritance was within the inheritance of the children of Jūdah.

2 And they had in their inheritance Be'er–shē'ba, and Shē'ba, and Mŏl'a-dah,

3 And Hā'zar–shū'al, and Bā'lah, and Ā'zem,

4 And Ĕl'tō-lăd, and Bĕth–ul, and Hôr'mah,

5 And Ziklag, and Bĕth–mär'ca-bôth, and Hā'zar–sū'sah,

6 And Bĕth–leb'ā-ŏth, and Sha-rū'-hen; thirteen cities and their villages:

7 Ā'ĭn, Rĕm'mon, and Ē'ther, and Ā'shan; four cities and their villages:

8 And all the villages that *were* round about these cities to Bā'al-ăth–bē'er, Rā'math of the south. This *is* the inheritance of the tribe of the children of Simeon according to their families.

9 Out of the portion of the children of Jūdah *was* the inheritance of the children of Simeon: for the part of the children of Jūdah was too much for them: therefore the children of Simeon had their inheritance within the inheritance of them.

10 ¶And the third lot came up for the children of Zĕb'u-lun according to their families: and the border of their inheritance was unto Sâ'rĭd:

11 And their border went up toward the sea, and Mär'a-lah, and reached to Dăb'ba-shĕth, and reached to the river that *is* before Jŏk'ne-am;

12 And turned from Sâ'rĭd eastward toward the sunrising unto the border of Chĭs'lŏth–tā'bor, and then goeth out to Dăb'e-răth, and goeth up to Ja-phī'a,

13 And from thence passeth on along on the east to Gĭt'tah–hē'pher, to Ĭt'tah–kā'zĭn, and goeth out to Rĕm'-mon–mĕth'ō-är to Nē'ah;

14 And the border compasseth it on the north side to Hăn'na-thŏn: and the outgoings thereof are in the valley of Jĭph'thah–ĕl:

15 And Kăt'tăth, and Na-hăl'lal, and Shĭm'rŏn, and Ĭd'a-lah, and Bĕth–lehĕm: twelve cities with their villages.

16 This *is* the inheritance of the children of Zĕb'u-lun according to their families, these cities with their villages.

17 ¶*And* the fourth lot came out to Ĭs'sa-char, for the children of Ĭs'sa-char according to their families.

18 And their border was toward Jĕz′re-el, and Che-sŭl′lŏth, and Shū′nem,
19 And Hăph-rā′im, and Shī′hŏn, and An-ā-ha′răth,
20 And Răb′bĭth, and Kĭsh′ī-on, and Abĕz,
21 And Rē′meth, and Ĕn–găn′nĭm, and Ĕn–hăd′dah, and Bĕth–păz′zez;
22 And the coast reacheth to Tā′bor, and Shā-haz′ī-mah, and Bĕth–shĕ′mesh; and the outgoings of their border were at Jordan: sixteen cities with their villages.
23 This *is* the inheritance of the tribe of the children of Ĭs′sa-char according to their families, the cities and their villages.
24 ¶And the fifth lot came out for the tribe of the children of Asher according to their families.
25 And their border was Hĕl′kăth, and Hā′lī, and Bē′ten, and Ăch′shăph,
26 And A-lăm′me-lĕch, and Ā′măd, and Mĭsh′e-al; and reacheth to Carmel westward, and to Shī′hôr–lĭb′nath;
27 And turneth toward the sunrising to Bĕth–dā′gon, and reacheth to Zĕb′u-lun, and to the valley of Jĭph′thah–ĕl toward the north side of Bĕth–e′mĕk, and Nē-ī′el, and goeth out to Cā′bul on the left hand,
28 And Hēbron, and Rē′hŏb, and Hăm′mon, and Kā′nah, *even* unto great Zī′don;
29 And *then* the coast turneth to Rā′mah, and to the strong city Tyre; and the coast turneth to Hō′sah; and the outgoings thereof are at the sea from the coast to Ăch′zĭb:
30 Ŭm′mah also, and Ā′phĕk, and Rē′hŏb: twenty and two cities with their villages.
31 This *is* the inheritance of the tribe of the children of Asher according to their families, these cities with their villages.
32 ¶The sixth lot came out to the children of Năph′ta-lī, *even* for the children of Năph′ta-lī according to their families.
33 And their coast was from Hē′lĕph, from Ăl′lon to Zā-a-năn′nĭm, and Ăd′a-mi, Nĕ′kĕb, and Jăb′ne-el, unto Lă′kum; and the outgoings thereof were at Jordan:
34 And *then* the coast turneth westward to Ăz′nŏth–tā′bor, and goeth out from thence to Hŭk′kŏk, and reacheth to Zĕb′u-lun on the south side, and reacheth to Asher on the west side, and to Jūdah upon Jordan toward the sunrising.
35 And the fenced cities *are* Zĭd′dĭm, Zer, and Hăm′măth, Răk′kath, and Chĭn′ne-rĕth,
36 And Ăd′a-mah, and Rā′mah, and Hā′zôr,
37 And Kē′dĕsh, and Ĕd′re-ī, and Ĕn–hā′zôr,
38 And Ī′ron, and Mĭg′dal–ĕl, Hô′rĕm, and Bĕth–ā′năth, and Bĕth–shĕ′mesh; nineteen cities with their villages.
39 This *is* the inheritance of the tribe of the children of Năph′ta-lī according to their families, the cities and their villages.
40 ¶*And* the seventh lot came out for the tribe of the children of Dan according to their families.
41 And the coast of their inheritance was Zô′rah, and Ĕsh′ta-ol, and Ĭr–shĕ′mesh,
42 And Shā-al-ăb′bin, and Ăj′a-lŏn, and Jĕth′lah,
43 And Ē′lŏn, and Thĭm′na-thah, and Ĕkron,
44 And Ĕl′te-keh, and Gĭb′be-thŏn, and Bā′al-ăth,
45 And Jehud, and Bĕn′e–be′răk, and Găth–rĭm′mon,
46 And Mē–jăr′kŏn, and Răk′kŏn, with the border before Jā′phō.
47 And the coast of the children of Dan went out *too little* for them: therefore the children of Dan went up to fight against Lē′shem, and took it, and smote it with the edge of the sword, and possessed it, and dwelt therein, and called Lē′shem, Dan, after the name of Dan their father.
48 This *is* the inheritance of the tribe of the children of Dan according to their families, these cities with their villages.
49 ¶When they had made an end of dividing the land for inheritance by their coasts, the children of Israel gave an inheritance to Joshua the son of Nun among them:
50 According to the word of the LORD they gave him the city which he asked, *even* Tĭm′năth–se′rah in mount Ē′phra-im: and he built the city, and dwelt therein.
51 These *are* the inheritances, which Ē-le-ā′zar the priest, and Joshua the son of Nun, and the heads of the fathers of the tribes of the children of Israel, divided for an inheritance by lot in Shī′lōh before the LORD, at the door of the tabernacle of the congregation. So they made an end of dividing the country.

CHAPTER 20

THE LORD also spake unto Joshua, saying,
2 Speak to the children of Israel, saying, Appoint out for you cities of refuge, whereof I spake unto you by the hand of Moses:

3 That the slayer that killeth *any* person unawares *and* unwittingly may flee thither: and they shall be your refuge from the avenger of blood.

4 And when he that doth flee unto one of those cities shall stand at the entering of the gate of the city, and shall declare his cause in the ears of the elders of that city, they shall take him into the city unto them, and give him a place, that he may dwell among them.

5 And if the avenger of blood pursue after him, then they shall not deliver the slayer up into his hand; because he smote his neighbour unwittingly, and hated him not beforetime.

6 And he shall dwell in that city, until he stand before the congregation for judgment, *and* until the death of the high priest that shall be in those days: then shall the slayer return, and come unto his own city, and unto his own house, unto the city from whence he fled.

7 ¶And they appointed Kē'dĕsh in Galilee in mount Năph'ta-lī, and Shĕ'chem in mount Ē'phra-im, and Kĭr'jath-ăr'ba, which *is* Hēbron, in the mountain of Jūdah.

8 And on the other side Jordan by Jericho eastward, they assigned Bē'zer in the wilderness upon the plain out of the tribe of Reuben, and Rā'mŏth in Gilead out of the tribe of Gad, and Gō'lan in Bā'shan out of the tribe of Ma-năs'seh.

9 These were the cities appointed for all the children of Israel, and for the stranger that sojourneth among them, that whosoever killeth *any* person at unawares might flee thither, and not die by the hand of the avenger of blood, until he stood before the congregation.

CHAPTER 21

THEN came near the heads of the fathers of the Lēvītes unto Ē-le-ā'zar the priest, and unto Joshua the son of Nun, and unto the heads of the fathers of the tribes of the children of Israel;

2 And they spake unto them at Shī'lōh in the land of Canaan, saying, The LORD commanded by the hand of Moses to give us cities to dwell in, with the suburbs thereof for our cattle.

3 And the children of Israel gave unto the Lēvītes out of their inheritance, at the commandment of the LORD, these cities and their suburbs.

4 And the lot came out for the families of the Kō'hăth-ītes: and the children of Aaron the priest, *which were* of the Lēvītes, had by lot out of the tribe of Jūdah, and out of the tribe of Simeon, and out of the tribe of Benjamin, thirteen cities.

5 And the rest of the children of Kō'hăth *had* by lot out of the families of the tribe of Ē'phra-im, and out of the tribe of Dan, and out of the half tribe of Ma-năs'seh, ten cities.

6 And the children of Ger'shon *had* by lot out of the families of the tribe of Ĭs'sa-char, and out of the tribe of Asher, and out of the tribe of Năph'ta-lī, and out of the half tribe of Ma-năs'seh in Bā'shan, thirteen cities.

7 The children of Me-râ'rī by their families *had* out of the tribe of Reuben, and out of the tribe of Gad, and out of the tribe of Zĕb'u-lun, twelve cities.

8 And the children of Israel gave by lot unto the Lēvītes these cities with their suburbs, as the LORD commanded by the hand of Moses.

9 ¶And they gave out of the tribe of the children of Jūdah, and out of the tribe of the children of Simeon, these cities which are *here* mentioned by name,

10 Which the children of Aaron, *being* of the families of the Kō'hăth-ītes, *who were* of the children of Levi, had: for theirs was the first lot.

11 And they gave them the city of Ăr'ba the father of Anak, which *city is* Hēbron, in the hill *country* of Jūdah, with the suburbs thereof round about it.

12 But the fields of the city, and the villages thereof, gave they to Caleb the son of Je-phŭn'neh for his possession.

13 Thus they gave to the children of Aaron the priest Hēbron with her suburbs, *to be* a city of refuge for the slayer; and Lĭb'nah with her suburbs,

14 And Jăt'tir with her suburbs, and Ĕsh-te-mō'a with her suburbs,

15 And Hō'lŏn with her suburbs, and Dē'bir with her suburbs,

16 And Ā'ĭn with her suburbs, and Jŭt'tah with her suburbs, *and* Bĕth-shĕmesh with her suburbs; nine cities out of those two tribes.

17 And out of the tribe of Benjamin, Gĭbeon with her suburbs, Gē'ba with her suburbs,

18 Ăn'a-thŏth with her suburbs, and Ăl'mon with her suburbs; four cities.

19 All the cities of the children of Aaron, the priests, *were* thirteen cities with their suburbs.

20 ¶And the families of the children of Kō'hăth, the Lēvītes which remained of the children of Kō'hăth, even they had the cities of their lot out of the tribe of Ē'phra-im.

21 For they gave them Shĕ'chem with her suburbs in mount Ē'phra-im,

to be a city of refuge for the slayer; and
Gē′zer with her suburbs,
22 And Kĭb′zā-im with her suburbs,
and Bĕth–hô′ron with her suburbs; four
cities.
23 And out of the tribe of Dan, Ĕl′te-
keh with her suburbs, Gĭb′be-thŏn with
her suburbs,
24 Āij′a-lŏn with her suburbs,
Găth–rĭm′mon with her suburbs; four
cities.
25 And out of the half tribe of Ma-
năs′seh, Tā′năch with her suburbs, and
Găth–rĭm′mon with her suburbs; two
cities.
26 All the cities *were* ten with their
suburbs for the families of the children
of Kō′hăth that remained.
27 ¶And unto the children of
Ger′shon, of the families of the Lē′vītes,
out of the *other* half tribe of Ma-năs′seh
they gave Gō′lan in Bā′shan with her
suburbs, *to be* a city of refuge for the
slayer; and Bē-ĕsh′–te-rah with her sub-
urbs; two cities.
28 And out of the tribe of Ĭs′sa-char,
Kī′shŏn with her suburbs, Dăb′a-reh
with her suburbs,
29 Jär′mŭth with her suburbs,
Ĕn–găn′nĭm with her suburbs; four
cities.
30 And out of the tribe of Asher, Mī′-
shal with her suburbs, Ăbdŏn with her
suburbs,
31 Hĕl′kăth with her suburbs, and
Rē′hŏb with her suburbs; four cities.
32 And out of the tribe of Năph′ta-lī,
Kē′dĕsh in Galilee with her suburbs, *to
be* a city of refuge for the slayer; and
Hăm′moth–dôr with her suburbs, and
Kär′tăn with her suburbs; three cities.
33 All the cities of the Ger′shon-ītes
according to their families *were* thir-
teen cities with their suburbs.
34 ¶And unto the families of the
children of Me-râ′rī, the rest of the
Lēvītes, out of the tribe of Zĕb′u-lun,
Jŏk′ne-am with her suburbs, and Kär′-
tah with her suburbs,
35 Dĭm′nah with her suburbs, Nā′ha-
lăl with her suburbs; four cities.
36 And out of the tribe of Reuben,
Bē′zer with her suburbs, and Ja-hā′zah
with her suburbs,
37 Kĕd′e-mŏth with her suburbs, and
Mĕph′a-ăth with her suburbs; four
cities.
38 And out of the tribe of Gad, Rā′-
mŏth in Gilead with her suburbs, *to be*
a city of refuge for the slayer; and
Mā′ha-nā′im with her suburbs,
39 Hĕsh′bŏn with her suburbs, Jā′zer
with her suburbs; four cities in all.
40 So all the cities for the children of
Me-râ′rī by their families, which were
remaining of the families of the Lē-
vītes, were *by* their lot twelve cities.
41 All the cities of the Lēvītes within
the possession of the children of Israel
were forty and eight cities with their
suburbs.
42 These cities were every one with
their suburbs round about them: thus
were all these cities.
43 ¶And the LORD gave unto Israel all
the land which he sware to give unto
their fathers; and they possessed it, and
dwelt therein.
44 And the LORD gave them rest
round about, according to all that he
sware unto their fathers: and there
stood not a man of all their enemies be-
fore them; the LORD delivered all their
enemies into their hand.
45 There failed not ought of any good
thing which the LORD had spoken unto
the house of Israel; all came to pass.

CHAPTER 22

THEN Joshua called the Reubenites,
and the Gădītes, and the half tribe of
Ma-năs′seh,
2 And said unto them, Ye have kept
all that Moses the servant of the LORD
commanded you, and have obeyed my
voice in all that I commanded you:
3 Ye have not left your brethren these
many days unto this day, but have kept
the charge of the commandment of the
LORD your God.
4 And now the LORD your God hath
given rest unto your brethren, as he
promised them: therefore now return
ye, and get you unto your tents, *and*
unto the land of your possession, which
Moses the servant of the LORD gave you
on the other side Jordan.
5 But take diligent heed to do the
commandment and the law, which
Moses the servant of the LORD charged
you, to love the LORD your God, and to
walk in all his ways, and to keep his
commandments, and to cleave unto
him, and to serve him with all your
heart and with all your soul.
6 So Joshua blessed them, and sent
them away: and they went unto their
tents.
7 ¶Now to the *one* half of the tribe of
Ma-năs′seh Moses had given *posses-
sion* in Bā′shan: but unto the *other* half
thereof gave Joshua among their breth-
ren on this side Jordan westward.
And when Joshua sent them away also
unto their tents, then he blessed them,
8 And he spake unto them, saying,
Return with much riches unto your
tents, and with very much cattle, with
silver, and with gold, and with brass,
and with iron, and with very much rai-

ment: divide the spoil of your enemies
with your brethren.
9 And the children of Reuben and the
children of Gad and the half tribe of
Ma-năs'seh returned, and departed
from the children of Israel out of Shī'-
lōh, which *is* in the land of Canaan, to
go unto the country of Gilead, to the
land of their possession, whereof they
were possessed, according to the word
of the LORD by the hand of Moses.
10 ¶And when they came unto the
borders of Jordan, that *are* in the land
of Canaan, the children of Reuben and
the children of Gad and the half tribe of
Ma-năs'seh built there an altar by Jor-
dan, a great altar to see to.
11 ¶And the children of Israel heard
say, Behold, the children of Reuben
and the children of Gad and the half
tribe of Ma-năs'seh have built an altar
over against the land of Canaan, in the
borders of Jordan, at the passage of the
children of Israel.
12 And when the children of Israel
heard *of it*, the whole congregation of
the children of Israel gathered them-
selves together at Shī'lōh, to go up to
war against them.
13 And the children of Israel sent
unto the children of Reuben, and to the
children of Gad, and to the half tribe of
Ma-năs'seh, into the land of Gilead,
Phĭn'e-has the son of Ĕ-le-ā'zar the
priest,
14 And with him ten princes, of each
chief house a prince throughout all the
tribes of Israel; and each one *was* an
head of the house of their fathers
among the thousands of Israel.
15 And they came unto the children
of Reuben, and to the children of Gad,
and to the half tribe of Ma-năs'seh,
unto the land of Gilead, and they spake
with them, saying,
16 Thus saith the whole congregation
of the LORD, What trespass *is* this that
ye have committed against the God of
Israel, to turn away this day from follow-
ing the LORD, in that ye have builded
you an altar, that ye might rebel this
day against the LORD?
17 *Is* the iniquity of Pē'or too little for
us, from which we are not cleansed un-
til this day, although there was a plague
in the congregation of the LORD,
18 But that ye must turn away this
day from following the LORD? and it
will be, *seeing* ye rebel to day against
the LORD, that to morrow he will be
wroth with the whole congregation of
Israel.
19 Notwithstanding, if the land of
your possession *be* unclean, *then* pass
ye over unto the land of the possession
of the LORD, wherein the LORD's taber-
nacle dwelleth, and take possession
among us: but rebel not against the
LORD, nor rebel against us, in building
you an altar beside the altar of the LORD
our God.
20 Did not Ā'chăn the son of Ze'rah
commit a trespass in the accursed
thing, and wrath fell on all the congre-
gation of Israel? and that man perished
not alone in his iniquity.
21 ¶Then the children of Reuben and
the children of Gad and the half tribe of
Ma-năs'seh answered, and said unto
the heads of the thousands of Israel,
22 The LORD God of gods, the LORD
God of gods, he knoweth, and Israel he
shall know; if *it be* in rebellion, or if in
transgression against the LORD, (save
us not this day,)
23 That we have built us an altar to
turn from following the LORD, or if to
offer thereon burnt offering or meat of-
fering, or if to offer peace offerings
thereon, let the LORD himself require *it*;
24 And if we have not *rather* done it
for fear of *this* thing, saying, In time to
come your children might speak unto
our children, saying, What have ye to
do with the LORD God of Israel?
25 For the LORD hath made Jordan a
border between us and you, ye children
of Reuben and children of Gad; ye have
no part in the LORD: so shall your chil-
dren make our children cease from
fearing the LORD.
26 Therefore we said, Let us now pre-
pare to build us an altar, not for burnt
offering, nor for sacrifice:
27 But *that* it *may be* a witness be-
tween us and you, and our generations
after us, that we might do the service of
the LORD before him with our burnt of-
ferings, and with our sacrifices, and
with our peace offerings; that your
children may not say to our children in
time to come, Ye have no part in the
LORD.
28 Therefore said we, that it shall be,
when they should *so* say to us or to our
generations in time to come, that we
may say *again*, Behold the pattern of
the altar of the LORD, which our fathers
made, not for burnt offerings, nor for
sacrifices; but it *is* a witness between
us and you.
29 God forbid that we should rebel
against the LORD, and turn this day
from following the LORD, to build an al-
tar for burnt offerings, for meat offer-
ings, or for sacrifices, beside the altar
of the LORD our God that *is* before his
tabernacle.
30 ¶And when Phĭn'e-has the priest,
and the princes of the congregation and

heads of the thousands of Israel which
were with him, heard the words that
the children of Reuben and the children
of Gad and the children of Ma-năs'seh
spake, it pleased them.
31 And Phĭn'e-has the son of Ĕ-le-ā'zar
the priest said unto the children of
Reuben, and to the children of Gad, and
to the children of Ma-năs'seh, This day
we perceive that the LORD *is* among us,
because ye have not committed this
trespass against the LORD: now ye have
delivered the children of Israel out of
the hand of the LORD.
32 And Phĭn'e-has the son of Ĕ-le-ā'zar
the priest, and the princes, returned
from the children of Reuben, and from
the children of Gad, out of the land of
Gilead, unto the land of Canaan, to the
children of Israel, and brought them
word again.
33 And the thing pleased the children
of Israel; and the children of Israel
blessed God, and did not intend to go
up against them in battle, to destroy
the land wherein the children of Reu-
ben and Gad dwelt.
34 And the children of Reuben and
the children of Gad called the altar *Ed:*
for it *shall be* a witness between us that
the LORD *is* God.

CHAPTER 23

AND it came to pass a long time after
that the LORD had given rest unto Israel
from all their enemies round about,
that Joshua waxed old *and* stricken in
age.
2 And Joshua called for all Israel, *and*
for their elders, and for their heads, and
for their judges, and for their officers,
and said unto them, I am old *and* strick-
en in age:
3 And ye have seen all that the LORD
your God hath done unto all these na-
tions because of you; for the LORD your
God *is* he that hath fought for you.
4 Behold, I have divided unto you by
lot these nations that remain, to be an
inheritance for your tribes, from Jor-
dan, with all the nations that I have cut
off, even unto the great sea westward.
5 And the LORD your God, he shall ex-
pel them from before you, and drive
them from out of your sight; and ye
shall possess their land, as the LORD
your God hath promised unto you.
6 Be ye therefore very courageous to
keep and to do all that is written in the
book of the law of Moses, that ye turn
not aside therefrom *to* the right hand or
to the left;
7 That ye come not among these na-
tions, these that remain among you;
neither make mention of the name of
their gods, nor cause to swear *by them,*
neither serve them, nor bow yourselves
unto them:
8 But cleave unto the LORD your God,
as ye have done unto this day.
9 For the LORD hath driven out from
before you great nations and strong:
but *as for* you, no man hath been able to
stand before you unto this day.
10 One man of you shall chase a thou-
sand: for the LORD your God, he *it is*
that fighteth for you, as he hath prom-
ised you.
11 Take good heed therefore unto
yourselves, that ye love the LORD your
God.
12 Else if ye do in any wise go back,
and cleave unto the remnant of these
nations, *even* these that remain among
you, and shall make marriages with
them, and go in unto them, and they to
you:
13 Know for a certainty that the LORD
your God will no more drive out *any of*
these nations from before you; but they
shall be snares and traps unto you, and
scourges in your sides, and thorns in
your eyes, until ye perish from off this
good land which the LORD your God
hath given you.
14 And, behold, this day I *am* going
the way of all the earth: and ye know in
all your hearts and in all your souls,
that not one thing hath failed of all the
good things which the LORD your God
spake concerning you; all are come to
pass unto you, *and* not one thing hath
failed thereof.
15 Therefore it shall come to pass,
that as all good things are come upon
you, which the LORD your God prom-
ised you; so shall the LORD bring upon
you all evil things, until he have de-
stroyed you from off this good land
which the LORD your God hath given
you.
16 When ye have transgressed the
covenant of the LORD your God, which
he commanded you, and have gone and
served other gods, and bowed your-
selves to them; then shall the anger of
the LORD be kindled against you, and ye
shall perish quickly from off the good
land which he hath given unto you.

CHAPTER 24

AND Joshua gathered all the tribes of
Israel to Shĕ'chem, and called for the
elders of Israel, and for their heads, and
for their judges, and for their officers;
and they presented themselves before
God.
2 And Joshua said unto all the people,
Thus saith the LORD God of Israel, Your
fathers dwelt on the other side of the

flood in old time, *even* Te'rah, the
father of Abraham, and the father of
Nā'chôr: and they served other gods.
3 And I took your father Abraham
from the other side of the flood, and led
him throughout all the land of Canaan,
and multiplied his seed, and gave him
Isaac.
4 And I gave unto Isaac Jacob and
Esau: and I gave unto Esau mount Sē'ir,
to possess it; but Jacob and his children
went down into Egypt.
5 I sent Moses also and Aaron, and I
plagued Egypt, according to that which
I did among them: and afterward I
brought you out.
6 And I brought your fathers out of
Egypt: and ye came unto the sea; and
the Egyptians pursued after your fa-
thers with chariots and horsemen unto
the Red sea.
7 And when they cried unto the LORD,
he put darkness between you and the
Egyptians, and brought the sea upon
them, and covered them; and your eyes
have seen what I have done in Egypt:
and ye dwelt in the wilderness a long
season.
8 And I brought you into the land of
the Ămorītes, which dwelt on the other
side Jordan; and they fought with you:
and I gave them into your hand, that ye
might possess their land; and I de-
stroyed them from before you.
9 Then Bā'lăk the son of Zippor, king
of Moab, arose and warred against
Israel, and sent and called Bā'laam the
son of Bē'ôr to curse you:
10 But I would not hearken unto Bā'-
laam; therefore he blessed you still: so I
delivered you out of his hand.
11 And ye went over Jordan, and
came unto Jericho: and the men of
Jericho fought against you, the Ămor-
ītes, and the Pĕr'iz-zītes, and the Ca-
naanites, and the Hittites, and the
Gir'ga-shītes, the Hī'vītes, and the
Jēb'u-sītes; and I delivered them into
your hand.
12 And I sent the hornet before you,
which drave them out from before you,
even the two kings of the Ămorītes; *but*
not with thy sword, nor with thy bow.
13 And I have given you a land for
which ye did not labour, and cities
which ye built not, and ye dwell in
them; of the vineyards and oliveyards
which ye planted not do ye eat.
14 ¶Now therefore fear the LORD, and
serve him in sincerity and in truth: and
put away the gods which your fathers
served on the other side of the flood,
and in Egypt; and serve ye the LORD.
15 And if it seem evil unto you to
serve the LORD, choose you this day
whom ye will serve; whether the gods
which your fathers served that *were* on
the other side of the flood, or the gods
of the Ămorītes, in whose land ye
dwell: but as for me and my house, we
will serve the LORD.
16 And the people answered and
said, God forbid that we should forsake
the LORD, to serve other gods;
17 For the LORD our God, he *it is* that
brought us up and our fathers out of the
land of Egypt, from the house of bond-
age, and which did those great signs
in our sight, and preserved us in all the
way wherein we went, and among all
the people through whom we passed:
18 And the LORD drave out from be-
fore us all the people, even the Ămor-
ītes which dwelt in the land: *therefore*
will we also serve the LORD; for he *is*
our God.
19 And Joshua said unto the people,
Ye cannot serve the LORD: for he *is* an
holy God; he *is* a jealous God; he will
not forgive your transgressions nor
your sins.
20 If ye forsake the LORD, and serve
strange gods, then he will turn and do
you hurt, and consume you, after that
he hath done you good.
21 And the people said unto Joshua,
Nay; but we will serve the LORD.
22 And Joshua said unto the people,
Ye *are* witnesses against yourselves
that ye have chosen you the LORD, to
serve him. And they said, *We are* wit-
nesses.
23 Now therefore put away, *said he,*
the strange gods which *are* among you,
and incline your heart unto the LORD
God of Israel.
24 And the people said unto Joshua,
The LORD our God will we serve, and
his voice will we obey.
25 So Joshua made a covenant with
the people that day, and set them a stat-
ute and an ordinance in Shĕ'chem.
26 And Joshua wrote these words in
the book of the law of God, and took a
great stone, and set it up there under an
oak, that *was* by the sanctuary of the
LORD.
27 And Joshua said unto all the peo-
ple, Behold, this stone shall be a wit-
ness unto us; for it hath heard all the
words of the LORD which he spake unto
us: it shall be therefore a witness unto
you, lest ye deny your God.
28 So Joshua let the people depart,
every man unto his inheritance.
29 ¶And it came to pass after these
things, that Joshua the son of Nun, the
servant of the LORD, died, *being* an
hundred and ten years old.
30 And they buried him in the border

of his inheritance in Tĭm′năth-se′rah,
which *is* in mount Ē′phra-im, on the
north side of the hill of Gā′ash.
31 And Israel served the LORD all the
days of Joshua, and all the days of the
elders that overlived Joshua, and
which had known all the works of the
LORD, that he had done for Israel.
32 ¶And the bones of Joseph, which
the children of Israel brought up out of
Egypt, buried they in Shĕ′chem, in a
parcel of ground which Jacob bought
of the sons of Hā′môr the father of
Shĕ′chem for an hundred pieces of sil-
ver: and it became the inheritance of
the children of Joseph.
33 ¶And Ē-le-ā′zar the son of Aaron
died; and they buried him in a hill *that*
pertained to Phĭn′e-has his son, which
was given him in mount Ē′phra-im.

THE BOOK OF JUDGES

CHAPTER 1

NOW after the death of Joshua it came
to pass, that the children of Israel
asked the LORD, saying, Who shall go
up for us against the Canaanites first,
to fight against them?
2 And the LORD said, Jūdah shall go
up: behold, I have delivered the land
into his hand.
3 And Jūdah said unto Simeon his
brother, Come up with me into my lot,
that we may fight against the Canaan-
ites; and I likewise will go with thee
into thy lot. So Simeon went with him.
4 And Jūdah went up; and the LORD
delivered the Canaanites and the Pĕr′-
iz-zītes into their hand: and they slew
of them in Bē′zĕk ten thousand men.
5 And they found A-dō′nī-bē′zĕk in
Bē′zĕk: and they fought against him,
and they slew the Canaanites and the
Pĕr′iz-zītes.
6 But A-dō′nī-bē′zĕk fled; and they
pursued after him, and caught him, and
cut off his thumbs and his great toes.
7 And A-dō′nī-bē′zĕk said, Threescore
and ten kings, having their thumbs and
their great toes cut off, gathered *their*
meat under my table: as I have done, so
God hath requited me. And they
brought him to Jerusalem, and there he
died.
8 ¶Now the children of Jūdah had
fought against Jerusalem, and had
taken it, and smitten it with the edge of
the sword, and set the city on fire.
9 And afterward the children of Jū-
dah went down to fight against the Ca-
naanites, that dwelt in the mountain,
and in the south, and in the valley.
10 And Judah went against the Ca-
naanites that dwelt in Hēbron: (now the
name of Hēbron before *was* Kĭr′-
jath-är′ba:) and they slew Shē′shaī,
and A-hī′man, and Tăl′maī.
11 And from thence he went against
the inhabitants of Dē′bir: and the
name of Dē′bir before *was* Kĭr′-
jath-sē′pher:
12 And Caleb said, He that smiteth
Kir′jath-sē′pher, and taketh it, to him
will I give Ăch′sah my daughter to wife.
13 And Ŏth′nī-el the son of Kē′năz,
Caleb's younger brother, took it: and
he gave him Ăch′sah his daughter to
wife.
14 And it came to pass, when she
came *to him*, that she moved him to ask
of her father a field: and she lighted
from off *her* ass; and Caleb said unto
her, What wilt thou?
15 And she said unto him, Give me a
blessing: for thou hast given me a south
land; give me also springs of water.
And Caleb gave her the upper springs
and the nether springs.
16 ¶And the children of the Kēn′īte,
Moses' father in law, went up out of the
city of palm trees with the children of
Jūdah into the wilderness of Jūdah,
which *lieth* in the south of Â′răd; and
they went and dwelt among the people.
17 And Jūdah went with Simeon his
brother, and they slew the Canaanites
that inhabited Zē′phăth, and utterly
destroyed it. And the name of the city
was called Hôr′mah.
18 Also Jūdah took Gā′za with the
coast thereof, and Ăs′ke-lŏn with the
coast thereof, and Ĕk-ron with the
coast thereof.
19 And the LORD was with Jūdah; and
he drave out *the inhabitants of* the
mountain; but could not drive out the
inhabitants of the valley, because they
had chariots of iron.
20 And they gave Hēbron unto Caleb,
as Moses said: and he expelled thence
the three sons of Anak.
21 ¶And the children of Benjamin did
not drive out the Jēb′u-sītes that
inhabited Jerusalem; but the Jēb′u-
sītes dwell with the children of Ben-
jamin in Jerusalem unto this day.
22 ¶And the house of Joseph, they
also went up against Bĕth-el: and the
LORD *was* with them.
23 And the house of Joseph sent to
descry Bĕth-el. (Now the name of the
city before *was* Luz.)
24 And the spies saw a man come

forth out of the city, and they said unto him, Shew us, we pray thee, the entrance into the city, and we will shew thee mercy.

25 And when he shewed them the entrance into the city, they smote the city with the edge of the sword; but they let go the man and all his family.

26 And the man went into the land of the Hittites, and built a city, and called the name thereof Luz: which *is* the name thereof unto this day.

27 ¶Neither did Ma-năs'seh drive out *the inhabitants of* Bĕth-shē'an and her towns, nor Tā'a-năch and her towns, nor the inhabitants of Dor and her towns, nor the inhabitants of Ĭb'le-am and her towns, nor the inhabitants of Me-gĭd'dō and her towns: but the Canaanites would dwell in that land.

28 And it came to pass, when Israel was strong, that they put the Canaanites to tribute, and did not utterly drive them out.

29 Neither did Ē'phra-im drive out the Canaanites that dwelt in Gē'zer; but the Canaanites dwelt in Gē'zer among them.

30 Neither did Zĕb'u-lun drive out the inhabitants of Kĭt'rŏn, nor the inhabitants of Nā'ha-lŏl; but the Canaanites dwelt among them, and became tributaries.

31 Neither did Asher drive out the inhabitants of Ăc'chō, nor the inhabitants of Zī'don, nor of Äh'lăb, nor of Ăch'zĭb, nor of Hĕl'bah, nor of Ā'phĭk, nor of Rē'hŏb:

32 But the Asherites dwelt among the Canaanites, the inhabitants of the land: for they did not drive them out.

33 Neither did Năph'ta-lī drive out the inhabitants of Bĕth-shĕ'mesh, nor the inhabitants of Bĕth-ā'năth; but he dwelt among the Canaanites, the inhabitants of the land: nevertheless the inhabitants of Bĕth-shĕ'mesh and of Bĕth-ā'năth became tributaries unto them.

34 And the Ămorītes forced the children of Dan into the mountain: for they would not suffer them to come down to the valley:

35 But the Ămorītes would dwell in mount He'res in Āij'a-lŏn, and in Shā-ăl'bĭm: yet the hand of the house of Joseph prevailed, so that they became tributaries.

36 And the coast of the Ămorītes *was* from the going up to Ā-krăb'bĭm, from the rock, and upward.

CHAPTER 2

AND an angel of the LORD came up from Gilgal to Bō'chĭm, and said, I made you to go up out of Egypt, and have brought you unto the land which I sware unto your fathers; and I said, I will never break my covenant with you.

2 And ye shall make no league with the inhabitants of this land; ye shall throw down their altars: but ye have not obeyed my voice: why have ye done this?

3 Wherefore I also said, I will not drive them out from before you; but they shall be *as thorns* in your sides, and their gods shall be a snare unto you.

4 And it came to pass, when the angel of the LORD spake these words unto all the children of Israel, that the people lifted up their voice, and wept.

5 And they called the name of that place Bō'chĭm: and they sacrificed there unto the LORD.

6 ¶And when Joshua had let the people go, the children of Israel went every man unto his inheritance to possess the land.

7 And the people served the LORD all the days of Joshua, and all the days of the elders that outlived Joshua, who had seen all the great works of the LORD, that he did for Israel.

8 And Joshua the son of Nun, the servant of the LORD, died, *being* an hundred and ten years old.

9 And they buried him in the border of his inheritance in Tĭm'năth-he'reś, in the mount of Ē'phra-im, on the north side of the hill Gā'ash.

10 And also all that generation were gathered unto their fathers: and there arose another generation after them, which knew not the LORD, nor yet the works which he had done for Israel.

11 ¶And the children of Israel did evil in the sight of the LORD, and served Bā'al-ĭm:

12 And they forsook the LORD God of their fathers, which brought them out of the land of Egypt, and followed other gods, of the gods of the people that *were* round about them, and bowed themselves unto them, and provoked the LORD to anger.

13 And they forsook the LORD, and served Bā'al and Ăsh'ta-rŏth.

14 And the anger of the LORD was hot against Israel, and he delivered them into the hands of spoilers that spoiled them, and he sold them into the hands of their enemies round about, so that they could not any longer stand before their enemies.

15 Whithersoever they went out, the hand of the LORD was against them for evil, as the LORD had said, and as the

LORD had sworn unto them: and they
were greatly distressed.
16 ¶Nevertheless the LORD raised up
judges, which delivered them out of the
hand of those that spoiled them.
17 And yet they would not hearken
unto their judges, but they went a
whoring after other gods, and bowed
themselves unto them: they turned
quickly out of the way which their fa-
thers walked in, obeying the command-
ments of the LORD; *but* they did not so.
18 And when the LORD raised them
up judges, then the LORD was with the
judge, and delivered them out of the
hand of their enemies all the days of the
judge: for it repented the LORD because
of their groanings by reason of them
that oppressed them and vexed them.
19 And it came to pass, when the
judge was dead, *that* they returned,
and corrupted *themselves* more than
their fahers, in following other gods to
serve them, and to bow down unto
them; they ceased not from their own
doings, nor from their stubborn way.
20 ¶And the anger of the LORD was
hot against Israel; and he said, Because
that this people hath transgressed my
covenant which I commanded their
fathers, and have not hearkened unto
my voice;
21 I also will not henceforth drive out
any from before them of the nations
which Joshua left when he died:
22 That through them I may prove
Israel, whether they will keep the way
of the LORD to walk therein, as their
fathers did keep *it*, or not.
23 Therefore the LORD left those na-
tions, without driving them out hastily;
neither delivered he them into the hand
of Joshua.

CHAPTER 3

NOW these *are* the nations which the
LORD left, to prove Israel by them, *even*
as many *of Israel* as had not known all
the wars of Canaan;
2 Only that the generations of the
children of Israel might know, to teach
them war, at the least such as before
knew nothing thereof;
3 *Namely*, five lords of the Philis-
tines, and all the Canaanites, and the
Si-dō′ni-anṡ, and the Hī′vītes that
dwelt in mount Lebanon, from mount
Ba′al–her′mon unto the entering in of
Hā′măth.
4 And they were to prove Israel by
them, to know whether they would
hearken unto the commandments of
the LORD, which he commanded their
fathers by the hand of Moses.
5 ¶And the children of Israel dwelt
among the Canaanites, Hittites, and
Ămorītes, and Pĕr′iz-zītes, and Hī′vītes,
and Jēb′u-sītes:
6 And they took their daughters to be
their wives, and gave their daughters to
their sons, and served their gods.
7 And the children of Israel did evil in
the sight of the LORD, and forgat the
LORD their God, and served Bā′al-ĭm
and the groves.
8 Therefore the anger of the LORD
was hot against Israel, and he sold
them into the hand of Chū′shăn–rĭsh-a-
thā′im king of Mĕs-o-po-tā′mĭ-a: and
the children of Israel served Chū′-
shăn–rĭsh-a-thā′im eight years.
9 And when the children of Israel
cried unto the LORD, the LORD raised up
a deliverer to the children of Israel,
who delivered them, *even* Ŏth′nī-el the
son of Kē′năz, Caleb's younger brother.
10 And the Spirit of the LORD came
upon him, and he judged Israel, and
went out to war: and the LORD de-
livered Chū′shăn–rĭsh-a-thā′im king of
Mĕs-o-po-tā′mĭ-a into his hand; and his
hand prevailed against Chū′shăn–rĭsh-
a-thā′im.
11 And the land had rest forty years.
And Ŏth′nī-el the son of Kē′năz died.
12 ¶And the children of Israel did evil
again in the sight of the LORD: and the
LORD strengthened Ĕg′lŏn the king of
Moab against Israel, because they had
done evil in the sight of the LORD.
13 And he gathered unto him the
children of Ammon and Ăm′a-lĕk, and
went and smote Israel, and possessed
the city of palm trees.
14 So the children of Israel served
Ĕg′lŏn the king of Moab eighteen years.
15 But when the children of Israel
cried unto the LORD, the LORD raised
them up a deliverer, Ē′hŭd the son of
Ge′ra, a Benjamite, a man left-handed:
and by him the children of Israel sent a
present unto Ĕg′lŏn the king of Moab.
16 But Ē′hŭd made him a dagger
which had two edges, of a cubit length;
and he did gird it under his raiment
upon his right thigh.
17 And he brought the present unto
Ĕg′lŏn king of Moab: and Ĕg′lŏn *was* a
very fat man.
18 And when he had made an end to
offer the present, he sent away the
people that bare the present.
19 But he himself turned again from
the quarries that *were* by Gilgal, and
said, I have a secret errand unto thee, O
king: who said, Keep silence. And all
that stood by him went out from him.
20 And Ē′hŭd came unto him; and he
was sitting in a summer parlour, which
he had for himself alone. And Ē′hŭd

said, I have a message from God unto thee. And he arose out of *his* seat.

21 And Ē'hŭd put forth his left hand, and took the dagger from his right thigh, and thrust it into his belly:

22 And the haft also went in after the blade; and the fat closed upon the blade, so that he could not draw the dagger out of his belly; and the dirt came out.

23 Then Ē'hŭd went forth through the porch, and shut the doors of the parlour upon him, and locked them.

24 When he was gone out, his servants came; and when they saw that, behold, the doors of the parlour *were* locked, they said, Surely he covereth his feet in his summer chamber.

25 And they tarried till they were ashamed: and, behold, he opened not the doors of the parlour; therefore they took a key, and opened *them:* and, behold, their lord *was* fallen down dead on the earth.

26 And Ē'hŭd escaped while they tarried, and passed beyond the quarries, and escaped unto Sē'i-răth.

27 And it came to pass, when he was come, that he blew a trumpet in the mountain of Ē'phra-im, and the children of Israel went down with him from the mount, and he before them.

28 And he said unto them, Follow after me: for the LORD hath delivered your enemies the Moabites into your hand. And they went down after him, and took the fords of Jordan toward Moab, and suffered not a man to pass over.

29 And they slew of Moab at that time about ten thousand men, all lusty, and all men of valour; and there escaped not a man.

30 So Moab was subdued that day under the hand of Israel. And the land had rest fourscore years.

31 ¶And after him was Shăm'găr the son of Ā'năth, which slew of the Philistines six hundred men with an ox goad: and he also delivered Israel.

CHAPTER 4

AND the children of Israel again did evil in the sight of the LORD, when Ē'hŭd was dead.

2 And the LORD sold them into the hand of Jā'bin king of Canaan, that reigned in Hā'zôr; the captain of whose host *was* Sĭs'e-ra, which dwelt in Ha-rō'shĕth of the Gentiles.

3 And the children of Israel cried unto the LORD: for he had nine hundred chariots of iron; and twenty years he mightily oppressed the children of Israel.

4 ¶And Dĕb'o-rah, a prophetess, the wife of Lăp'i-dŏth, she judged Israel at that time.

5 And she dwelt under the palm tree of Dĕb'o-rah between Rā'mah and Bĕth–el in mount Ē'phra-im: and the children of Israel came up to her for judgment.

6 And she sent and called Bâ'rak the son of A-bĭn'ō-am out of Kē'dĕsh-năph'ta-lī, and said unto him, Hath not the LORD God of Israel commanded, *saying,* Go and draw toward mount Tā'bor, and take with thee ten thousand men of the children of Năph'ta-lī and of the children of Zĕb'u-lun?

7 And I will draw unto thee to the river Kī'shŏn Sĭs'e-ra, the captain of Jā'bin's army, with his chariots and his multitude; and I will deliver him into thine hand.

8 And Bâ'rak said unto her, If thou wilt go with me, then I will go: but if thou wilt not go with me, *then* I will not go.

9 And she said, I will surely go with thee: notwithstanding the journey that thou takest shall not be for thine honour; for the LORD shall sell Sĭs'e-ra into the hand of a woman. And Dĕb'o-rah arose, and went with Bâ'rak to Kē'dĕsh.

10 And Bâ'rak called Zĕb'u-lun and Năph'ta-lī to Kē'dĕsh; and he went up with ten thousand men at his feet: and Dĕb'o-rah went up with him.

11 Now Hē'ber the Kēn'īte, *which was* of the children of Hō'băb the father in law of Moses, had severed himself from the Kēn'ītes, and pitched his tent unto the plain of Zā-a-nā'im, which *is* by Kē'dĕsh.

12 And they shewed Sĭs'e-ra that Bâ'rak the son of A-bĭn'ō-am was gone up to mount Tā'bor.

13 And Sĭs'e-ra gathered together all his chariots, *even* nine hundred chariots of iron, and all the people that *were* with him, from Ha-rō'shĕth of the Gentiles unto the river of Kī'shŏn.

14 And Dĕb'o-rah said unto Bâ'rak, Up; for this *is* the day in which the LORD hath delivered Sĭs'e-ra into thine hand: is not the LORD gone out before thee? So Bâ'rak went down from mount Tā'bor, and ten thousand men after him.

15 And the LORD discomfited Sĭs'e-ra, and all *his* chariots, and all *his* host, with the edge of the sword before Bâ'rak; so that Sĭs'e-ra lighted down off *his* chariot, and fled away on his feet.

16 But Bâ'rak pursued after the chariots, and after the host, unto Ha-rō'shĕth of the Gentiles: and all the host of

Sĭs′e-ra fell upon the edge of the sword;
and there was not a man left.
17 Howbeit Sĭs′e-ra fled away on his
feet to the tent of Jā′el the wife of Hē′-
ber the Kēn′īte: for *there was* peace
between Jā′bin the king of Hā′zôr and
the house of Hē′ber the Kēn′īte.
18 And Jā′el went out to meet Sĭs′e-
ra, and said unto him, Turn in, my lord,
turn in to me; fear not. And when he
had turned in unto her into the tent, she
covered him with a mantle.
19 And he said unto her, Give me, I
pray thee, a little water to drink; for I
am thirsty. And she opened a bottle of
milk, and gave him drink, and covered
him.
20 Again he said unto her, Stand in
the door of the tent, and it shall be,
when any man doth come and enquire
of thee, and say, Is there any man here?
that thou shalt say, No.
21 Then Jā′el Hē′ber's wife took a nail
of the tent, and took an hammer in her
hand, and went softly unto him, and
smote the nail into his temples, and fas-
tened it into the ground: for he was fast
asleep and weary. So he died.
22 And, behold, as Bâ′rak pursued
Sĭs′e-ra, Jā′el came out to meet him,
and said unto him, Come, and I will
shew thee the man whom thou seekest.
And when he came into her *tent*, be-
hold, Sĭs′e-ra lay dead, and the nail *was*
in his temples.
23 So God subdued on that day Jā′bin
the king of Canaan before the children
of Israel.
24 And the hand of the children of
Israel prospered, and prevailed against
Jā′bin the king of Canaan, until they
had destroyed Jā′bin king of Canaan.

CHAPTER 5

THEN sang Dĕb′o-rah and Bâ′rak the
son of A-bĭn′ō-am on that day, saying,
2 Praise ye the LORD for the avenging
of Israel, when the people willingly of-
fered themselves.
3 Hear, O ye kings; give ear, O ye
princes; I, *even* I, will sing unto the
LORD; I will sing *praise* to the LORD God
of Israel.
4 LORD, when thou wentest out of
Sē′ir, when thou marchedst out of the
field of Ē′dom, the earth trembled, and
the heavens dropped, the clouds also
dropped water.
5 The mountains melted from before
the LORD, *even* that Sī′naī from before
the LORD God of Israel.
6 In the days of Shăm′gär the son of
Ā′năth, in the days of Jā′el, the high-
ways were unoccupied, and the travel-
lers walked through byways.
7 *The inhabitants of* the villages
ceased, they ceased in Israel, until that
I Dĕb′o-rah arose, that I arose a mother
in Israel.
8 They chose new gods; then *was* war
in the gates: was there a shield or spear
seen among forty thousand in Israel?
9 My heart *is* toward the governors of
Israel, that offered themselves willing-
ly among the people. Bless ye the
LORD.
10 Speak, ye that ride on white asses,
ye that sit in judgment, and walk by the
way.
11 *They that are delivered* from the
noise of archers in the places of
drawing water, there shall they re-
hearse the righteous acts of the LORD,
even the righteous acts *toward the
inhabitants* of his villages in Israel:
then shall the people of the LORD go
down to the gates.
12 Awake, awake, Dĕb′o-rah: awake,
awake, utter a song: arise, Bâ′rak, and
lead thy captivity captive, thou son of
A-bĭn′ō-am.
13 Then he made him that remaineth
have dominion over the nobles among
the people: the LORD made me have
dominion over the mighty.
14 Out of Ē′phra-im *was there* a root
of them against Ăm′a-lĕk; after thee,
Benjamin, among thy people; out of
Mā′chĭr came down governors, and out
of Zĕb′u-lun they that handle the pen of
the writer.
15 And the princes of Ĭs′sa-char *were*
with Dĕb′o-rah; even Ĭs′sa-char, and
also Bâ′rak: he was sent on foot into the
valley. For the divisions of Reuben
there were great thoughts of heart.
16 Why abodest thou among the
sheepfolds, to hear the bleatings of the
flocks? For the divisions of Reuben
there were great searchings of heart.
17 Gilead abode beyond Jordan: and
why did Dan remain in ships? Asher
continued on the sea shore, and abode
in his breaches.
18 Zĕb′u-lun and Năph′ta-lī *were* a
people *that* jeoparded their lives unto
the death in the high places of the field.
19 The kings came *and* fought, then
fought the kings of Canaan in Ta′a-
năch by the waters of Me-gĭd′dō; they
took no gain of money.
20 They fought from heaven; the
stars in their courses fought against
Sĭs′e-ra.
21 The river of Kī′shŏn swept them
away, that ancient river, the river
Kī′shŏn. O my soul, thou hast trodden
down strength.
22 Then were the horsehoofs broken

by the means of the pransings, the pransings of their mighty ones.

23 Curse ye Me'rŏz, said the angel of the LORD, curse ye bitterly the inhabitants thereof; because they came not to the help of the LORD, to the help of the LORD against the mighty.

24 Blessed above women shall Jā'el the wife of Hē'ber the Kēn'īte be, blessed shall she be above women in the tent.

25 He asked water, *and* she gave *him* milk; she brought forth butter in a lordly dish.

26 She put her hand to the nail, and her right hand to the workmen's hammer; and with the hammer she smote Sĭs'e-ra, she smote off his head, when she had pierced and stricken through his temples.

27 At her feet he bowed, he fell, he lay down: at her feet he bowed, he fell: where he bowed, there he fell down dead.

28 The mother of Sĭs'e-ra looked out at a window, and cried through the lattice, Why is his chariot *so* long in coming? why tarry the wheels of his chariots?

29 Her wise ladies answered her, yea, she returned answer to herself,

30 Have they not sped? have they *not* divided the prey; to every man a damsel *or* two; to Sĭs'e-ra a prey of divers colours, a prey of divers colours of needlework, of divers colours of needlework on both sides, *meet* for the necks of *them that take* the spoil?

31 So let all thine enemies perish, O LORD: but *let* them that love him *be* as the sun when he goeth forth in his might. And the land had rest forty years.

CHAPTER 6

AND the children of Israel did evil in the sight of the LORD: and the LORD delivered them into the hand of Mĭd'ĭ-an seven years.

2 And the hand of Mĭd'ĭ-an prevailed against Israel: *and* because of the Mĭd'ĭ-an-ītes the children of Israel made them the dens which *are* in the mountains, and caves, and strong holds.

3 And *so* it was, when Israel had sown, that the Mĭd'ĭ-an-ītes came up, and the Am'ă-lek-ītes, and the children of the east, even they came up against them;

4 And they encamped against them, and destroyed the increase of the earth, till thou come unto Gā'za, and left no sustenance for Israel, neither sheep, nor ox, nor ass.

5 For they came up with their cattle and their tents, and they came as grasshoppers for multitude; *for* both they and their camels were without number: and they entered into the land to destroy it.

6 And Israel was greatly impoverished because of the Mĭd'ĭ-an-ītes; and the children of Israel cried unto the LORD.

7 ¶And it came to pass, when the children of Israel cried unto the LORD because of the Mĭd'ĭ-an-ītes,

8 That the LORD sent a prophet unto the children of Israel, which said unto them, Thus saith the LORD God of Israel, I brought you up from Egypt, and brought you forth out of the house of bondage;

9 And I delivered you out of the hand of the Egyptians, and out of the hand of all that oppressed you, and drave them out from before you, and gave you their land;

10 And I said unto you, I *am* the LORD your God; fear not the gods of the Ăm'or-ītes, in whose land ye dwell: but ye have not obeyed my voice.

11 ¶And there came an angel of the LORD, and sat under an oak which *was* in Ŏph'rah, that *pertained* unto Jō'ăsh the Ă'bĭ–ĕz'rīte: and his son Gideon threshed wheat by the winepress, to hide *it* from the Mĭd'ĭ-an-ītes.

12 And the angel of the LORD appeared unto him, and said unto him, The LORD *is* with thee, thou mighty man of valour.

13 And Gideon said unto him, Oh my Lord, if the LORD be with us, why then is all this befallen us? and where *be* all his miracles which our fathers told us of, saying, Did not the LORD bring us up from Egypt? but now the LORD hath forsaken us, and delivered us into the hands of the Mĭd'ĭ-an-ītes.

14 And the LORD looked upon him, and said, Go in this thy might, and thou shalt save Israel from the hand of the Mĭd'ĭ-an-ītes: have not I sent thee?

15 And he said unto him, Oh my Lord, wherewith shall I save Israel? behold, my family *is* poor in Ma-năs'seh, and I *am* the least in my father's house.

16 And the LORD said unto him, Surely I will be with thee, and thou shalt smite the Mĭd'ĭ-an-ītes as one man.

17 And he said unto him, If now I have found grace in thy sight, then shew me a sign that thou talkest with me.

18 Depart not hence, I pray thee, until I come unto thee, and bring forth my present, and set *it* before thee. And he said, I will tarry until thou come again.

19 And Gideon went in, and made

ready a kid, and unleavened cakes of an ephah of flour: the flesh he put in a basket, and he put the broth in a pot, and brought *it* out unto him under the oak, and presented *it*.
20 And the angel of God said unto him, Take the flesh and the unleavened cakes, and lay *them* upon this rock, and pour out the broth. And he did so.
21 Then the angel of the LORD put forth the end of the staff that *was* in his hand, and touched the flesh and the unleavened cakes; and there rose up fire out of the rock, and consumed the flesh and the unleavened cakes. Then the angel of the LORD departed out of his sight.
22 And when Gideon perceived that he *was* an angel of the LORD, Gideon said, Alas, O Lord GOD! for because I have seen an angel of the LORD face to face.
23 And the LORD said unto him, Peace *be* unto thee; fear not: thou shalt not die.
24 Then Gideon built an altar there unto the LORD, and called it Je-hō'-vah-shā'lom: unto this day it *is* yet in Ŏph'rah of the Ā'bī-ĕz'rītes.
25 ¶And it came to pass the same night, that the LORD said unto him, Take thy father's young bullock, even the second bullock of seven years old, and throw down the altar of Bā'al that thy father hath, and cut down the grove that *is* by it:
26 And build an altar unto the LORD thy God upon the top of this rock, in the ordered place, and take the second bullock, and offer a burnt sacrifice with the wood of the grove which thou shalt cut down.
27 Then Gideon took ten men of his servants, and did as the LORD had said unto him: and *so* it was, because he feared his father's household, and the men of the city, that he could not do *it* by day, that he did *it* by night.
28 ¶And when the men of the city arose early in the morning, behold, the altar of Bā'al was cast down, and the grove was cut down that *was* by it, and the second bullock was offered upon the altar *that was* built.
29 And they said one to another, Who hath done this thing? And when they enquired and asked, they said, Gideon the son of Jō'ăsh hath done this thing.
30 Then the men of the city said unto Jō'ăsh, Bring out thy son, that he may die: because he hath cast down the altar of Bā'al, and because he hath cut down the grove that *was* by it.
31 And Jō'ăsh said unto all that stood against him, Will ye plead for Bā'al? will ye save him? he that will plead for him, let him be put to death whilst *it is yet* morning: if he *be* a god, let him plead for himself, because *one* hath cast down his altar.
32 Therefore on that day he called him Je-rŭb'ba-al, saying, Let Bā'al plead against him, because he hath thrown down his altar.
33 ¶Then all the Mĭd'ĭ-an-ītes and the Am'ă-lek-ītes and the children of the east were gathered together, and went over, and pitched in the valley of Jĕz're-el.
34 But the Spirit of the LORD came upon Gideon, and he blew a trumpet; and Ā'bī-ē'zer was gathered after him.
35 And he sent messengers throughout all Ma-năs'seh; who also was gathered after him: and he sent messengers unto Asher, and unto Zĕb'u-lun, and unto Năph'ta-lī; and they came up to meet them.
36 ¶And Gideon said unto God, If thou wilt save Israel by mine hand, as thou hast said,
37 Behold, I will put a fleece of wool in the floor; *and* if the dew be on the fleece only, and *it be* dry upon all the earth *beside*, then shall I know that thou wilt save Israel by mine hand, as thou hast said.
38 And it was so: for he rose up early on the morrow, and thrust the fleece together, and wringed the dew out of the fleece, a bowl full of water.
39 And Gideon said unto God, Let not thine anger be hot against me, and I will speak but this once: let me prove, I pray thee, but this once with the fleece; let it now be dry only upon the fleece, and upon all the ground let there be dew.
40 And God did so that night: for it was dry upon the fleece only, and there was dew on all the ground.

CHAPTER 7

THEN Je-rŭb'ba-al, who *is* Gideon, and all the people that *were* with him, rose up early, and pitched beside the well of Hâ'rŏd: so that the host of the Mĭd'ĭ-an-ītes were on the north side of them, by the hill of Mô'reh, in the valley.
2 And the LORD said unto Gideon, The people that *are* with thee *are* too many for me to give the Mĭd'ĭ-an-ītes into their hands, lest Israel vaunt themselves against me, saying, Mine own hand hath saved me.
3 Now therefore go to, proclaim in the ears of the people, saying, Whosoever *is* fearful and afraid, let him return and depart early from mount Gilead. And there returned of the people

twenty and two thousand; and there re-
mained ten thousand.
4 And the LORD said unto Gideon, The
people *are* yet *too* many; bring them
down unto the water, and I will try
them for thee there: and it shall be, *that*
of whom I say unto thee, This shall go
with thee, the same shall go with thee;
and of whomsoever I say unto thee,
This shall not go with thee, the same
shall not go.
5 So he brought down the people
unto the water: and the LORD said unto
Gideon, Every one that lappeth of the
water with his tongue, as a dog lappeth,
him shalt thou set by himself; likewise
every one that boweth down upon his
knees to drink.
6 And the number of them that
lapped, *putting* their hand to their
mouth, were three hundred men: but
all the rest of the people bowed down
upon their knees to drink water.
7 And the LORD said unto Gideon, By
the three hundred men that lapped will
I save you, and deliver the Mĭd'ī-an-ītes
into thine hand: and let all the *other*
people go every man unto his place.
8 So the people took victuals in their
hand, and their trumpets: and he sent
all *the rest of* Israel every man unto his
tent, and retained those three hundred
men: and the host of Mĭd'ī-an was be-
neath him in the valley.
9 ¶And it came to pass the same
night, that the LORD said unto him,
Arise, get thee down unto the host; for I
have delivered it into thine hand.
10 But if thou fear to go down, go
thou with Phū'rah thy servant down to
the host:
11 And thou shalt hear what they say;
and afterward shall thine hands be
strengthened to go down unto the host.
Then went he down with Phū'rah his
servant unto the outside of the armed
men that *were* in the host.
12 And the Mĭd'ī-an-ītes and the
Am'ă-lek-ītes and all the children of the
east lay along in the valley like
grasshoppers for multitude; and their
camels *were* without number, as the
sand by the sea side for multitude.
13 And when Gideon was come, be-
hold, *there was* a man that told a dream
unto his fellow, and said, Behold, I
dreamed a dream, and, lo, a cake of
barley bread tumbled into the host of
Mĭd'ī-an, and came unto a tent, and
smote it that it fell, and overturned it,
that the tent lay along.
14 And his fellow answered and said,
This *is* nothing else save the sword of
Gideon the son of Jō'ăsh, a man of
Israel: *for* into his hand hath God deliv-
ered Mĭd'ī-an, and all the host.
15 ¶And it was *so*, when Gideon
heard the telling of the dream, and the
interpretation thereof, that he wor-
shipped, and returned into the host of
Israel, and said, Arise; for the LORD
hath delivered into your hand the host
of Mĭd'ī-an.
16 And he divided the three hundred
men *into* three companies, and he put a
trumpet in every man's hand, with
empty pitchers, and lamps within the
pitchers.
17 And he said unto them, Look on
me, and do likewise: and, behold, when
I come to the outside of the camp, it
shall be *that*, as I do, so shall ye do.
18 When I blow with a trumpet, I and
all that *are* with me, then blow ye the
trumpets also on every side of all the
camp, and say, *The sword* of the LORD,
and of Gideon.
19 ¶So Gideon, and the hundred men
that *were* with him, came unto the out-
side of the camp in the beginning of the
middle watch; and they had but newly
set the watch: and they blew the trum-
pets, and brake the pitchers that *were*
in their hands.
20 And the three companies blew the
trumpets, and brake the pitchers, and
held the lamps in their left hands, and
the trumpets in their right hands to
blow *withal*: and they cried, The sword
of the LORD, and of Gideon.
21 And they stood every man in his
place round about the camp: and all the
host ran, and cried, and fled.
22 And the three hundred blew the
trumpets, and the LORD set every man's
sword against his fellow, even
throughout all the host: and the host
fled to Bĕth–shĭt'tah in Zĕr'e-răth, *and*
to the border of Ā'bel–mĕ-hō'lah, unto
Tăb'bath.
23 And the men of Israel gathered
themselves together out of Năph'ta-lī,
and out of Asher, and out of all Ma-
năs'seh, and pursued after the Mĭd'ī-
an-ītes.
24 And Gideon sent messengers
throughout all mount Ē'phra-im,
saying, Come down against the Mĭd'ī-
an-ītes, and take before them the waters
unto Bĕth–bâ'rah and Jordan. Then
all the men of Ē'phra-im gathered
themselves together, and took the wa-
ters unto Bĕth–bâ'rah and Jordan.
25 And they took two princes of the
Mĭd'ī-an-ītes, Ô'reb and Zē'eb; and they
slew Ô'reb upon the rock Ô'reb, and
Zē'eb they slew at the winepress of
Zē'eb, and pursued Mĭd'ī-an, and

brought the heads of Ô'reb and Zē'eb to Gideon on the other side Jordan.

CHAPTER 8

AND the men of Ē'phra-im said unto him, Why hast thou served us thus, that thou calledst us not, when thou wentest to fight with the Mĭd'ĭ-an-ītes? And they did chide with him sharply.

2 And he said unto them, What have I done now in comparison of you? *Is* not the gleaning of the grapes of Ē'phra-im better than the vintage of Ă'bĭ-ē'zer?

3 God hath delivered into your hands the princes of Mĭd'ĭ-an, Ô'reb and Zē'eb: and what was I able to do in comparison of you? Then their anger was abated toward him, when he had said that.

4 ¶And Gideon came to Jordan, *and* passed over, he, and the three hundred men that *were* with him, faint, yet pursuing *them.*

5 And he said unto the men of Sŭc'coth, Give, I pray you, loaves of bread unto the people that follow me: for they *be* faint, and I am pursuing after Zē'bah and Zăl-mŭn'na, kings of Mĭd'ĭ-an.

6 And the princes of Sŭc'coth said, *Are* the hands of Zē'bah and Zăl-mŭn'na now in thine hand, that we should give bread unto thine army?

7 And Gideon said, Therefore when the LORD hath delivered Zē'bah and Zăl-mŭn'na into mine hand, then I will tear your flesh with the thorns of the wilderness and with briers.

8 And he went up thence to Pe-nū'el, and spake unto them likewise: and the men of Pe-nū'el answered him as the men of Sŭc'coth had answered *him.*

9 And he spake also unto the men of Pe-nū'el, saying, When I come again in peace, I will break down this tower.

10 ¶Now Zē'bah and Zăl-mŭn'na *were* in Kär'kôr, and their hosts with them, about fifteen thousand *men,* all that were left of all the hosts of the children of the east: for there fell an hundred and twenty thousand men that drew sword.

11 ¶And Gideon went up by the way of them that dwelt in tents on the east of Nō'bah and Jŏg'be-hah, and smote the host: for the host was secure.

12 And when Zē'bah and Zăl-mŭn'na fled, he pursued after them, and took the two kings of Mĭd'ĭ-an, Zē'bah and Zăl-mŭn'na, and discomfited all the host.

13 ¶And Gideon the son of Jō'ăsh returned from battle before the sun *was up,*

14 And caught a young man of the men of Sŭc'coth, and enquired of him: and he described unto him the princes of Sŭc'coth, and the elders thereof, *even* threescore and seventeen men.

15 And he came unto the men of Sŭc'coth, and said, Behold Zē'bah and Zăl-mŭn'na, with whom ye did upbraid me, saying, *Are* the hands of Zē'bah and Zăl-mŭn'na now in thine hand, that we should give bread unto thy men *that are* weary?

16 And he took the elders of the city, and thorns of the wilderness and briers, and with them he taught the men of Sŭc'coth.

17 And he beat down the tower of Pe-nū'el, and slew the men of the city.

18 ¶Then said he unto Zē'bah and Zăl'mŭn'na, What manner of men *were they* whom ye slew at Tā'bor? And they answered, As thou *art,* so *were* they; each one resembled the children of a king.

19 And he said, They *were* my brethren, *even* the sons of my mother: *as* the LORD liveth, if ye had saved them alive, I would not slay you.

20 And he said unto Jē'ther his firstborn, Up, *and* slay them. But the youth drew not his sword: for he feared, because he *was* yet a youth.

21 Then Zē'bah and Zăl-mŭn'na said, Rise thou, and fall upon us: for as the man *is, so is* his strength. And Gideon arose, and slew Zē'bah and Zăl-mŭn'na, and took away the ornaments that *were* on their camels' necks.

22 ¶Then the men of Israel said unto Gideon, Rule thou over us, both thou, and thy son, and thy son's son also: for thou hast delivered us from the hand of Mĭd'ĭ-an.

23 And Gideon said unto them, I will not rule over you, neither shall my son rule over you: the LORD shall rule over you.

24 And Gideon said unto them, I would desire a request of you, that ye would give me every man the earrings of his prey. (For they had golden earrings, because they *were* Īsh'ma-el-ītes.)

25 And they answered, We will willingly give *them.* And they spread a garment, and did cast therein every man the earrings of his prey.

26 And the weight of the golden earrings that he requested was a thousand and seven hundred *shekels* of gold; beside ornaments, and collars, and purple raiment that *was* on the kings of Mĭd'ĭ-an, and beside the chains that *were* about their camels' necks.

27 And Gideon made an ephod thereof, and put it in his city, *even* in Ŏph'rah: and all Israel went thither a

whoring after it: which thing became a
snare unto Gideon, and to his house.
28 ¶Thus was Mĭd'ĭan subdued be-
fore the children of Israel, so that they
lifted up their heads no more. And the
country was in quietness forty years in
the days of Gideon.
29 And Je-rŭb'ba-al the son of Jō'ăsh
went and dwelt in his own house.
30 And Gideon had threescore and
ten sons of his body begotten: for he
had many wives.
31 And his concubine that *was* in
Shĕ'chem, she also bare him a son,
whose name he called A-bĭm'e-lĕch.
32 And Gideon the son of Jō'ăsh died
in a good old age, and was buried in the
sepulchre of Jō'ăsh his father, in Ŏph'rah
of the Ă'bī-ĕz'rītes.
33 And it came to pass, as soon as Gid-
eon was dead, that the children of
Israel turned again, and went a whor-
ing after Bā'al-ĭm, and made Bā'al-
bĕ'rĭth their god.
34 And the children of Israel remem-
bered not the LORD their God, who had
delivered them out of the hands of all
their enemies on every side:
35 Neither shewed they kindness to
the house of Je-rŭb'ba-al, *namely*, Gid-
eon, according to all the goodness
which he had shewed unto Israel.

CHAPTER 9

AND A'bĭm'e-lĕch the son of Je-rŭb'ba-
al went to Shĕ'-chem unto his mother's
brethren, and communed with them,
and with all the family of the house of
his mother's father, saying,
2 Speak, I pray you, in the ears of all
the men of Shĕ'chem, Whether *is* bet-
ter for you, either that all the sons of Je-
rŭb'ba-al, *which are* threescore and ten
persons, reign over you, or that one
reign over you? remember also that I
am your bone and your flesh.
3 And his mother's brethren spake of
him in the ears of all the men of Shĕ'-
chem all these words: and their hearts
inclined to follow A-bĭm'e-lĕch; for
they said, He *is* our brother.
4 And they gave him threescore and
ten *pieces* of silver out of the house of
Bā'al-bĕ'rĭth, wherewith A-bĭm'e-lĕch
hired vain and light persons, which fol-
lowed him.
5 And he went unto his father's house
at Ŏph'rah, and slew his brethren the
sons of Je-rŭb'ba-al, *being* threescore
and ten persons, upon one stone: not-
withstanding yet Jō'tham the youngest
son of Je-rŭb'ba-al was left; for he hid
himself.
6 And all the men of Shĕ'chem gath-
ered together, and all the house of
Mĭl'lō, and went, and made A-bĭm'e-
lĕch king, by the plain of the pillar that
was in Shĕ'chem.
7 And when they told *it* to Jō'tham,
he went and stood in the top of mount
Gĕr'i-zĭm, and lifted up his voice, and
cried, and said unto them, Hearken
unto me, ye men of Shĕ'chem, that God
may hearken unto you.
8 The trees went forth *on a time* to
anoint a king over them; and they said
unto the olive tree, Reign thou over us.
9 But the olive tree said unto them,
Should I leave my fatness, wherewith
by me they honour God and man, and
go to be promoted over the trees?
10 And the trees said to the fig tree,
Come thou, *and* reign over us.
11 But the fig tree said unto them,
Should I forsake my sweetness, and my
good fruit, and go to be promoted over
the trees?
12 Then said the trees unto the vine,
Come thou, *and* reign over us.
13 And the vine said unto them,
Should I leave my wine, which cheer-
eth God and man, and go to be pro-
moted over the trees?
14 Then said all the trees unto the
bramble, Come thou, *and* reign over us.
15 And the bramble said unto the
trees, If in truth ye anoint me king over
you, *then* come *and* put your trust in
my shadow: and if not, let fire come out
of the bramble, and devour the cedars
of Lebanon.
16 Now therefore, if ye have done
truly and sincerely, in that ye have
made A-bĭm'e-lĕch king, and if ye have
dealt well with Je-rŭb'ba-al and his
house, and have done unto him accord-
ing to the deserving of his hands;
17 (For my father fought for you, and
adventured his life far, and delivered
you out of the hand of Mĭd'ĭ-an:
18 And ye are risen up against my
father's house this day, and have slain
his sons, threescore and ten persons,
upon one stone, and have made A-
bĭm'e-lĕch, the son of his maidservant,
king over the men of Shĕ'chem, be-
cause he *is* your brother;)
19 If ye then have dealt truly and sin-
cerely with Je-rŭb'ba-al and with his
house this day, *then* rejoice ye in A-
bĭm'e-lĕch, and let him also rejoice in
you:
20 But if not, let fire come out from A-
bĭm'e-lĕch, and devour the men of
Shĕ'chem, and the house of Mĭl'lō; and
let fire come out from the men of Shĕ'-
chem, and from the house of Mĭl'lō, and
devour A-bĭm'e-lĕch.
21 And Jō'tham ran away, and fled,

and went to Beer, and dwelt there, for
fear of A-bĭm′e-lĕch his brother.
22 ¶When A-bĭm′e-lĕch had reigned
three years over Israel,
23 Then God sent an evil spirit be-
tween A-bĭm′e-lĕch and the men of
Shĕ′chem; and the men of Shĕ′chem
dealt treacherously with A-bĭm′e-lĕch:
24 That the cruelty *done* to the
threescore and ten sons of Je-rŭb′ba-al
might come, and their blood be laid
upon A-bĭm′e-lĕch their brother, which
slew them; and upon the men of Shĕ′-
chem, which aided him in the killing of
his brethren.
25 And the men of Shĕ′chem set liers
in wait for him in the top of the moun-
tains, and they robbed all that came
along that way by them: and it was told
A-bĭm′e-lĕch.
26 And Gā′al the son of Ē′bĕd came
with his brethren, and went over to
Shĕ′chem: and the men of Shĕ′chem
put their confidence in him.
27 And they went out into the fields,
and gathered their vineyards, and
trode *the grapes,* and made merry, and
went into the house of their god, and
did eat and drink, and cursed A-bĭm′e-
lĕch.
28 And Gā′al the son of Ē′bĕd said,
Who *is* A-bĭm′e-lĕch, and who *is* Shĕ′-
chem, that we should serve him? *is* not
he the son of Je-rŭb′ba-al? and Zē′bul
his officer? serve the men of Hā′môr
the father of Shĕ′chem: for why should
we serve him?
29 And would to God this people
were under my hand! then would I re-
move A-bĭm′e-lĕch. And he said to A-
bĭm′e-lĕch, Increase thine army, and
come out.
30 ¶And when Zē′bul the ruler of the
city heard the words of Gā′al the son of
Ē′bĕd, his anger was kindled.
31 And he sent messengers unto A-
bĭm′e-lĕch privily, saying, Behold, Gā′al
the son of Ē′bĕd and his brethren be
come to Shĕ′chem; and, behold, they
fortify the city against thee.
32 Now therefore up by night, thou
and the people that *is* with thee, and lie
in wait in the field:
33 And it shall be, *that* in the morn-
ing, as soon as the sun is up, thou shalt
rise early, and set upon the city: and,
behold, *when* he and the people that *is*
with him come out against thee, then
mayest thou do to them as thou shalt
find occasion.
34 ¶And A-bĭm′e-lĕch rose up, and all
the people that *were* with him, by
night, and they laid wait against Shĕ′-
chem in four companies.
35 And Gā′al the son of Ē′bĕd went
out, and stood in the entering of the
gate of the city: and A-bĭm′e-lĕch rose
up, and the people that *were* with him,
from lying in wait.
36 And when Gā′al saw the people,
he said to Zē′bul, Behold, there come
people down from the top of the moun-
tains. And Zē′bul said unto him, Thou
seest the shadow of the mountains as *if*
they were men.
37 And Gā′al spake again and said,
See there come people down by the
middle of the land, and another com-
pany come along by the plain of Mē-
ŏn′e-nĭm.
38 Then said Zē′bul unto him, Where
is now thy mouth, wherewith thou
saidst, Who *is* A-bĭm′e-lĕch, that we
should serve him? *is* not this the people
that thou hast despised? go out, I pray
now, and fight with them.
39 And Gā′al went out before the
men of Shĕ′chem, and fought with A-
bĭm′e-lĕch.
40 And A-bĭm′e-lĕch chased him, and
he fled before him, and many were
overthrown *and* wounded, *even* unto
the entering of the gate.
41 And A-bĭm′e-lĕch dwelt at A-rŭ′-
mah: and Zē′bul thrust out Gā′al and
his brethren, that they should not dwell
in Shĕ′chem.
42 And it came to pass on the
morrow, that the people went out into
the field; and they told A-bĭm′e-lĕch.
43 And he took the people, and di-
vided them into three companies, and
laid wait in the field, and looked, and,
behold, the people *were* come forth out
of the city; and he rose up against them,
and smote them.
44 And A-bĭm′e-lĕch, and the com-
pany that *was* with him, rushed for-
ward, and stood in the entering of the
gate of the city: and the two *other* com-
panies ran upon all *the people* that
were in the fields, and slew them.
45 And A-bĭm′e-lĕch fought against
the city all that day; and he took the
city, and slew the people that *was* there-
in, and beat down the city, and
sowed it with salt.
46 ¶And when all the men of the tow-
er of Shĕ′chem heard *that,* they en-
tered into an hold of the house of the
god Be′rĭth.
47 And it was told A-bĭm′e-lĕch, that
all the men of the tower of Shĕ′chem
were gathered together.
48 And A-bĭm′e-lĕch gat him up to
mount Zăl′mon, he and all the people
that *were* with him; and A-bĭm′e-lĕch
took an axe in his hand, and cut down a
bough from the trees, and took it, and
laid *it* on his shoulder, and said unto the

people that *were* with him, What ye have seen me do, make haste, *and* do as I *have done*.

49 And all the people likewise cut down every man his bough, and followed A-bĭm'e-lĕch, and put *them* to the hold, and set the hold on fire upon them; so that all the men of the tower of Shĕ'chem died also, about a thousand men and women.

50 ¶Then went A-bĭm'e-lĕch to Thē'bez, and encamped against Thē'bez, and took it.

51 But there was a strong tower within the city, and thither fled all the men and women, and all they of the city, and shut *it* to them, and gat them up to the top of the tower.

52 And A-bĭm'e-lĕch came unto the tower, and fought against it, and went hard unto the door of the tower to burn it with fire.

53 And a certain woman cast a piece of a millstone upon A-bĭm'e-lĕch's head, and all to brake his skull.

54 Then he called hastily unto the young man his armourbearer, and said unto him, Draw thy sword, and slay me, that men say not of me, A woman slew him. And his young man thrust him through, and he died.

55 And when the men of Israel saw that A-bĭm'e-lĕch was dead, they departed every man unto his place.

56 ¶Thus God rendered the wickedness of A-bĭm'e-lĕch, which he did unto his father, in slaying his seventy brethren:

57 And all the evil of the men of Shĕ'chem did God render upon their heads: and upon them came the curse of Jō'tham the son of Je'rŭb'ba-al.

CHAPTER 10

AND after A-bĭm'e-lĕch there arose to defend Israel Tō'la the son of Pū'ah, the sone of Dodo, a man of Ĭs'sa-char; and he dwelt in Shā'mir in mount Ē'phra-im.

2 And he judged Israel twenty and three years, and died, and was buried in Shā'mir.

3 ¶And after him arose Jā'ir, a Gileadite, and judged Israel twenty and two years.

4 And he had thirty sons that rode on thirty ass colts, and they had thirty cities, which are called Hă'vŏth–jā'ir unto this day, which *are* in the land of Gilead.

5 And Jā'ir died, and was buried in Cā'mon.

6 ¶And the children of Israel did evil again in the sight of the LORD, and served Bā'al-ĭm, and Ăsh'ta-rŏth, and the gods of Syria, and the gods of Zī'don, and the gods of Moab, and the gods of the children of Ammon, and the gods of the Philistines, and forsook the LORD, and served not him.

7 And the anger of the LORD was hot against Israel, and he sold them into the hands of the Philistines, and into the hands of the children of Ammon.

8 And that year they vexed and oppressed the children of Israel: eighteen years, all the children of Israel that *were* on the other side Jordan in the land of the Ămorites, which *is* in Gilead.

9 Moreover the children of Ammon passed over Jordan to fight also against Jūdah, and against Benjamin, and against the house of Ē'phra-im; so that Israel was sore distressed.

10 ¶And the children of Israel cried unto the LORD, saying, We have sinned against thee, both because we have forsaken our God, and also served Bā'al-ĭm.

11 And the LORD said unto the children of Israel, *Did* not *I deliver you* from the Egyptians, and from the Ămorītes, from the children of Ammon, and from the Philistines?

12 The Zī-dō'nĭ-ans also, and the Am'ă-lek-ītes, and the Mā'on-ītes, did oppress you; and ye cried to me, and I delivered you out of their hand.

13 Yet ye have forsaken me, and served other gods: wherefore I will deliver you no more.

14 Go and cry unto the gods which ye have chosen; let them deliver you in the time of your tribulation.

15 And the children of Israel said unto the LORD, We have sinned: do thou unto us whatsoever seemeth good unto thee; deliver us only, we pray thee, this day.

16 And they put away the strange gods from among them, and served the LORD: and his soul was grieved for the misery of Israel.

17 Then the children of Ammon were gathered together, and encamped in Gilead. And the children of Israel assembled themselves together, and encamped in Mĭz'peh.

18 And the people *and* princes of Gilead said one to another, What man *is he* that will begin to fight against the children of Ammon? he shall be head over all the inhabitants of Gilead.

CHAPTER 11

NOW Jĕph'thah the Gileadite was a mighty man of valour, and he *was* the son of an harlot: and Gilead begat Jĕph'thah.

2 And Gilead's wife bare him sons; and his wife's sons grew up, and they thrust out Jĕph'thah, and said unto him, Thou shalt not inherit in our father's house; for thou *art* the son of a strange woman.

3 Then Jĕph'thah fled from his brethren, and dwelt in the land of Tob: and there were gathered vain men to Jĕph'thah, and went out with him.

4 ¶And it came to pass in process of time, that the children of Ammon made war against Israel.

5 And it was so, that when the children of Ammon made war against Israel, the elders of Gilead went to fetch Jĕph'thah out of the land of Tob:

6 And they said unto Jĕph'thah, Come, and be our captain, that we may fight with the children of Ammon.

7 And Jĕph'thah said unto the elders of Gilead, Did not ye hate me, and expel me out of my father's house? and why are ye come unto me now when ye are in distress?

8 And the elders of Gilead said unto Jĕph'thah, Therefore we turn again to thee now, that thou mayest go with us, and fight against the children of Ammon, and be our head over all the inhabitants of Gilead.

9 And Jĕph'thah said unto the elders of Gilead, If ye bring me home again to fight against the children of Ammon, and the LORD deliver them before me, shall I be your head?

10 And the elders of Gilead said unto Jĕph'thah, The LORD be witness between us, if we do not so according to thy words.

11 Then Jĕph'thah went with the elders of Gilead, and the people made him head and captain over them: and Jĕph'thah uttered all his words before the LORD in Mĭz'peh.

12 ¶And Jĕph'thah sent messengers unto the king of the children of Ammon, saying, What hast thou to do with me, that thou art come against me to fight in my land?

13 And the king of the children of Ammon answered unto the messengers of Jĕph'thah, Because Israel took away my land, when they came up out of Egypt, from Arnon even unto Jabbok, and unto Jordan: now therefore restore those *lands* again peaceably.

14 And Jĕph'thah sent messengers again unto the king of the children of Ammon:

15 And said unto him, Thus saith Jĕph'thah, Israel took not away the land of Moab, nor the land of the children of Ammon:

16 But when Israel came up from Egypt, and walked through the wilderness unto the Red sea, and came to Kā'desh;

17 Then Israel sent messengers unto the king of Ēdom, saying, Let me, I pray thee, pass through thy land: but the king of Ēdom would not hearken *thereto.* And in like manner they sent unto the king of Moab: but he would not *consent:* and Israel abode in Kā'desh.

18 Then they went along through the wilderness, and compassed the land of Edom, and the land of Moab, and came by the east side of the land of Moab, and pitched on the other side of Arnon, but came not within the border of Moab: for Arnon *was* the border of Moab.

19 And Israel sent messengers unto Sihon king of the Ămorītes, the king of Hĕsh'bŏn; and Israel said unto him, Let us pass, we pray thee, through thy land into my place.

20 But Sihon trusted not Israel to pass through his coast: but Sihon gathered all his people together, and pitched in Jā'hăz, and fought against Israel.

21 And the LORD God of Israel delivered Sihon and all his people into the hand of Israel, and they smote them: so Israel possessed all the land of the Ămorītes, the inhabitants of that country.

22 And they possessed all the coasts of the Ămorītes, from Arnon even unto Jabbok, and from the wilderness even unto Jordan.

23 So now the LORD God of Israel hath dispossessed the Ămorītes from before his people Israel, and shouldest thou possess it?

24 Wilt not thou possess that which Chē'mŏsh thy god giveth thee to possess? So whomsoever the LORD our God shall drive out from before us, them will we possess.

25 And now *art* thou any thing better than Bā'lăk the son of Zippor, king of Moab? did he ever strive against Israel, or did he ever fight against them,

26 While Israel dwelt in Hĕsh'bŏn and her towns, and in Ar'ō-er and her towns, and in all the cities that *be* along by the coasts of Arnon, three hundred years? why therefore did ye not recover *them* within that time?

27 Wherefore I have not sinned against thee, but thou doest me wrong to war against me: the LORD the Judge be judge this day between the children of Israel and the children of Ammon.

28 Howbeit the king of the children of

Ammon hearkened not unto the words
of Jĕph'thah which he sent him.
29 ¶Then the Spirit of the LORD came
upon Jĕph'thah, and he passed over Gil-
ead, and Ma-năs'seh, and passed over
Mĭz'peh of Gilead, and from Mĭz'peh of
Gilead he passed over *unto* the children
of Ammon.
30 And Jĕph'thah vowed a vow unto
the LORD, and said, If thou shalt
without fail deliver the children of Am-
mon into mine hands,
31 Then it shall be, that whatsoever
cometh forth of the doors of my house
to meet me, when I return in peace
from the children of Ammon, shall sure-
ly be the LORD's, and I will offer it up
for a burnt offering.
32 ¶So Jĕph'thah passed over unto
the children of Ammon to fight against
them; and the LORD delivered them into
his hands.
33 And he smote them from Ar'ō-er,
even till thou come to Mĭn'nĭth, *even*
twenty cities, and unto the plain of the
vineyards, with a very great slaughter.
Thus the children of Ammon were sub-
dued before the children of Israel.
34 ¶And Jĕph'thah came to Mĭz'peh
unto his house, and, behold, his
daughter came out to meet him with
timbrels and with dances: and she *was*
his only child; beside her he had neither
son nor daughter.
35 And it came to pass, when he saw
her, that he rent his clothes, and said,
Alas, my daughter! thou hast brought
me very low, and thou art one of them
that trouble me: for I have opened my
mouth unto the LORD, and I cannot go
back.
36 And she said unto him, My father,
if thou hast opened thy mouth unto the
LORD, do to me according to that which
hath proceeded out of thy mouth; for-
asmuch as the LORD hath taken ven-
geance for thee of thine enemies, *even* of
the children of Ammon.
37 And she said unto her father, Let
this thing be done for me: let me alone
two months, that I may go up and down
upon the mountains, and bewail my
virginity, I and my fellows.
38 And he said, Go. And he sent her
away *for* two months: and she went
with her companions, and bewailed her
virginity upon the mountains.
39 And it came to pass at the end of
two months, that she returned unto her
father, who did with her *according* to
his vow which he had vowed: and she
knew no man. And it was a custom in
Israel,
40 *That* the daughters of Israel went
yearly to lament the daughter of Jĕph'-
thah the Gileadite four days in a
year.

CHAPTER 12

AND the men of Ē'phra-im gathered
themselves together, and went north-
ward, and said unto Jĕph'thah, Where-
fore passedst thou over to fight against
the children of Ammon, and didst not
call us to go with thee? we will burn
thine house upon thee with fire.
2 And Jĕph'thah said unto them, I
and my people were at great strife with
the children of Ammon; and when I
called you, ye delivered me not out of
their hands.
3 And when I saw that ye delivered
me not, I put my life in my hands, and
passed over against the children of
Ammon, and the LORD delivered them
into my hand: wherefore then are ye
come up unto me this day, to fight
against me?
4 The Jĕph'thah gathered together all
the men of Gilead, and fought with
Ē'phra-im: and the men of Gilead
smote Ē'phra-im, because they said, Ye
Gileadites *are* fugitives of Ē'phra-im
among the Ē'phra-im-ītes, *and* among
the Ma-năs'sītes.
5 And the Gileadites took the pas-
sages of Jordan before the Ē'phra-im-
ītes: and it was *so*, that when those
Ē'phra-im-ītes which were escaped
said, Let me go over; that the men of
Gilead said unto him, *Art* thou an
Ē'phra-im-īte? If he said, Nay;
6 Then said they unto him, Say now
Shĭb'bo-leth: and he said Sĭb'bo-leth:
for he could not frame to pronounce *it*
right. Then they took him, and slew
him at the passages of Jordan: and
there fell at that time of the Ē'phra-im-
ītes forty and two thousand.
7 And Jĕph'thah judged Israel six
years. Then died Jĕph'thah the Gilead-
ite, and was buried in *one of* the cities
of Gilead.
8 ¶And after him Ĭb'zăn of Bĕth-lehĕm
judged Israel.
9 And he had thirty sons, and thirty
daughters, *whom* he sent abroad, and
took in thirty daughters from abroad
for his sons. And he judged Israel seven
years.
10 Then died Ĭb'zăn, and was buried
at Bĕth-lehĕm.
11 ¶And after him Ē'lŏn, a Zĕb'u-lon-
īte, judged Israel; and he judged Israel
ten years.
12 And Ē'lŏn the Zĕb'u-lon-īte died,
and was buried in Āij'a-lŏn in the
country of Zĕb'u-lun.

13 ¶And after him Ăb′dŏn the son of
Hĭl′lel, a Pĭr′a-thŏn-īte, judged Israel.
14 And he had forty sons and thirty
nephews, that rode on threescore and
ten ass colts: and he judged Israel eight
years.
15 And Ăb′dŏn the son of Hĭl′lel the
Pĭr′a-thŏn-īte died, and was buried in
Pĭr′a-thŏn in the land of Ē′phra-im, in
the mount of the Am′ă-lek-ītes.

CHAPTER 13

AND the children of Israel did evil
again in the sight of the LORD; and the
LORD delivered them into the hand of
the Philistines forty years.
2 ¶And there was a certain man of
Zō′rah, of the family of the Danites,
whose name *was* Ma-nō′ah; and his
wife *was* barren, and bare not.
3 And the angel of the LORD appeared
unto the woman, and said unto her, Be-
hold now, thou *art* barren, and bearest
not: but thou shalt conceive, and bear a
son.
4 Now therefore beware, I pray thee,
and drink not wine nor strong drink,
and eat not any unclean *thing:*
5 For, lo, thou shalt conceive, and
bear a son; and no razor shall come on
his head: for the child shall be a Naza-
rite unto God from the womb: and he
shall begin to deliver Israel out of the
hand of the Philistines.
6 ¶Then the woman came and told
her husband, saying, A man of God
came unto me, and his countenance
was like the countenance of an angel of
God, very terrible: but I asked him not
whence he *was,* neither told he me his
name:
7 But he said unto me, Behold, thou
shalt conceive, and bear a son; and now
drink no wine nor strong drink, neither
eat any unclean *thing:* for the child
shall be a Nazarite to God from the
womb to the day of his death.
8 ¶Then Ma-nō′ah intreated the LORD,
and said, O my Lord, let the man of God
which thou didst send come again unto
us, and teach us what we shall do unto
the child that shall be born.
9 And God hearkened to the voice of
Ma-nō′ah; and the angel of God came
again unto the woman as she sat in the
field: but Ma-nō′ah her husband *was*
not with her.
10 And the woman made haste, and
ran, and shewed her husband, and said
unto him, Behold, the man hath ap-
peared unto me, that came unto me the
other day.
11 And Ma-nō′ah arose, and went af-
ter his wife, and came to the man, and
said unto him, *Art* thou the man that
spakest unto the woman? And he said, I
am.
12 And Ma-nō′ah said, Now let thy
words come to pass. How shall we or-
der the child, and *how* shall we do unto
him?
13 And the angel of the LORD said
unto Ma-nō′ah, Of all that I said unto
the woman let her beware.
14 She may not eat of any *thing* that
cometh of the vine, neither let her drink
wine or strong drink, nor eat any un-
clean *thing:* all that I commanded her
let her observe.
15 ¶And Ma-nō′ah said unto the an-
gel of the LORD, I pray thee, let us detain
thee, until we shall have made ready a
kid for thee.
16 And the angel of the LORD said
unto Ma-nō′ah, Though thou detain
me, I will not eat of thy bread: and if
thou wilt offer a burnt offering, thou
must offer it unto the LORD. For Ma-
nō′ah knew not that he *was* an angel of
the LORD.
17 And Ma-nō′ah said unto the angel
of the LORD, What *is* thy name, that
when thy sayings come to pass we may
do thee honour?
18 And the angel of the LORD said
unto him, Why askest thou thus after
my name, seeing it *is* secret?
19 So Ma-nō′ah took a kid with a
meat offering, and offered *it* upon a
rock unto the LORD: and *the angel* did
wonderously; and Ma-nō′ah and his
wife looked on.
20 For it came to pass, when the
flame went up toward heaven from off
the altar, that the angel of the LORD as-
cended in the flame of the altar. And
Ma-nō′ah and his wife looked on *it,* and
fell on their faces to the ground.
21 But the angel of the LORD did no
more appear to Ma-nō′ah and to his
wife. Then Ma-nō′ah knew that he *was*
an angel of the LORD.
22 And Ma-nō′ah said unto his wife,
We shall surely die, because we have
seen God.
23 But his wife said unto him, If the
LORD were pleased to kill us, he would
not have received a burnt offering and
a meat offering at our hands, neither
would he have shewed us all these
things, nor would as at this time have
told us *such things* as these.
24 ¶And the woman bare a son, and
called his name Samson: and the child
grew, and the LORD blessed him.
25 And the Spirit of the LORD began
to move him at times in the camp of
Dan between Zō′rah and Ĕsh′ta-ol.

CHAPTER 14

AND Samson went down to Tĭm′năth,
and saw a woman in Tĭm′năth of the
daughters of the Philistines.
2 And he came up, and told his father
and his mother, and said, I have seen a
woman in Tĭm′năth of the daughters of
the Philistines: now therefore get her
for me to wife.
3 Then his father and his mother said
unto him, *Is there* never a woman
among the daughters of thy brethren,
or among all my people, that thou goest
to take a wife of the uncircumcised
Philistines? And Samson said unto his
father, Get her for me; for she pleaseth
me well.
4 But his father and his mother knew
not that it *was* of the LORD, that he
sought an occasion against the Philis-
tines: for at that time the Philistines
had dominion over Israel.
5 Then went Samson down, and his
father and his mother, to Tĭm′năth, and
came to the vineyards of Tĭm′năth:
and, behold, a young lion roared
against him.
6 And the Spirit of the LORD came
mightily upon him, and he rent him as
he would have rent a kid, and *he had*
nothing in his hand: but he told not his
father or his mother what he had done.
7 And he went down, and talked with
the woman; and she pleased Samson
well.
8 ¶And after a time he returned to
take her, and he turned aside to see the
carcase of the lion: and, behold, *there*
was a swarm of bees and honey in the
carcase of the lion.
9 And he took thereof in his hands,
and went on eating, and came to his
father and mother, and he gave them,
and they did eat: but he told not them
that he had taken the honey out of the
carcase of the lion.
10 ¶So his father went down unto the
woman: and Samson made there a
feast; for so used the young men to do.
11 And it came to pass, when they
saw him, that they brought thirty com-
panions to be with him.
12 And Samson said unto them, I will
now put forth a riddle unto you: if ye
can certainly declare it me within the
seven days of the feast, and find *it* out,
then I will give you thirty sheets and
thirty change of garments:
13 But if ye cannot declare *it* me, then
shall ye give me thirty sheets and thirty
change of garments. And they said
unto him, Put forth thy riddle, that we
may hear it.
14 And he said unto them, Out of the
eater came forth meat, and out of the
strong came forth sweetness. And they
could not in three days expound the
riddle.
15 And it came to pass on the seventh
day, that they said unto Samson's wife,
Entice thy husband, that he may declare
unto us the riddle, lest we burn
thee and thy father's house with fire:
have ye called us to take that we have?
is it not *so?*
16 And Samson's wife wept before
him, and said, Thou dost but hate me,
and lovest me not: thou hast put forth a
riddle unto the children of my people,
and hast not told *it* me. And he said
unto her, Behold, I have not told *it* my
father nor my mother, and shall I tell *it*
thee?
17 And she wept before him the
seven days, while their feast lasted:
and it came to pass on the seventh day,
that he told her, because she lay sore
upon him: and she told the riddle to the
children of her people.
18 And the men of the city said unto
him on the seventh day before the sun
went down, What *is* sweeter than
honey? and what *is* stronger than a
lion? And he said unto them, If ye had
not plowed with my heifer, ye had not
found out my riddle.
19 And the Spirit of the LORD came
upon him, and he went down to Ăsh′ke-
lŏn, and slew thirty men of them, and
took their spoil, and gave change of
garments unto them which expounded
the riddle. And his anger was kindled,
and he went up to his father's house.
20 But Samson's wife was *given* to
his companion, whom he had used as
his friend.

CHAPTER 15

BUT it came to pass within a while af-
ter, in the time of wheat harvest, that
Samson visited his wife with a kid; and
he said, I will go in to my wife into the
chamber. But her father would not suf-
fer him to go in.
2 And her father said, I verily thought
that thou hadst utterly hated her; there-
fore I gave her to thy companion: *is*
not her younger sister fairer than she?
take her, I pray thee, instead of her.
3 ¶And Samson said concerning
them, Now shall I be more blameless
than the Philistines, though I do them a
displeasure.
4 And Samson went and caught three
hundred foxes, and took firebrands,
and turned tail to tail, and put a fire-
brand in the midst between two tails.
5 And when he had set the brands on
fire, he let *them* go into the standing

corn of the Philistines, and burnt up
both the shocks, and also the standing
corn, with the vineyards *and* olives.
6 Then the Philistines said, Who hath
done this? And they answered, Sam-
son, the son in law of the Tĭm'nīte, be-
cause he had taken his wife, and given
her to his companion. And the Philis-
tines came up, and burnt her and her
father with fire.
7 ¶And Samson said unto them,
Though ye have done this, yet will I be
avenged of you, and after that I will
cease.
8 And he smote them hip and thigh
with a great slaughter: and he went
down and dwelt in the top of the rock
Ē'tam.
9 ¶Then the Philistines went up, and
pitched in Jūdah, and spread them-
selves in Lē'hī.
10 And the men of Jūdah said, Why
are ye come up against us? And they
answered, To bind Samson are we
come up, to do to him as he hath done
to us.
11 Then three thousand men of Jūdah
went to the top of the rock Ē'tam, and
said to Samson, Knowest thou not that
the Philistines *are* rulers over us? what
is this *that* thou hast done unto us? And
he said unto them, As they did unto me,
so have I done unto them.
12 And they said unto him, We are
come down to bind thee, that we may
deliver thee into the hand of the Philis-
tines. And Samson said unto them,
Swear unto me, that ye will not fall
upon me yourselves.
13 And they spake unto him, saying,
No; but we will bind thee fast, and de-
liver thee into their hand: but surely we
will not kill thee. And they bound him
with two new cords, and brought him
up from the rock.
14 ¶*And* when he came unto Lē'hī,
the Philistines shouted against him:
and the Spirit of the LORD came
mightily upon him, and the cords that
were upon his arms became as flax that
was burnt with fire, and his bands
loosed from off his hands.
15 And he found a new jawbone of an
ass, and put forth his hand, and took it,
and slew a thousand men therewith.
16 And Samson said, With the jaw-
bone of an ass, heaps upon heaps, with
the jaw of an ass have I slain a thou-
sand men.
17 And it came to pass, when he had
made an end of speaking, that he cast
away the jawbone out of his hand, and
called that place Rā'math-lē'hī.
18 ¶And he was sore athirst, and
called on the LORD, and said, Thou hast
given this great deliverance into the
hand of thy servant: and now shall I die
for thirst, and fall into the hand of the
uncircumcised?
19 But God clave an hollow place that
was in the jaw, and there came water
thereout; and when he had drunk, his
spirit came again, and he revived: where-
fore he called the name thereof
Ĕn-hăk'ko-re, which *is* in Lē'hī unto this
day.
20 And he judged Israel in the days of
the Philistines twenty years.

CHAPTER 16

THEN went Samson to Gā'za, and saw
there an harlot, and went in unto her.
2 *And it was told* the Gā'zītes, saying,
Samson is come hither. And they com-
passed *him* in, and laid wait for him all
night in the gate of the city, and were
quiet all the night, saying, In the morn-
ing, when it is day, we shall kill him.
3 And Samson lay till midnight, and
arose at midnight, and took the doors
of the gate of the city, and the two
posts, and went away with them, bar
and all, and put *them* upon his shoul-
ders, and carried them up to the top of
an hill that *is* before Hēbron.
4 ¶And it came to pass afterward,
that he loved a woman in the valley of
Sô'rĕk, whose name *was* De-lī'lah.
5 And the lords of the Philistines
came up unto her, and said unto her,
Entice him, and see wherein his great
strength *lieth,* and by what *means* we
may prevail against him, that we may
bind him to afflict him: and we will give
thee every one of us eleven hundred
pieces of silver.
6 And De-lī'lah said to Samson, Tell
me, I pray thee, wherein thy great
strength *lieth,* and wherewith thou
mightest be bound to afflict thee.
7 And Samson said unto her, If they
bind me with seven green withs that
were never dried, then shall I be weak,
and be as another man.
8 Then the lords of the Philistines
brought up to her seven green withs
which had not been dried, and she
bound him with them.
9 Now *there were* men lying in wait,
abiding with her in the chamber. And
she said unto him, The Philistines *be*
upon thee, Samson. And he brake the
withs, as a thread of tow is broken
when it toucheth the fire. So his
strength was not known.
10 And De-lī'lah said unto Samson,
Behold, thou hast mocked me, and told
me lies: now tell me, I pray thee, where-
with thou mightest be bound.
11 And he said unto her, If they bind

me fast with new ropes that never were
occupied, then shall I be weak, and be
as another man.
12 De-lī'lah therefore took new
ropes, and bound him therewith, and
said unto him, The Philistines *be* upon
thee, Samson. And *there were* liers in
wait abiding in the chamber. And he
brake them from off his arms like a
thread.
13 And De-lī'lah said unto Samson,
Hitherto thou hast mocked me, and
told me lies: tell me wherewith thou
mightest be bound. And he said unto
her, If thou weavest the seven locks of
my head with the web.
14 And she fastened *it* with the pin,
and said unto him, The Philistines *be*
upon thee, Samson. And he awaked out
of his sleep, and went away with the
pin of the beam, and with the web.
15 ¶And she said unto him, How
canst thou say, I love thee, when thine
heart *is* not with me? thou hast mocked
me these three times, and hast not told
me wherein thy great strength *lieth*.
16 And it came to pass, when she
pressed him daily with her words, and
urged him, *so* that his soul was vexed
unto death;
17 That he told her all his heart, and
said unto her, There hath not come a
razor upon mine head; for I *have been* a
Nazarite unto God from my mother's
womb: if I be shaven, then my strength
will go from me, and I shall become
weak, and be like any *other* man.
18 And when De-lī'lah saw that he
had told her all his heart, she sent and
called for the lords of the Philistines,
saying, Come up this once, for he hath
shewed me all his heart. Then the lords
of the Philistines came up unto her, and
brought money in their hand.
19 And she made him sleep upon her
knees; and she called for a man, and
she caused him to shave off the seven
locks of his head; and she began to af-
flict him, and his strength went from
him.
20 And she said, The Philistines *be*
upon thee, Samson. And he awoke out
of his sleep, and said, I will go out as at
other times before, and shake myself.
And he wist not that the LORD was de-
parted from him.
21 But the Philistines took him, and
put out his eyes, and brought him down
to Gā'za, and bound him with fetters of
brass; and he did grind in the prison
house.
22 Howbeit the hair of his head began
to grow again after he was shaven.
23 Then the lords of the Philistines
gathered them together for to offer a
great sacrifice unto Dā'gŏn their god,
and to rejoice: for they said, Our god
hath delivered Samson our enemy into
our hand.
24 And when the people saw him,
they praised their god: for they said,
Our god hath delivered into our hands
our enemy, and the destroyer of our
country, which slew many of us.
25 And it came to pass, when their
hearts were merry, that they said, Call
for Samson, that he may make us sport.
And they called for Samson out of the
prison house; and he made them sport:
and they set him between the pillars.
26 And Samson said unto the lad that
held him by the hand, Suffer me that I
may feel the pillars whereupon the
house standeth, that I may lean upon
them.
27 Now the house was full of men and
women; and all the lords of the Philis-
tines *were* there; and *there were* upon
the roof about three thousand men and
women, that beheld while Samson
made sport.
28 And Samson called unto the LORD,
and said, O Lord GOD, remember me, I
pray thee, and strengthen me, I pray
thee, only this once, O God, that I may
be at once avenged of the Philistines
for my two eyes.
29 And Samson took hold of the two
middle pillars upon which the house
stood, and on which it was borne up, of
the one with his right hand, and of the
other with his left.
30 And Samson said, Let me die with
the Philistines. And he bowed himself
with *all his* might; and the house fell
upon the lords, and upon all the people
that *were* therein. So the dead which he
slew at his death were more than *they*
which he slew in his life.
31 Then his brethren and all the
house of his father came down, and
took him, and brought *him* up, and
buried him between Zō'rah and Ĕsh'ta-
ol in the buryingplace of Ma-nō'ah his
father. And he judged Israel twenty
years.

CHAPTER 17

AND there was a man of mount Ē'phra-
im, whose name *was* Mī'cah.
2 And he said unto his mother, The
eleven hundred *shekels* of silver that
were taken from thee, about which
thou cursedst, and spakest of also in
mine ears, behold, the silver *is* with me;
I took it. And his mother said, Blessed
be thou of the LORD, my son.
3 And when he had restored the
eleven hundred *shekels* of silver to his
mother, his mother said, I had wholly

dedicated the silver unto the LORD from my hand for my son, to make a graven image and a molten image: now therefore I will restore it unto thee.

4 Yet he restored the money unto his mother; and his mother took two hundred *shekels* of silver, and gave them to the founder, who made thereof a graven image and a molten image: and they were in the house of Mī'cah.

5 And the man Mī'cah had an house of gods, and made an ephod, and teraphim, and consecrated one of his sons, who became his priest.

6 In those days *there was* no king in Israel, *but* every man did *that which was* right in his own eyes.

7 ¶And there was a young man out of Bĕth-lehĕm-jūdah of the family of Jūdah, who *was* a Levite, and he sojourned there.

8 And the man departed out of the city from Bĕth-lehĕm-jūdah to sojourn where he could find *a place:* and he came to mount Ē'phra-im to the house of Mī'cah, as he journeyed.

9 And Mī'cah said unto him, Whence comest thou? And he said unto him, I *am* a Levite of Bĕth-lehĕm-jūdah, and I go to sojourn where I may find *a place.*

10 And Mī'cah said unto him, Dwell with me, and be unto me a father and a priest, and I will give thee ten *shekels* of silver by the year, and a suit of apparel, and thy victuals. So the Levite went in.

11 And the Levite was content to dwell with the man; and the young man was unto him as one of his sons.

12 And Mī'cah consecrated the Levite; and the young man became his priest, and was in the house of Mī'cah.

13 Then said Mī'cah, Now know I that the LORD will do me good, seeing I have a Levite to *my* priest.

CHAPTER 18

IN those days *there was* no king in Israel: and in those days the tribe of the Danites sought them an inheritance to dwell in; for unto that day *all their* inheritance had not fallen unto them among the tribes of Israel.

2 And the children of Dan sent of their family five men from their coasts, men of valour, from Zô'rah, and from Ĕsh'ta-ol, to spy out the land, and to search it; and they said unto them, Go, search the land: who when they came to mount Ē'phra-im, to the house of Mī'cah, they lodged there.

3 When they *were* by the house of Mī'cah, they knew the voice of the young man the Levite: and they turned in thither, and said unto him, Who brought thee hither? and what makest thou in this *place?* and what hast thou here?

4 And he said unto them, Thus and thus dealeth Mī'cah with me, and hath hired me, and I am his priest.

5 And they said unto him, Ask counsel, we pray thee, of God, that we may know whether our way which we go shall be prosperous.

6 And the priest said unto them, Go in peace: before the LORD *is* your way wherein ye go.

7 ¶Then the five men departed, and came to Lā'ĭsh, and saw the people that *were* therein, how they dwelt careless, after the manner of the Zī-dō'nĭ-ans, quiet and secure; and *there was* no magistrate in the land, that might put *them* to shame in *any* thing; and they *were* far from the Zī-dō'nĭ-ans, and had no business with *any* man.

8 And they came unto their brethren to Zô'rah and Ĕsh'ta-ol: and their brethren said unto them, What *say* ye?

9 And they said, Arise, that we may go up against them: for we have seen the land, and, behold, it *is* very good: and *are* ye still? be not slothful to go, *and* to enter to possess the land.

10 When ye go, ye shall come unto a people secure, and to a large land: for God hath given it into your hands; a place where *there is* no want of any thing that *is* in the earth.

11 ¶And there went from thence of the family of the Danites, out of Zô'rah and out of Ĕsh'ta-ol, six hundred men appointed with weapons of war.

12 And they went up, and pitched in Kir'jath-jē'a-rĭm, in Judah: wherefore they called that place Mā'ha-neh-dăn unto this day: behold, *it is* behind Kir'jath-jē'a-rĭm.

13 And they passed thence unto mount Ē'phra-im, and came unto the house of Mī'cah.

14 Then answered the five men that went to spy out the country of Lā'ĭsh, and said unto their brethren, Do ye know that there is in these houses an ephod, and teraphim, and a graven image, and a molten image? now therefore consider what ye have to do.

15 And they turned thitherward, and came to the house of the young man the Levite, *even* unto the house of Mī'cah, and saluted him.

16 And the six hundred men appointed with their weapons of war, which *were* of the children of Dan, stood by the entering of the gate.

17 And the five men that went to spy out the land went up, *and* came in thither, *and* took the graven image, and

the ephod, and the teraphim, and the molten image: and the priest stood in the entering of the gate with the six hundred men *that were* appointed with weapons of war.

18 And these went into Mī'cah'ṡ house, and fetched the carved image, the ephod, and the teraphim, and the molten image. Then said the priest unto them, What do ye?

19 And they said unto him, Hold thy peace, lay thine hand upon thy mouth, and go with us, and be to us a father and a priest: *is it* better for thee to be a priest unto the house of one man, or that thou be a priest unto a tribe and a family in Israel?

20 And the priest's heart was glad, and he took the ephod, and the teraphim, and the graven image, and went in the midst of the people.

21 So they turned and departed, and put the little ones and the cattle and the carriage before them.

22 ¶*And* when they were a good way from the house of Mī'cah, the men that *were* in the houses near to Mī'cah'ṡ house were gathered together, and overtook the children of Dan.

23 And they cried unto the children of Dan. And they turned their faces, and said unto Mī'cah, What aileth thee, that thou comest with such a company?

24 And he said, Ye have taken away my gods which I made, and the priest, and ye are gone away: and what have I more? and what *is* this *that* ye say unto me, What aileth thee?

25 And the children of Dan said unto him, Let not thy voice be heard among us, lest angry fellows run upon thee, and thou lose thy life, with the lives of thy household.

26 And the children of Dan went their way: and when Mī'cah saw that they *were* too strong for him, he turned and went back unto his house.

27 And they took *the things* which Mī'cah had made, and the priest which he had, and came unto Lā'ĭsh, unto a people *that were* at quiet and secure: and they smote them with the edge of the sword, and burnt the city with fire.

28 And *there was* no deliverer, because it *was* far from Zī'don, and they had no business with *any* man; and it was in the valley that *lieth* by Bĕth-rē'hŏb. And they built a city, and dwelt therein.

29 And they called the name of the city Dan, after the name of Dan their father, who was born unto Israel: howbeit the name of the city *was* Lā'ĭsh at the first.

30 And the children of Dan set up the graven image: and Jonathan, the son of Ger'shom, the son of Ma-năs'seh, he and his sons were priests to the tribe of Dan until the day of the captivity of the land.

31 And they set them up Mī'cah'ṡ graven image, which he made, all the time that the house of God was in Shī'-lōh.

CHAPTER 19

AND it came to pass in those days, when *there was* no king in Israel, that there was a certain Levite sojourning on the side of mount Ē'phra-im, who took to him a concubine out of Bĕth-lehĕm-jūdah.

2 And his concubine played the whore against him, and went away from him unto her father's house to Bĕth-lehĕm-jūdah, and was there four whole months.

3 And her husband arose, and went after her, to speak friendly unto her, *and* to bring her again, having his servant with him, and a couple of asses: and she brought him into her father's house: and when the father of the damsel saw him, he rejoiced to meet him.

4 And his father in law, the damsel's father, retained him; and he abode with him three days: so they did eat and drink, and lodged there.

5 And it came to pass on the fourth day, when they arose early in the morning, that he rose up to depart: and the damsel's father said unto his son in law, Comfort thine heart with a morsel of bread, and afterward go your way.

6 And they sat down, and did eat and drink both of them together: for the damsel's father had said unto the man, Be content, I pray thee, and tarry all night, and let thine heart be merry.

7 And when the man rose up to depart, his father in law urged him: therefore he lodged there again.

8 And he arose early in the morning on the fifth day to depart: and the damsel's father said, Comfort thine heart, I pray thee. And they tarried until afternoon, and they did eat both of them.

9 And when the man rose up to depart, he, and his concubine, and his servant, his father in law, the damsel's father, said unto him, Behold, now the day draweth toward evening, I pray you tarry all night: behold, the day groweth to an end, lodge here, that thine heart may be merry; and to morrow get you early on your way, that thou mayest go home.

10 But the man would not tarry that night, but he rose up and departed, and

came over against Jē'bus, which *is* Jerusalem; and *there were* with him two asses saddled, his concubine also *was* with him.

11 *And* when they *were* by Jē'bus, the day was far spent; and the servant said unto his master, Come, I pray thee, and let us turn in into this city of the Jēb'u-sītes, and lodge in it.

12 And his master said unto him, We will not turn aside hither into the city of a stranger, that *is* not of the children of Israel; we will pass over to Gĭb'e-ah.

13 And he said unto his servant, Come, and let us draw near to one of these places to lodge all night, in Gĭb'e-ah, or in Rā'mah.

14 And they passed on and went their way; and the sun went down upon them *when they were* by Gĭb'e-ah, which *belongeth* to Benjamin.

15 And they turned aside thither, to go in *and* to lodge in Gĭb'e-ah: and when he went in, he sat him down in a street of the city: for *there was* no man that took them into his house to lodging.

16 ¶And, behold, there came an old man from his work out of the field at even, which *was* also of mount Ē'phra-im; and he sojourned in Gĭb'e-ah: but the men of the place *were* Benjamites.

17 And when he had lifted up his eyes, he saw a wayfaring man in the street of the city: and the old man said, Whither goest thou? and whence comest thou?

18 And he said unto him, We *are* passing from Bĕth–lehĕm–jūdah toward the side of mount E'phra-im; from thence *am* I: and I went to Bĕth–lehĕm–jūdah, but I *am now* going to the house of the Lord; and there *is* no man that receiveth me to house.

19 Yet there is both straw and provender for our asses; and there is bread and wine also for me, and for thy handmaid, and for the young man *which is* with thy servants: *there is* no want of any thing.

20 And the old man said, Peace *be* with thee; howsoever *let* all thy wants *lie* upon me; only lodge not in the street.

21 So he brought him into his house, and gave provender unto the asses: and they washed their feet, and did eat and drink.

22 ¶*Now* as they were making their hearts merry, behold, the men of the city, certain sons of Bē'lĭ-al, beset the house round about, *and* beat at the door, and spake to the master of the house, the old man, saying, Bring forth the man that came into thine house, that we may know him.

23 And the man, the master of the house, went out unto them, and said unto them, Nay, my brethren, *nay,* I pray you, do not *so* wickedly; seeing that this man is come into mine house, do not this folly.

24 Behold, *here is* my daughter a maiden, and his concubine; them I will bring out now, and humble ye them, and do with them what seemeth good unto you: but unto this man do not so vile a thing.

25 But the men would not hearken to him: so the man took his concubine, and brought her forth unto them; and they knew her, and abused her all the night until the morning: and when the day began to spring, they let her go.

26 Then came the woman in the dawning of the day, and fell down at the door of the man's house where her lord *was,* till it was light.

27 And her lord rose up in the morning, and opened the doors of the house, and went out to go his way: and, behold, the woman his concubine was fallen down *at* the door of the house, and her hands *were* upon the threshold.

28 And he said unto her, Up, and let us be going. But none answered. Then the man took her *up* upon an ass, and the man rose up, and gat him unto his place.

29 ¶And when he was come into his house, he took a knife, and laid hold on his concubine, and divided her, *together* with her bones, into twelve pieces, and sent her into all the coasts of Israel.

30 And it was so, that all that saw it said, There was no such deed done nor seen from the day that the children of Israel came up out of the land of Egypt unto this day: consider of it, take advice, and speak *your minds.*

CHAPTER 20

THEN all the children of Israel went out, and the congregation was gathered together as one man, from Dan even to Be'er–shē'ba, with the land of Gilead, unto the Lord in Mĭz'peh.

2 And the chief of all the people, *even* of all the tribes of Israel, presented themselves in the assembly of the people of God, four hundred thousand footmen that drew sword.

3 (Now the children of Benjamin heard that the children of Israel were gone up to Mĭz'peh.) Then said the children of Israel, Tell *us,* how was this wickedness?

4 And the Levite, the husband of the woman that was slain, answered and

said, I came into Gĭb′e-ah that *belong-*
eth to Benjamin, I and my concubine,
to lodge.
5 And the men of Gĭb′e-ah rose
against me, and beset the house round
about upon me by night, *and* thought to
have slain me: and my concubine have
they forced, that she is dead.
6 And I took my concubine, and cut
her in pieces, and sent her throughout
all the country of the inheritance of
Israel: for they have committed lewd-
ness and folly in Israel.
7 Behold, ye *are* all children of Israel:
give here your advice and counsel.
8 ¶And all the people arose as one
man, saying, We will not any *of us* go to
his tent, neither will we any *of us* turn
into his house.
9 But now this *shall be* the thing
which we will do to Gĭb′e-ah; *we will go*
up by lot against it;
10 And we will take ten men of an
hundred throughout all the tribes of
Israel, and an hundred of a thousand,
and a thousand out of ten thousand, to
fetch victual for the people, that they
may do, when they come to Gĭb′e-ah of
Benjamin, according to all the folly
that they have wrought in Israel.
11 So all the men of Israel were gath-
ered against the city, knit together as
one man.
12 ¶And the tribes of Israel sent men
through all the tribe of Benjamin,
saying, What wickedness *is* this that is
done among you?
13 Now therefore deliver *us* the men,
the children of Bē′lĭ-al, which *are* in
Gĭb′e-ah, that we may put them to
death, and put away evil from Israel.
But the children of Benjamin would not
hearken to the voice of their brethren
the children of Israel:
14 But the children of Benjamin gath-
ered themselves together out of the
cities unto Gĭb′e-ah, to go out to battle
against the children of Israel.
15 And the children of Benjamin
were numbered at that time out of the
cities twenty and six thousand men
that drew sword, beside the inhabi-
tants of Gĭb′e-ah, which were num-
bered seven hundred chosen men.
16 Among all this people *there were*
seven hundred chosen men lefthanded;
every one could sling stones at an hair
breadth, and not miss.
17 And the men of Israel, beside Ben-
jamin, were numbered four hundred
thousand men that drew sword: all
these *were* men of war.
18 ¶And the children of Israel arose,
and went up to the house of God, and
asked counsel of God, and said, Which
of us shall go up first to the battle
against the children of Benjamin? An
the LORD said, Jūdah *shall go up* first.
19 And the children of Israel rose up
in the morning, and encamped against
Gĭb′e-ah.
20 And the men of Israel went out to
battle against Benjamin; and the men
of Israel put themselves in array to
fight against them at Gĭb′e-ah.
21 And the children of Benjamin
came forth out of Gĭb′e-ah, and de-
stroyed down to the ground of the
Israelites that day twenty and two
thousand men.
22 And the people the men of Israel
encouraged themselves, and set their
battle again in array in the place where
they put themselves in array the first
day.
23 (And the children of Israel went up
and wept before the LORD until even,
and asked counsel of the LORD, saying,
Shall I go up again to battle against the
children of Benjamin my brother? And
the LORD said, Go up against him.)
24 And the children of Israel came
near against the children of Benjamin
the second day.
25 And Benjamin went forth against
them out of Gĭb′e-ah the second day,
and destroyed down to the ground of
the children of Israel again eighteen
thousand men; all these drew the
sword.
26 ¶Then all the children of Israel,
and all the people, went up, and came
unto the house of God, and wept, and
sat there before the LORD, and fasted
that day until even, and offered burnt
offerngs and peace offerings before the
LORD.
27 And the children of Israel en-
quired of the LORD, (for the ark of the
covenant of God *was* there in those
days,
28 And Phĭn′e-has, the son of Ĕ-le-
ā′zar, the son of Aaron, stood before it in
those days,) saying, Shall I yet again go
out to battle against the children of
Benjamin my brother, or shall I cease?
And the LORD said, Go up; for to
morrow I will deliver them into thine
hand.
29 ¶And Israel set liers in wait round
about Gĭb′e-ah.
30 And the children of Israel went up
against the children of Benjamin on the
third day, and put themselves in array
against Gĭb′e-ah, as at other times.
31 And the children of Benjamin
went out against the people, *and* were
drawn away from the city; and they be-
gan to smite of the people, *and* kill, as
at other times, in the highways, of

which one goeth up to the house of
God, and the other to Gĭb'e-ah in the
field, about thirty men of Israel.
32 And the children of Benjamin said,
They *are* smitten down before us, as at
the first. But the children of Israel said,
Let us flee, and draw them from the
city unto the highways.
33 And all the men of Israel rose up
out of their place, and put themselves
in array at Bā'al-tā'mar: and the liers in
wait of Israel came forth out of their
places, *even* out of the meadows of
Gĭb'e-ah.
34 And there came against Gĭb'e-ah
ten thousand chosen men out of all
Israel, and the battle was sore: but they
knew not that evil *was* near them.
35 And the LORD smote Benjamin be-
fore Israel: and the children of Israel
destroyed of the Benjamites that day
twenty and five thousand and an
hundred men: all these drew the sword.
36 So the children of Benjamin saw
that they were smitten: for the men of
Israel gave place to the Benjamites,
bcause they trusted unto the liers in
wait which they had set beside Gĭb'e-
ah.
37 And the liers in wait hasted, and
rushed upon Gĭb'e-ah; and the liers in
wait drew *themselves* along, and smote
all the city with the edge of the sword.
38 Now there was an appointed sign
between the men of Israel and the liers
in wait, that they should make a great
flame with smoke rise up out of the
city.
39 And when the men of Israel retired
in the battle, Benjamin began to smite
and kill of the men of Israel about thirty
persons: for they said, Surely they are
smitten down before us, as *in* the first
battle.
40 But when the flame began to arise
up out of the city with a pillar of smoke,
the Benjamites looked behind them,
and, behold, the flame of the city as-
cended up to heaven.
41 And when the men of Israel turned
again, the men of Benjamin were
amazed: for they saw that evil was
come upon them.
42 Therefore they turned *their backs*
before the men of Israel unto the way of
the wilderness; but the battle overtook
them; and them which *came* out of the
cities they destroyed in the midst of
them.
43 *Thus* they inclosed the Benjamites
round about, *and* chased them, *and*
trode them down with ease over
against Gĭb'e-ah toward the sunrising.
44 And there fell of Benjamin
eighteen thousand men; all these *were*
men of valour.
45 And they turned and fled toward
the wilderness unto the rock of Rim-
mon: and they gleaned of them in the
highways five thousand men: and
pursued hard after them unto Gī'dom,
and slew two thousand men of them.
46 So that all which fell that day of
Benjamin were twenty and five thou-
sand men that drew the sword; all
these *were* men of valour.
47 But six hundred men turned and
fled to the wilderness unto the rock
Rimmon, and abode in the rock Rim-
mon four months.
48 And the men of Israel turned again
upon the children of Benjamin, and
smote them with the edge of the sword,
as well the men of *every* city, as the
beast, and all that came to hand: also
they set on fire all the cities that they
came to.

CHAPTER 21

NOW the men of Israel had sworn in
Mĭz'peh, saying, There shall not any of
us give his daughter unto Benjamin to
wife.
2 And the people came to the house
of God, and abode there till even before
God, and lifted up their voices, and
wept sore;
3 And said, O LORD God of Israel, why
is this come to pass in Israel, that there
should be to day one tribe lacking in
Israel?
4 And it came to pass on the morrow,
that the people rose early, and built
there an altar, and offered burnt offer-
ings and peace offerings.
5 And the children of Israel said, Who
is there among all the tribes of Israel
that came not up with the congregation
unto the LORD? For they had made a
great oath concerning him that came
not up to the LORD to Mĭz'peh, saying,
He shall surely be put to death.
6 And the children of Israel repented
them for Benjamin their brother, and
said, There is one tribe cut off from
Israel this day.
7 How shall we do for wives for them
that remain, seeing we have sworn by
the LORD that we will not give them of
our daughters to wives?
8 ¶And they said, What one *is there*
of the tribes of Israel that came not up
to Mĭz'peh to the LORD? And, behold,
there came none to the camp from Jā'-
besh–gĭl'e-ad to the assembly.
9 For the people were numbered,
and, behold, *there were* none of the
inhabitants of Jā'besh–gĭl'e-ad there.
10 And the congregation sent thither

twelve thousand men of the valiantest, and commanded them, saying, Go and smite the inhabitants of Jā'besh-gĭl'e-ad with the edge of the sword, with the women and the children.
11 And this *is* the thing that ye shall do, Ye shall utterly destroy every male, and every woman that hath lain by man.
12 And they found among the inhabitants of Jā'besh-gĭl'e-ad four hundred young virgins, that had known no man by lying with any male: and they brought them unto the camp to Shī'lōh, which *is* in the land of Canaan.
13 And the whole congregation sent *some* to speak to the children of Benjamin that *were* in the rock Rimmon, and to call peaceably unto them.
14 And Benjamin came again at that time; and they gave them wives which they had saved alive of the women of Jā'besh-gĭl'e-ad: and yet so they sufficed them not.
15 And the people repented them for Benjamin, because that the LORD had made a breach in the tribes of Israel.
16 ¶Then the elders of the congregation said, How shall we do for wives for them that remain, seeing the women are destroyed out of Benjamin?
17 And they said, *There must be* an inheritance for them that be escaped of Benjamin, that a tribe be not destroyed out of Israel.
18 Howbeit we may not give them wives of our daughters: for the children of Israel have sworn, saying, Cursed *be* he that giveth a wife to Benjamin.
19 Then they said, Behold, *there is* a feast of the LORD in Shī'lōh yearly *in a place* which *is* on the north side of Bĕth-el, on the east side of the highway that goeth up from Bĕth-el to Shĕ'chem, and on the south of Le-bō'nah.
20 Therefore they commanded the children of Benjamin, saying, Go and lie in wait in the vineyards;
21 And see, and, behold, if the daughters of Shī'lōh come out to dance in dances, then come ye out of the vineyards, and catch you every man his wife of the daughters of Shī'lōh, and go to the land of Benjamin.
22 And it shall be, when their fathers or their brethren come unto us to complain, that we will say unto them, Be favourable unto them for our sakes: because we reserved not to each man his wife in the war: for ye did not give unto them at this time, *that* ye should be guilty.
23 And the children of Benjamin did so, and took *them* wives, according to their number, of them that danced, whom they caught: and they went and returned unto their inheritance, and repaired the cities, and dwelt in them.
24 And the children of Israel departed thence at that time, every man to his tribe and to his family, and they went out from thence every man to his inheritance.
25 In those days *there was* no king in Israel: every man did *that which was* right in his own eyes.

THE BOOK OF RUTH

CHAPTER 1

NOW it came to pass in the days when the judges ruled, that there was a famine in the land. And a certain man of Bĕth-lehĕm-jūdah went to sojourn in the country of Moab, he, and his wife, and his two sons.
2 And the name of the man *was* E-lĭm'e-lĕch, and the name of his wife Naomi, and the name of his two sons Māh'lon and Chĭl'ĭ-on, Ĕph'rath-ītes of Bĕth-lehĕm-jūdah. And they came into the country of Moab, and continued there.
3 And E-lĭm'e-lĕch Naomi's husband died; and she was left, and her two sons.
4 And they took them wives of the women of Moab; the name of the one *was* Ôr'pah, and the name of the other Ruth: and they dwelled there about ten years.
5 And Māh'lon and Chĭl'ĭ-on died also both of them; and the woman was left of her two sons and her husband.
6 ¶Then she arose with her daughters in law, that she might return from the country of Moab: for she had heard in the country of Moab how that the LORD had visited his people in giving them bread.
7 Wherefore she went forth out of the place where she was, and her two daughters in law with her; and they went on the way to return unto the land of Judah.
8 And Naomi said unto her two daughters in law, Go, return each to her mother's house: the LORD deal kindly with you, as ye have dealt with the dead, and with me.
9 The LORD grant you that ye may find rest, each *of you* in the house of her husband. Then she kissed them; and they lifted up their voice, and wept.

10 And they said unto her, Surely we
will return with thee unto thy people.
11 And Naomi said, Turn again, my
daughters: why will ye go with me? *are*
there yet *any more* sons in my womb,
that they may be your husbands?
12 Turn again, my daughters, go *your*
way; for I am too old to have an husband.
If I should say, I have hope, *if* I
should have an husband also to night,
and should also bear sons;
13 Would ye tarry for them till they
were grown? would ye stay for them
from having husbands? nay, my
daughters; for it grieveth me much for
your sakes that the hand of the LORD is
gone out against me.
14 And they lifted up their voice, and
wept again: and Ôr'pah kissed her
mother in law; but Ruth clave unto her.
15 And she said, Behold, thy sister in
law is gone back unto her people, and
unto her gods: return thou after thy sis-
ter in law.
16 And Ruth said, Intreat me not to
leave thee, *or* to return from following
after thee: for whither thou goest, I will
go; and where thou lodgest, I will
lodge: thy people *shall be* my people,
and thy God my God:
17 Where thou diest, will I die, and
there will I be buried: the LORD do so to
me, and more also, *if ought* but death
part thee and me.
18 When she saw that she was sted-
fastly minded to go with her, then she
left speaking unto her.
19 ¶So they two went until they came
to Bĕth-lehĕm. And it came to pass,
when they were come to Bĕth-lehĕm,
that all the city was moved about them,
and they said, *Is* this Naomi?
20 And she said unto them, Call me
not Naomi, call me Mâ'ra: for the Al-
mighty hath dealt very bitterly with
me.
21 I went out full, and the LORD hath
brought me home again empty: why
then call ye me Naomi, seeing the LORD
hath testified against me, and the Al-
mighty hath afflicted me?
22 So Naomi returned, and Ruth the
Moabitess, her daughter in law, with
her, which returned out of the country
of Moab: and they came to Bĕth-lehĕm
in the beginning of barley harvest.

CHAPTER 2

AND Naomi had a kinsman of her hus-
band's, a mighty man of wealth, of the
family of E-lĭm'e-lĕch; and his name
was Bō'ăz.
2 And Ruth the Moabitess said unto
Naomi, Let me now go to the field, and
glean ears of corn after *him* in whose
sight I shall find grace. And she said
unto her, Go, my daughter.
3 And she went, and came, and
gleaned in the field after the reapers:
and her hap was to light on a part of the
field *belonging* unto Bō'ăz, who *was* of
the kindred of E-lĭm'e-lĕch.
4 ¶And, behold, Bō'ăz came from
Bĕth-lehĕm, and said unto the reapers,
The LORD *be* with you. And they an-
swered him, The LORD bless thee.
5 Then said Bō'ăz unto his servant
that was set over the reapers, Whose
damsel *is* this?
6 And the servant that was set over
the reapers answered and said, It *is* the
Moabitish damsel that came back with
Naomi out of the country of Moab:
7 And she said, I pray you, let me
glean and gather after the reapers
among the sheaves: so she came, and
hath continued even from the morning
until now, that she tarried a little in the
house.
8 Then said Bō'ăz unto Ruth, Hearest
thou not, my daughter? Go not to glean
in another field, neither go from hence,
but abide here fast by my maidens:
9 *Let* thine eyes *be* on the field that
they do reap, and go thou after them:
have I not charged the young men that
they shall not touch thee? and when
thou art athirst, go unto the vessels,
and drink of *that* which the young men
have drawn.
10 Then she fell on her face, and
bowed herself to the ground, and said
unto him, Why have I found grace in
thine eyes, that thou shouldest take
knowledge of me, seeing I *am* a
stranger?
11 And Bō'ăz answered and said unto
her, It hath fully been shewed me, all
that thou hast done unto thy mother in
law since the death of thine husband:
and *how* thou hast left thy father and
thy mother, and the land of thy nativ-
ity, and art come unto a people which
thou knewest not heretofore.
12 The LORD recompense thy work,
and a full reward be given thee of the
LORD God of Israel, under whose wings
thou art come to trust.
13 Then she said, Let me find favour
in thy sight, my lord; for that thou hast
comforted me, and for that thou hast
spoken friendly unto thine handmaid,
though I be not like unto one of thine
handmaidens.
14 And Bō'ăz said unto her, At meal-
time come thou hither, and eat of the
bread, and dip thy morsel in the vinegar.
And she sat beside the reapers: and
he reached her parched *corn*, and she
did eat, and was sufficed, and left.

15 And when she was risen up to
glean, Bō'ăz commanded his young
men, saying, Let her glean even among
the sheaves, and reproach her not:
16 And let fall also *some* of the hand-
fuls of purpose for her, and leave *them*,
that she may glean *them*, and rebuke
her not.
17 So she gleaned in the field until
even, and beat out that she had
gleaned: and it was about an ephah of
barley.
18 ¶And she took *it* up, and went into
the city: and her mother in law saw
what she had gleaned: and she brought
forth, and gave to her that she had re-
served after she was sufficed.
19 And her mother in law said unto
her, Where hast thou gleaned to day?
and where wroughtest thou? blessed be
he that did take knowledge of thee.
And she shewed her mother in law with
whom she had wrought, and said, The
man's name with whom I wrought to
day *is* Bō'ăz.
20 And Naomi said unto her daughter
in law, Blessed *be* he of the LORD, who
hath not left off his kindness to the liv-
ing and to the dead. And Naomi said
unto her, The man *is* near of kin unto
us, one of our next kinsmen.
21 And Ruth the Moabitess said, He
said unto me also, Thou shalt keep fast
by my young men, until they have
ended all my harvest.
22 And Naomi said unto Ruth her
daughter in law, *It is* good, my
daughter, that thou go out with his
maidens, that they meet thee not in any
other field.
23 So she kept fast by the maidens of
Bō'ăz to glean unto the end of barley
harvest and of wheat harvest; and
dwelt with her mother in law.

CHAPTER 3

THEN Naomi her mother in law said
unto her, My daughter, shall I not seek
rest for thee, that it may be well with
thee?
2 And now *is* not Bō'ăz of our
kindred, with whose maidens thou
wast? Behold, he winnoweth barley to
night in the threshingfloor.
3 Wash thyself therefore, and anoint
thee, and put thy raiment upon thee,
and get thee down to the floor: *but*
make not thyself known unto the man,
until he shall have done eating and
drinking.
4 And it shall be, when he lieth down,
that thou shalt mark the place where he
shall lie, and thou shalt go in, and un-
cover his feet, and lay thee down; and
he will tell thee what thou shalt do.
5 And she said unto her, All that thou
sayest unto me I will do.
6 ¶And she went down unto the floor,
and did according to all that her mother
in law bade her.
7 And when Bō'ăz had eaten and
drunk, and his heart was merry, he
went to lie down at the end of the heap
of corn: and she came softly, and un-
covered his feet, and laid her down.
8 ¶And it came to pass at midnight,
that the man was afraid, and turned
himself: and, behold, a woman lay at
his feet.
9 And he said, Who *art* thou? And she
answered, I *am* Ruth thine handmaid:
spread therefore thy skirt over thine
handmaid; for thou *art* a near kinsman.
10 And he said, Blessed *be* thou of the
LORD, my daughter: *for* thou hast
shewed more kindness in the latter end
than at the beginning, inasmuch as
thou followedst not young men,
whether poor or rich.
11 And now, my daughter, fear not; I
will do to thee all that thou requirest:
for all the city of my people doth know
that thou *art* a virtuous woman.
12 And now it is true that I *am thy*
near kinsman: howbeit there is a kins-
man nearer than I.
13 Tarry this night, and it shall be in
the morning, *that* if he will perform
unto thee the part of a kinsman, well;
let him do the kinsman's part: but if he
will not do the part of a kinsman to
thee, then will I do the part of a kins-
man to thee, as the LORD liveth: lie
down until the morning.
14 ¶And she lay at his feet until the
morning: and she rose up before one
could know another. And he said, Let it
not be known that a woman came into
the floor.
15 Also he said, Bring the vail that
thou hast upon thee, and hold it. And
when she held it, he measured six *mea-
sures* of barley, and laid *it* on her: and
she went into the city.
16 And when she came to her mother
in law, she said, Who *art* thou, my
daughter? And she told her all that the
man had done to her.
17 And she said, These six *measures*
of barley gave he me; for he said to me,
Go not empty unto thy mother in law.
18 Then said she, Sit still, my
daughter, until thou know how the
matter will fall: for the man will not be
in rest, until he have finished the thing
this day.

CHAPTER 4

THEN went Bō'ăz up to the gate, and
sat him down there: and, behold, the
kinsman of whom Bō'ăz spake came

by; unto whom he said, Ho, such a one! turn aside, sit down here. And he turned aside, and sat down.

2 And he took ten men of the elders of the city, and said, Sit ye down here. And they sat down.

3 And he said unto the kinsman, Naomi, that is come again out of the country of Moab, selleth a parcel of land, which *was* our brother E-lĭm′e-lĕch's:

4 And I thought to advertise thee, saying, Buy *it* before the inhabitants, and before the elders of my people. If thou wilt redeem *it*, redeem *it*: but if thou wilt not redeem *it*, *then* tell me, that I may know: for *there is* none to redeem *it* beside thee; and I *am* after thee. And he said, I will redeem *it*.

5 Then said Bō′ăz, What day thou buyest the field of the hand of Naomi, thou must buy *it* also of Ruth the Moabitess, the wife of the dead, to raise up the name of the dead upon his inheritance.

6 And the kinsman said, I cannot redeem *it* for myself, lest I mar mine own inheritance: redeem thou my right to thyself; for I cannot redeem *it*.

7 Now this *was the manner* in former time in Israel concerning redeeming and concerning changing, for to confirm all things; a man plucked off his shoe, and gave *it* to his neighbour: and this *was* a testimony in Israel.

8 Therefore the kinsman said unto Bō′ăz, Buy *it* for thee. So he drew off his shoe.

9 ¶And Bō′ăz said unto the elders, and *unto* all the people, Ye *are* witnesses this day, that I have bought all that *was* E-lĭm′e-lĕch's, and all that *was* Chĭl′ĭ-on's and Măh′lon's, of the hand of Naomi.

10 Moreover Ruth the Moabitess, the wife of Măh′lon, have I purchased to be my wife, to raise up the name of the dead upon his inheritance, that the name of the dead be not cut off from among his brethren, and from the gate of his place: ye *are* witnesses this day.

11 And all the people that *were* in the gate, and the elders, said, *We are* witnesses. The LORD make the woman that is come into thine house like Rāchel and like Leah, which two did build the house of Israel: and do thou worthily in Ĕph′ra-tah, and be famous in Bĕth-lehĕm:

12 And let thy house be like the house of Phâ′rĕz, whom Tā′mar bare unto Jūdah, of the seed which the LORD shall give thee of this young woman.

13 ¶So Bō′ăz took Ruth, and she was his wife: and when he went in unto her, the LORD gave her conception, and she bare a son.

14 And the women said unto Naomi, Blessed *be* the LORD, which hath not left thee this day without a kinsman, that his name may be famous in Israel.

15 And he shall be unto thee a restorer of *thy* life, and a nourisher of thine old age: for thy daughter in law, which loveth thee, which is better to thee than seven sons, hath born him.

16 And Naomi took the child, and laid it in her bosom, and became nurse unto it.

17 And the women her neighbours gave it a name, saying, There is a son born to Naomi; and they called his name Ō′bed: he *is* the father of Jesse, the father of David.

18 ¶Now these *are* the generations of Phâ′rĕz: Phâ′rĕz begat Hĕz′ron,

19 And Hĕz′ron begat Ram, and Ram begat Am-mĭn′a-dăb,

20 And Am-mĭn′a-dăb begat Năh′shŏn, and Năh′shŏn begat Săl′mon,

21 And Săl′mon begat Bō′ăz, and Bō′ăz begat Ō′bed,

22 And Ō′bed begat Jesse, and Jesse begat David.

THE

FIRST BOOK OF SAMUEL

OTHERWISE CALLED

THE FIRST BOOK OF THE KINGS

CHAPTER 1

NOW there was a certain man of Ră-math-ā′im-zō′phĭm, of mount Ē′phra-im, and his name *was* Ĕl′kā-nah, the son of Jer′ō-hăm, the son of E-lī′hū, the son of Tō′hū, the son of Zuph, an Ĕph′-rath-īte:

2 And he had two wives; the name of the one *was* Hannah, and the name of the other Pe-nĭn′nah: and Pe-nĭn′nah had children, but Hannah had no children.

3 And this man went up out of his city yearly to worship and to sacrifice unto the LORD of hosts in Shī′lōh. And the two sons of Eli, Hŏph′nī and Phĭn′e-has, the priests of the LORD, *were* there.

4 And when the time was that Ĕl′kā-nah offered, he gave to Pe-nĭn′nah his

wife, and to all her sons and her daughters, portions:

5 But unto Hannah he gave a worthy portion; for he loved Hannah: but the LORD had shut up her womb.

6 And her adversary also provoked her sore, for to make her fret, because the LORD had shut up her womb.

7 And *as* he did so year by year, when she went up to the house of the LORD, so she provoked her; therefore she wept, and did not eat.

8 Then said Ĕl'kā-nah her husband to her, Hannah, why weepest thou? and why eatest thou not? and why is thy heart grieved? *am* not I better to thee than ten sons?

9 ¶So Hannah rose up after they had eaten in Shī'lōh, and after they had drunk. Now Eli the priest sat upon a seat by a post of the temple of the LORD.

10 And she *was* in bitterness of soul, and prayed unto the LORD, and wept sore.

11 And she vowed a vow, and said, O LORD of hosts, if thou wilt indeed look on the affliction of thine handmaid, and remember me, and not forget thine handmaid, but wilt give unto thine handmaid a man child, then I will give him unto the LORD all the days of his life, and there shall no razor come upon his head.

12 ¶And it came to pass, as she continued praying before the LORD, that Eli marked her mouth.

13 Now Hannah, she spake in her heart; only her lips moved, but her voice was not heard: therefore Eli thought she had been drunken.

14 And Eli said unto her, How long wilt thou be drunken? put away thy wine from thee.

15 And Hannah answered and said, No, my lord, I *am* a woman of a sorrowful spirit: I have drunk neither wine nor strong drink, but have poured out my soul before the LORD.

16 Count not thine handmaid for a daughter of Bē'lī-al: for out of the abundance of my complaint and grief have I spoken hitherto.

17 Then Eli answered and said, Go in peace: and the God of Israel grant *thee* thy petition that thou hast asked of him.

18 And she said, Let thine handmaid find grace in thy sight. So the woman went her way, and did eat, and her countenance was no more *sad*.

19 ¶And they rose up in the morning early, and worshipped before the LORD, and returned, and came to their house to Rā'mah: and Ĕl'kā-nah knew Hannah his wife; and the LORD remembered her.

20 Wherefore it came to pass, when the time was come about after Hannah had conceived, that she bare a son, and called his name Samuel, *saying*, Because I have asked him of the LORD.

21 And the man Ĕl'kā-nah, and all his house, went up to offer unto the LORD the yearly sacrifice, and his vow.

22 But Hannah went not up; for she said unto her husband, *I will not go up* until the child be weaned, and *then* I will bring him, that he may appear before the LORD, and there abide for ever.

23 And Ĕl'kā-nah her husband said unto her, Do what seemeth thee good; tarry until thou have weaned him; only the LORD establish his word. So the woman abode, and gave her son suck until she weaned him.

24 ¶And when she had weaned him, she took him up with her, with three bullocks, and one ephah of flour, and a bottle of wine, and brought him unto the house of the LORD in Shī'lōh: and the child *was* young.

25 And they slew a bullock, and brought the child to Eli.

26 And she said, Oh my lord, *as* thy soul liveth, my lord, I *am* the woman that stood by thee here, praying unto the LORD.

27 For this child I prayed; and the LORD hath given me my petition which I asked of him:

28 Therefore also I have lent him to the LORD; as long as he liveth he shall be lent to the LORD. And he worshipped the LORD there.

CHAPTER 2

AND Hannah prayed, and said, My heart rejoiceth in the LORD, mine horn is exalted in the LORD: my mouth is enlarged over mine enemies; because I rejoice in thy salvation.

2 *There is* none holy as the LORD: for *there is* none beside thee: neither *is there* any rock like our God.

3 Talk no more so exceeding proudly; let *not* arrogancy come out of your mouth: for the LORD *is* a God of knowledge, and by him actions are weighed.

4 The bows of the mighty men *are* broken, and they that stumbled are girded with strength.

5 *They that were* full have hired out themselves for bread; and *they that were* hungry ceased: so that the barren hath born seven; and she that hath many children is waxed feeble.

6 The LORD killeth, and maketh alive: he bringeth down to the grave, and bringeth up.

7 The LORD maketh poor, and maketh rich: he bringeth low, and lifteth up.

8 He raiseth up the poor out of the dust, *and* lifteth up the beggar from the dunghill, to set *them* among princes, and to make them inherit the throne of glory: for the pillars of the earth *are* the LORD's, and he hath set the world upon them.

9 He will keep the feet of his saints, and the wicked shall be silent in darkness; for by strength shall no man prevail.

10 The adversaries of the LORD shall be broken to pieces; out of heaven shall he thunder upon them: the LORD shall judge the ends of the earth; and he shall give strength unto his king, and exalt the horn of his anointed.

11 ¶And Ĕl′kā-nah went to Rā′mah to his house. And the child did minister unto the LORD before Eli the priest.

12 Now the sons of Eli *were* sons of Bē′lĭ-al; they knew not the LORD.

13 And the priest's custom with the people *was, that,* when any man offered sacrifice, the priest's servant came, while the flesh was in seething, with a fleshhook of three teeth in his hand;

14 And he struck *it* into the pan, or kettle, or caldron, or pot; all that the fleshhook brought up the priest took for himself. So they did in Shī′lōh unto all the Israelites that came thither.

15 Also before they burnt the fat, the priest's servant came, and said to the man that sacrificed, Give flesh to roast for the priest; for he will not have sodden flesh of thee, but raw.

16 And *if* any man said unto him, Let them not fail to burn the fat presently, and *then* take *as much* as thy soul desireth; then he would answer him, *Nay;* but thou shalt give *it me* now: and if not, I will take *it* by force.

17 Wherefore the sin of the young men was very great before the LORD: for men abhorred the offering of the LORD.

18 ¶But Samuel ministered before the LORD, *being* a child, girded with a linen ephod.

19 Moreover his mother made him a little coat, and brought *it* to him from year to year, when she came up with her husband to offer the yearly sacrifice.

20 And Eli blessed Ĕl′kā-nah and his wife, and said, The LORD give thee seed of this woman for the loan which is lent to the LORD. And they went unto their own home.

21 And the LORD visited Hannah, so that she conceived, and bare three sons and two daughters. And the child Samuel grew before the LORD.

22 ¶Now Eli was very old, and heard all that his sons did unto all Israel; and how they lay with the women that assembled *at* the door of the tabernacle of the congregation.

23 And he said unto them, Why do ye such things? for I hear of your evil dealings by all this people.

24 Nay, my sons; for *it is* no good report that I hear: ye make the LORD's people to transgress.

25 If one man sin against another, the judge shall judge him: but if a man sin against the LORD, who shall intreat for him? Notwithstanding they hearkened not unto the voice of their father, because the LORD would slay them.

26 And the child Samuel grew on, and was in favour both with the LORD, and also with men.

27 ¶And there came a man of God unto Eli, and said unto him, Thus saith the LORD, Did I plainly appear unto the house of thy father, when they were in Egypt in Pharaoh's house?

28 And did I choose him out of all the tribes of Israel *to be* my priest, to offer upon mine altar, to burn incense, to wear an ephod before me? and did I give unto the house of thy father all the offerings made by fire of the children of Israel?

29 Wherefore kick ye at my sacrifice and at mine offering, which I have commanded *in my* habitation; and honourest thy sons above me, to make yourselves fat with the chiefest of all the offerings of Israel my people?

30 Wherefore the LORD God of Israel saith, I said indeed *that* thy house, and the house of thy father, should walk before me for ever: but now the LORD saith, Be it far from me; for them that honour me I will honour, and they that despise me shall be lightly esteemed.

31 Behold, the days come, that I will cut off thine arm, and the arm of thy father's house, that there shall not be an old man in thine house.

32 And thou shalt see an enemy *in my* habitation, in all *the wealth* which *God* shall give Israel: and there shall not be an old man in thine house for ever.

33 And the man of thine, *whom* I shall not cut off from mine altar, *shall be* to consume thine eyes, and to grieve thine heart: and all the increase of thine house shall die in the flower of their age.

34 And this *shall be* a sign unto thee, that shall come upon thy two sons, on Hŏph′nī and Phĭn′e-has; in one day they shall die both of them.

35 And I will raise me up a faithful priest, *that* shall do according to *that* which *is* in mine heart and in my mind: and I will build him a sure house; and he shall walk before mine anointed for ever.

36 And it shall come to pass, *that* every one that is left in thine house shall come *and* crouch to him for a piece of silver and a morsel of bread, and shall say, Put me, I pray thee, into one of the priests' offices, that I may eat a piece of bread.

CHAPTER 3

AND the child Samuel ministered unto the LORD before Eli. And the word of the LORD was precious in those days; *there was* no open vision.

2 And it came to pass at that time, when Eli *was* laid down in his place, and his eyes began to wax dim, *that* he could not see;

3 And ere the lamp of God went out in the temple of the LORD, where the ark of God *was*, and Samuel was laid down *to sleep;*

4 That the LORD called Samuel: and he answered, Here *am* I.

5 And he ran unto Eli, and said, Here *am* I; for thou calledst me. And he said, I called not; lie down again. And he went and lay down.

6 And the LORD called yet again, Samuel. And Samuel arose and went to Eli, and said, Here *am* I; for thou didst call me. And he answered, I called not, my son; lie down again.

7 Now Samuel did not yet know the LORD, neither was the word of the LORD yet revealed unto him.

8 And the LORD called Samuel again the third time. And he arose and went to Eli, and said, Here *am* I; for thou didst call me. And Eli perceived that the LORD had called the child.

9 Therefore Eli said unto Samuel, Go, lie down: and it shall be, if he call thee, that thou shalt say, Speak, LORD; for thy servant heareth. So Samuel went and lay down in his place.

10 And the LORD came, and stood, and called as at other times, Samuel, Samuel. Then Samuel answered, Speak; for thy servant heareth.

11 ¶And the LORD said to Samuel, Behold, I will do a thing in Israel, at which both the ears of every one that heareth it shall tingle.

12 In that day I will perform against Eli all *things* which I have spoken concerning his house: when I begin, I will also make an end.

13 For I have told him that I will judge his house for ever for the iniquity which he knoweth; because his sons made themselves vile, and he restrained them not.

14 And therefore I have sworn unto the house of Eli, that the iniquity of Eli's house shall not be purged with sacrifice nor offering for ever.

15 ¶And Samuel lay until the morning, and opened the doors of the house of the LORD. And Samuel feared to shew Eli the vision.

16 Then Eli called Samuel, and said, Samuel, my son. And he answered, Here *am* I.

17 And he said, What *is* the thing that *the* LORD hath said unto thee? I pray thee hide *it* not from me: God do so to thee, and more also, if thou hide *any* thing from me of all the things that he said unto thee.

18 And Samuel told him every whit, and hid nothing from him. And he said, It *is* the LORD: let him do what seemeth him good.

19 And Samuel grew, and the LORD was with him, and did let none of his words fall to the ground.

20 And all Israel from Dan even to Be´er–shē´ba knew that Samuel *was* established *to be* a prophet of the LORD.

21 And the LORD appeared again in Shī´lōh: for the LORD revealed himself to Samuel in Shī´lōh by the word of the LORD.

CHAPTER 4

AND the word of Samuel came to all Israel. Now Israel went out against the Philistines to battle, and pitched beside Ĕb´en–ē´zer: and the Philistines pitched in Ā´phĕk.

2 And the Philistines put themselves in array against Israel: and when they joined battle, Israel was smitten before the Philistines: and they slew of the army in the field about four thousand men.

3 ¶And when the people were come into the camp, the elders of Israel said, Wherefore hath the LORD smitten us to day before the Philistines? Let us fetch the ark of the covenant of the LORD out of Shī´lōh unto us, that, when it cometh among us, it may save us out of the hand of our enemies.

4 So the people sent to Shī´lōh, that they might bring from thence the ark of the covenant of the LORD of hosts, which dwelleth *between* the cherubims: and the two sons of Eli, Hŏph´nī and Phĭn´e-has, *were* there with the ark of the covenant of God.

5 And when the ark of the covenant of the LORD came into the camp, all

Israel shouted with a great shout, so
that the earth rang again.
6 And when the Philistines heard the
noise of the shout, they said, What
meaneth the noise of this great shout in
the camp of the Hebrews? And they
understood that the ark of the LORD was
come into the camp.
7 And the Philistines were afraid, for
they said, God is come into the camp.
And they said, Woe unto us! for there
hath not been such a thing heretofore.
8 Woe unto us! who shall deliver us
out of the hand of these mighty Gods?
these *are* the Gods that smote the
Egyptians with all the plagues in the
wilderness.
9 Be strong, and quit yourselves like
men, O ye Philistines, that ye be not
servants unto the Hebrews, as they
have been to you: quit yourselves like
men, and fight.
10 ¶And the Philistines fought, and
Israel was smitten, and they fled every
man into his tent: and there was a very
great slaughter; for there fell of Israel
thirty thousand footmen.
11 And the ark of God was taken; and
the two sons of Eli, Hŏph′nī and Phĭn′e-
has, were slain.
12 ¶And there ran a man of Benjamin
out of the army, and came to Shī′lōh the
same day with his clothes rent, and
with earth upon his head.
13 And when he came, lo, Eli sat upon
a seat by the wayside watching: for his
heart trembled for the ark of God. And
when the man came into the city, and
told *it*, all the city cried out.
14 And when Eli heard the noise of
the crying, he said, What *meaneth* the
noise of this tumult? And the man came
in hastily, and told Eli.
15 Now Eli was ninety and eight
years old; and his eyes were dim, that
he could not see.
16 And the man said unto Eli, I *am* he
that came out of the army, and I fled to
day out of the army. And he said, What
is there done, my son?
17 And the messenger answered and
said, Israel is fled before the Philis-
tines, and there hath been also a great
slaughter among the people, and thy
two sons also, Hŏph′nī and Phĭn′e-has,
are dead, and the ark of God is taken.
18 And it came to pass, when he
made mention of the ark of God, that he
fell from off the seat backward by the
side of the gate, and his neck brake, and
he died: for he was an old man, and
heavy. And he had judged Israel forty
years.
19 ¶And his daughter in law, Phĭn′e-
has' wife, was with child, *near* to be de-
livered: and when she heard the tidings
that the ark of God was taken, and that
her father in law and her husband were
dead, she bowed herself and travailed;
for her pains came upon her.
20 And about the time of her death
the women that stood by her said unto
her, Fear not; for thou hast born a son.
But she answered not, neither did she
regard *it*.
21 And she named the child Ī′-cha-
bŏd, saying, The glory is departed from
Israel: because the ark of God was
taken, and because of her father in law
and her husband.
22 And she said, The glory is de-
parted from Israel: for the ark of God is
taken.

CHAPTER 5

AND the Philistines took the ark of
God, and brought it from Ĕb′en-ē′zer
unto Ăsh′dŏd.
2 When the Philistines took the ark of
God, they brought it into the house of
Dā′gŏn, and set it by Dā′gŏn.
3 ¶And when they of Ăsh′dŏd arose
early on the morrow, behold, Dā′gŏn
was fallen upon his face to the earth be-
fore the ark of the LORD. And they took
Dā′gŏn, and set him in his place again.
4 And when they arose early on the
morrow morning, behold, Dā′gŏn *was*
fallen upon his face to the ground be-
fore the ark of the LORD; and the head
of Dā′gŏn and both the palms of his
hands *were* cut off upon the threshold;
only *the stump of* Dā′gŏn was left to
him.
5 Therefore neither the priests of Dā′-
gŏn, nor any that come into Da′gŏn's
house, tread on the threshold of Dā′gŏn
in Ăsh′dŏd unto this day.
6 ¶But the hand of the LORD was heavy
upon them of Ăsh′dŏd, and he destroyed
them, and smote them with emer-
ods, *even* Ăsh′dŏd and the coasts there-
of.
7 And when the men of Ăsh′dŏd saw
that *it was* so, they said, The ark of the
God of Israel shall not abide with us:
for his hand is sore upon us, and upon
Dā′gŏn our god.
8 They sent therefore and gathered
all the lords of the Philistines unto
them, and said, What shall we do with
the ark of the God of Israel? And they
answered, Let the ark of the God of
Israel be carried about unto Gath. And
they carried the ark of the God of Israel
about *thither*.
9 And it was *so*, that, after they had
carried it about, the hand of the LORD
was against the city with a very great
destruction: and he smote the men of

the city, both small and great, and they
had emerods in their secret parts.
10 ¶Therefore they sent the ark of
God to Ĕkron. And it came to pass, as
the ark of God came to Ĕkron, that the
Ĕkronītes cried out, saying, They have
brought about the ark of the God of
Israel to us, to slay us and our people.
11 So they sent and gathered togeth-
er all the lords of the Philistines, and
said, Send away the ark of the God of
Israel, and let it go again to his own
place, that it slay us not, and our
people: for there was a deadly destruc-
tion throughout all the city; the hand of
God was very heavy there.
12 And the men that died not were
smitten with the emerods: and the cry
of the city went up to heaven.

CHAPTER 6

AND the ark of the LORD was in the
country of the Philistines seven
months.
2 And the Philistines called for the
priests and the diviners, saying, What
shall we do to the ark of the LORD? tell
us wherewith we shall send it to his
place.
3 And they said, If ye send away the
ark of the God of Israel, send it not
empty; but in any wise return him a
trespass offering: then ye shall be
healed, and it shall be known to you
why his hand is not removed from you.
4 Then said they, What *shall be* the
trespass offering which we shall return
to him? They answered, Five golden
emerods, and five golden mice, *accord-*
ing to the number of the lords of the
Philistines: for one plague *was* on you
all, and on your lords.
5 Wherefore ye shall make images of
your emerods, and images of your mice
that mar the land; and ye shall give
glory unto the God of Israel: peradven-
ture he will lighten his hand from off
you, and from off your gods, and from
off your land.
6 Wherefore then do ye harden your
hearts, as the Egyptians and Pharaoh
hardened their hearts? when he had
wrought wonderfully among them, did
they not let the people go, and they de-
parted?
7 Now therefore make a new cart,
and take two milch kine, on which
there hath come no yoke, and tie the
kine to the cart, and bring their calves
home from them:
8 And take the ark of the LORD, and
lay it upon the cart; and put the jewels
of gold, which ye return him *for* a tres-
pass offering, in a coffer by the side
thereof; and send it away, that it may
go.
9 And see, if it goeth up by the way of
his own coast to Bĕth-shĕmesh, *then* he
hath done us this great evil: but if not,
then we shall know that *it is* not his
hand *that* smote us; it *was* a chance
that happened to us.
10 ¶And the men did so; and took two
milch kine, and tied them to the cart,
and shut up their calves at home:
11 And they laid the ark of the LORD
upon the cart, and the coffer with the
mice of gold and the images of their
emerods.
12 And the kine took the straight way
to the way of Bĕth-shĕmesh, *and* went
along the highway, lowing as they
went, and turned not aside *to* the right
hand or *to* the left; and the lords of the
Philistines went after them unto the
border of Bĕth-shĕmesh.
13 And *they of* Bĕth-shĕmesh *were*
reaping their wheat harvest in the val-
ley: and they lifted up their eyes, and
saw the ark, and rejoiced to see *it*.
14 And the cart came into the field of
Joshua, a Bĕth-shĕmīte, and stood
there, where *there was* a great stone:
and they clave the wood of the cart, and
offered the kine a burnt offering unto
the LORD.
15 And the Levites took down the ark
of the LORD, and the coffer that *was*
with it, wherein the jewels of gold
were, and put *them* on the great stone:
and the men of Bĕth-shĕmesh offered
burnt offerings and sacrificed sacri-
fices the same day unto the LORD.
16 And when the five lords of the
Philistines had seen *it*, they returned to
Ĕkron the same day.
17 And these *are* the golden emerods
which the Philistines returned *for* a
trespass offering unto the LORD; for
Ăsh'dŏd one, for Gā'za one, for Ăs'ke-
lŏn one, for Gath one, for Ĕkron one;
18 And the golden mice, *according to*
the number of all the cities of the Philis-
tines *belonging* to the five lords, *both* of
fenced cities, and of country villages,
even unto the great *stone of* Abel, where-
on they set down the ark of the
LORD: *which stone remaineth* unto this
day in the field of Joshua, the
Bĕth-shĕmīte.
19 ¶And he smote the men of
Bĕth-shĕmesh, because they had looked
into the ark of the LORD, even he smote
of the people fifty thousand and three-
score and ten men: and the people la-
mented, because the LORD had smitten
many of the people with a great
slaughter.
20 And the men of Bĕth-shĕmesh said,

Who is able to stand before this holy LORD God? and to whom shall he go up from us?
21 And they sent messengers to the inhabitants of Kir'jath–jĕ'a-rĭm, saying, The Philistines have brought again the ark of the LORD; come ye down, *and* fetch it up to you.

CHAPTER 7

AND the men of Kir'jath–jĕ'a-rĭm came, and fetched up the ark of the LORD, and brought it into the house of A-bĭn'a-dăb in the hill, and sanctified Ĕ-le-ā'zar his son to keep the ark of the LORD.
2 And it came to pass, while the ark abode in Kir'jath–jĕ'a-rĭm, that the time was long; for it was twenty years: and all the house of Israel lamented after the LORD.
3 ¶And Samuel spake unto all the house of Israel, saying, If ye do return unto the LORD with all your hearts, *then* put away the strange gods and Ăsh'ta-rŏth from among you, and prepare your hearts unto the LORD, and serve him only: and he will deliver you out of the hand of the Philistines.
4 Then the children of Israel did put away Bā'al-ĭm and Ăsh'ta-rŏth, and served the LORD only.
5 And Samuel said, Gather all Israel to Mĭz'peh, and I will pray for you unto the LORD.
6 And they gathered together to Mĭz'peh, and drew water, and poured *it* out before the LORD, and fasted on that day, and said there, We have sinned against the LORD. And Samuel judged the children of Israel in Mĭz'peh.
7 And when the Philistines heard that the children of Israel were gathered together to Mĭz'peh, the lords of the Philistines went up against Israel. And when the children of Israel heard *it*, they were afraid of the Philistines.
8 And the children of Israel said to Samuel, Cease not to cry unto the LORD our God for us, that he will save us out of the hand of the Philistines.
9 And Samuel took a sucking lamb, and offered *it for* a burnt offering wholly unto the LORD: and Samuel cried unto the LORD for Israel; and the LORD heard him.
10 And as Samuel was offering up the burnt offering, the Philistines drew near to battle against Israel: but the LORD thundered with a great thunder on that day upon the Philistines, and discomfited them; and they were smitten before Israel.
11 And the men of Israel went out of Mĭz'peh, and pursued the Philistines, and smote them, until *they came* under Bĕth-cär.
12 Then Samuel took a stone, and set *it* between Mĭz'peh and Shen, and called the name of it Ĕb'en–ĕ'zer, saying, Hitherto hath the LORD helped us.
13 So the Philistines were subdued, and they came no more into the coast of Israel: and the hand of the LORD was against the Philistines all the days of Samuel.
14 And the cities which the Philistines had taken from Israel were restored to Israel, from Ĕkron even unto Gath; and the coasts thereof did Israel deliver out of the hands of the Philistines. And there was peace between Israel and the Ămorītes.
15 ¶And Samuel judged Israel all the days of his life.
16 And he went from year to year in circuit to Bĕth-el, and Gilgal, and Mĭz'peh, and judged Israel in all those places.
17 And his return *was* to Rā'mah; for there *was* his house; and there he judged Israel; and there he built an altar unto the LORD.

CHAPTER 8

AND it came to pass, when Samuel was old, that he made his sons judges over Israel.
2 Now the name of his firstborn was Jō'el; and the name of his second, Ă-bī'ah: *they were* judges in Be'er–shē'ba.
3 And his sons walked not in his ways, but turned aside after lucre, and took bribes, and perverted judgment.
4 Then all the elders of Israel gathered themselves together, and came to Samuel unto Rā'mah,
5 And said unto him, Behold, thou art old, and thy sons walk not in thy ways: now make us a king to judge us like all the nations.
6 ¶But the thing displeased Samuel, when they said, Give us a king to judge us. And Samuel prayed unto the LORD.
7 And the LORD said unto Samuel, Hearken unto the voice of the people in all that they say unto thee: for they have not rejected thee, but they have rejected me, that I should not reign over them.
8 According to all the works which they have done since the day that I brought them up out of Egypt even unto this day, wherewith they have forsaken me, and served other gods, so do they also unto thee.
9 Now therefore hearken unto their voice: howbeit yet protest solemnly unto them, and shew them the manner of the king that shall reign over them.

10 ¶And Samuel told all the words of the LORD unto the people that asked of him a king.
11 And he said, This will be the manner of the king that shall reign over you: He will take your sons, and appoint *them* for himself, for his chariots, and *to be* his horsemen; and *some* shall run before his chariots.
12 And he will appoint him captains over thousands, and captains over fifties; and *will set them* to ear his ground, and to reap his harvest, and to make his instruments of war, and instruments of his chariots.
13 And he will take your daughters *to be* confectionaries, and *to be* cooks, and *to be* bakers.
14 And he will take your fields, and your vineyards, and your oliveyards, *even* the best *of them*, and give *them* to his servants.
15 And he will take the tenth of your seed, and of your vineyards, and give to his officers, and to his servants.
16 And he will take your menservants, and your maidservants, and your goodliest young men, and your asses, and put *them* to his work.
17 He will take the tenth of your sheep: and ye shall be his servants.
18 And ye shall cry out in that day because of your king which ye shall have chosen you; and the LORD will not hear you in that day.
19 ¶Nevertheless the people refused to obey the voice of Samuel; and they said, Nay; but we will have a king over us;
20 That we also may be like all the nations; and that our king may judge us, and go out before us, and fight our battles.
21 And Samuel heard all the words of the people, and he rehearsed them in the ears of the LORD.
22 And the LORD said to Samuel, Hearken unto their voice, and make them a king. And Samuel said unto the men of Israel, Go ye every man unto his city.

CHAPTER 9

NOW there was a man of Benjamin, whose name *was* Kish, the son of Ā'bī'-el, the son of Ze'rôr, the son of Be-chô'-răth, the son of A-phī'ah, a Benjamite, a mighty man of power.
2 And he had a son, whose name *was* Saul, a choice young man, and a goodly: and *there was* not among the children of Israel a goodlier person than he: from his shoulders and upward *he was* higher than any of the people.
3 And the asses of Kish Saul's father were lost. And Kish said to Saul his son, Take now one of the servants with thee, and arise, go seek the asses.
4 And he passed through mount Ē'phra-im, and passed through the land of Shal'ī-sha, but they found *them* not: then they passed through the land of Shā'lĭm, and *there they were* not: and he passed through the land of the Benjamites, but they found *them* not.
5 *And* when they were come to the land of Zuph, Saul said to his servant that *was* with him, Come, and let us return; lest my father leave *caring* for the asses, and take thought for us.
6 And he said unto him, Behold now, *there is* in this city a man of God, and *he is* an honourable man; all that he saith cometh surely to pass: now let us go thither; peradventure he can shew us our way that we should go.
7 Then said Saul to his servant, But, behold, *if* we go, what shall we bring the man? for the bread is spent in our vessels, and *there is* not a present to bring to the man of God: what have we?
8 And the servant answered Saul again, and said, Behold, I have here at hand the fourth part of a shekel of silver: *that* will I give to the man of God, to tell us our way.
9 (Beforetime in Israel, when a man went to enquire of God, thus he spake, Come, and let us go to the seer: for *he that is* now *called* a Prophet was beforetime called a Seer.)
10 Then said Saul to his servant, Well said; come, let us go. So they went unto the city where the man of God *was*.
11 ¶*And* as they went up the hill to the city, they found young maidens going out to draw water, and said unto them, Is the seer here?
12 And they answered them, and said, He is; behold, *he is* before you: make haste now, for he came to day to the city; for *there is* a sacrifice of the people to day in the high place:
13 As soon as ye be come into the city, ye shall straightway find him, before he go up to the high place to eat: for the people will not eat until he come, because he doth bless the sacrifice; *and* afterwards they eat that be bidden. Now therefore get you up; for about this time ye shall find him.
14 And they went up into the city: *and* when they were come into the city, behold, Samuel came out against them, for to go up to the high place.
15 ¶Now the LORD had told Samuel in his ear a day before Saul came, saying,
16 To morrow about this time I will

The Shepherd David Kills a Lion (1 Sam 17)

Solomon's Wisdom in Judgment (1 Kings 3)

send thee a man out of the land of Benjamin, and thou shalt anoint him *to be* captain over my people Israel, that he may save my people out of the hand of the Philistines: for I have looked upon my people, because their cry is come unto me.
17 And when Samuel saw Saul, the LORD said unto him, Behold the man whom I spake to thee of! this same shall reign over my people.
18 Then Saul drew near to Samuel in the gate, and said, Tell me, I pray thee, where the seer's house *is*.
19 And Samuel answered Saul, and said, I *am* the seer: go up before me unto the high place; for ye shall eat with me to day, and to morrow I will let thee go, and will tell thee all that *is* in thine heart.
20 And as for thine asses that were lost three days ago, set not thy mind on them; for they are found. And on whom *is* all the desire of Israel? *Is it* not on thee, and on all thy father's house?
21 And Saul answered and said, *Am* not I a Benjamite, of the smallest of the tribes of Israel? and my family the least of all the families of the tribe of Benjamin? wherefore then speakest thou so to me?
22 And Samuel took Saul and his servant, and brought them into the parlour, and made them sit in the chiefest place among them that were bidden, which *were* about thirty persons.
23 And Samuel said unto the cook, Bring the portion which I gave thee, of which I said unto thee, Set it by thee.
24 And the cook took up the shoulder, and *that* which *was* upon it, and set *it* before Saul. And Samuel said, Behold that which is left! set *it* before thee, *and* eat: for unto this time hath it been kept for thee since I said, I have invited the people. So Saul did eat with Samuel that day.
25 ¶And when they were come down from the high place into the city, *Samuel* communed with Saul upon the top of the house.
26 And they arose early: and it came to pass about the spring of the day, that Samuel called Saul to the top of the house, saying, Up, that I may send thee away. And Saul arose, and they went out both of them, he and Samuel, abroad.
27 *And* as they were going down to the end of the city, Samuel said to Saul, Bid the servant pass on before us, (and he passed on,) but stand thou still a while, that I may shew thee the word of God.

CHAPTER 10

THEN Samuel took a vial of oil, and poured *it* upon his head, and kissed him, and said, *Is it* not because the LORD hath anointed thee *to be* captain over his inheritance?
2 When thou art departed from me to day, then thou shalt find two men by Rāchel's sepulchre in the border of Benjamin at Zĕl'zah; and they will say unto thee, The asses which thou wentest to seek are found: and, lo, thy father hath left the care of the asses, and sorroweth for you, saying, What shall I do for my son?
3 Then shalt thou go on forward from thence, and thou shalt come to the plain of Tā'bor, and there shall meet thee three men going up to God to Bĕth-el, one carrying three kids, and another carrying three loaves of bread, and another carrying a bottle of wine:
4 And they will salute thee, and give thee two *loaves* of bread; which thou shalt receive of their hands.
5 After that thou shalt come to the hill of God, where *is* the garrison of the Philistines: and it shall come to pass, when thou art come thither to the city, that thou shalt meet a company of prophets coming down from the high place with a psaltery, and a tabret, and a pipe, and a harp, before them; and they shall prophesy:
6 And the Spirit of the LORD will come upon thee, and thou shalt prophesy with them, and shalt be turned into another man.
7 And let it be, when these signs are come unto thee, *that* thou do as occasion serve thee; for God *is* with thee.
8 And thou shalt go down before me to Gilgal; and, behold, I will come down unto thee, to offer burnt offerings, *and* to sacrifice sacrifices of peace offerings: seven days shalt thou tarry, till I come to thee, and shew thee what thou shalt do.
9 ¶And it was *so*, that when he had turned his back to go from Samuel, God gave him another heart: and all those signs came to pass that day.
10 And when they came thither to the hill, behold, a company of prophets met him; and the Spirit of God came upon him, and he prophesied among them.
11 And it came to pass, when all that knew him beforetime saw that, behold, he prophesied among the prophets, then the people said one to another, What *is* this *that* is come unto the son of Kish? *Is* Saul also among the prophets?
12 And one of the same place an-

swered and said, But who *is* their
father? Therefore it became a proverb,
Is Saul also among the prophets?
13 And when he had made an end of
prophesying, he came to the high place.
14 ¶And Saul's uncle said unto him
and to his servant, Whither went ye?
And he said, To seek the asses: and
when we saw that *they were* no where,
we came to Samuel.
15 And Saul's uncle said, Tell me, I
pray thee, what Samuel said unto you.
16 And Saul said unto his uncle, He
told us plainly that the asses were
found. But of the matter of the king-
dom, whereof Samuel spake, he told
him not.
17 ¶And Samuel called the people
together unto the LORD to Mĭz'peh;
18 And said unto the children of
Israel, Thus saith the LORD God of
Israel, I brought up Israel out of Egypt,
and delivered you out of the hand of the
Egyptians, and out of the hand of all
kingdoms, *and* of them that oppressed
you:
19 And ye have this day rejected your
God, who himself saved you out of all
your adversities and your tribulations;
and ye have said unto him, *Nay*, but set
a king over us. Now therefore present
yourselves before the LORD by your
tribes, and by your thousands.
20 And when Samuel had caused all
the tribes of Israel to come near, the
tribe of Benjamin was taken.
21 When he had caused the tribe of
Benjamin to come near by their fam-
ilies, the family of Mă'trī was taken,
and Saul the son of Kish was taken: and
when they sought him, he could not be
found.
22 Therefore they enquired of the
LORD further, if the man should yet
come thither. And the LORD answered,
Behold, he hath hid himself among the
stuff.
23 And they ran and fetched him
thence: and when he stood among the
people, he was higher than any of the
people from his shoulders and upward.
24 And Samuel said to all the people,
See ye him whom the LORD hath cho-
sen, that *there is* none like him among
all the people? And all the people
shouted, and said, God save the king.
25 Then Samuel told the people the
manner of the kingdom, and wrote *it* in
a book, and laid *it* up before the LORD.
And Samuel sent all the people away,
every man to his house.
26 And Saul also went home to Gĭb'e-
ah; and there went with him a band of
men, whose hearts God had touched.
27 But the children of Bē'lī-al said,
How shall this man save us? And they
despised him, and brought him no pres-
ents. But he held his peace.

CHAPTER 11

THEN Nāhāsh the Ammonite came up,
and encamped against Jā'besh-gĭl'e-ad:
and all the men of Jā'besh said unto
Nāhăsh, Make a covenant with us, and
we will serve thee.
2 And Nāhăsh the Ammonite an-
swered them, On this *condition* will I
make *a covenant* with you, that I may
thrust out all your right eyes, and lay it
for a reproach upon all Israel.
3 And the elders of Jā'besh said unto
him, Give us seven days' respite, that
we may send messengers unto all the
coasts of Israel: and then, if *there be* no
man to save us, we will come out to
thee.
4 ¶Then came the messengers to
Gĭb'e-ah of Saul, and told the tidings in
the ears of the people: and all the peo-
ple lifted up their voices, and wept.
5 And, behold, Saul came after the
herd out of the field; and Saul said,
What *aileth* the people that they weep?
And they told him the tidings of the
men of Jā'besh.
6 And the Spirit of God came upon
Saul when he heard those tidings, and
his anger was kindled greatly.
7 And he took a yoke of oxen, and
hewed them in pieces, and sent *them*
throughout all the coasts of Israel by
the hands of messengers, saying,
Whosoever cometh not forth after Saul
and after Samuel, so shall it be done
unto his oxen. And the fear of the LORD
fell on the people, and they came out
with one consent.
8 And when he numbered them in
Bē'zĕk, the children of Israel were
three hundred thousand, and the men
of Jūdah thirty thousand.
9 And they said unto the messengers
that came, Thus shall ye say unto the
men of Jā'besh–gĭl'e-ad, To morrow, by
that time the sun be hot, ye shall have
help. And the messengers came and
shewed *it* to the men of Jā'besh; and
they were glad.
10 Therefore the men of Jā'besh said,
To morrow we will come out unto you,
and ye shall do with us all that seemeth
good unto you.
11 And it was *so* on the morrow, that
Saul put the people in three companies;
and they came into the midst of the
host in the morning watch, and slew
the Ammonites until the heat of the
day: and it came to pass, that they
which remained were scattered, so that
two of them were not left together.

12 ¶And the people said unto Samuel, Who *is* he that said, Shall Saul reign over us? bring the men, that we may put them to death.

13 And Saul said, There shall not a man be put to death this day: for to day the LORD hath wrought salvation in Israel.

14 ¶Then said Samuel to the people, Come, and let us go to Gilgal, and renew the kingdom there.

15 And all the people went to Gilgal; and there they made Saul king before the LORD in Gilgal; and there they sacrificed sacrifices of peace offerings before the LORD; and there Saul and all the men of Israel rejoiced greatly.

CHAPTER 12

AND Samuel said unto all Israel, Behold, I have hearkened unto your voice in all that ye said unto me, and have made a king over you.

2 And now, behold, the king walketh before you: and I am old and grayheaded; and, behold, my sons *are* with you: and I have walked before you from my childhood unto this day.

3 Behold, here I *am*: witness against me before the LORD, and before his anointed: whose ox have I taken? or whose ass have I taken? or whom have I defrauded? whom have I oppressed? or of whose hand have I received *any* bribe to blind mine eyes therewith? and I will restore it you.

4 And they said, Thou hast not defrauded us, nor oppressed us, neither hast thou taken ought of any man's hand.

5 And he said unto them, The LORD *is* witness against you, and his anointed *is* witness this day, that ye have not found ought in my hand. And they answered, *He is* witness.

6 ¶And Samuel said unto the people, *It is* the LORD that advanced Moses and Aaron, and that brought your fathers up out of the land of Egypt.

7 Now therefore stand still, that I may reason with you before the LORD of all the righteous acts of the LORD, which he did to you and to your fathers.

8 When Jacob was come into Egypt, and your fathers cried unto the LORD, then the LORD sent Moses and Aaron, which brought forth your fathers out of Egypt, and made them dwell in this place.

9 And when they forgat the LORD their God, he sold them into the hand of Sĭs'e-ra, captain of the host of Hā'zôr, and into the hand of the Philistines, and into the hand of the king of Moab, and they fought against them.

10 And they cried unto the LORD, and said, We have sinned, because we have forsaken the LORD, and have served Bā'al-ĭm and Ăsh'ta-rŏth: but now deliver us out of the hand of our enemies, and we will serve thee.

11 And the LORD sent Je-rŭb'ba-al, and Bē'dăn, and Jĕph'thah, and Samuel, and delivered you out of the hand of your enemies on every side, and ye dwelled safe.

12 And when ye saw that Nāhăsh the king of the children of Ammon came against you, ye said unto me, Nay; but a king shall reign over us: when the LORD your God *was* your king.

13 Now therefore behold the king whom ye have chosen, *and* whom ye have desired! and, behold, the LORD hath set a king over you.

14 If ye will fear the LORD, and serve him, and obey his voice, and not rebel against the commandment of the LORD, then shall both ye and also the king that reigneth over you continue following the LORD your God:

15 But if ye will not obey the voice of the LORD, but rebel against the commandment of the LORD, then shall the hand of the LORD be against you, as *it was* against your fathers.

16 Now therefore stand and see this great thing, which the LORD will do before your eyes.

17 *Is it* not wheat harvest to day? I will call unto the LORD, and he shall send thunder and rain; that ye may perceive and see that your wickedness *is* great, which ye have done in the sight of the LORD, in asking you a king.

18 So Samuel called unto the LORD; and the LORD sent thunder and rain that day: and all the people greatly feared the LORD and Samuel.

19 And all the people said unto Samuel, Pray for thy servants unto the LORD thy God, that we die not: for we have added unto all our sins *this* evil, to ask us a king.

20 And Samuel said unto the people, Fear not: ye have done all this wickedness: yet turn not aside from following the LORD, but serve the LORD with all your heart;

21 And turn ye not aside: for *then should ye go* after vain *things*, which cannot profit nor deliver; for they *are* vain.

22 For the LORD will not forsake his people for his great name's sake: because it hath pleased the LORD to make you his people.

23 Moreover as for me, God forbid that I should sin against the LORD in

ceasing to pray for you: but I will teach you the good and the right way:

24 Only fear the LORD, and serve him in truth with all your heart: for consider how great *things* he hath done for you.

25 But if ye shall still do wickedly, ye shall be consumed, both ye and your king.

CHAPTER 13

SAUL reigned one year; and when he had reigned two years over Israel,

2 Saul chose him three thousand *men* of Israel; *whereof* two thousand were with Saul in Mĭch'măsh and in mount Bĕth-el, and a thousand were with Jonathan in Gĭb'e-ah of Benjamin: and the rest of the people he sent every man to his tent.

3 And Jonathan smote the garrison of the Philistines that *was* in Gē'ba, and the Philistines heard *of it.* And Saul blew the trumpet throughout all the land, saying, Let the Hebrews hear.

4 And all Israel heard say *that* Saul had smitten a garrison of the Philistines, and *that* Israel also was had in abomination with the Philistines. And the people were called together after Saul to Gilgal.

5 And the Philistines gathered themselves together to fight with Israel, thirty thousand chariots, and six thousand horsemen, and people as the sand which *is* on the sea shore in multitude: and they came up, and pitched in Mĭch'măsh, eastward from Bĕth-ā'ven.

6 When the men of Israel saw that they were in a strait, (for the people were distressed,) then the people did hide themselves in caves, and in thickets, and in rocks, and in high places, and in pits.

7 And *some of* the Hebrews went over Jordan to the land of Gad and Gilead. As for Saul, he *was* yet in Gilgal, and all the people followed him trembling.

8 And he tarried seven days, according to the set time that Samuel *had appointed:* but Samuel came not to Gilgal; and the people were scattered from him.

9 And Saul said, Bring hither a burnt offering to me, and peace offerings. And he offered the burnt offering.

10 And it came to pass, that as soon as he had made an end of offering the burnt offering, behold, Samuel came; and Saul went out to meet him, that he might salute him.

11 And Samuel said, What hast thou done? And Saul said, Because I saw that the people were scattered from me, and *that* thou camest not within the days appointed, and *that* the Philistines gathered themselves together at Mĭch'măsh;

12 Therefore said I, The Philistines will come down now upon me to Gilgal, and I have not made supplication unto the LORD: I forced myself therefore, and offered a burnt offering.

13 And Samuel said to Saul, Thou hast done foolishly: thou hast not kept the commandment of the LORD thy God, which he commanded thee: for now would the LORD have established thy kingdom upon Israel for ever.

14 But now thy kingdom shall not continue: the LORD hath sought him a man after his own heart, and the LORD hath commanded him *to be* captain over his people, because thou hast not kept *that* which the LORD commanded thee.

15 And Samuel arose, and gat him up from Gilgal unto Gĭb'e-ah of Benjamin. And Saul numbered the people *that were* present with him, about six hundred men.

16 And Saul, and Jonathan his son, and the people *that were* present with them, abode in Gĭb'e-ah of Benjamin: but the Philistines encamped in Mĭch'-măsh.

17 ¶And the spoilers came out of the camp of the Philistines in three companies: one company turned unto the way *that leadeth to* Ŏph'rah, unto the land of Shū'al:

18 And another company turned the way *to* Bĕth-hô'ron: and another company turned *to* the way of the border that looketh to the valley of Ze-bō'im toward the wilderness.

19 ¶Now there was no smith found throughout all the land of Israel: for the Philistines said, Lest the Hebrews make *them* swords or spears:

20 But all the Israelites went down to the Philistines, to sharpen every man his share, and his coulter, and his axe, and his mattock.

21 Yet they had a file for the mattocks, and for the coulters, and for the forks, and for the axes, and to sharpen the goads.

22 So it came to pass in the day of battle, that there was neither sword nor spear found in the hand of any of the people that *were* with Saul and Jonathan: but with Saul and with Jonathan his son was there found.

23 And the garrison of the Philistines went out to the passage of Mĭch'măsh.

CHAPTER 14

NOW it came to pass upon a day, that Jonathan the son of Saul said unto the young man that bare his armour, Come, and let us go over to the Philistines' garrison, that *is* on the other side. But he told not his father.

2 And Saul tarried in the uttermost part of Gĭb′e-ah under a pomegranate tree which *is* in Mĭg′rŏn: and the people that *were* with him *were* about six hundred men;

3 And A-hī′ah, the son of A-hī′tŭb, Ī′-cha-bŏd's brother, the son of Phĭn′e-has, the son of Eli, the LORD's priest in Shī′lōh, wearing an ephod. And the people knew not that Jonathan was gone.

4 ¶And between the passages, by which Jonathan sought to go over unto the Philistines' garrison, *there was* a sharp rock on the one side, and a sharp rock on the other side: and the name of the one *was* Bō′zez, and the name of the other Sĕ′neh.

5 The forefront of the one *was* situate northward over against Mĭch′măsh, and the other southward over against Gĭb′e-ah.

6 And Jonathan said to the young man that bare his armour, Come, and let us go over unto the garrison of these uncircumcised: it may be that the LORD will work for us: for *there is* no restraint to the LORD to save by many or by few.

7 And his armourbearer said unto him, Do all that *is* in thine heart: turn thee; behold, I *am* with thee according to thy heart.

8 Then said Jonathan, Behold, we will pass over unto *these* men, and we will discover ourselves unto them.

9 If they say thus unto us, Tarry until we come to you; then we will stand still in our place, and will not go up unto them.

10 But if they say thus, Come up unto us; then we will go up: for the LORD hath delivered them into our hand: and this *shall be* a sign unto us.

11 And both of them discovered themselves unto the garrison of the Philistines: and the Philistines said, Behold, the Hebrews come forth out of the holes where they had hid themselves.

12 And the men of the garrison answered Jonathan and his armourbearer, and said, Come up to us, and we will shew you a thing. And Jonathan said unto his armourbearer, Come up after me: for the LORD hath delivered them into the hand of Israel.

13 And Jonathan climbed up upon his hands and upon his feet, and his armourbearer after him: and they fell before Jonathan; and his armourbearer slew after him.

14 And that first slaughter, which Jonathan and his armourbearer made, was about twenty men, within as it were an half acre of land, *which* a yoke *of oxen might plow*.

15 ¶And there was trembling in the host, in the field, and among all the people: the garrison, and the spoilers, they also trembled, and the earth quaked: so it was a very great trembling.

16 And the watchmen of Saul in Gĭb′e-ah of Benjamin looked; and, behold, the multitude melted away, and they went on beating down *one another*.

17 ¶Then said Saul unto the people that *were* with him, Number now, and see who is gone from us. And when they had numbered, behold, Jonathan and his armourbearer *were* not *there*.

18 And Saul said unto A-hī′ah, Bring hither the ark of God. For the ark of God was at that time with the children of Israel.

19 ¶And it came to pass, while Saul talked unto the priest, that the noise that *was* in the host of the Philistines went on and increased: and Saul said unto the priest, Withdraw thine hand.

20 And Saul and all the people that *were* with him assembled themselves, and they came to the battle: and, behold, every man's sword was against his fellow, *and there was* a very great discomfiture.

21 Moreover the Hebrews *that* were with the Philistines before that time, which went up with them into the camp *from the country* round about, even they also *turned* to be with the Israelites that *were* with Saul and Jonathan.

22 Likewise all the men of Israel which had hid themselves in mount Ē′phra-im, *when* they heard that the Philistines fled, even they also followed hard after them in the battle.

23 So the LORD saved Israel that day: and the battle passed over unto Bĕth-ā′ven.

24 ¶And the men of Israel were distressed that day: for Saul had adjured the people, saying, Cursed *be* the man that eateth *any* food until evening, that I may be avenged on mine enemies. So none of the people tasted *any* food.

25 And all *they of* the land came to a wood; and there was honey upon the ground.

26 And when the people were come into the wood, behold, the honey

dropped; but no man put his hand to his mouth: for the people feared the oath.

27 But Jonathan heard not when his father charged the people with the oath: wherefore he put forth the end of the rod that *was* in his hand, and dipped it in an honeycomb, and put his hand to his mouth; and his eyes were enlightened.

28 Then answered one of the people, and said, Thy father straitly charged the people with an oath, saying, Cursed *be* the man that eateth *any* food this day. And the people were faint.

29 Then said Jonathan, My father hath troubled the land: see, I pray you, how mine eyes have been enlightened, because I tasted a little of this honey.

30 How much more, if haply the people had eaten freely to day of the spoil of their enemies which they found? for had there not been now a much greater slaughter among the Philistines?

31 And they smote the Philistines that day from Mĭch'măsh to Āij'a-lŏn: and the people were very faint.

32 And the people flew upon the spoil, and took sheep, and oxen, and calves, and slew *them* on the ground: and the people did eat *them* with the blood.

33 Then they told Saul, saying, Behold, the people sin against the LORD, in that they eat with the blood. And he said, Ye have transgressed: roll a great stone unto me this day.

34 And Saul said, Disperse yourselves among the people, and say unto them, Bring me hither every man his ox, and every man his sheep, and slay *them* here, and eat; and sin not against the LORD in eating with the blood. And all the people brought every man his ox with him that night, and slew *them* there.

35 And Saul built an altar unto the LORD: the same was the first altar that he built unto the LORD.

36 ¶And Saul said, Let us go down after the Philistines by night, and spoil them until the morning light, and let us not leave a man of them. And they said, Do whatsoever seemeth good unto thee. Then said the priest, Let us draw near hither unto God.

37 And Saul asked counsel of God, Shall I go down after the Philistines? wilt thou deliver them into the hand of Israel? But he answered him not that day.

38 And Saul said, Draw ye near hither, all the chief of the people: and know and see wherein this sin hath been this day.

39 For, *as* the LORD liveth, which saveth Israel, though it be in Jonathan my son, he shall surely die. But *there was* not a man among all the people *that* answered him.

40 Then said he unto all Israel, Be ye on one side, and I and Jonathan my son will be on the other side. And the people said unto Saul, Do what seemeth good unto thee.

41 Therefore Saul said unto the LORD God of Israel, Give a perfect *lot*. And Saul and Jonathan were taken: but the people escaped.

42 And Saul said, Cast *lots* between me and Jonathan my son. And Jonathan was taken.

43 Then Saul said to Jonathan, Tell me what thou hast done. And Jonathan told him, and said, I did but taste a little honey with the end of the rod that *was* in mine hand, *and*, lo, I must die.

44 And Saul answered, God do so and more also: for thou shalt surely die, Jonathan.

45 And the people said unto Saul, Shall Jonathan die, who hath wrought this great salvation in Israel? God forbid: *as* the LORD liveth, there shall not one hair of his head fall to the ground; for he hath wrought with God this day. So the people rescued Jonathan, that he died not.

46 Then Saul went up from following the Philistines: and the Philistines went to their own place.

47 ¶So Saul took the kingdom over Israel, and fought against all his enemies on every side, against Moab, and against the children of Ammon, and against Ēdom, and against the kings of Zōbah, and against the Philistines: and whithersoever he turned himself, he vexed *them*.

48 And he gathered an host, and smote the Am'ă-lek-ītes, and delivered Israel out of the hands of them that spoiled them.

49 ¶Now the sons of Saul were Jonathan, and Ĭsh'ū-ī, and Měl'chī-shū'a: and the names of his two daughters *were these;* the name of the firstborn Me'răb, and the name of the younger Mī'chal:

50 And the name of Saul's wife *was* A-hĭn'ō-am, the daughter of A-hĭm'ă-az: and the name of the captain of his host *was* Abner, the son of Ner, Saul's uncle.

51 And Kish *was* the father of Saul; and Ner the father of Abner *was* the son of Ā'bĭ-el.

52 And there was sore war against the Philistines all the days of Saul: and

when Saul saw any strong man, or any
valiant man, he took him unto him.

CHAPTER 15

SAMUEL also said unto Saul, The LORD
sent me to anoint thee *to be* king over
his people, over Israel: now therefore
hearken thou unto the voice of the
words of the LORD.
2 Thus saith the LORD of hosts, I
remember *that* which Ăm′a-lĕk did to
Israel, how he laid *wait* for him in the
way, when he came up from Egypt.
3 Now go and smite Ăm′a-lĕk, and ut-
terly destroy all that they have, and
spare them not; but slay both man and
woman, infant and suckling, ox and
sheep, camel and ass.
4 And Saul gathered the people to-
gether, and numbered them in Tel′ā-im,
two hundred thousand footmen, and
ten thousand men of Judah.
5 And Saul came to a city of Ăm′a-
lĕk, and laid wait in the valley.
6 ¶And Saul said unto the Kēn′ītes,
Go, depart, get you down from among
the Am′ă-lek-ītes, lest I destroy you
with them: for ye shewed kindness to
all the children of Israel, when they
came up out of Egypt. So the Kēn′ītes
departed from among the Am′ă-lek-
ītes.
7 And Saul smote the Am′ă-lek-ītes
from Hăv′i-lah *until* thou comest to
Shur, that *is* over against Egypt.
8 And he took Agăg the king of the
Am′ă-lek-ītes alive, and utterly de-
stroyed all the people with the edge of
the sword.
9 But Saul and the people spared
Agăg, and the best of the sheep, and of
the oxen, and of the fatlings, and the
lambs, and all *that was* good, and
would not utterly destroy them: but
every thing *that was* vile and refuse,
that they destroyed utterly.
10 ¶Then came the word of the LORD
unto Samuel, saying,
11 It repenteth me that I have set up
Saul *to be* king: for he is turned back
from following me, and hath not per-
formed my commandments. And it
grieved Samuel; and he cried unto the
LORD all night.
12 And when Samuel rose early to
meet Saul in the morning, it was told
Samuel, saying, Saul came to Carmel,
and, behold, he set him up a place, and
is gone about, and passed on, and gone
down to Gilgal.
13 And Samuel came to Saul: and
Saul said unto him, Blessed *be* thou of
the LORD: I have performed the com-
mandment of the LORD.
14 And Samuel said, What *meaneth*
then this bleating of the sheep in mine
ears, and the lowing of the oxen which I
hear?
15 And Saul said, They have brought
them from the Am′ă-lek-ītes: for the
people spared the best of the sheep and
of the oxen, to sacrifice unto the LORD
thy God; and the rest we have utterly
destroyed.
16 Then Samuel said unto Saul, Stay,
and I will tell thee what the LORD hath
said to me this night. And he said unto
him, Say on.
17 And Samuel said, When thou *wast*
little in thine own sight, *wast* thou not
made the head of the tribes of Israel,
and the LORD anointed thee king over
Israel?
18 And the LORD sent thee on a jour-
ney, and said, Go and utterly destroy
the sinners the Am′ă-lek-ītes, and
fight against them until they be con-
sumed.
19 Wherefore then didst thou not
obey the voice of the LORD, but didst fly
upon the spoil, and didst evil in the
sight of the LORD?
20 And Saul said unto Samuel, Yea, I
have obeyed the voice of the LORD, and
have gone the way which the LORD sent
me, and have brought Agăg the king of
Ăm′a-lĕk, and have utterly destroyed
the Am′ă-lek-ītes.
21 But the people took of the spoil,
sheep and oxen, the chief of the things
which should have been utterly de-
stroyed, to sacrifice unto the LORD thy
God in Gilgal.
22 And Samuel said, Hath the LORD
as great delight in burnt offerings and
sacrifices, as in obeying the voice of the
LORD? Behold, to obey *is* better than
sacrifice, *and* to hearken than the fat of
rams.
23 For rebellion *is as* the sin of
witchcraft, and stubbornness *is as* iniq-
uity and idolatry. Because thou hast re-
jected the word of the LORD, he hath
also rejected thee from *being* king.
24 And Saul said unto Samuel, I have
sinned: for I have transgressed the
commandment of the LORD, and thy
words: because I feared the people, and
obeyed their voice.
25 Now therefore, I pray thee, pardon
my sin, and turn again with me, that I
may worship the LORD.
26 And Samuel said unto Saul, I will
not return with thee: for thou hast re-
jected the word of the LORD, and the
LORD hath rejected thee from being
king over Israel.
27 And as Samuel turned about to go
away, he laid hold upon the skirt of his
mantle, and it rent.

28 And Samuel said unto him, The LORD hath rent the kingdom of Israel from thee this day, and hath given it to a neighbour of thine, *that is* better than thou.

29 And also the Strength of Israel will not lie nor repent: for he *is* not a man, that he should repent.

30 Then he said, I have sinned: *yet* honour me now, I pray thee, before the elders of my people, and before Israel, and turn again with me, that I may worship the LORD thy God.

31 So Samuel turned again after Saul; and Saul worshipped the LORD.

32 ¶Then said Samuel, Bring ye hither to me Agag the king of the Am'ă-lek-ītes. And Agag came unto him delicately. And Agag said, Surely the bitterness of death is past.

33 And Samuel said, As thy sword hath made women childless, so shall thy mother be childless among women. And Samuel hewed Agag in pieces before the LORD in Gilgal.

34 ¶Then Samuel went to Rā'mah; and Saul went up to his house to Gĭb'e-ah of Saul.

35 And Samuel came no more to see Saul until the day of his death: nevertheless Samuel mourned for Saul: and the LORD repented that he had made Saul king over Israel.

CHAPTER 16

AND the LORD said unto Samuel, How long wilt thou mourn for Saul, seeing I have rejected him from reigning over Israel? fill thine horn with oil, and go, I will send thee to Jesse the Bĕth-lehĕmīte: for I have provided me a king among his sons.

2 And Samuel said, How can I go? if Saul hear *it*, he will kill me. And the LORD said, Take an heifer with thee, and say, I am come to sacrifice to the LORD.

3 And call Jesse to the sacrifice, and I will shew thee what thou shalt do: and thou shalt anoint unto me *him* whom I name unto thee.

4 And Samuel did that which the LORD spake, and came to Bĕth-lehĕm. And the elders of the town trembled at his coming, and said, Comest thou peaceably?

5 And he said, Peaceably: I am come to sacrifice unto the LORD: sanctify yourselves, and come with me to the sacrifice. And he sanctified Jesse and his sons, and called them to the sacrifice.

6 And it came to pass, when they were come, that he looked on E-lī'ab, and said, Surely the LORD's anointed *is* before him.

7 But the LORD said unto Samuel, Look not on his countenance, or on the height of his stature; because I have refused him: for *the LORD seeth* not as man seeth; for man looketh on the outward appearance, but the LORD looketh on the heart.

8 Then Jesse called A-bĭn'a-dăb, and made him pass before Samuel. And he said, Neither hath the LORD chosen this.

9 Then Jesse made Shăm'mah to pass by. And he said, Neither hath the LORD chosen this.

10 Again, Jesse made seven of his sons to pass before Samuel. And Samuel said unto Jesse, The LORD hath not chosen these.

11 And Samuel said unto Jesse, Are here all *thy* children? And he said, There remaineth yet the youngest, and, behold, he keepeth the sheep. And Samuel said unto Jesse, Send and fetch him: for we will not sit down till he come hither.

12 And he sent, and brought him in. Now he *was* ruddy, *and* withal of a beautiful countenance, and goodly to look to. And the LORD said, Arise, anoint him: for this *is* he.

13 Then Samuel took the horn of oil, and anointed him in the midst of his brethren: and the Spirit of the LORD came upon David from that day forward. So Samuel rose up, and went to Rā'mah.

14 ¶But the Spirit of the LORD departed from Saul, and an evil spirit from the LORD troubled him.

15 And Saul's servants said unto him, Behold now, an evil spirit from God troubleth thee.

16 Let our lord now command thy servants, *which are* before thee, to seek out a man, *who is* a cunning player on an harp: and it shall come to pass, when the evil spirit from God is upon thee, that he shall play with his hand, and thou shalt be well.

17 And Saul said unto his servants, Provide me now a man that can play well, and bring *him* to me.

18 Then answered one of the servants, and said, Behold, I have seen a son of Jesse the Bĕth-lehĕmīte, *that is* cunning in playing, and a mighty valiant man, and a man of war, and prudent in matters, and a comely person, and the LORD *is* with him.

19 ¶Wherefore Saul sent messengers unto Jesse, and said, Send me David thy son, which *is* with the sheep.

20 And Jesse took an ass *laden* with

bread, and a bottle of wine, and a kid,
and sent *them* by David his son unto
Saul.
21 And David came to Saul, and
stood before him: and he loved him
greatly; and he became his armour-
bearer.
22 And Saul sent to Jesse, saying, Let
David, I pray thee, stand before me; for
he hath found favour in my sight.
23 And it came to pass, when the *evil*
spirit from God was upon Saul, that
David took an harp, and played with
his hand: so Saul was refreshed, and
was well, and the evil spirit departed
from him.

CHAPTER 17

NOW the Philistines gathered together
their armies to battle, and were gath-
ered together at Shō'chōh, which *be-
longeth* to Judah, and pitched between
Shō'chōh and A-zē'kah, in Ē'phes-
dăm'mīm.
2 And Saul and the men of Israel
were gathered together, and pitched by
the valley of Ē'lah, and set the battle in
array against the Philistines.
3 And the Philistines stood on a
mountain on the one side, and Israel
stood on a mountain on the other side:
and *there was* a valley between them.
4 And there went out a champion out
of the camp of the Philistines, named
Golīath, of Gath, whose height *was* six
cubits and a span.
5 And *he had* an helmet of brass upon
his head, and he *was* armed with a coat
of mail; and the weight of the coat *was*
five thousand shekels of brass.
6 And *he had* greaves of brass upon
his legs, and a target of brass between
his soulders.
7 And the staff of his spear *was* like a
weaver's beam; and his spear's head
weighed six hundred shekels of iron:
and one bearing a shield went before
him.
8 And he stood and cried unto the ar-
mies of Israel, and said unto them, Why
are ye come out to set *your* battle in
array? *am* not I a Philistine, and ye ser-
vants to Saul? choose you a man for
you, and let him come down to me.
9 If he be able to fight with me, and to
kill me, then will we be your servants:
but if I prevail against him, and kill
him, then shall ye be our servants, and
serve us.
10 And the Philistine said, I defy the
armies of Israel this day; give me a
man, that we may fight together.
11 When Saul and all Israel heard
those words of the Philistine, they were
dismayed, and greatly afraid.
12 ¶Now David *was* the son of that
Ĕph'rath-īte of Bĕth-lehĕm-jūdah,
whose name *was* Jesse; and he had
eight sons: and the man went among
men *for* an old man in the days of Saul.
13 And the three eldest sons of Jesse
went *and* followed Saul to the battle:
and the names of his three sons that
went to the battle *were* E-lī'ab the first-
born, and next unto him A-bīn'a-dăb,
and the third Shăm'mah.
14 And David *was* the youngest: and
the three eldest followed Saul.
15 But David went and returned from
Saul to feed his father's sheep at
Bĕth-lehĕm.
16 And the Philistine drew near morn-
ing and evening, and presented him-
self forty days.
17 And Jesse said unto David his son,
Take now for thy brethren an ephah of
this parched *corn*, and these ten loaves,
and run to the camp to thy brethren;
18 And carry these ten cheeses unto
the captain of *their* thousand, and look
how thy brethren fare, and take their
pledge.
19 Now Saul, and they, and all the
men of Israel, *were* in the valley of Ē'lah,
fighting with the Philistines.
20 And David rose up early in the
morning, and left the sheep with a keep-
er, and took, and went, as Jesse had
commanded him; and he came to the
trench, as the host was going forth to
the fight, and shouted for the battle.
21 For Israel and the Philistines had
put the battle in array, army against
army.
22 And David left his carriage in the
hand of the keeper of the carriage, and
ran into the army, and came and sa-
luted his brethren.
23 And as he talked with them, be-
hold, there came up the champion, the
Philistine of Gath, Golīath by name, out
of the armies of the Philistines, and
spake according to the same words:
and David heard *them*.
24 And all the men of Israel, when
they saw the man, fled from him, and
were sore afraid.
25 And the men of Israel said, Have
ye seen this man that is come up? sure-
ly to defy Israel is he come up: and it
shall be, *that* the man who killeth him,
the king will enrich him with great
riches, and will give him his daughter,
and make his father's house free in
Israel.
26 And David spake to the men that
stood by him, saying, What shall be
done to the man that killeth this Philis-
tine, and taketh away the reproach
from Israel? for who *is* this uncircum-

cised Philistine, that he should defy the armies of the living God?

27 And the people answered him after this manner, saying, So shall it be done to the man that killeth him.

28 And E-lī′ab his eldest brother heard when he spake unto the men; and E-lī′ab's anger was kindled against David, and he said, Why camest thou down hither? and with whom hast thou left those few sheep in the wilderness? I know thy pride, and the naughtiness of thine heart; for thou art come down that thou mightest see the battle.

29 And David said, What have I now done? *Is there* not a cause?

30 And he turned from him toward another, and spake after the same manner: and the people answered him again after the former manner.

31 And when the words were heard which David spake, they rehearsed *them* before Saul: and he sent for him.

32 ¶And David said to Saul, Let no man's heart fail because of him; thy servant will go and fight with this Philistine.

33 And Saul said to David, Thou art not able to go against this Philistine to fight with him: for thou *art but* a youth, and he a man of war from his youth.

34 And David said unto Saul, Thy servant kept his father's sheep, and there came a lion, and a bear, and took a lamb out of the flock:

35 And I went out after him, and smote him, and delivered *it* out of his mouth: and when he arose against me, I caught *him* by his beard, and smote him, and slew him.

36 Thy servant slew both the lion and the bear: and this uncircumcised Philistine shall be as one of them, seeing he hath defied the armies of the living God.

37 David said moreover, The LORD that delivered me out of the paw of the lion, and out of the paw of the bear, he will deliver me out of the hand of this Philistine. And Saul said unto David, Go, and the LORD be with thee.

38 ¶And Saul armed David with his armour, and he put an helmet of brass upon his head; also he armed him with a coat of mail.

39 And David girded his sword upon his armour, and he assayed to go; for he had not proved *it*. And David said unto Saul, I cannot go with these; for I have not proved *them*. And David put them off him.

40 And he took his staff in his hand, and chose him five smooth stones out of the brook, and put them in a shepherd's bag which he had, even in a scrip; and his sling *was* in his hand: and he drew near to the Philistine.

41 And the Philistine came on and drew near unto David; and the man that bare the shield *went* before him.

42 And when the Philistine looked about, and saw David, he disdained him: for he was *but* a youth, and ruddy, and of a fair countenance.

43 And the Philistine said unto David, *Am* I a dog, that thou comest to me with staves? And the Philistine cursed David by his gods.

44 And the Philistine said to David, Come to me, and I will give thy flesh unto the fowls of the air, and to the beasts of the field.

45 Then said David to the Philistine, Thou comest to me with a sword, and with a spear, and with a shield: but I come to thee in the name of the LORD of hosts, the God of the armies of Israel, whom thou hast defied.

46 This day will the LORD deliver thee into mine hand; and I will smite thee, and take thine head from thee; and I will give the carcases of the host of the Philistines this day unto the fowls of the air, and to the wild beasts of the earth; that all the earth may know that there is a God in Israel.

47 And all this assembly shall know that the LORD saveth not with sword and spear: for the battle *is* the LORD's, and he will give you into our hands.

48 And it came to pass, when the Philistine arose, and came and drew nigh to meet David, that David hasted, and ran toward the army to meet the Philistine.

49 And David put his hand in his bag, and took thence a stone, and slang *it*, and smote the Philistine in his forehead, that the stone sunk into his forehead; and he fell upon his face to the earth.

50 So David prevailed over the Philistine with a sling and with a stone, and smote the Philistine, and slew him; but *there was* no sword in the hand of David.

51 Therefore David ran, and stood upon the Philistine, and took his sword, and drew it out of the sheath thereof, and slew him, and cut off his head therewith. And when the Philistines saw their champion was dead, they fled.

52 And the men of Israel and of Jūdah arose, and shouted, and pursued the Philistines, until thou come to the valley, and to the gates of Ĕkron. And the wounded of the Philistines fell down by the way to Shā-a-rā′im, even unto Gath, and unto Ĕkron.

53 And the children of Israel returned

from chasing after the Philistines, and they spoiled their tents.

54 And David took the head of the Philistine, and brought it to Jerusalem; but he put his armour in his tent.

55 ¶And when Saul saw David go forth against the Philistine, he said unto Abner, the captain of the host, Abner, whose son *is* this youth? And Abner said, *As* thy soul liveth, O king, I cannot tell.

56 And the king said, Enquire thou whose son the stripling *is.*

57 And as David returned from the slaughter of the Philistine, Abner took him, and brought him before Saul with the head of the Philistine in his hand.

58 And Saul said to him, Whose son *art* thou, *thou* young man? And David answered, I *am* the son of thy servant Jesse the Bĕth–lehĕmīte.

CHAPTER 18

AND it came to pass, when he had made an end of speaking unto Saul, that the soul of Jonathan was knit with the soul of David, and Jonathan loved him as his own soul.

2 And Saul took him that day, and would let him go no more home to his father's house.

3 Then Jonathan and David made a covenant, because he loved him as his own soul.

4 And Jonathan stripped himself of the robe that *was* upon him, and gave it to David, and his garments, even to his sword, and to his bow, and to his girdle.

5 ¶And David went out whithersoever Saul sent him, *and* behaved himself wisely: and Saul set him over the men of war, and he was accepted in the sight of all the people, and also in the sight of Saul's servants.

6 ¶And it came to pass as they came, when David was returned from the slaughter of the Philistine, that the women came out of all cities of Israel, singing and dancing, to meet king Saul, with tabrets, with joy, and with instruments of musick.

7 And the women answered *one another* as they played, and said, Saul hath slain his thousands, and David his ten thousands.

8 And Saul was very wroth, and the saying displeased him; and he said, They have ascribed unto David ten thousands, and to me they have ascribed *but* thousands: and *what* can he have more but the kingdom?

9 And Saul eyed David from that day and forward.

10 ¶And it came to pass on the morrow, that the evil spirit from God came upon Saul, and he prophesied in the midst of the house: and David played with his hand, as at other times: and *there was* a javelin in Saul's hand.

11 And Saul cast the javelin; for he said, I will smite David even to the wall *with it.* And David avoided out of his presence twice.

12 ¶And Saul was afraid of David, because the LORD was with him, and was departed from Saul.

13 Therefore Saul removed him from him, and made him his captain over a thousand; and he went out and came in before the people.

14 And David behaved himself wisely in all his ways; and the LORD *was* with him.

15 Wherefore when Saul saw that he behaved himself very wisely, he was afraid of him.

16 But all Israel and Jūdah loved David, because he went out and came in before them.

17 ¶And Saul said to David, Behold my elder daughter Me'răb, her will I give thee to wife: only be thou valiant for me, and fight the LORD's battles. For Saul said, Let not mine hand be upon him, but let the hand of the Philistines be upon him.

18 And David said unto Saul, Who *am* I? and what *is* my life, *or* my father's family in Israel, that I should be son in law to the king?

19 But it came to pass at the time when Me'răb Saul's daughter should have been given to David, that she was given unto Ā'drĭ-el the Me-hōl'ath-īte to wife.

20 And Mī'chal Saul's daughter loved David: and they told Saul, and the thing pleased him.

21 And Saul said, I will give him her, that she may be a snare to him, and that the hand of the Philistines may be against him. Wherefore Saul said to David, Thou shalt this day be my son in law in *the one of* the twain.

22 And Saul commanded his servants, *saying,* Commune with David secretly, and say, Behold, the king hath delight in thee, and all his servants love thee: now therefore be the king's son in law.

23 And Saul's servants spake those words in the ears of David. And David said, Seemeth it to you *a* light *thing* to be a king's son in law, seeing that I *am* a poor man, and lightly esteemed?

24 And the servants of Saul told him, saying, On this manner spake David.

25 And Saul said, Thus shall ye say to David, The king desireth not any dowry, but an hundred foreskins of the

Philistines, to be avenged of the king's
enemies. But Saul thought to make Da-
vid fall by the hand of the Philistines.
26 And when his servants told David
these words, it pleased David well to be
the king's son in law: and the days were
not expired.
27 Wherefore David arose and went,
he and his men, and slew of the Philis-
tines two hundred men; and David
brought their foreskins, and they gave
them in full tale to the king, that he
might be the king's son in law. And
Saul gave him Mī'chal his daughter to
wife.
28 And Saul saw and knew that the
LORD *was* with David, and *that* Mī'chal
Saul's daughter loved him.
29 And Saul was yet the more afraid
of David; and Saul became David's en-
emy continually.
30 Then the princes of the Philistines
went forth: and it came to pass, after
they went forth, *that* David behaved
himself more wisely than all the ser-
vants of Saul; so that his name was
much set by.

CHAPTER 19

AND Saul spake to Jonathan his son,
and to all his servants, that they should
kill David.
2 But Jonathan Saul's son delighted
much in David: and Jonathan told Da-
vid, saying, Saul my father seeketh to
kill thee: now therefore, I pray thee,
take heed to thyself until the morning,
and abide in a secret *place*, and hide
thyself:
3 And I will go out and stand beside
my father in the field where thou *art*,
and I will commune with my father of
thee; and what I see, that I will tell thee.
4 And Jonathan spake good of David
unto Saul his father, and said unto him,
Let not the king sin against his servant,
against David; because he hath not
sinned against thee, and because his
works *have been* to thee-ward very
good:
5 For he did put his life in his hand,
and slew the Philistine, and the LORD
wrought a great salvation for all Israel:
thou sawest *it*, and didst rejoice: where-
fore then wilt thou sin against inno-
cent blood, to slay David without a
cause?
6 And Saul hearkened unto the voice
of Jonathan: and Saul sware, *As* the
LORD liveth, he shall not be slain.
7 And Jonathan called David, and
Jonathan shewed him all those things.
And Jonathan brought David to Saul,
and he was in his presence, as in times
past.
8 ¶And there was war again: and Da-
vid went out, and fought with the Philis-
tines, and slew them with a great
slaughter; and they fled from him.
9 And the evil spirit from the LORD
was upon Saul, as he sat in his house
with his javelin in his hand: and David
played with *his* hand.
10 And Saul sought to smite David
even to the wall with the javelin; but he
slipped away out of Saul's presence,
and he smote the javelin into the wall:
and David fled, and escaped that night.
11 Saul also sent messengers unto
David's house, to watch him, and to
slay him in the morning: and Mī'chal
David's wife told him, saying, If thou
save not thy life to night, to morrow
thou shalt be slain.
12 So Mī'chal let David down
through a window: and he went, and
fled, and escaped.
13 And Mī'chal took an image, and
laid *it* in the bed, and put a pillow of
goats' *hair* for his bolster, and covered
it with a cloth.
14 And when Saul sent messengers
to take David, she said, He *is* sick.
15 And Saul sent the messengers
again to see David, saying, Bring him
up to me in the bed, that I may slay him.
16 And when the messengers were
come in, behold, *there was* an image in
the bed, with a pillow of goats' *hair* for
his bolster.
17 And Saul said unto Mī'chal, Why
hast thou deceived me so, and sent
away mine enemy, that he is escaped?
And Mī'chal answered Saul, He said
unto me, Let me go; why should I kill
thee?
18 ¶So David fled, and escaped, and
came to Samuel to Rā'mah, and told
him all that Saul had done to him. And
he and Samuel went and dwelt in Nā'-
iŏth.
19 And it was told Saul, saying, Be-
hold, David *is* at Nā'iŏth in Rā'mah.
20 And Saul sent messengers to take
David: and when they saw the com-
pany of the prophets prophesying, and
Samuel standing *as* appointed over
them, the Spirit of God was upon the
messengers of Saul, and they also
prophesied.
21 And when it was told Saul, he sent
other messengers, and they prophesied
likewise. And Saul sent messengers
again the third time, and they proph-
esied also.
22 Then went he also to Rā'mah, and
came to a great well that *is* in Sē'chū:
and he asked and said, Where *are* Sam-
uel and David? And *one* said, Behold,
they be at Nā'iŏth in Rā'mah.

23 And he went thither to Nā'iŏth in Rā'mah: and the Spirit of God was upon him also, and he went on, and prophesied, until he came to Nā'iŏth in Rā'mah.

24 And he stripped off his clothes also, and prophesied before Samuel in like manner, and lay down naked all that day and all that night. Wherefore they say, *Is* Saul also among the prophets?

CHAPTER 20

AND David fled from Nā'iŏth in Rā'-mah, and came and said before Jonathan, What have I done? what *is* mine iniquity? and what *is* my sin before thy father, that he seeketh my life?

2 And he said unto him, God forbid; thou shalt not die: behold, my father will do nothing either great or small, but that he will shew it me: and why should my father hide this thing from me? it *is* not *so*.

3 And David sware moreover, and said, Thy father certainly knoweth that I have found grace in thine eyes; and he saith, Let not Jonathan know this, lest he be grieved: but truly *as* the LORD liveth, and *as* thy soul liveth, *there is* but a step between me and death.

4 Then said Jonathan unto David, Whatsoever thy soul desireth, I will even do *it* for thee.

5 And David said unto Jonathan, Behold, to morrow *is* the new moon, and I should not fail to sit with the king at meat: but let me go, that I may hide myself in the field unto the third *day* at even.

6 If thy father at all miss me, then say, David earnestly asked *leave* of me that he might run to Bĕth-lehĕm his city: for *there is* a yearly sacrifice there for all the family.

7 If he say thus, *It is* well; thy servant shall have peace: but if he be very wroth, *then* be sure that evil is determined by him.

8 Therefore thou shalt deal kindly with thy servant; for thou hast brought thy servant into a covenant of the LORD with thee: notwithstanding, if there be in me iniquity, slay me thyself; for why shouldest thou bring me to thy father?

9 And Jonathan said, Far be it from thee: for if I knew certainly that evil were determined by my father to come upon thee, then would not I tell it thee?

10 Then said David to Jonathan, Who shall tell me? or what *if* thy father answer thee roughly?

11 And Jonathan said unto David, Come, and let us go out into the field. And they went out both of them into the field.

12 And Jonathan said unto David, O LORD God of Israel, when I have sounded my father about to morrow any time, *or* the third *day*, and, behold, *if there be* good toward David, and I then send not unto thee, and shew it thee;

13 The LORD do so and much more to Jonathan: but if it please my father *to do* thee evil, then I will shew it thee, and send thee away, that thou mayest go in peace: and the LORD be with thee, as he hath been with my father.

14 And thou shalt not only while yet I live shew me the kindness of the LORD, that I die not:

15 But *also* thou shalt not cut off thy kindness from my house for ever: no, not when the LORD hath cut off the enemies of David every one from the face of the earth.

16 So Jonathan made *a covenant* with the house of David, *saying*, Let the LORD even require *it* at the hand of David's enemies.

17 And Jonathan caused David to swear again, because he loved him: for he loved him as he loved his own soul.

18 Then Jonathan said to David, To morrow *is* the new moon: and thou shalt be missed, because thy seat will be empty.

19 And *when* thou hast stayed three days, *then* thou shalt go down quickly, and come to the place where thou didst hide thyself when the business was *in hand*, and shalt remain by the stone Ē'zel.

20 And I will shoot three arrows on the side *thereof*, as though I shot at a mark.

21 And, behold, I will send a lad, *saying*, Go, find out the arrows. If I expressly say unto the lad, Behold, the arrows *are* on this side of thee, take them; then come thou: for *there is* peace to thee, and no hurt; *as* the LORD liveth.

22 But if I say thus unto the young man, Behold, the arrows *are* beyond thee; go thy way: for the LORD hath sent thee away.

23 And *as touching* the matter which thou and I have spoken of, behold, the LORD *be* between thee and me for ever.

24 ¶So David hid himself in the field: and when the new moon was come, the king sat him down to eat meat.

25 And the king sat upon his seat, as at other times, *even* upon a seat by the wall: and Jonathan arose, and Abner sat by Saul's side, and David's place was empty.

26 Nevertheless Saul spake not any thing that day: for he thought, Something hath befallen him, he *is* not clean; surely he *is* not clean.

27 And it came to pass on the morrow, *which was* the second *day* of the month, that David's place was empty: and Saul said unto Jonathan his son, Wherefore cometh not the son of Jesse to meat, neither yesterday, nor to day?

28 And Jonathan answered Saul, David earnestly asked *leave* of me *to go* to Bĕth-lehĕm:

29 And he said, Let me go, I pray thee; for our family hath a sacrifice in the city; and my brother, he hath commanded me *to be there:* and now, if I have found favour in thine eyes, let me get away, I pray thee, and see my brethren. Therefore he cometh not unto the king's table.

30 Then Saul's anger was kindled against Jonathan, and he said unto him, Thou son of the perverse rebellious *woman,* do not I know that thou hast chosen the son of Jesse to thine own confusion, and unto the confusion of thy mother's nakedness?

31 For as long as the son of Jesse liveth upon the ground, thou shalt not be established, nor thy kingdom. Wherefore now send and fetch him unto me, for he shall surely die.

32 And Jonathan answered Saul his father, and said unto him, Wherefore shall he be slain? what hath he done?

33 And Saul cast a javelin at him to smite him: whereby Jonathan knew that it was determined of his father to slay David.

34 So Jonathan arose from the table in fierce anger, and did eat no meat the second day of the month: for he was grieved for David, because his father had done him shame.

35 ¶And it came to pass in the morning, that Jonathan went out into the field at the time appointed with David, and a little lad with him.

36 And he said unto his lad, Run, find out now the arrows which I shoot. *And* as the lad ran, he shot an arrow beyond him.

37 And when the lad was come to the place of the arrow which Jonathan had shot, Jonathan cried after the lad, and said, *Is* not the arrow beyond thee?

38 And Jonathan cried after the lad, Make speed, haste, stay not. And Jonathan's lad gathered up the arrows, and came to his master.

39 But the lad knew not any thing: only Jonathan and David knew the matter.

40 And Jonathan gave his artillery unto his lad, and said unto him, Go, carry *them* to the city.

41 ¶*And* as soon as the lad was gone, David arose out of *a place* toward the south, and fell on his face to the ground, and bowed himself three times: and they kissed one another, and wept one with another, until David exceeded.

42 And Jonathan said to David, Go in peace, forasmuch as we have sworn both of us in the name of the LORD, saying, The LORD be between me and thee, and between my seed and thy seed for ever. And he arose and departed: and Jonathan went into the city.

CHAPTER 21

THEN came David to Nob to A-hĭm'e-lĕch the priest: and A-hĭm'e-lĕch was afraid at the meeting of David, and said unto him, Why *art* thou alone, and no man with thee?

2 And David said unto A-hĭm'e-lĕch the priest, The king hath commanded me a business, and hath said unto me, Let no man know any thing of the business whereabout I send thee, and what I have commanded thee: and I have appointed *my* servants to such and such a place.

3 Now therefore what is under thine hand? give *me* five *loaves of* bread in mine hand, or what there is present.

4 And the priest answered David, and said, *There is* no common bread under mine hand, but there is hallowed bread; if the young men have kept themselves at least from women.

5 And David answered the priest, and said unto him, Of a truth women *have been* kept from us about these three days, since I came out, and the vessels of the young men are holy, and *the bread is* in a manner common, yea, though it were sanctified this day in the vessel.

6 So the priest gave him hallowed *bread:* for there was no bread there but the shewbread, that was taken from before the LORD, to put hot bread in the day when it was taken away.

7 Now a certain man of the servants of Saul *was* there that day, detained before the LORD; and his name *was* Dō'eg, and Edomite, the chiefest of the herdmen that *belonged* to Saul.

8 And David said unto A-hĭm'e-lĕch, And is there not here under thine hand spear or sword? for I have neither brought my sword nor my weapons with me, because the king's business required haste.

9 And the priest said, The sword of Golīath the Philistine, whom thou slewest in the valley of Ē'lah, behold, it *is here* wrapped in a cloth behind the ephod: if thou wilt take that, take *it:* for *there is* no other save that here. And David said, *There is* none like that; give it me.

10 ¶And David arose, and fled that day for fear of Saul, and went to Ā'chĭsh the king of Gath.

11 And the servants of Ā'chĭsh said unto him, *Is* not this David the king of the land? did they not sing one to another of him in dances, saying, Saul hath slain his thousands, and David his ten thousands?

12 And David laid up these words in his heart, and was sore afraid of Ā'chĭsh the king of Gath.

13 And he changed his behavior before them, and feigned himself mad in their hands, and scrabbled on the doors of the gate, and let his spittle fall down upon his beard.

14 Then said Ā'chĭsh unto his servants, Lo, ye see the man is mad: wherefore *then* have ye brought him to me?

15 Have I need of mad men, that ye have brought this *fellow* to play the mad man in my presence? shall this *fellow* come into my house?

CHAPTER 22

DAVID therefore departed thence, and escaped to the cave A-dŭl'lam: and when his brethren and all his father's house heard *it,* they went down thither to him.

2 And every one *that was* in distress, and every one that *was* in debt, and every one *that was* discontented, gathered themselves unto him; and he became a captain over them: and there were with him about four hundred men.

3 ¶And David went thence to Mĭz'peh of Moab: and he said unto the king of Moab, Let my father and my mother, I pray thee, come forth, *and be* with you, till I know what God will do for me.

4 And he brought them before the king of Moab: and they dwelt with him all the while that David was in the hold.

5 ¶And the prophet Gad said unto David, Abide not in the hold; depart, and get thee into the land of Jūdah. Then David departed, and came into the forest of Hā'rĕth.

6 ¶When Saul heard that David was discovered, and the men that *were* with him, (now Saul abode in Gĭb'e-ah under a tree in Rā'mah, having his spear in his hand, and all his servants *were* standing about him;)

7 Then Saul said unto his servants that stood about him, Hear now, ye Benjamites; will the son of Jesse give every one of you fields and vineyards, *and* make you all captains of thousands, and captains of hundreds;

8 That all of you have conspired against me, and *there is* none that sheweth me that my son hath made a league with the son of Jesse, and *there is* none of you that is sorry for me, or sheweth unto me that my son hath stirred up my servant against me, to lie in wait, as at this day?

9 ¶Then answered Dō'eg the Edomite, which was set over the servants of Saul, and said, I saw the son of Jesse coming to Nob, to A-hĭm'e-lĕch the son of A-hī'tŭb.

10 And he enquired of the LORD for him and gave him victuals, and gave him the sword of Golīath the Philistine.

11 ¶Then the king sent to call A-hĭm'e-lĕch the priest, the son of A-hī'tŭb, and all his father's house, the priests that *were* in Nob: and they came all of them to the king.

12 And Saul said, Here now, thou son of A-hī'tŭb. And he answered, Here I *am,* my lord.

13 And Saul said unto him, Why have ye conspired against me, thou and the son of Jesse, in that thou hast given him bread, and a sword, and hast enquired of God for him, that he should rise against me, to lie in wait, as at this day?

14 Then A-hĭm'e-lĕch answered the king, and said, And who *is so* faithful among all thy servants as David, which is the king's son in law, and goeth at thy bidding, and is honourable in thine house?

15 Did I then begin to enquire of God for him? be it far from me: let not the king impute *any*thing unto his servant, *nor* to all the house of my father: for thy servant knew nothing of all this, less or more.

16 And the king said, Thou shalt surely die, A-hĭm'e-lĕch, thou, and all thy father's house.

17 And the king said unto the footmen that stood about him, Turn, and slay the priests of the LORD; because their hand also *is* with David, and because they knew when he fled, and did not shew it to me. But the servants of the king would not put forth their hand to fall upon the priests of the LORD.

18 And the king said to Dō'eg, Turn thou, and fall upon the priests. And Dō'eg the Edomite turned, and he fell upon the priests, and slew on that day

fourscore and five persons that did
wear a linen ephod.
19 And Nob, the city of the priests,
smote he with the edge of the sword,
both men and women, children and
sucklings, and oxen, and asses, and
sheep, with the edge of the sword.
20 ¶And one of the sons of A-hĭm′e-
lĕch the son of A-hī′tŭb, named Ă-bī′a-
thar, escaped, and fled after David.
21 And Ă-bī′a-thar shewed David
that Saul had slain the LORD's priests.
22 And David said unto Ă-bī′a-thar, I
knew *it* that day, when Dō′eg the
Edomite *was* there, that he would sure-
ly tell Saul: I have occasioned *the
death* of all the persons of thy father's
house.
23 Abide thou with me, fear not: for
he that seeketh my life seeketh thy life:
but with me thou *shalt be* in safeguard.

CHAPTER 23

THEN they told David, saying, Behold,
the Philistines fight against Keī′lah,
and they rob the threshingfloors.
2 Therefore David enquired of the
LORD, saying, Shall I go and smite these
Philistines? And the LORD said unto Da-
vid, Go, and smite the Philistines, and
save Keī′lah.
3 And David's men said unto him, Be-
hold, we be afraid here in Jūdah: how
much more then if we come to Keī′lah
against the armies of the Philistines?
4 Then David enquired of the LORD
yet again. And the LORD answered him
and said, Arise, go down to Keī′lah; for
I will deliver the Philistines into thine
hand.
5 So David and his men went to Keī′-
lah, and fought with the Philistines,
and brought away their cattle, and
smote them with a great slaughter. So
David saved the inhabitants of Keī′lah.
6 And it came to pass, when Ă-bī′a-
thar the son of A-hĭm′e-lĕch fled to Da-
vid to Keī′lah, *that* he came down *with*
an ephod in his hand.
7 ¶And it was told Saul that David
was come to Keī′lah. And Saul said,
God hath delivered him into mine
hand; for he is shut in, by entering into
a town that hath gates and bars.
8 And Saul called all the people to-
gether to war, to go down to Keī′lah, to
besiege David and his men.
9 And David knew that Saul secretly
practised mischief against him; and he
said to Ă-bī′a-thar the priest, Bring
hither the ephod.
10 Then said David, O LORD God of
Israel, thy servant hath certainly heard
that Saul seeketh to come to Keī′lah, to
destroy the city for my sake.
11 Will the men of Keī′lah deliver me
up into his hand? will Saul come down,
as thy servant hath heard? O LORD God
of Israel, I beseech thee, tell thy ser-
vant. And the LORD said, He will come
down.
12 Then said David, Will the men of
Keī′lah deliver me and my men into the
hand of Saul? And the LORD said, They
will deliver *thee* up.
13 Then David and his men, *which
were* about six hundred, arose and de-
parted out of Keī′lah, and went whith-
ersoever they could go. And it was told
Saul that David was escaped from
Keī′lah; and he forbare to go forth.
14 And David abode in the wilder-
ness in strong holds, and remained in a
mountain in the wilderness of Ziph.
And Saul sought him every day, but
God delivered him not into his hand.
15 And David saw that Saul was
come out to seek his life: and David
was in the wilderness of Ziph in a
wood.
16 ¶And Jonathan Saul's son arose,
and went to David into the wood, and
strengthened his hand in God.
17 And he said unto him, Fear not: for
the hand of Saul my father shall not
find thee; and thou shalt be king over
Israel, and I shall be next unto thee; and
that also Saul my father knoweth.
18 And they two made a covenant be-
fore the LORD: and David abode in the
wood, and Jonathan went to his house.
19 ¶Then came up the Zīph′ītes to
Saul to Gĭb′e-ah, saying, Doth not Da-
vid hide himself with us in strong holds
in the wood, in the hill of Hach′ī-lah,
which *is* on the south of Jesh′ī-mon?
20 Now therefore, O king, come
down according to all the desire of thy
soul to come down; and our part *shall
be* to deliver him into the king's hand.
21 And Saul said, Blessed *be* ye of the
LORD; for ye have compassion on me.
22 Go, I pray you, prepare yet, and
know and see his place where his haunt
is, *and* who hath seen him there: for it is
told me *that* he dealeth very subtilly.
23 See therefore, and take knowl-
edge of all the lurking places where he
hideth himself, and come ye again to
me with the certainty, and I will go with
you: and it shall come to pass, if he be in
the land, that I will search him out
throughout all the thousands of Jūdah.
24 And they arose, and went to Ziph
before Saul: but David and his men
were in the wilderness of Mā′on, in the
plain on the south of Jesh′ī-mon.
25 Saul also and his men went to seek
him. And they told David: wherefore he
came down into a rock, and abode in

the wilderness of Mā′on. And when Saul heard *that*, he pursued after David in the wilderness of Mā′on.
26 And Saul went on this side of the mountain, and David and his men on that side of the mountain: and David made haste to get away for fear of Saul; for Saul and his men compassed David and his men round about to take them.
27 ¶But there came a messenger unto Saul, saying, Haste thee, and come; for the Philistines have invaded the land.
28 Wherefore Saul returned from pursuing after David, and went against the Philistines: therefore they called that place Sē′la-ham′māh-le′kŏth.
29 ¶And David went up from thence, and dwelt in strong holds at Ĕn-gĕ′dī.

CHAPTER 24

AND it came to pass, when Saul was returned from following the Philistines, that it was told him, saying, Behold, David *is* in the wilderness of Ĕn-gĕ′dī.
2 Then Saul took three thousand chosen men out of all Israel, and went to seek David and his men upon the rocks of the wild goats.
3 And he came to the sheepcotes by the way, where *was* a cave; and Saul went in to cover his feet: and David and his men remained in the sides of the cave.
4 And the men of David said unto him, Behold the day of which the LORD said unto thee, Behold, I will deliver thine enemy into thine hand, that thou mayest do to him as it shall seem good unto thee. Then David arose, and cut off the skirt of Saul's robe privily.
5 And it came to pass afterward, that David's heart smote him, because he had cut off Saul's skirt.
6 And he said unto his men, The LORD forbid that I should do this thing unto my master, the LORD's anointed, to stretch forth mine hand against him, seeing he *is* the anointed of the LORD.
7 So David stayed his servants with these words, and suffered them not to rise against Saul. But Saul rose up out of the cave, and went on *his* way.
8 ¶David also arose afterward, and went out of the cave, and cried after Saul, saying, My lord the king. And when Saul looked behind him, David stooped with his face to the earth, and bowed himself.
9 And David said to Saul, Wherefore hearest thou men's words, saying, Behold, David seeketh thy hurt?
10 Behold, this day thine eyes have seen how that the LORD had delivered thee to day into mine hand in the cave: and *some* bade *me* kill thee: but *mine eye* spared thee; and I said, I will not put forth mine hand against my lord; for he *is* the LORD's anointed.
11 Moreover, my father, see, yea, see the skirt of thy robe in my hand: for in that I cut off the skirt of thy robe, and killed thee not, know thou and see that *there is* neither evil nor transgression in mine hand, and I have not sinned against thee; yet thou huntest my soul to take it.
12 The LORD judge between me and thee, and the LORD avenge me of thee: but mine hand shall not be upon thee.
13 As saith the proverb of the ancients, Wickedness proceedeth from the wicked: but mine hand shall not be upon thee.
14 After whom is the king of Israel come out? after whom dost thou pursue? after a dead dog, after a flea.
15 The LORD therefore be judge, and judge between me and thee, and see, and plead my cause, and deliver me out of thine hand.
16 ¶And it came to pass, when David had made an end of speaking these words unto Saul, that Saul said, *Is* this thy voice, my son David? And Saul lifted up his voice, and wept.
17 And he said to David, Thou *art* more righteous than I: for thou hast rewarded me good, whereas I have rewarded thee evil.
18 And thou hast shewed this day how that thou hast dealt well with me: forasmuch as when the LORD had delivered me into thine hand, thou killedst me not.
19 For if a man find his enemy, will he let him go well away? wherefore the LORD reward thee good for that thou hast done unto me this day.
20 And now, behold, I know well that thou shalt surely be king, and that the kingdom of Israel shall be established in thine hand.
21 Swear now therefore unto me by the LORD, that thou wilt not cut off my seed after me, and that thou wilt not destroy my name out of my father's house.
22 And David sware unto Saul. And Saul went home; but David and his men gat them up unto the hold.

CHAPTER 25

AND Samuel died; and all the Israelites were gathered together, and lamented him, and buried him in his house at Rā′-mah. And David arose, and went down to the wilderness of Paran.
2 And *there was* a man in Mā′on, whose possessions *were* in Carmel;

and the man *was* very great, and he had three thousand sheep, and a thousand goats: and he was shearing his sheep in Carmel.

3 Now the name of the man *was* Nā'bal; and the name of his wife Ăb'i-gāil: and *she was* a woman of good understanding, and of a beautiful countenance: but the man *was* churlish and evil in his doings; and he *was* of the house of Caleb.

4 And David heard in the wilderness that Nā'bal did shear his sheep.

5 And David sent out ten young men, and David said unto the young men, Get you up to Carmel, and go to Nā'bal, and greet him in my name:

6 And thus shall ye say to him that liveth *in prosperity,* Peace *be* both to thee, and peace *be* to thine house, and peace *be* unto all that thou hast.

7 And now I have heard that thou hast shearers: now thy shepherds which were with us, we hurt them not, neither was there ought missing unto them, all the while they were in Carmel.

8 Ask thy young men, and they will shew thee. Wherefore let the young men find favour in thine eyes: for we come in a good day: give, I pray thee, whatsoever cometh to thine hand unto thy servants, and to thy son David.

9 And when David's young men came, they spake to Nā'bal according to all those words in the name of David, and ceased.

10 And Nā'bal answered David's servants, and said, Who *is* David? and who *is* the son of Jesse? there be many servants now a days that break away every man from his master.

11 Shall I then take my bread, and my water, and my flesh that I have killed for my shearers, and give *it* unto men, whom I know not whence they *be?*

12 So David's young men turned their way, and went again, and came and told him all those sayings.

13 And David said unto his men, Gird ye on every man his sword. And they girded on every man his sword; and David also girded on his sword: and there went up after David about four hundred men; and two hundred abode by the stuff.

14 ¶But one of the young men told Ăb'i-gāil, Nā'bal's wife, saying, Behold, David sent messengers out of the wilderness to salute our master; and he railed on them.

15 But the men *were* very good unto us, and we were not hurt, neither missed we any thing, as long as we were conversant with them, when we were in the fields:

16 They were a wall unto us both by night and day, all the while we were with them keeping the sheep.

17 Now therefore know and consider what thou wilt do; for evil is determined against our master, and against all his household: for he *is such* a son of Bē'lĭ-al, that *a man* cannot speak to him.

18 Then Ăb'i-gāil made haste, and took two hundred loaves, and two bottles of wine, and five sheep ready dressed, and five measures of parched *corn,* and an hundred clusters of raisins, and two hundred cakes of figs, and laid *them* on asses.

19 And she said unto her servants, Go on before me; behold, I come after you. But she told not her husband Nā'bal.

20 And it was *so, as* she rode on the ass, that she came down by the covert of the hill, and, behold, David and his men came down against her; and she met them.

21 Now David had said, Surely in vain have I kept all that this *fellow* hath in the wilderness, so that nothing was missed of all that *pertained* unto him: and he hath requited me evil for good.

22 So and more also do God unto the enemies of David, if I leave of all that *pertain* to him by the morning light any that pisseth against the wall.

23 And when Ăb'i-gāil saw David, she hasted, and lighted off the ass, and fell before David on her face, and bowed herself to the ground,

24 And fell at his feet, and said, Upon me, my lord, *upon* me *let this* iniquity *be:* and let thine handmaid, I pray thee, speak in thine audience, and hear the words of thine handmaid.

25 Let not my lord, I pray thee, regard this man of Bē'lĭ-al, *even* Nā'bal: for as his name *is,* so *is* he; Nā'bal *is* his name, and folly *is* with him: but I thine handmaid saw not the young men of my lord, whom thou didst send.

26 Now therefore, my lord, *as* the LORD liveth, and *as* thy soul liveth, seeing the LORD hath withholden thee from coming to *shed* blood, and from avenging thyself with thine own hand, now let thine enemies, and they that seek evil to my lord, be as Nā'bal.

27 And now this blessing which thine handmaid hath brought unto my lord, let it even be given unto the young men that follow my lord.

28 I pray thee, forgive the trespass of thine handmaid: for the LORD will certainly make my lord a sure house; because my lord fighteth the battles of

the LORD, and evil hath not been found in thee *all* thy days.

29 Yet a man is risen to pursue thee, and to seek thy soul: but the soul of my lord shall be bound in the bundle of life with the LORD thy God; and the souls of thine enemies, them shall he sling out, *as out* of the middle of a sling.

30 And it shall come to pass, when the LORD shall have done to my lord according to all the good that he hath spoken concerning thee, and shall have appointed thee ruler over Israel;

31 That this shall be no grief unto thee, nor offence of heart unto my lord, either that thou hast shed blood causeless, or that my lord hath avenged himself: but when the LORD shall have dealt well with my lord, then remember thine handmaid.

32 ¶And David said to Ăb'i-gāil, Blessed *be* the LORD God of Israel, which sent thee this day to meet me:

33 And blessed *be* thy advice, and blessed *be* thou, which hast kept me this day from coming to *shed* blood, and from avenging myself with mine own hand.

34 For in very deed, *as* the LORD God of Israel liveth, which hath kept me back from hurting thee, except thou hadst hasted and come to meet me, surely there had not been left unto Nā'bal by the morning light any that pisseth against the wall.

35 So David received of her hand *that* which she had brought him, and said unto her, Go up in peace to thine house; see, I have hearkened to thy voice, and have accepted thy person.

36 ¶And Ăb'i-gāil came to Nā'bal; and, behold, he held a feast in his house, like the feast of a king; and Nā'bal's heart *was* merry within him, for he *was* very drunken: wherefore she told him nothing, less or more, until the morning light.

37 But it came to pass in the morning, when the wine was gone out of Nā'bal, and his wife had told him these things, that his heart died within him, and he became *as* a stone.

38 And it came to pass about ten days *after*, that the LORD smote Nā'bal, that he died.

39 And when David heard that Nā'bal was dead, he said, Blessed *be* the LORD, that hath pleaded the cause of my reproach from the hand of Nā'bal, and hath kept his servant from evil: for the LORD hath returned the wickedness of Nā'bal upon his own head. And David sent and communed with Ăb'i-gāil, to take her to him to wife.

40 And when the servants of David were come to Ăb'i-gāil to Carmel, they spake unto her, saying, David sent us unto thee, to take thee to him to wife.

41 And she arose, and bowed herself on *her* face to the earth, and said, Behold, *let* thine handmaid *be* a servant to wash the feet of the servants of my lord.

42 And Ăb'i-gāil hasted, and arose, and rode upon an ass, with five damsels of hers that went after her; and she went after the messengers of David, and became his wife.

43 David also took A-hĭn'ō-am of Jĕz're-el; and they were also both of them his wives.

44 But Saul had given Mī'chal his daughter, David's wife, to Phăl'tī the son of Lā'ĭsh, which *was* of Găl'lĭm.

CHAPTER 26

AND the Zīph'ītes came unto Saul to Gĭb'e-ah, saying, Doth not David hide himself in the hill of Hach'ī-lah, *which is* before Jesh'-ī-mon?

2 Then Saul arose, and went down to the wilderness of Ziph, having three thousand chosen men of Israel with him, to seek David in the wilderness of Ziph.

3 And Saul pitched in the hill of Hach'ī-lah, which *is* before Jesh'-ī-mon, by the way. But David abode in the wilderness, and he saw that Saul came after him into the wilderness.

4 David therefore sent out spies, and understood that Saul was come in very deed.

5 ¶And David arose, and came to the place where Saul had pitched: and David beheld the place where Saul lay, and Abner the son of Ner, the captain of his host: and Saul lay in the trench, and the people pitched round about him.

6 Then answered David and said to A-hĭm'e-lĕch the Hittite, and to A-bī'-shaī the son of Zer-ū-i'ah, brother to Jō'ăb, saying, Who will go down with me to Saul to the camp? And A-bī'shaī said, I will go down with thee.

7 So David and A-bī'shaī came to the people by night: and, behold, Saul lay sleeping within the trench, and his spear stuck in the ground at his bolster: but Abner and the people lay round about him.

8 Then said A-bī'shaī to David, God hath delivered thine enemy into thine hand this day: now therefore let me smite him, I pray thee, with the spear even to the earth at once, and I will not *smite* him the second time.

9 And David said to A-bī'shaī, Destroy him not: for who can stretch forth

his hand against the LORD's anointed, and be guiltless?

10 David said furthermore, *As* the LORD liveth, the LORD shall smite him; or his day shall come to die; or he shall descend into battle, and perish.

11 The LORD forbid that I should stretch forth mine hand against the LORD's anointed: but, I pray thee, take thou now the spear that *is* at his bolster, and the cruse of water, and let us go.

12 So David took the spear and the cruse of water from Saul's bolster; and they gat them away, and no man saw *it*, nor knew *it*, neither awaked: for they *were* all asleep; because a deep sleep from the LORD was fallen upon them.

13 ¶Then David went over to the other side, and stood on the top of an hill afar off; a great space *being* between them:

14 And David cried to the people, and to Abner the son of Ner, saying, Answerest thou not, Abner? Then Abner answered and said, Who *art* thou *that* criest to the king?

15 And David said to Abner, *Art* not thou a *valiant* man? and who *is* like to thee in Israel? wherefore then hast thou not kept thy lord the king? for there came one of the people in to destroy the king thy lord.

16 This thing *is* not good that thou hast done. *As* the LORD liveth, ye *are* worthy to die, because ye have not kept your master, the LORD's anointed. And now see where the king's spear *is*, and the cruse of water that *was* at his bolster.

17 And Saul knew David's voice, and said, *Is* this thy voice, my son David? And David said, *It is* my voice, my lord, O king.

18 And he said, Wherefore doth my lord thus pursue after his servant? for what have I done? or what evil *is* in mine hand?

19 Now therefore, I pray thee, let my lord the king hear the words of his servant. If the LORD have stirred thee up against me, let him accept an offering: but if *they be* the children of men, cursed *be* they before the LORD; for they have driven me out this day from abiding in the inheritance of the LORD, saying, Go, serve other gods.

20 Now therefore, let not my blood fall to the earth before the face of the LORD: for the king of Israel is come out to seek a flea, as when one doth hunt a partridge in the mountains.

21 ¶Then said Saul, I have sinned: return, my son David: for I will no more do thee harm, because my soul was precious in thine eyes this day: behold, I have played the fool, and have erred exceedingly.

22 And David answered and said, Behold the king's spear! and let one of the young men come over and fetch it.

23 The LORD render to every man his righteousness and his faithfulness: for the LORD delivered thee into *my* hand to day, but I would not stretch forth mine hand against the LORD's anointed.

24 And, behold, as thy life was much set by this day in mine eyes, so let my life be much set by in the eyes of the LORD, and let him deliver me out of all tribulation.

25 Then Saul said to David, Blessed *be* thou, my son David: thou shalt both do great *things*, and also shalt still prevail. So David went on his way, and Saul returned to his place.

CHAPTER 27

AND David said in his heart, I shall now perish one day by the hand of Saul: *there is* nothing better for me than that I should speedily escape into the land of the Philistines; and Saul shall despair of me, to seek me any more in any coast of Israel: so shall I escape out of his hand.

2 And David arose, and he passed over with the six hundred men that *were* with him unto Ā'chĭsh, the son of Mā'och, king of Gath.

3 And David dwelt with Ā'chĭsh at Gath, he and his men, every man with his household, *even* David with his two wives, A-hĭn'ō-am the Jĕz're-el-īt-ess, and Ăb'i-gāil the Carmelitess, Nā'bal's wife.

4 And it was told Saul that David was fled to Gath: and he sought no more again for him.

5 ¶And David said unto Ā'chĭsh, If I have now found grace in thine eyes, let them give me a place in some town in the country, that I may dwell there: for why should thy servant dwell in the royal city with thee?

6 Then Ā'chĭsh gave him Ziklag that day: wherefore Ziklag pertaineth unto the kings of Jūdah unto this day.

7 And the time that David dwelt in the country of the Philistines was a full year and four months.

8 ¶And David and his men went up, and invaded the Gĕsh'u-rītes, and the Gĕz'rītes, and the Am'ă-lek-ītes: for those *nations were* of old the inhabitants of the land, as thou goest to Shur, even unto the land of Egypt.

9 And David smote the land, and left neither man nor woman alive, and took away the sheep, and the oxen, and the

asses, and the camels, and the apparel, and returned, and came to Ā'chĭsh.
10 And Ā'chĭsh said, Whither have ye made a road to day? And David said, Against the south of Jūdah, and against the south of the Je-räh'me-el-ītes, and against the south of the Kēn'ītes.
11 And David saved neither man nor woman alive, to bring *tidings* to Gath, saying, Lest they should tell on us, saying, So did David, and so *will be* his manner all the while he dwelleth in the country of the Philistines.
12 And Ā'chĭsh believed David, saying, He hath made his people Israel utterly to abhor him; therefore he shall be my servant for ever.

CHAPTER 28

AND it came to pass in those days, that the Philistines gathered their armies together for warfare, to fight with Israel. And Ā'chĭsh said unto David, Know thou assuredly, that thou shalt go out with me to battle, thou and thy men.
2 And David said to Ā'chĭsh, Surely thou shalt know what thy servant can do. And Ā'chĭsh said to David, Therefore will I make thee keeper of mine head for ever.
3 ¶Now Samuel was dead, and all Israel had lamented him, and buried him in Rā'mah, even in his own city. And Saul had put away those that had familiar spirits, and the wizards, out of the land.
4 And the Philistines gathered themselves together, and came and pitched in Shū'nem: and Saul gathered all Israel together, and they pitched in Gĭl-bō'a.
5 And when Saul saw the host of the Philistines, he was afraid, and his heart greatly trembled.
6 And when Saul enquired of the LORD, the LORD answered him not, neither by dreams, nor by Û'rĭm, nor by prophets.
7 Then said Saul unto his servants, Seek me a woman that hath a familiar spirit, that I may go to her, and enquire of her. And his servants said to him, Behold, *there is* a woman that hath a familiar spirit at Ĕn-dôr.
8 And Saul disguised himself, and put on other raiment, and he went, and two men with him, and they came to the woman by night: and he said, I pray thee, divine unto me by the familiar spirit, and bring me *him* up, whom I shall name unto thee.
9 And the woman said unto him, Behold, thou knowest what Saul hath done, how he hath cut off those that have familiar spirits, and the wizards, out of the land: wherefore then layest thou a snare for my life, to cause me to die?
10 And Saul sware to her by the LORD, saying, *As* the LORD liveth, there shall no punishment happen to thee for this thing.
11 Then said the woman, Whom shall I bring up unto thee? And he said, Bring me up Samuel.
12 And when the woman saw Samuel, she cried with a loud voice: and the woman spake to Saul, saying, Why hast thou deceived me? for thou *art* Saul.
13 And the king said unto her, Be not afraid: for what sawest thou? And the woman said unto Saul, I saw gods ascending out of the earth.
14 And he said unto her, What form *is* he of? And she said, An old man cometh up; and he *is* covered with a mantle. And Saul perceived that it *was* Samuel, and he stooped with *his* face to the ground, and bowed himself.
15 And Samuel said to Saul, Why hast thou disquieted me, to bring me up? And Saul answered, I am sore distressed; for the Philistines make war against me, and God is departed from me, and answereth me no more, neither by prophets, nor by dreams: therefore I have called thee, that thou mayest make known unto me what I shall do.
16 Then said Samuel, Wherefore then dost thou ask of me, seeing the LORD is departed from thee, and is become thine enemy?
17 And the LORD hath done to him, as he spake by me: for the LORD hath rent the kingdom out of thine hand, and given it to thy neighbour, *even* to David:
18 Because thou obeyedst not the voice of the LORD, nor executedst his fierce wrath upon Ăm'a-lĕk, therefore hath the LORD done this thing unto thee this day.
19 Moreover the LORD will also deliver Israel with thee into the hand of the Philistines: and to morrow *shalt* thou and thy sons *be* with me: the LORD also shall deliver the host of Israel into the hand of the Philistines.
20 Then Saul fell straightway all along on the earth, and was sore afraid, because of the words of Samuel: and there was no strength in him; for he had eaten no bread all the day, nor all the night.
21 ¶And the woman came unto Saul, and saw that he was sore troubled, and said unto him, Behold, thine handmaid hath obeyed thy voice, and I have put my life in my hand, and have hear-

kened unto thy words which thou spak-
est unto me.
22 Now therefore, I pray thee, hear-
ken thou also unto the voice of thine
handmaid, and let me set a morsel of
bread before thee; and eat, that thou
mayest have strength, when thou goest
on thy way.
23 But he refused, and said, I will not
eat. But his servants, together with the
woman, compelled him; and he hear-
kened unto their voice. So he arose
from the earth, and sat upon the bed.
24 And the woman had a fat calf in
the house; and she hasted, and killed it,
and took flour, and kneaded *it*, and did
bake unleavened bread thereof:
25 And she brought *it* before Saul,
and before his servants; and they did
eat. Then they rose up, and went away
that night.

CHAPTER 29

NOW the Philistines gathered together
all their armies to Ā'phĕk: and the
Israelites pitched by a fountain which
is in Jĕz're-el.
2 And the lords of the Philistines
passed on by hundreds, and by thou-
sands: but David and his men passed
on in the rereward with Ā'chĭsh.
3 Then said the princes of the Philis-
tines, What *do* these Hebrews *here*?
And Ā'chĭsh said unto the princes of
the Philistines, *Is* not this David, the
servant of Saul the king of Israel, which
hath been with me these days, or these
years, and I have found no fault in him
since he fell *unto me* unto this day?
4 And the princes of the Philistines
were wroth with him; and the princes
of the Philistines said unto him, Make
this fellow return, that he may go again
to his place which thou hast appointed
him, and let him not go down with us to
battle, lest in the battle he be an adver-
sary to us: for wherewith should he rec-
oncile himself unto his master? *should*
it not *be* with the heads of these men?
5 *Is* not this David, of whom they
sang one to another in dances, saying,
Saul slew his thousands, and David his
ten thousands?
6 ¶Then Ā'chĭsh called David, and
said unto him, Surely, *as* the LORD
liveth, thou hast been upright, and thy
going out and thy coming in with me in
the host *is* good in my sight: for I have
not found evil in thee since the day of
thy coming unto me unto this day:
nevertheless the lords favour thee not.
7 Wherefore now return, and go in
peace, that thou displease not the lords
of the Philistines.
8 And David said unto Ā'chĭsh, But
what have I done? and what hast thou
found in thy servant so long as I have
been with thee unto this day, that I may
not go fight against the enemies of my
lord the king?
9 And Ā'chĭsh answered and said to
David, I know that thou *art* good in my
sight, as an angel of God: notwith-
standing the princes of the Philistines
have said, He shall not go up with us to
the battle.
10 Wherefore now rise up early in the
morning with thy master's servants
that are come with thee: and as soon as
ye be up early in the morning, and have
light, depart.
11 So David and his men rose up
early to depart in the morning, to re-
turn into the land of the Philistines.
And the Philistines went up to Jĕz're-el.

CHAPTER 30

AND it came to pass, when David and
his men were come to Ziklag on the
third day, that the Am'ă-lek-ītes had in-
vaded the south, and Ziklag, and smit-
ten Ziklag, and burned it with fire;
2 And had taken the women captives,
that *were* therein: they slew not any,
either great or small, but carried *them*
away, and went on their way.
3 So David and his men came to the
city, and, behold, *it was* burned with
fire; and their wives, and their sons,
and their daughters, were taken cap-
tives.
4 Then David and the people that
were with him lifted up their voice and
wept, until they had no more power to
weep.
5 And David's two wives were taken
captives, A-hĭn'ō-am the Jĕz're-el-īt-
ess, and Ăb'i-gāil the wife of Nā'bal the
Carmelite.
6 And David was greatly distressed;
for the people spake of stoning him, be-
cause the soul of all the people was
grieved, every man for his sons and for
his daughters: but David encouraged
himself in the LORD his God.
7 And David said to Ă-bī'a-thar the
priest, A-hĭm'e-lĕch's son, I pray thee,
bring me hither the ephod. And Ă-bī'a-
thar brought thither the ephod to Da-
vid.
8 And David enquired at the LORD,
saying, Shall I pursue after this troop?
shall I overtake them? And he an-
swered him, Pursue: for thou shalt sure-
ly overtake *them*, and without fail re-
cover *all*.
9 So David went, he and the six
hundred men that *were* with him, and
came to the brook Bē'ṡôr, where those
that were left behind stayed.

10 But David pursued, he and four
hundred men: for two hundred abode
behind, which were so faint that they
could not go over the brook Bē′ŝôr.
11 ¶And they found an Egyptian in
the field, and brought him to David,
and gave him bread, and he did eat; and
they made him drink water;
12 And they gave him a piece of a
cake of figs, and two clusters of raisins:
and when he had eaten, his spirit came
again to him: for he had eaten no bread,
nor drunk *any* water, three days and
three nights.
13 And David said unto him, To
whom *belongest* thou? and whence *art*
thou? And he said, I *am* a young man of
Egypt, servant to an Am′ă-lek-īte; and
my master left me, because three days
agone I fell sick.
14 We made an invasion *upon* the
south of the Chĕr′e-thītes, and upon *the*
coast which *belongeth* to Jūdah, and
upon the south of Caleb; and we
burned Ziklag with fire.
15 And David said to him, Canst thou
bring me down to this company? And
he said, Swear unto me by God, that
thou wilt neither kill me, nor deliver me
into the hands of my master, and I will
bring thee down to this company.
16 And when he had brought him
down, behold, *they were* spread abroad
upon all the earth, eating and drinking,
and dancing, because of all the great
spoil that they had taken out of the
land of the Philistines, and out of the
land of Jūdah.
17 And David smote them from the
twilight even unto the evening of the
next day: and there escaped not a man
of them, save four hundred young men,
which rode upon camels, and fled.
18 And David recovered all that the
Am′ă-lek-ītes had carried away: and
David rescued his two wives.
19 And there was nothing lacking to
them, neither small nor great, neither
sons nor daughters, neither spoil, nor
any *thing* that they had taken to them:
David recovered all.
20 And David took all the flocks and
the herds, *which* they drave before
those *other* cattle, and said, This *is* Da-
vid's spoil.
21 ¶And David came to the two
hundred men, which were so faint that
they could not follow David, whom
they had made also to abide at the
brook Bē′ŝôr: and they went forth to
meet David, and to meet the people
that *were* with him: and when David
came near to the people, he saluted
them.
22 Then answered all the wicked men
and *men* of Bē′lĭ-al, of those that went
with David, and said, Because they
went not with us, we will not give them
ought of the spoil that we have re-
covered, save to every man his wife
and his children, that they may lead
them away, and depart.
23 Then said David, Ye shall not do
so, my brethren, with that which the
LORD hath given us, who hath pre-
served us, and delivered the company
that came against us into our hand.
24 For who will hearken unto you in
this matter? but as his part *is* that go-
eth down to the battle, so *shall* his part
be that tarrieth by the stuff: they shall
part alike.
25 And it was *so* from that day for-
ward, that he made it a statute and an
ordinance for Israel unto this day.
26 ¶And when David came to Ziklag,
he sent of the spoil unto the elders of
Jūdah, *even* to his friends, saying, Be-
hold a present for you of the spoil of the
enemies of the LORD;
27 To *them* which *were* in Bĕth–el, and
to *them* which *were* in south Rā′mŏth,
and to *them* which *were* in Jăt′tir,
28 And to *them* which *were* in Ar′ō-
er, and to *them* which *were* in Sĭph′-
mŏth, and to *them* which *were* in
Ĕsh-te-mō′a,
29 And to *them* which *were* in Rā′-
chăl, and to *them* which *were* in the
cities of the Je-räh′me-el-ītes, and to
them which *were* in the cities of the
Kēn′-ītes,
30 And to *them* which *were* in Hôr′-
mah, and to *them* which *were* in
Chôr–ā′shan, and to *them* which *were* in
Ā′thăch,
31 And to *them* which *were* in Hē-
bron, and to all the places where David
himself and his men were wont to
haunt.

CHAPTER 31

NOW the Philistines fought against
Israel: and the men of Israel fled from
before the Philistines, and fell down
slain in mount Gĭl-bō′a.
2 And the Philistines followed hard
upon Saul and upon his sons; and the
Philistines slew Jonathan, and A-bĭn′a-
dăb, and Mĕl′chī–shū′a, Saul's sons.
3 And the battle went sore against
Saul, and the archers hit him; and he
was sore wounded of the archers.
4 Then said Saul unto his armour-
bearer, Draw thy sword, and thrust me
through therewith; lest these uncir-
cumcised come and thrust me through,
and abuse me. But his armourbearer
would not; for he was sore afraid. There-

fore Saul took a sword, and fell upon it.

5 And when his armourbearer saw that Saul was dead, he fell likewise upon his sword, and died with him.

6 So Saul died, and his three sons, and his armourbearer, and all his men, that same day together.

7 ¶And when the men of Israel that *were* on the other side of the valley, and *they* that *were* on the other side Jordan, saw that the men of Israel fled, and that Saul and his sons were dead, they forsook the cities, and fled; and the Philistines came and dwelt in them.

8 ¶And it came to pass on the morrow, when the Philistines came to strip the slain, that they found Saul and his three sons fallen in mount Gĭl-bō'a.

9 And they cut off his head, and stripped off his armour, and sent into the land of the Philistines round about, to publish *it in* the house of their idols, and among the people.

10 And they put his armour in the house of Ăsh'ta-rŏth: and they fastened his body to the wall of Bĕth'-shăn.

11 And when the inhabitants of Jā'-besh-gĭl'e-ad heard of that which the Philistines had done to Saul;

12 All the valiant men arose, and went all night, and took the body of Saul and the bodies of his sons from the wall of Bĕth'-shăn, and came to Jā'-besh, and burnt them there.

13 And they took their bones, and buried *them* under a tree at Jā'besh, and fasted seven days.

THE

SECOND BOOK OF SAMUEL

OTHERWISE CALLED

THE SECOND BOOK OF THE KINGS

CHAPTER 1

NOW it came to pass after the death of Saul, when David was returned from the slaughter of the Am'ă-lek-ītes, and David had abode two days in Ziklag;

2 It came even to pass on the third day, that, behold, a man came out of the camp from Saul with his clothes rent, and earth upon his head: and *so* it was, when he came to David, that he fell to the earth, and did obeisance.

3 And David said unto him, From whence comest thou? And he said unto him, Out of the camp of Israel am I escaped.

4 And David said unto him, How went the matter? I pray thee, tell me. And he answered, That the people are fled from the battle, and many of the people also are fallen and dead; and Saul and Jonathan his son are dead also.

5 And David said unto the young man that told him, How knowest thou that Saul and Jonathan his son be dead?

6 And the young man that told him said, As I happened by chance upon mount Gĭl-bō'a, behold, Saul leaned upon his spear; and, lo, the chariots and horsemen followed hard after him.

7 And when he looked behind him, he saw me, and called unto me. And I answered, Here *am* I.

8 And he said unto me, Who *art* thou? And I answered him, I *am* an Am'ă-lek-īte.

9 He said unto me again, Stand, I pray thee, upon me, and slay me: for anguish is come upon me, because my life *is* yet whole in me.

10 So I stood upon him, and slew him, because I was sure that he could not live after that he was fallen: and I took the crown that *was* upon his head, and the bracelet that *was* on his arm, and have brought them hither unto my lord.

11 Then David took hold on his clothes, and rent them; and likewise all the men that *were* with him:

12 And they mourned, and wept, and fasted until even, for Saul, and for Jonathan his son, and for the people of the LORD, and for the house of Israel; because they were fallen by the sword.

13 ¶And David said unto the young man that told him, Whence *art* thou? And he answered, I *am* the son of a stranger, an Am'ă-lek-īte.

14 And David said unto him, How wast thou not afraid to stretch forth thine hand to destroy the LORD's anointed?

15 And David called one of the young men, and said, Go near, *and* fall upon him. And he smote him that he died.

16 And David said unto him, Thy blood *be* upon thy head; for thy mouth hath testified against thee, saying, I have slain the LORD's anointed.

17 ¶And David lamented with this lamentation over Saul and over Jonathan his son:

18 (Also he bade them teach the children of Jūdah *the use of* the bow: behold, *it is* written in the book of Jā'-sher.)

19 The beauty of Israel is slain upon

thy high places: how are the mighty fallen!

20 Tell *it* not in Gath, publish *it* not in the streets of Ăs′ke-lŏn; lest the daughters of the Philistines rejoice, lest the daughters of the uncircumcised triumph.

21 Ye mountains of Gĭl-bō′a, *let there be* no dew, neither *let there be* rain, upon you, nor fields of offerings: for there the shield of the mighty is vilely cast away, the shield of Saul, *as though he had* not *been* anointed with oil.

22 From the blood of the slain, from the fat of the mighty, the bow of Jonathan turned not back, and the sword of Saul returned not empty.

23 Saul and Jonathan *were* lovely and pleasant in their lives, and in their death they were not divided: they were swifter than eagles, they were stronger than lions.

24 Ye daughters of Israel, weep over Saul, who clothed you in scarlet, with *other* delights, who put on ornaments of gold upon your apparel.

25 How are the mighty fallen in the midst of the battle! O Jonathan, *thou wast* slain in thine high places.

26 I am distressed for thee, my brother Jonathan: very pleasant hast thou been unto me: thy love to me was wonderful, passing the love of women.

27 How are the mighty fallen, and the weapons of war perished!

CHAPTER 2

AND it came to pass after this, that David enquired of the LORD, saying, Shall I go up into any of the cities of Jūdah? And the LORD said unto him, Go up. And David said, Whither shall I go up? And he said, Unto Hēbron.

2 So David went up thither, and his two wives also, A-hĭn′ō-am the Jĕz′re-el-īt-ess, and Ăb′i-gāil Nā′bal's wife the Carmelite.

3 And his men that *were* with him did David bring up, every man with his household: and they dwelt in the cities of Hēbron.

4 And the men of Jūdah came, and there they anointed David king over the house of Jūdah. And they told David, saying, *That* the men of Jā′besh-gĭl′e-ad *were they* that buried Saul.

5 ¶And David sent messengers unto the men of Jā′besh-gĭl′e-ad, and said unto them, Blessed *be* ye of the LORD, that ye have shewed this kindness unto your lord, *even* unto Saul, and have buried him.

6 And now the LORD shew kindness and truth unto you: and I also will requite you this kindness, because ye have done this thing.

7 Therefore now let your hands be strengthened, and be ye valiant: for your master Saul is dead, and also the house of Jūdah have anointed me king over them.

8 ¶But Abner the son of Ner, captain of Saul's host, took Ĭsh-bō′sheth the son of Saul, and brought him over to Mā-ha-nā′im;

9 And made him king over Gilead, and over the Ăsh′ur-ītes, and over Jĕz′-re-el, and over Ē′phra-im, and over Benjamin, and over all Israel.

10 Ĭsh-bō′sheth Saul's son *was* forty years old when he began to reign over Israel, and reigned two years. But the house of Jūdah followed David.

11 And the time that David was king in Hēbron over the house of Jūdah was seven years and six months.

12 ¶And Abner the son of Ner, and the servants of Ĭsh-bō′sheth the son of Saul, went out from Mā-ha-nā′im to Gĭb′-e-on.

13 And Jō′ăb the son of Zer-ū-i′ah, and the servants of David, went out, and met together by the pool of Gĭb′-e-on: and they sat down, the one on the one side of the pool, and the other on the other side of the pool.

14 And Abner said to Jō′ăb, Let the young men now arise, and play before us. And Jō′ăb said, Let them arise.

15 Then there arose and went over by number twelve of Benjamin, which *pertained* to Ĭsh-bō′sheth the son of Saul, and twelve of the servants of David.

16 And they caught every one his fellow by the head, and *thrust* his sword in his fellow's side; so they fell down together: wherefore that place was called Hĕl′kăth-hăz′zu-rĭm, which *is* in Gĭb′e-on.

17 And there was a very sore battle that day; and Abner was beaten, and the men of Israel, before the servants of David.

18 ¶And there were three sons of Zer-ū-i′ah there, Jō′ăb, and A-bī′shaī, and Ă′sa-hĕl: and Ă′sa-hĕl *was as* light of foot as a wild roe.

19 And Ă′sa-hĕl pursued after Abner; and in going he turned not to the right hand nor to the left from following Abner.

20 Then Abner looked behind him, and said, *Art* thou Ă′sa-hĕl? And he answered, I *am*.

21 And Abner said to him, Turn thee aside to thy right hand or to thy left, and lay thee hold on one of the young men, and take thee his armour. But

Ă'sa-hĕl would not turn aside from fol-
lowing of him.
22 And Abner said again to Ă'sa-hĕl,
Turn thee aside from following me:
wherefore should I smite thee to the
ground? how then should I hold up my
face to Jō'ăb thy brother?
23 Howbeit he refused to turn aside:
wherefore Abner with the hinder end
of the spear smote him under the fifth
rib, that the spear came out behind
him; and he fell down there, and died in
the same place: and it came to pass,
that as many as came to the place
where Ă'sa-hĕl fell down and died
stood still.
24 Jō'ăb also and A-bī'shaī pursued
after Abner: and the sun went down
when they were come to the hill of Ăm'-
mah, that *lieth* before Gī'ah by the way
of the wilderness of Gĭbeon.
25 ¶And the children of Benjamin
gathered themselves together after Ab-
ner, and became one troop, and stood
on the top of an hill.
26 Then Abner called to Jō'ăb, and
said, Shall the sword devour for ever?
knowest thou not that it will be bitter-
ness in the latter end? how long shall it
be then, ere thou bid the people return
from following their brethren?
27 And Jō'ăb said, *As* God liveth, un-
less thou hadst spoken, surely then in
the morning the people had gone up
every one from following his brother.
28 So Jō'ăb blew a trumpet, and all
the people stood still, and pursued after
Israel no more, neither fought they any
more.
29 And Abner and his men walked all
that night through the plain, and
passed over Jordan, and went through
all Bĭth'rŏn, and they came to Mā-ha-
nā'im.
30 And Jō'ăb returned from follow-
ing Abner: and when he had gathered
all the people together, there lacked of
David's servants nineteen men and
Ă'sa-hĕl.
31 But the servants of David had
smitten of Benjamin, and of Abner's
men, *so that* three hundred and three-
score men died.
32 ¶And they took up Ă'sa-hĕl, and
buried him in the sepulchre of his
father, which *was in* Bĕth-lehĕm. And
Jō'ăb and his men went all night, and
they came to Hēbron at break of day.

CHAPTER 3

NOW there was long war between the
house of Saul and the house of David:
but David waxed stronger and stron-
ger, and the house of Saul waxed
weaker and weaker.
2 ¶And unto David were sons born in
Hēbron: and his firstborn was Ăm'nŏn,
of A-hĭn'ō-am the Jĕz're-el-īt-ess;
3 And his second, Chĭl'e-ăb, of Ăb'i-
gāil the wife of Nā'bal the Carmelite;
and the third, Ăb'sa-lom the son of
Mā'a-cah the daughter of Tăl'maī king
of Gĕ'shur;
4 And the fourth, Ăd-o-nī'jah the son
of Hăg'gĭth; and the fifth, Shĕph-a-tī'ah
the son of Ăb'i-tal;
5 And the sixth, Ĭth're-am, by Ĕg'lah
David's wife. These were born to David
in Hēbron.
6 ¶And it came to pass, while there
was war between the house of Saul and
the house of David, that Abner made
himself strong for the house of Saul.
7 And Saul had a concubine, whose
name *was* Rĭz'pah, the daughter of Ā-
ĭ'ah: and *Ish-bo'sheth* said to Abner,
Wherefore hast thou gone in unto my
father's concubine?
8 Then was Abner very wroth for the
words of Ĭsh-bō'sheth, and said, *Am* I a
dog's head, which against Jūdah do
shew kindness this day unto the house
of Saul thy father, to his brethren, and
to his friends, and have not delivered
thee into the hand of David, that thou
chargest me to day with a fault concern-
ing this woman?
9 So do God to Abner, and more also,
except, as the LORD hath sworn to Da-
vid, even so I do to him;
10 To translate the kingdom from the
house of Saul, and to set up the throne
of David over Israel and over Jūdah,
from Dan even to Be'er-shē'ba.
11 And he could not answer Abner a
word again, because he feared him.
12 ¶And Abner sent messengers to
David on his behalf, saying, Whose *is*
the land? saying *also,* Make thy league
with me, and, behold, my hand *shall be*
with thee, to bring about all Israel unto
thee.
13 And he said, Well; I will make a
league with thee: but one thing I re-
quire of thee, that is, Thou shalt not see
my face, except thou first bring Mī'chal
Saul's daughter, when thou comest to
see my face.
14 And David sent messengers to
Ĭsh-bō'sheth Saul's son, saying, Deliver
me my wife Mī'chal, which I espoused
to me for an hundred foreskins of the
Philistines.
15 And Ĭsh-bō'sheth sent, and took
her from *her* husband, *even* from Phăl'-
tĭ-el the son of Lā'ĭsh.
16 And her husband went with her
along weeping behind her to Ba-hû'rĭm.
Then said Abner unto him, Go, return.
And he returned.

17 ¶And Abner had communication with the elders of Israel, saying, Ye sought for David in times past *to be* king over you:
18 Now then do *it*: for the LORD hath spoken of David, saying, By the hand of my servant David I will save my people Israel out of the hand of the Philistines, and out of the hand of all their enemies.
19 And Abner also spake in the ears of Benjamin: and Abner went also to speak in the ears of David in Hḗbron all that seemed good to Israel, and that seemed good to the whole house of Benjamin.
20 So Abner came to David to Hē-bron, and twenty men with him. And David made Abner and the men that *were* with him a feast.
21 And Abner said unto David, I will arise and go, and will gather all Israel unto my lord the king, that they may make a league with thee, and that thou mayest reign over all that thine heart desireth. And David sent Abner away; and he went in peace.
22 ¶And, behold, the servants of David and Jō'ăb came from *pursuing* a troop, and brought in a great spoil with them: but Abner *was* not with David in Hĕbron; for he had sent him away, and he was gone in peace.
23 When Jō'ăb and all the host that *was* with him were come, they told Jō'ăb, saying, Abner the son of Ner came to the king, and he hath sent him away, and he is gone in peace.
24 Then Jō'ăb came to the king, and said, What hast thou done? behold, Abner came unto thee; why *is* it *that* thou hast sent him away, and he is quite gone?
25 Thou knowest Abner the son of Ner, that he came to deceive thee, and to know thy going out and thy coming in, and to know all that thou doest.
26 And when Jō'ăb was come out from David, he sent messengers after Abner, which brought him again from the well of Sī'rah: but David knew *it* not.
27 And when Abner was returned to Hĕbron, Jō'ăb took him aside in the gate to speak with him quietly, and smote him there under the fifth *rib*, that he died, for the blood of Ă'sa-hĕl his brother.
28 ¶And afterward when David heard *it*, he said, I and my kingdom *are* guiltless before the LORD for ever from the blood of Abner the son of Ner:
29 Let it rest on the head of Jō'ăb, and on all his father's house; and let there not fail from the house of Jō'ăb one that hath an issue, or that is a leper, or that leaneth on a staff, or that falleth on the sword, or that lacketh bread.
30 So Jō'ăb and A-bī'shaī his brother slew Abner, because he had slain their brother Ă'sa-hĕl at Gĭbeon in the battle.
31 ¶And David said to Jō'ăb, and to all the people that *were* with him, Rend your clothes, and gird you with sackcloth, and mourn before Abner. And king David *himself* followed the bier.
32 And they buried Abner in Hēbron: and the king lifted up his voice, and wept at the grave of Abner; and all the people wept.
33 And the king lamented over Abner, and said, Died Abner as a fool dieth?
34 Thy hands *were* not bound, nor thy feet put into fetters: as a man falleth before wicked men, *so* fellest thou. And all the people wept again over him.
35 And when all the people came to cause David to eat meat while it was yet day, David sware, saying, So do God to me, and more also, if I taste bread, or ought else, till the sun be down.
36 And all the people took notice *of it*, and it pleased them: as whatsoever the king did pleased all the people.
37 For all the people and all Israel understood that day that it was not of the king to slay Abner the son of Ner.
38 And the king said unto his servants, Know ye not that there is a prince and a great man fallen this day in Israel?
39 And I *am* this day weak, though anointed king; and these men the sons of Zer-ū-i'ah *be* too hard for me: the LORD shall reward the doer of evil according to his wickedness.

CHAPTER 4

AND when Saul's son heard that Abner was dead in Hēbron, his hands were feeble, and all the Israelites were troubled.
2 And Saul's son had two men *that were* captains of bands: the name of the one *was* Bā'a-nah, and the name of the other Rē'chăb, the sons of Rimmon a Bē-ē'rŏth-īte, of the children of Benjamin: (for Bē-ē'rŏth also was reckoned to Benjamin.
3 And the Bē-ē'rŏth-ītes fled to Gĭt'ta-im, and were sojourners there until this day.)
4 And Jonathan, Saul's son, had a son *that was* lame of *his* feet. He was five years old when the tidings came of Saul and Jonathan out of Jĕz're-el, and his nurse took him up, and fled: and it came to pass, as she made haste to flee,

that he fell, and became lame. And his name *was* Me-phĭb′o-shĕth.

5 ¶And the sons of Rimmon the Bē-ē′rŏth-īte, Rē′chăb and Bā′a-nah, went, and came about the heat of the day to the house of Ĭsh–bō′sheth, who lay on a bed at noon.

6 And they came thither into the midst of the house, *as though* they would have fetched wheat; and they smote him under the fifth *rib:* and Rē′-chăb and Bā′a-nah his brother escaped.

7 For when they came into the house, he lay on his bed in his bedchamber, and they smote him, and slew him, and beheaded him, and took his head, and gat them away through the plain all night.

8 And they brought the head of Ĭsh–bō′sheth unto David to Hēbron, and said to the king, Behold the head of Ĭsh–bō′sheth the son of Saul thine enemy, which sought thy life; and the LORD hath avenged my lord the king this day of Saul, and of his seed.

9 ¶And David answered Rē′chăb and Bā′a-nah his brother, the sons of Rimmon the Bē-ē′rŏth-īte, and said unto them, *As* the LORD liveth, who hath redeemed my soul out of all adversity,

10 When one told me, saying, Behold, Saul is dead, thinking to have brought good tidings, I took hold of him, and slew him in Ziklag, who *thought* that I would have given him a reward for his tidings:

11 How much more, when wicked men have slain a righteous person in his own house upon his bed? shall I not therefore now require his blood of your hand, and take you away from the earth?

12 And David commanded his young men, and they slew them, and cut off their hands and their feet, and hanged *them* up over the pool in Hēbron. But they took the head of Ĭsh–bō′sheth, and buried *it* in the sepulchre of Abner in Hēbron.

CHAPTER 5

THEN came all the tribes of Israel to David unto Hēbron, and spake, saying, Behold, we *are* thy bone and thy flesh.

2 Also in time past, when Saul was king over us, thou wast he that leddest out and broughtest in Israel: and the LORD said to thee, Thou shalt feed my people Israel, and thou shalt be a captain over Israel.

3 So all the elders of Israel came to the king to Hēbron; and king David made a league with them in Hēbron before the LORD: and they anointed David king over Israel.

4 David *was* thirty years old when he began to reign, *and* he reigned forty years.

5 In Hēbron he reigned over Jūdah seven years and six months: and in Jerusalem he reigned thirty and three years over all Israel and Jūdah.

6 ¶And the king and his men went to Jerusalem unto the Jēb′u-sītes, the inhabitants of the land: which spake unto David, saying, Except thou take away the blind and the lame, thou shalt not come in hither: thinking, David cannot come in hither.

7 Nevertheless David took the strong hold of Zion: the same *is* the city of David.

8 And David said on that day, Whosoever getteth up to the gutter, and smiteth the Jēb′u-sītes, and the lame and the blind, *that are* hated of David's soul, *he shall be chief and captain.* Wherefore they said, The blind and the lame shall not come into the house.

9 So David dwelt in the fort, and called it the city of David. And David built round about from Mĭl′lō and inward.

10 And David went on, and grew great, and the LORD God of hosts *was* with him.

11 ¶And Hiram king of Tyre sent messengers to David, and cedar trees, and carpenters, and masons: and they built David an house.

12 And David perceived that the LORD had established him king over Israel, and that he had exalted his kingdom for his people Israel's sake.

13 ¶And David took *him* more concubines and wives out of Jerusalem, after he was come from Hēbron: and there were yet sons and daughters born to David.

14 And these *be* the names of those that were born unto him in Jerusalem; Shām-mū′ah, and Shō′băb, and Nā′-than, and Sŏlomon,

15 Ĭb′hār also and Ĕl-i-shū′a, and Nē′phĕg, and Ja-phī′a,

16 And E-lĭsh′a-ma, and E-lī′a-da, and E-lĭph′a-lĕt.

17 ¶But when the Philistines heard that they had anointed David king over Israel, all the Philistines came up to seek David; and David heard *of it,* and went down to the hold.

18 The Philistines also came and spread themselves in the valley of Rĕph′a-im.

19 And David enquired of the LORD, saying, Shall I go up to the Philistines? wilt thou deliver them into mine hand? And the LORD said unto David, Go up:

for I will doubtless deliver the Philistines into thine hand.
20 And David came to Bā'al-per'a-zĭm, and David smote them there, and said, the LORD hath broken forth upon mine enemies before me, as the breach of waters. Therefore he called the name of that place Bā'al-per'a-zĭm.
21 And there they left their images, and David and his men burned them.
22 ¶And the Philistines came up yet again, and spread themselves in the valley of Rĕph'a-im.
23 And when David enquired of the LORD, he said, Thou shalt not go up; *but* fetch a compass behind them, and come upon them over against the mulberry trees.
24 And let it be, when thou hearest the sound of a going in the tops of the mulberry trees, that then thou shalt bestir thyself: for then shall the LORD go out before thee, to smite the host of the Philistines.
25 And David did so, as the LORD had commanded him; and smote the Philistines from Gē'ba until thou come to Gā'zer.

CHAPTER 6

AGAIN, David gathered together all *the* chosen *men* of Israel, thirty thousand.
2 And David arose, and went with all the people that *were* with him from Bā'-al-e of Jūdah, to bring up from thence the ark of God, whose name is called by the name of the LORD of hosts that dwelleth *between* the cherubims.
3 And they set the ark of God upon a new cart, and brought it out of the house of A-bĭn'a-dăb that *was* in Gĭb'e-ah: and Ŭz'zah and A-hī'o, the sons of A-bĭn'a-dăb, drave the new cart.
4 And they brought it out of the house of A-bĭn'a-dăb which *was* at Gĭb'e-ah, accompanying the ark of God: and A-hī'o went before the ark.
5 And David and all the house of Israel played before the LORD on all manner of *instruments made of* fir wood, even on harps, and on psalteries, and on timbrels, and on cornets, and on cymbals.
6 And when they came to Nā'chŏn's threshingfloor, Ŭz'zah put forth *his hand* to the ark of God, and took hold of it; for the oxen shook *it*.
7 And the anger of the LORD was kindled against Ŭz'zah; and God smote him there for *his* error; and there he died by the ark of God.
8 And David was displeased, because the LORD had made a breach upon Ŭz'-zah: and he called the name of the place Pe'rĕz-ūz'zah to this day.
9 And David was afraid of the LORD that day, and said, How shall the ark of the LORD come to me?
10 So David would not remove the ark of the LORD unto him into the city of David: but David carried it aside into the house of Ō'bed-ē'dom the Gĭt'tīte.
11 And the ark of the LORD continued in the house of Ō'bed-ē'dom the Gĭt'tīte three months: and the LORD blessed Ō'bed-ē'dom, and all his household.
12 ¶And it was told king David, saying, The LORD hath blessed the house of Ō'bed-ē'dom, and all that *pertaineth* unto him, because of the ark of God. So David went and brought up the ark of God from the house of Ō'bed-ē'dom into the city of David with gladness.
13 And it was *so*, that when they that bare the ark of the LORD had gone six paces, he sacrificed oxen and fatlings.
14 And David danced before the LORD with all *his* might; and David *was* girded with a linen ephod.
15 So David and all the house of Israel brought up the ark of the LORD with shouting, and with the sound of the trumpet.
16 And as the ark of the LORD came into the city of David, Mī'chal Saul's daughter looked through a window, and saw king David leaping and dancing before the LORD; and she despised him in her heart.
17 ¶And they brought in the ark of the LORD, and set it in his place, in the midst of the tabernacle that David had pitched for it: and David offered burnt offerings and peace offerings before the LORD.
18 And as soon as David had made an end of offering burnt offerings and peace offerings, he blessed the people in the name of the LORD of hosts.
19 And he dealt among all the people, *even* among the whole multitude of Israel, as well to the women as men, to every one a cake of bread, and a good piece *of flesh*, and a flagon *of wine*. So all the people departed every one to his house.
20 ¶Then David returned to bless his household. And Mī'chal the daughter of Saul came out to meet David, and said, How glorious was the king of Israel to day, who uncovered himself to day in the eyes of the handmaids of his servants, as one of the vain fellows shamelessly uncovereth himself!
21 And David said unto Mī'chal, *It was* before the LORD, which chose me before thy father, and before all his

house, to appoint me ruler over the people of the LORD, over Israel: therefore will I play before the LORD.

22 And I will yet be more vile than thus, and will be base in mine own sight: and of the maidservants which thou hast spoken of, of them shall I be had in honour.

23 Therefore Mī'chal the daughter of Saul had no child unto the day of her death.

CHAPTER 7

AND it came to pass, when the king sat in his house, and the LORD had given him rest round about from all his enemies;

2 That the king said unto Nāthan the prophet, See now, I dwell in an house of cedar, but the ark of God dwelleth within curtains.

3 And Nāthan said to the king, Go, do all that *is* in thine heart; for the LORD *is* with thee.

4 ¶And it came to pass that night, that the word of the LORD came unto Nāthan, saying,

5 Go and tell my servant David, Thus saith the LORD, Shalt thou build me an house for me to dwell in?

6 Whereas I have not dwelt in *any* house since the time that I brought up the children of Israel out of Egypt, even to this day, but have walked in a tent and in a tabernacle.

7 In all *the places* wherein I have walked with all the children of Israel spake I a word with any of the tribes of Israel, whom I commanded to feed my people Israel, saying, Why build ye not me an house of cedar?

8 Now therefore so shalt thou say unto my servant David, Thus saith the LORD of hosts, I took thee from the sheepcote, from following the sheep, to be ruler over my people, over Israel:

9 And I was with thee whithersoever thou wentest, and have cut off all thine enemies out of thy sight, and have made thee a great name, like unto the name of the great *men* that *are* in the earth.

10 Moreover I will appoint a place for my people Israel, and will plant them, that they may dwell in a place of their own, and move no more; neither shall the children of wickedness afflict them any more, as beforetime,

11 And as since the time that I commanded judges *to be* over my people Israel, and have caused thee to rest from all thine enemies. Also the LORD telleth thee that he will make thee an house.

12 And when thy days be fulfilled, and thou shalt sleep with thy fathers, I will set up thy seed after thee, which shall proceed out of thy bowels, and I will establish his kingdom.

13 He shall build an house for my name, and I will stablish the throne of his kingdom for ever.

14 I will be his father, and he shall be my son. If he commit iniquity, I will chasten him with the rod of men, and with the stripes of the children of men:

15 But my mercy shall not depart away from him, as I took *it* from Saul, whom I put away before thee.

16 And thine house and thy kingdom shall be established for ever before thee: thy throne shall be established for ever.

17 According to all these words, and according to all this vision, so did Nāthan speak unto David.

18 ¶Then went king David in, and sat before the LORD, and he said, Who *am* I, O Lord GOD? and what *is* my house, that thou hast brought me hitherto?

19 And this was yet a small thing in thy sight, O Lord GOD; but thou hast spoken also of thy servant's house for a great while to come. And *is* this the manner of man, O Lord GOD?

20 And what can David say more unto thee? for thou, Lord GOD, knowest thy servant.

21 For thy word's sake, and according to thine own heart, hast thou done all these great things, to make thy servant know *them*.

22 Wherefore thou art great, O LORD God: for *there is* none like thee, neither *is there any* God beside thee, according to all that we have heard with our ears.

23 And what one nation in the earth *is* like thy people, *even* like Israel, whom God went to redeem for a people to himself, and to make him a name, and to do for you great things and terrible, for thy land, before thy people, which thou redeemedst to thee from Egypt, *from* the nations and their gods?

24 For thou hast confirmed to thyself thy people Israel *to be* a people unto thee for ever: and thou, LORD, art become their God.

25 And now, O LORD God, the word that thou hast spoken concerning thy servant, and concerning his house, establish *it* for ever, and do as thou hast said.

26 And let thy name be magnified for ever, saying, The LORD of hosts *is* the God over Israel: and let the house of thy servant David be established before thee.

27 For thou, O LORD of hosts, God of Israel, hast revealed to thy servant,

saying, I will build thee an house: therefore hath thy servant found in his heart to pray this prayer unto thee.

28 And now, O Lord GOD, thou *art* that God, and thy words be true, and thou hast promised this goodness unto thy servant:

29 Therefore now let it please thee to bless the house of thy servant, that it may continue for ever before thee: for thou, O Lord GOD, hast spoken *it*: and with thy blessing let the house of thy servant be blessed for ever.

CHAPTER 8

AND after this it came to pass, that David smote the Philistines, and subdued them: and David took Mē'thĕg-ăm'-mah out of the hand of the Philistines.

2 And he smote Moab, and measured them with a line, casting them down to the ground; even with two lines measured he to put to death, and with one full line to keep alive. And *so* the Moabites became David's servants, *and* brought gifts.

3 ¶David smote also Hăd-ad-ē'zer, the son of Rē'hŏb, king of Zōbah, as he went to recover his border at the river Eū-phrā'tēš.

4 And David took from him a thousand *chariots*, and seven hundred horsemen, and twenty thousand footmen: and David houghed all the chariot *horses*, but reserved of them *for* an hundred chariots.

5 And when the Syrians of Damascus came to succour Hăd-ad-ē'zer king of Zōbah, David slew of the Syrians two and twenty thousand men.

6 Then David put garrisons in Syria of Damascus: and the Syrians became servants to David, *and* brought gifts. And the LORD preserved David whithersoever he went.

7 And David took the shields of gold that were on the servants of Hăd-ad-ē'zer, and brought them to Jerusalem.

8 And from Bē'tah, and from Ber'ō-thaī, cities of Hăd-ad-ē'zer, king David took exceeding much brass.

9 ¶When Tō'ī king of Hā'măth heard that David had smitten all the host of Hăd-ad-ē'zer,

10 Then Tō'ī sent Joram his son unto king David, to salute him, and to bless him, because he had fought against Hăd-ad-ē'zer, and smitten him: for Hăd-ad-ē'zer had wars with Tō'ī. And *Joram* brought with him vessels of silver, and vessels of gold, and vessels of brass:

11 Which also king David did dedicate unto the LORD, with the silver and gold that he had dedicated of all nations which he subdued;

12 Of Syria, and of Moab, and of the children of Ammon, and of the Philistines, and of Ăm'a-lĕk, and of the spoil of Hăd-ad-ē'zer, son of Rē'hŏb, king of Zōbah.

13 And David gat *him* a name when he returned from smiting of the Syrians in the valley of salt, *being* eighteen thousand *men*.

14 ¶And he put garrisons in Ēdom; throughout all Ēdom put he garrisons, and all they of Ēdom became David's servants. And the LORD preserved David whithersoever he went.

15 And David reigned over all Israel; and David executed judgment and justice unto all his people.

16 And Jō'ăb the son of Zer-ū-i'ah *was* over the host; and Je-hŏsh'a-phăt the son of A-hī'lud *was* recorder;

17 And Ză'dŏk the son of A-hī'tŭb, and A-hĭm'e-lĕch the son of Ă-bī'a-thar, *were* the priests; and Se-ra-ī'ah *was* the scribe;

18 And Be-nā'iah the son of Je-hoi'a-da *was over* both the Chĕr'e-thītes and the Pĕl'e-thītes; and David's sons were chief rulers.

CHAPTER 9

AND David said, Is there yet any that is left of the house of Saul, that I may shew him kindness for Jonathan's sake?

2 And *there was* of the house of Saul a servant whose name *was* Zī'ba. And when they had called him unto David, the king said unto him, *Art* thou Zī'ba? And he said, Thy servant *is he*.

3 And the king said, *Is* there not yet any of the house of Saul, that I may shew the kindness of God unto him? And Zī'ba said unto the king, Jonathan hath yet a son, *which is* lame on *his* feet.

4 And the king said unto him, Where *is* he? And Zī'ba said unto the king, Behold, he *is* in the house of Mā'chĭr, the son of Ăm'mī-el, in Lō-dē'bar.

5 Then king David sent, and fetched him out of the house of Mā'chĭr, the son of Ăm'mī-el, from Lō-dē'bar.

6 Now when Me-phĭb'o-shĕth, the son of Jonathan, the son of Saul, was come unto David, he fell on his face, and did reverence. And David said, Me-phĭb'o-shĕth. And he answered, Behold thy servant!

7 ¶And David said unto him, Fear not: for I will surely shew thee kindness for Jonathan thy father's sake, and will restore thee all the land of Saul thy

father; and thou shalt eat bread at my
table continually.
8 And he bowed himself, and said,
What *is* thy servant, that thou should-
est look upon such a dead dog as I *am?*
9 ¶Then the king called to Zī′ba,
Saul's servant, and said unto him, I
have given unto thy master's son all
that pertained to Saul and to all his
house.
10 Thou therefore, and thy sons, and
thy servants, shall till the land for him,
and thou shalt bring in *the fruits,* that
thy master's son may have food to eat:
but Me-phĭb′o-shĕth thy master's son
shall eat bread alway at my table. Now
Zī′ba had fifteen sons and twenty ser-
vants.
11 Then said Zī′ba unto the king, Ac-
cording to all that my lord the king hath
commanded his servant, so shall thy
servant do. As for Me-phĭb′o-shĕth,
said the king, he shall eat at my table,
as one of the king's sons.
12 And Me-phĭb′o-shĕth had a young
son, whose name *was* Mī′cha. And all
that dwelt in the house of Zī′ba *were*
servants unto Me-phĭb′o-shĕth.
13 So Me-phĭb′o-shĕth dwelt in Jeru-
salem: for he did eat continually at the
king's table; and was lame on both his
feet.

CHAPTER 10

AND it came to pass after this, that the
king of the children of Ammon died,
and Hā′nun his son reigned in his stead.
2 Then said David, I will shew kind-
ness unto Hā′nun the son of Nā′hăsh, as
his father shewed kindness unto me.
And David sent to comfort him by the
hand of his servants for his father. And
David's servants came into the land of
the children of Ammon.
3 And the princes of the children of
Ammon said unto Hā′nun their lord,
Thinkest thou that David doth honour
thy father, that he hath sent comforters
unto thee? hath not David *rather* sent
his servants unto thee to search the
city, and to spy it out, and to overthrow
it?
4 Wherefore Hā′nun took David's
servants, and shaved off the one half of
their beards, and cut off their garments
in the middle, *even* to their buttocks,
and sent them away.
5 When they told *it* unto David, he
sent to meet them, because the men
were greatly ashamed: and the king
said, Tarry at Jericho until your beards
be grown, and *then* return.
6 ¶And when the children of Ammon
saw that they stank before David, the
children of Ammon sent and hired the
Syrians of Bĕth-rē′hŏb, and the Syrians
of Zō′ba, twenty thousand footmen,
and of king Mā′a-cah a thousand men,
and of Ĭsh′-tŏb twelve thousand men.
7 And when David heard of *it,* he sent
Jō′ăb, and all the host of the mighty
men.
8 And the children of Ammon came
out, and put the battle in array at the
entering in of the gate: and the Syrians
of Zō′ba, and of Rē′hŏb, and Ĭsh′-tŏb,
and Mā′a-cah, *were* by themselves in
the field.
9 When Jō′ăb saw that the front of
the battle was against him before and
behind, he chose of all the choice *men*
of Israel, and put *them* in array against
the Syrians:
10 And the rest of the people he deliv-
ered into the hand of A-bī′shaī his
brother, that he might put *them* in ar-
ray against the children of Ammon.
11 And he said, If the Syrians be too
strong for me, then thou shalt help me:
but if the children of Ammon be too
strong for thee, then I will come and
help thee.
12 Be of good courage, and let us play
the men for our people, and for the
cities of our God: and the LORD do that
which seemeth him good.
13 And Jō′ăb drew nigh, and the
people that *were* with him, unto the
battle against the Syrians: and they
fled before him.
14 And when the children of Ammon
saw that the Syrians were fled, then
fled they also before A-bī′shaī, and en-
tered into the city. So Jō′ăb returned
from the children of Ammon, and came
to Jerusalem.
15 ¶And when the Syrians saw that
they were smitten before Israel, they
gathered themselves together.
16 And Hăd-ar-ē′zer sent, and
brought out the Syrians that *were*
beyond the river: and they came to Hē′-
lam; and Shō′băch the captain of the
host of Hăd-ar-ē′zer *went* before them.
17 And when it was told David, he
gathered all Israel together, and passed
over Jordan, and came to Hē′lam. And
the Syrians set themselves in array
against David, and fought with him.
18 And the Syrians fled before Israel;
and David slew *the men of* seven
hundred chariots of the Syrians, and
forty thousand horsemen, and smote
Shō′băch the captain of their host, who
died there.
19 And when all the kings *that were*
servants to Hăd-ar-ē′zer saw that they
were smitten before Israel, they made
peace with Israel, and served them. So

the Syrians feared to help the children
of Ammon any more.

CHAPTER 11

AND it came to pass, after the year was
expired, at the time when kings go
forth *to battle*, that David sent Jō'ăb,
and his servants with him, and all
Israel; and they destroyed the children
of Ammon, and besieged Răb'bah. But
David tarried still at Jerusalem.
2 ¶And it came to pass in an evening-
tide, that David arose from off his bed,
and walked upon the roof of the king's
house: and from the roof he saw a wom-
an washing herself; and the woman
was very beautiful to look upon.
3 And David sent and enquired after
the woman. And *one* said, *Is* not this
Băth'-shē-ba, the daughter of E-lī'am,
the wife of Ū-rī'ah the Hittite?
4 And David sent messengers, and
took her; and she came in unto him, and
he lay with her; for she was purified
from her uncleanness: and she re-
turned unto her house.
5 And the woman conceived, and
sent and told David, and said, I *am* with
child.
6 And David sent to Jō'ăb, *saying*,
Send me Ū-rī'ah the Hittite. And Jō'ăb
sent Ū-rī'ah to David.
7 And when Ū-rī'ah was come unto
him, David demanded *of him* how Jō'ăb
did, and how the people did, and
how the war prospered.
8 And David said to Ū-rī'ah, Go down
to thy house, and wash thy feet. And Ū-
rī'ah departed out of the king's house,
and there followed him a mess *of meat*
from the king.
9 But Ū-rī'ah slept at the door of the
king's house with all the servants of his
lord, and went not down to his house.
10 And when they had told David,
saying, Ū-rī'ah went not down unto his
house, David said unto Ū-rī'ah, Camest
thou not from *thy* journey? why *then*
didst thou not go down unto thine
house?
11 And Ū-rī'ah said unto David, The
ark, and Israel, and Jūdah, abide in
tents; and my lord Jō'ăb, and the ser-
vants of my lord, are encamped in the
open fields; shall I then go into mine
house, to eat and to drink, and to lie
with my wife? *as* thou livest, and *as* thy
soul liveth, I will not do this thing.
12 And David said to Ū-rī'ah, Tarry
here to day also, and tomorrow I will let
thee depart. So Ū-rī'ah abode in Jeru-
salem that day, and the morrow.
13 And when David had called him,
he did eat and drink before him; and he
made him drunk: and at even he went
out to lie on his bed with the servants of
his lord, but went not down to his
house.
14 ¶And it came to pass in the morn-
ing, that David wrote a letter to Jō'ăb,
and sent *it* by the hand of Ū-rī'ah.
15 And he wrote in the letter, saying,
Set ye Ū-rī'ah in the forefront of the
hottest battle, and retire ye from him,
that he may be smitten, and die.
16 And it came to pass, when Jō'ăb
observed the city, that he assigned Ū-
rī'ah unto a place where he knew that
valiant men *were*.
17 And the men of the city went out,
and fought with Jō'ăb: and there fell
some of the people of the servants of
David; and Ū-rī'ah the Hittite died also.
18 ¶Then Jō'ăb sent and told David
all the things concerning the war;
19 And charged the messenger,
saying, When thou hast made an end of
telling the matters of the war unto the
king,
20 And if so be that the king's wrath
arise, and he say unto thee, Wherefore
approached ye so nigh unto the city
when ye did fight? knew ye not that
they would shoot from the wall?
21 Who smote A-bĭm'e-lĕch the son
of Je-rŭb'be-shĕth? did not a woman
cast a piece of a millstone upon him
from the wall, that he died in Thē'bez?
why went ye nigh the wall? then say
thou, Thy servant Ū-rī'ah the Hittite is
dead also.
22 ¶So the messenger went, and
came and shewed David all that Jō'ăb
had sent him for.
23 And the messenger said unto Da-
vid, Surely the men prevailed against
us, and came out unto us into the field,
and we were upon them even unto the
entering of the gate.
24 And the shooters shot from off the
wall upon thy servants; and *some* of the
king's servants be dead, and thy ser-
vant Ū-rī'ah the Hittite is dead also.
25 Then David said unto the messen-
ger, Thus shalt thou say unto Jō'ăb, Let
not this thing displease thee, for the
sword devoureth one as well as an-
other: make thy battle more strong
against the city, and overthrow it: and
encourage thou him.
26 ¶And when the wife of Ū-rī'ah
heard that Ū-rī'ah her husband was
dead, she mourned for her husband.
27 And when the mourning was past,
David sent and fetched her to his
house, and she became his wife, and
bare him a son. But the thing that David
had done displeased the LORD.

CHAPTER 12

AND the LORD sent Nāthan unto David.
And he came unto him, and said unto
him, There were two men in one city;
the one rich, and the other poor.
2 The rich *man* had exceeding many
flocks and herds:
3 But the poor *man* had nothing, save
one little ewe lamb, which he had
bought and nourished up: and it grew
up together with him, and with his
children; it did eat of his own meat, and
drank of his own cup, and lay in his bo-
som, and was unto him as a daughter.
4 And there came a traveller unto the
rich man, and he spared to take of his
own flock and of his own herd, to dress
for the wayfaring man that was come
unto him; but took the poor man's
lamb, and dressed it for the man that
was come to him.
5 And David's anger was greatly
kindled against the man; and he said to
Nāthan, *As* the LORD liveth, the man
that hath done this *thing* shall surely
die:
6 And he shall restore the lamb four-
fold, because he did this thing, and be-
cause he had no pity.
7 ¶And Nāthan said to David, Thou
art the man. Thus saith the LORD God of
Israel, I anointed thee king over Israel,
and I delivered thee out of the hand of
Saul;
8 And I gave thee thy master's house,
and thy master's wives into thy bosom,
and gave thee the house of Israel and of
Jūdah; and if *that had been* too little, I
would moreover have given unto thee
such and such things.
9 Wherefore hast thou despised the
commandment of the LORD, to do evil
in his sight? thou hast killed Ū-rī'ah the
Hittite with the sword, and hast taken
his wife *to be* thy wife, and hast slain
him with the sword of the children of
Ammon.
10 Now therefore the sword shall nev-
er depart from thine house; because
thou hast despised me, and hast taken
the wife of Ū-rī'ah the Hittite to be thy
wife.
11 Thus saith the LORD, Behold, I will
raise up evil against thee out of thine
own house, and I will take thy wives
before thine eyes, and give *them* unto
thy neighbour, and he shall lie with thy
wives in the sight of this sun.
12 For thou didst *it* secretly: but I will
do this thing before all Israel, and be-
fore the sun.
13 And David said unto Nāthan, I
have sinned against the LORD. And Nā-
than said unto David, The LORD also
hath put away thy sin; thou shalt not
die.
14 Howbeit, because by this deed
thou hast given great occasion to the
enemies of the LORD to blaspheme, the
child also *that is* born unto thee shall
surely die.
15 ¶And Nāthan departed unto his
house. And the LORD struck the child
that Ū-rī'ah's wife bare unto David, and
it was very sick.
16 David therefore besought God for
the child; and David fasted, and went
in, and lay all night upon the earth.
17 And the elders of his house arose,
and went to him, to raise him up from
the earth: but he would not, neither did
he eat bread with them.
18 And it came to pass on the seventh
day, that the child died. And the ser-
vants of David feared to tell him that
the child was dead: for they said, Be-
hold, while the child was yet alive, we
spake unto him, and he would not hear-
ken unto our voice: how will he then
vex himself, if we tell him that the child
is dead?
19 But when David saw that his ser-
vants whispered, David perceived that
the child was dead: therefore David
said unto his servants, Is the child
dead? And they said, He is dead.
20 Then David arose from the earth,
and washed, and anointed *himself*, and
changed his apparel, and came into the
house of the LORD, and worshipped:
then he came to his own house; and
when he required, they set bread be-
fore him, and he did eat.
21 Then said his servants unto him,
What thing *is* this that thou hast done?
thou didst fast and weep for the child,
while it was alive; but when the child
was dead, thou didst rise and eat bread.
22 And he said, While the child was
yet alive, I fasted and wept: for I said,
Who can tell *whether* GOD will be gra-
cious to me, that the child may live?
23 But now he is dead, wherefore
should I fast? can I bring him back
again? I shall go to him, but he shall not
return to me.
24 ¶And David comforted Băth'-shē-
ba his wife, and went in unto her, and
lay with her: and she bare a son, and he
called his name Sŏlomon: and the LORD
loved him.
25 And he sent by the hand of Nāthan
the prophet; and he called his name
Jĕd-i-dī'ah, because of the LORD.
26 ¶And Jō'ăb fought against Răb'-
bah of the children of Ammon, and
took the royal city.
27 And Jō'ăb sent messengers to Da-
vid, and said, I have fought against

Răb'bah, and have taken the city of waters.

28 Now therefore gather the rest of the people together, and encamp against the city, and take it: lest I take the city, and it be called after my name.

29 And David gathered all the people together, and went to Răb'bah, and fought against it, and took it.

30 And he took their king's crown from off his head, the weight whereof *was* a talent of gold with the precious stones: and it was *set* on David's head. And he brought forth the spoil of the city in great abundance.

31 And he brought forth the people that *were* therein, and put *them* under saws, and under harrows of iron, and under axes of iron, and made them pass through the brick-kiln: and thus did he unto all the cities of the children of Ammon. So David and all the people returned unto Jerusalem.

CHAPTER 13

AND it came to pass after this, that Ăb'sa-lom the son of David had a fair sister, whose name *was* Tā'mar; and Ămnŏn the son of David loved her.

2 And Ămnŏn was so vexed, that he fell sick for his sister Tā'mar; for she *was* a virgin; and Ămnŏn thought it hard for him to do anything to her.

3 But Ămnŏn had a friend, whose name *was* Jōn'a-dăb, the son of Shĭm'e-ah David's brother: and Jōn'a-dăb *was* a very subtil man.

4 And he said unto him, Why *art* thou, *being* the king's son, lean from day to day? wilt thou not tell me? And Ămnŏn said unto him, I love Tā'mar, my brother Ăb'sa-lom's sister.

5 And Jōn'a-dăb said unto him, Lay thee down on thy bed, and make thyself sick: and when thy father cometh to see thee, say unto him, I pray thee, let my sister Tā'mar come, and give me meat, and dress the meat in my sight, that I may see *it*, and eat *it* at her hand.

6 So Ămnŏn lay down, and made himself sick: and when the king was come to see him, Ămnŏn said unto the king, I pray thee, let Tā'mar my sister come, and make me a couple of cakes in my sight, that I may eat at her hand.

7 Then David sent home to Tā'mar, saying, Go now to thy brother Ămnŏn's house, and dress him meat.

8 So Tā'mar went to her brother Ămnŏn's house; and he was laid down. And she took flour, and kneaded *it*, and made cakes in his sight, and did bake the cakes.

9 And she took a pan, and poured *them* out before him; but he refused to eat. And Ămnŏn said, Have out all men from me. And they went out every man from him.

10 And Ămnŏn said unto Tā'mar, Bring the meat into the chamber, that I may eat of thine hand. And Tā'mar took the cakes which she had made, and brought *them* into the chamber to Ămnŏn her brother.

11 And when she had brought *them* unto him to eat, he took hold of her, and said unto her, Come lie with me, my sister.

12 And she answered him, Nay, my brother, do not force me; for no such thing ought to be done in Israel: do not thou this folly.

13 And I, whither shall I cause my shame to go? and as for thee, thou shalt be as one of the fools in Israel. Now therefore, I pray thee, speak unto the king; for he will not withhold me from thee.

14 Howbeit he would not hearken unto her voice: but, being stronger than she, forced her, and lay with her.

15 ¶Then Ămnŏn hated her exceedingly; so that the hatred wherewith he hated her *was* greater than the love wherewith he had loved her. And Ămnŏn said unto her, Arise, be gone.

16 And she said unto him, *There is* no cause: this evil in sending me away *is* greater than the other that thou didst unto me. But he would not hearken unto her.

17 Then he called his servant that ministered unto him, and said, Put now this *woman* out from me, and bolt the door after her.

18 And *she had* a garment of divers colours upon her: for with such robes were the king's daughters *that were* virgins apparelled. Then his servant brought her out, and bolted the door after her.

19 ¶And Tā'mar put ashes on her head, and rent her garment of divers colours that *was* on her, and laid her hand on her head, and went on crying.

20 And Ăb'sa-lom her brother said unto her, Hath Ămnŏn thy brother been with thee? but hold now thy peace, my sister: he *is* thy brother; regard not this thing. So Tā'mar remained desolate in her brother Ăb'sa-lom's house.

21 ¶But when king David heard of all these things, he was very wroth.

22 And Ăb'sa-lom spake unto his brother Ămnŏn neither good nor bad: for Ăb'sa-lom hated Ămnŏn, because he had forced his sister Tā'mar.

23 ¶And it came to pass after two full years, that Ăb'sa-lom had sheepshearers in Bā'al-hā'zôr, which *is* beside

Ē'phra-im: and Ăb'sa-lom invited all the king's sons.

24 And Ăb'sa-lom came to the king, and said, Behold now, thy servant hath sheepshearers; let the king, I beseech thee, and his servants go with thy servant.

25 And the king said to Ăb'sa-lom, Nay, my son, let us not all now go, lest we be chargeable unto thee. And he pressed him: howbeit he would not go, but blessed him.

26 Then said Ăb'sa-lom, If not, I pray thee, let my brother Ămnŏn go with us. And the king said unto him, Why should he go with thee?

27 But Ăb'sa-lom pressed him, that he let Ămnŏn and all the king's sons go with him.

28 ¶Now Ăb'sa-lom had commanded his servants, saying, Mark ye now when Ămnŏn's heart is merry with wine, and when I say unto you, Smite Ămnŏn; then kill him, fear not: have not I commanded you? be courageous, and be valiant.

29 And the servants of Ăb'sa-lom did unto Ămnŏn as Ăb'sa-lom had commanded. Then all the king's sons arose, and every man gat him up upon his mule, and fled.

30 ¶And it came to pass, while they were in the way, that tidings came to David, saying, Ăb'sa-lom hath slain all the king's sons, and there is not one of them left.

31 Then the king arose, and tare his garments, and lay on the earth; and all his servants stood by with their clothes rent.

32 And Jōn'a-dăb, the son of Shĭm'e-ah David's brother, answered and said, Let not my lord suppose *that* they have slain all the young men the king's sons; for Ămnŏn only is dead: for by the appointment of Ăb'sa-lom this hath been determined from the day that he forced his sister Tā'mar.

33 Now therefore let not my lord the king take the thing to his heart, to think that all the king's sons are dead: for Ămnŏn only is dead.

34 But Ăb'sa-lom fled. And the young man that kept the watch lifted up his eyes, and looked, and, behold, there came much people by the way of the hill side behind him.

35 And Jōn'a-dăb said unto the king, Behold, the king's sons come: as thy servant said, so it is.

36 And it came to pass, as soon as he had made an end of speaking, that, behold, the king's sons came, and lifted up their voice and wept: and the king also and all his servants wept very sore.

37 ¶But Ăb'sa-lom fled, and went to Tăl'maī, the son of Ăm-mī'hŭd, king of Gĕ'shur. And *David* mourned for his son every day.

38 So Ăb'sa-lom fled, and went to Gĕ'shur, and was there three years.

39 And *the soul of* king David longed to go forth unto Ăb'sa-lom: for he was comforted concerning Ămnŏn, seeing he was dead.

CHAPTER 14

NOW Jō'ăb the son of Zer-ū-i'ah perceived that the king's heart *was* toward Ăb'sa-lom.

2 And Jō'ăb sent to Te-kō'ah, and fetched thence a wise woman, and said unto her, I pray thee, feign thyself to be a mourner, and put on now mourning apparel, and anoint not thyself with oil, but be as a woman that had a long time mourned for the dead:

3 And come to the king, and speak on this manner unto him. So Jō'ăb put the words in her mouth.

4 ¶And when the woman of Te-kō'ah spake to the king, she fell on her face to the ground, and did obeisance, and said, Help, O king.

5 And the king said unto her, What aileth thee? And she answered, I *am* indeed a widow woman, and mine husband is dead.

6 And thy handmaid had two sons, and they two strove together in the field, and *there was* none to part them, but the one smote the other, and slew him.

7 And, behold, the whole family is risen against thine handmaid, and they said, Deliver him that smote his brother, that we may kill him, for the life of his brother whom he slew; and we will destroy the heir also: and so they shall quench my coal which is left, and shall not leave to my husband *neither* name nor remainder upon the earth.

8 And the king said unto the woman, Go to thine house, and I will give charge concerning thee.

9 And the woman of Te-kō'ah said unto the king, My lord, O king, the iniquity *be* on me, and on my father's house: and the king and his throne *be* guiltless.

10 And the king said, Whosoever saith *ought* unto thee, bring him to me, and he shall not touch thee any more.

11 Then said she, I pray thee, let the king remember the LORD thy God, that thou wouldest not suffer the revengers of blood to destroy any more, lest they destroy my son. And he said, *As* the

LORD liveth, there shall not one hair of thy son fall to the earth.

12 Then the woman said, Let thine handmaid, I pray thee, speak *one* word unto my lord the king. And he said, Say on.

13 And the woman said, Wherefore then hast thou thought such a thing against the people of God? for the king doth speak this thing as one which is faulty, in that the king doth not fetch home again his banished.

14 For we must needs die, and *are* as water spilt on the ground, which cannot be gathered up again; neither doth God respect *any* person: yet doth he devise means, that his banished be not expelled from him.

15 Now therefore that I am come to speak of this thing unto my lord the king, *it is* because the people have made me afraid: and thy handmaid said, I will now speak unto the king; it may be that the king will perform the request of his handmaid.

16 For the king will hear, to deliver his handmaid out of the hand of the man *that would* destroy me and my son together out of the inheritance of God.

17 Then thine handmaid said, The word of my lord the king shall now be comfortable: for as an angel of God, so *is* my lord the king to discern good and bad: therefore the LORD thy God will be with thee.

18 Then the king answered and said unto the woman, Hide not from me, I pray thee, the thing that I shall ask thee. And the woman said, Let my lord the king now speak.

19 And the king said, *Is not* the hand of Jō'ăb with thee in all this? And the woman answered and said, *As* thy soul liveth, my lord the king, none can turn to the right hand or to the left from ought that my lord the king hath spoken: for thy servant Jō'ăb, he bade me, and he put all these words in the mouth of thine handmaid:

20 To fetch about this form of speech hath thy servant Jō'ăb done this thing: and my lord *is* wise, according to the wisdom of an angel of God, to know all *things* that *are* in the earth.

21 ¶And the king said unto Jō'ăb, Behold now, I have done this thing: go therefore, bring the young man Ăb'sa-lom again.

22 And Jō'ăb fell to the ground on his face, and bowed himself, and thanked the king: and Jō'ăb said, To day thy servant knoweth that I have found grace in thy sight, my lord, O king, in that the king hath fulfilled the request of his servant.

23 So Jō'ăb arose and went to Gĕ'-shur, and brought Ăb'sa-lom to Jerusalem.

24 And the king said, Let him turn to his own house, and let him not see my face. So Ăb'sa-lom returned to his own house, and saw not the king's face.

25 ¶But in all Israel there was none to be so much praised as Ăb'sa-lom for his beauty: from the sole of his foot even to the crown of his head there was no blemish in him.

26 And when he polled his head, (for it was at every year's end that he polled *it:* because *the hair* was heavy on him, therefore he polled it:) he weighed the hair of his head at two hundred shekels after the king's weight.

27 And unto Ăb'sa-lom there were born three sons, and one daughter, whose name *was* Tā'mar: she was a woman of a fair countenance.

28 ¶So Ăb'sa-lom dwelt two full years in Jerusalem, and saw not the king's face.

29 Therefore Ăb'sa-lom sent for Jō'ăb, to have sent him to the king; but he would not come to him: and when he sent again the second time, he would not come.

30 Therefore he said unto his servants, See, Jō'ăb's field is near mine, and he hath barley there; go and set it on fire. And Ăb'sa-lom's servants set the field on fire.

31 Then Jō'ăb arose, and came to Ăb'sa-lom unto *his* house, and said unto him, Wherefore have thy servants set my field on fire?

32 And Ăb'sa-lom answered Jō'ăb, Behold, I sent unto thee, saying, Come hither, that I may send thee to the king, to say, Wherefore am I come from Gĕ'shur? *it had been* good for me *to have been* there still: now therefore let me see the king's face; and if there be *any* iniquity in me, let him kill me.

33 So Jō'ăb came to the king, and told him: and when he had called for Ăb'salom, he came to the king, and bowed himself on his face to the ground before the king: and the king kissed Ăb'salom.

CHAPTER 15

AND it came to pass after this, that Ăb'sa-lom prepared him chariots and horses, and fifty men to run before him.

2 And Ăb'sa-lom rose up early, and stood beside the way of the gate: and it was *so,* that when any man that had a controversy came to the king for judgment, then Ăb'sa-lom called unto him, and said, Of what city *art* thou? And he

said, Thy servant *is* of one of the tribes of Israel.

3 And Ăb′sa-lom said unto him, See, thy matters *are* good and right; but *there is* no man *deputed* of the king to hear thee.

4 Ăb′sa-lom said moreover, Oh that I were made judge in the land, that every man which hath any suit or cause might come unto me, and I would do him justice!

5 And it was *so*, that when any man came nigh *to him* to do him obeisance, he put forth his hand, and took him, and kissed him.

6 And on this manner did Ăb′sa-lom to all Israel that came to the king for judgment: so Ăb′sa-lom stole the hearts of the men of Israel.

7 ¶And it came to pass after forty years, that Ăb′sa-lom said unto the king, I pray thee, let me go and pay my vow, which I have vowed unto the LORD, in Hēbron.

8 For thy servant vowed a vow while I abode at Gĕ′shur in Syria, saying, If the LORD shall bring me again indeed to Jerusalem, then I will serve the LORD.

9 And the king said unto him, Go in peace. So he arose, and went to Hē-bron.

10 ¶But Ăb′sa-lom sent spies throughout all the tribes of Israel, saying, As soon as ye hear the sound of the trumpet, then ye shall say, Ăb′sa-lom reigneth in Hēbron.

11 And with Ăb′sa-lom went two hundred men out of Jerusalem, *that were* called; and they went in their simplicity, and they knew not any thing.

12 And Ăb′sa-lom sent for A-hĭth′o-phĕl the Gī′lo-nīte, David's counsellor, from his city, *even* from Gī′lōh, while he offered sacrifices. And the conspiracy was strong; for the people increased continually with Ăb′sa-lom.

13 ¶And there came a messenger to David, saying, The hearts of the men of Israel are after Ăb′sa-lom.

14 And David said unto all his servants that *were* with him at Jerusalem, Arise, and let us flee; for we shall not *else* escape from Ăb′sa-lom: make speed to depart, lest he overtake us suddenly, and bring evil upon us, and smite the city with the edge of the sword.

15 And the king's servants said unto the king, Behold, thy servants *are ready to do* whatsoever my lord the king shall appoint.

16 And the king went forth, and all his household after him. And the king left ten women, *which were* concubines, to keep the house.

17 And the king went forth, and all the people after him, and tarried in a place that was far off.

18 And all his servants passed on beside him; and all the Chĕr′e-thītes, and all the Pĕl′e-thītes, and all the Gĭt′tītes, six hundred men which came after him from Gath, passed on before the king.

19 ¶Then said the king to Ĭt′ta-ī the Gĭt′tīte, Wherefore goest thou also with us? return to thy place, and abide with the king: for thou *art* a stranger, and also an exile.

20 Whereas thou camest *but* yesterday, should I this day make thee go up and down with us? seeing I go whither I may, return thou, and take back thy brethren: mercy and truth *be* with thee.

21 And Ĭt′ta-ī answered the king, and said, *As* the LORD liveth, and *as* my lord the king liveth, surely in what place my lord the king shall be, whether in death or life, even there also will thy servant be.

22 And David said to Ĭt′ta-ī, Go and pass over. And Ĭt′ta-ī the Gĭt′tīte passed over, and all his men, and all the little ones that *were* with him.

23 And all the country wept with a loud voice, and all the people passed over: the king also himself passed over the brook Kidron, and all the people passed over, toward the way of the wilderness.

24 ¶And lo Zā′dŏk also, and all the Lēvītes *were* with him, bearing the ark of the covenant of God: and they set down the ark of God; and Ă-bī′a-thar went up, until all the people had done passing out of the city.

25 And the king said unto Zā′dŏk, Carry back the ark of God into the city: if I shall find favour in the eyes of the LORD, he will bring me again, and shew me *both* it, and his habitation:

26 But if he thus say, I have no delight in thee; behold, *here am* I, let him do to me as seemeth good unto him.

27 The king said also unto Zā′dŏk the priest, *Art not* thou a seer? return into the city in peace, and your two sons with you, A-hĭm′ă-az thy son, and Jonathan the son of Ă-bī′a-thar.

28 See, I will tarry in the plain of the wilderness, until there come word from you to certify me.

29 Zā′dŏk therefore and Ă-bī′a-thar carried the ark of God again to Jerusalem: and they tarried there.

30 ¶And David went up by the ascent of *mount* Olivet, and wept as he went up, and had his head covered, and he went barefoot: and all the people that

was with him covered every man his head, and they went up, weeping as they went up.

31 And *one* told David, saying, A-hĭth'o-phĕl *is* among the conspirators with Ăb'sa-lom. And David said, O LORD, I pray thee, turn the counsel of A-hĭth'o-phĕl into foolishness.

32 ¶And it came to pass, that *when* David was come to the top *of the mount*, where he worshipped God, behold, Hu'shaī the Ăr'chīte came to meet him with his coat rent, and earth upon his head:

33 Unto whom David said, If thou passest on with me, then thou shalt be a burden unto me:

34 But if thou return to the city, and say unto Ăb'sa-lom, I will be thy servant, O king; *as* I *have been* thy father's servant hitherto, so *will* I now also *be* thy servant: then mayest thou for me defeat the counsel of A-hĭth'o-phĕl.

35 And *hast thou* not there with thee Zā'dŏk and Ă-bī'a-thar the priests? therefore it shall be, *that* what thing soever thou shalt hear out of the king's house, thou shalt tell *it* to Zā'dŏk and Ă-bī'a-thar the priests.

36 Behold, *they have* there with them their two sons, A-hĭm'ā-az Zā'dŏk's *son*, and Jonathan Ă-bī'a-thar's *son*; and by them ye shall send unto me every thing that ye can hear.

37 So Hu'shaī David's friend came into the city, and Ăb'sa-lom came into Jerusalem.

CHAPTER 16

AND when David was a little past the top *of the hill*, behold, Zī'ba the servant of Me-phĭb'o-shĕth met him, with a couple of asses saddled, and upon them two hundred *loaves* of bread, and an hundred bunches of raisins, and an hundred of summer fruits, and a bottle of wine.

2 And the king said unto Zī'ba, What meanest thou by these? And Zī'ba said, The asses *be* for the king's household to ride on; and the bread and summer fruit for the young men to eat; and the wine, that such as be faint in the wilderness may drink.

3 And the king said, And where *is* thy master's son? And Zī'ba said unto the king, Behold, he abideth at Jerusalem: for he said, To day shall the house of Israel restore me the kingdom of my father.

4 Then said the king to Zī'ba, Behold, thine *are* all that *pertained* unto Me-phĭb'o-shĕth. And Zī'ba said, I humbly beseech thee *that* I may find grace in thy sight, my lord, O king.

5 ¶And when king David came to Ba-hû'rĭm, behold, thence came out a man of the family of the house of Saul, whose name *was* Shĭm'e-ī, the son of Gē'ra: he came forth, and cursed still as he came.

6 And he cast stones at David, and at all the servants of king David: and all the people and all the mighty men *were* on his right hand and on his left.

7 And thus said Shĭm'e-ī when he cursed, Come out, come out, thou bloody man, and thou man of Bē'lĭ-al:

8 The LORD hath returned upon thee all the blood of the house of Saul, in whose stead thou hast reigned; and the LORD hath delivered the kingdom into the hand of Ăb'sa-lom thy son: and, behold, thou *art taken* in thy mischief, because thou *art* a bloody man.

9 ¶Then said A-bī'shaī the son of Zer-ū-i'ah unto the king, Why should this dead dog curse my lord the king? let me go over, I pray thee, and take off his head.

10 And the king said, What have I to do with you, ye sons of Zer-ū-i'ah? so let him curse, because the LORD hath said unto him, Curse David. Who shall then say, Wherefore hast thou done so?

11 And David said to A-bī'shaī, and to all his servants, Behold, my son, which came forth of my bowels, seeketh my life: how much more now *may this* Benjamite *do it?* let him alone, and let him curse; for the LORD hath bidden him.

12 It may be that the LORD will look on mine affliction, and that the LORD will requite me good for his cursing this day.

13 And as David and his men went by the way, Shĭm'e-ī went along on the hill's side over against him, and cursed as he went, and threw stones at him, and cast dust.

14 And the king, and all the people that *were* with him, came weary, and refreshed themselves there.

15 ¶And Ăb'sa-lom, and all the people the men of Israel, came to Jerusalem, and A-hĭth'o-phĕl with him.

16 And it came to pass, when Hu'shaī the Ăr'chīte, David's friend, was come unto Ăb'sa-lom, that Hu'shaī said unto Ăb'sa-lom, God save the king, God save the king.

17 And Ăb'sa-lom said to Hu'shaī, *Is* this thy kindness to thy friend? why wentest thou not with thy friend?

18 And Hu'shaī said unto Ăb'sa-lom, Nay; but whom the LORD, and this people, and all the men of Israel, choose, his will I be, and with him will I abide.

19 And again, whom should I serve?
should I not *serve* in the presence of his
son? as I have served in thy father's
presence, so will I be in thy presence.
20 ¶Then said Ăb′sa-lom to A-hĭth′o-
phĕl, Give counsel among you what we
shall do.
21 And A-hĭth′o-phĕl said unto Ăb′sa-
lom, Go in unto thy father's concu-
bines, which he hath left to keep the
house; and all Israel shall hear that
thou art abhorred of thy father: then
shall the hands of all that *are* with thee
be strong.
22 So they spread Ăb′sa-lom a tent
upon the top of the house; and Ăb′sa-
lom went in unto his father's concu-
bines in the sight of all Israel.
23 And the counsel of A-hĭth′o-phĕl,
which he counselled in those days, *was*
as if a man had enquired at the oracle of
God: so *was* all the counsel of A-hĭth′o-
phĕl both with David and with Ăb′sa-
lom.

CHAPTER 17

MOREOVER A-hĭth′o-phĕl said unto
Ăb′sa-lom, Let me now choose out
twelve thousand men, and I will arise
and pursue after David this night:
2 And I will come upon him while he
is weary and weak handed, and will
make him afraid: and all the people
that *are* with him shall flee; and I will
smite the king only:
3 And I will bring back all the people
unto thee: the man whom thou seekest
is as if all returned: *so* all the people
shall be in peace.
4 And the saying pleased Ăb′sa-lom
well, and all the elders of Israel.
5 Then said Ăb′sa-lom, Call now
Hu′shaī the Är′chīte also, and let us
hear likewise what he saith.
6 And when Hu′shaī was come to
Ăb′sa-lom, Ăb′sa-lom spake unto him,
saying, A-hĭth′o-phĕl hath spoken after
this manner: shall we do *after* his
saying? if not; speak thou.
7 And Hu′shaī said unto Ăb′sa-lom,
The counsel that A-hĭth′o-phĕl hath giv-
en *is* not good at this time.
8 For, said Hu′shaī, thou knowest thy
father and his men, that they *be* mighty
men, and they *be* chafed in their minds,
as a bear robbed of her whelps in the
field: and thy father *is* a man of war,
and will not lodge with the people.
9 Behold, he is hid now in some pit, or
in some *other* place: and it will come to
pass, when some of them be over-
thrown at the first, that whosoever
heareth it will say, There is a slaughter
among the people that follow Ăb′sa-
lom.
10 And he also *that is* valiant, whose
heart *is* as the heart of a lion, shall ut-
terly melt: for all Israel knoweth that
thy father *is* a mighty man, and *they*
which *be* with him *are* valiant men.
11 Therefore I counsel that all Israel
be generally gathered unto thee, from
Dan even to Be′er–shē′ba, as the sand
that *is* by the sea for multitude; and
that thou go to battle in thine own per-
son.
12 So shall we come upon him in
some place where he shall be found,
and we will light upon him as the dew
falleth on the ground: and of him and of
all the men that *are* with him there shall
not be left so much as one.
13 Moreover, if he be gotten into a
city, then shall all Israel bring ropes to
that city, and we will draw it into the
river, until there be not one small stone
found there.
14 And Ăb′sa-lom and all the men of
Israel said, The counsel of Hu′shaī the
Är′chīte *is* better than the counsel of A-
hĭth′o-phĕl. For the Lord had ap-
pointed to defeat the good counsel of
A-hĭth′o-phĕl, to the intent that the
Lord might bring evil upon Ăb′sa-lom.
15 ¶Then said Hu′shaī unto Zā′dŏk
and to Ā-bī′a-thar the priests, Thus and
thus did A-hĭth′o-phĕl counsel Ăb′sa-
lom and the elders of Israel; and thus
and thus have I counselled.
16 Now therefore send quickly, and
tell David, saying, Lodge not this night
in the plains of the wilderness, but
speedily pass over; lest the king be
swallowed up, and all the people that
are with him.
17 Now Jonathan and A-hĭm′ă-az
stayed by Ĕn-rō′gel; for they might not
be seen to come into the city: and a
wench went and told them; and they
went and told king David.
18 Nevertheless a lad saw them, and
told Ăb′sa-lom: but they went both of
them away quickly, and came to a
man's house in Ba-hû′rĭm, which had a
well in his court; whither they went
down.
19 And the woman took and spread a
covering over the well's mouth, and
spread ground corn thereon; and the
thing was not known.
20 And when Ăb′sa-lom's servants
came to the woman to the house, they
said, Where *is* A-hĭm′ă-az and Jona-
than? And the woman said unto
them, They be gone over the brook of
water. And when they had sought and
could not find *them*, they returned to
Jerusalem.
21 And it came to pass, after they
were departed, that they came up out

of the well, and went and told king David, and said unto David, Arise, and pass quickly over the water: for thus hath A-hĭth'o-phĕl counselled against you.

22 Then David arose, and all the people that *were* with him, and they passed over Jordan: by the morning light there lacked not one of them that was not gone over Jordan.

23 ¶And when A-hĭth'o-phĕl saw that his counsel was not followed, he saddled *his* ass, and arose, and gat him home to his house, to his city, and put his household in order, and hanged himself, and died, and was buried in the sepulchre of his father.

24 Then David came to Mā-ha-nā'im. And Ăb'sa-lom passed over Jordan, he and all the men of Israel with him.

25 And Ăb'sa-lom made Am'ā-sa captain of the host instead of Jō'ăb: which Am'ā-sa *was* a man's son, whose name *was* Ĭth'ra an Israelite, that went in to Ăb'i-gāil the daughter of Nā'hăsh, sister to Zer-ū-i'ah Jō'ăb's mother.

26 So Israel and Ăb'sa-lom pitched in the land of Gilead.

27 ¶And it came to pass, when David was come to Mā-ha-nā'im, that Shō'bī the son of Nā'hăsh of Răb'bah of the children of Ammon, and Mā'chĭr the son of Ăm'mī-el of Lō-dē'bar, and Bärzĭl'la-ī the Gileadite of Rō-ge'lĭm,

28 Brought beds, and basons, and earthen vessels, and wheat, and barley, and flour, and parched *corn*, and beans, and lentiles, and parched *pulse*,

29 And honey, and butter, and sheep, and cheese of kine, for David, and for the people that *were* with him, to eat: for they said, The people *is* hungry, and weary, and thirsty, in the wilderness.

CHAPTER 18

AND David numbered the people that *were* with him, and set captains of thousands and captains of hundreds over them.

2 And David sent forth a third part of the people under the hand of Jō'ăb, and a third part under the hand of A-bī'shaī the son of Zer-ū-i'ah, Jō'ăb's brother, and a third part under the hand of Ĭt'ta-ī the Gĭt'tīte, And the king said unto the people, I will surely go forth with you myself also.

3 But the people answered, Thou shalt not go forth: for if we flee away, they will not care for us; neither if half of us die, will they care for us: but now *thou art* worth ten thousand of us: therefore now *it is* better that thou succour us out of the city.

4 And the king said unto them, What seemeth you best I will do. And the king stood by the gate side, and all the people came out by hundreds and by thousands.

5 And the king commanded Jō'ăb and A-bī'shaī and Ĭt'ta-ī, saying, *Deal* gently for my sake with the young man, *even* with Ăb'sa-lom. And all the people heard when the king gave all the captains charge concerning Ăb'sa-lom.

6 ¶So the people went out into the field against Israel: and the battle was in the wood of Ē'phra-im;

7 Where the people of Israel were slain before the servants of David, and there was there a great slaughter that day of twenty thousand *men*.

8 For the battle was there scattered over the face of all the country: and the wood devoured more people that day than the sword devoured.

9 ¶And Ăb'sa-lom met the servants of David. And Ăb'sa-lom rode upon a mule, and the mule went under the thick boughs of a great oak, and his head caught hold of the oak, and he was taken up between the heaven and the earth; and the mule that *was* under him went away.

10 And a certain man saw *it*, and told Jō'ăb, and said, Behold, I saw Ăb'salom hanged in an oak.

11 And Jō'ăb said unto the man that told him, And, behold, thou sawest *him*, and why didst thou not smite him there to the ground? and I would have given thee ten *shekels* of silver, and a girdle.

12 And the man said unto Jō'ăb, Though I should receive a thousand *shekels* of silver in mine hand, *yet* would I not put forth mine hand against the king's son: for in our hearing the king charged thee and A-bī'shaī and Ĭt'ta-ī, saying, Beware that none *touch* the young man Ăb'sa-lom.

13 Otherwise I should have wrought falsehood against mine own life: for there is no matter hid from the king, and thou thyself wouldest have set thyself against *me*.

14 Then said Jō'ăb, I may not tarry thus with thee. And he took three darts in his hand, and thrust them through the heart of Ăb'sa-lom, while he *was* yet alive in the midst of the oak.

15 And ten young men that bare Jō'ăb's armour compassed about and smote Ăb'sa-lom, and slew him.

16 And Jō'ăb blew the trumpet, and the people returned from pursuing after Israel: for Jō'ăb held back the people.

17 And they took Ăb'sa-lom, and cast him into a great pit in the wood, and

laid a very great heap of stones upon him: and all Israel fled every one to his tent.

18 ¶Now Ăb'sa-lom in his lifetime had taken and reared up for himself a pillar, which *is* in the king's dale: for he said, I have no son to keep my name in remembrance: and he called the pillar after his own name: and it is called unto this day, Ăb'sa-lom's place.

19 ¶Then said A-hĭm'ă-az the son of Ză'dŏk, Let me now run, and bear the king tidings, how that the LORD hath avenged him of his enemies.

20 And Jō'ăb said unto him, Thou shalt not bear tidings this day, but thou shalt bear tidings another day: but this day thou shalt bear no tidings, because the king's son is dead.

21 Then said Jō'ăb to Cū'shī, Go tell the king what thou hast seen. And Cū'shī bowed himself unto Jō'ăb, and ran.

22 Then said A-hĭm'ă-az the son of Ză'dŏk yet again to Jō'ăb, But howsoever, let me, I pray thee, also run after Cū'shī. And Jō'ăb said, Wherefore wilt thou run, my son, seeing that thou hast no tidings ready?

23 But howsoever, *said he*, let me run. And he said unto him, Run. Then A-hĭm'ă-az ran by the way of the plain, and overran Cū'shī.

24 And David sat between the two gates: and the watchman went up to the roof over the gate unto the wall, and lifted up his eyes, and looked, and behold a man running alone.

25 And the watchman cried, and told the king. And the king said, If he *be* alone, *there is* tidings in his mouth. And he came apace, and drew near.

26 And the watchman saw another man running: and the watchman called unto the porter, and said, Behold *another* man running alone. And the king said, He also bringeth tidings.

27 And the watchman said, Me thinketh the running of the foremost is like the running of A-hĭm'ă-az the son of Ză'dŏk. And the king said, He *is* a good man, and cometh with good tidings.

28 And A-hĭm'ă-az called, and said unto the king, All is well. And he fell down to the earth upon his face before the king, and said, Blessed *be* the LORD thy God, which hath delivered up the men that lifted up their hand against my lord the king.

29 And the king said, Is the young man Ăb'sa-lom safe? And A-hĭm'ă-az answered, When Jō'ăb sent the king's servant, and *me* thy servant, I saw a great tumult, but I knew not what *it was*.

30 And the king said *unto him*, Turn aside, *and* stand here. And he turned aside, and stood still.

31 And, behold, Cū'shī came; and Cū'shī said, Tidings, my lord the king: for the LORD hath avenged thee this day of all them that rose up against thee.

32 And the king said unto Cū'shī, *Is* the young man Ăb'sa-lom safe? And Cū'shī answered, The enemies of my lord the king, and all that rise against thee to do *thee* hurt, be as *that* young man *is*.

33 ¶And the king was much moved, and went up to the chamber over the gate, and wept: and as he went, thus he said, O my son Ăb'sa-lom, my son, my son Ăb'sa-lom! would God I had died for thee, O Ăb'sa-lom, my son, my son!

CHAPTER 19

AND it was told Jō'ăb, Behold, the king weepeth and mourneth for Ăb'sa-lom.

2 And the victory that day was *turned* into mourning unto all the people: for the people heard say that day how the king was grieved for his son.

3 And the people gat them by stealth that day into the city, as people being ashamed steal away when they flee in battle.

4 But the king covered his face, and the king cried with a loud voice, O my son Ăb'sa-lom, O Ăb'sa-lom, my son, my son!

5 And Jō'ăb came into the house to the king, and said, Thou hast shamed this day the faces of all thy servants, which this day have saved thy life, and the lives of thy sons and of thy daughters, and the lives of thy wives, and the lives of thy concubines;

6 In that thou lovest thine enemies, and hatest thy friends. For thou hast declared this day, that thou regardest neither princes nor servants: for this day I perceive, that if Ăb'sa-lom had lived, and all we had died this day, then it had pleased thee well.

7 Now therefore arise, go forth, and speak comfortably unto thy servants: for I swear by the LORD, if thou go not forth, there will not tarry one with thee this night: and that will be worse unto thee than all the evil that befell thee from thy youth until now.

8 Then the king arose, and sat in the gate. And they told unto all the people, saying, Behold, the king doth sit in the gate. And all the people came before the king: for Israel had fled every man to his tent.

9 ¶And all the people were at strife throughout all the tribes of Israel, saying, The king saved us out of the hand of our enemies, and he delivered

us out of the hand of the Philistines;
and now he is fled out of the land for
Ăb'sa-lom.
10 And Ăb'sa-lom, whom we
anointed over us, is dead in battle. Now
therefore why speak ye not a word of
bringing the king back?
11 ¶And king David sent to Zā'dŏk
and to Ā-bī'a-thar the priests, saying,
Speak unto the elders of Jūdah, saying,
Why are ye the last to bring the king
back to his house? seeing the speech of
all Israel is come to the king, *even* to his
house.
12 Ye *are* my brethren, ye *are* my
bones and my flesh: wherefore then are
ye the last to bring back the king?
13 And say ye to Am'ā-sa, *Art* thou
not of my bone, and of my flesh? God
do so to me, and more also, if thou be
not captain of the host before me con-
tinually in the room of Jō'ăb.
14 And he bowed the heart of all the
men of Jūdah, even as *the heart of* one
man; so that they sent *this word* unto
the king, Return thou, and all thy ser-
vants.
15 So the king returned, and came to
Jordan. And Jūdah came to Gilgal, to
go to meet the king, to conduct the king
over Jordan.
16 ¶And Shĭm'e-ī the son of Ge'ra, a
Benjamite, which *was* of Ba-hû'rĭm,
hasted and came down with the men of
Jūdah to meet king David.
17 And *there were* a thousand men of
Benjamin with him, and Zī'ba the ser-
vant of the house of Saul, and his fif-
teen sons and his twenty servants with
him; and they went over Jordan before
the king.
18 And there went over a ferry boat
to carry over the king's household, and
to do what he thought good. And
Shĭm'e-ī the son of Ge'ra fell down be-
fore the king, as he was come over Jor-
dan;
19 And said unto the king, Let not my
lord impute iniquity unto me, neither
do thou remember that which they ser-
vant did perversely the day that my
lord the king went out of Jerusalem,
that the king should take it to his heart.
20 For thy servant doth know that I
have sinned: therefore, behold, I am
come the first this day of all the house
of Joseph to go down to meet my lord
the king.
21 But A-bī'shaī the son of Zer-ū-i'ah
answered and said, Shall not Shĭm'e-ī
be put to death for this, because he
cursed the LORD's anointed?
22 And David said, What have I to do
with you, ye sons of Zer-ū-i'ah, that ye
should this day be adversaries unto
me? shall there any man be put to death
this day in Israel? for do not I know that
I *am* this day king over Israel?
23 Therefore the king said unto
Shĭm'e-ī, Thou shalt not die. And the
king sware unto him.
24 ¶And Me-phĭb'o-shĕth the son of
Saul came down to meet the king, and
had neither dressed his feet, nor
trimmed his beard, nor washed his
clothes, from the day the king departed
until the day he came *again* in peace.
25 And it came to pass, when he was
come to Jerusalem to meet the king,
that the king said unto him, Wherefore
wentest not thou with me, Me-phĭb'o-
shĕth?
26 And he answered, My lord, O king,
my servant deceived me: for thy ser-
vant said, I will saddle me an ass, that I
may ride thereon, and go to the king;
because thy servant *is* lame.
27 And he hath slandered thy servant
unto my lord the king; but my lord the
king *is* as an angel of God: do therefore
what is good in thine eyes.
28 For all *of* my father's house were
but dead men before my lord the king:
yet didst thou set thy servant among
them that did eat at thine own table.
What right therefore have I yet to cry
any more unto the king?
29 And the king said unto him, Why
speakest thou any more of thy matters?
I have said, Thou and Zī'ba divide the
land.
30 And Me-phĭb'o-shĕth said unto
the king, Yea, let him take all, foras-
much as my lord the king is come again
in peace unto his own house.
31 ¶And Bär-zĭl'la-ī the Gĭleadīte
came down from Rō-ge'lĭm, and went
over Jordan with the king, to conduct
him over Jordan.
32 Now Bär-zĭl'la-ī was a very aged
man, *even* fourscore years old: and he
had provided the king of sustenance
while he lay at Mā-ha-nā'im; for he *was*
a very great man.
33 And the king said unto Bär-zĭl'la-ī,
Come thou over with me, and I will
feed thee with me in Jerusalem.
34 And Bär-zĭl'la-ī said unto the king,
How long have I to live, that I should go
up with the king unto Jerusalem?
35 I *am* this day fourscore years old:
and can I discern between good and
evil? can thy servant taste what I eat or
what I drink? can I hear any more the
voice of singing men and singing wom-
en? wherefore then should thy ser-
vant be yet a burden unto my lord the
king?
36 Thy servant will go a little way
over Jordan with the king: and why

should the king recompense it me with such a reward?
37 Let thy servant, I pray thee, turn back again, that I may die in mine own city, *and be buried* by the grave of my father and of my mother. But behold thy servant Chĭm′hăm; let him go over with my lord the king; and do to him what shall seem good unto thee.
38 And the king answered, Chĭm′hăm shall go over with me, and I will do to him that which shall seem good unto thee: and whatsoever thou shalt require of me, *that* will I do for thee.
39 And all the people went over Jordan. And when the king was come over, the king kissed Bär-zĭl′la-ī, and blessed him; and he returned unto his own place.
40 Then the king went on to Gilgal, and Chĭm′hăm went on with him: and all the people of Jūdah conducted the king, and also half the people of Israel.
41 ¶And, behold, all the men of Israel came to the king, and said unto the king, Why have our brethren the men of Jūdah stolen thee away, and have brought the king, and his household, and all David's men with him, over Jordan?
42 And all the men of Jūdah answered the men of Israel, Because the king *is* near of kin to us: wherefore then be ye angry for this matter? have we eaten at all of the king's *cost?* or hath he given us any gift?
43 And the men of Israel answered the men of Jūdah, and said, We have ten parts in the king, and we have also more *right* in David than ye: why then did ye despise us, that our advice should not be first had in bringing back our king? And the words of the men of Jūdah were fiercer than the words of the men of Israel.

CHAPTER 20

AND there happened to be there a man of Bē′lĭ-al, whose name *was* Shē′ba, the son of Bĭch′rī, a Benjamite: and he blew a trumpet, and said, We have no part in David, neither have we inheritance in the son of Jesse: every man to his tents, O Israel.
2 So every man of Israel went up from after David, *and* followed Shē′ba the son of Bĭch′rī: but the men of Jūdah clave unto their king, from Jordan even to Jerusalem.
3 ¶And David came to his house at Jerusalem; and the king took the ten women *his* concubines, whom he had left to keep the house, and put them in ward, and fed them, but went not in unto them. So they were shut up unto the day of their death, living in widowhood.
4 ¶Then said the king to Am′ā-sa, Assemble me the men of Jūdah within three days, and be thou here present.
5 So Am′ā-sa went to assemble *the men of* Jūdah: but he tarried longer than the set time which he had appointed him.
6 And David said to A-bī′shaī, Now shall Shē′ba the son of Bĭch′rī do us more harm than *did* Ăb′sa-lom: take thou thy lord's servants, and pursue after him, lest he get him fenced cities, and escape us.
7 And there went out after him Jō′ăb's men, and the Chĕr′e-thītes, and the Pĕl′e-thītes, and all the mighty men: and they went out of Jerusalem, to pursue after Shē′ba the son of Bĭch′rī.
8 When they *were* at the great stone which *is* in Gĭbeon, Am′ā-sa went before them. And Jō′ăb's garment that he had put on was girded unto him, and upon it a girdle *with* a sword fastened upon his loins in the sheath thereof; and as he went forth it fell out.
9 And Jō′ăb said to Am′ā-sa, *Art* thou in health, my brother? And Jō′ăb took Am′ā-sa by the beard with the right hand to kiss him.
10 But Am′ā-sa took no heed to the sword that *was* in Jō′ăb's hand: so he smote him therewith in the fifth *rib,* and shed out his bowels to the ground, and struck him not again; and he died. So Jō′ăb and A-bī′shaī his brother pursued after Shē′ba the son of Bĭch′rī.
11 And one of Jō′ăb's men stood by him, and said, He that favoureth Jō′ăb, and he that *is* for David, *let him go* after Jō′ăb.
12 And Am′ā-sa wallowed in blood in the midst of the highway. And when the man saw that all the people stood still, he removed Am′ā-sa out of the highway into the field, and cast a cloth upon him, when he saw that every one that came by him stood still.
13 When he was removed out of the highway, all the people went on after Jō′ăb, to pursue after Shē′ba the son of Bĭch′rī.
14 ¶And he went through all the tribes of Israel unto Abel, and to Bĕth–mā′a-chah, and all the Bē′rītes: and they were gathered together, and went also after him.
15 And they came and besieged him in Abel of Bĕth–mā′a-chah, and they cast up a bank against the city, and it stood in the trench: and all the people that *were* with Jō′ăb battered the wall, to throw it down.
16 ¶Then cried a wise woman out of

the city, Hear, hear; say, I pray you, unto Jō′ăb, Come near hither, that I may speak with thee.

17 And when he was come near unto her, the woman said, *Art* thou Jō′ăb? And he answered, I *am he.* Then she said unto him, Hear the words of thine handmaid. And he answered, I do hear.

18 Then she spake, saying, They were wont to speak in old time, saying, They shall surely ask *counsel* at Abel: and so they ended *the matter.*

19 I *am one of them that are* peaceable *and* faithful in Israel: thou seekest to destroy a city and a mother in Israel: why wilt thou swallow up the inheritance of the LORD?

20 And Jō′ăb answered and said, Far be it, far be it from me, that I should swallow up or destroy.

21 The matter *is* not so: but a man of mount Ē′phra-im, Shē′ba the son of Bĭch′rī by name, hath lifted up his hand against the king, *even* against David: deliver him only, and I will depart from the city. And the woman said unto Jō′ăb, Behold, his head shall be thrown to thee over the wall.

22 Then the woman went unto all the people in her wisdom. And they cut off the head of Shē′ba the son of Bĭch′rī, and cast *it* out to Jō′ăb. And he blew a trumpet, and they retired from the city, every man to his tent. And Jō′ăb returned to Jerusalem unto the king.

23 ¶Now Jō′ăb *was* over all the host of Israel: and Be-nā′iah the son of Jehoi′a-da *was* over the Chĕr′e-thītes and over the Pĕl′e-thītes:

24 And Ă-dô′ram *was* over the tribute: and Je-hŏsh′a-phăt the son of A-hī′lud *was* recorder:

25 And Shē′va *was* scribe: and Zā′dŏk and Ă-bī′a-thar *were* the priests:

26 And Īra also the Jā′ir-īte was a chief ruler about David.

CHAPTER 21

THEN there was a famine in the days of David three years, year after year; and David enquired of the LORD. And the LORD answered, *It is* for Saul, and for *his* bloody house, because he slew the Gĭb′e-o-nītes.

2 And the king called the Gĭb′e-o-nītes, and said unto them; (now the Gĭb′e-o-nītes *were* not of the children of Israel, but of the remnant of the Ămor-ītes; and the children of Israel had sworn unto them: and Saul sought to slay them in his zeal to the children of Israel and Jūdah.)

3 Wherefore David said unto the Gĭb′e-o-nītes, What shall I do for you? and wherewith shall I make the atonement, that ye may bless the inheritance of the LORD?

4 And the Gĭb′e-o-nītes said unto him, We will have no silver nor gold of Saul, nor of his house; neither for us shalt thou kill any man in Israel. And he said, What ye shall say, *that* will I do for you.

5 And they answered the king, The man that consumed us, and that devised against us *that* we should be destroyed from remaining in any of the coasts of Israel,

6 Let seven men of his sons be delivered unto us, and we will hang them up unto the LORD in Gĭb′e-ah of Saul, *whom* the LORD did choose. And the king said, I will give *them.*

7 But the king spared Me-phĭb′o-shĕth, the son of Jonathan the son of Saul, because of the LORD's oath that *was* between them, between David and Jonathan the son of Saul.

8 But the king took the two sons of Rĭz′pah the daughter of Ă-ī′ah, whom she bare unto Saul, Är-mō′nī and Me-phĭb′o-shĕth; and the five sons of Mī′-chal the daughter of Saul, whom she brought up for Ā′drī-el the son of Bär-zĭl′la-ī the Me-hōl′ath-īte:

9 And he delivered them into the hands of the Gĭb′e-o-nītes and they hanged them in the hill before the LORD: and they fell *all* seven together, and were put to death in the days of harvest, in the first *days,* in the beginning of barley harvest.

10 ¶And Rĭz′pah the daughter of Ă-ī′ah took sackcloth, and spread it for her upon the rock, from the beginning of harvest until water dropped upon them out of heaven, and suffered neither the birds of the air to rest on them by day, nor the beasts of the field by night.

11 And it was told David what Rĭz′-pah the daughter of Ă-ī′ah, the concubine of Saul, had done.

12 And David went and took the bones of Saul and the bones of Jonathan his son from the men of Jā′-besh–gĭl′e-ad, which had stolen them from the street of Bĕth′–shăn, where the Philistines had hanged them, when the Philistines had slain Saul in Gĭl-bō′a:

13 And he brought up from thence the bones of Saul and the bones of Jonathan his son; and they gathered the bones of them that were hanged.

14 And the bones of Saul and Jonathan his son buried they in the country of Benjamin in Zē′lah, in the sepulchre of Kish his father: and they performed all that the king commanded.

And after that God was intreated for the land.

15 ¶Moreover the Philistines had yet war again with Israel; and David went down, and his servants with him, and fought against the Philistines: and David waxed faint.

16 And Ĭsh′bī–bē′nŏb, which *was* of the sons of the giant, the weight of whose spear *weighed* three hundred *shekels* of brass in weight, he being girded with a new *sword,* thought to have slain David.

17 But A-bī′shaī the son of Zer-ū-i′ah succoured him, and smote the Philistine, and killed him. Then the men of David sware unto him, saying, Thou shalt go no more out with us to battle, that thou quench not the light of Israel.

18 And it came to pass after this, that there was again a battle with the Philistines at Gob: then Sĭb′be-chaī the Hu′shath-īte slew Saph, which *was* of the sons of the giant.

19 And there was again a battle in Gob with the Philistines, where Ĕl-hā′-nan the son of Jā-ar′e-ôr′e-gĭm, a Bĕth–lehĕmīte, slew *the brother of* Go-lī′ath the Gĭt′tīte, the staff of whose spear *was* like a weaver's beam.

20 And there was yet a battle in Gath, where was a man of *great* stature, that had on every hand six fingers, and on every foot six toes, four and twenty in number; and he also was born to the giant.

21 And when he defied Israel, Jonathan the son of Shĭm′e-ah the brother of David slew him.

22 These four were born to the giant in Gath, and fell by the hand of David, and by the hand of his servants.

CHAPTER 22

AND David spake unto the LORD the words of this song in the day *that* the LORD had delivered him out of the hand of all his enemies, and out of the hand of Saul:

2 And he said, The LORD *is* my rock, and my fortress, and my deliverer;

3 The God of my rock; in him will I trust: *he is* my shield, and the horn of my salvation, my high tower, and my refuge, my saviour; thou savest me from violence.

4 I will call on the LORD, *who is* worthy to be praised: so shall I be saved from mine enemies.

5 When the waves of death compassed me, the floods of ungodly men made me afraid;

6 The sorrows of hell compassed me about; the snares of death prevented me;

7 In my distress I called upon the LORD, and cried to my God: and he did hear my voice out of his temple, and my cry *did enter* into his ears.

8 Then the earth shook and trembled; the foundations of heaven moved and shook, because he was wroth.

9 There went up a smoke out of his nostrils, and fire out of his mouth devoured: coals were kindled by it.

10 He bowed the heavens also, and came down; and darkness *was* under his feet.

11 And he rode upon a cherub, and did fly: and he was seen upon the wings of the wind.

12 And he made darkness pavilions round about him, dark waters, *and* thick clouds of the skies.

13 Through the brightness before him were coals of fire kindled.

14 The LORD thundered from heaven, and the most High uttered his voice.

15 And he sent out arrows, and scattered them; lightning, and discomfited them.

16 And the channels of the sea appeared, the foundations of the world were discovered, at the rebuking of the LORD, at the blast of the breath of his nostrils.

17 He sent from above, he took me; he drew me out of many waters;

18 He delivered me from my strong enemy, *and* from them that hated me: for they were too strong for me.

19 They prevented me in the day of my calamity: but the LORD was my stay.

20 He brought me forth also into a large place: he delivered me, because he delighted in me.

21 The LORD rewarded me according to my righteousness: according to the cleanness of my hands hath he recompensed me.

22 For I have kept the ways of the LORD, and have not wickedly departed from my God.

23 For all his judgments *were* before me: and *as for* his statutes, I did not depart from them.

24 I was also upright before him, and have kept myself from mine iniquity.

25 Therefore the LORD hath recompensed me according to my righteousness; according to my cleanness in his eye sight.

26 With the merciful thou wilt shew thyself merciful, *and* with the upright man thou wilt shew thyself upright.

27 With the pure thou wilt shew thyself pure; and with the froward thou wilt shew thyself unsavoury.

28 And the afflicted people thou wilt

save: but thine eyes *are* upon the
haughty, *that* thou mayest bring *them*
down.
29 For thou *art* my lamp, O LORD: and
the LORD will lighten my darkness.
30 For by thee I have run through a
troop: by my God have I leaped over a
wall.
31 *As for* God, his way *is* perfect; the
word of the LORD *is* tried: he *is* a buckler to all them that trust in him.
32 For who *is* God, save the LORD?
and who *is* a rock, save our God?
33 God *is* my strength *and* power:
and he maketh my way perfect.
34 He maketh my feet like hinds' *feet*:
and setteth me upon my high places.
35 He teacheth my hands to war; so
that a bow of steel is broken by mine
arms.
36 Thou hast also given me the shield
of thy salvation: and thy gentleness
hath made me great.
37 Thou hast enlarged my steps under me; so that my feet did not slip.
38 I have pursued mine enemies, and
destroyed them; and turned not again
until I had consumed them.
39 And I have consumed them, and
wounded them, that they could not
arise: yea, they are fallen under my
feet.
40 For thou hast girded me with
strength to battle: them that rose up
against me hast thou subdued under
me.
41 Thou hast also given me the necks
of mine enemies, that I might destroy
them that hate me.
42 They looked, but *there was* none
to save; *even* unto the LORD, but he answered them not.
43 Then did I beat them as small as
the dust of the earth, I did stamp them
as the mire of the street, *and* did spread
them abroad.
44 Thou also hast delivered me from
the strivings of my people, thou hast
kept me *to be* head of the heathen: a
people *which* I knew not shall serve
me.
45 Strangers shall submit themselves
unto me: as soon as they hear, they
shall be obedient unto me.
46 Strangers shall fade away, and
they shall be afraid out of their close
places.
47 The LORD liveth; and blessed *be*
my rock; and exalted be the God of the
rock of my salvation.
48 It *is* God that avengeth me, and
that bringeth down the people under
me,
49 And that bringeth me forth from
mine enemies: thou also hast lifted me
up on high above them that rose up
against me: thou hast delivered me
from the violent man.
50 Therefore I will give thanks unto
thee, O LORD, among the heathen, and I
will sing praises unto thy name.
51 *He is* the tower of salvation for his
king: and sheweth mercy to his
anointed, unto David, and to his seed
for evermore.

CHAPTER 23

NOW these *be* the last words of David.
David the son of Jesse said, and the
man *who was* raised up on high, the
anointed of the God of Jacob, and the
sweet psalmist of Israel, said,
2 The Spirit of the LORD spake by me,
and his word *was* in my tongue.
3 The God of Israel said, the Rock of
Israel spake to me, He that ruleth over
men *must be* just, ruling in the fear of
God.
4 And *he shall be* as the light of the
morning, *when* the sun riseth, *even* a
morning without clouds; *as* the tender
grass *springing* out of the earth by clear
shining after rain.
5 Although my house *be* not so with
God; yet he hath made with me an everlasting covenant, ordered in all *things*,
and sure: for *this is* all my salvation,
and all *my* desire, although he make *it*
not to grow.
6 But *the sons* of Bē'lī-al *shall be* all of
them as thorns thrust away, because
they cannot be taken with hands:
7 But the man *that* shall touch them
must be fenced with iron and the staff
of a spear; and they shall be utterly
burned with fire in the *same* place.
8 ¶These *be* the names of the mighty
men whom David had: The Tăch'mo-nīte that sat in the seat, chief among the
captains; the same *was* Ăd'i-nō the Ĕz'-nīte: *he lift up his spear* against eight
hundred, whom he slew at one time.
9 And after him *was* Ĕ-le-ā'zar the
son of Dodo the A-hō'hīte, *one* of the
three mighty men with David, when
they defied the Philistines *that* were
there gathered together to battle, and
the men of Israel were gone away:
10 He arose, and smote the Philistines until his hand was weary, and his
hand clave unto the sword: and the
LORD wrought a great victory that day;
and the people returned after him only
to spoil.
11 And after him *was* Shăm'mah the
son of Ăg'ee the Hâ'ra-rīte. And the
Philistines were gathered together into
a troop, where was a piece of ground
full of lentiles: and the people fled from
the Philistines.
12 But he stood in the midst of the

ground, and defended it, and slew the Philistines: and the LORD wrought a great victory.

13 And three of the thirty chief went down, and came to David in the harvest time unto the cave of Adŭllam: and the troop of the Philistines pitched in the valley of Rĕph′a-im.

14 And David *was* then in an hold, and the garrison of the Philistines *was* then *in* Bĕth–lehĕm.

15 And David longed, and said, Oh that one would give me drink of the water of the well of Bĕth–lehĕm, which *is* by the gate!

16 And the three mighty men brake through the host of the Philistines, and drew water out of the well of Bĕth–lehĕm, that *was* by the gate, and took *it*, and brought *it* to David: nevertheless he would not drink thereof, but poured it out unto the LORD.

17 And he said, Be it far from me, O LORD, that I should do this: *is not this* the blood of the men that went in jeopardy of their lives? therefore he would not drink it. These things did these three mighty men.

18 And A-bī′shaī, the brother of Jō′ăb, the son of Zer-ū-i′ah, was chief among three. And he lifted up his spear against three hundred, *and* slew *them*, and had the name among three.

19 Was he not most honourable of three? therefore he was their captain: howbeit he attained not unto the *first* three.

20 And Be-nā′iah the son of Je-hoi′a-da, the son of a valiant man, of Kăb′ze-el, who had done many acts, he slew two lionlike men of Moab: he went down also and slew a lion in the midst of a pit in time of snow:

21 And he slew an Egyptian, a goodly man: and the Egyptian had a spear in his hand; but he went down to him with a staff, and plucked the spear out of the Egyptian's hand, and slew him with his own spear.

22 These *things* did Be-nā′iah the son of Je-hoi′a-da, and had the name among three mighty men.

23 He was more honourable than the thirty, but he attained not to the *first* three. And David set him over his guard.

24 Ă′sa-hĕl the brother of Jō′ăb *was* one of the thirty; Ĕl-hā′nan the son of Dodo of Bĕth–lehĕm,

25 Shăm′mah the Hâ′rod-īte, E-lī′ka the Hâ′rod-īte,

26 Hĕ′lĕz the Păl′tīte, Īra the son of Īk′kesh the Te-kō′īte,

27 Ă-bi-ē′zer the Ăn′e-thŏth-īte, Me-bŭn′naī the Hu′shath-īte,

28 Zăl′mon the A-hō′hīte, Mā-har′a-ī the Ne-tōph′a-thīte,

29 Hē′lĕb the son of Bā′a-nah, a Ne-tōph′a-thīte, Īt′ta-ī the son of Rī′baī out of Gĭb′e-ah of the children of Benjamin,

30 Be-nā′iah the Pĭr′a-thŏn-īte, Hĭd′-da-ī of the brooks of Gā′ash,

31 Ā′bī–ăl′bon the Är′bath-īte, Ăz′ma-vĕth the Bär-hū′mīte,

32 E-lī′ah-ba the Shā-ăl′bo-nīte, of the sons of Jā′shen, Jonathan,

33 Shăm′mah the Hâ′ra-rīte, A-hī′am the son of Shâ′rär the Hâ′ra-rīte,

34 E-lĭph′e-lĕt the son of A-hăs′ba-ī, the son of the Mā-ăch′a-thīte, E-lī′am the son of A-hĭth′o-phĕl the Gī′lo-nīte,

35 Hĕz′ra-ī the Carmelite, Pā′a-raī the Är′bīte,

36 Ī′găl the son of Nāthan of Zōbah, Bā′nī the Gădīte,

37 Zē′lĕk the Ammonite, Nā′ha-rī the Bē-ē′rŏth-īte, armourbearer to Jō′ăb the son of Zer-ū-i′ah,

38 Īra an Īth′rīte, Gâ′rĕb an Īth′rīte,

39 Ū-rī′ah the Hittite: thirty and seven in all.

CHAPTER 24

AND again the anger of the LORD was kindled against Israel, and he moved David against them to say, Go, number Israel and Judah.

2 For the king said to Jō′ăb the captain of the host, which *was* with him, Go now through all the tribes of Israel, from Dan even to Be′er–shē′ba, and number ye the people, that I may know the number of the people.

3 And Jō′ăb said unto the king, Now the LORD thy God add unto the people, how many soever they be, an hundredfold, and that the eyes of my lord the king may see *it*: but why doth my lord the king delight in this thing?

4 Notwithstanding the king's word prevailed against Jō′ăb, and against the captains of the host. And Jō′ăb and the captains of the host went out from the presence of the king, to number the people of Israel.

5 And they passed over Jordan, and pitched in Ar′ō-er, on the right side of the city that *lieth* in the midst of the river of Gad, and toward Jā′zer:

6 Then they came to Gilead, and to the land of Tăh′tĭm–hŏd′shī; and they came to Dăn–jā′an, and about to Zī′don,

7 And came to the strong hold of Tyre, and to all the cities of the Hī′vītes, and of the Canaanites: and they went out to the south of Jūdah, *even* to Be′er–shē′ba.

8 So when they had gone through all the land, they came to Jerusalem at the end of nine months and twenty days.

9 And Jō'ăb gave up the sum of the number of the people unto the king: and there were in Israel eight hundred thousand valiant men that drew the sword; and the men of Jūdah *were* five hundred thousand men.
10 ¶And David's heart smote him after that he had numbered the people. And David said unto the LORD, I have sinned greatly in that I have done: and now, I beseech thee, O LORD, take away the iniquity of thy servant; for I have done very foolishly.
11 For when David was up in the morning, the word of the LORD came unto the prophet Gad, David's seer, saying,
12 Go and say unto David, Thus saith the LORD, I offer thee three *things;* choose thee one of them, that I may *do it* unto thee.
13 So Gad came to David, and told him, and said unto him, Shall seven years of famine come unto thee in thy land? or wilt thou flee three months before thine enemies, while they pursue thee? or that there be three days' pestilence in thy land? now advise, and see what answer I shall return to him that sent me.
14 And David said unto Gad, I am in a great strait: let us fall now into the hand of the LORD; for his mercies *are* great: and let me not fall into the hand of man.
15 ¶So the LORD sent a pestilence upon Israel from the morning even to the time appointed: and there died of the people from Dan even to Be'er-shē'ba seventy thousand men.
16 And when the angel stretched out his hand upon Jerusalem to destroy it, the LORD repented him of the evil, and said to the angel that destroyed the people, It is enough: stay now thine hand. And the angel of the LORD was by the threshingplace of A-rau'nah the Jēb'u-sīte.
17 And David spake unto the LORD when he saw the angel that smote the people, and said, Lo, I have sinned, and I have done wickedly: but these sheep, what have they done? let thine hand, I pray thee, be against me, and against my father's house.
18 ¶And Gad came that day to David, and said unto him, Go up, rear an altar unto the LORD in the threshingfloor of A-rau'nah the Jēb'u-sīte.
19 And David, according to the saying of Gad, went up as the LORD commanded.
20 And A-rau'nah looked, and saw the king and his servants coming on toward him: and A-rau'nah went out, and bowed himself before the king on his face upon the ground.
21 And A-rau'nah said, Wherefore is my lord the king come to his servant? And David said, To buy the threshingfloor of thee, to build an altar unto the LORD, that the plague may be stayed from the people.
22 And A-rau'nah said unto David, Let my lord the king take and offer up what *seemeth* good unto him: behold, *here be* oxen for burnt sacrifice, and threshing instruments and *other* instruments of the oxen for wood.
23 All these *things* did A-rau'nah, *as* a king, give unto the king. And A-rau'nah said unto the king, The LORD thy God accept thee.
24 And the king said unto A-rau'nah, Nay; but I will surely buy *it* of thee at a price: neither will I offer burnt offerings unto the LORD my God of that which doth cost me nothing. So David bought the threshingfloor and the oxen for fifty shekels of silver.
25 And David built there an altar unto the LORD, and offered burnt offerings and peace offerings. So the LORD was intreated for the land, and the plague was stayed from Israel.

THE

FIRST BOOK OF THE KINGS

COMMONLY CALLED

THE THIRD BOOK OF THE KINGS

CHAPTER 1

NOW king David was old *and* stricken in years; and they covered him with clothes, but he gat no heat.
2 Wherefore his servants said unto him, Let there be sought for my lord the king a young virgin: and let her stand before the king, and let her cherish him, and let her lie in thy bosom, that my lord the king may get heat.
3 So they sought for a fair damsel throughout all the coasts of Israel, and found Ăb'i-shăg a Shū'nam-mīte, and brought her to the king.
4 And the damsel *was* very fair, and cherished the king, and ministered to him: but the king knew her not.
5 ¶Then Ăd-o-nī'jah the son of Hăg'gīth exalted himself, saying, I will be king: and he prepared him chariots and

horsemen, and fifty men to run before him.

6 And his father had not displeased him at any time in saying, Why hast thou done so? and he also *was a* very goodly *man;* and *his mother* bare him after Ăb'sa-lom.

7 And he conferred with Jō'ăb the son of Zer-ū-i'ah, and with Ā-bī'a-thar the priest: and they following Ăd-o-nī'jah helped *him.*

8 But Zā'dŏk the priest, and Be-nā'iah the son of Je-hoi'a-da, and Nāthan the prophet, and Shĭm'e-ī, and Rē'ī, and the mighty men which *belonged* to David, were not with Ăd-o-nī'jah.

9 And Ăd-o-nī'jah slew sheep and oxen and fat cattle by the stone of Zō'he-lĕth, which *is* by Ĕn–rō'gel, and called all his brethren the king's sons, and all the men of Jūdah the king's servants:

10 But Nāthan the prophet, and Be-nā'iah, and the mighty men, and Sŏlomon his brother, he called not.

11 ¶Wherefore Nāthan spake unto Băth'–shē-ba the mother of Sŏlomon, saying, Hast thou not heard that Ăd-o-nī'jah the son of Hăg'gĭth doth reign, and David our lord knoweth *it* not?

12 Now therefore come, let me, I pray thee, give thee counsel, that thou mayest save thine own life, and the life of thy son Sŏlomon.

13 Go and get thee in unto king David, and say unto him, Didst not thou, my lord, O king, swear unto thine handmaid, saying, Assuredly Sŏlomon thy son shall reign after me, and he shall sit upon my throne? why then doth Ăd-o-nī'jah reign?

14 Behold, while thou yet talkest there with the king, I also will come in after thee, and confirm thy words.

15 ¶And Băth'–shē-ba went in unto the king into the chamber: and the king was very old; and Ăb'i-shăg the Shū'-nam-mīte ministered unto the king.

16 And Băth'–shē-ba bowed, and did obeisance unto the king. And the king said, What wouldest thou?

17 And she said unto him, My lord, thou swarest by the LORD thy God unto thine handmaid, *saying,* Assuredly Sŏlomon thy son shall reign after me, and he shall sit upon my throne.

18 And now, behold, Ăd-o-nī'jah reigneth; and now, my lord the king, thou knowest *it* not:

19 And he hath slain oxen and fat cattle and sheep in abundance, and hath called all the sons of the king, and Ā-bī'a-thar the priest, and Jō'ăb the captain of the host: but Sŏlomon thy servant hath he not called.

20 And thou, my lord, O king, the eyes of all Israel *are* upon thee, that thou shouldest tell them who shall sit on the throne of my lord the king after him.

21 Otherwise it shall come to pass, when my lord the king shall sleep with his fathers, that I and my son Sŏlomon shall be counted offenders.

22 ¶And, lo, while she yet talked with the king, Nāthan the prophet also came in.

23 And they told the king, saying, Behold Nāthan the prophet. And when he was come in before the king, he bowed himself before the king with his face to the ground.

24 And Nāthan said, My lord, O king, hast thou said, Ăd-o-nī'jah shall reign after me, and he shall sit upon my throne?

25 For he is gone down this day, and hath slain oxen and fat cattle and sheep in abundance, and hath called all the king's sons, and the captains of the host, and Ā-bī'a-thar the priest; and, behold, they eat and drink before him, and say, God save king Ăd-o-nī'jah.

26 But me, *even* me thy servant, and Zā'dŏk the priest, and Be-nā'iah the son of Je-hoi'a-da, and thy servant Sŏlomon, hath he not called.

27 Is this thing done by my lord the king, and thou hast not shewed *it* unto thy servant, who should sit on the throne of my lord the king after him?

28 ¶Then king David answered and said, Call me Băth'–shē-ba. And she came into the king's presence, and stood before the king.

29 And the king sware, and said, *As* the LORD liveth, that hath redeemed my soul out of all distress,

30 Even as I sware unto thee by the LORD God of Israel, saying, Assuredly Sŏlomon thy son shall reign after me, and he shall sit upon my throne in my stead; even so will I certainly do this day.

31 Then Băth'–shē-ba bowed with *her* face to the earth, and did reverence to the king, and said, Let my lord king David live for ever.

32 ¶And king David said, Call me Zā'-dŏk the priest, and Nāthan the prophet, and Be-nā'iah the son of Je-hoi'a-da. And they came before the king.

33 The king also said unto them, Take with you the servants of your lord, and cause Sŏlomon my son to ride upon mine own mule, and bring him down to Gī'hŏn:

34 And let Zā'dŏk the priest and Nāthan the prophet anoint him there king

over Israel: and blow ye with the trumpet, and say, God save king Sŏlomon.
35 Then ye shall come up after him, that he may come and sit upon my throne; for he shall be king in my stead: and I have appointed him to be ruler over Israel and over Jūdah.
36 And Be-nā'iah the son of Je-hoi'a-da answered the king, and said, Amen: the LORD God of my lord the king say so *too.*
37 As the LORD hath been with my lord the king, even so be he with Sŏlomon, and make his throne greater than the throne of my lord king David.
38 So Zā'dŏk the priest, and Nāthan the prophet, and Be-nā'iah the son of Je-hoi'a-da, and the Chĕr'e-thītes, and the Pĕl'e-thītes, went down, and caused Sŏlomon to ride upon king David's mule, and brought him to Gī'hŏn.
39 And Zā'dŏk the priest took an horn of oil out of the tabernacle, and anointed Sŏlomon. And they blew the trumpet; and all the people said, God save king Sŏlomon.
40 And all the people came up after him, and the people piped with pipes, and rejoiced with great joy, so that the earth rent with the sound of them.
41 ¶And Ăd-o-nī'jah and all the guests that *were* with him heard *it* as they had made an end of eating. And when Jō'ăb heard the sound of the trumpet, he said, Wherefore *is this* noise of the city being in an uproar?
42 And while he yet spake, behold, Jonathan the son of Ă-bī'a-thar the priest came; and Ăd-o-nī'jah said unto him, Come in; for thou *art* a valiant man, and bringest good tidings.
43 And Jonathan answered and said to Ăd-o-nī'jah, Verily our lord king David hath made Sŏlomon king.
44 And the king hath sent with him Zā'dŏk the priest, and Nāthan the prophet, and Be-nā'iah the son of Jehoi'a-da, and the Chĕr'e-thītes, and the Pĕl'e-thītes, and they have caused him to ride upon the king's mule:
45 And Zā'dŏk the priest and Nāthan the prophet have anointed him king in Gī'hŏn: and they are come up from thence rejoicing, so that the city rang again. This *is* the noise that ye have heard.
46 And also Sŏlomon sitteth on the throne of the kingdom.
47 And moreover the king's servants came to bless our lord king David, saying, God make the name of Sŏlomon better than thy name, and make his throne greater than thy throne. And the king bowed himself upon the bed.
48 And also thus said the king, Blessed *be* the LORD God of Israel, which hath given *one* to sit on my throne this day, mine eyes even seeing *it.*
49 And all the guests that *were* with Ăd-o-nī'jah were afraid, and rose up, and went every man his way.
50 And Ăd-o-nī'jah feared because of Sŏlomon, and arose, and went, and caught hold on the horns of the altar.
51 And it was told Sŏlomon, saying, Behold, Ăd-o-nī'jah feareth king Sŏlomon: for, lo, he hath caught hold on the horns of the altar, saying, Let king Sŏlomon swear unto me today that he will not slay his servant with the sword.
52 And Sŏlomon said, If he will shew himself a worthy man, there shall not an hair of him fall to the earth: but if wickedness shall be found in him, he shall die.
53 So king Sŏlomon sent, and they brought him down from the altar. And he came and bowed himself to king Sŏlomon: and Sŏlomon said unto him, Go to thine house.

CHAPTER 2

NOW the days of David drew nigh that he should die; and he charged Sŏlomon his son, saying,
2 I go the way of all the earth: be thou strong therefore, and shew thyself a man;
3 And keep the charge of the LORD thy God, to walk in his ways, to keep his statutes, and his commandments, and his judgments, and his testimonies, as it is written in the law of Moses, that thou mayest prosper in all that thou doest, and whithersoever thou turnest thyself:
4 That the LORD may continue his word which he spake concerning me, saying, If thy children take heed to their way, to walk before me in truth with all their heart and with all their soul, there shall not fail thee (said he) a man on the throne of Israel.
5 Moreover thou knowest also what Jō'ăb the son of Zer-ū-i'ah did to me, *and* what he did to the two captains of the hosts of Israel, unto Abner the son of Ner, and unto Am'ā-sa the son of Jē'ther, whom he slew, and shed the blood of war in peace, and put the blood of war upon his girdle that *was* about his loins, and in his shoes that *were* on his feet.
6 Do therefore according to thy wisdom, and let not his hoar head go down to the grave in peace.
7 But shew kindness unto the sons of Bär-zĭl'la-ī the Gīleadīte, and let them

be of those that eat at thy table: for so
they came to me when I fled because of
Ăb′sa-lom thy brother.
8 And, behold, *thou hast* with thee
Shĭm′e-ī the son of Ge′ra, a Benjamite
of Ba-hû′rĭm, which cursed me with a
grievous curse in the day when I went
to Mā-ha-nā′im: but he came down to
meet me at Jordan, and I sware to him
by the LORD, saying, I will not put thee
to death with the sword.
9 Now therefore hold him not guilt-
less: for thou *art* a wise man, and know-
est what thou oughtest to do unto
him; but his hoar head bring thou down
to the grave with blood.
10 ¶So David slept with his fathers,
and was buried in the city of David.
11 And the days that David reigned
over Israel *were* forty years: seven
years reigned he in Hēbron, and thirty
and three years reigned he in Jeru-
salem.
12 ¶Then sat Sŏlomon upon the
throne of David his father; and his
kingdom was established greatly.
13 ¶And Ăd-o-nī′jah the son of Hăg′-
gĭth came to Băth′-shē-ba the mother of
Sŏlomon. And she said, Comest thou
peaceably? And he said, Peaceably.
14 He said moreover, I have
somewhat to say unto thee. And she
said, Say on.
15 And he said, Thou knowest that
the kingdom was mine, and *that* all
Israel set their faces on me, that I
should reign: howbeit the kingdom is
turned about, and is become my broth-
er's: for it was his from the LORD.
16 And now I ask one petition of thee,
deny me not. And she said unto him,
Say on.
17 And he said, Speak, I pray thee,
unto Sŏlomon the king, (for he will not
say thee nay,) that he give me Ăb′i-shăg
the Shū′nam-mīte to wife.
18 And Băth′-shē-ba said, Well; I will
speak for thee unto the king.
19 ¶Băth′-shē-ba therefore went unto
king Sŏlomon, to speak unto him for
Ăd-o-nī′jah. And the king rose up to
meet her, and bowed himself unto her,
and sat down on his throne, and caused
a seat to be set for the king's mother;
and she sat on his right hand.
20 Then she said, I desire one small
petition of thee; *I pray thee,* say me not
nay. And the king said unto her, Ask
on, my mother: for I will not say thee
nay.
21 And she said, Let Ăb′i-shăg the
Shū′nam-mīte be given to Ăd-o-nī′jah
thy brother to wife.
22 And king Sŏlomon answered and
said unto his mother, And why dost
thou ask Ăb′i-shăg the Shū′nam-mīte
for Ăd-o-nī′jah? ask for him the king-
dom also; for he *is* mine elder brother;
even for him, and for Ă-bī′a-thar the
priest, and for Jō′ăb the son of Zer-ū-
i′ah.
23 Then king Sŏlomon sware by the
LORD, saying, God do so to me, and
more also, if Ăd-o-nī′jah have not spo-
ken this word against his own life.
24 Now therefore, *as* the LORD liveth,
which hath established me, and set me
on the throne of David my father, and
who hath made me an house, as he prom-
ised, Ăd-o-nī′jah shall be put to death
this day.
25 And king Sŏlomon sent by the
hand of Be-nā′iah the son of Je-hoi′a-
da; and he fell upon him that he died.
26 ¶And unto Ă-bī′a-thar the priest
said the king, Get thee to Ăn′a-thŏth,
unto thine own fields; for thou *art*
worthy of death: but I will not at this
time put thee to death, because thou
barest the ark of the Lord GOD before
David my father, and because thou
hast been afflicted in all wherein my
father was afflicted.
27 So Sŏlomon thrust out Ă-bī′a-thar
from being priest unto the LORD; that
he might fulfil the word of the LORD,
which he spake concerning the house
of Eli in Shī′lōh.
28 ¶Then tidings came to Jō′ăb: for
Jō′ăb had turned after Ăd-o-nī′jah,
though he turned not after Ăb′sa-lom.
And Jō′ăb fled unto the tabernacle of
the LORD, and caught hold on the horns
of the altar.
29 And it was told king Sŏlomon that
Jō′ăb was fled unto the tabernacle of
the LORD; and, behold, *he is* by the altar.
Then Sŏlomon sent Be-nā′iah the son of
Je-hoi′a-da, saying, Go, fall upon him.
30 And Be-nā′iah came to the taber-
nacle of the LORD, and said unto him,
Thus saith the king, Come forth. And
he said, Nay; but I will die here. And
Be-nā′iah brought the king word again,
saying, Thus said Jō′ăb, and thus he
answered me.
31 And the king said unto him, Do as
he hath said, and fall upon him, and
bury him; that thou mayest take away
the innocent blood, which Jō′ăb shed,
from me, and from the house of my
father.
32 And the LORD shall return his
blood upon his own head, who fell upon
two men more righteous and better
than he, and slew them with the sword,
my father David not knowing *thereof,*
to wit, Abner the son of Ner, captain of
the host of Israel, and Am′ā-sa the son
of Jē′ther, captain of the host of Jūdah.

33 Their blood shall therefore return
upon the head of Jō'ăb, and upon the
head of his seed for ever: but upon Da-
vid, and upon his seed, and upon his
house, and upon his throne, shall there
be peace for ever from the LORD.
34 So Be-nā'iah the son of Je-hoi'a-da
went up, and fell upon him, and slew
him: and he was buried in his own
house in the wilderness.
35 ¶And the king put Be-nā'iah the
son of Je-hoi'a-da in his room over the
host: and Zā'dŏk the priest did the king
put in the room of Ā-bī'a-thar.
36 ¶And the king sent and called for
Shĭm'e-ī, and said unto him, Build thee
an house in Jerusalem, and dwell there,
and go not forth thence any whither.
37 For it shall be, *that* on the day thou
goest out, and passest over the brook
Kidron, thou shalt know for certain
that thou shalt surely die: thy blood
shall be upon thine own head.
38 And Shĭm'e-ī said unto the king,
The saying *is* good: as my lord the king
hath said, so will thy servant do. And
Shĭm'e-ī dwelt in Jerusalem many
days.
39 And it came to pass at the end of
three years, that two of the servants of
Shĭm'e-ī ran away unto Ā'chĭsh son of
Mā'a-chah king of Gath. And they told
Shĭm'e-ī, saying, Behold, thy servants
be in Gath.
40 And Shĭm'e-ī arose, and saddled
his ass, and went to Gath to Ā'chĭsh to
seek his servants: and Shĭm'e-ī went,
and brought his servants from Gath.
41 And it was told Sŏlomon that
Shĭm'e-ī had gone from Jerusalem to
Gath, and was come again.
42 And the king sent and called for
Shĭm'e-ī, and said unto him, Did I not
make thee to swear by the LORD, and
protested unto thee, saying, Know for a
certain, on the day thou goest out, and
walkest abroad any whither, that thou
shalt surely die? and thou saidst unto
me, The word *that* I have heard *is* good.
43 Why then hast thou not kept the
oath of the LORD, and the command-
ment that I have charged thee with?
44 The king said moreover to Shĭm'-
e-ī, Thou knowest all the wickedness
which thine heart is privy to, that thou
didst to David my father: therefore the
LORD shall return thy wickedness upon
thine own head;
45 And king Sŏlomon *shall be*
blessed, and the throne of David shall
be established before the LORD for ever.
46 So the king commanded Be-nā'iah
the son of Je-hoi'a-da; which went out,
and fell upon him, that he died. And the
kingdom was established in the hand of
Sŏlomon.

CHAPTER 3

AND Sŏlomon made affinity with
Pharaoh king of Egypt, and took
Pharaoh's daughter, and brought her
into the city of David, until he had
made an end of building his own house,
and the house of the LORD, and the wall
of Jerusalem round about.
2 Only the people sacrificed in high
places, because there was no house
built unto the name of the LORD, until
those days.
3 And Sŏlomon loved the LORD,
walking in the statutes of David his
father: only he sacrificed and burnt in-
cense in high places.
4 And the king went to Gĭbeon to sac-
rifice there; for that *was* the great high
place: a thousand burnt offerings did
Sŏlomon offer upon that altar.
5 ¶In Gĭbeon the LORD appeared to
Sŏlomon in a dream by night: and God
said, Ask what I shall give thee.
6 And Sŏlomon said, Thou hast
shewed unto thy servant David my
father great mercy, according as he
walked before thee in truth, and in
righteousness, and in uprightness of
heart with thee; and thou hast kept for
him this great kindness, that thou hast
given him a son to sit on his throne, as *it*
is this day.
7 And now, O LORD my God, thou
hast made thy servant king instead of
David my father: and I *am but* a little
child: I know not *how* to go out or come
in.
8 And thy servant *is* in the midst of
thy people which thou hast chosen, a
great people, that cannot be numbered
nor counted for multitude.
9 Give therefore thy servant an under-
standing heart to judge thy people,
that I may discern between good and
bad: for who is able to judge this thy so
great a people?
10 And the speech pleased the LORD,
that Sŏlomon had asked this thing.
11 And God said unto him, Because
thou hast asked this thing, and hast not
asked for thyself long life; neither hast
asked riches for thyself, nor hast asked
the life of thine enemies; but hast asked
for thyself understanding to discern
judgment;
12 Behold, I have done according to
thy words: lo, I have given thee a wise
and an understanding heart; so that
there was none like thee before thee,
neither after thee shall any arise like
unto thee.
13 And I have also given thee that

which thou hast not asked, both riches, and honour: so that there shall not be any among the kings like unto thee all thy days.

14 And if thou wilt walk in my ways, to keep my statutes and my commandments, as thy father David did walk, then I will lengthen thy days.

15 And Sŏlomon awoke; and, behold, *it was* a dream. And he came to Jerusalem, and stood before the ark of the covenant of the Lord, and offered up burnt offerings, and offered peace offerings, and made a feast to all his servants.

16 ¶Then came there two women, *that were* harlots, unto the king, and stood before him.

17 And the one woman said, O my lord, I and this woman dwell in one house; and I was delivered of a child with her in the house.

18 And it came to pass the third day after that I was delivered, that this woman was delivered also: and we *were* together; *there was* no stranger with us in the house, save we two in the house.

19 And this woman's child died in the night; because she overlaid it.

20 And she arose at midnight, and took my son from beside me, while thine handmaid slept, and laid it in her bosom, and laid her dead child in my bosom.

21 And when I rose in the morning to give my child suck, behold, it was dead: but when I had considered it in the morning, behold, it was not my son, which I did bear.

22 And the other woman said, Nay; but the living *is* my son, and the dead *is* thy son. And this said, No; but the dead *is* thy son, and the living *is* my son. Thus they spake before the king.

23 Then said the king, The one saith, This *is* my son that liveth, and thy son *is* the dead: and the other saith, Nay; but thy son *is* the dead, and my son *is* the living.

24 And the king said, Bring me a sword. And they brought a sword before the king.

25 And the king said, Divide the living child in two, and give half to the one, and half to the other.

26 Then spake the woman whose the living child *was* unto the king, for her bowels yearned upon her son, and she said, O my lord, give her the living child, and in no wise slay it. But the other said, Let it be neither mine nor thine, *but* divide *it*.

27 Then the king answered and said, Give her the living child, and in no wise slay it: she *is* the mother thereof.

28 And all Israel heard of the judgment which the king had judged; and they feared the king: for they saw that the wisdom of God *was* in him, to do judgment.

CHAPTER 4

SO king Sŏlomon was king over all Israel.

2 And these *were* the princes which he had; Ăz-a-rī'ah the son of Zā'dŏk the priest,

3 Ĕl-i-hô'reph and A-hī'ah, the sons of Shī'sha, scribes; Je-hŏsh'a-phăt the son of A-hī'lud, the recorder.

4 And Be-nā'iah the son of Je-hoi'a-da *was* over the host: and Zā'dŏk and Ā-bī'a-thar *were* the priests:

5 And Ăz-a-rī'ah the son of Nāthan *was* over the officers: and Zā'bŭd the son of Nāthan *was* principal officer, *and* the king's friend:

6 And A-hī'shär *was* over the household: and Ăd-o-nī'ram the son of Ăb'da *was* over the tribute.

7 ¶And Sŏlomon had twelve officers over all Israel, which provided victuals for the king and his household: each man his month in a year made provision.

8 And these *are* their names: The son of Hur, in mount Ē'phra-im:

9 The son of Dē'kar, in Mā'kăz, and in Shā-ăl'bĭm, and Bĕth-shĕ'mesh, and Ē'lon-bĕth-hā'nan:

10 The son of Hē'sed, in Ar'ŭ-bŏth; to him *pertained* Sō'chōh, and all the land of Hē'pher:

11 The son of A-bĭn'a-dăb, in all the region of Dor; which had Tā'phăth the daughter of Sŏlomon to wife:

12 Bā'a-na the son of A-hī'lud; *to him pertained* Tā'a-năch and Me-gĭd'dō, and all Bĕth-shē'an, which *is* by Zär'ta-nah beneath Jĕz're-el, from Bĕth-shē'-an to Ā'bel-mĕ-hō'lah, *even* unto *the place that is* beyond Jŏk'ne-am:

13 The son of Gē'ber, in Rā'moth-gĭl'e-ad; to him *pertained* the towns of Jā'ir the son of Ma-năs'seh, which *are* in Gilead; to him *also pertained* the region of Är'gŏb, which *is* in Bā'shan, threescore great cities with walls and brasen bars:

14 A-hĭn'a-dăb the son of Ĭd'dō *had* Mā-ha-nā'im:

15 A-hĭm'ă-az *was* in Năph'ta-lī; he also took Băs'măth the daughter of Sŏlomon to wife:

16 Bā'a-nah the son of Hu'shaī *was* in Asher and in Ā'lŏth:

17 Je-hŏsh'a-phăt the son of Par'ū-ah, in Ĭs'sa-char:

18 Shĭm'e-ī the son of Ē'lah, in Benjamin:

19 Gē'ber the son of Ū'rī *was* in the

country of Gilead, *in* the country of Si-
hon king of the Ămorītes, and of Og
king of Bā'shan; and *he was* the only
officer which *was* in the land.
20 ¶Jūdah and Israel *were* many, as
the sand which *is* by the sea in multi-
tude, eating and drinking, and making
merry.
21 And Sŏlomon reigned over all
kingdoms from the river unto the land
of the Philistines, and unto the border
of Egypt: they brought presents, and
served Sŏlomon all the days of his life.
22 ¶And Sŏlomon's provision for one
day was thirty measures of fine flour,
and threescore measures of meal,
23 Ten fat oxen, and twenty oxen out
of the pastures, and an hundred sheep,
beside harts, and roebucks, and fallow-
deer, and fatted fowl.
24 For he had dominion over all *the
region* on this side the river, from Tīph'-
sah even to Ăz'zah, over all the
kings on this side the river: and he had
peace on all sides round about him.
25 And Jūdah and Israel dwelt safely,
every man under his vine and under his
fig tree, from Dan even to Be'er–shē'ba,
all the days of Sŏlomon.
26 ¶And Sŏlomon had forty thousand
stalls of horses for his chariots, and
twelve thousand horsemen.
27 And those officers provided vic-
tual for king Sŏlomon, and for all that
came unto king Sŏlomon's table, every
man in his month: they lacked nothing.
28 Barley also and straw for the
horses and dromedaries brought they
unto the place where *the officers* were,
every man according to his charge.
29 ¶And God gave Sŏlomon wisdom
and understanding exceeding much,
and largeness of heart, even as the sand
that *is* on the sea shore.
30 And Sŏlomon's wisdom excelled
the wisdom of all the children of the
east country, and all the wisdom of
Egypt.
31 For he was wiser than all men;
than Ethan the Ĕz'ra-hīte, and Hē'măn,
and Chăl'cŏl, and Där'da, the sons of
Mā'hŏl: and his fame was in all nations
round about.
32 And he spake three thousand prov-
erbs: and his songs were a thousand
and five.
33 And he spake of trees, from the ce-
dar tree that *is* in Lebanon even unto
the hyssop that springeth out of the
wall: he spake also of beasts, and of
fowl, and of creeping things, and of
fishes.
34 And there came of all people to
hear the wisdom of Sŏlomon, from all
kings of the earth, which had heard of
his wisdom.

CHAPTER 5

AND Hiram king of Tyre sent his ser-
vants unto Sŏlomon; for he had heard
that they had anointed him king in the
room of his father: for Hiram was ever
a lover of David.
2 And Sŏlomon sent to Hiram,
saying,
3 Thou knowest how that David my
father could not build an house unto
the name of the LORD his God for the
wars which were about him on every
side, until the LORD put them under the
soles of his feet.
4 But now the LORD my God hath giv-
en me rest on every side, *so that there
is* neither adversary nor evil occurrent.
5 And, behold, I purpose to build an
house unto the name of the LORD my
God, as the LORD spake unto David my
father, saying, Thy son, whom I will set
upon thy throne in thy room, he shall
build an house unto my name.
6 Now therefore command thou that
they hew me cedar trees out of Leba-
non; and my servants shall be with thy
servants: and unto thee will I give hire
for thy servants according to all that
thou shalt appoint: for thou knowest
that *there is* not among us any that can
skill to hew timber like unto the Si-dō'ni-
ans.
7 ¶And it came to pass, when Hiram
heard the words of Sŏlomon, that he re-
joiced greatly, and said, Blessed *be* the
LORD this day, which hath given unto
David a wise son over this great people.
8 And Hiram sent to Sŏlomon,
saying, I have considered the things
which thou sentest to me for: *and* I will
do all thy desire concerning timber of
cedar, and concerning timber of fir.
9 My servants shall bring *them* down
from Lebanon unto the sea: and I will
convey them by sea in floats unto the
place that thou shalt appoint me, and
will cause them to be discharged there,
and thou shalt receive *them:* and thou
shalt accomplish my desire, in giving
food for my household.
10 So Hiram gave Sŏlomon cedar
trees and fir trees *according to* all his
desire.
11 And Sŏlomon gave Hiram twenty
thousand measures of wheat *for* food
to his household, and twenty measures
of pure oil: thus gave Sŏlomon to
Hiram year by year.
12 And the LORD gave Sŏlomon wis-
dom, as he promised him: and there
was peace between Hiram and Sŏlo-

mon; and they two made a league to-
gether.
13 ¶And king Sŏlomon raised a levy
out of all Israel; and the levy was thirty
thousand men.
14 And he sent them to Lebanon, ten
thousand a month by courses: a month
they were in Lebanon, *and* two months
at home: and Ăd-o-nī'ram *was* over the
levy.
15 And Sŏlomon had threescore and
ten thousand that bare burdens, and
fourscore thousand hewers in the
mountains;
16 Beside the chief of Sŏlomon's offi-
cers which *were* over the work, three
thousand and three hundred, which
ruled over the people that wrought in
the work.
17 And the king commanded, and
they brought great stones, costly
stones, *and* hewed stones, to lay the
foundation of the house.
18 And Sŏlomon's builders and
Hiram's builders did hew *them*, and the
stonesquarers: so they prepared timber
and stones to build the house.

CHAPTER 6

AND it came to pass in the four
hundred and eightieth year after the
children of Israel were come out of the
land of Egypt, in the fourth year of Sŏl-
omon's reign over Israel, in the month
Zif, which *is* the second month, that he
began to build the house of the LORD.
2 And the house which king Sŏlomon
built for the LORD, the length thereof
was threescore cubits, and the breadth
thereof twenty *cubits*, and the height
thereof thirty cubits.
3 And the porch before the temple of
the house, twenty cubits *was* the length
thereof, according to the breadth of the
house; *and* ten cubits *was* the breadth
thereof before the house.
4 And for the house he made win-
dows of narrow lights.
5 And against the wall of the house he
built chambers round about, *against*
the walls of the house round about,
both of the temple and of the oracle:
and he made chambers round about:
6 The nethermost chamber *was* five
cubits broad, and the middle *was* six
cubits broad, and the third *was* seven
cubits broad: for without *in the wall* of
the house he made narrowed rests
round about, that *the beams* should not
be fastened in the walls of the house.
7 And the house, when it was in build-
ing, was built of stone made ready be-
fore it was brought thither: so that
there was neither hammer nor axe *nor*
any tool of iron heard in the house,
while it was in building.
8 The door for the middle chamber
was in the right side of the house: and
they went up with winding stairs into
the middle *chamber*, and out of the
middle into the third.
9 So he built the house, and finished
it; and covered the house with beams
and boards of cedar.
10 And *then* he built chambers
against all the house, five cubits high:
and they rested on the house with tim-
ber of cedar.
11 ¶And the word of the LORD came
to Sŏlomon, saying,
12 *Concerning* this house which thou
art in building, if thou wilt walk in my
statutes, and execute my judgments,
and keep all my commandments to
walk in them; then will I perform my
word with thee, which I spake unto Da-
vid thy father:
13 And I will dwell among the chil-
dren of Israel, and will not forsake my
people Israel.
14 So Sŏlomon built the house, and
finished it.
15 And he built the walls of the house
within with boards of cedar, both the
floor of the house, and the walls of the
ceiling: *and* he covered *them* on the in-
side with wood, and covered the floor
of the house with planks of fir.
16 And he built twenty cubits on the
sides of the house, both the floor and
the walls with boards of cedar: he even
built *them* for it within, *even* for the
oracle, *even* for the most holy *place*.
17 And the house, that *is*, the temple
before it, was forty cubits *long*.
18 And the cedar of the house within
was carved with knops and open flow-
ers: all *was* cedar; there was no stone
seen.
19 And the oracle he prepared in the
house within, to set there the ark of the
covenant of the LORD.
20 And the oracle in the forepart *was*
twenty cubits in length, and twenty cu-
bits in breadth, and twenty cubits in the
height thereof: and he overlaid it with
pure gold; and *so* covered the altar
which was of cedar.
21 So Sŏlomon overlaid the house
within with pure gold: and he made a
partition by the chains of gold before
the oracle; and he overlaid it with gold.
22 And the whole house he overlaid
with gold, until he had finished all the
house: also the whole altar that *was* by
the oracle he overlaid with gold.
23 ¶And within the oracle he made
two cherubims *of* olive tree, *each* ten
cubits high.

24 And five cubits *was* the one wing
of the cherub, and five cubits the other
wing of the cherub: from the uttermost
part of the one wing unto the uttermost
part of the other *were* ten cubits.
25 And the other cherub *was* ten cu-
bits: both the cherubims *were* of one
measure and one size.
26 The height of the one cherub *was*
ten cubits, and so *was it* of the other
cherub.
27 And he set the cherubims within
the inner house: and they stretched
forth the wings of the cherubims, so
that the wing of the one touched the
one wall, and the wing of the other
cherub touched the other wall; and
their wings touched one another in the
midst of the house.
28 And he overlaid the cherubims
with gold.
29 And he carved all the walls of the
house round about with carved figures
of cherubims and palm trees and open
flowers, within and without.
30 And the floor of the house he over-
laid with gold, within and without.
31 ¶And for the entering of the oracle
he made doors *of* olive tree: the lintel
and side posts *were* a fifth part *of the
wall*.
32 The two doors also *were of* olive
tree; and he carved upon them carvings
of cherubims and palm trees and open
flowers, and overlaid *them* with gold,
and spread gold upon the cherubims,
and upon the palm trees.
33 So also made he for the door of the
temple posts *of* olive tree, a fourth part
of the wall.
34 And the two doors *were of* fir tree:
the two leaves of the one door *were*
folding, and the two leaves of the other
door *were* folding.
35 And he carved *thereon* cherubims
and palm trees and open flowers: and
covered *them* with gold fitted upon the
carved work.
36 And he built the inner court with
three rows of hewed stone, and a row of
cedar beams.
37 ¶In the fourth year was the foun-
dation of the house of the LORD laid, in
the month Zif:
38 And in the eleventh year, in the
month Bul, which *is* the eighth month,
was the house finished throughout all
the parts thereof, and according to all
the fashion of it. So was he seven years
in building it.

CHAPTER 7

BUT Sŏlomon was building his own
house thirteen years, and he finished
all his house.
2 ¶He built also the house of the
forest of Lebanon; the length thereof
was an hundred cubits, and the breadth
thereof fifty cubits, and the height
thereof thirty cubits, upon four rows of
cedar pillars, with cedar beams upon
the pillars.
3 And *it was* covered with cedar
above upon the beams, that *lay* on forty
five pillars, fifteen *in* a row.
4 And *there were* windows *in* three
rows, and light *was* against light *in*
three ranks.
5 And all the doors and posts *were*
square, with the windows: and light
was against light *in* three ranks.
6 ¶And he made a porch of pillars; the
length thereof *was* fifty cubits, and the
breadth thereof thirty cubits: and the
porch *was* before them: and the *other*
pillars and the thick beam *were* before
them.
7 Then he made a porch for the
throne where he might judge, *even* the
porch of judgment: and *it was* covered
with cedar from one side of the floor to
the other.
8 And his house where he dwelt *had*
another court within the porch, *which*
was of the like work. Sŏlomon made
also an house for Pharaoh's daughter,
whom he had taken *to wife*, like unto
this porch.
9 All these *were of* costly stones, ac-
cording to the measures of hewed
stones, sawed with saws, within and
without, even from the foundation unto
the coping, and *so* on the outside to-
ward the great court.
10 And the foundation *was of* costly
stones, even great stones, stones of ten
cubits, and stones of eight cubits.
11 And above *were* costly stones, af-
ter the measures of hewed stones, and
cedars.
12 And the great court round about
was with three rows of hewed stones,
and a row of cedar beams, both for the
inner court of the house of the LORD,
and for the porch of the house.
13 ¶And king Sŏlomon sent and
fetched Hiram out of Tyre.
14 He *was* a widow's son of the tribe
of Năph'ta-lī, and his father *was* a man
of Tyre, a worker in brass: and he was
filled with wisdom, and understanding,
and cunning to work all works in brass.
And he came to king Sŏlomon, and
wrought all his work.
15 For he cast two pillars of brass, of
eighteen cubits high apiece: and a line
of twelve cubits did compass either of
them about.
16 And he made two chapiters *of*
molten brass, to set upon the tops of

the pillars: the height of the one chapiter *was* five cubits, and the height of the other chapiter *was* five cubits:
17 *And* nets of checker work, and wreaths of chain work, for the chapiters which *were* upon the top of the pillars; seven for the one chapiter, and seven for the other chapiter.
18 And he made the pillars, and two rows round about upon the one network, to cover the chapiters that *were* upon the top, with pomegranates: and so did he for the other chapiter.
19 And the chapiters that *were* upon the top of the pillars *were* of lily work in the porch, four cubits.
20 And the chapiters upon the two pillars *had pomegranates* also above, over against the belly which *was* by the network: and the pomegranates *were* two hundred in rows round about upon the other chapiter.
21 And he set up the pillars in the porch of the temple: and he set up the right pillar, and called the name thereof Jā'chin: and he set up the left pillar, and called the name thereof Bō'ăz.
22 And upon the top of the pillars *was* lily work: so was the work of the pillars finished.
23 ¶And he made a molten sea, ten cubits from the one brim to the other: *it was* round all about, and his height *was* five cubits: and a line of thirty cubits did compass it round about.
24 And under the brim of it round about *there were* knops compassing it, ten in a cubit, compassing the sea round about: the knops *were* cast in two rows, when it was cast.
25 It stood upon twelve oxen, three looking toward the north, and three looking toward the west, and three looking toward the south, and three looking toward the east: and the sea *was set* above upon them, and all their hinder parts *were* inward.
26 And it *was* an hand breadth thick, and the brim thereof was wrought like the brim of a cup, with flowers of lilies: it contained two thousand baths.
27 ¶And he made ten bases of brass; four cubits *was* the length of one base, and four cubits the breadth thereof, and three cubits the height of it.
28 And the work of the bases *was* on this *manner*: they had borders, and the borders *were* between the ledges:
29 And on the borders that *were* between the ledges *were* lions, oxen, and cherubims: and upon the ledges *there was* a base above: and beneath the lions and oxen *were* certain additions made of thin work.
30 And every base had four brasen wheels, and plates of brass: and the four corners thereof had undersetters: under the laver *were* undersetters molten, at the side of every addition.
31 And the mouth of it within the chapiter and above *was* a cubit: but the mouth thereof *was* round *after* the work of the base, a cubit and an half: and also upon the mouth of it *were* gravings with their borders, foursquare, not round.
32 And under the borders *were* four wheels; and the axletrees of the wheels *were joined* to the base: and the height of a wheel *was* a cubit and half a cubit.
33 And the work of the wheels *was* like the work of a chariot wheel: their axletrees, and their naves, and their felloes, and their spokes, *were* all molten.
34 And *there were* four undersetters to the four corners of one base: *and* the undersetters *were* of the very base itself.
35 And in the top of the base *was there* a round compass of half a cubit high: and on the top of the base the ledges thereof and the borders thereof *were* of the same.
36 For on the plates of the ledges thereof, and on the borders thereof, he graved cherubims, lions, and palm trees, according to the proportion of every one, and additions round about.
37 After this *manner* he made the ten bases: all of them had one casting, one measure, *and* one size.
38 Then made he ten lavers of brass: one laver contained forty baths: *and* every laver was four cubits: *and* upon every one of the ten bases one laver.
39 And he put five bases on the right side of the house, and five on the left side of the house: and he set the sea on the right side of the house eastward over against the south.
40 ¶And Hiram made the lavers, and the shovels, and the basons. So Hiram made an end of doing all the work that he made king Sŏlomon for the house of the LORD:
41 The two pillars, and the *two* bowls of the chapiters that *were* on the top of the two pillars; and the two networks, to cover the two bowls of the chapiters which *were* upon the top of the pillars;
42 And four hundred pomegranates for the two networks, *even* two rows of pomegranates for one network, to cover the two bowls of the chapiters that *were* upon the pillars;
43 And the ten bases, and ten lavers on the bases;
44 And one sea, and twelve oxen under the sea;
45 And the pots, and the shovels, and

the basons: and all these vessels, which
Hiram made to king Sŏlomon for the
house of the LORD, *were of* bright brass.
46 In the plain of Jordan did the king
cast them, in the clay ground between
Sŭc'coth and Zär'thăn,
47 And Sŏlomon left all the vessels
unweighed, because they were exceed-
ing many: neither was the weight of the
brass found out.
48 And Sŏlomon made all the vessels
that *pertained* unto the house of the
LORD: the altar of gold, and the table of
gold, whereupon the shewbread *was*,
49 And the candlesticks of pure gold,
five on the right *side*, and five on the
left, before the oracle, with the flowers,
and the lamps, and the tongs *of* gold,
50 And the bowls, and the snuffers,
and the basons, and the spoons, and the
censers *of* pure gold; and the hinges *of*
gold, *both* for the doors of the inner
house, the most holy *place*, *and* for the
doors of the house, *to wit*, of the
temple.
51 So was ended all the work that
king Sŏlomon made for the house of
the LORD. And Sŏlomon brought in the
things which David his father had dedi-
cated; *even* the silver, and the gold, and
the vessels, did he put among the trea-
sures of the house of the LORD.

CHAPTER 8

THEN Sŏlomon assembled the elders
of Israel, and all the heads of the tribes,
the chief of the fathers of the children
of Israel, unto king Sŏlomon in Jeru-
salem, that they might bring up the ark
of the covenant of the LORD out of the
city of David, which *is* Zion.
2 And all the men of Israel assembled
themselves unto king Sŏlomon at the
feast in the month Ĕth'a-nĭm, which *is*
the seventh month.
3 And all the elders of Israel came,
and the priests took up the ark.
4 And they brought up the ark of the
LORD, and the tabernacle of the congre-
gation, and all the holy vessels that
were in the tabernacle, even those did
the priests and the Levites bring up.
5 And king Sŏlomon, and all the
congregation of Israel, that were as-
sembled unto him, *were* with him be-
fore the ark, sacrificing sheep and
oxen, that could not be told nor num-
bered for multitude.
6 And the priests brought in the ark
of the covenant of the LORD unto his
place, into the oracle of the house, to
the most holy *place*, *even* under the
wings of the cherubims.
7 For the cherubims spread forth
their two wings over the place of the
ark, and the cherubims covered the ark
and the staves thereof above.
8 And they drew out the staves, that
the ends of the staves were seen out in
the holy *place* before the oracle, and
they were not seen without: and there
they are unto this day.
9 *There was* nothing in the ark save
the two tables of stone, which Moses
put there at Hô'rĕb, when the LORD
made *a covenant* with the children of
Israel, when they came out of the land
of Egypt.
10 And it came to pass, when the
priests were come out of the holy *place*,
that the cloud filled the house of the
LORD,
11 So that the priests could not stand
to minister because of the cloud: for the
glory of the LORD had filled the house of
the LORD.
12 ¶Then spake Sŏlomon, The LORD
said that he would dwell in the thick
darkness.
13 I have surely built thee an house to
dwell in, a settled place for thee to
abide in for ever.
14 And the king turned his face
about, and blessed all the congregation
of Israel: (and all the congregation of
Israel stood;)
15 And he said, Blessed *be* the LORD
God of Israel, which spake with his
mouth unto David my father, and hath
with his hand fulfilled *it*, saying,
16 Since the day that I brought forth
my people Israel out of Egypt, I chose
no city out of all the tribes of Israel to
build an house, that my name might be
therein; but I chose David to be over
my people Israel.
17 And it was in the heart of David
my father to build an house for the
name of the LORD God of Israel.
18 And the LORD said unto David my
father, Whereas it was in thine heart to
build an house unto my name, thou
didst well that it was in thine heart.
19 Nevertheless thou shalt not build
the house; but thy son that shall come
forth out of thy loins, he shall build the
house unto my name.
20 And the LORD hath performed his
word that he spake, and I am risen up in
the room of David my father, and sit on
the throne of Israel, as the LORD prom-
ised, and have built an house for the
name of the LORD God of Israel.
21 And I have set there a place for the
ark, wherein *is* the covenant of the
LORD, which he made with our fathers,
when he brought them out of the land
of Egypt.
22 ¶And Sŏlomon stood before the al-
tar of the LORD in the presence of all the

congregation of Israel, and spread
forth his hands toward heaven:
23 And he said, LORD God of Israel,
there is no God like thee, in heaven
above, or on earth beneath, who keep-
est covenant and mercy with thy ser-
vants that walk before thee with all
their heart:
24 Who hast kept with thy servant
David my father that thou promisedst
him: thou spakest also with thy mouth,
and hast fulfilled *it* with thine hand, as
it is this day.
25 Therefore now, LORD God of
Israel, keep with thy servant David my
father that thou promisedst him,
saying, There shall not fail thee a man
in my sight to sit on the throne of Israel;
so that thy children take heed to their
way, that they walk before me as thou
hast walked before me.
26 And now, O God of Israel, let thy
word, I pray thee, be verified, which
thou spakest unto thy servant David
my father.
27 But will God indeed dwell on the
earth? behold, the heaven and heaven
of heavens cannot contain thee; how
much less this house that I have
builded?
28 Yet have thou respect unto the
prayer of thy servant, and to his suppli-
cation, O LORD my God, to hearken
unto the cry and to the prayer, which
thy servant prayeth before thee to day:
29 That thine eyes may be open to-
ward this house night and day, *even* to-
ward the place of which thou hast said,
My name shall be there: that thou
mayest hearken unto the prayer which
thy servant shall make toward this
place.
30 And hearken thou to the supplica-
tion of thy servant, and of thy people
Israel, when they shall pray toward this
place: and hear thou in heaven thy
dwelling place: and when thou hearest,
forgive.
31 ¶If any man trespass against his
neighbour, and an oath be laid upon
him to cause him to swear, and the oath
come before thine altar in this house:
32 Then hear thou in heaven, and do,
and judge thy servants, condemning
the wicked, to bring his way upon his
head; and justifying the righteous, to
give him according to his righteous-
ness.
33 ¶When thy people Israel be smit-
ten down before the enemy, because
they have sinned against thee, and
shall turn again to thee, and confess thy
name, and pray, and make supplication
unto thee in this house:
34 Then hear thou in heaven, and for-
give the sin of thy people Israel, and
bring them again unto the land which
thou gavest unto their fathers.
35 ¶When heaven is shut up, and
there is no rain, because they have
sinned against thee; if they pray to-
ward this place, and confess thy name,
and turn from their sin, when thou af-
flictest them:
36 Then hear thou in heaven, and for-
give the sin of thy servants, and of thy
people Israel, that thou teach them the
good way wherein they should walk,
and give rain upon thy land, which thou
hast given to thy people for an inheri-
tance.
37 ¶If there be in the land famine, if
there be pestilence, blasting, mildew,
locust, *or* if there be caterpiller; if their
enemy besiege them in the land of their
cities; whatsoever plague, whatsoever
sickness *there be;*
38 What prayer and supplication so-
ever be *made* by any man, *or* by all thy
people Israel, which shall know every
man the plague of his own heart, and
spread forth his hands toward this
house:
39 Then hear thou in heaven thy
dwelling place, and forgive, and do,
and give to every man according to his
ways, whose heart thou knowest; (for
thou, *even* thou only, knowest the
hearts of all the children of men;)
40 That they may fear thee all the
days that they live in the land which
thou gavest unto our fathers.
41 ¶Moreover concerning a stranger,
that *is* not of thy people Israel, but
cometh out of a far country for thy
name's sake;
42 (For they shall hear of thy great
name, and of thy strong hand, and of
thy stretched out arm;) when he shall
come and pray toward this house;
43 Hear thou in heaven thy dwelling
place, and do according to all that the
stranger calleth to thee for: that all
people of the earth may know thy
name, to fear thee, as *do* thy people
Israel; and that they may know that
this house, which I have builded, is
called by thy name.
44 ¶If thy people go out to battle
against their enemy, whithersoever
thou shalt send them, and shall pray
unto the LORD toward the city which
thou hast chosen, and *toward* the
house that I have built for thy name:
45 Then hear thou in heaven their
prayer and their supplication, and
maintain their cause.
46 If they sin against thee, (for *there*
is no man that sinneth not,) and thou be
angry with them, and deliver them to

the enemy, so that they carry them away captives unto the land of the enemy, far or near;
47 *Yet* if they shall bethink themselves in the land whither they were carried captives, and repent, and make supplication unto thee in the land of them that carried them captives, saying, We have sinned, and have done perversely, we have committed wickedness;
48 And *so* return unto thee with all their heart, and with all their soul, in the land of their enemies, which led them away captive, and pray unto thee toward their land, which thou gavest unto their fathers, the city which thou hast chosen, and the house which I have built for thy name:
49 Then hear thou their prayer and their supplication in heaven thy dwelling place, and maintain their cause,
50 And forgive thy people that have sinned against thee, and all their transgressions wherein they have transgressed against thee, and give them compassion before them who carried them captive, that they may have compassion on them:
51 For they *be* thy people, and thine inheritance, which thou broughtest forth out of Egypt, from the midst of the furnace of iron:
52 That thine eyes may be open unto the supplication of thy servant, and unto the supplication of thy people Israel, to hearken unto them in all that they call for unto thee.
53 For thou didst separate them from among all the people of the earth, *to be* thine inheritance, as thou spakest by the hand of Moses thy servant, when thou broughtest our fathers out of Egypt, O Lord GOD.
54 ¶And it was *so*, that when Sŏlomon had made an end of praying all this prayer and supplication unto the LORD, he arose from before the altar of the LORD, from kneeling on his knees with his hands spread up to heaven.
55 And he stood, and blessed all the congregation of Israel with a loud voice, saying,
56 Blessed *be* the LORD, that hath given rest unto his people Israel, according to all that he promised: there hath not failed one word of all his good promise, which he promised by the hand of Moses his servant.
57 The LORD our God be with us, as he was with our fathers: let him not leave us, nor forsake us:
58 That he may incline our hearts unto him, to walk in all his ways, and to keep his commandments, and his statutes, and his judgments, which he commanded our fathers.
59 And let these my words, wherewith I have made supplication before the LORD, be nigh unto the LORD our God day and night, that he maintain the cause of his servant, and the cause of his people Israel at all times, as the matter shall require:
60 That all the people of the earth may know that the LORD *is* God, *and that there is* none else.
61 Let your heart therefore be perfect with the LORD our God, to walk in his statutes, and to keep his commandments, as at this day.
62 ¶And the king, and all Israel with him, offered sacrifice before the LORD.
63 And Sŏlomon offered a sacrifice of peace offerings, which he offered unto the LORD, two and twenty thousand oxen, and an hundred and twenty thousand sheep. So the king and all the children of Israel dedicated the house of the LORD.
64 The same day did the king hallow the middle of the court that *was* before the house of the LORD: for there he offered burnt offerings, and meat offerings, and the fat of the peace offerings: because the brasen altar that *was* before the LORD *was* too little to receive the burnt offerings, and meat offerings, and the fat of the peace offerings.
65 ¶And at that time Sŏlomon held a feast, and all Israel with him, a great congregation, from the entering in of Hā′măth unto the river of Egypt, before the LORD our God, seven days and seven days, *even* fourteen days.
66 On the eighth day he sent the people away: and they blessed the king, and went unto their tents joyful and glad of heart for all the goodness that the LORD had done for David his servant, and for Israel his people.

CHAPTER 9

AND it came to pass, when Sŏlomon had finished the building of the house of the LORD, and the king's house, and all Sŏlomon's desire which he was pleased to do,
2 That the LORD appeared to Sŏlomon the second time, as he had appeared unto him at Gĭbeon.
3 And the LORD said unto him, I have heard thy prayer and thy supplication, that thou hast made before me: I have hallowed this house, which thou hast built, to put my name there for ever; and mine eyes and mine heart shall be there perpetually.
4 And if thou wilt walk before me, as David thy father walked, in integrity of

heart, and in uprightness, to do according to all that I have commanded thee, *and* wilt keep my statutes and my judgments:

5 Then I will establish the throne of thy kingdom upon Israel for ever, as I promised to David thy father, saying, There shall not fail thee a man upon the throne of Israel.

6 *But* if ye shall at all turn from following me, ye or your children, and will not keep my commandments *and* my statutes which I have set before you, but go and serve other gods, and worship them:

7 Then will I cut off Israel out of the land which I have given them; and this house, which I have hallowed for my name, will I cast out of my sight; and Israel shall be a proverb and a byword among all people:

8 And at this house, *which* is high, every one that passeth by it shall be astonished, and shall hiss; and they shall say, Why hath the LORD done thus unto this land, and to this house?

9 And they shall answer, Because they forsook the LORD their God, who brought forth their fathers out of the land of Egypt, and have taken hold upon other gods, and have worshipped them, and served them: therefore hath the LORD brought upon them all this evil.

10 ¶And it came to pass at the end of twenty years, when Sŏlomon had built the two houses, the house of the LORD, and the king's house,

11 (*Now* Hiram the king of Tyre had furnished Sŏlomon with cedar trees and fir trees, and with gold, according to all his desire,) that then king Sŏlomon gave Hiram twenty cities in the land of Galilee.

12 And Hiram came out from Tyre to see the cities which Sŏlomon had given him; and they pleased him not.

13 And he said, What cities *are* these which thou hast given me, my brother? And he called them the land of Cā'bul unto this day.

14 And Hiram sent to the king sixscore talents of gold.

15 ¶And this *is* the reason of the levy which king Sŏlomon raised; for to build the house of the LORD, and his own house, and Mĭl'lō, and the wall of Jerusalem, and Hā'zôr, and Me-gĭd'dō, and Gē'zer.

16 *For* Pharaoh king of Egypt had gone up, and taken Gē'zer, and burnt it with fire, and slain the Canaanites that dwelt in the city, and given it *for* a present unto his daughter, Sŏlomon's wife.

17 And Sŏlomon built Gē'zer, and Bĕth-hô'ron the nether,

18 And Bā'al-ăth, and Tăd'môr in the wilderness, in the land,

19 And all the cities of store that Sŏlomon had, and cities for his chariots, and cities for his horsemen, and that which Sŏlomon desired to build in Jerusalem, and in Lebanon, and in all the land of his dominion.

20 *And* all the people *that were* left of the Ămorītes, Hittites, Pĕr'iz-zītes, Hī'vītes, and Jēb'u-sītes, which *were* not of the children of Israel,

21 Their children that were left after them in the land, whom the children of Israel also were not able utterly to destroy, upon those did Sŏlomon levy a tribute of bondservice unto this day.

22 But of the children of Israel did Sŏlomon make no bondmen: but they *were* men of war, and his servants, and his princes, and his captains, and rulers of his chariots, and his horsemen.

23 These *were* the chief of the officers that *were* over Sŏlomon's work, five hundred and fifty, which bare rule over the people that wrought in the work.

24 ¶But Pharaoh's daughter came up out of the city of David unto her house which *Solomon* had built for her: then did he build Mĭl'lō.

25 ¶And three times in a year did Sŏlomon offer burnt offerings and peace offerings upon the altar which he built unto the LORD, and he burnt incense upon the altar that *was* before the LORD. So he finished the house.

26 ¶And king Sŏlomon made a navy of ships in Ĕ'zĭ-on-gē'ber, which *is* beside Ē'lŏth, on the shore of the Red sea, in the land of Ē'dom.

27 And Hiram sent in the navy his servants, shipmen that had knowledge of the sea, with the servants of Sŏlomon.

28 And they came to Ō'phir, and fetched from thence gold, four hundred and twenty talents, and brought *it* to king Sŏlomon.

CHAPTER 10

AND when the queen of Shēba heard of the fame of Sŏlomon concerning the name of the LORD, she came to prove him with hard questions.

2 And she came to Jerusalem with a very great train, with camels that bare spices, and very much gold, and precious stones: and when she was come to Sŏlomon, she communed with him of all that was in her heart.

3 And Sŏlomon told her all her ques-

tions: there was not *any* thing hid from the king, which he told her not.

4 And when the queen of Shēba had seen all Sŏlomon's wisdom, and the house that he had built,

5 And the meat of his table, and the sitting of his servants, and the attendance of his ministers, and their apparel, and his cupbearers, and his ascent by which he went up unto the house of the LORD; there was no more spirit in her.

6 And she said to the king, It was a true report that I heard in mine own land of thy acts and of thy wisdom.

7 Howbeit I believed not the words, until I came, and mine eyes had seen *it:* and, behold, the half was not told me: thy wisdom and prosperity exceedeth the fame which I heard.

8 Happy *are* thy men, happy *are* these thy servants, which stand continually before thee, *and* that hear thy wisdom.

9 Blessed be the LORD thy God, which delighted in thee, to set thee on the throne of Israel: because the LORD loved Israel for ever, therefore made he thee king, to do judgment and justice.

10 And she gave the king an hundred and twenty talents of gold, and of spices very great store, and precious stones: there came no more such abundance of spices as these which the queen of Shēba gave to king Sŏlomon.

11 And the navy also of Hiram, that brought gold from Ō'phir, brought in from Ō'phir great plenty of almug trees, and precious stones.

12 And the king made of the almug trees pillars for the house of the LORD, and for the king's house, harps also and psalteries for singers: there came no such almug trees, nor were seen unto this day.

13 And king Sŏlomon gave unto the queen of Shēba all her desire, whatsoever she asked, beside *that* which Sŏlomon gave her of his royal bounty. So she turned and went to her own country, she and her servants.

14 ¶Now the weight of gold that came to Sŏlomon in one year was six hundred threescore and six talents of gold,

15 Beside *that he had* of the merchantmen, and of the traffick of the spice merchants, and of all the kings of Arabia, and of the governors of the country.

16 ¶And king Sŏlomon made two hundred targets *of* beaten gold: six hundred *shekels* of gold went to one target.

17 And *he made* three hundred shields *of* beaten gold; three pound of gold went to one shield: and the king put them in the house of the forest of Lebanon.

18 ¶Moreover the king made a great throne of ivory, and overlaid it with the best gold.

19 The throne had six steps, and the top of the throne *was* round behind: and *there were* stays on either side on the place of the seat, and two lions stood beside the stays.

20 And twelve lions stood there on the one side and on the other upon the six steps: there was not the like made in any kingdom.

21 And all king Sŏlomon's drinking vessels *were of* gold, and all the vessels of the house of the forest of Lebanon *were of* pure gold; none *were of* silver: it was nothing accounted of in the days of Sŏlomon.

22 For the king had at sea a navy of Thär'shĭsh with the navy of Hiram: once in three years came the navy of Thär'shĭsh, bringing gold, and silver, ivory, and apes, and peacocks.

23 So king Sŏlomon exceeded all the kings of the earth for riches and for wisdom.

24 ¶And all the earth sought to Sŏlomon, to hear his wisdom, which God had put in his heart.

25 And they brought every man his present, vessels of silver, and vessels of gold, and garments, and armour, and spices, horses, and mules, a rate year by year.

26 ¶And Sŏlomon gathered together chariots and horsemen: and he had a thousand and four hundred chariots, and twelve thousand horsemen, whom he bestowed in the cities for chariots, and with the king at Jerusalem.

27 And the king made silver *to be* in Jerusalem as stones, and cedars made he *to be* as the sycomore trees that *are* in the vale, for abundance.

28 ¶And Sŏlomon had horses brought out of Egypt, and linen yarn: the king's merchants received the linen yarn at a price.

29 And a chariot came up and went out of Egypt for six hundred *shekels* of silver, and an horse for an hundred and fifty: and so for all the kings of the Hittites, and for the kings of Syria, did they bring *them* out by their means.

CHAPTER 11

BUT king Sŏlomon loved many strange women, together with the daughter of Pharaoh, women of the Moabites, Ammonites, Edomites, Zī-dō'nĭ-ans, *and* Hittites;

2 Of the nations *concerning* which

the LORD said unto the children of
Israel, Ye shall not go in to them,
neither shall they come in unto you: *for*
surely they will turn away your heart
after their gods: Sŏlomon clave unto
these in love.
3 And he had seven hundred wives,
princesses, and three hundred concu-
bines: and his wives turned away his
heart.
4 For it came to pass, when Sŏlomon
was old, *that* his wives turned away his
heart after other gods: and his heart
was not perfect with the LORD his God,
as *was* the heart of David his father.
5 For Sŏlomon went after Ăsh′to-rĕth
the goddess of the Zī-dō′nĭ-ans, and af-
ter Mĭl′com the abomination of the
Ammonites.
6 And Sŏlomon did evil in the sight of
the LORD, and went not fully after the
LORD, as *did* David his father.
7 Then did Sŏlomon build an high
place for Chē′mŏsh, the abomination of
Moab, in the hill that *is* before Jeru-
salem, and for Mō′lĕch, the abomina-
tion of the children of Ammon.
8 And likewise did he for all his
strange wives, which burnt incense
and sacrificed unto their gods.
9 ¶And the LORD was angry with Sŏl-
omon, because his heart was turned
from the LORD God of Israel, which had
appeared unto him twice,
10 And had commanded him concern-
ing this thing, that he should not go
after other gods: but he kept not that
which the LORD commanded.
11 Wherefore the LORD said unto Sŏl-
omon, Forasmuch as this is done of
thee, and thou hast not kept my cove-
nant and my statutes, which I have
commanded thee, I will surely rend the
kingdom from thee, and will give it to
thy servant.
12 Notwithstanding in thy days I will
not do it for David thy father's sake:
but I will rend it out of the hand of thy
son.
13 Howbeit I will not rend away all
the kingdom; *but* will give one tribe to
thy son for David my servant's sake,
and for Jerusalem's sake which I have
chosen.
14 ¶And the LORD stirred up an adver-
sary unto Sŏlomon, Hā′dăd the
Edomite: he *was* of the king's seed in
Ēdom.
15 For it came to pass, when David
was in Ēdom, and Jō′ăb the captain of
the host was gone up to bury the slain,
after he had smitten every male in
Ēdom;
16 (For six months did Jō′ăb remain
there with all Israel, until he had cut off
every male in Ēdom:)
17 That Hā′dăd fled, he and certain
Edomites of his father's servants with
him, to go into Egypt; Hā′dăd *being* yet
a little child.
18 And they arose out of Mĭd′ĭ-an,
and came to Paran: and they took men
with them out of Paran, and they came
to Egypt, unto Pharaoh king of Egypt;
which gave him an house, and ap-
pointed him victuals, and gave him
land.
19 And Hā′dăd found great favour in
the sight of Pharaoh, so that he gave
him to wife the sister of his own wife,
the sister of Täh′pen-ēṡ the queen.
20 And the sister of Täh′pen-ēṡ bare
him Ge-nū′băth his son, whom
Täh′pen-ēṡ weaned in Pharaoh's house:
and Ge-nū′băth was in Pharaoh's
household among the sons of Pharaoh.
21 And when Hā′dăd heard in Egypt
that David slept with his fathers, and
that Jō′ăb the captain of the host was
dead, Hā′dăd said to Pharaoh, Let me
depart, that I may go to mine own
country.
22 Then Pharaoh said unto him, But
what hast thou lacked with me, that,
behold, thou seekest to go to thine own
country? And he answered, Nothing:
howbeit let me go in any wise.
23 ¶And God stirred him up *another*
adversary, Rē′zon the son of E-lī′a-dah,
which fled from his lord Hăd-ad-ē′zer
king of Zōbah:
24 And he gathered men unto him,
and became captain over a band, when
David slew them *of Zōbah*: and they
went to Damascus, and dwelt therein,
and reigned in Damascus.
25 And he was an adversary to Israel
all the days of Sŏlomon, beside the
mischief that Hā′dăd *did*: and he
abhorred Israel, and reigned over Syr-
ia.
26 ¶And Jĕr-o-bō′am the son of Nē′-
băt, an Ĕph′rath-īte of Zĕr′e-da, Sŏlo-
mon's servant, whose mother's name
was Ze-rū′ah, a widow woman, even he
lifted up *his* hand against the king.
27 And this *was* the cause that he
lifted up *his* hand against the king: Sŏl-
omon built Mĭl′lō, *and* repaired the
breaches of the city of David his father.
28 And the man Jĕr-o-bō′am *was* a
mighty man of valour: and Sŏlomon
seeing the young man that he was in-
dustrious, he made him ruler over all
the charge of the house of Joseph.
29 And it came to pass at that time
when Jĕr-o-bō′am went out of Jeru-
salem, that the prophet A-hī′jah the
Shī′lo-nīte found him in the way; and

he had clad himself with a new garment; and they two *were* alone in the field:

30 And A-hī'jah caught the new garment that *was* on him, and rent it *in* twelve pieces:

31 And he said to Jĕr-o-bō'am, Take thee ten pieces: for thus saith the LORD, the God of Israel, Behold, I will rend the kingdom out of the hand of Sŏlomon, and will give ten tribes to thee:

32 (But he shall have one tribe for my servant David's sake, and for Jerusalem's sake, the city which I have chosen out of all the tribes of Israel:)

33 Because that they have forsaken me, and have worshipped Ăsh'to-rĕth the goddess of the Zī-dō'nī-ans, Chē'-mŏsh the god of the Moabites, and Mĭl'-com the god of the children of Ammon, and have not walked in my ways, to do *that which is* right in mine eyes, and *to keep* my statutes and my judgments, as *did* David his father.

34 Howbeit I will not take the whole kingdom out of his hand: but I will make him prince all the days of his life for David my servant's sake, whom I chose, because he kept my commandments and my statutes:

35 But I will take the kingdom out of his son's hand, and will give it unto thee, *even* ten tribes.

36 And unto his son will I give one tribe, that David my servant may have a light alway before me in Jerusalem, the city which I have chosen me to put my name there.

37 And I will take thee, and thou shalt reign according to all that thy soul desireth, and shalt be king over Israel.

38 And it shall be, if thou wilt hearken unto all that I command thee, and wilt walk in my ways, and do *that is* right in my sight, to keep my statutes and my commandments, as David my servant did; that I will be with thee, and build thee a sure house, as I built for David, and will give Israel unto thee.

39 And I will for this afflict the seed of David, but not for ever.

40 Sŏlomon sought therefore to kill Jĕr-o-bō'am. And Jĕr-o-bō'am arose, and fled into Egypt, unto Shī'shăk king of Egypt, and was in Egypt until the death of Sŏlomon.

41 ¶And the rest of the acts of Sŏlomon, and all that he did, and his wisdom, *are* they not written in the book of the acts of Sŏlomon?

42 And the time that Sŏlomon reigned in Jerusalem over all Israel *was* forty years.

43 And Sŏlomon slept with his fathers, and was buried in the city of David his father: and Rē-ho-bō'am his son reigned in his stead.

CHAPTER 12

AND Rē-ho-bō'am went to Shĕ'chem: for all Israel were come to Shĕ'chem to make him king.

2 And it came to pass, when Jĕr-o-bō'am the son of Nē'băt, who was yet in Egypt, heard *of it*, (for he was fled from the presence of king Sŏlomon, and Jĕr-o-bō'am dwelt in Egypt;)

3 That they sent and called him. And Jĕr-o-bō'am and all the congregation of Israel came, and spake unto Rē-ho-bō'am, saying,

4 Thy father made our yoke grievous: now therefore make thou the grievous service of thy father, and his heavy yoke which he put upon us, lighter, and we will serve thee.

5 And he said unto them, Depart yet *for* three days, then come again to me. And the people departed.

6 ¶And king Rē-ho-bō'am consulted with the old men, that stood before Sŏlomon his father while he yet lived, and said, How do ye advise that I may answer this people?

7 And they spake unto him, saying, If thou wilt be a servant unto this people this day, and wilt serve them, and answer them, and speak good words to them, then they will be thy servants for ever.

8 But he forsook the counsel of the old men, which they had given him, and consulted with the young men that were grown up with him, *and* which stood before him:

9 And he said unto them, What counsel give ye that we may answer this people, who have spoken to me, saying, Make the yoke which thy father did put upon us lighter?

10 And the young men that were grown up with him spake unto him, saying, Thus shalt thou speak unto this people that spake unto thee, saying, Thy father made our yoke heavy, but make thou *it* lighter unto us; thus shalt thou say unto them, My little *finger* shall be thicker than my father's loins.

11 And now whereas my father did lade you with a heavy yoke, I will add to your yoke: my father hath chastised you with whips, but I will chastise you with scorpions.

12 ¶So Jĕr-o-bō'am and all the people came to Rē-ho-bō'am the third day, as the king had appointed, saying, Come to me again the third day.

13 And the king answered the people roughly, and forsook the old men's counsel that they gave him;

14 And spake to them after the coun-
sel of the young men, saying, My father
made your yoke heavy, and I will add to
your yoke: my father *also* chastised
you with whips, but I will chastise you
with scorpions.
15 Wherefore the king hearkened not
unto the people; for the cause was from
the LORD, that he might perform his
saying, which the LORD spake by A-hī'-
jah the Shī'lo-nīte unto Jĕr-o-bō'am the
son of Nĕ'băt.
16 ¶So when all Israel saw that the
king hearkened not unto them, the
people answered the king, saying,
What portion have we in David?
neither *have we* inheritance in the son
of Jesse: to your tents, O Israel: now
see to thine own house, David. So Israel
departed unto their tents.
17 But *as for* the children of Israel
which dwelt in the cities of Jūdah, Rē-
ho-bō'am reigned over them.
18 Then king Rē-ho-bō'am sent Ă-
dô'ram, who *was* over the tribute; and
all Israel stoned him with stones, that
he died. Therefore king Rē-ho-bō'am
made speed to get him up to his chariot,
to flee to Jerusalem.
19 So Israel rebelled against the
house of David unto this day.
20 ¶And it came to pass, when all
Israel heard that Jĕr-o-bō'am was
come again, that they sent and called
him unto the congregation, and made
him king over all Israel: there was none
that followed the house of David, but
the tribe of Jūdah only.
21 ¶And when Rē-ho-bō'am was
come to Jerusalem, he assembled all
the house of Jūdah, with the tribe of
Benjamin, an hundred and fourscore
thousand chosen men, which were
warriors, to fight against the house of
Israel, to bring the kingdom again to
Rē-ho-bō'am the son of Sŏlomon.
22 But the word of God came unto
Shem-a-i'ah the man of God, saying,
23 Speak unto Rē-ho-bō'am, the son
of Sŏlomon, king of Jūdah, and unto all
the house of Jūdah and Benjamin, and
to the remnant of the people, saying,
24 Thus saith the LORD, Ye shall not
go up, nor fight against your brethren
the children of Israel: return every man
to his house; for this thing is from me.
They hearkened therefore to the word
of the LORD, and returned to depart, ac-
cording to the word of the LORD.
25 ¶Then Jĕr-o-bō'am built Shĕ'chem
in mount Ē'phra-im, and dwelt therein;
and went out from thence, and built Pe-
nū'el.
26 ¶And Jĕr-o-bō'am said in his
heart, Now shall the kingdom return to
the house of David:
27 If this people go up to do sacrifice
in the house of the LORD at Jerusalem,
then shall the heart of this people turn
again unto their lord, *even* unto Rē-ho-
bō'am king of Jūdah, and they shall kill
me, and go again to Rē-ho-bō'am king
of Jūdah.
28 Whereupon the king took counsel,
and made two calves *of* gold, and said
unto them, It is too much for you to go
up to Jerusalem: behold thy gods, O
Israel, which brought thee up out of the
land of Egypt.
29 And he set the one in Bĕth-el, and
the other put he in Dan.
30 And this thing became a sin: for
the people went *to worship* before the
one, *even* unto Dan.
31 And he made an house of high
places, and made priests of the lowest
of the people, which were not of the
sons of Levi.
32 And Jĕr-o-bō'am ordained a feast
in the eighth month, on the fifteenth
day of the month, like unto the feast
that *is* in Jūdah, and he offered upon
the altar. So did he in Bĕth-el, sacrific-
ing unto the calves that he had made:
and he placed in Bĕth-el the priests of
the high places which he had made.
33 So he offered upon the altar which
he had made in Bĕth-el the fifteenth day
of the eighth month, *even* in the month
which he had devised of his own heart;
and ordained a feast unto the children
of Israel: and he offered upon the altar,
and burnt incense.

CHAPTER 13

AND, behold, there came a man of God
out of Jūdah by the word of the LORD
unto Bĕth-el: and Jĕr-o-bō'am stood by
the altar to burn incense.
2 And he cried against the altar in the
word of the LORD, and said, O altar, al-
tar, thus saith the LORD; Behold, a child
shall be born unto the house of David,
Jō-sī'ah by name; and upon thee shall
he offer the priests of the high places
that burn incense upon thee, and men's
bones shall be burnt upon thee.
3 And he gave a sign the same day,
saying, This *is* the sign which the LORD
hath spoken; Behold, the altar shall be
rent, and the ashes that *are* upon it shall
be poured out.
4 ¶And it came to pass, when king
Jĕr-o-bō'am heard the saying of the
man of God, which had cried against
the altar in Bĕth-el, that he put forth his
hand from the altar, saying, Lay hold
on him. And his hand, which he put

forth against him, dried up, so that he
could not pull it in again to him.
5 The altar also was rent, and the
ashes poured out from the altar, according
to the sign which the man of God
had given by the word of the LORD.
6 And the king answered and said
unto the man of God, Intreat now the
face of the LORD thy God, and pray for
me, that my hand may be restored me
again. And the man of God besought
the LORD, and the king's hand was restored
him again, and became as *it was*
before.
7 ¶And the king said unto the man of
God, Come home with me, and refresh
thyself, and I will give thee a reward.
8 And the man of God said unto the
king, If thou wilt give me half thine
house, I will not go in with thee, neither
will I eat bread nor drink water in this
place:
9 For so was it charged me by the
word of the LORD, saying, Eat no bread,
nor drink water, nor turn again by the
same way that thou camest.
10 So he went another way, and returned
not by the way that he came to
Bĕth-el.
11 ¶Now there dwelt an old prophet
in Bĕth-el; and his sons came and told
him all the works that the man of God
had done that day in Bĕth-el: the words
which he had spoken unto the king,
them they told also to their father.
12 And their father said unto them,
What way went he? For his sons had
seen what way the man of God went,
which came from Jūdah.
13 And he said unto his sons, Saddle
me the ass. So they saddled him the
ass: and he rode thereon,
14 And went after the man of God,
and found him sitting under an oak:
and he said unto him, *Art* thou the man
of God that camest from Jūdah? And he
said, I *am*.
15 Then he said unto him, Come
home with me, and eat bread.
16 And he said, I may not return with
thee, nor go in with thee: neither will I
eat bread nor drink water with thee in
this place:
17 For it was said to me by the word
of the LORD, Thou shalt eat no bread nor
drink water there, nor turn again to go
by the way that thou camest.
18 He said unto him, I *am* a prophet
also as thou *art;* and an angel spake
unto me by the word of the LORD,
saying, Bring him back with thee into
thine house, that he may eat bread and
drink water. *But* he lied unto him.
19 So he went back with him, and did
eat bread in his house, and drank water.
20 ¶And it came to pass, as they sat at
the table, that the word of the LORD
came unto the prophet that brought
him back:
21 And he cried unto the man of God
that came from Jūdah, saying, Thus
saith the LORD, Forasmuch as thou hast
disobeyed the mouth of the LORD, and
hast not kept the commandment which
the LORD thy God commanded thee,
22 But camest back, and hast eaten
bread and drunk water in the place, of
the which *the LORD* did say to thee, Eat
no bread, and drink no water; thy carcase
shall not come unto the sepulchre
of thy fathers.
23 ¶And it came to pass, after he had
eaten bread, and after he had drunk,
that he saddled for him the ass, *to wit*,
for the prophet whom he had brought
back.
24 And when he was gone, a lion met
him by the way, and slew him: and his
carcase was cast in the way, and the
ass stood by it, the lion also stood by
the carcase.
25 And, behold, men passed by, and
saw the carcase cast in the way, and
the lion standing by the carcase: and
they came and told *it* in the city where
the old prophet dwelt.
26 ¶And when the prophet that
brought him back from the way heard
thereof, he said, It *is* the man of God,
who was disobedient unto the word of
the LORD: therefore the LORD hath delivered
him unto the lion, which hath
torn him, and slain him, according to
the word of the LORD, which he spake
unto him.
27 And he spake to his sons, saying,
Saddle me the ass. And they saddled
him.
28 And he went and found his carcase
cast in the way, and the ass and
the lion standing by the carcase: the
lion had not eaten the carcase, nor torn
the ass.
29 And the prophet took up the carcase
of the man of God, and laid it upon
the ass, and brought it back: and the old
prophet came to the city, to mourn and
to bury him.
30 And he laid his carcase in his own
grave; and they mourned over him,
saying, Alas, my brother!
31 And it came to pass, after he had
buried him, that he spake to his sons,
saying, When I am dead, then bury me
in the sepulchre wherein the man of
God *is* buried; lay my bones beside his
bones:
32 For the saying which he cried by

the word of the LORD against the altar in Bĕth–el, and against all the houses of the high places which *are* in the cities of Sa-mâ'rĭ-a, shall surely come to pass.

33 ¶After this thing Jĕr-o-bō'am returned not from his evil way, but made again of the lowest of the people priests of the high places: whosoever would, he consecrated him, and he became *one* of the priests of the high places.

34 And this thing became sin unto the house of Jĕr-o-bō'am, even to cut *it* off, and to destroy *it* from off the face of the earth.

CHAPTER 14

AT that time A-bī'jah the son of Jĕr-o-bō'am fell sick.

2 And Jĕr-o-bō'am said to his wife, Arise, I pray thee, and disguise thyself, that thou be not known to be the wife of Jĕr-o-bō'am; and get thee to Shī'lōh: behold, there *is* A-hī'jah the prophet, which told me that *I should be* king over this people.

3 And take with thee ten loaves, and cracknels, and a cruse of honey, and go to him: he shall tell thee what shall become of the child.

4 And Jĕr-o-bō'am's wife did so, and arose, and went to Shī'lōh, and came to the house of A-hī'jah. But A-hī'jah could not see; for his eyes were set by reason of his age.

5 ¶And the LORD said unto A-hī'jah, Behold, the wife of Jĕr-o-bō'am cometh to ask a thing of thee for her son; for he *is* sick: thus and thus shalt thou say unto her: for it shall be, when she cometh in, that she shall feign herself *to be* another *woman*.

6 And it was *so*, when A-hī'jah heard the sound of her feet, as she came in at the door, that he said, Come in, thou wife of Jĕr-o-bō'am; why feignest thou thyself *to be* another? for I *am* sent to thee *with* heavy *tidings*.

7 Go, tell Jĕr-o-bō'am, Thus saith the LORD God of Israel, Forasmuch as I exalted thee from among the people, and made thee prince over my people Israel,

8 And rent the kingdom away from the house of David, and gave it thee: and *yet* thou hast not been as my servant David, who kept my commandments, and who followed me with all his heart, to do *that* only *which was* right in mine eyes;

9 But hast done evil above all that were before thee: for thou hast gone and made thee other gods, and molten images, to provoke me to anger, and hast cast me behind thy back:

10 Therefore, behold, I will bring evil upon the house of Jĕr-o-bō'am, and will cut off from Jĕr-o-bō'am him that pisseth against the wall, *and* him that is shut up and left in Israel, and will take away the remnant of the house of Jĕr-o-bō'am, as a man taketh away dung, till it be all gone.

11 Him that dieth of Jĕr-o-bō'am in the city shall the dogs eat; and him that dieth in the field shall the fowls of the air eat: for the LORD hath spoken *it*.

12 Arise thou therefore, get thee to thine own house: *and* when thy feet enter into the city, the child shall die.

13 And all Israel shall mourn for him, and bury him: for he only of Jĕr-o-bō'am shall come to the grave, because in him there is found *some* good thing toward the LORD God of Israel in the house of Jĕr-o-bō'am.

14 Moreover the LORD shall raise him up a king over Israel, who shall cut off the house of Jĕr-o-bō'am that day: but what? even now.

15 For the LORD shall smite Israel, as a reed is shaken in the water, and he shall root up Israel out of this good land, which he gave to their fathers, and shall scatter them beyond the river, because they have made their groves, provoking the LORD to anger.

16 And he shall give Israel up because of the sins of Jĕr-o-bō'am, who did sin, and who made Israel to sin.

17 ¶And Jĕr-o-bō'am's wife arose, and departed, and came to Tir'zah: *and* when she came to the threshold of the door, the child died;

18 And they buried him; and all Israel mourned for him, according to the word of the LORD, which he spake by the hand of his servant A-hī'jah the prophet.

19 And the rest of the acts of Jĕr-o-bō'am, how he warred, and how he reigned, behold, they *are* written in the book of the chronicles of the kings of Israel.

20 And the days which Jĕr-o-bō'am reigned *were* two and twenty years: and he slept with his fathers, and Nā'dăb his son reigned in his stead.

21 ¶And Rē-ho-bō'am the son of Sŏlomon reigned in Jūdah. Rē-ho-bō'am *was* forty and one years old when he began to reign, and he reigned seventeen years in Jerusalem, the city which the LORD did choose out of all the tribes of Israel, to put his name there. And his mother's name *was* Nā'a-mah an Ammonitess.

22 And Jūdah did evil in the sight of the LORD, and they provoked him to jealousy with their sins which they had

committed, above all that their fathers
had done.
23 For they also built them high
places, and images, and groves, on
every high hill, and under every green
tree.
24 And there were also sodomites in
the land: *and* they did according to all
the abominations of the nations which
the LORD cast out before the children of
Israel.
25 ¶And it came to pass in the fifth
year of king Rē-ho-bō'am, *that* Shī'-
shăk king of Egypt came up against Je-
rusalem:
26 And he took away the treasures of
the house of the LORD, and the trea-
sures of the king's house; he even took
away all: and he took away all the
shields of gold which Sŏlomon had
made.
27 And king Rē-ho-bō'am made in
their stead brasen shields, and com-
mitted *them* unto the hands of the chief
of the guard, which kept the door of the
king's house.
28 And it was *so*, when the king went
into the house of the LORD, that the
guard bare them, and brought them
back into the guard chamber.
29 ¶Now the rest of the acts of Rē-ho-
bō'am, and all that he did, *are* they not
written in the book of the chronicles of
the kings of Jūdah?
30 And there was war between Rē-
ho-bō'am and Jĕr-o-bō'am all *their*
days.
31 And Rē-ho-bō'am slept with his
fathers, and was buried with his fathers
in the city of David. And his mother's
name *was* Nā'a-mah an Ammonitess.
And A-bī'jam his son reigned in his
stead.

CHAPTER 15

NOW in the eighteenth year of king
Jĕr-o-bō'am the son of Nē'băt reigned
A-bī'jam over Jūdah.
2 Three years reigned he in Jeru-
salem. And his mother's name *was*
Mā'a-chah, the daughter of A-bĭsh'a-
lom.
3 And he walked in all the sins of his
father, which he had done before him:
and his heart was not perfect with the
LORD his God, as the heart of David his
father.
4 Nevertheless for David's sake did
the LORD his God give him a lamp in
Jerusalem, to set up his son after him,
and to establish Jerusalem:
5 Because David did *that which was*
right in the eyes of the LORD, and
turned not aside from any *thing* that he
commanded him all the days of his life,
save only in the matter of Ū-rī'ah the
Hittite.
6 And there was war between Rē-ho-
bō'am and Jĕr-o-bō'am all the days of
his life.
7 Now the rest of the acts of A-bī'jam,
and all that he did, *are* they not written
in the book of the chronicles of the
kings of Jūdah? And there was war be-
tween A-bī'jam and Jĕr-o-bō'am.
8 And A-bī'jam slept with his fathers;
and they buried him in the city of Da-
vid: and Āsa his son reigned in his
stead.
9 ¶And in the twentieth year of Jĕr-o-
bō'am king of Israel reigned Āsa over
Jūdah.
10 And forty and one years reigned
he in Jerusalem. And his mother's
name *was* Mā'a-chah, the daughter of
A-bĭsh'a-lom.
11 And Āsa did *that which was* right
in the eyes of the LORD, as *did* David his
father.
12 And he took away the sodomites
out of the land, and removed all the
idols that his fathers had made.
13 And also Mā'a-chah his mother,
even her he removed from *being* queen,
because she had made an idol in a
grove; and Āsa destroyed her idol, and
burnt *it* by the brook Kidron.
14 But the high places were not re-
moved: nevertheless Āsa's heart was
perfect with the LORD all his days.
15 And he brought in the things
which his father had dedicated, and the
things which himself had dedicated,
into the house of the LORD, silver, and
gold, and vessels.
16 ¶And there was war between Āsa
and Bā'a-sha king of Israel all their
days.
17 And Bā'a-sha king of Israel went
up against Jūdah, and built Rā'mah,
that he might not suffer any to go out or
come in to Āsa king of Jūdah.
18 Then Āsa took all the silver and
the gold *that were* left in the treasures
of the house of the LORD, and the trea-
sures of the king's house, and delivered
them into the hand of his servants: and
king Āsa sent them to Bĕn-hā'dăd, the
son of Tăb'rĭ-mon, the son of Hē'zi-ŏn,
king of Syria, that dwelt at Damascus,
saying,
19 *There is* a league between me and
thee, *and* between my father and thy
father: behold, I have sent unto thee a
present of silver and gold; come and
break thy league with Bā'a-sha king of
Israel, that he may depart from me.
20 So Bĕn-hā'dăd hearkened unto
king Āsa, and sent the captains of the
hosts which he had against the cities of

Israel, and smote Ī′jŏn, and Dan, and
Ā′bel–bĕth–mā′a-chah, and all Cĭn′-
ne-rŏth, with all the land of Năph′ta-lī.
21 And it came to pass, when Bā′a-
sha heard *thereof*, that he left off build-
ing of Rā′mah, and dwelt in Tir′zah.
22 Then king Āsa made a proclama-
tion throughout all Jūdah; none *was* ex-
empted: and they took away the stones
of Rā′mah, and the timber thereof,
wherewith Bā′a-sha had builded; and
king Āsa built with them Gē′ba of Ben-
jamin, and Miz′pah.
23 The rest of all the acts of Āsa, and
all his might, and all that he did, and the
cities which he built, *are* they not writ-
ten in the book of the chronicles of the
kings of Jūdah? Nevertheless in the
time of his old age he was diseased in
his feet.
24 And Āsa slept with his fathers, and
was buried with his fathers in the city
of David his father: and Je-hŏsh′a-phăt
his son reigned in his stead.
25 ¶And Nā′dăb the son of Jĕr-o-bō′am
began to reign over Israel in the sec-
ond year of Āsa king of Jūdah, and
reigned over Israel two years.
26 And he did evil in the sight of the
LORD, and walked in the way of his
father, and in his sin wherewith he
made Israel to sin.
27 ¶And Bā′a-sha the son of A-hī′jah,
of the house of Ĭs′sa-char, conspired
against him; and Bā′a-sha smote him at
Gĭb′be-thŏn, which *belonged* to the
Philistines; for Nā′dăb and all Israel
laid siege to Gĭb′be-thŏn.
28 Even in the third year of Āsa king
of Jūdah did Bā′a-sha slay him, and
reigned in his stead.
29 And it came to pass, when he
reigned, *that* he smote all the house of
Jĕr-o-bō′am; he left not to Jĕr-o-bō′am
any that breathed, until he had de-
stroyed him, according unto the saying
of the LORD, which he spake by his ser-
vant A-hī′jah the Shī′lo-nīte:
30 Because of the sins of Jĕr-o-bō′am
which he sinned, and which he made
Israel sin, by his provocation wherewith
he provoked the LORD God of Israel
to anger.
31 ¶Now the rest of the acts of Na′-
dăb, and all that he did, *are* they not
written in the book of the chronicles of
the kings of Israel?
32 And there was war between Āsa
and Bā′a-sha king of Israel all their
days.
33 ¶In the third year of Āsa king of
Jūdah began Bā′a-sha the son of A-hī′-
jah to reign over all Israel in Tir′zah,
twenty and four years.
34 And he did evil in the sight of the
LORD, and walked in the way of Jĕr-o-
bō′am, and in his sin wherewith he
made Israel to sin.

CHAPTER 16

THEN the word of the LORD came to
Jehu the son of Ha-nā′nī against Bā′a-
sha, saying,
2 Forasmuch as I exalted thee out of
the dust, and made thee prince over my
people Israel; and thou hast walked in
the way of Jĕr-o-bō′am, and hast made
my people Israel to sin, to provoke me
to anger with their sins;
3 Behold, I will take away the poster-
ity of Bā′a-sha, and the posterity of his
house; and will make thy house like the
house of Jĕr-o-bō′am the son of Nē′băt.
4 Him that dieth of Bā′a-sha in the
city shall the dogs eat; and him that
dieth of his in the fields shall the fowls
of the air eat.
5 Now the rest of the acts of Bā′a-sha,
and what he did, and his might *are* they
not written in the book of the chron-
icles of the kings of Israel?
6 So Bā′a-sha slept with his fathers,
and was buried in Tir′zah: and Ē′lah his
son reigned in his stead.
7 And also by the hand of the prophet
Jehu the son of Ha-nā′nī came the word
of the LORD against Bā′a-sha, and
against his house, even for all the evil
that he did in the sight of the LORD, in
provoking him to anger with the work
of his hands, in being like the house of
Jĕr-o-bō′am; and because he killed
him.
8 ¶In the twenty and sixth year of Āsa
king of Jūdah began Ē′lah the son of
Bā′a-sha to reign over Israel in Tir′zah,
two years.
9 And his servant Zimri, captain of
half *his* chariots, conspired against
him, as he was in Tir′zah, drinking him-
self drunk in the house of Är′za steward
of *his* house in Tir′zah.
10 And Zimri went in and smote him,
and killed him, in the twenty and
seventh year of Āsa king of Jūdah, and
reigned in his stead.
11 ¶And it came to pass, when he be-
gan to reign, as soon as he sat on his
throne, *that* he slew all the house of
Bā′a-sha: he left him not one that piss-
eth against a wall, neither of his
kinsfolks, nor of his friends.
12 Thus did Zimri destroy all the
house of Bā′a-sha, according to the
word of the LORD, which he spake
against Bā′a-sha by Jehu the prophet,
13 For all the sins of Bā′a-sha, and the
sins of Ē′lah his son, by which they
sinned, and by which they made Israel

to sin, in provoking the LORD God of Israel to anger with their vanities.

14 Now the rest of the acts of Ē′lah, and all that he did, *are* they not written in the book of the chronicles of the kings of Israel?

15 ¶In the twenty and seventh year of Ā′sa king of Jū′dah did Zimri reign seven days in Tir′zah. And the people *were* encamped against Gĭb′be-thŏn, which *belonged* to the Philistines.

16 And the people *that were* encamped heard say, Zimri hath conspired, and hath also slain the king: wherefore all Israel made Omri, the captain of the host, king over Israel that day in the camp.

17 And Omri went up from Gĭb′be-thŏn, and all Israel with him, and they besieged Tir′zah.

18 And it came to pass, when Zimri saw that the city was taken, that he went into the palace of the king's house, and burnt the king's house over him with fire, and died.

19 For his sins which he sinned in doing evil in the sight of the LORD, in walking in the way of Jĕr-o-bō′am, and in his sin which he did, to make Israel to sin.

20 Now the rest of the acts of Zimri, and his treason that he wrought, *are* they not written in the book of the chronicles of the kings of Israel?

21 ¶Then were the people of Israel divided into two parts: half of the people followed Tĭb′nī the son of Gī′năth, to make him king; and half followed Omri.

22 But the people that followed Omri prevailed against the people that followed Tĭb′nī the son of Gī′năth: so Tĭb′nī died, and Omri reigned.

23 ¶In the thirty and first year of Ā′sa king of Jū′dah began Omri to reign over Israel, twelve years: six years reigned he in Tir′zah.

24 And he bought the hill Sa-mâ′rĭ-a of Shē′mer for two talents of silver, and built on the hill, and called the name of the city which he built, after the name of Shē′mer, owner of the hill, Sa-mâ′rĭ-a.

25 ¶But Omri wrought evil in the eyes of the LORD, and did worse than all that *were* before him.

26 For he walked in all the way of Jĕr-o-bō′am the son of Nē′băt, and in his sin wherewith he made Israel to sin, to provoke the LORD God of Israel to anger with their vanities.

27 Now the rest of the acts of Omri which he did, and his might that he shewed, *are* they not written in the book of the chronicles of the kings of Israel?

28 So Omri slept with his fathers, and was buried in Sa′mâ′rĭ-a: and Ahab his son reigned in his stead.

29 ¶And in the thirty and eighth year of Ā′sa king of Jū′dah began Ahab the son of Omri to reign over Israel: and Ahab the son of Omri reigned over Israel in Sa′mâ′rĭ-a twenty and two years.

30 And Ahab the son of Omri did evil in the sight of the LORD above all that *were* before him.

31 And it came to pass, as if it had been a light thing for him to walk in the sins of Jĕr-o-bō′am the son of Nē′băt, that he took to wife Jĕz′e-bel the daughter of Ĕth-bā′al king of the Zī-dō′nĭ-ans, and went and served Bā′al, and worshipped him.

32 And he reared up an altar for Bā′al in the house of Bā′al, which he had built in Sa′mâ′rĭ-a.

33 And Ahab made a grove; and Ahab did more to provoke the LORD God of Israel to anger than all the kings of Israel that were before him.

34 ¶In his days did Hī′el the Bethelite build Jericho: he laid the foundation thereof in A-bī′ram his firstborn, and set up the gates thereof in his youngest *son* Sē′gŭb, according to the word of the LORD, which he spake by Joshua the son of Nun.

CHAPTER 17

AND E-lī′jah the Tĭsh′bīte, *who was* of the inhabitants of Gilead, said unto Ahab, *As* the LORD God of Israel liveth, before whom I stand, there shall not be dew nor rain these years, but according to my word.

2 And the word of the LORD came unto him, saying,

3 Get thee hence, and turn thee eastward, and hide thyself by the brook Chĕ′rĭth, that *is* before Jordan.

4 And it shall be, *that* thou shalt drink of the brook; and I have commanded the ravens to feed thee there.

5 So he went and did according unto the word of the LORD: for he went and dwelt by the brook Chĕ′rĭth, that *is* before Jordan.

6 And the ravens brought him bread and flesh in the morning, and bread and flesh in the evening; and he drank of the brook.

7 And it came to pass after a while, that the brook dried up, because there had been no rain in the land.

8 ¶And the word of the LORD came unto him, saying,

9 Arise, get thee to Zăr′e-phăth,

which *belongeth* to Zī'don, and dwell there: behold, I have commanded a widow woman there to sustain thee.
10 So he arose and went to Zăr'e-phăth. And when he came to the gate of the city, behold, the widow woman *was* there gathering of sticks: and he called to her, and said, Fetch me, I pray thee, a little water in a vessel, that I may drink.
11 And as she was going to fetch *it*, he called to her, and said, Bring me, I pray thee, a morsel of bread in thine hand.
12 And she said, *As* the LORD thy God liveth, I have not a cake, but an handful of meal in a barrel, and a little oil in a cruse: and, behold, I *am* gathering two sticks, that I may go in and dress it for me and my son, that we may eat it, and die.
13 And E-lī'jah said unto her, Fear not; go *and* do as thou hast said: but make me thereof a little cake first, and bring *it* unto me, and after make for thee and for thy son.
14 For thus saith the LORD God of Israel, The barrel of meal shall not waste, neither shall the cruse of oil fail, until the day *that* the LORD sendeth rain upon the earth.
15 And she went and did according to the saying of E-lī'jah: and she, and he, and her house, did eat *many* days.
16 *And* the barrel of meal wasted not, neither did the cruse of oil fail, according to the word of the LORD, which he spake by E-lī'jah.
17 ¶And it came to pass after these things, *that* the son of the woman, the mistress of the house, fell sick; and his sickness was so sore, that there was no breath left in him.
18 And she said unto E-lī'jah, What have I to do with thee, O thou man of God? art thou come unto me to call my sin to remembrance, and to slay my son?
19 And he said unto her, Give me thy son. And he took him out of her bosom, and carried him up into a loft, where he abode, and laid him upon his own bed.
20 And he cried unto the LORD, and said, O LORD my God, hast thou also brought evil upon the widow with whom I sojourn, by slaying her son?
21 And he stretched himself upon the child three times, and cried unto the LORD, and said, O LORD my God, I pray thee, let this child's soul come into him again.
22 And the LORD heard the voice of E-lī'jah; and the soul of the child came into him again, and he revived.
23 And E-lī'jah took the child, and brought him down out of the chamber into the house, and delivered him unto his mother: and E-lī'jah said, See, thy son liveth.
24 And the woman said to E-lī'jah, Now by this I know that thou *art* a man of God, *and* that the word of the LORD in thy mouth *is* truth.

CHAPTER 18

AND it came to pass *after* many days, that the word of the LORD came to E-lī'jah in the third year, saying, Go, shew thyself unto Ahab; and I will send rain upon the earth.
2 And E-lī'jah went to shew himself unto Ahab. And *there was* a sore famine in Sa-mâ'rī-a.
3 And Ahab called Ō-ba-dī'ah, which *was* the governor of *his* house. (Now Ō-ba-dī'ah feared the LORD greatly:
4 For it was *so*, when Jĕz'e-bel cut off the prophets of the LORD, that Ō-ba-dī'ah took an hundred prophets, and hid them by fifty in a cave, and fed them with bread and water.)
5 And Ahab said unto Ō-ba-dī'ah, Go into the land, unto all fountains of water, and unto all brooks: peradventure we may find grass to save the horses and mules alive, that we lose not all the beasts.
6 So they divided the land between them to pass throughout it: Ahab went one way by himself, and Ō-ba-dī'ah went another way by himself.
7 ¶And as Ō'ba-dī'ah was in the way, behold, E-lī'jah met him: and he knew him, and fell on his face, and said, *Art* thou that my lord E-lī'jah?
8 And he answered him, I *am*: go, tell thy lord, Behold, E-lī'jah *is here*.
9 And he said, What have I sinned, that thou wouldest deliver thy servant into the hand of Ahab, to slay me?
10 *As* the LORD thy God liveth, there is no nation or kingdom, whither my lord hath not sent to seek thee: and when they said, *He is* not *there;* he took an oath of the kingdom and nation, that they found thee not.
11 And now thou sayest, Go, tell thy lord, Behold, E-lī'jah *is here*.
12 And it shall come to pass, *as soon as* I am gone from thee, that the Spirit of the LORD shall carry thee whither I know not; and *so* when I come and tell Ahab, and he cannot find thee, he shall slay me: but I thy servant fear the LORD from my youth.
13 Was it not told my lord what I did when Jĕz'e-bel slew the prophets of the LORD, how I hid an hundred men of the LORD's prophets by fifty in a cave, and fed them with bread and water?
14 And now thou sayest, Go, tell thy

lord, Behold, E-lī'jah *is here:* and he shall slay me.
15 And E-lī'jah said, *As* the LORD of hosts liveth, before whom I stand, I will surely shew myself unto him to day.
16 So Ō-ba-dī'ah went to meet Ahab, and told him: and Ahab went to meet E-lī'jah.
17 ¶And it came to pass, when Ahab saw E-lī'jah, that Ahab said unto him, *Art* thou he that troubleth Israel?
18 And he answered, I have not troubled Israel; but thou, and thy father's house, in that ye have forsaken the commandments of the LORD, and thou hast followed Bā'al-īm.
19 Now therefore send, *and* gather to me all Israel unto mount Carmel, and the prophets of Bā'al four hundred and fifty, and the prophets of the groves four hundred, which eat at Jĕz'e-bel's table.
20 So Ahab sent unto all the children of Israel, and gathered the prophets together unto mount Carmel.
21 ¶And E-lī'jah came unto all the people, and said, How long halt ye between two opinions? if the LORD *be* God, follow him: but if Bā'al, *then* follow him. And the people answered him not a word.
22 Then said E-lī'jah unto the people, I, *even* I only, remain a prophet of the LORD; but Bā'al's prophets *are* four hundred and fifty men.
23 Let them therefore give us two bullocks; and let them choose one bullock for themselves, and cut it in pieces, and lay *it* on wood, and put no fire *under:* and I will dress the other bullock, and lay *it* on wood, and put no fire *under:*
24 And call ye on the name of your gods, and I will call on the name of the LORD: and the God that answereth by fire, let him be God. And all the people answered and said, It is well spoken.
25 And E-lī'jah said unto the prophets of Bā'al, Choose you one bullock for yourselves, and dress *it* first; for ye *are* many; and call on the name of your gods, but put no fire *under.*
26 And they took the bullock which was given them, and they dressed *it,* and called on the name of Bā'al from morning even until noon, saying, O Bā'al, hear us. But *there was* no voice, nor any that answered. And they leaped upon the altar which was made.
27 And it came to pass at noon, that E-lī'jah mocked them, and said, Cry aloud: for he *is* a god; either he is talking, or he is pursuing, or he is in a journey, *or* peradventure he sleepeth, and must be awaked.
28 And they cried aloud, and cut themselves after their manner with knives and lancets, till the blood gushed out upon them.
29 And it came to pass, when midday was past, and they prophesied until the *time* of the offering of the *evening* sacrifice, that *there was* neither voice, nor any to answer, nor any that regarded.
30 And E-lī'jah said unto all the people, Come near unto me. And all the people came near unto him. And he repaired the altar of the LORD *that was* broken down.
31 And E-lī'jah took twelve stones, according to the number of the tribes of the sons of Jacob, unto whom the word of the LORD came, saying, Israel shall be thy name:
32 And with the stones he built an altar in the name of the LORD: and he made a trench about the altar, as great as would contain two measures of seed.
33 And he put the wood in order, and cut the bullock in pieces, and laid *him* on the wood, and said, Fill four barrels with water, and pour *it* on the burnt sacrifice, and on the wood.
34 And he said, Do *it* the second time. And they did *it* the second time. And he said, Do *it* the third time. And they did *it* the third time.
35 And the water ran round about the altar; and he filled the trench also with water.
36 And it came to pass at *the time of* the offering of the *evening* sacrifice, that E-lī'jah the prophet came near, and said, LORD God of Abraham, Isaac, and of Israel, let it be known this day that thou *art* God in Israel, and *that* I *am* thy servant, and *that* I have done all these things at thy word.
37 Hear me, O LORD, hear me, that this people may know that thou *art* the LORD God, and *that* thou hast turned their heart back again.
38 Then the fire of the LORD fell, and consumed the burnt sacrifice, and the wood, and the stones, and the dust, and licked up the water that *was* in the trench.
39 And when all the people saw *it,* they fell on their faces: and they said, The LORD, he *is* the God; the LORD, he *is* the God.
40 And E-lī'jah said unto them, Take the prophets of Bā'al; let not one of them escape. And they took them: and E-lī'jah brought them down to the brook Kī'shŏn, and slew them there.
41 ¶And E-lī'jah said unto Ahab, Get thee up, eat and drink; for *there is* a sound of abundance of rain.

42 So Ahab went up to eat and to drink. And E-lī'jah went up to the top of Carmel; and he cast himself down upon the earth, and put his face between his knees,

43 And said to his servant, Go up now, look toward the sea. And he went up, and looked, and said, *There is* nothing. And he said, Go again seven times.

44 And it came to pass at the seventh time, that he said, Behold, there ariseth a little cloud out of the sea, like a man's hand. And he said, Go up, say unto Ahab, Prepare *thy chariot,* and get thee down, that the rain stop thee not.

45 And it came to pass in the mean while, that the heaven was black with clouds and wind, and there was a great rain. And Ahab rode, and went to Jĕz'-re-el.

46 And the hand of the LORD was on E-lī'jah; and he girded up his loins, and ran before Ahab to the entrance of Jĕz'-re-el.

CHAPTER 19

AND Ahab told Jĕz'e-bel all that E-lī'-jah had done, and withal how he had slain all the prophets with the sword.

2 Then Jĕz'e-bel sent a messenger unto E-lī'jah, saying, So let the gods do *to me,* and more also, if I make not thy life as the life of one of them by to morrow about this time.

3 And when he saw *that,* he arose, and went for his life, and came to Be'er-shē'ba, which *belongeth* to Jūdah, and left his servant there.

4 ¶But he himself went a day's journey into the wilderness, and came and sat down under a juniper tree: and he requested for himself that he might die; and said, It is enough; now, O LORD, take away my life; for I *am* not better than my fathers.

5 And as he lay and slept under a juniper tree, behold, then an angel touched him, and said unto him, Arise *and* eat.

6 And he looked, and, behold, *there was* a cake baken on the coals, and a cruse of water at his head. And he did eat and drink, and laid him down again.

7 And the angel of the LORD came again the second time, and touched him, and said, Arise *and* eat; because the journey *is* too great for thee.

8 And he arose, and did eat and drink, and went in the strength of that meat forty days and forty nights unto Hô'rĕb the mount of God.

9 ¶And he came thither unto a cave, and lodged there; and, behold, the word of the LORD *came* to him, and he said unto him, What doest thou here, E-lī'jah?

10 And he said, I have been very jealous for the LORD God of hosts: for the children of Israel have forsaken thy covenant, thrown down thine altars, and slain thy prophets with the sword; and I, *even* I only, am left; and they seek my life, to take it away.

11 And he said, Go forth, and stand upon the mount before the LORD. And, behold, the LORD passed by, and a great and strong wind rent the mountains, and brake in pieces the rocks before the LORD; *but* the LORD *was* not in the wind: and after the wind an earthquake; *but* the LORD *was* not in the earthquake:

12 And after the earthquake a fire; *but* the LORD *was* not in the fire: and after the fire a still small voice.

13 And it was *so,* when E-lī'jah heard *it,* that he wrapped his face in his mantle, and went out, and stood in the entering in of the cave. And, behold, *there came* a voice unto him, and said, What doest thou here, E-lī'jah?

14 And he said, I have been very jealous for the LORD God of hosts: because the children of Israel have forsaken thy covenant, thrown down thine altars, and slain thy prophets with the sword; and I, *even* I only, am left; and they seek my life, to take it away.

15 And the LORD said unto him, Go, return on thy way to the wilderness of Damascus: and when thou comest, anoint Hāz'a-el *to be* king over Syria:

16 And Jehu the son of Nĭm'shī shalt thou anoint *to be* king over Israel: and E-lī'sha the son of Shā'phat of Ā'bel-mĕ-hō'lah shalt thou anoint *to be* prophet in thy room.

17 And it shall come to pass, *that* him that escapeth the sword of Hāz'a-el shall Jehu slay: and him that escapeth from the sword of Jehu shall E-lī'sha slay.

18 Yet I have left *me* seven thousand in Israel, all the knees which have not bowed unto Bā'al, and every mouth which hath not kissed him.

19 ¶So he departed thence, and found E-lī'sha the son of Shā'phat, who *was* plowing *with* twelve yoke *of oxen* before him, and he with the twelfth: and E-lī'jah passed by him, and cast his mantle upon him.

20 And he left the oxen, and ran after E-lī'jah, and said, Let me, I pray thee, kiss my father and my mother, and *then* I will follow thee. And he said unto him, Go back again: for what have I done to thee?

21 And he returned back from him, and took a yoke of oxen, and slew them, and boiled their flesh with the

instruments of the oxen, and gave unto the people, and they did eat. Then he arose, and went after E-lī'jah, and ministered unto him.

CHAPTER 20

AND Bĕn-hā'dăd the king of Syria gathered all his host together: and *there were* thirty and two kings with him, and horses, and chariots: and he went up and besieged Sa-mâ'rĭ-a, and warred against it.

2 And he sent messengers to Ahab king of Israel into the city, and said unto him, Thus saith Bĕn-hā'dăd,

3 Thy silver and thy gold *is* mine; thy wives also and thy children, *even* the goodliest, *are* mine.

4 And the king of Israel answered and said, My lord, O king, according to thy saying, I *am* thine, and all that I have.

5 And the messengers came again, and said, Thus speaketh Bĕn-hā'dăd, saying, Although I have sent unto thee, saying, Thou shalt deliver me thy silver, and thy gold, and thy wives, and thy children;

6 Yet I will send my servants unto thee to morrow about this time, and they shall search thine house, and the houses of thy servants; and it shall be, *that* whatsoever is pleasant in thine eyes, they shall put *it* in their hand, and take *it* away.

7 Then the king of Israel called all the elders of the land, and said, Mark, I pray you, and see how this *man* seeketh mischief: for he sent unto me for my wives, and for my children, and for my silver, and for my gold; and I denied him not.

8 And all the elders and all the people said unto him, Hearken not *unto him*, nor consent.

9 Wherefore he said unto the messengers of Bĕn-hā'dăd, Tell my lord the king, All that thou didst send for to thy servant at the first I will do: but this thing I may not do. And the messengers departed, and brought him word again.

10 And Bĕn-hā'dăd sent unto him, and said, The gods do so unto me, and more also, if the dust of Sa-mâ'rĭ-a shall suffice for handfuls for all the people that follow me.

11 And the king of Israel answered and said, Tell *him*, Let not him that girdeth on *his harness* boast himself as he that putteth it off.

12 And it came to pass, when *Ben-ha'dad* heard this message, as he *was* drinking, he and the kings in the pavilions, that he said unto his servants, Set *yourselves in array*. And they set *themselves in array* against the city.

13 ¶And, behold, there came a prophet unto Ahab king of Israel, saying, Thus saith the LORD, Hast thou seen all this great multitude? behold, I will deliver it into thine hand this day; and thou shalt know that I *am* the LORD.

14 And Ahab said, By whom? And he said, Thus saith the LORD, *Even* by the young men of the princes of the provinces. Then he said, Who shall order the battle? And he answered, Thou.

15 Then he numbered the young men of the princes of the provinces, and they were two hundred and thirty two: and after them he numbered all the people, *even* all the children of Israel, *being* seven thousand.

16 And they went out at noon. But Bĕn-hā'dăd *was* drinking himself drunk in the pavilions, he and the kings, the thirty and two kings that helped him.

17 And the young men of the princes of the provinces went out first; and Bĕn-hā'dăd sent out, and they told him, saying, There are men come out of Sa-mâ'rĭ-a.

18 And he said, Whether they be come out for peace, take them alive; or whether they be come out for war, take them alive.

19 So these young men of the princes of the provinces came out of the city, and the army which followed them.

20 And they slew every one his man: and the Syrians fled; and Israel pursued them: and Bĕn-hā'dăd the king of Syria escaped on an horse with the horsemen.

21 And the king of Israel went out, and smote the horses and chariots, and slew the Syrians with a great slaughter.

22 ¶And the prophet came to the king of Israel, and said unto him, Go, strengthen thyself, and mark, and see what thou doest: for at the return of the year the king of Syria will come up against thee.

23 And the servants of the king of Syria said unto him, Their gods *are* gods of the hills; therefore they were stronger than we; but let us fight against them in the plain, and surely we shall be stronger than they.

24 And do this thing, Take the kings away, every man out of his place, and put captains in their rooms:

25 And number thee an army, like the army that thou hast lost, horse for horse, and chariot for chariot: and we will fight against them in the plain, *and* surely we shall be stronger than they. And he hearkened unto their voice, and did so.

26 And it came to pass at the return of the year, that Bĕn-hā'dăd numbered the Syrians, and went up to Ā'phĕk, to fight against Israel.
27 And the children of Israel were numbered, and were all present, and went against them: and the children of Israel pitched before them like two little flocks of kids; but the Syrians filled the country.
28 ¶And there came a man of God, and spake unto the king of Israel, and said, Thus saith the LORD, Because the Syrians have said, The LORD *is* God of the hills, but he *is* not God of the valleys, therefore will I deliver all this great multitude into thine hand, and ye shall know that I *am* the LORD.
29 And they pitched one over against the other seven days. And *so* it was, that in the seventh day the battle was joined: and the children of Israel slew of the Syrians an hundred thousand footmen in one day.
30 But the rest fled to Ā'phĕk, into the city; and *there* a wall fell upon twenty and seven thousand of the men *that were* left. And Bĕn-hā'dăd fled, and came into the city, into an inner chamber.
31 ¶And his servants said unto him, Behold now, we have heard that the kings of the house of Israel *are* merciful kings: let us, I pray thee, put sackcloth on our loins, and ropes upon our heads, and go out to the king of Israel: peradventure he will save thy life.
32 So they girded sackcloth on their loins, and *put* ropes on their heads, and came to the king of Israel, and said, Thy servant Bĕn-hā'dăd saith, I pray thee, let me live. And he said, *Is* he yet alive? he *is* my brother.
33 Now the men did diligently observe whether *any thing would come* from him, and did hastily catch *it:* and they said, Thy brother Bĕn-hā'dăd. Then he said, Go ye, bring him. Then Bĕn-hā'dăd came forth to him; and he caused him to come up into the chariot.
34 And *Ben-ha'dad* said unto him, The cities, which my father took from thy father, I will restore; and thou shalt make streets for thee in Damascus, as my father made in Sa-mâ'rĭ-a. Then *said Ahab,* I will send thee away with this covenant. So he made a covenant with him, and sent him away.
35 ¶And a certain man of the sons of the prophets said unto his neighbour in the word of the LORD, Smite me, I pray thee. And the man refused to smite him.
36 Then said he unto him, Because thou hast not obeyed the voice of the LORD, behold, as soon as thou art departed from me, a lion shall slay thee. And as soon as he was departed from him, a lion found him, and slew him.
37 Then he found another man, and said, Smite me, I pray thee. And the man smote him, so that in smiting he wounded *him.*
38 So the prophet departed, and waited for the king by the way, and disguised himself with ashes upon his face.
39 And as the king passed by, he cried unto the king: and he said, Thy servant went out into the midst of the battle; and, behold, a man turned aside, and brought a man unto me, and said, Keep this man: if by any means he be missing, then shall thy life be for his life, or else thou shalt pay a talent of silver.
40 And as thy servant was busy here and there, he was gone. And the king of Israel said unto him, So *shall* thy judgment *be;* thyself hast decided *it.*
41 And he hasted, and took the ashes away from his face; and the king of Israel discerned him that he *was* of the prophets.
42 And he said unto him, Thus saith the LORD, Because thou hast let go out of *thy* hand a man whom I appointed to utter destruction, therefore thy life shall go for his life, and thy people for his people.
43 And the king of Israel went to his house heavy and displeased, and came to Sa-mâ'rĭ-a.

CHAPTER 21

AND it came to pass after these things, *that* Nā'bŏth the Jĕz're-el-īte had a vineyard, which *was* in Jĕz're-el, hard by the palace of Ahab king of Sa-mâ'rĭ-a.
2 And Ahab spake unto Nā'bŏth, saying, Give me thy vineyard, that I may have it for a garden of herbs, because it *is* near unto my house: and I will give thee for it a better vineyard than it; *or,* if it seem good to thee, I will give thee the worth of it in money.
3 And Nā'bŏth said to Ahab, The LORD forbid it me, that I should give the inheritance of my fathers unto thee.
4 And Ahab came into his house heavy and displeased because of the word which Nā'bŏth the Jĕz're-el-īte had spoken to him: for he had said, I will not give thee the inheritance of my fathers. And he laid him down upon his bed, and turned away his face, and would eat no bread.
5 ¶But Jĕz'e-bel his wife came to him, and said unto him, Why is thy spirit so sad, that thou eatest no bread?

6 And he said unto her, Because I
spake unto Nā'bŏth the Jĕz're-el-īte,
and said unto him, Give me thy vineyard
for money; or else, if it please thee, I
will give thee *another* vineyard for it:
and he answered, I will not give thee
my vineyard.
7 And Jĕz'e-bel his wife said unto
him, Dost thou now govern the king-
dom of Israel? arise, *and* eat bread, and
let thine heart be merry: I will give thee
the vineyard of Nā'bŏth the Jĕz're-el-
īte.
8 So she wrote letters in Ahab's
name, and sealed *them* with his seal,
and sent the letters unto the elders and
to the nobles that *were* in his city, dwell-
ing with Nā'bŏth.
9 And she wrote in the letters, saying,
Proclaim a fast, and set Nā'bŏth on
high among the people:
10 And set two men, sons of Bē'lī-al,
before him, to bear witness against
him, saying, Thou didst blaspheme
God and the king. And *then* carry him
out, and stone him, that he may die.
11 And the men of his city, *even* the
elders and the nobles who were the
inhabitants in his city, did as Jĕz'e-bel
had sent unto them, *and* as it *was* writ-
ten in the letters which she had sent
unto them.
12 They proclaimed a fast, and set
Nā'bŏth on high among the people.
13 And there came in two men, chil-
dren of Bē'lī-al, and sat before him: and
the men of Bē'lī-al witnessed against
him, *even* against Nā'bŏth, in the pres-
ence of the people, saying, Nā'bŏth did
blaspheme God and the king. Then
they carried him forth out of the city,
and stoned him with stones, that he
died.
14 Then they sent to Jĕz'e-bel,
saying, Nā'bŏth is stoned, and is dead.
15 ¶And it came to pass, when Jĕz'e-
bel heard that Nā'bŏth was stoned, and
was dead, that Jĕz'e-bel said to Ahab,
Arise, take possession of the vineyard
of Nā'bŏth the Jĕz're-el-īte, which he
refused to give thee for money: for Nā'-
bŏth is not alive, but dead.
16 And it came to pass, when Ahab
heard that Nā'bŏth was dead, that
Ahab rose up to go down to the vineyard
of Nā'bŏth the Jĕz're-el-īte, to take
possession of it.
17 ¶And the word of the LORD came
to E-lī'jah the Tĭsh'bīte, saying,
18 Arise, go down to meet Ahab king
of Israel, which *is* in Sa-mâ'rĭ-a: behold,
he is in the vineyard of Nā'bŏth,
whither he is gone down to possess it.
19 And thou shalt speak unto him,
saying, Thus saith the LORD, Hast thou
killed, and also taken possession? And
thou shalt speak unto him, saying,
Thus saith the LORD, In the place where
dogs licked the blood of Nā'bŏth shall
dogs lick thy blood, even thine.
20 And Ahab said to E-lī'jah, Hast
thou found me, O mine enemy? And he
answered, I have found *thee:* because
thou hast sold thyself to work evil in
the sight of the LORD.
21 Behold, I will bring evil upon thee,
and will take away thy posterity, and
will cut off from Ahab him that pisseth
against the wall, and him that is shut up
and left in Israel,
22 And will make thine house like the
house of Jĕr-o-bō'am the son of Nē'băt,
and like the house of Bā'a-sha the son
of A-hī'jah, for the provocation where-
with thou hast provoked *me* to an-
ger, and made Israel to sin.
23 And of Jĕz'e-bel also spake the
LORD, saying, The dogs shall eat Jĕz'e-
bel by the wall of Jĕz're-el.
24 Him that dieth of Ahab in the city
the dogs shall eat; and him that dieth in
the field shall the fowls of the air eat.
25 But there was none like unto
Ahab, which did sell himself to work
wickedness in the sight of the LORD,
whom Jĕz'e-bel his wife stirred up.
26 And he did very abominably in fol-
lowing idols, according to all *things* as
did the Amorites, whom the LORD cast
out before the children of Israel.
27 And it came to pass, when Ahab
heard those words, that he rent his
clothes, and put sackcloth upon his
flesh, and fasted, and lay in sackcloth,
and went softly.
28 And the word of the LORD came to
E-lī'jah the Tĭsh'bīte, saying,
29 Seest thou how Ahab humbleth
himself before me? because he hum-
bleth himself before me, I will not bring
the evil in his days: *but* in his son's days
will I bring the evil upon his house.

CHAPTER 22

AND they continued three years
without war between Syria and Israel.
2 And it came to pass in the third
year, that Je-hŏsh'a-phăt the king of
Jūdah came down to the king of Israel.
3 And the king of Israel said unto his
servants, Know ye that Rā'mŏth in Gil-
ead *is* ours, and we *be* still, *and* take it
not out of the hand of the king of Syria?
4 And he said unto Je-hŏsh'a-phăt,
Wilt thou go with me to battle to Rā'-
moth-gĭl'e-ad? And Je-hŏsh'a-phăt said
to the king of Israel, I *am* as thou *art*,
my people as thy people, my horses as
thy horses.
5 ¶And Je-hŏsh'a-phăt said unto the

king of Israel, Enquire, I pray thee, at the word of the LORD to day.

6 Then the king of Israel gathered the prophets together, about four hundred men, and said unto them, Shall I go against Ră'moth-gĭl'e-ad to battle, or shall I forbear? And they said, Go up; for the Lord shall deliver *it* into the hand of the king.

7 And Je-hŏsh'a-phăt said, *Is there* not here a prophet of the LORD besides, that we might enquire of him?

8 And the king of Israel said unto Je-hŏsh'a-phăt, *There is* yet one man, Mī-cā'iah the son of Ĭm'lah, by whom we may enquire of the LORD: but I hate him; for he doth not prophesy good concerning me, but evil. And Je-hŏsh'a-phăt said, Let not the king say so.

9 Then the king of Israel called an officer, and said, Hasten *hither* Mī-cā'iah the son of Ĭm'lah.

10 And the king of Israel and Je-hŏsh'a-phăt the king of Jūdah sat each on his throne, having put on their robes, in a void place in the entrance of the gate of Sa-mâ'rī-a; and all the prophets prophesied before them.

11 And Zĕd-e-kī'ah the son of Che-nā'a-nah made him horns of iron: and he said, Thus saith the LORD, With these shalt thou push the Syrians, until thou have consumed them.

12 And all the prophets prophesied so, saying, Go up to Ră'moth-gĭl'e-ad, and prosper: for the LORD shall deliver *it* into the king's hand.

13 And the messenger that was gone to call Mī-cā'iah spake unto him, saying, Behold now, the words of the prophets *declare* good unto the king with one mouth: let thy word, I pray thee, be like the word of one of them, and speak *that which is* good.

14 And Mī-cā'iah said, *As* the LORD liveth, what the LORD saith unto me, that will I speak.

15 So he came to the king. And the king said unto him, Mī-cā'iah, shall we go against Ră'moth-gĭl'e-ad to battle, or shall we forbear? And he answered him, Go, and prosper: for the LORD shall deliver *it* into the hand of the king.

16 And the king said unto him, How many times shall I adjure thee that thou tell me nothing but *that which is* true in the name of the LORD?

17 And he said, I saw all Israel scattered upon the hills, as sheep that have not a shepherd: and the LORD said, These have no master: let them return every man to his house in peace.

18 And the king of Israel said unto Je-hŏsh'a-phăt, Did I not tell thee that he would prophesy no good concerning me, but evil?

19 And he said, Hear thou therefore the word of the LORD: I saw the LORD sitting on his throne, and all the host of heaven standing by him on his right hand and on his left.

20 And the LORD said, Who shall persuade Ahab, that he may go up and fall at Ră'moth-gĭl'e-ad? And one said on this manner, and another said on that manner.

21 And there came forth a spirit, and stood before the LORD, and said, I will persuade him.

22 And the LORD said unto him, Wherewith? And he said, I will go forth, and I will be a lying spirit in the mouth of all his prophets. And he said, Thou shalt persuade *him*, and prevail also: go forth, and do so.

23 Now therefore, behold, the LORD hath put a lying spirit in the mouth of all these thy prophets, and the LORD hath spoken evil concerning thee.

24 ¶But Zĕd-e-kī'ah the son of Che-nā'a-nah went near, and smote Mī-cā'iah on the cheek, and said, Which way went the Spirit of the LORD from me to speak unto thee?

25 And Mī-cā'iah said, Behold, thou shalt see in that day, when thou shalt go into an inner chamber to hide thyself.

26 And the king of Israel said, Take Mī-cā'iah, and carry him back unto Ā'mon the governor of the city, and to Jō'ăsh the king's son;

27 And say, Thus saith the king, Put this *fellow* in the prison, and feed him with bread of affliction and with water of affliction, until I come in peace.

28 And Mī-cā'iah said, If thou return at all in peace, the LORD hath not spoken by me. And he said, Hearken, O people, every one of you.

29 So the king of Israel and Je-hŏsh'a-phăt the king of Jūdah went up to Ră'moth-gĭl'e-ad.

30 And the king of Israel said unto Je-hŏsh'a-phăt, I will disguise myself, and enter into the battle; but put thou on thy robes. And the king of Israel disguised himself, and went into the battle.

31 But the king of Syria commanded his thirty and two captains that had rule over his chariots, saying, Fight neither with small nor great, save only with the king of Israel.

32 And it came to pass, when the captains of the chariots saw Je-hŏsh'a-phăt, that they said, Surely it *is* the king of Israel. And they turned aside to fight

against him: and Je-hŏsh'a-phăt cried out.

33 And it came to pass, when the captains of the chariots perceived that it *was* not the king of Israel, that they turned back from pursuing him.

34 ¶And a *certain* man drew a bow at a venture, and smote the king of Israel between the joints of the harness: wherefore he said unto the driver of his chariot, Turn thine hand, and carry me out of the host; for I am wounded.

35 And the battle increased that day: and the king was stayed up in his chariot against the Syrians, and died at even: and the blood ran out of the wound into the midst of the chariot.

36 And there went a proclamation throughout the host about the going down of the sun, saying, Every man to his city, and every man to his own country.

37 So the king died, and was brought to Sa-mâ'rī-a; and they buried the king in Sa-mâ'rī-a.

38 And *one* washed the chariot in the pool of Sa-mâ'rī-a; and the dogs licked up his blood; and they washed his armour; according unto the word of the LORD which he spake.

39 Now the rest of the acts of Ahab, and all that he did, and the ivory house which he made, and all the cities that he built, *are* they not written in the book of the chronicles of the kings of Israel?

40 So Ahab slept with his fathers; and Ā-ha-zī'ah his son reigned in his stead.

41 ¶And Je-hŏsh'a-phăt the son of Āsa began to reign over Jūdah in the fourth year of Ahab king of Israel.

42 Je-hŏsh'a-phăt *was* thirty and five years old when he began to reign; and he reigned twenty and five years in Jerusalem. And his mother's name *was* A-zū'bah the daughter of Shĭl'hī.

43 And he walked in all the ways of Āsa his father; he turned not aside from it, doing *that which was* right in the eyes of the LORD: nevertheless the high places were not taken away; *for* the people offered and burnt incense yet in the high places.

44 And Je-hŏsh'a-phăt made peace with the king of Israel.

45 Now the rest of the acts of Je-hŏsh'a-phăt, and his might that he shewed, and how he warred, *are* they not written in the book of the chronicles of the kings of Jūdah?

46 And the remnant of the sodomites, which remained in the days of his father Āsa, he took out of the land.

47 *There was* then no king in Ēdom: a deputy *was* king.

48 Je-hŏsh'a-phăt made ships of Thär'shĭsh to go to Ō'phir for gold: but they went not; for the ships were broken at Ē'zĭ-on–gē'ber.

49 Then said Ā-ha-zī'ah the son of Ahab unto Je-hŏsh'a-phăt, Let my servants go with thy servants in the ships. But Je-hŏsh'a-phăt would not.

50 ¶And Je-hŏsh'a-phăt slept with his fathers, and was buried with his fathers in the city of David his father: and Je-hô'ram his son reigned in his stead.

51 ¶Ā-ha-zī'ah the son of Ahab began to reign over Israel in Sa-mâ'rī-a the seventeenth year of Je-hŏsh'a-phăt king of Jūdah, and reigned two years over Israel.

52 And he did evil in the sight of the LORD, and walked in the way of his father, and in the way of his mother, and in the way of Jĕr-o-bō'am the son of Nē'băt, who made Israel to sin:

53 For he served Bā'al, and worshipped him, and provoked to anger the LORD God of Israel, according to all that his father had done.

THE

SECOND BOOK OF THE KINGS

COMMONLY CALLED THE FOURTH BOOK OF THE KINGS

CHAPTER 1

THEN Moab rebelled against Israel after the death of Ahab.

2 And Ā-ha-zī'ah fell down through a lattice in his upper chamber that *was* in Sa-mâ'rī-a, and was sick: and he sent messengers, and said unto them, Go, enquire of Bā'al–zē'bŭb the god of Ĕkron whether I shall recover of this disease.

3 But the angel of the LORD said to E-lī'jah the Tĭsh'bīte, Arise, go up to meet the messengers of the king of Sa-mâ'rī-a, and say unto them, *Is it* not because *there is* not a God in Israel, *that* ye go to enquire of Bā'al–zē'bŭb the god of Ĕkron?

4 Now therefore thus saith the LORD, Thou shalt not come down from that

bed on which thou art gone up, but
shalt surely die. And E-lī'jah departed.
5 ¶And when the messengers turned
back unto him, he said unto them, Why
are ye now turned back?
6 And they said unto him, There
came a man up to meet us, and said
unto us, Go, turn again unto the king
that sent you, and say unto him, Thus
saith the LORD, *Is it* not because *there is*
not a God in Israel, *that* thou sendest to
enquire of Bā'al–zē'bŭb the god of
Ēkron? therefore thou shalt not come
down from that bed on which thou art
gone up, but shalt surely die.
7 And he said unto them, What manner
of man *was he* which came up to
meet you, and told you these words?
8 And they answered him, *He was* an
hairy man, and girt with a girdle of
leather about his loins. And he said, It *is*
E-lī'jah the Tĭsh'bīte.
9 Then the king sent unto him a captain
of fifty with his fifty. And he went
up to him: and, behold, he sat on the top
of an hill. And he spake unto him, Thou
man of God, the king hath said, Come
down.
10 And E-lī'jah answered and said to
the captain of fifty, If I *be* a man of God,
then let fire come down from heaven,
and consume thee and thy fifty. And
there came down fire from heaven, and
consumed him and his fifty.
11 Again also he sent unto him another
captain of fifty with his fifty. And
he answered and said unto him, O man
of God, thus hath the king said, Come
down quickly.
12 And E-lī'jah answered and said
unto them, If I *be* a man of God, let fire
come down from heaven, and consume
thee and thy fifty. And the fire of God
came down from heaven, and consumed
him and his fifty.
13 And he sent again a captain of the
third fifty with his fifty. And the third
captain of fifty went up, and came and
fell on his knees before E-lī'jah, and besought
him, and said unto him, O man
of God, I pray thee, let my life, and the
life of these fifty thy servants, be precious
in thy sight.
14 Behold, there came fire down
from heaven, and burnt up the two captains
of the former fifties with their
fifties: therefore let my life now be precious
in thy sight.
15 And the angel of the LORD said
unto E-lī'jah, Go down with him: be not
afraid of him. And he arose, and went
down with him unto the king.
16 And he said unto him, Thus saith
the LORD, Forasmuch as thou hast sent
messengers to enquire of Bā'al–zē'bŭb
the God of Ĕkron, *is it* not because
there is no God in Israel to enquire of
his word? therefore thou shalt not
come down off that bed on which thou
art gone up, but shalt surely die.
17 ¶So he died according to the word
of the LORD which E-lī'jah had spoken.
And Je-hô'ram reigned in his stead in
the second year of Je-hô'ram the son of
Je-hŏsh'a-phăt king of Jūdah; because
he had no son.
18 Now the rest of the acts of Ā-ha-
zī'ah which he did, *are* they not written
in the book of the chronicles of the
kings of Israel?

CHAPTER 2

AND it came to pass, when the LORD
would take up E-lī'jah into heaven by a
whirlwind, that E-lī'jah went with
E-lī'sha from Gilgal.
2 And E-lī'jah said unto E-lī'sha,
Tarry here, I pray thee; for the LORD
hath sent me to Bĕth–el. And E-lī'sha
said *unto him, As* the LORD liveth, and
as thy soul liveth, I will not leave thee.
So they went down to Bĕth–el.
3 And the sons of the prophets that
were at Bĕth–el came forth to E-lī'sha,
and said unto him, Knowest thou that
the LORD will take away thy master
from thy head to day? And he said, Yea,
I know *it;* hold ye your peace.
4 And E-lī'jah said unto him, E-lī'sha,
tarry here, I pray thee; for the LORD
hath sent me to Jericho. And he said,
As the LORD liveth, and *as* thy soul
liveth, I will not leave thee. So they
came to Jericho.
5 And the sons of the prophets that
were at Jericho came to E-lī'sha, and
said unto him, Knowest thou that the
LORD will take away thy master from
thy head to day? And he answered,
Yea, I know *it:* hold ye your peace.
6 And E-lī'jah said unto him, Tarry, I
pray thee, here; for the LORD hath sent
me to Jordan. And he said, *As* the LORD
liveth, and *as* thy soul liveth, I will not
leave thee. And they two went on.
7 And fifty men of the sons of the
prophets went, and stood to view afar
off: and they two stood by Jordan.
8 And E-lī'jah took his mantle, and
wrapped *it* together, and smote the waters,
and they were divided hither and
thither, so that they two went over on
dry ground.
9 ¶And it came to pass, when they
were gone over, that E-lī'jah said unto
E-lī'sha, Ask what I shall do for thee,
before I be taken away from thee. And

E-lī'sha said, I pray thee, let a double
portion of thy spirit be upon me.
10 And he said, Thou hast asked a
hard thing: *nevertheless,* if thou see me
when I am taken from thee, it shall be
so unto thee; but if not, it shall not be
so.
11 And it came to pass, as they still
went on, and talked, that, behold, *there*
appeared a chariot of fire, and horses of
fire, and parted them both asunder;
and E-lī'jah went up by a whirlwind
into heaven.
12 And E-lī'sha saw *it,* and he cried,
My father, my father, the chariot of
Israel, and the horsemen thereof. And
he saw him no more: and he took hold
of his own clothes, and rent them in
two pieces.
13 He took up also the mantle of E-lī'-
jah that fell from him, and went back,
and stood by the bank of Jordan;
14 And he took the mantle of E-lī'jah
that fell from him, and smote the waters,
and said, Where *is* the LORD God of
E-lī'jah? and when he also had smitten
the waters, they parted hither and
thither: and E-lī'sha went over.
15 And when the sons of the prophets
which *were* to view at Jericho saw him,
they said, The spirit of E-lī'jah doth rest
on E-lī'sha. And they came to meet
him, and bowed themselves to the
ground before him.
16 And they said unto him, Behold
now, there be with thy servants fifty
strong men; let them go, we pray thee,
and seek thy master: lest peradventure
the Spirit of the LORD hath taken him
up, and cast him upon some mountain,
or into some valley. And he said, Ye
shall not send.
17 And when they urged him till he
was ashamed, he said, Send. They sent
therefore fifty men; and they sought
three days, but found him not.
18 And when they came again to him,
(for he tarried at Jericho,) he said unto
them, Did I not say unto you, Go not?
19 ¶And the men of the city said unto
E-lī'sha, Behold, I pray thee, the situ-
ation of this city *is* pleasant, as my lord
seeth: but the water *is* naught, and the
ground barren.
20 And he said, Bring me a new cruse,
and put salt therein. And they brought
it to him.
21 And he went forth unto the spring
of the waters, and cast the salt in there,
and said, Thus saith the LORD, I have
healed these waters; there shall not be
from thence any more death or barren
land.
22 So the waters were healed unto
this day, according to the saying of E-
lī'sha which he spake.
23 ¶And he went up from thence unto
Bĕth-el: and as he was going up by the
way, there came forth little children
out of the city, and mocked him and
said unto him, Go up, thou bald head;
go up, thou bald head.
24 And he turned back, and looked on
them, and cursed them in the name of
the LORD. And there came forth two she
bears out of the wood, and tare forty
and two children of them.
25 And he went from thence to
mount Carmel, and from thence he re-
turned to Sa-mâ'rĭ-a.

CHAPTER 3

NOW Je-hô'ram the son of Ahab began
to reign over Israel in Sa-mâ'rĭ-a the
eighteenth year of Je-hŏsh'a-phăt king
of Jūdah, and reigned twelve years.
2 And he wrought evil in the sight of
the LORD; but not like his father, and
like his mother: for he put away the
image of Bā'al that his father had made.
3 Nevertheless he cleaved unto the
sins of Jĕr-o-bō'am the son of Nē'băt,
which made Israel to sin; he departed
not therefrom.
4 ¶And Mē'sha king of Moab was a
sheepmaster, and rendered unto the
king of Israel an hundred thousand
lambs, and an hundred thousand rams,
with the wool.
5 But it came to pass, when Ahab was
dead, that the king of Moab rebelled
against the king of Israel.
6 ¶And king Je-hô'ram went out of
Sa-mâ'rĭ-a the same time, and num-
bered all Israel.
7 And he went and sent to Je-hŏsh'a-
phăt the king of Jūdah, saying, The
king of Moab hath rebelled against me:
wilt thou go with me against Moab to
battle? And he said, I will go up: I *am* as
thou *art,* my people as thy people, *and*
my horses as thy horses.
8 And he said, Which way shall we go
up? And he answered, The way through
the wilderness of Ēdom.
9 So the king of Israel went, and the
king of Jūdah, and the king of Ēdom:
and they fetched a compass of seven
days' journey: and there was no water
for the host, and for the cattle that fol-
lowed them.
10 And the king of Israel said, Alas!
that the LORD hath called these three
kings together, to deliver them into the
hand of Moab!
11 But Je-hŏsh'a-phăt said, *Is there*
not here a prophet of the LORD, that we
may enquire of the LORD by him? And
one of the king of Israel's servants an-

swered and said, Here *is* E-lī'sha the son of Shā'phat, which poured water on the hands of E-lī'jah.
12 And Je-hŏsh'a-phăt said, The word of the LORD is with him. So the king of Israel and Je-hŏsh'a-phăt and the king of Ēdom went down to him.
13 And E-lī'sha said unto the king of Israel, What have I to do with thee? get thee to the prophets of thy father, and to the prophets of thy mother. And the king of Israel said unto him, Nay: for the LORD hath called these three kings together, to deliver them into the hand of Moab.
14 And E-lī'sha said, *As* the LORD of hosts liveth, before whom I stand, surely, were it not that I regard the presence of Je-hŏsh'a-phăt the king of Jū-dah, I would not look toward thee, nor see thee.
15 But now bring me a minstrel. And it came to pass, when the minstrel played, that the hand of the LORD came upon him.
16 And he said, Thus saith the LORD, Make this valley full of ditches.
17 For thus saith the LORD, Ye shall not see wind, neither shall ye see rain; yet that valley shall be filled with water, that ye may drink, both ye, and your cattle, and your beasts.
18 And this is *but* a light thing in the sight of the LORD: he will deliver the Moabites also into your hand.
19 And ye shall smite every fenced city, and every choice city, and shall fell every good tree, and stop all wells of water, and mar every good piece of land with stones.
20 And it came to pass in the morning, when the meat offering was offered, that, behold, there came water by the way of Ēdom, and the country was filled with water.
21 ¶And when all the Moabites heard that the kings were come up to fight against them, they gathered all that were able to put on armour, and upward, and stood in the border.
22 And they rose up early in the morning, and the sun shone upon the water, and the Moabites saw the water on the other side *as* red as blood:
23 And they said, This *is* blood: the kings are surely slain, and they have smitten one another: now therefore, Moab, to the spoil.
24 And when they came to the camp of Israel, the Israelites rose up and smote the Moabites, so that they fled before them: but they went forward smiting the Moabites, even in *their* country.
25 And they beat down the cities, and on every good piece of land cast every man his stone, and filled it; and they stopped all the wells of water, and felled all the good trees: only in Kĭr–hăr'a-sĕth left they the stones thereof; howbeit the slingers went about *it*, and smote it.
26 ¶And when the king of Moab saw that the battle was too sore for him, he took with him seven hundred men that drew swords, to break through *even* unto the king of Ēdom: but they could not.
27 Then he took his eldest son that should have reigned in his stead, and offered him *for* a burnt offering upon the wall. And there was great indignation against Israel: and they departed from him, and returned to *their own* land.

CHAPTER 4

NOW there cried a certain woman of the wives of the sons of the prophets unto E-lī'sha, saying, Thy servant my husband is dead; and thou knowest that thy servant did fear the LORD: and the creditor is come to take unto him my two sons to be bondmen.
2 And E-lī'sha said unto her, What shall I do for thee? tell me, what hast thou in the house? And she said, Thine handmaid hath not any thing in the house, save a pot of oil.
3 Then he said, Go, borrow thee vessels abroad of all thy neighbours, *even* empty vessels; borrow not a few.
4 And when thou art come in, thou shalt shut the door upon thee and upon thy sons, and shalt pour out into all those vessels, and thou shalt set aside that which is full.
5 So she went from him, and shut the door upon her and upon her sons, who brought *the vessels* to her; and she poured out.
6 And it came to pass, when the vessels were full, that she said unto her son, Bring me yet a vessel. And he said unto her, *There is* not a vessel more. And the oil stayed.
7 Then she came and told the man of God. And he said, Go, sell the oil, and pay thy debt, and live thou and thy children of the rest.
8 ¶And it fell on a day, that E-lī'sha passed to Shū'nem, where *was* a great woman; and she constrained him to eat bread. And *so* it was, *that* as oft as he passed by, he turned in thither to eat bread.
9 And she said unto her husband, Behold now, I perceive that this *is* an holy man of God, which passeth by us continually.

10 Let us make a little chamber, I pray thee, on the wall; and let us set for him there a bed, and a table, and a stool, and a candlestick: and it shall be, when he cometh to us, that he shall turn in thither.
11 And it fell on a day, that he came thither, and he turned into the chamber, and lay there.
12 And he said to Ge-hā'zī his servant, Call this Shū'nam-mīte. And when he had called her, she stood before him.
13 And he said unto him, Say now unto her, Behold, thou hast been careful for us with all this care; what *is* to be done for thee? wouldest thou be spoken for to the king, or to the captain of the host? And she answered, I dwell among mine own people.
14 And he said, What then *is* to be done for her? and Ge-hā'zī answered, Verily she hath no child, and her husband is old.
15 And he said, Call her. And when he had called her, she stood in the door.
16 And he said, About this season, according to the time of life, thou shalt embrace a son. And she said, Nay, my lord, *thou* man of God, do not lie unto thine handmaid.
17 And the woman conceived, and bare a son at that season that E-lī'sha had said unto her, according to the time of life.
18 ¶And when the child was grown, it fell on a day, that he went out to his father to the reapers.
19 And he said unto his father, My head, my head. And he said to a lad, Carry him to his mother.
20 And when he had taken him, and brought him to his mother, he sat on her knees till noon, and *then* died.
21 And she went up, and laid him on the bed of the man of God, and shut *the door* upon him, and went out.
22 And she called unto her husband, and said, Send me, I pray thee, one of the young men, and one of the asses, that I may run to the man of God, and come again.
23 And he said, Wherefore wilt thou go to him to day? *it is* neither new moon, nor sabbath. And she said, *It shall be* well.
24 Then she saddled an ass, and said to her servant, Drive, and go forward; slack not *thy* riding for me, except I bid thee.
25 So she went and came unto the man of God to mount Carmel. And it came to pass, when the man of God saw her afar off, that he said to Ge-hā'zī his servant, Behold, *yonder is* that Shū'nam-mīte:
26 Run now, I pray thee, to meet her, and say unto her, *Is it* well with thee? *is it* well with thy husband? *is it* well with the child? And she answered, *It is* well.
27 And when she came to the man of God to the hill, she caught him by the feet: but Ge-hā'zī came near to thrust her away. And the man of God said, Let her alone; for her soul *is* vexed within her: and the LORD hath hid *it* from me, and hath not told me.
28 Then she said, Did I desire a son of my lord? did I not say, Do not deceive me?
29 Then he said to Ge-hā'zī, Gird up thy loins, and take my staff in thine hand, and go thy way: if thou meet any man, salute him not; and if any salute thee, answer him not again: and lay my staff upon the face of the child.
30 And the mother of the child said, *As* the LORD liveth, and *as* thy soul liveth, I will not leave thee. And he arose, and followed her.
31 And Ge-hā'zī passed on before them, and laid the staff upon the face of the child; but *there was* neither voice, nor hearing. Wherefore he went again to meet him, and told him, saying, The child is not awaked.
32 And when E-lī'sha was come into the house, behold, the child was dead, *and* laid upon his bed.
33 He went in therefore, and shut the door upon them twain, and prayed unto the LORD.
34 And he went up, and lay upon the child, and put his mouth upon his mouth, and his eyes upon his eyes, and his hands upon his hands: and he stretched himself upon the child; and the flesh of the child waxed warm.
35 Then he returned, and walked in the house to and fro; and went up, and stretched himself upon him: and the child sneezed seven times, and the child opened his eyes.
36 And he called Ge-hā'zī, and said, Call this Shū'nam-mīte. So he called her. And when she was come in unto him, he said, Take up thy son.
37 Then she went in, and fell at his feet, and bowed herself to the ground, and took up her son, and went out.
38 ¶And E-lī'sha came again to Gilgal: and *there was* a dearth in the land; and the sons of the prophets *were* sitting before him: and he said unto his servant, Set on the great pot, and seethe pottage for the sons of the prophets.
39 And one went out into the field to gather herbs, and found a wild vine,

and gathered thereof wild gourds his
lap full, and came and shred *them* into
the pot of pottage: for they knew *them*
not.
40 So they poured out for the men to
eat. And it came to pass, as they were
eating of the pottage, that they cried
out, and said, O *thou* man of God, *there*
is death in the pot. And they could not
eat *thereof.*
41 But he said, Then bring meal. And
he cast *it* into the pot; and he said, Pour
out for the people, that they may eat.
And there was no harm in the pot.
42 ¶And there came a man from Bā'-
al–shăl'i-sha, and brought the man of
God bread of the firstfruits, twenty
loaves of barley, and full ears of corn in
the husk thereof. And he said, Give
unto the people, that they may eat.
43 And his servitor said, What,
should I set this before an hundred
men? He said again, Give the people,
that they may eat: for thus saith the
LORD, They shall eat, and shall leave
thereof.
44 So he set *it* before them, and they
did eat, and left *thereof,* according to
the word of the LORD.

CHAPTER 5

NOW Nā'a-man, captain of the host of
the king of Syria, was a great man with
his master, and honourable, because by
him the LORD had given deliverance
unto Syria: he was also a mighty man in
valour, *but he was* a leper.
2 And the Syrians had gone out by
companies, and had brought away cap-
tive out of the land of Israel a little
maid; and she waited on Nā'a-man's
wife.
3 And she said unto her mistress,
Would God my lord *were* with the
prophet that *is* in Sa-mâ'rĭ-a! for he
would recover him of his leprosy.
4 And *one* went in, and told his lord,
saying, Thus and thus said the maid
that *is* of the land of Israel.
5 And the king of Syria said, Go to,
go, and I will send a letter unto the king
of Israel. And he departed, and took
with him ten talents of silver, and six
thousand *pieces* of gold, and ten
changes of raiment.
6 And he brought the letter to the
king of Israel, saying, Now when this
letter is come unto thee, behold, I have
therewith sent Nā'a-man my servant to
thee, that thou mayest recover him of
his leprosy.
7 And it came to pass, when the king
of Israel had read the letter, that he rent
his clothes, and said, *Am* I God, to kill
and to make alive, that this man doth
send unto me to recover a man of his
leprosy? wherefore consider, I pray
you, and see how he seeketh a quarrel
against me.
8 ¶And it was *so,* when E-lī'sha the
man of God had heard that the king of
Israel had rent his clothes, that he sent
to the king, saying, Wherefore hast
thou rent thy clothes? let him come
now to me, and he shall know that
there is a prophet in Israel.
9 So Nā'a-man came with his horses
and with his chariot, and stood at the
door of the house of E-lī'sha.
10 And E-lī'sha sent a messenger
unto him, saying, Go and wash in Jor-
dan seven times, and thy flesh shall
come again to thee, and thou shalt be
clean.
11 But Nā'a-man was wroth, and
went away, and said, Behold, I thought,
He will surely come out to me, and
stand, and call on the name of the LORD
his God, and strike his hand over the
place, and recover the leper.
12 *Are* not Ăb'a-na and Phär'pär, riv-
ers of Damascus, better than all the wa-
ters of Israel? may I not wash in them,
and be clean? So he turned and went
away in a rage.
13 And his servants came near, and
spake unto him, and said, My father, *if*
the prophet had bid thee *do some* great
thing, wouldest thou not have done *it?*
how much rather then, when he saith to
thee, Wash, and be clean?
14 Then went he down, and dipped
himself seven times in Jordan, accord-
ing to the saying of the man of God:
and his flesh came again like unto the
flesh of a little child, and he was clean.
15 ¶And he returned to the man of
God, he and all his company, and came,
and stood before him: and he said, Be-
hold, now I know that *there is* no God in
all the earth, but in Israel: now there-
fore, I pray thee, take a blessing of thy
servant.
16 But he said, *As* the LORD liveth, be-
fore whom I stand, I will receive none.
And he urged him to take *it;* but he re-
fused.
17 And Nā'a-man said, Shall there
not then, I pray thee, be given to thy
servant two mules' burden of earth? for
thy servant will henceforth offer
neither burnt offering nor sacrifice
unto other gods, but unto the LORD.
18 In this thing the LORD pardon thy
servant, *that* when my master goeth
into the house of Rimmon to worship
there, and he leaneth on my hand, and I
bow myself in the house of Rimmon:
when I bow down myself in the house

of Rimmon, the LORD pardon thy servant in this thing.
19 And he said unto him, Go in peace.
So he departed from him a little way.
20 ¶But Ge-hā'zī, the servant of E-lī'-sha the man of God, said, Behold, my master hath spared Nā'a-man this Syrian, in not receiving at his hands that which he brought: but, *as* the LORD liveth, I will run after him, and take somewhat of him.
21 So Ge-hā'zī followed after Nā'a-man. And when Nā'a-man saw *him* running after him, he lighted down from the chariot to meet him, and said, *Is* all well?
22 And he said, All *is* well. My master hath sent me, saying, Behold, even now there be come to me from mount Ē'phra-im two young men of the sons of the prophets: give them, I pray thee, a talent of silver, and two changes of garments.
23 And Nā'a-man said, Be content, take two talents. And he urged him, and bound two talents of silver in two bags, with two changes of garments, and laid *them* upon two of his servants; and they bare *them* before him.
24 And when he came to the tower, he took *them* from their hand, and bestowed *them* in the house: and he let the men go, and they departed.
25 But he went in, and stood before his master. And E-lī'sha said unto him, Whence *comest thou,* Ge-hā'zī? And he said, Thy servant went no whither.
26 And he said unto him, Went not mine heart *with thee,* when the man turned again from his chariot to meet thee? *Is it* a time to receive money, and to receive garments, and oliveyards, and vineyards, and sheep, and oxen, and menservants, and maidservants?
27 The leprosy therefore of Nā'a-man shall cleave unto thee, and unto thy seed for ever. And he went out from his presence a leper *as white* as snow.

CHAPTER 6

AND the sons of the prophets said unto E-lī'sha, Behold now, the place where we dwell with thee is too strait for us.
2 Let us go, we pray thee, unto Jordan, and take thence every man a beam, and let us make us a place there, where we may dwell. And he answered, Go ye.
3 And one said, Be content, I pray thee, and go with thy servants. And he answered, I will go.
4 So he went with them. And when they came to Jordan, they cut down wood.
5 But as one was felling a beam, the axe head fell into the water: and he cried, and said, Alas, master! for it was borrowed.
6 And the man of God said, Where fell it? And he shewed him the place. And he cut down a stick, and cast *it* in thither; and the iron did swim.
7 Therefore said he, Take *it* up to thee. And he put out his hand, and took it.
8 ¶Then the king of Syria warred against Israel, and took counsel with his servants, saying, In such and such a place *shall be* my camp.
9 And the man of God sent unto the king of Israel, saying, Beware that thou pass not such a place; for thither the Syrians are come down.
10 And the king of Israel sent to the place which the man of God told him and warned him of, and saved himself there, not once nor twice.
11 Therefore the heart of the king of Syria was sore troubled for this thing; and he called his servants, and said unto them, Will ye not shew me which of us *is* for the king of Israel?
12 And one of his servants said, None, my lord, O king: but E-lī'sha, the prophet that *is* in Israel, telleth the king of Israel the words that thou speakest in thy bedchamber.
13 And he said, Go and spy where he *is,* that I may send and fetch him. And it was told him, saying, Behold, *he is* in Dō'than.
14 Therefore sent he thither horses, and chariots, and a great host: and they came by night, and compassed the city about.
15 And when the servant of the man of God was risen early, and gone forth, behold, an host compassed the city both with horses and chariots. And his servant said unto him, Alas, my master! how shall we do?
16 And he answered, Fear not: for they that *be* with us *are* more than they that *be* with them.
17 And E-lī'sha prayed, and said, LORD, I pray thee, open his eyes, that he may see. And the LORD opened the eyes of the young man; and he saw: and, behold, the mountain *was* full of horses and chariots of fire round about E-lī'-sha.
18 And when they came down to him, E-lī'sha prayed unto the LORD, and said, Smite this people, I pray thee, with blindness. And he smote them with blindness according to the word of E-lī'sha.
19 And E-lī'sha said unto them, This *is* not the way, neither *is* this the city: follow me, and I will bring you to the

man whom ye seek. But he led them to Sa-mâ'rĭ-a.
20 And it came to pass, when they were come into Sā-mâ'rĭ-a, that E-lī'-sha said, LORD, open the eyes of these *men*, that they may see. And the LORD opened their eyes, and they saw; and, behold, *they were* in the midst of Sā-mâ'rĭ-a.
21 And the king of Israel said unto E-lī'sha, when he saw them, My father, shall I smite *them?* shall I smite *them?*
22 And he answered, Thou shalt not smite *them:* wouldest thou smite those whom thou hast taken captive with thy sword and with thy bow? set bread and water before them, that they may eat and drink, and go to their master.
23 And he prepared great provision for them: and when they had eaten and drunk, he sent them away, and they went to their master. So the bands of Syria came no more into the land of Israel.
24 ¶And it came to pass after this, that Bĕn-hā'dăd king of Syria gathered all his host, and went up, and besieged Sā-mâ'rĭ-a.
25 And there was a great famine in Sā-mâ'rĭ-a: and, behold, they besieged it, until an ass's head was *sold* for fourscore *pieces* of silver, and the fourth part of a cab of dove's dung for five *pieces* of silver.
26 ¶And as the king of Israel was passing by upon the wall, there cried a woman unto him, saying, Help, my lord, O king.
27 And he said, If the LORD do not help thee, whence shall I help thee? out of the barnfloor, or out of the winepress?
28 And the king said unto her, What aileth thee? And she answered, This woman said unto me, Give thy son, that we may eat him to day, and we will eat my son to morrow.
29 So we boiled my son, and did eat him: and I said unto her on the next day, Give thy son, that we may eat him: and she hath hid her son.
30 And it came to pass, when the king heard the words of the woman, that he rent his clothes; and he passed by upon the wall, and the people looked, and, behold, *he had* sackcloth within upon his flesh.
31 Then he said, God do so and more also to me, if the head of E-lī'sha the son of Shā'phat shall stand on him this day.
32 But E-lī'sha sat in his house, and the elders sat with him; and *the king* sent a man from before him: but ere the messenger came to him, he said to the elders, See ye how this son of a murderer hath sent to take away mine head? look, when the messenger cometh, shut the door, and hold him fast at the door: *is* not the sound of his master's feet behind him?
33 And while he yet talked with them, behold, the messenger came down unto him: and he said, Behold, this evil *is* of the LORD; what should I wait for the LORD any longer?

CHAPTER 7

THEN E-lī'sha said, Hear ye the word of the LORD; Thus saith the LORD, To morrow about this time *shall* a measure of fine flour *be sold* for a shekel, and two measures of barley for a shekel, in the gate of Sā-mâ'rĭ-a.
2 Then a lord on whose hand the king leaned answered the man of God, and said, Behold, *if* the LORD would make windows in heaven, might this thing be? And he said, Behold, thou shalt see *it* with thine eyes, but shalt not eat thereof.
3 ¶And there were four leprous men at the entering in of the gate: and they said one to another, Why sit we here until we die?
4 If we say, We will enter into the city, then the famine *is* in the city, and we shall die there: and if we sit still here, we die also. Now therefore come, and let us fall unto the host of the Syrians: if they save us alive, we shall live; and if they kill us, we shall but die.
5 And they rose up in the twilight, to go unto the camp of the Syrians: and when they were come to the uttermost part of the camp of Syria, behold, *there was* no man there.
6 For the Lord had made the host of the Syrians to hear a noise of chariots, and a noise of horses, *even* the noise of a great host: and they said one to another, Lo, the king of Israel hath hired against us the kings of the Hittites, and the kings of the Egyptians, to come upon us.
7 Wherefore they arose and fled in the twilight, and left their tents, and their horses, and their asses, even the camp as it *was,* and fled for their life.
8 And when these lepers came to the uttermost part of the camp, they went into one tent, and did eat and drink, and carried thence silver, and gold, and raiment, and went and hid *it;* and came again, and entered into another tent, and carried thence *also,* and went and hid *it.*
9 Then they said one to another, We do not well: this day *is* a day of good tidings, and we hold our peace: if we

tarry till the morning light, some mis-
chief will come upon us: now therefore
come, that we may go and tell the
king's household.
10 So they came and called unto the
porter of the city: and they told them,
saying, We came to the camp of the Syr-
ians, and, behold, *there was* no man
there, neither voice of man, but horses
tied, and asses tied, and the tents as
they *were*.
11 And he called the porters; and
they told *it* to the king's house within.
12 ¶And the king arose in the night,
and said unto his servants, I will now
shew you what the Syrians have done
to us. They know that we *be* hungry;
therefore are they gone out of the camp
to hide themselves in the field, saying,
When they come out of the city, we
shall catch them alive, and get into the
city.
13 And one of his servants answered
and said, Let *some* take, I pray thee,
five of the horses that remain, which
are left in the city, (behold, they *are* as
all the multitude of Israel that are left in
it: behold, *I say*, they *are* even as all the
multitude of the Israelites that are con-
sumed:) and let us send and see.
14 They took therefore two chariot
horses; and the king sent after the host
of the Syrians, saying, Go and see.
15 And they went after them unto
Jordan: and, lo, all the way *was* full of
garments and vessels, which the Syr-
ians had cast away in their haste. And
the messengers returned, and told the
king.
16 And the people went out, and
spoiled the tents of the Syrians. So a
measure of fine flour was *sold* for a
shekel, and two measures of barley for
a shekel, according to the word of the
LORD.
17 ¶And the king appointed the lord
on whose hand he leaned to have the
charge of the gate: and the people trode
upon him in the gate, and he died, as
the man of God had said, who spake
when the king came down to him.
18 And it came to pass as the man of
God had spoken to the king, saying,
Two measures of barley for a shekel,
and a measure of fine flour for a shekel,
shall be to morrow about this time in
the gate of Sā-mâ'rĭ-a:
19 And that lord answered the man of
God, and said, Now, behold, *if* the LORD
should make windows in heaven,
might such a thing be? And he said, Be-
hold, thou shalt see it with thine eyes,
but shalt not eat thereof.
20 And so it fell out unto him: for the
people trode upon him in the gate, and
he died.

CHAPTER 8

THEN spake E-lī'sha unto the woman,
whose son he had restored to life,
saying, Arise, and go thou and thine
household, and sojourn wheresoever
thou canst sojourn: for the LORD hath
called for a famine; and it shall also
come upon the land seven years.
2 And the woman arose, and did after
the saying of the man of God: and she
went with her household, and so-
journed in the land of the Philistines
seven years.
3 And it came to pass at the seven
years' end, that the woman returned
out of the land of the Philistines: and
she went forth to cry unto the king for
her house and for her land.
4 And the king talked with Ge-hā'zī
the servant of the man of God, saying,
Tell me, I pray thee, all the great things
that E-lī'sha hath done.
5 And it came to pass, as he was tell-
ing the king how he had restored a
dead body to life, that, behold, the wom-
an, whose son he had restored to life,
cried to the king for her house and for
her land. And Ge-hā'zī said, My lord, O
king, this *is* the woman, and this *is* her
son, whom E-lī'sha restored to life.
6 And when the king asked the wom-
an, she told him. So the king ap-
pointed unto her a certain officer,
saying, Restore all that *was* hers, and
all the fruits of the field since the day
that she left the land, even until now.
7 ¶And E-lī'sha came to Damascus;
and Bĕn-hā'dăd the king of Syria was
sick; and it was told him, saying, The
man of God is come hither.
8 And the king said unto Hāz'a-el,
Take a present in thine hand, and go,
meet the man of God, and enquire of
the LORD by him, saying, Shall I recover
of this disease?
9 So Hāz'a-el went to meet him, and
took a present with him, even of every
good thing of Damascus, forty camels'
burden, and came and stood before
him, and said, Thy son Bĕn-hā'dăd king
of Syria hath sent me to thee, saying,
Shall I recover of this disease?
10 And E-lī'sha said unto him, Go,
say unto him, Thou mayest certainly
recover: howbeit the LORD hath
shewed me that he shall surely die.
11 And he settled his countenance
stedfastly, until he was ashamed: and
the man of God wept.
12 And Hāz'a-el said, Why weepeth
my lord? And he answered, Because I
know the evil that thou wilt do unto the
children of Israel: their strong holds

wilt thou set on fire, and their young men wilt thou slay with the sword, and wilt dash their children, and rip up their women with child.

13 And Hāz'a-el said, But what, *is* thy servant a dog, that he should do this great thing? And E-lī'sha answered, The LORD hath shewed me that thou *shalt be* king over Syria.

14 So he departed from E-lī'sha, and came to his master; who said to him, What said E-lī'sha to thee? And he answered, He told me *that* thou shouldest surely recover.

15 And it came to pass on the morrow, that he took a thick cloth, and dipped *it* in water, and spread *it* on his face, so that he died: and Hāz'a-el reigned in his stead.

16 ¶And in the fifth year of Joram the son of Ahab king of Israel, Je-hŏsh'a-phăt *being* then king of Jūdah, Je-hô'-ram the son of Je-hŏsh'a-phăt king of Jūdah began to reign.

17 Thirty and two years old was he when he began to reign; and he reigned eight years in Jerusalem.

18 And he walked in the way of the kings of Israel, as did the house of Ahab: for the daughter of Ahab was his wife: and he did evil in the sight of the LORD.

19 Yet the LORD would not destroy Jūdah for David his servant's sake, as he promised him to give him alway a light, *and* to his children.

20 ¶In his days Ēdom revolted from under the hand of Jūdah, and made a king over themselves.

21 So Joram went over to Zā'ir, and all the chariots with him: and he rose by night, and smote the Edomites which compassed him about, and the captains of the chariots: and the people fled into their tents.

22 Yet Ēdom revolted from under the hand of Jūdah unto this day. Then Lĭb'-nah revolted at the same time.

23 And the rest of the acts of Joram, and all that he did, *are* they not written in the book of the chronicles of the kings of Jūdah?

24 And Joram slept with his fathers, and was buried with his fathers in the city of David: and Ā-ha-zī'ah his son reigned in his stead.

25 ¶In the twelfth year of Joram the son of Ahab king of Israel did Ā-ha-zī'ah the son of Je-hô'ram king of Jūdah begin to reign.

26 Two and twenty years old *was* Ā-ha-zī'ah when he began to reign; and he reigned one year in Jerusalem. And his mother's name *was* Ăth-a-lī'ah, the daughter of Omri king of Israel.

27 And he walked in the way of the house of Ahab, and did evil in the sight of the LORD, as *did* the house of Ahab: for he *was* the son in law of the house of Ahab.

28 ¶And he went with Joram the son of Ahab to the war against Hāz'a-el king of Syria in Ră'moth-gĭl'e-ad; and the Syrians wounded Joram.

29 And king Joram went back to be healed in Jĕz're-el of the wounds which the Syrians had given him at Rā'mah, when he fought against Hāz'a-el king of Syria. And Ā-ha-zī'ah the son of Je-hô'ram king of Jūdah went down to see Joram the son of Ahab in Jĕz're-el, because he was sick.

CHAPTER 9

AND E-lī'sha the prophet called one of the children of the prophets, and said unto him, Gird up thy loins, and take this box of oil in thine hand, and go to Ră'moth-gĭl'e-ad:

2 And when thou comest thither, look out there Jehu the son of Je'-hŏsh'a-phăt the son of Nĭm'shī, and go in, and make him arise up from among his brethren, and carry him to an inner chamber;

3 Then take the box of oil, and pour *it* on his head, and say, Thus saith the LORD, I have anointed thee king over Israel. Then open the door, and flee, and tarry not.

4 So the young man, *even* the young man the prophet, went to Ră'moth-gĭl'e-ad.

5 And when he came, behold, the captains of the host *were* sitting; and he said, I have an errand to thee, O captain. And Jehu said, Unto which of all us? And he said, To thee, O captain.

6 And he arose, and went into the house; and he poured the oil on his head, and said unto him, Thus saith the LORD God of Israel, I have anointed thee king over the people of the LORD, *even* over Israel.

7 And thou shalt smite the house of Ahab thy master, that I may avenge the blood of my servants the prophets, and the blood of all the servants of the LORD, at the hand of Jĕz'e-bel.

8 For the whole house of Ahab shall perish: and I will cut off from Ahab him that pisseth against the wall, and him that is shut up and left in Israel:

9 And I will make the house of Ahab like the house of Jĕr-o-bō'am the son of Nē'băt, and like the house of Bā'a-sha the son of A-hī'jah:

10 And the dogs shall eat Jĕz'e-bel in the portion of Jĕz're-el, and *there shall*

be none to bury *her*. And he opened the door, and fled.

11 ¶Then Jehu came forth to the servants of his lord: and *one* said unto him, *Is* all well? wherefore came this mad *fellow* to thee? And he said unto them, Ye know the man, and his communication.

12 And they said, *It is* false; tell us now. And he said, Thus and thus spake he to me, saying, Thus saith the LORD, I have anointed thee king over Israel.

13 Then they hasted, and took every man his garment, and put *it* under him on the top of the stairs, and blew with trumpets, saying, Jehu is king.

14 So Jehu the son of Je-hŏsh′a-phăt the son of Nĭm′shī conspired against Joram. (Now Joram had kept Ră′-moth–gĭl′e-ad, he and all Israel, because of Hāz′a-el king of Syria.

15 But king Joram was returned to be healed in Jĕz′re-el of the wounds which the Syrians had given him, when he fought with Hāz′a-el king of Syria.) And Jehu said, If it be your minds, *then* let none go forth *nor* escape out of the city to go to tell *it* in Jĕz′re-el.

16 So Jehu rode in a chariot, and went to Jĕz′re-el; for Joram lay there. And Ā-ha-zī′ah king of Jūdah was come down to see Joram.

17 And there stood a watchman on the tower in Jĕz′re-el, and he spied the company of Jehu as he came, and said, I see a company. And Joram said, Take an horseman, and send to meet them, and let him say, *Is it* peace?

18 So there went one on horseback to meet him, and said, Thus saith the king, *Is it* peace? And Jehu said, What hast thou to do with peace? turn thee behind me. And the watchman told, saying, The messenger came to them, but he cometh not again.

19 Then he sent out a second on horseback, which came to them, and said, Thus saith the king, *Is it* peace? And Jehu answered, What hast thou to do with peace? turn thee behind me.

20 And the watchman told, saying, He came even unto them, and cometh not again: and the driving *is* like the driving of Jehu the son of Nĭm′shī; for he driveth furiously.

21 And Joram said, Make ready. And his chariot was made ready. And Joram king of Israel and Ā-ha-zī′ah king of Jūdah went out, each in his chariot, and they went out against Jehu, and met him in the portion of Nā′bŏth the Jĕz′re-el-īte.

22 And it came to pass, when Joram saw Jehu, that he said, *Is it* peace, Jehu? And he answered, What peace, so long as the whoredoms of thy mother Jĕz′e-bel and her witchcrafts *are so* many?

23 And Joram turned his hands, and fled, and said to Ā-ha-zī′ah, *There is* treachery, O Ā-ha-zī′ah.

24 And Jehu drew a bow with his full strength, and smote Je-hô′ram between his arms, and the arrow went out at his heart, and he sunk down in his chariot.

25 Then said *Jehu* to Bĭd′kär his captain, Take up, *and* cast him in the portion of the field of Nā′bŏth the Jĕz′re-el-īte: for remember how that, when I and thou rode together after Ahab his father, the LORD laid this burden upon him;

26 Surely I have seen yesterday the blood of Nā′bŏth, and the blood of his sons, saith the LORD; and I will requite thee in this plat, saith the LORD. Now therefore take *and* cast him into the plat *of ground*, according to the word of the LORD.

27 ¶But when Ā-ha-zī′ah the king of Jūdah saw *this*, he fled by the way of the garden house. And Jehu followed after him, and said, Smite him also in the chariot. *And they did so* at the going up to Gur, which *is* by Ĭb′le-am. And he fled to Me-gĭd′dō, and died there.

28 And his servants carried him in a chariot to Jerusalem, and buried him in his sepulchre with his fathers in the city of David.

29 And in the eleventh year of Joram the son of Ahab began Ā-ha-zī′ah to reign over Jūdah.

30 ¶And when Jehu was come to Jĕz′-re-el, Jĕz′e-bel heard *of it;* and she painted her face, and tired her head, and looked out at a window.

31 And as Jehu entered in at the gate, she said, *Had* Zimri peace, who slew his master?

32 And he lifted up his face to the window, and said, Who *is* on my side? who? And there looked out to him two *or* three eunuchs.

33 And he said, Throw her down. So they threw her down: and *some* of her blood was sprinkled on the wall, and on the horses: and he trode her under foot.

34 And when he was come in, he did eat and drink, and said, Go, see now this cursed *woman*, and bury her: for she *is* a king's daughter.

35 And they went to bury her: but they found no more of her than the skull, and the feet, and the palms of *her* hands.

36 Wherefore they came again, and told him. And he said, This *is* the word

of the LORD, which he spake by his servant E-lī'jah the Tĭsh'bīte, saying, In the portion of Jĕz're-el shall dogs eat the flesh of Jĕz'e-bel:
37 And the carcase of Jĕz'e-bel shall be as dung upon the face of the field in the portion of Jĕz're-el; *so* that they shall not say, This *is* Jĕz'e-bel.

CHAPTER 10

AND Ahab had seventy sons in Sa-mâ'-rĭ-a. And Jehu wrote letters, and sent to Sa-mâ'rĭ-a, unto the rulers of Jĕz're-el, to the elders, and to them that brought up Ahab's *children*, saying,
2 Now as soon as this letter cometh to you, seeing your master's sons *are* with you, and *there are* with you chariots and horses, a fenced city also, and armour;
3 Look even out the best and meetest of your master's sons, and set *him* on his father's throne, and fight for your master's house.
4 But they were exceedingly afraid, and said, Behold, two kings stood not before him: how then shall we stand?
5 And he that *was* over the house, and he that *was* over the city, the elders also, and the bringers up *of the children*, sent to Jehu, saying, We *are* thy servants, and will do all that thou shalt bid us; we will not make any king: do thou *that which is* good in thine eyes.
6 Then he wrote a letter the second time to them, saying, If ye *be* mine, and *if* ye will hearken unto my voice, take ye the heads of the men your master's sons, and come to me to Jĕz're-el by to morrow this time. Now the king's sons, *being* seventy persons, *were* with the great men of the city, which brought them up.
7 And it came to pass, when the letter came to them, that they took the king's sons, and slew seventy persons, and put their heads in baskets, and sent him *them* to Jĕz're-el.
8 And there came a messenger, and told him, saying, They have brought the heads of the king's sons. And he said, Lay ye them in two heaps at the entering in of the gate until the morning.
9 And it came to pass in the morning, that he went out, and stood, and said to all the people, Ye *be* righteous: behold, I conspired against my master, and slew him: but who slew all these?
10 Know now that there shall fall unto the earth nothing of the word of the LORD, which the LORD spake concerning the house of Ahab: for the LORD hath done *that* which he spake by his servant E-lī'jah.
11 So Jehu slew all that remained of the house of Ahab in Jĕz're-el, and all his great men, and his kinsfolks, and his priests, until he left him none remaining.
12 ¶And he arose and departed, and came to Sa-mâ'rĭ-a. *And* as he *was* at the shearing house in the way,
13 Jehu met with the brethren of A-ha-zī'ah king of Jūdah, and said, Who *are* ye? And they answered, We *are* the brethren of A-ha-zī'ah; and we go down to salute the children of the king and the children of the queen.
14 And he said, Take them alive. And they took them alive, and slew them at the pit of the shearing house, *even* two and forty men; neither left he any of them.
15 ¶And when he was departed thence, he lighted on Je-hōn'a-dăb the son of Rē'chăb *coming* to meet him: and he saluted him, and said to him, Is thine heart right, as my heart *is* with thy heart? And Je-hōn'a-dăb answered, It is. If it be, give *me* thine hand. And he gave *him* his hand; and he took him up to him into the chariot.
16 And he said, Come with me, and see my zeal for the LORD. So they made him ride in his chariot.
17 And when he came to Sa-mâ'rĭ-a, he slew all that remained unto Ahab in Sa-mâ'rĭ-a, till he had destroyed him, according to the saying of the LORD, which he spake to E-lī'jah.
18 ¶And Jehu gathered all the people together, and said unto them, Ahab served Bā'al a little; *but* Jehu shall serve him much.
19 Now therefore call unto me all the prophets of Bā'al, all his servants, and all his priests; let none be wanting: for I have a great sacrifice *to do* to Bā'al; whosoever shall be wanting, he shall not live. But Jehu did *it* in subtilty, to the intent that he might destroy the worshippers of Bā'al.
20 And Jehu said, Proclaim a solemn assembly for Bā'al. And they proclaimed *it*.
21 And Jehu sent through all Israel: and all the worshippers of Bā'al came, so that there was not a man left that came not. And they came into the house of Bā'al; and the house of Bā'al was full from one end to another.
22 And he said unto him that *was* over the vestry, Bring forth vestments for all the worshippers of Bā'al. And he brought them forth vestments.
23 And Jehu went, and Je-hōn'a-dăb the son of Rē'chăb, into the house of Bā'al, and said unto the worshippers of

Bā'al. Search, and look that there be here with you none of the servants of the LORD, but the worshippers of Bā'al only.
24 And when they went in to offer sacrifices and burnt offerings, Jehu appointed fourscore men without, and said, *If* any of the men whom I have brought into your hands escape, *he that letteth him go,* his life *shall be* for the life of him.
25 And it came to pass, as soon as he had made an end of offering the burnt offering, that Jehu said to the guard and to the captains, Go in, *and* slay them; let none come forth. And they smote them with the edge of the sword; and the guard and the captains cast *them* out, and went to the city of the house of Bā'al.
26 And they brought forth the images out of the house of Bā'al, and burned them.
27 And they brake down the image of Bā'al, and brake down the house of Bā'al, and made it a draught house unto this day.
28 Thus Jehu destroyed Bā'al out of Israel.
29 Howbeit *from* the sins of Jĕr-o-bō'am the son of Nē'băt, who made Israel to sin, Jehu departed not from after them, *to wit,* the golden calves that *were* in Bĕth–el, and that *were* in Dan.
30 And the LORD said unto Jehu, Because thou hast done well in executing *that which is* right in mine eyes, *and* hast done unto the house of Ahab according to all that *was* in mine heart, thy children of the fourth *generation* shall sit on the throne of Israel.
31 But Jehu took no heed to walk in the law of the LORD God of Israel with all his heart: for he departed not from the sins of Jĕr-o-bō'am, which made Israel to sin.
32 ¶In those days the LORD began to cut Israel short: and Hăz'a-el smote them in all the coasts of Israel;
33 From Jordan eastward, all the land of Gilead, the Gădītes, and the Reubenites, and the Ma-năs'sītes, from Ar'ō-er, which *is* by the river Arnon, even Gilead and Bā'shan.
34 Now the rest of the acts of Jehu, and all that he did, and all his might, *are* they not written in the book of the chronicles of the kings of Israel?
35 And Jehu slept with his fathers: and they buried him in Sa-mâ'rĭ-a. And Je-hō'a-hăz his son reigned in his stead.
36 And the time that Jehu reigned over Israel in Sa-mâ'rĭ-a *was* twenty and eight years.

CHAPTER 11

AND when Ăth-a-lī'ah the mother of Ā-ha-zī'ah saw that her son was dead, she arose and destroyed all the seed royal.
2 But Je-hŏsh'e-ba, the daughter of king Joram, sister of Ā-ha-zī'ah, took Jō'ăsh the son of Ā-ha-zī'ah, and stole him from among the king's sons *which were* slain; and they hid him, *even* him and his nurse, in the bedchamber from Ăth-a-lī'ah, so that he was not slain.
3 And he was with her hid in the house of the LORD six years. And Ăth-a-lī'ah did reign over the land.
4 ¶And the seventh year Je-hoi'a-da sent and fetched the rulers over hundreds, with the captains and the guard, and brought them to him into the house of the LORD, and made a covenant with them, and took an oath of them in the house of the LORD, and shewed them the king's son.
5 And he commanded them, saying, This *is* the thing that ye shall do; A third part of you that enter in on the sabbath shall even be keepers of the watch of the king's house;
6 And a third part *shall be* at the gate of Sur; and a third part at the gate behind the guard: so shall ye keep the watch of the house, that it be not broken down.
7 And two parts of all you that go forth on the sabbath, even they shall keep the watch of the house of the LORD about the king.
8 And ye shall compass the king round about, every man with his weapons in his hand: and he that cometh within the ranges, let him be slain: and be ye with the king as he goeth out and as he cometh in.
9 And the captains over the hundreds did according to all *things* that Je-hoi'a-da the priest commanded: and they took every man his men that were to come in on the sabbath, with them that should go out on the sabbath, and came to Je-hoi'a-da the priest.
10 And to the captains over hundreds did the priest give king David's spears and shields, that *were* in the temple of the LORD.
11 And the guard stood, every man with his weapons in his hand, round about the king, from the right corner of the temple to the left corner of the temple, *along* by the altar and the temple.
12 And he brought forth the king's son, and put the crown upon him, and *gave him* the testimony; and they made him king, and anointed him; and they clapped their hands, and said, God save the king.

13 ¶And when Ăth-a-lī'ah heard the noise of the guard *and* of the people, she came to the people into the temple of the LORD.

14 And when she looked, behold, the king stood by a pillar, as the manner *was,* and the princes and the trumpeters by the king, and all the people of the land rejoiced, and blew with trumpets: and Ăth-a-lī'ah rent her clothes, and cried, Treason, Treason.

15 But Je-hoi'a-da the priest commanded the captains of the hundreds, the officers of the host, and said unto them, Have her forth without the ranges: and him that followeth her kill with the sword. For the priest had said, Let her not be slain in the house of the LORD.

16 And they laid hands on her; and she went by the way by the which the horses came into the king's house: and there was she slain.

17 ¶And Je-hoi'a-da made a covenant between the LORD and the king and the people, that they should be the LORD's people; between the king also and the people.

18 And all the people of the land went into the house of Bā'al, and brake it down; his altars and his images brake they in pieces thoroughly, and slew Măt'tan the priest of Bā'al before the altars. And the priest appointed officers over the house of the LORD.

19 And he took the rulers over hundreds, and the captains, and the guard, and all the people of the land; and they brought down the king from the house of the LORD, and came by the way of the gate of the guard to the king's house. And he sat on the throne of the kings.

20 And all the people of the land rejoiced, and the city was in quiet: and they slew Ăth-a-lī'ah with the sword *beside* the king's house.

21 Seven years old *was* Je-hō'ăsh when he began to reign.

CHAPTER 12

IN the seventh year of Jehu Je-hō'ăsh began to reign; and forty years reigned he in Jerusalem. And his mother's name *was* Zĭb'ĭ-ah of Be'er–shē'ba.

2 And Je-hō'ăsh did *that which was* right in the sight of the LORD all his days wherein Je-hoi'a-da the priest instructed him.

3 But the high places were not taken away: the people still sacrificed and burnt incense in the high places.

4 ¶And Je-hō'ăsh said to the priests, All the money of the dedicated things that is brought into the house of the LORD, *even* the money of every one that passeth *the account,* the money that every man is set at, *and* all the money that cometh into any man's heart to bring into the house of the LORD,

5 Let the priests take *it* to them, every man of his acquaintance: and let them repair the breaches of the house, wheresoever any breach shall be found.

6 But it was *so, that* in the three and twentieth year of king Je-hō'ăsh the priests had not repaired the breaches of the house.

7 Then king Je-hō'ăsh called for Je-hoi'a-da the priest, and the *other* priests, and said unto them, Why repair ye not the breaches of the house? now therefore receive no *more* money of your acquaintance, but deliver it for the breaches of the house.

8 And the priests consented to receive no *more* money of the people, neither to repair the breaches of the house.

9 But Je-hoi'a-da the priest took a chest, and bored a hole in the lid of it, and set it beside the altar, on the right side as one cometh into the house of the LORD: and the priests that kept the door put therein all the money *that was* brought into the house of the LORD.

10 And it was *so,* when they saw that *there was* much money in the chest, that the king's scribe and the high priest came up, and they put up in bags, and told the money that was found in the house of the LORD.

11 And they gave the money, being told, into the hands of them that did the work, that had the oversight of the house of the LORD: and they laid it out to the carpenters and builders, that wrought upon the house of the LORD,

12 And to masons, and hewers of stone, and to buy timber and hewed stone to repair the breaches of the house of the LORD, and for all that was laid out for the house to repair *it.*

13 Howbeit there were not made for the house of the LORD bowls of silver, snuffers, basons, trumpets, any vessels of gold, or vessels of silver, of the money *that was* brought into the house of the LORD:

14 But they gave that to the workmen, and repaired therewith the house of the LORD.

15 Moreover they reckoned not with the men, into whose hand they delivered the money to be bestowed on workmen: for they dealt faithfully.

16 The trespass money and sin money was not brought into the house of the LORD: it was the priests'.

17 ¶Then Hāz'a-el king of Syria went
up, and fought against Gath, and took
it: and Hāz'a-el set his face to go up to
Jerusalem.
18 And Je-hō'ăsh king of Jūdah took
all the hallowed things that Je-hŏsh'a-
phăt, and Je-hô'ram, and Ā-ha-zī'ah,
his fathers, kings of Jūdah, had dedi-
cated, and his own hallowed things,
and all the gold *that was* found in the
treasures of the house of the LORD, and
in the king's house, and sent *it* to Hāz'a-
el king of Syria: and he went away from
Jerusalem.
19 ¶And the rest of the acts of Jō'ăsh,
and all that he did, *are* they not written
in the book of the chronicles of the
kings of Jūdah?
20 And his servants arose, and made
a conspiracy, and slew Jō'ăsh in the
house of Mĭl'lō, which goeth down to
Sĭl'la.
21 For Jōz'a-chär the son of Shĭm'e-
ăth, and Je-hōz'a-băd the son of Shō'-
mer, his servants, smote him, and he
died; and they buried him with his fa-
thers in the city of David: and Ăm-a-zī'ah
his son reigned in his stead.

CHAPTER 13

IN the three and twentieth year of Jō'ăsh
the son of Ā-ha-zī'ah king of Jūdah
Je-hō'a-hăz the son of Jehu began to
reign over Israel in Sa-mâ'rĭ-a, *and
reigned* seventeen years.
2 And he did *that which was* evil in
the sight of the LORD, and followed the
sins of Jĕr-o-bō'am the son of Nē'băt,
which made Israel to sin; he departed
not therefrom.
3 And the anger of the LORD was
kindled against Israel, and he delivered
them into the hand of Hāz'a-el king of
Syria, and into the hand of Bĕn–hā'dăd
the son of Hāz'a-el, all *their* days.
4 And Je-hō'a-hăz besought the
LORD, and the LORD hearkened unto
him: for he saw the oppression of
Israel, because the king of Syria op-
pressed them.
5 (And the LORD gave Israel a saviour,
so that they went out from under
the hand of the Syrians: and the chil-
dren of Israel dwelt in their tents, as
beforetime.
6 Nevertheless they departed not
from the sins of the house of Jĕr-o-bō'-
am, who made Israel sin, *but* walked
therein: and there remained the grove
also in Sa-mâ'rĭ-a.)
7 Neither did he leave of the people to
Je-hō'a-hăz but fifty horsemen, and ten
chariots, and ten thousand footmen;
for the king of Syria had destroyed
them, and had made them like the dust
by threshing.
8 ¶Now the rest of the acts of Je-hō'a-
hăz, and all that he did, and his might,
are they not written in the book of the
chronicles of the kings of Israel?
9 And Je-hō'a-hăz slept with his fa-
thers; and they buried him in Sa-mâ'rĭ-a:
and Jō'ăsh his son reigned in his stead.
10 ¶In the thirty and seventh year of
Jō'ăsh king of Jūdah began Je-hō'ăsh
the son of Je-hō'a-hăz to reign over
Israel in Sa-mâ'rĭ-a, *and reigned* six-
teen years.
11 And he did *that which was* evil in
the sight of the LORD; he departed not
from all the sins of Jĕr-o-bō'am the son
of Nē'băt, who made Israel sin: *but* he
walked therein.
12 And the rest of the acts of Jō'ăsh,
and all that he did, and his might where-
with he fought against Ăm-a-zī'ah
king of Jūdah, *are* they not written in
the book of the chronicles of the kings
of Israel?
13 And Jō'ăsh slept with his fathers;
and Jĕr-o-bō'am sat upon his throne:
and Jō'ăsh was buried in Sa-mâ'rĭ-a
with the kings of Israel.
14 ¶Now E-lī'sha was fallen sick of
his sickness whereof he died. And Jō'-
ăsh the king of Israel came down unto
him, and wept over his face, and said, O
my father, my father, the chariot of
Israel, and the horsemen thereof.
15 And E-lī'sha said unto him, Take
bow and arrows. And he took unto him
bow and arrows.
16 And he said to the king of Israel,
Put thine hand upon the bow. And he
put his hand *upon it:* and E-lī'sha put
his hands upon the king's hands.
17 And he said, Open the window
eastward. And he opened *it.* Then E-
lī'sha said, Shoot. And he shot. And he
said, The arrow of the LORD's deliver-
ance, and the arrow of deliverance
from Syria: for thou shalt smite the Syr-
ians in Ā'phĕk, till thou have con-
sumed *them.*
18 And he said, Take the arrows. And
he took *them.* And he said unto the king
of Israel, Smite upon the ground. And
he smote thrice, and stayed.
19 And the man of God was wroth
with him, and said, Thou shouldest
have smitten five or six times; then
hadst thou smitten Syria till thou hadst
consumed *it:* whereas now thou shalt
smite Syria *but* thrice.
20 ¶And E-lī'sha died, and they
buried him. And the bands of the Moab-
ites invaded the land at the coming in
of the year.
21 And it came to pass, as they were

burying a man, that, behold, they spied
a band *of men;* and they cast the man
into the sepulchre of E-lī'sha: and when
the man was let down, and touched the
bones of E-lī'sha, he revived, and stood
up on his feet.
22 ¶But Hāz'a-el king of Syria op-
pressed Israel all the days of Je-hō'a-
hăz.
23 And the LORD was gracious unto
them, and had compassion on them,
and had respect unto them, because of
his covenant with Abraham, Isaac, and
Jacob, and would not destroy them,
neither cast he them from his presence
as yet.
24 So Hāz'a-el king of Syria died; and
Běn-hā'dăd his son reigned in his stead.
25 And Je-hō'ăsh the son of Je-hō'a-
hăz took again out of the hand of
Běn-hā'dăd the son of Hāz'a-el the
cities, which he had taken out of the
hand of Je-hō'a-hăz his father by war.
Three times did Jō'ăsh beat him, and
recovered the cities of Israel.

CHAPTER 14

IN the second year of Jō'ăsh son of Je-
hō'a-hăz king of Israel reigned Ăm-a-
zī'ah the son of Jō'ăsh king of Jūdah.
2 He was twenty and five years old
when he began to reign, and reigned
twenty and nine years in Jerusalem.
And his mother's name *was* Je-hō-ad'-
dan of Jerusalem.
3 And he did *that which was* right in
the sight of the LORD, yet not like David
his father: he did according to all things
as Jō'ăsh his father did.
4 Howbeit the high places were not
taken away: as yet the people did sacri-
fice and burnt incense on the high
places.
5 ¶And it came to pass, as soon as the
kingdom was confirmed in his hand,
that he slew his servants which had
slain the king his father.
6 But the children of the murderers
he slew not: according unto that which
is written in the book of the law of
Moses, wherein the LORD commanded,
saying, The fathers shall not be put to
death for the children, nor the children
be put to death for the fathers; but
every man shall be put to death for his
own sin.
7 He slew of Ēdom in the valley of salt
ten thousand, and took Sē'lah by war,
and called the name of it Jŏk'the-el
unto this day.
8 ¶Then Ăm-a-zī'ah sent messengers
to Je-hō'ăsh, the son of Je-hō'a-hăz son
of Jehu, king of Israel, saying, Come,
let us look one another in the face.
9 And Je-hō'ăsh the king of Israel
sent to Ăm-a-zī'ah king of Jūdah,
saying, The thistle that *was* in Leba-
non sent to the cedar that *was* in Leba-
non, saying, Give thy daughter to my
son to wife: and there passed by a wild
beast that *was* in Lebanon, and trode
down the thistle.
10 Thou hast indeed smitten Ēdom,
and thine heart hath lifted thee up:
glory *of this,* and tarry at home: for
why shouldest thou meddle to *thy* hurt,
that thou shouldest fall, *even* thou, and
Jūdah with thee?
11 But Ăm-a-zī'ah would not hear.
Therefore Je-hō'ăsh king of Israel went
up; and he and Ăm-a-zī'ah king of Jū-
dah looked one another in the face at
Běth-shě'mesh, which *belongeth* to Jū-
dah.
12 And Jūdah was put to the worse
before Israel; and they fled every man
to their tents.
13 And Je-hō'ăsh king of Israel took
Ăm-a-zī'ah king of Jūdah, the son of
Je-hō'ăsh the son of Ă-ha-zī'ah, at
Běth-shě'mesh, and came to Jerusalem,
and brake down the wall of Jerusalem
from the gate of Ē'phra-im unto the cor-
ner gate, four hundred cubits.
14 And he took all the gold and silver,
and all the vessels that were found in
the house of the LORD, and in the trea-
sures of the king's house, and hostages,
and returned to Sa-mâ'rĭ-a.
15 ¶Now the rest of the acts of Je-hō'-
ăsh which he did, and his might, and
how he fought with Ăm-a-zī'ah king of
Jūdah, *are* they not written in the book
of the chronicles of the kings of Israel?
16 And Je-hō'ăsh slept with his fa-
thers, and was buried in Sa-mâ'rĭ-a with
the kings of Israel; and Jěr-o-bō'am his
son reigned in his stead.
17 ¶And Ăm-a-zī'ah the son of Jō'ăsh
king of Jūdah lived after the death of
Je-hō'ăsh son of Je-hō'a-hăz king of
Israel fifteen years.
18 And the rest of the acts of Ăm-a-
zī'ah, *are* they not written in the book
of the chronicles of the kings of Jūdah?
19 Now they made a conspiracy
against him in Jerusalem: and he fled to
Lā'chĭsh; but they sent after him to
Lā'chĭsh, and slew him there.
20 And they brought him on horses:
and he was buried at Jerusalem with
his fathers in the city of David.
21 ¶And all the people of Jūdah took
Ăz-a-rī'ah, which *was* sixteen years
old, and made him king instead of his
father Ăm-a-zī'ah.
22 He built Ē'lăth, and restored it to
Jūdah, after that the king slept with his
fathers.
23 ¶In the fifteenth year of Ăm-a-

zī'ah the son of Jō'ăsh king of Jūdah
Jĕr-o-bō'am the son of Jō'ăsh king of
Israel began to reign in Sa-mâ'rĭ-a, *and*
reigned forty and one years.
24 And he did *that which was* evil in
the sight of the LORD: he departed not
from all the sins of Jĕr-o-bō'am the son
of Nē'băt, who made Israel to sin.
25 He restored the coast of Israel
from the entering of Hā'măth unto the
sea of the plain, according to the word
of the LORD God of Israel, which he
spake by the hand of his servant Jonah,
the son of A-mĭt'ta-ī, the prophet,
which *was* of Găth-hē'pher.
26 For the LORD saw the affliction of
Israel, *that it was* very bitter: for *there*
was not any shut up, nor any left, nor
any helper for Israel.
27 And the LORD said not that he
would blot out the name of Israel from
under heaven: but he saved them by
the hand of Jĕr-o-bō'am the son of Jō'-
ăsh.
28 ¶Now the rest of the acts of Jĕr-o-
bō'am, and all that he did, and his
might, how he warred, and how he re-
covered Damascus, and Hā'măth,
which belonged to Jūdah, for Israel, *are*
they not written in the book of the
chronicles of the kings of Israel?
29 And Jĕr-o-bō'am slept with his
fathers, *even* with the kings of Israel;
and Zăch-a-rī'ah his son reigned in his
stead.

CHAPTER 15

IN the twenty and seventh year of Jĕr-
o-bō'am king of Israel began Ăz-a-rī'ah
son of Ăm-a-zī'ah king of Jūdah to
reign.
2 Sixteen years old was he when he
began to reign, and he reigned two and
fifty years in Jerusalem. And his moth-
er's name *was* Jĕch-o-lī'ah of Jeru-
salem.
3 And he did *that which was* right in
the sight of the LORD, according to all
that his father Ăm-a-zī'ah had done;
4 Save that the high places were not
removed: the people sacrificed and
burnt incense still on the high places.
5 ¶And the LORD smote the king, so
that he was a leper unto the day of his
death, and dwelt in a several house.
And Jō'tham the king's son *was* over
the house, judging the people of the
land.
6 And the rest of the acts of Ăz-a-rī'ah,
and all that he did, *are* they not
written in the book of the chronicles of
the kings of Jūdah?
7 So Ăz-a-rī'ah slept with his fathers;
and they buried him with his fathers in
the city of David: and Jō'tham his son
reigned in his stead.
8 ¶In the thirty and eighth year of Ăz-
a-rī'ah king of Jūdah did Zăch-a-rī'ah
the son of Jĕr-o-bō'am reign over Israel
in Sa-mâ'rĭ-a six months.
9 And he did *that which was* evil in
the sight of the LORD, as his fathers had
done: he departed not from the sins of
Jĕr-o-bō'am the son of Nē'băt, who
made Israel to sin.
10 And Shăl'lum the son of Jā'besh
conspired against him, and smote him
before the people, and slew him, and
reigned in his stead.
11 And the rest of the acts of Zăch-a-
rī'ah, behold, they *are* written in the
book of the chronicles of the kings of
Israel.
12 This *was* the word of the LORD
which he spake unto Jehu, saying, Thy
sons shall sit on the throne of Israel
unto the fourth *generation.* And so it
came to pass.
13 ¶Shăl'lum the son of Jā'besh be-
gan to reign in the nine and thirtieth
year of Uz-zī'ah king of Jūdah; and he
reigned a full month in Sa-mâ'rĭ-a.
14 For Mĕn'a-hĕm the son of Gā'dī
went up from Tir'zah, and came to Sa-
mâ'rĭ-a, and smote Shăl'lum the son of
Jā'besh in Sa-mâ'rĭ-a, and slew him,
and reigned in his stead.
15 And the rest of the acts of Shăl'-
lum, and his conspiracy which he
made, behold, they *are* written in the
book of the chronicles of the kings of
Israel.
16 Then Mĕn'a-hĕm smote Tĭph'sah,
and all that *were* therein, and the
coasts thereof from Tir'zah: because
they opened not *to him,* therefore he
smote *it; and* all the women therein
that were with child he ripped up.
17 ¶In the nine and thirtieth year of
Ăz-a-rī'ah king of Jūdah began Mĕn'a-
hĕm the son of Gā'dī to reign over
Israel, *and reigned* ten years in Sa-mâ'-
rĭ-a.
18 And he did *that which was* evil in
the sight of the LORD: he departed not
all his days from the sins of Jĕr-o-bō'am
the son of Nē'băt, who made Israel
to sin.
19 *And* Pul the king of Assyria came
against the land: and Mĕn'a-hĕm gave
Pul a thousand talents of silver, that his
hand might be with him to confirm the
kingdom in his hand.
20 And Mĕn'a-hĕm exacted the mon-
ey of Israel, *even* of all the mighty
men of wealth, of each man fifty
shekels of silver, to give to the king of
Assyria. So the king of Assyria turned
back, and stayed not there in the land.

21 ¶And the rest of the acts of Mĕn′a-hĕm, and all that he did, *are* they not written in the book of the chronicles of the kings of Israel?

22 And Mĕn′a-hĕm slept with his fathers; and Pĕk-a-hī′ah his son reigned in his stead.

23 ¶In the fiftieth year of Ăz-a-rī′ah king of Jūdah Pĕk-a-hī′ah the son of Mĕn′a-hĕm began to reign over Israel in Sa-mâ′rĭ-a, *and reigned* two years.

24 And he did *that which was* evil in the sight of the LORD: he departed not from the sins of Jĕr-o-bō′am the son of Nē′băt, who made Israel to sin.

25 But Pē′kah the son of Rĕm-a-lī′ah, a captain of his, conspired against him, and smote him in Sa-mâ′rĭ-a, in the palace of the king's house, with Är′gŏb and Â-rī′eh, and with him fifty men of the Gileadites: and he killed him, and reigned in his room.

26 And the rest of the acts of Pĕk-a-hī′ah, and all that he did, behold, they *are* written in the book of the chronicles of the kings of Israel.

27 ¶In the two and fiftieth year of Ăz-a-rī′ah king of Jūdah Pē′kah the son of Rĕm-a-lī′ah began to reign over Israel in Sa-mâ′rĭ-a, *and reigned* twenty years.

28 And he did *that which was* evil in the sight of the LORD: he departed not from the sins of Jĕr-o-bō′am the son of Nē′băt, who made Israel to sin.

29 In the days of Pē′kah king of Israel came Tĭg′lăth-pĭ-lē′ṡer king of Assyria, and took Ī′jŏn, and Ā′bel-bĕth-mā′a-chah, and Ja-nō′ah, and Kē′dĕsh, and Hā′zôr, and Gilead, and Galilee, all the land of Năph′ta-lī, and carried them captive to Assyria.

30 And Hō-shē′a the son of Ē′lah made a conspiracy against Pē′kah the son of Rĕm-a-lī′ah, and smote him, and slew him, and reigned in his stead, in the twentieth year of Jō′tham the son of Uz-zī′ah.

31 And the rest of the acts of Pē′kah, and all that he did, behold, they *are* written in the book of the chronicles of the kings of Israel.

32 ¶In the second year of Pē′kah the son of Rĕm-a-lī′ah king of Israel began Jō′tham the son of Uz-zī′ah king of Jūdah to reign.

33 Five and twenty years old was he when he began to reign, and he reigned sixteen years in Jerusalem. And his mother's name *was* Je-rū′sha, the daughter of Zā′dŏk.

34 And he did *that which was* right in the sight of the LORD: he did according to all that his father Uz-zī′ah had done.

35 Howbeit the high places were not removed: the people sacrificed and burned incense still in the high places. He built the higher gate of the house of the LORD.

36 ¶Now the rest of the acts of Jō′tham, and all that he did, *are* they not written in the book of the chronicles of the kings of Jūdah?

37 In those days the LORD began to send against Jūdah Rē′zĭn the king of Syria, and Pē′kah the son of Rĕm-a-lī′ah.

38 And Jō′tham slept with his fathers, and was buried with his fathers in the city of David his father: and Ahaz his son reigned in his stead.

CHAPTER 16

IN the seventeenth year of Pē′kah the son of Rĕm-a-lī′ah Ahaz the son of Jō′tham king of Jūdah began to reign.

2 Twenty years old *was* Ahaz when he began to reign, and reigned sixteen years in Jerusalem, and did not *that which was* right in the sight of the LORD his God, like David his father.

3 But he walked in the way of the kings of Israel, yea, and made his son to pass through the fire, according to the abominations of the heathen, whom the LORD cast out from before the children of Israel.

4 And he sacrificed and burnt incense in the high places, and on the hills, and under every green tree.

5 ¶Then Rē′zĭn king of Syria and Pē′kah son of Rĕm-a-lī′ah king of Israel came up to Jerusalem to war: and they besieged Ahaz, but could not overcome *him*.

6 At that time Rē′zĭn king of Syria recovered Ē′lăth to Syria, and drave the Jews from Ē′lăth: and the Syrians came to Ē′lăth, and dwelt there unto this day.

7 So Ahaz sent messengers to Tĭg′lăth-pĭ-lē′ṡer king of Assyria, saying, I *am* thy servant and thy son: come up, and save me out of the hand of the king of Syria, and out of the hand of the king of Israel, which rise up against me.

8 And Ahaz took the silver and gold that was found in the house of the LORD, and in the treasures of the king's house, and sent *it for* a present to the king of Assyria.

9 And the king of Assyria hearkened unto him: for the king of Assyria went up against Damascus, and took it, and carried *the people of* it captive to Kir, and slew Rē′zĭn.

10 ¶And king Ahaz went to Damascus to meet Tĭg′lăth-pĭ-lē′ṡer king of Asyria, and saw an altar that *was* at Damascus: and king Ahaz sent to Ū-rī′jah the priest the fashion of the altar,

and the pattern of it, according to all the workmanship thereof.

11 And Ū-rī'jah the priest built an altar according to all that king Ahaz had sent from Damascus: so Ū-rī'jah the priest made *it* against king Ahaz came from Damascus.

12 And when the king was come from Damascus, the king saw the altar: and the king approached to the altar, and offered thereon.

13 And he burnt his burnt offering and his meat offering, and poured his drink offering, and sprinkled the blood of his peace offerings, upon the altar.

14 And he brought also the brasen altar, which *was* before the LORD, from the forefront of the house, from between the altar and the house of the LORD, and put it on the north side of the altar.

15 And king Ahaz commanded Ū-rī'-jah the priest, saying, Upon the great altar burn the morning burnt offering, and the evening meat offering, and the king's burnt sacrifice, and his meat offering, with the burnt offering of all the people of the land, and their meat offering, and their drink offerings; and sprinkle upon it all the blood of the burnt offering, and all the blood of the sacrifice: and the brasen altar shall be for me to enquire *by*.

16 Thus did Ū-rī'jah the priest, according to all that king Ahaz commanded.

17 ¶And king Ahaz cut off the borders of the bases, and removed the laver from off them; and took down the sea from off the brasen oxen that *were* under it, and put it upon a pavement of stones.

18 And the covert for the sabbath that they had built in the house, and the king's entry without, turned he from the house of the LORD for the king of Assyria.

19 ¶Now the rest of the acts of Ahaz which he did, *are* they not written in the book of the chronicles of the kings of Jūdah?

20 And Ahaz slept with his fathers, and was buried with his fathers in the city of David: and Hĕz-e-kī'ah his son reigned in his stead.

CHAPTER 17

IN the twelfth year of Ahaz king of Jūdah began Hō-shē'a the son of Ē'lah to reign in Sa-mâ'rī-a over Israel nine years.

2 And he did *that which was* evil in the sight of the LORD, but not as the kings of Israel that were before him.

3 Against him came up Shăl-man-ē'ser king of Assyria; and Hō-shē'a became his servant, and gave him presents.

4 And the king of Assyria found conspiracy in Hō-shē'a: for he had sent messengers to So king of Egypt, and brought no present to the king of Assyria, as *he had done* year by year: therefore the king of Assyria shut him up, and bound him in prison.

5 Then the king of Assyria came up throughout all the land, and went up to Sa-mâ'rī-a, and besieged it three years.

6 In the ninth year of Hō-shē'a the king of Assyria took Sa-mâ'rī-a, and carried Israel away into Assyria, and placed them in Hā'lah and in Hā'bôr *by* the river of Gō'zăn, and in the cities of the Medes.

7 For *so* it was, that the children of Israel had sinned against the LORD their God, which had brought them up out of the land of Egypt, from under the hand of Pharaoh king of Egypt, and had feared other gods,

8 And walked in the statutes of the heathen, whom the LORD cast out from before the children of Israel, and of the kings of Israel, which they had made.

9 And the children of Israel did secretly *those* things that *were* not right against the LORD their God, and they built them high places in all their cities, from the tower of the watchmen to the fenced city.

10 And they set them up images and groves in every high hill, and under every green tree:

11 And there they burnt incense in all the high places, as *did* the heathen whom the LORD carried away before them; and wrought wicked things to provoke the LORD to anger:

12 For they served idols, whereof the LORD had said unto them, Ye shall not do this thing.

13 Yet the LORD testified against Israel, and against Jūdah, by all the prophets, *and by* all the seers, saying, Turn ye from your evil ways, and keep my commandments *and* my statutes, according to all the law which I commanded your fathers, and which I sent to you by my servants the prophets.

14 Notwithstanding they would not hear, but hardened their necks, like to the neck of their fathers, that did not believe in the LORD their God.

15 And they rejected his statutes, and his covenant that he made with their fathers, and his testimonies which he testified against them; and they followed vanity, and became vain, and went after the heathen that *were* round about them, *concerning* whom the

LORD had charged them, that they
should not do like them.
16 And they left all the command-
ments of the LORD their God, and made
them molten images, *even* two calves,
and made a grove, and worshipped all
the host of heaven, and served Bā'al.
17 And they caused their sons and
their daughters to pass through the
fire, and used divination and enchant-
ments, and sold themselves to do evil in
the sight of the LORD, to provoke him to
anger.
18 Therefore the LORD was very
angry with Israel, and removed them
out of his sight: there was none left but
the tribe of Jūdah only.
19 Also Jūdah kept not the com-
mandments of the LORD their God, but
walked in the statutes of Israel which
they made.
20 And the LORD rejected all the seed
of Israel, and afflicted them, and deliv-
ered them into the hand of spoilers, un-
til he had cast them out of his sight.
21 For he rent Israel from the house
of David; and they made Jĕr-o-bō'am
the son of Nē'băt king: and Jĕr-o-bō'am
drave Israel from following the LORD,
and made them sin a great sin.
22 For the children of Israel walked
in all the sins of Jĕr-o-bō'am which he
did; they departed not from them;
23 Until the LORD removed Israel out
of his sight, as he had said by all his
servants the prophets. So was Israel
carried away out of their own land to
Assyria unto this day.
24 ¶And the king of Assyria brought
men from Babylon, and from Cū'thah,
and from Ā'va, and from Hā'măth, and
from Sĕph-ar-vā'im, and placed *them*
in the cities of Sa-mâ'rĭ-a instead of the
children of Israel: and they possessed
Sa-mâ'rĭ-a, and dwelt in the cities there-
of.
25 And *so* it was at the beginning of
their dwelling there, *that* they feared
not the LORD: therefore the LORD sent
lions among them, which slew *some* of
them.
26 Wherefore they spake to the king
of Assyria, saying, The nations which
thou hast removed, and placed in the
cities of Sa-mâ'rĭ-a, know not the man-
ner of the God of the land: therefore he
hath sent lions among them, and, be-
hold, they slay them, because they
know not the manner of the God of the
land.
27 Then the king of Assyria com-
manded, saying, Carry thither one of
the priests whom ye brought from
thence; and let them go and dwell
there, and let him teach them the man-
ner of the God of the land.
28 Then one of the priests whom they
had carried away from Sa-mâ'rĭ-a
came and dwelt in Bĕth-el, and taught
them how they should fear the LORD.
29 Howbeit every nation made gods
of their own, and put *them* in the
houses of the high places which the Sa-
măr'i-tanṡ had made, every nation in
their cities wherein they dwelt.
30 And the men of Babylon made
Sŭc'coth–bē'nŏth, and the men of Cuth
made Ner'găl, and the men of Hā'măth
made Ash'ĭ-ma,
31 And the Ā'vītes made Nĭb'hăz and
Tär'tăk, and the Sĕph'ar-vītes burnt
their children in fire to A-drăm'me-lĕch
and A-năm'me-lĕch, the gods of Sĕph-
ar-vā'im.
32 So they feared the LORD, and made
unto themselves of the lowest of them
priests of the high places, which sacri-
ficed for them in the houses of the high
places.
33 They feared the LORD, and served
their own gods, after the manner of the
nations whom they carried away from
thence.
34 Unto this day they do after the for-
mer manners: they fear not the LORD,
neither do they after their statutes, or
after their ordinances, or after the law
and commandment which the LORD
commanded the children of Jacob,
whom he named Israel;
35 With whom the LORD had made a
covenant, and charged them, saying,
Ye shall not fear other gods, nor bow
yourselves to them, nor serve them,
nor sacrifice to them:
36 But the LORD, who brought you up
out of the land of Egypt with great pow-
er and a stretched out arm, him shall
ye fear, and him shall ye worship, and
to him shall ye do sacrifice.
37 And the statutes, and the ordi-
nances, and the law, and the command-
ment, which he wrote for you, ye shall
observe to do for evermore; and ye
shall not fear other gods.
38 And the covenant that I have
made with you ye shall not forget;
neither shall ye fear other gods.
39 But the LORD your God ye shall
fear; and he shall deliver you out of the
hand of all your enemies.
40 Howbeit they did not hearken, but
they did after their former manner.
41 So these nations feared the LORD,
and served their graven images, both
their children, and their children's
children: as did their fathers, so do they
unto this day.

CHAPTER 18

NOW it came to pass in the third year
of Hŏ-shē′a son of Ē′lah king of Israel,
that Hĕz-e-kī′ah the son of Ahaz king of
Jūdah began to reign.
2 Twenty and five years old was he
when he began to reign; and he reigned
twenty and nine years in Jerusalem.
His mother's name also *was* Ā′bī, the
daughter of Zăch-a-rī′ah.
3 And he did *that which was* right in
the sight of the LORD, according to all
that David his father did.
4 He removed the high places, and
brake the images, and cut down the
groves, and brake in pieces the brasen
serpent that Moses had made: for unto
those days the children of Israel did
burn incense to it: and he called it Ne-
hūsh′tan.
5 He trusted in the LORD God of
Israel; so that after him was none like
him among all the kings of Jūdah, nor
any that were before him.
6 For he clave to the LORD, *and* de-
parted not from following him, but
kept his commandments, which the
LORD commanded Moses.
7 And the LORD was with him; *and* he
prospered whithersoever he went
forth: and he rebelled against the king
of Assyria, and served him not.
8 He smote the Philistines, *even* unto
Gā′za, and the borders thereof, from
the tower of the watchmen to the
fenced city.
9 And it came to pass in the fourth
year of king Hĕz-e-kī′ah, which *was* the
seventh year of Hō-shē′a son of Ē′lah
king of Israel, *that* Shăl-man-ē′-ṡer
king of Assyria came up against Sa-
mâ′rī-a, and besieged it.
10 And at the end of three years they
took it: *even* in the sixth year of Hĕz-e-
kī′ah, that *is* the ninth year of Hō-shē′a
king of Israel, Sa-mâ′rī-a was taken.
11 And the king of Assyria did carry
away Israel unto Assyria, and put them
in Hā′lah and in Hā′bôr *by* the river of
Gō′zăn, and in the cities of the Medes:
12 Because they obeyed not the voice
of the LORD their God, but transgressed
his covenant, *and* all that Moses the
servant of the LORD commanded, and
would not hear *them*, nor do *them*.
13 ¶Now in the fourteenth year of
king Hĕz-e-kī′ah did Sen-năch′e-rĭb
king of Assyria come up against all the
fenced cities of Jūdah, and took them.
14 And Hĕz-e-kī′ah king of Jūdah
sent to the king of Assyria to Lā′chĭsh,
saying, I have offended; return from
me: that which thou puttest on me will I
bear. And the king of Assyria ap-
pointed unto Hĕz-e-kī′ah king of Jūdah
three hundred talents of silver and
thirty talents of gold.
15 And Hĕz-e-kī′ah gave *him* all the
silver that was found in the house of the
LORD, and in the treasures of the king's
house.
16 At that time did Hĕz-e-kī′ah cut
off *the gold from* the doors of the
temple of the LORD, and *from* the pillars
which Hĕz-e-kī′ah king of Jūdah had
overlaid, and gave it to the king of As-
syria.
17 And the king of Assyria sent Tar-
tan and Răb′-sa-rĭs and Răb′-sha-keh
from Lā′chĭsh to king Hĕz-e-kī′ah with
a great host against Jerusalem. And
they went up and came to Jerusalem.
And when they were come up, they
came and stood by the conduit of the
upper pool, which *is* in the highway of
the fuller's field.
18 And when they had called to the
king, there came out to them E-lī′a-kĭm
the son of Hĭl-kī′ah, which *was* over the
household, and Shĕb′na the scribe, and
Jō′ah the son of Ā′săph the recorder.
19 And Răb′-sha-keh said unto them,
Speak ye now to Hĕz-e-kī′ah, Thus
saith the great king, the king of Assyr-
ia, What confidence *is* this wherein
thou trustest?
20 Thou sayest, (but *they are but* vain
words,) *I have* counsel and strength for
the war. Now on whom dost thou trust,
that thou rebellest against me?
21 Now, behold, thou trustest upon
the staff of this bruised reed, *even* upon
Egypt, on which if a man lean, it will go
into his hand, and pierce it: so *is*
Pharaoh king of Egypt unto all that
trust on him.
22 But if ye say unto me, We trust in
the LORD our God: *is* not that he, whose
high places and whose altars Hĕz-e-kī′-
ah hath taken away, and hath said to
Jūdah and Jerusalem, Ye shall worship
before this altar in Jerusalem?
23 Now therefore, I pray thee, give
pledges to my lord the king of Assyria,
and I will deliver thee two thousand
horses, if thou be able on thy part to set
riders upon them.
24 How then wilt thou turn away the
face of one captain of the least of my
master's servants, and put thy trust on
Egypt for chariots and for horsemen?
25 Am I now come up without the
LORD against this place to destroy it?
The LORD said to me, Go up against this
land, and destroy it.
26 Then said E-lī′a-kĭm the son of Hĭl-
kī′ah, and Shĕb′na and Jō′ah, unto
Răb′-sha-keh, Speak, I pray thee, to
thy servants in the Syrian language; for

we understand *it:* and talk not with us in the Jews' language in the ears of the people that *are* on the wall.

27 But Răb'-sha-keh said unto them, Hath my master sent me to thy master, and to thee, to speak these words? *hath he* not *sent me* to the men which sit on the wall, that they may eat their own dung, and drink their own piss with you?

28 ¶Then Răb'-sha-keh stood and cried with a loud voice in the Jews' language, and spake, saying, Hear the word of the great king, the king of Assyria:

29 Thus saith the king, Let not Hĕz-e-kī'ah deceive you: for he shall not be able to deliver you out of his hand:

30 Neither let Hĕz-e-kī'ah make you trust in the LORD, saying, The LORD will surely deliver us, and this city shall not be delivered into the hand of the king of Assyria.

31 Hearken not to Hĕz-e-kī'ah: for thus saith the king of Assyria, Make *an agreement* with me by a present, and come out to me, and *then* eat ye every man of his own vine, and every one of his fig tree, and drink ye every one the waters of his cistern:

32 Until I come and take you away to a land like your own land, a land of corn and wine, a land of bread and vineyards, a land of oil olive and of honey, that ye may live, and not die: and hearken not unto Hĕz-e-kī'ah, when he persuadeth you, saying, The LORD will deliver us.

33 Hath any of the gods of the nations delivered at all his land out of the hand of the king of Assyria?

34 Where *are* the gods of Hā'măth, and of Är'păd? where *are* the gods of Sĕph-ar-vā'im, Hĕ'na, and Ī'vah? have they delivered Sa-mâ'rĭ-a out of mine hand?

35 Who *are* they among all the gods of the countries, that have delivered their country out of mine hand, that the LORD should deliver Jerusalem out of mine hand?

36 But the people held their peace, and answered him not a word: for the king's commandment was, saying, Answer him not.

37 Then came E-lī'a-kĭm the son of Hĭl-kī'ah, which *was* over the household, and Shĕb'na the scribe, and Jō'ah the son of Ā'săph the recorder, to Hĕz-e-kī'ah with *their* clothes rent, and told him the words of Răb'-sha-keh.

CHAPTER 19

AND it came to pass, when king Hĕz-e-kī'ah heard *it*, that he rent his clothes, and covered himself with sackcloth, and went into the house of the LORD.

2 And he sent E-lī'a-kĭm, which *was* over the household, and Shĕb'na the scribe, and the elders of the priests, covered with sackcloth, to Isaiah the prophet the son of Amoz.

3 And they said unto him, Thus saith Hĕz-e-kī'ah, This day *is* a day of trouble, and of rebuke, and blasphemy: for the children are come to the birth, and *there is* not strength to bring forth.

4 It may be the LORD thy God will hear all the words of Răb'-sha-keh, whom the king of Assyria his master hath sent to reproach the living God; and will reprove the words which the LORD thy God hath heard: wherefore lift up *thy* prayer for the remnant that are left.

5 So the servants of king Hĕz-e-kī'ah came to Isaiah.

6 ¶And Isaiah said unto them, Thus shall ye say to your master, Thus saith the LORD, Be not afraid of the words which thou hast heard, with which the servants of the king of Assyria have blasphemed me.

7 Behold, I will send a blast upon him, and he shall hear a rumour, and shall return to his own land; and I will cause him to fall by the sword in his own land.

8 ¶So Răb'-sha-keh returned, and found the king of Assyria warring against Lĭb'nah: for he had heard that he was departed from Lā'chĭsh.

9 And when he heard say of Tir'hā-kah king of Ē-thĭ-ō'pĭ-a, Behold, he is come out to fight against thee: he sent messengers again unto Hĕz-e-kī'ah, saying,

10 Thus shall ye speak to Hĕz-e-kī'ah king of Judah, saying, Let not thy God in whom thou trustest deceive thee, saying, Jerusalem shall not be delivered into the hand of the king of Assyria.

11 Behold, thou hast heard what the kings of Assyria have done to all lands, by destroying them utterly: and shalt thou be delivered?

12 Have the gods of the nations delivered them which my fathers have destroyed; *as* Gō'zăn, and Hâ'ran, and Rē'zĕph, and the children of Eden which *were* in The-lā'sar?

13 Where *is* the king of Hā'măth, and the king of Är'păd, and the king of the city of Sĕph-ar-vā'im, of Hĕ'na, and Ī'vah?

14 ¶And Hĕz-e-kī'ah received the letter of the hand of the messengers, and read it: and Hĕz-e-kī'ah went up into the house of the LORD, and spread it before the LORD.

15 And Hĕz-e-kī'ah prayed before the LORD, and said, O LORD God of Israel, which dwellest *between* the cherubims, thou art the God, *even* thou alone, of all the kingdoms of the earth; thou hast made heaven and earth.

16 LORD, bow down thine ear, and hear: open, LORD, thine eyes, and see: and hear the words of Sen-năch'e-rĭb, which hath sent him to reproach the living God.

17 Of a truth, LORD, the kings of Assyria have destroyed the nations and their lands,

18 And have cast their gods into the fire: for they *were* no gods, but the work of men's hands, wood and stone: therefore they have destroyed them.

19 Now therefore, O LORD our God, I beseech thee, save thou us out of his hand, that all the kingdoms of the earth may know that thou *art* the LORD God, *even* thou only.

20 ¶Then Isaiah the son of Amoz sent to Hĕz-e-kī'ah, saying, Thus saith the LORD God of Israel, *That* which thou hast prayed to me against Sen-năch'e-rĭb king of Assyria I have heard.

21 This *is* the word that the LORD hath spoken concerning him; The virgin the daughter of Zion hath despised thee, *and* laughed thee to scorn; the daughter of Jerusalem hath shaken her head at thee.

22 Whom hast thou reproached and blasphemed? and against whom hast thou exalted *thy* voice, and lifted up thine eyes on high? *even* against the Holy *One* of Israel.

23 By thy messengers thou hast reproached the Lord, and hast said, With the multitude of my chariots I am come up to the height of the mountains, to the sides of Lebanon, and will cut down the tall cedar trees thereof, *and* the choice fir trees thereof: and I will enter into the lodgings of his borders, *and into* the forest of his Carmel.

24 I have digged and drunk strange waters, and with the sole of my feet have I dried up all the rivers of besieged places.

25 Hast thou not heard long ago *how* I have done it, *and* of ancient times that I have formed it? now have I brought it to pass, that thou shouldest be to lay waste fenced cities *into* ruinous heaps.

26 Therefore their inhabitants were of small power, they were dismayed and confounded; they were *as* the grass of the field, and *as* the green herb, *as* the grass on the house tops, and *as corn* blasted before it be grown up.

27 But I know thy abode, and thy going out, and thy coming in, and thy rage against me.

28 Because thy rage against me and thy tumult is come up into mine ears, therefore I will put my hook in thy nose, and my bridle in thy lips, and I will turn thee back by the way by which thou camest.

29 And this *shall be* a sign unto thee, Ye shall eat this year such things as grow of themselves, and in the second year that which springeth of the same; and in the third year sow ye, and reap, and plant vineyards, and eat the fruits thereof.

30 And the remnant that is escaped of the house of Jūdah shall yet again take root downward, and bear fruit upward.

31 For out of Jerusalem shall go forth a remnant, and they that escape out of mount Zion: the zeal of the LORD *of hosts* shall do this.

32 Therefore thus saith the LORD concerning the king of Assyria, He shall not come into this city, nor shoot an arrow there, nor come before it with shield, nor cast a bank against it.

33 By the way that he came, by the same shall he return, and shall not come into this city, saith the LORD.

34 For I will defend this city, to save it, for mine own sake, and for my servant David's sake.

35 ¶And it came to pass that night, that the angel of the LORD went out, and smote in the camp of the Assyrians an hundred fourscore and five thousand: and when they arose early in the morning, behold, they *were* all dead corpses.

36 So Sen-năch'e-rĭb king of Assyria departed, and went and returned, and dwelt at Nĭn'e-veh.

37 And it came to pass, as he was worshipping in the house of Nĭs'rŏch his god, that A-drăm'me-lĕch and Sha-rē'zer his sons smote him with the sword: and they escaped into the land of Är-mē'nĭa. And Ē'sar-hăd'don his son reigned in his stead.

CHAPTER 20

IN those days was Hĕz-e-kī'ah sick unto death. And the prophet Isaiah the son of Amoz came to him, and said unto him, Thus saith the LORD, Set thine house in order; for thou shalt die, and not live.

2 Then he turned his face to the wall, and prayed unto the LORD, saying,

3 I beseech thee, O LORD, remember now how I have walked before thee in truth and with a perfect heart, and have done *that which is* good in thy sight. And Hĕz-e-kī'ah wept sore.

4 And it came to pass, afore Isaiah was gone out into the middle court, that the word of the LORD came to him, saying,

5 Turn again, and tell Hĕz-e-kī'ah the captain of my people, Thus saith the LORD, the God of David thy father, I have heard thy prayer, I have seen thy tears: behold, I will heal thee: on the third day thou shalt go up unto the house of the LORD.

6 And I will add unto thy days fifteen years; and I will deliver thee and this city out of the hand of the king of Assyria; and I will defend this city for mine own sake, and for my servant David's sake.

7 And Isaiah said, Take a lump of figs. And they took and laid *it* on the boil, and he recovered.

8 ¶And Hĕz-e-kī'ah said unto Isaiah, What *shall be* the sign that the LORD will heal me, and that I shall go up into the house of the LORD the third day?

9 And Isaiah said, This sign shalt thou have of the LORD, that the LORD will do the thing that he hath spoken: shall the shadow go forward ten degrees, or go back ten degrees?

10 And Hĕz-e-kī'ah answered, It is a light thing for the shadow to go down ten degrees: nay, but let the shadow return backward ten degrees.

11 And Isaiah the prophet cried unto the LORD: and he brought the shadow ten degrees backward, by which it had gone down in the dial of Ahaz.

12 ¶At that time Be-rō'dăch-băl'a-dan, the son of Băl'a-dan, king of Babylon, sent letters and a present unto Hĕz-e-kī'ah: for he had heard that Hĕz-e-kī'ah had been sick.

13 And Hĕz-e-kī'ah hearkened unto them, and shewed them all the house of his precious things, the silver, and the gold, and the spices, and the precious ointment, and *all* the house of his armour, and all that was found in his treasures: there was nothing in his house, nor in all his dominion, that Hĕz-e-kī'ah shewed them not.

14 ¶Then came Isaiah the prophet unto king Hĕz-e-kī'ah, and said unto him, What said these men? and from whence came they unto thee? And Hĕz-e-kī'ah said, They are come from a far country, *even* from Babylon.

15 And he said, What have they seen in thine house? And Hĕz-e-kī'ah answered, All *the things* that *are* in mine house have they seen: there is nothing among my treasures that I have not shewed them.

16 And Isaiah said unto Hĕz-e-kī'ah, Hear the word of the LORD.

17 Behold, the days come, that all that *is* in thine house, and that which thy fathers have laid up in store unto this day, shall be carried into Babylon: nothing shall be left, saith the LORD.

18 And of thy sons that shall issue from thee, which thou shalt beget, shall they take away; and they shall be eunuchs in the palace of the king of Babylon.

19 Then said Hĕz-e-kī'ah unto Isaiah, Good *is* the word of the LORD which thou hast spoken. And he said, *Is it* not *good,* if peace and truth be in my days?

20 ¶And the rest of the acts of Hĕz-e-kī'ah, and all his might, and how he made a pool, and a conduit, and brought water into the city, *are* they not written in the book of the chronicles of the kings of Jūdah?

21 And Hĕz-e-kī'ah slept with his fathers: and Ma-năs'seh his son reigned in his stead.

CHAPTER 21

MA-NĂS'SEH *was* twelve years old when he began to reign, and reigned fifty and five years in Jerusalem. And his mother's name *was* Hĕph'zĭ-bah.

2 And he did *that which was* evil in the sight of the LORD, after the abominations of the heathen, whom the LORD cast out before the children of Israel.

3 For he built up again the high places which Hĕz-e-kī'ah his father had destroyed; and he reared up altars for Bā'al, and made a grove, as did Ahab king of Israel; and worshipped all the host of heaven, and served them.

4 And he built altars in the house of the LORD, of which the LORD said, In Jerusalem will I put my name.

5 And he built altars for all the host of heaven in the two courts of the house of the LORD.

6 And he made his son pass through the fire, and observed times, and used enchantments, and dealt with familiar spirits and wizards: he wrought much wickedness in the sight of the LORD, to provoke *him* to anger.

7 And he set a graven image of the grove that he had made in the house, of which the LORD said to David, and to Solomon his son, In this house, and in Jerusalem, which I have chosen out of all tribes of Israel, will I put my name for ever:

8 Neither will I make the feet of Israel move any more out of the land which I gave their fathers; only if they will observe to do according to all that I have commanded them, and according to all the law that my servant Moses commanded them.

9 But they hearkened not: and Ma-
năs'seh seduced them to do more evil
than did the nations whom the LORD
destroyed before the children of Israel.
10 ¶And the LORD spake by his ser-
vants the prophets, saying,
11 Because Ma-năs'seh king of Jūdah
hath done these abominations, *and*
hath done wickedly above all that the
Ămorītes did, which *were* before him,
and hath made Jūdah also to sin with
his idols:
12 Therefore thus saith the LORD God
of Israel, Behold, I *am* bringing *such*
evil upon Jerusalem and Jūdah, that
whosoever heareth of it, both his ears
shall tingle.
13 And I will stretch over Jerusalem
the line of Sa-mâ'rĭ-a, and the plummet
of the house of Ahab: and I will wipe
Jerusalem as *a man* wipeth a dish, wip-
ing *it*, and turning *it* upside down.
14 And I will forsake the remnant of
mine inheritance, and deliver them into
the hand of their enemies; and they
shall become a prey and a spoil to all
their enemies;
15 Because they have done *that*
which was evil in my sight, and have
provoked me to anger, since the day
their fathers came forth out of Egypt,
even unto this day.
16 Moreover Ma-năs'seh shed inno-
cent blood very much, till he had filled
Jerusalem from one end to another; be-
side his sin wherewith he made Jūdah
to sin, in doing *that which was* evil in
the sight of the LORD.
17 ¶Now the rest of the acts of Ma-
năs'seh, and all that he did, and his sin
that he sinned, *are* they not written in
the book of the chronicles of the kings
of Jūdah?
18 And Ma-năs'seh slept with his
fathers, and was buried in the garden of
his own house, in the garden of Ŭz'za:
and Ămon his son reigned in his stead.
19 ¶Ămon *was* twenty and two years
old when he began to reign, and he
reigned two years in Jerusalem. And
his mother's name *was* Me-shŭl'le-
mĕth, the daughter of Hâ'rŭz of Jŏt'-
bah.
20 And he did *that which was* evil in
the sight of the LORD, as his father Ma-
năs'seh did.
21 And he walked in all the way that
his father walked in, and served the
idols that his father served, and wor-
shipped them:
22 And he forsook the LORD God of
his fathers, and walked not in the way
of the LORD.
23 And the servants of Ămon con-
spired against him, and slew the king in
his own house.
24 And the people of the land slew all
them that had conspired against king
Ămon; and the people of the land made
Jō-sī'ah his son king in his stead.
25 Now the rest of the acts of Ămon
which he did, *are* they not written in the
book of the chronicles of the kings of
Jūdah?
26 And he was buried in his sepulchre
in the garden of Ŭz'za: and Jō-sī'ah his
son reigned in his stead.

CHAPTER 22

JŌ-SĪ'AH *was* eight years old when he
began to reign, and he reigned thirty
and one years in Jerusalem. And his
mother's name *was* Je-dī'dah, the
daughter of Ăd-a-ī'ah of Bŏs'căth.
2 And he did *that which was* right in
the sight of the LORD, and walked in all
the way of David his father, and turned
not aside to the right hand or to the left.
3 ¶And it came to pass in the
eighteenth year of king Jō-sī'ah, *that*
the king sent Shā'phan the son of Ăz-a-
lī'ah, the son of Me-shŭl'lam, the
scribe, to the house of the LORD, saying,
4 Go up to Hĭl-kī'ah the high priest,
that he may sum the silver which is
brought into the house of the LORD,
which the keepers of the door have gath-
ered of the people:
5 And let them deliver it into the hand
of the doers of the work, that have the
oversight of the house of the LORD: and
let them give it to the doers of the work
which *is* in the house of the LORD, to
repair the breaches of the house,
6 Unto carpenters, and builders, and
masons, and to buy timber and hewn
stone to repair the house.
7 Howbeit there was no reckoning
made with them of the money that was
delivered into their hand, because they
dealt faithfully.
8 ¶And Hĭl-kī'ah the high priest said
unto Shā'phan the scribe, I have found
the book of the law in the house of the
LORD. And Hĭl-kī'ah gave the book to
Shā'phan, and he read it.
9 And Shā'phan the scribe came to
the king, and brought the king word
again, and said, Thy servants have gath-
ered the money that was found in the
house, and have delivered it into the
hand of them that do the work, that
have the oversight of the house of the
LORD.
10 And Shā'phan the scribe shewed
the king, saying, Hĭl-kī'ah the priest
hath delivered me a book. And Shā'-
phan read it before the king.
11 And it came to pass, when the king

had heard the words of the book of the law, that he rent his clothes.
12 And the king commanded Hĭl-kī'-
ah the priest, and A-hī'kam the son of
Shā'phan, and Ăch'bôr the son of Mī-
chā'iah, and Shā'phan the scribe, and
Aṡā̆hiah a servant of the king's, saying,
13 Go ye, enquire of the LORD for me,
and for the people, and for all Jūdah, concerning the words of this book that is found: for great *is* the wrath of the LORD that is kindled against us, because our fathers have not hearkened unto the words of this book, to do according unto all that which is written concerning us.
14 So Hĭl-kī'ah the priest, and A-
hī'kam, and Ăch'bôr, and Shā'phan, and Aṡā̆hiah, went unto Hŭl'dah the prophetess, the wife of Shăl'lum the son of Tĭk'vah, the son of Här'hăs, keeper of the wardrobe; (now she dwelt in Jerusalem in the college;) and they communed with her.
15 And she said unto them, Thus
saith the LORD God of Israel, Tell the man that sent you to me,
16 Thus saith the LORD, Behold, I will
bring evil upon this place, and upon the inhabitants thereof, *even* all the words of the book which the king of Jūdah hath read:
17 Because they have forsaken me,
and have burned incense unto other gods, that they might provoke me to anger with all the works of their hands; therefore my wrath shall be kindled against this place, and shall not be quenched.
18 But to the king of Jūdah which
sent you to enquire of the LORD, thus shall ye say to him, Thus saith the LORD God of Israel, *As touching* the words which thou hast heard;
19 Because thine heart was tender,
and thou hast humbled thyself before the LORD, when thou heardest what I spake against this place, and against the inhabitants thereof, that they should become a desolation and a curse, and hast rent thy clothes, and wept before me; I also have heard *thee*, saith the LORD.
20 Behold therefore, I will gather
thee unto thy fathers, and thou shalt be gathered into thy grave in peace; and thine eyes shall not see all the evil which I will bring upon this place. And they brought the king word again.

CHAPTER 23

AND the king sent, and they gathered unto him all the elders of Jūdah and of Jerusalem.
2 And the king went up into the house
of the LORD, and all the men of Jūdah and all the inhabitants of Jerusalem with him, and the priests, and the prophets, and all the people, both small and great: and he read in their ears all the words of the book of the covenant which was found in the house of the LORD.
3 And the king stood by a pillar, and
made a covenant before the LORD, to walk after the LORD, and to keep his commandments and his testimonies and his statutes with all *their* heart and all *their* soul, to perform the words of this covenant that were written in this book. And all the people stood to the covenant.
4 And the king commanded Hĭl-kī'ah
the high priest, and the priests of the second order, and the keepers of the door, to bring forth out of the temple of the LORD all the vessels that were made for Bā'al, and for the grove, and for all the host of heaven: and he burned them without Jerusalem in the fields of Kidron, and carried the ashes of them unto Bĕth-el.
5 And he put down the idolatrous
priests, whom the kings of Jūdah had ordained to burn incense in the high places in the cities of Jūdah, and in the places round about Jerusalem; them also that burned incense unto Bā'al, to the sun, and to the moon, and to the planets, and to all the host of heaven.
6 And he brought out the grove from
the house of the LORD, without Jerusalem, unto the brook Kidron, and burned it at the brook Kidron, and stamped *it* small to powder, and cast the powder thereof upon the graves of the children of the people.
7 And he brake down the houses of
the sodomites, that *were* by the house of the LORD, where the women wove hangings for the grove.
8 And he brought all the priests out of
the cities of Jūdah, and defiled the high places where the priests had burned incense, from Gē'ba to Be'er–shē'ba, and brake down the high places of the gates that *were* in the entering in of the gate of Joshua the governor of the city, which *were* on a man's left hand at the gate of the city.
9 Nevertheless the priests of the high
places came not up to the altar of the LORD in Jerusalem, but they did eat of the unleavened bread among their brethren.
10 And he defiled Tō'pheth, which *is*
in the valley of the children of Hĭn'nom, that no man might make his son or his daughter to pass through the fire to Mō'lĕch.

11 And he took away the horses that the kings of Jūdah had given to the sun, at the entering in of the house of the LORD, by the chamber of Nā′-thăn-mĕ′lech the chamberlain, which *was* in the suburbs, and burned the chariots of the sun with fire.
12 And the altars that *were* on the top of the upper chamber of Ahaz, which the kings of Jūdah had made, and the altars which Ma-năs′seh had made in the two courts of the house of the LORD, did the king beat down, and brake *them* down from thence, and cast the dust of them into the brook Kidron.
13 And the high places that *were* before Jerusalem, which *were* on the right hand of the mount of corruption, which Sŏlomon the king of Israel had builded for Ăsh′to-rĕth the abomination of the Zī-dō′nĭ-ans, and for Chē′-mŏsh the abomination of the Moabites, and for Mĭl′com the abomination of the children of Ammon, did the king defile.
14 And he brake in pieces the images, and cut down the groves, and filled their places with the bones of men.
15 ¶Moreover the altar that *was* at Bĕth-el, *and* the high place which Jĕr-o-bō′am the son of Nē′băt, who made Israel to sin, had made, both that altar and the high place he brake down, and burned the high place, *and* stamped *it* small to powder, and burned the grove.
16 And as Jō-sī′ah turned himself, he spied the sepulchres that *were* there in the mount, and sent, and took the bones out of the sepulchres, and burned *them* upon the altar, and polluted it, according to the word of the LORD which the man of God proclaimed, who proclaimed these words.
17 Then he said, What title *is* that that I see? And the men of the city told him, *It is* the sepulchre of the man of God, which came from Jūdah, and proclaimed these things that thou hast done against the altar of Bĕth-el.
18 And he said, Let him alone; let no man move his bones. So they let his bones alone, with the bones of the prophet that came out of Sa-mâ′rĭ-a.
19 And all the houses also of the high places that *were* in the cities of Sa-mâ′-rĭ-a, which the kings of Israel had made to provoke *the LORD* to anger, Jō-sī′ah took away, and did to them according to all the acts that he had done in Bĕth-el.
20 And he slew all the priests of the high places that *were* there upon the altars, and burned men's bones upon them, and returned to Jerusalem.
21 ¶And the king commanded all the people, saying, Keep the passover unto the LORD your God, as *it is* written in the book of this covenant.
22 Surely there was not holden such a passover from the days of the judges that judged Israel, nor in all the days of the kings of Israel, nor of the kings of Jūdah;
23 But in the eighteenth year of king Jō-sī′ah, *wherein* this passover was holden to the LORD in Jerusalem.
24 ¶Moreover the *workers with* familiar spirits, and the wizards, and the images, and the idols, and all the abominations that were spied in the land of Jūdah and in Jerusalem, did Jō-sī′ah put away, that he might perform the words of the law which were written in the book that Hĭl-kī′ah the priest found in the house of the LORD.
25 And like unto him was there no king before him, that turned to the LORD with all his heart, and with all his soul, and with all his might, according to all the law of Moses; neither after him arose there *any* like him.
26 Notwithstanding the LORD turned not from the fierceness of his great wrath, wherewith his anger was kindled against Jūdah, because of all the provocations that Ma-năs′seh had provoked him withal.
27 And the LORD said, I will remove Jūdah also out of my sight, as I have removed Israel, and will cast off this city Jerusalem which I have chosen, and the house of which I said, My name shall be there.
28 Now the rest of the acts of Jō-sī′ah, and all that he did, *are* they not written in the book of the chronicles of the kings of Jūdah?
29 In his days Phâraōh-nēchōh king of Egypt went up against the king of Assyria to the river Eū-phrā′tēṡ: and king Jō-sī′ah went against him; and he slew him at Me-gĭd′dō, when he had seen him.
30 And his servants carried him in a chariot dead from Me-gĭd′dō, and brought him to Jerusalem, and buried him in his own sepulchre. And the people of the land took Je-hō′a-hăz the son of Jō-sī′ah, and anointed him, and made him king in his father's stead.
31 ¶Je-hō′a-hăz *was* twenty and three years old when he began to reign; and he reigned three months in Jerusalem. And his mother's name *was* Ha-mū′tal, the daughter of Jĕr-e-mī′ah of Lĭb′nah.
32 And he did *that which was* evil in the sight of the LORD, according to all that his fathers had done.
33 And Phâraōh-nēchōh put him in bands at Rĭb′lah in the land of Hā′măth,

that he might not reign in Jerusalem;
and put the land to a tribute of an
hundred talents of silver, and a talent
of gold.
34 And Phâraōh-nēchōh made E-lī'a-
kĭm the son of Jō-sī'ah king in the room
of Jō-sī'ah his father, and turned his
name to Je-hoi'a-kĭm, and took Je-hō'a-
hăz away: and he came to Egypt, and
died there.
35 And Je-hoi'a-kĭm gave the silver
and the gold to Pharaoh; but he taxed
the land to give the money according to
the commandment of Pharaoh: he ex-
acted the silver and the gold of the
people of the land, of every one accord-
ing to his taxation, to give *it* unto Phâr-
aōh-nēchōh.
36 ¶Je-hoi'a-kĭm *was* twenty and five
years old when he began to reign; and
he reigned eleven years in Jerusalem.
And his mother's name *was* Ze-bū'dah,
the daughter of Pe-dā'iah of Rū'mah.
37 And he did *that which was* evil in
the sight of the LORD, according to all
that his fathers had done.

CHAPTER 24

IN his days Nĕb-u-chad-nĕz'zar king of
Babylon came up, and Je-hoi'a-kĭm be-
came his servant three years: then he
turned and rebelled against him.
2 And the LORD sent against him
bands of the Chăl'deeṡ, and bands of
the Syrians, and bands of the Moabites,
and bands of the children of Ammon,
and sent them against Jūdah to destroy
it, according to the word of the LORD,
which he spake by his servants the
prophets.
3 Surely at the commandment of the
LORD came *this* upon Jūdah, to remove
them out of his sight, for the sins of Ma-
năs'seh, according to all that he did;
4 And also for the innocent blood that
he shed: for he filled Jerusalem with in-
nocent blood; which the LORD would
not pardon.
5 ¶Now the rest of the acts of Je-
hoi'a-kĭm, and all that he did, *are* they
not written in the book of the chron-
icles of the kings of Jūdah?
6 So Je-hoi'a-kĭm slept with his fa-
thers: and Je-hoi'a-chĭn his son reigned
in his stead.
7 And the king of Egypt came not
again any more out of his land: for the
king of Babylon had taken from the riv-
er of Egypt unto the river Eū-phrā'tēṡ
all that pertained to the king of Egypt.
8 ¶Je-hoi'a-chĭn *was* eighteen years
old when he began to reign, and he
reigned in Jerusalem three months.
And his mother's name *was* Ne-
hūsh'ta, the daughter of Ĕl'nā-than of
Jerusalem.
9 And he did *that which was* evil in
the sight of the LORD, according to all
that his father had done.
10 ¶At that time the servants of Nĕb-
u-chad-nĕz'zar king of Babylon came
up against Jerusalem, and the city was
besieged.
11 And Nĕb-u-chad-nĕz'zar king of
Babylon came against the city, and his
servants did besiege it.
12 And Je-hoi'a-chĭn the king of Jū-
dah went out to the king of Babylon, he,
and his mother, and his servants, and
his princes, and his officers: and the
king of Babylon took him in the eighth
year of his reign.
13 And he carried out thence all the
treasures of the house of the LORD, and
the treasures of the king's house, and
cut in pieces all the vessels of gold
which Sŏlomon king of Israel had made
in the temple of the LORD, as the LORD
had said.
14 And he carried away all Jeru-
salem, and all the princes, and all the
mighty men of valour, *even* ten thou-
sand captives, and all the craftsmen
and smiths: none remained, save the
poorest sort of the people of the land.
15 And he carried away Je-hoi'a-chĭn
to Babylon, and the king's mother, and
the king's wives, and his officers, and
the mighty of the land, *those* carried he
into captivity from Jerusalem to Baby-
lon.
16 And all the men of might, *even*
seven thousand, and craftsmen and
smiths a thousand, all *that were* strong
and apt for war, even them the king of
Babylon brought captive to Babylon.
17 And the king of Babylon made
Măt-ta-nī'ah his father's brother king
in his stead, and changed his name to
Zĕd-e-kī'ah.
18 ¶Zĕd-e-kī'ah *was* twenty and one
years old when he began to reign, and
he reigned eleven years in Jerusalem.
And his mother's name *was* Ha-mū'tal,
the daughter of Jĕr-e-mī'ah of Lĭb'nah.
19 And he did *that which was* evil in
the sight of the LORD, according to all
that Je-hoi'a-kĭm had done.
20 For through the anger of the LORD
it came to pass in Jerusalem and Jūdah,
until he had cast them out from his pres-
ence, that Zĕd-e-kī'ah rebelled against
the king of Babylon.

CHAPTER 25

AND it came to pass in the ninth year of
his reign, in the tenth month, in the
tenth *day* of the month, *that* Nĕb-u-
chad-nĕz'zar king of Babylon came, he,

and all his host, against Jerusalem, and pitched against it; and they built forts against it round about.

2 And the city was besieged unto the eleventh year of king Zĕd-e-kī′ah.

3 And on the ninth *day* of the *fourth* month the famine prevailed in the city, and there was no bread for the people of the land.

4 And the city was broken up, and all the men of war *fled* by night by the way of the gate between two walls, which *is* by the king's garden: (now the Chăl′deeṡ *were* against the city round about:) and *the king* went the way toward the plain.

5 And the army of the Chăl′deeṡ pursued after the king, and overtook him in the plains of Jericho: and all his army were scattered from him.

6 So they took the king, and brought him up to the king of Babylon to Rĭb′-lah; and they gave judgment upon him.

7 And they slew the sons of Zĕd-e-kī′-ah before his eyes, and put out the eyes of Zĕd-e-kī′ah, and bound him with fetters of brass, and carried him to Babylon.

8 ¶And in the fifth month, on the seventh *day* of the month, which *is* the nineteenth year of king Nĕb-u-chad-nĕz′zar king of Babylon, came Nĕb′u-zar–ā′dan, captain of the guard, a servant of the king of Babylon, unto Jerusalem:

9 And he burnt the house of the LORD, and the king's house, and all the houses of Jerusalem, and every great *man's* house burnt he with fire.

10 And all the army of the Chăl′deeṡ, that *were with* the captain of the guard, brake down the walls of Jerusalem round about.

11 Now the rest of the people *that were* left in the city, and the fugitives that fell away to the king of Babylon, with the remnant of the multitude, did Nĕb′u-zar–ā′dan the captain of the guard carry away.

12 But the captain of the guard left of the poor of the land *to be* vinedressers and husbandmen.

13 And the pillars of brass that *were* in the house of the LORD, and the bases, and the brasen sea that *was* in the house of the LORD, did the Chăl′deeṡ break in pieces, and carried the brass of them to Babylon.

14 And the pots, and the shovels, and the snuffers, and the spoons, and all the vessels of brass wherewith they ministered, took they away.

15 And the firepans, and the bowls, *and* such things as *were* of gold, *in* gold, and of silver, *in* silver, the captain of the guard took away.

16 The two pillars, one sea, and the bases which Sŏlomon had made for the house of the LORD; the brass of all these vessels was without weight.

17 The height of the one pillar *was* eighteen cubits, and the chapiter upon it *was* brass: and the height of the chapiter three cubits; and the wreathen work, and pomegranates upon the chapiter round about, all of brass: and like unto these had the second pillar with wreathen work.

18 ¶And the captain of the guard took Se-ra-ī′ah the chief priest, and Zĕph-a-nī′ah the second priest, and the three keepers of the door:

19 And out of the city he took an officer that was set over the men of war, and five men of them that were in the king's presence, which were found in the city, and the principal scribe of the host, which mustered the people of the land, and threescore men of the people of the land *that were* found in the city:

20 And Nĕb′u-zar–ā′dan captain of the guard took these, and brought them to the king of Babylon to Rĭb′lah:

21 And the king of Babylon smote them, and slew them at Rĭb′lah in the land of Hā′măth. So Jūdah was carried away out of their land.

22 ¶And *as for* the people that remained in the land of Jūdah, whom Nĕb-u-chad-nĕz′zar king of Babylon had left, even over them he made Gĕd-a-lī′ah the son of A-hī′kam, the son of Shā′phan, ruler.

23 And when all the captains of the armies, they and their men, heard that the king of Babylon had made Gĕd-a-lī′ah governor, there came to Gĕd-a-lī′ah to Miz′pah, even Ĭsh′ma-el the son of Nĕth-a-nī′ah, and Jō-hā′nan the son of Ca-rē′ah, and Se-ra-ī′ah the son of Tăn′-hū-meth the Ne-tōph′a-thīte, and Jā-ăz-a-nī′ah the son of a Mā-ăch′a-thīte, they and their men.

24 And Gĕd-a-lī′ah sware to them, and to their men, and said unto them, Fear not to be the servants of the Chăl′-deeṡ: dwell in the land, and serve the king of Babylon; and it shall be well with you.

25 But it came to pass in the seventh month, that Ĭsh′ma-el the son of Nĕth-a-nī′ah, the son of E-lĭsh′a-ma, of the seed royal, came, and ten men with him, and smote Gĕd-a-lī′ah, that he died, and the Jews and the Chăl′deeṡ that were with him at Miz′pah.

26 And all the people, both small and great, and the captains of the armies,

arose, and came to Egypt: for they were afraid of the Chăl′deeṣ.
27 ¶And it came to pass in the seven and thirtieth year of the captivity of Je-hoi′a-chĭn king of Jūdah, in the twelfth month, on the seven and twentieth *day* of the month, *that* Ē′vil–mĕ-ro′dăch king of Babylon in the year that he began to reign did lift up the head of Je-hoi′a-chĭn king of Jūdah out of prison;
28 And he spake kindly to him, and set his throne above the throne of the kings that *were* with him in Babylon;
29 And changed his prison garments: and he did eat bread continually before him all the days of his life.
30 And his allowance *was* a continual allowance given him of the king, a daily rate for every day, all the days of his life.

THE FIRST BOOK OF THE

CHRONICLES

CHAPTER 1

ADAM, Sheth, Ē′nŏsh,
2 Ke′nan, Ma-hă′la-le-el, Je′rĕd,
3 Hē′nŏch, Me-thū′se-lah, Lā′mech,
4 Noah, Shem, Ham, and Jā′pheth.
5 ¶The sons of Jā′pheth; Gō′mer, and Mā′gŏg, and Măd′a-ī, and Jā′van, and Tū′bal, and Mē′shĕch, and Tī′ras.
6 And the sons of Gō′mer; Ăsh′che-năz, and Rī′phăth, and Tō-gär′mah.
7 And the sons of Jā′van; E-lī′shah, and Tär′shĭsh, Kĭt′tĭm, and Dō′da-nĭm.
8 ¶The sons of Ham; Cush, and Mĭz′-ra-im, Put, and Canaan.
9 And the sons of Cush; Sē′ba, and Hăv′i-lah, and Săb′ta, and Rā′a-mah, and Săb′te-cha. And the sons of Rā′a-mah; Shē′ba, and Dē′dan.
10 And Cush begat Nimrod: he began to be mighty upon the earth.
11 And Mĭz′ra-im begat Lū′dim, and Ăn′a-mĭm, and Le′hā-bĭm, and Năph′-tu-hĭm,
12 And Path-rū′sĭm, and Căs′lu-hĭm, (of whom came the Philistines,) and Căph′tho-rĭm.
13 And Canaan begat Zī′don his first-born, and Heth,
14 The Jĕb′u-sīte also, and the Ămor-īte, and the Gir′ga-shīte,
15 And the Hī′vīte, and the Ärk′īte, and the Sīn′īte,
16 And the Är′vad-īte, and the Zĕm′a-rīte, and the Hā′math-īte.
17 ¶The sons of Shem; Ē′lam, and Asshur, and Är-phăx′ăd, and Lud and Â′ram, and Uz, and Hul, and Gē′ther, and Mē′shĕch.
18 And Är-phăx′ăd begat Shē′lah, and Shē′lah begat Ē′ber.
19 And unto Ē′ber were born two sons: the name of the one *was* Pē′lĕg; because in his days the earth was divided: and his brother's name *was* Jŏk′-tăn.
20 And Jŏk′tăn begat Ăl-mō′dăd, and Shē′leph, and Hā′zar–mā′veth, and Je′rah,
21 Ha-dō′ram also, and Ū′zal, and Dĭk′lah,
22 And Ebal, and A-bĭm′a-el, and Shē′ba,
23 And Ō′phir, and Hăv′i-lah, and Jō′-băb. All these *were* the sons of Jŏk′tăn.
24 ¶Shem, Är-phăx′ăd, Shē′lah,
25 Ē′ber, Pē′lĕg, Rē′ū,
26 Se′rŭg, Nahor, Te′rah,
27 Abram; the same *is* Abraham.
28 The sons of Abraham; Isaac, and Ĭsh′ma-el.
29 ¶These *are* their generations: The firstborn of Ĭsh′ma-el, Ne-bā′iŏth; then Kē′dar, and Ăd′be-el, and Mĭb′săm,
30 Mĭsh′ma, and Dū′mah, Măs′sa, Hā′dăd, and Tē′ma,
31 Jē′tur, Nā′phĭsh, and Kĕd′e-mah. These are the sons of Ĭsh′ma-el.
32 ¶Now the sons of Ke-tū′rah, Abraham's concubine: she bare Zĭm′răn, and Jŏk′shăn, and Mē′dăn, and Mĭd′ī-an, and Ĭsh′băk, and Shū′ah. And the sons of Jŏk′shăn; Shē′ba, and Dē′dan.
33 And the sons of Mĭd′ī-an; Ē′phah, and Ē′pher, and Hē′nŏch, and A-bī′da, and Ĕl′dā-ah. All these *are* the sons of Ke-tū′rah.
34 And Abraham begat Isaac. The sons of Isaac; Esau and Israel.
35 ¶The sons of Esau; Ĕl′i-phăz, Reū′-el, and Jē′ŭsh, and Jā-a′lam, and Kôrah.
36 The sons of Ĕl′i-phăz; Tē′man, and Ōmär, Zē′phī, and Gă′tam, Kē′năz, and Tĭm′na, and Ăm′a-lĕk.
37 The sons of Reū′el; Nā′hăth, Ze′rah, Shăm′mah, and Mĭz′zah.
38 And the sons of Sē′ir; Lō′tăn, and Shō′bal, and Zĭb′e-on, and Ā′nah, and Dī′shŏn, and Ē′zar, and Dī′shăn.
39 And the sons of Lō′tăn; Hô′rī, and Hō′măm: and Tĭm′na *was* Lō′tăn's sister.
40 The sons of Shō′bal; Ā-lī′an, and Măn′a-hăth, and Ebal, Shē′phī, and Ō′nam, and the sons of Zĭb′e-on; Ā-ī′ah, and Ā′nah.
41 The sons of Ā′nah; Dī′shŏn. And

the sons of Dī′shŏn; Ăm-răm, and Ĕsh′-băn, and Ĭth′răn, and Chĕ′ran.

42 The sons of Ē′zer; Bĭl′hăn, and Zā′-van, *and* Jā′kan. The sons of Dī′shăn; Uz, and Â′răn.

43 ¶Now these *are* the kings that reigned in the land of Ēdom before *any* king reigned over the children of Israel; Bĕ′la the son of Bĕ′ôr: and the name of his city *was* Dĭn′ha-bah.

44 And when Bē′la was dead, Jō′băb the son of Ze′rah of Bŏz′rah reigned in his stead.

45 And when Jō′băb was dead, Hu′sham of the land of the Tē′man-ītes reigned in his stead.

46 And when Hu′sham was dead, Hă′dăd the son of Bē′dăd, which smote Mĭd′ī-an in the field of Moab, reigned in his stead: and the name of his city *was* Ā′vĭth.

47 And when Hā′dăd was dead, Săm′lah of Măs′re-kah reigned in his stead.

48 And when Săm′lah was dead, Shā′-ul of Re-hō′bŏth by the river reigned in his stead.

49 And when Shā′ul was dead, Bā′al-hā′nan the son of Ăch′bôr reigned in his stead.

50 And when Bā′al-hā′nan was dead, Hā′dăd reigned in his stead: and the name of his city *was* Pā′ī; and his wife's name *was* Me-hĕt′a-bĕl, the daughter of Mā′tred, the daughter of Mĕz′a-hăb.

51 Hā′dăd died also. And the dukes of Ēdom were; duke Tĭm′nah, duke Ă-lĭ′ah, duke Jē′thĕth,

52 Duke A-hōl-ī-bā′mah, duke Ē′lah, duke Pī′nŏn,

53 Duke Kē′năz, duke Tē′man, duke Mĭb′zär,

54 Duke Măg′dĭ-el, duke Ī′răm. These *are* the dukes of Ēdom.

CHAPTER 2

THESE *are* the sons of Israel; Reuben, Simeon, Levi, and Jūdah, Ĭs′sa-char, and Zĕb′u-lun,

2 Dan, Joseph, and Benjamin, Năph′-ta-lī, Gad, and Asher.

3 ¶The sons of Jūdah; Er, and Ō′nan, and Shē′lah: *which* three were born unto him of the daughter of Shū′a the Canaanitess. And Er, the firstborn of Jūdah, was evil in the sight of the LORD; and he slew him.

4 And Tā′mar his daughter in law bore him Phā′rĕz and Ze′rah. All the sons of Jūdah *were* five.

5 The sons of Phā′rĕz; Hĕz′ron, and Hā′mul.

6 And the sons of Ze′rah; Zimri, and Ē′than, and Hē′măn, and Căl′cŏl, and Dâ′ra: five of them in all.

7 And the sons of Cär′mī; Ā′chär, the troubler of Israel, who transgressed in the thing accursed.

8 And the sons of Ē′than; Ăz-a-rī′ah.

9 The sons also of Hĕz′ron, that were born unto him; Je-räh′me-el, and Ram, and Che-lū′baī.

10 And Ram begat Am-mĭn′a-dăb; and Am-mĭn′a-dăb begat Näh′shŏn, prince of the children of Jūdah;

11 And Näh′shŏn begat Săl′ma, and Săl′ma begat Bō′ăz,

12 And Bō′ăz begat Ō′bed, and Ō′bed begat Jesse,

13 And Jesse begat his firstborn E-lī′ab, and A-bĭn′a-dăb the second, and Shĭm′ma the third,

14 Ne-thăn′e-el the fourth, Răd′da-ī the fifth,

15 Ō′zem the sixth, David the seventh:

16 Whose sisters *were* Zer-ū-i′ah, and Ăb′i-gāil. And the sons of Zer-ū-i′ah; A-bī′shaī, and Jō′ăb, and Ă′sa-hĕl, three.

17 And Ăb′i-gāil bare Am′ā-sa: and the father of Am′ā-sa *was* Jē′ther the Ĭsh′me-el-īte.

18 ¶And Caleb the son of Hĕz′ron begat *children* of A-zū′bah *his* wife, and of Jĕ′rī-ŏth: her sons *are* these; Jē′sher, and Shō′băb, and Ardon.

19 And when A-zū′bah was dead, Caleb took unto him Ĕph′rath, which bare him Hur.

20 And Hur begat Ū′rī, and Ū′rī begat Be-zăl′e-el.

21 And afterward Hĕz′ron went in to the daughter of Mā′chĭr the father of Gilead, whom he married when he *was* threescore years old; and she bare him Sē′gŭb.

22 And Sē′gŭb begat Jā′ir, who had three and twenty cities in the land of Gilead.

23 And he took Gē′shur, and Â′ram, with the towns of Jā′ir, from them, with Kē′năth, and the towns thereof, *even* threescore cities. All these *belonged to* the sons of Mā′chĭr the father of Gilead.

24 And after that Hĕz′ron was dead in Cā′leb–ĕph′ra-täh, then Ă-bī′ah Hĕz′-ron's wife bare him Ashur the father of Te-kō′a.

25 ¶And the sons of Je-räh′me-el the firstborn of Hĕz′ron were, Ram the firstborn, and Bū′nah, and Ô′ren, and Ō′zem, *and* A-hī′jah.

26 Je-räh′me-el had also another wife, whose name *was* Ăt′a-rah; she *was* the mother of Ō′nam.

27 And the sons of Ram the firstborn of Je-räh′me-el were, Mā′ăz, and Jā′-mĭn, and Ē′ker.

28 And the sons of Ō′nam were,

Shăm′ma-ī, and Jā′da. And the sons of
Shăm′ma-ī; Nādăb, and Ab′ī-shur.
29 And the name of the wife of Ab′ī-
shur *was* Ăb-i-hā′il, and she bare him
Ăh′băn, and Mō′lĭd.
30 And the sons of Nādăb; Sē′lĕd, and
Ăp′pa-im: but Sē′lĕd died without
children.
31 And the sons of Ăp′pa-im; Ĭ′shī.
And the sons of Ĭ′shī; Shē′shăn. And the
children of Shē′shăn; Ăh′laī.
32 And the sons of Jā′da the brother
of Shăm′ma-ī; Jē′ther, and Jonathan:
and Jē′ther died without children.
33 And the sons of Jonathan; Pē′lĕth,
and Zā′za. These were the sons of Je-
răh′me-el.
34 ¶Now Shē′shăn had no sons, but
daughters. And Shē′shăn had a ser-
vant, an Egyptian, whose name *was*
Jär′ha.
35 And Shē′shăn gave his daughter to
Jär′ha his servant to wife; and she bare
him Ăt′taī.
36 And Ăt′taī begat Nāthan, and Nā-
than begat Zā′băd,
37 And Zā′băd begat Ĕph′lăl, and
Ĕph′lăl begat Ō′bed.
38 And Ō′bed begat Jehu, and Jehu
begat Ăz-a-rī′ah,
39 And Ăz-a-rī′ah begat Hē′lĕz, and
Hē′lĕz begat Ē-le′ā-sah,
40 And Ē-le′ā-sah begat Sĭ-sam′a-ī,
and Sĭ-sam′a-ī begat Shăl′lum,
41 And Shăl′lum begat Jĕk-a-mī′ah,
and Jĕk-a-mī′ah begat E-lĭsh′a-ma.
42 ¶Now the sons of Caleb the
brother of Je-răh′me-el *were*, Mē′sha
his firstborn, which *was* the father of
Ziph; and the sons of Ma-rē′shah the
father of Hēbron.
43 And the sons of Hēbron; Kôrah,
and Tăp′pū-ah, and Rē′kem, and
Shē′ma.
44 And Shē′ma begat Raham, the
father of Jôr′kō-am: and Rē′kem begat
Shăm′ma-ī.
45 And the son of Shăm′ma-ī *was*
Mā′on: and Mā′on *was* the father of
Bĕth′-zûr.
46 And Ē′phah, Caleb's concubine,
bare Hâ′ran, and Mō′za, and Gā′zez:
and Hâ′ran begat Gā′zez.
47 And the sons of Jăh′da-ī; Rē′gem,
and Jō′tham, and Gē′sham, and Pē′let,
and Ē′phah, and Shā′ăph.
48 Mā′a-chah, Caleb's concubine,
bare Shē′ber, and Tir′hā-nah.
49 She bare also Shā′ăph the father of
Măd-măn′nah, Shē′va the father of
Măch′bē-nah, and the father of Gĭb′e-a:
and the daughter of Caleb *was* Ăch′sa.
50 ¶These were the sons of Caleb the
son of Hur, the firstborn of Ĕph′ra-tăh;
Shō′bal the father of Kir′jath-jē′a-rĭm,
51 Săl′ma the father of Bĕth-lehĕm,
Hâ′rĕph the father of Bĕth-gā′der.
52 And Shō′bal the father of Kir′-
jath-jē′a-rĭm had sons; Har′ō-eh, *and*
half of the Mă-na′hĕth-ītes.
53 And the families of Kir′jath-jē′a-
rĭm; the Ĭth′rītes, and the Pū′hītes, and
the Shū′math-ītes, and the Mĭsh′ra-
ītes; of them came the Zâ′re-ath-ītes,
and the Ĕsh′ta-ul-ītes.
54 The sons of Săl′ma; Bĕth-lehĕm,
and the Ne-tōph′a-thītes, Ăt′a-rŏth, the
house of Jō′ăb, and half of the Mă-na′-
hĕth-ītes, the Zô′rītes.
55 And the families of the scribes
which dwelt at Jā′bez; the Tī′rath-ītes,
the Shĭm′e-ath-ītes, *and* Sū′chath-ītes.
These *are* the Kēn′ītes that came of
Hē′măth, the father of the house of
Rē′chăb.

CHAPTER 3

NOW these were the sons of David,
which were born unto him in Hēbron;
the firstborn Ăm′nŏn, of A-hĭn′ō-am
the Jĕz′re-el-īt-ess; the second Daniel,
of Ăb′i-gāil the Carmelitess:
2 The third, Ăb′sa-lom the son of
Mā′a-chah the daughter of Tăl′maī king
of Gē′shur: the fourth, Ăd-o-nī′jah the
son of Hăg′gĭth:
3 The fifth, Shĕph-a-tī′ah of Ăb′ı-tal:
the sixth, Ĭth′re-am by Ĕg′lah his wife.
4 *These* six were born unto him in
Hēbron; and there he reigned seven
years and six months: and in Jerusalem
he reigned thirty and three years.
5 And these were born unto him in Je-
rusalem; Shĭm′e-a, and Shō′băb, and
Nāthan, and Solomon, four, of
Băth′-shū-a the daughter of Ăm′mī-el:
6 Ĭb′här also, and E-lĭsh′a-ma, and E-
lĭph′e-lĕt,
7 And Nō′gah, and Nē′phĕg, and Ja-
phī′a,
8 And E-lĭsh′a-ma, and E-lī′a-da, and
E-lĭph′e-lĕt, nine.
9 *These were* all the sons of David,
beside the sons of the concubines, and
Tā′mar their sister.
10 ¶And Solomon's son *was* Rē-ho-
bō′am, Ā-bī′a his son, Ā′sa his son, Je-
hŏsh′a-phăt his son,
11 Joram his son, Ā-ha-zī′ah his son,
Jō′ăsh his son,
12 Ăm-a-zī′ah his son, Ăz-a-rī′ah his
son, Jō′tham his son,
13 Ahaz his son, Hĕz-e-kī′ah his son,
Ma-năs′seh his son,
14 Ămon his son, Jō-sī′ah his son.
15 And the sons of Jō-sī′ah *were*, the
firstborn Jō-hā′nan, the second Je-
hoi′a-kĭm, the third Zĕd-e-kī′ah, the
fourth Shăl′lum.
16 And the sons of Je-hoi′a-kĭm: Jĕc-
o-nī′ah his son, Zĕd-e-kī′ah his son.

17 ¶And the sons of Jĕc-o-nī′ah; Ăs′-
sir, Sa-lā′thĭ-el his son,
18 Măl-chī′ram also, and Pe-dā′iah,
and She-nă′zar, Jĕc-a-mī′ah, Hŏsh′a-
ma, and Nĕd-a-bī′ah.
19 And the sons of Pe-dā′iah *were*,
Ze-rŭb′ba-bel, and Shĭm′e-ī: and the
sons of Ze-rŭb′ba-bel; Me-shŭl′lam,
and Hăn-a-nī′ah, and Shel′ō-mĭth their
sister:
20 And Ha-shū′bah, and Ō′hĕl, and
Bĕr-e-chī′ah, and Hăs-a-dī′ah, Jū′-
shab-hĕ′sĕd, five.
21 And the sons of Hăn-a-nī′ah; Pĕl-
a-tī′ah, and Je-sā′iah: the sons of Reph-
ā-i′ah, the sons of Arnan, the sons of Ō-
ba-dī′ah, the sons of Shĕch-a-nī′ah.
22 And the sons of Shĕch-a-nī′ah;
Shem-ā-i′ah: and the sons of Shem-ā-i-
ah; Hăt′tŭsh, and Ĭg′e-al, and Ba-rī′ah,
and Nē-a-rī′ah, and Shā′phat, six.
23 And the sons of Nē′a-rī′ah; Ē-lī-ō-
ĕ′na-ī, and Hĕz-e-kī′ah, and Ăz′ri-kam,
three.
24 And the sons of Ē-lī-ō-ē′na-ī *were*,
Hŏd-ā-i′ah, and E-lī′a-shĭb, and Pel-ā-
i′ah, and Ăk′kŭb, and Jō-hā′nan, and
Dal-ā-i′ah, and An-ā′nī, seven.

CHAPTER 4

THE sons of Jūdah; Phâ′rĕz, Hĕz′ron,
and Căr′mī, and Hur, and Shō′bal.
2 And Rē-ā-i′ah the son of Shō′bal be-
gat Jă′hăth; and Jă′hăth begat A-
hū′ma-ī, and Lā′hăd. These *are* the fam-
ilies of the Zô′rath-ītes.
3 And these *were of* the father of
Ē′tam; Jĕz′re-el, and Ĭsh′ma, and Ĭd′-
băsh: and the name of their sister *was*
Hăz′e-lĕl-pō′nī:
4 And Pe-nū′el the father of Gē′dôr,
and Ē′zer the father of Hu′shah. These
are the sons of Hur, the firstborn of
Ĕph′ra-tăh, the father of Bĕth-lehĕm.
5 ¶And Ashur the father of Te-kō′a
had two wives, Hē′lah and Nā′a-rah.
6 And Nā′a-rah bare him A-hū′zam,
and Hē′pher, and Tĕm′e-nī, and Hā-a-
hăsh′ta-rī. These *were* the sons of Nā′a-
rah.
7 And the sons of Hē′lah *were*, Ze′-
reth, and Je-zō′ar, and Ĕth′nan.
8 And Coz begat Ā′nŭb, and Zō-
bĕ′bah, and the families of A-hâr′hĕl the
son of Hâ′rum.
9 ¶And Jā′bez was more honourable
than his brethren: and his mother
called his name Jā′bez, saying, Because
I bare him with sorrow.
10 And Jā′bez called on the God of
Israel, saying, Oh that thou wouldest
bless me indeed, and enlarge my coast,
and that thine hand might be with me,
and that thou wouldest keep *me* from
evil, that it may not grieve me! And
God granted him that which he re-
quested.
11 ¶And Chē′lŭb the brother of Shū′-
ah begat Mē′hir, which *was* the father
of Ĕsh′ton.
12 And Ĕsh′ton begat Bĕth-rā′pha,
and Pa-sē′ah, and Te-hĭn′nah the father
of Ĭr-nā′hăsh. These *are* the men of Rē′-
chăh.
13 And the sons of Kē′năz; Ŏth′nī-el,
and Se-ra-ī′ah: and the sons of Ŏth′nī-
el; Hā′thăth.
14 And Mē-ŏn′o-thaī begat Ŏph′rah:
and Se-ra-ī′ah begat Jō′ăb, the father of
the valley of Chăr′a-shĭm; for they
were craftsmen.
15 And the sons of Caleb the son of
Je-phŭn′neh; Ī′rū, Ē′lah, and Nā′am:
and the sons of Ē′lah, even Kē′năz.
16 And the sons of Jē′ha-lē′le-el;
Ziph, and Zī′phah, Tĭr′ī-a, and A-sâ′rē-
el.
17 And the sons of Ezra *were*, Jē′ther,
and Me′rĕd, and Ē′pher, and Jăl′ŏn: and
she bare Miriam, and Shăm′ma-ī, and
Ĭsh′bah the father of Ĕsh-te-mō′a.
18 And his wife Jē-hu-dī′jah bare
Je′rĕd the father of Gē′dôr, and Hē′ber
the father of Sō′chō, and Je-kū′thĭ-el
the father of Za-nō′ah. And these *are*
the sons of Bĭth′ī-ah the daughter of
Pharaoh, which Me′rĕd took.
19 And the sons of *his* wife Hō-dī′ah
the sister of Naham, the father of Keī′-
lah the Găr′mīte, and Ĕsh-te-mō′a the
Mā-ăch′a-thīte.
20 And the sons of Shī′mon *were*,
Ăm′nŏn, and Rĭn′nah, Bĕn-hā′nan, and
Tī′lon. And the sons of Ī′shī *were*, Zō′-
hĕth, and Bĕn-zō′hĕth.
21 ¶The sons of Shē′lah the son of Jū-
dah *were*, Er the father of Lē′cah, and
Lā′a-dah the father of Ma-rē′shah, and
the families of the house of them that
wrought fine linen, of the house of Ăsh-
bē′a,
22 And Jō′kĭm, and the men of Chō-
zē′ba, and Jō′ăsh, and Sâ′raph, who
had the dominion in Moab, and Jash′ū-
bī-lē′hĕm. And *these are* ancient
things.
23 These *were* the potters, and those
that dwelt among plants and hedges:
there they dwelt with the king for his
work.
24 ¶The sons of Simeon *were*, Nĕ-
mū′el, and Jā′mĭn, Jâ′rĭb, Ze′rah, *and*
Shā′ul:
25 Shăl′lum his son, Mĭb′săm his son,
Mĭsh′ma his son.
26 And the sons of Mĭsh′ma; Hă-
mu′ĕl his son, Zăc′chur his son, Shĭm′-
e-ī his son.
27 And Shĭm′e-ī had sixteen sons and
six daughters; but his brethren had not

many children, neither did all their family multiply, like to the children of Jūdah.
28 And they dwelt at Be'er-shē'ba, and Mŏl'a-dah, and Hā'zar-shū'al,
29 And at Bĭl'hah, and at Ē'zem, and at Tō'lăd,
30 And at Beth-ū'el, and at Hôr'mah, and at Ziklag,
31 And at Bĕth-mär'ca-bôth, and Hā'-zar-sū'sĭm, and at Bĕth-bir'e-ī, and at Shā'a-rā'im. These *were* their cities unto the reign of David.
32 And their villages *were*, Ē'tam, and Ā'ĭn, Rimmon, and Tō'chen, and Ā'shan, five cities:
33 And all their villages that *were* round about the same cities, unto Bā'al. These *were* their habitations, and their genealogy.
34 And Me-shō'băb, and Jăm-lĕch, and Jŏ'shah the son of Ăm-a-zī'ah,
35 And Jō'el, and Jehu the son of Jŏs-i-bī'ah, the son of Se-ra-ī'ah, the son of Ă'sī-el,
36 And Ĕ-lī-ō-ē'na-ī, and Jā-ak'ō-bah, and Jĕsh-o-hā'iah, and Aṡ-ā'iah, and Ā'-dī-el, and Jesim'ī-el, and Be-nā'iah,
37 And Zī'za the son of Shī'phī, the son of Ăl'lon, the son of Je-dā'iah, the son of Shĭm'rī, the son of Shem-ā-i'ah;
38 These mentioned by *their* names *were* princes in their families: and the house of their fathers increased greatly.
39 ¶And they went to the entrance of Gĕ'dôr, *even* unto the east side of the valley, to seek pasture for their flocks.
40 And they found fat pasture and good, and the land *was* wide, and quiet, and peaceable; for *they* of Ham had dwelt there of old.
41 And these written by name came in the days of Hĕz-e-kī'ah king of Jūdah, and smote their tents, and the habitations that were found there, and destroyed them utterly unto this day, and dwelt in their rooms: because *there was* pasture there for their flocks.
42 And *some* of them, *even* of the sons of Simeon, five hundred men, went to mount Sē'ir, having for their captains Pĕl-a-tī'ah, and Nē'a-rī'ah, and Reph-ā-i'ah, and Ŭz'zī-el, the sons of I'shī.
43 And they smote the rest of the Am'ā-lek-ītes that were escaped, and dwelt there unto this day.

CHAPTER 5

NOW the sons of Reuben the firstborn of Israel, (for he *was* the firstborn; but, forasmuch as he defiled his father's bed, his birthright was given unto the sons of Joseph the son of Israel: and the genealogy is not to be reckoned after the birthright.
2 For Jūdah prevailed above his brethren, and of him *came* the chief ruler; but the birthright *was* Joseph's:)
3 The sons, *I say*, of Reuben the firstborn of Israel *were*, Hā'nŏch, and Păl'-lū, Hĕz'ron, and Cär'mī.
4 The sons of Jō'el; Shem-ā-i'ah his son, Gog his son, Shĭm'e-ī his son,
5 Mī'cah his son, Rē-ā-ī'a his son, Bā'al his son,
6 Bē-ē'rah his son, whom Tĭl'găth-pĭl-nē'ṡer king of Assyria carried away *captive*: he *was* prince of the Reubenites.
7 And his brethren by their families, when the genealogy of their generations was reckoned, *were* the chief, Je-ī'el, and Zĕch-a-rī'ah,
8 And Bē'la the son of Ā'zăz, the son of Shē'ma, the son of Jō'el, who dwelt in Ar'ō-er, even unto Nebo and Bā'al-mē'on:
9 And eastward he inhabited unto the entering in of the wilderness from the river Eū-phrā'tēṡ: because their cattle were multiplied in the land of Gilead.
10 And in the days of Saul they made wa. with the Hă'gar-ītes, who fell by their hand: and they dwelt in their tents throughout all the east *land* of Gilead.
11 ¶And the children of Gad dwelt over against them, in the land of Bā'-shan unto Săl'cah:
12 Jō'el the chief, and Shā'pham the next, and Jā-a'naī, and Shā'phat in Bā'shan.
13 And their brethren of the house of their fathers *were*, Michael, and Me-shūl'lam, and Shē'ba, and Jô'raī, and Jā'chan, and Zī'a, and Hē'ber, seven.
14 These *are* the children of Ăb-i-hā'il the son of Hū'rī, the son of Ja-rō'ah, the son of Gilead, the son of Michael, the son of Je-shĭsh'a-ī, the son of Jăh'dō, the son of Buz;
15 Ā'hī the son of Ăb'dī-el, the son of Gū'nī, chief of the house of their fathers.
16 And they dwelt in Gilead in Bā'-shan, and in her towns, and in all the suburbs of Shâr'on, upon their borders.
17 All these were reckoned by genealogies in the days of Jō'tham king of Jūdah, and in the days of Jĕr-o-bō'am king of Israel.
18 ¶The sons of Reuben, and the Găd'-ītes, and half the tribe of Ma-năs'seh, of valiant men, men able to bear buckler and sword, and to shoot with bow, and skilful in war, *were* four and forty thousand seven hundred and threescore, that went out to the war.
19 And they made war with the Hā'-

gar-ītes, with Jē'tur, and Nē'phĭsh, and Nō'dăb.
20 And they were helped against them, and the Hă'gar-ītes were delivered into their hand, and all that *were* with them: for they cried to God in the battle, and he was intreated of them; because they put their trust in him.
21 And they took away their cattle; of their camels fifty thousand, and of sheep two hundred and fifty thousand, and of asses two thousand, and of men an hundred thousand.
22 For there fell down many slain, because the war *was* of God. And they dwelt in their steads until the captivity.
23 ¶And the children of the half tribe of Ma-năs'seh dwelt in the land: they increased from Bā'shan unto Bā'al-hermon and Sē'nir, and unto mount Hermon.
24 And these *were* the heads of the house of their fathers, even Ē'pher, and I'shī, and E-lī'el, and Ăz'rī-el, and Jĕr-e-mī'ah, and Hŏd-a-vī'ah, and Jăh'dī-el, mighty men of valour, famous men, *and* heads of the house of their fathers.
25 ¶And they transgressed against the God of their fathers, and went a whoring after the gods of the people of the land, whom God destroyed before them.
26 And the God of Israel stirred up the spirit of Pul king of Assyria, and the spirit of Tĭl'găth-pĭl-nē'ser king of Assyria and he carried them away, even the Reubenites, and the Găd'ītes, and the half tribe of Ma-năs'seh, and brought them unto Hā'lah, and Hā'bôr, and Hâ'ra, and to the river Gō'zăn, unto this day.

CHAPTER 6

THE sons of Levi; Ger'shon, Kō'hăth, and Me-râ'rī.
2 And the sons of Kō'hăth; Ăm'răm, Ĭz'här, and Hē'bron, and Ŭz'zī-el.
3 And the children of Ăm'răm; Aaron, and Moses, and Miriam. The sons also of Aaron; Nā'dăb, and A-bī'hū, Ĕ-le-ā'zar, and Ĭth'a-mär.
4 Ĕ-le-ā'zar begat Phĭn'e-has, Phĭn'e-has begat A-bĭsh'ū-a,
5 And A-bĭsh'ū-a begat Bŭk'kī, and Bŭk'kī begat Ŭz'zi,
6 And Ŭz'zi begat Zĕr-a-hī'ah, and Zĕr-a-hī'ah begat Me-rā'ioth,
7 Me-rā'ioth begat Ăm-a-rī'ah, and Ăm-a-rī'ah begat A-hī'tŭb,
8 And A-hī'tŭb begat Zā'dŏk, and Zā'dŏk begat A-hĭm'ă-az,
9 And A-hĭm'ă-az begat Ăz-a-rī'ah, and Ăz-a-rī'ah begat Jō-hā'nan,
10 And Jō-hā'nan begat Ăz-a-rī'ah, (he *it is* that executed the priest's office in the temple that Solomon built in Jerusalem:)
11 And Ăz-a-rī'ah begat Ăm-a-rī'ah, and Ăm-a-rī'ah begat A-hī'tŭb,
12 And A-hī'tŭb begat Zā'dŏk, and Zā'dŏk begat Shăl'lum,
13 And Shăl'lum begat Hĭl-kī'ah, and Hĭl-kī'ah begat Ăz-a-rī'ah,
14 And Ăz-a-rī'ah begat Se-ra-ī'ah, and Se-ra-ī'ah begat Je-hōz'a-dăk.
15 And Je-hōz'a-dăk went *into captivity*, when the LORD carried away Jū'dah and Jerusalem by the hand of Nĕb-u-chad-nĕz'zar.
16 ¶The sons of Levi; Ger'shom, Kō'hăth, and Me-râ'rī.
17 And these *be* the names of the sons of Ger'shom; Lĭb'nī, and Shĭm'e-ī.
18 And the sons of Kō'hăth *were*, Ăm'răm, and Ĭz'här, and Hē'bron, and Ŭz'zī-el.
19 The sons of Me-râ'rī; Măh'lī, and Mū'shī. And these *are* the families of the Lē'vītes according to their fathers.
20 Of Ger'shom; Lĭb'nī his son, Jā'hăth his son, Zimmah his son,
21 Jō'ah his son, Ĭd'dō his son, Ze'rah his son, Jē-ăt'e-raī his son.
22 The sons of Kō'hăth; Am-mĭn'a-dăb his son, Kô'rah his son, Ăs'sir his son,
23 Ĕl'kā-nah his son, and E-bī'a-săph his son, and Ăs'sir his son,
24 Tā'hăth his son, Ū'rī-el his son, Uz-zī'ah his son, and Shā'ul his son.
25 And the sons of Ĕl'kā-nah; A-măs'a-ī, and A-hī'moth.
26 *As for* Ĕl'kā-nah: the sons of Ĕl'kā-nah; Zō'phaī his son, and Nā'hăth his son,
27 E-lī'ab his son, Jer'ō-hăm his son, Ĕl'kā-nah his son.
28 And the sons of Samuel; the firstborn Văsh'nī, and Ā-bī'ah.
29 The sons of Me-râ'rī; Măh'lī, Lĭb'nī his son, Shĭm'e-ī his son, Ŭz'za his son,
30 Shĭm'e-a his son, Hăg-gī'ah his son, Aṡ-ā'iah his son.
31 And these *are they* whom David set over the service of song in the house of the LORD, after that the ark had rest.
32 And they ministered before the dwelling place of the tabernacle of the congregation with singing, until Solomon had built the house of the LORD in Jerusalem: and *then* they waited on their office according to their order.
33 And these *are* they that waited with their children. Of the sons of the Kō'hăth-ītes: Hē'man a singer, the son of Jō'el the son of Shĕ-mū'el,
34 The son of Ĕl'kā-nah, the son of Jer'ō-hăm, the son of E-lī'el, the son of Tō'ah,

35 The son of Zuph, the son of Ĕl′kā-
nah, the son of Mā′hăth, the son of A-
măs′a-ī,
36 The son of Ĕl′kā-nah, the son of
Jō′el, the son of Ăz-a-rī′ah, the son of
Zĕph-a-nī′ah,
37 The son of Tā′hăth, the son of Ăs′-
sir, the son of E-bī′a-săph, the son of
Kô′rah,
38 The son of Īz′här, the son of Kō′hăth,
the son of Levi, the son of Israel.
39 And his brother Ā′săph, who stood
on his right hand, *even* Ā′săph the son
of Bĕr-a-chī′ah, the son of Shĭm′e-a,
40 The son of Michael, the son of
Bā′a-sē′iah, the son of Măl-chī′ah,
41 The son of Ĕth′nī, the son of
Ze′rah, the son of Ăd-a-ī′ah,
42 The son of Ē′than, the son of Zim-
mah, the son of Shĭm′e-ī,
43 The son of Jā′hăth, the son of
Ger′shom, the son of Levi.
44 And their brethren the sons of Me-
râ′rī *stood* on the left hand: Ē′than the
son of Kĭsh′ī, the son of Ăb′dī, the son of
Măl′luch,
45 The son of Hăsh-a-bī′ah, the son of
Ăm-a-zī′ah, the son of Hĭl-kī′ah,
46 The son of Ăm′zī, the son of Bā′nī,
the son of Shā′mer,
47 The son of Măh′lī, the son of Mū′-
shī, the son of Me-râ′rī, the son of Levi.
48 Their brethren also the Lē′vītes
were appointed unto all manner of ser-
vice of the tabernacle of the house of
God.
49 ¶But Aaron and his sons offered
upon the altar of the burnt offering, and
on the altar of incense, *and were ap-
pointed* for all the work of the *place*
most holy, and to make an atonement
for Israel, according to all that Moses
the servant of God had commanded.
50 And these *are* the sons of Aaron;
Ĕ-le-ā′zar his son, Phĭn′e-has his son,
A-bĭsh′ū-a his son,
51 Bŭk′kī his son, Ūz′zi his son, Zĕr-a-
hī′ah his son,
52 Me-rā′ioth his son, Ăm-a-rī′ah his
son, A-hī′tūb his son,
53 Zā′dŏk his son, A-hĭm′ā-az his son.
54 ¶Now these *are* their dwelling
places throughout their castles in their
coasts, of the sons of Aaron, of the fam-
ilies of the Kō′hăth-ītes: for theirs
was the lot.
55 And they gave them Hē′bron in
the land of Jū′dah, and the suburbs
thereof round about it.
56 But the fields of the city, and the
villages thereof, they gave to Caleb the
son of Je-phŭn′neh.
57 And to the sons of Aaron they
gave the cities of Jū′dah, *namely*, Hē′-
bron, *the city* of refuge, and Lĭb′nah
with her suburbs, and Jăt′tir, and Ĕsh-
te-mō′a, with their suburbs,
58 And Hī′len with her suburbs, Dē′-
bir with her suburbs,
59 And Ā′shan with her suburbs, and
Bĕth-shĕ′mesh with her suburbs:
60 And out of the tribe of Benjamin;
Gē′ba with her suburbs, and Ăl′e-meth
with her suburbs, and Ăn′a-thŏth with
her suburbs. All their cities throughout
their families *were* thirteen cities.
61 And unto the sons of Kō′hăth,
which were left of the family of that
tribe, *were cities given* out of the half
tribe, *namely, out of* the half *tribe* of
Ma-năs′seh, by lot, ten cities.
62 And to the sons of Ger′shom
throughout their families out of the
tribe of Ĭs′sa-char, and out of the tribe
of Asher, and out of the tribe of Năph′-
ta-lī, and out of the tribe of Ma-năs′-
seh in Bā′shan, thirteen cities.
63 Unto the sons of Me-râ′rī *were giv-
en* by lot, throughout their families,
out of the tribe of Reuben, and out of
the tribe of Gad, and out of the tribe of
Zĕb′u-lun, twelve cities.
64 And the children of Israel gave to
the Lē′vītes *these* cities with their sub-
urbs.
65 And they gave by lot out of the
tribe of the children of Jū′dah, and out
of the tribe of the children of Simeon,
and out of the tribe of the children of
Benjamin, these cities, which are called
by *their* names.
66 And *the residue* of the families of
the sons of Kō′hăth had cities of their
coasts out of the tribe of Ē′phra-im.
67 And they gave unto them, *of* the
cities of refuge, Shĕ′chem in mount
Ē′phra-im with her suburbs; *they gave*
also Gē′zer with her suburbs,
68 And Jŏk′me-am with her suburbs,
and Bĕth-hô′ron with her suburbs,
69 And Āij′a-lŏn with her suburbs,
and Găth-rĭm′mon with her suburbs:
70 And out of the half tribe of Ma-
năs′seh; Aner with her suburbs, and
Bĭl′e-am with her suburbs, for the fam-
ily of the remnant of the sons of Kō′-
hăth.
71 Unto the sons of Ger′shom *were
given* out of the family of the half tribe
of Ma-năs′seh, Gō′lan in Bā′shan with
her suburbs, and Ăsh′ta-rŏth with her
suburbs:
72 And out of the tribe of Ĭs′sa-char;
Kē′dĕsh with her suburbs, Dăb′e-răth
with her suburbs,
73 And Rā′mŏth with her suburbs,
and Ā′nem with her suburbs:
74 And out of the tribe of Asher;
Mā′shal with her suburbs, and Ăb′dŏn
with her suburbs,

75 And Hū'kŏk with her suburbs, and Rē'hŏb with her suburbs:
76 And out of the tribe of Năph'ta-lī; Kē'dĕsh in Galilee with her suburbs, and Hăm'mon with her suburbs, and Kĭr-jath-ā'ĭm with her suburbs.
77 Unto the rest of the children of Me-râ'rī *were given* out of the tribe of Zĕb'u-lun, Rimmon with her suburbs, Tā'bor with her suburbs:
78 And on the other side Jordan by Jericho, on the east side of Jordan, *were given them* out of the tribe of Reuben, Bē'zer in the wilderness with her suburbs, and Jăh'zah with her suburbs,
79 Kĕd'e-mŏth also with her suburbs, and Mĕph'a-ăth with her suburbs:
80 And out of the tribe of Gad; Rā'mŏth in Gilead with her suburbs, and Mā'ha-nā'im with her suburbs,
81 And Hĕsh'bŏn with her suburbs, and Jā'zer with her suburbs.

CHAPTER 7

NOW the sons of Ĭs'sa-char *were*, Tō'la, and Pū'ah, Jāsh'ub, and Shĭm'rŏm, four.
2 And the sons of Tō'la; Ūz'zi, and Reph-ā-i'ah, and Je'rī-el, and Jăh'ma-ī, and Jĭb'săm, and Shĕ-mū'el, heads of their father's house, *to wit*, of Tō'la: *they were* valiant men of might in their generations; whose number *was* in the days of David two and twenty thousand and six hundred.
3 And the sons of Ūz'zi; Ĭz-ra-hī'ah: and the sons of Ĭz-ra-hī'ah; Michael, and Ō-ba-dī'ah, and Jō'el, Ī-shī'ah, five: all of them chief men.
4 And with them, by their generations, after the house of their fathers, *were* bands of soldiers for war, six and thirty thousand *men*: for they had many wives and sons.
5 And their brethren among all the families of Ĭs'sa-char *were* valiant men of might, reckoned in all by their genealogies fourscore and seven thousand.
6 ¶*The sons* of Benjamin; Bē'la, and Bē'cher, and Je-dī'a-el, three.
7 And the sons of Bē'la; Ĕz'bŏn, and Ūz'zi, Ŭz'zī-el, and Jĕr'ī-mŏth, and Ī'rī, five; heads of the house of *their* fathers, mighty men of valour; and were reckoned by their genealogies twenty and two thousand and thirty and four.
8 And the sons of Bē'cher; Ze-mī'ra, and Jō'ăsh, and Ē-lī-ē'zer, and Ē-lī-ō-ē'na-ī, and Omri, and Jĕr'ī-mŏth, and Ă-bī'ah, and Ăn'a-thŏth, and Ăl'a-meth. All these *are* the sons of Bē'cher.
9 And the number of them, after their genealogy by their generations, heads of the house of their fathers, mighty men of valour, *was* twenty thousand and two hundred.
10 The sons also of Je-dī'a-el; Bĭl'hăn: and the sons of Bĭl'hăn; Jē'ŭsh, and Benjamin, and Ē'hŭd, and Che-nā'a-nah, and Zē'than, and Thär'shĭsh, and A-hĭsh'a-här.
11 All these the sons of Je-dī'a-el, by the heads of their fathers, mighty men of valour, *were* seventeen thousand and two hundred *soldiers*, fit to go out for war *and* battle.
12 Shŭp'pĭm also, and Hŭp'pĭm, the children of Ir, *and* Hu'shĭm, the sons of Ā'her.
13 ¶The sons of Năph'ta-lī; Jăh'zī-el, and Gū'nī, and Jē'zer, and Shăl'lum, the sons of Bĭl'hah.
14 ¶The sons of Ma-năs'seh; Ăsh'rī-el, whom she bare: (*but* his concubine the Ă'ram-ĭt-ess bare Mā'chĭr the father of Gilead:
15 And Mā'chĭr took to wife *the sister* of Hŭp'pĭm and Shŭp'pĭm, whose sister's name *was* Mā'a-chah;) and the name of the second *was* Ze-lō'phe-hăd: and Ze-lō'phe-hăd had daughters.
16 And Mā'a-chah the wife of Mā'chĭr bare a son, and she called his name Pe'rĕsh; and the name of his brother *was* She'rĕsh; and his sons *were* Ū'lam and Rā'kĕm.
17 And the sons of Ū'lam; Bē'dăn. These *were* the sons of Gilead, the son of Mā'chĭr, the son of Ma-năs'seh.
18 And his sister Hăm-mŏl'e-kĕth bare Ī'shŏd, and Ă-bī-ē'zer, and Mă-hā'lăh.
19 And the sons of She-mī'dah were, A-hī'an, and Shĕ'chem, and Lĭk'hī, and A'nī-am.
20 ¶And the sons of Ē'phra-im; Shū'the-lah, and Be'rĕd his son, and Tā'hăth his son, and Ĕl'a-dah his son, and Tā'hăth his son,
21 And Zā'băd his son, and Shū'the-lah his son, and Ē'zer, and Ĕ'le-ad, whom the men of Gath *that were* born in *that* land slew, because they came down to take away their cattle.
22 And Ē'phra-im their father mourned many days, and his brethren came to comfort him.
23 ¶And when he went in to his wife, she conceived, and bare a son, and he called his name Be-rī'ah, because it went evil with his house.
24 (And his daughter *was* Shĕ'rah, who built Bĕth–hō'ron the nether, and the upper, and Ŭz'zen–shē'rah.)
25 And Rē'phah *was* his son, also Rē'shĕph, and Tē'lah his son, and Tā'hăn his son,
26 Lā'a-dan his son, Ăm-mī'hŭd his son, E-lĭsh'a-ma his son,

27 Non his son, Je-hŏsh'u-ah his son.
28 ¶And their possessions and habi-
tations *were*, Bĕth-el and the towns
thereof, and eastward Nā'a-răn, and
westward Gē'zer, with the towns there-
of; Shĕ'chem also and the towns
thereof, unto Gā'za and the towns
thereof:
29 And by the borders of the children
of Ma-năs'seh, Bĕth-shē'an and her
towns, Tā'a-năch and her towns, Me-
gĭd'dō and her towns, Dor and her
towns. In these dwelt the children of
Joseph the son of Israel.
30 ¶The sons of Asher; Ĭm'nah, and
Ĭs'ū-ah, and Ĭsh'ū-ai, and Be-rī'ah, and
Se'rah their sister.
31 And the sons of Be-rī'ah; Hē'ber,
and Măl'chĭ-el, who *is* the father of Bir'-
zā-vĭth.
32 And Hē'ber begat Jăph'let, and
Shō'mer, and Hō'tham, and Shū'a their
sister.
33 And the sons of Jăph'let; Pā'săch,
and Bĭm'hăl, and Ăsh'văth. These *are*
the children of Jăph'let.
34 And the sons of Shā'mer; Ā'hī, and
Rōh'gah, Je-hub'bah, and Â'ram.
35 And the sons of his brother Hē'-
lĕm; Zō'phah, and Ĭm'na, and Shē'lesh,
and Ā'mal.
36 The sons of Zō'phah; Sū'ah, and
Här'ne-pher, and Shū'al, and Be'rī, and
Ĭm'rah,
37 Bē'zer, and Hod, and Shăm'ma,
and Shĭl'shah, and Ĭth'răn, and Be-ē'ra.
38 And the sons of Jē'ther; Je-phŭn'-
neh, and Pĭs'pah, and Â'ra.
39 And the sons of Ūl'la; Ā'rah, and
Hăn'ī-el, and Re-zī'a.
40 All these *were* the children of
Asher, heads of *their* father's house,
choice *and* mighty men of valour, chief
of the princes. And the number
throughout the genealogy of them that
were apt to the war *and* to battle *was*
twenty and six thousand men.

CHAPTER 8

NOW Benjamin begat Bē'la his first-
born, Ăsh'bĕl the second, and A-hâr'ah
the third,
2 Nō'hah the fourth, and Rā'pha the
fifth.
3 And the sons of Bē'la were, Ăd'där,
and Ge'ra, and A-bī'hŭd,
4 And A-bĭsh'ū-a, and Nā'a-man, and
A-hō'ah,
5 And Ge'ra, and She-phū'phan, and
Hū'ram.
6 And these *are* the sons of Ē'hŭd:
these are the heads of the fathers of the
inhabitants of Gē'ba, and they removed
them to Măn'a-hăth:
7 And Nā'a-man, and A-hī'ah, and
Ge'ra, he removed them, and begat
Ŭz'za, and A-hī'hŭd.
8 And Shā-ha-rā'im begat *children* in
the country of Moab, after he had sent
them away; Hu'shĭm and Bā'a-ra *were*
his wives.
9 And he begat of Hō'dĕsh his wife,
Jō'băb, and Zĭb'ī-a, and Mē'sha, and
Măl'chăm,
10 And Jē'ŭz, and Sha-chī'a, and
Mir'ma. These *were* his sons, heads of
the fathers.
11 And of Hu'shĭm he begat Ab'ī-tŭb,
and Ĕl'pā-al.
12 The sons of Ĕl'pā-al; Ē'ber, and
Mī'shăm, and Shā'med, who built Ō'nō,
and Lod, with the towns thereof:
13 Be-rī'ah also, and Shē'ma, who
were heads of the fathers of the inhabi-
tants of Āij'a-lŏn, who drove away the
inhabitants of Gath:
14 And A-hī'o, Shā'shăk, and Jĕr'e-
mŏth,
15 And Zĕb-a-dī'ah, and Â'răd and
Ā'der,
16 And Michael, and Ĭs'pah, and
Jō'ha, the sons of Be-rī'ah;
17 And Zĕb-a-dī'ah, and Me-shŭl'-
lam, and Hez'e-kī, and Hē'ber,
18 Ĭsh'me-raī also, and Jez-lī'ah, and
Jō'băb, the sons of Ĕl'pā-al;
19 And Jakim, and Zĭch'rī, and Zăb'-
dī,
20 And Ĕ-lī-ē'na-ī, and Zĭl'thaī, and
E-lī'el,
21 And Ăd-a-ī'ah, and Bĕr-a-ī'ah, and
Shĭm'răth, the sons of Shĭm'hī;
22 And Ĭsh'păn, and Hē'ber, and
E-lī'el,
23 And Ăbdŏn, and Zĭch'rī, and Hā'-
nan,
24 And Hăn-a-nī'ah, and Ē'lam, and
Ăn-tō-thī'jah,
25 And Ĭph-e-dē'iah, and Pe-nū'el, the
sons of Shā'shăk;
26 And Shăm-she-ra'ī, and Shē-ha-
rī'ah, and Ăth-a-lī'ah,
27 And Jâr-e-sī'ah, and E-lī'ah, and
Zĭch'rī, the sons of Jer'ō-hăm.
28 These *were* heads of the fathers,
by their generations, chief *men*. These
dwelt in Jerusalem.
29 And at Gibeon dwelt the father of
Gibeon; whose wife's name *was* Mā'a-
chah:
30 And his firstborn son Ăbdŏn, and
Zur, and Kish, and Bā'al, and Nā'dăb,
31 And Gē'dôr, and A-hī'o, and Zā'-
cher,
32 And Mĭk'lŏth begat Shĭm'e-ah.
And these also dwelt with their breth-
ren in Jerusalem, over against them.
33 ¶And Ner begat Kish, and Kish be-
gat Saul, and Saul begat Jonathan, and

Măl′chī–shu′a, and A-bĭn′a-dăb, and
Ĕsh–bā′al.
34 And the son of Jonathan *was* Mĕr′-
ib–bā′al; and Mĕr′ib–bā′al begat Mī′cah.
35 And the sons of Mī′cah *were*, Pī′-
thŏn, and Mē′lĕch, and Tâ′re-a, and
Ahaz.
36 And Ahaz begat Je-hō′a-dah; and
Je-hō′a-dah begat Ăl′e-meth, and
Ăz′ma-vĕth, and Zimri; and Zimri be-
gat Mō′za.
37 And Mō′za begat Bĭn′e-a: Rā′pha
was his son, Ĕ-le′ā-sah his son, Ā′zel his
son:
38 And Ā′zel had six sons, whose
names *are* these, Ăz′ri-kam, Bōch′e-rū,
and Ĭsh′ma-el, and Shē-a-rī′ah, and Ō-
ba-dī′ah, and Hā′nan. All these *were*
the sons of Ā′zel.
39 And the sons of Ē′shĕk his brother
were, Ū′lam his firstborn, Jē′hŭsh the
second, and E-lĭph′e-lĕt the third.
40 And the sons of Ū′lam were
mighty men of valour, archers, and had
many sons, and sons' sons, an hundred
and fifty. All these *are* of the sons of
Benjamin.

CHAPTER 9

SO all Israel were reckoned by gene-
alogies; and, behold, they *were* written
in the book of the kings of Israel and
Jū′dah, *who* were carried away to Baby-
lon for their transgression.
2 ¶Now the first inhabitants that
dwelt in their possessions in their cities
were, the Israelites, the priests, Lē′-
vītes, and the Nĕth′i-nĭms.
3 And in Jerusalem dwelt of the
children of Jū′dah, and of the children
of Benjamin, and of the children of
Ē′phra-im, and Ma-năs′seh;
4 Ū′tha-ī the son of Ăm-mī′hŭd, the
son of Omri, the son of Ĭm′rī, the son of
Bā′nī, of the children of Phâ′rĕz the son
of Jū′dah.
5 And of the Shī′lo-nītes; A-ṡā′iah
the firstborn, and his sons.
6 And of the sons of Ze′rah; Je-ū′el,
and their brethren, six hundred and
ninety.
7 And of the sons of Benjamin; Săl′lū
the son of Me-shŭl′lam, the son of Hŏd-
a-vī′ah, the son of Hăs-e-nū′ah,
8 And Ĭb-nē′iah the son of Jer′ō-hăm,
and Ē′lah the son of Ŭz′zi, the son of
Mĭch′rī, and Me-shŭl′lam the son of
Sheph-a-thi′ah, the son of Re-ū′el, the
son of Ĭb-nī′jah;
9 And their brethren, according to
their generations, nine hundred and
fifty and six. All these men *were* chief
of the fathers in the house of their fa-
thers.
10 ¶And of the priests; Je-dā′iah, and
Je-hoi′a-rĭb, and Jā′chin,
11 And Ăz-a-rī′ah the son of Hĭl-kī′-
ah, the son of Me-shŭl′lam, the son of
Zā′dŏk, the son of Me-rā′ioth, the son
of A-hī′tŭb, the ruler of the house of
God;
12 And Ăd-a-ī′ah the son of Jer′ō-
hăm, the son of Păsh′ur, the son of Măl-
chī′jah, and Mā-ăs′ī-aī the son of Ā′dĭ-
el, the son of Jăh′ze-rah, the son of Me-
shŭl′lam, the son of Me-shĭl′le-mĭth,
the son of Ĭm′mer;
13 And their brethren, heads of the
house of their fathers, a thousand and
seven hundred and threescore; very
able men for the work of the service of
the house of God.
14 ¶And of the Lē′vītes; Shem-ā-i′ah
the son of Hăs′shub, the son of Ăz′ri-
kam, the son of Hăsh-a-bī′ah, of the
sons of Me-râ′rī;
15 And Băk-băk′kar, He′rĕsh, and Gā′-
lăl, and Măt-ta-nī′ah the son of Mī′cah,
the son of Zĭch′rī, the son of Ā′săph;
16 And Ō-ba-dī′ah the son of Shem-ā-
i′ah, the son of Gā′lăl, the son of Jed′ū-
thun, and Bĕr-e-chī′ah the son of Ā′sa,
the son of Ĕl′kā-nah, that dwelt in the
villages of the Ne-tōph′a-thītes.
17 And the porters *were*, Shăl′lum,
and Ăk′kŭb, and Tăl′mon, and A-hī′-
man, and their brethren: Shăl′lum *was*
the chief;
18 Who hitherto *waited* in the king's
gate eastward: they *were* porters in the
companies of the children of Levi.
19 And Shăl′lum the son of Kô′re, the
son of E-bī′a-săph, the son of Kô′rah,
and his brethren, of the house of his
father, the Kô′rah-ītes, *were* over the
work of the service, keepers of the
gates of the tabernacle: and their fa-
thers, *being* over the host of the LORD,
were keepers of the entry.
20 And Phĭn′e-has the son of Ĕ-le-ā′-
zar was the ruler over them in time
past, *and* the LORD *was* with him.
21 *And* Zĕch-a-rī′ah the son of Me-
shĕl-e-mī′ah *was* porter of the door of
the tabernacle of the congregation.
22 All these *which were* chosen to be
porters in the gates *were* two hundred
and twelve. These were reckoned by
their genealogy in their villages, whom
David and Samuel the seer did ordain
in their set office.
23 So they and their children *had* the
oversight of the gates of the house of
the LORD, *namely*, the house of the tab-
ernacle, by wards.
24 In four quarters were the porters,
toward the east, west, north, and south.
25 And their brethren, *which were* in
their villages, *were* to come after seven
days from time to time with them.
26 For these Lē′vītes, the four chief

porters, were in *their* set office, and were over the chambers and treasuries of the house of God.

27 And they lodged round about the house of God, because the charge *was* upon them, and the opening thereof every morning *pertained* to them.

28 And *certain* of them had the charge of the ministering vessels, that they should bring them in and out by tale.

29 *Some* of them also *were* appointed to oversee the vessels, and all the instruments of the sanctuary, and the fine flour, and the wine, and the oil, and the frankincense, and the spices.

30 And *some* of the sons of the priests made the ointment of the spices.

31 And Măt-ti-thī'ah, *one* of the Lē'vītes, who *was* the firstborn of Shăl'lum the Kô'rah-īte, had the set office over the things that were made in the pans.

32 And *other* of their brethren, of the sons of the Kō'hăth-ītes, *were* over the shewbread, to prepare *it* every sabbath.

33 And these *are* the singers, chief of the fathers of the Lē'vītes, *who remaining* in the chambers *were* free: for they were employed in *that* work day and night.

34 These chief fathers of the Lē'vītes *were* chief throughout their generations; these dwelt at Jerusalem.

35 ¶And in Gibeon dwelt the father of Gibeon, Je-hī'el, whose wife's name *was* Mā'a-chah:

36 And his firstborn son Ăb'dŏn, then Zur, and Kish, and Bā'al, and Ner, and Nā'dăb,

37 And Gē'dôr, and A-hī'o, and Zĕch-a-rī'ah, and Mĭk'lŏth.

38 And Mĭk'lŏth begat Shim'e-am. And they also dwelt with their brethren at Jerusalem, over against their brethren.

39 And Ner begat Kish; and Kish begat Saul; and Saul begat Jonathan, and Măl'chī-shu'a, and A-bĭn'a-dăb, and Ĕsh-bā'al.

40 And the son of Jonathan *was* Mĕr'-ib-bā'al: and Mĕr'ib-bā'al begat Mī'cah.

41 And the sons of Mī'cah *were*, Pī'thŏn, and Mē'lĕch, and Täh're-a, *and Ahaz.*

42 And Ahaz begat Jâ'rah; and Jâ'rah begat Ăl'e-meth, and Ăz'ma-vĕth, and Zimri; and Zimri begat Mō'za;

43 And Mō'za begat Bĭn'e-a; and Reph-ā-i'ah his son, Ē-le'ā-sah his son, Ā'zel his son.

44 And Ā'zel had six sons, whose names *are* these, Ăz'ri-kam, Bōch'e-rū, and Ĭsh'ma-el, and Shē'a-rī-ah, and Ō-ba-dī'ah, and Hā'nan: these *were* the sons of Ā'zel.

CHAPTER 10

NOW the Philistines fought against Israel; and the men of Israel fled from before the Philistines, and fell down slain in mount Gĭl-bō'a.

2 And the Philistines followed hard after Saul, and after his sons; and the Philistines slew Jonathan, and A-bĭn'a-dăb, and Mal'chi-shu'a, the sons of Saul.

3 And the battle went sore against Saul, and the archers hit him, and he was wounded of the archers.

4 Then said Saul to his armourbearer, Draw thy sword, and thrust me through therewith; lest these uncircumcised come and abuse me. But his armourbearer would not; for he was sore afraid. So Saul took a sword, and fell upon it.

5 And when his armourbearer saw that Saul was dead, he fell likewise on the sword, and died.

6 So Saul died, and his three sons, and all his house died together.

7 And when all the men of Israel that *were* in the valley saw that they fled, and that Saul and his sons were dead, then they forsook their cities, and fled: and the Philistines came and dwelt in them.

8 ¶And it came to pass on the morrow, when the Philistines came to strip the slain, that they found Saul and his sons fallen in mount Gĭl-bō'a.

9 And when they had stripped him, they took his head, and his armour, and sent into the land of the Philistines round about, to carry tidings unto their idols, and to the people.

10 And they put his armour in the house of their gods, and fastened his head in the temple of Dā'gŏn.

11 ¶And when all Jā'besh-gĭl'e-ad heard all that the Philistines had done to Saul,

12 They arose, all the valiant men, and took away the body of Saul, and the bodies of his sons, and brought them to Jā'besh, and buried their bones under the oak in Jā'besh, and fasted seven days.

13 ¶So Saul died for his transgression which he committed against the LORD, *even* against the word of the LORD, which he kept not, and also for asking *counsel* of *one that had* a familiar spirit, to enquire *of it;*

14 And enquired not of the LORD: therefore he slew him, and turned the kingdom unto David the son of Jesse.

CHAPTER 11

THEN all Israel gathered themselves to David unto Hē'bron, saying, Behold, we *are* thy bone and thy flesh.

2 And moreover in time past, even when Saul was king, thou *wast* he that leddest out and broughtest in Israel: and the LORD thy God said unto thee, Thou shalt feed my people Israel, and thou shalt be ruler over my people Israel.

3 Therefore came all the elders of Israel to the king to Hē'bron; and David made a covenant with them in Hē'bron before the LORD; and they anointed David king over Israel, according to the word of the LORD by Samuel.

4 ¶And David and all Israel went to Jerusalem, which *is* Jē'bus; where the Jēb'u-sītes *were*, the inhabitants of the land.

5 And the inhabitants of Jē'bus said to David, Thou shalt not come hither. Nevertheless David took the castle of Zion, which *is* the city of David.

6 And David said, Whosoever smiteth the Jēb'u-sītes first shall be chief and captain. So Jō'ăb the son of Zer-ū-i'ah went first up, and was chief.

7 And David dwelt in the castle; therefore they called it the city of David.

8 And he built the city round about, even from Mĭl'lō round about: and Jō'ăb repaired the rest of the city.

9 So David waxed greater and greater: for the LORD of hosts *was* with him.

10 ¶These also *are* the chief of the mighty men whom David had, who strengthened themselves with him in his kingdom, *and* with all Israel, to make him king, according to the word of the LORD concerning Israel.

11 And this *is* the number of the mighty men whom David had; Jashō'be-am, an Hăch'mō-nīte, the chief of the captains: he lifted up his spear against three hundred slain *by him* at one time.

12 And after him *was* Ĕ-le-ā'zar the son of Dodo, the A-hō'hīte, who *was one* of the three mighties.

13 He was with David at Păs-dăm'mĭm, and there the Philistines where gathered together to battle, where was a parcel of ground full of barley; and the people fled from before the Philistines.

14 And they set themselves in the midst of *that* parcel, and delivered it, and slew the Philistines; and the LORD saved *them* by a great deliverance.

15 Now three of the thirty captains went down to the rock to David, into the cave of A-dŭl'lam; and the host of the Philistines encamped in the valley of Rĕph'a-im.

16 And David *was* then in the hold, and the Philistines' garrison *was* then at Bĕth-lehĕm.

17 And David longed, and said, Oh that one would give me drink of the water of the well of Bĕth-lehĕm, that *is* at the gate!

18 And the three brake through the host of the Philistines, and drew water out of the well of Bĕth-lehĕm, that *was* by the gate, and took *it*, and brought *it* to David: but David would not drink *of* it, but poured it out to the LORD,

19 And said, My God forbid it me, that I should do this thing: shall I drink the blood of these men that have put their lives in jeopardy? for with *the jeopardy of* their lives they brought it. Therefore he would not drink it. These things did these three mightiest.

20 And A-bī'shaī the brother of Jō'ăb, he was chief of the three: for lifting up his spear against three hundred, he slew *them*, and had a name among the three.

21 Of the three, he was more honourable than the two; for he was their captain: howbeit he attained not to the *first* three.

22 Be-nā'iah the son of Je-hoi'a-da, the son of a valiant man of Kăb'ze-el, who had done many acts; he slew two lionlike men of Moab: also he went down and slew a lion in a pit in a snowy day.

23 And he slew an Egyptian, a man of *great* stature, five cubits high; and in the Egyptian's hand *was* a spear like a weaver's beam; and he went down to him with a staff, and plucked the spear out of the Egyptian's hand, and slew him with his own spear.

24 These *things* did Be-nā'iah the son of Je-hoi'a-da, and had the name among the three mighties.

25 Behold, he was honourable among the thirty, but attained not to the *first* three: and David set him over his guard.

26 Also the valiant men of the armies *were*, Ă'sa-hĕl the brother of Jō'ăb, Ĕl-hā'nan the son of Dodo of Bĕth-lehĕm,

27 Shăm'mŏth the Hâ'ro-rīte, Hē'lĕz the Pĕl'o-nīte,

28 Ī'ra the son of Ĭk'kesh the Te-kō'-īte, Ă'bī-e'zer the Ăn'toth-īte,

29 Sĭb'be-caī the Hu'shath-īte, Ī'laī the A-hō'hīte,

30 Mā-har'a-ī the Ne-tōph'a-thīte, Hē'lĕd the son of Bā'a-nah the Ne-tōph'a-thīte,

31 Ĭth'a-ī the son of Rī'baī of Gĭb'e-ah,

that pertained to the children of Benjamin, Be-nā'iah the Pĭr'a-thŏn-īte,
32 Hū'raī of the brooks of Gā'ash, Ā'bī-el the Är'bath-īte,
33 Ăz'ma-vĕth the Ba'hâ'rūm-īte, E-lī'ah-ba the Shā-ăl'bo-nīte,
34 The sons of Hā'shĕm the Gī'zo-nīte, Jonathan the son of Shā'ge the Hâ'ra-rīte,
35 A-hī'am the son of Sa'car the Hâ'ra-rīte, El'ī-phal the son of Ur,
36 Hē'pher the Me-chĕ'rath-īte, A-hī'jah the Pĕl'o-nīte,
37 Hĕz'rō the Carmelite, Nā'a-raī the son of Ĕz'ba-ī,
38 Jō'el the brother of Nā'than, Mĭb'här the son of Hăg'ge-rī,
39 Zē'lĕk the Ammonite, Nā-har'a-ī the Be'roth-īte, the armourbearer of Jō'ăb the son of Zer-ū-ī'ah,
40 Ī'ra the Ĭth'rīte, Gâ'rĕb the Ĭth'rīte,
41 Ū-rī'ah the Hittite, Zā'băd the son of Äh'laī,
42 Ăd'i-na the son of Shī'za the Reubenite, a captain of the Reubenites, and thirty with him,
43 Hā'nan the son of Mā'a-chah, and Jŏsh'a-phăt the Mĭth'nīte,
44 Uz-zī'a the Ăsh'te-răth-īte, Shā'ma and Je-hī'el the sons of Hō'than the Ar'ō-er-īte,
45 Je-dī'a-el the son of Shĭm'rī, and Jō'ha his brother, the Tī'zīte,
46 E-lī'el the Mā'ha-vīte, and Jĕr'i-baī, and Jŏsh-a-vī'ah, the sons of Ĕl'nā-am, and Ĭth'mah the Moabite,
47 E-lī'el, and Ō'bed, and Jā'sĭ-el the Me-sō'ba-īte.

CHAPTER 12

NOW these *are* they that came to David to Ziklag, while he yet kept himself close because of Saul the son of Kish: and they *were* among the mighty men, helpers of the war.
2 *They were* armed with bows, and could use both the right hand and the left in *hurling* stones and *shooting* arrows out of a bow, *even* of Saul's brethren of Benjamin.
3 The chief *was* Ā-hī'e-zer, then Jō'ăsh, the sons of She-mā'ah the Gĭb'e-ath-īte; and Jē'zi-el, and Pē'let, the sons of Ăz'ma-vĕth; and Bĕr'a-chah, and Jehu the An'toth-ite,
4 And Ĭs-mā-i'ah the Gĭb'e-o-nīte, a mighty man among the thirty, and over the thirty; and Jĕr-e-mī'ah, and Ja-hā'ziel, and Jō-hā'nan, and Jō's'a-băd the Gĕd'e-rath-īte,
5 E-lū'za-ī, and Jĕr'ī-mŏth, and Bē-a-lī'ah, and Shĕm-a-rī'ah, and Shĕph-a-tī'ah the Har'ū-phīte,
6 Ĕl'kā-nah, and Je-sī'ah, and A-zar'e-el, and Jō-ē'zer, and Ja-shō'be-am, the Kōr-hītes,
7 And Jō-ē'lah, and Zĕb-a-dī'ah, the sons of Jer'ō-hăm of Gē'dôr.
8 And of the Găd'ītes there separated themselves unto David into the hold to the wilderness men of might, *and* men of war *fit* for the battle, that could handle shield and buckler, whose faces *were like* the faces of lions, and *were* as swift as the roes upon the mountains;
9 Ē'zer the first, Ō-ba-dī'ah the second, E-lī'ab the third,
10 Mĭsh-măn'nah the fourth, Jĕr-e-mī'ah the fifth,
11 Ăt'taī the sixth, E-lī'el the seventh,
12 Jō-hā'nan the eighth, Ĕl'zā-băd the ninth,
13 Jĕr-e-mī'ah the tenth, Măch'bă-naī the eleventh.
14 These *were* of the sons of Gad, captains of the host: one of the least *was* over an hundred, and the greatest over a thousand.
15 These *are* they that went over Jordan in the first month, when it had overflown all his banks; and they put to flight all *them* of the valleys, *both* toward the east, and toward the west.
16 And there came of the children of Benjamin and Jū'dah to the hold unto David.
17 And David went out to meet them, and answered and said unto them, If ye be come peaceably unto me to help me, mine heart shall be knit unto you: but if *ye be come* to betray me to mine enemies, seeing *there is* no wrong in mine hands, the God of our fathers look *thereon*, and rebuke *it*.
18 Then the spirit came upon A-măs'a-ī, *who was* chief of the captains, *and he said*, Thine *are we*, David, and on thy side, thou son of Jesse: peace, peace *be* unto thee, and peace *be* to thine helpers; for thy God helpeth thee. Then David received them and made them captains of the band.
19 And there fell *some* of Ma-năs'seh to David, when he came with the Philistines against Saul to battle: but they helped them not: for the lords of the Philistines upon advisement sent him away, saying, He will fall to his master Saul to *the jeopardy of* our heads.
20 As he went to Ziklag, there fell to him of Ma-năs'seh, Ăd'nah, and Jōz'a-băd, and Je-dī'a-el, and Michael, and Jōz'a-băd, and E-lī'hū, and Zĭl'thaī, captains of the thousands that *were* of Ma-năs'seh.
21 And they helped David against the band *of the rovers* for they *were* all mighty men of valour, and were captains in the host.

22 For at *that* time day by day there
came to David to help him, until *it was*
a great host, like the host of God.
23 ¶And these *are* the numbers of the
bands *that were* ready armed to the
war, *and* came to David to Hē'bron, to
turn the kingdom of Saul to him, accord-
ing to the word of the LORD.
24 The children of Jū'dah that bare
shield and spear *were* six thousand and
eight hundred, ready armed to the war.
25 Of the children of Simeon, mighty
men of valour for the war, seven thou-
sand and one hundred.
26 Of the children of Levi four thou-
sand and six hundred.
27 And Je-hoi'a-da *was* the leader of
the Aăr'o-nītes, and with him *were*
three thousand and seven hundred;
28 And Zā'dŏk, a young man mighty
of valour, and of his father's house
twenty and two captains.
29 And of the children of Benjamin,
the kindred of Saul, three thousand: for
hitherto the greatest part of them had
kept the ward of the house of Saul.
30 And of the children of Ē'phra-im
twenty thousand and eight hundred,
mighty men of valour, famous
throughout the house of their fathers.
31 And of the half tribe of Ma-năs'seh
eighteen thousand, which were ex-
pressed by name, to come and make
David king.
32 And of the children of Ĭs'sa-char,
which were men that had understand-
ing of the times, to know what
Israel ought to do; the heads of them
were two hundred; and all their breth-
ren *were* at their commandment.
33 Of Zĕb'u-lun, such as went forth to
battle, expert in war, with all instru-
ments of war, fifty thousand, which
could keep rank: *they were* not of
double heart.
34 And of Năph'ta-lī a thousand cap-
tains, and with them with shield and
spear thirty and seven thousand.
35 And of the Danites expert in war
twenty and eight thousand and six
hundred.
36 And of Asher, such as went forth
to battle, expert in war, forty thousand.
37 And on the other side of Jordan, of
the Reubenites, and the Găd'ītes, and
of the half tribe of Ma-năs'seh, with all
manner of instruments of war for the
battle, an hundred and twenty thou-
sand.
38 All these men of war, that could
keep rank, came with a perfect heart to
Hē'bron, to make David king over all
Israel and all the rest also of Israel *were*
of one heart to make David king.
39 And there they were with David
three days, eating and drinking: for
their brethren had prepared for them.
40 Moreover they that were nigh
them, *even* unto Ĭs'sa-char and Zĕb'u-
lun and Năph'ta-lī, brought bread on
asses, and on camels, and on mules,
and on oxen, *and* meat, meal, cakes of
figs, and bunches of raisins, and wine,
and oil, and oxen, and sheep abundant-
ly: for *there was* joy in Israel.

CHAPTER 13

AND David consulted with the cap-
tains of thousands and hundreds, *and*
with every leader.
2 And David said unto all the congre-
gation of Israel, If *it seem* good unto
you, and *that it be* of the LORD our God,
let us send abroad unto our brethren
every where, *that are* left in all the land
of Israel, and with them *also* to the
priests and Lē'vītes *which are* in their
cities *and* suburbs, that they may gath-
er themselves unto us:
3 And let us bring again the ark of our
God to us: for we enquired not at it in
the days of Saul.
4 And all the congregation said that
they would do so: for the thing was
right in the eyes of all the people.
5 So David gathered all Israel togeth-
er, from Shī'hôr of Egypt even unto
the entering of Hē'măth, to bring the
ark of God from Kir'jath–jē'a-rĭm.
6 And David went up, and all Israel,
to Bā'al-ah, *that is*, to Kir'jath–jē'a-rĭm,
which *belonged* to Jū'dah, to bring up
thence the ark of God the LORD, that
dwelleth *between* the cherubims,
whose name is called *on it.*
7 And they carried the ark of God in a
new cart out of the house of A-bĭn'a-
dăb: and Ŭz'za and A-hī'o drave the
cart.
8 And David and all Israel played be-
fore God with all *their* might, and with
singing, and with harps, and with psal-
teries, and with timbrels, and with
cymbals, and with trumpets.
9 ¶And when they came unto the
threshingfloor of Chī'don, Ŭz'za put
forth his hand to hold the ark; for the
oxen stumbled.
10 And the anger of the LORD was
kindled against Ŭz'za, and he smote
him, because he put his hand to the ark:
and there he died before God.
11 And David was displeased, be-
cause the LORD had made a breach
upon Ŭz'za: wherefore that place is
called Pe'rĕz–ŭz'za to this day.
12 And David was afraid of God that
day, saying, How shall I bring the ark of
God *home* to me?
13 So David brought not the ark

home to himself to the city of David,
but carried it aside into the house of
Ō'bed-ē'dom the Gĭt'tīte.
14 And the ark of God remained with
the family of Ō'bed-ē'dom in his house
three months. And the LORD blessed
the house of Ō'bed-ē'dom, and all that
he had.

CHAPTER 14

NOW Hiram king of Tyre sent messen-
gers to David, and timber of cedars,
with masons and carpenters, to build
him an house.
2 And David perceived that the LORD
had confirmed him king over Israel, for
his kingdom was lifted up on high, be-
cause of his people Israel.
3 ¶And David took more wives at Jeru-
salem: and David begat more sons
and daughters.
4 Now these *are* the names of *his*
children which he had in Jerusalem;
Shăm-mū'a, and Shō'băb, Nā'than, and
Sŏl'o-mon,
5 And Ĭb'hăr, and Ĕl-i-shū'a, and Ĕl'pă-
let,
6 And Nō'gah, and Nē'phĕg, and Ja-
phī'a,
7 And E-lĭsh'a-ma, and Bē-el-ī'a-da,
and E-lĭph'a-lĕt.
8 ¶And when the Philistines heard
that David was anointed king over all
Israel, all the Philistines went up to
seek David. And David heard *of it*, and
went out against them.
9 And the Philistines came and
spread themselves in the valley of
Rĕph'a-im.
10 And David enquired of God,
saying, Shall I go up against the Philis-
tines? And wilt thou deliver them into
mine hand? And the LORD said unto
him, Go up; for I will deliver them into
thine hand.
11 So they came up to Bā'al-per'a-zĭm;
and David smote them there. Then Da-
vid said, God hath broken in upon mine
enemies by mine hand like the break-
ing forth of waters: therefore they
called the name of that place Bā'al-
per'a-zĭm.
12 And when they had left their gods
there, David gave a commandment,
and they were burned with fire.
13 And the Philistines yet again
spread themselves abroad in the valley.
14 Therefore David enquired again of
God; and God said unto him, Go not up
after them; turn away from them, and
come upon them over against the mul-
berry trees.
15 And it shall be, when thou shalt
hear a sound of going in the tops of the
mulberry trees, *that* then thou shalt go
out to battle: for God is gone forth be-
fore thee to smite the host of the Philis-
tines.
16 David therefore did as God com-
manded him: and they smote the host
of the Philistines from Gĭb'e-on even to
Gā'zer.
17 And the fame of David went out
into all lands; and the LORD brought the
fear of him upon all nations.

CHAPTER 15

AND *David* made him houses in the
city of David, and prepared a place for
the ark of God, and pitched for it a tent.
2 Then David said, None ought to
carry the ark of God but the Lē'vītes:
for them hath the LORD chosen to carry
the ark of God, and to minister unto
him for ever.
3 And David gathered all Israel to-
gether to Jerusalem, to bring up the ark
of the LORD unto his place, which he
had prepared for it.
4 And David assembled the children
of Aaron, and the Lē'vītes:
5 Of the sons of Kō'hăth; Ū'rĭ-el the
chief, and his brethren an hundred and
twenty:
6 Of the sons of Me-râ'rī; Aṡ-ā'iah
the chief, and his brethren two hundred
and twenty:
7 Of the sons of Ger'shom; Jō'el the
chief, and his brethren an hundred and
thirty:
8 Of the sons of Ĕ-liz'ā-phan; Shem-ā-
i'ah the chief, and his brethren two
hundred:
9 Of the sons of Hē'bron; E-lī'el the
chief, and his brethren fourscore:
10 Of the sons of Ŭz'zĭ-el; Am-mĭn'a-
dăb the chief, and his brethren an
hundred and twelve.
11 And David called for Zā'dŏk and
Ā-bī'a-thar the priests, and for the Lē'-
vītes, for Ū'rĭ-el, Aṡ-ā'iah, and Jō'el,
Shem-ā-i'ah, and E-lī'el, and Am-mĭn'a-
dăb,
12 And said unto them, Ye *are* the
chief of the fathers of the Lē'vītes:
sanctify yourselves, *both* ye and your
brethren, that ye may bring up the ark
of the LORD God of Israel unto *the place*
that I have prepared for it.
13 For because ye *did it* not at the
first, the LORD our God made a breach
upon us, for that we sought him not af-
ter the due order.
14 So the priests and the Lē'vītes
sanctified themselves to bring up the
ark of the LORD God of Israel.
15 And the children of the Lē'vītes
bare the ark of God upon their shoulders
with the staves thereon, as Moses

commanded according to the word of
the LORD.
16 And David spake to the chief of
the Lē'vītes to appoint their brethren *to
be* the singers with instruments of mu-
sick, psalteries and harps and cymbals,
sounding, by lifting up the voice with
joy.
17 So the Lē'vītes appointed Hē'man
the son of Jō'el; and of his brethren,
Ā'săph the son of Bĕr-e-chī'ah; and of
the sons of Me-râ'rī their brethren, Ē'-
than the son of Kū-shā'iah;
18 And with them their brethren of
the second *degree*, Zĕch-a-rī'ah, Ben,
and Jā-a'zī-el, and She-mĭr'a-mŏth, and
Je-hī'el, and Ŭn'nī, E-lī'ab, and Be-nā'-
iah, and Mā-a-sē'iah, and Măt-ti-thī'ah,
and E-lĭph'e-leh, and Mĭk-nē'iah, and
Ō'bed-ē'dom, and Je-ī'el, the porters.
19 So the singers, Hē'măn, Ā'săph,
and Ē'than, *were appointed* to sound
with cymbals of brass;
20 And Zĕch-a-rī'ah, and Ā'zī-el, and
She-mĭr'a-mŏth, and Je-hī'el, and Ŭn'nī,
and E-lī'ab, and Mā-a-sē'iah, and Be-
nā'iah, with psalteries on Ăl'a-mŏth;
21 And Măt-ti-thī'ah, and E-lĭph'e-
leh, and Mĭk-nē'iah, and Ō'bed-ē'dom,
and Je-ī'el, and Ăz-a-zī'ah, with harps
on the Shem'i-nith to excel.
22 And Chĕn-a-nī'ah, chief of the Lē'-
vītes, *was* for song: he instructed about
the song, because he *was* skilful.
23 And Bĕr-e-chī'ah and Ĕl'kâ-nah
were doorkeepers for the ark.
24 And Shĕb-a-nī'ah, and Je-hŏsh'a-
phăt, and Ne-thăn'e-el, and A-măs'a-ī,
and Zĕch-a-rī'ah, and Be-nā'iah, and Ĕ-
lī-ē'zer, the priests, did blow with the
trumpets before the ark of God: and
Ō'bed-ē'dom and Je-hī'ah *were*
doorkeepers for the ark.
25 ¶So David, and the elders of Israel,
and the captains over thousands, went
to bring up the ark of the covenant of
the LORD out of the house of
Ō'bed-ē'dom with joy.
26 And it came to pass, when God
helped the Lē'vītes that bare the ark of
the covenant of the LORD, that they of-
fered seven bullocks and seven rams.
27 And David *was* clothed with a
robe of fine linen, and all the Lē'vītes
that bare the ark, and the singers, and
Chĕn-a-nī'ah the master of the song
with the singers: David also *had* upon
him an ephod of linen.
28 Thus all Israel brought up the ark
of the covenant of the LORD with
shouting, and with sound of the cornet,
and with trumpets, and with cymbals,
making a noise with psalteries and
harps.
29 And it came to pass, *as* the ark of
the covenant of the LORD came to the
city of David, that Mī'chal the daughter
of Saul looking out at a window saw
king David dancing and playing: and
she despised him in her heart.

CHAPTER 16

SO they brought the ark of God, and set
it in the midst of the tent that David had
pitched for it: and they offered burnt
sacrifices and peace offerings before
God.
2 And when David had made an end
of offering the burnt offerings and the
peace offerings, he blessed the people
in the name of the LORD.
3 And he dealt to every one of Israel,
both man and woman, to every one a
loaf of bread, and a good piece of flesh,
and a flagon *of wine*.
4 ¶And he appointed *certain* of the
Lē'vītes to minister before the ark of
the LORD, and to record, and to thank
and praise the LORD God of Israel:
5 Ā'săph the chief, and next to him
Zĕch-a-rī'ah, Je-ī'el, and She-mĭr'a-
mŏth, and Je-hī'el, and Măt-ti-thī'ah,
and E-lī'ab, and Be-nā'iah, and
Ō'bed-ē'dom: and Je-ī'el with psalteries
and with harps; but Ā'săph made a
sound with cymbals;
6 Be-nā'iah also and Ja-hā'zi-el the
priests with trumpets continually be-
fore the ark of the covenant of God.
7 ¶Then on that day David delivered
first *this psalm* to thank the LORD into
the hand of Ā'săph and his brethren.
8 Give thanks unto the LORD, call
upon his name, make known his deeds
among the people.
9 Sing unto him, sing psalms unto
him, talk ye of all his wondrous works.
10 Glory ye in his holy name: let the
heart of them rejoice that seek the
LORD.
11 Seek the LORD and his strength,
seek his face continually.
12 Remember his marvellous works
that he hath done, his wonders, and the
judgments of his mouth;
13 O ye seed of Israel his servant, ye
children of Jacob, his chosen ones.
14 He *is* the LORD our God; his judg-
ments *are* in all the earth.
15 Be ye mindful always of his cov-
enant; the word *which* he commanded to
a thousand generations;
16 *Even of the covenant* which he
made with Abraham, and of his oath
unto Isaac;
17 And hath confirmed the same to
Jacob for a law, *and* to Israel *for* an ever-
lasting covenant,
18 Saying, Unto thee will I give the

land of Canaan, the lot of your inheritance;
19 When ye were but few, even a few, and strangers in it.
20 And *when* they went from nation to nation, and from *one* kingdom to another people;
21 He suffered no man to do them wrong: yea, he reproved kings for their sakes,
22 *Saying*, Touch not mine anointed, and do my prophets no harm.
23 Sing unto the LORD, all the earth; shew forth from day to day his salvation.
24 Declare his glory among the heathen; his marvellous works among all nations.
25 For great *is* the LORD, and greatly to be praised: he also *is* to be feared above all gods.
26 For all the gods of the people *are* idols: but the LORD made the heavens.
27 Glory and honour *are* in his presence; strength and gladness *are* in his place.
28 Give unto the LORD, ye kindreds of the people, give unto the LORD glory and strength.
29 Give unto the LORD the glory *due* unto his name: bring an offering, and come before him: worship the LORD in the beauty of holiness.
30 Fear before him, all the earth: the world also shall be stable, that it be not moved.
31 Let the heavens be glad, and let the earth rejoice: and let *men* say among the nations, The LORD reigneth.
32 Let the sea roar, and the fulness thereof: let the fields rejoice, and all that *is* therein.
33 Then shall the trees of the wood sing out at the presence of the LORD, because he cometh to judge the earth.
34 O give thanks unto the LORD; for *he is* good; for his mercy *endureth* for ever.
35 And say ye, Save us, O God of our salvation, and gather us together, and deliver us from the heathen, that we may give thanks to thy holy name, *and* glory in thy praise.
36 Blessed *be* the LORD God of Israel for ever and ever. And all the people said, Amen, and praised the LORD.
37 ¶So he left there before the ark of the covenant of the LORD Ā′săph and his brethren, to minister before the ark continually, as every day's work required:
38 And Ō′bed-ē′dom with their brethren, threescore and eight; Ō′bed-ē′dom also the son of Jed′ū-thun and Hō′sah *to be* porters:
39 And Zā′dŏk the priest, and his brethren the priests, before the tabernacle of the LORD in the high place that *was* at Gĭb′e-on,
40 To offer burnt offerings unto the LORD upon the altar of the burnt offering continually morning and evening, and *to do* according to all that is written in the law of the LORD, which he commanded Israel;
41 And with them Hē′man and Jed′ū-thun, and the rest that were chosen, who were expressed by name, to give thanks to the LORD, because his mercy *endureth* for ever;
42 And with them Hē′man and Jed′ū-thun with trumpets and cymbals for those that should make a sound, and with musical instruments of God. And the sons of Jed′ū-thun *were* porters.
43 And all the people departed every man to his house: and David returned to bless his house.

CHAPTER 17

NOW it came to pass, as David sat in his house, that David said to Nā′than the prophet, Lo, I dwell in an house of cedars, but the ark of the covenant of the LORD *remaineth* under curtains.
2 Then Nā′than said unto David, Do all that *is* in thine heart; for God *is* with thee.
3 ¶And it came to pass the same night, that the word of God came to Nā′than, saying,
4 Go and tell David my servant, Thus saith the LORD, Thou shalt not build me an house to dwell in:
5 For I have not dwelt in an house since the day that I brought up Israel unto this day; but have gone from tent to tent, and from *one* tabernacle *to another*.
6 Wheresoever I have walked with all Israel, spake I a word to any of the judges of Israel, whom I commanded to feed my people, saying, Why have ye not built me an house of cedars?
7 Now therefore thus shalt thou say unto my servant David, Thus saith the LORD of hosts, I took thee from the sheepcote, *even* from following the sheep, that thou shouldest be ruler over my people Israel:
8 And I have been with thee whithersoever thou hast walked, and have cut off all thine enemies from before thee, and have made thee a name like the name of the great men that *are* in the earth.
9 Also I will ordain a place for my people Israel, and will plant them, and they shall dwell in their place, and shall be moved no more; neither shall the

children of wickedness waste them any
more, as at the beginning,
10 And since the time that I commanded judges *to be* over my people
Israel. Moreover I will subdue all thine
enemies. Furthermore I tell thee that
the LORD will build thee an house.
11 And it shall come to pass, when
thy days be expired that thou must go
to be with thy fathers, that I will raise
up thy seed after thee, which shall be of
thy sons; and I will establish his kingdom.
12 He shall build me an house, and I
will stablish his throne for ever.
13 I will be his father, and he shall be
my son: and I will not take my mercy
away from him, as I took *it* from *him*
that was before thee:
14 But I will settle him in mine house
and in my kingdom for ever: and his
throne shall be established for evermore.
15 According to all these words, and
according to all this vision, so did Nā'than speak unto David.
16 ¶And David the king came and sat
before the LORD, and said, Who *am* I, O
LORD God, and what *is* mine house, that
thou hast brought me hitherto?
17 And *yet* this was a small thing in
thine eyes, O God; for thou hast *also*
spoken of thy servant's house for a
great while to come, and hast regarded
me according to the estate of a man of
high degree, O LORD God.
18 What can David *speak* more to
thee for the honour of thy servant? for
thou knowest thy servant.
19 O LORD, for thy servant's sake, and
according to thine own heart, hast thou
done all this greatness, in making
known all *these* great things.
20 O LORD, *there is* none like thee,
neither *is there any* God beside thee,
according to all that we have heard
with our ears.
21 And what one nation in the earth *is*
like thy people Israel, whom God went
to redeem *to be* his own people, to
make thee a name of greatness and terribleness, by driving out nations from
before thy people, whom thou hast redeemed out of Egypt?
22 For thy people Israel didst thou
make thine own people for ever; and
thou, LORD, becamest their God.
23 Therefore now, LORD, let the thing
that thou hast spoken concerning thy
servant and concerning his house be
established for ever, and do as thou
hast said.
24 Let it even be established, that thy
name may be magnified for ever,
saying, The LORD of hosts *is* the God of
Israel, *even* a God to Israel: and *let* the
house of David thy servant *be* established before thee.
25 For thou, O my God, hast told thy
servant that thou wilt build him an
house: therefore thy servant hath
found *in his heart* to pray before thee.
26 And now, LORD, thou art God, and
hast promised this goodness unto thy
servant:
27 Now therefore let it please thee to
bless the house of thy servant, that it
may be before thee for ever: for thou
blessest, O LORD, and *it shall be* blessed
for ever.

CHAPTER 18

NOW after this it came to pass, that
David smote the Philistines, and subdued them, and took Gath and her
towns out of the hand of the Philistines.
2 And he smote Moab; and the Moabites became David's servants, *and*
brought gifts.
3 ¶And David smote Hād-ar-ē'zer
king of Zō'bah unto Hā'măth, as he
went to stablish his dominion by the river Eū-phrā'tēs.
4 And David took from him a thousand chariots, and seven thousand
horsemen, and twenty thousand footmen: David also houghed all the
chariot *horses*, but reserved of them an
hundred chariots.
5 And when the Syrians of Damascus
came to help Hād-ar-ē'zer king of Zō'bah, David slew of the Syrians two and
twenty thousand men.
6 Then David put *garrisons* in Syria–damascus; and the Syrians became
David's servants, *and* brought gifts.
Thus the LORD preserved David whithersoever he went.
7 And David took the shields of gold
that were on the servants of Hād-ar-ē'zer, and brought them to Jerusalem.
8 Likewise from Tĭb'hăth, and from
Chun, cities of Hād-ar-ē'zer, brought
David very much brass, wherewith Sŏl-omon made the brasen sea, and the pillars, and the vessels of brass.
9 ¶Now when Tō'ū king of Hā'măth
heard how David had smitten all the
host of Hād-ar-ē'zer king of Zō'bah;
10 He sent Ha'dō'ram his son to king
David, to enquire of his welfare, and to
congratulate him, because he had
fought against Hād-ar-ē'zer, and smitten him; (for Hād-ar-ē'zer had war with
Tō'ū;) and *with him* all manner of vessels of gold and silver and brass.
11 Them also king David dedicated
unto the LORD, with the silver and the
gold that he brought from all *these* nations; from Ē'dom, and from Moab, and

from the children of Ammon, and from the Philistines, and from Ăm'a-lĕk.

12 Moreover, A-bī'shaī the son of Zer-ū-i'ah slew of the Edomites in the valley of salt eighteen thousand.

13 And he put garrisons in Ē'dom; and all the Edomites became David's servants. Thus the LORD preserved David whithersoever he went.

14 ¶So David reigned over all Israel, and executed judgment and justice among all his people.

15 And Jō'ăb the son of Zer-ū-i'ah *was* over the host; and Je-hŏsh'a-phăt the son of A-hī'lud, recorder.

16 And Zā'dŏk the son of A-hī'tŭb, and A-bĭm'e-lĕch the son of Ā-bī'a-thar, *were* the priests; and Shăv'sha was scribe;

17 And Be-nā'iah the son of Je-hoi'a-da *was* over the Chĕr'e-thītes and the Pĕl'e-thītes; and the sons of David *were* chief about the king.

CHAPTER 19

NOW it came to pass after this, that Nā'hăsh the king of the children of Ammon died, and his son reigned in his stead.

2 And David said, I will shew kindness unto Hā'nun the son of Nā'hăsh, because his father shewed kindness to me. And David sent messengers to comfort him concerning his father. So the servants of David came into the land of the children of Ammon to Hā'nun, to comfort him.

3 But the princes of the children of Ammon said to Hā'nun, Thinkest thou that David doth honour thy father, that he hath sent comforters unto thee? are not his servants come unto thee for to search, and to overthrow, and to spy out the land?

4 Wherefore Hā'nun took David's servants, and shaved them, and cut off their garments in the midst hard by their buttocks, and sent them away.

5 Then there went *certain*, and told David how the men were served. And he sent to meet them: for the men were greatly ashamed. And the king said, Tarry at Jericho until your beards be grown, and *then* return.

6 ¶And when the children of Ammon saw that they had made themselves odious to David, Hā'nun and the children of Ammon sent a thousand talents of silver to hire them chariots and horsemen out of Mĕs-o-po-tā'mĭ-a and out of Sỹr'ĭ-a-mā'a-chăh, and out of Zō'bah.

7 So they hired thirty and two thousand chariots, and the king of Mā'a-chah and his people; who came and pitched before Mĕd'e-ba. And the children of Ammon gathered themselves together from their cities, and came to battle.

8 And when David heard *of it*, he sent Jō'ăb, and all the host of the mighty men.

9 And the children of Ammon came out, and put the battle in array before the gate of the city: and the kings that were come *were* by themselves in the field.

10 Now when Jō'ăb saw that the battle was set against him before and behind, he chose out of all the choice of Israel, and put *them* in array against the Syrians.

11 And the rest of the people he delivered unto the hand of A-bī'shaī his brother, and they set *themselves* in array against the children of Ammon.

12 And he said, If the Syrians be too strong for me, then thou shalt help me: but if the children of Ammon be too strong for thee, then I will help thee.

13 Be of good courage, and let us behave ourselves valiantly for our people, and for the cities of our God: and let the LORD do *that which is* good in his sight.

14 So Jō'ăb and the people that *were* with him drew nigh before the Syrians unto the battle; and they fled before him.

15 And when the children of Ammon saw that the Syrians were fled, they likewise fled before A-bī'shaī his brother, and entered into the city. Then Jō'ăb came to Jerusalem.

16 ¶And when the Syrians saw that they were put to the worse before Israel, they sent messengers, and drew forth the Syrians that *were* beyond the river: and Shō'phăch the captain of the host of Hăd-ar-ē'zer *went* before them.

17 And it was told David; and he gathered all Israel, and passed over Jordan, and came upon them, and set *the battle* in array against them. So when David had put the battle in array against the Syrians, they fought with him.

18 But the Syrians fled before Israel; and David slew of the Syrians seven thousand *men which fought in* chariots, and forty thousand footmen, and killed Shō'phăch the captain of the host.

19 And when the servants of Hăd-ar-ē'zer saw that they were put to the worse before Israel, they made peace with David, and became his servants: neither would the Syrians help the children of Ammon any more.

CHAPTER 20

AND it came to pass, that after the year was expired, at the time that kings go out *to battle,* Jō′ăb led forth the power of the army, and wasted the country of the children of Ammon, and came and besieged Răb′bah. But David tarried at Jerusalem. And Jō′ăb smote Răb′bah, and destroyed it.

2 And David took the crown of their king from off his head, and found it to weigh a talent of gold, and *there were* precious stones in it; and it was set upon David's head: and he brought also exceeding much spoil out of the city.

3 And he brought out the people that *were* in it, and cut *them* with saws, and with harrows of iron, and with axes. Even so dealt David with all the cities of the children of Ammon. And David and all the people returned to Jerusalem.

4 ¶And it came to pass after this, that there arose war at Gē′zer with the Philistines; at which time Sĭb′be-chaī the Hu′shath-īte slew Sĭp′paī, *that was* of the children of the giant: and they were subdued.

5 And there was war again with the Philistines; and Ĕl-hā′nan the son of Jā′ir slew Läh′mī the brother of Goliath the Gĭt′tīte, whose spear staff *was* like a weaver's beam.

6 And yet again there was war at Gath, where was a man of *great* stature, whose fingers and toes *were* four and twenty, six *on each hand,* and six *on each foot* and he also was the son of the giant.

7 But when he defied Israel, Jonathan the son of Shĭm′e-a David's brother slew him.

8 These were born unto the giant in Gath; and they fell by the hand of David, and by the hand of his servants.

CHAPTER 21

AND Satan stood up against Israel, and provoked David to number Israel.

2 And David said to Jō′ăb and to the rulers of the people, Go, number Israel from Be′er-shē′ba even to Dan; and bring the number of them to me, that I may know *it.*

3 And Jō′ăb answered, The LORD make his people an hundred times so many more as they *be:* but, my lord the king, *are* they not all my lord's servants? why then doth my lord require this thing? why will he be a cause of trespass to Israel?

4 Nevertheless the king's word prevailed against Jō′ăb. Wherefore Jō′ăb departed, and went throughout all Israel, and came to Jerusalem.

5 And Jō′ăb gave the sum of the number of the people unto David. And all *they of* Israel were a thousand thousand and an hundred thousand men that drew sword: and Judah *was* four hundred threescore and ten thousand men that drew sword.

6 But Levi and Benjamin counted he not among them: for the king's word was abominable to Jō′ăb.

7 And God was displeased with this thing; therefore he smote Israel.

8 And David said unto God, I have sinned greatly, because I have done this thing: but now, I beseech thee, do away the iniquity of thy servant; for I have done very foolishly.

9 ¶And the LORD spake unto Gad, David's seer, saying,

10 Go and tell David, saying, Thus saith the LORD, I offer thee three *things:* choose thee one of them, that I may do *it* unto thee.

11 So Gad came to David, and said unto him, Thus saith the LORD, Choose thee

12 Either three years' famine; or three months to be destroyed before thy foes, while that the sword of thine enemies overtaketh *thee;* or else three days the sword of the LORD, even the pestilence, in the land, and the angel of the LORD destroying throughout all the coasts of Israel. Now therefore advise thyself what word I shall bring again to him that sent me.

13 And David said unto Gad, I am in a great strait: let me fall now into the hand of the LORD; for very great *are* his mercies: but let me not fall into the hand of man.

14 ¶So the LORD sent pestilence upon Israel: and there fell of Israel seventy thousand men.

15 And God sent an angel unto Jerusalem to destroy it: and as he was destroying, the LORD beheld, and he repented him of the evil, and said to the angel that destroyed, It is enough, stay now thine hand. And the angel of the LORD stood by the threshingfloor of Ôr′nan the Jēb′u-sīte.

16 And David lifted up his eyes, and saw the angel of the LORD stand between the earth and the heaven, having a drawn sword in his hand stretched out over Jerusalem. Then David and the elders *of Israel, who were* clothed in sackcloth, fell upon their faces.

17 And David said unto God, *Is it* not I *that* commanded the people to be numbered? even I it is that have sinned and done evil indeed; but *as for* these

sheep, what have they done? let thine hand, I pray thee, O LORD my God, be on me, and on my father's house; but not on thy people, that they should be plagued.

18 ¶Then the angel of the LORD commanded Gad to say to David, that David should go up, and set up an altar unto the LORD in the threshingfloor of Ôr′nan the Jēb′u-sīte.

19 And David went up at the saying of Gad, which he spake in the name of the LORD.

20 And Ôr′nan turned back, and saw the angel; and his four sons with him hid themselves. Now Ôr′nan was threshing wheat.

21 And as David came to Ôr′nan, Ôr′nan looked and saw David, and went out of the threshingfloor, and bowed himself to David with *his* face to the ground.

22 Then David said to Ôr′nan, Grant me the place of *this* threshingfloor, that I may build an altar therein unto the LORD: thou shalt grant it me for the full price: that the plague may be stayed from the people.

23 And Ôr′nan said unto David, Take *it* to thee, and let my lord the king do *that which is* good in his eyes: lo, I give *thee* the oxen *also* for burnt offerings, and the threshing instruments for wood, and the wheat for the meat offering; I give it all.

24 And king David said to Ôr′nan, Nay; but I will verily buy it for the full price: for I will not take *that* which *is* thine for the LORD, nor offer burnt offerings without cost.

25 So David gave to Ôr′nan for the place six hundred shekels of gold by weight.

26 And David built there an altar unto the LORD, and offered burnt offerings and peace offerings, and called upon the LORD; and he answered him from heaven by fire upon the altar of burnt offering.

27 And the LORD commanded the angel; and he put up his sword again into the sheath thereof.

28 ¶At that time when David saw that the LORD had answered him in the threshingfloor of Ôr′nan the Jēb′u-sīte, then he sacrificed there.

29 For the tabernacle of the LORD, which Moses made in the wilderness, and the altar of the burnt offering, *were* at that season in the high place at Gĭb′-e-on.

30 But David could not go before it to enquire of God: for he was afraid because of the sword of the angel of the LORD.

CHAPTER 22

THEN David said, This *is* the house of the LORD God, and this *is* the altar of the burnt offering for Israel.

2 And David commanded to gather together the strangers that *were* in the land of Israel; and he set masons to hew wrought stones to build the house of God.

3 And David prepared iron in abundance for the nails for the doors of the gates, and for the joinings; and brass in abundance without weight;

4 Also cedar trees in abundance: for the Zīd-ō′nĭ-ans and they of Tyre brought much cedar wood to David.

5 And David said, Sŏlomon my son *is* young and tender, and the house *that is* to be builded for the LORD *must be* exceeding magnifical, of fame and of glory throughout all countries: I will *therefore* now make preparation for it. So David prepared abundantly before his death.

6 ¶Then he called for Sŏlomon his son, and charged him to build an house for the LORD God of Israel.

7 And David said to Sŏlomon, My son, as for me, it was in my mind to build an house unto the name of the LORD my God:

8 But the word of the LORD came to me, saying, Thou hast shed blood abundantly, and hast made great wars: thou shalt not build an house unto my name, because thou hast shed much blood upon the earth in my sight.

9 Behold, a son shall be born to thee, who shall be a man of rest; and I will give him rest from all his enemies round about: for his name shall be Sŏlomon, and I will give peace and quietness unto Israel in his days.

10 He shall build an house for my name; and he shall be my son, and I *will be* his father; and I will establish the throne of his kingdom over Israel for ever.

11 Now, my son, the LORD be with thee; and prosper thou, and build the house of the LORD thy God, as he hath said of thee.

12 Only the LORD give thee wisdom and understanding, and give thee charge concerning Israel, that thou mayest keep the law of the LORD thy God.

13 Then shalt thou prosper, if thou takest heed to fulfil the statutes and judgments which the LORD charged Moses with concerning Israel: be strong, and of good courage; dread not, nor be dismayed.

14 Now, behold, in my trouble I have

prepared for the house of the LORD an
hundred thousand talents of gold, and a
thousand thousand talents of silver;
and of brass and iron without weight;
for it is in abundance: timber also and
stone have I prepared; and thou mayest
add thereto.
15 Moreover *there are* workmen with
thee in abundance, hewers and work-
ers of stone and timber, and all manner
of cunning men for every manner of
work.
16 Of the gold, the silver, and the
brass, and the iron, *there is* no number.
Arise *therefore*, and be doing, and the
LORD be with thee.
17 ¶David also commanded all the
princes of Israel to help Sŏlomon his
son, *saying*,
18 *Is* not the LORD your God with
you? and hath he *not* given you rest on
every side? for he hath given the
inhabitants of the land into mine hand;
and the land is subdued before the
LORD, and before his people.
19 Now set your heart and your soul
to seek the LORD your God; arise there-
fore, and build ye the sanctuary of the
LORD God, to bring the ark of the cove-
nant of the LORD, and the holy vessels
of God, into the house that is to be built
to the name of the LORD.

CHAPTER 23

SO when David was old and full of
days, he made Sŏlomon his son king
over Israel.
2 ¶And he gathered together all the
princes of Israel, with the priests and
the Lē′vītes.
3 Now the Lē′vītes were numbered
from the age of thirty years and up-
ward: and their number by their polls,
man by man, was thirty and eight thou-
sand.
4 Of which, twenty and four thou-
sand *were* to set forward the work of
the house of the LORD; and six thousand
were officers and judges:
5 Moreover four thousand *were* por-
ters; and four thousand praised the
LORD with the instruments which I
made, *said David* to praise *therewith*.
6 And David divided them into
courses among the sons of Levi, *name-
ly*, Ger′shon, Kō′hăth, and Me-râ′rī.
7 ¶Of the Ger′shon-ītes *were*, Lā′a-
dan, and Shĭm′e-ī.
8 The sons of Lā′a-dan; the chief *was*
Je-hī′el, and Zē′tham, and Jō′el, three.
9 The sons of Shĭm′e-ī; Shel′ô-mīth,
and Hā′zī-el, and Hâ′ran, three. These
were the chief of the fathers of Lā′a-
dan.
10 And the sons of Shĭm′e-ī *were*,
Jā′hăth, Zī′na, and Jē′ŭsh, and Be-rī′ah.
These four *were* the sons of Shĭm′e-ī.
11 And Jā′hăth was the chief, and Zī′-
zah the second: but Jē′ŭsh and Be-rī′ah
had not many sons; therefore they
were in one reckoning, according to
their father's house.
12 ¶The sons of Kō′hăth; Ăm′răm, Ĭz′-
här, Hē′bron, and Ŭz′zī-el, four.
13 The sons of Ăm′răm; Aaron and
Moses: and Aaron was separated, that
he should sanctify the most holy
things, he and his sons for ever, to burn
incense before the LORD, to minister
unto him, and to bless in his name for
ever.
14 Now *concerning* Moses the man of
God, his sons were named of the tribe
of Levi.
15 The sons of Moses *were*, Ger′-
shom, and Ĕ-lī-ē′zer.
16 Of the sons of Ger′shom, Shĕb′ū-el
was the chief.
17 And the sons of Ĕ-lī-ē′zer *were*,
Rē-ha-bī′ah the chief. And Ĕ-lī-ē′zer
had none other sons; but the sons of Rē-
ha-bī′ah were very many.
18 Of the sons of Ĭz′här; Shel′ō-mīth
the chief.
19 Of the sons of Hē′bron; Je-rī′ah the
first, Ăm-a-rī′ah the second, Ja-hā′zi-el
the third, and Jĕk-a-mē′am the fourth.
20 Of the sons of Ŭz′zī-el; Mī′cah the
first, and Je-sī′ah the second.
21 ¶The sons of Me-râ′rī; Māh′lī, and
Mū′shī. The sons of Māh′lī; Ĕ-le-ā′zar,
and Kish.
22 And Ĕ-le-ā′zar died, and had no
sons, but daughters: and their brethren
the sons of Kish took them.
23 The sons of Mū′shī; Māh′lī, and
Ē′der, and Jĕr′e-mŏth, three.
24 ¶These *were* the sons of Levi after
the house of their fathers; *even* the
chief of the fathers, as they were
counted by number of names by their
polls, that did the work for the service
of the house of the LORD, from the age
of twenty years and upward.
25 For David said, The LORD God of
Israel hath given rest unto his people,
that they may dwell in Jerusalem for
ever:
26 And also unto the Lē′vītes; they
shall no *more* carry the tabernacle, nor
any vessels of it for the service thereof.
27 For by the last words of David the
Lē′vītes *were* numbered from twenty
years old and above:
28 Because their office *was* to wait on
the sons of Aaron for the service of the
house of the LORD, in the courts, and in
the chambers, and in the purifying of

all holy things, and the work of the ser-
vice of the house of God;
29 Both for the shewbread, and for
the fine flour for meat offering, and for
the unleavened cakes, and for *that
which is baked in* the pan, and for that
which is fried, and for all manner of
measure and size;
30 And to stand every morning to
thank and praise the LORD, and like-
wise at even;
31 And to offer all burnt sacrifices
unto the LORD in the sabbaths, in the
new moons, and on the set feasts, by
number, according to the order com-
manded unto them, continually before
the LORD:
32 And that they should keep the
charge of the tabernacle of the congre-
gation, and the charge of the holy
place, and the charge of the sons of
Aaron their brethren, in the service of
the house of the LORD.

CHAPTER 24

NOW *these are* the divisions of the
sons of Aaron. The sons of Aaron; Nā'-
dăb, and A-bī'hū, Ĕ-le-ā'zar, and Ĭth'a-
mär.
2 But Nā'dăb and A-bī'hū died before
their father, and had no children: there-
fore Ĕ-le-ā'zar and Ĭth'a-mär executed
the priest's office.
3 And David distributed them, both
Zā'dŏk of the sons of Ĕ-le-ā'zar, and A-
hĭm'e-lĕch of the sons of Ĭth'a-mär, ac-
cording to their offices in their service.
4 And there were more chief men
found of the sons of Ĕ-le-ā'zar than of
the sons of Ĭth'a-mär; and *thus* were
they divided. Among the sons of Ĕ-le-
ā'zar *there were* sixteen chief men of
the house of *their* fathers, and eight
among the sons of Ĭth'a-mär according
to the house of their fathers.
5 Thus were they divided by lot, one
sort with another; for the governors of
the sanctuary, and governors *of the
house* of God, were of the sons of Ĕ-le-
ā'zar, and of the sons of Ĭth'a-mär.
6 And Shem-ā-i'ah the son of Ne-
thăn'e-el the scribe, *one* of the Lē'vītes,
wrote them before the king, and the
princes, and Zā'dŏk the priest, and A-
hĭm'e-lĕch the son of Ă-bī'a-thar, and
before the chief of the fathers of the
priests and Lē'vītes: one principal
household being taken for Ĕ-le-ā'zar,
and *one* taken for Ĭth'a-mär.
7 Now the first lot came forth to Je-
hoi'a-rĭb, the second to Je-dā'iah,
8 The third to Hâ'rĭm, the fourth to
Sē-ô'rĭm,
9 The fifth to Măl-chī'jah, the sixth to
Mĭj'a-mĭn,
10 The seventh to Hăk'kŏz, the eighth
to A-bī'jah,
11 The ninth to Jĕsh'u-ah, the tenth to
Shĕc-a-nī'ah,
12 The eleventh to E-lī'a-shĭb, the
twelfth to Jā'kĭm,
13 The thirteenth to Hŭp'pah, the
fourteenth to Je-shĕb'e-ăb,
14 The fifteenth to Bĭl'gah, the six-
teenth to Ĭm'mer,
15 The seventeenth to Hē'zir, the
eighteenth to Ăph'sēs,
16 The nineteenth to Pĕth-a-hī'ah, the
twentieth to Je-hĕz'e-kĕl,
17 The one and twentieth to Jā'chin,
the two and twentieth to Gā'mul,
18 The three and twentieth to Dĕl-a-
ī'ah, the four and twentieth to Mā-a-
zī'ah.
19 These *were* the orderings of them
in their service to come into the house
of the LORD, according to their manner,
under Aaron their father, as the LORD
God of Israel had commanded him.
20 ¶And the rest of the sons of Levi
were these: Of the sons of Ăm'răm;
Shū'ba-el: of the sons of Shū'ba-el; Jĕh-
dē'iah.
21 Concerning Rē-ha-bī'ah: of the
sons of Rē-ha-bī'ah, the first *was* Ĭs-
shī'ah.
22 Of the Ĭz'har-ītes; Shel'ō-mŏth: of
the sons of Shel'ō-mŏth; Jā'ăth.
23 And the sons *of Hē'bron;* Je-rī'ah
the first, Ăm-a-rī'ah the second, Ja-
hā'zi-el the third, Jĕk-a-mē'am the
fourth.
24 *Of* the sons of Ŭz'zī-el; Mī'chah: of
the sons of Mī'chah; Shā'mir.
25 The brother of Mī'chah *was* Ĭs-shī'-
ah: of the sons of Ĭs-shī'ah; Zĕch-a-
rī'ah.
26 The sons of Me-râ'rī *were* Māh'lī
and Mū'shī: the sons of Jā'a-zī'ah;
Bē'nō.
27 The sons of Me-râ'rī by Jā-a-zī'ah;
Bē'nō, and Shō'hăm, and Zăc'cur, and
Ĭb'rī.
28 Of Māh'lī *came* Ĕ-le-ā'zar, who
had no sons.
29 Concerning Kish: the son of Kish
was Je-răh'me-el.
30 The sons also of Mū'shī; Māh'lī,
and Ē'der, and Jĕr'ī-mŏth. These *were*
the sons of the Lē'vītes after the house
of their fathers.
31 These likewise cast lots over
against their brethren the sons of
Aaron in the presence of David the
king, and Zā'dŏk, and A-hĭm'e-lĕch,
and the chief of the fathers of the
priests and Lē'vītes, even the principal
fathers over against their younger
brethren.

CHAPTER 25

MOREOVER David and the captains of
the host separated to the service of the
sons of Ā'săph, and of Hē'măn, and of
Jed'ū-thun, who should prophesy with
harps, with psalteries, and with cym-
bals: and the number of the workmen
according to their service was:
2 Of the sons of Ā'săph; Zăc'cur, and
Joseph, and Něth-a-nī'ah, and Ăs-a-rē'-
lah, the sons of Ā'săph under the hands
of Ā'săph, which prophesied according
to the order of the king.
3 Of Jed'ū-thun: the sons of Jed'ū-
thun; Gĕd-a-lī'ah, and Ze'rī, and Je-shā'-
iah, Hăsh-a-bī'ah, and Măt-ti-thī'ah,
six, under the hands of their father Jed'ū-
thun, who prophesied with a harp,
to give thanks and to praise the LORD.
4 Of Hē'man: the sons of Hē'man:
Buk-kī'ah, Măt-ta-nī'ah, Ŭz'zī-el,
Shĕb'ū-el, and Jĕr'ī-mŏth, Hăn-a-nī'ah,
Ha-nā'nī, E-lī'a-thah, Gid-dăl'tī, and Rō-
măm'tī-ēzer, Jŏsh-bek'ā-shah, Măl'-
lothī, Hō'thir, *and* Ma-hā'zī-ŏth:
5 All these *were* the sons of Hē'man
the king's seer in the words of God, to
lift up the horn. And God gave to Hē'-
man fourteen sons and three daugh-
ters.
6 All these *were* under the hands of
their father for song *in* the house of the
LORD, with cymbals, psalteries, and
harps, for the service of the house of
God, according to the king's order to
Ā'săph, Jed'ū-thun, and Hē'man.
7 So the number of them, with their
brethren that were instructed in the
songs of the LORD, *even* all that were
cunning, was two hundred fourscore
and eight.
8 ¶And they cast lots, ward against
ward, as well the small as the great, the
teacher as the scholar.
9 Now the first lot came forth for
Ā'săph to Joseph: the second to Gĕd-a-
lī'ah, who with his brethren and sons
were twelve:
10 The third to Zăc'cur, *he*, his sons,
and his brethren, *were* twelve:
11 The fourth to Iz'rī, *he*, his sons, and
his brethren, *were* twelve:
12 The fifth to Nĕth-a-nī'ah, *he*, his
sons, and his brethren, *were* twelve:
13 The sixth to Buk-kī'ah, *he*, his
sons, and his brethren, *were* twelve:
14 The seventh to Jĕ-shar'ē-lah, *he*,
his sons, and his brethren, *were* twelve:
15 The eighth to Je-shā'iah, *he*, his
sons, and his brethren, *were* twelve:
16 The ninth to Măt-ta-nī'ah, *he*, his
sons, and his brethren, *were* twelve:
17 The tenth to Shĭm'e-ī, *he*, his sons,
and his brethren, *were* twelve:
18 The eleventh to Ă-zar'e-el, *he*, his
sons, and his brethren, *were* twelve:
19 The twelfth to Hăsh-a-bī'ah, *he*,
his sons, and his brethren, *were* twelve:
20 The thirteenth to Shū'ba-el, *he*, his
sons, and his brethren, *were* twelve:
21 The fourteenth to Măt-ti-thī'ah,
he, his sons, and his brethren, *were*
twelve:
22 The fifteenth to Jĕr'e-mŏth, *he*, his
sons, and his brethren, *were* twelve:
23 The sixteenth to Hăn-a-nī'ah, *he*,
his sons, and his brethren, *were* twelve:
24 The seventeenth to Jŏsh-bek'a-
shah, *he*, his sons, and his brethren,
were twelve:
25 The eighteenth to Ha-nā'nī, *he*, his
sons, and his brethren, *were* twelve:
26 The nineteenth to Măl'lo-thī, *he*,
his sons, and his brethren, *were* twelve:
27 The twentieth to E-lī'a-thah, *he*,
his sons, and his brethren, *were* twelve:
28 The one and twentieth to Hō'thir,
he, his sons, and his brethren, *were*
twelve:
29 The two and twentieth to Gid-dăl'-
tī, *he*, his sons, and his brethren, *were*
twelve:
30 The three and twentieth to Ma-hā'-
zī-ŏth, *he*, his sons, and his brethren,
were twelve:
31 The four and twentieth to Rō-
măm'tī-ē'zer, *he*, his sons, and his
brethren, *were* twelve.

CHAPTER 26

CONCERNING the divisions of the
porters: Of the Kôr'hītes *was* Me-shĕl-
e-mī'ah the son of Kô're, of the sons of
Ā'săph.
2 And the sons of Me-shĕl-e-mī'ah
were, Zĕch-a-rī'ah the firstborn, Je-
dī'a-el the second, Zĕb-a-dī'ah the
third, Jăth'nī-el the fourth,
3 Ē'lam the fifth, Je-hō-hā'nan the
sixth, Ĕ-lī-ō-ē'na-ī the seventh.
4 Moreover the sons of Ō'bed-ē'dom
were, Shem-ā-i'ah the firstborn, Je-
hōz'a-băd the second, Jō'ah the third,
and Sā'căr the fourth, and Ne-thăn'e-el
the fifth,
5 Ăm'mī-el the sixth, Is'sa-char the
seventh, Pē-ŭl'thaī the eighth: for God
blessed him.
6 Also unto Shem-ā-i'ah his son were
sons born, that ruled throughout the
house of their father: for they *were*
mighty men of valour.
7 The sons of Shem-ā-i'ah; Ŏth'nī,
and Rĕ'pha-el and Ō'bed, Ĕl'zā-băd,
whose brethren *were* strong men, E-
lī'hū, and Sĕm-a-chī'ah.
8 All these of the sons of
Ō'bed-ē'dom: they and their sons and
their brethren, able men for strength

for the service, *were* threescore and
two of Ō'bed–ĕ'dom.
9 And Me-shĕl-e-mī'ah had sons and
brethren, strong men, eighteen.
10 Also Hō'sah, of the children of Me-
râ'rī, had sons; Sĭm'rī the chief, (for
though he was not the firstborn, yet his
father made him the chief;)
11 Hĭl-kī'ah the second, Tĕb-a-lī'ah
the third, Zĕch-a-rī'ah the fourth: all
the sons and brethren of Hō'sah *were*
thirteen.
12 Among these *were* the divisions of
the porters, *even* among the chief men,
having wards one against another, to
minister in the house of the LORD.
13 ¶And they cast lots, as well the
small as the great, according to the
house of their fathers, for every gate.
14 And the lot eastward fell to Shĕl-e-
mī'ah. Then for Zĕch-a-rī'ah his son, a
wise counsellor, they cast lots; and his
lot came out northward.
15 To Ō'bed–ĕ'dom southward; and
to his sons the house of A-sŭp'pĭm.
16 To Shŭp'pĭm and Hō'sah *the lot
came forth* westward, with the gate
Shăl'le-chĕth, by the causeway of the
going up, ward against ward.
17 Eastward *were* six Lē'vītes, north-
ward four a day, southward four a day,
and toward A-sŭp'pĭm two *and* two.
18 At Pär'bar westward, four at the
causeway, *and* two at Pär'bar.
19 These *are* the divisions of the por-
ters among the sons of Kô're, and
among the sons of Me-râ'rī.
20 ¶And of the Lē'vītes, A-hī'jah *was*
over the treasures of the house of God,
and over the treasures of the dedicated
things.
21 *As concerning* the sons of Lā'a-
dan; the sons of the Ger'shon-īte Lā'a-
dan, chief fathers, *even* of Lā'a-dan the
Ger'shon-īte, *were* Je-hī'e-lī.
22 The sons of Je-hī'e-lī; Zē'tham,
and Jō'el his brother, *which were* over
the treasures of the house of the LORD.
23 Of the Ăm'ra-mītes, *and* the Ĭz'-
har-ītes, the Hē'bro-nītes, *and* the
Ŭz'zĭ-el-ītes:
24 And Shĕb'ū-el the son of
Ger'shom, the son of Moses, *was* ruler
of the treasures.
25 And his brethren by Ĕ-lī-ē'zer; Rē-
ha-bī'ah his son, and Je-shā'iah his son,
and Joram his son, and Zĭch'rī his son,
and Shel'ō-mĭth his son.
26 Which Shel'ō-mĭth and his breth-
ren *were* over all the treasures of the
dedicated things, which David the
king, and the chief fathers, the captains
over thousands and hundreds, and the
captains of the host, had dedicated.
27 Out of the spoils won in battles did
they dedicate to maintain the house of
the LORD.
28 And all that Samuel the seer, and
Saul the son of Kish, and Abner the son
of Ner, and Jō'ăb the son of Zer-ū-i'ah,
had dedicated; *and* whosoever had dedi-
cated *any thing, it was* under the
hand of Shel'ō-mĭth, and of his breth-
ren.
29 ¶Of the Ĭz'har-ītes, Chĕn-a-nī'ah
and his sons *were* for the outward busi-
ness over Israel, for officers and
judges.
30 *And* of the Hē'bro-nītes, Hăsh-a-
bī'ah and his brethren, men of valour, a
thousand and seven hundred, *were* of-
ficers among them of Israel on this side
Jordan westward in all the business of
the LORD, and in the service of the king.
31 Among the Hē'bro-nītes *was* Je-
rī'jah the chief, *even* among the Hē'bro-
nītes, according to the generations of
his fathers. In the fortieth year of the
reign of David they were sought for,
and there were found among them
mighty men of valour at Jā'zer of Gil-
ead.
32 And his brethren, men of valour,
were two thousand and seven hundred
chief fathers, whom king David made
rulers over the Reubenites, the Găd'-
ītes, and the half tribe of Ma-năs'seh,
for every matter pertaining to God, and
affairs of the king.

CHAPTER 27

NOW the children of Israel after their
number, *to wit,* the chief fathers and
captains of thousands and hundreds,
and their officers that served the king
in any matter of the courses, which
came in and went out month by month
throughout all the months of the year,
of every course *were* twenty and four
thousand.
2 Over the first course for the first
month *was* Ja-shō'be-am the son of
Zăb'dĭ-el: and in his course *were*
twenty and four thousand.
3 Of the children of Pe'rĕz *was* the
chief of all the captains of the host for
the first month.
4 And over the course of the second
month *was* Dō'da-ī an A-hō'hīte, and of
his course *was* Mĭk'lŏth also the ruler:
in his course likewise *were* twenty and
four thousand.
5 The third captain of the host for the
third month *was* Be-nā'iah the son of
Je-hoi'a-da, a chief priest: and in his
course *were* twenty and four thousand.
6 This *is that* Be-nā'iah, *who was*
mighty *among* the thirty, and above the
thirty: and in his course *was* Am-mĭz'a-
băd his son.

7 The fourth *captain* for the fourth month *was* Ā'sa-hĕl the brother of Jō'ăb, and Zĕb-a-dī'ah his son after him: and in his course *were* twenty and four thousand.
8 The fifth captain for the fifth month *was* Shăm'hŭth the Ĭz'ra-hīte: and in his course *were* twenty and four thousand.
9 The sixth *captain* for the sixth month *was* Ī'ra the son of Ĭk'kesh the Te-kō'īte: and in his course *were* twenty and four thousand.
10 The seventh *captain* for the seventh month *was* Hē'lĕz the Pĕl'o-nīte, of the children of Ē'phra-im: and in his course *were* twenty and four thousand.
11 The eighth *captain* for the eighth month *was* Sĭb'be-caī the Hu'shath-īte, of the Zär'hītes: and in his course *were* twenty and four thousand.
12 The ninth *captain* for the ninth month *was* Ā-bĭ-ē'zer the Ăn-e-tŏth'īte, of the Benjamites: and in his course *were* twenty and four thousand.
13 The tenth *captain* for the tenth month *was* Mā-har'a-ī the Ne-tōph'a-thīte, of the Zär'hītes: and in his course *were* twenty and four thousand.
14 The eleventh *captain* for the eleventh month *was* Be-nā'iah the Pĭr'-a-thŏn-īte, of the children of Ē'phra-im: and in his course *were* twenty and four thousand.
15 The twelfth *captain* for the twelfth month *was* Hĕl'da-ī the Ne-tōph'a-thīte, of Ŏth'nĭ-el: and in his course *were* twenty and four thousand.
16 ¶Furthermore over the tribes of Israel: the ruler of the Reubenites *was* Ē-lĭ-ē'zer the son of Zĭch'rī: of the Simeonites, Shĕph-a-tī'ah the son of Mā'a-chah:
17 Of the Lē'vītes, Hăsh-a-bī'ah the son of Kē-mū'el: of the Aăr'ŏ-nītes, Zā'-dŏk:
18 Of Jū'dah, E-lī'hū, *one* of the brethren of David: of Ĭs'sa-char, Omri the son of Michael:
19 Of Zĕb'u-lun, Ĭsh-mā-i'ah the son of Ō-ba-dī'ah: of Năph'ta-lī, Jĕr'ī-mŏth the son of Ăz'rĭ-el:
20 Of the children of Ē'phra-im, Hō-shē'a the son of Ăz-a-zī'ah: of the half tribe of Ma-năs'seh, Jō'el the son of Pe-dā'iah:
21 Of the half *tribe* of Ma-năs'seh in Gilead, Ĭd'dō the son of Zĕch-a-rī'ah: of Benjamin, Jā-ā'sĭ-el the son of Abner:
22 Of Dan, Ā-zar'e-el the son of Jer'ō-hăm. These were the princes of the tribes of Israel.
23 ¶But David took not the number of them from twenty years old and under: because the LORD had said he would increase Israel like to the stars of the heavens.
24 Jō'ăb the son of Zer-ū-i'ah began to number, but he finished not, because there fell wrath for it against Israel; neither was the number put in the account of the chronicles of king David.
25 ¶And over the king's treasures *was* Ăz'ma-vĕth the son of Ā'dĭ-el: and over the storehouses in the fields, in the cities, and in the villages, and in the castles, *was* Je-hŏn'a-than the son of Uz-zī'ah:
26 And over them that did the work of the field for tillage of the ground *was* Ĕz'rī the son of Chē'lŭb:
27 And over the vineyards *was* Shĭm'e-ī the Rā'math-īte: over the increase of the vineyards for the wine cellars *was* Zăb'dī the Shĭph'mīte:
28 And over the olive trees and the sycomore trees that *were* in the low plains *was* Bā'al–hā'nan the Gĕd'e-rīte: and over the cellars of oil *was* Jō'ăsh:
29 And over the herds that fed in Shâr'on *was* Shĭt'ra-ī the Shâr'on-īte: and over the herds *that were* in the valleys *was* Shā'phat the son of Ăd'la-ī:
30 Over the camels also *was* Ō'bĭl the Ĭsh'ma-el-īte: and over the asses *was* Jĕh-dē'iah the Me-rŏn'o-thīte:
31 And over the flocks *was* Jā'zĭz the Hă'ger-īte. All these *were* the rulers of the substance which *was* king David's.
32 Also Jonathan David's uncle was a counsellor, a wise man, and a scribe: and Je-hī'el the son of Hăch'mō-nī *was* with the king's sons:
33 And A-hĭth'o-phĕl *was* the king's counsellor: and Hu'shaī the Är'chīte *was* the king's companion:
34 And after A-hĭth'o-phĕl *was* Je-hoi'a-da the son of Be-nā'iah, and Ā-bī'a-thar: and the general of the king's army *was* Jō'ăb.

CHAPTER 28

AND David assembled all the princes of Israel, the princes of the tribes, and the captains of the companies that ministered to the king by course, and the captains over the thousands, and captains over the hundreds, and the stewards over all the substance and possession of the king, and of his sons, with the officers, and with the mighty men, and with all the valiant men, unto Jerusalem.
2 Then David the king stood up upon his feet, and said, Hear me, my brethren, and my people: *As for me,* I *had* in mine heart to build an house of rest for the ark of the covenant of the LORD, and for the footstool of our God, and had made ready for the building:

3 But God said unto me, Thou shalt
not build an house for my name, be-
cause thou *hast been* a man of war, and
hast shed blood.
4 Howbeit the LORD God of Israel
chose me before all the house of my
father to be king over Israel for ever:
for he hath chosen Jū'dah *to be* the rul-
er; and of the house of Jū'dah, the
house of my father; and among the
sons of my father he liked me to make
me king over all Israel:
5 And of all my sons, (for the LORD
hath given me many sons,) he hath cho-
sen Sŏlomon my son to sit upon the
throne of the kingdom of the LORD over
Israel.
6 And he said unto me, Sŏlomon thy
son, he shall build my house and my
courts: for I have chosen him *to be* my
son, and I will be his father.
7 Moreover I will establish his king-
dom for ever, if he be constant to do my
commandments and my judgments, as
at this day.
8 Now therefore in the sight of all
Israel the congregation of the LORD,
and in the audience of our God, keep
and seek for all the commandments of
the LORD your God: that ye may pos-
sess this good land, and leave *it* for an
inheritance for your children after you
for ever.
9 ¶And thou, Sŏlomon my son, know
thou the God of thy father, and serve
him with a perfect heart and with a will-
ing mind: for the LORD searcheth all
hearts, and understandeth all the imagi-
nations of the thoughts: if thou seek
him, he will be found of thee: but if thou
forsake him, he will cast thee off for
ever.
10 Take heed now; for the LORD hath
chosen thee to build an house for the
sanctuary: be strong, and do *it*.
11 ¶Then David gave to Sŏlomon his
son the pattern of the porch, and of the
houses thereof, and of the treasuries
thereof, and of the upper chambers
thereof, and of the inner parlours there-
of, and of the place of the mercy seat,
12 And the pattern of all that he had
by the spirit, of the courts of the house
of the LORD, and of all the chambers
round about, of the treasuries of the
house of God, and of the treasuries of
the dedicated things:
13 Also for the courses of the priests
and the Levites, and for all the work of
the service of the house of the LORD,
and for all the vessels of service in the
house of the LORD.
14 *He gave* of gold by weight for
things of gold, for all instruments of all
manner of service; *silver also* for all
instruments of silver by weight, for all
instruments of every kind of service:
15 Even the weight for the candle-
sticks of gold, and for their lamps of
gold, by weight for every candlestick,
and for the lamps thereof: and for the
candlesticks of silver by weight, *both*
for the candlestick, and *also* for the
lamps thereof, according to the use of
every candlestick.
16 And by weight *he gave* gold for the
tables of shewbread, for every table;
and *likewise* silver for the tables of sil-
ver:
17 Also pure gold for the fleshhooks,
and the bowls, and the cups: and for the
golden basons *he gave gold* by weight
for every bason; and *likewise silver* by
weight for every bason of silver:
18 And for the altar of incense
refined gold by weight; and gold for the
pattern of the chariot of the cherubims,
that spread out *their wings*, and
covered the ark of the covenant of the
LORD.
19 All *this, said David*, the LORD
made me understand in writing by *his*
hand upon me, *even* all the works of
this pattern.
20 And David said to Sŏlomon his
son, Be strong and of good courage,
and do *it*: fear not, nor be dismayed: for
the LORD God, *even* my God, *will be*
with thee; he will not fail thee, nor for-
sake thee, until thou hast finished all
the work for the service of the house of
the LORD.
21 And, behold, the courses of the
priests and the Lē'vītes, *even they shall*
be with thee for all the service of the
house of God: and *there shall be* with
thee for all manner of workmanship
every willing skilful man, for any man-
ner of service: also the princes and all
the people *will be* wholly at thy com-
mandment.

CHAPTER 29

FURTHERMORE David the king said
unto all the congregation, Sŏlomon my
son, whom alone God hath chosen, *is*
yet young and tender, and the work *is*
great: for the palace *is* not for man, but
for the LORD God.
2 Now I have prepared with all my
might for the house of my God the gold
for *things to be made* of gold, and the
silver for *things* of silver, and the brass
for *things* of brass, the iron for *things* of
iron, and wood for *things* of wood;
onyx stones, and *stones* to be set, glis-
tering stones, and of divers colours,
and all manner of precious stones, and
marble stones in abundance.

3 Moreover, because I have set my affection to the house of my God, I have of mine own proper good, of gold and silver, *which* I have given to the house of my God, over and above all that I have prepared for the holy house,
4 *Even* three thousand talents of gold, of the gold of Ō'phir, and seven thousand talents of refined silver, to overlay the walls of the houses *withal:*
5 The gold for *things* of gold, and the silver for *things* of silver, and for all manner of work *to be made* by the hands of artificers. And who *then* is willing to consecrate his service this day unto the LORD?
6 ¶Then the chief of the fathers and princes of the tribes of Israel, and the captains of thousands and of hundreds, with the rulers of the king's work, offered willingly,
7 And gave for the service of the house of God of gold five thousand talents and ten thousand drams, and of silver ten thousand talents, and of brass eighteen thousand talents, and one hundred thousand talents of iron.
8 And they with whom *precious* stones were found gave *them* to the treasure of the house of the LORD, by the hand of Je-hī'el the Ger'shon-īte.
9 Then the people rejoiced, for that they offered willingly, because with perfect heart they offered willingly to the LORD: and David the king also rejoiced with great joy.
10 ¶Wherefore David blessed the LORD before all the congregation: and David said, Blessed *be* thou, LORD God of Israel our father, for ever and ever.
11 Thine, O LORD, *is* the greatness, and the power, and the glory, and the victory, and the majesty: for all *that is* in the heaven and in the earth *is thine;* thine *is* the kingdom, O LORD, and thou art exalted as head above all.
12 Both riches and honour *come* of thee, and thou reignest over all; and in thine hand *is* power and might; and in thine hand *it is* to make great, and to give strength unto all.
13 Now therefore, our God, we thank thee, and praise thy glorious name.
14 But who *am* I, and what *is* my people, that we should be able to offer so willingly after this sort? for all things *come* of thee, and of thine own have we given thee.
15 For we *are* strangers before thee, and sojourners, as *were* all our fathers: our days on the earth *are* as a shadow, and *there is* none abiding.
16 O LORD our God, all this store that we have prepared to build thee an house for thine holy name *cometh* of thine hand, and *is* all thine own.
17 I know also, my God, that thou triest the heart, and hast pleasure in uprightness. As for me, in the uprightness of mine heart I have willingly offered all these things: and now have I seen with joy thy people, which are present here, to offer willingly unto thee.
18 O LORD God of Abraham, Isaac, and of Israel, our fathers, keep this for ever in the imagination of the thoughts of the heart of thy people, and prepare their heart unto thee:
19 And give unto Sŏlomon my son a perfect heart, to keep thy commandments, thy testimonies, and thy statutes, and to do all *these things,* and to build the palace, *for* the which I have made provision.
20 ¶And David said to all the congregation, Now bless the LORD your God. And all the congregation blessed the LORD God of their fathers, and bowed down their heads, and worshipped the LORD, and the king.
21 And they sacrificed sacrifices unto the LORD, and offered burnt offerings unto the LORD, on the morrow after that day, *even* a thousand bullocks, a thousand rams, *and* a thousand lambs, with their drink offerings, and sacrifices in abundance for all Israel:
22 And did eat and drink before the LORD on that day with great gladness. And they made Sŏlomon the son of David king the second time, and anointed *him* unto the LORD *to be* the chief governor, and Zā'dŏk *to be* priest.
23 Then Sŏlomon sat on the throne of the LORD as king instead of David his father, and prospered; and all Israel obeyed him.
24 And all the princes, and the mighty men, and all the sons likewise of king David, submitted themselves unto Sŏlomon the king.
25 And the LORD magnified Sŏlomon exceedingly in the sight of all Israel, and bestowed upon him *such* royal majesty as had not been on any king before him in Israel.
26 ¶Thus David the son of Jesse reigned over all Israel.
27 And the time that he reigned over Israel *was* forty years; seven years reigned he in Hēbron, and thirty and three *years* reigned he in Jerusalem.
28 And he died in a good old age, full of days, riches, and honour: and Sŏlomon his son reigned in his stead.
29 Now the acts of David the king, first and last, behold, they *are* written in the book of Samuel the seer, and in

the book of Nāthan the prophet, and in the book of Gad the seer,

30 With all his reign and his might, and the times that went over him, and over Israel, and over all the kingdoms of the countries.

THE SECOND BOOK OF THE

CHRONICLES

CHAPTER 1

AND Sŏlomon the son of David was strengthened in his kingdom, and the LORD his God *was* with him, and magnified him exceedingly.

2 Then Sŏlomon spake unto all Israel, to the captains of thousands and of hundreds, and to the judges, and to every governor in all Israel, the chief of the fathers.

3 So Sŏlomon, and all the congregation with him, went to the high place that *was* at Gĭbeon; for there was the tabernacle of the congregation of God, which Moses the servant of the LORD had made in the wilderness.

4 But the ark of God had David brought up from Kir'jath–jē'a-rĭm to *the place which* David had prepared for it: for he had pitched a tent for it at Jerusalem.

5 Moreover the brasen altar, that Be-zăl'e-el the son of Ū'rī, the son of Hur, had made, he put before the tabernacle of the LORD: and Sŏlomon and the congregation sought unto it.

6 And Sŏlomon went up thither to the brasen altar before the LORD, which *was* at the tabernacle of the congregation, and offered a thousand burnt offerings upon it.

7 ¶In that night did God appear unto Sŏlomon, and said unto him, Ask what I shall give thee.

8 And Sŏlomon said unto God, Thou hast shewed great mercy unto David my father, and hast made me to reign in his stead.

9 Now, O LORD God, let thy promise unto David my father be established: for thou hast made me king over a people like the dust of the earth in multitude.

10 Give me now wisdom and knowledge, that I may go out and come in before this people: for who can judge this thy people, *that is so* great?

11 And God said to Sŏlomon, Because this was in thine heart, and thou hast not asked riches, wealth, or honour, nor the life of thine enemies, neither yet hast asked long life; but hast asked wisdom and knowledge for thyself, that thou mayest judge my people, over whom I have made thee king:

12 Wisdom and knowledge *is* granted unto thee; and I will give thee riches, and wealth, and honour, such as none of the kings have had that *have been* before thee, neither shall there any after thee have the like.

13 ¶Then Sŏlomon came *from his journey* to the high place that *was* at Gĭbeon to Jerusalem, from before the tabernacle of the congregation, and reigned over Israel.

14 And Sŏlomon gathered chariots and horsemen: and he had a thousand and four hundred chariots, and twelve thousand horsemen, which he placed in the chariot cities, and with the king at Jerusalem.

15 And the king made silver and gold at Jerusalem *as plenteous* as stones, and cedar trees made he as the sycomore trees that *are* in the vale for abundance.

16 And Sŏlomon had horses brought out of Egypt, and linen yarn: the king's merchants received the linen yarn at a price.

17 And they fetched up, and brought forth out of Egypt a chariot for six hundred *shekels* of silver, and an horse for an hundred and fifty: and so brought they out *horses* for all the kings of the Hittites, and for the kings of Syria, by their means.

CHAPTER 2

AND Sŏlomon determined to build an house for the name of the LORD, and an house for his kingdom.

2 And Sŏlomon told out threescore and ten thousand men to bear burdens, and fourscore thousand to hew in the mountain, and three thousand and six hundred to oversee them.

3 ¶And Sŏlomon sent to Hū'ram the king of Tyre, saying, As thou didst deal with David my father, and didst send him cedars to build him an house to dwell therein, *even so deal with me.*

4 Behold, I build an house to the name of the LORD my God, to dedicate *it* to him, *and* to burn before him sweet incense, and for the continual shewbread, and for the burnt offerings morning and evening, on the sabbaths, and on the new moons, and on the solemn feasts of the LORD our God. This *is an ordinance* for ever to Israel.

5 And the house which I build *is*

great: for great *is* our God above all
gods.
6 But who is able to build him an
house, seeing the heaven and heaven of
heavens cannot contain him? who *am* I
then, that I should build him an house,
save only to burn sacrifice before him?
7 Send me now therefore a man cun-
ning to work in gold, and in silver, and
in brass, and in iron, and in purple, and
crimson, and blue, and that can skill to
grave with the cunning men that *are*
with me in Jūdah and in Jerusalem,
whom David my father did provide.
8 Send me also cedar trees, fir trees,
and algum trees, out of Lebanon: for I
know that thy servants can skill to cut
timber in Lebanon; and, behold, my
servants *shall be* with thy servants,
9 Even to prepare me timber in abun-
dance: for the house which I am about
to build *shall be* wonderful great.
10 And, behold, I will give to thy ser-
vants, the hewers that cut timber,
twenty thousand measures of beaten
wheat, and twenty thousand measures
of barley, and twenty thousand baths
of wine, and twenty thousand baths of
oil.
11 ¶Then Hū'ram the king of Tyre
answered in writing, which he sent to
Sŏlomon, Because the LORD hath loved
his people, he hath made thee king over
them.
12 Hū'ram said moreover, Blessed *be*
the LORD God of Israel, that made
heaven and earth, who hath given to
David the king a wise son, endued with
prudence and understanding, that
might build an house for the LORD, and
an house for his kingdom.
13 And now I have sent a cunning
man, endued with understanding, of
Hū'ram my father's,
14 The son of a woman of the daugh-
ters of Dan, and his father *was* a man of
Tyre, skilful to work in gold, and in sil-
ver, in brass, in iron, in stone, and in
timber, in purple, in blue, and in fine
linen, and in crimson; also to grave any
manner of graving, and to find out
every device which shall be put to him,
with thy cunning men, and with the
cunning men of my lord David thy
father.
15 Now therefore the wheat, and the
barley, the oil, and the wine, which my
lord hath spoken of, let him send unto
his servants:
16 And we will cut wood out of Leba-
non, as much as thou shalt need: and
we will bring it to thee in floats by sea
to Jŏppa; and thou shalt carry it up to
Jerusalem.
17 ¶And Sŏlomon numbered all the
strangers that *were* in the land of
Israel, after the numbering wherewith
David his father had numbered them;
and they were found an hundred and
fifty thousand and three thousand and
six hundred.
18 And he set threescore and ten
thousand of them *to be* bearers of bur-
dens, and fourscore thousand *to be* hew-
ers in the mountain, and three thou-
sand and six hundred overseers to set
the people a work.

CHAPTER 3

THEN Sŏlomon began to build the
house of the LORD at Jerusalem in
mount Mō-rī'ah, where *the LORD* ap-
peared unto David his father, in the
place that David had prepared in the
threshingfloor of Ôr'nan the Jēb'u-sīte.
2 And he began to build in the second
day of the second month, in the fourth
year of his reign.
3 ¶Now these *are the things wherein*
Sŏlomon was instructed for the build-
ing of the house of God. The length by
cubits after the first measure *was*
threescore cubits, and the breadth
twenty cubits.
4 And the porch that *was* in the front
of the house, the length *of it was* accord-
ing to the breadth of the house,
twenty cubits, and the height *was* an
hundred and twenty: and he overlaid it
within with pure gold.
5 And the greater house he cieled
with fir tree, which he overlaid with
fine gold, and set thereon palm trees
and chains.
6 And he garnished the house with
precious stones for beauty: and the
gold *was* gold of Pär-vā'im.
7 He overlaid also the house, the
beams, the posts, and the walls thereof,
and the doors thereof, with gold; and
graved cherubims on the walls.
8 And he made the most holy house,
the length whereof *was* according to
the breadth of the house, twenty cubits,
and the breadth thereof twenty cu-
bits: and he overlaid it with fine gold,
amounting to six hundred talents.
9 And the weight of the nails *was* fifty
shekels of gold. And he overlaid the up-
per chambers with gold.
10 And in the most holy house he
made two cherubims of image work,
and overlaid them with gold.
11 And the wings of the cherubims
were twenty cubits long: one wing *of
the one cherub was* five cubits, reach-
ing to the wall of the house: and the
other wing *was likewise* five cubits,
reaching to the wing of the other
cherub.

12 And *one* wing of the other cherub *was* five cubits, reaching to the wall of the house: and the other wing *was* five cubits *also*, joining to the wing of the other cherub.
13 The wings of these cherubims spread themselves forth twenty cubits: and they stood on their feet, and their faces *were* inward.
14 And he made the vail *of* blue, and purple, and crimson, and fine linen, and wrought cherubims thereon.
15 Also he made before the house two pillars of thirty and five cubits high, and the chapiter that *was* on the top of each of them *was* five cubits.
16 And he made chains, *as* in the oracle, and put *them* on the heads of the pillars; and made an hundred pomegranates, and put *them* on the chains.
17 And he reared up the pillars before the temple, one on the right hand, and the other on the left; and called the name of that on the right hand Jā'chin, and the name of that on the left Bō'ăz.

CHAPTER 4

MOREOVER he made an altar of brass, twenty cubits the length thereof, and twenty cubits the breadth thereof, and ten cubits the height thereof.
2 ¶Also he made a molten sea of ten cubits from brim to brim, round in compass, and five cubits the height thereof; and a line of thirty cubits did compass it round about.
3 And under it *was* the similitude of oxen, which did compass it round about: ten in a cubit, compassing the sea round about. Two rows of oxen *were* cast, when it was cast.
4 It stood upon twelve oxen, three looking toward the north, and three looking toward the west, and three looking toward the south, and three looking toward the east: and the sea *was set* above upon them, and all their hinder parts *were* inward.
5 And the thickness of it *was* an handbreadth, and the brim of it like the work of the brim of a cup, with flowers of lilies; *and* it received and held three thousand baths.
6 ¶He made also ten lavers, and put five on the right hand, and five on the left, to wash in them: such things as they offered for the burnt offering they washed in them; but the sea *was* for the priests to wash in.
7 And he made ten candlesticks of gold according to their form, and set *them* in the temple, five on the right hand, and five on the left.
8 He made also ten tables, and placed *them* in the temple, five on the right side, and five on the left. And he made an hundred basons of gold.
9 ¶Furthermore he made the court of the priests, and the great court, and doors for the court, and overlaid the doors of them with brass.
10 And he set the sea on the right side of the east end, over against the south.
11 ¶And Hū'ram made the pots, and the shovels, and the basons. And Hū'ram finished the work that he was to make for king Sŏlomon for the house of God;
12 *To wit*, the two pillars, and the pommels, and the chapiters *which were* on the top of the two pillars, and the two wreaths to cover the two pommels of the chapiters which *were* on the top of the pillars;
13 And four hundred pomegranates on the two wreaths; two rows of pomegranates on each wreath, to cover the two pommels of the chapiters which *were* upon the pillars.
14 He made also bases, and lavers made he upon the bases;
15 One sea, and twelve oxen under it.
16 The pots also, and the shovels, and the fleshhooks, and all their instruments, did Hū'ram his father make to king Sŏlomon for the house of the LORD of bright brass.
17 In the plain of Jordan did the king cast them, in the clay ground between Sŭc'coth and Zĕ-red'ā-thah.
18 Thus Sŏlomon made all these vessels in great abundance: for the weight of the brass could not be found out.
19 ¶And Sŏlomon made all the vessels that *were for* the house of God, the golden altar also, and the tables whereon the shewbread *was set*;
20 Moreover the candlesticks with their lamps, that they should burn after the manner before the oracle, of pure gold;
21 And the flowers, and the lamps, and the tongs, *made he of* gold, *and* that perfect gold;
22 And the snuffers, and the basons, and the spoons, and the censers, *of* pure gold: and the entry of the house, the inner doors thereof for the most holy *place*, and the doors of the house of the temple, *were of* gold.

CHAPTER 5

THUS all the work that Sŏlomon made for the house of the LORD was finished: and Sŏlomon brought in *all* the things that David his father had dedicated; and the silver, and the gold, and all the instruments, put he among the treasures of the house of God.

2 ¶Then Sŏlomon assembled the elders of Israel, and all the heads of the tribes, the chief of the fathers of the children of Israel, unto Jerusalem, to bring up the ark of the covenant of the LORD out of the city of David, which *is* Zion.

3 Wherefore all the men of Israel assembled themselves unto the king in the feast which *was* in the seventh month.

4 And all the elders of Israel came; and the Lē'vītes took up the ark.

5 And they brought up the ark, and the tabernacle of the congregation, and all the holy vessels that *were* in the tabernacle, these did the priests *and* the Lē'vītes bring up.

6 Also king Sŏlomon, and all the congregation of Israel that were assembled unto him before the ark, sacrificed sheep and oxen, which could not be told nor numbered for multitude.

7 And the priests brought in the ark of the covenant of the LORD unto his place, to the oracle of the house, into the most holy *place, even* under the wings of the cherubims:

8 For the cherubims spread forth *their* wings over the place of the ark, and the cherubims covered the ark and the staves thereof above.

9 And they drew out the staves *of the ark*, that the ends of the staves were seen from the ark before the oracle; but they were not seen without. And there it is unto this day.

10 *There was* nothing in the ark save the two tables which Moses put *therein* at Hô'rĕb, when the LORD made *a covenant* with the children of Israel, when they came out of Egypt.

11 ¶And it came to pass, when the priests were come out of the holy *place*: (for all the priests *that were* present were sanctified, *and* did not *then* wait by course:

12 Also the Lē'vītes *which were* the singers, all of them of Ā'săph, of Hē'măn, of Jed'ū-thun, with their sons and their brethren, *being* arrayed in white linen, having cymbals and psalteries and harps, stood at the east end of the altar, and with them an hundred and twenty priests sounding with trumpets:)

13 It came even to pass, as the trumpeters and singers *were* as one, to make one sound to be heard in praising and thanking the LORD; and when they lifted up *their* voice with the trumpets and cymbals and instruments of musick, and praised the LORD, *saying*, For *he is* good; for his mercy *endureth* for ever: that *then* the house was filled with a cloud, *even* the house of the LORD;

14 So that the priests could not stand to minister by reason of the cloud: for the glory of the LORD had filled the house of God.

CHAPTER 6

THEN said Sŏlomon, The LORD hath said that he would dwell in the thick darkness.

2 But I have built an house of habitation for thee, and a place for thy dwelling for ever.

3 And the king turned his face, and blessed the whole congregation of Israel: and all the congregation of Israel stood.

4 And he said, Blessed *be* the LORD God of Israel, who hath with his hands fulfilled *that* which he spake with his mouth to my father David, saying,

5 Since the day that I brought forth my people out of the land of Egypt I chose no city among all the tribes of Israel to build an house in, that my name might be there; neither chose I any man to be a ruler over my people Israel:

6 But I have chosen Jerusalem, that my name might be there; and have chosen David to be over my people Israel.

7 Now it was in the heart of David my father to build an house for the name of the LORD God of Israel.

8 But the LORD said to David my father, Forasmuch as it was in thine heart to build an house for my name, thou didst well in that it was in thine heart:

9 Notwithstanding thou shalt not build the house; but thy son which shall come forth out of thy loins, he shall build the house for my name.

10 The LORD therefore hath performed his word that he hath spoken: for I am risen up in the room of David my father, and am set on the throne of Israel, as the LORD promised, and have built the house for the name of the LORD God of Israel.

11 And in it have I put the ark, wherein *is* the covenant of the LORD, that he made with the children of Israel.

12 ¶And he stood before the altar of the LORD in the presence of all the congregation of Israel, and spread forth his hands:

13 For Sŏlomon had made a brasen scaffold of five cubits long, and five cubits broad, and three cubits high, and had set it in the midst of the court: and upon it he stood, and kneeled down upon his knees before all the congrega-

tion of Israel, and spread forth his hands toward heaven,

14 And said, O LORD God of Israel, *there is* no God like thee in the heaven, nor in the earth; which keepest covenant, and *shewest* mercy unto thy servants, that walk before thee with all their hearts:

15 Thou which hast kept with thy servant David my father that which thou hast promised him; and spakest with thy mouth, and hast fulfilled *it* with thine hand, as *it is* this day.

16 Now therefore, O LORD God of Israel, keep with thy servant David my father that which thou hast promised him, saying, There shall not fail thee a man in my sight to sit upon the throne of Israel; yet so that thy children take heed to their way to walk in my law, as thou hast walked before me.

17 Now then, O LORD God of Israel, let thy word be verified, which thou hast spoken unto thy servant David.

18 But will God in very deed dwell with men on the earth? behold, heaven and the heaven of heavens cannot contain thee; how much less this house which I have built!

19 Have respect therefore to the prayer of thy servant, and to his supplication, O LORD my God, to hearken unto the cry and the prayer which thy servant prayeth before thee:

20 That thine eyes may be open upon this house day and night, upon the place whereof thou hast said that thou wouldest put thy name there; to hearken unto the prayer which thy servant prayeth toward this place.

21 Hearken therefore unto the supplications of thy servant, and of thy people Israel, which they shall make toward this place: hear thou from thy dwelling place, *even* from heaven; and when thou hearest, forgive.

22 ¶If a man sin against his neighbour, and an oath be laid upon him to make him swear, and the oath come before thine altar in this house;

23 Then hear thou from heaven, and do, and judge thy servants, by requiting the wicked, by recompensing his way upon his own head; and by justifying the righteous, by giving him according to his righteousness.

24 ¶And if thy people Israel be put to the worse before the enemy, because they have sinned against thee; and shall return and confess thy name, and pray and make supplication before thee in this house;

25 Then hear thou from the heavens, and forgive the sin of thy people Israel, and bring them again unto the land which thou gavest to them and to their fathers.

26 ¶When the heaven is shut up, and there is no rain, because they have sinned against thee; *yet* if they pray toward this place, and confess thy name, and turn from their sin, when thou dost afflict them;

27 Then hear thou from heaven, and forgive the sin of thy servants, and of thy people Israel, when thou hast taught them the good way, wherein they should walk; and send rain upon thy land, which thou hast given unto thy people for an inheritance.

28 ¶If there be dearth in the land, if there be pestilence, if there be blasting, or mildew, locusts, or caterpillers; if their enemies besiege them in the cities of their land; whatsoever sore or whatsoever sickness *there be*:

29 *Then* what prayer *or* what supplication soever shall be made of any man, or of all thy people Israel, when every one shall know his own sore and his own grief, and shall spread forth his hands in this house:

30 Then hear thou from heaven thy dwelling place, and forgive, and render unto every man according unto all his ways, whose heart thou knowest; (for thou only knowest the hearts of the children of men:)

31 That they may fear thee, to walk in thy ways, so long as they live in the land which thou gavest unto our fathers.

32 ¶Moreover concerning the stranger, which is not of thy people Israel, but is come from a far country for thy great name's sake, and thy mighty hand, and thy stretched out arm; if they come and pray in this house;

33 Then hear thou from the heavens, *even* from thy dwelling place, and do according to all that the stranger calleth to thee for; that all people of the earth may know thy name, and fear thee, as *doth* thy people Israel, and may know that this house which I have built is called by thy name.

34 ¶If thy people go out to war against their enemies by the way that thou shalt send them, and they pray unto thee toward this city which thou hast chosen, and the house which I have built for thy name;

35 Then hear thou from the heavens their prayer and their supplication, and maintain their cause.

36 ¶If they sin against thee, (for *there is* no man which sinneth not,) and thou be angry with them, and deliver them over before *their* enemies, and they

carry them away captives unto a land far off or near;

37 Yet *if* they bethink themselves in the land whither they are carried captive, and turn and pray unto thee in the land of their captivity, saying, We have sinned, we have done amiss, and have dealt wickedly;

38 If they return to thee with all their heart and with all their soul in the land of their captivity, whither they have carried them captives, and pray toward their land, which thou gavest unto their fathers, and *toward* the city which thou hast chosen, and toward the house which I have built for thy name:

39 Then hear thou from the heavens, *even* from thy dwelling place, their prayer and their supplications, and maintain their cause, and forgive thy people which have sinned against thee.

40 Now, my God, let, I beseech thee, thine eyes be open, and *let* thine ears *be* attent unto the prayer *that is made* in this place.

41 Now therefore arise, O Lord God, into thy resting place, thou, and the ark of thy strength: let thy priests, O Lord God, be clothed with salvation, and let thy saints rejoice in goodness.

42 O Lord God, turn not away the face of thine anointed: remember the mercies of David thy servant.

CHAPTER 7

NOW when Sŏlomon had made an end of praying, the fire came down from heaven, and consumed the burnt offering and the sacrifices; and the glory of the Lord filled the house.

2 And the priests could not enter into the house of the Lord, because the glory of the Lord had filled the Lord's house.

3 And when all the children of Israel saw how the fire came down, and the glory of the Lord upon the house, they bowed themselves with their faces to the ground upon the pavement, and worshipped, and praised the Lord, *saying*, For *he is* good; for his mercy *endureth* for ever.

4 ¶Then the king and all the people offered sacrifices before the Lord.

5 And king Sŏlomon offered a sacrifice of twenty and two thousand oxen, and an hundred and twenty thousand sheep; so the king and all the people dedicated the house of God.

6 And the priests waited on their offices: the Lē′vītes also with instruments of musick of the Lord, which David the king had made to praise the Lord, because his mercy *endureth* for ever, when David praised by their ministry; and the priests sounded trumpets before them, and all Israel stood.

7 Moreover Sŏlomon hallowed the middle of the court that *was* before the house of the Lord: for there he offered burnt offerings, and the fat of the peace offerings, because the brasen altar which Solomon had made was not able to receive the burnt offerings, and the meat offerings, and the fat.

8 ¶Also at the same time Sŏlomon kept the feast seven days, and all Israel with him, a very great congregation, from the entering in of Hā′măth unto the river of Egypt.

9 And in the eighth day they made a solemn assembly: for they kept the dedication of the altar seven days, and the feast seven days.

10 And on the three and twentieth day of the seventh month he sent the people away into their tents, glad and merry in heart for the goodness that the Lord had shewed unto David, and to Sŏlomon, and to Israel his people.

11 Thus Sŏlomon finished the house of the Lord, and the king's house: and all that came into Sŏlomon's heart to make in the house of the Lord, and in his own house, he prosperously effected.

12 ¶And the Lord appeared to Sŏlomon by night, and said unto him, I have heard thy prayer, and have chosen this place to myself for an house of sacrifice.

13 If I shut up heaven that there be no rain, or if I command the locusts to devour the land, or if I send pestilence among my people;

14 If my people, which are called by my name, shall humble themselves, and pray, and seek my face, and turn from their wicked ways; then will I hear from heaven, and will forgive their sin, and will heal their land.

15 Now mine eyes shall be open, and mine ears attent unto the prayer *that is made* in this place.

16 For now have I chosen and sanctified this house, that my name may be there for ever: and mine eyes and mine heart shall be there perpetually.

17 And as for thee, if thou wilt walk before me, as David thy father walked, and do according to all that I have commanded thee, and shalt observe my statutes and my judgments;

18 Then will I stablish the throne of thy kingdom, according as I have covenanted with David thy father, saying, There shall not fail thee a man *to be* ruler in Israel.

19 But if ye turn away, and forsake my statutes and my commandments,

which I have set before you, and shall go and serve other gods, and worship them;

20 Then will I pluck them up by the roots out of my land which I have given them; and this house, which I have sanctified for my name, will I cast out of my sight, and will make it *to be* a proverb and a byword among all nations.

21 And this house, which is high, shall be an astonishment to every one that passeth by it; so that he shall say, Why hath the LORD done thus unto this land, and unto this house?

22 And it shall be answered, Because they forsook the LORD God of their fathers, which brought them forth out of the land of Egypt, and laid hold on other gods, and worshipped them, and served them: therefore hath he brought all this evil upon them.

CHAPTER 8

AND it came to pass at the end of twenty years, wherein Sŏlomon had built the house of the LORD, and his own house,

2 That the cities which Hū'ram had restored to Sŏlomon, Sŏlomon built them, and caused the children of Israel to dwell there.

3 And Sŏlomon went to Hā'măth-zō'bah, and prevailed against it.

4 And he built Tăd'môr in the wilderness, and all the store cities, which he built in Hā'măth.

5 Also he built Bĕth-hô'ron the upper, and Bĕth-hô'ron the nether, fenced cities, with walls, gates, and bars;

6 And Bā'al-ăth, and all the store cities that Sŏlomon had, and all the chariot cities, and the cities of the horsemen, and all that Sŏlomon desired to build in Jerusalem, and in Lebanon, and throughout all the land of his dominion.

7 ¶*As for* all the people *that were* left of the Hittites, and the Ămorītes, and the Pĕr'iz-zītes, and the Hī'vītes, and the Jēb'u-sītes, which *were* not of Israel,

8 *But* of their children, who were left after them in the land, whom the children of Israel consumed not, them did Sŏlomon make to pay tribute until this day.

9 But of the children of Israel did Sŏlomon make no servants for his work; but they *were* men of war, and chief of his captains, and captains of his chariots and horsemen.

10 And these *were* the chief of king Sŏlomon's officers, *even* two hundred and fifty, that bare rule over the people.

11 ¶And Sŏlomon brought up the daughter of Pharaoh out of the city of David unto the house that he had built for her: for he said, My wife shall not dwell in the house of David king of Israel, because *the places are* holy, whereunto the ark of the LORD hath come.

12 ¶Then Sŏlomon offered burnt offerings unto the LORD on the altar of the LORD, which he had built before the porch,

13 Even after a certain rate every day, offering according to the commandment of Moses, on the sabbaths, and on the new moons, and on the solemn feasts, three times in the year, *even* in the feast of unleavened bread, and in the feast of weeks, and in the feast of tabernacles.

14 And he appointed, according to the order of David his father, the courses of the priests to their service, and the Lē'vītes to their charges, to praise and minister before the priests, as the duty of every day required: the porters also by their courses at every gate: for so had David the man of God commanded.

15 And they departed not from the commandment of the king unto the priests and Lē'vītes concerning any matter, or concerning the treasures.

16 Now all the work of Sŏlomon was prepared unto the day of the foundation of the house of the LORD, and until it was finished. *So* the house of the LORD was perfected.

17 ¶Then went Sŏlomon to Ē'zĭ-on-gē'ber, and to Ē'lŏth, at the sea side in the land of Ēdom.

18 And Hū'ram sent him by the hands of his servants ships, and servants that had knowledge of the sea; and they went with the servants of Sŏlomon to Ō'phir, and took thence four hundred and fifty talents of gold, and brought *them* to king Sŏlomon.

CHAPTER 9

AND when the queen of Shēba heard of the fame of Sŏlomon, she came to prove Sŏlomon with hard questions at Jerusalem, with a very great company, and camels that bare spices, and gold in abundance, and precious stones: and when she was come to Sŏlomon, she communed with him of all that was in her heart.

2 And Sŏlomon told her all her questions: and there was nothing hid from Sŏlomon which he told her not.

3 And when the queen of Shēba had seen the wisdom of Sŏlomon, and the house that he had built,

4 And the meat of his table, and the
sitting of his servants, and the attendance of his ministers, and their apparel; his cupbearers also, and their apparel; and his ascent by which he went up into the house of the LORD; there was no more spirit in her.
5 And she said to the king, *It was* a
true report which I heard in mine own land of thine acts, and of thy wisdom:
6 Howbeit I believed not their words,
until I came, and mine eyes had seen *it:* and, behold, the one half of the greatness of thy wisdom was not told me: *for* thou exceedest the fame that I heard.
7 Happy *are* thy men, and happy *are*
these thy servants, which stand continually before thee, and hear thy wisdom.
8 Blessed be the LORD thy God, which
delighted in thee to set thee on his throne, *to be* king for the LORD thy God: because thy God loved Israel, to establish them for ever, therefore made he thee king over them, to do judgment and justice.
9 And she gave the king an hundred
and twenty talents of gold, and of spices great abundance, and precious stones: neither was there any such spice as the queen of Shēba gave king Sŏlomon.
10 And the servants also of Hū'ram,
and the servants of Sŏlomon, which brought gold from Ō'phir, brought algum trees and precious stones.
11 And the king made *of* the algum
trees terraces to the house of the LORD, and to the king's palace, and harps and psalteries for singers: and there were none such seen before in the land of Jūdah.
12 And king Sŏlomon gave to the
queen of Shēba all her desire, whatsoever she asked, beside *that* which she had brought unto the king. So she turned, and went away to her own land, she and her servants.
13 ¶Now the weight of gold that
came to Sŏlomon in one year was six hundred and three score and six talents of gold;
14 Beside *that which* chapmen and
merchants brought. And all the kings of Arabia and governors of the country brought gold and silver to Sŏlomon.
15 ¶And king Sŏlomon made two
hundred targets *of* beaten gold: six hundred *shekels* of beaten gold went to one target.
16 And three hundred shields *made*
he of beaten gold: three hundred *shekels* of gold went to one shield. And the king put them in the house of the forest of Lebanon.
17 ¶Moreover the king made a great
throne of ivory, and overlaid it with pure gold.
18 And *there were* six steps to the
throne, with a footstool of gold, *which were* fastened to the throne, and stays on each side of the sitting place, and two lions standing by the stays:
19 And twelve lions stood there on
the one side and on the other upon the six steps. There was not the like made in any kingdom.
20 ¶And all the drinking vessels of
king Sŏlomon *were of* gold, and all the vessels of the house of the forest of Lebanon *were of* pure gold: none *were of* silver; it was *not* any thing accounted of in the days of Sŏlomon.
21 For the king's ships went to Tär-
shĭsh with the servants of Hū'ram: every three years once came the ships of Tärshĭsh bringing gold, and silver, ivory, and apes, and peacocks.
22 And king Sŏlomon passed all the
kings of the earth in riches and wisdom.
23 ¶And all the kings of the earth
sought the presence of Sŏlomon, to hear his wisdom, that God had put in his heart.
24 And they brought every man his
present, vessels of silver, and vessels of gold, and raiment, harness, and spices, horses, and mules, a rate year by year.
25 ¶And Sŏlomon had four thousand
stalls for horses and chariots, and twelve thousand horsemen; whom he bestowed in the chariot cities, and with the king at Jerusalem.
26 ¶And he reigned over all the kings
from the river even unto the land of the Philistines, and to the border of Egypt.
27 And the king made silver in Jeru-
salem as stones, and cedar trees made he as the sycomore trees that *are* in the low plains in abundance.
28 And they brought unto Sŏlomon
horses out of Egypt, and out of all lands.
29 ¶Now the rest of the acts of Sŏlo-
mon, first and last, *are* they not written in the book of Nāthan the prophet, and in the prophecy of A-hī'jah the Shī'lo-nīte, and in the visions of Ĭd'dō the seer against Jĕr-o-bō'am the son of Nē'băt?
30 And Sŏlomon reigned in Jeru-
salem over all Israel forty years.
31 And Sŏlomon slept with his fa-
thers, and he was buried in the city of David his father: and Rē-ho-bō'am his son reigned in his stead.

CHAPTER 10

AND Rē-ho-bō'am went to Shĕ'chem: for to Shĕ'chem were all Israel come to make him king.

2 And it came to pass, when Jĕr-o-bō'am the son of Nē'băt, who *was* in Egypt, whither he had fled from the presence of Sŏlomon the king, heard *it*, that Jĕr-o-bō'am returned out of Egypt.
3 And they sent and called him. So Jĕr-o-bō'am and all Israel came and spake to Rē'ho-bō'am, saying,
4 Thy father made our yoke grievous: now therefore ease thou somewhat the grievous servitude of thy father, and his heavy yoke that he put upon us, and we will serve thee.
5 And he said unto them, Come again unto me after three days. And the people departed.
6 ¶And king Rē-ho-bō'am took counsel with the old men that had stood before Sŏlomon his father while he yet lived, saying, What counsel give ye *me* to return answer to this people?
7 And they spake unto him, saying, If thou be kind to this people, and please them, and speak good words to them, they will be thy servants for ever.
8 But he forsook the counsel which the old men gave him, and took counsel with the young men that were brought up with him, that stood before him.
9 And he said unto them, What advice give ye that we may return answer to this people, which have spoken to me, saying, Ease somewhat the yoke that thy father did put upon us?
10 And the young men that were brought up with him spake unto him, saying, Thus shalt thou answer the people that spake unto thee, saying, Thy father made our yoke heavy, but make thou *it* somewhat lighter for us; thus shalt thou say unto them, My little *finger* shall be thicker than my father's loins.
11 For whereas my father put a heavy yoke upon you, I will put more to your yoke: my father chastised you with whips, but I *will chastise you* with scorpions.
12 ¶So Jĕr-o-bo'am and all the people came to Rē-ho-bō'am on the third day, as the king bade, saying, Come again to me on the third day.
13 And the king answered them roughly; and king Rē-ho-bō'am forsook the counsel of the old men,
14 And answered them after the advice of the young men, saying, My father made your yoke heavy, but I will add thereto: my father chastised you with whips, but I *will chastise you* with scorpions.
15 So the king hearkened not unto the people: for the cause was of God, that the LORD might perform his word, which he spake by the hand of A-hī'jah the Shī'lo-nīte to Jĕr-o-bō'am the son of Nē'băt.
16 And when all Israel *saw* that the king would not hearken unto them, the people answered the king, saying, What portion have we in David? and *we have* none inheritance in the son of Jesse: every man to your tents, O Israel: *and* now, David, see to thine own house. So all Israel went to their tents.
17 But *as for* the children of Israel that dwelt in the cities of Jūdah, Rē-ho-bō'am reigned over them.
18 Then king Rē-ho-bō'am sent Ha-dō'ram that *was* over the tribute; and the children of Israel stoned him with stones, that he died. But king Rē-ho-bō'am made speed to get him up to *his* chariot, to flee to Jerusalem.
19 And Israel rebelled against the house of David unto this day.

CHAPTER 11

AND when Rē-ho-bō'am was come to Jerusalem, he gathered of the house of Jūdah and Benjamin an hundred and fourscore thousand chosen *men*, which were warriors, to fight against Israel, that he might bring the kingdom again to Rē-ho-bō'am.
2 But the word of the LORD came to Shem-ā-i'ah the man of God, saying,
3 Speak unto Rē-ho-bō'am the son of Sŏlomon, king of Jūdah, and to all Israel in Jūdah and Benjamin, saying,
4 Thus saith the LORD, Ye shall not go up, nor fight against your brethren: return every man to his house: for this thing is done of me. And they obeyed the words of the LORD, and returned from going against Jĕr-o-bō'am.
5 And Rē-ho-bō'am dwelt in Jerusalem, and built cities for defence in Jūdah.
6 He built even Bĕth-lehĕm, and Ē'tam, and Te-kō'a,
7 And Bĕth'-zûr, and Shō'cō, and Adullam,
8 And Gath, and Ma-rē'shah, and Ziph,
9 And Ăd-o-rā'im, and Lā'chĭsh, and A-zē'kah,
10 And Zō'rah, and Āij'a-lŏn, and Hēbron, which *are* in Jūdah and in Benjamin fenced cities.
11 And he fortified the strong holds, and put captains in them, and store of victual, and of oil and wine.
12 And in every several city *he put* shields and spears, and made them exceeding strong, having Jūdah and Benjamin on his side.
13 And the priests and the Lēvītes

that *were* in all Israel resorted to him
out of all their coasts.
14 For the Lēvītes left their suburbs
and their possession, and came to Jū-
dah and Jerusalem: for Jĕr-o-bō'am
and his sons had cast them off from ex-
ecuting the priest's office unto the
LORD:
15 And he ordained him priests for
the high places, and for the devils, and
for the calves which he had made.
16 And after them out of all the tribes
of Israel such as set their hearts to seek
the LORD God of Israel came to Jeru-
salem, to sacrifice unto the LORD God
of their fathers.
17 So they strengthened the kingdom
of Jūdah, and made Rē-ho-bō'am the
son of Sōlomon strong, three years: for
three years they walked in the way of
David and Sōlomon.
18 ¶And Rē-ho-bō'am took him
Mā'ha-lăth the daughter of Jĕr'ī-mŏth
the son of David to wife, *and* Ăb-i-hā'il
the daughter of E-lī'ab the son of Jesse;
19 Which bare him children; Jē'ŭsh,
and Shĕm-a-rī'ah, and Zā'hăm.
20 And after her he took Mā'a-chah
the daughter of Ăb'sa-lom; which bare
him A-bī'jah, and Ăt'taī, and Zī'za, and
Shel'ō-mĭth.
21 And Rē-ho-bō'am loved Mā'a-
chah the daughter of Ăb'sa-lom above
all his wives and his concubines: (for he
took eighteen wives, and threescore
concubines; and begat twenty and
eight sons, and threescore daughters.)
22 And Rē-ho-bō'am made A-bī'jah
the son of Mā'a-chah the chief, *to be*
ruler among his brethren: for *he*
thought to make him king.
23 And he dealt wisely, and dispersed
of all his children throughout all the
countries of Jūdah and Benjamin, unto
every fenced city: and he gave them
victual in abundance. And he desired
many wives.

CHAPTER 12

AND it came to pass, when Rē-ho-bō'am
had established the kingdom, and
had strengthened himself, he forsook
the law of the LORD, and all Israel with
him.
2 And it came to pass, *that* in the fifth
year of king Rē-ho-bō'am Shī'shăk king
of Egypt came up against Jerusalem,
because they had transgressed against
the LORD,
3 With twelve hundred chariots, and
threescore thousand horsemen: and
the people *were* without number that
came with him out of Egypt; the Lū'-
bĭms, the Sŭk'kĭ-ĭms, and the Ē-thĭ-
ō'pĭ-ans.
4 And he took the fenced cities which
pertained to Jūdah, and came to Jeru-
salem.
5 Then came Shem-ā-i'ah the prophet
to Rē-ho-bō'am, and *to* the princes of
Jūdah, that were gathered together to
Jerusalem because of Shī'shăk, and
said unto them, Thus saith the LORD, Ye
have forsaken me, and therefore have I
also left you in the hand of Shī'shăk.
6 Whereupon the princes of Israel
and the king humbled themselves; and
they said, The LORD *is* righteous.
7 And when the LORD saw that they
humbled themselves, the word of the
LORD came to Shem-ā-i'ah, saying,
They have humbled themselves; *there-*
fore I will not destroy them, but I will
grant them some deliverance; and my
wrath shall not be poured out upon Jeru-
salem by the hand of Shī'shăk.
8 Nevertheless they shall be his ser-
vants; that they may know my service,
and the service of the kingdoms of the
countries.
9 So Shī'shăk king of Egypt came up
against Jerusalem, and took away the
treasures of the house of the LORD, and
the treasures of the king's house; he
took all: he carried away also the
shields of gold which Sōlomon had
made.
10 Instead of which king Rē-ho-bō'am
made shields of brass, and com-
mitted *them* to the hands of the chief of
the guard, that kept the entrance of the
king's house.
11 And when the king entered into
the house of the LORD, the guard came
and fetched them, and brought them
again into the guard chamber.
12 And when he humbled himself,
the wrath of the LORD turned from him,
that he would not destroy *him* altogeth-
er: and also in Jū'dah things went
well.
13 ¶So king Rē-ho-bō'am strength-
ened himself in Jerusalem, and reign-
ed: for Rē-ho-bō'am *was* one and forty
years old when he began to reign, and
he reigned seventeen years in Jeru-
salem, the city which the LORD had cho-
sen out of all the tribes of Israel, to put
his name there. And his mother's name
was Nā'a-mah an Ammonitess.
14 And he did evil, because he pre-
pared not his heart to seek the LORD.
15 Now the acts of Rē-ho-bō'am, first
and last, *are* they not written in the
book of Shem-ā-i'ah the prophet, and
of Ĭd'dō the seer concerning gene-
alogies? And *there were* wars between
Rē-ho-bō'am and Jĕr-o-bō'am continu-
ally.
16 And Rē-ho-bō'am slept with his

fathers, and was buried in the city of David: and A-bī'jah his son reigned in his stead.

CHAPTER 13

NOW in the eighteenth year of king Jĕr-o-bō'am began A-bī'jah to reign over Jūdah.

2 He reigned three years in Jerusalem. His mother's name also *was* Mī-chā'iah the daughter of Ū'rĭ-el of Gĭb'e-ah. And there was war between A-bī'-jah and Jĕr-o-bō'am.

3 And A-bī'jah set the battle in array with an army of valiant men of war, *even* four hundred thousand chosen men: Jĕr-o-bō'am also set the battle in array against him with eight hundred thousand chosen men, *being* mighty men of valour.

4 ¶And A-bī'jah stood up upon mount Zĕm-a-rā'im, which *is* in mount Ē'phra-im, and said, Hear me, thou Jĕr-o-bō'am, and all Israel;

5 Ought ye not to know that the LORD God of Israel gave the kingdom over Israel to David for ever, *even* to him and to his sons by a covenant of salt?

6 Yet Jĕr-o-bō'am the son of Nē'băt, the servant of Sŏlomon the son of David, is risen up, and hath rebelled against his lord.

7 And there are gathered unto him vain men, the children of Bē'lî-al, and have strengthened themselves against Rē-ho-bō'am the son of Sŏlomon, when Rē-ho-bō'am was young and tenderhearted, and could not withstand them.

8 And now ye think to withstand the kingdom of the LORD in the hand of the sons of David; and ye *be* a great multitude, and *there are* with you golden calves, which Jĕr-o-bō'am made you for gods.

9 Have ye not cast out the priests of the LORD, the sons of Aaron, and the Lē'vītes, and have made you priests after the manner of the nations of *other* lands? so that whosoever cometh to consecrate himself with a young bullock and seven rams, *the same* may be a priest of *them that are* no gods.

10 But as for us, the LORD *is* our God, and we have not forsaken him; and the priests, which minister unto the LORD, *are* the sons of Aaron, and the Lē'vītes *wait* upon *their* business:

11 And they burn unto the LORD every morning and every evening burnt sacrifices and sweet incense: the shewbread also *set they in order* upon the pure table; and the candlestick of gold with the lamps thereof, to burn every evening: for we keep the charge of the LORD our God; but ye have forsaken him.

12 And, behold, God himself *is* with us for *our* captain, and his priests with sounding trumpets to cry alarm against you. O children of Israel, fight ye not against the LORD God of your fathers; for ye shall not prosper.

13 ¶But Jĕr-o-bō'am caused an ambushment to come about behind them: so they were before Jūdah, and the ambushment *was* behind them.

14 And when Jūdah looked back, behold, the battle *was* before and behind: and they cried unto the LORD, and the priests sounded with the trumpets.

15 Then the men of Jūdah gave a shout: and as the men of Jūdah shouted, it came to pass, that God smote Jĕr-o-bō'am and all Israel before A-bī'jah and Jūdah.

16 And the children of Israel fled before Jūdah: and God delivered them into their hand.

17 And A-bī'jah and his people slew them with a great slaughter: so there fell down slain of Israel five hundred thousand chosen men.

18 Thus the children of Israel were brought under at that time, and the children of Jūdah prevailed, because they relied upon the LORD God of their fathers.

19 And A-bī'jah pursued after Jĕr-o-bō'am, and took cities from him, Bĕth-el with the towns thereof, and Jĕsh'a-nah with the towns thereof, and Ē'phra-in with the towns thereof.

20 Neither did Jĕr-o-bō'am recover strength again in the days of A-bī'jah: and the LORD struck him, and he died.

21 ¶But A-bī'jah waxed mighty, and married fourteen wives, and begat twenty and two sons, and sixteen daughters.

22 And the rest of the acts of A-bī'jah, and his ways, and his sayings, *are* written in the story of the prophet Ĭd'dō.

CHAPTER 14

SO A-bī'jah slept with his fathers, and they buried him in the city of David: and Āsa his son reigned in his stead. In his days the land was quiet ten years.

2 And Āsa did *that which was* good and right in the eyes of the LORD his God:

3 For he took away the altars of the strange *gods*, and the high places, and brake down the images, and cut down the groves:

4 And commanded Jūdah to seek the LORD God of their fathers, and to do the law and the commandment.

5 Also he took away out of all the

cities of Jūdah the high places and the
images: and the kingdom was quiet be-
fore him.
6 ¶And he built fenced cities in Jū-
dah: for the land had rest, and he had
no war in those years; because the
LORD had given him rest.
7 Therefore he said unto Jūdah, Let
us build these cities, and make about
them walls, and towers, gates, and
bars, *while* the land *is* yet before us; be-
cause we have sought the LORD our
God, we have sought *him*, and he hath
given us rest on every side. So they
built and prospered.
8 And Āsa had an army *of men* that
bare targets and spears, out of Jūdah
three hundred thousand; and out of
Benjamin, that bare shields and drew
bows, two hundred and fourscore thou-
sand: all these *were* mighty men of val-
our.
9 ¶And there came out against them
Ze'rah the Ē-thĭ-ō'pĭ-an with an host of
a thousand thousand, and three
hundred chariots; and came unto Ma-
rē'shah.
10 Then Āsa went out against him,
and they set the battle in array in the
valley of Zĕph'a-thah at Ma-rē'shah.
11 And Āsa cried unto the LORD his
God, and said, LORD, *it is* nothing with
thee to help, whether with many, or
with them that have no power: help us,
O LORD our God; for we rest on thee,
and in thy name we go against this mul-
titude. O LORD, thou *art* our God; let not
man prevail against thee.
12 So the LORD smote the Ē-thĭ-ō'pĭ-
ans before Āsa, and before Jūdah; and
the Ē-thĭ-ō'pĭ-ans fled.
13 And Āsa and the people that *were*
with him pursued them unto Ge'rär:
and the Ē-thĭ-ō'pĭ-ans were over-
thrown, that they could not recover
themselves; for they were destroyed
before the LORD, and before his host;
and they carried away very much spoil.
14 And they smote all the cities round
about Ge'rär; for the fear of the LORD
came upon them: and they spoiled all
the cities; for there was exceeding
much spoil in them.
15 They smote also the tents of cattle,
and carried away sheep and camels in
abundance, and returned to Jerusalem.

CHAPTER 15

AND the Spirit of God came upon Ăz-a-
rī'ah the son of Ō'ded:
2 And he went out to meet Āsa, and
said unto him, Hear ye me, Āsa, and all
Jūdah and Benjamin; The LORD *is* with
you, while ye be with him; and if ye
seek him, he will be found of you; but if
ye forsake him, he will forsake you.
3 Now for a long season Israel *hath
been* without the true God, and without
a teaching priest, and without law.
4 But when they in their trouble did
turn unto the LORD God of Israel, and
sought him, he was found of them.
5 And in those times *there was* no
peace to him that went out, nor to him
that came in, but great vexations *were*
upon all the inhabitants of the coun-
tries.
6 And nation was destroyed of na-
tion, and city of city: for God did vex
them with all adversity.
7 Be ye strong therefore, and let not
your hands be weak: for your work
shall be rewarded.
8 ¶And when Āsa heard these words,
and the prophecy of Ō'ded the prophet,
he took courage, and put away the
abominable idols out of all the land of
Jūdah and Benjamin, and out of the
cities which he had taken from mount
Ē'phra-im, and renewed the altar of the
LORD, that *was* before the porch of the
LORD.
9 And he gathered all Jūdah and Ben-
jamin, and the strangers with them out
of Ē'phra-im and Ma-năs'seh, and out
of Simeon: for they fell to him out of
Israel in abundance, when they saw
that the LORD his God *was* with him.
10 So they gathered themselves to-
gether at Jerusalem in the third month,
in the fifteenth year of the reign of Āsa.
11 And they offered unto the LORD
the same time, of the spoil *which* they
had brought, seven hundred oxen and
seven thousand sheep.
12 And they entered into a covenant
to seek the LORD God of their fathers
with all their heart and with all their
soul;
13 That whosoever would not seek
the LORD God of Israel should be put to
death, whether small or great, whether
man or woman.
14 And they sware unto the LORD
with a loud voice, and with shouting,
and with trumpets, and with cornets.
15 And all Jūdah rejoiced at the oath:
for they had sworn with all their heart,
and sought him with their whole de-
sire; and he was found of them: and the
LORD gave them rest round about.
16 ¶And also *concerning* Mā'a-chah
the mother of Āsa the king, he removed
her from *being* queen, because she had
made an idol in a grove: and Āsa cut
down her idol, and stamped *it*, and
burnt *it* at the brook Kidron.
17 But the high places were not taken

away out of Israel: nevertheless the heart of Āsa was perfect all his days.

18 And he brought into the house of God the things that his father had dedicated, and that he himself had dedicated, silver, and gold, and vessels.

19 And there was no *more* war unto the five and thirtieth year of the reign of Āsa.

CHAPTER 16

IN the six and thirtieth year of the reign of Āsa Bā′a-sha king of Israel came up against Jū′dah, and built Rā′mah, to the intent that he might let none go out or come in to Āsa king of Jū′dah.

2 Then Āsa brought out silver and gold out of the treasures of the house of the LORD and of the king's house, and sent to Běn–hā′dăd king of Syria, that dwelt at Damascus, saying,

3 *There is* a league between me and thee, as *there was* between my father and thy father: behold, I have sent thee silver and gold; go, break thy league with Bā′a-sha king of Israel, that he may depart from me.

4 And Běn–hā′dăd hearkened unto king Āsa, and sent the captains of his armies against the cities of Israel; and they smote Ī′jŏn, and Dan, and Ā′bel–mā′Ĭm, and all the store cities of Năph′ta-lī.

5 And it came to pass, when Bā′a-sha heard *it*, that he left off building of Rā′mah, and let his work cease.

6 Then Āsa the king took all Jū′dah; and they carried away the stones of Rā′mah, and the timber thereof, wherewith Bā′a-sha was building; and he built therewith Gē′ba and Mizpah.

7 ¶And at that time Ha-nā′nī the seer came to Āsa king of Jū′dah, and said unto him, Because thou hast relied on the king of Syria, and not relied on the LORD thy God, therefore is the host of the king of Syria escaped out of thine hand.

8 Were not the Ē-thĭ-ō′pĭ-ans and the Lū′bĭms a huge host, with very many chariots and horsemen? yet, because thou didst rely on the LORD, he delivered them into thine hand.

9 For the eyes of the LORD run to and fro throughout the whole earth, to shew himself strong in the behalf of *them* whose heart *is* perfect toward him. Herein thou hast done foolishly: therefore from henceforth thou shalt have wars.

10 Then Āsa was wroth with the seer, and put him in a prison house; for *he was* in a rage with him because of this *thing*. And Āsa oppressed *some* of the people the same time.

11 ¶And, behold, the acts of Āsa, first and last, lo, they *are* written in the book of the kings of Jū′dah and Israel.

12 And Āsa in the thirty and ninth year of his reign was diseased in his feet, until his disease *was* exceeding *great:* yet in his disease he sought not to the LORD, but to the physicians.

13 And Āsa slept with his fathers, and died in the one and fortieth year of his reign.

14 And they buried him in his own sepulchres, which he had made for himself in the city of David, and laid him in the bed which was filled with sweet odours and divers kinds *of spices* prepared by the apothecaries' art: and they made a very great burning for him.

CHAPTER 17

AND Je-hŏsh′a-phăt his son reigned in his stead, and strengthened himself against Israel.

2 And he placed forces in all the fenced cities of Jū′dah, and set garrisons in the land of Jū′dah, and in the cities of Ē′phra-im, which Āsa his father had taken.

3 And the LORD was with Je-hŏsh′a-phăt, because he walked in the first ways of his father David, and sought not unto Bā′al-Ĭm;

4 But sought to the *LORD* God of his father, and walked in his commandments, and not after the doings of Israel.

5 Therefore the LORD stablished the kingdom in his hand; and all Jū′dah brought to Je-hŏsh′a-phăt presents; and he had riches and honour in abundance.

6 And his heart was lifted up in the ways of the LORD: moreover he took away the high places and groves out of Jū′dah.

7 ¶Also in the third year of his reign he sent to his princes, *even* to Běn-hā′il, and to Ō-ba-dī′ah, and to Zĕch-a-rī′ah, and to Ne-thăn′-e-el, and to Mī-chā′iah, to teach in the cities of Jū′dah.

8 And with them *he sent* Lēvītes, *even* Shem-ā-i′ah, and Něth-a-nī′ah, and Zěb-a-dī′ah, and Ā′sa-hěl, and Shemĭr′a-mŏth, and Je-hŏn′a-than, and Ăd-o-nī′jah, and Tō-bī′jah, and Tŏb′-ăd-o-nī′jah, Lēvītes; and with them E-lĭsh′a-ma and Je-hô′ram, priests.

9 And they taught in Jū′dah, and *had* the book of the law of the LORD with them, and went about throughout all the cities of Jū′dah, and taught the people.

10 ¶And the fear of the LORD fell upon all the kingdoms of the lands that *were*

round about Jū'dah, so that they made
no war against Je-hŏsh'a-phăt.
11 Also *some* of the Philistines
brought Je-hŏsh'a-phăt presents, and
tribute silver; and the Arabians
brought him flocks, seven thousand
and seven hundred rams, and seven
thousand and seven hundred he goats.
12 ¶And Je-hŏsh'a-phăt waxed great
exceedingly; and he built in Jū'dah
castles, and cities of store.
13 And he had much business in the
cities of Jū'dah: and the men of war,
mighty men of valour, *were* in Jeru-
salem.
14 And these *are* the numbers of
them according to the house of their
fathers: Of Jū'dah, the captains of thou-
sands; Ăd'nah the chief, and with him
mighty men of valour three hundred
thousand.
15 And next to him *was* Je-hō-hā'nan
the captain, and with him two hundred
and fourscore thousand.
16 And next him *was* Ăm-a-sī'ah the
son of Zĭch'rī, who willingly offered
himself unto the LORD; and with him
two hundred thousand mighty men of
valour.
17 And of Benjamin; E-lī'a-da a
mighty man of valour, and with him
armed men with bow and shield two
hundred thousand.
18 And next him *was* Je-hōz'a-băd,
and with him an hundred and fourscore
thousand ready prepared for the war.
19 These waited on the king, beside
those whom the king put in the fenced
cities throughout all Jū'dah.

CHAPTER 18

NOW Je-hŏsh'a-phăt had riches and
honour in abundance, and joined affin-
ity with Ahab.
2 And after *certain* years he went
down to Ahab to Sa-mâ'rĭ-a. And Ahab
killed sheep and oxen for him in abun-
dance, and for the people that *he had*
with him, and persuaded him to go up
with him to Rā'moth-gĭl'e-ad.
3 And Ahab king of Israel said unto
Je-hŏsh'a-phăt king of Jū'dah, Wilt
thou go with me to Rā'moth-gĭl'e-ad?
And he answered him, I *am* as thou *art*,
and my people as thy people; and *we
will be* with thee in the war.
4 ¶And Je-hŏsh'a-phăt said unto the
king of Israel, Enquire, I pray thee, at
the word of the LORD to day.
5 Therefore the king of Israel gath-
ered together of prophets four
hundred men, and said unto them,
Shall we go to Rā'moth-gĭl'e-ad to
battle, or shall I forbear? And they said,
Go up; for God will deliver *it* into the
king's hand.
6 ¶But Je-hŏsh'a-phăt said, *Is there*
not here a prophet of the LORD besides,
that we might enquire of him?
7 And the king of Israel said unto Je-
hŏsh'a-phăt, *There is* yet one man, by
whom we may enquire of the LORD: but
I hate him; for he never prophesied
good unto me, but always evil: the
same *is* Mī-cā'iah the son of Ĭm'la. And
Je-hŏsh'a-phăt said, Let not the king
say so.
8 And the king of Israel called for one
of his officers, and said, Fetch quickly
Mī-cā'iah the son of Ĭm'la.
9 And the king of Israel and Je-
hŏsh'a-phăt king of Jū'dah sat either of
them on his throne, clothed in *their*
robes, and they sat in a void place at the
entering in of the gate of Sa-mâ'rĭ-a;
and all the prophets prophesied before
them.
10 And Zĕd-e-kī'ah the son of Che-
nā'a-nah had made him horns of iron,
and said, Thus saith the LORD, With
these thou shalt push Syria until they
be consumed.
11 And all the prophets prophesied
so, saying, Go up to Rā'moth-gĭl'e-ad,
and prosper: for the LORD shall deliver
it into the hand of the king.
12 And the messenger that went to
call Mī-cā'iah spake to him, saying, Be-
hold, the words of the prophets *declare*
good to the king with one assent; let thy
word therefore, I pray thee, be like one
of theirs, and speak thou good.
13 And Mī-cā'iah said, *As* the LORD
liveth, even what my God saith, that
will I speak.
14 And when he was come to the
king, the king said unto him, Mī-cā'iah,
shall we go to Rā'moth-gĭl'e-ad to
battle, or shall I forbear? And he said,
Go ye up, and prosper, and they shall
be delivered into your hand.
15 And the king said to him, How
many times shall I adjure thee that
thou say nothing but the truth to me in
the name of the LORD?
16 Then he said, I did see all Israel
scattered upon the mountains, as sheep
that have no shepherd: and the LORD
said, These have no master; let them re-
turn *therefore* every man to his house
in peace.
17 And the king of Israel said to Je-
hŏsh'a-phăt, Did I not tell thee *that* he
would not prophesy good unto me, but
evil?
18 Again he said, Therefore hear the
word of the LORD; I saw the LORD sitting
upon his throne, and all the host of

heaven standing on his right hand and *on* his left.

19 And the LORD said, Who shall entice Ahab king of Israel, that he may go up and fall at Ră'moth-gĭl-e-ad? And one spake saying after this manner, and another saying after that manner.

20 Then there came out a spirit, and stood before the LORD, and said, I will entice him. And the LORD said unto him, Wherewith?

21 And he said, I will go out, and be a lying spirit in the mouth of all his prophets. And *the* LORD said, Thou shalt entice *him*, and thou shalt also prevail: go out, and do *even* so.

22 Now therefore, behold, the LORD hath put a lying spirit in the mouth of these thy prophets, and the LORD hath spoken evil against thee.

23 ¶Then Zĕd-e-kī'ah the son of Che-nā'a-nah came near, and smote Mī-cā'iah upon the cheek, and said, Which way went the Spirit of the LORD from me to speak unto thee?

24 And Mī-cā'iah said, Behold, thou shalt see on that day when thou shalt go into an inner chamber to hide thyself.

25 Then the king of Israel said, Take ye Mī-cā'iah, and carry him back to Ā̆mon the governor of the city, and to Jō'ăsh the king's son;

26 And say, Thus saith the king, Put this *fellow* in the prison, and feed him with bread of affliction and with water of affliction, until I return in peace.

27 And Mī-cā'iah said, If thou certainly return in peace, *then* hath not the LORD spoken by me. And he said, Hearken, all ye people.

28 So the king of Israel and Je-hŏsh'a-phăt the king of Jū'dah went up to Ră'moth-gĭl'e-ad.

29 And the king of Israel said unto Je-hŏsh'a-phăt, I will disguise myself, and will go to the battle; but put thou on thy robes. So the king of Israel disguised himself; and they went to the battle.

30 Now the king of Syria had commanded the captains of the chariots that *were* with him, saying, Fight ye not with small or great, save only with the king of Israel.

31 And it came to pass, when the captains of the chariots saw Je-hŏsh'a-phăt, that they said, It *is* the king of Israel. Therefore they compassed about him to fight: but Je-hŏsh'a-phăt cried out, and the LORD helped him; and God moved them *to depart* from him.

32 For it came to pass, that, when the captains of the chariots perceived that it was not the king of Israel, they turned back again from pursuing him.

33 And a *certain* man drew a bow at a venture, and smote the king of Israel between the joints of the harness: therefore he said to his chariot man, Turn thine hand, that thou mayest carry me out of the host; for I am wounded.

34 And the battle increased that day: howbeit the king of Israel stayed *himself* up in *his* chariot against the Syrians until the even: and about the time of the sun going down he died.

CHAPTER 19

AND Je-hŏsh'a-phăt the king of Jū'dah returned to his house in peace to Jerusalem.

2 And Jehu the son of Ha-nā'nī the seer went out to meet him, and said to king Je-hŏsh'a-phăt, Shouldest thou help the ungodly, and love them that hate the LORD? therefore *is* wrath upon thee from before the LORD.

3 Nevertheless there are good things found in thee, in that thou hast taken away the groves out of the land, and hast prepared thine heart to seek God.

4 And Je-hŏsh'a-phăt dwelt at Jerusalem: and he went out again through the people from Be'er-shē'ba to mount Ē'phra-im, and brought them back unto the LORD God of their fathers.

5 And he set judges in the land throughout all the fenced cities of Jū'dah, city by city,

6 And said to the judges, Take heed what ye do: for ye judge not for man, but for the LORD, who *is* with you in the judgment.

7 Wherefore now let the fear of the LORD be upon you; take heed and do *it*: for *there is* no iniquity with the LORD our God, nor respect of persons, nor taking of gifts.

8 Moreover in Jerusalem did Je-hŏsh'a-phăt set of the Lē'vītes, and *of* the priests, and of the chief of the fathers of Israel, for the judgment of the LORD, and for controversies, when they returned to Jerusalem.

9 And he charged them, saying, Thus shall ye do in the fear of the LORD, faithfully, and with a perfect heart.

10 And what cause soever shall come to you of your brethren that dwell in their cities, between blood and blood, between law and commandment, statutes and judgments, ye shall even warn them that they trespass not against the LORD, and *so* wrath come upon you, and upon your brethren: this do, and ye shall not trespass.

11 And, behold, Ā̆m-a-rī'ah the chief priest *is* over you in all matters of the LORD; and Zĕb-a-dī'ah the son of Ĭsh'ma-el, the ruler of the house of Jū'-

dah, for all the king's matters: also the
Lē'vītes *shall be* officers before you.
Deal courageously, and the LORD shall
be with the good.

CHAPTER 20

IT came to pass after this also, *that* the
children of Moab, and the children of
Ammon, and with them *other* beside
the Ammonites, came against Je-
hŏsh'a-phăt to battle.
2 Then there came some that told Je-
hŏsh'a-phăt, saying, There cometh a
great multitude against thee from
beyond the sea on this side Syria; and,
behold, they *be* in Hăz'a-zŏn–tā'mar,
which *is* Ēn–gĕ'dī.
3 And Je-hŏsh'a-phăt feared, and set
himself to seek the LORD, and pro-
claimed a fast throughout all Jū'dah.
4 And Jū'dah gathered themselves
together, to ask *help* of the LORD: even
out of all the cities of Jū'dah they came
to seek the LORD.
5 ¶And Je-hŏsh'a-phăt stood in the
congregation of Jū'dah and Jerusalem,
in the house of the LORD, before the
new court,
6 And said, O LORD God of our fathers,
art not thou God in heaven? and
rulest *not* thou over all the kingdoms of
the heathen? and in thine hand *is there*
not power and might, so that none is
able to withstand thee?
7 *Art* not thou our God, *who* didst
drive out the inhabitants of this land
before thy people Israel, and gavest it
to the seed of Abraham thy friend for
ever?
8 And they dwelt therein, and have
built thee a sanctuary therein for thy
name, saying,
9 If, *when* evil cometh upon us, *as* the
sword, judgment, or pestilence, or
famine, we stand before this house, and
in thy presence, (for thy name *is* in this
house,) and cry unto thee in our afflic-
tion, then thou wilt hear and help.
10 And now, behold, the children of
Ammon and Moab and mount Sē'ir,
whom thou wouldest not let Israel in-
vade, when they came out of the land of
Egypt, but they turned from them, and
destroyed them not;
11 Behold, *I say, how* they reward us,
to come to cast us out of thy posses-
sion, which thou hast given us to in-
herit.
12 O our God, wilt thou not judge
them? for we have no might against
this great company that cometh
against us; neither know we what to
do: but our eyes *are* upon thee.
13 And all Jū'dah stood before the
LORD, with their little ones, their wives,
and their children.
14 Then upon Ja-hā'zi-el the son of
Zĕch-a-rī'ah, the son of Be-nā'iah, the
son of Je-ī'el, the son of Măt-ta-nī'ah, a
Levite of the sons of Ā'săph, came the
Spirit of the LORD in the midst of the
congregation;
15 And he said, Hearken ye, all Jū'-
dah, and ye inhabitants of Jerusalem,
and thou king Je-hŏsh'a-phăt, Thus
saith the LORD unto you, Be not afraid
nor dismayed by reason of this great
multitude; for the battle *is* not yours,
but God's.
16 To morrow go ye down against
them: behold, they come up by the cliff
of Ziz; and ye shall find them at the end
of the brook, before the wilderness of
Jer'ū-el.
17 Ye shall not *need* to fight in this
battle: set yourselves, stand ye *still,*
and see the salvation of the LORD with
you, O Jū'dah and Jerusalem: fear not,
nor be dismayed; to morrow go out
against them: for the LORD *will be* with
you.
18 And Je-hŏsh'a-phăt bowed his
head with *his* face to the ground: and
all Jū'dah and the inhabitants of Jeru-
salem fell before the LORD, worship-
ping the LORD.
19 And the Lē'vītes, of the children of
the Kō'hăth-ītes, and of the children of
the Kŏr'hītes, stood up to praise the
LORD God of Israel with a loud voice on
high.
20 ¶And they rose early in the morn-
ing, and went forth into the wilderness
of Te-kō'a: and as they went forth, Je-
hŏsh'a-phăt stood and said, Hear me, O
Jū'dah, and ye inhabitants of Jeru-
salem; Believe in the LORD your God, so
shall ye be established; believe his
prophets, so shall ye prosper.
21 And when he had consulted with
the people, he appointed singers unto
the LORD, and that should praise the
beauty of holiness, as they went out be-
fore the army, and to say, Praise the
LORD; for his mercy *endureth* for ever.
22 ¶And when they began to sing and
to praise, the LORD set ambushments
against the children of Ammon, Moab,
and mount Sē'ir, which were come
against Jū'dah; and they were smitten.
23 For the children of Ammon and
Moab stood up against the inhabitants
of mount Sē'ir, utterly to slay and de-
stroy *them:* and when they had made an
end of the inhabitants of Sē'ir, every
one helped to destroy another.
24 And when Jū'dah came toward the
watch tower in the wilderness, they
looked unto the multitude, and, behold,

they *were* dead bodies fallen to the earth, and none escaped.

25 And when Je-hŏsh′a-phăt and his people came to take away the spoil of them, they found among them in abundance both riches with the dead bodies, and precious jewels, which they stripped off for themselves, more than they could carry away: and they were three days in gathering of the spoil, it was so much.

26 And on the fourth day they assembled themselves in the valley of Bĕr′a-chah; for there they blessed the LORD: therefore the name of the same place was called, The valley of Bĕr′a-chah, unto this day.

27 Then they returned, every man of Jū′dah and Jerusalem, and Je-hŏsh′a-phăt in the forefront of them, to go again to Jerusalem with joy; for the LORD had made them to rejoice over their enemies.

28 And they came to Jerusalem with psalteries and harps and trumpets unto the house of the LORD.

29 And the fear of God was on all the kingdoms of *those* countries, when they had heard that the LORD fought against the enemies of Israel.

30 So the realm of Je-hŏsh′a-phăt was quiet: for his God gave him rest round about.

31 ¶And Je-hŏsh′a-phăt reigned over Jū′dah: *he was* thirty and five years old when he began to reign, and he reigned twenty and five years in Jerusalem. And his mother's name *was* A-zū′bah the daughter of Shĭl′hī.

32 And he walked in the way of Ā̆sa his father, and departed not from it, doing *that which was* right in the sight of the LORD.

33 Howbeit the high places were not taken away: for as yet the people had not prepared their hearts unto the God of their fathers.

34 Now the rest of the acts of Je-hŏsh′a-phăt, first and last, behold, they *are* written in the book of Jehu the son of Ha-nā′nī, who *is* mentioned in the book of the kings of Israel.

35 ¶And after this did Je-hŏsh′a-phăt king of Jū′dah join himself with Ā-ha-zī′ah king of Israel, who did very wickedly:

36 And he joined himself with him to make ships to go to Tärshĭsh: and they made the ships in Ĕ′zī-on–gā′ber.

37 Then Ē-lĭ-ē′zer the son of Dō′da-vah of Ma-rē′shah prophesied against Je-hŏsh′a-phăt, saying, Because thou hast joined thyself with Ā-ha-zī′ah, the LORD hath broken thy works. And the ships were broken, that they were not able to go to Tärshĭsh.

CHAPTER 21

NOW Je-hŏsh′a-phăt slept with his fathers, and was buried with his fathers in the city of David. And Je-hô′ram his son reigned in his stead.

2 And he had brethren the sons of Je-hŏsh′a-phăt, Ăz-a-rī′ah, and Je-hī′el, and Zĕch-a-rī′ah, and Ăz-a-rī′ah, and Michael, and Shĕph-a-tī′ah: all these *were* the sons of Je-hŏsh′a-phăt king of Israel.

3 And their father gave them great gifts of silver, and of gold, and of precious things, with fenced cities in Jū′dah: but the kingdom gave he to Je-hô′ram; because he *was* the firstborn.

4 Now when Je-hô′ram was risen up to the kingdom of his father, he strengthened himself, and slew all his brethren with the sword, and *divers* also of the princes of Israel.

5 ¶Je-hô′ram *was* thirty and two years old when he began to reign, and he reigned eight years in Jerusalem.

6 And he walked in the way of the kings of Israel, like as did the house of Ahab: for he had the daughter of Ahab to wife: and he wrought *that which was* evil in the eyes of the LORD.

7 Howbeit the LORD would not destroy the house of David, because of the covenant that he had made with David, and as he promised to give a light to him and to his sons for ever.

8 ¶In his days the Edomites revolted from under the dominion of Jū′dah, and made themselves a king.

9 Then Je-hô′ram went forth with his princes, and all his chariots with him: and he rose up by night, and smote the Edomites which compassed him in, and the captains of the chariots.

10 So the Edomites revolted from under the hand of Jū′dah unto this day. The same time *also* did Lĭb′nah revolt from under his hand; because he had forsaken the LORD God of his fathers.

11 Moreover he made high places in the mountains of Jū′dah, and caused the inhabitants of Jerusalem to commit fornication, and compelled Jū′dah *thereto*.

12 ¶And there came a writing to him from E-lī′jah the prophet, saying, Thus saith the LORD God of David thy father, Because thou hast not walked in the ways of Je-hŏsh′a-phăt thy father, nor in the ways of Ā̆sa king of Jū′dah,

13 But hast walked in the way of the kings of Israel, and hast made Jū′dah and the inhabitants of Jerusalem to go a whoring, like to the whoredoms of the

house of Ahab, and also hast slain thy brethren of thy father's house, *which were* better than thyself:

14 Behold, with a great plague will the LORD smite thy people, and thy children, and thy wives, and all thy goods:

15 And thou *shalt have* great sickness by disease of thy bowels, until thy bowels fall out by reason of the sickness day by day.

16 ¶Moreover the LORD stirred up against Je-hô'ram the spirit of the Philistines, and of the Arabians, that *were* near the Ē-thĭ-ō'pĭ-ans:

17 And they came up into Jū'dah, and brake into it, and carried away all the substance that was found in the king's house, and his sons also, and his wives; so that there was never a son left him, save Je-hō'a-hăz, the youngest of his sons.

18 And after all this the LORD smote him in his bowels with an incurable disease.

19 And it came to pass, that in process of time, after the end of two years, his bowels fell out by reason of his sickness: so he died of sore diseases. And his people made no burning for him, like the burning of his fathers.

20 Thirty and two years old was he when he began to reign, and he reigned in Jerusalem eight years, and departed without being desired. Howbeit they buried him in the city of David, but not in the sepulchres of the kings.

CHAPTER 22

AND the inhabitants of Jerusalem made Ā-ha-zī'ah his youngest son king in his stead: for the band of men that came with the Arabians to the camp had slain all the eldest. So Ā-ha-zī'ah the son of Je-hô'ram king of Jū'dah reigned.

2 Forty and two years old *was* Ā-ha-zī'ah when he began to reign, and he reigned one year in Jerusalem. His mother's name also *was* Ăth-a-lī'ah, the daughter of Omri.

3 He also walked in the ways of the house of Ahab: for his mother was his counsellor to do wickedly.

4 Wherefore he did evil in the sight of the LORD like the house of Ahab: for they were his counsellors after the death of his father to his destruction.

5 He walked also after their counsel, and went with Je-hô'ram the son of Ahab king of Israel to war against Hāz'a-el king of Syria at Rā'moth-gĭl'e-ad: and the Syrians smote Joram.

6 And he returned to be healed in Jĕz're-el because of the wounds which were given him at Rā'mah, when he fought with Hāz'a-el king of Syria. And Ăz-a-rī'ah the son of Je-hô'ram king of Jū'dah went down to see Je-hô'ram the son of Ahab at Jĕz're-el, because he was sick.

7 And the destruction of Ā-ha-zī'ah was of God by coming to Joram: for when he was come, he went out with Je-hô'ram against Jehu the son of Nĭmshī, whom the LORD had anointed to cut off the house of Ahab.

8 And it came to pass, that, when Jehu was executing judgment upon the house of Ahab, and found the princes of Jū'dah, and the sons of the brethren of Ā-ha-zī'ah, that ministered to Ā-ha-zī'ah, he slew them.

9 And he sought Ā-ha-zī'ah: and they caught him, (for he was hid in Sa-mâ'-rĭ-a,) and brought him to Jehu: and when they had slain him, they buried him: Because, said they, he *is* the son of Je-hŏsh'a-phăt, who sought the LORD with all his heart. So the house of Ā-ha-zī'ah had no power to keep still the kingdom.

10 ¶But when Ăth-a-lī'ah the mother of Ā-ha-zī'ah saw that her son was dead, she arose and destroyed all the seed royal of the house of Jū'dah.

11 But Jē-hō-shăb'e-ath, the daughter of the king, took Jō'ăsh the son of Ā-ha-zī'ah, and stole him from among the king's sons that were slain, and put him and his nurse in a bedchamber. So Jē-hō-shăb'e-ath, the daughter of king Je-hô'ram, the wife of Je-hoi'a-da the priest, (for she was the sister of Ā-ha-zī'ah,) hid him from Ăth-a-lī'ah, so that she slew him not.

12 And he was with them hid in the house of God six years: and Ăth-a-lī'ah reigned over the land.

CHAPTER 23

AND in the seventh year Je-hoi'a-da strengthened himself, and took the captains of hundreds, Ăz-a-rī'ah the son of Jer'ō-hăm, and Ĭsh'ma-el the son of Je-hō-hā'nan, and Ăz-a-rī'ah the son of Ō'bed, and Mā-a-sē'iah the son of Ăd-a-ī'ah, and E-lĭsh'a-phăt the son of Zĭch'rī, into covenant with him.

2 And they went about in Jū'dah, and gathered the Lē'vītes out of all the cities of Jū'dah, and the chief of the fathers of Israel, and they came to Jerusalem.

3 And all the congregation made a covenant with the king in the house of God. And he said unto them, Behold, the king's son shall reign, as the LORD hath said of the sons of David.

4 This *is* the thing that ye shall do; A

third part of you entering on the sabbath, of the priests and of the Lē′vītes, *shall be* porters of the doors;

5 And a third part *shall be* at the king's house; and a third part at the gate of the foundation: and all the people *shall be* in the courts of the house of the LORD.

6 But let none come into the house of the LORD, save the priests, and they that minister of the Lē′vītes; they shall go in, for they *are* holy: but all the people shall keep the watch of the LORD.

7 And the Lē′vītes shall compass the king round about, every man with his weapons in his hand; and whosoever *else* cometh into the house, he shall be put to death: but be ye with the king when he cometh in, and when he goeth out.

8 So the Lē′vītes and all Jū′dah did according to all things that Je-hoi′a-da the priest had commanded, and took every man his men that were to come in on the sabbath, with them that were to go *out* on the sabbath: for Je-hoi′a-da the priest dismissed not the courses.

9 Moreover Je-hoi′a-da the priest delivered to the captains of hundreds spears, and bucklers, and shields, that *had been* king David's, which *were* in the house of God.

10 And he set all the people, every man having his weapon in his hand, from the right side of the temple to the left side of the temple, along by the altar and the temple, by the king round about.

11 Then they brought out the king's son, and put upon him the crown, and *gave him* the testimony, and made him king. And Je-hoi′a-da and his sons anointed him, and said, God save the king.

12 ¶Now when Ăth-a-lī′ah heard the noise of the people running and praising the king, she came to the people into the house of the LORD:

13 And she looked, and, behold, the king stood at his pillar at the entering in, and the princes and the trumpets by the king: and all the people of the land rejoiced, and sounded with trumpets, also the singers with instruments of musick, and such as taught to sing praise. Then Ăth-a-lī′ah rent her clothes, and said, Treason, Treason.

14 Then Je-hoi′a-da the priest brought out the captains of hundreds that were set over the host, and said unto them, Have her forth of the ranges: and whoso followeth her, let him be slain with the sword. For the priest said, Slay her not in the house of the LORD.

15 So they laid hands on her; and when she was come to the entering of the horse gate by the king's house, they slew her there.

16 ¶And Je-hoi′a-da made a covenant between him, and between all the people, and between the king, that they should be the LORD's people.

17 Then all the people went to the house of Bā′al, and brake it down, and brake his altars and his images in pieces, and slew Măt′tan the priest of Bā′al before the altars.

18 Also Je-hoi′a-da appointed the offices of the house of the LORD by the hand of the priests the Lē′vītes, whom David had distributed in the house of the LORD, to offer the burnt offerings of the LORD, as *it is* written in the law of Moses, with rejoicing and with singing, *as it was ordained* by David.

19 And he set the porters at the gates of the house of the LORD, that none *which was* unclean in any thing should enter in.

20 And he took the captains of hundreds, and the nobles, and the governors of the people, and all the people of the land, and brought down the king from the house of the LORD: and they came through the high gate into the king's house, and set the king upon the throne of the kingdom.

21 And all the people of the land rejoiced: and the city was quiet, after that they had slain Ăth-a-lī′ah with the sword.

CHAPTER 24

JŌ′ĂSH *was* seven years old when he began to reign, and he reigned forty years in Jerusalem. His mother's name also *was* Zĭb′ī-ah of Be′er–shē′ba.

2 And Jō′ăsh did *that which was* right in the sight of the LORD all the days of Je-hoi′a-da the priest.

3 And Je-hoi′a-da took for him two wives; and he begat sons and daughters.

4 ¶And it came to pass after this, *that* Jō′ăsh was minded to repair the house of the LORD.

5 And he gathered together the priests and the Lē′vītes, and said to them, Go out unto the cities of Jū′dah, and gather of all Israel money to repair the house of your God from year to year, and see that ye hasten the matter. Howbeit the Lē′vītes hastened *it* not.

6 And the king called for Je-hoi′a-da the chief, and said unto him, Why hast thou not required of the Lē′vītes to bring in out of Jū′dah and out of Jerusalem the collection, *according to the commandment* of Moses the servant of

the LORD, and of the congregation of Israel, for the tabernacle of witness?

7 For the sons of Ăth-a-lī'ah, that wicked woman, had broken up the house of God; and also all the dedicated things of the house of the LORD did they bestow upon Bā'al-ĭm.

8 And at the king's commandment they made a chest, and set it without at the gate of the house of the LORD.

9 And they made a proclamation through Jū'dah and Jerusalem, to bring in to the LORD the collection *that* Moses the servant of God *laid* upon Israel in the wilderness.

10 And all the princes and all the people rejoiced, and brought in, and cast into the chest, until they had made an end.

11 Now it came to pass, that at what time the chest was brought unto the king's office by the hand of the Lē'vītes, and when they saw that *there was* much money, the king's scribe and the high priest's officer came and emptied the chest, and took it, and carried it to his place again. Thus they did day by day, and gathered money in abundance.

12 And the king and Je-hoi'a-da gave it to such as did the work of the service of the house of the LORD, and hired masons and carpenters to repair the house of the LORD, and also such as wrought iron and brass to mend the house of the LORD.

13 So the workmen wrought, and the work was perfected by them, and they set the house of God in his state, and strengthened it.

14 And when they had finished *it*, they brought the rest of the money before the king and Je-hoi'a-da, whereof were made vessels for the house of the LORD, *even* vessels to minister, and to offer *withal*, and spoons, and vessels of gold and silver. And they offered burnt offerings in the house of the LORD continually all the days of Je-hoi'a-da.

15 ¶But Je-hoi'a-da waxed old, and was full of days when he died; an hundred and thirty years old *was he* when he died.

16 And they buried him in the city of David among the kings, because he had done good in Israel, both toward God, and toward his house.

17 Now after the death of Je-hoi'a-da came the princes of Jū'dah, and made obeisance to the king. Then the king hearkened unto them.

18 And they left the house of the LORD God of their fathers, and served groves and idols: and wrath came upon Jū'dah and Jerusalem for this their trespass.

19 Yet he sent prophets to them, to bring them again unto the LORD; and they testified against them: but they would not give ear.

20 And the Spirit of God came upon Zĕch-a-rī'ah the son of Je-hoi'a-da the priest, which stood above the people, and said unto them, Thus saith God, Why transgress ye the commandments of the LORD, that ye cannot prosper? because ye have forsaken the LORD, he hath also forsaken you.

21 And they conspired against him, and stoned him with stones at the commandment of the king in the court of the house of the LORD.

22 Thus Jō'ăsh the king remembered not the kindness which Je-hoi'a-da his father had done to him, but slew his son. And when he died, he said, The LORD look upon *it*, and require *it*.

23 ¶And it came to pass at the end of the year, *that* the host of Syria came up against him: and they came to Jū'dah and Jerusalem, and destroyed all the princes of the people from among the people, and sent all the spoil of them unto the king of Damascus.

24 For the army of the Syrians came with a small company of men, and the LORD delivered a very great host into their hand, because they had forsaken the LORD God of their fathers. So they executed judgment against Jō'ăsh.

25 And when they were departed from him, (for they left him in great diseases,) his own servants conspired against him for the blood of the sons of Je-hoi'a-da the priest, and slew him on his bed, and he died: and they buried him in the city of David, but they buried him not in the sepulchres of the kings.

26 And these are they that conspired against him; Zā'băd the son of Shĭm'e-ăth an Ammonitess, and Je-hōz'a-băd the son of Shĭm'rĭth a Moabitess.

27 Now *concerning* his sons, and the greatness of the burdens *laid* upon him, and the repairing of the house of God, behold, they *are* written in the story of the book of the kings. And Ăm-a-zī'ah his son reigned in his stead.

CHAPTER 25

ĂM-A-ZĪ'AH *was* twenty and five years old *when* he began to reign, and he reigned twenty and nine years in Jerusalem. And his mother's name *was* Je-hō-ad'dan of Jerusalem.

2 And he did *that which was* right in the sight of the LORD, but not with a perfect heart.

3 Now it came to pass, when the king-

dom was established to him, that he slew his servants that had killed the king his father.

4 But he slew not their children, but *did* as *it is* written in the law in the book of Moses, where the LORD commanded, saying, The fathers shall not die for the children, neither shall the children die for the fathers, but every man shall die for his own sin.

5 ¶Moreover Ăm-a-zī'ah gathered Jū'dah together, and made them captains over thousands, and captains over hundreds, according to the houses of *their* fathers, throughout all Jū'dah and Benjamin: and he numbered them from twenty years old and above, and found them three hundred thousand choice *men, able* to go forth to war, that could handle spear and shield.

6 He hired also an hundred thousand mighty men of valour out of Israel for an hundred talents of silver.

7 But there came a man of God to him, saying, O king, let not the army of Israel go with thee; for the LORD *is* not with Israel, *to wit, with* all the children of Ē'phra-im.

8 But if thou wilt go, do *it*, be strong for the battle: God shall make thee fall before the enemy: for God hath power to help, and to cast down.

9 And Ăm-a-zī'ah said to the man of God, But what shall we do for the hundred talents which I have given to the army of Israel? And the man of God answered, The LORD is able to give thee much more than this.

10 Then Ăm-a-zī'ah separated them, *to wit,* the army that was come to him out of Ē'phra-im, to go home again: wherefore their anger was greatly kindled against Jū'dah, and they returned home in great anger.

11 And Ăm-a-zī'ah strengthened himself, and led forth his people, and went to the valley of salt, and smote of the children of Sē'ir ten thousand.

12 And *other* ten thousand *left* alive did the children of Jū'dah carry away captive, and brought them unto the top of the rock, and cast them down from the top of the rock, that they all were broken in pieces.

13 But the soldiers of the army which Ăm-a-zī'ah sent back, that they should not go with him to battle, fell upon the cities of Jū'dah, from Sa-mâ'rĭ-a even unto Bĕth-hô'ron, and smote three thousand of them, and took much spoil.

14 ¶Now it came to pass, after that Ăm-a-zī'ah was come from the slaughter of the Edomites, that he brought the gods of the children of Sē'ir, and set them up *to be* his gods, and bowed down himself before them, and burned incense unto them.

15 Wherefore the anger of the LORD was kindled against Ăm-a-zī'ah, and he sent unto him a prophet, which said unto him, Why hast thou sought after the gods of the people, which could not deliver their own people out of thine hand?

16 And it came to pass, as he talked with him, that *the king* said unto him, Art thou made of the king's counsel? forbear; why shouldest thou be smitten? Then the prophet forbare, and said, I know that God hath determined to destroy thee, because thou hast done this, and hast not hearkened unto my counsel.

17 ¶Then Ăm-a-zī'ah king of Jū'dah took advice, and sent to Jō'ăsh, the son of Je-hō'a-hăz, the son of Jehu, king of Israel, saying, Come, let us see one another in the face.

18 And Jō'ăsh king of Israel sent to Ăm-a-zī'ah king of Jū'dah, saying, The thistle that *was* in Lebanon sent to the cedar that *was* in Lebanon, saying, Give thy daughter to my son to wife: and there passed by a wild beast that *was* in Lebanon, and trode down the thistle.

19 Thou sayest, Lo, thou hast smitten the Edomites; and thine heart lifteth thee up to boast: abide now at home; why shouldest thou meddle to *thine* hurt, that thou shouldest fall, *even* thou, and Jū'dah with thee?

20 But Ăm-a-zī'ah would not hear; for it *came* of God, that he might deliver them into the hand *of their enemies,* because they sought after the gods of Edom.

21 So Jō'ăsh the king of Israel went up; and they saw one another in the face, *both* he and Ăm-a-zī'ah king of Jū'dah, at Bĕth-shĕ'mesh, which *belongeth* to Jū'dah.

22 And Jū'dah was put to the worse before Israel, and they fled every man to his tent.

23 And Jō'ăsh the king of Israel took Ăm-a-zī'ah king of Jū'dah, the son of Jō'ăsh, the son of Je-hō'a-hăz, at Bĕth-shĕ'mesh, and brought him to Jerusalem, and brake down the wall of Jerusalem from the gate of Ē'phra-im to the corner gate, four hundred cubits.

24 And *he took* all the gold and the silver, and all the vessels that were found in the house of God with Ō'bed-ē'dom, and the treasures of the king's house, the hostages also, and returned to Sa-mâ'rĭ-a.

25 ¶And Ăm-a-zī'ah the son of Jō'ăsh king of Jū'dah lived after the death of

Jō'ăsh son of Je-hō'a-hăz king of Israel
fifteen years.
26 Now the rest of the acts of Ăm-a-
zī'ah, first and last, behold, *are* they not
written in the book of the kings of Jū'-
dah and Israel?
27 Now after the time that Ăm-a-
zī'ah did turn away from following the
LORD they made a conspiracy against
him in Jerusalem; and he fled to Lā'-
chĭsh: but they sent to Lā'chĭsh after
him, and slew him there.
28 And they brought him upon
horses, and buried him with his fathers
in the city of Jū'dah.

CHAPTER 26

THEN all the people of Jū'dah took Uz-
zī'ah, who *was* sixteen years old, and
made him king in the room of his father
Ăm-a-zī'ah.
2 He built Ē'lŏth, and restored it to
Jū'dah, after that the king slept with his
fathers.
3 Sixteen years old *was* Uz-zī'ah
when he began to reign, and he reigned
fifty and two years in Jerusalem. His
mother's name also *was* Jĕc-o-lī'ah of
Jerusalem.
4 And he did *that which was* right in
the sight of the LORD, according to all
that his father Ăm-a-zī'ah did.
5 And he sought God in the days of
Zĕch-a-rī'ah, who had understanding
in the visions of God: and as long as he
sought the LORD, God made him to
prosper.
6 And he went forth and warred
against the Philistines, and brake down
the wall of Gath, and the wall of Jăb'neh,
and the wall of Ăsh'dŏd, and built
cities about Ăsh'dod, and among the
Philistines.
7 And God helped him against the
Philistines, and against the Arabians
that dwelt in Gûr–bā'al, and the Me-hū'-
nĭms.
8 And the Ammonites gave gifts to
Uz-zī'ah: and his name spread abroad
even to the entering in of Egypt; for he
strengthened *himself* exceedingly.
9 Moreover Uz-zī'ah built towers in
Jerusalem at the corner gate, and at the
valley gate, and at the turning *of the*
wall, and fortified them.
10 Also he built towers in the desert,
and digged many wells: for he had
much cattle, both in the low country,
and in the plains: husbandmen *also*,
and vine dressers in the mountains, and
in Carmel: for he loved husbandry.
11 ¶Moreover Uz-zī'ah had an host of
fighting men, that went out to war by
bands, according to the number of their
account by the hand of Je-ī'el the scribe
and Mā'a-sē'iah the ruler, under the
hand of Hăn-a-nī'ah, *one* of the king's
captains.
12 The whole number of the chief of
the fathers of the mighty men of valour
were two thousand and six hundred.
13 And under their hand *was* an
army, three hundred thousand and
seven thousand and five hundred, that
made war with mighty power, to help
the king against the enemy.
14 And Uz-zī'ah prepared for them
throughout all the host shields, and
spears, and helmets, and habergeons,
and bows, and slings *to cast* stones.
15 And he made in Jerusalem en-
gines, invented by cunning men, to be
on the towers and upon the bulwarks,
to shoot arrows and great stones
withal. And his name spread far
abroad; for he was marvellously
helped, till he was strong.
16 ¶But when he was strong, his
heart was lifted up to *his* destruction:
for he transgressed against the LORD
his God, and went into the temple of
the LORD to burn incense upon the altar
of incense.
17 And Ăz-a-rī'ah the priest went in
after him, and with him fourscore
priests of the LORD, *that were* valiant
men:
18 And they withstood Uz-zī'ah the
king and said unto him, *It appertaineth*
not unto thee, Uz-zī'ah, to burn incense
unto the LORD, but to the priests the
sons of Aaron, that are consecrated to
burn incense: go out of the sanctuary;
for thou hast trespassed; neither *shall it*
be for thine honour from the LORD God.
19 Then Uz-zī'ah was wroth, and *had*
a censer in his hand to burn incense:
and while he was wroth with the
priests, the leprosy even rose up in his
forehead before the priests in the house
of the LORD, from beside the incense al-
tar.
20 And Ăz-a-rī'ah the chief priest,
and all the priests, looked upon him,
and, behold, he *was* leprous in his fore-
head, and they thrust him out from
thence; yea, himself hasted also to go
out, because the LORD had smitten him.
21 And Uz-zi'ah the king was a leper
unto the day of his death, and dwelt in a
several house, *being* a leper; for he was
cut off from the house of the LORD: and
Jō'tham his son *was* over the king's
house, judging the people of the land.
22 ¶Now the rest of the acts of Uz-
zī'ah, first and last, did Isaiah the
prophet, the son of Amoz, write.
23 So Uz-zī'ah slept with his fathers,
and they buried him with his fathers in
the field of the burial which *belonged*

to the kings; for they said, He *is* a leper: and Jō'tham his son reigned in his stead.

CHAPTER 27

JŌ'THAM *was* twenty and five years old when he began to reign, and he reigned sixteen years in Jerusalem. His mother's name also *was* Je-rū'shah, the daughter of Zā'dŏk.

2 And he did *that which was* right in the sight of the LORD, according to all that his father Uz-zī'ah did: howbeit he entered not into the temple of the LORD. And the people did yet corruptly.

3 He built the high gate of the house of the LORD, and on the wall of Ō'phĕl he built much.

4 Moreover he built cities in the mountains of Jū'dah, and in the forests he built castles and towers.

5 He fought also with the king of the Ammonites, and prevailed against them. And the children of Ammon gave him the same year an hundred talents of silver, and ten thousand measures of wheat, and ten thousand of barley. So much did the children of Ammon pay unto him, both the second year, and the third.

6 So Jō'tham became mighty, because he prepared his ways before the LORD his God.

7 ¶Now the rest of the acts of Jō'tham, and all his wars, and his ways, lo, they *are* written in the book of the kings of Israel and Jū'dah.

8 He was five and twenty years old when he began to reign, and reigned sixteen years in Jerusalem.

9 And Jō'tham slept with his fathers, and they buried him in the city of David: and Ahaz his son reigned in his stead.

CHAPTER 28

AHAZ *was* twenty years old when he began to reign, and he reigned sixteen years in Jerusalem: but he did not *that which was* right in the sight of the LORD, like David his father:

2 For he walked in the ways of the kings of Israel, and made also molten images for Bā'al-ĭm.

3 Moreover he burnt incense in the valley of the son of Hĭn'nom, and burnt his children in the fire, after the abominations of the heathen whom the LORD had cast out before the children of Israel.

4 He sacrificed also and burnt incense in the high places, and on the hills, and under every green tree.

5 Wherefore the LORD his God delivered him into the hand of the king of Syria; and they smote him, and carried away a great multitude of them captives, and brought *them* to Damascus. And he was also delivered into the hand of the king of Israel, who smote him with a great slaughter.

6 For Pē'kah the son of Rĕm-a-lī'ah slew in Jū'dah an hundred and twenty thousand in one day, *which were* all valiant men; because they had forsaken the LORD God of their fathers.

7 And Zĭch'rī, a mighty man of Ē'phra'im, slew Mā'a-sē'iah the king's son, and Ăz'ri-kam the governor of the house, and Ĕl'kā-nah *that was* next to the king.

8 And the children of Israel carried away captive of their brethren two hundred thousand, women, sons, and daughters, and took also away much spoil from them, and brought the spoil to Sa-mâ'rī-a.

9 But a prophet of the LORD was there, whose name *was* O'ded: and he went out before the host that came to Sa-mâ'rī-a, and said unto them, Behold, because the LORD God of your fathers was wroth with Jū'dah, he hath delivered them into your hand, and ye have slain them in a rage *that* reacheth up unto heaven.

10 And now ye purpose to keep under the children of Jū'dah and Jerusalem for bondmen, and bondwomen unto you: *but are there* not with you, even with you, sins against the LORD your God?

11 Now hear me therefore, and deliver the captives again, which ye have taken captive of your brethren: for the fierce wrath of the LORD *is* upon you.

12 Then certain of the heads of the children of Ē'phra-im, Ăz-a-rī'ah the son of Jo-ha'nan, Ber-e-chi'ah the son of Me-shĭl'le-mŏth, and Jĕ'hĭz-kī'ah the son of Shăl'lum, and Am'ā-sa the son of Hăd'la-ī, stood up against them that came from the war,

13 And said unto them, Ye shall not bring in the captives hither: for whereas we have offended against the LORD *already,* ye intend to add *more* to our sins and to our trespass: for our trespass is great, and *there is* fierce wrath against Israel.

14 So the armed men left the captives and the spoil before the princes and all the congregation.

15 And the men which were expressed by name rose up, and took the captives, and with the spoil clothed all that were naked among them, and arrayed them, and shod them, and gave them to eat and to drink, and anointed them, and carried all the feeble of them

upon asses, and brought them to
Jericho, the city of palm trees, to their
brethren: then they returned to Sa-
mâ'rĭ-a.
16 ¶At that time did king Ahaz send
unto the kings of Assyria to help him.
17 For again the Edomites had come
and smitten Jū'dah, and carried away
captives.
18 The Philistines also had invaded
the cities of the low country, and of the
south of Jū'dah, and had taken
Bĕth-shĕ'-mesh, and Ăj'a-lŏn, and Ge-
de'-rŏth, and Shō'chō with the villages
thereof, and Tĭm'nah with the villages
thereof, Gĭm'zō also and the villages
thereof: and they dwelt there.
19 For the LORD brought Jū'dah low
because of Ahaz king of Israel; for he
made Jū'dah naked, and transgressed
sore against the LORD.
20 And Tĭl'găth-pĭl-nē'ṡer king of As-
syria came unto him, and distressed
him, but strengthened him not.
21 For Ahaz took away a portion *out*
of the house of the LORD, and *out* of the
house of the king, and of the princes,
and gave *it* unto the king of Assyria:
but he helped him not.
22 And in the time of his distress did
he trespass yet more against the LORD:
this *is that* king Ahaz.
23 For he sacrificed unto the gods of
Damascus, which smote him: and he
said, Because the gods of the kings of
Syria help them, *therefore* will I sacri-
fice to them, that they may help me.
But they were the ruin of him, and of all
Israel.
24 And Ahaz gathered together the
vessels of the house of God, and cut in
pieces the vessels of the house of God,
and shut up the doors of the house of
the LORD, and he made him altars in
every corner of Jerusalem.
25 And in every several city of Jū'dah
he made high places to burn incense
unto other gods, and provoked to anger
the LORD God of his fathers.
26 ¶Now the rest of his acts and of all
his ways, first and last, behold, they *are*
written in the book of the kings of Jū'-
dah and Israel.
27 And Ahaz slept with his fathers,
and they buried him in the city, *even* in
Jerusalem: but they brought him not
into the sepulchres of the kings of
Israel: and Hĕz-e-kī'ah his son reigned
in his stead.

CHAPTER 29

HĔZ-E-KĪ'AH began to reign *when he
was* five and twenty years old, and he
reigned nine and twenty years in Jeru-
salem. And his mother's name *was*
A-bī'jah, the daughter of Zĕch-a-rī'ah.
2 And he did *that which was* right in
the sight of the LORD, according to all
that David his father had done.
3 ¶He in the first year of his reign, in
the first month, opened the doors of the
house of the LORD, and repaired them.
4 And he brought in the priests and
the Lē'vītes, and gathered them togeth-
er into the east street,
5 And said unto them, Hear me, ye
Lē'vītes, sanctify now yourselves, and
sanctify the house of the LORD God of
your fathers, and carry forth the filthi-
ness out of the holy *place*.
6 For our fathers have trespassed,
and done *that which was* evil in the
eyes of the LORD our God, and have for-
saken him, and have turned away their
faces from the habitation of the LORD,
and turned *their* backs.
7 Also they have shut up the doors of
the porch, and put out the lamps, and
have not burned incense nor offered
burnt offerings in the holy *place* unto
the God of Israel.
8 Wherefore the wrath of the LORD
was upon Jū'dah and Jerusalem, and he
hath delivered them to trouble, to aston-
ishment, and to hissing, as ye see with
your eyes.
9 For, lo, our fathers have fallen by
the sword, and our sons and our
daughters and our wives *are* in captiv-
ity for this.
10 Now *it is* in mine heart to make a
covenant with the LORD God of Israel,
that his fierce wrath may turn away
from us.
11 My sons, be not now negligent: for
the LORD hath chosen you to stand be-
fore him, to serve him, and that ye
should minister unto him, and burn in-
cense.
12 ¶Then the Lē'vītes arose, Mā'hăth
the son of A-măs'a-ī, and Jō'el the son
of Ăz-a-rī'ah, of the sons of the Kō'hăth-
ītes: and of the sons of Me-râ'rī, Kish
the son of Ăb'dī, and Ăz-a-rī'ah the son
of Je-hăl'e-lel: and of the Ger'shon-ītes;
Jō'ah the son of Zimmah, and Eden the
son of Jō'ah:
13 And of the sons of Ĕ-liz'ā-phan;
Shĭm'rī, and Je-ī'el: and of the sons of
Ā'săph; Zĕch-a-rī'ah, and Măt-ta-nī'ah:
14 And of the sons of Hē'măn; Je-
hī'el, and Shĭm'e-ī: and of the sons of
Jed'ū-thun; Shem-a-i'ah, and Ŭz'zī-el.
15 And they gathered their brethren,
and sanctified themselves, and came,
according to the commandment of the
king, by the words of the LORD, to
cleanse the house of the LORD.
16 And the priests went into the inner

part of the house of the LORD, to cleanse
it, and brought out all the uncleanness
that they found in the temple of the
LORD into the court of the house of the
LORD. And the Lē'vītes took *it,* to carry
it out abroad into the brook Kidron.
17 Now they began on the first *day* of
the first month to sanctify, and on the
eighth day of the month came they to
the porch of the LORD: so they sanc-
tified the house of the LORD in eight
days; and in the sixteenth day of the
first month they made an end.
18 Then they went in to Hĕz-e-kī'ah
the king, and said, We have cleansed all
the house of the LORD, and the altar of
burnt offering, with all the vessels there-
of, and the shewbread table, with all
the vessels thereof.
19 Moreover all the vessels, which
king Ahaz in his reign did cast away in
his transgression, have we prepared
and sanctified, and, behold, they *are*
before the altar of the LORD.
20 ¶Then Hĕz-e-kī'ah the king rose
early, and gathered the rulers of the
city, and went up to the house of the
LORD.
21 And they brought seven bullocks,
and seven rams, and seven lambs, and
seven he goats, for a sin offering for the
kingdom, and for the sanctuary, and
for Jū'dah. And he commanded the
priests the sons of Aaron to offer *them*
on the altar of the LORD.
22 So they killed the bullocks, and
the priests received the blood, and
sprinkled *it* on the altar: likewise, when
they had killed the rams, they sprinkled
the blood upon the altar: they killed
also the lambs, and they sprinkled the
blood upon the altar.
23 And they brought forth the he
goats *for* the sin offering before the
king and the congregation; and they
laid their hands upon them:
24 And the priests killed them, and
they made reconciliation with their
blood upon the altar, to make an atone-
ment for all Israel: for the king com-
manded *that* the burnt offering and the
sin offering *should be made* for all
Israel.
25 And he set the Lē'vītes in the
house of the LORD with cymbals, with
psalteries, and with harps, according to
the commandment of David, and of
Gad the king's seer, and Nā'than the
prophet: for *so was* the commandment
of the LORD by his prophets.
26 And the Lē'vītes stood with the
instruments of David, and the priests
with the trumpets.
27 And Hĕz-e-kī'ah commanded to
offer the burnt offering upon the altar.
And when the burnt offering began, the
song of the LORD began *also* with the
trumpets, and with the instruments *or-
dained* by David king of Israel.
28 And all the congregation wor-
shipped, and the singers sang, and the
trumpeters sounded: *and* all *this contin-
ued* until the burnt offering was fin-
ished.
29 And when they had made an end
of offering, the king and all that were
present with him bowed themselves,
and worshipped.
30 Moreover Hĕz-e-kī'ah the king
and the princes commanded the Lē'-
vītes to sing praise unto the LORD with
the words of David, and of Ā'săph the
seer. And they sang praises with glad-
ness, and they bowed their heads and
worshipped.
31 Then Hĕz-e-kī'ah answered and
said, Now ye have consecrated your-
selves unto the LORD, come near and
bring sacrifices and thank offerings
into the house of the LORD. And the
congregation brought in sacrifices and
thank offerings; and as many as were
of a free heart burnt offerings.
32 And the number of the burnt offer-
ings, which the congregation brought,
was threescore and ten bullocks, an
hundred rams, *and* two hundred lambs:
all these *were* for a burnt offering to the
LORD.
33 And the consecrated things *were*
six hundred oxen and three thousand
sheep.
34 But the priests were too few, so
that they could not flay all the burnt of-
ferings: wherefore their brethren the
Lē'vītes did help them, till the work
was ended, and until the *other* priests
had sanctified themselves: for the Lē'-
vītes *were* more upright in heart to
sanctify themselves than the priests.
35 And also the burnt offerings *were*
in abundance, with the fat of the peace
offerings, and the drink offerings for
every burnt offering. So the service of
the house of the LORD was set in order.
36 And Hĕz-e-kī'ah rejoiced, and all
the people, that God had prepared the
people: for the thing was *done* sud-
denly.

CHAPTER 30

AND Hĕz-e-kī'ah sent to all Israel and
Jū'dah, and wrote letters also to
Ē'phra-im and Ma-năs'seh, that they
should come to the house of the LORD at
Jerusalem, to keep the passover unto
the LORD God of Israel.
2 For the king had taken counsel, and
his princes, and all the congregation in

Jerusalem, to keep the passover in the
second month.
3 For they could not keep it at that
time, because the priests had not sanc-
tified themselves sufficiently, neither
had the people gathered themselves
together to Jerusalem.
4 And the thing pleased the king and
all the congregation.
5 So they established a decree to
make proclamation throughout all
Israel, from Bē'er–shē'ba even to Dan,
that they should come to keep the pass-
over unto the LORD God of Israel at Je-
rusalem: for they had not done *it* of a
long *time in such sort* as it was written.
6 So the posts went with the letters
from the king and his princes
throughout all Israel and Jū'dah, and
according to the commandment of the
king, saying, Ye children of Israel, turn
again unto the LORD God of Abraham,
Isaac, and Israel, and he will return to
the remnant of you, that are escaped
out of the hand of the kings of Assyria.
7 And be not ye like your fathers, and
like your brethren, which trespassed
against the LORD God of their fathers,
who therefore gave them up to desola-
tion, as ye see.
8 Now be ye not stiffnecked, as your
fathers *were, but* yield yourselves unto
the LORD, and enter into his sanctuary,
which he hath sanctified for ever: and
serve the LORD your God, that the fierce-
ness of his wrath may turn away from
you.
9 For if ye turn again unto the LORD,
your brethren and your children *shall
find* compassion before them that lead
them captive, so that they shall come
again into this land: for the LORD your
God *is* gracious and merciful, and will
not turn away *his* face from you, if ye
return unto him.
10 So the posts passed from city to
city through the country of Ē'phra-im
and Ma-năs'seh even unto Zĕb'u-lun:
but they laughed them to scorn, and
mocked them.
11 Nevertheless divers of Asher and
Ma-năs'seh and of Zĕb'u-lun humbled
themselves, and came to Jerusalem.
12 Also in Jū'dah the hand of God
was to give them one heart to do the
commandment of the king and of the
princes, by the word of the LORD.
13 ¶And there assembled at Jeru-
salem much people to keep the feast of
unleavened bread in the second month,
a very great congregation.
14 And they arose and took away the
altars that *were* in Jerusalem, and all
the altars for incense took they away,
and cast *them* into the brook Kidron.
15 Then they killed the passover on
the fourteenth *day* of the second
month: and the priests and the Lē'vītes
were ashamed, and sanctified them-
selves, and brought in the burnt offer-
ings into the house of the LORD.
16 And they stood in their place after
their manner, according to the law of
Moses the man of God: the priests
sprinkled the blood, *which they re-
ceived* of the hand of the Lē'vītes.
17 For *there were* many in the con-
gregation that were not sanctified:
therefore the Lē'vītes had the charge of
the killing of the passovers for every
one *that was* not clean, to sanctify
them unto the LORD.
18 For a multitude of the people, *even*
many of Ē'phra-im, and Ma-năs'seh,
Is'sa-char, and Zĕb'u-lun, had not
cleansed themselves, yet did they eat
the passover otherwise than it was
written. But Hĕz-e-kī'ah prayed for
them, saying, The good LORD pardon
every one
19 *That* prepareth his heart to seek
God, the LORD God of his fathers,
though *he be* not *cleansed* according to
the purification of the sanctuary.
20 And the LORD hearkened to Hĕz-e-
kī'ah, and healed the people.
21 And the children of Israel that
were present at Jerusalem, kept the
feast of unleavened bread seven days
with great gladness: and the Lē'vītes
and the priests praised the LORD day by
day, *singing* with loud instruments
unto the LORD.
22 And Hĕz-e-kī'ah spake comfort-
ably unto all the Lē'vītes that taught
the good knowledge of the LORD: and
they did eat throughout the feast seven
days, offering peace offerings, and
making confession to the LORD God of
their fathers.
23 And the whole assembly took
counsel to keep other seven days: and
they kept *other* seven days with glad-
ness.
24 For Hĕz-e-kī'ah king of Jū'dah did
give to the congregation a thousand
bullocks and seven thousand sheep;
and the princes gave to the congrega-
tion a thousand bullocks and ten thou-
sand sheep: and a great number of
priests sanctified themselves.
25 And all the congregation of Jū'-
dah, with the priests and the Lē'vītes,
and all the congregation that came out
of Israel, and the strangers that came
out of the land of Israel, and that dwelt
in Jū'dah, rejoiced.
26 So there was great joy in Jeru-
salem: for since the time of Sŏl'o-mon

the son of David king of Israel *there*
was not the like in Jerusalem.
27 Then the priests the Lē´vītes arose
and blessed the people: and their voice
was heard, and their prayer came *up* to
his holy dwelling place, *even* unto
heaven.

CHAPTER 31

NOW when all this was finished, all
Israel that were present went out to the
cities of Jū´dah, and brake the images
in pieces, and cut down the groves, and
threw down the high places and the altars
out of all Jū´dah and Benjamin, in
Ē´phra-im also and Ma-nǎs´seh, until
they had utterly destroyed them all.
Then all the children of Israel returned,
every man to his possession, into their
own cities.
2 ¶And Hěz-e-kī´ah appointed the
courses of the priests and the Lē´vītes
after their courses, every man according
to his service, the priests and
Lē´vītes for burnt offerings and for
peace offerings, to minister, and to give
thanks, and to praise in the gates of the
tents of the LORD.
3 *He appointed* also the king's portion
of his substance for the burnt offerings,
to wit, for the morning and evening
burnt offerings, and the burnt offerings
for the sabbaths, and for the
new moons, and for the set feasts, as *it*
is written in the law of the LORD.
4 Moreover he commanded the people
that dwelt in Jerusalem to give the
portion of the priests and the Lē´vītes,
that they might be encouraged in the
law of the LORD.
5 And as soon as the commandment
came abroad, the children of Israel
brought in abundance the firstfruits of
corn, wine, and oil, and honey, and of
all the increase of the field; and the
tithe of all *things* brought they in abundantly.
6 And *concerning* the children of
Israel and Jū´dah, that dwelt in the
cities of Jū´dah, they also brought in
the tithe of oxen and sheep, and the
tithe of holy things which were
consecrated unto the LORD their God,
and laid *them* by heaps.
7 In the third month they began to lay
the foundation of the heaps, and finished
them in the seventh month.
8 And when Hěz-e-kī´ah and the
princes came and saw the heaps, they
blessed the LORD, and his people Israel.
9 Then Hěz-e-kī´ah questioned with
the priests and the Lē´vītes concerning
the heaps.
10 And Ǎz-a-rī´ah the chief priest of
the house of Zā´dǒk answered him, and
said, Since *the people* began to bring
the offerings into the house of the
LORD, we have had enough to eat, and
have left plenty: for the LORD hath
blessed his people; and that which is
left *is* this great store.
11 ¶Then Hěz-e-kī´ah commanded to
prepare chambers in the house of the
LORD; and they prepared *them,*
12 And brought in the offerings and
the tithes and the dedicated *things*
faithfully: over which Cǒn-o-nī´ah the
Lē´vīte *was* ruler, and Shǐm´e-ī his
brother *was* the next.
13 And Je-hī´el, and Ǎz-a-zī´ah, and
Na´hǎth, and A´sa-hěl, and Jěr´ī-mǒth,
and Jōz´a-bǎd, and E-lī´el, and Ǐs-ma-chī´ah,
and Ma´hath, and Be-nā´iah,
were overseers under the hand of Cǒn-o-nī´ah
and Shǐm´e-ī his brother, at the
commandment of Hěz-e-kī´ah the king,
and Ǎz-a-rī´ah the ruler of the house of
God.
14 And Kō´re the son of Ǐm´nah the
Lē´vīte, the porter toward the east, *was*
over the freewill offerings of God, to
distribute the oblations of the LORD,
and the most holy things.
15 And next him *were* Eden, and
Mǐn´i-a-mǐn, and Jěsh´u-a, and Shem-ā-i´ah,
Ǎm-a-rī´ah, and Shěc-a-nī´ah, in
the cities of the priests, in *their* set office,
to give to their brethren by
courses, as well to the great as to the
small:
16 Beside their genealogy of males,
from three years old and upward, *even*
unto every one that entereth into the
house of the LORD, his daily portion for
their service in their charges according
to their courses;
17 Both to the genealogy of the
priests by the house of their fathers,
and the Lē´vītes from twenty years old
and upward, in their charges by their
courses;
18 And to the genealogy of all their
little ones, their wives, and their sons,
and their daughters, through all the
congregation: for in their set office
they sanctified themselves in holiness:
19 Also of the sons of Aaron the
priests, *which were* in the fields of the
suburbs of their cities, in every several
city, the men that were expressed by
name, to give portions to all the males
among the priests, and to all that were
reckoned by genealogies among the
Lē´vītes.
20 And thus did Hěz-e-kī´ah
throughout all Jū´dah, and wrought
that which was good and right and
truth before the LORD his God.
21 And in every work that he began
in the service of the house of God, and

in the law, and in the commandments,
to seek his God, he did *it* with all his
heart, and prospered.

CHAPTER 32

AFTER these things, and the establish-
ment thereof, Sen-năch'e-rĭb king of
Assyria came, and entered into Jū'dah,
and encamped against the fenced
cities, and thought to win them for him-
self.
2 And when Hĕz-e-kī'ah saw that
Sen-năch'e-rĭb was come, and that he
was purposed to fight against Jeru-
salem,
3 He took counsel with his princes
and his mighty men to stop the waters
of the fountains which *were* without
the city: and they did help him.
4 So there was gathered much people
together, who stopped all the foun-
tains, and the brook that ran through
the midst of the land, saying, Why
should the kings of Assyria come, and
find much water?
5 Also he strengthened himself, and
built up all the wall that was broken,
and raised *it* up to the towers, and an-
other wall without, and repaired Mĭl'lō
in the city of David, and made darts and
shields in abundance.
6 And he set captains of war over the
people, and gathered them together to
him in the street of the gate of the city,
and spake comfortably to them,
saying,
7 Be strong and courageous, be not
afraid nor dismayed for the king of As-
syria, nor for all the multitude that *is*
with him: for *there be* more with us
than with him:
8 With him *is* an arm of flesh; but
with us *is* the LORD our God to help us,
and to fight our battles. And the people
rested themselves upon the words of
Hĕz-e-kī'ah king of Jū'dah.
9 ¶After this did Sen-năch'e-rĭb king
of Assyria send his servants to Jeru-
salem, (but he *himself laid siege*
against Lā'chĭsh, and all his power with
him,) unto Hĕz-e-kī'ah king of Jū'dah,
and unto all Jū'dah that *were* at Jeru-
salem, saying,
10 Thus saith Sen-năch'e-rĭb king of
Assyria, Whereon do ye trust, that ye
abide in the siege in Jerusalem?
11 Doth not Hĕz-e-kī'ah persuade
you to give over yourselves to die by
famine and by thirst, saying, The LORD
our God shall deliver us out of the hand
of the king of Assyria?
12 Hath not the same Hĕz-e-kī'ah
taken away his high places and his al-
tars, and commanded Jū'dah and Jeru-
salem, saying, Ye shall worship before
one altar, and burn incense upon it?
13 Know ye not what I and my fathers
have done unto all the people of
other lands? were the gods of the na-
tions of those lands any ways able to
deliver their lands out of mine hand?
14 Who *was there* among all the gods
of those nations that my fathers utterly
destroyed, that could deliver his people
out of mine hand, that your God should
be able to deliver you out of mine hand?
15 Now therefore let not Hĕz-e-kī'ah
deceive you, nor persuade you on this
manner, neither yet believe him: for no
god of any nation or kingdom was able
to deliver his people out of mine hand,
and out of the hand of my fathers: how
much less shall your God deliver you
out of mine hand?
16 And his servants spake yet *more*
against the LORD God, and against his
servant Hĕz-e-kī'ah.
17 He wrote also letters to rail on the
LORD God of Israel, and to speak
against him, saying, As the gods of the
nations of *other* lands have not de-
livered their people out of mine hand,
so shall not the God of Hĕz-e-kī'ah de-
liver his people out of mine hand.
18 Then they cried with a loud voice
in the Jews' speech unto the people of
Jerusalem that *were* on the wall, to af-
fright them, and to trouble them; that
they might take the city.
19 And they spake against the God of
Jerusalem, as against the gods of the
people of the earth, *which were* the
work of the hands of man.
20 And for this *cause* Hĕz-e-kī'ah the
king, and the prophet Isaiah the son of
Amoz, prayed and cried to heaven.
21 And the LORD sent an angel, which
cut off all the mighty men of valour,
and the leaders and captains in the
camp of the king of Assyria. So he re-
turned with shame of face to his own
land. And when he was come into the
house of his god, they that came forth
of his own bowels slew him there with
the sword.
22 Thus the LORD saved Hĕz-e-kī'ah
and the inhabitants of Jerusalem from
the hand of Sen-năch'e-rĭb the king of
Assyria, and from the hand of all *other*,
and guided them on every side.
23 And many brought gifts unto the
LORD to Jerusalem, and presents to
Hĕz-e-kī'ah king of Judah: so that he
was magnified in the sight of all nations
from thenceforth.
24 ¶In those days Hĕz-e-kī'ah was
sick to the death, and prayed unto the
LORD: and he spake unto him, and he
gave him a sign.

25 But Hĕz-e-kī'ah rendered not
again according to the benefit *done*
unto him; for his heart was lifted up:
therefore there was wrath upon him,
and upon Jū'dah and Jerusalem.
26 Notwithstanding Hĕz-e-kī'ah
humbled himself for the pride of his
heart, *both* he and the inhabitants of Je-
rusalem, so that the wrath of the LORD
came not upon them in the days of Hĕz-
e-kī'ah.
27 ¶And Hĕz-e-kī'ah had exceeding
much riches and honour: and he made
himself treasuries for silver, and for
gold, and for precious stones, and for
spices, and for shields, and for all man-
ner of pleasant jewels;
28 Storehouses also for the increase
of corn, and wine, and oil; and stalls for
all manner of beasts, and cotes for
flocks.
29 Moreover he provided him cities,
and possessions of flocks and herds in
abundance: for God had given him
substance very much.
30 This same Hĕz-e-kī'ah also
stopped the upper watercourse of
Gī'hŏn, and brought it straight down to
the west side of the city of David. And
Hĕz-e-kī'ah prospered in all his works.
31 Howbeit in *the business of* the am-
bassadors of the princes of Babylon,
who sent unto him to enquire of the
wonder that was *done* in the land, God
left him, to try him, that he might know
all *that was* in his heart.
32 ¶Now the rest of the acts of Hĕz-e-
kī'ah, and his goodness, behold, they
are written in the vision of Isaiah the
prophet, the son of Amoz, *and* in the
book of the kings of Jū'dah and Israel.
33 And Hĕz-e-kī'ah slept with his
fathers, and they buried him in the
chiefest of the sepulchres of the sons of
David: and all Judah and the inhabi-
tants of Jerusalem did him honour at
his death. And Ma-năs'seh his son
reigned in his stead.

CHAPTER 33

MA-NĂS'SEH *was* twelve years old
when he began to reign, and he reigned
fifty and five years in Jerusalem:
2 But did *that which was* evil in the
sight of the LORD, like unto the abomi-
nations of the heathen, whom the LORD
had cast out before the children of
Israel.
3 For he built again the high places
which Hĕz-e-kī'ah his father had broken
down, and he reared up altars for
Bā'al-ĭm, and made groves, and wor-
shipped all the host of heaven, and
served them.
4 Also he built altars in the house of
the LORD, whereof the LORD had said, In
Jerusalem shall my name be for ever.
5 And he built altars for all the host of
heaven in the two courts of the house of
the LORD.
6 And he caused his children to pass
through the fire in the valley of the son
of Hĭn'nom: also he observed times,
and used enchantments, and used
witchcraft, and dealt with a familiar
spirit, and with wizards: he wrought
much evil in the sight of the LORD, to
provoke him to anger.
7 And he set a carved image, the idol
which he had made, in the house of
God, of which God had said to David
and to Sŏl'o-mon his son, In this house,
and in Jerusalem, which I have chosen
before all the tribes of Israel, will I put
my name for ever:
8 Neither will I any more remove the
foot of Israel from out of the land which
I have appointed for your fathers; so
that they will take heed to do all that I
have commanded them, according to
the whole law and the statutes and the
ordinances by the hand of Moses.
9 So Ma-năs'seh made Jū'dah and the
inhabitants of Jerusalem to err, *and* to
do worse than the heathen, whom the
LORD had destroyed before the children
of Israel.
10 ¶And the LORD spake to Ma-năs'-
seh, and to his people: but they would
not hearken.
11 Wherefore the LORD brought upon
them the captains of the host of the
king of Assyria, which took Ma-năs'seh
among the thorns, and bound him with
fetters, and carried him to Babylon.
12 And when he was in affliction, he
besought the LORD his God, and
humbled himself greatly before the
God of his fathers,
13 And prayed unto him: and he was
intreated of him, and heard his suppli-
cation, and brought him again to Jeru-
salem into his kingdom. Then Ma-năs'-
seh knew that the LORD he *was* God.
14 ¶Now after this he built a wall
without the city of David, on the west
side of Gī'hŏn, in the valley, even to the
entering in at the fish gate, and com-
passed about Ō'phĕl, and raised it up a
very great height, and put captains of
war in all the fenced cities of Jū'dah.
15 And he took away the strange
gods, and the idol out of the house of
the LORD, and all the altars that he had
built in the mount of the house of the
LORD, and in Jerusalem, and cast *them*
out of the city.
16 And he repaired the altar of the
LORD, and sacrificed thereon peace of-
ferings and thank offerings and com-

manded Jū'dah to serve the LORD God of Israel.

17 Nevertheless the people did sacrifice still in the high places, *yet* unto the LORD their God only.

18 ¶Now the rest of the acts of Ma-năs'seh, and his prayer unto his God, and the words of the seers that spake to him in the name of the LORD God of Israel, behold, they *are written* in the book of the kings of Israel.

19 His prayer also, and *how God* was intreated of him, and all his sins, and his trespass, and the places wherein he built high places, and set up groves and graven images, before he was humbled: behold, they *are* written among the sayings of the seers.

20 So Ma-năs'seh slept with his fathers, and they buried him in his own house: and Ā'mon his son reigned in his stead.

21 ¶Ā'mon *was* two and twenty years old when he began to reign, and reigned two years in Jerusalem.

22 But he did *that which was* evil in the sight of the LORD, as did Ma-năs'seh his father: for Ā'mon sacrificed unto all the carved images which Ma-năs'seh his father had made, and served them;

23 And humbled not himself before the LORD, as Ma-năs'seh his father had humbled himself; but Ā'mon trespassed more and more.

24 And his servants conspired against him, and slew him in his own house.

25 But the people of the land slew all them that had conspired against king Ā'mon; and the people of the land made Jō-sī'ah his son king in his stead.

CHAPTER 34

JŌ-SĪ'AH *was* eight years old when he began to reign, and he reigned in Jerusalem one and thirty years.

2 And he did *that which was* right in the sight of the LORD, and walked in the ways of David his father, and declined *neither* to the right hand, nor to the left.

3 For in the eighth year of his reign, while he was yet young, he began to seek after the God of David his father: and in the twelfth year he began to purge Jū'dah and Jerusalem from the high places, and the groves, and the carved images, and the molten images.

4 And they brake down the altars of Bā'al-īm in his presence; and the images, that *were* on high above them, he cut down; and the groves, and the carved images, and the molten images, he brake in pieces, and made dust *of them*, and strowed *it* upon the graves of them that had sacrificed unto them.

5 And he burnt the bones of the priests upon their altars, and cleansed Jū'dah and Jerusalem.

6 And *so did he* in the cities of Ma-năs'seh, and Ē'phra-im, and Simeon, even unto Năph'ta-lī, with their mattocks round about.

7 And when he had broken down the altars and the groves, and had beaten the graven images into powder, and cut down all the idols throughout all the land of Israel, he returned to Jerusalem.

8 ¶Now in the eighteenth year of his reign, when he had purged the land, and the house, he sent Shā'phan the son of Ăz-a-lī'ah, and Mā-a-sē'iah the governor of the city, and Jō'ah the son of Jō'a-hăz the recorder, to repair the house of the LORD his God.

9 And when they came to Hĭl-kī'ah the high priest, they delivered the money that was brought into the house of God, which the Lē'vītes that kept the doors had gathered of the hand of Ma-năs'seh and Ē'phra-im, and of all the remnant of Israel, and of all Jū'dah and Benjamin; and they returned to Jerusalem.

10 And they put *it* in the hand of the workmen that had the oversight of the house of the LORD, and they gave it to the workmen that wrought in the house of the LORD, to repair and amend the house:

11 Even to the artificers and builders gave they *it*, to buy hewn stone, and timber for couplings, and to floor the houses which the kings of Jū'dah had destroyed.

12 And the men did the work faithfully: and the overseers of them *were* Jā'hăth and Ō-ba-dī'ah, the Lē'vītes, of the sons of Me-râ'rī; and Zĕch-a-rī'ah and Me-shŭl'lam, of the sons of the Kō'hăth-ītes, to set *it* forward; and *other of* the Lē'vītes, all that could skill of instruments of musick.

13 Also *they were* over the bearers of burdens, and *were* overseers of all that wrought the work in any manner of service: and of the Lē'vītes *there were* scribes, and officers, and porters.

14 ¶And when they brought out the money that was brought into the house of the LORD, Hĭl-kī'ah the priest found a book of the law of the LORD *given* by Moses.

15 And Hĭl-kī'ah answered and said to Shā'phan the scribe, I have found the book of the law in the house of the LORD. And Hĭl-kī'ah delivered the book to Shā'phan.

16 And Shā'phan carried the book to the king, and brought the king word

back again, saying, All that was com-
mitted to thy servants, they do *it*.
17 And they have gathered together
the money that was found in the house
of the LORD, and have delivered it into
the hand of the overseers, and to the
hand of the workmen.
18 Then Shā'phan the scribe told the
king, saying, Hĭl-kī'ah the priest hath
given me a book. And Shā'phan read it
before the king.
19 And it came to pass, when the king
had heard the words of the law, that he
rent his clothes.
20 And the king commanded Hĭl-ki'-
ah, and A-hī'kam the son of Shā'phan,
and Ăb'dŏn the son of Mī'cah, and
Shā'phan the scribe, and Ȧs-ā'iah a ser-
vant of the king's, saying,
21 Go, enquire of the LORD for me,
and for them that are left in Israel and
in Jū'dah, concerning the words of the
book that is found: for great *is* the
wrath of the LORD that is poured out
upon us, because our fathers have not
kept the word of the LORD, to do after
all that is written in this book.
22 And Hĭl-kī'ah, and *they* that the
king *had appointed*, went to Hŭl'dah
the prophetess, the wife of Shăl'lum
the son of Tĭk'vath, the son of Hăs'rah,
keeper of the wardrobe; (now she
dwelt in Jerusalem in the college:) and
they spake to her to that *effect*.
23 And she answered them, Thus
saith the LORD God of Israel, Tell ye the
man that sent you to me,
24 Thus saith the LORD, Behold, I will
bring evil upon this place, and upon the
inhabitants thereof, *even* all the curses
that are written in the book which they
have read before the king of Jū'dah:
25 Because they have forsaken me,
and have burned incense unto other
gods, that they might provoke me to
anger with all the works of their hands;
therefore my wrath shall be poured out
upon this place, and shall not be
quenched.
26 And as for the king of Jū'dah, who
sent you to enquire of the LORD, so shall
ye say unto him, Thus saith the LORD
God of Israel *concerning* the words
which thou hast heard;
27 Because thine heart was tender,
and thou didst humble thyself before
God, when thou heardest his words
against this place, and against the
inhabitants thereof, and humbledst
thyself before me, and didst rend thy
clothes, and weep before me; I have
even heard *thee* also, saith the LORD.
28 Behold, I will gather thee to thy
fathers, and thou shalt be gathered to
thy grave in peace, neither shall thine
eyes see all the evil that I will bring
upon this place, and upon the inhabi-
tants of the same. So they brought the
king word again.
29 ¶Then the king sent and gathered
together all the elders of Jū'dah and Je-
rusalem.
30 And the king went up into the
house of the LORD, and all the men of
Jū'dah, and the inhabitants of Jeru-
salem, and the priests, and the Lē'vītes,
and all the people, great and small: and
he read in their ears all the words of the
book of the covenant that was found in
the house of the LORD.
31 And the king stood in his place,
and made a covenant before the LORD,
to walk after the LORD, and to keep his
commandments, and his testimonies,
and his statutes, with all his heart, and
with all his soul, to perform the words
of the covenant which are written in
this book.
32 And he caused all that were pres-
ent in Jerusalem and Benjamin to
stand *to it*. And the inhabitants of Jeru-
salem did according to the covenant of
God, the God of their fathers.
33 And Jō-sī'ah took away all the
abominations out of all the countries
that *pertained* to the children of Israel,
and made all that were present in Israel
to serve, *even* to serve the LORD their
God. *And* all his days they departed not
from following the LORD, the God of
their fathers.

CHAPTER 35

MOREOVER Jō-sī'ah kept a passover
unto the LORD in Jerusalem: and they
killed the passover on the fourteenth
day of the first month.
2 And he set the priests in their
charges, and encouraged them to the
service of the house of the LORD,
3 And said unto the Levites that
taught all Israel, which were holy unto
the LORD, Put the holy ark in the house
which Sŏl'o-mon the son of David king
of Israel did build; *it shall* not *be* a bur-
den upon *your* shoulders: serve now
the LORD your God, and his people
Israel,
4 And prepare *yourselves* by the
houses of your fathers, after your
courses, according to the writing of Da-
vid king of Israel, and according to the
writing of Sŏl'o-mon his son.
5 And stand in the holy *place* accord-
ing to the divisions of the families of
the fathers of your brethren the people,
and *after* the division of the families of
the Lē'vītes.
6 So kill the passover, and sanctify
yourselves, and prepare your brethren,

that *they* may do according to the word of the LORD by the hand of Moses.

7 And Jō-sī′ah gave to the people, of the flock, lambs and kids, all for the passover offerings, for all that were present, to the number of thirty thousand, and three thousand bullocks: these *were* of the king's substance.

8 And his princes gave willingly unto the people, to the priests, and to the Lē′vītes: Hĭl-kī′ah and Zĕch-a-rī′ah and Je-hī′el, rulers of the house of God, gave unto the priests for the passover offerings two thousand and six hundred *small cattle*, and three hundred oxen.

9 Cŏn-a-nī′ah also, and Shem-ā-i′ah and Ne-thăn′e-el, his brethren, and Hăsh-a-bī′ah and Je-ī′el and Jōz′a-băd, chief of the Lē′vītes, gave unto the Lē′vītes for passover offerings five thousand *small cattle*, and five hundred oxen.

10 So the service was prepared, and the priests stood in their place, and the Lē′vītes in their courses, according to the king's commandment.

11 And they killed the passover, and the priests sprinkled *the blood* from their hands, and the Lē′vītes flayed *them*.

12 And they removed the burnt offerings, that they might give according to the divisions of the families of the people, to offer unto the LORD, as *it is* written in the book of Moses. And so *did they* with the oxen.

13 And they roasted the passover with fire according to the ordinance: but the *other* holy *offerings* sod they in pots, and in caldrons, and in pans, and divided *them* speedily among all the people.

14 And afterward they made ready for themselves, and for the priests: because the priests the sons of Aaron *were busied* in offering of burnt offerings and the fat until night; therefore the Lē′vītes prepared for themselves, and for the priests the sons of Aaron.

15 And the singers the sons of Ā′săph *were* in their place, according to the commandment of David, and Ā′săph, and Hē′măn, and Jed′ū-thun the king's seer; and the porters *waited* at every gate; they might not depart from their service; for their brethren the Lē′vītes prepared for them.

16 So all the service of the LORD was prepared the same day, to keep the passover, and to offer burnt offerings upon the altar of the LORD, according to the commandment of king Jō-sī′ah.

17 And the children of Israel that were present kept the passover at that time, and the feast of unleavened bread seven days.

18 And there was no passover like to that kept in Israel from the days of Samuel the prophet; neither did all the kings of Israel keep such a passover as Jō-sī′ah kept, and the priests, and the Lē′vītes, and all Jū′dah and Israel that were present, and the inhabitants of Jerusalem.

19 In the eighteenth year of the reign of Jō-sī′ah was this passover kept.

20 ¶After all this, when Jō-sī′ah had prepared the temple, Nē′chō king of Egypt came up to fight against Cär′che-mĭsh by Eū-phrā′tēṡ: and Jō-sī′ah went out against him.

21 But he sent ambassadors to him, saying, What have I to do with thee, thou king of Jū′dah? *I come* not against thee this day, but against the house wherewith I have war: for God commanded me to make haste: forbear thee from *meddling with* God, who *is* with me, that he destroy thee not.

22 Nevertheless Jō-sī′ah would not turn his face from him, but disguised himself, that he might fight with him, and hearkened not unto the words of Nē′chō from the mouth of God, and came to fight in the valley of Me-gĭd′dō.

23 And the archers shot at king Jō-sī′ah; and the king said to his servants, Have me away; for I am sore wounded.

24 His servants therefore took him out of that chariot, and put him in the second chariot that he had; and they brought him to Jerusalem, and he died, and was buried in *one of* the sepulchres of his fathers. And all Jū′dah and Jerusalem mourned for Jō-sī′ah.

25 And Jĕr-e-mī′ah lamented for Jō-sī′ah: and all the singing men and the singing women spake of Jō-sī′ah in their lamentations to this day, and made them an ordinance in Israel: and, behold, they *are* written in the lamentations.

26 Now the rest of the acts of Jō-sī′ah, and his goodness, according to *that which was* written in the law of the LORD,

27 And his deeds, first and last, behold, they *are* written in the book of the kings of Israel and Jū′dah.

CHAPTER 36

THEN the people of the land took Je-hō′a-hăz the son of Jō-sī′ah, and made him king in his father's stead in Jerusalem.

2 Je-hō′a-hăz *was* twenty and three years old when he began to reign, and he reigned three months in Jerusalem.

3 And the king of Egypt put him

down at Jerusalem, and condemned the land in an hundred talents of silver and a talent of gold.

4 And the king of Egypt made E-lī'a-kĭm his brother king over Jū'dah and Jerusalem, and turned his name to Je-hoi'a-kĭm. And Nē'chō took Je-hō'a-hăz his brother, and carried him to Egypt.

5 ¶Je-hoi'a-kĭm *was* twenty and five years old when he began to reign, and he reigned eleven years in Jerusalem: and he did *that which was* evil in the sight of the LORD his God.

6 Against him came up Nĕb-u-chad-nĕz'zar king of Babylon, and bound him in fetters, to carry him to Babylon.

7 Nĕb-u-chad-nĕz'zar also carried of the vessels of the house of the LORD to Babylon, and put them in his temple at Babylon.

8 Now the rest of the acts of Je-hoi'a-kĭm, and his abominations which he did, and that which was found in him, behold, they *are* written in the book of the kings of Israel and Jū'dah: and Je-hoi'a-chĭn his son reigned in his stead.

9 ¶Je-hoi'a-chĭn *was* eight years old when he began to reign, and he reigned three months and ten days in Jerusalem: and he did *that which was* evil in the sight of the LORD.

10 And when the year was expired, king Nĕb-u-chad-nĕz'zar sent, and brought him to Babylon, with the goodly vessels of the house of the LORD, and made Zĕd-e-kī'ah his brother king over Jū'dah and Jerusalem.

11 Zĕd-e-kī'ah *was* one and twenty years old when he began to reign, and reigned eleven years in Jerusalem.

12 And he did *that which was* evil in the sight of the LORD his God, *and* humbled not himself before Jĕr-e-mī'-ah the prophet *speaking* from the mouth of the LORD.

13 And he also rebelled against king Nĕb-u-chad-nĕz'zar, who had made him swear by God: but he stiffened his neck, and hardened his heart from turning unto the LORD God of Israel.

14 Moreover all the chief of the priests, and the people, transgressed very much after all the abominations of the heathen; and polluted the house of the LORD which he had hallowed in Jerusalem.

15 And the LORD God of their fathers sent to them by his messengers, rising up betimes, and sending; because he had compassion on his people, and on his dwelling place:

16 But they mocked the messengers of God, and despised his words, and misused his prophets, until the wrath of the LORD arose against his people, till *there was* no remedy.

17 Therefore he brought upon them the king of the Chăl'dees, who slew their young men with the sword in the house of their sanctuary, and had no compassion upon young man or maiden, old man, or him that stooped for age: he gave *them* all into his hand.

18 And all the vessels of the house of God, great and small, and the treasures of the house of the LORD, and the treasures of the king, and of his princes; all *these* he brought to Babylon.

19 And they burnt the house of God, and brake down the wall of Jerusalem, and burnt all the palaces thereof with fire, and destroyed all the goodly vessels thereof.

20 And them that had escaped from the sword carried he away to Babylon; where they were servants to him and his sons until the reign of the kingdom of Persia:

21 To fulfil the word of the LORD by the mouth of Jĕr-e-mī'ah, until the land had enjoyed her sabbaths: *for* as long as she lay desolate she kept sabbath, to fulfil threescore and ten years.

22 ¶Now in the first year of Cyrus king of Persia, that the word of the LORD *spoken* by the mouth of Jĕr-e-mī'ah might be accomplished, the LORD stirred up the spirit of Cyrus king of Persia, that he made a proclamation throughout all his kingdom, and *put it* also in writing, saying,

23 Thus saith Cyrus king of Persia, All the kingdoms of the earth hath the LORD God of heaven given me; and he hath charged me to build him an house in Jerusalem, which *is* in Jū'dah. Who *is there* among you of all his people? The LORD his God *be* with him, and let him go up.

EZRA

CHAPTER 1

NOW in the first year of Cyrus king of Persia, that the word of the LORD by the mouth of Jĕr-e-mī'ah might be fulfilled, the LORD stirred up the spirit of Cyrus king of Persia, that he made a proclamation throughout all his kingdom, and *put it* also in writing, saying,

2 Thus saith Cyrus king of Persia, The LORD God of heaven hath given me all the kingdoms of the earth; and he hath

charged me to build him an house at Jerusalem, which *is* in Jū'dah.
3 Who *is there* among you of all his people? his God be with him, and let him go up to Jerusalem, which *is* in Jū'dah, and build the house of the LORD God of Israel, (he *is* the God,) which *is* in Jerusalem.
4 And whosoever remaineth in any place where he sojourneth, let the men of his place help him with silver, and with gold, and with goods, and with beasts, beside the freewill offering for the house of God that *is* in Jerusalem.
5 ¶Then rose up the chief of the fathers of Jū'dah and Benjamin, and the priests, and the Lē'vītes, with all *them* whose spirit God had raised, to go up to build the house of the LORD which *is* in Jerusalem.
6 And all they that *were* about them strengthened their hands with vessels of silver, with gold, with goods, and with beasts, and with precious things, beside all *that* was willingly offered.
7 ¶Also Cyrus the king brought forth the vessels of the house of the LORD, which Nĕb-u-chad-nĕz'zar had brought forth out of Jerusalem, and had put them in the house of his gods;
8 Even those did Cyrus king of Persia bring forth by the hand of Mĭth're-dăth the treasurer, and numbered them unto Shĕsh-băz-zar, the prince of Jū'dah.
9 And this *is* the number of them: thirty chargers of gold, a thousand chargers of silver, nine and twenty knives,
10 Thirty basons of gold, silver basons of a second *sort* four hundred and ten, *and* other vessels a thousand.
11 All the vessels of gold and of silver *were* five thousand and four hundred. All *these* did Shĕsh-băz'zar bring up with *them of* the captivity that were brought up from Babylon unto Jerusalem.

CHAPTER 2

NOW these *are* the children of the province that went up out of the captivity, of those which had been carried away, whom Nĕb-u-chad-nĕz'zar the king of Babylon had carried away unto Babylon, and came again unto Jerusalem and Jū'dah, every one unto his city;
2 Which came with Ze-rŭb'ba-bel: Jĕsh'u-a, Nē-he-mī'ah, Se-ra-ī'ah, Rē-el-a'īah, Môr'de-caī, Bĭl-shăn, Mĭz'păr, Bĭg'va-ī, Rē'hum, Bā'a-nah. The number of the men of the people of Israel:
3 The children of Pâ'rŏsh, two thousand an hundred seventy and two.
4 The children of Shĕph-a-tī'ah, three hundred seventy and two.
5 The children of Ā'rah, seven hundred seventy and five.
6 The children of Pā'hăth-mō'ăb, of the children of Jĕsh'u-a *and* Jō'ăb, two thousand eight hundred and twelve.
7 The children of Ē'lam, a thousand two hundred fifty and four.
8 The children of Zăt'tū, nine hundred forty and five.
9 The children of Zăc'ca-ī, seven hundred and threescore.
10 The children of Bā'nī, six hundred forty and two.
11 The children of Bĕb'a-ī, six hundred twenty and three.
12 The children of Ăz'găd, a thousand two hundred twenty and two.
13 The children of Ăd-on-ī'kam, six hundred sixty and six.
14 The children of Bĭg'va-ī, two thousand fifty and six.
15 The children of Ā'din, four hundred fifty and four.
16 The children of Ā'ter of Hĕz-e-kī'-ah, ninety and eight.
17 The children of Bē'zaī, three hundred twenty and three.
18 The children of Jô'rah, an hundred and twelve.
19 The children of Hā'shum, two hundred twenty and three.
20 The children of Gĭb'băr, ninety and five.
21 The children of Bĕth-le-hĕm, an hundred twenty and three.
22 The men of Ne-tō'phah, fifty and six.
23 The men of Ăn'a-thŏth, an hundred twenty and eight.
24 The children of Ăz-ma-vĕth, forty and two.
25 The children of Kir'jath-ā'rĭm, Che-phī'rah, and Bē-ē'rŏth, seven hundred and forty and three.
26 The children of Rā'mah and Gā'ba, six hundred twenty and one.
27 The men of Mĭch'măs, an hundred twenty and two.
28 The men of Bĕth-el and Ā'ī, two hundred twenty and three.
29 The children of Nebo, fifty and two.
30 The children of Măg'bĭsh, an hundred fifty and six.
31 The children of the other Ē'lam, a thousand two hundred fifty and four.
32 The children of Hā'rĭm, three hundred and twenty.
33 The children of Lod, Hā'dĭd, and Ō'nō, seven hundred twenty and five.
34 The children of Jericho, three hundred forty and five.

35 The children of Se-nā′ah, three thousand and six hundred and thirty.

36 ¶The priests: the children of Je-dā′-iah, of the house of Jĕsh′u-a, nine hundred seventy and three.

37 The children of Ĭm′mer, a thousand fifty and two.

38 The children of Păsh′ur, a thousand two hundred forty and seven.

39 The children of Hâ′rĭm, a thousand and seventeen.

40 ¶The Lē′vītes: the children of Jĕsh′u-a and Kăd′mĭ-el, of the children of Hŏd-a-vī′ah, seventy and four.

41 ¶The singers: the children of Ā′săph, an hundred twenty and eight.

42 ¶The children of the porters: the children of Shăl′lum, the children of Ā′ter, the children of Tăl′mon, the children of Ăk′kŭb, the children of Hat′ī-ta, the children of Shō′ba-ī, *in* all an hundred thirty and nine.

43 ¶The Nĕth′i-nĭmṡ: the children of Zī′ha, the children of Ha-sū′pha, the children of Tăb′ba-ŏth,

44 The children of Ke′rŏs, the children of Sī′a-ha, the children of Pā′don,

45 The children of Lĕb′a-nah, the children of Hăg′a-bah, the children of Ăk′kŭb,

46 The children of Hā′găb, the children of Shăl′ma-ī, the children of Hā′-nan,

47 The children of Gĭd′del, the children of Gā′här, the children of Rē-ā-i′ah,

48 The children of Rē′zĭn, the children of Ne-kō′da, the children of Găz′-zam,

49 The children of Ŭz′za, the children of Pa-sē′ah, the children of Bē′ṡaī,

50 The children of Ăs′nah, the children of Me-hū′nĭm, the children of Ne-phū′sĭm,

51 The children of Băk′bŭk, the children of Ha-kū′pha, the children of Här′hûr,

52 The children of Băz′luth, the children of Me-hī′da, the children of Här′-sha,

53 The children of Bär′kŏs, the children of Sĭs′e-ra, the children of Thā′-mah,

54 The children of Ne-zī′ah, the children of Hat′ī-pha.

55 The children of Solomon's servants: the children of Sō′ta-ī, the children of Sŏph′e-rĕth, the children of Pe-rū′da,

56 The children of Jā-a′lah, the children of Där′kŏn, the children of Gĭd′-del,

57 The children of Shĕph-a-tī′ah, the children of Hăt′til, the children of Pŏch′e-rĕth of Ze-bā′im, the children of Ā′mī.

58 All the Nĕth′i-nĭmṡ, and the children of Solomon's servants, *were* three hundred ninety and two.

59 And these *were* they which went up from Tĕl-mē′lah, Tĕl-här′sa, Cherub, Ăd′dan, *and* Ĭm′mer: but they could not shew their father's house, and their seed, whether they *were* of Israel.

60 The children of Dĕl-a-ī′ah, the children of Tō-bī′ah, the children of Ne-kō′da, six hundred fifty and two.

61 And of the children of the priests: the children of Ha-bā′iah, the children of Koz, the children of Bär-zĭl′la-ī; which took a wife of the daughters of Bär-zĭl′la-ī the Gĭl′e-ad-īte, and was called after their name:

62 These sought their register *among* those that were reckoned by genealogy, but they were not found: therefore were they, as polluted, put from the priesthood.

63 And the Tir′shā-tha said unto them, that they should not eat of the most holy things, till there stood up a priest with Û′rĭm and with Thŭm′mĭm.

64 ¶The whole congregation together *was* forty and two thousand three hundred *and* threescore,

65 Beside their servants and their maids, of whom *there were* seven thousand three hundred thirty and seven: and *there were* among them two hundred singing men and singing women.

66 Their horses *were* seven hundred thirty and six; their mules, two hundred forty and five;

67 Their camels, four hundred thirty and five; *their* asses, six thousand seven hundred and twenty.

68 ¶And *some* of the chief of the fathers, when they came to the house of the LORD which *is* at Jerusalem, offered freely for the house of God to set it up in his place:

69 They gave after their ability unto the treasure of the work threescore and one thousand drams of gold, and five thousand pound of silver, and one hundred priests' garments.

70 So the priests, and the Lē′vītes, and *some* of the people, and the singers, and the porters, and the Nĕth′i-nĭmṡ, dwelt in their cities, and all Israel in their cities.

CHAPTER 3

AND when the seventh month was come, and the children of Israel *were* in the cities, the people gathered themselves together as one man to Jerusalem.

2 Then stood up Jĕsh′u-a the son of Jōz′a-dăk, and his brethren the priests, and Ze-rŭb′ba-bel the son of Shē-ăl′tī-el, and his brethren, and builded the altar of the God of Israel, to offer burnt offerings thereon, as *it is* written in the law of Moses the man of God.

3 And they set the altar upon his bases; for fear *was* upon them because of the people of those countries: and they offered burnt offerings thereon unto the Lord, *even* burnt offerings morning and evening.

4 They kept also the feast of tabernacles, as *it is* written, and *offered* the daily burnt offerings by number, according to the custom, as the duty of every day required;

5 And afterward *offered* the continual burnt offering, both of the new moons, and of all the set feasts of the LORD that were consecrated, and of every one that willingly offered a freewill offering unto the LORD.

6 From the first day of the seventh month began they to offer burnt offerings unto the LORD. But the foundation of the temple of the LORD was not *yet* laid.

7 They gave money also unto the masons, and to the carpenters; and meat, and drink, and oil, unto them of Zī′don, and to them of Tyre, to bring cedar trees from Lebanon to the sea of Jŏp′pa, according to the grant that they had of Cyrus king of Persia.

8 ¶Now in the second year of their coming unto the house of God at Jerusalem, in the second month, began Ze-rŭb′ba-bel the son of Shē-ăl′tī-el, and Jĕsh′u-a the son of Jōz′a-dăk, and the remnant of their brethren the priests and the Lē′vītes, and all they that were come out of the captivity unto Jerusalem; and appointed the Lē′vītes, from twenty years old and upward, to set forward the work of the house of the LORD.

9 Then stood Jĕsh′u-a *with* his sons and his brethren, Kăd′mī-el and his sons, the sons of Jū′dah, together, to set forward the workmen in the house of God: the sons of Hĕn′a-dăd, *with* their sons and their brethren the Lē′vītes.

10 And when the builders laid the foundation of the temple of the LORD, they set the priests in their apparel with trumpets, and the Lē′vītes the sons of Ā′săph with cymbals, to praise the LORD, after the ordinance of David king of Israel.

11 And they sang together by course in praising and giving thanks unto the LORD; because *he is* good, for his mercy *endureth* for ever toward Israel. And all the people shouted with a great shout, when they praised the LORD, because the foundation of the house of the LORD was laid.

12 But many of the priests and Lē′vītes and chief of the fathers, *who were* ancient men, that had seen the first house, when the foundation of this house was laid before their eyes, wept with a loud voice; and many shouted aloud for joy:

13 So that the people could not discern the noise of the shout of joy from the noise of the weeping of the people: for the people shouted with a loud shout, and the noise was heard afar off.

CHAPTER 4

NOW when the adversaries of Jū′dah and Benjamin heard that the children of the captivity builded the temple unto the LORD God of Israel;

2 Then they came to Ze-rŭb′ba-bel, and to the chief of the fathers, and said unto them, Let us build with you: for we seek your God, as ye *do;* and we do sacrifice unto him since the days of Ē′sar-hăd′don king of Assur, which brought us up hither.

3 But Ze-rŭb′ba-bel, and Jĕsh′u-a, and the rest of the chief of the fathers of Israel, said unto them, Ye have nothing to do with us to build an house unto our God; but we ourselves together will build unto the LORD God of Israel, as king Cyrus the king of Persia hath commanded us.

4 Then the people of the land weakened the hands of the people of Jū′dah, and troubled them in building,

5 And hired counsellors against them, to frustrate their purpose, all the days of Cyrus king of Persia, even until the reign of Darius king of Persia.

6 And in the reign of A-haṡ-ū-ē′rus, in the beginning of his reign, wrote they *unto him* an accusation against the inhabitants of Jū′dah and Jerusalem.

7 And in the days of Är-ta-ẋer′ẋēṡ wrote Bĭsh′lam, Mĭth′re-dăth, Tă′be-el, and the rest of their companions, unto Är-ta-ẋer′ẋēṡ king of Persia; and the writing of the letter *was* written in the Syrian tongue, and interpreted in the Syrian tongue.

8 Rē′hum the chancellor and Shĭm′shaī the scribe wrote a letter against Jerusalem to Är-ta-ẋer′ẋēṡ the king in this sort:

9 Then *wrote* Rē′hum the chancellor, and Shĭm′shaī the scribe, and the rest of their companions; the Dī′na-ītes, the A-phär′sath-chītes, the Tär′pel-ītes, the A-phär′sītes, the Är′che-vītes, the Baby-

lonians, the Sū'san-chītes, the De-hā'-vītes, *and* the Ē'lam-ītes,

10 And the rest of the nations whom the great and noble Ăs-năp'per brought over, and set in the cities of Sa-mâ'ri-a, and the rest *that are* on this side the river, and at such a time.

11 This *is* the copy of the letter that they sent unto him, *even* unto Är-ta-ẋer'ẋēs the king; Thy servants the men on this side the river, and at such a time.

12 Be it known unto the king, that the Jews which came up from thee to us are come unto Jerusalem, building the rebellious and the bad city, and have set up the walls *thereof*, and joined the foundations.

13 Be it known now unto the king, that, if this city be builded, and the walls set up *again, then* will they not pay toll, tribute, and custom, and *so* thou shalt endamage the revenue of the kings.

14 Now because we have maintenance from *the king's* palace, and it was not meet for us to see the king's dishonour, therefore have we sent and certified the king;

15 That search may be made in the book of the records of thy fathers: so shalt thou find in the book of the records, and know that this city *is* a rebellious city, and hurtful unto kings and provinces, and that they have moved sedition within the same of old time: for which cause was this city destroyed.

16 We certify the king that, if this city be builded *again*, and the walls thereof set up, by this means thou shalt have no portion on this side the river.

17 ¶*Then* sent the king an answer unto Rē'hum the chancellor, and *to* Shĭm'shaī the scribe, and *to* the rest of their companions that dwell in Sa-mâ'ri-a, and *unto* the rest beyond the river, Peace, and at such a time.

18 The letter which ye sent unto us hath been plainly read before me.

19 And I commanded, and search hath been made, and it is found that this city of old time hath made insurrection against kings, and *that* rebellion and sedition have been made therein.

20 There have been mighty kings also over Jerusalem, which have ruled over all *countries* beyond the river; and toll, tribute, and custom, was paid unto them.

21 Give ye now commandment to cause these men to cease, and that this city be not builded, until *another* commandment shall be given from me.

22 Take heed now that ye fail not to do this: why should damage grow to the hurt of the kings?

23 ¶Now when the copy of king Är-ta-ẋer'ẋēs' letter *was* read before Rē'hum, and Shĭm'shaī the scribe, and their companions, they went up in haste to Jerusalem unto the Jews, and made them to cease by force and power.

24 Then ceased the work of the house of God which *is* at Jerusalem. So it ceased unto the second year of the reign of Darius king of Persia.

CHAPTER 5

THEN the prophets, Hăg'ga-ī the prophet, and Zĕch-a-rī'ah the son of Ĭd'-dō, prophesied unto the Jews that *were* in Jū'dah and Jerusalem in the name of the God of Israel, *even* unto them.

2 Then rose up Ze-rŭb'ba-bel the son of Shē-ăl'tī-el, and Jĕsh'u-a the son of Jōz'a-dăk, and began to build the house of God which *is* at Jerusalem: and with them *were* the prophets of God helping them.

3 ¶At the same time came to them Tăt'na-ī, governor on this side the river, and Shē'thär-bōz'na-ī and their companions, and said thus unto them, Who hath commanded you to build this house, and to make up this wall?

4 Then said we unto them after this manner, What are the names of the men that make this building?

5 But the eye of their God was upon the elders of the Jews, that they could not cause them to cease, till the matter came to Darius: and then they returned answer by letter concerning this *matter*.

6 ¶The copy of the letter that Tăt'na-ī, governor on this side the river, and Shē'thär-bōz'na-ī and his companions the A-phär'sach-ītes, which *were* on this side the river, sent unto Darius the king:

7 They sent a letter unto him, wherein was written thus; Unto Darius the king, all peace.

8 Be it known unto the king, that we went into the province of Judea, to the house of the great God, which is builded with great stones, and timber is laid in the walls, and this work goeth fast on, and prospereth in their hands.

9 Then asked we those elders, *and* said unto them thus, Who commanded you to build this house, and to make up these walls?

10 We asked their names also, to certify thee, that we might write the names of the men that *were* the chief of them.

11 And thus they returned us answer, saying, We are the servants of the God of heaven and earth, and build the house that was builded these many years ago, which a great king of Israel builded and set up.

12 But after that our fathers had provoked the God of heaven unto wrath, he gave them into the hand of Nĕb-u-chad-nĕz'zar the king of Babylon, the Chăl-dē'an, who destroyed this house, and carried the people away into Babylon.

13 But in the first year of Cyrus the king of Babylon *the same* king Cyrus made a decree to build this house of God.

14 And the vessels also of gold and silver of the house of God, which Nĕb-u-chad-nĕz'zar took out of the temple that *was* in Jerusalem, and brought them into the temple of Babylon, those did Cyrus the king take out of the temple of Babylon, and they were delivered unto *one*, whose name *was* Shĕsh-băz'zar, whom he had made governor;

15 And said unto him, Take these vessels, go, carry them into the temple that *is* in Jerusalem, and let the house of God be builded in his place.

16 Then came the same Shĕsh-băz'zar, *and* laid the foundation of the house of God which *is* in Jerusalem: and since that time even until now hath it been in building, and *yet* it is not finished.

17 Now therefore, if *it seem* good to the king, let there be search made in the king's treasure house, which *is* there at Babylon, whether it be *so*, that a decree was made of Cyrus the king to build this house of God at Jerusalem, and let the king send his pleasure to us concerning this matter.

CHAPTER 6

THEN Darius the king made a decree, and search was made in the house of the rolls, where the treasures were laid up in Babylon.

2 And there was found at Ăch'me-tha, in the palace that *is* in the province of the Medes, a roll, and therein *was* a record thus written:

3 In the first year of Cyrus the king *the same* Cyrus the king made a decree *concerning* the house of God at Jerusalem, Let the house be builded, the place where they offered sacrifices, and let the foundations thereof be strongly laid; the height thereof threescore cubits, *and* the breadth thereof threescore cubits;

4 *With* three rows of great stones, and a row of new timber: and let the expenses be given out of the king's house:

5 And also let the golden and silver vessels of the house of God, which Nĕb-u-chad-nĕz'zar took forth out of the temple which *is* at Jerusalem, and brought unto Babylon, be restored, and brought again unto the temple which *is* at Jerusalem, *every one* to his place, and place *them* in the house of God.

6 Now *therefore* Tăt'na-ī, governor beyond the river, Shē'thär–bōz'na-ī, and your companions the A-phär'sach-ītes, which *are* beyond the river, be ye far from thence:

7 Let the work of this house of God alone; let the governor of the Jews and the elders of the Jews build this house of God in his place.

8 Moreover I make a decree what ye shall do to the elders of these Jews for the building of this house of God: that of the king's goods, *even* of the tribute beyond the river, forthwith expenses be given unto these men, that they be not hindered.

9 And that which they have need of, both young bullocks, and rams, and lambs, for the burnt offerings of the God of heaven, wheat, salt, wine, and oil, according to the appointment of the priests which *are* at Jerusalem, let it be given them day by day without fail:

10 That they may offer sacrifices of sweet savours unto the God of heaven, and pray for the life of the king, and of his sons.

11 Also I have made a decree, that whosoever shall alter this word, let timber be pulled down from his house, and being set up, let him be hanged thereon; and let his house be made a dunghill for this.

12 And the God that hath caused his name to dwell there destroy all kings and people, that shall put to their hand to alter *and* to destroy this house of God which *is* at Jerusalem. I Darius have made a decree; let it be done with speed.

13 ¶Then Tăt'na-ī, governor on this side the river, Shē'thär–bōz'na-ī, and their companions, according to that which Darius the king had sent, so they did speedily.

14 And the elders of the Jews builded, and they prospered through the prophesying of Hăg'ga-ī the prophet and Zĕch-a-rī'ah the son of Ĭd'dō. And they builded, and finished *it*, according to the commandment of the God of Israel, and according to the commandment of Cyrus, and Darius, and Är-ta-ẋer'ẋēs king of Persia.

15 And this house was finished on the third day of the month Ā'där, which was in the sixth year of the reign of Darius the king.

16 ¶And the children of Israel, the priests, and the Lē'vītes and the rest of the children of the captivity, kept the dedication of this house of God with joy,

17 And offered at the dedication of this house of God an hundred bullocks, two hundred rams, four hundred lambs; and for a sin offering for all Israel, twelve he goats, according to the number of the tribes of Israel.

18 And they set the priests in their divisions, and the Lē'vītes in their courses, for the service of God, which *is* at Jerusalem; as it is written in the book of Moses.

19 ¶And the children of the captivity kept the passover upon the fourteenth *day* of the first month.

20 For the priests and the Lē'vītes were purified together, all of them *were* pure, and killed the passover for all the children of the captivity, and for their brethren the priests, and for themselves.

21 And the children of Israel, which were come again out of captivity, and all such as had separated themselves unto them from the filthiness of the heathen of the land, to seek the LORD God of Israel, did eat,

22 And kept the feast of unleavened bread seven days with joy: for the LORD had made them joyful, and turned the heart of the king of Assyria unto them, to strengthen their hands in the work of the house of God, the God of Israel.

CHAPTER 7

NOW after these things, in the reign of Är-ta-ẋer'ẋēṡ king of Persia, Ezra the son of Se-ra-ī'ah, the son of Ăz-a-rī'ah, the son of Hĭl-kī'ah,

2 The son of Shăl'lum, the son of Zā'-dŏk, the son of A-hī'tŭb,

3 The son of Ăm-a-rī'ah, the son of Ăz-a-rī'ah, the son of Me-rā'ioth,

4 The son of Zĕr-a-hī'ah, the son of Ŭz'zi, the son of Bŭk'kī,

5 The son of A-bĭsh'ū-a, the son of Phĭn'e-has, the son of Ē-le-ā'zar, the son of Aaron the chief priest:

6 This Ezra went up from Babylon; and he *was* a ready scribe in the law of Moses, which the LORD God of Israel had given: and the king granted him all his request, according to the hand of the LORD his God upon him.

7 And there went up *some* of the children of Israel, and of the priests, and the Lē'vītes, and the singers, and the porters, and the Nĕth'i-nĭmṡ, unto Jerusalem, in the seventh year of Är-ta-ẋer'ẋēṡ the king.

8 And he came to Jerusalem in the fifth month, which *was* in the seventh year of the king.

9 For upon the first *day* of the first month began he to go up from Babylon, and on the first *day* of the fifth month came he to Jerusalem, according to the good hand of his God upon him.

10 For Ezra had prepared his heart to seek the law of the LORD, and to do *it*, and to teach in Israel statutes and judgments.

11 ¶Now this *is* the copy of the letter that the king Är-ta-ẋer'ẋēṡ gave unto Ezra the priest, the scribe, *even* a scribe of the words of the commandments of the LORD, and of his statutes to Israel.

12 Är-ta-ẋer'ẋēṡ, king of kings, unto Ezra the priest, a scribe of the law of the God of heaven, perfect *peace*, and at such a time.

13 I make a decree, that all they of the people of Israel, and *of* his priests and Lē'vītes, in my realm, which are minded of their own freewill to go up to Jerusalem, go with thee.

14 Forasmuch as thou art sent of the king, and of his seven counsellors, to enquire concerning Jū'dah and Jerusalem, according to the law of thy God which *is* in thine hand;

15 And to carry the silver and gold, which the king and his counsellors have freely offered unto the God of Israel, whose habitation *is* in Jerusalem,

16 And all the silver and gold that thou canst find in all the province of Babylon, with the freewill offering of the people, and of the priests, offering willingly for the house of their God which *is* in Jerusalem:

17 That thou mayest buy speedily with this money bullocks, rams, lambs, with their meat offerings and their drink offerings, and offer them upon the altar of the house of your God which *is* in Jerusalem.

18 And whatsoever shall seem good to thee, and to thy brethren, to do with the rest of the silver and the gold, that do after the will of your God.

19 The vessels also that are given thee for the service of the house of thy God, *those* deliver thou before the God of Jerusalem.

20 And whatsoever more shall be needful for the house of thy God, which thou shalt have occasion to bestow, bestow *it* out of the king's treasure house.

21 And I, *even* I Är-ta-ẋer'ẋēṡ the

king, do make a decree to all the treasurers which *are* beyond the river, that whatsoever Ezra the priest, the scribe of the law of the God of heaven, shall require of you, it be done speedily,

22 Unto an hundred talents of silver, and to an hundred measures of wheat, and to an hundred baths of wine, and to an hundred baths of oil, and salt without prescribing *how much*.

23 Whatsoever is commanded by the God of heaven, let it be diligently done for the house of the God of heaven: for why should there be wrath against the realm of the king and his sons?

24 Also we certify you, that touching any of the priests and Lē′vītes, singers, porters, Nĕth′i-nīmṡ, or ministers of this house of God, it shall not be lawful to impose toll, tribute, or custom, upon them.

25 And thou, Ezra, after the wisdom of thy God, that *is* in thine hand, set magistrates and judges, which may judge all the people that *are* beyond the river, all such as know the laws of thy God; and teach ye them that know *them* not.

26 And whosoever will not do the law of thy God, and the law of the king, let judgment be executed speedily upon him, whether *it be* unto death, or to banishment, or to confiscation of goods, or to imprisonment.

27 ¶Blessed *be* the LORD God of our fathers, which hath put *such a thing* as this in the king's heart, to beautify the house of the LORD which *is* in Jerusalem:

28 And hath extended mercy unto me before the king, and his counsellors, and before all the king's mighty princes. And I was strengthened as the hand of the LORD my God *was* upon me, and I gathered together out of Israel chief men to go up with me.

CHAPTER 8

THESE *are* now the chief of their fathers, and *this is* the genealogy of them that went up with me from Babylon, in the reign of Är-ta-xer′xēṡ the king.

2 Of the sons of Phĭn′e-has; Ger′shom: of the sons of Ĭth′a-mär; Daniel: of the sons of David; Hăt′tŭsh.

3 Of the sons of Shĕch-a-nī′ah, of the sons of Phâ′rŏsh; Zĕch-a-rī′ah: and with him were reckoned by genealogy of the males an hundred and fifty.

4 Of the sons of Pā′hăth–mō′ăb; Ĕ-li-hō-ē′na-ī the son of Zĕr-a-hī′ah, and with him two hundred males.

5 Of the sons of Shĕch-a-nī′ah; the son of Ja-hā′zi-el, and with him three hundred males.

6 Of the sons also of Ā′din; Ē′bĕd the son of Jonathan, and with him fifty males.

7 And of the sons of Ē′lam; Je-shā′iah the son of Ăth-a-lī′ah, and with him seventy males.

8 And of the sons of Shĕph-a-tī′ah; Zĕb-a-dī′ah the son of Michael, and with him fourscore males.

9 Of the sons of Jō′ăb; Ō-ba-dī′ah the son of Je-hī′el, and with him two hundred and eighteen males.

10 And of the sons of Shel′ō-mīth; the son of Jŏs-i-phī′ah, and with him an hundred and threescore males.

11 And the sons of Bĕb′a-ī; Zĕch-a-rī′ah the son of Bĕb′a-ī, and with him twenty and eight males.

12 And of the sons of Ăz′găd; Jō-hā′nan the son of Hăk′ka-tăn, and with him an hundred and ten males.

13 And of the last sons of Ăd-on-ī′kam, whose names *are* these, E-lĭph′e-lĕt, Je-ī′el, and Shem-ā-i′ah, and with them threescore males.

14 Of the sons also of Bĭg′va-ī; Ū′tha-ī, and Zāb′bŭd, and with them seventy males.

15 ¶And I gathered them together to the river that runneth to A-hā′va; and there abode we in tents three days: and I viewed the people, and the priests, and found there none of the sons of Levi.

16 Then sent I for Ĕ-lī-ē′zer, for Â′rī-el, for Shem-ā-i′ah, and for Ĕl′nā-than, and for Jâ′rīb, and for Ĕl′nā-than, and for Nā′than, and for Zĕch-a-rī′ah, and for Me-shŭl′lam, chief men; also for Joi′a-rīb, and for Ĕl′nā-than, men of understanding.

17 And I sent them with commandment unto Ĭd′dō the chief at the place Ca-sĭph′ī-a, and I told them what they should say unto Ĭd′dō, *and* to his brethren the Nĕth′i-nīmṡ, at the place Ca-sĭph′ī-a, that they should bring unto us ministers for the house of our God.

18 And by the good hand of our God upon us they brought us a man of understanding, of the sons of Mäh′lī, the son of Levi, the son of Israel; and Shĕr-e-bī′ah, with his sons and his brethren, eighteen;

19 And Hăsh-a-bī′ah, and with him Je-shā′iah of the sons of Me-râ′rī, his brethren and their sons, twenty;

20 Also of the Nĕth′i-nīmṡ, whom David and the princes had appointed for the service of the Lē′vītes, two hundred and twenty Nĕth′i-nīmṡ: all of them were expressed by name.

21 ¶Then I proclaimed a fast there, at the river of A-hā′va, that we might afflict ourselves before our God, to seek

of him a right way for us, and for our little ones, and for all our substance.

22 For I was ashamed to require of the king a band of soldiers and horsemen to help us against the enemy in the way: because we had spoken unto the king, saying, The hand of our God *is* upon all them for good that seek him; but his power and his wrath *is* against all them that forsake him.

23 So we fasted and besought our God for this: and he was intreated of us.

24 ¶Then I separated twelve of the chief of the priests, Shĕr-e-bī'ah, Hăsh-a-bī'ah, and ten of their brethren with them,

25 And weighed unto them the silver, and the gold, and the vessels, *even* the offering of the house of our God, which the king, and his counsellors, and his lords, and all Israel *there* present, had offered:

26 I even weighed unto their hand six hundred and fifty talents of silver, and silver vessels an hundred talents, *and* of gold an hundred talents;

27 Also twenty basons of gold, of a thousand drams; and two vessels of fine copper, precious as gold.

28 And I said unto them, Ye *are* holy unto the LORD; the vessels *are* holy also; and the silver and the gold *are* a freewill offering unto the LORD God of your fathers.

29 Watch ye, and keep *them*, until ye weigh *them* before the chief of the priests and the Lē'vītes, and chief of the fathers of Israel, at Jerusalem, in the chambers of the house of the LORD.

30 So took the priests and the Lē'vītes the weight of the silver, and the gold, and the vessels, to bring *them* to Jerusalem unto the house of our God.

31 ¶Then we departed from the river of A-hā'va on the twelfth *day* of the first month, to go unto Jerusalem: and the hand of our God was upon us, and he delivered us from the hand of the enemy, and of such as lay in wait by the way.

32 And we came to Jerusalem, and abode there three days.

33 ¶Now on the fourth day was the silver and the gold and the vessels weighed in the house of our God by the hand of Mĕr'e-mŏth the son of Ū-rī'ah the priest; and with him *was* Ĕ-le-ā'zar the son of Phĭn'e-has; and with them *was* Jōz'a-băd the son of Jĕsh'u-a, and Nō-a-dī'ah the son of Bĭn'nū-ī, Lē'vītes;

34 By number *and* by weight of every one: and all the weight was written at that time.

35 *Also* the children of those that had been carried away, which were come out of the captivity, offered burnt offerings unto the God of Israel, twelve bullocks for all Israel, ninety and six rams, seventy and seven lambs, twelve he goats *for* a sin offering: all *this was* a burnt offering unto the LORD.

36 And they delivered the king's commissions unto the king's lieutenants, and to the governors on this side the river: and they furthered the people, and the house of God.

CHAPTER 9

NOW when these things were done, the princes came to me, saying, The people of Israel, and the priests, and the Lē'vītes, have not separated themselves from the people of the lands, *doing* according to their abominations, *even* of the Canaanites, the Hittites, the Pĕr'iz-zītes, the Jĕb'u-sītes, the Ammonites, the Moabites, the Egyptians, and the Ăm'ō-rites.

2 For they have taken of their daughters for themselves, and for their sons: so that the holy seed have mingled themselves with the people of *those* lands: yea, the hand of the princes and rulers hath been chief in this trespass.

3 And when I heard this thing, I rent my garment and my mantle, and plucked off the hair of my head and of my beard, and sat down astonied.

4 Then were assembled unto me every one that trembled at the words of the God of Israel, because of the transgression of those that had been carried away; and I sat astonied until the evening sacrifice.

5 ¶And at the evening sacrifice I arose up from my heaviness; and having rent my garment and my mantle, I fell upon my knees, and spread out my hands unto the LORD my God,

6 And said, O my God, I am ashamed and blush to lift up my face to thee, my God: for our iniquities are increased over *our* head, and our trespass is grown up unto the heavens.

7 Since the days of our fathers *have* we *been* in a great trespass unto this day; and for our iniquities have we, our kings, *and* our priests, been delivered into the hand of the kings of the lands, to the sword, to captivity, and to a spoil, and to confusion of face, as *it is* this day.

8 And now for a little space grace hath been *shewed* from the LORD our God, to leave us a remnant to escape, and to give us a nail in his holy place, that our God may lighten our eyes, and give us a little reviving in our bondage.

9 For we *were* bondmen; yet our God hath not forsaken us in our bondage,

but hath extended mercy unto us in the
sight of the kings of Persia, to give us a
reviving, to set up the house of our God,
and to repair the desolations thereof,
and to give us a wall in Jū'dah and in
Jerusalem.
10 And now, O our God, what shall
we say after this? for we have forsaken
thy commandments,
11 Which thou hast commanded by
thy servants the prophets, saying, The
land, unto which ye go to possess it, is
an unclean land with the filthiness of
the people of the lands, with their
abominations, which have filled it from
one end to another with their unclean-
ness.
12 Now therefore give not your
daughters unto their sons, neither take
their daughters unto your sons, nor
seek their peace or their wealth for
ever: that ye may be strong, and eat the
good of the land, and leave *it* for an in-
heritance to your children for ever.
13 And after all that is come upon us
for our evil deeds, and for our great
trespass, seeing that thou our God hast
punished us less than our iniquities *de-
serve*, and hast given us *such* deliver-
ance as this;
14 Should we again break thy com-
mandments, and join in affinity with
the people of these abominations?
wouldest not thou be angry with us till
thou hadst consumed *us*, so that *there
should be* no remnant nor escaping?
15 O LORD God of Israel, thou *art*
righteous: for we remain yet escaped,
as *it is* this day: behold, we *are* before
thee in our trespasses: for we cannot
stand before thee because of this.

CHAPTER 10

NOW when Ezra had prayed, and when
he had confessed, weeping and casting
himself down before the house of God,
there assembled unto him out of Israel
a very great congregation of men and
women and children: for the people
wept very sore.
2 And Shĕch-a-nī'ah the son of Je-
hī'el, *one* of the sons of Ē'lam, an-
swered and said unto Ezra, We have
trespassed against our God, and have
taken strange wives of the people of the
land: yet now there is hope in Israel
concerning this thing.
3 Now therefore let us make a cov-
enant with our God to put away all the
wives, and such as are born of them,
according to the counsel of my lord,
and of those that tremble at the com-
mandment of our God; and let it be
done according to the law.
4 Arise; for *this* matter *belongeth*
unto thee: we also *will be* with thee: be
of good courage, and do *it*.
5 Then arose Ezra, and made the
chief priests, the Lē'vītes, and all Israel,
to swear that they should do according
to this word. And they sware.
6 Then Ezra rose up from before the
house of God, and went into the cham-
ber of Jō-hā'nan the son of E-lī'a-shīb:
and *when* he came thither, he did eat no
bread, nor drink water: for he mourned
because of the transgression of them
that had been carried away.
7 And they made proclamation
throughout Jū'dah and Jerusalem unto
all the children of the captivity, that
they should gather themselves togeth-
er unto Jerusalem;
8 And that whosoever would not
come within three days, according to
the counsel of the princes and the elders,
all his substance should be for-
feited, and himself separated from the
congregation of those that had been
carried away.
9 ¶Then all the men of Jū'dah and
Benjamin gathered themselves togeth-
er unto Jerusalem within three days.
It *was* the ninth month, on the twen-
tieth *day* of the month; and all the
people sat in the street of the house of
God, trembling because of *this* matter,
and for the great rain.
10 And Ezra the priest stood up, and
said unto them, Ye have transgressed,
and have taken strange wives, to in-
crease the trespass of Israel.
11 Now therefore make confession
unto the LORD God of your fathers, and
do his pleasure: and separate your-
selves from the people of the land, and
from the strange wives.
12 Then all the congregation an-
swered and said with a loud voice, As
thou hast said, so must we do.
13 But the people *are* many, and *it is* a
time of much rain, and we are not able
to stand without, neither *is this* a work
of one day or two: for we are many that
have transgressed in this thing.
14 Let now our rulers of all the con-
gregation stand, and let all them which
have taken strange wives in our cities
come at appointed times, and with
them the elders of every city, and the
judges thereof, until the fierce wrath of
our God for this matter be turned from
us.
15 Only Jonathan the son of Ă'sa-hĕl
and Jă-ha-zī'ah the son of Tĭk'vah were
employed about this *matter*: and Me-
shŭl'lam and Shăb'be-thaī the Lē'vīte
helped them.
16 And the children of the captivity

did so. And Ezra the priest, *with* certain chief of the fathers, after the house of their fathers, and all of them by *their* names, were separated, and sat down in the first day of the tenth month to examine the matter.

17 And they made an end with all the men that had taken strange wives by the first day of the first month.

18 ¶And among the sons of the priests there were found that had taken strange wives: *namely,* of the sons of Jĕsh′u-a the son of Jōz′a-dăk, and his brethren; Mā-a-sē′iah, and Ē-lĭ-ē′zer, and Jâ′rĭb, and Gĕd-a-lī′ah.

19 And they gave their hands that they would put away their wives; and *being* guilty, *they offered* a ram of the flock for their trespass.

20 And of the sons of Ĭm′mer; Ha-nā′nī, and Zĕb-a-dī′ah.

21 And of the sons of Hâ′rĭm; Mā-a-sē′iah, and E-lī′jah, and Shem-ā-i′ah, and Je-hī′el, and Uz-zī′ah.

22 And of the sons of Păsh′ur; Ē-lī-ō-ē′na-ī, Mā-a-sē′iah, Ĭsh′ma-el, Ne-thăn′e-el, Jōz′a-băd, and Ĕl′a-sah.

23 Also of the Lē′vītes; Jōz′a-băd, and Shĭm′e-ī, and Ke-lā′iah, (the same *is* Kel′ī-ta,) Pĕth-a-hī′ah, Jū′dah, and Ē-lĭ-ē′zer.

24 Of the singers also; E-lī′a-shĭb: and of the porters; Shăl′lum, and Tē′lĕm, and Ū′rī.

25 Moreover of Israel: of the sons of Pâ′rŏsh; Ra-mī′ah, and Je-zī′ah, and Măl-chī′ah, and Mī′a-mĭn, and Ē-le-ā′zar, and Măl-chī′jah, and Be-nā′iah.

26 And of the sons of Ē′lam; Măt-ta-nī′ah, Zĕch-a-rī′ah, and Je-hī′el, and Ăb′dī, and Jĕr′e-mŏth, and E-lī′ah.

27 And of the sons of Zăt′tū; Ē-lī-ō-ē′na-ī, E-lī′a-shĭb, Măt-ta-nī′ah, and Jĕr′e-mŏth, and Zā′băd, and A-zī′za.

28 Of the sons also of Bĕb′a-ī; Je-hō-hā′nan, Hăn-a-nī′ah, Zăb′baī, *and* Ăth′laī.

29 And of the sons of Bā′nī; Me-shŭl′lam, Măl′luch, and Ăd-a-ī′ah, Jāsh′ub, and Shē′al, and Rā′moth.

30 And of the sons of Pā′hăth-mō′ăb; Ăd′na, and Chē′lăl, Be-nā′iah, Mā-a-sē′iah, Măt-ta-nī′ah, Be-zăl′e-el, and Bĭn′nū-ī, and Ma-năs′seh.

31 And *of* the sons of Hâ′rĭm; Ē-lĭ-ē′zer, Ĭ-shī′jah, Mal-chī′ah, Shem-ā-i′ah, Shĭm′e-on,

32 Benjamin, Măl′luch, *and* Shĕm-a-rī′ah.

33 Of the sons of Hā′shum; Mat-te-na′ī, Măt-ta-thah, Zā′băd, E-lĭph′e-lĕt, Jĕr′e-maī, Ma-năs′seh, *and* Shĭm′e-ī.

34 Of the sons of Bā′nī; Mā-ad′aī, Amram, and Ū′el,

35 Be-nā′iah, Be-dē′iah, Chĕl′luh,

36 Va-nī′ah, Mĕr′e-mŏth, E-lī′a-shĭb,

37 Măt-ta-nī′ah, Măt-te-na′ī, and Jā′a-sau,

38 And Bā′nī, and Bĭn′nū-ī, Shĭm′e-ī,

39 And Shĕl-e-mī′ah, and Nathan, and Ăd-a-ī′ah,

40 Măch-nă-de′baī, Shăsh′a-ī, Shâr′a-ī,

41 Ā-zar′e-el, and Shĕl-e-mī′ah, Shĕm-a-rī′ah,

42 Shăl′lum, Ăm-a-rī′ah, *and* Joseph.

43 Of the sons of Nebo; Je-ī′el, Măt-ti-thī′ah, Zā′băd, Ze-bī′na, Jā′dau, and Jō′el, Be-nā′iah.

44 All these had taken strange wives: and *some* of them had wives by whom they had children.

THE

BOOK OF NEHEMIAH

CHAPTER 1

THE words of Nē-he-mī′ah the son of Hăch-a-lī′ah. And it came to pass in the month Chĭs′leu, in the twentieth year, as I was in Shū′shăn the palace,

2 That Ha-nā′nī, one of my brethren, came, he and *certain* men of Jū′dah; and I asked them concerning the Jews that had escaped, which were left of the captivity, and concerning Jerusalem.

3 And they said unto me, The remnant that are left of the captivity there in the province *are* in great affliction and reproach: the wall of Jerusalem also *is* broken down, and the gates thereof are burned with fire.

4 ¶And it came to pass, when I heard these words, that I sat down and wept, and mourned *certain* days, and fasted, and prayed before the God of heaven,

5 And said, I beseech thee, O LORD God of heaven, the great and terrible God, that keepeth covenant and mercy for them that love him and observe his commandments:

6 Let thine ear now be attentive, and thine eyes open, that thou mayest hear the prayer of thy servant, which I pray before thee now, day and night, for the children of Israel thy servants, and confess the sins of the children of Israel, which we have sinned against thee: both I and my father's house have sinned.

7 We have dealt very corruptly against thee, and have not kept the

commandments, nor the statutes, nor
the judgments, which thou commandedst thy servant Moses.
8 Remember, I beseech thee, the
word that thou commandedst thy servant Moses, saying, *If* ye transgress, I
will scatter you abroad among the nations:
9 But *if* ye turn unto me, and keep my
commandments, and do them; though
there were of you cast out unto the uttermost part of heaven, *yet* will I gather
them from thence, and will bring them
unto the place that I have chosen to set
my name there.
10 Now these *are* thy servants and
thy people, whom thou hast redeemed
by thy great power, and by thy strong
hand.
11 O Lord, I beseech thee, let now
thine ear be attentive to the prayer of
thy servant, and to the prayer of thy
servants, who desire to fear thy name:
and prosper, I pray thee, thy servant
this day, and grant him mercy in the
sight of this man. For I was the king's
cupbearer.

CHAPTER 2

AND it came to pass in the month Nī'-
săn, in the twentieth year of Är-ta-xer'-
xēs the king, *that* wine *was* before him:
and I took up the wine, and gave *it* unto
the king. Now I had not been *beforetime* sad in his presence.
2 Wherefore the king said unto me,
Why *is* thy countenance sad, seeing
thou *art* not sick? this *is* nothing *else*
but sorrow of heart. Then I was very
sore afraid,
3 And said unto the king, Let the king
live for ever: why should not my countenance be sad, when the city, the place
of my fathers' sepulchres, *lieth* waste,
and the gates thereof are consumed
with fire?
4 Then the king said unto me, For
what dost thou make request? So I
prayed to the God of heaven.
5 And I said unto the king, If it please
the king, and if thy servant have found
favour in thy sight, that thou wouldest
send me unto Jū'dah, unto the city of
my fathers' sepulchres, that I may
build it.
6 And the king said unto me, (the
queen also sitting by him,) For how
long shall thy journey be? and when
wilt thou return? So it pleased the king
to send me; and I set him a time.
7 Moreover I said unto the king, If it
please the king, let letters be given me
to the governors beyond the river, that
they may convey me over till I come
into Jū'dah;
8 And a letter unto Ā'săph the keeper
of the king's forest, that he may give
me timber to make beams for the gates
of the palace which *appertained* to the
house, and for the wall of the city, and
for the house that I shall enter into. And
the king granted me, according to the
good hand of my God upon me.
9 ¶Then I came to the governors
beyond the river, and gave them the
king's letters. Now the king had sent
captains of the army and horsemen
with me.
10 When Săn-băl'lat the Hôr'o-nīte,
and Tō-bī'ah the servant, the Ammonite, heard *of it*, it grieved them exceedingly that there was come a man to
seek the welfare of the children of
Israel.
11 ¶So I came to Jerusalem, and was
there three days.
12 And I arose in the night, I and
some few men with me; neither told I
any man what my God had put in my
heart to do at Jerusalem: neither *was*
there any beast with me, save the beast
that I rode upon.
13 And I went out by night by the
gate of the valley, even before the dragon well, and to the dung port, and
viewed the walls of Jerusalem, which
were broken down, and the gates thereof were consumed with fire.
14 Then I went on to the gate of the
fountain, and to the king's pool: but
there was no place for the beast *that*
was under me to pass.
15 Then went I up in the night by the
brook, and viewed the wall, and turned
back, and entered by the gate of the
valley, and *so* returned.
16 And the rulers knew not whither I
went, or what I did; neither had I as yet
told *it* to the Jews, nor to the priests,
nor to the nobles, nor to the rulers, nor
to the rest that did the work.
17 Then said I unto them, Ye see the
distress that we *are* in, how Jerusalem
lieth waste, and the gates thereof are
burned with fire: come, and let us build
up the wall of Jerusalem, that we be no
more a reproach.
18 Then I told them of the hand of my
God which was good upon me; as also
the king's words that he had spoken
unto me. And they said, Let us rise up
and build. So they strengthened their
hands for *this* good *work*.
19 But when Săn-băl'lat the Hôr'onīte, and Tō-bī'ah the servant, the
Ammonite, and Gĕ'shem the Arabian,
heard *it*, they laughed us to scorn, and
despised us, and said, What *is* this
thing that ye do? will ye rebel against
the king?

20 Then answered I them, and said unto them, the God of heaven, he will prosper us; therefore we his servants will arise and build: but ye have no portion, nor right, nor memorial, in Jerusalem.

CHAPTER 3

THEN E-lī′a-shīb the high priest rose up with his brethren the priests, and they builded the sheep gate; they sanctified it, and set up the doors of it; even unto the tower of Mē′ah they sanctified it, unto the tower of Hă-nan′ē-el.

2 And next unto him builded the men of Jericho. And next to them builded Zăc′cur the son of Imri.

3 But the fish gate did the sons of Hăs-se-nā′ah build, who *also* laid the beams thereof, and set up the doors thereof, the locks thereof, and the bars thereof.

4 And next unto them repaired Mĕr′e-mŏth the son of Ū-rī′jah, the son of Koz. And next unto them repaired Me-shŭl′lam the son of Bĕr-e-chī′ah, the son of Me-shĕz′a-beel. And next unto them repaired Zā′dŏk the son of Bā′a-na.

5 And next unto them the Te-kō′ītes repaired; but their nobles put not their necks to the work of their Lord.

6 Moreover the old gate repaired Je-hoi′a-da the son of Pa-sē′ah, and Me-shŭl′lam the son of Bĕs-o-dē′iah; they laid the beams thereof, and set up the doors thereof, and the locks thereof, and the bars thereof.

7 And next unto them repaired Mĕl-a-tī′ah the Gĭb′e-o-nīte, and Jā′dŏn the Me-rŏn′o-thīte, the men of Gĭb′e-on, and of Mizpah, unto the throne of the governor on this side the river.

8 Next unto him repaired Ŭz′zĭ-el the son of Hăr-hā-i′ah, of the goldsmiths. Next unto him also repaired Hăn-a-ni′-ah the son of *one of* the apothecaries, and they fortified Jerusalem unto the broad wall.

9 And next unto them repaired Reph-ā-i′ah the son of Hur, the ruler of the half part of Jerusalem.

10 And next unto them repaired Je-dā′iah the son of Ha-rū′măph, even over against his house. And next unto him repaired Hăt′tŭsh the son of Hăsh-ab-nī′ah.

11 Măl-chī′jah the son of Hā′rĭm, and Hā′shŭb the son of Pā′hăth–mō′ăb, repaired the other piece, and the tower of the furnaces.

12 And next unto him repaired Shăl′-lum the son of Hă-lō′hĕsh, the ruler of the half part of Jerusalem, he and his daughters.

13 The valley gate repaired Hā′nun, and the inhabitants of Za-nō′ah; they built it, and set up the doors thereof, the locks thereof, and the bars thereof, and a thousand cubits on the wall unto the dung gate.

14 But the dung gate repaired Măl-chī′ah the son of Rē′chăb, the ruler of part of Bĕth–hăc′ce-rem; he built it, and set up the doors thereof, the locks thereof, and the bars thereof.

15 But the gate of the fountain repaired Shăl′lun the son of Cŏl–hō′zeh, the ruler of part of Mizpah; he built it, and covered it, and set up the doors thereof, the locks thereof, and the bars thereof, and the wall of the pool of Sī-lō′ah by the king's garden, and unto the stairs that go down from the city of David.

16 After him repaired Nē-he-mī′ah the son of Ăz′bŭk, the ruler of the half part of Bĕth′–zûr, unto *the place* over against the sepulchres of David, and to the pool that was made, and unto the house of the mighty.

17 After him repaired the Lē′vītes, Rē′hum the son of Bā′nī. Next unto him repaired Hăsh-a-bī′ah, the ruler of the half part of Keī′lah, in his part.

18 After him repaired their brethren, Băv′a-ī the son of Hĕn′a-dăd, the ruler of the half part of Keī′lah.

19 And next to him repaired Ē′zer the son of Jĕsh′u-a, the ruler of Mizpah, another piece over against the going up to the armoury at the turning *of the wall*.

20 After him Bā′ruch the son of Zăb′-baī earnestly repaired the other piece, from the turning *of the wall* unto the door of the house of E-lī′a-shīb the high priest.

21 After him repaired Mĕr′e-mŏth the son of Ū-rī′jah the son of Koz another piece, from the door of the house of E-lī′a-shīb even to the end of the house of E-lī′a-shīb.

22 And after him repaired the priests, the men of the plain.

23 After him repaired Benjamin and Hā′shŭb over against their house. After him repaired Ăz-a-rī′ah the son of Mā-a-sē′iah the son of Ăn-a-nī′ah by his house.

24 After him repaired Bĭn′nū-ī the son of Hĕn′a-dăd another piece, from the house of Ăz-a-rī′ah unto the turning *of the wall*, even unto the corner.

25 Pā′lăl the son of Ū′za-ī, over against the turning *of the wall*, and the tower which lieth out from the king's high house, that *was* by the court of the prison. After him Pe-dā′iah the son of Pā′rŏsh.

26 Moreover the Nĕth′i-nĭmṡ dwelt in

Ō'phĕl, unto *the place* over against the water gate toward the east, and the tower that lieth out.
27 After them the Te-kō'ītes repaired another piece, over against the great tower that lieth out, even unto the wall of Ō'phĕl.
28 From above the horse gate repaired the priests, every one over against the house.
29 After them repaired Zā'dŏk the son of Ĭm'mer over against his house. After him repaired also Shem-ā-i'ah the son of Shĕch-a-nī'ah, the keeper of the east gate.
30 After him repaired Hăn-a-nī'ah the son of Shĕl-e-mī'ah, and Hā'nun the sixth son of Zā'lăph, another piece. After him repaired Me-shūl'lam the son of Bĕr-e-chī'ah over against his chamber.
31 After him repaired Măl-chī'ah the goldsmith's son unto the place of the Nĕth'i-nĭmṡ, and of the merchants, over against the gate Mĭph'kăd, and to the going up of the corner.
32 And between the going up of the corner unto the sheep gate repaired the goldsmiths and the merchants.

CHAPTER 4

BUT it came to pass, that when Săn-băl'lat heard that we builded the wall, he was wroth, and took great indignation, and mocked the Jews.
2 And he spake before his brethren and the army of Sa-mâ'rĭ-a, and said, What do these feeble Jews? will they fortify themselves? will they sacrifice? will they make an end in a day? will they revive the stones out of the heaps of the rubbish which are burned?
3 Now Tō-bī'ah the Ammonite *was* by him, and he said, Even that which they build, if a fox go up, he shall even break down their stone wall.
4 Hear, O our God; for we are despised: and turn their reproach upon their own head, and give them for a prey in the land of captivity:
5 And cover not their iniquity, and let not their sin be blotted out from before thee: for they have provoked *thee* to anger before the builders.
6 So built we the wall; and all the wall was joined together unto the half thereof: for the people had a mind to work.
7 ¶But it came to pass, *that* when Săn-băl'lat, and Tō-bī'ah, and the Arabians, and the Ammonites, and the Ăsh'dŏd-ītes, heard that the walls of Jerusalem were made up, *and* that the breaches began to be stopped, then they were very wroth,
8 And conspired all of them together to come *and* to fight against Jerusalem, and to hinder it.
9 Nevertheless we made our prayer unto our God, and set a watch against them day and night, because of them.
10 And Jū'dah said, The strength of the bearers of burdens is decayed, and *there is* much rubbish; so that we are not able to build the wall.
11 And our adversaries said, They shall not know, neither see, till we come in the midst among them, and slay them, and cause the work to cease.
12 ¶And it came to pass, that when the Jews which dwelt by them came, they said unto us ten times, From all places whence ye shall return unto us *they will be upon you.*
13 Therefore set I in the lower places behind the wall, *and* on the higher places, I even set the people after their families with their swords, their spears, and their bows.
14 And I looked, and rose up, and said unto the nobles, and to the rulers, and to the rest of the people, Be not ye afraid of them: remember the Lord, *which is* great and terrible, and fight for your brethren, your sons, and your daughters, your wives, and your houses.
15 And it came to pass, when our enemies heard that it was known unto us, and God had brought their counsel to nought, that we returned all of us to the wall, every one unto his work.
16 And it came to pass from that time forth, *that* the half of my servants wrought in the work, and the other half of them held both the spears, the shields, and the bows, and the habergeons; and the rulers *were* behind all the house of Jū'dah.
17 They which builded on the wall, and they that bare burdens, with those that laded, *every one* with one of his hands wrought in the work, and with the other *hand* held a weapon.
18 For the builders, every one had his sword girded by his side, and *so* builded. And he that sounded the trumpet *was* by me.
19 And I said unto the nobles, and to the rulers, and to the rest of the people, The work *is* great and large, and we are separated upon the wall, one far from another.
20 In what place *therefore* ye hear the sound of the trumpet, resort ye thither unto us: our God shall fight for us.
21 So we laboured in the work: and half of them held the spears from the rising of the morning till the stars appeared.
22 Likewise at the same time said I

unto the people, Let every one with his servant lodge within Jerusalem, that in the night they may be a guard to us, and labour on the day.

23 So neither I, nor my brethren, nor my servants, nor the men of the guard which followed me, none of us put off our clothes, *saving that* every one put them off for washing.

CHAPTER 5

AND there was a great cry of the people and of their wives against their brethren the Jews.

2 For there were that said, We, our sons, and our daughters, *are* many: therefore we take up corn *for them*, that we may eat, and live.

3 *Some* also there were that said, We have mortgaged our lands, vineyards, and houses, that we might buy corn, because of the dearth.

4 There were also that said, We have borrowed money for the king's tribute, *and that upon* our lands and vineyards.

5 Yet now our flesh *is* as the flesh of our brethren, our children as their children: and, lo, we bring into bondage our sons and our daughters to be servants, and *some* of our daughters are brought unto bondage *already:* neither *is it* in our power *to redeem them;* for other men have our lands and vineyards.

6 ¶And I was very angry when I heard their cry and these words.

7 Then I consulted with myself, and I rebuked the nobles, and the rulers, and said unto them, Ye exact usury, every one of his brother. And I set a great assembly against them.

8 And I said unto them, We after our ability have redeemed our brethren the Jews, which were sold unto the heathen; and will ye even sell your brethren? or shall they be sold unto us? Then held they their peace, and found nothing *to answer*.

9 Also I said, It *is* not good that ye do: ought ye not to walk in the fear of our God because of the reproach of the heathen our enemies?

10 I likewise, *and* my brethren, and my servants, might exact of them money and corn: I pray you, let us leave off this usury.

11 Restore, I pray you, to them even this day, their lands, their vineyards, their oliveyards, and their houses, also the hundredth *part* of the money, and of the corn, the wine, and the oil, that ye exact of them.

12 Then said they, We will restore *them*, and will require nothing of them; so will we do as thou sayest. Then I called the priests, and took an oath of them, that they should do according to this promise.

13 Also I shook my lap, and said, So God shake out every man from his house, and from his labour, that performeth not this promise, even thus be he shaken out, and emptied. And all the congregation said, Amen, and praised the LORD. And the people did according to this promise.

14 ¶Moreover from the time that I was appointed to be their governor in the land of Jū'dah, from the twentieth year even unto the two and thirtieth year of Är-ta-ẋer'ẋēs the king, *that is*, twelve years, I and my brethren have not eaten the bread of the governor.

15 But the former governors that *had been* before me were chargeable unto the people, and had taken of them bread and wine, beside forty shekels of silver; yea, even their servants bare rule over the people: but so did not I, because of the fear of God.

16 Yea, also I continued in the work of this wall, neither bought we any land: and all my servants *were* gathered thither unto the work.

17 Moreover *there were* at my table an hundred and fifty of the Jews and rulers, beside those that came unto us from among the heathen that *are* about us.

18 Now *that* which was prepared *for me* daily *was* one ox *and* six choice sheep; also fowls were prepared for me, and once in ten days store of all sorts of wine: yet for all this required not I the bread of the governor, because the bondage was heavy upon this people.

19 Think upon me, my God, for good, *according* to all that I have done for this people.

CHAPTER 6

NOW it came to pass, when Săn-băl'lat, and Tō-bī'ah, and Gĕ'shem the Arabian, and the rest of our enemies, heard that I had builded the wall, and *that* there was no breach left therein; (though at that time I had not set up the doors upon the gates;)

2 That Săn-băl'lat and Gĕ'shem sent unto me, saying, Come, let us meet together in *some one of* the villages in the plain of Ō'nō. But they thought to do me mischief.

3 And I sent messengers unto them, saying, I *am* doing a great work, so that I cannot come down: why should the work cease, whilst I leave it, and come down to you?

4 Yet they sent unto me four times af-

ter this sort; and I answered them after
the same manner.
5 ¶Then sent Săn-băl'lat his servant
unto me in like manner the fifth time
with an open letter in his hand;
6 Wherein *was* written, It is reported
among the heathen, and Găsh'mū saith
it, that thou and the Jews think to rebel:
for which cause thou buildest the wall,
that thou mayest be their king, according
to these words.
7 And thou hast also appointed
prophets to preach of thee at Jerusalem,
saying, *There is* a king in Jū'dah:
and now shall it be reported to the king
according to these words. Come now
therefore, and let us take counsel together.
8 Then I sent unto him, saying, There
are no such things done as thou sayest,
but thou feignest them out of thine own
heart.
9 For they all made us afraid, saying,
Their hands shall be weakened from
the work, that it be not done. Now therefore,
O God, strengthen my hands.
10 ¶Afterward I came unto the house
of Shem-ā-i'ah the son of Dĕl-a-ī'ah the
son of Me-hĕt'a-beel, who *was* shut up;
and he said, Let us meet together in the
house of God, within the temple, and
let us shut the doors of the temple: for
they will come to slay thee; yea, in the
night will they come to slay thee.
11 And I said, Should such a man as I
flee? and who *is there,* that, *being* as I
am, would go into the temple to save
his life? I will not go in.
12 And, lo, I perceived that God had
not sent him; but that he pronounced
this prophecy against me: for Tō-bī'ah
and Săn-băl'lat had hired him.
13 Therefore *was* he hired, that I
should be afraid, and do so, and sin, and
that they might have *matter* for an evil
report, that they might reproach me.
14 My God, think thou upon Tō-bī'ah
and Săn-băl'lat according to these their
works, and on the prophetess Nō-a-dī'ah,
and the rest of the prophets, that
would have put me in fear.
15 ¶So the wall was finished in the
twenty and fifth *day* of *the month* Ē'lŭl,
in fifty and two days.
16 And it came to pass, that when all
our enemies heard *thereof,* and all the
heathen that *were* about us saw *these
things,* they were much cast down in
their own eyes: for they perceived that
this work was wrought of our God.
17 ¶Moreover in those days the
nobles of Jū'dah sent many letters unto
Tō-bī'ah, and *the letters* of Tō-bī'ah
came unto them.
18 For *there were* many in Jū'dah
sworn unto him, because he *was* the
son in law of Shĕch-a-nī'ah the son of
Â'rah; and his son Jō-hā'nan had taken
the daughter of Me-shŭl'lam the son of
Bĕr-e-chī'ah.
19 Also they reported his good deeds
before me, and uttered my words to
him. *And* Tō-bī'ah sent letters to put me
in fear.

CHAPTER 7

NOW it came to pass, when the wall
was built, and I had set up the doors,
and the porters and the singers and the
Lē'vītes were appointed,
2 That I gave my brother Ha-nā'nī,
and Hăn-a-nī'ah the ruler of the palace,
charge over Jerusalem: for he *was* a
faithful man, and feared God above
many.
3 And I said unto them, Let not the
gates of Jerusalem be opened until the
sun be hot; and while they stand by, let
them shut the doors, and bar *them:* and
appoint watches of the inhabitants of
Jerusalem, every one in his watch, and
every one *to be* over against his house.
4 ¶Now the city *was* large and great:
but the people *were* few therein, and
the houses *were* not builded.
5 And my God put into mine heart to
gather together the nobles, and the rulers,
and the people, that they might be
reckoned by genealogy. And I found a
register of the genealogy of them
which came up at the first and found
written therein,
6 These *are* the children of the
province, that went up out of the captivity,
of those that had been carried
away, whom Nĕb-u-chad-nĕz'zar the
king of Babylon had carried away, and
came again to Jerusalem and to Jū'dah,
every one unto his city;
7 Who came with Ze-rŭb'ba-bel,
Jĕsh'u-a, Nē-he-mī'ah, Ăz-a-rī'ah, Rā-a-mī'ah,
Na-hăm'a-nī, Môr'de-caī,
Bĭl'shăn, Mĭs'pe-rĕth, Bĭg'va-ī, Nē'hŭm,
Bā'a-nah. The number, *I say,* of the men
of the people of Israel *was this;*
8 The children of Pâ'rŏsh, two thousand
an hundred seventy and two.
9 The children of Shĕph-a-tī'ah, three
hundred seventy and two.
10 The children of Â'rah, six hundred
fifty and two.
11 The children of Pā'hăth-mō'ăb, of
the children of Jĕsh'u-a and Jō'ăb, two
thousand and eight hundred *and*
eighteen.
12 The children of Ē'lam, a thousand
two hundred fifty and four.
13 The children of Zăt'tū, eight
hundred forty and five.

14 The children of Zăc'ca-ī, seven hundred and threescore.
15 The children of Bĭn'nū-ī, six hundred forty and eight.
16 The children of Bĕb'a-ī, six hundred twenty and eight.
17 The children of Ăz'găd, two thousand three hundred twenty and two.
18 The children of Ăd-on-ī'kam, six hundred threescore and seven.
19 The children of Bĭg'va-ī, two thousand threescore and seven.
20 The children of Ā'din, six hundred fifty and five.
21 The children of Ā'ter of Hĕz-e-kī'ah, ninety and eight.
22 The children of Hā'shum, three hundred twenty and eight.
23 The children of Bē'zaī, three hundred twenty and four.
24 The children of Hâ'rĭph, an hundred and twelve.
25 The children of Gĭbeon, ninety and five.
26 The men of Bĕth-lehĕm and Ne-tō'phah, an hundred fourscore and eight.
27 The men of Ăn'a-thŏth, an hundred twenty and eight.
28 The men of Bĕth-ăz'ma-vĕth, forty and two.
29 The men of Kir'jath-jē'a-rĭm, Che-phī'rah, and Bē-ē'rŏth, seven hundred forty and three.
30 The men of Rā'mah and Gā'ba, six hundred twenty and one.
31 The men of Mĭch'măs, an hundred and twenty and two.
32 The men of Bĕth-el and Ā'ī, an hundred twenty and three.
33 The men of the other Nebo, fifty and two.
34 The children of the other Ē'lam, a thousand two hundred fifty and four.
35 The children of Hâ'rĭm, three hundred and twenty.
36 The children of Jericho, three hundred forty and five.
37 The children of Lod, Hā'dĭd, and Ō'nō, seven hundred twenty and one.
38 The children of Se-nā'ah, three thousand nine hundred and thirty.
39 ¶The priests: the children of Je-dā'-iah, of the house of Jĕsh'u-a, nine hundred seventy and three.
40 The children of Ĭm'mer, a thousand fifty and two.
41 The children of Păsh'ur, a thousand two hundred forty and seven.
42 The children of Hâ'rĭm, a thousand and seventeen.
43 ¶The Lēvītes: the children of Jĕsh'-u-a, of Kăd'mī-el, *and* of the children of Hō-dē'vah, seventy and four.
44 ¶The singers: the children of Ā'săph, an hundred forty and eight.
45 ¶The porters: the children of Shăl'-lum, the children of Ā'ter, the children of Tal'mon, the children of Ăk'kŭb, the children of Hat'ī-ta, the children of Shō'ba-ī, an hundred thirty and eight.
46 ¶The Nĕth'i-nĭmṡ: the children of Zī'ha, the children of Ha-shū'pha, the children of Tăb'ba-ŏth,
47 The children of Ke'rŏs, the children of Sī'a, the children of Pā'don,
48 The children of Lĕb'a-na, the children of Hăg'a-ba, the children of Shăl'ma-ī,
49 The children of Hā'nan, the children of Gĭd'del, the children of Gā'här,
50 The children of Rē-ā-i'ah, the children of Rē'zĭn, the children of Ne-kō'da,
51 The children of Găz'zam, the children of Ŭz'za, the children of Pha-sē'ah,
52 The children of Bē'ṡaī, the children of Me-ū'nĭm, the children of Ne-phĭsh'-e-sĭm,
53 The children of Băk'bŭk, the children of Ha-kū'pha, the children of Här'hûr,
54 The children of Băz'lĭth, the children of Me-hī'da, the children of Här'-sha,
55 The children of Bär'kŏs, the children of Sĭs'e-ra, the children of Tā'mah,
56 The children of Ne-zī'ah, the children of Hat'ī-pha.
57 The children of Sŏlomon's servants: the children of Sō'ta-ī, the children of Sŏph'e-rĕth, the children of Pe-rī'da,
58 The children of Jā-a'la, the children of Där'kŏn, the children of Gĭd'-del,
59 The children of Shĕph-a-tī'ah, the children of Hăt'til, the children of Pŏch'e-rĕth of Ze-bā'im, the children of Ămon.
60 All the Nĕth'i-nĭmṡ, and the children of Sŏlomon's servants, *were* three hundred ninety and two.
61 And these *were* they which went up *also* from Tĕl-mē'lah, Tĕl-hä-re'sha, Cherub, Ăd'dŏn, and Ĭm'mer: but they could not shew their father's house, nor their seed, whether they *were* of Israel.
62 The children of Dĕl-a-ī'ah, the children of Tō-bī'ah, the children of Ne-kō'da, six hundred forty and two.
63 ¶And of the priests: the children of Ha-bā'iah, the children of Koz, the children of Bar-zĭl'la-ī, which took *one* of the daughters of Bär-zĭl'la-ī the Gĭleadīte to wife, and was called after their name.
64 These sought their register *among*

those that were reckoned by gene-
alogy, but it was not found: therefore
were they, as polluted, put from the
priesthood.
65 And the Tir′shā-tha said unto
them, that they should not eat of the
most holy things, till there stood *up* a
priest with Ū′rĭm and Thŭm′mĭm.
66 ¶The whole congregation together
was forty and two thousand three
hundred and threescore,
67 Beside their manservants and
their maidservants, of whom *there*
were seven thousand three hundred
thirty and seven: and they had two
hundred forty and five singing men and
singing women.
68 Their horses, seven hundred thirty
and six: their mules, two hundred forty
and five:
69 *Their* camels, four hundred thirty
and five: six thousand seven hundred
and twenty asses.
70 ¶And some of the chief of the fa-
thers gave unto the work. The Tir′shā-
tha gave to the treasure a thousand
drams of gold, fifty basons, five
hundred and thirty priests' garments.
71 And *some* of the chief of the fathers
gave to the treasure of the work
twenty thousand drams of gold, and
two thousand and two hundred pound
of silver.
72 And *that* which the rest of the
people gave *was* twenty thousand
drams of gold, and two thousand
pound of silver, and threescore and
seven priests' garments.
73 So the priests, and the Lēvites,
and the porters, and the singers, and
some of the people, and the Nĕth′i-
nĭmṡ, and all Israel, dwelt in their
cities; and when the seventh month
came, the children of Israel *were* in
their cities.

CHAPTER 8

AND all the people gathered them-
selves together as one man into the
street that *was* before the water gate;
and they spake unto Ezra the scribe to
bring the book of the law of Moses,
which the LORD had commanded to
Israel.
2 And Ezra the priest brought the law
before the congregation both of men
and women, and all that could hear
with understanding, upon the first day
of the seventh month.
3 And he read therein before the
street that *was* before the water gate
from the morning until midday, before
the men and the women, and those that
could understand; and the ears of all
the people *were attentive* unto the
book of the law.
4 And Ezra the scribe stood upon a
pulpit of wood, which they had made
for the purpose; and beside him stood
Măt-ti-thī′ah, and Shē′ma, and An-a-
ī′ah, and Ū-rī′jah, and Hĭl-kī′ah, and
Mā-a-sē′iah, on his right hand; and on
his left hand, Pe-dā′iah, and Mĭsh′a-el,
and Măl-chī′ah, and Hā′shum, and
Hăsh-băd′a-na, Zĕch-a-rī′ah, *and* Me-
shŭl′lam.
5 And Ezra opened the book in the
sight of all the people; (for he was
above all the people;) and when he
opened it, all the people stood up:
6 And Ezra blessed the LORD, the
great God. And all the people an-
swered, Amen, Amen, with lifting up
their hands: and they bowed their
heads, and worshipped the LORD with
their faces to the ground.
7 Also Jĕsh′u-a, and Bā′nī, and Shĕr-
e-bī′ah, Jā′mĭn, Ăk′kŭb, Shăb′be-thaī,
Hō-dī′jah, Mā-a-sē′iah, Kel′ī-ta, Ăz-a-
rī′ah, Jōz′a-băd, Hā′nan, Pel-ā-i′ah, and
the Lēvītes, caused the people to under-
stand the law: and the people *stood*
in their place.
8 So they read in the book in the law
of God distinctly, and gave the sense,
and caused *them* to understand the
reading.
9 ¶And Nē-he-mī′ah, which *is* the
Tir′shā-tha, and Ezra the priest the
scribe, and the Lēvītes that taught the
people, said unto all the people, This
day *is* holy unto the LORD your God;
mourn not, nor weep. For all the people
wept, when they heard the words of the
law.
10 Then he said unto them, Go your
way, eat the fat, and drink the sweet,
and send portions unto them for whom
nothing is prepared: for *this* day *is* holy
unto our Lord: neither be ye sorry; for
the joy of the LORD is your strength.
11 So the Lēvītes stilled all the peo-
ple, saying, Hold your peace, for the
day *is* holy; neither be ye grieved.
12 And all the people went their way
to eat, and to drink, and to send por-
tions, and to make great mirth, because
they had understood the words that
were declared unto them.
13 ¶And on the second day were gath-
ered together the chief of the fathers
of all the people, the priests, and the
Lēvītes unto Ezra the scribe, even to
understand the words of the law.
14 And they found written in the law
which the LORD had commanded by
Moses, that the children of Israel
should dwell in booths in the feast of
the seventh month:
15 And that they should publish and
proclaim in all their cities, and in Jeru-

salem, saying, Go forth unto the
mount, and fetch olive branches, and
pine branches, and myrtle branches,
and palm branches, and branches of
thick trees, to make booths, as *it is*
written.
16 So the people went forth, and
brought *them*, and made themselves
booths, every one upon the roof of his
house, and in their courts, and in the
courts of the house of God, and in the
street of the water gate, and in the
street of the gate of Ē'phra-im.
17 And all the congregation of them
that were come again out of the captiv-
ity made booths, and sat under the
booths: for since the days of Jĕsh'u-a
the son of Nun unto that day had not
the children of Israel done so. And
there was very great gladness.
18 Also day by day, from the first day
unto the last day, he read in the book of
the law of God. And they kept the feast
seven days; and on the eighth day *was* a
solemn assembly, according unto the
manner.

CHAPTER 9

NOW in the twenty and fourth day of
this month the children of Israel were
assembled with fasting, and with
sackclothes, and earth upon them.
2 And the seed of Israel separated
themselves from all strangers, and
stood and confessed their sins, and the
iniquities of their fathers.
3 And they stood up in their place,
and read in the book of the law of the
LORD their God *one* fourth part of the
day; and *another* fourth part they con-
fessed, and worshipped the LORD their
God.
4 Then stood up upon the stairs, of
the Lēvītes, Jĕsh'u-a, and Bā'nī, Kăd'-
mĭ-el, Shĕb-a-nī'ah, Bŭn'nī, Shĕr-e-
bī'ah, Bā'nī, *and* Chen'ā-nī, and cried
with a loud voice unto the LORD their
God.
5 Then the Lēvītes, Jĕsh'u-a, and
Kăd'mĭ-el, Bā'nī, Hăsh-ab-nī'ah, Shĕr-
e-bī'ah, Hō-dī'jah, Shĕb-a-nī'ah, *and*
Pĕth-a-hī'ah, said, Stand up *and* bless
the LORD your God for ever and ever:
and blessed be thy glorious name,
which is exalted above all blessing and
praise.
6 Thou, *even* thou, *art* LORD alone;
thou hast made heaven, the heaven of
heavens, with all their host, the earth,
and all *things* that *are* therein, the seas,
and all that *is* therein, and thou preserv-
est them all; and the host of heaven
worshippeth thee.
7 Thou *art* the LORD the God, who
didst choose Abram, and broughtest
him forth out of Ur of the Chăl-deeṡ,
and gavest him the name of Abraham;
8 And foundest his heart faithful be-
fore thee, and madest a covenant with
him to give the land of the Canaanites,
the Hittites, the Ămorītes, and the Pĕr'-
iz-zītes, and the Jēb'u-sītes, and the
Gir'ga-shītes, to give *it, I say*, to his
seed, and hast performed thy words;
for thou *art* righteous:
9 And didst see the affliction of our
fathers in Egypt, and heardest their cry
by the Red sea;
10 And shewedst signs and wonders
upon Pharaoh, and on all his servants,
and on all the people of his land: for
thou knewest that they dealt proudly
against them. So didst thou get thee a
name, as *it is* this day.
11 And thou didst divide the sea be-
fore them, so that they went through
the midst of the sea on the dry land; and
their persecutors thou threwest into
the deeps, as a stone into the mighty
waters.
12 Moreover thou leddest them in the
day by a cloudy pillar; and in the night
by a pillar of fire, to give them light in
the way wherein they should go.
13 Thou camest down also upon
mount Sī'naī, and spakest with them
from heaven, and gavest them right
judgments, and true laws, good stat-
utes and commandments:
14 And madest known unto them thy
holy sabbath, and commandedst them
precepts, statutes, and laws, by the
hand of Moses thy servant:
15 And gavest them bread from
heaven for their hunger, and
broughtest forth water for them out of
the rock for their thirst, and promisedst
them that they should go in to possess
the land which thou hadst sworn to
give them.
16 But they and our fathers dealt
proudly, and hardened their necks, and
hearkened not to thy commandments,
17 And refused to obey, neither were
mindful of thy wonders that thou didst
among them; but hardened their necks,
and in their rebellion appointed a cap-
tain to return to their bondage: but
thou *art* a God ready to pardon, gra-
cious and merciful, slow to anger, and
of great kindness, and forsookest them
not.
18 Yea, when they had made them a
molten calf, and said, This *is* thy god
that brought thee up out of Egypt, and
had wrought great provocations;
19 Yet thou in thy manifold mercies
forsookest them not in the wilderness:
the pillar of the cloud departed not
from them by day, to lead them in the

way; neither the pillar of fire by night, to shew them light, and the way wherein they should go.
20 Thou gavest also thy good spirit to instruct them, and withheldest not thy manna from their mouth, and gavest them water for their thirst.
21 Yea, forty years didst thou sustain them in the wilderness, *so that* they lacked nothing; their clothes waxed not old, and their feet swelled not.
22 Moreover thou gavest them kingdoms and nations, and didst divide them into corners: so they possessed the land of Sihon, and the land of the king of Hĕsh'bŏn, and the land of Og king of Bā'shan.
23 Their children also multipliedst thou as the stars of heaven, and broughtest them into the land, concerning which thou hadst promised to their fathers, that they should go in to possess *it*.
24 So the children went in and possessed the land, and thou subduedst before them the inhabitants of the land, the Canaanites, and gavest them into their hands, with their kings, and the people of the land, that they might do with them as they would.
25 And they took strong cities, and a fat land, and possessed houses full of all goods, wells digged, vineyards, and oliveyards, and fruit trees in abundance: so they did eat, and were filled, and became fat, and delighted themselves in thy great goodness.
26 Nevertheless they were disobedient, and rebelled against thee, and cast thy law behind their backs, and slew thy prophets which testified against them to turn them to thee, and they wrought great provocations.
27 Therefore thou deliveredst them into the hand of their enemies, who vexed them: and in the time of their trouble, when they cried unto thee, thou heardest *them* from heaven; and according to thy manifold mercies thou gavest them saviours, who saved them out of the hand of their enemies.
28 But after they had rest, they did evil again before thee: therefore leftest thou them in the hand of their enemies, so that they had the dominion over them: yet when they returned, and cried unto thee, thou heardest *them* from heaven; and many times didst thou deliver them according to thy mercies;
29 And testifiedst against them, that thou mightest bring them again unto thy law: yet they dealt proudly, and hearkened not unto thy commandments, but sinned against thy judgments, (which if a man do, he shall live in them;) and withdrew the shoulder, and hardened their neck, and would not hear.
30 Yet many years didst thou forbear them, and testifiedst against them by thy spirit in thy prophets: yet would they not give ear: therefore gavest thou them into the hand of the people of the lands.
31 Nevertheless for thy great mercies' sake thou didst not utterly consume them, nor forsake them; for thou *art* a gracious and merciful God.
32 Now therefore, our God, the great, the mighty, and the terrible God, who keepest covenant and mercy, let not all the trouble seem little before thee, that hath come upon us, on our kings, on our princes, and on our priests, and on our prophets, and on our fathers, and on all thy people, since the time of the kings of Assyria unto this day.
33 Howbeit thou *art* just in all that is brought upon us; for thou hast done right, but we have done wickedly:
34 Neither have our kings, our princes, our priests, nor our fathers, kept thy law, nor hearkened unto thy commandments and thy testimonies, wherewith thou didst testify against them.
35 For they have not served thee in their kingdom, and in thy great goodness that thou gavest them, and in the large and fat land which thou gavest before them, neither turned they from their wicked works.
36 Behold, we *are* servants this day, and *for* the land that thou gavest unto our fathers to eat the fruit thereof and the good thereof, behold, we *are* servants in it:
37 And it yieldeth much increase unto the kings whom thou hast set over us because of our sins: also they have dominion over our bodies, and over our cattle, at their pleasure, and we *are* in great distress.
38 And because of all this we make a sure *covenant*, and write *it*; and our princes, Lēvītes, *and* priests, seal *unto it*.

CHAPTER 10

NOW those that sealed *were*, Nē-he-mī'ah, the Tir'shā-tha, the son of Hăch-a-lī'ah, and Zĭd-kī'jah,
2 Se-ra-ī'ah, Ăz-a-rī'ah, Jĕr-e-mī'ah,
3 Păsh'ur, Ăm-a-rī'ah, Măl-chī'jah,
4 Hăt'tŭsh, Shĕb-a-nī'ah, Măl'luch,
5 Hâ'rĭm, Mĕr'e-mŏth, Ō-ba-dī'ah,
6 Daniel, Gĭn'ne-thŏn, Bâ'ruch,
7 Me-shŭl'lam, A-bī'jah, Mĭj'a-mĭn,

8 Mā-a-zī'ah, Bĭl'ga-ī, Shem-a-i'ah:
these *were* the priests.
9 And the Lēvītes: both Jĕsh'u-a the
son of Ăz-a-nī'ah, Bĭn'nū-ī of the sons of
Hĕn'a-dăd, Kăd'mĭ-el;
10 And their brethren, Shĕb-a-nī'ah,
Hō-dī'jah, Kel'ī-ta, Pel-ā-i'ah, Hā'nan,
11 Mī'cha, Rē'hŏb, Hăsh-a-bī'ah,
12 Zăc'cur, Shĕr-e-bī'ah, Shĕb-a-ni'-
ah,
13 Hō-dī'jah, Bā'nī, Ben'ī-nū.
14 The chief of the people; Pâ'rŏsh,
Pā'hăth–mō'ăb, Ē'lam, Zăt'thū, Bā'nī,
15 Bŭn'nī, Ăz'găd, Bĕb'a-ī,
16 Ăd-o-nī'jah, Bĭg'va-ī, Ā'din,
17 Ā'ter, Hĭz-kī'jah, Ăz'zur,
18 Hō-dī'jah, Hā'shum, Bē'zaī,
19 Hâ'rĭph, Ăn'a-thŏth, Nēb'a-ī,
20 Măg'pĭ-ăsh, Me-shŭl'lam, Hē'zir,
21 Me-shĕz'a-beel, Zā'dŏk, Jăd-du'a,
22 Pĕl-a-tī'ah, Hā'nan, An-a-ī'ah,
23 Hō-shē'a, Hăn-a-nī'ah, Hā'shŭb,
24 Hăl-lō'hĕsh, Pĭl'e-hä, Shō'bĕk,
25 Rē'hum, Ha-shăb'nah, Mā-a-sē'-
iah,
26 And A-hī'jah, Hā'nan, Ā-nan,
27 Măl'luch, Hâ'rĭm, Bā'a-nah.
28 ¶And the rest of the people, the
priests, the Lēvītes, the porters, the sing-
ers, the Nĕth'i-nĭmṡ, and all they that
had separated themselves from the
people of the lands unto the law of God,
their wives, their sons, and their
daughters, every one having knowl-
edge, and having understanding;
29 They clave to their brethren, their
nobles, and entered into a curse, and
into an oath, to walk in God's law,
which was given by Moses the servant
of God, and to observe and do all the
commandments of the LORD our Lord,
and his judgments and his statutes;
30 And that we would not give our
daughters unto the people of the land,
nor take their daughters for our sons:
31 And *if* the people of the land bring
ware or any victuals on the sabbath day
to sell, *that* we would not buy it of them
on the sabbath, or on the holy day: and
that we would leave the seventh year,
and the exaction of every debt.
32 Also we made ordinances for us,
to charge ourselves yearly with the
third part of a shekel for the service of
the house of our God;
33 For the shewbread, and for the
continual meat offering, and for the
continual burnt offering, of the sab-
baths, of the new moons, for the set
feasts, and for the holy *things*, and for
the sin offerings to make an atonement
for Israel, and *for* all the work of the
house of our God.
34 And we cast the lots among the
priests, the Lēvītes, and the people, for
the wood offering, to bring *it* into the
house of our God, after the houses of
our fathers, at times appointed year by
year, to burn upon the altar of the LORD
our God, as *it is* written in the law:
35 And to bring the firstfruits of our
ground, and the firstfruits of all fruit of
all trees, year by year, unto the house of
the LORD:
36 Also the firstborn of our sons, and
of our cattle, as *it is* written in the law,
and the firstlings of our herds and of
our flocks, to bring to the house of our
God, unto the priests that minister in
the house of our God:
37 And *that* we should bring the
firstfruits of our dough, and our offer-
ings, and the fruit of all manner of
trees, of wine and of oil, unto the
priests, to the chambers of the house of
our God; and the tithes of our ground
unto the Lēvītes, that the same Lēvītes
might have the tithes in all the cities of
our tillage.
38 And the priest the son of Aaron
shall be with the Lēvītes, when the Lē-
vītes take tithes: and the Lēvītes shall
bring up the tithe of the tithes unto the
house of our God, to the chambers,
unto the treasure house.
39 For the children of Israel and the
children of Levi shall bring the offering
of the corn, of the new wine, and the oil,
unto the chambers, where *are* the ves-
sels of the sanctuary, and the priests
that minister, and the porters, and the
singers: and we will not forsake the
house of our God.

CHAPTER 11

AND the rulers of the people dwelt at
Jerusalem: the rest of the people also
cast lots, to bring one of ten to dwell in
Jerusalem the holy city, and nine parts
to dwell in *other* cities.
2 And the people blessed all the men,
that willingly offered themselves to
dwell at Jerusalem.
3 ¶Now these *are* the chief of the
province that dwelt in Jerusalem: but
in the cities of Jūdah dwelt every one in
his possession in their cities, *to wit*,
Israel, the priests, and the Lēvītes, and
the Nĕth'i-nĭmṡ, and the children of Sŏl-
omon's servants.
4 And at Jerusalem dwelt *certain* of
the children of Jūdah, and of the chil-
dren of Benjamin. Of the children of Jū-
dah; Ăth-a-ī'ah the son of Uz-zī'ah, the
son of Zĕch-a-rī'ah, the son of Ăm-a-
rī'ah, the son of Shĕph-a-tī'ah, the son of
Ma-hă'la-le-el, of the children of Pe'rĕz;
5 And Mā'a-sē'iah the son of Bâ'ruch,
the son of Cŏl-hō'zeh, the son of Ha-
zā'iah, the son of Ăd-a-ī'ah, the son of

Joi'a-rĭb, the son of Zĕch-a-rī'ah, the son of Shī-lō'nī.

6 All the sons of Pe'rĕz that dwelt at Jerusalem *were* four hundred threescore and eight valiant men.

7 And these *are* the sons of Benjamin; Săl'lū the son of Me-shŭl'lam, the son of Jō'ĕd, the son of Pe-dā'iah, the son of Kō-la-ī'ah, the son of Mā-a-sē'iah, the son of Ĭth'ī-el, the son of Je-sā'iah.

8 And after him Găb'ba-ī, Săl'la-ī, nine hundred twenty and eight.

9 And Jō'el the son of Zĭch'rī *was* their overseer: and Jūdah the son of Se-nū'ah *was* second over the city.

10 Of the priests: Je-dā'iah the son of Joi'a-rĭb, Jā'chin.

11 Se-ra-ī'ah the son of Hĭl-kī'ah, the son of Me-shŭl'lam, the son of Zā'dŏk, the son of Me-rā'ioth, the son of A-hī'tŭb, *was* the ruler of the house of God.

12 And their brethren that did the work of the house *were* eight hundred twenty and two: and Ăd-a-ī'ah the son of Jer'ō-hăm, the son of Pĕl-a-lī'ah, the son of Ăm'zī, the son of Zĕch-a-rī'ah, the son of Păsh'ur, the son of Măl-chī'ah,

13 And his brethren, chief of the fathers, two hundred forty and two: and A-măsh'a-ī the son of Ā-zar'e-el, the son of A-hās'a-ī, the son of Me-shĭl'le-mŏth, the son of Ĭm'mer,

14 And their brethren, mighty men of valour, an hundred twenty and eight: and their overseer *was* Zăb'dī-el, the son of *one of* the great men.

15 Also of the Lēvītes: Shem-ā-i'ah the son of Hā'shŭb, the son of Ăz'ri-kam, the son of Hăsh-a-bī'ah, the son of Bŭn'nī;

16 And Shăb'be-thaī and Jōz'a-băd, of the chief of the Lēvītes, *had* the oversight of the outward business of the house of God.

17 And Măt-ta-nī'ah the son of Mī'cha, the son of Zăb'dī, the son of Ā'săph *was* the principal to begin the thanksgiving in prayer: and Băk-buk-ī'ah the second among his brethren, and Ăb'da the son of Shăm-mū'a, the son of Gā'lăl, the son of Jed'ū-thun.

18 All the Lēvītes in the holy city *were* two hundred fourscore and four.

19 Moreover the porters, Ăk'kŭb, Tăl'mon, and their brethren that kept the gates, *were* an hundred seventy and two.

20 ¶And the residue of Israel, of the priests, *and* the Lēvītes, *were* in all the cities of Jūdah, every one in his inheritance.

21 But the Nĕth'i-nĭmṡ dwelt in Ō'phĕl: and Zī'ha and Gĭs'pa *were* over the Nĕth'i-nĭmṡ.

22 The overseer also of the Lēvītes at Jerusalem *was* Ŭz'zi the son of Bā'nī, the son of Hăsh-a-bī'ah, the son of Măt-ta-nī'ah, the son of Mī'cha. Of the sons of Ā'săph, the singers *were* over the business of the house of God.

23 For *it was* the king's commandment concerning them, that a certain portion should be for the singers, due for every day.

24 And Pĕth-a-hī'ah the son of Me-shĕz'a-beel, of the children of Ze'rah the son of Jūdah, *was* at the king's hand in all matters concerning the people.

25 And for the villages, with their fields, *some* of the children of Jūdah dwelt at Kir'jath–är'ba, and *in* the villages thereof, and at Dī'bŏn, and *in* the villages thereof, and at Je-kăb'ze-ĕl, and *in* the villages thereof,

26 And at Jĕsh'u-a, and at Mŏl'a-dah, and at Bĕth-phē'let,

27 And at Hā'zar–shū'al, and at Be'er–shē'ba, and *in* the villages thereof,

28 And at Ziklag, and at Mek'ō-nah, and in the villages thereof,

29 And at Ĕn-rĭm'mon, and at Zâ're-ah, and at Jär'mŭth,

30 Za-nō'ah, Adŭllam, and *in* their villages, at Lā'chĭsh, and the fields thereof, at A-zē'kah, and *in* the villages thereof. And they dwelt from Be'er–shē'ba unto the valley of Hĭn'nom.

31 The children also of Benjamin from Gē'ba *dwelt* at Mĭch'măsh, and A-ī'ja, and Bĕth-el, and *in* their villages,

32 *And* at Ăn'a-thŏth, Nob, Ăn-a-nī'ah,

33 Hā'zôr, Rā'mah, Gĭt'ta-im,

34 Hā'dĭd, Ze-bō'im, Ne-băl'lat,

35 Lod, and Ō'nō, the valley of craftsmen.

36 And of the Lēvītes *were* divisions *in* Jūdah, *and* in Benjamin.

CHAPTER 12

NOW these *are* the priests and the Lēvītes that went up with Ze-rŭb'ba-bel the son of Shē-ăl'tī-el, and Jĕsh'u-a: Se-ra-ī'ah, Jĕr-e-mī'ah, Ezra,

2 Ăm-a-rī'ah, Măl'luch, Hăt'tŭsh,

3 Shĕch-a-nī'ah, Rē'hum, Mĕr'e-mŏth,

4 Ĭd'dō, Gĭn'ne-thō, A-bī'jah,

5 Mī'a-mĭn, Mā-a-dī'ah, Bĭl'gah,

6 Shem-ā-i'ah, and Joi'a-rĭb, Je-dā'iah,

7 Săl'lū, Ā'mŏk, Hĭl-kī'ah, Je-dā'iah. These *were* the chief of the priests and of their brethren in the days of Jĕsh'u-a.

8 Moreover the Lēvītes: Jĕsh'u-a, Bĭn'nū-ī, Kăd'mī-el, Shĕr-e-bī'ah, Jūdah, *and* Măt-ta-nī'ah, *which was* over the thanksgiving, he and his brethren.

9 Also Băk-buk-ī'ah and Ŭn'nī, their

brethren, *were* over against them in the
watches.
10 ¶And Jĕsh′u-a begat Joi′a-kĭm,
Joi′a-kĭm also begat E-lī′a-shĭb, and E-
lī′a-shĭb begat Joi′a-da,
11 And Joi′a-da begat Jonathan, and
Jonathan begat Jăd-du′a.
12 And in the days of Joi′a-kĭm were
priests, the chief of the fathers: of Se-
ra-ī′ah, Mĕr-a-ī′ah; of Jĕr-e-mī′ah, Hăn-
a-nī′ah;
13 Of Ezra, Me-shŭl′lam; of Ăm-a-
rī′ah, Je-hō-hā′nan;
14 Of Mĕl′i-cu, Jonathan; of Shĕb-a-
nī′ah, Joseph;
15 Of Hā′rĭm, Ăd′na; of Me-rā′ioth,
Hĕl′ka-ī;
16 Of Ĭd′dō, Zĕch-a-rī′ah; of Gĭn′ne-
thŏn, Me-shŭl′lam;
17 Of A-bī′jah, Zĭch′rī; of Mĭn′i-a-
mĭn, of Mō-a-dī′ah, Pĭl′taī;
18 Of Bĭl′gah, Shăm-mū′a; of Shem-
ā-i′ah, Je-hŏn′a-than;
19 And of Joi′a-rĭb, Măt-te-na′ī; of Je-
dā′iah, Ŭz′zi;
20 Of Săl′la-ī, Kăl′la-ī; of Ā′mŏk,
Ē′ber;
21 Of Hĭl-kī′ah, Hăsh-a-bī′ah; of Je-
dā′iah, Ne-thăn′e-el.
22 ¶The Lēvītes in the days of E-lī′a-
shĭb, Joi′a-da, and Jō-hā′nan, and Jăd-
du′a, *were* recorded chief of the fathers:
also the priests, to the reign of
Darius the Persian.
23 The sons of Levi, the chief of the
fathers, *were* written in the book of the
chronicles, even until the days of Jō-
hā′nan the son of E-lī′a-shĭb.
24 And the chief of the Lēvītes: Hăsh-
a-bī′ah, Shĕr-e-bī′ah, and Jĕsh′u-a the
son of Kăd′mī-el, with their brethren
over against them, to praise *and* to give
thanks, according to the command-
ment of David the man of God, ward
over against ward.
25 Măt-ta-nī′ah, and Băk-buk-ī′ah,
Ō-ba-dī′ah, Me-shŭl′lam, Tăl′mon,
Ăk′kŭb, *were* porters keeping the ward
at the thresholds of the gates.
26 These *were* in the days of Joi′a-
kĭm the son of Jĕsh′u-a, the son of
Jōz′a-dăk, and in the days of Nē-he-mī′-
ah the governor, and of Ezra the priest,
the scribe.
27 ¶And at the dedication of the wall
of Jerusalem they sought the Lēvītes
out of all their places, to bring them to
Jerusalem, to keep the dedication with
gladness, both with thanksgivings, and
with singing, *with* cymbals, psalteries,
and with harps.
28 And the sons of the singers gath-
ered themselves together, both out of
the plain country round about Jeru-
salem, and from the villages of Ne-
tōph′a-thī;
29 Also from the house of Gilgal, and
out of the fields of Gē′ba and Ăz′ma-
vĕth: for the singers had builded them
villages round about Jerusalem.
30 And the priests and the Lēvītes pu-
rified themselves, and purified the
people, and the gates, and the wall.
31 Then I brought up the princes of
Jūdah upon the wall, and appointed
two great *companies of them that gave*
thanks, *whereof one* went on the right
hand upon the wall toward the dung
gate:
32 And after them went Hō-sha-ī′ah,
and half of the princes of Jūdah,
33 And Ăz-a-rī′ah, Ezra, and Me-
shŭl′lam,
34 Jūdah, and Benjamin, and Shem-
ā-i′ah, and Jĕr-e-mī′ah,
35 And *certain* of the priests' sons
with trumpets; *namely,* Zĕch-a-rī′ah
the son of Jonathan, the son of Shem-a-
i′ah, the son of Măt-ta-nī′ah, the son of
Mī-chā′iah, the son of Zăc′cur, the son
Ā′săph:
36 And his brethren, Shem-ā-i′ah,
and Ă-zar′ā-ĕl, Mĭl-a-la′ī, Gĭl′ā-laī, Ma-
ā′ī, Ne-thăn′e-el, and Jūdah, Ha-nā′nī,
with the musical instruments of David
the man of God, and Ezra the scribe be-
fore them.
37 And at the fountain gate, which
was over against them, they went up by
the stairs of the city of David, at the
going up of the wall, above the house of
David, even unto the water gate east-
ward.
38 And the other *company of them
that gave* thanks went over against
them, and I after them, and the half of
the people upon the wall, from beyond
the tower of the furnaces even unto the
broad wall;
39 And from above the gate of
Ē′phra-im, and above the old gate, and
above the fish gate, and the tower of
Hă-nan′ē-el, and the tower of Mē′ah,
even unto the sheep gate: and they
stood still in the prison gate.
40 So stood the two *companies of
them that gave* thanks in the house of
God, and I, and the half of the rulers
with me:
41 And the priests; E-lī′a-kĭm, Mā-a-
sē′iah, Mĭn′i-a-mĭn, Mī-chā′iah, Ĕ-lĭ-ō-
ē′na-ī, Zĕch-a-rī′ah, *and* Hăn-a-nī′ah,
with trumpets;
42 And Mā-a-sē′iah, and Shem-ā-i′ah,
and Ĕ-le-ā′zar, and Ŭz′zi, and Je-hō-hā′-
nan, and Măl-chī′jah, and Ē′lam, and
Ē′zer. And the singers sang loud, with
Jĕz-ra-hī′ah *their* overseer.
43 Also that day they offered great

sacrifices, and rejoiced: for God had
made them rejoice with great joy: the
wives also and the children rejoiced: so
that the joy of Jerusalem was heard
even afar off.
44 ¶And at that time were some ap-
pointed over the chambers for the trea-
sures, for the offerings, for the
firstfruits, and for the tithes, to gather
into them out of the fields of the cities
the portions of the law for the priests
and Lēvītes: for Jūdah rejoiced for the
priests and for the Lēvītes that waited.
45 And both the singers and the por-
ters kept the ward of their God, and the
ward of the purification, according to
the commandment of David, *and* of
Sŏl'o-mon his son.
46 For in the days of David and Ā'săph
of old *there were* chief of the sing-
ers, and songs of praise and thanksgiv-
ing unto God.
47 And all Israel in the days of Ze-
rŭb'ba-bel, and in the days of Nē-he-
mi'ah, gave the portions of the singers
and the porters, every day his portion:
and they sanctified *holy things* unto the
Lēvītes; and the Lēvītes sanctified
them unto the children of Aaron.

CHAPTER 13

ON that day they read in the book of
Moses in the audience of the people;
and therein was found written, that the
Ammonite and the Moabite should not
come into the congregation of God for
ever;
2 Because they met not the children
of Israel with bread and with water, but
hired Bā'laam against them, that he
should curse them: howbeit our God
turned the curse into a blessing.
3 Now it came to pass, when they had
heard the law, that they separated from
Israel all the mixed multitude.
4 ¶And before this, E-lī'a-shīb the
priest, having the oversight of the
chamber of the house of our God, *was*
allied unto Tō-bī'ah:
5 And he had prepared for him a
great chamber, where aforetime they
laid the meat offerings, the frankin-
cense, and the vessels, and the tithes of
the corn, the new wine, and the oil,
which was commanded *to be given* to
the Lēvītes, and the singers, and the
porters; and the offerings of the priests.
6 But in all this *time* was not I at Jeru-
salem: for in the two and thirtieth year
of Är-ta-xĕr'xēs king of Babylon came I
unto the king, and after certain days
obtained I leave of the king:
7 And I came to Jerusalem, and under-
stood of the evil that E-lī'a-shīb did
for Tō-bī'ah, in preparing him a cham-
ber in the courts of the house of God.
8 And it grieved me sore: therefore I
cast forth all the household stuff of Tō-
bī'ah out of the chamber.
9 Then I commanded, and they
cleansed the chambers: and thither
brought I again the vessels of the house
of God, with the meat offering and the
frankincense.
10 ¶And I perceived that the portions
of the Lēvītes had not been given *them*:
for the Lēvītes and the singers, that did
the work, were fled every one to his
field.
11 Then contended I with the rulers,
and said, Why is the house of God for-
saken? And I gathered them together,
and set them in their place.
12 Then brought all Jūdah the tithe
of the corn and the new wine and the oil
unto the treasuries.
13 And I made treasurers over the
treasuries, Shĕl-e-mī'ah the priest, and
Zā'dŏk the scribe, and of the Lēvītes,
Pe-dā'iah: and next to them *was* Hā-
nan the son of Zăc'cur, the son of Măt-
ta-nī'ah: for they were counted faithful,
and their office *was* to distribute unto
their brethren.
14 Remember me, O my God, concern-
ing this, and wipe not out my good
deeds that I have done for the house of
my God, and for the offices thereof.
15 ¶In those days saw I in Jūdah
some treading wine presses on the sab-
bath, and bringing in sheaves, and lad-
ing asses; as also wine, grapes, and figs,
and all *manner of* burdens, which they
brought into Jerusalem on the sabbath
day: and I testified *against them* in the
day wherein they sold victuals.
16 There dwelt men of Tyre also there-
in, which brought fish, and all man-
ner of ware, and sold on the sabbath
unto the children of Jūdah, and in
Jerusalem.
17 Then I contended with the nobles
of Jūdah, and said unto them, What
evil thing *is* this that ye do, and profane
the sabbath day?
18 Did not your fathers thus, and did
not our God bring all this evil upon us,
and upon this city? yet ye bring more
wrath upon Israel by profaning the sab-
bath.
19 And it came to pass, that when the
gates of Jerusalem began to be dark be-
fore the sabbath, I commanded that the
gates should be shut, and charged that
they should not be opened till after the
sabbath: and *some* of my servants set I
at the gates, *that* there should no bur-
den be brought in on the sabbath day.
20 So the merchants and sellers of all
kind of ware lodged without Jerusalem
once or twice.

21 Then I testified against them, and said unto them, Why lodge ye about the wall? if ye do *so* again, I will lay hands on you. From that time forth came they no *more* on the sabbath.
22 And I commanded the Lē'vītes that they should cleanse themselves, and *that* they should come *and* keep the gates, to sanctify the sabbath day. Remember me, O my God, *concerning* this also, and spare me according to the greatness of thy mercy.
23 ¶In those days also saw I Jews *that* had married wives of Ăsh'dŏd, of Ammon, *and* of Moab:
24 And their children spake half in the speech of Ăsh'dŏd, and could not speak in the Jews' language, but according to the language of each people.
25 And I contended with them, and cursed them, and smote certain of them, and plucked off their hair, and made them swear by God, *saying*, Ye shall not give your daughters unto their sons, nor take their daughters unto your sons, or for yourselves.
26 Did not Sŏl'o-mon king of Israel sin by these things? yet among many nations was there no king like him, who was beloved of his God, and God made him king over all Israel: nevertheless even him did outlandish women cause to sin.
27 Shall we then hearken unto you to do all this great evil, to transgress against our God in marrying strange wives?
28 And *one* of the sons of Joi'a-da, the son of E-lī'a-shīb the high priest, *was* son in law to Săn-băl'lat the Hôr'o-nīte: therefore I chased him from me.
29 Remember them, O my God, because they have defiled the priesthood, and the covenant of the priesthood, and of the Lē'vītes.
30 Thus cleansed I them from all strangers, and appointed the wards of the priests and the Lē'vītes, every one in his business;
31 And for the wood offering, at times appointed, and for the firstfruits. Remember me, O my God, for good.

THE

BOOK OF ESTHER

CHAPTER 1

NOW it came to pass in the days of A-haś-ū-ĕ'rus, (this *is* A-haś-ū-ĕ'rus which reigned, from India even unto Ē-thĭ-ō'pĭ-a, *over* an hundred and seven and twenty provinces:)
2 *That* in those days, when the king A-haś-ū-ĕ'rus sat on the throne of his kingdom, which *was* in Shū'shăn the palace,
3 In the third year of his reign, he made a feast unto all his princes and his servants; the power of Persia and Mē'-dĭ-a, the nobles and princes of the provinces, *being* before him:
4 When he shewed the riches of his glorious kingdom and the honour of his excellent majesty many days, *even* an hundred and fourscore days.
5 And when these days were expired, the king made a feast unto all the people that were present in Shū'shăn the palace, both unto great and small, seven days, in the court of the garden of the king's palace;
6 *Where were* white, green, and blue, *hangings*, fastened with cords of fine linen and purple to silver rings and pillars of marble: the beds *were of* gold and silver, upon a pavement of red, and blue, and white, and black, marble.
7 And they gave *them* drink in vessels of gold, (the vessels being diverse one from another,) and royal wine in abundance, according to the state of the king.
8 And the drinking *was* according to the law; none did compel: for so the king had appointed to all the officers of his house, that they should do according to every man's pleasure.
9 Also Văsh'tī the queen made a feast for the women *in* the royal house which *belonged* to king A-haś-ū-ĕ'rus.
10 ¶On the seventh day, when the heart of the king was merry with wine, he commanded Me-hū'man, Bĭz'tha, Här-bō'na, Bĭg'tha, and A-băg'tha, Zē'thär, and Cär'cas, the seven chamberlains that served in the presence of A-haś-ū-ĕ'rus the king,
11 To bring Văsh'tī the queen before the king with the crown royal, to shew the people and the princes her beauty: for she *was* fair to look on.
12 But the queen Văsh'tī refused to come at the king's commandment by *his* chamberlains: therefore was the king very wroth, and his anger burned in him.
13 ¶Then the king said to the wise men, which knew the times, (for so *was* the king's manner toward all that knew law and judgment:
14 And the next unto him *was* Cär-

shē'na, Shē'thär, Ăd'mā-tha, Tär'shĭsh, Me'rēs, Mär'sē-na, *and* Me-mū'can, the seven princes of Persia and Mē'dĭ-a, which saw the king's face, *and* which sat the first in the kingdom;)
15 What shall we do unto the queen Văsh'tī according to law because she hath not performed the commandment of the king A-haś-ū-ĕ'rus by the chamberlains?
16 And Me-mū'can answered before the king and the princes, Văsh'tī the queen hath not done wrong to the king only, but also to all the princes, and to all the people that *are* in all the provinces of the king A-haś-ū-ĕ'rus.
17 For *this* deed of the queen shall come abroad unto all women, so that they shall despise their husbands in their eyes, when it shall be reported, The king A-haś-ū-ĕ'rus commanded Văsh'tī the queen to be brought in before him, but she came not.
18 *Likewise* shall the ladies of Persia and Mē'dĭ-a say this day unto all the king's princes, which have heard of the deed of the queen. Thus *shall there arise* too much contempt and wrath.
19 If it please the king, let there go a royal commandment from him, and let it be written among the laws of the Persians and the Medes, that it be not altered, That Văsh'tī come no more before king A-haś-ū-ĕ'rus; and let the king give her royal estate unto another that is better than she.
20 And when the king's decree which he shall make shall be published throughout all his empire, (for it is great,) all the wives shall give to their husbands honour, both to great and small.
21 And the saying pleased the king and the princes; and the king did according to the word of Me-mū'can:
22 For he sent letters into all the king's provinces, into every province according to the writing thereof, and to every people after their language, that every man should bear rule in his own house, and that *it* should be published according to the language of every people.

CHAPTER 2

AFTER these things, when the wrath of king A-haś-ū-ĕ'rus was appeased, he remembered Văsh'tī, and what she had done, and what was decreed against her.
2 Then said the king's servants that ministered unto him, Let there be fair young virgins sought for the king:
3 And let the king appoint officers in all the provinces of his kingdom, that they may gather together all the fair young virgins unto Shū'shăn the palace, to the house of the women, unto the custody of Hē'ge the king's chamberlain, keeper of the women; and let their things for purification be given *them:*
4 And let the maiden which pleaseth the king be queen instead of Văsh'tī. And the thing pleased the king; and he did so.
5 ¶*Now* in Shū'shăn the palace there was a certain Jew, whose name *was* Môr'de-caī, the son of Jā'ir, the son of Shĭm'e-ī, the son of Kish, a Benjamite;
6 Who had been carried away from Jerusalem with the captivity which had been carried away with Jĕc-o-nī'ah king of Jū'dah, whom Nĕb-u-chad-nĕz'zar the king of Babylon had carried away.
7 And he brought up Ha-dăs'sah, that *is,* Esther, his uncle's daughter: for she had neither father nor mother, and the maid *was* fair and beautiful; whom Môr'de-caī, when her father and mother were dead, took for his own daughter.
8 ¶So it came to pass, when the king's commandment and his decree was heard, and when many maidens were gathered together unto Shū'shăn the palace, to the custody of Hĕg'a-ī, that Esther was brought also unto the king's house, to the custody of Hĕg'a-ī, keeper of the women.
9 And the maiden pleased him, and she obtained kindness of him; and he speedily gave her her things for purification, with such things as belonged to her, and seven maidens, *which were* meet to be given her, out of the king's house: and he preferred her and her maids unto the best *place* of the house of the women.
10 Esther had not shewed her people nor her kindred: for Môr'de-caī had charged her that she should not shew *it.*
11 And Môr'de-caī walked every day before the court of the women's house, to know how Esther did, and what should become of her.
12 ¶Now when every maid's turn was come to go in to king A-haś-ū-ĕ'rus, after that she had been twelve months, according to the manner of the women, (for so were the days of their purifications accomplished, *to wit,* six months with oil of myrrh, and six months with sweet odours, and with *other* things for the purifying of the women;)
13 Then thus came *every* maiden unto the king; whatsoever she desired was given her to go with her out of the

house of the women unto the king's house.

14 In the evening she went, and on the morrow she returned into the second house of the women, to the custody of Shā-ăsh'găz, the king's chamberlain, which kept the concubines: she came in unto the king no more, except the king delighted in her, and that she were called by name.

15 ¶Now when the turn of Esther, the daughter of Ăb-i-hā'il the uncle of Môr'de-caī, who had taken her for his daughter, was come to go in unto the king, she required nothing but what Hĕg'a-ī the king's chamberlain, the keeper of the women, appointed. And Esther obtained favour in the sight of all them that looked upon her.

16 So Esther was taken unto king A-haś-ū-ĕ'rus into his house royal in the tenth month, which *is* the month Tē'bĕth, in the seventh year of his reign.

17 And the king loved Esther above all the women, and she obtained grace and favour in his sight more than all the virgins; so that he set the royal crown upon her head, and made her queen instead of Văsh'tī.

18 Then the king made a great feast unto all his princes and his servants, *even* Esther's feast; and he made a release to the provinces, and gave gifts, according to the state of the king.

19 And when the virgins were gathered together the second time, then Môr'de-caī sat in the king's gate.

20 Esther had not *yet* shewed her kindred nor her people; as Môr'de-caī had charged her: for Esther did the commandment of Môr'de-caī, like as when she was brought up with him.

21 ¶In those days, while Môr'de-caī sat in the king's gate, two of the king's chamberlains, Bĭg'than and Te'rĕsh, of those which kept the door, were wroth, and sought to lay hand on the king A-haś-ū-ĕ'rus.

22 And the thing was known to Môr'de-caī, who told *it* unto Esther the queen; and Esther certified the king *thereof* in Môr'de-caī's name.

23 And when inquisition was made of the matter, it was found out; therefore they were both hanged on a tree: and it was written in the book of the chronicles before the king.

CHAPTER 3

AFTER these things did king A-haś-ū-ĕ'rus promote Hā'man the son of Hăm-med'ā-tha the Ā'gag-īte, and advanced him, and set his seat above all the princes that *were* with him.

2 And all the king's servants, that *were* in the king's gate, bowed, and reverenced Hā'man: for the king had so commanded concerning him. But Môr'de-caī bowed not, nor did *him* reverence.

3 Then the king's servants, which *were* in the king's gate, said unto Môr'de-caī, Why transgressest thou the king's commandment?

4 Now it came to pass, when they spake daily unto him, and he hearkened not unto them, that they told Hā'man, to see whether Môr'de-caī's matters would stand: for he had told them that he *was* a Jew.

5 And when Hā'man saw that Môr'de-caī bowed not, nor did him reverence, then was Hā'man full of wrath.

6 And he thought scorn to lay hands on Môr'de-caī alone; for they had shewed him the people of Môr'de-caī: wherefore Hā'man sought to destroy all the Jews that *were* throughout the whole kingdom of A-haś-ū-ĕ'rus, *even* the people of Môr'de-caī.

7 ¶In the first month, that *is,* the month Nī'săn, in the twelfth year of king A-haś-ū-ĕ'rus, they cast Pur, that *is,* the lot, before Hā'man from day to day, and from month to month, *to* the twelfth *month,* that *is,* the month Ā'där.

8 ¶And Hā'man said unto king A-haś-ū-ĕ'rus, There is a certain people scattered abroad and dispersed among the people in all the provinces of thy kingdom; and their laws *are* diverse from all people; neither keep they the king's laws: therefore it *is* not for the king's profit to suffer them.

9 If it please the king, let it be written that they may be destroyed: and I will pay ten thousand talents of silver to the hands of those that have the charge of the business, to bring *it* into the king's treasuries.

10 And the king took his ring from his hand, and gave it unto Hā'man the son of Hăm-med'ā-tha the Ā'gag-īte, the Jews' enemy.

11 And the king said unto Hā'man, The silver *is* given to thee, the people also, to do with them as it seemeth good to thee.

12 Then were the king's scribes called on the thirteenth day of the first month, and there was written according to all that Hā'man had commanded unto the king's lieutenants, and to the governors that *were* over every province, and to the rulers of every people of every province according to the writing thereof, and *to* every people after their language; in

the name of king A-haś-ū-ĕ′rus was it written, and sealed with the king's ring.

13 And the letters were sent by posts into all the king's provinces, to destroy, to kill, and to cause to perish, all Jews, both young and old, little children and women, in one day, *even* upon the thirteenth *day* of the twelfth month, which *is* the month Ā′dăr, and *to take* the spoil of them for a prey.

14 The copy of the writing for a commandment to be given in every province was published unto all people, that they should be ready against that day.

15 The posts went out, being hastened by the king's commandment, and the decree was given in Shū′shăn the palace. And the king and Hā′man sat down to drink; but the city Shū′shăn was perplexed.

CHAPTER 4

WHEN Môr′de-caī perceived all that was done, Môr′de-caī rent his clothes, and put on sackcloth with ashes, and went out into the midst of the city, and cried with a loud and a bitter cry;

2 And came even before the king's gate: for none *might* enter into the king's gate clothed with sackcloth.

3 And in every province, whithersoever the king's commandment and his decree came, *there was* great mourning among the Jews, and fasting, and weeping, and wailing; and many lay in sackcloth and ashes.

4 ¶So Esther's maids and her chamberlains came and told *it* her. Then was the queen exceedingly grieved; and she sent raiment to clothe Môr′de-caī, and to take away his sackcloth from him: but he received *it* not.

5 Then called Esther for Hă′tach, *one* of the king's chamberlains, whom he had appointed to attend upon her, and gave him a commandment to Môr′de-caī, to know what it *was,* and why it *was.*

6 So Hă′tach went forth to Môr′de-caī unto the street of the city, which *was* before the king's gate.

7 And Môr′de-caī told him of all that had happened unto him, and of the sum of the money that Hā′man had promised to pay to the king's treasuries for the Jews, to destroy them.

8 Also he gave him the copy of the writing of the decree that was given at Shū′shăn to destroy them, to shew *it* unto Esther, and to declare *it* unto her, and to charge her that she should go in unto the king, to make supplication unto him, and to make request before him for her people.

9 And Hă′tach came and told Esther the words of Môr′de-caī.

10 ¶Again Esther spake unto Hă′tach, and gave him commandment unto Môr′de-caī;

11 All the king's servants, and the people of the king's provinces, do know, that whosoever, whether man or woman, shall come unto the king into the inner court, who is not called, *there is* one law of his to put *him* to death, except such to whom the king shall hold out the golden sceptre, that he may live: but I have not been called to come in unto the king these thirty days.

12 And they told to Môr′de-caī Esther's words.

13 Then Môr′de-caī commanded to answer Esther, Think not with thyself that thou shalt escape in the king's house, more than all the Jews.

14 For if thou altogether holdest thy peace at this time, *then* shall there enlargement and deliverance arise to the Jews from another place; but thou and thy father's house shall be destroyed: and who knoweth whether thou art come to the kingdom for *such* a time as this?

15 ¶Then Esther bade *them* return Môr′de-caī *this answer,*

16 Go, gather together all the Jews that are present in Shū′shăn, and fast ye for me, and neither eat nor drink three days, night or day: I also and my maidens will fast likewise; and so will I go in unto the king, which *is* not according to the law: and if I perish, I perish.

17 So Môr′de-caī went his way, and did according to all that Esther had commanded him.

CHAPTER 5

NOW it came to pass on the third day, that Esther put on *her* royal *apparel,* and stood in the inner court of the king's house, over against the king's house: and the king sat upon his royal throne in the royal house, over against the gate of the house.

2 And it was so, when the king saw Esther the queen standing in the court, *that* she obtained favour in his sight: and the king held out to Esther the golden sceptre that *was* in his hand. So Esther drew near, and touched the top of the sceptre.

3 Then said the king unto her, What wilt thou, queen Esther? and what *is* thy request? it shall be even given thee to the half of the kingdom.

4 And Esther answered, If *it seem* good unto the king, let the king and Hā′man come this day unto the banquet that I have prepared for him.

5 Then the king said, Cause Hā'man to make haste, that he may do as Esther hath said. So the king and Hā'man came to the banquet that Esther had prepared.
6 ¶And the king said unto Esther at the banquet of wine, What *is* thy petition? and it shall be granted thee: and what *is* thy request? even to the half of the kingdom it shall be performed.
7 Then answered Esther, and said, My petition and my request *is;*
8 If I have found favour in the sight of the king, and if it please the king to grant my petition, and to perform my request, let the king and Hā'man come to the banquet that I shall prepare for them, and I will do to morrow as the king hath said.
9 ¶Then went Hā'man forth that day joyful and with a glad heart: but when Hā'man saw Môr'de-caī in the king's gate, that he stood not up, nor moved for him, he was full of indignation against Môr'de-caī.
10 Nevertheless Hā'man refrained himself: and when he came home, he sent and called for his friends, and Ze'resh his wife.
11 And Hā'man told them of the glory of his riches, and the multitude of his children, and all *the things* wherein the king had promoted him, and how he had advanced him above the princes and servants of the king.
12 Hā'man said moreover, Yea, Esther the queen did let no man come in with the king unto the banquet that she had prepared but myself; and to morrow am I invited unto her also with the king.
13 Yet all this availeth me nothing, so long as I see Môr'de-caī the Jew sitting at the king's gate.
14 Then said Ze'resh his wife and all his friends unto him, Let a gallows be made of fifty cubits high, and to morrow speak thou unto the king that Môr'de-caī may be hanged thereon: then go thou in merrily with the king unto the banquet. And the thing pleased Hā'man; and he caused the gallows to be made.

CHAPTER 6

ON that night could not the king sleep, and he commanded to bring the book of records of the chronicles; and they were read before the king.
2 And it was found written, that Môr'de-caī had told of Bĭg'tha-na and Te'rĕsh, two of the king's chamberlains, the keepers of the door, who sought to lay hand on the king A-haś-ū-ĕ'rus.
3 And the king said, What honour and dignity hath been done to Môr'de-caī for this? Then said the king's servants that ministered unto him, There is nothing done for him.
4 And the king said, Who *is* in the court? Now Hā'man was come into the outward court of the king's house, to speak unto the king to hang Môr'de-caī on the gallows that he had prepared for him.
5 And the king's servants said unto him, Behold, Hā'man standeth in the court. And the king said, Let him come in.
6 So Hā'man came in. And the king said unto him, What shall be done unto the man whom the king delighteth to honour? Now Hā'man thought in his heart, To whom would the king delight to do honour more than to myself?
7 And Hā'man answered the king, For the man whom the king delighteth to honour,
8 Let the royal apparel be brought which the king *useth* to wear, and the horse that the king rideth upon, and the crown royal which is set upon his head:
9 And let this apparel and horse be delivered to the hand of one of the king's most noble princes, that they may array the man *withal* whom the king delighteth to honour, and bring him on horseback through the street of the city, and proclaim before him, Thus shall it be done to the man whom the king delighteth to honour.
10 Then the king said to Hā'man, Make haste, *and* take the apparel and the horse, as thou hast said, and do even so to Môr'de-caī the Jew, that sitteth at the king's gate: let nothing fail of all that thou hast spoken.
11 Then took Hā'man the apparel and the horse, and arrayed Môr'de-caī, and brought him on horseback through the street of the city, and proclaimed before him, Thus shall it be done unto the man whom the king delighteth to honour.
12 ¶And Môr'de-caī came again to the king's gate. But Hā'man hasted to his house mourning, and having his head covered.
13 And Hā'man told Ze'resh his wife and all his friends every *thing* that had befallen him. Then said his wise men and Ze'resh his wife unto him, If Môr'de-caī *be* of the seed of the Jews, before whom thou hast begun to fall, thou shalt not prevail against him, but shalt surely fall before him.
14 And while they *were* yet talking with him, came the king's chamber-

lains, and hasted to bring Hā′man unto the banquet that Esther had prepared.

CHAPTER 7

SO the king and Hā′man came to banquet with Esther the queen.

2 And the king said again unto Esther on the second day at the banquet of wine, What *is* thy petition, queen Esther? and it shall be granted thee: and what *is* thy request? and it shall be performed, *even* to the half of the kingdom.

3 Then Esther the queen answered and said, If I have found favour in thy sight, O king, and if it please the king, let my life be given me at my petition, and my people at my request:

4 For we are sold, I and my people, to be destroyed, to be slain, and to perish. But if we had been sold for bondmen and bondwomen, I had held my tongue, although the enemy could not countervail the king's damage.

5 ¶Then the king A-haṡ-ū-ĕ′rus answered and said unto Esther the queen, Who is he, and where is he, that durst presume in his heart to do so?

6 And Esther said, The adversary and enemy *is* this wicked Hā′man. Then Hā′man was afraid before the king and the queen.

7 ¶And the king arising from the banquet of wine in his wrath *went* into the palace garden: and Hā′man stood up to make request for his life to Esther the queen; for he saw that there was evil determined against him by the king.

8 Then the king returned out of the palace garden into the place of the banquet of wine; and Hā′man was fallen upon the bed whereon Esther *was*. Then said the king, Will he force the queen also before me in the house? As the word went out of the king's mouth, they covered Hā′man's face.

9 And Här-bō′nah, one of the chamberlains, said before the king, Behold also, the gallows fifty cubits high, which Hā′man had made for Môr′de-caī, who had spoken good for the king, standeth in the house of Hā′man. Then the king said, Hang him thereon.

10 So they hanged Hā′man on the gallows that he had prepared for Môr′de-caī. Then was the king's wrath pacified.

CHAPTER 8

ON that day did the king A-haṡ-ū-ĕ′rus give the house of Hā′man the Jews' enemy unto Esther the queen. And Môr′de-caī came before the king; for Esther had told what he *was* unto her.

2 And the king took off his ring, which he had taken from Hā′man, and gave it unto Môr′de-caī. And Esther set Môr′de-caī over the house of Hā′man.

3 ¶And Esther spake yet again before the king, and fell down at his feet, and besought him with tears to put away the mischief of Hā′man the Ā′gag-īte, and his device that he had devised against the Jews.

4 Then the king held out the golden sceptre toward Esther. So Esther arose, and stood before the king,

5 And said, If it please the king, and if I have found favour in his sight, and the thing *seem* right before the king, and I *be* pleasing in his eyes, let it be written to reverse the letters devised by Hā′man the son of Hăm-med′ā-tha the Ā′gag-īte, which he wrote to destroy the Jews which *are* in all the king's provinces:

6 For how can I endure to see the evil that shall come unto my people? or how can I endure to see the destruction of my kindred?

7 ¶Then the king A-haṡ-ū-ĕ′rus said unto Esther the queen and to Môr′de-caī the Jew, Behold, I have given Esther the house of Hā′man, and him they have hanged upon the gallows, because he laid his hand upon the Jews.

8 Write ye also for the Jews, as it liketh you, in the king's name, and seal *it* with the king's ring: for the writing which is written in the king's name, and sealed with the king's ring, may no man reverse.

9 Then were the king's scribes called at that time in the third month, that *is*, the month Sī′văn, on the three and twentieth *day* thereof; and it was written according to all that Môr′de-caī commanded unto the Jews, and to the lieutenants, and the deputies and rulers of the provinces which *are* from India unto Ē-thĭ-ō′pĭ-a, an hundred twenty and seven provinces, unto every province according to the writing thereof, and unto every people after their language, and to the Jews according to their writing, and according to their language.

10 And he wrote in the king A-haṡ-ū-ĕ′rus' name, and sealed *it* with the king's ring, and sent letters by posts on horseback, *and* riders on mules, camels, *and* young dromedaries:

11 Wherein the king granted the Jews which *were* in every city to gather themselves together, and to stand for their life, to destroy, to slay, and to cause to perish, all the power of the people and province that would assault them, *both* little ones and women, and *to take* the spoil of them for a prey,

12 Upon one day in all the provinces

of king A-haš-ū-ĕ'rus, *namely,* upon the thirteenth *day* of the twelfth month, which *is* the month Ā'där.

13 The copy of the writing for a commandment to be given in every province *was* published unto all people, and that the Jews should be ready against that day to avenge themselves on their enemies.

14 *So* the posts that rode upon mules *and* camels went out, being hastened and pressed on by the king's commandment. And the decree was given at Shū'shăn the palace.

15 ¶And Môr'de-caī went out from the presence of the king in royal apparel of blue and white, and with a great crown of gold, and with a garment of fine linen and purple: and the city of Shū'shăn rejoiced and was glad.

16 The Jews had light, and gladness, and joy, and honour.

17 And in every province, and in every city, whithersoever the king's commandment and his decree came, the Jews had joy and gladness, a feast and a good day. And many of the people of the land became Jews; for the fear of the Jews fell upon them.

CHAPTER 9

NOW in the twelfth month, that *is,* the month Ā'där, on the thirteenth day of the same, when the king's commandment and his decree drew near to be put in execution, in the day that the enemies of the Jews hoped to have power over them, (though it was turned to the contrary, that the Jews had rule over them that hated them;)

2 The Jews gathered themselves together in their cities throughout all the provinces of the king A-haš-ū-ĕ'rus, to lay hand on such as sought their hurt: and no man could withstand them; for the fear of them fell upon all people.

3 And all the rulers of the provinces, and the lieutenants, and the deputies, and officers of the king, helped the Jews; because the fear of Môr'de-caī fell upon them.

4 For Môr'de-caī *was* great in the king's house, and his fame went out throughout all the provinces: for this man Môr'de-caī waxed greater and greater.

5 Thus the Jews smote all their enemies with the stroke of the sword, and slaughter, and destruction, and did what they would unto those that hated them.

6 And in Shū'shăn the palace the Jews slew and destroyed five hundred men.

7 And Pär-shăn'da-tha, and Dăl'phŏn, and Ăs'pā-tha,

8 And Pŏr'ā-tha, and Ad-ā-lī'a, and Ă-rĭd'ā-tha,

9 And Pär-măsh'ta, and Â-ris'a-ī, and Â-rid'a-ī, and Va-jĕz'a-tha.

10 The ten sons of Hā'man the son of Hăm-med'ā-tha, the enemy of the Jews, slew they; but on the spoil laid they not their hand.

11 On that day the number of those that were slain in Shū'shăn the palace was brought before the king.

12 ¶And the king said unto Esther the queen, The Jews have slain and destroyed five hundred men in Shū'shăn the palace, and the ten sons of Hā'man; what have they done in the rest of the king's provinces? now what *is* thy petition? and it shall be granted thee: or what *is* thy request further? and it shall be done.

13 Then said Esther, If it please the king, let it be granted to the Jews which *are* in Shū'shăn to do to morrow also according unto this day's decree, and let Hā'man's ten sons be hanged upon the gallows.

14 And the king commanded it so to be done: and the decree was given at Shū'shăn; and they hanged Hā'man's ten sons.

15 For the Jews that *were* in Shū'shăn gathered themselves together on the fourteenth day also of the month Ā'där, and slew three hundred men at Shū'shăn; but on the prey they laid not their hand.

16 But the other Jews that *were* in the king's provinces gathered themselves together, and stood for their lives, and had rest from their enemies, and slew of their foes seventy and five thousand, but they laid not their hands on the prey,

17 On the thirteenth day of the month Ā'där; and on the fourteenth day of the same rested they, and made it a day of feasting and gladness.

18 But the Jews that *were* at Shū'shăn assembled together on the thirteenth *day* thereof, and on the fourteenth thereof; and on the fifteenth *day* of the same they rested, and made it a day of feasting and gladness.

19 Therefore the Jews of the villages that dwelt in the unwalled towns, made the fourteenth day of the month Ā'där *a day of* gladness and feasting, and a good day, and of sending portions one to another.

20 ¶And Môr'de-caī wrote these things, and sent letters unto all the Jews that *were* in all the provinces of

the king A-haṡ-ū-ĕ'rus, *both* nigh and far,

21 To stablish *this* among them, that they should keep the fourteenth day of the month Ā'där, and the fifteenth day of the same, yearly,

22 As the days wherein the Jews rested from their enemies, and the month which was turned unto them from sorrow to joy, and from mourning into a good day: that they should make them days of feasting and joy, and of sending portions one to another, and gifts to the poor.

23 And the Jews undertook to do as they had begun, and as Môr'de-caī had written unto them;

24 Because Hā'man the son of Hăm-med'ā-tha, the Ā'gag-īte, the enemy of all the Jews, had devised against the Jews to destroy them, and had cast Pur, that *is*, the lot, to consume them, and to destroy them;

25 But when *Esther* came before the king, he commanded by letters that his wicked device, which he devised against the Jews, should return upon his own head, and that he and his sons should be hanged on the gallows.

26 Wherefore they called these days Pū'rĭm after the name of Pur. Therefore for all the words of this letter, and *of that* which they had seen concerning this matter, and which had come unto them,

27 The Jews ordained, and took upon them, and upon their seed, and upon all such as joined themselves unto them, so as it should not fail, that they would keep these two days according to their writing, and according to their *appointed* time every year;

28 And *that* these days *should be* remembered and kept throughout every generation, every family, every province, and every city; and *that* these days of Pū'rĭm should not fail from among the Jews, nor the memorial of them perish from their seed.

29 Then Esther the queen, the daughter of Ăb-i-hā'il, and Môr'de-caī the Jew, wrote with all authority, to confirm this second letter of Pū'rĭm.

30 And he sent the letters unto all the Jews, to the hundred twenty and seven provinces of the kingdom of A-haṡ-ū-ĕ'rus, *with* words of peace and truth,

31 To confirm these days of Pū'rĭm in their times *appointed*, according as Môr'de-caī the Jew and Esther the queen had enjoined them, and as they had decreed for themselves and for their seed, the matters of the fastings and their cry.

32 And the decree of Esther confirmed these matters of Pū'rĭm; and it was written in the book.

CHAPTER 10

AND the king A-haṡ-ū-ĕ'rus laid a tribute upon the land, and *upon* the isles of the sea.

2 And all the acts of his power and of his might, and the declaration of the greatness of Môr'de-caī, whereunto the king advanced him, *are* they not written in the book of the chronicles of the kings of Mē'dĭ-a and Persia?

3 For Môr'de-caī the Jew *was* next unto king A-haṡ-ū-ĕ'rus, and great among the Jews, and accepted of the multitude of his brethren, seeking the wealth of his people, and speaking peace to all his seed.

THE BOOK OF JOB

CHAPTER 1

THERE was a man in the land of Uz, whose name *was* Job; and that man was perfect and upright, and one that feared God, and eschewed evil.

2 And there were born unto him seven sons and three daughters.

3 His substance also was seven thousand sheep, and three thousand camels, and five hundred yoke of oxen, and five hundred she asses, and a very great household; so that this man was the greatest of all the men of the east.

4 And his sons went and feasted *in their* houses, every one his day; and sent and called for their three sisters to eat and to drink with them.

5 And it was so, when the days of *their* feasting were gone about, that Job sent and sanctified them, and rose up early in the morning, and offered burnt offerings *according* to the number of them all: for Job said, It may be that my sons have sinned, and cursed God in their hearts. Thus did Job continually.

6 ¶Now there was a day when the sons of God came to present themselves before the LORD, and Satan came also among them.

7 And the LORD said unto Satan, Whence comest thou? Then Satan answered the LORD, and said, From going to and fro in the earth, and from walking up and down in it.

8 And the LORD said unto Satan, Hast thou considered my servant Job, that *there is* none like him in the earth, a perfect and an upright man, one that feareth God, and escheweth evil?

9 Then Satan answered the LORD, and said, Doth Job fear God for nought?

10 Hast not thou made an hedge about him, and about his house, and about all that he hath on every side? thou hast blessed the work of his hands, and his substance is increased in the land.

11 But put forth thine hand now, and touch all that he hath, and he will curse thee to thy face.

12 And the LORD said unto Satan, Behold, all that he hath *is* in thy power; only upon himself put not forth thine hand. So Satan went forth from the presence of the LORD.

13 ¶And there was a day when his sons and his daughters *were* eating and drinking wine in their eldest brother's house:

14 And there came a messenger unto Job, and said, The oxen were plowing, and the asses feeding beside them:

15 And the Sa-bē'anṡ fell *upon them*, and took them away; yea, they have slain the servants with the edge of the sword; and I only am escaped alone to tell thee.

16 While he *was* yet speaking, there came also another, and said, The fire of God is fallen from heaven, and hath burned up the sheep, and the servants, and consumed them; and I only am escaped alone to tell thee.

17 While he *was* yet speaking, there came also another, and said, The Chăl-dē'anṡ made out three bands, and fell upon the camels, and have carried them away, yea, and slain the servants with the edge of the sword; and I only am escaped alone to tell thee.

18 While he *was* yet speaking, there came also another, and said, Thy sons and thy daughters *were* eating and drinking wine in their eldest brother's house:

19 And, behold, there came a great wind from the wilderness, and smote the four corners of the house, and it fell upon the young men, and they are dead; and I only am escaped alone to tell thee.

20 Then Job arose, and rent his mantle, and shaved his head, and fell down upon the ground, and worshipped,

21 And said, Naked came I out of my mother's womb, and naked shall I return thither: the LORD gave, and the LORD hath taken away; blessed be the name of the LORD.

22 In all this Job sinned not, nor charged God foolishly.

CHAPTER 2

AGAIN there was a day when the sons of God came to present themselves before the LORD, and Satan came also among them to present himself before the LORD.

2 And the LORD said unto Satan, From whence comest thou? And Satan answered the LORD, and said, From going to and fro in the earth, and from walking up and down in it.

3 And the LORD said unto Satan, Hast thou considered my servant Job, that *there is* none like him in the earth, a perfect and an upright man, one that feareth God, and escheweth evil? and still he holdeth fast his integrity, although thou movedst me against him, to destroy him without cause.

4 And Satan answered the LORD, and said, Skin for skin, yea, all that a man hath will he give for his life.

5 But put forth thine hand now, and touch his bone and his flesh, and he will curse thee to thy face.

6 And the LORD said unto Satan, Behold, he *is* in thine hand; but save his life.

7 ¶So went Satan forth from the presence of the LORD, and smote Job with sore boils from the sole of his foot unto his crown.

8 And he took him a potsherd to scrape himself withal; and he sat down among the ashes.

9 ¶Then said his wife unto him, Dost thou still retain thine integrity? curse God, and die.

10 But he said unto her, Thou speakest as one of the foolish women speaketh. What? shall we receive good at the hand of God, and shall we not receive evil? In all this did not Job sin with his lips.

11 ¶Now when Job's three friends heard of all this evil that was come upon him, they came every one from his own place: Ĕl'i-phăz the Tē'man-īte, and Bildad the Shū'hīte, and Zō'phar the Nā'a-math-īte; for they had made an appointment together to come to mourn with him and to comfort him.

12 And when they lifted up their eyes afar off, and knew him not, they lifted up their voice, and wept; and they rent every one his mantle, and sprinkled dust upon their heads toward heaven.

13 So they sat down with him upon the ground seven days and seven nights, and none spake a word unto

him: for they saw that *his* grief was very great.

CHAPTER 3

AFTER this opened Job his mouth, and cursed his day.

2 And Job spake, and said,

3 Let the day perish wherein I was born, and the night *in which* it was said, There is a man child conceived.

4 Let that day be darkness; let not God regard it from above, neither let the light shine upon it.

5 Let darkness and the shadow of death stain it; let a cloud dwell upon it; let the blackness of the day terrify it.

6 *As for* that night, let darkness seize upon it; let it not be joined unto the days of the year, let it not come into the number of the months.

7 Lo, let that night be solitary, let no joyful voice come therein.

8 Let them curse it that curse the day, who are ready to raise up their mourning.

9 Let the stars of the twilight thereof be dark; let it look for light, but *have* none; neither let it see the dawning of the day:

10 Because it shut not up the doors of my *mother's* womb, nor hid sorrow from mine eyes.

11 Why died I not from the womb? *why* did I *not* give up the ghost when I came out of the belly?

12 Why did the knees prevent me? or why the breasts that I should suck?

13 For now should I have lain still and been quiet, I should have slept: then had I been at rest,

14 With kings and counsellors of the earth, which built desolate places for themselves;

15 Or with princes that had gold, who filled their houses with silver:

16 Or as an hidden untimely birth I had not been; as infants *which* never saw light.

17 There the wicked cease *from* troubling; and there the weary be at rest.

18 *There* the prisoners rest together; they hear not the voice of the oppressor.

19 The small and great are there; and the servant *is* free from his master.

20 Wherefore is light given to him that is in misery, and life unto the bitter *in* soul;

21 Which long for death, but it *cometh* not; and dig for it more than for hid treasures;

22 Which rejoice exceedingly, *and* are glad, when they can find the grave?

23 *Why is light given* to a man whose way is hid, and whom God hath hedged in?

24 For my sighing cometh before I eat, and my roarings are poured out like the waters.

25 For the thing which I greatly feared is come upon me, and that which I was afraid of is come unto me.

26 I was not in safety, neither had I rest, neither was I quiet; yet trouble came.

CHAPTER 4

THEN Ĕl'i-phăz the Tē'man-īte answered and said,

2 *If* we assay to commune with thee, wilt thou be grieved? but who can withhold himself from speaking?

3 Behold, thou hast instructed many, and thou hast strengthened the weak hands.

4 Thy words have upholden him that was falling, and thou hast strengthened the feeble knees.

5 But now it is come upon thee, and thou faintest; it toucheth thee, and thou art troubled.

6 *Is* not *this* thy fear, thy confidence, thy hope, and the uprightness of thy ways?

7 Remember, I pray thee, who *ever* perished, being innocent? or where were the righteous cut off ?

8 Even as I have seen, they that plow iniquity, and sow wickedness, reap the same.

9 By the blast of God they perish, and by the breath of his nostrils are they consumed.

10 The roaring of the lion, and the voice of the fierce lion, and the teeth of the young lions, are broken.

11 The old lion perisheth for lack of prey, and the stout lion's whelps are scattered abroad.

12 Now a thing was secretly brought to me, and mine ear received a little thereof.

13 In thoughts from the visions of the night, when deep sleep falleth on men,

14 Fear came upon me, and trembling, which made all my bones to shake.

15 Then a spirit passed before my face; the hair of my flesh stood up:

16 It stood still, but I could not discern the form thereof: an image *was* before mine eyes, *there was* silence, and I heard a voice, *saying,*

17 Shall mortal man be more just than God? shall a man be more pure than his maker?

18 Behold, he put no trust in his servants; and his angels he charged with folly:

19 How much less *in* them that dwell in houses of clay, whose foundation *is* in the dust, *which* are crushed before the moth?

20 They are destroyed from morning to evening: they perish for ever without any regarding *it*.

21 Doth not their excellency *which is* in them go away? they die, even without wisdom.

CHAPTER 5

CALL now, if there be any that will answer thee; and to which of the saints wilt thou turn?

2 For wrath killeth the foolish man, and envy slayeth the silly one.

3 I have seen the foolish taking root: but suddenly I cursed his habitation.

4 His children are far from safety, and they are crushed in the gate, neither *is there* any to deliver *them*.

5 Whose harvest the hungry eateth up, and taketh it even out of the thorns, and the robber swalloweth up their substance.

6 Although affliction cometh not forth of the dust, neither doth trouble spring out of the ground;

7 Yet man is born unto trouble, as the sparks fly upward.

8 I would seek unto God, and unto God would I commit my cause:

9 Which doeth great things and unsearchable; marvellous things without number:

10 Who giveth rain upon the earth, and sendeth waters upon the fields:

11 To set up on high those that be low; that those which mourn may be exalted to safety.

12 He disappointeth the devices of the crafty, so that their hands cannot perform *their* enterprise.

13 He taketh the wise in their own craftiness: and the counsel of the froward is carried headlong.

14 They meet with darkness in the daytime, and grope in the noonday as in the night.

15 But he saveth the poor from the sword, from their mouth, and from the hand of the mighty.

16 So the poor hath hope, and iniquity stoppeth her mouth.

17 Behold, happy *is* the man whom God correcteth: therefore despise not thou the chastening of the Almighty:

18 For he maketh sore, and bindeth up: he woundeth, and his hands make whole.

19 He shall deliver thee in six troubles: yea, in seven there shall no evil touch thee.

20 In famine he shall redeem thee from death: and in war from the power of the sword.

21 Thou shalt be hid from the scourge of the tongue: neither shalt thou be afraid of destruction when it cometh.

22 At destruction and famine thou shalt laugh: neither shalt thou be afraid of the beasts of the earth.

23 For thou shalt be in league with the stones of the field: and the beasts of the field shall be at peace with thee.

24 And thou shalt know that thy tabernacle *shall be* in peace; and thou shalt visit thy habitation, and shalt not sin.

25 Thou shalt know also that thy seed *shall be* great, and thine offspring as the grass of the earth.

26 Thou shalt come to *thy* grave in a full age, like as a shock of corn cometh in in his season.

27 Lo this, we have searched it, so it *is*; hear it, and know thou *it* for thy good.

CHAPTER 6

BUT Job answered and said,

2 Oh that my grief were throughly weighed, and my calamity laid in the balances together!

3 For now it would be heavier than the sand of the sea: therefore my words are swallowed up.

4 For the arrows of the Almighty *are* within me, the poison whereof drinketh up my spirit: the terrors of God do set themselves in array against me.

5 Doth the wild ass bray when he hath grass? or loweth the ox over his fodder?

6 Can that which is unsavoury be eaten without salt? or is there *any* taste in the white of an egg?

7 The things *that* my soul refused to touch *are* as my sorrowful meat.

8 Oh that I might have my request; and that God would grant *me* the thing that I long for!

9 Even that it would please God to destroy me; that he would let loose his hand, and cut me off!

10 Then should I yet have comfort; yea, I would harden myself in sorrow: let him not spare; for I have not concealed the words of the Holy One.

11 What *is* my strength, that I should hope? and what *is* mine end, that I should prolong my life?

12 *Is* my strength the strength of stones? or *is* my flesh of brass?

13 *Is* not my help in me? and is wisdom driven quite from me?

14 To him that is afflicted pity *should be shewed* from his friend; but he forsaketh the fear of the Almighty.

15 My brethren have dealt deceitfully
as a brook, *and* as the stream of brooks
they pass away;
16 Which are blackish by reason of
the ice, *and* wherein the snow is hid:
17 What time they wax warm, they
vanish: when it is hot, they are con-
sumed out of their place.
18 The paths of their way are turned
aside; they go to nothing, and perish.
19 The troops of Tē'ma looked, the
companies of Shē'ba waited for them.
20 They were confounded because
they had hoped; they came thither, and
were ashamed.
21 For now ye are nothing; ye see *my*
casting down, and are afraid.
22 Did I say, Bring unto me? or, Give
a reward for me of your substance?
23 Or, Deliver me from the enemy's
hand? or, Redeem me from the hand of
the mighty?
24 Teach me, and I will hold my
tongue: and cause me to understand
wherein I have erred.
25 How forcible are right words! but
what doth your arguing reprove?
26 Do ye imagine to reprove words,
and the speeches of one that is des-
perate, *which are* as wind?
27 Yea, ye overwhelm the fatherless,
and ye dig *a pit* for your friend.
28 Now therefore be content, look
upon me; for *it is* evident unto you if I
lie.
29 Return, I pray you, let it not be iniq-
uity; yea, return again, my righteous-
ness *is* in it.
30 Is there iniquity in my tongue?
cannot my taste discern perverse
things?

CHAPTER 7

IS there not an appointed time to man
upon earth? *are not* his days also like
the days of an hireling?
2 As a servant earnestly desireth the
shadow, and as an hireling looketh for
the reward of his work:
3 So am I made to possess months of
vanity, and wearisome nights are ap-
pointed to me.
4 When I lie down, I say, When shall I
arise, and the night be gone? and I am
full of tossings to and fro unto the dawn-
ing of the day.
5 My flesh is clothed with worms and
clods of dust; my skin is broken, and
become loathsome.
6 My days are swifter than a weaver's
shuttle, and are spent without hope.
7 O remember that my life *is* wind:
mine eye shall no more see good.
8 The eye of him that hath seen me
shall see me no *more:* thine eyes *are*
upon me, and I *am* not.
9 *As* the cloud is consumed and van-
isheth away: so he that goeth down to
the grave shall come up no *more.*
10 He shall return no more to his
house, neither shall his place know him
any more.
11 Therefore I will not refrain my
mouth; I will speak in the anguish of
my spirit; I will complain in the bitter-
ness of my soul.
12 *Am* I a sea, or a whale, that thou
settest a watch over me?
13 When I say, My bed shall comfort
me, my couch shall ease my complaint;
14 Then thou scarest me with
dreams, and terrifiest me through vi-
sions:
15 So that my soul chooseth stran-
gling, *and* death rather than my life.
16 I loathe *it;* I would not live alway:
let me alone; for my days *are* vanity.
17 What *is* man, that thou shouldest
magnify him? and that thou shouldest
set thine heart upon him?
18 And *that* thou shouldest visit him
every morning, *and* try him every mo-
ment?
19 How long wilt thou not depart
from me, nor let me alone till I swallow
down my spittle?
20 I have sinned; what shall I do unto
thee, O thou preserver of men? why
hast thou set me as a mark against
thee, so that I am a burden to myself?
21 And why dost thou not pardon my
transgression, and take away mine iniq-
uity? for now shall I sleep in the dust;
and thou shalt seek me in the morning,
but I *shall* not *be.*

CHAPTER 8

THEN answered Bildad the Shū'hīte,
and said,
2 How long wilt thou speak these
things? and *how long shall* the words of
thy mouth *be like* a strong wind?
3 Doth God pervert judgment? or
doth the Almighty pervert justice?
4 If thy children have sinned against
him, and he have cast them away for
their transgression;
5 If thou wouldest seek unto God be-
times, and make thy supplication to the
Almighty;
6 If thou *wert* pure and upright; sure-
ly now he would awake for thee, and
make the habitation of thy righteous-
ness prosperous.
7 Though thy beginning was small,
yet thy latter end should greatly in-
crease.
8 For enquire, I pray thee, of the for-

mer age, and prepare thyself to the
search of their fathers:
9 (For we *are but of* yesterday, and
know nothing, because our days upon
earth *are* a shadow:)
10 Shall not they teach thee, *and* tell
thee, and utter words out of their
heart?
11 Can the rush grow up without
mire? can the flag grow without water?
12 Whilst it *is* yet in his greenness,
and not cut down, it withereth before
any *other* herb.
13 So *are* the paths of all that forget
God; and the hypocrite's hope shall
perish:
14 Whose hope shall be cut off, and
whose trust *shall be* a spider's web.
15 He shall lean upon his house, but it
shall not stand: he shall hold it fast, but
it shall not endure.
16 He *is* green before the sun, and his
branch shooteth forth in his garden.
17 His roots are wrapped about the
heap, *and* seeth the place of stones.
18 If he destroy him from his place,
then *it* shall deny him, *saying,* I have
not seen thee.
19 Behold, this *is* the joy of his way,
and out of the earth shall others grow.
20 Behold, God will not cast away a
perfect *man,* neither will he help the
evil doers:
21 Till he fill thy mouth with laughing
and thy lips with rejoicing.
22 They that hate thee shall be
clothed with shame; and the dwelling
place of the wicked shall come to
nought.

CHAPTER 9

THEN Job answered and said,
2 I know *it is* so of a truth: but how
should man be just with God?
3 If he will contend with him, he can-
not answer him one of a thousand.
4 *He is* wise in heart, and mighty in
strength: who hath hardened *himself*
against him, and hath prospered?
5 Which removeth the mountains,
and they know not: which overturneth
them in his anger.
6 Which shaketh the earth out of her
place, and the pillars thereof tremble.
7 Which commandeth the sun, and it
riseth not; and sealeth up the stars.
8 Which alone spreadeth out the
heavens, and treadeth upon the waves
of the sea.
9 Which maketh Ărc-tû'rus, Ō-rī'on,
and Plē'ia-dēs, and the chambers of the
south.
10 Which doeth great things past
finding out; yea, and wonders without
number.
11 Lo, he goeth by me, and I see *him*
not: he passeth on also, but I perceive
him not.
12 Behold, he taketh away, who can
hinder him? who will say unto him,
What doest thou?
13 *If* God will not withdraw his anger,
the proud helpers do stoop under him.
14 How much less shall I answer him,
and choose out my words *to reason*
with him?
15 Whom, though I were righteous,
yet would I not answer, *but* I would
make supplication to my judge.
16 If I had called, and he had an-
swered me; *yet* would I not believe that
he had hearkened unto my voice.
17 For he breaketh me with a tem-
pest, and multiplieth my wounds
without cause.
18 He will not suffer me to take my
breath, but filleth me with bitterness.
19 If *I speak* of strength, lo, *he is*
strong: and if of judgment, who shall
set me a time *to plead?*
20 If I justify myself, mine own
mouth shall condemn me: *if I say,* I *am*
perfect, it shall also prove me perverse.
21 *Though* I *were* perfect, *yet* would I
not know my soul: I would despise my
life.
22 This *is* one *thing,* therefore I said
it, He destroyeth the perfect and the
wicked.
23 If the scourge slay suddenly, he
will laugh at the trial of the innocent.
24 The earth is given into the hand of
the wicked: he covereth the faces of the
judges thereof; if not, where, *and* who
is he?
25 Now my days are swifter than a
post: they flee away, they see no good.
26 They are passed away as the swift
ships: as the eagle *that* hasteth to the
prey.
27 If I say, I will forget my complaint,
I will leave off my heaviness, and com-
fort *myself:*
28 I am afraid of all my sorrows, I
know that thou wilt not hold me inno-
cent.
29 *If* I be wicked, why then labour I in
vain?
30 If I wash myself with snow water,
and make my hands never so clean;
31 Yet shalt thou plunge me in the
ditch, and mine own clothes shall
abhor me.
32 For *he is* not a man, as I *am, that* I
should answer him, *and* we should
come together in judgment.
33 Neither is there any daysman be-
twixt us, *that* might lay his hand upon
us both.
34 Let him take his rod away from

me, and let not his fear terrify me:
35 *Then* would I speak, and not fear him; but *it is* not so with me.

CHAPTER 10

MY soul is weary of my life; I will leave my complaint upon myself; I will speak in the bitterness of my soul.
2 I will say unto God, Do not condemn me; shew me wherefore thou contendest with me.
3 *Is it* good unto thee that thou shouldest oppress, that thou shouldest despise the work of thine hands, and shine upon the counsel of the wicked?
4 Hast thou eyes of flesh? or seest thou as man seeth?
5 *Are* thy days as the days of man? *are* thy years as man's days,
6 That thou enquirest after mine iniquity, and searchest after my sin?
7 Thou knowest that I am not wicked; and *there is* none that can deliver out of thine hand.
8 Thine hands have made me and fashioned me together round about; yet thou dost destroy me.
9 Remember, I beseech thee, that thou hast made me as the clay; and wilt thou bring me into dust again?
10 Hast thou not poured me out as milk, and curdled me like cheese?
11 Thou hast clothed me with skin and flesh, and hast fenced me with bones and sinews.
12 Thou hast granted me life and favour, and thy visitation hath preserved my spirit.
13 And these *things* hast thou hid in thine heart: I know that this *is* with thee.
14 If I sin, then thou markest me, and thou wilt not acquit me from mine iniquity.
15 If I be wicked, woe unto me; and *if* I be righteous, *yet* will I not lift up my head. *I am* full of confusion; therefore see thou mine affliction;
16 For it increaseth. Thou huntest me as a fierce lion: and again thou shewest thyself marvellous upon me.
17 Thou renewest thy witnesses against me, and increasest thine indignation upon me; changes and war *are* against me.
18 Wherefore then hast thou brought me forth out of the womb? Oh that I had given up the ghost, and no eye had seen me!
19 I should have been as though I had not been; I should have been carried from the womb to the grave.
20 *Are* not my days few? cease *then, and* let me alone, that I may take comfort a little,
21 Before I go *whence* I shall not return, *even* to the land of darkness and the shadow of death;
22 A land of darkness, as darkness *itself; and* of the shadow of death, without any order, and *where* the light *is* as darkness.

CHAPTER 11

THEN answered Zō'phar the Nā'a-math-īte, and said,
2 Should not the multitude of words be answered? and should a man full of talk be justified?
3 Should thy lies make men hold their peace? and when thou mockest, shall no man make thee ashamed?
4 For thou hast said, My doctrine *is* pure, and I am clean in thine eyes.
5 But oh that God would speak, and open his lips against thee;
6 And that he would shew thee the secrets of wisdom, that *they are* double to that which is! Know therefore that God exacteth of thee *less* than thine iniquity *deserveth.*
7 Canst thou by searching find out God? canst thou find out the Almighty unto perfection?
8 *It is* as high as heaven; what canst thou do? deeper than hell; what canst thou know?
9 The measure thereof *is* longer than the earth, and broader than the sea.
10 If he cut off, and shut up, or gather together, then who can hinder him?
11 For he knoweth vain men: he seeth wickedness also; will he not then consider *it*?
12 For vain man would be wise, though man be born *like* a wild ass's colt.
13 If thou prepare thine heart, and stretch out thine hands toward him;
14 If iniquity *be* in thine hand, put it far away, and let not wickedness dwell in thy tabernacles.
15 For then shalt thou lift up thy face without spot; yea, thou shalt be stedfast, and shalt not fear:
16 Because thou shalt forget *thy* misery, *and* remember *it* as waters *that* pass away:
17 And *thine* age shall be clearer than the noonday; thou shalt shine forth, thou shalt be as the morning.
18 And thou shalt be secure, because there is hope; yea, thou shalt dig *about thee, and* thou shalt take thy rest in safety.
19 Also thou shalt lie down, and none shall make *thee* afraid; yea, many shall make suit unto thee.
20 But the eyes of the wicked shall fail, and they shall not escape, and their

hope *shall be as* the giving up of the ghost.

CHAPTER 12

AND Job answered and said,

2 No doubt but ye *are* the people, and wisdom shall die with you.

3 But I have understanding as well as you; I *am* not inferior to you: yea, who knoweth not such things as these?

4 I am *as* one mocked of his neighbour, who calleth upon God, and he answereth him: the just upright *man is* laughed to scorn.

5 He that is ready to slip with *his* feet *is as* a lamp despised in the thought of him that is at ease.

6 The tabernacles of robbers prosper, and they that provoke God are secure; into whose hand God bringeth *abundantly*.

7 But ask now the beasts, and they shall teach thee; and the fowls of the air, and they shall tell thee:

8 Or speak to the earth, and it shall teach thee: and the fishes of the sea shall declare unto thee.

9 Who knoweth not in all these that the hand of the LORD hath wrought this?

10 In whose hand *is* the soul of every living thing, and the breath of all mankind.

11 Doth not the ear try words? and the mouth taste his meat?

12 With the ancient *is* wisdom; and in length of days understanding.

13 With him *is* wisdom and strength, he hath counsel and understanding.

14 Behold, he breaketh down, and it cannot be built again: he shutteth up a man, and there can be no opening.

15 Behold, he withholdeth the waters, and they dry up: also he sendeth them out, and they overturn the earth.

16 With him *is* strength and wisdom: the deceived and the deceiver *are* his.

17 He leadeth counsellors away spoiled, and maketh the judges fools.

18 He looseth the bond of kings, and girdeth their loins with a girdle.

19 He leadeth princes away spoiled, and overthroweth the mighty.

20 He removeth away the speech of the trusty, and taketh away the understanding of the aged.

21 He poureth contempt upon princes, and weakeneth the strength of the mighty.

22 He discovereth deep things out of darkness, and bringeth out to light the shadow of death.

23 He increaseth the nations, and destroyeth them: he enlargeth the nations, and straiteneth them *again*.

24 He taketh away the heart of the chief of the people of the earth, and causeth them to wander in a wilderness *where there is* no way.

25 They grope in the dark without light, and he maketh them to stagger like *a* drunken *man*.

CHAPTER 13

LO, mine eye hath seen all *this*, mine ear hath heard and understood it.

2 What ye know, *the same* do I know also: I *am* not inferior unto you.

3 Surely I would speak to the Almighty, and I desire to reason with God.

4 But ye *are* forgers of lies, ye *are* all physicians of no value.

5 O that ye would altogether hold your peace! and it should be your wisdom.

6 Hear now my reasoning, and hearken to the pleadings of my lips.

7 Will ye speak wickedly for God? and talk deceitfully for him?

8 Will ye accept his person? will ye contend for God?

9 Is it good that he should search you out? or as one man mocketh another, do ye *so* mock him?

10 He will surely reprove you, if ye do secretly accept persons.

11 Shall not his excellency make you afraid? and his dread fall upon you?

12 Your remembrances *are* like unto ashes, your bodies to bodies of clay.

13 Hold your peace, let me alone, that I may speak, and let come on me what *will*.

14 Wherefore do I take my flesh in my teeth, and put my life in mine hand?

15 Though he slay me, yet will I trust in him: but I will maintain mine own ways before him.

16 He also *shall be* my salvation: for an hypocrite shall not come before him.

17 Hear diligently my speech, and my declaration with your ears.

18 Behold now, I have ordered *my* cause; I know that I shall be justified.

19 Who *is* he *that* will plead with me? for now, if I hold my tongue, I shall give up the ghost.

20 Only do not two *things* unto me: then will I not hide myself from thee.

21 Withdraw thine hand far from me: and let not thy dread make me afraid.

22 Then call thou, and I will answer: or let me speak, and answer thou me.

23 How many *are* mine iniquities and sins? make me to know my transgression and my sin.

24 Wherefore hidest thou thy face, and holdest me for thine enemy?

25 Wilt thou break a leaf driven to

and fro? and wilt thou pursue the dry
stubble?
26 For thou writest bitter things
against me, and makest me to possess
the iniquities of my youth.
27 Thou puttest my feet also in the
stocks, and lookest narrowly unto all
my paths; thou settest a print upon the
heels of my feet.
28 And he, as a rotten thing, con-
sumeth, as a garment that is moth
eaten.

CHAPTER 14

MAN *that is* born of a woman *is* of few
days, and full of trouble.
2 He cometh forth like a flower, and
is cut down: he fleeth also as a shadow,
and continueth not.
3 And dost thou open thine eyes upon
such an one, and bringest me into judg-
ment with thee?
4 Who can bring a clean *thing* out of
an unclean? not one.
5 Seeing his days *are* determined, the
number of his months *are* with thee,
thou hast appointed his bounds that he
cannot pass;
6 Turn from him, that he may rest, till
he shall accomplish, as an hireling, his
day.
7 For there is hope of a tree, if it be
cut down, that it will sprout again, and
that the tender branch thereof will not
cease.
8 Though the root thereof wax old in
the earth, and the stock thereof die in
the ground;
9 *Yet* through the scent of water it
will bud, and bring forth boughs like a
plant.
10 But man dieth, and wasteth away:
yea, man giveth up the ghost, and
where *is* he?
11 *As* the waters fail from the sea,
and the flood decayeth and drieth up:
12 So man lieth down, and riseth not:
till the heavens *be* no more, they shall
not awake, nor be raised out of their
sleep.
13 O that thou wouldest hide me in
the grave, that thou wouldest keep me
secret, until thy wrath be past, that
thou wouldest appoint me a set time,
and remember me!
14 If a man die, shall he live *again?* all
the days of my appointed time will I
wait, till my change come.
15 Thou shalt call, and I will answer
thee: thou wilt have a desire to the
work of thine hands.
16 For now thou numberest my
steps: dost thou not watch over my sin?
17 My transgression *is* sealed up in a
bag, and thou sewest up mine iniquity.
18 And surely the mountain falling
cometh to nought, and the rock is re-
moved out of his place.
19 The waters wear the stones: thou
washest away the things which grow
out of the dust of the earth; and thou
destroyest the hope of man.
20 Thou prevailest for ever against
him, and he passeth: thou changest his
countenance, and sendest him away.
21 His sons come to honour, and he
knoweth *it* not; and they are brought
low, but he perceiveth *it* not of them.
22 But his flesh upon him shall have
pain, and his soul within him shall
mourn.

CHAPTER 15

THEN answered Ĕl′i-phăz the Tē′man-
īte, and said,
2 Should a wise man utter vain knowl-
edge, and fill his belly with the east
wind?
3 Should he reason with unprofitable
talk? or with speeches wherewith he
can do no good?
4 Yea, thou castest off fear, and re-
strainest prayer before God.
5 For thy mouth uttereth thine iniq-
uity, and thou choosest the tongue of
the crafty.
6 Thine own mouth condemneth
thee, and not I: yea, thine own lips tes-
tify against thee.
7 *Art* thou the first man *that* was
born? or wast thou made before the
hills?
8 Hast thou heard the secret of God?
and dost thou restrain wisdom to thy-
self?
9 What knowest thou, that we know
not? *what* understandest thou, which *is*
not in us?
10 With us *are* both the gray headed
and very aged men, much elder than
thy father.
11 *Are* the consolations of God small
with thee? is there any secret thing
with thee?
12 Why doth thine heart carry thee
away? and what do thy eyes wink at,
13 That thou turnest thy spirit
against God, and lettest *such* words go
out of thy mouth?
14 What *is* man, that he should be
clean? and *he which is* born of a wom-
an, that he should be righteous?
15 Behold, he putteth no trust in his
saints; yea, the heavens are not clean in
his sight.
16 How much more abominable and
filthy *is* man, which drinketh iniquity
like water?
17 I will shew thee, hear me; and that
which I have seen I will declare;

18 Which wise men have told from their fathers, and have not hid *it:*

19 Unto whom alone the earth was given, and no stranger passed among them.

20 The wicked man travaileth with pain all *his* days, and the number of years is hidden to the oppressor.

21 A dreadful sound *is* in his ears: in prosperity the destroyer shall come upon him.

22 He believeth not that he shall return out of darkness, and he is waited for of the sword.

23 He wandereth abroad for bread, *saying,* Where *is it?* he knoweth that the day of darkness is ready at his hand.

24 Trouble and anguish shall make him afraid; they shall prevail against him, as a king ready to the battle.

25 For he stretcheth out his hand against God, and strengtheneth himself against the Almighty.

26 He runneth upon him, *even* on *his* neck, upon the thick bosses of his bucklers:

27 Because he covereth his face with his fatness, and maketh collops of fat on *his* flanks.

28 And he dwelleth in desolate cities, *and* in houses which no man inhabiteth, which are ready to become heaps.

29 He shall not be rich, neither shall his substance continue, neither shall he prolong the perfection thereof upon the earth.

30 He shall not depart out of darkness; the flame shall dry up his branches, and by the breath of his mouth shall he go away.

31 Let not him that is deceived trust in vanity: for vanity shall be his recompence.

32 It shall be accomplished before his time, and his branch shall not be green.

33 He shall shake off his unripe grape as the vine, and shall cast off his flower as the olive.

34 For the congregation of hypocrites *shall be* desolate, and fire shall consume the tabernacles of bribery.

35 They conceive mischief, and bring forth vanity, and their belly prepareth deceit.

CHAPTER 16

THEN Job answered and said,

2 I have heard many such things: miserable comforters *are* ye all.

3 Shall vain words have an end? or what emboldeneth thee that thou answerest?

4 I also could speak as ye *do:* if your soul were in my soul's stead, I could heap up words against you, and shake mine head at you.

5 *But* I would strengthen you with my mouth, and the moving of my lips should asswage *your grief.*

6 Though I speak, my grief is not asswaged: and *though* I forbear, what am I eased?

7 But now he hath made me weary: thou hast made desolate all my company.

8 And thou hast filled me with wrinkles, *which* is a witness *against me:* and my leanness rising up in me beareth witness to my face.

9 He teareth *me* in his wrath, who hateth me: he gnasheth upon me with his teeth; mine enemy sharpeneth his eyes upon me.

10 They have gaped upon me with their mouth; they have smitten me upon the cheek reproachfully; they have gathered themselves together against me.

11 God hath delivered me to the ungodly, and turned me over into the hands of the wicked.

12 I was at ease, but he hath broken me asunder: he hath also taken *me* by my neck, and shaken me to pieces, and set me up for his mark.

13 His archers compass me round about, he cleaveth my reins asunder, and doth not spare; he poureth out my gall upon the ground.

14 He breaketh me with breach upon breach, he runneth upon me like a giant.

15 I have sewed sackcloth upon my skin, and defiled my horn in the dust.

16 My face is foul with weeping, and on my eyelids *is* the shadow of death;

17 Not for *any* injustice in mine hands: also my prayer *is* pure.

18 O earth, cover not thou my blood, and let my cry have no place.

19 Also now, behold, my witness *is* in heaven, and my record *is* on high.

20 My friends scorn me: *but* mine eye poureth out *tears* unto God.

21 O that one might plead for a man with God, as a man *pleadeth* for his neighbour!

22 When a few years are come, then I shall go the way *whence* I shall not return.

CHAPTER 17

MY breath is corrupt, my days are extinct, the graves *are ready* for me.

2 *Are there* not mockers with me? and doth not mine eye continue in their provocation?

3 Lay down now, put me in a surety

with thee; who *is* he *that* will strike hands with me?

4 For thou hast hid their heart from understanding: therefore shalt thou not exalt *them*.

5 He that speaketh flattery to *his* friends, even the eyes of his children shall fail.

6 He hath made me also a byword of the people; and aforetime I was as a tabret.

7 Mine eye also is dim by reason of sorrow, and all my members *are* as a shadow.

8 Upright *men* shall be astonied at this, and the innocent shall stir up himself against the hypocrite.

9 The righteous also shall hold on his way, and he that hath clean hands shall be stronger and stronger.

10 But as for you all, do ye return, and come now: for I cannot find *one* wise *man* among you.

11 My days are past, my purposes are broken off, *even* the thoughts of my heart.

12 They change the night into day: the light *is* short because of darkness.

13 If I wait, the grave *is* mine house: I have made my bed in the darkness.

14 I have said to corruption, Thou *art* my father: to the worm, *Thou art* my mother, and my sister.

15 And where *is* now my hope? as for my hope, who shall see it?

16 They shall go down to the bars of the pit, when *our* rest together *is* in the dust.

CHAPTER 18

THEN answered Bildad the Shū'hīte, and said,

2 How long *will it be ere* ye make an end of words? mark, and afterwards we will speak.

3 Wherefore are we counted as beasts, *and* reputed vile in your sight?

4 He teareth himself in his anger: shall the earth be forsaken for thee? and shall the rock be removed out of his place?

5 Yea, the light of the wicked shall be put out, and the spark of his fire shall not shine.

6 The light shall be dark in his tabernacle, and his candle shall be put out with him.

7 The steps of his strength shall be straitened, and his own counsel shall cast him down.

8 For he is cast into a net by his own feet, and he walketh upon a snare.

9 The gin shall take *him* by the heel, *and* the robber shall prevail against him.

10 The snare *is* laid for him in the ground, and a trap for him in the way.

11 Terrors shall make him afraid on every side, and shall drive him to his feet.

12 His strength shall be hungerbitten, and destruction *shall be* ready at his side.

13 It shall devour the strength of his skin: *even* the firstborn of death shall devour his strength.

14 His confidence shall be rooted out of his tabernacle, and it shall bring him to the king of terrors.

15 It shall dwell in his tabernacle, because *it is* none of his: brimstone shall be scattered upon his habitation.

16 His roots shall be dried up beneath, and above shall his branch be cut off.

17 His remembrance shall perish from the earth, and he shall have no name in the street.

18 He shall be driven from light into darkness, and chased out of the world.

19 He shall neither have son nor nephew among his people, nor any remaining in his dwellings.

20 They that come after *him* shall be astonied at his day, as they that went before were affrighted.

21 Surely such *are* the dwellings of the wicked, and this *is* the place *of him that* knoweth not God.

CHAPTER 19

THEN Job answered and said,

2 How long will ye vex my soul, and break me in pieces with words?

3 These ten times have ye reproached me: ye are not ashamed *that* ye make yourselves strange to me.

4 And be it indeed *that* I have erred, mine error remaineth with myself.

5 If indeed ye will magnify *yourselves* against me, and plead against me my reproach:

6 Know now that God hath overthrown me, and hath compassed me with his net.

7 Behold, I cry out of wrong, but I am not heard: I cry aloud, but *there is* no judgment.

8 He hath fenced up my way that I cannot pass, and he hath set darkness in my paths.

9 He hath stripped me of my glory, and taken the crown *from* my head.

10 He hath destroyed me on every side, and I am gone: and mine hope hath he removed like a tree.

11 He hath also kindled his wrath against me, and he counteth me unto him as *one of* his enemies.

12 His troops come together, and

raise up their way against me, and encamp round about my tabernacle.
13 He hath put my brethren far from me, and mine acquaintance are verily estranged from me.
14 My kinsfolk have failed, and my familiar friends have forgotten me.
15 They that dwell in mine house, and my maids, count me for a stranger: I am an alien in their sight.
16 I called my servant, and he gave *me* no answer; I intreated him with my mouth.
17 My breath is strange to my wife, though I intreated for the children's *sake* of mine own body.
18 Yea, young children despised me; I arose, and they spake against me.
19 All my inward friends abhorred me: and they whom I loved are turned against me.
20 My bone cleaveth to my skin and to my flesh, and I am escaped with the skin of my teeth.
21 Have pity upon me, have pity upon me, O ye my friends; for the hand of God hath touched me.
22 Why do ye persecute me as God, and are not satisfied with my flesh?
23 Oh that my words were now written! oh that they were printed in a book!
24 That they were graven with an iron pen and lead in the rock for ever!
25 For I know *that* my redeemer liveth, and *that* he shall stand at the latter *day* upon the earth:
26 And *though* after my skin *worms* destroy this *body*, yet in my flesh shall I see God:
27 Whom I shall see for myself, and mine eyes shall behold, and not another; *though* my reins be consumed within me.
28 But ye should say, Why persecute we him, seeing the root of the matter is found in me?
29 Be ye afraid of the sword: for wrath *bringeth* the punishments of the sword, that ye may know *there is* a judgment.

CHAPTER 20

THEN answered Zō'phar the Nā'a-math-īte, and said,
2 Therefore do my thoughts cause me to answer, and for *this* I make haste.
3 I have heard the check of my reproach, and the spirit of my understanding causeth me to answer.
4 Knowest thou *not* this of old, since man was placed upon earth,
5 That the triumphing of the wicked *is* short, and the joy of the hypocrite *but* for a moment?
6 Though his excellency mount up to the heavens, and his head reach unto the clouds;
7 *Yet* he shall perish for ever like his own dung: they which have seen him shall say, Where *is* he?
8 He shall fly away as a dream, and shall not be found: yea, he shall be chased away as a vision of the night.
9 The eye also *which* saw him shall *see him* no more; neither shall his place any more behold him.
10 His children shall seek to please the poor, and his hands shall restore their goods.
11 His bones are full *of the sin* of his youth, which shall lie down with him in the dust.
12 Though wickedness be sweet in his mouth, *though* he hide it under his tongue;
13 *Though* he spare it, and forsake it not; but keep it still within his mouth:
14 *Yet* his meat in his bowels is turned, *it is* the gall of asps within him.
15 He hath swallowed down riches, and he shall vomit them up again: God shall cast them out of his belly.
16 He shall suck the poison of asps: the viper's tongue shall slay him.
17 He shall not see the rivers, the floods, the brooks of honey and butter.
18 That which he laboured for shall he restore, and shall not swallow *it* down: according to *his* substance *shall* the restitution *be*, and he shall not rejoice *therein*.
19 Because he hath oppressed *and* hath forsaken the poor; *because* he hath violently taken away an house which he builded not;
20 Surely he shall not feel quietness in his belly, he shall not save of that which he desired.
21 There shall none of his meat be left; therefore shall no man look for his goods.
22 In the fulness of his sufficiency he shall be in straits: every hand of the wicked shall come upon him.
23 *When* he is about to fill his belly, *God* shall cast the fury of his wrath upon him, and shall rain *it* upon him while he is eating.
24 He shall flee from the iron weapon, *and* the bow of steel shall strike him through.
25 It is drawn, and cometh out of the body; yea, the glittering sword cometh out of his gall: terrors *are* upon him.
26 All darkness *shall be* hid in his secret places: a fire not blown shall consume him; it shall go ill with him that is left in his tabernacle.
27 The heaven shall reveal his iniq-

uity; and the earth shall rise up against
him.
28 The increase of his house shall de-
part, *and his goods* shall flow away in
the day of his wrath.
29 This *is* the portion of a wicked man
from God, and the heritage appointed
unto him by God.

CHAPTER 21

BUT Job answered and said,
2 Hear diligently my speech, and let
this be your consolations.
3 Suffer me that I may speak; and af-
ter that I have spoken, mock on.
4 As for me, *is* my complaint to man?
and if *it were so*, why should not my
spirit be troubled?
5 Mark me, and be astonished, and
lay *your* hand upon *your* mouth.
6 Even when I remember I am afraid,
and trembling taketh hold on my flesh.
7 Wherefore do the wicked live, be-
come old, yea, are mighty in power?
8 Their seed is established in their
sight with them, and their offspring be-
fore their eyes.
9 Their houses *are* safe from fear,
neither *is* the rod of God upon them.
10 Their bull gendereth, and faileth
not; their cow calveth, and casteth not
her calf.
11 They send forth their little ones
like a flock, and their children dance.
12 They take the timbrel and harp,
and rejoice at the sound of the organ.
13 They spend their days in wealth,
and in a moment go down to the grave.
14 Therefore they say unto God, De-
part from us; for we desire not the
knowledge of thy ways.
15 What *is* the Almighty, that we
should serve him? and what profit
should we have, if we pray unto him?
16 Lo, their good *is* not in their hand:
the counsel of the wicked is far from
me.
17 How oft is the candle of the
wicked put out! and *how oft* cometh
their destruction upon them! *God* dis-
tributeth sorrows in his anger.
18 They are as stubble before the
wind, and as chaff that the storm carri-
eth away.
19 God layeth up his iniquity for his
children: he rewardeth him, and he
shall know *it*.
20 His eyes shall see his destruction,
and he shall drink of the wrath of the
Almighty.
21 For what pleasure *hath* he in his
house after him, when the number of
his months is cut off in the midst?
22 Shall *any* teach God knowledge?
seeing he judgeth those that are high.
23 One dieth in his full strength,
being wholly at ease and quiet.
24 His breasts are full of milk, and his
bones are moistened with marrow.
25 And another dieth in the bitter-
ness of his soul, and never eateth with
pleasure.
26 They shall lie down alike in the
dust, and the worms shall cover them.
27 Behold, I know your thoughts, and
the devices *which* ye wrongfully
imagine against me.
28 For ye say, Where *is* the house of
the prince? and where *are* the dwelling
places of the wicked?
29 Have ye not asked them that go by
the way? and do ye not know their to-
kens,
30 That the wicked is reserved to the
day of destruction? they shall be
brought forth to the day of wrath.
31 Who shall declare his way to his
face? and who shall repay him *what* he
hath done?
32 Yet shall he be brought to the
grave, and shall remain in the tomb.
33 The clods of the valley shall be
sweet unto him, and every man shall
draw after him, as *there are* innumer-
able before him.
34 How then comfort ye me in vain,
seeing in your answers there remaineth
falsehood?

CHAPTER 22

THEN Ĕl'i-phăz the Tē'man-īte an-
swered and said,
2 Can a man be profitable unto God,
as he that is wise may be profitable
unto himself?
3 *Is it* any pleasure to the Almighty,
that thou art righteous? or *is it* gain *to*
him, that thou makest thy ways per-
fect?
4 Will he reprove thee for fear of
thee? will he enter with thee into judg-
ment?
5 *Is* not thy wickedness great? and
thine iniquities infinite?
6 For thou hast taken a pledge from
thy brother for nought, and stripped
the naked of their clothing.
7 Thou hast not given water to the
weary to drink, and thou hast with-
holden bread from the hungry.
8 But *as for* the mighty man, he had
the earth; and the honourable man
dwelt in it.
9 Thou hast sent widows away emp-
ty, and the arms of the fatherless have
been broken.
10 Therefore snares *are* round about
thee, and sudden fear troubleth thee;
11 Or darkness, *that* thou canst not

see; and abundance of waters cover
thee.
12 *Is* not God in the height of heaven?
and behold the height of the stars, how
high they are!
13 And thou sayest, How doth God
know? can he judge through the dark
cloud?
14 Thick clouds *are* a covering to
him, that he seeth not; and he walketh
in the circuit of heaven.
15 Hast thou marked the old way
which wicked men have trodden?
16 Which were cut down out of time,
whose foundation was overflown with
a flood:
17 Which said unto God, Depart from
us: and what can the Almighty do for
them?
18 Yet he filled their houses with
good *things:* but the counsel of the
wicked is far from me.
19 The righteous see *it*, and are glad:
and the innocent laugh them to scorn.
20 Whereas our substance is not cut
down, but the remnant of them the fire
consumeth.
21 Acquaint now thyself with him,
and be at peace: thereby good shall
come unto thee.
22 Receive, I pray thee, the law from
his mouth, and lay up his words in thine
heart.
23 If thou return to the Almighty,
thou shalt be built up, thou shalt put
away iniquity far from thy tabernacles.
24 Then shalt thou lay up gold as
dust, and the *gold* of Ō'phir as the
stones of the brooks.
25 Yea, the Almighty shall be thy de-
fence, and thou shalt have plenty of sil-
ver.
26 For then shalt thou have thy de-
light in the Almighty, and shalt lift up
thy face unto God.
27 Thou shalt make thy prayer unto
him, and he shall hear thee, and thou
shalt pay thy vows.
28 Thou shalt also decree a thing, and
it shall be established unto thee: and
the light shall shine upon thy ways.
29 When *men* are cast down, then
thou shalt say, *There is* lifting up; and
he shall save the humble person.
30 He shall deliver the island of the
innocent: and it is delivered by the pure-
ness of thine hands.

CHAPTER 23

THEN Job answered and said,
2 Even to day *is* my complaint bitter:
my stroke is heavier than my groaning.
3 Oh that I knew where I might find
him! *that* I might come *even* to his seat!
4 I would order *my* cause before him,
and fill my mouth with arguments.
5 I would know the words *which* he
would answer me, and understand
what he would say unto me.
6 Will he plead against me with *his*
great power? No; but he would put
strength in me.
7 There the righteous might dispute
with him; so should I be delivered for
ever from my judge.
8 Behold, I go forward, but he *is* not
there; and backward, but I cannot per-
ceive him:
9 On the left hand, where he doth
work, but I cannot behold *him;* he
hideth himself on the right hand, that I
cannot see *him;*
10 But he knoweth the way that I
take: *when* he hath tried me, I shall
come forth as gold.
11 My foot hath held his steps, his
way have I kept, and not declined.
12 Neither have I gone back from the
commandment of his lips; I have
esteemed the words of his mouth more
than my necessary *food.*
13 But he *is* in one *mind*, and who can
turn him? and *what* his soul desireth,
even *that* he doeth.
14 For he performeth *the thing that is*
appointed for me: and many such
things are with him.
15 Therefore am I troubled at his
presence: when I consider, I am afraid
of him.
16 For God maketh my heart soft,
and the Almighty troubleth me:
17 Because I was not cut off before
the darkness, *neither* hath he covered
the darkness from my face.

CHAPTER 24

WHY, seeing times are not hidden
from the Almighty, do they that know
him not see his days?
2 *Some* remove the landmarks; they
violently take away flocks, and feed
thereof.
3 They drive away the ass of the
fatherless, they take the widow's ox for
a pledge.
4 They turn the needy out of the way:
the poor of the earth hide themselves
together.
5 Behold, *as* wild asses in the desert,
go they forth to their work; rising be-
times for a prey: the wilderness *yield-
eth* food for them *and* for *their* chil-
dren.
6 They reap *every one* his corn in the
field: and they gather the vintage of the
wicked.
7 They cause the naked to lodge

without clothing, that *they have* no covering in the cold.
8 They are wet with the showers of the mountains, and embrace the rock for want of a shelter.
9 They pluck the fatherless from the breast, and take a pledge of the poor.
10 They cause *him* to go naked without clothing, and they take away the sheaf *from* the hungry;
11 *Which* make oil within their walls, *and* tread *their* winepresses, and suffer thirst.
12 Men groan from out of the city, and the soul of the wounded crieth out: yet God layeth not folly *to them*.
13 They are of those that rebel against the light; they know not the ways thereof, nor abide in the paths thereof.
14 The murderer rising with the light killeth the poor and needy, and in the night is as a thief.
15 The eye also of the adulterer waiteth for the twilight, saying, No eye shall see me: and disguiseth *his* face.
16 In the dark they dig through houses, *which* they had marked for themselves in the daytime: they know not the light.
17 For the morning *is* to them even as the shadow of death: if *one* know *them, they are in* the terrors of the shadow of death.
18 He *is* swift as the waters; their portion is cursed in the earth: he beholdeth not the way of the vineyards.
19 Drought and heat consume the snow waters: *so doth* the grave *those which* have sinned.
20 The womb shall forget him; the worm shall feed sweetly on him; he shall be no more remembered; and wickedness shall be broken as a tree.
21 He evil entreateth the barren *that* beareth not: and doeth not good to the widow.
22 He draweth also the mighty with his power: he riseth up, and no *man* is sure of life.
23 *Though* it be given him *to be* in safety, whereon he resteth; yet his eyes *are* upon their ways.
24 They are exalted for a little while, but are gone and brought low; they are taken out of the way as all *other*, and cut off as the tops of the ears of corn.
25 And if *it be* not *so* now, who will make me a liar, and make my speech nothing worth?

CHAPTER 25

THEN answered Bildad the Shū'hīte, and said,
2 Dominion and fear *are* with him, he maketh peace in his high places.
3 Is there any number of his armies? and upon whom doth not his light arise?
4 How then can man be justified with God? or how can he be clean *that is* born of a woman?
5 Behold even to the moon, and it shineth not; yea, the stars are not pure in his sight.
6 How much less man, *that is* a worm? and the son of man, *which is* a worm?

CHAPTER 26

BUT Job answered and said,
2 How hast thou helped *him that is* without power? *how* savest thou the arm *that hath* no strength?
3 How hast thou counselled *him that hath* no wisdom? and *how* hast thou plentifully declared the thing as it is?
4 To whom hast thou uttered words? and whose spirit came from thee?
5 Dead *things* are formed from under the waters, and the inhabitants thereof.
6 Hell *is* naked before him, and destruction hath no covering.
7 He stretcheth out the north over the empty place, *and* hangeth the earth upon nothing.
8 He bindeth up the waters in his thick clouds; and the cloud is not rent under them.
9 He holdeth back the face of his throne, *and* spreadeth his cloud upon it.
10 He hath compassed the waters with bounds, until the day and night come to an end.
11 The pillars of heaven tremble and are astonished at his reproof.
12 He divideth the sea with his power, and by his understanding he smiteth through the proud.
13 By his spirit he hath garnished the heavens; his hand hath formed the crooked serpent.
14 Lo, these *are* parts of his ways: but how little a portion is heard of him? but the thunder of his power who can understand?

CHAPTER 27

MOREOVER Job continued his parable, and said,
2 *As* God liveth, *who* hath taken away my judgment; and the Almighty, *who* hath vexed my soul;
3 All the while my breath *is* in me, and the spirit of God *is* in my nostrils;
4 My lips shall not speak wickedness, nor my tongue utter deceit.
5 God forbid that I should justify you:

till I die I will not remove mine integrity
from me.
6 My righteousness I hold fast, and
will not let it go: my heart shall not
reproach *me* so long as I live.
7 Let mine enemy be as the wicked,
and he that riseth up against me as the
unrighteous.
8 For what *is* the hope of the hypo-
crite, though he hath gained, when God
taketh away his soul?
9 Will God hear his cry when trouble
cometh upon him?
10 Will he delight himself in the Al-
mighty? will he always call upon God?
11 I will teach you by the hand of
God: *that* which *is* with the Almighty
will I not conceal.
12 Behold, all ye yourselves have
seen *it;* why then are ye thus altogether
vain?
13 This *is* the portion of a wicked man
with God, and the heritage of oppres-
sors, *which* they shall receive of the Al-
mighty.
14 If his children be multiplied, *it is*
for the sword: and his offspring shall
not be satisfied with bread.
15 Those that remain of him shall be
buried in death: and his widows shall
not weep.
16 Though he heap up silver as the
dust, and prepare raiment as the clay;
17 He may prepare *it,* but the just
shall put *it* on, and the innocent shall
divide the silver.
18 He buildeth his house as a moth,
and as a booth *that* the keeper maketh.
19 The rich man shall lie down, but he
shall not be gathered: he openeth his
eyes, and he *is* not.
20 Terrors take hold on him as wa-
ters, a tempest stealeth him away in the
night.
21 The east wind carrieth him away,
and he departeth: and as a storm
hurleth him out of his place.
22 For *God* shall cast upon him, and
not spare: he would fain flee out of his
hand.
23 *Men* shall clap their hands at him,
and shall hiss him out of his place.

CHAPTER 28

SURELY there is a vein for the silver,
and a place for gold *where* they fine *it.*
2 Iron is taken out of the earth, and
brass *is* molten *out of* the stone.
3 He setteth an end to darkness, and
searcheth out all perfection: the stones
of darkness, and the shadow of death.
4 The flood breaketh out from the
inhabitant: *even the waters* forgotten
of the foot: they are dried up, they are
gone away from men.
5 *As for* the earth, out of it cometh
bread: and under it is turned up as it
were fire.
6 The stones of it *are* the place of
sapphires: and it hath dust of gold.
7 *There is* a path which no fowl
knoweth, and which the vulture's eye
hath not seen:
8 The lion's whelps have not trodden
it, nor the fierce lion passed by it.
9 He putteth forth his hand upon the
rock; he overturneth the mountains by
the roots.
10 He cutteth out rivers among the
rocks; and his eye seeth every precious
thing.
11 He bindeth the floods from over-
flowing; and *the thing that is* hid bring-
eth he forth to light.
12 But where shall wisdom be found?
and where *is* the place of understand-
ing?
13 Man knoweth not the price there-
of; neither is it found in the land of
the living.
14 The depth saith, It *is* not in me: and
the sea saith, *It is* not with me.
15 It cannot be gotten for gold,
neither shall silver be weighed *for* the
price thereof.
16 It cannot be valued with the gold
of Ōphir, with the precious onyx, or the
sapphire.
17 The gold and the crystal cannot
equal it: and the exchange of it *shall not
be for* jewels of fine gold.
18 No mention shall be made of coral,
or of pearls: for the price of wisdom *is*
above rubies.
19 The topaz of Ē-thĭ-ō′pĭ-a shall not
equal it, neither shall it be valued with
pure gold.
20 Whence then cometh wisdom?
and where *is* the place of understand-
ing?
21 Seeing it is hid from the eyes of all
living, and kept close from the fowls of
the air.
22 Destruction and death say, We
have heard the fame thereof with our
ears.
23 God understandeth the way there-
of, and he knoweth the place there-
of.
24 For he looketh to the ends of the
earth, *and* seeth under the whole
heaven;
25 To make the weight for the winds;
and he weigheth the waters by mea-
sure.
26 When he made a decree for the
rain, and a way for the lightning of the
thunder:
27 Then did he see it, and declare it;
he prepared it, yea, and searched it out.

28 And unto man he said, Behold, the
fear of the Lord, that *is* wisdom; and to
depart from evil *is* understanding.

CHAPTER 29

MOREOVER Job continued his para-
ble, and said,
2 Oh that I were as *in* months past, as
in the days *when* God preserved me;
3 When his candle shined upon my
head, *and when* by his light I walked
through darkness;
4 As I was in the days of my youth,
when the secret of God *was* upon my
tabernacle;
5 When the Almighty *was* yet with
me, *when* my children *were* about me;
6 When I washed my steps with but-
ter, and the rock poured me out rivers
of oil;
7 When I went out to the gate
through the city, *when* I prepared my
seat in the street!
8 The young men saw me, and hid
themselves: and the aged arose, *and*
stood up.
9 The princes refrained talking, and
laid *their* hand on their mouth.
10 The nobles held their peace, and
their tongue cleaved to the roof of their
mouth.
11 When the ear heard *me*, then it
blessed me; and when the eye saw *me*,
it gave witness to me:
12 Because I delivered the poor that
cried, and the fatherless, and *him that*
had none to help him.
13 The blessing of him that was ready
to perish came upon me: and I caused
the widow's heart to sing for joy.
14 I put on righteousness, and it
clothed me: my judgment *was* as a robe
and a diadem.
15 I was eyes to the blind, and feet
was I to the lame.
16 I *was* a father to the poor: and the
cause *which* I knew not I searched out.
17 And I brake the jaws of the
wicked, and plucked the spoil out of his
teeth.
18 Then I said, I shall die in my nest,
and I shall multiply *my* days as the
sand.
19 My root *was* spread out by the wa-
ters, and the dew lay all night upon my
branch.
20 My glory *was* fresh in me, and my
bow was renewed in my hand.
21 Unto me *men* gave ear, and
waited, and kept silence at my counsel.
22 After my words they spake not
again; and my speech dropped upon
them.
23 And they waited for me as for the
rain; and they opened their mouth wide
as for the latter rain.
24 *If* I laughed on them, they believed
it not; and the light of my countenance
they cast not down.
25 I chose out their way, and sat
chief, and dwelt as a king in the army,
as one *that* comforteth the mourners.

CHAPTER 30

BUT now *they that are* younger than I
have me in derision, whose fathers I
would have disdained to have set with
the dogs of my flock.
2 Yea, whereto *might* the strength of
their hands *profit* me, in whom old age
was perished?
3 For want and famine *they were* soli-
tary; fleeing into the wilderness in for-
mer time desolate and waste.
4 Who cut up mallows by the bushes,
and juniper roots *for* their meat.
5 They were driven forth from among
men, (they cried after them as *after* a
thief;)
6 To dwell in the cliffs of the valleys,
in caves of the earth, and *in* the rocks.
7 Among the bushes they brayed; un-
der the nettles they were gathered
together.
8 *They were* children of fools, yea,
children of base men: they were viler
than the earth.
9 And now am I their song, yea, I am
their byword.
10 They abhor me, they flee far from
me, and spare not to spit in my face.
11 Because he hath loosed my cord,
and afflicted me, they have also let
loose the bridle before me.
12 Upon *my* right *hand* rise the
youth; they push away my feet, and
they raise up against me the ways of
their destruction.
13 They mar my path, they set for-
ward my calamity, they have no helper.
14 They came *upon me* as a wide
breaking in *of waters:* in the desolation
they rolled themselves *upon me*.
15 Terrors are turned upon me: they
pursue my soul as the wind: and my
welfare passeth away as a cloud.
16 And now my soul is poured out
upon me; the days of affliction have
taken hold upon me.
17 My bones are pierced in me in the
night season: and my sinews take no
rest.
18 By the great force *of my disease* is
my garment changed: it bindeth me
about as the collar of my coat.
19 He hath cast me into the mire, and
I am become like dust and ashes.
20 I cry unto thee, and thou dost not

hear me: I stand up, and thou regardest me *not*.
21 Thou art become cruel to me: with thy strong hand thou opposest thyself against me.
22 Thou liftest me up to the wind; thou causest me to ride *upon it*, and dissolvest my substance.
23 For I know *that* thou wilt bring me *to* death, and *to* the house appointed for all living.
24 Howbeit he will not stretch out *his* hand to the grave, though they cry in his destruction.
25 Did not I weep for him that was in trouble? was *not* my soul grieved for the poor?
26 When I looked for good, then evil came *unto me*: and when I waited for light, there came darkness.
27 My bowels boiled, and rested not: the days of affliction prevented me.
28 I went mourning without the sun: I stood up, *and* I cried in the congregation.
29 I am a brother to dragons, and a companion to owls.
30 My skin is black upon me, and my bones are burned with heat.
31 My harp also is *turned* to mourning, and my organ into the voice of them that weep.

CHAPTER 31

I MADE a covenant with mine eyes: why then should I think upon a maid?
2 For what portion of God *is there* from above? and *what* inheritance of the Almighty from on high?
3 *Is* not destruction to the wicked? and a strange *punishment* to the workers of iniquity?
4 Doth not he see my ways, and count all my steps?
5 If I have walked with vanity, or if my foot hath hasted to deceit;
6 Let me be weighed in an even balance that God may know mine integrity.
7 If my step hath turned out of the way, and mine heart walked after mine eyes, and if any blot hath cleaved to mine hands;
8 *Then* let me sow, and let another eat; yea, let my offspring be rooted out.
9 If mine heart have been deceived by a woman, or *if* I have laid wait at my neighbour's door;
10 *Then* let my wife grind unto another, and let others bow down upon her.
11 For this *is* an heinous crime; yea, it *is* an iniquity *to be punished by* the judges.
12 For it *is* a fire *that* consumeth to destruction, and would root out all mine increase.
13 If I did despise the cause of my manservant or of my maidservant, when they contended with me;
14 What then shall I do when God riseth up? and when he visiteth, what shall I answer him?
15 Did not he that made me in the womb make him? and did not one fashion us in the womb?
16 If I have withheld the poor from *their* desire, or have caused the eyes of the widow to fail;
17 Or have eaten my morsel myself alone, and the fatherless hath not eaten thereof;
18 (For from my youth he was brought up with me, as *with* a father, and I have guided her from my mother's womb;)
19 If I have seen any perish for want of clothing, or any poor without covering;
20 If his loins have not blessed me, and *if* he were *not* warmed with the fleece of my sheep;
21 If I have lifted up my hand against the fatherless, when I saw my help in the gate:
22 *Then* let mine arm fall from my shoulder blade, and mine arm be broken from the bone.
23 For destruction *from* God *was* a terror to me, and by reason of his highness I could not endure.
24 If I have made gold my hope, or have said to the fine gold, *Thou art* my confidence;
25 If I rejoiced because my wealth *was* great, and because mine hand had gotten much;
26 If I beheld the sun when it shined, or the moon walking *in* brightness;
27 And my heart hath been secretly enticed, or my mouth hath kissed my hand:
28 This also *were* an iniquity *to be punished by* the judge: for I should have denied the God *that is* above.
29 If I rejoiced at the destruction of him that hated me, or lifted up myself when evil found him:
30 Neither have I suffered my mouth to sin by wishing a curse to his soul.
31 If the men of my tabernacle said not, Oh that we had of his flesh! we cannot be satisfied.
32 The stranger did not lodge in the street: *but* I opened my doors to the traveller.
33 If I covered my transgressions as Adam, by hiding mine iniquity in my bosom:
34 Did I fear a great multitude, or did

the contempt of families terrify me, that I kept silence, *and* went not out of the door?

35 Oh that one would hear me! behold, my desire *is, that* the Almighty would answer me, and *that* mine adversary had written a book.

36 Surely I would take it upon my shoulder, *and* bind it *as* a crown to me.

37 I would declare unto him the number of my steps; as a prince would I go near unto him.

38 If my land cry against me, or that the furrows likewise thereof complain;

39 If I have eaten the fruits thereof without money, or have caused the owners thereof to lose their life:

40 Let thistles grow instead of wheat, and cockle instead of barley. The words of Job are ended.

CHAPTER 32

SO these three men ceased to answer Job, because he *was* righteous in his own eyes.

2 Then was kindled the wrath of E-lī'hū the son of Băr'a-chĕl the Bū'zīte, of the kindred of Ram: against Job was his wrath kindled, because he justified himself rather than God.

3 Also against his three friends was his wrath kindled, because they had found no answer, and *yet* had condemned Job.

4 Now E-lī'hū had waited till Job had spoken, because they *were* elder than he.

5 When E-lī'hū saw that *there was* no answer in the mouth of *these* three men, then his wrath was kindled.

6 And E-lī'hū the son of Băr'a-chĕl the Bū'zīte answered and said, I *am* young, and ye *are* very old; wherefore I was afraid, and durst not shew you mine opinion.

7 I said, Days should speak, and multitude of years should teach wisdom.

8 But *there is* a spirit in man: and the inspiration of the Almighty giveth them understanding.

9 Great men are not *always* wise: neither do the aged understand judgment.

10 Therefore I said, Hearken to me; I also will shew mine opinion.

11 Behold, I waited for your words; I gave ear to your reasons, whilst ye searched out what to say.

12 Yea, I attended unto you, and, behold, *there was* none of you that convinced Job, *or* that answered his words:

13 Lest ye should say, We have found out wisdom: God thrusteth him down, not man.

14 Now he hath not directed *his* words against me: neither will I answer him with your speeches.

15 They were amazed, they answered no more: they left off speaking.

16 When I had waited, (for they spake not, but stood still, *and* answered no more;)

17 *I said,* I will answer also my part, I also will shew mine opinion.

18 For I am full of matter, the spirit within me constraineth me.

19 Behold, my belly *is* as wine *which* hath no vent; it is ready to burst like new bottles.

20 I will speak, that I may be refreshed: I will open my lips and answer.

21 Let me not, I pray you, accept any man's person, neither let me give flattering titles unto man.

22 For I know not to give flattering titles; *in so doing* my maker would soon take me away.

CHAPTER 33

WHEREFORE, Job, I pray thee, hear my speeches, and hearken to all my words.

2 Behold, now I have opened my mouth, my tongue hath spoken in my mouth.

3 My words *shall be of* the uprightness of my heart: and my lips shall utter knowledge clearly.

4 The spirit of God hath made me, and the breath of the Almighty hath given me life.

5 If thou canst answer me, set *thy words* in order before me, stand up.

6 Behold, I *am* according to thy wish in God's stead: I also am formed out of the clay.

7 Behold, my terror shall not make thee afraid, neither shall my hand be heavy upon thee.

8 Surely thou hast spoken in mine hearing, and I have heard the voice of *thy* words, *saying,*

9 I am clean without transgression, I *am* innocent; neither *is there* iniquity in me.

10 Behold, he findeth occasions against me, he counteth me for his enemy,

11 He putteth my feet in the stocks, he marketh all my paths.

12 Behold, *in* this thou art not just: I will answer thee, that God is greater than man.

13 Why dost thou strive against him? for he giveth not account of any of his matters.

14 For God speaketh once, yea twice, *yet man* perceiveth it not.

15 In a dream, in a vision of the night, when deep sleep falleth upon men, in slumberings upon the bed;
16 Then he openeth the ears of men, and sealeth their instruction,
17 That he may withdraw man *from his* purpose, and hide pride from man.
18 He keepeth back his soul from the pit, and his life from perishing by the sword.
19 He is chastened also with pain upon his bed, and the multitude of his bones with strong *pain:*
20 So that his life abhorreth bread, and his soul dainty meat.
21 His flesh is consumed away, that it cannot be seen; and his bones *that* were not seen stick out.
22 Yea, his soul draweth near unto the grave, and his life to the destroyers.
23 If there be a messenger with him, an interpreter, one among a thousand, to shew unto man his uprightness:
24 Then he is gracious unto him, and saith, Deliver him from going down to the pit: I have found a ransom.
25 His flesh shall be fresher than a child's: he shall return to the days of his youth:
26 He shall pray unto God, and he will be favourable unto him: and he shall see his face with joy: for he will render unto man his righteousness.
27 He looketh upon men, and *if any* say, I have sinned, and perverted *that which was* right, and it profited me not;
28 He will deliver his soul from going into the pit, and his life shall see the light.
29 Lo, all these *things* worketh God oftentimes with man,
30 To bring back his soul from the pit, to be enlightened with the light of the living.
31 Mark well, O Job, hearken unto me: hold thy peace, and I will speak.
32 If thou hast anything to say, answer me: speak, for I desire to justify thee.
33 If not, hearken unto me: hold thy peace, and I shall teach thee wisdom.

CHAPTER 34

FURTHERMORE E-lī'hū answered and said,
2 Hear my words, O ye wise *men;* and give ear unto me, ye that have knowledge.
3 For the ear trieth words, as the mouth tasteth meat.
4 Let us choose to us judgment: let us know among ourselves what *is* good.
5 For Job hath said, I am righteous: and God hath taken away my judgment.
6 Should I lie against my right? my wound *is* incurable without transgression.
7 What man *is* like Job, *who* drinketh up scorning like water?
8 Which goeth in company with the workers of iniquity, and walketh with wicked men.
9 For he hath said, It profiteth a man nothing that he should delight himself with God.
10 Therefore hearken unto me ye men of understanding: far be it from God, *that he should do* wickedness; and *from* the Almighty, *that he should commit* iniquity.
11 For the work of a man shall he render unto him, and cause every man to find according to *his* ways.
12 Yea, surely God will not do wickedly, neither will the Almighty pervert judgment.
13 Who hath given him a charge over the earth? or who hath disposed the whole world?
14 If he set his heart upon man *if* he gather unto himself his spirit and his breath;
15 All flesh shall perish together, and man shall turn again unto dust.
16 If now *thou hast* understanding, hear this: hearken to the voice of my words.
17 Shall even he that hateth right govern? and wilt thou condemn him that is most just?
18 *Is it fit* to say to a king, *Thou art* wicked? *and* to princes, *Ye are* ungodly?
19 *How much less to him* that accepteth not the persons of princes, nor regardeth the rich more than the poor? for they all *are* the work of his hands.
20 In a moment shall they die, and the people shall be troubled at midnight, and pass away: and the mighty shall be taken away without hand.
21 For his eyes *are* upon the ways of man, and he seeth all his goings.
22 *There is* no darkness, nor shadow of death, where the workers of iniquity may hide themselves.
23 For he will not lay upon man more *than right;* that he should enter into judgment with God.
24 He shall break in pieces mighty men without number, and set others in their stead.
25 Therefore he knoweth their works, and he overturneth *them* in the night, so that they are destroyed.
26 He striketh them as wicked men in the open sight of others;
27 Because they turned back from

him, and would not consider any of his ways:
28 So that they cause the cry of the poor to come unto him, and he heareth the cry of the afflicted.
29 When he giveth quietness, who then can make trouble? and when he hideth *his* face, who then can behold him? whether *it be done* against a nation, or against a man only:
30 That the hypocrite reign not, lest the people be ensnared.
31 Surely it is meet to be said unto God, I have borne *chastisement*, I will not offend *any more*:
32 *That which* I see not teach thou me: if I have done iniquity, I will do no more.
33 *Should it be* according to thy mind? he will recompense it, whether thou refuse, or whether thou choose; and not I: therefore speak what thou knowest.
34 Let men of understanding tell me, and let a wise man hearken unto me.
35 Job hath spoken without knowledge, and his words *were* without wisdom.
36 My desire *is that* Job may be tried unto the end because of *his* answers for wicked men.
37 For he addeth rebellion unto his sin, he clappeth *his hands* among us, and multiplieth his words against God.

CHAPTER 35

E-LĪ'HŪ spake moreover, and said,
2 Thinkest thou this to be right, *that* thou saidst, My righteousness *is* more than God's?
3 For thou saidst, What advantage will it be unto thee? *and*, What profit shall I have, *if I be cleansed* from my sin?
4 I will answer thee, and thy companions with thee.
5 Look unto the heavens, and see; and behold the clouds *which* are higher than thou.
6 If thou sinnest, what doest thou against him? or *if* thy transgressions be multiplied, what doest thou unto him?
7 If thou be righteous, what givest thou him? or what receiveth he of thine hand?
8 Thy wickedness *may hurt* a man as thou *art*; and thy righteousness *may profit* the son of man.
9 By reason of the multitude of oppressions they make *the oppressed* to cry: they cry out by reason of the arm of the mighty.
10 But none saith, Where *is* God my maker, who giveth songs in the night;
11 Who teacheth us more than the beasts of the earth, and maketh us wiser than the fowls of heaven?
12 There they cry, but none giveth answer, because of the pride of evil men.
13 Surely God will not hear vanity, neither will the Almighty regard it.
14 Although thou sayest thou shalt not see him, *yet* judgment *is* before him; therefore trust thou in him.
15 But now, because *it is* not *so*, he hath visited in his anger; yet he knoweth *it* not in great extremity:
16 Therefore doth Job open his mouth in vain; he multiplieth words without knowledge.

CHAPTER 36

E-LĪ'HŪ also proceeded, and said,
2 Suffer me a little, and I will shew thee that *I have* yet to speak on God's behalf.
3 I will fetch my knowledge from afar, and will ascribe righteousness to my Maker.
4 For truly my words *shall* not *be* false: he that is perfect in knowledge *is* with thee.
5 Behold, God *is* mighty, and despiseth not *any*: *he is* mighty in strength *and* wisdom.
6 He preserveth not the life of the wicked: but giveth right to the poor.
7 He withdraweth not his eyes from the righteous: but with kings *are they* on the throne; yea, he doth establish them for ever, and they are exalted.
8 And if *they be* bound in fetters, *and* be holden in cords of affliction;
9 Then he sheweth them their work, and their transgressions that they have exceeded.
10 He openeth also their ear to discipline, and commandeth that they return from iniquity.
11 If they obey and serve *him*, they shall spend their days in prosperity, and their years in pleasures.
12 But if they obey not, they shall perish by the sword, and they shall die without knowledge.
13 But the hypocrites in heart heap up wrath: they cry not when he bindeth them.
14 They die in youth, and their life *is* among the unclean.
15 He delivereth the poor in his affliction, and openeth their ears in oppression.
16 Even so would he have removed thee out of the strait *into* a broad place, where *there is* no straitness: and that which should be set on thy table *should be* full of fatness.
17 But thou hast fulfilled the judg-

ment of the wicked: judgment and justice take hold *on thee.*

18 Because *there is* wrath, *beware* lest he take thee away with *his* stroke: then a great ransom cannot deliver thee.

19 Will he esteem thy riches? *no,* not gold, nor all the forces of strength.

20 Desire not the night, when people are cut off in their place.

21 Take heed, regard not iniquity: for this hast thou chosen rather than affliction.

22 Behold, God exalteth by his power: who teacheth like him?

23 Who hath enjoined him his way? or who can say, Thou hast wrought iniquity?

24 Remember that thou magnify his work, which men behold.

25 Every man may see it; man may behold *it* afar off.

26 Behold, God *is* great, and we know *him* not, neither can the number of his years be searched out.

27 For he maketh small the drops of water: they pour down rain according to the vapour thereof:

28 Which the clouds do drop *and* distil upon man abundantly.

29 Also can *any* understand the spreadings of the clouds, *or* the noise of his tabernacle?

30 Behold, he spreadeth his light upon it, and covereth the bottom of the sea.

31 For by them judgeth he the people; he giveth meat in abundance.

32 With clouds he covereth the light; and commandeth it *not to shine* by *the cloud* that cometh betwixt.

33 The noise thereof sheweth concerning it, the cattle also concerning the vapour.

CHAPTER 37

AT this also my heart trembleth, and is moved out of his place.

2 Hear attentively the noise of his voice, and the sound *that* goeth out of his mouth.

3 He directeth it under the whole heaven, and his lightning unto the ends of the earth.

4 After it a voice roareth: he thundereth with the voice of his excellency; and he will not stay them when his voice is heard.

5 God thundereth marvellously with his voice; great things doeth he, which we cannot comprehend.

6 For he saith to the snow, Be thou *on* the earth; likewise to the small rain, and to the great rain of his strength.

7 He sealeth up the hand of every man; that all men may know his work.

8 Then the beasts go into dens, and remain in their places.

9 Out of the south cometh the whirlwind: and cold out of the north.

10 By the breath of God frost is given: and the breadth of the waters is straitened.

11 Also by watering he wearieth the thick cloud: he scattereth his bright cloud:

12 And it is turned round about by his counsels: that they may do whatsoever he commandeth them upon the face of the world in the earth.

13 He causeth it to come, whether for correction, or for his land, or for mercy.

14 Hearken unto this, O Job: stand still, and consider the wondrous works of God.

15 Dost thou know when God disposed them, and caused the light of his cloud to shine?

16 Dost thou know the balancings of the clouds, the wondrous works of him which is perfect in knowledge?

17 How thy garments *are* warm, when he quieteth the earth by the south *wind?*

18 Hast thou with him spread out the sky, *which is* strong, *and* as a molten looking glass?

19 Teach us what we shall say unto him; *for* we cannot order *our speech* by reason of darkness.

20 Shall it be told him that I speak? if a man speak, surely he shall be swallowed up.

21 And now *men* see not the bright light which *is* in the clouds: but the wind passeth, and cleanseth them.

22 Fair weather cometh out of the north: with God *is* terrible majesty.

23 *Touching* the Almighty, we cannot find him out: *he is* excellent in power, and in judgment, and in plenty of justice: he will not afflict.

24 Men do therefore fear him: he respecteth not any *that are* wise of heart.

CHAPTER 38

THEN the LORD answered Job out of the whirlwind, and said,

2 Who *is* this that darkeneth counsel by words without knowledge?

3 Gird up now thy loins like a man: for I will demand of thee, and answer thou me.

4 Where wast thou when I laid the foundations of the earth? declare, if thou hast understanding.

5 Who hath laid the measures thereof, if thou knowest? or who hath stretched the line upon it?

6 Whereupon are the foundations thereof fastened? or who laid the corner stone thereof;

7 When the morning stars sang together, and all the sons of God shouted for joy?

8 Or *who* shut up the sea with doors, when it brake forth, *as if* it had issued out of the womb?

9 When I made the cloud the garment thereof, and thick darkness a swaddlingband for it,

10 And brake up for it my decreed *place*, and set bars and doors,

11 And said, Hitherto shalt thou come, but no further: and here shall thy proud waves be stayed?

12 Hast thou commanded the morning since thy days; *and* caused the dayspring to know his place;

13 That it might take hold of the ends of the earth, that the wicked might be shaken out of it?

14 It is turned as clay *to* the seal; and they stand as a garment.

15 And from the wicked their light is withholden, and the high arm shall be broken.

16 Hast thou entered into the springs of the sea? or hast thou walked in the search of the depth?

17 Have the gates of death been opened unto thee? or hast thou seen the doors of the shadow of death?

18 Hast thou perceived the breadth of the earth? declare if thou knowest it all.

19 Where *is* the way *where* light dwelleth? and *as for* darkness, where *is* the place thereof,

20 That thou shouldest take it to the bound thereof, and that thou shouldest know the paths *to* the house thereof?

21 Knowest thou *it*, because thou wast then born? or *because* the number of thy days *is* great?

22 Hast thou entered into the treasures of the snow? or hast thou seen the treasures of the hail,

23 Which I have reserved against the time of trouble, against the day of battle and war?

24 By what way is the light parted, *which* scattereth the east wind upon the earth?

25 Who hath divided a watercourse for the overflowing of waters, or a way for the lightning of thunder;

26 To cause it to rain on the earth, *where* no man *is*; *on* the wilderness, wherein *there is* no man;

27 To satisfy the desolate and waste *ground;* and to cause the bud of the tender herb to spring forth?

28 Hath the rain a father? or who hath begotten the drops of dew?

29 Out of whose womb came the ice? and the hoary frost of heaven, who hath gendered it?

30 The waters are hid as *with* a stone, and the face of the deep is frozen.

31 Canst thou bind the sweet influences of Plē'ia-dēṡ, or loose the bands of Ō-rī'on?

32 Canst thou bring forth Măz'za-rŏth in his season? or canst thou guide Ärc-tū'rus with his sons?

33 Knowest thou the ordinances of heaven? canst thou set the dominion thereof in the earth?

34 Canst thou lift up thy voice to the clouds, that abundance of waters may cover thee?

35 Canst thou send lightnings, that they may go, and say unto thee, Here we *are?*

36 Who hath put wisdom in the inward parts? or who hath given understanding to the heart?

37 Who can number the clouds in wisdom? or who can stay the bottles of heaven,

38 When the dust groweth into hardness, and the clods cleave fast together?

39 Wilt thou hunt the prey for the lion? or fill the appetite of the young lions,

40 When they couch in *their* dens, *and* abide in the covert to lie in wait?

41 Who provideth for the raven his food? when his young ones cry unto God, they wander for lack of meat.

CHAPTER 39

KNOWEST thou the time when the wild goats of the rock bring forth? *or* canst thou mark when the hinds do calve?

2 Canst thou number the months *that* they fulfil? or knowest thou the time when they bring forth?

3 They bow themselves, they bring forth their young ones, they cast out their sorrows.

4 Their young ones are in good liking, they grow up with corn; they go forth, and return not unto them.

5 Who hath sent out the wild ass free? or who hath loosed the bands of the wild ass?

6 Whose house I have made the wilderness, and the barren land his dwellings.

7 He scorneth the multitude of the city, neither regardeth he the crying of the driver.

8 The range of the mountains *is* his

pasture, and he searcheth after every green thing.

9 Will the unicorn be willing to serve thee, or abide by thy crib?

10 Canst thou bind the unicorn with his band in the furrow? or will he harrow the valleys after thee?

11 Wilt thou trust him, because his strength *is* great? or wilt thou leave thy labour to him?

12 Wilt thou believe him, that he will bring home thy seed, and gather *it into* thy barn?

13 *Gavest thou* the goodly wings unto the peacocks? or wings and feathers unto the ostrich?

14 Which leaveth her eggs in the earth, and warmeth them in dust,

15 And forgetteth that the foot may crush them, or that the wild beast may break them.

16 She is hardened against her young ones, as though *they were* not hers: her labour is in vain without fear;

17 Because God hath deprived her of wisdom, neither hath he imparted to her understanding.

18 What time she lifteth up herself on high, she scorneth the horse and his rider.

19 Hast thou given the horse strength? hast thou clothed his neck with thunder?

20 Canst thou make him afraid as a grasshopper? the glory of his nostrils *is* terrible.

21 He paweth in the valley, and rejoiceth in *his* strength: he goeth on to meet the armed men.

22 He mocketh at fear, and is not affrighted; neither turneth he back from the sword.

23 The quiver rattleth against him, the glittering spear and the shield.

24 He swalloweth the ground with fierceness and rage: neither believeth he that *it is* the sound of the trumpet.

25 He saith among the trumpets, Ha, ha; and he smelleth the battle afar off, the thunder of the captains, and the shouting.

26 Doth the hawk fly by thy wisdom, *and* stretch her wings toward the south?

27 Doth the eagle mount up at thy command, and make her nest on high?

28 She dwelleth and abideth on the rock, upon the crag of the rock, and the strong place.

29 From thence she seeketh the prey, *and* her eyes behold afar off.

30 Her young ones also suck up blood: and where the slain *are*, there *is* she.

CHAPTER 40

MOREOVER the LORD answered Job, and said,

2 Shall he that contendeth with the Almighty instruct *him?* he that reproveth God, let him answer it.

3 ¶Then Job answered the LORD, and said,

4 Behold, I am vile; what shall I answer thee? I will lay mine hand upon my mouth.

5 Once have I spoken; but I will not answer: yea, twice; but I will proceed no further.

6 ¶Then answered the LORD unto Job out of the whirlwind, and said,

7 Gird up thy loins now like a man: I will demand of thee, and declare thou unto me.

8 Wilt thou also disannul my judgment? wilt thou condemn me, that thou mayest be righteous?

9 Hast thou an arm like God? or canst thou thunder with a voice like him?

10 Deck thyself now *with* majesty and excellency; and array thyself with glory and beauty.

11 Cast abroad the rage of thy wrath: and behold every one *that is* proud, and abase him.

12 Look on every one *that is* proud, *and* bring him low; and tread down the wicked in their place.

13 Hide them in the dust together; *and* bind their faces in secret.

14 Then will I also confess unto thee that thine own right hand can save thee.

15 ¶Behold now behemoth, which I made with thee; he eateth grass as an ox.

16 Lo now, his strength *is* in his loins, and his force *is* in the navel of his belly.

17 He moveth his tail like a cedar: the sinews of his stones are wrapped together.

18 His bones *are as* strong pieces of brass; his bones *are* like bars of iron.

19 He *is* the chief of the ways of God: he that made him can make his sword to approach *unto him.*

20 Surely the mountains bring him forth food, where all the beasts of the field play.

21 He lieth under the shady trees, in the covert of the reed, and fens.

22 The shady trees cover him *with* their shadow; the willows of the brook compass him about.

23 Behold, he drinketh up a river, *and* hasteth not: he trusteth that he can draw up Jordan into his mouth.

24 He taketh it with his eyes: *his* nose pierceth through snares.

CHAPTER 41

CANST thou draw out leviathan with an hook? or his tongue with a cord *which* thou lettest down?

2 Canst thou put an hook into his nose? or bore his jaw through with a thorn?

3 Will he make many supplications unto thee? will he speak soft *words* unto thee?

4 Will he make a covenant with thee? wilt thou take him for a servant for ever?

5 Wilt thou play with him as *with* a bird? or wilt thou bind him for thy maidens?

6 Shall the companions make a banquet of him? shall they part him among the merchants?

7 Canst thou fill his skin with barbed irons? or his head with fish spears?

8 Lay thine hand upon him, remember the battle, do no more.

9 Behold, the hope of him is in vain: shall not *one* be cast down even at the sight of him?

10 None *is so* fierce that dare stir him up: who then is able to stand before me?

11 Who hath prevented me, that I should repay *him? whatsoever is* under the whole heaven is mine.

12 I will not conceal his parts, nor his power, nor his comely proportion.

13 Who can discover the face of his garment? *or* who can come *to him* with his double bridle?

14 Who can open the doors of his face? his teeth *are* terrible round about.

15 *His* scales *are his* pride, shut up together *as with* a close seal.

16 One is so near to another, that no air can come between them.

17 They are joined one to another, they stick together, that they cannot be sundered.

18 By his neesings a light doth shine, and his eyes *are* like the eyelids of the morning.

19 Out of his mouth go burning lamps, *and* sparks of fire leap out.

20 Out of his nostrils goeth smoke, as *out* of a seething pot or caldron.

21 His breath kindleth coals, and a flame goeth out of his mouth.

22 In his neck remaineth strength, and sorrow is turned into joy before him.

23 The flakes of his flesh are joined together: they are firm in themselves; they cannot be moved.

24 His heart is as firm as a stone; yea, as hard as a piece of the nether *millstone.*

25 When he raiseth up himself, the mighty are afraid: by reason of breakings they purify themselves.

26 The sword of him that layeth at him cannot hold: the spear, the dart, nor the habergeon.

27 He esteemeth iron as straw, *and* brass as rotten wood.

28 The arrow cannot make him flee: slingstones are turned with him into stubble.

29 Darts are counted as stubble: he laugheth at the shaking of a spear.

30 Sharp stones *are* under him: he spreadeth sharp pointed things upon the mire.

31 He maketh the deep to boil like a pot: he maketh the sea like a pot of ointment.

32 He maketh a path to shine after him; *one* would think the deep *to be* hoary.

33 Upon earth there is not his like, who is made without fear.

34 He beholdeth all high *things:* he *is* a king over all the children of pride.

CHAPTER 42

THEN Job answered the LORD, and said,

2 I know that thou canst do every *thing,* and *that* no thought can be withholden from thee.

3 Who *is* he that hideth counsel without knowledge? therefore have I uttered that I understood not; things too wonderful for me, which I knew not.

4 Hear, I beseech thee, and I will speak: I will demand of thee, and declare thou unto me.

5 I have heard of thee by the hearing of the ear: but now mine eye seeth thee.

6 Wherefore I abhor *myself,* and repent in dust and ashes.

7 ¶And it was *so,* that after the LORD had spoken these words unto Job, the LORD said to Ĕl'i-phăz the Tē'man-īte, My wrath is kindled against thee, and against thy two friends: for ye have not spoken of me *the thing that is* right, as my servant Job *hath.*

8 Therefore take unto you now seven bullocks and seven rams, and go to my servant Job, and offer up for yourselves a burnt offering; and my servant Job shall pray for you: for him will I accept: lest I deal with you *after your* folly, in that ye have not spoken of me *the thing which is* right, like my servant Job.

9 ¶So Ĕl'i-phăz the Tē'man-īte and Bildad the Shū'hīte *and* Zō'phar the

Nā'a-math-īte went, and did according as the LORD commanded them: the LORD also accepted Job.
10 And the LORD turned the captivity of Job, when he prayed for his friends: also the LORD gave Job twice as much as he had before.
11 Then came there unto him all his brethren, and all his sisters, and all they that had been of his acquaintance before, and did eat bread with him in his house: and they bemoaned him, and comforted him over all the evil that the LORD had brought upon him: every man also gave him a piece of money, and every one an earring of gold.
12 So the LORD blessed the latter end of Job more than his beginning: for he had fourteen thousand sheep, and six thousand camels, and a thousand yoke of oxen, and a thousand she asses.
13 He had also seven sons and three daughters.
14 And he called the name of the first, Je-mī'ma; and the name of the second, Ke-zī'a; and the name of the third, Kĕr'en-hăp'puch.
15 And in all the land were no women found *so* fair as the daughters of Job: and their father gave them inheritance among their brethren.
16 After this lived Job an hundred and forty years, and saw his sons, and his sons' sons, *even* four generations.
17 So Job died, *being* old and full of days.

THE

BOOK OF PSALMS

PSALM 1

BLESSED *is* the man that walketh not in the counsel of the ungodly, nor standeth in the way of sinners, nor sitteth in the seat of the scornful.
2 But his delight *is* in the law of the LORD; and in his law doth he meditate day and night.
3 And he shall be like a tree planted by the rivers of water, that bringeth forth his fruit in his season; his leaf also shall not wither; and whatsoever he doeth shall prosper.
4 The ungodly *are* not so: but *are* like the chaff which the wind driveth away.
5 Therefore the ungodly shall not stand in the judgment, nor sinners in the congregation of the righteous.
6 For the LORD knoweth the way of the righteous: but the way of the ungodly shall perish.

PSALM 2

WHY do the heathen rage, and the people imagine a vain thing?
2 The kings of the earth set themselves, and the rulers take counsel together, against the LORD, and against his anointed, *saying*,
3 Let us break their bands asunder, and cast away their cords from us.
4 He that sitteth in the heavens shall laugh: the LORD shall have them in derision.
5 Then shall he speak unto them in his wrath, and vex them in his sore displeasure.
6 Yet have I set my king upon my holy hill of Zion.
7 I will declare the decree: the LORD hath said unto me, Thou *art* my Son; this day have I begotten thee.
8 Ask of me, and I shall give *thee* the heathen *for* thine inheritance, and the uttermost parts of the earth *for* thy possession.
9 Thou shalt break them with a rod of iron; thou shalt dash them in pieces like a potter's vessel.
10 Be wise now therefore, O ye kings: be instructed, ye judges of the earth.
11 Serve the LORD with fear, and rejoice with trembling.
12 Kiss the Son, lest he be angry, and ye perish *from* the way, when his wrath is kindled but a little. Blessed *are* all they that put their trust in him.

PSALM 3

LORD, how are they increased that trouble me! many *are* they that rise up against me.
2 Many *there be* which say of my soul, *There is* no help for him in God. Sē'lah.
3 But thou, O LORD, *art* a shield for me; my glory, and the lifter up of mine head.
4 I cried unto the LORD with my voice, and he heard me out of his holy hill. Sē'lah.
5 I laid me down and slept; I awaked; for the LORD sustained me.
6 I will not be afraid of ten thousands of people, that have set *themselves* against me round about.
7 Arise, O LORD; save me, O my God: for thou hast smitten all mine enemies *upon* the cheek bone; thou hast broken the teeth of the ungodly.
8 Salvation *belongeth* unto the LORD: thy blessing *is* upon thy people. Sē'lah.

PSALM 4

HEAR me when I call, O God of my
righteousness: thou hast enlarged me
when I was in distress; have mercy
upon me, and hear my prayer.
2 O ye sons of men, how long *will ye
turn* my glory into shame? *how long*
will ye love vanity, *and* seek after
leasing? Sē'lah.
3 But know that the LORD hath set
apart him that is godly for himself: the
LORD will hear when I call unto him.
4 Stand in awe, and sin not: com-
mune with your own heart upon your
bed, and be still. Sē'lah.
5 Offer the sacrifices of righteous-
ness, and put your trust in the LORD.
6 *There be* many that say, Who will
shew us *any* good? LORD, lift thou up
the light of thy countenance upon us.
7 Thou hast put gladness in my heart,
more than in the time *that* their corn
and their wine increased.
8 I will both lay me down in peace,
and sleep: for thou, LORD, only makest
me dwell in safety.

PSALM 5

GIVE ear to my words, O LORD, con-
sider my meditation.
2 Hearken unto the voice of my cry,
my King, and my God: for unto thee
will I pray.
3 My voice shalt thou hear in the
morning, O LORD; in the morning will I
direct *my prayer* unto thee, and will
look up.
4 For thou *art* not a God that hath
pleasure in wickedness: neither shall
evil dwell with thee.
5 The foolish shall not stand in thy
sight: thou hatest all workers of iniq-
uity.
6 Thou shalt destroy them that speak
leasing: the LORD will abhor the bloody
and deceitful man.
7 But as for me, I will come *into* thy
house in the multitude of thy mercy:
and in thy fear will I worship toward
thy holy temple.
8 Lead me, O LORD, in thy righteous-
ness because of mine enemies; make
thy way straight before my face.
9 For *there is* no faithfulness in their
mouth; their inward part *is* very
wickedness; their throat *is* an open
sepulchre; they flatter with their
tongue.
10 Destroy thou them, O God; let
them fall by their own counsels; cast
them out in the multitude of their
transgressions; for they have rebelled
against thee.
11 But let all those that put their trust
in thee rejoice: let them ever shout for
joy, because thou defendest them: let
them also that love thy name be joyful
in thee.
12 For thou, LORD, wilt bless the
righteous; with favour wilt thou com-
pass him as *with* a shield.

PSALM 6

O LORD, rebuke me not in thine anger,
neither chasten me in thy hot displeas-
ure.
2 Have mercy upon me, O LORD; for I
am weak: O LORD, heal me; for my
bones are vexed.
3 My soul is also sore vexed: but
thou, O LORD, how long?
4 Return, O LORD, deliver my soul: oh
save me for thy mercies' sake.
5 For in death *there is* no remem-
brance of thee: in the grave who shall
give thee thanks?
6 I am weary with my groaning; all
the night make I my bed to swim; I wa-
ter my couch with my tears.
7 Mine eye is consumed because of
grief; it waxeth old because of all mine
enemies.
8 Depart from me, all ye workers of
iniquity; for the LORD hath heard the
voice of my weeping.
9 The LORD hath heard my supplica-
tion; the LORD will receive my prayer.
10 Let all mine enemies be ashamed
and sore vexed: let them return *and* be
ashamed suddenly.

PSALM 7

O LORD my God, in thee do I put my
trust: save me from all them that perse-
cute me, and deliver me:
2 Lest he tear my soul like a lion,
rending *it* in pieces, while *there is* none
to deliver.
3 O LORD my God, if I have done this;
if there be iniquity in my hands;
4 If I have rewarded evil unto him
that was at peace with me; (yea, I have
delivered him that without cause is
mine enemy:)
5 Let the enemy persecute my soul,
and take *it;* yea, let him tread down my
life upon the earth, and lay mine hon-
our in the dust. Sē'lah.
6 Arise, O LORD, in thine anger, lift up
thyself because of the rage of mine en-
emies: and awake for me *to* the judg-
ment *that* thou hast commanded.
7 So shall the congregation of the
people compass thee about: for their
sakes therefore return thou on high.
8 The LORD shall judge the people:
judge me, O LORD, according to my
righteousness, and according to mine
integrity *that is* in me.

9 Oh let the wickedness of the wicked come to an end; but establish the just: for the righteous God trieth the hearts and reins.
10 My defence *is* of God, which saveth the upright in heart.
11 God judgeth the righteous, and God is angry *with the wicked* every day.
12 If he turn not, he will whet his sword; he hath bent his bow, and made it ready.
13 He hath also prepared for him the instruments of death; he ordaineth his arrows against the persecutors.
14 Behold, he travaileth with iniquity, and hath conceived mischief, and brought forth falsehood.
15 He made a pit, and digged it, and is fallen into the ditch *which* he made.
16 His mischief shall return upon his own head, and his violent dealing shall come down upon his own pate.
17 I will praise the LORD according to his righteousness: and will sing praise to the name of the LORD most high.

PSALM 8

O LORD our Lord, how excellent *is* thy name in all the earth! who hast set thy glory above the heavens.
2 Out of the mouth of babes and sucklings hast thou ordained strength because of thine enemies, that thou mightest still the enemy and the avenger.
3 When I consider thy heavens, the work of thy fingers, the moon and the stars, which thou hast ordained;
4 What is man, that thou art mindful of him? and the son of man, that thou visitest him?
5 For thou hast made him a little lower than the angels, and hast crowned him with glory and honour.
6 Thou madest him to have dominion over the works of thy hands: thou hast put all *things* under his feet:
7 All sheep and oxen, yea, and the beasts of the field;
8 The fowl of the air, and the fish of the sea, *and whatsoever* passeth through the paths of the seas.
9 O LORD our Lord, how excellent *is* thy name in all the earth!

PSALM 9

I WILL praise *thee*, O LORD, with my whole heart; I will shew forth all thy marvellous works.
2 I will be glad and rejoice in thee: I will sing praise to thy name, O thou most High.
3 When mine enemies are turned back, they shall fall and perish at thy presence.
4 For thou hast maintained my right and my cause; thou satest in the throne judging right.
5 Thou hast rebuked the heathen, thou hast destroyed the wicked, thou hast put out their name for ever and ever.
6 O thou enemy, destructions are come to a perpetual end: and thou hast destroyed cities; their memorial is perished with them.
7 But the LORD shall endure for ever: he hath prepared his throne for judgment.
8 And he shall judge the world in righteousness, he shall minister judgment to the people in uprightness.
9 The LORD also will be a refuge for the oppressed, a refuge in times of trouble.
10 And they that know thy name will put their trust in thee: for thou, LORD, hast not forsaken them that seek thee.
11 Sing praises to the LORD, which dwelleth in Zion: declare among the people his doings.
12 When he maketh inquisition for blood, he remembereth them: he forgetteth not the cry of the humble.
13 Have mercy upon me, O LORD; consider my trouble *which I suffer* of them that hate me, thou that liftest me up from the gates of death:
14 That I may shew forth all thy praise in the gates of the daughter of Zion: I will rejoice in thy salvation.
15 The heathen are sunk down in the pit *that* they made: in the net which they hid is their own foot taken.
16 The LORD is known *by* the judgment *which* he executeth: the wicked is snared in the work of his own hands. Hĭg-gā'iŏn. Sē'lah.
17 The wicked shall be turned into hell, *and* all the nations that forget God.
18 For the needy shall not alway be forgotten: the expectation of the poor shall *not* perish for ever.
19 Arise, O LORD; let not man prevail: let the heathen be judged in thy sight.
20 Put them in fear, O LORD: *that* the nations may know themselves *to be but* men. Sē'lah.

PSALM 10

WHY standest thou afar off, O LORD? *why* hidest thou *thyself* in times of trouble?
2 The wicked in *his* pride doth persecute the poor: let them be taken in the devices that they have imagined.
3 For the wicked boasteth of his

heart's desire, and blesseth the covet-
ous, *whom* the Lord abhorreth.
4 The wicked, through the pride of
his countenance, will not seek *after*
God: God *is* not in all his thoughts.
5 His ways are always grievous; thy
judgments *are* far above out of his
sight: *as for* all his enemies, he puffeth
at them.
6 He hath said in his heart, I shall not
be moved: for *I shall* never *be* in adver-
sity.
7 His mouth is full of cursing and de-
ceit and fraud: under his tongue *is*
mischief and vanity.
8 He sitteth in the lurking places of
the villages: in the secret places doth he
murder the innocent: his eyes are priv-
ily set against the poor.
9 He lieth in wait secretly as a lion in
his den: he lieth in wait to catch the
poor: he doth catch the poor, when he
draweth him into his net.
10 He croucheth, *and* humbleth him-
self, that the poor may fall by his strong
ones.
11 He hath said in his heart, God hath
forgotten: he hideth his face; he will
never *see it.*
12 Arise, O Lord; O God, lift up thine
hand: forget not the humble.
13 Wherefore doth the wicked con-
temn God? he hath said in his heart,
Thou wilt not require *it.*
14 Thou hast seen *it;* for thou behold-
est mischief and spite, to requite *it*
with thy hand: the poor committeth
himself unto thee; thou art the helper of
the fatherless.
15 Break thou the arm of the wicked
and the evil *man:* seek out his wicked-
ness *till* thou find none.
16 The Lord *is* King for ever and
ever: the heathen are perished out of
his land.
17 Lord, thou hast heard the desire of
the humble: thou wilt prepare their
heart, thou wilt cause thine ear to hear:
18 To judge the fatherless and the
oppressed, that the man of the earth
may no more oppress.

PSALM 11

IN the Lord put I my trust: how say ye
to my soul, Flee *as* a bird to your moun-
tain?
2 For, lo, the wicked bend *their* bow,
they make ready their arrow upon the
string, that they may privily shoot at
the upright in heart.
3 If the foundations be destroyed,
what can the righteous do?
4 The Lord *is* in his holy temple, the
Lord's throne *is* in heaven: his eyes be-
hold, his eyelids try, the children of
men.
5 The Lord trieth the righteous: but
the wicked and him that loveth vio-
lence his soul hateth.
6 Upon the wicked he shall rain
snares, fire and brimstone, and an hor-
rible tempest: *this shall be* the portion
of their cup.
7 For the righteous Lord loveth
righteousness; his countenance doth
behold the upright.

PSALM 12

HELP, Lord; for the godly man ceas-
eth; for the faithful fail from among the
children of men.
2 They speak vanity every one with
his neighbour: *with* flattering lips *and*
with a double heart do they speak.
3 The Lord shall cut off all flattering
lips, *and* the tongue that speaketh
proud things:
4 Who have said, With our tongue
will we prevail; our lips *are* our own:
who *is* lord over us?
5 For the oppression of the poor, for
the sighing of the needy, now will I
arise, saith the Lord; I will set *him* in
safety *from him that* puffeth at him.
6 The words of the Lord *are* pure
words: *as* silver tried in a furnace of
earth, purified seven times.
7 Thou shalt keep them, O Lord, thou
shalt preserve them from this genera-
tion for ever.
8 The wicked walk on every side,
when the vilest men are exalted.

PSALM 13

HOW long wilt thou forget me, O
Lord? for ever? how long wilt thou hide
thy face from me?
2 How long shall I take counsel in my
soul, *having* sorrow in my heart daily?
how long shall mine enemy be exalted
over me?
3 Consider *and* hear me, O Lord my
God: lighten mine eyes, lest I sleep the
sleep of death;
4 Lest mine enemy say, I have pre-
vailed against him; *and* those that
trouble me rejoice when I am moved.
5 But I have trusted in thy mercy; my
heart shall rejoice in thy salvation.
6 I will sing unto the Lord, because
he hath dealt bountifully with me.

PSALM 14

THE fool hath said in his heart, *There is*
no God. They are corrupt, they have
done abominable works, *there is* none
that doeth good.
2 The Lord looked down from heaven
upon the children of men, to see if there

were any that did understand, *and* seek God.

3 They are all gone aside, they are *all* together become filthy: *there is* none that doeth good, no, not one.

4 Have all the workers of iniquity no knowledge? who eat up my people *as* they eat bread, and call not upon the LORD.

5 There were they in great fear: for God *is* in the generation of the righteous.

6 Ye have shamed the counsel of the poor, because the LORD *is* his refuge.

7 Oh that the salvation of Israel *were come* out of Zion! when the LORD bringeth back the captivity of his people, Jacob shall rejoice, *and* Israel shall be glad.

PSALM 15

LORD, who shall abide in thy tabernacle? who shall dwell in thy holy hill?

2 He that walketh uprightly, and worketh righteousness, and speaketh the truth in his heart.

3 *He that* backbiteth not with his tongue, nor doeth evil to his neighbour, nor taketh up a reproach against his neighbour.

4 In whose eyes a vile person is contemned; but he honoureth them that fear the LORD. *He that* sweareth to *his own* hurt, and changeth not.

5 *He that* putteth not out his money to usury, nor taketh reward against the innocent. He that doeth these *things* shall never be moved.

PSALM 16

PRESERVE me, O God: for in thee do I put my trust.

2 *O my soul,* thou hast said unto the LORD, Thou *art* my Lord: my goodness *extendeth* not to thee;

3 *But* to the saints that *are* in the earth, and *to* the excellent, in whom *is* all my delight.

4 Their sorrows shall be multiplied *that* hasten *after* another *god:* their drink offerings of blood will I not offer, nor take up their names into my lips.

5 The LORD *is* the portion of mine inheritance and of my cup: thou maintainest my lot.

6 The lines are fallen unto me in pleasant *places;* yea, I have a goodly heritage.

7 I will bless the LORD, who hath given me counsel: my reins also instruct me in the night seasons.

8 I have set the LORD always before me: because *he is* at my right hand, I shall not be moved.

9 Therefore my heart is glad, and my glory rejoiceth: my flesh also shall rest in hope.

10 For thou wilt not leave my soul in hell; neither wilt thou suffer thine Holy One to see corruption.

11 Thou wilt shew me the path of life: in thy presence *is* fulness of joy; at thy right hand *there are* pleasures for evermore.

PSALM 17

HEAR the right, O LORD, attend unto my cry, give ear unto my prayer, *that goeth* not out of feigned lips.

2 Let my sentence come forth from thy presence; let thine eyes behold the things that are equal.

3 Thou hast proved mine heart; thou hast visited *me* in the night; thou hast tried me, *and* shalt find nothing; I am purposed *that* my mouth shall not transgress.

4 Concerning the works of men, by the word of thy lips I have kept *me from* the paths of the destroyer.

5 Hold up my goings in thy paths, *that* my footsteps slip not.

6 I have called upon thee, for thou wilt hear me, O God: incline thine ear unto me, *and hear* my speech.

7 Shew thy marvellous lovingkindness, O thou that savest by thy right hand them which put their trust *in thee* from those that rise up *against them.*

8 Keep me as the apple of the eye, hide me under the shadow of thy wings,

9 From the wicked that oppress me, *from* my deadly enemies, *who* compass me about.

10 They are inclosed in their own fat: with their mouth they speak proudly.

11 They have now compassed us in our steps: they have set their eyes bowing down to the earth;

12 Like as a lion *that* is greedy of his prey, and as it were a young lion lurking in secret places.

13 Arise, O LORD, disappoint him, cast him down: deliver my soul from the wicked, *which is* thy sword:

14 From men *which are* thy hand, O LORD, from men of the world, *which have* their portion in *this* life, and whose belly thou fillest with thy hid *treasure:* they are full of children, and leave the rest of their *substance* to their babes.

15 As for me, I will behold thy face in righteousness: I shall be satisfied, when I awake, with thy likeness.

PSALM 18

I WILL love thee, O LORD, my strength.
2 The LORD *is* my rock, and my for-
tress, and my deliverer; my God, my
strength, in whom I will trust; my
buckler, and the horn of my salvation,
and my high tower.
3 I will call upon the LORD, *who is
worthy* to be praised: so shall I be saved
from mine enemies.
4 The sorrows of death compassed
me, and the floods of ungodly men
made me afraid.
5 The sorrows of hell compassed me
about: the snares of death prevented
me.
6 In my distress I called upon the
LORD, and cried unto my God: he heard
my voice out of his temple, and my cry
came before him, *even* into his ears.
7 Then the earth shook and trembled;
the foundations also of the hills moved
and were shaken, because he was
wroth.
8 There went up a smoke out of his
nostrils, and fire out of his mouth de-
voured: coals were kindled by it.
9 He bowed the heavens also, and
came down: and darkness *was* under
his feet.
10 And he rode upon a cherub, and
did fly: yea, he did fly upon the wings of
the wind.
11 He made darkness his secret
place; his pavilion round about him
were dark waters *and* thick clouds of
the skies.
12 At the brightness *that was* before
him his thick clouds passed, hail *stones*
and coals of fire.
13 The LORD also thundered in the
heavens, and the Highest gave his
voice; hail *stones* and coals of fire.
14 Yea, he sent out his arrows, and
scattered them; and he shot out light-
nings, and discomfited them.
15 Then the channels of waters were
seen, and the foundations of the world
were discovered at thy rebuke, O LORD,
at the blast of the breath of thy nostrils.
16 He sent from above, he took me,
he drew me out of many waters.
17 He delivered me from my strong
enemy, and from them which hated
me: for they were too strong for me.
18 They prevented me in the day of
my calamity: but the LORD was my
stay.
19 He brought me forth also into a
large place; he delivered me, because
he delighted in me.
20 The LORD rewarded me according
to my righteousness; according to the
cleanness of my hands hath he recom-
pensed me.
21 For I have kept the ways of the
LORD, and have not wickedly departed
from my God.
22 For all his judgments *were* before
me, and I did not put away his statutes
from me.
23 I was also upright before him, and
I kept myself from mine iniquity.
24 Therefore hath the LORD recom-
pensed me according to my righteous-
ness, according to the cleanness of my
hands in his eyesight.
25 With the merciful thou wilt shew
thyself merciful; with an upright man
thou wilt shew thyself upright;
26 With the pure thou wilt shew thy-
self pure; and with the froward thou
wilt shew thyself froward.
27 For thou wilt save the afflicted
people; but wilt bring down high looks.
28 For thou wilt light my candle: the
LORD my God will enlighten my dark-
ness.
29 For by thee I have run through a
troop; and by my God have I leaped
over a wall.
30 *As for* God, his way *is* perfect: the
word of the LORD is tried: he *is* a buck-
ler to all those that trust in him.
31 For who *is* God save the LORD? or
who *is* a rock save our God?
32 *It is* God that girdeth me with
strength, and maketh my way perfect.
33 He maketh my feet like hinds' *feet*,
and setteth me upon my high places.
34 He teacheth my hands to war, so
that a bow of steel is broken by mine
arms.
35 Thou hast also given me the shield
of thy salvation: and thy right hand
hath holden me up, and thy gentleness
hath made me great.
36 Thou hast enlarged my steps un-
der me, that my feet did not slip.
37 I have pursued mine enemies, and
overtaken them: neither did I turn
again till they were consumed.
38 I have wounded them that they
were not able to rise: they are fallen un-
der my feet.
39 For thou hast girded me with
strength unto the battle: thou hast sub-
dued under me those that rose up
against me.
40 Thou hast also given me the necks
of mine enemies; that I might destroy
them that hate me.
41 They cried, *but there was* none to
save *them: even* unto the LORD, but he
answered them not.
42 Then did I beat them small as the
dust before the wind: I did cast them
out as the dirt in the streets.
43 Thou hast delivered me from the
strivings of the people; *and* thou hast

made me the head of the heathen: a people *whom* I have not known shall serve me.

44 As soon as they hear of me, they shall obey me: the strangers shall submit themselves unto me.

45 The strangers shall fade away, and be afraid out of their close places.

46 The LORD liveth; and blessed *be* my rock; and let the God of my salvation be exalted.

47 *It is* God that avengeth me, and subdueth the people under me.

48 He delivereth me from mine enemies: yea, thou liftest me up above those that rise up against me: thou hast delivered me from the violent man.

49 Therefore will I give thanks unto thee, O LORD, among the heathen, and sing praises unto thy name.

50 Great deliverance giveth he to his king; and sheweth mercy to his anointed, to David, and to his seed for evermore.

PSALM 19

THE heavens declare the glory of God; and the firmament sheweth his handywork.

2 Day unto day uttereth speech, and night unto night sheweth knowledge.

3 *There is* no speech nor language, *where* their voice is not heard.

4 Their line is gone out through all the earth, and their words to the end of the world. In them hath he set a tabernacle for the sun,

5 Which *is* as a bridegroom coming out of his chamber, *and* rejoiceth as a strong man to run a race.

6 His going forth *is* from the end of the heaven, and his circuit unto the ends of it: and there is nothing hid from the heat thereof.

7 The law of the LORD *is* perfect, converting the soul: the testimony of the LORD *is* sure, making wise the simple.

8 The statutes of the LORD *are* right, rejoicing the heart: the commandment of the LORD *is* pure, enlightening the eyes.

9 The fear of the LORD *is* clean, enduring for ever: the judgments of the LORD *are* true *and* righteous altogether.

10 More to be desired *are they* than gold, yea, than much fine gold: sweeter also than honey and the honeycomb.

11 Moreover by them is thy servant warned: *and* in keeping of them *there is* great reward.

12 Who can understand *his* errors? cleanse thou me from secret *faults*.

13 Keep back thy servant also from presumptuous *sins*; let them not have dominion over me: then shall I be upright, and I shall be innocent from the great transgression.

14 Let the words of my mouth, and the meditation of my heart, be acceptable in thy sight, O LORD, my strength, and my redeemer.

PSALM 20

THE LORD hear thee in the day of trouble; the name of the God of Jacob defend thee;

2 Send thee help from the sanctuary, and strengthen thee out of Zion;

3 Remember all thy offerings, and accept thy burnt sacrifice; Sē'lah.

4 Grant thee according to thine own heart, and fulfil all thy counsel.

5 We will rejoice in thy salvation, and in the name of our God we will set up *our* banners: the LORD fulfil all thy petitions.

6 Now know I that the LORD saveth his anointed; he will hear him from his holy heaven with the saving strength of his right hand.

7 Some *trust* in chariots, and some in horses: but we will remember the name of the LORD our God.

8 They are brought down and fallen: but we are risen, and stand upright.

9 Save, LORD: let the king hear us when we call.

PSALM 21

THE king shall joy in thy strength, O LORD; and in thy salvation how greatly shall he rejoice!

2 Thou hast given him his heart's desire, and hast not withholden the request of his lips. Sē'lah.

3 For thou preventest him with the blessings of goodness: thou settest a crown of pure gold on his head.

4 He asked life of thee, *and* thou gavest *it* him, *even* length of days for ever and ever.

5 His glory *is* great in thy salvation: honour and majesty hast thou laid upon him.

6 For thou hast made him most blessed for ever: thou hast made him exceeding glad with thy countenance.

7 For the king trusteth in the LORD, and through the mercy of the most High he shall not be moved.

8 Thine hand shall find out all thine enemies: thy right hand shall find out those that hate thee.

9 Thou shalt make them as a fiery oven in the time of thine anger: the LORD shall swallow them up in his wrath, and the fire shall devour them.

10 Their fruit shalt thou destroy from

the earth, and their seed from among the children of men.

11 For they intended evil against thee: they imagined a mischievous device, *which* they are not able *to perform*.

12 Therefore shalt thou make them turn their back, *when* thou shalt make ready *thine arrows* upon thy strings against the face of them.

13 Be thou exalted, LORD, in thine own strength: *so* will we sing and praise thy power.

PSALM 22

MY God, my God, why hast thou forsaken me? *why art thou so* far from helping me, *and from* the words of my roaring?

2 O my God, I cry in the daytime, but thou hearest not; and in the night season, and am not silent.

3 But thou *art* holy, *O thou* that inhabitest the praises of Israel.

4 Our fathers trusted in thee: they trusted, and thou didst deliver them.

5 They cried unto thee, and were delivered: they trusted in thee, and were not confounded.

6 But I *am* a worm, and no man; a reproach of men, and despised of the people.

7 All they that see me laugh me to scorn: they shoot out the lip, they shake the head, *saying*,

8 He trusted on the LORD *that* he would deliver him: let him deliver him, seeing he delighted in him.

9 But thou *art* he that took me out of the womb: thou didst make me hope *when I was* upon my mother's breasts.

10 I was cast upon thee from the womb: thou *art* my God from my mother's belly.

11 Be not far from me; for trouble *is* near; for *there is* none to help.

12 Many bulls have compassed me: strong *bulls* of Bā'shan have beset me round.

13 They gaped upon me *with* their mouths, *as* a ravening and a roaring lion.

14 I am poured out like water, and all my bones are out of joint: my heart is like wax; it is melted in the midst of my bowels.

15 My strength is dried up like a potsherd; and my tongue cleaveth to my jaws; and thou hast brought me into the dust of death.

16 For dogs have compassed me: the assembly of the wicked have inclosed me: they pierced my hands and my feet.

17 I may tell all my bones: they look *and* stare upon me.

18 They part my garments among them, and cast lots upon my vesture.

19 But be not thou far from me, O LORD: O my strength, haste thee to help me.

20 Deliver my soul from the sword; my darling from the power of the dog.

21 Save me from the lion's mouth: for thou hast heard me from the horns of the unicorns.

22 I will declare thy name unto my brethren: in the midst of the congregation will I praise thee.

23 Ye that fear the LORD, praise him; all ye the seed of Jacob, glorify him; and fear him, all ye the seed of Israel.

24 For he hath not despised nor abhorred the affliction of the afflicted; neither hath he hid his face from him; but when he cried unto him, he heard.

25 My praise *shall be* of thee in the great congregation: I will pay my vows before them that fear him.

26 The meek shall eat and be satisfied: they shall praise the LORD that seek him: your heart shall live for ever.

27 All the ends of the world shall remember and turn unto the LORD: and all the kindreds of the nations shall worship before thee.

28 For the kingdom *is* the LORD's: and he *is* the governor among the nations.

29 All *they that be* fat upon earth shall eat and worship: all they that go down to the dust shall bow before him: and none can keep alive his own soul.

30 A seed shall serve him; it shall be accounted to the Lord for a generation.

31 They shall come, and shall declare his righteousness unto a people that shall be born, that he hath done *this*.

PSALM 23

THE LORD *is* my shepherd; I shall not want.

2 He maketh me to lie down in green pastures: he leadeth me beside the still waters.

3 He restoreth my soul: he leadeth me in the paths of righteousness for his name's sake.

4 Yea, though I walk through the valley of the shadow of death, I will fear no evil: for thou *art* with me; thy rod and thy staff they comfort me.

5 Thou preparest a table before me in the presence of mine enemies: thou anointest my head with oil; my cup runneth over.

6 Surely goodness and mercy shall follow me all the days of my life: and I will dwell in the house of the LORD for ever.

PSALM 24

THE earth *is* the LORD's, and the fulness thereof; the world, and they that dwell therein.
2 For he hath founded it upon the seas, and established it upon the floods.
3 Who shall ascend into the hill of the LORD? or who shall stand in his holy place?
4 He that hath clean hands, and a pure heart; who hath not lifted up his soul unto vanity, nor sworn deceitfully.
5 He shall receive the blessing from the LORD, and righteousness from the God of his salvation.
6 This *is* the generation of them that seek him, that seek thy face, O Jacob. Sē'lah.
7 Lift up your heads, O ye gates; and be ye lift up, ye everlasting doors; and the King of glory shall come in.
8 Who *is* this King of glory? The LORD strong and mighty, the LORD mighty in battle.
9 Lift up your heads, O ye gates; even lift *them* up, ye everlasting doors; and the King of glory shall come in.
10 Who is this King of glory? The LORD of hosts, he *is* the King of glory. Sē'lah.

PSALM 25

UNTO thee, O LORD, do I lift up my soul.
2 O my God, I trust in thee: let me not be ashamed, let not mine enemies triumph over me.
3 Yea, let none that wait on thee be ashamed: let them be ashamed which transgress without cause.
4 Shew me thy ways, O LORD; teach me thy paths.
5 Lead me in thy truth, and teach me: for thou *art* the God of my salvation; on thee do I wait all the day.
6 Remember, O LORD, thy tender mercies and thy lovingkindnesses; for they *have been* ever of old.
7 Remember not the sins of my youth, nor my transgressions: according to thy mercy remember thou me for thy goodness' sake, O LORD.
8 Good and upright *is* the LORD: therefore will he teach sinners in the way.
9 The meek will he guide in judgment: and the meek will he teach his way.
10 All the paths of the LORD *are* mercy and truth unto such as keep his covenant and his testimonies.
11 For thy name's sake, O LORD, pardon mine iniquity; for it *is* great.
12 What man *is* he that feareth the LORD? him shall he teach in the way *that* he shall choose.
13 His soul shall dwell at ease; and his seed shall inherit the earth.
14 The secret of the LORD *is* with them that fear him; and he will shew them his covenant.
15 Mine eyes *are* ever toward the LORD; for he shall pluck my feet out of the net.
16 Turn thee unto me, and have mercy upon me; for I *am* desolate and afflicted.
17 The troubles of my heart are enlarged: *O* bring thou me out of my distresses.
18 Look upon mine affliction and my pain; and forgive all my sins.
19 Consider mine enemies; for they are many; and they hate me with cruel hatred.
20 O keep my soul, and deliver me: let me not be ashamed; for I put my trust in thee.
21 Let integrity and uprightness preserve me; for I wait on thee.
22 Redeem Israel, O God, out of all his troubles.

PSALM 26

JUDGE me, O LORD; for I have walked in mine integrity: I have trusted also in the LORD; *therefore* I shall not slide.
2 Examine me, O LORD, and prove me; try my reins and my heart.
3 For thy lovingkindness *is* before mine eyes: and I have walked in thy truth.
4 I have not sat with vain persons, neither will I go in with dissemblers.
5 I have hated the congregation of evil doers; and will not sit with the wicked.
6 I will wash mine hands in innocency: so will I compass thine altar, O LORD:
7 That I may publish with the voice of thanksgiving, and tell of all thy wondrous works.
8 LORD, I have loved the habitation of thy house, and the place where thine honour dwelleth.
9 Gather not my soul with sinners, nor my life with bloody men:
10 In whose hands *is* mischief, and their right hand is full of bribes.
11 But as for me, I will walk in mine integrity: redeem me, and be merciful unto me.
12 My foot standeth in an even place: in the congregations will I bless the LORD.

PSALM 27

THE LORD *is* my light and my salvation; whom shall I fear? the LORD *is* the strength of my life; of whom shall I be afraid?
2 When the wicked, *even* mine enemies and my foes, came upon me to eat up my flesh, they stumbled and fell.
3 Though an host should encamp against me, my heart shall not fear: though war should rise against me, in this *will* I *be* confident.
4 One *thing* have I desired of the LORD, that will I seek after; that I may dwell in the house of the LORD all the days of my life, to behold the beauty of the LORD, and to enquire in his temple.
5 For in the time of trouble he shall hide me in his pavilion: in the secret of his tabernacle shall he hide me; he shall set me up upon a rock.
6 And now shall mine head be lifted up above mine enemies round about me: therefore will I offer in his tabernacle sacrifices of joy; I will sing, yea, I will sing praises unto the LORD.
7 Hear, O LORD, *when* I cry with my voice: have mercy also upon me, and answer me.
8 *When thou saidst,* Seek ye my face; my heart said unto thee, Thy face, LORD, will I seek.
9 Hide not thy face *far* from me; put not thy servant away in anger: thou hast been my help; leave me not, neither forsake me, O God of my salvation.
10 When my father and my mother forsake me, then the LORD will take me up.
11 Teach me thy way, O LORD, and lead me in a plain path, because of mine enemies.
12 Deliver me not over unto the will of mine enemies: for false witnesses are risen up against me, and such as breathe out cruelty.
13 *I had fainted,* unless I had believed to see the goodness of the LORD in the land of the living.
14 Wait on the LORD: be of good courage, and he shall strengthen thine heart: wait, I say, on the LORD.

PSALM 28

UNTO thee will I cry, O LORD my rock; be not silent to me: lest, *if* thou be silent to me, I become like them that go down into the pit.
2 Hear the voice of my supplications, when I cry unto thee, when I lift up my hands toward thy holy oracle.
3 Draw me not away with the wicked, and with the workers of iniquity, which speak peace to their neighbours, but mischief *is* in their hearts.
4 Give them according to their deeds, and according to the wickedness of their endeavours: give them after the work of their hands; render to them their desert.
5 Because they regard not the works of the LORD, nor the operation of his hands, he shall destroy them, and not build them up.
6 Blessed *be* the LORD, because he hath heard the voice of my supplications.
7 The LORD *is* my strength and my shield; my heart trusted in him, and I am helped: therefore my heart greatly rejoiceth; and with my song will I praise him.
8 The LORD *is* their strength, and he *is* the saving strength of his anointed.
9 Save thy people, and bless thine inheritance: feed them also, and lift them up for ever.

PSALM 29

GIVE unto the LORD, O ye mighty, give unto the LORD glory and strength.
2 Give unto the LORD the glory due unto his name; worship the LORD in the beauty of holiness.
3 The voice of the LORD *is* upon the waters: the God of glory thundereth: the LORD *is* upon many waters.
4 The voice of the LORD *is* powerful; the voice of the LORD *is* full of majesty.
5 The voice of the LORD breaketh the cedars; yea, the LORD breaketh the cedars of Lebanon.
6 He maketh them also to skip like a calf; Lebanon and Sĭr′i-on like a young unicorn.
7 The voice of the LORD divideth the flames of fire.
8 The voice of the LORD shaketh the wilderness; the LORD shaketh the wilderness of Kā′desh.
9 The voice of the LORD maketh the hinds to calve, and discovereth the forests: and in his temple doth every one speak of *his* glory.
10 The LORD sitteth upon the flood; yea, the LORD sitteth King for ever.
11 The LORD will give strength unto his people; the LORD will bless his people with peace.

PSALM 30

I WILL extol thee, O LORD; for thou hast lifted me up, and hast not made my foes to rejoice over me.
2 O LORD my God, I cried unto thee, and thou hast healed me.
3 O LORD, thou hast brought up my soul from the grave: thou hast kept me

alive, that I should not go down to the
pit.
4 Sing unto the LORD, O ye saints of
his, and give thanks at the remem-
brance of his holiness.
5 For his anger *endureth but* a mo-
ment; in his favour *is* life: weeping may
endure for a night, but joy *cometh* in
the morning.
6 And in my prosperity I said, I shall
never be moved.
7 LORD, by thy favour thou hast made
my mountain to stand strong: thou
didst hide thy face, *and* I was troubled.
8 I cried to thee, O LORD; and unto the
LORD I made supplication.
9 What profit *is there* in my blood,
when I go down to the pit? Shall the
dust praise thee? shall it declare thy
truth?
10 Hear, O LORD, and have mercy
upon me: LORD, be thou my helper.
11 Thou hast turned for me my
mourning into dancing: thou hast put
off my sackcloth, and girded me with
gladness;
12 To the end that *my* glory may sing
praise to thee, and not be silent. O LORD
my God, I will give thanks unto thee for
ever.

PSALM 31

IN thee, O LORD, do I put my trust; let
me never be ashamed: deliver me in thy
righteousness.
2 Bow down thine ear to me; deliver
me speedily: be thou my strong rock,
for an house of defence to save me.
3 For thou *art* my rock and my for-
tress; therefore for thy name's sake
lead me, and guide me.
4 Pull me out of the net that they have
laid privily for me: for thou *art* my
strength.
5 Into thine hand I commit my spirit:
thou hast redeemed me, O LORD God of
truth.
6 I have hated them that regard lying
vanities: but I trust in the LORD.
7 I will be glad and rejoice in thy
mercy: for thou hast considered my
trouble; thou hast known my soul in ad-
versities;
8 And hast not shut me up into the
hand of the enemy: thou hast set my
feet in a large room.
9 Have mercy upon me, O LORD, for I
am in trouble: mine eye is consumed
with grief, *yea* my soul and my belly.
10 For my life is spent with grief, and
my years with sighing: my strength
faileth because of mine iniquity, and
my bones are consumed.
11 I was a reproach among all mine
enemies, but especially among my
neighbours, and a fear to mine acquaint-
ance: they that did see me without fled
from me.
12 I am forgotten as a dead man out
of mind: I am like a broken vessel.
13 For I have heard the slander of
many: fear *was* on every side: while
they took counsel together against me,
they devised to take away my life.
14 But I trusted in thee, O LORD: I
said, Thou *art* my God.
15 My times *are* in thy hand: deliver
me from the hand of mine enemies, and
from them that persecute me.
16 Make thy face to shine upon thy
servant: save me for thy mercies' sake.
17 Let me not be ashamed, O LORD;
for I have called upon thee: let the
wicked be ashamed, *and* let them be
silent in the grave.
18 Let the lying lips be put to silence;
which speak grievous things proudly
and contemptuously against the
righteous.
19 *Oh* how great *is* thy goodness,
which thou hast laid up for them that
fear thee; *which* thou hast wrought for
them that trust in thee before the sons
of men!
20 Thou shalt hide them in the secret
of thy presence from the pride of man:
thou shalt keep them secretly in a pavil-
ion from the strife of tongues.
21 Blessed *be* the LORD: for he hath
shewed me his marvellous kindness in
a strong city.
22 For I said in my haste, I am cut off
from before thine eyes: nevertheless
thou heardest the voice of my supplica-
tions when I cried unto thee.
23 O love the LORD, all ye his saints:
for the LORD preserveth the faithful,
and plentifully rewardeth the proud
doer.
24 Be of good courage, and he shall
strengthen your heart, all ye that hope
in the LORD.

PSALM 32

BLESSED *is he whose* transgression *is*
forgiven, *whose* sin *is* covered.
2 Blessed *is* the man unto whom the
LORD imputeth not iniquity, and in
whose spirit *there is* no guile.
3 When I kept silence, my bones
waxed old through my roaring all the
day long.
4 For day and night thy hand was
heavy upon me: my moisture is turned
into the drought of summer. Sē'lah.
5 I acknowledged my sin unto thee,
and mine iniquity have I not hid. I said,
I will confess my transgressions unto
the LORD; and thou forgavest the iniq-
uity of my sin. Sē'lah.

6 For this shall every one that is godly
pray unto thee in a time when thou
mayest be found: surely in the floods of
great waters they shall not come nigh
unto him.
7 Thou *art* my hiding place; thou
shalt preserve me from trouble; thou
shalt compass me about with songs of
deliverance. Sē'lah.
8 I will instruct thee and teach thee in
the way which thou shalt go: I will
guide thee with mine eye.
9 Be ye not as the horse, *or* as the
mule, *which* have no understanding:
whose mouth must be held in with bit
and bridle, lest they come near unto
thee.
10 Many sorrows *shall be* to the
wicked: but he that trusteth in the
LORD, mercy shall compass him about.
11 Be glad in the LORD, and rejoice, ye
righteous: and shout for joy, all *ye that
are* upright in heart.

PSALM 33

REJOICE in the LORD, O ye righteous:
for praise is comely for the upright.
2 Praise the LORD with harp: sing
unto him with the psaltery *and* an in-
strument of ten strings.
3 Sing unto him a new song; play skil-
fully with a loud noise.
4 For the word of the LORD *is* right;
and all his works *are done* in truth.
5 He loveth righteousness and judg-
ment: the earth is full of the goodness
of the LORD.
6 By the word of the LORD were the
heavens made; and all the host of them
by the breath of his mouth.
7 He gathereth the waters of the sea
together as an heap: he layeth up the
depth in storehouses.
8 Let all the earth fear the LORD: let all
the inhabitants of the world stand in
awe of him.
9 For he spake, and it was *done;* he
commanded, and it stood fast.
10 The LORD bringeth the counsel of
the heathen to nought: he maketh the
devices of the people of none effect.
11 The counsel of the LORD standeth
for ever, the thoughts of his heart to all
generations.
12 Blessed *is* the nation whose God *is*
the LORD: *and* the people *whom* he hath
chosen for his own inheritance.
13 The LORD looketh from heaven; he
beholdeth all the sons of men.
14 From the place of his habitation he
looketh upon all the inhabitants of the
earth.
15 He fashioneth their hearts alike;
he considereth all their works.
16 There is no king saved by the mul-
titude of an host: a mighty man is not
delivered by much strength.
17 An horse *is* a vain thing for safety:
neither shall he deliver *any* by his great
strength.
18 Behold, the eye of the LORD *is* upon
them that fear him, upon them that
hope in his mercy;
19 To deliver their soul from death,
and to keep them alive in famine.
20 Our soul waiteth for the LORD: he
is our help and our shield.
21 For our heart shall rejoice in him,
because we have trusted in his holy
name.
22 Let thy mercy, O LORD, be upon us,
according as we hope in thee.

PSALM 34

I WILL bless the LORD at all times: his
praise *shall* continually *be* in my
mouth.
2 My soul shall make her boast in the
LORD: the humble shall hear *thereof,*
and be glad.
3 O magnify the LORD with me, and
let us exalt his name together.
4 I sought the LORD, and he heard me,
and delivered me from all my fears.
5 They looked unto him, and were
lightened: and their faces were not
ashamed.
6 This poor man cried, and the LORD
heard *him,* and saved him out of all his
troubles.
7 The angel of the LORD encampeth
round about them that fear him, and
delivereth them.
8 O taste and see that the LORD *is*
good: blessed *is* the man *that* trusteth
in him.
9 O fear the LORD, ye his saints: for
there is no want to them that fear him.
10 The young lions do lack, and suffer
hunger: but they that seek the LORD
shall not want any good *thing.*
11 Come, ye children, hearken unto
me: I will teach you the fear of the
LORD.
12 What man *is he that* desireth life,
and loveth *many* days, that he may see
good?
13 Keep thy tongue from evil, and thy
lips from speaking guile.
14 Depart from evil, and do good;
seek peace, and pursue it.
15 The eyes of the LORD *are* upon the
righteous, and his ears *are open* unto
their cry.
16 The face of the LORD *is* against
them that do evil, to cut off the remem-
brance of them from the earth.
17 *The righteous* cry, and the LORD
heareth, and delivereth them out of all
their troubles.

18 The LORD *is* nigh unto them that
are of a broken heart; and saveth such
as be of a contrite spirit.
19 Many *are* the afflictions of the
righteous: but the LORD delivereth him
out of them all.
20 He keepeth all his bones: not one
of them is broken.
21 Evil shall slay the wicked: and
they that hate the righteous shall be
desolate.
22 The LORD redeemeth the soul of
his servants: and none of them that
trust in him shall be desolate.

PSALM 35

PLEAD *my cause,* O LORD, with them
that strive with me: fight against them
that fight against me.
2 Take hold of shield and buckler,
and stand up for mine help.
3 Draw out also the spear, and stop
the way against them that persecute
me: say unto my soul, I *am* thy salva-
tion.
4 Let them be confounded and put to
shame that seek after my soul: let them
be turned back and brought to confu-
sion that devise my hurt.
5 Let them be as chaff before the
wind: and let the angel of the LORD
chase *them.*
6 Let their way be dark and slippery:
and let the angel of the LORD persecute
them.
7 For without cause have they hid for
me their net *in* a pit, *which* without
cause they have digged for my soul.
8 Let destruction come upon him at
unawares; and let his net that he hath
hid catch himself: into that very destruc-
tion let him fall.
9 And my soul shall be joyful in the
LORD: it shall rejoice in his salvation.
10 All my bones shall say, LORD, who
is like unto thee, which deliverest the
poor from him that is too strong for
him, yea, the poor and the needy from
him that spoileth him?
11 False witnesses did rise up; they
laid to my charge *things* that I knew
not.
12 They rewarded me evil for good *to*
the spoiling of my soul.
13 But as for me, when they were
sick, my clothing *was* sackcloth: I
humbled my soul with fasting; and my
prayer returned into mine own bosom.
14 I behaved myself as though *he had*
been my friend *or* brother: I bowed
down heavily, as one that mourneth *for*
his mother.
15 But in mine adversity they re-
joiced, and gathered themselves togeth-
er: *yea,* the abjects gathered them-
selves together against me, and I knew
it not; they did tear *me,* and ceased not:
16 With hypocritical mockers in
feasts, they gnashed upon me with
their teeth.
17 Lord, how long wilt thou look on?
rescue my soul from their destructions,
my darling from the lions.
18 I will give thee thanks in the great
congregation: I will praise thee among
much people.
19 Let not them that are mine en-
emies wrongfully rejoice over me:
neither let them wink with the eye that
hate me without a cause.
20 For they speak not peace: but they
devise deceitful matters against *them*
that are quiet in the land.
21 Yea, they opened their mouth
wide against me, *and* said, Aha, aha,
our eye hath seen *it.*
22 *This* thou hast seen, O LORD: keep
not silence: O Lord, be not far from me.
23 Stir up thyself, and awake to my
judgment, *even* unto my cause, my
God and my Lord.
24 Judge me, O LORD my God, accord-
ing to thy righteousness; and let them
not rejoice over me.
25 Let them not say in their hearts,
Ah, so would we have it: let them not
say, We have swallowed him up.
26 Let them be ashamed and brought
to confusion together that rejoice at
mine hurt: let them be clothed with
shame and dishonour that magnify
themselves against me.
27 Let them shout for joy, and be
glad, that favour my righteous cause:
yea, let them say continually, Let the
LORD be magnified, which hath plea-
sure in the prosperity of his servant.
28 And my tongue shall speak of thy
righteousness *and* of thy praise all the
day long.

PSALM 36

THE transgression of the wicked saith
within my heart, *that there is* no fear of
God before his eyes.
2 For he flattereth himself in his own
eyes, until his iniquity be found to be
hateful.
3 The words of his mouth *are* iniquity
and deceit: he hath left off to be wise,
and to do good.
4 He deviseth mischief upon his bed;
he setteth himself in a way *that is* not
good; he abhorreth not evil.
5 Thy mercy, O LORD, *is* in the heav-
ens; *and* thy faithfulness *reacheth* unto
the clouds.
6 Thy righteousness *is* like the great
mountains; thy judgments *are* a great

deep: O LORD, thou preservest man and beast.
7 How excellent *is* thy lovingkindness, O God! therefore the children of men put their trust under the shadow of thy wings.
8 They shall be abundantly satisfied with the fatness of thy house; and thou shalt make them drink of the river of thy pleasures.
9 For with thee *is* the fountain of life: in thy light shall we see light.
10 O continue thy lovingkindness unto them that know thee; and thy righteousness to the upright in heart.
11 Let not the foot of pride come against me, and let not the hand of the wicked remove me.
12 There are the workers of iniquity fallen: they are cast down, and shall not be able to rise.

PSALM 37

FRET not thyself because of evildoers, neither be thou envious against the workers of iniquity.
2 For they shall soon be cut down like the grass, and wither as the green herb.
3 Trust in the LORD, and do good; *so* shalt thou dwell in the land, and verily thou shalt be fed.
4 Delight thyself also in the LORD; and he shall give thee the desires of thine heart.
5 Commit thy way unto the LORD; trust also in him; and he shall bring *it* to pass.
6 And he shall bring forth thy righteousness as the light, and thy judgment as the noonday.
7 Rest in the LORD, and wait patiently for him: fret not thyself because of him who prospereth in his way, because of the man who bringeth wicked devices to pass.
8 Cease from anger, and forsake wrath: fret not thyself in any wise to do evil.
9 For evildoers shall be cut off: but those that wait upon the LORD, they shall inherit the earth.
10 For yet a little while, and the wicked *shall* not *be;* yea, thou shalt diligently consider his place, and it *shall* not *be.*
11 But the meek shall inherit the earth; and shall delight themselves in the abundance of peace.
12 The wicked plotteth against the just, and gnasheth upon him with his teeth.
13 The Lord shall laugh at him: for he seeth that his day is coming.
14 The wicked have drawn out the sword, and have bent their bow, to cast down the poor and needy, *and* to slay such as be of upright conversation.
15 Their sword shall enter into their own heart, and their bows shall be broken.
16 A little that a righteous man hath *is* better than the riches of many wicked.
17 For the arms of the wicked shall be broken: but the LORD upholdeth the righteous.
18 The LORD knoweth the days of the upright: and their inheritance shall be for ever.
19 They shall not be ashamed in the evil time: and in the days of famine they shall be satisfied.
20 But the wicked shall perish, and the enemies of the LORD *shall be* as the fat of lambs: they shall consume; into smoke shall they consume away.
21 The wicked borroweth, and payeth not again: but the righteous sheweth mercy, and giveth.
22 For *such as be* blessed of him shall inherit the earth; and *they that be* cursed of him shall be cut off.
23 The steps of a *good* man are ordered by the LORD: and he delighteth in his way.
24 Though he fall, he shall not be utterly cast down: for the LORD upholdeth *him with* his hand.
25 I have been young, and *now* am old; yet have I not seen the righteous forsaken, nor his seed begging bread.
26 *He is* ever merciful, and lendeth; and his seed *is* blessed.
27 Depart from evil, and do good; and dwell for evermore.
28 For the LORD loveth judgment, and forsaketh not his saints; they are preserved for ever: but the seed of the wicked shall be cut off.
29 The righteous shall inherit the land, and dwell therein for ever.
30 The mouth of the righteous speaketh wisdom, and his tongue talketh of judgment.
31 The law of his God *is* in his heart; none of his steps shall slide.
32 The wicked watcheth the righteous, and seeketh to slay him.
33 The LORD will not leave him in his hand, nor condemn him when he is judged.
34 Wait on the LORD, and keep his way, and he shall exalt thee to inherit the land: when the wicked are cut off, thou shalt see *it.*
35 I have seen the wicked in great power, and spreading himself like a green bay tree.
36 Yet he passed away, and, lo, he

was not: yea, I sought him, but he could
not be found.
37 Mark the perfect *man*, and behold
the upright: for the end of *that* man *is*
peace.
38 But the transgressors shall be
destroyed together: the end of the
wicked shall be cut off.
39 But the salvation of the righteous
is of the LORD: *he is* their strength in the
time of trouble.
40 And the LORD shall help them, and
deliver them: he shall deliver them
from the wicked, and save them, be-
cause they trust in him.

PSALM 38

O LORD, rebuke me not in thy wrath:
neither chasten me in thy hot displeas-
ure.
2 For thine arrows stick fast in me,
and thy hand presseth me sore.
3 *There is* no soundness in my flesh
because of thine anger; neither *is there*
any rest in my bones because of my sin.
4 For mine iniquities are gone over
mine head: as an heavy burden they are
too heavy for me.
5 My wounds stink *and* are corrupt
because of my foolishness.
6 I am troubled; I am bowed down
greatly; I go mourning all the day long.
7 For my loins are filled with a
loathsome *disease:* and *there is* no
soundness in my flesh.
8 I am feeble and sore broken: I have
roared by reason of the disquietness of
my heart.
9 Lord, all my desire *is* before thee;
and my groaning is not hid from thee.
10 My heart panteth, my strength
faileth me: as for the light of mine eyes,
it also is gone from me.
11 My lovers and my friends stand
aloof from my sore; and my kinsmen
stand afar off.
12 They also that seek after my life
lay snares *for me:* and they that seek
my hurt speak mischievous things, and
imagine deceits all the day long.
13 But I, as a deaf *man*, heard not;
and *I was* as a dumb man *that* openeth
not his mouth.
14 Thus I was as a man that heareth
not, and in whose mouth *are* no re-
proofs.
15 For in thee, O LORD, do I hope:
thou wilt hear, O Lord my God.
16 For I said, *Hear me*, lest *otherwise*
they should rejoice over me: when my
foot slippeth, they magnify *themselves*
against me.
17 For I *am* ready to halt, and my
sorrow *is* continually before me.
18 For I will declare mine iniquity; I
will be sorry for my sin.
19 But mine enemies *are* lively, *and*
they are strong: and they that hate me
wrongfully are multiplied.
20 They also that render evil for good
are mine adversaries; because I follow
the thing that good *is*.
21 Forsake me not, O LORD: O my
God, be not far from me.
22 Make haste to help me, O Lord my
salvation.

PSALM 39

I SAID, I will take heed to my ways,
that I sin not with my tongue: I will
keep my mouth with a bridle, while the
wicked is before me.
2 I was dumb with silence, I held my
peace, *even* from good; and my sorrow
was stirred.
3 My heart was hot within me, while I
was musing the fire burned: *then* spake
I with my tongue,
4 LORD, make me to know mine end,
and the measure of my days, what it *is:*
that I may know how frail I *am*.
5 Behold, thou hast made my days *as*
an handbreadth; and mine age *is* as
nothing before thee: verily every man
at his best state *is* altogether vanity.
Sē′lah.
6 Surely every man walketh in a vain
shew: surely they are disquieted in
vain: he heapeth up *riches*, and
knoweth not who shall gather them.
7 And now, Lord, what wait I for? my
hope *is* in thee.
8 Deliver me from all my transgres-
sions: make me not the reproach of the
foolish.
9 I was dumb, I opened not my
mouth; because thou didst *it*.
10 Remove thy stroke away from me:
I am consumed by the blow of thine
hand.
11 When thou with rebukes dost cor-
rect man for iniquity, thou makest his
beauty to consume away like a moth:
surely every man *is* vanity. Sē′lah.
12 Hear my prayer, O LORD, and give
ear unto my cry; hold not thy peace at
my tears: for I *am* a stranger with thee,
and a sojourner, as all my fathers *were*.
13 O spare me, that I may recover
strength, before I go hence, and be no
more.

PSALM 40

I WAITED patiently for the LORD; and
he inclined unto me, and heard my cry.
2 He brought me up also out of an
horrible pit, out of the miry clay, and
set my feet upon a rock, *and* estab-
lished my goings.

3 And he hath put a new song in my
mouth, *even* praise unto our God:
many shall see *it*, and fear, and shall
trust in the LORD.
4 Blessed *is* that man that maketh the
LORD his trust, and respecteth not the
proud, nor such as turn aside to lies.
5 Many, O LORD my God, *are* thy
wonderful works *which* thou hast
done, and thy thoughts *which are* to us-
ward: they cannot be reckoned up in
order unto thee: *if* I would declare and
speak *of them*, they are more than can
be numbered.
6 Sacrifice and offering thou didst
not desire; mine ears hast thou opened:
burnt offering and sin offering hast
thou not required.
7 Then said I, Lo, I come: in the vol-
ume of the book *it is* written of me,
8 I delight to do thy will, O my God:
yea, thy law *is* within my heart.
9 I have preached righteousness in
the great congregation: lo, I have not
refrained my lips, O LORD, thou know-
est.
10 I have not hid thy righteousness
within my heart; I have declared thy
faithfulness and thy salvation: I have
not concealed thy lovingkindness and
thy truth from the great congregation.
11 Withhold not thou thy tender
mercies from me, O LORD: let thy lov-
ing kindness and thy truth continu-
ally preserve me.
12 For innumerable evils have com-
passed me about: mine iniquities have
taken hold upon me, so that I am not
able to look up; they are more than the
hairs of mine head: therefore my heart
faileth me.
13 Be pleased, O LORD, to deliver me:
O LORD, make haste to help me.
14 Let them be ashamed and con-
founded together that seek after my
soul to destroy it; let them be driven
backward and put to shame that wish
me evil.
15 Let them be desolate for a reward
of their shame that say unto me, Aha,
aha.
16 Let all those that seek thee rejoice
and be glad in thee: let such as love thy
salvation say continually, The LORD be
magnified.
17 But I *am* poor and needy; *yet* the
Lord thinketh upon me: thou *art* my
help and my deliverer; make no tarry-
ing, O my God.

PSALM 41

BLESSED *is* he that considereth the
poor: the LORD will deliver him in time
of trouble.
2 The LORD will preserve him, and
keep him alive; *and* he shall be blessed
upon the earth: and thou wilt not de-
liver him unto the will of his enemies.
3 The LORD will strengthen him upon
the bed of languishing: thou wilt make
all his bed in his sickness.
4 I said, LORD, be merciful unto me:
heal my soul; for I have sinned against
thee.
5 Mine enemies speak evil of me,
When shall he die, and his name per-
ish?
6 And if he come to see *me*, he
speaketh vanity: his heart gathereth
iniquity to itself; *when* he goeth
abroad, he telleth *it*.
7 All that hate me whisper together
against me: against me do they devise
my hurt.
8 An evil disease, *say they*, cleaveth
fast unto him: and *now* that he lieth he
shall rise up no more.
9 Yea, mine own familiar friend, in
whom I trusted, which did eat of my
bread, hath lifted up *his* heel against
me.
10 But thou, O LORD, be merciful unto
me, and raise me up, that I may requite
them.
11 By this I know that thou favourest
me, because mine enemy doth not
triumph over me.
12 And as for me, thou upholdest me
in mine integrity, and settest me before
thy face for ever.
13 Blessed *be* the LORD God of Israel
from everlasting, and to everlasting.
Amen, and Amen.

PSALM 42

AS the hart panteth after the water
brooks, so panteth my soul after thee,
O God.
2 My soul thirsteth for God, for the
living God: when shall I come and ap-
pear before God?
3 My tears have been my meat day
and night, while they continually say
unto me, Where *is* thy God?
4 When I remember these *things*, I
pour out my soul in me: for I had gone
with the multitude, I went with them to
the house of God, with the voice of joy
and praise, with a multitude that kept
holyday.
5 Why art thou cast down, O my
soul? and *why* art thou disquieted in
me? hope thou in God: for I shall yet
praise him *for* the help of his counte-
nance.
6 O my God, my soul is cast down
within me: therefore will I remember
thee from the land of Jordan, and of the
Her′mon-ītes, from the hill Mī′zär.
7 Deep calleth unto deep at the noise

of thy waterspouts: all thy waves and
thy billows are gone over me.
8 *Yet* the LORD will command his
lovingkindness in the daytime, and
in the night his song *shall be* with me,
and my prayer unto the God of my life.
9 I will say unto God my rock, Why
hast thou forgotten me? why go I mourning because of the oppression of the
enemy?
10 *As* with a sword in my bones, mine
enemies reproach me; while they say
daily unto me, Where *is* thy God?
11 Why art thou cast down, O my
soul? and why art thou disquieted
within me? hope thou in God: for I shall
yet praise him, *who is* the health of my
countenance, and my God.

PSALM 43

JUDGE me, O God, and plead my cause
against an ungodly nation: O deliver
me from the deceitful and unjust man.
2 For thou *art* the God of my
strength: why dost thou cast me off?
why go I mourning because of the oppression of the enemy?
3 O send out thy light and thy truth:
let them lead me; let them bring me
unto thy holy hill, and to thy tabernacles.
4 Then will I go unto the altar of God,
unto God my exceeding joy: yea, upon
the harp will I praise thee, O God my
God.
5 Why art thou cast down, O my
soul? and why art thou disquieted
within me? hope in God: for I shall yet
praise him, *who is* the health of my
countenance, and my God.

PSALM 44

WE have heard with our ears, O God,
our fathers have told us, *what* work
thou didst in their days, in the times of
old.
2 *How* thou didst drive out the
heathen with thy hand, and plantedst
them; *how* thou didst afflict the people,
and cast them out.
3 For they got not the land in possession by their own sword, neither did
their own arm save them: but thy right
hand, and thine arm, and the light of
thy countenance, because thou hadst a
favour unto them.
4 Thou art my King, O God: command deliverances for Jacob.
5 Through thee will we push down
our enemies: through thy name will we
tread them under that rise up against
us.
6 For I will not trust in my bow,
neither shall my sword save me.
7 But thou hast saved us from our enemies, and hast put them to shame that
hated us.
8 In God we boast all the day long,
and praise thy name for ever. Sē'lah.
9 But thou hast cast off, and put us to
shame; and goest not forth with our armies.
10 Thou makest us to turn back from
the enemy: and they which hate us
spoil for themselves.
11 Thou hast given us like sheep *appointed* for meat; and hast scattered us
among the heathen.
12 Thou sellest thy people for nought,
and dost not increase *thy wealth* by
their price.
13 Thou makest us a reproach to our
neighbours, a scorn and a derision to
them that are round about us.
14 Thou makest us a byword among
the heathen, a shaking of the head
among the people.
15 My confusion *is* continually before me, and the shame of my face hath
covered me,
16 For the voice of him that reproacheth and blasphemeth; by reason of the
enemy and avenger.
17 All this is come upon us; yet have
we not forgotten thee, neither have we
dealt falsely in thy covenant.
18 Our heart is not turned back,
neither have our steps declined from
thy way;
19 Though thou hast sore broken us
in the place of dragons, and covered us
with the shadow of death.
20 If we have forgotten the name of
our God, or stretched out our hands to a
strange god;
21 Shall not God search this out? for
he knoweth the secrets of the heart.
22 Yea, for thy sake are we killed all
the day long; we are counted as sheep
for the slaughter.
23 Awake, why sleepest thou, O
Lord? arise, cast *us* not off for ever.
24 Wherefore hidest thou thy face,
and forgettest our affliction and our
oppression?
25 For our soul is bowed down to the
dust: our belly cleaveth unto the earth.
26 Arise for our help, and redeem us
for thy mercies' sake.

PSALM 45

MY heart is inditing a good matter: I
speak of the things which I have made
touching the king: my tongue *is* the pen
of a ready writer.
2 Thou art fairer than the children of
men: grace is poured into thy lips: therefore God hath blessed thee for ever.
3 Gird thy sword upon *thy* thigh, O

most mighty, with thy glory and thy majesty.
4 And in thy majesty ride prosperously because of truth and meekness *and* righteousness; and thy right hand shall teach thee terrible things.
5 Thine arrows *are* sharp in the heart of the king's enemies; *whereby* the people fall under thee.
6 Thy throne, O God, *is* for ever and ever: the sceptre of thy kingdom *is* a right sceptre.
7 Thou lovest righteousness, and hatest wickedness: therefore God, thy God, hath anointed thee with the oil of gladness above thy fellows.
8 All thy garments *smell* of myrrh, and aloes, *and* cassia, out of the ivory palaces, whereby they have made thee glad.
9 Kings' daughters *were* among thy honourable women: upon thy right hand did stand the queen in gold of Ō'phir.
10 Hearken, O daughter, and consider, and incline thine ear; forget also thine own people, and thy father's house;
11 So shall the king greatly desire thy beauty: for he *is* thy Lord; and worship thou him.
12 And the daughter of Tyre *shall be there* with a gift; *even* the rich among the people shall intreat thy favour.
13 The king's daughter *is* all glorious within: her clothing *is* of wrought gold.
14 She shall be brought unto the king in raiment of needlework: the virgins her companions that follow her shall be brought unto thee.
15 With gladness and rejoicing shall they be brought: they shall enter into the king's palace.
16 Instead of thy fathers shall be thy children, whom thou mayest make princes in all the earth.
17 I will make thy name to be remembered in all generations: therefore shall the people praise thee for ever and ever.

PSALM 46

GOD *is* our refuge and strength, a very present help in trouble.
2 Therefore will not we fear, though the earth be removed, and though the mountains be carried into the midst of the sea;
3 *Though* the waters thereof roar *and* be troubled, *though* the mountains shake with the swelling thereof. Sē'lah.
4 *There is* a river, the streams whereof shall make glad the city of God, the holy *place* of the tabernacles of the most High.
5 God *is* in the midst of her; she shall not be moved: God shall help her, *and that* right early.
6 The heathen raged, the kingdoms were moved: he uttered his voice, the earth melted.
7 The LORD of hosts *is* with us; the God of Jacob *is* our refuge. Sē'lah.
8 Come, behold the works of the LORD, what desolations he hath made in the earth.
9 He maketh wars to cease unto the end of the earth; he breaketh the bow, and cutteth the spear in sunder; he burneth the chariot in the fire.
10 Be still, and know that I *am* God: I will be exalted among the heathen, I will be exalted in the earth.
11 The LORD of hosts *is* with us; the God of Jacob *is* our refuge. Sē'lah.

PSALM 47

O CLAP your hands, all ye people; shout unto God with the voice of triumph.
2 For the LORD most high *is* terrible; *he is* a great King over all the earth.
3 He shall subdue the people under us, and the nations under our feet.
4 He shall choose our inheritance for us, the excellency of Jacob whom he loved. Sē'lah.
5 God is gone up with a shout, the LORD with the sound of a trumpet.
6 Sing praises to God, sing praises: sing praises unto our King, sing praises.
7 For God *is* the King of all the earth: sing ye praises with understanding.
8 God reigneth over the heathen: God sitteth upon the throne of his holiness.
9 The princes of the people are gathered together, *even* the people of the God of Abraham: for the shields of the earth *belong* unto God: he is greatly exalted.

PSALM 48

GREAT *is* the LORD, and greatly to be praised in the city of our God, *in* the mountain of his holiness.
2 Beautiful for situation, the joy of the whole earth, *is* mount Zion, *on* the sides of the north, the city of the great King.
3 God is known in her palaces for a refuge.
4 For, lo, the kings were assembled, they passed by together.
5 They saw *it*, *and* so they marvelled; they were troubled, *and* hasted away.
6 Fear took hold upon them there, *and* pain, as of a woman in travail.
7 Thou breakest the ships of Tärshĭsh with an east wind.

8 As we have heard, so have we seen
in the city of the LORD of hosts, in the
city of our God: God will establish it for
ever. Sē'lah.
9 We have thought of thy lovingkind-
ness, O God, in the midst of thy temple.
10 According to thy name, O God, so
is thy praise unto the ends of the earth:
thy right hand is full of righteousness.
11 Let mount Zion rejoice, let the
daughters of Jūdah be glad, because of
thy judgments.
12 Walk about Zion, and go round
about her: tell the towers thereof.
13 Mark ye well her bulwarks, con-
sider her palaces; that ye may tell *it* to
the generation following.
14 For this God *is* our God for ever
and ever: he will be our guide *even* unto
death.

PSALM 49

HEAR this, all *ye* people; give ear, all *ye*
inhabitants of the world:
2 Both low and high, rich and poor,
together.
3 My mouth shall speak of wisdom;
and the meditation of my heart *shall be*
of understanding.
4 I will incline mine ear to a parable: I
will open my dark saying upon the
harp.
5 Wherefore should I fear in the days
of evil, *when* the iniquity of my heels
shall compass me about?
6 They that trust in their wealth, and
boast themselves in the multitude of
their riches;
7 None *of them* can by any means re-
deem his brother, nor give to God a ran-
som for him:
8 (For the redemption of their soul *is*
precious, and it ceaseth for ever:)
9 That he should still live for ever,
and not see corruption.
10 For he seeth *that* wise men die,
likewise the fool and the brutish person
perish, and leave their wealth to others.
11 Their inward thought *is, that* their
houses *shall continue* for ever, *and*
their dwelling places to all generations;
they call *their* lands after their own
names.
12 Nevertheless man *being* in honour
abideth not: he is like the beasts *that*
perish.
13 This their way *is* their folly: yet
their posterity approve their sayings.
Sē'lah.
14 Like sheep they are laid in the
grave; death shall feed on them; and
the upright shall have dominion over
them in the morning; and their beauty
shall consume in the grave from their
dwelling.
15 But God will redeem my soul from
the power of the grave: for he shall re-
ceive me. Sē'lah.
16 Be not thou afraid when one is
made rich, when the glory of his house
is increased;
17 For when he dieth he shall carry
nothing away: his glory shall not de-
scend after him.
18 Though while he lived he blessed
his soul: and *men* will praise thee, when
thou doest well to thyself.
19 He shall go to the generation of his
fathers; they shall never see light.
20 Man *that is* in honour, and under-
standeth not, is like the beasts *that* per-
ish.

PSALM 50

THE mighty God, *even* the LORD, hath
spoken, and called the earth from the
rising of the sun unto the going down
thereof.
2 Out of Zion, the perfection of
beauty, God hath shined.
3 Our God shall come, and shall not
keep silence: a fire shall devour before
him, and it shall be very tempestuous
round about him.
4 He shall call to the heavens from
above, and to the earth, that he may
judge his people.
5 Gather my saints together unto me;
those that have made a covenant with
me by sacrifice.
6 And the heavens shall declare his
righteousness: for God *is* judge him-
self. Sē'lah.
7 Hear, O my people, and I will speak;
O Israel, and I will testify against thee: I
am God, *even* thy God.
8 I will not reprove thee for thy sacri-
fices or thy burnt offerings, *to have been*
continually before me.
9 I will take no bullock out of thy
house, *nor* he goats out of thy folds.
10 For every beast of the forest *is*
mine, *and* the cattle upon a thousand
hills.
11 I know all the fowls of the moun-
tains: and the wild beasts of the field
are mine.
12 If I were hungry, I would not tell
thee: for the world *is* mine, and the ful-
ness thereof.
13 Will I eat the flesh of bulls, or
drink the blood of goats?
14 Offer unto God thanksgiving; and
pay thy vows unto the most High:
15 And call upon me in the day of
trouble: I will deliver thee, and thou
shalt glorify me.
16 But unto the wicked God saith,
What hast thou to do to declare my stat-

utes, or *that* thou shouldest take my
covenant in thy mouth?
17 Seeing thou hatest instruction,
and casteth my words behind thee.
18 When thou sawest a thief, then
thou consentedst with him, and hast
been partaker with adulterers.
19 Thou givest thy mouth to evil, and
thy tongue frameth deceit.
20 Thou sittest *and* speakest against
thy brother; thou slanderest thine own
mother's son.
21 These *things* hast thou done, and I
kept silence; thou thoughtest that I was
altogether *such an one* as thyself: *but* I
will reprove thee, and set *them* in order
before thine eyes.
22 Now consider this, ye that forget
God, lest I tear *you* in pieces, and *there*
be none to deliver.
23 Whoso offereth praise glorifieth
me: and to him that ordereth *his* con-
versation *aright* will I shew the salva-
tion of God.

PSALM 51

HAVE mercy upon me, O God, accord-
ing to thy lovingkindness: according
unto the multitude of thy tender
mercies blot out my transgressions.
2 Wash me throughly from mine iniq-
uity, and cleanse me from my sin.
3 For I acknowledge my transgres-
sions: and my sin *is* ever before me.
4 Against thee, thee only, have I
sinned, and done *this* evil in thy sight:
that thou mightest be justified when
thou speakest, *and* be clear when thou
judgest.
5 Behold, I was shapen in iniquity;
and in sin did my mother conceive me.
6 Behold, thou desirest truth in the in-
ward parts: and in the hidden *part* thou
shalt make me to know wisdom.
7 Purge me with hyssop, and I shall
be clean: wash me, and I shall be whiter
than snow.
8 Make me to hear joy and gladness;
that the bones *which* thou hast broken
may rejoice.
9 Hide thy face from my sins, and
blot out all mine iniquities.
10 Create in me a clean heart, O God;
and renew a right spirit within me.
11 Cast me not away from thy pres-
ence; and take not thy holy spirit from
me.
12 Restore unto me the joy of thy sal-
vation; and uphold me *with thy* free
spirit.
13 *Then* will I teach transgressors thy
ways; and sinners shall be converted
unto thee.
14 Deliver me from bloodguiltiness,
O God, thou God of my salvation: *and*
my tongue shall sing aloud of thy
righteousness.
15 O Lord, open thou my lips; and my
mouth shall shew forth thy praise.
16 For thou desirest not sacrifice;
else would I give *it:* thou delightest not
in burnt offering.
17 The sacrifices of God *are* a broken
spirit: a broken and a contrite heart, O
God, thou wilt not despise.
18 Do good in thy good pleasure unto
Zion: build thou the walls of Jerusalem.
19 Then shalt thou be pleased with
the sacrifices of righteousness, with
burnt offering and whole burnt offer-
ing: then shall they offer bullocks upon
thine altar.

PSALM 52

WHY boastest thou thyself in mischief,
O mighty man? the goodness of God
endureth continually.
2 Thy tongue deviseth mischiefs; like
a sharp razor, working deceitfully.
3 Thou lovest evil more than good;
and lying rather than to speak
righteousness. Sē'lah.
4 Thou lovest all devouring words, O
thou deceitful tongue.
5 God shall likewise destroy thee for
ever, he shall take thee away, and pluck
thee out of *thy* dwelling place, and root
thee out of the land of the living. Sē'lah.
6 The righteous also shall see, and
fear, and shall laugh at him:
7 Lo, *this is* the man *that* made not
God his strength; but trusted in the
abundance of his riches, *and*
strengthened himself in his wicked-
ness.
8 But I *am* like a green olive tree in
the house of God: I trust in the mercy of
God for ever and ever.
9 I will praise thee for ever, because
thou hast done *it:* and I will wait on thy
name; for *it is* good before thy saints.

PSALM 53

THE fool hath said in his heart, *There is*
no God. Corrupt are they, and have
done abominable iniquity: *there is*
none that doeth good.
2 God looked down from heaven
upon the children of men, to see if there
were *any* that did understand, that did
seek God.
3 Every one of them is gone back:
they are altogether become filthy;
there is none that doeth good, no, not
one.
4 Have the workers of iniquity no
knowledge? who eat up my people *as*
they eat bread: they have not called
upon God.
5 There were they in great fear,

where no fear was: for God hath scattered the bones of him that encampeth *against* thee: thou hast put *them* to shame, because God hath despised them.

6 Oh that the salvation of Israel *were come* out of Zion! When God bringeth back the captivity of his people, Jacob shall rejoice, *and* Israel shall be glad.

PSALM 54

SAVE me, O God, by thy name, and judge me by thy strength.

2 Hear my prayer, O God; give ear to the words of my mouth.

3 For strangers are risen up against me, and oppressors seek after my soul: they have not set God before them. Sē′lah.

4 Behold, God *is* mine helper: the Lord *is* with them that uphold my soul.

5 He shall reward evil unto mine enemies: cut them off in thy truth.

6 I will freely sacrifice unto thee: I will praise thy name, O LORD; for *it is* good.

7 For he hath delivered me out of all trouble: and mine eye hath seen *his desire* upon mine enemies.

PSALM 55

GIVE ear to my prayer, O God; and hide not thyself from my supplication.

2 Attend unto me, and hear me: I mourn in my complaint, and make a noise;

3 Because of the voice of the enemy, because of the oppression of the wicked: for they cast iniquity upon me, and in wrath they hate me.

4 My heart is sore pained within me: and the terrors of death are fallen upon me.

5 Fearfulness and trembling are come upon me, and horror hath overwhelmed me.

6 And I said, Oh that I had wings like a dove! *for then* would I fly away, and be at rest.

7 Lo, *then* would I wander far off, *and* remain in the wilderness. Sē′lah.

8 I would hasten my escape from the windy storm *and* tempest.

9 Destroy, O Lord, *and* divide their tongues: for I have seen violence and strife in the city.

10 Day and night they go about it upon the walls thereof: mischief also and sorrow *are* in the midst of it.

11 Wickedness *is* in the midst thereof: deceit and guile depart not from her streets.

12 For *it was* not an enemy *that* reproached me; then I could have borne *it:* neither *was it* he that hated me *that* did magnify *himself* against me; then I would have hid myself from him:

13 But *it was* thou, a man mine equal, my guide, and mine acquaintance.

14 We took sweet counsel together, *and* walked unto the house of God in company.

15 Let death seize upon them, *and* let them go down quick into hell: for wickedness *is* in their dwellings, *and* among them.

16 As for me, I will call upon God; and the LORD shall save me.

17 Evening, and morning, and at noon, will I pray, and cry aloud: and he shall hear my voice.

18 He hath delivered my soul in peace from the battle *that was* against me: for there were many with me.

19 God shall hear, and afflict them, even he that abideth of old. Sē′lah. Because they have no changes, therefore they fear not God.

20 He hath put forth his hands against such as be at peace with him: he hath broken his covenant.

21 *The words* of his mouth were smoother than butter, but war *was* in his heart: his words were softer than oil, yet *were* they drawn swords.

22 Cast thy burden upon the LORD, and he shall sustain thee: he shall never suffer the righteous to be moved.

23 But thou, O God, shalt bring them down into the pit of destruction: bloody and deceitful men shall not live out half their days; but I will trust in thee.

PSALM 56

BE merciful unto me, O God: for man would swallow me up; he fighting daily oppresseth me.

2 Mine enemies would daily swallow *me* up: for *they be* many that fight against me, O thou most High.

3 What time I am afraid, I will trust in thee.

4 In God I will praise his word, in God I have put my trust; I will not fear what flesh can do unto me.

5 Every day they wrest my words: all their thoughts *are* against me for evil.

6 They gather themselves together, they hide themselves, they mark my steps, when they wait for my soul.

7 Shall they escape by iniquity? in *thine* anger cast down the people, O God.

8 Thou tellest my wanderings: put thou my tears into thy bottle: *are they* not in thy book?

9 When I cry *unto thee*, then shall mine enemies turn back: this I know; for God *is* for me.

10 In God will I praise *his* word: in the
LORD will I praise *his* word.
11 In God have I put my trust: I will
not be afraid what man can do unto me.
12 Thy vows *are* upon me, O God: I
will render praises unto thee.
13 For thou hast delivered my soul
from death: *wilt* not *thou deliver* my
feet from falling, that I may walk be-
fore God in the light of the living?

PSALM 57

BE merciful unto me, O God, be merci-
ful unto me: for my soul trusteth in
thee: yea, in the shadow of thy wings
will I make my refuge, until *these* ca-
lamities be overpast.
2 I will cry unto God most high; unto
God that performeth *all things* for me.
3 He shall send from heaven, and
save me *from* the reproach of him that
would swallow me up. Sē'lah. God shall
send forth his mercy and his truth.
4 My soul *is* among lions: *and* I lie
even among them that are set on fire,
even the sons of men, whose teeth *are*
spears and arrows, and their tongue a
sharp sword.
5 Be thou exalted, O God, above the
heavens; *let* thy glory *be* above all the
earth.
6 They have prepared a net for my
steps; my soul is bowed down: they
have digged a pit before me, into the
midst whereof they are fallen *them-
selves*. Sē'lah.
7 My heart is fixed, O God, my heart
is fixed: I will sing and give praise.
8 Awake up, my glory; awake, psal-
tery and harp: I *myself* will awake
early.
9 I will praise thee, O Lord, among
the people: I will sing unto thee among
the nations.
10 For thy mercy *is* great unto the
heavens, and thy truth unto the clouds.
11 Be thou exalted, O God, above the
heavens: *let* thy glory *be* above all the
earth.

PSALM 58

DO ye indeed speak righteousness, O
congregation? do ye judge uprightly, O
ye sons of men?
2 Yea, in heart ye work wickedness;
ye weigh the violence of your hands in
the earth.
3 The wicked are estranged from the
womb: they go astray as soon as they
be born, speaking lies.
4 Their poison *is* like the poison of a
serpent: *they are* like the deaf adder
that stoppeth her ear;
5 Which will not hearken to the voice
of charmers, charming never so wisely.
6 Break their teeth, O God, in their
mouth: break out the great teeth of the
young lions, O LORD.
7 Let them melt away as waters
which run continually: *when* he bend-
eth *his bow to shoot* his arrows, let
them be as cut in pieces.
8 As a snail *which* melteth, let *every
one of them* pass away: *like* the untime-
ly birth of a woman, *that* they may not
see the sun.
9 Before your pots can feel the
thorns, he shall take them away as with
a whirlwind, both living, and in *his*
wrath.
10 The righteous shall rejoice when
he seeth the vengeance: he shall wash
his feet in the blood of the wicked.
11 So that a man shall say, Verily
there is a reward for the righteous:
verily he is a God that judgeth in the
earth.

PSALM 59

DELIVER me from mine enemies, O
my God: defend me from them that rise
up against me.
2 Deliver me from the workers of iniq-
uity, and save me from bloody men.
3 For, lo, they lie in wait for my soul:
the mighty are gathered against me;
not *for* my transgression, nor *for* my
sin, O LORD.
4 They run and prepare themselves
without *my* fault: awake to help me,
and behold.
5 Thou therefore, O LORD God of
hosts, the God of Israel, awake to visit
all the heathen: be not merciful to any
wicked transgressors. Sē'lah.
6 They return at evening: they make a
noise like a dog, and go round about the
city.
7 Behold, they belch out with their
mouth: swords *are* in their lips: for
who, *say they*, doth hear?
8 But thou, O LORD, shalt laugh at
them; thou shalt have all the heathen in
derision.
9 *Because of* his strength will I wait
upon thee: for God *is* my defence.
10 The God of my mercy shall pre-
vent me: God shall let me see *my desire*
upon mine enemies.
11 Slay them not, lest my people for-
get: scatter them by thy power; and
bring them down, O Lord our shield.
12 *For* the sin of their mouth *and* the
words of their lips let them even be
taken in their pride: and for cursing and
lying *which* they speak.
13 Consume *them* in wrath, consume
them, that they *may* not *be*: and let
them know that God ruleth in Jacob
unto the ends of the earth. Sē'lah.

14 And at evening let them return; *and* let them make a noise like a dog, and go round about the city.
15 Let them wander up and down for meat, and grudge if they be not satisfied.
16 But I will sing of thy power; yea, I will sing aloud of thy mercy in the morning: for thou hast been my defence and refuge in the day of my trouble.
17 Unto thee, O my strength, will I sing: for God *is* my defence, *and* the God of my mercy.

PSALM 60

O GOD, thou hast cast us off, thou hast scattered us, thou hast been displeased; O turn thyself to us again.
2 Thou hast made the earth to tremble; thou hast broken it: heal the breaches thereof; for it shaketh.
3 Thou hast shewed thy people hard things: thou hast made us to drink the wine of astonishment.
4 Thou hast given a banner to them that fear thee, that it may be displayed because of the truth. Sē'lah.
5 That thy beloved may be delivered; save *with* thy right hand, and hear me.
6 God hath spoken in his holiness; I will rejoice, I will divide Shĕ'chem, and mete out the valley of Sŭc'coth.
7 Gilead *is* mine, and Ma-năs'seh *is* mine; Ē'phra-im also *is* the strength of mine head; Jū'dah *is* my lawgiver;
8 Moab *is* my washpot; over Edom will I cast out my shoe: Philistia, triumph thou because of me.
9 Who will bring me *into* the strong city? who will lead me into Edom?
10 *Wilt* not thou, O God, *which* hadst cast us off? and *thou,* O God, *which* didst not go out with our armies?
11 Give us help from trouble: for vain *is* the help of man.
12 Through God we shall do valiantly: for he *it is that* shall tread down our enemies.

PSALM 61

HEAR my cry, O God; attend unto my prayer.
2 From the end of the earth will I cry unto thee, when my heart is overwhelmed: lead me to the rock *that* is higher than I.
3 For thou hast been a shelter for me, *and* a strong tower from the enemy.
4 I will abide in thy tabernacle for ever: I will trust in the covert of thy wings. Sē'lah.
5 For thou, O God, hast heard my vows: thou hast given *me* the heritage of those that fear thy name.
6 Thou wilt prolong the king's life: *and* his years as many generations.
7 He shall abide before God for ever: O prepare mercy and truth, *which* may preserve him.
8 So will I sing praise unto thy name for ever, that I may daily perform my vows.

PSALM 62

TRULY my soul waiteth upon God: from him *cometh* my salvation.
2 He only *is* my rock and my salvation; *he is* my defence; I shall not be greatly moved.
3 How long will ye imagine mischief against a man? ye shall be slain all of you: as a bowing wall *shall ye be, and as* a tottering fence.
4 They only consult to cast *him* down from his excellency: they delight in lies: they bless with their mouth, but they curse inwardly. Sē'lah.
5 My soul, wait thou only upon God; for my expectation *is* from him.
6 He only *is* my rock and my salvation: *he is* my defence; I shall not be moved.
7 In God *is* my salvation and my glory: the rock of my strength, *and* my refuge, *is* in God.
8 Trust in him at all times; ye people, pour out your heart before him: God *is* a refuge for us. Sē'lah.
9 Surely men of low degree *are* vanity, *and* men of high degree *are* a lie: to be laid in the balance, they *are* altogether *lighter* than vanity.
10 Trust not in oppression, and become not vain in robbery: if riches increase, set not your heart *upon them.*
11 God hath spoken once; twice have I heard this; that power *belongeth* unto God.
12 Also unto thee, O Lord, *belongeth* mercy: for thou renderest to every man according to his work.

PSALM 63

O GOD, thou *art* my God; early will I seek thee: my soul thirsteth for thee, my flesh longeth for thee in a dry and thirsty land, where no water is;
2 To see thy power and thy glory, so *as* I have seen thee in the sanctuary.
3 Because thy lovingkindness *is* better than life, my lips shall praise thee.
4 Thus will I bless thee while I live: I will lift up my hands in thy name.
5 My soul shall be satisfied as *with* marrow and fatness; and my mouth shall praise *thee* with joyful lips:
6 When I remember thee upon my bed, *and* meditate on thee in the *night* watches.

7 Because thou hast been my help,
therefore in the shadow of thy wings
will I rejoice.
8 My soul followeth hard after thee:
thy right hand upholdeth me.
9 But those *that* seek my soul, to de-
stroy *it*, shall go into the lower parts of
the earth.
10 They shall fall by the sword: they
shall be a portion for foxes.
11 But the king shall rejoice in God;
every one that sweareth by him shall
glory: but the mouth of them that speak
lies shall be stopped.

PSALM 64

HEAR my voice, O God, in my prayer:
preserve my life from fear of the en-
emy.
2 Hide me from the secret counsel of
the wicked; from the insurrection of
the workers of iniquity:
3 Who whet their tongue like a
sword, *and* bend *their bows to shoot*
their arrows, *even* bitter words:
4 That they may shoot in secret at the
perfect: suddenly do they shoot at him,
and fear not.
5 They encourage themselves *in* an
evil matter: they commune of laying
snares privily; they say, Who shall see
them?
6 They search out iniquities; they ac-
complish a diligent search: both the in-
ward *thought* of every one *of them*, and
the heart, *is* deep.
7 But God shall shoot at them *with* an
arrow; suddenly shall they be
wounded.
8 So they shall make their own
tongue to fall upon themselves: all that
see them shall flee away.
9 And all men shall fear, and shall
declare the work of God; for they shall
wisely consider of his doing.
10 The righteous shall be glad in the
LORD, and shall trust in him; and all the
upright in heart shall glory.

PSALM 65

PRAISE waiteth for thee, O God, in
Sion: and unto thee shall the vow be
performed.
2 O thou that hearest prayer, unto
thee shall all flesh come.
3 Iniquities prevail against me: *as for*
our transgressions, thou shalt purge
them away.
4 Blessed *is the man whom* thou
choosest, and causest to approach *unto*
thee, that he may dwell in thy courts:
we shall be satisfied with the goodness
of thy house, *even* of thy holy temple.
5 *By* terrible things in righteousness
wilt thou answer us, O God of our sal-
vation; *who art* the confidence of all the
ends of the earth, and of them that are
afar off *upon* the sea:
6 Which by his strength setteth fast
the mountains; *being* girded with pow-
er:
7 Which stilleth the noise of the seas,
the noise of their waves, and the tumult
of the people.
8 They also that dwell in the utter-
most parts are afraid at thy tokens:
thou makest the outgoings of the morn-
ing and evening to rejoice.
9 Thou visitest the earth, and water-
est it: thou greatly enrichest it with the
river of God, *which* is full of water:
thou preparest them corn, when thou
hast so provided for it.
10 Thou waterest the ridges thereof
abundantly: thou settlest the furrows
thereof: thou makest it soft with show-
ers: thou blessest the springing thereof.
11 Thou crownest the year with thy
goodness; and thy paths drop fatness.
12 They drop *upon* the pastures of the
wilderness: and the little hills rejoice
on every side.
13 The pastures are clothed with
flocks; the valleys also are covered
over with corn; they shout for joy, they
also sing.

PSALM 66

MAKE a joyful noise unto God, all ye
lands:
2 Sing forth the honour of his name:
make his praise glorious.
3 Say unto God, How terrible *art thou*
in thy works! through the greatness of
thy power shall thine enemies submit
themselves unto thee.
4 All the earth shall worship thee,
and shall sing unto thee; they shall sing
to thy name. Sē'lah.
5 Come and see the works of God: *he*
is terrible *in his* doing toward the chil-
dren of men.
6 He turned the sea into dry *land*:
they went through the flood on foot:
there did we rejoice in him.
7 He ruleth by his power for ever; his
eyes behold the nations: let not the re-
bellious exalt themselves. Sē'lah.
8 O bless our God, ye people, and
make the voice of his praise to be
heard:
9 Which holdeth our soul in life, and
suffereth not our feet to be moved.
10 For thou, O God, hast proved us:
thou hast tried us, as silver is tried.
11 Thou broughtest us into the net;
thou laidst affliction upon our loins.
12 Thou hast caused men to ride over
our heads; we went through fire and

through water: but thou broughtest us
out into a wealthy *place*.
13 I will go into thy house with burnt
offerings: I will pay thee my vows,
14 Which my lips have uttered, and
my mouth hath spoken, when I was in
trouble.
15 I will offer unto thee burnt sacri-
fices of fatlings, with the incense of
rams; I will offer bullocks with goats.
Sē'lah.
16 Come *and* hear, all ye that fear
God, and I will declare what he hath
done for my soul.
17 I cried unto him with my mouth,
and he was extolled with my tongue.
18 If I regard iniquity in my heart, the
Lord will not hear *me*:
19 *But* verily God hath heard *me*; he
hath attended to the voice of my
prayer.
20 Blessed *be* God, which hath not
turned away my prayer, nor his mercy
from me.

PSALM 67

GOD be merciful unto us, and bless us;
and cause his face to shine upon us; Sē'-
lah.
2 That thy way may be known upon
earth, thy saving health among all na-
tions.
3 Let the people praise thee, O God;
let all the people praise thee.
4 O let the nations be glad and sing
for joy: for thou shalt judge the people
righteously, and govern the nations
upon earth. Sē'lah.
5 Let the people praise thee, O God;
let all the people praise thee.
6 *Then* shall the earth yield her in-
crease; *and* God, *even* our own God,
shall bless us.
7 God shall bless us; and all the ends
of the earth shall fear him.

PSALM 68

LET God arise, let his enemies be scat-
tered: let them also that hate him flee
before him.
2 As smoke is driven away, *so* drive
them away: as wax melteth before the
fire, *so* let the wicked perish at the pres-
ence of God.
3 But let the righteous be glad; let
them rejoice before God: yea, let them
exceedingly rejoice.
4 Sing unto God, sing praises to his
name: extol him that rideth upon the
heavens by his name JAH, and rejoice
before him.
5 A father of the fatherless, and a
judge of the widows, *is* God in his holy
habitation.
6 God setteth the solitary in families:
he bringeth out those which are bound
with chains: but the rebellious dwell in
a dry *land*.
7 O God, when thou wentest forth be-
fore thy people, when thou didst march
through the wilderness; Sē'lah:
8 The earth shook, the heavens also
dropped at the presence of God: *even*
Sī'naī itself *was moved* at the presence
of God, the God of Israel.
9 Thou, O God, didst send a plentiful
rain, whereby thou didst confirm thine
inheritance, when it was weary.
10 Thy congregation hath dwelt
therein: thou, O God, hast prepared of
thy goodness for the poor.
11 The Lord gave the word: great *was*
the company of those that published *it*.
12 Kings of armies did flee apace:
and she that tarried at home divided
the spoil.
13 Though ye have lien among the
pots, *yet shall ye be as* the wings of a
dove covered with silver, and her feath-
ers with yellow gold.
14 When the Almighty scattered
kings in it, it was *white* as snow in Săl'-
mon.
15 The hill of God *is as* the hill of Bā'-
shan; an high hill *as* the hill of Bā'shan.
16 Why leap ye, ye high hills? *this is*
the hill *which* God desireth to dwell in;
yea, the LORD will dwell *in it* for ever.
17 The chariots of God *are* twenty
thousand, *even* thousands of angels:
the Lord *is* among them, *as in* Sī'naī, in
the holy *place*.
18 Thou hast ascended on high, thou
hast led captivity captive: thou hast re-
ceived gifts for men; yea, *for* the rebel-
lious also, that the LORD God might
dwell *among them*.
19 Blessed *be* the Lord, *who* daily
loadeth us *with benefits, even* the God
of our salvation. Sē'lah.
20 *He that is* our God *is* the God of
salvation; and unto GOD the Lord *belong*
the issues from death.
21 But God shall wound the head of
his enemies, *and* the hairy scalp of such
an one as goeth on still in his tres-
passes.
22 The Lord said, I will bring again
from Bā'shan, I will bring *my people*
again from the depths of the sea:
23 That thy foot may be dipped in the
blood of *thine* enemies, *and* the tongue
of thy dogs in the same.
24 They have seen thy goings, O God;
even the goings of my God, my King, in
the sanctuary.
25 The singers went before, the
players on instruments *followed* after;
among *them were* the damsels playing
with timbrels.

26 Bless ye God in the congregations, *even* the Lord, from the fountain of Israel.

27 There *is* little Benjamin *with* their ruler, the princes of Jū'dah *and* their council, the princes of Zĕb'u-lun, *and* the princes of Năph'ta-lī.

28 Thy God hath commanded thy strength: strengthen, O God, that which thou hast wrought for us.

29 Because of thy temple at Jerusalem shall kings bring presents unto thee.

30 Rebuke the company of spearmen, the multitude of the bulls, with the calves of the people, *till every one* submit himself with pieces of silver: scatter thou the people *that* delight in war.

31 Princes shall come out of Egypt; Ē-thĭ-ō'pĭ-a shall soon stretch out her hands unto God.

32 Sing unto God, ye kingdoms of the earth; O sing praises unto the Lord; Sē'-lah:

33 To him that rideth upon the heavens of heavens, *which were* of old; lo, he doth send out his voice, *and that* a mighty voice.

34 Ascribe ye strength unto God: his excellency *is* over Israel, and his strength *is* in the clouds.

35 O God, *thou art* terrible out of thy holy places: the God of Israel *is* he that giveth strength and power unto *his* people. Blessed *be* God.

PSALM 69

SAVE me, O God; for the waters are come in unto *my* soul.

2 I sink in deep mire, where *there is* no standing: I am come into deep waters, where the floods overflow me.

3 I am weary of my crying: my throat is dried: mine eyes fail while I wait for my God.

4 They that hate me without a cause are more than the hairs of mine head: they that would destroy me, *being* mine enemies wrongfully, are mighty: then I restored *that* which I took not away.

5 O God, thou knowest my foolishness; and my sins are not hid from thee.

6 Let not them that wait on thee, O Lord GOD of hosts, be ashamed for my sake: let not those that seek thee be confounded for my sake, O God of Israel.

7 Because for thy sake I have borne reproach; shame hath covered my face.

8 I am become a stranger unto my brethren, and an alien unto my mother's children.

9 For the zeal of thine house hath eaten me up; and the reproaches of them that reproached thee are fallen upon me.

10 When I wept, *and chastened* my soul with fasting, that was to my reproach.

11 I made sackcloth also my garment; and I became a proverb to them.

12 They that sit in the gate speak against me; and I *was* the song of the drunkards.

13 But as for me, my prayer *is* unto thee, O LORD, *in* an acceptable time: O God, in the multitude of thy mercy hear me, in the truth of thy salvation.

14 Deliver me out of the mire, and let me not sink: let me be delivered from them that hate me, and out of the deep waters.

15 Let not the waterflood overflow me, neither let the deep swallow me up, and let not the pit shut her mouth upon me.

16 Hear me, O LORD; for thy lovingkindness *is* good: turn unto me according to the multitude of thy tender mercies.

17 And hide not thy face from thy servant; for I am in trouble: hear me speedily.

18 Draw nigh unto my soul, *and* redeem it: deliver me because of mine enemies.

19 Thou hast known my reproach, and my shame, and my dishonour: mine adversaries *are* all before thee.

20 Reproach hath broken my heart; and I am full of heaviness: and I looked *for some* to take pity, but *there was* none; and for comforters, but I found none.

21 They gave me also gall for my meat; and in my thirst they gave me vinegar to drink.

22 Let their table become a snare before them: and *that which should have been* for *their* welfare, *let it become* a trap.

23 Let their eyes be darkened, that they see not; and make their loins continually to shake.

24 Pour out thine indignation upon them, and let thy wrathful anger take hold of them.

25 Let their habitation be desolate; *and* let none dwell in their tents.

26 For they persecute *him* whom thou hast smitten; and they talk to the grief of those whom thou hast wounded.

27 Add iniquity unto their iniquity: and let them not come into thy righteousness.

28 Let them be blotted out of the

book of the living, and not be written
with the righteous.
29 But I *am* poor and sorrowful: let
thy salvation, O God, set me up on high.
30 I will praise the name of God with
a song, and will magnify him with
thanksgiving.
31 *This* also shall please the LORD bet-
ter than an ox *or* bullock that hath
horns and hoofs.
32 The humble shall see *this, and* be
glad: and your heart shall live that seek
God.
33 For the LORD heareth the poor, and
despiseth not his prisoners.
34 Let the heaven and earth praise
him, the seas, and every thing that
moveth therein.
35 For God will save Zion, and will
build the cities of Jū'dah: that they may
dwell there, and have it in possession.
36 The seed also of his servants shall
inherit it: and they that love his name
shall dwell therein.

PSALM 70

MAKE *haste,* O God, to deliver me;
make haste to help me, O LORD.
2 Let them be ashamed and con-
founded that seek after my soul: let
them be turned backward, and put to
confusion, that desire my hurt.
3 Let them be turned back for a re-
ward of their shame that say, Aha, aha.
4 Let all those that seek thee rejoice
and be glad in thee: and let such as love
thy salvation say continually, Let God
be magnified.
5 But I *am* poor and needy: make
haste unto me, O God: thou *art* my help
and my deliverer; O LORD, make no
tarrying.

PSALM 71

IN thee, O LORD, do I put my trust: let
me never be put to confusion.
2 Deliver me in thy righteousness,
and cause me to escape: incline thine
ear unto me, and save me.
3 Be thou my strong habitation,
whereunto I may continually resort:
thou hast given commandment to save
me; for thou *art* my rock and my
fortress.
4 Deliver me, O my God, out of the
hand of the wicked, out of the hand of
the unrighteous and cruel man.
5 For thou *art* my hope, O Lord GOD:
thou art my trust from my youth.
6 By thee have I been holden up from
the womb: thou art he that took me out
of my mother's bowels: my praise *shall
be* continually of thee.
7 I am as a wonder unto many; but
thou *art* my strong refuge.
8 Let my mouth be filled *with* thy
praise *and with* thy honour all the day.
9 Cast me not off in the time of old
age; forsake me not when my strength
faileth.
10 For mine enemies speak against
me; and they that lay wait for my soul
take counsel together,
11 Saying, God hath forsaken him:
persecute and take him; for *there is*
none to deliver *him.*
12 O God, be not far from me: O my
God, make haste for my help.
13 Let them be confounded *and* con-
sumed that are adversaries to my soul;
let them be covered *with* reproach and
dishonour that seek my hurt.
14 But I will hope continually, and
will yet praise thee more and more.
15 My mouth shall shew forth thy
righteousness *and* thy salvation all the
day; for I know not the numbers *there-
of.*
16 I will go in the strength of the Lord
GOD: I will make mention of thy
righteousness, *even* of thine only.
17 O God, thou hast taught me from
my youth: and hitherto have I declared
thy wondrous works.
18 Now also when I am old and
greyheaded, O God, forsake me not;
until I have shewed thy strength unto
this generation, *and* thy power to every
one *that* is to come.
19 Thy righteousness also, O God, *is*
very high, who hast done great things:
O God, who *is* like unto thee!
20 *Thou,* which hast shewed me great
and sore troubles, shalt quicken me
again, and shalt bring me up again from
the depths of the earth.
21 Thou shalt increase my greatness,
and comfort me on every side.
22 I will also praise thee with the
psaltery, *even* thy truth, O my God:
unto thee will I sing with the harp, O
thou Holy One of Israel.
23 My lips shall greatly rejoice when
I sing unto thee; and my soul, which
thou hast redeemed.
24 My tongue also shall talk of thy
righteousness all the day long: for they
are confounded, for they are brought
unto shame, that seek my hurt.

PSALM 72

GIVE the king thy judgments, O God,
and thy righteousness unto the king's
son.
2 He shall judge thy people with
righteousness, and thy poor with judg-
ment.
3 The mountains shall bring peace to
the people, and the little hills, by
righteousness.

4 He shall judge the poor of the peo-
ple, he shall save the children of the
needy, and shall break in pieces the
oppressor.
5 They shall fear thee as long as the
sun and moon endure, throughout all
generations.
6 He shall come down like rain upon
the mown grass: as showers *that* water
the earth.
7 In his days shall the righteous
flourish; and abundance of peace so
long as the moon endureth.
8 He shall have dominion also from
sea to sea, and from the river unto the
ends of the earth.
9 They that dwell in the wilderness
shall bow before him; and his enemies
shall lick the dust.
10 The kings of Tärshĭsh and of the
isles shall bring presents: the kings of
Shē′ba and Sē′ba shall offer gifts.
11 Yea, all kings shall fall down be-
fore him: all nations shall serve him.
12 For he shall deliver the needy
when he crieth; the poor also, and *him*
that hath no helper.
13 He shall spare the poor and needy,
and shall save the souls of the needy.
14 He shall redeem their soul from
deceit and violence: and precious shall
their blood be in his sight.
15 And he shall live, and to him shall
be given of the gold of Shē′ba: prayer
also shall be made for him continually;
and daily shall he be praised.
16 There shall be an handful of corn
in the earth upon the top of the moun-
tains; the fruit thereof shall shake like
Lebanon: and *they* of the city shall
flourish like grass of the earth.
17 His name shall endure for ever: his
name shall be continued as long as the
sun: and *men* shall be blessed in him:
all nations shall call him blessed.
18 Blessed *be* the LORD God, the God
of Israel, who only doeth wondrous
things.
19 And blessed *be* his glorious name
for ever: and let the whole earth be
filled *with* his glory; Amen, and Amen.
20 The prayers of David the son of
Jesse are ended.

PSALM 73

TRULY God *is* good to Israel, *even* to
such as are of a clean heart.
2 But as for me, my feet were almost
gone; my steps had well nigh slipped.
3 For I was envious at the foolish,
when I saw the prosperity of the
wicked.
4 For *there are* no bands in their
death: but their strength *is* firm.
5 They *are* not in trouble as *other*
men; neither are they plagued like
other men.
6 Therefore pride compasseth them
about as a chain; violence covereth
them *as* a garment.
7 Their eyes stand out with fatness:
they have more than heart could wish.
8 They are corrupt, and speak
wickedly *concerning* oppression: they
speak loftily.
9 They set their mouth against the
heavens, and their tongue walketh
through the earth.
10 Therefore his people return hither:
and waters of a full *cup* are wrung out
to them.
11 And they say, How doth God
know? and is there knowledge in the
most High?
12 Behold, these *are* the ungodly,
who prosper in the world; they increase
in riches.
13 Verily I have cleansed my heart *in*
vain, and washed my hands in inno-
cency.
14 For all the day long have I been
plagued, and chastened every morning.
15 If I say, I will speak thus; behold, I
should offend *against* the generation of
thy children.
16 When I thought to know this, it
was too painful for me;
17 Until I went into the sanctuary of
God; *then* understood I their end.
18 Surely thou didst set them in slip-
pery places: thou castedst them down
into destruction.
19 How are they *brought* into desola-
tion, as in a moment! they are utterly
consumed with terrors.
20 As a dream when *one* awaketh; *so*,
O Lord, when thou awakest, thou shalt
despise their image.
21 Thus my heart was grieved, and I
was pricked in my reins.
22 So foolish *was* I, and ignorant: I
was *as* a beast before thee.
23 Nevertheless I *am* continually
with thee: thou hast holden *me* by my
right hand.
24 Thou shalt guide me with thy
counsel, and afterward receive me *to*
glory.
25 Whom have I in heaven *but thee?*
and *there is* none upon earth *that* I de-
sire beside thee.
26 My flesh and my heart faileth: *but*
God *is* the strength of my heart, and my
portion for ever.
27 For, lo, they that are far from thee
shall perish: thou hast destroyed all
them that go a whoring from thee.
28 But *it is* good for me to draw near
to God: I have put my trust in the Lord
GOD, that I may declare all thy works.

PSALM 74

O GOD, why hast thou cast *us* off for
ever? *why* doth thine anger smoke
against the sheep of thy pasture?
2 Remember thy congregation,
which thou hast purchased of old; the
rod of thine inheritance, *which* thou
hast redeemed; this mount Zion, where-
in thou hast dwelt.
3 Lift up thy feet unto the perpetual
desolations; *even* all *that* the enemy
hath done wickedly in the sanctuary.
4 Thine enemies roar in the midst of
thy congregations; they set up their en-
signs *for* signs.
5 *A man* was famous according as he
had lifted up axes upon the thick trees.
6 But now they break down the
carved work thereof at once with axes
and hammers.
7 They have cast fire into thy sanc-
tuary, they have defiled *by casting
down* the dwelling place of thy name to
the ground.
8 They said in their hearts, Let us
destroy them together: they have
burned up all the synagogues of God in
the land.
9 We see not our signs: *there is* no
more any prophet: neither *is there*
among us any that knoweth how long.
10 O God, how long shall the adver-
sary reproach? shall the enemy blas-
pheme thy name for ever?
11 Why withdrawest thou thy hand,
even thy right hand? pluck *it* out of thy
bosom.
12 For God *is* my King of old, work-
ing salvation in the midst of the earth.
13 Thou didst divide the sea by thy
strength: thou brakest the heads of the
dragons in the waters.
14 Thou brakest the heads of le-
viathan in pieces, *and* gavest him *to be*
meat to the people inhabiting the wil-
derness.
15 Thou didst cleave the fountain and
the flood: thou driedst up mighty riv-
ers.
16 The day *is* thine, the night also *is*
thine: thou hast prepared the light and
the sun.
17 Thou hast set all the borders of the
earth: thou hast made summer and
winter.
18 Remember this, *that* the enemy
hath reproached, O LORD, and *that* the
foolish people have blasphemed thy
name.
19 O deliver not the soul of thy turtle-
dove unto the multitude *of the wicked*:
forget not the congregation of thy poor
for ever.
20 Have respect unto the covenant:
for the dark places of the earth are full
of the habitations of cruelty.
21 O let not the oppressed return
ashamed: let the poor and needy praise
thy name.
22 Arise, O God, plead thine own
cause: remember how the foolish man
reproacheth thee daily.
23 Forget not the voice of thine en-
emies: the tumult of those that rise up
against thee increaseth continually.

PSALM 75

UNTO thee, O God, do we give thanks,
unto thee do we give thanks: for *that*
thy name is near thy wondrous works
declare.
2 When I shall receive the congrega-
tion I will judge uprightly.
3 The earth and all the inhabitants
thereof are dissolved: I bear up the pil-
lars of it. Sē'lah.
4 I said unto the fools, Deal not foolish-
ly: and to the wicked, Lift not up the
horn:
5 Lift not up your horn on high: speak
not with a stiff neck.
6 For promotion *cometh* neither from
the east, nor from the west, nor from
the south.
7 But God *is* the judge: he putteth
down one, and setteth up another.
8 For in the hand of the LORD *there is*
a cup, and the wine is red; it is full of
mixture; and he poureth out of the
same: but the dregs thereof, all the
wicked of the earth shall wring *them*
out, *and* drink *them*.
9 But I will declare for ever; I will sing
praises to the God of Jacob.
10 All the horns of the wicked also
will I cut off; *but* the horns of the
righteous shall be exalted.

PSALM 76

IN Jū'dah *is* God known: his name *is*
great in Israel.
2 In Sā'lem also is his tabernacle, and
his dwelling place in Zion.
3 There brake he the arrows of the
bow, the shield, and the sword, and the
battle. Sē'lah.
4 Thou *art* more glorious *and* excel-
lent than the mountains of prey.
5 The stouthearted are spoiled, they
have slept their sleep: and none of the
men of might have found their hands.
6 At thy rebuke, O God of Jacob, both
the chariot and horse are cast into a
dead sleep.
7 Thou, *even* thou, *art* to be feared:
and who may stand in thy sight when
once thou art angry?
8 Thou didst cause judgment to be

heard from heaven; the earth feared, and was still,
9 When God arose to judgment, to save all the meek of the earth. Sē'lah.
10 Surely the wrath of man shall praise thee: the remainder of wrath shalt thou restrain.
11 Vow, and pay unto the LORD your God: let all that be round about him bring presents unto him that ought to be feared.
12 He shall cut off the spirit of princes: *he is* terrible to the kings of the earth.

PSALM 77

I CRIED unto God with my voice, *even* unto God with my voice; and he gave ear unto me.
2 In the day of my trouble I sought the Lord: my sore ran in the night, and ceased not: my soul refused to be comforted.
3 I remembered God, and was troubled: I complained, and my spirit was overwhelmed. Sē'lah.
4 Thou holdest mine eyes waking: I am so troubled that I cannot speak.
5 I have considered the days of old, the years of ancient times.
6 I call to remembrance my song in the night: I commune with mine own heart: and my spirit made diligent search.
7 Will the Lord cast off for ever? and will he be favourable no more?
8 Is his mercy clean gone for ever? doth *his* promise fail for evermore?
9 Hath God forgotten to be gracious? hath he in anger shut up his tender mercies? Sē'lah.
10 And I said, This *is* my infirmity: *but I will remember* the years of the right hand of the most High.
11 I will remember the works of the LORD: surely I will remember thy wonders of old.
12 I will meditate also of all thy work, and talk of thy doings.
13 Thy way, O God, *is* in the sanctuary: who *is so* great a God as *our* God?
14 Thou *art* the God that doest wonders: thou hast declared thy strength among the people.
15 Thou hast with *thine* arm redeemed thy people, the sons of Jacob and Joseph. Sē'lah.
16 The waters saw thee, O God, the waters saw thee; they were afraid: the depths also were troubled.
17 The clouds poured out water: the skies sent out a sound: thine arrows also went abroad.
18 The voice of thy thunder *was* in the heaven: the lightnings lightened the world: the earth trembled and shook.
19 Thy way *is* in the sea, and thy path in the great waters, and thy footsteps are not known.
20 Thou leddest thy people like a flock by the hand of Moses and Aaron.

PSALM 78

GIVE ear, O my people, *to* my law: incline your ears to the words of my mouth.
2 I will open my mouth in a parable: I will utter dark sayings of old:
3 Which we have heard and known, and our fathers have told us.
4 We will not hide *them* from their children, shewing to the generation to come the praises of the LORD, and his strength, and his wonderful works that he hath done.
5 For he established a testimony in Jacob, and appointed a law in Israel, which he commanded our fathers, that they should make them known to their children:
6 That the generation to come might know *them, even* the children *which* should be born; *who* should arise and declare *them* to their children:
7 That they might set their hope in God, and not forget the works of God, but keep his commandments:
8 And might not be as their fathers, a stubborn and rebellious generation; a generation *that* set not their heart aright, and whose spirit was not stedfast with God.
9 The children of Ē'phra-im, *being* armed, *and* carrying bows, turned back in the day of battle.
10 They kept not the covenant of God, and refused to walk in his law;
11 And forgat his works, and his wonders that he had shewed them.
12 Marvellous things did he in the sight of their fathers, in the land of Egypt, *in* the field of Zō'an.
13 He divided the sea, and caused them to pass through; and he made the waters to stand as an heap.
14 In the daytime also he led them with a cloud, and all the night with a light of fire.
15 He clave the rocks in the wilderness, and gave *them* drink as *out of* the great depths.
16 He brought streams also out of the rock, and caused waters to run down like rivers.
17 And they sinned yet more against him by provoking the most High in the wilderness.
18 And they tempted God in their heart by asking meat for their lust.

19 Yea, they spake against God; they
said, Can God furnish a table in the wilderness?
20 Behold, he smote the rock, that the
waters gushed out, and the streams
overflowed; can he give bread also?
can he provide flesh for his people?
21 Therefore the LORD heard *this*, and
was wroth: so a fire was kindled
against Jacob, and anger also came up
against Israel;
22 Because they believed not in God,
and trusted not in his salvation:
23 Though he had commanded the
clouds from above, and opened the
doors of heaven,
24 And had rained down manna upon
them to eat, and had given them of the
corn of heaven.
25 Man did eat angels' food: he sent
them meat to the full.
26 He caused an east wind to blow in
the heaven: and by his power he
brought in the south wind.
27 He rained flesh also upon them as
dust, and feathered fowls like as the
sand of the sea:
28 And he let *it* fall in the midst of
their camp, round about their habitations.
29 So they did eat, and were well
filled: for he gave them their own desire;
30 They were not estranged from
their lust. But while their meat *was* yet
in their mouths,
31 The wrath of God came upon
them, and slew the fattest of them, and
smote down the chosen *men* of Israel.
32 For all this they sinned still, and
believed not for his wondrous works.
33 Therefore their days did he consume in vanity, and their years in
trouble.
34 When he slew them, then they
sought him: and they returned and enquired early after God.
35 And they remembered that God
was their rock, and the high God their
redeemer.
36 Nevertheless they did flatter him
with their mouth, and they lied unto
him with their tongues.
37 For their heart was not right with
him, neither were they stedfast in his
covenant.
38 But he, *being* full of compassion,
forgave *their* iniquity, and destroyed
them not: yea, many a time turned he
his anger away, and did not stir up all
his wrath.
39 For he remembered that they *were*
but flesh; a wind that passeth away,
and cometh not again.
40 How oft did they provoke him in
the wilderness, *and* grieve him in the
desert!
41 Yea, they turned back and
tempted God, and limited the Holy One
of Israel.
42 They remembered not his hand,
nor the day when he delivered them
from the enemy.
43 How he had wrought his signs in
Egypt, and his wonders in the field of
Zō'an:
44 And had turned their rivers into
blood; and their floods that they could
not drink.
45 He sent divers sorts of flies among
them, which devoured them; and frogs,
which destroyed them.
46 He gave also their increase unto
the caterpiller, and their labour unto
the locust.
47 He destroyed their vines with hail,
and their sycomore trees with frost.
48 He gave up their cattle also to the
hail, and their flocks to hot thunderbolts.
49 He cast upon them the fierceness
of his anger, wrath, and indignation,
and trouble, by sending evil angels
among them.
50 He made a way to his anger; he
spared not their soul from death, but
gave their life over to the pestilence;
51 And smote all the firstborn in
Egypt; the chief of *their* strength in the
tabernacles of Ham:
52 But made his own people to go
forth like sheep, and guided them in the
wilderness like a flock.
53 And he led them on safely, so that
they feared not: but the sea overwhelmed their enemies.
54 And he brought them to the border
of his sanctuary, *even to* this mountain,
which his right hand had purchased.
55 He cast out the heathen also before them, and divided them an inheritance by line, and made the tribes of
Israel to dwell in their tents.
56 Yet they tempted and provoked
the most high God, and kept not his testimonies:
57 But turned back, and dealt unfaithfully like their fathers: they were
turned aside like a deceitful bow.
58 For they provoked him to anger
with their high places, and moved him
to jealousy with their graven images.
59 When God heard *this*, he was
wroth, and greatly abhorred Israel:
60 So that he forsook the tabernacle
of Shī'lōh, the tent *which* he placed
among men;
61 And delivered his strength into
captivity, and his glory into the enemy's hand.

62 He gave his people over also unto the sword; and was wroth with his inheritance.

63 The fire consumed their young men; and their maidens were not given to marriage.

64 Their priests fell by the sword; and their widows made no lamentation.

65 Then the LORD awaked as one out of sleep, *and* like a mighty man that shouteth by reason of wine.

66 And he smote his enemies in the hinder parts: he put them to a perpetual reproach.

67 Moreover he refused the tabernacle of Joseph, and chose not the tribe of Ē′phra-im:

68 But chose the tribe of Jū′dah, the mount Zion which he loved.

69 And he built his sanctuary like high *palaces*, like the earth which he hath established for ever.

70 He chose David also his servant, and took him from the sheepfolds:

71 From following the ewes great with young he brought him to feed Jacob his people, and Israel his inheritance.

72 So he fed them according to the integrity of his heart; and guided them by the skilfulness of his hands.

PSALM 79

O GOD, the heathen are come into thine inheritance; thy holy temple have they defiled; they have laid Jerusalem on heaps.

2 The dead bodies of thy servants have they given *to be* meat unto the fowls of the heaven, the flesh of thy saints unto the beasts of the earth.

3 Their blood have they shed like water round about Jerusalem; and *there was* none to bury *them*.

4 We are become a reproach to our neighbours, a scorn and derision to them that are round about us.

5 How long, LORD? wilt thou be angry for ever? shall thy jealousy burn like fire?

6 Pour out thy wrath upon the heathen that have not known thee, and upon the kingdoms that have not called upon thy name.

7 For they have devoured Jacob, and laid waste his dwelling place.

8 O remember not against us former iniquities: let thy tender mercies speedily prevent us: for we are brought very low.

9 Help us, O God of our salvation, for the glory of thy name: and deliver us, and purge away our sins, for thy name's sake.

10 Wherefore should the heathen say, Where *is* their God? let him be known among the heathen in our sight *by* the revenging of the blood of thy servants *which is* shed.

11 Let the sighing of the prisoner come before thee; according to the greatness of thy power preserve thou those that are appointed to die;

12 And render unto our neighbours sevenfold into their bosom their reproach, wherewith they have reproached thee, O Lord.

13 So we thy people and sheep of thy pasture will give thee thanks for ever: we will shew forth thy praise to all generations.

PSALM 80

GIVE ear, O Shepherd of Israel, thou that leadest Joseph like a flock; thou that dwellest *between* the cherubims, shine forth.

2 Before Ē′phra-im and Benjamin and Ma-năs′seh stir up thy strength, and come *and* save us.

3 Turn us again, O God, and cause thy face to shine; and we shall be saved.

4 O LORD God of hosts, how long wilt thou be angry against the prayer of thy people?

5 Thou feedest them with the bread of tears; and givest them tears to drink in great measure.

6 Thou makest us a strife unto our neighbours: and our enemies laugh among themselves.

7 Turn us again, O God of hosts, and cause thy face to shine; and we shall be saved.

8 Thou hast brought a vine out of Egypt: thou hast cast out the heathen, and planted it.

9 Thou preparedst *room* before it, and didst cause it to take deep root, and it filled the land.

10 The hills were covered with the shadow of it, and the boughs thereof *were like* the goodly cedars.

11 She sent out her boughs unto the sea, and her branches unto the river.

12 Why hast thou *then* broken down her hedges, so that all they which pass by the way do pluck her?

13 The boar out of the wood doth waste it, and the wild beast of the field doth devour it.

14 Return, we beseech thee, O God of hosts: look down from heaven, and behold, and visit this vine;

15 And the vineyard which thy right hand hath planted, and the branch *that* thou madest strong for thyself.

16 *It is* burned with fire, *it is* cut

down: they perish at the rebuke of thy
countenance.
17 Let thy hand be upon the man of
thy right hand, upon the son of man
whom thou madest strong for thyself.
18 So will not we go back from thee:
quicken us, and we will call upon thy
name.
19 Turn us again, O LORD God of
hosts, cause thy face to shine; and we
shall be saved.

PSALM 81

SING aloud unto God our strength:
make a joyful noise unto the God of Ja-
cob.
2 Take a psalm, and bring hither the
timbrel, the pleasant harp with the
psaltery.
3 Blow up the trumpet in the new
moon, in the time appointed, on our
solemn feast day.
4 For this *was* a statute for Israel, *and*
a law of the God of Jacob.
5 This he ordained in Joseph *for* a tes-
timony, when he went out through the
land of Egypt: *where* I heard a language
that I understood not.
6 I removed his shoulder from the
burden: his hands were delivered from
the pots.
7 Thou calledst in trouble, and I deliv-
ered thee; I answered thee in the secret
place of thunder: I proved thee at the
waters of Mĕr′i-bah. Sē′lah.
8 Hear, O my people, and I will testify
unto thee: O Israel, if thou wilt hearken
unto me;
9 There shall no strange god be in
thee; neither shalt thou worship any
strange god.
10 I *am* the LORD thy God, which
brought thee out of the land of Egypt:
open thy mouth wide, and I will fill it.
11 But my people would not hearken
to my voice; and Israel would none of
me.
12 So I gave them up unto their own
hearts' lust: *and* they walked in their
own counsels.
13 Oh that my people had hearkened
unto me, *and* Israel had walked in my
ways!
14 I should soon have subdued their
enemies, and turned my hand against
their adversaries.
15 The haters of the LORD should
have submitted themselves unto him:
but their time should have endured for
ever.
16 He should have fed them also with
the finest of the wheat: and with honey
out of the rock should I have satisfied
thee.

PSALM 82

GOD standeth in the congregation of
the mighty; he judgeth among the
gods.
2 How long will ye judge unjustly,
and accept the persons of the wicked?
Sē′lah.
3 Defend the poor and fatherless: do
justice to the afflicted and needy.
4 Deliver the poor and needy: rid
them out of the hand of the wicked.
5 They know not, neither will they
understand; they walk on in darkness:
all the foundations of the earth are out
of course.
6 I have said, Ye *are* gods; and all of
you *are* children of the most High.
7 But ye shall die like men, and fall
like one of the princes.
8 Arise, O God, judge the earth: for
thou shalt inherit all nations.

PSALM 83

KEEP not thou silence, O God: hold not
thy peace, and be not still, O God.
2 For, lo, thine enemies make a tu-
mult: and they that hate thee have
lifted up the head.
3 They have taken crafty counsel
against thy people, and consulted
against thy hidden ones.
4 They have said, Come, and let us
cut them off from *being* a nation; that
the name of Israel may be no more in
remembrance.
5 For they have consulted together
with one consent: they are confederate
against thee:
6 The tabernacles of Edom, and the
Ĭsh′ma-el-ītes; of Moab, and the Hă′-
gar-ēnes;
7 Gē′bal, and Ammon, and Ăm′a-lĕk;
the Philistines with the inhabitants of
Tyre;
8 Assur also is joined with them: they
have holpen the children of Lot. Sē′lah.
9 Do unto them as *unto* the Mĭd′ĭ-an-
ītes; as *to* Sĭs′e-ra, as *to* Jā′bin, at the
brook of Kĭ′son:
10 *Which* perished at Ĕn-dôr: they
became *as* dung for the earth.
11 Make their nobles like Ō′reb, and
like Zē′eb: yea, all their princes as Zē′-
bah, and as Zăl-mŭn′na:
12 Who said, Let us take to ourselves
the houses of God in possession.
13 O my God, make them like a
wheel; as the stubble before the wind.
14 As the fire burneth a wood, and as
the flame setteth the mountains on fire;
15 So persecute them with thy tem-
pest, and make them afraid with thy
storm.

16 Fill their faces with shame; that they may seek thy name, O LORD.

17 Let them be confounded and troubled for ever; yea, let them be put to shame, and perish:

18 That *men* may know that thou, whose name alone *is* JE-HŌ'VAH, *art* the most high over all the earth.

PSALM 84

HOW amiable *are* thy tabernacles, O LORD of hosts!

2 My soul longeth, yea, even fainteth for the courts of the LORD: my heart and my flesh crieth out for the living God.

3 Yea, the sparrow hath found an house, and the swallow a nest for herself, where she may lay her young, *even* thine altars, O LORD of hosts, my King, and my God.

4 Blessed *are* they that dwell in thy house: they will be still praising thee. Sē'lah.

5 Blessed *is* the man whose strength *is* in thee; in whose heart *are* the ways *of them*.

6 *Who* passing through the valley of Bā'ca make it a well; the rain also filleth the pools.

7 They go from strength to strength, *every one of them* in Zion appeareth before God.

8 O LORD God of hosts, hear my prayer: give ear, O God of Jacob. Sē'lah.

9 Behold, O God our shield, and look upon the face of thine anointed.

10 For a day in thy courts *is* better than a thousand. I had rather be a doorkeeper in the house of my God, than to dwell in the tents of wickedness.

11 For the LORD God *is* a sun and shield: the LORD will give grace and glory: no good *thing* will he withhold from them that walk uprightly.

12 O LORD of hosts, blessed *is* the man that trusteth in thee.

PSALM 85

LORD, thou hast been favourable unto thy land: thou hast brought back the captivity of Jacob.

2 Thou hast forgiven the iniquity of thy people, thou hast covered all their sin. Sē'lah.

3 Thou hast taken away all thy wrath: thou hast turned *thyself* from the fierceness of thine anger.

4 Turn us, O God of our salvation, and cause thine anger toward us to cease.

5 Wilt thou be angry with us for ever? wilt thou draw out thine anger to all generations?

6 Wilt thou not revive us again: that thy people may rejoice in thee?

7 Shew us thy mercy, O LORD, and grant us thy salvation.

8 I will hear what God the LORD will speak: for he will speak peace unto his people, and to his saints: but let them not turn again to folly.

9 Surely his salvation *is* nigh them that fear him; that glory may dwell in our land.

10 Mercy and truth are met together; righteousness and peace have kissed *each other*.

11 Truth shall spring out of the earth; and righteousness shall look down from heaven.

12 Yea, the LORD shall give *that which is* good; and our land shall yield her increase.

13 Righteousness shall go before him; and shall set *us* in the way of his steps.

PSALM 86

BOW down thine ear, O LORD, hear me: for I *am* poor and needy.

2 Preserve my soul; for I *am* holy: O thou my God, save thy servant that trusteth in thee.

3 Be merciful unto me, O Lord: for I cry unto thee daily.

4 Rejoice the soul of thy servant: for unto thee, O Lord, do I lift up my soul.

5 For thou, Lord, *art* good, and ready to forgive; and plenteous in mercy unto all them that call upon thee.

6 Give ear, O LORD, unto my prayer; and attend to the voice of my supplications.

7 In the day of my trouble I will call upon thee: for thou wilt answer me.

8 Among the gods *there is* none like unto thee, O Lord; neither *are there any works* like unto thy works.

9 All nations whom thou hast made shall come and worship before thee, O Lord; and shall glorify thy name.

10 For thou *art* great, and doest wondrous things: thou *art* God alone.

11 Teach me thy way, O LORD; I will walk in thy truth: unite my heart to fear thy name.

12 I will praise thee, O Lord my God, with all my heart: and I will glorify thy name for evermore.

13 For great *is* thy mercy toward me: and thou hast delivered my soul from the lowest hell.

14 O God, the proud are risen against me, and the assemblies of violent *men* have sought after my soul; and have not set thee before them.

15 But thou, O Lord, *art* a God full of

compassion, and gracious, longsuffering, and plenteous in mercy and truth.

16 O turn unto me, and have mercy upon me; give thy strength unto thy servant, and save the son of thine handmaid.

17 Shew me a token for good; that they which hate me may see *it*, and be ashamed: because thou, Lord, hast holpen me, and comforted me.

PSALM 87

HIS foundation *is* in the holy mountains.

2 The Lord loveth the gates of Zion more than all the dwellings of Jacob.

3 Glorious things are spoken of thee, O city of God. Sē'lah.

4 I will make mention of Rahab and Babylon to them that know me: behold Philistia, and Tyre, with Ē-thĭ-ō'pĭ-a; this *man* was born there.

5 And of Zion it shall be said, This and that man was born in her: and the highest himself shall establish her.

6 The Lord shall count, when he writeth up the people, *that* this *man* was born there. Sē'lah.

7 As well the singers as the players on instruments *shall be there*: all my springs *are* in thee.

PSALM 88

O LORD God of my salvation, I have cried day *and* night before thee:

2 Let my prayer come before thee: incline thine ear unto my cry;

3 For my soul is full of troubles: and my life draweth nigh unto the grave.

4 I am counted with them that go down into the pit: I am as a man *that hath* no strength:

5 Free among the dead, like the slain that lie in the grave, whom thou rememberest no more: and they are cut off from thy hand.

6 Thou hast laid me in the lowest pit, in darkness, in the deeps.

7 Thy wrath lieth hard upon me, and thou hast afflicted *me* with all thy waves. Sē'lah.

8 Thou hast put away mine acquaintance far from me; thou hast made me an abomination unto them: *I am* shut up, and I cannot come forth.

9 Mine eye mourneth by reason of affliction: Lord, I have called daily upon thee, I have stretched out my hands unto thee.

10 Wilt thou shew wonders to the dead? shall the dead arise *and* praise thee? Sē'lah.

11 Shall thy lovingkindness be declared in the grave? *or* thy faithfulness in destruction?

12 Shall thy wonders be known in the dark? and thy righteousness in the land of forgetfulness?

13 But unto thee have I cried, O Lord; and in the morning shall my prayer prevent thee.

14 Lord, why castest thou off my soul? *why* hidest thou thy face from me?

15 I *am* afflicted and ready to die from *my* youth up: *while* I suffer thy terrors I am distracted.

16 Thy fierce wrath goeth over me; thy terrors have cut me off.

17 They came round about me daily like water; they compassed me about together.

18 Lover and friend hast thou put far from me, *and* mine acquaintance into darkness.

PSALM 89

I WILL sing of the mercies of the Lord for ever: with my mouth will I make known thy faithfulness to all generations.

2 For I have said, Mercy shall be built up for ever: thy faithfulness shalt thou establish in the very heavens.

3 I have made a covenant with my chosen, I have sworn unto David my servant,

4 Thy seed will I establish for ever, and build up thy throne to all generations. Sē'lah.

5 And the heavens shall praise thy wonders, O Lord: thy faithfulness also in the congregation of the saints.

6 For who in the heaven can be compared unto the Lord? *who* among the sons of the mighty can be likened unto the Lord?

7 God is greatly to be feared in the assembly of the saints, and to be had in reverence of all *them that are* about him.

8 O Lord God of hosts, who *is* a strong Lord like unto thee? or to thy faithfulness round about thee?

9 Thou rulest the raging of the sea: when the waves thereof arise, thou stillest them.

10 Thou hast broken Rahab in pieces, as one that is slain; thou hast scattered thine enemies with thy strong arm.

11 The heavens *are* thine, the earth also *is* thine: *as for* the world and the fulness thereof, thou hast founded them.

12 The north and the south thou hast created them: Tā'bor and Her'mon shall rejoice in thy name.

13 Thou hast a mighty arm: strong is thy hand, *and* high is thy right hand.

14 Justice and judgment *are* the habi-

tation of thy throne: mercy and truth
shall go before thy face.
15 Blessed *is* the people that know
the joyful sound: they shall walk, O
LORD, in the light of thy countenance.
16 In thy name shall they rejoice all
the day: and in thy righteousness shall
they be exalted.
17 For thou *art* the glory of their
strength: and in thy favour our horn
shall be exalted.
18 For the LORD *is* our defence; and
the Holy One of Israel *is* our king.
19 Then thou spakest in vision to thy
holy one, and saidst, I have laid help
upon *one that is* mighty; I have exalted
one chosen out of the people.
20 I have found David my servant;
with my holy oil have I anointed him:
21 With whom my hand shall be es-
tablished: mine arm also shall
strengthen him.
22 The enemy shall not exact upon
him; nor the son of wickedness afflict
him.
23 And I will beat down his foes be-
fore his face, and plague them that hate
him.
24 But my faithfulness and my mercy
shall be with him: and in my name shall
his horn be exalted.
25 I will set his hand also in the sea,
and his right hand in the rivers.
26 He shall cry unto me, Thou *art* my
father, my God, and the rock of my sal-
vation.
27 Also I will make him *my* firstborn,
higher than the kings of the earth.
28 My mercy will I keep for him for
evermore, and my covenant shall stand
fast with him.
29 His seed also will I make *to endure*
for ever, and his throne as the days of
heaven.
30 If his children forsake my law, and
walk not in my judgments;
31 If they break my statutes, and
keep not my commandments;
32 Then will I visit their transgres-
sion with the rod, and their iniquity
with stripes.
33 Nevertheless my lovingkindness
will I not utterly take from him, nor suf-
fer my faithfulness to fail.
34 My covenant will I not break, nor
alter the thing that is gone out of my
lips.
35 Once have I sworn by my holiness
that I will not lie unto David.
36 His seed shall endure for ever, and
his throne as the sun before me.
37 It shall be established for ever as
the moon, and *as* a faithful witness in
heaven. Sē'lah.
38 But thou hast cast off and
abhorred, thou hast been wroth with
thine anointed.
39 Thou hast made void the covenant
of thy servant: thou hast profaned his
crown *by casting it* to the ground.
40 Thou hast broken down all his
hedges; thou hast brought his strong
holds to ruin.
41 All that pass by the way spoil him:
he is a reproach to his neighbours.
42 Thou hast set up the right hand of
his adversaries; thou hast made all his
enemies to rejoice.
43 Thou hast also turned the edge of
his sword, and hast not made him to
stand in the battle.
44 Thou hast made his glory to cease,
and cast his throne down to the ground.
45 The days of his youth hast thou
shortened: thou hast covered him with
shame. Sē'lah.
46 How long, LORD? wilt thou hide
thyself for ever? shall thy wrath burn
like fire?
47 Remember how short my time is:
wherefore hast thou made all men in
vain?
48 What man *is he that* liveth, and
shall not see death? shall he deliver his
soul from the hand of the grave? Sē'lah.
49 Lord, where *are* thy former loving-
kindnesses, *which* thou swarest unto
David in thy truth?
50 Remember, Lord, the reproach of
thy servants; *how* I do bear in my bo-
som *the reproach of* all the mighty
people;
51 Wherewith thine enemies have
reproached, O LORD; wherewith they
have reproached the footsteps of thine
anointed.
52 Blessed *be* the LORD for evermore.
Amen, and Amen.

PSALM 90

LORD, thou hast been our dwelling
place in all generations.
2 Before the mountains were brought
forth, or ever thou hadst formed the
earth and the world, even from ever-
lasting to everlasting, thou *art* God.
3 Thou turnest man to destruction;
and sayest, Return, ye children of men.
4 For a thousand years in thy sight
are but as yesterday when it is past,
and *as* a watch in the night.
5 Thou carriest them away as with a
flood; they are *as* a sleep: in the morn-
ing *they are* like grass *which* groweth
up.
6 In the morning it flourisheth, and
groweth up; in the evening it is cut
down, and withereth.
7 For we are consumed by thine an-
ger, and by thy wrath are we troubled.

8 Thou hast set our iniquities before
thee, our secret *sins* in the light of thy
countenance.
9 For all our days are passed away in
the wrath: we spend our years as a tale
that is told.
10 The days of our years *are* three-
score years and ten; and if by reason of
strength *they be* fourscore years, yet *is*
their strength labour and sorrow; for it
is soon cut off, and we fly away.
11 Who knoweth the power of thine
anger? even according to thy fear, *so is*
thy wrath.
12 So teach *us* to number our days,
that we may apply *our* hearts unto wis-
dom.
13 Return, O LORD, how long? and let
it repent thee concerning thy servants.
14 O satisfy us early with thy mercy;
that we may rejoice and be glad all our
days.
15 Make us glad according to the
days *wherein* thou hast afflicted us,
and the years *wherein* we have seen
evil.
16 Let thy work appear unto thy ser-
vants, and thy glory unto their chil-
dren.
17 And let the beauty of the LORD our
God be upon us: and establish thou the
work of our hands upon us; yea, the
work of our hands establish thou it.

PSALM 91

HE that dwelleth in the secret place of
the most High shall abide under the
shadow of the Almighty.
2 I will say of the LORD, *He is* my ref-
uge and my fortress: my God; in him
will I trust.
3 Surely he shall deliver thee from
the snare of the fowler, *and* from the
noisome pestilence.
4 He shall cover thee with his feath-
ers, and under his wings shalt thou
trust: his truth *shall be thy* shield and
buckler.
5 Thou shalt not be afraid for the ter-
ror by night; *nor* for the arrow *that*
flieth by day;
6 *Nor* for the pestilence *that* walketh
in darkness; *nor* for the destruction
that wasteth at noonday.
7 A thousand shall fall at thy side,
and ten thousand at thy right hand; *but*
it shall not come nigh thee.
8 Only with thine eyes shalt thou be-
hold and see the reward of the wicked.
9 Because thou hast made the LORD,
which is my refuge, *even* the most
High, thy habitation;
10 There shall no evil befall thee,
neither shall any plague come nigh thy
dwelling.
11 For he shall give his angels charge
over thee, to keep thee in all thy ways.
12 They shall bear thee up in *their*
hands, lest thou dash thy foot against a
stone.
13 Thou shalt tread upon the lion and
adder: the young lion and the dragon
shalt thou trample under feet.
14 Because he hath set his love upon
me, therefore will I deliver him: I will
set him on high, because he hath
known my name.
15 He shall call upon me, and I will
answer him: I *will be* with him in
trouble; I will deliver him, and honour
him.
16 With long life will I satisfy him,
and shew him my salvation.

PSALM 92

IT is a good *thing* to give thanks unto
the LORD, and to sing praises unto thy
name, O most High:
2 To shew forth thy lovingkindness in
the morning, and thy faithfulness every
night,
3 Upon an instrument of ten strings,
and upon the psaltery; upon the harp
with a solemn sound.
4 For thou, LORD, hast made me glad
through thy work: I will triumph in the
works of thy hands.
5 O LORD, how great are thy works!
and thy thoughts are very deep.
6 A brutish man knoweth not; neither
doth a fool understand this.
7 When the wicked spring as the
grass, and when all the workers of iniq-
uity do flourish; *it is* that they shall be
destroyed for ever:
8 But thou, LORD, *art most* high for
evermore.
9 For, lo, thine enemies, O LORD, for,
lo, thine enemies shall perish; all the
workers of iniquity shall be scattered.
10 But my horn shalt thou exalt like
the horn of an unicorn: I shall be
anointed with fresh oil.
11 Mine eye also shall see *my desire*
on mine enemies, *and* mine ears shall
hear *my desire* of the wicked that rise
up against me.
12 The righteous shall flourish like
the palm tree: he shall grow like a cedar
in Lebanon.
13 Those that be planted in the house
of the LORD shall flourish in the courts
of our God.
14 They shall still bring forth fruit in
old age; they shall be fat and
flourishing;
15 To shew that the LORD *is* upright:
he is my rock, and *there is* no un-
righteousness in him.

PSALM 93

THE LORD reigneth, he is clothed with
majesty; the LORD is clothed with
strength, *wherewith* he hath girded
himself: the world also is stablished,
that it cannot be moved.
2 Thy throne *is* established of old:
thou *art* from everlasting.
3 The floods have lifted up, O LORD,
the floods have lifted up their voice; the
floods lift up their waves.
4 The LORD on high *is* mightier than
the noise of many waters, *yea, than* the
mighty waves of the sea.
5 Thy testimonies are very sure: holi-
ness becometh thine house, O LORD, for
ever.

PSALM 94

O LORD God, to whom vengeance be-
longeth; O God, to whom vengeance be-
longeth, shew thyself.
2 Lift up thyself, thou judge of the
earth: render a reward to the proud.
3 LORD, how long shall the wicked,
how long shall the wicked triumph?
4 *How long* shall they utter *and* speak
hard things? *and* all the workers of iniq-
uity boast themselves?
5 They break in pieces thy people, O
LORD, and afflict thine heritage.
6 They slay the widow and the
stranger, and murder the fatherless.
7 Yet they say, The LORD shall not
see, neither shall the God of Jacob re-
gard *it*.
8 Understand, ye brutish among the
people: and *ye* fools, when will ye be
wise?
9 He that planted the ear, shall he not
hear? he that formed the eye, shall he
not see?
10 He that chastiseth the heathen,
shall not he correct? he that teacheth
man knowledge, *shall not he know?*
11 The LORD knoweth the thoughts of
man, that they *are* vanity.
12 Blessed *is* the man whom thou
chastenest, O LORD, and teachest him
out of thy law;
13 That thou mayest give him rest
from the days of adversity, until the pit
be digged for the wicked.
14 For the LORD will not cast off his
people, neither will he forsake his in-
heritance.
15 But judgment shall return unto
righteousness: and all the upright in
heart shall follow it.
16 Who will rise up for me against the
evildoers? *or* who will stand up for me
against the workers of iniquity?
17 Unless the LORD *had been* my help,
my soul had almost dwelt in silence.
18 When I said, My foot slippeth; thy
mercy, O LORD, held me up.
19 In the multitude of my thoughts
within me thy comforts delight my
soul.
20 Shall the throne of iniquity have
fellowship with thee, which frameth
mischief by a law?
21 They gather themselves together
against the soul of the righteous, and
condemn the innocent blood.
22 But the LORD is my defence; and
my God *is* the rock of my refuge.
23 And he shall bring upon them their
own iniquity, and shall cut them off in
their own wickedness; *yea*, the LORD
our God shall cut them off.

PSALM 95

O COME, let us sing unto the LORD: let
us make a joyful noise to the rock of
our salvation.
2 Let us come before his presence
with thanksgiving, and make a joyful
noise unto him with psalms.
3 For the LORD *is* a great God, and a
great King above all gods.
4 In his hand *are* the deep places of
the earth: the strength of the hills *is* his
also.
5 The sea *is* his, and he made it: and
his hands formed the dry *land*.
6 O come, let us worship and bow
down: let us kneel before the LORD our
maker.
7 For he *is* our God; and we *are* the
people of his pasture, and the sheep of
his hand. To day if ye will hear his
voice,
8 Harden not your heart, as in the
provocation, *and* as *in* the day of temp-
tation in the wilderness:
9 When your fathers tempted me,
proved me, and saw my work.
10 Forty years long was I grieved
with *this* generation, and said, It *is* a
people that do err in their heart, and
they have not known my ways:
11 Unto whom I sware in my wrath
that they should not enter into my rest.

PSALM 96

O SING unto the LORD a new song: sing
unto the LORD, all the earth.
2 Sing unto the LORD, bless his name;
shew forth his salvation from day to
day.
3 Declare his glory among the
heathen, his wonders among all people.
4 For the LORD *is* great, and greatly to
be praised: he *is* to be feared above all
gods.
5 For all the gods of the nations *are*
idols: but the LORD made the heavens.
6 Honour and majesty *are* before

him: strength and beauty *are* in his sanctuary.

7 Give unto the LORD, O ye kindreds of the people, give unto the LORD glory and strength.

8 Give unto the LORD the glory *due unto* his name: bring an offering, and come into his courts.

9 O worship the LORD in the beauty of holiness: fear before him, all the earth.

10 Say among the heathen *that* the LORD reigneth: the world also shall be established that it shall not be moved: he shall judge the people righteously.

11 Let the heavens rejoice, and let the earth be glad; let the sea roar, and the fulness thereof.

12 Let the field be joyful, and all that *is* therein: then shall all the trees of the wood rejoice

13 Before the LORD: for he cometh, for he cometh to judge the earth: he shall judge the world with righteousness, and the people with his truth.

PSALM 97

THE LORD reigneth; let the earth rejoice; let the multitude of isles be glad *thereof.*

2 Clouds and darkness *are* round about him: righteousness and judgment *are* the habitation of his throne.

3 A fire goeth before him, and burneth up his enemies round about.

4 His lightnings enlightened the world: the earth saw, and trembled.

5 The hills melted like wax at the presence of the LORD, at the presence of the Lord of the whole earth.

6 The heavens declare his righteousness, and all the people see his glory.

7 Confounded be all they that serve graven images, that boast themselves of idols: worship him, all *ye* gods.

8 Zion heard, and was glad; and the daughters of Jū'dah rejoiced because of thy judgments, O LORD.

9 For thou, LORD, *art* high above all the earth: thou art exalted far above all gods.

10 Ye that love the LORD, hate evil: he preserveth the souls of his saints; he delivereth them out of the hand of the wicked.

11 Light is sown for the righteous, and gladness for the upright in heart.

12 Rejoice in the LORD, ye righteous; and give thanks at the remembrance of his holiness.

PSALM 98

O SING unto the LORD a new song; for he hath done marvellous things: his right hand, and his holy arm, hath gotten him the victory.

2 The LORD hath made known his salvation: his righteousness hath he openly shewed in the sight of the heathen.

3 He hath remembered his mercy and his truth toward the house of Israel: all the ends of the earth have seen the salvation of our God.

4 Make a joyful noise unto the LORD, all the earth: make a loud noise, and rejoice, and sing praise.

5 Sing unto the LORD with the harp; with the harp, and the voice of a psalm.

6 With trumpets and sound of cornets make a joyful noise before the LORD, the King.

7 Let the sea roar, and the fulness thereof; the world, and they that dwell therein.

8 Let the floods clap *their* hands: let the hills be joyful together

9 Before the LORD; for he cometh to judge the earth: with righteousness shall he judge the world, and the people with equity.

PSALM 99

THE LORD reigneth; let the people tremble: he sitteth *between* the cherubims; let the earth be moved.

2 The LORD *is* great in Zion; and he *is* high above all the people.

3 Let them praise thy great and terrible name; *for* it *is* holy.

4 The king's strength also loveth judgment; thou dost establish equity, thou executest judgment and righteousness in Jacob.

5 Exalt ye the LORD our God, and worship at his footstool; *for* he *is* holy.

6 Moses and Aaron among his priests, and Samuel among them that call upon his name; they called upon the LORD, and he answered them.

7 He spake unto them in the cloudy pillar: they kept his testimonies, and the ordinance *that* he gave them.

8 Thou answeredst them, O LORD our God: thou wast a God that forgavest them, though thou tookest vengeance of their inventions.

9 Exalt the LORD our God, and worship at his holy hill; for the LORD our God *is* holy.

PSALM 100

MAKE a joyful noise unto the LORD, all ye lands.

2 Serve the LORD with gladness: come before his presence with singing.

3 Know ye that the LORD he *is* God: *it is* he *that* hath made us, and not we ourselves; *we are* his people, and the sheep of his pasture.

4 Enter into his gates with thanksgiv-

ing, *and* into his courts with praise: be thankful unto him, *and* bless his name.

5 For the Lord *is* good; his mercy *is* everlasting; and his truth *endureth* to all generations.

PSALM 101

I WILL sing of mercy and judgment: unto thee, O Lord, will I sing.

2 I will behave myself wisely in a perfect way. O when wilt thou come unto me? I will walk within my house with a perfect heart.

3 I will set no wicked thing before mine eyes: I hate the work of them that turn aside; *it* shall not cleave to me.

4 A froward heart shall depart from me: I will not know a wicked *person*.

5 Whoso privily slandereth his neighbour, him will I cut off: him that hath an high look and a proud heart will not I suffer.

6 Mine eyes *shall be* upon the faithful of the land, that they may dwell with me: he that walketh in a perfect way, he shall serve me.

7 He that worketh deceit shall not dwell within my house: he that telleth lies shall not tarry in my sight.

8 I will early destroy all the wicked of the land; that I may cut off all wicked doers from the city of the Lord.

PSALM 102

HEAR my prayer, O Lord, and let my cry come unto thee.

2 Hide not thy face from me in the day *when* I am in trouble; incline thine ear unto me: in the day *when* I call answer me speedily.

3 For my days are consumed like smoke, and my bones are burned as an hearth.

4 My heart is smitten, and withered like grass; so that I forget to eat my bread.

5 By reason of the voice of my groaning my bones cleave to my skin.

6 I am like a pelican of the wilderness: I am like an owl of the desert.

7 I watch, and am as a sparrow alone upon the house top.

8 Mine enemies reproach me all the day; *and* they that are mad against me are sworn against me.

9 For I have eaten ashes like bread, and mingled my drink with weeping,

10 Because of thine indignation and thy wrath: for thou hast lifted me up, and cast me down.

11 My days *are* like a shadow that declineth; and I am withered like grass.

12 But thou, O Lord, shalt endure for ever; and thy remembrance unto all generations.

13 Thou shalt arise, *and* have mercy upon Zion: for the time to favour her, yea, the set time, is come.

14 For thy servants take pleasure in her stones, and favour the dust thereof.

15 So the heathen shall fear the name of the Lord, and all the kings of the earth thy glory.

16 When the Lord shall build up Zion, he shall appear in his glory.

17 He will regard the prayer of the destitute, and not despise their prayer.

18 This shall be written for the generation to come: and the people which shall be created shall praise the Lord.

19 For he hath looked down from the height of his sanctuary; from heaven did the Lord behold the earth;

20 To hear the groaning of the prisoner; to loose those that are appointed to death;

21 To declare the name of the Lord in Zion, and his praise in Jerusalem;

22 When the people are gathered together, and the kingdoms, to serve the Lord.

23 He weakened my strength in the way; he shortened my days.

24 I said, O my God, take me not away in the midst of my days: thy years *are* throughout all generations.

25 Of old hast thou laid the foundation of the earth: and the heavens *are* the work of thy hands.

26 They shall perish, but thou shalt endure: yea, all of them shall wax old like a garment; as a vesture shalt thou change them, and they shall be changed:

27 But thou *art* the same, and thy years shall have no end.

28 The children of thy servants shall continue, and their seed shall be established before thee.

PSALM 103

BLESS the Lord, O my soul: and all that is within me, *bless* his holy name.

2 Bless the Lord, O my soul, and forget not all his benefits:

3 Who forgiveth all thine iniquities; who healeth all thy diseases;

4 Who redeemeth thy life from destruction; who crowneth thee with lovingkindness and tender mercies;

5 Who satisfieth thy mouth with good *things; so that* thy youth is renewed like the eagle's.

6 The Lord executeth righteousness and judgment for all that are oppressed.

7 He made known his ways unto Moses, his acts unto the children of Israel.

8 The LORD *is* merciful and gracious, slow to anger, and plenteous in mercy.
9 He will not always chide: neither will he keep *his anger* for ever.
10 He hath not dealt with us after our sins; nor rewarded us according to our iniquities.
11 For as the heaven is high above the earth, *so* great is his mercy toward them that fear him.
12 As far as the east is from the west, *so* far hath he removed our transgressions from us.
13 Like as a father pitieth *his* children, *so* the LORD pitieth them that fear him.
14 For he knoweth our frame; he remembereth that we *are* dust.
15 *As for* man, his days *are* as grass: as a flower of the field, so he flourisheth.
16 For the wind passeth over it, and it is gone; and the place thereof shall know it no more.
17 But the mercy of the LORD *is* from everlasting to everlasting upon them that fear him, and his righteousness unto children's children;
18 To such as keep his covenant, and to those that remember his commandments to do them.
19 The LORD hath prepared his throne in the heavens; and his kingdom ruleth over all.
20 Bless the LORD, ye his angels, that excel in strength, that do his commandments, hearkening unto the voice of his word.
21 Bless ye the LORD, all *ye* his hosts; *ye* ministers of his, that do his pleasure.
22 Bless the LORD, all his works in all places of his dominion: bless the LORD, O my soul.

PSALM 104

BLESS the LORD, O my soul. O LORD my God, thou art very great; thou art clothed with honour and majesty.
2 Who coverest *thyself* with light as *with* a garment: who stretchest out the heavens like a curtain:
3 Who layeth the beams of his chambers in the waters: who maketh the clouds his chariot: who walketh upon the wings of the wind:
4 Who maketh his angels spirits; his ministers a flaming fire:
5 *Who* laid the foundations of the earth, *that* it should not be removed for ever.
6 Thou coveredst it with the deep as *with* a garment: the waters stood above the mountains.
7 At thy rebuke they fled; at the voice of thy thunder they hasted away.
8 They go up by the mountains; they go down by the valleys unto the place which thou hast founded for them.
9 Thou hast set a bound that they may not pass over; that they turn not again to cover the earth.
10 He sendeth the springs into the valleys, *which* run among the hills.
11 They give drink to every beast of the field: the wild asses quench their thirst.
12 By them shall the fowls of the heaven have their habitation, *which* sing among the branches.
13 He watereth the hills from his chambers: the earth is satisfied with the fruit of thy works.
14 He causeth the grass to grow for the cattle, and herb for the service of man: that he may bring forth food out of the earth;
15 And wine *that* maketh glad the heart of man, *and* oil to make *his* face to shine, and bread *which* strengtheneth man's heart.
16 The trees of the LORD are full *of sap;* the cedars of Lebanon, which he hath planted;
17 Where the birds make their nests: *as for* the stork, the fir trees *are* her house.
18 The high hills *are* a refuge for the wild goats; *and* the rocks for the conies.
19 He appointed the moon for seasons: the sun knoweth his going down.
20 Thou makest darkness and it is night: wherein all the beasts of the forest do creep *forth.*
21 The young lions roar after their prey, and seek their meat from God.
22 The sun ariseth, they gather themselves together, and lay them down in their dens.
23 Man goeth forth unto his work and to his labour until the evening.
24 O LORD, how manifold are thy works! in wisdom hast thou made them all: the earth is full of thy riches.
25 *So is* this great and wide sea, wherein *are* things creeping innumerable, both small and great beasts.
26 There go the ships: *there is* that leviathan, *whom* thou hast made to play therein.
27 These wait all upon thee; that thou mayest give *them* their meat in due season.
28 *That* thou givest them they gather: thou openest thine hand, they are filled with good.
29 Thou hidest thy face, they are troubled: thou takest away their breath, they die, and return to their dust.
30 Thou sendest forth thy spirit, they

are created: and thou renewest the face
of the earth.
31 The glory of the LORD shall endure
for ever: the LORD shall rejoice in his
works.
32 He looketh on the earth, and it
trembleth: he toucheth the hills, and
they smoke.
33 I will sing unto the LORD as long as
I live: I will sing praise to my God while
I have my being.
34 My meditation of him shall be
sweet: I will be glad in the LORD.
35 Let the sinners be consumed out of
the earth, and let the wicked be no
more. Bless thou the LORD, O my soul.
Praise ye the LORD.

PSALM 105

O GIVE thanks unto the LORD; call
upon his name: make known his deeds
among the people.
2 Sing unto him, sing psalms unto
him: talk ye of all his wondrous works.
3 Glory ye in his holy name: let the
heart of them rejoice that seek the
LORD.
4 Seek the LORD, and his strength:
seek his face evermore.
5 Remember his marvellous works
that he hath done; his wonders, and the
judgments of his mouth;
6 O ye seed of Abraham his servant,
ye children of Jacob his chosen.
7 He *is* the LORD our God: his judg-
ments *are* in all the earth.
8 He hath remembered his covenant
for ever, the word *which* he com-
manded to a thousand generations.
9 Which *covenant* he made with
Abraham, and his oath unto Isaac;
10 And confirmed the same unto Ja-
cob for a law, *and* to Israel *for* an ever-
lasting covenant:
11 Saying, Unto thee will I give the
land of Canaan, the lot of your inheri-
tance:
12 When they were *but* a few men in
number; yea, very few, and strangers in
it.
13 When they went from one nation
to another, from *one* kingdom to an-
other people;
14 He suffered no man to do them
wrong: yea, he reproved kings for their
sakes;
15 *Saying*, Touch not mine anointed,
and do my prophets no harm.
16 Moreover he called for a famine
upon the land: he brake the whole staff
of bread.
17 He sent a man before them, *even*
Joseph, *who* was sold for a servant:
18 Whose feet they hurt with fetters:
he was laid in iron:
19 Until the time that his word came:
the word of the LORD tried him.
20 The king sent and loosed him;
even the ruler of the people, and let him
go free.
21 He made him lord of his house,
and ruler of all his substance:
22 To bind his princes at his pleasure;
and teach his senators wisdom.
23 Israel also came into Egypt; and
Jacob sojourned in the land of Ham.
24 And he increased his people great-
ly; and made them stronger than
their enemies.
25 He turned their heart to hate his
people, to deal subtilly with his ser-
vants.
26 He sent Moses his servant; *and*
Aaron whom he had chosen.
27 They shewed his signs among
them, and wonders in the land of Ham.
28 He sent darkness, and made it
dark; and they rebelled not against his
word.
29 He turned their waters into blood,
and slew their fish.
30 Their land brought forth frogs in
abundance, in the chambers of their
kings.
31 He spake, and there came divers
sorts of flies, *and* lice in all their coasts.
32 He gave them hail for rain, *and*
flaming fire in their land.
33 He smote their vines also and their
fig trees; and brake the trees of their
coasts.
34 He spake, and the locusts came,
and caterpillers, and that without num-
ber,
35 And did eat up all the herbs in their
land, and devoured the fruit of their
ground.
36 He smote also all the firstborn in
their land, the chief of all their strength.
37 He brought them forth also with
silver and gold: and *there was* not one
feeble *person* among their tribes.
38 Egypt was glad when they de-
parted: for the fear of them fell upon
them.
39 He spread a cloud for a covering;
and fire to give light in the night.
40 *The people* asked, and he brought
quails, and satisfied them with the
bread of heaven.
41 He opened the rock, and the waters
gushed out; they ran in the dry
places *like* a river.
42 For he remembered his holy prom-
ise, *and* Abraham his servant.
43 And he brought forth his people
with joy, *and* his chosen with gladness:
44 And gave them the lands of the
heathen: and they inherited the labour
of the people;

45 That they might observe his statutes, and keep his laws. Praise ye the LORD.

PSALM 106

PRAISE ye the LORD. O give thanks unto the LORD; for *he is* good: for his mercy *endureth* for ever.

2 Who can utter the mighty acts of the LORD? *who* can shew forth all his praise?

3 Blessed *are* they that keep judgment, *and* he that doeth righteousness at all times.

4 Remember me, O LORD, with the favour *that thou bearest unto* thy people: O visit me with thy salvation;

5 That I may see the good of thy chosen, that I may rejoice in the gladness of thy nation, that I may glory with thine inheritance.

6 We have sinned with our fathers, we have committed iniquity, we have done wickedly.

7 Our fathers understood not thy wonders in Egypt; they remembered not the multitude of thy mercies; but provoked *him* at the sea, *even* at the Red sea.

8 Nevertheless he saved them for his name's sake, that he might make his mighty power to be known.

9 He rebuked the Red sea also, and it was dried up: so he led them through the depths, as through the wilderness.

10 And he saved them from the hand of him that hated *them*, and redeemed them from the hand of the enemy.

11 And the waters covered their enemies: there was not one of them left.

12 Then believed they his words; they sang his praise.

13 They soon forgat his works; they waited not for his counsel:

14 But lusted exceedingly in the wilderness, and tempted God in the desert.

15 And he gave them their request; but sent leanness into their soul.

16 They envied Moses also in the camp, *and* Aaron the saint of the LORD.

17 The earth opened and swallowed up Dā'than, and covered the company of A-bī'ram.

18 And a fire was kindled in their company; the flame burned up the wicked.

19 They made a calf in Hô'rĕb, and worshipped the molten image.

20 Thus they changed their glory into the similitude of an ox that eateth grass.

21 They forgat God their saviour, which had done great things in Egypt;

22 Wondrous works in the land of Ham, *and* terrible things by the Red sea.

23 Therefore he said that he would destroy them, had not Moses his chosen stood before him in the breach, to turn away his wrath, lest he should destroy *them*.

24 Yea, they despised the pleasant land, they believed not his word:

25 But murmured in their tents, *and* hearkened not unto the voice of the LORD.

26 Therefore he lifted up his hand against them, to overthrow them in the wilderness:

27 To overthrow their seed also among the nations, and to scatter them in the lands.

28 They joined themselves also unto Bā'al-pē'ôr, and ate the sacrifices of the dead.

29 Thus they provoked *him* to anger with their inventions: and the plague brake in upon them.

30 Then stood up Phĭn'e-has, and executed judgment: and *so* the plague was stayed.

31 And that was counted unto him for righteousness unto all generations for evermore.

32 They angered *him* also at the waters of strife, so that it went ill with Moses for their sakes:

33 Because they provoked his spirit, so that he spake unadvisedly with his lips.

34 They did not destroy the nations, concerning whom the LORD commanded them:

35 But were mingled among the heathen, and learned their works.

36 And they served their idols: which were a snare unto them.

37 Yea, they sacrificed their sons and their daughters unto devils,

38 And shed innocent blood, *even* the blood of their sons and of their daughters, whom they sacrificed unto the idols of Canaan: and the land was polluted with blood.

39 Thus were they defiled with their own works, and went a whoring with their own inventions.

40 Therefore was the wrath of the LORD kindled against his people, insomuch that he abhorred his own inheritance.

41 And he gave them into the hand of the heathen; and they that hated them ruled over them.

42 Their enemies also oppressed them, and they were brought into subjection under their hand.

43 Many times did he deliver them; but they provoked *him* with their coun-

sel, and were brought low for their iniquity.
44 Nevertheless he regarded their
affliction, when he heard their cry:
45 And he remembered for them his
covenant, and repented according to
the multitude of his mercies.
46 He made them also to be pitied of
all those that carried them captives.
47 Save us, O LORD our God, and gather
us from among the heathen, to
give thanks unto thy holy name, *and* to
triumph in thy praise.
48 Blessed *be* the LORD God of Israel
from everlasting to everlasting: and let
all the people say, Amen. Praise ye the
LORD.

PSALM 107

O GIVE thanks unto the LORD, for *he is*
good: for his mercy *endureth* for ever.
2 Let the redeemed of the LORD say
so, whom he hath redeemed from the
hand of the enemy;
3 And gathered them out of the lands,
from the east, and from the west, from
the north, and from the south.
4 They wandered in the wilderness in
a solitary way; they found no city to
dwell in.
5 Hungry and thirsty, their soul
fainted in them.
6 Then they cried unto the LORD in
their trouble, *and* he delivered them
out of their distresses.
7 And he led them forth by the right
way, that they might go to a city of
habitation.
8 Oh that *men* would praise the LORD
for his goodness, and *for* his wonderful
works to the children of men!
9 For he satisfieth the longing soul,
and filleth the hungry soul with goodness.
10 Such as sit in darkness and in the
shadow of death, *being* bound in affliction
and iron;
11 Because they rebelled against the
words of God, and contemned the
counsel of the most High:
12 Therefore he brought down their
heart with labour; they fell down and
there was none to help.
13 Then they cried unto the LORD in
their trouble, *and* he saved them out of
their distresses.
14 He brought them out of darkness
and the shadow of death, and brake
their bands in sunder.
15 Oh that *men* would praise the
LORD *for* his goodness, and *for* his wonderful
works to the children of men!
16 For he hath broken the gates of
brass, and cut the bars of iron in sunder.
17 Fools because of their transgression,
and because of their iniquities, are
afflicted.
18 Their soul abhorreth all manner of
meat; and they draw near unto the
gates of death.
19 Then they cry unto the LORD in
their trouble, *and* he saveth them out of
their distresses.
20 He sent his word, and healed
them, and delivered *them* from their
destructions.
21 Oh that *men* would praise the
LORD *for* his goodness, and *for* his wonderful
works to the children of men!
22 And let them sacrifice the sacrifices
of thanksgiving, and declare his
works with rejoicing.
23 They that go down to the sea in
ships, that do business in great waters;
24 These see the works of the LORD,
and his wonders in the deep.
25 For he commandeth, and raiseth
the stormy wind, which lifteth up the
waves thereof.
26 They mount up to the heaven, they
go down again to the depths: their soul
is melted because of trouble.
27 They reel to and fro, and stagger
like a drunken man, and are at their
wit's end.
28 Then they cry unto the LORD in
their trouble, and he bringeth them out
of their distresses.
29 He maketh the storm a calm, so
that the waves thereof are still.
30 Then are they glad because they
be quiet; so he bringeth them unto their
desired haven.
31 Oh that *men* would praise the
LORD *for* his goodness, and *for* his wonderful
works to the children of men!
32 Let them exalt him also in the
congregation of the people, and praise
him in the assembly of the elders.
33 He turneth rivers into a wilderness,
and the watersprings into dry
ground;
34 A fruitful land into barrenness, for
the wickedness of them that dwell therein.
35 He turneth the wilderness into a
standing water, and dry ground into
watersprings.
36 And there he maketh the hungry
to dwell, that they may prepare a city
for habitation;
37 And sow the fields, and plant vineyards,
which may yield fruits of increase.
38 He blesseth them also, so that they
are multiplied greatly; and suffereth
not their cattle to decrease.
39 Again, they are minished and

brought low through oppression, affliction, and sorrow.

40 He poureth contempt upon princes, and causeth them to wander in the wilderness, *where there is* no way.

41 Yet setteth he the poor on high from affliction, and maketh *him* families like a flock.

42 The righteous shall see *it*, and rejoice: and all iniquity shall stop her mouth.

43 Whoso *is* wise, and will observe these *things*, even they shall understand the lovingkindness of the LORD.

PSALM 108

O GOD, my heart is fixed: I will sing and give praise, even with my glory.

2 Awake, psaltery and harp: I *myself* will awake early.

3 I will praise thee, O LORD, among the people: and I will sing praises unto thee among the nations.

4 For thy mercy *is* great above the heavens: and thy truth *reacheth* unto the clouds.

5 Be thou exalted, O God, above the heavens: and thy glory above all the earth;

6 That thy beloved may be delivered: save *with* thy right hand, and answer me.

7 God hath spoken in his holiness; I will rejoice, I will divide Shĕ′chem, and mete out the valley of Sŭc′coth.

8 Gilead *is* mine; Ma-năs′seh *is* mine; Ē′phra-im also *is* the strength of mine head; Jū′dah *is* my lawgiver;

9 Moab *is* my washpot; over Edom will I cast out my shoe; over Philistia will I triumph.

10 Who will bring me into the strong city? who will lead me into Edom?

11 *Wilt* not *thou*, O God, *who* hast cast us off? and wilt not thou, O God, go forth with our hosts?

12 Give us help from trouble: for vain *is* the help of man.

13 Through God we shall do valiantly: for he *it is that* shall tread down our enemies.

PSALM 109

HOLD not thy peace, O God of my praise;

2 For the mouth of the wicked and the mouth of the deceitful are opened against me: they have spoken against me with a lying tongue.

3 They compassed me about also with words of hatred; and fought against me without *a* cause.

4 For my love they are my adversaries: but I *give myself unto* prayer.

5 And they have rewarded me evil for good, and hatred for my love.

6 Set thou a wicked man over him: and let Satan stand at his right hand.

7 When he shall be judged, let him be condemned: and let his prayer become sin.

8 Let his days be few; *and* let another take his office.

9 Let his children be fatherless, and his wife a widow.

10 Let his children be continually vagabonds, and beg: let them seek *their bread* also out of their desolate places.

11 Let the extortioner catch all that he hath; and let the strangers spoil his labour.

12 Let there be none to extend mercy unto him: neither let there be any to favour his fatherless children.

13 Let his posterity be cut off; *and* in the generation following let their name be blotted out.

14 Let the iniquity of his fathers be remembered with the LORD; and let not the sin of his mother be blotted out.

15 Let them be before the LORD continually, that he may cut off the memory of them from the earth.

16 Because that he remembered not to shew mercy, but persecuted the poor and needy man, that he might even slay the broken in heart.

17 As he loved cursing, so let it come unto him: as he delighted not in blessing, so let it be far from him.

18 As he clothed himself with cursing like as with his garment, so let it come into his bowels like water, and like oil into his bones.

19 Let it be unto him as the garment *which* covereth him, and for a girdle wherewith he is girded continually.

20 *Let* this *be* the reward of mine adversaries from the LORD, and of them that speak evil against my soul.

21 But do thou for me, O GOD the Lord, for thy name's sake: because thy mercy *is* good, deliver thou me.

22 For I *am* poor and needy, and my heart is wounded within me.

23 I am gone like the shadow when it declineth: I am tossed up and down as the locust.

24 My knees are weak through fasting; and my flesh faileth of fatness.

25 I became also a reproach unto them: *when* they looked upon me they shaked their heads.

26 Help me, O LORD my God: O save me according to thy mercy:

27 That they may know that this *is* thy hand; *that* thou, LORD, hast done it.

28 Let them curse, but bless thou:

when they arise, let them be ashamed; but let thy servant rejoice.
29 Let mine adversaries be clothed with shame, and let them cover themselves with their own confusion, as with a mantle.
30 I will greatly praise the LORD with my mouth; yea, I will praise him among the multitude.
31 For he shall stand at the right hand of the poor, to save *him* from those that condemn his soul.

PSALM 110

THE LORD said unto my Lord, Sit thou at my right hand, until I make thine enemies thy footstool.
2 The LORD shall send the rod of thy strength out of Zion: rule thou in the midst of thine enemies.
3 Thy people *shall be* willing in the day of thy power, in the beauties of holiness from the womb of the morning: thou hast the dew of thy youth.
4 The LORD hath sworn, and will not repent, Thou *art* a priest for ever after the order of Mĕl-chĭz'e-dĕk.
5 The Lord at thy right hand shall strike through kings in the day of his wrath.
6 He shall judge among the heathen, he shall fill *the places* with the dead bodies; he shall wound the heads over many countries.
7 He shall drink of the brook in the way: therefore shall he lift up the head.

PSALM 111

PRAISE ye the LORD. I will praise the LORD with *my* whole heart, in the assembly of the upright, and *in* the congregation.
2 The works of the LORD *are* great, sought out of all them that have pleasure therein.
3 His work *is* honourable and glorious: and his righteousness endureth for ever.
4 He hath made his wonderful works to be remembered: the LORD *is* gracious and full of compassion.
5 He hath given meat unto them that fear him: he will ever be mindful of his covenant.
6 He hath shewed his people the power of his works, that he may give them the heritage of the heathen.
7 The works of his hands *are* verity and judgment; all his commandments *are* sure.
8 They stand fast for ever and ever, *and are* done in truth and uprightness.
9 He sent redemption unto his people: he hath commanded his covenant for ever: holy and reverend *is* his name.
10 The fear of the LORD *is* the beginning of wisdom: a good understanding have all they that do *his commandments*: his praise endureth for ever.

PSALM 112

PRAISE ye the LORD. Blessed *is* the man *that* feareth the LORD, *that* delighteth greatly in his commandments.
2 His seed shall be mighty upon earth: the generation of the upright shall be blessed.
3 Wealth and riches *shall be* in his house: and his righteousness endureth for ever.
4 Unto the upright there ariseth light in the darkness: *he is* gracious, and full of compassion, and righteous.
5 A good man sheweth favour, and lendeth: he will guide his affairs with discretion.
6 Surely he shall not be moved for ever: the righteous shall be in everlasting remembrance.
7 He shall not be afraid of evil tidings: his heart is fixed, trusting in the LORD.
8 His heart *is* established, he shall not be afraid, until he see *his desire* upon his enemies.
9 He hath dispersed, he hath given to the poor; his righteousness endureth for ever; his horn shall be exalted with honour.
10 The wicked shall see *it*, and be grieved; he shall gnash with his teeth, and melt away: the desire of the wicked shall perish.

PSALM 113

PRAISE ye the LORD. Praise, O ye servants of the LORD, praise the name of the LORD.
2 Blessed be the name of the LORD from this time forth and for evermore.
3 From the rising of the sun unto the going down of the same the LORD's name *is* to be praised.
4 The LORD *is* high above all nations, *and* his glory above the heavens.
5 Who *is* like unto the LORD our God, who dwelleth on high,
6 Who humbleth *himself* to behold *the things that are* in heaven, and in the earth!
7 He raiseth up the poor out of the dust, *and* lifteth the needy out of the dunghill;
8 That he may set *him* with princes, *even* with the princes of his people.
9 He maketh the barren woman to keep house, *and to be* a joyful mother of children. Praise ye the LORD.

PSALM 114

WHEN Israel went out of Egypt, the house of Jacob from a people of strange language;
2 Jū´dah was his sanctuary, *and* Israel his dominion.
3 The sea saw *it*, and fled: Jordan was driven back.
4 The mountains skipped like rams, *and* the little hills like lambs.
5 What *ailed* thee, O thou sea, that thou fleddest? thou Jordan, *that* thou wast driven back?
6 Ye mountains, *that* ye skipped like rams; *and* ye little hills, like lambs?
7 Tremble, thou earth, at the presence of the Lord, at the presence of the God of Jacob;
8 Which turned the rock *into* a standing water, the flint into a fountain of waters.

PSALM 115

NOT unto us, O LORD, not unto us, but unto thy name give glory, for thy mercy, *and* for thy truth's sake.
2 Wherefore should the heathen say, Where *is* now their God?
3 But our God *is* in the heavens: he hath done whatsoever he hath pleased.
4 Their idols *are* silver and gold, the work of men's hands.
5 They have mouths, but they speak not: eyes have they, but they see not:
6 They have ears, but they hear not: noses have they, but they smell not:
7 They have hands, but they handle not: feet have they, but they walk not: neither speak they through their throat.
8 They that make them are like unto them; *so is* every one that trusteth in them.
9 O Israel, trust thou in the LORD: he *is* their help and their shield.
10 O house of Aaron, trust in the LORD: he *is* their help and their shield.
11 Ye that fear the LORD, trust in the LORD: he *is* their help and their shield.
12 The LORD hath been mindful of us: he will bless *us*; he will bless the house of Israel; he will bless the house of Aaron.
13 He will bless them that fear the LORD, *both* small and great.
14 The LORD shall increase you more and more, you and your children.
15 Ye *are* blessed of the LORD which made heaven and earth.
16 The heaven, *even* the heavens, *are* the LORD's: but the earth hath he given to the children of men.
17 The dead praise not the LORD, neither any that go down into silence.
18 But we will bless the LORD from this time forth and for evermore. Praise the LORD.

PSALM 116

I LOVE the LORD, because he hath heard my voice *and* my supplications.
2 Because he hath inclined his ear unto me, therefore will I call upon *him* as long as I live.
3 The sorrows of death compassed me, and the pains of hell gat hold upon me: I found trouble and sorrow.
4 Then called I upon the name of the LORD; O LORD, I beseech thee, deliver my soul.
5 Gracious *is* the LORD, and righteous; yea, our God *is* merciful.
6 The LORD preserveth the simple: I was brought low, and he helped me.
7 Return unto thy rest, O my soul; for the LORD hath dealt bountifully with thee.
8 For thou hast delivered my soul from death, mine eyes from tears, *and* my feet from falling.
9 I will walk before the LORD in the land of the living.
10 I believed, therefore have I spoken: I was greatly afflicted:
11 I said in my haste, All men *are* liars.
12 What shall I render unto the LORD *for* all his benefits toward me?
13 I will take the cup of salvation, and call upon the name of the LORD.
14 I will pay my vows unto the LORD now in the presence of all his people.
15 Precious in the sight of the LORD *is* the death of his saints.
16 O LORD, truly I *am* thy servant; I *am* thy servant, *and* the son of thine handmaid: thou hast loosed my bonds.
17 I will offer to thee the sacrifice of thanksgiving, and will call upon the name of the LORD.
18 I will pay my vows unto the LORD now in the presence of all his people,
19 In the courts of the LORD's house, in the midst of thee, O Jerusalem. Praise ye the LORD.

PSALM 117

O PRAISE the LORD, all ye nations: praise him, all ye people.
2 For his merciful kindness is great toward us: and the truth of the LORD *endureth* for ever. Praise ye the LORD.

PSALM 118

O GIVE thanks unto the LORD; for *he is* good: because his mercy *endureth* for ever.
2 Let Israel now say, that his mercy *endureth* for ever.

3 Let the house of Aaron now say, that his mercy *endureth* for ever.
4 Let them now that fear the LORD say, that his mercy *endureth* for ever.
5 I called upon the LORD in distress: the LORD answered me, *and set me* in a large place.
6 The LORD *is* on on my side; I will not fear: what can man do unto me?
7 The LORD taketh my part with them that help me: therefore shall I see *my desire* upon them that hate me.
8 *It is* better to trust in the LORD than to put confidence in man.
9 *It is* better to trust in the LORD than to put confidence in princes.
10 All nations compassed me about: but in the name of the LORD will I destroy them.
11 They compassed me about; yea, they compassed me about: but in the name of the LORD I will destroy them.
12 They compassed me about like bees; they are quenched as the fire of thorns: for in the name of the LORD I will destroy them.
13 Thou hast thrust sore at me that I might fall: but the LORD helped me.
14 The LORD *is* my strength and song, and is become my salvation.
15 The voice of rejoicing and salvation *is* in the tabernacles of the righteous: the right hand of the LORD doeth valiantly.
16 The right hand of the LORD is exalted: the right hand of the LORD doeth valiantly.
17 I shall not die, but live, and declare the works of the LORD.
18 The LORD hath chastened me sore: but he hath not given me over unto death.
19 Open to me the gates of righteousness: I will go into them, *and* I will praise the LORD:
20 This gate of the LORD, into which the righteous shall enter.
21 I will praise thee: for thou hast heard me, and art become my salvation.
22 The stone *which* the builders refused is become the head *stone* of the corner.
23 This is the LORD's doing; *it is* marvellous in our eyes.
24 This *is* the day *which* the LORD hath made; we will rejoice and be glad in it.
25 Save now, I beseech thee, O LORD: O LORD, I beseech thee, send now prosperity.
26 Blessed *be* he that cometh in the name of the LORD: we have blessed you out of the house of the LORD.
27 God *is* the LORD, which hath shewed us light: bind the sacrifice with cords, *even* unto the horns of the altar.
28 Thou *art* my God, and I will praise thee: *thou art* my God, I will exalt thee.
29 O give thanks unto the LORD; for *he is* good: for his mercy *endureth* for ever.

PSALM 119

ALEPH

BLESSED *are* the undefiled in the way, who walk in the law of the LORD.
2 Blessed *are* they that keep his testimonies, *and that* seek him with the whole heart.
3 They also do no iniquity: they walk in his ways.
4 Thou hast commanded *us* to keep thy precepts diligently.
5 O that my ways were directed to keep thy statutes!
6 Then shall I not be ashamed, when I have respect unto all thy commandments.
7 I will praise thee with uprightness of heart, when I shall have learned thy righteous judgments.
8 I will keep thy statutes: O forsake me not utterly.

BETH

9 Wherewithal shall a young man cleanse his way? by taking heed *thereto* according to thy word.
10 With my whole heart have I sought thee: O let me not wander from thy commandments.
11 Thy word have I hid in mine heart, that I might not sin against thee.
12 Blessed *art* thou, O LORD: teach me thy statutes.
13 With my lips have I declared all the judgments of thy mouth.
14 I have rejoiced in the way of thy testimonies, as *much as* in all riches.
15 I will meditate in thy precepts, and have respect unto thy ways.
16 I will delight myself in thy statutes: I will not forget thy word.

GIMEL

17 Deal bountifully with thy servant, *that* I may live, and keep thy word.
18 Open thou mine eyes, that I may behold wondrous things out of thy law.
19 I am a stranger in the earth: hide not thy commandments from me.
20 My soul breaketh for the longing *that it hath* unto thy judgments at all times.
21 Thou hast rebuked the proud *that are* cursed, which do err from thy commandments.
22 Remove from me reproach and contempt; for I have kept thy testimonies.

23 Princes also did sit *and* speak against me: *but* thy servant did meditate in thy statutes.
24 Thy testimonies also *are* my delight *and* my counsellors.

DALETH

25 My soul cleaveth unto the dust: quicken thou me according to thy word.
26 I have declared my ways, and thou heardest me: teach me thy statutes.
27 Make me to understand the way of thy precepts: so shall I talk of thy wondrous works.
28 My soul melteth for heaviness: strengthen thou me according unto thy word.
29 Remove from me the way of lying: and grant me thy law graciously.
30 I have chosen the way of truth: thy judgments have I laid *before me.*
31 I have stuck unto thy testimonies: O LORD, put me not to shame.
32 I will run the way of thy commandments, when thou shalt enlarge my heart.

HE

33 Teach me, O LORD, the way of thy statutes; and I shall keep it *unto* the end.
34 Give me understanding, and I shall keep thy law; yea, I shall observe it with *my* whole heart.
35 Make me to go in the path of thy commandments; for therein do I delight.
36 Incline my heart unto thy testimonies, and not to covetousness.
37 Turn away mine eyes from beholding vanity; *and* quicken thou me in thy way.
38 Stablish thy word unto thy servant, who *is devoted* to thy fear.
39 Turn away my reproach which I fear: for thy judgments *are* good.
40 Behold, I have longed after thy precepts: quicken me in thy righteousness.

VAU

41 Let thy mercies come also unto me, O LORD, *even* thy salvation, according to thy word.
42 So shall I have wherewith to answer him that reproacheth me: for I trust in thy word.
43 And take not the word of truth utterly out of my mouth; for I have hoped in thy judgments.
44 So shall I keep thy law continually for ever and ever.
45 And I will walk at liberty: for I seek thy precepts.
46 I will speak of thy testimonies also before kings, and will not be ashamed.
47 And I will delight myself in thy commandments, which I have loved.
48 My hands also will I lift up unto thy commandments, which I have loved; and I will meditate in thy statutes.

ZAIN

49 Remember the word unto thy servant, upon which thou hast caused me to hope.
50 This *is* my comfort in my affliction: for thy word hath quickened me.
51 The proud have had me greatly in derision: *yet* have I not declined from thy law.
52 I remembered thy judgments of old, O LORD; and have comforted myself.
53 Horror hath taken hold upon me because of the wicked that forsake thy law.
54 Thy statutes have been my songs in the house of my pilgrimage.
55 I have remembered thy name, O LORD, in the night, and have kept thy law.
56 This I had, because I kept thy precepts.

CHETH

57 *Thou art* my portion, O LORD: I have said that I would keep thy words.
58 I intreated thy favour with *my* whole heart: be merciful unto me according to thy word.
59 I thought on my ways, and turned my feet unto thy testimonies.
60 I made haste, and delayed not to keep thy commandments.
61 The bands of the wicked have robbed me: *but* I have not forgotten thy law.
62 At midnight I will rise to give thanks unto thee because of thy righteous judgments.
63 I *am* a companion of all *them* that fear thee, and of them that keep thy precepts.
64 The earth, O LORD, is full of thy mercy: teach me thy statutes.

TETH

65 Thou hast dealt well with thy servant, O LORD, according unto thy word.
66 Teach me good judgment and knowledge: for I have believed thy commandments.
67 Before I was afflicted I went astray: but now have I kept thy word.
68 Thou *art* good, and doest good; teach me thy statutes.
69 The proud have forged a lie

against me: *but* I will keep thy precepts with *my* whole heart.

70 Their heart is as fat as grease; *but* I delight in thy law.

71 *It is* good for me that I have been afflicted; that I might learn thy statutes.

72 The law of thy mouth *is* better unto me than thousands of gold and silver.

JOD

73 Thy hands have made me and fashioned me: give me understanding, that I may learn thy commandments.

74 They that fear thee will be glad when they see me; because I have hoped in thy word.

75 I know, O LORD, that thy judgments *are* right, and *that* thou in faithfulness hast afflicted me.

76 Let, I pray thee, thy merciful kindness be for my comfort, according to thy word unto thy servant.

77 Let thy tender mercies come unto me, that I may live: for thy law *is* my delight.

78 Let the proud be ashamed; for they dealt perversely with me without a cause: *but* I will meditate in thy precepts.

79 Let those that fear thee turn unto me, and those that have known thy testimonies.

80 Let my heart be sound in thy statutes; that I be not ashamed.

CAPH

81 My soul fainteth for thy salvation: *but* I hope in thy word.

82 Mine eyes fail for thy word, saying, When wilt thou comfort me?

83 For I am become like a bottle in the smoke; *yet* do I not forget thy statutes.

84 How many *are* the days of thy servant? when wilt thou execute judgment on them that persecute me?

85 The proud have digged pits for me, which *are* not after thy law.

86 All thy commandments *are* faithful: they persecute me wrongfully; help thou me.

87 They had almost consumed me upon earth; but I forsook not thy precepts.

88 Quicken me after thy lovingkindness; so shall I keep the testimony of thy mouth.

LAMED

89 For ever, O LORD, thy word is settled in heaven.

90 Thy faithfulness *is* unto all generations: thou hast established the earth, and it abideth.

91 They continue this day according to thine ordinances: for all *are* thy servants.

92 Unless thy law *had been* my delights, I should then have perished in mine affliction.

93 I will never forget thy precepts: for with them thou hast quickened me.

94 I *am* thine, save me; for I have sought thy precepts.

95 The wicked have waited for me to destroy me: *but* I will consider thy testimonies.

96 I have seen an end of all perfection: *but* thy commandment *is* exceeding broad.

MEM

97 O how I love thy law! it *is* my meditation all the day.

98 Thou through thy commandments hast made me wiser than mine enemies: for they *are* ever with me.

99 I have more understanding than all my teachers: for thy testimonies *are* my meditation.

100 I understand more than the ancients, because I keep thy precepts.

101 I have refrained my feet from every evil way, that I might keep thy word.

102 I have not departed from thy judgments: for thou hast taught me.

103 How sweet are thy words unto my taste! *yea, sweeter* than honey to my mouth!

104 Through thy precepts I get understanding: therefore I hate every false way.

NUN

105 Thy word *is* a lamp unto my feet, and a light unto my path.

106 I have sworn, and I will perform *it*, that I will keep thy righteous judgments.

107 I am afflicted very much: quicken me, O LORD, according unto thy word.

108 Accept, I beseech thee, the freewill offerings of my mouth, O LORD, and teach me thy judgments.

109 My soul *is* continually in my hand: yet do I not forget thy law.

110 The wicked have laid a snare for me: yet I erred not from thy precepts.

111 Thy testimonies have I taken as an heritage for ever: for they *are* the rejoicing of my heart.

112 I have inclined mine heart to perform thy statutes alway, *even unto* the end.

SAMECH

113 I hate *vain* thoughts: but thy law do I love.
114 Thou *art* my hiding place and my shield: I hope in thy word.
115 Depart from me, ye evildoers: for I will keep the commandments of my God.
116 Uphold me according unto thy word, that I may live: and let me not be ashamed of my hope.
117 Hold thou me up, and I shall be safe: and I will have respect unto thy statutes continually.
118 Thou hast trodden down all them that err from thy statutes: for their deceit *is* falsehood.
119 Thou puttest away all the wicked of the earth *like* dross: therefore I love thy testimonies.
120 My flesh trembleth for fear of thee; and I am afraid of thy judgments.

AIN

121 I have done judgment and justice: leave me not to mine oppressors.
122 Be surety for thy servant for good: let not the proud oppress me.
123 Mine eyes fail for thy salvation, and for the word of thy righteousness.
124 Deal with thy servant according unto thy mercy, and teach me thy statutes.
125 I *am* thy servant; give me understanding, that I may know thy testimonies.
126 *It is* time for *thee*, LORD, to work: *for* they have made void thy law.
127 Therefore I love thy commandments above gold; yea, above fine gold.
128 Therefore I esteem all *thy* precepts *concerning* all *things to be* right; *and* I hate every false way.

PE

129 Thy testimonies *are* wonderful: therefore doth my soul keep them.
130 The entrance of thy words giveth light; it giveth understanding unto the simple.
131 I opened my mouth, and panted: for I longed for thy commandments.
132 Look thou upon me, and be merciful unto me, as thou usest to do unto those that love thy name.
133 Order my steps in thy word: and let not any iniquity have dominion over me.
134 Deliver me from the oppression of man: so will I keep thy precepts.
135 Make thy face to shine upon thy servant; and teach me thy statutes.
136 Rivers of waters run down mine eyes, because they keep not thy law.

TZADDI

137 Righteous *art* thou, O LORD, and upright *are* thy judgments.
138 Thy testimonies *that* thou hast commanded *are* righteous and very faithful.
139 My zeal hath consumed me, because mine enemies have forgotten thy words.
140 Thy word *is* very pure: therefore thy servant loveth it.
141 I *am* small and despised: *yet* do not I forget thy precepts.
142 Thy righteousness *is* an everlasting righteousness, and thy law *is* the truth.
143 Trouble and anguish have taken hold on me: *yet* thy commandments *are* my delights.
144 The righteousness of thy testimonies *is* everlasting: give me understanding, and I shall live.

KOPH

145 I cried with *my* whole heart; hear me, O LORD: I will keep thy statutes.
146 I cried unto thee; save me, and I shall keep thy testimonies.
147 I prevented the dawning of the morning, and cried: I hoped in thy word.
148 Mine eyes prevent the *night* watches, that I might meditate in thy word.
149 Hear my voice according unto thy lovingkindness: O LORD, quicken me according to thy judgment.
150 They draw nigh that follow after mischief: they are far from thy law.
151 Thou *art* near, O LORD; and all thy commandments *are* truth.
152 Concerning thy testimonies, I have known of old that thou hast founded them for ever.

RESH

153 Consider mine affliction, and deliver me: for I do not forget thy law.
154 Plead my cause, and deliver me: quicken me according to thy word.
155 Salvation *is* far from the wicked: for they seek not thy statutes.
156 Great *are* thy tender mercies, O LORD: quicken me according to thy judgments.
157 Many *are* my persecutors and mine enemies; *yet* do I not decline from thy testimonies.
158 I beheld the transgressors, and was grieved; because they kept not thy word.
159 Consider how I love thy precepts: quicken me, O LORD, according to thy lovingkindness.

160 Thy word *is* true *from* the beginning: and every one of thy righteous judgments *endureth* for ever.

SCHIN

161 Princes have persecuted me without a cause: but my heart standeth in awe of thy word.
162 I rejoice at thy word, as one that findeth great spoil.
163 I hate and abhor lying: *but* thy law do I love.
164 Seven times a day do I praise thee because of thy righteous judgments.
165 Great peace have they which love thy law: and nothing shall offend them.
166 LORD, I have hoped for thy salvation, and done thy commandments.
167 My soul hath kept thy testimonies; and I love them exceedingly.
168 I have kept thy precepts and thy testimonies: for all my ways *are* before thee.

TAU

169 Let my cry come near before thee, O LORD: give me understanding according to thy word.
170 Let my supplication come before thee: deliver me according to thy word.
171 My lips shall utter praise, when thou hast taught me thy statutes.
172 My tongue shall speak of thy word: for all thy commandments *are* righteousness.
173 Let thine hand help me; for I have chosen thy precepts.
174 I have longed for thy salvation, O LORD; and thy law *is* my delight.
175 Let my soul live, and it shall praise thee; and let thy judgments help me.
176 I have gone astray like a lost sheep; seek thy servant; for I do not forget thy commandments.

PSALM 120

IN my distress I cried unto the LORD, and he heard me.
2 Deliver my soul, O LORD, from lying lips, *and* from a deceitful tongue.
3 What shall be given unto thee? or what shall be done unto thee, thou false tongue?
4 Sharp arrows of the mighty, with coals of juniper.
5 Woe is me, that I sojourn in Mē′sĕch, *that* I dwell in the tents of Kē′dar!
6 My soul hath long dwelt with him that hateth peace.
7 I *am for* peace: but when I speak, they *are* for war.

PSALM 121

I WILL lift up mine eyes unto the hills, from whence cometh my help.
2 My help *cometh* from the LORD, which made heaven and earth.
3 He will not suffer thy foot to be moved: he that keepeth thee will not slumber.
4 Behold, he that keepeth Israel shall neither slumber nor sleep.
5 The LORD *is* thy keeper: the LORD *is* thy shade upon thy right hand.
6 The sun shall not smite thee by day, nor the moon by night.
7 The LORD shall preserve thee from all evil: he shall preserve thy soul.
8 The LORD shall preserve thy going out and thy coming in from this time forth, and even for evermore.

PSALM 122

I WAS glad when they said unto me, Let us go into the house of the LORD.
2 Our feet shall stand within thy gates, O Jerusalem.
3 Jerusalem is builded as a city that is compact together:
4 Whither the tribes go up, the tribes of the LORD, unto the testimony of Israel, to give thanks unto the name of the LORD.
5 For there are set thrones of judgment, the thrones of the house of David.
6 Pray for the peace of Jerusalem: they shall prosper that love thee.
7 Peace be within thy walls, *and* prosperity within thy palaces.
8 For my brethren and companions' sakes, I will now say, Peace *be* within thee.
9 Because of the house of the LORD our God I will seek thy good.

PSALM 123

UNTO thee lift I up mine eyes, O thou that dwellest in the heavens.
2 Behold, as the eyes of servants *look* unto the hand of their masters, *and* as the eyes of a maiden unto the hand of her mistress; so our eyes *wait* upon the LORD our God, until that he have mercy upon us.
3 Have mercy upon us, O LORD, have mercy upon us: for we are exceedingly filled with contempt.
4 Our soul is exceedingly filled with the scorning of those that are at ease, *and* with the contempt of the proud.

PSALM 124

IF *it had not been* the LORD who was on our side, now may Israel say;
2 If *it had not been* the LORD who was

on our side, when men rose up against us:

3 Then they had swallowed us up quick, when their wrath was kindled against us:

4 Then the waters had overwhelmed us, the stream had gone over our soul:

5 Then the proud waters had gone over our soul.

6 Blessed *be* the LORD, who hath not given us *as* a prey to their teeth.

7 Our soul is escaped as a bird out of the snare of the fowlers: the snare is broken, and we are escaped.

8 Our help *is* in the name of the LORD, who made heaven and earth.

PSALM 125

THEY that trust in the LORD *shall be* as mount Zion *which* cannot be removed, *but* abideth for ever.

2 *As* the mountains *are* round about Jerusalem, so the LORD *is* round about his people from henceforth even for ever.

3 For the rod of the wicked shall not rest upon the lot of the righteous; lest the righteous put forth their hands unto iniquity.

4 Do good, O LORD, unto *those that be* good, and to *them that are* upright in their hearts.

5 As for such as turn aside unto their crooked ways, the LORD shall lead them forth with the workers of iniquity: *but* peace *shall be* upon Israel.

PSALM 126

WHEN the LORD turned again the captivity of Zion, we were like them that dream.

2 Then was our mouth filled with laughter, and our tongue with singing: then said they among the heathen, The LORD hath done great things for them.

3 The LORD hath done great things for us; *whereof* we are glad.

4 Turn again our captivity, O LORD, as the streams in the south.

5 They that sow in tears shall reap in joy.

6 He that goeth forth and weepeth, bearing precious seed, shall doubtless come again with rejoicing, bringing his sheaves *with him*.

PSALM 127

EXCEPT the LORD build the house, they labour in vain that build it: except the LORD keep the city, the watchman waketh *but* in vain.

2 *It is* vain for you to rise up early, to sit up late, to eat the bread of sorrows: *for* so he giveth his beloved sleep.

3 Lo, children *are* an heritage of the LORD: *and* the fruit of the womb *is his* reward.

4 As arrows *are* in the hand of a mighty man; so *are* children of the youth.

5 Happy *is* the man that hath his quiver full of them: they shall not be ashamed, but they shall speak with the enemies in the gate.

PSALM 128

BLESSED *is* every one that feareth the LORD; that walketh in his ways.

2 For thou shalt eat the labour of thine hands: happy *shalt* thou *be*, and *it shall be* well with thee.

3 Thy wife *shall be* as a fruitful vine by the sides of thine house: thy children like olive plants round about thy table.

4 Behold, that thus shall the man be blessed that feareth the LORD.

5 The LORD shall bless thee out of Zion: and thou shalt see the good of Jerusalem all the days of thy life.

6 Yea, thou shalt see thy children's children, *and* peace upon Israel.

PSALM 129

MANY a time have they afflicted me from my youth, may Israel now say:

2 Many a time have they afflicted me from my youth: yet they have not prevailed against me.

3 The plowers plowed upon my back: they made long their furrows.

4 The LORD *is* righteous: he hath cut asunder the cords of the wicked.

5 Let them all be confounded and turned back that hate Zion.

6 Let them be as the grass *upon* the housetops, which withereth afore it groweth up:

7 Wherewith the mower filleth not his hand; nor he that bindeth sheaves his bosom.

8 Neither do they which go by say, The blessing of the LORD *be* upon you: we bless you in the name of the LORD.

PSALM 130

OUT of the depths have I cried unto thee, O LORD.

2 Lord, hear my voice: let thine ears be attentive to the voice of my supplications.

3 If thou, LORD, shouldst mark iniquities, O LORD, who shall stand?

4 But *there is* forgiveness with thee, that thou mayest be feared.

5 I wait for the LORD, my soul doth wait, and in his word do I hope.

6 My soul *waiteth* for the Lord more than they that watch for the morning: *I say, more than* they that watch for the morning.

7 Let Israel hope in the LORD: for with
the LORD *there is* mercy, and with him
is plenteous redemption.
8 And he shall redeem Israel from all
his iniquities.

PSALM 131

LORD, my heart is not haughty, nor
mine eyes lofty: neither do I exercise
myself in great matters, or in things too
high for me.
2 Surely I have behaved and quieted
myself, as a child that is weaned of his
mother: my soul *is* even as a weaned
child.
3 Let Israel hope in the LORD from
henceforth and for ever.

PSALM 132

LORD, remember David, *and* all his
afflictions:
2 How he sware unto the LORD, *and*
vowed unto the mighty *God* of Jacob;
3 Surely I will not come into the tab-
ernacle of my house, nor go up into
my bed;
4 I will not give sleep to mine eyes, *or*
slumber to mine eyelids,
5 Until I find out a place for the LORD,
an habitation for the mighty *God* of Ja-
cob.
6 Lo, we heard of it at Ĕph'ra-tăh: we
found it in the fields of the wood.
7 We will go into his tabernacles: we
will worship at his footstool.
8 Arise, O LORD, into thy rest; thou,
and the ark of thy strength.
9 Let thy priests be clothed with
righteousness; and let thy saints shout
for joy.
10 For thy servant David's sake turn
not away the face of thine anointed.
11 The LORD hath sworn *in* truth unto
David; he will not turn from it; Of the
fruit of thy body will I set upon thy
throne.
12 If thy children will keep my cov-
enant and my testimony that I shall
teach them, their children shall also sit
upon thy throne for evermore.
13 For the LORD hath chosen Zion; he
hath desired *it* for his habitation.
14 This *is* my rest for ever: here will I
dwell; for I have desired it.
15 I will abundantly bless her provi-
sion: I will satisfy her poor with bread.
16 I will also clothe her priests with
salvation: and her saints shall shout
aloud for joy.
17 There will I make the horn of Da-
vid to bud: I have ordained a lamp for
mine anointed.
18 His enemies will I clothe with
shame: but upon himself shall his
crown flourish.

PSALM 133

BEHOLD, how good and how pleasant
it is for brethren to dwell together in
unity!
2 *It is* like the precious ointment upon
the head, that ran down upon the
beard, *even* Aaron's beard: that went
down to the skirts of his garments;
3 As the dew of Her'mon, *and as the*
dew that descended upon the moun-
tains of Zion: for there the LORD com-
manded the blessing, *even* life for ever-
more.

PSALM 134

BEHOLD, bless ye the LORD, all *ye* ser-
vants of the LORD, which by night stand
in the house of the LORD.
2 Lift up your hands *in* the sanctuary,
and bless the LORD.
3 The LORD that made heaven and
earth bless thee out of Zion.

PSALM 135

PRAISE ye the LORD. Praise ye the
name of the LORD; praise *him*, O ye ser-
vants of the LORD.
2 Ye that stand in the house of the
LORD, in the courts of the house of our
God,
3 Praise the LORD; for the LORD *is*
good: sing praises unto his name; for *it*
is pleasant.
4 For the LORD hath chosen Jacob
unto himself, *and* Israel for his peculiar
treasure.
5 For I know that the LORD *is* great,
and *that* our Lord *is* above all gods.
6 Whatsoever the LORD pleased, *that*
did he in heaven, and in earth, in the
seas, and all deep places.
7 He causeth the vapours to ascend
from the ends of the earth; he maketh
lightnings for the rain; he bringeth the
wind out of his treasuries.
8 Who smote the firstborn of Egypt,
both of man and beast.
9 *Who* sent tokens and wonders into
the midst of thee, O Egypt, upon
Pharaoh, and upon all his servants.
10 Who smote great nations, and
slew mighty kings;
11 Sihon king of the Ăm'o-rītes, and
Og king of Bā'shan, and all the king-
doms of Canaan:
12 And gave their land *for* an heri-
tage, an heritage unto Israel his people.
13 Thy name, O LORD, *endureth* for
ever; *and* thy memorial, O LORD,
throughout all generations.
14 For the LORD will judge his people,
and he will repent himself concerning
his servants.

15 The idols of the heathen *are* silver and gold, the work of men's hands.

16 They have mouths, but they speak not; eyes have they, but they see not;

17 They have ears, but they hear not; neither is there *any* breath in their mouths.

18 They that make them are like unto them: *so is* every one that trusteth in them.

19 Bless the LORD, O house of Israel: bless the LORD, O house of Aaron:

20 Bless the LORD, O house of Levi: ye that fear the LORD, bless the LORD.

21 Blessed be the LORD out of Zion, which dwelleth at Jerusalem. Praise ye the LORD.

PSALM 136

O GIVE thanks unto the LORD; for *he is* good: for his mercy *endureth* for ever.

2 O give thanks unto the God of gods: for his mercy *endureth* for ever.

3 O give thanks to the Lord of lords: for his mercy *endureth* for ever.

4 To him who alone doeth great wonders: for his mercy *endureth* for ever.

5 To him that by wisdom made the heavens: for his mercy *endureth* for ever.

6 To him that stretched out the earth above the waters: for his mercy *endureth* for ever.

7 To him that made great lights: for his mercy *endureth* for ever:

8 The sun to rule by day: for his mercy *endureth* for ever:

9 The moon and stars to rule by night: for his mercy *endureth* for ever.

10 To him that smote Egypt in their firstborn: for his mercy *endureth* for ever:

11 And brought out Israel from among them: for his mercy *endureth* for ever:

12 With a strong hand, and with a stretched out arm: for his mercy *endureth* for ever.

13 To him which divided the Red sea into parts: for his mercy *endureth* for ever:

14 And made Israel to pass through the midst of it: for his mercy *endureth* for ever:

15 But overthrew Pharaoh and his host in the Red sea: for his mercy *endureth* for ever.

16 To him which led his people through the wilderness: for his mercy *endureth* for ever.

17 To him which smote great kings: for his mercy *endureth* for ever:

18 And slew famous kings: for his mercy *endureth* for ever:

19 Sihon king of the Ăm'o-rītes: for his mercy *endureth* for ever:

20 And Og the king of Bā'shan: for his mercy *endureth* for ever:

21 And gave their land for an heritage: for his mercy *endureth* for ever:

22 *Even* an heritage unto Israel his servant: for his mercy *endureth* for ever.

23 Who remembered us in our low estate: for his mercy *endureth* for ever:

24 And hath redeemed us from our enemies: for his mercy *endureth* for ever.

25 Who giveth food to all flesh: for his mercy *endureth* for ever.

26 O give thanks unto the God of heaven: for his mercy *endureth* for ever.

PSALM 137

BY the rivers of Babylon, there we sat down, yea, we wept, when we remembered Zion.

2 We hanged our harps upon the willows in the midst thereof.

3 For there they that carried us away captive required of us a song; and they that wasted us *required of us* mirth, *saying,* Sing us *one* of the songs of Zion.

4 How shall we sing the LORD's song in a strange land?

5 If I forget thee, O Jerusalem, let my right hand forget *her cunning.*

6 If I do not remember thee, let my tongue cleave to the roof of my mouth; if I prefer not Jerusalem above my chief joy.

7 Remember, O LORD, the children of Ē'dom in the day of Jerusalem; who said, Rase *it,* rase *it, even* to the foundation thereof.

8 O daughter of Babylon, who art to be destroyed; happy *shall he be,* that rewardeth thee as thou hast served us.

9 Happy *shall he be,* that taketh and dasheth thy little ones against the stones.

PSALM 138

I WILL praise thee with my whole heart: before the gods will I sing praise unto thee.

2 I will worship toward thy holy temple, and praise thy name for thy lovingkindness and for thy truth: for thou hast magnified thy word above all thy name.

3 In the day when I cried thou answeredst me, *and* strengthenedst me *with* strength in my soul.

4 All the kings of the earth shall praise thee, O LORD, when they hear the words of thy mouth.

5 Yea, they shall sing in the ways of the LORD: for great *is* the glory of the LORD.
6 Though the LORD *be* high, yet hath he respect unto the lowly: but the proud he knoweth afar off.
7 Though I walk in the midst of trouble, thou wilt revive me: thou shalt stretch forth thine hand against the wrath of mine enemies, and thy right hand shall save me.
8 The LORD will perfect *that which* concerneth me: thy mercy, O LORD, *endureth* for ever: forsake not the works of thine own hands.

PSALM 139

O LORD, thou hast searched me, and known *me*.
2 Thou knowest my downsitting and mine uprising, thou understandest my thought afar off.
3 Thou compassest my path and my lying down, and art acquainted *with* all my ways.
4 For *there is* not a word in my tongue, *but*, lo, O LORD, thou knowest it altogether.
5 Thou hast beset me behind and before, and laid thine hand upon me.
6 *Such* knowledge *is* too wonderful for me; it is high, I cannot *attain* unto it.
7 Whither shall I go from thy spirit? or whither shall I flee from thy presence?
8 If I ascend up into heaven, thou *art* there: if I make my bed in hell, behold, thou *art there*.
9 *If* I take the wings of the morning, *and* dwell in the uttermost parts of the sea;
10 Even there shall thy hand lead me, and thy right hand shall hold me.
11 If I say, Surely the darkness shall cover me; even the night shall be light about me.
12 Yea, the darkness hideth not from thee; but the night shineth as the day: the darkness and the light *are* both alike *to thee*.
13 For thou hast possessed my reins: thou hast covered me in my mother's womb.
14 I will praise thee; for I am fearfully *and* wonderfully made: marvellous *are* thy works; and *that* my soul knoweth right well.
15 My substance was not hid from thee, when I was made in secret, *and* curiously wrought in the lowest parts of the earth.
16 Thine eyes did see my substance, yet being unperfect; and in thy book all *my members* were written, *which* in continuance were fashioned, when *as yet there was* none of them.
17 How precious also are thy thoughts unto me, O God! how great is the sum of them!
18 *If* I should count them, they are more in number than the sand: when I awake, I am still with thee.
19 Surely thou wilt slay the wicked, O God: depart from me therefore, ye bloody men.
20 For they speak against thee wickedly, *and* thine enemies take *thy name* in vain.
21 Do not I hate them, O LORD, that hate thee? and am not I grieved with those that rise up against thee?
22 I hate them with perfect hatred: I count them mine enemies.
23 Search me, O God, and know my heart: try me, and know my thoughts:
24 And see if *there be any* wicked way in me, and lead me in the way everlasting.

PSALM 140

DELIVER me, O LORD, from the evil man: preserve me from the violent man;
2 Which imagine mischiefs in *their* heart; continually are they gathered together *for* war.
3 They have sharpened their tongues like a serpent; adders' poison *is* under their lips. Sē'lah.
4 Keep me, O LORD, from the hands of the wicked; preserve me from the violent man; who have purposed to overthrow my goings.
5 The proud have hid a snare for me, and cords; they have spread a net by the wayside; they have set gins for me. Sē'lah.
6 I said unto the LORD, Thou *art* my God: hear the voice of my supplications, O LORD.
7 O GOD the Lord, the strength of my salvation, thou hast covered my head in the day of battle.
8 Grant not, O LORD, the desires of the wicked: further not his wicked device; *lest* they exalt themselves. Sē'lah.
9 *As for* the head of those that compass me about, let the mischief of their own lips cover them.
10 Let burning coals fall upon them: let them be cast into the fire; into deep pits, that they rise not up again.
11 Let not an evil speaker be established in the earth: evil shall hunt the violent man to overthrow *him*.
12 I know that the LORD will maintain

the cause of the afflicted, *and* the right
of the poor.
13 Surely the righteous shall give
thanks unto thy name: the upright shall
dwell in thy presence.

PSALM 141

LORD, I cry unto thee: make haste unto
me; give ear unto my voice, when I cry
unto thee.
2 Let my prayer be set forth before
thee *as* incense; *and* the lifting up of my
hands *as* the evening sacrifice.
3 Set a watch, O LORD, before my
mouth; keep the door of my lips.
4 Incline not my heart to *any* evil
thing, to practise wicked works with
men that work iniquity: and let me not
eat of their dainties.
5 Let the righteous smite me; *it shall
be* a kindness: and let him reprove me;
it shall be an excellent oil, *which* shall
not break my head: for yet my prayer
also *shall be* in their calamities.
6 When their judges are overthrown
in stony places, they shall hear my
words; for they are sweet.
7 Our bones are scattered at the
grave's mouth, as when one cutteth
and cleaveth *wood* upon the earth.
8 But mine eyes *are* unto thee, O GOD
the Lord: in thee is my trust; leave not
my soul destitute.
9 Keep me from the snares *which*
they have laid for me, and the gins of
the workers of iniquity.
10 Let the wicked fall into their own
nets, whilst that I withal escape.

PSALM 142

I CRIED unto the LORD with my voice;
with my voice unto the LORD did I make
my supplication.
2 I poured out my complaint before
him; I shewed before him my trouble.
3 When my spirit was overwhelmed
within me, then thou knewest my path.
In the way wherein I walked have they
privily laid a snare for me.
4 I looked on *my* right hand, and be-
held, but *there was* no man that would
know me: refuge failed me; no man
cared for my soul.
5 I cried unto thee, O LORD: I said,
Thou *art* my refuge *and* my portion in
the land of the living.
6 Attend unto my cry; for I am
brought very low: deliver me from
my persecutors; for they are stronger
than I.
7 Bring my soul out of prison, that I
may praise thy name: the righteous
shall compass me about; for thou shalt
deal bountifully with me.

PSALM 143

HEAR my prayer, O LORD, give ear to
my supplications: in thy faithfulness
answer me, *and* in thy righteousness.
2 And enter not into judgment with
thy servant: for in thy sight shall no
man living be justified.
3 For the enemy hath persecuted my
soul; he hath smitten my life down to
the ground; he hath made me to dwell
in darkness, as those that have been
long dead.
4 Therefore is my spirit overwhelmed
within me; my heart within me is deso-
late.
5 I remember the days of old; I medi-
tate on all thy works; I muse on the
work of thy hands.
6 I stretch forth my hands unto thee:
my soul *thirsteth* after thee, as a thirsty
land. Sē'lah.
7 Hear me speedily, O LORD: my spirit
faileth: hide not thy face from me, lest I
be like unto them that go down into the
pit.
8 Cause me to hear thy lovingkind-
ness in the morning; for in thee do I
trust: cause me to know the way where-
in I should walk; for I lift up my soul
unto thee.
9 Deliver me, O LORD, from mine en-
emies: I flee unto thee to hide me.
10 Teach me to do thy will; for thou
art my God: thy spirit *is* good; lead me
into the land of uprightness.
11 Quicken me, O LORD, for thy
name's sake: for thy righteousness'
sake bring my soul out of trouble.
12 And of thy mercy cut off mine en-
emies, and destroy all them that afflict
my soul: for I *am* thy servant.

PSALM 144

BLESSED *be* the LORD my strength,
which teacheth my hands to war, *and*
my fingers to fight:
2 My goodness, and my fortress; my
high tower, and my deliverer; my
shield, and *he* in whom I trust; who
subdueth my people under me.
3 LORD, what *is* man, that thou takest
knowledge of him! *or* the son of man,
that thou makest account of him!
4 Man is like to vanity: his days *are* as
a shadow that passeth away.
5 Bow thy heavens, O LORD, and
come down: touch the mountains, and
they shall smoke.
6 Cast forth lightning, and scatter
them: shoot out thine arrows, and de-
stroy them.
7 Send thine hand from above; rid
me, and deliver me out of great waters,
from the hand of strange children;

8 Whose mouth speaketh vanity, and their right hand *is* a right hand of falsehood.
9 I will sing a new song unto thee, O God: upon a psaltery *and* an instrument of ten strings will I sing praises unto thee.
10 *It is he* that giveth salvation unto kings: who delivereth David his servant from the hurtful sword.
11 Rid me, and deliver me from the hand of strange children, whose mouth speaketh vanity, and their right hand *is* a right hand of falsehood:
12 That our sons *may be* as plants grown up in their youth; *that* our daughters *may be* as corner stones, polished *after* the similitude of a palace:
13 *That* our garners *may be* full, affording all manner of store: *that* our sheep may bring forth thousands and ten thousands in our streets:
14 *That* our oxen *may be* strong to labour; *that there be* no breaking in, nor going out; that *there be* no complaining in our streets.
15 Happy *is that* people, that is in such a case: *yea*, happy *is that* people, whose God *is* the LORD.

PSALM 145

I WILL extol thee, my God, O king; and I will bless thy name for ever and ever.
2 Every day will I bless thee; and I will praise thy name for ever and ever.
3 Great *is* the LORD, and greatly to be praised; and his greatness *is* unsearchable.
4 One generation shall praise thy works to another, and shall declare thy mighty acts.
5 I will speak of the glorious honour of thy majesty, and of thy wondrous works.
6 And *men* shall speak of the might of thy terrible acts: and I will declare thy greatness.
7 They shall abundantly utter the memory of thy great goodness, and shall sing of thy righteousness.
8 The LORD *is* gracious, and full of compassion; slow to anger, and of great mercy.
9 The LORD *is* good to all: and his tender mercies *are* over all his works.
10 All thy works shall praise thee, O LORD; and thy saints shall bless thee.
11 They shall speak of the glory of thy kingdom, and talk of thy power;
12 To make known to the sons of men his mighty acts, and the glorious majesty of his kingdom.
13 Thy kingdom *is* an everlasting kingdom, and thy dominion *endureth* throughout all generations.
14 The LORD upholdeth all that fall, and raiseth up all *those that be* bowed down.
15 The eyes of all wait upon thee; and thou givest them their meat in due season.
16 Thou openest thine hand, and satisfiest the desire of every living thing.
17 The LORD *is* righteous in all his ways, and holy in all his works.
18 The LORD *is* nigh unto all them that call upon him, to all that call upon him in truth.
19 He will fulfil the desire of them that fear him: he also will hear their cry, and will save them.
20 The LORD preserveth all them that love him: but all the wicked will he destroy.
21 My mouth shall speak the praise of the LORD: and let all flesh bless his holy name for ever and ever.

PSALM 146

PRAISE ye the LORD. Praise the LORD, O my soul.
2 While I live will I praise the LORD: I will sing praises unto my God while I have any being.
3 Put not your trust in princes, *nor* in the son of man, in whom *there is* no help.
4 His breath goeth forth, he returneth to his earth; in that very day his thoughts perish.
5 Happy *is he* that *hath* the God of Jacob for his help, whose hope *is* in the LORD his God:
6 Which made heaven, and earth, the sea, and all that therein *is*: which keepeth truth for ever:
7 Which executeth judgment for the oppressed: which giveth food to the hungry. The LORD looseth the prisoners:
8 The LORD openeth *the eyes of* the blind: the LORD raiseth them that are bowed down: the LORD loveth the righteous:
9 The LORD preserveth the strangers; he relieveth the fatherless and widow: but the way of the wicked he turneth upside down.
10 The LORD shall reign for ever, *even* thy God, O Zion, unto all generations. Praise ye the LORD.

PSALM 147

PRAISE ye the LORD: for *it is* good to sing praises unto our God; for *it is* pleasant; *and* praise is comely.
2 The LORD doth build up Jerusalem: he gathereth together the outcasts of Israel.
3 He healeth the broken in heart, and bindeth up their wounds.

4 He telleth the number of the stars; he calleth them all by *their* names.

5 Great *is* our Lord, and of great power: his understanding *is* infinite.

6 The LORD lifteth up the meek: he casteth the wicked down to the ground.

7 Sing unto the LORD with thanksgiving; sing praise upon the harp unto our God:

8 Who covereth the heaven with clouds, who prepareth rain for the earth, who maketh grass to grow upon the mountains.

9 He giveth to the beast his food, *and* to the young ravens which cry.

10 He delighteth not in the strength of the horse: he taketh not pleasure in the legs of a man.

11 The LORD taketh pleasure in them that fear him, in those that hope in his mercy.

12 Praise the LORD, O Jerusalem; praise thy God, O Zion.

13 For he hath strengthened the bars of thy gates; he hath blessed thy children within thee.

14 He maketh peace *in* thy borders, *and* filleth thee with the finest of the wheat.

15 He sendeth forth his commandment *upon* earth: his word runneth very swiftly.

16 He giveth snow like wool: he scattereth the hoarfrost like ashes.

17 He casteth forth his ice like morsels: who can stand before his cold?

18 He sendeth out his word, and melteth them: he causeth his wind to blow, *and* the waters flow.

19 He sheweth his word unto Jacob, his statutes and his judgments unto Israel.

20 He hath not dealt so with any nation: and *as for his* judgments, they have not known them. Praise ye the LORD.

PSALM 148

PRAISE ye the LORD. Praise ye the LORD from the heavens: praise him in the heights.

2 Praise ye him, all his angels: praise ye him, all his hosts.

3 Praise ye him, sun and moon: praise him, all ye stars of light.

4 Praise him, ye heavens of heavens, and ye waters that *be* above the heavens.

5 Let them praise the name of the LORD: for he commanded, and they were created.

6 He hath also stablished them for ever and ever: he hath made a decree which shall not pass.

7 Praise the LORD from the earth, ye dragons, and all deeps:

8 Fire, and hail; snow, and vapours; stormy wind fulfilling his word:

9 Mountains, and all hills; fruitful trees, and all cedars:

10 Beasts, and all cattle; creeping things, and flying fowl:

11 Kings of the earth, and all people; princes, and all judges of the earth:

12 Both young men, and maidens; old men, and children:

13 Let them praise the name of the LORD: for his name alone is excellent; his glory *is* above the earth and heaven.

14 He also exalteth the horn of his people, the praise of all his saints; *even* of the children of Israel, a people near unto him. Praise ye the LORD.

PSALM 149

PRAISE ye the LORD. Sing unto the LORD a new song, *and* his praise in the congregation of saints.

2 Let Israel rejoice in him that made him: let the children of Zion be joyful in their King.

3 Let them praise his name in the dance: let them sing praises unto him with the timbrel and harp.

4 For the LORD taketh pleasure in his people: he will beautify the meek with salvation.

5 Let the saints be joyful in glory: let them sing aloud upon their beds.

6 *Let* the high *praises* of God *be* in their mouth, and a two-edged sword in their hand;

7 To execute vengeance upon the heathen, *and* punishments upon the people;

8 To bind their kings with chains, and their nobles with fetters of iron;

9 To execute upon them the judgment written: this honour have all his saints. Praise ye the LORD.

PSALM 150

PRAISE ye the LORD. Praise God in his sanctuary: praise him in the firmament of his power.

2 Praise him for his mighty acts: praise him according to his excellent greatness.

3 Praise him with the sound of the trumpet: praise him with the psaltery and harp.

4 Praise him with the timbrel and dance: praise him with stringed instruments and organs.

5 Praise him upon the loud cymbals: praise him upon the high sounding cymbals.

6 Let every thing that hath breath praise the LORD. Praise ye the LORD.

THE PROVERBS

CHAPTER 1

THE proverbs of Sŏl'o-mon the son of David, king of Israel;

2 To know wisdom and instruction; to perceive the words of understanding;

3 To receive the instruction of wisdom, justice, and judgment, and equity;

4 To give subtilty to the simple, to the young man knowledge and discretion.

5 A wise *man* will hear, and will increase learning; and a man of understanding shall attain unto wise counsels:

6 To understand a proverb, and the interpretation; the words of the wise, and their dark sayings.

7 ¶The fear of the LORD *is* the beginning of knowledge: *but* fools despise wisdom and instruction.

8 My son, hear the instruction of thy father, and forsake not the law of thy mother:

9 For they *shall be* an ornament of grace unto thy head, and chains about thy neck.

10 ¶My son, if sinners entice thee, consent thou not.

11 If they say, Come with us, let us lay wait for blood, let us lurk privily for the innocent without cause:

12 Let us swallow them up alive as the grave; and whole, as those that go down into the pit:

13 We shall find all precious substance, we shall fill our houses with spoil:

14 Cast in thy lot among us; let us all have one purse:

15 My son, walk not thou in the way with them; refrain thy foot from their path:

16 For their feet run to evil, and make haste to shed blood.

17 Surely in vain the net is spread in the sight of any bird.

18 And they lay wait for their *own* blood; they lurk privily for their *own* lives.

19 So *are* the ways of every one that is greedy of gain; *which* taketh away the life of the owners thereof.

20 ¶Wisdom crieth without; she uttereth her voice in the streets:

21 She crieth in the chief place of concourse, in the openings of the gates: in the city she uttereth her words, *saying,*

22 How long, ye simple ones, will ye love simplicity? and the scorners delight in their scorning, and fools hate knowledge?

23 Turn you at my reproof: behold, I will pour out my spirit unto you, I will make known my words unto you.

24 ¶Because I have called, and ye refused; I have stretched out my hand, and no man regarded;

25 But ye have set at nought all my counsel, and would none of my reproof:

26 I also will laugh at your calamity; I will mock when your fear cometh;

27 When your fear cometh as desolation, and your destruction cometh as a whirlwind; when distress and anguish cometh upon you.

28 Then shall they call upon me, but I will not answer; they shall seek me early, but they shall not find me:

29 For that they hated knowledge, and did not choose the fear of the LORD:

30 They would none of my counsel: they despised all my reproof.

31 Therefore shall they eat of the fruit of their own way, and be filled with their own devices.

32 For the turning away of the simple shall slay them, and the prosperity of fools shall destroy them.

33 But whoso hearkeneth unto me shall dwell safely, and shall be quiet from fear of evil.

CHAPTER 2

MY son, if thou wilt receive my words, and hide my commandments with thee;

2 So that thou incline thine ear unto wisdom, *and* apply thine heart to understanding;

3 Yea, if thou criest after knowledge, *and* liftest up thy voice for understanding;

4 If thou seekest her as silver, and searchest for her as *for* hid treasures;

5 Then shalt thou understand the fear of the LORD, and find the knowledge of God.

6 For the LORD giveth wisdom: out of his mouth *cometh* knowledge and understanding.

7 He layeth up sound wisdom for the righteous: *he is* a buckler to them that walk uprightly.

8 He keepeth the paths of judgment, and preserveth the way of his saints.

9 Then shalt thou understand righteousness, and judgment, and equity; *yea,* every good path.

10 ¶When wisdom entereth into thine heart, and knowledge is pleasant unto thy soul;

11 Discretion shall preserve thee, understanding shall keep thee:

12 To deliver thee from the way of the evil *man,* from the man that speaketh froward things;

13 Who leave the paths of uprightness, to walk in the ways of darkness;

14 Who rejoice to do evil, *and* delight in the frowardness of the wicked;

15 Whose ways *are* crooked, and *they* froward in their paths:

16 To deliver thee from the strange woman, *even* from the stranger *which* flattereth with her words;

17 Which forsaketh the guide of her youth, and forgetteth the covenant of her God.

18 For her house inclineth unto death, and her paths unto the dead.

19 None that go unto her return again, neither take they hold of the paths of life.

20 That thou mayest walk in the way of good *men,* and keep the paths of the righteous.

21 For the upright shall dwell in the land, and the perfect shall remain in it.

22 But the wicked shall be cut off from the earth, and the transgressors shall be rooted out of it.

CHAPTER 3

MY son, forget not my law; but let thine heart keep my commandments:

2 For length of days, and long life, and peace, shall they add to thee.

3 Let not mercy and truth forsake thee: bind them about thy neck; write them upon the table of thine heart:

4 So shalt thou find favour and good understanding in the sight of God and man.

5 ¶Trust in the LORD with all thine heart; and lean not unto thine own understanding.

6 In all thy ways acknowledge him, and he shall direct thy paths.

7 Be not wise in thine own eyes: fear the LORD, and depart from evil.

8 It shall be health to thy navel, and marrow to thy bones.

9 Honour the LORD with thy substance, and with the firstfruits of all thine increase:

10 So shall thy barns be filled with plenty, and thy presses shall burst out with new wine.

11 ¶My son, despise not the chastening of the LORD; neither be weary of his correction:

12 For whom the LORD loveth he correcteth; even as a father the son *in whom* he delighteth.

13 ¶Happy *is* the man *that* findeth wisdom, and the man *that* getteth understanding.

14 For the merchandise of it *is* better than the merchandise of silver, and the gain thereof than fine gold.

15 She *is* more precious than rubies: and all the things thou canst desire are not to be compared unto her.

16 Length of days *is* in her right hand; *and* in her left hand riches and honour.

17 Her ways *are* ways of pleasantness, and all her paths *are* peace.

18 She *is* a tree of life to them that lay hold upon her: and happy *is every one* that retaineth her.

19 The LORD by wisdom hath founded the earth; by understanding hath he established the heavens.

20 By his knowledge the depths are broken up, and the clouds drop down the dew.

21 ¶My son, let not them depart from thine eyes: keep sound wisdom and discretion:

22 So shall they be life unto thy soul, and grace to thy neck.

23 Then shalt thou walk in thy way safely, and thy foot shall not stumble.

24 When thou liest down, thou shalt not be afraid: yea, thou shalt lie down, and thy sleep shall be sweet.

25 Be not afraid of sudden fear, neither of the desolation of the wicked, when it cometh.

26 For the LORD shall be thy confidence, and shall keep thy foot from being taken.

27 ¶Withhold not good from them to whom it is due, when it is in the power of thine hand to do *it.*

28 Say not unto thy neighbour, Go, and come again, and to morrow I will give; when thou hast it by thee.

29 Devise not evil against thy neighbour, seeing he dwelleth securely by thee.

30 Strive not with a man without cause, if he have done thee no harm.

31 ¶Envy thou not the oppressor, and choose none of his ways.

32 For the froward *is* abomination to the LORD: but his secret *is* with the righteous.

33 The curse of the LORD *is* in the house of the wicked: but he blesseth the habitation of the just.

34 Surely he scorneth the scorners: but he giveth grace unto the lowly.

35 The wise shall inherit glory: but shame shall be the promotion of fools.

CHAPTER 4

HEAR, ye children, the instruction of a father, and attend to know understanding.

2 For I give you good doctrine, forsake ye not my law.

3 For I was my father's son, tender and only *beloved* in the sight of my mother.
4 He taught me also, and said unto me, Let thine heart retain my words: keep my commandments, and live.
5 Get wisdom, get understanding: forget *it* not; neither decline from the words of my mouth.
6 Forsake her not, and she shall preserve thee: love her, and she shall keep thee.
7 Wisdom *is* the principal thing; *therefore* get wisdom: and with all thy getting get understanding.
8 Exalt her, and she shall promote thee: she shall bring thee to honour, when thou dost embrace her.
9 She shall give to thine head an ornament of grace: a crown of glory shall she deliver to thee.
10 Hear, O my son, and receive my sayings; and the years of thy life shall be many.
11 I have taught thee in the way of wisdom; I have led thee in right paths.
12 When thou goest, thy steps shall not be straitened; and when thou runnest, thou shalt not stumble.
13 Take fast hold of instruction; let *her* not go: keep her; for she *is* thy life.
14 ¶Enter not into the path of the wicked, and go not in the way of evil *men*.
15 Avoid it, pass not by it, turn from it, and pass away.
16 For they sleep not, except they have done mischief; and their sleep is taken away, unless they cause *some* to fall.
17 For they eat the bread of wickedness, and drink the wine of violence.
18 But the path of the just *is* as the shining light, that shineth more and more unto the perfect day.
19 The way of the wicked *is* as darkness: they know not at what they stumble.
20 ¶My son, attend to my words; incline thine ear unto my sayings.
21 Let them not depart from thine eyes; keep them in the midst of thine heart.
22 For they *are* life unto those that find them, and health to all their flesh.
23 ¶Keep thy heart with all diligence; for out of it *are* the issues of life.
24 Put away from thee a froward mouth, and perverse lips put far from thee.
25 Let thine eyes look right on, and let thine eyelids look straight before thee.
26 Ponder the path of thy feet, and let all thy ways be established.
27 Turn not to the right hand nor to the left: remove thy foot from evil.

CHAPTER 5

MY son, attend unto my wisdom, *and* bow thine ear to my understanding:
2 That thou mayest regard discretion, and *that* thy lips may keep knowledge.
3 ¶For the lips of a strange woman drop *as* an honeycomb, and her mouth *is* smoother than oil:
4 But her end is bitter as wormwood, sharp as a two-edged sword.
5 Her feet go down to death; her steps take hold on hell.
6 Lest thou shouldest ponder the path of life, her ways are moveable, *that* thou canst not know *them*.
7 Hear me now therefore, O ye children, and depart not from the words of my mouth.
8 Remove thy way far from her, and come not nigh the door of her house:
9 Lest thou give thine honour unto others, and thy years unto the cruel:
10 Lest strangers be filled with thy wealth; and thy labours *be* in the house of a stranger;
11 And thou mourn at the last, when thy flesh and thy body are consumed,
12 And say, How have I hated instruction, and my heart despised reproof;
13 And have not obeyed the voice of my teachers, nor inclined mine ear to them that instructed me!
14 I was almost in all evil in the midst of the congregation and assembly.
15 ¶Drink waters out of thine own cistern, and running waters out of thine own well.
16 Let thy fountains be dispersed abroad, *and* rivers of waters in the streets.
17 Let them be only thine own, and not strangers' with thee.
18 Let thy fountain be blessed: and rejoice with the wife of thy youth.
19 *Let her be as* the loving hind and pleasant roe; let her breasts satisfy thee at all times; and be thou ravished always with her love.
20 And why wilt thou, my son, be ravished with a strange woman, and embrace the bosom of a stranger?
21 For the ways of man *are* before the eyes of the LORD, and he pondereth all his goings.
22 His own iniquities shall take the wicked himself, and he shall be holden with the cords of his sins.
23 He shall die without instruction;

and in the greatness of his folly he shall go astray.

CHAPTER 6

MY son, if thou be surety for thy friend, *if* thou hast stricken thy hand with a stranger,

2 Thou art snared with the words of thy mouth, thou art taken with the words of thy mouth.

3 Do this now, my son, and deliver thyself, when thou art come into the hand of thy friend; go, humble thyself, and make sure thy friend.

4 Give not sleep to thine eyes, nor slumber to thine eyelids.

5 Deliver thyself as a roe from the hand *of the hunter*, and as a bird from the hand of the fowler.

6 ¶Go to the ant, thou sluggard; consider her ways, and be wise:

7 Which having no guide, overseer, or ruler,

8 Provideth her meat in the summer, *and* gathereth her food in the harvest.

9 How long wilt thou sleep, O sluggard? when wilt thou arise out of thy sleep?

10 *Yet* a little sleep, a little slumber, a little folding of the hands to sleep:

11 So shall thy poverty come as one that travelleth, and thy want as an armed man.

12 ¶A naughty person, a wicked man, walketh with a froward mouth.

13 He winketh with his eyes, he speaketh with his feet, he teacheth with his fingers;

14 Frowardness *is* in his heart, he deviseth mischief continually; he soweth discord.

15 Therefore shall his calamity come suddenly; suddenly shall he be broken without remedy.

16 ¶These six *things* doth the LORD hate: yea, seven *are* an abomination unto him:

17 A proud look, a lying tongue, and hands that shed innocent blood,

18 An heart that deviseth wicked imaginations, feet that be swift in running to mischief,

19 A false witness *that* speaketh lies, and he that soweth discord among brethren.

20 ¶My son, keep thy father's commandment, and forsake not the law of thy mother:

21 Bind them continually upon thine heart, *and* tie them about thy neck.

22 When thou goest, it shall lead thee; when thou sleepest, it shall keep thee; and *when* thou awakest, it shall talk with thee.

23 For the commandment *is* a lamp; and the law *is* light; and reproofs of instruction *are* the way of life:

24 To keep thee from the evil woman, from the flattery of the tongue of a strange woman.

25 Lust not after her beauty in thine heart; neither let her take thee with her eyelids.

26 For by means of a whorish woman *a man is brought* to a piece of bread: and the adulteress will hunt for the precious life.

27 Can a man take fire in his bosom, and his clothes not be burned?

28 Can one go upon hot coals, and his feet not be burned?

29 So he that goeth in to his neighbour's wife; whosoever toucheth her shall not be innocent.

30 *Men* do not despise a thief, if he steal to satisfy his soul when he is hungry;

31 But *if* he be found, he shall restore sevenfold; he shall give all the substance of his house.

32 *But* whoso committeth adultery with a woman lacketh understanding: he *that* doeth it destroyeth his own soul.

33 A wound and dishonour shall he get; and his reproach shall not be wiped away.

34 For jealousy *is* the rage of a man: therefore he will not spare in the day of vengeance.

35 He will not regard any ransom; neither will he rest content, though thou givest many gifts.

CHAPTER 7

MY son, keep my words, and lay up my commandments with thee.

2 Keep my commandments, and live; and my law as the apple of thine eye.

3 Bind them upon thy fingers, write them upon the table of thine heart.

4 Say unto wisdom, Thou *art* my sister; and call understanding *thy* kinswoman:

5 That they may keep thee from the strange woman, from the stranger *which* flattereth with her words.

6 ¶For at the window of my house I looked through my casement,

7 And beheld among the simple ones, I discerned among the youths, a young man void of understanding,

8 Passing through the street near her corner; and he went the way to her house,

9 In the twilight, in the evening, in the black and dark night:

10 And, behold, there met him a wom-

an *with* the attire of an harlot, and
subtil of heart.
11 (She *is* loud and stubborn; her feet
abide not in her house:
12 Now *is she* without, now in the
streets, and lieth in wait at every cor-
ner.)
13 So she caught him, and kissed
him, *and* with an impudent face said
unto him,
14 *I have* peace offerings with me;
this day have I payed my vows.
15 Therefore came I forth to meet
thee, diligently to seek thy face, and I
have found thee.
16 I have decked my bed with cover-
ings of tapestry, with carved *works*,
with fine linen of Egypt.
17 I have perfumed my bed with
myrrh, aloes, and cinnamon.
18 Come, let us take our fill of love
until the morning: let us solace our-
selves with loves.
19 For the goodman *is* not at home,
he is gone a long journey:
20 He hath taken a bag of money with
him, *and* will come home at the day ap-
pointed.
21 With her much fair speech she
caused him to yield, with the flattering
of her lips she forced him.
22 He goeth after her straightway, as
an ox goeth to the slaughter, or as a fool
to the correction of the stocks;
23 Till a dart strike through his liver;
as a bird hasteth to the snare, and
knoweth not that it *is* for his life.
24 ¶Hearken unto me now therefore,
O ye children, and attend to the words
of my mouth.
25 Let not thine heart decline to her
ways, go not astray in her paths.
26 For she hath cast down many
wounded: yea, many strong *men* have
been slain by her.
27 Her house *is* the way to hell, going
down to the chambers of death.

CHAPTER 8

DOTH not wisdom cry? and under-
standing put forth her voice?
2 She standeth in the top of high
places, by the way in the places of the
paths.
3 She crieth at the gates, at the entry
of the city, at the coming in at the
doors.
4 Unto you, O men, I call; and my
voice *is* to the sons of man.
5 O ye simple, understand wisdom:
and, ye fools, be ye of an understanding
heart.
6 Hear; for I will speak of excellent
things; and the opening of my lips *shall
be* right things.
7 For my mouth shall speak truth;
and wickedness *is* an abomination to
my lips.
8 All the words of my mouth *are* in
righteousness; *there is* nothing fro-
ward or perverse in them.
9 They *are* all plain to him that under-
standeth, and right to them that find
knowledge.
10 Receive my instruction, and not
silver; and knowledge rather than
choice gold.
11 For wisdom *is* better than rubies;
and all the things that may be desired
are not to be compared to it.
12 I wisdom dwell with prudence,
and find out knowledge of witty inven-
tions.
13 The fear of the LORD *is* to hate evil:
pride, and arrogancy, and the evil way,
and the froward mouth, do I hate.
14 Counsel *is* mine, and sound wis-
dom: I *am* understanding; I have
strength.
15 By me kings reign, and princes
decree justice.
16 By me princes rule, and nobles,
even all the judges of the earth.
17 I love them that love me; and those
that seek me early shall find me.
18 Riches and honour *are* with me;
yea, durable riches and righteousness.
19 My fruit *is* better than gold, yea,
than fine gold; and my revenue than
choice silver.
20 I lead in the way of righteousness,
in the midst of the paths of judgment:
21 That I may cause those that love
me to inherit substance; and I will fill
their treasures.
22 The LORD possessed me in the
beginning of his way, before his works
of old.
23 I was set up from everlasting,
from the beginning, or ever the earth
was.
24 When *there were* no depths, I was
brought forth; when *there were* no
fountains abounding with water.
25 Before the mountains were
settled, before the hills was I brought
forth:
26 While as yet he had not made the
earth, nor the fields, nor the highest
part of the dust of the world.
27 When he prepared the heavens, I
was there: when he set a compass upon
the face of the depth:
28 When he established the clouds
above: when he strengthened the foun-
tains of the deep:
29 When he gave to the sea his

decree, that the waters should not pass
his commandment: when he appointed
the foundations of the earth:
30 Then I was by him, *as* one brought
up *with him:* and I was daily *his* delight,
rejoicing always before him;
31 Rejoicing in the habitable part of
his earth; and my delights *were* with
the sons of men.
32 Now therefore hearken unto me,
O ye children: for blessed *are they that*
keep my ways.
33 Hear instruction, and be wise, and
refuse it not.
34 Blessed *is* the man that heareth
me, watching daily at my gates, wait-
ing at the posts of my doors.
35 For whoso findeth me findeth life,
and shall obtain favour of the LORD.
36 But he that sinneth against me
wrongeth his own soul: all they that
hate me love death.

CHAPTER 9

WISDOM hath builded her house, she
hath hewn out her seven pillars:
2 She hath killed her beasts; she hath
mingled her wine; she hath also fur-
nished her table.
3 She hath sent forth her maidens:
she crieth upon the highest places of
the city,
4 Whoso *is* simple, let him turn in
hither: *as for* him that wanteth under-
standing, she saith to him,
5 Come, eat of my bread, and drink of
the wine *which* I have mingled.
6 Forsake the foolish, and live; and go
in the way of understanding.
7 He that reproveth a scorner getteth
to himself shame: and he that rebuketh
a wicked *man getteth* himself a blot.
8 Reprove not a scorner, lest he hate
thee: rebuke a wise man, and he will
love thee.
9 Give *instruction* to a wise *man*, and
he will be yet wiser: teach a just *man*,
and he will increase in learning.
10 The fear of the LORD *is* the begin-
ning of wisdom: and the knowledge of
the holy *is* understanding.
11 For by me thy days shall be mul-
tiplied, and the years of thy life shall be
increased.
12 If thou be wise, thou shalt be wise
for thyself: but *if* thou scornest, thou
alone shalt bear *it*.
13 ¶A foolish woman *is* clamorous:
she is simple, and knoweth nothing.
14 For she sitteth at the door of her
house, on a seat in the high places of
the city,
15 To call passengers who go right on
their ways:
16 Whoso *is* simple, let him turn in
hither: and *as for* him that wanteth
understanding, she saith to him,
17 Stolen waters are sweet, and
bread *eaten* in secret is pleasant.
18 But he knoweth not that the dead
are there; *and that* her guests *are* in the
depths of hell.

CHAPTER 10

THE proverbs of Sŏl'o-mon. A wise son
maketh a glad father: but a foolish son
is the heaviness of his mother.
2 Treasures of wickedness profit
nothing: but righteousness delivereth
from death.
3 The LORD will not suffer the soul of
the righteous to famish: but he casteth
away the substance of the wicked.
4 He becometh poor that dealeth
with a slack hand: but the hand of the
diligent maketh rich.
5 He that gathereth in summer *is* a
wise son: *but* he that sleepeth in har-
vest *is* a son that causeth shame.
6 Blessings *are* upon the head of the
just: but violence covereth the mouth
of the wicked.
7 The memory of the just *is* blessed:
but the name of the wicked shall rot.
8 The wise in heart will receive com-
mandments: but a prating fool shall
fall.
9 He that walketh uprightly walketh
surely: but he that perverteth his ways
shall be known.
10 He that winketh with the eye caus-
eth sorrow: but a prating fool shall
fall.
11 The mouth of a righteous *man is* a
well of life: but violence covereth the
mouth of the wicked.
12 Hatred stirreth up strifes: but love
covereth all sins.
13 In the lips of him that hath under-
standing wisdom is found: but a rod *is*
for the back of him that is void of under-
standing.
14 Wise *men* lay up knowledge: but
the mouth of the foolish *is* near destruc-
tion.
15 The rich man's wealth *is* his strong
city: the destruction of the poor *is* their
poverty.
16 The labour of the righteous *tend-
eth* to life: the fruit of the wicked to
sin.
17 He *is in* the way of life that keep-
eth instruction: but he that refuseth
reproof erreth.
18 He that hideth hatred *with* lying
lips, and he that uttereth a slander, *is* a
fool.
19 In the multitude of words there

wanteth not sin: but he that refraineth
his lips *is* wise.
20 The tongue of the just *is as* choice
silver: the heart of the wicked *is* little
worth.
21 The lips of the righteous feed
many: but fools die for want of wis-
dom.
22 The blessing of the LORD, it
maketh rich, and he addeth no sorrow
with it.
23 *It is* as sport to a fool to do mis-
chief: but a man of understanding hath
wisdom.
24 The fear of the wicked, it shall
come upon him: but the desire of the
righteous shall be granted.
25 As the whirlwind passeth, so *is* the
wicked no *more:* but the righteous *is* an
everlasting foundation.
26 As vinegar to the teeth, and as
smoke to the eyes, so *is* the sluggard to
them that send him.
27 The fear of the LORD prolongeth
days: but the years of the wicked shall
be shortened.
28 The hope of the righteous *shall be*
gladness: but the expectation of the
wicked shall perish.
29 The way of the LORD *is* strength to
the upright: but destruction *shall be* to
the workers of iniquity.
30 The righteous shall never be re-
moved: but the wicked shall not inhabit
the earth.
31 The mouth of the just bringeth
forth wisdom: but the froward tongue
shall be cut out.
32 The lips of the righteous know
what is acceptable: but the mouth of
the wicked *speaketh* frowardness.

CHAPTER 11

A FALSE balance *is* abomination to
the LORD: but a just weight *is* his de-
light.
2 *When* pride cometh, then cometh
shame: but with the lowly *is* wisdom.
3 The integrity of the upright shall
guide them: but the perverseness of
transgressors shall destroy them.
4 Riches profit not in the day of
wrath: but righteousness delivereth
from death.
5 The righteousness of the perfect
shall direct his way: but the wicked
shall fall by his own wickedness.
6 The righteousness of the upright
shall deliver them: but transgressors
shall be taken in *their own* naughtiness.
7 When a wicked man dieth, *his* ex-
pectation shall perish: and the hope of
unjust *men* perisheth.
8 The righteous is delivered out of
trouble, and the wicked cometh in his
stead.
9 An hypocrite with *his* mouth de-
stroyeth his neighbour: but through
knowledge shall the just be delivered.
10 When it goeth well with the
righteous, the city rejoiceth: and when
the wicked perish, *there is* shouting.
11 By the blessing of the upright the
city is exalted: but it is overthrown by
the mouth of the wicked.
12 He that is void of wisdom despis-
eth his neighbour: but a man of under-
standing holdeth his peace.
13 A talebearer revealeth secrets: but
he that is of a faithful spirit concealeth
the matter.
14 Where no counsel *is*, the people
fall: but in the multitude of counsellors
there is safety.
15 He that is surety for a stranger
shall smart *for it:* and he that hateth
suretiship is sure.
16 A gracious woman retaineth hon-
our: and strong *men* retain riches.
17 The merciful man doeth good to
his own soul: but *he that is* cruel trou-
bleth his own flesh.
18 The wicked worketh a deceitful
work: but to him that soweth
righteousness *shall be* a sure reward.
19 As righteousness *tendeth* to life:
so he that pursueth evil *pursueth it* to
his own death.
20 They that are of a froward heart
are abomination to the LORD: but *such
as are* upright in *their* way *are* his de-
light.
21 *Though* hand *join* in hand, the
wicked shall not be unpunished: but
the seed of the righteous shall be deliv-
ered.
22 *As* a jewel of gold in a swine's
snout, *so is* a fair woman which is
without discretion.
23 The desire of the righteous *is* only
good: *but* the expectation of the wicked
is wrath.
24 There is that scattereth, and yet
increaseth; and *there is* that withhold-
eth more than is meet, but *it tendeth*
to poverty.
25 The liberal soul shall be made fat:
and he that watereth shall be watered
also himself.
26 He that withholdeth corn, the
people shall curse him: but blessing
shall be upon the head of him that sell-
eth *it*.
27 He that diligently seeketh good
procureth favour: but he that seeketh
mischief, it shall come unto him.
28 He that trusteth in his riches shall
fall; but the righteous shall flourish as a
branch.

29 He that troubleth his own house shall inherit the wind: and the fool *shall be* servant to the wise of heart.

30 The fruit of the righteous *is* a tree of life; and he that winneth souls *is* wise.

31 Behold, the righteous shall be recompensed in the earth: much more the wicked and the sinner.

CHAPTER 12

WHOSO loveth instruction loveth knowledge: but he that hateth reproof *is* brutish.

2 A good *man* obtaineth favour of the LORD: but a man of wicked devices will he condemn.

3 A man shall not be established by wickedness: but the root of the righteous shall not be moved.

4 A virtuous woman *is* a crown to her husband: but she that maketh ashamed *is* as rottenness in his bones.

5 The thoughts of the righteous *are* right: *but* the counsels of the wicked *are* deceit.

6 The words of the wicked *are* to lie in wait for blood: but the mouth of the upright shall deliver them.

7 The wicked are overthrown, and *are* not: but the house of the righteous shall stand.

8 A man shall be commended according to his wisdom: but he that is of a perverse heart shall be despised.

9 *He that is* despised, and hath a servant, *is* better than he that honoureth himself, and lacketh bread.

10 A righteous *man* regardeth the life of his beast: but the tender mercies of the wicked *are* cruel.

11 He that tilleth his land shall be satisfied with bread: but he that followeth vain *persons is* void of understanding.

12 The wicked desireth the net of evil *men:* but the root of the righteous yieldeth *fruit*.

13 The wicked is snared by the transgression of *his* lips: but the just shall come out of trouble.

14 A man shall be satisfied with good by the fruit of *his* mouth: and the recompence of a man's hands shall be rendered unto him.

15 The way of a fool *is* right in his own eyes: but he that hearkeneth unto counsel *is* wise.

16 A fool's wrath is presently known: but a prudent *man* covereth shame.

17 *He that* speaketh truth sheweth forth righteousness: but a false witness deceit.

18 There is that speaketh like the piercings of a sword: but the tongue of the wise *is* health.

19 The lip of truth shall be established for ever: but a lying tongue *is* but for a moment.

20 Deceit *is* in the heart of them that imagine evil: but to the counsellors of peace *is* joy.

21 There shall no evil happen to the just: but the wicked shall be filled with mischief.

22 Lying lips *are* abomination to the LORD: but they that deal truly *are* his delight.

23 A prudent man concealeth knowledge: but the heart of fools proclaimeth foolishness.

24 The hand of the diligent shall bear rule: but the slothful shall be under tribute.

25 Heaviness in the heart of man maketh it stoop: but a good word maketh it glad.

26 The righteous *is* more excellent than his neighbour: but the way of the wicked seduceth them.

27 The slothful *man* roasteth not that which he took in hunting: but the substance of a diligent man *is* precious.

28 In the way of righteousness *is* life: and *in* the pathway *thereof there is* no death.

CHAPTER 13

A WISE son *heareth* his father's instruction: but a scorner heareth not rebuke.

2 A man shall eat good by the fruit of *his* mouth: but the soul of the transgressors *shall eat* violence.

3 He that keepeth his mouth keepeth his life: *but* he that openeth wide his lips shall have destruction.

4 The soul of the sluggard desireth, and *hath* nothing: but the soul of the diligent shall be made fat.

5 A righteous *man* hateth lying: but a wicked *man* is loathsome, and cometh to shame.

6 Righteousness keepeth *him that is* upright in the way: but wickedness overthroweth the sinner.

7 There is that maketh himself rich, yet *hath* nothing: *there is* that maketh himself poor, yet *hath* great riches.

8 The ransom of a man's life *are* his riches: but the poor heareth not rebuke.

9 The light of the righteous rejoiceth: but the lamp of the wicked shall be put out.

10 Only by pride cometh contention: but with the well advised *is* wisdom.

11 Wealth *gotten* by vanity shall be diminished: but he that gathereth by labour shall increase.

12 Hope deferred maketh the heart
sick: but *when* the desire cometh, *it is* a
tree of life.
13 Whoso despiseth the word shall
be destroyed: but he that feareth the
commandment shall be rewarded.
14 The law of the wise *is* a fountain of
life, to depart from the snares of death.
15 Good understanding giveth fa-
vour: but the way of transgressors *is*
hard.
16 Every prudent *man* dealeth with
knowledge: but a fool layeth open *his*
folly.
17 A wicked messenger falleth into
mischief: but a faithful ambassador *is*
health.
18 Poverty and shame *shall be to* him
that refuseth instruction: but he that
regardeth reproof shall be honoured.
19 The desire accomplished is sweet
to the soul: but *it is* abomination to
fools to depart from evil.
20 He that walketh with wise *men*
shall be wise: but a companion of fools
shall be destroyed.
21 Evil pursueth sinners: but to the
righteous good shall be repayed.
22 A good *man* leaveth an inheri-
tance to his children's children: and the
wealth of the sinner *is* laid up for the
just.
23 Much food *is in* the tillage of the
poor: but there is *that is* destroyed for
want of judgment.
24 He that spareth his rod hateth his
son: but he that loveth him chasteneth
him betimes.
25 The righteous eateth to the satis-
fying of his soul: but the belly of the
wicked shall want.

CHAPTER 14

EVERY wise woman buildeth her
house: but the foolish plucketh it down
with her hands.
2 He that walketh in his uprightness
feareth the LORD: but *he that is* perverse
in his ways despiseth him.
3 In the mouth of the foolish *is* a rod
of pride: but the lips of the wise shall
preserve them.
4 Where no oxen *are*, the crib *is*
clean: but much increase *is* by the
strength of the ox.
5 A faithful witness will not lie: but a
false witness will utter lies.
6 A scorner seeketh wisdom, and *find-
eth it* not: but knowledge *is* easy unto
him that understandeth.
7 Go from the presence of a foolish
man, when thou perceivest not *in him*
the lips of knowledge.
8 The wisdom of the prudent *is* to
understand his way: but the folly of
fools *is* deceit.
9 Fools make a mock at sin: but
among the righteous *there is* favour.
10 The heart knoweth his own bitter-
ness; and a stranger doth not inter-
meddle with his joy.
11 The house of the wicked shall be
overthrown: but the tabernacle of the
upright shall flourish.
12 There is a way which seemeth
right unto a man, but the end thereof
are the ways of death.
13 Even in laughter the heart is
sorrowful; and the end of that mirth *is*
heaviness.
14 The backslider in heart shall be
filled with his own ways: and a good
man *shall be satisfied* from himself.
15 The simple believeth every word:
but the prudent *man* looketh well to his
going.
16 A wise *man* feareth, and departeth
from evil: but the fool rageth, and is
confident.
17 *He that is* soon angry dealeth
foolishly: and a man of wicked devices
is hated.
18 The simple inherit folly: but the
prudent are crowned with knowledge.
19 The evil bow before the good; and
the wicked at the gates of the
righteous.
20 The poor is hated even of his own
neighbour: but the rich *hath* many
friends.
21 He that despiseth his neighbour
sinneth: but he that hath mercy on the
poor, happy *is* he.
22 Do they not err that devise evil?
but mercy and truth *shall be* to them
that devise good.
23 In all labour there is profit: but the
talk of the lips *tendeth* only to penury.
24 The crown of the wise *is* their
riches: *but* the foolishness of fools *is*
folly.
25 A true witness delivereth souls:
but a deceitful *witness* speaketh lies.
26 In the fear of the LORD *is* strong
confidence: and his children shall have
a place of refuge.
27 The fear of the LORD *is* a fountain
of life, to depart from the snares of
death.
28 In the multitude of people *is* the
king's honour: but in the want of people
is the destruction of the prince.
29 *He that is* slow to wrath *is* of great
understanding: but *he that is* hasty of
spirit exalteth folly.
30 A sound heart *is* the life of the
flesh: but envy the rottenness of the
bones.
31 He that oppresseth the poor

reproacheth his Maker: but he that honoureth him hath mercy on the poor.

32 The wicked is driven away in his wickedness: but the righteous hath hope in his death.

33 Wisdom resteth in the heart of him that hath understanding: but *that which is* in the midst of fools is made known.

34 Righteousness exalteth a nation: but sin *is* a reproach to any people.

35 The king's favour *is* toward a wise servant: but his wrath is *against* him that causeth shame.

CHAPTER 15

A SOFT answer turneth away wrath: but grievous words stir up anger.

2 The tongue of the wise useth knowledge aright: but the mouth of fools poureth out foolishness.

3 The eyes of the LORD *are* in every place, beholding the evil and the good.

4 A wholesome tongue *is* a tree of life: but perverseness therein *is* a breach in the spirit.

5 A fool despiseth his father's instruction: but he that regardeth reproof is prudent.

6 In the house of the righteous *is* much treasure: but in the revenues of the wicked is trouble.

7 The lips of the wise disperse knowledge: but the heart of the foolish *doeth* not so.

8 The sacrifice of the wicked *is* an abomination to the LORD: but the prayer of the upright *is* his delight.

9 The way of the wicked *is* an abomination unto the LORD: but he loveth him that followeth after righteousness.

10 Correction *is* grievous unto him that forsaketh the way: *and* he that hateth reproof shall die.

11 Hell and destruction *are* before the LORD: how much more then the hearts of the children of men?

12 A scorner loveth not one that reproveth him: neither will he go unto the wise.

13 A merry heart maketh a cheerful countenance: but by sorrow of the heart the spirit is broken.

14 The heart of him that hath understanding seeketh knowledge: but the mouth of fools feedeth on foolishness.

15 All the days of the afflicted *are* evil: but he that is of a merry heart *hath* a continual feast.

16 Better *is* little with the fear of the LORD than great treasure and trouble therewith.

17 Better *is* a dinner of herbs where love is, than a stalled ox and hatred therewith.

18 A wrathful man stirreth up strife: but *he that is* slow to anger appeaseth strife.

19 The way of the slothful *man is* as an hedge of thorns: but the way of the righteous *is* made plain.

20 A wise son maketh a glad father: but a foolish man despiseth his mother.

21 Folly *is* joy to *him that is* destitute of wisdom: but a man of understanding walketh uprightly.

22 Without counsel purposes are disappointed: but in the multitude of counsellors they are established.

23 A man hath joy by the answer of his mouth: and a word *spoken* in due season, how good *is it!*

24 The way of life *is* above to the wise, that he may depart from hell beneath.

25 The LORD will destroy the house of the proud: but he will establish the border of the widow.

26 The thoughts of the wicked *are* an abomination to the LORD: but *the words* of the pure *are* pleasant words.

27 He that is greedy of gain troubleth his own house; but he that hateth gifts shall live.

28 The heart of the righteous studieth to answer: but the mouth of the wicked poureth out evil things.

29 The LORD *is* far from the wicked: but he heareth the prayer of the righteous.

30 The light of the eyes rejoiceth the heart: *and* a good report maketh the bones fat.

31 The ear that heareth the reproof of life abideth among the wise.

32 He that refuseth instruction despiseth his own soul: but he that heareth reproof getteth understanding.

33 The fear of the LORD *is* the instruction of wisdom; and before honour *is* humility.

CHAPTER 16

THE preparations of the heart in man, and the answer of the tongue, *is* from the LORD.

2 All the ways of a man *are* clean in his own eyes; but the LORD weigheth the spirits.

3 Commit thy works unto the LORD, and thy thoughts shall be established.

4 The LORD hath made all *things* for himself: yea, even the wicked for the day of evil.

5 Every one *that is* proud in heart *is* an abomination to the LORD: *though* hand *join* in hand, he shall not be unpunished.

6 By mercy and truth iniquity is

purged: and by the fear of the LORD *men* depart from evil.
7 When a man's ways please the LORD, he maketh even his enemies to be at peace with him.
8 Better *is* a little with righteousness than great revenues without right.
9 A man's heart deviseth his way: but the LORD directeth his steps.
10 A devine sentence *is* in the lips of the king: his mouth transgresseth not in judgment.
11 A just weight and balance *are* the LORD's: all the weights of the bag *are* his work.
12 *It is* an abomination to kings to commit wickedness: for the throne is established by righteousness.
13 Righteous lips *are* the delight of kings; and they love him that speaketh right.
14 The wrath of a king *is as* messengers of death: but a wise man will pacify it.
15 In the light of the king's countenance *is* life; and his favour *is* as a cloud of the latter rain.
16 How much better *is it* to get wisdom than gold! and to get understanding rather to be chosen than silver!
17 The highway of the upright *is* to depart from evil: he that keepeth his way preserveth his soul.
18 Pride *goeth* before destruction, and an haughty spirit before a fall.
19 Better *it is to be* of an humble spirit with the lowly, than to divide the spoil with the proud.
20 He that handleth a matter wisely shall find good: and whoso trusteth in the LORD, happy *is* he.
21 The wise in heart shall be called prudent: and the sweetness of the lips increaseth learning.
22 Understanding *is* a wellspring of life unto him that hath it: but the instruction of fools *is* folly.
23 The heart of the wise teacheth his mouth, and addeth learning to his lips.
24 Pleasant words *are as* an honeycomb, sweet to the soul, and health to the bones.
25 There is a way that seemeth right unto a man, but the end thereof *are* the ways of death.
26 He that laboureth laboureth for himself; for his mouth craveth it of him.
27 An ungodly man diggeth up evil: and in his lips *there is* as a burning fire.
28 A froward man soweth strife: and a whisperer separateth chief friends.
29 A violent man enticeth his neighbour, and leadeth him into the way *that is* not good.
30 He shutteth his eyes to devise froward things: moving his lips he bringeth evil to pass.
31 The hoary head *is* a crown of glory, *if* it be found in the way of righteousness.
32 *He that is* slow to anger *is* better than the mighty; and he that ruleth his spirit than he that taketh a city.
33 The lot is cast into the lap; but the whole disposing thereof *is* of the LORD.

CHAPTER 17

BETTER *is* a dry morsel, and quietness therewith, than an house full of sacrifices *with* strife.
2 A wise servant shall have rule over a son that causeth shame, and shall have part of the inheritance among the brethren.
3 The fining pot *is* for silver, and the furnace for gold: but the LORD trieth the hearts.
4 A wicked doer giveth heed to false lips; *and* a liar giveth ear to a naughty tongue.
5 Whoso mocketh the poor reproacheth his Maker: *and* he that is glad at calamities shall not be unpunished.
6 Children's children *are* the crown of old men; and the glory of children *are* their fathers.
7 Excellent speech becometh not a fool: much less do lying lips a prince.
8 A gift *is as* a precious stone in the eyes of him that hath it: whithersoever it turneth, it prospereth.
9 He that covereth a transgression seeketh love; but he that repeateth a matter separateth *very* friends.
10 A reproof entereth more into a wise man than an hundred stripes into a fool.
11 An evil *man* seeketh only rebellion: therefore a cruel messenger shall be sent against him.
12 Let a bear robbed of her whelps meet a man, rather than a fool in his folly.
13 Whoso rewardeth evil for good, evil shall not depart from his house.
14 The beginning of strife *is as* when one letteth out water: therefore leave off contention, before it be meddled with.
15 He that justifieth the wicked, and he that condemneth the just, even they both *are* abomination to the LORD.
16 Wherefore *is there* a price in the hand of a fool to get wisdom, seeing *he hath* no heart *to it?*
17 A friend loveth at all times, and a brother is born for adversity.
18 A man void of understanding striketh hands, *and* becometh surety in the presence of his friend.

19 He loveth transgression that loveth strife: *and* he that exalteth his gate seeketh destruction.
20 He that hath a froward heart findeth no good: and he that hath a perverse tongue falleth into mischief.
21 He that begetteth a fool *doeth it* to his sorrow: and the father of a fool hath no joy.
22 A merry heart doeth good *like* a medicine: but a broken spirit drieth the bones.
23 A wicked *man* taketh a gift out of the bosom to pervert the ways of judgment.
24 Widsom *is* before him that hath understanding; but the eyes of a fool *are* in the ends of the earth.
25 A foolish son *is* a grief to his father, and bitterness to her that bare him.
26 Also to punish the just *is* not good, *nor* to strike princes for equity.
27 He that hath knowledge spareth his words: *and* a man of understanding is of an excellent spirit.
28 Even a fool, when he holdeth his peace, is counted wise: *and* he that shutteth his lips *is esteemed* a man of understanding.

CHAPTER 18

THROUGH desire a man, having separated himself, seeketh *and* intermeddleth with all wisdom.
2 A fool hath no delight in understanding, but that his heart may discover itself.
3 When the wicked cometh, *then* cometh also contempt, and with ignominy reproach.
4 The words of a man's mouth *are as* deep waters, *and* the wellspring of wisdom *as* a flowing brook.
5 *It is* not good to accept the person of the wicked, to overthrow the righteous in judgment.
6 A fool's lips enter into contention, and his mouth calleth for strokes.
7 A fool's mouth *is* his destruction, and his lips *are* the snare of his soul.
8 The words of a talebearer *are* as wounds, and they go down into the innermost parts of the belly.
9 He also that is slothful in his work is brother to him that is a great waster.
10 The name of the LORD *is* a strong tower: the righteous runneth into it, and is safe.
11 The rich man's wealth *is* his strong city, and as an high wall in his own conceit.
12 Before destruction the heart of man is haughty, and before honour *is* humility.
13 He that answereth a matter before he heareth *it*, it *is* folly and shame unto him.
14 The spirit of a man will sustain his infirmity; but a wounded spirit who can bear?
15 The heart of the prudent getteth knowledge; and the ear of the wise seeketh knowledge.
16 A man's gift maketh room for him, and bringeth him before great men.
17 *He that is* first in his own cause *seemeth* just; but his neighbour cometh and searcheth him.
18 The lot causeth contentions to cease, and parteth between the mighty.
19 A brother offended *is harder to be won* than a strong city: and *their* contentions *are* like the bars of a castle.
20 A man's belly shall be satisfied with the fruit of his mouth; *and* with the increase of his lips shall he be filled.
21 Death and life *are* in the power of the tongue: and they that love it shall eat the fruit thereof.
22 *Whoso* findeth a wife findeth a good *thing*, and obtaineth favour of the LORD.
23 The poor useth intreaties; but the rich answereth roughly.
24 A man *that hath* friends must shew himself friendly: and there is a friend *that* sticketh closer than a brother.

CHAPTER 19

BETTER *is* the poor that walketh in his integrity, than *he that is* perverse in his lips, and is a fool.
2 Also, *that* the soul *be* without knowledge, *it is* not good; and he that hasteth with *his* feet sinneth.
3 The foolishness of man perverteth his way: and his heart fretteth against the LORD.
4 Wealth maketh many friends; but the poor is separated from his neighbour.
5 A false witness shall not be unpunished, and *he that* speaketh lies shall not escape.
6 Many will intreat the favour of the prince: and every man *is* a friend to him that giveth gifts.
7 All the brethren of the poor do hate him: how much more do his friends go far from him? he pursueth *them with* words, *yet* they *are* wanting *to him*.
8 He that getteth wisdom loveth his own soul: he that keepeth understanding shall find good.
9 A false witness shall not be unpunished, and *he that* speaketh lies shall perish.
10 Delight is not seemly for a fool;

much less for a servant to have rule over princes.

11 The discretion of a man deferreth his anger; and *it is* his glory to pass over a transgression.

12 The king's wrath *is* as the roaring of a lion; but his favour *is* as dew upon the grass.

13 A foolish son *is* the calamity of his father: and the contentions of a wife *are* a continual dropping.

14 House and riches *are* the inheritance of fathers: and a prudent wife *is* from the LORD.

15 Slothfulness casteth into a deep sleep; and an idle soul shall suffer hunger.

16 He that keepeth the commandment keepeth his own soul; *but* he that despiseth his ways shall die.

17 He that hath pity upon the poor lendeth unto the LORD; and that which he hath given will he pay him again.

18 Chasten thy son while there is hope, and let not thy soul spare for his crying.

19 A man of great wrath shall suffer punishment: for if thou deliver *him*, yet thou must do it again.

20 Hear counsel, and receive instruction, that thou mayest be wise in thy latter end.

21 *There are* many devices in a man's heart; nevertheless the counsel of the LORD, that shall stand.

22 The desire of a man *is* his kindness: and a poor man *is* better than a liar.

23 The fear of the LORD *tendeth* to life: and *he that hath it* shall abide satisfied; he shall not be visited with evil.

24 A slothful *man* hideth his hand in *his* bosom, and will not so much as bring it to his mouth again.

25 Smite a scorner, and the simple will beware: and reprove one that hath understanding, *and* he will understand knowledge.

26 He that wasteth *his* father, *and* chaseth away *his* mother, *is* a son that causeth shame, and bringeth reproach.

27 Cease, my son, to hear the instruction *that causeth* to err from the words of knowledge.

28 An ungodly witness scorneth judgment: and the mouth of the wicked devoureth iniquity.

29 Judgments are prepared for scorners, and stripes for the back of fools.

CHAPTER 20

WINE *is* a mocker, strong drink *is* raging: and whosoever is deceived thereby is not wise.

2 The fear of a king *is* as the roaring of a lion: *whoso* provoketh him to anger sinneth *against* his own soul.

3 *It is* an honour for a man to cease from strife: but every fool will be meddling.

4 The sluggard will not plow by reason of the cold; *therefore* shall he beg in harvest, and *have* nothing.

5 Counsel in the heart of man *is like* deep water; but a man of understanding will draw it out.

6 Most men will proclaim every one his own goodness: but a faithful man who can find?

7 The just *man* walketh in his integrity: his children *are* blessed after him.

8 A king that sitteth in the throne of judgment scattereth away all evil with his eyes.

9 Who can say, I have made my heart clean, I am pure from my sin?

10 Divers weights, *and* divers measures, both of them *are* alike abomination to the LORD.

11 Even a child is known by his doings, whether his work *be* pure, and whether *it be* right.

12 The hearing ear, and the seeing eye, the LORD hath made even both of them.

13 Love not sleep, lest thou come to poverty; open thine eyes, *and* thou shalt be satisfied with bread.

14 *It is* naught, *it is* naught, saith the buyer: but when he is gone his way, then he boasteth.

15 There is gold, and a multitude of rubies: but the lips of knowledge *are* a precious jewel.

16 Take his garment that is surety *for* a stranger: and take a pledge of him for a strange woman.

17 Bread of deceit *is* sweet to a man; but afterwards his mouth shall be filled with gravel.

18 *Every* purpose is established by counsel: and with good advice make war.

19 He that goeth about *as* a talebearer revealeth secrets: therefore meddle not with him that flattereth with his lips.

20 Whoso curseth his father or his mother, his lamp shall be put out in obscure darkness.

21 An inheritance *may be* gotten hastily at the beginning; but the end thereof shall not be blessed.

22 Say not thou, I will recompense evil; *but* wait on the LORD, and he shall save thee.

23 Divers weights are an abomination unto the LORD; and a false balance *is* not good.

24 Man's goings *are* of the LORD; how

can a man then understand his own way?

25 *It is* a snare to the man *who* devoureth *that which is* holy, and after vows to make enquiry.

26 A wise king scattereth the wicked, and bringeth the wheel over them.

27 The spirit of man *is* the candle of the LORD, searching all the inward parts of the belly.

28 Mercy and truth preserve the king: and his throne is upholden by mercy.

29 The glory of young men *is* their strength: and the beauty of old men *is* the grey head.

30 The blueness of a wound cleanseth away evil: so *do* stripes the inward parts of the belly.

CHAPTER 21

THE king's heart *is* in the hand of the LORD, *as* the rivers of water: he turneth it whithersoever he will.

2 Every way of a man *is* right in his own eyes: but the LORD pondereth the hearts.

3 To do justice and judgment *is* more acceptable to the LORD than sacrifice.

4 An high look, and a proud heart, *and* the plowing of the wicked, *is* sin.

5 The thoughts of the diligent *tend* only to plenteousness; but of every one *that is* hasty only to want.

6 The getting of treasures by a lying tongue *is* a vanity tossed to and fro of them that seek death.

7 The robbery of the wicked shall destroy them; because they refuse to do judgment.

8 The way of man *is* froward and strange: but *as for* the pure, his work *is* right.

9 *It is* better to dwell in a corner of the housetop, than with a brawling woman in a wide house.

10 The soul of the wicked desireth evil: his neighbour findeth no favour in his eyes.

11 When the scorner is punished, the simple is made wise: and when the wise is instructed, he receiveth knowledge.

12 The righteous *man* wisely considereth the house of the wicked: *but God* overthroweth the wicked for *their* wickedness.

13 Whoso stoppeth his ears at the cry of the poor, he also shall cry himself, but shall not be heard.

14 A gift in secret pacifieth anger: and a reward in the bosom strong wrath.

15 *It is* joy to the just to do judgment: but destruction *shall be* to the workers of iniquity.

16 The man that wandereth out of the way of understanding shall remain in the congregation of the dead.

17 He that loveth pleasure *shall be* a poor man: he that loveth wine and oil shall not be rich.

18 The wicked *shall be* a ransom for the righteous, and the transgressor for the upright.

19 *It is* better to dwell in the wilderness, than with a contentious and an angry woman.

20 *There is* treasure to be desired and oil in the dwelling of the wise; but a foolish man spendeth it up.

21 He that followeth after righteousness and mercy findeth life, righteousness, and honour.

22 A wise *man* scaleth the city of the mighty, and casteth down the strength of the confidence thereof.

23 Whoso keepeth his mouth and his tongue keepeth his soul from troubles.

24 Proud *and* haughty scorner *is* his name, who dealeth in proud wrath.

25 The desire of the slothful killeth him; for his hands refuse to labour.

26 He coveteth greedily all the day long: but the righteous giveth and spareth not.

27 The sacrifice of the wicked *is* abomination: how much more, *when* he bringeth it with a wicked mind?

28 A false witness shall perish: but the man that heareth speaketh constantly.

29 A wicked man hardeneth his face: but *as for* the upright, he directeth his way.

30 *There is* no wisdom nor understanding nor counsel against the LORD.

31 The horse *is* prepared against the day of battle: but safety *is* of the LORD.

CHAPTER 22

A *GOOD* name *is* rather to be chosen than great riches, *and* loving favour rather than silver and gold.

2 The rich and poor meet together: the LORD *is* the maker of them all.

3 A prudent *man* forseeth the evil, and hideth himself: but the simple pass on, and are punished.

4 By humility *and* the fear of the LORD *are* riches, and honour, and life.

5 Thorns *and* snares *are* in the way of the froward: he that doth keep his soul shall be far from them.

6 Train up a child in the way he should go: and when he is old, he will not depart from it.

7 The rich ruleth over the poor, and the borrower *is* servant to the lender.

8 He that soweth iniquity shall reap vanity: and the rod of his anger shall fail.

9 He that hath a bountiful eye shall be blessed; for he giveth of his bread to the poor.

10 Cast out the scorner, and contention shall go out; yea, strife and reproach shall cease.

11 He that loveth pureness of heart, *for* the grace of his lips the king *shall be* his friend.

12 The eyes of the LORD preserve knowledge, and he overthroweth the words of the transgressor.

13 The slothful *man* saith, *There is* a lion without, I shall be slain in the streets.

14 The mouth of strange women *is* a deep pit: he that is abhorred of the LORD shall fall therein.

15 Foolishness *is* bound in the heart of a child; *but* the rod of correction shall drive it far from him.

16 He that oppresseth the poor to increase his *riches, and* he that giveth to the rich, *shall* surely *come* to want.

17 ¶Bow down thine ear, and hear the words of the wise, and apply thine heart unto my knowledge.

18 For *it is* a pleasant thing if thou keep them within thee; they shall withal be fitted in thy lips.

19 That thy trust may be in the LORD, I have made known to thee this day, even to thee.

20 Have not I written to thee excellent things in counsels and knowledge,

21 That I might make thee know the certainty of the words of truth; that thou mightest answer the words of truth to them that send unto thee?

22 Rob not the poor, because he *is* poor: neither oppress the afflicted in the gate:

23 For the LORD will plead their cause, and spoil the soul of those that spoiled them.

24 Make no friendship with an angry man; and with a furious man thou shalt not go:

25 Lest thou learn his ways, and get a snare to thy soul.

26 Be not thou *one* of them that strike hands, *or* of them that are sureties for debts.

27 If thou hast nothing to pay, why should he take away thy bed from under thee?

28 Remove not the ancient landmark, which thy fathers have set.

29 Seest thou a man diligent in his business? he shall stand before kings; he shall not stand before mean *men*.

CHAPTER 23

WHEN thou sittest to eat with a ruler, consider diligently what *is* before thee:

2 And put a knife to thy throat, if thou *be* a man given to appetite.

3 Be not desirous of his dainties: for they *are* deceitful meat.

4 Labour not to be rich: cease from thine own wisdom.

5 Wilt thou set thine eyes upon that which is not? for *riches* certainly make themselves wings; they fly away as an eagle toward heaven.

6 Eat thou not the bread of *him that hath* an evil eye, neither desire thou his dainty meats:

7 For as he thinketh in his heart, so *is* he: Eat and drink, saith he to thee; but his heart *is* not with thee.

8 The morsel *which* thou hast eaten shalt thou vomit up, and lose thy sweet words.

9 Speak not in the ears of a fool: for he will despise the wisdom of thy words.

10 Remove not the old landmark; and enter not into the fields of the fatherless:

11 For their redeemer *is* mighty; he shall plead their cause with thee.

12 Apply thine heart unto instruction, and thine ears to the words of knowledge.

13 Withhold not correction from the child: for *if* thou beatest him with the rod, he shall not die.

14 Thou shalt beat him with the rod, and shalt deliver his soul from hell.

15 My son, if thine heart be wise, my heart shall rejoice, even mine.

16 Yea, my reins shall rejoice, when thy lips speak right things.

17 Let not thine heart envy sinners: but *be thou* in the fear of the LORD all the day long.

18 For surely there is an end; and thine expectation shall not be cut off.

19 Hear thou, my son, and be wise, and guide thine heart in the way.

20 Be not among winebibbers; among riotous eaters of flesh:

21 For the drunkard and the glutton shall come to poverty: and drowsiness shall clothe *a man* with rags.

22 Hearken unto thy father that begat thee, and despise not thy mother when she is old.

23 Buy the truth, and sell *it* not; *also* wisdom, and instruction, and understanding.

24 The father of the righteous shall greatly rejoice: and he that begetteth a wise *child* shall have joy of him.

25 Thy father and thy mother shall be

glad, and she that bare thee shall rejoice.

26 My son, give me thine heart, and let thine eyes observe my ways.

27 For a whore *is* a deep ditch; and a strange woman *is* a narrow pit.

28 She also lieth in wait as *for* a prey, and increaseth the transgressors among men.

29 Who hath woe? who hath sorrow? who hath contentions? who hath babbling? who hath wounds without cause? who hath redness of eyes?

30 They that tarry long at the wine; they that go to seek mixed wine.

31 Look not thou upon the wine when it is red, when it giveth his colour in the cup, *when* it moveth itself aright.

32 At the last it biteth like a serpent, and stingeth like an adder.

33 Thine eyes shall behold strange women, and thine heart shall utter perverse things.

34 Yea, thou shalt be as he that lieth down in the midst of the sea, or as he that lieth upon the top of a mast.

35 They have stricken me, *shalt thou say, and* I was not sick; they have beaten me, *and* I felt *it* not: when shall I awake? I will seek it yet again.

CHAPTER 24

BE not thou envious against evil men, neither desire to be with them.

2 For their heart studieth destruction, and their lips talk of mischief.

3 Through wisdom is an house builded; and by understanding it is established:

4 And by knowledge shall the chambers be filled with all precious and pleasant riches.

5 A wise man *is* strong; yea, a man of knowledge increaseth strength.

6 For by wise counsel thou shalt make thy war: and in multitude of counsellors *there is* safety.

7 Wisdom *is* too high for a fool: he openeth not his mouth in the gate.

8 He that deviseth to do evil shall be called a mischievous person.

9 The thought of foolishness *is* sin: and the scorner *is* an abomination to men.

10 *If* thou faint in the day of adversity, thy strength *is* small.

11 If thou forbear to deliver *them that are* drawn unto death, and *those that are* ready to be slain;

12 If thou sayest, Behold, we knew it not; doth not he that pondereth the heart consider *it?* and he that keepeth thy soul, doth *not* he know *it?* and shall *not* he render to *every* man according to his works?

13 My son, eat thou honey, because *it is* good; and the honeycomb, *which is* sweet to thy taste:

14 So *shall* the knowledge of wisdom *be* unto thy soul: when thou hast found *it,* then there shall be a reward, and thy expectation shall not be cut off.

15 Lay not wait, O wicked *man,* against the dwelling of the righteous; spoil not his resting place:

16 For a just *man* falleth seven times, and riseth up again: but the wicked shall fall into mischief.

17 Rejoice not when thine enemy falleth, and let not thine heart be glad when he stumbleth:

18 Lest the LORD see *it,* and it displease him, and he turn away his wrath from him.

19 Fret not thyself because of evil *men,* neither be thou envious at the wicked:

20 For there shall be no reward to the evil *man;* the candle of the wicked shall be put out.

21 My son, fear thou the LORD and the king: *and* meddle not with them that are given to change:

22 For their calamity shall rise suddenly; and who knoweth the ruin of them both?

23 These *things* also *belong* to the wise. *It is* not good to have respect of persons in judgment.

24 He that saith unto the wicked, Thou *art* righteous; him shall the people curse, nations shall abhor him:

25 But to them that rebuke *him* shall be delight, and a good blessing shall come upon them.

26 *Every man* shall kiss *his* lips that giveth a right answer.

27 Prepare thy work without, and make it fit for thyself in the field; and afterwards build thine house.

28 Be not a witness against thy neighbour without cause; and deceive *not* with thy lips.

29 Say not, I will do so to him as he hath done to me: I will render to the man according to his work.

30 I went by the field of the slothful, and by the vineyard of the man void of understanding;

31 And, lo, it was all grown over with thorns, *and* nettles had covered the face thereof, and the stone wall thereof was broken down.

32 Then I saw, *and* considered *it* well: I looked upon *it, and* received instruction.

33 *Yet* a little sleep, a little slumber, a little folding of the hands to sleep:

34 So shall thy poverty come *as* one

that travelleth; and thy want as an armed man.

CHAPTER 25

THESE *are* also proverbs of Sŏl'o-mon, which the men of Hĕz-e-kī'ah king of Jū'dah copied out.
2 *It is* the glory of God to conceal a thing: but the honour of kings *is* to search out a matter.
3 The heaven for height, and the earth for depth, and the heart of kings *is* unsearchable.
4 Take away the dross from the silver, and there shall come forth a vessel for the finer.
5 Take away the wicked *from* before the king, and his throne shall be established in righteousness.
6 Put not forth thyself in the presence of the king, and stand not in the place of great *men:*
7 For better *it is* that it be said unto thee, Come up hither; than that thou shouldest be put lower in the presence of the prince whom thine eyes have seen.
8 Go not forth hastily to strive, lest *thou know not* what to do in the end thereof, when thy neighbour hath put thee to shame.
9 Debate thy cause with thy neighbour *himself;* and discover not a secret to another:
10 Lest he that heareth *it* put thee to shame, and thine infamy turn not away.
11 A word fitly spoken *is like* apples of gold in pictures of silver.
12 *As* an earring of gold, and an ornament of fine gold, *so is* a wise reprover upon an obedient ear.
13 As the cold of snow in the time of harvest, *so is* a faithful messenger to them that send him: for he refresheth the soul of his masters.
14 Whoso boasteth himself of a false gift *is like* clouds and wind without rain.
15 By long forbearing is a prince persuaded, and a soft tongue breaketh the bone.
16 Hast thou found honey? eat so much as is sufficient for thee, lest thou be filled therewith, and vomit it.
17 Withdraw thy foot from thy neighbour's house; lest he be weary of thee, and *so* hate thee.
18 A man that beareth false witness against his neighbour *is* a maul, and a sword, and a sharp arrow.
19 Confidence in an unfaithful man in time of trouble *is like* a broken tooth, and a foot out of joint.
20 *As* he that taketh away a garment in cold weather, *and as* vinegar upon nitre, so *is* he that singeth songs to an heavy heart.
21 If thine enemy be hungry, give him bread to eat; and if he be thirsty, give him water to drink:
22 For thou shalt heap coals of fire upon his head, and the LORD shall reward thee.
23 The north wind driveth away rain: so *doth* an angry countenance a backbiting tongue.
24 *It is* better to dwell in the corner of the housetop, than with a brawling woman and in a wide house.
25 *As* cold waters to a thirsty soul, so *is* good news from a far country.
26 A righteous man falling down before the wicked *is as* a troubled fountain, and a corrupt spring.
27 *It is* not good to eat much honey: so *for men* to search their own glory *is not* glory.
28 He that *hath* no rule over his own spirit *is like* a city *that is* broken down, *and* without walls.

CHAPTER 26

AS snow in summer, and as rain in harvest, so honour is not seemly for a fool.
2 As the bird by wandering, as the swallow by flying, so the curse causeless shall not come.
3 A whip for the horse, a bridle for the ass, and a rod for the fool's back.
4 Answer not a fool according to his folly, lest thou also be like unto him.
5 Answer a fool according to his folly, lest he be wise in his own conceit.
6 He that sendeth a message by the hand of a fool cutteth off the feet, *and* drinketh damage.
7 The legs of the lame are not equal: so *is* a parable in the mouth of fools.
8 As he that bindeth a stone in a sling, so *is* he that giveth honour to a fool.
9 *As* a thorn goeth up into the hand of a drunkard, so *is* a parable in the mouth of fools.
10 The great *God* that formed all *things* both rewardeth the fool, and rewardeth transgressors.
11 As a dog returneth to his vomit, *so* a fool returneth to his folly.
12 Seest thou a man wise in his own conceit? *there is* more hope of a fool than of him.
13 The slothful *man* saith, *There is* a lion in the way; a lion *is* in the streets.
14 *As* the door turneth upon his hinges, so *doth* the slothful upon his bed.
15 The slothful hideth his hand in *his* bosom; it grieveth him to bring it again to his mouth.

16 The sluggard *is* wiser in his own conceit than seven men that can render a reason.

17 He that passeth by, *and* meddleth with strife *belonging* not to him, *is like* one that taketh a dog by the ears.

18 As a mad *man* who casteth firebrands, arrows, and death,

19 So *is* the man *that* deceiveth his neighbour, and saith, Am not I in sport?

20 Where no wood is, *there* the fire goeth out: so where *there is* no talebearer, the strife ceaseth.

21 *As* coals *are* to burning coals, and wood to fire; so *is* a contentious man to kindle strife.

22 The words of a talebearer *are* as wounds, and they go down into the innermost parts of the belly.

23 Burning lips and a wicked heart *are like* a potsherd covered with silver dross.

24 He that hateth dissembleth with his lips, and layeth up deceit within him;

25 When he speaketh fair, believe him not: for *there are* seven abominations in his heart.

26 *Whose* hatred is covered by deceit, his wickedness shall be shewed before the *whole* congregation.

27 Whoso diggeth a pit shall fall therein: and he that rolleth a stone, it will return upon him.

28 A lying tongue hateth *those that are* afflicted by it; and a flattering mouth worketh ruin.

CHAPTER 27

BOAST not thyself of to morrow; for thou knowest not what a day may bring forth.

2 Let another man praise thee, and not thine own mouth; a stranger, and not thine own lips.

3 A stone *is* heavy, and the sand weighty; but a fool's wrath *is* heavier than them both.

4 Wrath *is* cruel, and anger *is* outrageous; but who *is* able to stand before envy?

5 Open rebuke *is* better than secret love.

6 Faithful *are* the wounds of a friend; but the kisses of an enemy *are* deceitful.

7 The full soul loatheth an honeycomb; but to the hungry soul every bitter thing is sweet.

8 As a bird that wandereth from her nest, so *is* a man that wandereth from his place.

9 Ointment and perfume rejoice the heart: so *doth* the sweetness of a man's friend by hearty counsel.

10 Thine own friend, and thy father's friend, forsake not; neither go into thy brother's house in the day of thy calamity: *for* better *is* a neighbour *that is* near than a brother far off.

11 My son, be wise, and make my heart glad, that I may answer him that reproacheth me.

12 A prudent *man* foreseeth the evil, *and* hideth himself; *but* the simple pass on, *and* are punished.

13 Take his garment that is surety for a stranger, and take a pledge of him for a strange woman.

14 He that blesseth his friend with a loud voice, rising early in the morning, it shall be counted a curse to him.

15 A continual dropping in a very rainy day and a contentious woman are alike.

16 Whosoever hideth her hideth the wind, and the ointment of his right hand, *which* bewrayeth *itself*.

17 Iron sharpeneth iron; so a man sharpeneth the countenance of his friend.

18 Whoso keepeth the fig tree shall eat the fruit thereof: so he that waiteth on his master shall be honoured.

19 As in water face *answereth* to face, so the heart of man to man.

20 Hell and destruction are never full; so the eyes of man are never satisfied.

21 *As* the fining pot for silver, and the furnace for gold; so *is* a man to his praise.

22 Though thou shouldest bray a fool in a mortar among wheat with a pestle, *yet* will not his foolishness depart from him.

23 Be thou diligent to know the state of thy flocks, *and* look well to thy herds.

24 For riches *are* not for ever: and doth the crown *endure* to every generation?

25 The hay appeareth, and the tender grass sheweth itself, and herbs of the mountains are gathered.

26 The lambs *are* for thy clothing, and the goats *are* the price of the field.

27 And *thou shalt have* goats' milk enough for thy food, for the food of thy household, and *for* the maintenance for thy maidens.

CHAPTER 28

THE wicked flee when no man pursueth: but the righteous are bold as a lion.

2 For the transgression of a land many *are* the princes thereof: but by a man of understanding *and* knowledge the state *thereof* shall be prolonged.

3 A poor man that oppresseth the

poor *is like* a sweeping rain which leav-
eth no food.
4 They that forsake the law praise the
wicked: but such as keep the law con-
tend with them.
5 Evil men understand not judgment:
but they that seek the LORD understand
all *things*.
6 Better *is* the poor that walketh in
his uprightness, than *he that is* perverse
in his ways, though he *be* rich.
7 Whoso keepeth the law *is* a wise
son: but he that is a companion of riot-
ous *men* shameth his father.
8 He that by usury and unjust gain
increaseth his substance, he shall gath-
er it for him that will pity the poor.
9 He that turneth away his ear from
hearing the law, even his prayer *shall
be* abomination.
10 Whoso causeth the righteous to go
astray in an evil way, he shall fall him-
self into his own pit: but the upright
shall have good *things* in possession.
11 The rich man *is* wise in his own
conceit; but the poor that hath under-
standing searcheth him out.
12 When righteous *men* do rejoice,
there is great glory: but when the
wicked rise, a man is hidden.
13 He that covereth his sins shall not
prosper: but whoso confesseth and for-
saketh *them* shall have mercy.
14 Happy *is* the man that feareth
alway: but he that hardeneth his heart
shall fall into mischief.
15 *As* a roaring lion, and a ranging
bear; *so is* a wicked ruler over the poor
people.
16 The prince that wanteth under-
standing *is* also a great oppressor: *but* he
that hateth covetousness shall prolong
his days.
17 A man that doeth violence to the
blood of *any* person shall flee to the pit;
let no man stay him.
18 Whoso walketh uprightly shall be
saved: but *he that is* perverse *in his*
ways shall fall at once.
19 He that tilleth his land shall have
plenty of bread: but he that followeth
after vain *persons* shall have poverty
enough.
20 A faithful man shall abound with
blessings: but he that maketh haste to
be rich shall not be innocent.
21 To have respect of persons *is* not
good: for for a piece of bread *that* man
will transgress.
22 He that hasteth to be rich *hath* an
evil eye, and considereth not that pov-
erty shall come upon him.
23 He that rebuketh a man after-
wards shall find more favour than he
that flattereth with the tongue.
24 Whoso robbeth his father or his
mother, and saith, *It is* no transgres-
sion; the same *is* the companion of a
destroyer.
25 He that is of a proud heart stirreth
up strife: but he that putteth his trust in
the LORD shall be made fat.
26 He that trusteth in his own heart is
a fool: but whoso walketh wisely, he
shall be delivered.
27 He that giveth unto the poor shall
not lack: but he that hideth his eyes
shall have many a curse.
28 When the wicked rise, men hide
themselves: but when they perish, the
righteous increase.

CHAPTER 29

HE, that being often reproved hard-
eneth *his* neck, shall suddenly be
destroyed, and that without remedy.
2 When the righteous are in au-
thority, the people rejoice: but when
the wicked beareth rule, the people
mourn.
3 Whoso loveth wisdom rejoiceth his
father: but he that keepeth company
with harlots spendeth *his* substance.
4 The king by judgment establisheth
the land: but he that receiveth gifts
overthroweth it.
5 A man that flattereth his neighbour
spreadeth a net for his feet.
6 In the transgression of an evil man
there is a snare: but the righteous doth
sing and rejoice.
7 The righteous considereth the
cause of the poor: *but* the wicked re-
gardeth not to know *it*.
8 Scornful men bring a city into a
snare: but wise *men* turn away wrath.
9 *If* a wise man contendeth with a
foolish man, whether he rage or laugh,
there is no rest.
10 The bloodthirsty hate the upright:
but the just seek his soul.
11 A fool uttereth all his mind: but a
wise *man* keepeth it in till afterwards.
12 If a ruler hearken to lies, all his ser-
vants *are* wicked.
13 The poor and the deceitful man
meet together: the LORD lighteneth
both their eyes.
14 The king that faithfully judgeth
the poor, his throne shall be established
for ever.
15 The rod and reproof give wisdom:
but a child left *to himself* bringeth his
mother to shame.
16 When the wicked are multiplied,
transgression increaseth: but the
righteous shall see their fall.
17 Correct thy son, and he shall give
thee rest; yea, he shall give delight unto
thy soul.

18 Where *there is* no vision, the peo-
ple perish: but he that keepeth the
law, happy *is* he.
19 A servant will not be corrected by
words: for though he understand he
will not answer.
20 Seest thou a man *that is* hasty in
his words? *there is* more hope of a fool
than of him.
21 He that delicately bringeth up his
servant from a child shall have him be-
come *his* son at the length.
22 An angry man stirreth up strife,
and a furious man aboundeth in trans-
gression.
23 A man's pride shall bring him low:
but honour shall uphold the humble in
spirit.
24 Whoso is partner with a thief
hateth his own soul: he heareth
cursing, and bewrayeth *it* not.
25 The fear of man bringeth a snare:
but whoso putteth his trust in the LORD
shall be safe.
26 Many seek the ruler's favour; but
every man's judgment *cometh* from
the LORD.
27 An unjust man *is* an abomination
to the just: and *he that is* upright in the
way *is* abomination to the wicked.

CHAPTER 30

THE words of Ā'gur the son of Jā'keh,
even the prophecy: the man spake unto
Ith'ī-el, even unto Ith'ī-el and Ū'cal,
2 Surely I *am* more brutish than *any*
man, and have not the understanding
of a man.
3 I neither learned wisdom, nor have
the knowledge of the holy.
4 Who hath ascended up into heaven,
or descended? who hath gathered the
wind in his fists? who hath bound the
waters in a garment? who hath estab-
lished all the ends of the earth? what *is*
his name, and what *is* his son's name, if
thou canst tell?
5 Every word of God *is* pure: he *is* a
shield unto them that put their trust in
him.
6 Add thou not unto his words, lest he
reprove thee, and thou be found a liar.
7 Two *things* have I required of thee;
deny me *them* not before I die:
8 Remove far from me vanity and
lies: give me neither poverty nor riches;
feed me with food convenient for me:
9 Lest I be full, and deny *thee,* and
say, Who *is* the LORD? or lest I be poor,
and steal, and take the name of my God
in vain.
10 Accuse not a servant unto his mas-
ter, lest he curse thee, and thou be
found guilty.
11 *There is* a generation *that* curseth
their father, and doth not bless their
mother.
12 *There is* a generation *that are* pure
in their own eyes, and *yet* is not washed
from their filthiness.
13 *There is* a generation, O how lofty
are their eyes! and their eyelids are
lifted up.
14 *There is* a generation, whose teeth
are as swords, and their jaw teeth *as*
knives, to devour the poor from off the
earth, and the needy from *among* men.
15 The horseleach hath two daugh-
ters, *crying,* Give, give. There are three
things that are never satisfied, *yea,*
four *things* say not, *It is* enough:
16 The grave; and the barren womb;
the earth *that* is not filled with water;
and the fire *that* saith not, *It is* enough.
17 The eye *that* mocketh at *his* father,
and despiseth to obey *his* mother, the
ravens of the valley shall pick it out,
and the young eagles shall eat it.
18 There be three *things which* are
too wonderful for me, yea, four which I
know not:
19 The way of an eagle in the air; the
way of a serpent upon a rock; the way
of a ship in the midst of the sea; and the
way of a man with a maid.
20 Such *is* the way of an adulterous
woman; she eateth, and wipeth her
mouth, and saith, I have done no
wickedness.
21 For three *things* the earth is dis-
quieted, and for four *which* it cannot
bear:
22 For a servant when he reigneth;
and a fool when he is filled with meat;
23 For an odious *woman* when she is
married; and an handmaid that is heir
to her mistress.
24 There be four *things which are*
little upon the earth, but they *are* ex-
ceeding wise:
25 The ants *are* a people not strong,
yet they prepare their meat in the sum-
mer;
26 The conies *are but* a feeble folk,
yet make they their houses in the rocks;
27 The locusts have no king, yet go
they forth all of them by bands;
28 The spider taketh hold with her
hands, and is in kings' palaces.
29 There be three *things* which go
well, yea, four are comely in going:
30 A lion *which is* strongest among
beasts, and turneth not away for any;
31 A greyhound; an he goat also; and
a king, against whom *there is* no rising
up.
32 If thou hast done foolishly in lift-
ing up thyself, or if thou hast thought
evil, *lay* thine hand upon thy mouth.
33 Surely the churning of milk bring-

eth forth butter, and the wringing of the nose bringeth forth blood: so the forcing of wrath bringeth forth strife.

CHAPTER 31

THE words of king Lĕm'ū-el, the prophecy that his mother taught him.
2 What, my son? and what, the son of my womb? and what, the son of my vows?
3 Give not thy strength unto women, nor thy ways to that which destroyeth kings.
4 *It is* not for kings, O Lĕm'ū-el, *it is* not for kings to drink wine; nor for princes strong drink:
5 Lest they drink, and forget the law, and pervert the judgment of any of the afflicted.
6 Give strong drink unto him that is ready to perish, and wine unto those that be of heavy hearts.
7 Let him drink, and forget his poverty, and remember his misery no more.
8 Open thy mouth for the dumb in the cause of all such as are appointed to destruction.
9 Open thy mouth, judge righteously, and plead the cause of the poor and needy.
10 ¶Who can find a virtuous woman? for her price *is* far above rubies.
11 The heart of her husband doth safely trust in her, so that he shall have no need of spoil.
12 She will do him good and not evil all the days of her life.
13 She seeketh wool, and flax, and worketh willingly with her hands.
14 She is like the merchants' ships; she bringeth her food from afar.
15 She riseth also while it is yet night, and giveth meat to her household, and a portion to her maidens.
16 She considereth a field, and buyeth it: with the fruit of her hands she planteth a vineyard.
17 She girdeth her loins with strength, and strengtheneth her arms.
18 She perceiveth that her merchandise *is* good: her candle goeth not out by night.
19 She layeth her hands to the spindle, and her hands hold the distaff.
20 She stretcheth out her hand to the poor; yea, she reacheth forth her hands to the needy.
21 She is not afraid of the snow for her household: for all her household *are* clothed with scarlet.
22 She maketh herself coverings of tapestry; her clothing *is* silk and purple.
23 Her husband is known in the gates, when he sitteth among the elders of the land.
24 She maketh fine linen, and selleth *it;* and delivereth girdles unto the merchant.
25 Strength and honour *are* her clothing; and she shall rejoice in time to come.
26 She openeth her mouth with wisdom; and in her tongue *is* the law of kindness.
27 She looketh well to the ways of her household, and eateth not the bread of idleness.
28 Her children arise up, and call her blessed; her husband *also,* and he praiseth her.
29 Many daughters have done virtuously, but thou excellest them all.
30 Favour *is* deceitful, and beauty *is* vain: *but* a woman *that* feareth the LORD, she shall be praised.
31 Give her of the fruit of her hands; and let her own works praise her in the gates.

ECCLESIASTES;

OR, THE PREACHER

CHAPTER 1

THE words of the Preacher, the son of David, king in Jerusalem.
2 Vanity of vanities, saith the Preacher, vanity of vanities; all *is* vanity.
3 What profit hath a man of all his labour which he taketh under the sun?
4 *One* generation passeth away, and *another* generation cometh: but the earth abideth for ever.
5 The sun also ariseth, and the sun goeth down, and hasteth to his place where he arose.
6 The wind goeth toward the south, and turneth about unto the north; it whirleth about continually, and the wind returneth again according to his circuits.
7 All the rivers run into the sea; yet the sea *is* not full; unto the place from whence the rivers come, thither they return again.
8 All things *are* full of labour; man cannot utter *it:* the eye is not satisfied with seeing, nor the ear filled with hearing.

9 The thing that hath been, it *is that*
which shall be; and that which is done
is that which shall be done: and *there is*
no new *thing* under the sun.
10 Is there *any* thing whereof it may
be said, See, this *is* new? it hath been
already of old time, which was before
us.
11 *There is* no remembrance of former *things;* neither shall there be *any*
remembrance of *things* that are to
come with *those* that shall come after.
12 ¶I the Preacher was king over
Israel in Jerusalem.
13 And I gave my heart to seek and
search out by wisdom concerning all
things that are done under heaven: this
sore travail hath God given to the sons
of man to be exercised therewith.
14 I have seen all the works that are
done under the sun; and, behold, all *is*
vanity and vexation of spirit.
15 *That which is* crooked cannot be
made straight: and that which is
wanting cannot be numbered.
16 I communed with mine own heart,
saying, Lo, I am come to great estate,
and have gotten more wisdom than all
they that have been before me in Jerusalem: yea, my heart had great experience of wisdom and knowledge.
17 And I gave my heart to know wisdom, and to know madness and folly: I
perceived that this also is vexation of
spirit.
18 For in much wisdom *is* much grief:
and he that increaseth knowledge increaseth sorrow.

CHAPTER 2

I SAID in mine heart, Go to now, I will
prove thee with mirth, therefore enjoy
pleasure: and, behold, this also *is* vanity.
2 I said of laughter, *It is* mad: and of
mirth, What doeth it?
3 I sought in mine heart to give myself unto wine, yet acquainting mine
heart with wisdom; and to lay hold on
folly, till I might see what *was* that
good for the sons of men, which they
should do under the heaven all the days
of their life.
4 I made me great works; I builded
me houses; I planted me vineyards:
5 I made me gardens and orchards,
and I planted trees in them of all *kind of*
fruits:
6 I made me pools of water, to water
therewith the wood that bringeth forth
trees:
7 I got *me* servants and maidens, and
had servants born in my house; also I
had great possessions of great and
small cattle above all that were in Jerusalem before me:
8 I gathered me also silver and gold,
and the peculiar treasure of kings and
of the provinces: I gat me men singers
and women singers, and the delights of
the sons of men, *as* musical instruments, and that of all sorts.
9 So I was great, and increased more
than all that were before me in Jerusalem: also my wisdom remained with
me.
10 And whatsoever mine eyes desired I kept not from them, I withheld
not my heart from any joy; for my heart
rejoiced in all my labour: and this was
my portion of all my labour.
11 Then I looked on all the works that
my hands had wrought, and on the
labour that I had laboured to do: and, behold, all *was* vanity and vexation of
spirit, and *there was* no profit under the
sun.
12 ¶And I turned myself to behold
wisdom, and madness, and folly: for
what *can* the man *do* that cometh after
the king? *even* that which hath been already done.
13 Then I saw that wisdom excelleth
folly, as far as light excelleth darkness.
14 The wise man's eyes *are* in his
head; but the fool walketh in darkness:
and I myself perceived also that one
event happeneth to them all.
15 Then said I in my heart, As it happeneth to the fool, so it happeneth even
to me; and why was I then more wise?
Then I said in my heart, that this also *is*
vanity.
16 For *there is* no remembrance of
the wise more than of the fool for ever;
seeing that which now *is* in the days to
come shall all be forgotten. And how
dieth the wise *man?* as the fool.
17 Therefore I hated life; because the
work that is wrought under the sun *is*
grievous unto me: for all *is* vanity and
vexation of spirit.
18 ¶Yea, I hated all my labour which I
had taken under the sun: because I
should leave it unto the man that shall
be after me.
19 And who knoweth whether he
shall be a wise *man* or a fool? yet shall
he have rule over all my labour wherein
I have laboured, and wherein I have
shewed myself wise under the sun.
This *is* also vanity.
20 Therefore I went about to cause
my heart to despair of all the labour
which I took under the sun.
21 For there is a man whose labour *is*
in wisdom, and in knowledge, and in
equity; yet to a man that hath not la-

boured therein shall he leave it *for* his portion. This also *is* vanity and a great evil.
22 For what hath man of all his labour, and of the vexation of his heart, wherein he hath laboured under the sun?
23 For all his days *are* sorrows, and his travail grief; yea, his heart taketh not rest in the night. This is also vanity.
24 ¶*There is* nothing better for a man, *than* that he should eat and drink, and *that* he should make his soul enjoy good in his labour. This also I saw, that it *was* from the hand of God.
25 For who can eat, or who else can hasten *hereunto,* more than I?
26 For *God* giveth to a man that *is* good in his sight wisdom, and knowledge, and joy: but to the sinner he giveth travail, to gather and to heap up, that he may give to *him that is* good before God. This also *is* vanity and vexation of spirit.

CHAPTER 3

TO every *thing there is* a season, and a time to every purpose under the heaven:
2 A time to be born, and a time to die; a time to plant, and a time to pluck up *that which is* planted;
3 A time to kill, and a time to heal; a time to break down, and a time to build up;
4 A time to weep, and a time to laugh; a time to mourn, and a time to dance;
5 A time to cast away stones, and a time to gather stones together; a time to embrace, and a time to refrain from embracing;
6 A time to get, and a time to lose; a time to keep, and a time to cast away;
7 A time to rend, and a time to sew; a time to keep silence, and a time to speak;
8 A time to love, and a time to hate; a time of war, and a time of peace.
9 What profit hath he that worketh in that wherein he laboureth?
10 I have seen the travail, which God hath given to the sons of men to be exercised in it.
11 He hath made every *thing* beautiful in his time: also he hath set the world in their heart, so that no man can find out the work that God maketh from the beginning to the end.
12 I know that *there is* no good in them, but for *a man* to rejoice, and to do good in his life.
13 And also that every man should eat and drink, and enjoy the good of all his labour, it *is* the gift of God.
14 I know that, whatsoever God doeth, it shall be for ever: nothing can be put to it, nor any thing taken from it: and God doeth *it,* that *men* should fear before him.
15 That which hath been is now; and that which is to be hath already been; and God requireth that which is past.
16 And moreover I saw under the sun the place of judgment, *that* wickedness *was* there; and the place of righteousness, *that* iniquity *was* there.
17 I said in mine heart, God shall judge the righteous and the wicked: for *there is* a time there for every purpose and for every work.
18 I said in mine heart concerning the estate of the sons of men, that God might manifest them, and that they might see that they themselves are beasts.
19 For that which befalleth the sons of men befalleth beasts; even one thing befalleth them: as the one dieth, so dieth the other; yea, they have all one breath; so that a man hath no preeminence above a beast: for all *is* vanity.
20 All go unto one place; all are of the dust, and all turn to dust again.
21 Who knoweth the spirit of man that goeth upward, and the spirit of the beast that goeth downward to the earth?
22 Wherefore I perceive that *there is* nothing better, than that a man should rejoice in his own works; for that *is* his portion: for who shall bring him to see what shall be after him?

CHAPTER 4

SO I returned, and considered all the oppressions that are done under the sun: and behold the tears of *such as were* oppressed, and they had no comforter; and on the side of their oppressors *there was* power; but they had no comforter.
2 Wherefore I praised the dead which are already dead more than the living which are yet alive.
3 Yea, better *is he* than both they, which hath not yet been, who hath not seen the evil work that is done under the sun.
4 ¶Again, I considered all travail, and every right work, that for this a man is envied of his neighbour. This *is* also vanity and vexation of spirit.
5 ¶The fool foldeth his hands together, and eateth his own flesh.
6 Better *is* an handful *with* quietness, than both the hands full *with* travail and vexation of spirit.
7 ¶Then I returned, and I saw vanity under the sun.
8 There is one *alone,* and *there is* not a

second; yea, he hath neither child nor brother: yet *is there* no end of all his labour; neither is his eye satisfied with riches; neither *saith he*, For whom do I labour, and bereave my soul of good? This *is* also vanity, yea, it *is* a sore travail.

9 ¶Two *are* better than one; because they have a good reward for their labour.

10 For if they fall, the one will lift up his fellow: but woe to him *that is* alone when he falleth; for *he hath* not another to help him up.

11 Again, if two lie together, then they have heat: but how can one be warm *alone?*

12 And if one prevail against him, two shall withstand him; and a threefold cord is not quickly broken.

13 ¶Better *is* a poor and a wise child than an old and foolish king, who will no more be admonished.

14 For out of prison he cometh to reign; whereas also *he that is* born in his kingdom becometh poor.

15 I considered all the living which walk under the sun, with the second child that shall stand up in his stead.

16 *There is* no end of all the people, *even* of all that have been before them: they also that come after shall not rejoice in him. Surely this also *is* vanity and vexation of spirit.

CHAPTER 5

KEEP thy foot when thou goest to the house of God, and be more ready to hear, than to give the sacrifice of fools: for they consider not that they do evil.

2 Be not rash with thy mouth, and let not thine heart be hasty to utter *any* thing before God: for God *is* in heaven, and thou upon earth: therefore let thy words be few.

3 For a dream cometh through the multitude of business; and a fool's voice *is known* by multitude of words.

4 When thou vowest a vow unto God, defer not to pay it; for *he hath* no pleasure in fools: pay that which thou hast vowed.

5 Better *is it* that thou shouldest not vow, than that thou shouldest vow and not pay.

6 Suffer not thy mouth to cause thy flesh to sin; neither say thou before the angel, that it *was* an error: wherefore should God be angry at thy voice, and destroy the work of thine hands?

7 For in the multitude of dreams and many words *there are* also *divers* vanities: but fear thou God.

8 ¶If thou seest the oppression of the poor, and violent perverting of judgment and justice in a province, marvel not at the matter: for *he that is* higher than the highest regardeth; and *there be* higher than they.

9 ¶Moreover the profit of the earth is for all: the king *himself* is served by the field.

10 He that loveth silver shall not be satisfied with silver; nor he that loveth abundance with increase: this *is* also vanity.

11 When goods increase, they are increased that eat them: and what good *is there* to the owners thereof, saving the beholding *of them* with their eyes?

12 The sleep of a labouring man *is* sweet, whether he eat little or much: but the abundance of the rich will not suffer him to sleep.

13 There is a sore evil *which* I have seen under the sun, *namely* riches kept for the owners thereof to their hurt.

14 But those riches perish by evil travail: and he begetteth a son, and *there is* nothing in his hand.

15 As he came forth of his mother's womb, naked shall he return to go as he came, and shall take nothing of his labour, which he may carry away in his hand.

16 And this also *is* a sore evil, *that* in all points as he came, so shall he go: and what profit hath he that hath laboured for the wind?

17 All his days also he eateth in darkness, and *he hath* much sorrow and wrath with his sickness.

18 ¶Behold *that* which I have seen: *it is* good and comely *for one* to eat and to drink, and to enjoy the good of all his labour that he taketh under the sun all the days of his life, which God giveth him: for it *is* his portion.

19 Every man also to whom God hath given riches and wealth, and hath given him power to eat thereof, and to take his portion, and to rejoice in his labour; this *is* the gift of God.

20 For he shall not much remember the days of his life; because God answereth *him* in the joy of his heart.

CHAPTER 6

THERE is an evil which I have seen under the sun, and it *is* common among men:

2 A man to whom God hath given riches, wealth, and honour, so that he wanteth nothing for his soul of all that he desireth, yet God giveth him not power to eat thereof, but a stranger eateth it: this *is* vanity, and it *is* an evil disease.

3 ¶If a man beget an hundred *children*, and live many years, so that the days of his years be many, and his soul

be not filled with good, and also *that* he
have no burial; I say, *that* an untimely
birth *is* better than he.
4 For he cometh in with vanity, and
departeth in darkness, and his name
shall be covered with darkness.
5 Moreover he hath not seen the sun,
nor known *any thing:* this hath more
rest than the other.
6 Yea, though he live a thousand
years twice *told,* yet hath he seen no
good: do not all go to one place?
7 All the labour of man *is* for his
mouth, and yet the appetite is not filled.
8 For what hath the wise more than
the fool? what hath the poor, that
knoweth to walk before the living?
9 Better *is* the sight of the eyes than
the wandering of the desire: this *is* also
vanity and vexation of spirit.
10 ¶That which hath been is named
already, and it is known that it *is* man:
neither may he contend with him that
is mightier than he.
11 Seeing there be many things that
increase vanity, what *is* man the bet-
ter?
12 For who knoweth what *is* good for
man in *this* life, all the days of his vain
life which he spendeth as a shadow? for
who can tell a man what shall be after
him under the sun?

CHAPTER 7

A GOOD name *is* better than precious
ointment; and the day of death than the
day of one's birth.
2 ¶*It is* better to go to the house of
mourning, than to go to the house of
feasting: for that *is* the end of all men;
and the living will lay *it* to his heart.
3 Sorrow *is* better than laughter: for
by the sadness of the countenance the
heart is made better.
4 The heart of the wise *is* in the house
of mourning; but the heart of fools *is* in
the house of mirth.
5 *It is* better to hear the rebuke of the
wise, than for a man to hear the song of
fools.
6 For as the crackling of thorns under
a pot, so *is* the laughter of the fool: this
also *is* vanity.
7 ¶Surely oppression maketh a wise
man mad; and a gift destroyeth the
heart.
8 Better *is* the end of a thing than the
beginning thereof: *and* the patient in
spirit *is* better than the proud in spirit.
9 Be not hasty in thy spirit to be
angry: for anger resteth in the bosom of
fools.
10 Say not thou, What is *the cause*
that the former days were better than
these? for thou dost not enquire wisely
concerning this.
11 ¶Wisdom *is* good with an inheri-
tance: and *by it there is* profit to them
that see the sun.
12 For wisdom *is* a defence, *and* mon-
ey *is* a defence: but the excellency of
knowledge *is, that* wisdom giveth life
to them that have it.
13 Consider the work of God: for who
can make *that* straight, which he hath
made crooked?
14 In the day of prosperity be joyful,
but in the day of adversity consider:
God also hath set the one over against
the other, to the end that man should
find nothing after him.
15 All *things* have I seen in the days
of my vanity: there is a just *man* that
perisheth in his righteousness, and
there is a wicked *man* that prolongeth
his life in his wickedness.
16 Be not righteous over much;
neither make thyself over wise: why
shouldest thou destroy thyself?
17 Be not over much wicked, neither
be thou foolish: why shouldest thou die
before thy time?
18 *It is* good that thou shouldest take
hold of this; yea, also from this with-
draw not thine hand: for he that feareth
God shall come forth of them all.
19 Wisdom strengtheneth the wise
more than ten mighty *men* which are in
the city.
20 For *there is* not a just man upon
earth, that doeth good, and sinneth not.
21 Also take no heed unto all words
that are spoken; lest thou hear thy ser-
vant curse thee:
22 For oftentimes also thine own
heart knoweth that thou thyself like-
wise hast cursed others.
23 All this have I proved by wisdom: I
said, I will be wise; but it *was* far from
me.
24 That which is far off, and exceed-
ing deep, who can find it out?
25 I applied mine heart to know and
to search, and to seek out wisdom, and
the reason *of things,* and to know the
wickedness of folly, even of foolishness
and madness:
26 And I find more bitter than death
the woman, whose heart *is* snares and
nets, *and* her hands *as* bands: whoso
pleaseth God shall escape from her; but
the sinner shall be taken by her.
27 Behold, this have I found, saith the
preacher, *counting* one by one, to find
out the account:
28 Which yet my soul seeketh, but I
find not: one man among a thousand
have I found; but a woman among all
those have I not found.

29 Lo, this only have I found, that God hath made man upright; but they have sought out many inventions.

CHAPTER 8

WHO *is* as the wise *man?* and who knoweth the interpretation of a thing? a man's wisdom maketh his face to shine, and the boldness of his face shall be changed.

2 I *counsel thee* to keep the king's commandment, and *that* in regard of the oath of God.

3 Be not hasty to go out of his sight: stand not in an evil thing; for he doeth whatsoever pleaseth him.

4 Where the word of a king *is, there is* power: and who may say unto him, What doest thou?

5 Whoso keepeth the commandment shall feel no evil thing: and a wise man's heart discerneth both time and judgment.

6 Because to every purpose there is time and judgment, therefore the misery of man *is* great upon him.

7 For he knoweth not that which shall be: for who can tell him when it shall be?

8 *There is* no man that hath power over the spirit to retain the spirit; neither *hath he* power in the day of death: and *there is* no discharge in *that* war; neither shall wickedness deliver those that are given to it.

9 All this have I seen, and applied my heart unto every work that is done under the sun: *there is* a time wherein one man ruleth over another to his own hurt.

10 And so I saw the wicked buried, who had come and gone from the place of the holy, and they were forgotten in the city where they had so done: this *is* also vanity.

11 Because sentence against an evil work is not executed speedily, therefore the heart of the sons of men is fully set in them to do evil.

12 Though a sinner do evil an hundred times, and his *days* be prolonged, yet surely I know that it shall be well with them that fear God, which fear before him:

13 But it shall not be well with the wicked, neither shall he prolong *his* days, *which are* as a shadow; because he feareth not before God.

14 There is a vanity which is done upon the earth; that there be just *men,* unto whom it happeneth according to the work of the wicked; again, there be wicked *men,* to whom it happeneth according to the work of the righteous: I said that this also *is* vanity.

15 Then I commended mirth, because a man hath no better thing under the sun, than to eat, and to drink, and to be merry: for that shall abide with him of his labour the days of his life, which God giveth him under the sun.

16 ¶When I applied mine heart to know wisdom, and to see the business that is done upon the earth: (for also *there is that* neither day nor night seeth sleep with his eyes:)

17 Then I beheld all the work of God, that a man cannot find out the work that is done under the sun: because though a man labour to seek *it* out, yet he shall not find *it;* yea farther; though a wise *man* think to know *it,* yet shall he not be able to find *it.*

CHAPTER 9

FOR all this I considered in my heart even to declare all this, that the righteous, and the wise, and their works, *are* in the hand of God: no man knoweth either love or hatred *by* all *that is* before them.

2 All *things come* alike to all: *there is* one event to the righteous, and to the wicked; to the good and to the clean, and to the unclean; to him that sacrificeth, and to him that sacrificeth not: as *is* the good, so *is* the sinner; *and* he that sweareth, as *he* that feareth an oath.

3 This *is* an evil among all *things* that are done under the sun, that *there is* one event unto all: yea, also the heart of the sons of men is full of evil, and madness *is* in their heart while they live, and after that *they go* to the dead.

4 For to him that is joined to all the living there is hope: for a living dog is better than a dead lion.

5 For the living know that they shall die: but the dead know not any thing, neither have they any more a reward; for the memory of them is forgotten.

6 Also their love, and their hatred, and their envy, is now perished; neither have they any more a portion for ever in any *thing* that is done under the sun.

7 ¶Go thy way, eat thy bread with joy, and drink thy wine with a merry heart; for God now accepteth thy works.

8 Let thy garments be always white; and let thy head lack no ointment.

9 Live joyfully with the wife whom thou lovest all the days of the life of thy vanity, which he hath given thee under the sun, all the days of thy vanity: for that *is* thy portion in *this* life, and in thy labour which thou takest under the sun.

10 Whatsoever thy hand findeth to do, do *it* with thy might; for *there is* no

work, nor device, nor knowledge, nor wisdom, in the grave, whither thou goest.
11 ¶I returned, and saw under the sun, that the race *is* not to the swift, nor the battle to the strong, neither yet bread to the wise, nor yet riches to men of understanding, nor yet favour to men of skill; but time and chance happeneth to them all.
12 For man also knoweth not his time: as the fishes that are taken in an evil net, and as the birds that are caught in the snare; so *are* the sons of men snared in an evil time, when it falleth suddenly upon them.
13 ¶This wisdom have I seen also under the sun, and it *seemed* great unto me:
14 *There was* a little city, and few men within it; and there came a great king against it, and besieged it, and built great bulwarks against it:
15 Now there was found in it a poor wise man, and he by his wisdom delivered the city; yet no man remembered that same poor man.
16 Then said I, Wisdom *is* better than strength: nevertheless the poor man's wisdom *is* despised, and his words are not heard.
17 The words of wise *men are* heard in quiet more than the cry of him that ruleth among fools.
18 Wisdom *is* better than weapons of war: but one sinner destroyeth much good.

CHAPTER 10

DEAD flies cause the ointment of the apothecary to send forth a stinking savour: *so doth* a little folly him that is in reputation for wisdom *and* honour.
2 A wise man's heart *is* at his right hand; but a fool's heart at his left.
3 Yea also, when he that is a fool walketh by the way, his wisdom faileth *him*, and he saith to every one *that* he *is* a fool.
4 If the spirit of the ruler rise up against thee, leave not thy place; for yielding pacifieth great offences.
5 There is an evil *which* I have seen under the sun, as an error *which* proceedeth from the ruler:
6 Folly is set in great dignity, and the rich sit in low place.
7 I have seen servants upon horses, and princes walking as servants upon the earth.
8 He that diggeth a pit shall fall into it; and whoso breaketh an hedge, a serpent shall bite him.
9 Whoso removeth stones shall be hurt therewith; *and* he that cleaveth wood shall be endangered thereby.
10 If the iron be blunt, and he do not whet the edge, then must he put to more strength: but wisdom *is* profitable to direct.
11 Surely the serpent will bite without enchantment; and a babbler is no better.
12 The words of a wise man's mouth *are* gracious; but the lips of a fool will swallow up himself.
13 The beginning of the words of his mouth *is* foolishness: and the end of his talk *is* mischievous madness.
14 A fool also is full of words: a man cannot tell what shall be; and what shall be after him, who can tell him?
15 The labour of the foolish wearieth every one of them, because he knoweth not how to go to the city.
16 ¶Woe to thee, O land, when thy king *is* a child, and thy princes eat in the morning!
17 Blessed *art* thou, O land, when thy king *is* the son of nobles, and thy princes eat in due season, for strength, and not for drunkenness!
18 ¶By much slothfulness the building decayeth; and through idleness of the hands the house droppeth through.
19 ¶A feast is made for laughter, and wine maketh merry: but money answereth all *things*.
20 ¶Curse not the king, no not in thy thought; and curse not the rich in thy bedchamber: for a bird of the air shall carry the voice, and that which hath wings shall tell the matter.

CHAPTER 11

CAST thy bread upon the waters: for thou shalt find it after many days.
2 Give a portion to seven, and also to eight; for thou knowest not what evil shall be upon the earth.
3 If the clouds be full of rain, they empty *themselves* upon the earth: and if the tree fall toward the south, or toward the north, in the place where the tree falleth, there it shall be.
4 He that observeth the wind shall not sow; and he that regardeth the clouds shall not reap.
5 As thou knowest not what *is* the way of the spirit, *nor* how the bones *do grow* in the womb of her that is with child: even so thou knowest not the works of God who maketh all.
6 In the morning sow thy seed, and in the evening withhold not thine hand: for thou knowest not whether shall prosper, either this or that, or whether they both *shall be* alike good.

7 ¶Truly the light *is* sweet, and a pleasant *thing it is* for the eyes to behold the sun:
8 But if a man live many years, *and* rejoice in them all; yet let him remember the days of darkness; for they shall be many. All that cometh *is* vanity.
9 ¶Rejoice, O young man, in thy youth; and let thy heart cheer thee in the days of thy youth, and walk in the ways of thine heart, and in the sight of thine eyes: but know thou, that for all these *things* God will bring thee into judgment.
10 Therefore remove sorrow from thy heart, and put away evil from thy flesh: for childhood and youth *are* vanity.

CHAPTER 12

REMEMBER now thy Creator in the days of thy youth, while the evil days come not, nor the years draw nigh, when thou shalt say, I have no pleasure in them;
2 While the sun, or the light, or the moon, or the stars, be not darkened, nor the clouds return after the rain:
3 In the day when the keepers of the house shall tremble, and the strong men shall bow themselves, and the grinders cease because they are few, and those that look out of the windows be darkened,
4 And the doors shall be shut in the streets, when the sound of the grinding is low, and he shall rise up at the voice of the bird, and all the daughters of musick shall be brought low;
5 Also *when* they shall be afraid of *that which is* high, and fears *shall be* in the way, and the almond tree shall flourish, and the grasshopper shall be a burden, and desire shall fail: because man goeth to his long home, and the mourners go about the streets:
6 Or ever the silver cord be loosed, or the golden bowl be broken, or the pitcher be broken at the fountain, or the wheel broken at the cistern.
7 Then shall the dust return to the earth as it was: and the spirit shall return unto God who gave it.
8 ¶Vanity of vanities, saith the preacher; all *is* vanity.
9 And moreover, because the preacher was wise, he still taught the people knowledge; yea, he gave good heed, and sought out, *and* set in order many proverbs.
10 The preacher sought to find out acceptable words: and *that which was* written *was* upright, *even* words of truth.
11 The words of the wise *are* as goads, and as nails fastened *by* the masters of assemblies, *which* are given from one shepherd.
12 And further, by these, my son, be admonished: of making many books *there is* no end; and much study *is* a weariness of the flesh.
13 ¶Let us hear the conclusion of the whole matter: Fear God, and keep his commandments: for this is the whole *duty* of man.
14 For God shall bring every work into judgment, with every secret thing, whether *it be* good, or whether *it be* evil.

THE SONG OF SOLOMON

CHAPTER 1

THE song of songs, which *is* Sŏl′o-mon's.
2 Let him kiss me with the kisses of his mouth: for thy love *is* better than wine.
3 Because of the savour of thy good ointments thy name *is as* ointment poured forth, therefore do the virgins love thee.
4 Draw me, we will run after thee: the king hath brought me into his chambers: we will be glad and rejoice in thee, we will remember thy love more than wine: the upright love thee.
5 ¶I *am* black, but comely, O ye daughters of Jerusalem, as the tents of Kē′dar, as the curtains of Sŏl′o-mon.
6 Look not upon me, because I *am* black, because the sun hath looked upon me: my mother's children were angry with me; they made me the keeper of the vineyards; *but* mine own vineyard have I not kept.
7 Tell me, O thou whom my soul loveth, where thou feedest, where thou makest *thy flock* to rest at noon: for why should I be as one that turneth aside by the flocks of thy companions?
8 ¶If thou know not, O thou fairest among women, go thy way forth by the footsteps of the flock, and feed thy kids beside the shepherds' tents.
9 I have compared thee, O my love, to a company of horses in Pharaoh's chariots.
10 Thy cheeks are comely with rows of *jewels*, thy neck with chains *of gold*.

11 We will make thee borders of gold with studs of silver.

12 ¶While the king *sitteth* at his table, my spikenard sendeth forth the smell thereof.

13 A bundle of myrrh *is* my well-beloved unto me; he shall lie all night betwixt my breasts.

14 My beloved *is* unto me *as* a cluster of camphire in the vineyard of Ĕn–gē'dī.

15 Behold, thou *art* fair, my love; behold, thou *art* fair; thou *hast* doves' eyes.

16 Behold, thou *art* fair, my beloved, yea, pleasant: also our bed *is* green.

17 The beams of our house *are* cedar, *and* our rafters of fir.

CHAPTER 2

I *AM* the rose of Shâ'ron, *and* the lily of the valleys.

2 As the lily among thorns, so *is* my love among the daughters.

3 As the apple tree among the trees of the wood, so *is* my beloved among the sons. I sat down under his shadow with great delight, and his fruit *was* sweet to my taste.

4 He brought me to the banqueting house, and his banner over me *was* love.

5 Stay me with flagons, comfort me with apples: for I *am* sick of love.

6 His left hand *is* under my head, and his right hand doth embrace me.

7 I charge you, O ye daughters of Jerusalem, by the roes, and by the hinds of the field, that ye stir not up, nor awake *my* love, till he please.

8 ¶The voice of my beloved! behold, he cometh leaping upon the mountains, skipping upon the hills.

9 My beloved is like a roe or a young hart: behold, he standeth behind our wall, he looketh forth at the windows, shewing himself through the lattice.

10 My beloved spake, and said unto me, Rise up, my love, my fair one, and come away.

11 For, lo, the winter is past, the rain is over *and* gone;

12 The flowers appear on the earth; the time of the singing *of birds* is come, and the voice of the turtle is heard in our land;

13 The fig tree putteth forth her green figs, and the vines *with* the tender grape give a *good* smell. Arise, my love, my fair one, and come away.

14 O my dove, *that art* in the clefts of the rock, in the secret *places* of the stairs, let me see thy countenance, let me hear thy voice; for sweet *is* thy voice, and thy countenance *is* comely.

15 Take us the foxes, the little foxes, that spoil the vines: for our vines *have* tender grapes.

16 ¶My beloved *is* mine, and I *am* his: he feedeth among the lilies.

17 Until the day break, and the shadows flee away, turn, my beloved, and be thou like a roe or a young hart upon the mountains of Bē'ther.

CHAPTER 3

BY night on my bed I sought him whom my soul loveth: I sought him, but I found him not.

2 I will rise now, and go about the city in the streets, and in the broad ways I will seek him whom my soul loveth: I sought him, but I found him not.

3 The watchmen that go about the city found me: *to whom I said,* Saw ye him whom my soul loveth?

4 *It was* but a little that I passed from them, but I found him whom my soul loveth: I held him, and would not let him go, until I had brought him into my mother's house, and into the chamber of her that conceived me.

5 I charge you, O ye daughters of Jerusalem, by the roes, and by the hinds of the field, that ye stir not up, nor awake *my* love, till he please.

6 ¶Who *is* this that cometh out of the wilderness like pillars of smoke, perfumed with myrrh and frankincense, with all powders of the merchant?

7 Behold his bed, which is Sŏl'o-mon's; threescore valiant men *are* about it, of the valiant of Israel.

8 They all hold swords, *being* expert in war: every man *hath* his sword upon his thigh because of fear in the night.

9 King Sŏl'o-mon made himself a chariot of the wood of Lebanon.

10 He made the pillars thereof *of* silver, the bottom thereof *of* gold, the covering of it *of* purple, the midst thereof being paved *with* love, for the daughters of Jerusalem.

11 Go forth, O ye daughters of Zion, and behold king Sŏl'o-mon with the crown wherewith his mother crowned him in the day of his espousals, and in the day of the gladness of his heart.

CHAPTER 4

BEHOLD, thou *art* fair, my love; behold, thou *art* fair; thou *hast* doves' eyes within thy locks: thy hair *is* as a flock of goats, that appear from mount Gilead.

2 Thy teeth *are* like a flock *of sheep that are even* shorn, which came up from the washing; whereof every one bear twins, and none *is* barren among them.

3 Thy lips *are* like a thread of scarlet,

and thy speech *is* comely: thy temples
are like a piece of a pomegranate
within thy locks.
4 Thy neck *is* like the tower of David
builded for an armoury, whereon there
hang a thousand bucklers, all shields of
mighty men.
5 Thy two breasts *are* like two young
roes that are twins, which feed among
the lilies.
6 Until the day break, and the shad-
ows flee away, I will get me to the
mountain of myrrh, and to the hill of
frankincense.
7 Thou *art* all fair, my love; *there is* no
spot in thee.
8 ¶Come with me from Lebanon, *my*
spouse, with me from Lebanon: look
from the top of A-mā′na, from the top
of She′nir and Her′mon, from the lions'
dens, from the mountains of the leop-
ards.
9 Thou hast ravished my heart, my
sister, *my* spouse; thou hast ravished
my heart with one of thine eyes, with
one chain of thy neck.
10 How fair is thy love, my sister, *my*
spouse! how much better is thy love
than wine! and the smell of thine oint-
ments than all spices!
11 Thy lips, O *my* spouse, drop *as* the
honeycomb: honey and milk *are* under
thy tongue; and the smell of thy gar-
ments *is* like the smell of Lebanon.
12 A garden inclosed *is* my sister, *my*
spouse; a spring shut up, a fountain
sealed.
13 Thy plants *are* an orchard of pome-
granates, with pleasant fruits;
camphire, with spikenard,
14 Spikenard and saffron; calamus
and cinnamon, with all trees of frankin-
cense; myrrh and aloes, with all the
chief spices:
15 A fountain of gardens, a well of liv-
ing waters, and streams from Leba-
non.
16 ¶Awake, O north wind; and come,
thou south; blow upon my garden, *that*
the spices thereof may flow out. Let my
beloved come into his garden, and eat
his pleasant fruits.

CHAPTER 5

I AM come into my garden, my sister,
my spouse: I have gathered my myrrh
with my spice; I have eaten my honey-
comb with my honey; I have drunk my
wine with my milk: eat, O friends;
drink, yea, drink abundantly, O be-
loved.
2 ¶I sleep, but my heart waketh: *it is*
the voice of my beloved that knocketh,
saying, Open to me, my sister, my love,
my dove, my undefiled: for my head is
filled with dew, *and* my locks with the
drops of the night.
3 I have put off my coat; how shall I
put it on? I have washed my feet; how
shall I defile them?
4 My beloved put in his hand by the
hole *of the door*, and my bowels were
moved for him.
5 I rose up to open to my beloved; and
my hands dropped *with* myrrh, and my
fingers *with* sweet smelling myrrh,
upon the handles of the lock.
6 I opened to my beloved; but my be-
loved had withdrawn himself, *and* was
gone: my soul failed when he spake: I
sought him, but I could not find him; I
called him, but he gave me no answer.
7 The watchmen that went about the
city found me, they smote me, they
wounded me; the keepers of the walls
took away my vail from me.
8 I charge you, O daughters of Jeru-
salem, if ye find my beloved, that ye tell
him, that I *am* sick of love.
9 ¶What *is* thy beloved more than *an-*
other beloved, O thou fairest among
women? what *is* thy beloved more than
another beloved, that thou dost so
charge us?
10 ¶My beloved *is* white and ruddy,
the chiefest among ten thousand.
11 His head *is as* the most fine gold,
his locks *are* bushy, *and* black as a ra-
ven.
12 His eyes *are* as *the eyes* of doves
by the rivers of waters, washed with
milk, *and* fitly set.
13 His cheeks *are* as a bed of spices,
as sweet flowers: his lips *like* lilies,
dropping sweet smelling myrrh.
14 His hands *are as* gold rings set
with the beryl: his belly *is as* bright
ivory overlaid *with* sapphires.
15 His legs *are as* pillars of marble,
set upon sockets of fine gold: his coun-
tenance *is* as Lebanon, excellent as the
cedars.
16 His mouth *is* most sweet: yea, he *is*
altogether lovely. This *is* my beloved,
and this *is* my friend, O daughters of
Jerusalem.

CHAPTER 6

WHITHER is thy beloved gone, O thou
fairest among women? whither is thy
beloved turned aside? that we may
seek him with thee.
2 ¶My beloved is gone down into his
garden, to the beds of spices, to feed in
the gardens, and to gather lilies.
3 I *am* my beloved's, and my beloved
is mine: he feedeth among the lilies.
4 ¶Thou *art* beautiful, O my love, as
Tir′zah, comely as Jerusalem, terrible
as *an army* with banners.

5 Turn away thine eyes from me, for
they have overcome me: thy hair *is* as a
flock of goats that appear from Gilead.
6 Thy teeth *are* as a flock of sheep
which go up from the washing, where-
of every one beareth twins, and
there is not one barren among them.
7 As a piece of a pomegranate *are* thy
temples within thy locks.
8 There are threescore queens, and
fourscore concubines, and virgins
without number.
9 My dove, my undefiled is *but* one;
she *is* the *only* one of her mother, she *is*
the choice *one* of her that bare her. The
daughters saw her, and blessed her;
yea, the queens and the concubines,
and they praised her.
10 ¶Who *is* she *that* looketh forth as
the morning, fair as the moon, clear as
the sun, *and* terrible as *an army* with
banners?
11 I went down into the garden of
nuts to see the fruits of the valley, *and*
to see whether the vine flourished, *and*
the pomegranates budded.
12 Or ever I was aware, my soul
made me *like* the chariots of Am-mĭ'-
na-dĭb.
13 Return, return, O Shū'lam-īte; re-
turn, return, that we may look upon
thee. What will ye see in the Shū'lam-
īte? As it were the company of two ar-
mies.

CHAPTER 7

HOW beautiful are thy feet with shoes,
O prince's daughter! the joints of thy
thighs *are* like jewels, the work of the
hands of a cunning workman.
2 Thy navel *is like* a round goblet,
which wanteth not liquor: thy belly *is*
like an heap of wheat set about with
lilies.
3 Thy two breasts *are* like two young
roes *that are* twins.
4 Thy neck *is* as a tower of ivory;
thine eyes *like* the fishpools in Hĕsh'-
bŏn, by the gate of Băth-răb'bĭm: thy
nose *is* as the tower of Lebanon which
looketh toward Damascus.
5 Thine head upon thee *is* like Car-
mel, and the hair of thine head like
purple; the king *is* held in the galleries.
6 How fair and how pleasant art thou,
O love, for delights!
7 This thy stature is like to a palm
tree, and thy breasts to clusters *of*
grapes.
8 I said, I will go up to the palm tree, I
will take hold of the boughs thereof:
now also thy breasts shall be as clusters
of the vine, and the smell of thy
nose like apples;
9 And the roof of thy mouth like the
best wine for my beloved, that goeth
down sweetly, causing the lips of those
that are asleep to speak.
10 ¶I *am* my beloved's, and his desire
is toward me.
11 Come, my beloved, let us go forth
into the field; let us lodge in the vil-
lages.
12 Let us get up early to the vine-
yards; let us see if the vine flourish,
whether the tender grape appear, *and*
the pomegranates bud forth: there will
I give thee my loves.
13 The mandrakes give a smell, and
at our gates *are* all manner of pleasant
fruits, new and old, *which* I have laid up
for thee, O my beloved.

CHAPTER 8

O THAT thou *wert* as my brother, that
sucked the breasts of my mother! *when*
I should find thee without, I would kiss
thee; yea, I should not be despised.
2 I would lead thee, *and* bring thee
into my mother's house, *who* would
instruct me: I would cause thee to drink
of spiced wine of the juice of my pome-
granate.
3 His left hand *should be* under my
head, and his right hand should em-
brace me.
4 I charge you, O daughters of Jeru-
salem, that ye stir not up, nor awake
my love, until he please.
5 ¶Who *is* this that cometh up from
the wilderness, leaning upon her be-
loved? I raised thee up under the apple
tree: there thy mother brought thee
forth: there she brought thee forth *that*
bare thee.
6 Set me as a seal upon thine heart, as
a seal upon thine arm: for love *is* strong
as death; jealousy *is* cruel as the grave:
the coals thereof *are* coals of fire,
which hath a most vehement flame.
7 Many waters cannot quench love,
neither can the floods drown it: if a man
would give all the substance of his
house for love, it would utterly be con-
temned.
8 ¶We have a little sister, and she
hath no breasts: what shall we do for
our sister in the day when she shall be
spoken for?
9 If she *be* a wall, we will build upon
her a palace of silver: and if she *be* a
door, we will inclose her with boards of
cedar.
10 I *am* a wall, and my breasts like
towers: then was I in his eyes as one
that found favour.
11 Sŏl'o-mon had a vineyard at Bā'al-
hā'mon; he let out the vineyard unto
keepers; every one for the fruit thereof

was to bring a thousand *pieces* of sil-
ver.
12 My vineyard, which *is* mine, *is* be-
fore me: thou, O Sŏl'o-mon, *must have*
a thousand, and those that keep the
fruit thereof two hundred.
13 Thou that dwellest in the gardens,
the companions hearken to thy voice:
cause me to hear *it*.
14 ¶Make haste, my beloved, and be
thou like to a roe or to a young hart
upon the mountains of spices.

THE BOOK OF THE PROPHET

ISAIAH

CHAPTER 1

THE vision of Isaiah the son of Amoz,
which he saw concerning Jū'dah and
Jerusalem in the days of Uz-zī'ah, Jō'-
tham, Ahaz, *and* Hĕz-e-kī'ah, kings of
Jū'dah.
2 ¶Hear, O heavens, and give ear, O
earth: for the LORD hath spoken, I have
nourished and brought up children,
and they have rebelled against me.
3 The ox knoweth his owner, and the
ass his master's crib: *but* Israel doth
not know, my people doth not consider.
4 Ah sinful nation, a people laden
with iniquity, a seed of evildoers, chil-
dren that are corrupters: they have for-
saken the LORD, they have provoked
the Holy One of Israel unto anger, they
are gone away backward.
5 Why should ye be stricken any
more? ye will revolt more and more:
the whole head is sick, and the whole
heart faint.
6 From the sole of the foot even unto
the head *there is* no soundness in it; *but*
wounds, and bruises, and putrifying
sores: they have not been closed,
neither bound up, neither mollified
with ointment.
7 Your country *is* desolate, your
cities *are* burned with fire: your land,
strangers devour it in your presence,
and *it is* desolate, as overthrown by
strangers.
8 And the daughter of Zion is left as a
cottage in a vineyard, as a lodge in a
garden of cucumbers, as a besieged
city.
9 Except the LORD of hosts had left
unto us a very small remnant, we
should have been as Sodom, *and* we
should have been like unto Go-mŏr'rah.
10 ¶Hear the word of the LORD, ye rul-
ers of Sodom; give ear unto the law of
our God, ye people of Go-mŏr'rah.
11 To what purpose *is* the multitude
of your sacrifices unto me? saith the
LORD: I am full of the burnt offerings of
rams, and the fat of fed beasts; and I
delight not in the blood of bullocks, or
of lambs, or of he goats.
12 When ye come to appear before
me, who hath required this at your
hand, to tread my courts?
13 Bring no more vain oblations; in-
cense is an abomination unto me; the
new moons and sabbaths, the calling of
assemblies, I cannot away with; *it is*
iniquity, even the solemn meeting.
14 Your new moons and your ap-
pointed feasts my soul hateth: they are
a trouble unto me; I am weary to bear
them.
15 And when ye spread forth your
hands, I will hide mine eyes from you:
yea, when ye make many prayers, I will
not hear: your hands are full of blood.
16 Wash you, make you clean; put
away the evil of your doings from be-
fore mine eyes; cease to do evil;
17 Learn to do well; seek judgment,
relieve the oppressed, judge the father-
less, plead for the widow.
18 ¶Come now, and let us reason
together, saith the LORD: though your
sins be as scarlet, they shall be as white
as snow; though they be red like crim-
son, they shall be as wool.
19 If ye be willing and obedient, ye
shall eat the good of the land:
20 But if ye refuse and rebel, ye shall
be devoured with the sword: for the
mouth of the LORD hath spoken *it*.
21 ¶How is the faithful city become
an harlot! it was full of judgment;
righteousness lodged in it; but now
murderers.
22 Thy silver is become dross, thy
wine mixed with water:
23 Thy princes *are* rebellious, and
companions of thieves: every one lov-
eth gifts, and followeth after rewards:
they judge not the fatherless, neither
doth the cause of the widow come unto
them.
24 Therefore saith the Lord, the LORD
of hosts, the mighty One of Israel, Ah, I
will ease me of mine adversaries, and
avenge me of mine enemies:
25 And I will turn my hand upon thee,
and purely purge away thy dross, and
take away all thy tin:
26 And I will restore thy judges as at
the first, and thy counsellors as at the
beginning: afterward thou shalt be

called, The city of righteousness, the faithful city.

27 Zion shall be redeemed with judgment, and her converts with righteousness.

28 And the destruction of the transgressors and of the sinners *shall be* together, and they that forsake the LORD shall be consumed.

29 For they shall be ashamed of the oaks which ye have desired, and ye shall be confounded for the gardens that ye have chosen.

30 For ye shall be as an oak whose leaf fadeth, and as a garden that hath no water.

31 And the strong shall be as tow, and the maker of it as a spark, and they shall both burn together, and none shall quench *them*.

CHAPTER 2

THE word that Isaiah the son of Amoz saw concerning Jū'dah and Jerusalem.

2 And it shall come to pass in the last days, *that* the mountain of the LORD's house shall be established in the top of the mountains, and shall be exalted above the hills; and all nations shall flow unto it.

3 And many people shall go and say, Come ye, and let us go up to the mountain of the LORD, to the house of the God of Jacob; and he will teach us of his ways, and we will walk in his paths: for out of Zion shall go forth the law, and the word of the LORD from Jerusalem.

4 And he shall judge among the nations, and shall rebuke many people: and they shall beat their swords into plowshares, and their spears into pruninghooks: nation shall not lift up sword against nation, neither shall they learn war any more.

5 ¶O house of Jacob, come ye, and let us walk in the light of the LORD.

6 Therefore thou hast forsaken thy people the house of Jacob, because they be replenished from the east, and *are* soothsayers like the Philistines, and they please themselves in the children of strangers.

7 Their land also is full of silver and gold, neither *is there any* end of their treasures; their land is also full of horses, neither *is there any* end of their chariots:

8 Their land also is full of idols; they worship the work of their own hands, that which their own fingers have made:

9 And the mean man boweth down, and the great man humbleth himself: therefore forgive them not.

10 ¶Enter into the rock, and hide thee in the dust, for fear of the LORD, and for the glory of his majesty.

11 The lofty looks of man shall be humbled, and the haughtiness of men shall be bowed down, and the LORD alone shall be exalted in that day.

12 For the day of the LORD of hosts *shall be* upon every *one that is* proud and lofty, and upon every *one that is* lifted up; and he shall be brought low:

13 And upon all the cedars of Lebanon, *that are* high and lifted up, and upon all the oaks of Bā'shan,

14 And upon all the high mountains, and upon all the hills *that are* lifted up,

15 And upon every high tower, and upon every fenced wall,

16 And upon all the ships of Tär'shĭsh, and upon all pleasant pictures.

17 And the loftiness of man shall be bowed down, and the haughtiness of men shall be made low: and the LORD alone shall be exalted in that day.

18 And the idols he shall utterly abolish.

19 And they shall go into the holes of the rocks, and into the caves of the earth, for fear of the LORD, and for the glory of his majesty, when he ariseth to shake terribly the earth.

20 In that day a man shall cast his idols of silver, and his idols of gold, which they made *each one* for himself to worship, to the moles and to the bats;

21 To go into the clefts of the rocks, and into the tops of the ragged rocks, for fear of the LORD, and for the glory of his majesty, when he ariseth to shake terribly the earth.

22 Cease ye from man, whose breath *is* in his nostrils: for wherein is he to be accounted of?

CHAPTER 3

FOR, behold, the Lord, the LORD of hosts, doth take away from Jerusalem and from Jū'dah the stay and the staff, the whole stay of bread, and the whole stay of water.

2 The mighty man, and the man of war, the judge, and the prophet, and the prudent, and the ancient,

3 The captain of fifty, and the honourable man, and the counsellor, and the cunning artificer, and the eloquent orator.

4 And I will give children *to be* their princes, and babes shall rule over them.

5 And the people shall be oppressed, every one by another, and every one by his neighbour: the child shall behave himself proudly against the ancient, and the base against the honourable.

6 When a man shall take hold of his

brother of the house of his father, *saying*, Thou hast clothing, be thou our ruler, and *let* this ruin *be* under thy hand:
7 In that day shall he swear, saying, I will not be an healer: for in my house *is* neither bread nor clothing: make me not a ruler of the people.
8 For Jerusalem is ruined, and Jū'dah is fallen: because their tongue and their doings *are* against the LORD, to provoke the eyes of his glory.
9 The shew of their countenance doth witness against them; and they declare their sin as Sodom, they hide *it* not. Woe unto their soul! for they have rewarded evil unto themselves.
10 Say ye to the righteous, that *it shall be* well *with him:* for they shall eat the fruit of their doings.
11 Woe unto the wicked! *it shall be* ill *with him:* for the reward of his hands shall be given him.
12 *As for* my people, children *are* their oppressors, and women rule over them. O my people, they which lead thee cause *thee* to err, and destroy the way of thy paths.
13 ¶The LORD standeth up to plead, and standeth to judge the people.
14 The LORD will enter into judgment with the ancients of his people, and the princes thereof: for ye have eaten up the vineyard; the spoil of the poor *is* in your houses.
15 What mean ye *that* ye beat my people to pieces, and grind the faces of the poor? saith the Lord GOD of hosts.
16 ¶Moreover the LORD saith, Because the daughters of Zion are haughty, and walk with stretched forth necks and wanton eyes, walking and mincing *as* they go, and making a tinkling with their feet:
17 Therefore the Lord will smite with a scab the crown of the head of the daughters of Zion, and the LORD will discover their secret parts.
18 In that day the Lord will take away the bravery of *their* tinkling ornaments *about their feet*, and *their* cauls, and *their* round tires like the moon,
19 The chains, and the bracelets, and the mufflers,
20 The bonnets, and the ornaments of the legs, and the headbands, and the tablets, and the earrings,
21 The rings, and nose jewels,
22 The changeable suits of apparel, and the mantles, and the wimples, and the crisping pins,
23 The glasses, and the fine linen, and the hoods, and the vails.
24 And it shall come to pass, *that* instead of sweet smell there shall be stink; and instead of a girdle a rent; and instead of well set hair baldness; and instead of a stomacher a girding of sackcloth; *and* burning instead of beauty.
25 Thy men shall fall by the sword, and thy mighty in the war.
26 And her gates shall lament and mourn; and she *being* desolate shall sit upon the ground.

CHAPTER 4

AND in that day seven women shall take hold of one man, saying, We will eat our own bread, and wear our own apparel: only let us be called by thy name, to take away our reproach.
2 ¶In that day shall the branch of the LORD be beautiful and glorious, and the fruit of the earth *shall be* excellent and comely for them that are escaped of Israel.
3 And it shall come to pass, *that he that is* left in Zion, and *he that* remaineth in Jerusalem, shall be called holy, *even* every one that is written among the living in Jerusalem:
4 When the Lord shall have washed away the filth of the daughters of Zion, and shall have purged the blood of Jerusalem from the midst thereof by the spirit of judgment, and by the spirit of burning.
5 And the LORD will create upon every dwelling place of mount Zion, and upon her assemblies, a cloud and smoke by day, and the shining of a flaming fire by night: for upon all the glory *shall be* a defence.
6 And there shall be a tabernacle for a shadow in the daytime from the heat, and for a place of refuge, and for a covert from storm and from rain.

CHAPTER 5

NOW will I sing to my wellbeloved a song of my beloved touching his vineyard. My wellbeloved hath a vineyard in a very fruitful hill:
2 And he fenced it, and gathered out the stones thereof, and planted it with the choicest vine, and built a tower in the midst of it, and also made a winepress therein: and he looked that it should bring forth grapes, and it brought forth wild grapes.
3 And now, O inhabitants of Jerusalem, and men of Jū'dah, judge, I pray you, betwixt me and my vineyard.
4 What could have been done more to my vineyard, that I have not done in it? wherefore, when I looked that it should bring forth grapes, brought it forth wild grapes?
5 And now go to; I will tell you what I

will do to my vineyard: I will take away
the hedge thereof, and it shall be eaten
up; *and* break down the wall thereof,
and it shall be trodden down:
6 And I will lay it waste: it shall not be
pruned, nor digged; but there shall
come up briers and thorns: I will also
command the clouds that they rain no
rain upon it.
7 For the vineyard of the LORD of
hosts *is* the house of Israel, and the
men of Jū'dah his pleasant plant: and
he looked for judgment, but behold op-
pression; for righteousness, but behold
a cry.
8 ¶Woe unto them that join house to
house, *that* lay field to field, till *there be*
no place, that they may be placed alone
in the midst of the earth!
9 In mine ears *said* the LORD of hosts,
Of a truth many houses shall be deso-
late, *even* great and fair, without
inhabitant.
10 Yea, ten acres of vineyard shall
yield one bath, and the seed of an
homer shall yield an ephah.
11 ¶Woe unto them that rise up early
in the morning, *that* they may follow
strong drink; that continue until night,
till wine inflame them!
12 And the harp, and the viol, the
tabret, and pipe, and wine, are in their
feasts: but they regard not the work of
the LORD, neither consider the opera-
tion of his hands.
13 Therefore my people are gone into
captivity, because *they have* no knowl-
edge: and their honourable men *are*
famished, and their multitude dried up
with thirst.
14 Therefore hell hath enlarged her-
self, and opened her mouth without
measure: and their glory, and their
multitude, and their pomp, and he that
rejoiceth, shall descend into it.
15 And the mean man shall be
brought down, and the mighty man
shall be humbled, and the eyes of the
lofty shall be humbled:
16 But the LORD of hosts shall be ex-
alted in judgment, and God that is holy
shall be sanctified in righteousness.
17 Then shall the lambs feed after
their manner, and the waste places of
the fat ones shall strangers eat.
18 ¶Woe unto them that draw iniq-
uity with cords of vanity, and sin as it
were with a cart rope:
19 That say, Let him make speed, *and*
hasten his work, that we may see *it:*
and let the counsel of the Holy One of
Israel draw nigh and come, that we
may know *it!*
20 Woe unto them that call evil good,
and good evil; that put darkness for
light, and light for darkness; that put
bitter for sweet, and sweet for bitter!
21 Woe unto *them that are* wise in
their own eyes, and prudent in their
own sight!
22 Woe unto *them that are* mighty to
drink wine, and men of strength to
mingle strong drink:
23 Which justify the wicked for re-
ward, and take away the righteousness
of the righteous from him!
24 Therefore as the fire devoureth the
stubble, and the flame consumeth the
chaff, *so* their root shall be as rotten-
ness, and their blossom shall go up as
dust: because they have cast away the
law of the LORD of hosts, and despised
the word of the Holy One of Israel.
25 Therefore is the anger of the LORD
kindled against his people, and he hath
stretched forth his hand against them,
and hath smitten them: and the hills did
tremble, and their carcases *were* torn
in the midst of the streets. For all this
his anger is not turned away, but his
hand *is* stretched out still.
26 ¶And he will lift up an ensign to
the nations from far, and will hiss unto
them from the end of the earth: and,
behold, they shall come with speed
swiftly:
27 None shall be weary nor stumble
among them; none shall slumber nor
sleep; neither shall the girdle of their
loins be loosed, nor the latchet of their
shoes be broken:
28 Whose arrows *are* sharp, and all
their bows bent, their horses' hoofs
shall be counted like flint, and their
wheels like a whirlwind:
29 Their roaring *shall be* like a lion,
they shall roar like young lions: yea,
they shall roar, and lay hold of the prey,
and shall carry *it* away safe, and none
shall deliver *it.*
30 And in that day they shall roar
against them like the roaring of the sea:
and if *one* look unto the land, behold
darkness *and* sorrow, and the light is
darkened in the heavens thereof.

CHAPTER 6

IN the year that king Uz-zī'ah died I
saw also the Lord sitting upon a throne,
high and lifted up, and his train filled
the temple.
2 Above it stood the seraphims: each
one had six wings; with twain he
covered his face, and with twain he
covered his feet, and with twain he did
fly.
3 And one cried unto another, and
said, Holy, holy, holy, *is* the LORD of
hosts: the whole earth *is* full of his
glory.

4 And the posts of the door moved at the voice of him that cried, and the house was filled with smoke.

5 Then said I, Woe *is* me! for I am undone; because I *am* a man of unclean lips, and I dwell in the midst of a people of unclean lips: for mine eyes have seen the King, the LORD of hosts.

6 Then flew one of the seraphims unto me, having a live coal in his hand, *which* he had taken with the tongs from off the altar:

7 And he laid *it* upon my mouth, and said, Lo, this hath touched thy lips; and thine iniquity is taken away, and thy sin purged.

8 Also I heard the voice of the Lord, saying, Whom shall I send, and who will go for us? Then said I, Here *am* I; send me.

9 And he said, Go, and tell this people, Hear ye indeed, but understand not; and see ye indeed, but perceive not.

10 Make the heart of this people fat, and make their ears heavy, and shut their eyes; lest they see with their eyes, and hear with their ears, and understand with their heart, and convert, and be healed.

11 Then said I, Lord, how long? And he answered, Until the cities be wasted without inhabitant, and the houses without man, and the land be utterly desolate,

12 And the LORD have removed men far away, and *there be* a great forsaking in the midst of the land.

13 But yet in it *shall be* a tenth, and *it* shall return, and shall be eaten: as a teil tree, and as an oak, whose substance *is* in them, when they cast *their leaves: so* the holy seed *shall be* the substance thereof.

CHAPTER 7

AND it came to pass in the days of Ahaz the son of Jō'tham, the son of Uzzī'ah, king of Jū'dah, *that* Rē'zĭn the king of Syria, and Pē'kah the son of Rĕm-a-lī'ah, king of Israel, went up toward Jerusalem to war against it, but could not prevail against it.

2 And it was told the house of David, saying, Syria is confederate with Ē'phra-im. And his heart was moved, and the heart of his people, as the trees of the wood are moved with the wind.

3 Then said the LORD unto Isaiah, Go forth now to meet Ahaz, thou, and Shē'ar–jā'shub thy son, at the end of the conduit of the upper pool in the highway of the fuller's field;

4 And say unto him, Take heed, and be quiet; fear not, neither be fainthearted for the two tails of these smoking firebrands, for the fierce anger of Rē'zĭn with Syria, and of the son of Rĕm-a-lī'ah.

5 Because Syria, Ē'phra-im, and the son of Rĕm-a-lī'ah, have taken evil counsel against thee, saying,

6 Let us go up against Jū'dah, and vex it, and let us make a breach therein for us, and set a king in the midst of it, *even* the son of Tā'be-al:

7 Thus saith the Lord GOD, It shall not stand, neither shall it come to pass.

8 For the head of Syria *is* Damascus, and the head of Damascus *is* Rē'zĭn; and within threescore and five years shall Ē'phra-im be broken, that it be not a people.

9 And the head of Ē'phra-im *is* Sa-mâ'rĭ-a, and the head of Sa-mâ'rĭ-a *is* Rĕm-a-lī'ah's son. If ye will not believe, surely ye shall not be established.

10 ¶Moreover the LORD spake again unto Ahaz, saying,

11 Ask thee a sign of the LORD thy God; ask it either in the depth, or in the height above.

12 But Ahaz said, I will not ask, neither will I tempt the LORD.

13 And he said, Hear ye now, O house of David; *Is it* a small thing for you to weary men, but will ye weary my God also?

14 Therefore the Lord himself shall give you a sign; Behold, a virgin shall conceive, and bear a son, and shall call his name Ĭm-măn'ū-el.

15 Butter and honey shall he eat, that he may know to refuse the evil, and choose the good.

16 For before the child shall know to refuse the evil, and choose the good, the land that thou abhorrest shall be forsaken of both her kings.

17 ¶The LORD shall bring upon thee, and upon thy people, and upon thy father's house, days that have not come from the day that Ē'phra-im departed from Jū'dah; *even* the king of Assyria.

18 And it shall come to pass in that day, *that* the LORD shall hiss for the fly that *is* in the uttermost part of the rivers of Egypt, and for the bee that *is* in the land of Assyria.

19 And they shall come, and shall rest all of them in the desolate valleys, and in the holes of the rocks, and upon all thorns, and upon all bushes.

20 In the same day shall the Lord shave with a razor that is hired, *namely*, by them beyond the river, by the king of Assyria, the head, and the hair of the feet: and it shall also consume the beard.

21 And it shall come to pass in that

day, *that* a man shall nourish a young cow, and two sheep;
22 And it shall come to pass, for the abundance of milk *that* they shall give he shall eat butter: for butter and honey shall every one eat that is left in the land.
23 And it shall come to pass in that day, *that* every place shall be, where there were a thousand vines at a thousand silverlings, it shall *even* be for briers and thorns.
24 With arrows and with bows shall *men* come thither; because all the land shall become briers and thorns.
25 And *on* all hills that shall be digged with the mattock, there shall not come thither the fear of briers and thorns: but it shall be for the sending forth of oxen, and for the treading of lesser cattle.

CHAPTER 8

MOREOVER the LORD said unto me, Take thee a great roll, and write in it with a man's pen concerning Mā'-her-shăl'al-hăsh'-băz.
2 And I took unto me faithful witnesses to record, Ū-rī'ah the priest, and Zĕch-a-rī'ah the son of Je-bĕr-e-chī'ah.
3 And I went unto the prophetess; and she conceived, and bare a son. Then said the LORD to me, Call his name Mā'her-shăl'al-hăsh'-băz.
4 For before the child shall have knowledge to cry, My father, and my mother, the riches of Damascus and the spoil of Sa-mâ'rī-a shall be taken away before the king of Assyria.
5 ¶The LORD spake also unto me again, saying,
6 Forasmuch as this people refuseth the waters of Shī-lō'ah that go softly, and rejoice in Rē'zīn and Rĕm-a-lī'ah's son;
7 Now therefore, behold, the Lord bringeth up upon them the waters of the river, strong and many, *even* the king of Assyria, and all his glory: and he shall come up over all his channels, and go over all his banks:
8 And he shall pass through Jū'dah; he shall overflow and go over, he shall reach *even* to the neck; and the stretching out of his wings shall fill the breadth of thy land, O Ĭm-măn'ū-el.
9 ¶Associate yourselves, O ye people, and ye shall be broken in pieces; and give ear, all ye of far countries: gird yourselves, and ye shall be broken in pieces; gird yourselves, and ye shall be broken in pieces.
10 Take counsel together, and it shall come to nought; speak the word, and it shall not stand: for God *is* with us.
11 For the LORD spake thus to me with a strong hand, and instructed me that I should not walk in the way of this people, saying,
12 Say ye not, A confederacy, to all *them to* whom this people shall say, A confederacy; neither fear ye their fear, nor be afraid.
13 Sanctify the LORD of hosts himself; and *let* him *be* your fear, and *let* him *be* your dread.
14 And he shall be for a sanctuary; but for a stone of stumbling and for a rock of offence to both the houses of Israel, for a gin and for a snare to the inhabitants of Jerusalem.
15 And many among them shall stumble, and fall, and be broken, and be snared, and be taken.
16 Bind up the testimony, seal the law among my disciples.
17 And I will wait upon the LORD, that hideth his face from the house of Jacob, and I will look for him.
18 Behold, I and the children whom the LORD hath given me *are* for signs and for wonders in Israel from the LORD of hosts, which dwelleth in mount Zion.
19 And when they shall say unto you, Seek unto them that have familiar spirits, and unto wizards that peep, and that mutter: should not a people seek unto their God? for the living to the dead?
20 To the law and to the testimony: if they speak not according to this word, *it is* because *there is* no light in them.
21 And they shall pass through it, hardly bestead and hungry: and it shall come to pass, that when they shall be hungry, they shall fret themselves, and curse their king and their God, and look upward.
22 And they shall look unto the earth; and behold trouble and darkness, dimness of anguish; and *they shall be* driven to darkness.

CHAPTER 9

NEVERTHELESS the dimness *shall* not *be* such as *was* in her vexation, when at the first he lightly afflicted the land of Zĕb'u-lun and the land of Năph'ta-lī, and afterward did more grievously afflict *her by* the way of the sea, beyond Jordan, in Galilee of the nations.
2 The people that walked in darkness have seen a great light: they that dwell in the land of the shadow of death, upon them hath the light shined.
3 Thou hast multiplied the nation, *and* not increased the joy: they joy before thee according to the joy in har-

vest, *and* as *men* rejoice when they di-
vide the spoil.
4 For thou hast broken the yoke of his
burden, and the staff of his shoulder,
the rod of his oppressor, as in the day of
Mĭd'ĭ-an.
5 For every battle of the warrior *is*
with confused noise, and garments
rolled in blood; but *this* shall be with
burning *and* fuel of fire.
6 For unto us a child is born, unto us a
son is given: and the government shall
be upon his shoulder: and his name
shall be called Wonderful, Counsellor,
The mighty God, The everlasting
Father, The Prince of Peace.
7 Of the increase of *his* government
and peace *there shall be* no end, upon
the throne of David, and upon his king-
dom, to order it, and to establish it with
judgment and with justice from hence-
forth even for ever. The zeal of the
LORD of hosts will perform this.
8 ¶The Lord sent a word into Jacob,
and it hath lighted upon Israel.
9 And all the people shall know, *even*
Ē'phra-im and the inhabitant of Sa-
mâ'rĭ-a, that say in the pride and stout-
ness of heart,
10 The bricks are fallen down, but we
will build with hewn stones: the syco-
mores are cut down, but we will change
them into cedars.
11 Therefore the LORD shall set up the
adversaries of Rē'zĭn against him, and
join his enemies together;
12 The Syrians before, and the Philis-
tines behind; and they shall devour
Israel with open mouth. For all this his
anger is not turned away, but his hand
is stretched out still.
13 ¶For the people turneth not unto
him that smiteth them, neither do they
seek the LORD of hosts.
14 Therefore the LORD will cut off
from Israel head and tail, branch and
rush, in one day.
15 The ancient and honourable, he *is*
the head; and the prophet that teacheth
lies, he *is* the tail.
16 For the leaders of this people
cause *them* to err; and *they that are* led
of them *are* destroyed.
17 Therefore the Lord shall have no
joy in their young men, neither shall
have mercy on their fatherless and wid-
ows: for every one *is* an hypocrite and
an evildoer, and every mouth speaketh
folly. For all this his anger is not turned
away, but his hand *is* stretched out still.
18 ¶For wickedness burneth as the
fire: it shall devour the briers and
thorns, and shall kindle in the thickets
of the forest, and they shall mount up
like the lifting up of smoke.
19 Through the wrath of the LORD of
hosts is the land darkened, and the
people shall be as the fuel of the fire: no
man shall spare his brother.
20 And he shall snatch on the right
hand, and be hungry; and he shall eat
on the left hand, and they shall not be
satisfied: they shall eat every man the
flesh of his own arm:
21 Ma-năs'seh, Ē'phra-im; and Ē'
phra-im, Ma-năs'seh: *and* they togeth-
er *shall be* against Jū'dah. For all this
his anger is not turned away, but his
hand *is* stretched out still.

CHAPTER 10

WOE unto them that decree un-
righteous decrees, and that write griev-
ousness *which* they have prescribed.
2 To turn aside the needy from judg-
ment, and to take away the right from
the poor of my people, that widows
may be their prey, and *that* they may
rob the fatherless!
3 And what will ye do in the day of
visitation, and in the desolation *which*
shall come from far? to whom will ye
flee for help? and where will ye leave
your glory?
4 Without me they shall bow down
under the prisoners, and they shall fall
under the slain. For all this his anger is
not turned away, but his hand *is*
stretched out still.
5 ¶O Assyrian, the rod of mine anger,
and the staff in their hand is mine indig-
nation.
6 I will send him against an hypocriti-
cal nation, and against the people of my
wrath will I give him a charge, to take
the spoil, and to take the prey, and to
tread them down like the mire of the
streets.
7 Howbeit he meaneth not so, neither
doth his heart think so; but *it is* in his
heart to destroy and cut off nations not
a few.
8 For he saith, *Are* not my princes al-
together kings?
9 *Is* not Căl'nō as Cär'che-mĭsh? *is*
not Hā'măth as Är'păd? *is* not Sa-mâ'-
rĭ-a as Damascus?
10 As my hand hath found the king-
doms of the idols, and whose graven
images did excel them of Jerusalem
and of Sa-mâ'rĭ-a:
11 Shall I not, as I have done unto Sa-
mâ'rĭ-a and her idols, so do to Jeru-
salem and her idols?
12 Wherefore it shall come to pass,
that when the Lord hath performed his
whole work upon mount Zion and on
Jerusalem, I will punish the fruit of the
stout heart of the king of Assyria, and
the glory of his high looks.

13 For he saith, By the strength of my hand I have done *it*, and by my wisdom; for I am prudent: and I have removed the bounds of the people, and have robbed their treasures, and I have put down the inhabitants like a valiant *man:*

14 And my hand hath found as a nest the riches of the people: and as one gathereth eggs *that are* left, have I gathered all the earth; and there was none that moved the wing, or opened the mouth, or peeped.

15 Shall the axe boast itself against him that heweth therewith? *or* shall the saw magnify itself against him that shaketh it? as if the rod should shake *itself* against them that lift it up, *or* as if the staff should lift up *itself, as if it were* no wood.

16 Therefore shall the Lord, the Lord of hosts, send among his fat ones leanness; and under his glory he shall kindle a burning like the burning of a fire.

17 And the light of Israel shall be for a fire, and his Holy One for a flame: and it shall burn and devour his thorns and his briers in one day;

18 And shall consume the glory of his forest, and of his fruitful field, both soul and body: and they shall be as when a standardbearer fainteth.

19 And the rest of the trees of his forest shall be few, that a child may write them.

20 ¶And it shall come to pass in that day, *that* the remnant of Israel, and such as are escaped of the house of Jacob, shall no more again stay upon him that smote them; but shall stay upon the LORD, the Holy One of Israel, in truth.

21 The remnant shall return, *even* the remnant of Jacob, unto the mighty God.

22 For though thy people Israel be as the sand of the sea, *yet* a remnant of them shall return: the consumption decreed shall overflow with righteousness.

23 For the Lord GOD of hosts shall make a consumption, even determined, in the midst of all the land.

24 ¶Therefore thus saith the Lord GOD of hosts, O my people that dwellest in Zion, be not afraid of the Assyrian: he shall smite thee with a rod, and shall lift up his staff against thee, after the manner of Egypt.

25 For yet a very little while, and the indignation shall cease, and mine anger in their destruction.

26 And the LORD of hosts shall stir up a scourge for him according to the slaughter of Mĭd'ĭ-an at the rock of Ō'reb: and *as* his rod *was* upon the sea, so shall he lift it up after the manner of Egypt.

27 And it shall come to pass in that day, *that* his burden shall be taken away from off thy shoulder, and his yoke from off thy neck, and the yoke shall be destroyed because of the anointing.

28 He is come to Ā-i'āth, he is passed to Mĭg'rŏn; at Mĭch'măsh he hath laid up his carriages:

29 They are gone over the passage: they have taken up their lodging at Gē'ba; Rā'mah is afraid; Gĭb'e-ah of Saul is fled.

30 Lift up thy voice, O daughter of Găl'lĭm: cause it to be heard unto Lā'ĭsh, O poor Ăn'a-thŏth.

31 Măd-mē'nah is removed; the inhabitants of Gē'bĭm gather themselves to flee.

32 As yet shall he remain at Nob that day: he shall shake his hand *against* the mount of the daughter of Zion, the hill of Jerusalem.

33 Behold, the Lord, the LORD of hosts, shall lop the bough with terror: and the high ones of stature *shall* be hewn down, and the haughty shall be humbled.

34 And he shall cut down the thickets of the forest with iron, and Lebanon shall fall by a mighty one.

CHAPTER 11

AND there shall come forth a rod out of the stem of Jesse, and a Branch shall grow out of his roots:

2 And the spirit of the LORD shall rest upon him, the spirit of wisdom and understanding, the spirit of counsel and might, the spirit of knowledge and of the fear of the LORD;

3 And shall make him of quick understanding in the fear of the LORD: and he shall not judge after the sight of his eyes, neither reprove after the hearing of his ears:

4 But with righteousness shall he judge the poor, and reprove with equity for the meek of the earth: and he shall smite the earth: with the rod of his mouth, and with the breath of his lips shall he slay the wicked.

5 And righteousness shall be the girdle of his loins, and faithfulness the girdle of his reins.

6 The wolf also shall dwell with the lamb, and the leopard shall lie down with the kid; and the calf and the young lion and the fatling together; and a little child shall lead them.

7 And the cow and the bear shall

feed; their young ones shall lie down together: and the lion shall eat straw like the ox.

8 And the sucking child shall play on the hole of the asp, and the weaned child shall put his hand on the cockatrice' den.

9 They shall not hurt nor destroy in all my holy mountain: for the earth shall be full of the knowledge of the LORD, as the waters cover the sea.

10 And in that day there shall be a root of Jesse, which shall stand for an ensign of the people; to it shall the Gentiles seek: and his rest shall be glorious.

11 And it shall come to pass in that day, *that* the Lord shall set his hand again the second time to recover the remnant of his people, which shall be left, from Assyria, and from Egypt, and from Păth'rŏs, and from Cush, and from Ē'lam, and from Shī'när, and from Hā'măth, and from the islands of the sea.

12 And he shall set up an ensign for the nations, and shall assemble the outcasts of Israel, and gather together the dispersed of Jū'dah from the four corners of the earth.

13 The envy also of Ē'phra-im shall depart, and the adversaries of Jū'dah shall be cut off: Ē'phra-im shall not envy Jū'dah, and Jū'dah shall not vex Ē'phra-im.

14 But they shall fly upon the shoulders of the Philistines toward the west; they shall spoil them of the east together: they shall lay their hand upon Ē'dom and Moab; and the children of Ammon shall obey them.

15 And the LORD shall utterly destroy the tongue of the Egyptian sea; and with his mighty wind shall he shake his hand over the river, and shall smite it in the seven streams, and make *men* go over dryshod.

16 And there shall be an highway for the remnant of his people, which shall be left, from Assyria; like as it was to Israel in the day that he came up out of the land of Egypt.

CHAPTER 12

AND in that day thou shalt say, O LORD, I will praise thee: though thou wast angry with me, thine anger is turned away, and thou comfortedst me.

2 Behold, God *is* my salvation; I will trust, and not be afraid: for the LORD JEHOVAH *is* my strength and *my* song; he also is become my salvation.

3 Therefore with joy shall ye draw water out of the wells of salvation.

4 And in that day shall ye say, Praise the LORD, call upon his name, declare his doings among the people, make mention that his name is exalted.

5 Sing unto the LORD; for he hath done excellent things: this *is* known in all the earth.

6 Cry out and shout, thou inhabitant of Zion: for great *is* the Holy One of Israel in the midst of thee.

CHAPTER 13

THE burden of Babylon, which Isaiah the son of Amoz did see.

2 Lift ye up a banner upon the high mountain, exalt the voice unto them, shake the hand, that they may go into the gates of the nobles.

3 I have commanded my sanctified ones, I have also called my mighty ones for mine anger, *even* them that rejoice in my highness.

4 The noise of a multitude in the mountains, like as of a great people; a tumultuous noise of the kingdoms of nations gathered together: the LORD of hosts mustereth the host of the battle.

5 They come from a far country, from the end of heaven, *even* the LORD, and the weapons of his indignation, to destroy the whole land.

6 ¶Howl ye; for the day of the LORD *is* at hand; it shall come as a destruction from the Almighty.

7 Therefore shall all hands be faint, and every man's heart shall melt:

8 And they shall be afraid: pangs and sorrows shall take hold of them; they shall be in pain as a woman that travaileth: they shall be amazed one at another; their faces *shall be as* flames.

9 Behold, the day of the LORD cometh, cruel both with wrath and fierce anger, to lay the land desolate: and he shall destroy the sinners thereof out of it.

10 For the stars of heaven and the constellations thereof shall not give their light: the sun shall be darkened in his going forth, and the moon shall not cause her light to shine.

11 And I will punish the world for *their* evil, and the wicked for their iniquity; and I will cause the arrogancy of the proud to cease, and will lay low the haughtiness of the terrible.

12 I will make a man more precious than fine gold; even a man than the golden wedge of Ō'phir.

13 Therefore I will shake the heavens, and the earth shall remove out of her place, in the wrath of the LORD of hosts, and in the day of his fierce anger.

14 And it shall be as the chased roe, and as a sheep that no man taketh up: they shall every man turn to his own people, and flee every one into his own land.

15 Every one that is found shall be
thrust through; and every one that is
joined *unto them* shall fall by the
sword.
16 Their children also shall be dashed
to pieces before their eyes; their houses
shall be spoiled, and their wives rav-
ished.
17 Behold, I will stir up the Medes
against them, which shall not regard
silver; and *as for* gold, they shall not
delight in it.
18 *Their* bows also shall dash the
young men to pieces; and they shall
have no pity on the fruit of the womb;
their eye shall not spare children.
19 And Babylon, the glory of king-
doms, the beauty of the Chăl′deēs′ ex-
cellency, shall be as when God over-
threw Sodom and Go-mŏr′rah.
20 It shall never be inhabited, neither
shall it be dwelt in from generation to
generation: neither shall the Arabian
pitch tent there; neither shall the
shepherds make their fold there.
21 But wild beasts of the desert shall
lie there; and their houses shall be full
of doleful creatures; and owls shall
dwell there, and satyrs shall dance
there.
22 And the wild beasts of the islands
shall cry in their desolate houses, and
dragons in *their* pleasant palaces: and
her time *is* near to come, and her days
shall not be prolonged.

CHAPTER 14

FOR the LORD will have mercy on Ja-
cob, and will yet choose Israel, and set
them in their own land: and the strang-
ers shall be joined with them, and they
shall cleave to the house of Jacob.
2 And the people shall take them, and
bring them to their place: and the house
of Israel shall possess them in the land
of the LORD for servants and hand-
maids: and they shall take them cap-
tives, whose captives they were; and
they shall rule over their oppressors.
3 And it shall come to pass in the day
that the LORD shall give thee rest from
thy sorrow, and from thy fear, and
from the hard bondage wherein thou
wast made to serve,
4 That thou shalt take up this proverb
against the king of Babylon, and say,
How hath the oppressor ceased! the
golden city ceased!
5 The LORD hath broken the staff of
the wicked, *and* the sceptre of the rul-
ers.
6 He who smote the people in wrath
with a continual stroke, he that ruled
the nations in anger, is persecuted, *and*
none hindereth.
7 The whole earth is at rest, *and* is
quiet: they break forth into singing.
8 Yea, the fir trees rejoice at thee, *and*
the cedars of Lebanon, *saying,* Since
thou art laid down, no feller is come up
against us.
9 Hell from beneath is moved for thee
to meet *thee* at thy coming: it stirreth
up the dead for thee, *even* all the chief
ones of the earth; it hath raised up from
their thrones all the kings of the na-
tions.
10 All they shall speak and say unto
thee, Art thou also become weak as
we? art thou become like unto us?
11 Thy pomp is brought down to the
grave, *and* the noise of thy viols: the
worm is spread under thee, and the
worms cover thee.
12 How art thou fallen from heaven,
O Lū′cĭf-er, son of the morning! *how* art
thou cut down to the ground, which
didst weaken the nations!
13 For thou hast said in thine heart, I
will ascend into heaven, I will exalt my
throne above the stars of God: I will sit
also upon the mount of the congrega-
tion, in the sides of the north:
14 I will ascend above the heights of
the clouds; I will be like the most High.
15 Yet thou shalt be brought down to
hell, to the sides of the pit.
16 They that see thee shall narrowly
look upon thee, *and* consider thee,
saying, Is this the man that made the
earth to tremble, that did shake king-
doms;
17 *That* made the world as a wilder-
ness, and destroyed the cities thereof;
that opened not the house of his prison-
ers?
18 All the kings of the nations, *even*
all of them, lie in glory, every one in his
own house.
19 But thou art cast out of thy grave
like an abominable branch, *and as* the
raiment of those that are slain, thrust
through with a sword, that go down to
the stones of the pit; as a carcase trod-
den under feet.
20 Thou shalt not be joined with them
in burial, because thou hast destroyed
thy land, *and* slain thy people: the seed
of evildoers shall never be renowned.
21 Prepare slaughter for his children
for the iniquity of their fathers; that
they do not rise, nor possess the land,
nor fill the face of the world with cities.
22 For I will rise up against them,
saith the LORD of hosts, and cut off
from Babylon the name, and remnant,
and son, and nephew, saith the LORD.
23 I will also make it a possession for
the bittern, and pools of water: and I

will sweep it with the besom of destruc-
tion, saith the LORD of hosts.
24 ¶The LORD of hosts hath sworn,
saying, Surely as I have thought, so
shall it come to pass; and as I have pur-
posed, *so* shall it stand:
25 That I will break the Assyrian in
my land, and upon my mountains tread
him under foot: then shall his yoke de-
part from off them, and his burden de-
part from off their shoulders.
26 This *is* the purpose that is pur-
posed upon the whole earth: and this *is*
the hand that is stretched out upon all
the nations.
27 For the LORD of hosts hath pur-
posed, and who shall disannul *it?* and
his hand *is* stretched out, and who shall
turn it back?
28 ¶In the year that king Ahaz died
was this burden.
29 ¶Rejoice not thou, whole Pales-
tina, because the rod of him that smote
thee is broken: for out of the serpent's
root shall come forth a cockatrice, and
his fruit *shall be* a fiery flying serpent.
30 And the firstborn of the poor shall
feed, and the needy shall lie down in
safety: and I will kill thy root with
famine, and he shall slay thy remnant.
31 Howl, O gate; cry, O city; thou,
whole Palestina, *art* dissolved: for
there shall come from the north a
smoke, and none *shall be* alone in his
appointed times.
32 What shall *one* then answer the
messengers of the nation? That the
LORD hath founded Zion, and the poor
of his people shall trust in it.

CHAPTER 15

THE burden of Moab. Because in the
night Ar of Moab is laid waste, *and*
brought to silence; because in the night
Kir of Moab is laid waste, *and* brought
to silence;
2 He is gone up to Bā'jĭth, and to Dī'-
bŏn, the high places, to weep: Moab
shall howl over Nebo, and over Mĕd'e-
ba: on all their heads *shall be* baldness,
and every beard cut off.
3 In their streets they shall gird them-
selves with sackcloth: on the tops of
their houses, and in their streets, every
one shall howl, weeping abundantly.
4 And Hĕsh'bŏn shall cry, and Ĕ-le-
ā'leh: their voices shall be heard *even*
unto Jā'hăz: therefore the armed sol-
diers of Moab shall cry out; his life shall
be grievous unto him.
5 My heart shall cry out for Moab; his
fugitives *shall flee* unto Zō'ar, an heifer
of three years old: for by the mounting
up of Lū'hĭth with weeping shall they
go it up; for in the way of Hôr-o-nā'im
they shall raise up a cry of destruction.
6 For the waters of Nĭm'rĭm shall be
desolate: for the hay is withered away,
the grass faileth, there is no green
thing.
7 Therefore the abundance they have
gotten, and that which they have laid
up, shall they carry away to the brook
of the willows.
8 For the cry is gone round about the
borders of Moab; the howling thereof
unto Ĕg'la-im, and the howling thereof
unto Be'er–ē'lĭm.
9 For the waters of Dī'mon shall be
full of blood: for I will bring more upon
Dī'mon, lions upon him that escapeth
of Moab, and upon the remnant of the
land.

CHAPTER 16

SEND ye the lamb to the ruler of the
land from Sē'la to the wilderness, unto
the mount of the daughter of Zion.
2 For it shall be, *that*, as a wandering
bird cast out of the nest, *so* the daugh-
ters of Moab shall be at the fords of
Arnon.
3 Take counsel, execute judgment;
make thy shadow as the night in the
midst of the noonday; hide the out-
casts; bewray not him that wandereth.
4 Let mine outcasts dwell with thee,
Moab; be thou a covert to them from
the face of the spoiler: for the extortion-
er is at an end, the spoiler ceaseth, the
oppressors are consumed out of the
land.
5 And in mercy shall the throne be es-
tablished: and he shall sit upon it in
truth in the tabernacle of David, judg-
ing, and seeking judgment, and hasting
righteousness.
6 ¶We have heard of the pride of
Moab; *he is* very proud: *even* of his
haughtiness, and his pride, and his
wrath: *but* his lies *shall* not *be* so.
7 Therefore shall Moab howl for
Moab, every one shall howl: for the
foundations of Kĭr–hăr'e-sĕth shall ye
mourn; surely *they are* stricken.
8 For the fields of Hĕsh'bŏn languish,
and the vine of Sĭb'mah: the lords of the
heathen have broken down the prin-
cipal plants thereof, they are come
even unto Jā'zer, they wandered
through the wilderness: her branches
are stretched out, they are gone over
the sea.
9 Therefore I will bewail with the
weeping of Jā'zer the vine of Sĭb'mah: I
will water thee with my tears, O Hĕsh'-
bŏn, and Ĕ-le-ā'leh: for the shouting for
thy summer fruits and for thy harvest
is fallen.

10 And gladness is taken away, and joy out of the plentiful field; and in the vineyards there shall be no singing, neither shall there be shouting: the treaders shall tread out no wine in *their* presses; I have made *their vintage* shouting to cease.

11 Wherefore my bowels shall sound like an harp for Moab, and mine inward parts for Kĭr–hă'rĕsh.

12 And it shall come to pass, when it is seen that Moab is weary on the high place, that he shall come to his sanctuary to pray; but he shall not prevail.

13 This *is* the word that the Lord hath spoken concerning Moab since that time.

14 But now the Lord hath spoken, saying, Within three years, as the years of an hireling, and the glory of Moab shall be contemned, with all that great multitude; and the remnant *shall be* very small *and* feeble.

CHAPTER 17

THE burden of Damascus. Behold, Damascus is taken away from *being* a city, and it shall be a ruinous heap.

2 The cities of Ar'ō-er *are* forsaken: they shall be for flocks, which shall lie down, and none shall make *them* afraid.

3 The fortress also shall cease from Ē'phra-im, and the kingdom from Damascus, and the remnant of Syria: they shall be as the glory of the children of Israel, saith the Lord of hosts.

4 And in that day it shall come to pass, *that* the glory of Jacob shall be made thin, and the fatness of his flesh shall wax lean.

5 And it shall be as when the harvestman gathereth the corn, and reapeth the ears with his arm; and it shall be as he that gathereth ears in the valley of Rĕph'a-im.

6 Yet gleaning grapes shall be left in it, as the shaking of an olive tree, two *or* three berries in the top of the uppermost bough, four *or* five in the outmost fruitful branches thereof, saith the Lord God of Israel.

7 At that day shall a man look to his Maker, and his eyes shall have respect to the Holy One of Israel.

8 And he shall not look to the altars, the work of his hands, neither shall respect *that* which his fingers have made, either the groves, or the images.

9 In that day shall his strong cities be as a forsaken bough, and an uppermost branch, which they left because of the children of Israel: and there shall be desolation.

10 Because thou hast forgotten the God of thy salvation, and hast not been mindful of the rock of thy strength, therefore shalt thou plant pleasant plants, and shalt set it with strange slips:

11 In the day shalt thou make thy plant to grow, and in the morning shalt thou make thy seed to flourish: *but* the harvest *shall be* a heap in the day of grief and of desperate sorrow.

12 ¶Woe to the multitude of many people, *which* make a noise like the noise of the seas; and to the rushing of nations, *that* make a rushing like the rushing of mighty waters!

13 The nations shall rush like the rushing of many waters: but *God* shall rebuke them, and they shall flee far off, and shall be chased as the chaff of the mountains before the wind, and like a rolling thing before the whirlwind.

14 And behold at eveningtide trouble; *and* before the morning he *is* not. This *is* the portion of them that spoil us, and the lot of them that rob us.

CHAPTER 18

WOE to the land shadowing with wings, which *is* beyond the rivers of Ē-thĭ-ō'pĭ-a:

2 That sendeth ambassadors by the sea, even in vessels of bulrushes upon the waters, *saying*, Go, ye swift messengers, to a nation scattered and peeled, to a people terrible from their beginning hitherto; a nation meted out and trodden down, whose land the rivers have spoiled!

3 All ye inhabitants of the world, and dwellers on the earth, see ye, when he lifteth up an ensign on the mountains; and when he bloweth a trumpet, hear ye.

4 For so the Lord said unto me, I will take my rest, and I will consider in my dwelling place like a clear heat upon herbs, *and* like a cloud of dew in the heat of harvest.

5 For afore the harvest, when the bud is perfect, and the sour grape is ripening in the flower, he shall both cut off the sprigs with pruning hooks, and take away *and* cut down the branches.

6 They shall be left together unto the fowls of the mountains, and to the beasts of the earth: and the fowls shall summer upon them, and all the beasts of the earth shall winter upon them.

7 ¶In that time shall the present be brought unto the Lord of hosts of a people scattered and peeled, and from a people terrible from their beginning hitherto; a nation meted out and trodden under foot, whose land the rivers

have spoiled, to the place of the name of the LORD of hosts, the mount Zion.

CHAPTER 19

THE burden of Egypt. Behold, the LORD rideth upon a swift cloud, and shall come into Egypt: and the idols of Egypt shall be moved at his presence, and the heart of Egypt shall melt in the midst of it.

2 And I will set the Egyptians against the Egyptians: and they shall fight every one against his brother, and every one against his neighbour; city against city, *and* kingdom against kingdom.

3 And the spirit of Egypt shall fail in the midst thereof; and I will destroy the counsel thereof: and they shall seek to the idols, and to the charmers, and to them that have familiar spirits, and to the wizards.

4 And the Egyptians will I give over into the hand of a cruel lord; and a fierce king shall rule over them, saith the Lord, the LORD of hosts.

5 And the waters shall fail from the sea, and the river shall be wasted and dried up.

6 And they shall turn the rivers far away; *and* the brooks of defence shall be emptied and dried up: the reeds and flags shall wither.

7 The paper reeds by the brooks, by the mouth of the brooks, and every thing sown by the brooks, shall wither, be driven away, and be no *more*.

8 The fishers also shall mourn, and all they that cast angle into the brooks shall lament, and they that spread nets upon the waters shall languish.

9 Moreover they that work in fine flax, and they that weave networks, shall be confounded.

10 And they shall be broken in the purposes thereof, all that make sluices *and* ponds for fish.

11 Surely the princes of Zō'an *are* fools, the counsel of the wise counsellors of Pharaoh is become brutish: how say ye unto Pharaoh, I *am* the son of the wise, the son of ancient kings?

12 Where *are* they? where *are* thy wise *men?* and let them tell thee now, and let them know what the LORD of hosts hath purposed upon Egypt.

13 The princes of Zō'an are become fools, the princes of Noph are deceived; they have also seduced Egypt, *even they that are* the stay of the tribes thereof.

14 The LORD hath mingled a perverse spirit in the midst thereof: and they have caused Egypt to err in every work thereof, as a drunken *man* staggereth in his vomit.

15 Neither shall there be *any* work for Egypt, which the head or tail, branch or rush, may do.

16 In that day shall Egypt be like unto women: and it shall be afraid and fear because of the shaking of the hand of the LORD of hosts, which he shaketh over it.

17 And the land of Jū'dah shall be a terror unto Egypt, every one that maketh mention thereof shall be afraid in himself, because of the counsel of the LORD of hosts, which he hath determined against it.

18 In that day shall five cities in the land of Egypt speak the language of Canaan, and swear to the LORD of hosts; one shall be called, The city of destruction.

19 In that day shall there be an altar to the LORD in the midst of the land of Egypt, and a pillar at the border thereof to the LORD.

20 And it shall be for a sign and for a witness unto the LORD of hosts in the land of Egypt: for they shall cry unto the LORD because of the oppressors, and he shall send them a saviour, and a great one, and he shall deliver them.

21 And the LORD shall be known to Egypt, and the Egyptians shall know the LORD in that day, and shall do sacrifice and oblation; yea, they shall vow a vow unto the LORD, and perform *it*.

22 And the LORD shall smite Egypt: he shall smite and heal *it:* and they shall return *even* to the LORD, and he shall be intreated of them, and shall heal them.

23 In that day shall there be a highway out of Egypt to Assyria, and the Assyrian shall come into Egypt, and the Egyptian into Assyria, and the Egyptians shall serve with the Assyrians.

24 In that day shall Israel be the third with Egypt and with Assyria, *even* a blessing in the midst of the land:

25 Whom the LORD of hosts shall bless, saying, Blessed *be* Egypt my people, and Assyria the work of my hands, and Israel mine inheritance.

CHAPTER 20

IN the year that Tartan came unto Ăsh'dŏd, (when Sär'gŏn the king of Assyria sent him,) and fought against Ăsh'dŏd, and took it.

2 At the same time spake the LORD by Isaiah the son of Amoz, saying, Go and loose the sackcloth from off thy loins, and put off thy shoe from thy foot. And he did so, walking naked and barefoot.

3 And the LORD said, Like as my ser-

vant Isaiah hath walked naked and barefoot three years *for* a sign and wonder upon Egypt and upon Ē-thĭ-ō'pĭ-a;
4 So shall the king of Assyria lead away the Egyptians prisoners, and the Ē-thĭ-ō'pĭ-ans captives, young and old, naked and barefoot, even with *their* buttocks uncovered, to the shame of Egypt.
5 And they shall be afraid and ashamed of Ē-thĭ-ō'pĭ-a their expectation, and of Egypt their glory.
6 And the inhabitant of this isle shall say in that day, Behold, such *is* our expectation, whither we flee for help to be delivered from the king of Assyria: and how shall we escape?

CHAPTER 21

THE burden of the desert of the sea. As whirlwinds in the south pass through; *so* it cometh from the desert, from a terrible land.
2 A grievous vision is declared unto me; the treacherous dealer dealeth treacherously, and the spoiler spoileth. Go up, O Ē'lam: besiege, O Mē'dĭ-a; all the sighing thereof have I made to cease.
3 Therefore are my loins filled with pain: pangs have taken hold upon me, as the pangs of a woman that travaileth: I was bowed down at the hearing *of it;* I was dismayed at the seeing *of it.*
4 My heart panted, fearfulness affrighted me: the night of my pleasure hath he turned into fear unto me.
5 Prepare the table, watch in the watchtower, eat, drink: arise, ye princes, *and* anoint the shield.
6 For thus hath the LORD said unto me, Go, set a watchman, let him declare what he seeth.
7 And he saw a chariot *with* a couple of horsemen, a chariot of asses, *and* a chariot of camels; and he hearkened diligently with much heed:
8 And he cried, A lion: My lord, I stand continually upon the watchtower in the daytime, and I am set in my ward whole nights:
9 And, behold, here cometh a chariot of men, *with* a couple of horsemen. And he answered and said, Babylon is fallen, is fallen; and all the graven images of her gods he hath broken unto the ground.
10 O my threshing, and the corn of my floor: that which I have heard of the LORD of hosts, the God of Israel, have I declared unto you.
11 ¶The burden of Dū'mah. He calleth to me out of Sē'ir, Watchman, what of the night? Watchman, what of the night?
12 The watchman said, The morning cometh, and also the night: if ye will enquire, enquire ye: return, come.
13 ¶The burden upon Arabia. In the forest in Arabia shall ye lodge, O ye travelling companies of Dēd'a-nĭm.
14 The inhabitants of the land of Tē'ma brought water to him that was thirsty, they prevented with their bread him that fled.
15 For they fled from the swords, from the drawn sword, and from the bent bow, and from the grievousness of war.
16 For thus hath the LORD said unto me, Within a year, according to the years of an hireling, and all the glory of Kē'dar shall fail:
17 And the residue of the number of archers, the mighty men of the children of Kē'dar, shall be diminished: for the LORD God of Israel hath spoken *it.*

CHAPTER 22

THE burden of the valley of vision. What aileth thee now, that thou art wholly gone up to the housetops?
2 Thou that art full of stirs, a tumultuous city, a joyous city: thy slain *men are* not slain with the sword, nor dead in battle.
3 All thy rulers are fled together, they are bound by the archers: all that are found in thee are bound together, *which* have fled from far.
4 Therefore said I, Look away from me; I will weep bitterly, labour not to comfort me, because of the spoiling of the daughter of my people.
5 For *it is* a day of trouble, and of treading down, and of perplexity by the Lord GOD of hosts in the valley of vision, breaking down the walls, and of crying to the mountains.
6 And Ē'lam bare the quiver with chariots of men *and* horsemen, and Kir uncovered the shield.
7 And it shall come to pass, *that* thy choicest valleys shall be full of chariots, and the horsemen shall set themselves in array at the gate.
8 ¶And he discovered the covering of Jŭ'dah, and thou didst look in that day to the armour of the house of the forest.
9 Ye have seen also the breaches of the city of David, that they are many: and ye gathered together the waters of the lower pool.
10 And ye have numbered the houses of Jerusalem, and the houses have ye broken down to fortify the wall.
11 Ye made also a ditch between the

two walls for the water of the old pool:
but ye have not looked unto the maker
thereof, neither had respect unto him
that fashioned it long ago.
12 And in that day did the Lord GOD
of hosts call to weeping, and to mourning,
and to baldness, and to girding
with sackcloth:
13 And behold joy and gladness,
slaying oxen, and killing sheep, eating
flesh, and drinking wine: let us eat and
drink; for tomorrow we shall die.
14 And it was revealed in mine ears
by the LORD of hosts, Surely this iniquity
shall not be purged from you till ye
die, saith the Lord GOD of hosts.
15 ¶Thus saith the Lord GOD of hosts,
Go, get thee unto this treasurer, *even*
unto Shĕb'na, which *is* over the house,
and say,
16 What hast thou here? and whom
hast thou here, that thou hast hewed
thee out a sepulchre here, *as* he that
heweth him out a sepulchre on high,
and that graveth an habitation for himself
in a rock?
17 Behold, the LORD will carry thee
away with a mighty captivity, and will
surely cover thee.
18 He will surely violently turn and
toss thee *like* a ball into a large country:
there shalt thou die, and there the
chariots of thy glory *shall be* the shame
of thy lord's house.
19 And I will drive thee from thy station,
and from thy state shall he pull
thee down.
20 ¶And it shall come to pass in that
day, that I will call my servant E-lī'a-kĭm
the son of Hĭl-ki'ah:
21 And I will clothe him with thy
robe, and strengthen him with thy
girdle, and I will commit thy government
into his hand: and he shall be a
father to the inhabitants of Jerusalem,
and to the house of Jū'dah.
22 And the key of the house of David
will I lay upon his shoulder; so he shall
open, and none shall shut; and he shall
shut, and none shall open.
23 And I will fasten him *as* a nail in a
sure place; and he shall be for a glorious
throne to his father's house.
24 And they shall hang upon him all
the glory of his father's house, the
offspring and the issue, all vessels of
small quantity, from the vessels of
cups, even to all the vessels of flagons.
25 In that day, saith the LORD of
hosts, shall the nail that is fastened in
the sure place be removed, and be cut
down, and fall; and the burden that *was*
upon it shall be cut off: for the LORD
hath spoken *it*.

CHAPTER 23

THE burden of Tyre. Howl, ye ships of
Tär'shĭsh; for it is laid waste, so that
there is no house, no entering in: from
the land of Chĭt'tĭm it is revealed to
them.
2 Be still, ye inhabitants of the isle;
thou whom the merchants of Zī'don,
that pass over the sea, have replenished.
3 And by great waters the seed of
Sī'hôr, the harvest of the river, *is* her
revenue; and she is a mart of nations.
4 Be thou ashamed, O Zī'don: for the
sea hath spoken, *even* the strength of
the sea, saying, I travail not, nor bring
forth children, neither do I nourish up
young men, *nor* bring up virgins.
5 As at the report concerning Egypt,
so shall they be sorely pained at the report
of Tyre.
6 Pass ye over to Tär'shĭsh; howl, ye
inhabitants of the isle.
7 *Is* this your joyous *city*, whose antiquity
is of ancient days? her own feet
shall carry her afar off to sojourn.
8 Who hath taken this counsel
against Tyre, the crowning *city*, whose
merchants *are* princes, whose traffickers
are the honourable of the earth?
9 The LORD of hosts hath purposed it,
to stain the pride of all glory, *and* to
bring into contempt all the honourable
of the earth.
10 Pass through thy land as a river, O
daughter of Tär'shĭsh: *there is* no more
strength.
11 He stretched out his hand over the
sea, he shook the kingdoms: the LORD
hath given a commandment against
the merchant *city*, to destroy the strong
holds thereof.
12 And he said, Thou shalt no more
rejoice, O thou oppressed virgin,
daughter of Zī'don: arise, pass over to
Chĭt'tĭm; there also shalt thou have no
rest.
13 Behold the land of the Chăl-dē'-anṡ;
this people was not, *till* the Assyrian
founded it for them that dwell in
the wilderness: they set up the towers
thereof, they raised up the palaces
thereof; *and* he brought it to ruin.
14 Howl, ye ships of Tär'shĭsh: for
your strength is laid waste.
15 And it shall come to pass in that
day, that Tyre shall be forgotten
seventy years, according to the days of
one king: after the end of seventy years
shall Tyre sing as an harlot.
16 Take an harp, go about the city,
thou harlot that hast been forgotten;
make sweet melody, sing many songs,
that thou mayest be remembered.

17 ¶And it shall come to pass after the end of seventy years, that the LORD will visit Tyre, and she shall turn to her hire, and shall commit fornication with all the kingdoms of the world upon the face of the earth.
18 And her merchandise and her hire shall be holiness to the LORD: it shall not be treasured nor laid up; for her merchandise shall be for them that dwell before the LORD, to eat sufficiently, and for durable clothing.

CHAPTER 24

BEHOLD, the LORD maketh the earth empty, and maketh it waste, and turneth it upside down, and scattereth abroad the inhabitants thereof.
2 And it shall be, as with the people, so with the priest; as with the servant, so with his master; as with the maid, so with her mistress; as with the buyer, so with the seller; as with the lender, so with the borrower; as with the taker of usury, so with the giver of usury to him.
3 The land shall be utterly emptied, and utterly spoiled: for the LORD hath spoken this word.
4 The earth mourneth *and* fadeth away, the world languisheth *and* fadeth away, the haughty people of the earth do languish.
5 The earth also is defiled under the inhabitants thereof; because they have transgressed the laws, changed the ordinance, broken the everlasting covenant.
6 Therefore hath the curse devoured the earth, and they that dwell therein are desolate: therefore the inhabitants of the earth are burned, and few men left.
7 The new wine mourneth, the vine languisheth, all the merryhearted do sigh.
8 The mirth of tabrets ceaseth, the noise of them that rejoice endeth, the joy of the harp ceaseth.
9 They shall not drink wine with a song; strong drink shall be bitter to them that drink it.
10 The city of confusion is broken down: every house is shut up, that no man may come in.
11 *There is* a crying for wine in the streets; all joy is darkened, the mirth of the land is gone.
12 In the city is left desolation, and the gate is smitten with destruction.
13 ¶When thus it shall be in the midst of the land among the people, *there shall be* as the shaking of an olive tree, *and* as the gleaning grapes when the vintage is done.
14 They shall lift up their voice, they shall sing for the majesty of the LORD, they shall cry aloud from the sea.
15 Wherefore glorify ye the LORD in the fires, *even* the name of the LORD God of Israel in the isles of the sea.
16 ¶From the uttermost part of the earth have we heard songs, *even* glory to the righteous. But I said, My leanness, my leanness, woe unto me! the treacherous dealers have dealt treacherously; yea, the treacherous dealers have dealt very treacherously.
17 Fear, and the pit, and the snare, *are* upon thee, O inhabitant of the earth.
18 And it shall come to pass, *that* he who fleeth from the noise of the fear shall fall into the pit; and he that cometh up out of the midst of the pit shall be taken in the snare: for the windows from on high are open, and the foundations of the earth do shake.
19 The earth is utterly broken down, the earth is clean dissolved, the earth is moved exceedingly.
20 The earth shall reel to and fro like a drunkard, and shall be removed like a cottage; and the transgression thereof shall be heavy upon it; and it shall fall, and not rise again.
21 And it shall come to pass in that day, *that* the LORD shall punish the host of the high ones *that are* on high, and the kings of the earth upon the earth.
22 And they shall be gathered together, *as* prisoners are gathered in the pit, and shall be shut up in the prison, and after many days shall they be visited.
23 Then the moon shall be confounded, and the sun ashamed, when the LORD of hosts shall reign in mount Zion, and in Jerusalem, and before his ancients gloriously.

CHAPTER 25

O LORD, thou *art* my God; I will exalt thee, I will praise thy name; for thou hast done wonderful *things; thy* counsels of old *are* faithfulness *and* truth.
2 For thou hast made of a city an heap; *of* a defenced city a ruin: a palace of strangers to be no city; it shall never be built.
3 Therefore shall the strong people glorify thee, the city of the terrible nations shall fear thee.
4 For thou hast been a strength to the poor, a strength to the needy in his distress, a refuge from the storm, a shadow from the heat, when the blast of the terrible ones *is* as a storm *against* the wall.
5 Thou shalt bring down the noise of strangers, as the heat in a dry place;

even the heat with the shadow of a
cloud: the branch of the terrible ones
shall be brought low.
6 ¶And in this mountain shall the
LORD of hosts make unto all people a
feast of fat things, a feast of wines on
the lees, of fat things full of marrow, of
wines on the lees well refined.
7 And he will destroy in this moun-
tain the face of the covering cast over
all people, and the vail that is spread
over all nations.
8 He will swallow up death in victory;
and the Lord GOD will wipe away tears
from off all faces; and the rebuke of his
people shall he take away from off all
the earth: for the LORD hath spoken *it*.
9 ¶And it shall be said in that day, Lo,
this *is* our God; we have waited for him,
and he will save us: this *is* the LORD; we
have waited for him, we will be glad
and rejoice in his salvation.
10 For in this mountain shall the hand
of the LORD rest, and Moab shall be
trodden down under him, even as straw
is trodden down for the dunghill.
11 And he shall spread forth his
hands in the midst of them, as he that
swimmeth spreadeth forth *his hands* to
swim: and he shall bring down their
pride together with the spoils of their
hands.
12 And the fortress of the high fort of
thy walls shall he bring down, lay low,
and bring to the ground, *even* to the
dust.

CHAPTER 26

IN THAT day shall this song be sung in
the land of Jū'dah; We have a strong
city; salvation will *God* appoint *for*
walls and bulwarks.
2 Open ye the gates, that the righ-
teous nation which keepeth the truth
may enter in.
3 Thou wilt keep *him* in perfect
peace, *whose* mind *is* stayed *on thee*:
because he trusteth in thee.
4 Trust ye in the LORD for ever: for in
the LORD JE-HŌ'VAH *is* everlasting
strength:
5 ¶For he bringeth down them that
dwell on high; the lofty city, he layeth it
low; he layeth it low, *even* to the
ground; he bringeth it *even* to the dust.
6 The foot shall tread it down, *even*
the feet of the poor, *and* the steps of the
needy.
7 The way of the just *is* uprightness:
thou, most upright, dost weigh the path
of the just.
8 Yea, in the way of thy judgments, O
LORD, have we waited for thee; the de-
sire of *our* soul *is* to thy name, and to
the remembrance of thee.
9 With my soul have I desired thee in
the night; yea, with my spirit within me
will I seek thee early: for when thy
judgments *are* in the earth, the inhabi-
tants of the world will learn righteous-
ness.
10 Let favour be shewed to the
wicked, *yet* will he not learn righteous-
ness; in the land of uprightness will he
deal unjustly, and will not behold the
majesty of the LORD.
11 LORD, *when* thy hand is lifted up,
they will not see: *but* they shall see, and
be ashamed for *their* envy at the peo-
ple; yea, the fire of thine enemies shall
devour them.
12 ¶LORD, thou wilt ordain peace for
us: for thou also hast wrought all our
works in us.
13 O LORD our God, *other* lords be-
side thee have had dominion over us:
but by thee only will we make mention
of thy name.
14 *They are* dead, they shall not live;
they are deceased, they shall not rise:
therefore hast thou visited and de-
stroyed them, and made all their mem-
ory to perish.
15 Thou hast increased the nation, O
LORD, thou hast increased the nation:
thou art glorified: thou hadst removed
it far *unto* all the ends of the earth.
16 LORD, in trouble have they visited
thee, they poured out a prayer *when*
thy chastening *was* upon them.
17 Like as a woman with child, *that*
draweth near the time of her delivery,
is in pain, *and* crieth out in her pangs;
so have we been in thy sight, O LORD.
18 We have been with child, we have
been in pain, we have as it were
brought forth wind; we have not
wrought any deliverance in the earth;
neither have the inhabitants of the
world fallen.
19 Thy dead *men* shall live, *together
with* my dead body shall they arise.
Awake and sing, ye that dwell in dust:
for thy dew *is as* the dew of herbs, and
the earth shall cast out the dead.
20 ¶Come, my people, enter thou into
thy chambers, and shut thy doors
about thee: hide thyself as it were for a
little moment, until the indignation be
overpast.
21 For, behold, the LORD cometh out
of his place to punish the inhabitants of
the earth for their iniquity: the earth
also shall disclose her blood, and shall
no more cover her slain.

CHAPTER 27

IN that day the LORD with his sore and
great and strong sword shall punish le-
viathan the piercing serpent, even le-

viathan that crooked serpent; and he
shall slay the dragon that *is* in the sea.
2 ¶In that day sing ye unto her, A vine-
yard of red wine.
3 I the LORD do keep it; I will water it
every moment: lest *any* hurt it, I will
keep it night and day.
4 Fury *is* not in me: who would set the
briers *and* thorns against me in battle? I
would go through them, I would burn
them together.
5 Or let him take hold of my strength,
that he may make peace with me; *and*
he shall make peace with me.
6 He shall cause them that come of
Jacob to take root: Israel shall blossom
and bud, and fill the face of the world
with fruit.
7 Hath he smitten him, as he smote
those that smote him? *or* is he slain ac-
cording to the slaughter of them that
are slain by him?
8 In measure, when it shooteth forth,
thou wilt debate with it: he stayeth his
rough wind in the day of the east wind.
9 By this therefore shall the iniquity
of Jacob be purged; and this *is* all the
fruit to take away his sin; when he
maketh all the stones of the altar as
chalkstones that are beaten in sunder,
the groves and images shall not stand
up.
10 Yet the defenced city *shall be* deso-
late, *and* the habitation forsaken,
and left like a wilderness: there shall
the calf feed, and there shall he lie
down, and consume the branches there-
of.
11 When the boughs thereof are
withered, they shall be broken off: the
women come, *and* set them on fire: for
it *is* a people of no understanding: there-
fore he that made them will not
have mercy on them, and he that
formed them will shew them no favour.
12 And it shall come to pass in that
day, *that* the LORD shall beat off from
the channel of the river unto the stream
of Egypt, and ye shall be gathered one
by one, O ye children of Israel.
13 And it shall come to pass in that
day, *that* the great trumpet shall be
blown, and they shall come which were
ready to perish in the land of Assyria,
and the outcasts in the land of Egypt,
and shall worship the LORD in the holy
mount at Jerusalem.

CHAPTER 28

WOE to the crown of pride, to the
drunkards of Ē'phra-im, whose glori-
ous beauty *is* a fading flower, which *are*
on the head of the fat valleys of them
that are overcome with wine!
2 Behold, the Lord hath a mighty and
strong one, which as a tempest of hail
and a destroying storm, as a flood of
mighty waters overflowing, shall cast
down to the earth with the hand.
3 The crown of pride, the drunkards
of Ē'phra-im, shall be trodden under
feet:
4 And the glorious beauty, which *is*
on the head of the fat valley, shall be a
fading flower, *and* as the hasty fruit be-
fore the summer; which *when* he that
looketh upon it seeth, while it is yet in
his hand he eateth it up.
5 ¶In that day shall the LORD of hosts
be for a crown of glory, and for a dia-
dem of beauty, unto the residue of his
people,
6 And for a spirit of judgment to him
that sitteth in judgment, and for
strength to them that turn the battle to
the gate.
7 But they also have erred through
wine, and through strong drink are out
of the way; the priest and the prophet
have erred through strong drink, they
are swallowed up of wine, they are out
of the way through strong drink; they
err in vision, they stumble *in* judgment.
8 For all tables are full of vomit *and*
filthiness, *so that there is* no place
clean.
9 Whom shall he teach knowledge?
and whom shall he make to understand
doctrine? *them that are* weaned from
the milk, *and* drawn from the breasts.
10 For precept *must be* upon precept,
precept upon precept; line upon line,
line upon line; here a little, *and* there a
little:
11 For with stammering lips and an-
other tongue will he speak to this peo-
ple.
12 To whom he said, This *is* the rest
wherewith ye may cause the weary to
rest; and this *is* the refreshing: yet they
would not hear.
13 But the word of the LORD was unto
them precept upon precept, precept
upon precept; line upon line, line upon
line; here a little, *and* there a little; that
they might go, and fall backward, and
be broken, and snared, and taken.
14 ¶Wherefore hear the word of the
LORD, ye scornful men, that rule this
people which *is* in Jerusalem.
15 Because ye have said, We have
made a covenant with death, and with
hell are we at agreement; when the
overflowing scourge shall pass
through, it shall not come unto us: for
we have made lies our refuge, and un-
der falsehood have we hid ourselves;
16 Therefore thus saith the Lord GOD,
Behold, I lay in Zion for a foundation a
stone, a tried stone, a precious corner

stone, a sure foundation: he that believeth shall not make haste.
17 Judgment also will I lay to the line, and righeousness to the plummet: and the hail shall sweep away the refuge of lies, and the waters shall overflow the hiding place.
18 And your covenant with death shall be disannulled, and your agreement with hell shall not stand; when the overflowing scourge shall pass through, then ye shall be trodden down by it.
19 From the time that it goeth forth it shall take you: for morning by morning shall it pass over, by day and by night: and it shall be a vexation only *to* understand the report.
20 For the bed is shorter than that *a man* can stretch himself *on it:* and the covering narrower than that he can wrap himself *in it.*
21 For the LORD shall rise up as *in* mount Per'ā-zĭm, he shall be wroth as *in* the valley of Gĭb'e-on, that he may do his work, his strange work; and bring to pass his act, his strange act.
22 Now therefore be ye not mockers, lest your bands be made strong: for I have heard from the Lord GOD of hosts a consumption, even determined upon the whole earth.
23 ¶Give ye ear, and hear my voice; hearken, and hear my speech.
24 Doth the plowman plow all day to sow? doth he open and break the clods of his ground?
25 When he hath made plain the face thereof, doth he not cast abroad the fitches, and scatter the cummin, and cast in the principal wheat and the appointed barley and the rie in their place?
26 For his God doth instruct him to discretion, *and* doth teach him.
27 For the fitches are not threshed with a threshing instrument, neither is a cart wheel turned about upon the cummin; but the fitches are beaten out with a staff, and the cummin with a rod.
28 Bread *corn* is bruised; because he will not ever be threshing it, nor break *it with* the wheel of his cart, nor bruise it *with* his horsemen.
29 This also cometh forth from the LORD of hosts, *which* is wonderful in counsel, *and* excellent in working.

CHAPTER 29

WOE to Â'rĭ-el, to Â'rĭ-el, the city *where* David dwelt! add ye year to year; let them kill sacrifices.
2 Yet I will distress Â'rĭ-el, and there shall be heaviness and sorrow: and it shall be unto me as Â'rĭ-el.
3 And I will camp against thee round about, and will lay siege against thee with a mount, and I will raise forts against thee.
4 And thou shalt be brought down, *and* shalt speak out of the ground, and thy speech shall be low out of the dust, and thy voice shall be, as of one that hath a familiar spirit, out of the ground, and thy speech shall whisper out of the dust.
5 Moreover the multitude of thy strangers shall be like small dust, and the multitude of the terrible ones *shall be* as chaff that passeth away: yea, it shall be at an instant suddenly.
6 Thou shalt be visited of the LORD of hosts with thunder, and with earthquake, and great noise, with storm and tempest, and the flame of devouring fire.
7 And the multitude of all the nations that fight against Â'rĭ-el, even all that fight against her and her munition, and that distress her, shall be as a dream of a night vision.
8 It shall even be as when an hungry *man* dreameth, and, behold, he eateth; but he awaketh, and his soul is empty: or as when a thirsty man dreameth, and, behold, he drinketh; but he awaketh, and, behold, *he is* faint, and his soul hath appetite: so shall the multitude of all the nations be, that fight against mount Zion.
9 ¶Stay yourselves, and wonder; cry ye out, and cry: they are drunken, but not with wine; they stagger, but not with strong drink.
10 For the LORD hath poured out upon you the spirit of deep sleep, and hath closed your eyes: the prophets and your rulers, the seers hath he covered.
11 And the vision of all is become unto you as the words of a book that is sealed, which *men* deliver to one that is learned, saying, Read this, I pray thee: and he saith, I cannot; for it *is* sealed:
12 And the book is delivered to him that is not learned, saying, Read this, I pray thee: and he saith, I am not learned.
13 ¶Wherefore the Lord said, Forasmuch as this people draw near *me* with their mouth, and with their lips do honour me, but have removed their heart far from me, and their fear toward me is taught by the precept of men:
14 Therefore, behold, I will proceed to do a marvellous work among this people, *even* a marvellous work and a wonder: for the wisdom of their wise

men shall perish, and the understanding of their prudent *men* shall be hid.
15 Woe unto them that seek deep to hide their counsel from the LORD, and their works are in the dark, and they say, Who seeth us? and who knoweth us?
16 Surely your turning of things upside down shall be esteemed as the potter's clay: for shall the work say of him that made it, He made me not? or shall the thing framed say of him that framed it, He had no understanding?
17 ¶*Is* it not yet a very little while, and Lebanon shall be turned into a fruitful field, and the fruitful field shall be esteemed as a forest?
18 And in that day shall the deaf hear the words of the book, and the eyes of the blind shall see out of obscurity, and out of darkness.
19 The meek also shall increase *their* joy in the LORD, and the poor among men shall rejoice in the Holy One of Israel.
20 For the terrible one is brought to nought, and the scorner is consumed, and all that watch for iniquity are cut off:
21 That make a man an offender for a word, and lay a snare for him that reproveth in the gate, and turn aside the just for a thing of nought.
22 Therefore thus saith the LORD, who redeemed Abraham, concerning the house of Jacob, Jacob shall not now be ashamed, neither shall his face now wax pale.
23 But when he seeth his children, the work of mine hands, in the midst of him, they shall sanctify my name, and sanctify the Holy One of Jacob, and shall fear the God of Israel.
24 They also that erred in spirit shall come to understanding, and they that murmured shall learn doctrine.

CHAPTER 30

WOE to the rebellious children, saith the LORD, that take counsel, but not of me; and that cover with a covering, but not of my spirit, that they may add sin to sin:
2 That walk to go down into Egypt, and have not asked at my mouth; to strengthen themselves in the strength of Pharaoh, and to trust in the shadow of Egypt!
3 Therefore shall the strength of Pharaoh be your shame, and the trust in the shadow of Egypt *your* confusion.
4 For his princes were at Zō'an, and his ambassadors came to Hā'nēs.
5 They were all ashamed of a people *that* could not profit them, nor be an help nor profit, but a shame, and also a reproach.
6 The burden of the beasts of the south: into the land of trouble and anguish, from whence *come* the young and old lion, the viper and fiery flying serpent, they will carry their riches upon the shoulders of young asses, and their treasures upon the bunches of camels, to a people *that* shall not profit *them*.
7 For the Egyptians shall help in vain, and to no purpose: therefore have I cried concerning this, Their strength *is* to sit still.
8 ¶Now go, write it before them in a table, and note it in a book, that it may be for the time to come for ever and ever:
9 That this *is* a rebellious people, lying children, children *that* will not hear the law of the LORD:
10 Which say to the seers, See not; and to the prophets, Prophesy not unto us right things, speak unto us smooth things, prophesy deceits:
11 Get you out of the way, turn aside out of the path, cause the Holy One of Israel to cease from before us.
12 Wherefore thus saith the Holy One of Israel, Because ye despise this word, and trust in oppression and perverseness, and stay thereon:
13 Therefore this iniquity shall be to you as a breach ready to fall, swelling out in a high wall, whose breaking cometh suddenly at an instant.
14 And he shall break it as the breaking of the potters' vessel that is broken in pieces; he shall not spare: so that there shall not be found in the bursting of it a sherd to take fire from the hearth, or to take water *withal* out of the pit.
15 For thus saith the Lord GOD, the Holy One of Israel; In returning and rest shall ye be saved; in quietness and in confidence shall be your strength: and ye would not.
16 But ye said, No; for we will flee upon horses; therefore shall ye flee: and, We will ride upon the swift; therefore shall they that pursue you be swift.
17 One thousand *shall flee* at the rebuke of one; at the rebuke of five shall ye flee: till ye be left as a beacon upon the top of a mountain, and as an ensign on an hill.
18 And therefore will the LORD wait, that he may be gracious unto you, and therefore will he be exalted, that he may have mercy upon you: for the LORD *is* a God of judgment: blessed *are* all they that wait for him.
19 ¶For the people shall dwell in Zion

at Jerusalem: thou shalt weep no more:
he will be very gracious unto thee at the
voice of thy cry; when he shall hear it,
he will answer thee.
20 And *though* the Lord give you the
bread of adversity, and the water of af-
fliction, yet shall not thy teachers be re-
moved into a corner any more, but
thine eyes shall see thy teachers:
21 And thine ears shall hear a word
behind thee, saying, This *is* the way,
walk ye in it, when ye turn to the right
hand, and when ye turn to the left.
22 Ye shall defile also the covering of
thy graven images of silver, and the or-
nament of thy molten images of gold:
thou shalt cast them away as a men-
struous cloth; thou shalt say unto it,
Get thee hence.
23 Then shall he give the rain of thy
seed, that thou shalt sow the ground
withal; and bread of the increase of the
earth, and it shall be fat and plenteous:
in that day shall thy cattle feed in large
pastures.
24 The oxen likewise and the young
asses that ear the ground shall eat
clean provender, which hath been win-
nowed with the shovel and with the
fan.
25 And there shall be upon every high
mountain, and upon every high hill, riv-
ers *and* streams of waters in the day of
the great slaughter, when the towers
fall.
26 Moreover the light of the moon
shall be as the light of the sun, and the
light of the sun shall be sevenfold, as
the light of seven days, in the day that
the LORD bindeth up the breach of his
people, and healeth the stroke of their
wound.
27 ¶Behold, the name of the LORD
cometh from far, burning *with* his an-
ger, and the burden *thereof is* heavy:
his lips are full of indignation, and his
tongue as a devouring fire:
28 And his breath, as an overflowing
stream, shall reach to the midst of the
neck, to sift the nations with the sieve
of vanity: and *there shall be* a bridle in
the jaws of the people, causing *them* to
err.
29 Ye shall have a song, as in the
night *when* a holy solemnity is kept;
and gladness of heart, as when one
goeth with a pipe to come into the
mountain of the LORD, to the mighty
One of Israel.
30 And the LORD shall cause his glori-
ous voice to be heard, and shall shew
the lighting down of his arm, with the
indignation of *his* anger, and *with* the
flame of a devouring fire, *with* scatter-
ing, and tempest, and hailstones.
31 For through the voice of the LORD
shall the Assyrian be beaten down,
which smote with a rod.
32 And *in* every place where the
grounded staff shall pass, which the
LORD shall lay upon him, *it* shall be with
tabrets and harps: and in battles of
shaking will he fight with it.
33 For Tō'phet *is* ordained of old; yea,
for the king it is prepared; he hath
made *it* deep *and* large: the pile thereof
is fire and much wood; the breath of the
LORD, like a stream of brimstone, doth
kindle it.

CHAPTER 31

WOE to them that go down to Egypt for
help; and stay on horses, and trust in
chariots, because *they are* many; and in
horsemen, because they are very
strong; but they look not unto the Holy
One of Israel, neither seek the LORD!
2 Yet he also *is* wise, and will bring
evil, and will not call back his words:
but will arise against the house of the
evildoers, and against the help of them
that work iniquity.
3 Now the Egyptians *are* men, and
not God; and their horses flesh, and not
spirit. When the LORD shall stretch out
his hand, both he that helpeth shall fall,
and he that is holpen shall fall down,
and they all shall fail together.
4 For thus hath the LORD spoken unto
me, Like as the lion and the young lion
roaring on his prey, when a multitude
of shepherds is called forth against
him, *he* will not be afraid of their voice,
nor abase himself for the noise of them:
so shall the LORD of hosts come down to
fight for mount Zion, and for the hill
thereof.
5 As birds flying, so will the LORD of
hosts defend Jerusalem; defending also
he will deliver *it; and* passing over he
will preserve it.
6 ¶Turn ye unto *him from* whom the
children of Israel have deeply revolted.
7 For in that day every man shall cast
away his idols of silver, and his idols of
gold, which your own hands have made
unto you *for* a sin.
8 Then shall the Assyrian fall with the
sword, not of a mighty man; and the
sword, not of a mean man, shall devour
him: but he shall flee from the sword,
and his young men shall be discom-
fited.
9 And he shall pass over to his strong
hold for fear, and his princes shall be
afraid of the ensign, saith the LORD,
whose fire *is* in Zion, and his furnace in
Jerusalem.

CHAPTER 32

BEHOLD, a king shall reign in righteousness, and princes shall rule in judgment.

2 And a man shall be as an hiding place from the wind, and a covert from the tempest; as rivers of water in a dry place, as the shadow of a great rock in a weary land.

3 And the eyes of them that see shall not be dim, and the ears of them that hear shall hearken.

4 The heart also of the rash shall understand knowledge, and the tongue of the stammerers shall be ready to speak plainly.

5 The vile person shall be no more called liberal, nor the churl said *to be* bountiful.

6 For the vile person will speak villany, and his heart will work iniquity, to practise hypocrisy, and to utter error against the LORD, to make empty the soul of the hungry, and he will cause the drink of the thirsty to fail.

7 The instruments also of the churl *are* evil: he deviseth wicked devices to destroy the poor with lying words, even when the needy speaketh right.

8 But the liberal deviseth liberal things; and by liberal things shall he stand.

9 ¶Rise up, ye women that are at ease; hear my voice, ye careless daughters; give ear unto my speech.

10 Many days and years shall ye be troubled, ye careless women: for the vintage shall fail, the gathering shall not come.

11 Tremble, ye women that are at ease; be troubled, ye careless ones: strip you, and make you bare, and gird *sackcloth* upon *your* loins.

12 They shall lament for the teats, for the pleasant fields, for the fruitful vine.

13 Upon the land of my people shall come up thorns *and* briers; yea, upon all the houses of joy *in* the joyous city:

14 Because the palaces shall be forsaken; the multitude of the city shall be left; the forts and towers shall be for dens for ever, a joy of wild asses, a pasture of flocks;

15 Until the spirit be poured upon us from on high, and the wilderness be a fruitful field, and the fruitful field be counted for a forest.

16 Then judgment shall dwell in the wilderness, and righteousness remain in the fruitful field.

17 And the work of righteousness shall be peace; and the effect of righteousness quietness and assurance for ever.

18 And my people shall dwell in a peaceable habitation, and in sure dwellings, and in quiet resting places;

19 When it shall hail, coming down on the forest; and the city shall be low in a low place.

20 Blessed *are* ye that sow beside all waters, that send forth *thither* the feet of the ox and the ass.

CHAPTER 33

WOE to thee that spoilest, and thou *wast* not spoiled; and dealest treacherously, and they dealt not treacherously with thee! when thou shalt cease to spoil, thou shalt be spoiled; *and* when thou shalt make an end to deal treacherously, they shall deal treacherously with thee.

2 O LORD, be gracious unto us; we have waited for thee: be thou their arm every morning, our salvation also in the time of trouble.

3 At the noise of the tumult the people fled; at the lifting up of thyself the nations were scattered.

4 And your spoil shall be gathered *like* the gathering of the caterpiller: as the running to and fro of locusts shall he run upon them.

5 The LORD is exalted; for he dwelleth on high: he hath filled Zion with judgment and righteousness.

6 And wisdom and knowledge shall be the stability of thy times, *and* strength of salvation: the fear of the LORD *is* his treasure.

7 Behold, their valiant ones shall cry without: the ambassadors of peace shall weep bitterly.

8 The highways lie waste, the wayfaring man ceaseth: he hath broken the covenant, he hath despised the cities, he regardeth no man.

9 The earth mourneth *and* languisheth: Lebanon is ashamed *and* hewn down: Shâr'on is like a wilderness; and Bā'shan and Carmel shake off *their fruits*.

10 ¶Now will I rise, saith the LORD; now will I be exalted; now will I lift up myself.

11 Ye shall conceive chaff, ye shall bring forth stubble: your breath, *as* fire, shall devour you.

12 And the people shall be *as* the burnings of lime: *as* thorns cut up shall they be burned in the fire.

13 ¶Hear, ye *that are* far off, what I have done; and, ye *that are* near, acknowledge my might.

14 The sinners in Zion are afraid; fearfulness hath surprised the hypocrites. Who among us shall dwell with

the devouring fire? who among us shall dwell with everlasting burnings?

15 He that walketh righteously, and speaketh uprightly; he that despiseth the gain of oppressions, that shaketh his hands from holding of bribes, that stoppeth his ears from hearing of blood, and shutteth his eyes from seeing evil;

16 He shall dwell on high: his place of defence *shall be* the munitions of rocks: bread shall be given him; his waters *shall be* sure.

17 Thine eyes shall see the king in his beauty: they shall behold the land that is very far off.

18 Thine heart shall meditate terror. Where *is* the scribe? where *is* the receiver? where *is* he that counted the towers?

19 Thou shalt not see a fierce people, a people of a deeper speech than thou canst perceive; of a stammering tongue, *that thou canst* not understand.

20 Look upon Zion, the city of our solemnities: thine eyes shall see Jerusalem a quiet habitation, a tabernacle *that* shall not be taken down; not one of the stakes thereof shall ever be removed, neither shall any of the cords thereof be broken.

21 But there the glorious Lord *will be* unto us a place of broad rivers *and* streams; wherein shall go no galley with oars, neither shall gallant ship pass thereby.

22 For the Lord *is* our judge, the Lord *is* our lawgiver, the Lord *is* our king; he will save us.

23 Thy tacklings are loosed; they could not well strengthen their mast, they could not spread the sail: then is the prey of a great spoil divided; the lame take the prey.

24 And the inhabitant shall not say, I am sick: the people that dwell therein *shall be* forgiven *their* iniquity.

CHAPTER 34

COME near, ye nations, to hear; and hearken, ye people: let the earth hear, and all that is therein; the world, and all things that come forth of it.

2 For the indignation of the Lord *is* upon all nations, and *his* fury upon all their armies: he hath utterly destroyed them, he hath delivered them to the slaughter.

3 Their slain also shall be cast out, and their stink shall come up out of their carcases, and the mountains shall be melted with their blood.

4 And all the host of heaven shall be dissolved, and the heavens shall be rolled together as a scroll: and all their host shall fall down, as the leaf falleth off from the vine, and as a falling *fig* from the fig tree.

5 For my sword shall be bathed in heaven: behold, it shall come down upon Ī-dū-mē'a, and upon the people of my curse, to judgment.

6 The sword of the Lord is filled with blood, it is made fat with fatness, *and* with the blood of lambs and goats, with the fat of the kidneys of rams: for the Lord hath a sacrifice in Bŏz'rah, and a great slaughter in the land of Ī-dū-mē'a.

7 And the unicorns shall come down with them, and the bullocks with the bulls; and their land shall be soaked with blood, and their dust made fat with fatness.

8 For *it is* the day of the Lord's vengeance, *and* the year of recompences for the controversy of Zion.

9 And the streams thereof shall be turned into pitch, and the dust thereof into brimstone, and the land thereof shall become burning pitch.

10 It shall not be quenched night nor day; the smoke thereof shall go up for ever: from generation to generation it shall lie waste; none shall pass through it for ever and ever.

11 But the cormorant and the bittern shall possess it; the owl also and the raven shall dwell in it: and he shall stretch out upon it the line of confusion, and the stones of emptiness.

12 They shall call the nobles thereof to the kingdom, but none *shall be* there, and all her princes shall be nothing.

13 And thorns shall come up in her palaces, nettles and brambles in the fortresses thereof: and it shall be an habitation of dragons, *and* a court for owls.

14 The wild beasts of the desert shall also meet with the wild beasts of the island, and the satyr shall cry to his fellow; the screech owl also shall rest there, and find for herself a place of rest.

15 There shall the great owl make her nest, and lay, and hatch, and gather under her shadow: there shall the vultures also be gathered, every one with her mate.

16 ¶Seek ye out of the book of the Lord, and read: no one of these shall fail, none shall want her mate: for my mouth it hath commanded, and his spirit it hath gathered them.

17 And he hath cast the lot for them, and his hand hath divided it unto them by line: they shall possess it for ever, from generation to generation shall they dwell therein.

CHAPTER 35

THE wilderness and the solitary place shall be glad for them; and the desert shall rejoice, and blossom as the rose.

2 It shall blossom abundantly, and rejoice even with joy and singing: the glory of Lebanon shall be given unto it, the excellency of Carmel and Shâr′on, they shall see the glory of the LORD, *and* the excellency of our God.

3 Strengthen ye the weak hands, and confirm the feeble knees.

4 Say to them *that are* of a fearful heart, Be strong, fear not: behold, your God will come *with* vengeance, *even* God *with* a recompence; he will come and save you.

5 Then the eyes of the blind shall be opened, and the ears of the deaf shall be unstopped.

6 Then shall the lame *man* leap as an hart, and the tongue of the dumb sing: for in the wilderness shall waters break out, and streams in the desert.

7 And the parched ground shall become a pool, and the thirsty land springs of water: in the habitation of dragons, where each lay, *shall be* grass with reeds and rushes.

8 And an highway shall be there, and a way, and it shall be called The way of holiness; the unclean shall not pass over it; but it *shall be* for those: the wayfaring men, though fools, shall not err *therein.*

9 No lion shall be there, nor *any* ravenous beast shall go up thereon, it shall not be found there; but the redeemed shall walk *there:*

10 And the ransomed of the LORD shall return, and come to Zion with songs and everlasting joy upon their heads: they shall obtain joy and gladness, and sorrow and sighing shall flee away.

CHAPTER 36

NOW it came to pass in the fourteenth year of king Hĕz-e-kī′ah, *that* Sen-năch′e-rĭb king of Assyria came up against all the defenced cities of Jū′dah, and took them.

2 And the king of Assyria sent Răb′sha-keh from Lā′chĭsh to Jerusalem unto king Hĕz-e-kī′ah with a great army. And he stood by the conduit of the upper pool in the highway of the fuller's field.

3 Then came forth unto him E-lī′a-kĭm, Hĭl-kī′ah's son, which was over the house, and Shĕb′na the scribe, and Jō′ah, Ā′săph's son, the recorder.

4 And Răb′sha-keh said unto them, Say ye now to Hĕz-e-kī′ah, Thus saith the great king, the king of Assyria, What confidence *is* this wherein thou trustest?

5 I say, *sayest thou,* (but *they are but* vain words) *I have* counsel and strength for war: now on whom dost thou trust, that thou rebellest against me?

6 Lo, thou trustest in the staff of this broken reed, on Egypt; whereon if a man lean, it will go into his hand, and pierce it: so *is* Pharaoh king of Egypt to all that trust in him.

7 But if thou say to me, We trust in the LORD our God: *is it* not he, whose high places and whose altars Hĕz-e-kī′ah hath taken away, and said to Jū′dah and to Jerusalem, Ye shall worship before this altar?

8 Now therefore give pledges, I pray thee, to my master the king of Assyria, and I will give thee two thousand horses, if thou be able on thy part to set riders upon them.

9 How then wilt thou turn away the face of one captain of the least of my master's servants, and put thy trust on Egypt for chariots and for horsemen?

10 And am I now come up without the LORD against this land to destroy it? the LORD said unto me, Go up against this land, and destroy it.

11 Then said E-lī′a-kĭm and Shĕb′na and Jō′ah unto Răb′sha-keh, Speak, I pray thee, unto thy servants in the Syrian language; for we understand *it:* and speak not to us in the Jews' language, in the ears of the people that *are* on the wall.

12 But Răb′sha-keh said, Hath my master sent me to thy master and to thee to speak these words? *hath he* not *sent me* to the men that sit upon the wall, that they may eat their own dung, and drink their own piss with you?

13 Then Răb′sha-keh stood, and cried with a loud voice in the Jews' language, and said, Hear ye the words of the great king, the king of Assyria.

14 Thus saith the king, Let not Hĕz-e-kī′ah deceive you: for he shall not be able to deliver you.

15 Neither let Hĕz-e-kī′ah make you trust in the LORD, saying, The LORD will surely deliver us: this city shall not be delivered into the hand of the king of Assyria.

16 Hearken not to Hĕz-e-kī′ah: for thus saith the king of Assyria, Make *an agreement* with me *by* a present, and come out to me: and eat ye every one of his vine, and every one of his fig tree, and drink ye every one the waters of his own cistern;

17 Until I come and take you away to

a land like your own land, a land of corn
and wine, a land of bread and vine-
yards.
18 *Beware* lest Hĕz-e-kī'ah persuade
you, saying, The LORD will deliver us.
Hath any of the gods of the nations de-
livered his land out of the hand of the
king of Assyria?
19 Where *are* the gods of Hā'măth
and Är'phăd? where *are* the gods of
Sĕph-ar-vā'im? and have they de-
livered Sa-mâ'rĭ-a out of my hand?
20 Who *are they* among all the gods
of these lands, that have delivered their
land out of my hand, that the LORD
should deliver Jerusalem out of my
hand?
21 But they held their peace, and an-
swered him not a word: for the king's
commandment was, saying, Answer
him not.
22 Then came E-lī'a-kĭm, the son of
Hĭl-kī'ah, that *was* over the household,
and Shĕb'na the scribe, and Jō'ah, the
son of Ā'săph, the recorder, to Hĕz-e-
kī'ah with their clothes rent, and told
him the words of Răb'sha-keh.

CHAPTER 37

AND it came to pass, when king Hĕz-e-
kī'ah heard *it*, that he rent his clothes,
and covered himself with sackcloth,
and went into the house of the LORD.
2 And he sent E-lī'a-kĭm, who *was*
over the household, and Shĕb'na the
scribe, and the elders of the priests cov-
ered with sackcloth, unto Isaiah the
prophet the son of Amoz.
3 And they said unto him, Thus saith
Hĕz-e-kī'ah, This day *is* a day of
trouble, and of rebuke, and of blas-
phemy: for the children are come to the
birth, and *there is* not strength to bring
forth.
4 It may be the LORD thy God will
hear the words of Răb'sha-keh, whom
the king of Assyria his master hath sent
to reproach the living God, and will
reprove the words which the LORD thy
God hath heard: wherefore lift up *thy*
prayer for the remnant that is left.
5 So the servants of king Hĕz-e-kī'ah
came to Isaiah.
6 And Isaiah said unto them, Thus
shall ye say unto your master, Thus
saith the LORD, Be not afraid of the
words that thou hast heard, wherewith
the servants of the king of Assyria have
blasphemed me.
7 Behold, I will send a blast upon him,
and he shall hear a rumour, and return
to his own land; and I will cause him to
fall by the sword in his own land.
8 ¶So Răb'sha-keh returned, and
found the king of Assyria warring
against Lĭb'nah: for he had heard that
he was departed from Lā'chĭsh.
9 And he heard say concerning
Tir'hā-kah king of Ē-thĭ-ō'pĭ-a, He is
come forth to make war with thee. And
when he heard *it*, he sent messengers to
Hĕz-e-kī'ah, saying,
10 Thus shall ye speak to Hĕz-e-kī'ah
king of Jū'dah, saying, Let not thy God,
in whom thou trustest, deceive thee,
saying, Jerusalem shall not be given
into the hand of the king of Assyria.
11 Behold, thou hast heard what the
kings of Assyria have done to all lands
by destroying them utterly; and shalt
thou be delivered?
12 Have the gods of the nations deliv-
ered them which my fathers have de-
stroyed, *as* Gō'zăn, and Hâ'ran, and Rē'-
zĕph, and the children of Eden which
were in Te-lăs'sar?
13 Where *is* the king of Hā'măth,
and the king of Är'phăd, and the king of
the city of Sĕph-ar-vā'im, Hē'na, and
Ī'vah?
14 ¶And Hĕz-e-kī'ah received the let-
ter from the hand of the messengers,
and read it: and Hĕz-e-kī'ah went up
unto the house of the LORD, and spread
it before the LORD.
15 And Hĕz-e-kī'ah prayed unto the
LORD, saying,
16 O LORD of hosts, God of Israel, that
dwellest *between* the cherubims, that
art the God, *even* thou alone, of all the
kingdoms of the earth: thou hast made
heaven and earth.
17 Incline thine ear, O LORD, and
hear; open thine eyes, O LORD, and see:
and hear all the words of Sen-năch'e-
rĭb, which hath sent to reproach the liv-
ing God.
18 Of a truth, LORD, the kings of As-
syria have laid waste all the nations,
and their countries.
19 And have cast their gods into the
fire: for they *were* no gods, but the
work of men's hands, wood and stone:
therefore they have destroyed them.
20 Now therefore, O LORD our God,
save us from his hand, that all the king-
doms of the earth may know that thou
art the LORD, *even* thou only.
21 ¶Then Isaiah the son of Amoz sent
unto Hĕz-e-kī'ah, saying, Thus saith
the LORD God of Israel, Whereas thou
hast prayed to me against Sen-năch'e-
rĭb king of Assyria:
22 This *is* the word which the LORD
hath spoken concerning him; The vir-
gin, the daughter of Zion, hath despised
thee, *and* laughed thee to scorn;
the daughter of Jerusalem hath shaken
her head at thee.
23 Whom hast thou reproached and

blasphemed? and against whom hast
thou exalted *thy* voice, and lifted up
thine eyes on high? *even* against the
Holy One of Israel.
24 By thy servants hast thou
reproached the Lord, and hast said, By
the multitude of my chariots am I come
up to the height of the mountains, to
the sides of Lebanon; and I will cut
down the tall cedars thereof, *and* the
choice fir trees thereof: and I will enter
into the height of his border, *and* the
forest of his Carmel.
25 I have digged, and drunk water;
and with the sole of my feet have I dried
up all the rivers of the besieged places.
26 Hast thou not heard long ago, *how*
I have done it; *and* of ancient times,
that I have formed it? now have I
brought it to pass, that thou shouldest
be to lay waste defenced cities *into*
ruinous heaps.
27 Therefore their inhabitants *were*
of small power, they were dismayed
and confounded: they were *as* the grass
of the field, and *as* the green herb, *as*
the grass on the housetops, and *as corn*
blasted before it be grown up.
28 But I know thy abode, and thy
going out, and thy coming in, and thy
rage against me.
29 Because thy rage against me, and
thy tumult, is come up into mine ears,
therefore will I put my hook in thy
nose, and my bridle in thy lips, and I
will turn thee back by the way by which
thou camest.
30 And this *shall be* a sign unto thee,
Ye shall eat *this* year such as groweth
of itself; and the second year that
which springeth of the same: and in the
third year sow ye, and reap, and plant
vineyards, and eat the fruit thereof.
31 And the remnant that is escaped
of the house of Jū'dah shall again take
root downward, and bear fruit upward:
32 For out of Jerusalem shall go forth
a remnant, and they that escape out of
mount Zion: the zeal of the LORD of
hosts shall do this.
33 Therefore thus saith the LORD con-
cerning the king of Assyria, He shall
not come into this city, nor shoot an
arrow there, nor come before it with
shields, nor cast a bank against it.
34 By the way that he came, by the
same shall he return, and shall not
come into this city, saith the LORD.
35 For I will defend this city to save it
for mine own sake, and for my servant
David's sake.
36 ¶Then the angel of the LORD went
forth, and smote in the camp of the As-
syrians a hundred and fourscore and
five thousand: and when they arose
early in the morning, behold, they *were*
all dead corpses.
37 So Sen-năch'e-rĭb king of Assyria
departed, and went and returned, and
dwelt at Nĭn'e-veh.
38 And it came to pass, as he was
worshipping in the house of Nĭs'rŏch
his god, that A-drăm'me-lĕch and Sha-
rē'zer his sons smote him with the
sword; and they escaped into the land
of Ăr-mē'nĭ-a: and Ē'sar-hăd'don his
son reigned in his stead.

CHAPTER 38

IN those days was Hĕz-e-kī'ah sick
unto death. And Isaiah the prophet the
son of Amoz came unto him, and said
unto him, Thus saith the LORD, Set
thine house in order: for thou shalt die,
and not live.
2 Then Hĕz-e-kī'ah turned his face to-
ward the wall, and prayed unto the
LORD,
3 And said, Remember now, O LORD,
I beseech thee, how I have walked be-
fore thee in truth and with a perfect
heart, and have done *that which is* good
in thy sight. And Hĕz-e-kī'ah wept sore.
4 Then came the word of the LORD to
Isaiah, saying,
5 Go, and say to Hĕz-e-kī'ah, Thus
saith the LORD, the God of David thy
father, I have heard thy prayer, I have
seen thy tears: behold, I will add unto
thy days fifteen years.
6 And I will deliver thee and this city
out of the hand of the king of Assyria:
and I will defend this city.
7 And this *shall be* a sign unto thee
from the LORD, that the LORD will do
this thing that he hath spoken;
8 Behold, I will bring again the shad-
ow of the degrees, which is gone
down in the sun dial of Ahaz, ten
degrees backward. So the sun returned
ten degrees, by which degrees it was
gone down.
9 ¶The writing of Hĕz-e-kī'ah king of
Jū'dah, when he had been sick, and was
recovered of his sickness:
10 I said in the cutting off of my days,
I shall go to the gates of the grave: I am
deprived of the residue of my years.
11 I said, I shall not see the LORD,
even the LORD, in the land of the living:
I shall behold man no more with the
inhabitants of the world.
12 Mine age is departed, and is re-
moved from me as a shepherd's tent: I
have cut off like a weaver my life: he
will cut me off with pining sickness:
from day *even* to night wilt thou make
an end of me.
13 I reckoned till morning, *that*, as a
lion, so will he break all my bones: from

day *even* to night wilt thou make an end of me.
14 Like a crane *or* a swallow, so did I chatter: I did mourn as a dove: mine eyes fail *with looking* upward: O LORD, I am oppressed; undertake for me.
15 What shall I say? he hath both spoken unto me, and himself hath done *it:* I shall go softly all my years in the bitterness of my soul.
16 O LORD, by these *things men* live, and in all these *things is* the life of my spirit: so wilt thou recover me, and make me to live.
17 Behold, for peace I had great bitterness: but thou hast in love to my soul *delivered it* from the pit of corruption: for thou hast cast all my sins behind thy back.
18 For the grave cannot praise thee, death can *not* celebrate thee: they that go down into the pit cannot hope for thy truth.
19 The living, the living, he shall praise thee, as I *do* this day: the father to the children shall make known thy truth.
20 The LORD *was ready* to save me: therefore we will sing my songs to the stringed instruments all the days of our life in the house of the LORD.
21 For Isaiah had said, Let them take a lump of figs, and lay *it* for a plaister upon the boil, and he shall recover.
22 Hĕz-e-kī'ah also had said, What *is* the sign that I shall go up to the house of the LORD?

CHAPTER 39

AT that time Me-rō'dăch-băl'a-dan, the son of Băl'a-dan, king of Babylon, sent letters and a present to Hĕz-e-kī'ah: for he had heard that he had been sick, and was recovered.
2 And Hĕz-e-kī'ah was glad of them, and shewed them the house of his precious things, the silver, and the gold, and the spices, and the precious ointment, and all the house of his armour, and all that was found in his treasures: there was nothing in his house, nor in all his dominion, that Hĕz-e-kī'ah, shewed them not.
3 ¶Then came Isaiah the prophet unto king Hĕz-e-kī'ah, and said unto him, What said these men? and from whence came they unto thee? And Hĕz-e-kī'ah said, They are come from a far country unto me, *even* from Babylon.
4 Then said he, What have they seen in thine house? And Hĕz-e-kī'ah answered, All that *is* in mine house have they seen: there is nothing among my treasures that I have not shewed them.
5 Then said Isaiah to Hĕz-e-kī'ah, Hear the word of the LORD of hosts:
6 Behold, the days come, that all that *is* in thine house, and *that* which thy fathers have laid up in store until this day, shall be carried to Babylon: nothing shall be left, saith the LORD.
7 And of thy sons that shall issue from thee, which thou shalt beget, shall they take away; and they shall be eunuchs in the palace of the king of Babylon.
8 Then said Hĕz-e-kī'ah to Isaiah, Good *is* the word of the LORD which thou hast spoken. He said moreover, For there shall be peace and truth in my days.

CHAPTER 40

COMFORT ye, confort ye my people, saith your God.
2 Speak ye comfortably to Jerusalem, and cry unto her, that her warfare is accomplished, that her iniquity is pardoned: for she hath received of the LORD's hand double for all her sins.
3 ¶The voice of him that crieth in the wilderness, Prepare ye the way of the LORD, make straight in the desert a highway for our God.
4 Every valley shall be exalted, and every mountain and hill shall be made low: and the crooked shall be made straight, and the rough places plain:
5 And the glory of the LORD shall be revealed, and all flesh shall see *it* together: for the mouth of the LORD hath spoken *it*.
6 The voice said, Cry. And he said, What shall I cry? All flesh *is* grass, and all the goodliness thereof *is* as the flower of the field:
7 The grass withereth, the flower fadeth: because the spirit of the LORD bloweth upon it: surely the people *is* grass.
8 The grass withereth, the flower fadeth: but the word of our God shall stand for ever.
9 ¶O Zion, that bringest good tidings, get thee up into the high mountain; O Jerusalem, that bringest good tidings, lift up thy voice with strength; lift *it* up, be not afraid; say unto the cities of Jū'dah, Behold your God!
10 Behold, the Lord GOD will come with strong *hand*, and his arm shall rule for him: behold, his reward *is* with him, and his work before him.
11 He shall feed his flock like a shepherd: he shall gather the lambs with his arm, and carry *them* in his bosom, *and* shall gently lead those that are with young.
12 ¶Who hath measured the waters

in the hollow of his hand, and meted
out heaven with the span, and compre-
hended the dust of the earth in a mea-
sure, and weighed the mountains in
scales, and the hills in a balance?
13 Who hath directed the Spirit of the
LORD, or *being* his counsellor hath
taught him?
14 With whom took he counsel, and
who instructed him, and taught him in
the path of judgment, and taught him
knowledge, and shewed to him the way
of understanding?
15 Behold, the nations *are* as a drop
of a bucket, and are counted as the
small dust of the balance: behold, he
taketh up the isles as a very little thing.
16 And Lebanon *is* not sufficient to
burn, nor the beasts thereof sufficient
for a burnt offering.
17 All nations before him *are* as noth-
ing; and they are counted to him less
than nothing, and vanity.
18 ¶To whom then will ye liken God?
or what likeness will ye compare unto
him?
19 The workman melteth a graven
image, and the goldsmith spreadeth it
over with gold, and casteth silver
chains.
20 He that *is* so impoverished that he
hath no oblation chooseth a tree *that*
will not rot; he seeketh unto him a cun-
ning workman to prepare a graven
image, *that* shall not be moved.
21 Have ye not known? have ye not
heard? hath it not been told you from
the beginning? have ye not understood
from the foundations of the earth?
22 *It is* he that sitteth upon the circle
of the earth, and the inhabitants
thereof *are* as grasshoppers; that
stretcheth out the heavens as a curtain,
and spreadeth them out as a tent to
dwell in:
23 That bringeth the princes to noth-
ing; he maketh the judges of the earth
as vanity.
24 Yea, they shall not be planted; yea,
they shall not be sown: yea, their stock
shall not take root in the earth: and he
shall also blow upon them, and they
shall wither, and the whirlwind shall
take them away as stubble.
25 To whom then will ye liken me, or
shall I be equal? saith the Holy One.
26 Lift up your eyes on high, and be-
hold who hath created these *things*,
that bringeth out their host by number:
he calleth them all by names by the
greatness of his might, for that *he is*
strong in power; not one faileth.
27 Why sayest thou, O Jacob, and
speakest, O Israel, My way is hid from
the LORD, and my judgment is passed
over from my God?
28 Hast thou not known? hast thou
not heard, *that* the everlasting God, the
LORD, the Creator of the ends of the
earth, fainteth not, neither is weary?
there is no searching of his understand-
ing.
29 He giveth power to the faint; and
to *them that have* no might he increas-
eth strength.
30 Even the youths shall faint and be
weary, and the young men shall utterly
fall:
31 But they that wait upon the LORD
shall renew their strength; they shall
mount up with wings as eagles; they
shall run, and not be weary; *and* they
shall walk, and not faint.

CHAPTER 41

KEEP silence before me, O islands; and
let the people renew *their* strength: let
them come near; then let them speak:
let us come near together to judgment.
2 Who raised up the righteous *man*
from the east, called him to his foot,
gave the nations before him, and made
him rule over kings? he gave *them* as
the dust to his sword, *and* as driven
stubble to his bow.
3 He pursued them, *and* passed safely;
even by the way *that* he had not
gone with his feet.
4 Who hath wrought and done *it*, call-
ing the generations from the beginning?
I the LORD, the first, and with the
last; I *am* he.
5 The isles saw *it*, and feared; the
ends of the earth were afraid, drew
near, and came.
6 They helped every one his neigh-
bour; and *every one* said to his
brother, Be of good courage.
7 So the carpenter encouraged the
goldsmith, *and* he that smootheth *with*
the hammer him that smote the anvil,
saying, It *is* ready for the sodering: and
he fastened it with nails, *that* it should
not be moved.
8 But thou, Israel, *art* my servant, Ja-
cob whom I have chosen, the seed of
Abraham my friend.
9 *Thou* whom I have taken from the
ends of the earth, and called thee from
the chief men thereof, and said unto
thee, Thou *art* my servant; I have cho-
sen thee, and not cast thee away.
10 ¶Fear thou not; for I *am* with thee:
be not dismayed; for I *am* thy God: I
will strengthen thee; yea, I will help
thee; yea, I will uphold thee with the
right hand of my righteousness.
11 Behold, all they that were incensed
against thee shall be ashamed

and confounded: they shall be as noth-
ing; and they that strive with thee shall
perish.
12 Thou shalt seek them, and shalt
not find them, *even* them that con-
tended with thee: they that war against
thee shall be as nothing, and as a thing
of nought.
13 For I the LORD thy God will hold
thy right hand, saying unto thee, Fear
not; I will help thee.
14 Fear not, thou worm Jacob, *and* ye
men of Israel; I will help thee, saith the
LORD, and thy redeemer, the Holy One
of Israel.
15 Behold, I will make thee a new
sharp threshing instrument having
teeth: thou shalt thresh the mountains,
and beat *them* small, and shalt make
the hills as chaff.
16 Thou shalt fan them, and the wind
shall carry them away, and the whirl-
wind shall scatter them: and thou shalt
rejoice in the LORD, *and* shalt glory in
the Holy One of Israel.
17 *When* the poor and needy seek
water, and *there is* none, *and* their
tongue faileth for thirst, I the LORD will
hear them, I the God of Israel will not
forsake them.
18 I will open rivers in high places,
and fountains in the midst of the val-
leys: I will make the wilderness a pool
of water, and the dry land springs of
water.
19 I will plant in the wilderness the
cedar, the shittah tree, and the myrtle,
and the oil tree; I will set in the desert
the fir tree, *and* the pine, and the box
tree together:
20 That they may see, and know, and
consider, and understand together,
that the hand of the LORD hath done
this, and the Holy One of Israel hath
created it.
21 ¶Produce your cause, saith the
LORD; bring forth your strong *reasons*,
saith the King of Jacob.
22 Let them bring *them* forth, and
shew us what shall happen: let them
shew the former things, what they *be*,
that we may consider them, and know
the latter end of them; or declare us
things for to come.
23 Shew the things that are to come
hereafter, that we may know that ye
are gods: yea, do good, or do evil, that
we may be dismayed, and behold *it*
together.
24 Behold, ye *are* of nothing, and
your work of nought: an abomination *is*
he that chooseth you.
25 I have raised up *one* from the
north, and he shall come: from the ris-
ing of the sun shall he call upon my
name: and he shall come upon princes
as *upon* morter, and as the potter tread-
eth clay.
26 Who hath declared from the
beginning, that we may know? and
beforetime, that we may say, *He is*
righteous? yea, *there is* none that shew-
eth, yea, *there is* none that declareth,
yea, *there is* none that heareth your
words.
27 The first *shall say* to Zion, Behold,
behold them: and I will give to Jeru-
salem one that bringeth good tidings.
28 For I beheld, and *there was* no
man; even among them, and *there was*
no counsellor, that, when I asked of
them, could answer a word.
29 Behold, they *are* all vanity; their
works *are* nothing: their molten images
are wind and confusion.

CHAPTER 42

BEHOLD my servant, whom I uphold;
mine elect, *in whom* my soul de-
lighteth; I have put my spirit upon him:
he shall bring forth judgment to the
Gentiles.
2 He shall not cry, nor lift up, nor
cause his voice to be heard in the street.
3 A bruised reed shall he not break,
and the smoking flax shall he not
quench: he shall bring forth judgment
unto truth.
4 He shall not fail nor be discouraged,
till he have set judgment in the earth:
and the isles shall wait for his law.
5 ¶Thus saith God the LORD, he that
created the heavens, and stretched
them out; he that spread forth the
earth, and that which cometh out of it;
he that giveth breath unto the people
upon it, and spirit to them that walk
therein:
6 I the LORD have called thee in
righteousness, and will hold thine
hand, and will keep thee, and give thee
for a covenant of the people, for a light
of the Gentiles;
7 To open the blind eyes, to bring out
the prisoners from the prison, *and*
them that sit in darkness out of the pris-
on house.
8 I am the LORD: that *is* my name: and
my glory will I not give to another,
neither my praise to graven images.
9 Behold, the former things are come
to pass, and new things do I declare:
before they spring forth I tell you of
them.
10 ¶Sing unto the LORD a new song,
and his praise from the end of the earth,
ye that go down to the sea, and all that
is therein; the isles, and the inhabitants
thereof.

11 Let the wilderness and the cities
thereof lift up *their voice*, the villages
that Kē'dar doth inhabit: let the inhabi-
tants of the rock sing, let them shout
from the top of the mountains.
12 Let them give glory unto the LORD,
and declare his praise in the islands.
13 The LORD shall go forth as a
mighty man, he shall stir up jealousy
like a man of war: he shall cry, yea,
roar; he shall prevail against his en-
emies.
14 I have long time holden my peace;
I have been still, *and* refrained myself:
now will I cry like a travailing woman; I
will destroy and devour at once.
15 I will make waste mountains and
hills, and dry up all their herbs; and I
will make the rivers islands, and I will
dry up the pools.
16 And I will bring the blind by a way
that they knew not; I will lead them in
paths *that* they have not known: I will
make darkness light before them, and
crooked things straight. These things
will I do unto them, and not forsake
them.
17 They shall be turned back, they
shall be greatly ashamed, that trust in
graven images, that say to the molten
images, Ye *are* our gods.
18 ¶Hear, ye deaf; and look, ye blind,
that ye may see.
19 Who *is* blind, but my servant? or
deaf, as my messenger *that* I sent? who
is blind as *he that is* perfect, and blind
as the LORD's servant?
20 Seeing many things, but thou ob-
servest not; opening the ears, but he
heareth not.
21 The LORD is well pleased for his
righteousness' sake; he will magnify
the law, and make *it* honourable.
22 But this *is* a people robbed and
spoiled; *they are* all of them snared in
holes, and they are hid in prison
houses: they are for a prey, and none
delivereth; for a spoil, and none saith,
Restore.
23 Who among you will give ear to
this? *who* will hearken and hear for the
time to come?
24 Who gave Jacob for a spoil, and
Israel to the robbers? did not the LORD,
he against whom we have sinned? for
they would not walk in his ways,
neither were they obedient unto his
law.
25 Therefore he hath poured upon
him the fury of his anger, and the
strength of battle: and it hath set him
on fire round about, yet he knew not;
and it burned him, yet he laid *it* not to
heart.

CHAPTER 43

BUT now thus saith the LORD that
created thee, O Jacob, and he that
formed thee, O Israel, Fear not: for I
have redeemed thee, I have called *thee*
by thy name; thou *art* mine.
2 When thou passest through the wa-
ters, I *will be* with thee; and through
the rivers, they shall not overflow thee:
when thou walkest through the fire,
thou shalt not be burned; neither shall
the flame kindle upon thee.
3 For I *am* the LORD thy God, the Holy
One of Israel, thy Saviour: I gave Egypt
for thy ransom, Ē-thĭ-ō'pĭ-a and Sē'ba
for thee.
4 Since thou wast precious in my
sight, thou hast been honourable, and I
have loved thee: therefore will I give
men for thee, and people for thy life.
5 Fear not: for I *am* with thee: I will
bring thy seed from the east, and gath-
er thee from the west;
6 I will say to the north, Give up; and
to the south, Keep not back: bring my
sons from far, and my daughters from
the ends of the earth;
7 *Even* every one that is called by my
name: for I have created him for my
glory, I have formed him; yea, I have
made him.
8 ¶Bring forth the blind people that
have eyes, and the deaf that have ears.
9 Let all the nations be gathered to-
gether, and let the people be assembled:
who among them can declare this, and
shew us former things? let them bring
forth their witnesses, that they may be
justified: or let them hear, and say, *It is*
truth.
10 Ye *are* my witnesses, saith the
LORD, and my servant whom I have
chosen: that ye may know and believe
me, and understand that I *am* he: be-
fore me there was no God formed,
neither shall there be after me.
11 I, *even* I, *am* the LORD; and beside
me *there is* no saviour.
12 I have declared, and have saved,
and I have shewed, when *there was* no
strange *god* among you: therefore ye
are my witnesses, saith the LORD, that I
am God.
13 Yea, before the day *was* I *am* he;
and *there is* none that can deliver out of
my hand: I will work, and who shall let
it?
14 ¶Thus saith the LORD, your redeem-
er, the Holy One of Israel; For your
sake I have sent to Babylon, and have
brought down all their nobles, and the
Chăl-dē'ans, whose cry *is* in the ships.
15 I *am* the LORD, your Holy One, the
creator of Israel, your King.

16 Thus saith the LORD, which maketh a way in the sea, and a path in the mighty waters;
17 Which bringeth forth the chariot and horse, the army and the power; they shall lie down together, they shall not rise: they are extinct, they are quenched as tow.
18 Remember ye not the former things, neither consider the things of old.
19 Behold, I will do a new thing; now it shall spring forth; shall ye not know it? I will even make a way in the wilderness, *and* rivers in the desert.
20 The beast of the field shall honour me, the dragons and the owls: because I give waters in the wilderness, *and* rivers in the desert, to give drink to my people, my chosen.
21 This people have I formed for myself; they shall shew forth my praise.
22 ¶But thou hast not called upon me, O Jacob; but thou hast been weary of me, O Israel.
23 Thou hast not brought me the small cattle of thy burnt offerings; neither hast thou honoured me with thy sacrifices. I have not caused thee to serve with an offering, nor wearied thee with incense.
24 Thou hast bought me no sweet cane with money, neither hast thou filled me with the fat of thy sacrifices: but thou hast made me to serve with thy sins, thou hast wearied me with thine iniquities.
25 I, *even* I, *am* he that blotteth out thy transgressions for mine own sake, and will not remember thy sins.
26 Put me in remembrance: let us plead together: declare thou, that thou mayest be justified.
27 Thy first father hath sinned, and thy teachers have transgressed against me.
28 Therefore I have profaned the princes of the sanctuary, and have given Jacob to the curse, and Israel to reproaches.

CHAPTER 44

YET now hear, O Jacob my servant; and Israel, whom I have chosen:
2 Thus saith the LORD that made thee, and formed thee from the womb, *which* will help thee; Fear not, O Jacob, my servant; and thou, Jĕs'u-run, whom I have chosen.
3 For I will pour water upon him that is thirsty, and floods upon the dry ground: I will pour my spirit upon thy seed, and my blessing upon thine offspring:
4 And they shall spring up *as* among the grass, as willows by the water courses.
5 One shall say, I *am* the LORD's; and another shall call *himself* by the name of Jacob; and another shall subscribe *with* his hand unto the LORD, and surname *himself* by the name of Israel.
6 Thus saith the LORD the King of Israel, and his redeemer the LORD of hosts; I *am* the first, and I *am* the last; and beside me *there is* no God.
7 And who, as I, shall call, and shall declare it, and set it in order for me, since I appointed the ancient people? and the things that are coming, and shall come, let them shew unto them.
8 Fear ye not, neither be afraid: have not I told thee from that time, and have declared *it?* ye *are* even my witnesses. Is there a God beside me? yea, *there is* no God; I know not *any*.
9 They that make a graven image *are* all of them vanity; and their delectable things shall not profit; and they *are* their own witnesses; they see not, nor know; that they may be ashamed.
10 Who hath formed a god, or molten a graven image *that* is profitable for nothing?
11 Behold, all his fellows shall be ashamed: and the workmen, they *are* of men: let them all be gathered together, let them stand up; *yet* they shall fear, *and* they shall be ashamed together.
12 The smith with the tongs both worketh in the coals, and fashioneth it with hammers, and worketh it with the strength of his arms: yea, he is hungry, and his strength faileth: he drinketh no water, and is faint.
13 The carpenter stretcheth out *his* rule; he marketh it out with a line; he fitteth it with planes, and he marketh it out with the compass, and maketh it after the figure of a man, according to the beauty of a man; that it may remain in the house.
14 He heweth him down cedars, and taketh the cypress and the oak, which he strengtheneth for himself among the trees of the forest: he planteth an ash, and the rain doth nourish *it*.
15 Then shall it be for a man to burn: for he will take thereof, and warm himself; yea, he kindleth *it,* and baketh bread; yea, he maketh a god, and worshippeth *it;* he maketh it a graven image, and falleth down thereto.
16 He burneth part thereof in the fire; with part thereof he eateth flesh; he roasteth roast, and is satisfied: yea, he warmeth *himself,* and saith, Aha, I am warm, I have seen the fire:
17 And the residue thereof he maketh a god, *even* his graven image: he falleth

down unto it, and worshippeth *it*, and prayeth unto it, and saith, Deliver me; for thou *art* my god.

18 They have not known nor understood: for he hath shut their eyes, that they cannot see; *and* their hearts, that they cannot understand.

19 And none considereth in his heart, neither *is there* knowledge nor understanding to say, I have burned part of it in the fire; yea, also I have baked bread upon the coals thereof; I have roasted flesh, and eaten *it:* and shall I make the residue thereof an abomination? shall I fall down to the stock of a tree?

20 He feedeth on ashes: a deceived heart hath turned him aside, that he cannot deliver his soul, nor say, *Is there* not a lie in my right hand?

21 ¶Remember these, O Jacob and Israel; for thou *art* my servant: I have formed thee; thou *art* my servant: O Israel, thou shalt not be forgotten of me.

22 I have blotted out, as a thick cloud, thy transgressions, and, as a cloud, thy sins: return unto me; for I have redeemed thee.

23 Sing, O ye heavens; for the LORD hath done *it:* shout, ye lower parts of the earth: break forth into singing, ye mountains, O forest, and every tree therein: for the LORD hath redeemed Jacob, and glorified himself in Israel.

24 Thus saith the LORD, thy redeemer, and he that formed thee from the womb, I *am* the LORD that maketh all *things;* that stretcheth forth the heavens alone; that spreadeth abroad the earth by myself;

25 That frustrateth the tokens of the liars, and maketh diviners mad; that turneth wise *men* backward, and maketh their knowledge foolish;

26 That confirmeth the word of his servant, and performeth the counsel of his messengers; that saith to Jerusalem, Thou shalt be inhabited; and to the cities of Jū'dah, Ye shall be built, and I will raise up the decayed places thereof:

27 That saith to the deep, Be dry, and I will dry up thy rivers:

28 That saith of Cyrus, *He is* my shepherd, and shall perform all my pleasure: even saying to Jerusalem, Thou shalt be built; and to the temple, Thy foundation shall be laid.

CHAPTER 45

THUS saith the LORD to his anointed, to Cyrus, whose right hand I have holden, to subdue nations before him; and I will loose the loins of kings, to open before him the two leaved gates; and the gates shall not be shut;

2 I will go before thee, and make the crooked places straight: I will break in pieces the gates of brass, and cut in sunder the bars of iron:

3 And I will give thee the treasures of darkness, and hidden riches of secret places, that thou mayest know that I, the LORD, which call *thee* by thy name, *am* the God of Israel.

4 For Jacob my servant's sake, and Israel mine elect, I have even called thee by thy name: I have surnamed thee, though thou hast not known me.

5 I *am* the LORD, and *there is* none else, *there is* no God beside me: I girded thee, though thou hast not known me:

6 That they may know from the rising of the sun, and from the west, that *there is* none beside me. I *am* the LORD, and *there is* none else.

7 I form the light, and create darkness: I make peace, and create evil: I the LORD do all these *things*.

8 Drop down, ye heavens, from above, and let the skies pour down righteousness: let the earth open, and let them bring forth salvation, and let righteousness spring up together; I the LORD have created it.

9 Woe unto him that striveth with his Maker! *Let* the potsherd *strive* with the potsherds of the earth. Shall the clay say to him that fashioneth it, What makest thou? or thy work, He hath no hands?

10 Woe unto him that saith unto *his* father, What begettest thou? or to the woman, What hast thou brought forth?

11 Thus saith the LORD, the Holy One of Israel, and his Maker, Ask me of things to come concerning my sons, and concerning the work of my hands command ye me.

12 I have made the earth, and created man upon it: I, *even* my hands, have stretched out the heavens, and all their host have I commanded.

13 I have raised him up in righteousness, and I will direct all his ways: he shall build my city, and he shall let go my captives, not for price nor reward, saith the LORD of hosts.

14 Thus saith the LORD, The labour of Egypt, and merchandise of Ē-thĭ-ō'pĭ-a and of the Sa-bē'anṡ, men of stature, shall come over unto thee, and they shall be thine: they shall come after thee; in chains they shall come over, and they shall fall down unto thee, they shall make supplication unto thee, *saying*, Surely God *is* in thee; and *there is* none else, *there is* no God.

15 Verily thou *art* a God that hidest
thyself, O God of Israel, the Saviour.
16 They shall be ashamed, and also
confounded, all of them: they shall go
to confusion together *that are* makers
of idols.
17 *But* Israel shall be saved in the
LORD with an everlasting salvation: ye
shall not be ashamed nor confounded
world without end.
18 For thus saith the LORD that
created the heavens; God himself that
formed the earth and made it; he hath
established it, he created it not in vain,
he formed it to be inhabited: I *am* the
LORD; and *there is* none else.
19 I have not spoken in secret, in a
dark place of the earth: I said not unto
the seed of Jacob, Seek ye me in vain: I
the LORD speak righteousness, I declare
things that are right.
20 ¶Assemble yourselves and come;
draw near together, ye *that are* escaped
of the nations: they have no knowledge
that set up the wood of their graven
image, and pray unto a god *that* cannot
save.
21 Tell ye, and bring *them* near; yea,
let them take counsel together: who
hath declared this from ancient time?
who hath told it from that time? *have*
not I the LORD? and *there is* no God else
beside me; a just God and a Saviour;
there is none beside me.
22 Look unto me, and be ye saved, all
the ends of the earth: for I *am* God, and
there is none else.
23 I have sworn by myself, the word
is gone out of my mouth *in* righteous-
ness, and shall not return, That unto me
every knee shall bow, every tongue
shall swear.
24 Surely, shall *one* say, in the LORD
have I righteousness and strength:
even to him shall *men* come; and all
that are incensed against him shall be
ashamed.
25 In the LORD shall all the seed of
Israel be justified, and shall glory.

CHAPTER 46

BEL boweth down, Nebo stoopeth,
their idols were upon the beasts, and
upon the cattle: your carriages *were*
heavy loaden; *they are* a burden to the
weary *beast*.
2 They stoop, they bow down togeth-
er; they could not deliver the burden,
but themselves are gone into captivity.
3 ¶Hearken unto me, O house of Ja-
cob, and all the remnant of the house of
Israel, which are borne *by me* from the
belly, which are carried from the
womb:
4 And *even* to *your* old age I *am* he;
and *even* to hoar hairs will I carry *you*: I
have made, and I will bear; even I will
carry, and will deliver *you*.
5 ¶To whom will ye liken me, and
make *me* equal, and compare me, that
we may be like?
6 They lavish gold out of the bag, and
weigh silver in the balance, *and* hire a
goldsmith; and he maketh it a god: they
fall down, yea, they worship.
7 They bear him upon the shoulder,
they carry him, and set him in his place,
and he standeth; from his place shall he
not remove: yea, *one* shall cry unto
him, yet can he not answer, nor save
him out of his trouble.
8 Remember this, and shew your-
selves men: bring *it* again to mind, O ye
transgressors.
9 Remember the former things of old:
for I *am* God, and *there is* none else; I
am God, and *there is* none like me,
10 Declaring the end from the begin-
ning, and from ancient times *the things*
that are not *yet* done, saying, My coun-
sel shall stand, and I will do all my plea-
sure:
11 Calling a ravenous bird from the
east, the man that executeth my coun-
sel from a far country: yea, I have spok-
en *it*, I will also bring it to pass; I have
purposed *it*, I will also do it.
12 ¶Hearken unto me, ye stout-
hearted, that *are* far from righ-
teousness:
13 I bring near my righteousness: it
shall not be far off, and my salvation
shall not tarry: and I will place salva-
tion in Zion for Israel my glory.

CHAPTER 47

COME down, and sit in the dust, O vir-
gin daughter of Babylon, sit on the
ground: *there is* no throne, O daughter
of the Chăl-dē'anṡ: for thou shalt no
more be called tender and delicate.
2 Take the millstones, and grind
meal; uncover thy locks, make bare the
leg, uncover the thigh, pass over the riv-
ers.
3 Thy nakedness shall be uncovered,
yea, thy shame shall be seen: I will take
vengeance, and I will not meet *thee as* a
man.
4 ¶*As for* our redeemer, the LORD of
hosts *is* his name, the Holy One of
Israel.
5 Sit thou silent, and get thee into
darkness, O daughter of the Chăl-dē'-
anṡ: for thou shalt no more be called,
The lady of kingdoms.
6 I was wroth with my people, I have
polluted mine inheritance, and given
them into thine hand: thou didst shew

them no mercy; upon the ancient hast
thou very heavily laid thy yoke.
7 And thou saidst, I shall be a lady for
ever: *so* that thou didst not lay these
things to thy heart, neither didst
remember the latter end of it.
8 Therefore hear now this, *thou that*
art given to pleasures, that dwellest
carelessly, that sayest in thine heart, I
am, and none else beside me; I shall not
sit *as* a widow, neither shall I know the
loss of children:
9 But these two *things* shall come to
thee in a moment in one day, the loss of
children, and widowhood: they shall
come upon thee in their perfection for
the multitude of thy sorceries, *and* for
the great abundance of thine enchant-
ments.
10 For thou hast trusted in thy
wickedness: thou hast said, None seeth
me. Thy wisdom and thy knowledge, it
hath perverted thee; and thou hast said
in thine heart, I *am*, and none else be-
side me.
11 Therefore shall evil come upon
thee; thou shalt not know from whence
it riseth: and mischief shall fall upon
thee; thou shalt not be able to put it off:
and desolation shall come upon thee
suddenly, *which* thou shalt not know.
12 Stand now with thine enchant-
ments, and with the multitude of thy
sorceries, wherein thou hast laboured
from thy youth; if so be thou shalt be
able to profit, if so be thou mayest pre-
vail.
13 Thou art wearied in the multitude
of thy counsels. Let now the astrologers,
the stargazers, the monthly prog-
nosticators, stand up, and save thee
from *these things* that shall come upon
thee.
14 Behold, they shall be as stubble;
the fire shall burn them; they shall not
deliver themselves from the power of
the flame: *there shall* not *be* a coal to
warm at, *nor* fire to sit before it.
15 Thus shall they be unto thee with
whom thou hast laboured, *even* thy
merchants, from thy youth: they shall
wander every one to his quarter; none
shall save thee.

CHAPTER 48

HEAR ye this, O house of Jacob, which
are called by the name of Israel, and are
come forth out of the waters of Jū'dah,
which swear by the name of the LORD,
and make mention of the God of Israel,
but not in truth, nor in righteousness.
2 For they call themselves of the holy
city, and stay themselves upon the God
of Israel; The LORD of hosts *is* his name.
3 I have declared the former things
from the beginning; and they went
forth out of my mouth, and I shewed
them; I did *them* suddenly, and they
came to pass.
4 Because I knew that thou *art* obsti-
nate, and thy neck *is* an iron sinew, and
thy brow brass;
5 I have even from the beginning de-
clared *it* to thee; before it came to pass I
shewed *it* thee: lest thou shouldest say,
Mine idol hath done them, and my grav-
en image, and my molten image, hath
commanded them.
6 Thou hast heard, see all this; and
will not ye declare *it?* I have shewed
thee new things from this time, even
hidden things, and thou didst not know
them.
7 They are created now, and not from
the beginning; even before the day
when thou heardest them not; lest thou
shouldest say, Behold, I knew them.
8 Yea, thou heardest not; yea, thou
knewest not; yea, from that time *that*
thine ear was not opened: for I knew
that thou wouldest deal very treach-
erously, and wast called a transgres-
sor from the womb.
9 ¶For my name's sake will I defer
mine anger, and for my praise will I re-
frain for thee, that I cut thee not off.
10 Behold, I have refined thee, but
not with silver; I have chosen thee in
the furnace of affliction.
11 For mine own sake, *even* for mine
own sake, will I do *it:* for how should
my name be polluted? and I will not
give my glory unto another.
12 ¶Hearken unto me, O Jacob and
Israel, my called; I *am* he; I *am* the first,
I also *am* the last.
13 Mine hand also hath laid the foun-
dation of the earth, and my right hand
hath spanned the heavens: *when* I call
unto them, they stand up together.
14 All ye, assemble yourselves, and
hear; which among them hath declared
these *things?* The LORD hath loved him:
he will do his pleasure on Babylon, and
his arm *shall be on* the Chăl-dē'ans.
15 I, *even* I, have spoken; yea, I have
called him: I have brought him, and he
shall make his way prosperous.
16 ¶Come ye near unto me, hear ye
this; I have not spoken in secret from
the beginning; from the time that it
was, there *am* I: and now the Lord GOD,
and his Spirit, hath sent me.
17 Thus saith the LORD, thy Redeem-
er, the Holy One of Israel; I *am* the
LORD thy God which teacheth thee to
profit, which leadeth thee by the way
that thou shouldest go.
18 O that thou hadst hearkened to my
commandments! then had thy peace

been as a river and thy righteousness as the waves of the sea:

19 Thy seed also had been as the sand, and the offspring of thy bowels like the gravel thereof; his name should not have been cut off nor destroyed from before me.

20 ¶Go ye forth of Babylon, flee ye from the Chăl-dē′anṡ, with a voice of singing declare ye, tell this, utter it *even* to the end of the earth; say ye, The LORD hath redeemed his servant Jacob.

21 And they thirsted not *when* he led them through the deserts: he caused the waters to flow out of the rock for them: he clave the rock also, and the waters gushed out.

22 *There is* no peace, saith the LORD, unto the wicked.

CHAPTER 49

LISTEN, O isles, unto me; and hearken, ye people, from far; The LORD hath called me from the womb; from the bowels of my mother hath he made mention of my name.

2 And he hath made my mouth like a sharp sword; in the shadow of his hand hath he hid me, and made me a polished shaft; in his quiver hath he hid me;

3 And said unto me, Thou *art* my servant, O Israel, in whom I will be glorified.

4 Then I said, I have laboured in vain, I have spent my strength for nought, and in vain: *yet* surely my judgment *is* with the LORD, and my work with my God.

5 And now, saith the LORD that formed me from the womb *to be* his servant, to bring Jacob again to him, Though Israel be not gathered, yet shall I be glorious in the eyes of the LORD, and my God shall be my strength.

6 And he said, It is a light thing that thou shouldest be my servant to raise up the tribes of Jacob, and to restore the preserved of Israel: I will also give thee for a light to the Gentiles, that thou mayest be my salvation unto the end of the earth.

7 ¶Thus saith the LORD, the Redeemer of Israel, *and* his Holy One, to him whom man despiseth, to him whom the nation abhorreth, to a servant of rulers, Kings shall see and arise, princes also shall worship, because of the LORD that is faithful, *and* the Holy One of Israel, and he shall choose thee.

8 Thus saith the LORD, In an acceptable time have I heard thee, and in a day of salvation have I helped thee: and I will preserve thee, and give thee for a covenant of the people, to establish the earth, to cause to inherit the desolate heritages;

9 That thou mayest say to the prisoners, Go forth; to them that *are* in darkness, Shew yourselves. They shall feed in the ways, and their pastures *shall be* in all high places.

10 They shall not hunger nor thirst; neither shall the heat nor sun smite them: for he that hath mercy on them shall lead them, even by the springs of water shall he guide them.

11 And I will make all my mountains a way, and my highways shall be exalted.

12 Behold, these shall come from far: and, lo, these from the north and from the west; and these from the land of Sī′nim.

13 ¶Sing, O heavens; and be joyful, O earth; and break forth into singing, O mountains: for the LORD hath comforted his people, and will have mercy upon his afflicted.

14 But Zion said, The LORD hath forsaken me, and my Lord hath forgotten me.

15 Can a woman forget her sucking child, that she should not have compassion on the son of her womb? yea, they may forget, yet will I not forget thee.

16 Behold, I have graven thee upon the palms of *my* hands; thy walls *are* continually before me.

17 Thy children shall make haste; thy destroyers and they that made thee waste shall go forth of thee.

18 Lift up thine eyes round about, and behold: all these gather themselves together, *and* come to thee. *As* I live, saith the LORD, thou shalt surely clothe thee with them all, as with an ornament, and bind them *on thee*, as a bride *doeth*.

19 For thy waste and thy desolate places, and the land of thy destruction, shall even now be too narrow by reason of the inhabitants, and they that swallowed thee up shall be far away.

20 The children which thou shalt have, after thou hast lost the other, shall say again in thine ears, The place *is* too strait for me: give place to me that I may dwell.

21 Then shalt thou say in thine heart, who hath begotten me these, seeing I have lost my children, and am desolate, a captive, and removing to and fro? and who hath brought up these? Behold, I was left alone; these, where *had* they *been?*

22 Thus saith the Lord GOD, Behold, I will lift up mine hand to the Gentiles, and set up my standard to the people: and they shall bring thy sons in *their*

arms, and thy daughters shall be carried upon *their* shoulders.

23 And kings shall be thy nursing fathers, and their queens thy nursing mothers: they shall bow down to thee with *their* face toward the earth, and lick up the dust of thy feet; and thou shalt know that I *am* the LORD: for they shall not be ashamed that wait for me.

24 ¶Shall the prey be taken from the mighty, or the lawful captive delivered?

25 But thus saith the LORD, Even the captives of the mighty shall be taken away, and the prey of the terrible shall be delivered: for I will contend with him that contendeth with thee, and I will save thy children.

26 And I will feed them that oppress thee with their own flesh; and they shall be drunken with their own blood, as with sweet wine: and all flesh shall know that I the LORD *am* thy Saviour and thy Redeemer, the mighty One of Jacob.

CHAPTER 50

THUS saith the LORD, Where *is* the bill of your mother's divorcement, whom I have put away? or which of my creditors *is it* to whom I have sold you? Behold, for your iniquities have ye sold yourselves, and for your transgressions is your mother put away.

2 Wherefore, when I came, *was there* no man? when I called, *was there* none to answer? Is my hand shortened at all, that it cannot redeem? or have I no power to deliver? behold, at my rebuke I dry up the sea, I make the rivers a wilderness: their fish stinketh, because *there is* no water, and dieth for thirst.

3 I clothe the heavens with blackness, and I make sackcloth their covering.

4 ¶The Lord GOD hath given me the tongue of the learned, that I should know how to speak a word in season to *him that is* weary: he wakeneth morning by morning, he wakeneth mine ear to hear as the learned.

5 The Lord GOD hath opened mine ear, and I was not rebellious, neither turned away back.

6 I gave my back to the smiters, and my cheeks to them that plucked off the hair: I hid not my face from shame and spitting.

7 For the Lord GOD will help me; therefore shall I not be confounded: therefore have I set my face like a flint, and I know that I shall not be ashamed.

8 *He is* near that justifieth me; who will contend with me? let us stand together: who *is* mine adversary? let him come near to me.

9 Behold, the Lord GOD will help me; who *is* he *that* shall condemn me? lo, they all shall wax old as a garment; the moth shall eat them up.

10 ¶Who *is* among you that feareth the LORD, that obeyeth the voice of his servant, that walketh *in* darkness, and hath no light? let him trust in the name of the LORD, and stay upon his God.

11 Behold, all ye that kindle a fire, that compass *yourselves* about with sparks: walk in the light of your fire, and in the sparks *that* ye have kindled. This shall ye have of mine hand; ye shall lie down in sorrow.

CHAPTER 51

HEARKEN to me, ye that follow after righteousness, ye that seek the LORD: look unto the rock *whence* ye are hewn, and to the hole of the pit *whence* ye are digged.

2 Look unto Abraham your father, and unto Sarah *that* bare you: for I called him alone, and blessed him, and increased him.

3 For the LORD shall comfort Zion: he will comfort all her waste places; and he will make her wilderness like Eden, and her desert like the garden of the LORD; joy and gladness shall be found therein, thanksgiving, and the voice of melody.

4 ¶Hearken unto me, my people; and give ear unto me, O my nation: for a law shall proceed from me, and I will make my judgment to rest for a light of the people.

5 My righteousness *is* near; my salvation is gone forth, and mine arms shall judge the people; the isles shall wait upon me, and on mine arm shall they trust.

6 Lift up your eyes to the heavens, and look upon the earth beneath: for the heavens shall vanish away like smoke, and the earth shall wax old like a garment, and they that dwell therein shall die in like manner: but my salvation shall be for ever, and my righteousness shall not be abolished.

7 ¶Hearken unto me, ye that know righteousness, the people in whose heart *is* my law; fear ye not the reproach of men, neither be ye afraid of their revilings.

8 For the moth shall eat them up like a garment, and the worm shall eat them like wool: but my righteousness shall be for ever, and my salvation from generation to generation.

9 ¶Awake, awake, put on strength, O arm of the LORD; awake, as in the an-

cient days, in the generations of old. *Art* thou not it that hath cut Rahab, *and* wounded the dragon?

10 *Art* thou not it which hath dried the sea, the waters of the great deep; that hath made the depths of the sea a way for the ransomed to pass over?

11 Therefore the redeemed of the LORD shall return, and come with singing unto Zion; and everlasting joy *shall be* upon their head: they shall obtain gladness and joy; *and* sorrow and mourning shall flee away.

12 I, *even* I, *am* he that comforteth you: who *art* thou, that thou shouldest be afraid of a man *that* shall die, and of the son of man *which* shall be made *as* grass;

13 And forgettest the LORD thy maker, that hath stretched forth the heavens, and laid the foundations of the earth; and hast feared continually every day because of the fury of the oppressor, as if he were ready to destroy? and where *is* the fury of the oppressor?

14 The captive exile hasteneth that he may be loosed, and that he should not die in the pit, nor that his bread should fail.

15 But I *am* the LORD thy God, that divided the sea, whose waves roared: The LORD of hosts *is* his name.

16 And I have put my words in thy mouth, and I have covered thee in the shadow of mine hand, that I may plant the heavens, and lay the foundations of the earth, and say unto Zion, Thou *art* my people.

17 ¶Awake, awake, stand up, O Jerusalem, which hast drunk at the hand of the LORD the cup of his fury; thou hast drunken the dregs of the cup of trembling, *and* wrung *them* out.

18 *There is* none to guide her among all the sons *whom* she hath brought forth; neither *is there any* that taketh her by the hand of all the sons *that* she hath brought up.

19 These two *things* are come unto thee; who shall be sorry for thee? desolation, and destruction, and the famine, and the sword: by whom shall I comfort thee?

20 Thy sons have fainted, they lie at the head of all the streets, as a wild bull in a net: they are full of the fury of the LORD, the rebuke of thy God.

21 ¶Therefore hear now this, thou afflicted, and drunken, but not with wine:

22 Thus saith thy Lord the LORD, and thy God *that* pleadeth the cause of his people, Behold, I have taken out of thine hand the cup of trembling, *even* the dregs of the cup of my fury; thou shalt no more drink it again:

23 But I will put it into the hand of them that afflict thee; which have said to thy soul, Bow down, that we may go over: and thou hast laid thy body as the ground, and as the street, to them that went over.

CHAPTER 52

AWAKE, awake; put on thy strength, O Zion; put on thy beautiful garments, O Jerusalem, the holy city: for henceforth there shall no more come into thee the uncircumcised and the unclean.

2 Shake thyself from the dust; arise, *and* sit down, O Jerusalem: loose thyself from the bands of thy neck, O captive daughter of Zion.

3 For thus saith the LORD, Ye have sold yourselves for nought; and ye shall be redeemed without money.

4 For thus saith the Lord GOD, My people went down aforetime into Egypt to sojourn there; and the Assyrian oppressed them without cause.

5 Now therefore, what have I here, saith the LORD, that my people is taken away for nought? they that rule over them make them to howl, saith the LORD; and my name continually every day *is* blasphemed.

6 Therefore my people shall know my name: therefore *they shall know* in that day that I *am* he that doth speak: behold, *it is* I.

7 ¶How beautiful upon the mountains are the feet of him that bringeth good tidings, that publisheth peace; that bringeth good tidings of good, that publisheth salvation; that saith unto Zion, Thy God reigneth!

8 Thy watchmen shall lift up the voice; with the voice together shall they sing: for they shall see eye to eye, when the LORD shall bring again Zion.

9 Break forth into joy, sing together, ye waste places of Jerusalem: for the LORD hath comforted his people, he hath redeemed Jerusalem.

10 The LORD hath made bare his holy arm in the eyes of all the nations; and all the ends of the earth shall see the salvation of our God.

11 ¶Depart ye, depart ye, go ye out from thence, touch no unclean *thing;* go ye out of the midst of her; be ye clean, that bear the vessels of the LORD.

12 For ye shall not go out with haste, nor go by flight: for the LORD will go before you; and the God of Israel *will be* your rereward.

13 ¶Behold, my servant shall deal

prudently, he shall be exalted and ex-
tolled, and be very high.
14 As many were astonied at thee; his
visage was so marred more than any
man, and his form more than the sons
of men:
15 So shall he sprinkle many nations;
the kings shall shut their mouths at
him: for *that* which had not been told
them shall they see; and *that* which
they had not heard shall they consider.

CHAPTER 53

WHO hath believed our report? and to
whom is the arm of the LORD revealed?
2 For he shall grow up before him as a
tender plant, and as a root out of a dry
ground: he hath no form nor comeli-
ness; and when we shall see him, *there
is* no beauty that we should desire him.
3 He is despised and rejected of men;
a man of sorrows, and acquainted with
grief: and we hid as it were *our* faces
from him; he was despised, and we
esteemed him not.
4 ¶Surely he hath borne our griefs,
and carried our sorrows: yet we did
esteem him stricken, smitten of God,
and afflicted.
5 But he *was* wounded for our trans-
gressions, *he was* bruised for our iniqui-
ties: the chastisement of our peace
was upon him; and with his stripes we
are healed.
6 All we like sheep have gone astray;
we have turned every one to his own
way; and the LORD hath laid on him the
iniquity of us all.
7 He was oppressed, and he was af-
flicted, yet he opened not his mouth: he
is brought as a lamb to the slaughter,
and as a sheep before her shearers is
dumb, so he openeth not his mouth.
8 He was taken from prison and from
judgment: and who shall declare his
generation? for he was cut off out of the
land of the living: for the transgression
of my people was he stricken.
9 And he made his grave with the
wicked, and with the rich in his death;
because he had done no violence,
neither *was any* deceit in his mouth.
10 Yet it pleased the LORD to bruise
him; he hath put *him* to grief: when
thou shalt make his soul an offering for
sin, he shall see *his* seed, he shall pro-
long *his* days, and the pleasure of the
LORD shall prosper in his hand.
11 He shall see of the travail of his
soul, *and* shall be satisfied: by his
knowledge shall my righteous servant
justify many; for he shall bear their in-
iquities.
12 Therefore will I divide him *a por-
tion* with the great, and he shall divide
the spoil with the strong; because he
hath poured out his soul unto death:
and he was numbered with the trans-
gressors; and he bare the sin of many,
and made intercession for the trans-
gressors.

CHAPTER 54

SING, O barren, thou *that* didst not
bear; break forth into singing, and cry
aloud, thou *that* didst not travail with
child: for more *are* the children of the
desolate than the children of the
married wife, saith the LORD.
2 Enlarge the place of thy tent, and let
them stretch forth the curtains of thine
habitations: spare not, lengthen thy
cords, and strengthen thy stakes;
3 For thou shalt break forth on the
right hand and on the left; and thy seed
shall inherit the Gentiles, and make the
desolate cities to be inhabited.
4 Fear not; for thou shalt not be
ashamed: neither be thou confounded;
for thou shalt not be put to shame: for
thou shalt forget the shame of thy
youth, and shalt not remember the
reproach of thy widowhood any more.
5 For thy Maker *is* thine husband; the
LORD of hosts *is* his name; and thy Re-
deemer the Holy One of Israel; The God
of the whole earth shall he be called.
6 For the LORD hath called thee as a
woman forsaken and grieved in spirit,
and a wife of youth, when thou wast
refused, saith thy God.
7 For a small moment have I forsaken
thee; but with great mercies will I gath-
er thee.
8 In a little wrath I hid my face from
thee for a moment; but with everlasting
kindness will I have mercy on thee,
saith the LORD thy Redeemer.
9 For this *is as* the waters of Noah
unto me: for *as* I have sworn that the
waters of Noah should no more go over
the earth; so have I sworn that I would
not be wroth with thee, nor rebuke
thee.
10 For the mountains shall depart,
and the hills be removed; but my kind-
ness shall not depart from thee, neither
shall the covenant of my peace be re-
moved, saith the LORD that hath mercy
on thee.
11 ¶O thou afflicted, tossed with tem-
pest, *and* not comforted, behold, I will
lay thy stones with fair colours, and lay
thy foundations with sapphires.
12 And I will make thy windows of
agates, and thy gates of carbuncles,
and all thy borders of pleasant stones.
13 And all thy children *shall be*
taught of the LORD; and great *shall be*
the peace of thy children.

14 In righteousness shalt thou be established: thou shalt be far from oppression; for thou shalt not fear: and from terror; for it shall not come near thee.

15 Behold, they shall surely gather together, *but* not by me: whosoever shall gather together against thee shall fall for thy sake.

16 Behold, I have created the smith that bloweth the coals in the fire, and that bringeth forth an instrument for his work; and I have created the waster to destroy.

17 No weapon that is formed against thee shall prosper; and every tongue *that* shall rise against thee in judgment thou shalt condemn. This *is* the heritage of the servants of the LORD, and their righteousness *is* of me, saith the LORD.

CHAPTER 55

HO, every one that thirsteth, come ye to the waters, and he that hath no money; come ye, buy, and eat; yea, come, buy wine and milk without money and without price.

2 Wherefore do ye spend money for *that which is* not bread? and your labour for *that which* satisfieth not? hearken diligently unto me, and eat ye *that which is* good, and let your soul delight itself in fatness.

3 Incline your ear, and come unto me: hear, and your soul shall live; and I will make an everlasting covenant with you, *even* the sure mercies of David.

4 Behold, I have given him *for* a witness to the people, a leader and commander to the people.

5 Behold, thou shalt call a nation *that* thou knowest not, and nations *that* knew not thee shall run unto thee because of the LORD thy God, and for the Holy One of Israel; for he hath glorified thee.

6 ¶Seek ye the LORD while he may be found, call ye upon him while he is near:

7 Let the wicked forsake his way, and the unrighteous man his thoughts: and let him return unto the LORD, and he will have mercy upon him; and to our God, for he will abundantly pardon.

8 ¶For my thoughts *are* not your thoughts, neither *are* your ways my ways, saith the LORD.

9 For *as* the heavens are higher than the earth, so are my ways higher than your ways, and my thoughts than your thoughts.

10 For as the rain cometh down, and the snow from heaven, and returneth not thither, but watereth the earth, and maketh it bring forth and bud, that it may give seed to the sower, and bread to the eater:

11 So shall my word be that goeth forth out of my mouth: it shall not return unto me void, but it shall accomplish that which I please, and it shall prosper *in the thing* whereto I sent it.

12 For ye shall go out with joy, and be led forth with peace: the mountains and the hills shall break forth before you into singing, and all the trees of the field shall clap *their* hands.

13 Instead of the thorn shall come up the fir tree, and instead of the brier shall come up the myrtle tree: and it shall be to the LORD for a name, for an everlasting sign *that* shall not be cut off.

CHAPTER 56

THUS saith the LORD, Keep ye judgment, and do justice: for my salvation *is* near to come, and my righteousness to be revealed.

2 Blessed *is* the man *that* doeth this, and the son of man *that* layeth hold on it; that keepeth the sabbath from polluting it, and keepeth his hand from doing any evil.

3 ¶Neither let the son of the stranger, that hath joined himself to the LORD, speak, saying, The LORD hath utterly separated me from his people: neither let the eunuch say, Behold, I *am* a dry tree.

4 For thus saith the LORD unto the eunuchs that keep my sabbaths, and choose *the things* that please me, and take hold of my covenant;

5 Even unto them will I give in mine house and within my walls a place and a name better than of sons and of daughters: I will give them an everlasting name, that shall not be cut off.

6 Also the sons of the stranger, that join themselves to the LORD, to serve him, and to love the name of the LORD, to be his servants, every one that keepeth the sabbath from polluting it, and taketh hold of my covenant;

7 Even them will I bring to my holy mountain, and make them joyful in my house of prayer: their burnt offerings and their sacrifices *shall be* accepted upon mine altar; for mine house shall be called an house of prayer for all people.

8 The Lord GOD which gathereth the outcasts of Israel saith, Yet will I gather *others* to him, beside those that are gathered unto him.

9 ¶All ye beasts of the field, come to devour, *yea,* all ye beasts in the forest.

10 His watchmen *are* blind: they are

all ignorant, they *are* all dumb dogs, they cannot bark; sleeping, lying down, loving to slumber.
11 Yea, *they are* greedy dogs *which* can never have enough, and they *are* shepherds *that* cannot understand: they all look to their own way, every one for his gain, from his quarter.
12 Come ye, *say they,* I will fetch wine, and we will fill ourselves with strong drink; and to morrow shall be as this day, *and* much more abundant.

CHAPTER 57

THE righteous perisheth, and no man layeth *it* to heart: and merciful men *are* taken away, none considering that the righteous is taken away from the evil *to come.*
2 He shall enter into peace: they shall rest in their beds, *each one* walking *in* his uprightness.
3 ¶But draw near hither, ye sons of the sorceress, the seed of the adulterer and the whore.
4 Against whom do ye sport yourselves? against whom make ye a wide mouth, *and* draw out the tongue? *are* ye not children of transgression, a seed of falsehood,
5 Enflaming yourselves with idols under every green tree, slaying the children in the valleys under the clifts of the rocks?
6 Among the smooth *stones* of the stream *is* thy portion; they, they *are* thy lot: even to them hast thou poured a drink offering, thou hast offered a meat offering. Should I receive comfort in these?
7 Upon a lofty and high mountain hast thou set thy bed: even thither wentest thou up to offer sacrifice.
8 Behind the doors also and the posts hast thou set up thy remembrance: for thou hast discovered *thyself to another* than me, and art gone up; thou hast enlarged thy bed, and made thee *a covenant* with them; thou lovedst their bed where thou sawest *it.*
9 And thou wentest to the king with ointment, and didst increase thy perfumes, and didst send thy messengers far off, and didst debase *thyself even* unto hell.
10 Thou art wearied in the greatness of thy way; *yet* saidst thou not, There is no hope: thou hast found the life of thine hand; therefore thou wast not grieved.
11 And of whom hast thou been afraid or feared, that thou hast lied, and hast not remembered me, nor laid *it* to thy heart? have not I held my peace even of old, and thou fearest me not?
12 I will declare thy righteousness, and thy works; for they shall not profit thee.
13 When thou criest, let thy companies deliver thee; but the wind shall carry them all away; vanity shall take *them:* but he that putteth his trust in me shall possess the land, and shall inherit my holy mountain;
14 And shall say, Cast ye up, cast ye up, prepare the way, take up the stumblingblock out of the way of my people.
15 For thus saith the high and lofty One that inhabiteth eternity, whose name *is* Holy; I dwell in the high and holy *place,* with him also *that is* of a contrite and humble spirit, to revive the spirit of the humble, and to revive the heart of the contrite ones.
16 For I will not contend for ever, neither will I be always wroth: for the spirit should fail before me, and the souls *which* I have made.
17 For the iniquity of his covetousness was I wroth, and smote him: I hid me, and was wroth, and he went on frowardly in the way of his heart.
18 I have seen his ways, and will heal him: I will lead him also, and restore comforts unto him and to his mourners.
19 I create the fruit of the lips; Peace, peace to *him that is* far off, and to *him that is* near, saith the LORD; and I will heal him.
20 But the wicked *are* like the troubled sea, when it cannot rest, whose waters cast up mire and dirt.
21 *There is* no peace, saith my God, to the wicked.

CHAPTER 58

CRY aloud, spare not, lift up thy voice like a trumpet, and shew my people their transgression, and the house of Jacob their sins.
2 Yet they seek me daily, and delight to know my ways, as a nation that did righteousness, and forsook not the ordinance of their God: they ask of me the ordinances of justice; they take delight in approaching to God.
3 Wherefore have we fasted, *say they,* and thou seest not? *wherefore* have we afflicted our soul, and thou takest no knowledge? Behold, in the day of your fast ye find pleasure, and exact all your labours.
4 Behold, ye fast for strife and debate, and to smite with the fist of wickedness: ye shall not fast as *ye do this* day, to make your voice to be heard on high.
5 Is it such a fast that I have chosen? a

day for a man to afflict his soul? *is it* to bow down his head as a bulrush, and to spread sackcloth and ashes *under him?* wilt thou call this a fast, and an acceptable day to the LORD?

6 *Is* not this the fast that I have chosen? to loose the bands of wickedness, to undo the heavy burdens, and to let the oppressed go free, and that ye break every yoke?

7 *Is it* not to deal thy bread to the hungry, and that thou bring the poor that are cast out to thy house? when thou seest the naked, that thou cover him; and that thou hide not thyself from thine own flesh?

8 ¶Then shall thy light break forth as the morning, and thine health shall spring forth speedily: and thy righteousness shall go before thee; the glory of the LORD shall be thy rereward.

9 Then shalt thou call, and the LORD shall answer; thou shalt cry, and he shall say, Here I *am*. If thou take away from the midst of thee the yoke, the putting forth of the finger, and speaking vanity;

10 And *if* thou draw out thy soul to the hungry, and satisfy the afflicted soul; then shall thy light rise in obscurity, and thy darkness *be* as the noon day:

11 And the LORD shall guide thee continually, and satisfy thy soul in drought, and make fat thy bones: and thou shalt be like a watered garden, and like a spring of water, whose waters fail not.

12 And *they that shall be* of thee shall build the old waste places: thou shalt raise up the foundations of many generations; and thou shalt be called, The repairer of the breach, The restorer of paths to dwell in.

13 ¶If thou turn away thy foot from the sabbath, *from* doing thy pleasure on my holy day; and call the sabbath a delight, the holy of the LORD, honourable; and shalt honour him, not doing thine own ways, nor finding thine own pleasure, nor speaking *thine own* words:

14 Then shalt thou delight thyself in the LORD; and I will cause thee to ride upon the high places of the earth, and feed thee with the heritage of Jacob thy father: for the mouth of the LORD hath spoken *it*.

CHAPTER 59

BEHOLD, the LORD'S hand is not shortened, that it cannot save; neither his ear heavy, that it cannot hear:

2 But your iniquities have separated between you and your God, and your sins have hid *his* face from you, that he will not hear.

3 For your hands are defiled with blood, and your fingers with iniquity; your lips have spoken lies, your tongue hath muttered perverseness.

4 None calleth for justice, nor *any* pleadeth for truth: they trust in vanity, and speak lies; they conceive mischief, and bring forth iniquity.

5 They hatch cockatrice' eggs, and weave the spider's web: he that eateth of their eggs dieth, and that which is crushed breaketh out into a viper.

6 Their webs shall not become garments, neither shall they cover themselves with their works: their works *are* works of iniquity, and the act of violence *is* in their hands.

7 Their feet run to evil, and they make haste to shed innocent blood: their thoughts *are* thoughts of iniquity; wasting and destruction *are* in their paths.

8 The way of peace they know not; and *there is* no judgment in their goings: they have made them crooked paths: whosoever goeth therein shall not know peace.

9 ¶Therefore is judgment far from us, neither doth justice overtake us: we wait for light, but behold obscurity; for brightness, *but* we walk in darkness.

10 We grope for the wall like the blind, and we grope as if *we had* no eyes: we stumble at noon day as in the night; *we are* in desolate places as dead *men*.

11 We roar all like bears, and mourn sore like doves: we look for judgment, but *there is* none; for salvation, *but* it is far off from us.

12 For our transgressions are multiplied before thee, and our sins testify against us: for our transgressions *are* with us; and *as for* our iniquities, we know them;

13 In transgressing and lying against the LORD, and departing away from our God, speaking oppression and revolt, conceiving and uttering from the heart words of falsehood.

14 And judgment is turned away backward, and justice standeth afar off: for truth is fallen in the street, and equity cannot enter.

15 Yea, truth faileth; and he *that* departeth from evil maketh himself a prey: and the LORD saw *it*, and it displeased him that *there was* no judgment.

16 ¶And he saw that *there was* no man, and wondered that *there was* no intercessor: therefore his arm brought salvation unto him; and his righteousness, it sustained him.

17 For he put on righteousness as a breastplate, and an helmet of salvation upon his head; and he put on the garments of vengeance *for* clothing, and was clad with zeal as a cloak.

18 According to *their* deeds, accordingly he will repay, fury to his adversaries, recompence to his enemies; to the islands he will repay recompence.

19 So shall they fear the name of the LORD from the west, and his glory from the rising of the sun. When the enemy shall come in like a flood, the Spirit of the LORD shall lift up a standard against him.

20 ¶And the Redeemer shall come to Zion, and unto them that turn from transgression in Jacob, saith the LORD.

21 As for me, this *is* my covenant with them, saith the LORD; My spirit that *is* upon thee, and my words which I have put in thy mouth, shall not depart out of thy mouth, nor out of the mouth of thy seed, nor out of the mouth of thy seed's seed, saith the LORD, from henceforth and for ever.

CHAPTER 60

ARISE, shine; for thy light is come, and the glory of the LORD is risen upon thee.

2 For, behold, the darkness shall cover the earth, and gross darkness the people: but the LORD shall arise upon thee, and his glory shall be seen upon thee.

3 And the Gentiles shall come to thy light, and kings to the brightness of thy rising.

4 Lift up thine eyes round about, and see: all they gather themselves together, they come to thee: thy sons shall come from far, and thy daughters shall be nursed at *thy* side.

5 Then thou shalt see, and flow together, and thine heart shall fear, and be enlarged; because the abundance of the sea shall be converted unto thee, the forces of the Gentiles shall come unto thee.

6 The multitude of camels shall cover thee, the dromedaries of Mĭd'ĭ-an and Ē'phah; all they from Shē'ba shall come: they shall bring gold and incense; and they shall shew forth the praises of the LORD.

7 All the flocks of Kē'dar shall be gathered together unto thee, the rams of Ne-bā'iŏth shall minister unto thee: they shall come up with acceptance on mine altar, and I will glorify the house of my glory.

8 Who *are* these *that* fly as a cloud, and as the doves to their windows?

9 Surely the isles shall wait for me, and the ships of Tär'shĭsh first, to bring thy sons from far, their silver and their gold with them, unto the name of the LORD thy God, and to the Holy One of Israel, because *he* hath glorified thee.

10 And the sons of strangers shall build up thy walls, and their kings shall minister unto thee: for in my wrath I smote thee, but in my favour have I had mercy on thee.

11 Therefore thy gates shall be open continually; they shall not be shut day nor night; that *men* may bring unto thee the forces of the Gentiles, and *that* their kings *may be* brought.

12 For the nation and kingdom that will not serve thee shall perish; yea, *those* nations shall be utterly wasted.

13 The glory of Lebanon shall come unto thee, the fir tree, the pine tree, and the box together, to beautify the place of my sanctuary; and I will make the place of my feet glorious.

14 The sons also of them that afflicted thee shall come bending unto thee; and all they that despised thee shall bow themselves down at the soles of thy feet; and they shall call thee, The city of the LORD, The Zion of the Holy One of Israel.

15 Whereas thou hast been forsaken and hated, so that no man went through *thee,* I will make thee an eternal excellency, a joy of many generations.

16 Thou shalt also suck the milk of the Gentiles, and shalt suck the breast of kings: and thou shalt know that I the LORD *am* thy Saviour and thy Redeemer, the mighty One of Jacob.

17 For brass I will bring gold, and for iron I will bring silver, and for wood brass, and for stones iron: I will also make thy officers peace, and thine exactors righteousness.

18 Violence shall no more be heard in thy land, wasting nor destruction within thy borders; but thou shalt call thy walls Salvation, and thy gates Praise.

19 The sun shall be no more thy light by day; neither for brightness shall the moon give light unto thee: but the LORD shall be unto thee an everlasting light, and thy God thy glory.

20 Thy sun shall no more go down; neither shall thy moon withdraw itself: for the LORD shall be thine everlasting light, and the days of thy mourning shall be ended.

21 Thy people also *shall be* all righteous: they shall inherit the land for ever, the branch of my planting, the work of my hands, that I may be glorified.

22 A little one shall become a thou-

sand, and a small one a strong nation: I the LORD will hasten it in his time.

CHAPTER 61

THE Spirit of the Lord GOD *is* upon me; because the LORD hath anointed me to preach good tidings unto the meek; he hath sent me to bind up the brokenhearted, to proclaim liberty to the captives, and the opening of the prison to *them that are* bound;

2 To proclaim the acceptable year of the LORD, and the day of vengeance of our God; to comfort all that mourn;

3 To appoint unto them that mourn in Zion, to give unto them beauty for ashes, the oil of joy for mourning, the garment of praise for the spirit of heaviness; that they might be called trees of righteousness, the planting of the LORD, that he might be glorified.

4 ¶And they shall build the old wastes, they shall raise up the former desolations, and they shall repair the waste cities, the desolations of many generations.

5 And strangers shall stand and feed your flocks, and the sons of the alien *shall be* your plowmen and your vinedressers.

6 But ye shall be named the Priests of the LORD: *men* shall call you the Ministers of our God: ye shall eat the riches of the Gentiles, and in their glory shall ye boast yourselves.

7 For your shame *ye shall have* double; and *for* confusion they shall rejoice in their portion: therefore in their land they shall possess the double: everlasting joy shall be unto them.

8 For I the LORD love judgment, I hate robbery for burnt offering; and I will direct their work in truth, and I will make an everlasting covenant with them.

9 And their seed shall be known among the Gentiles, and their offspring among the people: all that see them shall acknowledge them, that they *are* the seed *which* the LORD hath blessed.

10 I will greatly rejoice in the LORD, my soul shall be joyful in my God; for he hath clothed me with the garments of salvation, he hath covered me with the robe of righteousness, as a bridegroom decketh *himself* with ornaments, and as a bride adorneth *herself* with her jewels.

11 For as the earth bringeth forth her bud, and as the garden causeth the things that are sown in it to spring forth; so the Lord GOD will cause righteousness and praise to spring forth before all the nations.

CHAPTER 62

FOR Zion's sake will I not hold my peace, and for Jerusalem's sake I will not rest, until the righteousness thereof go forth as brightness, and the salvation thereof as a lamp *that* burneth.

2 And the Gentiles shall see thy righteousness, and all kings thy glory: and thou shalt be called by a new name, which the mouth of the LORD shall name.

3 Thou shalt also be a crown of glory in the hand of the LORD, and a royal diadem in the hand of thy God.

4 Thou shalt no more be termed Forsaken; neither shall thy land any more be termed Desolate: but thou shalt be called Hĕph′zĭ-bah, and thy land Beū′-lah: for the LORD delighteth in thee, and thy land shall be married.

5 For *as* a young man marrieth a virgin, *so* shall thy sons marry thee: and *as* the bridegroom rejoiceth over the bride, *so* shall thy God rejoice over thee.

6 ¶I have set watchmen upon thy walls, O Jerusalem, *which* shall never hold their peace day nor night: ye that make mention of the LORD, keep not silence,

7 And give him no rest, till he establish, and till he make Jerusalem a praise in the earth.

8 The LORD hath sworn by his right hand, and by the arm of his strength, Surely I will no more give thy corn *to be* meat for thine enemies; and the sons of the stranger shall not drink thy wine, for the which thou hast laboured:

9 But they that have gathered it shall eat it, and praise the LORD; and they that have brought it together shall drink it in the courts of my holiness.

10 ¶Go through, go through the gates; prepare ye the way of the people; cast up, cast up the highway; gather out the stones; lift up a standard for the people.

11 Behold, the LORD hath proclaimed unto the end of the world, Say ye to the daughter of Zion, Behold, thy salvation cometh; behold, his reward *is* with him, and his work before him.

12 And they shall call them, The holy people, The redeemed of the LORD: and thou shalt be called, Sought out, A city not forsaken.

CHAPTER 63

WHO *is* this that cometh from Ē′dom, with dyed garments from Bŏz′rah? this *that is* glorious in his apparel, travelling in the greatness of his strength? I

that speak in righteousness, mighty to
save.
2 Wherefore *art thou* red in thine apparel, and thy garments like him that treadeth in the winefat?
3 I have trodden the winepress alone; and of the people *there was* none with me: for I will tread them in mine anger, and trample them in my fury; and their blood shall be sprinkled upon my garments, and I will stain all my raiment.
4 For the day of vengeance *is* in mine heart, and the year of my redeemed is come.
5 And I looked, and *there was* none to help; and I wondered that *there was* none to uphold: therefore mine own arm brought salvation unto me; and my fury, it upheld me.
6 And I will tread down the people in mine anger, and make them drunk in my fury, and I will bring down their strength to the earth.
7 ¶I will mention the lovingkindnesses of the LORD, *and* the praises of the LORD, according to all that the LORD hath bestowed on us, and the great goodness toward the house of Israel, which he hath bestowed on them according to his mercies, and according to the multitude of his lovingkindnesses.
8 For he said, Surely they *are* my people, children *that* will not lie: so he was their Saviour.
9 In all their affliction he was afflicted, and the angel of his presence saved them: in his love and in his pity he redeemed them; and he bare them, and carried them all the days of old.
10 But they rebelled, and vexed his holy Spirit: therefore he was turned to be their enemy, *and* he fought against them.
11 ¶Then he remembered the days of old, Moses *and* his people, *saying,* Where *is* he that brought them up out of the sea with the shepherd of his flock? where *is* he that put his holy Spirit within him?
12 That led *them* by the right hand of Moses with his glorious arm, dividing the water before them, to make himself an everlasting name?
13 That led them through the deep, as an horse in the wilderness, *that* they should not stumble?
14 As a beast goeth down into the valley, the Spirit of the LORD caused him to rest: so didst thou lead thy people, to make thyself a glorious name.
15 ¶Look down from heaven, and behold from the habitation of thy holiness and of thy glory: where *is* thy zeal and thy strength, the sounding of thy bowels and of thy mercies toward me? are they restrained?
16 Doubtless thou *art* our father, though Abraham be ignorant of us, and Israel acknowledge us not: thou, O LORD, *art* our father, our redeemer; thy name *is* from everlasting.
17 ¶O LORD, why hast thou made us to err from thy ways, *and* hardened our heart from thy fear? Return for thy servants' sake, the tribes of thine inheritance.
18 The people of thy holiness have possessed *it* but a little while: our adversaries have trodden down thy sanctuary.
19 We are *thine:* thou never barest rule over them; they were not called by thy name.

CHAPTER 64

OH that thou wouldest rend the heavens, that thou wouldest come down, that the mountains might flow down at thy presence,
2 As *when* the melting fire burneth, the fire causeth the waters to boil, to make thy name known to thine adversaries, *that* the nations may tremble at thy presence!
3 When thou didst terrible things *which* we looked not for, thou camest down, the mountains flowed down at thy presence.
4 For since the beginning of the world *men* have not heard, nor perceived by the ear, neither hath the eye seen, O God, beside thee, *what* he hath prepared for him that waiteth for him.
5 Thou meetest him that rejoiceth and worketh righteousness, *those that* remember thee in thy ways: behold, thou art wroth; for we have sinned: in those is continuance, and we shall be saved.
6 But we are all as an unclean *thing,* and all our righteousnesses *are* as filthy rags; and we all do fade as a leaf; and our iniquities, like the wind, have taken us away.
7 And *there is* none that calleth upon thy name, that stirreth up himself to take hold of thee: for thou hast hid thy face from us, and hast consumed us, because of our iniquities.
8 But now, O LORD, thou *art* our father; we *are* the clay, and thou our potter; and we all *are* the work of thy hand.
9 Be not wroth very sore, O LORD, neither remember iniquity for ever: behold, see, we beseech thee, we *are* all thy people.

10 Thy holy cities are a wilderness, Zion is a wilderness, Jerusalem a desolation.

11 Our holy and our beautiful house, where our fathers praised thee, is burned up with fire: and all our pleasant things are laid waste.

12 Wilt thou refrain thyself for these *things,* O Lord? wilt thou hold thy peace, and afflict us very sore?

CHAPTER 65

I AM sought of *them that* asked not *for me;* I am found of *them that* sought me not: I said, Behold me, behold me, unto a nation *that* was not called by my name.

2 I have spread out my hands all the day unto a rebellious people, which walketh in a way *that was* not good, after their own thoughts;

3 A people that provoketh me to anger continually to my face; that sacrificeth in gardens, and burneth incense upon altars of brick;

4 Which remain among the graves, and lodge in the monuments, which eat swine's flesh, and broth of abominable *things is in* their vessels;

5 Which say, Stand by thyself, come not near to me: for I am holier than thou. These *are* a smoke in my nose, a fire that burneth all the day.

6 Behold, *it is* written before me: I will not keep silence, but will recompense, even recompense into their bosom,

7 Your iniquities, and the iniquities of your fathers together, saith the Lord, which have burned incense upon the mountains, and blasphemed me upon the hills: therefore will I measure their former work into their bosom.

8 ¶Thus saith the Lord, As the new wine is found in the cluster, and *one* saith, Destroy it not; for a blessing *is* in it: so will I do for my servants' sakes, that I may not destroy them all.

9 And I will bring forth a seed out of Jacob, and out of Jū'dah an inheritor of my mountains: and mine elect shall inherit it, and my servants shall dwell there.

10 And Shâr'on shall be a fold of flocks, and the valley of Ā'chôr a place for the herds to lie down in, for my people that have sought me.

11 ¶But ye *are* they that forsake the Lord, that forget my holy mountain, that prepare a table for that troop, and that furnish the drink offering unto that number.

12 Therefore will I number you to the sword, and ye shall all bow down to the slaughter: because when I called, ye did not answer; when I spake, ye did not hear; but did evil before mine eyes, and did choose *that* wherein I delighted not.

13 Therefore thus saith the Lord God, Behold, my servants shall eat, but ye shall be hungry: behold, my servants shall drink, but ye shall be thirsty: behold, my servants shall rejoice, but ye shall be ashamed:

14 Behold, my servants shall sing for joy of heart, but ye shall cry for sorrow of heart, and shall howl for vexation of spirit.

15 And ye shall leave your name for a curse unto my chosen: for the Lord God shall slay thee, and call his servants by another name:

16 That he who blesseth himself in the earth shall bless himself in the God of truth; and he that sweareth in the earth shall swear by the God of truth; because the former troubles are forgotten, and because they are hid from mine eyes.

17 ¶For, behold, I create new heavens and a new earth: and the former shall not be remembered, nor come into mind.

18 But be ye glad and rejoice for ever *in that* which I create: for, behold, I create Jerusalem a rejoicing, and her people a joy.

19 And I will rejoice in Jerusalem, and joy in my people: and the voice of weeping shall be no more heard in her, nor the voice of crying.

20 There shall be no more thence an infant of days, nor an old man that hath not filled his days: for the child shall die an hundred years old; but the sinner *being* an hundred years old shall be accursed.

21 And they shall build houses, and inhabit *them;* and they shall plant vineyards, and eat the fruit of them.

22 They shall not build, and another inhabit; they shall not plant, and another eat: for as the days of a tree *are* the days of my people, and mine elect shall long enjoy the work of their hands.

23 They shall not labour in vain, nor bring forth for trouble; for they *are* the seed of the blessed of the Lord, and their offspring with them.

24 And it shall come to pass, that before they call, I will answer; and while they are yet speaking, I will hear.

25 The wolf and the lamb shall feed together, and the lion shall eat straw like the bullock: and dust *shall be* the

serpent's meat. They shall not hurt nor destroy in all my holy mountain, saith the LORD.

CHAPTER 66

THUS saith the LORD, The heaven *is* my throne, and the earth *is* my footstool: where *is* the house that ye build unto me? and where *is* the place of my rest?

2 For all those *things* hath mine hand made, and all those *things* have been, saith the LORD: but to this *man* will I look, *even* to *him that is* poor and of a contrite spirit, and trembleth at my word.

3 He that killeth an ox *is as if* he slew a man; he that sacrificeth a lamb, *as if* he cut off a dog's neck; he that offereth an oblation, *as if he offered* swine's blood; he that burneth incense, *as if* he blessed an idol. Yea, they have chosen their own ways, and their soul delighteth in their abominations.

4 I also will choose their delusions, and will bring their fears upon them; because when I called, none did answer; when I spake, they did not hear: but they did evil before mine eyes, and chose *that* in which I delighted not.

5 ¶Hear the word of the LORD, ye that tremble at his word; Your brethren that hated you, that cast you out for my name's sake, said, Let the LORD be glorified: but he shall appear to your joy, and they shall be ashamed.

6 A voice of noise from the city, a voice from the temple, a voice of the LORD that rendereth recompence to his enemies.

7 Before she travailed, she brought forth; before her pain came, she was delivered of a man child.

8 Who hath heard such a thing? who hath seen such things? Shall the earth be made to bring forth in one day? *or* shall a nation be born at once? for as soon as Zion travailed, she brought forth her children.

9 Shall I bring to the birth, and not cause to bring forth? saith the LORD: shall I cause to bring forth, and shut *the womb?* saith thy God.

10 Rejoice ye with Jerusalem, and be glad with her, all ye that love her: rejoice for joy with her, all ye that mourn for her:

11 That ye may suck, and be satisfied with the breasts of her consolations; that ye may milk out, and be delighted with the abundance of her glory.

12 For thus saith the LORD, Behold, I will extend peace to her like a river, and the glory of the Gentiles like a flowing stream: then shall ye suck, ye shall be borne upon *her* sides, and be dandled upon *her* knees.

13 As one whom his mother comforteth, so will I comfort you; and ye shall be comforted in Jerusalem.

14 And when ye see *this*, your heart shall rejoice, and your bones shall flourish like an herb: and the hand of the LORD shall be known toward his servants, and *his* indignation toward his enemies.

15 For, behold, the LORD will come with fire, and with his chariots like a whirlwind, to render his anger with fury, and his rebuke with flames of fire.

16 For by fire and by his sword will the LORD plead with all flesh: and the slain of the LORD shall be many.

17 They that sanctify themselves, and purify themselves in the gardens behind one *tree* in the midst, eating swine's flesh, and the abomination, and the mouse, shall be consumed together, saith the LORD.

18 For I *know* their works and their thoughts: it shall come, that I will gather all nations and tongues; and they shall come, and see my glory.

19 And I will set a sign among them, and I will send those that escape of them unto the nations, *to* Tär'shĭsh, Pul, and Lud, that draw the bow, *to* Tū'bal, and Jā'van, *to* the isles afar off, that have not heard my fame, neither have seen my glory; and they shall declare my glory among the Gentiles.

20 And they shall bring all your brethren *for* an offering unto the LORD out of all nations upon horses, and in chariots, and in litters, and upon mules, and upon swift beasts, to my holy mountain Jerusalem, saith the LORD, as the children of Israel bring an offering in a clean vessel into the house of the LORD.

21 And I will also take of them for priests *and* for Lē'vītes, saith the LORD.

22 For as the new heavens and the new earth, which I will make, shall remain before me, saith the LORD, so shall your seed and your name remain.

23 And it shall come to pass, *that* from one new moon to another, and from one sabbath to another, shall all flesh come to worship before me, saith the LORD.

24 And they shall go forth, and look upon the carcases of the men that have transgressed against me: for their worm shall not die, neither shall their fire be quenched; and they shall be an abhorring unto all flesh.

THE BOOK OF THE PROPHET

JEREMIAH

CHAPTER 1

THE words of Jĕr′e-mī′ah the son of Hilkī′ah, of the priests that *were* in Ăn′a-thŏth in the land of Benjamin:

2 To whom the word of the LORD came in the days of Jō-sī′ah the son of Ămon king of Jū′dah, in the thirteenth year of his reign.

3 It came also in the days of Je-hoi′a-kĭm the son of Jō-sī′ah king of Jū′dah, unto the end of the eleventh year of Zĕd-e-kī′ah the son of Jō-sī′ah king of Jū′dah, unto the carrying away of Jerusalem captive in the fifth month.

4 ¶Then the word of the LORD came unto me, saying,

5 Before I formed thee in the belly I knew thee; and before thou camest forth out of the womb I sanctified thee, *and* I ordained thee a prophet unto the nations.

6 Then said I, Ah, Lord GOD! behold, I cannot speak: for I *am* a child.

7 But the LORD said unto me, Say not, I *am* a child: for thou shalt go to all that I shall send thee, and whatsoever I command thee thou shalt speak.

8 Be not afraid of their faces: for I *am* with thee to deliver thee, saith the LORD.

9 Then the LORD put forth his hand, and touched my mouth. And the LORD said unto me, Behold, I have put my words in thy mouth.

10 See, I have this day set thee over the nations and over the kingdoms, to root out, and to pull down, and to destroy, and to throw down, to build, and to plant.

11 ¶Moreover the word of the LORD came unto me, saying, Jĕr′e-mī′ah, what seest thou? And I said, I see a rod of an almond tree.

12 Then said the LORD unto me, Thou hast well seen: for I will hasten my word to perform it.

13 And the word of the LORD came unto me the second time, saying, What seest thou? And I said, I see a seething pot; and the face thereof *is* toward the north.

14 Then the LORD said unto me, Out of the north an evil shall break forth upon all the inhabitants of the land.

15 For, lo, I will call all the families of the kingdoms of the north, saith the LORD; and they shall come, and they shall set every one his throne at the entering of the gates of Jerusalem, and against all the walls thereof round about, and against all the cities of Jū′dah.

16 And I will utter my judgments against them touching all their wickedness, who have forsaken me, and have burned incense unto other gods, and worshipped the works of their own hands.

17 ¶Thou therefore gird up thy loins, and arise, and speak unto them all that I command thee: be not dismayed at their faces, lest I confound thee before them.

18 For, behold, I have made thee this day a defenced city, and an iron pillar, and brasen walls against the whole land, against the kings of Jū′dah, against the princes thereof, against the priests thereof, and against the people of the land.

19 And they shall fight against thee; but they shall not prevail against thee; for I *am* with thee, saith the LORD, to deliver thee.

CHAPTER 2

MOREOVER the word of the LORD came to me, saying,

2 Go and cry in the ears of Jerusalem, saying, Thus saith the LORD; I remember thee, the kindness of thy youth, the love of thine espousals, when thou wentest after me in the wilderness, in a land *that was* not sown.

3 Israel *was* holiness unto the LORD, *and* the firstfruits of his increase: all that devour him shall offend; evil shall come upon them, saith the LORD.

4 ¶Hear ye the word of the LORD, O house of Jacob, and all the families of the house of Israel:

5 Thus saith the LORD, What iniquity have your fathers found in me, that they are gone far from me, and have walked after vanity, and are become vain?

6 Neither said they, Where *is* the LORD that brought us up out of the land of Egypt, that led us through the wilderness, through a land of deserts and of pits, through a land of drought, and of the shadow of death, through a land that no man passed through, and where no man dwelt?

7 And I brought you into a plentiful country, to eat the fruit thereof and the goodness thereof; but when ye entered, ye defiled my land, and made mine heritage an abomination.

8 The priests said not, Where *is* the LORD? and they that handle the law

knew me not: the pastors also trans-
gressed against me, and the prophets
prophesied by Bā'al, and walked after
things that do not profit.
9 ¶Wherefore I will yet plead with
you, saith the LORD, and with your
children's children will I plead.
10 For pass over the isles of Chĭt'tĭm,
and see; and send unto Kē'dar, and con-
sider diligently, and see if there be such
a thing.
11 Hath a nation changed *their* gods,
which *are* yet no gods? but my people
have changed their glory for *that which*
doth not profit.
12 Be astonished, O ye heavens, at
this, and be horribly afraid, be ye very
desolate, saith the LORD.
13 For my people have committed
two evils; they have forsaken me the
fountain of living waters, *and* hewed
them out cisterns, broken cisterns, that
can hold no water.
14 ¶*Is* Israel a servant? *is* he a home-
born *slave?* why is he spoiled?
15 The young lions roared upon him,
and yelled, and they made his land
waste: his cities are burned without
inhabitant.
16 Also the children of Noph and Tä-
hăp'a-nēṡ have broken the crown of thy
head.
17 Hast thou not procured this unto
thyself, in that thou hast forsaken the
LORD thy God, when he led thee by the
way?
18 And now what hast thou to do in
the way of Egypt, to drink the waters of
Sī'hôr? or what hast thou to do in the
way of Assyria, to drink the waters of
the river?
19 Thine own wickedness shall cor-
rect thee, and thy backslidings shall
reprove thee: know therefore and see
that *it is* an evil *thing* and bitter, that
thou hast forsaken the LORD thy God,
and that my fear *is* not in thee, saith the
Lord GOD of hosts.
20 For of old time I have broken thy
yoke, *and* burst thy bands; and thou
saidst, I will not transgress; when upon
every high hill and under every green
tree thou wanderest, playing the har-
lot.
21 Yet I had planted thee a noble
vine, wholly a right seed: how then art
thou turned into the degenerate plant
of a strange vine unto me?
22 For though thou wash thee with
nitre, and take thee much soap, *yet*
thine iniquity is marked before me,
saith the Lord GOD.
23 How canst thou say, I am not pol-
luted, I have not gone after Bā'al-ĭm?
see thy way in the valley, know what
thou hast done: *thou art* a swift drom-
edary traversing her ways;
24 A wild ass used to the wilderness,
that snuffeth up the wind at her plea-
sure; in her occasion who can turn her
away? all they that seek her will not
weary themselves; in her month they
shall find her.
25 Withhold thy foot from being un-
shod, and thy throat from thirst: but
thou saidst, There is no hope: no; for I
have loved strangers, and after them
will I go.
26 As the thief is ashamed when he is
found, so is the house of Israel
ashamed; they, their kings, their
princes, and their priests, and their
prophets,
27 Saying to a stock, Thou *art* my
father; and to a stone, Thou hast
brought me forth: for they have turned
their back unto me, and not *their* face:
but in the time of their trouble they will
say, Arise, and save us.
28 But where *are* thy gods that thou
hast made thee? let them arise, if they
can save thee in the time of thy trouble:
for *according to* the number of thy
cities are thy gods, O Jū'dah.
29 Wherefore will ye plead with me?
ye all have transgressed against me,
saith the LORD.
30 In vain have I smitten your chil-
dren; they received no correction: your
own sword hath devoured your
prophets, like a destroying lion.
31 ¶O generation, see ye the word of
the LORD. Have I been a wilderness
unto Israel? a land of darkness? where-
fore say my people, We are lords; we
will come no more unto thee?
32 Can a maid forget her ornaments,
or a bride her attire? yet my people
have forgotten me days without num-
ber.
33 Why trimmest thou thy way to
seek love? therefore hast thou also
taught the wicked ones thy ways.
34 Also in thy skirts is found the
blood of the souls of the poor inno-
cents: I have not found it by secret
search, but upon all these.
35 Yet thou sayest, Because I am in-
nocent, surely his anger shall turn from
me. Behold, I will plead with thee, be-
cause thou sayest, I have not sinned.
36 Why gaddest thou about so much
to change thy way? thou also shalt be
ashamed of Egypt, as thou wast
ashamed of Assyria.
37 Yea, thou shalt go forth from him,
and thine hands upon thine head: for
the LORD hath rejected thy confidences,
and thou shalt not prosper in
them.

CHAPTER 3

THEY say, If a man put away his wife,
and she go from him, and become an-
other man's, shall he return unto her
again? shall not that land be greatly
polluted? but thou hast played the har-
lot with many lovers; yet return again
to me, saith the LORD.
2 Lift up thine eyes unto the high
places, and see where thou hast not
been lien with. In the ways hast thou
sat for them, as the Arabian in the wil-
derness; and thou hast polluted the
land with thy whoredoms and with thy
wickedness.
3 Therefore the showers have been
withholden, and there hath been no lat-
ter rain; and thou hadst a whore's fore-
head, thou refusedst to be ashamed.
4 Wilt thou not from this time cry
unto me, My father, thou *art* the guide
of my youth?
5 Will he reserve *his anger* for ever?
will he keep *it* to the end? Behold, thou
hast spoken and done evil things as
thou couldest.
6 ¶The LORD said also unto me in the
days of Jō-sī'ah the king, Hast thou
seen *that* which backsliding Israel hath
done? she is gone up upon every high
mountain and under every green tree,
and there hath played the harlot.
7 And I said after she had done all
these *things*, Turn thou unto me. But
she returned not. And her treacherous
sister Jū'dah saw *it*.
8 And I saw, when for all the causes
whereby backsliding Israel committed
adultery I had put her away, and given
her a bill of divorce; yet her treach-
erous sister Jū'dah feared not, but
went and played the harlot also.
9 And it came to pass through the
lightness of her whoredom, that she de-
filed the land, and committed adultery
with stones and with stocks.
10 And yet for all this her treacherous
sister Jū'dah hath not turned unto me
with her whole heart, but feignedly,
saith the LORD.
11 ¶And the LORD said unto me, The
backsliding Israel hath justified herself
more than treacherous Jū'dah.
12 Go and proclaim these words to-
ward the north, and say, Return, thou
backsliding Israel, saith the LORD; *and* I
will not cause mine anger to fall upon
you: for I *am* merciful, saith the LORD,
and I will not keep *anger* for ever.
13 Only acknowledge thine iniquity,
that thou hast transgressed against the
LORD thy God, and hast scattered thy
ways to the strangers under every
green tree, and ye have not obeyed my
voice, saith the LORD.
14 Turn, O backsliding children, saith
the LORD; for I am married unto you:
and I will take you one of a city, and
two of a family, and I will bring you to
Zion:
15 And I will give you pastors accord-
ing to mine heart, which shall feed
you with knowledge and understand-
ing.
16 And it shall come to pass, when ye
be multiplied and increased in the land,
in those days, saith the LORD, they shall
say no more, The ark of the covenant of
the LORD: neither shall it come to mind:
neither shall they remember it; neither
shall they visit *it;* neither shall *that* be
done any more.
17 At that time they shall call Jeru-
salem the throne of the LORD; and all
the nations shall be gathered unto it, to
the name of the LORD, to Jerusalem:
neither shall they walk any more after
the imagination of their evil heart.
18 In those days the house of Jū'dah
shall walk with the house of Israel, and
they shall come together out of the land
of the north to the land that I have giv-
en for an inheritance unto your fa-
thers.
19 But I said, How shall I put thee
among the children, and give thee a
pleasant land, a goodly heritage of the
hosts of nations? and I said, Thou shalt
call me, My father; and shalt not turn
away from me.
20 Surely *as* a wife treacherously de-
parteth from her husband, so have ye
dealt treacherously with me, O house
of Israel, saith the LORD.
21 ¶A voice was heard upon the high
places, weeping *and* supplications of
the children of Israel: for they have per-
verted their way, *and* they have for-
gotten the LORD their God.
22 Return, ye backsliding children,
and I will heal your backslidings. Be-
hold, we come unto thee; for thou *art*
the LORD our God.
23 Truly in vain *is salvation hoped for*
from the hills, *and from* the multitude
of mountains: truly in the LORD our God
is the salvation of Israel.
24 For shame hath devoured the la-
bour of our fathers from our youth;
their flocks and their herds, their sons
and their daughters.
25 We lie down in our shame, and our
confusion covereth us: for we have
sinned against the LORD our God, we
and our fathers, from our youth even
unto this day, and have not obeyed the
voice of the LORD our God.

CHAPTER 4

IF thou wilt return, O Israel, saith the
LORD, return unto me: and if thou wilt
put away thine abominations out of my
sight, then shalt thou not remove.
2 And thou shalt swear, The LORD
liveth, in truth, in judgment, and in
righteousness; and the nations shall
bless themselves in him, and in him
shall they glory.
3 ¶For thus saith the LORD to the men
of Jū'dah and Jerusalem, Break up your
fallow ground, and sow not among
thorns.
4 Circumcise yourselves to the LORD,
and take away the foreskins of your
heart, ye men of Jū'dah and inhabitants
of Jerusalem: lest my fury come forth
like fire, and burn that none can quench
it, because of the evil of your doings.
5 Declare ye in Jū'dah, and publish in
Jerusalem; and say, Blow ye the trum-
pet in the land: cry, gather together,
and say, Assemble yourselves, and let
us go into the defenced cities.
6 Set up the standard toward Zion:
retire, stay not: for I will bring evil from
the north, and a great destruction.
7 The lion is come up from his thick-
et, and the destroyer of the Gentiles is
on his way; he is gone forth from his
place to make thy land desolate; *and*
thy cities shall be laid waste, without
an inhabitant.
8 For this gird you with sackcloth, la-
ment and howl: for the fierce anger of
the LORD is not turned back from us.
9 And it shall come to pass at that
day, saith the LORD, *that* the heart of
the king shall perish, and the heart of
the princes; and the priests shall be as-
tonished, and the prophets shall won-
der.
10 Then said I, Ah, Lord GOD! surely
thou hast greatly deceived this people
and Jerusalem, saying, Ye shall have
peace; whereas the sword reacheth
unto the soul.
11 At that time shall it be said to this
people and to Jerusalem, A dry wind of
the high places in the wilderness to-
ward the daughter of my people, not to
fan, nor to cleanse,
12 *Even* a full wind from those *places*
shall come unto me: now also will I give
sentence against them.
13 Behold, he shall come up as
clouds, and his chariots *shall be* as a
whirlwind: his horses are swifter than
eagles. Woe unto us! for we are spoiled.
14 O Jerusalem, wash thine heart
from wickedness, that thou mayest be
saved. How long shall thy vain
thoughts lodge within thee?
15 For a voice declareth from Dan,
and publisheth affliction from mount
Ē'phra-im.
16 Make ye mention to the nations;
behold, publish against Jerusalem, *that*
watchers come from a far country, and
give out their voice against the cities of
Jū'dah.
17 As keepers of a field, are they
against her round about; because she
hath been rebellious against me, saith
the LORD.
18 Thy way and thy doings have pro-
cured these *things* unto thee; this *is* thy
wickedness, because it is bitter, be-
cause it reacheth unto thine heart.
19 ¶My bowels, my bowels! I am
pained at my very heart; my heart
maketh a noise in me; I cannot hold my
peace, because thou hast heard, O my
soul, the sound of the trumpet, the
alarm of war.
20 Destruction upon destruction is
cried; for the whole land is spoiled: sud-
denly are my tents spoiled, *and* my cur-
tains in a moment.
21 How long shall I see the standard,
and hear the sound of the trumpet?
22 For my people *is* foolish, they have
not known me; they *are* sottish chil-
dren, and they have none understand-
ing: they *are* wise to do evil, but to
do good they have no knowledge.
23 I beheld the earth, and, lo, *it was*
without form, and void; and the heav-
ens, and they *had* no light.
24 I beheld the mountains, and, lo,
they trembled, and all the hills moved
lightly.
25 I beheld, and, lo, *there was* no
man, and all the birds of the heavens
were fled.
26 I beheld, and, lo, the fruitful place
was a wilderness, and all the cities
thereof were broken down at the
presence of the LORD, *and* by his fierce
anger.
27 For thus hath the LORD said, The
whole land shall be desolate; yet will I
not make a full end.
28 For this shall the earth mourn, and
the heavens above be black: because I
have spoken *it*, I have purposed *it*, and
will not repent, neither will I turn back
from it.
29 The whole city shall flee for the
noise of the horsemen and bowmen;
they shall go into thickets, and climb
up upon the rocks: every city *shall be*
forsaken, and not a man dwell therein.
30 And *when* thou *art* spoiled, what
wilt thou do? Though thou clothest thy-
self with crimson, though thou deckest
thee with ornaments of gold, though
thou rentest thy face with painting, in

vain shalt thou make thyself fair; *thy* lovers will despise thee, they will seek thy life.

31 For I have heard a voice as of a woman in travail, *and* the anguish as of her that bringeth forth her first child, the voice of the daughter of Zion, *that* bewaileth herself, *that* spreadeth her hands, *saying*, Woe *is* me now! for my soul is wearied because of murderers.

CHAPTER 5

RUN ye to and fro through the streets of Jerusalem, and see now, and know, and seek in the broad places thereof, if ye can find a man, if there be *any* that executeth judgment, that seeketh the truth; and I will pardon it.

2 And though they say, The LORD liveth; surely they swear falsely.

3 O LORD, *are* not thine eyes upon the truth? thou hast stricken them, but they have not grieved; thou hast consumed them, *but* they have refused to receive correction: they have made their faces harder than a rock; they have refused to return.

4 Therefore I said, Surely these *are* poor; they are foolish: for they know not the way of the LORD, *nor* the judgment of their God.

5 I will get me unto the great men, and will speak unto them; for they have known the way of the LORD, *and* the judgment of their God: but these have altogether broken the yoke, *and* burst the bonds.

6 Wherefore a lion out of the forest shall slay them, *and* a wolf of the evenings shall spoil them, a leopard shall watch over their cities: every one that goeth out thence shall be torn in pieces: because their transgressions are many, *and* their backslidings are increased.

7 How shall I pardon thee for this? thy children have forsaken me, and sworn by *them that are* no gods: when I had fed them to the full, they then committed adultery, and assembled themselves by troops in the harlots' houses.

8 They were *as* fed horses in the morning: every one neighed after his neighbour's wife.

9 Shall I not visit for these *things*? saith the LORD: and shall not my soul be avenged on such a nation as this?

10 ¶Go ye up upon her walls, and destroy; but make not a full end: take away her battlements; for they *are* not the LORD's.

11 For the house of Israel and the house of Jū'dah have dealt very treacherously against me, saith the LORD.

12 They have belied the LORD, and said, *It is* not he; neither shall evil come upon us; neither shall we see sword nor famine:

13 And the prophets shall become wind, and the word *is* not in them: thus shall it be done unto them.

14 Wherefore thus saith the LORD God of hosts, Because ye speak this word, behold, I will make my words in thy mouth fire, and this people wood, and it shall devour them.

15 Lo, I will bring a nation upon you from far, O house of Israel, saith the LORD; it *is* a mighty nation, it *is* an ancient nation, a nation whose language thou knowest not, neither understandest what they say.

16 Their quiver *is* as an open sepulchre, they *are* all mighty men.

17 And they shall eat up thine harvest, and thy bread, *which* thy sons and thy daughters should eat: they shall eat up thy flocks and thine herds: they shall eat up thy vines and thy fig trees: they shall impoverish thy fenced cities, wherein thou trustedst, with the sword.

18 Nevertheless in those days, saith the LORD, I will not make a full end with you.

19 And it shall come to pass, when ye shall say, Wherefore doeth the LORD our God all these *things* unto us? then shalt thou answer them, Like as ye have forsaken me, and served strange gods in your land, so shall ye serve strangers in a land *that is* not yours.

20 ¶Declare this in the house of Jacob, and publish it in Jū'dah, saying,

21 Hear now this, O foolish people, and without understanding; which have eyes, and see not; which have ears, and hear not:

22 Fear ye not me? saith the LORD: will ye not tremble at my presence, which have placed the sand *for* the bound of the sea by a perpetual decree, that it cannot pass it: and though the waves thereof toss themselves, yet can they not prevail; though they roar, yet can they not pass over it?

23 But this people hath a revolting and a rebellious heart; they are revolted and gone.

24 Neither say they in their heart, Let us now fear the LORD our God, that giveth rain, both the former and the latter, in his season: he reserveth unto us the appointed weeks of the harvest.

25 ¶Your iniquities have turned away these *things*, and your sins have withholden good *things* from you.

26 For among my people are found wicked *men*: they lay wait, as he that setteth snares; they set a trap, they catch men.

27 As a cage is full of birds, so *are*
their houses full of deceit: therefore
they are become great, and waxen rich.
28 They are waxen fat, they shine:
yea, they overpass the deeds of the
wicked: they judge not the cause, the
cause of the fatherless, yet they pros-
per; and the right of the needy do they
not judge.
29 Shall I not visit for these *things?*
saith the LORD: shall not my soul be
avenged on such a nation as this?
30 ¶A wonderful and horrible thing is
committed in the land;
31 The prophets prophesy falsely,
and the priests bear rule by their
means; and my people love *to have it*
so: and what will ye do in the end there-
of?

CHAPTER 6

O YE children of Benjamin, gather
yourselves to flee out of the midst of
Jerusalem, and blow the trumpet in Te-
kō'a, and set up a sign of fire in Bĕth-
hăc'ce-rem: for evil appeareth out of
the north, and great destruction.
2 I have likened the daughter of Zion
to a comely and delicate *woman*.
3 The shepherds with their flocks
shall come unto her; they shall pitch
their tents against her round about;
they shall feed every one in his place.
4 Prepare ye war against her; arise,
and let us go up at noon. Woe unto us!
for the day goeth away, for the shad-
ows of the evening are stretched out.
5 Arise, and let us go by night, and let
us destroy her palaces.
6 ¶For thus hath the LORD of hosts
said, Hew ye down trees, and cast a
mount against Jerusalem: this *is* the
city to be visited; she *is* wholly oppres-
sion in the midst of her.
7 As a fountain casteth out her waters,
so she casteth out her wickedness:
violence and spoil is heard in her; be-
fore me continually *is* grief and
wounds.
8 Be thou instructed, O Jerusalem,
lest my soul depart from thee; lest I
make thee desolate, a land not
inhabited.
9 ¶Thus saith the LORD of hosts, They
shall throughly glean the remnant of
Israel as a vine: turn back thine hand as
a grapegatherer into the baskets.
10 To whom shall I speak, and give
warning, that they may hear? behold,
their ear *is* uncircumcised, and they
cannot hearken: behold, the word of
the LORD is unto them a reproach; they
have no delight in it.
11 Therefore I am full of the fury of
the LORD; I am weary with holding in: I
will pour it out upon the children
abroad, and upon the assembly of
young men together: for even the hus-
band with the wife shall be taken, the
aged with *him that is* full of days.
12 And their houses shall be turned
unto others, *with their* fields and wives
together: for I will stretch out my hand
upon the inhabitants of the land, saith
the LORD.
13 For from the least of them even
unto the greatest of them every one *is*
given to covetousness; and from the
prophet even unto the priest every one
dealeth falsely.
14 They have healed also the hurt *of
the daughter* of my people slightly,
saying, Peace, peace; when *there is* no
peace.
15 Were they ashamed when they
had committed abomination? nay, they
were not at all ashamed, neither could
they blush: therefore they shall fall
among them that fall: at the time *that* I
visit them they shall be cast down,
saith the LORD.
16 Thus saith the LORD, Stand ye in
the ways, and see, and ask for the old
paths, where *is* the good way, and walk
therein, and ye shall find rest for your
souls. But they said, We will not walk
therein.
17 Also I set watchmen over you,
saying, Hearken to the sound of the
trumpet. But they said, We will not
hearken.
18 ¶Therefore hear, ye nations, and
know, O congregation, what *is* among
them.
19 Hear, O earth: behold, I will bring
evil upon this people, *even* the fruit of
their thoughts, because they have not
hearkened unto my words, nor to my
law, but rejected it.
20 To what purpose cometh there to
me incense from Shē'ba, and the sweet
cane from a far country? your burnt of-
ferings *are* not acceptable, nor your
sacrifices sweet unto me.
21 Therefore thus saith the LORD, Be-
hold, I will lay stumblingblocks before
this people, and the fathers and the
sons together shall fall upon them; the
neighbour and his friend shall perish.
22 Thus saith the LORD, Behold, a
people cometh from the north country,
and a great nation shall be raised from
the sides of the earth.
23 They shall lay hold on bow and
spear; they *are* cruel, and have no
mercy; their voice roareth like the sea;
and they ride upon horses, set in array
as men for war against thee, O
daughter of Zion.
24 We have heard the fame thereof:

our hands wax feeble: anguish hath
taken hold of us, *and* pain, as of a wom-
an in travail.
25 Go not forth into the field, nor
walk by the way; for the sword of the
enemy *and* fear *is* on every side.
26 ¶O daughter of my people, gird
thee with sackcloth, and wallow thy-
self in ashes: make thee mourning, *as*
for an only son, most bitter lamenta-
tion: for the spoiler shall suddenly
come upon us.
27 I have set thee *for* a tower *and* a
fortress among my people, that thou
mayest know and try their way.
28 They *are* all grievous revolters,
walking with slanders: *they are* brass
and iron; they *are* all corrupters.
29 The bellows are burned, the lead is
consumed of the fire; the founder melt-
eth in vain: for the wicked are not
plucked away.
30 Reprobate silver shall *men* call
them, because the Lord hath rejected
them.

CHAPTER 7

THE word that came to Jĕr′e-mī′ah
from the Lord, saying,
2 Stand in the gate of the Lord's
house, and proclaim there this word,
and say, Hear the word of the Lord, all
ye of Jū′dah, that enter in at these gates
to worship the Lord.
3 Thus saith the Lord of hosts, the
God of Israel, Amend your ways and
your doings, and I will cause you to
dwell in this place.
4 Trust ye not in lying words, saying,
The temple of the Lord, The temple of
the Lord, The temple of the Lord, *are*
these.
5 For if ye throughly amend your
ways and your doings; if ye throughly
execute judgment between a man and
his neighbour;
6 *If* ye oppress not the stranger, the
fatherless, and the widow, and shed not
innocent blood in this place, neither
walk after other gods to your hurt:
7 Then will I cause you to dwell in this
place, in the land that I gave to your
fathers, for ever and ever.
8 ¶Behold, ye trust in lying words,
that cannot profit.
9 Will ye steal, murder, and commit
adultery, and swear falsely, and burn
incense unto Bā′al, and walk after
other gods whom ye know not;
10 And come and stand before me in
this house, which is called by my name,
and say, We are delivered to do all
these abominations?
11 Is this house, which is called by
my name, become a den of robbers in
your eyes? Behold, even I have seen *it*,
saith the Lord.
12 But go ye now unto my place
which *was* in Shī′lōh, where I set my
name at the first, and see what I did to it
for the wickedness of my people Israel.
13 And now, because ye have done all
these works, saith the Lord, and I
spake unto you, rising up early and
speaking, but ye heard not; and I called
you, but ye answered not;
14 Therefore will I do unto *this* house,
which is called by my name, wherein ye
trust, and unto the place which I gave
to you and to your fathers, as I have
done to Shī′lōh.
15 And I will cast you out of my sight,
as I have cast out all your brethren,
even the whole seed of Ē′phra-im.
16 Therefore pray not thou for this
people, neither lift up cry nor prayer for
them, neither make intercession to me:
for I will not hear thee.
17 ¶Seest thou not what they do in
the cities of Jū′dah and in the streets of
Jerusalem?
18 The children gather wood, and the
fathers kindle the fire, and the women
knead *their* dough, to make cakes to
the queen of heaven, and to pour out
drink offerings unto other gods, that
they may provoke me to anger.
19 Do they provoke me to anger?
saith the Lord: *do they* not *provoke*
themselves to the confusion of their
own faces?
20 Therefore thus saith the Lord God;
Behold, mine anger and my fury shall
be poured out upon this place, upon
man, and upon beast, and upon the
trees of the field, and upon the fruit of
the ground; and it shall burn, and shall
not be quenched.
21 ¶Thus saith the Lord of hosts, the
God of Israel; Put your burnt offerings
unto your sacrifices and eat flesh.
22 For I spake not unto your fathers,
nor commanded them in the day that I
brought them out of the land of Egypt,
concerning burnt offerings or sacri-
fices:
23 But this thing commanded I them,
saying, Obey my voice, and I will be
your God, and ye shall be my people:
and walk ye in all the ways that I have
commanded you, that it may be well
unto you.
24 But they hearkened not, nor in-
clined their ear, but walked in the coun-
sels *and* in the imagination of their evil
heart, and went backward, and not for-
ward.
25 Since the day that your fathers
came forth out of the land of Egypt
unto this day I have even sent unto you

all my servants the prophets, daily rising up early and sending *them:*

26 Yet they hearkened not unto me, nor inclined their ear, but hardened their neck: they did worse than their fathers.

27 Therefore thou shalt speak all these words unto them; but they will not hearken to thee: thou shalt also call unto them; but they will not answer thee.

28 But thou shalt say unto them, This *is* a nation that obeyeth not the voice of the LORD their God, nor receiveth correction: truth is perished, and is cut off from their mouth.

29 ¶Cut off thine hair, *O Jerusalem,* and cast *it* away, and take up a lamentation on high places; for the LORD hath rejected and forsaken the generation of his wrath.

30 For the children of Jū'dah have done evil in my sight, saith the LORD: they have set their abominations in the house which is called by my name, to pollute it.

31 And they have built the high places of Tō'phet, which *is* in the valley of the son of Hĭn'nom, to burn their sons and their daughters in the fire; which I commanded *them* not, neither came it into my heart.

32 ¶Therefore, behold, the days come, saith the LORD, that it shall no more be called Tō'phet, nor the valley of the son of Hĭn'nom, but the valley of slaughter: for they shall bury in Tō'phet, till there be no place.

33 And the carcases of this people shall be meat for the fowls of the heaven, and for the beasts of the earth; and none shall fray *them* away.

34 Then will I cause to cease from the cities of Jū'dah, and from the streets of Jerusalem, the voice of mirth, and the voice of gladness, the voice of the bridegroom, and the voice of the bride: for the land shall be desolate.

CHAPTER 8

AT that time, saith the LORD, they shall bring out the bones of the kings of Jū'dah, and the bones of his princes, and the bones of the priests, and the bones of the prophets, and the bones of the inhabitants of Jerusalem, out of their graves:

2 And they shall spread them before the sun, and the moon, and all the host of heaven, whom they have loved, and whom they have served, and after whom they have walked, and whom they have sought, and whom they have worshipped: they shall not be gathered, nor be buried; they shall be for dung upon the face of the earth.

3 And death shall be chosen rather than life by all the residue of them that remain of this evil family, which remain in all the places whither I have driven them, saith the LORD of hosts.

4 ¶Moreover thou shalt say unto them, Thus saith the LORD; Shall they fall, and not arise? shall he turn away, and not return?

5 Why *then* is this people of Jerusalem slidden back by a perpetual backsliding? they hold fast deceit, they refuse to return.

6 I hearkened and heard, *but* they spake not aright: no man repented him of his wickedness, saying, What have I done? every one turned to his course, as the horse rusheth into the battle.

7 Yea, the stork in the heaven knoweth her appointed times; and the turtle and the crane and the swallow observe the time of their coming; but my people know not the judgment of the LORD.

8 How do ye say, We *are* wise, and the law of the LORD *is* with us? Lo, certainly in vain made he *it;* the pen of the scribes *is* in vain.

9 The wise *men* are ashamed, they are dismayed and taken: lo, they have rejected the word of the LORD; and what wisdom *is* in them?

10 Therefore will I give their wives unto others, *and* their fields to them that shall inherit *them:* for every one from the least even unto the greatest is given to covetousness, from the prophet even unto the priest every one dealeth falsely.

11 For they have healed the hurt of the daughter of my people slightly, saying, Peace, peace; when *there is* no peace.

12 Were they ashamed when they had committed abomination? nay, they were not at all ashamed, neither could they blush: therefore shall they fall among them that fall: in the time of their visitation they shall be cast down, saith the LORD.

13 I will surely consume them, saith the LORD: *there shall be* no grapes on the vine, nor figs on the fig tree, and the leaf shall fade; and *the things that* I have given them shall pass away from them.

14 ¶Why do we sit still? assemble yourselves, and let us enter into the defenced cities, and let us be silent there: for the LORD our God hath put us to silence, and given us water of gall to drink, because we have sinned against the LORD.

15 We looked for peace, but no good
came; and for a time of health, and be-
hold trouble!
16 The snorting of his horses was
heard from Dan: the whole land
trembled at the sound of the neighing
of his strong ones; for they are come,
and have devoured the land, and all
that is in it; the city, and those that
dwell therein.
17 For, behold, I will send serpents,
cockatrices, among you, which *will* not
be charmed, and they shall bite you,
saith the LORD.
18 ¶*When* I would comfort myself
against sorrow, my heart *is* faint in me.
19 Behold the voice of the cry of the
daughter of my people because of them
that dwell in a far country: *Is* not the
LORD in Zion? *is* not her king in her?
Why have they provoked me to anger
with their graven images, *and* with
strange vanities?
20 The harvest is past, the summer is
ended, and we are not saved.
21 For the hurt of the daughter of my
people am I hurt; I am black; astonish-
ment hath taken hold on me.
22 *Is there* no balm in Gilead; *is there*
no physician there? why then is not the
health of the daughter of my people re-
covered?

CHAPTER 9

OH that my head were waters, and
mine eyes a fountain of tears, that I
might weep day and night for the slain
of the daughter of my people!
2 Oh that I had in the wilderness a
lodging place of wayfaring men; that I
might leave my people, and go from
them! for they *be* all adulterers, an as-
sembly of treacherous men.
3 And they bend their tongues *like*
their bow *for* lies: but they are not val-
iant for the truth upon the earth; for
they proceed from evil to evil, and they
know not me, saith the LORD.
4 Take ye heed every one of his neigh-
bour, and trust ye not in any
brother: for every brother will utterly
supplant, and every neighbour will
walk with slanders.
5 And they will deceive every one his
neighbour, and will not speak the truth:
they have taught their tongue to speak
lies, *and* weary themselves to commit
iniquity.
6 Thine habitation *is* in the midst of
deceit; through deceit they refuse to
know me, saith the LORD.
7 Therefore thus saith the LORD of
hosts, Behold, I will melt them, and try
them; for how shall I do for the
daughter of my people?
8 Their tongue *is as* an arrow shot
out; it speaketh deceit: *one* speaketh
peaceably to his neighbour with his
mouth, but in heart he layeth his wait.
9 ¶Shall I not visit them for these
things? saith the LORD: shall not my
soul be avenged on such a nation as
this?
10 For the mountains will I take up a
weeping and wailing, and for the habi-
tations of the wilderness a lamentation,
because they are burned up, so that
none can pass through *them;* neither
can *men* hear the voice of the cattle;
both the fowl of the heavens and the
beast are fled; they are gone.
11 And I will make Jerusalem heaps,
and a den of dragons; and I will make
the cities of Jū′dah desolate, without an
inhabitant.
12 ¶Who *is* the wise man, that may
understand this? and *who is he* to
whom the mouth of the LORD hath spok-
en, that he may declare it, for what the
land perisheth *and* is burned up like a
wilderness, that none passeth through?
13 And the LORD saith, Because they
have forsaken my law which I set be-
fore them, and have not obeyed my
voice, neither walked therein;
14 But have walked after the imagi-
nation of their own heart, and after Bā′-
al-īm, which their fathers taught them:
15 Therefore thus saith the LORD of
hosts, the God of Israel; Behold, I will
feed them, *even* this people, with
wormwood, and give them water of
gall to drink.
16 I will scatter them also among the
heathen, whom neither they nor their
fathers have known: and I will send a
sword after them, till I have consumed
them.
17 ¶Thus saith the LORD of hosts,
Consider ye, and call for the mourning
women, that they may come; and send
for cunning *women,* that they may
come:
18 And let them make haste, and take
up a wailing for us, that our eyes may
run down with tears, and our eyelids
gush out with waters.
19 For a voice of wailing is heard out
of Zion, How are we spoiled! we are
greatly confounded, because we have
forsaken the land, because our dwel-
lings have cast *us* out.
20 Yet hear the word of the LORD, O
ye women, and let your ear receive the
word of his mouth, and teach your
daughters wailing, and every one her
neighbour lamentation.
21 For death is come up into our win-
dows, *and* is entered into our palaces,

to cut off the children from without, *and* the young men from the streets.

22 Speak, Thus saith the LORD, Even the carcases of men shall fall as dung upon the open field, and as the handful after the harvestman, and none shall gather *them*.

23 ¶Thus saith the LORD, Let not the wise *man* glory in his wisdom, neither let the mighty *man* glory in his might, let not the rich *man* glory in his riches:

24 But let him that glorieth glory in this, that he understandeth and knoweth me, that I *am* the LORD which exercise lovingkindness, judgment, and righteousness, in the earth: for in these *things* I delight, saith the LORD.

25 ¶Behold, the days come, saith the LORD, that I will punish all *them which are* circumcised with the uncircumcised;

26 Egypt, and Jū'dah, and Edom, and the children of Ammon, and Moab, and all *that are* in the utmost corners, that dwell in the wilderness: for all *these* nations *are* uncircumcised, and all the house of Israel *are* uncircumcised in the heart.

CHAPTER 10

HEAR ye the word which the LORD speaketh unto you, O house of Israel:

2 Thus saith the LORD, Learn not the way of the heathen, and be not dismayed at the signs of heaven; for the heathen are dismayed at them.

3 For the customs of the people *are* vain: for *one* cutteth a tree out of the forest, the work of the hands of the workman, with the axe.

4 They deck it with silver and with gold; they fasten it with nails and with hammers, that it move not.

5 They *are* upright as the palm tree, but speak not: they must needs be borne, because they cannot go. Be not afraid of them; for they cannot do evil, neither also *is it* in them to do good.

6 Forasmuch as *there is* none like unto thee, O LORD; thou *art* great, and thy name *is* great in might.

7 Who would not fear thee, O King of nations? for to thee doth it appertain: forasmuch as among all the wise *men* of the nations, and in all their kingdoms, *there is* none like unto thee.

8 But they are altogether brutish and foolish: the stock *is* a doctrine of vanities.

9 Silver spread into plates is brought from Tär'shĭsh, and gold from Ū'phăz, the work of the workman, and of the hands of the founder: blue and purple *is* their clothing: they *are* all the work of cunning *men*.

10 But the LORD *is* the true God, he *is* the living God, and an everlasting king: at his wrath the earth shall tremble, and the nations shall not be able to abide his indignation.

11 Thus shall ye say unto them, The gods that have not made the heavens and the earth, *even* they shall perish from the earth, and from under these heavens.

12 He hath made the earth by his power, he hath established the world by his wisdom, and hath stretched out the heavens by his discretion.

13 When he uttereth his voice, *there is* a multitude of waters in the heavens, and he causeth the vapours to ascend from the ends of the earth; he maketh lightnings with rain, and bringeth forth the wind out of his treasures.

14 Every man is brutish in *his* knowledge: every founder is confounded by the graven image: for his molten image *is* falsehood, and *there is* no breath in them.

15 They *are* vanity, *and* the work of errors: in the time of their visitation they shall perish.

16 The portion of Jacob *is* not like them: for he *is* the former of all *things;* and Israel *is* the rod of his inheritance: The LORD of hosts *is* his name.

17 ¶Gather up thy wares out of the land, O inhabitant of the fortress.

18 For thus saith the LORD, Behold, I will sling out the inhabitants of the land at this once, and will distress them, that they may find *it so*.

19 ¶Woe is me for my hurt! my wound is grievous: but I said, Truly this *is* a grief, and I must bear it.

20 My tabernacle is spoiled, and all my cords are broken: my children are gone forth of me, and they *are* not: *there is* none to stretch forth my tent any more, and to set up my curtains.

21 For the pastors are become brutish, and have not sought the LORD: therefore they shall not prosper, and all their flocks shall be scattered.

22 Behold, the noise of the bruit is come, and a great commotion out of the north country, to make the cities of Jū'dah desolate, *and* a den of dragons.

23 ¶O LORD, I know that the way of man *is* not in himself: *it is* not in man that walketh to direct his steps.

24 O LORD, correct me, but with judgment; not in thine anger, lest thou bring me to nothing.

25 Pour out thy fury upon the heathen that know thee not, and upon the families that call not on thy name: for they have eaten up Jacob, and de-

voured him, and consumed him, and
have made his habitation desolate.

CHAPTER 11

THE word that came to Jĕr'e-mī'ah
from the LORD, saying,
2 Hear ye the words of this covenant,
and speak unto the men of Jū'dah, and
to the inhabitants of Jerusalem;
3 And say thou unto them, Thus saith
the LORD God of Israel; Cursed *be* the
man that obeyeth not the words of this
covenant,
4 Which I commanded your fathers
in the day *that* I brought them forth out
of the land of Egypt, from the iron fur-
nace, saying, Obey my voice, and do
them, according to all which I com-
mand you: so shall ye be my people,
and I will be your God:
5 That I may perform the oath which
I have sworn unto your fathers, to give
them a land flowing with milk and
honey, as *it is* this day. Then answered
I, and said, So be it, O LORD.
6 Then the LORD said unto me, Pro-
claim all these words in the cities of Jū'-
dah, and in the streets of Jerusalem,
saying, Hear ye the words of this cov-
enant, and do them.
7 For I earnestly protested unto your
fathers in the day *that* I brought them
up out of the land of Egypt, *even* unto
this day, rising early and protesting,
saying, Obey my voice.
8 Yet they obeyed not, nor inclined
their ear, but walked every one in the
imagination of their evil heart: there-
fore I will bring upon them all the
words of this covenant, which I com-
manded *them* to do; but they did *them*
not.
9 And the LORD said unto me, A con-
spiracy is found among the men of Jū'-
dah, and among the inhabitants of Jeru-
salem.
10 They are turned back to the iniqui-
ties of their forefathers, which refused
to hear my words; and they went after
other gods to serve them: the house of
Israel and the house of Jū'dah have
broken my covenant which I made with
their fathers.
11 Therefore thus saith the LORD, Be-
hold, I will bring evil upon them, which
they shall not be able to escape; and
though they shall cry unto me, I will not
hearken unto them.
12 Then shall the cities of Jū'dah and
inhabitants of Jerusalem go, and cry
unto the gods unto whom they offer in-
cense: but they shall not save them at
all in the time of their trouble.
13 For *according to* the number of
thy cities were thy gods, O Jū'dah; and
according to the number of the streets
of Jerusalem have ye set up altars to
that shameful thing, *even* altars to burn
incense unto Bā'al.
14 Therefore pray not thou for this
people, neither lift up a cry or prayer
for them: for I will not hear *them* in the
time that they cry unto me for their
trouble.
15 What hath my beloved to do in
mine house, *seeing* she hath wrought
lewdness with many, and the holy flesh
is passed from thee? when thou doest
evil, then thou rejoicest.
16 The LORD called thy name, A green
olive tree, fair, *and* of goodly fruit: with
the noise of a great tumult he hath
kindled fire upon it, and the branches
of it are broken.
17 For the LORD of hosts, that planted
thee, hath pronounced evil against
thee, for the evil of the house of Israel
and of the house of Jū'dah, which they
have done against themselves to pro-
voke me to anger in offering incense
unto Bā'al.
18 ¶And the LORD hath given me
knowledge *of it*, and I know *it:* then
thou shewedst me their doings.
19 But I *was* like a lamb *or* an ox *that*
is brought to the slaughter; and I knew
not that they had devised devices
against me, *saying*, Let us destroy the
tree with the fruit thereof, and let us cut
him off from the land of the living, that
his name may be no more remembered.
20 But, O LORD of hosts, that judgest
righteously, that triest the reins and the
heart, let me see thy vengeance on
them: for unto thee have I revealed my
cause.
21 Therefore thus saith the LORD of
the men of Ăn'a-thŏth, that seek thy
life, saying, Prophesy not in the name
of the LORD, that thou die not by our
hand:
22 Therefore thus saith the LORD of
hosts, Behold, I will punish them: the
young men shall die by the sword; their
sons and their daughters shall die by
famine:
23 And there shall be no remnant of
them: for I will bring evil upon the men
of Ăn'a-thŏth, *even* the year of their visi-
tation.

CHAPTER 12

RIGHTEOUS *art* thou, O LORD, when I
plead with thee: yet let me talk with
thee of *thy* judgments: Wherefore doth
the way of the wicked prosper? *where-
fore* are all they happy that deal very
treacherously?
2 Thou hast planted them, yea, they
have taken root: the grow, yea, they

bring forth fruit: thou *art* near in their
mouth, and far from their reins.
3 But thou, O LORD, knowest me:
thou hast seen me, and tried mine heart
toward thee: pull them out like sheep
for the slaughter, and prepare them for
the day of slaughter.
4 How long shall the land mourn, and
the herbs of every field wither, for the
wickedness of them that dwell therein?
the beasts are consumed, and the birds;
because they said, He shall not see our
last end.
5 ¶If thou hast run with the footmen,
and they have wearied thee, then how
canst thou contend with horses? and *if*
in the land of peace, *wherein* thou trust-
edst, *they wearied thee*, then how wilt
thou do in the swelling of Jordan?
6 For even thy brethren, and the
house of thy father, even they have
dealt treacherously with thee; yea, they
have called a multitude after thee: be-
lieve them not, though they speak fair
words unto thee.
7 ¶I have forsaken mine house, I have
left mine heritage; I have given the
dearly beloved of my soul into the hand
of her enemies.
8 Mine heritage is unto me as a lion in
the forest; it crieth out against me: there-
fore have I hated it.
9 Mine heritage *is* unto me *as* a
speckled bird, the birds round about
are against her; come ye, assemble all
the beasts of the field, come to devour.
10 Many pastors have destroyed my
vineyard, they have trodden my por-
tion under foot, they have made my
pleasant portion a desolate wilderness.
11 They have made it desolate, *and
being* desolate it mourneth unto me;
the whole land is made desolate, be-
cause no man layeth *it* to heart.
12 The spoilers are come upon all
high places through the wilderness: for
the sword of the LORD shall devour
from the *one* end of the land even to the
other end of the land: no flesh shall
have peace.
13 They have sown wheat, but shall
reap thorns: they have put themselves
to pain, *but* shall not profit: and they
shall be ashamed of your revenues be-
cause of the fierce anger of the LORD.
14 ¶Thus saith the LORD against all
mine evil neighbours, that touch the in-
heritance which I have caused my
people Israel to inherit; Behold, I will
pluck them out of their land, and pluck
out the house of Jū'dah from among
them.
15 And it shall come to pass, after
that I have plucked them out I will re-
turn, and have compassion on them,
and will bring them again, every man to
his heritage, and every man to his land.
16 And it shall come to pass, if they
will diligently learn the ways of my
people, to swear by my name, The LORD
liveth; as they taught my people to
swear by Bā'al; then shall they be built
in the midst of my people.
17 But if they will not obey, I will ut-
terly pluck up and destroy that nation,
saith the LORD.

CHAPTER 13

THUS saith the LORD unto me, Go and
get thee a linen girdle, and put it upon
thy loins, and put it not in water.
2 So I got a girdle according to the
word of the LORD, and put *it* on my
loins.
3 And the word of the LORD came
unto me the second time, saying,
4 Take the girdle that thou hast got,
which *is* upon thy loins, and arise, go to
Eū-phrā'tēs, and hide it there in a hole
of the rock.
5 So I went, and hid it by Eū-phrā'tēs,
as the LORD commanded me.
6 And it came to pass after many
days, that the LORD said unto me, Arise,
go to Eū-phrā'tēs, and take the girdle
from thence, which I commanded thee
to hide there.
7 Then I went to Eū-phrā'tēs, and
digged, and took the girdle from the
place where I had hid it: and, behold,
the girdle was marred, it was profitable
for nothing.
8 Then the word of the LORD came
unto me, saying,
9 Thus saith the LORD, After this
manner will I mar the pride of Jū'dah,
and the great pride of Jerusalem.
10 This evil people, which refuse to
hear my words, which walk in the
imagination of their heart, and walk af-
ter other gods, to serve them, and to
worship them, shall even be as this
girdle, which is good for nothing.
11 For as the girdle cleaveth to the
loins of a man, so have I caused to
cleave unto me the whole house of
Israel and the whole house of Jū'dah,
saith the LORD; that they might be unto
me for a people, and for a name, and for
a praise, and for a glory: but they would
not hear.
12 ¶Therefore thou shalt speak unto
them this word; Thus saith the LORD
God of Israel, Every bottle shall be
filled with wine: and they shall say unto
thee, Do we not certainly know that
every bottle shall be filled with wine?
13 Then shalt thou say unto them,
Thus saith the LORD, Behold, I will fill
all the inhabitants of this land, even the

kings that sit upon David's throne, and the priests, and the prophets, and all the inhabitants of Jerusalem, with drunkenness.

14 And I will dash them one against another, even the fathers and the sons together, saith the LORD: I will not pity, nor spare, nor have mercy, but destroy them.

15 ¶Hear ye, and give ear; be not proud: for the LORD hath spoken.

16 Give glory to the LORD your God, before he cause darkness, and before your feet stumble upon the dark mountains, and, while ye look for light, he turn it into the shadow of death, *and* make *it* gross darkness.

17 But if ye will not hear it, my soul shall weep in secret places for *your* pride; and mine eye shall weep sore, and run down with tears, because the LORD's flock is carried away captive.

18 Say unto the king and to the queen, Humble yourselves, sit down: for your principalities shall come down, *even* the crown of your glory.

19 The cities of the south shall be shut up, and none shall open *them:* Jū'dah shall be carried away captive all of it, it shall be wholly carried away captive.

20 Lift up your eyes, and behold them that come from the north: where *is* the flock *that* was given thee, thy beautiful flock?

21 What wilt thou say when he shall punish thee? for thou hast taught them *to be* captains, *and* as chief over thee: shall not sorrows take thee, as a woman in travail?

22 ¶And if thou say in thine heart, Wherefore come these things upon me? For the greatness of thine iniquity are thy skirts discovered, *and* thy heels made bare.

23 Can the Ē-thĭ-ō'pĭ-an change his skin, or the leopard his spots? *then* may ye also do good, that are accustomed to do evil.

24 Therefore will I scatter them as the stubble that passeth away by the wind of the wilderness.

25 This *is* thy lot, the portion of thy measures from me, saith the LORD; because thou hast forgotten me, and trusted in falsehood.

26 Therefore will I discover thy skirts upon thy face, that thy shame may appear.

27 I have seen thine adulteries and thy neighings, the lewdness of thy whoredom, *and* thine abominations on the hills in the fields. Woe unto thee, O Jerusalem! wilt thou not be made clean? when *shall it* once *be*?

CHAPTER 14

THE word of the LORD that came to Jĕr'e-mī'ah concerning the dearth.

2 Jū'dah mourneth, and the gates thereof languish; they are black unto the ground; and the cry of Jerusalem is gone up.

3 And their nobles have sent their little ones to the waters: they came to the pits, *and* found no water; they returned with their vessels empty; they were ashamed and confounded, and covered their heads.

4 Because the ground is chapt, for there was no rain in the earth, the plowmen were ashamed, they covered their heads.

5 Yea, the hind also calved in the field, and forsook *it,* because there was no grass.

6 And the wild asses did stand in the high places, they snuffed up the wind like dragons; their eyes did fail, because *there was* no grass.

7 ¶O LORD, though our iniquities testify against us, do thou *it* for thy name's sake: for our backslidings are many; we have sinned against thee.

8 O the hope of Israel, the saviour thereof in time of trouble, why shouldest thou be as a stranger in the land, and as a wayfaring man *that* turneth aside to tarry for a night?

9 Why shouldest thou be as a man astonied, as a mighty man *that* cannot save? yet thou, O LORD, *art* in the midst of us, and we are called by thy name; leave us not.

10 ¶Thus saith the LORD unto this people, Thus have they loved to wander, they have not refrained their feet, therefore the LORD doth not accept them; he will now remember their iniquity, and visit their sins.

11 Then said the LORD unto me, Pray not for this people for *their* good.

12 When they fast, I will not hear their cry; and when they offer burnt offering and an oblation, I will not accept them: but I will consume them by the sword, and by the famine, and by the pestilence.

13 ¶Then said I, Ah, Lord GOD! behold, the prophets say unto them, Ye shall not see the sword, neither shall ye have famine; but I will give you assured peace in this place.

14 Then the LORD said unto me, The prophets prophesy lies in my name: I sent them not, neither have I commanded them, neither spake unto them: they prophesy unto you a false vision and divination, and a thing of nought, and the deceit of their heart.

15 Therefore thus saith the LORD concerning the prophets that prophesy in my name, and I sent them not, yet they say, Sword and famine shall not be in this land; By sword and famine shall those prophets be consumed.

16 And the people to whom they prophesy shall be cast out in the streets of Jerusalem because of the famine and the sword; and they shall have none to bury them, them, their wives, nor their sons, nor their daughters: for I will pour their wickedness upon them.

17 Therefore thou shalt say this word unto them; Let mine eyes run down with tears night and day, and let them not cease: for the virgin daughter of my people is broken with a great breach, with a very grievous blow.

18 If I go forth into the field, then behold the slain with the sword! and if I enter into the city, then behold them that are sick with famine! yea, both the prophet and the priest go about into a land that they know not.

19 Hast thou utterly rejected Jū'dah? hath thy soul lothed Zion? why hast thou smitten us, and *there is* no healing for us? we looked for peace, and *there is* no good; and for the time of healing, and behold trouble!

20 We acknowledge, O LORD, our wickedness, *and* the iniquity of our fathers: for we have sinned against thee.

21 Do not abhor *us*, for thy name's sake, do not disgrace the throne of thy glory: remember, break not thy covenant with us.

22 Are there *any* among the vanities of the Gentiles that can cause rain? or can the heavens give showers? *art* not thou he, O LORD our God? therefore we will wait upon thee: for thou hast made all these *things*.

CHAPTER 15

THEN said the LORD unto me, Though Moses and Samuel stood before me, *yet* my mind *could* not *be* toward this people: cast *them* out of my sight, and let them go forth.

2 And it shall come to pass, if they say unto thee, Whither shall we go forth? then thou shalt tell them, Thus saith the LORD; Such as *are* for death, to death; and such as *are* for the sword, to the sword; and such as *are* for the famine, to the famine; and such as *are* for the captivity, to the captivity.

3 And I will appoint over them four kinds, saith the LORD: the sword to slay, and the dogs to tear, and the fowls of the heaven, and the beasts of the earth, to devour and destroy.

4 And I will cause them to be removed into all kingdoms of the earth, because of Ma-năs'seh the son of Hĕz-e-kī'ah king of Jū'dah, for *that* which he did in Jerusalem.

5 For who shall have pity upon thee, O Jerusalem? or who shall bemoan thee? or who shall go aside to ask how thou doest?

6 Thou hast forsaken me, saith the LORD, thou art gone backward: therefore will I stretch out my hand against thee, and destroy thee; I am weary with repenting.

7 And I will fan them with a fan in the gates of the land; I will bereave *them* of children, I will destroy my people, *since* they return not from their ways.

8 Their widows are increased to me above the sand of the seas: I have brought upon them against the mother of the young men a spoiler at noonday: I have caused *him* to fall upon it suddenly, and terrors upon the city.

9 She that hath borne seven languisheth: she hath given up the ghost; her sun is gone down while *it was* yet day: she hath been ashamed and confounded: and the residue of them will I deliver to the sword before their enemies, saith the LORD.

10 ¶Woe is me, my mother, that thou hast borne me a man of strife and a man of contention to the whole earth! I have neither lent on usury, nor men have lent to me on usury; *yet* every one of them doth curse me.

11 The LORD said, Verily it shall be well with thy remnant; verily I will cause the enemy to entreat thee *well* in the time of evil and in the time of affliction.

12 Shall iron break the northern iron and the steel?

13 Thy substance and thy treasures will I give to the spoil without price, and *that* for all thy sins, even in all thy borders.

14 And I will make *thee* to pass with thine enemies into a land *which* thou knowest not: for a fire is kindled in mine anger, *which* shall burn upon you.

15 ¶O LORD, thou knowest: remember me, and visit me, and revenge me of my persecutors; take me not away in thy longsuffering: know that for thy sake I have suffered rebuke.

16 Thy words were found, and I did eat them; and thy word was unto me the joy and rejoicing of mine heart: for I am called by thy name, O LORD God of hosts.

17 I sat not in the assembly of the mockers, nor rejoiced; I sat alone be-

cause of thy hand: for thou hast filled me with indignation.

18 Why is my pain perpetual, and my wound incurable, *which* refuseth to be healed? wilt thou be altogether unto me as a liar, *and as* waters *that* fail?

19 ¶Therefore thus saith the LORD, If thou return, then will I bring thee again, *and* thou shalt stand before me: and if thou take forth the precious from the vile, thou shalt be as my mouth: let them return unto thee; but return not thou unto them.

20 And I will make thee unto this people a fenced brasen wall: and they shall fight against thee, but they shall not prevail against thee: for I *am* with thee to save thee and to deliver thee, saith the LORD.

21 And I will deliver thee out of the hand of the wicked, and I will redeem thee out of the hand of the terrible.

CHAPTER 16

THE word of the LORD came also unto me, saying,

2 Thou shalt not take thee a wife, neither shalt thou have sons or daughters in this place.

3 For thus saith the LORD concerning the sons and concerning the daughters that are born in this place, and concerning their mothers that bare them, and concerning their fathers that begat them in this land;

4 They shall die of grievous deaths; they shall not be lamented; neither shall they be buried; *but* they shall be as dung upon the face of the earth: and they shall be consumed by the sword, and by famine; and their carcases shall be meat for the fowls of heaven, and for the beasts of the earth.

5 For thus saith the LORD, Enter not into the house of mourning, neither go to lament nor bemoan them: for I have taken away my peace from this people, saith the LORD, *even* lovingkindness and mercies.

6 Both the great and the small shall die in this land: they shall not be buried, neither shall *men* lament for them, nor cut themselves, nor make themselves bald for them:

7 Neither shall *men* tear *themselves* for them in mourning, to comfort them for the dead; neither shall *men* give them the cup of consolation to drink for their father or for their mother.

8 Thou shalt not also go into the house of feasting, to sit with them to eat and to drink.

9 For thus saith the LORD of hosts, the God of Israel; Behold, I will cause to cease out of this place in your eyes, and in your days, the voice of mirth, and the voice of gladness, the voice of the bridegroom, and the voice of the bride.

10 ¶And it shall come to pass, when thou shalt shew this people all these words, and they shall say unto thee, Wherefore hath the LORD pronounced all this great evil against us? or what *is* our iniquity? or what *is* our sin that we have committed against the LORD our God?

11 Then shalt thou say unto them, Because your fathers have forsaken me, saith the LORD, and have walked after other gods, and have served them, and have worshipped them, and have forsaken me, and have not kept my law;

12 And ye have done worse than your fathers; for, behold, ye walk every one after the imagination of his evil heart, that they may not hearken unto me:

13 Therefore will I cast you out of this land into a land that ye know not, *neither* ye nor your fathers; and there shall ye serve other gods day and night; where I will not shew you favour.

14 ¶Therefore, behold, the days come, saith the LORD, that it shall no more be said, The LORD liveth, that brought up the children of Israel out of the land of Egypt;

15 But, The LORD liveth, that brought up the children of Israel from the land of the north, and from all the lands whither he had driven them: and I will bring them again into their land that I gave unto their fathers.

16 ¶Behold, I will send for many fishers, saith the LORD, and they shall fish them; and after will I send for many hunters, and they shall hunt them from every mountain, and from every hill, and out of the holes of the rocks.

17 For mine eyes *are* upon all their ways: they are not hid from my face, neither is their iniquity hid from mine eyes.

18 And first I will recompense their iniquity and their sin double; because they have defiled my land, they have filled mine inheritance with the carcases of their detestable and abominable things.

19 O LORD, my strength, and my fortress, and my refuge in the day of affliction, the Gentiles shall come unto thee from the ends of the earth, and shall say, Surely our fathers have inherited lies, vanity, and *things* wherein *there is* no profit.

20 Shall a man make gods unto himself, and they *are* no gods?

21 Therefore, behold, I will this once cause them to know, I will cause them

to know mine hand and my might; and
they shall know that my name *is* The
LORD.

CHAPTER 17

THE sin of Jū'dah *is* written with a pen
of iron, *and* with the point of a dia-
mond: *it is* graven upon the table of
their heart, and upon the horns of your
altars;
2 Whilst their children remember
their altars and their groves by the
green trees upon the high hills.
3 O my mountain in the field, I will
give thy substance *and* all thy treasures
to the spoil, *and* thy high places for sin,
throughout all thy borders.
4 And thou, even thyself, shalt dis-
continue from thine heritage that I
gave thee; and I will cause thee to serve
thine enemies in the land which thou
knowest not; for ye have kindled a fire
in mine anger, *which* shall burn for
ever.
5 ¶Thus saith the LORD; Cursed *be* the
man that trusteth in man, and maketh
flesh his arm, and whose heart depart-
eth from the LORD.
6 For he shall be like the heath in the
desert, and shall not see when good
cometh; but shall inhabit the parched
places in the wilderness, *in* a salt land
and not inhabited.
7 Blessed *is* the man that trusteth in
the LORD, and whose hope the LORD is.
8 For he shall be as a tree planted by
the waters, and *that* spreadeth out her
roots by the river, and shall not see
when heat cometh, but her leaf shall be
green; and shall not be careful in the
year of drought, neither shall cease
from yielding fruit.
9 ¶The heart *is* deceitful above all
things, and desperately wicked: who
can know it?
10 I the LORD search the heart, *I* try
the reins, even to give every man accord-
ing to his ways, *and* according to the
fruit of his doings.
11 *As* the partridge sitteth *on eggs*,
and hatcheth *them* not; *so* he that get-
teth riches, and not by right, shall leave
them in the midst of his days, and at his
end shall be a fool.
12 ¶A glorious high throne from the
beginning *is* the place of our sanctuary.
13 O LORD, the hope of Israel, all that
forsake thee shall be ashamed, *and*
they that depart from me shall be writ-
ten in the earth, because they have for-
saken the LORD, the fountain of living
waters.
14 Heal me, O LORD, and I shall be
healed; save me, and I shall be saved:
for thou *art* my praise.
15 Behold, they say unto me, where *is*
the word of the LORD? let it come now.
16 As for me, I have not hastened
from *being* a pastor to follow thee:
neither have I desired the woeful day;
thou knowest: that which came out of
my lips was *right* before thee.
17 Be not a terror unto me: thou *art*
my hope in the day of evil.
18 Let them be confounded that per-
secute me, but let not me be con-
founded: let them be dismayed, but let
not me be dismayed: bring upon them
the day of evil, and destroy them with
double destruction.
19 ¶Thus said the LORD unto me; Go
and stand in the gate of the children of
the people, whereby the kings of Jū'dah
come in, and by the which they go out,
and in all the gates of Jerusalem;
20 And say unto them, Hear ye the
word of the LORD, ye kings of Jū'dah,
and all Jū'dah, and all the inhabitants
of Jerusalem, that enter in by these
gates:
21 Thus saith the LORD; Take heed to
yourselves, and bear no burden on the
sabbath day, nor bring *it* in by the gates
of Jerusalem;
22 Neither carry forth a burden out of
your houses on the sabbath day,
neither do ye any work, but hallow ye
the sabbath day, as I commanded your
fathers.
23 But they obeyed not, neither in-
clined their ear, but made their neck
stiff, that they might not hear, nor re-
ceive instruction.
24 And it shall come to pass, if ye dili-
gently hearken unto me, saith the
LORD, to bring in no burden through the
gates of this city on the sabbath day,
but hallow the sabbath day, to do no
work therein;
25 Then shall there enter into the
gates of this city kings and princes sit-
ting upon the throne of David, riding in
chariots and on horses, they, and their
princes, the men of Jū'dah, and the
inhabitants of Jerusalem: and this city
shall remain for ever.
26 And they shall come from the
cities of Jū'dah, and from the places
about Jerusalem, and from the land of
Benjamin, and from the plain, and from
the mountains, and from the south,
bringing burnt offerings, and sacri-
fices, and meat offerings, and incense,
and bringing sacrifices of praise, unto
the house of the LORD.
27 But if ye will not hearken unto me
to hallow the sabbath day, and not to
bear a burden, even entering in at the
gates of Jerusalem on the sabbath day;
then will I kindle a fire in the gates there-

of, and it shall devour the palaces of
Jerusalem, and it shall not be
quenched.

CHAPTER 18

THE word which came to Jĕr′e-mī′ah
from the LORD, saying,
2 Arise, and go down to the potter's
house, and there I will cause thee to
hear my words.
3 Then I went down to the potter's
house, and, behold, he wrought a work
on the wheels.
4 And the vessel that he made of clay
was marred in the hand of the potter: so
he made it again another vessel, as
seemed good to the potter to make *it*.
5 Then the word of the LORD came to
me, saying,
6 O house of Israel, cannot I do with
you as this potter? saith the LORD. Be-
hold, as the clay *is* in the potter's hand,
so *are* ye in mine hand, O house of
Israel.
7 *At what* instant I shall speak con-
cerning a nation, and concerning a
kingdom, to pluck up, and to pull down,
and to destroy *it;*
8 If that nation, against whom I have
pronounced, turn from their evil, I will
repent of the evil that I thought to do
unto them.
9 And *at what* instant I shall speak
concerning a nation, and concerning a
kingdom, to build and to plant *it;*
10 If it do evil in my sight, that it obey
not my voice, then I will repent of the
good, wherewith I said I would benefit
them.
11 Now therefore go to, speak to the
men of Jū′dah, and to the inhabitants of
Jerusalem, saying, Thus saith the LORD;
Behold, I frame evil against you, and
devise a device against you: return ye
now every one from his evil way, and
make your ways and your doings good.
12 And they said, There is no hope:
but we will walk after our own devices,
and we will every one do the imagina-
tion of his evil heart.
13 Therefore thus saith the LORD; Ask
ye now among the heathen, who hath
heard such things: the virgin of Israel
hath done a very horrible thing.
14 Will *a man* leave the snow of Leba-
non *which cometh* from the rock of the
field? *or* shall the cold flowing waters
that come from another place be for-
saken?
15 Because my people hath forgotten
me, they have burned incense to van-
ity, and they have caused them to
stumble in their ways *from* the ancient
paths, to walk in paths, *in* a way not
cast up;
16 To make their land desolate, *and* a
perpetual hissing; every one that pass-
eth thereby shall be astonished, and
wag his head.
17 I will scatter them as with an east
wind before the enemy; I will shew
them the back, and not the face, in the
day of their calamity.
18 ¶Then said they, Come, and let us
devise devices against Jĕr′e-mī′ah; for
the law shall not perish from the priest,
nor counsel from the wise, nor the
word from the prophet. Come, and let
us smite him with the tongue, and let us
not give heed to any of his words.
19 Give heed to me, O LORD, and
hearken to the voice of them that con-
tend with me.
20 Shall evil be recompensed for
good? for they have digged a pit for my
soul. Remember that I stood before
thee to speak good for them, *and* to
turn away thy wrath from them.
21 Therefore deliver up their children
to the famine, and pour out their *blood*
by the force of the sword; and let their
wives be bereaved of their children,
and *be* widows; and let their men be put
to death; *let* their young men *be* slain
by the sword in battle.
22 Let a cry be heard from their
houses, when thou shalt bring a troop
suddenly upon them: for they have
digged a pit to take me, and hid snares
for my feet.
23 Yet, LORD, thou knowest all their
counsel against me to slay *me:* forgive
not their iniquity, neither blot out their
sin from thy sight, but let them be over-
thrown before thee; deal *thus* with
them in the time of thine anger.

CHAPTER 19

THUS saith the LORD, Go and get a pot-
ter's earthen bottle, and *take* of the an-
cients of the people, and of the ancients
of the priests;
2 And go forth unto the valley of the
son of Hĭn′nom, which *is* by the entry of
the east gate, and proclaim there the
words that I shall tell thee,
3 And say, Hear ye the word of the
LORD, O kings of Jū′dah, and inhabi-
tants of Jerusalem; Thus saith the LORD
of hosts, the God of Israel; Behold, I
will bring evil upon this place, the
which whosoever heareth, his ears
shall tingle.
4 Because they have forsaken me,
and have estranged this place, and
have burned incense in it unto other
gods, whom neither they nor their fa-
thers have known, nor the kings of Jū′-
dah, and have filled this place with the
blood of innocents;

5 They have built also the high places
of Bā'al, to burn their sons with fire *for*
burnt offerings unto Bā'al, which I
commanded not, nor spake *it*, neither
came *it* into my mind:
6 Therefore, behold, the days come,
saith the LORD, that this place shall no
more be called Tō'phet, nor The valley
of the son of Hĭn'nom, but The valley of
slaughter.
7 And I will make void the counsel of
Jū'dah and Jerusalem in this place; and
I will cause them to fall by the sword
before their enemies, and by the hands
of them that seek their lives: and their
carcases will I give to be meat for the
fowls of the heaven, and for the beasts
of the earth.
8 And I will make this city desolate,
and an hissing; every one that passeth
thereby shall be astonished and hiss
because of all the plagues thereof.
9 And I will cause them to eat the
flesh of their sons and the flesh of their
daughters, and they shall eat every one
the flesh of his friend in the siege and
straitness, wherewith their enemies,
and they that seek their lives, shall
straiten them.
10 Then shalt thou break the bottle in
the sight of the men that go with thee,
11 And shalt say unto them, Thus
saith the LORD of hosts; Even so will I
break this people and this city, as *one*
breaketh a potter's vessel, that cannot
be made whole again: and they shall
bury *them* in Tō'phet, till *there be* no
place to bury.
12 Thus will I do unto this place, saith
the LORD, and to the inhabitants there-
of, and *even* make this city as Tō'-
phet:
13 And the houses of Jerusalem, and
the houses of the kings of Jū'dah, shall
be defiled as the place of Tō'phet, be-
cause of all the houses upon whose
roofs they have burned incense unto all
the host of heaven, and have poured
out drink offerings unto other gods.
14 Then came Jĕr'e-mī'ah from Tō'-
phet, whither the LORD had sent him to
prophesy; and he stood in the court of
the LORD's house; and said to all the
people,
15 Thus saith the LORD of hosts, the
God of Israel; Behold, I will bring upon
this city and upon all her towns all the
evil that I have pronounced against it,
because they have hardened their
necks, that they might not hear my
words.

CHAPTER 20

NOW Păsh'ur the son of Ĭm'mer the
priest, who *was* also chief governor in
the house of the LORD, heard that Jĕr'e-
mī'ah prophesied these things.
2 Then Păsh'ur smote Jĕr'e-mī'ah the
prophet, and put him in the stocks that
were in the high gate of Benjamin,
which *was* by the house of the LORD.
3 And it came to pass on the morrow,
that Păsh'ur brought forth Jĕr'e-mī'ah
out of the stocks. Then said Jĕr'e-mī'ah
unto him, The LORD hath not called thy
name Păsh'ur, but Mā'gôr-mĭs'sa-bĭb.
4 For thus saith the LORD, Behold, I
will make thee a terror to thyself, and
to all thy friends: and they shall fall by
the sword of their enemies, and thine
eyes shall behold *it*: and I will give all
Jū'dah into the hand of the king of Bab-
ylon, and he shall carry them captive
into Babylon, and shall slay them with
the sword.
5 Moreover I will deliver all the
strength of this city, and all the labours
thereof, and all the precious things
thereof, and all the treasures of the
kings of Jū'dah will I give into the hand
of their enemies, which shall spoil
them, and take them, and carry them to
Babylon.
6 And thou, Păsh'ur, and all that
dwell in thine house shall go into cap-
tivity: and thou shalt come to Babylon,
and there thou shalt die, and shalt be
buried there, thou, and all thy friends,
to whom thou hast prophesied lies.
7 ¶O LORD, thou hast deceived me,
and I was deceived: thou art stronger
than I, and hast prevailed: I am in deri-
sion daily, every one mocketh me.
8 For since I spake, I cried out, I cried
violence and spoil; because the word of
the LORD was made a reproach unto
me, and a derision, daily.
9 Then I said, I will not make mention
of him, nor speak any more in his name.
But *his word* was in mine heart as a
burning fire shut up in my bones, and I
was weary with forbearing, and I could
not *stay*.
10 For I heard the defaming of many,
fear on every side. Report, *say they*,
and we will report it. All my familiars
watched for my halting, *saying*, Perad-
venture he will be enticed, and we shall
prevail against him, and we shall take
our revenge on him.
11 But the LORD *is* with me as a
mighty terrible one: therefore my per-
secutors shall stumble, and they shall
not prevail: they shall be greatly
ashamed; for they shall not prosper:
their everlasting confusion shall never
be forgotten.
12 But, O LORD of hosts, that triest
the righteous, *and* seest the reins and
the heart, let me see thy vengeance on

them: for unto thee have I opened my cause.

13 Sing unto the LORD, praise ye the LORD: for he hath delivered the soul of the poor from the hand of evildoers.

14 ¶Cursed *be* the day wherein I was born: let not the day wherein my mother bare me be blessed.

15 Cursed *be* the man who brought tidings to my father, saying, A man child is born unto thee; making him very glad.

16 And let that man be as the cities which the LORD overthrew, and repented not: and let him hear the cry in the morning, and the shouting at noontide;

17 Because he slew me not from the womb; or that my mother might have been my grave, and her womb *to be* always great *with me.*

18 Wherefore came I forth out of the womb to see labour and sorrow, that my days should be consumed with shame?

CHAPTER 21

THE word which came unto Jĕr′e-mī′ah from the LORD, when king Zĕd-e-kī′ah sent unto him Păsh′ur the son of Mĕl-chī′ah, and Zĕph-a-nī′ah the son of Mā-a-sē′iah the priest, saying,

2 Enquire, I pray thee, of the LORD for us; for Nĕb-u-chad-rĕz′zar king of Babylon maketh war against us; if so be that the LORD will deal with us according to all his wondrous works, that he may go up from us.

3 ¶Then said Jĕr′e-mī′ah unto them, Thus shall ye say to Zĕd-e-kī′ah:

4 Thus saith the LORD God of Israel; Behold, I will turn back the weapons of war that *are* in your hands, wherewith ye fight against the king of Babylon, and *against* the Chăl-dē′anṡ, which besiege you without the walls, and I will assemble them into the midst of this city.

5 And I myself will fight against you with an outstretched hand and with a strong arm, even in anger, and in fury, and in great wrath.

6 And I will smite the inhabitants of this city, both man and beast: they shall die of a great pestilence.

7 And afterward, saith the LORD, I will deliver Zĕd-e-kī′ah king of Jū′dah, and his servants, and the people, and such as are left in this city from the pestilence, from the sword, and from the famine, into the hand of Nĕb-u-chad-rĕz′zar king of Babylon, and into the hand of their enemies, and into the hand of those that seek their life: and he shall smite them with the edge of the sword; he shall not spare them, neither have pity, nor have mercy.

8 ¶And unto this people thou shalt say, Thus saith the LORD; Behold, I set before you the way of life, and the way of death.

9 He that abideth in this city shall die by the sword, and by the famine, and by the pestilence: but he that goeth out, and falleth to the Chăl-dē′anṡ that besiege you, he shall live, and his life shall be unto him for a prey.

10 For I have set my face against this city for evil, and not for good, saith the LORD: it shall be given into the hand of the king of Babylon, and he shall burn it with fire.

11 ¶And touching the house of the king of Jū′dah, *say*, Hear ye the word of the LORD;

12 O house of David, thus saith the LORD; Execute judgment in the morning, and deliver *him that is* spoiled out of the hand of the oppressor, lest my fury go out like fire, and burn that none can quench *it*, because of the evil of your doings.

13 Behold, I *am* against thee, O inhabitant of the valley, *and* rock of the plain, saith the LORD; which say, Who shall come down against us? or who shall enter into our habitations?

14 But I will punish you according to the fruit of your doings, saith the LORD: and I will kindle a fire in the forest thereof, and it shall devour all things round about it.

CHAPTER 22

THUS saith the LORD; Go down to the house of the king of Jū′dah, and speak there this word,

2 And say, Hear the word of the LORD, O king of Jū′dah, that sittest upon the throne of David, thou, and thy servants, and thy people that enter in by these gates:

3 Thus saith the LORD; Execute ye judgment and righteousness, and deliver the spoiled out of the hand of the oppressor: and do no wrong, do no violence to the stranger, the fatherless, nor the widow, neither shed innocent blood in this place.

4 For if ye do this thing indeed, then shall there enter in by the gates of this house kings sitting upon the throne of David, riding in chariots and on horses, he, and his servants, and his people.

5 But if ye will not hear these words, I swear by myself, saith the LORD, that this house shall become a desolation.

6 For thus saith the LORD unto the king's house of Jū′dah; thou *art* Gilead unto me, *and* the head of Lebanon: *yet*

surely I will make thee a wilderness,
and cities *which* are not inhabited.
7 And I will prepare destroyers
against thee, every one with his weap-
ons: and they shall cut down thy choice
cedars, and cast *them* into the fire.
8 And many nations shall pass by this
city, and they shall say every man to his
neighbour, Wherefore hath the LORD
done thus unto this great city?
9 Then they shall answer, Because
they have forsaken the covenant of the
LORD their God, and worshipped other
gods, and served them.
10 ¶Weep ye not for the dead, neither
bemoan him: *but* weep sore for him
that goeth away: for he shall return no
more, nor see his native country.
11 For thus saith the LORD touching
Shăl′lum the son of Jō-sī′ah king of Jū′-
dah, which reigned instead of Jō-sī′ah
his father, which went forth out of this
place; He shall not return thither any
more:
12 But he shall die in the place
whither they have led him captive, and
shall see this land no more.
13 ¶Woe unto him that buildeth his
house by unrighteousness, and his
chambers by wrong; *that* useth his
neighbour's service without wages,
and giveth him not for his work;
14 That saith, I will build me a wide
house and large chambers, and cutteth
him out windows; and *it is* cieled with
cedar, and painted with vermilion.
15 Shalt thou reign, because thou clos-
est *thyself* in cedar? did not thy father
eat and drink, and do judgment and
justice, *and* then *it was* well with him?
16 He judged the cause of the poor
and needy; then *it was* well *with him*:
was not this to know me? saith the
LORD.
17 But thine eyes and thine heart *are*
not but for thy covetousness, and for to
shed innocent blood, and for oppres-
sion, and for violence, to do *it*.
18 Therefore thus saith the LORD con-
cerning Je-hoi′a-kĭm the son of Jō-sī′ah
king of Jū′dah; They shall not lament
for him, *saying*, Ah my brother! or, Ah
sister! they shall not lament for him,
saying, Ah lord! or, Ah his glory!
19 He shall be buried with the burial
of an ass, drawn and cast forth beyond
the gates of Jerusalem.
20 ¶Go up to Lebanon, and cry; and
lift up thy voice in Bā′shan, and cry
from the passages: for all thy lovers are
destroyed.
21 I spake unto thee in thy prosper-
ity; *but* thou saidst, I will not hear. This
hath been thy manner from thy youth,
that thou obeyedst not my voice.
22 The wind shall eat up all thy pas-
tors, and thy lovers shall go into captiv-
ity: surely then shalt thou be ashamed
and confounded for all thy wickedness.
23 O inhabitant of Lebanon, that mak-
est thy nest in the cedars, how gra-
cious shalt thou be when pangs come
upon thee, the pain as of a woman in
travail!
24 *As* I live, saith the LORD, though
Co-nī′ah the son of Je-hoi′a-kĭm king of
Jū′dah were the signet upon my right
hand, yet would I pluck thee thence;
25 And I will give thee into the hand
of them that seek thy life, and into the
hand *of them* whose face thou fearest,
even into the hand of Nĕb-u-chad-rĕz′-
zar king of Babylon, and into the hand
of the Chăl-dē′anṡ.
26 And I will cast thee out, and thy
mother that bare thee, into another
country, where ye were not born; and
there shall ye die.
27 But to the land whereunto they de-
sire to return, thither shall they not re-
turn.
28 *Is* this man Co-nī′ah a despised
broken idol? *is he* a vessel wherein *is* no
pleasure? wherefore are they cast out,
he and his seed, and are cast into a land
which they know not?
29 O earth, earth, earth, hear the
word of the LORD.
30 Thus saith the LORD, Write ye this
man childless, a man *that* shall not
prosper in his days: for no man of his
seed shall prosper, sitting upon the
throne of David, and ruling any more in
Jū′dah.

CHAPTER 23

WOE be unto the pastors that destroy
and scatter the sheep of my pasture!
saith the LORD.
2 Therefore thus saith the LORD God
of Israel against the pastors that feed
my people; Ye have scattered my flock,
and driven them away, and have not
visited them: behold, I will visit upon
you the evil of your doings, saith the
LORD.
3 And I will gather the remnant of my
flock out of all countries whither I have
driven them, and will bring them again
to their folds; and they shall be fruitful
and increase.
4 And I will set up shepherds over
them which shall feed them: and they
shall fear no more, nor be dismayed,
neither shall they be lacking, saith the
LORD.
5 Behold, the days come, saith the
LORD, that I will raise unto David a
righteous Branch, and a King shall

reign and prosper, and shall execute judgment and justice in the earth.

6 In his days Jū'dah shall be saved, and Israel shall dwell safely: and this *is* his name whereby he shall be called, THE LORD OUR RIGHTEOUSNESS.

7 Therefore, behold, the days, come, saith the LORD, that they shall no more say, The LORD liveth, which brought up the children of Israel out of the land of Egypt;

8 But, The LORD liveth, which brought up and which led the seed of the house of Israel out of the north country, and from all countries whither I had driven them; and they shall dwell in their own land.

9 ¶Mine heart within me is broken because of the prophets; all my bones shake; I am like a drunken man, and like a man whom wine hath overcome, because of the LORD, and because of the words of his holiness.

10 For the land is full of adulterers; for because of swearing the land mourneth; the pleasant places of the wilderness are dried up, and their course is evil, and their force *is* not right.

11 For both prophet and priest are profane; yea, in my house have I found their wickedness, saith the LORD.

12 Wherefore their way shall be unto them as slippery *ways* in the darkness: they shall be driven on, and fall therein: for I will bring evil upon them, *even* the year of their visitation, saith the LORD.

13 And I have seen folly in the prophets of Sa-mâ'rĭ-a; they prophesied in Bā'al, and caused my people Israel to err.

14 I have seen also in the prophets of Jerusalem an horrible thing: they commit adultery, and walk in lies: they strengthen also the hands of evildoers, that none doth return from his wickedness: they are all of them unto me as Sodom, and the inhabitants thereof as Go-mŏr'rah.

15 Therefore thus saith the LORD of hosts concerning the prophets; Behold, I will feed them with wormwood, and make them drink the water of gall: for from the prophets of Jerusalem is profaneness gone forth into all the land.

16 Thus saith the LORD of hosts, Hearken not unto the words of the prophets that prophesy unto you: they make you vain: they speak a vision of their own heart, *and* not out of the mouth of the LORD.

17 They say still unto them that despise me, The LORD hath said, Ye shall have peace; and they say unto every one that walketh after the imagination of his own heart, No evil shall come upon you.

18 For who hath stood in the counsel of the LORD, and hath perceived and heard his word? who hath marked his word, and heard *it?*

19 Behold, a whirlwind of the LORD is gone forth in fury, even a grievous whirlwind: it shall fall grievously upon the head of the wicked.

20 The anger of the LORD shall not return, until he have executed, and till he have performed the thoughts of his heart: in the latter days ye shall consider it perfectly.

21 I have not sent these prophets, yet they ran: I have not spoken to them, yet they prophesied.

22 But if they had stood in my counsel, and had caused my people to hear my words, then they should have turned them from their evil way, and from the evil of their doings.

23 *Am* I a God at hand, saith the LORD, and not a God afar off?

24 Can any hide himself in secret places that I shall not see him? saith the LORD. Do not I fill heaven and earth? saith the LORD.

25 I have heard what the prophets said, that prophesy lies in my name, saying, I have dreamed, I have dreamed.

26 How long shall *this* be in the heart of the prophets that prophesy lies? yea, *they are* prophets of the deceit of their own heart;

27 Which think to cause my people to forget my name by their dreams which they tell every man to his neighbour, as their fathers have forgotten my name for Bā'al.

28 The prophet that hath a dream, let him tell a dream; and he that hath my word, let him speak my word faithfully. What *is* the chaff to the wheat? saith the LORD.

29 *Is* not my word like as a fire? saith the LORD; and like a hammer *that* breaketh the rock in pieces?

30 Therefore, behold, I *am* against the prophets, saith the LORD, that steal my words every one from his neighbour.

31 Behold, I *am* against the prophets, saith the LORD, that use their tongues, and say, He saith.

32 Behold, I *am* against them that prophesy false dreams, saith the LORD, and do tell them, and cause my people to err by their lies, and by their lightness; yet I sent them not, nor commanded them: therefore they shall not profit this people at all, saith the LORD.

33 ¶And when this people, or the

prophet, or a priest, shall ask thee,
saying, What *is* the burden of the LORD?
thou shalt then say unto them, What
burden? I will even forsake you, saith
the LORD.
34 And *as for* the prophet, and the
priest, and the people, that shall say,
The burden of the LORD, I will even pun-
ish that man and his house.
35 Thus shall ye say every one to his
neighbour, and every one to his
brother, What hath the LORD an-
swered? and, What hath the LORD spo-
ken?
36 And the burden of the LORD shall
ye mention no more: for every man's
word shall be his burden; for ye have
perverted the words of the living God,
of the LORD of hosts our God.
37 Thus shalt thou say to the prophet,
What hath the LORD answered thee?
and, What hath the LORD spoken?
38 But since ye say, The burden of the
LORD; therefore thus saith the LORD;
Because ye say this word, The burden
of the LORD, and I have sent unto you,
saying, Ye shall not say, The burden of
the LORD;
39 Therefore, behold, I, even I, will
utterly forget you, and I will forsake
you, and the city that I gave you and
your fathers, *and cast you* out of my
presence:
40 And I will bring an everlasting
reproach upon you, and a perpetual
shame, which shall not be forgotten.

CHAPTER 24

THE LORD shewed me, and, behold,
two baskets of figs *were* set before the
temple of the LORD, after that Něb-u-
chad-rěz-zar king of Babylon had
carried away captive Jěc-o-nī'ah the
son of Je-hoi'a-kĭm king of Jū'dah, and
the princes of Jū'dah, with the carpen-
ters and smiths, from Jerusalem, and
had brought them to Babylon.
2 One basket *had* very good figs, *even*
like the figs *that are* first ripe: and the
other basket *had* very naughty figs,
which could not be eaten, they were so
bad.
3 Then said the LORD unto me, What
seest thou, Jěr'e-mī'ah? And I said,
Figs; the good figs, very good; and the
evil, very evil, that cannot be eaten,
they are so evil.
4 ¶Again the word of the LORD came
unto me, saying,
5 Thus saith the LORD, the God of
Israel; Like these good figs, so will I
acknowledge them that are carried
away captive of Jū'dah, whom I have
sent out of this place into the land of the
Chăl-dē'ans for *their* good.
6 For I will set mine eyes upon them
for good, and I will bring them again to
this land: and I will build them, and not
pull *them* down; and I will plant them,
and not pluck *them* up.
7 And I will give them an heart to
know me, that I *am* the LORD: and they
shall be my people, and I will be their
God: for they shall return unto me with
their whole heart.
8 ¶And as the evil figs, which cannot
be eaten, they are so evil; surely thus
saith the LORD, So will I give Zěd-e-kī'-
ah the king of Jū'dah, and his princes,
and the residue of Jerusalem, that re-
main in this land, and them that dwell
in the land of Egypt:
9 And I will deliver them to be re-
moved into all the kingdoms of the
earth for *their* hurt, *to be* a reproach
and a proverb, a taunt and a curse, in all
places whither I shall drive them.
10 And I will send the sword, the
famine, and the pestilence, among
them, till they be consumed from off
the land that I gave unto them and to
their fathers.

CHAPTER 25

THE word that came to Jěr'e-mī'ah
concerning all the people of Jū'dah in
the fourth year of Je-hoi'a-kĭm the son
of Jō-sī'ah king of Jū'dah, that *was* the
first year of Něb-u-chad-rěz'zar king of
Babylon;
2 The which Jěr'e-mī'ah the prophet
spake unto all the people of Jū'dah, and
to all the inhabitants of Jerusalem,
saying,
3 From the thirteenth year of Jō-sī'ah
the son of Ā'mon king of Jū'dah, even
unto this day, that *is* the three and
twentieth year, the word of the LORD
hath come unto me, and I have spoken
unto you, rising early and speaking; but
ye have not hearkened.
4 And the LORD hath sent unto you all
his servants the prophets, rising early
and sending *them;* but ye have not
hearkened, nor inclined your ear to
hear.
5 They said, Turn ye again now every
one from his evil way, and from the evil
of your doings, and dwell in the land
that the LORD hath given unto you and
to your fathers for ever and ever:
6 And go not after other gods to serve
them, and to worship them, and pro-
voke me not to anger with the works of
your hands; and I will do you no hurt.
7 Yet ye have not hearkened unto me,
saith the LORD; that ye might provoke
me to anger with the works of your
hands to your own hurt.
8 ¶Therefore thus saith the LORD of

hosts; Because ye have not heard my
words,
9 Behold, I will send and take all the
families of the north, saith the LORD,
and Něb-u-chad-rěz'zar the king of Bab-
ylon, my servant, and will bring them
against this land, and against the
inhabitants thereof, and against all
these nations round about, and will ut-
terly destroy them, and make them an
astonishment, and an hissing, and per-
petual desolations.
10 Moreover I will take from them
the voice of mirth, and the voice of
gladness, the voice of the bridegroom,
and the voice of the bride, the sound of
the millstones, and the light of the
candle.
11 And this whole land shall be a deso-
lation, *and* an astonishment; and
these nations shall serve the king of Bab-
ylon seventy years.
12 ¶And it shall come to pass, when
seventy years are accomplished, *that* I
will punish the king of Babylon, and
that nation, saith the LORD, for their iniq-
uity, and the land of the Chăl-dē'ans,
and will make it perpetual desolations.
13 And I will bring upon that land all
my words which I have pronounced
against it, *even* all that is written in this
book, which Jěr'e-mī'ah hath proph-
esied against all the nations.
14 For many nations and great kings
shall serve themselves of them also:
and I will recompense them according
to their deeds, and according to the
works of their own hands.
15 ¶For thus saith the LORD God of
Israel unto me; Take the wine cup of
this fury at my hand, and cause all the
nations, to whom I send thee, to drink
it.
16 And they shall drink, and be
moved, and be mad, because of the
sword that I will send among them.
17 Then took I the cup at the LORD's
hand, and made all the nations to drink,
unto whom the LORD had sent me:
18 *To wit,* Jerusalem, and the cities of
Jū'dah, and the kings thereof, and the
princes thereof, to make them a desola-
tion, an astonishment, an hissing, and a
curse; as *it is* this day;
19 Pharaoh king of Egypt, and his
servants, and his princes, and all his
people;
20 And all the mingled people, and all
the kings of the land of Uz, and all the
kings of the land of the Philistines, and
Ăsh'ke-lon, and Ăz'zah, and Ekron, and
the remnant of Ăsh'dŏd,
21 Edom, and Moab, and the children
of Ammon,
22 And all the kings of Tȳ'rus, and all
the kings of Zī'don, and the kings of the
isles which *are* beyond the sea,
23 Dē'dan, and Tē'ma, and Buz, and
all *that are* in the utmost corners,
24 And all the kings of Arabia, and all
the kings of the mingled people that
dwell in the desert,
25 And all the kings of Zimri, and all
the kings of Ē'lam, and all the kings of
the Medes,
26 And all the kings of the north, far
and near, one with another, and all the
kingdoms of the world, which *are* upon
the face of the earth: and the king of
Shē'shăch shall drink after them.
27 Therefore thou shalt say unto
them, Thus saith the LORD of hosts, the
God of Israel; Drink ye, and be
drunken, and spue, and fall, and rise no
more, because of the sword which I will
send among you.
28 And it shall be, if they refuse to
take the cup at thine hand to drink,
then shalt thou say unto them, Thus
saith the LORD of hosts; Ye shall cer-
tainly drink.
29 For, lo, I begin to bring evil on the
city which is called by my name, and
should ye be utterly unpunished? Ye
shall not be unpunished: for I will call
for a sword upon all the inhabitants of
the earth, saith the LORD of hosts.
30 Therefore prophesy thou against
them all these words, and say unto
them, The LORD shall roar from on high,
and utter his voice from his holy habi-
tation; he shall mightily roar upon his
habitation; he shall give a shout, as
they that tread *the grapes,* against all
the inhabitants of the earth.
31 A noise shall come *even* to the
ends of the earth; for the LORD hath a
controversy with the nations, he will
plead with all flesh; he will give them
that are wicked to the sword, saith the
LORD.
32 Thus saith the LORD of hosts, Be-
hold, evil shall go forth from nation to
nation, and a great whirlwind shall be
raised up from the coasts of the earth.
33 And the slain of the LORD shall be
at that day from *one* end of the earth
even unto the *other* end of the earth:
they shall not be lamented, neither gath-
ered, nor buried; they shall be dung
upon the ground.
34 ¶Howl, ye shepherds, and cry; and
wallow yourselves *in the ashes,* ye
principal of the flock: for the days of
your slaughter and of your dispersions
are accomplished; and ye shall fall like
a pleasant vessel.
35 And the shepherds shall have no
way to flee, nor the principal of the
flock to escape.

36 A voice of the cry of the
shepherds, and an howling of the prin-
cipal of the flock, *shall be heard:* for the
LORD hath spoiled their pasture.
37 And the peaceable habitations are
cut down because of the fierce anger of
the LORD.
38 He hath forsaken his covert, as the
lion: for their land is desolate because
of the fierceness of the oppressor, and
because of his fierce anger.

CHAPTER 26

IN the beginning of the reign of Je-
hoi'a-kĭm the son of Jō-sī'ah king of Jū'-
dah came this word from the LORD,
saying,
2 Thus saith the LORD; Stand in the
court of the LORD's house, and speak
unto all the cities of Jū'dah, which
come to worship in the LORD's house,
all the words that I command thee to
speak unto them; diminish not a word:
3 If so be they will hearken, and turn
every man from his evil way, that I may
repent me of the evil, which I purpose
to do unto them because of the evil of
their doings.
4 And thou shalt say unto them, Thus
saith the LORD; If ye will not hearken to
me, to walk in my law, which I have set
before you,
5 To hearken to the words of my ser-
vants the prophets, whom I sent unto
you, both rising up early, and sending
them, but ye have not hearkened;
6 Then will I make this house like
Shī'lōh, and will make this city a curse
to all the nations of the earth.
7 So the priests and the prophets and
all the people heard Jĕr'e-mī'ah speak-
ing these words in the house of the
LORD.
8 ¶Now it came to pass, when Jĕr'e-
mī'ah had made an end of speaking all
that the LORD had commanded *him* to
speak unto all the people, that the
priests and the prophets and all the
people took him, saying, Thou shalt
surely die.
9 Why hast thou prophesied in the
name of the LORD, saying, This house
shall be like Shī'lōh, and this city shall
be desolate without an inhabitant? And
all the people were gathered against
Jĕr'e-mī'ah in the house of the LORD.
10 ¶When the princes of Jū'dah heard
these things, then they came up from
the king's house unto the house of the
LORD, and sat down in the entry of the
new gate of the LORD's *house.*
11 Then spake the priests and the
prophets unto the princes and to all the
people, saying, This man *is* worthy to
die; for he hath prophesied against this
city, as ye have heard with your ears.
12 ¶Then spake Jĕr'e-mī'ah unto all
the princes and to all the people,
saying, The LORD sent me to prophesy
against this house and against this city
all the words that ye have heard.
13 Therefore now amend your ways
and your doings, and obey the voice of
the LORD your God; and the LORD will
repent him of the evil that he hath pro-
nounced against you.
14 As for me, behold, I *am* in your
hand: do with me as seemeth good and
meet unto you.
15 But know ye for certain, that if ye
put me to death, ye shall surely bring
innocent blood upon yourselves, and
upon this city, and upon the inhabi-
tants thereof: for of a truth the LORD
hath sent me unto you to speak all
these words in your ears.
16 ¶Then said the princes and all the
people unto the priests and to the
prophets; This man *is* not worthy to
die: for he hath spoken to us in the
name of the LORD our God.
17 Then rose up certain of the elders
of the land, and spake to all the as-
sembly of the people, saying,
18 Mī'cah the Mô'ras-thīte proph-
esied in the days of Hĕz-e-kī'ah king
of Jū'dah, and spake to all the people of
Jū'dah, saying, Thus saith the LORD of
hosts; Zion shall be plowed *like* a field,
and Jerusalem shall become heaps, and
the mountain of the house as the high
places of a forest.
19 Did Hĕz-e-kī'ah king of Jū'dah and
all Jū'dah put him at all to death? did he
not fear the LORD, and besought the
LORD, and the LORD repented him of the
evil which he had pronounced against
them? Thus might we procure great
evil against our souls.
20 And there was also a man that
prophesied in the name of the LORD, Ū-
rī'jah the son of Shĕm-a-ī'ah of Kir'jăth-
jē'a-rĭm, who prophesied against
this city and against this land accord-
ing to all the words of Jĕr'e-mī'ah:
21 And when Je-hoi'a-kĭm the king,
with all his mighty men, and all the
princes, heard his words, the king
sought to put him to death: but when Ū-
rī'jah heard it, he was afraid, and fled,
and went into Egypt;
22 And Je-hoi'a-kĭm the king sent
men into Egypt, *namely,* Ĕl'nā-than the
son of Ăch'bôr, and *certain* men with
him into Egypt.
23 And they fetched forth Ū-rī'jah out
of Egypt, and brought him unto Je-
hoi'a-kĭm the king; who slew him with

the sword, and cast his dead body into the graves of the common people.

24 Nevertheless the hand of A-hī'kam the son of Shā'phan was with Jĕr'e-mī'ah, that they should not give him into the hand of the people to put him to death.

CHAPTER 27

IN the beginning of the reign of Je-hoi'a-kĭm the son of Jō-sī'ah king of Jū'-dah came this word unto Jĕr'e-mī'ah from the LORD, saying,

2 Thus saith the LORD to me; Make thee bonds and yokes, and put them upon thy neck,

3 And send them to the king of Edom, and to the king of Moab, and to the king of the Ammonites, and to the king of Tȳ'rus, and to the king of Zī'don, by the hand of the messengers which come to Jerusalem unto Zĕd-e-kī'ah king of Jū'-dah;

4 And command them to say unto their masters, Thus saith the LORD of hosts, the God of Israel; Thus shall ye say unto your masters;

5 I have made the earth, the man and the beast that *are* upon the ground, by my great power and by my out-stretched arm, and have given it unto whom it seemed meet unto me.

6 And now have I given all these lands into the hand of Nĕb-u-chad-nĕz'zar the king of Babylon, my ser-vant; and the beasts of the field have I given him also to serve him.

7 And all nations shall serve him, and his son, and his son's son, until the very time of his land come: and then many nations and great kings shall serve themselves of him.

8 And it shall come to pass, *that* the nation and kingdom which will not serve the same Nĕb-u-chad-nĕz'zar the king of Babylon, and that will not put their neck under the yoke of the king of Babylon, that nation will I punish, saith the LORD, with the sword, and with the famine, and with the pestilence, until I have consumed them by his hand.

9 Therefore hearken not ye to your prophets, nor to your diviners, nor to your dreamers, nor to your enchanters, nor to your sorcerers, which speak unto you, saying, Ye shall not serve the king of Babylon:

10 For they prophesy a lie unto you, to remove you far from your land; and that I should drive you out, and ye should perish.

11 But the nations that bring their neck under the yoke of the king of Bab-ylon, and serve him, those will I let re-main still in their own land, saith the LORD; and they shall till it, and dwell therein.

12 ¶I spake also to Zĕd-e-kī'ah king of Jū'dah according to all these words, saying, Bring your necks under the yoke of the king of Babylon, and serve him and his people, and live.

13 Why will ye die, thou and thy people, by the sword, by the famine, and by the pestilence, as the LORD hath spoken against the nation that will not serve the king of Babylon?

14 Therefore hearken not unto the words of the prophets that speak unto you, saying, Ye shall not serve the king of Babylon: for they prophesy a lie unto you.

15 For I have not sent them, saith the LORD, yet they prophesy a lie in my name; that I might drive you out, and that ye might perish, ye, and the prophets that prophesy unto you.

16 Also I spake to the priests and to all this people, saying, Thus saith the LORD; Hearken not to the words of your prophets that prophesy unto you, saying, Behold, the vessels of the LORD's house shall now shortly be brought again from Babylon: for they prophesy a lie unto you.

17 Hearken not unto them; serve the king of Babylon, and live: wherefore should this city be laid waste?

18 But if they *be* prophets, and if the word of the LORD be with them, let them now make intercession to the LORD of hosts, that the vessels which are left in the house of the LORD, and *in* the house of the king of Jū'dah, and at Jerusalem, go not to Babylon.

19 ¶For thus saith the LORD of hosts concerning the pillars, and concerning the sea, and concerning the bases, and concerning the residue of the vessels that remain in this city,

20 Which Nĕb-u-chad-nĕz'zar king of Babylon took not, when he carried away captive Jĕc-o-nī'ah the son of Je-hoi'a-kĭm king of Jū'dah from Jeru-salem to Babylon, and all the nobles of Jū'dah and Jerusalem;

21 Yea, thus saith the LORD of hosts, the God of Israel, concerning the ves-sels that remain *in* the house of the LORD, and *in* the house of the king of Jū'dah and of Jerusalem;

22 They shall be carried to Babylon, and there shall they be until the day that I visit them, saith the LORD; then will I bring them up, and restore them to this place.

CHAPTER 28

AND it came to pass the same year, in the beginning of the reign of Zĕd-e-kī'-

ah king of Jū'dah, in the fourth year,
and in the fifth month, *that* Hăn-a-nī'ah
the son of Ā'zur the prophet, which *was*
of Gibeon, spake unto me in the house
of the LORD, in the presence of the
priests and of all the people, saying,
2 Thus speaketh the LORD of hosts,
the God of Israel, saying, I have broken
the yoke of the king of Babylon.
3 Within two full years will I bring
again into this place all the vessels of
the LORD's house, that Nĕb-u-chad-
nĕz'zar king of Babylon took away
from this place, and carried them to Bab-
ylon:
4 And I will bring again to this place
Jĕc-o-nī'ah the son of Je-hoi'a-kĭm king
of Jū'dah, with all the captives of Jū'-
dah, that went into Babylon, saith the
LORD: for I will break the yoke of the
king of Babylon.
5 ¶Then the prophet Jĕr'e-mī'ah said
unto the prophet Hăn-a-nī'ah in the
presence of the priests, and in the pres-
ence of all the people that stood in the
house of the LORD,
6 Even the prophet Jĕr'e-mī'ah said,
Amen: the LORD do so: the LORD per-
form thy words which thou hast proph-
esied, to bring again the vessels of the
LORD's house, and all that is carried
away captive, from Babylon into this
place.
7 Nevertheless hear thou now this
word that I speak in thine ears, and in
the ears of all the people;
8 The prophets that have been before
me and before thee of old prophesied
both against many countries, and
against great kingdoms, of war, and of
evil, and of pestilence.
9 The prophet which prophesieth of
peace, when the word of the prophet
shall come to pass, *then* shall the
prophet be known, that the LORD hath
truly sent him.
10 ¶Then Hăn-a-nī'ah the prophet
took the yoke from off the prophet
Jĕr'e-mī'ah's neck, and brake it.
11 And Hăn-a-nī'ah spake in the pres-
ence of all the people, saying, Thus
saith the LORD; Even so will I break the
yoke of Nĕb-u-chad-nĕz'zar king of Bab-
ylon from the neck of all nations
within the space of two full years. And
the prophet Jĕr'e-mī'ah went his way.
12 ¶Then the word of the LORD came
unto Jĕr'e-mī'ah *the prophet,* after that
Hăn-a-nī'ah the prophet had broken
the yoke from off the neck of the
prophet Jĕr'e-mī'ah, saying,
13 Go and tell Hăn-a-nī'ah, saying,
Thus saith the LORD; Thou hast broken
the yokes of wood; but thou shalt make
for them yokes of iron.
14 For thus saith the LORD of hosts,
the God of Israel; I have put a yoke of
iron upon the neck of all these nations,
that they may serve Nĕb-u-chad-nĕz'zar
king of Babylon; and they shall
serve him: and I have given him the
beasts of the field also.
15 ¶Then said the prophet Jĕr'e-mī'ah
unto Hăn-a-nī'ah the prophet, Hear
now, Hăn-a-nī'ah; The LORD hath not
sent thee; but thou makest this people
to trust in a lie.
16 Therefore thus saith the LORD; Be-
hold, I will cast thee from off the face of
the earth: this year thou shalt die, be-
cause thou hast taught rebellion
against the LORD.
17 So Hăn-a-nī'ah the prophet died
the same year in the seventh month.

CHAPTER 29

NOW these *are* the words of the letter
that Jĕr'e-mī'ah the prophet sent from
Jerusalem unto the residue of the elders
which were carried away captives,
and to the priests, and to the prophets,
and to all the people whom Nĕb-u-
chad-nĕz'zar had carried away captive
from Jerusalem to Babylon;
2 (After that Jĕc-o-nī'ah the king, and
the queen, and the eunuchs, the princes
of Jū'dah and Jerusalem, and the car-
penters, and the smiths, were departed
from Jerusalem;)
3 By the hand of Ĕl'a-sah the son of
Shā'phan, and Gĕm-a-rī'ah the son of
Hĭl-kī'ah, (whom Zĕd-e-kī'ah king of
Jū'dah sent unto Babylon to Nĕb-u-
chad-nĕz'zar king of Babylon) saying,
4 Thus saith the LORD of hosts, the
God of Israel, unto all that are carried
away captives, whom I have caused to
be carried away from Jerusalem unto
Babylon;
5 Build ye houses, and dwell *in them;*
and plant gardens, and eat the fruit of
them;
6 Take ye wives, and beget sons and
daughters; and take wives for your
sons, and give your daughters to hus-
bands, that they may bear sons and
daughters; that ye may be increased
there, and not diminished.
7 And seek the peace of the city
whither I have caused you to be carried
away captives, and pray unto the LORD
for it: for in the peace thereof shall ye
have peace.
8 ¶For thus saith the LORD of hosts,
the God of Israel; Let not your prophets
and your diviners, that *be* in the midst
of you, deceive you, neither hearken to
your dreams which ye cause to be
dreamed.
9 For they prophesy falsely unto you

in my name: I have not sent them, saith
the LORD.
10 ¶For thus saith the LORD, That af-
ter seventy years be accomplished at
Babylon I will visit you, and perform
my good word toward you, in causing
you to return to this place.
11 For I know the thoughts that I
think toward you, saith the LORD,
thoughts of peace, and not of evil, to
give you an expected end.
12 Then shall ye call upon me, and ye
shall go and pray unto me, and I will
hearken unto you.
13 And ye shall seek me, and find *me*,
when ye shall search for me with all
your heart.
14 And I will be found of you, saith
the LORD: and I will turn away your
captivity, and I will gather you from all
the nations, and from all the places
whither I have driven you, saith the
LORD; and I will bring you again into the
place whence I caused you to be
carried away captive.
15 ¶Because ye have said, The LORD
hath raised us up prophets in Babylon;
16 *Know* that thus saith the LORD of
the king that sitteth upon the throne of
David, and of all the people that dwel-
leth in this city, *and* of your brethren
that are not gone forth with you into
captivity;
17 Thus saith the LORD of hosts; Be-
hold, I will send upon them the sword,
the famine, and the pestilence, and will
make them like vile figs, that cannot be
eaten, they are so evil.
18 And I will persecute them with the
sword, with the famine, and with the
pestilence, and will deliver them to be
removed to all the kingdoms of the
earth, to be a curse, and an astonish-
ment, and an hissing, and a reproach,
among all the nations whither I have
driven them:
19 Because they have not hearkened
to my words, saith the LORD, which I
sent unto them by my servants the
prophets, rising up early and sending
them; but ye would not hear, saith the
LORD.
20 ¶Hear ye therefore the word of the
LORD, all ye of the captivity, whom I
have sent from Jerusalem to Babylon:
21 Thus saith the LORD of hosts, the
God of Israel, of Ahab the son of Kō-la-
ī'ah, and of Zĕd-e-kī'ah the son of Mā-a-
sē'iah, which prophesy a lie unto you in
my name; Behold, I will deliver them
into the hand of Nĕb-u-chad-rĕz'zar
king of Babylon; and he shall slay them
before your eyes;
22 And of them shall be taken up a
curse by all the captivity of Jū'dah
which *are* in Babylon, saying, The LORD
make thee like Zĕd-e-kī'ah and like
Ahab, whom the king of Babylon
roasted in the fire;
23 Because they have committed vil-
lany in Israel, and have committed
adultery with their neighbours' wives,
and have spoken lying words in my
name, which I have not commanded
them; even I know, and *am* a witness,
saith the LORD.
24 ¶*Thus* shalt thou also speak to
Shĕm-a-ī'ah the Ne-hĕl'a-mīte, saying,
25 Thus speaketh the LORD of hosts,
the God of Israel, saying, Because thou
hast sent letters in thy name unto all
the people that *are* at Jerusalem, and to
Zĕph-a-nī'ah the son of Mā-a-sē'iah the
priest, and to all the priests, saying,
26 The LORD hath made thee priest in
the stead of Je-hoi'a-da the priest, that
ye should be officers in the house of the
LORD, for every man *that is* mad, and
maketh himself a prophet, that thou
shouldest put him in prison, and in the
stocks.
27 Now therefore why hast thou not
reproved Jĕr'e-mī'ah of Ăn'a-thŏth,
which maketh himself a prophet to
you?
28 For therefore he sent unto us *in*
Babylon, saying, This *captivity is* long:
build ye houses, and dwell *in them*; and
plant gardens, and eat the fruit of them.
29 And Zĕph-a-nī'ah the priest read
this letter in the ears of Jĕr'e-mī'ah the
prophet.
30 ¶Then came the word of the LORD
unto Jĕr'e-mī'ah saying,
31 Send to all them of the captivity,
saying, Thus saith the LORD concerning
Shĕm-a-ī'ah the Ne-hĕl'a-mīte; Be-
cause that Shĕm-a-ī'ah hath proph-
esied unto you, and I sent him not, and
he caused you to trust in a lie:
32 Therefore thus saith the LORD; Be-
hold, I will punish Shĕm-a-ī'ah the Ne-
hĕl'a-mīte, and his seed: he shall not
have a man to dwell among this people;
neither shall he behold the good that I
will do for my people, saith the LORD,
because he hath taught rebellion
against the LORD.

CHAPTER 30

THE word that came to Jĕr'e-mī'ah
from the LORD, saying,
2 Thus speaketh the LORD God of
Israel, saying, Write thee all the words
that I have spoken unto thee in a book.
3 For, lo, the days come, saith the
LORD, that I will bring again the captiv-
ity of my people Israel and Jū'dah, saith
the LORD: and I will cause them to re-

turn to the land that I gave to their fa-
thers, and they shall possess it.
4 ¶And these *are* the words that the
LORD spake concerning Israel and con-
cerning Jū'dah.
5 For thus saith the LORD; We have
heard a voice of trembling, of fear, and
not of peace.
6 Ask ye now, and see whether a man
doth travail with child? wherefore do I
see every man with his hands on his
loins, as a woman in travail, and all
faces are turned into paleness?
7 Alas! for that day *is* great, so that
none *is* like it: it *is* even the time of Ja-
cob's trouble; but he shall be saved out
of it.
8 For it shall come to pass in that day,
saith the LORD of hosts, *that* I will break
his yoke from off thy neck, and will
burst thy bonds, and strangers shall no
more serve themselves of him:
9 But they shall serve the LORD their
God, and David their king, whom I will
raise up unto them.
10 Therefore fear thou not, O my ser-
vant Jacob, saith the LORD; neither be
dismayed, O Israel: for, lo, I will save
thee from afar, and thy seed from the
land of their captivity; and Jacob shall
return, and shall be in rest, and be
quiet, and none shall make *him* afraid.
11 For I *am* with thee, saith the LORD,
to save thee: though I make a full end of
all nations whither I have scattered
thee, yet will I not make a full end of
thee: but I will correct thee in measure,
and will not leave thee altogether un-
punished.
12 For thus saith the LORD, Thy
bruise *is* incurable, *and* thy wound *is*
grievous.
13 *There is* none to plead thy cause,
that thou mayest be bound up: thou
hast no healing medicines.
14 All thy lovers have forgotten thee;
they seek thee not; for I have wounded
thee with the wound of an enemy, with
the chastisement of a cruel one, for the
multitude of thine iniquity; *because* thy
sins were increased.
15 Why criest thou for thine afflic-
tion? thy sorrow *is* incurable for the
multitude of thine iniquity: *because* thy
sins were increased, I have done these
things unto thee.
16 Therefore all they that devour thee
shall be devoured; and all thine adver-
saries, every one of them, shall go into
captivity; and they that spoil thee shall
be a spoil, and all that prey upon thee
will I give for a prey.
17 For I will restore health unto thee,
and I will heal thee of thy wounds, saith
the LORD; because they called thee an
Outcast, *saying*, This *is* Zion, whom no
man seeketh after.
18 ¶Thus saith the LORD; Behold, I
will bring again the captivity of Jacob's
tents, and have mercy on his dwelling-
places; and the city shall be builded
upon her own heap, and the palace
shall remain after the manner thereof.
19 And out of them shall proceed
thanksgiving and the voice of them
that make merry: and I will multiply
them, and they shall not be few; I will
also glorify them, and they shall not be
small.
20 Their children also shall be as
aforetime, and their congregation shall
be established before me, and I will pun-
ish all that oppress them.
21 And their nobles shall be of them-
selves, and their governor shall
proceed from the midst of them; and I
will cause him to draw near, and he
shall approach unto me: for who *is* this
that engaged his heart to approach
unto me? saith the LORD.
22 And ye shall be my people, and I
will be your God.
23 ¶Behold, the whirlwind of the
LORD goeth forth with fury, a continu-
ing whirlwind: it shall fall with pain
upon the head of the wicked.
24 The fierce anger of the LORD shall
not return, until he have done *it*, and
until he have performed the intents of
his heart: in the latter days ye shall con-
sider it.

CHAPTER 31

AT the same time, saith the LORD, will I
be the God of all the families of Israel,
and they shall be my people.
2 Thus saith the LORD, The people
which were left of the sword found
grace in the wilderness; *even* Israel,
when I went to cause him to rest.
3 The LORD hath appeared of old unto
me, *saying*, Yea, I have loved thee with
an everlasting love: therefore with
lovingkindness have I drawn thee.
4 Again I will build thee, and thou
shalt be built, O virgin of Israel: thou
shalt again be adorned with thy
tabrets, and shalt go forth in the dances
of them that make merry.
5 Thou shalt yet plant vines upon the
mountains of Sa-mâ'rĭ-a: the planters
shall plant, and shall eat *them* as com-
mon things.
6 For there shall be a day, *that* the
watchman upon the mount Ē'phra-im
shall cry, Arise ye, and let us go up to
Zion unto the LORD our God.
7 For thus saith the LORD; Sing with
gladness for Jacob, and shout among
the chief of the nations: publish ye,

praise ye, and say, O LORD, save thy people, the remnant of Israel.

8 Behold, I will bring them from the north country, and gather them from the coasts of the earth, *and* with them the blind and the lame, the woman with child and her that travaileth with child together: a great company shall return thither.

9 They shall come with weeping, and with supplications will I lead them: I will cause them to walk by the rivers of waters in a straight way, wherein they shall not stumble: for I am a father to Israel, and Ē′phra-im *is* my firstborn.

10 ¶Hear the word of the LORD, O ye nations, and declare *it* in the isles afar off, and say, He that scattered Israel will gather him, and keep him, as a shepherd *doth* his flock.

11 For the LORD hath redeemed Jacob, and ransomed him from the hand of *him that was* stronger than he.

12 Therefore they shall come and sing in the height of Zion, and shall flow together to the goodness of the LORD, for wheat, and for wine, and for oil, and for the young of the flock and of the herd: and their soul shall be as a watered garden; and they shall not sorrow any more at all.

13 Then shall the virgin rejoice in the dance, both young men and old together: for I will turn their mourning into joy, and will comfort them, and make them rejoice from their sorrow.

14 And I will satiate the soul of the priests with fatness, and my people shall be satisfied with my goodness, saith the LORD.

15 ¶Thus saith the LORD; A voice was heard in Rā′mah, lamentation, *and* bitter weeping; Rahel weeping for her children refused to be comforted for her children, because they *were* not.

16 Thus saith the LORD; Refrain thy voice from weeping, and thine eyes from tears: for thy work shall be rewarded, saith the LORD; and they shall come again from the land of the enemy.

17 And there is hope in thine end, saith the LORD, that thy children shall come again to their own border.

18 ¶I have surely heard Ē′phra-im bemoaning himself *thus;* Thou hast chastised me, and I was chastised, as a bullock unaccustomed *to the yoke:* turn thou me, and I shall be turned; for thou *art* the LORD my God.

19 Surely after that I was turned, I repented; and after that I was instructed, I smote upon *my* thigh: I was ashamed, yea, even confounded, because I did bear the reproach of my youth.

20 *Is* Ē′phra-im my dear son? *is he* a pleasant child? for since I spake against him, I do earnestly remember him still: therefore my bowels are troubled for him; I will surely have mercy upon him, saith the LORD.

21 Set thee up waymarks, make thee high heaps: set thine heart toward the highway, *even* the way *which* thou wentest: turn again, O virgin of Israel, turn again to these thy cities.

22 ¶How long wilt thou go about, O thou backsliding daughter? for the LORD hath created a new thing in the earth, A woman shall compass a man.

23 Thus saith the LORD of hosts, the God of Israel; As yet they shall use this speech in the land of Jū′dah and in the cities thereof, when I shall bring again their captivity; The LORD bless thee, O habitation of justice, *and* mountain of holiness.

24 And there shall dwell in Jū′dah itself, and in all the cities thereof together, husbandmen, and they *that* go forth with flocks.

25 For I have satiated the weary soul, and I have replenished every sorrowful soul.

26 Upon this I awaked, and beheld; and my sleep was sweet unto me.

27 ¶Behold, the days come, saith the LORD, that I will sow the house of Israel and the house of Jū′dah with the seed of man, and with the seed of beast.

28 And it shall come to pass, *that* like as I have watched over them, to pluck up, and to break down, and to throw down, and to destroy, and to afflict; so will I watch over them to build, and to plant, saith the LORD.

29 In those days they shall say no more, The fathers have eaten a sour grape, and the children's teeth are set on edge.

30 But every one shall die for his own iniquity: every man that eateth the sour grape, his teeth shall be set on edge.

31 ¶Behold, the days come, saith the LORD, that I will make a new covenant with the house of Israel and with the house of Jū′dah:

32 Not according to the covenant that I made with their fathers in the day *that* I took them by the hand to bring them out of the land of Egypt; which my covenant they brake, although I was an husband unto them, saith the LORD:

33 But this *shall be* the covenant that I will make with the house of Israel; After those days, saith the LORD, I will put my law in their inward parts, and write it in their hearts; and will be their God, and they shall be my people.

34 And they shall teach no more

every man his neighbour, and every
man his brother, saying, Know the
LORD: for they shall all know me, from
the least of them unto the greatest of
them, saith the LORD: for I will forgive
their iniquity, and I will remember
their sin no more.
35 ¶Thus saith the LORD, which giv-
eth the sun for a light by day, *and* the
ordinances of the moon and of the stars
for a light by night, which divideth the
sea when the waves thereof roar; The
LORD of hosts *is* his name:
36 If those ordinances depart from
before me, saith the LORD, *then* the
seed of Israel also shall cease from
being a nation before me for ever.
37 Thus saith the LORD; If heaven
above can be measured, and the foun-
dations of the earth searched out be-
neath, I will also cast off all the seed of
Israel for all that they have done, saith
the LORD.
38 ¶Behold, the days come, saith the
LORD, that the city shall be built to the
LORD from the tower of Hă-nan'ē-el
unto the gate of the corner.
39 And the measuring line shall yet
go forth over against it upon the hill
Gâ'rĕb, and shall compass about to Gō'-
ăth.
40 And the whole valley of the dead
bodies, and of the ashes, and all the
fields unto the brook of Kidron, unto
the corner of the horse gate toward the
east, *shall be* holy unto the LORD; it
shall not be plucked up, nor thrown
down any more for ever.

CHAPTER 32

THE word that came to Jĕr'e-mī'ah
from the LORD in the tenth year of Zĕd-
e-kī'ah king of Jū'dah, which *was* the
eighteenth year of Nĕb-u-chad-rĕz-zar.
2 For then the king of Babylon's army
besieged Jerusalem: and Jĕr'e-mī'ah
the prophet was shut up in the court of
the prison, which *was* in the king of Jū'-
ah's house.
3 For Zĕd-e-kī'ah king of Jū'dah had
shut him up, saying, Wherefore dost
thou prophesy, and say, Thus saith the
LORD, Behold, I will give this city into
the hand of the king of Babylon, and he
shall take it;
4 And Zĕd-e-kī'ah king of Jū'dah
shall not escape out of the hand of the
Chăl-dē'anṡ, but shall surely be deliv-
ered into the hand of the king of Baby-
lon, and shall speak with him mouth to
mouth, and his eyes shall behold his
eyes;
5 And he shall lead Zĕd-e-kī'ah to Bab-
ylon, and there shall he be until I visit
him, saith the LORD: though ye fight
with the Chăl-dē'anṡ, ye shall not pros-
per.
6 ¶And Jĕr'e-mī'ah said, The word of
the LORD came unto me, saying,
7 Behold, Hă-nam'ē-el the son of
Shăl'lum thine uncle shall come unto
thee, saying, Buy thee my field that *is* in
Ăn'a-thŏth: for the right of redemption
is thine to buy *it*.
8 So Hă-nam'ē-el mine uncle's son
came to me in the court of the prison
according to the word of the LORD, and
said unto me, Buy my field, I pray thee,
that *is* in Ăn'a-thŏth, which *is* in the
country of Benjamin: for the right of in-
heritance *is* thine, and the redemption
is thine; buy *it* for thyself. Then I knew
that this *was* the word of the LORD.
9 And I bought the field of Hă-nam'ē-
el my uncle's son, that *was* in Ăn'a-
thŏth, and weighed him the money,
even seventeen shekels of silver.
10 And I subscribed the evidence,
and sealed *it*, and took witnesses, and
weighed *him* the money in the bal-
ances.
11 So I took the evidence of the pur-
chase, *both* that which was sealed *ac-
cording* to the law and custom, and that
which was open:
12 And I gave the evidence of the
purchase unto Bâ'ruch the son of Ne-rī'-
ah, the son of Mā-a-sē'iah, in the sight
of Hă-nam'ē-el mine uncle's *son*, and in
the presence of the witnesses that
subscribed the book of the purchase,
before all the Jews that sat in the court
of the prison.
13 ¶And I charged Bâ'ruch before
them, saying,
14 Thus saith the LORD of hosts, the
God of Israel; Take these evidences,
this evidence of the purchase, both
which is sealed, and this evidence
which is open; and put them in an earth-
en vessel, that they may continue
many days.
15 For thus saith the LORD of hosts,
the God of Israel; Houses and fields and
vineyards shall be possessed again in
this land.
16 ¶Now when I had delivered the
evidence of the purchase unto Bâ'ruch
the son of Ne-rī'ah, I prayed unto the
LORD, saying,
17 Ah Lord GOD! behold, thou hast
made the heaven and the earth by thy
great power and stretched out arm, *and*
there is nothing too hard for thee:
18 Thou shewest lovingkindness
unto thousands, and recompensest the
iniquity of the fathers into the bosom of
their children after them: the Great, the
Mighty God, the LORD of hosts, *is* his
name,

19 Great in counsel, and mighty in work: for thine eyes *are* open upon all the ways of the sons of men: to give every one according to his ways, and according to the fruit of his doings:
20 Which hast set signs and wonders in the land of Egypt, *even* unto this day, and in Israel, and among *other* men; and hast made thee a name, as at this day;
21 And hast brought forth thy people Israel out of the land of Egypt with signs, and with wonders, and with a strong hand, and with a stretched out arm, and with great terror;
22 And hast given them this land, which thou didst swear to their fathers to give them, a land flowing with milk and honey;
23 And they came in, and possessed it; but they obeyed not thy voice, neither walked in thy law; they have done nothing of all that thou commandedst them to do: therefore thou hast caused all this evil to come upon them:
24 Behold the mounts, they are come unto the city to take it: and the city is given into the hand of the Chăl-dē'anṡ, that fight against it, because of the sword, and of the famine, and of the pestilence: and what thou hast spoken is come to pass; and, behold, thou seest *it*.
25 And thou hast said unto me, O Lord GOD, Buy thee the field for money, and take witnesses; for the city is given into the hand of the Chăl-dē'anṡ.
26 ¶Then came the word of the LORD unto Jĕr'e-mī'ah, saying,
27 Behold, I *am* the LORD, the God of all flesh: is there any thing too hard for me?
28 Therefore thus saith the LORD; Behold, I will give this city into the hand of the Chăl-dē'anṡ, and into the hand of Nĕb-u-chad-rĕz'zar king of Babylon, and he shall take it:
29 And the Chăl-dē'anṡ, that fight against this city, shall come and set fire on this city, and burn it with the houses, upon whose roofs they have offered incense unto Bā'al, and poured out drink offerings unto other gods, to provoke me to anger.
30 For the children of Israel and the children of Jū'dah have only done evil before me from their youth: for the children of Israel have only provoked me to anger with the work of their hands, saith the LORD.
31 For this city hath been to me *as* a provocation of mine anger and of my fury from the day that they built it even unto this day; that I should remove it from before my face,
32 Because of all the evil of the children of Israel and of the children of Jū'dah, which they have done to provoke me to anger, they, their kings, their princes, their priests, and their prophets, and the men of Jū'dah, and the inhabitants of Jerusalem.
33 And they have turned unto me the back, and not the face: though I taught them, rising up early and teaching *them*, yet they have not hearkened to receive instruction.
34 But they set their abominations in the house, which is called by my name, to defile it.
35 And they built the high places of Bā'al, which *are* in the valley of the son of Hĭn'nom, to cause their sons and their daughters to pass through *the fire* unto Mō'lĕch; which I commanded them not, neither came it into my mind, that they should do this abomination, to cause Jū'dah to sin.
36 ¶And now therefore thus saith the LORD, the God of Israel, concerning this city, whereof ye say, It shall be delivered into the hand of the king of Babylon by the sword, and by the famine, and by the pestilence;
37 Behold, I will gather them out of all countries, whither I have driven them in mine anger, and in my fury, and in great wrath; and I will bring them again unto this place, and I will cause them to dwell safely:
38 And they shall be my people, and I will be their God:
39 And I will give them one heart, and one way, that they may fear me for ever, for the good of them, and of their children after them:
40 And I will make an everlasting covenant with them, that I will not turn away from them, to do them good; but I will put my fear in their hearts, that they shall not depart from me.
41 Yea, I will rejoice over them to do them good, and I will plant them in this land assuredly with my whole heart and with my whole soul.
42 For thus saith the LORD; Like as I have brought all this great evil upon this people, so will I bring upon them all the good that I have promised them.
43 And fields shall be bought in this land, whereof ye say, *It is* desolate without man or beast; it is given into the hand of the Chăl-dē'anṡ.
44 Men shall buy fields for money, and subscribe evidences, and seal *them*, and take witnesses in the land of Benjamin, and in the places about Jerusalem, and in the cities of Jū'dah, and in the cities of the mountains, and in the cities of the valley, and in the cities of

the south: for I will cause their captivity to return, saith the LORD.

CHAPTER 33

MOREOVER the word of the LORD came unto Jĕr'e-mī'ah the second time, while he was yet shut up in the court of the prison, saying,

2 Thus saith the LORD the maker thereof, the LORD that formed it, to establish it; the LORD *is* his name;

3 Call unto me, and I will answer thee, and shew thee great and mighty things, which thou knowest not.

4 For thus saith the LORD, the God of Israel, concerning the houses of this city, and concerning the houses of the kings of Jū'dah, which are thrown down by the mounts, and by the sword;

5 They come to fight with the Chăl-dē'anṡ, but *it is* to fill them with the dead bodies of men, whom I have slain in mine anger and in my fury, and for all whose wickedness I have hid my face from this city.

6 Behold, I will bring it health and cure, and I will cure them, and will reveal unto them the abundance of peace and truth.

7 And I will cause the captivity of Jū'dah and the captivity of Israel to return, and will build them, as at the first.

8 And I will cleanse them from all their iniquity, whereby they have sinned against me; and I will pardon all their iniquities, whereby they have sinned, and whereby they have transgressed against me.

9 And it shall be to me a name of joy, a praise and an honour before all the nations of the earth, which shall hear all the good that I do unto them: and they shall fear and tremble for all the goodness and for all the prosperity that I procure unto it.

10 ¶Thus saith the LORD; Again there shall be heard in this place, which ye say *shall be* desolate without man and without beast, *even* in the cities of Jū'dah, and in the streets of Jerusalem, that are desolate, without man, and without inhabitant, and without beast,

11 The voice of joy, and the voice of gladness, the voice of the bridegroom, and the voice of the bride, the voice of them that shall say, Praise the LORD of hosts: for the LORD *is* good; for his mercy *endureth* for ever: *and* of them that shall bring the sacrifice of praise into the house of the LORD. For I will cause to return the captivity of the land, as at the first, saith the LORD.

12 ¶Thus saith the LORD of hosts; Again in this place, which is desolate without man and without beast, and in all the cities thereof, shall be an habitation of shepherds causing *their* flocks to lie down.

13 In the cities of the mountains, in the cities of the vale, and in the cities of the south, and in the land of Benjamin, and in the places about Jerusalem, and in the cities of Jū'dah, shall the flocks pass again under the hands of him that telleth *them*, saith the LORD.

14 Behold, the days come, saith the LORD, that I will perform that good thing which I have promised unto the house of Israel and to the house of Jū'dah.

15 ¶In those days, and at that time, will I cause the Branch of righteousness to grow up unto David; and he shall execute judgment and righteousness in the land.

16 In those days shall Jū'dah be saved, and Jerusalem shall dwell safely: and this *is the name* wherewith she shall be called, The LORD our righteousness.

17 ¶For thus saith the LORD; David shall never want a man to sit upon the throne of the house of Israel;

18 Neither shall the priests the Levites want a man before me to offer burnt offerings, and to kindle meat offerings, and to do sacrifice continually.

19 ¶And the word of the LORD came unto Jeremiah, saying,

20 Thus saith the LORD, If ye can break my covenant of the day, and my covenant of the night, and that there should not be day and night in their season;

21 *Then* may also my covenant be broken with David my servant, that he should not have a son to reign upon his throne; and with the Levites the priests, my ministers.

22 As the host of heaven cannot be numbered, neither the sand of the sea measured: so will I multiply the seed of David my servant, and the Levites that minister unto me.

23 ¶Moreover the word of the LORD came to Jĕr'e-mī'ah, saying,

24 Considerest thou not what this people have spoken, saying, The two families which the LORD hath chosen, he hath even cast them off? thus they have despised my people, that they should be no more a nation before them.

25 Thus saith the LORD; If my covenant *be* not with day and night, *and if* I have not appointed the ordinances of heaven and earth;

26 Then will I cast away the seed of Jacob, and David my servant, *so* that I will not take *any* of his seed *to be* rulers

over the seed of Abraham, Isaac, and Jacob: for I will cause their captivity to return, and have mercy on them.

CHAPTER 34

THE word which came unto Jĕr′e-mī′ah from the LORD, when Nĕb-u-chad-nĕz′zar king of Babylon, and all his army, and all the kingdoms of the earth of his dominion, and all the people, fought against Jerusalem, and against all the cities thereof, saying,

2 Thus saith the LORD, the God of Israel; Go and speak to Zĕd-e-kī′ah king of Jū′dah, and tell him, Thus saith the LORD; Behold, I will give this city into the hand of the king of Babylon, and he shall burn it with fire:

3 And thou shalt not escape out of his hand, but shalt surely be taken, and delivered into his hand; and thine eyes shall behold the eyes of the king of Babylon, and he shall speak with thee mouth to mouth, and thou shalt go to Babylon.

4 Yet hear the word of the LORD, O Zĕd-e-kī′ah king of Jū′dah; Thus saith the LORD of thee, Thou shalt not die by the sword:

5 *But* thou shalt die in peace: and with the burnings of thy fathers, the former kings which were before thee, so shall they burn *odours* for thee; and they will lament thee, *saying,* Ah lord! for I have pronounced the word, saith the LORD.

6 Then Jĕr′e-mī′ah the prophet spake all these words unto Zĕd-e-kī′ah king of Jū′dah in Jerusalem,

7 When the king of Babylon's army fought against Jerusalem, and against all the cities of Jū′dah that were left, against Lā′chĭsh, and against A-zē′kah: for these defenced cities remained of the cities of Jū′dah.

8 ¶*This is* the word that came unto Jĕr′e-mī′ah from the LORD, after that the king Zĕd-e-kī′ah had made a covenant with all the people which *were* at Jerusalem, to proclaim liberty unto them;

9 That every man should let his manservant, and every man his maidservant, *being* an Hebrew or an Hebrewess, go free; that none should serve himself of them *to wit,* of a Jew his brother.

10 Now when all the princes, and all the people, which had entered into the covenant, heard that every one should let his manservant, and every one his maidservant, go free, that none should serve themselves of them any more, then they obeyed, and let *them* go.

11 But afterward they turned, and caused the servants and the handmaids, whom they had let go free, to return, and brought them into subjection for servants and for handmaids.

12 ¶Therefore the word of the LORD came to Jĕr′e-mī′ah from the LORD, saying,

13 Thus saith the LORD, the God of Israel; I made a covenant with your fathers in the day that I brought them forth out of the land of Egypt, out of the house of bondmen, saying,

14 At the end of seven years let ye go every man his brother an Hebrew, which hath been sold unto thee; and when he hath served thee six years, thou shalt let him go free from thee: but your fathers hearkened not unto me, neither inclined their ear.

15 And ye were now turned, and had done right in my sight, in proclaiming liberty every man to his neighbour; and ye had made a covenant before me in the house which is called by my name:

16 But ye turned and polluted my name, and caused every man his servant, and every man his handmaid, whom he had set at liberty at their pleasure, to return, and brought them into subjection, to be unto you for servants and for handmaids.

17 Therefore thus saith the LORD; Ye have not hearkened unto me, in proclaiming liberty, every one to his brother, and every man to his neighbour: behold, I proclaim a liberty for you, saith the LORD, to the sword, to the pestilence, and to the famine; and I will make you to be removed into all the kingdoms of the earth.

18 And I will give the men that have transgressed my covenant, which have not performed the words of the covenant which they had made before me, when they cut the calf in twain, and passed between the parts thereof,

19 The princes of Jū′dah, and the princes of Jerusalem, the eunuchs, and the priests, and all the people of the land, which passed between the parts of the calf;

20 I will even give them into the hand of their enemies, and into the hand of them that seek their life: and their dead bodies shall be for meat unto the fowls of the heaven, and to the beasts of the earth.

21 And Zĕd-e-kī′ah king of Jū′dah and his princes will I give into the hand of their enemies, and into the hand of them that seek their life, and into the hand of the king of Babylon's army, which are gone up from you.

22 Behold, I will command, saith the LORD, and cause them to return to this

city; and they shall fight against it, and take it, and burn it with fire: and I will make the cities of Jū'dah a desolation without an inhabitant.

CHAPTER 35

THE word which came unto Jĕr'e-mī'ah from the LORD in the days of Je-hoi'a-kĭm the son of Jō-sī'ah king of Jū'dah, saying,

2 Go unto the house of the Rĕ'chab-ītes, and speak unto them, and bring them into the house of the LORD, into one of the chambers, and give them wine to drink.

3 Then I took Jā-ăz-a-nī'ah the son of Jĕr'e-mī'ah, the son of Hăb-a-zī-nī'ah, and his brethren, and all his sons, and the whole house of the Rĕ'chab-ītes;

4 And I brought them into the house of the LORD, into the chamber of the sons of Hā'nan, the son of Ĭg-da-lī'ah, a man of God, which *was* by the chamber of the princes, which *was* above the chamber of Mā-a-sē'iah the son of Shăl'lum, the keeper of the door:

5 And I set before the sons of the house of the Rĕ'chab-ītes pots full of wine, and cups, and I said unto them, Drink ye wine.

6 But they said, We will drink no wine: for Jōn'a-dăb the son of Rē'chăb our father commanded us, saying, Ye shall drink no wine, *neither* ye, nor your sons for ever:

7 Neither shall ye build house, nor sow seed, nor plant vineyard, nor have *any:* but all your days ye shall dwell in tents; that ye may live many days in the land where ye *be* strangers.

8 Thus have we obeyed the voice of Jōn'a-dăb the son of Rē'chăb our father in all that he hath charged us, to drink no wine all our days, we, our wives, our sons, nor our daughters;

9 Nor to build houses for us to dwell in: neither have we vineyard, nor field, nor seed:

10 But we have dwelt in tents, and have obeyed, and done according to all that Jōn'a-dăb our father commanded us.

11 But it came to pass, when Nĕb-u-chad-rĕz'zar king of Babylon came up into the land, that we said, Come, and let us go to Jerusalem for fear of the army of the Chăl-dē'anṡ, and for fear of the army of the Syrians: so we dwell at Jerusalem.

12 ¶Then came the word of the LORD unto Jĕr'e-mī'ah, saying,

13 Thus saith the LORD of hosts, the God of Israel; Go and tell the men of Jū'dah and the inhabitants of Jerusalem, Will ye not receive instruction to hearken to my words? saith the LORD.

14 The words of Jōn'a-dăb the son of Rē'chăb, that he commanded his sons not to drink wine, are performed; for unto this day they drink none, but obey their father's commandment: notwithstanding I have spoken unto you, rising early and speaking; but ye hearkened not unto me.

15 I have sent also unto you all my servants the prophets, rising up early and sending *them*, saying, Return ye now every man from his evil way, and amend your doings, and go not after other gods to serve them, and ye shall dwell in the land which I have given to you and to your fathers: but ye have not inclined your ear, nor hearkened unto me.

16 Because the sons of Jōn'a-dăb the son of Rē'chăb have performed the commandment of their father, which he commanded them; but this people hath not hearkened unto me:

17 Therefore thus saith the LORD God of hosts, the God of Israel; Behold, I will bring upon Jū'dah and upon all the inhabitants of Jerusalem all the evil that I have pronounced against them: because I have spoken unto them, but they have not heard; and I have called unto them, but they have not answered.

18 ¶And Jĕr'e-mī'ah said unto the house of the Rĕ'chab-ītes, Thus saith the LORD of hosts, the God of Israel; Because ye have obeyed the commandment of Jōn'a-dăb your father, and kept all his precepts, and done according unto all that he hath commanded you:

19 Therefore thus saith the LORD of hosts, the God of Israel; Jōn'a-dăb the son of Rē'chăb shall not want a man to stand before me for ever.

CHAPTER 36

AND it came to pass in the fourth year of Je-hoi'a-kĭm the son of Jō-sī'ah king of Jū'dah, *that* this word came unto Jĕr'e-mī'ah from the LORD, saying,

2 Take thee a roll of a book, and write therein all the words that I have spoken unto thee against Israel, and against Jū'dah, and against all the nations, from the day I spake unto thee, from the days of Jō-sī'ah, even unto this day.

3 It may be that the house of Jū'dah will hear all the evil which I purpose to do unto them; that they may return every man from his evil way; that I may forgive their iniquity and their sin.

4 Then Jeremiah called Bâ'ruch the son of Ne-rī'ah: and Bâ'ruch wrote from the mouth of Jĕr'e-mī'ah all the

words of the LORD, which he had spok-
en unto him, upon a roll of a book.
5 And Jĕr′e-mī′ah commanded Bâ′-
ruch, saying, I *am* shut up; I cannot go
into the house of the LORD:
6 Therefore go thou, and read in the
roll, which thou hast written from my
mouth, the words of the LORD in the
ears of the people in the LORD's house
upon the fasting day: and also thou
shalt read them in the ears of all Jū′dah
that come out of their cities.
7 It may be they will present their
supplication before the LORD, and will
return every one from his evil way: for
great *is* the anger and the fury that the
LORD hath pronounced against this
people.
8 And Bâ′ruch the son of Ne-rī′ah did
according to all that Jĕr′e-mī′ah the
prophet commanded him, reading in
the book the words of the LORD in the
LORD's house.
9 And it came to pass in the fifth year
of Je-hoi′a-kĭm the son of Jō-sī′ah king
of Jū′dah, in the ninth month, *that* they
proclaimed a fast before the LORD to all
the people in Jerusalem, and to all the
people that came from the cities of Jū′-
dah unto Jerusalem.
10 Then read Bâ′ruch in the book the
words of Jĕr′e-mī′ah in the house of the
LORD, in the chamber of Gĕm-a-rī′ah
the son of Shā′phan the scribe, in the
higher court, at the entry of the new
gate of the LORD's house, in the ears of
all the people.
11 ¶When Mī-chā′iah the son of Gĕm-
a-rī′ah, the son of Shā′phan, had heard
out of the book all the words of the
LORD,
12 Then he went down into the king's
house, into the scribe's chamber: and,
lo, all the princes sat there, *even* E-lĭsh′-
a-ma the scribe, and Dĕl-a-ī′ah the
son of Shĕm-a-ī′ah, and Ĕl′nā-than the
son of Ăch′bôr, and Gĕm-a-rī′ah the
son of Shā′phan, and Zĕd-e-kī′ah the
son of Hăn-a-nī′ah, and all the princes.
13 Then Mī-chā′iah declared unto
them all the words that he had heard,
when Bâ′ruch read the book in the ears
of the people.
14 Therefore all the princes sent Je-
hū′dī the son of Nĕth-a-nī′ah, the son of
Shĕl-e-mī′ah, the son of Cū′shī, unto
Bâ′ruch, saying, Take in thine hand the
roll wherein thou hast read in the ears
of the people, and come. So Bâ′ruch the
son of Ne-rī′ah took the roll in his hand,
and came unto them.
15 And they said unto him, Sit down
now, and read it in our ears. So Bâ′ruch
read *it* in their ears.
16 Now it came to pass, when they
had heard all the words, they were
afraid both one and other, and said
unto Bâ′ruch, We will surely tell the
king of all these words.
17 And they asked Bâ′ruch, saying,
Tell us now, How didst thou write all
these words at his mouth?
18 Then Bâ′ruch answered them, He
pronounced all these words unto me
with his mouth, and I wrote *them* with
ink in the book.
19 Then said the princes unto Bâ′-
ruch, Go, hide thee, thou and Jĕr′e-mī′-
ah; and let no man know where ye be.
20 ¶And they went in to the king into
the court, but they laid up the roll in the
chamber of E-lĭsh′a-ma the scribe, and
told all the words in the ears of the
king.
21 So the king sent Je-hū′dī to fetch
the roll: and he took it out of E-lĭsh′a-
ma the scribe's chamber. And Je-hū′dī
read it in the ears of the king, and in the
ears of all the princes which stood be-
side the king.
22 Now the king sat in the win-
terhouse in the ninth month: and *there
was a fire* on the hearth burning before
him.
23 And it came to pass, *that* when Je-
hū′dī had read three or four leaves, he
cut it with the penknife, and cast *it* into
the fire that *was* on the hearth, until all
the roll was consumed in the fire that
was on the hearth.
24 Yet they were not afraid, nor rent
their garments, *neither* the king, nor
any of his servants that heard all these
words.
25 Nevertheless Ĕl′nā-than and Dĕl-
a-ī′ah and Gĕm-a-rī′ah had made inter-
cession to the king that he would not
burn the roll: but he would not hear
them.
26 But the king commanded Je-
răh′me-el the son of Hăm′me-lĕch, and
Se-ra-ī′ah the son of Ăz′rĭ-el, and Shĕl-
e-mī′ah the son of Ăb′de-el, to take Bâ′-
ruch the scribe and Jĕr′e-mī′ah the
prophet: but the LORD hid them.
27 ¶Then the word of the LORD came
to Jĕr′e-mī′ah, after that the king had
burned the roll, and the words which
Bâ′ruch wrote at the mouth of Jĕr′e-mī′-
ah, saying,
28 Take thee again another roll, and
write in it all the former words that
were in the first roll, which Je-hoi′a-
kĭm the king of Jū′dah hath burned.
29 And thou shalt say to Je-hoi′a-kĭm
king of Jū′dah, Thus saith the LORD;
Thou hast burned this roll, saying, Why
hast thou written therein, saying, The
king of Babylon shall certainly come

and destroy this land, and shall cause to cease from thence man and beast?

30 Therefore thus saith the LORD of Je-hoi'a-kĭm king of Jū'dah; He shall have none to sit upon the throne of David: and his dead body shall be cast out in the day to the heat, and in the night to the frost.

31 And I will punish him and his seed and his servants for their iniquity; and I will bring upon them, and upon the inhabitants of Jerusalem, and upon the men of Jū'dah, all the evil that I have pronounced against them; but they hearkened not.

32 ¶Then took Jĕr'e-mī'ah another roll, and gave it to Bâ'ruch the scribe, the son of Ne-rī'ah; who wrote therein from the mouth of Jĕr'e-mī'ah all the words of the book which Je-hoi'a-kĭm king of Jū'dah had burned in the fire: and there were added besides unto them many like words.

CHAPTER 37

AND king Zĕd-e-kī'ah the son of Jō-sī'-ah reigned instead of Co-nī'ah the son of Je-hoi'a-kĭm, whom Nĕb-u-chad-rĕz'zar king of Babylon made king in the land of Jū'dah.

2 But neither he, nor his servants, nor the people of the land, did hearken unto the words of the LORD, which he spake by the prophet Jĕr'e-mī'ah.

3 And Zĕd-e-kī'ah the king sent Je-hū'cal the son of Shĕl-e-mī'ah and Zĕph-a-nī'ah the son of Mā-a-sē'iah the priest to the prophet Jĕr'e-mī'ah saying, Pray now unto the LORD our God for us.

4 Now Jĕr'e-mī'ah came in and went out among the people: for they had not put him into prison.

5 Then Pharaoh's army was come forth out of Egypt: and when the Chăl-dē'anṡ that besieged Jerusalem heard tidings of them, they departed from Jerusalem.

6 ¶Then came the word of the LORD unto the prophet Jĕr'e-mī'ah, saying,

7 Thus saith the LORD, the God of Israel; Thus shall ye say to the king of Jū'dah, that sent you unto me to enquire of me; Behold, Pharaoh's army, which is come forth to help you, shall return to Egypt into their own land.

8 And the Chăl-dē'anṡ shall come again, and fight against this city, and take it, and burn it with fire.

9 Thus saith the LORD; Deceive not yourselves, saying, The Chăl-dē'anṡ shall surely depart from us: for they shall not depart.

10 For though ye had smitten the whole army of the Chăl-dē'anṡ that fight against you, and there remained *but* wounded men among them, *yet* should they rise up every man in his tent, and burn this city with fire.

11 ¶And it came to pass, that when the army of the Chăl-dē'anṡ was broken up from Jerusalem for fear of Pharaoh's army,

12 Then Jĕr'e-mī'ah went forth out of Jerusalem to go into the land of Benjamin, to separate himself thence in the midst of the people.

13 And when he was in the gate of Benjamin, a captain of the ward *was* there, whose name *was* Ī-rī'jah, the son of Shĕl-e-mī'ah, the son of Hăn-a-nī'ah; and he took Jĕr'e-mī'ah the prophet, saying, Thou fallest away to the Chăl-dē'anṡ.

14 Then said Jĕr'e-mī'ah, *It is* false; I fall not away to the Chăl-dē'anṡ. But he hearkened not to him: so Ī-rī'jah took Jĕr'e-mī'ah, and brought him to the princes.

15 Wherefore the princes were wroth with Jĕr'e-mī'ah, and smote him, and put him in prison in the house of Jonathan the scribe: for they had made that the prison.

16 ¶When Jĕr'e-mī'ah was entered into the dungeon, and into the cabins, and Jĕr'e-mī'ah had remained there many days;

17 Then Zĕd-e-kī'ah the king sent, and took him out: and the king asked him secretly in his house, and said, Is there *any* word from the LORD? And Jĕr'e-mī'ah said, There is: for, said he, thou shalt be delivered into the hand of the king of Babylon.

18 Moreover Jĕr'e-mī'ah said unto king Zĕd-e-kī'ah, What have I offended against thee, or against thy servants, or against this people, that ye have put me in prison?

19 Where *are* now your prophets which prophesied unto you, saying, The king of Babylon shall not come against you, nor against this land?

20 Therefore hear now, I pray thee, O my lord the king: let my supplication, I pray thee, be accepted before thee; that thou cause me not to return to the house of Jonathan the scribe, lest I die there.

21 Then Zĕd-e-kī'ah the king commanded that they should commit Jĕr'e-mī'ah into the court of the prison, and that they should give him daily a piece of bread out of the bakers' street, until all the bread in the city were spent. Thus Jĕr'e-mī'ah remained in the court of the prison.

CHAPTER 38

THEN Shĕph-a-tī'ah the son of Măt'-tan, and Gĕd-a-lī'ah the son of Păsh'ur, and Jū'cal the son of Shĕl-e-mī'ah, and Păsh'ur the son of Măl-chī'ah, heard the words that Jĕr'e-mī'ah had spoken unto all the people, saying,

2 Thus saith the LORD, He that remaineth in this city shall die by the sword, by the famine, and by the pestilence: but he that goeth forth to the Chăl-dē'anṡ shall live; for he shall have his life for a prey, and shall live.

3 Thus saith the LORD, This city shall surely be given into the hand of the king of Babylon's army, which shall take it.

4 Therefore the princes said unto the king, We beseech thee, let this man be put to death: for thus he weakeneth the hands of the men of war that remain in this city, and the hands of all the people, in speaking such words unto them: for this man seeketh not the welfare of this people, but the hurt.

5 Then Zĕd-e-kī'ah the king said, Behold, he *is* in your hand: for the king *is* not *he that* can do *any* thing against you.

6 Then took they Jĕr'e-mī'ah and cast him into the dungeon of Măl-chī'ah the son of Hăm'me-lĕch, that *was* in the court of the prison: and they let down Jĕr'e-mī'ah with cords. And in the dungeon *there was* no water, but mire: so Jĕr'e-mī'ah sunk in the mire.

7 ¶Now when Ē'bed-mĕ'lech the Ē-thī-ō'pī-an, one of the eunuchs which was in the king's house, heard that they had put Jĕr'e-mī'ah in the dungeon; the king then sitting in the gate of Benjamin;

8 Ē'bed-mĕ'lech went forth out of the king's house, and spake to the king, saying,

9 My lord the king, these men have done evil in all that they have done to Jĕr'e-mī'ah the prophet, whom they have cast into the dungeon; and he is like to die for hunger in the place where he is: for *there is* no more bread in the city.

10 Then the king commanded Ē'bed-mĕ'lech the Ē-thī-ō'pī-an, saying, Take from hence thirty men with thee, and take up Jĕr'e-mī'ah the prophet out of the dungeon, before he die.

11 So Ē'bed-mĕ'lech took the men with him, and went into the house of the king under the treasury, and took thence old cast clouts and old rotten rags, and let them down by cords into the dungeon to Jĕr'e-mī'ah.

12 And Ē'bed-mĕ'lech the Ē-thī-ō'pī-an said unto Jĕr'e-mī'ah, Put now *these* old cast clouts and rotten rags under thine armholes under the cords. And Jĕr'e-mī'ah did so.

13 So they drew up Jĕr'e-mī'ah with cords and took him up out of the dungeon: and Jĕr'e-mī'ah remained in the court of the prison.

14 ¶Then Zĕd-e-kī'ah the king sent, and took Jĕr'e-mī'ah the prophet unto him into the third entry that *is* in the house of the LORD: and the king said unto Jĕr'e-mī'ah, I will ask thee a thing; hide nothing from me.

15 Then Jĕr'e-mī'ah said unto Zĕd-e-kī'ah, If I declare *it* unto thee, wilt thou not surely put me to death? and if I give thee counsel, wilt thou not hearken unto me?

16 So Zĕd-e-kī'ah the king sware secretly unto Jĕr'e-mī'ah saying, *As* the LORD liveth, that made us this soul, I will not put thee to death, neither will I give thee into the hand of these men that seek thy life.

17 Then said Jĕr'e-mī'ah unto Zĕd-e-kī'ah, Thus saith the LORD, the God of hosts, the God of Israel; If thou wilt assuredly go forth unto the king of Babylon's princes, then thy soul shall live, and this city shall not be burned with fire; and thou shalt live, and thine house:

18 But if thou wilt not go forth to the king of Babylon's princes, then shall this city be given into the hand of the Chăl-dē'anṡ, and they shall burn it with fire, and thou shalt not escape out of their hand.

19 And Zĕd-e-kī'ah the king said unto Jĕr'e-mī'ah, I am afraid of the Jews that are fallen to the Chăl-dē'anṡ, lest they deliver me into their hand, and they mock me.

20 But Jĕr'e-mī'ah said, They shall not deliver *thee*. Obey, I beseech thee, the voice of the LORD, which I speak unto thee: so it shall be well unto thee, and thy soul shall live.

21 But if thou refuse to go forth, this *is* the word that the LORD hath shewed me:

22 And, behold, all the women that are left in the king of Jū'dah's house *shall be* brought forth to the king of Babylon's princes, and those *women* shall say, Thy friends have set thee on, and have prevailed against thee: thy feet are sunk in the mire, *and* they are turned away back.

23 So they shall bring out all thy wives and thy children to the Chăl-dē'anṡ: and thou shalt not escape out of their hand, but shalt be taken by the

hand of the king of Babylon: and thou shalt cause this city to be burned with fire.

24 ¶Then said Zĕd-e-kī'ah unto Jĕr'e-mī'ah, Let no man know of these words, and thou shalt not die.

25 But if the princes hear that I have talked with thee, and they come unto thee, and say unto thee, Declare unto us now what thou hast said unto the king, hide it not from us, and we will not put thee to death; also what the king said unto thee:

26 Then thou shalt say unto them, I presented my supplication before the king, that he would not cause me to return to Jonathan's house, to die there.

27 Then came all the princes unto Jĕr'e-mī'ah, and asked him: and he told them according to all these words that the king had commanded. So they left off speaking with him; for the matter was not perceived.

28 So Jĕr'e-mī'ah abode in the court of the prison until the day that Jerusalem was taken: and he was *there* when Jerusalem was taken.

CHAPTER 39

IN the ninth year of Zĕd-e-kī'ah king of Jū'dah, in the tenth month, came Nĕb-u-chad-rĕz'zar king of Babylon and all his army against Jerusalem, and they besieged it.

2 *And* in the eleventh year of Zĕd-e-kī'ah, in the fourth month, the ninth *day* of the month, the city was broken up.

3 And all the princes of the king of Babylon came in, and sat in the middle gate, *even* Ner'găl-sha-rē'zer, Săm'găr-nē'bō, Sär'se-kĭm, Răb'-sa-rĭs, Ner'-găl-sha-rē'zer, Răb'-măg, with all the residue of the princes of the king of Babylon.

4 ¶And it came to pass, *that* when Zĕd-e-kī'ah the king of Jū'dah saw them, and all the men of war, then they fled, and went forth out of the city by night, by the way of the king's garden, by the gate betwixt the two walls: and he went out the way of the plain.

5 But the Chăl-dē'anṡ' army pursued after them, and overtook Zĕd-e-kī'ah in the plains of Jericho: and when they had taken him, they brought him up to Nĕb-u-chad-rĕz'zar king of Babylon to Rĭb'lah in the land of Hā'măth, where he gave judgment upon him.

6 Then the king of Babylon slew the sons of Zĕd-e-kī'ah in Rĭb'lah before his eyes: also the king of Babylon slew all the nobles of Jū'dah.

7 Moreover he put out Zĕd-e-kī'ah's eyes, and bound him with chains, to carry him to Babylon.

8 And the Chăl-dē'anṡ burned the king's house, and the houses of the people, with fire, and brake down the walls of Jerusalem.

9 ¶Then Nĕb'u-zar-ā'dan the captain of the guard carried away captive into Babylon the remnant of the people that remained in the city, and those that fell away, that fell to him, with the rest of the people that remained.

10 But Nĕb'u-zar-ā'dan the captain of the guard left of the poor of the people, which had nothing, in the land of Jū'dah, and gave them vineyards and fields at the same time.

11 ¶Now Nĕb-u-chad-rĕz'zar king of Babylon gave charge concerning Jĕr'e-mī'ah to Nĕb'u-zar-ā'dan the captain of the guard, saying,

12 Take him, and look well to him, and do him no harm; but do unto him even as he shall say unto thee.

13 So Nĕb'u-zar-ā'dan the captain of the guard sent, and Nĕb-u-shăṡ'băn, Răb'-sa-rĭs, and Ner'găl-sha-rē'zer, Răb'-măg, and all the king of Babylon's princes;

14 Even they sent, and took Jĕr'e-mī'ah out of the court of the prison, and committed him unto Gĕd-a-lī'ah the son of A-hī'kam the son of Shā'phan, that he should carry him home: so he dwelt among the people.

15 ¶Now the word of the LORD came unto Jĕr'e-mī'ah, while he was shut up in the court of the prison, saying,

16 Go and speak to Ē'bed-mĕ'lech the Ē-thĭ-ō'pĭ-an, saying, Thus saith the LORD of hosts, the God of Israel; Behold, I will bring my words upon this city for evil, and not for good; and they shall be *accomplished* in that day before thee.

17 But I will deliver thee in that day, saith the LORD: and thou shalt not be given into the hand of the men of whom thou *art* afraid.

18 For I will surely deliver thee, and thou shalt not fall by the sword, but thy life shall be for a prey unto thee: because thou hast put thy trust in me, saith the LORD.

CHAPTER 40

THE word that came to Jĕr'e-mī'ah from the LORD, after that Nĕb'u-zar-ā'dan the captain of the guard had let him go from Rā'mah, when he had taken him being bound in chains among all that were carried away captive of Jerusalem and Jū'dah, which were carried away captive unto Babylon.

2 And the captain of the guard took Jĕr′e-mī′ah, and said unto him, The LORD thy God hath pronounced this evil upon this place.

3 Now the LORD hath brought *it*, and done according as he hath said: because ye have sinned against the LORD, and have not obeyed his voice, therefore this thing is come upon you.

4 And now, behold, I loose thee this day from the chains which *were* upon thine hand. If it seem good unto thee to come with me into Babylon, come; and I will look well unto thee: but if it seem ill unto thee to come with me into Babylon, forbear: behold, all the land *is* before thee: whither it seemeth good and convenient for thee to go, thither go.

5 Now while he was not yet gone back, *he said*, Go back also to Gĕd-a-lī′ah the son of A-hī′-kam the son of Shā′phan, whom the king of Babylon hath made governor over the cities of Jū′dah, and dwell with him among the people: or go wheresoever it seemeth convenient unto thee to go. So the captain of the guard gave him victuals and a reward, and let him go.

6 Then went Jĕr′e-mī′ah unto Gĕd-a-lī′ah the son of A-hī′kam to Mizpah; and dwelt with him among the people that were left in the land.

7 Now when all the captains of the forces which *were* in the fields, *even* they and their men, heard that the king of Babylon had made Gĕd-a-lī′ah the son of A-hī′kam governor in the land, and had committed unto him men, and women, and children, and of the poor of the land, of them that were not carried away captive to Babylon;

8 Then they came to Gĕd-a-lī′ah to Mizpah, even Ĭsh′ma-el the son of Nĕth-a-nī′ah, and Jō-hā′nan and Jonathan the sons of Ka-rē′ah, and Se-ra-ī′ah the son of Tăn′hū-meth, and the sons of Ē′phaī the Ne-tōph′a-thīte, and Jĕz-a-nī′ah the son of a Mā-ăch′a-thīte, they and their men.

9 And Gĕd-a-lī′ah the son of A-hī′kam the son of Shā′phan sware unto them and to their men, saying, Fear not to serve the Chăl-dē′anṡ: dwell in the land, and serve the king of Babylon, and it shall be well with you.

10 As for me, behold, I will dwell at Mizpah, to serve the Chăl-dē′anṡ, which will come unto us: but ye, gather ye wine, and summer fruits, and oil, and put *them* in your vessels, and dwell in your cities that ye have taken.

11 Likewise when all the Jews that *were* in Moab, and among the Ammonites, and in Edom, and that *were* in all the countries, heard that the king of Babylon had left a remnant of Jū′dah, and that he had set over them Gĕd-a-lī′ah the son of A-hī′kam the son of Shā′phan;

12 Even all the Jews returned out of all places whither they were driven, and came to the land of Jū′dah, to Gĕd-a-lī′ah, unto Mizpah, and gathered wine and summer fruits very much.

13 ¶Moreover Jō-hā′nan the son of Ka-rē′ah, and all the captains of the forces that *were* in the fields, came to Gĕd-a-lī′ah to Mizpah,

14 And said unto him, Dost thou certainly know that Bā′a-lĭs the king of the Ammonites hath sent Ĭsh′ma-el the son of Nĕth-a-nī′ah to slay thee? But Gĕd-a-lī′ah the son of A-hī′kam believed them not.

15 Then Jō-hā′nan the son of Ka-rē′ah spake to Gĕd-a-lī′ah in Mizpah secretly, saying, Let me go, I pray thee, and I will slay Ĭsh′ma-el the son of Nĕth-a-nī′ah, and no man shall know *it*: wherefore should he slay thee, that all the Jews which are gathered unto thee should be scattered, and the remnant in Jū′dah perish?

16 But Gĕd-a-lī′ah the son of A-hī′kam said unto Jō-hā′nan the son of Ka-rē′ah, Thou shalt not do this thing: for thou speakest falsely of Ĭsh′ma-el.

CHAPTER 41

NOW it came to pass in the seventh month, that Ĭsh′ma-el the son of Nĕth-a-nī′ah the son of E-lĭsh′a-ma, of the seed royal, and the princes of the king, even ten men with him, came unto Gĕd-a-lī′ah the son of A-hī′kam to Mizpah; and there they did eat bread together in Mizpah.

2 Then arose Ĭsh′ma-el the son of Nĕth-a-nī′ah, and the ten men that were with him, and smote Gĕd-a-lī′ah the son of A-hī′kam the son of Shā′phan with the sword, and slew him, whom the king of Babylon had made governor over the land.

3 Ĭsh′ma-el also slew all the Jews that were with him, *even* with Gĕd-a-lī′ah, at Mizpah, the Chăl-dē′anṡ that were found there, *and* the men of war.

4 And it came to pass the second day after he had slain Gĕd-a-lī′ah, and no man knew *it*,

5 That there came certain from Shĕ′chem, from Shī′lōh, and from Sa-mâ′rĭ-a, *even* fourscore men, having their beards shaven, and their clothes rent, and having cut themselves, with offerings and incense in their hand, to bring *them* to the house of the LORD.

6 And Ĭsh′ma-el the son of Nĕth-a-nī′ah went forth from Mizpah to meet

them, weeping all along as he went: and it came to pass, as he met them, he said unto them, Come to Gĕd-a-lī'ah the son of A-hī'kam.
7 And it was *so*, when they came into the midst of the city, that Ĭsh'ma-el the son of Nĕth-a-nī'ah slew them, *and cast them* into the midst of the pit, he, and the men that *were* with him.
8 But ten men were found among them that said unto Ĭsh'ma-el, Slay us not: for we have treasures in the field, of wheat, and of barley, and of oil, and of honey. So he forbare, and slew them not among their brethren.
9 Now the pit wherein Ĭsh'ma-el had cast all the dead bodies of the men, whom he had slain because of Gĕd-a-lī'ah, *was* it which Ā'sa the king had made for fear of Bā'a-sha king of Israel: *and* Ĭsh'ma-el the son of Nĕth-a-nī'ah filled it with *them that were* slain.
10 Then Ĭsh'ma-el carried away captive all the residue of the people that *were* in Mizpah, *even* the king's daughters, and all the people that remained in Mizpah, whom Nĕb'u-zar-ā'dan the captain of the guard had committed to Gĕd-a-lī'ah the son of A-hī'kam: and Ĭsh'ma-el the son of Nĕth-a-nī'ah carried them away captive, and departed to go over to the Ammonites.
11 ¶But when Jō-hā'nan the son of Ka-rē'ah, and all the captains of the forces that *were* with him, heard of all the evil that Ĭsh'ma-el the son of Nĕth-a-nī'ah had done,
12 Then they took all the men, and went to fight with Ĭsh'ma-el the son of Nĕth-a-nī'ah, and found him by the great waters that *are* in Gibeon.
13 Now it came to pass, *that* when all the people which *were* with Ĭsh'ma-el saw Jō-hā'nan the son of Ka-rē'ah, and all the captains of the forces that *were* with him, then they were glad.
14 So all the people that Ĭsh'ma-el had carried away captive from Mizpah cast about and returned, and went unto Jō-hā'nan the son of Ka-rē'ah.
15 But Ĭsh'ma-el the son of Nĕth-a-nī'ah escaped from Jō-hā'nan with eight men, and went to the Ammonites.
16 Then took Jō-hā'nan the son of Ka-rē'ah, and all the captains of the forces that *were* with him, all the remnant of the people whom he had recovered from Ĭsh'ma-el the son of Nĕth-a-nī'ah, from Mizpah, after *that* he had slain Gĕd-a-lī'ah the son of A-hī'kam, *even* mighty men of war, and the women, and the children, and the eunuchs, whom he had brought again from Gibeon:
17 And they departed, and dwelt in the habitation of Chĭm'hăm, which is by Bĕth'-le-hĕm, to go to enter into Egypt,
18 Because of the Chăl-dē'anṡ: for they were afraid of them, because Ĭsh'ma-el the son of Nĕth-a-nī'ah had slain Gĕd-a-lī'ah the son of A-hī'kam, whom the king of Babylon made governor in the land.

CHAPTER 42

THEN all the captains of the forces, and Jō-hā'nan the son of Ka-rē'ah, Jĕz-a-nī'ah the son of Hō-sha-ī'ah, and all the people from the least even unto the greatest, came near,
2 And said unto Jĕr'e-mī'ah the prophet, Let, we beseech thee, our supplication be accepted before thee, and pray for us unto the LORD thy God, *even* for all this remnant; (for we are left *but* a few of many, as thine eyes do behold us:)
3 That the LORD thy God may shew us the way wherein we may walk, and the thing that we may do.
4 Then Jĕr'e-mī'ah the prophet said unto them, I have heard *you;* behold, I will pray unto the LORD your God according to your words; and it shall come to pass, *that* whatsoever thing the LORD shall answer you, I will declare *it* unto you; I will keep nothing back from you.
5 Then they said to Jĕr'e-mī'ah, The LORD be a true and faithful witness between us, if we do not even according to all things for the which the LORD thy God shall send thee to us.
6 Whether *it be* good, or whether *it be* evil, we will obey the voice of the LORD our God, to whom we send thee; that it may be well with us, when we obey the voice of the LORD our God.
7 ¶And it came to pass after ten days, that the word of the LORD came unto Jĕr'e-mī'ah.
8 Then called he Jō-hā'nan the son of Ka-rē'ah, and all the captains of the forces which *were* with him, and all the people from the least even to the greatest,
9 And said unto them, Thus saith the LORD, the God of Israel, unto whom ye sent me to present your supplication before him;
10 If ye will still abide in this land, then will I build you, and not pull *you* down, and I will plant you, and not pluck *you* up: for I repent me of the evil that I have done unto you.
11 Be not afraid of the king of Babylon, of whom ye are afraid; be not afraid of him, saith the LORD: for I *am*

with you to save you, and to deliver you from his hand.

12 And I will shew mercies unto you, that he may have mercy upon you, and cause you to return to your own land.

13 But if ye say, We will not dwell in this land, neither obey the voice of the LORD your God,

14 Saying, No; but we will go into the land of Egypt, where we shall see no war, nor hear the sound of the trumpet, nor have hunger of bread; and there will we dwell:

15 And now therefore hear the word of the LORD, ye remnant of Jū'dah; Thus saith the LORD of hosts, the God of Israel; If ye wholly set your faces to enter into Egypt, and go to sojourn there;

16 Then it shall come to pass, *that* the sword, which ye feared, shall overtake you there in the land of Egypt, and the famine, whereof ye were afraid, shall follow close after you there in Egypt; and there ye shall die.

17 So shall it be with all the men that set their faces to go into Egypt to sojourn there; they shall die by the sword, by the famine, and by the pestilence: and none of them shall remain or escape from the evil that I will bring upon them.

18 For thus saith the LORD of hosts, the God of Israel; As mine anger and my fury hath been poured forth upon the inhabitants of Jerusalem; so shall my fury be poured forth upon you, when ye shall enter into Egypt: and ye shall be an execration, and an astonishment, and a curse, and a reproach; and ye shall see this place no more.

19 ¶The LORD hath said concerning you, O ye remnant of Jū'dah; Go ye not into Egypt: know certainly that I have admonished you this day.

20 For ye dissembled in your hearts, when ye sent me unto the LORD your God, saying, Pray for us unto the LORD our God; and according unto all that the LORD our God shall say, so declare unto us, and we will do *it*.

21 And *now* I have this day declared *it* to you; but ye have not obeyed the voice of the LORD your God, nor any *thing* for the which he hath sent me unto you.

22 Now therefore know certainly that ye shall die by the sword, by the famine, and by the pestilence, in the place whither ye desire to go *and* to sojourn.

CHAPTER 43

AND it came to pass, *that* when Jĕr'e-mī'ah had made an end of speaking unto all the people all the words of the LORD their God, for which the LORD their God had sent him to them, *even* all these words,

2 Then spake Ăz-a-rī'ah the son of Hō-sha-ī'ah, and Jō-hā'nan the son of Ka-rē'ah, and all the proud men, saying unto Jĕr'e-mī'ah, Thou speakest falsely: the LORD our God hath not sent thee to say, Go not into Egypt to sojourn there:

3 But Bâ'ruch the son of Ne-rī'ah setteth thee on against us, for to deliver us into the hand of the Chăl-dē'anṡ, that they might put us to death, and carry us away captives into Babylon.

4 So Jō-hā'nan the son of Ka-rē'ah, and all the captains of the forces, and all the people, obeyed not the voice of the LORD, to dwell in the land of Jū'dah.

5 But Jō-hā'nan the son of Ka-rē'ah, and all the captains of the forces, took all the remnant of Jū'dah, that were returned from all nations, whither they had been driven, to dwell in the land of Jū'dah;

6 *Even* men, and women, and children, and the king's daughters, and every person that Nĕb'u-zar-ā'dan the captain of the guard had left with Gĕd-a-lī'ah the son of A-hī'kam the son of Shā'phan, and Jĕr'e-mī'ah the prophet, and Bâ'ruch the son of Ne-rī'ah.

7 So they came into the land of Egypt: for they obeyed not the voice of the LORD: thus came they *even* to Tăh'pan-hēṡ.

8 ¶Then came the word of the LORD unto Jĕr'e-mī'ah in Tăh'pan-hēṡ, saying,

9 Take great stones in thine hand, and hide them in the clay in the brickkiln, which *is* at the entry of Pharaoh's house in Tăh'pan-hēṡ, in the sight of the men of Jū'dah;

10 And say unto them, Thus saith the LORD of hosts, the God of Israel; Behold, I will send and take Nĕb-u-chad-rĕz'zar the king of Babylon, my servant, and will set his throne upon these stones that I have hid; and he shall spread his royal pavilion over them.

11 And when he cometh, he shall smite the land of Egypt, *and deliver* such *as are* for death to death; and such *as are* for captivity to captivity; and such *as are* for the sword to the sword.

12 And I will kindle a fire in the houses of the gods of Egypt; and he shall burn them, and carry them away captives: and he shall array himself with the land of Egypt, as a shepherd putteth on his garment; and he shall go forth from thence in peace.

13 He shall break also the images of Bĕth-shĕ'mesh, that *is* in the land of

Egypt; and the houses of the gods of the Egyptians shall he burn with fire.

CHAPTER 44

THE word that came to Jĕr′e-mī′ah concerning all the Jews which dwell in the land of Egypt, which dwell at Mĭg′dŏl, and at Tăh′pan-hēs, and at Noph, and in the country of Păth′rŏs, saying,
2 Thus saith the LORD of hosts, the God of Israel; Ye have seen all the evil that I have brought upon Jerusalem, and upon all the cities of Jū′dah; and, behold, this day they *are* a desolation, and no man dwelleth therein,
3 Because of their wickedness which they have committed to provoke me to anger, in that they went to burn incense, *and* to serve other gods, whom they knew not, *neither* they, ye, nor your fathers.
4 Howbeit I sent unto you all my servants the prophets, rising early and sending *them*, saying, Oh, do not this abominable thing that I hate.
5 But they hearkened not, nor inclined their ear to turn from their wickedness, to burn no incense unto other gods.
6 Wherefore my fury and mine anger was poured forth, and was kindled in the cities of Jū′dah and in the streets of Jerusalem; and they are wasted *and* desolate, as at this day.
7 Therefore now thus saith the LORD, the God of hosts, the God of Israel; Wherefore commit ye *this* great evil against your souls, to cut off from you man and woman, child and suckling, out of Jū′dah, to leave you none to remain;
8 In that ye provoke me unto wrath with the works of your hands, burning incense unto other gods in the land of Egypt, whither ye be gone to dwell, that ye might cut yourselves off, and that ye might be a curse and a reproach among all the nations of the earth?
9 Have ye forgotten the wickedness of your fathers, and the wickedness of the kings of Jū′dah, and the wickedness of their wives, and your own wickedness, and the wickedness of your wives, which they have committed in the land of Jū′dah, and in the streets of Jerusalem?
10 They are not humbled *even* unto this day, neither have they feared, nor walked in my law, nor in my statutes, that I set before you and before your fathers.
11 ¶Therefore thus saith the LORD of hosts, the God of Israel; Behold, I will set my face against you for evil, and to cut off all Jū′dah.
12 And I will take the remnant of Jū′dah, that have set their faces to go into the land of Egypt to sojourn there, and they shall all be consumed, *and* fall in the land of Egypt; they shall *even* be consumed by the sword *and* by the famine: they shall die, from the least even unto the greatest, by the sword and by the famine: and they shall be an execration, *and* an astonishment, and a curse, and a reproach.
13 For I will punish them that dwell in the land of Egypt, as I have punished Jerusalem, by the sword, by the famine, and by the pestilence:
14 So that none of the remnant of Jū′dah, which are gone into the land of Egypt to sojourn there, shall escape or remain, that they should return into the land of Jū′dah, to the which they have a desire to return to dwell there: for none shall return but such as shall escape.
15 ¶Then all the men which knew that their wives had burned incense unto other gods, and all the women that stood by, a great multitude, even all the people that dwelt in the land of Egypt, in Păth′rŏs, answered Jĕr′e-mī′ah, saying,
16 As *for* the word that thou hast spoken unto us in the name of the LORD, we will not hearken unto thee.
17 But we will certainly do whatsoever thing goeth forth out of our own mouth, to burn incense unto the queen of heaven, and to pour out drink offerings unto her, as we have done, we, and our fathers, our kings, and our princes, in the cities of Jū′dah, and in the streets of Jerusalem: for *then* had we plenty of victuals, and were well, and saw no evil.
18 But since we left off to burn incense to the queen of heaven, and to pour out drink offerings unto her, we have wanted all *things*, and have been consumed by the sword and by the famine.
19 And when we burned incense to the queen of heaven, and poured out drink offerings unto her, did we make her cakes to worship her, and pour out drink offerings unto her, without our men?
20 ¶Then Jĕr′e-mī′ah said unto all the people, to the men, and to the women, and to all the people which had given him *that* answer, saying,
21 The incense that ye burned in the cities of Jū′dah, and in the streets of Jerusalem, ye, and your fathers, your kings, and your princes, and the people of the land, did not the LORD remember them, and came it *not* into his mind?
22 So that the LORD could no longer

bear, because of the evil of your doings, *and* because of the abominations which ye have committed; therefore is your land a desolation, and an astonishment, and a curse, without an inhabitant, as at this day.

23 Because ye have burned incense, and because ye have sinned against the LORD, and have not obeyed the voice of the LORD, nor walked in his law, nor in his statutes, nor in his testimonies; therefore this evil is happened unto you, as at this day.

24 Moreover Jĕr′e-mī′ah said unto all the people, and to all the women, Hear the word of the LORD, all Jū′dah that *are* in the land of Egypt:

25 Thus saith the LORD of hosts, the God of Israel, saying; Ye and your wives have both spoken with your mouths, and fulfilled with your hand, saying, We will surely perform our vows that we have vowed, to burn incense to the queen of heaven, and to pour out drink offerings unto her: ye will surely accomplish your vows, and surely perform your vows.

26 Therefore hear ye the word of the LORD, all Jū′dah that dwell in the land of Egypt; Behold, I have sworn by my great name, saith the LORD, that my name shall no more be named in the mouth of any man of Jū′dah in all the land of Egypt, saying, The Lord GOD liveth.

27 Behold, I will watch over them for evil, and not for good: and all the men of Jū′dah that *are* in the land of Egypt shall be consumed by the sword and by the famine, until there be an end of them.

28 Yet a small number that escape the sword shall return out of the land of Egypt into the land of Jū′dah, and all the remnant of Jū′dah, that are gone into the land of Egypt to sojourn there, shall know whose words shall stand, mine, or their's.

29 ¶And this *shall be* a sign unto you, saith the LORD, that I will punish you in this place, that ye may know that my words shall surely stand against you for evil:

30 Thus saith the LORD; Behold, I will give Phâ′raōh-hŏph′ra king of Egypt into the hand of his enemies, and into the hand of them that seek his life; as I gave Zĕd-e-kī′ah king of Jū′dah into the hand of Nĕb-u-chad-rĕz′zar king of Babylon, his enemy, and that sought his life.

CHAPTER 45

THE word that Jĕr′e-mī′ah the prophet spake unto Bâ′ruch the son of Ne-rī′ah, when he had written these words in a book at the mouth of Jĕr′e-mī′ah, in the fourth year of Je-hoi′a-kĭm the son of Jō-sī′ah king of Jū′dah, saying,

2 Thus saith the LORD, the God of Israel, unto thee, O Bâ′ruch;

3 Thou didst say, Woe is me now! for the LORD hath added grief to my sorrow; I fainted in my sighing, and I find no rest.

4 Thus shalt thou say unto him, The LORD saith thus; Behold, *that* which I have built will I break down, and that which I have planted I will pluck up, even this whole land.

5 And seekest thou great things for thyself? seek *them* not: for, behold, I will bring evil upon all flesh, saith the LORD: but thy life will I give unto thee for a prey in all places whither thou goest.

CHAPTER 46

THE word of the LORD which came to Jĕr′e-mī′ah the prophet against the Gentiles;

2 Against Egypt, against the army of Phâ′raōh–nē′chō king of Egypt, which was by the river Eū-phrā′tēṡ in Cär′chemĭsh, which Nĕb-u-chad-rĕz′zar king of Babylon smote in the fourth year of Je-hoi′a-kĭm the son of Jō-sī′ah king of Jū′dah.

3 Order ye the buckler and shield, and draw near to battle.

4 Harness the horses; and get up, ye horsemen, and stand forth with *your* helmets; furbish the spears, *and* put on the brigandines.

5 Wherefore have I seen them dismayed *and* turned away back? and their mighty ones are beaten down, and are fled apace, and look not back: *for* fear *was* round about, saith the LORD.

6 Let not the swift flee away, nor the mighty man escape; they shall stumble, and fall toward the north by the river Eū-phrā′tēṡ.

7 Who *is* this *that* cometh up as a flood, whose waters are moved as the rivers?

8 Egypt riseth up like a flood, and *his* waters are moved like the rivers; and he saith, I will go up, *and* will cover the earth; I will destroy the city and the inhabitants thereof.

9 Come up, ye horses; and rage, ye chariots; and let the mighty men come forth; the Ē-thĭ-ō′pĭ-ans and the Lĭb′ȳ-anṡ that handle the shield; and the Lȳd′ĭ-ans, that handle *and* bend the bow.

10 For this *is* the day of the Lord GOD of hosts, a day of vengeance, that he may avenge him of his adversaries: and the sword shall devour, and it shall be

satiate and made drunk with their
blood: for the Lord God of hosts hath a
sacrifice in the north country by the riv-
er Eū-phrā'tēṡ.
11 Go up into Gilead, and take balm,
O virgin, the daughter of Egypt: in vain
shalt thou use many medicines; *for*
thou shalt not be cured.
12 The nations have heard of thy
shame, and thy cry hath filled the land:
for the mighty man hath stumbled
against the mighty, *and* they are fallen
both together.
13 ¶The word that the LORD spake to
Jĕr'e-mī'ah the prophet, how Nĕb-u-
chad-rĕz'zar king of Babylon should
come *and* smite the land of Egypt.
14 Declare ye in Egypt, and publish in
Mĭg'dŏl, and publish in Noph and in
Täh'pan-hēṡ: say ye, Stand fast, and
prepare thee; for the sword shall de-
vour round about thee.
15 Why are thy valiant *men* swept
away? they stood not, because the
LORD did drive them.
16 He made many to fall, yea, one fell
upon another: and they said, Arise, and
let us go again to our own people, and
to the land of our nativity, from the
oppressing sword.
17 They did cry there, Pharaoh king
of Egypt *is but* a noise; he hath passed
the time appointed.
18 *As* I live, saith the King, whose
name *is* the LORD of hosts, Surely as
Tā'bor *is* among the mountains, and as
Carmel by the sea, *so* shall he come.
19 O thou daughter dwelling in
Egypt, furnish thyself to go into captiv-
ity: for Noph shall be waste and deso-
late without an inhabitant.
20 Egypt *is like* a very fair heifer, *but*
destruction cometh; it cometh out of
the north.
21 Also her hired men *are* in the
midst of her like fatted bullocks; for
they also are turned back, *and* are fled
away together: they did not stand, be-
cause the day of their calamity was
come upon them, *and* the time of their
visitation.
22 The voice thereof shall go like a
serpent; for they shall march with an
army, and come against her with axes,
as hewers of wood.
23 They shall cut down her forest,
saith the LORD, though it cannot be
searched; because they are more than
the grasshoppers, and *are* innumer-
able.
24 The daughter of Egypt shall be
confounded; she shall be delivered into
the hand of the people of the north.
25 The LORD of hosts, the God of
Israel, saith; Behold, I will punish the
multitude of No, and Pharaoh, and
Egypt, with their gods, and their kings;
even Pharaoh, and *all* them that trust in
him:
26 And I will deliver them into the
hand of those that seek their lives, and
into the hand of Nĕb-u-chad-rĕz'zar
king of Babylon, and into the hand of
his servants: and afterward it shall be
inhabited, as in the days of old, saith
the LORD.
27 ¶But fear not thou, O my servant
Jacob, and be not dismayed, O Israel:
for, behold, I will save thee from afar
off, and thy seed from the land of their
captivity; and Jacob shall return, and
be in rest and at ease, and none shall
make *him* afraid.
28 Fear thou not, O Jacob my ser-
vant, saith the LORD: for I *am* with thee;
for I will make a full end of all the na-
tions whither I have driven thee: but I
will not make a full end of thee, but cor-
rect thee in measure; yet will I not leave
thee wholly unpunished.

CHAPTER 47

THE word of the LORD that came to
Jĕr'e-mī'ah the prophet against the
Philistines, before that Pharaoh smote
Gā'za.
2 Thus saith the LORD; Behold, waters
rise up out of the north, and shall be an
overflowing flood, and shall overflow
the land, and all that is therein; the city,
and them that dwell therein: then the
men shall cry, and all the inhabitants of
the land shall howl.
3 At the noise of the stamping of the
hoofs of his strong *horses*, at the
rushing of his chariots, *and at* the
rumbling of his wheels, the fathers
shall not look back to *their* children for
feebleness of hands;
4 Because of the day that cometh to
spoil all the Philistines, *and* to cut off
from Tȳ'rus and Zī'don every helper
that remaineth: for the LORD will spoil
the Philistines, the remnant of the
country of Căph'tôr.
5 Baldness is come upon Gā'za;
Ăsh'ke-lon is cut off *with* the remnant
of their valley: how long wilt thou cut
thyself?
6 O thou sword of the LORD, how long
will it be ere thou be quiet? put up thy-
self into thy scabbard, rest, and be still.
7 How can it be quiet, seeing the
LORD hath given it a charge against
Ăsh'ke-lon, and against the sea shore?
there hath he appointed it.

CHAPTER 48

AGAINST Moab thus saith the LORD of
hosts, the God of Israel; Woe unto
Nebo! for it is spoiled: Kĭr-ī-a-thā'im is

confounded *and* taken: Mĭs'găb is confounded and dismayed.

2 *There shall be* no more praise of Moab: in Hĕsh'bŏn they have devised evil against it; come, and let us cut it off from *being* a nation. Also thou shalt be cut down, O Măd'mĕn; the sword shall pursue thee.

3 A voice of crying *shall be* from Hôr-o-nā'im, spoiling and great destruction.

4 Moab is destroyed; her little ones have caused a cry to be heard.

5 For in the going up of Lū'hīth continual weeping shall go up; for in the going down of Hôr-o-nā'im the enemies have heard a cry of destruction.

6 ¶Flee, save your lives, and be like the heath in the wilderness.

7 For because thou hast trusted in thy works and in thy treasures, thou shalt also be taken: and Chē'mŏsh shall go forth into captivity *with* his priests and his princes together.

8 And the spoiler shall come upon every city, and no city shall escape: the valley also shall perish, and the plain shall be destroyed, as the LORD hath spoken.

9 Give wings unto Moab, that it may flee and get away: for the cities thereof shall be desolate, without any to dwell therein.

10 Cursed *be* he that doeth the work of the LORD deceitfully, and cursed *be* he that keepeth back his sword from blood.

11 ¶Moab hath been at ease from his youth, and he hath settled on his lees, and hath not been emptied from vessel to vessel, neither hath he gone into captivity: therefore his taste remained in him, and his scent is not changed.

12 Therefore, behold, the days come, saith the LORD, that I will send unto him wanderers, that shall cause him to wander, and shall empty his vessels, and break their bottles.

13 And Moab shall be ashamed of Chē'mŏsh, as the house of Israel was ashamed of Bĕth-el their confidence.

14 ¶How say ye, We *are* mighty and strong men for the war?

15 Moab is spoiled, and gone up *out of* her cities, and his chosen young men are gone down to the slaughter, saith the King, whose name *is* the LORD of hosts.

16 The calamity of Moab *is* near to come, and his affliction hasteth fast.

17 All ye that are about him, bemoan him; and all ye that know his name, say, How is the strong staff broken, *and* the beautiful rod!

18 Thou daughter that dost inhabit Dī'bŏn, come down from *thy* glory, and sit in thirst; for the spoiler of Moab shall come upon thee, *and* he shall destroy thy strong holds.

19 O inhabitant of Ar'ō-er, stand by the way, and espy; ask him that fleeth, and her that escapeth, *and* say, What is done?

20 Moab is confounded; for it is broken down: howl and cry; tell ye it in Arnon, that Moab is spoiled,

21 And judgment is come upon the plain country; upon Hō'lŏn, and upon Ja-hā'zah, and upon Mĕph'a-āth,

22 And upon Dī'bŏn, and upon Nebo, and upon Bĕth-dĭb-la-thā'im,

23 And upon Kĭr-ī-a-thā'im, and upon Bĕth-gā'mul, and upon Bĕth-mē'ŏn,

24 And upon Kĕ'rĭ-ŏth, and upon Bŏz'rah, and upon all the cities of the land of Moab, far or near.

25 The horn of Moab is cut off, and his arm is broken, saith the LORD.

26 ¶Make ye him drunken: for he magnified *himself* against the LORD: Moab also shall wallow in his vomit, and he also shall be in derision.

27 For was not Israel a derision unto thee? was he found among thieves? for since thou spakest of him, thou skippedst for joy.

28 O ye that dwell in Moab, leave the cities, and dwell in the rock, and be like the dove *that* maketh her nest in the sides of the hole's mouth.

29 We have heard the pride of Moab, (he is exceeding proud) his loftiness, and his arrogancy, and his pride, and the haughtiness of his heart.

30 I know his wrath, saith the LORD, but *it shall* not *be* so; his lies shall not so effect *it*.

31 Therefore will I howl for Moab, and I will cry out for all Moab; *mine heart* shall mourn for the men of Kĭr-he'rĕs.

32 O vine of Sĭb'mah, I will weep for thee with the weeping of Jā'zer: thy plants are gone over the sea, they reach *even* to the sea of Jā'zer: the spoiler is fallen upon thy summer fruits and upon thy vintage.

33 And joy and gladness is taken from the plentiful field, and from the land of Moab; and I have caused wine to fail from the winepresses: none shall tread with shouting; *their* shouting *shall be* no shouting.

34 From the cry of Hĕsh'bŏn *even* unto Ē-le-ā'leh, *and even* unto Jā'hăz, have they uttered their voice, from Zō'ar *even* unto Hôr-o-nā'im, *as* an heifer of three years old: for the waters also of Nimrim shall be desolate.

35 Moreover I will cause to cease in

Moab, saith the LORD, him that offereth in the high places, and him that burneth incense to his gods.

36 Therefore mine heart shall sound for Moab like pipes, and mine heart shall sound like pipes for the men of Kĭr–he'rĕs: because the riches *that* he hath gotten are perished.

37 For every head *shall be* bald, and every beard clipped: upon all the hands *shall be* cuttings, and upon the loins sackcloth.

38 *There shall be* lamentation generally upon all the housetops of Moab, and in the streets thereof: for I have broken Moab like a vessel wherein *is* no pleasure, saith the LORD.

39 They shall howl, *saying*, How is it broken down! how hath Moab turned the back with shame! so shall Moab be a derision and a dismaying to all them about him.

40 For thus saith the LORD; Behold, he shall fly as an eagle, and shall spread his wings over Moab.

41 Kĕ'rĭ-ŏth is taken, and the strong holds are surprised, and the mighty men's hearts in Moab at that day shall be as the heart of a woman in her pangs.

42 And Moab shall be destroyed from *being* a people, because he hath magnified *himself* against the LORD.

43 Fear, and the pit, and the snare, *shall be* upon thee, O inhabitant of Moab, saith the LORD.

44 He that fleeth from the fear shall fall into the pit; and he that getteth up out of the pit shall be taken in the snare: for I will bring upon it, *even* upon Moab, the year of their visitation, saith the LORD.

45 They that fled stood under the shadow of Hĕsh'bŏn because of the force: but a fire shall come forth out of Hĕsh'bŏn, and a flame from the midst of Sihon, and shall devour the corner of Moab, and the crown of the head of the tumultuous ones.

46 Woe be unto thee, O Moab! the people of Chē'mŏsh perisheth: for thy sons are taken captives, and thy daughters captives.

47 Yet will I bring again the captivity of Moab in the latter days, saith the LORD. Thus far *is* the judgment of Moab.

CHAPTER 49

CONCERNING the Ammonites, thus saith the LORD; Hath Israel no sons? hath he no heir? why *then* doth their king inherit Gad, and his people dwell in his cities?

2 Therefore, behold, the days come, saith the LORD, that I will cause an alarm of war to be heard in Răb'bah of the Ammonites; and it shall be a desolate heap, and her daughters shall be burned with fire: then shall Israel be heir unto them that were his heirs, saith the LORD.

3 Howl, O Hĕsh'bŏn, for Ā'ī is spoiled: cry, ye daughters of Răb'bah, gird you with sackcloth; lament, and run to and fro by the hedges; for their king shall go into captivity, *and* his priests and his princes together.

4 Wherefore gloriest thou in the valleys, thy flowing valley, O backsliding daughter? that trusted in her treasures, *saying*, Who shall come unto me?

5 Behold, I will bring a fear upon thee, saith the Lord GOD of hosts from all those that be about thee; and ye shall be driven out every man right forth; and none shall gather up him that wandereth.

6 And afterward I will bring again the captivity of the children of Ammon, saith the LORD.

7 ¶Concerning Edom, thus saith the LORD of hosts; *Is* wisdom no more in Tē'man? is counsel perished from the prudent? is their wisdom vanished?

8 Flee ye, turn back, dwell deep, O inhabitants of Dē'dan; for I will bring the calamity of Esau upon him, the time *that* I will visit him.

9 If grapegatherers come to thee, would they not leave *some* gleaning grapes? if thieves by night, they will destroy till they have enough.

10 But I have made Esau bare, I have uncovered his secret places, and he shall not be able to hide himself: his seed is spoiled, and his brethren, and his neighbours, and he *is* not.

11 Leave thy fatherless children, I will preserve *them* alive; and let thy widows trust in me.

12 For thus saith the LORD; Behold, they whose judgment *was* not to drink of the cup have assuredly drunken; and *art* thou he *that* shall altogether go unpunished? thou shalt not go unpunished, but thou shalt surely drink *of it*.

13 For I have sworn by myself, saith the LORD, that Bŏz'rah shall become a desolation, a reproach, a waste, and a curse; and all the cities thereof shall be perpetual wastes.

14 I have heard a rumour from the LORD, and an ambassador is sent unto the heathen, *saying*, Gather ye together, and come against her, and rise up to the battle.

15 For, lo, I will make thee small among the heathen, *and* despised among men.

16 Thy terribleness hath deceived

thee, *and* the pride of thine heart, O
thou that dwellest in the clefts of the
rock, that holdest the height of the hill:
though thou shouldest make thy nest
as high as the eagle, I will bring thee
down from thence, saith the LORD.
17 Also Edom shall be a desolation:
every one that goeth by it shall be aston-
ished, and shall hiss at all the plagues
thereof.
18 As in the overthrow of Sodom and
Go-mŏr'rah and the neighbour *cities*
thereof, saith the LORD, no man shall
abide there, neither shall a son of man
dwell in it.
19 Behold, he shall come up like a lion
from the swelling of Jordan against the
habitation of the strong: but I will sud-
denly make him run away from her:
and who *is* a chosen *man, that* I may
appoint over her? for who *is* like me?
and who will appoint me the time? and
who *is* that shepherd that will stand be-
fore me?
20 Therefore hear the counsel of the
LORD, that he hath taken against Edom;
and his purposes, that he hath pur-
posed against the inhabitants of Tē'-
man: Surely the least of the flock shall
draw them out: surely he shall make
their habitations desolate with them.
21 The earth is moved at the noise of
their fall, at the cry the noise thereof
was heard in the Red sea.
22 Behold, he shall come up and fly as
the eagle, and spread his wings over
Bŏz'rah: and at that day shall the heart
of the mighty men of Edom be as the
heart of a woman in her pangs.
23 ¶Concerning Damascus. Hā'măth
is confounded, and Ärpăd: for they
have heard evil tidings: they are faint-
hearted; *there is* sorrow on the sea; it
cannot be quiet.
24 Damascus is waxed feeble, *and*
turneth herself to flee, and fear hath
seized on *her:* anguish and sorrows
have taken her, as a woman in travail.
25 How is the city of praise not left,
the city of my joy!
26 Therefore her young men shall fall
in her streets, and all the men of war
shall be cut off in that day, saith the
LORD of hosts.
27 And I will kindle a fire in the wall
of Damascus, and it shall consume the
palaces of Bĕn–hā'dăd.
28 ¶Concerning Kē'dar, and concern-
ing the kingdoms of Hā'zôr, which
Nĕb-u-chad-rĕz'zar king of Babylon
shall smite, thus saith the LORD; Arise
ye, go up to Kē'dar, and spoil the men
of the east.
29 Their tents and their flocks shall
they take away: they shall take to
themselves their curtains, and all their
vessels, and their camels; and they
shall cry unto them, Fear *is* on every
side.
30 ¶Flee, get you far off, dwell deep,
O ye inhabitants of Hā'zôr, saith the
LORD; for Nĕb-u-chad-rĕz'zar king of
Babylon hath taken counsel against
you, and hath conceived a purpose
against you.
31 Arise, get you up unto the wealthy
nation, that dwelleth without care,
saith the LORD, which have neither
gates nor bars, *which* dwell alone.
32 And their camels shall be a booty,
and the multitude of their cattle a spoil:
and I will scatter into all winds them
that are in the utmost corners; and I
will bring their calamity from all sides
thereof, saith the LORD.
33 And Hā'zôr shall be a dwelling for
dragons, *and* a desolation for ever:
there shall no man abide there, nor *any*
son of man dwell in it.
34 ¶The word of the LORD that came
to Jĕr'e-mī'ah the prophet against Ē'-
lam in the beginning of the reign of
Zĕd-e-kī'ah king of Jū'dah, saying,
35 Thus saith the LORD of hosts; Be-
hold, I will break the bow of Ē'lam, the
chief of their might.
36 And upon Ē'lam will I bring the
four winds from the four quarters of
heaven, and will scatter them toward
all those winds; and there shall be no
nation whither the outcasts of Ē'lam
shall not come.
37 For I will cause Ē'lam to be dis-
mayed before their enemies, and be-
fore them that seek their life: and I will
bring evil upon them, *even* my fierce
anger, saith the LORD; and I will send
the sword after them, till I have con-
sumed them:
38 And I will set my throne in Ē'lam,
and will destroy from thence the king
and the princes, saith the LORD.
39 ¶But it shall come to pass in the
latter days, *that* I will bring again the
captivity of Ē'lam, saith the LORD.

CHAPTER 50

THE word that the LORD spake against
Babylon *and* against the land of the
Chăl-dē'ans by Jĕr'e-mī'ah the prophet.
2 Declare ye among the nations, and
publish, and set up a standard; publish,
and conceal not: say, Babylon is taken,
Bel is confounded, Me-rō'dăch is broken
in pieces; her idols are confounded,
her images are broken in pieces.
3 For out of the north there cometh
up a nation against her, which shall
make her land desolate, and none shall

dwell therein: they shall remove, they
shall depart, both man and beast.
4 ¶In those days, and in that time,
saith the LORD, the children of Israel
shall come, they and the children of Jū'-
dah together, going and weeping: they
shall go, and seek the LORD their God.
5 They shall ask the way to Zion with
their faces thitherward, *saying*, Come,
and let us join ourselves to the LORD in
a perpetual covenant *that* shall not be
forgotten.
6 My people hath been lost sheep:
their shepherds have caused them to go
astray, they have turned them away *on*
the mountains: they have gone from
mountain to hill, they have forgotten
their restingplace.
7 All that found them have devoured
them: and their adversaries said, We
offend not, because they have sinned
against the LORD, the habitation of jus-
tice, even the LORD, the hope of their
fathers.
8 Remove out of the midst of Baby-
lon, and go forth out of the land of the
Chăl-dē'anṡ, and be as the he goats be-
fore the flocks.
9 ¶For, lo, I will raise and cause to
come up against Babylon an assembly
of great nations from the north
country: and they shall set themselves
in array against her; from thence she
shall be taken: their arrows *shall be* as
of a mighty expert man; none shall re-
turn in vain.
10 And Chăl-dē'a shall be a spoil: all
that spoil her shall be satisfied, saith
the LORD.
11 Because ye were glad, because ye
rejoiced, O ye destroyers of mine heri-
tage, because ye are grown fat as the
heifer at grass, and bellow as bulls;
12 Your mother shall be sore con-
founded; she that bare you shall be
ashamed: behold, the hindermost of
the nations *shall be* a wilderness, a dry
land, and a desert.
13 Because of the wrath of the LORD it
shall not be inhabited, but it shall be
wholly desolate: every one that goeth
by Babylon shall be astonished, and
hiss at all her plagues.
14 Put yourselves in array against
Babylon round about: all ye that bend
the bow, shoot at her, spare no arrows:
for she hath sinned against the LORD.
15 Shout against her round about:
she hath given her hand: her founda-
tions are fallen, her walls are thrown
down: for it *is* the vengeance of the
LORD: take vengeance upon her; as she
hath done, do unto her.
16 Cut off the sower from Babylon,
and him that handleth the sickle in the
time of harvest: for fear of the oppress-
ing sword they shall turn every one to
his people, and they shall flee every one
to his own land.
17 ¶Israel *is* a scattered sheep; the
lions have driven *him* away: first the
king of Assyria hath devoured him; and
last this Nĕb-u-chad-rĕz'zar king of Bab-
ylon hath broken his bones.
18 Therefore thus saith the LORD of
hosts, the God of Israel; Behold, I will
punish the king of Babylon and his
land, as I have punished the king of As-
syria.
19 And I will bring Israel again to his
habitation, and he shall feed on Carmel
and Bā'shan, and his soul shall be satis-
fied upon mount Ē'phra-im and Gilead.
20 In those days, and in that time,
saith the LORD, the iniquity of Israel
shall be sought for, and *there shall be*
none; and the sins of Jū'dah, and they
shall not be found: for I will pardon
them whom I reserve.
21 ¶Go up against the land of Mĕr-a-
thā'im, *even* against it, and against the
inhabitants of Pē'kŏd: waste and ut-
terly destroy after them, saith the
LORD, and do according to all that I
have commanded thee.
22 A sound of battle *is* in the land,
and of great destruction.
23 How is the hammer of the whole
earth cut asunder and broken! how is
Babylon become a desolation among
the nations!
24 I have laid a snare for thee, and
thou art also taken, O Babylon, and
thou wast not aware: thou art found,
and also caught, because thou hast striv-
en against the LORD.
25 The LORD hath opened his ar-
moury, and hath brought forth the
weapons of his indignation: for this *is*
the work of the Lord GOD of hosts in the
land of the Chăl-dē'anṡ.
26 Come against her from the utmost
border, open her storehouses: cast her
up as heaps, and destroy her utterly: let
nothing of her be left.
27 Slay all her bullocks; let them go
down to the slaughter: woe unto them!
for their day is come, the time of their
visitation.
28 The voice of them that flee and es-
cape out of the land of Babylon, to de-
clare in Zion the vengeance of the LORD
our God, the vengeance of his temple.
29 Call together the archers against
Babylon: all ye that bend the bow,
camp against it round about; let none
thereof escape: recompense her accord-
ing to her work; according to all that
she hath done, do unto her: for she hath

been proud against the LORD, against the Holy One of Israel.

30 Therefore shall her young men fall in the streets, and all her men of war shall be cut off in that day, saith the LORD.

31 Behold, I *am* against thee, *O thou* most proud, saith the Lord GOD of hosts: for thy day is come, the time *that* I will visit thee.

32 And the most proud shall stumble and fall, and none shall raise him up: and I will kindle a fire in his cities, and it shall devour all round about him.

33 ¶Thus saith the LORD of hosts; The children of Israel and the children of Jū'dah *were* oppressed together: and all that took them captives held them fast; they refused to let them go.

34 Their Redeemer *is* strong; the LORD of hosts *is* his name: he shall throughly plead their cause, that he may give rest to the land, and disquiet the inhabitants of Babylon.

35 ¶A sword *is* upon the Chăl-dē'anṡ, saith the LORD, and upon the inhabitants of Babylon, and upon her princes, and upon her wise *men.*

36 A sword *is* upon the liars; and they shall dote: a sword *is* upon her mighty men; and they shall be dismayed.

37 A sword *is* upon their horses, and upon their chariots, and upon all the mingled people that *are* in the midst of her; and they shall become as women: a sword *is* upon her treasures; and they shall be robbed.

38 A drought *is* upon her waters; and they shall be dried up: for it *is* the land of graven images, and they are mad upon *their* idols.

39 Therefore the wild beasts of the desert with the wild beasts of the islands shall dwell *there,* and the owls shall dwell therein: and it shall be no more inhabited for ever; neither shall it be dwelt in from generation to generation.

40 As God overthrew Sodom and Go-mŏr'rah and the neighbour *cities* thereof, saith the LORD; *so* shall no man abide there, neither shall any son of man dwell therein.

41 Behold, a people shall come from the north, and a great nation, and many kings shall be raised up from the coasts of the earth.

42 They shall hold the bow and the lance: they *are* cruel, and will not shew mercy: their voice shall roar like the sea, and they shall ride upon horses, *every one* put in array, like a man to the battle, against thee, O daughter of Babylon.

43 The king of Babylon hath heard the report of them, and his hands waxed feeble: anguish took hold of him, *and* pangs as of a woman in travail.

44 Behold, he shall come up like a lion from the swelling of Jordan unto the habitation of the strong: but I will make them suddenly run away from her: and who *is* a chosen *man, that* I may appoint over her? for who *is* like me? and who will appoint me the time? and who *is* that shepherd that will stand before me?

45 Therefore hear ye the counsel of the LORD, that he hath taken against Babylon; and his purposes, that he hath purposed against the land of the Chăl-dē'anṡ: Surely the least of the flock shall draw them out: surely he shall make *their* habitation desolate with them.

46 At the noise of the taking of Babylon the earth is moved, and the cry is heard among the nations.

CHAPTER 51

THUS saith the LORD; Behold, I will raise up against Babylon, and against them that dwell in the midst of them that rise up against me, a destroying wind;

2 And will send unto Babylon fanners, that shall fan her, and shall empty her land: for in the day of trouble they shall be against her round about.

3 Against *him that* bendeth let the archer bend his bow, and against *him that* lifteth himself up in his brigandine: and spare ye not her young men; destroy ye utterly all her host.

4 Thus the slain shall fall in the land of the Chăl-dē'anṡ, and *they that are* thrust through in her streets.

5 For Israel *hath* not *been* forsaken, nor Jū'dah of his God, of the LORD of hosts; though their land was filled with sin against the Holy One of Israel.

6 Flee out of the midst of Babylon, and deliver every man his soul: be not cut off in her iniquity; for this *is* the time of the LORD's vengeance; he will render unto her a recompence.

7 Babylon *hath been* a golden cup in the LORD's hand, that made all the earth drunken: the nations have drunken of her wine; therefore the nations are mad.

8 Babylon is suddenly fallen and destroyed: howl for her; take balm for her pain, if so be she may be healed.

9 We would have healed Babylon, but she is not healed: forsake her, and let us go every one into his own country: for her judgment reacheth

unto heaven, and is lifted up *even* to the skies.

10 The LORD hath brought forth our righteousness: come, and let us declare in Zion the work of the LORD our God.

11 Make bright the arrows; gather the shields: the LORD hath raised up the spirit of the kings of the Medes: for his device *is* against Babylon, to destroy it; because it *is* the vengeance of the LORD, the vengeance of his temple.

12 Set up the standard upon the walls of Babylon, make the watch strong, set up the watchmen, prepare the ambushes: for the LORD hath both devised and done that which he spake against the inhabitants of Babylon.

13 O thou that dwellest upon many waters, abundant in treasures, thine end is come, *and* the measure of thy covetousness.

14 The LORD of hosts hath sworn by himself, *saying,* Surely I will fill thee with men, as with caterpillers; and they shall lift up a shout against thee.

15 He hath made the earth by his power, he hath established the world by his wisdom, and hath stretched out the heaven by his understanding.

16 When he uttereth *his* voice, *there is* a multitude of waters in the heavens; and he causeth the vapours to ascend from the ends of the earth: he maketh lightnings with rain, and bringeth forth the wind out of his treasures.

17 Every man is brutish by *his* knowledge; every founder is confounded by the graven image: for his molten image *is* falsehood, and *there is* no breath in them.

18 They *are* vanity, the work of errors: in the time of their visitation they shall perish.

19 The portion of Jacob *is* not like them; for he *is* the former of all things: and *Israel is* the rod of his inheritance: the LORD of hosts *is* his name.

20 Thou *art* my battle axe *and* weapons of war: for with thee will I break in pieces the nations, and with thee will I destroy kingdoms;

21 And with thee will I break in pieces the horse and his rider; and with thee will I break in pieces the chariot and his rider;

22 With thee also will I break in pieces man and woman; and with thee will I break in pieces old and young; and with thee will I break in pieces the young man and the maid;

23 I will also break in pieces with thee the shepherd and his flock; and with thee will I break in pieces the husbandman and his yoke of oxen; and with thee will I break in pieces captains and rulers.

24 And I will render unto Babylon and to all the inhabitants of Chăl-dē'a all their evil that they have done in Zion in your sight, saith the LORD.

25 Behold, I *am* against thee, O destroying mountain, saith the LORD, which destroyest all the earth: and I will stretch out mine hand upon thee, and roll thee down from the rocks, and will make thee a burnt mountain.

26 And they shall not take of thee a stone for a corner, nor a stone for foundations; but thou shalt be desolate for ever, saith the LORD.

27 Set ye up a standard in the land, blow the trumpet among the nations, prepare the nations against her, call together against her the kingdoms of Ăr'a-răt, Mĭn'nī, and Ăsh'che-năz; appoint a captain against her; cause the horses to come up as the rough caterpillers.

28 Prepare against her the nations with the kings of the Medes, the captains thereof, and all the rulers thereof, and all the land of his dominion.

29 And the land shall tremble and sorrow: for every purpose of the LORD shall be performed against Babylon, to make the land of Babylon a desolation without an inhabitant.

30 The mighty men of Babylon have forborn to fight, they have remained in *their* holds: their might hath failed; they became as women: they have burned her dwellingplaces; her bars are broken.

31 One post shall run to meet another, and one messenger to meet another, to shew the king of Babylon that his city is taken at *one* end,

32 And that the passages are stopped, and the reeds they have burned with fire, and the men of war are affrighted.

33 For thus saith the LORD of hosts, the God of Israel; The daughter of Babylon *is* like a threshingfloor, *it is* time to thresh her: yet a little while, and the time of her harvest shall come.

34 Nĕb-u-chad-rĕz'zar the king of Babylon hath devoured me, he hath crushed me, he hath made me an empty vessel, he hath swallowed me up like a dragon, he hath filled his belly with my delicates, he hath cast me out.

35 The violence done to me and to my flesh *be* upon Babylon, shall the inhabitant of Zion say; and my blood upon the inhabitants of Chăl-dē'a, shall Jerusalem say.

36 Therefore thus saith the LORD; Be-

hold, I will plead thy cause, and take vengeance for thee; and I will dry up her sea, and make her springs dry.
37 And Babylon shall become heaps, a dwellingplace for dragons, and astonishment, and an hissing, without an inhabitant.
38 They shall roar together like lions: they shall yell as lions' whelps.
39 In their heat I will make their feasts, and I will make them drunken, that they may rejoice, and sleep a perpetual sleep, and not wake, saith the LORD.
40 I will bring them down like lambs to the slaughter, like rams with he goats.
41 How is Shē'shăch taken! and how is the praise of the whole earth surprised! how is Babylon become an astonishment among the nations!
42 The sea is come up upon Babylon: she is covered with the multitude of the waves thereof.
43 Her cities are a desolation, a dry land, and a wilderness, a land wherein no man dwelleth, neither doth *any* son of man pass thereby.
44 And I will punish Bel in Babylon, and I will bring forth out of his mouth that which he hath swallowed up: and the nations shall not flow together any more unto him: yea, the wall of Babylon shall fall.
45 My people, go ye out of the midst of her, and deliver ye every man his soul from the fierce anger of the LORD.
46 And lest your heart faint, and ye fear for the rumour that shall be heard in the land; a rumour shall both come *one* year, and after that in *another* year *shall come* a rumour, and violence in the land, ruler against ruler.
47 Therefore, behold, the days come, that I will do judgment upon the graven images of Babylon: and her whole land shall be confounded, and all her slain shall fall in the midst of her.
48 Then the heaven and the earth, and all that *is* therein, shall sing for Babylon: for the spoilers shall come unto her from the north, saith the LORD.
49 As Babylon *hath caused* the slain of Israel to fall, so at Babylon shall fall the slain of all the earth.
50 Ye that have escaped the sword, go away, stand not still: remember the LORD afar off, and let Jerusalem come into your mind.
51 We are confounded, because we have heard reproach: shame hath covered our faces: for strangers are come into the sanctuaries of the LORD's house.
52 Wherefore, behold, the days come, saith the LORD, that I will do judgment upon her graven images: and through all her land the wounded shall groan.
53 Though Babylon should mount up to heaven, and though she should fortify the height of her strength, *yet* from me shall spoilers come unto her, saith the LORD.
54 A sound of a cry *cometh* from Babylon, and great destruction from the land the of Chăl-dē'anṡ:
55 Because the LORD hath spoiled Babylon, and destroyed out of her the great voice; when her waves do roar like great waters, a noise of their voice is uttered:
56 Because the spoiler is come upon her, *even* upon Babylon, and her mighty men are taken, every one of their bows is broken: for the LORD God of recompences shall surely requite.
57 And I will make drunk her princes, and her wise *men*, her captains, and her rulers, and her mighty men: and they shall sleep a perpetual sleep, and not wake, saith the King, whose name *is* the LORD of hosts.
58 Thus saith the LORD of hosts; The broad walls of Babylon shall be utterly broken, and her high gates shall be burned with fire; and the people shall labour in vain, and the folk in the fire, and they shall be weary.
59 ¶The word which Jĕr'e-mī'ah the prophet commanded Se-ra-ī'ah the son of Ne-rī'ah, the son of Mā-a-sē'iah, when he went with Zĕd-e-kī'ah the king of Jū'dah into Babylon in the fourth year of his reign. And *this* Se-ra-ī'ah *was* a quiet prince.
60 So Jĕr'e-mī'ah wrote in a book all the evil that should come upon Babylon, *even* all these words that are written against Babylon.
61 And Jĕr'e-mī'ah said to Se-ra-ī'ah, When thou comest to Babylon, and shalt see, and shalt read all these words;
62 Then shalt thou say, O LORD, thou hast spoken against this place, to cut it off, that none shall remain in it, neither man nor beast, but that it shall be desolate for ever.
63 And it shall be, when thou hast made an end of reading this book, *that* thou shalt bind a stone to it, and cast it into the midst of Eū-phrā'tēṡ:
64 And thou shalt say, Thus shall Babylon sink, and shall not rise from the evil that I will bring upon her: and they shall be weary. Thus far *are* the words of Jĕr'e-mī'ah.

CHAPTER 52

ZĔD-E-KĪ'AH *was* one and twenty
years old when he began to reign, and
he reigned eleven years in Jerusalem.
And his mother's name *was* Ha-mū'tal
the daughter of Jĕr'e-mī'ah of Lĭb'nah.
2 And he did *that which was* evil in
the eyes of the LORD, according to all
that Je-hoi'a-kĭm had done.
3 For through the anger of the LORD it
came to pass in Jerusalem and Jū'dah,
till he had cast them out from his pres-
ence, that Zĕd-e-kī'ah rebelled against
the king of Babylon.
4 ¶And it came to pass in the ninth
year of his reign, in the tenth month, in
the tenth *day* of the month, *that* Nĕb-u-
chad-rĕz'zar king of Babylon came, he
and all his army, against Jerusalem,
and pitched against it, and built forts
against it round about.
5 So the city was besieged unto the
eleventh year of king Zĕd-e-kī'ah.
6 And in the fourth month, in the
ninth *day* of the month, the famine was
sore in the city, so that there was no
bread for the people of the land.
7 Then the city was broken up, and all
the men of war fled, and went forth out
of the city by night by the way of the
gate between the two walls, which *was*
by the king's garden; (now the Chăl-dē'-
anṡ *were* by the city round about:) and
they went by the way of the plain.
8 But the army of the Chăl-dē'anṡ
pursued after the king, and overtook
Zĕd-e-kī'ah in the plains of Jericho; and
all his army was scattered from him.
9 Then they took the king, and
carried him up unto the king of Baby-
lon to Rĭb'lah in the land of Hā'măth;
where he gave judgment upon him.
10 And the king of Babylon slew the
sons of Zĕd-e-kī'ah before his eyes: he
slew also all the princes of Jū'dah in
Rĭb'lah.
11 Then he put out the eyes of Zĕd-e-
kī'ah; and the king of Babylon bound
him in chains, and carried him to Baby-
lon, and put him in prison till the day of
his death.
12 ¶Now in the fifth month, in the
tenth *day* of the month, which *was* the
nineteenth year of Nĕb-u-chad-rĕz'zar
king of Babylon, came Nĕb-u-
zar-ā'dan, captain of the guard, *which*
served the king of Babylon, into Jeru-
salem,
13 And burned the house of the LORD,
and the king's house; and all the houses
of Jerusalem, and all the houses of the
great *men*, burned he with fire:
14 And all the army of the Chăl-dē'-
anṡ, that *were* with the captain of the
guard, brake down all the walls of Jeru-
salem round about.
15 Then Nĕb'u-zar-ā'dan the captain
of the guard carried away captive *cer-
tain* of the poor of the people, and the
residue of the people that remained in
the city, and those that fell away, that
fell to the king of Babylon, and the rest
of the multitude.
16 But Nĕb'u-zar-ā'dan the captain
of the guard left *certain* of the poor of
the land for vinedressers and for hus-
bandmen.
17 Also the pillars of brass that *were*
in the house of the LORD, and the bases,
and the brasen sea that *was* in the
house of the LORD, the Chăl-dē'anṡ
brake, and carried all the brass of them
to Babylon.
18 The caldrons also, and the shovels,
and the snuffers, and the bowls, and
the spoons, and all the vessels of brass
wherewith they ministered, took they
away.
19 And the basons, and the firepans,
and the bowls, and the caldrons, and
the candlesticks, and the spoons, and
the cups; *that* which *was* of gold *in*
gold, and *that* which *was* of silver *in* sil-
ver, took the captain of the guard away.
20 The two pillars, one sea, and
twelve brasen bulls that *were* under the
bases, which king Sŏlomon had made
in the house of the LORD: the brass of all
these vessels was without weight.
21 And *concerning* the pillars, the
height of one pillar *was* eighteen cubits;
and a fillet of twelve cubits did
compass it; and the thickness thereof
was four fingers: *it was* hollow.
22 And a chapiter of brass *was* upon
it; and the height of one chapiter *was*
five cubits, with network and pomegran-
ates upon the chapiters round about,
all *of* brass. The second pillar also and
the pomegranates *were* like unto these.
23 And there were ninety and six
pomegranates on a side; *and* all the
pomegranates upon the network *were*
an hundred round about.
24 ¶And the captain of the guard took
Se-ra-ī'ah the chief priest, and Zĕph-a-
nī'ah the second priest, and the three
keepers of the door:
25 He took also out of the city an eu-
nuch, which had the charge of the men
of war; and seven men of them that
were near the king's person, which
were found in the city; and the prin-
cipal scribe of the host, who mustered
the people of the land; and threescore
men of the people of the land, that were
found in the midst of the city.
26 So Nĕb'u-zar-ā'dan the captain of

the guard took them, and brought them to the king of Babylon to Rĭb'lah.

27 And the king of Babylon smote them, and put them to death in Rĭb'lah in the land of Hā'măth. Thus Jū'dah was carried away captive out of his own land.

28 This *is* the people whom Nĕb-u-chad-rĕz'zar carried away captive: in the seventh year three thousand Jews and three and twenty:

29 In the eighteenth year of Nĕb-u-chad-rĕz'zar he carried away captive from Jerusalem eight hundred thirty and two persons:

30 In the three and twentieth year of Nĕb-u-chad-rĕz'zar Nĕb'u-zar-ă'dan the captain of the guard carried away captive of the Jews seven hundred forty and five persons: all the persons *were* four thousand and six hundred.

31 ¶And it came to pass in the seven and thirtieth year of the captivity of Je-hoi'a-chĭn king of Jū'dah, in the twelfth month, in the five and twentieth *day* of the month, *that* Ē'vil-mĕ-ro'dăch king of Babylon in the *first* year of his reign lifted up the head of Je-hoi'a-chĭn king of Jū'dah, and brought him forth out of prison,

32 And spake kindly unto him, and set his throne above the throne of the kings that *were* with him in Babylon,

33 And changed his prison garments: and he did continually eat bread before him all the days of his life.

34 And *for* his diet, there was a continual diet given him of the king of Babylon, every day a portion until the day of his death, all the days of his life.

THE LAMENTATIONS of Jeremiah

CHAPTER 1

HOW doth the city sit solitary, *that was* full of people! *how* is she become as a widow! she *that was* great among the nations, *and* princess among the provinces, *how* is she become tributary!

2 She weepeth sore in the night, and her tears *are* on her cheeks: among all her lovers she hath none to comfort *her:* all her friends have dealt treacherously with her, they are become her enemies.

3 Jū'dah is gone into captivity because of affliction, and because of great servitude: she dwelleth among the heathen, she findeth no rest: all her persecutors overtook her between the straits.

4 The ways of Zion do mourn, because none come to the solemn feasts: all her gates are desolate: her priests sigh, her virgins are afflicted, and she *is* in bitterness.

5 Her adversaries are the chief, her enemies prosper; for the LORD hath afflicted her for the multitude of her transgressions: her children are gone into captivity before the enemy.

6 And from the daughter of Zion all her beauty is departed: her princes are become like harts *that* find no pasture, and they are gone without strength before the pursuer.

7 Jerusalem remembered in the days of her affliction and of her miseries all her pleasant things that she had in the days of old, when her people fell into the hand of the enemy, and none did help her: the adversaries saw her, *and* did mock at her sabbaths.

8 Jerusalem hath grievously sinned; therefore she is removed: all that honoured her despise her, because they have seen her nakedness: yea, she sigheth, and turneth backward.

9 Her filthiness *is* in her skirts; she remembereth not her last end; therefore she came down wonderfully: she had no comforter. O LORD, behold my affliction: for the enemy hath magnified *himself*.

10 The adversary hath spread out his hand upon all her pleasant things: for she hath seen *that* the heathen entered into her sanctuary, whom thou didst command *that* they should not enter into thy congregation.

11 All her people sigh, they seek bread; they have given their pleasant things for meat to relieve the soul: see, O LORD, and consider; for I am become vile.

12 ¶*Is it* nothing to you, all ye that pass by? behold, and see if there be any sorrow like unto my sorrow, which is done unto me, wherewith the LORD hath afflicted *me* in the day of his fierce anger.

13 From above hath he sent fire into my bones, and it prevaileth against them: he hath spread a net for my feet, he hath turned me back: he hath made me desolate *and* faint all the day.

14 The yoke of my transgressions is

bound by his hand: they are wreathed,
and come up upon my neck: he hath
made my strength to fall, the LORD hath
delivered me into *their* hands, *from*
whom I am not able to rise up.
15 The LORD hath trodden under foot
all my mighty *men* in the midst of me:
he hath called an assembly against me
to crush my young men: the LORD hath
trodden the virgin, the daughter of Jū′-
dah, *as* in a winepress.
16 For these *things* I weep; mine eye,
mine eye runneth down with water, be-
cause the comforter that should relieve
my soul is far from me: my children are
desolate, because the enemy prevailed.
17 Zion spreadeth forth her hands,
and there is none to comfort her: the
LORD hath commanded concerning Ja-
cob, *that* his adversaries *should be*
round about him: Jerusalem is as a
menstruous woman among them.
18 ¶The LORD is righteous; for I have
rebelled against his commandment:
hear, I pray you, all people, and behold
my sorrow: my virgins and my young
men are gone into captivity.
19 I called for my lovers, *but* they de-
ceived me: my priests and mine elders
gave up the ghost in the city, while they
sought their meat to relieve their souls.
20 Behold, O LORD; for I *am* in dis-
tress: my bowels are troubled; mine
heart is turned within me; for I have
grievously rebelled: abroad the sword
bereaveth, at home *there is* as death.
21 They have heard that I sigh: *there*
is none to comfort me: all mine enemies
have heard of my trouble; they are glad
that thou hast done *it*: thou wilt *bring*
the day *that* thou hast called, and they
shall be like unto me.
22 Let all their wickedness come be-
fore thee; and do unto them, as thou
hast done unto me for all my transgres-
sions: for my sighs *are* many, and my
heart *is* faint.

CHAPTER 2

HOW hath the LORD covered the
daughter of Zion with a cloud in his an-
ger, *and* cast down from heaven unto
the earth the beauty of Israel, and
remembered not his footstool in the
day of his anger!
2 The LORD hath swallowed up all the
habitations of Jacob, and hath not
pitied: he hath thrown down in his
wrath the strong holds of the daughter
of Jū′dah; he hath brought *them* down
to the ground: he hath polluted the
kingdom and the princes thereof.
3 He hath cut off in *his* fierce anger all
the horn of Israel: he hath drawn back
his right hand from before the enemy,
and he burned against Jacob like a
flaming fire, *which* devoureth round
about.
4 He hath bent his bow like an en-
emy: he stood with his right hand as an
adversary, and slew all *that were* pleas-
ant to the eye in the tabernacle of the
daughter of Zion: he poured out his
fury like fire.
5 The LORD was as an enemy: he hath
swallowed up Israel, he hath swal-
lowed up all her palaces: he hath de-
stroyed his strong holds, and hath in-
creased in the daughter of Jū′dah
mourning and lamentation.
6 And he hath violently taken away
his tabernacle, as *if it were of* a garden:
he hath destroyed his places of the as-
sembly: the LORD hath caused the sol-
emn feasts and sabbaths to be forgotten
in Zion, and hath despised in the
indignation of his anger the king and
the priest.
7 The LORD hath cast off his altar, he
hath abhorred his sanctuary, he hath
given up into the hand of the enemy the
walls of her palaces; they have made a
noise in the house of the LORD, as in the
day of a solemn feast.
8 The LORD hath purposed to destroy
the wall of the daughter of Zion: he
hath stretched out a line, he hath not
withdrawn his hand from destroying:
therefore he made the rampart and the
wall to lament; they languished togeth-
er.
9 Her gates are sunk into the ground;
he hath destroyed and broken her bars:
her king and her princes *are* among the
Gentiles: the law *is* no *more*; her
prophets also find no vision from the
LORD.
10 The elders of the daughter of Zion
sit upon the ground, *and* keep silence:
they have cast up dust upon their
heads; they have girded themselves
with sackcloth: the virgins of Jeru-
salem hang down their heads to the
ground.
11 Mine eyes do fail with tears, my
bowels are troubled, my liver is poured
upon the earth, for the destruction of
the daughter of my people; because the
children and the sucklings swoon in the
streets of the city.
12 They say to their mothers, Where
is corn and wine? when they swooned
as the wounded in the streets of the
city, when their soul was poured out
into their mothers' bosom.
13 What thing shall I take to witness
for thee? what thing shall I liken to
thee, O daughter of Jerusalem? what
shall I equal to thee, that I may comfort
thee, O virgin daughter of Zion? for thy

breach *is* great like the sea: who can
heal thee?
14 Thy prophets have seen vain and
foolish things for thee: and they have
not discovered thine iniquity, to turn
away thy captivity; but have seen for
thee false burdens and causes of ban-
ishment.
15 All that pass by clap *their* hands at
thee; they hiss and wag their head at
the daughter of Jerusalem, *saying*, *Is*
this the city that *men* call The perfec-
tion of beauty, The joy of the whole
earth?
16 All thine enemies have opened
their mouth against thee: they hiss and
gnash the teeth: they say, We have
swallowed *her* up: certainly this *is* the
day that we looked for; we have found,
we have seen *it*.
17 The LORD hath done *that* which he
had devised; he hath fulfilled his word
that he had commanded in the days of
old: he hath thrown down, and hath not
pitied: and he hath caused *thine* enemy
to rejoice over thee, he hath set up the
horn of thine adversaries.
18 Their heart cried unto the LORD, O
wall of the daughter of Zion, let tears
run down like a river day and night:
give thyself no rest; let not the apple of
thine eye cease.
19 Arise, cry out in the night: in the
beginning of the watches pour out
thine heart like water before the face of
the LORD: lift up thy hands toward him
for the life of thy young children, that
faint for hunger in the top of every
street.
20 Behold, O LORD, and consider to
whom thou hast done this. Shall the
women eat their fruit, *and* children of a
span long? shall the priest and the
prophet be slain in the sanctuary of the
Lord?
21 The young and the old lie on the
ground in the streets: my virgins and
my young men are fallen by the sword;
thou hast slain *them* in the day of thine
anger; thou hast killed, *and* not pitied.
22 Thou hast called as in a solemn
day my terrors round about, so that in
the day of the LORD's anger none es-
caped nor remained: those that I have
swaddled and brought up hath mine
enemy consumed.

CHAPTER 3

I *AM* the man *that* hath seen affliction
by the rod of his wrath.
2 He hath led me, and brought *me*
into darkness, but not *into* light.
3 Surely against me is he turned; he
turneth his hand *against me* all the day.
4 My flesh and my skin hath he made
old; he hath broken my bones.
5 He hath builded against me, and
compassed *me* with gall and travail.
6 He hath set me in dark places, as
they that be dead of old.
7 He hath hedged me about, that I
cannot get out: he hath made my chain
heavy.
8 Also when I cry and shout, he shut-
teth out my prayer.
9 He hath inclosed my ways with
hewn stone, he hath made my paths
crooked.
10 He *was* unto me *as* a bear lying in
wait, *and as* a lion in secret places.
11 He hath turned aside my ways,
and pulled me in pieces: he hath made
me desolate.
12 He hath bent his bow, and set me
as a mark for the arrow.
13 He hath caused the arrows of his
quiver to enter into my reins.
14 I was a derision to all my people;
and their song all the day.
15 He hath filled me with bitterness,
he hath made me drunken with worm-
wood.
16 He hath also broken my teeth with
gravel stones, he hath covered me with
ashes.
17 And thou hast removed my soul
far off from peace: I forgat prosperity.
18 And I said, My strength and my
hope is perished from the LORD:
19 Remembering mine affliction and
my misery, the wormwood and the
gall.
20 My soul hath *them* still in remem-
brance, and is humbled in me.
21 This I recall to my mind, therefore
have I hope.
22 ¶*It is of* the LORD's mercies that we
are not consumed, because his com-
passions fail not.
23 *They are* new every morning:
great *is* thy faithfulness.
24 The LORD *is* my portion, saith my
soul; therefore will I hope in him.
25 The LORD *is* good unto them that
wait for him, to the soul *that* seeketh
him.
26 *It is* good that *a man* should both
hope and quietly wait for the salvation
of the LORD.
27 *It is* good for a man that he bear
the yoke in his youth.
28 He sitteth alone and keepeth si-
lence, because he hath borne *it* upon
him.
29 He putteth his mouth in the dust; if
so be there may be hope.
30 He giveth *his* cheek to him that
smiteth him: he is filled full with
reproach.

31 For the Lord will not cast off for ever:
32 But though he cause grief, yet will he have compassion according to the multitude of his mercies.
33 For he doth not afflict willingly nor grieve the children of men.
34 To crush under his feet all the prisoners of the earth,
35 To turn aside the right of a man before the face of the most High,
36 To subvert a man in his cause, the Lord approveth not.
37 ¶Who *is* he *that* saith, and it cometh to pass, *when* the Lord commandeth *it* not?
38 Out of the mouth of the most High proceedeth not evil and good?
39 Wherefore doth a living man complain, a man for the punishment of his sins?
40 Let us search and try our ways, and turn again to the LORD.
41 Let us lift up our heart with *our* hands unto God in the heavens.
42 We have transgressed and have rebelled: thou hast not pardoned.
43 Thou hast covered with anger, and persecuted us: thou hast slain, thou hast not pitied.
44 Thou hast covered thyself with a cloud, that *our* prayer should not pass through.
45 Thou hast made us *as* the offscouring and refuse in the midst of the people.
46 All our enemies have opened their mouths against us.
47 Fear and a snare is come upon us, desolation and destruction.
48 Mine eye runneth down with rivers of water for the destruction of the daughter of my people.
49 Mine eye trickleth down, and ceaseth not, without any intermission,
50 Till the LORD look down, and behold from heaven.
51 Mine eye affecteth mine heart because of all the daughters of my city.
52 Mine enemies chased me sore, like a bird, without cause.
53 They have cut off my life in the dungeon, and cast a stone upon me.
54 Waters flowed over mine head; *then* I said, I am cut off.
55 ¶I called upon thy name, O LORD, out of the low dungeon.
56 Thou hast heard my voice: hide not thine ear at my breathing, at my cry.
57 Thou drewest near in the day *that* I called upon thee: thou saidst, Fear not.
58 O Lord, thou hast pleaded the causes of my soul; thou hast redeemed my life.
59 O LORD, thou hast seen my wrong: judge thou my cause.
60 Thou hast seen all their vengeance *and* all their imaginations against me.
61 Thou hast heard their reproach, O LORD, *and* all their imaginations against me;
62 The lips of those that rose up against me, and their device against me all the day.
63 Behold their sitting down, and their rising up; I *am* their musick.
64 Render unto them a recompence, O LORD, according to the work of their hands.
65 Give them sorrow of heart, thy curse unto them.
66 Persecute and destroy them in anger from under the heavens of the LORD.

CHAPTER 4

HOW is the gold become dim! *how* is the most fine gold changed! the stones of the sanctuary are poured out in the top of every street.
2 The precious sons of Zion, comparable to fine gold, how are they esteemed as earthen pitchers, the work of the hands of the potter!
3 Even the sea monsters draw out the breast, they give suck to their young ones: the daughter of my people *is become* cruel, like the ostriches in the wilderness.
4 The tongue of the sucking child cleaveth to the roof of his mouth for thirst: the young children ask bread, *and* no man breaketh *it* unto them.
5 They that did feed delicately are desolate in the streets: they that were brought up in scarlet embrace dunghills.
6 For the punishment of the iniquity of the daughter of my people is greater than the punishment of the sin of Sodom, that was overthrown as in a moment, and no hands stayed on her.
7 Her Nazarites were purer than snow, they were whiter than milk, they were more ruddy in body than rubies, their polishing *was* of sapphire:
8 Their visage is blacker than a coal; they are not known in the streets: their skin cleaveth to their bones; it is withered, it is become like a stick.
9 *They that be* slain with the sword are better than *they that be* slain with hunger: for these pine away, stricken through for *want of* the fruits of the field.
10 The hands of the pitiful women have sodden their own children: they

were their meat in the destruction of the daughter of my people.

11 The LORD hath accomplished his fury; he hath poured out his fierce anger, and hath kindled a fire in Zion, and it hath devoured the foundations thereof.

12 The kings of the earth, and all the inhabitants of the world, would not have believed that the adversary and the enemy should have entered into the gates of Jerusalem.

13 For the sins of her prophets, *and* the iniquities of her priests, that have shed the blood of the just in the midst of her,

14 They have wandered *as* blind *men* in the streets, they have polluted themselves with blood, so that men could not touch their garments.

15 They cried unto them, Depart ye; *it is* unclean; depart, depart, touch not: when they fled away and wandered, they said among the heathen, They shall no more sojourn *there*.

16 The anger of the LORD hath divided them; he will no more regard them: they respected not the persons of the priests, they favoured not the elders.

17 As for us, our eyes as yet failed for our vain help: in our watching we have watched for a nation *that* could not save *us*.

18 They hunt our steps, that we cannot go in our streets: our end is near, our days are fulfilled; for our end is come.

19 Our persecutors are swifter than the eagles of the heaven: they pursued us upon the mountains, they laid wait for us in the wilderness.

20 The breath of our nostrils, the anointed of the LORD, was taken in their pits, of whom we said, Under his shadow we shall live among the heathen.

21 Rejoice and be glad, O daughter of Edom, that dwellest in the land of Uz; the cup also shall pass through unto thee: thou shalt be drunken, and shalt make thyself naked.

22 The punishment of thine iniquity is accomplished, O daughter of Zion; he will no more carry thee away into captivity: he will visit thine iniquity, O daughter of Edom; he will discover thy sins.

CHAPTER 5

REMEMBER, O LORD, what is come upon us: consider, and behold our reproach.

2 Our inheritance is turned to strangers, our houses to aliens.

3 We are orphans and fatherless, our mothers *are* as widows.

4 We have drunken our water for money; our wood is sold unto us.

5 Our necks *are* under persecution: we labour, *and* have no rest.

6 We have given the hand *to* the Egyptians, *and to* the Assyrians, to be satisfied with bread.

7 Our fathers have sinned, *and are* not; and we have borne their iniquities.

8 Servants have ruled over us: *there is* none that doth deliver *us* out of their hand.

9 We gat our bread with *the peril of* our lives because of the sword of the wilderness.

10 Our skin was black like an oven because of the terrible famine.

11 They ravished the women in Zion, *and* the maids in the cities of Jū'dah.

12 Princes are hanged up by their hand: the faces of elders were not honoured.

13 They took the young men to grind, and the children fell under the wood.

14 The elders have ceased from the gate, the young men from their musick.

15 The joy of our heart is ceased; our dance is turned into mourning.

16 The crown is fallen *from* our head: woe unto us, that we have sinned!

17 For this our heart is faint; for these *things* our eyes are dim.

18 Because of the mountain of Zion, which is desolate, the foxes walk upon it.

19 Thou, O LORD, remainest for ever; thy throne from generation to generation.

20 Wherefore dost thou forget us for ever, *and* forsake us so long time?

21 Turn thou us unto thee, O LORD, and we shall be turned; renew our days as of old.

22 But thou hast utterly rejected us; thou art very wroth against us.

THE BOOK OF THE PROPHET

EZEKIEL

CHAPTER 1

NOW it came to pass in the thirtieth year, in the fourth *month*, in the fifth *day* of the month, as I *was* among the captives by the river of Chē'bär, *that* the heavens were opened, and I saw visions of God.

2 In the fifth *day* of the month, which

was the fifth year of king Je-hoi'a-chĭn's captivity,

3 The word of the LORD came expressly unto E-zē'ki-el the priest, the son of Bū'zī, in the land of the Chăl-dē'ans by the river Chē'bär; and the hand of the LORD was there upon him.

4 ¶And I looked, and, behold, a whirlwind came out of the north, a great cloud, and a fire infolding itself, and a brightness *was* about it, and out of the midst thereof as the colour of amber, out of the midst of the fire.

5 Also out of the midst thereof *came* the likeness of four living creatures. And this *was* their appearance; they had the likeness of a man.

6 And every one had four faces, and every one had four wings.

7 And their feet *were* straight feet; and the sole of their feet *was* like the sole of a calf's foot: and they sparkled like the colour of burnished brass.

8 And *they had* the hands of a man under their wings on their four sides; and they four had their faces and their wings.

9 Their wings *were* joined one to another; they turned not when they went; they went every one straight forward.

10 As for the likeness of their faces, they four had the face of a man, and the face of a lion, on the right side: and they four had the face of an ox on the left side; they four also had the face of an eagle.

11 Thus *were* their faces: and their wings *were* stretched upward; two *wings* of every one *were* joined one to another, and two covered their bodies.

12 And they went every one straight forward: whither the spirit was to go, they went; *and* they turned not when they went.

13 As for the likeness of the living creatures, their appearance *was* like burning coals of fire, *and* like the appearance of lamps: it went up and down among the living creatures; and the fire was bright, and out of the fire went forth lightning.

14 And the living creatures ran and returned as the appearance of a flash of lightning.

15 ¶Now as I beheld the living creatures, behold one wheel upon the earth by the living creatures, with his four faces.

16 The appearance of the wheels and their work *was* like unto the colour of a beryl: and they four had one likeness: and their appearance and their work *was* as it were a wheel in the middle of a wheel.

17 When they went, they went upon their four sides: *and* they turned not when they went.

18 As for their rings, they were so high that they were dreadful; and their rings *were* full of eyes round about them four.

19 And when the living creatures went, the wheels went by them: and when the living creatures were lifted up from the earth, the wheels were lifted up.

20 Whithersoever the spirit was to go, they went, thither *was their* spirit to go; and the wheels were lifted up over against them: for the spirit of the living creature *was* in the wheels.

21 When those went, *these* went; and when those stood, *these* stood; and when those were lifted up from the earth, the wheels were lifted up over against them: for the spirit of the living creature *was* in the wheels.

22 And the likeness of the firmament upon the heads of the living creature *was* as the colour of the terrible crystal, stretched forth over their heads above.

23 And under the firmament *were* their wings straight, the one toward the other: every one had two, which covered on this side, and every one had two, which covered on that side, their bodies.

24 And when they went, I heard the noise of their wings, like the noise of great waters, as the voice of the Almighty, the voice of speech, as the noise of an host: when they stood, they let down their wings.

25 And there was a voice from the firmament that *was* over their heads, when they stood, *and* had let down their wings.

26 ¶And above the firmament that *was* over their heads *was* the likeness of a throne, as the appearance of a sapphire stone: and upon the likeness of the throne *was* the likeness as the appearance of a man above upon it.

27 And I saw as the colour of amber, as the appearance of fire round about within it, from the appearance of his loins even upward, and from the appearance of his loins even downward, I saw as it were the appearance of fire, and it had brightness round about.

28 As the appearance of the bow that is in the cloud in the day of rain, so *was* the appearance of the brightness round about. This *was* the appearance of the likeness of the glory of the LORD. And when I saw *it*, I fell upon my face, and I heard a voice of one that spake.

CHAPTER 2

AND he said unto me, Son of man,

stand upon thy feet, and I will speak unto thee.

2 And the spirit entered into me when he spake unto me, and set me upon my feet, that I heard him that spake unto me.

3 And he said unto me, Son of man, I send thee to the children of Israel, to a rebellious nation that hath rebelled against me: they and their fathers have transgressed against me, *even* unto this very day.

4 For *they are* impudent children and stiffhearted. I do send thee unto them; and thou shalt say unto them, Thus saith the Lord GOD.

5 And they, whether they will hear, or whether they will forbear, (for they *are* a rebellious house,) yet shall know that there hath been a prophet among them.

6 ¶And thou, son of man, be not afraid of them, neither be afraid of their words, though briers and thorns *be* with thee, and thou dost dwell among scorpions: be not afraid of their words, nor be dismayed at their looks, though they *be* a rebellious house.

7 And thou shalt speak my words unto them, whether they will hear, or whether they will forbear: for they *are* most rebellious.

8 But thou, son of man, hear what I say unto thee; Be not thou rebellious like that rebellious house: open thy mouth, and eat that I give thee.

9 ¶And when I looked, behold, an hand *was* sent unto me; and, lo, a roll of a book *was* therein;

10 And he spread it before me; and it *was* written within and without: and *there was* written therein lamentations, and mourning, and woe.

CHAPTER 3

MOREOVER he said unto me, Son of man, eat that thou findest; eat this roll, and go speak unto the house of Israel.

2 So I opened my mouth, and he caused me to eat that roll.

3 And he said unto me, Son of man, cause thy belly to eat, and fill thy bowels with this roll that I give thee. Then did I eat *it;* and it was in my mouth as honey for sweetness.

4 ¶And he said unto me, Son of man, go, get thee unto the house of Israel, and speak with my words unto them.

5 For thou *art* not sent to a people of a strange speech and of an hard language, *but* to the house of Israel;

6 Not to many people of a strange speech and of an hard language, whose words thou canst not understand. Surely, had I sent thee to them, they would have hearkened unto thee.

7 But the house of Israel will not hearken unto thee; for they will not hearken unto me: for all the house of Israel *are* impudent and hardhearted.

8 Behold, I have made thy face strong against their faces, and thy forehead strong against their foreheads.

9 As an adamant harder than flint have I made thy forehead: fear them not, neither be dismayed at their looks, though they *be* a rebellious house.

10 Moreover he said unto me, Son of man, all my words that I shall speak unto thee receive in thine heart, and hear with thine ears.

11 And go, get thee to them of the captivity, unto the children of thy people, and speak unto them, and tell them, Thus saith the Lord GOD; whether they will hear, or whether they will forbear.

12 Then the spirit took me up, and I heard behind me a voice of a great rushing, *saying*, Blessed *be* the glory of the LORD from his place.

13 *I heard* also the noise of the wings of the living creatures that touched one another, and the noise of the wheels over against them, and a noise of a great rushing.

14 So the spirit lifted me up, and took me away, and I went in bitterness, in the heat of my spirit; but the hand of the LORD was strong upon me.

15 ¶Then I came to them of the captivity at Tĕl–a'bĭb, that dwelt by the river of Chē'bär, and I sat where they sat, and remained there astonished among them seven days.

16 And it came to pass at the end of seven days, that the word of the LORD came unto me, saying,

17 Son of man, I have made thee a watchman unto the house of Israel: therefore hear the word at my mouth, and give them warning from me.

18 When I say unto the wicked, Thou shalt surely die; and thou givest him not warning, nor speakest to warn the wicked from his wicked way, to save his life; the same wicked *man* shall die in his iniquity; but his blood will I require at thine hand.

19 Yet if thou warn the wicked, and he turn not from his wickedness, nor from his wicked way, he shall die in his iniquity; but thou hast delivered thy soul.

20 Again, When a righteous *man* doth turn from his righteousness, and commit iniquity, and I lay a stumblingblock before him, he shall die: because

thou hast not given him warning, he
shall die in his sin, and his righteous-
ness which he hath done shall not be
remembered; but his blood will I re-
quire at thine hand.
21 Nevertheless if thou warn the
righteous *man*, that the righteous sin
not, and he doth not sin, he shall surely
live, because he is warned; also thou
hast delivered thy soul.
22 ¶And the hand of the LORD was
there upon me; and he said unto me,
Arise, go forth into the plain, and I will
there talk with thee.
23 Then I arose, and went forth into
the plain: and, behold, the glory of the
LORD stood there, as the glory which I
saw by the river of Chē'bär: and I fell on
my face.
24 Then the spirit entered into me,
and set me upon my feet, and spake
with me, and said unto me, Go, shut
thyself within thine house.
25 But thou, O son of man, behold,
they shall put bands upon thee, and
shall bind thee with them, and thou
shalt not go out among them:
26 And I will make thy tongue cleave
to the roof of thy mouth, that thou shalt
be dumb, and shalt not be to them a
reprover: for they *are* a rebellious
house.
27 But when I speak with thee, I will
open thy mouth, and thou shalt say
unto them, Thus saith the Lord GOD; He
that heareth, let him hear; and he that
forbeareth, let him forbear: for they *are*
a rebellious house.

CHAPTER 4

THOU also, son of man, take thee a tile,
and lay it before thee, and pourtray
upon it the city, *even* Jerusalem:
2 And lay siege against it, and build a
fort against it, and cast a mount against
it; set the camp also against it, and set
battering rams against it round about.
3 Moreover take thou unto thee an
iron pan, and set it *for* a wall of iron
between thee and the city: and set thy
face against it, and it shall be besieged,
and thou shalt lay siege against it. This
shall be a sign to the house of Israel.
4 Lie thou also upon thy left side, and
lay the iniquity of the house of Israel
upon it: *according* to the number of the
days that thou shalt lie upon it thou
shalt bear their iniquity.
5 For I have laid upon thee the years
of their iniquity, according to the num-
ber of the days, three hundred and nine-
ty days: so shalt thou bear the iniquity
of the house of Israel.
6 And when thou hast accomplished
them, lie again on thy right side, and
thou shalt bear the iniquity of the house
of Jū'dah forty days: I have appointed
thee each day for a year.
7 Therefore thou shalt set thy face to-
ward the siege of Jerusalem, and thine
arm *shall be* uncovered, and thou shalt
prophesy against it.
8 And, behold, I will lay bands upon
thee, and thou shalt not turn thee from
one side to another, till thou hast ended
the days of thy siege.
9 ¶Take thou also unto thee wheat,
and barley, and beans, and lentiles, and
millet, and fitches, and put them in one
vessel, and make thee bread thereof,
according to the number of the days
that thou shalt lie upon thy side, three
hundred and ninety days shalt thou eat
thereof.
10 And thy meat which thou shalt eat
shall be by weight, twenty shekels a
day: from time to time shalt thou eat it.
11 Thou shalt drink also water by
measure, the sixth part of an hin: from
time to time shalt thou drink.
12 And thou shalt eat it *as* barley
cakes, and thou shalt bake it with dung
that cometh out of man, in their sight.
13 And the LORD said, Even thus shall
the children of Israel eat their defiled
bread among the Gentiles, whither I
will drive them.
14 Then said I, Ah Lord GOD! behold,
my soul hath not been polluted; for
from my youth up even till now have I
not eaten of that which dieth of itself,
or is torn in pieces; neither came there
abominable flesh into my mouth.
15 Then he said unto me, Lo, I have
given thee cow's dung for man's dung,
and thou shalt prepare thy bread there-
with.
16 Moreover he said unto me, Son of
man, behold, I will break the staff of
bread in Jerusalem: and they shall eat
bread by weight, and with care; and
they shall drink water by measure, and
with astonishment:
17 That they may want bread and wa-
ter, and be astonied one with another,
and consume away for their iniquity.

CHAPTER 5

AND thou, son of man, take thee a
sharp knife, take thee a barber's razor,
and cause *it* to pass upon thine head
and upon thy beard: then take thee bal-
ances to weigh, and divide the *hair*.
2 Thou shalt burn with fire a third
part in the midst of the city, when the
days of the siege are fulfilled: and thou
shalt take a third part, *and* smite about
it with a knife: and a third part thou
shalt scatter in the wind; and I will
draw out a sword after them.

3 Thou shalt also take thereof a few in number, and bind them in thy skirts.

4 Then take of them again, and cast them into the midst of the fire, and burn them in the fire; *for* thereof shall a fire come forth into all the house of Israel.

5 ¶Thus saith the Lord GOD; This *is* Jerusalem: I have set it in the midst of the nations and countries *that are* round about her.

6 And she hath changed my judgments into wickedness more than the nations, and my statutes more than the countries that *are* round about her: for they have refused my judgments and my statutes, they have not walked in them.

7 Therefore thus saith the Lord GOD; Because ye multiplied more than the nations that *are* round about you, *and* have not walked in my statutes, neither have kept my judgments, neither have done according to the judgments of the nations that *are* round about you;

8 Therefore thus saith the Lord GOD; Behold, I, even I, *am* against thee, and will execute judgments in the midst of thee in the sight of the nations.

9 And I will do in thee that which I have not done, and whereunto I will not do any more the like, because of all thine abominations.

10 Therefore the fathers shall eat the sons in the midst of thee, and the sons shall eat their fathers; and I will execute judgments in thee, and the whole remnant of thee will I scatter into all the winds.

11 Wherefore, *as* I live, saith the Lord GOD; surely, because thou hast defiled my sanctuary with all thy detestable things, and with all thine abominations, therefore will I also diminish *thee;* neither shall mine eye spare, neither will I have any pity.

12 ¶A third part of thee shall die with the pestilence, and with famine shall they be consumed in the midst of thee: and a third part shall fall by the sword round about thee; and I will scatter a third part into all the winds, and I will draw out a sword after them.

13 Thus shall mine anger be accomplished, and I will cause my fury to rest upon them, and I will be comforted: and they shall know that I the LORD have spoken *it* in my zeal, when I have accomplished my fury in them.

14 Moreover I will make thee waste, and a reproach among the nations that *are* round about thee, in the sight of all that pass by.

15 So it shall be a reproach and a taunt, an instruction and an astonishment unto the nations that *are* round about thee, when I shall execute judgments in thee in anger and in fury and in furious rebukes. I the LORD have spoken *it.*

16 When I shall send upon them the evil arrows of famine, which shall be for *their* destruction, *and* which I will send to destroy you: and I will increase the famine upon you, and will break your staff of bread:

17 So will I send upon you famine and evil beasts, and they shall bereave thee; and pestilence and blood shall pass through thee; and I will bring the sword upon thee. I the LORD have spoken *it.*

CHAPTER 6

AND the word of the LORD came unto me, saying,

2 Son of man, set thy face toward the mountains of Israel, and prophesy against them,

3 And say, Ye mountains of Israel, hear the word of the Lord GOD; Thus saith the Lord GOD to the mountains, and to the hills, to the rivers, and to the valleys; Behold, I, *even* I, will bring a sword upon you, and I will destroy your high places.

4 And your altars shall be desolate, and your images shall be broken: and I will cast down your slain *men* before your idols.

5 And I will lay the dead carcases of the children of Israel before their idols; and I will scatter your bones round about your altars.

6 In all your dwellingplaces the cities shall be laid waste, and the high places shall be desolate; that your altars may be laid waste and made desolate, and your idols may be broken and cease, and your images may be cut down, and your works may be abolished.

7 And the slain shall fall in the midst of you, and ye shall know that I *am* the LORD.

8 ¶Yet will I leave a remnant, that ye may have *some* that shall escape the sword among the nations, when ye shall be scattered through the countries.

9 And they that escape of you shall remember me among the nations whither they shall be carried captives, because I am broken with their whorish heart, which hath departed from me, and with their eyes, which go a whoring after their idols: and they shall lothe themselves for the evils which they have committed in all their abominations.

10 And they shall know that I *am* the

LORD, *and that* I have not said in vain
that I would do this evil unto them.
11 ¶Thus saith the Lord GOD; Smite
with thine hand, and stamp with thy
foot, and say, Alas for all the evil
abominations of the house of Israel! for
they shall fall by the sword, by the
famine, and by the pestilence.
12 He that is far off shall die of the
pestilence; and he that is near shall fall
by the sword; and he that remaineth
and is besieged shall die by the famine:
thus will I accomplish my fury upon
them.
13 Then shall ye know that I *am* the
LORD, when their slain *men* shall be
among their idols round about their al-
tars, upon every high hill, in all the tops
of the mountains, and under every
green tree, and under every thick oak,
the place where they did offer sweet
savour to all their idols.
14 So will I stretch out my hand upon
them, and make the land desolate, yea,
more desolate than the wilderness to-
ward Dĭb′lăth, in all their habitations:
and they shall know that I *am* the LORD.

CHAPTER 7

MOREOVER the word of the LORD
came unto me, saying,
2 Also, thou son of man, thus saith
the Lord GOD unto the land of Israel; An
end, the end is come upon the four cor-
ners of the land.
3 Now *is* the end *come* upon thee, and
I will send mine anger upon thee, and
will judge thee according to thy ways,
and will recompense upon thee all
thine abominations.
4 And mine eye shall not spare thee,
neither will I have pity: but I will rec-
ompense thy ways upon thee, and
thine abominations shall be in the
midst of thee: and ye shall know that I
am the LORD.
5 Thus saith the Lord GOD; An evil, an
only evil, behold, is come.
6 An end is come, the end is come: it
watcheth for thee; behold, it is come.
7 The morning is come unto thee, O
thou that dwellest in the land: the time
is come, the day of trouble *is* near, and
not the sounding again of the moun-
tains.
8 Now will I shortly pour out my fury
upon thee, and accomplish mine anger
upon thee: and I will judge thee accord-
ing to thy ways, and will recompense
thee for all thine abominations.
9 And mine eye shall not spare,
neither will I have pity: I will recompense
thee according to thy ways and
thine abominations *that* are in the
midst of thee; and ye shall know that I
am the LORD that smiteth.
10 Behold the day, behold, it is come:
the morning is gone forth; the rod hath
blossomed, pride hath budded.
11 Violence is risen up into a rod of
wickedness: none of them *shall remain*,
nor of their multitude, nor of any of
theirs: neither *shall there be* wailing for
them.
12 The time is come, the day draweth
near: let not the buyer rejoice, nor the
seller mourn: for wrath *is* upon all the
multitude thereof.
13 For the seller shall not return to
that which is sold, although they were
yet alive: for the vision *is* touching the
whole multitude thereof, *which* shall
not return; neither shall any strengthen
himself in the iniquity of his life.
14 They have blown the trumpet,
even to make all ready; but none goeth
to the battle: for my wrath *is* upon all
the multitude thereof.
15 The sword *is* without, and the pes-
tilence and the famine within: he that *is*
in the field shall die with the sword; and
he that *is* in the city, famine and pesti-
lence shall devour him.
16 ¶But they that escape of them
shall escape, and shall be on the moun-
tains like doves of the valleys, all of
them mourning, every one for his iniq-
uity.
17 All hands shall be feeble, and all
knees shall be weak *as* water.
18 They shall also gird *themselves*
with sackcloth, and horror shall cover
them; and shame *shall be* upon all
faces, and baldness upon all their
heads.
19 They shall cast their silver in the
streets, and their gold shall be re-
moved: their silver and their gold shall
not be able to deliver them in the day of
the wrath of the LORD: they shall not
satisfy their souls, neither fill their bow-
els: because it is the stumblingblock
of their iniquity.
20 As for the beauty of his ornament,
he set it in majesty: but they made the
images of their abominations *and* of
their detestable things therein: there-
fore have I set it far from them.
21 And I will give it into the hands of
the strangers for a prey, and to the
wicked of the earth for a spoil; and they
shall pollute it.
22 My face will I turn also from them,
and they shall pollute my secret *place*:
for the robbers shall enter into it, and
defile it.
23 ¶Make a chain: for the land is full
of bloody crimes, and the city is full of
violence.

24 Wherefore I will bring the worst of the heathen, and they shall possess their houses: I will also make the pomp of the strong to cease; and their holy places shall be defiled.

25 Destruction cometh; and they shall seek peace, and *there shall be* none.

26 Mischief shall come upon mischief, and rumour shall be upon rumour; then shall they seek a vision of the prophet; but the law shall perish from the priest, and counsel from the ancients.

27 The king shall mourn, and the prince shall be clothed with desolation, and the hands of the people of the land shall be troubled: I will do unto them after their way, and according to their deserts will I judge them; and they shall know that I *am* the LORD.

CHAPTER 8

AND it came to pass in the sixth year, in the sixth *month*, in the fifth *day* of the month, *as* I sat in mine house, and the elders of Jū′dah sat before me, that the hand of the Lord GOD fell there upon me.

2 Then I beheld, and lo a likeness as the appearance of fire: from the appearance of his loins even downward, fire; and from his loins even upward, as the appearance of brightness, as the colour of amber.

3 And he put forth the form of an hand, and took me by a lock of mine head; and the spirit lifted me up between the earth and the heaven, and brought me in the visions of God to Jerusalem, to the door of the inner gate that looketh toward the north; where *was* the seat of the image of jealousy, which provoketh to jealousy.

4 And, behold, the glory of the God of Israel *was* there, according to the vision that I saw in the plain.

5 ¶Then said he unto me, Son of man, lift up thine eyes now the way toward the north. So I lifted up mine eyes the way toward the north, and behold northward at the gate of the altar this image of jealousy in the entry.

6 He said furthermore unto me, Son of man, seest thou what they do? *even* the great abominations that the house of Israel committeth here, that I should go far off from my sanctuary? but turn thee yet again, *and* thou shalt see greater abominations.

7 ¶And he brought me to the door of the court; and when I looked, behold a hole in the wall.

8 Then said he unto me, Son of man, dig now in the wall: and when I had digged in the wall, behold a door.

9 And he said unto me, Go in, and behold the wicked abominations that they do here.

10 So I went in and saw; and behold every form of creeping things, and abominable beasts, and all the idols of the house of Israel, pourtrayed upon the wall round about.

11 And there stood before them seventy men of the ancients of the house of Israel, and in the midst of them stood Jā-ăz-a-nī′ah the son of Shā′phan, with every man his censer in his hand; and a thick cloud of incense went up.

12 Then said he unto me, Son of man, hast thou seen what the ancients of the house of Israel do in the dark, every man in the chambers of his imagery? for they say, The LORD seeth us not; the LORD hath forsaken the earth.

13 ¶He said also unto me, Turn thee yet again, *and* thou shalt see greater abominations that they do.

14 Then he brought me to the door of the gate of the LORD's house which *was* toward the north; and, behold, there sat women weeping for Tăm′mŭz.

15 ¶Then said he unto me, Hast thou seen *this*, O son of man? turn thee yet again, *and* thou shalt see greater abominations than these.

16 And he brought me into the inner court of the LORD's house, and, behold, at the door of the temple of the LORD, between the porch and the altar, *were* about five and twenty men, with their backs toward the temple of the LORD, and their faces toward the east; and they worshipped the sun toward the east.

17 ¶Then he said unto me, Hast thou seen *this*, O son of man? Is it a light thing to the house of Jū′dah that they commit the abominations which they commit here? for they have filled the land with violence, and have returned to provoke me to anger: and, lo, they put the branch to their nose.

18 Therefore will I also deal in fury: mine eye shall not spare, neither will I have pity: and though they cry in mine ears with a loud voice, *yet* will I not hear them.

CHAPTER 9

HE cried also in mine ears with a loud voice, saying, Cause them that have charge over the city to draw near, even every man *with* his destroying weapon in his hand.

2 And, behold, six men came from the way of the higher gate, which lieth

toward the north, and every man a slaughter weapon in his hand; and one man among them *was* clothed with linen, with a writer's inkhorn by his side: and they went in, and stood beside the brasen altar.

3 And the glory of the God of Israel was gone up from the cherub, whereupon he was, to the threshold of the house. And he called to the man clothed with linen, which *had* the writer's inkhorn by his side;

4 And the LORD said unto him, Go through the midst of the city, through the midst of Jerusalem, and set a mark upon the foreheads of the men that sigh and that cry for all the abominations that be done in the midst thereof.

5 And to the others he said in mine hearing, Go ye after him through the city, and smite: let not your eye spare, neither have ye pity:

6 Slay utterly old *and* young, both maids, and little children, and women: but come not near any man upon whom *is* the mark; and begin at my sanctuary. Then they began at the ancient men which *were* before the house.

7 And he said unto them, Defile the house, and fill the courts with the slain: go ye forth. And they went forth, and slew in the city.

8 ¶And it came to pass, while they were slaying them, and I was left, that I fell upon my face, and cried, and said, Ah Lord GOD! wilt thou destroy all the residue of Israel in thy pouring out of thy fury upon Jerusalem?

9 Then said he unto me, The iniquity of the house of Israel and Jū'dah *is* exceeding great, and the land is full of blood, and the city full of perverseness: for they say, The LORD hath forsaken the earth, and the LORD seeth not.

10 And as for me also, mine eye shall not spare, neither will I have pity, *but* I will recompense their way upon their head.

11 And, behold, the man clothed with linen, which *had* the inkhorn by his side, reported the matter, saying, I have done as thou hast commanded me.

CHAPTER 10

THEN I looked, and, behold, in the firmament that was above the head of the cherubims there appeared over them as it were a sapphire stone, as the appearance of the likeness of a throne.

2 And he spake unto the man clothed with linen, and said, Go in between the wheels, *even* under the cherub, and fill thine hand with coals of fire from between the cherubims, and scatter *them* over the city. And he went in in my sight.

3 Now the cherubims stood on the right side of the house, when the man went in; and the cloud filled the inner court.

4 Then the glory of the LORD went up from the cherub, *and stood* over the threshold of the house; and the house was filled with the cloud, and the court was full of the brightness of the LORD's glory.

5 And the sound of the cherubims' wings was heard *even* to the outer court, as the voice of the Almighty God when he speaketh.

6 And it came to pass, *that* when he had commanded the man clothed with linen, saying, Take fire from between the wheels, from between the cherubims; then he went in, and stood beside the wheels.

7 And *one* cherub stretched forth his hand from between the cherubims unto the fire that *was* between the cherubims, and took *thereof*, and put *it* into the hands of *him that was* clothed with linen: who took *it*, and went out.

8 ¶And there appeared in the cherubims the form of a man's hand under their wings.

9 And when I looked, behold the four wheels by the cherubims, one wheel by one cherub, and another wheel by another cherub: and the appearance of the wheels *was* as the colour of a beryl stone.

10 And *as for* their appearances, they four had one likeness, as if a wheel had been in the midst of a wheel.

11 When they went, they went upon their four sides; they turned not as they went, but to the place whither the head looked they followed it; they turned not as they went.

12 And their whole body, and their backs, and their hands, and their wings, and the wheels, *were* full of eyes round about, *even* the wheels that they four had.

13 As for the wheels, it was cried unto them in my hearing, O wheel.

14 And every one had four faces: the first face *was* the face of a cherub, and the second face *was* the face of a man, and the third the face of a lion, and the fourth the face of an eagle.

15 And the cherubims were lifted up. This *is* the living creature that I saw by the river of Chē'bär.

16 And when the cherubims went, the wheels went by them: and when the cherubims lifted up their wings to mount up from the earth, the same

wheels also turned not from beside them.

17 When they stood, *these* stood; and when they were lifted up, *these* lifted up themselves *also:* for the spirit of the living creature *was* in them.

18 Then the glory of the LORD departed from off the threshold of the house, and stood over the cherubims.

19 And the cherubims lifted up their wings, and mounted up from the earth in my sight: when they went out, the wheels also *were* beside them, and *every one* stood at the door of the east gate of the LORD'S house; and the glory of the God of Israel *was* over them above.

20 This *is* the living creature that I saw under the God of Israel by the river of Chē'bär; and I knew that they *were* the cherubims.

21 Every one had four faces apiece, and every one four wings; and the likeness of the hands of a man *was* under their wings.

22 And the likeness of their faces *was* the same faces which I saw by the river of Chē'bär, their appearances and themselves: they went every one straight forward.

CHAPTER 11

MOREOVER the spirit lifted me up, and brought me unto the east gate of the LORD'S house, which looketh eastward: and behold at the door of the gate five and twenty men; among whom I saw Jā-ăz-a-nī'ah the son of Ā'zur, and Pĕl-a-tī'ah the son of Be-nā'iah, princes of the people.

2 Then said he unto me, Son of man, these *are* the men that devise mischief, and give wicked counsel in this city:

3 Which say, *It is* not near; let us build houses: this *city is* the caldron, and we *be* the flesh.

4 ¶Therefore prophesy against them, prophesy, O son of man.

5 And the Spirit of the LORD fell upon me, and said unto me, Speak; Thus saith the LORD; Thus have ye said, O house of Israel: for I know the things that come into your mind, *every one of* them.

6 Ye have multiplied your slain in this city, and ye have filled the streets thereof with the slain.

7 Therefore thus saith the Lord GOD; Your slain whom ye have laid in the midst of it, they *are* the flesh, and this *city is* the caldron: but I will bring you forth out of the midst of it.

8 Ye have feared the sword; and I will bring a sword upon you, saith the Lord GOD.

9 And I will bring you out of the midst thereof, and deliver you into the hands of strangers, and will execute judgments among you.

10 Ye shall fall by the sword; I will judge you in the border of Israel; and ye shall know that I *am* the LORD.

11 This *city* shall not be your caldron, neither shall ye be the flesh in the midst thereof; *but* I will judge you in the border of Israel:

12 And ye shall know that I *am* the LORD: for ye have not walked in my statutes, neither executed my judgments, but have done after the manners of the heathen that *are* round about you.

13 ¶And it came to pass, when I prophesied, that Pĕl-a-tī'ah the son of Be-nā'iah died. Then fell I down upon my face, and cried with a loud voice, and said, Ah Lord GOD! wilt thou make a full end of the remnant of Israel?

14 ¶Again the word of the LORD came unto me, saying,

15 Son of man, thy brethren, *even* thy brethren, the men of thy kindred, and all the house of Israel wholly, *are* they unto whom the inhabitants of Jerusalem have said, Get you far from the LORD: unto us is this land given in possession.

16 Therefore say, Thus saith the Lord GOD; Although I have cast them far off among the heathen, and although I have scattered them among the countries, yet will I be to them as a little sanctuary in the countries where they shall come.

17 Therefore say, Thus saith the Lord GOD; I will even gather you from the people, and assemble you out of the countries where ye have been scattered, and I will give you the land of Israel.

18 And they shall come thither, and they shall take away all the detestable things thereof and all the abominations thereof from thence.

19 And I will give them one heart, and I will put a new spirit within you; and I will take the stony heart out of their flesh, and will give them an heart of flesh:

20 That they may walk in my statutes, and keep mine ordinances, and do them: and they shall be my people, and I will be their God.

21 But *as for them* whose heart walketh after the heart of their detestable things and their abominations, I will recompense their way upon their own heads, saith the Lord GOD.

22 ¶Then did the cherubims lift up their wings, and the wheels beside

them; and the glory of the God of Israel *was* over them above.

23 And the glory of the LORD went up from the midst of the city, and stood upon the mountain which *is* on the east side of the city.

24 ¶Afterwards the spirit took me up, and brought me in a vision by the Spirit of God into Chăl-dē'a, to them of the captivity. So the vision that I had seen went up from me.

25 Then I spake unto them of the captivity all the things that the LORD had shewed me.

CHAPTER 12

THE word of the LORD also came unto me, saying,

2 Son of man, thou dwellest in the midst of a rebellious house, which have eyes to see, and see not; they have ears to hear, and hear not: for they *are* a rebellious house.

3 Therefore, thou son of man, prepare thee stuff for removing, and remove by day in their sight; and thou shalt remove from thy place to another place in their sight: it may be they will consider, though they *be* a rebellious house.

4 Then shalt thou bring forth thy stuff by day in their sight, as stuff for removing: and thou shalt go forth at even in their sight, as they that go forth into captivity.

5 Dig thou through the wall in their sight, and carry out thereby.

6 In their sight shalt thou bear *it* upon *thy* shoulders, *and* carry *it* forth in the twilight: thou shalt cover thy face, that thou see not the ground: for I have set thee *for* a sign unto the house of Israel.

7 And I did so as I was commanded: I brought forth my stuff by day, as stuff for captivity, and in the even I digged through the wall with mine hand; I brought *it* forth in the twilight, *and* I bare *it* upon *my* shoulder in their sight.

8 And in the morning came the word of the LORD unto me, saying,

9 Son of man, hath not the house of Israel, the rebellious house, said unto thee, What doest thou?

10 Say thou unto them, Thus saith the Lord GOD; This burden *concerneth* the prince in Jerusalem, and all the house of Israel that *are* among them.

11 Say, I *am* your sign: like as I have done, so shall it be done unto them: they shall remove *and* go into captivity.

12 And the prince that *is* among them shall bear upon *his* shoulder in the twilight, and shall go forth: they shall dig through the wall to carry out thereby: he shall cover his face, that he see not the ground with *his* eyes.

13 My net also will I spread upon him, and he shall be taken in my snare: and I will bring him to Babylon *to* the land of the Chăl-dē'ans; yet shall he not see it, though he shall die there.

14 And I will scatter toward every wind all that *are* about him to help him, and all his bands; and I will draw out the sword after them.

15 And they shall know that I *am* the LORD, when I shall scatter them among the nations, and disperse them in the countries.

16 But I will leave a few men of them from the sword, from the famine, and from the pestilence; that they may declare all their abominations among the heathen whither they come; and they shall know that I *am* the LORD.

17 ¶Moreover the word of the LORD came to me, saying,

18 Son of man, eat thy bread with quaking, and drink thy water with trembling and with carefulness;

19 And say unto the people of the land, Thus saith the Lord GOD of the inhabitants of Jerusalem, *and* of the land of Israel; They shall eat their bread with carefulness, and drink their water with astonishment, that her land may be desolate from all that is therein, because of the violence of all them that dwell therein.

20 And the cities that are inhabited shall be laid waste, and the land shall be desolate; and ye shall know that I *am* the LORD.

21 ¶And the word of the LORD came unto me, saying,

22 Son of man, what *is* that proverb *that* ye have in the land of Israel, saying, The days are prolonged, and every vision faileth?

23 Tell them therefore, Thus saith the Lord GOD; I will make this proverb to cease, and they shall no more use it as a proverb in Israel; but say unto them, The days are at hand, and the effect of every vision.

24 For there shall be no more any vain vision nor flattering divination within the house of Israel.

25 For I *am* the LORD: I will speak, and the word that I shall speak shall come to pass; it shall be no more prolonged: for in your days, O rebellious house, will I say the word, and will perform it, saith the Lord GOD.

26 ¶Again the word of the LORD came to me, saying,

27 Son of man, behold, *they of* the house of Israel say, The vision that he seeth *is* for many days *to come*, and he

prophesieth of the times *that are* far off.

28 Therefore say unto them, Thus saith the Lord GOD; There shall none of my words be prolonged any more, but the word which I have spoken shall be done, saith the Lord GOD.

CHAPTER 13

AND the word of the LORD came unto me, saying,

2 Son of man, prophesy against the prophets of Israel that prophesy, and say thou unto them that prophesy out of their own hearts, Hear ye the word of the LORD;

3 Thus saith the Lord GOD; Woe unto the foolish prophets, that follow their own spirit, and have seen nothing!

4 O Israel, thy prophets are like the foxes in the deserts.

5 Ye have not gone up into the gaps, neither made up the hedge for the house of Israel to stand in the battle in the day of the LORD.

6 They have seen vanity and lying divination, saying, The LORD saith: and the LORD hath not sent them: and they have made *others* to hope that they would confirm the word.

7 Have ye not seen a vain vision, and have ye not spoken a lying divination, whereas ye say, The LORD saith *it;* albeit I have not spoken?

8 Therefore thus saith the Lord GOD; Because ye have spoken vanity, and seen lies, therefore, behold, I *am* against you, saith the Lord GOD.

9 And mine hand shall be upon the prophets that see vanity, and that divine lies: they shall not be in the assembly of my people, neither shall they be written in the writing of the house of Israel, neither shall they enter into the land of Israel; and ye shall know that I *am* the Lord GOD.

10 Because, even because they have seduced my people, saying, Peace; and *there was* no peace; and one built up a wall, and, lo, others daubed it with untempered *morter:*

11 Say unto them which daub *it* with untempered *morter,* that it shall fall: there shall be an overflowing shower; and ye, O great hailstones, shall fall; and a stormy wind shall rend *it.*

12 Lo, when the wall is fallen, shall it not be said unto you, Where *is* the daubing wherewith ye have daubed *it?*

13 Therefore thus saith the Lord GOD; I will even rend *it* with a stormy wind in my fury; and there shall be an overflowing shower in mine anger, and great hailstones in *my* fury to consume *it.*

14 So will I break down the wall that ye have daubed with untempered *morter,* and bring it down to the ground, so that the foundation thereof shall be discovered, and it shall fall, and ye shall be consumed in the midst thereof: and ye shall know that I *am* the LORD.

15 Thus will I accomplish my wrath upon the wall, and upon them that have daubed it with untempered *morter,* and will say unto you, The wall *is* no *more,* neither they that daubed it;

16 *To wit,* the prophets of Israel which prophesy concerning Jerusalem, and which see visions of peace for her, and *there is* no peace, saith the Lord GOD.

17 ¶Likewise, thou son of man, set thy face against the daughters of thy people, which prophesy out of their own heart; and prophesy thou against them,

18 And say, Thus saith the Lord GOD; Woe to the *women* that sew pillows to all armholes, and make kerchiefs upon the head of every stature to hunt souls! Will ye hunt the souls of my people, and will ye save the souls alive *that come* unto you?

19 And will ye pollute me among my people for handfuls of barley and for pieces of bread, to slay the souls that should not die, and to save the souls alive that should not live, by your lying to my people that hear *your* lies?

20 Wherefore thus saith the Lord GOD; Behold, I *am* against your pillows, wherewith ye there hunt the souls to make *them* fly, and I will tear them from your arms, and will let the souls go, *even* the souls that ye hunt to make *them* fly.

21 Your kerchiefs also will I tear, and deliver my people out of your hand, and they shall be no more in your hand to be hunted; and ye shall know that I *am* the LORD.

22 Because with lies ye have made the heart of the righteous sad, whom I have not made sad; and strengthened the hands of the wicked, that he should not return from his wicked way, by promising him life:

23 Therefore ye shall see no more vanity, nor divine divinations: for I will deliver my people out of your hand: and ye shall know that I *am* the LORD.

CHAPTER 14

THEN came certain of the elders of Israel unto me, and sat before me.

2 And the word of the LORD came unto me, saying,

3 Son of man, these men have set up their idols in their heart, and put the stumblingblock of their iniquity before

their face: should I be enquired of at all
by them?
4 Therefore speak unto them, and say
unto them, Thus saith the Lord GOD;
Every man of the house of Israel that
setteth up his idols in his heart, and
putteth the stumblingblock of his iniq-
uity before his face, and cometh to the
prophet; I the LORD will answer him
that cometh according to the multitude
of his idols;
5 That I may take the house of Israel
in their own heart, because they are all
estranged from me through their idols.
6 ¶Therefore say unto the house of
Israel, Thus saith the Lord GOD; Re-
pent, and turn *yourselves* from your
idols; and turn away your faces from all
your abominations.
7 For every one of the house of Israel,
or of the stranger that sojourneth in
Israel, which separateth himself from
me, and setteth up his idols in his heart,
and putteth the stumblingblock of his
iniquity before his face, and cometh to
a prophet to enquire of him concerning
me; I the LORD will answer him by my-
self:
8 And I will set my face against that
man, and will make him a sign and a
proverb, and I will cut him off from the
midst of my people; and ye shall know
that I *am* the LORD.
9 And if the prophet be deceived
when he hath spoken a thing, I the LORD
have deceived that prophet, and I will
stretch out my hand upon him, and will
destroy him from the midst of my
people Israel.
10 And they shall bear the punish-
ment of their iniquity: the punishment
of the prophet shall be even as the pun-
ishment of him that seeketh *unto him;*
11 That the house of Israel may go no
more astray from me, neither be pol-
luted any more with all their transgres-
sions; but that they may be my people,
and I may be their God, saith the Lord
GOD.
12 ¶The word of the LORD came again
to me, saying,
13 Son of man, when the land sinneth
against me by trespassing grievously,
then will I stretch out mine hand upon
it, and will break the staff of the bread
thereof, and will send famine upon it,
and will cut off man and beast from it:
14 Though these three men, Noah,
Daniel, and Job, were in it, they should
deliver *but* their own souls by their
righteousness, saith the Lord GOD.
15 ¶If I cause noisome beasts to pass
through the land, and they spoil it, so
that it be desolate, that no man may
pass through because of the beasts:
16 *Though* these three men *were* in it,
as I live, saith the Lord GOD, they shall
deliver neither sons nor daughters;
they only shall be delivered, but the
land shall be desolate.
17 ¶Or *if* I bring a sword upon that
land, and say, Sword, go through the
land; so that I cut off man and beast
from it:
18 Though these three men *were* in it,
as I live, saith the Lord GOD, they shall
deliver neither sons nor daughters, but
they only shall be delivered them-
selves.
19 ¶Or *if* I send a pestilence into that
land, and pour out my fury upon it in
blood, to cut off from it man and beast:
20 Though Noah, Daniel, and Job,
were in it, *as* I live, saith the Lord GOD,
they shall deliver neither son nor
daughter; they shall *but* deliver their
own souls by their righteousness.
21 For thus saith the Lord GOD; How
much more when I send my four sore
judgments upon Jerusalem, the sword,
and the famine, and the noisome beast,
and the pestilence, to cut off from it
man and beast?
22 Yet, behold, therein shall be left a
remnant that shall be brought forth,
both sons and daughters: behold, they
shall come forth unto you, and ye shall
see their way and their doings: and ye
shall be comforted concerning the evil
that I have brought upon Jerusalem,
even concerning all that I have brought
upon it.
23 And they shall comfort you, when
ye see their ways and their doings: and
ye shall know that I have not done
without cause all that I have done in it,
saith the Lord GOD.

CHAPTER 15

AND the word of the LORD came unto
me, saying,
2 Son of man, What is the vine tree
more than any tree, *or than* a branch
which is among the trees of the forest?
3 Shall wood be taken thereof to do
any work? or will *men* take a pin of it to
hang any vessel thereon?
4 Behold, it is cast into the fire for
fuel; the fire devoureth both the ends of
it, and the midst of it is burned. Is it
meet for *any* work?
5 Behold, when it was whole, it was
meet for no work: how much less shall
it be meet yet for *any* work, when the
fire hath devoured it, and it is burned?
6 ¶Therefore thus saith the Lord GOD;
As the vine tree among the trees of the
forest, which I have given to the fire for
fuel, so will I give the inhabitants of Je-
rusalem.

7 And I will set my face against them;
they shall go out from *one* fire, and *another* fire shall devour them; and ye shall know that I *am* the LORD, when I set my face against them.
8 And I will make the land desolate,
because they have committed a trespass, saith the Lord GOD.

CHAPTER 16

AGAIN the word of the LORD came unto me, saying,
2 Son of man, cause Jerusalem to
know her abominations,
3 And say, Thus saith the Lord GOD
unto Jerusalem; Thy birth and thy nativity *is* of the land of Canaan; thy father *was* an Ămorīte, and thy mother an Hittite.
4 And *as for* thy nativity, in the day
thou wast born thy navel was not cut, neither wast thou washed in water to supple *thee;* thou wast not salted at all, nor swaddled at all.
5 None eye pitied thee, to do any of
these unto thee, to have compassion upon thee; but thou wast cast out in the open field, to the lothing of thy person, in the day that thou wast born.
6 ¶And when I passed by thee, and
saw thee polluted in thine own blood, I said unto thee *when thou wast* in thy blood, Live; yea, I said unto thee *when thou wast* in thy blood, Live.
7 I have caused thee to multiply as
the bud of the field, and thou hast increased and waxen great, and thou art come to excellent ornaments: *thy* breasts are fashioned, and thine hair is grown, whereas thou *wast* naked and bare.
8 Now when I passed by thee, and
looked upon thee, behold, thy time *was* the time of love; and I spread my skirt over thee, and covered thy nakedness: yea, I sware unto thee, and entered into a covenant with thee, saith the Lord GOD, and thou becamest mine.
9 Then washed I thee with water; yea,
I throughly washed away thy blood from thee, and I anointed thee with oil.
10 I clothed thee also with broidered
work, and shod thee with badgers' skin, and I girded thee about with fine linen, and I covered thee with silk.
11 I decked thee also with ornaments, and I put bracelets upon thy hands, and a chain on thy neck.
12 And I put a jewel on thy forehead,
and earrings in thine ears, and a beautiful crown upon thine head.
13 Thus wast thou decked with gold
and silver; and thy raiment *was of* fine linen, and silk, and broidered work; thou didst eat fine flour, and honey, and oil: and thou wast exceeding beautiful, and thou didst prosper into a kingdom.
14 And thy renown went forth among
the heathen for thy beauty: for it *was* perfect through my comeliness, which I had put upon thee, saith the Lord GOD.
15 ¶But thou didst trust in thine own
beauty, and playedst the harlot because of thy renown, and pouredst out thy fornications on every one that passed by; his it was.
16 And of thy garments thou didst
take, and deckedst thy high places with divers colours, and playedst the harlot thereupon: *the like things* shall not come, neither shall it be *so.*
17 Thou hast also taken thy fair
jewels of my gold and of my silver, which I had given thee, and madest to thyself images of men, and didst commit whoredom with them,
18 And tookest thy broidered garments, and coveredst them: and thou hast set mine oil and mine incense before them.
19 My meat also which I gave thee,
fine flour, and oil, and honey, *wherewith* I fed thee, thou hast even set it before them for a sweet savour: and *thus* it was, saith the Lord GOD.
20 Moreover thou hast taken thy sons
and thy daughters, whom thou hast borne unto me, and these hast thou sacrificed unto them to be devoured. *Is this* of thy whoredoms a small matter,
21 That thou hast slain my children,
and delivered them to cause them to pass through *the fire* for them?
22 And in all thine abominations and
thy whoredoms thou hast not remembered the days of thy youth, when thou wast naked and bare, *and* wast polluted in thy blood.
23 And it came to pass after all thy
wickedness, (woe, woe unto thee! saith the Lord GOD;)
24 *That* thou hast also built unto thee
an eminent place, and hast made thee an high place in every street.
25 Thou hast built thy high place at
every head of the way, and hast made thy beauty to be abhorred, and hast opened thy feet to every one that passed by, and multiplied thy whoredoms.
26 Thou hast also committed fornication with the Egyptians thy neighbours, great of flesh; and hast increased thy whoredoms, to provoke me to anger.
27 Behold, therefore I have stretched
out my hand over thee, and have diminished thine ordinary *food,* and delivered thee unto the will of them that hate thee, the daughters of the Philis-

tines, which are ashamed of thy lewd way.

28 Thou hast played the whore also with the Assyrians, because thou wast unsatiable; yea, thou hast played the harlot with them, and yet couldest not be satisfied.

29 Thou hast moreover multiplied thy fornication in the land of Canaan unto Chăl-dē'a; and yet thou wast not satisfied herewith.

30 How weak is thine heart, saith the Lord God, seeing thou doest all these *things*, the work of an imperious whorish woman;

31 In that thou buildest thine eminent place in the head of every way, and makest thine high place in every street; and hast not been as an harlot, in that thou scornest hire;

32 *But as* a wife that committeth adultery, *which* taketh strangers instead of her husband!

33 They give gifts to all whores: but thou givest thy gifts to all thy lovers, and hirest them, that they may come unto thee on every side for thy whoredom.

34 And the contrary is in thee from *other* women in thy whoredoms, whereas none followeth thee to commit whoredoms: and in that thou givest a reward, and no reward is given unto thee, therefore thou art contrary.

35 ¶Wherefore, O harlot, hear the word of the Lord:

36 Thus saith the Lord God; Because thy filthiness was poured out, and thy nakedness discovered through thy whoredoms with thy lovers, and with all the idols of thy abominations, and by the blood of thy children, which thou didst give unto them;

37 Behold, therefore I will gather all thy lovers, with whom thou hast taken pleasure, and all *them* that thou hast loved, with all *them* that thou hast hated; I will even gather them round about against thee, and will discover thy nakedness unto them, that they may see all thy nakedness.

38 And I will judge thee, as women that break wedlock and shed blood are judged; and I will give thee blood in fury and jealousy.

39 And I will also give thee into their hand, and they shall throw down thine eminent place, and shall break down thy high places: they shall strip thee also of thy clothes, and shall take thy fair jewels, and leave thee naked and bare.

40 They shall also bring up a company against thee, and they shall stone thee with stones, and thrust thee through with their swords.

41 And they shall burn thine houses with fire, and execute judgment upon thee in the sight of many women: and I will cause thee to cease from playing the harlot, and thou also shalt give no hire any more.

42 So will I make my fury toward thee to rest, and my jealousy shall depart from thee, and I will be quiet, and will be no more angry.

43 Because thou hast not remembered the days of thy youth, but hast fretted me in all these *things;* behold, therefore I also will recompense thy way upon *thine* head, saith the Lord God: and thou shalt not commit this lewdness above all thine abominations.

44 ¶Behold, every one that useth proverbs shall use *this* proverb against thee, saying, As *is* the mother, *so is* her daughter.

45 Thou *art* thy mother's daughter, that lotheth her husband and her children; and thou *art* the sister of thy sisters, which lothed their husbands and their children: your mother *was* an Hittite, and your father an Ămorīte.

46 And thine elder sister *is* Sa-mâ'-rĭ-a, she and her daughters that dwell at thy left hand: and thy younger sister, that dwelleth at thy right hand, *is* Sodom and her daughters.

47 Yet hast thou not walked after their ways, nor done after their abominations: but, as *if that were* a very little *thing*, thou wast corrupted more than they in all thy ways.

48 *As* I live, saith the Lord God, Sodom thy sister hath not done, she nor her daughters, as thou hast done, thou and thy daughters.

49 Behold, this was the iniquity of thy sister Sodom, pride, fulness of bread, and abundance of idleness was in her and in her daughters, neither did she strengthen the hand of the poor and needy.

50 And they were haughty, and committed abomination before me: therefore I took them away as I saw *good*.

51 Neither hath Sa-mâ'rĭ-a committed half of thy sins; but thou hast multiplied thine abominations more than they, and hast justified thy sisters in all thine abominations which thou hast done.

52 Thou also, which hast judged thy sisters, bear thine own shame for thy sins that thou hast committed more abominable than they: they are more righteous than thou: yea, be thou confounded also, and bear thy shame, in that thou hast justified thy sisters.

53 When I shall bring again their cap-
tivity, the captivity of Sodom and her
daughters, and the captivity of Sa-mâ'-
rĭ-a and her daughters, then *will I bring
again* the captivity of thy captives in
the midst of them:
54 That thou mayest bear thine own
shame, and mayest be confounded in
all that thou hast done, in that thou art
a comfort unto them.
55 When thy sisters, Sodom and her
daughters, shall return to their former
estate, and Sa-mâ'rĭ-a and her daughters
shall return to their former estate,
then thou and thy daughters shall re-
turn to your former estate.
56 For thy sister Sodom was not
mentioned by thy mouth in the day of
thy pride,
57 Before thy wickedness was dis-
covered, as at the time of *thy* reproach
of the daughters of Syria, and all *that
are* round about her, the daughters of
the Philistines, which despise thee
round about.
58 Thou hast borne thy lewdness and
thine abominations, saith the LORD.
59 For thus saith the Lord GOD; I will
even deal with thee as thou hast done,
which hast despised the oath in break-
ing the covenant.
60 Nevertheless I will remember my
covenant with thee in the days of thy
youth, and I will establish unto thee an
everlasting covenant.
61 Then thou shalt remember thy
ways, and be ashamed, when thou
shalt receive thy sisters, thine elder and
thy younger: and I will give them unto
thee for daughters, but not by thy cov-
enant.
62 And I will establish my covenant
with thee; and thou shalt know that I
am the LORD:
63 That thou mayest remember, and
be confounded, and never open thy
mouth any more because of thy shame,
when I am pacified toward thee for all
that thou hast done, saith the Lord GOD.

CHAPTER 17

AND the word of the LORD came unto
me, saying,
2 Son of man, put forth a riddle, and
speak a parable unto the house of
Israel;
3 And say, Thus saith the Lord GOD;
A great eagle with great wings, long-
winged, full of feathers, which had di-
vers colours, came unto Lebanon, and
took the highest branch of the cedar:
4 He cropped off the top of his young
twigs, and carried it into a land of traf-
fick; he set it in a city of merchants.
5 He took also of the seed of the land,
and planted it in a fruitful field; he
placed *it* by great waters, *and* set it *as* a
willow tree.
6 And it grew, and became a spread-
ing vine of low stature, whose branches
turned toward him, and the roots there-
of were under him: so it became a
vine, and brought forth branches, and
shot forth sprigs.
7 There was also another great eagle
with great wings and many feathers:
and, behold, this vine did bend her
roots toward him, and shot forth her
branches toward him, that he might
water it by the furrows of her planta-
tion.
8 It was planted in a good soil by
great waters, that it might bring forth
branches, and that it might bear fruit,
that it might be a goodly vine.
9 Say thou, Thus saith the Lord GOD;
Shall it prosper? shall he not pull up the
roots thereof, and cut off the fruit there-
of, that it wither? it shall wither in
all the leaves of her spring, even
without great power or many people to
pluck it up by the roots thereof.
10 Yea, behold, *being* planted, shall it
prosper? shall it not utterly wither,
when the east wind toucheth it? it shall
wither in the furrows where it grew.
11 ¶Moreover the word of the LORD
came unto me, saying,
12 Say now to the rebellious house,
Know ye not what these *things mean?*
tell *them,* Behold, the king of Babylon
is come to Jerusalem, and hath taken
the king thereof, and the princes there-
of, and led them with him to Baby-
lon;
13 And hath taken of the king's seed,
and made a covenant with him, and
hath taken an oath of him: he hath also
taken the mighty of the land:
14 That the kingdom might be base,
that it might not lift itself up, *but* that
by keeping of his covenant it might
stand.
15 But he rebelled against him in
sending his ambassadors into Egypt,
that they might give him horses and
much people. Shall he prosper? shall he
escape that doeth such *things?* or shall
he break the covenant, and be de-
livered?
16 *As* I live, saith the Lord GOD, sure-
ly in the place *where* the king *dwelleth*
that made him king, whose oath he de-
spised, and whose covenant he brake,
even with him in the midst of Babylon
he shall die.
17 Neither shall Pharaoh with *his*
mighty army and great company make
for him in the war, by casting up

mounts, and building forts, to cut off many persons:

18 Seeing he despised the oath by breaking the covenant, when, lo, he had given his hand, and hath done all these *things*, he shall not escape.

19 Therefore thus saith the Lord GOD; *As* I live, surely mine oath that he hath despised, and my covenant that he hath broken, even it will I recompense upon his own head.

20 And I will spread my net upon him, and he shall be taken in my snare, and I will bring him to Babylon, and will plead with him there for his trespass that he hath trespassed against me.

21 And all his fugitives with all his bands shall fall by the sword, and they that remain shall be scattered toward all winds: and ye shall know that I the LORD have spoken *it*.

22 ¶Thus saith the Lord GOD; I will also take of the highest branch of the high cedar, and will set *it*; I will crop off from the top of his young twigs a tender one, and will plant *it* upon an high mountain and eminent:

23 In the mountain of the height of Israel will I plant it: and it shall bring forth boughs, and bear fruit, and be a goodly cedar: and under it shall dwell all fowl of every wing; in the shadow of the branches thereof shall they dwell.

24 And all the trees of the field shall know that I the LORD have brought down the high tree, have exalted the low tree, have dried up the green tree, and have made the dry tree to flourish: I the LORD have spoken and have done *it*.

CHAPTER 18

THE word of the LORD came unto me again, saying,

2 What mean ye, that ye use this proverb concerning the land of Israel, saying, The fathers have eaten sour grapes, and the children's teeth are set on edge?

3 *As* I live, saith the Lord GOD, ye shall not have *occasion* any more to use this proverb in Israel.

4 Behold, all souls are mine; as the soul of the father, so also the soul of the son is mine: the soul that sinneth, it shall die.

5 But if a man be just, and do that which is lawful and right,

6 *And* hath not eaten upon the mountains, neither hath lifted up his eyes to the idols of the house of Israel, neither hath defiled his neighbour's wife, neither hath come near to a menstruous woman,

7 And hath not oppressed any, *but* hath restored to the debtor his pledge, hath spoiled none by violence, hath given his bread to the hungry, and hath covered the naked with a garment;

8 He *that* hath not given forth upon usury, neither hath taken any increase, *that* hath withdrawn his hand from iniquity, hath executed true judgment between man and man,

9 Hath walked in my statutes, and hath kept my judgments, to deal truly; he *is* just, he shall surely live, saith the Lord GOD.

10 ¶If he beget a son *that is* a robber, a shedder of blood, and *that* doeth the like to *any* one of these *things*,

11 And that doeth not any of those *duties*, but even hath eaten upon the mountains, and defiled his neighbour's wife,

12 Hath oppressed the poor and needy, hath spoiled by violence, hath not restored the pledge, and hath lifted up his eyes to the idols, hath committed abomination,

13 Hath given forth upon usury, and hath taken increase: shall he then live? he shall not live; he hath done all these abominations; he shall surely die; his blood shall be upon him.

14 ¶Now, lo, *if* he beget a son, that seeth all his father's sins which he hath done, and considereth, and doeth not such like,

15 *That* hath not eaten upon the mountains, neither hath lifted up his eyes to the idols of the house of Israel, hath not defiled his neighbour's wife,

16 Neither hath oppressed any, hath not withholden the pledge, neither hath spoiled by violence, *but* hath given his bread to the hungry, and hath covered the naked with a garment,

17 *That* hath taken off his hand from the poor, *that* hath not received usury nor increase, hath executed my judgments, hath walked in my statutes; he shall not die for the iniquity of his father, he shall surely live.

18 *As for* his father, because he cruelly oppressed, spoiled his brother by violence, and did *that* which *is* not good among his people, lo, even he shall die in his iniquity.

19 ¶Yet say ye, Why? doth not the son bear the iniquity of the father? When the son hath done that which is lawful and right, *and* hath kept all my statutes, and hath done them, he shall surely live.

20 The soul that sinneth, it shall die. The son shall not bear the iniquity of the father, neither shall the father bear the iniquity of the son: the righteous-

ness of the righteous shall be upon him, and the wickedness of the wicked shall be upon him.

21 But if the wicked will turn from all his sins that he hath committed, and keep all my statutes, and do that which is lawful and right, he shall surely live, he shall not die.

22 All his transgressions that he hath committed, they shall not be mentioned unto him: in his righteousness that he hath done he shall live.

23 Have I any pleasure at all that the wicked should die? saith the Lord GOD: *and* not that he should return from his ways, and live?

24 ¶But when the righteous turneth away from his righteousness, and committeth iniquity, *and* doeth according to all the abominations that the wicked *man* doeth, shall he live? All his righteousness that he hath done shall not be mentioned: in his trespass that he hath trespassed, and in his sin that he hath sinned, in them shall he die.

25 ¶Yet ye say, The way of the Lord is not equal. Hear now, O house of Israel; Is not my way equal? are not your ways unequal?

26 When a righteous *man* turneth away from his righteousness, and committeth iniquity, and dieth in them; for his iniquity that he hath done shall he die.

27 Again, when the wicked *man* turneth away from his wickedness that he hath committed, and doeth that which is lawful and right, he shall save his soul alive.

28 Because he considereth, and turneth away from all his transgressions that he hath committed, he shall surely live, he shall not die.

29 Yet saith the house of Israel, The way of the Lord is not equal. O house of Israel, are not my ways equal? are not your ways unequal?

30 Therefore I will judge you, O house of Israel, every one according to his ways, saith the Lord GOD. Repent, and turn *yourselves* from all your transgressions; so iniquity shall not be your ruin.

31 ¶Cast away from you all your transgressions, whereby ye have transgressed; and make you a new heart and a new spirit: for why will ye die, O house of Israel?

32 For I have no pleasure in the death of him that dieth, saith the Lord GOD: wherefore turn *yourselves*, and live ye.

CHAPTER 19

MOREOVER take thou up a lamentation for the princes of Israel,

2 And say, What *is* thy mother? A lioness: she lay down among lions, she nourished her whelps among young lions.

3 And she brought up one of her whelps: it became a young lion, and it learned to catch the prey; it devoured men.

4 The nations also heard of him; he was taken in their pit, and they brought him with chains unto the land of Egypt.

5 Now when she saw that she had waited, *and* her hope was lost, then she took another of her whelps, *and* made him a young lion.

6 And he went up and down among the lions, he became a young lion, and learned to catch the prey, *and* devoured men.

7 And he knew their desolate palaces, and he laid waste their cities; and the land was desolate, and the fulness thereof, by the noise of his roaring.

8 Then the nations set against him on every side from the provinces, and spread their net over him: he was taken in their pit.

9 And they put him in ward in chains, and brought him to the king of Babylon: they brought him into holds, that his voice should no more be heard upon the mountains of Israel.

10 ¶Thy mother *is* like a vine in thy blood, planted by the waters: she was fruitful and full of branches by reason of many waters.

11 And she had strong rods for the sceptres of them that bare rule, and her stature was exalted among the thick branches, and she appeared in her height with the multitude of her branches.

12 But she was plucked up in fury, she was cast down to the ground, and the east wind dried up her fruit: her strong rods were broken and withered; the fire consumed them.

13 And now she *is* planted in the wilderness, in a dry and thirsty ground.

14 And fire is gone out of a rod of her branches, *which* hath devoured her fruit, so that she hath no strong rod *to be* a sceptre to rule. This *is* a lamentation, and shall be for a lamentation.

CHAPTER 20

AND it came to pass in the seventh year, in the fifth *month*, the tenth *day* of the month, *that* certain of the elders of Israel came to enquire of the LORD, and sat before me.

2 Then came the word of the LORD unto me, saying,

3 Son of man, speak unto the elders of Israel, and say unto them, Thus saith

the Lord GOD; Are ye come to enquire
of me? *As* I live, saith the Lord GOD, I
will not be enquired of by you.
4 Wilt thou judge them, son of man,
wilt thou judge *them?* cause them to
know the abominations of their fa-
thers:
5 And say unto them, Thus saith the
Lord GOD; In the day when I chose
Israel, and lifted up mine hand unto the
seed of the house of Jacob, and made
myself known unto them in the land of
Egypt, when I lifted up mine hand unto
them, saying, I *am* the LORD your God;
6 In the day *that* I lifted up mine hand
unto them, to bring them forth of the
land of Egypt into a land that I had
espied for them, flowing with milk and
honey, which *is* the glory of all lands:
7 Then said I unto them, Cast ye
away every man the abominations of
his eyes, and defile not yourselves with
the idols of Egypt: I *am* the LORD your
God.
8 But they rebelled against me, and
would not hearken unto me: they did
not every man cast away the abomina-
tions of their eyes, neither did they for-
sake the idols of Egypt: then I said, I
will pour out my fury upon them, to ac-
complish my anger against them in the
midst of the land of Egypt.
9 But I wrought for my name's sake,
that it should not be polluted before the
heathen, among whom they *were*, in
whose sight I made myself known unto
them, in bringing them forth out of the
land of Egypt.
10 Wherefore I caused them to go
forth out of the land of Egypt, and
brought them into the wilderness.
11 And I gave them my statutes, and
shewed them my judgments, which *if* a
man do, he shall even live in them.
12 Moreover also I gave them my
sabbaths, to be a sign between me and
them, that they might know that I *am*
the LORD that sanctify them.
13 But the house of Israel rebelled
against me in the wilderness: they
walked not in my statutes, and they
despised my judgments, which *if* a man
do, he shall even live in them; and my
sabbaths they greatly polluted: then I
said, I would pour out my fury upon
them in the wilderness, to consume
them.
14 But I wrought for my name's sake,
that it should not be polluted before the
heathen, in whose sight I brought them
out.
15 Yet also I lifted up my hand unto
them in the wilderness, that I would not
bring them into the land which I had
given *them*, flowing with milk and
honey, which *is* the glory of all lands;
16 Because they despised my judg-
ments, and walked not in my statutes,
but polluted my sabbaths: for their
heart went after their idols.
17 Nevertheless mine eye spared
them from destroying them, neither
did I make an end of them in the wilder-
ness.
18 But I said unto their children in the
wilderness, Walk ye not in the statutes
of your fathers, neither observe their
judgments, nor defile yourselves with
their idols:
19 I *am* the LORD your God; walk in
my statutes, and keep my judgments,
and do them;
20 And hallow my sabbaths; and they
shall be a sign between me and you,
that ye may know that I *am* the LORD
your God.
21 Notwithstanding the children re-
belled against me: they walked not in
my statutes, neither kept my judg-
ments to do them, which *if* a man do, he
shall even live in them; they polluted
my sabbaths: then I said, I would pour
out my fury upon them, to accomplish
my anger against them in the wilder-
ness.
22 Nevertheless I withdrew mine
hand, and wrought for my name's sake,
that it should not be polluted in the
sight of the heathen, in whose sight I
brought them forth.
23 I lifted up mine hand unto them
also in the wilderness, that I would
scatter them among the heathen, and
disperse them through the countries;
24 Because they had not executed my
judgments, but had despised my stat-
utes, and had polluted my sabbaths,
and their eyes were after their fathers'
idols.
25 Wherefore I gave them also stat-
utes *that were* not good, and judg-
ments whereby they should not live;
26 And I polluted them in their own
gifts, in that they caused to pass
through *the fire* all that openeth the
womb, that I might make them deso-
late, to the end that they might know
that I *am* the LORD.
27 ¶Therefore, son of man, speak
unto the house of Israel, and say unto
them, Thus saith the Lord GOD; Yet in
this your fathers have blasphemed me,
in that they have committed a trespass
against me.
28 *For* when I had brought them into
the land, *for* the which I lifted up mine
hand to give it to them, then they saw
every high hill, and all the thick trees,
and they offered there their sacrifices,

and there they presented the provocation of their offering: there also they made their sweet savour, and poured out there their drink offerings.

29 Then I said unto them, What *is* the high place whereunto ye go? And the name thereof is called Bā'mah unto this day.

30 Wherefore say unto the house of Israel, Thus saith the Lord GOD; Are ye polluted after the manner of your fathers? and commit ye whoredom after their abominations?

31 For when ye offer your gifts, when ye make your sons to pass through the fire, ye pollute yourselves with all your idols, even unto this day: and shall I be enquired of by you, O house of Israel? *As* I live, saith the Lord GOD, I will not be enquired of by you.

32 And that which cometh into your mind shall not be at all, that ye say, We will be as the heathen, as the families of the countries, to serve wood and stone.

33 *As* I live, saith the Lord GOD, surely with a mighty hand, and with a stretched out arm, and with fury poured out, will I rule over you:

34 And I will bring you out from the people, and will gather you out of the countries wherein ye are scattered, with a mighty hand, and with a stretched out arm, and with fury poured out.

35 And I will bring you into the wilderness of the people, and there will I plead with you face to face.

36 Like as I pleaded with your fathers in the wilderness of the land of Egypt, so will I plead with you, saith the Lord GOD.

37 And I will cause you to pass under the rod, and I will bring you into the bond of the covenant:

38 And I will purge out from among you the rebels, and them that transgress against me: I will bring them forth out of the country where they sojourn, and they shall not enter into the land of Israel: and ye shall know that I *am* the LORD.

39 As for you, O house of Israel thus saith the Lord GOD; Go ye, serve ye every one his idols, and hereafter *also*, if ye will not hearken unto me: but pollute ye my holy name no more with your gifts, and with your idols.

40 For in mine holy mountain, in the mountain of the height of Israel, saith the Lord GOD, there shall all the house of Israel, all of them in the land, serve me: there will I accept them, and there will I require your offerings, and the firstfruits of your oblations, with all your holy things.

41 I will accept you with your sweet savour, when I bring you out from the people, and gather you out of the countries wherein ye have been scattered; and I will be sanctified in you before the heathen.

42 And ye shall know that I *am* the LORD, when I shall bring you into the land of Israel, into the country *for* the which I lifted up mine hand to give it to your fathers.

43 And there shall ye remember your ways, and all your doings, wherein ye have been defiled; and ye shall lothe yourselves in your own sight for all your evils that ye have committed.

44 And ye shall know that I *am* the LORD, when I have wrought with you for my name's sake, not according to your wicked ways, nor according to your corrupt doings, O ye house of Israel, saith the Lord GOD.

45 ¶Moreover the word of the LORD came unto me, saying,

46 Son of man, set thy face toward the south, and drop *thy word* toward the south, and prophesy against the forest of the south field;

47 And say to the forest of the south, Hear the word of the LORD; Thus saith the Lord GOD; Behold, I will kindle a fire in thee, and it shall devour every green tree in thee, and every dry tree: the flaming flame shall not be quenched, and all faces from the south to the north shall be burned therein.

48 And all flesh shall see that I the LORD have kindled it: it shall not be quenched.

49 Then said I, Ah Lord GOD! they say of me, Doth he not speak parables?

CHAPTER 21

AND the word of the LORD came unto me, saying,

2 Son of man, set thy face toward Jerusalem, and drop *thy word* toward the holy places, and prophesy against the land of Israel,

3 And say to the land of Israel, Thus saith the LORD; Behold, I *am* against thee, and will draw forth my sword out of his sheath, and will cut off from thee the righteous and the wicked.

4 Seeing then that I will cut off from thee the righteous and the wicked, therefore shall my sword go forth out of his sheath against all flesh from the south to the north:

5 That all flesh may know that I the LORD have drawn forth my sword out of his sheath: it shall not return any more.

6 Sigh therefore, thou son of man, with the breaking of *thy* loins; and with bitterness sigh before their eyes.

7 And it shall be, when they say unto thee, Wherefore sighest thou? that thou shalt answer, For the tidings; because it cometh: and every heart shall melt, and all hands shall be feeble, and every spirit shall faint, and all knees shall be weak *as* water: behold, it cometh, and shall be brought to pass, saith the Lord GOD.

8 ¶Again the word of the LORD came unto me, saying,

9 Son of man, prophesy, and say, Thus saith the LORD; Say, A sword, a sword is sharpened, and also furbished:

10 It is sharpened to make a sore slaughter; it is furbished that it may glitter: should we then make mirth? it contemneth the rod of my son, *as* every tree.

11 And he hath given it to be furbished, that it may be handled: this sword is sharpened, and it is furbished, to give it into the hand of the slayer.

12 Cry and howl, son of man: for it shall be upon my people, it *shall be* upon all the princes of Israel: terrors by reason of the sword shall be upon my people: smite therefore upon *thy* thigh.

13 Because *it is* a trial, and what if *the sword* contemn even the rod? it shall be no *more*, saith the Lord GOD.

14 Thou therefore, son of man, prophesy, and smite *thine* hands together, and let the sword be doubled the third time, the sword of the slain: it *is* the sword of the great *men that are* slain, which entereth into their privy chambers.

15 I have set the point of the sword against all their gates, that *their* heart may faint, and *their* ruins be multiplied: ah! *it is* made bright, *it is* wrapped up for the slaughter.

16 Go thee one way or other, *either* on the right hand, *or* on the left, whithersoever thy face *is* set.

17 I will also smite mine hands together, and I will cause my fury to rest: I the LORD have said *it*.

18 ¶The word of the LORD came unto me again, saying,

19 Also, thou son of man, appoint thee two ways, that the sword of the king of Babylon may come: both twain shall come forth out of one land: and choose thou a place, choose *it* at the head of the way to the city.

20 Appoint a way, that the sword may come to Răb′bath of the Ammonites, and to Jū′dah in Jerusalem the defenced.

21 For the king of Babylon stood at the parting of the way, at the head of the two ways, to use divination: he made *his* arrows bright, he consulted with images, he looked in the liver.

22 At his right hand was the divination for Jerusalem, to appoint captains, to open the mouth in the slaughter, to lift up the voice with shouting, to appoint *battering* rams against the gates, to cast a mount, *and* to build a fort.

23 And it shall be unto them as a false divination in their sight, to them that have sworn oaths: but he will call to remembrance the iniquity, that they may be taken.

24 Therefore thus saith the Lord GOD; Because ye have made your iniquity to be remembered, in that your transgressions are discovered, so that in all your doings your sins do appear; because, *I say*, that ye are come to remembrance, ye shall be taken with the hand.

25 ¶And thou, profane wicked prince of Israel, whose day is come, when iniquity *shall have* an end,

26 Thus saith the Lord GOD; Remove the diadem, and take off the crown: this *shall* not *be* the same: exalt *him that is* low, and abase *him that is* high.

27 I will overturn, overturn, overturn, it: and it shall be no *more*, until he come whose right it is; and I will give it *him*.

28 ¶And thou, son of man, prophesy and say, Thus saith the Lord GOD concerning the Ammonites, and concerning their reproach; even say thou, The sword, the sword *is* drawn: for the slaughter *it is* furbished, to consume because of the glittering:

29 Whiles they see vanity unto thee, whiles they divine a lie unto thee, to bring thee upon the necks of *them that are* slain, of the wicked, whose day is come, when their iniquity *shall have* an end.

30 Shall I cause *it* to return into his sheath? I will judge thee in the place where thou wast created, in the land of thy nativity.

31 And I will pour out mine indignation upon thee, I will blow against thee in the fire of my wrath, and deliver thee into the hand of brutish men, *and* skilful to destroy.

32 Thou shalt be for fuel to the fire; thy blood shall be in the midst of the land; thou shalt be no *more* remembered: for I the LORD have spoken *it*.

CHAPTER 22

MOREOVER the word of the LORD came unto me, saying,

2 Now, thou son of man, wilt thou judge, wilt thou judge the bloody city? yea, thou shalt shew her all her abominations.

3 Then say thou, Thus saith the Lord

GOD, The city sheddeth blood in the
midst of it, that her time may come,
and maketh idols against herself to de-
file herself.
4 Thou art become guilty in thy blood
that thou hast shed; and hast defiled
thyself in thine idols which thou hast
made; and thou hast caused thy days to
draw near, and art come *even* unto thy
years: therefore have I made thee a
reproach unto the heathen, and a
mocking to all countries.
5 *Those that be* near, and *those that
be* far from thee, shall mock thee,
which art infamous *and* much vexed.
6 Behold, the princes of Israel, every
one were in thee to their power to shed
blood.
7 In thee have they set light by father
and mother: in the midst of thee have
they dealt by oppression with the
stranger: in thee have they vexed the
fatherless and the widow.
8 Thou hast despised mine holy
things, and hast profaned my sabbaths.
9 In thee are men that carry tales to
shed blood: and in thee they eat upon
the mountains: in the midst of thee they
commit lewdness.
10 In thee have they discovered their
fathers' nakedness: in thee have they
humbled her that was set apart for pol-
lution.
11 And one hath committed abomi-
nation with his neighbour's wife; and
another hath lewdly defiled his
daughter in law; and another in thee
hath humbled his sister, his father's
daughter.
12 In thee have they taken gifts to
shed blood; thou hast taken usury and
increase, and thou hast greedily gained
of thy neighbours by extortion, and
hast forgotten me, saith the Lord GOD.
13 Behold, therefore I have smitten
mine hand at thy dishonest gain which
thou hast made, and at thy blood which
hath been in the midst of thee.
14 Can thine heart endure, or can
thine hands be strong, in the days that I
shall deal with thee? I the LORD have
spoken *it*, and will do *it*.
15 And I will scatter thee among the
heathen, and disperse thee in the
countries, and will consume thy filthi-
ness out of thee.
16 And thou shalt take thine inheri-
tance in thyself in the sight of the
heathen, and thou shalt know that I *am*
the LORD.
17 ¶And the word of the LORD came
unto me, saying,
18 Son of man, the house of Israel is
to me become dross: all they *are* brass,
and tin, and iron, and lead, in the midst
of the furnace; they are *even* the dross
of silver.
19 Therefore thus saith the Lord GOD;
Because ye are all become dross, be-
hold, therefore I will gather you into
the midst of Jerusalem.
20 *As* they gather silver, and brass,
and iron, and lead, and tin, into the
midst of the furnace, to blow the fire
upon it, to melt *it*; so will I gather *you* in
mine anger and in my fury, and I will
leave *you there*, and melt you.
21 Yea, I will gather you, and blow
upon you in the fire of my wrath, and ye
shall be melted in the midst thereof.
22 As silver is melted in the midst of
the furnace, so shall ye be melted in the
midst thereof; and ye shall know that I
the LORD have poured out my fury upon
you.
23 ¶And the word of the LORD came
unto me, saying,
24 Son of man, say unto her, Thou *art*
the land that is not cleansed, nor rained
upon in the day of indignation.
25 *There is* a conspiracy of her
prophets in the midst thereof, like a
roaring lion ravening the prey; they
have devoured souls; they have taken
the treasure and precious things; they
have made her many widows in the
midst thereof.
26 Her priests have violated my law,
and have profaned mine holy things:
they have put no difference between
the holy and profane, neither have they
shewed *difference* between the un-
clean and the clean, and have hid their
eyes from my sabbaths, and I am pro-
faned among them.
27 Her princes in the midst thereof
are like wolves ravening the prey, to
shed blood, *and* to destroy souls, to get
dishonest gain.
28 And her prophets have daubed
them with untempered *morter*, seeing
vanity, and divining lies unto them,
saying, Thus saith the Lord GOD, when
the LORD hath not spoken.
29 The people of the land have used
oppression, and exercised robbery, and
have vexed the poor and needy: yea,
they have oppressed the stranger
wrongfully.
30 And I sought for a man among
them, that should make up the hedge,
and stand in the gap before me for the
land, that I should not destroy it: but I
found none.
31 Therefore have I poured out mine
indignation upon them; I have con-
sumed them with the fire of my wrath:
their own way have I recompensed
upon their heads, saith the Lord GOD.

CHAPTER 23

THE word of the LORD came again unto
me, saying,
2 Son of man, there were two women,
the daughters of one mother:
3 And they committed whoredoms in
Egypt; they committed whoredoms in
their youth: there were their breasts
pressed, and there they bruised the
teats of their virginity.
4 And the names of them *were* A-hō'-
lah the elder, and A-hōl'ĭ-bah her sister:
and they were mine, and they bare sons
and daughters. Thus *were* their names;
Sa-mâ'rĭ-a *is* A-hō'lah, and Jerusalem
A-hōl'ĭ-bah.
5 And A-hō'lah played the harlot
when she was mine; and she doted on
her lovers, on the Assyrians *her* neigh-
bours,
6 Which *were* clothed with blue, cap-
tains and rulers, all of them desirable
young men, horsemen riding upon
horses.
7 Thus she committed her whore-
doms with them, with all them *that*
were the chosen men of Assyria, and
with all on whom she doted: with all
their idols she defiled herself.
8 Neither left she her whoredoms
brought from Egypt: for in her youth
they lay with her, and they bruised the
breasts of her virginity, and poured
their whoredom upon her.
9 Wherefore I have delivered her into
the hand of her lovers, into the hand of
the Assyrians, upon whom she doted.
10 These discovered her nakedness:
they took her sons and her daughters,
and slew her with the sword: and she
became famous among women; for
they had executed judgment upon her.
11 And when her sister A-hōl'ĭ-bah
saw *this*, she was more corrupt in her
inordinate love than she, and in her
whoredoms more than her sister in *her*
whoredoms.
12 She doted upon the Assyrians *her*
neighbours, captains and rulers
clothed most gorgeously, horsemen
riding upon horses, all of them desir-
able young men.
13 Then I saw that she was defiled,
that they *took* both one way,
14 And *that* she increased her whore-
doms: for when she saw men pour-
trayed upon the wall, the images of the
Chăl-dē'anś pourtrayed with vermil-
ion,
15 Girded with girdles upon their
loins, exceeding in dyed attire upon
their heads, all of them princes to look
to, after the manner of the Babylonians
of Chăl-dē'a, the land of their nativity:
16 And as soon as she saw them with
her eyes, she doted upon them, and
sent messengers unto them into Chăl-
dē'a.
17 And the Babylonians came to her
into the bed of love, and they defiled
her with their whoredom, and she was
polluted with them, and her mind was
alienated from them.
18 So she discovered her whore-
doms, and discovered her nakedness:
then my mind was alienated from her,
like as my mind was alienated from her
sister.
19 Yet she multiplied her whore-
doms, in calling to remembrance the
days of her youth, wherein she had
played the harlot in the land of Egypt.
20 For she doted upon their para-
mours, whose flesh *is as* the flesh of
asses, and whose issue *is like* the issue
of horses.
21 Thus thou calledst to remem-
brance the lewdness of thy youth, in
bruising thy teats by the Egyptians for
the paps of thy youth.
22 ¶Therefore, O A-hōl'ĭ-bah, thus
saith the Lord GOD; Behold, I will raise
up thy lovers against thee, from whom
thy mind is alienated, and I will bring
them against thee on every side;
23 The Babylonians, and all the Chăl-
dē'anś, Pē'kŏd, and Shō'a, and Kō'a,
and all the Assyrians with them: all of
them desirable young men, captains
and rulers, great lords and renowned,
all of them riding upon horses.
24 And they shall come against thee
with chariots, wagons, and wheels, and
with an assembly of people, *which*
shall set against thee buckler and
shield and helmet round about: and I
will set judgment before them, and
they shall judge thee according to their
judgments.
25 And I will set my jealousy against
thee, and they shall deal furiously with
thee: they shall take away thy nose and
thine ears; and thy remnant shall fall by
the sword: they shall take thy sons and
thy daughters; and thy residue shall be
devoured by the fire.
26 They shall also strip thee out of thy
clothes, and take away thy fair jewels.
27 Thus will I make thy lewdness to
cease from thee, and thy whoredom
brought from the land of Egypt: so that
thou shalt not lift up thine eyes unto
them, nor remember Egypt any more.
28 For thus saith the Lord GOD; Be-
hold, I will deliver thee into the hand *of*
them whom thou hatest, into the hand
of them from whom thy mind is alien-
ated:
29 And they shall deal with thee hate-

fully, and shall take away all thy la-
bour, and shall leave thee naked and
bare: and the nakedness of thy whore-
doms shall be discovered, both thy
lewdness and thy whoredoms.
30 I will do these *things* unto thee, be-
cause thou hast gone a whoring after
the heathen, *and* because thou art pol-
luted with their idols.
31 Thou hast walked in the way of thy
sister; therefore will I give her cup into
thine hand.
32 Thus saith the Lord GOD; Thou
shalt drink of thy sister's cup deep and
large: thou shalt be laughed to scorn
and had in derision; it containeth
much.
33 Thou shalt be filled with drunken-
ness and sorrow, with the cup of aston-
ishment and desolation, with the cup
of thy sister Sa-mâ'rĭ-a.
34 Thou shalt even drink it and suck
it out, and thou shalt break the sherds
thereof, and pluck off thine own
breasts: for I have spoken *it*, saith the
Lord GOD.
35 Therefore thus saith the Lord GOD;
Because thou hast forgotten me, and
cast me behind thy back, therefore
bear thou also thy lewdness and thy
whoredoms.
36 ¶The LORD said moreover unto me;
Son of man, wilt thou judge A-hō'lah
and A-hōl'ĭ-bah? yea, declare unto
them their abominations;
37 That they have committed adul-
tery, and blood *is* in their hands, and
with their idols have they committed
adultery, and have also caused their
sons, whom they bare unto me, to pass
for them through *the fire*, to devour
them.
38 Moreover this they have done
unto me: they have defiled my sanc-
tuary in the same day, and have pro-
faned my sabbaths.
39 For when they had slain their
children to their idols, then they came
the same day into my sanctuary to pro-
fane it; and, lo, thus have they done in
the midst of mine house.
40 And furthermore, that ye have
sent for men to come from far, unto
whom a messenger *was* sent; and, lo,
they came: for whom thou didst wash
thyself, paintedst thy eyes, and
deckedst thyself with ornaments,
41 And satest upon a stately bed, and
a table prepared before it, whereupon
thou hast set mine incense and mine
oil.
42 And a voice of a multitude being at
ease *was* with her: and with the men of
the common sort *were* brought Sa-bē'-
anṡ from the wilderness, which put
bracelets upon their hands, and beauti-
ful crowns upon their heads.
43 Then said I unto *her that was* old in
adulteries, Will they now commit
whoredoms with her, and she *with
them*?
44 Yet they went in unto her, as they
go in unto a woman that playeth the
harlot: so went they in unto A-hō'lah
and unto A-hōl'ĭ-bah, the lewd women.
45 ¶And the righteous men, they
shall judge them after the manner of
adulteresses, and after the manner of
women that shed blood; because they
are adulteresses, and blood *is* in their
hands.
46 For thus saith the Lord GOD; I will
bring up a company upon them, and
will give them to be removed and
spoiled.
47 And the company shall stone them
with stones, and dispatch them with
their swords; they shall slay their sons
and their daughters, and burn up their
houses with fire.
48 Thus will I cause lewdness to
cease out of the land, that all women
may be taught not to do after your
lewdness.
49 And they shall recompense your
lewdness upon you, and ye shall bear
the sins of your idols: and ye shall know
that I *am* the Lord GOD.

CHAPTER 24

AGAIN in the ninth year, in the tenth
month, in the tenth *day* of the month,
the word of the LORD came unto me,
saying,
2 Son of man, write thee the name of
the day, *even* of this same day: the king
of Babylon set himself against Jeru-
salem this same day.
3 And utter a parable unto the rebel-
lious house, and say unto them, Thus
saith the Lord GOD; Set on a pot, set *it*
on, and also pour water into it:
4 Gather the pieces thereof into it,
even every good piece, the thigh, and
the shoulder; fill *it* with the choice
bones.
5 Take the choice of the flock, and
burn also the bones under it, *and* make
it boil well, and let them seethe the
bones of it therein.
6 ¶Wherefore thus saith the Lord
GOD; Woe to the bloody city, to the pot
whose scum *is* therein, and whose
scum is not gone out of it! bring it out
piece by piece; let no lot fall upon it.
7 For her blood is in the midst of her;
she set it upon the top of a rock; she
poured it not upon the ground, to cover
it with dust;
8 That it might cause fury to come up
to take vengeance; I have set her blood

upon the top of a rock, that it should
not be covered.
9 Therefore thus saith the Lord GOD;
Woe to the bloody city! I will even
make the pile for fire great.
10 Heap on wood, kindle the fire,
consume the flesh, and spice it well,
and let the bones be burned.
11 Then set it empty upon the coals
thereof, that the brass of it may be hot,
and may burn, and *that* the filthiness of
it may be molten in it, *that* the scum of
it may be consumed.
12 She hath wearied *herself* with lies,
and her great scum went not forth out
of her: her scum *shall be* in the fire.
13 In thy filthiness *is* lewdness: be-
cause I have purged thee, and thou
wast not purged, thou shalt not be
purged from thy filthiness any more,
till I have caused my fury to rest upon
thee.
14 I the LORD have spoken *it:* it shall
come to pass, and I will do *it;* I will not
go back, neither will I spare, neither
will I repent; according to thy ways,
and according to thy doings, shall they
judge thee, saith the LORD GOD.
15 ¶Also the word of the LORD came
unto me, saying,
16 Son of man, behold, I take away
from thee the desire of thine eyes with
a stroke: yet neither shalt thou mourn
nor weep, neither shall thy tears run
down.
17 Forbear to cry, make no mourning
for the dead, bind the tire of thine head
upon thee, and put on thy shoes upon
thy feet, and cover not *thy* lips, and eat
not the bread of men.
18 So I spake unto the people in the
morning: and at even my wife died; and
I did in the morning as I was com-
manded.
19 ¶And the people said unto me,
Wilt thou not tell us what these *things*
are to us, that thou doest *so?*
20 Then I answered them, The word
of the LORD came unto me, saying,
21 Speak unto the house of Israel,
Thus saith the Lord GOD; Behold, I will
profane my sanctuary, the excellency
of your strength, the desire of your
eyes, and that which your soul pitieth;
and your sons and your daughters
whom ye have left shall fall by the
sword.
22 And ye shall do as I have done: ye
shall not cover *your* lips, nor eat the
bread of men.
23 And your tires *shall be* upon your
heads, and your shoes upon your feet:
ye shall not mourn nor weep; but ye
shall pine away for your iniquities, and
mourn one toward another.
24 Thus E-zē'ki-el is unto you a sign:
according to all that he hath done shall
ye do: and when this cometh, ye shall
know that I *am* the Lord GOD.
25 Also, thou son of man, *shall it* not
be in the day when I take from them
their strength, the joy of their glory, the
desire of their eyes, and that whereupon
they set their minds, their sons and
their daughters,
26 *That* he that escapeth in that day
shall come unto thee, to cause *thee* to
hear *it* with *thine* ears?
27 In that day shall thy mouth be
opened to him which is escaped, and
thou shalt speak, and be no more
dumb: and thou shalt be a sign unto
them; and they shall know that I *am* the
LORD.

CHAPTER 25

THE word of the LORD came again unto
me, saying,
2 Son of man, set thy face against the
Ammonites, and prophesy against
them;
3 And say unto the Ammonites, Hear
the word of the Lord GOD; Thus saith
the Lord GOD; Because thou saidst,
Aha, against my sanctuary, when it
was profaned; and against the land of
Israel, when it was desolate; and
against the house of Jū'dah, when they
went into captivity;
4 Behold, therefore I will deliver thee
to the men of the east for a possession,
and they shall set their palaces in thee,
and make their dwellings in thee: they
shall eat thy fruit, and they shall drink
thy milk.
5 And I will make Răb'bah a stable
for camels, and the Ammonites a
couching place for flocks: and ye shall
know that I *am* the LORD.
6 For thus saith the Lord GOD; Be-
cause thou hast clapped *thine* hands,
and stamped with the feet, and rejoiced
in heart with all thy despite against the
land of Israel;
7 Behold, therefore I will stretch out
mine hand upon thee, and will deliver
thee for a spoil to the heathen; and I
will cut thee off from the people, and I
will cause thee to perish out of the
countries: I will destroy thee; and thou
shalt know that I *am* the LORD.
8 ¶Thus saith the Lord GOD; Because
that Moab and Sēir do say, Behold, the
house of Jū'dah *is* like unto all the
heathen;
9 Therefore, behold, I will open the
side of Moab from the cities, from his
cities *which are* on his frontiers, the
glory of the country, Bĕth-jĕsh'i-mŏth,
Bā'al-mē'ŏn, and Kĭr-ĭ-a-thā'im,

10 Unto the men of the east with the Ammonites, and will give them in possession, that the Ammonites may not be remembered among the nations.
11 And I will execute judgments upon Moab; and they shall know that I *am* the LORD.
12 ¶Thus saith the Lord GOD; Because that Edom hath dealt against the house of Jū'dah by taking vengeance, and hath greatly offended, and revenged himself upon them;
13 Therefore thus saith the Lord GOD; I will also stretch out mine hand upon Edom, and will cut off man and beast from it; and I will make it desolate from Tē'man; and they of Dē'dan shall fall by the sword.
14 And I will lay my vengeance upon Edom by the hand of my people Israel: and they shall do in Edom according to mine anger and according to my fury; and they shall know my vengeance, saith the Lord GOD.
15 ¶Thus saith the Lord GOD; Because the Philistines have dealt by revenge, and have taken vengeance with a despiteful heart, to destroy *it* for the old hatred;
16 Therefore thus saith the Lord GOD; Behold, I will stretch out mine hand upon the Philistines, and I will cut off the Chĕr'e-thĭms and destroy the remnant of the sea coast.
17 And I will execute great vengeance upon them with furious rebukes; and they shall know that I *am* the LORD, when I shall lay my vengeance upon them.

CHAPTER 26

AND it came to pass in the eleventh year, in the first *day* of the month, *that* the word of the LORD came unto me, saying,
2 Son of man, because that Tyrus hath said against Jerusalem, Aha, she is broken *that was* the gates of the people: she is turned unto me: I shall be replenished, *now* she is laid waste:
3 Therefore thus saith the Lord GOD; Behold, I *am* against thee, O Tyrus, and will cause many nations to come up against thee, as the sea causeth his waves to come up.
4 And they shall destroy the walls of Tyrus, and break down her towers: I will also scrape her dust from her, and make her like the top of a rock.
5 It shall be *a place for* the spreading of nets in the midst of the sea: for I have spoken *it*, saith the Lord GOD: and it shall become a spoil to the nations.
6 And her daughters which *are* in the field shall be slain by the sword; and they shall know that I *am* the LORD.
7 ¶For thus saith the Lord GOD; Behold, I will bring upon Tyrus Nĕb-u-chad-rĕz'zar king of Babylon, a king of kings, from the north, with horses, and with chariots, and with horsemen and companies, and much people.
8 He shall slay with the sword thy daughters in the field: and he shall make a fort against thee, and cast a mount against thee, and lift up the buckler against thee.
9 And he shall set engines of war against thy walls, and with his axes he shall break down thy towers.
10 By reason of the abundance of his horses their dust shall cover thee: thy walls shall shake at the noise of the horsemen, and of the wheels, and of the chariots, when he shall enter into thy gates, as men enter into a city wherein is made a breach.
11 With the hoofs of his horses shall he tread down all thy streets: he shall slay thy people by the sword, and thy strong garrisons shall go down to the ground.
12 And they shall make a spoil of thy riches, and make a prey of thy merchandise: and they shall break down thy walls, and destroy thy pleasant houses: and they shall lay thy stones and thy timber and thy dust in the midst of the water.
13 And I will cause the noise of thy songs to cease; and the sound of thy harps shall be no more heard.
14 And I will make thee like the top of a rock: thou shalt be *a place* to spread nets upon; thou shalt be built no more: for I the LORD have spoken *it*, saith the Lord GOD.
15 ¶Thus saith the Lord GOD to Tyrus; Shall not the isles shake at the sound of thy fall, when the wounded cry, when the slaughter is made in the midst of thee?
16 Then all the princes of the sea shall come down from their thrones, and lay away their robes, and put off their broidered garments: they shall clothe themselves with trembling; they shall sit upon the ground, and shall tremble at *every* moment, and be astonished at thee.
17 And they shall take up a lamentation for thee, and say to thee, How art thou destroyed, *that wast* inhabited of seafaring men, the renowned city, which wast strong in the sea, she and her inhabitants, which cause their terror *to be* on all that haunt it!
18 Now shall the isles tremble in the day of thy fall; yea, the isles that *are* in

the sea shall be troubled at thy departure.

19 For thus saith the Lord GOD; When I shall make thee a desolate city, like the cities that are not inhabited; when I shall bring up the deep upon thee, and great waters shall cover thee;

20 When I shall bring thee down with them that descend into the pit, with the people of old time, and shall set thee in the low parts of the earth, in places desolate of old, with them that go down to the pit, that thou be not inhabited; and I shall set glory in the land of the living;

21 I will make thee a terror, and thou *shalt be* no *more:* though thou be sought for, yet shalt thou never be found again, saith the Lord GOD.

CHAPTER 27

THE word of the LORD came again unto me, saying,

2 Now, thou son of man, take up a lamentation for Tyrus;

3 And say unto Tyrus, O thou that art situate at the entry of the sea, *which art* a merchant of the people for many isles, Thus saith the Lord GOD; O Tyrus, thou hast said, I *am* of perfect beauty.

4 Thy borders *are* in the midst of the seas, thy builders have perfected thy beauty.

5 They have made all thy *ship* boards of fir trees of Sē'nir: they have taken cedars from Lebanon to make masts for thee.

6 *Of* the oaks of Bā'shan have they made thine oars; the company of the Āshurītes have made thy benches *of* ivory, *brought* out of the isles of Chĭt'tĭm.

7 Fine linen with broidered work from Egypt was that which thou spreadest forth to be thy sail; blue and purple from the isles of E-lī'shah was that which covered thee.

8 The inhabitants of Zī'don and Är'väd were thy mariners: thy wise *men,* O Tyrus, *that* were in thee, were thy pilots.

9 The ancients of Gē'bal and the wise *men* thereof were in thee thy calkers: and all the ships of the sea with their mariners were in thee to occupy thy merchandise.

10 They of Persia and of Lud and of Phut were in thine army, thy men of war: they hanged the shield and helmet in thee; they set forth thy comeliness.

11 The men of Är'väd with thine army *were* upon thy walls round about, and the Găm'ma-dĭms were in thy towers: they hanged their shields upon thy walls round about; they have made thy beauty perfect.

12 Tär'shĭsh *was* thy merchant by reason of the multitude of all *kind of* riches; with silver, iron, tin, and lead, they traded in thy fairs.

13 Jā'van, Tū'bal, and Mē'shĕch, they *were* thy merchants: they traded the persons of men and vessels of brass in thy market.

14 They of the house of Tō-gär'mah traded in thy fairs with horses and horsemen and mules.

15 The men of Dē'dan *were* thy merchants; many isles *were* the merchandise of thine hand: they brought thee *for* a present horns of ivory and ebony.

16 Syria *was* thy merchant by reason of the multitude of the wares of thy making: they occupied in thy fairs with emeralds, purple, and broidered work, and fine linen, and coral, and agate.

17 Jū'dah, and the land of Israel, they *were* thy merchants: they traded in thy market wheat of Mĭn'nĭth, and Păn'năg, and honey, and oil, and balm.

18 Damascus *was* thy merchant in the multitude of the wares of thy making, for the multitude of all riches; in the wine of Hĕl'bŏn, and white wool.

19 Dan also and Jā'van going to and fro occupied in thy fairs: bright iron, cassia, and calamus, were in thy market.

20 Dē'dan *was* thy merchant in precious clothes for chariots.

21 Arabia, and all the princes of Kē'dar, they occupied with thee in lambs, and rams, and goats: in these *were they* thy merchants.

22 The merchants of Shē'ba and Rā'a-mah, they *were* thy merchants: they occupied in thy fairs with chief of all spices, and with all precious stones, and gold.

23 Hâ'ran, and Căn'neh, and Eden, the merchants of Shē'ba, Asshur, *and* Chĭl'măd, *were* thy merchants.

24 These *were* thy merchants in all sorts *of things,* in blue clothes, and broidered work, and in chests of rich apparel, bound with cords, and made of cedar, among thy merchandise.

25 The ships of Tär'shĭsh did sing of thee in thy market: and thou wast replenished, and made very glorious in the midst of the seas.

26 ¶Thy rowers have brought thee into great waters: the east wind hath broken thee in the midst of the seas.

27 Thy riches, and thy fairs, thy merchandise, thy mariners, and thy pilots, thy calkers, and the occupiers of thy merchandise, and all thy men of war, that *are* in thee, and in all thy company which *is* in the midst of thee, shall

fall into the midst of the seas in the day of thy ruin.

28 The suburbs shall shake at the sound of the cry of thy pilots.

29 And all that handle the oar, the mariners, *and* all the pilots of the sea, shall come down from their ships, they shall stand upon the land;

30 And shall cause their voice to be heard against thee, and shall cry bitterly, and shall cast up dust upon their heads, they shall wallow themselves in the ashes:

31 And they shall make themselves utterly bald for thee, and gird them with sackcloth, and they shall weep for thee with bitterness of heart *and* bitter wailing.

32 And in their wailing they shall take up a lamentation for thee, and lament over thee, *saying*, What *city is* like Tyrus, like the destroyed in the midst of the sea?

33 When thy wares went forth out of the seas, thou filledst many people; thou didst enrich the kings of the earth with the multitude of thy riches and of thy merchandise.

34 In the time *when* thou shalt be broken by the seas in the depths of the waters thy merchandise and all thy company in the midst of thee shall fall.

35 All the inhabitants of the isles shall be astonished at thee, and their kings shall be sore afraid, they shall be troubled in *their* countenance.

36 The merchants among the people shall hiss at thee; thou shalt be a terror, and never *shalt be* any more.

CHAPTER 28

THE word of the LORD came again unto me, saying,

2 Son of man, say unto the prince of Tyrus, Thus saith the Lord GOD; Because thine heart *is* lifted up, and thou hast said, I *am* a God, I sit *in* the seat of God, in the midst of the seas; yet thou *art* a man, and not God, though thou set thine heart as the heart of God:

3 Behold, thou *art* wiser than Daniel; there is no secret that they can hide from thee:

4 With thy wisdom and with thine understanding thou hast gotten thee riches, and hast gotten gold and silver into thy treasures:

5 By thy great wisdom *and* by thy traffick hast thou increased thy riches, and thine heart is lifted up because of thy riches:

6 Therefore thus saith the Lord GOD; Because thou hast set thine heart as the heart of God;

7 Behold, therefore I will bring strangers upon thee, the terrible of the nations: and they shall draw their swords against the beauty of thy wisdom, and they shall defile thy brightness.

8 They shall bring thee down to the pit, and thou shalt die the deaths of *them that are* slain in the midst of the seas.

9 Wilt thou yet say before him that slayeth thee, I *am* God? but thou *shalt be* a man, and no God, in the hand of him that slayeth thee.

10 Thou shalt die the deaths of the uncircumcised by the hand of strangers: for I have spoken *it*, saith the Lord GOD.

11 ¶Moreover the word of the LORD came unto me, saying,

12 Son of man, take up a lamentation upon the king of Tyrus, and say unto him, Thus saith the Lord GOD; Thou sealest up the sum, full of wisdom, and perfect in beauty.

13 Thou hast been in Eden the garden of God; every precious stone *was* thy covering, the sardius, topaz, and the diamond, the beryl, the onyx, and the jasper, the sapphire, the emerald, and the carbuncle, and gold: the workmanship of thy tabrets and of thy pipes was prepared in thee in the day that thou wast created.

14 Thou *art* the anointed cherub that covereth; and I have set thee *so*: thou wast upon the holy mountain of God; thou hast walked up and down in the midst of the stones of fire.

15 Thou *wast* perfect in thy ways from the day that thou wast created, till iniquity was found in thee.

16 By the multitude of thy merchandise they have filled the midst of thee with violence, and thou hast sinned: therefore I will cast thee as profane out of the mountain of God: and I will destroy thee, O covering cherub, from the midst of the stones of fire.

17 Thine heart was lifted up because of thy beauty, thou hast corrupted thy wisdom by reason of thy brightness: I will cast thee to the ground, I will lay thee before kings, that they may behold thee.

18 Thou hast defiled thy sanctuaries by the multitude of thine iniquities, by the iniquity of thy traffick; therefore will I bring forth a fire from the midst of thee, it shall devour thee, and I will bring thee to ashes upon the earth in the sight of all them that behold thee.

19 All they that know thee among the people shall be astonished at thee: thou shalt be a terror, and never *shalt* thou *be* any more.

20 ¶Again the word of the LORD came
unto me, saying,
21 Son of man, set thy face against
Zī′don, and prophesy against it,
22 And say, Thus saith the Lord GOD:
Behold, I *am* against thee, O Zī′don;
and I will be glorified in the midst of
thee: and they shall know that I *am* the
LORD, when I shall have executed judgments in her, and shall be sanctified in
her.
23 For I will send into her pestilence,
and blood into her streets; and the
wounded shall be judged in the midst
of her by the sword upon her on every
side; and they shall know that I *am* the
LORD.
24 ¶And there shall be no more a
pricking brier unto the house of Israel,
nor *any* grieving thorn of all *that are*
round about them, that despised them;
and they shall know that I *am* the Lord
GOD.
25 Thus saith the Lord GOD; When I
shall have gathered the house of Israel
from the people among whom they are
scattered, and shall be sanctified in
them in the sight of the heathen, then
shall they dwell in their land that I have
given to my servant Jacob.
26 And they shall dwell safely therein, and shall build houses, and plant
vineyards; yea, they shall dwell with
confidence, when I have executed
judgments upon all those that despise
them round about them; and they shall
know that I *am* the LORD their God.

CHAPTER 29

IN the tenth year, in the tenth *month*, in
the twelfth *day* of the month, the word
of the LORD came unto me, saying,
2 Son of man, set thy face against
Pharaoh king of Egypt, and prophesy
against him, and against all Egypt:
3 Speak, and say, Thus saith the Lord
GOD; Behold, I *am* against thee,
Pharaoh king of Egypt, the great dragon that lieth in the midst of his rivers,
which hath said, My river *is* mine own,
and I have made *it* for myself.
4 But I will put hooks in thy jaws, and
I will cause the fish of thy rivers to stick
unto thy scales, and I will bring thee up
out of the midst of thy rivers, and all the
fish of thy rivers shall stick unto thy
scales.
5 And I will leave thee *thrown* into
the wilderness, thee and all the fish of
thy rivers: thou shalt fall upon the open
fields; thou shalt not be brought together, nor gathered: I have given thee for
meat to the beasts of the field and to the
fowls of the heaven.
6 And all the inhabitants of Egypt
shall know that I *am* the LORD, because
they have been a staff of reed to the
house of Israel.
7 When they took hold of thee by thy
hand, thou didst break, and rend all
their shoulder: and when they leaned
upon thee, thou brakest, and madest all
their loins to be at a stand.
8 ¶Therefore thus saith the Lord GOD;
Behold, I will bring a sword upon thee,
and cut off man and beast out of thee.
9 And the land of Egypt shall be desolate and waste; and they shall know
that I *am* the LORD: because he hath
said, The river *is* mine, and I have made
it.
10 Behold, therefore I *am* against
thee, and against thy rivers, and I will
make the land of Egypt utterly waste
and desolate, from the tower of Sȳ-ē′ne
even unto the border of Ē-thĭ-ō′pĭ-a.
11 No foot of man shall pass through
it, nor foot of beast shall pass through
it, neither shall it be inhabited forty
years.
12 And I will make the land of Egypt
desolate in the midst of the countries
that are desolate, and her cities among
the cities *that are* laid waste shall be
desolate forty years: and I will scatter
the Egyptians among the nations, and
will disperse them through the countries.
13 ¶Yet thus saith the Lord GOD; At
the end of forty years will I gather the
Egyptians from the people whither
they were scattered:
14 And I will bring again the captivity
of Egypt, and will cause them to return
into the land of Păth′rŏs, into the land
of their habitation; and they shall be
there a base kingdom.
15 It shall be the basest of the kingdoms; neither shall it exalt itself any
more above the nations: for I will diminish them, that they shall no more rule
over the nations.
16 And it shall be no more the confidence of the house of Israel, which
bringeth *their* iniquity to remembrance, when they shall look after
them: but they shall know that I *am* the
Lord GOD.
17 ¶And it came to pass in the seven
and twentieth year, in the first *month*,
in the first *day* of the month, the word
of the LORD came unto me, saying,
18 Son of man, Nĕb-u-chad-rĕz′zar
king of Babylon caused his army to
serve a great service against Tyrus:
every head *was* made bald, and every
shoulder *was* peeled: yet had he no
wages, nor his army, for Tyrus, for the
service that he had served against it:
19 Therefore thus saith the Lord GOD;
Behold, I will give the land of Egypt

unto Nĕb-u-chad-rĕz'zar king of Babylon; and he shall take her multitude, and take her spoil, and take her prey; and it shall be the wages for his army.

20 I have given him the land of Egypt *for* his labour wherewith he served against it, because they wrought for me, saith the Lord GOD.

21 In that day will I cause the horn of the house of Israel to bud forth, and I will give thee the opening of the mouth in the midst of them; and they shall know that I *am* the LORD.

CHAPTER 30

THE word of the LORD came again unto me, saying,

2 Son of man, prophesy and say, Thus saith the Lord GOD; Howl ye, Woe worth the day!

3 For the day *is* near, even the day of the LORD *is* near, a cloudy day; it shall be the time of the heathen.

4 And the sword shall come upon Egypt, and great pain shall be in Ē-thĭ-ō'pĭ-a, when the slain shall fall in Egypt, and they shall take away her multitude, and her foundations shall be broken down.

5 Ē-thĭ-ō'pĭ-a, and Libya, and Lydia, and all the mingled people, and Chub, and the men of the land that is in league, shall fall with them by the sword.

6 Thus saith the LORD; They also that uphold Egypt shall fall; and the pride of her power shall come down: from the tower of Sȳ-ē'ne shall they fall in it by the sword, saith the Lord GOD.

7 And they shall be desolate in the midst of the countries *that are* desolate, and her cities shall be in the midst of the cities *that are* wasted.

8 And they shall know that I *am* the LORD, when I have set a fire in Egypt, and *when* all her helpers shall be destroyed.

9 In that day shall messengers go forth from me in ships to make the careless Ē-thĭ-ō'pĭ-ans afraid, and great pain shall come upon them, as in the day of Egypt: for, lo, it cometh.

10 Thus saith the Lord GOD; I will also make the multitude of Egypt to cease by the hand of Nĕb-u-chad-rĕz'zar king of Babylon.

11 He and his people with him, the terrible of the nations, shall be brought to destroy the land: and they shall draw their swords against Egypt, and fill the land with the slain.

12 And I will make the rivers dry, and sell the land into the hand of the wicked: and I will make the land waste, and all that is therein, by the hand of strangers: I the LORD have spoken *it*.

13 Thus saith the Lord GOD; I will also destroy the idols, and I will cause *their* images to cease out of Noph; and there shall be no more a prince of the land of Egypt: and I will put a fear in the land of Egypt.

14 And I will make Păth'rŏs desolate, and will set fire in Zō'an, and will execute judgments in No.

15 And I will pour my fury upon Sin, the strength of Egypt; and I will cut off the multitude of No.

16 And I will set fire in Egypt: Sin shall have great pain, and No shall be rent asunder, and Noph *shall have* distresses daily.

17 The young men of Ā'ven and of Pī-bē'ṡeth shall fall by the sword: and these *cities* shall go into captivity.

18 At Te-hăph'ne-hĕs also the day shall be darkened, when I shall break there the yokes of Egypt: and the pomp of her strength shall cease in her: as for her, a cloud shall cover her, and her daughters shall go into captivity.

19 Thus will I execute judgments in Egypt: and they shall know that I *am* the LORD.

20 ¶And it came to pass in the eleventh year, in the first *month*, in the seventh *day* of the month, *that* the word of the LORD came unto me, saying,

21 Son of man, I have broken the arm of Pharaoh king of Egypt; and, lo, it shall not be bound up to be healed, to put a roller to bind it, to make it strong to hold the sword.

22 Therefore thus saith the Lord GOD; Behold, I *am* against Pharaoh king of Egypt, and will break his arms, the strong, and that which was broken; and I will cause the sword to fall out of his hand.

23 And I will scatter the Egyptians among the nations, and will disperse them through the countries.

24 And I will strengthen the arms of the king of Babylon, and put my sword in his hand: but I will break Pharaoh's arms, and he shall groan before him with the groanings of a deadly wounded *man*.

25 But I will strengthen the arms of the king of Babylon, and the arms of Pharaoh shall fall down; and they shall know that I *am* the LORD, when I shall put my sword into the hand of the king of Babylon, and he shall stretch it out upon the land of Egypt.

26 And I will scatter the Egyptians among the nations, and disperse them

among the countries; and they shall know that I *am* the LORD.

CHAPTER 31

AND it came to pass in the eleventh year, in the third *month*, in the first *day* of the month, *that* the word of the LORD came unto me, saying,

2 Son of man, speak unto Pharaoh king of Egypt, and to his multitude; Whom art thou like in thy greatness?

3 Behold, the Assyrian *was* a cedar in Lebanon with fair branches, and with a shadowing shroud, and of an high stature; and his top was among the thick boughs.

4 The waters made him great, the deep set him up on high with her rivers running round about his plants, and sent out her little rivers unto all the trees of the field.

5 Therefore his height was exalted above all the trees of the field, and his boughs were multiplied, and his branches became long because of the multitude of waters, when he shot forth.

6 All the fowls of heaven made their nests in his boughs, and under his branches did all the beasts of the field bring forth their young, and under his shadow dwelt all great nations.

7 Thus was he fair in his greatness, in the length of his branches: for his root was by great waters.

8 The cedars in the garden of God could not hide him: the fir trees were not like his boughs, and the chesnut trees were not like his branches; nor any tree in the garden of God was like unto him in his beauty.

9 I have made him fair by the multitude of his branches: so that all the trees of Eden, that *were* in the garden of God, envied him.

10 ¶Therefore thus saith the Lord GOD; Because thou hast lifted up thyself in height, and he hath shot up his top among the thick boughs, and his heart is lifted up in his height;

11 I have therefore delivered him into the hand of the mighty one of the heathen; he shall surely deal with him: I have driven him out for his wickedness.

12 And strangers, the terrible of the nations, have cut him off, and have left him: upon the mountains and in all the valleys his branches are fallen, and his boughs are broken by all the rivers of the land; and all the people of the earth are gone down from his shadow, and have left him.

13 Upon his ruin shall all the fowls of the heaven remain, and all the beasts of the field shall be upon his branches:

14 To the end that none of all the trees by the waters exalt themselves for their height, neither shoot up their top among the thick boughs, neither their trees stand up in their height, all that drink water: for they are all delivered unto death, to the nether parts of the earth, in the midst of the children of men, with them that go down to the pit.

15 Thus saith the Lord GOD; In the day when he went down to the grave I caused a mourning: I covered the deep for him, and I restrained the floods thereof, and the great waters were stayed: and I caused Lebanon to mourn for him, and all the trees of the field fainted for him.

16 I made the nations to shake at the sound of his fall, when I cast him down to hell with them that descend into the pit: and all the trees of Eden, the choice and best of Lebanon, all that drink water, shall be comforted in the nether parts of the earth.

17 They also went down into hell with him unto *them that be* slain with the sword; and *they that were* his arm, *that* dwelt under his shadow in the midst of the heathen.

18 ¶To whom art thou thus like in glory and in greatness among the trees of Eden? yet shalt thou be brought down with the trees of Eden unto the nether parts of the earth: thou shalt lie in the midst of the uncircumcised with *them that be* slain by the sword. This *is* Pharaoh and all his multitude, saith the Lord GOD.

CHAPTER 32

AND it came to pass in the twelfth year, in the twelfth month, in the first *day* of the month, *that* the word of the LORD came unto me, saying,

2 Son of man, take up a lamentation for Pharaoh king of Egypt, and say unto him, Thou art like a young lion of the nations, and thou *art* as a whale in the seas: and thou camest forth with thy rivers, and troubledst the waters with thy feet, and fouledst their rivers.

3 Thus saith the Lord GOD; I will therefore spread out my net over thee with a company of many people; and they shall bring thee up in my net.

4 Then will I leave thee upon the land, I will cast thee forth upon the open field, and will cause all the fowls of the heaven to remain upon thee, and I will fill the beasts of the whole earth with thee.

5 And I will lay thy flesh upon the

mountains, and fill the valleys with thy
height.
6 I will also water with thy blood the
land wherein thou swimmest, *even* to
the mountains; and the rivers shall be
full of thee.
7 And when I shall put thee out, I will
cover the heaven, and make the stars
thereof dark; I will cover the sun with a
cloud, and the moon shall not give her
light.
8 All the bright lights of heaven will I
make dark over thee, and set darkness
upon thy land, saith the Lord God.
9 I will also vex the hearts of many
people, when I shall bring thy destruc-
tion among the nations, into the coun-
tries which thou hast not known.
10 Yea, I will make many people
amazed at thee, and their kings shall be
horribly afraid for thee, when I shall
brandish my sword before them; and
they shall tremble at *every* moment,
every man for his own life, in the day of
thy fall.
11 ¶For thus saith the Lord God; The
sword of the king of Babylon shall
come upon thee.
12 By the swords of the mighty will I
cause thy multitude to fall, the terrible
of the nations, all of them: and they
shall spoil the pomp of Egypt, and all
the multitude thereof shall be de-
stroyed.
13 I will destroy also all the beasts
thereof from beside the great waters;
neither shall the foot of man trouble
them any more, nor the hoofs of beasts
trouble them.
14 Then will I make their waters
deep, and cause their rivers to run like
oil, saith the Lord God.
15 When I shall make the land of
Egypt desolate, and the country shall
be destitute of that whereof it was full,
when I shall smite all them that dwell
therein, then shall they know that I *am*
the Lord.
16 This *is* the lamentation wherewith
they shall lament her: the daughters of
the nations shall lament her: they shall
lament for her, *even* for Egypt, and for
all her multitude, saith the Lord God.
17 ¶It came to pass also in the twelfth
year, in the fifteenth *day* of the month,
that the word of the Lord came unto
me, saying,
18 Son of man, wail for the multitude
of Egypt, and cast them down, *even*
her, and the daughters of the famous
nations, unto the nether parts of the
earth, with them that go down into the
pit.
19 Whom dost thou pass in beauty?
go down, and be thou laid with the un-
circumcised.
20 They shall fall in the midst of *them*
that are slain by the sword: she is deliv-
ered to the sword: draw her and all her
multitudes.
21 The strong among the mighty
shall speak to him out of the midst of
hell with them that help him: they are
gone down, they lie uncircumcised,
slain by the sword.
22 Asshur *is* there and all her com-
pany: his graves *are* about him: all of
them slain, fallen by the sword:
23 Whose graves are set in the sides
of the pit, and her company is round
about her grave: all of them slain, fallen
by the sword, which caused terror in
the land of the living.
24 There *is* Ē'lam and all her multi-
tude round about her grave, all of them
slain, fallen by the sword, which are
gone down uncircumcised into the
nether parts of the earth, which caused
their terror in the land of the living; yet
have they borne their shame with them
that go down to the pit.
25 They have set her a bed in the
midst of the slain with all her multi-
tude: her graves *are* round about him:
all of them uncircumcised, slain by the
sword: though their terror was caused
in the land of the living, yet have they
borne their shame with them that go
down to the pit: he is put in the midst of
them that be slain.
26 There *is* Mē'shĕch, Tū'bal, and all
her multitude: her graves *are* round
about him: all of them uncircumcised,
slain by the sword, though they caused
their terror in the land of the living.
27 And they shall not lie with the
mighty *that are* fallen of the uncircum-
cised, which are gone down to hell with
their weapons of war: and they have
laid their swords under their heads, but
their iniquities shall be upon their
bones, though *they were* the terror of
the mighty in the land of the living.
28 Yea, thou shalt be broken in the
midst of the uncircumcised, and shalt
lie with *them that are* slain with the
sword.
29 There *is* Edom, her kings, and all
her princes, which with their might are
laid by *them that were* slain by the
sword: they shall lie with the uncir-
cumcised, and with them that go down
to the pit.
30 There *be* the princes of the north,
all of them, and all the Zī-dō'nĭ-ans,
which are gone down with the slain;
with their terror they are ashamed of
their might; and they lie uncircumcised
with *them that be* slain by the sword,

and bear their shame with them that go
down to the pit.
31 Pharaoh shall see them, and shall
be comforted over all his multitude,
even Pharaoh and all his army slain by
the sword, saith the Lord GOD.
32 For I have caused my terror in the
land of the living: and he shall be laid in
the midst of the uncircumcised with
them that are slain with the sword,
even Pharaoh and all his multitude,
saith the Lord GOD.

CHAPTER 33

AGAIN the word of the LORD came
unto me, saying,
2 Son of man, speak to the children of
thy people, and say unto them, When I
bring the sword upon a land, if the
people of the land take a man of their
coasts, and set him for their watchman:
3 If when he seeth the sword come
upon the land, he blow the trumpet,
and warn the people;
4 Then whosoever heareth the sound
of the trumpet, and taketh not warning;
if the sword come, and take him away,
his blood shall be upon his own head.
5 He heard the sound of the trumpet,
and took not warning; his blood shall
be upon him. But he that taketh warn-
ing shall deliver his soul.
6 But if the watchman see the sword
come, and blow not the trumpet, and
the people be not warned; if the sword
come, and take *any* person from among
them, he is taken away in his iniquity;
but his blood will I require at the
watchman's hand.
7 So thou, O son of man, I have set
thee a watchman unto the house of
Israel; therefore thou shalt hear the
word at my mouth, and warn them
from me.
8 When I say unto the wicked, O
wicked *man*, thou shalt surely die; if
thou dost not speak to warn the wicked
from his way, that wicked *man* shall
die in his iniquity; but his blood will I
require at thine hand.
9 Nevertheless, if thou warn the
wicked of his way to turn from it; if he
do not turn from his way, he shall die in
his iniquity; but thou hast delivered thy
soul.
10 Therefore O thou son of man,
speak unto the house of Israel; Thus ye
speak, saying, If our transgressions
and our sins *be* upon us, and we pine
away in them, how should we then live?
11 Say unto them, *As* I live, saith the
Lord GOD, I have no pleasure in the
death of the wicked; but that the
wicked turn from his way and live: turn
ye, turn ye from your evil ways; for
why will ye die, O house of Israel?
12 Therefore, thou son of man, say
unto the children of thy people, The
righteousness of the righteous shall not
deliver him in the day of his transgres-
sion: as for the wickedness of the
wicked, he shall not fall thereby in the
day that he turneth from his wicked-
ness; neither shall the righteous be able
to live for his *righteousness* in the day
that he sinneth.
13 When I shall say to the righteous,
that he shall surely live; if he trust to his
own righteousness, and commit iniq-
uity, all his righteousnesses shall not be
remembered; but for his iniquity that
he hath committed, he shall die for it.
14 Again, when I say unto the
wicked, Thou shalt surely die; if he turn
from his sin, and do that which is law-
ful and right;
15 *If* the wicked restore the pledge,
give again that he had robbed, walk in
the statutes of life, without committing
iniquity; he shall surely live, he shall
not die.
16 None of his sins that he hath com-
mitted shall be mentioned unto him: he
hath done that which is lawful and
right; he shall surely live.
17 ¶Yet the children of thy people
say, The way of the Lord is not equal:
but as for them, their way is not equal.
18 When the righteous turneth from
his righteousness, and committeth iniq-
uity, he shall even die thereby.
19 But if the wicked turn from his
wickedness, and do that which is law-
ful and right, he shall live thereby.
20 Yet ye say, The way of the Lord is
not equal. O ye house of Israel, I will
judge you every one after his ways.
21 ¶And it came to pass in the twelfth
year of our captivity, in the tenth
month, in the fifth *day* of the month,
that one that had escaped out of Jeru-
salem came unto me, saying, The city is
smitten.
22 Now the hand of the LORD was
upon me in the evening, afore he that
was escaped came; and had opened my
mouth, until he came to me in the morn-
ing; and my mouth was opened, and I
was no more dumb.
23 Then the word of the LORD came
unto me, saying,
24 Son of man, they that inhabit
those wastes of the land of Israel speak,
saying, Abraham was one, and he in-
herited the land: but we *are* many; the
land is given us for inheritance.
25 Wherefore say unto them, Thus
saith the Lord GOD; Ye eat with the
blood, and lift up your eyes toward

your idols, and shed blood: and shall ye
possess the land?
26 Ye stand upon your sword, ye
work abomination, and ye defile every
one his neighbour's wife: and shall ye
possess the land?
27 Say thou thus unto them, Thus
saith the Lord GOD; *As* I live, surely
they that *are* in the wastes shall fall by
the sword, and him that *is* in the open
field will I give to the beasts to be de-
voured, and they that *be* in the forts
and in the caves shall die of the pesti-
lence.
28 For I will lay the land most deso-
late, and the pomp of her strength shall
cease; and the mountains of Israel shall
be desolate, that none shall pass
through.
29 Then shall they know that I *am* the
LORD, when I have laid the land most
desolate because of all their abomina-
tions which they have committed.
30 ¶Also, thou son of man, the chil-
dren of thy people still are talking
against thee by the walls and in the
doors of the houses, and speak one to
another, every one to his brother,
saying, Come, I pray you, and hear
what is the word that cometh forth
from the LORD.
31 And they come unto thee as the
people cometh, and they sit before thee
as my people, and they hear thy words,
but they will not do them: for with their
mouth they shew much love, *but* their
heart goeth after their covetousness.
32 And, lo, thou *art* unto them as a
very lovely song of one that hath a pleas-
ant voice, and can play well on an in-
strument: for they hear thy words, but
they do them not.
33 And when this cometh to pass, (lo,
it will come,) then shall they know that
a prophet hath been among them.

CHAPTER 34

AND the word of the LORD came unto
me, saying,
2 Son of man, prophesy against the
shepherds of Israel, prophesy, and say
unto them, Thus saith the Lord GOD
unto the shepherds; Woe *be* to the
shepherds of Israel that do feed them-
selves! should not the shepherds feed
the flocks?
3 Ye eat the fat, and ye clothe you
with the wool, ye kill them that are fed:
but ye feed not the flock.
4 The diseased have ye not
strengthened, neither have ye healed
that which was sick, neither have ye
bound up *that which was* broken,
neither have ye brought again that
which was driven away, neither have
ye sought that which was lost; but with
force and with cruelty have ye ruled
them.
5 And they were scattered, because
there is no shepherd: and they became
meat to all the beasts of the field, when
they were scattered.
6 My sheep wandered through all the
mountains, and upon every high hill:
yea, my flock was scattered upon all
the face of the earth, and none did
search or seek *after them*.
7 ¶Therefore, ye shepherds, hear the
word of the LORD;
8 *As* I live, saith the Lord GOD, surely
because my flock became a prey, and
my flock became meat to every beast
of the field, because *there was* no
shepherd, neither did my shepherds
search for my flock, but the shepherds
fed themselves, and fed not my flock;
9 Therefore, O ye shepherds, hear the
word of the LORD;
10 Thus saith the Lord GOD; Behold, I
am against the shepherds; and I will re-
quire my flock at their hand, and cause
them to cease from feeding the flock;
neither shall the shepherds feed them-
selves any more; for I will deliver my
flock from their mouth, that they may
not be meat for them.
11 ¶For thus saith the Lord GOD; Be-
hold, I, *even* I, will both search my
sheep, and seek them out.
12 As a shepherd seeketh out his
flock in the day that he is among his
sheep *that are* scattered; so will I seek
out my sheep, and will deliver them out
of all places where they have been scat-
tered in the cloudy and dark day.
13 And I will bring them out from the
people, and gather them from the
countries, and will bring them to their
own land, and feed them upon the
mountains of Israel by the rivers, and in
all the inhabited places of the country.
14 I will feed them in a good pasture,
and upon the high mountains of Israel
shall their fold be: there shall they lie in
a good fold, and *in* a fat pasture shall
they feed upon the mountains of Israel.
15 I will feed my flock, and I will
cause them to lie down, saith the Lord
GOD.
16 I will seek that which was lost, and
bring again that which was driven
away, and will bind up *that which was*
broken, and will strengthen that which
was sick: but I will destroy the fat and
the strong; I will feed them with judg-
ment.
17 And *as for* you, O my flock, thus
saith the Lord GOD; Behold, I judge be-

tween cattle and cattle, between the
rams and the he goats.
18 *Seemeth it* a small thing unto you
to have eaten up the good pasture, but
ye must tread down with your feet the
residue of your pastures? and to have
drunk of the deep waters, but ye must
foul the residue with your feet?
19 And *as for* my flock, they eat that
which ye have trodden with your feet;
and they drink that which ye have
fouled with your feet.
20 ¶Therefore thus saith the Lord
God unto them; Behold, I, *even* I, will
judge between the fat cattle and be-
tween the lean cattle.
21 Because ye have thrust with side
and with shoulder, and pushed all the
diseased with your horns, till ye have
scattered them abroad;
22 Therefore will I save my flock, and
they shall no more be a prey; and I will
judge between cattle and cattle.
23 And I will set up one shepherd
over them, and he shall feed them, *even*
my servant David; he shall feed them,
and he shall be their shepherd.
24 And I the Lord will be their God,
and my servant David a prince among
them; I the Lord have spoken *it*.
25 And I will make with them a cov-
enant of peace, and will cause the evil
beasts to cease out of the land: and they
shall dwell safely in the wilderness, and
sleep in the woods.
26 And I will make them and the
places round about my hill a blessing;
and I will cause the shower to come
down in his season; there shall be
showers of blessing.
27 And the tree of the field shall yield
her fruit, and the earth shall yield her
increase, and they shall be safe in their
land, and shall know that I *am* the
Lord, when I have broken the bands of
their yoke, and delivered them out of
the hand of those that served them-
selves of them.
28 And they shall no more be a prey
to the heathen, neither shall the beast
of the land devour them; but they shall
dwell safely, and none shall make *them*
afraid.
29 And I will raise up for them a plant
of renown, and they shall be no more
consumed with hunger in the land,
neither bear the shame of the heathen
any more.
30 Thus shall they know that I the
Lord their God *am* with them, and *that*
they, *even* the house of Israel, *are* my
people, saith the Lord God.
31 And ye my flock, the flock of my
pasture, *are* men, *and* I *am* your God,
saith the Lord God.

CHAPTER 35

MOREOVER the word of the Lord
came unto me, saying,
2 Son of man, set thy face against
mount Sē'ir, and prophesy against it,
3 And say unto it, Thus saith the Lord
God; Behold, O mount Sē'ir, I *am*
against thee, and I will stretch out mine
hand against thee, and I will make thee
most desolate.
4 I will lay thy cities waste, and thou
shalt be desolate, and thou shalt know
that I *am* the Lord.
5 Because thou hast had a perpetual
hatred, and hast shed *the blood of* the
children of Israel by the force of the
sword in the time of their calamity, in
the time *that their* iniquity *had* an end:
6 Therefore, *as* I live, saith the Lord
God, I will prepare thee unto blood, and
blood shall pursue thee: sith thou hast
not hated blood, even blood shall
pursue thee.
7 Thus will I make mount Sē'ir most
desolate, and cut off from it him that
passeth out and him that returneth.
8 And I will fill his mountains with his
slain *men*: in thy hills, and in thy val-
leys, and in all thy rivers, shall they fall
that are slain with the sword.
9 I will make thee perpetual desola-
tions, and thy cities shall not return:
and ye shall know that I *am* the Lord.
10 Because thou hast said, These two
nations and these two countries shall
be mine, and we will possess it; where-
as the Lord was there:
11 Therefore, *as* I live, saith the Lord
God, I will even do according to thine
anger, and according to thine envy
which thou hast used out of thy hatred
against them; and I will make myself
known among them, when I have
judged thee.
12 And thou shalt know that I *am* the
Lord, *and that* I have heard all thy
blasphemies which thou hast spoken
against the mountains of Israel, saying,
They are laid desolate, they are given
us to consume.
13 Thus with your mouth ye have
boasted against me, and have mul-
tiplied your words against me: I have
heard *them*.
14 Thus saith the Lord God; When
the whole earth rejoiceth, I will make
thee desolate.
15 As thou didst rejoice at the inheri-
tance of the house of Israel, because it
was desolate, so will I do unto thee:
thou shalt be desolate, O mount Sē'ir,
and all Ĭ-dū-mē'a, *even* all of it: and
they shall know that I *am* the Lord.

CHAPTER 36

ALSO, thou son of man, prophesy unto
the mountains of Israel, and say, Ye
mountains of Israel, hear the word of
the LORD:
2 Thus saith the Lord GOD; Because
the enemy hath said against you, Aha,
even the ancient high places are ours in
possession:
3 Therefore prophesy and say, Thus
saith the Lord GOD; Because they have
made *you* desolate, and swallowed you
up on every side, that ye might be a
possession unto the residue of the
heathen, and ye are taken up in the lips
of talkers, and *are* an infamy of the
people:
4 Therefore, ye mountains of Israel,
hear the word of the Lord GOD; thus
saith the Lord GOD to the mountains,
and to the hills, to the rivers, and to the
valleys, to the desolate wastes, and to
the cities that are forsaken, which be-
came a prey and derision to the residue
of the heathen that *are* round about;
5 Therefore thus saith the Lord GOD;
Surely in the fire of my jealousy have I
spoken against the residue of the
heathen, and against all Ī-dū-mē′a,
which have appointed my land into
their possession with the joy of all *their*
heart, with the despiteful minds, to cast
it out for a prey.
6 Prophesy therefore concerning the
land of Israel, and say unto the moun-
tains, and to the hills, to the rivers, and
to the valleys, Thus saith the Lord GOD;
Behold, I have spoken in my jealousy
and in my fury, because ye have borne
the shame of the heathen:
7 Therefore thus saith the Lord GOD; I
have lifted up mine hand, Surely the
heathen that *are* about you, they shall
bear their shame.
8 ¶But ye, O mountains of Israel, ye
shall shoot forth your branches, and
yield your fruit to my people of Israel;
for they are at hand to come.
9 For, behold, I *am* for you, and I will
turn unto you, and ye shall be tilled and
sown:
10 And I will multiply men upon you,
all the house of Israel, *even* all of it: and
the cities shall be inhabited, and the
wastes shall be builded:
11 And I will multiply upon you man
and beast; and they shall increase and
bring fruit: and I will settle you after
your old estates, and will do better *unto*
you than at your beginnings: and ye
shall know that I *am* the LORD.
12 Yea, I will cause men to walk upon
you, *even* my people Israel; and they
shall possess thee, and thou shalt be
their inheritance, and thou shalt no
more henceforth bereave them *of men.*
13 Thus saith the Lord GOD; Because
they say unto you, Thou *land* devourest
up men, and hast bereaved thy nations;
14 Therefore thou shalt devour men
no more, neither bereave thy nations
any more, saith the Lord GOD.
15 Neither will I cause *men* to hear in
thee the shame of the heathen any
more, neither shalt thou bear the
reproach of the people any more,
neither shalt thou cause thy nations to
fall any more, saith the Lord GOD.
16 ¶Moreover the word of the LORD
came unto me, saying,
17 Son of man, when the house of
Israel dwelt in their own land, they de-
filed it by their own way and by their
doings: their way was before me as the
uncleanness of a removed woman.
18 Wherefore I poured my fury upon
them for the blood that they had shed
upon the land, and for their idols *where-*
with they had polluted it:
19 And I scattered them among the
heathen, and they were dispersed
through the countries: according to
their way and according to their doings
I judged them.
20 And when they entered unto the
heathen, whither they went, they pro-
faned my holy name, when they said to
them, These *are* the people of the LORD,
and are gone forth out of his land.
21 ¶But I had pity for mine holy
name, which the house of Israel had
profaned among the heathen, whither
they went.
22 Therefore say unto the house of
Israel, Thus saith the LORD GOD; I do
not *this* for your sakes, O house of
Israel, but for mine holy name's sake,
which ye have profaned among the
heathen, whither ye went.
23 And I will sanctify my great name,
which was profaned among the
heathen, which ye have profaned in the
midst of them; and the heathen shall
know that I *am* the LORD, saith the Lord
GOD, when I shall be sanctified in you
before their eyes.
24 For I will take you from among the
heathen, and gather you out of all
countries, and will bring you into your
own land.
25 Then will I sprinkle clean water
upon you, and ye shall be clean: from
all your filthiness, and from all your
idols, will I cleanse you.
26 A new heart also will I give you,
and a new spirit will I put within you:
and I will take away the stony heart out
of your flesh, and I will give you an
heart of flesh.

27 And I will put my spirit within you, and cause you to walk in my statutes, and ye shall keep my judgments, and do *them.*
28 And ye shall dwell in the land that I gave to your fathers; and ye shall be my people, and I will be your God.
29 I will also save you from all your uncleannesses: and I will call for the corn, and will increase it, and lay no famine upon you.
30 And I will multiply the fruit of the tree, and the increase of the field, that ye shall receive no more reproach of famine among the heathen.
31 Then shall ye remember your own evil ways, and your doings that *were* not good, and shall lothe yourselves in your own sight for your iniquities and for your abominations.
32 Not for your sakes do I *this,* saith the Lord GOD, be it known unto you: be ashamed and confounded for your own ways, O house of Israel.
33 Thus saith the Lord GOD; In the day that I shall have cleansed you from all your iniquities I will also cause *you* to dwell in the cities, and the wastes shall be builded.
34 And the desolate land shall be tilled, whereas it lay desolate in the sight of all that passed by.
35 And they shall say, This land that was desolate is become like the garden of Eden; and the waste and desolate and ruined cities *are become* fenced, *and* are inhabited.
36 Then the heathen that are left round about you shall know that I the LORD build the ruined *places, and* plant that that was desolate: I the LORD have spoken *it,* and I will do *it.*
37 Thus saith the Lord GOD; I will yet *for* this be enquired of by the house of Israel, to do *it* for them; I will increase them with men like a flock.
38 As the holy flock, as the flock of Jerusalem in her solemn feasts; so shall the waste cities be filled with flocks of men: and they shall know that I *am* the LORD.

CHAPTER 37

THE hand of the LORD was upon me, and carried me out in the spirit of the LORD, and set me down in the midst of the valley which *was* full of bones,
2 And caused me to pass by them round about: and, behold, *there were* very many in the open valley; and, lo, *they were* very dry.
3 And he said unto me, Son of man, can these bones live? And I answered, O Lord GOD, thou knowest.
4 Again he said unto me, Prophesy upon these bones, and say unto them, O ye dry bones, hear the word of the LORD.
5 Thus saith the Lord GOD unto these bones; Behold, I will cause breath to enter into you, and ye shall live:
6 And I will lay sinews upon you, and will bring up flesh upon you, and cover you with skin, and put breath in you, and ye shall live; and ye shall know that I *am* the LORD.
7 So I prophesied as I was commanded: and as I prophesied, there was a noise, and behold a shaking, and the bones came together, bone to his bone.
8 And when I beheld, lo, the sinews and the flesh came up upon them, and the skin covered them above: but *there was* no breath in them.
9 Then said he unto me, Prophesy unto the wind, prophesy, son of man, and say to the wind, thus saith the Lord GOD; Come from the four winds, O breath, and breathe upon these slain, that they may live.
10 So I prophesied as he commanded me, and the breath came into them, and they lived, and stood up upon their feet, an exceeding great army.
11 Then he said unto me, Son of man, these bones are the whole house of Israel: behold, they say, Our bones are dried, and our hope is lost: we are cut off for our parts.
12 Therefore prophesy and say unto them, Thus saith the Lord GOD; Behold, O my people, I will open your graves, and cause you to come up out of your graves, and bring you into the land of Israel.
13 And ye shall know that I *am* the LORD, when I have opened your graves, O my people, and brought you up out of your graves,
14 And shall put my spirit in you, and ye shall live, and I shall place you in your own land: then shall ye know that I the LORD have spoken *it,* and performed *it,* saith the LORD.
15 ¶The word of the LORD came again unto me, saying,
16 Moreover, thou son of man, take thee one stick, and write upon it, For Jū'dah, and for the children of Israel his companions: then take another stick, and write upon it, For Joseph, the stick of Ē'phra-im, and *for* all the house of Israel his companions:
17 And join them one to another into one stick; and they shall become one in thine hand.
18 And when the children of thy people shall speak unto thee, saying, Wilt thou not shew us what thou *meanest* by these?

19 Say unto them, Thus saith the
Lord God; Behold, I will take the stick
of Joseph, which *is* in the hand of Ē'-
phra-im, and the tribes of Israel his fel-
lows, and will put them with him, *even*
with the stick of Jū'dah, and make
them one stick, and they shall be one in
mine hand.
20 And the sticks whereon thou writ-
est shall be in thine hand before their
eyes.
21 ¶And say unto them, Thus saith
the Lord God; Behold, I will take the
children of Israel from among the
heathen, whither they be gone, and will
gather them on every side, and bring
them into their own land:
22 And I will make them one nation
in the land upon the mountains of
Israel; and one king shall be king to
them all: and they shall be no more two
nations, neither shall they be divided
into two kingdoms any more at all:
23 Neither shall they defile them-
selves any more with their idols, nor
with their detestable things, nor with
any of their transgressions: but I will
save them out of all their dwelling-
places, wherein they have sinned, and
will cleanse them: so shall they be my
people, and I will be their God.
24 And David my servant *shall be*
king over them; and they all shall have
one shepherd: they shall also walk in
my judgments, and observe my stat-
utes, and do them.
25 And they shall dwell in the land
that I have given unto Jacob my ser-
vant, wherein your fathers have dwelt;
and they shall dwell therein, *even* they,
and their children, and their children's
children for ever: and my servant Da-
vid *shall be* their prince for ever.
26 Moreover I will make a covenant
of peace with them; it shall be an ever-
lasting covenant with them: and I will
place them, and multiply them, and
will set my sanctuary in the midst of
them for evermore.
27 My tabernacle also shall be with
them: yea, I will be their God, and they
shall be my people.
28 And the heathen shall know that I
the Lord do sanctify Israel, when my
sanctuary shall be in the midst of them
for evermore.

CHAPTER 38

AND the word of the Lord came unto
me, saying,
2 Son of man, set thy face against
Gog, the land of Mā'gŏg, the chief
prince of Mē'shĕch and Tū'bal, and
prophesy against him,
3 And say, Thus saith the Lord God;
Behold, I *am* against thee, O Gog, the
chief prince of Mē'shĕch and Tū'bal:
4 And I will turn thee back, and put
hooks into thy jaws, and I will bring
thee forth, and all thine army, horses
and horsemen, all of them clothed with
all sorts *of armour, even* a great com-
pany *with* bucklers and shields, all of
them handling swords:
5 Persia, Ē-thĭ-ō'pĭ-a, and Libya with
them; all of them with shield and hel-
met:
6 Gō'mer, and all his bands; the house
of Tō-gär'mah of the north quarters,
and all his bands: *and* many people
with thee.
7 Be thou prepared, and prepare for
thyself, thou, and all thy company that
are assembled unto thee, and be thou a
guard unto them.
8 After many days thou shalt be
visited: in the latter years thou shalt
come into the land *that is* brought back
from the sword, *and is* gathered out of
many people, against the mountains of
Israel, which have been always waste:
but it is brought forth out of the na-
tions, and they shall dwell safely all of
them.
9 Thou shalt ascend and come like a
storm, thou shalt be like a cloud to
cover the land, thou, and all thy bands,
and many people with thee.
10 Thus saith the Lord God; It shall
also come to pass, *that* at the same time
shall things come into thy mind, and
thou shalt think an evil thought:
11 And thou shalt say, I will go up to
the land of unwalled villages; I will go
to them that are at rest that dwell safely,
all of them dwelling without walls,
and having neither bars nor gates,
12 To take a spoil, and to take a prey;
to turn thine hand upon the desolate
places *that are now* inhabited, and
upon the people *that are* gathered out
of the nations, which have gotten cattle
and goods, that dwell in the midst of
the land.
13 Shē'ba, and Dē'dan, and the mer-
chants of Tärshĭsh, with all the young
lions thereof, shall say unto thee, Art
thou come to take a spoil? hast thou
gathered thy company to take a prey?
to carry away silver and gold, to take
away cattle and goods, to take a great
spoil?
14 ¶Therefore, son of man, prophesy
and say unto Gog, Thus saith the Lord
God; In that day when my people of
Israel dwelleth safely, shalt thou not
know *it?*
15 And thou shalt come from thy
place out of the north parts, thou, and
many people with thee, all of them rid-

ing upon horses, a great company, and
a mighty army:
16 And thou shalt come up against
my people of Israel, as a cloud to cover
the land; it shall be in the latter days,
and I will bring thee against my land,
that the heathen may know me, when I
shall be sanctified in thee, O Gog, be-
fore their eyes.
17 Thus saith the Lord GOD; *Art* thou
he of whom I have spoken in old time
by my servants the prophets of Israel,
which prophesied in those days *many*
years that I would bring thee against
them?
18 And it shall come to pass at the
same time when Gog shall come
against the land of Israel, saith the Lord
GOD, *that* my fury shall come up in my
face.
19 For in my jealousy *and* in the fire
of my wrath have I spoken, Surely in
that day there shall be a great shaking
in the land of Israel;
20 So that the fishes of the sea, and
the fowls of the heaven, and the beasts
of the field, and all creeping things that
creep upon the earth, and all the men
that *are* upon the face of the earth, shall
shake at my presence, and the moun-
tains shall be thrown down, and the
steep places shall fall, and every wall
shall fall to the ground.
21 And I will call for a sword against
him throughout all my mountains,
saith the Lord GOD: every man's sword
shall be against his brother.
22 And I will plead against him with
pestilence and with blood; and I will
rain upon him, and upon his bands, and
upon the many people that *are* with
him, an overflowing rain, and great
hailstones, fire, and brimstone.
23 Thus will I magnify myself, and
sanctify myself; and I will be known in
the eyes of many nations, and they
shall know that I *am* the LORD.

CHAPTER 39

THEREFORE, thou son of man, proph-
esy against Gog, and say, Thus saith
the Lord GOD; behold, I *am* against
thee, O Gog, the chief prince of Mē´shĕch
and Tū´bal:
2 And I will turn thee back, and leave
but the sixth part of thee, and will
cause thee to come up from the north
parts, and will bring thee upon the
mountains of Israel:
3 And I will smite thy bow out of thy
left hand, and will cause thine arrows
to fall out of thy right hand.
4 Thou shalt fall upon the mountains
of Israel, thou, and all thy bands, and
the people that *is* with thee: I will give
thee unto the ravenous birds of every
sort, and *to* the beasts of the field to be
devoured.
5 Thou shalt fall upon the open field:
for I have spoken *it*, saith the Lord GOD.
6 And I will send a fire on Mā´gŏg,
and among them that dwell carelessly
in the isles: and they shall know that I
am the LORD.
7 So will I make my holy name
known in the midst of my people Israel;
and I will not *let them* pollute my holy
name any more: and the heathen shall
know that I *am* the LORD, the Holy One
in Israel.
8 ¶Behold, it is come, and it is done,
saith the Lord GOD; this *is* the day
whereof I have spoken.
9 And they that dwell in the cities of
Israel shall go forth, and shall set on
fire and burn the weapons, both the
shields and the bucklers, the bows and
the arrows, and the handstaves, and
the spears, and they shall burn them
with fire seven years:
10 So that they shall take no wood
out of the field, neither cut down *any*
out of the forests; for they shall burn
the weapons with fire: and they shall
spoil those that spoiled them, and rob
those that robbed them, saith the Lord
GOD.
11 ¶And it shall come to pass in that
day, *that* I will give unto Gog a place
there of graves in Israel, the valley of
the passengers on the east of the sea:
and it shall stop the *noses* of the pas-
sengers: and there shall they bury Gog
and all his multitude: and they shall call
it The valley of Hā´mon–gŏg.
12 And seven months shall the house
of Israel be burying of them, that they
may cleanse the land.
13 Yea, all the people of the land shall
bury *them*; and it shall be to them a re-
nown the day that I shall be glorified,
saith the Lord GOD.
14 And they shall sever out men
of continual employment, passing
through the land to bury with the pas-
sengers those that remain upon the
face of the earth, to cleanse it: after the
end of seven months shall they search.
15 And the passengers *that* pass
through the land, when *any* seeth a
man's bone, then shall he set up a sign
by it, till the buriers have buried it in
the valley of Hā´mon–gŏg.
16 And also the name of the city *shall*
be Ha-mō´nah. Thus shall they cleanse
the land.
17 ¶And, thou son of man, thus saith
the Lord GOD; Speak unto every
feathered fowl, and to every beast of
the field, Assemble yourselves, and

come; gather yourselves on every side to my sacrifice that I do sacrifice for you, *even* a great sacrifice upon the mountains of Israel, that ye may eat flesh, and drink blood.
18 Ye shall eat the flesh of the mighty, and drink the blood of the princes of the earth, of rams, of lambs, and of goats, of bullocks, all of them fatlings of Bā'shan.
19 And ye shall eat fat till ye be full, and drink blood till ye be drunken, of my sacrifice which I have sacrificed for you.
20 Thus ye shall be filled at my table with horses and chariots, with mighty men, and with all men of war, saith the Lord God.
21 And I will set my glory among the heathen, and all the heathen shall see my judgment that I have executed, and my hand that I have laid upon them.
22 So the house of Israel shall know that I *am* the LORD their God from that day and forward.
23 And the heathen shall know that the house of Israel went into captivity for their iniquity: because they trespassed against me, therefore hid I my face from them, and gave them into the hand of their enemies: so fell they all by the sword.
24 According to their uncleanness and according to their transgressions have I done unto them, and hid my face from them.
25 Therefore thus saith the Lord GOD; Now will I bring again the captivity of Jacob, and have mercy upon the whole house of Israel, and will be jealous for my holy name;
26 After that they have borne their shame, and all their trespasses whereby they have trespassed against me, when they dwelt safely in their land, and none made *them* afraid.
27 When I have brought them again from the people, and gathered them out of their enemies' lands, and am sanctified in them in the sight of many nations;
28 Then shall they know that I *am* the LORD their God, which caused them to be led into captivity among the heathen: but I have gathered them unto their own land, and have left none of them any more there.
29 Neither will I hide my face any more from them: for I have poured out my spirit upon the house of Israel, saith the Lord GOD.

CHAPTER 40

IN the five and twentieth year of our captivity, in the beginning of the year, in the tenth *day* of the month, in the fourteenth year after that the city was smitten, in the selfsame day the hand of the LORD was upon me, and brought me thither.
2 In the visions of God brought he me into the land of Israel, and set me upon a very high mountain, by which *was* as the frame of a city on the south.
3 And he brought me thither, and, behold, *there was* a man, whose appearance *was* like the appearance of brass, with a line of flax in his hand, and a measuring reed; and he stood in the gate.
4 And the man said unto me, Son of man, behold with thine eyes, and hear with thine ears, and set thine heart upon all that I shall shew thee; for to the intent that I might shew *them* unto thee *art* thou brought hither: declare all that thou seest to the house of Israel.
5 And behold a wall on the outside of the house round about, and in the man's hand a measuring reed of six cubits *long* by the cubit and an hand breadth: so he measured the breadth of the building, one reed; and the height, one reed.
6 ¶Then came he unto the gate which looketh toward the east, and went up the stairs thereof, and measured the threshold of the gate, *which was* one reed broad; and the other threshold *of the gate, which was* one reed broad.
7 And *every* little chamber *was* one reed long, and one reed broad; and between the little chambers *were* five cubits; and the threshold of the gate by the porch of the gate within *was* one reed.
8 He measured also the porch of the gate within, one reed.
9 Then measured he the porch of the gate, eight cubits; and the posts thereof, two cubits; and the porch of the gate *was* inward.
10 And the little chambers of the gate eastward *were* three on this side, and three on that side; they three *were* of one measure: and the posts had one measure on this side and on that side.
11 And he measured the breadth of the entry of the gate, ten cubits; *and* the length of the gate, thirteen cubits.
12 The space also before the little chambers *was* one cubit *on this side*, and the space *was* one cubit on that side: and the little chambers *were* six cubits on this side, and six cubits on that side.
13 He measured then the gate from the roof of *one* little chamber to the roof of another: the breadth *was* five and twenty cubits, door against door.

14 He made also posts of threescore
cubits, even unto the post of the court
round about the gate.
15 And from the face of the gate of
the entrance unto the face of the porch
of the inner gate *were* fifty cubits.
16 And *there were* narrow windows
to the little chambers, and to their
posts within the gate round about, and
likewise to the arches: and windows
were round about inward: and upon
each post *were* palm trees.
17 Then brought he me into the outward court, and, lo, *there were* chambers, and a pavement made for the
court round about: thirty chambers
were upon the pavement.
18 And the pavement by the side of
the gates over against the length of the
gates *was* the lower pavement.
19 Then he measured the breadth
from the forefront of the lower gate
unto the forefront of the inner court
without, an hundred cubits eastward
and northward.
20 ¶And the gate of the outward
court that looked toward the north, he
measured the length thereof, and the
breadth thereof.
21 And the little chambers thereof
were three on this side and three on
that side; and the posts thereof and the
arches thereof were after the measure
of the first gate: the length thereof *was*
fifty cubits, and the breadth five and
twenty cubits.
22 And their windows, and their
arches, and their palm trees, *were* after
the measure of the gate that looketh toward the east; and they went up unto it
by seven steps; and the arches thereof
were before them.
23 And the gate of the inner court
was over against the gate toward the
north, and toward the east; and he measured from gate to gate an hundred cubits.
24 ¶After that he brought me toward
the south, and behold a gate toward the
south: and he measured the posts thereof and the arches thereof according
to these measures.
25 And *there were* windows in it and
in the arches thereof round about, like
those windows: the length *was* fifty cubits, and the breadth five and twenty
cubits.
26 And *there were* seven steps to go
up to it, and the arches thereof *were* before them: and it had palm trees, one on
this side, and another on that side,
upon the posts thereof.
27 And *there was* a gate in the inner
court toward the south: and he measured from gate to gate toward the
south an hundred cubits.
28 And he brought me to the inner
court by the south gate: and he measured the south gate according to these
measures;
29 And the little chambers thereof,
and the posts thereof, and the arches
thereof, according to these measures:
and *there were* windows in it and in the
arches thereof round about: *it was* fifty
cubits long, and five and twenty cubits
broad.
30 And the arches round about *were*
five and twenty cubits long, and five
cubits broad.
31 And the arches thereof *were* toward the utter court; and palm trees
were upon the posts thereof: and the
going up to it *had* eight steps.
32 ¶And he brought me into the inner
court toward the east: and he measured
the gate according to these measures.
33 And the little chambers thereof,
and the posts thereof, and the arches
thereof, *were* according to these measures: and *there were* windows therein
and in the arches thereof round about:
it was fifty cubits long, and five and
twenty cubits broad.
34 And the arches thereof *were* toward the outward court; and palm
trees *were* upon the posts thereof, on
this side, and on that side: and the
going up to it *had* eight steps.
35 ¶And he brought me to the north
gate, and measured *it* according to
these measures;
36 The little chambers thereof, the
posts thereof, and the arches thereof,
and the windows to it round about: the
length *was* fifty cubits, and the breadth
five and twenty cubits.
37 And the posts thereof *were* toward the utter court; and palm trees
were upon the posts thereof, on this
side, and on that side: and the going up
to it *had* eight steps.
38 And the chambers and the entries
thereof *were* by the posts of the gates,
where they washed the burnt offering.
39 ¶And in the porch of the gate *were*
two tables on this side, and two tables
on that side, to slay thereon the burnt
offering and the sin offering and the
trespass offering.
40 And at the side without as one
goeth up to the entry of the north gate,
were two tables; and on the other side,
which *was* at the porch of the gate,
were two tables.
41 Four tables *were* on this side, and
four tables on that side, by the side of
the gate; eight tables, whereupon they
slew *their sacrifices.*

42 And the four tables *were* of hewn
stone for the burnt offering, of a cubit
and an half long, and a cubit and an half
broad, and one cubit high: whereupon
also they laid the instruments where-
with they slew the burnt offering and
the sacrifice.
43 And within *were* hooks, an hand
broad, fastened round about: and upon
the tables *was* the flesh of the offering.
44 ¶And without the inner gate *were*
the chambers of the singers in the inner
court, which *was* at the side of the
north gate; and their prospect *was* to-
ward the south: one at the side of the
east gate *having* the prospect toward
the north.
45 And he said unto me, This cham-
ber, whose prospect *is* toward the
south, *is* for the priests, the keepers of
the charge of the house.
46 And the chamber whose prospect
is toward the north *is* for the priests,
the keepers of the charge of the altar:
these *are* the sons of Zā'dŏk among the
sons of Levi, which come near to the
LORD to minister unto him.
47 So he measured the court, an
hundred cubits long, and an hundred
cubits broad, foursquare; and the altar
that was before the house.
48 ¶And he brought me to the porch
of the house, and measured *each* post
of the porch, five cubits on this side,
and five cubits on that side: and the
breadth of the gate *was* three cubits on
this side, and three cubits on that side.
49 The length of the porch *was*
twenty cubits, and the breadth eleven
cubits; and *he brought me* by the steps
whereby they went up to it: and *there
were* pillars by the posts, one on this
side, and another on that side.

CHAPTER 41

AFTERWARD he brought me to the
temple, and measured the posts, six cu-
bits broad on the one side, and six cubits
broad on the other side, *which* was
the breadth of the tabernacle.
2 And the breadth of the door *was* ten
cubits; and the sides of the door *were*
five cubits on the one side, and five cu-
bits on the other side: and he measured
the length thereof, forty cubits: and the
breadth, twenty cubits.
3 Then went he inward, and mea-
sured the post of the door, two cubits;
and the door, six cubits; and the
breadth of the door, seven cubits.
4 So he measured the length thereof,
twenty cubits; and the breadth, twenty
cubits, before the temple: and he said
unto me, This *is* the most holy *place*.
5 After he measured the wall of the
house, six cubits; and the breadth of
every side chamber, four cubits, round
about the house on every side.
6 And the side chambers *were* three,
one over another, and thirty in order;
and they entered into the wall which
was of the house for the side chambers
round about, that they might have
hold, but they had not hold in the wall
of the house.
7 And *there was* an enlarging, and a
winding about still upward to the side
chambers: for the winding about of the
house went still upward round about
the house: therefore the breadth of the
house *was still* upward, and so in-
creased *from* the lowest *chamber* to
the highest by the midst.
8 I saw also the height of the house
round about: the foundations of the
side chambers *were* a full reed of six
great cubits.
9 The thickness of the wall, which
was for the side chamber without, *was*
five cubits: and *that* which *was* left *was*
the place of the side chambers that
were within.
10 And between the chambers *was*
the wideness of twenty cubits round
about the house on every side.
11 And the doors of the side cham-
bers *were* toward *the place that was*
left, one door toward the north, and an-
other door toward the south: and the
breadth of the place that was left *was*
five cubits round about.
12 Now the building that *was* before
the separate place at the end toward
the west *was* seventy cubits broad; and
the wall of the building *was* five cubits
thick round about, and the length there-
of ninety cubits.
13 So he measured the house, an
hundred cubits long; and the separate
place, and the building, with the walls
thereof, an hundred cubits long;
14 Also the breadth of the face of the
house, and of the separate place to-
ward the east, an hundred cubits.
15 And he measured the length of the
building over against the separate
place which *was* behind it, and the gal-
leries thereof on the one side and on the
other side, an hundred cubits, with the
inner temple, and the porches of the
court;
16 The door posts, and the narrow
windows, and the galleries round about
on their three stories, over against the
door, cieled with wood round about,
and from the ground up to the win-
dows, and the windows *were* covered;
17 To that above the door, even unto
the inner house, and without, and by all

the wall round about within and
without, by measure.
18 And *it was* made with cherubims
and palm trees, so that a palm tree *was*
between a cherub and a cherub; and
every cherub had two faces;
19 So that the face of a man *was* to-
ward the palm tree on the one side, and
the face of a young lion toward the
palm tree on the other side: *it was* made
through all the house round about.
20 From the ground unto above the
door *were* cherubims and palm trees
made, and *on* the wall of the temple.
21 The posts of the temple *were*
squared, *and* the face of the sanctuary;
the appearance *of the one* as the appear-
ance *of the other.*
22 The altar of wood *was* three cubits
high, and the length thereof two cubits;
and the corners thereof, and the length
thereof, and the walls thereof, *were* of
wood: and he said unto me, This *is* the
table that *is* before the LORD.
23 And the temple and the sanctuary
had two doors.
24 And the doors had two leaves
apiece, two turning leaves; two *leaves*
for the one door, and two leaves for the
other *door.*
25 And *there were* made on them, on
the doors of the temple, cherubims and
palm trees, like as *were* made upon the
walls; and *there were* thick planks
upon the face of the porch without.
26 And *there were* narrow windows
and palm trees on the one side and on
the other side, on the sides of the porch,
and *upon* the side chambers of the
house, and thick planks.

CHAPTER 42

THEN he brought me forth into the ut-
ter court, the way toward the north:
and he brought me into the chamber
that *was* over against the separate
place, and which *was* before the build-
ing toward the north.
2 Before the length of an hundred cu-
bits *was* the north door, and the
breadth *was* fifty cubits.
3 Over against the twenty *cubits*
which *were* for the inner court, and
over against the pavement which *was*
for the utter court, *was* gallery against
gallery in three *stories.*
4 And before the chambers *was* a
walk of ten cubits breadth inward, a
way of one cubit; and their doors to-
ward the north.
5 Now the upper chambers *were*
shorter: for the galleries were higher
than these, than the lower, and than the
middlemost of the building.
6 For they *were* in three *stories,* but
had not pillars as the pillars of the
courts: therefore *the building* was
straitened more than the lowest and
the middlemost from the ground.
7 And the wall that *was* without over
against the chambers, toward the utter
court on the forepart of the chambers,
the length thereof *was* fifty cubits.
8 For the length of the chambers that
were in the utter court *was* fifty cubits:
and, lo, before the temple *were* an
hundred cubits.
9 And from under these chambers
was the entry on the east side, as one
goeth into them from the utter court.
10 The chambers *were* in the thick-
ness of the wall of the court toward the
east, over against the separate place,
and over against the building.
11 And the way before them *was* like
the appearance of the chambers which
were toward the north, as long as they,
and as broad as they: and all their
goings out *were* both according to their
fashions, and according to their doors.
12 And according to the doors of the
chambers that *were* toward the south
was a door in the head of the way, *even*
the way directly before the wall toward
the east, as one entereth into them.
13 ¶Then said he unto me, The north
chambers *and* the south chambers,
which *are* before the separate place,
they *be* holy chambers, where the
priests that approach unto the LORD
shall eat the most holy things: there
shall they lay the most holy things, and
the meat offering, and the sin offering,
and the trespass offering; for the place
is holy.
14 When the priests enter therein,
then shall they not go out of the holy
place into the utter court, but there
they shall lay their garments wherein
they minister; for they *are* holy; and
shall put on other garments, and shall
approach to *those things* which *are* for
the people.
15 ¶Now when he had made an end of
measuring the inner house, he brought
me forth toward the gate whose pros-
pect *is* toward the east, and measured it
round about.
16 He measured the east side with
the measuring reed, five hundred
reeds, with the measuring reed round
about.
17 He measured the north side, five
hundred reeds, with the measuring
reed round about.
18 He measured the south side, five
hundred reeds, with the measuring
reed.
19 He turned about to the west side,

and measured five hundred reeds with
the measuring reed.
20 He measured it by the four sides: it
had a wall round about, five hundred
reeds long, and five hundred broad, to
make a separation between the sanc-
tuary and the profane place.

CHAPTER 43

AFTERWARD he brought me to the
gate, *even* the gate that looketh toward
the east:
2 And, behold, the glory of the God of
Israel came from the way of the east:
and his voice *was* like a noise of many
waters: and the earth shined with his
glory.
3 And *it was* according to the appear-
ance of the vision which I saw, *even* ac-
cording to the vision that I saw when I
came to destroy the city: and the vi-
sions *were* like the vision that I saw by
the river Chē'bär; and I fell upon my
face.
4 And the glory of the LORD came into
the house by the way of the gate whose
prospect *is* toward the east.
5 So the spirit took me up, and
brought me into the inner court; and,
behold, the glory of the LORD filled the
house.
6 And I heard *him* speaking unto me
out of the house; and the man stood by
me.
7 ¶And he said unto me, Son of man,
the place of my throne, and the place of
the soles of my feet, where I will dwell
in the midst of the children of Israel for
ever, and my holy name, shall the
house of Israel no more defile, *neither*
they, nor their kings, by their whore-
dom, nor by the carcases of their kings
in their high places.
8 In their setting of their threshold by
my thresholds, and their post by my
posts, and the wall between me and
them, they have even defiled my holy
name by their abominations that they
have committed: wherefore I have con-
sumed them in mine anger.
9 Now let them put away their whore-
dom, and the carcases of their kings,
far from me, and I will dwell in the
midst of them for ever.
10 ¶Thou son of man, shew the house
to the house of Israel, that they may be
ashamed of their iniquities: and let
them measure the pattern.
11 And if they be ashamed of all that
they have done, shew them the form of
the house, and the fashion thereof, and
the goings out thereof, and the comings
in thereof, and all the forms thereof,
and all the ordinances thereof, and all
the forms thereof, and all the laws there-
of: and write *it* in their sight, that
they may keep the whole form thereof,
and all the ordinances thereof, and do
them.
12 This *is* the law of the house; Upon
the top of the mountain the whole limit
thereof round about *shall be* most holy.
Behold, this *is* the law of the house.
13 ¶And these *are* the measures of
the altar after the cubits: The cubit *is* a
cubit and an hand breadth; even the
bottom *shall be* a cubit, and the breadth
a cubit, and the border thereof by the
edge thereof round about *shall be* a
span: and this *shall be* the higher place
of the altar.
14 And from the bottom *upon* the
ground *even* to the lower settle *shall be*
two cubits, and the breadth one cubit;
and from the lesser settle *even* to the
greater settle *shall be* four cubits, and
the breadth *one* cubit.
15 So the altar *shall be* four cubits;
and from the altar and upward *shall be*
four horns.
16 And the altar *shall be* twelve *cubits*
long, twelve broad, square in the
four squares thereof.
17 And the settle *shall be* fourteen *cu-
bits* long and fourteen broad in the four
squares thereof; and the border about
it *shall be* half a cubit; and the bottom
thereof *shall be* a cubit about; and his
stairs shall look toward the east.
18 ¶And he said unto me, Son of man,
thus saith the Lord GOD; These *are* the
ordinances of the altar in the day when
they shall make it, to offer burnt offer-
ings thereon, and to sprinkle blood
thereon.
19 And thou shalt give to the priests
the Levites that be of the seed of Zā'-
dŏk, which approach unto me, to min-
ister unto me, saith the Lord GOD, a
young bullock for a sin offering.
20 And thou shalt take of the blood
thereof, and put *it* on the four horns of
it, and on the four corners of the settle,
and upon the border round about: thus
shalt thou cleanse and purge it.
21 Thou shalt take the bullock also of
the sin offering, and he shall burn it in
the appointed place of the house,
without the sanctuary.
22 And on the second day thou shalt
offer a kid of the goats without blemish
for a sin offering; and they shall cleanse
the altar, as they did cleanse *it* with the
bullock.
23 When thou hast made an end of
cleansing *it*, thou shalt offer a young
bullock without blemish, and a ram out
of the flock without blemish.
24 And thou shalt offer them before
the LORD, and the priests shall cast salt

upon them, and they shall offer them
up *for* a burnt offering unto the LORD.
25 Seven days shalt thou prepare
every day a goat *for* a sin offering: they
shall also prepare a young bullock, and
a ram out of the flock, without blemish.
26 Seven days shall they purge the al-
tar and purify it; and they shall
consecrate themselves.
27 And when these days are expired,
it shall be, *that* upon the eighth day,
and *so* forward, the priests shall make
your burnt offerings upon the altar, and
your peace offerings; and I will accept
you, saith the Lord GOD.

CHAPTER 44

THEN he brought me back the way of
the gate of the outward sanctuary
which looketh toward the east; and it
was shut.
2 Then said the LORD unto me; This
gate shall be shut, it shall not be
opened, and no man shall enter in by it;
because the LORD, the God of Israel,
hath entered in by it, therefore it shall
be shut.
3 *It is* for the prince; the prince, he
shall sit in it to eat bread before the
LORD; he shall enter by the way of the
porch of *that* gate, and shall go out by
the way of the same.
4 ¶Then brought he me the way of the
north gate before the house: and I
looked, and, behold, the glory of the
LORD filled the house of the LORD: and I
fell upon my face.
5 And the LORD said unto me, Son of
man, mark well, and behold with thine
eyes, and hear with thine ears all that I
say unto thee concerning all the ordi-
nances of the house of the LORD, and all
the laws thereof; and mark well the en-
tering in of the house, with every going
forth of the sanctuary.
6 And thou shalt say to the rebellious,
even to the house of Israel, Thus saith
the Lord GOD; O ye house of Israel, let it
suffice you of all your abominations,
7 In that ye have brought *into my
sanctuary* strangers, uncircumcised in
heart, and uncircumcised in flesh, to be
in my sanctuary, to pollute it, *even* my
house, when ye offer my bread, the fat
and the blood, and they have broken
my covenant because of all your
abominations.
8 And ye have not kept the charge of
mine holy things: but ye have set keep-
ers of my charge in my sanctuary for
yourselves.
9 ¶Thus saith the Lord GOD; No stran-
ger, uncircumcised in heart, nor uncir-
cumcised in flesh, shall enter into my
sanctuary, of any stranger that *is*
among the children of Israel.
10 And the Levites that are gone
away far from me, when Israel went
astray, which went astray away from
me after their idols; they shall even
bear their iniquity.
11 Yet they shall be ministers in my
sanctuary, *having* charge at the gates
of the house, and ministering to the
house: they shall slay the burnt offer-
ing and the sacrifice for the people, and
they shall stand before them to minis-
ter unto them.
12 Because they ministered unto
them before their idols, and caused the
house of Israel to fall into iniquity; there-
fore have I lifted up mine hand
against them, saith the Lord GOD, and
they shall bear their iniquity.
13 And they shall not come near unto
me, to do the office of a priest unto me,
nor to come near to any of my holy
things, in the most holy *place:* but they
shall bear their shame, and their
abominations which they have com-
mitted.
14 But I will make them keepers of
the charge of the house, for all the ser-
vice thereof, and for all that shall be
done therein.
15 ¶But the priests the Levites, the
sons of Zā'dŏk, that kept the charge of
my sanctuary when the children of
Israel went astray from me, they shall
come near to me to minister unto me,
and they shall stand before me to offer
unto me the fat and the blood, saith the
Lord GOD:
16 They shall enter into my sanc-
tuary, and they shall come near to my
table, to minister unto me, and they
shall keep my charge.
17 ¶And it shall come to pass, *that*
when they enter in at the gates of the
inner court, they shall be clothed with
linen garments; and no wool shall come
upon them, whiles they minister in the
gates of the inner court, and within.
18 They shall have linen bonnets
upon their heads, and shall have linen
breeches upon their loins; they shall
not gird *themselves* with any thing that
causeth sweat.
19 And when they go forth into the
utter court, *even* into the utter court to
the people, they shall put off their gar-
ments wherein they ministered, and
lay them in the holy chambers, and
they shall put on other garments; and
they shall not sanctify the people with
their garments.
20 Neither shall they shave their
heads, nor suffer their locks to grow
long; they shall only poll their heads.

21 Neither shall any priest drink wine, when they enter into the inner court.
22 Neither shall they take for their wives a widow, nor her that is put away: but they shall take maidens of the seed of the house of Israel, or a widow that had a priest before.
23 And they shall teach my people *the difference* between the holy and profane, and cause them to discern between the unclean and the clean.
24 And in controversy they shall stand in judgment; *and* they shall judge it according to my judgments: and they shall keep my laws and my statutes in all mine assemblies; and they shall hallow my sabbaths.
25 And they shall come at no dead person to defile themselves: but for father, or for mother, or for son, or for daughter, for brother, or for sister that hath had no husband, they may defile themselves.
26 And after he is cleansed, they shall reckon unto him seven days.
27 And in the day that he goeth into the sanctuary, unto the inner court, to minister in the sanctuary, he shall offer his sin offering, saith the Lord GOD.
28 And it shall be unto them for an inheritance: I *am* their inheritance: and ye shall give them no possession in Israel: I *am* their possession.
29 They shall eat the meat offering, and the sin offering, and the trespass offering; and every dedicated thing in Israel shall be theirs.
30 And the first of all the firstfruits of all *things*, and every oblation of all, of every *sort* of your oblations, shall be the priest's: ye shall also give unto the priest the first of your dough, that he may cause the blessing to rest in thine house.
31 The priests shall not eat of any thing that is dead of itself, or torn, whether it be fowl or beast.

CHAPTER 45

MOREOVER, when ye shall divide by lot the land for inheritance, ye shall offer an oblation unto the LORD, an holy portion of the land: the length *shall be* the length of five and twenty thousand *reeds*, and the breadth *shall be* ten thousand. This *shall be* holy in all the borders thereof round about.
2 Of this there shall be for the sanctuary five hundred *in length*, with five hundred *in breadth*, square round about; and fifty cubits round about for the suburbs thereof.
3 And of this measure shalt thou measure the length of five and twenty thousand, and the breadth of ten thousand: and in it shall be the sanctuary *and* the most holy *place*.
4 The holy *portion* of the land shall be for the priests the ministers of the sanctuary, which shall come near to minister unto the LORD: and it shall be a place for their houses, and an holy place for the sanctuary.
5 And the five and twenty thousand of length, and the ten thousand of breadth, shall also the Levites, the ministers of the house, have for themselves, for a possession for twenty chambers.
6 ¶And ye shall appoint the possession of the city five thousand broad, and five and twenty thousand long, over against the oblation of the holy *portion*: it shall be for the whole house of Israel.
7 ¶And *a portion shall be* for the prince on the one side and on the other side of the oblation of the holy *portion*, and of the possession of the city, before the oblation of the holy *portion*, and before the possession of the city, from the west side westward, and from the east side eastward: and the length *shall be* over against one of the portions, from the west border unto the east border.
8 In the land shall be his possession in Israel: and my princes shall no more oppress my people; and *the rest of* the land shall they give to the house of Israel according to their tribes.
9 ¶Thus saith the Lord GOD; Let it suffice you, O princes of Israel: remove violence and spoil, and execute judgment and justice, take away your exactions from my people, saith the Lord GOD.
10 Ye shall have just balances, and a just ephah, and a just bath.
11 The ephah and the bath shall be of one measure, that the bath may contain the tenth part of an homer, and the ephah the tenth part of an homer: the measure thereof shall be after the homer.
12 And the shekel *shall be* twenty gerahs: twenty shekels, five and twenty shekels, fifteen shekels, shall be your maneh.
13 This *is* the oblation that ye shall offer; the sixth part of an ephah of an homer of wheat, and ye shall give the sixth part of an ephah of an homer of barley:
14 Concerning the ordinance of oil, the bath of oil, *ye shall offer* the tenth part of a bath out of the cor, *which is* an homer of ten baths; for ten baths *are* an homer:
15 And one lamb out of the flock, out

of two hundred, out of the fat pastures
of Israel; for a meat offering, and for a
burnt offering, and for peace offerings,
to make reconciliation for them, saith
the Lord God.
16 All the people of the land shall give
this oblation for the prince in Israel.
17 And it shall be the prince's part *to*
give burnt offerings, and meat offer-
ings, and drink offerings, in the feasts,
and in the new moons, and in the sab-
baths, in all solemnities of the house of
Israel: he shall prepare the sin offering,
and the meat offering, and the burnt of-
fering, and the peace offerings, to make
reconciliation for the house of Israel.
18 Thus saith the Lord God; In the
first *month*, in the first *day* of the
month, thou shalt take a young bullock
without blemish, and cleanse the sanc-
tuary:
19 And the priest shall take of the
blood of the sin offering, and put *it*
upon the posts of the house, and upon
the four corners of the settle of the al-
tar, and upon the posts of the gate of
the inner court.
20 And so thou shalt do the seventh
day of the month for every one that er-
reth, and for *him that is* simple: so shall
ye reconcile the house.
21 In the first *month*, in the four-
teenth day of the month, ye shall have
the passover, a feast of seven days; un-
leavened bread shall be eaten.
22 And upon that day shall the prince
prepare for himself and for all the
people of the land a bullock *for* a sin
offering.
23 And seven days of the feast he
shall prepare a burnt offering to the
Lord, seven bullocks and seven rams
without blemish daily the seven days;
and a kid of the goats daily *for* a sin
offering.
24 And he shall prepare a meat offer-
ing of an ephah for a bullock, and an
ephah for a ram, and an hin of oil for an
ephah.
25 In the seventh *month*, in the fif-
teenth day of the month, shall he do the
like in the feast of the seven days, ac-
cording to the sin offering, according to
the burnt offering, and according to the
meat offering, and according to the oil.

CHAPTER 46

THUS saith the Lord God; The gate of
the inner court that looketh toward the
east shall be shut the six working days;
but on the sabbath it shall be opened,
and in the day of the new moon it shall
be opened.
2 And the prince shall enter by the
way of the porch of *that* gate without,
and shall stand by the post of the gate,
and the priests shall prepare his burnt
offering and his peace offerings, and he
shall worship at the threshold of the
gate: then he shall go forth; but the gate
shall not be shut until the evening.
3 Likewise the people of the land
shall worship at the door of this gate
before the Lord in the sabbaths and in
the new moons.
4 And the burnt offering that the
prince shall offer unto the Lord in the
sabbath day *shall be* six lambs without
blemish, and a ram without blemish.
5 And the meat offering *shall be* an
ephah for a ram, and the meat offering
for the lambs as he shall be able to give,
and an hin of oil to an ephah.
6 And in the day of the new moon *it*
shall be a young bullock without
blemish, and six lambs, and a ram: they
shall be without blemish.
7 And he shall prepare a meat offer-
ing, an ephah for a bullock, and an
ephah for a ram, and for the lambs ac-
cording as his hand shall attain unto,
and an hin of oil to an ephah.
8 And when the prince shall enter, he
shall go in by the way of the porch of
that gate, and he shall go forth by the
way thereof.
9 ¶But when the people of the land
shall come before the Lord in the sol-
emn feasts, he that entereth in by the
way of the north gate to worship shall
go out by the way of the south gate: and
he that entereth by the way of the south
gate shall go forth by the way of the
north gate: he shall not return by the
way of the gate whereby he came in,
but shall go forth over against it.
10 And the prince in the midst of
them, when they go in, shall go in; and
when they go forth, shall go forth.
11 And in the feasts and in the solem-
nities the meat offering shall be an
ephah to a bullock, and an ephah to a
ram, and to the lambs as he is able to
give, and an hin of oil to an ephah.
12 Now when the prince shall pre-
pare a voluntary burnt offering or
peace offerings voluntarily unto the
Lord, *one* shall then open him the gate
that looketh toward the east, and he
shall prepare his burnt offering and his
peace offerings, as he did on the sab-
bath day: then he shall go forth; and af-
ter his going forth *one* shall shut the
gate.
13 Thou shalt daily prepare a burnt
offering unto the Lord *of* a lamb of the
first year without blemish: thou shalt
prepare it every morning.
14 And thou shalt prepare a meat of-
fering for it every morning, the sixth

part of an ephah, and the third part of
an hin of oil, to temper with the fine
flour; a meat offering continually by a
perpetual ordinance unto the LORD.
15 Thus shall they prepare the lamb,
and the meat offering, and the oil,
every morning *for* a continual burnt offering.
16 ¶Thus saith the Lord GOD; If the
prince give a gift unto any of his sons,
the inheritance thereof shall be his
sons'; it *shall be* their possession by inheritance.
17 But if he give a gift of his inheritance to one of his servants, then it
shall be his to the year of liberty; after it
shall return to the prince: but his inheritance shall be his sons' for them.
18 Moreover the prince shall not take
of the people's inheritance by oppression, to thrust them out of their possession; *but* he shall give his sons inheritance out of his own possession: that
my people be not scattered every man
from his possession.
19 ¶After he brought me through the
entry, which *was* at the side of the gate,
into the holy chambers of the priests,
which looked toward the north: and,
behold, there *was* a place on the two
sides westward.
20 Then said he unto me, This *is* the
place where the priests shall boil the
trespass offering and the sin offering,
where they shall bake the meat offering; that they bear *them* not out into the
utter court, to sanctify the people.
21 Then he brought me forth into the
utter court, and caused me to pass by
the four corners of the court; and, behold, in every corner of the court *there
was* a court.
22 In the four corners of the court
there were courts joined of forty *cubits*
long and thirty broad: these four corners
were of one measure.
23 And *there was* a row *of building*
round about in them, round about them
four, and *it was* made with boiling
places under the rows round about.
24 Then said he unto me, these *are*
the places of them that boil, where the
ministers of the house shall boil the
sacrifice of the people.

CHAPTER 47

AFTERWARD he brought me again
unto the door of the house; and, behold,
waters issued out from under the
threshold of the house eastward: for
the forefront of the house *stood toward*
the east, and the waters came down
from under from the right side of the
house, at the south *side* of the altar.
2 Then brought he me out of the way
of the gate northward, and led me
about the way without unto the utter
gate by the way that looketh eastward;
and, behold, there ran out waters on
the right side.
3 And when the man that had the line
in his hand went forth eastward, he
measured a thousand cubits, and he
brought me through the waters; the
waters *were* to the ancles.
4 Again he measured a thousand, and
brought me through the waters; the
waters *were* to the knees. Again he
measured a thousand, and brought me
through; the waters *were* to the loins.
5 Afterward he measured a thousand; *and it was* a river that I could not
pass over: for the waters were risen,
waters to swim in, a river that could not
be passed over.
6 ¶And he said unto me, Son of man,
hast thou seen *this?* Then he brought
me, and caused me to return to the
brink of the river.
7 Now when I had returned, behold,
at the bank of the river *were* very many
trees on the one side and on the other.
8 Then said he unto me, These waters
issue out toward the east country, and
go down into the desert, and go into the
sea: *which being* brought forth into the
sea, the waters shall be healed.
9 And it shall come to pass, *that*
every thing that liveth, which moveth,
whithersoever the rivers shall come,
shall live: and there shall be a very
great multitude of fish, because these
waters shall come thither: for they
shall be healed; and every thing shall
live whither the river cometh.
10 And it shall come to pass, *that* the
fishers shall stand upon it from Ĕn-gĕdī
even unto Ĕn-ĕg'la-im; they shall be a
place to spread forth nets; their fish
shall be according to their kinds, as the
fish of the great sea, exceeding many.
11 But the miry places thereof and
the marishes thereof shall not be
healed; they shall be given to salt.
12 And by the river upon the bank
thereof, on this side and on that side,
shall grow all trees for meat, whose leaf
shall not fade, neither shall the fruit
thereof be consumed: it shall bring
forth new fruit according to his
months, because their waters they
issued out of the sanctuary: and the
fruit thereof shall be for meat, and the
leaf thereof for medicine.
13 ¶Thus saith the Lord GOD; This
shall be the border, whereby ye shall
inherit the land according to the twelve
tribes of Israel: Joseph *shall have two*
portions.
14 And ye shall inherit it, one as well

as another: *concerning* the which I lifted up mine hand to give it unto your fathers: and this land shall fall unto you for inheritance.
15 And this *shall be* the border of the land toward the north side, from the great sea, the way of Hĕth'lŏn, as men go to Zē'dăd;
16 Hā'măth, Be-rō'thah, Sĭb'rā-im, which *is* between the border of Damascus and the border of Hā'măth; Hā'-zar-hăt'ti-cŏn, which *is* by the coast of Hau'ran.
17 And the border from the sea shall be Hā'zar-ē'nan, the border of Damascus, and the north northward, and the border of Hā'măth. And *this is* the north side.
18 And the east side ye shall measure from Hau'ran, and from Damascus, and from Gilead, and from the land of Israel *by* Jordan, from the border unto the east sea. And *this is* the east side.
19 And the south side southward, from Tā'mar *even* to the waters of strife *in* Kā'desh, the river to the great sea. And *this is* the south side southward.
20 The west side also *shall be* the great sea from the border, till a man come over against Hā'măth. This *is* the west side.
21 So shall ye divide this land unto you according to the tribes of Israel.
22 And it shall come to pass, *that* ye shall divide it by lot for an inheritance unto you, and to the strangers that sojourn among you, which shall beget children among you: and they shall be unto you as born in the country among the children of Israel; they shall have inheritance with you among the tribes of Israel.
23 And it shall come to pass, *that* in what tribe the stranger sojourneth, there shall ye give *him* his inheritance, saith the Lord GOD.

CHAPTER 48

NOW these *are* the names of the tribes. From the north end to the coast of the way of Hĕth'lŏn, as one goeth to Hā'-măth, Hā'zar-ē'nan, the border of Damascus northward, to the coast of Hā'-măth; for these are his sides east *and* west; a *portion for* Dan.
2 And by the border of Dan, from the east side unto the west side, a *portion for* Asher.
3 And by the border of Asher, from the east side even unto the west side, a *portion for* Năph'ta-lī.
4 And by the border of Năph'ta-lī, from the east side unto the west side, a *portion for* Ma-năs'seh.
5 And by the border of Ma-năs'seh, from the east side unto the west side, a *portion for* Ē'phra-im.
6 And by the border of Ē'phra-im, from the east side even unto the west side, a *portion for* Reuben.
7 And by the border of Reuben, from the east side unto the west side, a *portion for* Judah.
8 And by the border of Judah, from the east side unto the west side, shall be the offering which ye shall offer of five and twenty thousand *reeds in* breadth, and *in* length as one of the *other* parts, from the east side unto the west side: and the sanctuary shall be in the midst of it.
9 The oblation that ye shall offer unto the LORD *shall be* of five and twenty thousand in length, and of ten thousand in breadth.
10 And for them, *even* for the priests, shall be *this* holy oblation; toward the north five and twenty thousand *in length,* and toward the west ten thousand in breadth, and toward the east ten thousand in breadth, and toward the south five and twenty thousand in length: and the sanctuary of the LORD shall be in the midst thereof.
11 *It shall be* for the priests that are sanctified of the sons of Zā'dŏk; which have kept my charge, which went not astray when the children of Israel went astray, as the Levites went astray.
12 And *this* oblation of the land that is offered shall be unto them a thing most holy by the border of the Levites.
13 And over against the border of the priests the Levites *shall have* five and twenty thousand in length, and ten thousand in breadth: all the length *shall be* five and twenty thousand, and the breadth ten thousand.
14 And they shall not sell of it, neither exchange, nor alienate the firstfruits of the land: for *it is* holy unto the LORD.
15 ¶And the five thousand, that are left in the breadth over against the five and twenty thousand, shall be a profane *place* for the city, for dwelling, and for suburbs: and the city shall be in the midst thereof.
16 And these *shall be* the measures thereof; the north side four thousand and five hundred, and the south side four thousand and five hundred, and on the east side four thousand and five hundred, and the west side four thousand and five hundred.
17 And the suburbs of the city shall be toward the north two hundred and fifty, and toward the south two hundred and fifty, and toward the east

two hundred and fifty, and toward the west two hundred and fifty.

18 And the residue in length over against the oblation of the holy *portion shall be* ten thousand eastward, and then thousand westward: and it shall be over against the oblation of the holy *portion;* and the increase thereof shall be for food unto them that serve the city.

19 And they that serve the city shall serve it out of all the tribes of Israel.

20 All the oblation *shall be* five and twenty thousand by five and twenty thousand: ye shall offer the holy oblation foursquare, with the possession of the city.

21 And the residue *shall be* for the prince, on the one side and on the other of the holy oblation, and of the possession of the city, over against the five and twenty thousand of the oblation toward the east border, and westward over against the five and twenty thousand toward the west border, over against the portions for the prince: and it shall be the holy oblation; and the sanctuary of the house *shall be* in the midst thereof.

22 Moreover from the possession of the Levites, and from the possession of the city, *being* in the midst *of that* which is the prince's, between the border of Judah and the border of Benjamin, shall be for the prince.

23 As for the rest of the tribes, from the east side unto the west side, Benjamin *shall have* a *portion.*

24 And by the border of Benjamin, from the east side unto the west side, Simeon *shall have* a *portion.*

25 And by the border of Simeon, from the east side unto the west side, Ĭs'sa-char a *portion.*

26 And by the border of Ĭs'sa-char, from the east side unto the west side, Zĕb'u-lun a *portion.*

27 And by the border of Zĕb'u-lun, from the east side unto the west side, Gad a *portion.*

28 And by the border of Gad, at the south side southward, the border shall be even from Tā'mar *unto* the waters of strife *in* Kā'desh, *and* to the river toward the great sea.

29 This *is* the land which ye shall divide by lot unto the tribes of Israel for inheritance, and these *are* their portions, saith the Lord God.

30 ¶And these *are* the goings out of the city on the north side, four thousand and five hundred measures.

31 And the gates of the city *shall be* after the names of the tribes of Israel: three gates northward; one gate of Reuben, one gate of Judah, one gate of Levi.

32 And at the east side four thousand and five hundred: and three gates; and one gate of Joseph, one gate of Benjamin, one gate of Dan.

33 And at the south side four thousand and five hundred measures: and three gates; one gate of Simeon, one gate of Ĭs'sa-char, one gate of Zĕb'u-lun.

34 At the west side four thousand and five hundred, *with* their three gates; one gate of Gad, one gate of Asher, one gate of Năph'ta-lī.

35 *It was* round about eighteen thousand *measures:* and the name of the city from *that* day *shall be,* The Lord *is* there.

THE BOOK OF DANIEL

CHAPTER 1

IN the third year of the reign of Je-hoi'a-kĭm king of Judah came Nĕb-u-chad-nĕz'zar king of Babylon unto Jerusalem, and besieged it.

2 And the Lord gave Je-hoi'a-kĭm king of Judah into his hand, with part of the vessels of the house of God: which he carried into the land of Shī'när to the house of his god; and he brought the vessels into the treasure house of his god.

3 ¶And the king spake unto Ăsh'pe-năz the master of his eunuchs, that he should bring *certain* of the children of Israel, and of the king's seed, and of the princes;

4 Children in whom *was* no blemish, but well favoured, and skilful in all wisdom, and cunning in knowledge, and understanding science, and such as *had* ability in them to stand in the king's palace, and whom they might teach the learning and the tongue of the Chăl-dē'anṡ.

5 And the king appointed them a daily provision of the king's meat, and of the wine which he drank: so nourishing them three years, that at the end thereof they might stand before the king.

6 Now among these were of the children of Judah, Daniel, Hăn-a-nī'ah, Mĭsh'a-el, and Ăz-a-rī'ah:

7 Unto whom the prince of the eu-

nuchs gave names: for he gave unto
Daniel *the name* of Bĕl-te-shăz′zar; and
to Hăn-a-nī′ah, of Shā′drăch; and to
Mĭsh′a-el, of Mē′shăch; and to Ăz-a-rī′-
ah, of A-bĕd′-ne-gō.
8 ¶But Daniel purposed in his heart
that he would not defile himself with
the portion of the king's meat, nor with
the wine which he drank: therefore he
requested of the prince of the eunuchs
that he might not defile himself.
9 Now God had brought Daniel into
favour and tender love with the prince
of the eunuchs.
10 And the prince of the eunuchs said
unto Daniel, I fear my lord the king,
who hath appointed your meat and
your drink: for why should he see your
faces worse liking than the children
which *are* of your sort? then shall ye
make *me* endanger my head to the
king.
11 Then said Daniel to Mĕl′zär,
whom the prince of the eunuchs had set
over Daniel, Hăn-a-nī′ah, Mĭsh′a-el,
and Ăz-a-rī′ah,
12 Prove thy servants, I beseech thee,
ten days; and let them give us pulse to
eat, and water to drink.
13 Then let our countenances be
looked upon before thee, and the coun-
tenance of the children that eat of the
portion of the king's meat: and as thou
seest, deal with thy servants.
14 So he consented to them in this
matter, and proved them ten days.
15 And at the end of ten days their
countenances appeared fairer and fat-
ter in flesh than all the children which
did eat the portion of the king's meat.
16 Thus Mĕl′zär took away the por-
tion of their meat, and the wine that
they should drink; and gave them
pulse.
17 ¶As for these four children, God
gave them knowledge and skill in all
learning and wisdom: and Daniel had
understanding in all visions and
dreams.
18 Now at the end of the days that the
king had said he should bring them in,
then the prince of the eunuchs brought
them in before Nĕb-u-chad-nĕz′zar.
19 And the king communed with
them; and among them all was found
none like Daniel, Hăn-a-nī′ah, Mĭsh′a-
el, and Ăz-a-rī′ah: therefore stood they
before the king.
20 And in all matters of wisdom *and*
understanding, that the king enquired
of them, he found them ten times better
than all the magicians *and* astrologers
that *were* in all his realm.
21 And Daniel continued *even* unto
the first year of king Cyrus.

CHAPTER 2

AND in the second year of the reign of
Nĕb-u-chad-nĕz′zar Nĕb-u-chad-nĕz′-
zar dreamed dreams, wherewith his
spirit was troubled, and his sleep brake
from him.
2 Then the king commanded to call
the magicians, and the astrologers, and
the sorcerers, and the Chăl-dē′anṡ, for
to shew the king his dreams. So they
came and stood before the king.
3 And the king said unto them, I have
dreamed a dream, and my spirit was
troubled to know the dream.
4 Then spake the Chăl-dē′anṡ to the
king in Sȳr′i-ăck, O king, live for ever:
tell thy servants the dream, and we will
shew the interpretation.
5 The king answered and said to the
Chăl-dē′anṡ, The thing is gone from
me: if ye will not make known unto me
the dream, with the interpretation there-
of, ye shall be cut in pieces, and your
houses shall be made a dunghill.
6 But if ye shew the dream, and the
interpretation thereof, ye shall receive
of me gifts and rewards and great
honour: therefore shew me the dream,
and the interpretation thereof.
7 They answered again and said, Let
the king tell his servants the dream,
and we will shew the interpretation of
it.
8 The king answered and said, I know
of certainty that ye would gain the
time, because ye see the thing is gone
from me.
9 But if ye will not make known unto
me the dream, *there is but* one decree
for you: for ye have prepared lying and
corrupt words to speak before me, till
the time be changed: therefore tell me
the dream, and I shall know that ye can
shew me the interpretation thereof.
10 ¶The Chăl-dē′anṡ answered before
the king, and said, There is not a man
upon the earth that can shew the king's
matter: therefore *there is* no king, lord,
nor ruler, *that* asked such things at any
magician, or astrologer, or Chăl-dē′an.
11 And *it is* a rare thing that the king
requireth, and there is none other that
can shew it before the king, except the
gods, whose dwelling is not with flesh.
12 For this cause the king was angry
and very furious, and commanded to
destroy all the wise *men* of Babylon.
13 And the decree went forth that the
wise *men* should be slain; and they
sought Daniel and his fellows to be
slain.
14 ¶Then Daniel answered with
counsel and wisdom to Â′rī-ŏch the
captain of the king's guard, which was

gone forth to slay the wise *men* of Babylon:

15 He answered and said to Ā'rĭ-ŏch the king's captain, Why *is* the decree *so* hasty from the king? Then Ā'rĭ-ŏch made the thing known to Daniel.

16 Then Daniel went in, and desired of the king that he would give him time, and that he would shew the king the interpretation.

17 Then Daniel went to his house, and made the thing known to Hăn-a-nī'-ah, Mĭsh'a-el, and Ăz-a-rī'ah, his companions:

18 That they would desire mercies of the God of heaven concerning this secret; that Daniel and his fellows should not perish with the rest of the wise *men* of Babylon.

19 ¶Then was the secret revealed unto Daniel in a night vision. Then Daniel blessed the God of heaven.

20 Daniel answered and said, Blessed be the name of God for ever and ever: for wisdom and might are his:

21 And he changeth the times and the seasons: he removeth kings, and setteth up kings: he giveth wisdom unto the wise, and knowledge to them that know understanding:

22 He revealeth the deep and secret things: he knoweth what *is* in the darkness, and the light dwelleth with him.

23 I thank thee, and praise thee, O thou God of my fathers, who hast given me wisdom and might, and hast made known unto me now what we desired of thee: for thou hast *now* made known unto us the king's matter.

24 ¶Therefore Daniel went in unto Ā'rĭ-ŏch, whom the king had ordained to destroy the wise *men* of Babylon: he went and said thus unto him; Destroy not the wise *men* of Babylon: bring me in before the king, and I will shew unto the king the interpretation.

25 Then Ā'rĭ-ŏch brought in Daniel before the king in haste, and said thus unto him, I have found a man of the captives of Judah, that will make known unto the king the interpretation.

26 The king answered and said to Daniel, whose name *was* Bĕl-te-shăz'zar, Art thou able to make known unto me the dream which I have seen, and the interpretation thereof?

27 Daniel answered in the presence of the king, and said, The secret which the king hath demanded cannot the wise *men*, the astrologers, the magicians, the soothsayers, shew unto the king;

28 But there is a God in heaven that revealeth secrets, and maketh known to the king Nĕb-u-chad-nĕz'zar what shall be in the latter days. Thy dream, and the visions of thy head upon thy bed, are these;

29 As for thee, O king, thy thoughts came *into thy mind* upon thy bed, what should come to pass hereafter: and he that revealeth secrets maketh known to thee what shall come to pass.

30 But as for me, this secret is not revealed to me for *any* wisdom that I have more than any living, but for *their* sakes that shall make known the interpretation to the king, and that thou mightest know the thoughts of thy heart.

31 ¶Thou, O king, sawest, and behold a great image. This great image, whose brightness *was* excellent, stood before thee; and the form thereof *was* terrible.

32 This image's head *was* of fine gold, his breast and his arms of silver, his belly and his thighs of brass,

33 His legs of iron, his feet part of iron and part of clay.

34 Thou sawest till that a stone was cut out without hands, which smote the image upon his feet *that were* of iron and clay, and brake them to pieces.

35 Then was the iron, the clay, the brass, the silver, and the gold, broken to pieces together, and became like the chaff of the summer threshingfloors; and the wind carried them away, that no place was found for them: and the stone that smote the image became a great mountain, and filled the whole earth.

36 ¶This *is* the dream; and we will tell the interpretation thereof before the king.

37 Thou, O king, *art* a king of kings: for the God of heaven hath given thee a kingdom, power, and strength, and glory.

38 And wheresoever the children of men dwell, the beasts of the field and the fowls of the heaven hath he given into thine hand, and hath made thee ruler over them all. Thou *art* this head of gold.

39 And after thee shall arise another kingdom inferior to thee, and another third kingdom of brass, which shall bear rule over all the earth.

40 And the fourth kingdom shall be strong as iron: forasmuch as iron breaketh in pieces and subdueth all *things:* and as iron that breaketh all these, shall it break in pieces and bruise.

41 And whereas thou sawest the feet and toes, part of potters' clay, and part of iron, the kingdom shall be divided; but there shall be in it of the strength of

the iron, forasmuch as thou sawest the iron mixed with miry clay.

42 And *as* the toes of the feet *were* part of iron, and part of clay, *so* the kingdom shall be partly strong, and partly broken.

43 And whereas thou sawest iron mixed with miry clay, they shall mingle themselves with the seed of men: but they shall not cleave one to another, even as iron is not mixed with clay.

44 And in the days of these kings shall the God of heaven set up a kingdom, which shall never be destroyed: and the kingdom shall not be left to other people, *but* it shall break in pieces and consume all these kingdoms, and it shall stand for ever.

45 Forasmuch as thou sawest that the stone was cut out of the mountain without hands, and that it brake in pieces the iron, the brass, the clay, the silver, and the gold; the great God hath made known to the king what shall come to pass hereafter: and the dream *is* certain, and the interpretation thereof sure.

46 ¶Then the king Nĕb-u-chad-nĕz'-zar fell upon his face, and worshipped Daniel, and commanded that they should offer an oblation and sweet odours unto him.

47 The king answered unto Daniel, and said, Of a truth *it is*, that your God *is* a God of gods, and a Lord of kings, and a revealer of secrets, seeing thou couldest reveal this secret.

48 Then the king made Daniel a great man, and gave him many great gifts, and made him ruler over the whole province of Babylon, and chief of the governors over all the wise *men* of Babylon.

49 Then Daniel requested of the king, and he set Shă'drăch, Mē'shăch, and A-bĕd'-ne-gō, over the affairs of the province of Babylon: but Daniel *sat* in the gate of the king.

CHAPTER 3

NĔB-U-CHAD-NĔZ'ZAR the king made an image of gold, whose height *was* threescore cubits, *and* the breadth thereof six cubits: he set it up in the plain of Dū'ra, in the province of Babylon.

2 Then Nĕb-u-chad-nĕz'zar the king sent to gather together the princes, the governors, and the captains, the judges, the treasurers, the counsellors, the sheriffs, and all the rulers of the provinces, to come to the dedication of the image which Nĕb-u-chad-nĕz'zar the king had set up.

3 Then the princes, the governors, and captains, the judges, the treasurers, the counsellors, the sheriffs, and all the rulers of the provinces, were gathered together unto the dedication of the image that Nĕb-u-chad-nĕz'zar the king had set up; and they stood before the image that Nĕb-u-chad-nĕz'zar had set up.

4 Then an herald cried aloud, To you it is commanded, O people, nations, and languages,

5 *That* at what time ye hear the sound of the cornet, flute, harp, sackbut, psaltery, dulcimer, and all kinds of musick, ye fall down and worship the golden image that Nĕb-u-chad-nĕz'zar the king hath set up:

6 And whoso falleth not down and worshippeth shall the same hour be cast into the midst of a burning fiery furnace.

7 Therefore at that time, when all the people heard the sound of the cornet, flute, harp, sackbut, psaltery, and all kinds of musick, all the people, the nations, and the languages, fell down *and* worshipped the golden image that Nĕb-u-chad-nĕz'zar the king had set up.

8 ¶Wherefore at that time certain Chăl-dē'anṡ came near, and accused the Jews.

9 They spake and said to the king Nĕb-u-chad-nĕz'zar, O king, live for ever.

10 Thou, O king, hast made a decree, that every man that shall hear the sound of the cornet, flute, harp, sackbut, psaltery, and dulcimer, and all kinds of musick, shall fall down and worship the golden image:

11 And whoso falleth not down and worshippeth, *that* he should be cast into the midst of a burning fiery furnace.

12 There are certain Jews whom thou hast set over the affairs of the province of Babylon, Shă'drăch, Mē'shăch, and A-bĕd'-ne-gō; these men, O king, have not regarded thee: they serve not thy gods, nor worship the golden image which thou hast set up.

13 ¶Then Nĕb-u-chad-nĕz'zar in *his* rage and fury commanded to bring Shă'drăch, Mē'shăch, and A-bĕd'-ne-gō. Then they brought these men before the king.

14 Nĕb-u-chad-nĕz'zar spake and said unto them, *Is it* true, O Shă'drăch, Mē'shăch, and A-bĕd'-ne-gō, do not ye serve my gods, nor worship the golden image which I have set up?

15 Now if ye be ready that at what time ye hear the sound of the cornet, flute, harp, sackbut, psaltery, and dul-

cimer, and all kinds of musick, ye fall down and worship the image which I have made; *well:* but if ye worship not, ye shall be cast the same hour into the midst of a burning fiery furnace; and who *is* that God that shall deliver you out of my hands?

16 Shă′drăch, Mē′shăch, and A-bĕd′-ne-gō, answered and said to the king, O Nĕb-u-chad-nĕz′zar, we *are* not careful to answer thee in this matter.

17 If it be *so*, our God whom we serve is able to deliver us from the burning fiery furnace, and he will deliver *us* out of thine hand, O king.

18 But if not, be it known unto thee, O king, that we will not serve thy gods, nor worship the golden image which thou hast set up.

19 ¶Then was Nĕb-u-chad-nĕz′zar full of fury, and the form of his visage was changed against Shă′drăch, Mē′shăch, and A-bĕd′-ne-gō: *therefore* he spake, and commanded that they should heat the furnace one seven times more than it was wont to be heated.

20 And he commanded the most mighty men that *were* in his army to bind Shă′drăch, Mē′shăch, and A-bĕd′-ne-gō, *and* to cast *them* into the burning fiery furnace.

21 Then these men were bound in their coats, their hosen, and their hats, and their *other* garments, and were cast into the midst of the burning fiery furnace.

22 Therefore because the king's commandment was urgent, and the furnace exceeding hot, the flame of the fire slew those men that took up Shă′drăch, Mē′shăch, and A-bĕd′-ne-gō.

23 And these three men, Shă′drăch, Mē′shăch, and A-bĕd′-ne-gō, fell down bound into the midst of the burning fiery furnace.

24 Then Nĕb-u-chad-nĕz′zar the king was astonied, and rose up in haste, *and* spake, and said unto his counsellors, Did not we cast three men bound into the midst of the fire? They answered and said unto the king, True, O king.

25 He answered and said, Lo, I see four men loose, walking in the midst of the fire, and they have no hurt; and the form of the fourth is like the Son of God.

26 ¶Then Nĕb-u-chad-nĕz′zar came near to the mouth of the burning fiery furnace, *and* spake, and said, Shă′drăch, Mē′shăch, and A-bĕd′-ne-gō, ye servants of the most high God, come forth, and come *hither*. Then Shă′drăch, Mē′shăch, and A-bĕd′-ne-gō, came forth of the midst of the fire.

27 And the princes, governors, and captains, and the king's counsellors, being gathered together, saw these men, upon whose bodies the fire had no power, nor was an hair of their head singed, neither were their coats changed, nor the smell of fire had passed on them.

28 *Then* Nĕb-u-chad-nĕz′zar spake, and said, Blessed *be* the God of Shă′drăch, Mē′shăch, and A-bĕd′-ne-gō, who hath sent his angel, and delivered his servants that trusted in him, and have changed the king's word, and yielded their bodies, that they might not serve nor worship any god, except their own God.

29 Therefore I make a decree, That every people, nation, and language, which speak any thing amiss against the God of Shă′drăch, Mē′shăch, and A-bĕd′-ne-gō, shall be cut in pieces, and their houses shall be made a dunghill: because there is no other God that can deliver after this sort.

30 ¶Then the king promoted Shă′drăch, Mē′shăch, and A-bĕd′-ne-gō, in the province of Babylon.

CHAPTER 4

NEB-U-CHAD-NEZ′ZAR the king, unto all people, nations, and languages, that dwell in all the earth; Peace be multiplied unto you.

2 I thought it good to shew the signs and wonders that the high God hath wrought toward me.

3 How great *are* his signs! and how mighty *are* his wonders! his kingdom *is* an everlasting kingdom, and his dominion *is* from generation to generation.

4 ¶I Nĕb-u-chad-nĕz′zar was at rest in mine house, and flourishing in my palace:

5 I saw a dream which made me afraid, and the thoughts upon my bed and the visions of my head troubled me.

6 Therefore made I a decree to bring in all the wise *men* of Babylon before me, that they might make known unto me the interpretation of the dream.

7 Then came in the magicians, the astrologers, the Chăl-dē′anṡ, and the soothsayers: and I told the dream before them; but they did not make known unto me the interpretation thereof.

8 But at the last Daniel came in before me, whose name *was* Bĕl-te-shăz′zar, according to the name of my god, and in whom *is* the spirit of the holy gods: and before him I told the dream, *saying*,

9 O Bĕl-te-shăz'zar, master of the magicians, because I know that the spirit of the holy gods *is* in thee, and no secret troubleth thee, tell me the visions of my dream that I have seen, and the interpretation thereof.
10 Thus *were* the visions of mine head in my bed; I saw, and behold a tree in the midst of the earth, and the height thereof *was* great.
11 The tree grew, and was strong, and the height thereof reached unto heaven, and the sight thereof to the end of all the earth:
12 The leaves thereof *were* fair, and the fruit thereof much, and in it *was* meat for all: the beasts of the field had shadow under it, and the fowls of the heaven dwelt in the boughs thereof, and all flesh was fed of it.
13 I saw in the visions of my head upon my bed, and, behold, a watcher and an holy one came down from heaven;
14 He cried aloud, and said thus, Hew down the tree, and cut off his branches, shake off his leaves, and scatter his fruit: let the beasts get away from under it, and the fowls from his branches:
15 Nevertheless leave the stump of his roots in the earth, even with a band of iron and brass, in the tender grass of the field; and let it be wet with the dew of heaven, and *let* his portion *be* with the beasts in the grass of the earth:
16 Let his heart be changed from man's, and let a beast's heart be given unto him; and let seven times pass over him.
17 This matter *is* by the decree of the watchers, and the demand by the word of the holy ones: to the intent that the living may know that the most High ruleth in the kingdom of men, and giveth it to whomsoever he will, and setteth up over it the basest of men.
18 This dream I king Nĕb-u-chad-nĕz'zar have seen. Now thou, O Bĕl-te-shăz'zar, declare the interpretation thereof, forasmuch as all the wise *men* of my kingdom are not able to make known unto me the interpretation: but thou *art* able; for the spirit of the holy gods *is* in thee.
19 ¶Then Daniel, whose name *was* Bĕl-te-shăz'zar, was astonied for one hour, and his thoughts troubled him. The king spake, and said, Bĕl-te-shăz'zar, let not the dream, or the interpretation thereof, trouble thee. Bĕl-te-shăz'zar answered and said, My lord, the dream *be* to them that hate thee, and the interpretation thereof to thine enemies.
20 The tree that thou sawest, which grew, and was strong, whose height reached unto the heaven, and the sight thereof to all the earth;
21 Whose leaves *were* fair, and the fruit thereof much, and in it *was* meat for all; under which the beasts of the field dwelt, and upon whose branches the fowls of the heaven had their habitation:
22 It *is* thou, O king, that art grown and become strong: for thy greatness is grown, and reacheth unto heaven, and thy dominion to the end of the earth.
23 And whereas the king saw a watcher and an holy one coming down from heaven, and saying, Hew the tree down, and destroy it; yet leave the stump of the roots thereof in the earth, even with a band of iron and brass, in the tender grass of the field; and let it be wet with the dew of heaven, and *let* his portion *be* with the beasts of the field, till seven times pass over him;
24 This *is* the interpretation, O king, and this *is* the decree of the most High, which is come upon my lord the king:
25 That they shall drive thee from men, and thy dwelling shall be with the beasts of the field, and they shall make thee to eat grass as oxen, and they shall wet thee with the dew of heaven, and seven times shall pass over thee, till thou know that the most High ruleth in the kingdom of men, and giveth it to whomsoever he will.
26 And whereas they commanded to leave the stump of the tree roots; thy kingdom shall be sure unto thee, after that thou shalt have known that the heavens do rule.
27 Wherefore, O king, let my counsel be acceptable unto thee, and break off thy sins by righteousness, and thine iniquities by shewing mercy to the poor; if it may be a lengthening of thy tranquillity.
28 ¶All this came upon the king Nĕb-u-chad-nĕz'zar.
29 At the end of twelve months he walked in the palace of the kingdom of Babylon.
30 The king spake, and said, Is not this great Babylon, that I have built for the house of the kingdom by the might of my power, and for the honour of my majesty?
31 While the word *was* in the king's mouth, there fell a voice from heaven, *saying*, O king Nĕb-u-chad-nĕz-zar, to thee it is spoken; The kingdom is departed from thee.
32 And they shall drive thee from men, and thy dwelling *shall be* with the beasts of the field: they shall make thee to eat grass as oxen, and seven times

shall pass over thee, until thou know that the most High ruleth in the kingdom of men, and giveth it to whomsoever he will.

33 The same hour was the thing fulfilled upon Nĕb-u-chad-nĕz′zar: and he was driven from men, and did eat grass as oxen, and his body was wet with the dew of heaven, till his hairs were grown like eagles' *feathers*, and his nails like birds' *claws*.

34 And at the end of the days I Nĕb-u-chad-nĕz′zar lifted up mine eyes unto heaven, and mine understanding returned unto me, and I blessed the most High, and I praised and honoured him that liveth for ever, whose dominion *is* an everlasting dominion, and his kingdom *is* from generation to generation:

35 And all the inhabitants of the earth *are* reputed as nothing: and he doeth according to his will in the army of heaven, and *among* the inhabitants of the earth: and none can stay his hand, or say unto him, What doest thou?

36 At the same time my reason returned unto me; and for the glory of my kingdom, mine honour and brightness returned unto me; and my counsellors and my lords sought unto me; and I was established in my kingdom, and excellent majesty was added unto me.

37 Now I Nĕb-u-chad-nĕz′zar praise and extol and honour the King of heaven, all whose works *are* truth, and his ways judgment: and those that walk in pride he is able to abase.

CHAPTER 5

BEL-SHAZ′ZAR the king made a great feast to a thousand of his lords, and drank wine before the thousand.

2 Bĕl-shăz′zar, whiles he tasted the wine, commanded to bring the golden and silver vessels which his father Nĕb-u-chad-nĕz′zar had taken out of the temple which *was* in Jerusalem; that the king, and his princes, his wives, and his concubines, might drink therein.

3 Then they brought the golden vessels that were taken out of the temple of the house of God which *was* at Jerusalem; and the king, and his princes, his wives, and his concubines, drank in them.

4 They drank wine, and praised the gods of gold, and of silver, of brass, of iron, of wood, and of stone.

5 ¶In the same hour came forth fingers of a man's hand, and wrote over against the candlestick upon the plaister of the wall of the king's palace: and the king saw the part of the hand that wrote.

6 Then the king's countenance was changed, and his thoughts troubled him, so that the joints of his loins were loosed, and his knees smote one against another.

7 The king cried aloud to bring in the astrologers, the Chăl-dē′anṡ, and the soothsayers. *And* the king spake, and said to the wise *men* of Babylon, Whosoever shall read this writing, and shew me the interpretation thereof, shall be clothed with scarlet, and *have* a chain of gold about his neck, and shall be the third ruler in the kingdom.

8 Then came in all the king's wise *men:* but they could not read the writing, nor make known to the king the interpretation thereof.

9 Then was king Bĕl-shăz′zar greatly troubled, and his countenance was changed in him, and his lords were astonied.

10 ¶*Now* the queen by reason of the words of the king and his lords came into the banquet house: *and* the queen spake and said, O king, live for ever: let not thy thoughts trouble thee, nor let thy countenance be changed:

11 There is a man in thy kingdom, in whom *is* the spirit of the holy gods; and in the days of thy father light and understanding and wisdom, like the wisdom of the gods, was found in him; whom the king Nĕb-u-chad-nĕz′zar thy father, the king, *I say*, thy father, made master of the magicians, astrologers, Chăl-dē′anṡ, *and* soothsayers;

12 Forasmuch as an excellent spirit, and knowledge, and understanding, interpreting of dreams, and shewing of hard sentences, and dissolving of doubts, were found in the same Daniel, whom the king named Bĕl-te-shăz′zar: now let Daniel be called, and he will shew the interpretation.

13 Then was Daniel brought in before the king. *And* the king spake and said unto Daniel, *Art* thou that Daniel, which *art* of the children of the captivity of Judah, whom the king my father brought out of Jewry?

14 I have even heard of thee, that the spirit of the gods *is* in thee, and *that* light and understanding and excellent wisdom is found in thee.

15 And now the wise *men*, the astrologers, have been brought in before me, that they should read this writing, and make known unto me the interpretation thereof: but they could not shew the interpretation of the thing:

16 And I have heard of thee, that thou canst make interpretations, and dissolve doubts: now if thou canst read the writing, and make known to me the interpretation thereof, thou shalt be

clothed with scarlet, and *have* a chain of gold about thy neck, and shalt be the third ruler in the kingdom.

17 ¶Then Daniel answered and said before the king, Let thy gifts be to thyself, and give thy rewards to another; yet I will read the writing unto the king, and make known to him the interpretation.

18 O thou king, the most high God gave Nĕb-u-chad-nĕz′zar thy father a kingdom, and majesty, and glory, and honour:

19 And for the majesty that he gave him, all people, nations, and languages, trembled and feared before him: whom he would he slew; and whom he would he kept alive; and whom he would he set up; and whom he would he put down.

20 But when his heart was lifted up, and his mind hardened in pride, he was deposed from his kingly throne, and they took his glory from him:

21 And he was driven from the sons of men; and his heart was made like the beasts, and his dwelling *was* with the wild asses: they fed him with grass like oxen, and his body was wet with the dew of heaven; till he knew that the most high God ruled in the kingdom of men, and *that* he appointeth over it whomsoever he will.

22 And thou his son, O Bĕl-shăz′zar, hast not humbled thine heart, though thou knewest all this;

23 But hast lifted up thyself against the Lord of heaven; and they have brought the vessels of his house before thee, and thou, and thy lords, thy wives, and thy concubines, have drunk wine in them; and thou hast praised the gods of silver, and gold, of brass, iron, wood, and stone, which see not, nor hear, nor know: and the God in whose hand thy breath *is*, and whose *are* all thy ways, hast thou not glorified:

24 Then was the part of the hand sent from him; and this writing was written.

25 ¶And this *is* the writing that was written, MĒ′NE, MĒ′NE, TĒ′KEL, Ū-PHÄR′SĬN.

26 This *is* the interpretation of the thing: MĒ′NE; God hath numbered thy kingdom, and finished it.

27 TĒ′KEL; Thou art weighed in the balances, and art found wanting.

28 PĒ′RES; Thy kingdom is divided, and given to the Medes and Persians.

29 Then commanded Bĕl-shăz′zar, and they clothed Daniel with scarlet, and *put* a chain of gold about his neck, and made a proclamation concerning him, that he should be the third ruler in the kingdom.

30 ¶In that night was Bĕl-shăz′zar the king of the Chăl-dē′ans slain.

31 And Darius the Mē′dĭ-an took the kingdom, *being* about threescore and two years old.

CHAPTER 6

IT pleased Darius to set over the kingdom an hundred and twenty princes, which should be over the whole kingdom;

2 And over these three presidents; of whom Daniel *was* first: that the princes might give accounts unto them, and the king should have no damage.

3 Then this Daniel was preferred above the presidents and princes, because an excellent spirit *was* in him; and the king thought to set him over the whole realm.

4 ¶Then the presidents and princes sought to find occasion against Daniel concerning the kingdom; but they could find none occasion nor fault; forasmuch as he *was* faithful, neither was there any error or fault found in him.

5 Then said these men, We shall not find any occasion against this Daniel, except we find *it* against him concerning the law of his God.

6 Then these presidents and princes assembled together to the king, and said thus unto him, King Darius, live for ever.

7 All the presidents of the kingdom, the governors, and the princes, the counsellors, and the captains, have consulted together to establish a royal statute, and to make a firm decree, that whosoever shall ask a petition of any God or man for thirty days, save of thee, O king, he shall be cast into the den of lions.

8 Now, O king, establish the decree, and sign the writing, that it be not changed, according to the law of the Medes and Persians, which altereth not.

9 Wherefore king Darius signed the writing and the decree.

10 ¶Now when Daniel knew that the writing was signed, he went into his house; and his windows being open in his chamber toward Jerusalem, he kneeled upon his knees three times a day, and prayed, and gave thanks before his God, as he did aforetime.

11 Then these men assembled, and found Daniel praying and making supplication before his God.

12 Then they came near, and spake before the king concerning the king's decree; Hast thou not signed a decree, that every man that shall ask *a petition* of any God or man within thirty days,

save of thee, O king, shall be cast into
the den of lions? The king answered
and said, The thing *is* true, according to
the law of the Medes and Persians,
which altereth not.
13 Then answered they and said be-
fore the king, That Daniel, which *is* of
the children of the captivity of Judah,
regardeth not thee, O king, nor the
decree that thou hast signed, but
maketh his petition three times a day.
14 Then the king, when he heard
these words, was sore displeased with
himself, and set *his* heart on Daniel to
deliver him: and he laboured till the
going down of the sun to deliver him.
15 Then these men assembled unto
the king, and said unto the king, Know,
O king, that the law of the Medes and
Persians *is*, That no decree nor statute
which the king establisheth may be
changed.
16 Then the king commanded, and
they brought Daniel, and cast *him* into
the den of lions. *Now* the king spake
and said unto Daniel, Thy God whom
thou servest continually, he will deliver
thee.
17 And a stone was brought, and laid
upon the mouth of the den; and the king
sealed it with his own signet, and with
the signet of his lords; that the purpose
might not be changed concerning Dan-
iel.
18 ¶Then the king went to his palace,
and passed the night fasting: neither
were instruments of musick brought
before him: and his sleep went from
him.
19 Then the king arose very early in
the morning, and went in haste unto
the den of lions.
20 And when he came to the den, he
cried with a lamentable voice unto Dan-
iel: *and* the king spake and said to Dan-
iel, O Daniel, servant of the living
God, is thy God, whom thou servest
continually, able to deliver thee from
the lions?
21 Then said Daniel unto the king, O
king, live for ever.
22 My God hath sent his angel, and
hath shut the lions' mouths, that they
have not hurt me: forasmuch as before
him innocency was found in me; and
also before thee, O king, have I done no
hurt.
23 Then was the king exceeding glad
for him, and commanded that they
should take Daniel up out of the den. So
Daniel was taken up out of the den, and
no manner of hurt was found upon him,
because he believed in his God.
24 ¶And the king commanded, and
they brought those men which had ac-
cused Daniel, and they cast *them* into
the den of lions, them, their children,
and their wives; and the lions had the
mastery of them, and brake all their
bones in pieces or ever they came at the
bottom of the den.
25 ¶Then king Darius wrote unto all
people, nations, and languages, that
dwell in all the earth; Peace be mul-
tiplied unto you.
26 I make a decree, That in every
dominion of my kingdom men tremble
and fear before the God of Daniel: for
he *is* the living God, and stedfast for
ever, and his kingdom *that* which shall
not be destroyed, and his dominion
shall be even unto the end.
27 He delivereth and rescueth, and he
worketh signs and wonders in heaven
and in earth, who hath delivered Daniel
from the power of the lions.
28 So this Daniel prospered in the
reign of Darius, and in the reign of Cy-
rus the Persian.

CHAPTER 7

IN the first year of Bĕl-shăz′zar king of
Babylon Daniel had a dream and vi-
sions of his head upon his bed: then he
wrote the dream, *and* told the sum of
the matters.
2 Daniel spake and said, I saw in my
vision by night, and, behold, the four
winds of the heaven strove upon the
great sea.
3 And four great beasts came up from
the sea, diverse one from another.
4 The first *was* like a lion, and had
eagle's wings: I beheld till the wings
thereof were plucked, and it was lifted
up from the earth, and made stand
upon the feet as a man, and a man's
heart was given to it.
5 And behold another beast, a sec-
ond, like to a bear, and it raised up it-
self on one side, and *it had* three ribs in
the mouth of it between the teeth of it:
and they said thus unto it, Arise, de-
vour much flesh.
6 After this I beheld, and lo another,
like a leopard, which had upon the back
of it four wings of a fowl; the beast had
also four heads; and dominion was giv-
en to it.
7 After this I saw in the night visions,
and behold a fourth beast, dreadful and
terrible, and strong exceedingly; and it
had great iron teeth: it devoured and
brake in pieces, and stamped the res-
idue with the feet of it: and it *was* di-
verse from all the beasts that *were* be-
fore it; and it had ten horns.
8 I considered the horns, and, behold,
there came up among them another
little horn, before whom there were

three of the first horns plucked up by
the roots: and, behold, in this horn *were*
eyes like the eyes of man, and a mouth
speaking great things.
9 ¶I beheld till the thrones were cast
down, and the Ancient of days did sit,
whose garment *was* white as snow, and
the hair of his head like the pure wool:
his throne *was like* the fiery flame, *and*
his wheels *as* burning fire.
10 A fiery stream issued and came
forth from before him: thousand thou-
sands ministered unto him, and ten
thousand times ten thousand stood be-
fore him: the judgment was set, and the
books were opened.
11 I beheld then because of the voice
of the great words which the horn
spake: I beheld *even* till the beast was
slain, and his body destroyed, and giv-
en to the burning flame.
12 As concerning the rest of the
beasts, they had their dominion taken
away: yet their lives were prolonged
for a season and time.
13 I saw in the night visions, and, be-
hold, *one* like the Son of man came
with the clouds of heaven, and came to
the Ancient of days, and they brought
him near before him.
14 And there was given him
dominion, and glory, and a kingdom,
that all people, nations, and languages,
should serve him: his dominion *is* an
everlasting dominion, which shall not
pass away, and his kingdom *that* which
shall not be destroyed.
15 ¶I Daniel was grieved in my spirit
in the midst of *my* body, and the visions
of my head troubled me.
16 I came near unto one of them that
stood by, and asked him the truth of all
this. So he told me, and made me know
the interpretation of the things.
17 These great beasts, which are
four, *are* four kings, *which* shall arise
out of the earth.
18 But the saints of the most High
shall take the kingdom, and possess the
kingdom for ever, even for ever and
ever.
19 Then I would know the truth of the
fourth beast, which was diverse from
all the others, exceeding dreadful,
whose teeth *were of* iron, and his nails
of brass; *which* devoured, brake in
pieces, and stamped the residue with
his feet;
20 And of the ten horns that *were* in
his head, and *of* the other which came
up, and before whom three fell; even *of*
that horn that had eyes, and a mouth
that spake very great things, whose
look *was* more stout than his fellows.
21 I beheld, and the same horn made
war with the saints, and prevailed
against them;
22 Until the Ancient of days came,
and judgment was given to the saints of
the most High; and the time came that
the saints possessed the kingdom.
23 Thus he said, The fourth beast
shall be the fourth kingdom upon earth,
which shall be diverse from all king-
doms, and shall devour the whole
earth, and shall tread it down, and
break it in pieces.
24 And the ten horns out of this king-
dom *are* ten kings *that* shall arise: and
another shall rise after them; and he
shall be diverse from the first, and he
shall subdue three kings.
25 And he shall speak *great* words
against the most High, and shall wear
out the saints of the most High, and
think to change times and laws: and
they shall be given into his hand until a
time and times and the dividing of time.
26 But the judgment shall sit, and
they shall take away his dominion, to
consume and to destroy *it* unto the end.
27 And the kingdom and dominion,
and the greatness of the kingdom un-
der the whole heaven, shall be given to
the people of the saints of the most
High, whose kingdom *is* an everlasting
kingdom, and all dominions shall serve
and obey him.
28 Hitherto *is* the end of the matter.
As for me Daniel, my cogitations much
troubled me, and my countenance
changed in me: but I kept the matter in
my heart.

CHAPTER 8

IN the third year of the reign of king
Bĕl-shăz'zar a vision appeared unto
me, *even unto* me Daniel, after that
which appeared unto me at the first.
2 And I saw in a vision; and it came to
pass, when I saw, that I *was* at Shū'-
shăn *in* the palace, which *is* in the
province of Ē'lam; and I saw in a vision,
and I was by the river of Ū'la-ī.
3 Then I lifted up mine eyes, and saw,
and, behold, there stood before the riv-
er a ram which had *two* horns: and the
two horns *were* high; but one *was* high-
er than the other, and the higher came
up last.
4 I saw the ram pushing westward,
and northward, and southward; so that
no beasts might stand before him,
neither *was there any* that could de-
liver out of his hand; but he did accord-
ing to his will, and became great.
5 And as I was considering, behold,
an he goat came from the west on the
face of the whole earth, and touched

not the ground: and the goat *had* a notable horn between his eyes.

6 And he came to the ram that had *two* horns, which I had seen standing before the river, and ran unto him in the fury of his power.

7 And I saw him come close unto the ram, and he was moved with choler against him, and smote the ram, and brake his two horns: and there was no power in the ram to stand before him, but he cast him down to the ground, and stamped upon him: and there was none that could deliver the ram out of his hand.

8 Therefore the he goat waxed very great: and when he was strong, the great horn was broken; and for it came up four notable ones toward the four winds of heaven.

9 And out of one of them came forth a little horn, which waxed exceeding great, toward the south, and toward the east, and toward the pleasant *land*.

10 And it waxed great, *even* to the host of heaven; and it cast down *some* of the host and of the stars to the ground, and stamped upon them.

11 Yea, he magnified *himself* even to the prince of the host, and by him the daily *sacrifice* was taken away, and the place of his sanctuary was cast down.

12 And an host was given *him* against the daily *sacrifice* by reason of transgression, and it cast down the truth to the ground; and it practised, and prospered.

13 ¶Then I heard one saint speaking, and another saint said unto that certain *saint* which spake, How long *shall be* the vision *concerning* the daily *sacrifice*, and the transgression of desolation, to give both the sanctuary and the host to be trodden under foot?

14 And he said unto me, Unto two thousand and three hundred days; then shall the sanctuary be cleansed.

15 ¶And it came to pass, when I, *even* I Daniel, had seen the vision, and sought for the meaning, then, behold, there stood before me as the appearance of a man.

16 And I heard a man's voice between *the banks of* Ū'la-ī, which called, and said, Gabriel, make this *man* to understand the vision.

17 So he came near where I stood: and when he came, I was afraid, and fell upon my face: but he said unto me, Understand, O son of man: for at the time of the end *shall be* the vision.

18 Now as he was speaking with me, I was in a deep sleep on my face toward the ground: but he touched me, and set me upright.

19 And he said, Behold, I will make thee know what shall be in the last end of the indignation: for at the time appointed the end *shall be*.

20 The ram which thou sawest having *two* horns *are* the kings of Mē'dĭ-a and Persia.

21 And the rough goat *is* the king of Grecia: and the great horn that *is* between his eyes *is* the first king.

22 Now that being broken, whereas four stood up for it, four kingdoms shall stand up out of the nation, but not in his power.

23 And in the latter time of their kingdom, when the transgressors are come to the full, a king of fierce countenance, and understanding dark sentences, shall stand up.

24 And his power shall be mighty, but not by his own power: and he shall destroy wonderfully, and shall prosper, and practise, and shall destroy the mighty and the holy people.

25 And through his policy also he shall cause craft to prosper in his hand; and he shall magnify *himself* in his heart, and by peace shall destroy many: he shall also stand up against the Prince of princes; but he shall be broken without hand.

26 And the vision of the evening and the morning which was told *is* true: wherefore shut thou up the vision; for it *shall be* for many days.

27 And I Daniel fainted, and was sick *certain* days; afterward I rose up, and did the king's business; and I was astonished at the vision, but none understood *it*.

CHAPTER 9

IN the first year of Darius the son of A-haś-ū-ē'rus, of the seed of the Medes, which was made king over the realm of the Chăl-dē'anś;

2 In the first year of his reign I Daniel understood by books the number of the years, whereof the word of the LORD came to Jeremiah the prophet, that he would accomplish seventy years in the desolations of Jerusalem.

3 ¶And I set my face unto the Lord God, to seek by prayer and supplications, with fasting, and sackcloth, and ashes:

4 And I prayed unto the LORD my God, and made my confession, and said, O Lord, the great and dreadful God, keeping the covenant and mercy to them that love him, and to them that keep his commandments;

5 We have sinned, and have committed iniquity, and have done wickedly, and have rebelled, even by

departing from thy precepts and from
thy judgments:
6 Neither have we hearkened unto
thy servants the prophets, which spake
in thy name to our kings, our princes,
and our fathers, and to all the people of
the land.
7 O Lord, righteousness *belongeth*
unto thee, but unto us confusion of
faces, as at this day; to the men of Ju-
dah, and to the inhabitants of Jeru-
salem, and unto all Israel, *that are* near,
and *that are* far off, through all the
countries whither thou hast driven
them, because of their trespass that
they have trespassed against thee.
8 O Lord, to us *belongeth* confusion
of face, to our kings, to our princes, and
to our fathers, because we have sinned
against thee.
9 To the Lord our God *belong* mercies
and forgivenesses, though we have re-
belled against him;
10 Neither have we obeyed the voice
of the LORD our God, to walk in his
laws, which he set before us by his ser-
vants the prophets.
11 Yea, all Israel have transgressed
thy law, even by departing, that they
might not obey thy voice; therefore the
curse is poured upon us, and the oath
that *is* written in the law of Moses the
servant of God, because we have
sinned against him.
12 And he hath confirmed his words,
which he spake against us, and against
our judges that judged us, by bringing
upon us a great evil: for under the
whole heaven hath not been done as
hath been done upon Jerusalem.
13 As *it is* written in the law of Moses,
all this evil is come upon us: yet made
we not our prayer before the LORD our
God, that we might turn from our iniqui-
ties, and understand thy truth.
14 Therefore hath the LORD watched
upon the evil, and brought it upon us:
for the LORD our God *is* righteous in all
his works which he doeth: for we
obeyed not his voice.
15 And now, O Lord our God, that
hast brought thy people forth out of the
land of Egypt with a mighty hand, and
hast gotten thee renown, as at this day;
we have sinned, we have done
wickedly.
16 ¶O Lord, according to all thy
righteousness, I beseech thee, let thine
anger and thy fury be turned away
from thy city Jerusalem, thy holy
mountain: because for our sins, and for
the iniquities of our fathers, Jerusalem
and thy people *are become* a reproach
to all *that are* about us.
17 Now therefore, O our God, hear
the prayer of thy servant, and his sup-
plications, and cause thy face to shine
upon thy sanctuary that is desolate, for
the Lord's sake.
18 O my God, incline thine ear, and
hear; open thine eyes, and behold our
desolations, and the city which is called
by thy name: for we do not present our
supplications before thee for our righ-
teousnesses, but for thy great mercies.
19 O Lord, hear; O Lord, forgive; O
Lord, hearken and do; defer not, for
thine own sake, O my God: for thy city
and thy people are called by thy name.
20 ¶And whiles I *was* speaking, and
praying, and confessing my sin and the
sin of my people Israel, and presenting
my supplication before the LORD my
God for the holy mountain of my God;
21 Yea, whiles I *was* speaking in
prayer, even the man Gabriel, whom I
had seen in the vision at the beginning,
being caused to fly swiftly, touched me
about the time of the evening oblation.
22 And he informed *me*, and talked
with me, and said, O Daniel, I am now
come forth to give thee skill and under-
standing.
23 At the beginning of thy supplica-
tions the commandment came forth,
and I am come to shew *thee*; for thou
art greatly beloved: therefore under-
stand the matter, and consider the
vision.
24 Seventy weeks are determined
upon thy people and upon thy holy city,
to finish the transgression, and to make
an end of sins, and to make reconciliation
for iniquity, and to bring in ever-
lasting righteousness, and to seal up
the vision and prophecy, and to anoint
the most Holy.
25 Know therefore and understand,
that from the going forth of the com-
mandment to restore and to build Jeru-
salem unto the Messiah the Prince *shall*
be seven weeks, and threescore and
two weeks: the street shall be built
again, and the wall, even in troublous
times.
26 And after threescore and two
weeks shall Messiah be cut off, but not
for himself: and the people of the
prince that shall come shall destroy the
city and the sanctuary; and the end there-
of *shall be* with a flood, and unto the
end of the war desolations are deter-
mined.
27 And he shall confirm the covenant
with many for one week: and in the
midst of the week he shall cause the
sacrifice and the oblation to cease, and
for the overspreading of abominations
he shall make *it* desolate, even until the

consummation, and that determined
shall be poured upon the desolate.

CHAPTER 10

IN the third year of Cyrus king of Per-
sia a thing was revealed unto Daniel,
whose name was called Bĕl-te-shăz′zar;
and the thing *was* true, but the
time appointed *was* long: and he under-
stood the thing, and had understand-
ing of the vision.
2 In those days I Daniel was mourn-
ing three full weeks.
3 I ate no pleasant bread, neither
came flesh nor wine in my mouth,
neither did I anoint myself at all, till
three whole weeks were fulfilled.
4 And in the four and twentieth day
of the first month, as I was by the side
of the great river, which *is* Hĭd′de-kĕl;
5 Then I lifted up mine eyes, and
looked, and behold, a certain man
clothed in linen, whose loins *were*
girded with fine gold of Ū′phăz:
6 His body also *was* like the beryl,
and his face as the appearance of light-
ning, and his eyes as lamps of fire, and
his arms and his feet like in colour to
polished brass, and the voice of his
words like the voice of a multitude.
7 And I Daniel alone saw the vision:
for the men that were with me saw not
the vision; but a great quaking fell upon
them, so that they fled to hide them-
selves.
8 Therefore I was left alone, and saw
this great vision, and there remained
no strength in me: for my comeliness
was turned in me into corruption, and I
retained no strength.
9 Yet heard I the voice of his words:
and when I heard the voice of his
words, then was I in a deep sleep on my
face, and my face toward the ground.
10 ¶And, behold, an hand touched
me, which set me upon my knees and
upon the palms of my hands.
11 And he said unto me, O Daniel, a
man greatly beloved, understand the
words that I speak unto thee, and stand
upright: for unto thee am I now sent.
And when he had spoken this word
unto me, I stood trembling.
12 Then said he unto me, Fear not,
Daniel: for from the first day that thou
didst set thine heart to understand, and
to chasten thyself before thy God, thy
words were heard, and I am come for
thy words.
13 But the prince of the kingdom of
Persia withstood me one and twenty
days: but, lo, Michael, one of the chief
princes, came to help me; and I re-
mained there with the kings of Persia.
14 Now I am come to make thee under-
stand what shall befall thy people in
the latter days: for yet the vision *is* for
many days.
15 And when he had spoken such
words unto me, I set my face toward
the ground, and I became dumb.
16 And, behold, *one* like the simili-
tude of the sons of men touched my
lips: then I opened my mouth, and
spake, and said unto him that stood be-
fore me, O my lord, by the vision my
sorrows are turned upon me, and I have
retained no strength.
17 For how can the servant of this my
lord talk with this my lord? for as for
me, straightway there remained no
strength in me, neither is there breath
left in me.
18 Then there came again and
touched me *one* like the appearance of
a man, and he strengthened me,
19 And said, O man greatly beloved,
fear not: peace *be* unto thee, be strong,
yea, be strong. And when he had spo-
ken unto me, I was strengthened, and
said, Let my lord speak; for thou hast
strengthened me.
20 Then said he, Knowest thou where-
fore I come unto thee? and now will
I return to fight with the prince of Per-
sia: and when I am gone forth, lo, the
prince of Grecia shall come.
21 But I will shew thee that which is
noted in the scripture of truth: and
there is none that holdeth with me in
these things, but Michael your prince.

CHAPTER 11

ALSO I in the first year of Darius the
Mede, *even* I, stood to confirm and to
strengthen him.
2 And now will I shew thee the truth.
Behold, there shall stand up yet three
kings in Persia; and the fourth shall be
far richer than *they* all: and by his
strength through his riches he shall stir
up all against the realm of Grecia.
3 And a mighty king shall stand up,
that shall rule with great dominion, and
do according to his will.
4 And when he shall stand up, his
kingdom shall be broken, and shall be
divided toward the four winds of
heaven; and not to his posterity, nor ac-
cording to his dominion which he
ruled: for his kingdom shall be plucked
up, even for others beside those.
5 ¶And the king of the south shall be
strong, and *one* of his princes; and he
shall be strong above him, and have
dominion; his dominion *shall be* a great
dominion.
6 And in the end of years they shall
join themselves together; for the king's
daughter of the south shall come to the

king of the north to make an agree-
ment: but she shall not retain the power
of the arm; neither shall he stand, nor
his arm: but she shall be given up, and
they that brought her, and he that be-
gat her, and he that strengthened her in
these times.
7 But out of a branch of her roots
shall *one* stand up in his estate, which
shall come with an army, and shall en-
ter into the fortress of the king of the
north, and shall deal against them, and
shall prevail:
8 And shall also carry captives into
Egypt their gods, with their princes,
and with their precious vessels of silver
and of gold; and he shall continue *more*
years than the king of the north.
9 So the king of the south shall come
into *his* kingdom, and shall return into
his own land.
10 But his sons shall be stirred up,
and shall assemble a multitude of great
forces: and *one* shall certainly come,
and overflow, and pass through: then
shall he return, and be stirred up, *even*
to his fortress.
11 And the king of the south shall be
moved with choler, and shall come
forth and fight with him, *even* with the
king of the north: and he shall set forth
a great multitude; but the multitude
shall be given into his hand.
12 *And* when he hath taken away the
multitude, his heart shall be lifted up;
and he shall cast down *many* ten thou-
sands: but he shall not be strengthened
by it.
13 For the king of the north shall re-
turn, and shall set forth a multitude
greater than the former, and shall cer-
tainly come after certain years with a
great army and with much riches.
14 And in those times there shall
many stand up against the king of the
south: also the robbers of thy people
shall exalt themselves to establish the
vision; but they shall fall.
15 So the king of the north shall
come, and cast up a mount, and take
the most fenced cities: and the arms of
the south shall notwithstand, neither
his chosen people, neither *shall there
be any* strength to withstand.
16 But he that cometh against him
shall do according to his own will, and
none shall stand before him: and he
shall stand in the glorious land, which
by his hand shall be consumed.
17 He shall also set his face to enter
with the strength of his whole king-
dom, and upright ones with him; thus
shall he do: and he shall give him the
daughter of women, corrupting her:
but she shall not stand *on his side,*
neither be for him.
18 After this shall he turn his face
unto the isles, and shall take many: but
a prince for his own behalf shall cause
the reproach offered by him to cease;
without his own reproach he shall
cause *it* to turn upon him.
19 Then he shall turn his face toward
the fort of his own land: but he shall
stumble and fall, and not be found.
20 Then shall stand up in his estate a
raiser of taxes *in* the glory of the king-
dom: but within few days he shall be
destroyed, neither in anger, nor in
battle.
21 And in his estate shall stand up a
vile person, to whom they shall not give
the honour of the kingdom: but he shall
come in peaceably, and obtain the
kingdom by flatteries.
22 And with the arms of a flood shall
they be overflown from before him,
and shall be broken; yea, also the
prince of the covenant.
23 And after the league *made* with
him he shall work deceitfully: for he
shall come up, and shall become strong
with a small people.
24 He shall enter peaceably even
upon the fattest places of the province;
and he shall do *that* which his fathers
have not done, nor his fathers' fathers;
he shall scatter among them the prey,
and spoil, and riches: *yea,* and he shall
forecast his devices against the strong
holds, even for a time.
25 And he shall stir up his power and
his courage against the king of the
south with a great army; and the king
of the south shall be stirred up to battle
with a very great and mighty army; but
he shall not stand: for they shall fore-
cast devices against him.
26 Yea, they that feed of the portion
of his meat shall destroy him, and his
army shall overflow: and many shall
fall down slain.
27 And both these kings' hearts *shall
be* to do mischief, and they shall speak
lies at one table; but it shall not pros-
per: for yet the end *shall be* at the time
appointed.
28 Then shall he return into his land
with great riches; and his heart *shall be*
against the holy covenant; and he shall
do *exploits,* and return to his own land.
29 At the time appointed he shall re-
turn, and come toward the south; but it
shall not be as the former, or as the lat-
ter.
30 For the ships of Chĭt'tĭm shall
come against him: therefore he shall be
grieved, and return, and have indigna-
tion against the holy covenant: so shall

he do; he shall even return, and have intelligence with them that forsake the holy covenant.

31 And arms shall stand on his part, and they shall pollute the sanctuary of strength, and shall take away the daily *sacrifice*, and they shall place the abomination that maketh desolate.

32 And such as do wickedly against the covenant shall he corrupt by flatteries: but the people that do know their God shall be strong, and do *exploits*.

33 And they that understand among the people shall instruct many: yet they shall fall by the sword, and by flame, by captivity, and by spoil, *many* days.

34 Now when they shall fall, they shall be holpen with a little help: but many shall cleave to them with flatteries.

35 And *some* of them of understanding shall fall, to try them, and to purge, and to make *them* white, *even* to the time of the end: because *it is* yet for a time appointed.

36 And the king shall do according to his will; and he shall exalt himself, and magnify himself above every god, and shall speak marvellous things against the God of gods, and shall prosper till the indignation be accomplished: for that that is determined shall be done.

37 Neither shall he regard the God of his fathers, nor the desire of women, nor regard any god: for he shall magnify himself above all.

38 But in his estate shall he honour the God of forces: and a god whom his fathers knew not shall he honour with gold, and silver, and with precious stones, and pleasant things.

39 Thus shall he do in the most strong holds with a strange god, whom he shall acknowledge *and* increase with glory: and he shall cause them to rule over many, and shall divide the land for gain.

40 And at the time of the end shall the king of the south push at him: and the king of the north shall come against him like a whirlwind, with chariots, and with horsemen, and with many ships; and he shall enter into the countries, and shall overflow and pass over.

41 He shall enter also into the glorious land, and many *countries* shall be overthrown: but these shall escape out of his hand, *even* Edom, and Moab, and the chief of the children of Ammon.

42 He shall stretch forth his hand also upon the countries: and the land of Egypt shall not escape.

43 But he shall have power over the treasures of gold and of silver, and over all the precious things of Egypt; and the Lĭb′y̆-anṡ and the Ē-thĭ-ō′pĭ-ans *shall be* at his steps.

44 But tidings out of the east and out of the north shall trouble him: therefore he shall go forth with great fury to destroy, and utterly to make away many.

45 And he shall plant the tabernacles of his palace between the seas in the glorious holy mountain; yet he shall come to his end, and none shall help him.

CHAPTER 12

AND at that time shall Michael stand up, the great prince which standeth for the children of thy people: and there shall be a time of trouble, such as never was since there was a nation *even* to that same time: and at that time thy people shall be delivered, every one that shall be found written in the book.

2 And many of them that sleep in the dust of the earth shall awake, some to everlasting life, and some to shame *and* everlasting contempt.

3 And they that be wise shall shine as the brightness of the firmament; and they that turn many to righteousness as the stars for ever and ever.

4 But thou, O Daniel, shut up the words, and seal the book, *even* to the time of the end: many shall run to and fro, and knowledge shall be increased.

5 ¶Then I Daniel looked, and, behold, there stood other two, the one on this side of the bank of the river, and the other on that side of the bank of the river.

6 And *one* said to the man clothed in linen, which *was* upon the waters of the river, How long *shall it be to* the end of these wonders?

7 And I heard the man clothed in linen, which *was* upon the waters of the river, when he held up his right hand and his left hand unto heaven, and sware by him that liveth for ever that *it shall be* for a time, times, and an half; and when he shall have accomplished to scatter the power of the holy people, all these *things* shall be finished.

8 And I heard, but I understood not: then said I, O my Lord, what *shall be* the end of these *things?*

9 And he said, Go thy way, Daniel: for the words *are* closed up and sealed till the time of the end.

10 Many shall be purified, and made white, and tried; but the wicked shall do wickedly: and none of the wicked shall understand; but the wise shall understand.

11 And from the time *that* the daily

sacrifice shall be taken away, and the abomination that maketh desolate set up, *there shall be* a thousand two hundred and ninety days.

12 Blessed *is* he that waiteth, and cometh to the thousand three hundred and five and thirty days.

13 But go thou thy way till the end *be:* for thou shalt rest, and stand in thy lot at the end of the days.

HOSEA

CHAPTER 1

THE word of the LORD that came unto Hō-sē'a, the son of Bē-ē'rī, in the days of Uz-zī'ah, Jō'tham, Ahaz, *and* Hĕz-e-kī'ah, kings of Judah, and in the days of Jĕr-o-bō'am the son of Jō'ash, king of Israel.

2 The beginning of the word of the LORD by Hō-sē'a. And the LORD said to Hō-sē'a, Go, take unto thee a wife of whoredoms and children of whoredoms: for the land hath committed great whoredom, *departing* from the LORD.

3 So he went and took Gō'mer the daughter of Dĭb'lā-im; which conceived, and bare him a son.

4 And the LORD said unto him, Call his name Jĕz're-el; for yet a little *while*, and I will avenge the blood of Jĕz're-el upon the house of Jehu, and will cause to cease the kingdom of the house of Israel.

5 And it shall come to pass at that day, that I will break the bow of Israel in the valley of Jĕz're-el.

6 ¶And she conceived again, and bare a daughter. And *God* said unto him, Call her name Lō-rū-hā'mah: for I will no more have mercy upon the house of Israel; but I will utterly take them away.

7 But I will have mercy upon the house of Judah, and will save them by the LORD their God, and will not save them by bow, nor by sword, nor by battle, by horses, nor by horsemen.

8 ¶Now when she had weaned Lō-rū-hā'mah, she conceived, and bare a son.

9 Then said *God*, Call his name Lō-ăm'mī: for ye *are* not my people, and I will not be your *God*.

10 Yet the number of the children of Israel shall be as the sand of the sea, which cannot be measured nor numbered; and it shall come to pass, *that* in the place where it was said unto them, Ye *are* not my people, *there* it shall be said unto them, *Ye are* the sons of the living God.

11 Then shall the children of Judah and the children of Israel be gathered together, and appoint themselves one head, and they shall come up out of the land: for great *shall be* the day of Jĕz're-el.

CHAPTER 2

SAY ye unto your brethren, Ăm'-mī; and to your sisters, Rū-hā'mah.

2 Plead with your mother, plead: for she *is* not my wife, neither *am* I her husband: let her therefore put away her whoredoms out of her sight, and her adulteries from between her breasts;

3 Lest I strip her naked, and set her as in the day that she was born, and make her as a wilderness, and set her like a dry land, and slay her with thirst.

4 And I will not have mercy upon her children; for they *be* the children of whoredoms.

5 For their mother hath played the harlot: she that conceived them hath done shamefully: for she said, I will go after my lovers, that give *me* my bread and my water, my wool and my flax, mine oil and my drink.

6 ¶Therefore, behold, I will hedge up thy way with thorns, and make a wall, that she shall not find her paths.

7 And she shall follow after her lovers, but she shall not overtake them; and she shall seek them, but shall not find *them:* then shall she say, I will go and return to my first husband; for then *was it* better with me than now.

8 For she did not know that I gave her corn, and wine, and oil, and multiplied her silver and gold, *which* they prepared for Bā'al.

9 Therefore will I return, and take away my corn in the time thereof, and my wine in the season thereof, and will recover my wool and my flax *given* to cover her nakedness.

10 And now will I discover her lewdness in the sight of her lovers, and none shall deliver her out of mine hand.

11 I will also cause all her mirth to cease, her feast days, her new moons, and her sabbaths, and all her solemn feasts.

12 And I will destroy her vines and her fig trees, whereof she hath said, These *are* my rewards that my lovers have given me: and I will make them a forest, and the beasts of the field shall eat them.

13 And I will visit upon her the days
of Bā'al-ĭm, wherein she burned incense
to them, and she decked herself
with her earrings and her jewels, and
she went after her lovers, and forgat
me, saith the LORD.
14 ¶Therefore, behold, I will allure
her, and bring her into the wilderness,
and speak comfortably unto her.
15 And I will give her her vineyards
from thence, and the valley of Ā'chôr
for a door of hope: and she shall sing
there, as in the days of her youth, and
as in the day when she came up out of
the land of Egypt.
16 And it shall be at that day, saith
the LORD, *that* thou shalt call me Ī'shī;
and shalt call me no more Bā'al-ī.
17 For I will take away the names of
Bā'al-ĭm out of her mouth, and they
shall no more be remembered by their
name.
18 And in that day will I make a cov-
enant for them with the beasts of the
field, and with the fowls of heaven, and
with the creeping things of the ground:
and I will break the bow and the sword
and the battle out of the earth, and will
make them to lie down safely.
19 And I will betroth thee unto me for
ever; yea, I will betroth thee unto me in
righteousness, and in judgment, and in
lovingkindness, and in mercies.
20 I will even betroth thee unto me in
faithfulness: and thou shalt know the
LORD.
21 And it shall come to pass in that
day, I will hear, saith the LORD, I will
hear the heavens, and they shall hear
the earth;
22 And the earth shall hear the corn,
and the wine, and the oil; and they shall
hear Jĕz're-el.
23 And I will sow her unto me in the
earth; and I will have mercy upon her
that had not obtained mercy; and I will
say to *them which were* not my people,
Thou *art* my people; and they shall say,
Thou art my God.

CHAPTER 3

THEN said the LORD unto me, Go yet,
love a woman beloved of *her* friend, yet
an adulteress, according to the love of
the LORD toward the children of Israel,
who look to other gods, and love flag-
ons of wine.
2 So I bought her to me for fifteen
pieces of silver, and *for* an homer of
barley, and an half homer of barley:
3 And I said unto her, Thou shalt
abide for me many days; thou shalt not
play the harlot, and thou shalt not be
for *another* man: so *will* I also *be* for
thee.
4 For the children of Israel shall abide
many days without a king, and without
a prince, and without a sacrifice, and
without an image, and without an
ephod, and *without* terephim:
5 Afterward shall the children of
Israel return, and seek the LORD their
God, and David their king; and shall
fear the LORD and his goodness in the
latter days.

CHAPTER 4

HEAR the word of the LORD, ye chil-
dren of Israel: for the LORD hath a con-
troversy with the inhabitants of the
land, because *there is* no truth, nor
mercy, nor knowledge of God in the
land.
2 By swearing, and lying, and killing,
and stealing, and committing adultery,
they break out, and blood toucheth
blood.
3 Therefore shall the land mourn, and
every one that dwelleth therein shall
languish, with the beasts of the field,
and with the fowls of heaven; yea, the
fishes of the sea also shall be taken
away.
4 Yet let no man strive, nor reprove
another: for thy people *are* as they that
strive with the priest.
5 Therefore shalt thou fall in the day,
and the prophet also shall fall with thee
in the night, and I will destroy thy
mother.
6 ¶My people are destroyed for lack
of knowledge: because thou hast re-
jected knowledge, I will also reject
thee, that thou shalt be no priest to me:
seeing thou hast forgotten the law of
thy God, I will also forget thy children.
7 As they were increased, so they
sinned against me: *therefore* will I
change their glory into shame.
8 They eat up the sin of my people,
and they set their heart on their iniq-
uity.
9 And there shall be, like people, like
priest: and I will punish them for their
ways, and reward them their doings.
10 For they shall eat, and not have
enough: they shall commit whoredom,
and shall not increase: because they
have left off to take heed to the LORD.
11 Whoredom and wine and new
wine take away the heart.
12 ¶My people ask counsel at their
stocks, and their staff declareth unto
them: for the spirit of whoredoms hath
caused *them* to err, and they have gone
a whoring from under their God.
13 They sacrifice upon the tops of the
mountains, and burn incense upon the
hills, under oaks and poplars and elms,
because the shadow thereof *is* good:

therefore your daughters shall commit
whoredom, and your spouses shall
commit adultery.
14 I will not punish your daughters
when they commit whoredom, nor
your spouses when they commit adul-
tery: for themselves are separated with
whores, and they sacrifice with harlots:
therefore the people *that* doth not
understand shall fall.
15 ¶Though thou, Israel, play the har-
lot, *yet* let not Judah offend; and come
not ye unto Gilgal, neither go ye up to
Bĕth–ā'ven, nor swear, The LORD
liveth.
16 For Israel slideth back as a back-
sliding heifer: now the LORD will feed
them as a lamb in a large place.
17 Ē'phra-im *is* joined to idols: let him
alone.
18 Their drink is sour: they have com-
mitted whoredom continually: her rul-
ers *with* shame do love, Give ye.
19 The wind hath bound her up in her
wings, and they shall be ashamed be-
cause of their sacrifices.

CHAPTER 5

HEAR ye this, O priests; and hearken,
ye house of Israel; and give ye ear, O
house of the king; for judgment *is* to-
ward you, because ye have been a
snare on Mizpah, and a net spread upon
Tā'bor.
2 And the revolters are profound to
make slaughter, though I *have been* a
rebuker of them all.
3 I know Ē'phra-im, and Israel is not
hid from me: for now, O Ē'phra-im,
thou committest whoredom, *and* Israel
is defiled.
4 They will not frame their doings to
turn unto their God: for the spirit of
whoredoms *is* in the midst of them, and
they have not known the LORD.
5 And the pride of Israel doth testify
to his face: therefore shall Israel and
Ē'phra-im fall in their iniquity; Judah
also shall fall with them.
6 They shall go with their flocks and
with their herds to seek the LORD; but
they shall not find *him;* he hath with-
drawn himself from them.
7 They have dealt treacherously
against the LORD: for they have begot-
ten strange children: now shall a month
devour them with their portions.
8 ¶Blow ye the cornet in Gĭb'e-ah,
and the trumpet in Rā'mah: cry aloud
at Bĕth–ā'ven, after thee, O Benjamin.
9 Ē'phra-im shall be desolate in the
day of rebuke: among the tribes of
Israel have I made known that which
shall surely be.
10 The princes of Judah were like
them that remove the bound: *therefore*
I will pour out my wrath upon them like
water.
11 Ē'phra-im *is* oppressed *and* broken
in judgment, because he willingly
walked after the commandment.
12 Therefore *will* I *be* unto Ē'phra-im
as a moth, and to the house of Judah as
rottenness.
13 When Ē'phra-im saw his sickness,
and Judah *saw* his wound, then went
Ē'phra-im to the Assyrian, and sent to
king Jâ'reb: yet could he not heal you,
nor cure you of your wound.
14 For I *will be* unto Ē'phra-im as a
lion, and as a young lion to the house of
Judah: I, *even* I, will tear and go away; I
will take away, and none shall rescue
him.
15 I will go *and* return to my place, till
they acknowledge their offence, and
seek my face: in their affliction they
will seek me early.

CHAPTER 6

COME, and let us return unto the LORD:
for he hath torn, and he will heal us; he
hath smitten, and he will bind us up.
2 After two days will he revive us: in
the third day he will raise us up, and we
shall live in his sight.
3 Then shall we know, *if* we follow on
to know the LORD: his going forth is
prepared as the morning; and he shall
come unto us as the rain, as the latter
and former rain unto the earth.
4 ¶O Ē'phra-im, what shall I do unto
thee? O Judah, what shall I do unto
thee? for your goodness *is* as a morning
cloud, and as the early dew it goeth
away.
5 Therefore have I hewed *them* by the
prophets; I have slain them by the
words of my mouth: and thy judgments
are as the light *that* goeth forth.
6 For I desired mercy, and not sacri-
fice; and the knowledge of God more
than burnt offerings.
7 But they like men have trans-
gressed the covenant: there have they
dealt treacherously against me.
8 Gilead *is* a city of them that work
iniquity, *and is* polluted with blood.
9 And as troops of robbers wait for a
man, *so* the company of priests murder
in the way by consent: for they commit
lewdness.
10 I have seen an horrible thing in the
house of Israel: there *is* the whoredom
of Ē'phra-im, Israel is defiled.
11 Also, O Judah, he hath set an har-
vest for thee, when I returned the cap-
tivity of my people.

CHAPTER 7

WHEN I would have healed Israel, then the iniquity of Ē'phra-im was discovered, and the wickedness of Sa-mâ'rĭ-a: for they commit falsehood; and the thief cometh in, *and* the troop of robbers spoileth without.

2 And they consider not in their hearts *that* I remember all their wickedness: now their own doings have beset them about; they are before my face.

3 They make the king glad with their wickedness, and the princes with their lies.

4 They *are* all adulterers, as an oven heated by the baker, *who* ceaseth from raising after he hath kneaded the dough, until it be leavened.

5 In the day of our king the princes have made *him* sick with bottles of wine; he stretched out his hand with scorners.

6 For they have made ready their heart like an oven, whiles they lie in wait: their baker sleepeth all the night; in the morning it burneth as a flaming fire.

7 They are all hot as an oven, and have devoured their judges; all their kings are fallen: *there is* none among them that calleth unto me.

8 ¶Ē'phra-im, he hath mixed himself among the people; Ē'phra-im is a cake not turned.

9 Strangers have devoured his strength, and he knoweth *it* not: yea, gray hairs are here and there upon him, yet he knoweth not.

10 And the pride of Israel testifieth to his face: and they do not return to the LORD their God, nor seek him for all this.

11 Ē'phra-im also is like a silly dove without heart: they call to Egypt, they go to Assyria.

12 When they shall go, I will spread my net upon them; I will bring them down as the fowls of the heaven; I will chastise them, as their congregation hath heard.

13 Woe unto them! for they have fled from me: destruction unto them! because they have transgressed against me: though I have redeemed them, yet they have spoken lies against me.

14 And they have not cried unto me with their heart, when they howled upon their beds: they assemble themselves for corn and wine, *and* they rebel against me.

15 Though I have bound *and* strengthened their arms, yet do they imagine mischief against me.

16 They return, *but* not to the most High: they are like a deceitful bow: their princes shall fall by the sword for the rage of their tongue: this *shall be* their derision in the land of Egypt.

CHAPTER 8

SET the trumpet to thy mouth. *He shall come* as an eagle against the house of the LORD, because they have transgressed my covenant, and trespassed against my law.

2 Israel shall cry unto me, My God, we know thee.

3 Israel hath cast off *the thing that is* good: the enemy shall pursue him.

4 They have set up kings, but not by me: they have made princes, and I knew *it* not: of their silver and their gold have they made them idols, that they may be cut off.

5 ¶Thy calf, O Sa-mâ'rĭ-a, hath cast *thee* off; mine anger is kindled against them: how long *will it be* ere they attain to innocency?

6 For from Israel *was* it also: the workman made it; therefore it *is* not God: but the calf of Sa-mâ'rĭ-a shall be broken in pieces.

7 For they have sown the wind, and they shall reap the whirlwind: it hath no stalk: the bud shall yield no meal: if so be it yield, the strangers shall swallow it up.

8 Israel is swallowed up: now shall they be among the Gentiles as a vessel wherein *is* no pleasure.

9 For they are gone up to Assyria, a wild ass alone by himself: Ē'phra-im hath hired lovers.

10 Yea, though they have hired among the nations, now will I gather them, and they shall sorrow a little for the burden of the king of princes.

11 Because Ē'phra-im hath made many altars to sin, altars shall be unto him to sin.

12 I have written to him the great things of my law, *but* they were counted as a strange thing.

13 They sacrifice flesh *for* the sacrifices of mine offerings, and eat *it; but* the LORD accepteth them not; now will he remember their iniquity, and visit their sins: they shall return to Egypt.

14 For Israel hath forgotten his Maker, and buildeth temples; and Judah hath multiplied fenced cities: but I will send a fire upon his cities, and it shall devour the palaces thereof.

CHAPTER 9

REJOICE not, O Israel, for joy, as *other* people: for thou hast gone a whoring from thy God, thou hast loved a reward upon every cornfloor.

2 The floor and the winepress shall not feed them, and the new wine shall fail in her.

3 They shall not dwell in the LORD's land; but Ē'phra-im shall return to Egypt, and they shall eat unclean *things* in Assyria.

4 They shall not offer wine *offerings* to the LORD, neither shall they be pleasing unto him: their sacrifices *shall be* unto them as the bread of mourners; all that eat thereof shall be polluted: for their bread for their soul shall not come into the house of the LORD.

5 What will ye do in the solemn day, and in the day of the feast of the LORD?

6 For, lo, they are gone because of destruction: Egypt shall gather them up, Mĕm'phĭs shall bury them: the pleasant *places* for their silver, nettles shall possess them: thorns *shall be* in their tabernacles.

7 The days of visitation are come, the days of recompence are come; Israel shall know *it:* the prophet *is* a fool, the spiritual man *is* mad, for the multitude of thine iniquity, and the great hatred.

8 The watchman of Ē'phra-im *was* with my God: *but* the prophet *is* a snare of a fowler in all his ways, *and* hatred in the house of his God.

9 They have deeply corrupted *themselves,* as in the days of Gĭb'e-ah: *therefore* he will remember their iniquity, he will visit their sins.

10 I found Israel like grapes in the wilderness; I saw your fathers as the firstripe in the fig tree at her first time: *but* they went to Bā'al-pē'ôr, and separated themselves unto *that* shame; and *their* abominations were according as they loved.

11 *As for* Ē'phra-im, their glory shall fly away like a bird, from the birth, and from the womb, and from the conception.

12 Though they bring up their children, yet will I bereave them, *that there shall* not *be* a man *left:* yea, woe also to them when I depart from them!

13 Ē'phra-im, as I saw Tyrus, *is* planted in a pleasant place: but Ē'phraim shall bring forth his children to the murderer.

14 Give them, O LORD: what wilt thou give? give them a miscarrying womb and dry breasts.

15 All their wickedness *is* in Gilgal: for there I hated them: for the wickedness of their doings I will drive them out of mine house, I will love them no more: all their princes *are* revolters.

16 Ē'phra-im is smitten, their root is dried up, they shall bear no fruit: yea, though they bring forth, yet will I slay *even* the beloved *fruit* of their womb.

17 My God will cast them away, because they did not hearken unto him: and they shall be wanderers among the nations.

CHAPTER 10

ISRAEL *is* an empty vine, he bringeth forth fruit unto himself: according to the multitude of his fruit he hath increased the altars; according to the goodness of his land they have made goodly images.

2 Their heart is divided; now shall they be found faulty: he shall break down their altars, he shall spoil their images.

3 For now they shall say, We have no king, because we feared not the LORD; what then should a king do to us?

4 They have spoken words, swearing falsely in making a covenant: thus judgment springeth up as hemlock in the furrows of the field.

5 The inhabitants of Sa-mâ'rĭ-a shall fear because of the calves of Bĕth-ā'-ven: for the people thereof shall mourn over it, and the priests thereof *that* rejoiced on it, for the glory thereof, because it is departed from it.

6 It shall be also carried unto Assyria *for* a present to king Jâ'reb: Ē'phra-im shall receive shame, and Israel shall be ashamed of his own counsel.

7 *As for* Sa-mâ'rĭ-a, her king is cut off as the foam upon the water.

8 The high places also of Ā'ven, the sin of Israel, shall be destroyed: the thorn and the thistle shall come up on their altars; and they shall say to the mountains, Cover us; and to the hills, Fall on us.

9 O Israel, thou hast sinned from the days of Gĭb'e-ah: there they stood: the battle in Gĭb'e-ah against the children of iniquity did not overtake them.

10 *It is* in my desire that I should chastise them; and the people shall be gathered against them, when they shall bind themselves in their two furrows.

11 And Ē'phra-im *is as* an heifer *that is* taught, *and* loveth to tread out *the corn;* but I passed over upon her fair neck: I will make Ē'phra-im to ride; Judah shall plow, *and* Jacob shall break his clods.

12 Sow to yourselves in righteousness, reap in mercy; break up your fallow ground: for *it is* time to seek the LORD, till he come and rain righteousness upon you.

13 Ye have plowed wickedness, ye

have reaped iniquity; ye have eaten the
fruit of lies: because thou didst trust in
thy way, in the multitude of thy mighty
men.
14 Therefore shall a tumult arise
among thy people, and all thy fortresses shall be spoiled, as Shăl'man
spoiled Běth-är'bel in the day of battle:
the mother was dashed in pieces upon
her children.
15 So shall Běth-el do unto you because of your great wickedness: in a
morning shall the king of Israel utterly
be cut off.

CHAPTER 11

WHEN Israel *was* a child, then I loved
him, and called my son out of Egypt.
2 *As* they called them, so they went
from them: they sacrificed unto Bā'alim, and burned incense to graven
images.
3 I taught Ē'phra-im also to go, taking
them by their arms; but they knew not
that I healed them.
4 I drew them with cords of a man,
with bands of love: and I was to them as
they that take off the yoke on their
jaws, and I laid meat unto them.
5 ¶He shall not return into the land of
Egypt, but the Assyrian shall be his
king, because they refused to return.
6 And the sword shall abide on his
cities, and shall consume his branches,
and devour *them*, because of their own
counsels.
7 And my people are bent to backsliding from me: though they called them
to the most High, none at all would exalt *him*.
8 How shall I give thee up, Ē'phra-im?
how shall I deliver thee, Israel? how
shall I make thee as Ăd'mah? *how* shall
I set thee as Ze-bō'im? mine heart is
turned within me, my repentings are
kindled together.
9 I will not execute the fierceness of
mine anger, I will not return to destroy
Ē'phra-im: for I *am* God, and not man;
the Holy One in the midst of thee: and I
will not enter into the city.
10 They shall walk after the LORD: he
shall roar like a lion: when he shall roar,
then the children shall tremble from
the west.
11 They shall tremble as a bird out of
Egypt, and as a dove out of the land of
Assyria: and I will place them in their
houses, saith the LORD.
12 Ē'phra-im compasseth me about
with lies, and the house of Israel with
deceit: but Judah yet ruleth with God,
and is faithful with the saints.

CHAPTER 12

Ē'PHRA-IM feedeth on wind, and followeth after the east wind: he daily increaseth lies and desolation; and they
do make a covenant with the Assyrians, and oil is carried into Egypt.
2 The LORD hath also a controversy
with Judah, and will punish Jacob according to his ways; according to his
doings will he recompense him.
3 ¶He took his brother by the heel in
the womb, and by his strength he had
power with God:
4 Yea, he had power over the angel,
and prevailed: he wept, and made
supplication unto him: he found him *in*
Běth-el, and there he spake with us;
5 Even the LORD God of hosts; the
LORD *is* his memorial.
6 Therefore turn thou to thy God:
keep mercy and judgment, and wait on
thy God continually.
7 ¶*He is* a merchant, the balances of
deceit *are* in his hand: he loveth to oppress.
8 And Ē'phra-im said, Yet I am become rich, I have found me out substance: *in* all my labours they shall find
none iniquity in me that *were* sin.
9 And I *that am* the LORD thy God
from the land of Egypt will yet make
thee to dwell in tabernacles, as in the
days of the solemn feast.
10 I have also spoken by the
prophets, and I have multiplied visions,
and used similitudes, by the ministry of
the prophets.
11 *Is there* iniquity *in* Gilead? surely
they are vanity: they sacrifice bullocks in Gilgal; yea, their altars *are* as
heaps in the furrows of the fields.
12 And Jacob fled into the country of
Syria, and Israel served for a wife, and
for a wife he kept *sheep*.
13 And by a prophet the LORD
brought Israel out of Egypt, and by a
prophet was he preserved.
14 Ē'phra-im provoked *him* to anger
most bitterly: therefore shall he leave
his blood upon him, and his reproach
shall his Lord return unto him.

CHAPTER 13

WHEN Ē'phra-im spake trembling, he
exalted himself in Israel; but when he
offended in Bā'al, he died.
2 And now they sin more and more,
and have made them molten images of
their silver, *and* idols according to their
own understanding, all of it the work of
the craftsmen: they say of them, Let
the men that sacrifice kiss the calves.
3 Therefore they shall be as the morning cloud, and as the early dew that

passeth away, as the chaff *that* is driv-
en with the whirlwind out of the floor,
and as the smoke out of the chimney.
4 Yet I *am* the LORD thy God from the
land of Egypt, and thou shalt know no
god but me: for *there is* no saviour be-
side me.
5 I did know thee in the wilderness, in
the land of great drought.
6 According to their pasture, so were
they filled; they were filled, and their
heart was exalted; therefore have they
forgotten me.
7 Therefore I will be unto them as a
lion: as a leopard by the way will I ob-
serve *them:*
8 I will meet them as a bear *that is*
bereaved *of her whelps,* and will rend
the caul of their heart, and there will I
devour them like a lion: the wild beast
shall tear them.
9 ¶O Israel, thou hast destroyed thy-
self; but in me *is* thine help.
10 I will be thy king: where *is any*
other that may save thee in all thy
cities? and thy judges of whom thou
saidst, Give me a king and princes?
11 I gave thee a king in mine anger,
and took *him* away in my wrath.
12 The iniquity of Ē'phra-im *is* bound
up; his sin *is* hid.
13 The sorrows of a travailing wom-
an shall come upon him: he *is* an un-
wise son; for he should not stay long in
the place of the breaking forth of chil-
dren.
14 I will ransom them from the power
of the grave; I will redeem them from
death: O death, I will be thy plagues; O
grave, I will be thy destruction: repen-
tance shall be hid from mine eyes.
15 ¶Though he be fruitful among *his*
brethren, an east wind shall come, the
wind of the LORD shall come up from
the wilderness, and his spring shall be-
come dry, and his fountain shall be
dried up: he shall spoil the treasure of
all pleasant vessels.
16 Sa-mâ'rĭ-a shall become desolate;
for she hath rebelled against her God:
they shall fall by the sword: their in-
fants shall be dashed in pieces, and
their women with child shall be ripped
up.

CHAPTER 14

O ISRAEL, return unto the LORD thy
God; for thou hast fallen by thine iniq-
uity.
2 Take with you words, and turn to
the LORD: say unto him, Take away all
iniquity, and receive *us* graciously: so
will we render the calves of our lips.
3 Asshur shall not save us; we will
not ride upon horses: neither will we
say any more to the work of our hands,
Ye are our gods: for in thee the father-
less findeth mercy.
4 ¶I will heal their backsliding, I will
love them freely; for mine anger is
turned away from him.
5 I will be as the dew unto Israel: he
shall grow as the lily, and cast forth his
roots as Lebanon.
6 His branches shall spread, and his
beauty shall be as the olive tree, and his
smell as Lebanon.
7 They that dwell under his shadow
shall return; they shall revive *as* the
corn, and grow as the vine: the scent
thereof *shall be* as the wine of Lebanon.
8 Ē'phra-im *shall say,* What have I to
do any more with idols? I have heard
him, and observed him: I *am* like a
green fir tree. From me is thy fruit
found.
9 Who *is* wise, and he shall understand
these *things?* prudent, and he shall
know them? for the ways of the LORD
are right, and the just shall walk in
them: but the transgressors shall fall
therein.

JOEL

CHAPTER 1

THE word of the LORD that came to
Jō'el the son of Pe-thū'el.
2 Hear this, ye old men, and give ear,
all ye inhabitants of the land. Hath this
been in your days, or even in the days of
your fathers?
3 Tell ye your children of it, and *let*
your children *tell* their children, and
their children another generation.
4 That which the palmerworm hath
left hath the locust eaten; and that
which the locust hath left hath the can-
kerworm eaten; and that which the
cankerworm hath left hath the caterpil-
ler eaten.
5 Awake, ye drunkards, and weep;
and howl, all ye drinkers of wine, be-
cause of the new wine; for it is cut off
from your mouth.
6 For a nation is come up upon my
land, strong, and without number,
whose teeth *are* the teeth of a lion, and
he hath the cheek teeth of a great lion.
7 He hath laid my vine waste, and
barked my fig tree: he hath made it
clean bare, and cast *it* away; the
branches thereof are made white.

8 ¶Lament like a virgin girded with sackcloth for the husband of her youth.

9 The meat offering and the drink offering is cut off from the house of the LORD; the priests, the LORD's ministers, mourn.

10 The field is wasted, the land mourneth; for the corn is wasted: the new wine is dried up, the oil languisheth.

11 Be ye ashamed, O ye husbandmen; howl, O ye vinedressers, for the wheat and for the barley; because the harvest of the field is perished.

12 The vine is dried up, and the fig tree languisheth; the pomegranate tree, the palm tree also, and the apple tree, *even* all the trees of the field, are withered: because joy is withered away from the sons of men.

13 ¶Gird yourselves, and lament, ye priests: howl, ye ministers of the altar: come, lie all night in sackcloth, ye ministers of my God: for the meat offering and the drink offering is withholden from the house of your God.

14 Sanctify ye a fast, call a solemn assembly, gather the elders *and* all the inhabitants of the land *into* the house of the LORD your God, and cry unto the LORD,

15 Alas for the day! for the day of the LORD *is* at hand, and as a destruction from the Almighty shall it come.

16 Is not the meat cut off before our eyes, *yea*, joy and gladness from the house of our God?

17 The seed is rotten under their clods, the garners are laid desolate, the barns are broken down; for the corn is withered.

18 How do the beasts groan! the herds of cattle are perplexed, because they have no pasture; yea, the flocks of sheep are made desolate.

19 O LORD, to thee will I cry: for the fire hath devoured the pastures of the wilderness, and the flame hath burned all the trees of the field.

20 The beasts of the field cry also unto thee: for the rivers of waters are dried up, and the fire hath devoured the pastures of the wilderness.

CHAPTER 2

BLOW ye the trumpet in Zion, and sound an alarm in my holy mountain: let all the inhabitants of the land tremble: for the day of the LORD cometh, for *it is* nigh at hand;

2 A day of darkness and of gloominess, a day of clouds and of thick darkness, as the morning spread upon the mountains: a great people and a strong; there hath not been ever the like, neither shall be any more after it, *even* to the years of many generations.

3 A fire devoureth before them; and behind them a flame burneth: the land *is* as the garden of Eden before them, and behind them a desolate wilderness; yea, and nothing shall escape them.

4 The appearance of them *is* as the appearance of horses; and as horsemen, so shall they run.

5 Like the noise of chariots on the tops of mountains shall they leap, like the noise of a flame of fire that devoureth the stubble, as a strong people set in battle array.

6 Before their face the people shall be much pained: all faces shall gather blackness.

7 They shall run like mighty men; they shall climb the wall like men of war; and they shall march every one on his ways, and they shall not break their ranks:

8 Neither shall one thrust another; they shall walk every one in his path: and *when* they fall upon the sword, they shall not be wounded.

9 They shall run to and fro in the city; they shall run upon the wall, they shall climb up upon the houses; they shall enter in at the windows like a thief.

10 The earth shall quake before them; the heavens shall tremble: the sun and the moon shall be dark, and the stars shall withdraw their shining:

11 And the LORD shall utter his voice before his army: for his camp *is* very great: for *he is* strong that executeth his word: for the day of the LORD *is* great and very terrible; and who can abide it?

12 ¶Therefore also now, saith the LORD, Turn ye *even* to me with all your heart, and with fasting, and with weeping, and with mourning:

13 And rend your heart, and not your garments, and turn unto the LORD your God: for he *is* gracious and merciful, slow to anger, and of great kindness, and repenteth him of the evil.

14 Who knoweth *if* he will return and repent, and leave a blessing behind him; *even* a meat offering and a drink offering unto the LORD your God?

15 ¶Blow the trumpet in Zion, sanctify a fast, call a solemn assembly:

16 Gather the people, sanctify the congregation, assemble the elders, gather the children, and those that suck the breasts: let the bridegroom go forth of his chamber, and the bride out of her closet.

17 Let the priests, the ministers of the LORD, weep between the porch and the altar, and let them say, Spare thy peo-

ple, O Lord, and give not thine heri-
tage to reproach, that the heathen
should rule over them: wherefore
should they say among the people,
Where *is* their God?
18 ¶Then will the Lord be jealous for
his land, and pity his people.
19 Yea, the Lord will answer and say
unto his people, Behold, I will send you
corn, and wine, and oil, and ye shall be
satisfied therewith: and I will no more
make you a reproach among the
heathen:
20 But I will remove far off from you
the northern *army*, and will drive him
into a land barren and desolate, with
his face toward the east sea, and his
hinder part toward the utmost sea, and
his stink shall come up, and his ill sav-
our shall come up, because he hath
done great things.
21 Fear not, O land; be glad and re-
joice: for the Lord will do great things.
22 Be not afraid, ye beasts of the
field: for the pastures of the wilderness
do spring, for the tree beareth her fruit,
the fig tree and the vine do yield their
strength.
23 Be glad then, ye children of Zion,
and rejoice in the Lord your God: for he
hath given you the former rain moder-
ately, and he will cause to come down
for you the rain, the former rain, and
the latter rain in the first *month*.
24 And the floors shall be full of
wheat, and the fats shall overflow with
wine and oil.
25 And I will restore to you the years
that the locust hath eaten, the canker-
worm, and the caterpiller, and the palm-
erworm, my great army which I sent
among you.
26 And ye shall eat in plenty, and be
satisfied, and praise the name of the
Lord your God, that hath dealt won-
drously with you: and my people shall
never be ashamed.
27 And ye shall know that I *am* in the
midst of Israel, and *that* I *am* the Lord
your God, and none else: and my peo-
ple shall never be ashamed.
28 ¶And it shall come to pass after-
ward, *that* I will pour out my spirit
upon all flesh; and your sons and your
daughters shall prophesy, your old
men shall dream dreams, your young
men shall see visions:
29 And also upon the servants and
upon the handmaids in those days will I
pour out my spirit.
30 And I will shew wonders in the
heavens and in the earth, blood, and
fire, and pillars of smoke.
31 The sun shall be turned into dark-
ness, and the moon into blood, before
the great and the terrible day of the
Lord come.
32 And it shall come to pass, *that*
whosoever shall call on the name of the
Lord shall be delivered: for in mount
Zion and in Jerusalem shall be deliver-
ance, as the Lord hath said, and in the
remnant whom the Lord shall call.

CHAPTER 3

FOR, behold, in those days, and in that
time, when I shall bring again the cap-
tivity of Judah and Jerusalem,
2 I will also gather all nations, and
will bring them down into the valley of
Je-hŏsh'a-phăt, and will plead with
them there for my people and *for* my
heritage Israel, whom they have scat-
tered among the nations, and parted
my land.
3 And they have cast lots for my
people; and have given a boy for an har-
lot, and sold a girl for wine, that they
might drink.
4 Yea, and what have ye to do with
me, O Tyre, and Zī'don, and all the
coasts of Palestine? will ye render me a
recompence? and if ye recompense me,
swiftly *and* speedily will I return your
recompence upon your own head;
5 Because ye have taken my silver
and my gold, and have carried into
your temples my goodly pleasant
things:
6 The children also of Judah and the
children of Jerusalem have ye sold unto
the Grecians, that ye might remove
them far from their border.
7 Behold, I will raise them out of the
place whither ye have sold them, and
will return your recompence upon your
own head:
8 And I will sell your sons and your
daughters into the hand of the children
of Judah, and they shall sell them to the
Sa-bē'ans, to a people far off: for the
Lord hath spoken *it*.
9 ¶Proclaim ye this among the Gen-
tiles; Prepare war, wake up the mighty
men, let all the men of war draw near;
let them come up:
10 Beat your plowshares into swords,
and your pruninghooks into spears: let
the weak say, I *am* strong.
11 Assemble yourselves, and come,
all ye heathen, and gather yourselves
together round about: thither cause thy
mighty ones to come down, O Lord.
12 Let the heathen be wakened, and
come up to the valley of Je-hŏsh'a-
phăt: for there will I sit to judge all the
heathen round about.
13 Put ye in the sickle, for the harvest
is ripe: come, get you down; for the

press is full, the fats overflow; for their
wickedness *is* great.
14 Multitudes, multitudes in the val-
ley of decision: for the day of the LORD
is near in the valley of decision.
15 The sun and the moon shall be dark-
ened, and the stars shall withdraw
their shining.
16 The LORD also shall roar out of
Zion, and utter his voice from Jeru-
salem; and the heavens and the earth
shall shake: but the LORD *will be* the
hope of his people, and the strength of
the children of Israel.
17 So shall ye know that I *am* the
LORD your God dwelling in Zion, my
holy mountain: then shall Jerusalem be
holy, and there shall no strangers pass
through her any more.
18 ¶And it shall come to pass in that
day, *that* the mountains shall drop
down new wine, and the hills shall flow
with milk, and all the rivers of Judah
shall flow with waters, and a fountain
shall come forth of the house of the
LORD, and shall water the valley of
Shĭt'tĭm.
19 Egypt shall be a desolation, and
Edom shall be a desolate wilderness,
for the violence *against* the children of
Judah, because they have shed inno-
cent blood in their land.
20 But Judah shall dwell for ever, and
Jerusalem from generation to genera-
tion.
21 For I will cleanse their blood *that* I
have not cleansed: for the LORD dwel-
leth in Zion.

AMOS

CHAPTER 1

THE words of Amos, who was among
the herdmen of Te-kō'a, which he saw
concerning Israel in the days of Uz-
zī'ah king of Judah, and in the days of
Jĕr-o-bō'am the son of Jō'ash king of
Israel, two years before the earth-
quake.
2 And he said, The LORD will roar
from Zion, and utter his voice from Jeru-
salem; and the habitations of the
shepherds shall mourn, and the top of
Carmel shall wither.
3 ¶Thus saith the LORD; For three
transgressions of Damascus, and for
four, I will not turn away *the punish-*
ment thereof; because they have
threshed Gilead with threshing instru-
ments of iron:
4 But I will send a fire into the house
of Hāz'a-el, which shall devour the pal-
aces of Bĕn-hā'dăd.
5 I will break also the bar of Damas-
cus, and cut off the inhabitant from the
plain of Ā'ven, and him that holdeth the
sceptre from the house of Eden: and the
people of Syria shall go into captivity
unto Kir, saith the LORD.
6 ¶Thus saith the LORD; For three
transgressions of Gā'za, and for four, I
will not turn away *the punishment*
thereof; because they carried away
captive the whole captivity, to deliver
them up to Edom:
7 But I will send a fire on the wall of
Gā'za, which shall devour the palaces
thereof:
8 And I will cut off the inhabitant
from Ăsh'dŏd, and him that holdeth the
sceptre from Ăsh'ke-lon, and I will turn
mine hand against Ekron: and the rem-
nant of the Philistines shall perish,
saith the Lord GOD.
9 ¶Thus saith the LORD; For three
transgressions of Tyrus, and for four, I
will not turn away *the punishment*
thereof; because they delivered up the
whole captivity to Edom, and remem-
bered not the brotherly covenant:
10 But I will send a fire on the wall of
Tyrus, which shall devour the palaces
thereof.
11 ¶Thus saith the LORD; For three
transgressions of Edom, and for four, I
will not turn away *the punishment*
thereof; because he did pursue his
brother with the sword, and did cast off
all pity, and his anger did tear perpetu-
ally, and he kept his wrath for ever:
12 But I will send a fire upon Tē'man,
which shall devour the palaces of Bŏz'-
rah.
13 ¶Thus saith the LORD; For three
transgressions of the children of Am-
mon, and for four, I will not turn away
the punishment thereof; because they
have ripped up the women with child of
Gilead, that they might enlarge their
border:
14 But I will kindle a fire in the wall of
Răb'bah, and it shall devour the pal-
aces thereof, with shouting in the day
of battle, with a tempest in the day of
the whirlwind:
15 And their king shall go into captiv-
ity, he and his princes together, saith
the LORD.

CHAPTER 2

THUS saith the LORD; For three trans-
gressions of Moab, and for four, I will
not turn away *the punishment* thereof;

because he burned the bones of the
king of Edom into lime:
2 But I will send a fire upon Moab,
and it shall devour the palaces of Kir'ĭ-
ŏth: and Moab shall die with tumult,
with shouting, *and* with the sound of
the trumpet:
3 And I will cut off the judge from the
midst thereof, and will slay all the
princes thereof with him, saith the
LORD.
4 ¶Thus saith the LORD; For three
transgressions of Judah, and for four, I
will not turn away *the punishment*
thereof; because they have despised
the law of the LORD, and have not kept
his commandments, and their lies
caused them to err, after the which
their fathers have walked:
5 But I will send a fire upon Judah,
and it shall devour the palaces of Jeru-
salem.
6 ¶Thus saith the LORD; For three
transgressions of Israel, and for four, I
will not turn away *the punishment*
thereof; because they sold the righ-
teous for silver, and the poor for a pair
of shoes;
7 That pant after the dust of the earth
on the head of the poor, and turn aside
the way of the meek: and a man and his
father will go in unto the *same* maid, to
profane my holy name:
8 And they lay *themselves* down
upon clothes laid to pledge by every al-
tar, and they drink the wine of the con-
demned *in* the house of their god.
9 ¶Yet destroyed I the Amorite be-
fore them, whose height *was* like the
height of the cedars, and he *was* strong
as the oaks; yet I destroyed his fruit
from above, and his roots from be-
neath.
10 Also I brought you up from the
land of Egypt, and led you forty years
through the wilderness, to possess the
land of the Amorite.
11 And I raised up of your sons for
prophets, and of your young men for
Nazarites. *Is it* not even thus, O ye
children of Israel? saith the LORD.
12 But ye gave the Nazarites wine to
drink; and commanded the prophets,
saying, Prophesy not.
13 Behold, I am pressed under you, as
a cart is pressed *that is* full of sheaves.
14 Therefore the flight shall perish
from the swift, and the strong shall not
strengthen his force, neither shall the
mighty deliver himself:
15 Neither shall he stand that hand-
leth the bow; and *he that is* swift of
foot shall not deliver *himself*: neither
shall he that rideth the horse deliver
himself.
16 And *he that is* courageous among
the mighty shall flee away naked in
that day, saith the LORD.

CHAPTER 3

HEAR this word that the LORD hath
spoken against you, O children of
Israel, against the whole family which I
brought up from the land of Egypt,
saying,
2 You only have I known of all the fam-
ilies of the earth: therefore I will pun-
ish you for all your iniquities.
3 Can two walk together, except they
be agreed?
4 Will a lion roar in the forest, when
he hath no prey? will a young lion cry
out of his den, if he have taken nothing?
5 Can a bird fall in a snare upon the
earth, where no gin *is* for him? shall *one*
take up a snare from the earth, and
have taken nothing at all?
6 Shall a trumpet be blown in the city,
and the people not be afraid? shall
there be evil in a city, and the LORD hath
not done *it?*
7 Surely the Lord GOD will do nothing
but he revealeth his secret unto his ser-
vants the prophets.
8 The lion hath roared, who will not
fear? the Lord GOD hath spoken, who
can but prophesy?
9 ¶Publish in the palaces at Ăsh'dŏd,
and in the palaces in the land of Egypt,
and say, Assemble yourselves upon the
mountains of Sa-mâ'rĭ-a, and behold
the great tumults in the midst thereof,
and the oppressed in the midst thereof.
10 For they know not to do right,
saith the LORD, who store up violence
and robbery in their palaces.
11 Therefore thus saith the Lord GOD;
An adversary *there shall be* even round
about the land; and he shall bring down
thy strength from thee, and thy palaces
shall be spoiled.
12 Thus saith the LORD; As the
shepherd taketh out of the mouth of the
lion two legs, or a piece of an ear; so
shall the children of Israel be taken out
that dwell in Sa-mâ'rĭ-a in the corner of
a bed, and in Damascus *in* a couch.
13 Hear ye, and testify in the house of
Jacob, saith the Lord GOD, the God of
hosts,
14 That in the day that I shall visit the
transgressions of Israel upon him I will
also visit the altars of Bĕth–el: and the
horns of the altar shall be cut off, and
fall to the ground.
15 And I will smite the winter house
with the summer house; and the houses
of ivory shall perish, and the great
houses shall have an end, saith the
LORD.

CHAPTER 4

HEAR this word, ye kine of Bā'shan, that *are* in the mountain of Sa-mâ'rĭ-a, which oppress the poor, which crush the needy, which say to their masters, Bring, and let us drink.

2 The Lord GOD hath sworn by his holiness, that, lo, the days shall come upon you, that he will take you away with hooks, and your posterity with fishhooks.

3 And ye shall go out at the breaches, every *cow at that which is* before her; and ye shall cast *them* into the palace, saith the LORD.

4 ¶Come to Bĕth-el, and transgress; at Gilgal multiply transgression; and bring your sacrifices every morning, *and* your tithes after three years:

5 And offer a sacrifice of thanksgiving with leaven, and proclaim *and* publish the free offerings: for this liketh you, O ye children of Israel, saith the Lord GOD.

6 ¶And I also have given you cleanness of teeth in all your cities, and want of bread in all your places: yet have ye not returned unto me, saith the LORD.

7 And also I have withholden the rain from you, when *there were* yet three months to the harvest: and I caused it to rain upon one city, and caused it not to rain upon another city: one piece was rained upon, and the piece whereupon it rained not withered.

8 So two *or* three cities wandered unto one city, to drink water; but they were not satisfied: yet have ye not returned unto me, saith the LORD.

9 I have smitten you with blasting and mildew: when your gardens and your vineyards and your fig trees and your olive trees increased, the palmerworm devoured *them:* yet have ye not returned unto me, saith the LORD.

10 I have sent among you the pestilence after the manner of Egypt: your young men have I slain with the sword, and have taken away your horses; and I have made the stink of your camps to come up unto your nostrils: yet have ye not returned unto me, saith the LORD.

11 I have overthrown *some* of you, as God overthrew Sodom and Gomŏr'rah, and ye were as a firebrand plucked out of the burning: yet have ye not returned unto me, saith the LORD.

12 Therefore thus will I do unto thee, O Israel: *and* because I will do this unto thee, prepare to meet thy God, O Israel.

13 For, lo, he that formeth the mountains, and createth the wind, and declareth unto man what *is* his thought, that maketh the morning darkness, and treadeth upon the high places of the earth, The LORD, The God of hosts, *is* his name.

CHAPTER 5

HEAR ye this word which I take up against you, *even* a lamentation, O house of Israel.

2 The virgin of Israel is fallen; she shall no more rise: she is forsaken upon her land; *there is* none to raise her up.

3 For thus saith the Lord GOD; The city that went out *by* a thousand shall leave an hundred, and that which went forth *by* an hundred shall leave ten, to the house of Israel.

4 ¶For thus saith the LORD unto the house of Israel, Seek ye me, and ye shall live:

5 But seek not Bĕth-el, nor enter into Gilgal, and pass not to Be'er-shē'ba: for Gilgal shall surely go into captivity, and Bĕth-el shall come to nought.

6 Seek the LORD, and ye shall live; lest he break out like fire in the house of Joseph, and devour *it,* and *there be* none to quench *it* in Bĕth-el.

7 Ye who turn judgment to wormwood, and leave off righteousness in the earth,

8 *Seek him* that maketh the seven stars and Ō-rī'on, and turneth the shadow of death into the morning, and maketh the day dark with night: that calleth for the waters of the sea, and poureth them out upon the face of the earth: The LORD *is* his name:

9 That strengtheneth the spoiled against the strong, so that the spoiled shall come against the fortress.

10 They hate him that rebuketh in the gate, and they abhor him that speaketh uprightly.

11 Forasmuch therefore as your treading *is* upon the poor, and ye take from him burdens of wheat: ye have built houses of hewn stone, but ye shall not dwell in them; ye have planted pleasant vineyards, but ye shall not drink wine of them.

12 For I know your manifold transgressions and your mighty sins: they afflict the just, they take a bribe, and they turn aside the poor in the gate *from their right.*

13 Therefore the prudent shall keep silence in that time; for it *is* an evil time.

14 Seek good, and not evil, that ye may live: and so the LORD, the God of hosts, shall be with you, as ye have spoken.

15 Hate the evil, and love the good, and establish judgment in the gate: it may be that the LORD God of hosts will

be gracious unto the remnant of Jo-
seph.
16 Therefore the LORD, the God of
hosts, the Lord, saith thus; Wailing
shall be in all streets; and they shall say
in all the highways, Alas! alas! and they
shall call the husbandman to mourn-
ing, and such as are skilful of lamenta-
tion to wailing.
17 And in all vineyards *shall be*
wailing: for I will pass through thee,
saith the LORD.
18 Woe unto you that desire the day
of the LORD! to what end *is* it for you?
the day of the LORD *is* darkness, and not
light.
19 As if a man did flee from a lion,
and a bear met him; or went into the
house, and leaned his hand on the wall,
and a serpent bit him.
20 *Shall* not the day of the LORD *be*
darkness, and not light? even very
dark, and no brightness in it?
21 ¶I hate, I despise your feast days,
and I will not smell in your solemn as-
semblies.
22 Though ye offer me burnt offer-
ings and your meat offerings, I will not
accept *them*: neither will I regard the
peace offerings of your fat beasts.
23 Take thou away from me the noise
of thy songs; for I will not hear the mel-
ody of thy viols.
24 But let judgment run down as wa-
ters, and righteousness as a mighty
stream.
25 Have ye offered unto me sacrifices
and offerings in the wilderness forty
years, O house of Israel?
26 But ye have borne the tabernacle
of your Moloch and Chī'un your
images, the star of your god, which ye
made to yourselves.
27 Therefore will I cause you to go
into captivity beyond Damascus, saith
the LORD, whose name *is* The God of
hosts.

CHAPTER 6

WOE to them *that are* at ease in Zion,
and trust in the mountain of Sa-mâ'rĭ-a,
which are named chief of the nations,
to whom the house of Israel came!
2 Pass ye unto Căl'nĕh, and see; and
from thence go ye to Hā'măth the
great: then go down to Gath of the Philis-
tines: *be they* better than these king-
doms? or their border greater than your
border?
3 Ye that put far away the evil day,
and cause the seat of violence to come
near;
4 That lie upon beds of ivory, and
stretch themselves upon their couches,
and eat the lambs out of the flock, and
the calves out of the midst of the stall;
5 That chant to the sound of the viol,
and invent to themselves instruments
of musick, like David;
6 That drink wine in bowls, and
anoint themselves with the chief oint-
ments: but they are not grieved for the
affliction of Joseph.
7 ¶Therefore now shall they go cap-
tive with the first that go captive, and
the banquet of them that stretched
themselves shall be removed.
8 The Lord GOD hath sworn by him-
self, saith the LORD the God of hosts, I
abhor the excellency of Jacob, and hate
his palaces: therefore will I deliver up
the city with all that is therein.
9 And it shall come to pass, if there
remain ten men in one house, that they
shall die.
10 And a man's uncle shall take him
up, and he that burneth him, to bring
out the bones out of the house, and
shall say unto him that *is* by the sides of
the house, *Is there* yet *any* with thee?
and he shall say, No. Then shall he say,
Hold thy tongue: for we may not make
mention of the name of the LORD.
11 For, behold, the LORD command-
eth, and he will smite the great house
with breaches, and the little house with
clefts.
12 ¶Shall horses run upon the rock?
will *one* plow *there* with oxen? for ye
have turned judgment into gall, and the
fruit of righteousness into hemlock:
13 Ye which rejoice in a thing of
nought, which say, Have we not taken
to us horns by our own strength?
14 But, behold, I will raise up against
you a nation, O house of Israel, saith
the LORD the God of hosts; and they
shall afflict you from the entering in of
Hē'măth unto the river of the wilder-
ness.

CHAPTER 7

THUS hath the Lord GOD shewed unto
me; and, behold, he formed grasshop-
pers in the beginning of the shooting up
of the latter growth; and, lo, *it was* the
latter growth after the king's mowings.
2 And it came to pass, *that* when they
had made an end of eating the grass of
the land, then I said, O Lord GOD, for-
give, I beseech thee: by whom shall Ja-
cob arise? for he *is* small.
3 The LORD repented for this: It shall
not be, saith the LORD.
4 ¶Thus hath the Lord GOD shewed
unto me: and, behold, the Lord GOD
called to contend by fire, and it de-
voured the great deep, and did eat up a
part.

5 Then said I, O Lord GOD, cease, I beseech thee: by whom shall Jacob arise? for he *is* small.

6 The LORD repented for this: This also shall not be, saith the Lord GOD.

7 ¶Thus he shewed me: and, behold, the Lord stood upon a wall *made* by a plumbline, with a plumbline in his hand.

8 And the LORD said unto me, Amos, what seest thou? And I said, A plumbline. Then said the Lord, Behold, I will set a plumbline in the midst of my people Israel: I will not again pass by them any more:

9 And the high places of Isaac shall be desolate, and the sanctuaries of Israel shall be laid waste; and I will rise against the house of Jĕr-o-bō'am with the sword.

10 ¶Then Ăm-a-zī'ah the priest of Bĕth–el sent to Jĕr-o-bō'am king of Israel, saying, Amos hath conspired against thee in the midst of the house of Israel: the land is not able to bear all his words.

11 For thus Amos saith, Jĕr-o-bō'am shall die by the sword, and Israel shall surely be led away captive out of their own land.

12 Also Ăm-a-zī'ah said unto Amos, O thou seer, go, flee thee away into the land of Judah, and there eat bread, and prophesy there:

13 But prophesy not again any more at Bĕth–el: for it *is* the king's chapel, and it *is* the king's court.

14 ¶Then answered Amos, and said to Ăm-a-zī'ah, I *was* no prophet, neither *was* I a prophet's son; but I *was* an herdman, and a gatherer of sycomore fruit:

15 And the LORD took me as I followed the flock, and the LORD said unto me, Go, prophesy unto my people Israel.

16 Now therefore hear thou the word of the LORD: Thou sayest, Prophesy not against Israel, and drop not *thy word* against the house of Isaac.

17 Therefore thus saith the LORD; Thy wife shall be an harlot in the city, and thy sons and thy daughters shall fall by the sword, and thy land shall be divided by line; and thou shalt die in a polluted land: and Israel shall surely go into captivity forth of his land.

CHAPTER 8

THUS hath the Lord GOD shewed unto me: and behold a basket of summer fruit.

2 And he said, Amos, what seest thou? And I said, A basket of summer fruit. Then said the LORD unto me, The end is come upon my people of Israel; I will not again pass by them any more.

3 And the songs of the temple shall be howlings in that day, saith the Lord GOD: *there shall be* many dead bodies in every place; they shall cast *them* forth with silence.

4 ¶Hear this, O ye that swallow up the needy, even to make the poor of the land to fail,

5 Saying, When will the new moon be gone, that we may sell corn? and the sabbath, that we may set forth wheat, making the ephah small, and the shekel great, and falsifying the balances by deceit?

6 That we may buy the poor for silver, and the needy for a pair of shoes; *yea*, and sell the refuse of the wheat?

7 The LORD hath sworn by the excellency of Jacob, Surely I will never forget any of their works.

8 Shall not the land tremble for this, and every one mourn that dwelleth therein? and it shall rise up wholly as a flood; and it shall be cast out and drowned, as *by* the flood of Egypt.

9 And it shall come to pass in that day, saith the Lord GOD, that I will cause the sun to go down at noon, and I will darken the earth in the clear day:

10 And I will turn your feasts into mourning, and all your songs into lamentation; and I will bring up sackcloth upon all loins, and baldness upon every head; and I will make it as the mourning of an only *son*, and the end thereof as a bitter day.

11 ¶Behold, the days come, saith the Lord GOD, that I will send a famine in the land, not a famine of bread, nor a thirst for water, but of hearing the words of the LORD:

12 And they shall wander from sea to sea, and from the north even to the east, they shall run to and fro to seek the word of the LORD, and shall not find *it*.

13 In that day shall the fair virgins and young men faint for thirst.

14 They that swear by the sin of Să-mâ'rĭ-a, and say, Thy God, O Dan, liveth; and, The manner of Be'er–shē'ba liveth; even they shall fall, and never rise up again.

CHAPTER 9

I SAW the Lord standing upon the altar: and he said, Smite the lintel of the door, that the posts may shake: and cut them in the head, all of them; and I will slay the last of them with the sword: he that fleeth of them shall not flee away, and he that escapeth of them shall not be delivered.

2 Though they dig into hell, thence
shall mine hand take them; though they
climb up to heaven, thence will I bring
them down:
3 And though they hide themselves in
the top of Carmel, I will search and
take them out thence; and though they
be hid from my sight in the bottom of
the sea, thence will I command the serpent, and he shall bite them:
4 And though they go into captivity
before their enemies, thence will I command the sword, and it shall slay them:
and I will set mine eyes upon them for
evil, and not for good.
5 And the Lord GOD of hosts *is* he that
toucheth the land, and it shall melt, and
all that dwell therein shall mourn: and
it shall rise up wholly like a flood; and
shall be drowned, as *by* the flood of
Egypt.
6 *It is* he that buildeth his stories in
the heaven, and hath founded his troop
in the earth; he that calleth for the waters
of the sea, and poureth them out
upon the face of the earth: The LORD *is*
his name.
7 *Are* ye not as children of the Ē-thĭ-ō'pĭ-ans unto me, O children of Israel?
saith the LORD. Have not I brought up
Israel out of the land of Egypt? and the
Philistines from Căph'tôr, and the Syrians from Kir?
8 Behold, the eyes of the Lord GOD
are upon the sinful kingdom, and I will
destroy it from off the face of the earth;
saving that I will not utterly destroy the
house of Jacob, saith the LORD.
9 For, lo, I will command, and I will
sift the house of Israel among all nations, like as *corn* is sifted in a sieve, yet
shall not the least grain fall upon the
earth.
10 All the sinners of my people shall
die by the sword, which say, The evil
shall not overtake nor prevent us.
11 ¶In that day will I raise up the tabernacle of David that is fallen, and
close up the breaches thereof; and I will
raise up his ruins, and I will build it as in
the days of old:
12 That they may possess the remnant of Edom, and of all the heathen,
which are called by my name, saith the
LORD that doeth this.
13 Behold, the days come, saith the
LORD, that the plowman shall overtake
the reaper, and the treader of grapes
him that soweth seed; and the mountains shall drop sweet wine, and all the
hills shall melt.
14 And I will bring again the captivity
of my people of Israel, and they shall
build the waste cities, and inhabit
them; and they shall plant vineyards,
and drink the wine thereof; they shall
also make gardens, and eat the fruit of
them.
15 And I will plant them upon their
land, and they shall no more be pulled
up out of their land which I have given
them, saith the LORD thy God.

OBADIAH

THE vision of Ō-ba-dī'ah. Thus saith
the Lord GOD concerning Edom; We
have heard a rumour from the LORD,
and an ambassador is sent among the
heathen, Arise ye, and let us rise up
against her in battle.
2 ¶Behold, I have made thee small
among the heathen: thou art greatly
despised.
3 The pride of thine heart hath deceived thee, thou that dwellest in the
clefts of the rock, whose habitation *is*
high; that saith in his heart, Who shall
bring me down to the ground?
4 Though thou exalt *thyself* as the
eagle, and though thou set thy nest
among the stars, thence will I bring
thee down, saith the LORD.
5 If thieves came to thee, if robbers
by night, (how art thou cut off!) would
they not have stolen till they had
enough? if the grapegatherers came to
thee, would they not leave *some*
grapes?
6 ¶How are *the things* of Esau
searched out! *how* are his hidden
things sought up!
7 All the men of thy confederacy
have brought thee *even* to the border:
the men that were at peace with thee
have deceived thee, *and* prevailed
against thee; *they that eat* thy bread
have laid a wound under thee: *there is*
none understanding in him.
8 Shall I not in that day, saith the
LORD, even destroy the wise *men* out of
Edom, and understanding out of the
mount of Esau?
9 And thy mighty *men*, O Tē'man,
shall be dismayed, to the end that every
one of the mount of Esau may be cut off
by slaughter.
10 For *thy* violence against thy
brother Jacob shame shall cover thee,
and thou shalt be cut off for ever.
11 In the day that thou stoodest on
the other side, in the day that the strangers carried away captive his forces,

and foreigners entered into his gates, and cast lots upon Jerusalem, even thou *wast* as one of them.

12 But thou shouldest not have looked on the day of thy brother in the day that he became a stranger; neither shouldest thou have rejoiced over the children of Judah in the day of their destruction; neither shouldest thou have spoken proudly in the day of distress.

13 Thou shouldest not have entered into the gate of my people in the day of their calamity; yea, thou shouldest not have looked on their affliction in the day of their calamity, nor have laid *hands* on their substance in the day of their calamity;

14 Neither shouldest thou have stood in the crossway, to cut off those of his that did escape; neither shouldest thou have delivered up those of his that did remain in the day of distress.

15 For the day of the LORD *is* near upon all the heathen: as thou hast done, it shall be done unto thee: thy reward shall return upon thine own head.

16 For as ye have drunk upon my holy mountain, *so* shall all the heathen drink continually, yea, they shall drink, and they shall swallow down, and they shall be as though they had not been.

17 ¶But upon mount Zion shall be deliverance, and there shall be holiness; and the house of Jacob shall possess their possessions.

18 And the house of Jacob shall be a fire, and the house of Joseph a flame, and the house of Esau for stubble, and they shall kindle in them, and devour them; and there shall not be *any* remaining of the house of Esau; for the LORD hath spoken *it*.

19 And *they of* the south shall possess the mount of Esau; and *they of* the plain the Philistines: and they shall possess the fields of Ē'phra-im, and the fields of Sa-mâ'rĭ-a: and Benjamin *shall possess* Gilead.

20 And the captivity of this host of the children of Israel *shall possess* that of the Canaanites, *even* unto Zăr'e-phăth; and the captivity of Jerusalem, which *is* in Sĕph'a-răd, shall possess the cities of the south.

21 And saviours shall come up on mount Zion to judge the mount of Esau; and the kingdom shall be the LORD's.

JONAH

CHAPTER 1

NOW the word of the LORD came unto Jonah the son of A-mĭt'ta-ī, saying,

2 Arise, go to Nĭn'e-veh, that great city, and cry against it; for their wickedness is come up before me.

3 But Jonah rose up to flee unto Tarshish from the presence of the LORD, and went down to Joppa; and he found a ship going to Tarshish: so he paid the fare thereof, and went down into it, to go with them unto Tarshish from the presence of the LORD.

4 ¶But the LORD sent out a great wind into the sea, and there was a mighty tempest in the sea, so that the ship was like to be broken.

5 Then the mariners were afraid, and cried every man unto his god, and cast forth the wares that *were* in the ship into the sea, to lighten *it* of them. But Jonah was gone down into the sides of the ship; and he lay, and was fast asleep.

6 So the shipmaster came to him, and said unto him, What meanest thou, O sleeper? arise, call upon thy God, if so be that God will think upon us, that we perish not.

7 And they said every one to his fellow, Come, and let us cast lots, that we may know for whose cause this evil *is* upon us. So they cast lots, and the lot fell upon Jonah.

8 Then said they unto him, Tell us, we pray thee, for whose cause this evil *is* upon us; What *is* thine occupation? and whence comest thou? what *is* thy country? and of what people *art* thou?

9 And he said unto them, I *am* an Hebrew; and I fear the LORD, the God of heaven, which hath made the sea and the dry *land*.

10 Then were the men exceedingly afraid, and said unto him, Why hast thou done this? For the men knew that he fled from the presence of the LORD, because he had told them.

11 Then said they unto him, What shall we do unto thee, that the sea may be calm unto us? for the sea wrought, and was tempestuous.

12 And he said unto them, Take me up, and cast me forth into the sea; so shall the sea be calm unto you: for I know that for my sake this great tempest *is* upon you.

13 Nevertheless the men rowed hard to bring *it* to the land; but they could not: for the sea wrought, and was tempestuous against them.

14 Wherefore they cried unto the

LORD, and said, We beseech thee, O LORD, we beseech thee, let us not perish for this man's life, and lay not upon us innocent blood: for thou, O LORD, hast done as it pleased thee.

15 So they took up Jonah, and cast him forth into the sea: and the sea ceased from her raging.

16 Then the men feared the LORD exceedingly, and offered a sacrifice unto the LORD, and made vows.

17 ¶Now the LORD had prepared a great fish to swallow up Jonah. And Jonah was in the belly of the fish three days and three nights.

CHAPTER 2

THEN Jonah prayed unto the LORD his God out of the fish's belly,

2 And said, I cried by reason of mine affliction unto the LORD, and he heard me; out of the belly of hell cried I, *and* thou heardest my voice.

3 For thou hadst cast me into the deep, in the midst of the seas; and the floods compassed me about: all thy billows and thy waves passed over me.

4 Then I said, I am cast out of thy sight; yet I will look again toward thy holy temple.

5 The waters compassed me about, *even* to the soul: the depth closed me round about, the weeds were wrapped about my head.

6 I went down to the bottoms of the mountains; the earth with her bars *was* about me for ever: yet hast thou brought up my life from corruption, O LORD my God.

7 When my soul fainted within me I remembered the LORD: and my prayer came in unto thee, into thine holy temple.

8 They that observe lying vanities forsake their own mercy.

9 But I will sacrifice unto thee with the voice of thanksgiving; I will pay *that* that I have vowed. Salvation *is* of the LORD.

10 ¶And the LORD spake unto the fish, and it vomited out Jonah upon the dry *land*.

CHAPTER 3

AND the word of the LORD came unto Jonah the second time, saying,

2 Arise, go unto Nĭn'e-veh, that great city, and preach unto it the preaching that I bid thee.

3 So Jonah arose, and went unto Nĭn'e-veh, according to the word of the LORD. Now Nĭn'e-veh was an exceeding great city of three days' journey.

4 And Jonah began to enter into the city a day's journey, and he cried, and said, Yet forty days, and Nĭn'e-veh shall be overthrown.

5 ¶So the people of Nĭn'e-veh believed God, and proclaimed a fast, and put on sackcloth, from the greatest of them even to the least of them.

6 For word came unto the king of Nĭn'e-veh, and he arose from his throne, and he laid his robe from him, and covered *him* with sackcloth, and sat in ashes.

7 And he caused *it* to be proclaimed and published through Nĭn'e-veh by the decree of the king and his nobles, saying, Let neither man nor beast, herd nor flock, taste anything: let them not feed, nor drink water:

8 But let man and beast be covered with sackcloth, and cry mightily unto God: yea, let them turn every one from his evil way, and from the violence that *is* in their hands.

9 Who can tell *if* God will turn and repent, and turn away from his fierce anger, that we perish not?

10 And God saw their works, that they turned from their evil way; and God repented of the evil, that he had said that he would do unto them; and he did *it* not.

CHAPTER 4

BUT it displeased Jonah exceedingly, and he was very angry.

2 And he prayed unto the LORD, and said, I pray thee, O LORD, *was* not this my saying, when I was yet in my country? Therefore I fled before unto Tarshish: for I knew that thou *art* a gracious God, and merciful, slow to anger, and of great kindness, and repentest thee of the evil.

3 Therefore now, O LORD, take, I beseech thee, my life from me; for *it is* better for me to die than to live.

4 ¶Then said the LORD, Doest thou well to be angry?

5 So Jonah went out of the city, and sat on the east side of the city, and there made him a booth, and sat under it in the shadow, till he might see what would become of the city.

6 And the LORD God prepared a gourd, and made *it* to come up over Jonah, that it might be a shadow over his head, to deliver him from his grief. So Jonah was exceeding glad of the gourd.

7 But God prepared a worm when the morning rose the next day, and it smote the gourd that it withered.

8 And it came to pass, when the sun did arise, that God prepared a vehement east wind; and the sun beat upon the head of Jonah, that he fainted, and

wished in himself to die, and said, *It is*
better for me to die than to live.
9 And God said to Jonah, Doest thou
well to be angry for the gourd? And he
said, I do well to be angry, *even* unto
death.
10 Then said the LORD, Thou hast had
pity on the gourd, for the which thou
hast not laboured, neither madest it
grow; which came up in a night, and
perished in a night:
11 And should not I spare Nĭn′e-veh,
that great city, wherein are more than
sixscore thousand persons that cannot
discern between their right hand and
their left hand; and *also* much cattle?

MICAH

CHAPTER 1

THE word of the LORD that came to Mī′-
cah the Mô′ras-thīte in the days of Jō′-
tham, Ahaz, *and* Hĕz-e-kī′ah, kings of
Judah, which he saw concerning Sa-
mâ′rĭ-a and Jerusalem.
2 ¶Hear, all ye people; hearken, O
earth, and all that therein is: and let the
Lord GOD be witness against you, the
Lord from his holy temple.
3 For, behold, the LORD cometh forth
out of his place, and will come down,
and tread upon the high places of the
earth.
4 And the mountains shall be molten
under him, and the valleys shall be
cleft, as wax before the fire, *and* as the
waters *that are* poured down a steep
place.
5 For the transgression of Jacob *is* all
this, and for the sins of the house of
Israel. What *is* the transgression of Ja-
cob? *is it* not Sa-mâ′rĭ-a? and what *are*
the high places of Judah? *are they* not
Jerusalem?
6 Therefore I will make Sa-mâ′rĭ-a as
an heap of the field, *and* as plantings of
a vineyard: and I will pour down the
stones thereof into the valley, and I will
discover the foundations thereof.
7 And all the graven images thereof
shall be beaten to pieces, and all the
hires thereof shall be burned with the
fire, and all the idols thereof will I lay
desolate: for she gathered *it* of the hire
of an harlot, and they shall return to the
hire of an harlot.
8 Therefore I will wail and howl, I will
go stripped and naked: I will make a
wailing like the dragons, and mourning
as the owls.
9 For her wound *is* incurable; for it is
come unto Judah; he is come unto the
gate of my people, *even* to Jerusalem.
10 Declare ye *it* not at Gath, weep ye
not at all: in the house of Ăph′rah roll
thyself in the dust.
11 Pass ye away, thou inhabitant of
Sā′phir, having thy shame naked: the
inhabitant of Zā′a-năn came not forth
in the mourning of Bĕth–ē′zel; he shall
receive of you his standing.
12 For the inhabitant of Mâ′rŏth
waited carefully for good: but evil
came down from the LORD unto the
gate of Jerusalem.
13 O thou inhabitant of Lā′chĭsh, bind
the chariot to the swift beast: she *is* the
beginning of the sin to the daughter of
Zion: for the transgressions of Israel
were found in thee.
14 Therefore shalt thou give presents
to Môr′esh-ĕth-găth: the houses of
Ăch′zĭb *shall be* a lie to the kings of
Israel.
15 Yet will I bring an heir unto thee, O
inhabitant of Ma-rē′shah: he shall
come unto A-dŭl′lam the glory of
Israel.
16 Make thee bald, and poll thee for
thy delicate children; enlarge thy bald-
ness as the eagle; for they are gone into
captivity from thee.

CHAPTER 2

WOE to them that devise iniquity, and
work evil upon their beds! when the
morning is light, they practise it, be-
cause it is in the power of their hand.
2 And they covet fields, and take
them by violence; and houses, and take
them away: so they oppress a man and
his house, even a man and his heritage.
3 Therefore thus saith the LORD; Be-
hold, against this family do I devise an
evil, from which ye shall not remove
your necks; neither shall ye go
haughtily: for this time *is* evil.
4 In that day shall *one* take up a
parable against you, and lament with a
doleful lamentation, *and* say, We be ut-
terly spoiled: he hath changed the por-
tion of my people: how hath he re-
moved *it* from me! turning away he
hath divided our fields.
5 Therefore thou shalt have none that
shall cast a cord by lot in the congrega-
tion of the LORD.
6 Prophesy ye not, *say they to them
that* prophesy: they shall not prophesy
to them, *that* they shall not take shame.
7 O *thou that art* named the house of
Jacob, is the spirit of the LORD
straitened? *are* these his doings? do not

my words do good to him that walketh
uprightly?
8 Even of late my people is risen up as
an enemy: ye pull off the robe with the
garment from them that pass by secure-
ly as men averse from war.
9 The women of my people have ye
cast out from their pleasant houses;
from their children have ye taken away
my glory for ever.
10 Arise ye, and depart; for this *is* not
your rest: because it is polluted, it shall
destroy *you*, even with a sore destruc-
tion.
11 If a man walking in the spirit and
falsehood do lie, *saying*, I will prophesy
unto thee of wine and of strong drink;
he shall even be the prophet of this
people.
12 ¶I will surely assemble, O Jacob,
all of thee; I will surely gather the rem-
nant of Israel; I will put them together
as the sheep of Bŏz′rah, as the flock in
the midst of their fold: they shall make
great noise by reason of *the multitude*
of men.
13 The breaker is come up before
them: they have broken up, and have
passed through the gate, and are gone
out by it: and their king shall pass be-
fore them, and the LORD on the head of
them.

CHAPTER 3

AND I said, Hear, I pray you, O heads
of Jacob, and ye princes of the house of
Israel; *Is it* not for you to know judg-
ment?
2 Who hate the good, and love the
evil; who pluck off their skin from off
them, and their flesh from off their
bones;
3 Who also eat the flesh of my people,
and flay their skin from off them; and
they break their bones, and chop them
in pieces, as for the pot, and as flesh
within the caldron.
4 Then shall they cry unto the LORD,
but he will not hear them: he will even
hide his face from them at that time, as
they have behaved themselves ill in
their doings.
5 ¶Thus saith the LORD concerning
the prophets that make my people err,
that bite with their teeth, and cry,
Peace; and he that putteth not into their
mouths, they even prepare war against
him.
6 Therefore night *shall be* unto you,
that ye shall not have a vision; and it
shall be dark unto you, that ye shall not
divine; and the sun shall go down over
the prophets, and the day shall be dark
over them.
7 Then shall the seers be ashamed,
and the diviners confounded: yea, they
shall all cover their lips; for *there is* no
answer of God.
8 But truly I am full of power by the
spirit of the LORD, and of judgment, and
of might, to declare unto Jacob his
transgression, and to Israel his sin.
9 ¶Hear this, I pray you, ye heads of
the house of Jacob, and princes of the
house of Israel, that abhor judgment,
and pervert all equity.
10 They build up Zion with blood,
and Jerusalem with iniquity.
11 The heads thereof judge for re-
ward, and the priests thereof teach for
hire, and the prophets thereof divine
for money: yet will they lean upon the
LORD, and say, *Is* not the LORD among
us? none evil can come upon us.
12 Therefore shall Zion for your sake
be plowed *as* a field, and Jerusalem
shall become heaps, and the mountain
of the house as the high places of the
forest.

CHAPTER 4

BUT in the last days it shall come to
pass, *that* the mountain of the house of
the LORD shall be established in the top
of the mountains, and it shall be ex-
alted above the hills; and people shall
flow unto it.
2 And many nations shall come, and
say, Come, and let us go up to the
mountain of the LORD, and to the house
of the God of Jacob; and he will teach
us of his ways, and we will walk in his
paths: for the law shall go forth of Zion,
and the word of the LORD from Jeru-
salem.
3 ¶And he shall judge among many
people, and rebuke strong nations afar
off; and they shall beat their swords
into plowshares, and their spears into
pruninghooks: nation shall not lift up a
sword against nation, neither shall they
learn war any more.
4 But they shall sit every man under
his vine and under his fig tree; and none
shall make *them* afraid: for the mouth
of the LORD of hosts hath spoken *it*.
5 For all people will walk every one in
the name of his god, and we will walk in
the name of the LORD our God for ever
and ever.
6 ¶In that day, saith the LORD, will I
assemble her that halteth, and I will
gather her that is driven out, and her
that I have afflicted;
7 And I will make her that halted a
remnant, and her that was cast far off a
strong nation: and the LORD shall reign
over them in mount Zion from hence-
forth, even for ever.
8 And thou, O tower of the flock, the

strong hold of the daughter of Zion,
unto thee shall it come, even the first
dominion; the kingdom shall come to
the daughter of Jerusalem.
9 ¶Now why dost thou cry out aloud?
is there no king in thee? is thy counsel-
lor perished? for pangs have taken thee
as a woman in travail.
10 Be in pain, and labour to bring
forth, O daughter of Zion, like a woman
in travail: for now shalt thou go forth
out of the city, and thou shalt dwell in
the field, and thou shalt go *even* to Bab-
ylon: there shalt thou be delivered;
there the Lord shall redeem thee from
the hand of thine enemies.
11 ¶Now also many nations are gath-
ered against thee, that say, Let her be
defiled, and let our eye look upon Zion.
12 But they know not the thoughts of
the Lord, neither understand they his
counsel: for he shall gather them as the
sheaves into the floor.
13 Arise and thresh, O daughter of
Zion: for I will make thine horn iron,
and I will make thy hoofs brass: and
thou shalt beat in pieces many people:
and I will consecrate their gain unto the
Lord, and their substance unto the
Lord of the whole earth.

CHAPTER 5

NOW gather thyself in troops, O
daughter of troops: he hath laid siege
against us: they shall smite the judge of
Israel with a rod upon the cheek.
2 But thou, Bĕth–lehĕm Ĕph'ra-tăh,
though thou be little among the thou-
sands of Judah, *yet* out of thee shall he
come forth unto me *that is* to be ruler in
Israel; whose goings forth *have been*
from of old, from everlasting.
3 Therefore will he give them up, un-
til the time *that* she which travaileth
hath brought forth: then the remnant of
his brethren shall return unto the chil-
dren of Israel.
4 And he shall stand and feed in the
strength of the Lord, in the majesty of
the name of the Lord his God; and they
shall abide: for now shall he be great
unto the ends of the earth.
5 And this *man* shall be the peace,
when the Assyrian shall come into our
land: and when he shall tread in our pal-
aces, then shall we raise against him
seven shepherds, and eight principal
men.
6 And they shall waste the land of As-
syria with the sword, and the land of
Nimrod in the entrances thereof: thus
shall he deliver *us* from the Assyrian,
when he cometh into our land, and
when he treadeth within our borders.
7 And the remnant of Jacob shall be
in the midst of many people as a dew
from the Lord, as the showers upon the
grass, that tarrieth not for man, nor
waiteth for the sons of men.
8 ¶And the remnant of Jacob shall be
among the Gentiles in the midst of
many people as a lion among the beasts
of the forest, as a young lion among the
flocks of sheep: who, if he go through,
both treadeth down, and teareth in
pieces, and none can deliver.
9 Thine hand shall be lifted up upon
thine adversaries, and all thine enemies
shall be cut off.
10 And it shall come to pass in that
day, saith the Lord, that I will cut off
thy horses out of the midst of thee, and
I will destroy thy chariots:
11 And I will cut off the cities of thy
land, and throw down all thy strong
holds:
12 And I will cut off witchcrafts out
of thine hand; and thou shalt have no
more soothsayers:
13 Thy graven images also will I cut
off, and thy standing images out of the
midst of thee; and thou shalt no more
worship the work of thine hands.
14 And I will pluck up thy groves out
of the midst of thee: so will I destroy
thy cities.
15 And I will execute vengeance in
anger and fury upon the heathen, such
as they have not heard.

CHAPTER 6

HEAR ye now what the Lord saith;
Arise, contend thou before the moun-
tains, and let the hills hear thy voice.
2 Hear ye, O mountains, the Lord's
controversy, and ye strong foundations
of the earth: for the Lord hath a contro-
versy with his people, and he will plead
with Israel.
3 O my people, what have I done unto
thee? and wherein have I wearied thee?
testify against me.
4 For I brought thee up out of the land
of Egypt, and redeemed thee out of the
house of servants; and I sent before
thee Moses, Aaron, and Miriam.
5 O my people, remember now what
Bā'lăk king of Moab consulted, and
what Bā'laam the son of Bē'ôr an-
swered him from Shĭt'tĭm unto Gilgal;
that ye may know the righteousness of
the Lord.
6 Wherewith shall I come before the
Lord, *and* bow myself before the high
God? shall I come before him with
burnt offerings, with calves of a year
old?
7 Will the Lord be pleased with thou-
sands of rams, *or* with ten thousands of
rivers of oil? shall I give my firstborn
for my transgression, the fruit of my
body *for* the sin of my soul?

8 He hath shewed thee, O man, what *is* good; and what doth the LORD require of thee, but to do justly, and to love mercy, and to walk humbly with thy God?

9 ¶The LORD's voice crieth unto the city, and *the man of* wisdom shall see thy name: hear ye the rod, and who hath appointed it.

10 Are there yet the treasures of wickedness in the house of the wicked, and the scant measure *that is* abominable?

11 Shall I count *them* pure with the wicked balances, and with the bag of deceitful weights?

12 For the rich men thereof are full of violence, and the inhabitants thereof have spoken lies, and their tongue *is* deceitful in their mouth.

13 Therefore also will I make *thee* sick in smiting thee, in making *thee* desolate because of thy sins.

14 Thou shalt eat, but not be satisfied; and thy casting down *shall be* in the midst of thee; and thou shalt take hold, but shalt not deliver; and *that* which thou deliverest will I give up to the sword.

15 Thou shalt sow, but thou shalt not reap; thou shalt tread the olives, but thou shalt not anoint thee with oil; and sweet wine, but shalt not drink wine.

16 For the statutes of Omri are kept, and all the works of the house of Ahab, and ye walk in their counsels; that I should make thee a desolation, and the inhabitants thereof an hissing: therefore ye shall bear the reproach of my people.

CHAPTER 7

WOE is me! for I am as when they have gathered the summer fruits, as the grapegleanings of the vintage: *there is* no cluster to eat: my soul desired the firstripe fruit.

2 The good *man* is perished out of the earth: and *there is* none upright among men: they all lie in wait for blood; they hunt every man his brother with a net.

3 That they may do evil with both hands earnestly, the prince asketh, and the judge *asketh* for a reward; and the great *man*, he uttereth his mischievous desire: so they wrap it up.

4 The best of them *is* as a brier: the most upright *is sharper* than a thorn hedge: the day of thy watchmen *and* thy visitation cometh; now shall be their perplexity.

5 Trust ye not in a friend, put ye not confidence in a guide: keep the doors of thy mouth from her that lieth in thy bosom.

6 For the son dishonoureth the father, the daughter riseth up against her mother, the daughter in law against her mother in law; a man's enemies *are* the men of his own house.

7 Therefore I will look unto the LORD; I will wait for the God of my salvation: my God will hear me.

8 ¶Rejoice not against me, O mine enemy: when I fall, I shall arise; when I sit in darkness, the LORD *shall be* a light unto me.

9 I will bear the indignation of the LORD, because I have sinned against him, until he plead my cause, and execute judgment for me: he will bring me forth to the light, *and* I shall behold his righteousness.

10 Then *she that is* mine enemy shall see *it*, and shame shall cover her which said unto me, Where is the LORD thy God? mine eyes shall behold her: now shall she be trodden down as the mire of the streets.

11 ¶*In* the day that thy walls are to be built, *in* that day shall the decree be far removed.

12 *In* that day *also* he shall come even to thee from Assyria, and *from* the fortified cities, and from the fortress even to the river, and from sea to sea, and *from* mountain to mountain.

13 Notwithstanding the land shall be desolate because of them that dwell therein, for the fruit of their doings.

14 ¶Feed thy people with thy rod, the flock of thine heritage, which dwell solitarily *in* the wood, in the midst of Carmel: let them feed *in* Bā'shan and Gilead, as in the days of old.

15 According to the days of thy coming out of the land of Egypt will I shew unto him marvellous *things*.

16 The nations shall see and be confounded at all their might: they shall lay *their* hand upon *their* mouth, their ears shall be deaf.

17 They shall lick the dust like a serpent, they shall move out of their holes like worms of the earth: they shall be afraid of the LORD our God, and shall fear because of thee.

18 ¶Who *is* a God like unto thee, that pardoneth iniquity, and passeth by the transgression of the remnant of his heritage? he retaineth not his anger for ever, because he delighteth *in* mercy.

19 He will turn again, he will have compassion upon us; he will subdue our iniquities; and thou wilt cast all their sins into the depths of the sea.

20 Thou wilt perform the truth to Jacob, *and* the mercy to Abraham, which thou hast sworn unto our fathers from the days of old.

NAHUM

CHAPTER 1

THE burden of Nĭn′e-veh. The book of the vision of Nahum the Ĕl′kosh-īte.

2 God *is* jealous, and the LORD revengeth; the LORD revengeth, and *is* furious; the LORD will take vengeance on his adversaries, and he reserveth *wrath* for his enemies.

3 The LORD *is* slow to anger, and great in power, and will not at all acquit *the wicked:* the LORD *hath* his way in the whirlwind and in the storm, and the clouds *are* the dust of his feet.

4 He rebuketh the sea, and maketh it dry, and drieth up all the rivers; Bā′-shan languisheth, and Carmel, and the flower of Lebanon languisheth.

5 The mountains quake at him, and the hills melt, and the earth is burned at his presence, yea, the world, and all that dwell therein.

6 Who can stand before his indignation? and who can abide in the fierceness of his anger? his fury is poured out like fire, and the rocks are thrown down by him.

7 ¶The LORD *is* good, a strong hold in the day of trouble; and he knoweth them that trust in him.

8 But with an overrunning flood he will make an utter end of the place thereof, and darkness shall pursue his enemies.

9 What do ye imagine against the LORD? he will make an utter end: affliction shall not rise up the second time.

10 For while *they be* folden together *as* thorns, and while they are drunken *as* drunkards, they shall be devoured as stubble fully dry.

11 There is *one* come out of thee, that imagineth evil against the LORD, a wicked counsellor.

12 Thus saith the LORD; Though *they be* quiet, and likewise many, yet thus shall they be cut down, when he shall pass through. Though I have afflicted thee, I will afflict thee no more.

13 For now will I break his yoke from off thee, and will burst thy bonds in sunder.

14 And the LORD hath given a commandment concerning thee, *that* no more of thy name be sown: out of the house of thy gods will I cut off the graven image and the molten image: I will make thy grave; for thou art vile.

15 Behold upon the mountains the feet of him that bringeth good tidings, that publisheth peace! O Judah, keep thy solemn feasts, perform thy vows: for the wicked shall no more pass through thee; he is utterly cut off.

CHAPTER 2

HE that dasheth in pieces is come up before thy face: keep the munition, watch the way, make *thy* loins strong, fortify *thy* power mightily.

2 For the LORD hath turned away the excellency of Jacob, as the excellency of Israel: for the emptiers have emptied them out, and marred their vine branches.

3 The shield of his mighty men is made red, the valiant men *are* in scarlet: the chariots *shall be* with flaming torches in the day of his preparation, and the fir trees shall be terribly shaken.

4 The chariots shall rage in the streets, they shall justle one against another in the broad ways: they shall seem like torches, they shall run like the lightnings.

5 He shall recount his worthies: they shall stumble in their walk; they shall make haste to the wall thereof, and the defence shall be prepared.

6 The gates of the rivers shall be opened, and the palace shall be dissolved.

7 And Hŭz′zab shall be led away captive, she shall be brought up, and her maids shall lead *her* as with the voice of doves, tabering upon their breasts.

8 But Nĭn′e-veh *is* of old like a pool of water: yet they shall flee away. Stand, stand, *shall they cry;* but none shall look back.

9 Take ye the spoil of silver, take the spoil of gold: for *there is* none end of the store *and* glory out of all the pleasant furniture.

10 She is empty, and void, and waste: and the heart melteth, and the knees smite together, and much pain *is* in all loins, and the faces of them all gather blackness.

11 Where *is* the dwelling of the lions, and the feedingplace of the young lions, where the lion, *even* the old lion, walked, *and* the lion's whelp, and none made *them* afraid?

12 The lion did tear in pieces enough for his whelps, and strangled for his lionesses, and filled his holes with prey, and his dens with ravin.

13 Behold, I *am* against thee, saith the LORD of hosts, and I will burn her chariots in the smoke, and the sword shall devour thy young lions: and I will cut off thy prey from the earth, and the

voice of thy messengers shall no more
be heard.

CHAPTER 3

WOE to the bloody city! it *is* all full of
lies *and* robbery; the prey departeth
not;
2 The noise of a whip, and the noise of
the rattling of the wheels, and of the
pransing horses, and of the jumping
chariots.
3 The horseman lifteth up both the
bright sword and the glittering spear:
and *there is* a multitude of slain, and a
great number of carcases; and *there is*
none end of *their* corpses; they stumble
upon their corpses:
4 Because of the multitude of the
whoredoms of the well-favoured harlot,
the mistress of witchcrafts, that
selleth nations through her whoredoms,
and families through her
witchcrafts.
5 Behold, I *am* against thee, saith the
LORD of hosts; and I will discover thy
skirts upon thy face, and I will shew the
nations thy nakedness, and the kingdoms
thy shame.
6 And I will cast abominable filth
upon thee, and make thee vile, and will
set thee as a gazingstock.
7 And it shall come to pass, *that* all
they that look upon thee shall flee from
thee, and say, Nĭn'e-veh is laid waste:
who will bemoan her? whence shall I
seek comforters for thee?
8 Art thou better than populous No,
that was situate among the rivers, *that
had* the waters round about it, whose
rampart *was* the sea, *and* her wall *was*
from the sea?
9 Ē-thĭ-ō'pĭ-a and Egypt *were* her
strength, and *it was* infinite; Put and
Lū'bim were thy helpers.
10 Yet *was* she carried away, she
went into captivity: her young children
also were dashed in pieces at the top of
all the streets: and they cast lots for her
honourable men, and all her great men
were bound in chains.
11 Thou also shalt be drunken: thou
shalt be hid, thou also shalt seek
strength because of the enemy.
12 All thy strong holds *shall be like*
fig trees with the firstripe figs: if they
be shaken, they shall even fall into the
mouth of the eater.
13 Behold, thy people in the midst of
thee *are* women: the gates of thy land
shall be set wide open unto thine enemies:
the fire shall devour thy bars.
14 Draw thee waters for the siege,
fortify thy strong holds: go into clay,
and tread the morter, make strong the
brickkiln.
15 There shall the fire devour thee;
the sword shall cut thee off, it shall eat
thee up like the cankerworm: make
thyself many as the cankerworm, make
thyself many as the locusts.
16 Thou hast multiplied thy merchants
above the stars of heaven: the
cankerworm spoileth, and fleeth away.
17 Thy crowned *are* as the locusts,
and thy captains as the great grasshoppers,
which camp in the hedges in
the cold day, *but* when the sun ariseth
they flee away, and their place is not
known where they *are*.
18 Thy shepherds slumber, O king of
Assyria: thy nobles shall dwell *in the
dust:* thy people is scattered upon the
mountains, and no man gathereth
them.
19 *There is* no healing of thy bruise;
thy wound is grievous: all that hear the
bruit of thee shall clap the hands over
thee: for upon whom hath not thy
wickedness passed continually?

HABAKKUK

CHAPTER 1

THE burden which Ha-băk'kuk the
prophet did see.
2 O LORD, how long shall I cry, and
thou wilt not hear! *even* cry out unto
thee *of* violence, and thou wilt not save!
3 Why dost thou shew me iniquity,
and cause *me* to behold grievance? for
spoiling and violence *are* before me:
and there are *that* raise up strife and
contention.
4 Therefore the law is slacked, and
judgment doth never go forth: for the
wicked doth compass about the
righteous; therefore wrong judgment
proceedeth.
5 ¶Behold ye among the heathen, and
regard, and wonder marvellously: for *I*
will work a work in your days, *which* ye
will not believe, though it be told *you*.
6 For, lo, I raise up the Chăl-dē'anṡ,
that bitter and hasty nation, which
shall march through the breadth of the
land, to possess the dwellingplaces
that are not theirs.
7 They *are* terrible and dreadful: their
judgment and their dignity shall
proceed of themselves.
8 Their horses also are swifter than

the leopards, and are more fierce than the evening wolves: and their horsemen shall spread themselves, and their horsemen shall come from far; they shall fly as the eagle *that* hasteth to eat.

9 They shall come all for violence: their faces shall sup up *as* the east wind, and they shall gather the captivity as the sand.

10 And they shall scoff at the kings, and the princes shall be a scorn unto them: they shall deride every strong hold; for they shall heap dust, and take it.

11 Then shall *his* mind change, and he shall pass over, and offend, *imputing* this his power unto his god.

12 ¶*Art* thou not from everlasting, O LORD my God, mine Holy One? we shall not die. O LORD, thou hast ordained them for judgment; and, O mighty God, thou hast established them for correction.

13 *Thou art* of purer eyes than to behold evil, and canst not look on iniquity: wherefore lookest thou upon them that deal treacherously, *and* holdest thy tongue when the wicked devoureth *the man that is* more righteous than he?

14 And makest men as the fishes of the sea, as the creeping things, *that have* no ruler over them?

15 They take up all of them with the angle, they catch them in their net, and gather them in their drag: therefore they rejoice and are glad.

16 Therefore they sacrifice unto their net, and burn incense unto their drag; because by them their portion *is* fat, and their meat plenteous.

17 Shall they therefore empty their net, and not spare continually to slay the nations?

CHAPTER 2

I WILL stand upon my watch, and set me upon the tower, and will watch to see what he will say unto me, and what I shall answer when I am reproved.

2 And the LORD answered me, and said, Write the vision, and make *it* plain upon tables, that he may run that readeth it.

3 For the vision *is* yet for an appointed time, but at the end it shall speak, and not lie: though it tarry, wait for it; because it will surely come, it will not tarry.

4 ¶Behold, his soul *which* is lifted up is not upright in him: but the just shall live by his faith.

5 Yea also, because he transgresseth by wine, *he is* a proud man, neither keepeth at home, who enlargeth his desire as hell, and *is* as death, and cannot be satisfied, but gathereth unto him all nations, and heapeth unto him all people:

6 Shall not all these take up a parable against him, and a taunting proverb against him, and say, Woe to him that increaseth *that which is* not his! how long? and to him that ladeth himself with thick clay!

7 Shall they not rise up suddenly that shall bite thee, and awake that shall vex thee, and thou shalt be for booties unto them?

8 Because thou hast spoiled many nations, all the remnant of the people shall spoil thee; because of men's blood, and *for* the violence of the land, of the city, and of all that dwell therein.

9 ¶Woe to him that coveteth an evil covetousness to his house, that he may set his nest on high, that he may be delivered from the power of evil!

10 Thou hast consulted shame to thy house by cutting off many people, and hast sinned *against* thy soul.

11 For the stone shall cry out of the wall, and the beam out of the timber shall answer it.

12 ¶Woe to him that buildeth a town with blood, and stablisheth a city by iniquity!

13 Behold, *is it* not of the LORD of hosts that the people shall labour in the very fire, and the people shall weary themselves for very vanity?

14 For the earth shall be filled with the knowledge of the glory of the LORD, as the waters cover the sea.

15 ¶Woe unto him that giveth his neighbour drink, that puttest thy bottle to *him*, and makest *him* drunken also, that thou mayest look on their nakedness!

16 Thou art filled with shame for glory: drink thou also, and let thy foreskin be uncovered: the cup of the LORD's right hand shall be turned unto thee, and shameful spewing *shall be* on thy glory.

17 For the violence of Lebanon shall cover thee, and the spoil of beasts, *which* made them afraid, because of men's blood, and for the violence of the land, of the city, and of all that dwell therein.

18 ¶What profiteth the graven image that the maker thereof hath graven it; the molten image, and a teacher of lies, that the maker of his work trusteth therein, to make dumb idols?

19 Woe unto him that saith to the

wood, Awake; to the dumb stone,
Arise, it shall teach! Behold, it *is* laid
over with gold and silver, and *there is*
no breath at all in the midst of it.
20 But the LORD *is* in his holy temple:
let all the earth keep silence before
him.

CHAPTER 3

A PRAYER of Ha-băk'kuk the prophet
upon Shĭ-gī'o-nŏth.
2 O LORD, I have heard thy speech,
and was afraid: O LORD, revive thy
work in the midst of the years, in the
midst of the years make known; in
wrath remember mercy.
3 ¶God came from Tē'man, and the
Holy One from mount Pâ'ran, Sē'lah.
His glory covered the heavens, and the
earth was full of his praise.
4 And *his* brightness was as the light;
he had horns *coming* out of his hand:
and there *was* the hiding of his power.
5 Before him went the pestilence, and
burning coals went forth at his feet.
6 He stood, and measured the earth:
he beheld, and drove asunder the na-
tions; and the everlasting mountains
were scattered, the perpetual hills did
bow: his ways *are* everlasting.
7 I saw the tents of Cū'shăn in afflic-
tion: *and* the curtains of the land of
Mĭd'ĭ-an did tremble.
8 Was the LORD displeased against
the rivers? *was* thine anger against the
rivers? *was* thy wrath against the sea,
that thou didst ride upon thine horses
and thy chariots of salvation?
9 Thy bow was made quite naked, *ac-
cording* to the oaths of the tribes, *even*
thy word. Sē'lah. Thou didst cleave the
earth with rivers.
10 The mountains saw thee, *and* they
trembled: the overflowing of the water
passed by: the deep uttered his voice,
and lifted up his hands on high.
trembled: the overflowing of the water
passed by: the deep uttered his voice,
and lifted up his hands on high.
11 The sun *and* moon stood still in
their habitation: at the light of thine
arrows they went, *and* at the shining of
thy glittering spear.
12 Thou didst march through the
land in indignation, thou didst thresh
the heathen in anger.
13 Thou wentest forth for the salva-
tion of thy people, *even* for salvation
with thine anointed; thou woundedst
the head out of the house of the wicked,
by discovering the foundation unto the
neck. Sē'lah.
14 Thou didst strike through with his
staves the head of his villages: they
came out as a whirlwind to scatter me:
their rejoicing *was* as to devour the
poor secretly.
15 Thou didst walk through the sea
with thine horses, *through* the heap of
great waters.
16 When I heard, my belly trembled;
my lips quivered at the voice: rotten-
ness entered into my bones, and I
trembled in myself, that I might rest in
the day of trouble: when he cometh up
unto the people, he will invade them
with his troops.
17 ¶Although the fig tree shall not
blossom, neither *shall* fruit *be* in the
vines; the labour of the olive shall fail,
and the fields shall yield no meat; the
flock shall be cut off from the fold, and
there shall be no herd in the stalls:
18 Yet I will rejoice in the LORD, I will
joy in the God of my salvation.
19 The LORD God *is* my strength, and
he will make my feet like hinds' *feet*,
and he will make me to walk upon mine
high places. To the chief singer on my
stringed instruments.

ZEPHANIAH

CHAPTER 1

THE word of the LORD which came
unto Zĕph-a-nī'ah the son of Cū'shī, the
son Gĕd-a-lī'ah, the son of Ăm-a-rī'ah,
the son of Hĭz-kī'ah, in the days of Jō-
sī'ah the son of Amon, king of Judah.
2 I will utterly consume all *things*
from off the land, saith the LORD.
3 I will consume man and beast; I will
consume the fowls of the heaven, and
the fishes of the sea, and the stumbling-
blocks with the wicked; and I will cut
off man from off the land, saith the
LORD.
4 I will also stretch out mine hand
upon Judah, and upon all the inhabi-
tants of Jerusalem; and I will cut off the
remnant of Bā'al from this place, *and*
the name of the Chĕm'a-rīms with the
priests;
5 And them that worship the host of
heaven upon the housetops; and them
that worship *and* that swear by the
LORD, and that swear by Măl'chăm;
6 And them that are turned back
from the LORD; and *those* that have not
sought the LORD, nor enquired for him.
7 Hold thy peace at the presence of
the Lord GOD: for the day of the LORD *is*
at hand: for the LORD hath prepared a
sacrifice, he hath bid his guests.

8 And it shall come to pass in the day of the LORD's sacrifice, that I will punish the princes, and the king's children, and all such as are clothed with strange apparel.
9 In the same day also will I punish all those that leap on the threshold, which fill their masters' houses with violence and deceit.
10 And it shall come to pass in that day, saith the LORD, *that there shall be* the noise of a cry from the fish gate, and an howling from the second, and a great crashing from the hills.
11 Howl, ye inhabitants of Măk'tĕsh, for all the merchant people are cut down; all they that bear silver are cut off.
12 ¶And it shall come to pass at that time, *that* I will search Jerusalem with candles, and punish the men that are settled on their lees: that say in their heart, The LORD will not do good, neither will he do evil.
13 Therefore their goods shall become a booty, and their houses a desolation: they shall also build houses, but not inhabit *them;* and they shall plant vineyards, but not drink the wine thereof.
14 The great day of the LORD *is* near, *it is* near, and hasteth greatly, *even* the voice of the day of the LORD: the mighty man shall cry there bitterly.
15 That day *is* a day of wrath, a day of trouble and distress, a day of wasteness and desolation, a day of darkness and gloominess, a day of clouds and thick darkness,
16 A day of the trumpet and alarm against the fenced cities, and against the high towers.
17 And I will bring distress upon men, that they shall walk like blind men, because they have sinned against the LORD: and their blood shall be poured out as dust, and their flesh as the dung.
18 Neither their silver nor their gold shall be able to deliver them in the day of the LORD's wrath; but the whole land shall be devoured by the fire of his jealousy: for he shall make even a speedy riddance of all them that dwell in the land.

CHAPTER 2

GATHER yourselves together, yea, gather together, O nation not desired;
2 Before the decree bring forth, *before* the day pass as the chaff, before the fierce anger of the LORD come upon you, before the day of the LORD's anger come upon you.
3 Seek ye the LORD, all ye meek of the earth, which have wrought his judgment; seek righteousness, seek meekness: it may be ye shall be hid in the day of the LORD's anger.
4 ¶For Gā'za shall be forsaken, and Ăsh'ke-lon a desolation: they shall drive out Ăsh'dŏd at the noon day, and Ekron shall be rooted up.
5 Woe unto the inhabitants of the sea coast, the nation of the Chĕr'e-thītes! the word of the LORD *is* against you; O Canaan, the land of the Philistines, I will even destroy thee, that there shall be no inhabitant.
6 And the sea coast shall be dwellings *and* cottages for shepherds, and folds for flocks.
7 And the coast shall be for the remnant of the house of Judah; they shall feed thereupon: in the houses of Ăsh'-ke-lon shall they lie down in the evening: for the LORD their God shall visit them and turn away their captivity.
8 ¶I have heard the reproach of Moab, and the revilings of the children of Ammon, whereby they have reproached my people, and magnified *themselves* against their border.
9 Therefore *as* I live, saith the LORD of hosts, the God of Israel, Surely Moab shall be as Sodom, and the children of Ammon as Go-mŏr'rah, *even* the breeding of nettles, and saltpits, and a perpetual desolation: the residue of my people shall spoil them, and the remnant of my people shall possess them.
10 This shall they have for their pride, because they have reproached and magnified *themselves* against the people of the LORD of hosts.
11 The LORD *will be* terrible unto them: for he will famish all the gods of the earth; and *men* shall worship him, every one from his place, *even* all the isles of the heathen.
12 ¶Ye Ē-thĭ-ō'pĭ-ans also, ye *shall be* slain by my sword.
13 And he will stretch out his hand against the north, and destroy Assyria; and will make Nĭn'e-veh a desolation, *and* dry like a wilderness.
14 And flocks shall lie down in the midst of her, all the beasts of the nations: both the cormorant and the bittern shall lodge in the upper lintels of it; *their* voice shall sing in the windows; desolation *shall be* in the thresholds: for he shall uncover the cedar work.
15 This *is* the rejoicing city that dwelt carelessly, that said in her heart, I *am,* and *there is* none beside me: how is she become a desolation, a place for beasts to lie down in! every one that passeth by her shall hiss, *and* wag his hand.

CHAPTER 3

WOE to her that is filthy and polluted, to the oppressing city!

2 She obeyed not the voice; she received not correction; she trusted not in the LORD; she drew not near to her God.

3 Her princes within her *are* roaring lions; her judges *are* evening wolves; they gnaw not the bones till the morrow.

4 Her prophets *are* light *and* treacherous persons: her priests have polluted the sanctuary, they have done violence to the law.

5 The just LORD *is* in the midst thereof; he will not do iniquity: every morning doth he bring his judgment to light, he faileth not; but the unjust knoweth no shame.

6 I have cut off the nations: their towers are desolate; I made their streets waste, that none passeth by: their cities are destroyed, so that there is no man, that there is none inhabitant.

7 I said, Surely thou wilt fear me, thou wilt receive instruction; so their dwelling should not be cut off, howsoever I punished them: but they rose early, *and* corrupted all their doings.

8 ¶Therefore wait ye upon me, saith the LORD, until the day that I rise up to the prey: for my determination *is* to gather the nations, that I may assemble the kingdoms, to pour upon them mine indignation, *even* all my fierce anger: for all the earth shall be devoured with the fire of my jealousy.

9 For then will I turn to the people a pure language, that they may all call upon the name of the LORD, to serve him with one consent.

10 From beyond the rivers of Ē-thĭ-ō′-pĭ-a my suppliants, *even* the daughter of my dispersed, shall bring mine offering.

11 In that day shalt thou not be ashamed for all thy doings, wherein thou hast transgressed against me: for then I will take away out of the midst of thee them that rejoice in thy pride, and thou shalt no more be haughty because of my holy mountain.

12 I will also leave in the midst of thee an afflicted and poor people, and they shall trust in the name of the LORD.

13 ¶The remnant of Israel shall not do iniquity, nor speak lies; neither shall a deceitful tongue be found in their mouth: for they shall feed and lie down, and none shall make *them* afraid.

14 ¶Sing, O daughter of Zion; shout, O Israel; be glad and rejoice with all the heart, O daughter of Jerusalem.

15 The LORD hath taken away thy judgments, he hath cast out thine enemy: the king of Israel, *even* the LORD, *is* in the midst of thee: thou shalt not see evil any more.

16 In that day it shall be said to Jerusalem, Fear thou not: *and to* Zion, Let not thine hands be slack.

17 The LORD thy God in the midst of thee *is* mighty; he will save, he will rejoice over thee with joy; he will rest in his love, he will joy over thee with singing.

18 I will gather *them that are* sorrowful for the solemn assembly, *who* are of thee, *to whom* the reproach of it *was* a burden.

19 Behold, at that time I will undo all that afflict thee: and I will save her that halteth, and gather her that was driven out; and I will get them praise and fame in every land where they have been put to shame.

20 At that time will I bring you *again*, even in the time that I gather you: for I will make you a name and a praise among all people of the earth, when I turn back your captivity before your eyes, saith the LORD.

HAGGAI

CHAPTER 1

IN the second year of Darius the king, in the sixth month, in the first day of the month, came the word of the LORD by Hăg′ga-ī the prophet unto Ze-rŭb′ba-bel the son of Shē-ăl′tĭ-el, governor of Judah, and to Joshua the son of Jŏs′e-dĕch, the high priest, saying,

2 Thus speaketh the LORD of hosts, saying, This people say, The time is not come, the time that the LORD's house should be built.

3 Then came the word of the LORD by Hăg′ga-ī the prophet, saying,

4 *Is it* time for you, O ye, to dwell in your cieled houses, and this house *lie* waste?

5 Now therefore thus saith the LORD of hosts; Consider your ways.

6 Ye have sown much, and bring in little; ye eat, but ye have not enough; ye drink, but ye are not filled with drink; ye clothe you, but there is none warm; and he that earneth wages earneth wages *to put it* into a bag with holes.

7 ¶Thus saith the LORD of hosts; Consider your ways.

8 Go up to the mountain, and bring wood, and build the house; and I will take pleasure in it, and I will be glorified, saith the LORD.

9 Ye looked for much, and, lo, *it came* to little; and when ye brought *it* home, I did blow upon it. Why? saith the LORD of hosts. Because of mine house that *is* waste, and ye run every man unto his own house.

10 Therefore the heaven over you is stayed from dew, and the earth is stayed *from* her fruit.

11 And I called for a drought upon the land, and upon the mountains, and upon the corn, and upon the new wine, and upon the oil, and upon *that* which the ground bringeth forth, and upon men, and upon cattle, and upon all the labour of the hands.

12 ¶Then Ze-rŭb′ba-bel the son of Shē-ăl′tī-el, and Joshua the son of Jōs′e-dĕch, the high priest, with all the remnant of the people, obeyed the voice of the LORD their God, and the words of Hăg′ga-ī the prophet, as the LORD their God had sent him, and the people did fear before the LORD.

13 Then spake Hăg′ga-ī the LORD's messenger in the LORD's message unto the people, saying, I *am* with you, saith the LORD.

14 And the LORD stirred up the spirit of Ze-rŭb′ba-bel the son of Shē-ăl′tī-el, governor of Judah, and the spirit of Joshua the son of Jōs′e-dĕch, the high priest, and the spirit of all the remnant of the people; and they came and did work in the house of the LORD of hosts, their God,

15 In the four and twentieth day of the sixth month, in the second year of Darius the king.

CHAPTER 2

IN the seventh *month,* in the one and twentieth *day* of the month, came the word of the LORD by the prophet Hăg′ga-ī, saying,

2 Speak now to Ze-rŭb′ba-bel the son of Shē-ăl′tī-el, governor of Judah, and to Joshua the son of Jōs′e-dĕch, the high priest, and to the residue of the people, saying,

3 Who *is* left among you that saw this house in her first glory? and how do ye see it now? *is it* not in your eyes in comparison of it as nothing?

4 Yet now be strong, O Ze-rŭb′ba-bel, saith the LORD; and be strong, O Joshua, son of Jōs′e-dĕch, the high priest; and be strong, all ye people of the land, saith the LORD, and work: for I *am* with you, saith the LORD of hosts:

5 *According to* the word that I covenanted with you when ye came out of Egypt, so my spirit remaineth among you: fear ye not.

6 For thus saith the LORD of hosts; Yet once, it *is* a little while, and I will shake the heavens, and the earth, and the sea, and the dry *land;*

7 And I will shake all nations, and the desire of all nations shall come: and I will fill this house with glory, saith the LORD of hosts.

8 The silver *is* mine, and the gold *is* mine, saith the LORD of hosts.

9 The glory of this latter house shall be greater than of the former, saith the LORD of hosts: and in this place will I give peace, saith the LORD of hosts.

10 ¶In the four and twentieth *day* of the ninth *month,* in the second year of Darius, came the word of the LORD by Hăg′ga-ī the prophet, saying,

11 Thus saith the LORD of hosts; Ask now the priests *concerning* the law, saying,

12 If one bear holy flesh in the skirt of his garment, and with his skirt do touch bread, or pottage, or wine, or oil, or any meat, shall it be holy? And the priests answered and said, No.

13 Then said Hăg′ga-ī, If *one that is* unclean by a dead body touch any of these, shall it be unclean? And the priests answered and said, It shall be unclean.

14 Then answered Hăg′ga-ī, and said, So *is* this people, and so *is* this nation before me, saith the LORD; and so *is* every work of their hands; and that which they offer there *is* unclean.

15 And now, I pray you, consider from this day and upward, from before a stone was laid upon a stone in the temple of the LORD:

16 Since those *days* were, when *one* came to an heap of twenty *measures,* there were *but* ten: when *one* came to the pressfat for to draw out fifty *vessels* out of the press, there were *but* twenty.

17 I smote you with blasting and with mildew and with hail in all the labours of your hands; yet ye *turned* not to me, saith the LORD.

18 ¶Consider now from this day and upward, from the four and twentieth day of the ninth *month, even* from the day that the foundation of the LORD's temple was laid, consider *it.*

19 Is the seed yet in the barn? yea, as yet the vine, and the fig tree, and the pomegranate, and the olive tree, hath

not brought forth: from this day will I bless *you.*

20 ¶And again the word of the LORD came unto Hăg'ga-ī in the four and twentieth *day* of the month, saying,

21 Speak to Ze-rŭb'ba-bel, governor of Judah, saying, I will shake the heavens and the earth;

22 And I will overthrow the throne of kingdoms, and I will destroy the strength of the kingdoms of the heathen; and I will overthrow the chariots, and those that ride in them; and the horses and their riders shall come down, every one by the sword of his brother.

23 In that day, saith the LORD of hosts, will I take thee, O Ze-rŭb'ba-bel, my servant, the son of Shē-ăl'tī-el, saith the LORD, and will make thee as a signet: for I have chosen thee, saith the LORD of hosts.

ZECHARIAH

CHAPTER 1

IN the eighth month, in the second year of Darius, came the word of the LORD unto Zĕch-a-rī'ah, the son of Bĕr-e-chī'-ah, the son of Ĭd'dō the prophet, saying,

2 The LORD hath been sore displeased with your fathers.

3 Therefore say thou unto them, Thus saith the LORD of hosts; Turn ye unto me, saith the LORD of hosts, and I will turn unto you, saith the LORD of hosts.

4 Be ye not as your fathers, unto whom the former prophets have cried, saying, Thus saith the LORD of hosts; Turn ye now from your evil ways, and *from* your evil doings: but they did not hear, nor hearken unto me, saith the LORD.

5 Your fathers, where *are* they? and the prophets, do they live for ever?

6 But my words and my statutes, which I commanded my servants the prophets, did they not take hold of your fathers? and they returned and said, Like as the LORD of hosts thought to do unto us, according to our ways, and according to our doings, so hath he dealt with us.

7 ¶Upon the four and twentieth day of the eleventh month, which *is* the month Sĕ'bat, in the second year of Darius, came the word of the LORD unto Zĕch-a-rī'ah, the son of Bĕr-e-chī'ah, the son of Ĭd'dō the prophet, saying,

8 I saw by night, and behold a man riding upon a red horse, and he stood among the myrtle trees that *were* in the bottom; and behind him *were there* red horses, speckled, and white.

9 Then said I, O my lord, what *are* these? And the angel that talked with me said unto me, I will shew thee what these *be.*

10 And the man that stood among the myrtle trees answered and said, These *are they* whom the LORD hath sent to walk to and fro through the earth.

11 And they answered the angel of the LORD that stood among the myrtle trees, and said, We have walked to and fro through the earth, and, behold, all the earth sitteth still, and is at rest.

12 ¶Then the angel of the LORD answered and said, O LORD of hosts, how long wilt thou not have mercy on Jerusalem and on the cities of Judah, against which thou hast had indignation these threescore and ten years?

13 And the LORD answered the angel that talked with me *with* good words *and* comfortable words.

14 So the angel that communed with me said unto me, Cry thou, saying, Thus saith the LORD of hosts; I am jealous for Jerusalem and for Zion with a great jealousy.

15 And I am very sore displeased with the heathen *that are* at ease: for I was but a little displeased, and they helped forward the affliction.

16 Therefore thus saith the LORD; I am returned to Jerusalem with mercies: my house shall be built in it, saith the LORD of hosts, and a line shall be stretched forth upon Jerusalem.

17 Cry yet, saying, Thus saith the LORD of hosts; My cities through prosperity shall yet be spread abroad; and the LORD shall yet comfort Zion, and shall yet choose Jerusalem.

18 ¶Then lifted I up mine eyes, and saw, and behold four horns.

19 And I said unto the angel that talked with me, What *be* these? And he answered me, These *are* the horns which have scattered Judah, Israel, and Jerusalem.

20 And the LORD shewed me four carpenters.

21 Then said I, What come these to do? And he spake, saying, These *are* the horns which have scattered Judah, so that no man did lift up his head: but these are come to fray them, to cast out the horns of the Gentiles, which lifted up *their* horn over the land of Judah to scatter it.

CHAPTER 2

I LIFTED up mine eyes again, and
looked, and behold a man with a measuring line in his hand.
2 Then said I, Whither goest thou?
And he said unto me, To measure Jerusalem, to see what *is* the breadth thereof, and what *is* the length thereof.
3 And, behold, the angel that talked
with me went forth, and another angel
went out to meet him,
4 And said unto him, Run, speak to
this young man, saying, Jerusalem
shall be inhabited *as* towns without
walls for the multitude of men and
cattle therein:
5 For I, saith the LORD, will be unto
her a wall of fire round about, and will
be the glory in the midst of her.
6 ¶Ho, ho, *come forth*, and flee from
the land of the north, saith the LORD: for
I have spread you abroad as the four
winds of the heaven, saith the LORD.
7 Deliver thyself, O Zion, that dwellest *with* the daughter of Babylon.
8 For thus saith the LORD of hosts; After the glory hath he sent me unto the
nations which spoiled you: for he that
toucheth you toucheth the apple of his
eye.
9 For, behold, I will shake mine hand
upon them, and they shall be a spoil to
their servants: and ye shall know that
the LORD of hosts hath sent me.
10 ¶Sing and rejoice, O daughter of
Zion: for, lo, I come, and I will dwell in
the midst of thee, saith the LORD.
11 And many nations shall be joined
to the LORD in that day, and shall be my
people: and I will dwell in the midst of
thee, and thou shalt know that the LORD
of hosts hath sent me unto thee.
12 And the LORD shall inherit Judah
his portion in the holy land, and shall
choose Jerusalem again.
13 Be silent, O all flesh, before the
LORD: for he is raised up out of his holy
habitation.

CHAPTER 3

AND he shewed me Joshua the high
priest standing before the angel of the
LORD, and Satan standing at his right
hand to resist him.
2 And the LORD said unto Satan, The
LORD rebuke thee, O Satan; even the
LORD that hath chosen Jerusalem rebuke thee: *is* not this a brand plucked
out of the fire?
3 Now Joshua was clothed with filthy
garments, and stood before the angel.
4 And he answered and spake unto
those that stood before him, saying,
Take away the filthy garments from
him. And unto him he said, Behold, I
have caused thine iniquity to pass from
thee, and I will clothe thee with change
of raiment.
5 And I said, Let them set a fair mitre
upon his head. So they set a fair mitre
upon his head, and clothed him with
garments. And the angel of the LORD
stood by.
6 And the angel of the LORD protested
unto Joshua, saying,
7 Thus saith the LORD of hosts; If thou
wilt walk in my ways, and if thou wilt
keep my charge, then thou shalt also
judge my house, and shalt also keep my
courts, and I will give thee places to
walk among these that stand by.
8 Hear now, O Joshua the high priest,
thou, and thy fellows that sit before
thee: for they *are* men wondered at: for,
behold, I will bring forth my servant
the BRANCH.
9 For behold the stone that I have laid
before Joshua; upon one stone *shall be*
seven eyes: behold, I will engrave the
graving thereof, saith the LORD of
hosts, and I will remove the iniquity of
that land in one day.
10 In that day, saith the LORD of
hosts, shall ye call every man his neighbour under the vine and under the
fig tree.

CHAPTER 4

AND the angel that talked with me
came again, and waked me, as a man
that is wakened out of his sleep,
2 And said unto me, What seest thou?
And I said, I have looked, and behold a
candlestick all *of* gold, with a bowl
upon the top of it, and his seven lamps
thereon, and seven pipes to the seven
lamps, which *are* upon the top thereof:
3 And two olive trees by it, one upon
the right *side* of the bowl, and the other
upon the left *side* thereof.
4 So I answered and spake to the angel that talked with me, saying, What
are these, my lord?
5 Then the angel that talked with me
answered and said unto me, Knowest
thou not what these be? And I said, No,
my lord.
6 Then he answered and spake unto
me, saying, This *is* the word of the LORD
unto Ze-rŭb'ba-bel, saying, Not by
might, nor by power, but by my spirit,
saith the LORD of hosts.
7 Who *art* thou, O great mountain?
before Ze-rŭb'ba-bel *thou shalt become* a plain: and he shall bring forth
the headstone *thereof with* shoutings,
crying, Grace, grace unto it.
8 Moreover the word of the LORD
came unto me, saying,

9 The hands of Ze-rŭb'ba-bel have
laid the foundation of this house; his
hands shall also finish it; and thou shalt
know that the LORD of hosts hath sent
me unto you.
10 For who hath despised the day of
small things? for they shall rejoice, and
shall see the plummet in the hand of
Ze-rŭb'ba-bel *with* those seven; they
are the eyes of the LORD, which run to
and fro through the whole earth.
11 ¶Then answered I, and said unto
him, What *are* these two olive trees
upon the right *side* of the candlestick
and upon the left *side* thereof?
12 And I answered again, and said
unto him, What *be these* two olive
branches which through the two gold-
en pipes empty the golden *oil* out of
themselves?
13 And he answered me and said,
knowest thou not what these *be?* And I
said, No, my lord.
14 Then said he, These *are* the two
anointed ones, that stand by the Lord
of the whole earth.

CHAPTER 5

THEN I turned, and lifted up mine eyes,
and looked, and behold a flying roll.
2 And he said unto me, What seest
thou? And I answered, I see a flying
roll; the length thereof *is* twenty cubits,
and the breadth thereof ten cubits.
3 Then said he unto me, This *is* the
curse that goeth forth over the face of
the whole earth: for every one that
stealeth shall be cut off *as* on this side
according to it; and every one that
sweareth shall be cut off *as* on that side
according to it.
4 I will bring it forth, saith the LORD of
hosts, and it shall enter into the house
of the thief, and into the house of him
that sweareth falsely by my name: and
it shall remain in the midst of his house,
and shall consume it with the timber
thereof and the stones thereof.
5 ¶Then the angel that talked with me
went forth, and said unto me, Lift up
now thine eyes, and see what *is* this
that goeth forth.
6 And I said, What *is* it? And he said,
This *is* an ephah that goeth forth. He
said moreover, This *is* their resem-
blance through all the earth.
7 And, behold, there was lifted up a
talent of lead: and this *is* a woman that
sitteth in the midst of the ephah.
8 And he said, This *is* wickedness.
And he cast it into the midst of the
ephah; and he cast the weight of lead
upon the mouth thereof.
9 Then lifted I up mine eyes, and
looked, and, behold, there came out
two women, and the wind *was* in their
wings; for they had wings like the
wings of a stork: and they lifted up the
ephah between the earth and the
heaven.
10 Then said I to the angel that talked
with me, Whither do these bear the
ephah?
11 And he said unto me, To build it an
house in the land of Shī'när: and it shall
be established, and set there upon her
own base.

CHAPTER 6

AND I turned, and lifted up mine eyes,
and looked, and, behold, there came
four chariots out from between two
mountains; and the mountains *were*
mountains of brass.
2 In the first chariot *were* red horses;
and in the second chariot black horses;
3 And in the third chariot white
horses; and in the fourth chariot grisled
and bay horses.
4 Then I answered and said unto the
angel that talked with me, What *are*
these, my lord?
5 And the angel answered and said
unto me, These *are* the four spirits of
the heavens, which go forth from stand-
ing before the Lord of all the earth.
6 The black horses which *are* therein
go forth into the north country; and the
white go forth after them; and the
grisled go forth toward the south
country.
7 And the bay went forth, and sought
to go that they might walk to and fro
through the earth: and he said, Get you
hence, walk to and fro through the
earth. So they walked to and fro
through the earth.
8 Then cried he upon me, and spake
unto me, saying, Behold, these that go
toward the north country have quieted
my spirit in the north country.
9 ¶And the word of the LORD came
unto me, saying,
10 Take of *them of* the captivity, *even*
of Hĕl'da-ī, of Tō-bī'jah, and of Je-dā'-
iah, which are come from Babylon,
and come thou the same day, and go
into the house of Josiah the son of
Zĕph-a-nī'ah;
11 Then take silver and gold, and
make crowns, and set *them* upon the
head of Joshua the son of Jōs'e-dĕch,
the high priest;
12 And speak unto him, saying, Thus
speaketh the LORD of hosts, saying, Be-
hold the man whose name *is* The
BRANCH; and he shall grow up out of
his place, and he shall build the temple
of the LORD:
13 Even he shall build the temple of

the LORD; and he shall bear the glory, and shall sit and rule upon his throne; and he shall be a priest upon his throne: and the counsel of peace shall be between them both.

14 And the crowns shall be to Hē′lĕm, and to Tō-bī′jah, and to Je-dā′iah, and to Hen the son of Zĕph-a-nī′ah, for a memorial in the temple of the LORD.

15 And they *that are* far off shall come and build in the temple of the LORD, and ye shall know that the LORD of hosts hath sent me unto you. And *this* shall come to pass, if ye will diligently obey the voice of the LORD your God.

CHAPTER 7

AND it came to pass in the fourth year of king Darius, *that* the word of the LORD came unto Zĕch-a-rī′ah in the fourth *day* of the ninth month, *even* in Chĭs′leu;

2 When they had sent unto the house of God She-rē′zer and Rē′gem-mĕ′lech, and their men, to pray before the LORD,

3 *And* to speak unto the priests which *were* in the house of the LORD of hosts, and to the prophets, saying, Should I weep in the fifth month, separating myself, as I have done these so many years?

4 ¶Then came the word of the LORD of hosts unto me, saying,

5 Speak unto all the people of the land, and to the priests, saying, When ye fasted and mourned in the fifth and seventh *month,* even those seventy years, did ye at all fast unto me, *even* to me?

6 And when ye did eat, and when ye did drink, did not ye eat *for yourselves,* and drink *for yourselves?*

7 *Should ye* not *hear* the words which the LORD hath cried by the former prophets, when Jerusalem was inhabited and in prosperity, and the cities thereof round about her, when *men* inhabited the south and the plain?

8 ¶And the word of the LORD came unto Zĕch-a-rī′ah, saying,

9 Thus speaketh the LORD of hosts, saying, Execute true judgment, and shew mercy and compassions every man to his brother.

10 And oppress not the widow, nor the fatherless, the stranger, nor the poor; and let none of you imagine evil against his brother in your heart.

11 But they refused to hearken, and pulled away the shoulder, and stopped their ears, that they should not hear.

12 Yea, they made their hearts *as* an adamant stone, lest they should hear the law, and the words which the LORD of hosts hath sent in his spirit by the former prophets: therefore came a great wrath from the LORD of hosts.

13 Therefore it is come to pass, *that* as he cried, and they would not hear; so they cried, and I would not hear, saith the LORD of hosts:

14 But I scattered them with a whirlwind among all the nations whom they knew not. Thus the land was desolate after them, that no man passed through nor returned: for they laid the pleasant land desolate.

CHAPTER 8

AGAIN the word of the LORD of hosts came *to me,* saying,

2 Thus saith the LORD of hosts; I was jealous for Zion with great jealousy, and I was jealous for her with great fury.

3 Thus saith the LORD; I am returned unto Zion, and will dwell in the midst of Jerusalem: and Jerusalem shall be called a city of truth; and the mountain of the LORD of hosts the holy mountain.

4 Thus saith the LORD of hosts; There shall yet old men and old women dwell in the streets of Jerusalem, and every man with his staff in his hand for very age.

5 And the streets of the city shall be full of boys and girls playing in the streets thereof.

6 Thus saith the LORD of hosts; If it be marvellous in the eyes of the remnant of this people in these days, should it also be marvellous in mine eyes? saith the LORD of hosts.

7 Thus saith the LORD of hosts; Behold, I will save my people from the east country, and from the west country;

8 And I will bring them, and they shall dwell in the midst of Jerusalem: and they shall be my people, and I will be their God, in truth and in righteousness.

9 ¶Thus saith the LORD of hosts; Let your hands be strong, ye that hear in these days these words by the mouth of the prophets, which *were* in the day *that* the foundation of the house of the LORD of hosts was laid, that the temple might be built.

10 For before these days there was no hire for man, nor any hire for beast; neither *was there any* peace to him that went out or came in because of the affliction: for I set all men every one against his neighbour.

11 But now I *will* not *be* unto the residue of this people as in the former days, saith the LORD of hosts.

12 For the seed *shall be* prosperous;

the vine shall give her fruit, and the ground shall give her increase, and the heavens shall give their dew; and I will cause the remnant of this people to possess all these *things*.

13 And it shall come to pass, *that* as ye were a curse among the heathen, O house of Judah, and house of Israel; so will I save you, and ye shall be a blessing: fear not, *but* let your hands be strong.

14 For thus saith the LORD of hosts; As I thought to punish you, when your fathers provoked me to wrath, saith the LORD of hosts, and I repented not:

15 So again have I thought in these days to do well unto Jerusalem and to the house of Judah: fear ye not.

16 ¶These *are* the things that ye shall do; Speak ye every man the truth to his neighbour; execute the judgment of truth and peace in your gates:

17 And let none of you imagine evil in your hearts against his neighbour; and love no false oath: for all these *are things* that I hate, saith the LORD.

18 ¶And the word of the LORD of hosts came unto me, saying,

19 Thus saith the LORD of hosts; The fast of the fourth *month*, and the fast of the fifth, and the fast of the seventh, and the fast of the tenth, shall be to the house of Judah joy and gladness, and cheerful feasts; therefore love the truth and peace.

20 Thus saith the LORD of hosts; *It shall* yet *come to pass*, that there shall come people, and the inhabitants of many cities:

21 And the inhabitants of one *city* shall go to another, saying, Let us go speedily to pray before the LORD, and to seek the LORD of hosts: I will go also.

22 Yea, many people and strong nations shall come to seek the LORD of hosts in Jerusalem, and to pray before the LORD.

23 Thus saith the LORD of hosts; In those days *it shall come to pass*, that ten men shall take hold out of all languages of the nations, even shall take hold of the skirt of him that is a Jew, saying, We will go with you: for we have heard *that* God *is* with you.

CHAPTER 9

THE burden of the word of the LORD in the land of Hā'drăch, and Damascus *shall be* the rest thereof: when the eyes of man, as of all the tribes of Israel, *shall be* toward the LORD.

2 And Hā'măth also shall border thereby; Tȳ'rus, and Zī'don, though it be very wise.

3 And Tȳ'rus did build herself a strong hold, and heaped up silver as the dust, and fine gold as the mire of the streets.

4 Behold, the Lord will cast her out, and he will smite her power in the sea; and she shall be devoured with fire.

5 Ăsh'ke-lon shall see *it*, and fear; Gā'za also *shall see it*, and be very sorrowful, and Ekron; for her expectation shall be ashamed; and the king shall perish from Gā'za, and Ăsh'ke-lon shall not be inhabited.

6 And a bastard shall dwell in Ăsh'dŏd, and I will cut off the pride of the Philistines.

7 And I will take away his blood out of his mouth, and his abominations from between his teeth: but he that remaineth, even he, *shall be* for our God, and he shall be as a governor in Judah, and Ekron as a Jēb'-u-sīte.

8 And I will encamp about mine house because of the army, because of him that passeth by, and because of him that returneth: and no oppressor shall pass through them any more: for now have I seen with mine eyes.

9 ¶Rejoice greatly, O daughter of Zion; shout, O daughter of Jerusalem: behold, thy King cometh unto thee: he *is* just, and having salvation; lowly, and riding upon an ass, and upon a colt the foal of an ass.

10 And I will cut off the chariot from Ē'phra-im, and the horse from Jerusalem, and the battle bow shall be cut off: and he shall speak peace unto the heathen: and his dominion *shall be* from sea *even* to sea, and from the river *even* to the ends of the earth.

11 As for thee also, by the blood of thy covenant I have sent forth thy prisoners out of the pit wherein *is* no water.

12 Turn you to the strong hold, ye prisoners of hope: even to day do I declare *that* I will render double unto thee;

13 When I have bent Judah for me, filled the bow with Ē'phra-im, and raised up thy sons, O Zion, against thy sons, O Greece, and made thee as the sword of a mighty man.

14 And the LORD shall be seen over them, and his arrow shall go forth as the lightning: and the Lord GOD shall blow the trumpet, and shall go with whirlwinds of the south.

15 The LORD of hosts shall defend them; and they shall devour, and subdue with sling stones; and they shall drink, *and* make a noise as through wine; and they shall be filled like bowls, *and* as the corners of the altar.

16 And the LORD their God shall save them in that day as the flock of his people: for *they shall be as* the stones of

a crown, lifted up as an ensign upon his land.

17 For how great *is* his goodness, and how great *is* his beauty! corn shall make the young men cheerful, and new wine the maids.

CHAPTER 10

ASK ye of the LORD rain in the time of the latter rain; *so* the LORD shall make bright clouds, and give them showers of rain, to every one grass in the field.

2 For the idols have spoken vanity, and the diviners have seen a lie, and have told false dreams; they comfort in vain: therefore they went their way as a flock, they were troubled, because *there was* no shepherd.

3 Mine anger was kindled against the shepherds, and I punished the goats: for the LORD of hosts hath visited his flock the house of Judah, and hath made them as his goodly horse in the battle.

4 Out of him came forth the corner, out of him the nail, out of him the battle bow, out of him every oppressor together.

5 And they shall be as mighty *men*, which tread down *their enemies* in the mire of the streets in the battle: and they shall fight, because the LORD *is* with them, and the riders on horses shall be confounded.

6 And I will strengthen the house of Judah, and I will save the house of Joseph, and I will bring them again to place them; for I have mercy upon them: and they shall be as though I had not cast them off: for I *am* the LORD their God, and will hear them.

7 And *they of* Ē'phra-im shall be like a mighty *man*, and their heart shall rejoice as through wine: yea, their children shall see *it*, and be glad; their heart shall rejoice in the LORD.

8 I will hiss for them, and gather them; for I have redeemed them: and they shall increase as they have increased.

9 And I will sow them among the people: and they shall remember me in far countries; and they shall live with their children, and turn again.

10 I will bring them again also out of the land of Egypt, and gather them out of Assyria; and I will bring them into the land of Gilead and Lebanon; and *place* shall not be found for them.

11 And he shall pass through the sea with affliction, and shall smite the waves in the sea, and all the deeps of the river shall dry up: and the pride of Assyria shall be brought down, and the sceptre of Egypt shall depart away.

12 And I will strengthen them in the LORD; and they shall walk up and down in his name, saith the LORD.

CHAPTER 11

OPEN thy doors, O Lebanon, that the fire may devour thy cedars.

2 Howl, fir tree; for the cedar is fallen; because the mighty are spoiled: howl, O ye oaks of Bā'shan; for the forest of the vintage is come down.

3 ¶*There is* a voice of the howling of the shepherds; for their glory is spoiled: a voice of the roaring of young lions; for the pride of Jordan is spoiled.

4 Thus saith the LORD my God; Feed the flock of the slaughter;

5 Whose possessors slay them, and hold themselves not guilty: and they that sell them say, Blessed *be* the LORD; for I am rich: and their own shepherds pity them not.

6 For I will no more pity the inhabitants of the land, saith the LORD: but, lo, I will deliver the men every one into his neighbour's hand, and into the hand of his king: and they shall smite the land, and out of their hand I will not deliver *them*.

7 And I will feed the flock of slaughter, *even* you, O poor of the flock. And I took unto me two staves; the one I called Beauty, and the other I called Bands; and I fed the flock.

8 Three shepherds also I cut off in one month; and my soul lothed them, and their soul also abhorred me.

9 Then said I, I will not feed you: that that dieth, let it die; and that that is to be cut off, let it be cut off; and let the rest eat every one the flesh of another.

10 ¶And I took my staff, *even* Beauty, and cut it asunder, that I might break my covenant which I had made with all the people.

11 And it was broken in that day: and so the poor of the flock that waited upon me knew that it *was* the word of the LORD.

12 And I said unto them, If ye think good, give *me* my price; and if not, forbear. So they weighed for my price thirty *pieces* of silver.

13 And the LORD said unto me, Cast it unto the potter: a goodly price that I was prised at of them. And I took the thirty *pieces* of silver, and cast them to the potter in the house of the LORD.

14 Then I cut asunder mine other staff, *even* Bands, that I might break the brotherhood between Judah and Israel.

15 ¶And the LORD said unto me, Take unto thee yet the instruments of a foolish shepherd.

Elijah Calls Down God's Fire (1 Kings 18)

Shepherds Visit the Baby Jesus (Luke 2)

16 For, lo, I will raise up a shepherd in the land, *which* shall not visit those that be cut off, neither shall seek the young one, nor heal that that is broken, nor feed that that standeth still: but he shall eat the flesh of the fat, and tear their claws in pieces.

17 Woe to the idol shepherd that leaveth the flock! the sword *shall be* upon his arm, and upon his right eye: his arm shall be clean dried up, and his right eye shall be utterly darkened.

CHAPTER 12

THE burden of the word of the LORD for Israel, saith the LORD, which stretcheth forth the heavens, and layeth the foundation of the earth, and formeth the spirit of man within him.

2 Behold, I will make Jerusalem a cup of trembling unto all the people round about, when they shall be in the siege both against Judah *and* against Jerusalem.

3 And in that day will I make Jerusalem a burdensome stone for all people: all that burden themselves with it shall be cut in pieces, though all the people of the earth be gathered together against it.

4 In that day, saith the LORD, I will smite every horse with astonishment, and his rider with madness: and I will open mine eyes upon the house of Judah, and will smite every horse of the people with blindness.

5 And the governors of Judah shall say in their heart, The inhabitants of Jerusalem *shall be* my strength in the LORD of hosts their God.

6 In that day will I make the governors of Judah like an hearth of fire among the wood, and like a torch of fire in a sheaf; and they shall devour all the people round about, on the right hand and on the left: and Jerusalem shall be inhabited again in her own place, *even* in Jerusalem.

7 The LORD also shall save the tents of Judah first, that the glory of the house of David and the glory of the inhabitants of Jerusalem do not magnify *themselves* against Judah.

8 In that day shall the LORD defend the inhabitants of Jerusalem; and he that is feeble among them at that day shall be as David; and the house of David *shall be* as God, as the angel of the LORD before them.

9 And it shall come to pass in that day, *that* I will seek to destroy all the nations that come against Jerusalem.

10 And I will pour upon the house of David, and upon the inhabitants of Jerusalem, the spirit of grace and of supplications: and they shall look upon me whom they have pierced, and they shall mourn for him, as one mourneth for *his* only *son*, and shall be in bitterness for him, as one that is in bitterness for *his* firstborn.

11 In that day shall there be a great mourning in Jerusalem, as the mourning of Hā-dăd-rĭm'mon in the valley of Me-gĭd'don.

12 And the land shall mourn, every family apart; the family of the house of David apart, and their wives apart; the family of the house of Nathan apart, and their wives apart;

13 The family of the house of Levi apart, and their wives apart; the family of Shĭm'e-ī apart, and their wives apart;

14 All the families that remain, every family apart, and their wives apart.

CHAPTER 13

IN that day there shall be a fountain opened to the house of David and to the inhabitants of Jerusalem for sin and for uncleanness.

2 And it shall come to pass in that day, saith the LORD of hosts, *that* I will cut off the names of the idols out of the land, and they shall no more be remembered: and also I will cause the prophets and the unclean spirit to pass out of the land.

3 And it shall come to pass, *that* when any shall yet prophesy, then his father and his mother that begat him shall say unto him, Thou shalt not live; for thou speakest lies in the name of the LORD: and his father and his mother that begat him shall thrust him through when he prophesieth.

4 And it shall come to pass in that day, *that* the prophets shall be ashamed every one of his vision, when he hath prophesied; neither shall they wear a rough garment to deceive:

5 But he shall say, I *am* no prophet, I *am* an husbandman; for man taught me to keep cattle from my youth.

6 And *one* shall say unto him, What *are* these wounds in thine hands? Then he shall answer, *Those* with which I was wounded *in* the house of my friends.

7 ¶Awake, O sword, against my shepherd, and against the man *that is* my fellow, saith the LORD of hosts: smite the shepherd, and the sheep shall be scattered: and I will turn mine hand upon the little ones.

8 And it shall come to pass, *that* in all

the land, saith the LORD, two parts therein shall be cut off *and* die; but the third shall be left therein.

9 And I will bring the third part through the fire, and will refine them as silver is refined, and will try them as gold is tried: they shall call on my name, and I will hear them: I will say, It *is* my people: and they shall say, The LORD *is* my God.

CHAPTER 14

BEHOLD, the day of the LORD cometh, and thy spoil shall be divided in the midst of thee.

2 For I will gather all nations against Jerusalem to battle; and the city shall be taken, and the houses rifled, and the women ravished; and half of the city shall go forth into captivity, and the residue of the people shall not be cut off from the city.

3 ¶Then shall the LORD go forth, and fight against those nations, as when he fought in the day of battle.

4 And his feet shall stand in that day upon the mount of Olives, which *is* before Jerusalem on the east, and the mount of Olives shall cleave in the midst thereof toward the east and toward the west, *and there shall be* a very great valley; and half of the mountain shall remove toward the north, and half of it toward the south.

5 And ye shall flee *to* the valley of the mountains; for the valley of the mountains shall reach unto Ā'zal: yea, ye shall flee, like as ye fled from before the earthquake in the days of Uz-zī'ah king of Judah: and the LORD my God shall come, *and* all the saints with thee.

6 And it shall come to pass in that day, *that* the light shall not be clear, *nor* dark:

7 But it shall be one day which shall be known to the LORD, not day, nor night: but it shall come to pass, *that* at evening time it shall be light.

8 And it shall be in that day, *that* living waters shall go out from Jerusalem; half of them toward the former sea, and half of them toward the hinder sea: in summer and in winter shall it be.

9 And the LORD shall be king over all the earth: in that day shall there be one LORD, and his name one.

10 All the land shall be turned as a plain from Gē'ba to Rimmon south of Jerusalem: and it shall be lifted up, and inhabited in her place, from Benjamin's gate unto the place of the first gate, unto the corner gate, and *from* the tower of Hă-nan'ē-el unto the king's winepresses.

11 And *men* shall dwell in it, and there shall be no more utter destruction; but Jerusalem shall be safely inhabited.

12 ¶And this shall be the plague wherewith the LORD will smite all the people that have fought against Jerusalem; Their flesh shall consume away while they stand upon their feet, and their eyes shall consume away in their holes, and their tongue shall consume away in their mouth.

13 And it shall come to pass in that day, *that* a great tumult from the LORD shall be among them; and they shall lay hold every one on the hand of his neighbour, and his hand shall rise up against the hand of his neighbour.

14 And Judah also shall fight at Jerusalem; and the wealth of all the heathen round about shall be gathered together, gold, and silver, and apparel, in great abundance.

15 And so shall be the plague of the horse, of the mule, of the camel, and of the ass, and of all the beasts that shall be in these tents, as this plague.

16 ¶And it shall come to pass, *that* every one that is left of all the nations which came against Jerusalem shall even go up from year to year to worship the King, the LORD of hosts, and to keep the feast of tabernacles.

17 And it shall be, *that* whoso will not come up of *all* the families of the earth unto Jerusalem to worship the King, the LORD of hosts, even upon them shall be no rain.

18 And if the family of Egypt go not up, and come not, that *have* no *rain;* there shall be the plague, wherewith the LORD will smite the heathen that come not up to keep the feast of tabernacles.

19 This shall be the punishment of Egypt, and the punishment of all nations that come not up to keep the feast of tabernacles.

20 ¶In that day shall there be upon the bells of the horses, HOLINESS UNTO THE LORD; and the pots in the LORD's house shall be like the bowls before the altar.

21 Yea, every pot in Jerusalem and in Judah shall be holiness unto the LORD of hosts: and all they that sacrifice shall come and take of them, and seethe therein: and in that day there shall be no more the Canaanite in the house of the LORD of hosts.

MALACHI

CHAPTER 1

THE burden of the word of the LORD to Israel by Măl′a-chī.

2 I have loved you, saith the LORD. Yet ye say, Wherein hast thou loved us? *Was* not Esau Jacob's brother? saith the LORD: yet I loved Jacob,

3 And I hated Esau, and laid his mountains and his heritage waste for the dragons of the wilderness.

4 Whereas Edom saith, We are impoverished, but we will return and build the desolate places; thus saith the LORD of hosts, They shall build, but I will throw down; and they shall call them, The border of wickedness, and, The people against whom the LORD hath indignation for ever.

5 And your eyes shall see, and ye shall say, The LORD will be magnified from the border of Israel.

6 ¶A son honoureth *his* father, and a servant his master: if then I *be* a father, where *is* mine honour? and if I *be* a master, where *is* my fear? saith the LORD of hosts unto you, O priests, that despise my name. And ye say, Wherein have we despised thy name?

7 Ye offer polluted bread upon mine altar; and ye say, Wherein have we polluted thee? In that ye say, The table of the LORD *is* contemptible.

8 And if ye offer the blind for sacrifice, *is it* not evil? and if ye offer the lame and sick, *is it* not evil? offer it now unto thy governor; will he be pleased with thee, or accept thy person? saith the LORD of hosts.

9 And now, I pray you, beseech God that he will be gracious unto us: this hath been by your means: will he regard your persons? saith the LORD of hosts.

10 Who *is there* even among you that would shut the doors *for nought?* neither do ye kindle *fire* on mine altar for nought. I have no pleasure in you, saith the LORD of hosts, neither will I accept an offering at your hand.

11 For from the rising of the sun even unto the going down of the same my name *shall be* great among the Gentiles; and in every place incense *shall be* offered unto my name, and a pure offering: for my name *shall be* great among the heathen, saith the LORD of hosts.

12 ¶But ye have profaned it, in that ye say, The table of the LORD *is* polluted; and the fruit thereof, *even* his meat, *is* contemptible.

13 Ye said also, Behold, what a weariness *is it!* and ye have snuffed at it, saith the LORD of hosts; and ye brought *that which was* torn, and the lame, and the sick; thus ye brought an offering: should I accept this of your hand? saith the LORD.

14 But cursed *be* the deceiver, which hath in his flock a male, and voweth, and sacrificeth unto the LORD a corrupt thing: for I *am* a great King, saith the LORD of hosts, and my name *is* dreadful among the heathen.

CHAPTER 2

AND now, O ye priests, this commandment *is* for you.

2 If ye will not hear, and if ye will not lay *it* to heart, to give glory unto my name, saith the LORD of hosts, I will even send a curse upon you, and I will curse your blessings: yea, I have cursed them already, because ye do not lay *it* to heart.

3 Behold, I will corrupt your seed, and spread dung upon your faces, *even* the dung of your solemn feasts; and *one* shall take you away with it.

4 And ye shall know that I have sent this commandment unto you, that my covenant might be with Levi, saith the LORD of hosts.

5 My covenant was with him of life and peace; and I gave them to him *for* the fear wherewith he feared me, and was afraid before my name.

6 The law of truth was in his mouth, and iniquity was not found in his lips: he walked with me in peace and equity, and did turn many away from iniquity.

7 For the priest's lips should keep knowledge, and they should seek the law at his mouth: for he *is* the messenger of the LORD of hosts.

8 But ye are departed out of the way; ye have caused many to stumble at the law; ye have corrupted the covenant of Levi, saith the LORD of hosts.

9 Therefore have I also made you contemptible and base before all the people, according as ye have not kept my ways, but have been partial in the law.

10 Have we not all one father? hath not one God created us? why do we deal treacherously every man against his brother, by profaning the covenant of our fathers?

11 ¶Judah hath dealt treacherously, and an abomination is committed in Israel and in Jerusalem; for Judah hath profaned the holiness of the LORD

which he loved, and hath married the
daughter of a strange god.
12 The LORD will cut off the man that
doeth this, the master and the scholar,
out of the tabernacles of Jacob, and
him that offereth an offering unto the
LORD of hosts.
13 And this have ye done again,
covering the altar of the LORD with
tears, with weeping, and with crying
out, insomuch that he regardeth not the
offering any more, or receiveth *it* with
good will at your hand.
14 Yet ye say, Wherefore? Because
the LORD hath been witness between
thee and the wife of thy youth, against
whom thou hast dealt treacherously:
yet *is* she thy companion, and the wife
of thy covenant.
15 And did not he make one? Yet had
he the residue of the spirit. And where-
fore one? That he might seek a godly
seed. Therefore take heed to your
spirit, and let none deal treacherously
against the wife of his youth.
16 For the LORD, the God of Israel,
saith that he hateth putting away: for
one covereth violence with his gar-
ment, saith the LORD of hosts: therefore
take heed to your spirit, that ye deal not
treacherously.
17 ¶Ye have wearied the LORD with
your words. Yet ye say, Wherein have
we wearied *him*? When ye say, Every
one that doeth evil *is* good in the sight
of the LORD, and he delighteth in them;
or, Where *is* the God of judgment?

CHAPTER 3

BEHOLD, I will send my messenger,
and he shall prepare the way before
me: and the Lord, whom ye seek, shall
suddenly come to his temple, even the
messenger of the covenant, whom ye
delight in: behold, he shall come, saith
the LORD of hosts.
2 But who may abide the day of his
coming? and who shall stand when he
appeareth? for he *is* like a refiner's fire,
and like fullers' soap:
3 And he shall sit *as* a refiner and pu-
rifier of silver: and he shall purify the
sons of Levi, and purge them as gold
and silver, that they may offer unto the
LORD an offering in righteousness.
4 Then shall the offering of Judah and
Jerusalem be pleasant unto the LORD,
as in the days of old, and as in former
years.
5 And I will come near to you to judg-
ment; and I will be a swift witness
against the sorcerers, and against the
adulterers, and against false swearers,
and against those that oppress the hire-
ling in *his* wages, the widow, and the
fatherless, and that turn aside the
stranger *from his right*, and fear not
me, saith the LORD of hosts.
6 For I *am* the LORD, I change not;
therefore ye sons of Jacob are not con-
sumed.
7 ¶Even from the days of your fathers
ye are gone away from mine ordi-
nances, and have not kept *them*. Re-
turn unto me, and I will return unto
you, saith the LORD of hosts. But ye
said, Wherein shall we return?
8 ¶Will a man rob God? Yet ye have
robbed me. But ye say, Wherein have
we robbed thee? In tithes and offerings.
9 Ye *are* cursed with a curse: for ye
have robbed me, *even* this whole na-
tion.
10 Bring ye all the tithes into the
storehouse, that there may be meat in
mine house, and prove me now here-
with, saith the LORD of hosts, if I will not
open you the windows of heaven, and
pour you out a blessing, that *there shall*
not *be room* enough *to receive it*.
11 And I will rebuke the devourer for
your sakes, and he shall not destroy the
fruits of your ground; neither shall your
vine cast her fruit before the time in the
field, saith the LORD of hosts.
12 And all nations shall call you
blessed: for ye shall be a delightsome
land, saith the LORD of hosts.
13 ¶Your words have been stout
against me, saith the LORD. Yet ye say,
What have we spoken *so much* against
thee?
14 Ye have said, It *is* vain to serve
God: and what profit *is it* that we have
kept his ordinance, and that we have
walked mournfully before the LORD of
hosts?
15 And now we call the proud happy;
yea, they that work wickedness are set
up; yea, *they that* tempt God are even
delivered.
16 Then they that feared the LORD
spake often one to another: and the
LORD hearkened, and heard *it*, and a
book of remembrance was written be-
fore him for them that feared the LORD,
and that thought upon his name.
17 And they shall be mine, saith the
LORD of hosts, in that day when I make
up my jewels; and I will spare them, as
a man spareth his own son that serveth
him.
18 Then shall ye return, and discern
between the righteous and the wicked,
between him that serveth God and him
that serveth him not.

CHAPTER 4

FOR, behold, the day cometh, that shall

burn as an oven; and all the proud, yea,
and all that do wickedly, shall be
stubble: and the day that cometh shall
burn them up, saith the LORD of hosts,
that it shall leave them neither root nor
branch.
2 ¶But unto you that fear my name
shall the Sun of righteousness arise
with healing in his wings; and ye shall
go forth, and grow up as calves of the
stall.
3 And ye shall tread down the
wicked; for they shall be ashes under
the soles of your feet in the day that I
shall do *this*, saith the LORD of hosts.
4 ¶Remember ye the law of Moses
my servant, which I commanded unto
him in Hô′rĕb for all Israel, *with* the stat-
utes and judgments.
5 Behold, I will send you E-lī′jah the
prophet before the coming of the great
and dreadful day of the LORD:
6 And he shall turn the heart of the
fathers to the children, and the heart of
the children to their fathers, lest I come
and smite the earth with a curse.

THE END OF THE OLD TESTAMENT

THE
NEW TESTAMENT

of

OUR LORD AND SAVIOUR
JESUS CHRIST

King James Version

TRANSLATED OUT OF THE ORIGINAL GREEK:
AND WITH THE FORMER TRANSLATIONS
DILIGENTLY COMPARED AND REVISED

Words of Christ in Red

THE GOSPEL ACCORDING TO

ST. MATTHEW

CHAPTER 1

THE book of the generation of Jesus Christ, the son of David, the son of Abraham.

2 Abraham begat Isaac; and Isaac begat Jacob; and Jacob begat Judas and his brethren;

3 And Judas begat Phâ'rĕś and Zâ'ra of Thā'mar; and Phâ'rĕś begat Ĕs'rŏm; and Ĕs'rŏm begat Â'ram;

4 And Â'ram begat A-mĭn'a-dăb; and A-mĭn'a-dăb begat Nā-ăs'son; and Nā-ăs'son begat Săl'mon;

5 And Săl'mon begat Bō'ŏz of Rā'-chăb; and Bō'ŏz begat Ō'bed of Ruth; and Ō'bed begat Jesse;

6 And Jesse begat David the king; and David the king begat Solomon of her *that had been the wife* of Ū-rī'as;

7 And Solomon begat Rō-bō'am; and Rō-bō'am begat Ă-bī'a; and Ă-bī'a begat Asa;

8 And Asa begat Jŏs'a-phăt; and Jŏs'a-phăt begat Joram; and Joram begat Ō-zī'as;

9 And Ō-zī'as begat Jō'a-tham; and Jō'a-tham begat Ā'chăz; and Ā'chăz begat Ĕz-e-kī'as;

10 And Ĕz-e-kī'as begat Ma-năs'sēs; and Ma-năs'sēs begat Amon; and Amon begat Jo-sī'as;

11 And Jo-sī'as begat Jĕch-o-nī'as and his brethren, about the time they were carried away to Babylon:

12 And after they were brought to Babylon, Jĕch-o-nī'as begat Sa-lā'thĭ-el; and Sa-lā'thĭ-el begat Zō-rŏb'a-bel;

13 And Zō-rŏb'a-bel begat A-bī'ud; and A-bī'ud begat E-lī'a-kĭm; and E-lī'a-kĭm begat Azor;

14 And Azor begat Sā'dŏc; and Sā'-dŏc begat Ā'chĭm; and Ā'chĭm begat E-lī'ud;

15 And E-lī'ud begat Ĕ-le-ā'zar; and Ĕ-le-ā'zar begat Măt'thăn; and Măt'-thăn begat Jacob;

16 And Jacob begat Joseph the husband of Mary, of whom was born Jesus, who is called Christ.

17 So all the generations from Abraham to David *are* fourteen generations; and from David until the carrying away into Babylon *are* fourteen generations; and from the carrying away into Babylon unto Christ *are* fourteen generations.

18 ¶Now the birth of Jesus Christ was on this wise: When as his mother Mary was espoused to Joseph, before they came together, she was found with child of the Holy Ghost.

19 Then Joseph her husband, being a just *man*, and not willing to make her a publick example, was minded to put her away privily.

20 But while he thought on these things, behold, the angel of the Lord appeared unto him in a dream, saying, Joseph, thou son of David, fear not to take unto thee Mary thy wife: for that which is conceived in her is of the Holy Ghost.

21 And she shall bring forth a son, and thou shalt call his name JESUS: for he shall save his people from their sins.

22 Now all this was done, that it might be fulfilled which was spoken of the Lord by the prophet, saying,

23 Behold, a virgin shall be with child, and shall bring forth a son, and they shall call his name Ĕm-măn'ū-el, which being interpreted is, God with us.

24 Then Joseph being raised from sleep did as the angel of the Lord had bidden him, and took unto him his wife:

25 And knew her not till she had brought forth her firstborn son: and he called his name JESUS.

CHAPTER 2

NOW when Jesus was born in Bĕth-lehĕm of Judæa in the days of Herod the king, behold, there came wise men from the east to Jerusalem,

2 Saying, Where is he that is born King of the Jews? for we have seen his star in the east, and are come to worship him.

3 When Herod the king had heard *these things*, he was troubled, and all Jerusalem with him.

4 And when he had gathered all the chief priests and scribes of the people together, he demanded of them where Christ should be born.

5 And they said unto him, In Bĕth-lehĕm of Judæa: for thus it is written by the prophet,

6 And thou Bĕth-lehĕm, *in* the land of Juda, art not the least among the princes of Juda: for out of thee shall come a Governor, that shall rule my people Israel.

7 Then Herod, when he had privily called the wise men, enquired of them diligently what time the star appeared.

8 And he sent them to Bĕth-lehĕm, and said, Go and search diligently for the young child; and when ye have

found *him*, bring me word again, that I
may come and worship him also.
9 When they had heard the king, they
departed; and, lo, the star, which they
saw in the east, went before them, till it
came and stood over where the young
child was.
10 When they saw the star, they re-
joiced with exceeding great joy.
11 ¶And when they were come into
the house, they saw the young child
with Mary his mother, and fell down,
and worshipped him: and when they
had opened their treasures, they pre-
sented unto him gifts; gold, and
frankincense, and myrrh.
12 And being warned of God in a
dream that they should not return to
Herod, they departed into their own
country another way.
13 ¶And when they were departed,
behold, the angel of the Lord appeareth
to Joseph in a dream, saying, Arise, and
take the young child and his mother,
and flee into Egypt, and be thou there
until I bring thee word: for Herod will
seek the young child to destroy him.
14 When he arose, he took the young
child and his mother by night, and de-
parted into Egypt:
15 And was there until the death of
Herod: that it might be fulfilled which
was spoken of the Lord by the prophet,
saying, Out of Egypt have I called my
son.
16 ¶Then Herod, when he saw that he
was mocked of the wise men, was ex-
ceeding wroth, and sent forth, and slew
all the children that were in Bĕth-lehĕm,
and in all the coasts thereof, from
two years old and under, according to
the time which he had diligently en-
quired of the wise men.
17 Then was fulfilled that which was
spoken by Jeremy the prophet, saying,
18 In Rā'ma was there a voice heard,
lamentation, and weeping, and great
mourning, Rachel weeping *for* her
children, and would not be comforted,
because they are not.
19 ¶But when Herod was dead, be-
hold, an angel of the Lord appeareth in
a dream to Joseph in Egypt,
20 Saying, Arise, and take the young
child and his mother, and go into the
land of Israel: for they are dead which
sought the young child's life.
21 And he arose, and took the young
child and his mother, and came into the
land of Israel.
22 But when he heard that Är-che-
lā'us did reign in Judæa in the room of
his father Herod, he was afraid to
go thither: notwithstanding, being
warned of God in a dream, he turned
aside into the parts of Galilee:
23 And he came and dwelt in a city
called Nazareth: that it might be ful-
filled which was spoken by the
prophets, He shall be called a Naza-
rene.

CHAPTER 3

IN those days came John the Baptist,
preaching in the wilderness of Judæa,
2 And saying, Repent ye: for the king-
dom of heaven is at hand.
3 For this is he that was spoken of by
the prophet E-ṡā'ias, saying, The voice
of one crying in the wilderness, Prepare
ye the way of the Lord, make his paths
straight.
4 And the same John had his raiment
of camel's hair, and a leathern girdle
about his loins; and his meat was lo-
custs and wild honey.
5 ¶Then went out to him Jerusalem,
and all Judæa, and all the region round
about Jordan,
6 And were baptized of him in Jor-
dan, confessing their sins.
7 But when he saw many of the Phari-
sees and Săd'du-ceeṡ come to his bap-
tism, he said unto them, O generation
of vipers, who hath warned you to flee
from the wrath to come?
8 Bring forth therefore fruits meet for
repentance:
9 And think not to say within your-
selves, We have Abraham to *our*
father: for I say unto you, that God is
able of these stones to raise up children
unto Abraham.
10 And now also the axe is laid unto
the root of the trees: therefore every
tree which bringeth not forth good fruit
is hewn down, and cast into the fire.
11 I indeed baptize you with water
unto repentance: but he that cometh af-
ter me is mightier than I, whose shoes I
am not worthy to bear: he shall baptize
you with the Holy Ghost, and *with* fire:
12 Whose fan *is* in his hand, and he
will throughly purge his floor, and gath-
er his wheat into the garner; but he
will burn up the chaff with unquench-
able fire.
13 ¶Then cometh Jesus from Galilee
to Jordan unto John, to be baptized of
him.
14 But John forbad him, saying, I
have need to be baptized of thee, and
comest thou to me?
15 And Jesus answering said unto
him, Suffer *it to be so* now: for thus it
becometh us to fulfil all righteousness.
Then he suffered him.
16 And Jesus, when he was baptized,
went up straightway out of the water:

and, lo, the heavens were opened unto him, and he saw the Spirit of God descending like a dove, and lighting upon him:

17 And lo a voice from heaven, saying, This is my beloved Son, in whom I am well pleased.

CHAPTER 4

THEN was Jesus led up of the spirit into the wilderness to be tempted of the devil.

2 And when he had fasted forty days and forty nights, he was afterward an hungred.

3 And when the tempter came to him, he said, If thou be the Son of God, command that these stones be made bread.

4 But he answered and said, It is written, Man shall not live by bread alone, but by every word that proceedeth out of the mouth of God.

5 Then the devil taketh him up into the holy city, and setteth him on a pinnacle of the temple,

6 And saith unto him, If thou be the Son of God, cast thyself down: for it is written, He shall give his angels charge concerning thee: and in *their* hands they shall bear thee up, lest at any time thou dash thy foot against a stone.

7 Jesus said unto him, It is written again, Thou shalt not tempt the Lord thy God.

8 Again, the devil taketh him up into an exceeding high mountain, and sheweth him all the kingdoms of the world, and the glory of them;

9 And saith unto him, All these things will I give thee, if thou wilt fall down and worship me.

10 Then saith Jesus unto him, Get thee hence, Satan: for it is written, Thou shalt worship the Lord thy God, and him only shalt thou serve.

11 Then the devil leaveth him, and, behold, angels came and ministered unto him.

12 ¶Now when Jesus had heard that John was cast into prison, he departed into Galilee;

13 And leaving Nazareth, he came and dwelt in Ca-per'na-um, which is upon the sea coast, in the borders of Zăb'u-lon and Nĕph'tha-lĭm:

14 That it might be fulfilled which was spoken by E-ṡā'ias the prophet, saying,

15 The land of Zăb'u-lon, and the land of Nĕph'tha-lĭm, *by* the way of the sea, beyond Jordan, Galilee of the Gentiles;

16 The people which sat in darkness saw great light; and to them which sat in the region and shadow of death light is sprung up.

17 From that time Jesus began to preach, and to say, Repent: for the kingdom of heaven is at hand.

18 ¶And Jesus, walking by the sea of Galilee, saw two brethren, Simon called Peter, and Andrew his brother, casting a net into the sea: for they were fishers.

19 And he saith unto them, Follow me, and I will make you fishers of men.

20 And they straightway left *their* nets, and followed him.

21 And going on from thence, he saw other two brethren, James *the son* of Zĕb'e-dee, and John his brother, in a ship with Zĕb'e-dee their father, mending their nets; and he called them.

22 And they immediately left the ship and their father, and followed him.

23 ¶And Jesus went about all Galilee, teaching in their synagogues, and preaching the gospel of the kingdom, and healing all manner of sickness and all manner of disease among the people.

24 And his fame went throughout all Syria: and they brought unto him all sick people that were taken with divers diseases and torments, and those which were possessed with devils, and those which were lunatick, and those that had the palsy; and he healed them.

25 And there followed him great multitudes of people from Galilee, and *from* De-căp'o-lĭs, and *from* Jerusalem, and *from* Judæa, and *from* beyond Jordan.

CHAPTER 5

AND seeing the multitudes, he went up into a mountain: and when he was set, his disciples came unto him:

2 And he opened his mouth, and taught them, saying,

3 Blessed *are* the poor in spirit: for theirs is the kingdom of heaven.

4 Blessed *are* they that mourn: for they shall be comforted.

5 Blessed *are* the meek: for they shall inherit the earth.

6 Blessed *are* they which do hunger and thirst after righteousness: for they shall be filled.

7 Blessed *are* the merciful: for they shall obtain mercy.

8 Blessed *are* the pure in heart: for they shall see God.

9 Blessed *are* the peacemakers: for they shall be called the children of God.

10 Blessed *are* they which are persecuted for righteousness' sake: for theirs is the kingdom of heaven.

11 Blessed are ye, when *men* shall revile you, and persecute *you*, and shall

say all manner of evil against you falsely, for my sake.

12 Rejoice, and be exceeding glad: for great *is* your reward in heaven: for so persecuted they the prophets which were before you.

13 ¶Ye are the salt of the earth: but if the salt have lost his savour, wherewith shall it be salted? it is thenceforth good for nothing, but to be cast out, and to be trodden under foot of men.

14 Ye are the light of the world. A city that is set on an hill cannot be hid.

15 Neither do men light a candle, and put it under a bushel, but on a candlestick; and it giveth light unto all that are in the house.

16 Let your light so shine before men, that they may see your good works, and glorify your Father which is in heaven.

17 ¶Think not that I am come to destroy the law, or the prophets: I am not come to destroy, but to fulfil.

18 For verily I say unto you, Till heaven and earth pass, one jot or one tittle shall in no wise pass from the law, till all be fulfilled.

19 Whosoever therefore shall break one of these least commandments, and shall teach men so, he shall be called the least in the kingdom of heaven: but whosoever shall do and teach *them*, the same shall be called great in the kingdom of heaven.

20 For I say unto you, That except your righteousness shall exceed *the righteousness* of the scribes and Pharisees, ye shall in no case enter into the kingdom of heaven.

21 ¶Ye have heard that it was said by them of old time, Thou shalt not kill; and whosoever shall kill shall be in danger of the judgment:

22 But I say unto you, That whosoever is angry with his brother without a cause shall be in danger of the judgment: and whosoever shall say to his brother, Raca, shall be in danger of the council: but whosoever shall say, Thou fool, shall be in danger of hell fire.

23 Therefore if thou bring thy gift to the altar, and there rememberest that thy brother hath ought against thee;

24 Leave there thy gift before the altar, and go thy way; first be reconciled to thy brother, and then come and offer thy gift.

25 Agree with thine adversary quickly, whiles thou art in the way with him; lest at any time the adversary deliver thee to the judge, and the judge deliver thee to the officer, and thou be cast into prison.

26 Verily I say unto thee, Thou shalt by no means come out thence, till thou hast paid the uttermost farthing.

27 ¶Ye have heard that it was said by them of old time, Thou shalt not commit adultery:

28 But I say unto you, That whosoever looketh on a woman to lust after her hath committed adultery with her already in his heart.

29 And if thy right eye offend thee, pluck it out, and cast *it* from thee: for it is profitable for thee that one of thy members should perish, and not *that* thy whole body should be cast into hell.

30 And if thy right hand offend thee, cut it off, and cast *it* from thee: for it is profitable for thee that one of thy members should perish, and not *that* thy whole body should be cast into hell.

31 ¶It hath been said, Whosoever shall put away his wife, let him give her a writing of divorcement:

32 But I say unto you, That whosoever shall put away his wife, saving for the cause of fornication, causeth her to commit adultery: and whosoever shall marry her that is divorced committeth adultery.

33 ¶Again, ye have heard that it hath been said by them of old time, Thou shalt not forswear thyself, but shalt perform unto the Lord thine oaths:

34 But I say unto you, Swear not at all; neither by heaven; for it is God's throne:

35 Nor by the earth; for it is his footstool: neither by Jerusalem; for it is the city of the great King.

36 Neither shalt thou swear by thy head, because thou canst not make one hair white or black.

37 But let your communication be, Yea, yea; Nay, nay: for whatsoever is more than these cometh of evil.

38 ¶Ye have heard that it hath been said, An eye for an eye, and a tooth for a tooth:

39 But I say unto you, That ye resist not evil: but whosoever shall smite thee on thy right cheek, turn to him the other also.

40 And if any man will sue thee at the law, and take away thy coat, let him have *thy* cloak also.

41 And whosoever shall compel thee to go a mile, go with him twain.

42 Give to him that asketh thee, and from him that would borrow of thee turn not thou away.

43 ¶Ye have heard that it hath been said, Thou shalt love thy neighbour, and hate thine enemy.

44 But I say unto you, Love your enemies, bless them that curse you, do good to them that hate you, and pray

for them which despitefully use you,
and persecute you;
45 That ye may be the children of
your Father which is in heaven: for he
maketh his sun to rise on the evil and
on the good, and sendeth rain on the
just and on the unjust.
46 For if ye love them which love you,
what reward have ye? do not even the
publicans the same?
47 And if ye salute your brethren
only, what do ye more *than others?* do
not even the publicans so?
48 Be ye therefore perfect, even as
your Father which is in heaven is per-
fect.

CHAPTER 6

TAKE heed that ye do not your alms
before men, to be seen of them: other-
wise ye have no reward of your Father
which is in heaven.
2 Therefore when thou doest *thine*
alms, do not sound a trumpet before
thee, as the hypocrites do in the syna-
gogues and in the streets, that they
may have glory of men. Verily I say
unto you, They have their reward.
3 But when thou doest alms, let not
thy left hand know what thy right hand
doeth:
4 That thine alms may be in secret:
and thy Father which seeth in secret
himself shall reward thee openly.
5 ¶ And when thou prayest, thou shalt
not be as the hypocrites *are:* for they
love to pray standing in the synagogues
and in the corners of the streets, that
they may be seen of men. Verily I say
unto you, They have their reward.
6 But thou, when thou prayest, enter
into thy closet, and when thou hast
shut thy door, pray to thy Father which
is in secret; and thy Father which seeth
in secret shall reward thee openly.
7 But when ye pray, use not vain rep-
etitions, as the heathen *do:* for they
think that they shall be heard for their
much speaking.
8 Be not ye therefore like unto them:
for your Father knoweth what things
ye have need of, before ye ask him.
9 After this manner therefore pray
ye: Our Father which art in heaven,
Hallowed be thy name.
10 Thy kingdom come. Thy will be
done in earth, as *it is* in heaven.
11 Give us this day our daily bread.
12 And forgive us our debts, as we
forgive our debtors.
13 And lead us not into temptation,
but deliver us from evil: For thine is the
kingdom, and the power, and the glory,
for ever. Amen.
14 For if ye forgive men their tres-
passes, your heavenly Father will also
forgive you:
15 But if ye forgive not men their
trespasses, neither will your Father
forgive your trespasses.
16 ¶ Moreover when ye fast, be not, as
the hypocrites, of a sad countenance:
for they disfigure their faces, that they
may appear unto men to fast. Verily I
say unto you, They have their reward.
17 But thou, when thou fastest,
anoint thine head, and wash thy face;
18 That thou appear not unto men to
fast, but unto thy Father which is in
secret: and thy Father, which seeth in
secret, shall reward thee openly.
19 ¶ Lay not up for yourselves trea-
sures upon earth, where moth and rust
doth corrupt, and where thieves break
through and steal:
20 But lay up for yourselves trea-
sures in heaven, where neither moth
nor rust doth corrupt, and where
thieves do not break through nor steal:
21 For where your treasure is, there
will your heart be also.
22 The light of the body is the eye: if
therefore thine eye be single, thy whole
body shall be full of light.
23 But if thine eye be evil, thy whole
body shall be full of darkness. If there-
fore the light that is in thee be dark-
ness, how great *is* that darkness!
24 No man can serve two masters: for
either he will hate the one, and love the
other; or else he will hold to the one,
and despise the other. Ye cannot serve
God and mammon.
25 Therefore I say unto you, Take no
thought for your life, what ye shall eat,
or what ye shall drink; nor yet for your
body, what ye shall put on. Is not the
life more than meat, and the body than
raiment?
26 Behold the fowls of the air: for
they sow not, neither do they reap, nor
gather into barns; yet your heavenly
Father feedeth them. Are ye not much
better than they?
27 Which of you by taking thought
can add one cubit unto his stature?
28 And why take ye thought for rai-
ment? Consider the lilies of the field,
how they grow; they toil not, neither do
they spin:
29 And yet I say unto you, That even
Solomon in all his glory was not ar-
rayed like one of these.
30 Wherefore, if God so clothe the
grass of the field, which to day is, and
to morrow is cast into the oven, *shall he*
not much more *clothe* you, O ye of little
faith?
31 Therefore take no thought, saying,
What shall we eat? or, What shall we

drink? or, Wherewithal shall we be clothed?

32 (For after all these things do the Gentiles seek:) for your heavenly Father knoweth that ye have need of all these things.

33 But seek ye first the kingdom of God, and his righteousness; and all these things shall be added unto you.

34 Take therefore no thought for the morrow: for the morrow shall take thought for the things of itself. Sufficient unto the day *is* the evil thereof.

CHAPTER 7

JUDGE not, that ye be not judged.

2 For with what judgment ye judge, ye shall be judged: and with what measure ye mete, it shall be measured to you again.

3 And why beholdest thou the mote that is in thy brother's eye, but considerest not the beam that is in thine own eye?

4 Or how wilt thou say to thy brother, Let me pull out the mote out of thine eye; and, behold, a beam *is* in thine own eye?

5 Thou hypocrite, first cast out the beam out of thine own eye; and then shalt thou see clearly to cast out the mote out of thy brother's eye.

6 ¶Give not that which is holy unto the dogs, neither cast ye your pearls before swine, lest they trample them under their feet, and turn again and rend you.

7 ¶Ask, and it shall be given you; seek, and ye shall find; knock, and it shall be opened unto you:

8 For every one that asketh receiveth; and he that seeketh findeth; and to him that knocketh it shall be opened.

9 Or what man is there of you, whom if his son ask bread, will he give him a stone?

10 Or if he ask a fish, will he give him a serpent?

11 If ye then, being evil, know how to give good gifts unto your children, how much more shall your Father which is in heaven give good things to them that ask him?

12 Therefore all things whatsoever ye would that men should do to you, do ye even so to them: for this is the law and the prophets.

13 ¶Enter ye in at the strait gate: for wide *is* the gate, and broad *is* the way, that leadeth to destruction, and many there be which go in thereat:

14 Because strait *is* the gate, and narrow *is* the way, which leadeth unto life, and few there be that find it.

15 ¶Beware of false prophets, which come to you in sheep's clothing, but inwardly they are ravening wolves.

16 Ye shall know them by their fruits. Do men gather grapes of thorns, or figs of thistles?

17 Even so every good tree bringeth forth good fruit; but a corrupt tree bringeth forth evil fruit.

18 A good tree cannot bring forth evil fruit, neither *can* a corrupt tree bring forth good fruit.

19 Every tree that bringeth not forth good fruit is hewn down, and cast into the fire.

20 Wherefore by their fruits ye shall know them.

21 ¶Not every one that saith unto me, Lord, Lord, shall enter into the kingdom of heaven; but he that doeth the will of my Father which is in heaven.

22 Many will say to me in that day, Lord, Lord, have we not prophesied in thy name? and in thy name have cast out devils? and in thy name done many wonderful works?

23 And then will I profess unto them, I never knew you: depart from me, ye that work iniquity.

24 ¶Therefore whosoever heareth these sayings of mine, and doeth them, I will liken him unto a wise man, which built his house upon a rock:

25 And the rain descended, and the floods came, and the winds blew, and beat upon that house; and it fell not: for it was founded upon a rock.

26 And every one that heareth these sayings of mine, and doeth them not, shall be likened unto a foolish man, which built his house upon the sand:

27 And the rain descended, and the floods came, and the winds blew, and beat upon that house; and it fell: and great was the fall of it.

28 ¶And it came to pass, when Jesus had ended these sayings, the people were astonished at his doctrine:

29 For he taught them as *one* having authority, and not as the scribes.

CHAPTER 8

WHEN he was come down from the mountain, great multitudes followed him.

2 And, behold, there came a leper and worshipped him, saying, Lord, if thou wilt, thou canst make me clean.

3 And Jesus put forth *his* hand, and touched him, saying, I will; be thou clean. And immediately his leprosy was cleansed.

4 And Jesus saith unto him, See thou tell no man; but go thy way, shew thyself to the priest, and offer the gift that

Moses commanded, for a testimony
unto them.
5 ¶And when Jesus was entered into
Ca-per'na-um, there came unto him a
centurion, beseeching him,
6 And saying, Lord, my servant lieth
at home sick of the palsy, grievously
tormented.
7 And Jesus saith unto him, I will
come and heal him.
8 The centurion answered and said,
Lord, I am not worthy that thou should-
est come under my roof: but speak the
word only, and my servant shall be
healed.
9 For I am a man under authority, hav-
ing soldiers under me: and I say to this
man, Go, and he goeth; and to another,
Come, and he cometh; and to my ser-
vant, Do this, and he doeth *it*.
10 When Jesus heard *it*, he mar-
velled, and said to them that followed,
Verily I say unto you, I have not found
so great faith, no, not in Israel.
11 And I say unto you, That many
shall come from the east and west, and
shall sit down with Abraham, and
Isaac, and Jacob, in the kingdom of
heaven.
12 But the children of the kingdom
shall be cast out into outer darkness:
there shall be weeping and gnashing of
teeth.
13 And Jesus said unto the centurion,
Go thy way; and as thou hast believed,
so be it done unto thee. And his servant
was healed in the selfsame hour.
14 ¶And when Jesus was come into
Peter's house, he saw his wife's mother
laid, and sick of a fever.
15 And he touched her hand, and the
fever left her: and she arose, and minis-
tered unto them.
16 ¶When the even was come, they
brought unto him many that were pos-
sessed with devils: and he cast out the
spirits with *his* word, and healed all
that were sick:
17 That it might be fulfilled which
was spoken by E-ṡā'ias the prophet,
saying, Himself took our infirmities,
and bare *our* sicknesses.
18 ¶Now when Jesus saw great mul-
titudes about him, he gave command-
ment to depart unto the other side.
19 And a certain scribe came, and
said unto him, Master, I will follow thee
whithersoever thou goest.
20 And Jesus saith unto him, The
foxes have holes, and the birds of the
air *have* nests; but the Son of man hath
not where to lay *his* head.
21 And another of his disciples said
unto him, Lord, suffer me first to go
and bury my father.
22 But Jesus said unto him, Follow
me; and let the dead bury their dead.
23 ¶And when he was entered into a
ship, his disciples followed him.
24 And, behold, there arose a great
tempest in the sea, insomuch that the
ship was covered with the waves: but
he was asleep.
25 And his disciples came to *him*, and
awoke him, saying, Lord, save us: we
perish.
26 And he saith unto them, Why are
ye fearful, O ye of little faith? Then he
arose, and rebuked the winds and the
sea; and there was a great calm.
27 But the men marvelled, saying,
What manner of man is this, that even
the winds and the sea obey him!
28 ¶And when he was come to the
other side into the country of the
Ger'ge-sēneṡ, there met him two pos-
sessed with devils, coming out of the
tombs, exceeding fierce, so that no
man might pass by that way.
29 And, behold, they cried out,
saying, What have we to do with thee,
Jesus, thou Son of God? art thou come
hither to torment us before the time?
30 And there was a good way off
from them an herd of many swine feed-
ing.
31 So the devils besought him,
saying, If thou cast us out, suffer us to
go away into the herd of swine.
32 And he said unto them, Go. And
when they were come out, they went
into the herd of swine: and, behold, the
whole herd of swine ran violently down
a steep place into the sea, and perished
in the waters.
33 And they that kept them fled, and
went their ways into the city, and told
every thing, and what was befallen to
the possessed of the devils.
34 And, behold, the whole city came
out to meet Jesus: and when they saw
him, they besought *him* that he would
depart out of their coasts.

CHAPTER 9

AND he entered into a ship, and passed
over, and came into his own city.
2 And, behold, they brought to him a
man sick of the palsy, lying on a bed:
and Jesus seeing their faith said unto
the sick of the palsy; Son, be of good
cheer; thy sins be forgiven thee.
3 And, behold, certain of the scribes
said within themselves, This *man*
blasphemeth.
4 And Jesus knowing their thoughts
said, Wherefore think ye evil in your
hearts?

5 For whether is easier, to say, *Thy*
sins be forgiven thee; or to say, Arise,
and walk?
6 But that ye may know that the Son
of man hath power on earth to forgive
sins, (then saith he to the sick of the
palsy,) Arise, take up thy bed, and go
unto thine house.
7 And he arose, and departed to his
house.
8 But when the multitudes saw *it*,
they marvelled, and glorified God,
which had given such power unto men.
9 ¶And as Jesus passed forth from
thence, he saw a man, named Matthew,
sitting at the receipt of custom: and he
saith unto him, Follow me. And he
arose, and followed him.
10 ¶And it came to pass, as Jesus sat
at meat in the house, behold, many
publicans and sinners came and sat
down with him and his disciples.
11 And when the Pharisees saw *it*,
they said unto his disciples, Why eat-
eth your Master with publicans and
sinners?
12 But when Jesus heard *that*, he said
unto them, They that be whole need not
a physician, but they that are sick.
13 But go ye and learn what *that*
meaneth, I will have mercy, and not
sacrifice: for I am not come to call the
righteous, but sinners to repentance.
14 ¶Then came to him the disciples of
John, saying, Why do we and the Phari-
sees fast oft, but thy disciples fast not?
15 And Jesus said unto them, Can the
children of the bridechamber mourn,
as long as the bridegroom is with them?
but the days will come, when the bride-
groom shall be taken from them, and
then shall they fast.
16 No man putteth a piece of new
cloth unto an old garment, for that
which is put in to fill it up taketh from
the garment, and the rent is made
worse.
17 Neither do men put new wine into
old bottles: else the bottles break, and
the wine runneth out, and the bottles
perish: but they put new wine into new
bottles, and both are preserved.
18 ¶While he spake these things unto
them, behold, there came a certain rul-
er, and worshipped him, saying, My
daughter is even now dead: but come
and lay thy hand upon her, and she
shall live.
19 And Jesus arose, and followed
him, and *so did* his disciples.
20 ¶And, behold, a woman, which
was diseased with an issue of blood
twelve years, came behind *him*, and
touched the hem of his garment:
21 For she said within herself, If I
may but touch his garment, I shall be
whole.
22 But Jesus turned him about, and
when he saw her, he said, Daughter, be
of good comfort; thy faith hath made
thee whole. And the woman was made
whole from that hour.
23 And when Jesus came into the rul-
er's house, and saw the minstrels and
the people making a noise,
24 He said unto them, Give place: for
the maid is not dead, but sleepeth. And
they laughed him to scorn.
25 But when the people were put
forth, he went in, and took her by the
hand, and the maid arose.
26 And the fame hereof went abroad
into all that land.
27 ¶And when Jesus departed
thence, two blind men followed him,
crying, and saying, *Thou* son of David,
have mercy on us.
28 And when he was come into the
house, the blind men came to him: and
Jesus saith unto them, Believe ye that I
am able to do this? They said unto him,
Yea, Lord.
29 Then touched he their eyes,
saying, According to your faith be it
unto you.
30 And their eyes were opened; and
Jesus straitly charged them, saying,
See *that* no man know *it*.
31 But they, when they were de-
parted, spread abroad his fame in all
that country.
32 ¶As they went out, behold, they
brought to him a dumb man possessed
with a devil.
33 And when the devil was cast out,
the dumb spake: and the multitudes
marvelled, saying, It was never so seen
in Israel.
34 But the Pharisees said, He casteth
out devils through the prince of the dev-
ils.
35 ¶And Jesus went about all the
cities and villages, teaching in their syna-
gogues, and preaching the gospel of
the kingdom, and healing every sick-
ness and every disease among the
people.
36 But when he saw the multitudes,
he was moved with compassion on
them, because they fainted, and were
scattered abroad, as sheep having no
shepherd.
37 Then saith he unto his disciples,
The harvest truly *is* plenteous, but the
labourers *are* few;
38 Pray ye therefore the Lord of the
harvest, that he will send forth labour-
ers into his harvest.

CHAPTER 10

AND when he had called unto *him* his twelve disciples, he gave them power *against* unclean spirits, to cast them out, and to heal all manner of sickness and all manner of disease.

2 Now the names of the twelve apostles are these; The first, Simon, who is called Peter, and Andrew his brother; James *the son* of Zĕb'e-dee, and John his brother;

3 Philip, and Bartholomew; Thomas, and Matthew the publican; James *the son* of Ăl-phæ'us, and Lĕb-bæ'us, whose surname was Thăd-dæ'us;

4 Simon the Canaanite, and Judas Iscariot, who also betrayed him.

5 These twelve Jesus sent forth, and commanded them, saying, Go not into the way of the Gentiles, and into *any* city of the Sa-măr'i-tans enter ye not:

6 But go rather to the lost sheep of the house of Israel.

7 And as ye go, preach, saying, The kingdom of heaven is at hand.

8 Heal the sick, cleanse the lepers, raise the dead, cast out devils: freely ye have received, freely give.

9 Provide neither gold, nor silver, nor brass in your purses,

10 Nor scrip for *your* journey, neither two coats, neither shoes, nor yet staves: for the workman is worthy of his meat.

11 And into whatsoever city or town ye shall enter, enquire who in it is worthy; and there abide till ye go thence.

12 And when ye come into an house, salute it.

13 And if the house be worthy, let your peace come upon it: but if it be not worthy, let your peace return to you.

14 And whosoever shall not receive you, nor hear your words, when ye depart out of that house or city, shake off the dust of your feet.

15 Verily I say unto you, It shall be more tolerable for the land of Sodom and Go-mŏr'rha in the day of judgment, than for that city.

16 Behold, I send you forth as sheep in the midst of wolves: be ye therefore wise as serpents, and harmless as doves.

17 But beware of men: for they will deliver you up to the councils, and they will scourge you in their synagogues;

18 And ye shall be brought before governors and kings for my sake, for a testimony against them and the Gentiles.

19 But when they deliver you up, take no thought how or what ye shall speak: for it shall be given you in that same hour what ye shall speak.

20 For it is not ye that speak, but the Spirit of your Father which speaketh in you.

21 And the brother shall deliver up the brother to death, and the father the child: and the children shall rise up against *their* parents, and cause them to be put to death.

22 And ye shall be hated of all *men* for my name's sake: but he that endureth to the end shall be saved.

23 But when they persecute you in this city, flee ye into another: for verily I say unto you, Ye shall not have gone over the cities of Israel, till the Son of man be come.

24 The disciple is not above *his* master, nor the servant above his lord.

25 It is enough for the disciple that he be as his master, and the servant as his lord. If they have called the master of the house Bē-ĕl'ze-bŭb, how much more *shall they call* them of his household?

26 Fear them not therefore: for there is nothing covered, that shall not be revealed; and hid, that shall not be known.

27 What I tell you in darkness, *that* speak ye in light: and what ye hear in the ear, *that* preach ye upon the housetops.

28 And fear not them which kill the body, but are not able to kill the soul: but rather fear him which is able to destroy both soul and body in hell.

29 Are not two sparrows sold for a farthing? and one of them shall not fall on the ground without your Father.

30 But the very hairs of your head are all numbered.

31 Fear ye not therefore, ye are of more value than many sparrows.

32 Whosoever therefore shall confess me before men, him will I confess also before my Father which is in heaven.

33 But whosoever shall deny me before men, him will I also deny before my Father which is in heaven.

34 Think not that I am come to send peace on earth: I came not to send peace, but a sword.

35 For I am come to set a man at variance against his father, and the daughter against her mother, and the daughter in law against her mother in law.

36 And a man's foes *shall be* they of his own household.

37 He that loveth father or mother more than me is not worthy of me: and

he that loveth son or daughter more
than me is not worthy of me.
38 And he that taketh not his cross,
and followeth after me, is not worthy of
me.
39 He that findeth his life shall lose it:
and he that loseth his life for my sake
shall find it.
40 He that receiveth you receiveth
me, and he that receiveth me receiveth
him that sent me.
41 He that receiveth a prophet in the
name of a prophet shall receive a
prophet's reward; and he that receiveth
a righteous man in the name of a
righteous man shall receive a righteous
man's reward.
42 And whosoever shall give to drink
unto one of these little ones a cup of
cold *water* only in the name of a dis-
ciple, verily I say unto you, he shall in
no wise lose his reward.

CHAPTER 11

AND it came to pass, when Jesus had
made an end of commanding his
twelve disciples, he departed thence to
teach and to preach in their cities.
2 ¶Now when John had heard in the
prison the works of Christ, he sent two
of his disciples,
3 And said unto him, Art thou he that
should come, or do we look for an-
other?
4 Jesus answered and said unto
them, Go and shew John again those
things which ye do hear and see:
5 The blind receive their sight, and
the lame walk, the lepers are cleansed,
and the deaf hear, the dead are raised
up, and the poor have the gospel
preached to them.
6 And blessed is *he*, whosoever shall
not be offended in me.
7 ¶And as they departed, Jesus began
to say unto the multitudes concerning
John, What went ye out into the wilder-
ness to see? A reed shaken with the
wind?
8 But what went ye out for to see? A
man clothed in soft raiment? behold,
they that wear soft *clothing* are in
kings' houses.
9 But what went ye out for to see? A
prophet? yea, I say unto you, and more
than a prophet.
10 For this is *he*, of whom it is writ-
ten, Behold, I send my messenger be-
fore thy face, which shall prepare thy
way before thee.
11 Verily I say unto you, Among
them that are born of women there
hath not risen a greater than John the
Baptist: notwithstanding he that is
least in the kingdom of heaven is great-
er than he.
12 And from the days of John the
Baptist until now the kingdom of
heaven suffereth violence, and the vio-
lent take it by force.
13 For all the prophets and the law
prophesied until John.
14 And if ye will receive *it*, this is E-
lī'as, which was for to come.
15 He that hath ears to hear, let him
hear.
16 But whereunto shall I liken this gen-
eration? It is like unto children sitting
in the markets, and calling unto their
fellows,
17 And saying, We have piped unto
you, and ye have not danced; we have
mourned unto you, and ye have not la-
mented.
18 For John came neither eating nor
drinking, and they say, He hath a devil.
19 The Son of man came eating and
drinking, and they say, Behold a man
gluttonous, and a winebibber, a friend
of publicans and sinners. But wisdom is
justified of her children.
20 ¶Then began he to upbraid the
cities wherein most of his mighty
works were done, because they re-
pented not:
21 Woe unto thee, Chō-rā'zĭn! woe
unto thee, Bĕth-sā'i-da! for if the
mighty works, which were done in you,
had been done in Tyre and Sī'don, they
would have repented long ago in sack-
cloth and ashes.
22 But I say unto you, It shall be more
tolerable for Tyre and Sī'don at the day
of judgment, than for you.
23 And thou, Ca-per'na-um, which
art exalted unto heaven, shalt be
brought down to hell: for if the mighty
works, which have been done in thee,
had been done in Sodom, it would have
remained until this day.
24 But I say unto you, That it shall be
more tolerable for the land of Sodom,
in the day of judgment, than for thee.
25 ¶At that time Jesus answered and
said, I thank thee, O Father, Lord of
heaven and earth, because thou hast
hid these things from the wise and pru-
dent, and hast revealed them unto
babes.
26 Even so, Father: for so it seemed
good in thy sight.
27 All things are delivered unto me of
my Father: and no man knoweth the
Son, but the Father; neither knoweth
any man the Father, save the Son, and
he to whomsoever the Son will reveal
him.
28 ¶Come unto me, all *ye* that labour

and are heavy laden, and I will give you rest.

29 Take my yoke upon you, and learn of me; for I am meek and lowly in heart: and ye shall find rest unto your souls.

30 For my yoke *is* easy, and my burden is light.

CHAPTER 12

AT that time Jesus went on the sabbath day through the corn; and his disciples were an hungred, and began to pluck the ears of corn, and to eat.

2 But when the Pharisees saw *it*, they said unto him, Behold, thy disciples do that which is not lawful to do upon the sabbath day.

3 But he said unto them, Have ye not read what David did, when he was an hungred, and they that were with him;

4 How he entered into the house of God, and did eat the shewbread, which was not lawful for him to eat, neither for them which were with him, but only for the priests?

5 Or have ye not read in the law, how that on the sabbath days the priests in the temple profane the sabbath, and are blameless?

6 But I say unto you, That in this place is *one* greater than the temple.

7 But if ye had known what *this* meaneth, I will have mercy, and not sacrifice, ye would not have condemned the guiltless.

8 For the Son of man is Lord even of the sabbath day.

9 ¶And when he was departed thence, he went into their synagogue:

10 And, behold, there was a man which had *his* hand withered. And they asked him, saying, Is it lawful to heal on the sabbath days? that they might accuse him.

11 And he said unto them, What man shall there be among you, that shall have one sheep, and if it fall into a pit on the sabbath day, will he not lay hold on it, and lift *it* out?

12 How much then is a man better than a sheep? Wherefore it is lawful to do well on the sabbath days.

13 Then saith he to the man, Stretch forth thine hand. And he stretched *it* forth; and it was restored whole, like as the other.

14 ¶Then the Pharisees went out, and held a council against him, how they might destroy him.

15 But when Jesus knew *it*, he withdrew himself from thence: and great multitudes followed him, and he healed them all;

16 And charged them that they should not make him known:

17 That it might be fulfilled which was spoken by E-ṡā'ias the prophet, saying,

18 Behold my servant, whom I have chosen; my beloved, in whom my soul is well pleased: I will put my spirit upon him, and he shall shew judgment to the Gentiles.

19 He shall not strive, nor cry; neither shall any man hear his voice in the streets.

20 A bruised reed shall he not break, and smoking flax shall he not quench, till he send forth judgment unto victory.

21 And in his name shall the Gentiles trust.

22 ¶Then was brought unto him one possessed with a devil, blind, and dumb: and he healed him, insomuch that the blind and dumb both spake and saw.

23 And all the people were amazed, and said, Is not this the son of David?

24 But when the Pharisees heard *it*, they said, This *fellow* doth not cast out devils, but by Bē-ĕl'ze-bŭb the prince of the devils.

25 And Jesus knew their thoughts, and said unto them, Every kingdom divided against itself is brought to desolation; and every city or house divided against itself shall not stand:

26 And if Satan cast out Satan, he is divided against himself; how shall then his kingdom stand?

27 And if I by Bē-ĕl'ze-bŭb cast out devils, by whom do your children cast *them* out? therefore they shall be your judges.

28 But if I cast out devils by the Spirit of God, then the kingdom of God is come unto you.

29 Or else how can one enter into a strong man's house, and spoil his goods, except he first bind the strong man? and then he will spoil his house.

30 He that is not with me is against me; and he that gathereth not with me scattereth abroad.

31 Wherefore I say unto you, All manner of sin and blasphemy shall be forgiven unto men: but the blasphemy *against* the *Holy* Ghost shall not be forgiven unto men.

32 And whosoever speaketh a word against the Son of man, it shall be forgiven him: but whosoever speaketh against the Holy Ghost, it shall not be forgiven him, neither in this world, neither in the *world* to come.

33 Either make the tree good, and his fruit good; or else make the tree corrupt, and his fruit corrupt: for the tree is known by *his* fruit.

34 O generation of vipers, how can ye, being evil, speak good things? for out of the abundance of the heart the mouth speaketh.

35 A good man out of the good treasure of the heart bringeth forth good things: and an evil man out of the evil treasure bringeth forth evil things.

36 But I say unto you, That every idle word that men shall speak, they shall give account thereof in the day of judgment.

37 For by thy words thou shalt be justified, and by thy words thou shalt be condemned.

38 ¶Then certain of the scribes and of the Pharisees answered, saying, Master, we would see a sign from thee.

39 But he answered and said unto them, An evil and adulterous generation seeketh after a sign; and there shall no sign be given to it, but the sign of the prophet Jonas:

40 For as Jonas was three days and three nights in the whale's belly; so shall the Son of man be three days and three nights in the heart of the earth.

41 The men of Nĭn'e-veh shall rise in judgment with this generation, and shall condemn it: because they repented at the preaching of Jonas; and, behold, a greater than Jonas *is* here.

42 The queen of the south shall rise up in the judgment with this generation, and shall condemn it: for she came from the uttermost parts of the earth to hear the wisdom of Solomon; and, behold, a greater than Solomon *is* here.

43 When the unclean spirit is gone out of a man, he walketh through dry places, seeking rest, and findeth none.

44 Then he saith, I will return into my house from whence I came out; and when he is come, he findeth *it* empty, swept, and garnished.

45 Then goeth he, and taketh with himself seven other spirits more wicked than himself, and they enter in and dwell there: and the last *state* of that man is worse than the first. Even so shall it be also unto this wicked generation.

46 ¶While he yet talked to the people, behold, *his* mother and his brethren stood without, desiring to speak with him.

47 Then one said unto him, Behold, thy mother and thy brethren stand without, desiring to speak with thee.

48 But he answered and said unto him that told him, Who is my mother? and who are my brethren?

49 And he stretched forth his hand toward his disciples, and said, Behold my mother and my brethren!

50 For whosoever shall do the will of my Father which is in heaven, the same is my brother, and sister, and mother.

CHAPTER 13

THE same day went Jesus out of the house, and sat by the sea side.

2 And great multitudes were gathered together unto him, so that he went into a ship, and sat; and the whole multitude stood on the shore.

3 And he spake many things unto them in parables, saying, Behold, a sower went forth to sow;

4 And when he sowed, some *seeds* fell by the way side, and the fowls came and devoured them up:

5 Some fell upon stony places, where they had not much earth: and forthwith they sprung up, because they had no deepness of earth:

6 And when the sun was up, they were scorched; and because they had no root, they withered away.

7 And some fell among thorns; and the thorns sprung up, and choked them:

8 But other fell into good ground, and brought forth fruit, some an hundredfold, some sixtyfold, some thirtyfold.

9 ¶Who hath ears to hear, let him hear.

10 ¶And the disciples came, and said unto him, Why speakest thou unto them in parables?

11 He answered and said unto them, Because it is given unto you to know the mysteries of the kingdom of heaven, but to them it is not given.

12 For whosoever hath, to him shall be given, and he shall have more abundance: but whosoever hath not, from him shall be taken away even that he hath.

13 Therefore speak I to them in parables: because they seeing see not; and hearing they hear not, neither do they understand.

14 And in them is fulfilled the prophecy of E-śā'ias, which saith, By hearing ye shall hear, and shall not understand; and seeing ye shall see, and shall not perceive:

15 For this people's heart is waxed gross, and *their* ears are dull of hearing, and their eyes they have closed; lest at any time they should see with *their* eyes, and hear with *their* ears, and should understand with *their* heart, and should be converted, and I should heal them.

16 But blessed *are* your eyes, for they see: and your ears, for they hear.

17 For verily I say unto you, That many prophets and righteous *men*

have desired to see *those things* which
ye see, and have not seen *them;* and to
hear *those things* which ye hear, and
have not heard *them.*
18 ¶Hear ye therefore the parable of
the sower.
19 When any one heareth the word of
the kingdom, and understandeth *it* not,
then cometh the wicked *one,* and
catcheth away that which was sown in
his heart. This is he which received
seed by the way side.
20 But he that received the seed into
stony places, the same is he that hear-
eth the word, and anon with joy receiv-
eth it;
21 Yet hath he not root in himself, but
dureth for a while: for when tribulation
or persecution ariseth because of the
word, by and by he is offended.
22 He also that received seed among
the thorns is he that heareth the word;
and the care of this world, and the de-
ceitfulness of riches, choke the word,
and he becometh unfruitful.
23 But he that received seed into the
good ground is he that heareth the
word, and understandeth *it;* which also
beareth fruit, and bringeth forth, some
an hundredfold, some sixty, some
thirty.
24 **¶Another parable put he forth
unto them, saying,** The kingdom of
heaven is likened unto a man which
sowed good seed in his field:
25 But while men slept, his enemy
came and sowed tares among the
wheat, and went his way.
26 But when the blade was sprung
up, and brought forth fruit, then ap-
peared the tares also.
27 So the servants of the householder
came and said unto him, Sir, didst not
thou sow good seed in thy field? from
whence then hath it tares?
28 He said unto them, An enemy hath
done this. The servants said unto him,
Wilt thou then that we go and gather
them up?
29 But he said, Nay; lest while ye gath-
er up the tares, ye root up also the
wheat with them.
30 Let both grow together until the
harvest: and in the time of harvest I will
say to the reapers, Gather ye together
first the tares, and bind them in
bundles to burn them: but gather the
wheat into my barn.
31 **¶Another parable put he forth
unto them, saying,** The kingdom of
heaven is like to a grain of mustard
seed, which a man took, and sowed in
his field:
32 Which indeed is the least of all
seeds: but when it is grown, it is the
greatest among herbs, and becometh a
tree, so that the birds of the air come
and lodge in the branches thereof.
33 **¶Another parable spake he unto
them;** The kingdom of heaven is like
unto leaven, which a woman took, and
hid in three measures of meal, till the
whole was leavened.
34 **All these things spake Jesus unto
the multitude in parables; and without
a parable spake he not unto them:**
35 **That it might be fulfilled which
was spoken by the prophet, saying,** I
will open my mouth in parables; I will
utter things which have been kept secret
from the foundation of the world.
36 **¶Then Jesus sent the multitude
away, and went into the house: and his
disciples came unto him, saying, De-
clare unto us the parable of the tares of
the field.**
37 **He answered and said unto them,**
He that soweth the good seed is the Son
of man;
38 The field is the world; the good
seed are the children of the kingdom;
but the tares are the children of the
wicked *one;*
39 The enemy that sowed them is the
devil; the harvest is the end of the
world; and the reapers are the angels.
40 As therefore the tares are gath-
ered and burned in the fire; so shall it
be in the end of this world.
41 The Son of man shall send forth
his angels, and they shall gather out of
his kingdom all things that offend, and
them which do iniquity;
42 And shall cast them into a furnace
of fire: there shall be wailing and
gnashing of teeth.
43 Then shall the righteous shine
forth as the sun in the kingdom of their
Father. Who hath ears to hear, let him
hear.
44 ¶Again, the kingdom of heaven is
like unto treasure hid in a field; the
which when a man hath found, he
hideth, and for joy thereof goeth and
selleth all that he hath, and buyeth that
field.
45 ¶Again, the kingdom of heaven is
like unto a merchant man, seeking
goodly pearls:
46 Who, when he had found one pearl
of great price, went and sold all that he
had, and bought it.
47 ¶Again, the kingdom of heaven is
like unto a net, that was cast into the
sea, and gathered of every kind:
48 Which, when it was full, they drew
to shore, and sat down, and gathered
the good into vessels, but cast the bad
away.
49 So shall it be at the end of the

world: the angels shall come forth, and sever the wicked from among the just,
50 And shall cast them into the furnace of fire: there shall be wailing and gnashing of teeth.
51 Jesus saith unto them, Have ye understood all these things? They say unto him, Yea, Lord.
52 Then said he unto them, Therefore every scribe *which is* instructed unto the kingdom of heaven is like unto a man *that is* an householder, which bringeth forth out of his treasure *things* new and old.
53 ¶And it came to pass, *that* when Jesus had finished these parables, he departed thence.
54 And when he was come into his own country, he taught them in their synagogue, insomuch that they were astonished, and said, Whence hath this *man* this wisdom, and *these* mighty works?
55 Is not this the carpenter's son? is not his mother called Mary? and his brethren, James, and Joses, and Simon, and Judas?
56 And his sisters, are they not all with us? Whence then hath this *man* all these things?
57 And they were offended in him. But Jesus said unto them, A prophet is not without honour, save in his own country, and in his own house.
58 And he did not many mighty works there because of their unbelief.

CHAPTER 14

AT that time Herod the tetrarch heard of the fame of Jesus,
2 And said unto his servants, This is John the Baptist; he is risen from the dead; and therefore mighty works do shew forth themselves in him.
3 ¶For Herod had laid hold on John, and bound him, and put *him* in prison for He-rō'dĭ-as' sake, his brother Philip's wife.
4 For John said unto him, It is not lawful for thee to have her.
5 And when he would have put him to death, he feared the multitude, because they counted him as a prophet.
6 But when Herod's birthday was kept, the daughter of He-rō'dĭ-as danced before them, and pleased Herod.
7 Whereupon he promised with an oath to give her whatsoever she would ask.
8 And she, being before instructed of her mother, said, Give me here John Baptist's head in a charger.
9 And the king was sorry: nevertheless for the oath's sake, and them which sat with him at meat, he commanded *it* to be given *her*.
10 And he sent, and beheaded John in the prison.
11 And his head was brought in a charger, and given to the damsel: and she brought *it* to her mother.
12 And his disciples came, and took up the body, and buried it, and went and told Jesus.
13 ¶When Jesus heard *of it*, he departed thence by ship into a desert place apart: and when the people had heard *thereof*, they followed him on foot out of the cities.
14 And Jesus went forth, and saw a great multitude, and was moved with compassion toward them, and he healed their sick.
15 ¶And when it was evening, his disciples came to him, saying, This is a desert place, and the time is now past; send the multitude away, that they may go into the villages, and buy themselves victuals.
16 But Jesus said unto them, They need not depart; give ye them to eat.
17 And they say unto him, We have here but five loaves, and two fishes.
18 He said, Bring them hither to me.
19 And he commanded the multitude to sit down on the grass, and took the five loaves, and the two fishes, and looking up to heaven, he blessed, and brake, and gave the loaves to *his* disciples, and the disciples to the multitude.
20 And they did all eat, and were filled: and they took up of the fragments that remained twelve baskets full.
21 And they that had eaten were about five thousand men, beside women and children.
22 ¶And straightway Jesus constrained his disciples to get into a ship, and to go before him unto the other side, while he sent the multitudes away.
23 And when he had sent the multitudes away, he went up into a mountain apart to pray: and when the evening was come, he was there alone.
24 But the ship was now in the midst of the sea, tossed with waves: for the wind was contrary.
25 And in the fourth watch of the night Jesus went unto them, walking on the sea.
26 And when the disciples saw him walking on the sea, they were troubled, saying, It is a spirit; and they cried out for fear.
27 But straightway Jesus spake unto

them, saying, Be of good cheer; it is I; be not afraid.
28 And Peter answered him and said, Lord, if it be thou, bid me come unto thee on the water.
29 And he said, Come. And when Peter was come down out of the ship, he walked on the water, to go to Jesus.
30 But when he saw the wind boisterous, he was afraid; and beginning to sink, he cried, saying, Lord, save me.
31 And immediately Jesus stretched forth *his* hand, and caught him, and said unto him, O thou of little faith, wherefore didst thou doubt?
32 And when they were come into the ship, the wind ceased.
33 Then they that were in the ship came and worshipped him, saying, Of a truth thou art the Son of God.
34 ¶And when they were gone over, they came into the land of Gĕn-nĕs′a-ret.
35 And when the men of that place had knowledge of him, they sent out into all that country round about, and brought unto him all that were diseased;
36 And besought him that they might only touch the hem of his garment: and as many as touched were made perfectly whole.

CHAPTER 15

THEN came to Jesus scribes and Pharisees, which were of Jerusalem, saying,
2 Why do thy disciples transgress the tradition of the elders? for they wash not their hands when they eat bread.
3 But he answered and said unto them, Why do ye also transgress the commandment of God by your tradition?
4 For God commanded, saying, Honour thy father and mother: and, He that curseth father or mother, let him die the death.
5 But ye say, Whosoever shall say to *his* father or *his* mother, *It is* a gift, by whatsoever thou mightest be profited by me;
6 And honour not his father or his mother, *he shall be free*. Thus have ye made the commandment of God of none effect by your tradition.
7 *Ye* hypocrites, well did E-să′ias prophesy of you, saying,
8 This people draweth nigh unto me with their mouth, and honoureth me with *their* lips; but their heart is far from me.
9 But in vain they do worship me, teaching *for* doctrines the commandments of men.
10 ¶And he called the multitude, and said unto them, Hear, and understand:
11 Not that which goeth into the mouth defileth a man; but that which cometh out of the mouth, this defileth a man.
12 Then came his disciples, and said unto him, Knowest thou that the Pharisees were offended, after they heard this saying?
13 But he answered and said, Every plant, which my heavenly Father hath not planted, shall be rooted up.
14 Let them alone: they be blind leaders of the blind. And if the blind lead the blind, both shall fall into the ditch.
15 Then answered Peter and said unto him, Declare unto us this parable.
16 And Jesus said, Are ye also yet without understanding?
17 Do not ye yet understand, that whatsoever entereth in at the mouth goeth into the belly, and is cast out into the draught?
18 But those things which proceed out of the mouth come forth from the heart; and they defile the man.
19 For out of the heart proceed evil thoughts, murders, adulteries, fornications, thefts, false witness, blasphemies:
20 These are *the things* which defile a man: but to eat with unwashen hands defileth not a man.
21 ¶Then Jesus went thence, and departed into the coasts of Tyre and Sī′don.
22 And, behold, a woman of Canaan came out of the same coasts, and cried unto him, saying, Have mercy on me, O Lord, *thou* son of David; my daughter is grievously vexed with a devil.
23 But he answered her not a word. And his disciples came and besought him, saying, Send her away; for she crieth after us.
24 But he answered and said, I am not sent but unto the lost sheep of the house of Israel.
25 Then came she and worshipped him, saying, Lord, help me.
26 But he answered and said, It is not meet to take the children's bread, and to cast *it* to dogs.
27 And she said, Truth, Lord: yet the dogs eat of the crumbs which fall from their masters' table.
28 Then Jesus answered and said unto her, O woman, great *is* thy faith: be it unto thee even as thou wilt. And her daughter was made whole from that very hour.
29 ¶And Jesus departed from thence, and came nigh unto the sea of Galilee;

and went up into a mountain, and sat
down there.
30 And great multitudes came unto
him, having with them *those that were*
lame, blind, dumb, maimed, and many
others, and cast them down at Jesus'
feet; and he healed them:
31 Insomuch that the multitude won-
dered, when they saw the dumb to
speak, the maimed to be whole, the
lame to walk, and the blind to see: and
they glorified the God of Israel.
32 ¶Then Jesus called his disciples
unto him, and said, I have compassion
on the multitude, because they con-
tinue with me now three days, and have
nothing to eat: and I will not send them
away fasting, lest they faint in the way.
33 And his disciples say unto him,
Whence should we have so much bread
in the wilderness, as to fill so great a
multitude?
34 And Jesus saith unto them, How
many loaves have ye? And they said,
Seven, and a few little fishes.
35 And he commanded the multitude
to sit down on the ground.
36 And he took the seven loaves and
the fishes, and gave thanks, and brake
them, and gave to his disciples, and the
disciples to the multitude.
37 And they did all eat, and were
filled: and they took up of the broken
meat that was left seven baskets full.
38 And they that did eat were four
thousand men, beside women and
children.
39 And he sent away the multitude,
and took ship, and came into the coasts
of Măg′da-la.

CHAPTER 16

THE Pharisees also with the Săd′du-
ceės came, and tempting desired him
that he would shew them a sign from
heaven.
2 He answered and said unto them,
When it is evening, ye say, *It will be* fair
weather: for the sky is red.
3 And in the morning, *It will be* foul
weather to day: for the sky is red and
lowring. O *ye* hypocrites, ye can dis-
cern the face of the sky; but can ye not
discern the signs of the times?
4 A wicked and adulterous genera-
tion seeketh after a sign; and there
shall no sign be given unto it, but the
sign of the prophet Jonas. And he left
them, and departed.
5 ¶And when his disciples were come
to the other side, they had forgotten to
take bread.
6 Then Jesus said unto them, Take
heed and beware of the leaven of the
Pharisees and of the Săd′du-ceės.
7 And they reasoned among them-
selves, saying, *It is* because we have
taken no bread.
8 *Which* when Jesus perceived, he
said unto them, O ye of little faith, why
reason ye among yourselves, because
ye have brought no bread?
9 Do ye not yet understand, neither
remember the five loaves of the five
thousand, and how many baskets ye
took up?
10 Neither the seven loaves of the
four thousand, and how many baskets
ye took up?
11 How is it that ye do not understand
that I spake *it* not to you concern-
ing bread, that ye should beware of the
leaven of the Pharisees and of the Săd′-
du-ceės?
12 Then understood they how that
he bade *them* not beware of the
leaven of bread, but of the doctrine
of the Pharisees and of the Săd′du-ceės.
13 ¶When Jesus came into the coasts
of Cæs-a-re′a Phĭ-lip′pī, he asked his
disciples, saying, Whom do men say
that I the Son of man am?
14 And they said, Some *say that thou*
art John the Baptist: some, E-lī′as; and
others, Jeremias, or one of the
prophets.
15 He saith unto them, But whom say
ye that I am?
16 And Simon Peter answered and
said, Thou art the Christ, the Son of the
living God.
17 And Jesus answered and said unto
him, Blessed art thou, Simon Bär-jō′na:
for flesh and blood hath not revealed *it*
unto thee, but my Father which is in
heaven.
18 And I say also unto thee, That thou
art Peter, and upon this rock I will build
my church; and the gates of hell shall
not prevail against it.
19 And I will give unto thee the keys
of the kingdom of heaven: and what-
soever thou shalt bind on earth shall be
bound in heaven: and whatsoever thou
shalt loose on earth shall be loosed in
heaven.
20 Then charged he his disciples that
they should tell no man that he was Je-
sus the Christ.
21 ¶From that time forth began Jesus
to shew unto his disciples, how that he
must go unto Jerusalem, and suffer
many things of the elders and chief
priests and scribes, and be killed, and
be raised again the third day.
22 Then Peter took him, and began to
rebuke him, saying, Be it far from thee,
Lord: this shall not be unto thee.
23 But he turned, and said unto Peter,
Get thee behind me, Satan: thou art an
offence unto me: for thou savourest not

the things that be of God, but those that be of men.

24 Then said Jesus unto his disciples, If any *man* will come after me, let him deny himself, and take up his cross, and follow me.

25 For whosoever will save his life shall lose it: and whosoever will lose his life for my sake shall find it.

26 For what is a man profited, if he shall gain the whole world, and lose his own soul? or what shall a man give in exchange for his soul?

27 For the Son of man shall come in the glory of his Father with his angels; and then he shall reward every man according to his works.

28 Verily I say unto you, There be some standing here, which shall not taste of death, till they see the Son of man coming in his kingdom.

CHAPTER 17

AND after six days Jesus taketh Peter, James, and John his brother, and bringeth them up into an high mountain apart,

2 And was transfigured before them: and his face did shine as the sun, and his raiment was white as the light.

3 And, behold, there appeared unto them Moses and E-lī'as talking with him.

4 Then answered Peter, and said unto Jesus, Lord, it is good for us to be here: if thou wilt, let us make here three tabernacles; one for thee, and one for Moses, and one for E-lī'as.

5 While he yet spake, behold, a bright cloud overshadowed them: and behold a voice out of the cloud, which said, This is my beloved Son, in whom I am well pleased; hear ye him.

6 And when the disciples heard *it*, they fell on their face, and were sore afraid.

7 And Jesus came and touched them, and said, Arise, and be not afraid.

8 And when they had lifted up their eyes, they saw no man, save Jesus only.

9 ¶And as they came down from the mountain, Jesus charged them, saying, Tell the vision to no man, until the Son of man be risen again from the dead.

10 And his disciples asked him, saying, Why then say the scribes that E-lī'as must first come?

11 And Jesus answered and said unto them, E-lī'as truly shall first come, and restore all things.

12 But I say unto you, That E-lī'as is come already, and they knew him not, but have done unto him whatsoever they listed. Likewise shall also the Son of man suffer of them.

13 Then the disciples understood that he spake unto them of John the Baptist.

14 ¶And when they were come to the multitude, there came to him a *certain* man, kneeling down to him, and saying,

15 Lord, have mercy on my son: for he is lunatick, and sore vexed: for ofttimes he falleth into the fire, and oft into the water.

16 And I brought him to thy disciples, and they could not cure him.

17 Then Jesus answered and said, O faithless and perverse generation, how long shall I be with you? how long shall I suffer you? bring him hither to me.

18 And Jesus rebuked the devil; and he departed out of him: and the child was cured from that very hour.

19 Then came the disciples to Jesus apart, and said, Why could not we cast him out?

20 And Jesus said unto them, Because of your unbelief: for verily I say unto you, If ye have faith as a grain of mustard seed, ye shall say unto this mountain, Remove hence to yonder place; and it shall remove; and nothing shall be impossible unto you.

21 Howbeit this kind goeth not out but by prayer and fasting.

22 ¶And while they abode in Galilee, Jesus said unto them, The Son of man shall be betrayed into the hands of men:

23 And they shall kill him, and the third day he shall be raised again. And they were exceeding sorry.

24 ¶And when they were come to Ca-per'na-um, they that received tribute *money* came to Peter, and said, Doth not your master pay tribute?

25 He saith, Yes. And when he was come into the house, Jesus prevented him, saying, What thinkest thou, Simon? of whom do the kings of the earth take custom or tribute? of their own children, or of strangers?

26 Peter saith unto him, Of strangers. Jesus saith unto him, Then are the children free.

27 Notwithstanding, lest we should offend them, go thou to the sea, and cast an hook, and take up the fish that first cometh up; and when thou hast opened his mouth, thou shalt find a piece of money: that take, and give unto them for me and thee.

CHAPTER 18

AT the same time came the disciples unto Jesus, saying, Who is the greatest in the kingdom of heaven?

2 And Jesus called a little child unto him, and set him in the midst of them,

3 **And said,** Verily I say unto you, Ex-
cept ye be converted, and become as
little children, ye shall not enter into
the kingdom of heaven.
4 Whosoever therefore shall humble
himself as this little child, the same is
greatest in the kingdom of heaven.
5 And whoso shall receive one such
little child in my name receiveth me.
6 But whoso shall offend one of these
little ones which believe in me, it were
better for him that a millstone were
hanged about his neck, and *that* he
were drowned in the depth of the sea.
7 ¶Woe unto the world because of of-
fences! for it must needs be that of-
fences come; but woe to that man by
whom the offence cometh!
8 Wherefore if thy hand or thy foot
offend thee, cut them off, and cast
them from thee: it is better for thee to
enter into life halt or maimed, rather
than having two hands or two feet to be
cast into everlasting fire.
9 And if thine eye offend thee, pluck
it out, and cast *it* from thee: it is better
for thee to enter into life with one eye,
rather than having two eyes to be cast
into hell fire.
10 ¶Take heed that ye despise not one
of these little ones; for I say unto you,
That in heaven their angels do always
behold the face of my Father which is
in heaven.
11 For the Son of man is come to save
that which was lost.
12 How think ye? if a man have an
hundred sheep, and one of them be
gone astray, doth he not leave the nine-
ty and nine, and goeth into the moun-
tains, and seeketh that which is gone
astray?
13 And if so be that he find it, verily I
say unto you, he rejoiceth more of that
sheep, than of the ninety and nine
which went not astray.
14 Even so it is not the will of your
Father which is in heaven, that one of
these little ones should perish.
15 ¶Moreover if thy brother shall
trespass against thee, go and tell him
his fault between thee and him alone: if
he shall hear thee, thou hast gained thy
brother.
16 But if he will not hear *thee, then*
take with thee one or two more, that in
the mouth of two or three witnesses
every word may be established.
17 And if he shall neglect to hear
them, tell *it* unto the church: but if he
neglect to hear the church, let him be
unto thee as an heathen man and a publi-
can.
18 Verily I say unto you, Whatsoever
ye shall bind on earth shall be bound in
heaven: and whatsoever ye shall loose
on earth shall be loosed in heaven.
19 Again I say unto you, That if two
of you shall agree on earth as touching
any thing that they shall ask, it shall be
done for them of my Father which is in
heaven.
20 For where two or three are gath-
ered together in my name, there am I
in the midst of them.
21 **¶Then came Peter to him, and
said, Lord, how oft shall my brother sin
against me, and I forgive him? till seven
times?**
22 **Jesus saith unto him,** I say not
unto thee, Until seven times: but, Until
seventy times seven.
23 ¶Therefore is the kingdom of
heaven likened unto a certain king,
which would take account of his ser-
vants.
24 And when he had begun to reckon,
one was brought unto him, which owed
him ten thousand talents.
25 But forasmuch as he had not to
pay, his lord commanded him to be
sold, and his wife, and children, and all
that he had, and payment to be made.
26 The servant therefore fell down,
and worshipped him, saying, Lord,
have patience with me, and I will pay
thee all.
27 Then the lord of that servant was
moved with compassion, and loosed
him, and forgave him the debt.
28 But the same servant went out,
and found one of his fellowservants,
which owed him an hundred pence:
and he laid hands on him, and took *him*
by the throat, saying, Pay me that thou
owest.
29 And his fellowservant fell down at
his feet, and besought him, saying,
Have patience with me, and I will pay
thee all.
30 And he would not: but went and
cast him into prison, till he should pay
the debt.
31 So when his fellowservants saw
what was done, they were very sorry,
and came and told unto their lord all
that was done.
32 Then his lord, after that he had
called him, said unto him, O thou
wicked servant, I forgave thee all that
debt, because thou desiredst me:
33 Shouldest not thou also have had
compassion on thy fellowservant, even
as I had pity on thee?
34 And his lord was wroth, and deliv-
ered him to the tormentors, till he
should pay all that was due unto him.
35 So likewise shall my heavenly
Father do also unto you, if ye from your

hearts forgive not every one his brother
their trespasses.

CHAPTER 19

AND it came to pass, *that* when Jesus
had finished these sayings, he departed
from Galilee, and came into the coasts
of Judæa beyond Jordan;
2 And great multitudes followed him;
and he healed them there.
3 ¶The Pharisees also came unto him,
tempting him, and saying unto him, Is
it lawful for a man to put away his wife
for every cause?
4 And he answered and said unto
them, Have ye not read, that he which
made *them* at the beginning made
them male and female,
5 And said, For this cause shall a man
leave father and mother, and shall
cleave to his wife: and they twain shall
be one flesh?
6 Wherefore they are no more twain,
but one flesh. What therefore God hath
joined together, let not man put asun-
der.
7 They say unto him, Why did Moses
then command to give a writing of di-
vorcement, and to put her away?
8 He saith unto them, Moses because
of the hardness of your hearts suffered
you to put away your wives: but from
the beginning it was not so.
9 And I say unto you, Whosoever
shall put away his wife, except *it be* for
fornication, and shall marry another,
committeth adultery: and whoso mar-
rieth her which is put away doth com-
mit adultery.
10 ¶His disciples say unto him, If the
case of the man be so with *his* wife, it is
not good to marry.
11 But he said unto them, All *men*
cannot receive this saying, save *they* to
whom it is given.
12 For there are some eunuchs,
which were so born from *their* moth-
er's womb: and there are some eu-
nuchs, which were made eunuchs of
men: and there be eunuchs, which have
made themselves eunuchs for the king-
dom of heaven's sake. He that is able to
receive *it*, let him receive *it*.
13 ¶Then were there brought unto
him little children, that he should put
his hands on them, and pray: and the
disciples rebuked them.
14 But Jesus said, Suffer little chil-
dren, and forbid them not, to come
unto me: for of such is the kingdom of
heaven.
15 And he laid *his* hands on them, and
departed thence.
16 ¶And, behold, one came and said
unto him, Good Master, what good
thing shall I do, that I may have eternal
life?
17 And he said unto him, Why callest
thou me good? *there is* none good but
one, *that is*, God: but if thou wilt enter
into life, keep the commandments.
18 He saith unto him, Which? Jesus
said, Thou shalt do no murder, Thou
shalt not commit adultery, Thou shalt
not steal, Thou shalt not bear false wit-
ness,
19 Honour thy father and *thy* mother:
and, Thou shalt love thy neighbour as
thyself.
20 The young man saith unto him, All
these things have I kept from my youth
up: what lack I yet?
21 Jesus said unto him, If thou wilt be
perfect, go *and* sell that thou hast, and
give to the poor, and thou shalt have
treasure in heaven: and come *and* fol-
low me.
22 But when the young man heard
that saying, he went away sorrowful:
for he had great possessions.
23 ¶Then said Jesus unto his dis-
ciples, Verily I say unto you, That a rich
man shall hardly enter into the king-
dom of heaven.
24 And again I say unto you, It is eas-
ier for a camel to go through the eye of
a needle, than for a rich man to enter
into the kingdom of God.
25 When his disciples heard *it*, they
were exceedingly amazed, saying,
Who then can be saved?
26 But Jesus beheld *them*, and said
unto them, With men this is impos-
sible; but with God all things are pos-
sible.
27 ¶Then answered Peter and said
unto him, Behold, we have forsaken all,
and followed thee; what shall we have
therefore?
28 And Jesus said unto them, Verily I
say unto you, That ye which have fol-
lowed me, in the regeneration when the
Son of man shall sit in the throne of his
glory, ye also shall sit upon twelve
thrones, judging the twelve tribes of
Israel.
29 And every one that hath forsaken
houses, or brethren, or sisters, or
father, or mother, or wife, or children,
or lands, for my name's sake, shall re-
ceive an hundredfold, and shall inherit
everlasting life.
30 But many *that are* first shall be
last; and the last *shall be* first.

CHAPTER 20

FOR the kingdom of heaven is like unto
a man *that is* an householder, which
went out early in the morning to hire
labourers into his vineyard.

2 And when he had agreed with the labourers for a penny a day, he sent them into his vineyard.

3 And he went out about the third hour, and saw others standing idle in the marketplace,

4 And said unto them; Go ye also into the vineyard, and whatsoever is right I will give you. And they went their way.

5 Again he went out about the sixth and ninth hour, and did likewise.

6 And about the eleventh hour he went out, and found others standing idle, and saith unto them, Why stand ye here all the day idle?

7 They say unto him, Because no man hath hired us. He saith unto them, Go ye also into the vineyard; and whatsoever is right, *that* shall ye receive.

8 So when even was come, the lord of the vineyard saith unto his steward, Call the labourers, and give them *their* hire, beginning from the last unto the first.

9 And when they came that *were hired* about the eleventh hour, they received every man a penny.

10 But when the first came, they supposed that they should have received more; and they likewise received every man a penny.

11 And when they had received *it*, they murmured against the goodman of the house,

12 Saying, These last have wrought *but* one hour, and thou hast made them equal unto us, which have borne the burden and heat of the day.

13 But he answered one of them, and said, Friend, I do thee no wrong: didst not thou agree with me for a penny?

14 Take *that* thine *is*, and go thy way: I will give unto this last, even as unto thee.

15 Is it not lawful for me to do what I will with mine own? Is thine eye evil, because I am good?

16 So the last shall be first, and the first last: for many be called, but few chosen.

17 ¶And Jesus going up to Jerusalem took the twelve disciples apart in the way, and said unto them,

18 Behold, we go up to Jerusalem; and the Son of man shall be betrayed unto the chief priests and unto the scribes, and they shall condemn him to death,

19 And shall deliver him to the Gentiles to mock, and to scourge, and to crucify *him*: and the third day he shall rise again.

20 ¶Then came to him the mother of Zĕb′e-dee's children with her sons, worshipping *him*, and desiring a certain thing of him.

21 And he said unto her, What wilt thou? She saith unto him, Grant that these my two sons may sit, the one on thy right hand, and the other on the left, in thy kingdom.

22 But Jesus answered and said, Ye know not what ye ask. Are ye able to drink of the cup that I shall drink of, and to be baptized with the baptism that I am baptized with? They say unto him, We are able.

23 And he saith unto them, Ye shall drink indeed of my cup, and be baptized with the baptism that I am baptized with: but to sit on my right hand, and on my left, is not mine to give, but *it shall be given to them* for whom it is prepared of my Father.

24 And when the ten heard *it*, they were moved with indignation against the two brethren.

25 But Jesus called them *unto him*, and said, Ye know that the princes of the Gentiles exercise dominion over them, and they that are great exercise authority upon them.

26 But it shall not be so among you: but whosoever will be great among you, let him be your minister;

27 And whosoever will be chief among you, let him be your servant:

28 Even as the Son of man came not to be ministered unto, but to minister, and to give his life a ransom for many.

29 ¶And as they departed from Jericho, a great multitude followed him.

30 And, behold, two blind men sitting by the way side, when they heard that Jesus passed by, cried out, saying, Have mercy on us, O Lord, *thou* son of David.

31 And the multitude rebuked them, because they should hold their peace: but they cried the more, saying, Have mercy on us, O Lord, *thou* son of David.

32 And Jesus stood still, and called them, and said, What will ye that I shall do unto you?

33 They say unto him, Lord, that our eyes may be opened.

34 So Jesus had compassion *on them*, and touched their eyes: and immediately their eyes received sight, and they followed him.

CHAPTER 21

AND when they drew nigh unto Jerusalem, and were come to Bĕth′pha-ġē, unto the mount of Olives, then sent Jesus two disciples,

2 Saying unto them, Go into the village over against you, and straightway

ye shall find an ass tied, and a colt with
her: loose *them*, and bring *them* unto
me.
3 And if any *man* say ought unto you,
ye shall say, The Lord hath need of
them; and straightway he will send
them.
4 All this was done, that it might be
fulfilled which was spoken by the
prophet, saying,
5 Tell ye the daughter of Sion, Be-
hold, thy King cometh unto thee, meek,
and sitting upon an ass, and a colt the
foal of an ass.
6 And the disciples went, and did as
Jesus commanded them,
7 And brought the ass, and the colt,
and put on them their clothes, and they
set *him* thereon.
8 And a very great multitude spread
their garments in the way; others cut
down branches from the trees, and
strawed *them* in the way.
9 And the multitudes that went be-
fore, and that followed, cried, saying,
Hosanna to the son of David: Blessed *is*
he that cometh in the name of the Lord;
Hosanna in the highest.
10 ¶And when he was come into Jeru-
salem, all the city was moved, saying,
Who is this?
11 And the multitude said, This is Je-
sus the prophet of Nazareth of Galilee.
12 ¶And Jesus went into the temple
of God, and cast out all them that sold
and bought in the temple, and over-
threw the tables of the moneychang-
ers, and the seats of them that sold
doves,
13 And said unto them, It is written,
My house shall be called the house of
prayer; but ye have made it a den of
thieves.
14 And the blind and the lame came
to him in the temple; and he healed
them.
15 And when the chief priests and
scribes saw the wonderful things that
he did, and the children crying in the
temple, and saying, Hosanna to the son
of David; they were sore displeased,
16 And said unto him, Hearest thou
what these say? And Jesus saith unto
them, Yea; have ye never read, Out of
the mouth of babes and sucklings thou
hast perfected praise?
17 And he left them, and went out of
the city into Bethany; and he lodged
there.
18 ¶Now in the morning as he re-
turned into the city, he hungered.
19 And when he saw a fig tree in the
way, he came to it, and found nothing
thereon, but leaves only, and said unto
it, Let no fruit grow on thee hence-
forward for ever. And presently the fig
tree withered away.
20 And when the disciples saw *it*,
they marvelled, saying, How soon is
the fig tree withered away!
21 Jesus answered and said unto
them, Verily I say unto you, If ye have
faith, and doubt not, ye shall not only
do this *which is done* to the fig tree, but
also if ye shall say unto this mountain,
Be thou removed, and be thou cast into
the sea; it shall be done.
22 And all things, whatsoever ye
shall ask in prayer, believing, ye shall
receive.
23 ¶And when he was come into the
temple, the chief priests and the elders
of the people came unto him as he was
teaching, and said, By what authority
doest thou these things? and who gave
thee this authority?
24 And Jesus answered and said unto
them, I also will ask you one thing,
which if ye tell me, I in like wise will tell
you by what authority I do these things.
25 The baptism of John, whence was
it? from heaven, or of men? And they
reasoned with themselves, saying, If
we shall say, From heaven; he will say
unto us, Why did ye not then believe
him?
26 But if we shall say, Of men; we
fear the people; for all hold John as a
prophet.
27 And they answered Jesus, and
said, We cannot tell. And he said unto
them, Neither tell I you by what au-
thority I do these things.
28 ¶But what think ye? A *certain* man
had two sons; and he came to the first,
and said, Son, go work to day in my vine-
yard.
29 He answered and said, I will not:
but afterward he repented, and went.
30 And he came to the second, and
said likewise. And he answered and
said, I *go*, sir: and went not.
31 Whether of them twain did the
will of *his* father? They say unto him,
The first. Jesus saith unto them, Verily
I say unto you, That the publicans and
the harlots go into the kingdom of God
before you.
32 For John came unto you in the way
of righteousness, and ye believed him
not; but the publicans and the harlots
believed him: and ye, when ye had seen
it, repented not afterward, that ye
might believe him.
33 ¶Hear another parable: There was
a certain householder, which planted a
vineyard, and hedged it round about,
and digged a winepress in it, and built a
tower, and let it out to husbandmen,
and went into a far country:

34 And when the time of the fruit
drew near, he sent his servants to the
husbandmen, that they might receive
the fruits of it.
35 And the husbandmen took his ser-
vants, and beat one, and killed another,
and stoned another.
36 Again, he sent other servants
more than the first: and they did unto
them likewise.
37 But last of all he sent unto them his
son, saying, They will reverence my
son.
38 But when the husbandmen saw
the son, they said among themselves,
This is the heir; come, let us kill him,
and let us seize on his inheritance.
39 And they caught him, and cast *him*
out of the vineyard, and slew *him*.
40 When the lord therefore of the vine-
yard cometh, what will he do unto
those husbandmen?
41 They say unto him, He will mis-
erably destroy those wicked men, and
will let out *his* vineyard unto other hus-
bandmen, which shall render him the
fruits in their seasons.
42 Jesus saith unto them, Did ye nev-
er read in the scriptures, The stone
which the builders rejected, the same is
become the head of the corner: this is
the Lord's doing, and it is marvellous in
our eyes?
43 Therefore say I unto you, The
kingdom of God shall be taken from
you, and given to a nation bringing
forth the fruits thereof.
44 And whosoever shall fall on this
stone shall be broken: but on whom-
soever it shall fall, it will grind him to
powder.
45 And when the chief priests and
Pharisees had heard his parables, they
perceived that he spake of them.
46 But when they sought to lay hands
on him, they feared the multitude, be-
cause they took him for a prophet.

CHAPTER 22

AND Jesus answered and spake unto
them again by parables, and said,
2 The kingdom of heaven is like unto
a certain king, which made a marriage
for his son,
3 And sent forth his servants to call
them that were bidden to the wedding:
and they would not come.
4 Again, he sent forth other servants,
saying, Tell them which are bidden, Be-
hold, I have prepared my dinner: my
oxen and *my* fatlings *are* killed, and all
things *are* ready: come unto the mar-
riage.
5 But they made light of *it*, and went
their ways, one to his farm, another to
his merchandise:
6 And the remnant took his servants,
and entreated *them* spitefully, and slew
them.
7 But when the king heard *thereof*, he
was wroth: and he sent forth his
armies, and destroyed those murder-
ers, and burned up their city.
8 Then saith he to his servants, The
wedding is ready, but they which were
bidden were not worthy.
9 Go ye therefore into the highways,
and as many as ye shall find, bid to the
marriage.
10 So those servants went out into
the highways, and gathered together
all as many as they found, both bad and
good: and the wedding was furnished
with guests.
11 And when the king came in to see
the guests, he saw there a man which
had not on a wedding garment:
12 And he saith unto him, Friend,
how camest thou in hither not having a
wedding garment? And he was speech-
less.
13 Then said the king to the servants,
Bind him hand and foot, and take him
away, and cast *him* into outer dark-
ness; there shall be weeping and
gnashing of teeth.
14 For many are called, but few *are*
chosen.
15 ¶Then went the Pharisees, and
took counsel how they might entangle
him in *his* talk.
16 And they sent out unto him their
disciples with the He-rō'di-ans, saying,
Master, we know that thou art true,
and teachest the way of God in truth,
neither carest thou for any *man*: for
thou regardest not the person of men.
17 Tell us therefore, What thinkest
thou? Is it lawful to give tribute unto
Cæsar, or not?
18 But Jesus perceived their wicked-
ness, and said, Why tempt ye me, *ye*
hypocrites?
19 Shew me the tribute money. And
they brought unto him a penny.
20 And he saith unto them, Whose *is*
this image and superscription?
21 They say unto him, Cæsar's. Then
saith he unto them, Render therefore
unto Cæsar the things which are
Cæsar's; and unto God the things that
are God's.
22 When they had heard *these words*,
they marvelled, and left him, and went
their way.
23 ¶The same day came to him the
Săd'du-ceeṡ, which say that there is no
resurrection, and asked him,
24 Saying, Master, Moses said, If a

man die, having no children, his
brother shall marry his wife, and raise
up seed unto his brother.
25 Now there were with us seven
brethren: and the first, when he had
married a wife, deceased, and, having
no issue, left his wife unto his brother:
26 Likewise the second also, and the
third, unto the seventh.
27 And last of all the woman died
also.
28 Therefore in the resurrection
whose wife shall she be of the seven?
for they all had her.
29 Jesus answered and said unto
them, Ye do err, not knowing the scriptures, nor the power of God.
30 For in the resurrection they
neither marry, nor are given in marriage, but are as the angels of God in
heaven.
31 But as touching the resurrection of
the dead, have ye not read that which
was spoken unto you by God, saying,
32 I am the God of Abraham, and the
God of Isaac, and the God of Jacob?
God is not the God of the dead, but of
the living.
33 And when the multitude heard
this, they were astonished at his doctrine.
34 ¶But when the Pharisees had
heard that he had put the Săd′du-ceės
to silence, they were gathered together.
35 Then one of them, *which was* a lawyer, asked *him a question*, tempting
him, and saying,
36 Master, which *is* the great commandment in the law?
37 Jesus said unto him, Thou shalt
love the Lord thy God with all thy
heart, and with all thy soul, and with all
thy mind.
38 This is the first and great commandment.
39 And the second *is* like unto it,
Thou shalt love thy neighbour as thyself.
40 On these two commandments
hang all the law and the prophets.
41 ¶While the Pharisees were gathered together, Jesus asked them,
42 Saying, What think ye of Christ?
whose son is he? They say unto him,
The son of David.
43 He saith unto them, How then
doth David in spirit call him Lord,
saying,
44 The LORD said unto my Lord, Sit
thou on my right hand, till I make thine
enemies thy footstool?
45 If David then call him Lord, how is
he his son?
46 And no man was able to answer
him a word, neither durst any *man*
from that day forth ask him any more
questions.

CHAPTER 23

THEN spake Jesus to the multitude,
and to his disciples,
2 Saying, The scribes and the
Pharisees sit in Moses' seat:
3 All therefore whatsoever they bid
you observe, *that* observe and do; but
do not ye after their works: for they
say, and do not.
4 For they bind heavy burdens and
grievous to be borne, and lay *them* on
men's shoulders; but they *themselves*
will not move them with one of their
fingers.
5 But all their works they do for to be
seen of men: they make broad their
phylacteries, and enlarge the borders
of their garments,
6 And love the uppermost rooms at
feasts, and the chief seats in the synagogues,
7 And greetings in the markets, and
to be called of men, Rabbi, Rabbi.
8 But be not ye called Rabbi: for one
is your Master, *even* Christ; and all ye
are brethren.
9 And call no *man* your father upon
the earth: for one is your Father, which
is in heaven.
10 Neither be ye called masters: for
one is your Master, *even* Christ.
11 But he that is greatest among you
shall be your servant.
12 And whosoever shall exalt himself
shall be abased; and he that shall
humble himself shall be exalted.
13 ¶But woe unto you, scribes and
Pharisees, hypocrites! for ye shut up
the kingdom of heaven against men:
for ye neither go in *yourselves*, neither
suffer ye them that are entering to go
in.
14 Woe unto you, scribes and
Pharisees, hypocrites! for ye devour
widows' houses, and for a pretence
make long prayer: therefore ye shall receive the greater damnation.
15 Woe unto you, scribes and
Pharisees, hypocrites! for ye compass
sea and land to make one proselyte,
and when he is made, ye make him
twofold more the child of hell than
yourselves.
16 Woe unto you, *ye* blind guides,
which say, Whosoever shall swear by
the temple, it is nothing; but whosoever
shall swear by the gold of the temple,
he is a debtor!
17 *Ye* fools and blind: for whether is
greater, the gold, or the temple that
sanctifieth the gold?

18 And, Whosoever shall swear by the altar, it is nothing; but whosoever sweareth by the gift that is upon it, he is guilty.
19 *Ye* fools and blind: for whether *is* greater, the gift, or the altar that sanctifieth the gift?
20 Whoso therefore shall swear by the altar, sweareth by it, and by all things thereon.
21 And whoso shall swear by the temple, sweareth by it, and by him that dwelleth therein.
22 And he that shall swear by heaven, sweareth by the throne of God, and by him that sitteth thereon.
23 Woe unto you, scribes and Pharisees, hypocrites! for ye pay tithe of mint and anise and cummin, and have omitted the weightier *matters* of the law, judgment, mercy, and faith: these ought ye to have done, and not to leave the other undone.
24 *Ye* blind guides, which strain at a gnat, and swallow a camel.
25 Woe unto you, scribes and Pharisees, hypocrites! for ye make clean the outside of the cup and of the platter, but within they are full of extortion and excess.
26 *Thou* blind Pharisee, cleanse first that *which is* within the cup and platter, that the outside of them may be clean also.
27 Woe unto you, scribes and Pharisees, hypocrites! for ye are like unto whited sepulchres, which indeed appear beautiful outward, but are within full of dead *men's* bones, and of all uncleanness.
28 Even so ye also outwardly appear righteous unto men, but within ye are full of hypocrisy and iniquity.
29 Woe unto you, scribes and Pharisees, hypocrites! because ye build the tombs of the prophets, and garnish the sepulchres of the righteous,
30 And say, If we had been in the days of our fathers, we would not have been partakers with them in the blood of the prophets.
31 Wherefore ye be witnesses unto yourselves, that ye are the children of them which killed the prophets.
32 Fill ye up then the measure of your fathers.
33 *Ye* serpents, *ye* generation of vipers, how can ye escape the damnation of hell?
34 Wherefore, behold, I send unto you prophets, and wise men, and scribes: and *some* of them ye shall kill and crucify; and *some* of them shall ye scourge in your synagogues, and persecute *them* from city to city:
35 That upon you may come all the righteous blood shed upon the earth, from the blood of righteous Abel unto the blood of Zăch-a-rī'as son of Băr-a-chī'as, whom ye slew between the temple and the altar.
36 Verily I say unto you, All these things shall come upon this generation.
37 O Jerusalem, Jerusalem, *thou* that killest the prophets, and stonest them which are sent unto thee, how often would I have gathered thy children together, even as a hen gathereth her chickens under *her* wings, and ye would not!
38 Behold, your house is left unto you desolate.
39 For I say unto you, Ye shall not see me henceforth, till ye shall say, Blessed *is* he that cometh in the name of the Lord.

CHAPTER 24

AND Jesus went out, and departed from the temple: and his disciples came to *him* for to shew him the buildings of the temple.
2 **And Jesus said unto them,** See ye not all these things? verily I say unto you, There shall not be left here one stone upon another, that shall not be thrown down.
3 **¶And as he sat upon the mount of Olives, the disciples came unto him privately, saying, Tell us, when shall these things be? and what *shall be* the sign of thy coming, and of the end of the world?**
4 **And Jesus answered and said unto them,** Take heed that no man deceive you.
5 For many shall come in my name, saying, I am Christ; and shall deceive many.
6 And ye shall hear of wars and rumours of wars: see that ye be not troubled: for all *these things* must come to pass, but the end is not yet.
7 For nation shall rise against nation, and kingdom against kingdom: and there shall be famines, and pestilences, and earthquakes, in divers places.
8 All these *are* the beginning of sorrows.
9 Then shall they deliver you up to be afflicted, and shall kill you: and ye shall be hated of all nations for my name's sake.
10 And then shall many be offended, and shall betray one another, and shall hate one another.
11 And many false prophets shall rise, and shall deceive many.
12 And because iniquity shall

abound, the love of many shall wax
cold.
13 But he that shall endure unto the
end, the same shall be saved.
14 And this gospel of the kingdom
shall be preached in all the world for a
witness unto all nations; and then shall
the end come.
15 When ye therefore shall see the
abomination of desolation, spoken of
by Daniel the prophet, stand in the holy
place, (whoso readeth, let him under-
stand:)
16 Then let them which be in Judæa
flee into the mountains:
17 Let him which is on the housetop
not come down to take any thing out of
his house:
18 Neither let him which is in the
field return back to take his clothes.
19 And woe unto them that are with
child, and to them that give suck in
those days!
20 But pray ye that your flight be not
in the winter, neither on the sabbath
day:
21 For then shall be great tribulation,
such as was not since the beginning of
the world to this time, no, nor ever shall
be.
22 And except those days should be
shortened, there should no flesh be
saved: but for the elect's sake those
days shall be shortened.
23 Then if any man shall say unto
you, Lo, here *is* Christ, or there; believe
it not.
24 For there shall arise false Christs,
and false prophets, and shall shew
great signs and wonders; insomuch
that, if *it were* possible, they shall de-
ceive the very elect.
25 Behold, I have told you before.
26 Wherefore if they shall say unto
you, Behold, he is in the desert; go not
forth: behold, *he is* in the secret cham-
bers; believe *it* not.
27 For as the lightning cometh out of
the east, and shineth even unto the
west; so shall also the coming of the
Son of man be.
28 For wheresoever the carcase is,
there will the eagles be gathered togeth-
er.
29 ¶Immediately after the tribulation
of those days shall the sun be darkened,
and the moon shall not give her light,
and the stars shall fall from heaven,
and the powers of the heavens shall be
shaken:
30 And then shall appear the sign of
the Son of man in heaven: and then
shall all the tribes of the earth mourn,
and they shall see the Son of man com-
ing in the clouds of heaven with pow-
er and great glory.
31 And he shall send his angels with a
great sound of a trumpet, and they
shall gather together his elect from the
four winds, from one end of heaven to
the other.
32 ¶Now learn a parable of the fig
tree; When his branch is yet tender,
and putteth forth leaves, ye know that
summer *is* nigh:
33 So likewise ye, when ye shall see
all these things, know that it is near,
even at the doors.
34 Verily I say unto you, This genera-
tion shall not pass, till all these things
be fulfilled.
35 Heaven and earth shall pass away,
but my words shall not pass away.
36 ¶But of that day and hour knoweth
no *man*, no, not the angels of heaven,
but my Father only.
37 But as the days of Nō'e *were*, so
shall also the coming of the Son of man
be.
38 For as in the days that were before
the flood they were eating and drink-
ing, marrying and giving in marriage,
until the day that Nō'e entered into the
ark,
39 And knew not until the flood
came, and took them all away; so shall
also the coming of the Son of man be.
40 Then shall two be in the field; the
one shall be taken, and the other left.
41 Two *women shall be* grinding at
the mill; the one shall be taken, and the
other left.
42 ¶Watch therefore: for ye know not
what hour your Lord doth come.
43 But know this, that if the goodman
of the house had known in what watch
the thief would come, he would have
watched, and would not have suffered
his house to be broken up.
44 Therefore be ye also ready: for in
such an hour as ye think not the Son of
man cometh.
45 Who then is a faithful and wise
servant, whom his lord hath made ruler
over his household, to give them meat
in due season?
46 Blessed *is* that servant, whom his
lord when he cometh shall find so
doing.
47 Verily I say unto you, That he shall
make him ruler over all his goods.
48 But and if that evil servant shall
say in his heart, My lord delayeth his
coming;
49 And shall begin to smite *his* fel-
lowservants, and to eat and drink with
the drunken;
50 The lord of that servant shall come

in a day when he looketh not for *him*,
and in an hour that he is not aware of,
51 And shall cut him asunder, and ap-
point *him* his portion with the hypo-
crites: there shall be weeping and
gnashing of teeth.

CHAPTER 25

THEN shall the kingdom of heaven be
likened unto ten virgins, which took
their lamps, and went forth to meet the
bridegroom.
2 And five of them were wise, and
five *were* foolish.
3 They that *were* foolish took their
lamps, and took no oil with them:
4 But the wise took oil in their vessels
with their lamps.
5 While the bridegroom tarried, they
all slumbered and slept.
6 And at midnight there was a cry
made, Behold, the bridegroom cometh;
go ye out to meet him.
7 Then all those virgins arose, and
trimmed their lamps.
8 And the foolish said unto the wise,
Give us of your oil; for our lamps are
gone out.
9 But the wise answered, saying, *Not
so;* lest there be not enough for us and
you: but go ye rather to them that sell,
and buy for yourselves.
10 And while they went to buy, the
bridegroom came; and they that were
ready went in with him to the marriage:
and the door was shut.
11 Afterward came also the other vir-
gins, saying, Lord, Lord, open to us.
12 But he answered and said, Verily I
say unto you, I know you not.
13 Watch therefore, for ye know
neither the day nor the hour wherein
the Son of man cometh.
14 ¶For *the kingdom of heaven is* as a
man travelling into a far country, *who*
called his own servants, and delivered
unto them his goods.
15 And unto one he gave five talents,
to another two, and to another one; to
every man according to his several
ability; and straightway took his jour-
ney.
16 Then he that had received the five
talents went and traded with the same,
and made *them* other five talents.
17 And likewise he that *had received*
two, he also gained other two.
18 But he that had received one went
and digged in the earth, and hid his
lord's money.
19 After a long time the lord of those
servants cometh, and reckoneth with
them.
20 And so he that had received five
talents came and brought other five
talents, saying, Lord, thou deliveredst
unto me five talents: behold, I have
gained beside them five talents more.
21 His lord said unto him, Well done,
thou good and faithful servant: thou
hast been faithful over a few things, I
will make thee ruler over many things:
enter thou into the joy of thy lord.
22 He also that had received two
talents came and said, Lord, thou deliv-
eredst unto me two talents: behold, I
have gained two other talents beside
them.
23 His lord said unto him, Well done,
good and faithful servant; thou hast
been faithful over a few things, I will
make thee ruler over many things: en-
ter thou into the joy of thy lord.
24 Then he which had received the
one talent came and said, Lord, I knew
thee that thou art an hard man, reaping
where thou hast not sown, and gather-
ing where thou hast not strawed:
25 And I was afraid, and went and hid
thy talent in the earth: lo, *there* thou
hast *that is* thine.
26 His lord answered and said unto
him, *Thou* wicked and slothful servant,
thou knewest that I reap where I sowed
not, and gather where I have not
strawed:
27 Thou oughtest therefore to have
put my money to the exchangers, and
then at my coming I should have re-
ceived mine own with usury.
28 Take therefore the talent from
him, and give *it* unto him which hath
ten talents.
29 For unto every one that hath shall
be given, and he shall have abundance:
but from him that hath not shall be
taken away even that which he hath.
30 And cast ye the unprofitable ser-
vant into outer darkness: there shall be
weeping and gnashing of teeth.
31 ¶When the Son of man shall come
in his glory, and all the holy angels with
him, then shall he sit upon the throne of
his glory:
32 And before him shall be gathered
all nations: and he shall separate them
one from another, as a shepherd divid-
eth *his* sheep from the goats:
33 And he shall set the sheep on his
right hand, but the goats on the left.
34 Then shall the King say unto them
on his right hand, Come, ye blessed of
my Father, inherit the kingdom pre-
pared for you from the foundation of
the world:
35 For I was an hungred, and ye gave
me meat: I was thirsty, and ye gave me
drink: I was a stranger, and ye took me
in:
36 Naked, and ye clothed me: I was

sick, and ye visited me: I was in prison,
and ye came unto me.
37 Then shall the righteous answer
him, saying, Lord, when saw we thee
an hungred, and fed *thee?* or thirsty,
and gave *thee* drink?
38 When saw we thee a stranger, and
took *thee* in? or naked, and clothed
thee?
39 Or when saw we thee sick, or in
prison, and came unto thee?
40 And the King shall answer and say
unto them, Verily I say unto you, Inas-
much as ye have done *it* unto one of the
least of these my brethren, ye have
done *it* unto me.
41 Then shall he say also unto them
on the left hand, Depart from me, ye
cursed, into everlasting fire, prepared
for the devil and his angels:
42 For I was an hungred, and ye gave
me no meat: I was thirsty, and ye gave
me no drink:
43 I was a stranger, and ye took me
not in: naked, and ye clothed me not:
sick, and in prison, and ye visited me
not.
44 Then shall they also answer him,
saying, Lord, when saw we thee an
hungred, or athirst, or a stranger, or
naked, or sick, or in prison, and did not
minister unto thee?
45 Then shall he answer them,
saying, Verily I say unto you, Inasmuch
as ye did *it* not to one of the least of
these, ye did *it* not to me.
46 And these shall go away into ever-
lasting punishment: but the righteous
into life eternal.

CHAPTER 26

AND it came to pass, when Jesus had
finished all these sayings, he said unto
his disciples,
2 Ye know that after two days is *the
feast of* the passover, and the Son of
man is betrayed to be crucified.
3 ¶Then assembled together the chief
priests, and the scribes, and the elders
of the people, unto the palace of the
high priest, who was called Cā'ia-phas,
4 And consulted that they might take
Jesus by subtilty, and kill *him.*
5 But they said, Not on the feast *day,*
lest there be an uproar among the
people.
6 ¶Now when Jesus was in Bethany,
in the house of Simon the leper,
7 There came unto him a woman hav-
ing an alabaster box of very precious
ointment, and poured it on his head, as
he sat *at meat.*
8 But when his disciples saw *it,* they
had indignation, saying, To what pur-
pose *is* this waste?
9 For this ointment might have been
sold for much, and given to the poor.
10 When Jesus understood *it,* he said
unto them, Why trouble ye the woman?
for she hath wrought a good work upon
me.
11 For ye have the poor always with
you; but me ye have not always.
12 For in that she hath poured this
ointment on my body, she did *it* for my
burial.
13 Verily I say unto you, Wheresoever
this gospel shall be preached in the
whole world, *there* shall also this, that
this woman hath done, be told for a me-
morial of her.
14 ¶Then one of the twelve, called Ju-
das Iscariot, went unto the chief
priests,
15 And said *unto them,* What will ye
give me, and I will deliver him unto
you? And they covenanted with him for
thirty pieces of silver.
16 And from that time he sought op-
portunity to betray him.
17 ¶Now the first *day* of the *feast of*
unleavened bread the disciples came to
Jesus, saying unto him, Where wilt
thou that we prepare for thee to eat the
passover?
18 And he said, Go into the city to
such a man, and say unto him, The
Master saith, My time is at hand; I will
keep the passover at thy house with my
disciples.
19 And the disciples did as Jesus had
appointed them; and they made ready
the passover.
20 ¶Now when the even was come, he
sat down with the twelve.
21 And as they did eat, he said, Verily
I say unto you, that one of you shall be-
tray me.
22 And they were exceeding sorrow-
ful, and began every one of them to say
unto him, Lord, is it I?
23 And he answered and said, He that
dippeth *his* hand with me in the dish,
the same shall betray me.
24 The Son of man goeth as it is writ-
ten of him: but woe unto that man by
whom the Son of man is betrayed! it
had been good for that man if he had
not been born.
25 Then Judas, which betrayed him,
answered and said, Master, is it I? He
said unto him, Thou hast said.
26 ¶And as they were eating, Jesus
took bread, and blessed *it,* and brake *it,*
and gave *it* to the disciples, and said,
Take, eat; this is my body.
27 And he took the cup, and gave
thanks, and gave *it* to them, saying,
Drink ye all of it;
28 For this is my blood of the new tes-

tament, which is shed for many for the
remission of sins.
29 But I say unto you, I will not drink
henceforth of this fruit of the vine, until
that day when I drink it new with you in
my Father's kingdom.
30 ¶And when they had sung an
hymn, they went out into the mount of
Olives.
31 Then saith Jesus unto them, All ye
shall be offended because of me this
night: for it is written, I will smite the
shepherd, and the sheep of the flock
shall be scattered abroad.
32 But after I am risen again, I will go
before you into Galilee.
33 Peter answered and said unto him,
Though all *men* shall be offended be-
cause of thee, *yet* will I never be of-
fended.
34 Jesus said unto him, Verily I say
unto thee, That this night, before the
cock crow, thou shalt deny me thrice.
35 Peter said unto him, Though I
should die with thee, yet will I not deny
thee. Likewise also said all the dis-
ciples.
36 ¶Then cometh Jesus with them
unto a place called Gĕth-sĕm′a-ne, and
saith unto the disciples, Sit ye here,
while I go and pray yonder.
37 And he took with him Peter and
the two sons of Zĕb′e-dee, and began to
be sorrowful and very heavy.
38 Then saith he unto them, My soul
is exceeding sorrowful, even unto
death: tarry ye here, and watch with
me.
39 And he went a little farther, and
fell on his face, and prayed, saying, O
my Father, if it be possible, let this cup
pass from me: nevertheless not as I
will, but as thou *wilt*.
40 And he cometh unto the disciples,
and findeth them asleep, and saith unto
Peter, What, could ye not watch with
me one hour?
41 Watch and pray, that ye enter not
into temptation: the spirit indeed *is* will-
ing, but the flesh *is* weak.
42 He went away again the second
time, and prayed, saying, O my Father,
if this cup may not pass away from me,
except I drink it, thy will be done.
43 And he came and found them asleep
again: for their eyes were heavy.
44 And he left them, and went away
again, and prayed the third time,
saying the same words.
45 Then cometh he to his disciples,
and saith unto them, Sleep on now, and
take *your* rest: behold, the hour is at
hand, and the Son of man is betrayed
into the hands of sinners.
46 Rise, let us be going: behold, he is
at hand that doth betray me.
47 ¶And while he yet spake, lo, Judas,
one of the twelve, came, and with him a
great multitude with swords and
staves, from the chief priests and elders
of the people.
48 Now he that betrayed him gave
them a sign, saying, Whomsoever I
shall kiss, that same is he: hold him
fast.
49 And forthwith he came to Jesus,
and said, Hail, master; and kissed him.
50 And Jesus said unto him, Friend,
wherefore art thou come? Then came
they, and laid hands on Jesus, and took
him.
51 And, behold, one of them which
were with Jesus stretched out *his* hand,
and drew his sword, and struck a ser-
vant of the high priest's, and smote off
his ear.
52 Then said Jesus unto him, Put up
again thy sword into his place: for all
they that take the sword shall perish
with the sword.
53 Thinkest thou that I cannot now
pray to my Father, and he shall present-
ly give me more than twelve legions of
angels?
54 But how then shall the scriptures
be fulfilled, that thus it must be?
55 In that same hour said Jesus to the
multitudes, Are ye come out as against
a thief with swords and staves for to
take me? I sat daily with you teaching
in the temple, and ye laid no hold on
me.
56 But all this was done, that the
scriptures of the prophets might be ful-
filled. Then all the disciples forsook
him, and fled.
57 ¶And they that had laid hold on Je-
sus led *him* away to Cā′ia-phas the high
priest, where the scribes and the elders
were assembled.
58 But Peter followed him afar off
unto the high priest's palace, and went
in, and sat with the servants, to see the
end.
59 Now the chief priests, and elders,
and all the council, sought false wit-
ness against Jesus, to put him to death;
60 But found none: yea, though many
false witnesses came, *yet* found they
none. At the last came two false wit-
nesses,
61 And said, This *fellow* said, I am
able to destroy the temple of God, and
to build it in three days.
62 And the high priest arose, and said
unto him, Answerest thou nothing?
what *is it which* these witness against
thee?
63 But Jesus held his peace. And the

high priest answered and said unto
him, I adjure thee by the living God,
that thou tell us whether thou be the
Christ, the Son of God.
64 Jesus saith unto him, Thou hast
said: nevertheless I say unto you,
Hereafter shall ye see the Son of man
sitting on the right hand of power, and
coming in the clouds of heaven.
65 Then the high priest rent his
clothes, saying, He hath spoken blas-
phemy; what further need have we of
witnesses? behold, now ye have heard
his blasphemy.
66 What think ye? They answered
and said, He is guilty of death.
67 Then did they spit in his face, and
buffeted him; and others smote *him*
with the palms of their hands,
68 Saying, Prophesy unto us, thou
Christ, Who is he that smote thee?
69 ¶Now Peter sat without in the pal-
ace: and a damsel came unto him,
saying, Thou also wast with Jesus of
Galilee.
70 But he denied before *them* all,
saying, I know not what thou sayest.
71 And when he was gone out into
the porch, another *maid* saw him, and
said unto them that were there, This
fellow was also with Jesus of Nazareth.
72 And again he denied with an oath,
I do not know the man.
73 And after a while came unto *him*
they that stood by, and said to Peter,
Surely thou also art *one* of them; for
thy speech bewrayeth thee.
74 Then began he to curse and to
swear, *saying*, I know not the man. And
immediately the cock crew.
75 And Peter remembered the word
of Jesus, which said unto him, Before
the cock crow, thou shalt deny me
thrice. And he went out, and wept bit-
terly.

CHAPTER 27

WHEN the morning was come, all the
chief priests and elders of the people
took counsel against Jesus to put him
to death:
2 And when they had bound him,
they led *him* away, and delivered him
to Pontius Pilate the governor.
3 ¶Then Judas, which had betrayed
him, when he saw that he was con-
demned, repented himself, and
brought again the thirty pieces of silver
to the chief priests and elders,
4 Saying, I have sinned in that I have
betrayed the innocent blood. And they
said, What *is that* to us? see thou *to
that*.
5 And he cast down the pieces of sil-
ver in the temple, and departed, and
went and hanged himself.
6 And the chief priests took the silver
pieces, and said, It is not lawful for to
put them into the treasury, because it is
the price of blood.
7 And they took counsel, and bought
with them the potter's field, to bury
strangers in.
8 Wherefore that field was called,
The field of blood, unto this day.
9 Then was fulfilled that which was
spoken by Jeremy the prophet, saying,
And they took the thirty pieces of sil-
ver, the price of him that was valued,
whom they of the children of Israel did
value;
10 And gave them for the potter's
field, as the Lord appointed me.
11 ¶And Jesus stood before the gov-
ernor: and the governor asked him,
saying, Art thou the King of the Jews?
And Jesus said unto him, Thou sayest.
12 And when he was accused of the
chief priests and elders, he answered
nothing.
13 Then said Pilate unto him, Hearest
thou not how many things they witness
against thee?
14 And he answered him to never a
word; insomuch that the governor mar-
velled greatly.
15 ¶Now at *that* feast the governor
was wont to release unto the people a
prisoner, whom they would.
16 And they had then a notable pris-
oner, called Ba-răb'bas.
17 Therefore when they were gath-
ered together, Pilate said unto them,
Whom will ye that I release unto you?
Ba-răb'bas, or Jesus which is called
Christ?
18 For he knew that for envy they had
delivered him.
19 ¶When he was set down on the
judgment seat, his wife sent unto him,
saying, Have thou nothing to do with
that just man: for I have suffered many
things this day in a dream because of
him.
20 But the chief priests and elders
persuaded the multitude that they
should ask Ba-răb'bas, and destroy Je-
sus.
21 The governor answered and said
unto them, Whether of the twain will
ye that I release unto you? They said,
Ba-răb'bas.
22 Pilate saith unto them, What shall
I do then with Jesus which is called
Christ? *They* all say unto him, Let him
be crucified.
23 And the governor said, Why, what
evil hath he done? But they cried out
the more, saying, Let him be crucified.

24 When Pilate saw that he could prevail nothing, but *that* rather a tumult was made, he took water, and washed *his* hands before the multitude, saying, I am innocent of the blood of this just person: see ye *to it*.
25 Then answered all the people, and said, His blood *be* on us, and on our children.
26 Then released he Ba-răb′bas unto them: and when he had scourged Jesus, he delivered *him* to be crucified.
27 ¶Then the soldiers of the governor took Jesus into the common hall, and gathered unto him the whole band *of soldiers*.
28 And they stripped him, and put on him a scarlet robe.
29 ¶And when they had platted a crown of thorns, they put *it* upon his head, and a reed in his right hand: and they bowed the knee before him, and mocked him, saying, Hail, King of the Jews!
30 And they spit upon him, and took the reed, and smote him on the head.
31 And after that they had mocked him, they took the robe off from him, and put his own raiment on him, and led him away to crucify *him*.
32 And as they came out, they found a man of Ċȳ-rē′ne, Simon by name: him they compelled to bear his cross.
33 And when they were come unto a place called Gŏl′go-tha, that is to say, a place of a skull,
34 They gave him vinegar to drink mingled with gall: and when he had tasted *thereof*, he would not drink.
35 And they crucified him, and parted his garments, casting lots: that it might be fulfilled which was spoken by the prophet, They parted my garments among them, and upon my vesture did they cast lots.
36 And sitting down they watched him there;
37 And set up over his head his accusation written, THIS IS JESUS THE KING OF THE JEWS.
38 Then were there two thieves crucified with him, one on the right hand, and another on the left.
39 ¶And they that passed by reviled him, wagging their heads,
40 And saying, Thou that destroyest the temple, and buildest *it* in three days, save thyself. If thou be the Son of God, come down from the cross.
41 Likewise also the chief priests mocking *him*, with the scribes and elders, said,
42 He saved others; himself he cannot save. If he be the King of Israel, let him now come down from the cross, and we will believe him.
43 He trusted in God; let him deliver him now, if he will have him: for he said, I am the Son of God.
44 The thieves also, which were crucified with him, cast the same in his teeth.
45 ¶Now from the sixth hour there was darkness over all the land unto the ninth hour.
46 And about the ninth hour Jesus cried with a loud voice, saying, Ē′lī, Ē′lī, lä′ma sa-bach′tha-ni? that is to say, My God, my God, why hast thou forsaken me?
47 Some of them that stood there, when they heard *that*, said, This *man* calleth for E-lī′as.
48 And straightway one of them ran, and took a spunge, and filled *it* with vinegar, and put *it* on a reed, and gave him to drink.
49 The rest said, Let be, let us see whether E-lī′as will come to save him.
50 ¶Jesus, when he had cried again with a loud voice, yielded up the ghost.
51 And, behold, the vail of the temple was rent in twain from the top to the bottom; and the earth did quake, and the rocks rent;
52 And the graves were opened; and many bodies of the saints which slept arose,
53 And came out of the graves after his resurrection, and went into the holy city, and appeared unto many.
54 Now when the centurion, and they that were with him, watching Jesus, saw the earthquake, and those things that were done, they feared greatly, saying, Truly this was the Son of God.
55 And many women were there beholding afar off, which followed Jesus from Galilee, ministering unto him:
56 Among which was Mary Magdalene, and Mary the mother of James and Joses, and the mother of Zĕb′e-dee's children.
57 ¶When the even was come, there came a rich man of Ăr-i-ma-thæ′a, named Joseph, who also himself was Jesus' disciple:
58 He went to Pilate, and begged the body of Jesus. Then Pilate commanded the body to be delivered.
59 And when Joseph had taken the body, he wrapped it in a clean linen cloth,
60 And laid it in his own new tomb, which he had hewn out in the rock: and he rolled a great stone to the door of the sepulchre, and departed.
61 And there was Mary Magdalene,

and the other Mary, sitting over against the sepulchre.
62 ¶Now the next day, that followed the day of the preparation, the chief priests and Pharisees came together unto Pilate,
63 Saying, Sir, we remember that that deceiver said, while he was yet alive, After three days I will rise again.
64 Command therefore that the sepulchre be made sure until the third day, lest his disciples come by night, and steal him away, and say unto the people, He is risen from the dead: so the last error shall be worse than the first.
65 Pilate said unto them, Ye have a watch: go your way, make *it* as sure as ye can.
66 So they went, and made the sepulchre sure, sealing the stone, and setting a watch.

CHAPTER 28

IN the end of the sabbath, as it began to dawn toward the first *day* of the week, came Mary Magdalene and the other Mary to see the sepulchre.
2 And, behold, there was a great earthquake: for the angel of the Lord descended from heaven, and came and rolled back the stone from the door, and sat upon it.
3 His countenance was like lightning, and his raiment white as snow:
4 And for fear of him the keepers did shake, and became as dead *men*.
5 And the angel answered and said unto the women, Fear not ye: for I know that ye seek Jesus, which was crucified.
6 He is not here: for he is risen, as he said. Come, see the place where the Lord lay.
7 And go quickly, and tell his disciples that he is risen from the dead; and, behold, he goeth before you into Galilee; there shall ye see him: lo, I have told you.
8 And they departed quickly from the sepulchre with fear and great joy; and did run to bring his disciples word.
9 ¶And as they went to tell his disciples, behold, Jesus met them, saying, All hail. And they came and held him by the feet, and worshipped him.
10 Then said Jesus unto them, Be not afraid: go tell my brethren that they go into Galilee, and there shall they see me.
11 ¶Now when they were going, behold, some of the watch came into the city, and shewed unto the chief priests all the things that were done.
12 And when they were assembled with the elders, and had taken counsel, they gave large money unto the soldiers,
13 Saying, Say ye, His disciples came by night, and stole him *away* while we slept.
14 And if this come to the governor's ears, we will persuade him, and secure you.
15 So they took the money, and did as they were taught: and this saying is commonly reported among the Jews until this day.
16 ¶Then the eleven disciples went away into Galilee, into a mountain where Jesus had appointed them.
17 And when they saw him, they worshipped him: but some doubted.
18 And Jesus came and spake unto them, saying, All power is given unto me in heaven and in earth.
19 Go ye therefore, and teach all nations, baptizing them in the name of the Father, and of the Son, and of the Holy Ghost:
20 Teaching them to observe all things whatsoever I have commanded you: and, lo, I am with you alway, *even* unto the end of the world. Amen.

THE GOSPEL ACCORDING TO

SAINT MARK

CHAPTER 1

THE beginning of the gospel of Jesus Christ, the Son of God;
2 As it is written in the prophets, Behold, I send my messenger before thy face, which shall prepare thy way before thee.
3 The voice of one crying in the wilderness, Prepare ye the way of the Lord, make his paths straight.
4 John did baptize in the wilderness, and preach the baptism of repentance for the remission of sins.
5 And there went out unto him all the land of Judæa, and they of Jerusalem, and were all baptized of him in the river of Jordan, confessing their sins.
6 And John was clothed with camel's hair, and with a girdle of a skin about his loins; and he did eat locusts and wild honey;
7 And preached, saying, There cometh one mightier than I after me,

the latchet of whose shoes I am not
worthy to stoop down and unloose.
8 I indeed have baptized you with
water: but he shall baptize you with the
Holy Ghost.
9 ¶And it came to pass in those days,
that Jesus came from Nazareth of Gali-
lee, and was baptized of John in Jor-
dan.
10 And straightway coming up out of
the water, he saw the heavens opened,
and the Spirit like a dove descending
upon him:
11 And there came a voice from
heaven, *saying*, Thou art my beloved
Son, in whom I am well pleased.
12 ¶And immediately the spirit driv-
eth him into the wilderness.
13 And he was there in the wilder-
ness forty days, tempted of Satan; and
was with the wild beasts; and the an-
gels ministered unto him.
14 ¶Now after that John was put in
prison, Jesus came into Galilee,
preaching the gospel of the kingdom of
God,
15 And saying, The time is fulfilled,
and the kingdom of God is at hand: re-
pent ye, and believe the gospel.
16 ¶Now as he walked by the sea of
Galilee, he saw Simon and Andrew his
brother casting a net into the sea: for
they were fishers.
17 And Jesus said unto them, Come
ye after me, and I will make you to be-
come fishers of men.
18 And straightway they forsook
their nets, and followed him.
19 And when he had gone a little far-
ther thence, he saw James the *son* of
Zĕb′e-dee, and John his brother, who
also were in the ship mending their
nets.
20 And straightway he called them:
and they left their father Zĕb′e-dee in
the ship with the hired servants, and
went after him.
21 And they went into Ca-per′na-um;
and straightway on the sabbath day he
entered into the synagogue, and
taught.
22 And they were astonished at his
doctrine: for he taught them as one that
had authority, and not as the scribes.
23 And there was in their synagogue
a man with an unclean spirit; and he
cried out,
24 Saying, Let *us* alone; what have
we to do with thee, thou Jesus of Naza-
reth? art thou come to destroy us? I
know thee who thou art, the Holy One
of God.
25 And Jesus rebuked him, saying,
Hold thy peace, and come out of him.
26 And when the unclean spirit had
torn him, and cried with a loud voice,
he came out of him.
27 And they were all amazed, inso-
much that they questioned among
themselves, saying, What thing is this?
what new doctrine *is* this? for with au-
thority commandeth he even the un-
clean spirits, and they do obey him.
28 And immediately his fame spread
abroad throughout all the region round
about Galilee.
29 ¶And forthwith, when they were
come out of the synagogue, they en-
tered into the house of Simon and
Andrew, with James and John.
30 But Simon's wife's mother lay sick
of a fever, and anon they tell him of her.
31 And he came and took her by the
hand, and lifted her up; and immediate-
ly the fever left her, and she minis-
tered unto them.
32 ¶And at even, when the sun did
set, they brought unto him all that were
diseased, and them that were pos-
sessed with devils.
33 And all the city was gathered to-
gether at the door.
34 And he healed many that were
sick of divers diseases, and cast out
many devils; and suffered not the dev-
ils to speak, because they knew him.
35 ¶And in the morning, rising up a
great while before day, he went out,
and departed into a solitary place, and
there prayed.
36 And Simon and they that were
with him followed after him.
37 And when they had found him,
they said unto him, All *men* seek for
thee.
38 And he said unto them, Let us go
into the next towns, that I may preach
there also: for therefore came I forth.
39 And he preached in their syna-
gogues throughout all Galilee, and cast
out devils.
40 ¶And there came a leper to him,
beseeching him, and kneeling down to
him, and saying unto him, If thou wilt,
thou canst make me clean.
41 And Jesus, moved with compas-
sion, put forth *his* hand, and touched
him, and saith unto him, I will; be thou
clean.
42 And as soon as he had spoken, im-
mediately the leprosy departed from
him, and he was cleansed.
43 And he straitly charged him, and
forthwith sent him away;
44 And saith unto him, See thou say
nothing to any man: but go thy way,
shew thyself to the priest, and offer for
thy cleansing those things which
Moses commanded, for a testimony
unto them.

45 But he went out, and began to pub-
lish *it* much, and to blaze abroad the
matter, insomuch that Jesus could no
more openly enter into the city, but was
without in desert places: and they
came to him from every quarter.

CHAPTER 2

AND again he entered into Ca-per'na-
um after *some* days; and it was noised
that he was in the house.
2 And straightway many were gath-
ered together, insomuch that there
was no room to receive *them*, no, not so
much as about the door: and he
preached the word unto them.
3 And they come unto him, bringing
one sick of the palsy, which was borne
of four.
4 And when they could not come nigh
unto him for the press, they uncovered
the roof where he was: and when they
had broken *it* up, they let down the bed
wherein the sick of the palsy lay.
5 When Jesus saw their faith, he said
unto the sick of the palsy, Son, thy sins
be forgiven thee.
6 But there were certain of the
scribes sitting there, and reasoning in
their hearts,
7 Why doth this *man* thus speak
blasphemies? who can forgive sins but
God only?
8 And immediately when Jesus per-
ceived in his spirit that they so rea-
soned within themselves, he said unto
them, Why reason ye these things in
your hearts?
9 Whether is it easier to say to the
sick of the palsy, *Thy* sins be forgiven
thee; or to say, Arise, and take up thy
bed, and walk?
10 But that ye may know that the Son
of man hath power on earth to forgive
sins, (he saith to the sick of the palsy,)
11 I say unto thee, Arise, and take up
thy bed, and go thy way into thine
house.
12 And immediately he arose, took
up the bed, and went forth before them
all; insomuch that they were all
amazed, and glorified God, saying, We
never saw it on this fashion.
13 ¶And he went forth again by the
sea side; and all the multitude resorted
unto him, and he taught them.
14 And as he passed by, he saw Levi
the *son* of Ăl-phæ'us sitting at the re-
ceipt of custom, and said unto him, Fol-
low me. And he arose and followed
him.
15 And it came to pass, that, as Jesus
sat at meat in his house, many publi-
cans and sinners sat also together with
Jesus and his disciples: for there were
many, and they followed him.
16 And when the scribes and
Pharisees saw him eat with publicans
and sinners, they said unto his dis-
ciples, How is it that he eateth and drink-
eth with publicans and sinners?
17 When Jesus heard *it*, he saith unto
them, They that are whole have no
need of the physician, but they that are
sick: I came not to call the righteous,
but sinners to repentance.
18 ¶And the disciples of John and of
the Pharisees used to fast: and they
come and say unto him, Why do the
disciples of John and of the Pharisees
fast, but thy disciples fast not?
19 And Jesus said unto them, Can the
children of the bridechamber fast,
while the bridegroom is with them? as
long as they have the bridegroom with
them, they cannot fast.
20 But the days will come, when the
bridegroom shall be taken away from
them, and then shall they fast in those
days.
21 No man also seweth a piece of new
cloth on an old garment: else the new
piece that filled it up taketh away from
the old, and the rent is made worse.
22 And no man putteth new wine into
old bottles: else the new wine doth
burst the bottles, and the wine is
spilled, and the bottles will be marred:
but new wine must be put into new
bottles.
23 ¶And it came to pass, that he went
through the corn fields on the sabbath
day; and his disciples began, as they
went, to pluck the ears of corn.
24 And the Pharisees said unto him,
Behold, why do they on the sabbath
day that which is not lawful?
25 And he said unto them, Have ye
never read what David did, when he
had need, and was an hungred, he, and
they that were with him?
26 How he went into the house of
God in the days of Ā-bī'a-thar the high
priest, and did eat the shewbread,
which is not lawful to eat but for the
priests, and gave also to them which
were with him?
27 And he said unto them, The sab-
bath was made for man, and not man
for the sabbath:
28 Therefore the Son of man is Lord
also of the sabbath.

CHAPTER 3

AND he entered again into the syna-
gogue; and there was a man there
which had a withered hand.
2 And they watched him, whether he

would heal him on the sabbath day;
that they might accuse him.
3 And he saith unto the man which
had the withered hand, Stand forth.
4 And he saith unto them, Is it lawful
to do good on the sabbath days, or to do
evil? to save life, or to kill? But they
held their peace.
5 And when he had looked round
about on them with anger, being
grieved for the hardness of their hearts,
he saith unto the man, Stretch forth
thine hand. And he stretched *it* out: and
his hand was restored whole as the
other.
6 And the Pharisees went forth, and
straightway took counsel with the He-
rō′di-ans against him, how they might
destroy him.
7 ¶But Jesus withdrew himself with
his disciples to the sea: and a great mul-
titude from Galilee followed him, and
from Judæa,
8 And from Jerusalem, and from Ī-
dū-mæ′a, and *from* beyond Jordan; and
they about Tyre and Sī′don, a great
multitude, when they had heard what
great things he did, came unto him.
9 And he spake to his disciples, that a
small ship should wait on him because
of the multitude, lest they should
throng him.
10 For he had healed many; inso-
much that they pressed upon him for to
touch him, as many as had plagues.
11 And unclean spirits, when they
saw him, fell down before him, and
cried, saying, Thou art the Son of God.
12 And he straitly charged them that
they should not make him known.
13 ¶And he goeth up into a mountain,
and calleth *unto him* whom he would:
and they came unto him.
14 And he ordained twelve, that they
should be with him, and that he might
send them forth to preach,
15 And to have power to heal sick-
nesses, and to cast out devils:
16 And Simon he surnamed Peter;
17 And James the *son* of Zĕb′e-dee,
and John the brother of James; and he
surnamed them Bō-a-ner′ġēs, which is,
The sons of thunder:
18 And Andrew, and Philip, and Bar-
tholomew, and Matthew, and Thomas,
and James the *son* of Ăl-phæ′us, and
Thăd-dæ′us, and Simon the Canaanite,
19 And Judas Iscariot, which also
betrayed him: and they went into an
house.
20 ¶And the multitude cometh togeth-
er again, so that they could not so
much as eat bread.
21 And when his friends heard *of it*,
they went out to lay hold on him: for
they said, He is beside himself.
22 ¶And the scribes which came
down from Jerusalem said, He hath Bē-
ĕl′ze-bŭb, and by the prince of the dev-
ils casteth he out devils.
23 And he called them *unto him*, and
said unto them in parables, How can
Satan cast out Satan?
24 And if a kingdom be divided
against itself, that kingdom cannot
stand.
25 And if a house be divided against
itself, that house cannot stand.
26 And if Satan rise up against him-
self, and be divided, he cannot stand,
but hath an end.
27 No man can enter into a strong
man's house, and spoil his goods, ex-
cept he will first bind the strong man;
and then he will spoil his house.
28 Verily I say unto you, All sins shall
be forgiven unto the sons of men, and
blasphemies wherewith soever they
shall blaspheme:
29 But he that shall blaspheme
against the Holy Ghost hath never for-
giveness, but is in danger of eternal
damnation:
30 Because they said, He hath an un-
clean spirit.
31 ¶There came then his brethren and
his mother, and, standing without, sent
unto him, calling him.
32 And the multitude sat about him,
and they said unto him, Behold, thy
mother and thy brethren without seek
for thee.
33 And he answered them, saying,
Who is my mother, or my brethren?
34 And he looked round about on
them which sat about him, and said,
Behold my mother and my brethren!
35 For whosoever shall do the will of
God, the same is my brother, and my
sister, and mother.

CHAPTER 4

AND he began again to teach by the sea
side: and there was gathered unto him
a great multitude, so that he entered
into a ship, and sat in the sea; and the
whole multitude was by the sea on the
land.
2 And he taught them many things by
parables, and said unto them in his
doctrine,
3 Hearken; Behold, there went out a
sower to sow:
4 And it came to pass, as he sowed,
some fell by the way side, and the fowls
of the air came and devoured it up.
5 And some fell on stony ground,
where it had not much earth; and im-

mediately it sprang up, because it had
no depth of earth:
6 But when the sun was up, it was
scorched; and because it had no root, it
withered away.
7 And some fell among thorns, and
the thorns grew up, and choked it, and
it yielded no fruit.
8 And other fell on good ground, and
did yield fruit that sprang up and in-
creased; and brought forth, some
thirty, and some sixty, and some an
hundred.
9 **And he said unto them,** He that hath
ears to hear, let him hear.
10 ¶**And when he was alone, they that
were about him with the twelve asked
of him the parable.**
11 **And he said unto them,** Unto you it
is given to know the mystery of the
kingdom of God: but unto them that
are without, all *these* things are done in
parables:
12 That seeing they may see, and not
perceive; and hearing they may hear,
and not understand; lest at any time
they should be converted, and *their*
sins should be forgiven them.
13 **And he said unto them,** Know ye
not this parable? and how then will ye
know all parables?
14 ¶The sower soweth the word.
15 And these are they by the way
side, where the word is sown; but when
they have heard, Satan cometh imme-
diately, and taketh away the word that
was sown in their hearts.
16 And these are they likewise which
are sown on stony ground; who, when
they have heard the word, immediately
receive it with gladness;
17 And have no root in themselves,
and so endure but for a time: after-
ward, when affliction or persecution
ariseth for the word's sake, immediate-
ly they are offended.
18 And these are they which are
sown among thorns; such as hear the
word,
19 And the cares of this world, and
the deceitfulness of riches, and the
lusts of other things entering in, choke
the word, and it becometh unfruitful.
20 And these are they which are
sown on good ground; such as hear the
word, and receive *it*, and bring forth
fruit, some thirtyfold, some sixty, and
some an hundred.
21 ¶**And he said unto them,** Is a
candle brought to be put under a
bushel, or under a bed? and not to be
set on a candlestick?
22 For there is nothing hid, which
shall not be manifested; neither was
any thing kept secret, but that it should
come abroad.
23 If any man have ears to hear, let
him hear.
24 **And he said unto them,** Take heed
what ye hear: with what measure ye
mete, it shall be measured to you: and
unto you that hear shall more be given.
25 For he that hath, to him shall be
given: and he that hath not, from him
shall be taken even that which he hath.
26 ¶**And he said,** So is the kingdom of
God, as if a man should cast seed into
the ground;
27 And should sleep, and rise night
and day, and the seed should spring
and grow up, he knoweth not how.
28 For the earth bringeth forth fruit
of herself; first the blade, then the ear,
after that the full corn in the ear.
29 But when the fruit is brought
forth, immediately he putteth in the
sickle, because the harvest is come.
30 ¶**And he said,** Whereunto shall we
liken the kingdom of God? or with what
comparison shall we compare it?
31 *It is* like a grain of mustard seed,
which, when it is sown in the earth, is
less than all the seeds that be in the
earth:
32 But when it is sown, it groweth up,
and becometh greater than all herbs,
and shooteth out great branches; so
that the fowls of the air may lodge un-
der the shadow of it.
33 **And with many such parables
spake he the word unto them, as they
were able to hear *it*.
34 But without a parable spake he not
unto them: and when they were alone,
he expounded all things to his dis-
ciples.
35 ¶And the same day, when the even
was come, he saith unto them,** Let us
pass over unto the other side.
36 **And when they had sent away the
multitude, they took him even as he
was in the ship. And there were also
with him other little ships.
37 And there arose a great storm of
wind, and the waves beat into the ship,
so that it was now full.
38 And he was in the hinder part of
the ship, asleep on a pillow: and they
awake him, and say unto him, Master,
carest thou not that we perish?
39 And he arose, and rebuked the
wind, and said unto the sea,** Peace, be
still. **And the wind ceased, and there
was a great calm.
40 And he said unto them,** Why are
ye so fearful? how is it that ye have no
faith?
41 **And they feared exceedingly, and
said one to another, What manner of**

man is this, that even the wind and the sea obey him?

CHAPTER 5

AND they came over unto the other side of the sea, into the country of the Găd′a-rēneṡ.

2 And when he was come out of the ship, immediately there met him out of the tombs a man with an unclean spirit,

3 Who had *his* dwelling among the tombs; and no man could bind him, no, not with chains:

4 Because that he had been often bound with fetters and chains, and the chains had been plucked asunder by him, and the fetters broken in pieces: neither could any *man* tame him.

5 And always, night and day, he was in the mountains, and in the tombs, crying, and cutting himself with stones.

6 But when he saw Jesus afar off, he ran and worshipped him,

7 And cried with a loud voice, and said, What have I to do with thee, Jesus, *thou* Son of the most high God? I adjure thee by God, that thou torment me not.

8 For he said unto him, Come out of the man, *thou* unclean spirit.

9 And he asked him, What *is* thy name? And he answered, saying, My name *is* Legion: for we are many.

10 And he besought him much that he would not send them away out of the country.

11 Now there was there nigh unto the mountains a great herd of swine feeding.

12 And all the devils besought him, saying, Send us into the swine, that we may enter into them.

13 And forthwith Jesus gave them leave. And the unclean spirits went out, and entered into the swine: and the herd ran violently down a steep place into the sea, (they were about two thousand;) and were choked in the sea.

14 And they that fed the swine fled, and told *it* in the city, and in the country. And they went out to see what it was that was done.

15 And they come to Jesus, and see him that was possessed with the devil, and had the legion, sitting, and clothed, and in his right mind: and they were afraid.

16 And they that saw *it* told them how it befell to him that was possessed with the devil, and *also* concerning the swine.

17 And they began to pray him to depart out of their coasts.

18 And when he was come into the ship, he that had been possessed with the devil prayed him that he might be with him.

19 Howbeit Jesus suffered him not, but saith unto him, Go home to thy friends, and tell them how great things the Lord hath done for thee, and hath had compassion on thee.

20 And he departed, and began to publish in De-căp′o-lĭs how great things Jesus had done for him: and all *men* did marvel.

21 ¶And when Jesus was passed over again by ship unto the other side, much people gathered unto him: and he was nigh unto the sea.

22 And, behold, there cometh one of the rulers of the synagogue, Jā-ī′rus by name; and when he saw him, he fell at his feet,

23 And besought him greatly, saying, My little daughter lieth at the point of death: *I pray thee,* come and lay thy hands on her, that she may be healed; and she shall live.

24 And *Jesus* went with him; and much people followed him, and thronged him.

25 ¶And a certain woman, which had an issue of blood twelve years,

26 And had suffered many things of many physicians, and had spent all that she had, and was nothing bettered, but rather grew worse,

27 When she had heard of Jesus, came in the press behind, and touched his garment.

28 For she said, If I may touch but his clothes, I shall be whole.

29 And straightway the fountain of her blood was dried up; and she felt in *her* body that she was healed of that plague.

30 And Jesus, immediately knowing in himself that virtue had gone out of him, turned him about in the press, and said, Who touched my clothes?

31 And his disciples said unto him, Thou seest the multitude thronging thee, and sayest thou, Who touched me?

32 And he looked round about to see her that had done this thing.

33 But the woman fearing and trembling, knowing what was done in her, came and fell down before him, and told him all the truth.

34 And he said unto her, Daughter, thy faith hath made thee whole; go in peace, and be whole of thy plague.

35 ¶While he yet spake, there came from the ruler of the synagogue's *house certain* which said, Thy daughter is dead: why troublest thou the Master any further?

36 As soon as Jesus heard the word
that was spoken, he saith unto the ruler
of the synagogue, Be not afraid, only
believe.
37 And he suffered no man to follow
him, save Peter, and James, and John
the brother of James.
38 And he cometh to the house of the
ruler of the synagogue, and seeth the
tumult, and them that wept and wailed
greatly.
39 And when he was come in, he saith
unto them, Why make ye this ado, and
weep? the damsel is not dead, but
sleepeth.
40 And they laughed him to scorn.
But when he had put them all out, he
taketh the father and the mother of the
damsel, and them that were with him,
and entereth in where the damsel was
lying.
41 And he took the damsel by the
hand, and said unto her, Tăl′i-tha cū′mī;
which is, being interpreted, Damsel, I
say unto thee, arise.
42 And straightway the damsel
arose, and walked; for she was *of the
age* of twelve years. And they were as-
tonished with a great astonishment.
43 And he charged them straitly that
no man should know it; and com-
manded that something should be giv-
en her to eat.

CHAPTER 6

AND he went out from thence, and
came into his own country; and his dis-
ciples follow him.
2 And when the sabbath day was
come, he began to teach in the syna-
gogue: and many hearing *him* were as-
tonished, saying, From whence hath
this *man* these things? and what wis-
dom *is* this which is given unto him,
that even such mighty works are
wrought by his hands?
3 Is not this the carpenter, the son of
Mary, the brother of James, and Joses,
and of Juda, and Simon? and are not his
sisters here with us? And they were of-
fended at him.
4 But Jesus said unto them, A
prophet is not without honour, but in
his own country, and among his own
kin, and in his own house.
5 And he could there do no mighty
work, save that he laid his hands upon a
few sick folk, and healed *them*.
6 And he marvelled because of their
unbelief. And he went round about the
villages, teaching.
7 ¶And he called *unto him* the twelve,
and began to send them forth by two
and two; and gave them power over
unclean spirits;
8 And commanded them that they
should take nothing for *their* journey,
save a staff only; no scrip, no bread, no
money in *their* purse:
9 But *be* shod with sandals; and not
put on two coats.
10 And he said unto them, In what
place soever ye enter into an house,
there abide till ye depart from that
place.
11 And whosoever shall not receive
you, nor hear you, when ye depart
thence, shake off the dust under your
feet for a testimony against them.
Verily I say unto you, It shall be more
tolerable for Sodom and Go-mŏr′rha in
the day of judgment, than for that city.
12 And they went out, and preached
that men should repent.
13 And they cast out many devils,
and anointed with oil many that were
sick, and healed *them*.
14 ¶And king Herod heard *of him;*
(for his name was spread abroad:) and
he said, That John the Baptist was risen
from the dead, and therefore mighty
works do shew forth themselves in
him.
15 Others said, That it is E-lī′as. And
others said, That it is a prophet, or as
one of the prophets.
16 But when Herod heard *thereof*, he
said, It is John, whom I beheaded: he is
risen from the dead.
17 For Herod himself had sent forth
and laid hold upon John, and bound
him in prison for He-rō′dĭ-as' sake, his
brother Philip's wife: for he had
married her.
18 For John had said unto Herod, It is
not lawful for thee to have thy broth-
er's wife.
19 Therefore He-rō′dĭ-as had a quar-
rel against him, and would have killed
him; but she could not:
20 For Herod feared John, knowing
that he was a just man and an holy, and
observed him; and when he heard him,
he did many things, and heard him
gladly.
21 And when a convenient day was
come, that Herod on his birthday made
a supper to his lords, high captains, and
chief *estates* of Galilee;
22 And when the daughter of the said
He-rō′dĭ-as came in, and danced, and
pleased Herod and them that sat with
him, the king said unto the damsel, Ask
of me whatsoever thou wilt, and I will
give *it* thee.
23 And he sware unto her, Whatsoever
thou shalt ask of me, I will give *it*
thee, unto the half of my kingdom.
24 And she went forth, and said unto

her mother, What shall I ask? And she said, The head of John the Baptist.

25 And she came in straightway with haste unto the king, and asked, saying, I will that thou give me by and by in a charger the head of John the Baptist.

26 And the king was exceeding sorry; *yet* for his oath's sake, and for their sakes which sat with him, he would not reject her.

27 And immediately the king sent an executioner, and commanded his head to be brought: and he went and beheaded him in the prison.

28 And brought his head in a charger, and gave it to the damsel: and the damsel gave it to her mother.

29 And when his disciples heard *of it*, they came and took up his corpse, and laid it in a tomb.

30 ¶And the apostles gathered themselves together unto Jesus, and told him all things, both what they had done, and what they had taught.

31 And he said unto them, Come ye yourselves apart into a desert place, and rest a while: for there were many coming and going, and they had no leisure so much as to eat.

32 And they departed into a desert place by ship privately.

33 And the people saw them departing, and many knew him, and ran afoot thither out of all cities, and outwent them, and came together unto him.

34 And Jesus, when he came out, saw much people, and was moved with compassion toward them, because they were as sheep not having a shepherd: and he began to teach them many things.

35 And when the day was now far spent, his disciples came unto him, and said, This is a desert place, and now the time *is* far passed:

36 Send them away, that they may go into the country round about, and into the villages, and buy themselves bread: for they have nothing to eat.

37 He answered and said unto them, Give ye them to eat. And they say unto him, Shall we go and buy two hundred pennyworth of bread, and give them to eat?

38 He saith unto them, How many loaves have ye? go and see. And when they knew, they say, Five, and two fishes.

39 And he commanded them to make all sit down by companies upon the green grass.

40 And they sat down in ranks, by hundreds, and by fifties.

41 And when he had taken the five loaves and the two fishes, he looked up to heaven, and blessed, and brake the loaves, and gave *them* to his disciples to set before them; and the two fishes divided he among them all.

42 And they did all eat, and were filled.

43 And they took up twelve baskets full of the fragments, and of the fishes.

44 And they that did eat of the loaves were about five thousand men.

45 ¶And straightway he constrained his disciples to get into the ship, and to go to the other side before unto Bĕth-sā'i-da, while he sent away the people.

46 And when he had sent them away, he departed into a mountain to pray.

47 And when even was come, the ship was in the midst of the sea, and he alone on the land.

48 And he saw them toiling in rowing; for the wind was contrary unto them: and about the fourth watch of the night he cometh unto them, walking upon the sea, and would have passed by them.

49 But when they saw him walking upon the sea, they supposed it had been a spirit, and cried out:

50 For they all saw him, and were troubled. And immediately he talked with them, and saith unto them, Be of good cheer: it is I; be not afraid.

51 And he went up unto them into the ship; and the wind ceased: and they were sore amazed in themselves beyond measure, and wondered.

52 For they considered not *the miracle* of the loaves: for their heart was hardened.

53 And when they had passed over, they came into the land of Gĕn-nĕs'a-ret, and drew to the shore.

54 And when they were come out of the ship, straightway they knew him,

55 And ran through that whole region round about, and began to carry about in beds those that were sick, where they heard he was.

56 And whithersoever he entered, into villages, or cities, or country, they laid the sick in the streets, and besought him that they might touch if it were but the border of his garment: and as many as touched him were made whole.

CHAPTER 7

THEN came together unto him the Pharisees, and certain of the scribes, which came from Jerusalem.

2 And when they saw some of his disciples eat bread with defiled, that is to say, with unwashen, hands, they found fault.

3 For the Pharisees, and all the Jews,
except they wash *their* hands oft, eat
not, holding the tradition of the elders.
4 And *when they come* from the mar-
ket, except they wash, they eat not.
And many other things there be, which
they have received to hold, *as* the
washing of cups, and pots, brasen ves-
sels, and of tables.
5 Then the Pharisees and scribes
asked him, Why walk not thy disciples
according to the tradition of the elders,
but eat bread with unwashen hands?
6 He answered and said unto them,
Well hath E-ṡā'ias prophesied of you
hypocrites, as it is written, This people
honoureth me with *their* lips, but their
heart is far from me.
7 Howbeit in vain do they worship
me, teaching *for* doctrines the com-
mandments of men.
8 For laying aside the commandment
of God, ye hold the tradition of men, *as*
the washing of pots and cups: and
many other such like things ye do.
9 And he said unto them, Full well ye
reject the commandment of God, that
ye may keep your own tradition.
10 For Moses said, Honour thy father
and thy mother; and, Whoso curseth
father or mother, let him die the death:
11 But ye say, If a man shall say to his
father or mother, *It is* Corban, that is to
say, a gift, by whatsoever thou
mightest be profited by me; *he shall be
free.*
12 And ye suffer him no more to do
ought for his father or his mother;
13 Making the word of God of none
effect through your tradition, which ye
have delivered: and many such like
things do ye.
14 ¶And when he had called all the
people *unto him,* he said unto them,
Hearken unto me every one *of you,* and
understand:
15 There is nothing from without a
man, that entering into him can defile
him: but the things which come out of
him, those are they that defile the man.
16 If any man have ears to hear, let
him hear.
17 And when he was entered into the
house from the people, his disciples
asked him concerning the parable.
18 And he saith unto them, Are ye so
without understanding also? Do ye not
perceive, that whatsoever thing from
without entereth into the man, *it* can-
not defile him;
19 Because it entereth not into his
heart, but into the belly, and goeth out
into the draught, purging all meats?
20 And he said, That which cometh
out of the man, that defileth the man.
21 For from within, out of the heart of
men, proceed evil thoughts, adulteries,
fornications, murders,
22 Thefts, covetousness, wickedness,
deceit, lasciviousness, an evil eye,
blasphemy, pride, foolishness:
23 All these evil things come from
within, and defile the man.
24 ¶And from thence he arose, and
went into the borders of Tyre and Sī'-
don, and entered into an house, and
would have no man know *it,* but he
could not be hid.
25 For a *certain* woman, whose
young daughter had an unclean spirit,
heard of him, and came and fell at his
feet:
26 The woman was a Greek, a Sȳ-rō-
phe-nī'cian by nation; and she be-
sought him that he would cast forth the
devil out of her daughter.
27 But Jesus said unto her, Let the
children first be filled: for it is not meet
to take the children's bread, and to cast
it unto the dogs.
28 And she answered and said unto
him, Yes, Lord: yet the dogs under the
table eat of the children's crumbs.
29 And he said unto her, For this
saying go thy way; the devil is gone out
of thy daughter.
30 And when she was come to her
house, she found the devil gone out,
and her daughter laid upon the bed.
31 ¶And again, departing from the
coasts of Tyre and Sī'don, he came unto
the sea of Galilee, through the midst of
the coasts of De-căp'o-lĭs.
32 And they bring unto him one that
was deaf, and had an impediment in his
speech; and they beseech him to put his
hand upon him.
33 And he took him aside from the
multitude, and put his fingers into his
ears, and he spit, and touched his
tongue;
34 And looking up to heaven, he
sighed, and saith unto him, Eph'pha-
tha, that is, Be opened.
35 And straightway his ears were
opened, and the string of his tongue was
loosed, and he spake plain.
36 And he charged them that they
should tell no man: but the more he
charged them, so much the more a
great deal they published *it;*
37 And were beyond measure aston-
ished, saying, He hath done all things
well: he maketh both the deaf to hear,
and the dumb to speak.

CHAPTER 8

IN those days the multitude being very
great, and having nothing to eat, Jesus

called his disciples *unto him,* and saith
unto them,
2 I have compassion on the multi-
tude, because they have now been with
me three days, and have nothing to eat:
3 And if I send them away fasting to
their own houses, they will faint by the
way: for divers of them came from far.
4 And his disciples answered him,
From whence can a man satisfy these
men with bread here in the wilderness?
5 And he asked them, How many
loaves have ye? And they said, Seven.
6 And he commanded the people to
sit down on the ground: and he took the
seven loaves, and gave thanks, and
brake, and gave to his disciples to set
before *them;* and they did set *them* be-
fore the people.
7 And they had a few small fishes:
and he blessed, and commanded to set
them also before *them.*
8 So they did eat, and were filled: and
they took up of the broken *meat* that
was left seven baskets.
9 And they that had eaten were about
four thousand: and he sent them away.
10 ¶And straightway he entered into
a ship with his disciples, and came into
the parts of Dăl-ma-nū'tha.
11 And the Pharisees came forth, and
began to question with him, seeking of
him a sign from heaven, tempting him.
12 And he sighed deeply in his spirit,
and saith, Why doth this generation
seek after a sign? verily I say unto you,
There shall no sign be given unto this
generation.
13 And he left them, and entering
into the ship again departed to the
other side.
14 ¶Now *the disciples* had forgotten
to take bread, neither had they in the
ship with them more than one loaf.
15 And he charged them, saying,
Take heed, beware of the leaven of the
Pharisees, and *of* the leaven of Herod.
16 And they reasoned among them-
selves, saying, *It is* because we have no
bread.
17 And when Jesus knew *it,* he saith
unto them, Why reason ye, because ye
have no bread? perceive ye not yet,
neither understand? have ye your heart
yet hardened?
18 Having eyes, see ye not? and hav-
ing ears, hear ye not? and do ye not
remember?
19 When I brake the five loaves
among five thousand, how many
baskets full of fragments took ye up?
They say unto him, Twelve.
20 And when the seven among four
thousand, how many baskets full of
fragments took ye up? And they said,
Seven.
21 And he said unto them, How is it
that ye do not understand?
22 ¶And he cometh to Bĕth-sā'i-da:
and they bring a blind man unto him,
and besought him to touch him.
23 And he took the blind man by the
hand, and led him out of the town; and
when he had spit on his eyes, and put
his hands upon him, he asked him if he
saw ought.
24 And he looked up, and said, I see
men as trees, walking.
25 After that he put *his* hands again
upon his eyes, and made him look up:
and he was restored, and saw every
man clearly.
26 And he sent him away to his
house, saying, Neither go into the
town, nor tell *it* to any in the town.
27 ¶And Jesus went out, and his dis-
ciples, into the towns of Cæs-a-re'a
Phĭ-lip'pī: and by the way he asked his
disciples, saying unto them, Whom do
men say that I am?
28 And they answered, John the Bap-
tist: but some *say,* E-lī'as; and others,
One of the prophets.
29 And he saith unto them, But whom
say ye that I am? And Peter answereth
and saith unto him, Thou art the Christ.
30 And he charged them that they
should tell no man of him.
31 ¶And he began to teach them, that
the Son of man must suffer many
things, and be rejected of the elders,
and *of* the chief priests, and scribes,
and be killed, and after three days rise
again.
32 And he spake that saying openly.
And Peter took him, and began to re-
buke him.
33 But when he had turned about and
looked on his disciples, he rebuked Pe-
ter, saying, Get thee behind me, Satan:
for thou savourest not the things that
be of God, but the things that be of
men.
34 ¶And when he had called the
people *unto him* with his disciples also,
he said unto them, Whosoever will
come after me, let him deny himself,
and take up his cross, and follow me.
35 For whosoever will save his life
shall lose it; but whosoever shall lose
his life for my sake and the gospel's, the
same shall save it.
36 For what shall it profit a man, if he
shall gain the whole world, and lose his
own soul?
37 Or what shall a man give in ex-
change for his soul?
38 Whosoever therefore shall be
ashamed of me and of my words in this

adulterous and sinful generation; of him also shall the Son of man be ashamed, when he cometh in the glory of his Father with the holy angels.

CHAPTER 9

AND he said unto them, Verily I say unto you, That there be some of them that stand here, which shall not taste of death, till they have seen the kingdom of God come with power.

2 ¶And after six days Jesus taketh *with him* Peter, and James, and John, and leadeth them up into an high mountain apart by themselves: and he was transfigured before them.

3 And his raiment became shining, exceeding white as snow; so as no fuller on earth can white them.

4 And there appeared unto them E-lī'-as with Moses: and they were talking with Jesus.

5 And Peter answered and said to Jesus, Master, it is good for us to be here: and let us make three tabernacles; one for thee, and one for Moses, and one for E-lī'as.

6 For he wist not what to say; for they were sore afraid.

7 And there was a cloud that overshadowed them: and a voice came out of the cloud, saying, This is my beloved Son: hear him.

8 And suddenly, when they had looked round about, they saw no man any more, save Jesus only with themselves.

9 And as they came down from the mountain, he charged them that they should tell no man what things they had seen, till the Son of man were risen from the dead.

10 And they kept that saying with themselves, questioning one with another what the rising from the dead should mean.

11 ¶And they asked him, saying, Why say the scribes that E-lī'as must first come?

12 And he answered and told them, E-lī'as verily cometh first, and restoreth all things; and how it is written of the Son of man, that he must suffer many things, and be set at nought.

13 But I say unto you, That E-lī'as is indeed come, and they have done unto him whatsoever they listed, as it is written of him.

14 ¶And when he came to *his* disciples, he saw a great multitude about them, and the scribes questioning with them.

15 And straightway all the people, when they beheld him, were greatly amazed, and running to *him* saluted him.

16 And he asked the scribes, What question ye with them?

17 And one of the multitude answered and said, Master, I have brought unto thee my son, which hath a dumb spirit;

18 And wheresoever he taketh him, he teareth him: and he foameth, and gnasheth with his teeth, and pineth away: and I spake to thy disciples that they should cast him out; and they could not.

19 He answereth him, and saith, O faithless generation, how long shall I be with you? how long shall I suffer you? bring him unto me.

20 And they brought him unto him: and when he saw him, straightway the spirit tare him; and he fell on the ground, and wallowed foaming.

21 And he asked his father, How long is it ago since this came unto him? And he said, Of a child.

22 And ofttimes it hath cast him into the fire, and into the waters, to destroy him: but if thou canst do any thing, have compassion on us, and help us.

23 Jesus said unto him, If thou canst believe, all things *are* possible to him that believeth.

24 And straightway the father of the child cried out, and said with tears, Lord, I believe; help thou mine unbelief.

25 When Jesus saw that the people came running together, he rebuked the foul spirit, saying unto him, *Thou* dumb and deaf spirit, I charge thee, come out of him, and enter no more into him.

26 And *the spirit* cried, and rent him sore, and came out of him: and he was as one dead; insomuch that many said, He is dead.

27 But Jesus took him by the hand, and lifted him up; and he arose.

28 And when he was come into the house, his disciples asked him privately, Why could not we cast him out?

29 And he said unto them, This kind can come forth by nothing, but by prayer and fasting.

30 ¶And they departed thence, and passed through Galilee; and he would not that any man should know *it*.

31 For he taught his disciples, and said unto them, The Son of man is delivered into the hands of men, and they shall kill him; and after that he is killed, he shall rise the third day.

32 But they understood not that saying, and were afraid to ask him.

33 ¶And he came to Ca-per'na-um: and being in the house he asked them,

What was it that ye disputed among yourselves by the way?

34 But they held their peace: for by the way they had disputed among themselves, who *should be* the greatest.

35 And he sat down, and called the twelve, and saith unto them, If any man desire to be first, *the same* shall be last of all, and servant of all.

36 And he took a child, and set him in the midst of them: and when he had taken him in his arms, he said unto them,

37 Whosoever shall receive one of such children in my name, receiveth me: and whosoever shall receive me, receiveth not me, but him that sent me.

38 ¶And John answered him, saying, Master, we saw one casting out devils in thy name, and he followeth not us: and we forbad him, because he followeth not us.

39 But Jesus said, Forbid him not: for there is no man which shall do a miracle in my name, that can lightly speak evil of me.

40 For he that is not against us is on our part.

41 For whosoever shall give you a cup of water to drink in my name, because ye belong to Christ, verily I say unto you, he shall not lose his reward.

42 And whosoever shall offend one of *these* little ones that believe in me, it is better for him that a millstone were hanged about his neck, and he were cast into the sea.

43 And if thy hand offend thee, cut it off: it is better for thee to enter into life maimed, than having two hands to go into hell, into the fire that never shall be quenched:

44 Where their worm dieth not, and the fire is not quenched.

45 And if thy foot offend thee, cut it off: it is better for thee to enter halt into life, than having two feet to be cast into hell, into the fire that never shall be quenched:

46 Where their worm dieth not, and the fire is not quenched.

47 And if thine eye offend thee, pluck it out: it is better for thee to enter into the kingdom of God with one eye, than having two eyes to be cast into hell fire:

48 Where their worm dieth not, and the fire is not quenched.

49 For every one shall be salted with fire, and every sacrifice shall be salted with salt.

50 Salt *is* good: but if the salt have lost his saltness, wherewith will ye season it? Have salt in yourselves, and have peace one with another.

CHAPTER 10

AND he arose from thence, and cometh into the coasts of Judæa by the farther side of Jordan: and the people resort unto him again; and, as he was wont, he taught them again.

2 ¶And the Pharisees came to him, and asked him, Is it lawful for a man to put away *his* wife? tempting him.

3 And he answered and said unto them, What did Moses command you?

4 And they said, Moses suffered to write a bill of divorcement, and to put *her* away.

5 And Jesus answered and said unto them, For the hardness of your heart he wrote you this precept.

6 But from the beginning of the creation God made them male and female.

7 For this cause shall a man leave his father and mother, and cleave to his wife;

8 And they twain shall be one flesh: so then they are no more twain, but one flesh.

9 What therefore God hath joined together, let not man put asunder.

10 And in the house his disciples asked him again of the same *matter*.

11 And he saith unto them, Whosoever shall put away his wife, and marry another, committeth adultery against her.

12 And if a woman shall put away her husband, and be married to another, she committeth adultery.

13 ¶And they brought young children to him, that he should touch them: and *his* disciples rebuked those that brought *them*.

14 But when Jesus saw *it*, he was much displeased, and said unto them, Suffer the little children to come unto me, and forbid them not: for of such is the kingdom of God.

15 Verily I say unto you, Whosoever shall not receive the kingdom of God as a little child, he shall not enter therein.

16 And he took them up in his arms, put *his* hands upon them, and blessed them.

17 ¶And when he was gone forth into the way, there came one running, and kneeled to him, and asked him, Good Master, what shall I do that I may inherit eternal life?

18 And Jesus said unto him, Why callest thou me good? *there is* none good but one, *that is*, God.

19 Thou knowest the commandments, Do not commit adultery, Do not kill, Do not steal, Do not bear false witness, Defraud not, Honour thy father and mother.

20 And he answered and said unto
him, Master, all these have I observed
from my youth.
21 Then Jesus beholding him loved
him, and said unto him, One thing thou
lackest: go thy way, sell whatsoever
thou hast, and give to the poor, and
thou shalt have treasure in heaven: and
come, take up the cross, and follow me.
22 And he was sad at that saying, and
went away grieved: for he had great
possessions.
23 ¶And Jesus looked round about,
and saith unto his disciples, How hard-
ly shall they that have riches enter
into the kingdom of God!
24 And the disciples were astonished
at his words. But Jesus answereth
again, and saith unto them, Children,
how hard is it for them that trust in
riches to enter into the kingdom of
God!
25 It is easier for a camel to go
through the eye of a needle, than for a
rich man to enter into the kingdom of
God.
26 And they were astonished out of
measure, saying among themselves,
Who then can be saved?
27 And Jesus looking upon them
saith, With men *it is* impossible, but not
with God: for with God all things are
possible.
28 ¶Then Peter began to say unto
him, Lo, we have left all, and have fol-
lowed thee.
29 And Jesus answered and said,
Verily I say unto you, There is no man
that hath left house, or brethren, or sis-
ters, or father, or mother, or wife, or
children, or lands, for my sake, and the
gospel's,
30 But he shall receive an hundred-
fold now in this time, houses, and
brethren, and sisters, and mothers, and
children, and lands, with persecutions;
and in the world to come eternal life.
31 But many *that are* first shall be
last; and the last first.
32 ¶And they were in the way going
up to Jerusalem; and Jesus went before
them: and they were amazed; and as
they followed, they were afraid. And he
took again the twelve, and began to tell
them what things should happen unto
him,
33 *Saying*, Behold, we go up to Jeru-
salem; and the Son of man shall be de-
livered unto the chief priests, and unto
the scribes; and they shall condemn
him to death, and shall deliver him to
the Gentiles:
34 And they shall mock him, and
shall scourge him, and shall spit upon
him, and shall kill him: and the third
day he shall rise again.
35 ¶And James and John, the sons of
Zĕb'e-dee, come unto him, saying,
Master, we would that thou shouldest
do for us whatsoever we shall desire.
36 And he said unto them, What
would ye that I should do for you?
37 They said unto him, Grant unto us
that we may sit, one on thy right hand,
and the other on thy left hand, in thy
glory.
38 But Jesus said unto them, Ye
know not what ye ask: can ye drink of
the cup that I drink of? and be baptized
with the baptism that I am baptized
with?
39 And they said unto him, We can.
And Jesus said unto them, Ye shall
indeed drink of the cup that I drink of;
and with the baptism that I am bap-
tized withal shall ye be baptized:
40 But to sit on my right hand and on
my left hand is not mine to give; but *it
shall be given to them* for whom it is
prepared.
41 And when the ten heard *it*, they
began to be much displeased with
James and John.
42 But Jesus called them *to him*, and
saith unto them, Ye know that they
which are accounted to rule over the
Gentiles exercise lordship over them;
and their great ones exercise authority
upon them.
43 But so shall it not be among you:
but whosoever will be great among
you, shall be your minister:
44 And whosoever of you will be the
chiefest, shall be servant of all.
45 For even the Son of man came not
to be ministered unto, but to minister,
and to give his life a ransom for many.
46 ¶And they came to Jericho: and as
he went out of Jericho with his dis-
ciples and a great number of people,
blind Bär-ti-mæ'us, the son of Tī-
mæ'us, sat by the highway side beg-
ging.
47 And when he heard that it was Je-
sus of Nazareth, he began to cry out,
and say, Jesus, *thou* son of David, have
mercy on me.
48 And many charged him that he
should hold his peace: but he cried the
more a great deal, *Thou* son of David,
have mercy on me.
49 And Jesus stood still, and com-
manded him to be called. And they call
the blind man, saying unto him, Be of
good comfort, rise; he calleth thee.
50 And he, casting away his garment,
rose, and came to Jesus.
51 And Jesus answered and said unto
him, What wilt thou that I should do

unto thee? The blind man said unto
him, Lord, that I might receive my
sight.
52 And Jesus said unto him, Go thy
way; thy faith hath made thee whole.
And immediately he received his sight,
and followed Jesus in the way.

CHAPTER 11

AND when they came nigh to Jerusalem, unto Běth'pha-ġē and Bethany,
at the mount of Olives, he sendeth forth
two of his disciples,
2 And saith unto them, Go your way
into the village over against you: and as
soon as ye be entered into it, ye shall
find a colt tied, whereon never man sat;
loose him, and bring *him*.
3 And if any man say unto you, Why
do ye this? say ye that the Lord hath
need of him; and straightway he will
send him hither.
4 And they went their way, and found
the colt tied by the door without in a
place where two ways met; and they
loose him.
5 And certain of them that stood
there said unto them, What do ye, loosing the colt?
6 And they said unto them even as Jesus had commanded: and they let them
go.
7 And they brought the colt to Jesus,
and cast their garments on him; and he
sat upon him.
8 And many spread their garments in
the way: and others cut down branches
off the trees, and strawed *them* in the
way.
9 And they that went before, and they
that followed, cried, saying, Hosanna;
Blessed *is* he that cometh in the name
of the Lord:
10 Blessed *be* the kingdom of our
father David, that cometh in the name
of the Lord: Hosanna in the highest.
11 And Jesus entered into Jerusalem,
and into the temple: and when he had
looked round about upon all things,
and now the eventide was come, he
went out unto Bethany with the twelve.
12 ¶And on the morrow, when they
were come from Bethany, he was hungry:
13 And seeing a fig tree afar off having leaves, he came, if haply he might
find anything thereon: and when he
came to it, he found nothing but leaves;
for the time of figs was not *yet*.
14 And Jesus answered and said unto
it, No man eat fruit of thee hereafter for
ever. And his disciples heard *it*.
15 ¶And they come to Jerusalem: and
Jesus went into the temple, and began
to cast out them that sold and bought in
the temple, and overthrew the tables of
the moneychangers, and the seats of
them that sold doves;
16 And would not suffer that any
man should carry *any* vessel through
the temple.
17 And he taught, saying unto them,
Is it not written, My house shall be
called of all nations the house of
prayer? but ye have made it a den of
thieves.
18 And the scribes and chief priests
heard *it*, and sought how they might
destroy him: for they feared him, because all the people was astonished at
his doctrine.
19 And when even was come, he
went out of the city.
20 ¶And in the morning, as they
passed by, they saw the fig tree dried
up from the roots.
21 And Peter calling to remembrance
saith unto him, Master, behold, the fig
tree which thou cursedst is withered
away.
22 And Jesus answering saith unto
them, Have faith in God.
23 For verily I say unto you, That
whosoever shall say unto this mountain, Be thou removed, and be thou cast
into the sea; and shall not doubt in his
heart, but shall believe that those
things which he saith shall come to
pass; he shall have whatsoever he
saith.
24 Therefore I say unto you, What
things soever ye desire, when ye pray,
believe that ye receive *them*, and ye
shall have *them*.
25 And when ye stand praying, forgive, if ye have ought against any: that
your Father also which is in heaven
may forgive you your trespasses.
26 But if ye do not forgive, neither
will your Father which is in heaven forgive your trespasses.
27 ¶And they come again to Jerusalem: and as he was walking in the
temple, there come to him the chief
priests, and the scribes, and the elders,
28 And say unto him, By what authority doest thou these things? and
who gave thee this authority to do
these things?
29 And Jesus answered and said unto
them, I will also ask of you one question, and answer me, and I will tell you
by what authority I do these things.
30 The baptism of John, was *it* from
heaven, or of men? answer me.
31 And they reasoned with themselves, saying, If we shall say, From
heaven; he will say, Why then did ye
not believe him?
32 But if we shall say, Of men; they

feared the people: for all *men* counted
John, that he was a prophet indeed.
33 And they answered and said unto
Jesus, We cannot tell. And Jesus an-
swering saith unto them, Neither do I
tell you by what authority I do these
things.

CHAPTER 12

AND he began to speak unto them by
parables. A *certain* man planted a vine-
yard, and set an hedge about *it,* and
digged *a place for* the winefat, and built
a tower, and let it out to husbandmen,
and went into a far country.
2 And at the season he sent to the
husbandmen a servant, that he might
receive from the husbandmen of the
fruit of the vineyard.
3 And they caught *him,* and beat him,
and sent *him* away empty.
4 And again he sent unto them an-
other servant; and at him they cast
stones, and wounded *him* in the head,
and sent *him* away shamefully
handled.
5 And again he sent another; and him
they killed, and many others; beating
some, and killing some.
6 Having yet therefore one son, his
wellbeloved, he sent him also last unto
them, saying, They will reverence my
son.
7 But those husbandmen said among
themselves, This is the heir; come, let
us kill him, and the inheritance shall be
ours.
8 And they took him, and killed *him,*
and cast *him* out of the vineyard.
9 What shall therefore the lord of the
vineyard do? he will come and destroy
the husbandmen, and will give the vine-
yard unto others.
10 And have ye not read this scrip-
ture; The stone which the builders re-
jected is become the head of the cor-
ner:
11 This was the Lord's doing, and it is
marvellous in our eyes?
12 And they sought to lay hold on
him, but feared the people: for they
knew that he had spoken the parable
against them: and they left him, and
went their way.
13 ¶And they send unto him certain
of the Pharisees and of the He-rō'di-
ans, to catch him in *his* words.
14 And when they were come, they
say unto him, Master, we know that
thou art true, and carest for no man: for
thou regardest not the person of men,
but teachest the way of God in truth: Is
it lawful to give tribute to Cæsar, or
not?
15 Shall we give, or shall we not give?
But he, knowing their hypocrisy, said
unto them, Why tempt ye me? bring me
a penny, that I may see *it.*
16 And they brought *it.* And he saith
unto them, Whose *is* this image and
superscription? And they said unto him,
Cæsar's.
17 And Jesus answering said unto
them, Render to Cæsar the things that
are Caesar's, and to God the things that
are God's. And they marvelled at him.
18 ¶Then come unto him the Săd'du-
ceės, which say there is no resurrec-
tion; and they asked him, saying,
19 Master, Moses wrote unto us, If a
man's brother die, and leave *his* wife
behind him, and leave no children, that
his brother should take his wife, and
raise up seed unto his brother.
20 Now there were seven brethren:
and the first took a wife, and dying left
no seed.
21 And the second took her, and died,
neither left he any seed: and the third
likewise.
22 And the seven had her, and left no
seed: last of all the woman died also.
23 In the resurrection therefore,
when they shall rise, whose wife shall
she be of them? for the seven had her to
wife.
24 And Jesus answering said unto
them, Do ye not therefore err, because
ye know not the scriptures, neither the
power of God?
25 For when they shall rise from the
dead, they neither marry, nor are given
in marriage; but are as the angels
which are in heaven.
26 And as touching the dead, that
they rise: have ye not read in the book
of Moses, how in the bush God spake
unto him, saying, I *am* the God of Abra-
ham, and the God of Isaac, and the God
of Jacob?
27 He is not the God of the dead, but
the God of the living: ye therefore do
greatly err.
28 ¶And one of the scribes came, and
having heard them reasoning together,
and perceiving that he had answered
them well, asked him, Which is the first
commandment of all?
29 And Jesus answered him, The first
of all the commandments *is,* Hear, O
Israel; The Lord our God is one Lord:
30 And thou shalt love the Lord thy
God with all thy heart, and with all thy
soul, and with all thy mind, and with all
thy strength: this *is* the first command-
ment.
31 And the second *is* like, *namely*
this, Thou shalt love thy neighbour as
thyself. There is none other command-
ment greater than these.

32 And the scribe said unto him,
Well, Master, thou hast said the truth:
for there is one God; and there is none
other but he:
33 And to love him with all the heart
and with all the understanding, and
with all the soul, and with all the
strength, and to love *his* neighbour as
himself, is more than all whole burnt
offerings and sacrifices.
34 And when Jesus saw that he answered discreetly, he said unto him,
Thou art not far from the kingdom of
God. And no man after that durst ask
him *any question*.
35 ¶And Jesus answered and said,
while he taught in the temple, How say
the scribes that Christ is the son of David?
36 For David himself said by the Holy
Ghost, The LORD said to my Lord, Sit
thou on my right hand, till I make thine
enemies thy footstool.
37 David therefore himself calleth
him Lord; and whence is he *then* his
son? And the common people heard
him gladly.
38 ¶And he said unto them in his
doctrine, Beware of the scribes, which
love to go in long clothing, and *love* salutations in the marketplaces,
39 And the chief seats in the synagogues, and the uppermost rooms at
feasts:
40 Which devour widows' houses,
and for a pretence make long prayers:
these shall receive greater damnation.
41 ¶And Jesus sat over against the
treasury, and beheld how the people
cast money into the treasury: and
many that were rich cast in much.
42 And there came a certain poor widow, and she threw in two mites, which
make a farthing.
43 And he called *unto him* his disciples, and saith unto them, Verily I say
unto you, That this poor widow hath
cast more in, than all they which have
cast into the treasury:
44 For all *they* did cast in of their
abundance; but she of her want did cast
in all that she had, *even* all her living.

CHAPTER 13

AND as he went out of the temple, one
of his disciples saith unto him, Master,
see what manner of stones and what
buildings *are here!*
2 And Jesus answering said unto
him, Seest thou these great buildings?
there shall not be left one stone upon
another, that shall not be thrown down.
3 And as he sat upon the mount of
Olives over against the temple, Peter
and James and John and Andrew asked
him privately,
4 Tell us, when shall these things be?
and what *shall be* the sign when all
these things shall be fulfilled?
5 And Jesus answering them began
to say, Take heed lest any *man* deceive
you:
6 For many shall come in my name,
saying, I am *Christ;* and shall deceive
many.
7 And when ye shall hear of wars and
rumours of wars, be ye not troubled:
for *such things* must needs be; but the
end *shall* not *be* yet.
8 For nation shall rise against nation,
and kingdom against kingdom: and
there shall be earthquakes in divers
places, and there shall be famines and
troubles: these *are* the beginnings of
sorrows.
9 ¶But take heed to yourselves: for
they shall deliver you up to councils;
and in the synagogues ye shall be beaten: and ye shall be brought before rulers and kings for my sake, for a testimony
against them.
10 And the gospel must first be published among all nations.
11 But when they shall lead *you*, and
deliver you up, take no thought beforehand what ye shall speak, neither do ye
premeditate: but whatsoever shall be
given you in that hour, that speak ye:
for it is not ye that speak, but the Holy
Ghost.
12 Now the brother shall betray the
brother to death, and the father the
son; and children shall rise up against
their parents, and shall cause them to
be put to death.
13 And ye shall be hated of all *men*
for my name's sake: but he that shall
endure unto the end, the same shall be
saved.
14 ¶But when ye shall see the abomination of desolation, spoken of by Daniel the prophet, standing where it
ought not, (let him that readeth understand,) then let them that be in Judæa
flee to the mountains:
15 And let him that is on the housetop
not go down into the house, neither enter *therein*, to take any thing out of his
house:
16 And let him that is in the field not
turn back again for to take up his garment.
17 But woe to them that are with
child, and to them that give suck in
those days!
18 And pray ye that your flight be not
in the winter.
19 For *in* those days shall be affliction, such as was not from the beginning

of the creation which God created
unto this time, neither shall be.
20 And except that the Lord had
shortened those days, no flesh should
be saved: but for the elect's sake,
whom he hath chosen, he hath short-
ened the days.
21 And then if any man shall say to
you, Lo, here *is* Christ; or, lo, *he is*
there; believe *him* not:
22 For false Christs and false
prophets shall rise, and shall shew
signs and wonders, to seduce, if *it were*
possible, even the elect.
23 But take ye heed: behold, I have
foretold you all things.
24 ¶But in those days, after that tribu-
lation, the sun shall be darkened, and
the moon shall not give her light,
25 And the stars of heaven shall fall,
and the powers that are in heaven shall
be shaken.
26 And then shall they see the Son of
man coming in the clouds with great
power and glory.
27 And then shall he send his angels,
and shall gather together his elect from
the four winds, from the uttermost part
of the earth to the uttermost part of
heaven.
28 Now learn a parable of the fig tree;
When her branch is yet tender, and put-
teth forth leaves, ye know that summer
is near:
29 So ye in like manner, when ye
shall see these things come to pass,
know that it is nigh, *even* at the doors.
30 Verily I say unto you, that this gen-
eration shall not pass, till all these
things be done.
31 Heaven and earth shall pass away:
but my words shall not pass away.
32 ¶But of that day and *that* hour
knoweth no man, no, not the angels
which are in heaven, neither the Son,
but the Father.
33 Take ye heed, watch and pray: for
ye know not when the time is.
34 *For the Son of man is* as a man tak-
ing a far journey, who left his house,
and gave authority to his servants, and
to every man his work, and com-
manded the porter to watch.
35 Watch ye therefore: for ye know
not when the master of the house
cometh, at even, or at midnight, or at
the cockcrowing, or in the morning:
36 Lest coming suddenly he find you
sleeping.
37 And what I say unto you I say unto
all, Watch.

CHAPTER 14

AFTER two days was *the feast of* the
passover, and of unleavened bread:
and the chief priests and the scribes
sought how they might take him by
craft, and put *him* to death.
2 But they said, Not on the feast *day*,
lest there be an uproar of the people.
3 ¶And being in Bethany in the house
of Simon the leper, as he sat at meat,
there came a woman having an alabas-
ter box of ointment of spikenard very
precious; and she brake the box, and
poured *it* on his head.
4 And there were some that had in-
dignation within themselves, and said,
Why was this waste of the ointment
made?
5 For it might have been sold for
more than three hundred pence, and
have been given to the poor. And they
murmured against her.
6 And Jesus said, Let her alone; why
trouble ye her? she hath wrought a
good work on me.
7 For ye have the poor with you al-
ways, and whensoever ye will ye may
do them good: but me ye have not al-
ways.
8 She hath done what she could: she
is come aforehand to anoint my body to
the burying.
9 Verily I say unto you, Wheresoever
this gospel shall be preached
throughout the whole world, this also
that she hath done shall be spoken of
for a memorial of her.
10 ¶And Judas Iscariot, one of the
twelve, went unto the chief priests, to
betray him unto them.
11 And when they heard *it*, they were
glad, and promised to give him money.
And he sought how he might convenient-
ly betray him.
12 ¶And the first day of unleavened
bread, when they killed the passover,
his disciples said unto him, Where wilt
thou that we go and prepare that thou
mayest eat the passover?
13 And he sendeth forth two of his
disciples, and saith unto them, Go ye
into the city, and there shall meet you a
man bearing a pitcher of water: follow
him.
14 And wheresoever he shall go in,
say ye to the goodman of the house,
The Master saith, Where is the guest-
chamber, where I shall eat the passover
with my disciples?
15 And he will shew you a large up-
per room furnished *and* prepared:
there make ready for us.
16 And his disciples went forth, and
came into the city, and found as he had
said unto them: and they made ready
the passover.

17 And in the evening he cometh with the twelve.

18 And as they sat and did eat, Jesus said, Verily I say unto you, One of you which eateth with me shall betray me.

19 And they began to be sorrowful, and to say unto him one by one, *Is* it I? and another *said, Is* it I?

20 And he answered and said unto them, *It is* one of the twelve, that dippeth with me in the dish.

21 The Son of man indeed goeth, as it is written of him: but woe to that man by whom the Son of man is betrayed! good were it for that man if he had never been born.

22 ¶And as they did eat, Jesus took bread, and blessed, and brake *it*, and gave to them, and said, Take, eat: this is my body.

23 And he took the cup, and when he had given thanks, he gave *it* to them: and they all drank of it.

24 And he said unto them, This is my blood of the new testament, which is shed for many.

25 Verily I say unto you, I will drink no more of the fruit of the vine, until that day that I drink it new in the kingdom of God.

26 ¶And when they had sung an hymn, they went out into the mount of Olives.

27 And Jesus saith unto them, All ye shall be offended because of me this night: for it is written, I will smite the shepherd, and the sheep shall be scattered.

28 But after that I am risen, I will go before you into Galilee.

29 But Peter said unto him, Although all shall be offended, yet *will* not I.

30 And Jesus saith unto him, Verily I say unto thee, That this day, *even* in this night, before the cock crow twice, thou shalt deny me thrice.

31 But he spake the more vehemently, If I should die with thee, I will not deny thee in any wise. Likewise also said they all.

32 ¶And they came to a place which was named Gĕth-sĕm′a-ne: and he saith to his disciples, Sit ye here, while I shall pray.

33 And he taketh with him Peter and James and John, and began to be sore amazed, and to be very heavy;

34 And saith unto them, My soul is exceeding sorrowful unto death: tarry ye here, and watch.

35 And he went forward a little, and fell on the ground, and prayed that, if it were possible, the hour might pass from him.

36 And he said, Abba, Father, all things *are* possible unto thee; take away this cup from me: nevertheless not what I will, but what thou wilt.

37 And he cometh, and findeth them sleeping, and saith unto Peter, Simon, sleepest thou? couldest not thou watch one hour?

38 Watch ye and pray, lest ye enter into temptation. The spirit truly *is* ready, but the flesh *is* weak.

39 And again he went away, and prayed, and spake the same words.

40 And when he returned, he found them asleep again, (for their eyes were heavy,) neither wist they what to answer him.

41 And he cometh the third time, and saith unto them, Sleep on now, and take *your* rest: it is enough, the hour is come; behold, the Son of man is betrayed into the hands of sinners.

42 Rise up, let us go; lo, he that betrayeth me is at hand.

43 ¶And immediately, while he yet spake, cometh Judas, one of the twelve, and with him a great multitude with swords and staves, from the chief priests and the scribes and the elders.

44 And he that betrayed him had given them a token, saying, Whomsoever I shall kiss, that same is he; take him, and lead *him* away safely.

45 And as soon as he was come, he goeth straightway to him, and saith, Master, master; and kissed him.

46 And they laid their hands on him, and took him.

47 And one of them that stood by drew a sword, and smote a servant of the high priest, and cut off his ear.

48 And Jesus answered and said unto them, Are ye come out, as against a thief, with swords and *with* staves to take me?

49 I was daily with you in the temple teaching, and ye took me not: but the scriptures must be fulfilled.

50 And they all forsook him, and fled.

51 And there followed him a certain young man, having a linen cloth cast about *his* naked *body;* and the young men laid hold on him:

52 And he left the linen cloth, and fled from them naked.

53 ¶And they led Jesus away to the high priest: and with him were assembled all the chief priests and the elders and the scribes.

54 And Peter followed him afar off, even into the palace of the high priest: and he sat with the servants, and warmed himself at the fire.

55 And the chief priests and all the council sought for witness against Je-

sus to put him to death; and found
none.
56 For many bare false witness
against him, but their witness agreed
not together.
57 And there arose certain, and bare
false witness against him, saying,
58 We heard him say, I will destroy
this temple that is made with hands,
and within three days I will build an-
other made without hands.
59 But neither so did their witness
agree together.
60 And the high priest stood up in the
midst, and asked Jesus, saying, An-
swerest thou nothing? what *is it which*
these witness against thee?
61 But he held his peace, and an-
swered nothing. Again the high priest
asked him, and said unto him, Art thou
the Christ, the Son of the Blessed?
62 And Jesus said, I am: and ye shall
see the Son of man sitting on the right
hand of power, and coming in the
clouds of heaven.
63 Then the high priest rent his
clothes, and saith, What need we any
further witnesses?
64 Ye have heard the blasphemy:
what think ye? And they all condemned
him to be guilty of death.
65 And some began to spit on him,
and to cover his face, and to buffet him,
and to say unto him, Prophesy: and the
servants did strike him with the palms
of their hands.
66 ¶And as Peter was beneath in the
palace, there cometh one of the maids
of the high priest:
67 And when she saw Peter warming
himself, she looked upon him, and said,
And thou also wast with Jesus of Naza-
reth.
68 But he denied, saying, I know not,
neither understand I what thou sayest.
And he went out into the porch; and the
cock crew.
69 And a maid saw him again, and be-
gan to say to them that stood by, This is
one of them.
70 And he denied it again. And a little
after, they that stood by said again to
Peter, Surely thou art *one* of them: for
thou art a Galilæan, and thy speech
agreeth *thereto.*
71 But he began to curse and to
swear, *saying,* I know not this man of
whom ye speak.
72 And the second time the cock
crew. And Peter called to mind the
word that Jesus said unto him, Before
the cock crow twice, thou shalt deny
me thrice. And when he thought there-
on, he wept.

CHAPTER 15

AND straightway in the morning the
chief priests held a consultation with
the elders and scribes and the whole
council, and bound Jesus, and carried
him away, and delivered *him* to Pilate.
2 And Pilate asked him, Art thou the
King of the Jews? And he answering
said unto him, Thou sayest *it.*
3 And the chief priests accused him
of many things: but he answered noth-
ing.
4 And Pilate asked him again, saying,
Answerest thou nothing? behold how
many things they witness against thee.
5 But Jesus yet answered nothing; so
that Pilate marvelled.
6 ¶Now at *that* feast he released unto
them one prisoner, whomsoever they
desired.
7 And there was *one* named Ba-răb'-
bas, *which lay* bound with them that
had made insurrection with him, who
had committed murder in the insurrec-
tion.
8 And the multitude crying aloud be-
gan to desire *him to do* as he had ever
done unto them.
9 But Pilate answered them, saying,
Will ye that I release unto you the King
of the Jews?
10 For he knew that the chief priests
had delivered him for envy.
11 But the chief priests moved the
people, that he should rather release
Ba-răb'bas unto them.
12 And Pilate answered and said
again unto them, What will ye then that
I shall do *unto him* whom ye call the
King of the Jews?
13 And they cried out again, Crucify
him.
14 Then Pilate said unto them, Why,
what evil hath he done? And they cried
out the more exceedingly, Crucify him.
15 And *so* Pilate, willing to content
the people, released Ba-răb'bas unto
them, and delivered Jesus, when he
had scourged *him,* to be crucified.
16 ¶And the soldiers led him away
into the hall, called Præ-tō'rĭ-um; and
they call together the whole band.
17 And they clothed him with purple,
and platted a crown of thorns, and put
it about his *head,*
18 And began to salute him, Hail,
King of the Jews!
19 And they smote him on the head
with a reed, and did spit upon him, and
bowing *their* knees worshipped him.
20 And when they had mocked him,
they took off the purple from him, and
put his own clothes on him, and led him
out to crucify him.

21 And they compel one Simon a Ċy̆-rē′nĭ-an, who passed by, coming out of the country, the father of Alexander and Rufus, to bear his cross.

22 And they bring him unto the place Gŏl′go-tha, which is, being interpreted, The place of a skull.

23 And they gave him to drink wine mingled with myrrh: but he received *it* not.

24 And when they had crucified him, they parted his garments, casting lots upon them, what every man should take.

25 And it was the third hour, and they crucified him.

26 And the superscription of his accusation was written over, THE KING OF THE JEWS.

27 And with him they crucify two thieves; the one on his right hand, and the other on his left.

28 And the scripture was fulfilled, which saith, And he was numbered with the transgressors.

29 ¶And they that passed by railed on him, wagging their heads, and saying, Ah, thou that destroyest the temple, and buildest *it* in three days,

30 Save thyself, and come down from the cross.

31 Likewise also the chief priests mocking said among themselves with the scribes, He saved others; himself he cannot save.

32 Let Christ the King of Israel descend now from the cross, that we may see and believe. And they that were crucified with him reviled him.

33 ¶And when the sixth hour was come, there was darkness over the whole land until the ninth hour.

34 And at the ninth hour Jesus cried with a loud voice, saying, Ē-lō′ī, Ē-lō′ī, lä′ma sa-bach′tha-ni? which is, being interpreted, My God, my God, why hast thou forsaken me?

35 And some of them that stood by, when they heard *it*, said, Behold, he calleth E-lī′as.

36 And one ran and filled a spunge full of vinegar, and put *it* on a reed, and gave him to drink, saying, Let alone; let us see whether E-lī′as will come to take him down.

37 And Jesus cried with a loud voice, and gave up the ghost.

38 And the vail of the temple was rent in twain from the top to the bottom.

39 ¶And when the centurion, which stood over against him, saw that he so cried out, and gave up the ghost, he said, Truly this man was the Son of God.

40 There were also women looking on afar off: among whom was Mary Magdalene, and Mary the mother of James the less and of Joses, and Sa-lō′me;

41 (Who also, when he was in Galilee, followed him, and ministered unto him;) and many other women which came up with him unto Jerusalem.

42 ¶And now when the even was come, because it was the preparation, that is, the day before the sabbath,

43 Joseph of Ăr-i-ma-thæ′a, an honourable counsellor, which also waited for the kingdom of God, came, and went in boldly unto Pilate, and craved the body of Jesus.

44 And Pilate marvelled if he were already dead: and calling *unto him* the centurion, he asked him whether he had been any while dead.

45 And when he knew *it* of the centurion, he gave the body to Joseph.

46 And he bought fine linen, and took him down, and wrapped him in the linen, and laid him in a sepulchre which was hewn out of a rock, and rolled a stone unto the door of the sepulchre.

47 And Mary Magdalene and Mary *the mother* of Joses beheld where he was laid.

CHAPTER 16

AND when the sabbath was past, Mary Magdalene, and Mary the *mother* of James, and Sa-lō′me, had bought sweet spices, that they might come and anoint him.

2 And very early in the morning the first *day* of the week, they came unto the sepulchre at the rising of the sun.

3 And they said among themselves, Who shall roll us away the stone from the door of the sepulchre?

4 And when they looked, they saw that the stone was rolled away: for it was very great.

5 And entering into the sepulchre, they saw a young man sitting on the right side, clothed in a long white garment; and they were affrighted.

6 And he saith unto them, Be not affrighted: Ye seek Jesus of Nazareth, which was crucified: he is risen; he is not here: behold the place where they laid him.

7 But go your way, tell his disciples and Peter that he goeth before you into Galilee: there shall ye see him, as he said unto you.

8 And they went out quickly, and fled from the sepulchre; for they trembled and were amazed: neither said they any thing to any *man*; for they were afraid.

9 ¶Now when *Jesus* was risen early

the first *day* of the week, he appeared
first to Mary Magdalene, out of whom
he had cast seven devils.
10 *And* she went and told them that
had been with him, as they mourned
and wept.
11 And they, when they had heard
that he was alive, and had been seen of
her, believed not.
12 ¶After that he appeared in another
form unto two of them, as they walked,
and went into the country.
13 And they went and told *it* unto the
residue: neither believed they them.
14 ¶Afterward he appeared unto the
eleven as they sat at meat, and up-
braided them with their unbelief and
hardness of heart, because they be-
lieved not them which had seen him af-
ter he was risen.
15 And he said unto them, Go ye into
all the world, and preach the gospel to
every creature.
16 He that believeth and is baptized
shall be saved; but he that believeth not
shall be damned.
17 And these signs shall follow them
that believe; In my name shall they cast
out devils; they shall speak with new
tongues;
18 They shall take up serpents; and if
they drink any deadly thing, it shall not
hurt them; they shall lay hands on the
sick, and they shall recover.
19 ¶So then after the Lord had spok-
en unto them, he was received up into
heaven, and sat on the right hand of
God.
20 And they went forth, and
preached every where, the Lord work-
ing with *them,* and confirming the
word with signs following. Amen.

THE GOSPEL ACCORDING TO

SAINT LUKE

CHAPTER 1

FORASMUCH as many have taken in
hand to set forth in order a declaration
of those things which are most surely
believed among us,
2 Even as they delivered them unto
us, which from the beginning were eye-
witnesses, and ministers of the word;
3 It seemed good to me also, having
had perfect understanding of all things
from the very first, to write unto thee in
order, most excellent Thē-ŏph'i-lus,
4 That thou mightest know the cer-
tainty of those things, wherein thou
hast been instructed.
5 ¶THERE was in the days of Herod,
the king of Judæa, a certain priest
named Zăch-a-rī'as, of the course of Ă-
bī'a: and his wife *was* of the daughters
of Aaron, and her name *was* Elisabeth.
6 And they were both righteous be-
fore God, walking in all the command-
ments and ordinances of the Lord
blameless.
7 And they had no child, because that
Elisabeth was barren, and they both
were *now* well stricken in years.
8 And it came to pass, that while he
executed the priest's office before God
in the order of his course,
9 According to the custom of the
priest's office, his lot was to burn incense
when he went into the temple of
the Lord.
10 And the whole multitude of the
people were praying without at the
time of incense.
11 And there appeared unto him an
angel of the Lord standing on the right
side of the altar of incense.
12 And when Zăch-a-rī'as saw *him,*
he was troubled, and fear fell upon him.
13 But the angel said unto him, Fear
not, Zăch-a-rī'as: for thy prayer is
heard; and thy wife Elisabeth shall bear
thee a son, and thou shalt call his name
John.
14 And thou shalt have joy and glad-
ness; and many shall rejoice at his
birth.
15 For he shall be great in the sight of
the Lord, and shall drink neither wine
nor strong drink; and he shall be filled
with the Holy Ghost, even from his
mother's womb.
16 And many of the children of Israel
shall he turn to the Lord their God.
17 And he shall go before him in the
spirit and power of E-lī'as, to turn the
hearts of the fathers to the children,
and the disobedient to the wisdom of
the just; to make ready a people pre-
pared for the Lord.
18 And Zăch-a-rī'as said unto the an-
gel, Whereby shall I know this? for I am
an old man and my wife well stricken in
years.
19 And the angel answering said unto
him, I am Gabriel, that stand in the pres-
ence of God; and am sent to speak
unto thee, and to shew thee these glad
tidings.
20 And, behold, thou shalt be dumb,
and not able to speak, until the day that
these things shall be performed, be-

cause thou believest not my words, which shall be fulfilled in their season.

21 And the people waited for Zăch-a-rī'as, and marvelled that he tarried so long in the temple.

22 And when he came out, he could not speak unto them: and they perceived that he had seen a vision in the temple: for he beckoned unto them, and remained speechless.

23 And it came to pass, that, as soon as the days of his ministration were accomplished, he departed to his own house.

24 And after those days his wife Elisabeth conceived, and hid herself five months, saying,

25 Thus hath the Lord dealt with me in the days wherein he looked on *me*, to take away my reproach among men.

26 ¶And in the sixth month the angel Gabriel was sent from God unto a city of Galilee, named Nazareth,

27 To a virgin espoused to a man whose name was Joseph, of the house of David; and the virgin's name *was* Mary.

28 And the angel came in unto her, and said, Hail, *thou that art* highly favoured, the Lord *is* with thee: blessed *art* thou among women.

29 And when she saw *him*, she was troubled at his saying, and cast in her mind what manner of salutation this should be.

30 And the angel said unto her, Fear not, Mary: for thou hast found favour with God.

31 And, behold, thou shalt conceive in thy womb, and bring forth a son, and shalt call his name JESUS.

32 He shall be great, and shall be called the Son of the Highest: and the Lord God shall give unto him the throne of his father David:

33 And he shall reign over the house of Jacob for ever; and of his kingdom there shall be no end.

34 Then said Mary unto the angel, How shall this be, seeing I know not a man?

35 And the angel answered and said unto her, The Holy Ghost shall come upon thee, and the power of the Highest shall overshadow thee: therefore also that holy thing which shall be born of thee shall be called the Son of God.

36 And, behold, thy cousin Elisabeth, she hath also conceived a son in her old age: and this is the sixth month with her, who was called barren.

37 For with God nothing shall be impossible.

38 And Mary said, Behold the handmaid of the Lord; be it unto me according to thy word. And the angel departed from her.

39 ¶And Mary arose in those days, and went into the hill country with haste, into a city of Juda;

40 And entered into the house of Zăch-a-rī'as, and saluted Elisabeth.

41 And it came to pass, that, when Elisabeth heard the salutation of Mary, the babe leaped in her womb; and Elisabeth was filled with the Holy Ghost:

42 And she spake out with a loud voice, and said, Blessed *art* thou among women, and blessed *is* the fruit of thy womb.

43 And whence *is* this to me, that the mother of my Lord should come to me?

44 For, lo, as soon as the voice of thy salutation sounded in mine ears, the babe leaped in my womb for joy.

45 And blessed *is* she that believed: for there shall be a performance of those things which were told her from the Lord.

46 ¶And Mary said, My soul doth magnify the Lord,

47 And my spirit hath rejoiced in God my Saviour.

48 For he hath regarded the low estate of his handmaiden: for, behold, from henceforth all generations shall call me blessed.

49 For he that is mighty hath done to me great things; and holy *is* his name.

50 And his mercy *is* on them that fear him from generation to generation.

51 He hath shewed strength with his arm; he hath scattered the proud in the imagination of their hearts.

52 He hath put down the mighty from *their* seats, and exalted them of low degree.

53 He hath filled the hungry with good things; and the rich he hath sent empty away.

54 He hath holpen his servant Israel, in remembrance of *his* mercy;

55 As he spake to our fathers, to Abraham, and to his seed for ever.

56 And Mary abode with her about three months, and returned to her own house.

57 ¶Now Elisabeth's full time came that she should be delivered; and she brought forth a son.

58 And her neighbours and her cousins heard how the Lord had shewed great mercy upon her; and they rejoiced with her.

59 And it came to pass, that on the eighth day they came to circumcise the child; and they called him Zăch-a-rī'as, after the name of his father.

high priests, the word of God came
unto John the son of Zăch-a-rī'as in the
wilderness.
3 And he came into all the country
about Jordan, preaching the baptism of
repentance for the remission of sins;
4 As it is written in the book of the
words of E-ṡā'ias the prophet, saying,
The voice of one crying in the wilder-
ness, Prepare ye the way of the Lord,
make his paths straight.
5 Every valley shall be filled, and
every mountain and hill shall be
brought low; and the crooked shall be
made straight, and the rough ways
shall be made smooth;
6 And all flesh shall see the salvation
of God.
7 Then said he to the multitude that
came forth to be baptized of him, O gen-
eration of vipers, who hath warned
you to flee from the wrath to come?
8 Bring forth therefore fruits worthy
of repentance, and begin not to say
within yourselves, We have Abraham
to *our* father: for I say unto you, That
God is able of these stones to raise up
children unto Abraham.
9 And now also the axe is laid unto
the root of the trees: every tree there-
fore which bringeth not forth good fruit
is hewn down, and cast into the fire.
10 And the people asked him, saying,
What shall we do then?
11 He answereth and saith unto
them, He that hath two coats, let him
impart to him that hath none; and he
that hath meat, let him do likewise.
12 Then came also publicans to be
baptized, and said unto him, Master,
what shall we do?
13 And he said unto them, Exact no
more than that which is appointed you.
14 And the soldiers likewise de-
manded of him, saying, And what shall
we do? And he said unto them, Do vio-
lence to no man, neither accuse *any* false-
ly; and be content with your wages.
15 ¶And as the people were in expec-
tation, and all men mused in their
hearts of John, whether he were the
Christ, or not;
16 John answered, saying unto *them*
all, I indeed baptize you with water; but
one mightier than I cometh, the latchet
of whose shoes I am not worthy to un-
loose: he shall baptize you with the
Holy Ghost and with fire:
17 Whose fan *is* in his hand, and he
will thoroughly purge his floor, and will
gather the wheat into his garner; but
the chaff he will burn with fire unquench-
able.
18 And many other things in his ex-
hortation preached he unto the people.
19 ¶But Herod the tetrarch, being
reproved by him for He-rō'dĭ-as his
brother Philip's wife, and for all the
evils which Herod had done,
20 Added yet this above all, that he
shut up John in prison.
21 ¶Now when all the people were
baptized, it came to pass, that Jesus
also being baptized, and praying, the
heaven was opened,
22 And the Holy Ghost descended in
a bodily shape like a dove upon him,
and a voice came from heaven, which
said, Thou art my beloved Son; in thee I
am well pleased.
23 ¶And Jesus himself began to be
about thirty years of age, being (as was
supposed) the son of Joseph, which
was *the son* of Hē'lī,
24 Which was *the son* of Măt'thăt,
which was *the son* of Levi, which was
the son of Mĕl'chī, which was *the son* of
Jăn'na, which was *the son* of Joseph,
25 Which was *the son* of Măt-ta-thī'-
as, which was *the son* of Amos, which
was *the son* of Nā'um, which was *the
son* of Ĕs'lī, which was *the son* of Năg'-
ge,
26 Which was *the son* of Mā'ath,
which was *the son* of Măt-ta-thī'as,
which was *the son* of Sĕm'e-ī, which
was *the son* of Joseph, which was *the
son* of Juda,
27 Which was *the son* of Jō-ăn'na,
which was *the son* of Rhē'sa, which
was *the son* of Zō-rŏb'a-bel, which was
the son of Sa-lā'thĭ-el, which was *the
son* of Ne'rī,
28 Which was *the son* of Mĕl'chī,
which was *the son* of Ăd'dī, which was
the son of Cō'sam, which was *the son* of
Ĕl-mō'dăm, which was *the son* of Er,
29 Which was *the son* of Jō'se, which
was *the son* of Ē-lĭ-ē'zer, which was *the
son* of Jō'rĭm, which was *the son* of
Măt'thăt, which was *the son* of Levi,
30 Which was *the son* of Sĭmeon,
which was *the son* of Juda, which was
the son of Joseph, which was *the son* of
Jō'nan, which was *the son* of E-lī'a-kĭm,
31 Which was *the son* of Mē'le-a,
which was *the son* of Mē'năn, which
was *the son* of Măt'ta-tha, which was
the son of Nathan, which was *the son* of
David,
32 Which was *the son* of Jesse, which
was *the son* of Ō'bed, which was *the
son* of Bō'ŏz, which was *the son* of Săl'-
mon, which was *the son* of Nā-ăs'son,
33 Which was *the son* of A-mĭn'a-
dăb, which was *the son* of Â'ram, which
was *the son* of Ĕs-rŏm, which was *the
son* of Phâ'rĕṡ, which was *the son* of
Juda,
34 Which was *the son* of Jacob,

which was *the son* of Isaac, which was
the son of Abraham, which was *the son*
of Thâ'ra, which was *the son* of Nā'-
chôr,
35 Which was *the son* of Sâ'ruch,
which was *the son* of Rā'gau, which
was *the son* of Phā'lec, which was *the
son* of Hē'ber, which was *the son* of
Sā'la,
36 Which was *the son* of Ca-ī'nan,
which was *the son* of Är-phăx'ăd,
which was *the son* of Sem, which was
the son of Nō'e, which was *the son* of
Lā'mech,
37 Which was *the son* of Ma-thū'ṡa-
la, which was *the son* of Ē'noch, which
was *the son* of Jâ'red, which was *the
son* of Ma-lē'le-el, which was *the son* of
Ca-ī'nan,
38 Which was *the son* of Enos, which
was *the son* of Seth, which was *the son*
of Adam, which was *the son* of God.

CHAPTER 4

AND Jesus being full of the Holy Ghost
returned from Jordan, and was led by
the Spirit into the wilderness,
2 Being forty days tempted of the dev-
il. And in those days he did eat noth-
ing: and when they were ended, he after-
ward hungered.
3 And the devil said unto him, If thou
be the Son of God, command this stone
that it be made bread.
4 And Jesus answered him, saying, It
is written, That man shall not live by
bread alone, but by every word of God.
5 And the devil, taking him up into an
high mountain, shewed unto him all the
kingdoms of the world in a moment of
time.
6 And the devil said unto him, All this
power will I give thee, and the glory of
them: for that is delivered unto me; and
to whomsoever I will I give it.
7 If thou therefore wilt worship me,
all shall be thine.
8 And Jesus answered and said unto
him, Get thee behind me, Satan: for it is
written, Thou shalt worship the Lord
thy God, and him only shalt thou serve.
9 And he brought him to Jerusalem,
and set him on a pinnacle of the temple,
and said unto him, If thou be the Son of
God, cast thyself down from hence:
10 For it is written, He shall give his
angels charge over thee, to keep thee:
11 And in *their* hands they shall bear
thee up, lest at any time thou dash thy
foot against a stone.
12 And Jesus answering said unto
him, It is said, Thou shalt not tempt the
Lord thy God.
13 And when the devil had ended all
the temptation, he departed from him
for a season.
14 ¶And Jesus returned in the power
of the Spirit into Galilee: and there
went out a fame of him through all the
region round about.
15 And he taught in their syna-
gogues, being glorified of all.
16 ¶And he came to Nazareth, where
he had been brought up: and, as his cus-
tom was, he went into the synagogue
on the sabbath day, and stood up for to
read.
17 And there was delivered unto him
the book of the prophet E-ṡā'ias. And
when he had opened the book, he found
the place where it was written,
18 The Spirit of the Lord *is* upon me,
because he hath anointed me to preach
the gospel to the poor; he hath sent me
to heal the brokenhearted, to preach
deliverance to the captives, and re-
covering of sight to the blind, to set at
liberty them that are bruised,
19 To preach the acceptable year of
the Lord.
20 And he closed the book, and he
gave *it* again to the minister, and sat
down. And the eyes of all them that
were in the synagogue were fastened
on him.
21 And he began to say unto them,
This day is this scripture fulfilled in
your ears.
22 And all bare him witness, and
wondered at the gracious words which
proceeded out of his mouth. And they
said, Is not this Joseph's son?
23 And he said unto them, Ye will
surely say unto me this proverb, Physi-
cian, heal thyself: whatsoever we have
heard done in Ca-per'na-um, do also
here in thy country.
24 And he said, Verily I say unto you,
No prophet is accepted in his own
country.
25 But I tell you of a truth, many wid-
ows were in Israel in the days of E-lī'-
as, when the heaven was shut up three
years and six months, when great
famine was throughout all the land;
26 But unto none of them was E-lī'as
sent, save unto Sar-ĕp'ta, *a city* of Sī'-
don, unto a woman *that was* a widow.
27 And many lepers were in Israel in
the time of Ĕl-i-sē'us the prophet; and
none of them was cleansed, saving
Nā'a-man the Syrian.
28 And all they in the synagogue,
when they heard these things, were
filled with wrath,
29 And rose up, and thrust him out of
the city, and led him unto the brow of
the hill whereon their city was built,

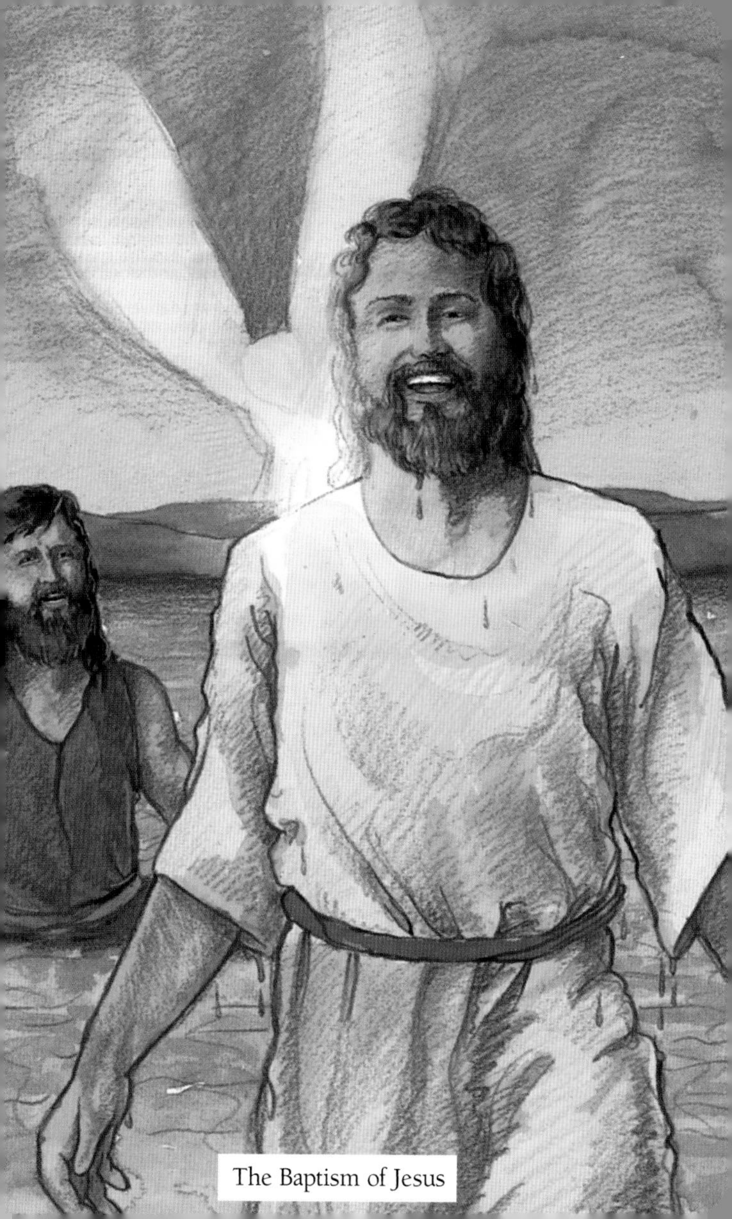

The Baptism of Jesus

The Lost Son Returns (Luke 15)

that they might cast him down headlong.

30 But he passing through the midst of them went his way,

31 And came down to Ca-per'na-um, a city of Galilee, and taught them on the sabbath days.

32 And they were astonished at his doctrine: for his word was with power.

33 ¶And in the synagogue there was a man, which had a spirit of an unclean devil, and cried out with a loud voice,

34 Saying, Let *us* alone; what have we to do with thee, *thou* Jesus of Nazareth? art thou come to destroy us? I know thee who thou art; the Holy One of God.

35 And Jesus rebuked him, saying, Hold thy peace, and come out of him. And when the devil had thrown him in the midst, he came out of him, and hurt him not.

36 And they were all amazed, and spake among themselves, saying, What a word *is* this! for with authority and power he commandeth the unclean spirits, and they come out.

37 And the fame of him went out into every place of the country round about.

38 ¶And he arose out of the synagogue, and entered into Simon's house. And Simon's wife's mother was taken with a great fever; and they besought him for her.

39 And he stood over her, and rebuked the fever; and it left her: and immediately she arose and ministered unto them.

40 ¶Now when the sun was setting, all they that had any sick with divers diseases brought them unto him; and he laid his hands on every one of them, and healed them.

41 And devils also came out of many, crying out, and saying, Thou art Christ the Son of God. And he rebuking *them* suffered them not to speak: for they knew that he was Christ.

42 And when it was day, he departed and went into a desert place: and the people sought him, and came unto him, and stayed him, that he should not depart from them.

43 And he said unto them, I must preach the kingdom of God to other cities also: for therefore am I sent.

44 And he preached in the synagogues of Galilee.

CHAPTER 5

AND it came to pass, that, as the people pressed upon him to hear the word of God, he stood by the lake of Gĕn-nĕs'-a-ret.

2 And saw two ships standing by the lake: but the fishermen were gone out of them, and were washing *their* nets.

3 And he entered into one of the ships, which was Simon's, and prayed him that he would thrust out a little from the land. And he sat down, and taught the people out of the ship.

4 Now when he had left speaking, he said unto Simon, Launch out into the deep, and let down your nets for a draught.

5 And Simon answering said unto him, Master, we have toiled all the night, and have taken nothing: nevertheless at thy word I will let down the net.

6 And when they had this done, they inclosed a great multitude of fishes: and their net brake.

7 And they beckoned unto *their* partners, which were in the other ship, that they should come and help them. And they came, and filled both the ships, so that they began to sink.

8 When Simon Peter saw *it*, he fell down at Jesus' knees, saying, Depart from me; for I am a sinful man, O Lord.

9 For he was astonished, and all that were with him, at the draught of the fishes which they had taken:

10 And so *was* also James, and John, the sons of Zĕb'e-dee, which were partners with Simon. And Jesus said unto Simon, Fear not; from henceforth thou shalt catch men.

11 And when they had brought their ships to land, they forsook all, and followed him.

12 ¶And it came to pass, when he was in a certain city, behold a man full of leprosy: who seeing Jesus fell on *his* face, and besought him, saying, Lord, if thou wilt, thou canst make me clean.

13 And he put forth *his* hand, and touched him, saying, I will: be thou clean. And immediately the leprosy departed from him.

14 And he charged him to tell no man: but go, and shew thyself to the priest, and offer for thy cleansing, according as Moses commanded, for a testimony unto them.

15 But so much the more went there a fame abroad of him: and great multitudes came together to hear, and to be healed by him of their infirmities.

16 And he withdrew himself into the wilderness, and prayed.

17 ¶And it came to pass on a certain day, as he was teaching, that there were Pharisees and doctors of the law sitting by, which were come out of every town of Galilee, and Judæa, and Jerusalem: and the power of the Lord was *present* to heal them.

18 ¶And, behold, men brought in a
bed a man which was taken with a
palsy: and they sought *means* to bring
him in, and to lay *him* before him.
19 And when they could not find by
what *way* they might bring him in be-
cause of the multitude, they went upon
the housetop, and let him down
through the tiling with *his* couch into
the midst before Jesus.
20 And when he saw their faith, he
said unto him, Man, thy sins are forgiven
thee.
21 And the scribes and the Pharisees
began to reason, saying, Who is this
which speaketh blasphemies? Who can
forgive sins, but God alone?
22 But when Jesus perceived their
thoughts, he answering said unto them,
What reason ye in your hearts?
23 Whether is easier, to say, Thy sins
be forgiven thee; or to say, Rise up and
walk?
24 But that ye may know that the Son
of man hath power upon earth to for-
give sins, (he said unto the sick of the
palsy,) I say unto thee, Arise, and take
up thy couch, and go into thine house.
25 And immediately he rose up be-
fore them, and took up that whereon he
lay, and departed to his own house,
glorifying God.
26 And they were all amazed, and
they glorified God, and were filled with
fear, saying, We have seen strange
things to day.
27 ¶And after these things he went
forth, and saw a publican, named Levi,
sitting at the receipt of custom: and he
said unto him, Follow me.
28 And he left all, rose up, and fol-
lowed him.
29 And Levi made him a great feast in
his own house: and there was a great
company of publicans and of others
that sat down with them.
30 But their scribes and Pharisees
murmured against his disciples,
saying, Why do ye eat and drink with
publicans and sinners?
31 And Jesus answering said unto
them, They that are whole need not a
physician; but they that are sick.
32 I came not to call the righteous,
but sinners to repentance.
33 ¶And they said unto him, Why do
the disciples of John fast often, and
make prayers, and likewise *the dis-
ciples* of the Pharisees; but thine eat
and drink?
34 And he said unto them, Can ye
make the children of the bridechamber
fast, while the bridegroom is with
them?
35 But the days will come, when the
bridegroom shall be taken away from
them, and then shall they fast in those
days.
36 ¶And he spake also a parable unto
them; No man putteth a piece of a new
garment upon an old; if otherwise, then
both the new maketh a rent, and the
piece that was *taken* out of the new
agreeth not with the old.
37 And no man putteth new wine into
old bottles; else the new wine will burst
the bottles, and be spilled, and the
bottles shall perish.
38 But new wine must be put into
new bottles; and both are preserved.
39 No man also having drunk old
wine straightway desireth new: for he
saith, The old is better.

CHAPTER 6

AND it came to pass on the second sab-
bath after the first, that he went
through the corn fields; and his dis-
ciples plucked the ears of corn, and did
eat, rubbing *them* in *their* hands.
2 And certain of the Pharisees said
unto them, Why do ye that which is not
lawful to do on the sabbath days?
3 And Jesus answering them said,
Have ye not read so much as this, what
David did, when himself was an
hungred, and they which were with
him;
4 How he went into the house of God,
and did take and eat the shewbread,
and gave also to them that were with
him; which it is not lawful to eat but for
the priests alone?
5 And he said unto them, That the
Son of man is Lord also of the sabbath.
6 ¶And it came to pass also on an-
other sabbath, that he entered into the
synagogue and taught: and there was a
man whose right hand was withered.
7 And the scribes and Pharisees
watched him, whether he would heal
on the sabbath day; that they might
find an accusation against him.
8 But he knew their thoughts, and
said to the man which had the withered
hand, Rise up, and stand forth in the
midst. And he arose and stood forth.
9 Then said Jesus unto them, I will
ask you one thing; Is it lawful on the
sabbath days to do good, or to do evil?
to save life, or to destroy *it?*
10 And looking round about upon
them all, he said unto the man, Stretch
forth thy hand. And he did so: and his
hand was restored whole as the other.
11 And they were filled with mad-
ness; and communed one with another
what they might do to Jesus.
12 ¶And it came to pass in those days,
that he went out into a mountain to

pray, and continued all night in prayer to God.

13 And when it was day, he called *unto him* his disciples: and of them he chose twelve, whom also he named apostles;

14 Simon, (whom he also named Peter,) and Andrew his brother, James and John, Philip and Bartholomew,

15 Matthew and Thomas, James the *son* of Al-phæ'us, and Simon called Ze-lō'tes,

16 And Judas *the brother* of James, and Judas Iscariot, which also was the traitor.

17 And he came down with them, and stood in the plain, and the company of his disciples, and a great multitude of people out of all Judæa and Jerusalem, and from the sea coast of Tyre and Sī'-don, which came to hear him, and to be healed of their diseases;

18 And they that were vexed with unclean spirits: and they were healed.

19 And the whole multitude sought to touch him: for there went virtue out of him, and healed *them* all.

20 ¶And he lifted up his eyes on his disciples, and said, Blessed *be ye* poor: for yours is the kingdom of God.

21 Blessed *are ye* that hunger now: for ye shall be filled. Blessed *are ye* that weep now: for ye shall laugh.

22 Blessed are ye, when men shall hate you, and when they shall separate you *from their company*, and shall reproach *you*, and cast out your name as evil, for the Son of man's sake.

23 Rejoice ye in that day, and leap for joy: for, behold, your reward *is* great in heaven: for in the like manner did their fathers unto the prophets.

24 But woe unto you that are rich! for ye have received your consolation.

25 Woe unto you that are full! for ye shall hunger. Woe unto you that laugh now! for ye shall mourn and weep.

26 Woe unto you, when all men shall speak well of you! for so did their fathers to the false prophets.

27 ¶But I say unto you which hear, Love your enemies, do good to them which hate you,

28 Bless them that curse you, and pray for them which despitefully use you.

29 And unto him that smiteth thee on the *one* cheek offer also the other; and him that taketh away thy cloak forbid not *to take thy* coat also.

30 Give to every man that asketh of thee; and of him that taketh away thy goods ask *them* not again.

31 And as ye would that men should do to you, do ye also to them likewise.

32 For if ye love them which love you, what thank have ye? for sinners also love those that love them.

33 And if ye do good to them which do good to you, what thank have ye? for sinners also do even the same.

34 And if ye lend *to them* of whom ye hope to receive, what thank have ye? for sinners also lend to sinners, to receive as much again.

35 But love ye your enemies, and do good, and lend, hoping for nothing again; and your reward shall be great, and ye shall be the children of the Highest: for he is kind unto the unthankful and *to* the evil.

36 Be ye therefore merciful, as your Father also is merciful.

37 Judge not, and ye shall not be judged: condemn not, and ye shall not be condemned: forgive, and ye shall be forgiven:

38 Give, and it shall be given unto you; good measure, pressed down, and shaken together, and running over, shall men give into your bosom. For with the same measure that ye mete withal it shall be measured to you again.

39 And he spake a parable unto them, Can the blind lead the blind? shall they not both fall into the ditch?

40 The disciple is not above his master: but every one that is perfect shall be as his master.

41 And why beholdest thou the mote that is in thy brother's eye, but perceivest not the beam that is in thine own eye?

42 Either how canst thou say to thy brother, Brother, let me pull out the mote that is in thine eye, when thou thyself beholdest not the beam that is in thine own eye? Thou hypocrite, cast out first the beam out of thine own eye, and then shalt thou see clearly to pull out the mote that is in thy brother's eye.

43 For a good tree bringeth not forth corrupt fruit; neither doth a corrupt tree bring forth good fruit.

44 For every tree is known by his own fruit. For of thorns men do not gather figs, nor of a bramble bush gather they grapes.

45 A good man out of the good treasure of his heart bringeth forth that which is good; and an evil man out of the evil treasure of his heart bringeth forth that which is evil: for of the abundance of the heart his mouth speaketh.

46 ¶And why call ye me, Lord, Lord, and do not the things which I say?

47 Whosoever cometh to me, and heareth my sayings, and doeth them, I will shew you to whom he is like:

48 He is like a man which built an house, and digged deep, and laid the foundation on a rock: and when the flood arose, the stream beat vehemently upon that house, and could not shake it: for it was founded upon a rock.

49 But he that heareth, and doeth not, is like a man that without a foundation built an house upon the earth; against which the stream did beat vehemently, and immediately it fell; and the ruin of that house was great.

CHAPTER 7

NOW when he had ended all his sayings in the audience of the people, he entered into Ca-per'na-um.

2 And a certain centurion's servant, who was dear unto him, was sick, and ready to die.

3 And when he heard of Jesus, he sent unto him the elders of the Jews, beseeching him that he would come and heal his servant.

4 And when they came to Jesus, they besought him instantly, saying, That he was worthy for whom he should do this:

5 For he loveth our nation, and he hath built us a synagogue.

6 Then Jesus went with them. And when he was now not far from the house, the centurion sent friends to him, saying unto him, Lord, trouble not thyself: for I am not worthy that thou shouldest enter under my roof:

7 Wherefore neither thought I myself worthy to come unto thee: but say in a word, and my servant shall be healed.

8 For I also am a man set under authority, having under me soldiers, and I say unto one, Go, and he goeth; and to another, Come, and he cometh; and to my servant, Do this, and he doeth *it*.

9 When Jesus heard these things, he marvelled at him, and turned him about, and said unto the people that followed him, I say unto you, I have not found so great faith, no, not in Israel.

10 And they that were sent, returning to the house, found the servant whole that had been sick.

11 ¶And it came to pass the day after, that he went into a city called Nain; and many of his disciples went with him, and much people.

12 Now when he came nigh to the gate of the city, behold, there was a dead man carried out, the only son of his mother, and she was a widow: and much people of the city was with her.

13 And when the Lord saw her, he had compassion on her, and said unto her, Weep not.

14 And he came and touched the bier: and they that bare *him* stood still. And he said, Young man, I say unto thee, Arise.

15 And he that was dead sat up, and began to speak. And he delivered him to his mother.

16 And there came a fear on all: and they glorified God, saying, That a great prophet is risen up among us; and, That God hath visited his people.

17 And this rumour of him went forth throughout all Judæa, and throughout all the region round about.

18 ¶And the disciples of John shewed him of all these things.

19 And John calling *unto him* two of his disciples sent *them* to Jesus, saying, Art thou he that should come? or look we for another?

20 When the men were come unto him, they said, John Baptist hath sent us unto thee, saying, Art thou he that should come? or look we for another?

21 And in that same hour he cured many of *their* infirmities and plagues, and of evil spirits; and unto many *that were* blind he gave sight.

22 Then Jesus answering said unto them, Go your way, and tell John what things ye have seen and heard; how that the blind see, the lame walk, the lepers are cleansed, the deaf hear, the dead are raised, to the poor the gospel is preached.

23 And blessed is *he*, whosoever shall not be offended in me.

24 ¶And when the messengers of John were departed, he began to speak unto the people concerning John, What went ye out into the wilderness for to see? A reed shaken with the wind?

25 But what went ye out for to see? A man clothed in soft raiment? Behold, they which are gorgeously apparelled, and live delicately, are in kings' courts.

26 But what went ye out for to see? A prophet? Yea, I say unto you, and much more than a prophet.

27 This is *he*, of whom it is written, Behold, I send my messenger before thy face, which shall prepare thy way before thee.

28 For I say unto you, Among those that are born of women there is not a greater prophet than John the Baptist: but he that is least in the kingdom of God is greater than he.

29 And all the people that heard *him*, and the publicans, justified God, being baptized with the baptism of John.

30 But the Pharisees and lawyers rejected the counsel of God against themselves, being not baptized of him.

31 ¶And the Lord said, Whereunto

then shall I liken the men of this generation? and to what are they like?
32 They are like unto children sitting in the marketplace, and calling one to another, and saying, We have piped unto you, and ye have not danced; we have mourned to you, and ye have not wept.
33 For John the Baptist came neither eating bread nor drinking wine; and ye say, He hath a devil.
34 The Son of man is come eating and drinking; and ye say, Behold a gluttonous man, and a winebibber, a friend of publicans and sinners!
35 But wisdom is justified of all her children.
36 ¶And one of the Pharisees desired him that he would eat with him. And he went into the Pharisee's house, and sat down to meat.
37 And, behold, a woman in the city, which was a sinner, when she knew that *Jesus* sat at meat in the Pharisee's house, brought an alabaster box of ointment,
38 And stood at his feet behind *him* weeping, and began to wash his feet with tears, and did wipe *them* with the hairs of her head, and kissed his feet, and anointed *them* with the ointment.
39 Now when the Pharisee which had bidden him saw *it*, he spake within himself, saying, This man, if he were a prophet, would have known who and what manner of woman *this is* that toucheth him: for she is a sinner.
40 And Jesus answering said unto him, Simon, I have somewhat to say unto thee. And he saith, Master, say on.
41 There was a certain creditor which had two debtors: the one owed five hundred pence, and the other fifty.
42 And when they had nothing to pay, he frankly forgave them both. Tell me therefore, which of them will love him most?
43 Simon answered and said, I suppose that *he*, to whom he forgave most. And he said unto him, Thou hast rightly judged.
44 And he turned to the woman, and said unto Simon, Seest thou this woman? I entered into thine house, thou gavest me no water for my feet: but she hath washed my feet with tears, and wiped *them* with the hairs of her head.
45 Thou gavest me no kiss: but this woman since the time I came in hath not ceased to kiss my feet.
46 My head with oil thou didst not anoint: but this woman hath anointed my feet with ointment.
47 Wherefore I say unto thee, Her sins, which are many, are forgiven; for she loved much: but to whom little is forgiven, *the same* loveth little.
48 And he said unto her, Thy sins are forgiven.
49 And they that sat at meat with him began to say within themselves, Who is this that forgiveth sins also?
50 And he said to the woman, Thy faith hath saved thee; go in peace.

CHAPTER 8

AND it came to pass afterward, that he went throughout every city and village, preaching and shewing the glad tidings of the kingdom of God: and the twelve *were* with him,
2 And certain women, which had been healed of evil spirits and infirmities, Mary called Magdalene, out of whom went seven devils,
3 And Jō′ăn-na the wife of Chū′za Herod's steward, and Susanna, and many others, which ministered unto him of their substance.
4 ¶And when much people were gathered together, and were come to him out of every city, he spake by a parable:
5 A sower went out to sow his seed: and as he sowed, some fell by the way side; and it was trodden down, and the fowls of the air devoured it.
6 And some fell upon a rock; and as soon as it was sprung up, it withered away, because it lacked moisture.
7 And some fell among thorns; and the thorns sprang up with it, and choked it.
8 And other fell on good ground, and sprang up, and bare fruit an hundredfold. And when he had said these things, he cried, He that hath ears to hear, let him hear.
9 ¶And his disciples asked him, saying, What might this parable be?
10 And he said, Unto you it is given to know the mysteries of the kingdom of God: but to others in parables; that seeing they might not see, and hearing they might not understand.
11 Now the parable is this: The seed is the word of God.
12 Those by the way side are they that hear; then cometh the devil, and taketh away the word out of their hearts, lest they should believe and be saved.
13 They on the rock *are they*, which, when they hear, receive the word with joy; and these have no root, which for a while believe, and in time of temptation fall away.
14 And that which fell among thorns are they, which, when they have heard, go forth, and are choked with cares and

riches and pleasures of *this* life, and
bring no fruit to perfection.
15 But that on the good ground are
they, which in an honest and good
heart, having heard the word, keep *it*,
and bring forth fruit with patience.
16 ¶No man, when he hath lighted a
candle, covereth it with a vessel, or put-
teth *it* under a bed; but setteth *it* on a
candlestick, that they which enter in
may see the light.
17 For nothing is secret, that shall not
be made manifest; neither *any thing*
hid, that shall not be known and come
abroad.
18 Take heed therefore how ye hear:
for whosoever hath, to him shall be giv-
en; and whosoever hath not, from him
shall be taken even that which he
seemeth to have.
19 ¶Then came to him *his* mother and
his brethren, and could not come at him
for the press.
20 And it was told him *by certain*
which said, Thy mother and thy breth-
ren stand without, desiring to see
thee.
21 And he answered and said unto
them, My mother and my brethren are
these which hear the word of God, and
do it.
22 ¶Now it came to pass on a certain
day, that he went into a ship with his
disciples: and he said unto them, Let us
go over unto the other side of the lake.
And they launched forth.
23 But as they sailed he fell asleep:
and there came down a storm of wind
on the lake; and they were filled *with*
water, and were in jeopardy.
24 And they came to him, and awoke
him, saying, Master, master, we perish.
Then he arose, and rebuked the wind
and the raging of the water: and they
ceased, and there was a calm.
25 And he said unto them, Where is
your faith? And they being afraid won-
dered, saying one to another, What
manner of man is this! for he command-
eth even the winds and water, and
they obey him.
26 ¶And they arrived at the country
of the Găd′a-rēneṡ, which is over
against Galilee.
27 And when he went forth to land,
there met him out of the city a certain
man, which had devils long time, and
ware no clothes, neither abode in *any*
house, but in the tombs.
28 When he saw Jesus, he cried out,
and fell down before him, and with a
loud voice said, What have I to do with
thee, Jesus, *thou* Son of God most high?
I beseech thee, torment me not.
29 (For he had commanded the un-
clean spirit to come out of the man. For
oftentimes it had caught him: and he
was kept bound with chains and in fet-
ters; and he brake the bands, and was
driven of the devil into the wilderness.)
30 And Jesus asked him, saying,
What is thy name? And he said, Legion:
because many devils were entered into
him.
31 And they besought him that he
would not command them to go out
into the deep.
32 And there was there an herd of
many swine feeding on the mountain:
and they besought him that he would
suffer them to enter into them. And he
suffered them.
33 Then went the devils out of the
man, and entered into the swine: and
the herd ran violently down a steep
place into the lake, and were choked.
34 When they that fed *them* saw
what was done, they fled, and went and
told *it* in the city and in the country.
35 Then they went out to see what
was done; and came to Jesus, and
found the man, out of whom the devils
were departed, sitting at the feet of Je-
sus, clothed, and in his right mind: and
they were afraid.
36 They also which saw *it* told them
by what means he that was possessed
of the devils was healed.
37 ¶Then the whole multitude of the
country of the Găd′a-rēneṡ round about
besought him to depart from them; for
they were taken with great fear: and he
went up into the ship, and returned
back again.
38 Now the man out of whom the dev-
ils were departed besought him that
he might be with him: but Jesus sent
him away, saying,
39 Return to thine own house, and
shew how great things God hath done
unto thee. And he went his way and
published throughout the whole city
how great things Jesus had done unto
him.
40 And it came to pass, that, when Je-
sus was returned, the people *gladly* re-
ceived him: for they were all waiting
for him.
41 ¶And, behold, there came a man
named Jā-ī′rus, and he was a ruler of
the synagogue: and he fell down at Je-
sus' feet, and besought him that he
would come into his house:
42 For he had one only daughter,
about twelve years of age, and she lay a
dying. But as he went the people
thronged him.
43 ¶And a woman having an issue of
blood twelve years, which had spent all

her living upon physicians, neither
could be healed of any,
44 Came behind *him*, and touched
the border of his garment: and immedi-
ately her issue of blood stanched.
45 And Jesus said, Who touched me?
When all denied, Peter and they that
were with him said, Master, the multi-
tude throng thee and press *thee*, and
sayest thou, Who touched me?
46 And Jesus said, Somebody hath
touched me: for I perceive that virtue is
gone out of me.
47 And when the woman saw that
she was not hid, she came trembling,
and falling down before him, she de-
clared unto him before all the people for
what cause she had touched him, and
how she was healed immediately.
48 And he said unto her, Daughter, be
of good comfort: thy faith hath made
thee whole; go in peace.
49 ¶While he yet spake, there cometh
one from the ruler of the synagogue's
house, saying to him, Thy daughter is
dead; trouble not the Master.
50 But when Jesus heard *it*, he an-
swered him, saying, Fear not: believe
only, and she shall be made whole.
51 And when he came into the house,
he suffered no man to go in, save Peter,
and James, and John, and the father
and the mother of the maiden.
52 And all wept, and bewailed her:
but he said, Weep not; she is not dead,
but sleepeth.
53 And they laughed him to scorn,
knowing that she was dead.
54 And he put them all out, and took
her by the hand, and called, saying,
Maid, arise.
55 And her spirit came again, and she
arose straightway: and he commanded
to give her meat.
56 And her parents were astonished:
but he charged them that they should
tell no man what was done.

CHAPTER 9

THEN he called his twelve disciples
together, and gave them power and
authority over all devils, and to cure dis-
eases.
2 And he sent them to preach the
kingdom of God, and to heal the sick.
3 And he said unto them, Take noth-
ing for *your* journey, neither staves,
nor scrip, neither bread, neither mon-
ey; neither have two coats apiece.
4 And whatsoever house ye enter
into, there abide, and thence depart.
5 And whosoever will not receive
you, when ye go out of that city, shake
off the very dust from your feet for a
testimony against them.
6 And they departed, and went
through the towns, preaching the gos-
pel, and healing every where.
7 ¶Now Herod the tetrarch heard of
all that was done by him: and he was
perplexed, because that it was said of
some, that John was risen from the
dead;
8 And of some, that E-lī'as had ap-
peared; and of others, that one of the
old prophets was risen again.
9 And Herod said, John have I be-
headed: but who is this, of whom I hear
such things? And he desired to see him.
10 ¶And the apostles, when they
were returned, told him all that they
had done. And he took them, and went
aside privately into a desert place be-
longing to the city called Bĕth-sā'i-da.
11 And the people, when they knew
it, followed him: and he received them,
and spake unto them of the kingdom of
God, and healed them that had need of
healing.
12 ¶And when the day began to wear
away, then came the twelve, and said
unto him, Send the multitude away,
that they may go into the towns and
country round about, and lodge, and
get victuals: for we are here in a desert
place.
13 But he said unto them, Give ye
them to eat. And they said, We have no
more but five loaves and two fishes; ex-
cept we should go and buy meat for all
this people.
14 For they were about five thousand
men. And he said to his disciples, Make
them sit down by fifties in a company.
15 And they did so, and made them
all sit down.
16 Then he took the five loaves and
the two fishes, and looking up to
heaven, he blessed them, and brake,
and gave to the disciples to set before
the multitude.
17 And they did eat, and were all
filled: and there was taken up of frag-
ments that remained to them twelve
baskets.
18 ¶And it came to pass, as he was
alone praying, his disciples were with
him: and he asked them, saying, Whom
say the people that I am?
19 They answering said, John the
Baptist; but some *say*, E-lī'as; and oth-
ers *say*, that one of the old prophets is
risen again.
20 He said unto them, But whom say
ye that I am? Peter answering said, The
Christ of God.
21 And he straitly charged them, and
commanded *them* to tell no man that
thing;
22 Saying, The Son of man must suf-

fer many things, and be rejected of the elders and chief priests and scribes, and be slain, and be raised the third day.

23 ¶And he said to *them* all, If any *man* will come after me, let him deny himself, and take up his cross daily, and follow me.

24 For whosoever will save his life shall lose it: but whosoever will lose his life for my sake, the same shall save it.

25 For what is a man advantaged, if he gain the whole world, and lose himself, or be cast away?

26 For whosoever shall be ashamed of me and of my words, of him shall the Son of man be ashamed, when he shall come in his own glory, and *in his* Father's, and of the holy angels.

27 But I tell you of a truth, there be some standing here, which shall not taste of death, till they see the kingdom of God.

28 ¶And it came to pass about an eight days after these sayings, he took Peter and John and James, and went up into a mountain to pray.

29 And as he prayed, the fashion of his countenance was altered, and his raiment *was* white *and* glistering.

30 And, behold, there talked with him two men, which were Moses and E-lī'as:

31 Who appeared in glory, and spake of his decease which he should accomplish at Jerusalem.

32 But Peter and they that were with him were heavy with sleep: and when they were awake, they saw his glory, and the two men that stood with him.

33 And it came to pass, as they departed from him, Peter said unto Jesus, Master, it is good for us to be here: and let us make three tabernacles; one for thee, and one for Moses, and one for E-lī'as: not knowing what he said.

34 While he thus spake, there came a cloud, and overshadowed them: and they feared as they entered into the cloud.

35 And there came a voice out of the cloud, saying, This is my beloved Son: hear him.

36 And when the voice was past, Jesus was found alone. And they kept *it* close, and told no man in those days any of those things which they had seen.

37 ¶And it came to pass, that on the next day, when they were come down from the hill, much people met him.

38 And, behold, a man of the company cried out, saying, Master, I beseech thee, look upon my son: for he is mine only child.

39 And, lo, a spirit taketh him, and he suddenly crieth out; and it teareth him that he foameth again, and bruising him hardly departeth from him.

40 And I besought thy disciples to cast him out; and they could not.

41 And Jesus answering said, O faithless and perverse generation, how long shall I be with you, and suffer you? Bring thy son hither.

42 And as he was yet a coming, the devil threw him down, and tare *him*. And Jesus rebuked the unclean spirit, and healed the child, and delivered him again to his father.

43 ¶And they were all amazed at the mighty power of God. But while they wondered every one at all things which Jesus did, he said unto his disciples,

44 Let these sayings sink down into your ears: for the Son of man shall be delivered into the hands of men.

45 But they understood not this saying, and it was hid from them, that they perceived it not: and they feared to ask him of that saying.

46 ¶Then there arose a reasoning among them, which of them should be greatest.

47 And Jesus, perceiving the thought of their heart, took a child, and set him by him,

48 And said unto them, Whosoever shall receive this child in my name receiveth me: and whosoever shall receive me receiveth him that sent me: for he that is least among you all, the same shall be great.

49 And John answered and said, Master, we saw one casting out devils in thy name; and we forbad him, because he followeth not with us.

50 And Jesus said unto him, Forbid *him* not: for he that is not against us is for us.

51 ¶And it came to pass, when the time was come that he should be received up, he stedfastly set his face to go to Jerusalem,

52 And sent messengers before his face: and they went, and entered into a village of the Sa-măr'i-tanṡ, to make ready for him.

53 And they did not receive him, because his face was as though he would go to Jerusalem.

54 And when his disciples James and John saw *this*, they said, Lord, wilt thou that we command fire to come down from heaven, and consume them, even as E-lī'as did?

55 But he turned, and rebuked them, and said, Ye know not what manner of spirit ye are of.

56 For the Son of man is not come to

destroy men's lives, but to save *them*. And they went to another village.

57 ¶And it came to pass, that, as they went in the way, a certain *man* said unto him, Lord, I will follow thee whithersoever thou goest.

58 And Jesus said unto him, Foxes have holes, and birds of the air *have* nests; but the Son of man hath not where to lay *his* head.

59 And he said unto another, Follow me. But he said, Lord, suffer me first to go and bury my father.

60 Jesus said unto him, Let the dead bury their dead: but go thou and preach the kingdom of God.

61 And another also said, Lord, I will follow thee; but let me first go bid them farewell, which are at home at my house.

62 And Jesus said unto him, No man, having put his hand to the plough, and looking back, is fit for the kingdom of God.

CHAPTER 10

AFTER these things the Lord appointed other seventy also, and sent them two and two before his face into every city and place, wither he himself would come.

2 Therefore said he unto them, The harvest truly *is* great, but the labourers *are* few: pray ye therefore the Lord of the harvest, that he would send forth labourers into his harvest.

3 Go your ways: behold, I send you forth as lambs among wolves.

4 Carry neither purse, nor scrip, nor shoes: and salute no man by the way.

5 And into whatsoever house ye enter, first say, Peace *be* to this house.

6 And if the son of peace be there, your peace shall rest upon it: if not, it shall turn to you again.

7 And in the same house remain, eating and drinking such things as they give: for the labourer is worthy of his hire. Go not from house to house.

8 And into whatsoever city ye enter, and they receive you, eat such things as are set before you:

9 And heal the sick that are therein, and say unto them, The kingdom of God is come nigh unto you.

10 But into whatsoever city ye enter, and they receive you not, go your ways out into the streets of the same, and say,

11 Even the very dust of your city, which cleaveth on us, we do wipe off against you: notwithstanding be ye sure of this, that the kingdom of God is come nigh unto you.

12 But I say unto you, that it shall be more tolerable in that day for Sodom, than for that city.

13 Woe unto thee, Chō-rā'zĭn! woe unto thee, Bĕth-sā'i-da! for if the mighty works had been done in Tyre and Sī'don, which have been done in you, they had a great while ago repented, sitting in sackcloth and ashes.

14 But it shall be more tolerable for Tyre and Sī'don at the judgment, than for you.

15 And thou, Ca-per'na-um, which art exalted to heaven, shalt be thrust down to hell.

16 He that heareth you heareth me; and he that despiseth you despiseth me; and he that despiseth me despiseth him that sent me.

17 ¶And the seventy returned again with joy, saying, Lord, even the devils are subject unto us through thy name.

18 And he said unto them, I beheld Satan as lightning fall from heaven.

19 Behold, I give unto you power to tread on serpents and scorpions, and over all the power of the enemy: and nothing shall by any means hurt you.

20 Notwithstanding in this rejoice not, that the spirits are subject unto you; but rather rejoice, because your names are written in heaven.

21 ¶In that hour Jesus rejoiced in spirit, and said, I thank thee, O Father, Lord of heaven and earth, that thou hast hid these things from the wise and prudent, and hast revealed them unto babes: even so, Father; for so it seemed good in thy sight.

22 All things are delivered to me of my Father: and no man knoweth who the Son is, but the Father; and who the Father is, but the Son, and *he* to whom the Son will reveal *him*.

23 ¶And he turned him unto *his* disciples, and said privately, Blessed *are* the eyes which see the things that ye see:

24 For I tell you, that many prophets and kings have desired to see those things which ye see, and have not seen *them;* and to hear those things which ye hear, and have not heard *them*.

25 ¶And, behold, a certain lawyer stood up, and tempted him, saying, Master, what shall I do to inherit eternal life?

26 He said unto him, What is written in the law? how readest thou?

27 And he answering said, Thou shalt love the Lord thy God with all thy heart, and with all thy soul, and with all thy strength, and with all thy mind; and thy neighbour as thyself.

28 And he said unto him, Thou hast

answered right: this do, and thou shalt live.

29 But he, willing to justify himself, said unto Jesus, And who is my neighbour?

30 And Jesus answering said, A certain *man* went down from Jerusalem to Jericho, and fell among thieves, which stripped him of his raiment, and wounded *him*, and departed, leaving *him* half dead.

31 And by chance there came down a certain priest that way: and when he saw him, he passed by on the other side.

32 And likewise a Levite, when he was at the place, came and looked *on him*, and passed by on the other side.

33 But a certain Sa-măr′i-tan, as he journeyed, came where he was: and when he saw him, he had compassion *on him*,

34 And went to *him*, and bound up his wounds, pouring in oil and wine, and set him on his own beast, and brought him to an inn, and took care of him.

35 And on the morrow when he departed, he took out two pence, and gave *them* to the host, and said unto him, Take care of him; and whatsoever thou spendest more, when I come again, I will repay thee.

36 Which now of these three, thinkest thou, was neighbour unto him that fell among the thieves?

37 And he said, He that shewed mercy on him. Then said Jesus unto him, Go, and do thou likewise.

38 ¶Now it came to pass, as they went, that he entered into a certain village: and a certain woman named Martha received him into her house.

39 And she had a sister called Mary, which also sat at Jesus' feet, and heard his word.

40 But Martha was cumbered about much serving, and came to him, and said, Lord, dost thou not care that my sister hath left me to serve alone? bid her therefore that she help me.

41 And Jesus answered and said unto her, Martha, Martha, thou art careful and troubled about many things:

42 But one thing is needful: and Mary hath chosen that good part, which shall not be taken away from her.

CHAPTER 11

AND it came to pass, that, as he was praying in a certain place, when he ceased, one of his disciples said unto him, Lord, teach us to pray, as John also taught his disciples.

2 And he said unto them, When ye pray, say, Our Father which art in heaven, Hallowed be thy name. Thy kingdom come. Thy will be done, as in heaven, so in earth.

3 Give us day by day our daily bread.

4 And forgive us our sins; for we also forgive every one that is indebted to us. And lead us not into temptation; but deliver us from evil.

5 And he said unto them, Which of you shall have a friend, and shall go unto him at midnight, and say unto him, Friend, lend me three loaves;

6 For a friend of mine in his journey is come to me, and I have nothing to set before him?

7 And he from within shall answer and say, Trouble me not: the door is now shut, and my children are with me in bed; I cannot rise and give thee.

8 I say unto you, Though he will not rise and give him, because he is his friend, yet because of his importunity he will rise and give him as many as he needeth.

9 And I say unto you, Ask, and it shall be given you; seek, and ye shall find; knock, and it shall be opened unto you.

10 For every one that asketh receiveth; and he that seeketh findeth; and to him that knocketh it shall be opened.

11 If a son shall ask bread of any of you that is a father, will he give him a stone? or if *he ask* a fish, will he for a fish give him a serpent?

12 Or if he shall ask an egg, will he offer him a scorpion?

13 If ye then, being evil, know how to give good gifts unto your children: how much more shall *your* heavenly Father give the Holy Spirit to them that ask him?

14 ¶And he was casting out a devil, and it was dumb. And it came to pass, when the devil was gone out, the dumb spake; and the people wondered.

15 But some of them said, He casteth out devils through Bē-ĕl′ze-bŭb the chief of the devils.

16 And others, tempting *him*, sought of him a sign from heaven.

17 But he, knowing their thoughts, said unto them, Every kingdom divided against itself is brought to desolation; and a house *divided* against a house falleth.

18 If Satan also be divided against himself, how shall his kingdom stand? because ye say that I cast out devils through Bē-ĕl′ze-bŭb.

19 And if I by Bē-ĕl′ze-bŭb cast out devils, by whom do your sons cast *them* out? therefore shall they be your judges.

20 But if I with the finger of God cast

out devils, no doubt the kingdom of
God is come upon you.
21 When a strong man armed keep-
eth his palace, his goods are in peace:
22 But when a stronger than he shall
come upon him, and overcome him, he
taketh from him all his armour wherein
he trusted, and divideth his spoils.
23 He that is not with me is against
me: and he that gathereth not with me
scattereth.
24 When the unclean spirit is gone
out of a man, he walketh through dry
places, seeking rest; and finding none,
he saith, I will return unto my house
whence I came out.
25 And when he cometh, he findeth *it*
swept and garnished.
26 Then goeth he, and taketh *to him*
seven other spirits more wicked than
himself; and they enter in, and dwell
there: and the last *state* of that man is
worse than the first.
27 ¶**And it came to pass, as he spake
these things, a certain woman of the
company lifted up her voice, and said
unto him, Blessed *is* the womb that
bare thee, and the paps which thou hast
sucked.**
28 **But he said,** Yea rather, blessed
are they that hear the word of God, and
keep it.
29 ¶**And when the people were gath-
ered thick together, he began to say,**
This is an evil generation: they seek a
sign; and there shall no sign be given it,
but the sign of Jonas the prophet.
30 For as Jonas was a sign unto the
Nīn'e-vītes, so shall also the Son of man
be to this generation.
31 The queen of the south shall rise
up in the judgment with the men of this
generation, and condemn them: for she
came from the utmost parts of the
earth to hear the wisdom of Solomon;
and, behold, a greater than Solomon *is*
here.
32 The men of Nīn'e-ve shall rise up
in the judgment with this generation,
and shall condemn it: for they repented
at the preaching of Jonas; and, behold,
a greater than Jonas *is* here.
33 No man, when he hath lighted a
candle, putteth *it* in a secret place,
neither under a bushel, but on a candle-
stick, that they which come in may
see the light.
34 The light of the body is the eye:
therefore when thine eye is single, thy
whole body also is full of light; but
when *thine eye* is evil, thy body also *is*
full of darkness.
35 Take heed therefore that the light
which is in thee be not darkness.
36 If thy whole body therefore *be* full
of light, having no part dark, the whole
shall be full of light, as when the bright
shining of a candle doth give thee light.
37 ¶**And as he spake, a certain
Pharisee besought him to dine with
him: and he went in, and sat down to
meat.**
38 **And when the Pharisee saw *it*, he
marvelled that he had not first washed
before dinner.**
39 **And the Lord said unto him,** Now
do ye Pharisees make clean the outside
of the cup and the platter; but your in-
ward part is full of ravening and
wickedness.
40 *Ye* fools, did not he that made that
which is without make that which is
within also?
41 But rather give alms of such things
as ye have; and, behold, all things are
clean unto you.
42 But woe unto you, Pharisees! for
ye tithe mint and rue and all manner of
herbs, and pass over judgment and the
love of God: these ought ye to have
done, and not to leave the other un-
done.
43 Woe unto you, Pharisees! for ye
love the uppermost seats in the syna-
gogues, and greetings in the markets.
44 Woe unto you, scribes and
Pharisees, hypocrites! for ye are as
graves which appear not, and the men
that walk over *them* are not aware *of
them.*
45 **Then answered one of the lawyers,
and said unto him, Master, thus saying
thou reproachest us also.**
46 **And he said,** Woe unto you also, *ye*
lawyers! for ye lade men with burdens
grievous to be borne, and ye yourselves
touch not the burdens with one of your
fingers.
47 Woe unto you! for ye build the
sepulchres of the prophets, and your
fathers killed them.
48 Truly ye bear witness that ye al-
low the deeds of your fathers: for they
indeed killed them, and ye build their
sepulchres.
49 Therefore also said the wisdom of
God, I will send them prophets and
apostles, and *some* of them they shall
slay and persecute:
50 That the blood of all the prophets,
which was shed from the foundation of
the world, may be required of this gen-
eration;
51 From the blood of Abel unto the
blood of Zăch-a-rī'as, which perished
between the altar and the temple:
verily I say unto you, It shall be re-
quired of this generation.
52 Woe unto you, lawyers! for ye
have taken away the key of knowledge:

ye entered not in yourselves, and them
that were entering in ye hindered.
53 And as he said these things unto
them, the scribes and the Pharisees be-
gan to urge *him* vehemently, and to
provoke him to speak of many things:
54 Laying wait for him, and seeking
to catch something out of his mouth,
that they might accuse him.

CHAPTER 12

IN the mean time, when there were gath-
ered together an innumerable multi-
tude of people, insomuch that they
trode one upon another, he began to
say unto his disciples first of all, Be-
ware ye of the leaven of the Pharisees,
which is hypocrisy.
2 For there is nothing covered, that
shall not be revealed; neither hid, that
shall not be known.
3 Therefore whatsoever ye have spok-
en in darkness shall be heard in the
light; and that which ye have spoken in
the ear in closets shall be proclaimed
upon the housetops.
4 And I say unto you my friends, Be
not afraid of them that kill the body,
and after that have no more that they
can do.
5 But I will forwarn you whom ye
shall fear: Fear him, which after he
hath killed hath power to cast into hell;
yea, I say unto you, Fear him.
6 Are not five sparrows sold for two
farthings, and not one of them is for-
gotten before God?
7 But even the very hairs of your head
are all numbered. Fear not therefore:
ye are of more value than many
sparrows.
8 Also I say unto you, Whosoever
shall confess me before men, him shall
the Son of man also confess before the
angels of God:
9 But he that denieth me before men
shall be denied before the angels of
God.
10 And whosoever shall speak a
word against the Son of man, it shall be
forgiven him: but unto him that blas-
phemeth against the Holy Ghost it shall
not be forgiven.
11 And when they bring you unto the
synagogues, and *unto* magistrates, and
powers, take ye no thought how or
what thing ye shall answer, or what ye
shall say:
12 For the Holy Ghost shall teach you
in the same hour what ye ought to say.
13 ¶And one of the company said
unto him, Master, speak to my brother,
that he divide the inheritance with me.
14 And he said unto him, Man, who
made me a judge or a divider over you?
15 And he said unto them, Take heed,
and beware of covetousness: for a
man's life consisteth not in the abun-
dance of the things which he possess-
eth.
16 And he spake a parable unto them,
saying, The ground of a certain rich
man brought forth plentifully:
17 And he thought within himself,
saying, What shall I do, because I have
no room where to bestow my fruits?
18 And he said, This will I do: I will
pull down my barns, and build greater;
and there will I bestow all my fruits and
my goods.
19 And I will say to my soul, Soul,
thou hast much goods laid up for many
years; take thine ease, eat, drink, *and*
be merry.
20 But God said unto him, *Thou* fool,
this night thy soul shall be required of
thee: then whose shall those things be,
which thou hast provided?
21 So *is* he that layeth up treasure for
himself, and is not rich toward God.
22 ¶And he said unto his disciples,
Therefore I say unto you, Take no
thought for your life, what ye shall eat;
neither for the body, what ye shall put
on.
23 The life is more than meat, and the
body *is more* than raiment.
24 Consider the ravens: for they
neither sow nor reap; which neither
have storehouse nor barn; and God feed-
eth them: how much more are ye bet-
ter than the fowls?
25 And which of you with taking
thought can add to his stature one cu-
bit?
26 If ye then be not able to do that
thing which is least, why take ye
thought for the rest?
27 Consider the lilies how they grow:
they toil not, they spin not; and yet I say
unto you, that Solomon in all his glory
was not arrayed like one of these.
28 If then God so clothe the grass,
which is to day in the field, and to
morrow is cast into the oven; how
much more *will he clothe* you, O ye of
little faith?
29 And seek not ye what ye shall eat,
or what ye shall drink, neither be ye of
doubtful mind.
30 For all these things do the nations
of the world seek after: and your Father
knoweth that ye have need of these
things.
31 But rather seek ye the kingdom of
God; and all these things shall be added
unto you.
32 Fear not, little flock; for it is your
Father's good pleasure to give you the
kingdom.

33 Sell that ye have, and give alms; provide yourselves bags which wax not old, a treasure in the heavens that faileth not, where no thief approacheth, neither moth corrupteth.

34 For where your treasure is, there will your heart be also.

35 Let your loins be girded about, and *your* lights burning;

36 And ye yourselves like unto men that wait for their lord, when he will return from the wedding; that when he cometh and knocketh, they may open unto him immediately.

37 Blessed *are* those servants, whom the lord when he cometh shall find watching: verily I say unto you, that he shall gird himself, and make them to sit down to meat, and will come forth and serve them.

38 And if he shall come in the second watch, or come in the third watch, and find *them* so, blessed are those servants.

39 And this know, that if the goodman of the house had known what hour the thief would come, he would have watched, and not have suffered his house to be broken through.

40 Be ye therefore ready also: for the Son of man cometh at an hour when ye think not.

41 ¶Then Peter said unto him, Lord, speakest thou this parable unto us, or even to all?

42 And the Lord said, Who then is that faithful and wise steward, whom *his* lord shall make ruler over his household, to give *them their* portion of meat in due season?

43 Blessed *is* that servant, whom his lord when he cometh shall find so doing.

44 Of a truth I say unto you, that he will make him ruler over all that he hath.

45 But and if that servant say in his heart, My lord delayeth his coming; and shall begin to beat the menservants and maidens, and to eat and drink, and to be drunken;

46 The lord of that servant will come in a day when he looketh not for *him*, and at an hour when he is not aware, and will cut him in sunder, and will appoint him his portion with the unbelievers.

47 And that servant, which knew his lord's will, and prepared not *himself*, neither did according to his will, shall be beaten with many *stripes*.

48 But he that knew not, and did commit things worthy of stripes, shall be beaten with few *stripes*. For unto whomsoever much is given, of him shall be much required: and to whom men have committed much, of him they will ask the more.

49 ¶I am come to send fire on the earth; and what will I, if it be already kindled?

50 But I have a baptism to be baptized with; and how am I straitened till it be accomplished!

51 Suppose ye that I am come to give peace on earth? I tell you, Nay; but rather division:

52 For from henceforth there shall be five in one house divided, three against two and two against three.

53 The father shall be divided against the son, and the son against the father; the mother against the daughter, and the daughter against the mother; the mother in law against her daughter in law, and the daughter in law against her mother in law.

54 ¶And he said also to the people, When ye see a cloud rise out of the west, straightway ye say, There cometh a shower; and so it is.

55 And when *ye see* the south wind blow, ye say, There will be heat; and it cometh to pass.

56 *Ye* hypocrites, ye can discern the face of the sky and of the earth; but how is it that ye do not discern this time?

57 Yea, and why even of yourselves judge ye not what is right?

58 ¶When thou goest with thine adversary to the magistrate, *as thou art* in the way, give diligence that thou mayest be delivered from him; lest he hale thee to the judge, and the judge deliver thee to the officer, and the officer cast thee into prison.

59 I tell thee, thou shalt not depart thence, till thou hast paid the very last mite.

CHAPTER 13

THERE were present at that season some that told him of the Galilæans, whose blood Pilate had mingled with their sacrifices.

2 And Jesus answering said unto them, Suppose ye that these Galilæans were sinners above all the Galilæans, because they suffered such things?

3 I tell you, Nay: but, except ye repent, ye shall all likewise perish.

4 Or those eighteen, upon whom the tower in Sī-lō'am fell, and slew them, think ye that they were sinners above all men that dwelt in Jerusalem?

5 I tell you, Nay: but, except ye repent, ye shall all likewise perish.

6 ¶He spake also this parable; A certain *man* had a fig tree planted in his

vineyard; and he came and sought fruit thereon, and found none.

7 Then said he unto the dresser of his vineyard, Behold, these three years I come seeking fruit on this fig tree, and find none: cut it down; why cumbereth it the ground?

8 And he answering said unto him, Lord, let it alone this year also, till I shall dig about it, and dung *it:*

9 And if it bear fruit, *well:* and if not, *then* after that thou shalt cut it down.

10 ¶And he was teaching in one of the synagogues on the sabbath.

11 And, behold, there was a woman which had a spirit of infirmity eighteen years, and was bowed together, and could in no wise lift up *herself.*

12 And when Jesus saw her, he called *her to him,* and said unto her, Woman, thou art loosed from thine infirmity.

13 And he laid *his* hands on her: and immediately she was made straight, and glorified God.

14 And the ruler of the synagogue answered with indignation, because that Jesus had healed on the sabbath day, and said unto the people, There are six days in which men ought to work: in them therefore come and be healed, and not on the sabbath day.

15 The Lord then answered him, and said, *Thou* hypocrite, doth not each one of you on the sabbath loose his ox or *his* ass from the stall, and lead *him* away to watering?

16 And ought not this woman, being a daughter of Abraham, whom Satan hath bound, lo, these eighteen years, be loosed from this bond on the sabbath day?

17 And when he had said these things, all his adversaries were ashamed: and all the people rejoiced for all the glorious things that were done by him.

18 ¶Then said he, Unto what is the kingdom of God like? and whereunto shall I resemble it?

19 It is like a grain of mustard seed, which a man took, and cast into his garden; and it grew, and waxed a great tree; and the fowls of the air lodged in the branches of it.

20 ¶And again he said, Whereunto shall I liken the kingdom of God?

21 It is like leaven, which a woman took and hid in three measures of meal, till the whole was leavened.

22 And he went through the cities and villages, teaching, and journeying toward Jerusalem.

23 ¶Then said one unto him, Lord, are there few that be saved? And he said unto them,

24 Strive to enter in at the strait gate: for many, I say unto you, will seek to enter in, and shall not be able.

25 When once the master of the house is risen up, and hath shut to the door, and ye begin to stand without, and to knock at the door, saying, Lord, Lord, open unto us; and he shall answer and say unto you, I know you not whence ye are:

26 Then shall ye begin to say, We have eaten and drunk in thy presence, and thou hast taught in our streets.

27 But he shall say, I tell you, I know you not whence ye are; depart from me, all *ye* workers of iniquity.

28 There shall be weeping and gnashing of teeth, when ye shall see Abraham, and Isaac, and Jacob, and all the prophets, in the kingdom of God, and you *yourselves* thrust out.

29 And they shall come from the east, and *from* the west, and from the north, and *from* the south, and shall sit down in the kingdom of God.

30 And, behold, there are last which shall be first, and there are first which shall be last.

31 ¶The same day there came certain of the Pharisees, saying unto him, Get thee out, and depart hence: for Herod will kill thee.

32 And he said unto them, Go ye, and tell that fox, Behold, I cast out devils, and I do cures to day and to morrow, and the third *day* I shall be perfected.

33 Nevertheless I must walk to day, and to morrow, and the *day* following: for it cannot be that a prophet perish out of Jerusalem.

34 O Jerusalem, Jerusalem, which killest the prophets, and stonest them that are sent unto thee; how often would I have gathered thy children together, as a hen *doth gather* her brood under *her* wings, and ye would not!

35 Behold, your house is left unto you desolate: and verily I say unto you, Ye shall not see me, until *the time* come when ye shall say, Blessed *is* he that cometh in the name of the Lord.

CHAPTER 14

AND it came to pass, as he went into the house of one of the chief Pharisees to eat bread on the sabbath day, that they watched him.

2 And, behold, there was a certain man before him which had the dropsy.

3 And Jesus answering spake unto the lawyers and Pharisees, saying, Is it lawful to heal on the sabbath day?

4 And they held their peace. And he

took *him*, and healed him, and let him
go;
5 And answered them, saying, Which
of you shall have an ass or an ox fallen
into a pit, and will not straightway pull
him out on the sabbath day?
6 And they could not answer him
again to these things.
7 ¶And he put forth a parable to those
which were bidden, when he marked
how they chose out the chief rooms;
saying unto them,
8 When thou art bidden of any *man* to
a wedding, sit not down in the highest
room; lest a more honourable man than
thou be bidden of him;
9 And he that bade thee and him
come and say to thee, Give this man
place; and thou begin with shame to
take the lowest room.
10 But when thou art bidden, go and
sit down in the lowest room; that when
he that bade thee cometh, he may say
unto thee, Friend, go up higher: then
shalt thou have worship in the pres-
ence of them that sit at meat with thee.
11 For whosoever exalteth himself
shall be abased; and he that humbleth
himself shall be exalted.
12 ¶Then said he also to him that
bade him, When thou makest a dinner
or a supper, call not thy friends, nor thy
brethren, neither thy kinsmen, nor *thy*
rich neighbours; lest they also bid thee
again, and a recompence be made thee.
13 But when thou makest a feast, call
the poor, the maimed, the lame, the
blind:
14 And thou shalt be blessed; for they
cannot recompense thee: for thou shalt
be recompensed at the resurrection of
the just.
15 ¶And when one of them that sat at
meat with him heard these things, he
said unto him, Blessed *is* he that shall
eat bread in the kingdom of God.
16 Then said he unto him, A certain
man made a great supper, and bade
many:
17 And sent his servant at supper
time to say to them that were bidden,
Come; for all things are now ready.
18 And they all with one *consent* be-
gan to make excuse. The first said unto
him, I have bought a piece of ground,
and I must needs go and see it: I pray
thee have me excused.
19 And another said, I have bought
five yoke of oxen, and I go to prove
them: I pray thee have me excused.
20 And another said, I have married a
wife, and therefore I cannot come.
21 So that servant came, and shewed
his lord these things. Then the master
of the house being angry said to his ser-
vant, Go out quickly into the streets
and lanes of the city, and bring in hither
the poor, and the maimed, and the halt,
and the blind.
22 And the servant said, Lord, it is
done as thou hast commanded, and yet
there is room.
23 And the lord said unto the servant,
Go out into the highways and hedges,
and compel *them* to come in, that my
house may be filled.
24 For I say unto you, That none of
those men which were bidden shall
taste of my supper.
25 ¶And there went great multitudes
with him: and he turned, and said unto
them.
26 If any *man* come to me, and hate
not his father, and mother, and wife,
and children, and brethren, and sisters,
yea, and his own life also, he cannot be
my disciple.
27 And whosoever doth not bear his
cross, and come after me, cannot be my
disciple.
28 For which of you, intending to
build a tower, sitteth not down first,
and counteth the cost, whether he have
sufficient to finish *it?*
29 Lest haply, after he hath laid the
foundation, and is not able to finish *it*,
all that behold *it* begin to mock him,
30 Saying, This man began to build,
and was not able to finish.
31 Or what king, going to make war
against another king, sitteth not down
first, and consulteth whether he be able
with ten thousand to meet him that
cometh against him with twenty thou-
sand?
32 Or else, while the other is yet a
great way off, he sendeth an ambas-
sage, and desireth conditions of peace.
33 So likewise, whosoever he be of
you that forsaketh not all that he hath,
he cannot be my disciple.
34 ¶Salt *is* good: but if the salt have
lost his savour, wherewith shall it be
seasoned?
35 It is neither fit for the land, nor yet
for the dunghill; *but* men cast it out. He
that hath ears to hear, let him hear.

CHAPTER 15

THEN drew near unto him all the publi-
cans and sinners for to hear him.
2 And the Pharisees and scribes mur-
mured, saying, This man receiveth sin-
ners, and eateth with them.
3 ¶And he spake this parable unto
them, saying,
4 What man of you, having an
hundred sheep, if he lose one of them,
doth not leave the ninety and nine in

the wilderness, and go after that which is lost, until he find it?

5 And when he hath found *it,* he layeth *it* on his shoulders, rejoicing.

6 And when he cometh home, he calleth together *his* friends and neighbours, saying unto them, Rejoice with me; for I have found my sheep which was lost.

7 I say unto you, that likewise joy shall be in heaven over one sinner that repenteth, more than over ninety and nine just persons, which need no repentance.

8 ¶Either what woman having ten pieces of silver, if she lose one piece, doth not light a candle, and sweep the house, and seek diligently till she find *it?*

9 And when she hath found *it,* she calleth *her* friends and *her* neighbours together, saying, Rejoice with me; for I have found the piece which I had lost.

10 Likewise, I say unto you there is joy in the presence of the angels of God over one sinner that repenteth.

11 ¶**And he said,** A certain man had two sons:

12 And the younger of them said to *his* father, Father, give me the portion of goods that falleth *to me.* And he divided unto them *his* living.

13 And not many days after the younger son gathered all together, and took his journey into a far country, and there wasted his substance with riotous living.

14 And when he had spent all, there arose a mighty famine in that land; and he began to be in want.

15 And he went and joined himself to a citizen of that country; and he sent him into his fields to feed swine.

16 And he would fain have filled his belly with the husks that the swine did eat: and no man gave unto him.

17 And when he came to himself, he said, How many hired servants of my father's have bread enough and to spare, and I perish with hunger!

18 I will arise and go to my father, and will say unto him, Father, I have sinned against heaven, and before thee,

19 And am no more worthy to be called thy son: make me as one of thy hired servants.

20 And he arose, and came to his father. But when he was yet a great way off, his father saw him, and had compassion, and ran, and fell on his neck, and kissed him.

21 And the son said unto him, Father, I have sinned against heaven, and in thy sight, and am no more worthy to be called thy son.

22 But the father said to his servants, Bring forth the best robe, and put *it* on him; and put a ring on his hand, and shoes on *his* feet:

23 And bring hither the fatted calf, and kill *it;* and let us eat, and be merry:

24 For this my son was dead, and is alive again; he was lost, and is found. And they began to be merry.

25 Now his elder son was in the field: and as he came and drew nigh to the house, he heard musick and dancing.

26 And he called one of the servants, and asked what these things meant.

27 And he said unto him, Thy brother is come; and thy father hath killed the fatted calf, because he hath received him safe and sound.

28 And he was angry, and would not go in: therefore came his father out, and intreated him.

29 And he answering said to *his* father, Lo, these many years do I serve thee, neither transgressed I at any time thy commandment: and yet thou never gavest me a kid, that I might make merry with my friends:

30 But as soon as this thy son was come, which hath devoured thy living with harlots, thou hast killed for him the fatted calf.

31 And he said unto him, Son, thou art ever with me, and all that I have is thine.

32 It was meet that we should make merry, and be glad: for this thy brother was dead, and is alive again; and was lost, and is found.

CHAPTER 16

AND he said also unto his disciples, There was a certain rich man, which had a steward; and the same was accused unto him that he had wasted his goods.

2 And he called him, and said unto him, How is it that I hear this of thee? give an account of thy stewardship; for thou mayest be no longer steward.

3 Then the steward said within himself, What shall I do? for my lord taketh away from me the stewardship: I cannot dig; to beg I am ashamed.

4 I am resolved what to do, that, when I am put out of the stewardship, they may receive me into their houses.

5 So he called every one of his lord's debtors *unto him,* and said unto the first, How much owest thou unto my lord?

6 And he said, An hundred measures of oil. And he said unto him, Take thy bill, and sit down quickly, and write fifty.

7 Then said he to another, And how

much owest thou? And he said, An hundred measures of wheat. And he said unto him, Take thy bill, and write fourscore.

8 And the lord commended the unjust steward, because he had done wisely: for the children of this world are in their generation wiser than the children of light.

9 And I say unto you, Make to yourselves friends of the mammon of unrighteousness; that, when ye fail, they may receive you into everlasting habitations.

10 He that is faithful in that which is least is faithful also in much: and he that is unjust in the least is unjust also in much.

11 If therefore ye have not been faithful in the unrighteous mammon, who will commit to your trust the true *riches?*

12 And if ye have not been faithful in that which is another man's, who shall give you that which is your own?

13 No servant can serve two masters: for either he will hate the one, and love the other; or else he will hold to the one, and despise the other. Ye cannot serve God and mammon.

14 **¶And the Pharisees also, who were covetous, heard all these things: and they derided him.**

15 **And he said unto them,** Ye are they which justify yourselves before men; but God knoweth your hearts: for that which is highly esteemed among men is abomination in the sight of God.

16 The law and the prophets *were* until John: since that time the kingdom of God is preached, and every man presseth into it.

17 And it is easier for heaven and earth to pass, than one tittle of the law to fail.

18 Whosoever putteth away his wife, and marrieth another, committeth adultery: and whosoever marrieth her that is put away from *her* husband committeth adultery.

19 ¶There was a certain rich man, which was clothed in purple and fine linen, and fared sumptuously every day:

20 And there was a certain beggar named Lazarus, which was laid at his gate, full of sores,

21 And desiring to be fed with the crumbs which fell from the rich man's table: moreover the dogs came and licked his sores.

22 And it came to pass, that the beggar died, and was carried by the angels into Abraham's bosom: the rich man also died, and was buried;

23 And in hell he lift up his eyes, being in torments, and seeth Abraham afar off, and Lazarus in his bosom.

24 And he cried and said, Father Abraham, have mercy on me, and send Lazarus, that he may dip the tip of his finger in water, and cool my tongue; for I am tormented in this flame.

25 But Abraham said, Son, remember that thou in thy lifetime receivedst thy good things, and likewise Lazarus evil things: but now he is comforted, and thou art tormented.

26 And beside all this, between us and you there is a great gulf fixed: so that they which would pass from hence to you cannot; neither can they pass to us, that *would come* from thence.

27 Then he said, I pray thee therefore, father, that thou wouldest send him to my father's house:

28 For I have five brethren; that he may testify unto them, lest they also come into this place of torment.

29 Abraham saith unto him, They have Moses and the prophets; let them hear them.

30 And he said, Nay, father Abraham: but if one went unto them from the dead, they will repent.

31 And he said unto him, If they hear not Moses and the prophets, neither will they be persuaded, though one rose from the dead.

CHAPTER 17

THEN said he unto the disciples, It is impossible but that offences will come: but woe *unto him,* through whom they come!

2 It were better for him that a millstone were hanged about his neck, and he cast into the sea, than that he should offend one of these little ones.

3 ¶Take heed to yourselves: If thy brother trespass against thee, rebuke him; and if he repent, forgive him.

4 And if he trespass against thee seven times in a day, and seven times in a day turn again to thee, saying, I repent; thou shalt forgive him.

5 **¶And the apostles said unto the Lord, Increase our faith.**

6 **And the Lord said,** If ye had faith as a grain of mustard seed, ye might say unto this sycamine tree, Be thou plucked up by the root, and be thou planted in the sea; and it should obey you.

7 But which of you, having a servant plowing or feeding cattle, will say unto him by and by, when he is come from the field, Go and sit down to meat?

8 And will not rather say unto him, Make ready wherewith I may sup, and

gird thyself, and serve me, till I have eaten and drunken; and afterward thou shalt eat and drink?

9 Doth he thank that servant because he did the things that were commanded him? I trow not.

10 So likewise ye, when ye shall have done all those things which are commanded you, say, We are unprofitable servants: we have done that which was our duty to do.

11 ¶And it came to pass, as he went to Jerusalem, that he passed through the midst of Sa-mâ'rĭ-a and Galilee.

12 And as he entered into a certain village, there met him ten men that were lepers, which stood afar off:

13 And they lifted up *their* voices, and said, Jesus, Master, have mercy on us.

14 And when he saw *them*, he said unto them, Go shew yourselves unto the priests. And it came to pass, that, as they went, they were cleansed.

15 And one of them, when he saw that he was healed, turned back, and with a loud voice glorified God,

16 And fell down on *his* face at his feet, giving him thanks: and he was a Sa-măr'i-tan.

17 And Jesus answering said, Were there not ten cleansed? but where *are* the nine?

18 There are not found that returned to give glory to God, save this stranger.

19 And he said unto him, Arise, go thy way: thy faith hath made thee whole.

20 ¶And when he was demanded of the Pharisees, when the kingdom of God should come, he answered them and said, The kingdom of God cometh not with observation:

21 Neither shall they say, Lo here! or, lo there! for, behold, the kingdom of God is within you.

22 ¶And he said unto the disciples, The days will come, when ye shall desire to see one of the days of the Son of man, and ye shall not see *it*.

23 And they shall say to you, See here; or, see there: go not after *them*, nor follow *them*.

24 For as the lightning, that lighteneth out of the one *part* under heaven, shineth unto the other *part* under heaven; so shall also the Son of man be in his day.

25 But first must he suffer many things, and be rejected of this generation.

26 And as it was in the days of Nō'e, so shall it be also in the days of the Son of man.

27 They did eat, they drank, they married wives, they were given in marriage, until the day that Nō'e entered into the ark, and the flood came, and destroyed them all.

28 Likewise also as it was in the days of Lot; they did eat, they drank, they bought, they sold, they planted, they builded;

29 But the same day that Lot went out of Sodom it rained fire and brimstone from heaven, and destroyed *them* all.

30 Even thus shall it be in the day when the Son of man is revealed.

31 In that day, he which shall be upon the housetop, and his stuff in the house, let him not come down to take it away: and he that is in the field, let him likewise not return back.

32 Remember Lot's wife.

33 Whosoever shall seek to save his life shall lose it; and whosoever shall lose his life shall preserve it.

34 I tell you, in that night there shall be two *men* in one bed; the one shall be taken, and the other shall be left.

35 Two *women* shall be grinding together; the one shall be taken, and the other left.

36 Two *men* shall be in the field; the one shall be taken, and the other left.

37 And they answered and said unto him, Where, Lord? And he said unto them, Wheresoever the body *is*, thither will the eagles be gathered together.

CHAPTER 18

AND he spake a parable unto them *to this end*, that men ought always to pray, and not to faint;

2 Saying, There was in a city a judge, which feared not God, neither regarded man:

3 And there was a widow in that city; and she came unto him, saying, Avenge me of mine adversary.

4 And he would not for a while: but afterward he said within himself, Though I fear not God, nor regard man;

5 Yet because this widow troubleth me, I will avenge her, lest by her continual coming she weary me.

6 And the Lord said, Hear what the unjust judge saith.

7 And shall not God avenge his own elect, which cry day and night unto him, though he bear long with them?

8 I tell you that he will avenge them speedily. Nevertheless when the Son of man cometh, shall he find faith on the earth?

9 ¶And he spake this parable unto certain which trusted in themselves that they were righteous, and despised others:

10 Two men went up into the temple to pray; the one a Pharisee, and the other a publican.
11 The Pharisee stood and prayed thus with himself, God, I thank thee, that I am not as other men *are*, extortioners, unjust, adulterers, or even as this publican.
12 I fast twice in the week, I give tithes of all that I possess.
13 And the publican, standing afar off, would not lift up so much as *his* eyes unto heaven, but smote upon his breast, saying, God be merciful to me a sinner.
14 I tell you, this man went down to his house justified *rather* than the other: for every one that exalteth himself shall be abased; and he that humbleth himself shall be exalted.
15 ¶And they brought unto him also infants, that he would touch them: but when *his* disciples saw *it*, they rebuked them.
16 But Jesus called them *unto him*, and said, Suffer little children to come unto me, and forbid them not: for of such is the kingdom of God.
17 Verily I say unto you, Whosoever shall not receive the kingdom of God as a little child shall in no wise enter therein.
18 ¶And a certain ruler asked him, saying, Good Master, what shall I do to inherit eternal life?
19 And Jesus said unto him, Why callest thou me good? none *is* good, save one, *that is*, God.
20 Thou knowest the commandments, Do not commit adultery, Do not kill, Do not steal, Do not bear false witness, Honour thy father and thy mother.
21 And he said, All these have I kept from my youth up.
22 Now when Jesus heard these things, he said unto him, Yet lackest thou one thing: sell all that thou hast, and distribute unto the poor, and thou shalt have treasure in heaven: and come, follow me.
23 And when he heard this, he was very sorrowful: for he was very rich.
24 And when Jesus saw that he was very sorrowful, he said, How hardly shall they that have riches enter into the kingdom of God!
25 For it is easier for a camel to go through a needle's eye, than for a rich man to enter into the kingdom of God.
26 And they that heard *it* said, Who then can be saved?
27 And he said, The things which are impossible with men are possible with God.
28 ¶Then Peter said, Lo, we have left all, and followed thee.
29 And he said unto them, Verily I say unto you, There is no man that hath left house, or parents, or brethren, or wife, or children, for the kingdom of God's sake,
30 Who shall not receive manifold more in this present time, and in the world to come life everlasting.
31 ¶Then he took *unto him* the twelve, and said unto them, Behold, we go up to Jerusalem, and all things that are written by the prophets concerning the Son of man shall be accomplished.
32 For he shall be delivered unto the Gentiles, and shall be mocked, and spitefully entreated, and spitted on:
33 And they shall scourge *him*, and put him to death: and the third day he shall rise again.
34 And they understood none of these things: and this saying was hid from them, neither knew they the things which were spoken.
35 ¶And it came to pass, that as he was come nigh unto Jericho, a certain blind man sat by the way side begging:
36 And hearing the multitude pass by, he asked what it meant.
37 And they told him, that Jesus of Nazareth passeth by.
38 And he cried, saying, Jesus, *thou* son of David, have mercy on me.
39 And they which went before rebuked him, that he should hold his peace: but he cried so much the more, *Thou* son of David, have mercy on me.
40 And Jesus stood, and commanded him to be brought unto him: and when he was come near, he asked him,
41 Saying, What wilt thou that I shall do unto thee? And he said, Lord, that I may receive my sight.
42 And Jesus said unto him, Receive thy sight: thy faith hath saved thee.
43 And immediately he received his sight, and followed him, glorifying God: and all the people, when they saw *it*, gave praise unto God.

CHAPTER 19

AND *Jesus* entered and passed through Jericho.
2 And, behold, *there was* a man named Zāc-chæ'us, which was the chief among the publicans, and he was rich.
3 And he sought to see Jesus who he was; and could not for the press, because he was little of stature.
4 And he ran before, and climbed up into a sycomore tree to see him: for he was to pass that *way*.
5 And when Jesus came to the place,

he looked up, and saw him, and said
unto him, Zāc-chæ'us, make haste, and
come down; for to day I must abide at
thy house.
6 And he made haste, and came
down, and received him joyfully.
7 And when they saw *it*, they all mur-
mured, saying, That he was gone to be
guest with a man that is a sinner.
8 And Zāc-chæ'us stood, and said
unto the Lord; Behold, Lord, the half of
my goods I give to the poor; and if I
have taken any thing from any man by
false accusation, I restore *him* fourfold.
9 And Jesus said unto him, This day is
salvation come to this house forso-
much as he also is a son of Abraham.
10 For the Son of man is come to seek
and to save that which was lost.
11 ¶And as they heard these things,
he added and spake a parable, because
he was nigh to Jerusalem, and because
they thought that the kingdom of God
should immediately appear.
12 He said therefore, A certain noble-
man went into a far country to receive
for himself a kingdom, and to return.
13 And he called his ten servants, and
delivered them ten pounds, and said
unto them, Occupy till I come.
14 But his citizens hated him, and
sent a message after him, saying, We
will not have this *man* to reign over us.
15 And it came to pass, that when he
was returned, having received the
kingdom, then he commanded these
servants to be called unto him, to
whom he had given the money, that he
might know how much every man had
gained by trading.
16 Then came the first, saying, Lord,
thy pound hath gained ten pounds.
17 And he said unto him, Well, thou
good servant: because thou hast been
faithful in a very little, have thou au-
thority over ten cities.
18 And the second came, saying,
Lord, thy pound hath gained five
pounds.
19 And he said likewise to him, Be
thou also over five cities.
20 And another came, saying, Lord,
behold, *here is* thy pound, which I have
kept laid up in a napkin:
21 For I feared thee, because thou art
an austere man: thou takest up that
thou layedst not down, and reapest
that thou didst not sow.
22 And he saith unto him, Out of
thine own mouth will I judge thee, *thou*
wicked servant. Thou knewest that I
was an austere man, taking up that I
laid not down, and reaping that I did
not sow:
23 Wherefore then gavest not thou
my money into the bank, that at my com-
ing I might have required mine own
with usury?
24 And he said unto them that stood
by, Take from him the pound, and give
it to him that hath ten pounds.
25 (And they said unto him, Lord, he
hath ten pounds.)
26 For I say unto you, That unto
every one which hath shall be given;
and from him that hath not, even that
he hath shall be taken away from him.
27 But those mine enemies, which
would not that I should reign over
them, bring hither, and slay *them* be-
fore me.
28 And when he had thus spoken he
went before, ascending up to Jeru-
salem.
29 ¶And it came to pass, when he was
come nigh to Bĕth'pha-ġē and Bethany,
at the mount called *the mount* of
Olives, he sent two of his disciples,
30 Saying, Go ye into the village over
against *you;* in the which at your enter-
ing ye shall find a colt tied, whereon yet
never man sat: loose him, and bring
him hither.
31 And if any man ask you, Why do
ye loose *him?* thus shall ye say unto
him, Because the Lord hath need of
him.
32 And they that were sent went their
way, and found even as he had said
unto them.
33 And as they were loosing the colt,
the owners thereof said unto them,
Why loose ye the colt?
34 And they said, The Lord hath need
of him.
35 And they brought him to Jesus:
and they cast their garments upon the
colt, and they set Jesus thereon.
36 And as he went, they spread their
clothes in the way.
37 And when he was come nigh, even
now at the descent of the mount of
Olives, the whole multitude of the dis-
ciples began to rejoice and praise God
with a loud voice for all the mighty
works that they had seen;
38 Saying, Blessed *be* the King that
cometh in the name of the Lord: peace
in heaven, and glory in the highest.
39 And some of the Pharisees from
among the multitude said unto him,
Master, rebuke thy disciples.
40 And he answered and said unto
them, I tell you that, if these should
hold their peace, the stones would im-
mediately cry out.
41 ¶And when he was come near, he
beheld the city, and wept over it,
42 Saying, If thou hadst known, even
thou, at least in this thy day, the things

which belong unto thy peace! but now
they are hid from thine eyes.
43 For the days shall come upon thee,
that thine enemies shall cast a trench
about thee, and compass thee round,
and keep thee in on every side,
44 And shall lay thee even with the
ground, and thy children within thee;
and they shall not leave in thee one
stone upon another; because thou knew-
est not the time of thy visitation.
45 And he went into the temple, and
began to cast out them that sold there-
in, and them that bought;
46 Saying unto them, It is written, My
house is the house of prayer: but ye
have made it a den of thieves.
47 And he taught daily in the temple.
But the chief priests and the scribes
and the chief of the people sought to
destroy him,
48 And could not find what they
might do: for all the people were very
attentive to hear him.

CHAPTER 20

AND it came to pass, *that* on one of
those days, as he taught the people in
the temple, and preached the gospel,
the chief priests and the scribes came
upon *him* with the elders,
2 And spake unto him, saying, Tell
us, by what authority doest thou these
things? or who is he that gave thee this
authority?
3 And he answered and said unto
them, I will also ask you one thing, and
answer me:
4 The baptism of John, was it from
heaven, or of men?
5 And they reasoned with them-
selves, saying, If we shall say, From
heaven; he will say, Why then believed
ye him not?
6 But and if we say, Of men; all the
people will stone us: for they be per-
suaded that John was a prophet.
7 And they answered, that they could
not tell whence *it was*.
8 And Jesus said unto them, Neither
tell I you by what authority I do these
things.
9 Then began he to speak to the peo-
ple this parable; A certain man
planted a vineyard, and let it forth to
husbandmen, and went into a far
country for a long time.
10 And at the season he sent a ser-
vant to the husbandmen, that they
should give him of the fruit of the vine-
yard: but the husbandmen beat him,
and sent *him* away empty.
11 And again he sent another ser-
vant: and they beat him also, and entreat-
ed *him* shamefully, and sent *him*
away empty.
12 And again he sent a third: and they
wounded him also, and cast *him* out.
13 Then said the lord of the vineyard,
What shall I do? I will send my beloved
son: it may be they will reverence *him*
when they see him.
14 But when the husbandmen saw
him, they reasoned among themselves,
saying, This is the heir: come, let us kill
him, that the inheritance may be ours.
15 So they cast him out of the vine-
yard, and killed *him*. What therefore
shall the lord of the vineyard do unto
them?
16 He shall come and destroy these
husbandmen, and shall give the vine-
yard to others. And when they heard *it*,
they said, God forbid.
17 And he beheld them, and said,
What is this then that is written, The
stone which the builders rejected, the
same is become the head of the corner?
18 Whosoever shall fall upon that
stone shall be broken; but on whom-
soever it shall fall, it will grind him to
powder.
19 And the chief priests and the
scribes the same hour sought to lay
hands on him; and they feared the
people: for they perceived that he had
spoken this parable against them.
20 ¶And they watched *him*, and sent
forth spies, which should feign them-
selves just men, that they might take
hold of his words, that so they might
deliver him unto the power and au-
thority of the governor.
21 And they asked him, saying, Mas-
ter, we know that thou sayest and
teachest rightly, neither acceptest thou
the person *of any*, but teachest the way
of God truly:
22 Is it lawful for us to give tribute
unto Cæsar, or no?
23 But he perceived their craftiness,
and said unto them, Why tempt ye me?
24 Shew me a penny. Whose image
and superscription hath it? They an-
swered and said, Cæsar's.
25 And he said unto them, Render
therefore unto Cæsar the things which
be Cæsar's, and unto God the things
which be God's.
26 And they could not take hold of his
words before the people: and they mar-
velled at his answer, and held their
peace.
27 ¶Then came to *him* certain of the
Săd′du-ceeṡ, which deny that there is
any resurrection: and they asked him,
28 Saying, Master, Moses wrote unto
us, If any man's brother die, having a

wife, and he die without children, that
his brother should take his wife, and
raise up seed unto his brother.
29 There were therefore seven brethren:
and the first took a wife, and
died without children.
30 And the second took her to wife,
and he died childless.
31 And the third took her; and in like
manner the seven also: and they left no
children, and died.
32 Last of all the woman died also.
33 Therefore in the resurrection
whose wife of them is she? for seven
had her to wife.
34 And Jesus answering said unto
them, The children of this world marry,
and are given in marriage:
35 But they which shall be accounted
worthy to obtain that world, and the resurrection
from the dead, neither
marry, nor are given in marriage:
36 Neither can they die any more: for
they are equal unto the angels; and are
the children of God, being the children
of the resurrection.
37 Now that the dead are raised, even
Moses shewed at the bush, when he
calleth the Lord the God of Abraham,
and the God of Isaac, and the God of
Jacob.
38 For he is not a God of the dead, but
of the living: for all live unto him.
39 Then certain of the scribes answering
said, Master, thou hast well
said.
40 And after that they durst not ask
him any *question at all.*
41 ¶And he said unto them, How say
they that Christ is David's son?
42 And David himself saith in the
book of Psalms, The LORD said unto my
Lord, Sit thou on my right hand,
43 Till I make thine enemies thy
footstool.
44 David therefore calleth him Lord,
how is he then his son?
45 ¶Then in the audience of all the
people he said unto his disciples,
46 Beware of the scribes, which desire
to walk in long robes, and love
greetings in the markets, and the
highest seats in the synagogues, and
the chief rooms at feasts;
47 Which devour widows' houses,
and for a shew make long prayers: the
same shall receive greater damnation.

CHAPTER 21

AND he looked up, and saw the rich
men casting their gifts into the treasury.
2 And he saw also a certain poor widow
casting in thither two mites.
3 And he said, Of a truth I say unto
you, that this poor widow hath cast in
more than they all:
4 For all these have of their abundance
cast in unto the offerings of God:
but she of her penury hath cast in all
the living that she had.
5 ¶And as some spake of the temple,
how it was adorned with goodly stones
and gifts, he said,
6 *As for* these things which ye behold,
the days will come, in the which
there shall not be left one stone upon
another, that shall not be thrown down.
7 And they asked him, saying, Master,
but when shall these things be? and
what sign *will there be* when these
things shall come to pass?
8 And he said, Take heed that ye be
not deceived: for many shall come in
my name, saying, I am *Christ;* and the
time draweth near: go ye not therefore
after them.
9 But when ye shall hear of wars and
commotions, be not terrified: for these
things must first come to pass; but the
end *is* not by and by.
10 Then said he unto them, Nation
shall rise against nation, and kingdom
against kingdom:
11 And great earthquakes shall be in
divers places, and famines, and pestilences;
and fearful sights and great
signs shall there be from heaven.
12 But before all these, they shall lay
their hands on you, and persecute *you,*
delivering *you* up to the synagogues,
and into prisons, being brought before
kings and rulers for my name's sake.
13 And it shall turn to you for a testimony.
14 Settle *it* therefore in your hearts,
not to meditate before what ye shall
answer:
15 For I will give you a mouth and
wisdom, which all your adversaries
shall not be able to gainsay nor resist.
16 And ye shall be betrayed both by
parents, and brethren, and kinsfolks,
and friends; and *some* of you shall they
cause to be put to death.
17 And ye shall be hated of all *men*
for my name's sake.
18 But there shall not an hair of your
head perish.
19 In your patience possess ye your
souls.
20 And when ye shall see Jerusalem
compassed with armies, then know
that the desolation thereof is nigh.
21 Then let them which are in Judæa
flee to the mountains; and let them
which are in the midst of it depart out;

and let not them that are in the coun-
tries enter thereinto.
22 For these be the days of vengeance,
that all things which are written
may be fulfilled.
23 But woe unto them that are with
child, and to them that give suck, in
those days! for there shall be great dis-
tress in the land, and wrath upon this
people.
24 And they shall fall by the edge of
the sword, and shall be led away cap-
tive into all nations: and Jerusalem
shall be trodden down of the Gentiles,
until the times of the Gentiles be ful-
filled.
25 ¶And there shall be signs in the
sun, and in the moon, and in the stars;
and upon the earth distress of nations,
with perplexity; the sea and the waves
roaring;
26 Men's hearts failing them for fear,
and for looking after those things
which are coming on the earth: for the
powers of heaven shall be shaken.
27 And then shall they see the Son of
man coming in a cloud with power and
great glory.
28 And when these things begin to
come to pass, then look up, and lift up
your heads; for your redemption draw-
eth nigh.
29 And he spake to them a parable;
Behold the fig tree, and all the trees;
30 When they now shoot forth, ye see
and know of your own selves that sum-
mer is now nigh at hand.
31 So likewise ye, when ye see these
things come to pass, know ye that the
kingdom of God is nigh at hand.
32 Verily I say unto you, This genera-
tion shall not pass away, till all be ful-
filled.
33 Heaven and earth shall pass away:
but my words shall not pass away.
34 ¶And take heed to yourselves, lest
at any time your hearts be overcharged
with surfeiting, and drunkenness, and
cares of this life, and *so* that day come
upon you unawares.
35 For as a snare shall it come on all
them that dwell on the face of the
whole earth.
36 Watch ye therefore, and pray al-
ways, that ye may be accounted
worthy to escape all these things that
shall come to pass, and to stand before
the Son of man.
37 And in the day time he was teach-
ing in the temple; and at night he went
out, and abode in the mount that is
called *the mount* of Olives.
38 And all the people came early in
the morning to him in the temple, for to
hear him.

CHAPTER 22

NOW the feast of unleavened bread
drew nigh, which is called the Pass-
over.
2 And the chief priests and scribes
sought how they might kill him; for
they feared the people.
3 ¶Then entered Satan into Judas sur-
named Iscariot, being of the number of
the twelve.
4 And he went his way, and com-
muned with the chief priests and cap-
tains, how he might betray him unto
them.
5 And they were glad, and cove-
nanted to give him money.
6 And he promised, and sought op-
portunity to betray him unto them in
the absence of the multitude.
7 ¶Then came the day of unleavened
bread, when the passover must be
killed.
8 And he sent Peter and John, saying,
Go and prepare us the passover, that
we may eat.
9 And they said unto him, Where wilt
thou that we prepare?
10 And he said unto them, Behold,
when ye are entered into the city, there
shall a man meet you, bearing a pitcher
of water; follow him into the house
where he entereth in.
11 And ye shall say unto the good-
man of the house, The Master saith
unto thee, Where is the guestchamber,
where I shall eat the passover with my
disciples?
12 And he shall shew you a large up-
per room furnished: there make ready.
13 And they went, and found as he
had said unto them: and they made ready
the passover.
14 And when the hour was come, he
sat down, and the twelve apostles with
him.
15 And he said unto them, With de-
sire I have desired to eat this passover
with you before I suffer:
16 For I say unto you, I will not any
more eat thereof, until it be fulfilled in
the kingdom of God.
17 And he took the cup, and gave
thanks, and said, Take this, and divide
it among yourselves:
18 For I say unto you, I will not drink
of the fruit of the vine, until the king-
dom of God shall come.
19 ¶And he took bread, and gave
thanks, and brake *it*, and gave unto
them, saying, This is my body which is
given for you: this do in remembrance
of me.
20 Likewise also the cup after sup-
per, saying, This cup *is* the new testa-

ment in my blood, which is shed for you.
21 ¶But, behold, the hand of him that betrayeth me *is* with me on the table.
22 And truly the Son of man goeth, as it was determined: but woe unto that man by whom he is betrayed!
23 And they began to enquire among themselves, which of them it was that should do this thing.
24 ¶And there was also a strife among them, which of them should be accounted the greatest.
25 And he said unto them, The kings of the Gentiles exercise lordship over them; and they that exercise authority upon them are called benefactors.
26 But ye *shall* not *be* so: but he that is greatest among you, let him be as the younger; and he that is chief, as he that doth serve.
27 For whether *is* greater, he that sitteth at meat, or he that serveth? *is* not he that sitteth at meat? but I am among you as he that serveth.
28 Ye are they which have continued with me in my temptations.
29 And I appoint unto you a kingdom, as my Father hath appointed unto me;
30 That ye may eat and drink at my table in my kingdom, and sit on thrones judging the twelve tribes of Israel.
31 ¶And the Lord said, Simon, Simon, behold, Satan hath desired *to have* you, that he may sift *you* as wheat:
32 But I have prayed for thee, that thy faith fail not: and when thou art converted, strengthen thy brethren.
33 And he said unto him, Lord, I am ready to go with thee, both into prison, and to death.
34 And he said, I tell thee, Peter, the cock shall not crow this day, before that thou shalt thrice deny that thou knowest me.
35 ¶And he said unto them, When I sent you without purse, and scrip, and shoes, lacked ye any thing? And they said, Nothing.
36 Then said he unto them, But now, he that hath a purse, let him take *it*, and likewise *his* scrip: and he that hath no sword, let him sell his garment, and buy one.
37 For I say unto you, that this that is written must yet be accomplished in me, And he was reckoned among the transgressors: for the things concerning me have an end.
38 And they said, Lord, behold, here *are* two swords. And he said unto them, It is enough.
39 ¶And he came out, and went, as he was wont, to the mount of Olives; and his disciples also followed him.
40 And when he was at the place, he said unto them, Pray that ye enter not into temptation.
41 And he was withdrawn from them about a stone's cast, and kneeled down, and prayed,
42 Saying, Father, if thou be willing, remove this cup from me: nevertheless not my will, but thine, be done.
43 And there appeared an angel unto him from heaven, strengthening him.
44 And being in an agony he prayed more earnestly: and his sweat was as it were great drops of blood falling down to the ground.
45 And when he rose up from prayer, and was come to his disciples, he found them sleeping for sorrow,
46 And said unto them, Why sleep ye? rise and pray, lest ye enter into temptation.
47 ¶And while he yet spake, behold a multitude, and he that was called Judas, one of the twelve, went before them, and drew near unto Jesus to kiss him.
48 But Jesus said unto him, Judas, betrayest thou the Son of man with a kiss?
49 When they which were about him saw what would follow, they said unto him, Lord, shall we smite with the sword?
50 ¶And one of them smote the servant of the high priest, and cut off his right ear.
51 And Jesus answered and said, Suffer ye thus far. And he touched his ear, and healed him.
52 Then Jesus said unto the chief priests, and captains of the temple, and the elders, which were come to him, Be ye come out, as against a thief, with swords and staves?
53 When I was daily with you in the temple, ye stretched forth no hands against me: but this is your hour, and the power of darkness.
54 ¶Then took they him, and led *him*, and brought him into the high priest's house. And Peter followed afar off.
55 And when they had kindled a fire in the midst of the hall, and were set down together, Peter sat down among them.
56 But a certain maid beheld him as he sat by the fire, and earnestly looked upon him, and said, This man was also with him.
57 And he denied him, saying, Woman, I know him not.
58 And after a little while another

saw him, and said, Thou art also of
them. And Peter said, Man, I am not.
59 And about the space of one hour
after another confidently affirmed,
saying, Of a truth this *fellow* also was
with him: for he is a Galilæan.
60 And Peter said, Man, I know not
what thou sayest. And immediately,
while he yet spake, the cock crew.
61 And the Lord turned, and looked
upon Peter. And Peter remembered the
word of the Lord, how he had said unto
him, Before the cock crow, thou shalt
deny me thrice.
62 And Peter went out and wept bit-
terly.
63 ¶And the men that held Jesus
mocked him, and smote him.
64 And when they had blindfolded
him, they struck him on the face, and
asked him, saying, Prophesy, who is it
that smote thee?
65 And many other things blasphe-
mously spake they against him.
66 ¶And as soon as it was day, the el-
ders of the people and the chief priests
and the scribes came together, and led
him into their council, saying,
67 Art thou the Christ? tell us. And he
said unto them, If I tell you, ye will not
believe:
68 And if I also ask *you*, ye will not
answer me, nor let *me* go.
69 Hereafter shall the Son of man sit
on the right hand of the power of God.
70 Then said they all, Art thou then
the Son of God? And he said unto them,
Ye say that I am.
71 And they said, What need we any
further witness? for we ourselves have
heard of his own mouth.

CHAPTER 23

AND the whole multitude of them
arose, and led him unto Pilate.
2 And they began to accuse him,
saying, We found this *fellow* per-
verting the nation, and forbidding to
give tribute to Cæsar, saying that he
himself is Christ a King.
3 And Pilate asked him, saying, Art
thou the King of the Jews? And he an-
swered him and said, Thou sayest *it*.
4 Then said Pilate to the chief priests
and *to* the people, I find no fault in this
man.
5 And they were the more fierce,
saying, He stirreth up the people,
teaching throughout all Jewry, begin-
ning from Galilee to this place.
6 When Pilate heard of Galilee, he
asked whether the man were a Gali-
læan.
7 And as soon as he knew that he be-
longed unto Herod's jurisdiction, he
sent him to Herod, who himself also
was at Jerusalem at that time.
8 ¶And when Herod saw Jesus, he
was exceeding glad: for he was desir-
ous to see him of a long *season*, be-
cause he had heard many things of him;
and he hoped to have seen some
miracle done by him.
9 Then he questioned with him in
many words; but he answered him
nothing.
10 And the chief priests and scribes
stood and vehemently accused him.
11 And Herod with his men of war set
him at nought, and mocked *him*, and
arrayed him in a gorgeous robe, and
sent him again to Pilate.
12 ¶And the same day Pilate and Her-
od were made friends together: for be-
fore they were at enmity between
themselves.
13 ¶And Pilate, when he had called
together the chief priests and the rulers
and the people,
14 Said unto them, Ye have brought
this man unto me, as one that pervert-
eth the people: and, behold, I, having
examined *him* before you, have found
no fault in this man touching those
things whereof ye accuse him:
15 No, nor yet Herod: for I sent you to
him; and, lo, nothing worthy of death is
done unto him.
16 I will therefore chastise him, and
release *him*.
17 (For of necessity he must release
one unto them at the feast.)
18 And they cried out all at once,
saying, Away with this *man*, and re-
lease unto us Ba-răb'bas:
19 (Who for a certain sedition made
in the city, and for murder, was cast
into prison.)
20 Pilate therefore, willing to release
Jesus, spake again to them.
21 But they cried, saying, Crucify
him, crucify him.
22 And he said unto them the third
time, Why, what evil hath he done? I
have found no cause of death in him: I
will therefore chastise him, and let *him*
go.
23 And they were instant with loud
voices, requiring that he might be
crucified. And the voices of them and
of the chief priests prevailed.
24 And Pilate gave sentence that it
should be as they required.
25 And he released unto them him
that for sedition and murder was cast
into prison, whom they had desired;
but he delivered Jesus to their will.
26 ¶And as they led him away, they
laid hold upon one Simon, a Çȳ-rē'nī-
an, coming out of the country, and on

him they laid the cross, that he might
bear *it* after Jesus.
27 And there followed him a great
company of people, and of women,
which also bewailed and lamented him.
28 But Jesus turning unto them said,
Daughters of Jerusalem, weep not for
me, but weep for yourselves, and for
your children.
29 For, behold, the days are coming,
in the which they shall say, Blessed *are*
the barren, and the wombs that never
bare, and the paps which never gave
suck.
30 Then shall they begin to say to the
mountains, Fall on us; and to the hills,
Cover us.
31 For if they do these things in a
green tree, what shall be done in the
dry?
32 ¶And there were also two other,
malefactors, led with him to be put to
death.
33 And when they were come to the
place, which is called Calvary, there
they crucified him, and the malefac-
tors, one on the right hand, and the
other on the left.
34 Then said Jesus, Father, forgive
them; for they know not what they do.
And they parted his raiment, and cast
lots.
35 And the people stood beholding.
And the rulers also with them derided
him, saying, He saved others; let him
save himself, if he be Christ, the chosen
of God.
36 And the soldiers also mocked him,
coming to him, and offering him vin-
egar,
37 And saying, If thou be the king of
the Jews, save thyself.
38 And a superscription also was
written over him in letters of Greek,
and Latin, and Hebrew, THIS IS THE
KING OF THE JEWS.
39 ¶And one of the malefactors
which were hanged railed on him,
saying, If thou be Christ, save thyself
and us.
40 But the other answering rebuked
him, saying, Dost not thou fear God,
seeing thou art in the same condemna-
tion?
41 And we indeed justly; for we re-
ceive the due reward of our deeds: but
this man hath done nothing amiss.
42 And he said unto Jesus, Lord,
remember me when thou comest into
thy kingdom.
43 And Jesus said unto him, Verily I
say unto thee, To day shalt thou be with
me in paradise.
44 ¶And it was about the sixth hour,
and there was a darkness over all the
earth until the ninth hour.
45 And the sun was darkened, and
the vail of the temple was rent in the
midst.
46 And when Jesus had cried with a
loud voice, he said, Father, into thy
hands I commend my spirit: and having
said thus, he gave up the ghost.
47 ¶Now when the centurion saw
what was done, he glorified God,
saying, Certainly this was a righteous
man.
48 And all the people that came togeth-
er to that sight, beholding the things
which were done, smote their breasts,
and returned.
49 And all his acquaintance, and the
women that followed him from Galilee,
stood afar off, beholding these things.
50 ¶And, behold, *there was* a man
named Joseph, a counsellor; *and he
was* a good man, and a just:
51 (The same had not consented to
the counsel and deed of them;) *he was*
of Ăr-i-ma-thæ'a, a city of the Jews:
who also himself waited for the king-
dom of God.
52 This *man* went unto Pilate, and
begged the body of Jesus.
53 And he took it down, and wrapped
it in linen, and laid it in a sepulchre that
was hewn in stone, wherein never man
before was laid.
54 And that day was the preparation,
and the sabbath drew on.
55 ¶And the women also, which came
with him from Galilee, followed after,
and beheld the sepulchre, and how his
body was laid.
56 And they returned, and prepared
spices and ointments; and rested the
sabbath day according to the com-
mandment.

CHAPTER 24

NOW upon the first *day* of the week,
very early in the morning, they came
unto the sepulchre, bringing the spices
which they had prepared, and certain
others with them.
2 And they found the stone rolled
away from the sepulchre.
3 And they entered in, and found not
the body of the Lord Jesus.
4 And it came to pass, as they were
much perplexed thereabout, behold,
two men stood by them in shining gar-
ments:
5 And as they were afraid, and bowed
down *their* faces to the earth, they said
unto them, Why seek ye the living
among the dead?

6 He is not here, but is risen: remem-
ber how he spake unto you when he
was yet in Galilee,

7 Saying, the Son of man must be de-
livered into the hands of sinful men,
and be crucified, and the third day rise
again.

8 And they remembered his words,

9 And returned from the sepulchre,
and told all these things unto the
eleven, and to all the rest.

10 It was Mary Magdalene, and Jō-
ăn'na, and Mary *the mother* of James,
and other *women that were* with them,
which told these things unto the
apostles.

11 And their words seemed to them
as idle tales, and they believed them
not.

12 Then arose Peter, and ran unto the
sepulchre; and stooping down, he be-
held the linen clothes laid by them-
selves, and departed, wondering in
himself at that which was come to
pass.

13 And, behold, two of them went
that same day to a village called Ĕm-
mā'us, which was from Jerusalem
about threescore furlongs.

14 And they talked together of all
these things which had happened.

15 And it came to pass, that, while
they communed *together* and rea-
soned, Jesus himself drew near, and
went with them.

16 But their eyes were holden that
they should not know him.

17 And he said unto them, What
manner of communications *are* these
that ye have one to another, as ye walk,
and are sad?

18 And the one of them, whose name
was Clē'o-pas, answering said unto
him, Art thou only a stranger in Jeru-
salem, and hast not known the things
which are come to pass there in these
days?

19 And he said unto them, What
things? And they said unto him, Con-
cerning Jesus of Nazareth, which was a
prophet mighty in deed and word be-
fore God and all the people:

20 And how the chief priests and our
rulers delivered him to be condemned
to death, and have crucified him.

21 But we trusted that it had been he
which should have redeemed Israel:
and beside all this, to day is the third
day since these things were done.

22 Yea, and certain women also of
our company made us astonished,
which were early at the sepulchre;

23 And when they found not his
body, they came, saying, that they had
also seen a vision of angels, which said
that he was alive.

24 And certain of them which were
with us went to the sepulchre, and
found *it* even so as the women had said:
but him they saw not.

25 Then he said unto them, O fools,
and slow of heart to believe all that the
prophets have spoken:

26 Ought not Christ to have suffered
these things, and to enter into his
glory?

27 And beginning at Moses and all
the prophets, he expounded unto them
in all the scriptures the things concern-
ing himself.

28 And they drew nigh unto the vil-
lage, whither they went: and he made
as though he would have gone further.

29 But they constrained him, saying,
Abide with us: for it is toward evening,
and the day is far spent. And he went in
to tarry with them.

30 And it came to pass, as he sat at
meat with them, he took bread, and
blessed *it*, and brake, and gave to them.

31 And their eyes were opened, and
they knew him; and he vanished out of
their sight.

32 And they said one to another, Did
not our heart burn within us, while he
talked with us by the way, and while he
opened to us the scriptures?

33 And they rose up the same hour,
and returned to Jerusalem, and found
the eleven gathered together, and them
that were with them,

34 Saying, The Lord is risen indeed,
and hath appeared to Simon.

35 And they told what things *were
done* in the way, and how he was
known of them in breaking of bread.

36 ¶And as they thus spake, Jesus
himself stood in the midst of them, and
saith unto them, Peace *be* unto you.

37 But they were terrified and af-
frighted, and supposed that they had
seen a spirit.

38 And he said unto them, Why are
ye troubled? and why do thoughts arise
in your hearts?

39 Behold my hands and my feet, that
it is I myself: handle me, and see; for a
spirit hath not flesh and bones, as ye
see me have.

40 And when he had thus spoken, he
shewed them *his* hands and *his* feet.

41 And while they yet believed not
for joy, and wondered, he said unto
them, Have ye here any meat?

42 And they gave him a piece of a
broiled fish, and of an honeycomb.

43 And he took *it*, and did eat before
them.

44 And he said unto them, These *are* the words which I spake unto you, while I was yet with you, that all things must be fulfilled, which were written in the law of Moses, and *in* the prophets, and *in* the psalms, concerning me.

45 Then opened he their understanding, that they might understand the scriptures,

46 And said unto them, Thus it is written, and thus it behoved Christ to suffer, and to rise from the dead the third day:

47 And that repentance and remission of sins should be preached in his name among all nations, beginning at Jerusalem.

48 And ye are witnesses of these things.

49 ¶And, behold, I send the promise of my Father upon you: but tarry ye in the city of Jerusalem, until ye be endued with power from on high.

50 ¶And he led them out as far as to Bethany, and he lifted up his hands, and blessed them.

51 And it came to pass, while he blessed them, he was parted from them, and carried up into heaven.

52 And they worshipped him, and returned to Jerusalem with great joy:

53 And were continually in the temple, praising and blessing God. Amen.

THE GOSPEL ACCORDING TO

SAINT JOHN

CHAPTER 1

IN the beginning was the Word, and the Word was with God, and the Word was God.

2 The same was in the beginning with God.

3 All things were made by him; and without him was not any thing made that was made.

4 In him was life; and the life was the light of men.

5 And the light shineth in darkness; and the darkness comprehended it not.

6 ¶There was a man sent from God, whose name *was* John.

7 The same came for a witness, to bear witness of the Light, that all *men* through him might believe.

8 He was not that Light, but *was sent* to bear witness of that Light.

9 *That* was the true Light, which lighteth every man that cometh into the world.

10 He was in the world, and the world was made by him, and the world knew him not.

11 He came unto his own, and his own received him not.

12 But as many as received him, to them gave he power to become the sons of God, *even* to them that believe on his name:

13 Which were born, not of blood, nor of the will of the flesh, nor of the will of man, but of God.

14 And the Word was made flesh, and dwelt among us, (and we beheld his glory, the glory as of the only begotten of the Father,) full of grace and truth.

15 ¶John bare witness of him, and cried, saying, This was he of whom I spake, He that cometh after me is preferred before me: for he was before me.

16 And of his fulness have all we received, and grace for grace.

17 For the law was given by Moses, *but* grace and truth came by Jesus Christ.

18 No man hath seen God at any time; the only begotten Son, which is in the bosom of the Father, he hath declared *him*.

19 ¶And this is the record of John, when the Jews sent priests and Levites from Jerusalem to ask him, Who art thou?

20 And he confessed, and denied not; but confessed, I am not the Christ.

21 And they asked him, What then? Art thou E-lĭ'as? And he saith, I am not. Art thou that prophet? And he answered, No.

22 Then said they unto him, Who art thou? that we may give an answer to them that sent us. What sayest thou of thyself?

23 He said, I *am* the voice of one crying in the wilderness, Make straight the way of the Lord, as said the prophet E-ṡā'ias.

24 And they which were sent were of the Pharisees.

25 And they asked him, and said unto him, Why baptizest thou then, if thou be not that Christ, nor E-lĭ'as, neither that prophet?

26 John answered them, saying, I baptize with water: but there standeth one among you, whom ye know not;

27 He it is, who coming after me is preferred before me, whose shoe's latchet I am not worthy to unloose.

28 These things were done in Bĕth-ăb'a-ra beyond Jordan, where John was baptizing.

29 ¶The next day John seeth Jesus coming unto him, and saith, Behold the Lamb of God, which taketh away the sin of the world.
30 This is he of whom I said, After me cometh a man which is preferred before me: for he was before me.
31 And I knew him not: but that he should be made manifest to Israel, therefore am I come baptizing with water.
32 And John bare record, saying, I saw the Spirit descending from heaven like a dove, and it abode upon him.
33 And I knew him not: but he that sent me to baptize with water, the same said unto me, Upon whom thou shalt see the Spirit descending, and remaining on him, the same is he which baptizeth with the Holy Ghost.
34 And I saw, and bare record that this is the Son of God.
35 ¶Again the next day after John stood, and two of his disciples;
36 And looking upon Jesus as he walked, he saith, Behold the Lamb of God!
37 And the two disciples heard him speak, and they followed Jesus.
38 Then Jesus turned, and saw them following, and saith unto them, What seek ye? They said unto him, Rabbi, (which is to say, being interpreted, Master,) where dwellest thou?
39 He saith unto them, Come and see. They came and saw where he dwelt, and abode with him that day: for it was about the tenth hour.
40 One of the two which heard John *speak*, and followed him, was Andrew, Simon Peter's brother.
41 He first findeth his own brother Simon, and saith unto him, We have found the Mes-sī'as, which is, being interpreted, the Christ.
42 And he brought him to Jesus. And when Jesus beheld him, he said, Thou art Simon the son of Jona: thou shalt be called Cē'phas, which is by interpretation, A stone.
43 ¶The day following Jesus would go forth into Galilee, and findeth Philip, and saith unto him, Follow me.
44 Now Philip was of Bĕth-sā'i-da, the city of Andrew and Peter.
45 Philip findeth Nathanael, and saith unto him, We have found him, of whom Moses in the law, and the prophets, did write, Jesus of Nazareth, the son of Joseph.
46 And Nathanael said unto him, Can there any good thing come out of Nazareth? Philip saith unto him, Come and see.
47 Jesus saw Nathanael coming to him, and saith of him, Behold an Israelite indeed, in whom is no guile!
48 Nathanael saith unto him, Whence knowest thou me? Jesus answered and said unto him, Before that Philip called thee, when thou wast under the fig tree, I saw thee.
49 Nathanael answered and saith unto him, Rabbi, thou art the Son of God; thou art the King of Israel.
50 Jesus answered and said unto him, Because I said unto thee, I saw thee under the fig tree, believest thou? thou shalt see greater things than these.
51 And he saith unto him, Verily, verily, I say unto you, Hereafter ye shall see heaven open, and the angels of God ascending and descending upon the Son of man.

CHAPTER 2

AND the third day there was a marriage in Cana of Galilee; and the mother of Jesus was there:
2 And both Jesus was called, and his disciples, to the marriage.
3 And when they wanted wine, the mother of Jesus saith unto him, They have no wine.
4 Jesus saith unto her, Woman, what have I to do with thee? mine hour is not yet come.
5 His mother saith unto the servants, Whatsoever he saith unto you, do *it*.
6 And there were set there six waterpots of stone, after the manner of the purifying of the Jews, containing two or three firkins apiece.
7 Jesus saith unto them, Fill the waterpots with water. And they filled them up to the brim.
8 And he saith unto them, Draw out now, and bear unto the governor of the feast. And they bare *it*.
9 When the ruler of the feast had tasted the water that was made wine, and knew not whence it was: (but the servants which drew the water knew;) the governor of the feast called the bridegroom,
10 And saith unto him, Every man at the beginning doth set forth good wine; and when men have well drunk, then that which is worse; *but* thou hast kept the good wine until now.
11 This beginning of miracles did Jesus in Cana of Galilee, and manifested forth his glory; and his disciples believed on him.
12 ¶After this he went down to Caper'na-um, he, and his mother, and his brethren, and his disciples: and they continued there not many days.
13 ¶And the Jews' passover was at hand, and Jesus went up to Jerusalem,

14 And found in the temple those that sold oxen and sheep and doves, and the changers of money sitting:

15 And when he had made a scourge of small cords, he drove them all out of the temple, and the sheep, and the oxen; and poured out the changers' money, and overthrew the tables;

16 And said unto them that sold doves, Take these things hence; make not my Father's house an house of merchandise.

17 And his disciples remembered that it was written, The zeal of thine house hath eaten me up.

18 ¶Then answered the Jews and said unto him, What sign shewest thou unto us, seeing that thou doest these things?

19 Jesus answered and said unto them, Destroy this temple, and in three days I will raise it up.

20 Then said the Jews, Forty and six years was this temple in building, and wilt thou rear it up in three days?

21 But he spake of the temple of his body.

22 When therefore he was risen from the dead, his disciples remembered that he had said this unto them; and they believed the scripture, and the word which Jesus had said.

23 ¶Now when he was in Jerusalem at the passover, in the feast *day*, many believed in his name, when they saw the miracles which he did.

24 But Jesus did not commit himself unto them, because he knew all *men*,

25 And needed not that any should testify of man: for he knew what was in man.

CHAPTER 3

THERE was a man of the Pharisees, named Nĭc-o-dē′mus, a ruler of the Jews:

2 The same came to Jesus by night, and said unto him, Rabbi, we know that thou art a teacher come from God: for no man can do these miracles that thou doest, except God be with him.

3 Jesus answered and said unto him, Verily, verily, I say unto thee, Except a man be born again, he cannot see the kingdom of God.

4 Nĭc-o-dē′mus saith unto him, How can a man be born when he is old? can he enter the second time into his mother's womb, and be born?

5 Jesus answered, Verily, verily, I say unto thee, Except a man be born of water and *of* the Spirit, he cannot enter into the kingdom of God.

6 That which is born of the flesh is flesh; and that which is born of the Spirit is spirit.

7 Marvel not that I said unto thee, Ye must be born again.

8 The wind bloweth where it listeth, and thou hearest the sound thereof, but canst not tell whence it cometh, and whither it goeth: so is every one that is born of the Spirit.

9 Nĭc-o-dē′mus answered and said unto him, How can these things be?

10 Jesus answered and said unto him Art thou a master of Israel, and knowest not these things?

11 Verily, verily, I say unto thee, We speak that we do know, and testify that we have seen; and ye receive not our witness.

12 If I have told you earthly things, and ye believe not, how shall ye believe, if I tell you *of* heavenly things?

13 And no man hath ascended up to heaven, but he that came down from heaven, *even* the Son of man which is in heaven.

14 And as Moses lifted up the serpent in the wilderness, even so must the Son of man be lifted up:

15 That whosoever believeth in him should not perish, but have eternal life.

16 For God so loved the world, that he gave his only begotten Son, that whosoever believeth in him should not perish, but have everlasting life.

17 For God sent not his Son into the world to condemn the world; but that the world through him might be saved.

18 He that believeth on him is not condemned: but he that believeth not is condemned already, because he hath not believed in the name of the only begotten Son of God.

19 And this is the condemnation, that light is come into the world, and men loved darkness rather than light, because their deeds were evil.

20 For every one that doeth evil hateth the light, neither cometh to the light, lest his deeds should be reproved.

21 But he that doeth truth cometh to the light, that his deeds may be made manifest, that they are wrought in God.

22 ¶After these things came Jesus and his disciples into the land of Judæa; and there he tarried with them, and baptized.

23 And John also was baptizing in Æ′nŏn near to Sā′lĭm, because there was much water there: and they came, and were baptized.

24 For John was not yet cast into prison.

25 ¶Then there arose a question between *some* of John's disciples and the Jews about purifying.

26 And they came unto John, and said unto him, Rabbi, he that was with

thee beyond Jordan, to whom thou barest witness, behold, the same baptizeth, and all *men* come to him.

27 John answered and said, A man can receive nothing, except it be given him from heaven.

28 Ye yourselves bear me witness, that I said, I am not the Christ, but that I am sent before him.

29 He that hath the bride is the bridegroom: but the friend of the bridegroom, which standeth and heareth him, rejoiceth greatly because of the bridegroom's voice: this my joy therefore is fulfilled.

30 He must increase, but I *must* decrease.

31 He that cometh from above is above all: he that is of the earth is earthly, and speaketh of the earth: he that cometh from heaven is above all.

32 And what he hath seen and heard, that he testifieth; and no man receiveth his testimony.

33 He that hath received his testimony hath set to his seal that God is true.

34 For he whom God hath sent speaketh the words of God: for God giveth not the Spirit by measure *unto him.*

35 The Father loveth the Son, and hath given all things into his hand.

36 He that believeth on the Son hath everlasting life: and he that believeth not the Son shall not see life; but the wrath of God abideth on him.

CHAPTER 4

WHEN therefore the Lord knew how the Pharisees had heard that Jesus made and baptized more disciples than John,

2 (Though Jesus himself baptized not, but his disciples,)

3 He left Judæa, and departed again into Galilee.

4 And he must needs go through Sa-mâ′rĭ-a.

5 Then cometh he to a city of Sa-mâ′-rĭ-a, which is called Sȳ′chär, near to the parcel of ground that Jacob gave to his son Joseph.

6 Now Jacob's well was there. Jesus therefore, being wearied with *his* journey, sat thus on the well: *and* it was about the sixth hour.

7 There cometh a woman of Sa-mâ′-rĭ-a to draw water: Jesus saith unto her, Give me to drink.

8 (For his disciples were gone away unto the city to buy meat.)

9 Then saith the woman of Sa-mâ′rĭ-a unto him, How is it that thou, being a Jew, askest drink of me, which am a woman of Sa-mâ′rĭ-a? for the Jews have no dealings with the Sa-măr′ĭ-tanṡ.

10 Jesus answered and said unto her, If thou knewest the gift of God, and who it is that saith to thee, Give me to drink; thou wouldest have asked of him, and he would have given thee living water.

11 The woman saith unto him, Sir, thou hast nothing to draw with, and the well is deep: from whence then hast thou that living water?

12 Art thou greater than our father Jacob, which gave us the well, and drank thereof himself, and his children, and his cattle?

13 Jesus answered and said unto her, Whosoever drinketh of this water shall thirst again:

14 But whosoever drinketh of the water that I shall give him shall never thirst; but the water that I shall give him shall be in him a well of water springing up into everlasting life.

15 The woman saith unto him, Sir, give me this water, that I thirst not, neither come hither to draw.

16 Jesus saith unto her, Go, call thy husband, and come hither.

17 The woman answered and said, I have no husband. Jesus said unto her, Thou hast well said, I have no husband:

18 For thou hast had five husbands; and he whom thou now hast is not thy husband: in that saidst thou truly.

19 The woman saith unto him, Sir, I perceive that thou art a prophet.

20 Our fathers worshipped in this mountain; and ye say, that in Jerusalem is the place where men ought to worship.

21 Jesus saith unto her, Woman, believe me, the hour cometh, when ye shall neither in this mountain, nor yet at Jerusalem, worship the Father.

22 Ye worship ye know not what: we know what we worship: for salvation is of the Jews.

23 But the hour cometh, and now is, when the true worshippers shall worship the Father in spirit and in truth: for the Father seeketh such to worship him.

24 God *is* a Spirit: and they that worship him must worship *him* in spirit and in truth.

25 The woman saith unto him, I know that Mes-sī′as cometh, which is called Christ: when he is come, he will tell us all things.

26 Jesus saith unto her, I that speak unto thee am *he.*

27 ¶And upon this came his disciples, and marvelled that he talked with the

woman: yet no man said, What seekest
thou? or, Why talkest thou with her?
28 The woman then left her waterpot,
and went her way into the city, and
saith to the men,
29 Come, see a man, which told me
all things that ever I did: is not this the
Christ?
30 Then they went out of the city, and
came unto him.
31 ¶In the mean while his disciples
prayed him, saying, Master, eat.
32 But he said unto them, I have meat
to eat that ye know not of.
33 Therefore said the disciples one to
another, Hath any man brought him
ought to eat?
34 Jesus saith unto them, My meat is
to do the will of him that sent me, and
to finish his work.
35 Say not ye, There are yet four
months, and *then* cometh harvest? behold,
I say unto you, Lift up your eyes,
and look on the fields; for they are
white already to harvest.
36 And he that reapeth receiveth
wages, and gathereth fruit unto life
eternal: that both he that soweth and
he that reapeth may rejoice together.
37 And herein is that saying true, One
soweth, and another reapeth.
38 I sent you to reap that whereon ye
bestowed no labour: other men laboured,
and ye are entered into their labours.
39 ¶And many of the Sa-măr′i-tanṡ of
that city believed on him for the saying
of the woman, which testified, He told
me all that ever I did.
40 So when the Sa-măr′i-tanṡ were
come unto him, they besought him that
he would tarry with them: and he
abode there two days.
41 And many more believed because
of his own word;
42 And said unto the woman, Now
we believe, not because of thy saying:
for we have heard *him* ourselves, and
know that this is indeed the Christ, the
Saviour of the world.
43 ¶Now after two days he departed
thence, and went into Galilee.
44 For Jesus himself testified, that a
prophet hath no honour in his own
country.
45 Then when he was come into Galilee,
the Galilæans received him, having
seen all the things that he did at Jerusalem
at the feast: for they also went
unto the feast.
46 So Jesus came again into Cana of
Galilee, where he made the water wine.
And there was a certain nobleman,
whose son was sick at Ca-per′na-um.
47 When he heard that Jesus was
come out of Judæa into Galilee, he
went unto him, and besought him that
he would come down, and heal his son:
for he was at the point of death.
48 Then said Jesus unto him, Except
ye see signs and wonders, ye will not
believe.
49 The nobleman saith unto him, Sir,
come down ere my child die.
50 Jesus saith unto him, Go thy way;
thy son liveth. And the man believed
the word that Jesus had spoken unto
him, and he went his way.
51 And as he was now going down,
his servants met him, and told *him*,
saying, Thy son liveth.
52 Then enquired he of them the hour
when he began to amend. And they
said unto him, Yesterday at the seventh
hour the fever left him.
53 So the father knew that *it was* at
the same hour, in the which Jesus said
unto him, Thy son liveth: and himself
believed, and his whole house.
54 This *is* again the second miracle
that Jesus did, when he was come out
of Judæa into Galilee.

CHAPTER 5

AFTER this there was a feast of the
Jews; and Jesus went up to Jerusalem.
2 Now there is at Jerusalem by the
sheep *market* a pool, which is called in
the Hebrew tongue Be-thĕṡ′da, having
five porches.
3 In these lay a great multitude of impotent
folk, of blind, halt, withered,
waiting for the moving of the water.
4 For an angel went down at a certain
season into the pool, and troubled the
water: whosoever then first after the
troubling of the water stepped in was
made whole of whatsoever disease he
had.
5 And a certain man was there, which
had an infirmity thirty and eight years.
6 When Jesus saw him lie, and knew
that he had been now a long time *in that
case*, he saith unto him, Wilt thou be
made whole?
7 The impotent man answered him,
Sir, I have no man, when the water is
troubled, to put me into the pool: but
while I am coming, another steppeth
down before me.
8 Jesus saith unto him, Rise, take up
thy bed, and walk.
9 And immediately the man was
made whole, and took up his bed, and
walked: and on the same day was the
sabbath.
10 ¶The Jews therefore said unto him
that was cured, It is the sabbath day: it
is not lawful for thee to carry *thy* bed.
11 He answered them, He that made

me whole, the same said unto me, Take
up thy bed, and walk.
12 Then asked they him, What man is
that which said unto thee, Take up thy
bed, and walk?
13 And he that was healed wist not
who it was: for Jesus had conveyed
himself away, a multitude being in *that*
place.
14 Afterward Jesus findeth him in
the temple, and said unto him, Behold,
thou art made whole: sin no more, lest a
worse thing come unto thee.
15 The man departed, and told the
Jews that it was Jesus, which had made
him whole.
16 And therefore did the Jews perse-
cute Jesus, and sought to slay him, be-
cause he had done these things on the
sabbath day.
17 ¶But Jesus answered them, My
Father worketh hitherto, and I work.
18 Therefore the Jews sought the
more to kill him, because he not only
had broken the sabbath, but said also
that God was his Father, making him-
self equal with God.
19 ¶Then answered Jesus and said
unto them, Verily, verily, I say unto
you, The Son can do nothing of himself,
but what he seeth the Father do: for
what things soever he doeth, these also
doeth the Son likewise.
20 For the Father loveth the Son, and
sheweth him all things that himself
doeth: and he will shew him greater
works than these, that ye may marvel.
21 For as the Father raiseth up the
dead, and quickeneth *them;* even so the
Son quickeneth whom he will.
22 For the Father judgeth no man,
but hath committed all judgment unto
the Son:
23 That all *men* should honour the
Son, even as they honour the Father.
He that honoureth not the Son hon-
oureth not the Father which hath sent
him.
24 Verily, verily, I say unto you, He
that heareth my word, and believeth on
him that sent me, hath everlasting life,
and shall not come into condemnation;
but is passed from death unto life.
25 Verily, verily, I say unto you, The
hour is coming, and now is, when the
dead shall hear the voice of the Son of
God: and they that hear shall live.
26 For as the Father hath life in him-
self; so hath he given to the Son to have
life in himself;
27 And hath given him authority to
execute judgment also, because he is
the Son of man.
28 Marvel not at this: for the hour is
coming, in the which all that are in the
graves shall hear his voice,
29 And shall come forth; they that
have done good, unto the resurrection
of life; and they that have done evil,
unto the resurrection of damnation.
30 I can of mine own self do nothing:
as I hear, I judge: and my judgment is
just; because I seek not mine own will,
but the will of the Father which hath
sent me.
31 If I bear witness of myself, my wit-
ness is not true.
32 There is another that beareth wit-
ness of me; and I know that the witness
which he witnesseth of me is true.
33 Ye sent unto John, and he bare
witness unto the truth.
34 But I receive not testimony from
man: but these things I say, that ye
might be saved.
35 He was a burning and a shining
light: and ye were willing for a season
to rejoice in his light.
36 But I have greater witness than
that of John: for the works which the
Father hath given me to finish, the
same works that I do, bear witness of
me, that the Father hath sent me.
37 And the Father himself, which
hath sent me, hath borne witness of
me. Ye have neither heard his voice at
any time, nor seen his shape.
38 And ye have not his word abiding
in you: for whom he hath sent, him ye
believe not.
39 Search the scriptures; for in them
ye think ye have eternal life: and they
are they which testify of me.
40 And ye will not come to me, that
ye might have life.
41 I receive not honour from men.
42 But I know you, that ye have not
the love of God in you.
43 I am come in my Father's name,
and ye receive me not: if another shall
come in his own name, him ye will re-
ceive.
44 How can ye believe, which receive
honour one of another, and seek not the
honour that *cometh* from God only?
45 Do not think that I will accuse you
to the Father: there is *one* that accuseth
you, *even* Moses in whom ye trust.
46 For had ye believed Moses, ye
would have believed me: for he wrote
of me.
47 But if ye believe not his writings,
how shall ye believe my words?

CHAPTER 6

AFTER these things Jesus went over
the sea of Galilee, which is *the sea* of Ti-
be'ri-as.

2 And a great multitude followed him, because they saw his miracles which he did on them that were diseased.

3 And Jesus went up into a mountain, and there he sat with his disciples.

4 And the passover, a feast of the Jews, was nigh.

5 When Jesus then lifted up *his* eyes, and saw a great company come unto him, he saith unto Philip, Whence shall we buy bread, that these may eat?

6 And this he said to prove him: for he himself knew what he would do.

7 Philip answered him, Two hundred pennyworth of bread is not sufficient for them, that every one of them may take a little.

8 One of his disciples, Andrew, Simon Peter's brother, saith unto him,

9 There is a lad here, which hath five barley loaves, and two small fishes: but what are they among so many?

10 And Jesus said, Make the men sit down. Now there was much grass in the place. So the men sat down, in number about five thousand.

11 And Jesus took the loaves; and when he had given thanks, he distributed to the disciples, and the disciples to them that were set down; and likewise of the fishes as much as they would.

12 When they were filled, he said unto his disciples, Gather up the fragments that remain, that nothing be lost.

13 Therefore they gathered *them* together, and filled twelve baskets with the fragments of the five barley loaves, which remained over and above unto them that had eaten.

14 ¶Then those men, when they had seen the miracle that Jesus did, said, This is of a truth that prophet that should come into the world.

15 When Jesus therefore perceived that they would come and take him by force, to make him a king, he departed again into a mountain himself alone.

16 ¶And when even was *now* come, his disciples went down unto the sea,

17 And entered into a ship, and went over the sea toward Ca-per′na-um. And it was now dark, and Jesus was not come to them.

18 And the sea arose by reason of a great wind that blew.

19 So when they had rowed about five and twenty or thirty furlongs, they see Jesus walking on the sea, and drawing nigh unto the ship: and they were afraid.

20 But he saith unto them, It is I; be not afraid.

21 Then they willingly received him into the ship: and immediately the ship was at the land whither they went.

22 ¶The day following, when the people which stood on the other side of the sea saw that there was none other boat there, save that one whereinto his disciples were entered, and that Jesus went not with his disciples into the boat, but *that* his disciples were gone away alone;

23 (Howbeit there came other boats from Ti-be′ri-as nigh unto the place where they did eat bread, after that the Lord had given thanks:)

24 When the people therefore saw that Jesus was not there, neither his disciples, they also took shipping, and came to Ca-per′na-um, seeking for Jesus.

25 And when they had found him on the other side of the sea they said unto him, Rabbi, when camest thou hither?

26 Jesus answered them and said, Verily, verily, I say unto you, Ye seek me, not because ye saw the miracles, but because ye did eat of the loaves, and were filled.

27 Labour not for the meat which perisheth, but for that meat which endureth unto everlasting life, which the Son of man shall give unto you: for him hath God the Father sealed.

28 Then said they unto him, What shall we do, that we might work the works of God?

29 Jesus answered and said unto them, This is the work of God, that ye believe on him whom he hath sent.

30 They said therefore unto him, What sign shewest thou then, that we may see, and believe thee? what dost thou work?

31 Our fathers did eat manna in the desert; as it is written, He gave them bread from heaven to eat.

32 Then Jesus said unto them, Verily, verily, I say unto you, Moses gave you not that bread from heaven; but my Father giveth you the true bread from heaven.

33 For the bread of God is he which cometh down from heaven, and giveth life unto the world.

34 Then said they unto him, Lord, evermore give us this bread.

35 And Jesus said unto them, I am the bread of life: he that cometh to me shall never hunger; and he that believeth on me shall never thirst.

36 But I said unto you, That ye also have seen me, and believe not.

37 All that the Father giveth me shall come to me; and him that cometh to me I will in no wise cast out.

38 For I came down from heaven, not to do mine own will, but the will of him that sent me.
39 And this is the Father's will which hath sent me, that of all which he hath given me I should lose nothing, but should raise it up again at the last day.
40 And this is the will of him that sent me, that every one which seeth the Son, and believeth on him, may have everlasting life: and I will raise him up at the last day.
41 The Jews then murmured at him, because he said, I am the bread which came down from heaven.
42 And they said, Is not this Jesus, the son of Joseph, whose father and mother we know? how is it then that he saith, I came down from heaven?
43 Jesus therefore answered and said unto them, Murmur not among yourselves.
44 No man can come to me, except the Father which hath sent me draw him: and I will raise him up at the last day.
45 It is written in the prophets, And they shall be all taught of God. Every man therefore that hath heard, and hath learned of the Father, cometh unto me.
46 Not that any man hath seen the Father, save he which is of God, he hath seen the Father.
47 Verily, verily, I say unto you, He that believeth on me hath everlasting life.
48 I am that bread of life.
49 Your fathers did eat manna in the wilderness, and are dead.
50 This is the bread which cometh down from heaven, that a man may eat thereof, and not die.
51 I am the living bread which came down from heaven: if any man eat of this bread, he shall live for ever: and the bread that I will give is my flesh, which I will give for the life of the world.
52 The Jews therefore strove among themselves, saying, How can this man give us *his* flesh to eat?
53 Then Jesus said unto them, Verily, verily, I say unto you, Except ye eat the flesh of the Son of man, and drink his blood, ye have no life in you.
54 Whoso eateth my flesh, and drinketh my blood, hath eternal life; and I will raise him up at the last day.
55 For my flesh is meat indeed, and my blood is drink indeed.
56 He that eateth my flesh, and drinketh my blood, dwelleth in me, and I in him.
57 As the living Father hath sent me, and I live by the Father: so he that eateth me, even he shall live by me.
58 This is that bread which came down from heaven: not as your fathers did eat manna, and are dead: he that eateth of this bread shall live for ever.
59 These things said he in the synagogue, as he taught in Ca-per'na-um.
60 Many therefore of his disciples, when they had heard *this*, said, This is an hard saying; who can hear it?
61 When Jesus knew in himself that his disciples murmured at it, he said unto them, Doth this offend you?
62 *What* and if ye shall see the Son of man ascend up where he was before?
63 It is the spirit that quickeneth; the flesh profiteth nothing: the words that I speak unto you, *they* are spirit, and *they* are life.
64 But there are some of you that believe not. For Jesus knew from the beginning who they were that believed not, and who should betray him.
65 And he said, Therefore said I unto you, that no man can come unto me, except it were given unto him of my Father.
66 ¶From that *time* many of his disciples went back, and walked no more with him.
67 Then said Jesus unto the twelve, Will ye also go away?
68 Then Simon Peter answered him, Lord, to whom shall we go? thou hast the words of eternal life.
69 And we believe and are sure that thou art that Christ, the Son of the living God.
70 Jesus answered them, Have not I chosen you twelve, and one of you is a devil?
71 He spake of Judas Iscariot *the son* of Simon: for he it was that should betray him, being one of the twelve.

CHAPTER 7

AFTER these things Jesus walked in Galilee: for he would not walk in Jewry, because the Jews sought to kill him.
2 ¶Now the Jews' feast of tabernacles was at hand.
3 His brethren therefore said unto him, Depart hence, and go into Judæa, that thy disciples also may see the works that thou doest.
4 For *there is* no man *that* doeth any thing in secret, and he himself seeketh to be known openly. If thou do these things, shew thyself to the world.
5 For neither did his brethren believe in him.
6 Then Jesus said unto them, My time

is not yet come: but your time is alway
ready.
7 The world cannot hate you; but me
it hateth, because I testify of it, that the
works thereof are evil.
8 Go ye up unto this feast: I go not up
yet unto this feast; for my time is not
yet full come.
9 When he had said these words unto
them, he abode *still* in Galilee.
10 ¶But when his brethren were gone
up, then went he also up unto the feast,
not openly, but as it were in secret.
11 Then the Jews sought him at the
feast, and said, Where is he?
12 And there was much murmuring
among the people concerning him: for
some said, He is a good man: others
said, Nay; but he deceiveth the people.
13 Howbeit no man spake openly of
him for fear of the Jews.
14 ¶Now about the midst of the feast
Jesus went up into the temple, and
taught.
15 And the Jews marvelled, saying,
How knoweth this man letters, having
never learned?
16 Jesus answered them, and said,
My doctrine is not mine, but his that
sent me.
17 If any man will do his will, he shall
know of the doctrine, whether it be of
God, or *whether* I speak of myself.
18 He that speaketh of himself
seeketh his own glory: but he that
seeketh his glory that sent him, the
same is true, and no unrighteousness is
in him.
19 Did not Moses give you the law,
and *yet* none of you keepeth the law?
Why go ye about to kill me?
20 The people answered and said,
Thou hast a devil: who goeth about to
kill thee?
21 Jesus answered and said unto
them, I have done one work, and ye all
marvel.
22 Moses therefore gave unto you
circumcision; (not because it is of
Moses, but of the fathers;) and ye on
the sabbath day circumcise a man.
23 If a man on the sabbath day re-
ceive circumcision, that the law of
Moses should not be broken; are ye
angry at me, because I have made a
man every whit whole on the sabbath
day?
24 Judge not according to the appear-
ance, but judge righteous judgment.
25 Then said some of them of Jeru-
salem, Is not this he, whom they seek to
kill?
26 But, lo, he speaketh boldly, and
they say nothing unto him. Do the rul-
ers know indeed that this is the very
Christ?
27 Howbeit we know this man
whence he is: but when Christ cometh,
no man knoweth whence he is.
28 Then cried Jesus in the temple as
he taught, saying, Ye both know me,
and ye know whence I am: and I am not
come of myself, but he that sent me is
true, whom ye know not.
29 But I know him: for I am from him,
and he hath sent me.
30 Then they sought to take him: but
no man laid hands on him, because his
hour was not yet come.
31 And many of the people believed
on him, and said, When Christ cometh,
will he do more miracles than these
which this *man* hath done?
32 ¶The Pharisees heard that the
people murmured such things concern-
ing him; and the Pharisees and the
chief priests sent officers to take him.
33 Then said Jesus unto them, Yet a
little while am I with you, and *then* I go
unto him that sent me.
34 Ye shall seek me, and shall not
find *me:* and where I am, *thither* ye can-
not come.
35 Then said the Jews among them-
selves, Whither will he go, that we shall
not find him? will he go unto the dis-
persed among the Gentiles, and teach
the Gentiles?
36 What *manner of* saying is this that
he said, Ye shall seek me, and shall not
find *me:* and where I am, *thither* ye can-
not come?
37 ¶In the last day, that great *day* of
the feast, Jesus stood and cried, saying,
If any man thirst, let him come unto
me, and drink.
38 He that believeth on me, as the
scripture hath said, out of his belly
shall flow rivers of living water.
39 (But this spake he of the Spirit,
which they that believe on him should
receive: for the Holy Ghost was not yet
given; because that Jesus was not yet
glorified.)
40 Many of the people therefore,
when they heard this saying, said, Of a
truth this is the Prophet.
41 Others said, This is the Christ. But
some said, Shall Christ come out of Gali-
lee?
42 Hath not the scripture said, That
Christ cometh of the seed of David, and
out of the town of Bethlehem, where
David was?
43 So there was a division among the
people because of him.
44 And some of them would have
taken him; but no man laid hands on
him.

45 ¶Then came the officers to the
chief priests and Pharisees; and they
said unto them, Why have ye not
brought him?
46 The officers answered, Never man
spake like this man.
47 Then answered them the Pha-
risees, Are ye also deceived?
48 Have any of the rulers or of the
Pharisees believed on him?
49 But this people who knoweth not
the law are cursed.
50 Nīc-o-dē'mus saith unto them, (he
that came to Jesus by night, being one
of them,)
51 Doth our law judge *any* man, be-
fore it hear him, and know what he
doeth?
52 They answered and said unto him,
Art thou also of Galilee? Search, and
look: for out of Galilee ariseth no
prophet.
53 And every man went unto his own
house.

CHAPTER 8

JESUS went unto the mount of Olives.
2 And early in the morning he came
again into the temple, and all the peo-
ple came unto him; and he sat down,
and taught them.
3 And the scribes and Pharisees
brought unto him a woman taken in
adultery; and when they had set her in
the midst,
4 They say unto him, Master, this
woman was taken in adultery, in the very
act.
5 Now Moses in the law commanded
us, that such should be stoned: but
what sayest thou?
6 This they said, tempting him, that
they might have to accuse him. But Je-
sus stooped down, and with *his* finger
wrote on the ground, *as though he
heard them not.*
7 So when they continued asking
him, he lifted up himself, and said unto
them, He that is without sin among
you, let him first cast a stone at her.
8 And again he stooped down, and
wrote on the ground.
9 And they which heard *it*, being con-
victed by *their own* conscience, went
out one by one, beginning at the eldest,
even unto the last: and Jesus was left
alone, and the woman standing in the
midst.
10 When Jesus had lifted up himself,
and saw none but the woman, he said
unto her, Woman, where are those
thine accusers? hath no man con-
demned thee?
11 She said, No man, Lord. And Jesus
said unto her, Neither do I condemn
thee: go, and sin no more.
12 ¶Then spake Jesus again unto
them, saying, I am the light of the
world: he that followeth me shall not
walk in darkness, but shall have the
light of life.
13 The Pharisees therefore said unto
him, Thou bearest record of thyself; thy
record is not true.
14 Jesus answered and said unto
them, Though I bear record of myself,
yet my record is true: for I know
whence I came, and whither I go; but ye
cannot tell whence I come, and whither
I go.
15 Ye judge after the flesh; I judge no
man.
16 And yet if I judge, my judgment is
true: for I am not alone, but I and the
Father that sent me.
17 It is also written in your law, that
the testimony of two men is true.
18 I am one that bear witness of my-
self, and the Father that sent me bear-
eth witness of me.
19 Then said they unto him, Where is
thy Father? Jesus answered, Ye neither
know me, nor my Father: if ye had
known me, ye should have known my
Father also.
20 These words spake Jesus in the
treasury, as he taught in the temple:
and no man laid hands on him; for his
hour was not yet come.
21 Then said Jesus again unto them, I
go my way, and ye shall seek me, and
shall die in your sins: whither I go, ye
cannot come.
22 Then said the Jews, Will he kill
himself? because he saith, Whither I
go, ye cannot come.
23 And he said unto them, Ye are
from beneath; I am from above: ye are
of this world; I am not of this world.
24 I said therefore unto you, that ye
shall die in your sins: for if ye believe
not that I am *he*, ye shall die in your
sins.
25 Then said they unto him, Who art
thou? And Jesus saith unto them, Even
the same that I said unto you from the
beginning.
26 I have many things to say and to
judge of you: but he that sent me is
true; and I speak to the world those
things which I have heard of him.
27 They understood not that he spake
to them of the Father.
28 Then said Jesus unto them, When
ye have lifted up the Son of man, then
shall ye know that I am *he*, and *that* I do
nothing of myself; but as my Father
hath taught me, I speak these things.
29 And he that sent me is with me:

the Father hath not left me alone; for I
do always those things that please him.
30 As he spake these words, many
believed on him.
31 Then said Jesus to those Jews
which believed on him, If ye continue
in my word, *then* are ye my disciples
indeed;
32 And ye shall know the truth, and
the truth shall make you free.
33 They answered him, We be Abra-
ham's seed, and were never in bondage
to any man: how sayest thou, Ye shall
be made free?
34 Jesus answered them, Verily,
verily, I say unto you, Whosoever com-
mitteth sin is the servant of sin.
35 And the servant abideth not in the
house for ever: *but* the Son abideth
ever.
36 If the Son therefore shall make
you free, ye shall be free indeed.
37 I know that ye are Abraham's
seed; but ye seek to kill me, because my
word hath no place in you.
38 I speak that which I have seen
with my Father: and ye do that which
ye have seen with your father.
39 They answered and said unto him,
Abraham is our father. Jesus saith unto
them, If ye were Abraham's children,
ye would do the works of Abraham.
40 But now ye seek to kill me, a man
that hath told you the truth, which I
have heard of God: this did not Abra-
ham.
41 Ye do the deeds of your father.
Then said they to him, We be not born
of fornication; we have one Father,
even God.
42 Jesus said unto them, If God were
your Father, ye would love me: for I
proceeded forth and came from God;
neither came I of myself, but he sent
me.
43 Why do ye not understand my
speech? *even* because ye cannot hear
my word.
44 Ye are of *your* father the devil, and
the lusts of your father ye will do. He
was a murderer from the beginning,
and abode not in the truth, because
there is no truth in him. When he
speaketh a lie, he speaketh of his own:
for he is a liar, and the father of it.
45 And because I tell *you* the truth, ye
believe me not.
46 Which of you convinceth me of
sin? And if I say the truth, why do ye
not believe me?
47 He that is of God heareth God's
words: ye therefore hear *them* not, be-
cause ye are not of God.
48 Then answered the Jews, and said
unto him, Say we not well that thou art
a Sa-mâr'i-tan, and hast a devil?
49 Jesus answered, I have not a devil;
but I honour my Father, and ye do
dishonour me.
50 And I seek not mine own glory:
there is one that seeketh and judgeth.
51 Verily, verily, I say unto you, If a
man keep my saying, he shall never see
death.
52 Then said the Jews unto him, Now
we know that thou hast a devil. Abra-
ham is dead, and the prophets; and
thou sayest, If a man keep my saying,
he shall never taste of death.
53 Art thou greater than our father
Abraham, which is dead? and the
prophets are dead: whom makest thou
thyself?
54 Jesus answered, If I honour my-
self, my honour is nothing: it is my
Father that honoureth me; of whom ye
say, that he is your God:
55 Yet ye have not known him; but I
know him: and if I should say, I know
him not, I shall be a liar like unto you:
but I know him, and keep his saying.
56 Your father Abraham rejoiced to
see my day: and he saw *it*, and was
glad.
57 Then said the Jews unto him, Thou
art not yet fifty years old, and hast thou
seen Abraham?
58 Jesus said unto them, Verily,
verily, I say unto you, Before Abraham
was, I am.
59 Then took they up stones to cast at
him: but Jesus hid himself, and went
out of the temple, going through the
midst of them, and so passed by.

CHAPTER 9

AND as *Jesus* passed by, he saw a man
which was blind from *his* birth.
2 And his disciples asked him,
saying, Master, who did sin, this man,
or his parents, that he was born blind?
3 Jesus answered, Neither hath this
man sinned, nor his parents: but that
the works of God should be made
manifest in him.
4 I must work the works of him that
sent me, while it is day: the night
cometh, when no man can work.
5 As long as I am in the world, I am
the light of the world.
6 When he had thus spoken, he spat
on the ground, and made clay of the
spittle, and he anointed the eyes of the
blind man with the clay,
7 And said unto him, Go, wash in the
pool of Sī-lō'am, (which is by interpre-
tation, Sent.) He went his way there-
fore, and washed, and came seeing.
8 ¶The neighbours therefore, and

they which before had seen him that he
was blind, said, Is not this he that sat
and begged?
9 Some said, This is he: others *said*,
He is like him: *but* he said, I am *he*.
10 Therefore said they unto him,
How were thine eyes opened?
11 He answered and said, A man that
is called Jesus made clay, and anointed
mine eyes, and said unto me, Go to the
pool of Sī-lō'am, and wash: and I went
and washed, and I received sight.
12 Then said they unto him, Where is
he? He said, I know not.
13 ¶They brought to the Pharisees
him that aforetime was blind.
14 And it was the sabbath day when
Jesus made the clay, and opened his
eyes.
15 Then again the Pharisees also
asked him how he had received his
sight. He said unto them, He put clay
upon mine eyes, and I washed, and do
see.
16 Therefore said some of the
Pharisees, This man is not of God, be-
cause he keepeth not the sabbath day.
Others said, How can a man that is a
sinner do such miracles? And there was
a division among them.
17 They say unto the blind man
again, What sayest thou of him, that he
hath opened thine eyes? He said, He is a
prophet.
18 But the Jews did not believe con-
cerning him, that he had been blind,
and received his sight, until they called
the parents of him that had received his
sight.
19 And they asked them, saying, Is
this your son, who ye say was born
blind? how then doth he now see?
20 His parents answered them and
said, We know that this is our son, and
that he was born blind:
21 But by what means he now seeth,
we know not; or who hath opened his
eyes, we know not: he is of age; ask
him: he shall speak for himself.
22 These *words* spake his parents,
because they feared the Jews: for the
Jews had agreed already, that if any
man did confess that he was Christ, he
should be put out of the synagogue.
23 Therefore said his parents, He is of
age; ask him.
24 Then again called they the man
that was blind, and said unto him, Give
God the praise: we know that this man
is a sinner.
25 He answered and said, Whether
he be a sinner *or no*, I know not: one
thing I know, that, whereas I was blind,
now I see.
26 Then said they to him again, What
did he to thee? how opened he thine
eyes?
27 He answered them, I have told you
already, and ye did not hear: wherefore
would ye hear *it* again? will ye also be
his disciples?
28 Then they reviled him, and said,
Thou art his disciple; but we are Moses'
disciples.
29 We know that God spake unto
Moses: *as for* this *fellow*, we know not
from whence he is.
30 The man answered and said unto
them, Why herein is a marvellous
thing, that ye know not from whence
he is, and *yet* he hath opened mine
eyes.
31 Now we know that God heareth
not sinners: but if any man be a wor-
shipper of God, and doeth his will, him
he heareth.
32 Since the world began was it not
heard that any man opened the eyes of
one that was born blind.
33 If this man were not of God, he
could do nothing.
34 They answered and said unto him,
Thou wast altogether born in sins, and
dost thou teach us? And they cast him
out.
35 ¶Jesus heard that they had cast
him out; and when he had found him,
he said unto him, Dost thou believe on
the Son of God?
36 He answered and said, Who is he,
Lord, that I might believe on him?
37 And Jesus said unto him, Thou
hast both seen him, and it is he that
talketh with thee.
38 And he said, Lord, I believe. And
he worshipped him.
39 ¶And Jesus said, For judgment I
am come into this world, that they
which see not might see; and that they
which see might be made blind.
40 And *some* of the Pharisees which
were with him heard these words, and
said unto him, Are we blind also?
41 Jesus said unto them, If ye were
blind, ye should have no sin: but now ye
say, We see; therefore your sin re-
maineth.

CHAPTER 10

VERILY, verily, I say unto you, He that
entereth not by the door into the sheep-
fold, but climbeth up some other way,
the same is a thief and a robber.
2 But he that entereth in by the door
is the shepherd of the sheep.
3 To him the porter openeth; and the
sheep hear his voice: and he calleth his
own sheep by name, and leadeth them
out.
4 And when he putteth forth his own

sheep, he goeth before them, and the sheep follow him: for they know his voice.

5 And a stranger will they not follow, but will flee from him: for they know not the voice of strangers.

6 This parable spake Jesus unto them: but they understood not what things they were which he spake unto them.

7 Then said Jesus unto them again, Verily, verily, I say unto you, I am the door of the sheep.

8 All that ever came before me are thieves and robbers: but the sheep did not hear them.

9 I am the door: by me if any man enter in, he shall be saved, and shall go in and out, and find pasture.

10 The thief cometh not, but for to steal, and to kill, and to destroy: I am come that they might have life, and that they might have *it* more abundantly.

11 I am the good shepherd: the good shepherd giveth his life for the sheep.

12 But he that is an hireling, and not the shepherd, whose own the sheep are not, seeth the wolf coming, and leaveth the sheep, and fleeth: and the wolf catcheth them, and scattereth the sheep.

13 The hireling fleeth, because he is an hireling, and careth not for the sheep.

14 I am the good shepherd, and know my *sheep*, and am known of mine.

15 As the Father knoweth me, even so know I the Father: and I lay down my life for the sheep.

16 And other sheep I have, which are not of this fold: them also I must bring, and they shall hear my voice; and there shall be one fold, *and* one shepherd.

17 Therefore doth my Father love me, because I lay down my life, that I might take it again.

18 No man taketh it from me, but I lay it down of myself. I have power to lay it down, and I have power to take it again. This commandment have I received of my Father.

19 ¶There was a division therefore again among the Jews for these sayings.

20 And many of them said, He hath a devil, and is mad; why hear ye him?

21 Others said, These are not the words of him that hath a devil. Can a devil open the eyes of the blind?

22 ¶And it was at Jerusalem the feast of the dedication, and it was winter.

23 And Jesus walked in the temple in Solomon's porch.

24 Then came the Jews round about him, and said unto him, How long dost thou make us to doubt? If thou be the Christ, tell us plainly.

25 Jesus answered them, I told you, and ye believed not: the works that I do in my Father's name, they bear witness of me.

26 But ye believe not, because ye are not of my sheep, as I said unto you.

27 My sheep hear my voice, and I know them, and they follow me:

28 And I give unto them eternal life; and they shall never perish, neither shall any *man* pluck them out of my hand.

29 My Father, which gave *them* me, is greater than all; and no *man* is able to pluck *them* out of my Father's hand.

30 I and *my* Father are one.

31 ¶Then the Jews took up stones again to stone him.

32 Jesus answered them, Many good works have I shewed you from my Father; for which of those works do ye stone me?

33 The Jews answered him, saying, For a good work we stone thee not; but for blasphemy; and because that thou, being a man, makest thyself God.

34 Jesus answered them, Is it not written in your law, I said, Ye are gods?

35 If he called them gods, unto whom the word of God came, and the scripture cannot be broken;

36 Say ye of him, whom the Father hath sanctified, and sent into the world, Thou blasphemest; because I said, I am the Son of God?

37 If I do not the works of my Father, believe me not.

38 But if I do, though ye believe not me, believe the works: that ye may know, and believe, that the Father *is* in me, and I in him.

39 ¶Therefore they sought again to take him: but he escaped out of their hand,

40 And went away again beyond Jordan into the place where John at first baptized; and there he abode.

41 And many resorted unto him, and said, John did no miracle: but all things that John spake of this man were true.

42 And many believed on him there.

CHAPTER 11

NOW a certain *man* was sick, *named* Lazarus, of Bethany, the town of Mary and her sister Martha.

2 (It was *that* Mary which anointed the Lord with ointment, and wiped his feet with her hair, whose brother Lazarus was sick.)

3 Therefore his sisters sent unto him,

saying, Lord, behold, he whom thou
lovest is sick.
4 When Jesus heard *that*, he said,
This sickness is not unto death, but for
the glory of God, that the Son of God
might be glorified thereby.
5 Now Jesus loved Martha, and her
sister, and Lazarus.
6 When he had heard therefore that
he was sick, he abode two days still in
the same place where he was.
7 Then after that saith he to *his* dis-
ciples, Let us go into Judæa again.
8 *His* disciples say unto him, Master,
the Jews of late sought to stone thee;
and goest thou thither again?
9 Jesus answered, Are there not
twelve hours in the day? If any man
walk in the day, he stumbleth not, be-
cause he seeth the light of this world.
10 But if a man walk in the night, he
stumbleth, because there is no light in
him.
11 These things said he: and after
that he saith unto them, Our friend Laza-
rus sleepeth; but I go, that I may
awake him out of sleep.
12 Then said his disciples, Lord, if he
sleep, he shall do well.
13 Howbeit Jesus spake of his death:
but they thought that he had spoken of
taking of rest in sleep.
14 Then said Jesus unto them plainly,
Lazarus is dead.
15 And I am glad for your sakes that I
was not there, to the intent ye may be-
lieve; nevertheless let us go unto him.
16 Then said Thomas, which is called
Dĭd'y-mus, unto his fellowdisciples,
Let us also go, that we may die with
him.
17 Then when Jesus came, he found
that he had *lain* in the grave four days
already.
18 Now Bethany was nigh unto Jeru-
salem, about fifteen furlongs off:
19 And many of the Jews came to
Martha and Mary, to comfort them
concerning their brother.
20 Then Martha, as soon as she heard
that Jesus was coming, went and met
him: but Mary sat *still* in the house.
21 Then said Martha unto Jesus,
Lord, if thou hadst been here, my
brother had not died.
22 But I know, that even now, what-
soever thou wilt ask of God, God will
give *it* thee.
23 Jesus saith unto her, Thy brother
shall rise again.
24 Martha saith unto him, I know
that he shall rise again in the resurrec-
tion at the last day.
25 Jesus said unto her, I am the resur-
rection, and the life: he that believeth in
me, though he were dead, yet shall he
live:
26 And whosoever liveth and believ-
eth in me shall never die. Believest
thou this?
27 She saith unto him, Yea, Lord: I
believe that thou art the Christ, the Son
of God, which should come into the
world.
28 And when she had so said, she
went her way, and called Mary her sis-
ter secretly, saying, The Master is
come, and calleth for thee.
29 As soon as she heard *that*, she
arose quickly, and came unto him.
30 Now Jesus was not yet come into
the town, but was in that place where
Martha met him.
31 The Jews then which were with
her in the house, and comforted her,
when they saw Mary, that she rose up
hastily and went out, followed her,
saying, She goeth unto the grave to
weep there.
32 Then when Mary was come where
Jesus was, and saw him, she fell down
at his feet, saying unto him, Lord, if
thou hadst been here, my brother had
not died.
33 When Jesus therefore saw her
weeping, and the Jews also weeping
which came with her, he groaned in the
spirit, and was troubled,
34 And said, Where have ye laid him?
They said unto him, Lord, come and
see.
35 Jesus wept.
36 Then said the Jews, Behold how he
loved him!
37 And some of them said, Could not
this man, which opened the eyes of the
blind, have caused that even this man
should not have died?
38 Jesus therefore again groaning in
himself cometh to the grave. It was a
cave, and a stone lay upon it.
39 Jesus said, Take ye away the
stone. Martha, the sister of him that
was dead, saith unto him, Lord, by this
time he stinketh: for he hath been *dead*
four days.
40 Jesus saith unto her, Said I not
unto thee, that, if thou wouldest be-
lieve, thou shouldest see the glory of
God?
41 Then they took away the stone
from the place where the dead was laid.
And Jesus lifted up *his* eyes, and said,
Father, I thank thee that thou hast
heard me.
42 And I knew that thou hearest me
always: but because of the people
which stand by I said *it*, that they may
believe that thou hast sent me.
43 And when he thus had spoken, he

cried with a loud voice, Lazarus, come forth.

44 And he that was dead came forth, bound hand and foot with graveclothes: and his face was bound about with a napkin. Jesus saith unto them, Loose him, and let him go.

45 Then many of the Jews which came to Mary, and had seen the things which Jesus did, believed on him.

46 But some of them went their ways to the Pharisees, and told them what things Jesus had done.

47 ¶Then gathered the chief priests and the Pharisees a council, and said, What do we? for this man doeth many miracles.

48 If we let him thus alone, all *men* will believe on him: and the Romans shall come and take away both our place and nation.

49 And one of them, *named* Cā′ia-phas, being the high priest that same year, said unto them, Ye know nothing at all,

50 Nor consider that it is expedient for us, that one man should die for the people, and that the whole nation perish not.

51 And this spake he not of himself: but being high priest that year, he prophesied that Jesus should die for that nation;

52 And not for that nation only, but that also he should gather together in one the children of God that were scattered abroad.

53 Then from that day forth they took counsel together for to put him to death.

54 Jesus therefore walked no more openly among the Jews; but went thence unto a country near to the wilderness, into a city called E′phra-im, and there continued with his disciples.

55 ¶And the Jews' passover was nigh at hand: and many went out of the country up to Jerusalem before the passover, to purify themselves.

56 Then sought they for Jesus, and spake among themselves, as they stood in the temple, What think ye, that he will not come to the feast?

57 Now both the chief priests and the Pharisees had given a commandment, that, if any man knew where he were, he should shew *it*, that they might take him.

CHAPTER 12

THEN Jesus six days before the passover came to Bethany, where Lazarus was which had been dead, whom he raised from the dead.

2 There they made him a supper; and Martha served: but Lazarus was one of them that sat at the table with him.

3 Then took Mary a pound of ointment of spikenard, very costly, and anointed the feet of Jesus, and wiped his feet with her hair: and the house was filled with the odour of the ointment.

4 Then saith one of his disciples, Judas Iscariot, Simon's *son*, which should betray him,

5 Why was not this ointment sold for three hundred pence, and given to the poor?

6 This he said, not that he cared for the poor; but because he was a thief, and had the bag, and bare what was put therein.

7 Then said Jesus, Let her alone: against the day of my burying hath she kept this.

8 For the poor always ye have with you; but me ye have not always.

9 ¶Much people of the Jews therefore knew that he was there: and they came not for Jesus' sake only, but that they might see Lazarus also, whom he had raised from the dead.

10 But the chief priests consulted that they might put Lazarus also to death;

11 Because that by reason of him many of the Jews went away, and believed on Jesus.

12 ¶On the next day much people that were come to the feast, when they heard that Jesus was coming to Jerusalem,

13 Took branches of palm trees, and went forth to meet him, and cried, Hosanna: Blessed *is* the King of Israel that cometh in the name of the Lord.

14 And Jesus, when he had found a young ass, sat thereon; as it is written,

15 Fear not, daughter of Sion; behold, thy King cometh, sitting on an ass's colt.

16 These things understood not his disciples at the first: but when Jesus was glorified, then remembered they that these things were written of him, and *that* they had done these things unto him.

17 The people therefore that was with him when he called Lazarus out of his grave, and raised him from the dead, bare record.

18 For this cause the people also met him, for that they heard that he had done this miracle.

19 The Pharisees therefore said among themselves, Perceive ye how ye prevail nothing? behold, the world is gone after him.

20 ¶And there were certain Greeks

among them that came up to worship
at the feast:
21 The same came therefore to Phil-
ip, which was of Bĕthsā'i-da of Galilee,
and desired him, saying, Sir, we would
see Jesus.
22 Philip cometh and telleth Andrew:
and again Andrew and Philip tell Jesus.
23 ¶And Jesus answered them,
saying, The hour is come, that the Son
of man should be glorified.
24 Verily, verily, I say unto you, Ex-
cept a corn of wheat fall into the
ground and die, it abideth alone: but if
it die, it bringeth forth much fruit.
25 He that loveth his life shall lose it;
and he that hateth his life in this world
shall keep it unto life eternal.
26 If any man serve me, let him fol-
low me; and where I am, there shall
also my servant be: if any man serve
me, him will *my* Father honour.
27 Now is my soul troubled; and what
shall I say? Father, save me from this
hour: but for this cause came I unto this
hour.
28 Father, glorify thy name. Then
came there a voice from heaven,
saying, I have both glorified *it*, and will
glorify *it* again.
29 The people therefore, that stood
by, and heard *it*, said that it thundered:
others said, An angel spake to him.
30 Jesus answered and said, This
voice came not because of me, but for
your sakes.
31 Now is the judgment of this world:
now shall the prince of this world be
cast out.
32 And I, if I be lifted up from the
earth, will draw all *men* unto me.
33 This he said, signifying what death
he should die.
34 The people answered him, We
have heard out of the law that Christ
abideth forever: and how sayest thou,
The Son of man must be lifted up? who
is this Son of man?
35 Then Jesus said unto them, Yet a
little while is the light with you. Walk
while ye have the light, lest darkness
come upon you: for he that walketh in
darkness knoweth not whither he
goeth.
36 While ye have light, believe in the
light, that ye may be the children of
light. These things spake Jesus, and de-
parted, and did hide himself from
them.
37 ¶But though he had done so many
miracles before them, yet they believed
not on him:
38 That the saying of E-ṡā'ias the
prophet might be fulfilled, which he
spake, Lord, who hath believed our re-
port? and to whom hath the arm of the
Lord been revealed?
39 Therefore they could not believe,
because that E-ṡā'ias said again,
40 He hath blinded their eyes, and
hardened their heart; that they should
not see with *their* eyes, nor understand
with *their* heart, and be converted, and
I should heal them.
41 These things said E-ṡā'ias, when
he saw his glory, and spake of him.
42 ¶Nevertheless among the chief rul-
ers also many believed on him; but be-
cause of the Pharisees they did not con-
fess *him*, lest they should be put out of
the synagogue:
43 For they loved the praise of men
more than the praise of God.
44 ¶Jesus cried and said, He that be-
lieveth on me, believeth not on me, but
on him that sent me.
45 And he that seeth me seeth him
that sent me.
46 I am come a light into the world,
that whosoever believeth on me should
not abide in darkness.
47 And if any man hear my words,
and believe not, I judge him not: for I
came not to judge the world, but to
save the world.
48 He that rejecteth me, and receiv-
eth not my words, hath one that judg-
eth him: the word that I have spoken,
the same shall judge him in the last
day.
49 For I have not spoken of myself;
but the Father which sent me, he gave
me a commandment, what I should
say, and what I should speak.
50 And I know that his command-
ment is life everlasting: whatsoever I
speak therefore, even as the Father
said unto me, so I speak.

CHAPTER 13

NOW before the feast of the passover,
when Jesus knew that his hour was
come that he should depart out of this
world unto the Father, having loved his
own which were in the world, he loved
them unto the end.
2 And supper being ended, the devil
having now put into the heart of Judas
Iscariot, Simon's *son*, to betray him;
3 Jesus knowing that the Father had
given all things into his hands, and that
he was come from God, and went to
God;
4 He riseth from supper, and laid
aside his garments; and took a towel
and girded himself.
5 After that he poureth water into a
bason, and began to wash the disciples'
feet, and to wipe *them* with the towel
wherewith he was girded.

6 Then cometh he to Simon Peter: and Peter saith unto him, Lord, dost thou wash my feet?
7 Jesus answered and said unto him, What I do thou knowest not now; but thou shalt know hereafter.
8 Peter saith unto him, Thou shalt never wash my feet. Jesus answered him, If I wash thee not, thou hast no part with me.
9 Simon Peter saith unto him, Lord, not my feet only, but also *my* hands and *my* head.
10 Jesus saith to him, He that is washed needeth not save to wash *his* feet, but is clean every whit: and ye are clean, but not all.
11 For he knew who should betray him; therefore said he, Ye are not all clean.
12 So after he had washed their feet, and had taken his garments, and was set down again, he said unto them, Know ye what I have done to you?
13 Ye call me Master and Lord: and ye say well; for *so* I am.
14 If I then, *your* Lord and Master, have washed your feet; ye also ought to wash one another's feet.
15 For I have given you an example, that ye should do as I have done to you.
16 Verily, verily, I say unto you, The servant is not greater than his lord; neither he that is sent greater than he that sent him.
17 If ye know these things, happy are ye if ye do them.
18 ¶I speak not of you all: I know whom I have chosen: but that the scripture may be fulfilled, He that eateth bread with me hath lifted up his heel against me.
19 Now I tell you before it come, that, when it is come to pass, ye may believe that I am *he*.
20 Verily, verily, I say unto you, He that receiveth whomsoever I send receiveth me; and he that receiveth me receiveth him that sent me.
21 When Jesus had thus said, he was troubled in spirit, and testified, and said, Verily, verily, I say unto you, that one of you shall betray me.
22 Then the disciples looked one on another, doubting of whom he spake.
23 Now there was leaning on Jesus' bosom one of his disciples, whom Jesus loved.
24 Simon Peter therefore beckoned to him, that he should ask who it should be of whom he spake.
25 He then lying on Jesus' breast saith unto him, Lord, who is it?
26 Jesus answered, He it is, to whom I shall give a sop, when I have dipped *it*. And when he had dipped the sop, he gave *it* to Judas Iscariot, *the son* of Simon.
27 And after the sop Satan entered into him. Then said Jesus unto him, That thou doest, do quickly.
28 Now no man at the table knew for what intent he spake this unto him.
29 For some *of them* thought, because Judas had the bag, that Jesus had said unto him, Buy *those things* that we have need of against the feast; or, that he should give something to the poor.
30 He then having received the sop went immediately out: and it was night.
31 ¶Therefore, when he was gone out, Jesus said, Now is the Son of man glorified, and God is glorified in him.
32 If God be glorified in him, God shall also glorify him in himself, and shall straightway glorify him.
33 Little children, yet a little while I am with you. Ye shall seek me: and as I said unto the Jews, Whither I go, ye cannot come; so now I say to you.
34 A new commandment I give unto you, That ye love one another; as I have loved you, that ye also love one another.
35 By this shall all *men* know that ye are my disciples, if ye have love one to another.
36 ¶Simon Peter said unto him, Lord, whither goest thou? Jesus answered him, Whither I go, thou canst not follow me now; but thou shalt follow me afterwards.
37 Peter said unto him, Lord, why cannot I follow thee now? I will lay down my life for thy sake.
38 Jesus answered him, Wilt thou lay down thy life for my sake? Verily, verily, I say unto thee, The cock shall not crow, till thou hast denied me thrice.

CHAPTER 14

LET not your heart be troubled: ye believe in God, believe also in me.
2 In my Father's house are many mansions: if *it were* not *so*, I would have told you. I go to prepare a place for you.
3 And if I go and prepare a place for you, I will come again, and receive you unto myself; that where I am, *there* ye may be also.
4 And whither I go ye know, and the way ye know.
5 ¶Thomas saith unto him, Lord, we know not whither thou goest; and how can we know the way?
6 Jesus saith unto him, I am the way,

the truth, and the life: no man cometh unto the Father, but by me.

7 If ye had known me, ye should have known my Father also: and from henceforth ye know him, and have seen him.

8 **¶Philip saith unto him, Lord, shew us the Father, and it sufficeth us.**

9 **Jesus saith unto him,** Have I been so long time with you, and yet hast thou not known me, Philip? he that hath seen me hath seen the Father; and how sayest thou *then*, Shew us the Father?

10 Believest thou not that I am in the Father, and the Father in me? the words that I speak unto you I speak not of myself: but the Father that dwelleth in me, he doeth the works.

11 Believe me that I *am* in the Father, and the Father in me: or else believe me for the very works' sake.

12 Verily, verily, I say unto you, He that believeth on me, the works that I do shall he do also; and greater *works* than these shall he do; because I go unto my Father.

13 And whatsoever ye shall ask in my name, that will I do, that the Father may be glorified in the Son.

14 If ye shall ask any thing in my name, I will do *it*.

15 ¶If ye love me, keep my commandments.

16 And I will pray the Father, and he shall give you another Comforter, that he may abide with you for ever;

17 *Even* the Spirit of truth; whom the world cannot receive, because it seeth him not, neither knoweth him: but ye know him; for he dwelleth with you, and shall be in you.

18 I will not leave you comfortless: I will come to you.

19 Yet a little while, and the world seeth me no more; but ye see me: because I live, ye shall live also.

20 At that day ye shall know that I *am* in my Father, and ye in me, and I in you.

21 He that hath my commandments, and keepeth them, he it is that loveth me: and he that loveth me shall be loved of my Father, and I will love him, and will manifest myself to him.

22 **Judas saith unto him, not Iscariot, Lord, how is it that thou wilt manifest thyself unto us, and not unto the world?**

23 **Jesus answered and said unto him,** If a man love me, he will keep my words: and my Father will love him, and we will come unto him, and make our abode with him.

24 He that loveth me not keepeth not my sayings: and the word which ye hear is not mine, but the Father's which sent me.

25 These things have I spoken unto you, being *yet* present with you.

26 But the Comforter, *which is* the Holy Ghost, whom the Father will send in my name, he shall teach you all things, and bring all things to your remembrance, whatsoever I have said unto you.

27 Peace I leave with you, my peace I give unto you: not as the world giveth, give I unto you. Let not your heart be troubled, neither let it be afraid.

28 Ye have heard how I said unto you, I go away, and come *again* unto you. If ye loved me, ye would rejoice, because I said, I go unto the Father: for my Father is greater than I.

29 And now I have told you before it come to pass, that, when it is come to pass, ye might believe.

30 Hereafter I will not talk much with you: for the prince of this world cometh, and hath nothing in me.

31 But that the world may know that I love the Father; and as the Father gave me commandment, even so I do. Arise, let us go hence.

CHAPTER 15

I AM the true vine, and my Father is the husbandman.

2 Every branch in me that beareth not fruit he taketh away: and every *branch* that beareth fruit, he purgeth it, that it may bring forth more fruit.

3 Now ye are clean through the word which I have spoken unto you.

4 Abide in me, and I in you. As the branch cannot bear fruit of itself, except it abide in the vine; no more can ye, except ye abide in me.

5 I am the vine, ye *are* the branches: He that abideth in me, and I in him, the same bringeth forth much fruit: for without me ye can do nothing.

6 If a man abide not in me, he is cast forth as a branch, and is withered; and men gather them, and cast *them* into the fire, and they are burned.

7 If ye abide in me, and my words abide in you, ye shall ask what ye will, and it shall be done unto you.

8 Herein is my Father glorified, that ye bear much fruit; so shall ye be my disciples.

9 As the Father hath loved me, so have I loved you: continue ye in my love.

10 If ye keep my commandments, ye shall abide in my love; even as I have kept my Father's commandments, and abide in his love.

11 These things have I spoken unto you, that my joy might remain in you, and *that* your joy might be full.

12 This is my commandment, That ye
love one another, as I have loved you.
13 Greater love hath no man than
this, that a man lay down his life for his
friends.
14 Ye are my friends, if ye do what-
soever I command you.
15 Henceforth I call you not servants;
for the servant knoweth not what his
lord doeth: but I have called you
friends; for all things that I have heard
of my Father I have made known unto
you.
16 Ye have not chosen me, but I have
chosen you, and ordained you, that ye
should go and bring forth fruit, and *that*
your fruit should remain: that whatso-
ever ye shall ask of the Father in my
name, he may give it you.
17 These things I command you, that
ye love one another.
18 ¶If the world hate you, ye know
that it hated me before *it hated* you.
19 If ye were of the world, the world
would love his own: but because ye are
not of the world, but I have chosen you
out of the world, therefore the world
hateth you.
20 Remember the word that I said
unto you, The servant is not greater
than his lord. If they have persecuted
me, they will also persecute you; if they
have kept my saying, they will keep
yours also.
21 But all these things will they do
unto you for my name's sake, because
they know not him that sent me.
22 If I had not come and spoken unto
them, they had not had sin: but now
they have no cloak for their sin.
23 He that hateth me hateth my
Father also.
24 If I had not done among them the
works which none other man did, they
had not had sin: but now have they
both seen and hated both me and my
Father.
25 But *this cometh to pass*, that the
word might be fulfilled that is written
in their law, They hated me without a
cause.
26 But when the Comforter is come,
whom I will send unto you from the
Father, *even* the Spirit of truth, which
proceedeth from the Father, he shall
testify of me:
27 And ye also shall bear witness, be-
cause ye have been with me from the
beginning.

CHAPTER 16

THESE things have I spoken unto you,
that ye should not be offended.
2 They shall put you out of the syna-
gogues: yea, the time cometh, that
whosoever killeth you will think that
he doeth God service.
3 And these things will they do unto
you, because they have not known the
Father, nor me.
4 But these things have I told you,
that when the time shall come, ye may
remember that I told you of them. And
these things I said not unto you at the
beginning, because I was with you.
5 But now I go my way to him that
sent me; and none of you asketh me,
Whither goest thou?
6 But because I have said these things
unto you, sorrow hath filled your heart.
7 Nevertheless I tell you the truth; It
is expedient for you that I go away: for
if I go not away, the Comforter will not
come unto you; but if I depart, I will
send him unto you.
8 And when he is come, he will
reprove the world of sin, and of
righteousness, and of judgment:
9 Of sin, because they believe not on
me;
10 Of righteousness, because I go to
my Father, and ye see me no more;
11 Of judgment, because the prince
of this world is judged.
12 I have yet many things to say unto
you, but ye cannot bear them now.
13 Howbeit when he, the Spirit of
truth, is come, he will guide you into all
truth: for he shall not speak of himself;
but whatsoever he shall hear, *that* shall
he speak: and he will shew you things
to come.
14 He shall glorify me: for he shall re-
ceive of mine, and shall shew *it* unto
you.
15 All things that the Father hath are
mine: therefore said I, that he shall take
of mine, and shall shew *it* unto you.
16 A little while, and ye shall not see
me: and again, a little while, and ye
shall see me, because I go to the Father.
17 Then said *some* of his disciples
among themselves, What is this that he
saith unto us, A little while, and ye shall
not see me: and again, a little while, and
ye shall see me: and, Because I go to the
Father?
18 They said therefore, What is this
that he saith, A little while? we cannot
tell what he saith.
19 Now Jesus knew that they were
desirous to ask him, and said unto
them, Do ye enquire among yourselves
of that I said, A little while, and ye shall
not see me: and again, a little while, and
ye shall see me?
20 Verily, verily, I say unto you, That
ye shall weep and lament, but the
world shall rejoice: and ye shall be

sorrowful, but your sorrow shall be
turned into joy.
21 A woman when she is in travail
hath sorrow, because her hour is come:
but as soon as she is delivered of the
child, she remembereth no more the
anguish, for joy that a man is born into
the world.
22 And ye now therefore have
sorrow: but I will see you again, and
your heart shall rejoice, and your joy
no man taketh from you.
23 And in that day ye shall ask me
nothing. Verily, verily, I say unto you,
Whatsoever ye shall ask the Father in
my name, he will give *it* you.
24 Hitherto have ye asked nothing in
my name: ask, and ye shall receive,
that your joy may be full.
25 These things have I spoken unto
you in proverbs: but the time cometh,
when I shall no more speak unto you in
proverbs, but I shall shew you plainly
of the Father.
26 At that day ye shall ask in my
name: and I say not unto you, that I will
pray the Father for you:
27 For the Father himself loveth you,
because ye have loved me, and have be-
lieved that I came out from God.
28 I came forth from the Father, and
am come into the world: again, I leave
the world, and go to the Father.
29 ¶His disciples said unto him, Lo,
now speakest thou plainly, and speak-
est no proverb.
30 Now are we sure that thou know-
est all things, and needest not that
any man should ask thee: by this we
believe that thou camest forth from
God.
31 Jesus answered them, Do ye now
believe?
32 Behold, the hour cometh, yea, is
now come, that ye shall be scattered,
every man to his own, and shall leave
me alone: and yet I am not alone, be-
cause the Father is with me.
33 These things I have spoken unto
you, that in me ye might have peace. In
the world ye shall have tribulation: but
be of good cheer; I have overcome the
world.

CHAPTER 17

THESE words spake Jesus, and lifted
up his eyes to heaven, and said, Father,
the hour is come; glorify thy Son, that
thy Son also may glorify thee:
2 As thou hast given him power over
all flesh, that he should give eternal life
to as many as thou hast given him.
3 And this is life eternal, that they
might know thee the only true God, and
Jesus Christ, whom thou hast sent.
4 I have glorified thee on the earth: I
have finished the work which thou gav-
est me to do.
5 And now, O Father, glorify thou me
with thine own self with the glory
which I had with thee before the world
was.
6 I have manifested thy name unto
the men which thou gavest me out of
the world: thine they were, and thou
gavest them me; and they have kept
thy word.
7 Now they have known that all
things whatsoever thou hast given me
are of thee.
8 For I have given unto them the
words which thou gavest me; and they
have received *them*, and have known
surely that I came out from thee, and
they have believed that thou didst send
me.
9 I pray for them: I pray not for the
world, but for them which thou hast giv-
en me; for they are thine.
10 And all mine are thine, and thine
are mine; and I am glorified in them.
11 And now I am no more in the
world, but these are in the world, and I
come to thee. Holy Father, keep
through thine own name those whom
thou hast given me, that they may be
one, as we *are*.
12 While I was with them in the
world, I kept them in thy name: those
that thou gavest me I have kept, and
none of them is lost, but the son of per-
dition; that the scripture might be ful-
filled.
13 And now come I to thee; and these
things I speak in the world, that they
might have my joy fulfilled in them-
selves.
14 I have given them thy word; and
the world hath hated them, because
they are not of the world, even as I am
not of the world.
15 I pray not that thou shouldest take
them out of the world, but that thou
shouldest keep them from the evil.
16 They are not of the world, even as I
am not of the world.
17 Sanctify them through thy truth:
thy word is truth.
18 As thou hast sent me into the
world, even so have I also sent them
into the world.
19 And for their sakes I sanctify my-
self, that they also might be sanctified
through the truth.
20 Neither pray I for these alone, but
for them also which shall believe on me
through their word;
21 That they all may be one; as thou,
Father, *art* in me, and I in thee, that
they also may be one in us: that the

world may believe that thou hast sent
me.
22 And the glory which thou gavest
me I have given them; that they may be
one, even as we are one:
23 I in them, and thou in me, that they
may be made perfect in one; and that
the world may know that thou hast
sent me, and hast loved them, as thou
hast loved me.
24 Father, I will that they also, whom
thou hast given me, be with me where I
am; that they may behold my glory,
which thou hast given me: for thou
lovedst me before the foundation of the
world.
25 O righteous Father, the world hath
not known thee: but I have known thee,
and these have known that thou hast
sent me.
26 And I have declared unto them thy
name, and will declare *it:* that the love
wherewith thou hast loved me may be
in them, and I in them.

CHAPTER 18

WHEN Jesus had spoken these words,
he went forth with his disciples over
the brook Ċē'dron, where was a garden,
into the which he entered, and his
disciples.
2 And Judas also, which betrayed
him, knew the place: for Jesus ofttimes
resorted thither with his disciples.
3 Judas then, having received a band
of men and officers from the chief
priests and Pharisees, cometh thither
with lanterns and torches and weapons.
4 Jesus therefore, knowing all things
that should come upon him, went forth,
and said unto them, Whom seek ye?
5 They answered him, Jesus of Nazareth.
Jesus saith unto them, I am *he.*
And Judas also, which betrayed him,
stood with them.
6 As soon then as he had said unto
them, I am *he,* they went backward,
and fell to the ground.
7 Then asked he them again, Whom
seek ye? And they said, Jesus of Nazareth.
8 Jesus answered, I have told you
that I am *he:* if therefore ye seek me, let
these go their way:
9 That the saying might be fulfilled,
which he spake, Of them which thou
gavest me have I lost none.
10 Then Simon Peter having a sword
drew it, and smote the high priest's servant,
and cut off his right ear. The servant's
name was Măl'chus.
11 Then said Jesus unto Peter, Put up
thy sword into the sheath: the cup
which my Father hath given me, shall I
not drink it?
12 Then the band and the captain and
officers of the Jews took Jesus, and
bound him,
13 And led him away to Ăn'nas first;
for he was father in law to Cā'ia-phas,
which was the high priest that same
year.
14 Now Cā'ia-phas was he, which
gave counsel to the Jews, that it was
expedient that one man should die for
the people.
15 ¶And Simon Peter followed Jesus,
and *so did* another disciple: that disciple
was known unto the high priest,
and went in with Jesus into the palace
of the high priest.
16 But Peter stood at the door
without. Then went out that other disciple,
which was known unto the high
priest, and spake unto her that kept the
door, and brought in Peter.
17 Then saith the damsel that kept
the door unto Peter, Art not thou also
one of this man's disciples? He saith, I
am not.
18 And the servants and officers
stood there, who had made a fire of
coals; for it was cold: and they warmed
themselves: and Peter stood with them,
and warmed himself.
19 ¶The high priest then asked Jesus
of his disciples, and of his doctrine.
20 Jesus answered him, I spake
openly to the world; I ever taught in the
synagogue, and in the temple, whither
the Jews always resort; and in secret
have I said nothing.
21 Why askest thou me? ask them
which heard me, what I have said unto
them: behold, they know what I said.
22 And when he had thus spoken, one
of the officers which stood by struck
Jesus with the palm of his hand, saying,
Answerest thou the high priest so?
23 Jesus answered him, If I have spoken
evil, bear witness of the evil: but if
well, why smitest thou me?
24 Now Ăn'nas had sent him bound
unto Cā'ia-phas the high priest.
25 ¶And Simon Peter stood and
warmed himself. They said therefore
unto him, Art not thou also *one* of his
disciples? He denied *it,* and said, I am
not.
26 One of the servants of the high
priest, being *his* kinsman whose ear Peter
cut off, saith, Did not I see thee in
the garden with him?
27 Peter then denied again: and immediately
the cock crew.
28 ¶Then led they Jesus from Cā'iaphas
unto the hall of judgment: and it
was early; and they themselves went

not into the judgment hall, lest they
should be defiled; but that they might
eat the passover.
29 Pilate then went out unto them,
and said, What accusation bring ye
against this man?
30 They answered and said unto him,
If he were not a malefactor, we would
not have delivered him up unto thee.
31 Then said Pilate unto them, Take
ye him, and judge him according to
your law. The Jews therefore said unto
him, It is not lawful for us to put any
man to death:
32 That the saying of Jesus might be
fulfilled, which he spake, signifying
what death he should die.
33 Then Pilate entered into the judgment hall again, and called Jesus, and
said unto him, Art thou the King of the
Jews?
34 Jesus answered him, Sayest thou
this thing of thyself, or did others tell it
thee of me?
35 Pilate answered, Am I a Jew?
Thine own nation and the chief priests
have delivered thee unto me: what hast
thou done?
36 Jesus answered, My kingdom is
not of this world: if my kingdom were
of this world, then would my servants
fight, that I should not be delivered to
the Jews: but now is my kingdom not
from hence.
37 Pilate therefore said unto him, Art
thou a king then? Jesus answered,
Thou sayest that I am a king. To this
end was I born, and for this cause came
I into the world, that I should bear witness unto the truth. Every one that is of
the truth heareth my voice.
38 Pilate saith unto him, What is
truth? And when he had said this, he
went out again unto the Jews, and saith
unto them, I find in him no fault *at all.*
39 But ye have a custom, that I
should release unto you one at the passover: will ye therefore that I release
unto you the King of the Jews?
40 Then cried they all again, saying,
Not this man, but Ba-răb'bas.
Now Ba-răb'bas was a robber.

CHAPTER 19

THEN Pilate therefore took Jesus, and
scourged *him.*
2 And the soldiers platted a crown of
thorns, and put *it* on his head, and they
put on him a purple robe,
3 And said, Hail, King of the Jews!
and they smote him with their hands.
4 Pilate therefore went forth again,
and saith unto them, Behold, I bring
him forth to you, that ye may know that
I find no fault in him.
5 Then came Jesus forth, wearing the
crown of thorns, and the purple robe.
And *Pilate* saith unto them, Behold the
man!
6 When the chief priests therefore
and officers saw him, they cried out,
saying, Crucify *him,* crucify *him.* Pilate
saith unto them, Take ye him, and
crucify *him:* for I find no fault in him.
7 The Jews answered him, We have a
law, and by our law he ought to die, because he made himself the Son of God.
8 ¶When Pilate therefore heard that
saying, he was the more afraid;
9 And went again into the judgment
hall, and saith unto Jesus, Whence art
thou? But Jesus gave him no answer.
10 Then saith Pilate unto him, Speakest thou not unto me? knowest thou not
that I have power to crucify thee, and
have power to release thee?
11 Jesus answered, Thou couldest
have no power *at all* against me, except
it were given thee from above: therefore he that delivered me unto thee
hath the greater sin.
12 And from thenceforth Pilate
sought to release him: but the Jews
cried out, saying, If thou let this man
go, thou art not Cæsar's friend:
whosoever maketh himself a king
speaketh against Cæsar.
13 ¶When Pilate therefore heard that
saying, he brought Jesus forth, and sat
down in the judgment seat in a place
that is called the Pavement, but in the
Hebrew, Găb'ba-tha.
14 And it was the preparation of the
passover, and about the sixth hour: and
he saith unto the Jews, Behold your
King!
15 But they cried out, Away with
him, away with *him,* crucify him. Pilate
saith unto them, Shall I crucify your
King? The chief priests answered, We
have no king but Cæsar.
16 Then delivered he him therefore
unto them to be crucified. And they
took Jesus, and led *him* away.
17 And he bearing his cross went
forth into a place called *the place* of a
skull, which is called in the Hebrew
Gŏl'go-tha:
18 Where they crucified him, and two
other with him, on either side one, and
Jesus in the midst.
19 ¶And Pilate wrote a title, and put *it*
on the cross. And the writing was, JESUS OF NAZARETH THE KING OF
THE JEWS.
20 This title then read many of the
Jews: for the place where Jesus was
crucified was nigh to the city: and it
was written in Hebrew, *and* Greek, *and*
Latin.

21 Then said the chief priests of the Jews to Pilate, Write not, The King of the Jews; but that he said, I am King of the Jews.

22 Pilate answered, What I have written I have written.

23 ¶Then the soldiers, when they had crucified Jesus, took his garments, and made four parts, to every soldier a part; and also *his* coat: now the coat was without seam, woven from the top throughout.

24 They said therefore among themselves, Let us not rend it, but cast lots for it, whose it shall be: that the scripture might be fulfilled, which saith, They parted my raiment among them, and for my vesture they did cast lots. These things therefore the soldiers did.

25 ¶Now there stood by the cross of Jesus his mother, and his mother's sister, Mary the *wife* of Clē'o-phas, and Mary Magdalene.

26 When Jesus therefore saw his mother, and the disciple standing by, whom he loved, he saith unto his mother, Woman, behold thy son!

27 Then saith he to the disciple, Behold thy mother! And from that hour that disciple took her unto his own *home*.

28 ¶After this, Jesus knowing that all things were now accomplished, that the scripture might be fulfilled, saith, I thirst.

29 Now there was set a vessel full of vinegar: and they filled a spunge with vinegar, and put *it* upon hyssop, and put *it* to his mouth.

30 When Jesus therefore had received the vinegar, he said, It is finished: and he bowed his head, and gave up the ghost.

31 ¶The Jews therefore, because it was the preparation, that the bodies should not remain upon the cross on the sabbath day, (for that sabbath day was an high day,) besought Pilate that their legs might be broken, and *that* they might be taken away.

32 Then came the soldiers, and brake the legs of the first, and of the other which was crucified with him.

33 But when they came to Jesus, and saw that he was dead already, they brake not his legs:

34 But one of the soldiers with a spear pierced his side, and forthwith came there out blood and water.

35 And he that saw *it* bare record, and his record is true: and he knoweth that he saith true, that ye might believe.

36 For these things were done, that the scripture should be fulfilled, A bone of him shall not be broken.

37 And again another scripture saith, They shall look on him whom they pierced.

38 ¶And after this Joseph of Ăr-i-ma-thæ'a, being a disciple of Jesus, but secretly for fear of the Jews, besought Pilate that he might take away the body of Jesus: and Pilate gave *him* leave. He came therefore, and took the body of Jesus.

39 And there came also Nĭc-o-dē'-mus, which at the first came to Jesus by night, and brought a mixture of myrrh and aloes, about an hundred pound *weight*.

40 Then took they the body of Jesus, and wound it in linen clothes with the spices, as the manner of the Jews is to bury.

41 Now in the place where he was crucified there was a garden; and in the garden a new sepulchre, wherein was never man yet laid.

42 There laid they Jesus therefore because of the Jews' preparation *day*; for the sepulchre was nigh at hand.

CHAPTER 20

THE first *day* of the week cometh Mary Magdalene early, when it was yet dark, unto the sepulchre, and seeth the stone taken away from the sepulchre.

2 Then she runneth, and cometh to Simon Peter, and to the other disciple, whom Jesus loved, and saith unto them, They have taken away the LORD out of the sepulchre, and we know not where they have laid him.

3 Peter therefore went forth, and that other disciple, and came to the sepulchre.

4 So they ran both together: and the other disciple did outrun Peter, and came first to the sepulchre.

5 And he stooping down, *and looking in,* saw the linen clothes lying; yet went he not in.

6 Then cometh Simon Peter following him, and went into the sepulchre, and seeth the linen clothes lie,

7 And the napkin, that was about his head, not lying with the linen clothes, but wrapped together in a place by itself.

8 Then went in also that other disciple, which came first to the sepulchre, and he saw, and believed.

9 For as yet they knew not the scripture, that he must rise again from the dead.

10 Then the disciples went away again unto their own home.

11 ¶But Mary stood without at the sepulchre weeping: and as she wept,

she stooped down, *and looked* into the
sepulchre,
12 And seeth two angels in white sit-
ting, the one at the head, and the other
at the feet, where the body of Jesus had
lain.
13 And they say unto her, Woman,
why weepest thou? She saith unto
them, Because they have taken away
my LORD, and I know not where they
have laid him.
14 And when she had thus said, she
turned herself back, and saw Jesus
standing, and knew not that it was Je-
sus.
15 Jesus saith unto her, Woman, why
weepest thou? whom seekest thou?
She, supposing him to be the gardener,
saith unto him, Sir, if thou have borne
him hence, tell me where thou hast laid
him, and I will take him away.
16 Jesus saith unto her, Mary. She
turned herself, and saith unto him,
Rab-bō'nī; which is to say, Master.
17 Jesus saith unto her, Touch me
not; for I am not yet ascended to my
Father: but go to my brethren, and say
unto them, I ascend unto my Father,
and your Father; and *to* my God, and
your God.
18 Mary Magdalene came and told
the disciples that she had seen the
LORD, and *that* he had spoken these
things unto her.
19 ¶Then the same day at evening,
being the first *day* of the week, when
the doors were shut where the disciples
were assembled for fear of the Jews,
came Jesus and stood in the midst, and
saith unto them, Peace *be* unto you.
20 And when he had so said, he
shewed unto them *his* hands and his
side. Then were the disciples glad,
when they saw the LORD.
21 Then said Jesus to them again,
Peace *be* unto you: as *my* Father hath
sent me, even so send I you.
22 And when he had said this, he
breathed on *them*, and saith unto them,
Receive ye the Holy Ghost:
23 Whose soever sins ye remit, they
are remitted unto them; *and* whose
soever *sins* ye retain, they are retained.
24 ¶But Thomas, one of the twelve,
called Dĭd'y-mus, was not with them
when Jesus came.
25 The other disciples therefore said
unto him, We have seen the LORD. But
he said unto them, Except I shall see in
his hands the print of the nails, and put
my finger into the print of the nails, and
thrust my hand into his side, I will not
believe.
26 ¶And after eight days again his
disciples were within, and Thomas
with them: *then* came Jesus, the doors
being shut, and stood in the midst, and
said, Peace *be* unto you.
27 Then saith he to Thomas, Reach
hither thy finger, and behold my hands;
and reach hither thy hand, and thrust *it*
into my side: and be not faithless, but
believing.
28 And Thomas answered and said
unto him, My LORD and my God.
29 Jesus saith unto him, Thomas, be-
cause thou hast seen me, thou hast be-
lieved: blessed *are* they that have not
seen, and *yet* have believed.
30 ¶And many other signs truly did
Jesus in the presence of his disciples,
which are not written in this book:
31 But these are written, that ye
might believe that Jesus is the Christ,
the Son of God; and that believing ye
might have life through his name.

CHAPTER 21

AFTER these things Jesus shewed him-
self again to the disciples at the sea of
Ti-be'ri-as; and on this wise shewed he
himself.
2 There were together Simon Peter,
and Thomas called Dĭd'y-mus, and
Nathanael of Cana in Galilee, and the
sons of Zĕb'e-dee, and two other of his
disciples.
3 Simon Peter saith unto them, I go a
fishing. They say unto him, We also go
with thee. They went forth, and entered
into a ship immediately: and that night
they caught nothing.
4 But when the morning was now
come, Jesus stood on the shore: but the
disciples knew not that it was Jesus.
5 Then Jesus saith unto them, Chil-
dren, have ye any meat? They an-
swered him, No.
6 And he said unto them, Cast the net
on the right side of the ship, and ye
shall find. They cast therefore, and now
they were not able to draw it for the
multitude of fishes.
7 Therefore that disciple whom Jesus
loved saith unto Peter, It is the Lord.
Now when Simon Peter heard that it
was the Lord, he girt *his* fisher's coat
unto him, (for he was naked,) and did
cast himself into the sea.
8 And the other disciples came in a
little ship; (for they were not far from
land, but as it were two hundred cubits,)
dragging the net with fishes.
9 As soon then as they were come to
land, they saw a fire of coals there, and
fish laid thereon, and bread.
10 Jesus saith unto them, Bring of the
fish which ye have now caught.
11 Simon Peter went up, and drew

the net to land full of great fishes, an hundred and fifty and three: and for all there were so many, yet was not the net broken.

12 Jesus saith unto them, Come *and* dine. And none of the disciples durst ask him, Who art thou? knowing that it was the Lord.

13 Jesus then cometh, and taketh bread, and giveth them, and fish likewise.

14 This is now the third time that Jesus shewed himself to his disciples, after that he was risen from the dead.

15 ¶So when they had dined, Jesus saith to Simon Peter, Simon, *son* of Jonas, lovest thou me more than these? He saith unto him, Yea, Lord; thou knowest that I love thee. He saith unto him, Feed my lambs.

16 He saith to him again the second time, Simon, *son* of Jonas, lovest thou me? He saith unto him, Yea, Lord; thou knowest that I love thee. He saith unto him, Feed my sheep.

17 He saith unto him the third time, Simon, *son* of Jonas, lovest thou me? Peter was grieved because he said unto him the third time, Lovest thou me? And he said unto him, Lord, thou knowest all things; thou knowest that I love thee. Jesus saith unto him, Feed my sheep.

18 Verily, verily, I say unto thee, When thou wast young, thou girdedst thyself, and walkedst whither thou wouldest: but when thou shalt be old, thou shalt stretch forth thy hands, and another shall gird thee, and carry *thee* whither thou wouldest not.

19 This spake he, signifying by what death he should glorify God. And when he had spoken this, he saith unto him, Follow me.

20 Then Peter, turning about, seeth the disciple whom Jesus loved following; which also leaned on his breast at supper, and said, Lord, which is he that betrayeth thee?

21 Peter seeing him saith to Jesus, Lord, and what *shall* this man *do?*

22 Jesus saith unto him, If I will that he tarry till I come, what *is that* to thee? follow thou me.

23 Then went this saying abroad among the brethren, that that disciple should not die: yet Jesus said not unto him, He shall not die; but, If I will that he tarry till I come, what *is that* to thee?

24 This is the disciple which testifieth of these things, and wrote these things: and we know that his testimony is true.

25 And there are also many other things which Jesus did, the which, if they should be written every one, I suppose that even the world itself could not contain the books that should be written. Amen.

THE

ACTS OF THE APOSTLES

CHAPTER 1

THE former treatise have I made, O Thē-ŏph′i-lus, of all that Jesus began both to do and teach,

2 Until the day in which he was taken up, after that he through the Holy Ghost had given commandments unto the apostles whom he had chosen:

3 To whom also he shewed himself alive after his passion by many infallible proofs, being seen of them forty days, and speaking of the things pertaining to the kingdom of God:

4 And, being assembled together with *them*, commanded them that they should not depart from Jerusalem, but wait for the promise of the Father, which, *saith he*, ye have heard of me.

5 For John truly baptized with water; but ye shall be baptized with the Holy Ghost not many days hence.

6 When they therefore were come together, they asked of him, saying, Lord, wilt thou at this time restore again the kingdom to Israel?

7 And he said unto them, It is not for you to know the times or the seasons, which the Father hath put in his own power.

8 But ye shall receive power, after that the Holy Ghost is come upon you: and ye shall be witnesses unto me both in Jerusalem, and in all Judaea, and in Sa-mâ′rĭ-a, and unto the uttermost part of the earth.

9 And when he had spoken these things, while they beheld, he was taken up; and a cloud received him out of their sight.

10 And while they looked stedfastly toward heaven as he went up, behold, two men stood by them in white apparel;

11 Which also said, Ye men of Galilee, why stand ye gazing up into heaven? this same Jesus, which is taken up from you into heaven, shall so come in like manner as ye have seen him go into heaven.

12 ¶Then returned they unto Jerusalem from the mount called Olivet,

which is from Jerusalem a sabbath
day's journey.
13 And when they were come in, they
went up into an upper room, where
abode both Peter, and James, and John,
and Andrew, Philip, and Thomas, Bar-
tholomew, and Matthew, James *the*
son of Ăl-phaē'us, and Simon Ze-lō'tēṡ,
and Judas *the brother* of James.
14 These all continued with one ac-
cord in prayer and supplication, with
the women, and Mary the mother of Je-
sus, and with his brethren.
15 ¶And in those days Peter stood up
in the midst of the disciples, and said,
(the number of names together were
about an hundred and twenty,)
16 Men *and* brethren, this scripture
must needs have been fulfilled, which
the Holy Ghost by the mouth of David
spake before concerning Judas, which
was guide to them that took Jesus.
17 For he was numbered with us, and
had obtained part of this ministry.
18 Now this man purchased a field
with the reward of iniquity; and falling
headlong, he burst asunder in the
midst, and all his bowels gushed out.
19 And it was known unto all the
dwellers at Jerusalem; insomuch as
that field is called in their proper
tongue, Acĕl'da-ma, that is to say, The
field of blood.
20 For it is written in the book of
Psalms, Let his habitation be desolate,
and let no man dwell therein: and his
bishoprick let another take.
21 Wherefore of these men which
have companied with us all the time
that the Lord Jesus went in and out
among us,
22 Beginning from the baptism of
John, unto that same day that he was
taken up from us, must one be ordained
to be a witness with us of his resurrec-
tion.
23 And they appointed two, Joseph
called Bär'să-bas, who was surnamed
Justus, and Mat-thī'as.
24 And they prayed, and said, Thou,
Lord, which knowest the hearts of all
men, shew whether of these two thou
hast chosen,
25 That he may take part of this min-
istry and apostleship, from which Ju-
das by transgression fell, that he might
go to his own place.
26 And they gave forth their lots; and
the lot fell upon Mat-thī'as; and he was
numbered with the eleven apostles.

CHAPTER 2

AND when the day of Pentecost was
fully come, they were all with one ac-
cord in one place.
2 And suddenly there came a sound
from heaven as of a rushing mighty
wind, and it filled all the house where
they were sitting.
3 And there appeared unto them clov-
en tongues like as of fire, and it sat
upon each of them.
4 And they were all filled with the
Holy Ghost, and began to speak with
other tongues, as the Spirit gave them
utterance.
5 And there were dwelling at Jeru-
salem Jews, devout men, out of every
nation under heaven.
6 Now when this was noised abroad,
the multitude came together, and were
confounded, because that every man
heard them speak in his own language.
7 And they were all amazed and mar-
velled, saying one to another, Behold,
are not all these which speak Galilæ-
ans?
8 And how hear we every man in our
own tongue, wherein we were born?
9 Pär'thĭ-anṡ, and Medes, and Ē'lam-
ītes, and the dwellers in Mĕs-o-po-tā'-
mĭ-a, and in Judæa, and Căp-pa-dō'-
ċi-a, in Pontus, and Asia,
10 Phrȳġ'ĭ-a, and Păm-phȳl'ĭ-a, in
Egypt, and in the parts of Lĭb'ȳ-a about
Ċȳ-rē'ne, and strangers of Rome, Jews
and proselytes,
11 Cretes and Arabians, we do hear
them speak in our tongues the wonder-
ful works of God.
12 And they were all amazed, and
were in doubt, saying one to another,
What meaneth this?
13 Others mocking said, These men
are full of new wine.
14 ¶But Peter, standing up with the
eleven, lifted up his voice, and said
unto them, Ye men of Judæa, and all *ye*
that dwell at Jerusalem, be this known
unto you, and hearken to my words:
15 For these are not drunken, as ye
suppose, seeing it is *but* the third hour
of the day.
16 But this is that which was spoken
by the prophet Jō'el;
17 And it shall come to pass in the
last days, saith God, I will pour out of
my Spirit upon all flesh: and your sons
and your daughters shall prophesy, and
your young men shall see visions, and
your old men shall dream dreams:
18 And on my servants and on my
handmaidens I will pour out in those
days of my Spirit; and they shall proph-
esy:
19 And I will shew wonders in heaven
above, and signs in the earth beneath;
blood, and fire, and vapour of smoke:
20 The sun shall be turned into dark-
ness, and the moon into blood, before

that great and notable day of the Lord come:

21 And it shall come to pass, *that* whosoever shall call on the name of the Lord shall be saved.

22 Ye men of Israel, hear these words; Jesus of Nazareth, a man approved of God among you by miracles and wonders and signs, which God did by him in the midst of you, as ye yourselves also know:

23 Him, being delivered by the determinate counsel and foreknowledge of God, ye have taken, and by wicked hands have crucified and slain:

24 Whom God hath raised up, having loosed the pains of death: because it was not possible that he should be holden of it.

25 For David speaketh concerning him, I foresaw the Lord always before my face, for he is on my right hand, that I should not be moved:

26 Therefore did my heart rejoice, and my tongue was glad; moreover also my flesh shall rest in hope:

27 Because thou wilt not leave my soul in hell, neither wilt thou suffer thine Holy One to see corruption.

28 Thou hast made known to me the ways of life; thou shalt make me full of joy with thy countenance.

29 Men *and* brethren, let me freely speak unto you of the patriarch David, that he is both dead and buried, and his sepulchre is with us unto this day.

30 Therefore being a prophet, and knowing that God had sworn with an oath to him, that of the fruit of his loins, according to the flesh, he would raise up Christ to sit on his throne;

31 He seeing this before spake of the resurrection of Christ, that his soul was not left in hell, neither his flesh did see corruption.

32 This Jesus hath God raised up, whereof we all are witnesses.

33 Therefore being by the right hand of God exalted, and having received of the Father the promise of the Holy Ghost, he hath shed forth this, which ye now see and hear.

34 For David is not ascended into the heavens: but he saith himself, The LORD said unto my Lord, Sit thou on my right hand,

35 Until I make thy foes thy footstool.

36 Therefore let all the house of Israel know assuredly, that God hath made that same Jesus, whom ye have crucified, both Lord and Christ.

37 ¶Now when they heard *this*, they were pricked in their heart, and said unto Peter and to the rest of the apostles, Men *and* brethren, what shall we do?

38 Then Peter said unto them, Repent, and be baptized every one of you in the name of Jesus Christ for the remission of sins, and ye shall receive the gift of the Holy Ghost.

39 For the promise is unto you, and to your children, and to all that are afar off, *even* as many as the Lord our God shall call.

40 And with many other words did he testify and exhort, saying, Save yourselves from this untoward generation.

41 ¶Then they that gladly received his word were baptized: and the same day there were added *unto them* about three thousand souls.

42 And they continued stedfastly in the apostles' doctrine and fellowship, and in breaking of bread, and in prayers.

43 And fear came upon every soul: and many wonders and signs were done by the apostles.

44 And all that believed were together, and had all things common;

45 And sold their possessions and goods, and parted them to all *men*, as every man had need.

46 And they, continuing daily with one accord in the temple, and breaking bread from house to house, did eat their meat with gladness and singleness of heart,

47 Praising God, and having favour with all the people. And the Lord added to the church daily such as should be saved.

CHAPTER 3

NOW Peter and John went up together into the temple at the hour of prayer, *being* the ninth *hour*.

2 And a certain man lame from his mother's womb was carried, whom they laid daily at the gate of the temple which is called Beautiful, to ask alms of them that entered into the temple;

3 Who seeing Peter and John about to go into the temple asked an alms.

4 And Peter, fastening his eyes upon him with John, said, Look on us.

5 And he gave heed unto them, expecting to receive something of them.

6 Then Peter said, Silver and gold have I none; but such as I have give I thee: In the name of Jesus Christ of Nazareth rise up and walk.

7 And he took him by the right hand, and lifted *him* up: and immediately his feet and ancle bones received strength.

8 And he leaping up stood, and walked, and entered with them into the

temple, walking, and leaping, and
praising God.
9 And all the people saw him walking
and praising God:
10 And they knew that it was he
which sat for alms at the Beautiful gate
of the temple: and they were filled with
wonder and amazement at that which
had happened unto him.
11 ¶And as the lame man which was
healed held Peter and John, all the
people ran together unto them in the
porch that is called Solomon's, greatly
wondering.
12 And when Peter saw *it*, he an-
swered unto the people, Ye men of
Israel, why marvel ye at this? or why
look ye so earnestly on us, as though by
our own power or holiness we had
made this man to walk?
13 The God of Abraham, and of Isaac,
and of Jacob, the God of our fathers,
hath glorified his Son Jesus; whom ye
delivered up, and denied him in the pres-
ence of Pilate, when he was deter-
mined to let *him* go.
14 But ye denied the Holy One and
the Just, and desired a murderer to be
granted unto you;
15 And killed the Prince of life, whom
God hath raised from the dead; where-
of we are witnesses.
16 And his name through faith in his
name hath made this man strong,
whom ye see and know: yea, the faith
which is by him hath given him this
perfect soundness in the presence of
you all.
17 And now, brethren, I wot that
through ignorance ye did *it*, as *did* also
your rulers.
18 But those things, which God be-
fore had shewed by the mouth of all his
prophets, that Christ should suffer, he
hath so fulfilled.
19 Repent ye therefore, and be con-
verted, that your sins may be blotted
out, when the times of refreshing shall
come from the presence of the Lord;
20 And he shall send Jesus Christ,
which before was preached unto you:
21 Whom the heaven must receive
until the times of restitution of all
things, which God hath spoken by the
mouth of all his holy prophets since the
world began.
22 For Moses truly said unto the fa-
thers, A prophet shall the Lord your God
raise up unto you of your brethren, like
unto me; him shall ye hear in all things
whatsoever he shall say unto you.
23 And it shall come to pass, *that*
every soul, which will not hear that
prophet, shall be destroyed from
among the people.
24 Yea, and all the prophets from Sam-
uel and those that follow after, as
many as have spoken, have likewise
foretold of these days.
25 Ye are the children of the
prophets, and of the covenant which
God made with our fathers, saying
unto Abraham, And in thy seed shall all
the kindreds of the earth be blessed.
26 Unto you first God, having raised
up his Son Jesus, sent him to bless you,
in turning away every one of you from
his iniquities.

CHAPTER 4

AND as they spake unto the people, the
priests, and the captain of the temple,
and the Săd′du-ceeṡ, came upon them,
2 Being grieved that they taught the
people, and preached through Jesus
the resurrection from the dead.
3 And they laid hands on them, and
put *them* in hold unto the next day: for
it was now eventide.
4 Howbeit many of them which
heard the word believed; and the num-
ber of the men was about five thou-
sand.
5 ¶And it came to pass on the
morrow, that their rulers, and elders,
and scribes,
6 And Ăn′nas the high priest, and Cā′-
ia-phas, and John, and Alexander, and
as many as were of the kindred of the
high priest, were gathered together at
Jerusalem.
7 And when they had set them in the
midst, they asked, By what power, or
by what name, have ye done this?
8 Then Peter, filled with the Holy
Ghost, said unto them, Ye rulers of the
people, and elders of Israel,
9 If we this day be examined of the
good deed done to the impotent man,
by what means he is made whole;
10 Be it known unto you all, and to all
the people of Israel, that by the name of
Jesus Christ of Nazareth, whom ye
crucified, whom God raised from the
dead, *even* by him doth this man stand
here before you whole.
11 This is the stone which was set at
nought of you builders which is be-
come the head of the corner.
12 Neither is there salvation in any
other: for there is none other name un-
der heaven given among men, whereby
we must be saved.
13 ¶Now when they saw the boldness
of Peter and John, and perceived that
they were unlearned and ignorant men,
they marvelled; and they took knowl-
edge of them, that they had been with
Jesus.
14 And beholding the man which was

healed standing with them, they could
say nothing against it.
15 But when they had commanded
them to go aside out of the council, they
conferred among themselves,
16 Saying, What shall we do to these
men? for that indeed a notable miracle
hath been done by them *is* manifest to
all them that dwell in Jerusalem; and
we cannot deny *it*.
17 But that it spread no further
among the people, let us straitly threat-
en them, that they speak henceforth
to no man in this name.
18 And they called them, and com-
manded them not to speak at all nor
teach in the name of Jesus.
19 But Peter and John answered and
said unto them, Whether it be right in
the sight of God to hearken unto you
more than unto God, judge ye.
20 For we cannot but speak the
things which we have seen and heard.
21 So when they had further threat-
ened them, they let them go, finding
nothing how they might punish them,
because of the people: for all *men* glori-
fied God for that which was done.
22 For the man was above forty years
old, on whom this miracle of healing
was shewed.
23 ¶And being let go, they went to
their own company, and reported all
that the chief priests and elders had
said unto them.
24 And when they heard that, they
lifted up their voice to God with one ac-
cord, and said, Lord, thou *art* God,
which hast made heaven, and earth,
and the sea, and all that in them is:
25 Who by the mouth of thy servant
David hast said, Why did the heathen
rage, and the people imagine vain
things?
26 The kings of the earth stood up,
and the rulers were gathered together
against the Lord, and against his
Christ.
27 For of a truth against thy holy
child Jesus, whom thou hast anointed,
both Herod, and Pontius Pilate, with
the Gentiles, and the people of Israel,
were gathered together,
28 For to do whatsoever thy hand and
thy counsel determined before to be
done.
29 And now, Lord, behold their threat-
enings: and grant unto thy servants,
that with all boldness they may speak
thy word,
30 By stretching forth thine hand to
heal; and that signs and wonders may
be done by the name of thy holy child
Jesus.
31 And when they had prayed, the
place was shaken where they were as-
sembled together; and they were all
filled with the Holy Ghost, and they
spake the word of God with boldness.
32 ¶And the multitude of them that
believed were of one heart and of one
soul: neither said any *of them* that
ought of the things which he possessed
was his own; but they had all things
common.
33 And with great power gave the
apostles witness of the resurrection of
the Lord Jesus: and great grace was
upon them all.
34 Neither was there any among
them that lacked: for as many as were
possessors of lands or houses sold
them, and brought the prices of the
things that were sold,
35 And laid *them* down at the
apostles' feet: and distribution was
made unto every man according as he
had need.
36 And Joses, who by the apostles
was surnamed Barnabas, (which is,
being interpreted, The son of consola-
tion,) a Levite, *and* of the country of
Cyprus,
37 Having land, sold *it*, and brought
the money, and laid *it* at the apostles'
feet.

CHAPTER 5

BUT a certain man named Ăn-a-nī'as,
with Sap-phī'ra his wife, sold a posses-
sion,
2 And kept back *part* of the price, his
wife also being privy *to it*, and brought
a certain part, and laid *it* at the
apostles' feet.
3 But Peter said, Ăn-a-nī'as, why hath
Satan filled thine heart to lie to the
Holy Ghost, and to keep back *part* of
the price of the land?
4 Whiles it remained, was it not thine
own? and after it was sold, was it not in
thine own power? why hast thou con-
ceived this thing in thine heart? thou
hast not lied unto men, but unto God.
5 And Ăn-a-nī'as hearing these words
fell down, and gave up the ghost: and
great fear came on all them that heard
these things.
6 And the young men arose, wound
him up, and carried *him* out, and buried
him.
7 And it was about the space of three
hours after, when his wife, not know-
ing what was done, came in.
8 And Peter answered unto her, Tell
me whether ye sold the land for so
much? And she said, Yea, for so much.
9 Then Peter said unto her, How is it
that ye have agreed together to tempt
the Spirit of the Lord? behold, the feet

of them which have buried thy husband *are* at the door, and shall carry thee out.

10 Then fell she down straightway at his feet, and yielded up the ghost: and the young men came in, and found her dead, and, carrying *her* forth, buried *her* by her husband.

11 And great fear came upon all the church, and upon as many as heard these things.

12 ¶And by the hands of the apostles were many signs and wonders wrought among the people; (and they were all with one accord in Solomon's porch.

13 And of the rest durst no man join himself to them: but the people magnified them.

14 And believers were the more added to the Lord, multitudes both of men and women.)

15 Insomuch that they brought forth the sick into the streets, and laid *them* on beds and couches, that at the least the shadow of Peter passing by might overshadow some of them.

16 There came also a multitude *out* of the cities round about unto Jerusalem, bringing sick folks, and them which were vexed with unclean spirits: and they were healed every one.

17 ¶Then the high priest rose up, and all they that were with him, (which is the sect of the Săd′du-ceeș,) and were filled with indignation,

18 And laid their hands on the apostles, and put them in the common prison.

19 But the angel of the Lord by night opened the prison doors, and brought them forth, and said,

20 Go, stand and speak in the temple to the people all the words of this life.

21 And when they heard *that* they entered into the temple early in the morning, and taught. But the high priest came, and they that were with him, and called the council together, and all the senate of the children of Israel, and sent to the prison to have them brought.

22 But when the officers came, and found them not in the prison, they returned, and told,

23 Saying, The prison truly found we shut with all safety, and the keepers standing without before the doors: but when we had opened, we found no man within.

24 Now when the high priest and the captain of the temple and the chief priests heard these things, they doubted of them whereunto this would grow.

25 Then came one and told them, saying, Behold, the men whom ye put in prison are standing in the temple, and teaching the people.

26 Then went the captain with the officers, and brought them without violence: for they feared the people, lest they should have been stoned.

27 And when they had brought them, they set *them* before the council: and the high priest asked them,

28 Saying, Did not we straitly command you that ye should not teach in this name? and, behold, ye have filled Jerusalem with your doctrine, and intend to bring this man's blood upon us.

29 Then Peter and the *other* apostles answered and said, We ought to obey God rather than men.

30 The God of our fathers raised up Jesus, whom ye slew and hanged on a tree.

31 Him hath God exalted with his right hand *to be* a Prince and a Saviour, for to give repentance to Israel, and forgiveness of sins.

32 And we are his witnesses of these things; and *so is* also the Holy Ghost, whom God hath given to them that obey him.

33 ¶When they heard *that*, they were cut *to the heart*, and took counsel to slay them.

34 Then stood there up one in the council, a Pharisee, named Ga-mā′lĭ-el, a doctor of the law, had in reputation among all the people, and commanded to put the apostles forth a little space;

35 And said unto them, Ye men of Israel, take heed to yourselves what ye intend to do as touching these men.

36 For before these days rose up Theū′das, boasting himself to be somebody; to whom a number of men, about four hundred, joined themselves: who was slain; and all, as many as obeyed him, were scattered, and brought to nought.

37 After this man rose up Judas of Galilee in the days of the taxing, and drew away much people after him: he also perished; and all, *even* as many as obeyed him, were dispersed.

38 And now I say unto you, Refrain from these men, and let them alone: for if this counsel or this work be of men, it will come to nought:

39 But if it be of God, ye cannot overthrow it; lest haply ye be found even to fight against God.

40 And to him they agreed: and when they had called the apostles, and beaten *them*, they commanded that they should not speak in the name of Jesus, and let them go.

41 And they departed from the pres-

ence of the council, rejoicing that they were counted worthy to suffer shame for his name.

42 And daily in the temple, and in every house, they ceased not to teach and preach Jesus Christ.

CHAPTER 6

AND in those days, when the number of the disciples was multiplied, there arose a murmuring of the Grecians against the Hebrews, because their widows were neglected in the daily ministration.

2 Then the twelve called the multitude of the disciples *unto them*, and said, It is not reason that we should leave the word of God, and serve tables.

3 Wherefore, brethren, look ye out among you seven men of honest report, full of the Holy Ghost and wisdom, whom we may appoint over this business.

4 But we will give ourselves continually to prayer, and to the ministry of the word.

5 And the saying pleased the whole multitude: and they chose Stephen, a man full of faith and of the Holy Ghost, and Philip, and Prŏch'o-rus, and Nī-cā'-nor, and Tī'mon, and Pär'me-nas, and Nicolas a proselyte of Antioch:

6 Whom they set before the apostles: and when they had prayed, they laid *their* hands on them.

7 And the word of God increased; and the number of the disciples multiplied in Jerusalem greatly; and a great company of the priests were obedient to the faith.

8 ¶And Stephen, full of faith and power, did great wonders and miracles among the people.

9 Then there arose certain of the synagogue, which is called *the synagogue* of the Lib'er-tines, and Ċȳ-rē'nī-anṡ, and Alexandrians, and of them of Ċī-lī'-ċia and of Asia, disputing with Stephen.

10 And they were not able to resist the wisdom and the spirit by which he spake.

11 Then they suborned men, which said, We have heard him speak blasphemous words against Moses, and *against* God.

12 And they stirred up the people, and the elders, and the scribes, and came upon *him*, and caught him, and brought *him* to the council,

13 And set up false witnesses, which said, This man ceaseth not to speak blasphemous words against this holy place, and the law:

14 For we have heard him say, that this Jesus of Nazareth shall destroy this place, and shall change the customs which Moses delivered us.

15 And all that sat in the council, looking stedfastly on him, saw his face as it had been the face of an angel.

CHAPTER 7

THEN said the high priest, Are these things so?

2 And he said, Men, brethren, and fathers, hearken; The God of glory appeared unto our father Abraham, when he was in Mĕs-o-po-tā'mi-a, before he dwelt in Chăr'ran,

3 And said unto him, Get thee out of thy country, and from thy kindred, and come into the land which I shall shew thee.

4 Then came he out of the land of the Chăl-dē'ans, and dwelt in Chăr'ran: and from thence, when his father was dead, he removed him into this land, wherein ye now dwell.

5 And he gave him none inheritance in it, no, not *so much as* to set his foot on: yet he promised that he would give it to him for a possession, and to his seed after him, when *as yet* he had no child.

6 And God spake on this wise, That his seed should sojourn in a strange land; and that they should bring them into bondage, and entreat *them* evil four hundred years.

7 And the nation to whom they shall be in bondage will I judge, said God: and after that shall they come forth, and serve me in this place.

8 And he gave him the covenant of circumcision: and so *Abraham* begat Isaac, and circumcised him the eighth day; and Isaac *begat* Jacob; and Jacob *begat* the twelve patriarchs.

9 And the patriarchs, moved with envy, sold Joseph into Egypt: but God was with him,

10 And delivered him out of all his afflictions, and gave him favour and wisdom in the sight of Pharaoh king of Egypt; and he made him governor over Egypt and all his house.

11 Now there came a dearth over all the land of Egypt and Chā'naan, and great affliction: and our fathers found no sustenance.

12 But when Jacob heard that there was corn in Egypt, he sent out our fathers first.

13 And at the second *time* Joseph was made known to his brethren; and Joseph's kindred was made known unto Pharaoh.

14 Then sent Joseph, and called his

father Jacob to *him*, and all his kindred,
threescore and fifteen souls.
15 So Jacob went down into Egypt,
and died, he, and our fathers,
16 And were carried over into Sȳ'-
chem, and laid in the sepulchre that
Abraham bought for a sum of money of
the sons of Ĕm'môr *the father* of Sȳ'-
chem.
17 But when the time of the promise
drew nigh, which God had sworn to
Abraham, the people grew and mul-
tiplied in Egypt,
18 Till another king arose, which
knew not Joseph.
19 The same dealt subtilly with our
kindred, and evil entreated our fathers,
so that they cast out their young chil-
dren, to the end they might not live.
20 In which time Moses was born,
and was exceeding fair, and nourished
up in his father's house three months:
21 And when he was cast out, Pha-
raoh's daughter took him up, and
nourished him for her own son.
22 And Moses was learned in all the
wisdom of the Egyptians, and was
mighty in words and in deeds.
23 And when he was full forty years
old, it came into his heart to visit his
brethren the children of Israel.
24 And seeing one *of them* suffer
wrong, he defended *him*, and avenged
him that was oppressed, and smote the
Egyptian:
25 For he supposed his brethren
would have understood how that God
by his hand would deliver them: but
they understood not.
26 And the next day he shewed him-
self unto them as they strove, and
would have set them at one again,
saying, Sirs, ye are brethren; why do ye
wrong one to another?
27 But he that did his neighbour
wrong thrust him away, saying, Who
made thee a ruler and a judge over us?
28 Wilt thou kill me, as thou diddest
the Egyptian yesterday?
29 Then fled Moses at this saying,
and was a stranger in the land of Mā'di-
an, where he begat two sons.
30 And when forty years were ex-
pired, there appeared to him in the wil-
derness of mount Sī'na an angel of the
Lord in a flame of fire in a bush.
31 When Moses saw *it*, he wondered
at the sight: and as he drew near to be-
hold *it*, the voice of the Lord came unto
him,
32 *Saying*, I *am* the God of thy fathers,
the God of Abraham, and the God
of Isaac, and the God of Jacob. Then
Moses trembled, and durst not behold.
33 Then said the Lord to him, Put off
thy shoes from thy feet: for the place
where thou standest is holy ground.
34 I have seen, I have seen the afflic-
tion of my people which is in Egypt,
and I have heard their groaning, and
am come down to deliver them. And
now come, I will send thee into Egypt.
35 This Moses whom they refused,
saying, Who made thee a ruler and a
judge? the same did God send *to be* a
ruler and a deliverer by the hand of the
angel which appeared to him in the
bush.
36 He brought them out, after that he
had shewed wonders and signs in the
land of Egypt, and in the Red sea, and in
the wilderness forty years.
37 This is that Moses, which said
unto the children of Israel, A prophet
shall the Lord your God raise up unto
you of your brethren, like unto me; him
shall ye hear.
38 This is he, that was in the church in
the wilderness with the angel which
spake to him in the mount Sī'na, and
with our fathers: who received the
lively oracles to give unto us:
39 To whom our fathers would not
obey, but thrust *him* from them, and in
their hearts turned back again into
Egypt,
40 Saying unto Aaron, Make us gods
to go before us: for *as for* this Moses,
which brought us out of the land of
Egypt, we wot not what is become of
him.
41 And they made a calf in those
days, and offered sacrifice unto the
idol, and rejoiced in the works of their
own hands.
42 Then God turned, and gave them
up to worship the host of heaven; as it
is written in the book of the prophets, O
ye house of Israel, have ye offered to
me slain beasts and sacrifices *by the*
space of forty years in the wilderness?
43 Yea, ye took up the tabernacle of
Mō'lŏch, and the star of your god
Rĕm'phan, figures which ye made to
worship them: and I will carry you
away beyond Băb'y-lon.
44 Our fathers had the tabernacle of
witness in the wilderness, as he had ap-
pointed, speaking unto Moses, that he
should make it according to the fashion
that he had seen.
45 Which also our fathers that came
after brought in with Jesus into the
possession of the Gentiles, whom God
drave out before the face of our fathers,
unto the days of David;
46 Who found favour before God,
and desired to find a tabernacle for the
God of Jacob.
47 But Solomon built him an house.

48 Howbeit the most High dwelleth not in temples made with hands; as saith the prophet,

49 Heaven *is* my throne, and earth *is* my footstool: what house will ye build me? saith the Lord: or what *is* the place of my rest?

50 Hath not my hand made all these things?

51 ¶Ye stiffnecked and uncircumcised in heart and ears, ye do always resist the Holy Ghost: as your fathers *did*, so *do* ye.

52 Which of the prophets have not your fathers persecuted? and they have slain them which shewed before of the coming of the Just One; of whom ye have been now the betrayers and murderers:

53 Who have received the law by the disposition of angels, and have not kept *it*.

54 ¶When they heard these things, they were cut to the heart, and they gnashed on him with *their* teeth.

55 But he, being full of the Holy Ghost, looked up stedfastly into heaven, and saw the glory of God, and Jesus standing on the right hand of God,

56 And said, Behold, I see the heavens opened, and the Son of man standing on the right hand of God.

57 Then they cried out with a loud voice, and stopped their ears, and ran upon him with one accord,

58 And cast *him* out of the city, and stoned *him*: and the witnesses laid down their clothes at a young man's feet, whose name was Saul.

59 And they stoned Stephen, calling upon *God*, and saying, Lord Jesus, receive my spirit.

60 And he kneeled down, and cried with a loud voice, Lord, lay not this sin to their charge. And when he had said this, he fell asleep.

CHAPTER 8

AND Saul was consenting unto his death. And at that time there was a great persecution against the church which was at Jerusalem; and they were all scattered abroad throughout the regions of Judæa and Sa-mâ'rĭ-a, except the apostles.

2 And devout men carried Stephen *to his burial*, and made great lamentation over him.

3 As for Saul, he made havock of the church, entering into every house, and haling men and women committed *them* to prison.

4 Therefore they that were scattered abroad went every where preaching the word.

5 ¶Then Philip went down to the city of Sa-mâ'rĭ-a, and preached Christ unto them.

6 And the people with one accord gave heed unto those things which Philip spake, hearing and seeing the miracles which he did.

7 For unclean spirits, crying with loud voice, came out of many that were possessed *with them*: and many taken with palsies, and that were lame, were healed.

8 And there was great joy in that city.

9 But there was a certain man, called Simon, which beforetime in the same city used sorcery, and bewitched the people of Sa-mâ'rĭ-a, giving out that himself was some great one:

10 To whom they all gave heed, from the least to the greatest, saying, This man is the great power of God.

11 And to him they had regard, because that of long time he had bewitched them with sorceries.

12 But when they believed Philip preaching the things concerning the kingdom of God, and the name of Jesus Christ, they were baptized, both men and women.

13 Then Simon himself believed also: and when he was baptized, he continued with Philip, and wondered, beholding the miracles and signs which were done.

14 ¶Now when the apostles which were at Jerusalem heard that Sa-mâ'rĭ-a had received the word of God, they sent unto them Peter and John:

15 Who, when they were come down, prayed for them, that they might receive the Holy Ghost:

16 (For as yet he was fallen upon none of them: only they were baptized in the name of the Lord Jesus.)

17 Then laid they *their* hands on them, and they received the Holy Ghost.

18 And when Simon saw that through laying on of the apostles' hands the Holy Ghost was given, he offered them money,

19 Saying, Give me also this power, that on whomsoever I lay hands, he may receive the Holy Ghost.

20 But Peter said unto him, Thy money perish with thee, because thou hast thought that the gift of God may be purchased with money.

21 Thou hast neither part nor lot in this matter: for thy heart is not right in the sight of God.

22 Repent therefore of this thy wickedness, and pray God, if perhaps

the thought of thine heart may be forgiven thee.
23 For I perceive that thou art in the
gall of bitterness, and *in* the bond of iniquity.
24 Then answered Simon, and said,
Pray ye to the Lord for me, that none of these things which ye have spoken come upon me.
25 And they, when they had testified
and preached the word of the Lord, returned to Jerusalem, and preached the gospel in many villages of the Sa-măr′i-tanṡ.
26 ¶And the angel of the Lord spake
unto Philip, saying, Arise, and go toward the south unto the way that goeth down from Jerusalem unto Gā′za, which is desert.
27 And he arose and went: and, behold, a man of Ē-thĭ-ō′pĭ-a, an eunuch of great authority under Căn′da-ċe queen of the Ē-thĭ-ō′pĭ-ans, who had the charge of all her treasure, and had come to Jerusalem for to worship,
28 Was returning, and sitting in his
chariot read E-ṡā′ias the prophet.
29 Then the Spirit said unto Philip,
Go near, and join thyself to this chariot.
30 And Philip ran thither to *him*, and
heard him read the prophet E-ṡā′ias, and said, Understandest thou what thou readest?
31 And he said, How can I, except
some man should guide me? And he desired Philip that he would come up and sit with him.
32 The place of the scripture which
he read was this, He was led as a sheep to the slaughter; and like a lamb dumb before his shearer, so opened he not his mouth:
33 In his humiliation his judgment
was taken away: and who shall declare his generation? for his life is taken from the earth.
34 And the eunuch answered Philip,
and said, I pray thee, of whom speaketh the prophet this? of himself, or of some other man?
35 Then Philip opened his mouth, and
began at the same scripture, and preached unto him Jesus.
36 And as they went on *their* way,
they came unto a certain water: and the eunuch said, See, *here is* water; what doth hinder me to be baptized?
37 And Philip said, If thou believest
with all thine heart, thou mayest. And he answered and said, I believe that Jesus Christ is the Son of God.
38 And he commanded the chariot to
stand still: and they went down both into the water, both Philip and the eunuch; and he baptized him.
39 And when they were come up out
of the water, the Spirit of the Lord caught away Philip, that the eunuch saw him no more: and he went on his way rejoicing.
40 But Philip was found at A-zō′tus:
and passing through he preached in all the cities, till he came to Cæs-a-re′a.

CHAPTER 9

AND Saul, yet breathing out threatenings and slaughter against the disciples of the Lord, went unto the high priest,
2 And desired of him letters to Damas-
cus to the synagogues, that if he found any of this way, whether they were men or women, he might bring them bound unto Jerusalem.
3 And as he journeyed, he came near
Damascus: and suddenly there shined round about him a light from heaven:
4 And he fell to the earth, and heard a
voice saying unto him, Saul, Saul, why persecutest thou me?
5 And he said, Who art thou, Lord?
And the Lord said, I am Jesus whom thou persecutest: *it is* hard for thee to kick against the pricks.
6 And he trembling and astonished
said, Lord, what wilt thou have me to do? And the Lord *said* unto him, Arise, and go into the city, and it shall be told thee what thou must do.
7 And the men which journeyed with
him stood speechless, hearing a voice, but seeing no man.
8 And Saul arose from the earth; and
when his eyes were opened, he saw no man: but they led him by the hand, and brought *him* into Damascus.
9 And he was three days without
sight, and neither did eat nor drink.
10 ¶And there was a certain disciple
at Damascus, named Ăn-a-nī′as; and to him said the Lord in a vision, Ăn-a-nī′-as. And he said, Behold, I *am here*, Lord.
11 And the Lord *said* unto him, Arise,
and go into the street which is called Straight, and enquire in the house of Judas for *one* called Saul of Tarsus: for, behold, he prayeth,
12 And hath seen in a vision a man
named Ăn-a-nī′as coming in, and putting *his* hand on him, that he might receive his sight.
13 Then Ăn-a-nī′as answered, Lord, I
have heard by many of this man, how much evil he hath done to thy saints at Jerusalem:
14 And here he hath authority from
the chief priests to bind all that call on thy name.
15 But the Lord said unto him, Go thy
way: for he is a chosen vessel unto me,

to bear my name before the Gentiles, and kings, and the children of Israel:

16 For I will shew him how great things he must suffer for my name's sake.

17 And Ăn-a-nī'as went his way, and entered into the house; and putting his hands on him said, Brother Saul, the Lord, *even* Jesus, that appeared unto thee in the way as thou camest, hath sent me, that thou mightest receive thy sight, and be filled with the Holy Ghost.

18 And immediately there fell from his eyes as it had been scales: and he received sight forthwith, and arose, and was baptized.

19 And when he had received meat, he was strengthened. Then was Saul certain days with the disciples which were at Damascus.

20 And straightway he preached Christ in the synagogues, that he is the Son of God.

21 But all that heard *him* were amazed, and said; Is not this he that destroyed them which called on this name in Jerusalem, and came hither for that intent, that he might bring them bound unto the chief priests?

22 But Saul increased the more in strength, and confounded the Jews which dwelt at Damascus, proving that this is very Christ.

23 ¶And after that many days were fulfilled, the Jews took counsel to kill him:

24 But their laying await was known of Saul. And they watched the gates day and night to kill him.

25 Then the disciples took him by night, and let *him* down by the wall in a basket.

26 And when Saul was come to Jerusalem, he assayed to join himself to the disciples: but they were all afraid of him, and believed not that he was a disciple.

27 But Barnabas took him, and brought *him* to the apostles, and declared unto them how he had seen the Lord in the way, and that he had spoken to him, and how he had preached boldly at Damascus in the name of Jesus.

28 And he was with them coming in and going out at Jerusalem.

29 And he spake boldly in the name of the Lord Jesus, and disputed against the Grecians: but they went about to slay him.

30 *Which* when the brethren knew, they brought him down to Cæs-a-re'a, and sent him forth to Tarsus.

31 Then had the churches rest throughout all Judæa and Galilee and Sa-mâ'rĭ-a, and were edified; and walking in the fear of the Lord, and in the comfort of the Holy Ghost, were multiplied.

32 ¶And it came to pass, as Peter passed throughout all *quarters*, he came down also to the saints which dwelt at Lyd'da.

33 And there he found a certain man named Æ'nē-as, which had kept his bed eight years, and was sick of the palsy.

34 And Peter said unto him, Æ'nē-as, Jesus Christ maketh thee whole: arise, and make thy bed. And he arose immediately.

35 And all that dwelt at Lyd'da and Sâ'ron saw him, and turned to the Lord.

36 ¶Now there was at Joppa a certain disciple named Tabitha, which by interpretation is called Dorcas: this woman was full of good works and almsdeeds which she did.

37 And it came to pass in those days, that she was sick, and died: whom when they had washed, they laid *her* in an upper chamber.

38 And forasmuch as Lyd'da was nigh to Joppa, and the disciples had heard that Peter was there, they sent unto him two men, desiring *him* that he would not delay to come to them.

39 Then Peter arose and went with them. When he was come, they brought him into the upper chamber: and all the widows stood by him weeping, and shewing the coats and garments which Dorcas made, while she was with them.

40 But Peter put them all forth, and kneeled down, and prayed; and turning *him* to the body said, Tabitha, arise. And she opened her eyes: and when she saw Peter, she sat up.

41 And he gave her *his* hand, and lifted her up, and when he had called the saints and widows, presented her alive.

42 And it was known throughout all Joppa; and many believed in the Lord.

43 And it came to pass, that he tarried many days in Joppa with one Simon a tanner.

CHAPTER 10

THERE was a certain man in Cæs-a-re'a called Cornelius, a centurion of the band called the Italian *band*,

2 A devout *man*, and one that feared God with all his house, which gave much alms to the people, and prayed to God alway.

3 He saw in a vision evidently about the ninth hour of the day an angel of

God coming in to him, and saying unto
him, Cornelius.
4 And when he looked on him, he was
afraid, and said, What is it, Lord? And
he said unto him, Thy prayers and thine
alms are come up for a memorial be-
fore God.
5 And now send men to Joppa, and
call for *one* Simon, whose surname is
Peter:
6 He lodgeth with one Simon a tan-
ner, whose house is by the sea side: he
shall tell thee what thou oughtest to do.
7 And when the angel which spake
unto Cornelius was departed, he called
two of his household servants, and a
devout soldier of them that waited on
him continually;
8 And when he had declared all *these*
things unto them, he sent them to
Joppa.
9 ¶On the morrow, as they went on
their journey, and drew nigh unto the
city, Peter went up upon the housetop
to pray about the sixth hour:
10 And he became very hungry, and
would have eaten: but while they made
ready, he fell into a trance,
11 And saw heaven opened, and a
certain vessel descending unto him, as
it had been a great sheet knit at the four
corners, and let down to the earth:
12 Wherein were all manner of four-
footed beasts of the earth, and wild
beasts, and creeping things, and fowls
of the air.
13 And there came a voice to him,
Rise, Peter; kill, and eat.
14 But Peter said, Not so, Lord; for I
have never eaten any thing that is com-
mon or unclean.
15 And the voice *spake* unto him
again the second time, What God hath
cleansed, *that* call not thou common.
16 This was done thrice: and the ves-
sel was received up again into heaven.
17 Now while Peter doubted in him-
self what this vision which he had seen
should mean, behold, the men which
were sent from Cornelius had made en-
quiry for Simon's house, and stood be-
fore the gate,
18 And called, and asked whether Si-
mon, which was surnamed Peter, were
lodged there.
19 While Peter thought on the vision,
the Spirit said unto him, Behold, three
men seek thee.
20 Arise therefore, and get thee
down, and go with them, doubting
nothing: for I have sent them.
21 Then Peter went down to the men
which were sent unto him from Corne-
lius; and said, Behold, I am he whom ye
seek: what *is* the cause wherefore ye
are come?
22 And they said, Cornelius the cen-
turion, a just man, and one that feareth
God, and of good report among all the
nation of the Jews, was warned from
God by an holy angel to send for thee
into his house, and to hear words of
thee.
23 Then called he them in, and lodged
them. And on the morrow Peter went
away with them, and certain brethren
from Joppa accompanied him.
24 And the morrow after they en-
tered into Cæs-a-re'a, And Cornelius
waited for them, and had called togeth-
er his kinsmen and near friends.
25 And as Peter was coming in, Cor-
nelius met him, and fell down at his
feet, and worshipped *him*.
26 But Peter took him up, saying,
Stand up; I myself also am a man.
27 And as he talked with him, he
went in, and found many that were
come together.
28 And he said unto them, Ye know
how that it is an unlawful thing for a
man that is a Jew to keep company, or
come unto one of another nation; but
God hath shewed me that I should not
call any man common or unclean.
29 Therefore came I *unto you*
without gainsaying, as soon as I was
sent for: I ask therefore for what intent
ye have sent for me?
30 And Cornelius said, Four days ago
I was fasting until this hour; and at the
ninth hour I prayed in my house, and,
behold, a man stood before me in
bright clothing,
31 And said, Cornelius, thy prayer is
heard, and thine alms are had in
remembrance in the sight of God.
32 Send therefore to Joppa, and call
hither Simon, whose surname is Peter;
he is lodged in the house of *one* Simon a
tanner by the sea side: who, when he
cometh, shall speak unto thee.
33 Immediately therefore I sent to
thee; and thou hast well done that thou
art come. Now therefore are we all here
present before God, to hear all things
that are commanded thee of God.
34 ¶Then Peter opened *his* mouth,
and said, Of a truth I perceive that God
is no respecter of persons:
35 But in every nation he that feareth
him, and worketh righteousness, is ac-
cepted with him.
36 The word which *God* sent unto the
children of Israel, preaching peace by
Jesus Christ: (he is Lord of all:)
37 That word, *I say*, ye know, which
was published throughout all Judæa,

and began from Galilee, after the baptism which John preached;

38 How God anointed Jesus of Nazareth with the Holy Ghost and with power: who went about doing good, and healing all that were oppressed of the devil; for God was with him.

39 And we are witnesses of all things which he did both in the land of the Jews, and in Jerusalem; whom they slew and hanged on a tree:

40 Him God raised up the third day, and shewed him openly;

41 Not to all the people, but unto witnesses chosen before of God, *even* to us, who did eat and drink with him after he rose from the dead.

42 And he commanded us to preach unto the people, and to testify that it is he which was ordained of God *to be* the Judge of quick and dead.

43 To him give all the prophets witness, that through his name whosoever believeth in him shall receive remission of sins.

44 ¶While Peter yet spake these words, the Holy Ghost fell on all them which heard the word.

45 And they of the circumcision which believed were astonished, as many as came with Peter, because that on the Gentiles also was poured out the gift of the Holy Ghost.

46 For they heard them speak with tongues, and magnify God. Then answered Peter,

47 Can any man forbid water, that these should not be baptized, which have received the Holy Ghost as well as we?

48 And he commanded them to be baptized in the name of the Lord. Then prayed they him to tarry certain days.

CHAPTER 11

AND the apostles and brethren that were in Judæa heard that the Gentiles had also received the word of God.

2 And when Peter was come up to Jerusalem, they that were of the circumcision contended with him,

3 Saying, Thou wentest in to men uncircumcised, and didst eat with them.

4 But Peter rehearsed *the matter* from the beginning, and expounded *it* by order unto them, saying,

5 I was in the city of Joppa praying: and in a trance I saw a vision, A certain vessel descend, as it had been a great sheet, let down from heaven by four corners; and it came even to me:

6 Upon the which when I had fastened mine eyes, I considered, and saw fourfooted beasts of the earth, and wild beasts, and creeping things, and fowls of the air.

7 And I heard a voice saying unto me, Arise, Peter; slay and eat.

8 But I said, Not so, Lord: for nothing common or unclean hath at any time entered into my mouth.

9 But the voice answered me again from heaven, What God hath cleansed, *that* call not thou common.

10 And this was done three times: and all were drawn up again into heaven.

11 And, behold, immediately there were three men already come unto the house where I was, sent from Cæs-a-re'a unto me.

12 And the spirit bade me go with them, nothing doubting. Moreover these six brethren accompanied me, and we entered into the man's house:

13 And he shewed us how he had seen an angel in his house, which stood and said unto him, Send men to Joppa, and call for Simon, whose surname is Peter;

14 Who shall tell thee words, whereby thou and all thy house shall be saved.

15 And as I began to speak, the Holy Ghost fell on them, as on us at the beginning.

16 Then remembered I the word of the Lord, how that he said, John indeed baptized with water; but ye shall be baptized with the Holy Ghost.

17 Forasmuch then as God gave them the like gift as *he did* unto us, who believed on the Lord Jesus Christ; what was I, that I could withstand God?

18 When they heard these things, they held their peace, and glorified God, saying, Then hath God also to the Gentiles granted repentance unto life.

19 ¶Now they which were scattered abroad upon the persecution that arose about Stephen travelled as far as Phe-nī'ċe, and Cyprus, and Antioch, preaching the word to none but unto the Jews only.

20 And some of them were men of Cyprus and Ċȳ-rē'ne, which, when they were come to Antioch, spake unto the Grecians, preaching the Lord Jesus.

21 And the hand of the Lord was with them: and a great number believed, and turned unto the Lord.

22 ¶Then tidings of these things came unto the ears of the church which was in Jerusalem: and they sent forth Barnabas, that he should go as far as Antioch.

23 Who, when he came, and had seen the grace of God, was glad, and ex-

Jesus Cleanses the Temple

The Crucifixion of Jesus

horted them all, that with purpose of
heart they would cleave unto the Lord.
24 For he was a good man, and full of
the Holy Ghost and of faith: and much
people was added unto the Lord.
25 Then departed Barnabas to Tar-
sus, for to seek Saul:
26 And when he had found him, he
brought him unto Antioch. And it came
to pass, that a whole year they as-
sembled themselves with the church,
and taught much people. And the dis-
ciples were called Christians first in
Antioch.
27 ¶And in these days came prophets
from Jerusalem unto Antioch.
28 And there stood up one of them
named Ăg'a-bus, and signified by the
spirit that there should be great dearth
throughout all the world: which came
to pass in the days of Claudius Cæsar.
29 Then the disciples, every man ac-
cording to his ability, determined to
send relief unto the brethren which
dwelt in Judæa:
30 Which also they did, and sent it to
the elders by the hands of Barnabas
and Saul.

CHAPTER 12

NOW about that time Herod the king
stretched forth *his* hands to vex certain
of the church.
2 And he killed James the brother of
John with the sword.
3 And because he saw it pleased the
Jews, he proceeded further to take Pe-
ter also. (Then were the days of unleav-
ened bread.)
4 And when he had apprehended
him, he put *him* in prison, and delivered
him to four quaternions of soldiers to
keep him; intending after Easter to
bring him forth to the people.
5 Peter therefore was kept in prison:
but prayer was made without ceasing
of the church unto God for him.
6 And when Herod would have
brought him forth, the same night Pe-
ter was sleeping between two soldiers,
bound with two chains: and the keep-
ers before the door kept the prison.
7 And, behold, the angel of the Lord
came upon *him*, and a light shined in
the prison: and he smote Peter on the
side, and raised him up, saying, Arise
up quickly. And his chains fell off from
his hands.
8 And the angel said unto him, Gird
thyself, and bind on thy sandals. And
so he did. And he saith unto him, Cast
thy garment about thee, and follow me.
9 And he went out, and followed him;
and wist not that it was true which was
done by the angel; but thought he saw a
vision.
10 When they were past the first and
the second ward, they came unto the
iron gate that leadeth unto the city;
which opened to them of his own ac-
cord: and they went out, and passed on
through one street; and forthwith the
angel departed from him.
11 And when Peter was come to him-
self, he said, Now I know of a surety,
that the Lord hath sent his angel, and
hath delivered me out of the hand of
Herod, and *from* all the expectation of
the people of the Jews.
12 And when he had considered *the
thing*, he came to the house of Mary the
mother of John, whose surname was
Mark; where many were gathered
together praying.
13 And as Peter knocked at the door
of the gate, a damsel came to hearken,
named Rhoda.
14 And when she knew Peter's voice,
she opened not the gate for gladness,
but ran in, and told how Peter stood be-
fore the gate.
15 And they said unto her, Thou art
mad. But she constantly affirmed that
it was even so. Then said they, It is his
angel.
16 But Peter continued knocking:
and when they had opened *the door*,
and saw him, they were astonished.
17 But he, beckoning unto them with
the hand to hold their peace, declared
unto them how the Lord had brought
him out of the prison. And he said, Go
shew these things unto James, and to
the brethren. And he departed, and
went into another place.
18 Now as soon as it was day, there
was no small stir among the soldiers,
what was become of Peter.
19 And when Herod had sought for
him, and found him not, he examined
the keepers, and commanded that *they*
should be put to death. And he went
down from Judæa to Cæs-a-re'a, and
there abode.
20 ¶And Herod was highly displeased
with them of Tyre and Sī'don: but they
came with one accord to him, and, hav-
ing made Blăs'tus the king's chamber-
lain their friend, desired peace; be-
cause their country was nourished by
the king's *country*.
21 And upon a set day Herod, arrayed
in royal apparel, sat upon his throne,
and made an oration unto them.
22 And the people gave a shout,
saying, *It is* the voice of a god, and not
of a man.
23 And immediately the angel of the
Lord smote him, because he gave not

God the glory: and he was eaten of worms, and gave up the ghost.

24 ¶But the word of God grew and multiplied.

25 And Barnabas and Saul returned from Jerusalem, when they had fulfilled *their* ministry, and took with them John, whose surname was Mark.

CHAPTER 13

NOW there were in the church that was at Antioch certain prophets and teachers; as Barnabas, and Simeon that was called Nī′ġer, and Lucius of Ċȳ-rē′ne, and Măn′a-en, which had been brought up with Herod the tetrarch, and Saul.

2 As they ministered to the Lord, and fasted, the Holy Ghost said, Separate me Barnabas and Saul for the work whereunto I have called them.

3 And when they had fasted and prayed, and laid *their* hands on them, they sent *them* away.

4 ¶So they, being sent forth by the Holy Ghost, departed unto Se-leū′ċi-a; and from thence they sailed to Cyprus.

5 And when they were at Săl′a-mĭs, they preached the word of God in the synagogues of the Jews: and they had also John to *their* minister.

6 And when they had gone through the isle unto Pā′phŏs, they found a certain sorcerer, a false prophet, a Jew, whose name *was* Bär-jē′sus:

7 Which was with the deputy of the country, Sergius Paulus, a prudent man; who called for Barnabas and Saul, and desired to hear the word of God.

8 But Ĕl′y-mas the sorcerer (for so is his name by interpretation) withstood them, seeking to turn away the deputy from the faith.

9 Then Saul, (who also *is called* Paul,) filled with the Holy Ghost, set his eyes on him,

10 And said, O full of all subtilty and all mischief, *thou* child of the devil, *thou* enemy of all righteousness, wilt thou not cease to pervert the right ways of the Lord?

11 And now, behold, the hand of the Lord *is* upon thee, and thou shalt be blind, not seeing the sun for a season. And immediately there fell on him a mist and a darkness; and he went about seeking some to lead him by the hand.

12 Then the deputy, when he saw what was done, believed, being astonished at the doctrine of the Lord.

13 ¶Now when Paul and his company loosed from Pā′phŏs, they came to Per′ga in Păm-phȳl′ĭ-a: and John departing from them returned to Jerusalem.

14 ¶But when they departed from Per′ga, they came to Antioch in Pĭ-sĭd′-ĭ-a, and went into the synagogue on the sabbath day, and sat down.

15 And after the reading of the law and the prophets the rulers of the synagogue sent unto them, saying, *Ye* men *and* brethren, if ye have any word of exhortation for the people, say on.

16 Then Paul stood up, and beckoning with *his* hand said, Men of Israel, and ye that fear God, give audience.

17 The God of this people of Israel chose our fathers, and exalted the people when they dwelt as strangers in the land of Egypt, and with an high arm brought he them out of it.

18 And about the time of forty years suffered he their manners in the wilderness.

19 And when he had destroyed seven nations in the land of Chā′naan, he divided their land to them by lot.

20 And after that he gave *unto them* judges about the space of four hundred and fifty years, until Samuel the prophet.

21 And afterward they desired a king: and God gave unto them Saul the son of Cis, a man of the tribe of Benjamin, by the space of forty years.

22 And when he had removed him, he raised up unto them David to be their king; to whom also he gave testimony, and said, I have found David the *son* of Jesse, a man after mine own heart, which shall fulfil all my will.

23 Of this man's seed hath God according to *his* promise raised unto Israel a Saviour, Jesus:

24 When John had first preached before his coming the baptism of repentance to all the people of Israel.

25 And as John fulfilled his course, he said, Whom think ye that I am? I am not *he*. But, behold, there cometh one after me, whose shoes of *his* feet I am not worthy to loose.

26 Men *and* brethren, children of the stock of Abraham, and whosoever among you feareth God, to you is the word of this salvation sent.

27 For they that dwell at Jerusalem, and their rulers, because they knew him not, nor yet the voices of the prophets which are read every sabbath day, they have fulfilled *them* in condemning *him*.

28 And though they found no cause of death *in him*, yet desired they Pilate that he should be slain.

29 And when they had fulfilled all that was written of him, they took *him*

down from the tree, and laid *him* in a
sepulchre.
30 But God raised him from the dead:
31 And he was seen many days of
them which came up with him from
Galilee to Jerusalem, who are his witnesses unto the people.
32 And we declare unto you glad tidings, how that the promise which was
made unto the fathers,
33 God hath fulfilled the same unto
us their children, in that he hath raised
up Jesus again; as it is also written in
the second psalm, Thou art my Son,
this day have I begotten thee.
34 And as concerning that he raised
him up from the dead, *now* no more to
return to corruption, he said on this
wise, I will give you the sure mercies of
David.
35 Wherefore he saith also in another
psalm, Thou shalt not suffer thine Holy
One to see corruption.
36 For David, after he had served his
own generation by the will of God, fell
on sleep, and was laid unto his fathers,
and saw corruption:
37 But he, whom God raised again,
saw no corruption.
38 ¶Be it known unto you therefore,
men *and* brethren, that through this
man is preached unto you the forgiveness of sins:
39 And by him all that believe are justified from all things, from which ye
could not be justified by the law of
Moses.
40 Beware therefore, lest that come
upon you, which is spoken of in the
prophets;
41 Behold, ye despisers, and wonder,
and perish: for I work a work in your
days, a work which ye shall in no wise
believe, though a man declare it unto
you.
42 ¶And when the Jews were gone
out of the synagogue, the Gentiles besought that these words might be
preached to them the next sabbath.
43 Now when the congregation was
broken up, many of the Jews and religious proselytes followed Paul and Barnabas: who, speaking to them, persuaded them to continue in the grace of
God.
44 ¶And the next sabbath day came
almost the whole city together to hear
the word of God.
45 But when the Jews saw the multitudes, they were filled with envy, and
spake against those things which were
spoken by Paul, contradicting and
blaspheming.
46 Then Paul and Barnabas waxed
bold, and said, It was necessary that
the word of God should first have been
spoken to you: but seeing ye put it from
you, and judge yourselves unworthy of
everlasting life, lo, we turn to the Gentiles.
47 For so hath the Lord commanded
us, *saying*, I have set thee to be a light
of the Gentiles, that thou shouldest be
for salvation unto the ends of the earth.
48 And when the Gentiles heard this,
they were glad, and glorified the word
of the Lord: and as many as were ordained to eternal life believed.
49 And the word of the Lord was published throughout all the region.
50 But the Jews stirred up the devout
and honourable women, and the chief
men of the city, and raised persecution
against Paul and Barnabas, and expelled them out of their coasts.
51 But they shook off the dust of their
feet against them, and came unto Ī-cō′-nĭ-um.
52 And the disciples were filled with
joy, and with the Holy Ghost.

CHAPTER 14

AND it came to pass in Ī-cō′nĭ-um, that
they went both together into the synagogue of the Jews, and so spake, that a
great multitude both of the Jews and
also of the Greeks believed.
2 But the unbelieving Jews stirred up
the Gentiles, and made their minds evil
affected against the brethren.
3 Long time therefore abode they
speaking boldly in the Lord, which
gave testimony unto the word of his
grace, and granted signs and wonders
to be done by their hands.
4 But the multitude of the city was divided: and part held with the Jews, and
part with the apostles.
5 And when there was an assault
made both of the Gentiles, and also of
the Jews with their rulers, to use *them*
despitefully, and to stone them,
6 They were ware of *it*, and fled unto
Lys′tra and Der′be, cities of Lyc-a-o′-ni-a, and unto the region that lieth
round about:
7 And there they preached the gospel.
8 ¶And there sat a certain man at
Lys′tra, impotent in his feet, being a
cripple from his mother's womb, who
never had walked:
9 The same heard Paul speak: who
stedfastly beholding him, and perceiving that he had faith to be healed,
10 Said with a loud voice, Stand
upright on thy feet. And he leaped and
walked.
11 And when the people saw what
Paul had done, they lifted up their

voices, saying in the speech of Lyc-a-o'ni-a, The gods are come down to us in the likeness of men.

12 And they called Barnabas, Jupiter; and Paul, Mer-cû'rĭ-us, because he was the chief speaker.

13 Then the priest of Jupiter, which was before their city, brought oxen and garlands unto the gates, and would have done sacrifice with the people.

14 *Which* when the apostles, Barnabas and Paul, heard *of*, they rent their clothes, and ran in among the people, crying out,

15 And saying, Sirs, why do ye these things? We also are men of like passions with you, and preach unto you that ye should turn from these vanities unto the living God, which made heaven, and earth, and the sea, and all things that are therein:

16 Who in times past suffered all nations to walk in their own ways.

17 Nevertheless he left not himself without witness, in that he did good, and gave us rain from heaven, and fruitful seasons, filling our hearts with food and gladness.

18 And with these sayings scarce restrained they the people, that they had not done sacrifice unto them.

19 ¶And there came thither *certain* Jews from Antioch and Ī-cō'nĭ-um, who persuaded the people, and, having stoned Paul, drew *him* out of the city, supposing he had been dead.

20 Howbeit, as the disciples stood round about him, he rose up, and came into the city: and the next day he departed with Barnabas to Der'be.

21 And when they had preached the gospel to that city, and had taught many, they returned again to Lys'tra, and *to* I-cō'nĭ-um, and Antioch,

22 Confirming the souls of the disciples, *and* exhorting them to continue in the faith, and that we must through much tribulation enter into the kingdom of God.

23 And when they had ordained them elders in every church, and had prayed with fasting, they commended them to the Lord, on whom they believed.

24 And after they had passed throughout Pĭ-sĭd'ĭ-a, they came to Păm-phȳl'ĭ-a.

25 And when they had preached the word in Per'ga, they went down into Ăt-ta'lī-a:

26 And thence sailed to Antioch, from whence they had been recommended to the grace of God for the work which they fulfilled.

27 And when they were come, and had gathered the church together, they rehearsed all that God had done with them, and how he had opened the door of faith unto the Gentiles.

28 And there they abode long time with the disciples.

CHAPTER 15

AND certain men which came down from Judæa taught the brethren, *and said*, Except ye be circumcised after the manner of Moses, ye cannot be saved.

2 When therefore Paul and Barnabas had no small dissension and disputation with them, they determined that Paul and Barnabas, and certain other of them, should go up to Jerusalem unto the apostles and elders about this question.

3 And being brought on their way by the church, they passed through Phenĭ'ce and Sa-mâ'rĭ-a, declaring the conversion of the Gentiles: and they caused great joy unto all the brethren.

4 And when they were come to Jerusalem, they were received of the church, and *of* the apostles and elders, and they declared all things that God had done with them.

5 ¶But there rose up certain of the sect of the Pharisees which believed, saying, That it was needful to circumcise them, and to command *them* to keep the law of Moses.

6 And the apostles and elders came together for to consider of this matter.

7 And when there had been much disputing, Peter rose up, and said unto them, Men *and* brethren, ye know how that a good while ago God made choice among us, that the Gentiles by my mouth should hear the word of the gospel, and believe.

8 And God, which knoweth the hearts, bare them witness, giving them the Holy Ghost, even as *he did* unto us;

9 And put no difference between us and them, purifying their hearts by faith.

10 Now therefore why tempt ye God, to put a yoke upon the neck of the disciples, which neither our fathers nor we were able to bear?

11 But we believe that through the grace of the Lord Jesus Christ we shall be saved, even as they.

12 ¶Then all the multitude kept silence, and gave audience to Barnabas and Paul, declaring what miracles and wonders God had wrought among the Gentiles by them.

13 ¶And after they had held their peace, James answered, saying, Men *and* brethren, hearken unto me:

14 Simeon hath declared how God at

the first did visit the Gentiles, to take
out of them a people for his name.
15 And to this agree the words of the
prophets; as it is written,
16 After this I will return, and will
build again the tabernacle of David,
which is fallen down; and I will build
again the ruins thereof, and I will set it
up:
17 That the residue of men might
seek after the Lord, and all the Gen-
tiles, upon whom my name is called,
saith the Lord, who doeth all these
things.
18 Known unto God are all his works
from the beginning of the world.
19 Wherefore my sentence is, that we
trouble not them, which from among
the Gentiles are turned to God:
20 But that we write unto them, that
they abstain from pollutions of idols,
and *from* fornication, and *from* things
strangled, and *from* blood.
21 For Moses of old time hath in
every city them that preach him, being
read in the synagogues every sabbath
day.
22 ¶Then pleased it the apostles and
elders, with the whole church, to send
chosen men of their own company to
Antioch with Paul and Barnabas; *name-*
ly, Judas surnamed Bär'să-bas, and
Silas, chief men among the brethren:
23 And they wrote *letters* by them af-
ter this manner; The apostles and elders
and brethren *send* greeting unto the
brethren which are of the Gentiles in
Antioch and Syria and Ċĭ-lĭ'ċia.
24 Forasmuch as we have heard, that
certain which went out from us have
troubled you with words, subverting
your souls, saying, *Ye must* be circum-
cised, and keep the law: to whom we
gave no *such* commandment:
25 It seemed good unto us, being as-
sembled with one accord, to send cho-
sen men unto you with our beloved
Barnabas and Paul,
26 Men that have hazarded their lives
for the name of our Lord Jesus Christ.
27 We have sent therefore Judas and
Silas, who shall also tell *you* the same
things by mouth.
28 For it seemed good to the Holy
Ghost, and to us, to lay upon you no
greater burden than these necessary
things;
29 That ye abstain from meats of-
fered to idols, and from blood, and
from things strangled, and from forni-
cation: from which if ye keep your-
selves, ye shall do well. Fare ye well.
30 So when they were dismissed,
they came to Antioch: and when they
had gathered the multitude together,
they delivered the epistle:
31 *Which* when they had read, they
rejoiced for the consolation.
32 And Judas and Silas, being
prophets also themselves, exhorted the
brethren with many words, and con-
firmed *them*.
33 And after they had tarried *there* a
space, they were let go in peace from
the brethren unto the apostles.
34 Notwithstanding it pleased Silas
to abide there still.
35 Paul also and Barnabas continued
in Antioch, teaching and preaching the
word of the Lord, with many others
also.
36 ¶And some days after Paul said
unto Barnabas, Let us go again and
visit our brethren in every city where
we have preached the word of the Lord,
and see how they do.
37 And Barnabas determined to take
with them John, whose surname was
Mark.
38 But Paul thought not good to take
him with them, who departed from
them from Păm-phȳl'ĭ-a, and went not
with them to the work.
39 And the contention was so sharp
between them, that they departed asun-
der one from the other: and so Bar-
nabas took Mark, and sailed unto Cy-
prus;
40 And Paul chose Silas, and de-
parted, being recommended by the
brethren unto the grace of God.
41 And he went through Syria and Ċĭ-
lĭ'ċia, confirming the churches.

CHAPTER 16

THEN came he to Der'be and Lys'tra:
and, behold, a certain disciple was
there, named Tĭ-mō'the-us, the son of a
certain woman, which was a Jewess,
and believed; but his father *was* a
Greek:
2 Which was well reported of by the
brethren that were at Lys'tra and Ī-cō'-
nĭ-um.
3 Him would Paul have to go forth
with him; and took and circumcised
him because of the Jews which were in
those quarters: for they knew all that
his father was a Greek.
4 And as they went through the
cities, they delivered them the decrees
for to keep, that were ordained of the
apostles and elders which were at Jeru-
salem.
5 And so were the churches estab-
lished in the faith, and increased in
number daily.
6 Now when they had gone

throughout Phrȳġ-ĭ-a and the region of Ga-lā'tia, and were forbidden of the Holy Ghost to preach the word in Asia,
7 After they were come to Mȳs'ĭa, they assayed to go into Bĭ-thȳn'ĭ-a: but the Spirit suffered them not.
8 And they passing by Mȳs'ĭa came down to Troas.
9 ¶And a vision appeared to Paul in the night; there stood a man of Macedonia, and prayed him, saying, Come over into Macedonia, and help us.
10 And after he had seen the vision, immediately we endeavoured to go into Macedonia, assuredly gathering that the Lord had called us for to preach the gospel unto them.
11 Therefore loosing from Troas, we came with a straight course to Săm-o-thrā'cia, and the next *day* to Nē-ăp'o-lĭs;
12 And from thence to Phĭ-lip'pī, which is the chief city of that part of Macedonia, *and* a colony: and we were in that city abiding certain days.
13 And on the sabbath we went out of the city by a river side, where prayer was wont to be made; and we sat down, and spake unto the women which resorted *thither*.
14 ¶And a certain woman named Lyd'i-a, a seller of purple, of the city of Thȳ-a-tī'ra, which worshipped God, heard *us:* whose heart the Lord opened, that she attended unto the things which were spoken of Paul.
15 And when she was baptized, and her household, she besought *us,* saying, If ye have judged me to be faithful to the Lord, come into my house, and abide *there.* And she constrained us.
16 ¶And it came to pass, as we went to prayer, a certain damsel possessed with a spirit of divination met us, which brought her masters much gain by soothsaying:
17 The same followed Paul and us, and cried, saying, These men are the servants of the most high God, which shew unto us the way of salvation.
18 And this did she many days. But Paul, being grieved, turned and said to the spirit, I command thee in the name of Jesus Christ to come out of her. And he came out the same hour.
19 ¶And when her masters saw that the hope of their gains was gone, they caught Paul and Silas, and drew *them* into the marketplace unto the rulers,
20 And brought them to the magistrates, saying, These men, being Jews, do exceedingly trouble our city,
21 And teach customs, which are not lawful for us to receive, neither to observe, being Romans.
22 And the multitude rose up together against them: and the magistrates rent off their clothes, and commanded to beat *them.*
23 And when they had laid many stripes upon them, they cast *them* into prison, charging the jailor to keep them safely:
24 Who, having received such a charge, thrust them into the inner prison, and made their feet fast in the stocks.
25 ¶And at midnight Paul and Silas prayed, and sang praises unto God: and the prisoners heard them.
26 And suddenly there was a great earthquake, so that the foundations of the prison were shaken: and immediately all the doors were opened, and every one's bands were loosed.
27 And the keeper of the prison awaking out of his sleep, and seeing the prison doors open, he drew out his sword, and would have killed himself, supposing that the prisoners had been fled.
28 But Paul cried with a loud voice, saying, Do thyself no harm: for we are all here.
29 Then he called for a light, and sprang in, and came trembling, and fell down before Paul and Silas,
30 And brought them out, and said, Sirs, what must I do to be saved?
31 And they said, Believe on the Lord Jesus Christ, and thou shalt be saved, and thy house.
32 And they spake unto him the word of the Lord, and to all that were in his house.
33 And he took them the same hour of the night, and washed *their* stripes; and was baptized, he and all his, straightway.
34 And when he had brought them into his house, he set meat before them, and rejoiced, believing in God with all his house.
35 And when it was day, the magistrates sent the serjeants, saying, Let those men go.
36 And the keeper of the prison told this saying to Paul, The magistrates have sent to let you go: now therefore depart, and go in peace.
37 But Paul said unto them, They have beaten us openly uncondemned, being Romans, and have cast *us* into prison; and now do they thrust us out privily? nay verily; but let them come themselves and fetch us out.
38 And the serjeants told these words

unto the magistrates: and they feared,
when they heard that they were Romans.
39 And they came and besought
them, and brought *them* out, and desired *them* to depart out of the city.
40 And they went out of the prison,
and entered into *the house of* Lyd'i-a:
and when they had seen the brethren,
they comforted them, and departed.

CHAPTER 17

NOW when they had passed through
Ăm-phĭp'o-lĭs and Ăp-ol-lō'nĭ-a, they
came to Thĕs-sa-lo-nī'ca, where was a
synagogue of the Jews:
2 And Paul, as his manner was, went
in unto them, and three sabbath days
reasoned with them out of the scriptures,
3 Opening and alleging, that Christ
must needs have suffered, and risen
again from the dead; and that this Jesus, whom I preach unto you, is Christ.
4 And some of them believed, and
consorted with Paul and Silas; and of
the devout Greeks a great multitude,
and of the chief women not a few.
5 ¶But the Jews which believed not,
moved with envy, took unto them certain lewd fellows of the baser sort, and
gathered a company, and set all the city
on an uproar, and assaulted the house
of Jason, and sought to bring them out
to the people.
6 And when they found them not,
they drew Jason and certain brethren
unto the rulers of the city, crying,
These that have turned the world upside down are come hither also;
7 Whom Jason hath received: and
these all do contrary to the decrees of
Cæsar, saying that there is another
king, *one* Jesus.
8 And they troubled the people and
the rulers of the city, when they heard
these things.
9 And when they had taken security
of Jason, and of the other, they let them
go.
10 ¶And the brethren immediately
sent away Paul and Silas by night unto
Be-rē'a: who coming *thither* went into
the synagogue of the Jews.
11 These were more noble than those
in Thĕs-sa-lo-nī'ca, in that they received the word with all readiness of
mind, and searched the scriptures
daily, whether those things were so.
12 Therefore many of them believed;
also of honourable women which were
Greeks, and of men, not a few.
13 But when the Jews of Thĕs-sa-lo-nī'ca had knowledge that the word of
God was preached of Paul at Be-rē'a,
they came thither also, and stirred up
the people.
14 And then immediately the brethren sent away Paul to go as it were to
the sea: but Silas and Tī-mō'the-us
abode there still.
15 And they that conducted Paul
brought him unto Athens: and receiving a commandment unto Silas and Tī-mō'the-us for to come to him with all
speed, they departed.
16 ¶Now while Paul waited for them
at Athens, his spirit was stirred in him,
when he saw the city wholly given to
idolatry.
17 Therefore disputed he in the synagogue with the Jews, and with the devout persons, and in the market daily
with them that met with him.
18 Then certain philosophers of the
Ĕp-i-cū-rē'ans, and of the Stō'ĭcks, encountered him. And some said, What
will this babbler say? other some, He
seemeth to be a setter forth of strange
gods: because he preached unto them
Jesus, and the resurrection.
19 And they took him, and brought
him unto Ăr-ē-ŏp'a-gus, saying, May
we know what this new doctrine, whereof thou speakest, *is?*
20 For thou bringest certain strange
things to our ears: we would know therefore what these things mean.
21 (For all the Athenians and strangers which were there spent their time in
nothing else, but either to tell, or to
hear some new thing.)
22 ¶Then Paul stood in the midst of
Mars' hill, and said, *Ye* men of Athens, I
perceive that in all things ye are too
superstitious.
23 For as I passed by, and beheld
your devotions, I found an altar with
this inscription, TO THE UNKNOWN
GOD. Whom therefore ye ignorantly
worship, him declare I unto you.
24 God that made the world and all
things therein, seeing that he is LORD of
heaven and earth, dwelleth not in
temples made with hands;
25 Neither is worshipped with men's
hands, as though he needed any thing,
seeing he giveth to all life, and breath,
and all things;
26 And hath made of one blood all nations of men for to dwell on all the face
of the earth, and hath determined the
times before appointed, and the
bounds of their habitation;
27 That they should seek the LORD, if
haply they might feel after him, and
find him, though he be not far from
every one of us:
28 For in him we live, and move, and
have our being; as certain also of your

own poets have said, For we are also
his offspring.
29 Forasmuch then as we are the
offspring of God, we ought not to think
that the Godhead is like unto gold, or
silver, or stone, graven by art and
man's device.
30 And the times of this ignorance
God winked at; but now commandeth
all men every where to repent:
31 Because he hath appointed a day,
in the which he will judge the world in
righteousness by *that* man whom he
hath ordained; *whereof* he hath given
assurance unto all *men*, in that he hath
raised him from the dead.
32 ¶And when they heard of the res-
urrection of the dead, some mocked:
and others said, We will hear thee
again of this *matter*.
33 So Paul departed from among
them.
34 Howbeit certain men clave unto
him, and believed: among the which
was Dī-o-nȳs'i-us the Ăr-ē-ŏp'a-gīte,
and a woman named Dăm'a-rĭs, and
others with them.

CHAPTER 18

AFTER these things Paul departed
from Athens and came to Corinth;
2 And found a certain Jew named
Ăq'ui-la, born in Pontus, lately come
from Italy, with his wife Priscilla; (be-
cause that Claudius had commanded
all Jews to depart from Rome:) and
came unto them.
3 And because he was of the same
craft, he abode with them, and
wrought: for by their occupation they
were tentmakers.
4 And he reasoned in the synagogue
every sabbath, and persuaded the Jews
and the Greeks.
5 And when Silas and Tī-mŏ'the-us
were come from Macedonia, Paul was
pressed in the spirit, and testified to the
Jews *that* Jesus *was* Christ.
6 And when they opposed them-
selves, and blasphemed, he shook *his*
raiment, and said unto them, Your
blood *be* upon your own heads; I *am*
clean: from henceforth I will go unto
the Gentiles.
7 And he departed thence, and en-
tered into a certain *man's* house,
named Justus, *one* that worshipped
God, whose house joined hard to the
synagogue.
8 And Crispus, the chief ruler of the
synagogue, believed on the LORD with
all his house; and many of the Co-rĭn'-
thĭ-anṡ hearing believed, and were
baptized.
9 Then spake the LORD to Paul in the
night by a vision, Be not afraid, but
speak, and hold not thy peace:
10 For I am with thee, and no man
shall set on thee to hurt thee: for I have
much people in this city.
11 And he continued *there* a year and
six months, teaching the word of God
among them.
12 ¶And when Găl'lĭ-ō was the dep-
uty of A-chā'ia, the Jews made insur-
rection with one accord against Paul,
and brought him to the judgment seat,
13 Saying, This *fellow* persuadeth
men to worship God contrary to the
law.
14 And when Paul was now about to
open *his* mouth, Găl'lĭ-ō said unto the
Jews, If it were a matter of wrong or
wicked lewdness, O *ye* Jews, reason
would that I should bear with you:
15 But if it be a question of words and
names, and *of* your law, look ye *to it;*
for I will be no judge of such *matters*.
16 And he drave them from the judg-
ment seat.
17 Then all the Greeks took Sŏs'the-
nēṡ, the chief ruler of the synagogue,
and beat *him* before the judgment seat.
And Găl'lĭ-ō cared for none of those
things.
18 ¶And Paul *after this* tarried *there*
yet a good while, and then took his
leave of the brethren, and sailed thence
into Syria, and with him Priscilla and
Ăq'ui-la; having shorn *his* head in
Ċĕn'chre-a: for he had a vow.
19 And he came to Ĕph'e-sus, and left
them there: but he himself entered into
the synagogue, and reasoned with the
Jews.
20 When they desired *him* to tarry
longer time with them, he consented
not;
21 But bade them farewell, saying, I
must by all means keep this feast that
cometh in Jerusalem: but I will return
again unto you, if God will. And he
sailed from Ĕph'e-sus.
22 And when he had landed at Cæs-a-
re'a, and gone up, and saluted the
church, he went down to Antioch.
23 And after he had spent some time
there, he departed, and went over *all*
the country of Ga-lā'tia and Phrȳġ'ĭ-a in
order, strengthening all the disciples.
24 ¶And a certain Jew named Apol-
los, born at Alexandria, an eloquent
man, *and* mighty in the scriptures,
came to Ĕph'e-sus.
25 This man was instructed in the
way of the LORD; and being fervent in
the spirit, he spake and taught diligent-
ly the things of the LORD, knowing
only the baptism of John.
26 And he began to speak boldly in

the synagogue: whom when Ăq'ui-la
and Priscilla had heard, they took him
unto *them*, and expounded unto him
the way of God more perfectly.
27 And when he was disposed to pass
into A-chā'ia, the brethren wrote, ex-
horting the disciples to receive him:
who, when he was come, helped them
much which had believed through
grace:
28 For he mightily convinced the
Jews, *and that* publickly, shewing by
the scriptures that Jesus was Christ.

CHAPTER 19

AND it came to pass, that, while Apol-
los was at Corinth, Paul having passed
through the upper coasts came to
Ĕph'e-sus: and finding certain dis-
ciples,
2 He said unto them, Have ye re-
ceived the Holy Ghost since ye be-
lieved? And they said unto him, We
have not so much as heard whether
there be any Holy Ghost.
3 And he said unto them, Unto what
then were ye baptized? And they said,
Unto John's baptism.
4 Then said Paul, John verily bap-
tized with the baptism of repentance,
saying unto the people, that they
should believe on him which should
come after him, that is, on Christ Jesus.
5 When they heard *this*, they were
baptized in the name of the Lord Jesus.
6 And when Paul had laid *his* hands
upon them, the Holy Ghost came on
them; and they spake with tongues,
and prophesied.
7 And all the men were about twelve.
8 And he went into the synagogue,
and spake boldly for the space of three
months, disputing and persuading the
things concerning the kingdom of God.
9 But when divers were hardened,
and believed not, but spake evil of that
way before the multitude, he departed
from them, and separated the disciples,
disputing daily in the school of one Tȳ-
răn'nus.
10 And this continued by the space of
two years; so that all they which dwelt
in Asia heard the word of the Lord Je-
sus, both Jews and Greeks.
11 And God wrought special
miracles by the hands of Paul:
12 So that from his body were
brought unto the sick handkerchiefs or
aprons, and the diseases departed from
them, and the evil spirits went out of
them.
13 ¶Then certain of the vagabond
Jews, exorcists, took upon them to call
over them which had evil spirits the
name of the Lord Jesus, saying, We ad-
jure you by Jesus whom Paul preach-
eth.
14 And there were seven sons of *one*
Scē'va, a Jew, *and* chief of the priests,
which did so.
15 And the evil spirit answered and
said, Jesus I know, and Paul I know;
but who are ye?
16 And the man in whom the evil
spirit was leaped on them, and over-
came them, and prevailed against
them, so that they fled out of that house
naked and wounded.
17 And this was known to all the
Jews and Greeks also dwelling at
Ĕph'e-sus; and fear fell on them all, and
the name of the Lord Jesus was magni-
fied.
18 And many that believed came, and
confessed, and shewed their deeds.
19 Many of them also which used cu-
rious arts brought their books together,
and burned them before all *men*: and
they counted the price of them, and
found *it* fifty thousand *pieces* of silver.
20 So mightily grew the word of God
and prevailed.
21 ¶After these things were ended,
Paul purposed in the spirit, when he
had passed through Macedonia and A-
chā'ia, to go to Jerusalem, saying, After
I have been there, I must also see
Rome.
22 So he sent into Macedonia two of
them that ministered unto him, Tĭ-
mō'the-us and E-răs'tus; but he himself
stayed in Asia for a season.
23 ¶And the same time there arose no
small stir about that way.
24 For a certain *man* named De-mē'-
trĭ-us, a silversmith which made silver
shrines for Diana, brought no small
gain unto the craftsmen;
25 Whom he called together with the
workmen of like occupation, and said,
Sirs, ye know that by this craft we have
our wealth.
26 Moreover ye see and hear, that not
alone at Ĕph'e-sus, but almost
throughout all Asia, this Paul hath per-
suaded and turned away much people,
saying that they be no gods, which are
made with hands:
27 So that not only this our craft is in
danger to be set at nought; but also that
the temple of the great goddess Diana
should be despised, and her magnifi-
cence should be destroyed, whom all
Asia and the world worshippeth.
28 And when they heard *these
sayings*, they were full of wrath, and
cried out, saying, Great *is* Diana of the
E-phē'ṡians.
29 And the whole city was filled with
confusion: and having caught Gaius

and Ăr-ĭs-tär′chus, men of Macedonia, Paul's companions in travel, they rushed with one accord into the theatre.

30 And when Paul would have entered in unto the people, the disciples suffered him not.

31 And certain of the chief of Asia, which were his friends, sent unto him, desiring *him* that he would not adventure himself into the theatre.

32 Some therefore cried one thing, and some another: for the assembly was confused; and the more part knew not wherefore they were come together.

33 And they drew Alexander out of the multitude, the Jews putting him forward. And Alexander beckoned with the hand, and would have made his defence unto the people.

34 But when they knew that he was a Jew, all with one voice about the space of two hours cried out, Great *is* Diana of the E-phē′ṡians.

35 And when the townclerk had appeased the people, he said, *Ye* men of Ĕph′e-sus, what man is there that knoweth not how that the city of the E-phē′ṡians is a worshipper of the great goddess Diana, and of the *image* which fell down from Jupiter?

36 Seeing then that these things cannot be spoken against, ye ought to be quiet, and to do nothing rashly.

37 For ye have brought hither these men, which are neither robbers of churches, nor yet blasphemers of your goddess.

38 Wherefore if De-mē′trĭ-us, and the craftsmen which are with him, have a matter against any man, the law is open, and there are deputies: let them implead one another.

39 But if ye enquire any thing concerning other matters, it shall be determined in a lawful assembly.

40 For we are in danger to be called in question for this day's uproar, there being no cause whereby we may give an account of this concourse.

41 And when he had thus spoken, he dismissed the assembly.

CHAPTER 20

AND after the uproar was ceased, Paul called unto *him* the disciples, and embraced *them,* and departed for to go into Macedonia.

2 And when he had gone over those parts, and had given them much exhortation, he came into Greece,

3 And *there* abode three months. And when the Jews laid wait for him, as he was about to sail into Syria, he purposed to return through Macedonia.

4 And there accompanied him into Asia Sōp′a-ter of Be-rē′a; and of the Thĕs-sa-lō′nī-anṡ, Ăr-ĭs-tär′chus and Se-cŭn′dus; and Gaius of Der′be, and Tī-mō′the-us; and of Asia, Tȳch′ĭ-cus and Trŏph′i-mus.

5 These going before tarried for us at Troas.

6 And we sailed away from Phī-lip′pī after the days of unleavened bread, and came unto them to Troas in five days; where we abode seven days.

7 ¶And upon the first *day* of the week, when the disciples came together to break bread, Paul preached unto them, ready to depart on the morrow; and continued his speech until midnight.

8 And there were many lights in the upper chamber, where they were gathered together.

9 And there sat in a window a certain young man named Eū′ty-chus, being fallen into a deep sleep: and as Paul was long preaching, he sunk down with sleep, and fell down from the third loft, and was taken up dead.

10 And Paul went down, and fell on him, and embracing *him* said, Trouble not yourselves; for his life is in him.

11 When he therefore was come up again, and had broken bread, and eaten, and talked a long while, even till break of day, so he departed.

12 And they brought the young man alive, and were not a little comforted.

13 ¶And we went before to ship, and sailed unto Ăs′sŏs, there intending to take in Paul: for so had he appointed, minding himself to go afoot.

14 And when he met with us at Ăs′sŏs, we took him in, and came to Mĭt-y-lē′ne.

15 And we sailed thence, and came the next *day* over against Chī′ŏs; and the next *day* we arrived at Sā′mŏs, and tarried at Trō-ġȳl′lĭ-um; and the next *day* we came to Mī-lē′tus.

16 For Paul had determined to sail by Ĕph′e-sus, because he would not spend the time in Asia: for he hasted, if it were possible for him, to be at Jerusalem the day of Pentecost.

17 ¶And from Mī-lē′tus he sent to Ĕph′e-sus, and called the elders of the church.

18 And when they were come to him, he said unto them, Ye know, from the first day that I came into Asia, after what manner I have been with you at all seasons,

19 Serving the Lord with all humility of mind, and with many tears, and

temptations, which befell me by the
lying in wait of the Jews:
20 *And* how I kept back nothing that
was profitable *unto you,* but have
shewed you, and have taught you pub-
lickly, and from house to house,
21 Testifying both to the Jews, and
also to the Greeks, repentance toward
God, and faith toward our Lord Jesus
Christ.
22 And now, behold, I go bound in the
spirit unto Jerusalem, not knowing the
things that shall befall me there:
23 Save that the Holy Ghost witness-
eth in every city, saying that bonds
and afflictions abide me.
24 But none of these things move me,
neither count I my life dear unto my-
self, so that I might finish my course
with joy, and the ministry, which I have
received of the Lord Jesus, to testify
the gospel of the grace of God.
25 And now, behold, I know that ye
all, among whom I have gone preach-
ing the kingdom of God, shall see my
face no more.
26 Wherefore I take you to record
this day, that I *am* pure from the blood
of all *men.*
27 For I have not shunned to declare
unto you all the counsel of God.
28 Take heed therefore unto your-
selves, and to all the flock, over the
which the Holy Ghost hath made you
overseers, to feed the church of God,
which he hath purchased with his own
blood.
29 For I know this, that after my de-
parting shall grievous wolves enter in
among you, not sparing the flock.
30 Also of your own selves shall men
arise, speaking perverse things, to
draw away disciples after them.
31 Therefore watch, and remember,
that by the space of three years I
ceased not to warn every one night and
day with tears.
32 And now, brethren, I commend
you to God, and to the word of his
grace, which is able to build you up,
and to give you an inheritance among
all them which are sanctified.
33 I have coveted no man's silver, or
gold, or apparel.
34 Yea, ye yourselves know, that
these hands have ministered unto my
necessities, and to them that were with
me.
35 I have shewed you all things, how
that so labouring ye ought to support
the weak, and to remember the words
of the Lord Jesus, how he said, It is
more blessed to give than to receive.
36 ¶And when he had thus spoken, he
kneeled down, and prayed with them
all.
37 And they all wept sore, and fell on
Paul's neck, and kissed him,
38 Sorrowing most of all for the
words which he spake, that they should
see his face no more. And they accom-
panied him unto the ship.

CHAPTER 21

AND it came to pass, that after we
were gotten from them, and had
launched, we came with a straight
course unto Cō'ŏs, and the *day* follow-
ing unto Rhodes, and from thence unto
Păt'a-ra:
2 And finding a ship sailing over unto
Phe-nī'ċia, we went aboard, and set
forth.
3 Now when we had discovered Cy-
prus, we left it on the left hand, and
sailed into Syria, and landed at Tyre:
for there the ship was to unlade her
burden.
4 And finding disciples, we tarried
there seven days: who said to Paul
through the Spirit, that he should not
go up to Jerusalem.
5 And when we had accomplished
those days, we departed and went our
way; and they all brought us on our
way, with wives and children, till *we
were* out of the city: and we kneeled
down on the shore, and prayed.
6 And when we had taken our leave
one of another, we took ship; and they
returned home again.
7 And when we had finished *our*
course from Tyre, we came to Ptŏl-e-
mā'is, and saluted the brethren, and
abode with them one day.
8 And the next *day* we that were of
Paul's company departed, and came
unto Cæs-a-re'a: and we entered into
the house of Philip the evangelist,
which was *one* of the seven; and abode
with him.
9 And the same man had four daugh-
ters, virgins, which did prophesy.
10 And as we tarried *there* many
days, there came down from Judæa a
certain prophet, named Ăg'a-bus.
11 And when he was come unto us,
he took Paul's girdle, and bound his
own hands and feet, and said, Thus
saith the Holy Ghost, So shall the Jews
at Jerusalem bind the man that owneth
this girdle, and shall deliver *him* into
the hands of the Gentiles.
12 And when we heard these things,
both we, and they of that place, be-
sought him not to go up to Jerusalem.
13 Then Paul answered, What mean
ye to weep and to break mine heart? for
I am ready not to be bound only, but

also to die at Jerusalem for the name of the Lord Jesus.

14 And when he would not be persuaded, we ceased, saying, The will of the Lord be done.

15 And after those days we took up our carriages, and went up to Jerusalem.

16 There went with us also *certain* of the disciples of Cæs-a-re'a, and brought with them one Mnā'son of Cyprus, an old disciple, with whom we should lodge.

17 And when we were come to Jerusalem, the brethren received us gladly.

18 And the *day* following Paul went in with us unto James; and all the elders were present.

19 And when he had saluted them, he declared particularly what things God had wrought among the Gentiles by his ministry.

20 And when they heard *it*, they glorified the Lord, and said unto him, Thou seest, brother, how many thousands of Jews there are which believe; and they are all zealous of the law:

21 And they are informed of thee, that thou teachest all the Jews which are among the Gentiles to forsake Moses, saying that they ought not to circumcise *their* children, neither to walk after the customs.

22 What is it therefore? the multitude must needs come together: for they will hear that thou art come.

23 Do therefore this that we say to thee: We have four men which have a vow on them;

24 Them take, and purify thyself with them, and be at charges with them, that they may shave *their* heads: and all may know that those things, whereof they were informed concerning thee, are nothing; but *that* thou thyself also walkest orderly, and keepest the law.

25 As touching the Gentiles which believe, we have written *and* concluded that they observe no such thing, save only that they keep themselves from *things* offered to idols, and from blood, and from strangled, and from fornication.

26 Then Paul took the men, and the next day purifying himself with them entered into the temple, to signify the accomplishment of the days of purification, until that an offering should be offered for every one of them.

27 And when the seven days were almost ended, the Jews which were of Asia, when they saw him in the temple, stirred up all the people, and laid hands on him,

28 Crying out, Men of Israel, help: This is the man, that teacheth all *men* every where against the people, and the law, and this place: and further brought Greeks also into the temple, and hath polluted this holy place.

29 (For they had seen before with him in the city Trŏph'i-mus an E-phē'-ṡian, whom they supposed that Paul had brought into the temple.)

30 And all the city was moved, and the people ran together: and they took Paul, and drew him out of the temple: and forthwith the doors were shut.

31 And as they went about to kill him, tidings came unto the chief captain of the band, that all Jerusalem was in an uproar.

32 Who immediately took soldiers and centurions, and ran down unto them: and when they saw the chief captain and the soldiers, they left beating of Paul.

33 Then the chief captain came near, and took him, and commanded *him* to be bound with two chains; and demanded who he was, and what he had done.

34 And some cried one thing, some another, among the multitude: and when he could not know the certainty for the tumult, he commanded him to be carried into the castle.

35 And when he came upon the stairs, so it was, that he was borne of the soldiers for the violence of the people.

36 For the multitude of the people followed after, crying, Away with him.

37 And as Paul was to be led into the castle, he said unto the chief captain, May I speak unto thee? Who said, Canst thou speak Greek?

38 Art not thou that Ē-gȳp'tian, which before these days madest an uproar, and leddest out into the wilderness four thousand men that were murderers?

39 But Paul said, I am a man *which am* a Jew of Tarsus, *a city* in Ċĭ-lĭ'ċia, a citizen of no mean city: and, I beseech thee, suffer me to speak unto the people.

40 And when he had given him licence, Paul stood on the stairs, and beckoned with the hand unto the people. And when there was made a great silence, he spake unto *them* in the Hebrew tongue, saying,

CHAPTER 22

MEN, brethren, and fathers, hear ye my defence *which I make* now unto you.

2 (And when they heard that he spake in the Hebrew tongue to them,

they kept the more silence: and he saith.)

3 I am verily a man *which am* a Jew, born in Tarsus, *a city* in Cĭ-lĭ'cia, yet brought up in this city at the feet of Ga-mā'lĭ-el, *and* taught according to the perfect manner of the law of the fathers, and was zealous toward God, as ye all are this day.

4 And I persecuted this way unto the death, binding and delivering into prisons both men and women.

5 As also the high priest doth bear me witness, and all the estate of the elders: from whom also I received letters unto the brethren, and went to Damascus, to bring them which were there bound unto Jerusalem, for to be punished.

6 And it came to pass, that as I made my journey, and was come nigh unto Damascus about noon, suddenly there shone from heaven a great light round about me.

7 And I fell unto the ground, and heard a voice saying unto me, Saul, Saul, why persecutest thou me?

8 And I answered, Who art thou, Lord? And he said unto me, I am Jesus of Nazareth, whom thou persecutest.

9 And they that were with me saw indeed the light, and were afraid; but they heard not the voice of him that spake to me.

10 And I said, What shall I do, Lord? And the Lord said unto me, Arise, and go into Damascus; and there it shall be told thee of all things which are appointed for thee to do.

11 And when I could not see for the glory of that light, being led by the hand of them that were with me, I came into Damascus.

12 And one Ăn-a-nī'as, a devout man according to the law, having a good report of all the Jews which dwelt *there*,

13 Came unto me, and stood, and said unto me, Brother Saul, receive thy sight. And the same hour I looked up upon him.

14 And he said, The God of our fathers hath chosen thee, that thou shouldest know his will, and see that Just One, and shouldest hear the voice of his mouth.

15 For thou shalt be his witness unto all men of what thou hast seen and heard.

16 And now why tarriest thou? arise, and be baptised, and wash away thy sins, calling on the name of the Lord.

17 And it came to pass, that, when I was come again to Jerusalem, even while I prayed in the temple, I was in a trance;

18 And saw him saying unto me, Make haste, and get thee quickly out of Jerusalem: for they will not receive thy testimony concerning me.

19 And I said, Lord, they know that I imprisoned and beat in every synagogue them that believed on thee:

20 And when the blood of thy martyr Stephen was shed, I also was standing by, and consenting unto his death, and kept the raiment of them that slew him.

21 And he said unto me, Depart: for I will send thee far hence unto the Gentiles.

22 ¶And they gave him audience unto this word, and *then* lifted up their voices, and said, Away with such a *fellow* from the earth: for it is not fit that he should live.

23 And as they cried out, and cast off *their* clothes, and threw dust into the air,

24 The chief captain commanded him to be brought into the castle, and bade that he should be examined by scourging; that he might know wherefore they cried so against him.

25 And as they bound him with thongs, Paul said unto the centurion that stood by, Is it lawful for you to scourge a man that is a Roman, and uncondemned?

26 When the centurion heard *that*, he went and told the chief captain, saying, Take heed what thou doest: for this man is a Roman.

27 Then the chief captain came, and said unto him, Tell me, art thou a Roman? He said, Yea.

28 And the chief captain answered, With a great sum obtained I this freedom. And Paul said, But I was *free* born.

29 Then straightway they departed from him which should have examined him: and the chief captain also was afraid, after he knew that he was a Roman, and because he had bound him.

30 On the morrow, because he would have known the certainty wherefore he was accused of the Jews, he loosed him from *his* bands, and commanded the chief priests and all their council to appear, and brought Paul down, and set him before them.

CHAPTER 23

AND Paul, earnestly beholding the council, said, Men *and* brethren, I have lived in all good conscience before God until this day.

2 And the high priest Ăn-a-nī'as commanded them that stood by him to smite him on the mouth.

3 Then said Paul unto him, God shall smite thee, *thou* whited wall: for sittest

thou to judge me after the law, and commandest me to be smitten contrary to the law?

4 And they that stood by said, Revilest thou God's high priest?

5 Then said Paul, I wist not, brethren, that he was the high priest: for it is written, Thou shalt not speak evil of the ruler of thy people.

6 But when Paul perceived that the one part were Săd′du-ceeṡ, and the other Pharisees, he cried out in the council, Men *and* brethren, I am a Pharisee, the son of a Pharisee: of the hope and resurrection of the dead I am called in question.

7 And when he had so said, there arose a dissension between the Pharisees and the Săd′du-ceeṡ: and the multitude was divided.

8 For the Săd′du-ceeṡ say that there is no resurrection, neither angel, nor spirit: but the Pharisees confess both.

9 And there arose a great cry: and the scribes *that were* of the Pharisees' part arose, and strove, saying, We find no evil in this man: but if a spirit or an angel hath spoken to him, let us not fight against God.

10 And when there arose a great dissension, the chief captain, fearing lest Paul should have been pulled in pieces of them, commanded the soldiers to go down, and to take him by force from among them, and to bring *him* into the castle.

11 And the night following the Lord stood by him, and said, Be of good cheer, Paul: for as thou hast testified of me in Jerusalem, so must thou bear witness also at Rome.

12 And when it was day, certain of the Jews banded together, and bound themselves under a curse, saying that they would neither eat nor drink till they had killed Paul.

13 And they were more than forty which had made this conspiracy.

14 And they came to the chief priests and elders, and said, We have bound ourselves under a great curse, that we will eat nothing until we have slain Paul.

15 Now therefore ye with the council signify to the chief captain that he bring him down unto you to morrow, as though ye would enquire something more perfectly concerning him: and we, or ever he come near, are ready to kill him.

16 And when Paul's sister's son heard of their lying in wait, he went and entered into the castle, and told Paul.

17 Then Paul called one of the centurions unto *him*, and said, Bring this young man unto the chief captain: for he hath a certain thing to tell him.

18 So he took him, and brought *him* to the chief captain, and said, Paul the prisoner called me unto *him*, and prayed me to bring this young man unto thee, who hath something to say unto thee.

19 Then the chief captain took him by the hand, and went *with him* aside privately, and asked *him*, What is that thou hast to tell me?

20 And he said, The Jews have agreed to desire thee that thou wouldest bring down Paul to morrow into the council, as though they would enquire somewhat of him more perfectly.

21 But do not thou yield unto them: for there lie in wait for him of them more than forty men, which have bound themselves with an oath, that they will neither eat nor drink till they have killed him: and now are they ready, looking for a promise from thee.

22 So the chief captain *then* let the young man depart, and charged *him*, *See thou* tell no man that thou hast shewed these things to me.

23 And he called unto *him* two centurions, saying, Make ready two hundred soldiers to go to Cæs-a-re′a, and horsemen threescore and ten, and spearmen two hundred, at the third hour of the night;

24 And provide *them* beasts, that they may set Paul on, and bring *him* safe unto Felix the governor.

25 And he wrote a letter after this manner:

26 Claudius Ly′si-as unto the most excellent governor Felix *sendeth* greeting.

27 This man was taken of the Jews, and should have been killed of them: then came I with an army, and rescued him, having understood that he was a Roman.

28 And when I would have known the cause wherefore they accused him, I brought him forth into their council:

29 Whom I perceived to be accused of questions of their law, but to have nothing laid to his charge worthy of death or of bonds.

30 And when it was told me how that the Jews laid wait for the man, I sent straightway to thee, and gave commandment to his accusers also to say before thee what *they had* against him. Farewell.

31 Then the soldiers, as it was commanded them, took Paul, and brought *him* by night to Ăn-tĭp′a-trĭs.

32 On the morrow they left the horse-

men to go with him, and returned to the castle:

33 Who, when they came to Cæs-a-re′a, and delivered the epistle to the governor, presented Paul also before him.

34 And when the governor had read *the letter,* he asked of what province he was. And when he understood that *he was* of Ċĭ-lĭ′ċia;

35 I will hear thee, said he, when thine accusers are also come. And he commanded him to be kept in Herod's judgment hall.

CHAPTER 24

AND after five days Ăn-a-nī′as the high priest descended with the elders, and *with* a certain orator *named* Ter-tŭl′lus, who informed the governor against Paul.

2 And when he was called forth, Ter-tŭl′lus began to accuse *him,* saying, Seeing that by thee we enjoy great quietness, and that very worthy deeds are done unto this nation by thy providence,

3 We accept *it* always, and in all places, most noble Felix, with all thankfulness.

4 Notwithstanding, that I be not further tedious unto thee, I pray thee that thou wouldest hear us of thy clemency a few words.

5 For we have found this man *a* pestilent *fellow,* and a mover of sedition among all the Jews throughout the world, and a ringleader of the sect of the Nazarenes:

6 Who also hath gone about to profane the temple: whom we took, and would have judged according to our law.

7 But the chief captain Ly′si-as came *upon us,* and with great violence took *him* away out of our hands,

8 Commanding his accusers to come unto thee: by examining of whom thyself mayest take knowledge of all these things, whereof we accuse him.

9 And the Jews also assented, saying that these things were so.

10 ¶Then Paul, after that the governor had beckoned unto him to speak, answered, Forasmuch as I know that thou hast been of many years a judge unto this nation, I do the more cheerfully answer for myself:

11 Because that thou mayest understand, that there are yet but twelve days since I went up to Jerusalem for to worship.

12 And they neither found me in the temple disputing with any man, neither raising up the people, neither in the synagogues, nor in the city:

13 Neither can they prove the things whereof they now accuse me.

14 But this I confess unto thee, that after the way which they call heresy, so worship I the God of my fathers, believing all things which are written in the law and in the prophets:

15 And have hope toward God, which they themselves also allow, that there shall be a resurrection of the dead, both of the just and unjust.

16 And herein do I exercise myself, to have always a conscience void of offence toward God, and *toward* men.

17 Now after many years I came to bring alms to my nation, and offerings.

18 Whereupon certain Jews from Asia found me purified in the temple, neither with multitude, nor with tumult.

19 Who ought to have been here before thee, and object, if they had ought against me.

20 Or else let these same *here* say, if they have found any evil doing in me, while I stood before the council,

21 Except it be for this one voice, that I cried standing among them, Touching the resurrection of the dead I am called in question by you this day.

22 ¶And when Felix heard these things, having more perfect knowledge of *that* way, he deferred them, and said, When Ly′si-as the chief captain shall come down, I will know the uttermost of your matter.

23 And he commanded a centurion to keep Paul, and to let *him* have liberty, and that he should forbid none of his acquaintance to minister or come unto him.

24 And after certain days, when Felix came with his wife Drū-sĭl′la, which was a Jewess, he sent for Paul, and heard him concerning the faith in Christ.

25 And as he reasoned of righteousness, temperance, and judgment to come, Felix trembled, and answered, Go thy way for this time; when I have a convenient season, I will call for thee.

26 He hoped also that money should have been given him of Paul, that he might loose him: wherefore he sent for him the oftener, and communed with him.

27 But after two years Pôr′ċi-us Fēs′-tus came into Felix' room: and Felix, willing to shew the Jews a pleasure, left Paul bound.

CHAPTER 25

NOW when Fēs′tus was come into the province, after three days he ascended from Cæs-a-re′a to Jerusalem.

2 Then the high priest and the chief of the Jews informed him against Paul, and besought him,

3 And desired favour against him, that he would send for him to Jerusalem, laying wait in the way to kill him.

4 But Fĕs'tus answered, that Paul should be kept at Cæs-a-re'a, and that he himself would depart shortly *thither*.

5 Let them therefore, said he, which among you are able, go down with *me*, and accuse this man, if there be any wickedness in him.

6 And when he had tarried among them more than ten days, he went down unto Cæs-a-re'a; and the next day sitting on the judgment seat commanded Paul to be brought.

7 And when he was come, the Jews which came down from Jerusalem stood round about, and laid many and grievous complaints against Paul, which they could not prove.

8 While he answered for himself, Neither against the law of the Jews, neither against the temple, nor yet against Cæsar, have I offended any thing at all.

9 But Fĕs'tus, willing to do the Jews a pleasure, answered Paul, and said, Wilt thou go up to Jerusalem, and there be judged of these things before me?

10 Then said Paul, I stand at Cæsar's judgment seat, where I ought to be judged: to the Jews have I done no wrong, as thou very well knowest.

11 For if I be an offender, or have committed any thing worthy of death, I refuse not to die: but if there be none of these things whereof these accuse me, no man may deliver me unto them. I appeal unto Cæsar.

12 Then Fĕs'tus, when he had conferred with the council, answered, Hast thou appealed unto Cæsar? unto Cæsar shalt thou go.

13 ¶And after certain days king A-grĭp'pa and Bernice came unto Cæs-a-re'a to salute Fĕs'tus.

14 And when they had been there many days, Fĕs'tus declared Paul's cause unto the king, saying, There is a certain man left in bonds by Felix:

15 About whom, when I was at Jerusalem, the chief priests and the elders of the Jews informed *me*, desiring *to have* judgment against him.

16 To whom I answered, It is not the manner of the Romans to deliver any man to die, before that he which is accused have the accusers face to face, and have licence to answer for himself concerning the crime laid against him.

17 Therefore, when they were come hither, without any delay on the morrow I sat on the judgment seat, and commanded the man to be brought forth.

18 Against whom when the accusers stood up, they brought none accusation of such things as I supposed:

19 But had certain questions against him of their own superstition, and of one Jesus, which was dead, whom Paul affirmed to be alive.

20 And because I doubted of such manner of questions, I asked *him* whether he would go to Jerusalem, and there be judged of these matters.

21 But when Paul had appealed to be reserved unto the hearing of Augustus, I commanded him to be kept till I might send him to Cæsar.

22 Then A-grĭp'pa said unto Fĕs'tus, I would also hear the man myself. To morrow, said he, thou shalt hear him.

23 And on the morrow, when A-grĭp'pa was come, and Bernice, with great pomp, and was entered into the place of hearing, with the chief captains, and principal men of the city, at Fĕs'tus' commandment Paul was brought forth.

24 And Fĕs'tus said, King A-grĭp'pa, and all men which are here present with us, ye see this man, about whom all the multitude of the Jews have dealt with me, both at Jerusalem, and *also* here, crying that he ought not to live any longer.

25 But when I found that he had committed nothing worthy of death, and that he himself hath appealed to Augustus, I have determined to send him.

26 Of whom I have no certain thing to write unto my lord. Wherefore I have brought him forth before you, and specially before thee, O king A-grĭp'pa, that, after examination had, I might have somewhat to write.

27 For it seemeth to me unreasonable to send a prisoner, and not withal to signify the crimes *laid* against him.

CHAPTER 26

THEN A-grĭp'pa said unto Paul, Thou art permitted to speak for thyself. Then Paul stretched forth the hand, and answered for himself:

2 I think myself happy, king A-grĭp'pa, because I shall answer for myself this day before thee touching all the things whereof I am accused of the Jews:

3 Especially *because I know* thee to be expert in all customs and questions which are among the Jews: wherefore I beseech thee to hear me patiently.

4 My manner of life from my youth,
which was at the first among mine own
nation at Jerusalem, know all the Jews;
5 Which knew me from the beginning,
if they would testify, that after the
most straitest sect of our religion I
lived a Pharisee.
6 And now I stand and am judged for
the hope of the promise made of God
unto our fathers:
7 Unto which *promise* our twelve
tribes, instantly serving *God* day and
night, hope to come. For which hope's
sake, king A-grĭp'pa, I am accused of
the Jews.
8 Why should it be thought a thing
incredible with you, that God should
raise the dead?
9 I verily thought with myself, that I
ought to do many things contrary to the
name of Jesus of Nazareth.
10 Which thing I also did in Jeru-
salem: and many of the saints did I shut
up in prison, having received authority
from the chief priests; and when they
were put to death, I gave my voice
against *them*.
11 And I punished them oft in every
synagogue, and compelled *them* to
blaspheme; and being exceedingly
mad against them, I persecuted *them*
even unto strange cities.
12 Whereupon as I went to Damas-
cus with authority and commission
from the chief priests,
13 At midday, O king, I saw in the
way a light from heaven, above the
brightness of the sun, shining round
about me and them which journeyed
with me.
14 And when we were all fallen to the
earth, I heard a voice speaking unto
me, and saying in the Hebrew tongue,
Saul, Saul, why persecutest thou me? *it
is* hard for thee to kick against the
pricks.
15 And I said, Who art thou, Lord?
And he said, I am Jesus whom thou per-
secutest.
16 But rise, and stand upon thy feet:
for I have appeared unto thee for this
purpose, to make thee a minister and a
witness both of these things which
thou hast seen, and of those things in
the which I will appear unto thee;
17 Delivering thee from the people,
and *from* the Gentiles, unto whom now
I send thee,
18 To open their eyes, *and* to turn
them from darkness to light, and *from*
the power of Satan unto God, that they
may receive forgiveness of sins, and in-
heritance among them which are sanc-
tified by faith that is in me.
19 Whereupon, O king A-grĭp'pa, I
was not disobedient unto the heavenly
vision:
20 But shewed first unto them of Da-
mascus, and at Jerusalem, and
throughout all the coasts of Judæa, and
then to the Gentiles, that they should
repent and turn to God, and do works
meet for repentance.
21 For these causes the Jews caught
me in the temple, and went about to kill
me.
22 Having therefore obtained help of
God, I continue unto this day, witness-
ing both to small and great, saying
none other things than those which the
prophets and Moses did say should
come:
23 That Christ should suffer, *and* that
he should be the first that should rise
from the dead, and should shew light
unto the people, and to the Gentiles.
24 ¶And as he thus spake for himself,
Fĕs'tus said with a loud voice, Paul,
thou art beside thyself; much learning
doth make thee mad.
25 But he said, I am not mad, most
noble Fĕs'tus; but speak forth the
words of truth and soberness.
26 For the king knoweth of these
things, before whom also I speak
freely: for I am persuaded that none of
these things are hidden from him; for
this thing was not done in a corner.
27 King A-grĭp'pa, believest thou the
prophets? I know that thou believest.
28 Then A-grĭp'pa said unto Paul, Al-
most thou persuadest me to be a Chris-
tian.
29 And Paul said, I would to God, that
not only thou, but also all that hear me
this day, were both almost, and altogeth-
er such as I am, except these bonds.
30 And when he had thus spoken, the
king rose up, and the governor, and
Bernice, and they that sat with them:
31 And when they were gone aside,
they talked between themselves,
saying, This man doeth nothing worthy
of death or of bonds.
32 Then said A-grĭp'pa unto Fĕs'tus,
This man might have been set at lib-
erty, if he had not appealed unto
Cæsar.

CHAPTER 27

AND when it was determined that we
should sail into Italy, they delivered
Paul and certain other prisoners unto
one named Julius a centurion of Augus-
tus' band.
2 And entering into a ship of Ăd-ra-
mўt'tĭ-um, we launched, meaning to
sail by the coasts of Asia; *one* Ăr-ĭs-
tär'chus, a Macedonian of Thĕs-sa-lo-
nī'ca, being with us.

3 And the next *day* we touched at Sī′don. And Julius courteously entreated Paul, and gave *him* liberty to go unto his friends to refresh himself.
4 And when we had launched from thence, we sailed under Cyprus, because the winds were contrary.
5 And when we had sailed over the sea of Ċĭ-lĭ′ċia and Păm-phȳl′ĭ-a, we came to Mȳ′ra, *a city* of Ly′cia.
6 And there the centurion found a ship of Alexandria sailing into Italy; and he put us therein.
7 And when we had sailed slowly many days, and scarce were come over against Cnī′dus, the wind not suffering us, we sailed under Crete, over against Săl-mō′ne;
8 And, hardly passing it, came unto a place which is called The fair havens; nigh whereunto was the city *of* La-sē′a.
9 ¶Now when much time was spent, and when sailing was now dangerous, because the fast was now already past, Paul admonished *them,*
10 And said unto them, Sirs, I perceive that this voyage will be with hurt and much damage, not only of the lading and ship, but also of our lives.
11 Nevertheless the centurion believed the master and the owner of the ship, more than those things which were spoken by Paul.
12 And because the haven was not commodious to winter in, the more part advised to depart thence also, if by any means they might attain to Phenī′ċe, *and there* to winter; *which is* an haven of Crete, and lieth toward the south west and north west.
13 And when the south wind blew softly, supposing that they had obtained *their* purpose, loosing *thence,* they sailed close by Crete.
14 But not long after there arose against it a tempestuous wind, called Eū-rŏc′lȳ-dŏn.
15 And when the ship was caught, and could not bear up into the wind, we let *her* drive.
16 And running under a certain island which is called Clau′da, we had much work to come by the boat:
17 Which when they had taken up, they used helps, undergirding the ship; and, fearing lest they should fall into the quicksands, strake sail, and so were driven.
18 And we being exceedingly tossed with a tempest, the next *day* they lightened the ship;
19 And the third *day* we cast out with our own hands the tackling of the ship.
20 And when neither sun nor stars in many days appeared, and no small tempest lay on *us,* all hope that we should be saved was then taken away.
21 ¶But after long abstinence Paul stood forth in the midst of them, and said, Sirs, ye should have hearkened unto me, and not have loosed from Crete, and to have gained this harm and loss.
22 And now I exhort you to be of good cheer: for there shall be no loss of *any man's* life among you, but of the ship.
23 For there stood by me this night the angel of God, whose I am, and whom I serve,
24 Saying, Fear not, Paul; thou must be brought before Cæsar: and, lo, God hath given thee all them that sail with thee.
25 Wherefore, sirs, be of good cheer: for I believe God, that it shall be even as it was told me.
26 Howbeit we must be cast upon a certain island.
27 But when the fourteenth night was come, as we were driven up and down in Ā′drĭ-a, about midnight the shipmen deemed that they drew near to some country;
28 And sounded, and found *it* twenty fathoms: and when they had gone a little further, they sounded again, and found *it* fifteen fathoms.
29 Then fearing lest we should have fallen upon rocks, they cast four anchors out of the stern, and wished for the day.
30 And as the shipmen were about to flee out of the ship, when they had let down the boat into the sea, under colour as though they would have cast anchors out of the foreship,
31 Paul said to the centurion and to the soldiers, Except these abide in the ship, ye cannot be saved.
32 Then the soldiers cut off the ropes of the boat, and let her fall off.
33 And while the day was coming on, Paul besought *them* all to take meat, saying, This day is the fourteenth day that ye have tarried and continued fasting, having taken nothing.
34 Wherefore I pray you to take *some* meat: for this is for your health: for there shall not an hair fall from the head of any of you.
35 And when he had thus spoken, he took bread, and gave thanks to God in presence of them all: and when he had broken *it,* he began to eat.
36 Then were they all of good cheer, and they also took *some* meat.
37 And we were in all in the ship two hundred threescore and sixteen souls.
38 And when they had eaten enough,

they lightened the ship, and cast out the wheat into the sea.

39 And when it was day, they knew not the land: but they discovered a certain creek with a shore, into the which they were minded, if it were possible, to thrust in the ship.

40 And when they had taken up the anchors, they committed *themselves* unto the sea, and loosed the rudder bands, and hoised up the mainsail to the wind, and made toward shore.

41 And falling into a place where two seas met, they ran the ship aground; and the forepart stuck fast, and remained unmoveable, but the hinder part was broken with the violence of the waves.

42 And the soldiers' counsel was to kill the prisoners, lest any of them should swim out, and escape.

43 But the centurion, willing to save Paul, kept them from *their* purpose; and commanded that they which could swim should cast *themselves* first *into the sea,* and get to land:

44 And the rest, some on boards, and some on *broken pieces* of the ship. And so it came to pass, that they escaped all safe to land.

CHAPTER 28

AND when they were escaped, then they knew that the island was called Mĕl'ĭ-ta.

2 And the barbarous people shewed us no little kindness: for they kindled a fire, and received us every one, because of the present rain, and because of the cold.

3 And when Paul had gathered a bundle of sticks, and laid *them* on the fire, there came a viper out of the heat, and fastened on his hand.

4 And when the barbarians saw the *venomous* beast hang on his hand, they said among themselves, No doubt this man is a murderer, whom, though he hath escaped the sea, yet vengeance suffereth not to live.

5 And he shook off the beast into the fire, and felt no harm.

6 Howbeit they looked when he should have swollen, or fallen down dead suddenly: but after they had looked a great while, and saw no harm come to him, they changed their minds, and said that he was a god.

7 ¶In the same quarters were possessions of the chief man of the island, whose name was Publius; who received us, and lodged us three days courteously.

8 And it came to pass, that the father of Publius lay sick of a fever and of a bloody flux: to whom Paul entered in, and prayed, and laid his hands on him, and healed him.

9 So when this was done, others also, which had diseases in the island, came, and were healed:

10 Who also honoured us with many honours; and when we departed, they laded *us* with such things as were necessary.

11 ¶And after three months we departed in a ship of Alexandria, which had wintered in the isle, whose sign was Castor and Pollux.

12 And landing at Syracuse, we tarried *there* three days.

13 And from thence we fetched a compass, and came to Rhē'gi-um: and after one day the south wind blew, and we came the next day to Pū-tē'o-lī:

14 Where we found brethren, and were desired to tarry with them seven days: and so we went toward Rome.

15 And from thence, when the brethren heard of us, they came to meet us as far as Ăp'pĭ-ī fō'rŭm, and The three taverns: whom when Paul saw, he thanked God, and took courage.

16 And when we came to Rome, the centurion delivered the prisoners to the captain of the guard: but Paul was suffered to dwell by himself with a soldier that kept him.

17 And it came to pass, that after three days Paul called the chief of the Jews together: and when they were come together, he said unto them, Men *and* brethren, though I have committed nothing against the people, or customs of our fathers, yet was I delivered prisoner from Jerusalem into the hands of the Romans.

18 Who, when they had examined me, would have let *me* go, because there was no cause of death in me.

19 But when the Jews spake against *it,* I was constrained to appeal unto Cæsar; not that I had ought to accuse my nation of.

20 For this cause therefore have I called for you, to see *you,* and to speak with *you:* because that for the hope of Israel I am bound with this chain.

21 And they said unto him, We neither received letters out of Judæa concerning thee, neither any of the brethren that came shewed or spake any harm of thee.

22 But we desire to hear of thee what thou thinkest: for as concerning this sect, we know that every where it is spoken against.

23 And when they had appointed him a day, there came many to him into *his* lodging; to whom he expounded and

testified the kingdom of God, persuading them concerning Jesus, both out of the law of Moses, and *out of* the prophets, from morning till evening.

24 And some believed the things which were spoken, and some believed not.

25 And when they agreed not among themselves, they departed, after that Paul had spoken one word, Well spake the Holy Ghost by E-śā'ias the prophet unto our fathers,

26 Saying, Go unto this people, and say, Hearing ye shall hear, and shall not understand; and seeing ye shall see, and not perceive:

27 For the heart of this people is waxed gross, and their ears are dull of hearing, and their eyes have they closed; lest they should see with *their* eyes, and hear with *their* ears, and understand with *their* heart, and should be converted, and I should heal them.

28 Be it known therefore unto you, that the salvation of God is sent unto the Gentiles, and *that* they will hear it.

29 And when he had said these words, the Jews departed, and had great reasoning among themselves.

30 ¶And Paul dwelt two whole years in his own hired house, and received all that came in unto him,

31 Preaching the kingdom of God, and teaching those things which concern the Lord Jesus Christ, with all confidence, no man forbidding him.

THE EPISTLE OF PAUL THE APOSTLE TO THE

ROMANS

CHAPTER 1

PAUL, a servant of Jesus Christ, called *to be* an apostle, separated unto the gospel of God,

2 (Which he had promised afore by his prophets in the holy scriptures,)

3 Concerning his Son Jesus Christ our Lord, which was made of the seed of David according to the flesh;

4 And declared *to be* the Son of God with power, according to the spirit of holiness, by the resurrection from the dead:

5 By whom we have received grace and apostleship, for obedience to the faith among all nations, for his name:

6 Among whom are ye also the called of Jesus Christ:

7 To all that be in Rome, beloved of God, called *to be* saints: Grace to you and peace from God our Father, and the Lord Jesus Christ.

8 First, I thank my God through Jesus Christ for you all, that your faith is spoken of throughout the whole world.

9 For God is my witness, whom I serve with my spirit in the gospel of his Son, that without ceasing I make mention of you always in my prayers;

10 Making request, if by any means now at length I might have a prosperous journey by the will of God to come unto you.

11 For I long to see you, that I may impart unto you some spiritual gift, to the end ye may be established;

12 That is, that I may be comforted together with you by the mutual faith both of you and me.

13 Now I would not have you ignorant, brethren, that oftentimes I purposed to come unto you, (but was let hitherto,) that I might have some fruit among you also, even as among other Gentiles.

14 I am debtor both to the Greeks, and to the Barbarians; both to the wise, and to the unwise.

15 So, as much as in me is, I am ready to preach the gospel to you that are at Rome also.

16 For I am not ashamed of the gospel of Christ: for it is the power of God unto salvation to every one that believeth; to the Jew first, and also to the Greek.

17 For therein is the righteousness of God revealed from faith to faith: as it is written, The just shall live by faith.

18 For the wrath of God is revealed from heaven against all ungodliness and unrighteousness of men, who hold the truth in unrighteousness;

19 Because that which may be known of God is manifest in them; for God hath shewed *it* unto them.

20 For the invisible things of him from the creation of the world are clearly seen, being understood by the things that are made, *even* his eternal power and Godhead; so that they are without excuse:

21 Because that, when they knew God, they glorified *him* not as God, neither were thankful; but became vain in their imaginations, and their foolish heart was darkened.

22 Professing themselves to be wise, they became fools,

23 And changed the glory of the uncorruptible God into an image made like to corruptible man, and to birds,

and fourfooted beasts, and creeping things.

24 Wherefore God also gave them up to uncleanness through the lusts of their own hearts, to dishonour their own bodies between themselves:

25 Who changed the truth of God into a lie, and worshipped and served the creature more than the Creator, who is blessed for ever. Amen.

26 For this cause God gave them up unto vile affections: for even their women did change the natural use into that which is against nature:

27 And likewise also the men, leaving the natural use of the woman, burned in their lust one toward another; men with men working that which is unseemly, and receiving in themselves that recompence of their error which was meet.

28 And even as they did not like to retain God in *their* knowledge, God gave them over to a reprobate mind, to do those things which are not convenient;

29 Being filled with all unrighteousness, fornication, wickedness, covetousness, maliciousness; full of envy, murder, debate, deceit, malignity; whisperers,

30 Backbiters, haters of God, despiteful, proud, boasters, inventors of evil things, disobedient to parents,

31 Without understanding, covenant breakers, without natural affection, implacable, unmerciful:

32 Who knowing the judgment of God, that they which commit such things are worthy of death, not only do the same, but have pleasure in them that do them.

CHAPTER 2

THEREFORE thou art inexcusable, O man, whosoever thou art that judgest: for wherein thou judgest another, thou condemnest thyself; for thou that judgest doest the same things.

2 But we are sure that the judgment of God is according to truth against them which commit such things.

3 And thinkest thou this, O man, that judgest them which do such things, and doest the same, that thou shalt escape the judgment of God?

4 Or despisest thou the riches of his goodness and forbearance and longsuffering; not knowing that the goodness of God leadeth thee to repentance?

5 But after thy hardness and impenitent heart treasurest up unto thyself wrath against the day of wrath and revelation of the righteous judgment of God;

6 Who will render to every man according to his deeds:

7 To them who by patient continuance in well doing seek for glory and honour and immortality, eternal life:

8 But unto them that are contentious, and do not obey the truth, but obey unrighteousness, indignation and wrath,

9 Tribulation and anguish, upon every soul of man that doeth evil, of the Jew first, and also of the Gentile;

10 But glory, honour, and peace, to every man that worketh good, to the Jew first, and also to the Gentile:

11 For there is no respect of persons with God.

12 For as many as have sinned without law shall also perish without law: and as many as have sinned in the law shall be judged by the law;

13 (For not the hearers of the law *are* just before God, but the doers of the law shall be justified.

14 For when the Gentiles, which have not the law, do by nature the things contained in the law, these, having not the law, are a law unto themselves:

15 Which shew the work of the law written in their hearts, their conscience also bearing witness, and *their* thoughts the mean while accusing or else excusing one another;)

16 In the day when God shall judge the secrets of men by Jesus Christ according to my gospel.

17 Behold, thou art called a Jew, and restest in the law, and makest thy boast of God,

18 And knowest *his* will, and approvest the things that are more excellent, being instructed out of the law;

19 And art confident that thou thyself art a guide of the blind, a light of them which are in darkness,

20 An instructor of the foolish, a teacher of babes, which hast the form of knowledge and of the truth in the law.

21 Thou therefore which teachest another, teachest thou not thyself? thou that preachest a man should not steal, dost thou steal?

22 Thou that sayest a man should not commit adultery, dost thou commit adultery? thou that abhorrest idols, dost thou commit sacrilege?

23 Thou that makest thy boast of the law, through breaking the law dishonourest thou God?

24 For the name of God is blasphemed among the Gentiles through you, as it is written.

25 For circumcision verily profiteth, if thou keep the law: but if thou be a breaker of the law, thy circumcision is made uncircumcision.

26 Therefore if the uncircumcision
keep the righteousness of the law, shall
not his uncircumcision be counted for
circumcision?
27 And shall not uncircumcision
which is by nature, if it fulfil the law,
judge thee, who by the letter and cir-
cumcision dost transgress the law?
28 For he is not a Jew, which is one
outwardly; neither *is that* circumci-
sion, which is outward in the flesh:
29 But he *is* a Jew, which is one in-
wardly; and circumcision *is that* of the
heart, in the spirit, *and* not in the letter;
whose praise *is* not of men, but of God.

CHAPTER 3

WHAT advantage then hath the Jew?
or what profit *is there* of circumcision?
2 Much every way: chiefly, because
that unto them were committed the
oracles of God.
3 For what if some did not believe?
shall their unbelief make the faith of
God without effect?
4 God forbid: yea, let God be true, but
every man a liar; as it is written, That
thou mightest be justified in thy
sayings, and mightest overcome when
thou art judged.
5 But if our unrighteousness com-
mend the righteousness of God, what
shall we say? *Is* God unrighteous who
taketh vengeance? (I speak as a man)
6 God forbid: for then how shall God
judge the world?
7 For if the truth of God hath more
abounded through my lie unto his
glory; why yet am I also judged as a
sinner?
8 And not *rather*, (as we be slan-
derously reported, and as some affirm
that we say,) Let us do evil, that good
may come? whose damnation is just.
9 What then? are we better *than
they?* No, in no wise: for we have before
proved both Jews and Gentiles, that
they are all under sin;
10 As it is written, There is none
righteous, no, not one:
11 There is none that understandeth,
there is none that seeketh after God.
12 They are all gone out of the way,
they are together become unprofitable;
there is none that doeth good, no, not
one.
13 Their throat *is* an open sepulchre;
with their tongues they have used de-
ceit; the poison of asps *is* under their
lips:
14 Whose mouth *is* full of cursing and
bitterness:
15 Their feet *are* swift to shed blood:
16 Destruction and misery *are* in
their ways:
17 And the way of peace have they
not known:
18 There is no fear of God before their
eyes.
19 Now we know that what things
soever the law saith, it saith to them
who are under the law: that every
mouth may be stopped, and all the
world may become guilty before God.
20 Therefore by the deeds of the law
there shall no flesh be justified in his
sight: for by the law *is* the knowledge of
sin.
21 But now the righteousness of God
without the law is manifested, being
witnessed by the law and the prophets;
22 Even the righteousness of God
which is by faith of Jesus Christ unto
all and upon all them that believe: for
there is no difference:
23 For all have sinned, and come
short of the glory of God;
24 Being justified freely by his grace
through the redemption that is in
Christ Jesus:
25 Whom God hath set forth *to be* a
propitiation through faith in his blood,
to declare his righteousness for the re-
mission of sins that are past, through
the forbearance of God;
26 To declare, *I say*, at this time his
righteousness: that he might be just,
and the justifier of him which believeth
in Jesus.
27 Where *is* boasting then? It is ex-
cluded. By what law? of works? Nay:
but by the law of faith.
28 Therefore we conclude that a man
is justified by faith without the deeds of
the law.
29 *Is he* the God of the Jews only? *is
he* not also of the Gentiles? Yes, of the
Gentiles also:
30 Seeing *it is* one God, which shall
justify the circumcision by faith, and
uncircumcision through faith.
31 Do we then make void the law
through faith? God forbid: yea, we es-
tablish the law.

CHAPTER 4

WHAT shall we say then that Abraham
our father, as pertaining to the flesh,
hath found?
2 For if Abraham were justified by
works, he hath *whereof* to glory; but
not before God.
3 For what saith the scripture? Abra-
ham believed God, and it was counted
unto him for righteousness.
4 Now to him that worketh is the re-
ward not reckoned of grace, but of
debt.
5 But to him that worketh not, but be-
lieveth on him that justifieth the un-

godly, his faith is counted for
righteousness.
6 Even as David also describeth the
blessedness of the man, unto whom
God imputeth righteousness without
works,
7 *Saying*, Blessed *are* they whose in-
iquities are forgiven, and whose sins are
covered.
8 Blessed *is* the man to whom the
Lord will not impute sin.
9 *Cometh* this blessedness then upon
the circumcision *only*, or upon the un-
circumcision also? for we say that faith
was reckoned to Abraham for
righteousness.
10 How was it then reckoned? when
he was in circumcision, or in uncircum-
cision? Not in circumcision, but in un-
circumcision.
11 And he received the sign of cir-
cumcision, a seal of the righteousness
of the faith which *he had yet* being un-
circumcised: that he might be the
father of all them that believe, though
they be not circumcised; that
righteousness might be imputed unto
them also:
12 And the father of circumcision to
them who are not of the circumcision
only, but who also walk in the steps of
that faith of our father Abraham, which
he had being *yet* uncircumcised.
13 For the promise, that he should be
the heir of the world, *was* not to Abra-
ham, or to his seed, through the law,
but through the righteousness of faith.
14 For if they which are of the law *be*
heirs, faith is made void, and the prom-
ise made of none effect:
15 Because the law worketh wrath:
for where no law is, *there is* no trans-
gression.
16 Therefore *it is* of faith, that *it*
might be by grace; to the end the prom-
ise might be sure to all the seed; not
to that only which is of the law, but to
that also which is of the faith of Abra-
ham; who is the father of us all,
17 (As it is written, I have made thee
a father of many nations,) before him
whom he believed, *even* God, who
quickeneth the dead, and calleth those
things which be not as though they
were.
18 Who against hope believed in
hope, that he might become the father
of many nations, according to that
which was spoken, So shall thy seed be.
19 And being not weak in faith, he
considered not his own body now dead,
when he was about an hundred years
old, neither yet the deadness of Sarah's
womb:
20 He staggered not at the promise of
God through unbelief; but was strong
in faith, giving glory to God;
21 And being fully persuaded that,
what he had promised, he was able also
to perform.
22 And therefore it was imputed to
him for righteousness.
23 Now it was not written for his sake
alone, that it was imputed to him;
24 But for us also, to whom it shall be
imputed, if we believe on him that
raised up Jesus our Lord from the dead;
25 Who was delivered for our of-
fences, and was raised again for our
justification.

CHAPTER 5

THEREFORE being justified by faith,
we have peace with God through our
Lord Jesus Christ:
2 By whom also we have access by
faith into this grace wherein we stand,
and rejoice in hope of the glory of God.
3 And not only *so*, but we glory in tribu-
lations also: knowing that tribula-
tion worketh patience;
4 And patience, experience; and ex-
perience, hope:
5 And hope maketh not ashamed; be-
cause the love of God is shed abroad in
our hearts by the Holy Ghost which is
given unto us.
6 For when we were yet without
strength, in due time Christ died for the
ungodly.
7 For scarcely for a righteous man
will one die: yet peradventure for a
good man some would even dare to die.
8 But God commendeth his love to-
ward us, in that, while we were yet sin-
ners, Christ died for us.
9 Much more then, being now jus-
tified by his blood, we shall be saved
from wrath through him.
10 For if, when we were enemies, we
were reconciled to God by the death of
his Son, much more, being reconciled,
we shall be saved by his life.
11 And not only *so*, but we also joy in
God through our Lord Jesus Christ, by
whom we have now received the atone-
ment.
12 Wherefore, as by one man sin en-
tered into the world, and death by sin;
and so death passed upon all men, for
that all have sinned:
13 (For until the law sin was in the
world: but sin is not imputed when
there is no law.
14 Nevertheless death reigned from
Adam to Moses, even over them that
had not sinned after the similitude of
Adam's transgression, who is the fig-
ure of him that was to come.
15 But not as the offence, so also *is*

the free gift. For if through the offence of one many be dead, much more the grace of God, and the gift by grace, *which is* by one man, Jesus Christ, hath abounded unto many.

16 And not as *it was* by one that sinned, *so is* the gift: for the judgment *was* by one to condemnation, but the free gift *is* of many offences unto justification.

17 For if by one man's offence death reigned by one; much more they which receive abundance of grace and of the gift of righteousness shall reign in life by one, Jesus Christ.)

18 Therefore as by the offence of one *judgment came* upon all men to condemnation; even so by the righteousness of one *the free gift came* upon all men unto justification of life.

19 For as by one man's disobedience many were made sinners, so by the obedience of one shall many be made righteous.

20 Moreover the law entered, that the offence might abound. But where sin abounded, grace did much more abound:

21 That as sin hath reigned unto death, even so might grace reign through righteousness unto eternal life by Jesus Christ our Lord.

CHAPTER 6

WHAT shall we say then? Shall we continue in sin, that grace may abound?

2 God forbid. How shall we, that are dead to sin, live any longer therein?

3 Know ye not, that so many of us as were baptized into Jesus Christ were baptized into his death?

4 Therefore we are buried with him by baptism into death: that like as Christ was raised up from the dead by the glory of the Father, even so we also should walk in newness of life.

5 For if we have been planted together in the likeness of his death, we shall be also *in the likeness* of *his* resurrection:

6 Knowing this, that our old man is crucified with *him*, that the body of sin might be destroyed, that henceforth we should not serve sin.

7 For he that is dead is freed from sin.

8 Now if we be dead with Christ, we believe that we shall also live with him:

9 Knowing that Christ being raised from the dead dieth no more; death hath no more dominion over him.

10 For in that he died, he died unto sin once: but in that he liveth, he liveth unto God.

11 Likewise reckon ye also yourselves to be dead indeed unto sin, but alive unto God through Jesus Christ our Lord.

12 Let not sin therefore reign in your mortal body, that ye should obey it in the lusts thereof.

13 Neither yield ye your members *as* instruments of unrighteousness unto sin: but yield yourselves unto God, as those that are alive from the dead, and your members *as* instruments of righteousness unto God.

14 For sin shall not have dominion over you: for ye are not under the law, but under grace.

15 What then? shall we sin, because we are not under the law, but under grace? God forbid.

16 Know ye not, that to whom ye yield yourselves servants to obey, his servants ye are to whom ye obey; whether of sin unto death, or of obedience unto righteousness?

17 But God be thanked, that ye were the servants of sin, but ye have obeyed from the heart that form of doctrine which was delivered you.

18 Being then made free from sin, ye became the servants of righteousness.

19 I speak after the manner of men because of the infirmity of your flesh: for as ye have yielded your members servants to uncleanness and to iniquity unto iniquity; even so now yield your members servants to righteousness unto holiness.

20 For when ye were the servants of sin, ye were free from righteousness.

21 What fruit had ye then in those things whereof ye are now ashamed? for the end of those things *is* death.

22 But now being made free from sin, and become servants to God, ye have your fruit unto holiness, and the end everlasting life.

23 For the wages of sin *is* death; but the gift of God *is* eternal life through Jesus Christ our Lord.

CHAPTER 7

KNOW ye not, brethren, (for I speak to them that know the law,) how that the law hath dominion over a man as long as he liveth?

2 For the woman which hath an husband is bound by the law to *her* husband so long as he liveth; but if the husband be dead, she is loosed from the law of *her* husband.

3 So then if, while *her* husband liveth, she be married to another man, she shall be called an adulteress: but if her husband be dead, she is free from that law; so that she is no adulteress, though she be married to another man.

4 Wherefore, my brethren, ye also
are become dead to the law by the body
of Christ; that ye should be married to
another, *even* to him who is raised from
the dead, that we should bring forth
fruit unto God.
5 For when we were in the flesh, the
motions of sins, which were by the law,
did work in our members to bring forth
fruit unto death.
6 But now we are delivered from the
law, that being dead wherein we were
held; that we should serve in newness
of spirit, and not *in* the oldness of the
letter.
7 What shall we say then? *Is* the law
sin? God forbid. Nay, I had not known
sin, but by the law: for I had not known
lust, except the law had said, Thou
shalt not covet.
8 But sin, taking occasion by the
commandment, wrought in me all
manner of concupiscence. For without
the law sin *was* dead.
9 For I was alive without the law
once: but when the commandment
came, sin revived, and I died.
10 And the commandment, which
was ordained to life, I found *to be* unto
death.
11 For sin, taking occasion by the
commandment, deceived me, and by it
slew *me*.
12 Wherefore the law *is* holy, and the
commandment holy, and just, and
good.
13 Was then that which is good made
death unto me? God forbid. But sin,
that it might appear sin, working death
in me by that which is good; that sin by
the commandment might become ex-
ceeding sinful.
14 For we know that the law is spiri-
tual: but I am carnal, sold under sin.
15 For that which I do I allow not: for
what I would, that do I not; but what I
hate, that do I.
16 If then I do that which I would not,
I consent unto the law that *it is* good.
17 Now then it is no more I that do it,
but sin that dwelleth in me.
18 For I know that in me (that is, in
my flesh,) dwelleth no good thing: for
to will is present with me; but *how* to
perform that which is good I find not.
19 For the good that I would I do not:
but the evil which I would not, that I do.
20 Now if I do that I would not, it is no
more I that do it, but sin that dwelleth
in me.
21 I find then a law, that, when I
would do good, evil is present with me.
22 For I delight in the law of God af-
ter the inward man:
23 But I see another law in my mem-
bers, warring against the law of my
mind, and bringing me into captivity to
the law of sin which is in my members.
24 O wretched man that I am! who
shall deliver me from the body of this
death?
25 I thank God through Jesus Christ
our Lord. So then with the mind I my-
self serve the law of God; but with the
flesh the law of sin.

CHAPTER 8

THERE is therefore now no condemna-
tion to them which are in Christ Jesus,
who walk not after the flesh, but after
the Spirit.
2 For the law of the Spirit of life in
Christ Jesus hath made me free from
the law of sin and death.
3 For what the law could not do, in
that it was weak through the flesh, God
sending his own Son in the likeness of
sinful flesh, and for sin, condemned sin
in the flesh:
4 That the righteousness of the law
might be fulfilled in us, who walk not
after the flesh, but after the Spirit.
5 For they that are after the flesh do
mind the things of the flesh; but they
that are after the Spirit the things of the
Spirit.
6 For to be carnally minded *is* death;
but to be spiritually minded *is* life and
peace.
7 Because the carnal mind *is* enmity
against God: for it is not subject to the
law of God, neither indeed can be.
8 So then they that are in the flesh
cannot please God.
9 But ye are not in the flesh, but in the
Spirit, if so be that the Spirit of God
dwell in you. Now if any man have not
the Spirit of Christ, he is none of his.
10 And if Christ *be* in you, the body *is*
dead because of sin; but the Spirit *is* life
because of righteousness.
11 But if the Spirit of him that raised
up Jesus from the dead dwell in you, he
that raised up Christ from the dead
shall also quicken your mortal bodies
by his Spirit that dwelleth in you.
12 Therefore, brethren, we are debt-
ors, not to the flesh, to live after the
flesh.
13 For if ye live after the flesh, ye
shall die: but if ye through the Spirit do
mortify the deeds of the body, ye shall
live.
14 For as many as are led by the
Spirit of God, they are the sons of God.
15 For ye have not received the spirit
of bondage again to fear; but ye have
received the Spirit of adoption, where-
by we cry, Abba, Father.
16 The Spirit itself beareth witness

with our spirit, that we are the children of God:

17 And if children, then heirs; heirs of God, and joint-heirs with Christ; if so be that we suffer with *him*, that we may be also glorified together.

18 For I reckon that the sufferings of this present time *are* not worthy *to be compared* with the glory which shall be revealed in us.

19 For the earnest expectation of the creature waiteth for the manifestation of the sons of God.

20 For the creature was made subject to vanity, not willingly, but by reason of him who hath subjected *the same* in hope,

21 Because the creature itself also shall be delivered from the bondage of corruption into the glorious liberty of the children of God.

22 For we know that the whole creation groaneth and travaileth in pain together until now.

23 And not only *they*, but ourselves also, which have the firstfruits of the Spirit, even we ourselves groan within ourselves, waiting for the adoption, *to wit*, the redemption of our body.

24 For we are saved by hope: but hope that is seen is not hope: for what a man seeth, why doth he yet hope for?

25 But if we hope for that we see not, *then* do we with patience wait for *it*.

26 Likewise the Spirit also helpeth our infirmities: for we know not what we should pray for as we ought: but the Spirit itself maketh intercession for us with groanings which cannot be uttered.

27 And he that searcheth the hearts knoweth what *is* the mind of the Spirit, because he maketh intercession for the saints according to *the will of* God.

28 And we know that all things work together for good to them that love God, to them who are the called according to *his* purpose.

29 For whom he did foreknow, he also did predestinate *to be* conformed to the image of his Son, that he might be the firstborn among many brethren.

30 Moreover whom he did predestinate, them he also called: and whom he called, them he also justified: and whom he justified, them he also glorified.

31 What shall we then say to these things? If God *be* for us, who *can be* against us?

32 He that spared not his own Son, but delivered him up for us all, how shall he not with him also freely give us all things?

33 Who shall lay any thing to the charge of God's elect? *It is* God that justifieth.

34 Who *is* he that condemneth? *It is* Christ that died, yea rather, that is risen again, who is even at the right hand of God, who also maketh intercession for us.

35 Who shall separate us from the love of Christ? *shall* tribulation, or distress, or persecution, or famine, or nakedness, or peril, or sword?

36 As it is written, For thy sake we are killed all the day long; we are accounted as sheep for the slaughter.

37 Nay, in all these things we are more than conquerors through him that loved us.

38 For I am persuaded, that neither death, nor life, nor angels, nor principalities, nor powers, nor things present, nor things to come,

39 Nor height, nor depth, nor any other creature, shall be able to separate us from the love of God, which is in Christ Jesus our Lord.

CHAPTER 9

I SAY the truth in Christ, I lie not, my conscience also bearing me witness in the Holy Ghost,

2 That I have great heaviness and continual sorrow in my heart.

3 For I could wish that myself were accursed from Christ for my brethren, my kinsmen according to the flesh:

4 Who are Israelites; to whom *pertaineth* the adoption, and the glory, and the covenants, and the giving of the law, and the service *of God*, and the promises;

5 Whose *are* the fathers, and of whom as concerning the flesh Christ *came*, who is over all, God blessed for ever. Amen.

6 Not as though the word of God hath taken none effect. For they *are* not all Israel, which are of Israel:

7 Neither, because they are the seed of Abraham, *are they* all children: but, In Isaac shall thy seed be called.

8 That is, They which are the children of the flesh, these *are* not the children of God: but the children of the promise are counted for the seed.

9 For this *is* the word of promise, At this time will I come, and Sarah shall have a son.

10 And not only *this;* but when Rebecca also had conceived by one, *even* by our father Isaac;

11 (For *the children* being not yet born, neither having done any good or evil, that the purpose of God according to election might stand, not of works, but of him that calleth;)

12 It was said unto her, The elder
shall serve the younger.
13 As it is written, Jacob have I loved,
but Esau have I hated.
14 What shall we say then? *Is there*
unrighteousness with God? God forbid.
15 For he saith to Moses, I will have
mercy on whom I will have mercy, and
I will have compassion on whom I will
have compassion.
16 So then *it is* not of him that willeth,
nor of him that runneth, but of God that
sheweth mercy.
17 For the scripture saith unto
Pharaoh, Even for this same purpose
have I raised thee up, that I might shew
my power in thee, and that my name
might be declared throughout all the
earth.
18 Therefore hath he mercy on whom
he will *have mercy*, and whom he will
he hardeneth.
19 Thou wilt say then unto me, Why
doth he yet find fault? For who hath re-
sisted his will?
20 Nay but, O man, who art thou that
repliest against God? Shall the thing
formed say to him that formed *it*, Why
hast thou made me thus?
21 Hath not the potter power over the
clay, of the same lump to make one ves-
sel unto honour, and another unto
dishonour?
22 *What* if God, willing to shew *his*
wrath, and to make his power known,
endured with much longsuffering the
vessels of wrath fitted to destruction:
23 And that he might make known
the riches of his glory on the vessels of
mercy, which he had afore prepared
unto glory,
24 Even us, whom he hath called, not
of the Jews only, but also of the Gen-
tiles?
25 As he saith also in Ō'ṡee, I will call
them my people, which were not my
people; and her beloved, which was not
beloved.
26 And it shall come to pass, *that* in
the place where it was said unto them,
Ye *are* not my people; there shall they
be called the children of the living God.
27 E-ṡā'ias also crieth concerning
Israel, Though the number of the chil-
dren of Israel be as the sand of the sea,
a remnant shall be saved:
28 For he will finish the work, and cut
it short in righteousness: because a
short work will the Lord make upon the
earth.
29 And as E-ṡā'ias said before, Ex-
cept the Lord of Săb'a-ŏth had left us a
seed, we had been as Sŏd'o-ma, and
been made like unto Go-mŏr'rha.
30 What shall we say then? That the
Gentiles, which followed not after
righteousness, have attained to
righteousness, even the righteousness
which is of faith.
31 But Israel, which followed after
the law of righteousness, hath not at-
tained to the law of righteousness.
32 Wherefore? Because *they sought
it* not by faith, but as it were by the
works of the law. For they stumbled at
that stumblingstone;
33 As it is written, Behold, I lay in
Sion a stumblingstone and rock of of-
fence: and whosoever believeth on him
shall not be ashamed.

CHAPTER 10

BRETHREN, my heart's desire and
prayer to God for Israel is, that they
might be saved.
2 For I bear them record that they
have a zeal of God, but not according to
knowledge.
3 For they being ignorant of God's
righteousness, and going about to es-
tablish their own righteousness, have
not submitted themselves unto the
righteousness of God.
4 For Christ *is* the end of the law for
righteousness to every one that believ-
eth.
5 For Moses describeth the right-
eousness which is of the law, That the
man which doeth those things shall live
by them.
6 But the righteousness which is of
faith speaketh on this wise, Say not in
thine heart, Who shall ascend into
heaven? (that is, to bring Christ down
from above:)
7 Or, Who shall descend into the
deep? (that is, to bring up Christ again
from the dead.)
8 But what saith it? The word is nigh
thee, *even* in thy mouth, and in thy
heart: that is, the word of faith, which
we preach;
9 That if thou shalt confess with thy
mouth the Lord Jesus, and shalt believe
in thine heart that God hath raised him
from the dead, thou shalt be saved.
10 For with the heart man believeth
unto righteousness; and with the
mouth confession is made unto salva-
tion.
11 For the scripture saith, Whosoever
believeth on him shall not be
ashamed.
12 For there is no difference between
the Jew and the Greek: for the same
Lord over all is rich unto all that call
upon him.
13 For whosoever shall call upon the
name of the Lord shall be saved.
14 How then shall they call on him in

whom they have not believed? and how
shall they believe in him of whom they
have not heard? and how shall they
hear without a preacher?
15 And how shall they preach, except
they be sent? as it is written, How beau-
tiful are the feet of them that preach the
gospel of peace, and bring glad tidings
of good things!
16 But they have not all obeyed the
gospel. For E-ṡā'ias saith, Lord, who
hath believed our report?
17 So then faith *cometh* by hearing,
and hearing by the word of God.
18 But I say, Have they not heard?
Yes verily, their sound went into all the
earth, and their words unto the ends of
the world.
19 But I say, Did not Israel know?
First Moses saith, I will provoke you to
jealousy by *them that are* no people,
and by a foolish nation I will anger you.
20 But E-ṡā'ias is very bold, and saith,
I was found of them that sought me
not; I was made manifest unto them
that asked not after me.
21 But to Israel he saith, All day long I
have stretched forth my hands unto a
disobedient and gainsaying people.

CHAPTER 11

I SAY then, Hath God cast away his
people? God forbid. For I also am an
Israelite, of the seed of Abraham, *of* the
tribe of Benjamin.
2 God hath not cast away his people
which he foreknew. Wot ye not what
the scripture saith of E-lī'as? how he
maketh intercession to God against
Israel, saying,
3 Lord, they have killed thy prophets,
and digged down thine altars; and I am
left alone, and they seek my life.
4 But what saith the answer of God
unto him? I have reserved to myself
seven thousand men, who have not
bowed the knee to *the image of* Bā'al.
5 Even so then at this present time
also there is a remnant according to the
election of grace.
6 And if by grace, then *is it* no more of
works: otherwise grace is no more
grace. But if *it be* of works, then is it no
more grace: otherwise work is no more
work.
7 What then? Israel hath not obtained
that which he seeketh for; but the elec-
tion hath obtained it, and the rest were
blinded
8 (According as it is written, God
hath given them the spirit of slumber,
eyes that they should not see, and ears
that they should not hear;) unto this
day.
9 And David saith, Let their table be
made a snare, and a trap, and a stum-
blingblock, and a recompence unto
them:
10 Let their eyes be darkened, that
they may not see, and bow down their
back alway.
11 I say then, Have they stumbled
that they should fall? God forbid: but
rather through their fall salvation *is*
come unto the Gentiles, for to provoke
them to jealousy.
12 Now if the fall of them *be* the
riches of the world, and the dimin-
ishing of them the riches of the Gen-
tiles; how much more their fulness?
13 For I speak to you Gentiles, inas-
much as I am the apostle of the Gen-
tiles, I magnify mine office:
14 If by any means I may provoke to
emulation *them which are* my flesh,
and might save some of them.
15 For if the casting away of them *be*
the reconciling of the world, what *shall*
the receiving *of them be*, but life from
the dead?
16 For if the firstfruit *be* holy, the
lump *is* also *holy:* and if the root *be*
holy, so *are* the branches.
17 And if some of the branches be
broken off, and thou, being a wild olive
tree, wert graffed in among them, and
with them partakest of the root and fat-
ness of the olive tree;
18 Boast not against the branches.
But if thou boast, thou bearest not the
root, but the root thee.
19 Thou wilt say then, The branches
were broken off, that I might be graffed
in.
20 Well; because of unbelief they
were broken off, and thou standest by
faith. Be not highminded, but fear:
21 For if God spared not the natural
branches, *take heed* lest he also spare
not thee.
22 Behold therefore the goodness
and severity of God: on them which
fell, severity; but toward thee, good-
ness, if thou continue in *his* goodness:
otherwise thou also shalt be cut off.
23 And they also, if they abide not
still in unbelief, shall be graffed in: for
God is able to graff them in again.
24 For if thou wert cut out of the olive
tree which is wild by nature, and wert
graffed contrary to nature into a good
olive tree: how much more shall these,
which be the natural *branches*, be
graffed into their own olive tree?
25 For I would not, brethren, that ye
should be ignorant of this mystery, lest
ye should be wise in your own conceits;
that blindness in part is happened to
Israel, until the fulness of the Gentiles
be come in.

26 And so all Israel shall be saved: as it is written, There shall come out of Sion the Deliverer, and shall turn away ungodliness from Jacob:

27 For this *is* my covenant unto them, when I shall take away their sins.

28 As concerning the gospel, *they are* enemies for your sakes: but as touching the election, *they are* beloved for the fathers' sakes.

29 For the gifts and calling of God *are* without repentance.

30 For as ye in times past have not believed God, yet have now obtained mercy through their unbelief:

31 Even so have these also now not believed, that through your mercy they also may obtain mercy.

32 For God hath concluded them all in unbelief, that he might have mercy upon all.

33 O the depth of the riches both of the wisdom and knowledge of God! how unsearchable *are* his judgments, and his ways past finding out!

34 For who hath known the mind of the Lord? or who hath been his counsellor?

35 Or who hath first given to him, and it shall be recompensed unto him again?

36 For of him, and through him, and to him, *are* all things: to whom *be* glory for ever. Amen.

CHAPTER 12

I BESEECH you therefore, brethren, by the mercies of God, that ye present your bodies a living sacrifice, holy, acceptable unto God, *which is* your reasonable service.

2 And be not conformed to this world: but be ye transformed by the renewing of your mind, that ye may prove what *is* that good, and acceptable, and perfect, will of God.

3 For I say, through the grace given unto me, to every man that is among you, not to think *of himself* more highly than he ought to think; but to think soberly, according as God hath dealt to every man the measure of faith.

4 For as we have many members in one body, and all members have not the same office:

5 So we, *being* many, are one body in Christ, and every one members one of another.

6 Having then gifts differing according to the grace that is given to us, whether prophecy, *let us prophesy* according to the proportion of faith;

7 Or ministry, *let us wait* on *our* ministering: or he that teacheth, on teaching;

8 Or he that exhorteth, on exhortation: he that giveth, *let him do it* with simplicity; he that ruleth, with diligence; he that sheweth mercy, with cheerfulness.

9 *Let* love be without dissimulation. Abhor that which is evil; cleave to that which is good.

10 *Be* kindly affectioned one to another with brotherly love; in honour preferring one another;

11 Not slothful in business; fervent in spirit; serving the Lord;

12 Rejoicing in hope; patient in tribulation; continuing instant in prayer;

13 Distributing to the necessity of saints; given to hospitality.

14 Bless them which persecute you: bless, and curse not.

15 Rejoice with them that do rejoice, and weep with them that weep.

16 *Be* of the same mind one toward another. Mind not high things, but condescend to men of low estate. Be not wise in your own conceits.

17 Recompense to no man evil for evil. Provide things honest in the sight of all men.

18 If it be possible, as much as lieth in you, live peaceably with all men.

19 Dearly beloved, avenge not yourselves, but *rather* give place unto wrath: for it is written, Vengeance *is* mine; I will repay, saith the Lord.

20 Therefore if thine enemy hunger, feed him; if he thirst, give him drink: for in so doing thou shalt heap coals of fire on his head.

21 Be not overcome of evil, but overcome evil with good.

CHAPTER 13

LET every soul be subject unto the higher powers. For there is no power but of God: the powers that be are ordained of God.

2 Whosoever therefore resisteth the power, resisteth the ordinance of God: and they that resist shall receive to themselves damnation.

3 For rulers are not a terror to good works, but to the evil. Wilt thou then not be afraid of the power? do that which is good, and thou shalt have praise of the same:

4 For he is the minister of God to thee for good. But if thou do that which is evil, be afraid; for he beareth not the sword in vain: for he is the minister of God, a revenger to *execute* wrath upon him that doeth evil.

5 Wherefore *ye* must needs be subject, not only for wrath, but also for conscience sake.

6 For for this cause pay ye tribute

also: for they are God's ministers, at-
tending continually upon this very
thing.
7 Render therefore to all their dues:
tribute to whom tribute *is due;* custom
to whom custom; fear to whom fear;
honour to whom honour.
8 Owe no man any thing, but to love
one another: for he that loveth another
hath fulfilled the law.
9 For this, Thou shalt not commit
adultery, Thou shalt not kill, Thou shalt
not steal, Thou shalt not bear false wit-
ness, Thou shalt not covet; and if *there
be* any other commandment, it is
briefly comprehended in this saying,
namely, Thou shalt love thy neighbour
as thyself.
10 Love worketh no ill to his neigh-
bour: therefore love *is* the fulfilling
of the law.
11 And that, knowing the time, that
now *it is* high time to awake out of
sleep: for now *is* our salvation nearer
than when we believed.
12 The night is far spent, the day is at
hand: let us therefore cast off the
works of darkness, and let us put on the
armour of light.
13 Let us walk honestly, as in the day;
not in rioting and drunkenness, not in
chambering and wantonness, not in
strife and envying.
14 But put ye on the Lord Jesus
Christ, and make not provision for the
flesh, to *fulfil* the lusts *thereof.*

CHAPTER 14

HIM that is weak in the faith receive ye,
but not to doubtful disputations.
2 For one believeth that he may eat
all things: another, who is weak, eateth
herbs.
3 Let not him that eateth despise him
that eateth not; and let not him which
eateth not judge him that eateth: for
God hath received him.
4 Who art thou that judgest another
man's servant? to his own master he
standeth or falleth. Yea, he shall be hold-
en up: for God is able to make him
stand.
5 One man esteemeth one day above
another: another esteemeth every day
alike. Let every man be fully persuaded
in his own mind.
6 He that regardeth the day, regard-
eth *it* unto the Lord; and he that regard-
eth not the day, to the Lord he doth
not regard *it.* He that eateth, eateth to
the Lord, for he giveth God thanks; and
he that eateth not, to the Lord he eateth
not, and giveth God thanks.
7 For none of us liveth to himself, and
no man dieth to himself.
8 For whether we live, we live unto
the Lord; and whether we die, we die
unto the Lord: whether we live there-
fore, or die, we are the Lord's.
9 For to this end Christ both died, and
rose, and revived, that he might be
Lord both of the dead and living.
10 But why dost thou judge thy
brother? or why dost thou set at nought
thy brother? for we shall all stand be-
fore the judgment seat of Christ.
11 For it is written, *As* I live, saith the
Lord, every knee shall bow to me, and
every tongue shall confess to God.
12 So then every one of us shall give
account of himself to God.
13 Let us not therefore judge one an-
other any more: but judge this rather,
that no man put a stumblingblock or an
occasion to fall in *his* brother's way.
14 I know, and am persuaded by the
Lord Jesus, that *there is* nothing un-
clean of itself: but to him that
esteemeth any thing to be unclean, to
him *it is* unclean.
15 But if thy brother be grieved with
thy meat, now walkest thou not chari-
tably. Destroy not him with thy meat,
for whom Christ died.
16 Let not then your good be evil spok-
en of:
17 For the kingdom of God is not
meat and drink; but righteousness, and
peace, and joy in the Holy Ghost.
18 For he that in these things serveth
Christ *is* acceptable to God, and ap-
proved of men.
19 Let us therefore follow after the
things which make for peace, and
things wherewith one may edify an-
other.
20 For meat destroy not the work of
God. All things indeed *are* pure; but *it is*
evil for that man who eateth with of-
fence.
21 *It is* good neither to eat flesh, nor
to drink wine, nor *any thing* whereby
thy brother stumbleth, or is offended,
or is made weak.
22 Hast thou faith? have *it* to thyself
before God. Happy *is* he that con-
demneth not himself in that thing
which he alloweth.
23 And he that doubteth is damned if
he eat, because *he eateth* not of faith:
for whatsoever *is* not of faith is sin.

CHAPTER 15

WE then that are strong ought to bear
the infirmities of the weak, and not to
please ourselves.
2 Let every one of us please *his* neigh-
bour for *his* good to edification.
3 For even Christ pleased not him-
self: but, as it is written, The

reproaches of them that reproached thee fell on me.

4 For whatsoever things were written aforetime were written for our learning, that we through patience and comfort of the scriptures might have hope.

5 Now the God of patience and consolation grant you to be likeminded one toward another according to Christ Jesus:

6 That ye may with one mind *and* one mouth glorify God, even the Father of our Lord Jesus Christ.

7 Wherefore receive ye one another, as Christ also received us to the glory of God.

8 Now I say that Jesus Christ was a minister of the circumcision for the truth of God, to confirm the promises *made* unto the fathers:

9 And that the Gentiles might glorify God for *his* mercy; as it is written, For this cause I will confess to thee among the Gentiles, and sing unto thy name.

10 And again he saith, Rejoice, ye Gentiles, with his people.

11 And again, Praise the Lord, all ye Gentiles; and laud him, all ye people.

12 And again, E-ṡā'ias saith, There shall be a root of Jesse, and he that shall rise to reign over the Gentiles; in him shall the Gentiles trust.

13 Now the God of hope fill you with all joy and peace in believing, that ye may abound in hope, through the power of the Holy Ghost.

14 And I myself also am persuaded of you, my brethren, that ye also are full of goodness, filled with all knowledge, able also to admonish one another.

15 Nevertheless, brethren, I have written the more boldly unto you in some sort, as putting you in mind, because of the grace that is given to me of God,

16 That I should be the minister of Jesus Christ to the Gentiles, ministering the gospel of God, that the offering up of the Gentiles might be acceptable, being sanctified by the Holy Ghost.

17 I have therefore whereof I may glory through Jesus Christ in those things which pertain to God.

18 For I will not dare to speak of any of those things which Christ hath not wrought by me, to make the Gentiles obedient, by word and deed,

19 Through mighty signs and wonders, by the power of the Spirit of God; so that from Jerusalem, and round about unto Ĭl-lўr'i-cum, I have fully preached the gospel of Christ.

20 Yea, so have I strived to preach the gospel, not where Christ was named, lest I should build upon another man's foundation:

21 But as it is written, To whom he was not spoken of, they shall see: and they that have not heard shall understand.

22 For which cause also I have been much hindered from coming to you.

23 But now having no more place in these parts, and having a great desire these many years to come unto you;

24 Whensoever I take my journey into Spain, I will come to you: for I trust to see you in my journey, and to be brought on my way thitherward by you, if first I be somewhat filled with your *company*.

25 But now I go unto Jerusalem to minister unto the saints.

26 For it hath pleased them of Macedonia and A-chā'ia to make a certain contribution for the poor saints which are at Jerusalem.

27 It hath pleased them verily; and their debtors they are. For if the Gentiles have been made partakers of their spiritual things, their duty is also to minister unto them in carnal things.

28 When therefore I have performed this, and have sealed to them this fruit, I will come by you into Spain.

29 And I am sure that, when I come unto you, I shall come in the fulness of the blessing of the gospel of Christ.

30 Now I beseech you, brethren, for the Lord Jesus Christ's sake, and for the love of the Spirit, that ye strive together with me in *your* prayers to God for me;

31 That I may be delivered from them that do not believe in Judæa; and that my service which *I have* for Jerusalem may be accepted of the saints;

32 That I may come unto you with joy by the will of God, and may with you be refreshed.

33 Now the God of peace *be* with you all. Amen.

CHAPTER 16

I COMMEND unto you Phebe our sister, which is a servant of the church which is at Ċĕn'chre-a:

2 That ye receive her in the Lord, as becometh saints, and that ye assist her in whatsoever business she hath need of you: for she hath been a succourer of many, and of myself also.

3 Greet Priscilla and Ăq'ui-la my helpers in Christ Jesus:

4 Who have for my life laid down their own necks: unto whom not only I give thanks, but also all the churches of the Gentiles.

5 Likewise *greet* the church that is in their house. Salute my well beloved E-pæn'e-tus, who is the first fruits of A-chā'ia unto Christ.

6 Greet Mary, who bestowed much labour on us.

7 Salute Ăn-drŏ-ni'cus and Junia, my kinsmen, and my fellowprisoners, who are of note among the apostles, who also were in Christ before me.

8 Greet Ăm'plĭ-as my beloved in the Lord.

9 Salute Ûr'bāne, our helper in Christ, and Stā'chȳs my beloved.

10 Salute A-pĕl'lēṡ approved in Christ. Salute them which are of Ăr-ĭs-tŏ-bū'lus' *household.*

11 Salute He-rō'dĭ-on my kinsman. Greet them that be of the *household* of När-ċĭs'sus, which are in the Lord.

12 Salute Trȳ-phē'na and Trȳ-phō'sa, who labour in the Lord. Salute the beloved Persis, which laboured much in the Lord.

13 Salute Rufus chosen in the Lord, and his mother and mine.

14 Salute A-sȳn'crĭ-tus, Phlĕ'gŏn, Her'mas, Păt'ro-bas, Her'mēs, and the brethren which are with them.

15 Salute Phĭ-lŏl'o-gus, and Julia, Ne're-us, and his sister, and Ō-lȳm'pas, and all the saints which are with them.

16 Salute one another with an holy kiss. The churches of Christ salute you.

17 Now I beseech you, brethren, mark them which cause divisions and offences contrary to the doctrine which ye have learned; and avoid them.

18 For they that are such serve not our Lord Jesus Christ, but their own belly; and by good words and fair speeches deceive the hearts of the simple.

19 For your obedience is come abroad unto all *men.* I am glad therefore on your behalf: but yet I would have you wise unto that which is good, and simple concerning evil.

20 And the God of peace shall bruise Satan under your feet shortly. The grace of our Lord Jesus Christ *be* with you. Amen.

21 Tĭ-mō'the-us my workfellow, and Lucius, and Jason, and Sō-sĭp'a-ter, my kinsmen, salute you.

22 I Ter'tĭus, who wrote *this* epistle, salute you in the Lord.

23 Gaius mine host, and of the whole church, saluteth you. E-răs'tus the chamberlain of the city saluteth you, and Quartus a brother.

24 The grace of our Lord Jesus Christ *be* with you all. Amen.

25 Now to him that is of power to stablish you according to my gospel, and the preaching of Jesus Christ, according to the revelation of the mystery, which was kept secret since the world began,

26 But now is made manifest, and by the scriptures of the prophets, according to the commandment of the everlasting God, made known to all nations for the obedience of faith:

27 To God only wise, *be* glory through Jesus Christ for ever. Amen.

Written to the Romans from Corinthus, *and sent* by Phebe servant of the church at Cenchrea.

THE FIRST EPISTLE OF PAUL THE APOSTLE TO THE

CORINTHIANS

CHAPTER 1

PAUL, called *to be* an apostle of Jesus Christ through the will of God, and Sŏs'the-nēṡ *our* brother,

2 Unto the church of God which is at Corinth, to them that are sanctified in Christ Jesus, called *to be* saints, with all that in every place call upon the name of Jesus Christ our Lord, both theirs and ours:

3 Grace *be* unto you, and peace, from God our Father, and *from* the Lord Jesus Christ.

4 I thank my God always on your behalf, for the grace of God which is given you by Jesus Christ;

5 That in every thing ye are enriched by him, in all utterance, and *in* all knowledge;

6 Even as the testimony of Christ was confirmed in you:

7 So that ye come behind in no gift; waiting for the coming of our Lord Jesus Christ:

8 Who shall also confirm you unto the end, *that ye may be* blameless in the day of our Lord Jesus Christ.

9 God *is* faithful, by whom ye were called unto the fellowship of his Son Jesus Christ our Lord.

10 Now I beseech you, brethren, by the name of our Lord Jesus Christ, that ye all speak the same thing, and *that* there be no divisions among you; but *that* ye be perfectly joined together in the same mind and in the same judgment.

11 For it hath been declared unto me of you, my brethren, by them *which are*

of the house of Chlō'e, that there are
contentions among you.
12 Now this I say, that every one of
you saith, I am of Paul; and I of Apollos;
and I of Cē'phas; and I of Christ.
13 Is Christ divided? was Paul
crucified for you? or were ye baptized
in the name of Paul?
14 I thank God that I baptized none of
you, but Crispus and Gaius;
15 Lest any should say that I had bap-
tized in mine own name.
16 And I baptized also the household
of Stĕph'a-nas: besides, I know not
whether I baptized any other.
17 For Christ sent me not to baptize,
but to preach the gospel: not with wis-
dom of words, lest the cross of Christ
should be made of none effect.
18 For the preaching of the cross is to
them that perish foolishness; but unto
us which are saved it is the power of
God.
19 For it is written, I will destroy the
wisdom of the wise, and will bring to
nothing the understanding of the pru-
dent.
20 Where *is* the wise? where *is* the
scribe? where *is* the disputer of this
world? hath not God made foolish the
wisdom of this world?
21 For after that in the wisdom of
God the world by wisdom knew not
God, it pleased God by the foolishness
of preaching to save them that believe.
22 For the Jews require a sign, and
the Greeks seek after wisdom:
23 But we preach Christ crucified,
unto the Jews a stumblingblock, and
unto the Greeks foolishness;
24 But unto them which are called,
both Jews and Greeks, Christ the pow-
er of God, and the wisdom of God.
25 Because the foolishness of God is
wiser than men; and the weakness of
God is stronger than men.
26 For ye see your calling, brethren,
how that not many wise men after the
flesh, not many mighty, not many
noble, *are called*:
27 But God hath chosen the foolish
things of the world to confound the
wise; and God hath chosen the weak
things of the world to confound the
things which are mighty;
28 And base things of the world, and
things which are despised, hath God
chosen, *yea*, and things which are not,
to bring to nought things that are:
29 That no flesh should glory in his
presence.
30 But of him are ye in Christ Jesus,
who of God is made unto us wisdom,
and righteousness, and sanctification,
and redemption:
31 That, according as it is written, He
that glorieth, let him glory in the Lord.

CHAPTER 2

AND I, brethren, when I came to you,
came not with excellency of speech or
of wisdom, declaring unto you the tes-
timony of God.
2 For I determined not to know any
thing among you, save Jesus Christ,
and him crucified.
3 And I was with you in weakness,
and in fear, and in much trembling.
4 And my speech and my preaching
was not with enticing words of man's
wisdom, but in demonstration of the
Spirit and of power:
5 That your faith should not stand in
the wisdom of men, but in the power of
God.
6 Howbeit we speak wisdom among
them that are perfect: yet not the wis-
dom of this world, nor of the princes of
this world, that come to nought:
7 But we speak the wisdom of God in
a mystery, *even* the hidden *wisdom*,
which God ordained before the world
unto our glory:
8 Which none of the princes of this
world knew: for had they known *it*,
they would not have crucified the Lord
of glory.
9 But as it is written, Eye hath not
seen, nor ear heard, neither have en-
tered into the heart of man, the things
which God hath prepared for them that
love him.
10 But God hath revealed *them* unto
us by his Spirit: for the Spirit searcheth
all things, yea, the deep things of God.
11 For what man knoweth the things
of a man, save the spirit of man which
is in him? even so the things of God
knoweth no man, but the Spirit of God.
12 Now we have received, not the
spirit of the world, but the spirit which
is of God; that we might know the
things that are freely given to us of
God.
13 Which things also we speak, not in
the words which man's wisdom teach-
eth, but which the Holy Ghost teach-
eth; comparing spiritual things with
spiritual.
14 But the natural man receiveth not
the things of the Spirit of God: for they
are foolishness unto him: neither can
he know *them*, because they are spiri-
tually discerned.
15 But he that is spiritual judgeth all
things, yet he himself is judged of no
man.
16 For who hath known the mind of
the Lord, that he may instruct him? But
we have the mind of Christ.

CHAPTER 3

AND I, brethren, could not speak unto you as unto spiritual, but as unto carnal, *even* as unto babes in Christ.

2 I have fed you with milk, and not with meat: for hitherto ye were not able *to bear it*, neither yet now are ye able.

3 For ye are yet carnal: for whereas *there is* among you envying, and strife, and divisions, are ye not carnal, and walk as men?

4 For while one saith, I am of Paul; and another, I *am* of Apollos; are ye not carnal?

5 Who then is Paul, and who *is* Apollos, but ministers by whom ye believed, even as the Lord gave to every man?

6 I have planted, Apollos watered; but God gave the increase.

7 So then neither is he that planteth any thing, neither he that watereth; but God that giveth the increase.

8 Now he that planteth and he that watereth are one: and every man shall receive his own reward according to his own labour.

9 For we are labourers together with God: ye are God's husbandry, *ye are* God's building.

10 According to the grace of God which is given unto me, as a wise masterbuilder, I have laid the foundation, and another buildeth thereon. But let every man take heed how he buildeth thereupon.

11 For other foundation can no man lay than that is laid, which is Jesus Christ.

12 Now if any man build upon this foundation gold, silver, precious stones, wood, hay, stubble;

13 Every man's work shall be made manifest: for the day shall declare it, because it shall be revealed by fire; and the fire shall try every man's work of what sort it is.

14 If any man's work abide which he hath built thereupon, he shall receive a reward.

15 If any man's work shall be burned, he shall suffer loss: but he himself shall be saved; yet so as by fire.

16 Know ye not that ye are the temple of God, and *that* the Spirit of God dwelleth in you?

17 If any man defile the temple of God, him shall God destroy; for the temple of God is holy, which *temple* ye are.

18 Let no man deceive himself. If any man among you seemeth to be wise in this world, let him become a fool, that he may be wise.

19 For the wisdom of this world is foolishness with God. For it is written, He taketh the wise in their own craftiness.

20 And again, The Lord knoweth the thoughts of the wise, that they are vain.

21 Therefore let no man glory in men. For all things are yours;

22 Whether Paul, or Apollos, or Cē'phas, or the world, or life, or death, or things present, or things to come; all are yours;

23 And ye are Christ's; and Christ *is* God's.

CHAPTER 4

LET a man so account of us, as of the ministers of Christ, and stewards of the mysteries of God.

2 Moreover it is required in stewards, that a man be found faithful.

3 But with me it is a very small thing that I should be judged of you, or of man's judgment: yea, ' judge not mine own self.

4 For I know nothing by myself; yet am I not hereby justified: but he that judgeth me is the Lord.

5 Therefore judge nothing before the time, until the Lord come, who both will bring to light the hidden things of darkness, and will make manifest the counsels of the hearts: and then shall every man have praise of God.

6 And these things, brethren, I have in a figure transferred to myself and *to* Apollos for your sakes; that ye might learn in us not to think *of men* above that which is written, that no one of you be puffed up for one against another.

7 For who maketh thee to differ *from another?* and what hast thou that thou didst not receive? now if thou didst receive *it*, why dost thou glory, as if thou hadst not received *it?*

8 Now ye are full, now ye are rich, ye have reigned as kings without us: and I would to God ye did reign, that we also might reign with you.

9 For I think that God hath set forth us the apostles last, as it were appointed to death: for we are made a spectacle unto the world, and to angels, and to men.

10 We *are* fools for Christ's sake, but ye *are* wise in Christ; we *are* weak, but ye *are* strong; ye *are* honourable, but we *are* despised.

11 Even unto this present hour we both hunger, and thirst, and are naked, and are buffeted, and have no certain dwellingplace;

12 And labour, working with our own hands: being reviled, we bless; being persecuted, we suffer it:

13 Being defamed, we intreat: we are

made as the filth of the world, *and are*
the offscouring of all things unto this
day.
14 I write not these things to shame
you, but as my beloved sons I warn
you.
15 For though ye have ten thousand
instructors in Christ, yet *have ye* not
many fathers: for in Christ Jesus I have
begotten you through the gospel.
16 Wherefore I beseech you, be ye
followers of me.
17 For this cause have I sent unto you
Tī-mō'the-us, who is my beloved son,
and faithful in the Lord, who shall bring
you into remembrance of my ways
which be in Christ, as I teach every
where in every church.
18 Now some are puffed up, as
though I would not come to you.
19 But I will come to you shortly, if
the Lord will, and will know, not the
speech of them which are puffed up,
but the power.
20 For the kingdom of God *is* not in
word, but in power.
21 What will ye? shall I come unto
you with a rod, or in love, and *in* the
spirit of meekness?

CHAPTER 5

IT is reported commonly *that there is*
fornication among you, and such forni-
cation as is not so much as named
among the Gentiles, that one should
have his father's wife.
2 And ye are puffed up, and have not
rather mourned, that he that hath done
this deed might be taken away from
among you.
3 For I verily, as absent in body, but
present in spirit, have judged already,
as though I were present, *concerning*
him that hath so done this deed,
4 In the name of our Lord Jesus
Christ, when ye are gathered together,
and my spirit, with the power of our
Lord Jesus Christ,
5 To deliver such an one unto Satan
for the destruction of the flesh, that the
spirit may be saved in the day of the
Lord Jesus.
6 Your glorying *is* not good. Know ye
not that a little leaven leaveneth the
whole lump?
7 Purge out therefore the old leaven,
that ye may be a new lump, as ye are
unleavened. For even Christ our pass-
over is sacrificed for us:
8 Therefore let us keep the feast, not
with old leaven, neither with the leaven
of malice and wickedness; but with the
unleavened *bread* of sincerity and
truth.
9 I wrote unto you in an epistle not to
company with fornicators:
10 Yet not altogether with the forni-
cators of this world, or with the covet-
ous, or extortioners, or with idolaters;
for then must ye needs go out of the
world.
11 But now I have written unto you
not to keep company, if any man that is
called a brother be a fornicator, or
covetous, or an idolater, or a railer, or a
drunkard, or an extortioner; with such
an one no not to eat.
12 For what have I to do to judge
them also that are without? do not ye
judge them that are within?
13 But them that are without God
judgeth. Therefore put away from
among yourselves that wicked person.

CHAPTER 6

DARE any of you, having a matter
against another, go to law before the
unjust, and not before the saints?
2 Do ye not know that the saints shall
judge the world? and if the world shall
be judged by you, are ye unworthy to
judge the smallest matters?
3 Know ye not that we shall judge an-
gels? how much more things that per-
tain to this life?
4 If then ye have judgments of things
pertaining to this life, set them to judge
who are least esteemed in the church.
5 I speak to your shame. Is it so, that
there is not a wise man among you? no,
not one that shall be able to judge be-
tween his brethren?
6 But brother goeth to law with
brother, and that before the unbeliev-
ers.
7 Now therefore there is utterly a
fault among you, because ye go to law
one with another. Why do ye not rather
take wrong? why do ye not rather *suf-*
fer yourselves to be defrauded?
8 Nay, ye do wrong, and defraud, and
that *your* brethren.
9 Know ye not that the unrighteous
shall not inherit the kingdom of God?
Be not deceived: neither fornicators,
nor idolaters, nor adulterers, nor ef-
feminate, nor abusers of themselves
with mankind,
10 Nor thieves, nor covetous, nor
drunkards, nor revilers, nor extortion-
ers, shall inherit the kingdom of God.
11 And such were some of you: but ye
are washed, but ye are sanctified, but
ye are justified in the name of the Lord
Jesus, and by the Spirit of our God.
12 All things are lawful unto me, but
all things are not expedient: all things
are lawful for me, but I will not be
brought under the power of any.

13 Meats for the belly, and the belly for meats: but God shall destroy both it and them. Now the body *is* not for fornication, but for the Lord; and the Lord for the body.

14 And God hath both raised up the Lord, and will also raise up us by his own power.

15 Know ye not that your bodies are the members of Christ? shall I then take the members of Christ, and make *them* the members of an harlot? God forbid.

16 What? know ye not that he which is joined to an harlot is one body? for two, saith he, shall be one flesh.

17 But he that is joined unto the Lord is one spirit.

18 Flee fornication. Every sin that a man doeth is without the body; but he that committeth fornication sinneth against his own body.

19 What? know ye not that your body is the temple of the Holy Ghost *which is* in you, which ye have of God, and ye are not your own?

20 For ye are bought with a price: therefore glorify God in your body, and in your spirit, which are God's.

CHAPTER 7

NOW concerning the things whereof ye wrote unto me: *It is* good for a man not to touch a woman.

2 Nevertheless, *to avoid* fornication, let every man have his own wife, and let every woman have her own husband.

3 Let the husband render unto the wife due benevolence: and likewise also the wife unto the husband.

4 The wife hath not power of her own body, but the husband: and likewise also the husband hath not power of his own body, but the wife.

5 Defraud ye not one the other, except *it be* with consent for a time, that ye may give yourselves to fasting and prayer; and come together again, that Satan tempt you not for your incontinency.

6 But I speak this by permission, *and* not of commandment.

7 For I would that all men were even as I myself. But every man hath his proper gift of God, one after this manner, and another after that.

8 I say therefore to the unmarried and widows, It is good for them if they abide even as I.

9 But if they cannot contain, let them marry: for it is better to marry than to burn.

10 And unto the married I command, *yet* not I, but the Lord, Let not the wife depart from *her* husband:

11 But and if she depart, let her remain unmarried, or be reconciled to *her* husband: and let not the husband put away *his* wife.

12 But to the rest speak I, not the Lord: If any brother hath a wife that believeth not, and she be pleased to dwell with him, let him not put her away.

13 And the woman which hath an husband that believeth not, and if he be pleased to dwell with her, let her not leave him.

14 For the unbelieving husband is sanctified by the wife, and the unbelieving wife is sanctified by the husband: else were your children unclean; but now are they holy.

15 But if the unbelieving depart, let him depart. A brother or a sister is not under bondage in such *cases:* but God hath called us to peace.

16 For what knowest thou, O wife, whether thou shalt save *thy* husband? or how knowest thou, O man, whether thou shalt save *thy* wife?

17 But as God hath distributed to every man, as the Lord hath called every one, so let him walk. And so ordain I in all churches.

18 Is any man called being circumcised? let him not become uncircumcised. Is any called in uncircumcision? let him not be circumcised.

19 Circumcision is nothing, and uncircumcision is nothing, but the keeping of the commandments of God.

20 Let every man abide in the same calling wherein he was called.

21 Art thou called *being* a servant? care not for it: but if thou mayest be made free, use *it* rather.

22 For he that is called in the Lord, *being* a servant, is the Lord's freeman: likewise also he that is called, *being* free, is Christ's servant.

23 Ye are bought with a price; be not ye the servants of men.

24 Brethren, let every man, wherein he is called, therein abide with God.

25 Now concerning virgins I have no commandment of the Lord: yet I give my judgment, as one that hath obtained mercy of the Lord to be faithful.

26 I suppose therefore that this is good for the present distress, *I say,* that *it is* good for a man so to be.

27 Art thou bound unto a wife? seek not to be loosed. Art thou loosed from a wife? seek not a wife.

28 But and if thou marry, thou hast not sinned; and if a virgin marry, she hath not sinned. Nevertheless such

shall have trouble in the flesh: but I
spare you.
29 But this I say, brethren, the time *is*
short: it remaineth, that both they that
have wives be as though they had none;
30 And they that weep, as though
they wept not; and they that rejoice, as
though they rejoiced not; and they that
buy, as though they possessed not;
31 And they that use this world, as
not abusing *it:* for the fashion of this
world passeth away.
32 But I would have you without
carefulness. He that is unmarried
careth for the things that belong to the
Lord, how he may please the Lord:
33 But he that is married careth for
the things that are of the world, how he
may please *his* wife.
34 There is difference *also* between a
wife and a virgin. The unmarried wom-
an careth for the things of the Lord,
that she may be holy both in body and
in spirit: but she that is married careth
for the things of the world, how she
may please *her* husband.
35 And this I speak for your own prof-
it; not that I may cast a snare upon
you, but for that which is comely, and
that ye may attend upon the Lord
without distraction.
36 But if any man think that he be-
haveth himself uncomely toward his
virgin, if she pass the flower of *her* age,
and need so require, let him do what he
will, he sinneth not: let them marry.
37 Nevertheless he that standeth
stedfast in his heart, having no neces-
sity, but hath power over his own will,
and hath so decreed in his heart that he
will keep his virgin, doeth well.
38 So then he that giveth *her* in mar-
riage doeth well; but he that giveth *her*
not in marriage doeth better.
39 The wife is bound by the law as
long as her husband liveth; but if her
husband be dead, she is at liberty to be
married to whom she will; only in the
Lord.
40 But she is happier if she so abide,
after my judgment: and I think also
that I have the Spirit of God.

CHAPTER 8

NOW as touching things offered unto
idols, we know that we all have knowl-
edge. Knowledge puffeth up, but char-
ity edifieth.
2 And if any man think that he
knoweth any thing, he knoweth noth-
ing yet as he ought to know.
3 But if any man love God, the same
is known of him.
4 As concerning therefore the eating
of those things that are offered in sacri-
fice unto idols, we know that an idol *is*
nothing in the world, and that *there is*
none other God but one.
5 For though there be that are called
gods, whether in heaven or in earth, (as
there be gods many, and lords many,)
6 But to us *there is but* one God, the
Father, of whom *are* all things, and we
in him; and one Lord Jesus Christ, by
whom *are* all things, and we by him.
7 Howbeit *there is* not in every man
that knowledge: for some with con-
science of the idol unto this hour eat *it*
as a thing offered unto an idol; and
their conscience being weak is defiled.
8 But meat commendeth us not to
God: for neither, if we eat, are we the
better; neither, if we eat not, are we the
worse.
9 But take heed lest by any means
this liberty of yours become a stum-
blingblock to them that are weak.
10 For if any man see thee which hast
knowledge sit at meat in the idol's
temple, shall not the conscience of him
which is weak be emboldened to eat
those things which are offered to idols;
11 And through thy knowledge shall
the weak brother perish, for whom
Christ died?
12 But when ye sin so against the
brethren, and wound their weak con-
science, ye sin against Christ.
13 Wherefore, if meat make my
brother to offend, I will eat no flesh
while the world standeth, lest I make
my brother to offend.

CHAPTER 9

AM I not an apostle? am I not free?
have I not seen Jesus Christ our Lord?
are not ye my work in the Lord?
2 If I be not an apostle unto others,
yet doubtless I am to you: for the seal of
mine apostleship are ye in the Lord.
3 Mine answer to them that do ex-
amine me is this,
4 Have we not power to eat and to
drink?
5 Have we not power to lead about a
sister, a wife, as well as other apostles,
and *as* the brethren of the Lord, and
Cē'phas?
6 Or I only and Barnabas, have not
we power to forbear working?
7 Who goeth a warfare any time at
his own charges? who planteth a vine-
yard, and eateth not of the fruit thereof?
or who feedeth a flock, and eateth not
of the milk of the flock?
8 Say I these things as a man? or saith
not the law the same also?
9 For it is written in the law of Moses,
Thou shalt not muzzle the mouth of the

ox that treadeth out the corn. Doth God
take care for oxen?
10 Or saith he *it* altogether for our
sakes? For our sakes, no doubt, *this* is
written: that he that ploweth should
plow in hope; and that he that
thresheth in hope should be partaker of
his hope.
11 If we have sown unto you spiritual
things, *is it* a great thing if we shall reap
your carnal things?
12 If others be partakers of *this* pow-
er over you, *are* not we rather? Never-
theless we have not used this power;
but suffer all things, lest we should hin-
der the gospel of Christ.
13 Do ye not know that they which
minister about holy things live *of the
things* of the temple? and they which
wait at the altar are partakers with the
altar?
14 Even so hath the Lord ordained
that they which preach the gospel
should live of the gospel.
15 But I have used none of these
things: neither have I written these
things, that it should be so done unto
me: for *it were* better for me to die, than
that any man should make my glorying
void.
16 For though I preach the gospel, I
have nothing to glory of: for necessity
is laid upon me; yea, woe is unto me, if I
preach not the gospel!
17 For if I do this thing willingly, I
have a reward: but if against my will, a
dispensation *of the gospel* is com-
mitted unto me.
18 What is my reward then? *Verily*
that, when I preach the gospel, I may
make the gospel of Christ without
charge, that I abuse not my power in
the gospel.
19 For though I be free from all *men*,
yet have I made myself servant unto
all, that I might gain the more.
20 And unto the Jews I became as a
Jew, that I might gain the Jews; to them
that are under the law, as under the
law, that I might gain them that are un-
der the law;
21 To them that are without law, as
without law, (being not without law to
God, but under the law to Christ,) that I
might gain them that are without law.
22 To the weak became I as weak,
that I might gain the weak: I am made
all things to all *men*, that I might by all
means save some.
23 And this I do for the gospel's sake,
that I might be partaker thereof with
you.
24 Know ye not that they which run
in a race run all, but one receiveth the
prize? So run, that ye may obtain.
25 And every man that striveth for
the mastery is temperate in all things.
Now they *do it* to obtain a corruptible
crown; but we an incorruptible.
26 I therefore so run, not as uncer-
tainly; so fight I, not as one that beateth
the air:
27 But I keep under my body, and
bring *it* into subjection: lest that by any
means, when I have preached to others,
I myself should be a castaway.

CHAPTER 10

MOREOVER, brethren, I would not
that ye should be ignorant, how that all
our fathers were under the cloud, and
all passed through the sea;
2 And were all baptized unto Moses
in the cloud and in the sea;
3 And did all eat the same spiritual
meat;
4 And did all drink the same spiritual
drink: for they drank of that spiritual
Rock that followed them: and that
Rock was Christ.
5 But with many of them God was not
well pleased: for they were overthrown
in the wilderness.
6 Now these things were our ex-
amples, to the intent we should not lust
after evil things, as they also lusted.
7 Neither be ye idolaters, as *were*
some of them; as it is written, The
people sat down to eat and drink, and
rose up to play.
8 Neither let us commit fornication,
as some of them committed, and fell in
one day three and twenty thousand.
9 Neither let us tempt Christ, as some
of them also tempted, and were de-
stroyed of serpents.
10 Neither murmur ye, as some of
them also murmured, and were de-
stroyed of the destroyer.
11 Now all these things happened
unto them for ensamples: and they are
written for our admonition, upon
whom the ends of the world are come.
12 Wherefore let him that thinketh
he standeth take heed lest he fall.
13 There hath no temptation taken
you but such as is common to man: but
God *is* faithful, who will not suffer you
to be tempted above that ye are able;
but will with the temptation also make
a way to escape, that ye may be able to
bear *it*.
14 Wherefore, my dearly beloved,
flee from idolatry.
15 I speak as to wise men; judge ye
what I say.
16 The cup of blessing which we
bless, is it not the communion of the
blood of Christ? The bread which we

break, is it not the communion of the
body of Christ?
17 For we *being* many are one bread,
and one body: for we are all partakers
of that one bread.
18 Behold Israel after the flesh: are
not they which eat of the sacrifices par-
takers of the altar?
19 What say I then? that the idol is
any thing, or that which is offered in
sacrifice to idols is any thing?
20 But *I say*, that the things which the
Gentiles sacrifice, they sacrifice to dev-
ils, and not to God: and I would not
that ye should have fellowship with dev-
ils.
21 Ye cannot drink the cup of the
Lord, and the cup of devils: ye cannot
be partakers of the Lord's table, and of
the table of devils.
22 Do we provoke the Lord to
jealousy? are we stronger than he?
23 All things are lawful for me, but all
things are not expedient: all things are
lawful for me, but all things edify not.
24 Let no man seek his own, but
every man another's *wealth*.
25 Whatsoever is sold in the
shambles, *that* eat, asking no question
for conscience sake:
26 For the earth *is* the Lord's, and the
fulness thereof.
27 If any of them that believe not bid
you *to a feast*, and ye be disposed to go;
whatsoever is set before you, eat,
asking no question for conscience
sake.
28 But if any man say unto you, This
is offered in sacrifice unto idols, eat not
for his sake that shewed it, and for
conscience sake: for the earth *is* the
Lord's, and the fulness thereof:
29 Conscience, I say, not thine own,
but of the other: for why is my liberty
judged of another *man's* conscience?
30 For if I by grace be a partaker, why
am I evil spoken of for that for which I
give thanks?
31 Whether therefore ye eat, or
drink, or whatsoever ye do, do all to the
glory of God.
32 Give none offence, neither to the
Jews, nor to the Gentiles, nor to the
church of God:
33 Even as I please all *men* in all
things, not seeking mine own profit,
but the *profit* of many, that they may be
saved.

CHAPTER 11

BE ye followers of me, even as I also *am*
of Christ.
2 Now I praise you, brethren, that ye
remember me in all things, and keep
the ordinances, as I delivered *them* to
you.
3 But I would have you know, that the
head of every man is Christ; and the
head of the woman *is* the man; and the
head of Christ *is* God.
4 Every man praying or prophesying,
having *his* head covered, dishonoureth
his head.
5 But every woman that prayeth or
prophesieth with *her* head uncovered
dishonoureth her head: for that is even
all one as if she were shaven.
6 For if the woman be not covered, let
her also be shorn: but if it be a shame
for a woman to be shorn or shaven, let
her be covered.
7 For a man indeed ought not to cover
his head, forasmuch as he is the image
and glory of God: but the woman is the
glory of the man.
8 For the man is not of the woman;
but the woman of the man.
9 Neither was the man created for the
woman; but the woman for the man.
10 For this cause ought the woman to
have power on *her* head because of the
angels.
11 Nevertheless neither is the man
without the woman, neither the wom-
an without the man, in the Lord.
12 For as the woman *is* of the man,
even so *is* the man also by the woman;
but all things of God.
13 Judge in yourselves: is it comely
that a woman pray unto God un-
covered?
14 Doth not even nature itself teach
you, that, if a man have long hair, it is a
shame unto him?
15 But if a woman have long hair, it is
a glory to her: for *her* hair is given her
for a covering.
16 But if any man seem to be conten-
tious, we have no such custom, neither
the churches of God.
17 Now in this that I declare *unto you*
I praise *you* not, that ye come together
not for the better, but for the worse.
18 For first of all, when ye come togeth-
er in the church, I hear that there be
divisions among you; and I partly be-
lieve it.
19 For there must be also heresies
among you, that they which are ap-
proved may be made manifest among
you.
20 When ye come together therefore
into one place, *this* is not to eat the
Lord's supper.
21 For in eating every one taketh be-
fore *other* his own supper: and one is
hungry, and another is drunken.
22 What? have ye not houses to eat
and to drink in? or despise ye the

church of God, and shame them that have not? What shall I say to you? shall I praise you in this? I praise *you* not.
23 For I have received of the Lord that which also I delivered unto you, That the Lord Jesus the *same* night in which he was betrayed took bread:
24 And when he had given thanks, he brake *it*, and said, Take, eat: this is my body, which is broken for you: this do in remembrance of me.
25 After the same manner also *he took* the cup, when he had supped, saying, This cup is the new testament in my blood: this do ye, as oft as ye drink *it*, in remembrance of me.
26 For as often as ye eat this bread, and drink this cup, ye do shew the Lord's death till he come.
27 Wherefore whosoever shall eat this bread, and drink *this* cup of the Lord, unworthily, shall be guilty of the body and blood of the Lord.
28 But let a man examine himself, and so let him eat of *that* bread, and drink of *that* cup.
29 For he that eateth and drinketh unworthily, eateth and drinketh damnation to himself, not discerning the Lord's body.
30 For this cause many *are* weak and sickly among you, and many sleep.
31 For if we would judge ourselves, we should not be judged.
32 But when we are judged, we are chastened of the Lord, that we should not be condemned with the world.
33 Wherefore, my brethren, when ye come together to eat, tarry one for another.
34 And if any man hunger, let him eat at home; that ye come not together unto condemnation. And the rest will I set in order when I come.

CHAPTER 12

NOW concerning spiritual *gifts*, brethren, I would not have you ignorant.
2 Ye know that ye were Gentiles, carried away unto these dumb idols, even as ye were led.
3 Wherefore I give you to understand, that no man speaking by the Spirit of God calleth Jesus accursed: and *that* no man can say that Jesus is the Lord, but by the Holy Ghost.
4 Now there are diversities of gifts, but the same Spirit.
5 And there are differences of administrations, but the same Lord.
6 And there are diversities of operations, but it is the same God which worketh all in all.
7 But the manifestation of the Spirit is given to every man to profit withal.
8 For to one is given by the Spirit the word of wisdom; to another the word of knowledge by the same Spirit;
9 To another faith by the same Spirit; to another the gifts of healing by the same Spirit;
10 To another the working of miracles; to another prophecy; to another discerning of spirits; to another *divers* kinds of tongues; to another the interpretation of tongues:
11 But all these worketh that one and the selfsame Spirit, dividing to every man severally as he will.
12 For as the body is one, and hath many members, and all the members of that one body, being many, are one body: so also *is* Christ.
13 For by one Spirit are we all baptized into one body, whether *we be* Jews or Gentiles, whether *we be* bond or free; and have been all made to drink into one Spirit.
14 For the body is not one member, but many.
15 If the foot shall say, Because I am not the hand, I am not of the body; is it therefore not of the body?
16 And if the ear shall say, Because I am not the eye, I am not of the body; is it therefore not of the body?
17 If the whole body *were* an eye, where *were* the hearing? If the whole *were* hearing, where *were* the smelling?
18 But now hath God set the members every one of them in the body, as it hath pleased him.
19 And if they were all one member, where *were* the body?
20 But now *are they* many members, yet but one body.
21 And the eye cannot say unto the hand, I have no need of thee: nor again the head to the feet, I have no need of you.
22 Nay, much more those members of the body, which seem to be more feeble, are necessary:
23 And those *members* of the body, which we think to be less honourable, upon these we bestow more abundant honour; and our uncomely *parts* have more abundant comeliness.
24 For our comely *parts* have no need: but God hath tempered the body together, having given more abundant honour to that *part* which lacked:
25 That there should be no schism in the body; but *that* the members should have the same care one for another.
26 And whether one member suffer, all the members suffer with it; or one member be honoured, all the members rejoice with it.

27 Now ye are the body of Christ, and members in particular.
28 And God hath set some in the church, first apostles, secondarily prophets, thirdly teachers, after that miracles, then gifts of healings, helps, governments, diversities of tongues.
29 *Are* all apostles? *are* all prophets? *are* all teachers? *are* all workers of miracles?
30 Have all the gifts of healing? do all speak with tongues? do all interpret?
31 But covet earnestly the best gifts: and yet shew I unto you a more excellent way.

CHAPTER 13

THOUGH I speak with the tongues of men and of angels, and have not charity, I am become *as* sounding brass, or a tinkling cymbal.
2 And though I have *the gift of* prophecy, and understand all mysteries, and all knowledge; and though I have all faith, so that I could remove mountains, and have not charity, I am nothing.
3 And though I bestow all my goods to feed *the poor*, and though I give my body to be burned, and have not charity, it profiteth me nothing.
4 Charity suffereth long, *and* is kind; charity envieth not; charity vaunteth not itself, is not puffed up,
5 Doth not behave itself unseemly, seeketh not her own, is not easily provoked, thinketh no evil;
6 Rejoiceth not in iniquity, but rejoiceth in the truth;
7 Beareth all things, believeth all things, hopeth all things, endureth all things.
8 Charity never faileth: but whether *there be* prophecies, they shall fail; whether *there be* tongues, they shall cease; whether *there be* knowledge, it shall vanish away.
9 For we know in part, and we prophesy in part.
10 But when that which is perfect is come, then that which is in part shall be done away.
11 When I was a child, I spake as a child, I understood as a child, I thought as a child: but when I became a man, I put away childish things.
12 For now we see through a glass, darkly; but then face to face: now I know in part; but then shall I know even as also I am known.
13 And now abideth faith, hope, charity, these three; but the greatest of these *is* charity.

CHAPTER 14

FOLLOW after charity, and desire spiritual *gifts*, but rather that ye may prophesy.
2 For he that speaketh in an *unknown* tongue speaketh not unto men, but unto God: for no man understandeth *him;* howbeit in the spirit he speaketh mysteries.
3 But he that prophesieth speaketh unto men *to* edification, and exhortation, and comfort.
4 He that speaketh in an *unknown* tongue edifieth himself; but he that prophesieth edifieth the church.
5 I would that ye all spake with tongues, but rather that ye prophesied: for greater *is* he that prophesieth than he that speaketh with tongues, except he interpret, that the church may receive edifying.
6 Now, brethren, if I come unto you speaking with tongues, what shall I profit you, except I shall speak to you either by revelation, or by knowledge, or by prophesying, or by doctrine?
7 And even things without life giving sound, whether pipe or harp, except they give a distinction in the sounds, how shall it be known what is piped or harped?
8 For if the trumpet give an uncertain sound, who shall prepare himself to the battle?
9 So likewise ye, except ye utter by the tongue words easy to be understood, how shall it be known what is spoken? for ye shall speak into the air.
10 There are, it may be, so many kinds of voices in the world, and none of them *is* without signification.
11 Therefore if I know not the meaning of the voice, I shall be unto him that speaketh a barbarian, and he that speaketh *shall be* a barbarian unto me.
12 Even so ye, forasmuch as ye are zealous of spiritual *gifts*, seek that ye may excel to the edifying of the church.
13 Wherefore let him that speaketh in an *unknown* tongue pray that he may interpret.
14 For if I pray in an *unknown* tongue, my spirit prayeth, but my understanding is unfruitful.
15 What is it then? I will pray with the spirit, and I will pray with the understanding also: I will sing with the spirit, and I will sing with the understanding also.
16 Else when thou shalt bless with the spirit, how shall he that occupieth the room of the unlearned say Amen at thy giving of thanks, seeing he understandeth not what thou sayest?

17 For thou verily givest thanks well,
but the other is not edified.
18 I thank my God, I speak with
tongues more than ye all:
19 Yet in the church I had rather
speak five words with my understand-
ing, that *by my voice* I might teach
others also, than ten thousand words in
an *unknown* tongue.
20 Brethren, be not children in under-
standing: howbeit in malice be ye
children, but in understanding be men.
21 In the law it is written, With *men
of* other tongues and other lips will I
speak unto this people; and yet for all
that will they not hear me, saith the
Lord.
22 Wherefore tongues are for a sign,
not to them that believe, but to them
that believe not: but prophesying *serv-
eth* not for them that believe not, but
for them which believe.
23 If therefore the whole church be
come together into one place, and all
speak with tongues, and there come in
those that are unlearned, or unbeliev-
ers, will they not say that ye are mad?
24 But if all prophesy, and there come
in one that believeth not, or *one* un-
learned, he is convinced of all, he is
judged of all:
25 And thus are the secrets of his
heart made manifest; and so falling
down on *his* face he will worship God,
and report that God is in you of a truth.
26 How is it then, brethren? when ye
come together, every one of you hath a
psalm, hath a doctrine, hath a tongue,
hath a revelation, hath an interpreta-
tion. Let all things be done unto edi-
fying.
27 If any man speak in an *unknown*
tongue, *let it be* by two, or at the most
by three, and *that* by course; and let
one interpret.
28 But if there be no interpreter, let
him keep silence in the church; and let
him speak to himself, and to God.
29 Let the prophets speak two or
three, and let the other judge.
30 If *any thing* be revealed to another
that sitteth by, let the first hold his
peace.
31 For ye may all prophesy one by
one, that all may learn, and all may be
comforted.
32 And the spirits of the prophets are
subject to the prophets.
33 For God is not *the author* of confu-
sion, but of peace, as in all churches of
the saints.
34 Let your women keep silence in
the churches: for it is not permitted
unto them to speak; but *they are com-
manded* to be under obedience, as also
saith the law.
35 And if they will learn any thing, let
them ask their husbands at home: for it
is a shame for women to speak in the
church.
36 What? came the word of God out
from you? or came it unto you only?
37 If any man think himself to be a
prophet, or spiritual, let him acknowl-
edge that the things that I write unto
you are the commandments of the
Lord.
38 But if any man be ignorant, let him
be ignorant.
39 Wherefore, brethren, covet to
prophesy, and forbid not to speak with
tongues.
40 Let all things be done decently and
in order.

CHAPTER 15

MOREOVER, brethren, I declare unto
you the gospel which I preached unto
you, which also ye have received, and
wherein ye stand;
2 By which also ye are saved, if ye
keep in memory what I preached unto
you, unless ye have believed in vain.
3 For I delivered unto you first of all
that which I also received, how that
Christ died for our sins according to the
scriptures;
4 And that he was buried, and that he
rose again the third day according to
the scriptures:
5 And that he was seen of Cē'phas,
then of the twelve:
6 After that he was seen of above five
hundred brethren at once; of whom the
greater part remain unto this present,
but some are fallen asleep.
7 After that, he was seen of James;
then of all the apostles.
8 And last of all he was seen of me
also, as of one born out of due time.
9 For I am the least of the apostles,
that am not meet to be called an
apostle, because I persecuted the
church of God.
10 But by the grace of God I am what
I am: and his grace which *was bestowed*
upon me was not in vain; but I
laboured more abundantly than they
all: yet not I, but the grace of God
which was with me.
11 Therefore whether *it were* I or
they, so we preach, and so ye believed.
12 Now if Christ be preached that he
rose from the dead, how say some
among you that there is no resurrection
of the dead?
13 But if there be no resurrection of
the dead, then is Christ not risen:
14 And if Christ be not risen, then *is*

our preaching vain, and your faith *is* also vain.
15 Yea, and we are found false witnesses of God; because we have testified of God that he raised up Christ: whom he raised not up, if so be that the dead rise not.
16 For if the dead rise not, then is not Christ raised:
17 And if Christ be not raised, your faith *is* vain; ye are yet in your sins.
18 Then they also which are fallen asleep in Christ are perished.
19 If in this life only we have hope in Christ, we are of all men most miserable.
20 But now is Christ risen from the dead, *and* become the firstfruits of them that slept.
21 For since by man *came* death, by man *came* also the resurrection of the dead.
22 For as in Adam all die, even so in Christ shall all be made alive.
23 But every man in his own order: Christ the firstfruits; afterward they that are Christ's at his coming.
24 Then *cometh* the end, when he shall have delivered up the kingdom to God, even the Father; when he shall have put down all rule and all authority and power.
25 For he must reign, till he hath put all enemies under his feet.
26 The last enemy *that* shall be destroyed *is* death.
27 For he hath put all things under his feet. But when he saith all things are put under *him, it is* manifest that he is excepted, which did put all things under him.
28 And when all things shall be subdued unto him, then shall the Son also himself be subject unto him that put all things under him, that God may be all in all.
29 Else what shall they do which are baptized for the dead, if the dead rise not at all? why are they then baptized for the dead?
30 And why stand we in jeopardy every hour?
31 I protest by your rejoicing which I have in Christ Jesus our Lord, I die daily.
32 If after the manner of men I have fought with beasts at Ĕph'e-sus, what advantageth it me, if the dead rise not? let us eat and drink; for to morrow we die.
33 Be not deceived: evil communications corrupt good manners.
34 Awake to righteousness, and sin not; for some have not the knowledge of God: I speak *this* to your shame.
35 But some *man* will say, How are the dead raised up? and with what body do they come?
36 *Thou* fool, that which thou sowest is not quickened, except it die:
37 And that which thou sowest, thou sowest not that body that shall be, but bare grain, it may chance of wheat, or of some other *grain:*
38 But God giveth it a body as it hath pleased him, and to every seed his own body.
39 All flesh *is* not the same flesh: but *there is* one *kind of* flesh of men, another flesh of beasts, another of fishes, *and* another of birds.
40 *There are* also celestial bodies, and bodies terrestrial: but the glory of the celestial *is* one, and the *glory* of the terrestrial *is* another.
41 *There is* one glory of the sun, and another glory of the moon, and another glory of the stars: for *one* star differeth from *another* star in glory.
42 So also *is* the resurrection of the dead. It is sown in corruption; it is raised in incorruption:
43 It is sown in dishonour; it is raised in glory: it is sown in weakness; it is raised in power:
44 It is sown a natural body; it is raised a spiritual body. There is a natural body, and there is a spiritual body.
45 And so it is written, The first man Adam was made a living soul; the last Adam *was made* a quickening spirit.
46 Howbeit that *was* not first which is spiritual, but that which is natural; and afterward that which is spiritual.
47 The first man *is* of the earth, earthy: the second man *is* the Lord from heaven.
48 As *is* the earthy, such *are* they also that are earthy: and as *is* the heavenly, such *are* they also that are heavenly.
49 And as we have borne the image of the earthy, we shall also bear the image of the heavenly.
50 Now this I say, brethren, that flesh and blood cannot inherit the kingdom of God; neither doth corruption inherit incorruption.
51 Behold, I shew you a mystery; We shall not all sleep, but we shall all be changed,
52 In a moment, in the twinkling of an eye, at the last trump: for the trumpet shall sound, and the dead shall be raised incorruptible, and we shall be changed.
53 For this corruptible must put on incorruption, and this mortal *must* put on immortality.
54 So when this corruptible shall

have put on incorruption, and this mor-
tal shall have put on immortality, then
shall be brought to pass the saying that
is written, Death is swallowed up in
victory.
55 O death, where *is* thy sting? O
grave, where *is* thy victory?
56 The sting of death *is* sin; and the
strength of sin *is* the law.
57 But thanks *be* to God, which giv-
eth us the victory through our Lord
Jesus Christ.
58 Therefore, my beloved brethren,
be ye stedfast, unmoveable, always
abounding in the work of the Lord, for-
asmuch as ye know that your labour is
not in vain in the Lord.

CHAPTER 16

NOW concerning the collection for the
saints, as I have given order to the
churches of Ga-lā′tia, even so do ye.
2 Upon the first *day* of the week let
every one of you lay by him in store, as
God hath prospered him, that there be
no gatherings when I come.
3 And when I come, whomsoever ye
shall approve by *your* letters, them will
I send to bring your liberality unto Jeru-
salem.
4 And if it be meet that I go also, they
shall go with me.
5 Now I will come unto you, when I
shall pass through Macedonia: for I do
pass through Macedonia.
6 And it may be that I will abide, yea,
and winter with you, that ye may bring
me on my journey whithersoever I go.
7 For I will not see you now by the
way; but I trust to tarry a while with
you, if the Lord permit.
8 But I will tarry at Ĕph′e-sus until
Pentecost.
9 For a great door and effectual is
opened unto me, and *there are* many ad-
versaries.
10 Now if Tī-mō′the-us come, see
that he may be with you without fear:
for he worketh the work of the Lord, as
I also *do*.
11 Let no man therefore despise him:
but conduct him forth in peace, that he
may come unto me: for I look for him
with the brethren.
12 As touching *our* brother Apollos, I
greatly desired him to come unto you
with the brethren: but his will was not
at all to come at this time; but he will
come when he shall have convenient
time.
13 Watch ye, stand fast in the faith,
quit you like men, be strong.
14 Let all your things be done with
charity.
15 I beseech you, brethren, (ye know
the house of Stĕph′a-nas, that it is the
firstfruits of A-chā′ia, and *that* they
have addicted themselves to the min-
istry of the saints,)
16 That ye submit yourselves unto
such, and to every one that helpeth
with *us*, and laboureth.
17 I am glad of the coming of Stĕph′a-
nas and Fôr-tu-nā′tus and A-chā′i-cus:
for that which was lacking on your part
they have supplied.
18 For they have refreshed my spirit
and yours: therefore acknowledge ye
them that are such.
19 The churches of Asia salute you.
Ăq′ui-la and Priscilla salute you much
in the Lord, with the church that is in
their house.
20 All the brethren greet you. Greet
ye one another with an holy kiss.
21 The salutation of *me* Paul with
mine own hand.
22 If any man love not the Lord Jesus
Christ, let him be A-năth′e-ma Măr′an-
ă′tha.
23 The grace of our Lord Jesus Christ
be with you.
24 My love *be* with you all in Christ
Jesus. Amen.

The first *epistle* to the Corinthians was written from Philippi by Stephanas, and Fortunatus, and Achaicus, and Timotheus.

THE SECOND EPISTLE OF PAUL THE APOSTLE
TO THE

CORINTHIANS

CHAPTER 1

PAUL, an apostle of Jesus Christ by the
will of God, and Timothy *our* brother,
unto the church of God which is at
Corinth, with all the saints which are in
all A-chā′ia:
2 Grace *be* to you and peace from
God our Father, and *from* the Lord Je-
sus Christ.
3 Blessed *be* God, even the Father of
our Lord Jesus Christ, the Father of
mercies, and the God of all comfort;
4 Who comforteth us in all our tribu-
lation, that we may be able to comfort
them which are in any trouble, by the
comfort wherewith we ourselves are
comforted of God.
5 For as the sufferings of Christ

abound in us, so our consolation also
aboundeth by Christ.
6 And whether we be afflicted, *it is*
for your consolation and salvation,
which is effectual in the enduring of the
same sufferings which we also suffer:
or whether we be comforted, *it is* for
your consolation and salvation.
7 And our hope of you *is* stedfast,
knowing, that as ye are partakers of the
sufferings, so *shall ye be* also of the
consolation.
8 For we would not, brethren, have
you ignorant of our trouble which came
to us in Asia, that we were pressed out
of measure, above strength, insomuch
that we despaired even of life:
9 But we had the sentence of death in
ourselves, that we should not trust in
ourselves, but in God which raiseth the
dead:
10 Who delivered us from so great a
death, and doth deliver: in whom we
trust that he will yet deliver *us;*
11 Ye also helping together by prayer
for us, that for the gift *bestowed* upon
us by the means of many persons
thanks may be given by many on our
behalf.
12 For our rejoicing is this, the testi-
mony of our conscience, that in sim-
plicity and godly sincerity, not with
fleshly wisdom, but by the grace of
God, we have had our conversation in
the world, and more abundantly to
you-ward.
13 For we write none other things
unto you, than what ye read or acknowl-
edge; and I trust ye shall acknowledge
even to the end;
14 As also ye have acknowledged us
in part, that we are your rejoicing, even
as ye also *are* ours in the day of the
Lord Jesus.
15 And in this confidence I was
minded to come unto you before, that
ye might have a second benefit;
16 And to pass by you into Macedo-
nia, and to come again out of Macedo-
nia unto you, and of you to be brought
on my way toward Judæa.
17 When I therefore was thus
minded, did I use lightness? or the
things that I purpose, do I purpose ac-
cording to the flesh, that with me there
should be yea yea, and nay nay?
18 But *as* God *is* true, our word to-
ward you was not yea and nay.
19 For the Son of God, Jesus Christ,
who was preached among you by us,
even by me and Sĭl-vā'nus and Tĭ-
mō'the-us, was not yea and nay, but in
him was yea.
20 For all the promises of God in him
are yea, and in him Amen, unto the
glory of God by us.
21 Now he which stablisheth us with
you in Christ, and hath anointed us, *is*
God;
22 Who hath also sealed us, and giv-
en the earnest of the Spirit in our
hearts.
23 Moreover I call God for a record
upon my soul, that to spare you I came
not as yet unto Corinth.
24 Not for that we have dominion
over your faith, but are helpers of your
joy: for by faith ye stand.

CHAPTER 2

BUT I determined this with myself,
that I would not come again to you in
heaviness.
2 For if I make you sorry, who is he
then that maketh me glad, but the same
which is made sorry by me?
3 And I wrote this same unto you,
lest, when I came, I should have sorrow
from them of whom I ought to rejoice;
having confidence in you all, that my
joy is *the joy* of you all.
4 For out of much affliction and an-
guish of heart I wrote unto you with
many tears; not that ye should be
grieved, but that ye might know the
love which I have more abundantly
unto you.
5 But if any have caused grief, he
hath not grieved me, but in part: that I
may not overcharge you all.
6 Sufficient to such a man *is* this pun-
ishment, which *was inflicted* of many.
7 So that contrariwise ye *ought* rath-
er to forgive *him*, and comfort *him*,
lest perhaps such a one should be swal-
lowed up with overmuch sorrow.
8 Wherefore I beseech you that ye
would confirm *your* love toward him.
9 For to this end also did I write, that I
might know the proof of you, whether
ye be obedient in all things.
10 To whom ye forgive any thing, I
forgive also: for if I forgave any thing,
to whom I forgave *it*, for your sakes *for-
gave I it* in the person of Christ;
11 Lest Satan should get an advan-
tage of us: for we are not ignorant of his
devices.
12 Furthermore, when I came to
Troas to *preach* Christ's gospel, and a
door was opened unto me of the Lord,
13 I had no rest in my spirit, because I
found not Titus my brother: but taking
my leave of them, I went from thence
into Macedonia.
14 Now thanks *be* unto God, which
always causeth us to triumph in Christ,
and maketh manifest the savour of his
knowledge by us in every place.

15 For we are unto God a sweet savour of Christ, in them that are saved, and in them that perish:
16 To the one *we are* the savour of death unto death; and to the other the savour of life unto life. And who *is* sufficient for these things?
17 For we are not as many, which corrupt the word of God: but as of sincerity, but as of God, in the sight of God speak we in Christ.

CHAPTER 3

DO we begin again to commend ourselves? or need we, as some *others*, epistles of commendation to you, or *letters* of commendation from you?
2 Ye are our epistle written in our hearts, known and read of all men:
3 *Forasmuch as ye are* manifestly declared to be the epistle of Christ ministered by us, written not with ink, but with the Spirit of the living God; not in tables of stone, but in fleshy tables of the heart.
4 And such trust have we through Christ to God-ward:
5 Not that we are sufficient of ourselves to think any thing as of ourselves; but our sufficiency *is* of God;
6 Who also hath made us able ministers of the new testament; not of the letter, but of the spirit: for the letter killeth, but the spirit giveth life.
7 But if the ministration of death, written *and* engraven in stones, was glorious, so that the children of Israel could not stedfastly behold the face of Moses for the glory of his countenance; which *glory* was to be done away:
8 How shall not the ministration of the spirit be rather glorious?
9 For if the ministration of condemnation *be* glory, much more doth the ministration of righteousness exceed in glory.
10 For even that which was made glorious had no glory in this respect, by reason of the glory that excelleth.
11 For if that which is done away *was* glorious, much more that which remaineth *is* glorious.
12 Seeing then that we have such hope, we use great plainness of speech:
13 And not as Moses, *which* put a vail over his face, that the children of Israel could not stedfastly look to the end of that which is abolished:
14 But their minds were blinded: for until this day remaineth the same vail untaken away in the reading of the old testament; which *vail* is done away in Christ.
15 But even unto this day, when Moses is read, the vail is upon their heart.
16 Nevertheless when it shall turn to the Lord, the vail shall be taken away.
17 Now the Lord is that Spirit: and where the Spirit of the Lord *is*, there *is* liberty.
18 But we all, with open face beholding as in a glass the glory of the Lord, are changed into the same image from glory to glory, *even* as by the Spirit of the Lord.

CHAPTER 4

THEREFORE seeing we have this ministry, as we have received mercy, we faint not;
2 But have renounced the hidden things of dishonesty, not walking in craftiness, nor handling the word of God deceitfully; but by manifestation of the truth commending ourselves to every man's conscience in the sight of God.
3 But if our gospel be hid, it is hid to them that are lost:
4 In whom the god of this world hath blinded the minds of them which believe not, lest the light of the glorious gospel of Christ, who is the image of God, should shine unto them.
5 For we preach not ourselves, but Christ Jesus the Lord; and ourselves your servants for Jesus' sake.
6 For God, who commanded the light to shine out of darkness, hath shined in our hearts, to *give* the light of the knowledge of the glory of God in the face of Jesus Christ.
7 But we have this treasure in earthen vessels, that the excellency of the power may be of God, and not of us.
8 *We are* troubled on every side, yet not distressed; *we are* perplexed, but not in despair;
9 Persecuted, but not forsaken; cast down, but not destroyed;
10 Always bearing about in the body the dying of the Lord Jesus, that the life also of Jesus might be made manifest in our body.
11 For we which live are alway delivered unto death for Jesus' sake, that the life also of Jesus might be made manifest in our mortal flesh.
12 So then death worketh in us, but life in you.
13 We having the same spirit of faith, according as it is written, I believed, and therefore have I spoken; we also believe, and therefore speak;
14 Knowing that he which raised up the Lord Jesus shall raise up us also by Jesus, and shall present *us* with you.

15 For all things *are* for your sakes, that the abundant grace might through the thanksgiving of many redound to the glory of God.

16 For which cause we faint not; but though our outward man perish, yet the inward *man* is renewed day by day.

17 For our light affliction, which is but for a moment, worketh for us a far more exceeding *and* eternal weight of glory;

18 While we look not at the things which are seen, but at the things which are not seen: for the things which are seen *are* temporal; but the things which are not seen *are* eternal.

CHAPTER 5

FOR we know that if our earthly house of *this* tabernacle were dissolved, we have a building of God, an house not made with hands, eternal in the heavens.

2 For in this we groan, earnestly desiring to be clothed upon with our house which is from heaven:

3 If so be that being clothed we shall not be found naked.

4 For we that are in *this* tabernacle do groan, being burdened: not for that we would be unclothed, but clothed upon, that mortality might be swallowed up of life.

5 Now he that hath wrought us for the selfsame thing *is* God, who also hath given unto us the earnest of the Spirit.

6 Therefore *we are* always confident, knowing that, whilst we are at home in the body, we are absent from the Lord:

7 (For we walk by faith, not by sight:)

8 We are confident, *I say*, and willing rather to be absent from the body, and to be present with the Lord.

9 Wherefore we labour, that, whether present or absent, we may be accepted of him.

10 For we must all appear before the judgment seat of Christ; that every one may receive the things *done* in *his* body, according to that he hath done, whether *it be* good or bad.

11 Knowing therefore the terror of the Lord, we persuade men; but we are made manifest unto God; and I trust also are made manifest in your consciences.

12 For we commend not ourselves again unto you, but give you occasion to glory on our behalf, that ye may have somewhat to *answer* them which glory in appearance, and not in heart.

13 For whether we be beside ourselves, *it is* to God: or whether we be sober, *it is* for your cause.

14 For the love of Christ constraineth us; because we thus judge, that if one died for all, then were all dead:

15 And *that* he died for all, that they which live should not henceforth live unto themselves, but unto him which died for them, and rose again.

16 Wherefore henceforth know we no man after the flesh: yea, though we have known Christ after the flesh, yet now henceforth know we *him* no more.

17 Therefore if any man *be* in Christ, *he is* a new creature: old things are passed away; behold, all things are become new.

18 And all things *are* of God, who hath reconciled us to himself by Jesus Christ, and hath given to us the ministry of reconciliation;

19 To wit, that God was in Christ, reconciling the world unto himself, not imputing their trespasses unto them; and hath committed unto us the word of reconciliation.

20 Now then we are ambassadors for Christ, as though God did beseech *you* by us: we pray *you* in Christ's stead, be ye reconciled to God.

21 For he hath made him *to be* sin for us, who knew no sin; that we might be made the righteousness of God in him.

CHAPTER 6

WE then, *as* workers together *with him*, beseech *you* also that ye receive not the grace of God in vain.

2 (For he saith, I have heard thee in a time accepted, and in the day of salvation have I succoured thee: behold, now *is* the accepted time; behold, now *is* the day of salvation.)

3 Giving no offence in any thing, that the ministry be not blamed:

4 But in all *things* approving ourselves as the ministers of God, in much patience, in afflictions, in necessities, in distresses,

5 In stripes, in imprisonments, in tumults, in labours, in watchings, in fastings;

6 By pureness, by knowledge, by longsuffering, by kindness, by the Holy Ghost, by love unfeigned,

7 By the word of truth, by the power of God, by the armour of righteousness on the right hand and on the left,

8 By honour and dishonour, by evil report and good report: as deceivers, and *yet* true;

9 As unknown, and *yet* well known; as dying, and, behold, we live; as chastened, and not killed;

10 As sorrowful, yet alway rejoicing; as poor, yet making many rich; as hav-

ing nothing, and *yet* possessing all things.

11 O *ye* Co-rĭnth′ĭ-anṡ, our mouth is open unto you, our heart is enlarged.

12 Ye are not straitened in us, but ye are straitened in your own bowels.

13 Now for a recompence in the same, (I speak as unto *my* children,) be ye also enlarged.

14 Be ye not unequally yoked together with unbelievers: for what fellowship hath righteousness with unrighteousness? and what communion hath light with darkness?

15 And what concord hath Christ with Bē′lĭ-al? or what part hath he that believeth with an infidel?

16 And what agreement hath the temple of God with idols? for ye are the temple of the living God; as God hath said, I will dwell in them, and walk in *them;* and I will be their God, and they shall be my people.

17 Wherefore come out from among them, and be ye separate, saith the Lord, and touch not the unclean *thing;* and I will receive you,

18 And will be a Father unto you, and ye shall be my sons and daughters, saith the Lord Almighty.

CHAPTER 7

HAVING therefore these promises, dearly beloved, let us cleanse ourselves from all filthiness of the flesh and spirit, perfecting holiness in the fear of God.

2 Receive us; we have wronged no man, we have corrupted no man, we have defrauded no man.

3 I speak not *this* to condemn *you:* for I have said before, that ye are in our hearts to die and live with *you.*

4 Great *is* my boldness of speech toward you, great *is* my glorying of you: I am filled with comfort, I am exceeding joyful in all our tribulation.

5 For, when we were come into Macedonia, our flesh had no rest, but we were troubled on every side; without *were* fightings, within *were* fears.

6 Nevertheless God, that comforteth those that are cast down, comforted us by the coming of Titus;

7 And not by his coming only, but by the consolation wherewith he was comforted in you, when he told us your earnest desire, your mourning, your fervent mind toward me, so that I rejoiced the more.

8 For though I made you sorry with a letter, I do not repent, though I did repent: for I perceive that the same epistle hath made you sorry, though *it were* but for a season.

9 Now I rejoice, not that ye were made sorry, but that ye sorrowed to repentance: for ye were made sorry after a godly manner, that ye might receive damage by us in nothing.

10 For godly sorrow worketh repentance to salvation not to be repented of: but the sorrow of the world worketh death.

11 For behold this selfsame thing, that ye sorrowed after a godly sort, what carefulness it wrought in you, yea, *what* clearing of yourselves, yea, *what* indignation, yea, *what* fear, yea, *what* vehement desire, yea, *what* zeal, yea, *what* revenge! In all *things* ye have approved yourselves to be clear in this matter.

12 Wherefore, though I wrote unto you, *I did it* not for his cause that had done the wrong, nor for his cause that suffered wrong, but that our care for you in the sight of God might appear unto you.

13 Therefore we were comforted in your comfort: yea, and exceedingly the more joyed we for the joy of Titus, because his spirit was refreshed by you all.

14 For if I have boasted any thing to him of you, I am not ashamed; but as we spake all things to you in truth, even so our boasting, which *I made* before Titus, is found a truth.

15 And his inward affection is more abundant toward you, whilst he remembereth the obedience of you all, how with fear and trembling ye received him.

16 I rejoice therefore that I have confidence in you in all *things.*

CHAPTER 8

MOREOVER, brethren, we do you to wit of the grace of God bestowed on the churches of Macedonia;

2 How that in a great trial of affliction the abundance of their joy and their deep poverty abounded unto the riches of their liberality.

3 For to *their* power, I bear record, yea, and beyond *their* power *they were* willing of themselves;

4 Praying us with much intreaty that we would receive the gift, and *take upon us* the fellowship of the ministering to the saints.

5 And *this they did,* not as we hoped, but first gave their own selves to the Lord, and unto us by the will of God.

6 Insomuch that we desired Titus, that as he had begun, so he would also finish in you the same grace also.

7 Therefore, as ye abound in every *thing, in* faith, and utterance, and

knowledge, and *in* all diligence, and *in*
your love to us, *see* that ye abound in
this grace also.
8 I speak not by commandment, but
by occasion of the forwardness of others,
and to prove the sincerity of your
love.
9 For ye know the grace of our Lord
Jesus Christ, that, though he was rich,
yet for your sakes he became poor, that
ye through his poverty might be rich.
10 And herein I give *my* advice: for
this is expedient for you, who have begun
before, not only to do, but also to
be forward a year ago.
11 Now therefore perform the doing
of it; that as *there was* a readiness to
will, so *there may be* a performance
also out of that which ye have.
12 For if there be first a willing mind,
it is accepted according to that a man
hath, *and* not according to that he hath
not.
13 For *I mean* not that other men be
eased, and ye burdened:
14 But by an equality, *that* now at this
time your abundance *may be a supply*
for their want, that their abundance
also may be *a supply* for your want:
that there may be equality:
15 As it is written, He that *had gathered*
much had nothing over; and he
that *had gathered* little had no lack.
16 But thanks *be* to God, which put
the same earnest care into the heart of
Titus for you.
17 For indeed he accepted the exhortation;
but being more forward, of his
own accord he went unto you.
18 And we have sent with him the
brother, whose praise *is* in the gospel
throughout all the churches;
19 And not *that* only, but who was
also chosen of the churches to travel
with us with this grace, which is administered
by us to the glory of the
same Lord, and *declaration of* your
ready mind:
20 Avoiding this, that no man should
blame us in this abundance which is administered
by us:
21 Providing for honest things, not
only in the sight of the Lord, but also in
the sight of men.
22 And we have sent with them our
brother, whom we have oftentimes
proved diligent in many things, but
now much more diligent, upon the
great confidence which *I have* in you.
23 Whether *any do enquire* of Titus,
he is my partner and fellowhelper concerning
you: or our brethren *be enquired of, they are* the messengers of
the churches, *and* the glory of Christ.
24 Wherefore shew ye to them, and
before the churches, the proof of your
love, and of our boasting on your behalf.

CHAPTER 9

FOR as touching the ministering to the
saints, it is superfluous for me to write
to you:
2 For I know the forwardness of your
mind, for which I boast of you to them
of Macedonia, that A-chā'ia was ready
a year ago; and your zeal hath provoked
very many.
3 Yet have I sent the brethren, lest
our boasting of you should be in vain in
this behalf; that, as I said, ye may be
ready:
4 Lest haply if they of Macedonia
come with me, and find you unprepared,
we (that we say not, ye) should
be ashamed in this same confident
boasting.
5 Therefore I thought it necessary to
exhort the brethren, that they would go
before unto you, and make up beforehand
your bounty, whereof ye had notice
before, that the same might be
ready, as *a matter of* bounty, and not as
of covetousness.
6 But this *I say,* He which soweth
sparingly shall reap also sparingly; and
he which soweth bountifully shall reap
also bountifully.
7 Every man according as he purposeth
in his heart, *so let him give;* not
grudgingly, or of necessity: for God loveth
a cheerful giver.
8 And God *is* able to make all grace
abound toward you; that ye, always having
all sufficiency in all *things,* may
abound to every good work:
9 (As it is written, He hath dispersed
abroad; he hath given to the poor: his
righteousness remaineth for ever.
10 Now he that ministereth seed to
the sower both minister bread for *your*
food, and multiply your seed sown, and
increase the fruits of your righteousness;)
11 Being enriched in every thing to all
bountifulness, which causeth through
us thanksgiving to God.
12 For the administration of this service
not only supplieth the want of the
saints, but is abundant also by many
thanksgivings unto God;
13 Whiles by the experiment of this
ministration they glorify God for your
professed subjection unto the gospel of
Christ, and for *your* liberal distribution
unto them, and unto all *men;*
14 And by their prayer for you, which
long after you for the exceeding grace
of God in you.

15 Thanks *be* unto God for his unspeakable gift.

CHAPTER 10

NOW I Paul myself beseech you by the meekness and gentleness of Christ, who in presence *am* base among you, but being absent am bold toward you:

2 But I beseech *you*, that I may not be bold when I am present with that confidence, wherewith I think to be bold against some, which think of us as if we walked according to the flesh.

3 For though we walk in the flesh, we do not war after the flesh:

4 (For the weapons of our warfare *are* not carnal, but mighty through God to the pulling down of strong holds;)

5 Casting down imaginations, and every high thing that exalteth itself against the knowledge of God, and bringing into captivity every thought to the obedience of Christ;

6 And having in a readiness to revenge all disobedience, when your obedience is fulfilled.

7 Do ye look on things after the outward appearance? If any man trust to himself that he is Christ's, let him of himself think this again, that, as he *is* Christ's, even so *are* we Christ's.

8 For though I should boast somewhat more of our authority, which the Lord hath given us for edification, and not for your destruction, I should not be ashamed:

9 That I may not seem as if I would terrify you by letters.

10 For *his* letters, say they, *are* weighty and powerful; but *his* bodily presence *is* weak, and *his* speech contemptible.

11 Let such an one think this, that, such as we are in word by letters when we are absent, such *will we be* also in deed when we are present.

12 For we dare not make ourselves of the number, or compare ourselves with some that commend themselves: but they measuring themselves by themselves, and comparing themselves among themselves, are not wise.

13 But we will not boast of things without *our* measure, but according to the measure of the rule which God hath distributed to us, a measure to reach even unto you.

14 For we stretch not ourselves beyond *our measure*, as though we reached not unto you: for we are come as far as to you also in *preaching* the gospel of Christ:

15 Not boasting of things without *our* measure, *that is*, of other men's labours; but having hope, when your faith is increased, that we shall be enlarged by you according to our rule abundantly,

16 To preach the gospel in the *regions* beyond you, *and* not to boast in another man's line of things made ready to our hand.

17 But he that glorieth, let him glory in the Lord.

18 For not he that commendeth himself is approved, but whom the Lord commendeth.

CHAPTER 11

WOULD to God ye could bear with me a little in *my* folly: and indeed bear with me.

2 For I am jealous over you with godly jealousy: for I have espoused you to one husband, that I may present *you as* a chaste virgin to Christ.

3 But I fear, lest by any means, as the serpent beguiled Eve through his subtilty, so your minds should be corrupted from the simplicity that is in Christ.

4 For if he that cometh preacheth another Jesus, whom we have not preached, or *if* ye receive another spirit, which ye have not received, or another gospel, which ye have not accepted, ye might well bear with *him*.

5 For I suppose I was not a whit behind the very chiefest apostles.

6 But though *I be* rude in speech, yet not in knowledge; but we have been throughly made manifest among you in all things.

7 Have I committed an offence in abasing myself that ye might be exalted, because I have preached to you the gospel of God freely?

8 I robbed other churches, taking wages *of them*, to do you service.

9 And when I was present with you, and wanted, I was chargeable to no man: for that which was lacking to me the brethren which came from Macedonia supplied: and in all *things* I have kept myself from being burdensome unto you, and *so* will I keep *myself*.

10 As the truth of Christ is in me, no man shall stop me of this boasting in the regions of A-chā'ia.

11 Wherefore? because I love you not? God knoweth.

12 But what I do, that I will do, that I may cut off occasion from them which desire occasion; that wherein they glory, they may be found even as we.

13 For such *are* false apostles, deceitful workers, transforming themselves into the apostles of Christ.

14 And no marvel; for Satan himself is transformed into an angel of light.

15 Therefore *it is* no great thing if his
ministers also be transformed as the
ministers of righteousness; whose end
shall be according to their works.
16 I say again, Let no man think me a
fool; if otherwise, yet as a fool receive
me, that I may boast myself a little.
17 That which I speak, I speak *it* not
after the Lord, but as it were foolishly,
in this confidence of boasting.
18 Seeing that many glory after the
flesh, I will glory also.
19 For ye suffer fools gladly, seeing
ye *yourselves* are wise.
20 For ye suffer, if a man bring you
into bondage, if a man devour *you*, if a
man take *of you*, if a man exalt himself,
if a man smite you on the face.
21 I speak as concerning reproach, as
though we had been weak. Howbeit
whereinsoever any is bold, (I speak
foolishly,) I am bold also.
22 Are they Hebrews? so *am* I. Are
they Israelites? so *am* I. Are they the
seed of Abraham? so *am* I.
23 Are they ministers of Christ? (I
speak as a fool) I *am* more; in labours
more abundant, in stripes above mea-
sure, in prisons more frequent, in
deaths oft.
24 Of the Jews five times received I
forty *stripes* save one.
25 Thrice was I beaten with rods,
once was I stoned, thrice I suffered
shipwreck, a night and a day I have
been in the deep;
26 *In* journeyings often, *in* perils of
waters, *in* perils of robbers, *in* perils by
mine own countrymen, *in* perils by the
heathen, *in* perils in the city, *in* perils in
the wilderness, *in* perils in the sea, *in*
perils among false brethren;
27 In weariness and painfulness, in
watchings often, in hunger and thirst,
in fastings often, in cold and naked-
ness.
28 Beside those things that are
without, that which cometh upon me
daily, the care of all the churches.
29 Who is weak, and I am not weak?
who is offended, and I burn not?
30 If I must needs glory, I will glory of
the things which concern mine infirmi-
ties.
31 The God and Father of our Lord
Jesus Christ, which is blessed for ever-
more, knoweth that I lie not.
32 In Damascus the governor under
Ăr′e-tas the king kept the city of the
Dăm′as-cēnes with a garrison, desirous
to apprehend me:
33 And through a window in a basket
was I let down by the wall, and escaped
his hands.

CHAPTER 12

IT is not expedient for me doubtless to
glory. I will come to visions and revela-
tions of the Lord.
2 I knew a man in Christ above four-
teen years ago, (whether in the body, I
cannot tell; or whether out of the body,
I cannot tell: God knoweth;) such an
one caught up to the third heaven.
3 And I knew such a man, (whether in
the body, or out of the body, I cannot
tell: God knoweth;)
4 How that he was caught up into
paradise, and heard unspeakable
words, which it is not lawful for a man
to utter.
5 Of such an one will I glory: yet of
myself I will not glory, but in mine infir-
mities.
6 For though I would desire to glory, I
shall not be a fool; for I will say the
truth: but *now* I forbear, lest any man
should think of me above that which he
seeth me *to be*, or *that* he heareth of
me.
7 And lest I should be exalted above
measure through the abundance of the
revelations, there was given to me a
thorn in the flesh, the messenger of Sa-
tan to buffet me, lest I should be ex-
alted above measure.
8 For this thing I besought the Lord
thrice, that it might depart from me.
9 And he said unto me, My grace is
sufficient for thee: for my strength is
made perfect in weakness. Most gladly
therefore will I rather glory in my infir-
mities, that the power of Christ may
rest upon me.
10 Therefore I take pleasure in infir-
mities, in reproaches, in necessities, in
persecutions, in distresses for Christ's
sake: for when I am weak, then am I
strong.
11 I am become a fool in glorying; ye
have compelled me: for I ought to have
been commended of you: for in nothing
am I behind the very chiefest apostles,
though I be nothing.
12 Truly the signs of an apostle were
wrought among you in all patience, in
signs, and wonders, and mighty deeds.
13 For what is it wherein ye were in-
ferior to other churches, except *it be*
that I myself was not burdensome to
you? forgive me this wrong.
14 Behold, the third time I am ready
to come to you; and I will not be bur-
densome to you: for I seek not yours,
but you: for the children ought not to
lay up for the parents, but the parents
for the children.
15 And I will very gladly spend and

be spent for you; though the more abundantly I love you, the less I be loved.

16 But be it so, I did not burden you: nevertheless, being crafty, I caught you with guile.

17 Did I make a gain of you by any of them whom I sent unto you?

18 I desired Titus, and with *him* I sent a brother. Did Titus make a gain of you? walked we not in the same spirit? *walked we* not in the same steps?

19 Again, think ye that we excuse ourselves unto you? we speak before God in Christ: but *we do* all things, dearly beloved, for your edifying.

20 For I fear, lest when I come, I shall not find you such as I would, and *that* I shall be found unto you such as ye would not: lest *there be* debates, envyings, wraths, strifes, backbitings, whisperings, swellings, tumults:

21 *And* lest, when I come again, my God will humble me among you, and *that* I shall bewail many which have sinned already, and have not repented of the uncleanness and fornication and lasciviousness which they have committed.

CHAPTER 13

THIS *is* the third *time* I am coming to you. In the mouth of two or three witnesses shall every word be established.

2 I told you before, and foretell you, as if I were present, the second time; and being absent now I write to them which heretofore have sinned, and to all other, that, if I come again, I will not spare:

3 Since ye seek a proof of Christ speaking in me, which to you-ward is not weak, but is mighty in you.

4 For though he was crucified through weakness, yet he liveth by the power of God. For we also are weak in him, but we shall live with him by the power of God toward you.

5 Examine yourselves, whether ye be in the faith; prove your own selves. Know ye not your own selves, how that Jesus Christ is in you, except ye be reprobates?

6 But I trust that ye shall know that we are not reprobates.

7 Now I pray to God that ye do no evil; not that we should appear approved, but that ye should do that which is honest, though we be as reprobates.

8 For we can do nothing against the truth, but for the truth.

9 For we are glad, when we are weak, and ye are strong: and this also we wish, *even* your perfection.

10 Therefore I write these things being absent, lest being present I should use sharpness, according to the power which the Lord hath given me to edification, and not to destruction.

11 Finally, brethren, farewell. Be perfect, be of good comfort, be of one mind, live in peace; and the God of love and peace shall be with you.

12 Greet one another with an holy kiss.

13 All the saints salute you.

14 The grace of the Lord Jesus Christ, and the love of God, and the communion of the Holy Ghost, *be* with you all. Amen.

The second *epistle* to the Corinthians was written from Philippi, *a city* of Macedonia, by Titus and Lucas.

THE EPISTLE OF PAUL THE APOSTLE TO THE

GALATIANS

CHAPTER 1

PAUL, an apostle, (not of men, neither by man, but by Jesus Christ, and God the Father, who raised him from the dead;)

2 And all the brethren which are with me, unto the churches of Ga-lā′tia:

3 Grace *be* to you and peace from God the Father, and *from* our Lord Jesus Christ,

4 Who gave himself for our sins, that he might deliver us from this present evil world, according to the will of God and our Father:

5 To whom *be* glory for ever and ever. Amen.

6 I marvel that ye are so soon removed from him that called you into the grace of Christ unto another gospel:

7 Which is not another; but there be some that trouble you, and would pervert the gospel of Christ.

8 But though we, or an angel from heaven, preach any other gospel unto you than that which we have preached unto you, let him be accursed.

9 As we said before, so say I now again, if any *man* preach any other gospel unto you than that ye have received, let him be accursed.

10 For do I now persuade men, or God? or do I seek to please men? for if I yet pleased men, I should not be the servant of Christ.

11 But I certify you, brethren, that
the gospel which was preached of me is
not after man.
12 For I neither received it of man,
neither was I taught *it*, but by the revela-
tion of Jesus Christ.
13 For ye have heard of my conversa-
tion in time past in the Jews' religion,
how that beyond measure I persecuted
the church of God, and wasted it:
14 And profited in the Jews' religion
above many my equals in mine own na-
tion, being more exceedingly zealous
of the traditions of my fathers.
15 But when it pleased God, who sepa-
rated me from my mother's womb,
and called *me* by his grace,
16 To reveal his Son in me, that I
might preach him among the heathen;
immediately I conferred not with flesh
and blood:
17 Neither went I up to Jerusalem to
them which were apostles before me;
but I went into Arabia, and returned
again unto Damascus.
18 Then after three years I went up to
Jerusalem to see Peter, and abode with
him fifteen days.
19 But other of the apostles saw I
none, save James the Lord's brother.
20 Now the things which I write unto
you, behold, before God, I lie not.
21 Afterwards I came into the regions
of Syria and Ċĭ-lĭ′ċia;
22 And was unknown by face unto
the churches of Judæa which were in
Christ:
23 But they had heard only, That he
which persecuted us in times past now
preacheth the faith which once he de-
stroyed.
24 And they glorified God in me.

CHAPTER 2

THEN fourteen years after I went up
again to Jerusalem with Barnabas, and
took Titus with *me* also.
2 And I went up by revelation, and
communicated unto them that gospel
which I preach among the Gentiles, but
privately to them which were of repu-
tation, lest by any means I should run,
or had run, in vain.
3 But neither Titus, who was with me,
being a Greek, was compelled to be cir-
cumcised:
4 And that because of false brethren
unawares brought in, who came in priv-
ily to spy out our liberty which we
have in Christ Jesus, that they might
bring us into bondage:
5 To whom we gave place by subjec-
tion, no, not for an hour; that the truth
of the gospel might continue with you.
6 But of these who seemed to be
somewhat, (whatsoever they were, it
maketh no matter to me: God accept-
eth no man's person:) for they who
seemed *to be somewhat* in conference
added nothing to me:
7 But contrariwise, when they saw
that the gospel of the uncircumcision
was committed unto me, as *the gospel*
of the circumcision *was* unto Peter;
8 (For he that wrought effectually in
Peter to the apostleship of the circum-
cision, the same was mighty in me to-
ward the Gentiles:)
9 And when James, Ċē′phas, and
John, who seemed to be pillars, per-
ceived the grace that was given unto
me, they gave to me and Barnabas the
right hands of fellowship; that we
should go unto the heathen, and they
unto the circumcision.
10 Only *they would* that we should
remember the poor; the same which I
also was forward to do.
11 But when Peter was come to An-
tioch, I withstood him to the face, be-
cause he was to be blamed.
12 For before that certain came from
James, he did eat with the Gentiles: but
when they were come, he withdrew
and separated himself, fearing them
which were of the circumcision.
13 And the other Jews dissembled
likewise with him; insomuch that Bar-
nabas also was carried away with their
dissimulation.
14 But when I saw that they walked
not uprightly according to the truth of
the gospel, I said unto Peter before
them all, If thou, being a Jew, livest af-
ter the manner of Gentiles, and not as
do the Jews, why compellest thou the
Gentiles to live as do the Jews?
15 We *who are* Jews by nature, and
not sinners of the Gentiles,
16 Knowing that a man is not jus-
tified by the works of the law, but by
the faith of Jesus Christ, even we have
believed in Jesus Christ, that we might
be justified by the faith of Christ, and
not by the works of the law: for by the
works of the law shall no flesh be jus-
tified.
17 But if, while we seek to be justified
by Christ, we ourselves also are found
sinners, *is* therefore Christ the minister
of sin? God forbid.
18 For if I build again the things
which I destroyed, I make myself a
transgressor.
19 For I through the law am dead to
the law, that I might live unto God.
20 I am crucified with Christ: never-
theless I live; yet not I, but Christ liveth
in me: and the life which I now live in
the flesh I live by the faith of the Son of

God, who loved me, and gave himself for me.

21 I do not frustrate the grace of God: for if righteousness *come* by the law, then Christ is dead in vain.

CHAPTER 3

O FOOLISH Ga-lā'tians, who hath bewitched you, that ye should not obey the truth, before whose eyes Jesus Christ hath been evidently set forth, crucified among you?

2 This only would I learn of you, Received ye the Spirit by the works of the law, or by the hearing of faith?

3 Are ye so foolish? having begun in the Spirit, are ye now made perfect by the flesh?

4 Have ye suffered so many things in vain? if *it be* yet in vain.

5 He therefore that ministereth to you the Spirit, and worketh miracles among you, *doeth he it* by the works of the law, or by the hearing of faith?

6 Even as Abraham believed God, and it was accounted to him for righteousness.

7 Know ye therefore that they which are of faith, the same are the children of Abraham.

8 And the scripture, foreseeing that God would justify the heathen through faith, preached before the gospel unto Abraham, *saying*, In thee shall all nations be blessed.

9 So then they which be of faith are blessed with faithful Abraham.

10 For as many as are of the works of the law are under the curse: for it is written, Cursed *is* every one that continueth not in all things which are written in the book of the law to do them.

11 But that no man is justified by the law in the sight of God, *it is* evident: for, The just shall live by faith.

12 And the law is not of faith: but, The man that doeth them shall live in them.

13 Christ hath redeemed us from the curse of the law, being made a curse for us: for it is written, Cursed *is* every one that hangeth on a tree:

14 That the blessing of Abraham might come on the Gentiles through Jesus Christ; that we might receive the promise of the Spirit through faith.

15 Brethren, I speak after the manner of men; Though *it be* but a man's covenant, yet *if it be* confirmed, no man disannulleth, or addeth thereto.

16 Now to Abraham and his seed were the promises made. He saith not, And to seeds, as of many; but as of one, And to thy seed, which is Christ.

17 And this I say, *that* the covenant, that was confirmed before of God in Christ, the law, which was four hundred and thirty years after, cannot disannul, that it should make the promise of none effect.

18 For if the inheritance *be* of the law, *it is* no more of promise: but God gave *it* to Abraham by promise.

19 Wherefore then *serveth* the law? It was added because of transgressions, till the seed should come to whom the promise was made; *and it was* ordained by angels in the hand of a mediator.

20 Now a mediator is not *a mediator* of one, but God is one.

21 *Is* the law then against the promises of God? God forbid: for if there had been a law given which could have given life, verily righteousness should have been by the law.

22 But the scripture hath concluded all under sin, that the promise by faith of Jesus Christ might be given to them that believe.

23 But before faith came, we were kept under the law, shut up unto the faith which should afterwards be revealed.

24 Wherefore the law was our schoolmaster *to bring us* unto Christ, that we might be justified by faith.

25 But after that faith is come, we are no longer under a schoolmaster.

26 For ye are all the children of God by faith in Christ Jesus.

27 For as many of you as have been baptized into Christ have put on Christ.

28 There is neither Jew nor Greek, there is neither bond nor free, there is neither male nor female: for ye are all one in Christ Jesus.

29 And if ye *be* Christ's, then are ye Abraham's seed, and heirs according to the promise.

CHAPTER 4

NOW I say, *That* the heir, as long as he is a child, differeth nothing from a servant, though he be lord of all;

2 But is under tutors and governors until the time appointed of the father.

3 Even so we, when we were children, were in bondage under the elements of the world:

4 But when the fulness of the time was come, God sent forth his Son, made of a woman, made under the law,

5 To redeem them that were under the law, that we might receive the adoption of sons.

6 And because ye are sons, God hath sent forth the Spirit of his Son into your hearts, crying, Abba, Father.

7 Wherefore thou art no more a ser-

vant, but a son; and if a son, then an
heir of God through Christ.
8 Howbeit then, when ye knew not
God, ye did service unto them which by
nature are no gods.
9 But now, after that ye have known
God, or rather are known of God, how
turn ye again to the weak and beggarly
elements, whereunto ye desire again to
be in bondage?
10 Ye observe days, and months, and
times, and years.
11 I am afraid of you, lest I have be-
stowed upon you labour in vain.
12 Brethren, I beseech you, be as I
am; for I *am* as ye *are:* ye have not in-
jured me at all.
13 Ye know how through infirmity of
the flesh I preached the gospel unto
you at the first.
14 And my temptation which was in
my flesh ye despised not, nor rejected;
but received me as an angel of God,
even as Christ Jesus.
15 Where is then the blessedness ye
spake of? for I bear you record, that, if
it had been possible, ye would have
plucked out your own eyes, and have
given them to me.
16 Am I therefore become your en-
emy, because I tell you the truth?
17 They zealously affect you, *but* not
well; yea, they would exclude you, that
ye might affect them.
18 But *it is* good to be zealously af-
fected always in *a* good *thing,* and not
only when I am present with you.
19 My little children, of whom I tra-
vail in birth again until Christ be
formed in you,
20 I desire to be present with you
now, and to change my voice; for I
stand in doubt of you.
21 Tell me, ye that desire to be under
the law, do ye not hear the law?
22 For it is written, that Abraham
had two sons, the one by a bondmaid,
the other by a freewoman.
23 But he *who was* of the bondwoman
was born after the flesh; but he of
the freewoman *was* by promise.
24 Which things are an allegory: for
these are the two covenants; the one
from the mount Sī′naī, which gen-
dereth to bondage, which is Ā′gär.
25 For this Ā′gär is mount Sī′naī in
Arabia, and answereth to Jerusalem
which now is, and is in bondage with
her children.
26 But Jerusalem which is above is
free, which is the mother of us all.
27 For it is written, Rejoice, *thou* bar-
ren that bearest not; break forth and
cry, thou that travailest not: for the deso-
late hath many more children than
she which hath an husband.
28 Now we, brethren, as Isaac was,
are the children of promise.
29 But as then he that was born after
the flesh persecuted him *that was born*
after the Spirit, even so *it is* now.
30 Nevertheless what saith the scrip-
ture? Cast out the bondwoman and her
son: for the son of the bondwoman
shall not be heir with the son of the
freewoman.
31 So then, brethren, we are not
children of the bondwoman, but of the
free.

CHAPTER 5

STAND fast therefore in the liberty
wherewith Christ hath made us free,
and be not entangled again with the
yoke of bondage.
2 Behold, I Paul say unto you, that if
ye be circumcised, Christ shall profit
you nothing.
3 For I testify again to every man that
is circumcised, that he is a debtor to do
the whole law.
4 Christ is become of no effect unto
you, whosoever of you are justified by
the law; ye are fallen from grace.
5 For we through the Spirit wait for
the hope of righteousness by faith.
6 For in Jesus Christ neither circum-
cision availeth any thing, nor uncir-
cumcision; but faith which worketh by
love.
7 Ye did run well; who did hinder you
that ye should not obey the truth?
8 This persuasion *cometh* not of him
that calleth you.
9 A little leaven leaveneth the whole
lump.
10 I have confidence in you through
the Lord, that ye will be none otherwise
minded: but he that troubleth you shall
bear his judgment, whosoever he be.
11 And I, brethren, if I yet preach cir-
cumcision, why do I yet suffer persecu-
tion? then is the offence of the cross
ceased.
12 I would they were even cut off
which trouble you.
13 For, brethren, ye have been called
unto liberty; only *use* not liberty for an
occasion to the flesh, but by love serve
one another.
14 For all the law is fulfilled in one
word, *even* in this; Thou shalt love thy
neighbour as thyself.
15 But if ye bite and devour one an-
other, take heed that ye be not con-
sumed one of another.
16 *This* I say then, Walk in the Spirit,

and ye shall not fulfil the lust of the flesh.

17 For the flesh lusteth against the Spirit, and the Spirit against the flesh: and these are contrary the one to the other: so that ye cannot do the things that ye would.

18 But if ye be led of the Spirit, ye are not under the law.

19 Now the works of the flesh are manifest, which are *these;* Adultery, fornication, uncleanness, lasciviousness,

20 Idolatry, witchcraft, hatred, variance, emulations, wrath, strife, seditions, heresies,

21 Envyings, murders, drunkenness, revellings, and such like: of the which I tell you before, as I have also told *you* in time past, that they which do such things shall not inherit the kingdom of God.

22 But the fruit of the Spirit is love, joy, peace, longsuffering, gentleness, goodness, faith,

23 Meekness, temperance: against such there is no law.

24 And they that are Christ's have crucified the flesh with the affections and lusts.

25 If we live in the Spirit, let us also walk in the Spirit.

26 Let us not be desirous of vain glory, provoking one another, envying one another.

CHAPTER 6

BRETHREN, if a man be overtaken in a fault, ye which are spiritual, restore such an one in the spirit of meekness; considering thyself, lest thou also be tempted.

2 Bear ye one another's burdens, and so fulfil the law of Christ.

3 For if a man think himself to be something, when he is nothing, he deceiveth himself.

4 But let every man prove his own work, and then shall he have rejoicing in himself alone, and not in another.

5 For every man shall bear his own burden.

6 Let him that is taught in the word communicate unto him that teacheth in all good things.

7 Be not deceived; God is not mocked: for whatsoever a man soweth, that shall he also reap.

8 For he that soweth to his flesh shall of the flesh reap corruption; but he that soweth to the Spirit shall of the Spirit reap life everlasting.

9 And let us not be weary in well doing: for in due season we shall reap, if we faint not.

10 As we have therefore opportunity, let us do good unto all *men,* especially unto them who are of the household of faith.

11 Ye see how large a letter I have written unto you with mine own hand.

12 As many as desire to make a fair shew in the flesh, they constrain you to be circumcised; only lest they should suffer persecution for the cross of Christ.

13 For neither they themselves who are circumcised keep the law; but desire to have you circumcised, that they may glory in your flesh.

14 But God forbid that I should glory, save in the cross of our Lord Jesus Christ, by whom the world is crucified unto me, and I unto the world.

15 For in Christ Jesus neither circumcision availeth any thing, nor uncircumcision, but a new creature.

16 And as many as walk according to this rule, peace *be* on them, and mercy, and upon the Israel of God.

17 From henceforth let no man trouble me: for I bear in my body the marks of the Lord Jesus.

18 Brethren, the grace of our Lord Jesus Christ *be* with your spirit. Amen.

Unto the Galatians written from Rome

THE EPISTLE OF PAUL THE APOSTLE TO THE

EPHESIANS

CHAPTER 1

PAUL, an apostle of Jesus Christ by the will of God, to the saints which are at Ĕph′e-sus, and to the faithful in Christ Jesus:

2 Grace *be* to you, and peace, from God our Father, and *from* the Lord Jesus Christ.

3 Blessed *be* the God and Father of our Lord Jesus Christ, who hath blessed us with all spiritual blessings in heavenly *places* in Christ:

4 According as he hath chosen us in him before the foundation of the world, that we should be holy and without blame before him in love:

5 Having predestinated us unto the adoption of children by Jesus Christ to

himself, according to the good pleasure
of his will,
6 To the praise of the glory of his
grace, wherein he hath made us accepted in the beloved.
7 In whom we have redemption
through his blood, the forgiveness of
sins, according to the riches of his
grace;
8 Wherein he hath abounded toward
us in all wisdom and prudence;
9 Having made known unto us the
mystery of his will, according to his
good pleasure which he hath purposed
in himself:
10 That in the dispensation of the fulness of times he might gather together
in one all things in Christ, both which
are in heaven, and which are on earth;
even in him:
11 In whom also we have obtained an
inheritance, being predestinated according to the purpose of him who
worketh all things after the counsel of
his own will:
12 That we should be to the praise of
his glory, who first trusted in Christ.
13 In whom ye also *trusted*, after that
ye heard the word of truth, the gospel
of your salvation: in whom also after
that ye believed, ye were sealed with
that holy Spirit of promise,
14 Which is the earnest of our inheritance until the redemption of the purchased possession, unto the praise of
his glory.
15 Wherefore I also, after I heard of
your faith in the Lord Jesus, and love
unto all the saints,
16 Cease not to give thanks for you,
making mention of you in my prayers,
17 That the God of our Lord Jesus
Christ, the Father of glory, may give
unto you the spirit of wisdom and revelation in the knowledge of him:
18 The eyes of your understanding
being enlightened; that ye may know
what is the hope of his calling, and
what the riches of the glory of his inheritance in the saints,
19 And what *is* the exceeding greatness of his power to usward who believe, according to the working of his
mighty power,
20 Which he wrought in Christ, when
he raised him from the dead, and set
him at his own right hand in the heavenly *places*,
21 Far above all principality, and power, and might, and dominion, and
every name that is named, not only in
this world, but also in that which is to
come:
22 And hath put all *things* under his
feet, and gave him *to be* the head over
all *things* to the church,
23 Which is his body, the fulness of
him that filleth all in all.

CHAPTER 2

AND you *hath he quickened*, who were
dead in trespasses and sins;
2 Wherein in time past ye walked according to the course of this world, according to the prince of the power of
the air, the spirit that now worketh in
the children of disobedience:
3 Among whom also we all had our
conversation in times past in the lusts
of our flesh, fulfilling the desires of the
flesh and of the mind; and were by nature the children of wrath, even as others.
4 But God, who is rich in mercy, for
his great love wherewith he loved us,
5 Even when we were dead in sins,
hath quickened us together with
Christ, (by grace ye are saved;)
6 And hath raised *us* up together, and
made *us* sit together in heavenly *places*
in Christ Jesus:
7 That in the ages to come he might
shew the exceeding riches of his grace
in *his* kindness toward us through
Christ Jesus.
8 For by grace are ye saved through
faith; and that not of yourselves: *it is*
the gift of God:
9 Not of works, lest any man should
boast.
10 For we are his workmanship,
created in Christ Jesus unto good
works, which God hath before ordained that we should walk in them.
11 Wherefore remember, that ye
being in time past Gentiles in the flesh,
who are called Uncircumcision by that
which is called the Circumcision in the
flesh made by hands;
12 That at that time ye were without
Christ, being aliens from the commonwealth of Israel, and strangers from the
covenants of promise, having no hope,
and without God in the world:
13 But now in Christ Jesus ye who
sometimes were far off are made nigh
by the blood of Christ.
14 For he is our peace, who hath
made both one, and hath broken down
the middle wall of partition *between*
us;
15 Having abolished in his flesh the
enmity, *even* the law of commandments *contained* in ordinances; for to
make in himself of twain one new man,
so making peace;
16 And that he might reconcile both

unto God in one body by the cross, hav-
ing slain the enmity thereby:
17 And came and preached peace to
you which were afar off, and to them
that were nigh.
18 For through him we both have ac-
cess by one Spirit unto the Father.
19 Now therefore ye are no more
strangers and foreigners, but fellowciti-
zens with the saints, and of the house-
hold of God;
20 And are built upon the foundation
of the apostles and prophets, Jesus
Christ himself being the chief corner
stone;
21 In whom all the building fitly
framed together groweth unto an holy
temple in the Lord:
22 In whom ye also are builded togeth-
er for an habitation of God through
the Spirit.

CHAPTER 3

FOR this cause I Paul, the prisoner of
Jesus Christ for you Gentiles,
2 If ye have heard of the dispensation
of the grace of God which is given me
to you-ward:
3 How that by revelation he made
known unto me the mystery; (as I
wrote afore in few words,
4 Whereby, when ye read, ye may un-
derstand my knowledge in the mystery
of Christ)
5 Which in other ages was not made
known unto the sons of men, as it is
now revealed unto his holy apostles
and prophets by the Spirit;
6 That the Gentiles should be fellow-
heirs, and of the same body, and
partakers of his promise in Christ by
the gospel:
7 Whereof I was made a minister, ac-
cording to the gift of the grace of God
given unto me by the effectual working
of his power.
8 Unto me, who am less than the least
of all saints, is this grace given, that I
should preach among the Gentiles the
unsearchable riches of Christ;
9 And to make all *men* see what *is* the
fellowship of the mystery, which from
the beginning of the world hath been
hid in God, who created all things by
Jesus Christ:
10 To the intent that now unto the
principalities and powers in heavenly
places might be known by the church
the manifold wisdom of God,
11 According to the eternal purpose
which he purposed in Christ Jesus our
Lord:
12 In whom we have boldness and ac-
cess with confidence by the faith of
him.
13 Wherefore I desire that ye faint
not at my tribulations for you, which is
your glory.
14 For this cause I bow my knees
unto the Father of our Lord Jesus
Christ,
15 Of whom the whole family in
heaven and earth is named,
16 That he would grant you, accord-
ing to the riches of his glory, to be
strengthened with might by his Spirit
in the inner man;
17 That Christ may dwell in your
hearts by faith; that ye, being rooted
and grounded in love,
18 May be able to comprehend with
all saints what *is* the breadth, and
length, and depth, and height;
19 And to know the love of Christ,
which passeth knowledge, that ye
might be filled with all the fulness of
God.
20 Now unto him that is able to do
exceeding abundantly above all that
we ask or think, according to the power
that worketh in us,
21 Unto him *be* glory in the church by
Christ Jesus throughout all ages, world
without end. Amen.

CHAPTER 4

I THEREFORE, the prisoner of the
Lord, beseech you that ye walk worthy
of the vocation wherewith ye are
called,
2 With all lowliness and meekness,
with longsuffering, forbearing one an-
other in love;
3 Endeavouring to keep the unity of
the Spirit in the bond of peace.
4 *There is* one body, and one Spirit,
even as ye are called in one hope of
your calling;
5 One Lord, one faith, one baptism,
6 One God and Father of all, who *is*
above all, and through all, and in you
all.
7 But unto every one of us is given
grace according to the measure of the
gift of Christ.
8 Wherefore he saith, When he as-
cended up on high, he led captivity cap-
tive, and gave gifts unto men.
9 (Now that he ascended, what is it
but that he also descended first into the
lower parts of the earth?
10 He that descended is the same also
that ascended up far above all heavens,
that he might fill all things.)
11 And he gave some, apostles; and
some, prophets; and some, evangelists;
and some, pastors and teachers;
12 For the perfecting of the saints, for

the work of the ministry, for the edi-
fying of the body of Christ:
13 Till we all come in the unity of the
faith, and of the knowledge of the Son
of God, unto a perfect man, unto the
measure of the stature of the fulness of
Christ:
14 That we *henceforth* be no more
children, tossed to and fro, and carried
about with every wind of doctrine, by
the sleight of men, *and* cunning crafti-
ness, whereby they lie in wait to de-
ceive;
15 But speaking the truth in love,
may grow up into him in all things,
which is the head, *even* Christ:
16 From whom the whole body fitly
joined together and compacted by that
which every joint supplieth, according
to the effectual working in the measure
of every part, maketh increase of the
body unto the edifying of itself in love.
17 This I say therefore, and testify in
the Lord, that ye henceforth walk not
as other Gentiles walk, in the vanity of
their mind,
18 Having the understanding dark-
ened, being alienated from the life of
God through the ignorance that is in
them, because of the blindness of their
heart:
19 Who being past feeling have given
themselves over unto lasciviousness,
to work all uncleanness with greedi-
ness.
20 But ye have not so learned Christ;
21 If so be that ye have heard him,
and have been taught by him, as the
truth is in Jesus:
22 That ye put off concerning the for-
mer conversation the old man, which is
corrupt according to the deceitful
lusts;
23 And be renewed in the spirit of
your mind;
24 And that ye put on the new man,
which after God is created in righteous-
ness and true holiness.
25 Wherefore putting away lying,
speak every man truth with his neigh-
bour: for we are members one of an-
other.
26 Be ye angry, and sin not: let not the
sun go down upon your wrath:
27 Neither give place to the devil.
28 Let him that stole steal no more:
but rather let him labour, working with
his hands the thing which is good, that
he may have to give to him that need-
eth.
29 Let no corrupt communication
proceed out of your mouth, but that
which is good to the use of edifying,
that it may minister grace unto the
hearers.
30 And grieve not the holy Spirit of
God, whereby ye are sealed unto the
day of redemption.
31 Let all bitterness, and wrath, and
anger, and clamour, and evil speaking,
be put away from you, with all malice:
32 And be ye kind one to another,
tenderhearted, forgiving one another,
even as God for Christ's sake hath for-
given you.

CHAPTER 5

BE ye therefore followers of God as
dear children:
2 And walk in love, as Christ also
hath loved us, and hath given himself
for us an offering and a sacrifice to God
for a sweetsmelling savour.
3 But fornication, and all unclean-
ness, or covetousness, let it not be once
named among you, as becometh saints;
4 Neither filthiness, nor foolish
talking, nor jesting, which are not con-
venient: but rather giving of thanks.
5 For this ye know, that no whore-
monger, nor unclean person, nor covet-
ous man, who is an idolater, hath any
inheritance in the kingdom of Christ
and of God.
6 Let no man deceive you with vain
words: for because of these things
cometh the wrath of God upon the
children of disobedience.
7 Be not ye therefore partakers with
them.
8 For ye were sometimes darkness,
but now *are ye* light in the Lord: walk
as children of light:
9 (For the fruit of the Spirit *is* in all
goodness and righteousness and
truth;)
10 Proving what is acceptable unto
the Lord.
11 And have no fellowship with the
unfruitful works of darkness, but rath-
er reprove *them*.
12 For it is a shame even to speak of
those things which are done of them in
secret.
13 But all things that are reproved are
made manifest by the light: for what-
soever doth make manifest is light.
14 Wherefore he saith, Awake thou
that sleepest, and arise from the dead,
and Christ shall give thee light.
15 See then that ye walk circumspect-
ly, not as fools, but as wise,
16 Redeeming the time, because the
days are evil.
17 Wherefore be ye not unwise, but
understanding what the will of the
Lord *is*.
18 And be not drunk with wine, where-
in is excess; but be filled with the
Spirit;

19 Speaking to yourselves in psalms and hymns and spiritual songs, singing and making melody in your heart to the Lord;

20 Giving thanks always for all things unto God and the Father in the name of our Lord Jesus Christ;

21 Submitting yourselves one to another in the fear of God.

22 Wives, submit yourselves unto your own husbands, as unto the Lord.

23 For the husband is the head of the wife, even as Christ is the head of the church: and he is the saviour of the body.

24 Therefore as the church is subject unto Christ, so *let* the wives *be* to their own husbands in every thing.

25 Husbands, love your wives, even as Christ also loved the church, and gave himself for it;

26 That he might sanctify and cleanse it with the washing of water by the word,

27 That he might present it to himself a glorious church, not having spot, or wrinkle, or any such thing; but that it should be holy and without blemish.

28 So ought men to love their wives as their own bodies. He that loveth his wife loveth himself.

29 For no man ever yet hated his own flesh; but nourisheth and cherisheth it, even as the Lord the church:

30 For we are members of his body, of his flesh, and of his bones.

31 For this cause shall a man leave his father and mother, and shall be joined unto his wife, and they two shall be one flesh.

32 This is a great mystery: but I speak concerning Christ and the church.

33 Nevertheless let every one of you in particular so love his wife even as himself; and the wife *see* that she reverence *her* husband.

CHAPTER 6

CHILDREN, obey your parents in the Lord: for this is right.

2 Honour thy father and mother; which is the first commandment with promise;

3 That it may be well with thee, and thou mayest live long on the earth.

4 And, ye fathers, provoke not your children to wrath: but bring them up in the nurture and admonition of the Lord.

5 Servants, be obedient to them that are *your* masters according to the flesh, with fear and trembling, in singleness of your heart, as unto Christ;

6 Not with eyeservice, as menpleasers; but as the servants of Christ, doing the will of God from the heart;

7 With good will doing service, as to the Lord, and not to men:

8 Knowing that whatsoever good thing any man doeth, the same shall he receive of the Lord, whether *he be* bond or free.

9 And, ye masters, do the same things unto them, forbearing threatening: knowing that your Master also is in heaven; neither is there respect of persons with him.

10 Finally, my brethren, be strong in the Lord, and in the power of his might.

11 Put on the whole armour of God, that ye may be able to stand against the wiles of the devil.

12 For we wrestle not against flesh and blood, but against principalities, against powers, against the rulers of the darkness of this world, against spiritual wickedness in high *places.*

13 Wherefore take unto you the whole armour of God, that ye may be able to withstand in the evil day, and having done all, to stand.

14 Stand therefore, having your loins girt about with truth, and having on the breastplate of righteousness;

15 And your feet shod with the preparation of the gospel of peace;

16 Above all, taking the shield of faith, wherewith ye shall be able to quench all the fiery darts of the wicked.

17 And take the helmet of salvation, and the sword of the Spirit, which is the word of God:

18 Praying always with all prayer and supplication in the Spirit, and watching thereunto with all perseverance and supplication for all saints;

19 And for me, that utterance may be given unto me, that I may open my mouth boldly, to make known the mystery of the gospel,

20 For which I am an ambassador in bonds: that therein I may speak boldly, as I ought to speak.

21 But that ye also may know my affairs, *and* how I do, Tȳch'ĭ-cus, a beloved brother and faithful minister in the Lord, shall make known to you all things:

22 Whom I have sent unto you for the same purpose, that ye might know our affairs, and *that* he might comfort your hearts.

23 Peace *be* to the brethren, and love with faith, from God the Father and the Lord Jesus Christ.

24 Grace *be* with all them that love our Lord Jesus Christ in sincerity. Amen.

Written from Rome unto the Ephesians by Tychicus

THE EPISTLE OF PAUL THE APOSTLE TO THE

PHILIPPIANS

CHAPTER 1

PAUL and Tī-mō'the-us, the servants of Jesus Christ, to all the saints in Christ Jesus which are at Phĭ-lip'pī, with the bishops and deacons:

2 Grace *be* unto you, and peace, from God our Father, and *from* the Lord Jesus Christ.

3 I thank my God upon every remembrance of you,

4 Always in every prayer of mine for you all making request with joy,

5 For your fellowship in the gospel from the first day until now;

6 Being confident of this very thing, that he which hath begun a good work in you will perform *it* until the day of Jesus Christ:

7 Even as it is meet for me to think this of you all, because I have you in my heart; inasmuch as both in my bonds, and in the defence and confirmation of the gospel, ye all are partakers of my grace.

8 For God is my record, how greatly I long after you all in the bowels of Jesus Christ.

9 And this I pray, that your love may abound yet more and more in knowledge and *in* all judgment;

10 That ye may approve things that are excellent; that ye may be sincere and without offence till the day of Christ;

11 Being filled with the fruits of righteousness, which are by Jesus Christ, unto the glory and praise of God.

12 But I would ye should understand, brethren, that the things *which happened* unto me have fallen out rather unto the furtherance of the gospel;

13 So that my bonds in Christ are manifest in all the palace, and in all other *places;*

14 And many of the brethren in the Lord, waxing confident by my bonds, are much more bold to speak the word without fear.

15 Some indeed preach Christ even of envy and strife; and some also of good will:

16 The one preach Christ of contention, not sincerely, supposing to add affliction to my bonds:

17 But the other of love, knowing that I am set for the defence of the gospel.

18 What then? notwithstanding, every way, whether in pretence, or in truth, Christ is preached; and I therein do rejoice, yea, and will rejoice.

19 For I know that this shall turn to my salvation through your prayer, and the supply of the Spirit of Jesus Christ,

20 According to my earnest expectation and *my* hope, that in nothing I shall be ashamed, but *that* with all boldness, as always, *so* now also Christ shall be magnified in my body, whether *it be* by life, or by death.

21 For to me to live *is* Christ, and to die *is* gain.

22 But if I live in the flesh, this *is* the fruit of my labour: yet what I shall choose I wot not.

23 For I am in a strait betwixt two, having a desire to depart, and to be with Christ; which is far better:

24 Nevertheless to abide in the flesh *is* more needful for you.

25 And having this confidence, I know that I shall abide and continue with you all for your furtherance and joy of faith;

26 That your rejoicing may be more abundant in Jesus Christ for me by my coming to you again.

27 Only let your conversation be as it becometh the gospel of Christ: that whether I come and see you, or else be absent, I may hear of your affairs, that ye stand fast in one spirit, with one mind striving together for the faith of the gospel;

28 And in nothing terrified by your adversaries: which is to them an evident token of perdition, but to you of salvation, and that of God.

29 For unto you it is given in the behalf of Christ, not only to believe on him, but also to suffer for his sake;

30 Having the same conflict which ye saw in me, and now hear *to be* in me.

CHAPTER 2

IF *there be* therefore any consolation in Christ, if any comfort of love, if any fellowship of the Spirit, if any bowels and mercies,

2 Fulfil ye my joy, that ye be likeminded, having the same love, *being* of one accord, of one mind.

3 *Let* nothing *be done* through strife or vainglory; but in lowliness of mind let each esteem other better than themselves.

4 Look not every man on his own things, but every man also on the things of others.

5 Let this mind be in you, which was
also in Christ Jesus:
6 Who, being in the form of God,
thought it not robbery to be equal with
God:
7 But made himself of no reputation,
and took upon him the form of a ser-
vant, and was made in the likeness of
men:
8 And being found in fashion as a
man, he humbled himself, and became
obedient unto death, even the death of
the cross.
9 Wherefore God also hath highly ex-
alted him, and given him a name which
is above every name:
10 That at the name of Jesus every
knee should bow, of *things* in heaven,
and *things* in earth, and *things* under
the earth;
11 And *that* every tongue should con-
fess that Jesus Christ *is* Lord, to the
glory of God the Father.
12 Wherefore, my beloved, as ye
have always obeyed, not as in my pres-
ence only, but now much more in my
absence, work out your own salvation
with fear and trembling.
13 For it is God which worketh in you
both to will and to do of *his* good plea-
sure.
14 Do all things without murmurings
and disputings:
15 That ye may be blameless and
harmless, the sons of God, without re-
buke, in the midst of a crooked and per-
verse nation, among whom ye shine as
lights in the world;
16 Holding forth the word of life; that
I may rejoice in the day of Christ, that I
have not run in vain, neither laboured
in vain.
17 Yea, and if I be offered upon the
sacrifice and service of your faith, I joy,
and rejoice with you all.
18 For the same cause also do ye joy,
and rejoice with me.
19 But I trust in the Lord Jesus to
send Tĭ-mō'the-us shortly unto you,
that I also may be of good comfort,
when I know your state.
20 For I have no man likeminded,
who will naturally care for your state.
21 For all seek their own, not the
things which are Jesus Christ's.
22 But ye know the proof of him, that,
as a son with the father, he hath served
with me in the gospel.
23 Him therefore I hope to send pres-
ently, so soon as I shall see how it will
go with me.
24 But I trust in the Lord that I also
myself shall come shortly.
25 Yet I supposed it necessary to
send to you E-păph-ro-dī'tus, my
brother, and companion in labour, and
fellowsoldier, but your messenger, and
he that ministered to my wants.
26 For he longed after you all, and
was full of heaviness, because that ye
had heard that he had been sick.
27 For indeed he was sick nigh unto
death: but God had mercy on him; and
not on him only, but on me also, lest I
should have sorrow upon sorrow.
28 I sent him therefore the more care-
fully, that, when ye see him again, ye
may rejoice, and that I may be the less
sorrowful.
29 Receive him therefore in the Lord
with all gladness; and hold such in repu-
tation:
30 Because for the work of Christ he
was nigh unto death, not regarding his
life, to supply your lack of service to-
ward me.

CHAPTER 3

FINALLY, my brethren, rejoice in the
Lord. To write the same things to you,
to me indeed *is* not grievous, but for
you *it is* safe.
2 Beware of dogs, beware of evil
workers, beware of the concision.
3 For we are the circumcision, which
worship God in the spirit, and rejoice in
Christ Jesus, and have no confidence in
the flesh.
4 Though I might also have confidence
in the flesh. If any other man think-
eth that he hath whereof he might
trust in the flesh, I more:
5 Circumcised the eighth day, of the
stock of Israel, *of* the tribe of Benjamin,
an Hebrew of the Hebrews; as touching
the law, a Pharisee;
6 Concerning zeal, persecuting the
church; touching the righteousness
which is in the law, blameless.
7 But what things were gain to me,
those I counted loss for Christ.
8 Yea doubtless, and I count all
things *but* loss for the excellency of the
knowledge of Christ Jesus my Lord: for
whom I have suffered the loss of all
things, and do count them *but* dung,
that I may win Christ,
9 And be found in him, not having
mine own righteousness, which is of
the law, but that which is through the
faith of Christ, the righteousness which
is of God by faith:
10 That I may know him, and the pow-
er of his resurrection, and the fellow-
ship of his sufferings, being made con-
formable unto his death;
11 If by any means I might attain
unto the resurrection of the dead.
12 Not as though I had already at-
tained, either were already perfect: but

I follow after, if that I may apprehend
that for which also I am apprehended
of Christ Jesus.
13 Brethren, I count not myself to
have apprehended: but *this* one thing *I*
do, forgetting those things which are
behind, and reaching forth unto those
things which are before,
14 I press toward the mark for the
prize of the high calling of God in
Christ Jesus.
15 Let us therefore, as many as be
perfect, be thus minded: and if in any
thing ye be otherwise minded, God
shall reveal even this unto you.
16 Nevertheless, whereto we have al-
ready attained, let us walk by the same
rule, let us mind the same thing.
17 Brethren, be followers together of
me, and mark them which walk so as ye
have us for an ensample.
18 (For many walk, of whom I have
told you often, and now tell you even
weeping, *that they are* the enemies of
the cross of Christ:
19 Whose end *is* destruction, whose
God *is their* belly, and *whose* glory *is* in
their shame, who mind earthly things.)
20 For our conversation is in heaven;
from whence also we look for the Sav-
iour, the Lord Jesus Christ:
21 Who shall change our vile body,
that it may be fashioned like unto his
glorious body, according to the work-
ing whereby he is able even to subdue
all things unto himself.

CHAPTER 4

THEREFORE, my brethren dearly be-
loved and longed for, my joy and
crown, so stand fast in the Lord, *my*
dearly beloved.
2 I beseech Eū-ŏ'dĭ-as, and beseech
Sȳn'tȳ-che, that they be of the same
mind in the Lord.
3 And I intreat thee also, true
yokefellow, help those women which
laboured with me in the gospel, with
Clement also, and *with* other my fel-
lowlabourers, whose names *are* in the
book of life.
4 Rejoice in the Lord alway: *and*
again I say, Rejoice.
5 Let your moderation be known
unto all men. The Lord *is* at hand.
6 Be careful for nothing; but in every
thing by prayer and supplication with
thanksgiving let your requests be made
known unto God.
7 And the peace of God, which pass-
eth all understanding, shall keep your
hearts and minds through Christ Jesus.
8 Finally, brethren, whatsoever
things are true, whatsoever things *are*
honest, whatsoever things *are* just,
whatsoever things *are* pure, whatso-
ever things *are* lovely, whatsoever
things *are* of good report; if *there be*
any virtue, and if *there be* any praise,
think on these things.
9 Those things, which ye have both
learned, and received, and heard, and
seen in me, do: and the God of peace
shall be with you.
10 But I rejoiced in the Lord greatly,
that now at the last your care of me
hath flourished again; wherein ye were
also careful, but ye lacked opportunity.
11 Not that I speak in respect of
want: for I have learned, in whatsoever
state I am, *therewith* to be content.
12 I know both how to be abased, and
I know how to abound: every where
and in all things I am instructed both to
be full and to be hungry, both to
abound and to suffer need.
13 I can do all things through Christ
which strengtheneth me.
14 Notwithstanding ye have well
done, that ye did communicate with
my affliction.
15 Now ye Phĭ-lĭp'pĭ-anṡ know also,
that in the beginning of the gospel,
when I departed from Macedonia, no
church communicated with me as con-
cerning giving and receiving, but ye
only.
16 For even in Thĕs-sa-lo-nī'ca ye
sent once and again unto my necessity.
17 Not because I desire a gift: but I
desire fruit that may abound to your
account.
18 But I have all, and abound: I am
full, having received of E-păph-ro-dī'-
tus the things *which were sent* from
you, an odour of a sweet smell, a sacri-
fice acceptable, wellpleasing to God.
19 But my God shall supply all your
need according to his riches in glory by
Christ Jesus.
20 Now unto God and our Father *be*
glory for ever and ever. Amen.
21 Salute every saint in Christ Jesus.
The brethren which are with me greet
you.
22 All the saints salute you, chiefly
they that are of Cæsar's household.
23 The grace of our Lord Jesus Christ
be with you all. Amen.

Written to the Philippians from Rome by Epaphroditus

THE EPISTLE OF PAUL THE APOSTLE TO THE

COLOSSIANS

CHAPTER 1

PAUL, an apostle of Jesus Christ by the will of God, and Tĭ-mō'the-us *our* brother,

2 To the saints and faithful brethren in Christ which are at Co-lŏs'se: Grace *be* unto you, and peace, from God our Father and the Lord Jesus Christ.

3 We give thanks to God and the Father of our Lord Jesus Christ, praying always for you,

4 Since we heard of your faith in Christ Jesus, and of the love *which ye have* to all the saints,

5 For the hope which is laid up for you in heaven, whereof ye heard before in the word of the truth of the gospel;

6 Which is come unto you, as *it is* in all the world; and bringeth forth fruit, as *it doth* also in you, since the day ye heard *of it*, and knew the grace of God in truth:

7 As ye also learned of Ĕp'a-phrăs our dear fellowservant, who is for you a faithful minister of Christ;

8 Who also declared unto us your love in the Spirit.

9 For this cause we also, since the day we heard *it*, do not cease to pray for you, and to desire that ye might be filled with the knowledge of his will in all wisdom and spiritual understanding;

10 That ye might walk worthy of the Lord unto all pleasing, being fruitful in every good work, and increasing in the knowledge of God;

11 Strengthened with all might, according to his glorious power, unto all patience and longsuffering with joyfulness;

12 Giving thanks unto the Father, which hath made us meet to be partakers of the inheritance of the saints in light:

13 Who hath delivered us from the power of darkness, and hath translated *us* into the kingdom of his dear Son:

14 In whom we have redemption through his blood, *even* the forgiveness of sins:

15 Who is the image of the invisible God, the firstborn of every creature:

16 For by him were all things created, that are in heaven, and that are in earth, visible and invisible, whether *they be* thrones, or dominions, or principalities, or powers: all things were created by him, and for him:

17 And he is before all things, and by him all things consist.

18 And he is the head of the body, the church: who is the beginning, the firstborn from the dead; that in all *things* he might have the preeminence.

19 For it pleased *the Father* that in him should all fulness dwell;

20 And, having made peace through the blood of his cross, by him to reconcile all things unto himself; by him, *I say*, whether *they be* things in earth, or things in heaven.

21 And you, that were sometime alienated and enemies in *your* mind by wicked works, yet now hath he reconciled

22 In the body of his flesh through death, to present you holy and unblameable and unreproveable in his sight:

23 If ye continue in the faith grounded and settled, and *be* not moved away from the hope of the gospel, which ye have heard, *and* which was preached to every creature which is under heaven; whereof I Paul am made a minister;

24 Who now rejoice in my sufferings for you, and fill up that which is behind of the afflictions of Christ in my flesh for his body's sake, which is the church:

25 Whereof I am made a minister, according to the dispensation of God which is given to me for you, to fulfil the word of God;

26 *Even* the mystery which hath been hid from ages and from generations, but now is made manifest to his saints:

27 To whom God would make known what *is* the riches of the glory of this mystery among the Gentiles; which is Christ in you, the hope of glory:

28 Whom we preach, warning every man, and teaching every man in all wisdom; that we may present every man perfect in Christ Jesus:

29 Whereunto I also labour, striving according to his working, which worketh in me mightily.

CHAPTER 2

FOR I would that ye knew what great conflict I have for you, and *for* them at La-od-i-ce'a, and *for* as many as have not seen my face in the flesh;

2 That their hearts might be comforted, being knit together in love, and unto all riches of the full assurance of understanding, to the acknowledge-

Breakfast with the Risen Christ (John 21)

Paul Raises the Young Man Who Fell (Acts 20)

ment of the mystery of God, and of the Father, and of Christ;

3 In whom are hid all the treasures of wisdom and knowledge.

4 And this I say, lest any man should beguile you with enticing words.

5 For though I be absent in the flesh, yet am I with you in the spirit, joying and beholding your order, and the stedfastness of your faith in Christ.

6 As ye have therefore received Christ Jesus the Lord, *so* walk ye in him:

7 Rooted and built up in him, and stablished in the faith, as ye have been taught, abounding therein with thanksgiving.

8 Beware lest any man spoil you through philosophy and vain deceit, after the tradition of men, after the rudiments of the world, and not after Christ.

9 For in him dwelleth all the fulness of the Godhead bodily.

10 And ye are complete in him, which is the head of all principality and power:

11 In whom also ye are circumcised with the circumcision made without hands, in putting off the body of the sins of the flesh by the circumcision of Christ:

12 Buried with him in baptism, wherein also ye are risen with *him* through the faith of the operation of God, who hath raised him from the dead.

13 And you, being dead in your sins and the uncircumcision of your flesh, hath he quickened together with him, having forgiven you all trespasses;

14 Blotting out the handwriting of ordinances that was against us, which was contrary to us, and took it out of the way, nailing it to his cross;

15 *And* having spoiled principalities and powers, he made a shew of them openly, triumphing over them in it.

16 Let no man therefore judge you in meat, or in drink, or in respect of an holyday, or of the new moon, or of the sabbath *days*:

17 Which are a shadow of things to come; but the body *is* of Christ.

18 Let no man beguile you of your reward in a voluntary humility and worshipping of angels, intruding into those things which he hath not seen, vainly puffed up by his fleshly mind,

19 And not holding the Head, from which all the body by joints and bands having nourishment ministered, and knit together, increaseth with the increase of God.

20 Wherefore if ye be dead with Christ from the rudiments of the world, why, as though living in the world, are ye subject to ordinances,

21 (Touch not; taste not; handle not;

22 Which all are to perish with the using;) after the commandments and doctrines of men?

23 Which things have indeed a shew of wisdom in will worship, and humility, and neglecting of the body; not in any honour to the satisfying of the flesh.

CHAPTER 3

IF ye then be risen with Christ, seek those things which are above, where Christ sitteth on the right hand of God.

2 Set your affection on things above, not on things on the earth.

3 For ye are dead, and your life is hid with Christ in God.

4 When Christ, *who is* our life, shall appear, then shall ye also appear with him in glory.

5 Mortify therefore your members which are upon the earth; fornication, uncleanness, inordinate affection, evil concupiscence, and covetousness, which is idolatry:

6 For which things' sake the wrath of God cometh on the children of disobedience:

7 In the which ye also walked some time, when ye lived in them.

8 But now ye also put off all these; anger, wrath, malice, blasphemy, filthy communication out of your mouth.

9 Lie not one to another, seeing that ye have put off the old man with his deeds;

10 And have put on the new *man*, which is renewed in knowledge after the image of him that created him:

11 Where there is neither Greek nor Jew, circumcision nor uncircumcision, Barbarian, Scy̆th'ĭ-an, bond *nor* free: but Christ *is* all, and in all.

12 Put on therefore, as the elect of God, holy and beloved, bowels of mercies, kindness, humbleness of mind, meekness, longsuffering;

13 Forbearing one another, and forgiving one another, if any man have a quarrel against any: even as Christ forgave you, so also *do* ye.

14 And above all these things *put on* charity, which is the bond of perfectness.

15 And let the peace of God rule in your hearts, to the which also ye are called in one body; and be ye thankful.

16 Let the word of Christ dwell in you richly in all wisdom; teaching and admonishing one another in psalms and hymns and spiritual songs, singing with grace in your hearts to the Lord.

17 And whatsoever ye do in word or deed, *do* all in the name of the Lord Jesus, giving thanks to God and the Father by him.

18 Wives, submit yourselves unto your own husbands, as it is fit in the Lord.

19 Husbands, love *your* wives, and be not bitter against them.

20 Children, obey *your* parents in all things: for this is well pleasing unto the Lord.

21 Fathers, provoke not your children *to anger*, lest they be discouraged.

22 Servants, obey in all things *your* masters according to the flesh; not with eyeservice, as menpleasers; but in singleness of heart, fearing God:

23 And whatsoever ye do, do *it* heartily, as to the Lord, and not unto men;

24 Knowing that of the Lord ye shall receive the reward of the inheritance: for ye serve the Lord Christ.

25 But he that doeth wrong shall receive for the wrong which he hath done: and there is no respect of persons.

CHAPTER 4

MASTERS, give unto *your* servants that which is just and equal; knowing that ye also have a Master in heaven.

2 Continue in prayer, and watch in the same with thanksgiving;

3 Withal praying also for us, that God would open unto us a door of utterance, to speak the mystery of Christ, for which I am also in bonds:

4 That I may make it manifest, as I ought to speak.

5 Walk in wisdom toward them that are without, redeeming the time.

6 Let your speech *be* alway with grace, seasoned with salt, that ye may know how ye ought to answer every man.

7 All my state shall Tȳch'ĭ-cus declare unto you, *who is* a beloved brother, and a faithful minister and fellowservant in the Lord:

8 Whom I have sent unto you for the same purpose, that he might know your estate, and comfort your hearts;

9 With O-nĕs'i-mus, a faithful and beloved brother, who is *one* of you. They shall make known unto you all things which *are done* here.

10 Ăr-ĭs-tär'chus my fellowprisoner saluteth you, and Marcus, sister's son to Barnabas, (touching whom ye received commandments: if he come unto you, receive him;)

11 And Jesus, which is called Justus, who are of the circumcision. These only *are my* fellowworkers unto the kingdom of God, which have been a comfort unto me.

12 Ĕp'a-phrăs, who is *one* of you, a servant of Christ, saluteth you, always labouring fervently for you in prayers, that ye may stand perfect and complete in all the will of God.

13 For I bear him record, that he hath a great zeal for you, and them *that are* in La-od-i-ce'a, and them in Hī-e-răp'o-lis.

14 Luke, the beloved physician, and Demas, greet you.

15 Salute the brethren which are in La-od-i-ce'a, and Nȳm'phas, and the church which is in his house.

16 And when this epistle is read among you, cause that it be read also in the church of the Lā-ŏd-i-çē'anṡ; and that ye likewise read the *epistle* from La-od-i-ce'a

17 And say to Ăr-chĭp'pus, Take heed to the ministry which thou hast received in the Lord, that thou fulfil it.

18 The salutation by the hand of me Paul. Remember my bonds. Grace *be* with you. Amen.

Written from Rome to the Colossians by Tychicus and Onesimus

THE FIRST EPISTLE OF PAUL THE APOSTLE TO THE

THESSALONIANS

CHAPTER 1

PAUL, and Sĭl-vā'nus, and Tĭ-mō'the-us, unto the church of the Thĕs-sa-lō'nĭ-anṡ *which is* in God the Father and *in* the Lord Jesus Christ: Grace *be* unto you, and peace, from God our Father, and the Lord Jesus Christ.

2 We give thanks to God always for you all, making mention of you in our prayers;

3 Remembering without ceasing your work of faith, and labour of love, and patience of hope in our Lord Jesus Christ, in the sight of God and our Father;

4 Knowing, brethren beloved, your election of God.

5 For our gospel came not unto you in word only, but also in power, and in the Holy Ghost, and in much assurance; as ye know what manner of men we were among you for your sake.

6 And ye became followers of us, and of the Lord, having received the word

in much affliction, with joy of the Holy
Ghost:
7 So that ye were ensamples to all
that believe in Macedonia and A-chā'-
ia.
8 For from you sounded out the word
of the Lord not only in Macedonia and
A-chā'ia, but also in every place your
faith to God-ward is spread abroad; so
that we need not to speak any thing.
9 For they themselves shew of us
what manner of entering in we had
unto you, and how ye turned to God
from idols to serve the living and true
God;
10 And to wait for his Son from
heaven, whom he raised from the dead,
even Jesus, which delivered us from
the wrath to come.

CHAPTER 2

FOR yourselves, brethren, know our
entrance in unto you, that it was not in
vain:
2 But even after that we had suffered
before, and were shamefully entreated,
as ye know, at Phĭ-lip'pī, we were bold
in our God to speak unto you the gospel
of God with much contention.
3 For our exhortation *was* not of de-
ceit, nor of uncleanness, nor in guile:
4 But as we were allowed of God to be
put in trust with the gospel, even so we
speak; not as pleasing men, but God,
which trieth our hearts.
5 For neither at any time used we
flattering words, as ye know, nor a
cloak of covetousness; God *is* witness:
6 Nor of men sought we glory,
neither of you, nor *yet* of others, when
we might have been burdensome, as
the apostles of Christ.
7 But we were gentle among you,
even as a nurse cherisheth her children:
8 So being affectionately desirous of
you, we were willing to have imparted
unto you, not the gospel of God only,
but also our own souls, because ye
were dear unto us.
9 For ye remember, brethren, our la-
bour and travail: for labouring night
and day, because we would not be
chargeable unto any of you, we
preached unto you the gospel of God.
10 Ye *are* witnesses, and God *also*,
how holily and justly and unblameably
we behaved ourselves among you that
believe:
11 As ye know how we exhorted and
comforted and charged every one of
you, as a father *doth* his children,
12 That ye would walk worthy of
God, who hath called you unto his king-
dom and glory.
13 For this cause also thank we God
without ceasing, because, when ye re-
ceived the word of God which ye heard
of us, ye received *it* not *as* the word of
men, but as it is in truth, the word of
God, which effectually worketh also in
you that believe.
14 For ye, brethren, became follow-
ers of the churches of God which in
Judæa are in Christ Jesus: for ye also
have suffered like things of your own
countrymen, even as they *have* of the
Jews:
15 Who both killed the Lord Jesus,
and their own prophets, and have per-
secuted us; and they please not God,
and are contrary to all men:
16 Forbidding us to speak to the Gen-
tiles that they might be saved, to fill up
their sins alway: for the wrath is come
upon them to the uttermost.
17 But we, brethren, being taken
from you for a short time in presence,
not in heart, endeavoured the more
abundantly to see your face with great
desire.
18 Wherefore we would have come
unto you, even I Paul, once and again;
but Satan hindered us.
19 For what *is* our hope, or joy, or
crown of rejoicing? *Are* not even ye in
the presence of our Lord Jesus Christ at
his coming?
20 For ye are our glory and joy.

CHAPTER 3

WHEREFORE when we could no long-
er forbear, we thought it good to be
left at Athens alone;
2 And sent Tī-mō'the-us, our brother,
and minister of God, and our fellow-
labourer in the gospel of Christ, to estab-
lish you, and to comfort you concern-
ing your faith:
3 That no man should be moved by
these afflictions: for yourselves know
that we are appointed thereunto.
4 For verily, when we were with you,
we told you before that we should suf-
fer tribulation; even as it came to pass,
and ye know.
5 For this cause, when I could no long-
er forbear, I sent to know your faith,
lest by some means the tempter have
tempted you, and our labour be in vain.
6 But now when Tī-mō'the-us came
from you unto us, and brought us good
tidings of your faith and charity, and
that ye have good remembrance of us
always, desiring greatly to see us, as we
also *to see* you:
7 Therefore, brethren, we were com-
forted over you in all our affliction and
distress by your faith:
8 For now we live, if ye stand fast in
the Lord.

9 For what thanks can we render to
God again for you, for all the joy where-
with we joy for your sakes before
our God;
10 Night and day praying exceeding-
ly that we might see your face, and
might perfect that which is lacking in
your faith?
11 Now God himself and our Father,
and our Lord Jesus Christ, direct our
way unto you.
12 And the Lord make you to in-
crease and abound in love one toward
another, and toward all *men*, even as
we *do* toward you:
13 To the end he may stablish your
hearts unblameable in holiness before
God, even our Father, at the coming of
our Lord Jesus Christ with all his
saints.

CHAPTER 4

FURTHERMORE then we beseech
you, brethren, and exhort *you* by the
Lord Jesus, that as ye have received of
us how ye ought to walk and to please
God, *so* ye would abound more and
more.
2 For ye know what commandments
we gave you by the Lord Jesus.
3 For this is the will of God, *even* your
sanctification, that ye should abstain
from fornication:
4 That every one of you should know
how to possess his vessel in sanctifica-
tion and honour;
5 Not in the lust of concupiscence,
even as the Gentiles which know not
God:
6 That no *man* go beyond and de-
fraud his brother in *any* matter: be-
cause that the Lord *is* the avenger of all
such, as we also have forewarned you
and testified.
7 For God hath not called us unto
uncleanness, but unto holiness.
8 He therefore that despiseth, despis-
eth not man, but God, who hath also
given unto us his holy Spirit.
9 But as touching brotherly love ye
need not that I write unto you: for ye
yourselves are taught of God to love
one another.
10 And indeed ye do it toward all the
brethren which are in all Macedonia:
but we beseech you, brethren, that ye
increase more and more;
11 And that ye study to be quiet, and
to do your own business, and to work
with your own hands, as we com-
manded you;
12 That ye may walk honestly toward
them that are without, and *that* ye may
have lack of nothing.
13 But I would not have you to be ig-
norant, brethren, concerning them
which are asleep, that ye sorrow not,
even as others which have no hope.
14 For if we believe that Jesus died
and rose again, even so them also
which sleep in Jesus will God bring
with him.
15 For this we say unto you by the
word of the Lord, that we which are
alive *and* remain unto the coming of the
Lord shall not prevent them which are
asleep.
16 For the Lord himself shall descend
from heaven with a shout, with the
voice of the archangel, and with the
trump of God: and the dead in Christ
shall rise first:
17 Then we which are alive *and* re-
main shall be caught up together with
them in the clouds to meet the Lord in
the air: and so shall we ever be with the
Lord.
18 Wherefore comfort one another
with these words.

CHAPTER 5

BUT of the times and the seasons,
brethren, ye have no need that I write
unto you.
2 For yourselves know perfectly that
the day of the Lord so cometh as a thief
in the night.
3 For when they shall say, Peace and
safety; then sudden destruction
cometh upon them, as travail upon a
woman with child; and they shall not
escape.
4 But ye, brethren, are not in dark-
ness, that that day should overtake you
as a thief.
5 Ye are all the children of light, and
the children of the day: we are not of
the night, nor of darkness.
6 Therefore let us not sleep, as *do* oth-
ers; but let us watch and be sober.
7 For they that sleep sleep in the
night; and they that be drunken are
drunken in the night.
8 But let us, who are of the day, be
sober, putting on the breastplate of
faith and love; and for an helmet, the
hope of salvation.
9 For God hath not appointed us to
wrath, but to obtain salvation by our
Lord Jesus Christ,
10 Who died for us, that, whether we
wake or sleep, we should live together
with him.
11 Wherefore comfort yourselves
together, and edify one another, even
as also ye do.
12 And we beseech you, brethren, to

know them which labour among you, and are over you in the Lord, and admonish you;
13 And to esteem them very highly in love for their work's sake. *And* be at peace among yourselves.
14 Now we exhort you, brethren, warn them that are unruly, comfort the feebleminded, support the weak, be patient toward all *men.*
15 See that none render evil for evil unto any *man;* but ever follow that which is good, both among yourselves, and to all *men.*
16 Rejoice evermore.
17 Pray without ceasing.
18 In every thing give thanks: for this is the will of God in Christ Jesus concerning you.
19 Quench not the Spirit.
20 Despise not prophesyings.
21 Prove all things; hold fast that which is good.
22 Abstain from all appearance of evil.
23 And the very God of peace sanctify you wholly; and *I pray God* your whole spirit and soul and body be preserved blameless unto the coming of our Lord Jesus Christ.
24 Faithful *is* he that calleth you, who also will do *it.*
25 Brethren, pray for us.
26 Greet all the brethren with an holy kiss.
27 I charge you by the Lord that this epistle be read unto all the holy brethren.
28 The grace of our Lord Jesus Christ *be* with you. Amen.

The first *epistle* unto the Thessalonians was written from Athens

THE SECOND EPISTLE OF PAUL THE APOSTLE TO THE

THESSALONIANS

CHAPTER 1

PAUL, and Sĭl-vā'nus, and Tĭ-mō'the-
us, unto the church of the Thĕs-sa-lō'nĭ-
anś in God our Father and the Lord Je-
sus Christ:
2 Grace unto you, and peace, from
God our Father and the Lord Jesus
Christ.
3 We are bound to thank God always
for you, brethren, as it is meet, because
that your faith groweth exceedingly,
and the charity of every one of you all
toward each other aboundeth;
4 So that we ourselves glory in you in
the churches of God for your patience
and faith in all your persecutions and
tribulations that ye endure:
5 *Which is* a manifest token of the
righteous judgment of God, that ye
may be counted worthy of the kingdom
of God, for which ye also suffer:
6 Seeing *it is* a righteous thing with
God to recompense tribulation to them
that trouble you;
7 And to you who are troubled rest
with us, when the Lord Jesus shall be
revealed from heaven with his mighty
angels,
8 In flaming fire taking vengeance on
them that know not God, and that obey
not the gospel of our Lord Jesus Christ:
9 Who shall be punished with ever-
lasting destruction from the presence
of the Lord, and from the glory of his
power;
10 When he shall come to be glorified
in his saints, and to be admired in all
them that believe (because our testi-
mony among you was believed) in that
day.
11 Wherefore also we pray always
for you, that our God would count you
worthy of *this* calling, and fulfil all the
good pleasure of *his* goodness, and the
work of faith with power:
12 That the name of our Lord Jesus
Christ may be glorified in you, and ye in
him, according to the grace of our God
and the Lord Jesus Christ.

CHAPTER 2

NOW we beseech you, brethren, by the
coming of our Lord Jesus Christ, and
by our gathering together unto him,
2 That ye be not soon shaken in mind,
or be troubled, neither by spirit, nor by
word, nor by letter as from us, as that
the day of Christ is at hand.
3 Let no man deceive you by any
means: for *that day shall not come,* ex-
cept there come a falling away first,
and that man of sin be revealed, the son
of perdition;
4 Who opposeth and exalteth himself
above all that is called God, or that is
worshipped; so that he as God sitteth in
the temple of God, shewing himself
that he is God.
5 Remember ye not, that, when I was
yet with you, I told you these things?
6 And now ye know what withhold-
eth that he might be revealed in his
time.
7 For the mystery of iniquity doth al-
ready work: only he who now letteth
will let, until he be taken out of the way.
8 And then shall that Wicked be re-

vealed, whom the Lord shall consume
with the spirit of his mouth, and shall
destroy with the brightness of his com-
ing:
9 *Even him*, whose coming is after
the working of Satan with all power
and signs and lying wonders,
10 And with all deceivableness of un-
righteousness in them that perish; be-
cause they received not the love of the
truth, that they might be saved.
11 And for this cause God shall send
them strong delusion, that they should
believe a lie:
12 That they all might be damned
who believed not the truth, but had
pleasure in unrighteousness.
13 But we are bound to give thanks
alway to God for you, brethren beloved
of the Lord, because God hath from the
beginning chosen you to salvation
through sanctification of the Spirit and
belief of the truth:
14 Whereunto he called you by our
gospel, to the obtaining of the glory of
our Lord Jesus Christ.
15 Therefore, brethren, stand fast,
and hold the traditions which ye have
been taught, whether by word, or our
epistle.
16 Now our Lord Jesus Christ him-
self, and God, even our Father, which
hath loved us, and hath given *us* ever-
lasting consolation and good hope
through grace,
17 Comfort your hearts, and stablish
you in every good word and work.

CHAPTER 3

FINALLY, brethren, pray for us, that
the word of the Lord may have *free*
course, and be glorified, even as *it is*
with you:
2 And that we may be delivered from
unreasonable and wicked men: for all
men have not faith.
3 But the Lord is faithful, who shall
stablish you, and keep *you* from evil.
4 And we have confidence in the Lord
touching you, that ye both do and will
do the things which we command you.
5 And the Lord direct your hearts
into the love of God, and into the pa-
tient waiting for Christ.
6 Now we command you, brethren, in
the name of our Lord Jesus Christ, that
ye withdraw yourselves from every
brother that walketh disorderly, and
not after the tradition which he re-
ceived of us.
7 For yourselves know how ye ought
to follow us: for we behaved not our-
selves disorderly among you;
8 Neither did we eat any man's bread
for nought; but wrought with labour
and travail night and day, that we
might not be chargeable to any of you:
9 Not because we have not power,
but to make ourselves an ensample
unto you to follow us.
10 For even when we were with you,
this we commanded you, that if any
would not work, neither should he eat.
11 For we hear that there are some
which walk among you disorderly,
working not at all, but are busybodies.
12 Now them that are such we com-
mand and exhort by our Lord Jesus
Christ, that with quietness they work,
and eat their own bread.
13 But ye, brethren, be not weary in
well doing.
14 And if any man obey not our word
by this epistle, note that man, and have
no company with him, that he may be
ashamed.
15 Yet count *him* not as an enemy,
but admonish *him* as a brother.
16 Now the Lord of peace himself
give you peace always by all means.
The Lord *be* with you all.
17 The salutation of Paul with mine
own hand, which is the token in every
epistle: so I write.
18 The grace of our Lord Jesus Christ
be with you all. Amen.

The second *epistle* to the Thessalonians was written from Athens

THE FIRST EPISTLE OF PAUL THE APOSTLE
TO

TIMOTHY

CHAPTER 1

PAUL, an apostle of Jesus Christ by the
commandment of God our Saviour,
and Lord Jesus Christ, *which is* our
hope;
2 Unto Timothy, *my* own son in the
faith: Grace, mercy, *and* peace, from
God our Father and Jesus Christ our
Lord.
3 As I besought thee to abide still at
Ĕph'e-sus, when I went into Macedo-
nia, that thou mightest charge some
that they teach no other doctrine,
4 Neither give heed to fables and end-
less genealogies, which minister ques-
tions, rather than godly edifying which
is in faith: *so do.*
5 Now the end of the commandment
is charity out of a pure heart, and *of* a

good conscience, and *of* faith un-
feigned:
6 From which some having swerved
have turned aside unto vain jangling;
7 Desiring to be teachers of the law;
understanding neither what they say,
nor whereof they affirm.
8 But we know that the law *is* good, if
a man use it lawfully;
9 Knowing this, that the law is not
made for a righteous man, but for the
lawless and disobedient, for the un-
godly and for sinners, for unholy and
profane, for murderers of fathers and
murderers of mothers, for manslayers,
10 For whoremongers, for them that
defile themselves with mankind, for
menstealers, for liars, for perjured per-
sons, and if there be any other thing
that is contrary to sound doctrine;
11 According to the glorious gospel
of the blessed God, which was com-
mitted to my trust.
12 And I thank Christ Jesus our Lord,
who hath enabled me, for that he
counted me faithful, putting me into
the ministry;
13 Who was before a blasphemer,
and a persecutor, and injurious: but I
obtained mercy, because I did *it* igno-
rantly in unbelief.
14 And the grace of our Lord was ex-
ceeding abundant with faith and love
which is in Christ Jesus.
15 This *is* a faithful saying, and
worthy of all acceptation, that Christ
Jesus came into the world to save sin-
ners; of whom I am chief.
16 Howbeit for this cause I obtained
mercy, that in me first Jesus Christ
might shew forth all longsuffering, for
a pattern to them which should here-
after believe on him to life everlasting.
17 Now unto the King eternal, im-
mortal, invisible, the only wise God, *be*
honour and glory for ever and ever.
Amen.
18 This charge I commit unto thee,
son Tĭm'o-thȳ, according to the
prophecies which went before on thee,
that thou by them mightest war a good
warfare;
19 Holding faith, and a good con-
science; which some having put away
concerning faith have made ship-
wreck:
20 Of whom is Hȳ-me-næ'us and Alex-
ander; whom I have delivered unto
Satan, that they may learn not to blas-
pheme.

CHAPTER 2

I EXHORT therefore, that, first of all,
supplications, prayers, intercessions,
and giving of thanks, be made for all
men;
2 For kings, and *for* all that are in au-
thority; that we may lead a quiet and
peaceable life in all godliness and
honesty.
3 For this *is* good and acceptable in
the sight of God our Saviour;
4 Who will have all men to be saved,
and to come unto the knowledge of the
truth.
5 For *there is* one God, and one media-
tor between God and men, the man
Christ Jesus;
6 Who gave himself a ransom for all,
to be testified in due time.
7 Whereunto I am ordained a preach-
er, and an apostle, (I speak the truth in
Christ, *and* lie not;) a teacher of the
Gentiles in faith and verity.
8 I will therefore that men pray every
where, lifting up holy hands, without
wrath and doubting.
9 In like manner also, that women ad-
orn themselves in modest apparel, with
shamefacedness and sobriety; not with
broided hair, or gold, or pearls, or
costly array;
10 But (which becometh women pro-
fessing godliness) with good works.
11 Let the woman learn in silence
with all subjection.
12 But I suffer not a woman to teach,
nor to usurp authority over the man,
but to be in silence.
13 For Adam was first formed, then
Eve.
14 And Adam was not deceived, but
the woman being deceived was in the
transgression.
15 Notwithstanding she shall be
saved in childbearing, if they continue
in faith and charity and holiness with
sobriety.

CHAPTER 3

THIS *is* a true saying, If a man desire
the office of a bishop, he desireth a
good work.
2 A bishop then must be blameless,
the husband of one wife, vigilant,
sober, of good behaviour, given to hos-
pitality, apt to teach;
3 Not given to wine, no striker, not
greedy of filthy lucre; but patient, not a
brawler, not covetous;
4 One that ruleth well his own house,
having his children in subjection with
all gravity;
5 (For if a man know not how to rule
his own house, how shall he take care
of the church of God?)
6 Not a novice, lest being lifted up
with pride he fall into the condemna-
tion of the devil.
7 Moreover he must have a good re-
port of them which are without; lest he

fall into reproach and the snare of the devil.

8 Likewise *must* the deacons *be* grave, not doubletongued, not given to much wine, not greedy of filthy lucre;

9 Holding the mystery of the faith in a pure conscience.

10 And let these also first be proved; then let them use the office of a deacon, being *found* blameless.

11 Even so *must their* wives *be* grave, not slanderers, sober, faithful in all things.

12 Let the deacons be the husbands of one wife, ruling their children and their own houses well.

13 For they that have used the office of a deacon well purchase to themselves a good degree, and great boldness in the faith which is in Christ Jesus.

14 These things write I unto thee, hoping to come unto thee shortly:

15 But if I tarry long, that thou mayest know how thou oughtest to behave thyself in the house of God, which is the church of the living God, the pillar and ground of the truth.

16 And without controversy great is the mystery of godliness: God was manifest in the flesh, justified in the Spirit, seen of angels, preached unto the Gentiles, believed on in the world, received up into glory.

CHAPTER 4

NOW the Spirit speaketh expressly, that in the latter times some shall depart from the faith, giving heed to seducing spirits, and doctrines of devils;

2 Speaking lies in hypocrisy; having their conscience seared with a hot iron;

3 Forbidding to marry, *and commanding* to abstain from meats, which God hath created to be received with thanksgiving of them which believe and know the truth.

4 For every creature of God *is* good, and nothing to be refused, if it be received with thanksgiving:

5 For it is sanctified by the word of God and prayer.

6 If thou put the brethren in remembrance of these things, thou shalt be a good minister of Jesus Christ, nourished up in the words of faith and of good doctrine, whereunto thou hast attained.

7 But refuse profane and old wives' fables, and exercise thyself *rather* unto godliness.

8 For bodily exercise profiteth little: but godliness is profitable unto all things, having promise of the life that now is, and of that which is to come.

9 This *is* a faithful saying and worthy of all acceptation.

10 For therefore we both labour and suffer reproach, because we trust in the living God, who is the Saviour of all men, specially of those that believe.

11 These things command and teach.

12 Let no man despise thy youth; but be thou an example of the believers, in word, in conversation, in charity, in spirit, in faith, in purity.

13 Till I come, give attendance to reading, to exhortation, to doctrine.

14 Neglect not the gift that is in thee, which was given thee by prophecy, with the laying on of the hands of the presbytery.

15 Meditate upon these things; give thyself wholly to them; that thy profiting may appear to all.

16 Take heed unto thyself, and unto the doctrine; continue in them: for in doing this thou shalt both save thyself, and them that hear thee.

CHAPTER 5

REBUKE not an elder, but intreat *him* as a father; *and* the younger men as brethren;

2 The elder women as mothers; the younger as sisters, with all purity.

3 Honour widows that are widows indeed.

4 But if any widow have children or nephews, let them learn first to shew piety at home, and to requite their parents: for that is good and acceptable before God.

5 Now she that is a widow indeed, and desolate, trusteth in God, and continueth in supplications and prayers night and day.

6 But she that liveth in pleasure is dead while she liveth.

7 And these things give in charge, that they may be blameless.

8 But if any provide not for his own, and specially for those of his own house, he hath denied the faith, and is worse than an infidel.

9 Let not a widow be taken into the number under threescore years old, having been the wife of one man,

10 Well reported of for good works; if she have brought up children, if she have lodged strangers, if she have washed the saints' feet, if she have relieved the afflicted, if she have diligently followed every good work.

11 But the younger widows refuse: for when they have begun to wax wanton against Christ, they will marry;

12 Having damnation, because they have cast off their first faith.

13 And withal they learn *to be* idle, wandering about from house to house;

and not only idle, but tattlers also and busybodies, speaking things which they ought not.

14 I will therefore that the younger women marry, bear children, guide the house, give none occasion to the adversary to speak reproachfully.

15 For some are already turned aside after Satan.

16 If any man or woman that believeth have widows, let them relieve them, and let not the church be charged; that it may relieve them that are widows indeed.

17 Let the elders that rule well be counted worthy of double honour, especially they who labour in the word and doctrine.

18 For the scripture saith, Thou shalt not muzzle the ox that treadeth out the corn. And, The labourer *is* worthy of his reward.

19 Against an elder receive not an accusation, but before two or three witnesses.

20 Them that sin rebuke before all, that others also may fear.

21 I charge *thee* before God, and the Lord Jesus Christ, and the elect angels, that thou observe these things without preferring one before another, doing nothing by partiality.

22 Lay hands suddenly on no man, neither be partaker of other men's sins: keep thyself pure.

23 Drink no longer water, but use a little wine for thy stomach's sake and thine often infirmities.

24 Some men's sins are open beforehand, going before to judgment; and some *men* they follow after.

25 Likewise also the good works *of some* are manifest beforehand; and they that are otherwise cannot be hid.

CHAPTER 6

LET as many servants as are under the yoke count their own masters worthy of all honour, that the name of God and *his* doctrine be not blasphemed.

2 And they that have believing masters, let them not despise *them*, because they are brethren; but rather do *them* service, because they are faithful and beloved, partakers of the benefit. These things teach and exhort.

3 If any man teach otherwise, and consent not to wholesome words, *even* the words of our Lord Jesus Christ, and to the doctrine which is according to godliness;

4 He is proud, knowing nothing, but doting about questions and strifes of words, whereof cometh envy, strife, railings, evil surmisings,

5 Perverse disputings of men of corrupt minds, and destitute of the truth, supposing that gain is godliness: from such withdraw thyself.

6 But godliness with contentment is great gain.

7 For we brought nothing into *this* world, *and it is* certain we can carry nothing out.

8 And having food and raiment let us be therewith content.

9 But they that will be rich fall into temptation and a snare, and *into* many foolish and hurtful lusts, which drown men in destruction and perdition.

10 For the love of money is the root of all evil: which while some coveted after, they have erred from the faith, and pierced themselves through with many sorrows.

11 But thou, O man of God, flee these things; and follow after righteousness, godliness, faith, love, patience, meekness.

12 Fight the good fight of faith, lay hold on eternal life, whereunto thou art also called, and hast professed a good profession before many witnesses.

13 I give thee charge in the sight of God, who quickeneth all things, and *before* Christ Jesus, who before Pontius Pilate witnessed a good confession;

14 That thou keep *this* commandment without spot, unrebukeable, until the appearing of our Lord Jesus Christ:

15 Which in his times he shall shew, *who is* the blessed and only Potentate, the King of kings, and Lord of lords;

16 Who only hath immortality, dwelling in the light which no man can approach unto; whom no man hath seen, nor can see: to whom *be* honour and power everlasting. Amen.

17 Charge them that are rich in this world, that they be not highminded, nor trust in uncertain riches, but in the living God, who giveth us richly all things to enjoy;

18 That they do good, that they be rich in good works, ready to distribute, willing to communicate;

19 Laying up in store for themselves a good foundation against the time to come, that they may lay hold on eternal life.

20 O Tĭm'o-thȳ, keep that which is committed to thy trust, avoiding profane *and* vain babblings, and oppositions of science falsely so called:

21 Which some professing have erred concerning the faith. Grace *be* with thee. Amen.

The first to Timothy was written from Laodicea, which is the chief city of Phrygia Pacatiana.

THE SECOND EPISTLE OF PAUL THE APOSTLE
TO

TIMOTHY

CHAPTER 1

PAUL, an apostle of Jesus Christ by the will of God, according to the promise of life which is in Christ Jesus,

2 To Tĭm'o-thy̆, *my* dearly beloved son: Grace, mercy, *and* peace, from God the Father and Christ Jesus our Lord.

3 I thank God, whom I serve from *my* forefathers with pure conscience, that without ceasing I have remembrance of thee in my prayers night and day;

4 Greatly desiring to see thee, being mindful of thy tears, that I may be filled with joy;

5 When I call to remembrance the unfeigned faith that is in thee, which dwelt first in thy grandmother Lois, and thy mother Eunice; and I am persuaded that in thee also.

6 Wherefore I put thee in remembrance that thou stir up the gift of God, which is in thee by the putting on of my hands.

7 For God hath not given us the spirit of fear; but of power, and of love, and of a sound mind.

8 Be not thou therefore ashamed of the testimony of our Lord, nor of me his prisoner: but be thou partaker of the afflictions of the gospel according to the power of God;

9 Who hath saved us, and called *us* with an holy calling, not according to our works, but according to his own purpose and grace, which was given us in Christ Jesus before the world began,

10 But is now made manifest by the appearing of our Saviour Jesus Christ, who hath abolished death, and hath brought life and immortality to light through the gospel:

11 Whereunto I am appointed a preacher, and an apostle, and a teacher of the Gentiles.

12 For the which cause I also suffer these things: nevertheless I am not ashamed: for I know whom I have believed, and am persuaded that he is able to keep that which I have committed unto him against that day.

13 Hold fast the form of sound words, which thou hast heard of me, in faith and love which is in Christ Jesus.

14 That good thing which was committed unto thee keep by the Holy Ghost which dwelleth in us.

15 This thou knowest, that all they which are in Asia be turned away from me; of whom are Phy̆-ġel'lus and Hĕr-mŏg'e-nēṡ.

16 The Lord give mercy unto the house of Ŏn-e-sĭph'o-rus; for he oft refreshed me, and was not ashamed of my chain:

17 But, when he was in Rome, he sought me out very diligently, and found *me*.

18 The Lord grant unto him that he may find mercy of the Lord in that day: and in how many things he ministered unto me at Ĕph'e-sus, thou knowest very well.

CHAPTER 2

THOU therefore, my son, be strong in the grace that is in Christ Jesus.

2 And the things that thou hast heard of me among many witnesses, the same commit thou to faithful men, who shall be able to teach others also.

3 Thou therefore endure hardness, as a good soldier of Jesus Christ.

4 No man that warreth entangleth himself with the affairs of *this* life; that he may please him who hath chosen him to be a soldier.

5 And if a man also strive for masteries, *yet* is he not crowned, except he strive lawfully.

6 The husbandman that laboureth must be first partaker of the fruits.

7 Consider what I say; and the Lord give thee understanding in all things.

8 Remember that Jesus Christ of the seed of David was raised from the dead according to my gospel:

9 Wherein I suffer trouble, as an evil doer, *even* unto bonds; but the word of God is not bound.

10 Therefore I endure all things for the elect's sakes, that they may also obtain the salvation which is in Christ Jesus with eternal glory.

11 *It is* a faithful saying: For if we be dead with *him*, we shall also live with *him*:

12 If we suffer, we shall also reign with *him*: if we deny *him*, he also will deny us:

13 If we believe not, *yet* he abideth faithful: he cannot deny himself.

14 Of these things put *them* in remembrance, charging *them* before the Lord that they strive not about words to no profit, *but* to the subverting of the hearers.

15 Study to shew thyself approved unto God, a workman that needeth not

to be ashamed, rightly dividing the word of truth.
16 But shun profane *and* vain babblings: for they will increase unto more ungodliness.
17 And their word will eat as doth a canker: of whom is Hȳ-me-næ'us and Phī-lē'tus;
18 Who concerning the truth have erred, saying that the resurrection is past already; and overthrow the faith of some.
19 Nevertheless the foundation of God standeth sure, having this seal, The Lord knoweth them that are his. And, Let every one that nameth the name of Christ depart from iniquity.
20 But in a great house there are not only vessels of gold and of silver, but also of wood and of earth; and some to honour, and some to dishonour.
21 If a man therefore purge himself from these, he shall be a vessel unto honour, sanctified, and meet for the master's use, *and* prepared unto every good work.
22 Flee also youthful lusts: but follow righteousness, faith, charity, peace, with them that call on the Lord out of a pure heart.
23 But foolish and unlearned questions avoid, knowing that they do gender strifes.
24 And the servant of the Lord must not strive; but be gentle unto all *men*, apt to teach, patient,
25 In meekness instructing those that oppose themselves; if God peradventure will give them repentance to the acknowledging of the truth;
26 And *that* they may recover themselves out of the snare of the devil, who are taken captive by him at his will.

CHAPTER 3

THIS know also, that in the last days perilous times shall come.
2 For men shall be lovers of their own selves, covetous, boasters, proud, blasphemers, disobedient to parents, unthankful, unholy,
3 Without natural affection, trucebreakers, false accusers, incontinent, fierce, despisers of those that are good,
4 Traitors, heady, highminded, lovers of pleasures more than lovers of God;
5 Having a form of godliness, but denying the power thereof: from such turn away.
6 For of this sort are they which creep into houses, and lead captive silly women laden with sins, led away with divers lusts,
7 Ever learning, and never able to come to the knowledge of the truth.
8 Now as Jăn'nēṡ and Jăm'brēṡ withstood Moses, so do these also resist the truth: men of corrupt minds, reprobate concerning the faith.
9 But they shall proceed no further: for their folly shall be manifest unto all *men*, as theirs also was.
10 But thou hast fully known my doctrine, manner of life, purpose, faith, longsuffering, charity, patience,
11 Persecutions, afflictions, which came unto me at Antioch, at Ī-cō'nĭ-um, at Lȳs'tra; what persecutions I endured: but out of *them* all the Lord delivered me.
12 Yea, and all that will live godly in Christ Jesus shall suffer persecution.
13 But evil men and seducers shall wax worse and worse, deceiving, and being deceived.
14 But continue thou in the things which thou hast learned and hast been assured of, knowing of whom thou hast learned *them*;
15 And that from a child thou hast known the holy scriptures, which are able to make thee wise unto salvation through faith which is in Christ Jesus.
16 All scripture *is* given by inspiration of God, and *is* profitable for doctrine, for reproof, for correction, for instruction in righteousness:
17 That the man of God may be perfect, throughly furnished unto all good works.

CHAPTER 4

I CHARGE *thee* therefore before God, and the Lord Jesus Christ, who shall judge the quick and the dead at his appearing and his kingdom;
2 Preach the word; be instant in season, out of season; reprove, rebuke, exhort with all longsuffering and doctrine.
3 For the time will come when they will not endure sound doctrine; but after their own lusts shall they heap to themselves teachers, having itching ears;
4 And they shall turn away *their* ears from the truth, and shall be turned unto fables.
5 But watch thou in all things, endure afflictions, do the work of an evangelist, make full proof of thy ministry.
6 For I am now ready to be offered, and the time of my departure is at hand.
7 I have fought a good fight, I have finished *my* course, I have kept the faith:

8 Henceforth there is laid up for me a crown of righteousness, which the Lord, the righteous judge, shall give me at that day: and not to me only, but unto all them also that love his appearing.
9 Do thy diligence to come shortly unto me:
10 For Demas hath forsaken me, having loved this present world, and is departed unto Thĕs-sa-lo-nī′ca; Crĕs′cenṡ to Ga-lā′tia, Titus unto Dăl-mā′ti-a.
11 Only Luke is with me. Take Mark, and bring him with thee: for he is profitable to me for the ministry.
12 And Tўch′ĭ-cus have I sent to Ĕph′e-sus.
13 The cloak that I left at Troas with Carpus, when thou comest, bring *with thee*, and the books, *but* especially the parchments.
14 Alexander the coppersmith did me much evil: the Lord reward him according to his works:
15 Of whom be thou ware also; for he hath greatly withstood our words.
16 At my first answer no man stood with me, but all *men* forsook me: *I pray God* that it may not be laid to their charge.
17 Notwithstanding the Lord stood with me, and strengthened me; that by me the preaching might be fully known, and *that* all the Gentiles might hear: and I was delivered out of the mouth of the lion.
18 And the Lord shall deliver me from every evil work, and will preserve *me* unto his heavenly kingdom: to whom *be* glory for ever and ever. Amen.
19 Salute Prĭs′ca and Ăq′ui-la, and the household of Ŏn-e-sĭph′o-rus.
20 E-răs′tus abode at Corinth: but Trŏph′i-mus have I left at Mī-lē′tum sick.
21 Do thy diligence to come before winter. Eū-bū′lus greeteth thee and Pū′dĕnṡ, and Li′nus, and Clau′dĭ-a, and all the brethren.
22 The Lord Jesus Christ *be* with thy spirit. Grace *be* with you. Amen.

The second *epistle* unto Timotheus, ordained the first bishop of the church of the Ephesians, was written from Rome, when Paul was brought before Nero the second time.

THE EPISTLE OF PAUL TO

TITUS

CHAPTER 1

PAUL, a servant of God, and an apostle of Jesus Christ, according to the faith of God's elect, and the acknowledging of the truth which is after godliness;
2 In hope of eternal life, which God, that cannot lie, promised before the world began;
3 But hath in due times manifested his word through preaching, which is committed unto me according to the commandment of God our Saviour;
4 To Titus, *mine* own son after the common faith: Grace, mercy, *and* peace, from God the Father and the Lord Jesus Christ our Saviour.
5 For this cause left I thee in Crete, that thou shouldest set in order the things that are wanting, and ordain elders in every city, as I had appointed thee:
6 If any be blameless, the husband of one wife, having faithful children not accused of riot or unruly.
7 For a bishop must be blameless, as the steward of God; not selfwilled, not soon angry, not given to wine, no striker, not given to filthy lucre;
8 But a lover of hospitality, a lover of good men, sober, just, holy, temperate;
9 Holding fast the faithful word as he hath been taught, that he may be able by sound doctrine both to exhort and to convince the gainsayers.
10 For there are many unruly and vain talkers and deceivers, specially they of the circumcision:
11 Whose mouths must be stopped, who subvert whole houses, teaching things which they ought not, for filthy lucre's sake.
12 One of themselves, *even* a prophet of their own, said, The Cretians *are* alway liars, evil beasts, slow bellies.
13 This witness is true. Wherefore rebuke them sharply, that they may be sound in the faith;
14 Not giving heed to Jewish fables, and commandments of men, that turn from the truth.
15 Unto the pure all things *are* pure: but unto them that are defiled and unbelieving *is* nothing pure; but even their mind and conscience is defiled.
16 They profess that they know God; but in works they deny *him*, being

abominable, and disobedient, and unto
every good work reprobate.

CHAPTER 2

BUT speak thou the things which be-
come sound doctrine:
2 That the aged men be sober, grave,
temperate, sound in faith, in charity, in
patience.
3 The aged women likewise, that *they*
be in behaviour as becometh holiness,
not false accusers, not given to much
wine, teachers of good things;
4 That they may teach the young wom-
en to be sober, to love their husbands,
to love their children,
5 *To be* discreet, chaste, keepers at
home, good, obedient to their own hus-
bands, that the word of God be not
blasphemed.
6 Young men likewise exhort to be
sober minded.
7 In all things shewing thyself a pat-
tern of good works: in doctrine
shewing uncorruptness, gravity, sin-
cerity,
8 Sound speech, that cannot be con-
demned; that he that is of the contrary
part may be ashamed, having no evil
thing to say of you.
9 *Exhort* servants to be obedient unto
their own masters, *and* to please *them*
well in all *things;* not answering again;
10 Not purloining, but shewing all
good fidelity; that they may adorn the
doctrine of God our Saviour in all
things.
11 For the grace of God that bringeth
salvation hath appeared to all men,
12 Teaching us that, denying ungodli-
ness and worldly lusts, we should live
soberly, righteously, and godly, in this
present world;
13 Looking for that blessed hope, and
the glorious appearing of the great God
and our Saviour Jesus Christ;
14 Who gave himself for us, that he
might redeem us from all iniquity, and
purify unto himself a peculiar people,
zealous of good works.
15 These things speak, and exhort,
and rebuke with all authority. Let no
man despise thee.

CHAPTER 3

PUT them in mind to be subject to prin-
cipalities and powers, to obey magis-
trates, to be ready to every good work,
2 To speak evil of no man, to be no
brawlers, *but* gentle, shewing all meek-
ness unto all men.
3 For we ourselves also were
sometimes foolish, disobedient, de-
ceived, serving divers lusts and plea-
sures, living in malice and envy, hate-
ful, *and* hating one another.
4 But after that the kindness and love
of God our Saviour toward man ap-
peared,
5 Not by works of righteousness
which we have done, but according to
his mercy he saved us, by the washing
of regeneration, and renewing of the
Holy Ghost;
6 Which he shed on us abundantly
through Jesus Christ our Saviour;
7 That being justified by his grace,
we should be made heirs according to
the hope of eternal life.
8 *This is* a faithful saying, and these
things I will that thou affirm constant-
ly, that they which have believed in
God might be careful to maintain good
works. These things are good and profit-
able unto men.
9 But avoid foolish questions, and ge-
nealogies, and contentions, and striv-
ings about the law; for they are unprofit-
able and vain.
10 A man that is an heretick after the
first and second admonition reject;
11 Knowing that he that is such is
subverted, and sinneth, being con-
demned of himself.
12 When I shall send Artemas unto
thee, or Ty̆ch'ĭ-cus, be diligent to come
unto me to Nī-cŏp'o-lĭs: for I have de-
termined there to winter.
13 Bring Zenas the lawyer and Apol-
los on their journey diligently, that
nothing be wanting unto them.
14 And let ours also learn to maintain
good works for necessary uses, that
they be not unfruitful.
15 All that are with me salute thee.
Greet them that love us in the faith.
Grace *be* with you all. Amen.

It was written to Titus, ordained the first bishop of the church of the Cretians, from Nicopolis of Macedonia.

THE EPISTLE OF PAUL TO

PHILEMON

PAUL, a prisoner of Jesus Christ, and
Tĭm'o-thy̆ *our* brother, unto Phī-lē'mon
our dearly beloved, and fellowlabour-
er,
2 And to *our* beloved Ăp'phĭ-a, and
Ăr-chĭp'pus our fellowsoldier, and to
the church in thy house:
3 Grace to you, and peace, from God

our Father and the Lord Jesus Christ.

4 I thank my God, making mention of thee always in my prayers,

5 Hearing of thy love and faith, which thou hast toward the Lord Jesus, and toward all saints;

6 That the communication of thy faith may become effectual by the acknowledging of every good thing which is in you in Christ Jesus.

7 For we have great joy and consolation in thy love, because the bowels of the saints are refreshed by thee, brother.

8 Wherefore, though I might be much bold in Christ to enjoin thee that which is convenient,

9 Yet for love's sake I rather beseech *thee*, being such an one as Paul the aged, and now also a prisoner of Jesus Christ.

10 I beseech thee for my son Ō-nĕs'i-mus, whom I have begotten in my bonds:

11 Which in time past was to thee unprofitable, but now profitable to thee and to me:

12 Whom I have sent again: thou therefore receive him, that is, mine own bowels:

13 Whom I would have retained with me, that in thy stead he might have ministered unto me in the bonds of the gospel:

14 But without thy mind would I do nothing; that thy benefit should not be as it were of necessity, but willingly.

15 For perhaps he therefore departed for a season, that thou shouldest receive him for ever;

16 Not now as a servant, but above a servant, a brother beloved, specially to me, but how much more unto thee, both in the flesh, and in the Lord?

17 If thou count me therefore a partner, receive him as myself.

18 If he hath wronged thee, or oweth *thee* ought, put that on mine account;

19 I Paul have written *it* with mine own hand, I will repay *it:* albeit I do not say to thee how thou owest unto me even thine own self besides.

20 Yea, brother, let me have joy of thee in the Lord: refresh my bowels in the Lord.

21 Having confidence in thy obedience I wrote unto thee, knowing that thou wilt also do more than I say.

22 But withal prepare me also a lodging: for I trust that through your prayers I shall be given unto you.

23 There salute thee Ĕp'a-phrăs, my fellowprisoner in Christ Jesus;

24 Marcus, Ăr-ĭs-tär'chus, Demas, Lucas, my fellowlabourers.

25 The grace of our Lord Jesus Christ *be* with your spirit. Amen.

Written from Rome to Philemon, by Onesimus, a bondservant

THE EPISTLE OF PAUL THE APOSTLE TO THE

HEBREWS

CHAPTER 1

GOD, who at sundry times and in divers manners spake in time past unto the fathers by the prophets,

2 Hath in these last days spoken unto us by *his* Son, whom he hath appointed heir of all things, by whom also he made the worlds;

3 Who being the brightness of *his* glory, and the express image of his person, and upholding all things by the word of his power, when he had by himself purged our sins, sat down on the right hand of the Majesty on high;

4 Being made so much better than the angels, as he hath by inheritance obtained a more excellent name than they.

5 For unto which of the angels said he at any time, Thou art my son, this day have I begotten thee? And again, I will be to him a Father, and he shall be to me a Son?

6 And again, when he bringeth in the firstbegotten into the world, he saith, And let all the angels of God worship him.

7 And of the angels he saith, Who maketh his angels spirits, and his ministers a flame of fire.

8 But unto the Son *he saith*, Thy throne, O God, *is* for ever and ever: a sceptre of righteousness *is* the sceptre of thy kingdom.

9 Thou hast loved righteousness, and hated iniquity; therefore God, *even* thy God, hath anointed thee with the oil of gladness above thy fellows.

10 And, Thou, Lord, in the beginning hast laid the foundation of the earth; and the heavens are the works of thine hands:

11 They shall perish; but thou remainest; and they all shall wax old as doth a garment;

12 And as a vesture shalt thou fold them up, and they shall be changed: but

thou art the same, and thy years shall not fail.

13 But to which of the angels said he at any time, Sit on my right hand, until I make thine enemies thy footstool?

14 Are they not all ministering spirits, sent forth to minister for them who shall be heirs of salvation?

CHAPTER 2

THEREFORE we ought to give the more earnest heed to the things which we have heard, lest at any time we should let *them* slip.

2 For if the word spoken by angels was stedfast, and every transgression and disobedience received a just recompence of reward;

3 How shall we escape, if we neglect so great salvation; which at the first began to be spoken by the Lord, and was confirmed unto us by them that heard *him*;

4 God also bearing *them* witness, both with signs and wonders, and with divers miracles, and gifts of the Holy Ghost, according to his own will?

5 For unto the angels hath he not put in subjection the world to come, whereof we speak.

6 But one in a certain place testified, saying, What is man, that thou art mindful of him? or the son of man, that thou visitest him?

7 Thou madest him a little lower than the angels; thou crownedst him with glory and honour, and didst set him over the works of thy hands:

8 Thou hast put all things in subjection under his feet. For in that he put all in subjection under him, he left nothing *that is* not put under him. But now we see not yet all things put under him.

9 But we see Jesus, who was made a little lower than the angels for the suffering of death, crowned with glory and honour; that he by the grace of God should taste death for every man.

10 For it became him, for whom *are* all things, and by whom *are* all things, in bringing many sons unto glory, to make the captain of their salvation perfect through sufferings.

11 For both he that sanctifieth and they who are sanctified *are* all of one: for which cause he is not ashamed to call them brethren,

12 Saying, I will declare thy name unto my brethren, in the midst of the church will I sing praise unto thee.

13 And again, I will put my trust in him. And again, Behold I and the children which God hath given me.

14 Forasmuch then as the children are partakers of flesh and blood, he also himself likewise took part of the same; that through death he might destroy him that had the power of death, that is, the devil;

15 And deliver them who through fear of death were all their lifetime subject to bondage.

16 For verily he took not on *him the nature of* angels; but he took on *him* the seed of Abraham.

17 Wherefore in all things it behoved him to be made like unto *his* brethren, that he might be a merciful and faithful high priest in things *pertaining* to God, to make reconciliation for the sins of the people.

18 For in that he himself hath suffered being tempted, he is able to succour them that are tempted.

CHAPTER 3

WHEREFORE, holy brethren, partakers of the heavenly calling, consider the Apostle and High Priest of our profession, Christ Jesus;

2 Who was faithful to him that appointed him, as also Moses *was faithful* in all his house.

3 For this *man* was counted worthy of more glory than Moses, inasmuch as he who hath builded the house hath more honour than the house.

4 For every house is builded by some *man;* but he that built all things *is* God.

5 And Moses verily *was* faithful in all his house, as a servant, for a testimony of those things which were to be spoken after;

6 But Christ as a son over his own house; whose house are we, if we hold fast the confidence and the rejoicing of the hope firm unto the end.

7 Wherefore (as the Holy Ghost saith, To day if ye will hear his voice,

8 Harden not your hearts, as in the provocation, in the day of temptation in the wilderness:

9 When your fathers tempted me, proved me, and saw my works forty years.

10 Wherefore I was grieved with that generation, and said, They do alway err in *their* heart; and they have not known my ways.

11 So I sware in my wrath, They shall not enter into my rest.)

12 Take heed, brethren, lest there be in any of you an evil heart of unbelief, in departing from the living God.

13 But exhort one another daily, while it is called To day; lest any of you be hardened through the deceitfulness of sin.

14 For we are made partakers of

Christ, if we hold the beginning of our confidence stedfast unto the end;
15 While it is said, To day if ye will hear his voice, harden not your hearts, as in the provocation.
16 For some, when they had heard, did provoke: howbeit not all that came out of Egypt by Moses.
17 But with whom was he grieved forty years? *was it* not with them that had sinned, whose carcases fell in the wilderness?
18 And to whom sware he that they should not enter into his rest, but to them that believed not?
19 So we see that they could not enter in because of unbelief.

CHAPTER 4

LET us therefore fear, lest, a promise being left *us* of entering into his rest, any of you should seem to come short of it.
2 For unto us was the gospel preached, as well as unto them: but the word preached did not profit them, not being mixed with faith in them that heard *it*.
3 For we which have believed do enter into rest, as he said, As I have sworn in my wrath, if they shall enter into my rest: although the works were finished from the foundation of the world.
4 For he spake in a certain place of the seventh *day* on this wise, And God did rest the seventh day from all his works.
5 And in this *place* again, If they shall enter into my rest.
6 Seeing therefore it remaineth that some must enter therein, and they to whom it was first preached entered not in because of unbelief:
7 Again, he limiteth a certain day, saying in David, To day, after so long a time; as it is said, To day if ye will hear his voice, harden not your hearts.
8 For if Jesus had given them rest, then would he not afterward have spoken of another day.
9 There remaineth therefore a rest to the people of God.
10 For he that is entered into his rest, he also hath ceased from his own works, as God *did* from his.
11 Let us labour therefore to enter into that rest, lest any man fall after the same example of unbelief.
12 For the word of God *is* quick, and powerful, and sharper than any twoedged sword, piercing even to the dividing asunder of soul and spirit, and of the joints and marrow, and *is* a discerner of the thoughts and intents of the heart.
13 Neither is there any creature that is not manifest in his sight: but all things *are* naked and opened unto the eyes of him with whom we have to do.
14 Seeing then that we have a great high priest, that is passed into the heavens, Jesus the Son of God, let us hold fast *our* profession.
15 For we have not an high priest which cannot be touched with the feeling of our infirmities; but was in all points tempted like as *we are, yet* without sin.
16 Let us therefore come boldly unto the throne of grace, that we may obtain mercy, and find grace to help in time of need.

CHAPTER 5

FOR every high priest taken from among men is ordained for men in things *pertaining* to God, that he may offer both gifts and sacrifices for sins:
2 Who can have compassion on the ignorant, and on them that are out of the way; for that he himself also is compassed with infirmity.
3 And by reason hereof he ought, as for the people, so also for himself, to offer for sins.
4 And no man taketh this honour unto himself, but he that is called of God, as *was* Aaron.
5 So also Christ glorified not himself to be made an high priest; but he that said unto him, Thou art my Son, to day have I begotten thee.
6 As he saith also in another *place*, Thou *art* a priest for ever after the order of Mĕl-chĭs'e-dĕc.
7 Who in the days of his flesh, when he had offered up prayers and supplications with strong crying and tears unto him that was able to save him from death, and was heard in that he feared;
8 Though he were a Son, yet learned he obedience by the things which he suffered;
9 And being made perfect, he became the author of eternal salvation unto all them that obey him;
10 Called of God an high priest after the order of Mĕl-chĭs'e-dĕc.
11 Of whom we have many things to say, and hard to be uttered, seeing ye are dull of hearing.
12 For when for the time ye ought to be teachers, ye have need that one teach you again which *be* the first principles of the oracles of God; and are become such as have need of milk, and not of strong meat.
13 For every one that useth milk *is* unskilful in the word of righteousness: for he is a babe.

14 But strong meat belongeth to them that are of full age, *even* those who by reason of use have their senses exercised to discern both good and evil.

CHAPTER 6

THEREFORE leaving the principles of the doctrine of Christ, let us go on unto perfection; not laying again the foundation of repentance from dead works, and of faith toward God,

2 Of the doctrine of baptisms, and of laying on of hands, and of resurrection of the dead, and of eternal judgment.

3 And this will we do, if God permit.

4 For *it is* impossible for those who were once enlightened, and have tasted of the heavenly gift, and were made partakers of the Holy Ghost,

5 And have tasted the good word of God, and the powers of the world to come,

6 If they shall fall away, to renew them again unto repentance; seeing they crucify to themselves the Son of God afresh, and put *him* to an open shame.

7 For the earth which drinketh in the rain that cometh oft upon it, and bringeth forth herbs meet for them by whom it is dressed, receiveth blessing from God:

8 But that which beareth thorns and briers *is* rejected, and *is* nigh unto cursing; whose end *is* to be burned.

9 But, beloved, we are persuaded better things of you, and things that accompany salvation, though we thus speak.

10 For God *is* not unrighteous to forget your work and labour of love, which ye have shewed toward his name, in that ye have ministered to the saints, and do minister.

11 And we desire that every one of you do shew the same diligence to the full assurance of hope unto the end:

12 That ye be not slothful, but followers of them who through faith and patience inherit the promises.

13 For when God made promise to Abraham, because he could swear by no greater, he sware by himself,

14 Saying, Surely blessing I will bless thee, and multiplying I will multiply thee.

15 And so, after he had patiently endured, he obtained the promise.

16 For men verily swear by the greater: and an oath for confirmation *is* to them an end of all strife.

17 Wherein God, willing more abundantly to shew unto the heirs of promise the immutability of his counsel, confirmed *it* by an oath:

18 That by two immutable things, in which *it was* impossible for God to lie, we might have a strong consolation, who have fled for refuge to lay hold upon the hope set before us:

19 Which *hope* we have as an anchor of the soul, both sure and stedfast, and which entereth into that within the vail;

20 Whither the forerunner is for us entered, *even* Jesus, made an high priest for ever after the order of Mĕl-chĭs'e-dĕc.

CHAPTER 7

FOR this Mĕl-chĭs'e-dĕc, king of Salem, priest of the most high God, who met Abraham returning from the slaughter of the kings, and blessed him;

2 To whom also Abraham gave a tenth part of all; first being by interpretation King of righteousness, and after that also King of Salem, which is, King of peace;

3 Without father, without mother, without descent, having neither beginning of days, nor end of life; but made like unto the Son of God; abideth a priest continually.

4 Now consider how great this man *was*, unto whom even the patriarch Abraham gave the tenth of the spoils.

5 And verily they that are of the sons of Levi, who receive the office of the priesthood, have a commandment to take tithes of the people according to the law, that is, of their brethren, though they come out of the loins of Abraham:

6 But he whose descent is not counted from them received tithes of Abraham, and blessed him that had the promises.

7 And without all contradiction the less is blessed of the better.

8 And here men that die receive tithes; but there he *receiveth them*, of whom it is witnessed that he liveth.

9 And as I may so say, Levi also, who receiveth tithes, payed tithes in Abraham.

10 For he was yet in the loins of his father, when Mĕl-chĭs'e-dĕc met him.

11 If therefore perfection were by the Le-vit'i-cal priesthood, (for under it the people received the law,) what further need *was there* that another priest should rise after the order of Mĕl-chĭs'e-dĕc, and not be called after the order of Aaron?

12 For the priesthood being changed, there is made of necessity a change also of the law.

13 For he of whom these things are spoken pertaineth to another tribe, of

which no man gave attendance at the
altar.
14 For *it is* evident that our Lord
sprang out of Juda; of which tribe
Moses spake nothing concerning
priesthood.
15 And it is yet far more evident: for
that after the similitude of Mĕl-chĭs'e-
dĕc there ariseth another priest,
16 Who is made, not after the law of a
carnal commandment, but after the
power of an endless life.
17 For he testifieth, Thou *art* a priest
for ever after the order of Mĕl-chĭs'e-
dĕc.
18 For there is verily a disannulling of
the commandment going before for the
weakness and unprofitableness there-
of.
19 For the law made nothing perfect,
but the bringing in of a better hope *did;*
by the which we draw nigh unto God.
20 And inasmuch as not without an
oath *he was made priest:*
21 (For those priests were made
without an oath; but this with an oath
by him that said unto him, The Lord
sware and will not repent, Thou *art* a
priest for ever after the order of Mĕl-
chĭs'e-dĕc:)
22 By so much was Jesus made a
surety of a better testament.
23 And they truly were many priests,
because they were not suffered to con-
tinue by reason of death:
24 But this *man,* because he continu-
eth ever, hath an unchangeable
priesthood.
25 Wherefore he is able also to save
them to the uttermost that come unto
God by him, seeing he ever liveth to
make intercession for them.
26 For such an high priest became us,
who is holy, harmless, undefiled, sepa-
rate from sinners, and made higher
than the heavens;
27 Who needeth not daily, as those
high priests, to offer up sacrifice, first
for his own sins, and then for the peo-
ple's: for this he did once, when he of-
fered up himself.
28 For the law maketh men high
priests which have infirmity; but the
word of the oath, which was since the
law, *maketh* the Son, who is
consecrated for evermore.

CHAPTER 8

NOW of the things which we have spok-
en *this is* the sum: We have such an
high priest, who is set on the right hand
of the throne of the Majesty in the
heavens;
2 A minister of the sanctuary, and of
the true tabernacle, which the Lord
pitched, and not man.
3 For every high priest is ordained to
offer gifts and sacrifices: wherefore *it*
is of necessity that this man have
somewhat also to offer.
4 For if he were on earth, he should
not be a priest, seeing that there are
priests that offer gifts according to the
law:
5 Who serve unto the example and
shadow of heavenly things, as Moses
was admonished of God when he was
about to make the tabernacle: for, See,
saith he, *that* thou make all things ac-
cording to the pattern shewed to thee
in the mount.
6 But now hath he obtained a more
excellent ministry, by how much also
he is the mediator of a better covenant,
which was established upon better
promises.
7 For if that first *covenant* had been
faultless, then should no place have
been sought for the second.
8 For finding fault with them, he
saith, Behold, the days come, saith the
Lord, when I will make a new covenant
with the house of Israel and with the
house of Judah:
9 Not according to the covenant that
I made with their fathers in the day
when I took them by the hand to lead
them out of the land of Egypt; because
they continued not in my covenant, and
I regarded them not, saith the Lord.
10 For this *is* the covenant that I will
make with the house of Israel after
those days, saith the Lord; I will put my
laws into their mind, and write them in
their hearts: and I will be to them a
God, and they shall be to me a people:
11 And they shall not teach every
man his neighbour, and every man his
brother, saying, Know the Lord: for all
shall know me, from the least to the
greatest.
12 For I will be merciful to their un-
righteousness, and their sins and their
iniquities will I remember no more.
13 In that he saith, A new *covenant,*
he hath made the first old. Now that
which decayeth and waxeth old *is* ready
to vanish away.

CHAPTER 9

THEN verily the first *covenant* had also
ordinances of divine service, and a
worldly sanctuary.
2 For there was a tabernacle made;
the first, wherein *was* the candlestick,
and the table, and the shewbread;
which is called the sanctuary.
3 And after the second vail, the taber-
nacle which is called the Holiest of all;

4 Which had the golden censer, and the ark of the covenant overlaid round about with gold, wherein *was* the golden pot that had manna, and Aaron's rod that budded, and the tables of the covenant;

5 And over it the cherubims of glory shadowing the mercyseat; of which we cannot now speak particularly.

6 Now when these things were thus ordained, the priests went always into the first tabernacle, accomplishing the service *of God*.

7 But into the second *went* the high priest alone once every year, not without blood, which he offered for himself, and *for* the errors of the people:

8 The Holy Ghost this signifying, that the way into the holiest of all was not yet made manifest, while as the first tabernacle was yet standing:

9 Which *was* a figure for the time then present, in which were offered both gifts and sacrifices, that could not make him that did the service perfect, as pertaining to the conscience;

10 *Which stood* only in meats and drinks, and divers washings, and carnal ordinances, imposed *on them* until the time of reformation.

11 But Christ being come an high priest of good things to come, by a greater and more perfect tabernacle, not made with hands, that is to say, not of this building;

12 Neither by the blood of goats and calves, but by his own blood he entered in once into the holy place, having obtained eternal redemption *for us*.

13 For if the blood of bulls and of goats, and the ashes of an heifer sprinkling the unclean, sanctifieth to the purifying of the flesh:

14 How much more shall the blood of Christ, who through the eternal Spirit offered himself without spot to God, purge your conscience from dead works to serve the living God?

15 And for this cause he is the mediator of the new testament, that by means of death, for the redemption of the transgressions *that were* under the first testament, they which are called might receive the promise of eternal inheritance.

16 For where a testament *is*, there must also of necessity be the death of the testator.

17 For a testament *is* of force after men are dead: otherwise it is of no strength at all while the testator liveth.

18 Whereupon neither the first *testament* was dedicated without blood.

19 For when Moses had spoken every precept to all the people according to the law, he took the blood of calves and of goats, with water, and scarlet wool, and hyssop, and sprinkled both the book, and all the people,

20 Saying, This *is* the blood of the testament which God hath enjoined unto you.

21 Moreover he sprinkled with blood both the tabernacle, and all the vessels of the ministry.

22 And almost all things are by the law purged with blood; and without shedding of blood is no remission.

23 *It was* therefore necessary that the patterns of things in the heavens should be purified with these; but the heavenly things themselves with better sacrifices than these.

24 For Christ is not entered into the holy places made with hands, *which are* the figures of the true; but into heaven itself, now to appear in the presence of God for us:

25 Nor yet that he should offer himself often, as the high priest entereth into the holy place every year with blood of others;

26 For then must he often have suffered since the foundation of the world: but now once in the end of the world hath he appeared to put away sin by the sacrifice of himself.

27 And as it is appointed unto men once to die, but after this the judgment:

28 So Christ was once offered to bear the sins of many; and unto them that look for him shall he appear the second time without sin unto salvation.

CHAPTER 10

FOR the law having a shadow of good things to come, *and* not the very image of the things, can never with those sacrifices which they offered year by year continually make the comers thereunto perfect.

2 For then would they not have ceased to be offered? because that the worshippers once purged should have had no more conscience of sins.

3 But in those *sacrifices there is* a remembrance again *made* of sins every year.

4 For *it is* not possible that the blood of bulls and of goats should take away sins.

5 Wherefore when he cometh into the world, he saith, Sacrifice and offering thou wouldest not, but a body hast thou prepared me:

6 In burnt offerings and *sacrifices* for sin thou hast had no pleasure.

7 Then said I, Lo, I come (in the vol-

ume of the book it is written of me,) to do thy will, O God.

8 Above when he said, Sacrifice and offering and burnt offerings and *offering* for sin thou wouldest not, neither hadst pleasure *therein;* which are offered by the law;

9 Then said he, Lo, I come to do thy will, O God. He taketh away the first, that he may establish the second.

10 By the which will we are sanctified through the offering of the body of Jesus Christ once *for all.*

11 And every priest standeth daily ministering and offering oftentimes the same sacrifices, which can never take away sins:

12 But this man, after he had offered one sacrifice for sins for ever, sat down on the right hand of God;

13 From henceforth expecting till his enemies be made his footstool.

14 For by one offering he hath perfected for ever them that are sanctified.

15 *Whereof* the Holy Ghost also is a witness to us: for after that he had said before,

16 This *is* the covenant that I will make with them after those days, saith the Lord, I will put my laws into their hearts, and in their minds will I write them;

17 And their sins and iniquities will I remember no more.

18 Now where remission of these *is, there is* no more offering for sin.

19 Having therefore, brethren, boldness to enter into the holiest by the blood of Jesus,

20 By a new and living way, which he hath consecrated for us, through the vail, that is to say, his flesh;

21 And *having* an high priest over the house of God;

22 Let us draw near with a true heart in full assurance of faith, having our hearts sprinkled from an evil conscience, and our bodies washed with pure water.

23 Let us hold fast the profession of *our* faith without wavering; (for he *is* faithful that promised;)

24 And let us consider one another to provoke unto love and to good works:

25 Not forsaking the assembling of ourselves together, as the manner of some *is;* but exhorting *one another:* and so much the more, as ye see the day approaching.

26 For if we sin wilfully after that we have received the knowledge of the truth, there remaineth no more sacrifice for sins,

27 But a certain fearful looking for of judgment and fiery indignation, which shall devour the adversaries.

28 He that despised Moses' law died without mercy under two or three witnesses:

29 Of how much sorer punishment, suppose ye, shall he be thought worthy, who hath trodden under foot the Son of God, and hath counted the blood of the covenant, wherewith he was sanctified, an unholy thing, and hath done despite unto the Spirit of grace?

30 For we know him that hath said, Vengeance *belongeth* unto me, I will recompense, saith the Lord. And again, The Lord shall judge his people.

31 *It is* a fearful thing to fall into the hands of the living God.

32 But call to remembrance the former days, in which, after ye were illuminated, ye endured a great fight of afflictions;

33 Partly, whilst ye were made a gazingstock both by reproaches and afflictions; and partly, whilst ye became companions of them that were so used.

34 For ye had compassion of me in my bonds, and took joyfully the spoiling of your goods, knowing in yourselves that ye have in heaven a better and an enduring substance.

35 Cast not away therefore your confidence, which hath great recompence of reward.

36 For ye have need of patience, that, after ye have done the will of God, ye might receive the promise.

37 For yet a little while, and he that shall come will come, and will not tarry.

38 Now the just shall live by faith: but if *any man* draw back, my soul shall have no pleasure in him.

39 But we are not of them who draw back unto perdition; but of them that believe to the saving of the soul.

CHAPTER 11

NOW faith is the substance of things hoped for, the evidence of things not seen.

2 For by it the elders obtained a good report.

3 Through faith we understand that the worlds were framed by the word of God, so that things which are seen were not made of things which do appear.

4 By faith Abel offered unto God a more excellent sacrifice than Cain, by which he obtained witness that he was righteous, God testifying of his gifts: and by it he being dead yet speaketh.

5 By faith Ē'noch was translated that he should not see death; and was not

found, because God had translated
him: for before his translation he had
this testimony, that he pleased God.
6 But without faith *it is* impossible to
please *him:* for he that cometh to God
must believe that he is, and *that* he is a
rewarder of them that diligently seek
him.
7 By faith Noah, being warned of God
of things not seen as yet, moved with
fear, prepared an ark to the saving of
his house; by the which he condemned
the world, and became heir of the
righteousness which is by faith.
8 By faith Abraham, when he was
called to go out into a place which he
should after receive for an inheritance,
obeyed; and he went out, not knowing
whither he went.
9 By faith he sojourned in the land of
promise, as *in* a strange country, dwell-
ing in tabernacles with Isaac and Ja-
cob, the heirs with him of the same prom-
ise:
10 For he looked for a city which hath
foundations, whose builder and maker
is God.
11 Through faith also Sara herself re-
ceived strength to conceive seed, and
was delivered of a child when she was
past age, because she judged him faith-
ful who had promised.
12 Therefore sprang there even of
one, and him as good as dead, *so many*
as the stars of the sky in multitude, and
as the sand which is by the sea shore
innumerable.
13 These all died in faith, not having
received the promises, but having seen
them afar off, and were persuaded of
them, and embraced *them,* and con-
fessed that they were strangers and
pilgrims on the earth.
14 For they that say such things de-
clare plainly that they seek a country.
15 And truly, if they had been mind-
ful of that *country* from whence they
came out, they might have had oppor-
tunity to have returned.
16 But now they desire a better
country, that is, an heavenly: where-
fore God is not ashamed to be called
their God: for he hath prepared for
them a city.
17 By faith Abraham, when he was
tried, offered up Isaac: and he that had
received the promises offered up his
only begotten *son,*
18 Of whom it was said, That in Isaac
shall thy seed be called:
19 Accounting that God *was* able to
raise *him* up, even from the dead; from
whence also he received him in a fig-
ure.
20 By faith Isaac blessed Jacob and
Esau concerning things to come.
21 By faith Jacob, when he was a
dying, blessed both the sons of Joseph;
and worshipped, *leaning* upon the top
of his staff.
22 By faith Joseph, when he died,
made mention of the departing of the
children of Israel; and gave command-
ment concerning his bones.
23 By faith Moses, when he was born,
was hid three months of his parents,
because they saw *he was* a proper
child; and they were not afraid of the
king's commandment.
24 By faith Moses, when he was come
to years, refused to be called the son of
Pharaoh's daughter;
25 Choosing rather to suffer afflic-
tion with the people of God, than to en-
joy the pleasures of sin for a season;
26 Esteeming the reproach of Christ
greater riches than the treasures in
Egypt: for he had respect unto the re-
compence of the reward.
27 By faith he forsook Egypt, not
fearing the wrath of the king: for he en-
dured, as seeing him who is invisible.
28 Through faith he kept the passover,
and the sprinkling of blood, lest he
that destroyed the firstborn should
touch them.
29 By faith they passed through the
Red sea as by dry *land:* which the Egyp-
tians assaying to do were drowned.
30 By faith the walls of Jericho fell
down, after they were compassed
about seven days.
31 By faith the harlot Rahab perished
not with them that believed not, when
she had received the spies with peace.
32 And what shall I more say? for the
time would fail me to tell of Gĕd'e-on,
and *of* Bâ'rak, and *of* Samson, and *of*
Jĕph'tha-ē: *of* David also, and Samuel,
and *of* the prophets:
33 Who through faith subdued king-
doms, wrought righteousness, ob-
tained promises, stopped the mouths of
lions,
34 Quenched the violence of fire, es-
caped the edge of the sword, out of
weakness were made strong, waxed
valiant in fight, turned to flight the ar-
mies of the aliens.
35 Women received their dead raised
to life again: and others were tortured,
not accepting deliverance; that they
might obtain a better resurrection:
36 And others had trial of *cruel*
mockings and scourgings, yea, more-
over of bonds and imprisonment:
37 They were stoned, they were sawn
asunder, were tempted, were slain with
the sword: they wandered about in

sheepskins and goatskins; being desti-
tute, afflicted, tormented;
38 (Of whom the world was not
worthy:) they wandered in deserts, and
in mountains, and *in* dens and caves of
the earth.
39 And these all, having obtained a
good report through faith, received not
the promise:
40 God having provided some better
thing for us, that they without us
should not be made perfect.

CHAPTER 12

WHEREFORE seeing we also are com-
passed about with so great a cloud of
witnesses, let us lay aside every
weight, and the sin which doth so easily
beset *us*, and let us run with patience
the race that is set before us,
2 Looking unto Jesus the author and
finisher of *our* faith; who for the joy
that was set before him endured the
cross, despising the shame, and is set
down at the right hand of the throne of
God.
3 For consider him that endured such
contradiction of sinners against him-
self, lest ye be wearied and faint in your
minds.
4 Ye have not yet resisted unto blood,
striving against sin.
5 And ye have forgotten the exhorta-
tion which speaketh unto you as unto
children, My son, despise not thou the
chastening of the Lord, nor faint when
thou art rebuked of him:
6 For whom the Lord loveth he chas-
teneth, and scourgeth every son whom
he receiveth.
7 If ye endure chastening, God deal-
eth with you as with sons; for what son
is he whom the father chasteneth not?
8 But if ye be without chastisement,
whereof all are partakers, then are ye
bastards, and not sons.
9 Furthermore we have had fathers
of our flesh which corrected *us*, and we
gave *them* reverence: shall we not
much rather be in subjection unto the
Father of spirits, and live?
10 For they verily for a few days
chastened *us* after their own pleasure;
but he for *our* profit, that *we* might be
partakers of his holiness.
11 Now no chastening for the present
seemeth to be joyous, but grievous:
nevertheless afterward it yieldeth the
peaceable fruit of righteousness unto
them which are exercised thereby.
12 Wherefore lift up the hands which
hang down, and the feeble knees;
13 And make straight paths for your
feet, lest that which is lame be turned
out of the way; but let it rather be
healed.
14 Follow peace with all *men*, and holi-
ness, without which no man shall see
the Lord:
15 Looking diligently lest any man
fail of the grace of God; lest any root of
bitterness springing up trouble *you*,
and thereby many be defiled;
16 Lest there *be* any fornicator, or
profane person, as Esau, who for one
morsel of meat sold his birthright.
17 For ye know how that afterward,
when he would have inherited the bless-
ing, he was rejected: for he found no
place of repentance, though he sought
it carefully with tears.
18 For ye are not come unto the
mount that might be touched, and that
burned with fire, nor unto blackness,
and darkness, and tempest,
19 And the sound of a trumpet, and
the voice of words; which *voice* they
that heard intreated that the word
should not be spoken to them any
more:
20 (For they could not endure that
which was commanded, And if so
much as a beast touch the mountain, it
shall be stoned, or thrust through with
a dart:
21 And so terrible was the sight, *that*
Moses said, I exceedingly fear and
quake:)
22 But ye are come unto mount Sion,
and unto the city of the living God, the
heavenly Jerusalem, and to an innumer-
able company of angels,
23 To the general assembly and
church of the firstborn, which are writ-
ten in heaven, and to God the Judge of
all, and to the spirits of just men made
perfect,
24 And to Jesus the mediator of the
new covenant, and to the blood of
sprinkling, that speaketh better things
than *that of* Abel.
25 See that ye refuse not him that
speaketh. For if they escaped not who
refused him that spake on earth, much
more *shall not* we *escape*, if we turn
away from him that *speaketh* from
heaven:
26 Whose voice then shook the earth:
but now he hath promised, saying, Yet
once more I shake not the earth only,
but also heaven.
27 And this *word*, Yet once more, sig-
nifieth the removing of those things
that are shaken, as of things that are
made, that those things which cannot
be shaken may remain.
28 Wherefore we receiving a king-

dom which cannot be moved, let us have grace, whereby we may serve God acceptably with reverence and godly fear:

29 For our God *is* a consuming fire.

CHAPTER 13

LET brotherly love continue.

2 Be not forgetful to entertain strangers: for thereby some have entertained angels unawares.

3 Remember them that are in bonds, as bound with them; *and* them which suffer adversity, as being yourselves also in the body.

4 Marriage *is* honourable in all, and the bed undefiled: but whoremongers and adulterers God will judge.

5 *Let your* conversation *be* without covetousness; *and be* content with such things as ye have: for he hath said, I will never leave thee, nor forsake thee.

6 So that we may boldly say, The Lord *is* my helper, and I will not fear what man shall do unto me.

7 Remember them which have the rule over you, who have spoken unto you the word of God: whose faith follow, considering the end of *their* conversation.

8 Jesus Christ the same yesterday, and to day, and for ever.

9 Be not carried about with divers and strange doctrines. For *it is* a good thing that the heart be established with grace; not with meats, which have not profited them that have been occupied therein.

10 We have an altar, whereof they have no right to eat which serve the tabernacle.

11 For the bodies of those beasts, whose blood is brought into the sanctuary by the high priest for sin, are burned without the camp.

12 Wherefore Jesus also, that he might sanctify the people with his own blood, suffered without the gate.

13 Let us go forth therefore unto him without the camp, bearing his reproach.

14 For here have we no continuing city, but we seek one to come.

15 By him therefore let us offer the sacrifice of praise to God continually, that is, the fruit of *our* lips giving thanks to his name.

16 But to do good and to communicate forget not: for with such sacrifices God is well pleased.

17 Obey them that have the rule over you, and submit yourselves: for they watch for your souls, as they that must give account, that they may do it with joy, and not with grief: for that *is* unprofitable for you.

18 Pray for us: for we trust we have a good conscience, in all things willing to live honestly.

19 But I beseech *you* the rather to do this, that I may be restored to you the sooner.

20 Now the God of peace, that brought again from the dead our Lord Jesus, that great shepherd of the sheep, through the blood of the everlasting covenant,

21 Make you perfect in every good work to do his will, working in you that which is wellpleasing in his sight, through Jesus Christ; to whom *be* glory for ever and ever. Amen.

22 And I beseech you, brethren, suffer the word of exhortation: for I have written a letter unto you in few words.

23 Know ye that *our* brother Tĭm'o-thy̆ is set at liberty; with whom, if he come shortly, I will see you.

24 Salute all them that have the rule over you, and all the saints. They of Italy salute you.

25 Grace *be* with you all. Amen.

Written to the Hebrews from Italy by Timothy

THE GENERAL EPISTLE OF

JAMES

CHAPTER 1

JAMES, a servant of God and of the Lord Jesus Christ, to the twelve tribes which are scattered abroad, greeting.

2 My brethren, count it all joy when ye fall into divers temptations;

3 Knowing *this*, that the trying of your faith worketh patience.

4 But let patience have *her* perfect work, that ye may be perfect and entire, wanting nothing.

5 If any of you lack wisdom, let him ask of God, that giveth to all *men* liberally, and upbraideth not; and it shall be given him.

6 But let him ask in faith, nothing wavering. For he that wavereth is like a wave of the sea driven with the wind and tossed.

7 For let not that man think that he shall receive any thing of the Lord.

8 A double minded man *is* unstable in all his ways.

9 Let the brother of low degree rejoice in that he is exalted:

10 But the rich, in that he is made
low: because as the flower of the grass
he shall pass away.
11 For the sun is no sooner risen with
a burning heat, but it withereth the
grass, and the flower thereof falleth,
and the grace of the fashion of it per-
isheth: so also shall the rich man fade
away in his ways.
12 Blessed *is* the man that endureth
temptation: for when he is tried, he
shall receive the crown of life, which
the Lord hath promised to them that
love him.
13 Let no man say when he is
tempted, I am tempted of God: for God
cannot be tempted with evil, neither
tempteth he any man:
14 But every man is tempted, when
he is drawn away of his own lust, and
enticed.
15 Then when lust hath conceived, it
bringeth forth sin: and sin, when it is
finished, bringeth forth death.
16 Do not err, my beloved brethren.
17 Every good gift and every perfect
gift is from above, and cometh down
from the Father of lights, with whom is
no variableness, neither shadow of turn-
ing.
18 Of his own will begat he us with
the word of truth, that we should be a
kind of firstfruits of his creatures.
19 Wherefore, my beloved brethren,
let every man be swift to hear, slow to
speak, slow to wrath:
20 For the wrath of man worketh not
the righteousness of God.
21 Wherefore lay apart all filthiness
and superfluity of naughtiness, and re-
ceive with meekness the engrafted
word, which is able to save your souls.
22 But be ye doers of the word, and
not hearers only, deceiving your own
selves.
23 For if any be a hearer of the word,
and not a doer, he is like unto a man
beholding his natural face in a glass:
24 For he beholdeth himself, and
goeth his way, and straightway forget-
teth what manner of man he was.
25 But whoso looketh into the perfect
law of liberty, and continueth *therein*,
he being not a forgetful hearer, but a
doer of the work, this man shall be
blessed in his deed.
26 If any man among you seem to be
religious, and bridleth not his tongue,
but deceiveth his own heart, this man's
religion *is* vain.
27 Pure religion and undefiled before
God and the Father is this, To visit the
fatherless and widows in their afflic-
tion, *and* to keep himself unspotted
from the world.

CHAPTER 2

MY brethren, have not the faith of our
Lord Jesus Christ, *the Lord* of glory,
with respect of persons.
2 For if there come unto your as-
sembly a man with a gold ring, in
goodly apparel, and there come in also
a poor man in vile raiment;
3 And ye have respect to him that
weareth the gay clothing, and say unto
him, Sit thou here in a good place; and
say to the poor, Stand thou there, or sit
here under my footstool:
4 Are ye not then partial in your-
selves, and are become judges of evil
thoughts?
5 Hearken, my beloved brethren,
Hath not God chosen the poor of this
world rich in faith, and heirs of the
kingdom which he hath promised to
them that love him?
6 But ye have despised the poor. Do
not rich men oppress you, and draw
you before the judgment seats?
7 Do not they blaspheme that worthy
name by the which ye are called?
8 If ye fulfil the royal law according
to the scripture, Thou shalt love thy
neighbour as thyself, ye do well:
9 But if ye have respect to persons, ye
commit sin, and are convinced of the
law as transgressors.
10 For whosoever shall keep the
whole law, and yet offend in one *point*,
he is guilty of all.
11 For he that said, Do not commit
adultery, said also, Do not kill. Now if
thou commit no adultery, yet if thou
kill, thou art become a transgressor of
the law.
12 So speak ye, and so do, as they
that shall be judged by the law of lib-
erty.
13 For he shall have judgment
without mercy, that hath shewed no
mercy; and mercy rejoiceth against
judgment.
14 What *doth it* profit, my brethren,
though a man say he hath faith, and
have not works? can faith save him?
15 If a brother or sister be naked, and
destitute of daily food,
16 And one of you say unto them, De-
part in peace, be *ye* warmed and filled;
notwithstanding ye give them not
those things which are needful to the
body; what *doth it* profit?
17 Even so faith, if it hath not works,
is dead, being alone.
18 Yea, a man may say, Thou hast
faith, and I have works: shew me thy
faith without thy works, and I will
shew thee my faith by my works.
19 Thou believest that there is one

God; thou doest well: the devils also believe, and tremble.
20 But wilt thou know, O vain man, that faith without works is dead?
21 Was not Abraham our father justified by works, when he had offered Isaac his son upon the altar?
22 Seest thou how faith wrought with his works, and by works was faith made perfect?
23 And the scripture was fulfilled which saith, Abraham believed God, and it was imputed unto him for righteousness: and he was called the Friend of God.
24 Ye see then how that by works a man is justified, and not by faith only.
25 Likewise also was not Rahab the harlot justified by works, when she had received the messengers, and had sent *them* out another way?
26 For as the body without the spirit is dead, so faith without works is dead also.

CHAPTER 3

MY brethren, be not many masters, knowing that we shall receive the greater condemnation.
2 For in many things we offend all. If any man offend not in word, the same *is* a perfect man, *and* able also to bridle the whole body.
3 Behold, we put bits in the horses' mouths, that they may obey us; and we turn about their whole body.
4 Behold also the ships, which though *they be* so great, and *are* driven of fierce winds, yet are they turned about with a very small helm, whithersoever the governor listeth.
5 Even so the tongue is a little member, and boasteth great things. Behold, how great a matter a little fire kindleth!
6 And the tongue *is* a fire, a world of iniquity: so is the tongue among our members, that it defileth the whole body, and setteth on fire the course of nature; and it is set on fire of hell.
7 For every kind of beasts, and of birds, and of serpents, and of things in the sea, is tamed, and hath been tamed of mankind:
8 But the tongue can no man tame; *it is* an unruly evil, full of deadly poison.
9 Therewith bless we God, even the Father; and therewith curse we men, which are made after the similitude of God.
10 Out of the same mouth proceedeth blessing and cursing. My brethren, these things ought not so to be.
11 Doth a fountain send forth at the same place sweet *water* and bitter?
12 Can the fig tree, my brethren, bear olive berries? either a vine, figs? so *can* no fountain both yield salt water and fresh.
13 Who *is* a wise man and endued with knowledge among you? let him shew out of a good conversation his works with meekness of wisdom.
14 But if ye have bitter envying and strife in your hearts, glory not, and lie not against the truth.
15 This wisdom descendeth not from above, but *is* earthly, sensual, devilish.
16 For where envying and strife *is*, there *is* confusion and every evil work.
17 But the wisdom that is from above is first pure, then peaceable, gentle, *and* easy to be intreated, full of mercy and good fruits, without partiality, and without hypocrisy.
18 And the fruit of righteousness is sown in peace of them that make peace.

CHAPTER 4

FROM whence *come* wars and fightings among you? *come they* not hence, *even* of your lusts that war in your members?
2 Ye lust, and have not: ye kill, and desire to have, and cannot obtain: ye fight and war, yet ye have not, because ye ask not.
3 Ye ask, and receive not, because ye ask amiss, that ye may consume *it* upon your lusts.
4 Ye adulterers and adulteresses, know ye not that the friendship of the world is enmity with God? whosoever therefore will be a friend of the world is the enemy of God.
5 Do ye think that the scripture saith in vain, The spirit that dwelleth in us lusteth to envy?
6 But he giveth more grace. Wherefore he saith, God resisteth the proud, but giveth grace unto the humble.
7 Submit yourselves therefore to God. Resist the devil, and he will flee from you.
8 Draw nigh to God, and he will draw nigh to you. Cleanse *your* hands, *ye* sinners; and purify *your* hearts, *ye* double minded.
9 Be afflicted, and mourn, and weep: let your laughter be turned to mourning, and *your* joy to heaviness.
10 Humble yourselves in the sight of the Lord, and he shall lift you up.
11 Speak not evil one of another, brethren. He that speaketh evil of *his* brother, and judgeth his brother, speaketh evil of the law, and judgeth the law: but if thou judge the law, thou art not a doer of the law, but a judge.
12 There is one lawgiver, who is able

to save and to destroy: who art thou that judgest another?

13 Go to now, ye that say, To day or to morrow we will go into such a city, and continue there a year, and buy and sell, and get gain:

14 Whereas ye know not what *shall be* on the morrow. For what *is* your life? It is even a vapour, that appeareth for a little time, and then vanisheth away.

15 For that ye *ought* to say, If the Lord will, we shall live, and do this, or that.

16 But now ye rejoice in your boastings: all such rejoicing is evil.

17 Therefore to him that knoweth to do good, and doeth *it* not, to him it is sin.

CHAPTER 5

GO to now, *ye* rich men, weep and howl for your miseries that shall come upon *you*.

2 Your riches are corrupted, and your garments are motheaten.

3 Your gold and silver is cankered; and the rust of them shall be a witness against you, and shall eat your flesh as it were fire. Ye have heaped treasure together for the last days.

4 Behold, the hire of the labourers who have reaped down your fields, which is of you kept back by fraud, crieth: and the cries of them which have reaped are entered into the ears of the Lord of Săb′a-ŏth.

5 Ye have lived in pleasure on the earth, and been wanton; ye have nourished your hearts, as in a day of slaughter.

6 Ye have condemned *and* killed the just; *and* he doth not resist you.

7 Be patient therefore, brethren, unto the coming of the Lord. Behold, the husbandman waiteth for the precious fruit of the earth, and hath long patience for it, until he receive the early and latter rain.

8 Be ye also patient; stablish your hearts: for the coming of the Lord draweth nigh.

9 Grudge not one against another, brethren, lest ye be condemned: behold, the judge standeth before the door.

10 Take, my brethren, the prophets, who have spoken in the name of the Lord, for an example of suffering affliction, and of patience.

11 Behold, we count them happy which endure. Ye have heard of the patience of Job, and have seen the end of the Lord; that the Lord is very pitiful, and of tender mercy.

12 But above all things, my brethren, swear not, neither by heaven, neither by the earth, neither by any other oath: but let your yea be yea; and *your* nay, nay; lest ye fall into condemnation.

13 Is any among you afflicted? let him pray. Is any merry? let him sing psalms.

14 Is any sick among you? let him call for the elders of the church; and let them pray over him, anointing him with oil in the name of the Lord:

15 And the prayer of faith shall save the sick, and the Lord shall raise him up; and if he have committed sins, they shall be forgiven him.

16 Confess *your* faults one to another, and pray one for another, that ye may be healed. The effectual fervent prayer of a righteous man availeth much.

17 E-lī′as was a man subject to like passions as we are, and he prayed earnestly that it might not rain: and it rained not on the earth by the space of three years and six months.

18 And he prayed again, and the heaven gave rain, and the earth brought forth her fruit.

19 Brethren, if any of you do err from the truth, and one convert him;

20 Let him know, that he which converteth the sinner from the error of his way shall save a soul from death, and shall hide a multitude of sins.

THE FIRST EPISTLE GENERAL OF

PETER

CHAPTER 1

PETER, an apostle of Jesus Christ, to the strangers scattered throughout Pontus, Ga-lā′tia, Căp-pa-dō′ci-a, Asia, and Bī-thy̆n′ĭ-a,

2 Elect according to the foreknowledge of God the Father, through sanctification of the Spirit, unto obedience and sprinkling of the blood of Jesus Christ: Grace unto you, and peace, be multiplied.

3 Blessed *be* the God and Father of our Lord Jesus Christ, which according to his abundant mercy hath begotten us again unto a lively hope by the resurrection of Jesus Christ from the dead,

4 To an inheritance incorruptible, and undefiled, and that fadeth not away, reserved in heaven for you,

5 Who are kept by the power of God through faith unto salvation ready to be revealed in the last time.
6 Wherein ye greatly rejoice, though now for a season, if need be, ye are in heaviness through manifold temptations:
7 That the trial of your faith, being much more precious than of gold that perisheth, though it be tried with fire, might be found unto praise and honour and glory at the appearing of Jesus Christ:
8 Whom having not seen, ye love; in whom, though now ye see *him* not, yet believing, ye rejoice with joy unspeakable and full of glory:
9 Receiving the end of your faith, *even* the salvation of *your* souls.
10 Of which salvation the prophets have enquired and searched diligently, who prophesied of the grace *that should come* unto you:
11 Searching what, or what manner of time the Spirit of Christ which was in them did signify, when it testified beforehand the sufferings of Christ, and the glory that should follow.
12 Unto whom it was revealed, that not unto themselves, but unto us they did minister the things, which are now reported unto you by them that have preached the gospel unto you with the Holy Ghost sent down from heaven; which things the angels desire to look into.
13 Wherefore gird up the loins of your mind, be sober, and hope to the end for the grace that is to be brought unto you at the revelation of Jesus Christ;
14 As obedient children, not fashioning yourselves according to the former lusts in your ignorance:
15 But as he which hath called you is holy, so be ye holy in all manner of conversation;
16 Because it is written, Be ye holy; for I am holy.
17 And if ye call on the Father, who without respect of persons judgeth according to every man's work, pass the time of your sojourning *here* in fear:
18 Forasmuch as ye know that ye were not redeemed with corruptible things, *as* silver and gold, from your vain conversation *received* by tradition from your fathers;
19 But with the precious blood of Christ, as of a lamb without blemish and without spot:
20 Who verily was foreordained before the foundation of the world, but was manifest in these last times for you,
21 Who by him do believe in God, that raised him up from the dead, and gave him glory; that your faith and hope might be in God.
22 Seeing ye have purified your souls in obeying the truth through the Spirit unto unfeigned love of the brethren, *see that ye* love one another with a pure heart fervently:
23 Being born again, not of corruptible seed, but of incorruptible, by the word of God, which liveth and abideth for ever.
24 For all flesh *is* as grass, and all the glory of man as the flower of grass. The grass withereth, and the flower thereof falleth away:
25 But the word of the Lord endureth for ever. And this is the word which by the gospel is preached unto you.

CHAPTER 2

WHEREFORE laying aside all malice, and all guile, and hypocrisies, and envies, and all evil speakings,
2 As newborn babes, desire the sincere milk of the word, that ye may grow thereby:
3 If so be ye have tasted that the Lord *is* gracious.
4 To whom coming, *as unto* a living stone, disallowed indeed of men, but chosen of God, *and* precious,
5 Ye also, as lively stones, are built up a spiritual house, an holy priesthood, to offer up spiritual sacrifices, acceptable to God by Jesus Christ.
6 Wherefore also it is contained in the scripture, Behold, I lay in Sion a chief corner stone, elect, precious: and he that believeth on him shall not be confounded.
7 Unto you therefore which believe *he is* precious: but unto them which be disobedient, the stone which the builders disallowed, the same is made the head of the corner,
8 And a stone of stumbling, and a rock of offence, *even to them* which stumble at the word, being disobedient: whereunto also they were appointed.
9 But ye *are* a chosen generation, a royal priesthood, an holy nation, a peculiar people; that ye should shew forth the praises of him who hath called you out of darkness into his marvellous light:
10 Which in time past *were* not a people, but *are* now the people of God: which had not obtained mercy, but now have obtained mercy.
11 Dearly beloved, I beseech *you* as strangers and pilgrims, abstain from

fleshly lusts, which war against the soul;
12 Having your conversation honest among the Gentiles: that, whereas they speak against you as evildoers, they may by *your* good works, which they shall behold, glorify God in the day of visitation.
13 Submit yourselves to every ordinance of man for the Lord's sake: whether it be to the king, as supreme;
14 Or unto governors, as unto them that are sent by him for the punishment of evildoers, and for the praise of them that do well.
15 For so is the will of God, that with well doing ye may put to silence the ignorance of foolish men:
16 As free, and not using *your* liberty for a cloak of maliciousness, but as the servants of God.
17 Honour all *men*. Love the brotherhood. Fear God. Honour the king.
18 Servants, *be* subject to *your* masters with all fear; not only to the good and gentle, but also to the froward.
19 For this *is* thankworthy, if a man for conscience toward God endure grief, suffering wrongfully.
20 For what glory *is it*, if, when ye be buffeted for your faults, ye shall take it patiently? but if, when ye do well, and suffer *for it*, ye take it patiently, this *is* acceptable with God.
21 For even hereunto were ye called: because Christ also suffered for us, leaving us an example, that ye should follow his steps:
22 Who did no sin, neither was guile found in his mouth:
23 Who, when he was reviled, reviled not again; when he suffered, he threatened not; but committed *himself* to him that judgeth righteously:
24 Who his own self bare our sins in his own body on the tree, that we, being dead to sins, should live unto righteousness: by whose stripes ye were healed.
25 For ye were as sheep going astray; but are now returned unto the Shepherd and Bishop of your souls.

CHAPTER 3

LIKEWISE, ye wives, *be* in subjection to your own husbands; that, if any obey not the word, they also may without the word be won by the conversation of the wives;
2 While they behold your chaste conversation *coupled* with fear.
3 Whose adorning let it not be that outward *adorning* of plaiting the hair, and of wearing of gold, or of putting on of apparel;
4 But *let it be* the hidden man of the heart, in that which is not corruptible, *even the ornament* of a meek and quiet spirit, which is in the sight of God of great price.
5 For after this manner in the old time the holy women also, who trusted in God, adorned themselves, being in subjection unto their own husbands:
6 Even as Sara obeyed Abraham, calling him lord: whose daughters ye are, as long as ye do well, and are not afraid with any amazement.
7 Likewise, ye husbands, dwell with *them* according to knowledge, giving honour unto the wife, as unto the weaker vessel, and as being heirs together of the grace of life; that your prayers be not hindered.
8 Finally, *be ye* all of one mind, having compassion one of another, love as brethren, *be* pitiful, *be* courteous:
9 Not rendering evil for evil, or railing for railing: but contrariwise blessing; knowing that ye are thereunto called, that ye should inherit a blessing.
10 For he that will love life, and see good days, let him refrain his tongue from evil, and his lips that they speak no guile:
11 Let him eschew evil, and do good; let him seek peace, and ensue it.
12 For the eyes of the Lord *are* over the righteous, and his ears *are open* unto their prayers: but the face of the Lord *is* against them that do evil.
13 And who *is* he that will harm you, if ye be followers of that which is good?
14 But and if ye suffer for righteousness' sake, happy *are ye*: and be not afraid of their terror, neither be troubled;
15 But sanctify the Lord God in your hearts: and *be* ready always to *give* an answer to every man that asketh you a reason of the hope that is in you with meekness and fear:
16 Having a good conscience; that, whereas they speak evil of you, as of evildoers, they may be ashamed that falsely accuse your good conversation in Christ.
17 For *it is* better, if the will of God be so, that ye suffer for well doing, than for evil doing.
18 For Christ also hath once suffered for sins, the just for the unjust, that he might bring us to God, being put to death in the flesh, but quickened by the Spirit:
19 By which also he went and preached unto the spirits in prison;
20 Which sometime were disobedi-

ent, when once the longsuffering of God waited in the days of Noah, while the ark was a preparing, wherein few, that is, eight souls were saved by water.

21 The like figure whereunto *even* baptism doth also now save us (not the putting away of the filth of the flesh, but the answer of a good conscience toward God,) by the resurrection of Jesus Christ:

22 Who is gone into heaven, and is on the right hand of God; angels and authorities and powers being made subject unto him.

CHAPTER 4

FORASMUCH then as Christ hath suffered for us in the flesh, arm yourselves likewise with the same mind: for he that hath suffered in the flesh hath ceased from sin;

2 That he no longer should live the rest of *his* time in the flesh to the lusts of men, but to the will of God.

3 For the time past of *our* life may suffice us to have wrought the will of the Gentiles, when we walked in lasciviousness, lusts, excess of wine, revellings, banquetings, and abominable idolatries:

4 Wherein they think it strange that ye run not with *them* to the same excess of riot, speaking evil of *you:*

5 Who shall give account to him that is ready to judge the quick and the dead.

6 For for this cause was the gospel preached also to them that are dead, that they might be judged according to men in the flesh, but live according to God in the spirit.

7 But the end of all things is at hand: be ye therefore sober, and watch unto prayer.

8 And above all things have fervent charity among yourselves: for charity shall cover the multitude of sins.

9 Use hospitality one to another without grudging.

10 As every man hath received the gift, *even so* minister the same one to another, as good stewards of the manifold grace of God.

11 If any man speak, *let him speak* as the oracles of God; if any man minister, *let him do it* as of the ability which God giveth: that God in all things may be glorified through Jesus Christ, to whom be praise and dominion for ever and ever. Amen.

12 Beloved, think it not strange concerning the fiery trial which is to try you, as though some strange thing happened unto you:

13 But rejoice, inasmuch as ye are partakers of Christ's sufferings; that, when his glory shall be revealed, ye may be glad also with exceeding joy.

14 If ye be reproached for the name of Christ, happy *are ye;* for the spirit of glory and of God resteth upon you: on their part he is evil spoken of, but on your part he is glorified.

15 But let none of you suffer as a murderer, or *as* a thief, or *as* an evildoer, or as a busybody in other men's matters.

16 Yet if *any man suffer* as a Christian, let him not be ashamed; but let him glorify God on this behalf.

17 For the time *is come* that judgment must begin at the house of God: and if *it* first *begin* at us, what shall the end *be* of them that obey not the gospel of God?

18 And if the righteous scarcely be saved, where shall the ungodly and the sinner appear?

19 Wherefore let them that suffer according to the will of God commit the keeping of their souls *to him* in well doing, as unto a faithful Creator.

CHAPTER 5

THE elders which are among you I exhort, who am also an elder, and a witness of the sufferings of Christ, and also a partaker of the glory that shall be revealed:

2 Feed the flock of God which is among you, taking the oversight *thereof,* not by constraint, but willingly; not for filthy lucre, but of a ready mind;

3 Neither as being lords over *God's* heritage, but being ensamples to the flock.

4 And when the chief Shepherd shall appear, ye shall receive a crown of glory that fadeth not away.

5 Likewise, ye younger, submit yourselves unto the elder. Yea, all *of you* be subject one to another, and be clothed with humility: for God resisteth the proud, and giveth grace to the humble.

6 Humble yourselves therefore under the mighty hand of God, that he may exalt you in due time:

7 Casting all your care upon him; for he careth for you.

8 Be sober, be vigilant; because your adversary the devil, as a roaring lion, walketh about, seeking whom he may devour:

9 Whom resist stedfast in the faith, knowing that the same afflictions are accomplished in your brethren that are in the world.

10 But the God of all grace, who hath called us unto his eternal glory by

Christ Jesus, after that ye have suf-
fered a while, make you perfect, stab-
lish, strengthen, settle *you.*
11 To him *be* glory and dominion for
ever and ever. Amen.
12 By Sĭl-vā′nus, a faithful brother
unto you, as I suppose, I have written
briefly, exhorting, and testifying that
this is the true grace of God wherein ye
stand.
13 The *church that is* at Babylon,
elected together with *you,* saluteth
you; and *so doth* Marcus my son.
14 Greet ye one another with a kiss of
charity. Peace *be* with you all that are
in Christ Jesus. Amen.

THE SECOND EPISTLE GENERAL OF

PETER

CHAPTER 1

SIMON Peter, a servant and an apostle
of Jesus Christ, to them that have ob-
tained like precious faith with us
through the righteousness of God and
our Saviour Jesus Christ:
2 Grace and peace be multiplied unto
you through the knowledge of God, and
of Jesus our Lord,
3 According as his divine power hath
given unto us all things that *pertain*
unto life and godliness, through the
knowledge of him that hath called us to
glory and virtue:
4 Whereby are given unto us exceed-
ing great and precious promises: that
by these ye might be partakers of the
divine nature, having escaped the cor-
ruption that is in the world through
lust.
5 And beside this, giving all diligence,
add to your faith virtue; and to
virtue knowledge;
6 And to knowledge temperance; and
to temperance patience; and to pa-
tience godliness;
7 And to godliness brotherly kind-
ness; and to brotherly kindness charity.
8 For if these things be in you, and
abound, they make *you that ye shall*
neither *be* barren nor unfruitful in the
knowledge of our Lord Jesus Christ.
9 But he that lacketh these things is
blind, and cannot see afar off, and hath
forgotten that he was purged from his
old sins.
10 Wherefore the rather, brethren,
give diligence to make your calling and
election sure: for if ye do these things,
ye shall never fall:
11 For so an entrance shall be minis-
tered unto you abundantly into the ever-
lasting kingdom of our Lord and Sav-
iour Jesus Christ.
12 Wherefore I will not be negligent
to put you always in remembrance of
these things, though ye know *them,*
and be established in the present truth.
13 Yea, I think it meet, as long as I am
in this tabernacle, to stir you up by put-
ting *you* in remembrance;
14 Knowing that shortly I must put
off *this* my tabernacle, even as our Lord
Jesus Christ hath shewed me.
15 Moreover I will endeavour that ye
may be able after my decease to have
these things always in remembrance.
16 For we have not followed cunning-
ly devised fables, when we made
known unto you the power and coming
of our Lord Jesus Christ, but were eye-
witnesses of his majesty.
17 For he received from God the
Father honour and glory, when there
came such a voice to him from the ex-
cellent glory, This is my beloved Son, in
whom I am well pleased.
18 And this voice which came from
heaven we heard, when we were with
him in the holy mount.
19 We have also a more sure word of
prophecy; whereunto ye do well that ye
take heed, as unto a light that shineth in
a dark place, until the day dawn, and
the day star arise in your hearts:
20 Knowing this first, that no
prophecy of the scripture is of any pri-
vate interpretation.
21 For the prophecy came not in old
time by the will of man: but holy men of
God spake *as they were* moved by the
Holy Ghost.

CHAPTER 2

BUT there were false prophets also
among the people, even as there shall
be false teachers among you, who priv-
ily shall bring in damnable heresies,
even denying the Lord that bought
them, and bring upon themselves swift
destruction.
2 And many shall follow their perni-
cious ways; by reason of whom the way
of truth shall be evil spoken of.
3 And through covetousness shall
they with feigned words make merchan-
dise of you: whose judgment now
of a long time lingereth not, and their
damnation slumbereth not.
4 For if God spared not the angels
that sinned, but cast *them* down to hell,
and delivered *them* into chains of dark-
ness, to be reserved unto judgment;

5 And spared not the old world, but saved Noah the eighth *person*, a preacher of righteousness, bringing in the flood upon the world of the ungodly;

6 And turning the cities of Sodom and Go-mŏr'rha into ashes condemned *them* with an overthrow, making *them* an ensample unto those that after should live ungodly;

7 And delivered just Lot, vexed with the filthy conversation of the wicked:

8 (For that righteous man dwelling among them, in seeing and hearing, vexed *his* righteous soul from day to day with *their* unlawful deeds);

9 The Lord knoweth how to deliver the godly out of temptations, and to reserve the unjust unto the day of judgment to be punished:

10 But chiefly them that walk after the flesh in the lust of uncleanness, and despise government. Presumptuous *are they*, selfwilled, they are not afraid to speak evil of dignities.

11 Whereas angels, which are greater in power and might, bring not railing accusation against them before the Lord.

12 But these, as natural brute beasts, made to be taken and destroyed, speak evil of the things that they understand not; and shall utterly perish in their own corruption;

13 And shall receive the reward of unrighteousness, *as* they that count it pleasure to riot in the day time. Spots *they are* and blemishes, sporting themselves with their own deceivings while they feast with you;

14 Having eyes full of adultery, and that cannot cease from sin; beguiling unstable souls: an heart they have exercised with covetous practices; cursed children:

15 Which have forsaken the right way, and are gone astray, following the way of Balaam *the son* of Bō'sôr, who loved the wages of unrighteousness;

16 But was rebuked for his iniquity: the dumb ass speaking with man's voice forbad the madness of the prophet.

17 These are wells without water, clouds that are carried with a tempest: to whom the mist of darkness is reserved for ever.

18 For when they speak great swelling *words* of vanity, they allure through the lusts of the flesh, *through much* wantonness, those that were clean escaped from them who live in error.

19 While they promise them liberty, they themselves are the servants of corruption: for of whom a man is overcome, of the same is he brought in bondage.

20 For if after they have escaped the pollutions of the world through the knowledge of the Lord and Saviour Jesus Christ, they are again entangled therein, and overcome, the latter end is worse with them than the beginning.

21 For it had been better for them not to have known the way of righteousness, than, after they have known *it*, to turn from the holy commandment delivered unto them.

22 But it is happened unto them according to the true proverb, The dog *is* turned to his own vomit again; and the sow that was washed to her wallowing in the mire.

CHAPTER 3

THIS second epistle, beloved, I now write unto you; in *both* which I stir up your pure minds by way of remembrance:

2 That ye may be mindful of the words which were spoken before by the holy prophets, and of the commandment of us the apostles of the Lord and Saviour:

3 Knowing this first, that there shall come in the last days scoffers, walking after their own lusts,

4 And saying, Where is the promise of his coming? for since the fathers fell asleep, all things continue as *they were* from the beginning of the creation.

5 For this they willingly are ignorant of, that by the word of God the heavens were of old, and the earth standing out of the water and in the water:

6 Whereby the world that then was, being overflowed with water, perished:

7 But the heavens and the earth, which are now, by the same word are kept in store, reserved unto fire against the day of judgment and perdition of ungodly men.

8 But, beloved, be not ignorant of this one thing, that one day *is* with the Lord as a thousand years, and a thousand years as one day.

9 The Lord is not slack concerning his promise, as some men count slackness; but is longsuffering to us-ward, not willing that any should perish, but that all should come to repentance.

10 But the day of the Lord will come as a thief in the night; in the which the heavens shall pass away with a great noise, and the elements shall melt with fervent heat, the earth also and the works that are therein shall be burned up.

11 *Seeing* then *that* all these things

shall be dissolved, what manner *of persons* ought ye to be in *all* holy conversation and godliness,

12 Looking for and hasting unto the coming of the day of God, wherein the heavens being on fire shall be dissolved, and the elements shall melt with fervent heat?

13 Nevertheless we, according to his promise, look for new heavens and a new earth, wherein dwelleth righteousness.

14 Wherefore, beloved, seeing that ye look for such things, be diligent that ye may be found of him in peace, without spot, and blameless.

15 And account *that* the longsuffering of our Lord *is* salvation; even as our beloved brother Paul also according to the wisdom given unto him hath written unto you;

16 As also in all *his* epistles, speaking in them of these things; in which are some things hard to be understood, which they that are unlearned and unstable wrest, as *they do* also the other scriptures, unto their own destruction.

17 Ye therefore, beloved, seeing ye know *these things* before, beware lest ye also, being led away with the error of the wicked, fall from your own stedfastness.

18 But grow in grace, and *in* the knowledge of our Lord and Saviour Jesus Christ. To him *be* glory both now and for ever. Amen.

THE FIRST EPISTLE GENERAL OF

JOHN

CHAPTER 1

THAT which was from the beginning, which we have heard, which we have seen with our eyes, which we have looked upon, and our hands have handled, of the Word of life;

2 (For the life was manifested, and we have seen *it*, and bear witness, and shew unto you that eternal life, which was with the Father, and was manifested unto us;)

3 That which we have seen and heard declare we unto you, that ye also may have fellowship with us: and truly our fellowship *is* with the Father, and with his Son Jesus Christ.

4 And these things write we unto you, that your joy may be full.

5 This then is the message which we have heard of him, and declare unto you, that God is light, and in him is no darkness at all.

6 If we say that we have fellowship with him, and walk in darkness, we lie, and do not the truth:

7 But if we walk in the light, as he is in the light, we have fellowship one with another, and the blood of Jesus Christ his Son cleanseth us from all sin.

8 If we say that we have no sin, we deceive ourselves, and the truth is not in us.

9 If we confess our sins, he is faithful and just to forgive us *our* sins, and to cleanse us from all unrighteousness.

10 If we say that we have not sinned, we make him a liar, and his word is not in us.

CHAPTER 2

MY little children, these things write I unto you, that ye sin not. And if any man sin, we have an advocate with the Father, Jesus Christ the righteous:

2 And he is the propitiation for our sins: and not for ours only, but also for *the sins of* the whole world.

3 And hereby we do know that we know him, if we keep his commandments.

4 He that saith, I know him, and keepeth not his commandments, is a liar, and the truth is not in him.

5 But whoso keepeth his word, in him verily is the love of God perfected: hereby know we that we are in him.

6 He that saith he abideth in him ought himself also so to walk, even as he walked.

7 Brethren, I write no new commandment unto you, but an old commandment which ye had from the beginning. The old commandment is the word which ye have heard from the beginning.

8 Again, a new commandment I write unto you, which thing is true in him and in you: because the darkness is past, and the true light now shineth.

9 He that saith he is in the light, and hateth his brother, is in darkness even until now.

10 He that loveth his brother abideth in the light, and there is none occasion of stumbling in him.

11 But he that hateth his brother is in darkness, and walketh in darkness, and knoweth not wither he goeth, because that darkness hath blinded his eyes.

12 I write unto you, little children, because your sins are forgiven you for his name's sake.

13 I write unto you, fathers, because ye have known him *that is* from the

beginning. I write unto you, young
men, because ye have overcome the
wicked one. I write unto you, little
children, because ye have known the
Father.
14 I have written unto you, fathers,
because ye have known him *that is*
from the beginning. I have written unto
you, young men, because ye are strong,
and the word of God abideth in you,
and ye have overcome the wicked one.
15 Love not the world, neither the
things *that are* in the world. If any man
love the world, the love of the Father is
not in him.
16 For all that *is* in the world, the lust
of the flesh, and the lust of the eyes, and
the pride of life, is not of the Father, but
is of the world.
17 And the world passeth away, and
the lust thereof: but he that doeth the
will of God abideth for ever.
18 Little children, it is the last time:
and as ye have heard that antichrist
shall come, even now are there many
antichrists; whereby we know that it is
the last time.
19 They went out from us, but they
were not of us: for if they had been of
us, they would *no doubt* have con-
tinued with us: but *they went out*, that
they might be made manifest that they
were not all of us.
20 But ye have an unction from the
Holy One, and ye know all things.
21 I have not written unto you be-
cause ye know not the truth, but be-
cause ye know it, and that no lie is of
the truth.
22 Who is a liar but he that denieth
that Jesus is the Christ? He is anti-
christ, that denieth the Father and the
Son.
23 Whosoever denieth the Son, the
same hath not the Father: *[but] he that
acknowledgeth the Son hath the Father
also.*
24 Let that therefore abide in you,
which ye have heard from the begin-
ning. If that which ye have heard from
the beginning shall remain in you, ye
also shall continue in the Son, and in
the Father.
25 And this is the promise that he
hath promised us, *even* eternal life.
26 These *things* have I written unto
you concerning them that seduce you.
27 But the anointing which ye have
received of him abideth in you, and ye
need not that any man teach you: but as
the same anointing teacheth you of all
things, and is truth, and is no lie, and
even as it hath taught you, ye shall
abide in him.
28 And now, little children, abide in
him; that, when he shall appear, we
may have confidence, and not be
ashamed before him at his coming.
29 If ye know that he is righteous, ye
know that every one that doeth
righteousness is born of him.

CHAPTER 3

BEHOLD, what manner of love the
Father hath bestowed upon us, that we
should be called the sons of God: there-
fore the world knoweth us not, because
it knew him not.
2 Beloved, now are we the sons of
God, and it doth not yet appear what
we shall be: but we know that, when he
shall appear, we shall be like him; for
we shall see him as he is.
3 And every man that hath this hope
in him purifieth himself, even as he is
pure.
4 Whosoever committeth sin trans-
gresseth also the law: for sin is the
transgression of the law.
5 And ye know that he was mani-
fested to take away our sins; and in him
is no sin.
6 Whosoever abideth in him sinneth
not: whosoever sinneth hath not seen
him, neither known him.
7 Little children, let no man deceive
you: he that doeth righteousness is
righteous, even as he is righteous.
8 He that committeth sin is of the dev-
il; for the devil sinneth from the begin-
ning. For this purpose the Son of God
was manifested, that he might destroy
the works of the devil.
9 Whosoever is born of God doth not
commit sin; for his seed remaineth in
him: and he cannot sin, because he is
born of God.
10 In this the children of God are
manifest, and the children of the devil:
whosoever doeth not righteousness is
not of God, neither he that loveth not
his brother.
11 For this is the message that ye
heard from the beginning, that we
should love one another.
12 Not as Cain, *who* was of that
wicked one, and slew his brother. And
wherefore slew he him? Because his
own works were evil, and his brother's
righteous.
13 Marvel not, my brethren, if the
world hate you.
14 We know that we have passed
from death unto life, because we love
the brethren. He that loveth not *his*
brother abideth in death.
15 Whosoever hateth his brother is a
murderer: and ye know that no mur-
derer hath eternal life abiding in him.
16 Hereby perceive we the love *of*

God, because he laid down his life for us: and we ought to lay down *our* lives for the brethren.

17 But whoso hath this world's good, and seeth his brother have need, and shutteth up his bowels *of compassion* from him, how dwelleth the love of God in him?

18 My little children, let us not love in word, neither in tongue; but in deed and in truth.

19 And hereby we know that we are of the truth, and shall assure our hearts before him.

20 For if our heart condemn us, God is greater than our heart, and knoweth all things.

21 Beloved, if our heart condemn us not, *then* have we confidence toward God.

22 And whatsoever we ask, we receive of him, because we keep his commandments, and do those things that are pleasing in his sight.

23 And this is his commandment, That we should believe on the name of his Son Jesus Christ, and love one another, as he gave us commandment.

24 And he that keepeth his commandments dwelleth in him, and he in him. And hereby we know that he abideth in us, by the Spirit which he hath given us.

CHAPTER 4

BELOVED, believe not every spirit, but try the spirits whether they are of God: because many false prophets are gone out into the world.

2 Hereby know ye the Spirit of God: Every spirit that confesseth that Jesus Christ is come in the flesh is of God:

3 And every spirit that confesseth not that Jesus Christ is come in the flesh is not of God: and this is that *spirit* of antichrist, whereof ye have heard that it should come; and even now already is it in the world.

4 Ye are of God, little children, and have overcome them: because greater is he that is in you, than he that is in the world.

5 They are of the world: therefore speak they of the world, and the world heareth them.

6 We are of God: he that knoweth God heareth us; he that is not of God heareth not us. Hereby know we the spirit of truth, and the spirit of error.

7 Beloved, let us love one another: for love is of God; and every one that loveth is born of God, and knoweth God.

8 He that loveth not knoweth not God; for God is love.

9 In this was manifested the love of God toward us, because that God sent his only begotten Son into the world, that we might live through him.

10 Herein is love, not that we loved God, but that he loved us, and sent his Son *to be* the propitiation for our sins.

11 Beloved, if God so loved us, we ought also to love one another.

12 No man hath seen God at any time. If we love one another, God dwelleth in us, and his love is perfected in us.

13 Hereby know we that we dwell in him, and he in us, because he hath given us of his Spirit.

14 And we have seen and do testify that the Father sent the Son *to be* the Saviour of the world.

15 Whosoever shall confess that Jesus is the Son of God, God dwelleth in him, and he in God.

16 And we have known and believed the love that God hath to us. God is love; and he that dwelleth in love dwelleth in God, and God in him.

17 Herein is our love made perfect, that we may have boldness in the day of judgment: because as he is, so are we in this world.

18 There is no fear in love; but perfect love casteth out fear: because fear hath torment. He that feareth is not made perfect in love.

19 We love him, because he first loved us.

20 If a man say, I love God, and hateth his brother, he is a liar: for he that loveth not his brother whom he hath seen, how can he love God whom he hath not seen?

21 And this commandment have we from him, That he who loveth God love his brother also.

CHAPTER 5

WHOSOEVER believeth that Jesus is the Christ is born of God: and every one that loveth him that begat loveth him also that is begotten of him.

2 By this we know that we love the children of God, when we love God, and keep his commandments.

3 For this is the love of God, that we keep his commandments: and his commandments are not grievous.

4 For whatsoever is born of God overcometh the world: and this is the victory that overcometh the world, *even* our faith.

5 Who is he that overcometh the world, but he that believeth that Jesus is the Son of God?

6 This is he that came by water and blood, *even* Jesus Christ; not by water only, but by water and blood. And it is

the Spirit that beareth witness, be-
cause the Spirit is truth.
7 For there are three that bear record
in heaven, the Father, the Word, and
the Holy Ghost: and these three are
one.
8 And there are three that bear wit-
ness in earth, the spirit, and the water,
and the blood: and these three agree in
one.
9 If we receive the witness of men,
the witness of God is greater: for this is
the witness of God which he hath tes-
tified of his Son.
10 He that believeth on the Son of
God hath the witness in himself: he that
believeth not God hath made him a liar;
because he believeth not the record
that God gave of his Son.
11 And this is the record, that God
hath given to us eternal life, and this
life is in his Son.
12 He that hath the Son hath life; *and*
he that hath not the Son of God hath
not life.
13 These things have I written unto
you that believe on the name of the Son
of God; that ye may know that ye have
eternal life, and that ye may believe on
the name of the Son of God.
14 And this is the confidence that we
have in him, that, if we ask any thing
according to his will, he heareth us:
15 And if we know that he hear us,
whatsoever we ask, we know that we
have the petitions that we desired of
him.
16 If any man see his brother sin a sin
which is not unto death, he shall ask,
and he shall give him life for them that
sin not unto death. There is a sin unto
death: I do not say that he shall pray for
it.
17 All unrighteousness is sin: and
there is a sin not unto death.
18 We know that whosoever is born
of God sinneth not; but he that is begot-
ten of God keepeth himself, and that
wicked one toucheth him not.
19 *And* we know that we are of God,
and the whole world lieth in wicked-
ness.
20 And we know that the Son of God
is come, and hath given us an under-
standing, that we may know him that is
true, and we are in him that is true,
even in his Son Jesus Christ. This is the
true God, and eternal life.
21 Little children, keep yourselves
from idols. Amen.

THE SECOND EPISTLE OF

JOHN

THE elder unto the elect lady and her
children, whom I love in the truth; and
not I only, but also all they that have
known the truth;
2 For the truth's sake, which dwell-
eth in us, and shall be with us for ever.
3 Grace be with you, mercy, *and*
peace, from God the Father, and from
the Lord Jesus Christ, the Son of the
Father, in truth and love.
4 I rejoiced greatly that I found of thy
children walking in truth, as we have
received a commandment from the
Father.
5 And now I beseech thee, lady, not
as though I wrote a new command-
ment unto thee, but that which we had
from the beginning, that we love one
another.
6 And this is love, that we walk after
his commandments. This is the com-
mandment, That, as ye have heard
from the beginning, ye should walk in
it.
7 For many deceivers are entered
into the world, who confess not that Je-
sus Christ is come in the flesh. This is a
deceiver and an antichrist.
8 Look to yourselves, that we lose not
those things which we have wrought,
but that we receive a full reward.
9 Whosoever transgresseth, and abid-
eth not in the doctrine of Christ, hath
not God. He that abideth in the doctrine
of Christ, he hath both the Father and
the Son.
10 If there come any unto you, and
bring not this doctrine, receive him not
into *your* house, neither bid him God
speed:
11 For he that biddeth him God speed
is partaker of his evil deeds.
12 Having many things to write unto
you, I would not *write* with paper and
ink: but I trust to come unto you, and
speak face to face, that our joy may be
full.
13 The children of thy elect sister
greet thee. Amen.

THE THIRD EPISTLE OF

JOHN

THE elder unto the well-beloved Gaius,
whom I love in the truth.
2 Beloved, I wish above all things
that thou mayest prosper and be in
health, even as thy soul prospereth.
3 For I rejoiced greatly, when the
brethren came and testified of the truth
that is in thee, even as thou walkest in
the truth.
4 I have no greater joy than to hear
that my children walk in truth.
5 Beloved, thou doest faithfully
whatsoever thou doest to the brethren,
and to strangers;
6 Which have borne witness of thy
charity before the church: whom if
thou bring forward on their journey af-
ter a godly sort, thou shalt do well:
7 Because that for his name's sake
they went forth, taking nothing of the
Gentiles.
8 We therefore ought to receive such,
that we might be fellow-helpers to the
truth.
9 I wrote unto the church: but Dĭ-
ŏt′re-phēs, who loveth to have the
preeminence among them, receiveth us
not.
10 Wherefore, if I come, I will
remember his deeds which he doeth,
prating against us with malicious
words: and not content therewith,
neither doth he himself receive the
brethren, and forbiddeth them that
would, and casteth *them* out of the
church.
11 Beloved, follow not that which is
evil, but that which is good. He that
doeth good is of God: but he that doeth
evil hath not seen God.
12 De-mē′trĭ-us hath good report of
all *men*, and of the truth itself: yea, and
we *also* bear record; and ye know that
our record is true.
13 I had many things to write, but I
will not with ink and pen write unto
thee:
14 But I trust I shall shortly see thee,
and we shall speak face to face. Peace
be to thee. *Our* friends salute thee.
Greet the friends by name.

THE GENERAL EPISTLE OF

JUDE

JUDE, the servant of Jesus Christ, and
brother of James, to them that are
sanctified by God the Father, and pre-
served in Jesus Christ, *and* called.
2 Mercy unto you, and peace, and
love, be multiplied.
3 Beloved, when I gave all diligence
to write unto you of the common salva-
tion, it was needful for me to write unto
you, and exhort *you* that ye should ear-
nestly contend for the faith which was
once delivered unto the saints.
4 For there are certain men crept in
unawares, who were before of old or-
dained to this condemnation, ungodly
men, turning the grace of our God into
lasciviousness, and denying the only
Lord God, and our Lord Jesus Christ.
5 I will therefore put you in remem-
brance, though ye once knew this, how
that the Lord, having saved the people
out of the land of Egypt, afterward
destroyed them that believed not.
6 And the angels which kept not their
first estate, but left their own habita-
tion, he hath reserved in everlasting
chains under darkness unto the judg-
ment of the great day.
7 Even as Sodom and Go-mŏr′rha,
and the cities about them in like man-
ner, giving themselves over to fornica-
tion, and going after strange flesh, are
set forth for an example, suffering the
vengeance of eternal fire.
8 Likewise also these *filthy* dreamers
defile the flesh, despise dominion, and
speak evil of dignities.
9 Yet Michael the archangel, when
contending with the devil he disputed
about the body of Moses, durst not
bring against him a railing accusation,
but said, The Lord rebuke thee.
10 But these speak evil of those
things which they know not: but what
they know naturally, as brute beasts, in
those things they corrupt themselves.
11 Woe unto them! for they have
gone in the way of Cain, and ran greed-
ily after the error of Balaam for reward,
and perished in the gainsaying of Cō′re.
12 These are spots in your feasts of
charity, when they feast with you, feed-
ing themselves without fear: clouds
they are without water, carried about
of winds; trees whose fruit withereth,
without fruit, twice dead, plucked up
by the roots;
13 Raging waves of the sea, foaming

out their own shame; wandering stars,
to whom is reserved the blackness of
darkness for ever.
14 And Ē'noch also, the seventh from
Adam, prophesied of these, saying, Be-
hold, the Lord cometh with ten thou-
sands of his saints,
15 To execute judgment upon all, and
to convince all that are ungodly among
them of all their ungodly deeds which
they have ungodly committed, and of
all their hard *speeches* which ungodly
sinners have spoken against him.
16 These are murmurers, complain-
ers, walking after their own lusts; and
their mouth speaketh great swelling
words, having men's persons in ad-
miration because of advantage.
17 But, beloved, remember ye the
words which were spoken before of the
apostles of our Lord Jesus Christ;
18 How that they told you there
should be mockers in the last time, who
should walk after their own ungodly
lusts.
19 These be they who separate them-
selves, sensual, having not the Spirit.
20 But ye, beloved, building up your-
selves on your most holy faith, praying
in the Holy Ghost,
21 Keep yourselves in the love of
God, looking for the mercy of our Lord
Jesus Christ unto eternal life.
22 And of some have compassion,
making a difference:
23 And others save with fear, pulling
them out of the fire; hating even the
garment spotted by the flesh.
24 Now unto him that is able to keep
you from falling, and to present *you*
faultless before the presence of his
glory with exceeding joy,
25 To the only wise God our Saviour,
be glory and majesty, dominion and
power, both now and ever. Amen.

THE REVELATION

OF SAINT JOHN THE DIVINE

CHAPTER 1

THE Revelation of Jesus Christ, which
God gave unto him, to shew unto his
servants things which must shortly
come to pass; and he sent and signified
it by his angel unto his servant John:
2 Who bare record of the word of
God, and of the testimony of Jesus
Christ, and of all things that he saw.
3 Blessed *is* he that readeth, and they
that hear the words of this prophecy,
and keep those things which are writ-
ten therein: for the time *is* at hand.
4 JOHN to the seven churches which
are in Asia: Grace *be* unto you, and
peace, from him which is, and which
was, and which is to come; and from
the seven Spirits which are before his
throne;
5 And from Jesus Christ, *who is* the
faithful witness, *and* the first begotten
of the dead, and the prince of the kings
of the earth. Unto him that loved us,
and washed us from our sins in his own
blood,
6 And hath made us kings and priests
unto God and his Father; to him *be*
glory and dominion for ever and ever.
Amen.
7 Behold, he cometh with clouds; and
every eye shall see him, and they *also*
which pierced him: and all kindreds of
the earth shall wail because of him.
Even so, Amen.
8 I am Alpha and Omega, the begin-
ning and the ending, saith the Lord,
which is, and which was, and which is
to come, the Almighty.
9 I John, who also am your brother,
and companion in tribulation, and in
the kingdom and patience of Jesus
Christ, was in the isle that is called Pat-
mos, for the word of God, and for the
testimony of Jesus Christ.
10 I was in the Spirit on the Lord's
day, and heard behind me a great voice,
as of a trumpet,
11 Saying, I am Alpha and Omega,
the first and the last: and, What thou
seest, write in a book, and send *it* unto
the seven churches which are in Asia;
unto Ĕph'e-sus, and unto Smyrna, and
unto Per'ga-mos, and unto Thȳ-a-tī'ra,
and unto Sardis, and unto Philadelphia,
and unto La-od-i-ce'a.
12 And I turned to see the voice that
spake with me. And being turned, I saw
seven golden candlesticks;
13 And in the midst of the seven
candlesticks *one* like unto the Son of
man, clothed with a garment down to
the foot, and girt about the paps with a
golden girdle.
14 His head and *his* hairs *were* white
like wool, as white as snow; and his
eyes *were* as a flame of fire;
15 And his feet like unto fine brass, as
if they burned in a furnace; and his
voice as the sound of many waters.
16 And he had in his right hand seven
stars: and out of his mouth went a
sharp twoedged sword: and his counte-

nance *was* as the sun shineth in his strength.

17 And when I saw him, I fell at his feet as dead. And he laid his right hand upon me, saying unto me, Fear not; I am the first and the last:

18 *I am* he that liveth, and was dead; and, behold, I am alive for evermore, Amen; and have the keys of hell and of death.

19 Write the things which thou hast seen, and the things which are, and the things which shall be hereafter;

20 The mystery of the seven stars which thou sawest in my right hand, and the seven golden candlesticks. The seven stars are the angels of the seven churches: and the seven candlesticks which thou sawest are the seven churches.

CHAPTER 2

UNTO the angel of the church of Ĕph'e-sus write; These things saith he that holdeth the seven stars in his right hand, who walketh in the midst of the seven golden candlesticks;

2 I know thy works, and thy labour, and thy patience, and how thou canst not bear them which are evil: and thou hast tried them which say they are apostles, and are not, and hast found them liars:

3 And hast borne, and hast patience, and for my name's sake hast laboured, and hast not fainted.

4 Nevertheless I have *somewhat* against thee, because thou hast left thy first love.

5 Remember therefore from whence thou art fallen, and repent, and do the first works; or else I will come unto thee quickly, and will remove thy candlestick out of his place, except thou repent.

6 But this thou hast, that thou hatest the deeds of the Nĭc-o-lā'i-tanes, which I also hate.

7 He that hath an ear, let him hear what the Spirit saith unto the churches; To him that overcometh will I give to eat of the tree of life, which is in the midst of the paradise of God.

8 And unto the angel of the church in Smyrna write; These things saith the first and the last, which was dead, and is alive;

9 I know thy works, and tribulation, and poverty, (but thou art rich) and *I know* the blasphemy of them which say they are Jews, and are not, but *are* the synagogue of Satan.

10 Fear none of those things which thou shalt suffer: behold, the devil shall cast *some* of you into prison, that ye may be tried; and ye shall have tribulation ten days: be thou faithful unto death, and I will give thee a crown of life.

11 He that hath an ear, let him hear what the Spirit saith unto the churches; He that overcometh shall not be hurt of the second death.

12 And to the angel of the church in Per'ga-mos write; These things saith he which hath the sharp sword with two edges;

13 I know thy works, and where thou dwellest, *even* where Satan's seat *is*: and thou holdest fast my name, and hast not denied my faith, even in those days wherein Ăn'ti-pas *was* my faithful martyr, who was slain among you, where Satan dwelleth.

14 But I have a few things against thee, because thou hast there them that hold the doctrine of Balaam, who taught Balac to cast a stumblingblock before the children of Israel, to eat things sacrificed unto idols, and to commit fornication.

15 So hast thou also them that hold the doctrine of the Nĭc-o-lā'i-tanes, which thing I hate.

16 Repent; or else I will come unto thee quickly, and will fight against them with the sword of my mouth.

17 He that hath an ear, let him hear what the Spirit saith unto the churches; To him that overcometh will I give to eat of the hidden manna, and will give him a white stone, and in the stone a new name written, which no man knoweth saving he that receiveth *it*.

18 And unto the angel of the church in Thȳ-a-tī'ra write; These things saith the Son of God, who hath his eyes like unto a flame of fire, and his feet *are* like fine brass;

19 I know thy works, and charity, and service, and faith, and thy patience, and thy works; and the last *to be* more than the first.

20 Notwithstanding I have a few things against thee, because thou sufferest that woman Jĕz'e-bel, which calleth herself a prophetess, to teach and to seduce my servants to commit fornication, and to eat things sacrificed unto idols.

21 And I gave her space to repent of her fornication; and she repented not.

22 Behold, I will cast her into a bed, and them that commit adultery with her into great tribulation, except they repent of their deeds.

23 And I will kill her children with death; and all the churches shall know that I am he which searcheth the reins

and hearts: and I will give unto every one of you according to your works.

24 But unto you I say, and unto the rest in Thy̆-a-tī′ra, as many as have not this doctrine, and which have not known the depths of Satan, as they speak; I will put upon you none other burden.

25 But that which ye have *already* hold fast till I come.

26 And he that overcometh, and keepeth my works unto the end, to him will I give power over the nations:

27 And he shall rule them with a rod of iron; as the vessels of a potter shall they be broken to shivers: even as I received of my Father.

28 And I will give him the morning star.

29 He that hath an ear, let him hear wnat the Spirit saith unto the churches.

CHAPTER 3

AND unto the angel of the church in Sardis write; These things saith he that hath the seven Spirits of God, and the seven stars; I know thy works, that thou hast a name that thou livest, and art dead.

2 Be watchful, and strengthen the things which remain, that are ready to die: for I have not found thy works perfect before God.

3 Remember therefore how thou hast received and heard, and hold fast, and repent. If therefore thou shalt not watch, I will come on thee as a thief, and thou shalt not know what hour I will come upon thee.

4 Thou hast a few names even in Sardis which have not defiled their garments; and they shall walk with me in white: for they are worthy.

5 He that overcometh, the same shall be clothed in white raiment; and I will not blot out his name out of the book of life, but I will confess his name before my Father, and before his angels.

6 He that hath an ear, let him hear what the Spirit saith unto the churches.

7 And to the angel of the church in Philadelphia write; These things saith he that is holy, he that is true, he that hath the key of David, he that openeth, and no man shutteth; and shutteth, and no man openeth;

8 I know thy works: behold, I have set before thee an open door, and no man can shut it: for thou hast a little strength, and hast kept my word, and hast not denied my name.

9 Behold, I will make them of the synagogue of Satan, which say they are Jews, and are not, but do lie; behold, I will make them to come and worship before thy feet, and to know that I have loved thee.

10 Because thou hast kept the word of my patience, I also will keep thee from the hour of temptation, which shall come upon all the world, to try them that dwell upon the earth.

11 Behold, I come quickly: hold that fast which thou hast, that no man take thy crown.

12 Him that overcometh will I make a pillar in the temple of my God, and he shall go no more out: and I will write upon him the name of my God, and the name of the city of my God, *which is* new Jerusalem, which cometh down out of heaven from my God: and *I will write upon him* my new name.

13 He that hath an ear, let him hear what the Spirit saith unto the churches.

14 And unto the angel of the church of the Lā-ŏd-i-ċē′anṡ write; These things saith the Amen, the faithful and true witness, the beginning of the creation of God;

15 I know thy works, that thou art neither cold nor hot: I would thou wert cold or hot.

16 So then because thou art lukewarm, and neither cold nor hot, I will spue thee out of my mouth.

17 Because thou sayest, I am rich, and increased with goods, and have need of nothing; and knowest not that thou art wretched, and miserable, and poor, and blind, and naked:

18 I counsel thee to buy of me gold tried in the fire, that thou mayest be rich; and white raiment, that thou mayest be clothed, and *that* the shame of thy nakedness do not appear; and anoint thine eyes with eye-salve, that thou mayest see.

19 As many as I love, I rebuke and chasten: be zealous therefore, and repent.

20 Behold, I stand at the door, and knock: if any man hear my voice, and open the door, I will come in to him, and will sup with him, and he with me.

21 To him that overcometh will I grant to sit with me in my throne, even as I also overcame, and am set down with my Father in his throne.

22 He that hath an ear, let him hear what the Spirit saith unto the churches.

CHAPTER 4

AFTER this I looked, and, behold, a door *was* opened in heaven: and the first voice which I heard *was* as it were of a trumpet talking with me; which said, Come up hither, and I will shew thee things which must be hereafter.

2 And immediately I was in the spirit:

and, behold, a throne was set in
heaven, and *one* sat on the throne.
3 And he that sat was to look upon
like a jasper and a sardine stone: and
there was a rainbow round about the
throne, in sight like unto an emerald.
4 And round about the throne *were*
four and twenty seats: and upon the
seats I saw four and twenty elders sit-
ting, clothed in white raiment; and they
had on their heads crowns of gold.
5 And out of the throne proceeded
lightnings and thunderings and voices:
and *there were* seven lamps of fire burn-
ing before the throne, which are the
seven Spirits of God.
6 And before the throne *there was* a
sea of glass like unto crystal: and in the
midst of the throne, and round about
the throne, *were* four beasts full of eyes
before and behind.
7 And the first beast *was* like a lion,
and the second beast like a calf, and the
third beast had a face as a man, and the
fourth beast *was* like a flying eagle.
8 And the four beasts had each of
them six wings about *him;* and *they
were* full of eyes within: and they rest
not day and night, saying, Holy, holy,
holy, Lord God Almighty, which was,
and is, and is to come.
9 And when those beasts give glory
and honour and thanks to him that sat
on the throne, who liveth for ever and
ever,
10 The four and twenty elders fall
down before him that sat on the throne,
and worship him that liveth for ever
and ever, and cast their crowns before
the throne, saying,
11 Thou art worthy, O Lord, to re-
ceive glory and honour and power: for
thou hast created all things, and for thy
pleasure they are and were created.

CHAPTER 5

AND I saw in the right hand of him that
sat on the throne a book written within
and on the backside, sealed with seven
seals.
2 And I saw a strong angel proclaim-
ing with a loud voice, Who is worthy to
open the book, and to loose the seals
thereof?
3 And no man in heaven, nor in earth,
neither under the earth, was able to
open the book, neither to look thereon.
4 And I wept much, because no man
was found worthy to open and to read
the book, neither to look thereon.
5 And one of the elders saith unto me,
Weep not: behold, the Lion of the tribe
of Juda, the Root of David, hath pre-
vailed to open the book, and to loose
the seven seals thereof.
6 And I beheld, and, lo, in the midst of
the throne and of the four beasts, and in
the midst of the elders, stood a Lamb as
it had been slain, having seven horns
and seven eyes, which are the seven
Spirits of God sent forth into all the
earth.
7 And he came and took the book out
of the right hand of him that sat upon
the throne.
8 And when he had taken the book,
the four beasts and four *and* twenty el-
ders fell down before the Lamb, having
every one of them harps, and golden
vials full of odours, which are the
prayers of saints.
9 And they sung a new song, saying,
Thou art worthy to take the book, and
to open the seals thereof: for thou wast
slain, and hast redeemed us to God by
thy blood out of every kindred, and
tongue, and people, and nation;
10 And hast made us unto our God
kings and priests: and we shall reign on
the earth.
11 And I beheld, and I heard the voice
of many angels round about the throne
and the beasts and the elders: and the
number of them was ten thousand
times ten thousand, and thousands of
thousands;
12 Saying with a loud voice, Worthy
is the Lamb that was slain to receive
power, and riches, and wisdom, and
strength, and honour, and glory, and
blessing.
13 And every creature which is in
heaven, and on the earth, and under the
earth, and such as are in the sea, and all
that are in them, heard I saying, Bless-
ing, and honour, and glory, and power,
be unto him that sitteth upon the
throne, and unto the Lamb for ever and
ever.
14 And the four beasts said, Amen.
And the four *and* twenty elders fell
down and worshipped him that liveth
for ever and ever.

CHAPTER 6

AND I saw when the Lamb opened one
of the seals, and I heard, as it were the
noise of thunder, one of the four beasts
saying, Come and see.
2 And I saw, and behold a white
horse: and he that sat on him had a
bow; and a crown was given unto him:
and he went forth conquering, and to
conquer.
3 And when he had opened the sec-
ond seal, I heard the second beast say,
Come and see.
4 And there went out another horse
that was red: and *power* was given to
him that sat thereon to take peace from

the earth, and that they should kill one
another: and there was given unto him
a great sword.
5 And when he had opened the third
seal, I heard the third beast say, Come
and see. And I beheld, and lo a black
horse; and he that sat on him had a pair
of balances in his hand.
6 And I heard a voice in the midst of
the four beasts say, A measure of
wheat for a penny, and three measures
of barley for a penny; and *see* thou hurt
not the oil and the wine.
7 And when he had opened the fourth
seal, I heard the voice of the fourth
beast say, Come and see.
8 And I looked, and behold a pale
horse: and his name that sat on him
was Death, and Hell followed with him.
And Power was given unto them over
the fourth part of the earth, to kill with
sword, and with hunger, and with
death, and with the beasts of the earth.
9 And when he had opened the fifth
seal, I saw under the altar the souls of
them that were slain for the word of
God, and for the testimony which they
held:
10 And they cried with a loud voice,
saying, How long, O Lord, holy and
true, dost thou not judge and avenge
our blood on them that dwell on the
earth?
11 And white robes were given unto
every one of them; and it was said unto
them, that they should rest yet for a
little season, until their fellowservants
also and their brethren, that should be
killed as they *were*, should be fulfilled.
12 And I beheld when he had opened
the sixth seal, and, lo, there was a great
earthquake; and the sun became black
as sackcloth of hair, and the moon be-
came as blood;
13 And the stars of heaven fell unto
the earth, even as a fig tree casteth her
untimely figs, when she is shaken of a
mighty wind.
14 And the heaven departed as a
scroll when it is rolled together; and
every mountain and island were moved
out of their places.
15 And the kings of the earth, and the
great men, and the rich men, and the
chief captains, and the mighty men,
and every bondman, and every free
man, hid themselves in the dens and in
the rocks of the mountains;
16 And said to the mountains and
rocks, Fall on us, and hide us from the
face of him that sitteth on the throne,
and from the wrath of the Lamb:
17 For the great day of his wrath is
come; and who shall be able to stand?

CHAPTER 7

AND after these things I saw four an-
gels standing on the four corners of the
earth, holding the four winds of the
earth, that the wind should not blow on
the earth, nor on the sea, nor on any
tree.
2 And I saw another angel ascending
from the east, having the seal of the liv-
ing God: and he cried with a loud voice
to the four angels, to whom it was given
to hurt the earth and the sea,
3 Saying, Hurt not the earth, neither
the sea, nor the trees, till we have
sealed the servants of our God in their
foreheads.
4 And I heard the number of them
which were sealed: *and there were*
sealed an hundred *and* forty *and* four
thousand of all the tribes of the chil-
dren of Israel.
5 Of the tribe of Juda *were* sealed
twelve thousand. Of the tribe of Reu-
ben *were* sealed twelve thousand. Of
the tribe of Gad *were* sealed twelve
thousand.
6 Of the tribe of Ā'ser *were* sealed
twelve thousand. Of the tribe of
Nĕph'tha-lĭm *were* sealed twelve thou-
sand. Of the tribe of Ma-năs'sēs *were*
sealed twelve thousand.
7 Of the tribe of Simeon *were* sealed
twelve thousand. Of the tribe of Levi
were sealed twelve thousand. Of the
tribe of Ĭs'sa-char *were* sealed twelve
thousand.
8 Of the tribe of Zăb'u-lon *were*
sealed twelve thousand. Of the tribe of
Joseph *were* sealed twelve thousand.
Of the tribe of Benjamin *were* sealed
twelve thousand.
9 After this I beheld, and, lo, a great
multitude, which no man could num-
ber, of all nations, and kindreds, and
people, and tongues, stood before the
throne, and before the Lamb, clothed
with white robes, and palms in their
hands;
10 And cried with a loud voice,
saying, Salvation to our God which sit-
teth upon the throne, and unto the
Lamb.
11 And all the angels stood round
about the throne, and *about* the elders
and the four beasts, and fell before the
throne on their faces, and worshipped
God,
12 Saying, Amen: Blessing, and
glory, and wisdom, and thanksgiving,
and honour, and power, and might, *be*
unto our God for ever and ever. Amen.
13 And one of the elders answered,
saying unto me, What are these which

are arrayed in white robes? and whence came they?

14 And I said unto him, Sir, thou knowest. And he said to me, These are they which came out of great tribulation, and have washed their robes, and made them white in the blood of the Lamb.

15 Therefore are they before the throne of God, and serve him day and night in his temple: and he that sitteth on the throne shall dwell among them.

16 They shall hunger no more, neither thirst any more; neither shall the sun light on them, nor any heat.

17 For the Lamb which is in the midst of the throne shall feed them, and shall lead them unto living fountains of waters: and God shall wipe away all tears from their eyes.

CHAPTER 8

AND when he had opened the seventh seal, there was silence in heaven about the space of half an hour.

2 And I saw the seven angels which stood before God; and to them were given seven trumpets.

3 And another angel came and stood at the altar, having a golden censer; and there was given unto him much incense, that he should offer *it* with the prayers of all saints upon the golden altar which was before the throne.

4 And the smoke of the incense, *which came* with the prayers of the saints, ascended up before God out of the angel's hand.

5 And the angel took the censer, and filled it with fire of the altar, and cast *it* into the earth: and there were voices, and thunderings, and lightnings, and an earthquake.

6 And the seven angels which had the seven trumpets prepared themselves to sound.

7 The first angel sounded, and there followed hail and fire mingled with blood, and they were cast upon the earth: and the third part of trees was burnt up, and all green grass was burnt up.

8 And the second angel sounded, and as it were a great mountain burning with fire was cast into the sea: and the third part of the sea became blood;

9 And the third part of the creatures which were in the sea, and had life, died; and the third part of the ships were destroyed.

10 And the third angel sounded, and there fell a great star from heaven, burning as it were a lamp, and it fell upon the third part of the rivers, and upon the fountains of waters;

11 And the name of the star is called Wormwood: and the third part of the waters became wormwood; and many men died of the waters, because they were made bitter.

12 And the fourth angel sounded, and the third part of the sun was smitten, and the third part of the moon, and the third part of the stars; so as the third part of them was darkened, and the day shone not for a third part of it, and the night likewise.

13 And I beheld, and heard an angel flying through the midst of heaven, saying with a loud voice, Woe, woe, woe, to the inhabiters of the earth by reason of the other voices of the trumpet of the three angels, which are yet to sound!

CHAPTER 9

AND the fifth angel sounded, and I saw a star fall from heaven unto the earth: and to him was given the key of the bottomless pit.

2 And he opened the bottomless pit; and there arose a smoke out of the pit, as the smoke of a great furnace; and the sun and the air were darkened by reason of the smoke of the pit.

3 And there came out of the smoke locusts upon the earth: and unto them was given power, as the scorpions of the earth have power.

4 And it was commanded them that they should not hurt the grass of the earth, neither any green thing, neither any tree; but only those men which have not the seal of God in their foreheads.

5 And to them it was given that they should not kill them, but that they should be tormented five months: and their torment *was* as the torment of a scorpion, when he striketh a man.

6 And in those days shall men seek death, and shall not find it; and shall desire to die, and death shall flee from them.

7 And the shapes of the locusts *were* like unto horses prepared unto battle; and on their heads *were* as it were crowns like gold, and their faces *were* as the faces of men.

8 And they had hair as the hair of women, and their teeth were as *the teeth* of lions.

9 And they had breastplates, as it were breastplates of iron; and the sound of their wings *was* as the sound of chariots of many horses running to battle.

10 And they had tails like unto scorpions, and there were stings in their tails: and their power *was* to hurt men five months.

11 And they had a king over them, *which is* the angel of the bottomless pit, whose name in the Hebrew tongue *is* A-băd′don, but in the Greek tongue hath *his* name A-pŏl′ly-on.
12 One woe is past; *and,* behold, there come two woes more hereafter.
13 And the sixth angel sounded, and I heard a voice from the four horns of the golden altar which is before God,
14 Saying to the sixth angel which had the trumpet, Loose the four angels which are bound in the great river Eū′phrā′tēṡ.
15 And the four angels were loosed, which were prepared for an hour, and a day, and a month, and a year, for to slay the third part of men.
16 And the number of the army of the horsemen *were* two hundred thousand thousand: and I heard the number of them.
17 And thus I saw the horses in the vision, and them that sat on them, having breastplates of fire, and of jacinth, and brimstone: and the heads of the horses *were* as the heads of lions; and out of their mouths issued fire and smoke and brimstone.
18 By these three was the third part of men killed, by the fire, and by the smoke, and by the brimstone, which issued out of their mouths.
19 For their power is in their mouth, and in their tails: for their tails *were* like unto serpents, and had heads, and with them they do hurt.
20 And the rest of the men which were not killed by these plagues yet repented not of the works of their hands, that they should not worship devils, and idols of gold, and silver, and brass, and stone, and of wood: which neither can see, nor hear, nor walk:
21 Neither repented they of their murders, nor of their sorceries, nor of their fornication, nor of their thefts.

CHAPTER 10

AND I saw another mighty angel come down from heaven, clothed with a cloud: and a rainbow *was* upon his head, and his face *was* as it were the sun, and his feet as pillars of fire:
2 And he had in his hand a little book open: and he set his right foot upon the sea, and *his* left *foot* on the earth,
3 And cried with a loud voice, as *when* a lion roareth: and when he had cried, seven thunders uttered their voices.
4 And when the seven thunders had uttered their voices, I was about to write: and I heard a voice from heaven saying unto me, Seal up those things which the seven thunders uttered, and write them not.
5 And the angel which I saw stand upon the sea and upon the earth lifted up his hand to heaven,
6 And sware by him that liveth for ever and ever, who created heaven, and the things that therein are, and the earth, and the things that therein are, and the sea, and the things which are therein, that there should be time no longer:
7 But in the days of the voice of the seventh angel, when he shall begin to sound, the mystery of God should be finished, as he hath declared to his servants the prophets.
8 And the voice which I heard from heaven spake unto me again, and said, Go *and* take the little book which is open in the hand of the angel which standeth upon the sea and upon the earth.
9 And I went unto the angel, and said unto him, Give me the little book. And he said unto me, Take *it,* and eat it up; and it shall make thy belly bitter, but it shall be in thy mouth sweet as honey.
10 And I took the little book out of the angel's hand, and ate it up; and it was in my mouth sweet as honey: and as soon as I had eaten it, my belly was bitter.
11 And he said unto me, Thou must prophesy again before many peoples, and nations, and tongues, and kings.

CHAPTER 11

AND there was given me a reed like unto a rod: and the angel stood, saying, Rise, and measure the temple of God, and the altar, and them that worship therein.
2 But the court which is without the temple leave out, and measure it not; for it is given unto the Gentiles: and the holy city shall they tread under foot forty *and* two months.
3 And I will give *power* unto my two witnesses, and they shall prophesy a thousand two hundred *and* threescore days, clothed in sackcloth.
4 These are the two olive trees, and the two candlesticks standing before the God of the earth.
5 And if any man will hurt them, fire proceedeth out of their mouth, and devoureth their enemies: and if any man will hurt them, he must in this manner be killed.
6 These have power to shut heaven, that it rain not in the days of their prophecy: and have power over waters to turn them to blood, and to smite the earth with all plagues, as often as they will.

7 And when they shall have finished
their testimony, the beast that ascend-
eth out of the bottomless pit shall
make war against them, and shall over-
come them, and kill them.
8 And their dead bodies *shall lie* in
the street of the great city, which spiri-
tually is called Sodom and Egypt,
where also our Lord was crucified.
9 And they of the people and
kindreds and tongues and nations shall
see their dead bodies three days and an
half, and shall not suffer their dead bod-
ies to be put in graves.
10 And they that dwell upon the earth
shall rejoice over them, and make
merry, and shall send gifts one to an-
other; because these two prophets tor-
mented them that dwelt on the earth.
11 And after three days and an half
the Spirit of life from God entered into
them, and they stood upon their feet;
and great fear fell upon them which
saw them.
12 And they heard a great voice from
heaven saying unto them, Come up
hither. And they ascended up to heaven
in a cloud; and their enemies beheld
them.
13 And the same hour was there a
great earthquake, and the tenth part of
the city fell, and in the earthquake were
slain of men seven thousand: and the
remnant were affrighted, and gave
glory to the God of heaven.
14 The second woe is past; *and*, be-
hold, the third woe cometh quickly.
15 And the seventh angel sounded;
and there were great voices in heaven,
saying, The kingdoms of this world are
become *the kingdoms* of our Lord, and
of his Christ; and he shall reign for ever
and ever.
16 And the four and twenty elders,
which sat before God on their seats, fell
upon their faces, and worshipped God,
17 Saying, We give thee thanks, O
Lord God Almighty, which art, and
wast, and art to come; because thou
hast taken to thee thy great power, and
hast reigned.
18 And the nations were angry, and
thy wrath is come, and the time of the
dead, that they should be judged, and
that thou shouldest give reward unto
thy servants the prophets, and to the
saints, and them that fear thy name,
small and great; and shouldest destroy
them which destroy the earth.
19 And the temple of God was
opened in heaven, and there was seen
in his temple the ark of his testament:
and there were lightnings, and voices,
and thunderings, and an earthquake,
and great hail.

CHAPTER 12

AND there appeared a great wonder in
heaven; a woman clothed with the sun,
and the moon under her feet, and upon
her head a crown of twelve stars:
2 And she being with child cried, tra-
vailing in birth, and pained to be de-
livered.
3 And there appeared another won-
der in heaven; and behold a great red
dragon, having seven heads and ten
horns, and seven crowns upon his
heads.
4 And his tail drew the third part of
the stars of heaven, and did cast them
to the earth: and the dragon stood be-
fore the woman which was ready to be
delivered, for to devour her child as
soon as it was born.
5 And she brought forth a man child,
who was to rule all nations with a rod of
iron: and her child was caught up unto
God, and *to* his throne.
6 And the woman fled into the wil-
derness, where she hath a place pre-
pared of God, that they should feed her
there a thousand two hundred *and*
threescore days.
7 And there was war in heaven:
Michael and his angels fought against
the dragon; and the dragon fought and
his angels,
8 And prevailed not; neither was
their place found any more in heaven.
9 And the great dragon was cast out,
that old serpent, called the Devil, and
Satan, which deceiveth the whole
world: he was cast out into the earth,
and his angels were cast out with him.
10 And I heard a loud voice saying in
heaven, Now is come salvation, and
strength, and the kingdom of our God,
and the power of his Christ: for the ac-
cuser of our brethren is cast down,
which accused them before our God
day and night.
11 And they overcame him by the
blood of the Lamb, and by the word of
their testimony; and they loved not
their lives unto the death.
12 Therefore rejoice, *ye* heavens, and
ye that dwell in them. Woe to the
inhabitants of the earth and of the sea!
for the devil is come down unto you,
having great wrath, because he
knoweth that he hath but a short time.
13 And when the dragon saw that he
was cast unto the earth, he persecuted
the woman which brought forth the
man *child*.
14 And to the woman were given two
wings of a great eagle, that she might
fly into the wilderness, into her place,
where she is nourished for a time, and

times, and half a time, from the face of the serpent.

15 And the serpent cast out of his mouth water as a flood after the woman, that he might cause her to be carried away of the flood.

16 And the earth helped the woman, and the earth opened her mouth, and swallowed up the flood which the dragon cast out of his mouth.

17 And the dragon was wroth with the woman, and went to make war with the remnant of her seed, which keep the commandments of God, and have the testimony of Jesus Christ.

CHAPTER 13

AND I stood upon the sand of the sea, and saw a beast rise up out of the sea, having seven heads and ten horns, and upon his horns ten crowns, and upon his heads the name of blasphemy.

2 And the beast which I saw was like unto a leopard, and his feet were as *the feet* of a bear, and his mouth as the mouth of a lion: and the dragon gave him his power, and his seat, and great authority.

3 And I saw one of his heads as it were wounded to death; and his deadly wound was healed: and all the world wondered after the beast.

4 And they worshipped the dragon which gave power unto the beast: and they worshipped the beast, saying, Who *is* like unto the beast? who is able to make war with him?

5 And there was given unto him a mouth speaking great things and blasphemies; and power was given unto him to continue forty *and* two months.

6 And he opened his mouth in blasphemy against God, to blaspheme his name, and his tabernacle, and them that dwell in heaven.

7 And it was given unto him to make war with the saints, and to overcome them: and power was given him over all kindreds, and tongues, and nations.

8 And all that dwell upon the earth shall worship him, whose names are not written in the book of life of the Lamb slain from the foundation of the world.

9 If any man have an ear, let him hear.

10 He that leadeth into captivity shall go into captivity: he that killeth with the sword must be killed with the sword. Here is the patience and the faith of the saints.

11 And I beheld another beast coming up out of the earth; and he had two horns like a lamb, and he spake as a dragon.

12 And he exerciseth all the power of the first beast before him, and causeth the earth and them which dwell therein to worship the first beast, whose deadly wound was healed.

13 And he doeth great wonders, so that he maketh fire come down from heaven on the earth in the sight of men,

14 And deceiveth them that dwell on the earth by *the means of* those miracles which he had power to do in the sight of the beast; saying to them that dwell on the earth, that they should make an image to the beast, which had the wound by a sword, and did live.

15 And he had power to give life unto the image of the beast, that the image of the beast should both speak, and cause that as many as would not worship the image of the beast should be killed.

16 And he causeth all, both small and great, rich and poor, free and bond, to receive a mark in their right hand, or in their foreheads:

17 And that no man might buy or sell, save he that had the mark, or the name of the beast, or the number of his name.

18 Here is wisdom. Let him that hath understanding count the number of the beast: for it is the number of a man; and his number *is* Six hundred threescore *and* six.

CHAPTER 14

AND I looked, and, lo, a Lamb stood on the mount Sion, and with him an hundred forty *and* four thousand, having his Father's name written in their foreheads.

2 And I heard a voice from heaven, as the voice of many waters, and as the voice of a great thunder: and I heard the voice of harpers harping with their harps:

3 And they sung as it were a new song before the throne, and before the four beasts, and the elders: and no man could learn that song but the hundred *and* forty *and* four thousand, which were redeemed from the earth.

4 These are they which were not defiled with women; for they are virgins. These are they which follow the Lamb whithersoever he goeth. These were redeemed from among men, *being* the firstfruits unto God and to the Lamb.

5 And in their mouth was found no guile: for they are without fault before the throne of God.

6 And I saw another angel fly in the midst of heaven, having the everlasting

gospel to preach unto them that dwell
on the earth, and to every nation, and
kindred, and tongue, and people,
7 Saying with a loud voice, Fear God,
and give glory to him; for the hour of
his judgment is come: and worship him
that made heaven, and earth, and the
sea, and the fountains of waters.
8 And there followed another angel,
saying, Băbylon is fallen, is fallen, that
great city, because she made all nations drink of the wine of the wrath of
her fornication.
9 And the third angel followed them,
saying with a loud voice, If any man
worship the beast and his image, and
receive *his* mark in his forehead, or in
his hand,
10 The same shall drink of the wine of
the wrath of God, which is poured out
without mixture into the cup of his indignation; and he shall be tormented
with fire and brimstone in the presence
of the holy angels, and in the presence
of the Lamb:
11 And the smoke of their torment
ascendeth up for ever and ever: and
they have no rest day nor night, who
worship the beast and his image, and
whosoever receiveth the mark of his
name.
12 Here is the patience of the saints:
here *are* they that keep the commandments of God, and the faith of Jesus.
13 And I heard a voice from heaven
saying unto me, Write, Blessed *are* the
dead which die in the Lord from henceforth: Yea, saith the Spirit, that they
may rest from their labours; and their
works do follow them.
14 And I looked, and behold a white
cloud, and upon the cloud *one* sat like
unto the Son of man, having on his
head a golden crown, and in his hand a
sharp sickle.
15 And another angel came out of the
temple, crying with a loud voice to him
that sat on the cloud, Thrust in thy
sickle, and reap: for the time is come
for thee to reap; for the harvest of the
earth is ripe.
16 And he that sat on the cloud thrust
in his sickle on the earth; and the earth
was reaped.
17 And another angel came out of the
temple which is in heaven, he also having a sharp sickle.
18 And another angel came out from
the altar, which had power over fire;
and cried with a loud cry to him that
had the sharp sickle, saying, Thrust in
thy sharp sickle, and gather the clusters
of the vine of the earth; for her
grapes are fully ripe.
19 And the angel thrust in his sickle
into the earth, and gathered the vine of
the earth, and cast *it* into the great winepress of the wrath of God.
20 And the winepress was trodden
without the city, and blood came out of
the winepress, even unto the horse
bridles, by the space of a thousand *and*
six hundred furlongs.

CHAPTER 15

AND I saw another sign in heaven,
great and marvellous, seven angels
having the seven last plagues; for in
them is filled up the wrath of God.
2 And I saw as it were a sea of glass
mingled with fire: and them that had
gotten the victory over the beast, and
over his image, and over his mark, *and*
over the number of his name, stand on
the sea of glass, having the harps of
God.
3 And they sing the song of Moses the
servant of God, and the song of the
Lamb, saying, Great and marvellous
are thy works, Lord God Almighty; just
and true *are* thy ways, thou King of
saints.
4 Who shall not fear thee, O Lord,
and glorify thy name? for *thou* only *art*
holy: for all nations shall come and
worship before thee; for thy judgments
are made manifest.
5 And after that I looked, and, behold, the temple of the tabernacle of
the testimony in heaven was opened:
6 And the seven angels came out of
the temple, having the seven plagues,
clothed in pure and white linen, and having their breasts girded with golden
girdles.
7 And one of the four beasts gave
unto the seven angels seven golden
vials full of the wrath of God, who
liveth for ever and ever.
8 And the temple was filled with
smoke from the glory of God, and from
his power; and no man was able to enter into the temple, till the seven
plagues of the seven angels were fulfilled.

CHAPTER 16

AND I heard a great voice out of the
temple saying to the seven angels, Go
your ways, and pour out the vials of the
wrath of God upon the earth.
2 And the first went, and poured out
his vial upon the earth; and there fell a
noisome and grievous sore upon the
men which had the mark of the beast,
and *upon* them which worshipped his
image.
3 And the second angel poured out
his vial upon the sea; and it became as

the blood of a dead *man:* and every living soul died in the sea.

4 And the third angel poured out his vial upon the rivers and fountains of waters; and they became blood.

5 And I heard the angel of the waters say, Thou art righteous, O Lord, which art, and wast, and shalt be, because thou hast judged thus.

6 For they have shed the blood of saints and prophets, and thou hast given them blood to drink; for they are worthy.

7 And I heard another out of the altar say, Even so, Lord God Almighty, true and righteous *are* thy judgments.

8 And the fourth angel poured out his vial upon the sun; and power was given unto him to scorch men with fire.

9 And men were scorched with great heat, and blasphemed the name of God, which hath power over these plagues: and they repented not to give him glory.

10 And the fifth angel poured out his vial upon the seat of the beast; and his kingdom was full of darkness; and they gnawed their tongues for pain,

11 And blasphemed the God of heaven because of their pains and their sores, and repented not of their deeds.

12 And the sixth angel poured out his vial upon the great river Eū-phrā′tēs; and the water thereof was dried up, that the way of the kings of the east might be prepared.

13 And I saw three unclean spirits like frogs *come* out of the mouth of the dragon, and out of the mouth of the beast, and out of the mouth of the false prophet.

14 For they are the spirits of devils, working miracles, *which* go forth unto the kings of the earth and of the whole world, to gather them to the battle of that great day of God Almighty.

15 ¶Behold, I come as a thief. Blessed *is* he that watcheth, and keepeth his garments, lest he walk naked, and they see his shame.

16 And he gathered them together into a place called in the Hebrew tongue Är-ma-gĕd′don.

17 And the seventh angel poured out his vial into the air; and there came a great voice out of the temple of heaven, from the throne, saying, It is done.

18 And there were voices, and thunders, and lightnings; and there was a great earthquake, such as was not since men were upon the earth, so mighty an earthquake, *and* so great.

19 And the great city was divided into three parts, and the cities of the nations fell: and great Băb′y-lon came in remembrance before God, to give unto her the cup of the wine of the fierceness of his wrath.

20 And every island fled away, and the mountains were not found.

21 And there fell upon men a great hail out of heaven, *every stone* about the weight of a talent: and men blasphemed God because of the plague of the hail; for the plague thereof was exceeding great.

CHAPTER 17

AND there came one of the seven angels which had the seven vials, and talked with me, saying unto me, Come hither; I will shew unto thee the judgment of the great whore that sitteth upon many waters:

2 With whom the kings of the earth have committed fornication, and the inhabitants of the earth have been made drunk with the wine of her fornication.

3 So he carried me away in the spirit into the wilderness: and I saw a woman sit upon a scarlet coloured beast, full of names of blasphemy, having seven heads and ten horns.

4 And the woman was arrayed in purple and scarlet colour, and decked with gold and precious stones and pearls, having a golden cup in her hand full of abominations and filthiness of her fornication:

5 And upon her forehead *was* a name written, MYSTERY, BABYLON THE GREAT, THE MOTHER OF HARLOTS AND ABOMINATIONS OF THE EARTH.

6 And I saw the woman drunken with the blood of the saints, and with the blood of the martyrs of Jesus: and when I saw her, I wondered with great admiration.

7 And the angel said unto me, Wherefore didst thou marvel? I will tell thee the mystery of the woman, and of the beast that carrieth her, which hath the seven heads and ten horns.

8 The beast that thou sawest was, and is not; and shall ascend out of the bottomless pit, and go into perdition: and they that dwell on the earth shall wonder, whose names were not written in the book of life from the foundation of the world, when they behold the beast that was, and is not, and yet is.

9 And here *is* the mind which hath wisdom. The seven heads are seven mountains, on which the woman sitteth.

10 And there are seven kings: five are fallen, and one is, *and* the other is not

yet come; and when he cometh, he must continue a short space.

11 And the beast that was, and is not, even he is the eighth, and is of the seven, and goeth into perdition.

12 And the ten horns which thou sawest are ten kings, which have received no kingdom as yet; but receive power as kings one hour with the beast.

13 These have one mind, and shall give their power and strength unto the beast.

14 These shall make war with the Lamb, and the Lamb shall overcome them: for he is Lord of lords, and King of kings: and they that are with him *are* called, and chosen, and faithful.

15 And he saith unto me, The waters which thou sawest, where the whore sitteth, are peoples, and multitudes, and nations, and tongues.

16 And the ten horns which thou sawest upon the beast, these shall hate the whore, and shall make her desolate and naked, and shall eat her flesh, and burn her with fire.

17 For God hath put in their hearts to fulfil his will, and to agree, and give their kingdom unto the beast, until the words of God shall be fulfilled.

18 And the woman which thou sawest is that great city, which reigneth over the kings of the earth.

CHAPTER 18

AND after these things I saw another angel come down from heaven, having great power; and the earth was lightened with his glory.

2 And he cried mightily with a strong voice, saying, Babylon the great is fallen, is fallen, and is become the habitation of devils, and the hold of every foul spirit, and a cage of every unclean and hateful bird.

3 For all nations have drunk of the wine of the wrath of her fornication, and the kings of the earth have committed fornication with her, and the merchants of the earth are waxed rich through the abundance of her delicacies.

4 And I heard another voice from heaven, saying, Come out of her, my people, that ye be not partakers of her sins, and that ye receive not of her plagues.

5 For her sins have reached unto heaven, and God hath remembered her iniquities.

6 Reward her even as she rewarded you, and double unto her double according to her works: in the cup which she hath filled fill to her double.

7 How much she hath glorified herself, and lived deliciously, so much torment and sorrow give her: for she saith in her heart, I sit a queen, and am no widow, and shall see no sorrow.

8 Therefore shall her plagues come in one day, death, and mourning, and famine; and she shall be utterly burned with fire: for strong *is* the Lord God who judgeth her.

9 And the kings of the earth, who have committed fornication and lived deliciously with her, shall bewail her, and lament for her, when they shall see the smoke of her burning,

10 Standing afar off for the fear of her torment, saying, Alas, alas that great city Babylon, that mighty city! for in one hour is thy judgment come.

11 And the merchants of the earth shall weep and mourn over her; for no man buyeth their merchandise any more:

12 The merchandise of gold, and silver, and precious stones, and of pearls, and fine linen, and purple, and silk, and scarlet, and all thyine wood, and all manner vessels of ivory, and all manner vessels of most precious wood, and of brass, and iron, and marble,

13 And cinnamon, and odours, and ointments, and frankincense, and wine, and oil, and fine flour, and wheat, and beasts, and sheep, and horses, and chariots, and slaves, and souls of men.

14 And the fruits that thy soul lusted after are departed from thee, and all things which were dainty and goodly are departed from thee, and thou shalt find them no more at all.

15 The merchants of these things, which were made rich by her, shall stand afar off for the fear of her torment, weeping and wailing,

16 And saying, Alas, alas that great city, that was clothed in fine linen, and purple, and scarlet, and decked with gold, and precious stones, and pearls!

17 For in one hour so great riches is come to nought. And every shipmaster, and all the company in ships, and sailors, and as many as trade by sea, stood afar off,

18 And cried when they saw the smoke of her burning, saying, What *city is* like unto this great city!

19 And they cast dust on their heads, and cried, weeping and wailing, saying, Alas, alas that great city, wherein were made rich all that had ships in the sea by reason of her costliness! for in one hour is she made desolate.

20 Rejoice over her, *thou* heaven, and *ye* holy apostles and prophets; for God hath avenged you on her.

21 And a mighty angel took up a

stone like a great millstone, and cast *it*
into the sea, saying, Thus with violence
shall that great city Babylon be thrown
down, and shall be found no more at all.
22 And the voice of harpers, and mu-
sicians, and of pipers, and trumpeters,
shall be heard no more at all in thee;
and no craftsman, of whatsoever craft
he be, shall be found any more in thee;
and the sound of a millstone shall be
heard no more at all in thee;
23 And the light of a candle shall
shine no more at all in thee; and the
voice of the bridegroom and of the
bride shall be heard no more at all in
thee: for thy merchants were the great
men of the earth; for by thy sorceries
were all nations deceived.
24 And in her was found the blood of
prophets, and of saints, and of all that
were slain upon the earth.

CHAPTER 19

AND after these things I heard a great
voice of much people in heaven,
saying, Alleluia; Salvation, and glory,
and honour, and power, unto the Lord
our God:
2 For true and righteous *are* his judg-
ments: for he hath judged the great
whore, which did corrupt the earth
with her fornication, and hath avenged
the blood of his servants at her hand.
3 And again they said, Alleluia. And
her smoke rose up for ever and ever.
4 And the four and twenty elders and
the four beasts fell down and wor-
shipped God that sat on the throne,
saying, Amen; Alleluia.
5 And a voice came out of the throne,
saying, Praise our God, all ye his ser-
vants, and ye that fear him, both small
and great.
6 And I heard as it were the voice of a
great multitude, and as the voice of
many waters, and as the voice of
mighty thunderings, saying, Alleluia:
for the Lord God omnipotent reigneth.
7 Let us be glad and rejoice, and give
honour to him: for the marriage of the
Lamb is come, and his wife hath made
herself ready.
8 And to her was granted that she
should be arrayed in fine linen, clean
and white: for the fine linen is the
righteousness of saints.
9 And he saith unto me, Write,
Blessed *are* they which are called unto
the marriage supper of the Lamb. And
he saith unto me, These are the true
sayings of God.
10 And I fell at his feet to worship
him. And he said unto me, See *thou do
it* not: I am thy fellowservant, and of
thy brethren that have the testimony of
Jesus: worship God: for the testimony
of Jesus is the spirit of prophecy.
11 And I saw heaven opened, and be-
hold a white horse; and he that sat upon
him *was* called Faithful and True, and
in righteousness he doth judge and
make war.
12 His eyes *were* as a flame of fire,
and on his head *were* many crowns;
and he had a name written, that no man
knew, but he himself.
13 And he *was* clothed with a vesture
dipped in blood: and his name is called
The Word of God.
14 And the armies *which were* in
heaven followed him upon white
horses, clothed in fine linen, white and
clean.
15 And out of his mouth goeth a
sharp sword, that with it he should
smite the nations: and he shall rule
them with a rod of iron: and he treadeth
the winepress of the fierceness and
wrath of Almighty God.
16 And he hath on *his* vesture and on
his thigh a name written, KING OF
KINGS, AND LORD OF LORDS.
17 And I saw an angel standing in the
sun; and he cried with a loud voice,
saying to all the fowls that fly in the
midst of heaven, Come and gather
yourselves together unto the supper of
the great God;
18 That ye may eat the flesh of kings,
and the flesh of captains, and the flesh
of mighty men, and the flesh of horses,
and of them that sit on them, and the
flesh of all *men, both* free and bond,
both small and great.
19 And I saw the beast, and the kings
of the earth, and their armies, gathered
together to make war against him that
sat on the horse, and against his army.
20 And the beast was taken, and with
him the false prophet that wrought
miracles before him, with which he de-
ceived them that had received the
mark of the beast, and them that wor-
shipped his image. These both were
cast alive into a lake of fire burning
with brimstone.
21 And the remnant were slain with
the sword of him that sat upon the
horse, which *sword* proceeded out of
his mouth: and all the fowls were filled
with their flesh.

CHAPTER 20

AND I saw an angel come down from
heaven, having the key of the bottom-
less pit and a great chain in his hand.
2 And he laid hold on the dragon, that
old serpent, which is the Devil, and Sa-
tan, and bound him a thousand years,
3 And cast him into the bottomless

pit, and shut him up, and set a seal upon
him, that he should deceive the nations
no more, till the thousand years should
be fulfilled: and after that he must be
loosed a little season.
4 And I saw thrones, and they sat
upon them, and judgment was given
unto them: and *I saw* the souls of them
that were beheaded for the witness of
Jesus, and for the word of God, and
which had not worshipped the beast,
neither his image, neither had received
his mark upon their foreheads, or in
their hands; and they lived and reigned
with Christ a thousand years.
5 But the rest of the dead lived not
again until the thousand years were finished. This *is* the first resurrection.
6 Blessed and holy *is* he that hath part
in the first resurrection: on such the second death hath no power, but they
shall be priests of God and of Christ,
and shall reign with him a thousand
years.
7 And when the thousand years are
expired, Satan shall be loosed out of his
prison,
8 And shall go out to deceive the nations which are in the four quarters of
the earth, Gog and Mā′gŏg, to gather
them together to battle: the number of
whom *is* as the sand of the sea.
9 And they went up on the breadth of
the earth, and compassed the camp of
the saints about, and the beloved city:
and fire came down from God out of
heaven, and devoured them.
10 And the devil that deceived them
was cast into the lake of fire and
brimstone, where the beast and the
false prophet *are,* and shall be tormented day and night for ever and
ever.
11 And I saw a great white throne,
and him that sat on it, from whose face
the earth and the heaven fled away;
and there was found no place for them.
12 And I saw the dead, small and
great, stand before God; and the books
were opened: and another book was
opened, which is *the book* of life: and
the dead were judged out of those
things which were written in the books,
according to their works.
13 And the sea gave up the dead
which were in it; and death and hell delivered up the dead which were in
them: and they were judged every man
according to their works.
14 And death and hell were cast into
the lake of fire. This is the second
death.
15 And whosoever was not found
written in the book of life was cast into
the lake of fire.

CHAPTER 21

AND I saw a new heaven and a new
earth: for the first heaven and the first
earth were passed away; and there was
no more sea.
2 And I John saw the holy city, new
Jerusalem, coming down from God out
of heaven, prepared as a bride adorned
for her husband.
3 And I heard a great voice out of
heaven saying, Behold, the tabernacle
of God *is* with men, and he will dwell
with them, and they shall be his people,
and God himself shall be with them,
and be their God.
4 And God shall wipe away all tears
from their eyes; and there shall be no
more death, neither sorrow, nor crying,
neither shall there be any more pain:
for the former things are passed away.
5 And he that sat upon the throne
said, Behold, I make all things new.
And he said unto me, Write: for these
words are true and faithful.
6 And he said unto me, It is done. I am
Alpha and Omega, the beginning and
the end. I will give unto him that is athirst
of the fountain of the water of life
freely.
7 He that overcometh shall inherit all
things; and I will be his God, and he
shall be my son.
8 But the fearful, and unbelieving,
and the abominable, and murderers,
and whoremongers, and sorcerers, and
idolaters, and all liars, shall have their
part in the lake which burneth with fire
and brimstone: which is the second
death.
9 And there came unto me one of the
seven angels which had the seven vials
full of the seven last plagues, and
talked with me, saying, Come hither, I
will shew thee the bride, the Lamb's
wife.
10 And he carried me away in the
spirit to a great and high mountain, and
shewed me that great city, the holy Jerusalem, descending out of heaven from
God,
11 Having the glory of God: and her
light *was* like unto a stone most precious, even like a jasper stone, clear as
crystal;
12 And had a wall great and high, *and*
had twelve gates, and at the gates
twelve angels, and names written thereon, which are *the names* of the
twelve tribes of the children of Israel:
13 On the east three gates; on the
north three gates; on the south three
gates; and on the west three gates.
14 And the wall of the city had twelve

foundations, and in them the names of
the twelve apostles of the Lamb.
15 And he that talked with me had a
golden reed to measure the city, and
the gates thereof, and the wall thereof.
16 And the city lieth foursquare, and
the length is as large as the breadth:
and he measured the city with the reed,
twelve thousand furlongs. The length
and the breadth and the height of it are
equal.
17 And he measured the wall thereof,
an hundred *and* forty *and* four cubits,
according to the measure of a man, that
is, of the angel.
18 And the building of the wall of it
was *of* jasper: and the city *was* pure
gold, like unto clear glass.
19 And the foundations of the wall of
the city *were* garnished with all man-
ner of precious stones. The first foun-
dation was jasper; the second, sap-
phire; the third, a chalcedony; the
fourth, an emerald;
20 The fifth, sardonyx; the sixth, sar-
dius; the seventh, chrysolyte; the
eighth, beryl; the ninth, a topaz; the
tenth, a chrysoprasus; the eleventh, a
jacinth; the twelfth, an amethyst.
21 And the twelve gates *were* twelve
pearls; every several gate was of one
pearl: and the street of the city *was*
pure gold, as it were transparent glass.
22 And I saw no temple therein: for
the Lord God Almighty and the Lamb
are the temple of it.
23 And the city had no need of the
sun, neither of the moon, to shine in it:
for the glory of God did lighten it, and
the Lamb *is* the light thereof.
24 And the nations of them which are
saved shall walk in the light of it: and
the kings of the earth do bring their
glory and honour into it.
25 And the gates of it shall not be
shut at all by day: for there shall be no
night there.
26 And they shall bring the glory and
honour of the nations into it.
27 And there shall in no wise enter
into it any thing that defileth, neither
whatsoever worketh abomination, or
maketh a lie: but they which are writ-
ten in the Lamb's book of life.

CHAPTER 22

AND he shewed me a pure river of wa-
ter of life, clear as crystal, proceeding
out of the throne of God and of the
Lamb.
2 In the midst of the street of it, and
on either side of the river, *was there* the
tree of life, which bare twelve *manner*
of fruits, *and* yielded her fruit every
month: and the leaves of the tree *were*
for the healing of the nations.
3 And there shall be no more curse:
but the throne of God and of the Lamb
shall be in it; and his servants shall
serve him:
4 And they shall see his face; and his
name *shall be* in their foreheads.
5 And there shall be no night there;
and they need no candle, neither light
of the sun; for the Lord God giveth
them light: and they shall reign for ever
and ever.
6 And he said unto me, These sayings
are faithful and true: and the Lord God
of the holy prophets sent his angel to
shew unto his servants the things
which must shortly be done.
7 Behold, I come quickly: blessed *is*
he that keepeth the sayings of the
prophecy of this book.
8 And I John saw these things, and
heard *them*. And when I had heard and
seen, I fell down to worship before the
feet of the angel which shewed me
these things.
9 Then saith he unto me, See *thou do*
it not: for I am thy fellowservant, and of
thy brethren the prophets, and of them
which keep the sayings of this book:
worship God.
10 And he saith unto me, Seal not the
sayings of the prophecy of this book:
for the time is at hand.
11 He that is unjust, let him be unjust
still: and he which is filthy, let him be
filthy still: and he that is righteous, let
him be righteous still: and he that is
holy, let him be holy still.
12 And, behold, I come quickly; and
my reward *is* with me, to give every
man according as his work shall be.
13 I am Alpha and Omega, the begin-
ning and the end, the first and the last.
14 Blessed *are* they that do his com-
mandments, that they may have right
to the tree of life, and may enter in
through the gates into the city.
15 For without *are* dogs, and sorcer-
ers, and whoremongers, and murder-
ers, and idolaters, and whosoever lov-
eth and maketh a lie.
16 I Jesus have sent mine angel to
testify unto you these things in the
churches. I am the root and the offspring
of David, *and* the bright and morn-
ing star.
17 And the Spirit and the bride say,
Come. And let him that heareth say,
Come. And let him that is athirst come.
And whosoever will, let him take the
water of life freely.
18 For I testify unto every man that
heareth the words of the prophecy of
this book, If any man shall add unto

these things, God shall add unto him the plagues that are written in this book:
19 And if any man shall take away from the words of the book of this prophecy, God shall take away his part out of the book of life, and out of the holy city, and *from* the things which are written in this book.
20 He which testifieth these things saith, Surely I come quickly. Amen. Even so, come, Lord Jesus.
21 The grace of our Lord Jesus Christ *be* with you all. Amen.

THE END OF THE NEW TESTAMENT

A Harmony of the Four Gospels

The publishers gratefully acknowledge the use of *Gospel Parallels, a Synopsis of the First Three Gospels*, edited by Burton H. Throckmorton, Jr., in preparing this chart of Gospel Harmony.

	Matthew	*Mark*	*Luke*	*John*
I. Gospel History before Jesus' Public Ministry				
Prologue to the gospel	—	—	1.1–4	1.1–18
The promise of John the Baptist's birth	—	—	1.5–25	—
The salutation of Mary; Mary visits Elizabeth	—	—	1.26–56	—
The birth of John the Baptist	—	—	1.57–80	—
The birth of Jesus; the shepherds	1.18–25	—	2.1–20	—
Visit of the wise men	2.1–12	—	—	
Circumcision of Jesus; presentation in the temple	—	—	2.21–40	—
Flight into Egypt; Herod slays the babies of Bethlehem; return from Egypt	2.13–23	—	—	
Jesus at twelve years of age	—	—	2.41–52	—
II. Preparation for Jesus' Public Ministry				
John the Baptist and his ministry	3.1–12	1.1–8	3.1–18	1.19–34
John's imprisonment	—	—	3.19–20	—
The baptism of Jesus	3.13–17	1.9–11	3.21–22	—
The genealogy of Jesus	1.1–17	—	3.23–38	—
The temptation of Jesus	4.1–11	1.12–13	4.1–13	—
III. Jesus' Public Ministry in Galilee				
Jesus' first miracle (water made wine); Jesus visits Capernaum	—	—	—	2.1–12
Jesus cleanses the temple during the Passover	—	—	—	2.13–25
Nicodemus visits Jesus at night ("God so loved the world")	—	—	—	3.1–21
Jesus baptizes, through his disciples, in Judea; John the Baptist again testifies to Jesus	—	—	—	3.22—4.3
Jesus converses with the woman of Samaria	—	—	—	4.4–42
Jesus arrives in Galilee; his first preaching there	4.12–17	1.14–15	4.14–15	4.43–45
Jesus' first rejection at Nazareth	—	—	4.16–30	—
The miraculous catch of fish; first disciples called	4.18–22	1.16–20	5.1–11	1.35–41
Jesus in the synagogue at Capernaum; heals a demoniac	7.28–29	1.21–28	4.31–37	7.46
Jesus heals Peter's mother-in-law and others	8.14–17	1.29–34	4.38–41	—
Jesus departs from Capernaum	—	1.35–38	4.42–43	—
A preaching journey in Galilee	4.23–25	1.39	4.44	—

A. The Sermon on the Mount (or, the Plain)

	Matthew	*Mark*	*Luke*	*John*
Introduction	5.1–2	—	6.20	—
The Beatitudes	5.3–12	—	6.20–23	—
The Woes	—	—	6.24–26	—
The parables of salt and of light	5.13–16	9.50	11.33–36; 14.34–35	—
On the law	5.17–20	—	16.16–17	—
On murder	5.21–26	—	12.57–59	—
On adultery and lust	5.27–30	—	—	—
On divorce	5.31–32	—	16.18	—
On swearing; on retaliation	5.33–42	—	6.29–30	—
On love of one's enemies	5.43–48	—	6.27–28, 32–36	—
On almsgiving; on prayer	6.1–8	—	—	—
The Lord's Prayer	6.9–15	—	11.1–4	—
On fasting; on treasures	6.16–21	—	12.33–34	—
The sound eye	6.22–23	—	11.34–36	—
On serving two masters	6.24	—	16.13	—
On anxiety	6.25–34	—	12.22–31	—
On judging	7.1–5	—	6.37–42	—
On profaning the holy	7.6	—	—	—
God's answering of prayer	7.7–11	—	11.9–13	—
The Golden Rule	7.12	—	6.31	—
The narrow gate	7.13–14	—	13.23–24	—
The test of a good man	7.15–20	—	6.43–45	—
Warning against self-deception	7.21–23	—	6.46; 13.26–27	—
Hearers and doers of the Word	7.24–27	—	6.47–49	—
The end of the Sermon	7.28–29	—	—	7.46

B. Continuing Jesus' Public Ministry in Galilee

Healing the leper	8.1–4	1.40–45	5.12–16	—
Healing the centurion's servant	8.5–13	—	7.1–10	4.46–54
Healing the widow's son at Naim	—	—	7.11–17	—
The nature of discipleship	8.18–22	—	9.57–62	—
The healing of the paralytic at Capernaum	9.1–8	2.1–12	5.17–26	5.8–9
The call of Levi (Matthew)	9.9–13	2.13–17	5.27–32	—
The question about fasting	9.14–17	2.18–22	5.33–39	—
Jesus heals the man at Bethesda; the testimony to Jesus	—	—	—	5.1–47
Two blind men healed	9.27–31	—	—	—
The healing of a dumb demoniac	9.32–34	3.22–27	11.14–23	—
The twelve disciples sent out	9.35—10.6	—	10.1–16	1.42; 4.35
The fate of the disciples	10.17–25	13.9–13	21.12–17	13.16; 14.26; 15.20
Exhortation to confession	10.26–33	—	12.2–12	14.26
Division in households	10.34–36	—	12.49–56	—
Conditions of discipleship	10.37–39	—	14.25–33	12.25
End of discourse to disciples	10.40–11.1	—	10.16	5.23; 12.44–45
John's question to Jesus	11.2–6	—	7.18–23	—
Jesus' words about John	11.7–19	—	7.24–35	—
Woes on the cities of Galilee	11.20–24	—	10.13–15	—
Jesus' thanksgiving to the Father	11.25–27	—	10.21–22	3.35; 7.29; 10.14–15; 17.2
Comfort for the heavy laden	11.28–30	—	—	—
Plucking grain on the sabbath	12.1–8	2.23–28	6.1–5	5.10
The healing of the man with a withered hand	12.9–14	3.1–6	6.6–11	—
Jesus heals the multitudes	12.15–21	3.7–12	6.17–19	—

	Matthew	*Mark*	*Luke*	*John*
The call of the twelve	10.1–4	3.13–19	6.12–16	1.42
The woman with the ointment	26.6–13	14.3–9	7.36–50	12.1–8
The ministering women	—	—	8.1–3	—
Accusations against Jesus; a house divided	12.22–37	3.20–30	11.14–23	7.20; 8.48, 52
Against seeking for signs	12.38–42	8.11–12	11.29–32	—
The return of the evil spirit	12.43–45	—	11.24–26	—
Jesus' true relatives	12.46–50	3.31–35	8.19–21	15.14
Jesus teaches by parables; the sower, the tares, the seed growing secretly, the mustard seed, the leaven, the hidden treasure, the pearl, the dragnet, the householder	13.1–52	4.1–34	8.4–18; 10.23–24; 13.18–21	12.40
The stilling of the storm	8.23–27	4.35–51	8.22–25	—
The Gadarene demoniac	8.28–34	5.1–20	8.26–39	—
Jairus' daughter and a woman's faith	9.18–26	5.21–43	8.40–56	—
Jesus is again rejected at Nazareth	13.53–58	6.1–6	—	4.44; 6.42; 7.5, 15
The sending out of the twelve	9.35; 10.1–11, 14	6.6–13	9.1–6	—
Herod thinks Jesus is John, risen	14.1–2	6.14–16	9.7–9	—
The death of John	14.3–12	6.17–29	—	—
The return of the twelve and the feeding of the 5,000	14.31–21	6.30–44	9.10–17	6.1–14
Walking on the water	14.22–33	6.45–52	—	6.15–21
Jesus' discourse on the bread of life	—	—	—	6.22–71
Healings at Gennesaret	14.34–36	6.53–56	—	—
What defiles a man	15.1–20	7.1–23	—	—
The Syrophenician woman	15.21–28	7.24–30	—	—
Healing of many; healing of the deaf mute	15.29–31	7.31–37	—	—
The feeding of the 4,000	15.32–39	8.1–10	—	—
The Pharisees seek a sign	16.1–4	8.11–13	11.29–32; 12.54–56	6.30
A discourse on leaven	16.5–12	8.14–21	12.1	—
The blind man at Bethsaida	—	8.22–26	—	9.1–7
Peter's confession at Caesarea Philippi; first prediction of the Passion	16.13–23	8.27–33	9.18–22	6.68–69; 20.21–23
The conditions of discipleship	16.24–28	8.34—9.1	9.23–27	12.25
The transfiguration	17.1–8	9.2–8	9.28–36	1.14
The coming of Elijah	17.9–13	9.9–13	—	
The epileptic boy healed	17.14–21	9.14–29	9.37–43a	14.9
The second prediction of the Passion	17.22–23	9.30–32	9.43b–45	7.1
The temple tax	17.24–27	—	—	—
The dispute about greatness	18.1–5	9.33–37	9.46–48	3.3, 5; 12.44–45; 13.20
The strange exorcist	—	9.38–41	9.49–50	—
On temptations	18.6–9	9.42–48	17.1–2	—
Concerning salt	5.13	9.49–50	14.34–35	—
The lost sheep	18.10–14	—	15.1–10	—
On reproving one's brother	18.15–20	—	17.3	20.23
On reconciliation	18.21–22	—	17.3–4	—
Parable of the unmerciful servant	18.23–35	—	—	—
Jesus goes to Jerusalem at the feast of Tabernacles; His discourses there	—	—	—	7.1–53
A woman taken in adultery is brought before Jesus	—	—	—	8.1–11
Jesus declares himself the light of the world; unbelieving Jews attempt to stone him	—	—	—	8.12–59
Jesus heals a blind beggar	—	—	—	9.1–41
The Good Shepherd	—	—	—	10.1–21

C. Luke's Special Section

	Matthew	*Mark*	*Luke*	*John*
The Samaritan villagers	—	—	9.51–56	—
The nature of discipleship	8.18–22	—	9.57–62	—
The sending out of the seventy	9.35—10.16	—	10.1–16	4.35; 5.23
The return of the seventy	—	—	10.17–20	12.31
Jesus' gratitude to the Father	11.25–27	—	10.21–22	10.15; 17.2
The blessedness of the disciples	13.16–17	—	10.23–24	—
The lawyer's question	22.34–40	12.28–31	10.25–28	—
Parable of the good Samaritan	—	—	10.29–37	—
Mary and Martha	—	—	10.38–42	11.1–3
The friend at midnight	—	—	11.5–8	—
The answer to prayer	7.7–11	—	11.9–13	—
The Beelzebub controversy	9.32–34; 12.22–30	—	11.14–23	—
The blessedness of Jesus' mother	—	—	11.27–28	—
The sign for this generation	12.38–42; 16.1–4	8.11–12	11.29–32	—
Concerning light	5.14–16; 6.22–23	—	11.33–36	—
Discourse against the Pharisees	23.1–36	12.37–40	11.37—12.1	—
Exhortation to fearless confession	10.19–20, 20–33; 12.32	4.22; 8.38	12.2–12	14.26
The parable of the rich fool	—	—	12.13–21	—
Cares about earthly things	6.16–21, 25–34	—	12.22–34	—
Watchfulness and faithfulness	24.43–51	13.32–33	12.35–46	13.4–5
The servant's wages	—	—	12.47–48	—
Interpreting the present time	10.34–36; 16.1–4	—	12.49–56	12.27
Agreement with one's accuser	5.25–26	—	12.57–59	—
Repentance or destruction	—	—	13.1–9	—
Healing of the woman with a spirit of infirmity	—	—	13.10–17	—
Parables of the mustard seed, of the leaven	13.31–33	4.30–32	13.18–21	—
Exclusion from the kingdom	7.13–14; 25.10–12; 7.22–23	—	13.22–30	—
The departure from Galilee	—	—	13.31–33	—
The lament over Jerusalem	22.37–39	—	13.34–35	—
The healing of a man with dropsy	—	—	14.1–6	—
Teaching on humility	—	—	14.7–14	—
The parable of the great supper	22.1–14	—	14.15–24	—
The cost of discipleship	10.26–33, 37–39	—	14.25–35	—
The lost sheep and the lost coin	18.12–14	—	15.1–10	—
The prodigal son	—	—	15.11–32	—
The unjust steward	6.24	—	16.1–13	—
The hypocrisy of the Pharisees	—	—	16.14–15	—
About the law and about divorce	5.17–20, 31–32; 11.12–13	—	16.16–18	—
The rich man and Lazarus	—	—	16.19–31	—
On causing sin	18.6–9	9.42–48	17.1–2	—
On forgiveness	18.15, 21–22	—	17.3–4	—
On faith	17.20	—	17.5–6	—
The servant's wages	—	—	17.7–10	—
The healing of ten lepers	—	—	17.11–19	—
On the kingdom of God	24.23–25	13.21–23	17.20–21	—
The day of the Son of man	24.26–28, 37–41	—	17.22–37	—

	Matthew	Mark	Luke	John
The parable of the unjust judge	—	—	18.1–8	—
The parable of the Pharisee and the publican	—	—	18.9–14	—

IV. The Judean Ministry

A. The Journey to Jerusalem

	Matthew	Mark	Luke	John
Marriage and divorce	19.1–12	10.1–12	—	—
Jesus blesses the children	19.13–15	10.13–16	18.15–17	3.3, 5
The rich young man	19.16–30	10.17–31	18.18–30	—
The parable of the laborers in the vineyard	20.1–10	—	—	—
The third prediction of the Passion	20.17–19	10.32–34	18.31–34	—
Jesus and the sons of Zebedee	20.20–28	10.35–45	22.24–27	—
The healing of Bartimeus	20.29–34	10.46–52	18.35–43	—
Zaccheus	—	—	19.1–10	—
The parable of the pounds	25.14–30	—	19.11–27	—

B. The Days in Jerusalem

	Matthew	Mark	Luke	John
The entry into Jerusalem; prediction of the destruction of Jerusalem; Jesus in the temple	21.1–17	11.1–11	19.28–46	12.21–50; 2.13–15
Jesus keeps the feast of Dedication at Jerusalem	—	—	—	10.22–39
Jesus goes to Bethany; raises Lazarus from the dead	—	—	—	10.40—11.44
A meeting of the chief priests and Pharisees	—	—	—	11.45–53
Jesus at Ephraim; the coming of the Passover	—	—	—	11.54–57
The cursing of the fig tree	21.18–19	11.12–14	—	—
The cleansing of the temple	21.12–13	11.15–19	19.45–48	2.13–17
The meaning of the withered fig tree	21.20–22	11.20–26	—	14.13–14
The question about authority	21.23–27	11.27–33	20.1–8	2.18
The parable of the two sons	21.28–32	—	—	—
The parable of the wicked tenants	21.33–46	12.1–12	20.9–19	—
The parable of the marriage feast (great supper)	22.1–14	—	14.16–24	—
Question on tribute to Caesar	22.15–22	12.13–17	20.20–26	3.2
Question on the resurrection	22.23–33	12.18–27	20.27–40	—
The great commandment	22.34–40	12.28–34	10.25–28	—
About David's son	22.41–46	12.35–37	20.41–44	—
Woes against the Pharisees	23.1–36	12.37–40	20.45–47; 11.37–52	—
The lament over Jerusalem	23.37–39	—	13.34–35	—
The widow's gift	—	12.41–44	21.1–4	—
Prediction of the destruction of the temple	24.1–3	13.1–4	21.5–7	—
The signs of the parousia	24.4–8	13.5–8	21.8–11	—
The beginning of the troubles	24.9–14	13.9–13	21.12–19	14.26; 15.21; 16.2
The desolating sacrilege	24.15–22	13.14–20	21.20–24	—
The culmination of the troubles	24.23–25	13.21–23	17.20–23	—
The day of the Son of man	24.26–28	—	17.23–24, 37	—
The parousia of the Son of man	24.29–31	13.24–27	21.25–28	—
The parable of the fig tree	24.32–33	13.28–29	21.29–31	—
The time of the parousia	24.34–36	13.30–32	21.32–33	—
Mark's ending to the discourse	—	13.33–37	—	—
Luke's ending to the discourse	—	—	21.34–36	—
The need for watchfulness	24.37–41	—	17.26–27, 34–35	—
Watchfulness and faithfulness	24.42–51	—	12.39–46	—

	Matthew	*Mark*	*Luke*	*John*
The parable of the ten maidens	25.1–13	—	—	—
The parable of the talents	25.14–30	—	19.12–27	—
The last judgment	25.31–46	—	—	5.28–29
A summary of the days spent in Jerusalem	—	—	21.37–38	—

C. The Passion Narrative

The conspiracy against Jesus	26.1–5	14.1–2	22.1–2	11.47–53
The anointing at Bethany	26.6–13	14.3–9	7.36–50	12.1–11
The betrayal by Judas	26.14–16	14.10–11	22.3–6	18.2–5
Preparation for the Passover	26.17–19	14.12–16	22.7–13	—
Jesus washes his disciples' feet	—	—	—	13.1–20
The traitor	26.20–25	14.17–21	22.14, 21–23	13.21–30
Institution of the Lord's Supper	26.26–29	14.22–25	22.15–20	—
Last words: the betrayal foretold; greatness in the kingdom of God; Peter's denial prophesied; the two swords	19.28; 20.25–28	10.42–45	22.21–38	13.4–5, 12–14, 36–38
Jesus' farewell discourse; His intercessory prayer	—	—	—	13.31—17.26
The way to Gethsemane; Peter's denial prophesied	26.30–35	14.26–31	22.39; 22.31–34	18.1; 13.36–38; 16.32
Jesus in Gethsemane	26.36–46	14.32–42	22.40–46	18.1; 12.27; 14.3; 18.11
Jesus taken captive	26.47–56	14.43–52	22.47–53	18.2–12, 20
Jesus before the Sanhedrin and others; Peter's denial	26.57–75	14.53–72	22.54–71	18.13–27
Jesus delivered to Pilate	27.1–2	15.1	23.1	18.28–32
The death of Judas	27.3–10	—	—	—
The trial before Pilate	27.11–14	15.2–5	23.2–5	18.33–37; 19.6, 9–10
Jesus before Herod	—	—	23.6–16	—
The sentence of death	27.15–26	15.6–15	23.17–25	18.38–40; 19.4–16
The mocking by the soldiers	27.27–31	15.16–20	—	19.1–3
The Crucifixion	27.32–44	15.21–32	23.26–43	19.17–24
The death on the cross; the burial of Jesus	27.45–61	15.33–47	23.44–56	19.25–42
The guard at the tomb	27.62–66	—	—	—

V. The Resurrection

The empty tomb	28.1–10	16.1–11	24.1–12	20.1–18
Bribing the Roman soldiers	28.11–15	—	—	—
Jesus appears to the two men on the road to Emmaus	—	16.12–13	24.13–35	—
Jesus appears in Jerusalem	—	—	24.36–49	—
Jesus appears to the disciples	—	—	—	20.19–29
Jesus appears at the sea of Tiberias	—	—	—	21.1–24
Jesus' appearance on the mountain in Galilee	28.16–20	16.14–16	—	—
Signs to accompany believers	—	16.17–18	—	—
The Ascension	—	16.19	24.50–53	—
The disciples go out into the world to preach	—	16.20	—	—
John's conclusion to the gospel	—	—	—	20.30–31; 21.25

Parables and Miracles in the Bible

Parables in the Old Testament

Parable	*By whom and to whom spoken*	*Reference*
The trees choosing a king	Jotham to the Shechemites	Judg. 9.7–15
Samson's riddle	Samson to his companions	Judg. 14.14
The poor man's ewe lamb	Nathan to David	2 Sam. 12.1–4
The two sons and avengers	the widow of Tekoah to David	2 Sam. 14.6–11
The escaped captive	a man of the sons of the prophets to Ahab	1 Kgs. 20.35–40
Micaiah's vision	Micaiah to Ahab	1 Kgs. 22.19–23
Thistle and cedar	Jehoash (Joash) to Amaziah	2 Kgs. 14.9; 2 Chr. 25.18
The drunkard	Solomon to the people of Israel	Prov. 23.29–35
The sluggard and his vineyard	Solomon to the people of Israel	Prov. 24.30–34
The unfruitful vineyard	Isaiah to Egypt	Isa. 5.1–7
The plowman	Isaiah to the people of Israel	Isa. 28.23–29
Eagles and the vine	Ezekiel to the people of Israel	Ezek. 17.2–10
Lion's whelps	Ezekiel to the people of Israel	Ezek. 19.2–9
The two harlots	Ezekiel to the people of Israel	Ezek. 23.1–49
The boiling pot	Ezekiel to the people of Israel	Ezek. 24.3–5
Cedar of Lebanon	Ezekiel to Egypt	Ezek. 31.3–18
Dragon in the seas	Ezekiel to Pharaoh	Ezek. 32.1–16
Shepherds and the flock	Ezekiel to the people of Israel	Ezek. 34.1–31
Dry bones in the valley	Ezekiel to the people of Israel	Ezek. 37.1–28
Living waters	Ezekiel to the people of Israel	Ezek. 47.1–23

For other parables see Amos 7.1—9.15; Zechariah 1.7—6.8; 11.3–17.

Miracles in the Old Testament

Preceding the Exodus

	Reference
Destruction of Sodom and Gomorrah	Gen. 19.24
Lot's wife turned into a pillar of salt	Gen. 19.26
The birth of Isaac	Gen. 21.1–3
The burning bush not consumed	Ex. 3.2

In Egypt

Aaron's rod turned into a serpent	Ex. 7.10–12
The ten plagues:	
1. Water made blood	Ex. 7.20–25
2. Frogs	Ex. 8.5–14
3. Lice	Ex. 8.16–18
4. Flies	Ex. 8.20–24
5. Murrain (death to cattle)	Ex. 9.3–6
6. Boils	Ex. 9.8–11
7. Thunder and hail	Ex. 9.22–26
8. Locusts	Ex. 10.12–19
9. Darkness	Ex. 10.21–23
10. The first-born slain	Ex. 12.29–30
Parting of the Red Sea	Ex. 14.21–31

In the Wilderness

The sweetening of the waters of Marah	Ex. 15.23–25
Feeding with manna	Ex. 16.14–35
Water from the rock at Rephidim	Ex. 17.5–7
Death of Nadab and Abihu for offering unholy fire	Lev. 10.1–2

	Reference
Burning of the camp at Taberah	Num. 11.1–3
Death of Korah, Dathan, and Abiram	Num. 16.31–35
Aaron's rod bears buds, blossoms, and almonds	Num. 17.8
Water from the rock at Meribah	Num. 20.7–11
The healing powers of the brass serpent	Num. 21.8–9
Stopping of the river Jordan	Josh. 3.14–17
In Canaan—under Joshua	
Fall of the walls of Jericho	Josh. 6.6–28
Staying of the sun and moon	Josh. 10.12–14
Strength of Samson	Judg. 14.1—16.30
The water flows from the hollow place at Lehi	Judg. 15.19
Men of Beth-shemesh slain for looking into the ark	1 Sam. 6.19
Thunderstorm causes panic in Philistine army	1 Sam. 7.10–12
Thunder and rain during wheat harvest	1 Sam. 12.17–18
Sound of marching in mulberry trees	2 Sam. 5.23–25
Under the Kings	
Death of Uzzah for touching the ark of God	2 Sam. 6.7
Withering of Jeroboam's hand and destruction of the altar at Beth-el	1 Kgs. 13.4–5
By Elijah	
Drought, fire from heaven, and rain at Elijah's prayer; Elijah wondrously fed	1 Kgs. 17.1–19.18
The increase of the oil and meal at Zarephath	1 Kgs. 17.14–16
The raising of the widow's son at Zarephath	1 Kgs. 17.17–24
Wall of Aphek falls upon thousands of Syrians	1 Kgs. 20.30
Burning of the captains and their companies	2 Kgs. 1.10–12
Dividing of the river Jordan	2 Kgs. 2.8
Elijah taken by a whirlwind into heaven	2 Kgs. 2.11
By Elisha	
Dividing of the river Jordan	2 Kgs. 2.14
The waters of Jericho made wholesome	2 Kgs. 2.21–22
Bears destroy forty-two mocking boys at Beth-el	2 Kgs. 2.24
Water supplied to the allied armies in Moab	2 Kgs. 3.16–20
Increase of the widow's oil	2 Kgs. 4.2–7
Raising of the Shunammite's son	2 Kgs. 4.32–37
The deadly pottage purified with meal	2 Kgs. 4.38–41
Feeding one hundred men with twenty loaves	2 Kgs. 4.42–44
Naaman's leprosy cured; the leprosy transferred to Gehazi	2 Kgs. 5.10–14, 27
An iron axe floats on the water	2 Kgs. 6.5–7
The Syrian army struck with blindness	2 Kgs. 6.18–20
Elisha's bones revive a dead man	2 Kgs. 13.21
Recorded by Isaiah	
Destruction of Sennacherib's army	2 Kgs. 19.35
The shadow goes back on the sundial of Ahaz	2 Kgs. 20.9–11
During Captivity	
Deliverance of Shadrach, Meshach, and Abed-nego from the furnace	Dan. 3.19–27
Daniel is saved from the den of lions	Dan. 6.16–23
Miscellaneous	
Dagon falls twice before the ark of God; Philistines afflicted by emerods	1 Sam. 5.1–12
Uzziah is smitten with leprosy	2 Chr. 26.16–21
Deliverance of Jonah from the great fish	Jon. 2.1–10

Parables of Our Lord

Parable	*Matthew*	*Mark*	*Luke*	*John*
Recorded in one gospel only				
Tares among the wheat	13.24–30			
The hidden treasure	13.44			
The pearl of great price				

	Matthew	Mark	Luke	John
The full net	13.47–48			
The unmerciful servant	18.23–34			
Laborers in the vineyard	20.1–16			
The father and two sons	21.28–32			
Marriage of the king's son	22.1–14			
Wise and foolish virgins	25.1–13			
The talents	25.14–30			
The sheep and the goats	25.31–46			
Growth of a seed of grain		4.26–29		
The watchful porter		13.34–36		
The two debtors			7.41–50	
The good Samaritan			10.30–37	
The friend at midnight			11.5–8	
The rich fool			12.16–21	
The waiting servants			12.35–40	
Faithful and wise steward			12.42–48	
The barren fig tree			13.6–9	
Places of honor			14.7–11	
The great supper			14.16–24	
The tower; the warring king			14.28–33	
The lost coin			15.8–10	
The prodigal son			15.11–32	
The dishonest steward			16.1–8	
The rich man and Lazarus			16.19–31	
The farmer and his servant			17.7–10	
The unrighteous judge			18.1–8	
Pharisee and publican			18.9–14	
Nobleman and the ten pounds			19.12–27	
The bread of life				6.25–59
Shepherd and the sheep				10.1–39
Vine and the branches				15.1–27
Recorded in two gospels				
Houses on rock and on sand	7.24–27		6.48–49	
The leaven	13.33		13.20–21	
The lost sheep	18.12–14		15.4–7	
Recorded in three gospels				
The lamp under a bushel	5.14–16	4.21–23	8.16–18	
New cloth on old garment; new wine in old wineskins	9.16–17	2.19–22	5.36–39	
The sower	13.18–30	4.3–9	8.5–8	
The mustard seed	13.31–32	4.31–32	13.18–19	
Vineyard and husbandmen	21.33–41	12.1–8	20.9–16	
Young leaves of the fig tree	24.32	13.38	21.29–30	
Other passages sometimes designated as parables				
The mote and the beam	7.3–5		6.41–42	
The wedding guests	9.15	2.19–20	5.34–35	
Children at play	11.16–17		7.31–32	
Seven unclean spirits	12.43–45		11.24–26	
Old and new treasures	13.52			
The rejected stones	21.42–45	12.10–11	20.17–18	
The shut door			13.25–27	

Miracles of Our Lord

	Matthew	Mark	Luke	John
Narrated in one gospel only				
Two blind men cured	9.27–31			
The dumb demoniac healed	9.32–33			
The shekel in the mouth of the fish	17.24–27			
A deaf and dumb man of Decapolis healed		7.31–37		
A blind man of Bethsaida cured		8.22–26		
Jesus passes unseen through the multitude			4.28–30	
The great catch of fish at Gennesaret			5.1–11	
The widow's son is raised from the dead			7.11–15	
A woman freed from her infirmity			13.11–13	

	Matthew	Mark	Luke	John
A man with dropsy cured			14.1–4	
Ten lepers cleansed			17.11–19	
Servant's ear healed (Malchus)			22.50–51	
Water changed to wine at Cana				2.1–11
Official's son healed of fever				4.46–54
Invalid man cured at pool of Bethesda				5.1–9
Jesus passes through the crowd in the temple				8.59
Man born blind cured at Jerusalem				9.1–7
Lazarus raised from the dead				11.38–44
Falling to the ground of soldiers				18.5–6
The catch of 153 fish				21.1–14
Narrated in two gospels				
Centurion's palsied servant cured	8.5–13		7.1–10	
The blind and dumb demoniac healed	12.22		11.14	
Daughter of the Syrophenician woman healed	15.21–28	7.24–30		
The four thousand fed	15.32–38	8.1–9		
The fig tree cursed by Jesus	21.19	11.14		
A demoniac in the synagogue cured		1.23–26	4.33–35	
Narrated in three gospels				
The leper cured	8.2–3	1.40–41	5.12–13	
Peter's mother-in-law cured of a fever	8.14–15	1.30–31	4.38–39	
The storm at sea stilled	8.23–26	4.35–39	8.22–24	
The devils entered into swine	8.28–32	5.1–13	8.26–33	
The palsied man cured	9.2–7	2.3–12	5.18–25	
Jairus' daughter raised to life	9.18–26	5.22–42	8.41–56	
A woman's hemorrhage cured	9.20–22	5.25–29	8.43–48	
A man's withered hand cured	12.10–13	3.1–5	6.6–11	
Jesus walks on the sea	14.25–27	6.48–51		6.19–20
The epileptic boy cured	17.14–18	9.17–27	9.37–42	
A blind man cured	20.30–34	10.46–52	18.35–43	
Narrated in four gospels				
Feeding the five thousand	14.15–21	6.35–44	9.10–17	6.1–14

Miracles Recorded in The Acts of the Apostles

	Reference
The disciples are filled with the Holy Spirit, with the accompanying signs	2.1–47
The gift of tongues	2.4–11; 10.44–48
Lame man at the Beautiful Gate of the temple	3.1–26
Death of Ananias and Sapphira	5.1–11
Peter healing the sick in the streets	5.12–16
Prison doors opened for the apostles by an angel	5.17–21
Stephen's vision of Christ at the right hand of God	7.55–56
Philip casts out unclean spirits	8.6–7
Christ appears to Saul on the way to Damascus	9.1–9; 22.6–11; 26.12–18
Saul's blindness healed by Ananias	9.17–19; 22.12–13
Eneas' palsy healed by Peter	9.33–34
Tabitha (Dorcas) raised to life by Peter	9.36–41
Vision of Cornelius	10.3–6, 30–32
Vision of Peter	10.10–16; 11.5–10
Prophecies of Agabus	11.27–28; 21.10–11
Peter's release from prison	12.6–10
Elymas blinded by Paul	13.9–11
Healing of the cripple at Lystra by Paul	14.8–10
Paul's vision of a man of Macedonia	16.9
Paul casts out spirit of divination from slave girl	16.16–18
Earthquake at Philippi	16.25–26
Special miracles done by Paul at Ephesus	19.11–12
Evil spirit puts Sceva's sons to flight	19.13–16
Paul raises Eutychus to life	20.9–12
Appearances of Christ to Paul	22.17–21; 23.11; 27.23–24
Paul unharmed by a viper's bite	28.3–6
Paul heals Publius' father and others at Malta	28.8–9

Miracles Referred to in the Epistles and Revelation

	Reference
Miracles by Paul and others	Rom. 15.18–19; 1 Cor. 12.8–10, 28–31; 14.18; Gal. 3.5; 1 Tim. 1.20
Miracle of tongues	1 Cor. 14.27–33
Appearances of Christ after His ressurection	1 Cor. 15.3–8
Visions and revelations of Paul	2 Cor. 12.1–4, 12
Powers of the age to come	Heb. 2.4; 6.5
The visions of John at Patmos	Rev. 1.10–11; 4.1—22.21

Dictionary-Concordance

This dictionary-concordance will help you to find the meanings of words used in the Bible and also to locate key passages in which those words occur.

The more difficult words show pronunciation. The meaning follows the word itself (or the pronunciation) and this is followed by the concordance listing. In the concordance listing only the first letter of the word is used—"l." for "love." The references give you the name of the Bible book, then the chapter, and then the verse or verses. Thus, Lk 24:30–51 would be Luke, chapter 24, verses 30 through 51. See the abbreviations for Bible books listed below.

Abbreviations for the Books of the Bible

Acts	Acts	James	Jas	Nehemiah	Neh		
Amos	Amos	Jeremiah	Jer	Numbers	Num		
I Chronicles	1 Chr	Job	Job	Obadiah	Obad		
II Chronicles	2 Chr	Joel	Joel	I Peter	1 Pet		
Colossians	Col	John (Gospel)	Jn	II Peter	2 Pet		
I Corinthians	1 Cor	I John	1 Jn	Philemon	Philem		
II Corinthians	2 Cor	II John	2 Jn	Philippians	Phil		
Daniel	Dan	III John	3 Jn	Proverbs	Prov		
Deuteronomy	Deut	Jonah	Jon	Psalms	Ps		
Ecclesiastes	Eccles	Joshua	Josh	Revelation	Rev		
Ephesians	Eph	Jude	Jude	Romans	Rom		
Esther	Esther	Judges	Judg	Ruth	Ruth		
Exodus	Ex	I Kings	1 Kgs	I Samuel	1 Sam		
Ezekiel	Ezek	II Kings	2 Kgs	II Samuel	2 Sam		
Ezra	Ezra	Lamentations	Lam	Song of Solomon	Song		
Galatians	Gal	Leviticus	Lev	I Thessalonians	1 Thess		
Genesis	Gen	Luke	Lk	II Thessalonians	2 Thess		
Habakkuk	Hab	Malachi	Mal	I Timothy	1 Tim		
Haggai	Hag	Mark	Mk	II Timothy	2 Tim		
Hebrews	Heb	Matthew	Mt	Titus	Tit		
Hosea	Hos	Micah	Mic	Zechariah	Zech		
Isaiah	Isa	Nahum	Nah	Zephaniah	Zeph		

Key to Pronunciation

ä	as in farm, father	ō	as in bone, boat
ă	as in cat	ŏ	as in bottle, gone
ā	as in fame	ô	as in shore, born
â	as in share, dare	ū	as in cute, tune
ĕ	as in jet, met	û	as in crude
ē	as in beat, street	ŭ	as in fuss
ī	as in kite, shine	u	as in burner
ĭ	as in sit, dim	o͞o	as in pool
		oo	as in foot
			ph is pronounced as f

A

Aaron (aar′on) The older brother of Moses (Ex 6:20; 7:7); the spokesman for Moses (Ex 7:1); brings on plagues with his rod (Ex 7:10—8:17); from him is descended the class of priests in Israel (Ex 29:9); he makes atonement and stops a plague (Num 16:41–50); his rod blossoms (Num 17:1–11); his death (Num 20:22–29).

Abba (äb′ba) Aramaic for "Father" (Mk 14:36; Rom 8:15; Gal 4:6).

Abed–nego (a-bĕd′–ne-gō) Babylonian name of one of Daniel's companions (Dan 1:7; 3:16 etc.).

Abel (ā′bel) Son of Adam; murdered by his brother Cain (Gen 4:2ff). He is described as righteous (Mt 23:35; 1 Jn 3:12). In Heb 11:4 he stands at the head of the heroes of faith.

Abiathar (a-bī′a-thar) A priest in the time of David (1 Sam 23:6ff).

Abner (ăb′ner) Commander of the Israelite army under Saul (1 Sam 14:50; 17:55; 26:5ff); murdered by Joab (2 Sam 3:27).

Abraham; Abram (ā′bra-hăm; ā′bram) Israel's first great patriarch or leader. Through faith in God's promise to make of him a great nation, he is led from Ur to Canaan (Gen 11:31—15:7). God makes a covenant with him (Gen 15:7–21); an angel of God promises that Sarah shall give birth to a son (Gen 18:10); God tests Abraham's faith (Gen 22:1–19). He stands as the father of all the faithful (Gal 3:7).

Absalom (ăb′sa-lom) Son of David and Maachah; turned the people against his father; was defeated and then slain by Joab, to the great sorrow of David (2 Sam 3:3; 13:20—19:10).

Adam The first man, from whom is descended all mankind. Created on the same day as the animals, he is particularly blessed by God (Gen 1:27, 28). He and Eve were driven from the Garden of Eden because of their disobedience (Gen 3:1–24).

adder

adder A poisonous snake.
stingeth like an a. Prov 23:32

Agrippa (a-grĭp′pa) King of Judea before whom Paul appeared to plead his defense (Acts 25:13—26:32).

Ahab (āhab) An evil king of the Northern Kingdom of Israel in the time of Elijah; married Jezebel, a Sidonian princess, which caused religious turmoil; robbed Naboth of his vineyard and then caused his death (1 Kgs 16:29—22:40).

Almighty, the God, as being all powerful.
I *m* the A. God Gen 17:1
name of God A. Ex 6:3
Holy, holy, holy, Lord God A. Rev 4:8

Alpha and Omega (ăl′pha; ō-mē′ga) The first and last letters of the Greek alphabet; hence, "the First and the Last." Applied to God (Rev 1:8, 11; 21:6) and to Christ (Rev 22:13).

altar Table of sacrifice.
Noah builded an a. Gen 8:20
Moses built an a. Ex 17:15

Am Exist; be. The reply to Moses' question for the name of the Deity, "I AM THAT I AM" (Ex 3:14), indicates that the Lord makes Himself present as He wills.

altar

Amen Verily; so be it (Mt 6:13; Rev 3:14).

Amos (ā'mos) A prophet of Israel; the first to proclaim that God is the ruler of the whole universe; foretold the downfall of the Northern Kingdom. The OT book of Amos is the third of the 12 Minor Prophets.

Ananias (ăn-a-nī-as) 1. A Christian of Jerusalem who lost his life for lying and attempting to hold back part of the price of property he had sold (Acts 5:1–10). 2. A Christian of Damascus who received Paul into Christian fellowship (Acts 9:10–17; 22:12–16). 3. A Jewish high priest before whom Paul was tried in Jerusalem (Acts 23:2; 24:1).

Ancient of Days The judge in Daniel's vision; probably intended to be God Himself (Dan 7:9, 13, 22).

Andrew One of the first of the 12 apostles of Jesus; brother of Simon Peter (Mt 4:18; 10:2–4; Mk 1:16–20, 29; 3:16–19; 13:3; Lk 6:14–16; Jn 1:35–42, 44; 6:5–9; 12:20–22; Acts 1:13). He was a former disciple of John the Baptist (Jn 1:35–40).

angel A heavenly messenger.
an a. spake unto me 1 Kgs 13:18
a little lower than the a. Ps 8:5
a. came and ministered Mt 4:11
the a. Gabriel was sent Lk 1:26
a. of the bottomless pit Rev 9:11

angel of the Lord The heavenly messenger whose presence is evidence of God Himself (Gen 16:7; Ex 3:2; Num 22:23; 1 Kgs 19:7; Mt 28:2; Lk 1:11; 2:9).

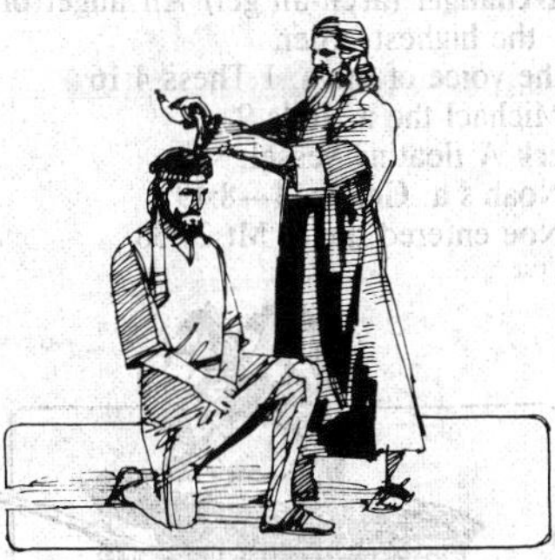

anoint

anoint To consecrate; to pour oil upon in a ceremony.
a. my head with oil Ps 23:5
to a. my body Mk 14:8
thou didst not a. Lk 7:46

antichrist (ăn'tĭ-chrīst) Opponent or enemy of Christ.
He is a., that denieth 1 Jn 2:22
deceiver and an a. 2 Jn 7

Antioch (ăn'tĭ-ŏch) 1. In Syria; the name "Christian" was first used here (Acts 11:26). 2. In Pisidia; visited by Paul and Barnabas (Acts 13:14–52).

apostle (a-pŏs'tle) One of the 12 disciples chosen by Jesus (Mt 10:2–4) or certain other early Christian leaders (Acts 14:14; Rom 16:7; Gal 1:1).

Arabia; Arabians The NW part of the large peninsula in SW Asia; scene of many biblical events. The peoples of the area were nomads.

Arameans (ăr-a-mē'ans) A Semitic people, traditionally descendants of Shem, the oldest son of Noah (Gen 10:22, 23). They were nomads, wandering along the W side of the Syrian desert.

Ararat (ăr′a-răt) The mountain on which the ark came to rest after the Flood (Gen 8:4); the land of Ararat is Armenia.

archangel (ärch-ān′gel) An angel of the highest order.
the voice of the a. 1 Thess 4:16
Michael the a. Jude 9

ark A floating vessel; ship.
Noah's a. Gen 6:14—8:19
Noe entered the a. Mt 24:38

ark of the covenant

ark of the covenant The chest which held the two stone tablets on which were inscribed the Ten Commandments (Ex 25:10; 1 Kgs 8:6; 2 Chr 5:2).

Armageddon (är-ma-gĕd′don) The place of the final great struggle between the forces of good and evil (Rev 16:16).

Artaxerxes (är-ta-xĕr′xes) The name of two Persian kings: the first, mentioned in Ezra 7 and Neh 2; 13; his grandson, the second, may have been the builder of the palace described in Esther 1:5, 6.

Ascension (a-scĕn′sion) The return of the risen Christ to heaven (Lk 24:51; Acts 1:9) on the fortieth day after the Resurrection.

Asher (ăsh′er) The eighth son of Jacob, the second by Zilpah; one of the 12 tribes of Israel (Gen 30:12ff).

Asia (ā′sia) A Roman province in the western part of what we call Asia Minor (Acts 16:6; 20:18; 1 Pet 1:1; Rev 1:4).

Assyria (as-syr′ĭ-a) One of the two civilizations that flourished in Mesopotamia from the third millennium B.C. till about 600 B.C.

B

Baal (bā′al) One of the fertility gods of Canaan. There were many local Baals. Elijah met the prophets of Baal in a contest (1 Kgs 18:1–40).

Babel (bā′bel) Hebrew form of the name "Babylon," capital of Babylonia; site of the tower of Babel (Gen 11:1–9).

Babylonia (băb-y-lō′nĭ-a) One of the two civilizations that flourished in Mesopotamia from the third millennium B.C. till about 600 B.C.

baptism A ceremony in which one enters the church family. It is a way of showing that you have been washed free of sin by the death and rising from the dead of Jesus Christ.
John's b. of Jesus Mt 3:13–17
b. by the disciples Jn 4:1, 2

Barabbas (ba-răb′bas) A robber held by the Roman authorities in prison at the time of Jesus' trial; Pilate freed him and condemned Jesus to death (Mt 27:20–26; Mk 15:7–15; Lk 23:18–25; Jn 18:39, 40).

Barnabas (bär′na-bas) The surname given by the apostles to Joses or Joseph, a Levite of Cyprus, who was sent by them to Antioch to confirm the church there. Accompanied Paul on his first missionary journey (Acts 4:36, 37; 9:27; 11:22, 25, 30; 12:25; 13:1–13, 43–52; 14:12, 14, 20; 15:2ff; 1 Cor 9:6; Gal 2:1, 9, 13; Col 4:10).

Bartholomew (bär-thŏl′o-mew) One of

the 12 apostles of Jesus (Mt 10:3; Mk 3:18; Lk 6:14; Acts 1:13).

Baruch (bâr'uch) Jeremiah's scribe, or secretary (Jer 36:4ff).

beam A log; a piece of timber.

cast out the b. Mt 7:5

beard The growth of hair on the lower part of a man's face. The Hebrews were forbidden to cut the edges of their beards (Lev 19:27). The shaving off of beards was an indignity (2 Sam 10:4, 5).

Beatitudes (bē-ăt'ĭ-tudes) The blessings listed by Jesus in the Sermon on the Mount (Mt 5:3–12; Lk 6:20–23).

Benjamin The youngest son of Jacob. His mother, Rachel, died at his birth (Gen 35:18). Especially beloved by his father and by Joseph, his only full brother (Gen 42:4, 36; 43:14–16, 29, 34; 44:12; 45:12, 14, 22). Ancestor of the tribe of Benjamin, the smallest of the 12 tribes of Israel.

Bethany (bĕth'a-ny) A small village on the E slope of the Mount of Olives, about one and one-half mi. E of Jerusalem. From here Jesus made His triumphal entry into Jerusalem (Mk 11:1–11); the home of Simon the leper (Mt 26:6; Mk 14:3); home of Lazarus, Mary, and Martha (Jn 11:1–44); site of Jesus' final parting from His disciples (Lk 24:50, 51).

Beth-el (bĕth-ĕl) City 14 mi. N of Jerusalem. Near here Abraham built an altar (Gen 12:8; 13:3, 4); here Jacob's name was changed to Israel (Gen 35:10–15); the ark of the covenant rested here (Judg 20:18–28); Jeroboam made it a place of idolatry (1 Kgs 12:29—13:32), which Josiah destroyed (2 Kgs 23:4–15).

Bethlehem A very old town about six mi. SSW of Jerusalem; the birthplace of Jesus (Mt 2:1–16; Lk 2:4–15; Jn 7:42); also associated with David (1 Sam 16:1–13; 17:12, 15; 20:6, 28), Ruth (1:1, 2, 19, 22; 2:4; 4:11), and other persons of the OT.

birthright Privilege of the firstborn of a family.

Esau despised his b. Gen 25:34

blood The life-giving fluid of the body. In the OT it is regarded as the seat of life; but since shed blood signifies death, the word is used of both life and death.

you shall eat no manner of b. Lev 7:26; Deut 12:16

this is my b. Mt 26:28; Mk 14:24

new testament in my b. Lk 22:20

eateth my flesh, and drinketh my b. Jn 6:54

redemption through his b. Eph 1:7; Col 1:14

precious b. of Christ 1 Pet 1:19

Boaz (bō'az) A wealthy Bethlehemite who married Ruth (2:1—4:22).

body The physical human being or animal. The church is called "the body of Christ" as the living spiritual community of which Christ is the head and all believers are members. At the Lord's Supper, Jesus broke bread to represent His body given in sacrifice for sinners.

touches the dead b. Num 19:11

light of the b. is the eye Mt 6:22

this is my b. Mt 26:26; Mk 14:22; Lk 22:19; 1 Cor 11:24

many members in one b. Rom 12:4

you are the b. of Christ 1 Cor 12:27

bread A food made of a dough of flour or meal and water and baked; sustenance in general. Often used in offerings by OT peoples. In the NT, also used in reference to the coming of the kingdom of God or to Jesus Himself.

not live by b. only Deut 8:3

shall eat unleavened b. Deut 16:8

Cast thy b. upon the Eccles 11:1

not live by b. alone Mt 4:4

Give us this day our daily b. Mt 6:11; Lk 11:3

eat b. in the kingdom Lk 14:15

the true b. from heaven Jn 6:32
I am the b. of life Jn 6:35
bread, breaking of Since the earliest form of the Lord's Supper involved the "breaking of bread," the term has been used for worship in general (Acts 2:42).

C

Cain Son of Adam; murdered his brother Abel (Gen 4:2ff); prototype of wicked men (1 Jn 3:12; Jude 11).
Calvary (căl'va-ry) Place of Jesus' crucifixion (Mk 15:22). *See* Golgotha.
Canaan; Canaanites (cā'naan; cā'naan-ītes) The land between the Jordan River and the Mediterranean Sea and that part of Syria along the coast (Phoenicia). Peopled by Semites with whom the Hebrews probably merged.

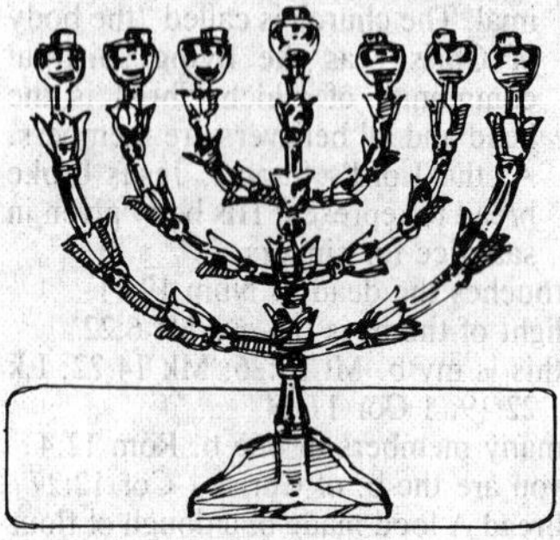

candlestick

candlestick Lampstand, particularly the seven-branched lampstand of the Tabernacle and the Temple, and the symbolic one of Revelation.
make a c. of pure gold Ex 25:31
I saw seven golden c. Rev 1:12
Capernaum (ca-pĕr'na-um) A city on the NW shore of the Sea of Galilee. Jesus lived there (Mk 2:1); home of Peter and Andrew (Mt 8:14); here Jesus healed the man with an unclean spirit (Mk 1:21–28) and the paralytic (Mk 2:1–12) and held discussions about true greatness (Mk 9:33–37) and paying the half-shekel tax (Mt 17:24–27).
child A young person of either sex.
a c. is known by his Prov 20:11
unto us a c. is born Isa 9:6
little c. shall lead Isa 11:6
children Young persons of either sex.
become as little c. Mt 18:3
Suffer little c., and Mt 19:14
Christians Followers of Christ.
called C. first in Antioch Acts 11:26
church The people of God; those destined to inherit the kingdom of God. Also, any local group of believers.
I will build my c. Mt 16:18
Christ is the head of the c. Eph 5:23
head of the body, the c. Col 1:18
the seven c. Rev 1:4, 11, 20
cloud A visible mass of water particles in the air above the earth.
pillar of a c. Ex 13:21; Num 12:5
c. covered the mount Ex 24:15
Colosse; Colossians (co-lŏs'se; co-lŏs'-sians) A city in Asia Minor. Paul wrote an epistle to the Christians of this city.
Comforter The Holy Ghost; the intercessor promised by Christ to help and guide believers (Jn 14:26; 15:26; 16:7).
commandment Any of the Ten Commandments or laws given to Moses by God at Mount Sinai (Ex 20:1–17; Deut 5:6–21); other OT laws.
keep the c. Mt 19:17
which is the great c. Mt 22:36
you love me, keep my c. Jn 14:15
congregation An assembly; gathering.
c. of the righteous Ps 1:5
God standeth in the c. Ps 82:1
in the c. of saints Ps 149:1
converted Changed, as one's religion or belief.
Except ye be c. Mt 18:3
Repent . . . and be c. Acts 3:19
Corinth; Corinthians (côr'ĭnth;

co-rĭn′-thĭ-ans) A city of S Greece, capital of the Roman province of Achaia. Paul wrote two epistles to the Christians of Corinth.

covenant (cŏv′e-nant) A binding agreement. The great covenant between God and Israel was made at Sinai (Ex 24:3–8); the tablets on which the Ten Commandments were engraved were called "the tables of the covenant" (Deut 9:11). The chest in which these tablets were placed was called the "ark of the covenant" (Ex 25:10). The new covenant came into being through the blood of Christ.

covet To long for; desire, particularly someone else's property.

shalt not c. Ex 20:17; Deut 5:21
Thou shalt not c. Rom 7:7; 13:9

creation The act of God in making heaven and earth and bringing forth all life; the whole universe.

the story of c. Gen 1:1—2:25
c. which God created Mk 13:19
the whole c. groaneth Rom 8:22

creator The maker; originator; hence, **Creator:** God; the Lord.

Remember now thy C. Eccles 12:1
C. of the ends of the Isa 40:28
creature more than the C. Rom 1:25

creature Any living thing that God has made.

every living c. Gen 1:21
called every living c. Gen 2:19
every c. of God is good 1 Tim 4:4

cross An upright post with cross-beam on which victims of execution were nailed; used by the Romans. A symbol of Christianity.

he that taketh not his c. Mt 10:38
take up his c. Mt 16:24; Mk 8:34
come down from the c. Mt 27:40
Simon . . . to bear his c. Mk 15:21
stood by the c. of Jesus Jn 19:25

crown A headdress of gold, precious stones, etc.; a wreath encircling the head.

a c. of glory Prov 4:9; 16:31
virtuous woman is a c. Prov 12:4
c. of thorns Mt 27:29; Mk 15:17; Jn 19:2, 5
corruptible c. 1 Cor 9:25

Crucifixion, the (crū-cĭ-fĭx′ion) Jesus' execution on the cross by the Romans at the instigation of the Jewish leaders (Mt 27; Mk 15; Lk 23; Jn 19).

crucify (crū′cĭ-fy) To put to death by fastening to a cross.

scourge, and to c. Mt 20:19
Let him be c. Mt 27:22
C. him Mk 15:13; Lk 23:21; Jn 19:6

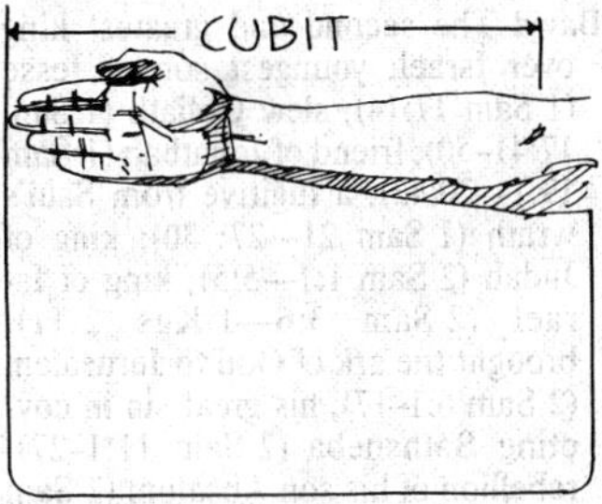

cubit

cubit A measure of length of about 18 inches.

add one c. unto Mt 6:27; Lk 12:25

cup A vessel from which to drink.

My c. runs over Ps 23:5
c. of cold water Mt 10:42; Mk 9:41
drink of the c. Mt 20:22; Mk 10:39
outside of the c. Mt 23:25
took the c. Mt 26:27; Mk 14:23; Lk 22:17; 1 Cor 11:25
c. pass from me Mt 26:39; Mk 14:36; Lk 22:42
c. which my Father Jn 18:11

Cyprus (cy′prus) A large island in the Mediterranean 41 mi. from the coast of Asia Minor; home of Barnabas (Acts 4:36); visited by Paul (Acts 13:4–12; 21:3).

D

Damascus (dă-măs′cus) A very ancient city, capital of Syria; in OT times the capital of the Aramean kingdom. Site of Saul's conversion (Acts 9:1–22).

Dan The fifth son of Jacob, born of Bilhah (Gen 30:1–6); one of the 12 tribes of Israel.

Daniel The Jewish prophet at the Babylonian court about whom the OT book of Daniel is written. Interpreted dreams (2:1–45) and the handwriting on the wall (5:17–30); saved by God from the lions (6:16–24).

David The second and greatest king over Israel; youngest son of Jesse (1 Sam 17:14); slew Goliath (1 Sam 17:41–50); friend of Jonathan (1 Sam 19:1—20:42); a fugitive from Saul's wrath (1 Sam 21—27; 30); king of Judah (2 Sam 1:1—5:5); king of Israel (2 Sam 3:6—1 Kgs 2:11); brought the ark of God to Jerusalem (2 Sam 6:1–17); his great sin in coveting Bathsheba (2 Sam 11:1–27); rebellion of his son Absalom (2 Sam 14–18); his psalm of thanksgiving (2 Sam 22); names Solomon, his son, to succeed him (1 Kgs 1:11—2:12).

day of the Lord In the OT, the day when God punishes evil (Amos 5:18–20); a day of universal disaster (Isa 2; 13; 24; Zeph 1:7–18; 2:2, 3; 3:8). In the NT, the day of the last judgment and the end of the world (1 Cor 4:5; 5:5; 1 Thess 5:2; Rev 16:14).

Dead Sea The salt lake at the mouth of the Jordan River. Biblical names: "Salt Sea" (Gen 14:3; Num 34:3, 12; Deut 3:17; Josh 3:16; 12:3; 15:2, 5; 18:19); "eastern sea" (Joel 2:20).

death The condition of being without life; the act of dying. Symbol of the final state of the unsaved (Jn 8:51; Rom 6:23; Rev 20:6), and of the power that rules over man in the age of sin (Rom 5:14; Rev 6:8).

valley of the shadow of d. Ps 23:4
swallow up d. in victory Isa 25:8
not taste of d. Mt 16:28; Mk 9:1; Lk 9:27
d., where is thy sting 1 Cor 15:55

Deborah 1. Rebekah's nurse and companion (Gen 35:8). 2. An early "judge" of Israel; aroused the scattered tribes to opposition to Canaanite oppression; Song of Deborah (Judg 5:2–31) celebrates her achievement.

debts Obligations; anything owed to another.

forgive us our d. Mt 6:12

Dedication, Feast of An eight-day festival observing the victories of Judas Maccabbeus and the purification and rededication of the Temple (Jn 10:22). *Also called* Feast of Lights; Hanukkah; Chanukah.

Delilah (de-lī′lah) A woman from the Valley of Sorek; betrayed Samson to the Philistines (Judg 16:4–22).

devil An evil spirit.

sacrifices unto d. Lev 17:7; Deut 32:17
possessed with d. Mt 4:24; 9:32; 12:22
He hath a d. Mt 11:18; Lk 7:33
one of you is a d. Jn 6:70

Devil The chief demon, Satan.

Jesus . . . tempted by the d. Mt 4:1–11
serpent of old, called the D. Rev 12:9; 20:2

disciple (dĭs-cī′ple) A learner; a follower, particularly one who follows Jesus Christ.

his twelve d. Mt 10:1; Lk 6:13
sent two of his d. Mt 11:2
d. rebuked them Mt 19:13
d. were called Christians first Acts 11:26

door Entrance way.

will pass over the d. Ex 12:23
and the d. was shut Mt 25:10
I am the d. Jn 10:9
d. was opened in heaven Rev 4:1

drink To swallow a liquid; the liquid so swallowed.

not d. wine nor strong d. Lev 10:9
strong d. is raging Prov 20:1

d.; for to morrow we shall die Isa 22:13
D. ye all of it Mt 26:27
shall d. neither wine Lk 1:15
dust Fine, dry, powdery earth.
God formed man of the d. Gen 2:7
d. thou art, and unto d. Gen 3:19

E

earth The planet on which we live; the soil.
God created the . . . e. Gen 1:1
The e. is the LORD's Ps 24:1
meek shall inherit the e. Ps 37:11
the e. is my footstool Isa 66:1
meek: . . . shall inherit the e. Mt 5:5
Thy will be done in e. Mt 6:10
on e. peace, good will Lk 2:14
new heaven and a new e. Rev 21:1
eat To consume food.
shall not e. of every Gen 3:1
e. and drink; for to morrow Isa 22:13
Take, e.; this is my body Mt 26:26
Eden, Garden of A garden of trees planted by the Lord (Gen 2:8) in which Adam and Eve first lived; actual site unknown; symbolically identified with Paradise.
Edom; Edomites (ē'dom; ē'do-mītes) A country to the E and S of Israel; its people had a close relationship to the Israelites, being descendants of Esau.
Egypt A land of NE Africa. Temporary home of Abraham (Gen 12:10–20); Joseph sold "into Egypt" (Gen 37:28, 36); Joseph as governor (Gen 41:37—47:26); Israel in bondage (Ex 1:1—12:36); the Exodus 12:37—14:31); Jesus taken there (Mt 2:13).
elders Seniors; among the Jews, the old and mature men who were civil and religious leaders; in the Christian church, leaders of the local church.
seventy of the e. of Israel Ex 24:9
tradition of the e. Mt 15:2; Mk 7:3
ordained them e. in every Acts 14:23
the e. who rule well 1 Tim 5:17
four and twenty e. Rev 4:4
Eli (ē'lī) The priest of Shiloh to whom the boy Samuel was brought (1 Sam 1—4).
Elijah; Elias (ē-lī'jah; ē-lī'as) A prophet from Tishbeh to Gilead in the Northern Kingdom; fed by ravens (1 Kgs 17:6); performs miracles (1 Kgs 17:14–16, 17–24; 20:30; 2 Kgs 1:10–12; 2:8); taken up by a whirlwind into heaven (2 Kgs 2:11). Malachi prophesies his return before the day of the Lord (Mal 4:5). In NT times, some thought Jesus to be Elijah (Mt 16:14; Lk 9:8); others thought John the Baptist to be Elijah (Jn 1:21). In the early church, John was regarded as the heir to the spirit and power of Elijah (Lk 1:17) or as Elijah reborn (Mt 11:14; 17:10–13). At the Transfiguration, Elijah appears with Moses (Mt 17:3, 4; Mk 9:4, 5).
Elisabeth (e-lĭs'a-bĕth) Wife of the priest, Zacharias, and mother of John the Baptist (Lk 1:5–66).
Elisha (ē-lī'sha) A prophet; disciple and successor to Elijah; performed many miracles (2 Kgs 2:14–24; 3:16–20; 4:2–7, 32–44; 5:10–14, 27; 6:5–7, 18–20); contact with his bones revives a dead man (2 Kgs 13:20, 21).
enemies Foes; opponents.
presence of my e. Ps 23:5
Love your e. Mt 5:44; Lk 6:27, 35
Ephesus; Ephesians (ĕph'e-sus; e-phē'-sians) A seaport in the Roman province of Asia; visited by Paul on his second and third journeys. Paul's NT epistle to the Ephesians seems to be a general letter to the churches of Asia Minor.
Ephraim (ē'phra-im) The younger son of Joseph; adopted by Jacob (Gen 48:1ff); ancestor of one of the most powerful of the 12 tribes of Israel.

Esau (ē′sau) Son of Isaac and Rebekah who traded his birthright to his younger twin brother Jacob for a bowl of pottage (Gen 25:22–34; 27; 33:1–16).

Esther A Jewess of Shushan who became Ahasuerus' queen and thwarted a plot to kill all the Jews, later commemorated by the Jewish festival of Purim. The book of Esther tells the story.

Eve The first woman; wife of Adam (Gen 2:21–25); tempted by the serpent (Gen 3:1–5).

everlasting Eternal; never ending.
the e. God Gen 21:33; Isa 40:28
underneath are the e. arms Deut 33:27
into e. fire Mt 18:8; 25:41
inherit e. life Mt 19:29
have e. life Jn 3:16, 36; 5:24

evil Wickedness; slanderous or injurious actions.
tree . . . of good and e. Gen 2:9
I will fear no e. Ps 23:4
Depart from e. Ps 37:27
deliver us from the e. Mt 6:13
what e. has he done Mt 27:23; Mk 15:14; Lk 23:22
love of money is a root of all kinds of e. 1 Tim 6:10

Exodus The going out of Israel from Egypt as recorded in the second book of the OT. It includes the deliverance from slavery, the wandering through the wilderness, the covenant with the Lord at Mount Sinai, and the provision of the tabernacle and ark of the covenant.

eye The organ of sight.
e. of them both were opened Gen 3:7
e. for e. Ex 21:24; Lev 24:20; Deut 19:21; Mt 5:38
lift up my e. to the hills Ps 121:1
wise in your own e. Prov 3:7
if thy right e. offend thee Mt 5:29; 18:9; Mk 9:47

Ezekiel (e-zē′kĭel) A major Jewish prophet; author of the OT book of Ezekiel; one of the captives of the Babylonian exile. Vision of God (1:4–28); parable of the two eagles and the vine (17:1–24); the fall of Jerusalem (24:1–27); various prophecies about other nations (25—32).

Ezra (ĕz′ra) A priest and scribe; supposed author of the OT book of Ezra, which details the first return of the Israelites from Babylon and the rebuilding of the Temple.

F

face The front of the head; the surface or top side; frequently used to indicate the presence of God. Among the Hebrews, "seeking the face of God" referred to attendance at public worship (Ps 27:8).
on the f. of the waters Gen 1:2
In the sweat of thy f. thou shalt Gen 3:19
LORD spake unto Moses f. to f. Ex 33:11
make his f. shine upon you Num 6:25
Seek ye my f. Ps 27:8
f. of the LORD is against Ps 34:16
the f. of my Father Mt 18:10
my messenger before thy f. Mk 1:2
but then f. to f. 1 Cor 13:12

faith Belief or trust in someone or something. Among Christians, belief in the Holy Trinity.
thy f. hath made thee Mt 9:22; Mk 5:34; 10:52; Lk 8:48; 17:19
f. as a . . . mustard seed Mt 17:20; Lk 17:6
just shall live by f. Rom 1:17
man is justified by f. Rom 3:28; 5:1; Gal 2:16; 3:24
f. is counted for righteousness Rom 4:5
saved through f. Eph 2:8
one Lord, one f., one Eph 4:5
f. is the substance of Heb 11:1
f. without works is dead Jas 2:17, 20

fast To go without food.
when ye f., be not Mt 6:16
Pharisees f. oft Mt 9:14; Mk 2:18

father The male parent or ancestor. In the OT, used of God as the One who made a covenant with the people of Israel.
be a f. of many nations Gen 17:4
Honour thy f. and Ex 20:12; Lev 19:3; Deut 5:16
that curseth his f. Ex 21:17; Lev 20:9
David slept with his f. 1 Kgs 2:10
f. of the fatherless, . . . is God Ps 68:5
LORD, thou art our f. Isa 64:8
Father The first Person of the Holy Trinity.
your F. which is in heaven Mt 5:16, 45
Our F. which art in Mt 6:9; Lk 11:2
Abba, F. Mk 14:36; Rom 8:15; Gal 4:6
baptizing them in the name of the F. Mt 28:19
about My F.'s business Lk 2:49
who the F., is but the Son Lk 10:22
the Promise of My F. Lk 24:49
the only begotten of the F. Jn 1:14
one F.—God Jn 8:41
I and My F. are one Jn 10:30
cometh unto the F., but by me Jn 14:6
ask of the F. in my name Jn 15:16
fear of the LORD The term used in the OT for "religion" (Deut 6:2; 10:20; 28:58; Ps 111:10; Prov 1:7; 8:13; Eccles 12:13). In the NT, "those who fear the Lord" are the faithful (Lk 1:50; 18:4) or converts to Judaism (Acts 10:2; 13:26)
fight Struggle against; do battle.
F. the good f. of faith 1 Tim 6:12
first and the last, the A title used by Isaiah (41:4; 44:6; 48:12) to convey the idea of God's everlasting sovereignty and eternal majesty and power. The same title is used in Revelation (1:11, 17; 2:8; 22:13) implying God's sovereign lordship manifest in Jesus Christ.
firstborn, firstfruits The eldest; the earliest fruits harvested. The consecration of the first of the male children, of animals, and of fruits was an important part of the religion of Israel.
LORD smote all the f. Ex 12:29
flesh The soft part of the human body; all mankind.
All f. is grass Isa 40:6; 1 Pet 1:24
but the f. is weak Mt 26:41; Mk 14:38
the Word was made f. Jn 1:14
Flood, the The covering of the earth with water because of man's wickedness. Noah's family and the animals of the earth are saved in an ark (Gen 6:1—8:19).
fool A silly or senseless person.
f. despise wisdom Prov 1:7
f. is right in his own eyes Prov 12:15
folly of f. is deceit Prov 14:8
f. for Christ's sake 1 Cor 4:10
foolish Silly; unwise. Parables of Jesus deal with:
f. and wise maidens Mt 25:1–13
f. rich man Lk 12:16–21
f. son returns Lk 15:11–32
forgive To pardon; show mercy to.
f. us . . . for we also f. Mt 6:12; Lk 11:4
f., and ye shall be Lk 6:37
Father, f. them Lk 23:34
fountain The source, as the spring from which water flows. The Lord is called "the fountain of living waters" (Jer 2:13; cf. Jn 4:14) and the "fountain of life" (Ps 36:9).
friend An associate whom one likes.
the rich hath many f. Prov 14:20
A f. loveth at all times Prov 17:17
a f. that sticketh closer Prov 18:24
furniture Equipment of any sort.
f. (= utensils) Ex 31:7–9

G

Gabriel (gā'brĭ-el) An angel of high rank (Dan 8:16; 9:21; Lk 1:19, 26).
Gad (găd) The seventh son of Jacob; born of Leah's maid Zilpah (Gen 30:11); ancestor of the tribe of Gad.
Galatia; Galatians (ga-lā'tia; ga-lā'-tians) a region and Roman province in Asia Minor. Paul, in the NT epis-

tle to the Galatians, tells of his own conversion.

Galilee (găl'i-lee) A region of N Palestine, including the Sea of Galilee on the E side. OT references include: Solomon gives 20 cities of Galilee to Hiram (1 Kgs 9:11); the prophecy of Isaiah (9:1) concerning "Galilee of the Gentiles" (cf. Mt 4:13). Called "land of Gennesaret" (Mt 14:34; Mk 6:53). Jesus' active ministry was almost entirely within its borders.

Galilee, Sea of The larger of the two fresh-water lakes on the Jordan River system. Site of miracles: the great catch of fish (Lk 5:1–11); Jesus stills the sea (Mt 8:23–26; Mk 4:35–39; Lk 8:22–24); Jesus walks on the sea (Mt 14:25–27; Mk 6:48–51; Jn 6:19–20). Also called "Chinnereth" (Num 34:11; Deut 3:17; Josh 13:27); "Chinneroth" (Josh 12:3); "Gennesaret" (Lk 5:1); and "Tiberias" (Jn 6:1; 21:1).

gate Doorway.
Enter into his g. with Ps 100:4
Enter ye in by the strait g. Mt 7:13

Gennesaret (gĕn-nĕs'a-rĕt) A fertile plain on the shore of the Sea of Galilee. *See also* Galilee.

Gethsemane (gĕth-sĕm'a-ne) A garden on the Mount of Olives where Jesus prayed and where He was betrayed by Judas (Mt 26:36; Mk 14:32).

Ghost, Holy The third Person of the Trinity; the Holy Spirit; that divine Spirit, referred to in the OT as "Spirit of the Lord" or "Spirit of God," through which men receive power, particularly effective through Jesus Christ in bringing men into fellowship with God. Some Bible translators use "Holy Spirit" rather than "Holy Ghost."
in the name of the Holy G. Mt 28:19
baptize with the Holy G. Mt 3:11; Mk 1:8; Lk 3:16; Jn 1:33
be filled with the Holy G. Lk 1:15
Holy G. was not yet given Jn 7:39
which is the Holy G. Jn 14:26
promise of the Holy G. Acts 2:33
witness in the Holy G. Rom 9:1
but by the Holy G. 1 Cor 12:3
communion of the Holy G. 2 Cor 13:14

Gideon (gĭd'e-on) A prophet of Israel especially favored by the Lord with revelations and unusual powers (Judg 6:11—8:35).

Gilead (gĭl'e-ad) A rugged, mountainous region E of the Jordan. Possibly also a city (Judg 10:17; Hos 6:8) and a tribe (Judg 5:17).

Gilgal (gĭl'găl) The name of several places in the OT, one of them a city of the tribe of Benjamin, near Jericho; site of the first encampment of the Israelites after crossing the Jordan (Josh 3; 4); there Saul was made king (1 Sam 11:14, 15).

give To bestow; hand over to another.
G. us this day our daily Mt 6:11
it shall be g. you Mt 7:7; Lk 6:38; 11:9
more blessed to g. than Acts 20:35

giver One who bestows.
God loveth a cheerful g. 2 Cor 9:7

glad tidings Good news; the gospel. (Used in Lk 1:19; 8:1; Acts 13:32; and Rom 10:15).

glory of the Lord The word *glory* is sometimes synonymous with "God" to avoid referring to God in human form (Ex 33:22); used of the fiery presence at Sinai (Ex 24:16) and of the radiance that filled the Tabernacle (Ex 40:34). In the NT, used of the divine Presence (Mk 8:38; Lk 2:9), of the quality of Jesus' appearance in His transfiguration (Lk 9:31), and of Jesus' second coming (Mt 25:31).

gods Idols.
have no other g. before Ex 20:3

Golden Rule A commandment given by Jesus in the Sermon on the Mount (Mt 7:12; Lk 6:31).

Golgotha (gŏl'go-tha) Place where

Jesus was crucified (Mt 27:33; Mk 15:22; Jn 19:17).

Gomorrah (go-môr′rah) One of the two cities destroyed by the Lord because of their wickedness (Gen 19:24–28).

gospel Good news; glad tidings. Hence, the teachings of Jesus and of the apostles. The NT books of Matthew, Mark, Luke, and John are called the Gospels.

g. of the kingdom Mt 4:23
the g. of Jesus Christ Mk 1:1
and believe the g. Mk 1:15
preach the g. Lk 4:18
hear the word of the g. Acts 15:7
the g. of Christ Rom 1:16

grace OT usage: "favor" in the expression "found g. in the eyes or sight" (Gen 6:8). In NT usage: "the unmerited and abundant gift of God's love and favor to man," particularly made effective in Jesus Christ for the Christian. Used by Paul as an opening and farewell greeting.

g. and truth came by Jesus Christ Jn 1:17
g. of God, and the gift by g. Rom 5:15
G. be unto you and 1 Cor 1:3; Eph 1:2
by the g. of God I am 1 Cor 15:10
g. of God in vain 2 Cor 6:1
g. of our Lord Jesus 2 Cor 8:9; 13:14
by g. ye are saved Eph 2:5

H

Habakkuk (ha-băk′kuk) A prophet of Judah; the OT book which bears his name is the eighth of the 12 Minor Prophets.

Haggai (hăg′gaī) A Jewish prophet contemporary with Zechariah; the tenth of the 12 Minor Prophets of the OT.

hallowed Made sacred; consecrated.

H. be thy name Mt 6:9

hands, laying on of A symbolic ritual: 1. Of divine blessing (Mt 19:15), sometimes accompanied by the gift of the Holy Spirit (Acts 19:6). 2. Of divine healing (Mk 7:32). 3. Of consecration of a man for a specific office (Acts 13:3; 1 Tim 4:14). 4. Of dedication of an animal as for sacrifice (Lev 16:21).

Hanukkah (hä′nuk-kah) Hebrew word for "dedication." *See* Dedication, Feast of.

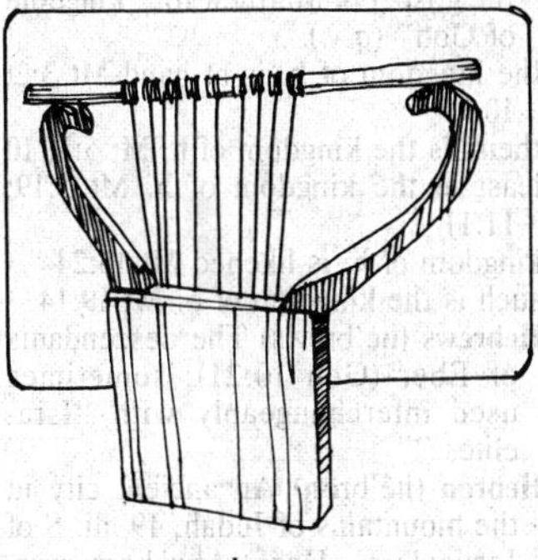

harp

harp A stringed musical instrument.

handle the h. and organ Gen 4:21
David took an h., and 1 Sam 16:23

heart The physical organ thought of as being the seat of the affections.

A broken and a contrite h. Ps 51:17
Blessed are the pure in h. Mt 5:8
not your h. be troubled Jn 14:1

heaven A term sometimes used for "God."

I have sinned against h. Lk 15:18
it be given him from h. Jn 3:27

heaven; heavens 1. The sky; the space in which the sun, the moon, and the stars move; the firmament.

God called the firmament H. Gen 1:8
he hath garnished the h. Job 26:13
h. declare the glory of God Ps 19:1
stretchest out the h. Ps 104:2; Isa 40:22
saw h. opened, and Acts 10:11

2. The place where God, the risen Christ, the angels, and the saints re-

side; the future home of the redeemed.
new h. and Isa 65:17; Rev 21:1
Till h. and earth pass Mt 5:18
Father which art in h. Mt 6:9; Lk 11:12
looked . . . toward h. as Acts 1:10
eternal in the h. 2 Cor 5:1

heaven, kingdom of Used throughout the gospel of Matthew for "kingdom of God" (q.v.).
the kingdom of h. is at hand Mt 3:2; 10:7
theirs is the kingdom of h. Mt 5:3, 10
least in the kingdom of h. Mt 5:19; 11:11
kingdom of h. is likened Mt 13:24
such is the kingdom of h. Mt 19:14

Hebrews (hē'brews) The descendants of Eber (Gen 10:21); sometimes used interchangeably with "Israelites."

Hebron (hē'bron) An ancient city in the mountains of Judah, 19 mi. S of Jerusalem. Here Abraham purchased a cave for a family burial place (Gen 23:1–20). David's capital city for the first seven and one-half years of his reign (2 Sam 2:1—5:5).

Herod (hĕr'od) 1. Ruler of Jewish Palestine under Rome (37–4 B.C.); sent the wise men to search out the infant Jesus (Mt 2:1–9). 2. **Herod Antipas:** Tetrarch of Galilee (4 B.C.–A.D. 39); put John the Baptist to death (Mt 14:1–12; Mk 6:14–29; Lk 3:19, 20; 9:7–9).

Hezekiah (hĕz-e-kī'ah) The name of four persons in the OT, one of whom was king of Judah 715–687 B.C. (2 Kgs 18—20; 2 Chr 29—32; Isa 36—39).

Holy Ghost *See* Ghost, Holy.

holy of holies The innermost room of the Temple or Tabernacle in which the ark of the Testimony was kept.

holy sepulchre The garden tomb belonging to Joseph of Arimathea where Jesus was buried after His crucifixion (Mt 27:60; Mk 15:46; Lk 23:53; Jn 19:41).

Holy Spirit *See* Ghost, Holy.

honour To esteem; to give respect.
H. thy father and thy mother Ex 20:12; Mt 15:4
before h. is humility Prov 15:33
prophet is not without h. Mt 13:57
h. to whom h. Rom 13:7

Horeb, Mount (hō'rĕb) A sacred mountain (Ex 3:1; Deut 1:2, 6, 9; 4:10; 5:2) which may be the same mountain as Mount Sinai.

Hosea (hō-se'a) A prophet of Israel; the first of the 12 Minor Prophets of the OT.

host Army.
chief captain of his h. Gen 21:22

host, heavenly 1. The celestial bodies—the sun, moon, and stars.
all the h. of heaven Deut 4:19
worshiped all the h. of 2 Kgs 17:16
all the h. of heaven Jer 8:2
2. The mighty army in God's service, including the angels.
all the h. of them Gen 2:1
heavens, with all their h. Neh 9:6
the h. of them by Ps 33:6
bringeth out their h. Isa 40:26
worship the h. of heaven Acts 7:42

hosts, LORD of God, first as Leader of the armies of Israel (1 Sam 17:45), then as Leader of the "heavenly host" (q.v.).
LORD of h., he is the King Ps 24:10
LORD of h. is his name Isa 47:4; 51:15; Jer 10:16; 31:35
name is The God of h. Amos 5:27

house 1. A dwelling place.
not covet thy neighbour's h. Ex 20:17
Set thine h. in order 2 Kgs 20:1
dwell in the h. of the LORD Ps 23:6
Father's h. are many mansions Jn 14:2
2. A family group; a nation.
me and my house, we will serve Josh 24:15
h. divided against itself Mt 12:25; Lk 11:17

I

idol A false god; an image or figure regarded as an object of worship.
Turn ye not unto i. Lev 19:4
that regard lying i. Ps 31:6
gods of the nations are i. Ps 96:5
and with strange i. Jer 8:19
keep yourselves from i. 1 Jn 5:21
image A likeness; an idol.
make man in our i. Gen 1:26
not make . . . any graven i. Ex 20:4
Immanuel (ĭm-măn'ū-el) A Hebrew name meaning "God-With-Us," used by Isaiah (7:14; 8:8) in foretelling the birth of the Messiah.
iniquity (ĭ-nĭq'ui-ty) Sin; wickedness. *See* sin.
the i. of the fathers Ex 20:5; Deut 5:9
pardon mine i. Ps 25:11
we have borne their i. Lam 5:7
Isaac (ī'saac) The son of Abraham and Sarah, and half-brother of Ishmael; by his wife Rebekah he was the father of Jacob and Esau (Gen 21:1–12; 22:1–19; 24:62–67; 25:9–11, 19, 20; 26:1—28:5; 35:27–29).
Isaiah; Esaias (ī-sai'ah; e-sai'as) A prophet of Israel; the first book of the OT Major Prophets.
Ishmael (ĭsh'ma-el) The name of six persons in the OT, one of them Abraham's son by Hagar (Gen 16; 17:18–27; 21:8–21; 25:12–18).
Israel (ĭs'rā-el) The name that Jacob received after his mysterious struggle at Jabbok (Gen 32:22–30); also the name of the whole people descended from him. After the separation into two kingdoms under Jeroboam, the name was confined to the Northern Kingdom of the ten tribes.
Israelites (ĭs'rā-el-ītes) A name applied to Israel (the people); also called "Hebrews," mostly by foreigners, as was the name "Jews"; the latter arose at the time when Judah, after the fall of the Northern Kingdom, represented the entire people.
Issachar (ĭs'sa-char) The ninth son of Jacob, the fifth by Leah (Gen 30:18); ancestor of the tribe of Issachar.

J

Jacob Son of Isaac and Rebekah; younger twin brother of Esau; father of the people of Israel. Gained by craft the blessing meant for Esau; married Leah and Rachel, the daughters of his uncle Laban; received the name Israel; finally found refuge in Egypt with his favorite son, Joseph (Gen 25:26—37:2; 47:28—49:33).
James The name of several persons in the NT. 1. "The elder," son of Zebedee and brother of John; one of the 12 apostles; martyred under Herod Agrippa (Mt 4:21; 10:2; 17:1; 20:20; 26:37; Mk 1:19, 20, 29; 3:17; 5:37; 9:2; 10:35, 41; 13:3; 14:33; Lk 5:10; 6:14; 8:51; 9:28, 54; Acts 1:13; 12:2). 2. The son of Alphaeus, also one of the 12 apostles (Mt 10:3; Mk 3:18; Lk 6:15; Acts 1:13). 3. One of the sons of Mary; known as "the less" (Mt 27:56; Mk 15:40; 16:1; Lk 24:10). Tradition regards James (3) to be the same person as James (2). 4. The father of Judas (Lk 6:16; Acts 1:13). 5. "The brother of the Lord"; a pillar of the church at Jerusalem; called "James the Just"; traditionally the author of the epistle of James (Mt 13:55; Mk 6:3; Acts 12:17; 15:13; 21:18; 1 Cor 15:7; Gal 1:19; 2:9, 12; Jas 1:1; Jude 1).
Jehovah (je-hō'vah) The LORD; God. Used by some Bible translators for the name of the covenant God of Israel (Ex 6:3; Ps 83:18; Isa 12:2; 26:4).
Jephthah (jĕph'thah) A warrior of Gilead; sacrificed his daughter in fulfillment of a vow (Judg 11:1—12:7).

Jeremiah; Jeremias (jĕr-e-mī'ah; jĕr-e-mī'as) The name of ten persons in the OT, one of them the prophet Jeremiah (c. 626–580 B.C.). His prophecies, visions, and life story are narrated in the second book of the OT Major Prophets, which bears his name. The almond rod and the seething pot (1:11–19); the potter's wheel (18:2–10); the good and bad figs (24:1–10); Baruch records his prophecies (36:4–32).

Jericho (jĕr'i-chō) An ancient city at the S end of the Jordan Valley; the fall of the city is told in Josh 6:1–25.

Jeroboam (jĕr-o-bō'am) 1. The first king of Israel (c. 922–901 B.C.); son of Nebat (1 Kgs 11:26—14:20; 2 Kgs 17:21, 22; 2 Chr 10:2–15; 13:1–20). 2. King of Israel (c. 786–747 B.C.); son and successor of Joash (2 Kgs 14:23–29).

Jerusalem (je-rū'sa-lem) The chief city of Palestine; most sacred city of both Jews and Christians; mentioned under one name or another (Shalem; Salem; City of David; Moriah; Jebus; Zion; Ariel) in about 40 of the 66 books of the Bible. David captured the city (2 Sam 5:6–9; 1 Chr 11:4–8) and made it his capital; brought the ark of God to the city (2 Sam 6). Solomon built the Temple and other buildings there (1 Kgs 5—7). Captured by Nebuchadnezzar (Jer 39); rebuilt by Ezra and Nehemiah. Several events in the life of Jesus occurred there: His presentation in the Temple (Lk 1:5–23); the cleansing of the Temple (Jn 2:13–25); the conversation with Nicodemus (Jn 3:1–21); and the events of the last week of His life (Mt 21—28; Mk 11—16; Lk 19—24; Jn 12—21).

Jesse (jĕs'se) Son of Obed; grandson of Boaz and Ruth; father of David (1 Sam 16:1–13; 17:12ff).

Jesus Christ The personal name of the one whose title gave its name to the Christian religion. Since "Jesus" was a fairly common name in the first century, distinguishing phrases were used when referring to Him (Jesus of Nazareth; Jesus, son of David; Christ Jesus; the Messiah Jesus; and Jesus Christ). The four Gospels detail His life and ministry: birth (Mt 1:18–25; Lk 2:1–20); baptism (Mt 3:13–17; Mk 1:9–11; Lk 3:21, 22); makes water into wine (Jn 2:1–12); the Sermon on the Mount (Mt 5:1—7:29; Lk 6:20–49); stilling of the storm (Mk 4:35–41; Lk 8:22–25); sending the unclean spirits into the swine (Mk 5:1–20); feeding of the 5,000 (Mt 14:13–21); Mk 6:30–44; Lk 9:10–17; Jn 6:1–14); walking on the water (Mt 14:22–33; Mk 6:45–52; Jn 6:15–21); feeding of the 4,000 (Mt 15:32–39; Mk 8:1–10); the Transfiguration (Mt 17:1–8; Mk 9:2–8; Lk 9:28–36); entry into Jerusalem (Mt 21:1–17; Mk 11:1–11; Lk 19:28–46; Jn 12:12–50); raises Lazarus from the dead (Jn 11:1–46); the Lord's Supper (Mt 26:26–29; Mk 14:22–25; Lk 22:15–20); is arrested (Mt 26:47–56; Mk 14:43–52; Lk 22:47–53; Jn 18:2–12); trial before Pilate (Mt 27:11–14; Mk 15:2–5; Lk 23:2–5; Jn 18:33–38); the Crucifixion (Mt 27:32–61; Mk 15:21–47; Lk 23:26–56; Jn 19:17–42); the Resurrection (Mt 28:1–20; Mk 16:1–20; Lk 24:1–53; Jn 20; 21).

Jews Hebrews. *See* Israelites.

Jesus, King of the J. Mt 27:11, 37; Mk 15:2, 12, 26; Lk 23:3, 38; Jn 18:33, 39; 19:3, 19

Jezebel (jĕz'e-bĕl) A Phoenician woman, wife of Ahab, king of Israel (1 Kgs 16:31; 21:5–25; 2 Kgs 9:30–37).

Job (jōb) Chief character in the OT book of Job; unknown otherwise.

Joel (jō'el) The name of several persons in the OT, including the prophet, son of Pethuel, author of the second book of the 12 Minor Prophets.

John The name of five persons in the NT, among them: 1. **John the Apostle:** A son of Zebedee, brother of James (Mt 4:21, 22; Mk 1:19, 20; Lk 5:10); sometimes called "the Beloved Disciple" and "Saint John"; traditional author of the Fourth Gospel, the three epistles of John, and the book of Revelation. 2. **John the Baptist:** The son of Elisabeth and Zacharias (Lk 1:5–66); a prophet, called the forerunner of Jesus (Jn 1:15–28); baptized Jesus (Mt 3:1–17; Mk 1:2–11; Lk 3:21, 22; Jn 1:29–34); imprisoned by Herod and beheaded (Mt 14:3–12; Mk 6:17–29). 3. **John Mark:** *See* Mark.

Jonah; Jonas (jō'nah; jō'nas) The name of two persons of the OT, one of whom was the prophet about whom the fifth book of the 12 Minor Prophets is written. Swallowed by a great fish (Jon 1:17—2:10).

Jonathan (jŏn'a-than) The name of 15 persons in the OT, one of whom was the oldest son of Saul; David's friend (1 Sam 13:2; 14:1–45; 19:1–7; 20).

Joppa; Japho The ancient seaport for Jerusalem (Josh 19:46; 2 Chr 2:16; Jon 1:3; Acts 9:36–43).

Jordan (jôr'dan) The chief river of Palestine, flowing from the slopes of Mount Hermon through Lake Huleh and the Sea of Galilee to the Dead Sea. The waters were miraculously stopped for the Israelites to pass (Josh 3:14—4:24). Jesus was baptized there (Mt 3:13–17; Mk 1:9–11; Lk 3:21—22).

Joseph; Joses (jō'seph; jō'ses) The name of 14 persons in the Bible, among them: 1. The son of Jacob and Rachel (Gen 30:22–24); his coat of many colors (Gen 37:3); sold into Egypt by his brothers (Gen 37:18–36); imprisoned on false accusations (Gen 39:20–23); interpreted Pharaoh's dreams, thus gaining favor (Gen 41:1–36); as administrator of Egypt (Gen 41:37—50:26); his brothers come to him for food (Gen 42—45). 2. The husband of Mary mother of Jesus; resident of Nazareth; descended from David (Mt 1:16–25; Lk 2:4–7; Jn 1:45). 3. **Joseph of Arimathea:** A member of the Sanhedrin; buried the body of Jesus on his own property (Mt 27:57–60; Mk 15:43–46; Lk 23:50–53; Jn 19:38–41).

Joshua; Jeshua (jŏsh'ū-a; jĕsh'ū-a) The name of several persons in the OT, the most important being Joshua, son of Nun, the central figure of the book of Joshua. This book tells the story of Moses' successor as leader of the Israelites, the conquest of Canaan, and the division of the country among the 12 tribes. His miraculous crossing of the Jordan (Josh 3:14—4:24); conquest of Jericho (Josh 6:1–20).

Judea (jū-de'a) An area of SW Palestine; formerly called **Judah.**

Judah (jū'dah) The fourth son of Jacob, by Leah (Gen 29:35); ancestor of the tribe of Judah.

Judas (jū'das) The name of six persons in the NT, including: 1. A brother of Jesus (Mt 13:55; Mk 6:3). *See* Jude. 2. **Judas Iscariot** (ĭs-cär'ĭ-ot): One of the 12 apostles; the betrayer of Jesus (Mt 26:20–25, 47–50; Mk 14:18–20, 43–46; Lk 22:47–49; Jn 13:21–26). 3. The son or brother of James; one of the 12 apostles (Lk 6:16; Jn 14:22 [?]; Acts 1:13). *See* Thaddaeus. 4. **Judas Barsabas** (bär'-sab-as): A Jewish Christian (Acts 15:22, 27, 32).

Jude, The General Epistle of (jūde) This NT letter designates its author as a "servant of Jesus Christ, and brother of James." *See* Judas (1).

judge To decide; form an opinion.

J. not, that ye be not Mt 7:1
judge One who forms an opinion. In the OT book of Judges, one chosen by God to save the people from foreign oppressors; a military leader with both legislative and executive authority.
made thee . . . a j. over us Ex 2:14
Judge God; Christ.
J. of all the earth Gen 18:25
J. of quick and dead Acts 10:42
to God the J. of all Heb 12:23

K

king A chief ruler; among ancient peoples, a religious leader often held to be divine. God and Jesus Christ are called "King."
trees . . . anoint a k. Judg 9:8
my K., and my God Ps 5:2; 84:3
the K. of glory shall Ps 24:7
seen the K., the LORD Isa 6:5
no k. but Caesar Jn 19:15
K. of kings, and Lord 1 Tim 6:15
kingdom of God The eternal sovereignty or kingly rule of God, manifested in its acceptance by men on earth and the hope for the future; the central theme of Jesus' teaching. The phrase does not occur in the OT, but the idea is present in "Thy kingdom," "My Kingdom," etc., which are also sometimes used in the NT. "Kingdom of heaven" is used in Matthew's gospel; "kingdom of his dear Son" (Col 1:13); "kingdom of our Lord and Saviour Jesus Christ" (2 Pet 1:11).
thine is the k., O LORD 1 Chr 29:11
the sceptre of thy k. Ps 45:6
Thy k. come Mt 6:10; Lk 11:2
seek ye first the k. of God Mt 6:33; Lk 12:31
with you in My Father's k. Mt 26:29
k. of God is at hand Mk 1:15
cannot see the k. of God Jn 3:3
inherit the k. of God 1 Cor 6:10; Gal 5:21

L

ladder A framework of uprights and cross-pieces on which one may ascend or descend.
Jacob dreams of a l. Gen 28:12
lamb The young of a sheep, commonly used as the sacrificial animal of the Passover.
God will provide . . . l. Gen 22:8
a l. to the slaughter Isa 53:7
wolf and the l. shall feed Isa 65:25
Feed my l. Jn 21:15
Lamb (of God) Christ, whose sacrificial death removed the sins of the world. By extension of "lamb" as the most common victim of OT sacrifices, particularly the "passover" (Christ our Passover 1 Cor 5:7).
Behold the L. of God Jn 1:29, 36
a l. without blemish 1 Pet 1:19
stood a L. as it had Rev 5:6
L. slain from the foundation Rev 13:8
L. shall overcome them Rev 17:14
lamp A device producing light.
ten virgins who took their l. Mt 25:1
last The final one.
first shall be l. Mt 19:30; Mk 10:31
I am the First and the L. Rev 1:17
latchet (lătch'et) Thong to fasten a sandal.
the l. of whose shoes Mk 1:7; Lk 3:16; Jn 1:27

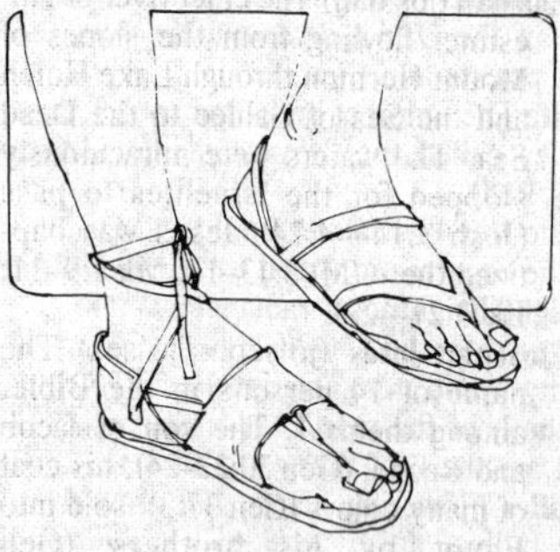

latchet

law Rules of conduct; particularly rules given by God to Moses by which the Israelites were to live and which were defined in the Pentateuch (the Law of Moses).
l. of the LORD is perfect Ps 19:7
not come to destroy L. Mt 5:17
l. was given by Moses Jn 1:17
Lazarus (lăz'a-rus) 1. The beggar in a parable told by Jesus (Lk 16:19–31). 2. A friend of Jesus; brother of Martha and Mary (Jn 11:1—12:11).
Leah (lē'ah) Elder daughter of Laban; Jacob's first wife to whom were born six of his sons (Gen 29:16—30:21).
leasing Lying; falsehood.
seek after l. Ps 4:2
them that speak l. Ps 5:6
leaven (leav'en) Yeast or other fermenting agent. It was forbidden to the Israelites in all offerings made with fire (Lev 2:11; 6:17) and at the Passover (Ex 12:19).
beware of the l. Mt 16:6
a little l. leaveneth 1 Cor 5:6
leopard (leop'ard) A wild animal of the cat family.
l. shall lie down with the Isa 11:6
Levi; Levites (lē'vī; lē'vītes) Third son of Jacob and Leah (Gen 29:34); ancestor of the tribe of Levites, who were charged with the care of the Tabernacle and the Temple.
Leviticus (le-vĭt'ĭ-cus) The third book of the OT; it deals mainly with the priests and their duties.
life The union of body and soul. Christ is called the "Prince of life" (Acts 3:15).
the tree of l. also Gen 2:9
the resurrection, and the l. Jn 11:25
light Brightness; radiance.
Let there be l. Gen 1:3
my l. and my salvation Ps 27:1
the l. of the world Mt 5:14
I am the l. of the world Jn 8:12
lilies Flowering plants that grow from bulbs.
he feeds his flock among the l. Song 6:3

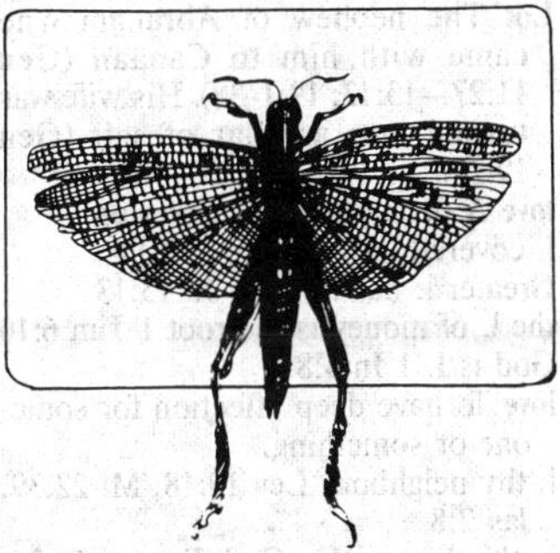

bald locust: referred to in Lev. 11:22

Consider the l. of the Mt 6:28
locusts Long-winged insects similar to grasshoppers.
east wind brought the l. Ex 10:13
ye may eat; the l. Lev 11:22
his meat was l. and Mt 3:4
lord One who has authority over persons or things; hence, **Lord:** God, as the Supreme Authority; Jesus, as Leader during His ministry and as the Son of God.
L. he is God Deut 4:35; 1 Kgs 18:39
the L. our God is one Deut 6:4
L. of the whole earth Ps 97:5
The L. said unto my L. Ps 110:1
saith unto me, L., L. Mt 7:21
L. of heaven and earth Mt 11:25
Son of man is L. also Mk 2:28
My L. and my God Jn 20:28
both L. and Christ Acts 2:36
crucified the L. of glory 1 Cor 2:8
is L. of l. and King Rev 17:14
Lord's Prayer The prayer, taught by Jesus to His disciples, that begins "Our Father" (Mt 6:9–13; Lk 11:2–4).
Lord's Supper 1. Holy Communion (1 Cor 11:20). 2. Last Supper.
lost Mislaid; not to be found.
the lost sheep Mt 18:12–14; Lk 15:4–7
the lost coin Lk 15:8–10
the lost (prodigal) son Lk 15:11–32

Lot The nephew of Abraham who came with him to Canaan (Gen 11:27—13:13; 19:1–38). His wife was turned into a pillar of salt (Gen 19:26).

love A deep affection; devotion.
l. covereth all sins Prov 10:12
Greater l. has no man Jn 15:13
the l. of money is the root 1 Tim 6:10
God is l. 1 Jn 4:8

love To have deep affection for someone or something.
l. thy neighbour Lev 19:18; Mt 22:39; Jas 2:8
l. the LORD thy God Deut 6:5; Mt 22:37
l. thy enemies Mt 5:44; Lk 6:27
God so l. the world Jn 3:16

Luke, Lucas The evangelist; a companion of Paul; a physician; traditional author of the NT books of Luke and Acts (Col 4:14; 2 Tim 4:11; Philem 24).

M

maker One who brings into being; creator; hence, **Maker:** God.
more pure than his M. Job 4:17
man look to his M. Isa 17:7
builder and m. is God Heb 11:10

Malachi (măl'a-chī) An OT prophet, author of the last book of the OT, one of the 12 Minor Prophets.

man A male human being; the whole human race.
God is not a m. Num 23:19
M. is born unto trouble Job 5:7
M. shall not live by Mt 4:4
not m. for the sabbath Mk 2:27

manna (măn'na) The food miraculously provided by God for the Israelites in their wanderings through the wilderness (Ex 16:15).

mark A sign.
set a m. upon Cain Gen 4:15
his m. in his forehead Rev 14:9

Mark; John Mark Son of Mary of Jerusalem; companion of Paul and other early Christian missionaries; the traditional author of the second Gospel (Acts 12:12, 25; 15:37).

marriage The union of one man and one woman. Explained by Jesus (Mk 10:6–9).
are given in m. Mt 22:30
M. is honourable in all Heb 13:4

Mary The name of seven persons in the NT, among them: 1. The mother of Jesus (Mt 1:16, 18–25; Lk 2:5–20). 2. **Mary Magdalene:** A Galilean follower of Jesus (Mt 27:56, 61; 28:1; Mk 15:40, 47; 16:1; Lk 8:2; 24:10; Jn 19:25; 20:1, 18). 3. The sister of Lazarus (Lk 10:38–42; Jn 11:1—12:8). 4. The mother of James "the less" (Mt 27:55, 56, 61; 28:1–10; Mk 15:40, 41, 47; 16:1–8; 23:49, 55, 56, 24:1–11). 5. The mother of John Mark (Acts 12:12).

master A male person in authority; one who controls someone or something; owner; teacher; hence: **Master,** used of Jesus during His ministry.
is free from his m. Job 3:19
can serve two m. Mt 6:24; Lk 16:13
disciple is not above his m. Mt 10:24
your M., even Christ Mt 23:8, 10
troublest thou the M. Mk 5:35
call me M. and Lord Jn 13:13

Matthew One of the 12 apostles; called "Levi the son of Alphaeus" in Mk 2:14; traditional author of the first Gospel.

meat Food in general; solid food in contrast to that which is drunk.
thou givest them their m. Ps 145:15
grow all trees for m. Ezek 47:12
life more than m. Mt 6:25
have ye any m. (= fish) Jn 21:5

mediator One who acts as a go-between in making an agreement between two parties. Moses is so designated (Gal 3:19) in making the covenant at Sinai. Christ is called the "one Mediator between God and men" (1 Tim 2:5).

meditate To study; contemplate.
he m. day and night Ps 1:2
meek Humble; gentle.
m. shall inherit the earth Ps 37:11
Blessed are the m. Mt 5:5
merciful Forgiving; unwilling to punish.
LORD God, m. and gracious Ex 34:6
God be m. unto us Ps 67:1
Blessed are the m. Mt 5:7
m. to me a sinner Lk 18:13
mercy Forgiveness or kindness, particularly to a wrongdoer.
His m. endureth forever Ezra 3:11
they shall obtain m. Mt 5:7
mercy seat Literally, "covering." The lid of the ark of the testimony, from above which God spoke to His people (Ex 25:22).
merry Joyous; happy.
m. heart maketh a cheerful Prov 15:13
m. heart doeth good Prov 17:22
to eat, and to drink, and to be m. Eccles 8:15; Lk 12:19
Meshach (mē′shăch) The Babylonian name of one of Daniel's friends (Dan 1:7; 3:12 et al.).
Messiah; Messias Literally, "anointed one"; one sent by God to save others. In Hebrew belief, the coming savior of the Jewish people; in Christianity, Jesus.
Methuselah (me-thū′se-lah) Noah's grandfather; lived for 969 years, the oldest person mentioned in the Bible (Gen 5:27).
Micah (mī′cah) A Judean prophet, contemporary of Isaiah, whose prophecies appear in the OT book of Micah, the sixth of the 12 Minor Prophets.
ministry God's service.
to the m. of the word Acts 6:4
m. of reconciliation 2 Cor 5:18
mite A copper coin of small value.
widow . . . threw in two m. Mk 12:42
money Riches; coins.
tables of the m. changers Mt 21:12
the tribute m. Mt 22:19
no m. in their purse Mk 6:8
love of m. is the root of all evil 1 Tim 6:10
Mordecai (môr′de-caī) The Jewish hero of the OT book of Esther.
Moses The great deliverer and lawgiver of Israel; born during the oppression of the Israelites in Egypt (Ex 2:2); brought up in Pharaoh's house (Ex 2:5–10); fled to Midian where he lived 40 years (Ex 2:15–25); called by God from the burning bush (Ex 3:2–5) to deliver the Israelites; after performing ten miracles of plagues (Ex 7:9—12:29) he got Pharaoh's consent to take the Israelites from Egypt; led them 40 years through the wilderness; received the Ten Commandments from God (Ex 20). The OT books of Exodus, Leviticus, Numbers, and Deuteronomy detail his life and deeds.
Most High, the A name used of God.
When the Most H. divided Deut 32:8
the most H. ruleth in Dan 4:25
the most H. dwelleth not Acts 7:48
mote A speck.
m. that is in thy brother's eye Mt 7:3; Lk 6:41
mother Female parent.
Honour . . . thy m. Ex 20:12; Mt 19:19
As is the m., . . . daughter Ezek 16:44
disciple, Behold thy m. Jn 19:27
mourn To grieve for.
Blessed are they that m. Mt 5:4

N

Nahum (nā′hum) A prophet, the prophecies of whom are given in the OT book of Nahum, the seventh of the 12 Minor Prophets.
name The word by which a person, place, or thing is called.
n. of the LORD thy God in vain Ex 20:7
how excellent is thy n. Ps 8:1

Hallowed be thy n. Mt 6:9; Lk 11:2
in my n. Mt 24:5; Mk 13:6; Lk 21:8
My n. is Legion Mk 5:9
ask of the Father in my n. Jn 15:16

Naphtali (năph'ta-li) The sixth son of Jacob, the second born of Bilhah (Gen 30:7, 8): ancestor of one of the 12 tribes of Israel.

narrow Not wide; small in width.
n. is the way, which Mt 7:14

Nathan (nā'than) The name of six persons in the OT, one of whom was a prophet contemporary of King David (2 Sam 7:1–17; 12:1–15, 25; 1 Kgs 1:5–48).

Nazareth (năz'a-rěth) The town in Lower Galilee where Jesus was brought up (Lk 2:39, 51).

Nebuchadnezzar; Nebuchadrezzar (něb-u-chad-něz'zar; —rěz'zar) King of Babylonia 605–562 B.C.

Nehemiah (nē-he-mī'ah) The name of three persons in the OT, one of whom was the rebuilder of Jerusalem after the Babylonian exile. The book of Nehemiah tells his story.

neighbour A person who lives near another.
false witness against thy n. Ex 20:16
love thy n. as thyself Lev 19:18; Mt 19:19

new Of recent origin.
no n. thing under the sun Eccles 1:9
n. heavens and a n. earth Isa 65:17
A n. commandment Jn 13:34
the n. man Eph 4:24; Col 3:10

Nineveh (nĭn'e-veh) One of the oldest and greatest cities of Mesopotamia; capital of Assyria; destroyed 612 B.C. (Gen 10:11, 12; 2 Kgs 19:36; Isa 37:37; Jon 1:2–7; 4:11; Nah 1:1; 2:8; 3:7).

Noah; Noe (nō'ah; nō'e) The ninth descendant of Adam; the survivor, with his family, of the Flood (Gen 6—9).

O

Obadiah (ō-ba-dī'ah) The name of 11 persons in the OT, none of whom can be assumed to be the author of the book of Obadiah, the shortest OT book and fourth of the 12 Minor Prophets.

offering Something given in worship. In the OT we find offerings of: 1. **grain** (Lev 2:1–16; 5:11; 6:14–23; Num 15:4, 6, 9). 2. **drink** (Num 6:17; 15:5, 10). 3. **animals,** or **sacrifice** (Lev 1:3). These were of three kinds: a. The **burnt offering** in which a male lamb, ram, goat, bullock, dove, or pigeon was entirely consumed on the altar (Lev 1; 6:9–13). b. The **sin offering** in which a bullock, a male or female goat, a female lamb, a dove, or a pigeon was given (Lev 4; 6:25–30) and the **trespass offering** in which a ram or a male lamb was used (Lev 5; 6:6; 7:1–8; 14:12, 21). c. The **peace offering,** including the giving of thanks (Lev 7:12–15), the payment of a vow (Ex 35:27–29; Lev 7:16; Num 6:10–21), and the voluntary or freewill offering (Lev 7:16–20); for these any animal without blemish of either sex could be used, but no birds (Lev 3; 7:11–27).

oil Any of several greasy liquids that can be burned.
anointest my head with o. Ps 23:5

Olives, Mount of; Olivet, mount called (ôl'i-vět) A mountain E of Jerusalem (2 Sam 15:30–32; Zech 14:4). Closely associated with the last days in the life of Jesus (in the four Gospels and Acts 1:12).

ordain 1. To appoint, consecrate, or set apart, as for the ministry.
o. them elders in every Acts 14:23
o. elders in every city Tit 1:5
2. To establish.
I will o. a place for 1 Chr 17:9

P

Palestine (păl'ĕs-tīne) The Greek and Roman names for Canaan; modern usage applies the name to the territory allotted to the 12 tribes of Israel.

Passover A seven-day Jewish festival held in Mar. or Apr., commemorating the slaying of the firstborn just before the Israelites were freed from slavery in Egypt (Ex 12); combined with the Feast of Unleavened Bread which commemorates the actual Exodus flight (Ex 13:3–16).

Passover The sacrificial lamb of the Passover (Ex 12:11, 27). Paul refers to Christ as the Paschal Lamb.

Christ, our p. was sacrificed 1 Cor 5:7

pasture Grassy land where cattle and sheep graze.

me to lie down in green p. Ps 23:2

Paul As Saul, the son of Hebrew parents, he persecuted the followers of Jesus (Acts 8:3; Gal 1:13). Miraculously converted (Acts 9:1ff) and name changed to Paul (Acts 13:9), he became the leading missionary of early Christianity. His life is detailed in the NT book of Acts. He founded many churches in Asia Minor and Greece and carried on extensive correspondence with them.

peace Freedom from turmoil and war.

of war, and a time of p. Eccles 3:8

is no p. . . . to the wicked Isa 57:21

came not to send p., but a sword. Mt 10:34

on earth, p., good will Lk 2:14

P. be unto you Lk 24:36; Jn 20:19

Pentecost (pĕn'te-côst) A Jewish festival on the fiftieth day after Passover; *also called* Feast of Weeks (Lev 23:15, 16). Observed by the Christian church as the day on which the gift of the Holy Ghost was given to the church (Acts 2:1).

perish To die; to be destroyed.

way of the ungodly shall p. Ps 1:6

believeth in him should not p. Jn 3:15

Peter; Simon Peter A fisherman on the Sea of Galilee who was called with his brother Andrew by Jesus (Mt 4:18–20; Mk 1:16–20; Lk 5:1–11; Jn 1:35–41). He became the "first" of the 12 apostles (Mt 10:2), and sometimes spoke for all the disciples. Jesus changed his name from Simon to Peter (Mt 16:18; Mk 3:16; Lk 6:14; Jn 1:42). His mother-in-law healed by Jesus (Mt 8:14; Mk 1:30; Lk 4:38); his confession that Jesus is the Christ (Mt 16:16; Mk 8:29; Lk 9:20); his denial of Jesus (Mt 26:69–75; Mk 14:66–72; Lk 22: 54–62). The traditional author of two NT epistles.

Pharaoh (phā-'raoh) A title used as a name, or prefixed to a name, of the king of Egypt. Joseph interprets Pharaoh's dream (Gen 41:1–36); the Pharaoh of the Exodus (Ex 7—14).

Pharisee (phăr'i-see) A member of a strict Jewish sect, holding the Mosaic Law and their own traditions as binding. The parable of the Pharisee and the publican (Lk 18:9–14).

Phenicia; Phenice (phĕ-nĭs'i-a; phe-nī'ce) A country W of the Lebanon range and Galilee on the coast of the Mediterranean Sea (Acts 11:19; 15:3; 21:2); its chief cities were Tyre and Sidon. *Also spelled* Phoenicia.

Philemon (phĭ-lē'mon) A Christian of Colosse to whom the NT epistle to Philemon was written by Paul. In the letter Paul asks Philemon to pardon Onesimus, a runaway slave whom Paul has converted.

Philip The name of four persons in the NT, among them: 1. The apostle (Mt 10:3; Mk 3:18; Lk 6:14; Jn 1:43–48; 6:5, 7; 12:21, 22; 14:8, 9; Acts 1:13). 2. The evangelist (Acts 6:5; 8:5–40; 21:8).

Philippi; Philippians (phĭl'ĭp-pī; phĭ-lĭp'pĭ-ans) A city of Macedonia where Paul founded his first Chris-

tian congregation in Europe. The NT epistle to the Philippians was written by Paul to the church there.
Philistines (phĭ-lĭs′tines; phĭl′i-stines) The people who lived along the S coast of Palestine; often at war with the Israelites. Goliath was a champion of the Philistines (1 Sam 17:23–51).
physician A medical doctor.
Is there no p. there Jer 8:22
They that be whole need not a p. Mt 9:12
P., heal thyself Lk 4:23
Luke the beloved p. Col 4:14
Pilate; Pontius Pilate (pī′late, pŏn′tĭ-us) The Roman governor of Judea A.D. 26–36; the judge in the trial and execution of Jesus (Mt 27:1–26; Mk 15:1–15; Lk 23:1–25; Jn 18:28—19:16).

plowshare

plowshare The cutting blade of a plow.
their swords into p. Isa 2:4
Beat your p. into swords Joel 3:10
poor Needy; having little or no goods or money.
the p. shall not give less Ex 30:15
Blessed are the p. in spirit Mt 5:3
have the p. always with you Mt 26:11; Mk 14:7
post Runner; courier; messenger.
letters were sent by p. Esther 3:13
p. that rode upon mules Esther 8:14
days swifter than a p. Job 9:25
pottage (pŏt′tāge) A thick soup.
Esau sells birthright for p. Gen 25:34
prayer Words addressed to God.
house of p. Isa 56:7; Mt 21:13; Mk 11:17; Lk 19:46
by p. and fasting Mt 17:21; Mk 9:29
you ask in p. Mt 21:22
presently Immediately; at once.
fool's wrath is p. known Prov 12:16
pride Conceit; vanity.
P. goeth before destruction Prov 16:18

priest

priest A minister. Aaron and his sons, of the tribe of Levi, were appointed to the priesthood at Sinai; the office became hereditary and restricted to that family (Ex 28:1; 40:12–15).
p. of the most high God Gen 14:18
prince One who has authority or influence; a ruler; hence, **Prince:** the Messiah; Christ.
made you a p. . . . over us Ex 2:14
Put not your trust in p. Ps 146:3
P. of Peace Isa 9:6
the P. of princes Dan 8:25
killed the P. of life Acts 3:15
prodigal (prŏd′i-gal) Wasteful. The parable of the prodigal son is given in Lk 15:11–32.
prophet (prŏph′et) A man called by God to be His spokesman.
I will raise them up a P. Deut 18:18

p. is not without honour Mt 13:57; Mk 6:4; Jn 4:44
No p. is accepted in his Lk 4:24
psalms (psälms) Songs of praise, particularly those from the OT book of Psalms.
joyful noise unto him with p. Ps 95:2
said in the book of P. Lk 20:42
let him sing p. Jas 5:13
publican Tax-collector.
Matthew the p. Mt 10:3
a friend of p. and sinners Mt 11:19
saw a p., named Levi Lk 5:27
Purim (pū'rĭm) A Jewish festival celebrating the deliverance from massacre (Esther 9:20–28).

Q

quick Alive; living.
swallowed us up q. Ps 124:3
the Judge of q. and dead Acts 10:42
the word of God is q. Heb 4:12
ready to judge the q. 1 Pet 4:5
quicken To make alive; revive.
Q. me, O LORD Ps 143:11
raiseth the dead, and q. Jn 5:21
God, who q. the dead Rom 4:17
q. by the Spirit 1 Pet 3:18

R

Rabbi (răb'bī) Master; Teacher.
They said to him, R. Jn 1:38
Rachel (rā'chel) The younger daughter of Laban; Jacob's second wife; mother of Joseph and Benjamin (Gen 29:1—31:35; 35:16–19).
Rebekah (re-bĕk'ah) Wife of Isaac; mother of Esau and Jacob (Gen 24:10–67; 25:20–26; 28; 26:6–11; 27:5–17).
redeemer One who buys back, rescues (as from sin), or ransoms. Jesus is called "the Redeemer," through His sacrificial death, although the word does not appear in the NT.
I know that my r. lives Job 19:25
LORD, my strength, and my r. Ps 19:14
R. shall come to Zion Isa 59:20
Red Sea; Sea of Reeds The body of water between Arabia and Africa; the miraculous parting of the sea (Ex 14:21–31) enabled the Israelites to escape the Egyptians.
repent To feel regret; to change one's mind about.
r. in dust and ashes Job 42:6
R. ye, for the kingdom Mt 3:2
except ye r., ye shall Lk 13:3
R., and be baptized Acts 2:38
R. ye therefore, and be Acts 3:19
rest Repose; quietness.
seventh day thou shalt r. Ex 23:12
the weary be at r. Job 3:17
R. in the LORD Ps 37:7
labour and have no r. Lam 5:5
I will give you r. Mt 11:28
resurrection (rĕs-ur-rĕc'tion) A rising from the dead; a return to life; hence, **Resurrection:** The rising of Christ from the dead (Mt 28; Mk 16; Lk 24; Jn 20; 1 Cor 15).
there is no r. Mt 22:23; Mk 12:18
I am the r. and the life Jn 11:25
This is the first r. Rev 20:5
Reuben; Reubenites (reu'ben; reu'benītes) The firstborn son of Jacob, by Leah (Gen 29:32); the ancestor of the tribe of Reuben.
revelation (rĕv-e-lā'tion) The making known of something previously concealed.
by the r. of Jesus Christ Gal 1:12
the R. of Jesus Christ Rev 1:1
reward To give payment for something done; used particularly of God's blessing upon the obedient and His punishment of the wicked.
r. in heaven Mt 5:12; Lk 6:23
receive his own r. 1 Cor 3:8
rich Wealthy; having money or property.
labour not to be r. Prov 23:4
for he was very r. Lk 18:23
riches Wealth; property; material goods.
r. are not forever Prov 27:24

deceitfulness of r. Mt 13:22; Mk 4:19
righteous One who does what is right; a virtuous person.
LORD knoweth the way of the r. Ps 1:6
come not to call the r. Mt 9:13
righteousness Virtue; right action; particularly, conformity to God's will.
in the paths of r. Ps 23:3
hunger and thirst after r. Mt 5:6
might grace reign through r. Rom 5:21
rock A mass of stone; anything hard like a rock.
art my r. and my fortress Ps 31:3
upon this r. I will build Mt 16:18
Rock The Lord.
Of the R. that begat you Deut 32:18
The LORD is my r. Ps 18:2
Rome; Romans The capital of the Roman Empire; Christianity probably came to Rome early in the apostolic age. Paul wrote the NT epistle to the Romans to the Christian community there.
Ruth A Moabite woman who became an ancestress of David through her second marriage, to Boaz. Her story of devotion is told in the OT book of Ruth.

S

sabbath The day of rest ordained by God; the day of divine worship (1 Cor 16:2).
Remember the s. day Ex 20:8
a s. of rest unto you Lev 16:31
s. was made for man Mk 2:27
sacrifice (săc′ri-fīce) An offering, usually of the life of a person or an animal, made to God.
s. to the LORD Ex 5:17
love . . . is more than . . . s. Mk 12:33
put away sin by the s. of Heb 9:26
Sadducees (săd′dū-cees) The aristocratic party of the Jews at the time of Christ. They collaborated with the Romans to maintain their favorable status.
salt A seasoning; a preservative.
became a pillar of s. Gen 19:26
Ye are the s. of the earth Mt 5:13
salvation Deliverance from evil, danger, or trouble; God's gift, through Christ, to save men's souls.
the God of my s. Ps 25:5
to the rock of our s. Ps 95:1
shall see the s. of God Lk 3:6
this shall turn to my s. Phil 1:19
grace of God that bringeth s. Tit 2:11
the author of their s. Heb 2:10
Samaria; Samaritans (sa-mâr′ĭ-a; sa-mâr′ĭ-tans) The capital city of the Northern Kingdom, Israel. Also the name of the territory near the city. The term "Samaritan" is usually applied to a member of a religious sect living in that area. The parable of the good Samaritan told by Jesus (Lk 10:30–37).
Samson A hero of the tribe of Dan, noted for his great strength (Judg 13—16).
Samuel The last "judge" of Israel; a prophet of the eleventh century B.C. The two OT books of Samuel record his life and deeds and the history of Israel through the reigns of Saul and David. The Lord calls Samuel (1 Sam 3); Samuel anoints David (1 Sam 16:11–13).
sanctify (sănc′tĭ-fy) To set apart as holy; to consecrate to religious use; to make holy.
seventh day and s. it Gen 2:3
s. by the Holy Ghost Rom 15:16
sanctuary (sănc′tū-a-ry) A building or place set apart for religious worship; in the OT, the Tabernacle (Ex 25:8) or the Temple (1 Chr 22:19).
sand Tiny particles of rock, especially as found in deserts and along seashores.
make thy seed as the s. of Gen 32:12
built his house upon the s. Mt 7:26
Sarah; Sarai (sâr′ah; sâr′aī) The wife of Abraham; mother of Isaac in accord with divine promise (Gen 17:15–21; 18:1–15).

Satan The Devil; the adversary of God and Christ.
S. casts out S. Mt 12:26; Mk 3:23
forty days, tempted of S. Mk 1:13
lest S. should get an advantage 2 Cor 2:11
S. will be released from Rev 20:7
Saul Son of Kish, of the tribe of Benjamin; first king over Israel. The prophet Samuel anoints him to be king (1 Sam 10:1); he disobeys the LORD (1 Sam 15); David enters his service (1 Sam 16:14–23); he tries to kill David (1 Sam 19:9, 10); David spares his life (1 Sam 26:6–24).
Saul of Tarsus *See* Paul.
Saviour Literally, "one who saves or delivers"; Christ, as the One who delivers us from the sins of this life and through whom salvation is obtained; God, as the Deliverer of the Israelites from oppression and as the Redeemer of all peoples.
my refuge; my s. 2 Sam 22:3
a just God and a S. Isa 45:21
rejoiced in God my S. Lk 1:47
Christ, the S. of the world Jn 4:42
Christ . . . the s. of the body Eph 5:23
S., the Lord Jesus Christ Phil 3:20
To the only wise God our S. Jude 25
scrip Bag; wallet.
stones . . . in a s. 1 Sam 17:40
Nor s. for your journey Mt 10:10
no s., no bread Mk 6:8; Lk 9:3
scripture Any writing, particularly that of a sacred nature; hence, **Scripture:** the Bible. Also "Scriptures"; "Holy Scripture"; "Holy Scriptures."
have you not read this s. Mk 12:10
search the s. Jn 5:39
s. is given by inspiration 2 Tim 3:16
seek To search for; to try to find.
s., and ye shall find Mt 7:7; Lk 11:9
none who s. after God Rom 3:11
Semites (sĕm′ītes) The people descended from Shem, the son of Noah (Gen 5:32), or those speaking one of the Semitic languages.

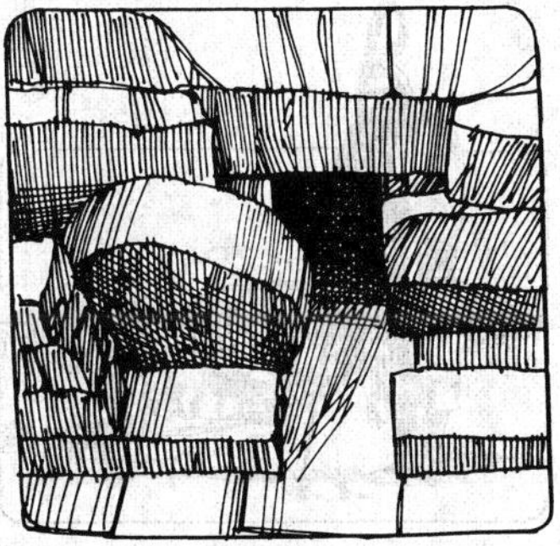

sepulchre

sepulchre (sĕp′ul-chre) Tomb. *See* holy sepulchre.
like unto whited s. Mt 23:27
serpent A snake; in biblical usage, many times synonymous with "Satan."
s. was more subtil than Gen 3:1
will take up s. Mk 16:18
s. beguiled Eve 2 Cor 11:3
that old s., who is the Devil Rev 20:2
Shadrach (shā′drăch) The Babylonian name of one of Daniel's companions (Dan 1:7; 3:12 et al.).
Sheba, Queen of (shē′ba) A queen, probably Arabian, who came to test Solomon's wisdom (1 Kgs 10:1–13; 2 Chr 3).
Shem (shĕm) The eldest son of Noah who stands as the ancestor of the Semites generally and of the Hebrews specifically (Gen 5:32; 9:18–27; 10:21–31; Lk 3:36).
shepherd One who herds and takes care of sheep; by extension, the ruler or king of a people. The Lord is the Shepherd of Israel; Christ is the Good Shepherd (Jn 10:7–18).
The LORD is my s. Ps 23:1
s. . . . keeping watch over Lk 2:8
one fold and one s. Jn 10:16
Lord Jesus that great s. Heb 13:20
Shiloh (shī′loh) A city of Ephraim, 10

shepherd with sheep

mi. NE of Bethel; site of the ark of the Testimony and the Tabernacle from the time of Joshua to Samuel.

Silas; Silvanus (sī'las; sil-vā'nus) One of the earliest of the apostolic missionaries, associated with both Paul (Acts 16:19ff; 1 Thess 1:1; 2:1, 2) and Peter (1 Pet 5:12).

Simeon (sĭm'e-on) The name of six persons in the Bible, including: 1. The second son of Jacob, by Leah (Gen 29:33); ancestor of the tribe of Simeon. 2. A devout man who blessed the infant Jesus when His parents presented Him in the Temple (Lk 2:25–35).

Simon (sī'mon) The name of nine persons in the NT, including: 1. **Simon Peter:** *See* Peter (Mt 16:17, 18; Jn 1:42). 2. **Simon the Zealot:** Also one of the 12 apostles (Lk 6:15). 3. **Simon the Pharisee,** in whose home Jesus was anointed by the sinful woman (Lk 7:36–50). 4. **Simon the leper,** in whose home Jesus was anointed by Mary (Mk 14:3–9; Jn 12:1–8). 5. **Simon of Cyrene,** who was forced to carry Jesus' cross (Mt 27:32; Mk 15:21; Lk 23:26). 6. **Simon the sorcerer,** who offered money to Peter and John for the power of the Holy Ghost (Acts 8:9–24).

sin An offense or revolt against God (as Adam and Eve in the Garden of Eden); deliberate defiance; wickedness; iniquity; ungodliness.

put to death for his own s. Deut 24:16
our s. testify against us Isa 59:12
power on earth to forgive s. Mt 9:6
who can forgive s. Mk 2:7; Lk 5:21
taketh away the s. of Jn 1:29
He who is without s. Jn 8:7
gave himself for our s. Gal 1:4

sin To commit an offense against God; to be wicked.

is no man that s. not 1 Kgs 8:46
soul that s., it shall die Ezek 18:4
S. no more, lest a Jn 5:14
cannot s., because he is born of God 1 Jn 3:9

Sinai, Mount (sī'naī) The sacred mountain where God made the covenant with Israel (Ex 19—24), near the S end of the Sinai Peninsula. May be the same place as Mount Horeb.

sinful Wicked; full of iniquity.

s. nation, a people laden Isa 1:4
in the likeness of s. flesh Rom 8:3

sinner One who commits an offense against God.

standeth in the way of s. Ps 1:1
Why does your Master eat with . . . s. Mt 9:11; Mk 2:16; Lk 5:30
come to call . . . s., to repentance Mt 9:13; Mk 2:17; Lk 5:32
over one s. that repenteth Lk 15:7
be merciful to me a s. Lk 18:13

Sodom (sŏd'om) One of the two cities destroyed by the Lord because of their wickedness (Gen 19:24–28).

Solomon (sŏl'o-mon) Son of David and Bathsheba; third king of Israel; under his reign the kingdom reached its zenith; noted for his wisdom (1 Kgs 3:16–28) and his gift of expressing himself. The OT books of Proverbs, Ecclesiastes, and Song of Solomon, and 72nd and 127th Psalms are attributed to him. He built the Temple (1 Kgs 6; 7; 2 Chr 3); was visited by the Queen of

Sheba (1 Kgs 10:1–13; 2 Chr 9:1–12).

son A male child or man as related to his parents; a male descendant.
wise s. maketh a glad Prov 10:1
unto us a S. is given Isa 9:6
not this the carpenter's s. Mt 13:55

Son; Son of God The second Person of the Trinity; Christ.
is my beloved S. Mt 3:17; 17:5; Mk 1:11; Lk 9:35
S. of the living God Mt 16:16; Jn 6:69
this is the S. of God Jn 1:34
gave his only begotten S. Jn 3:16

son of man Any human being (Ps 8:4); the prophet Ezekiel (used throughout the OT book of Ezekiel); in the Gospels, Jesus uses "Son of Man" as a self-designation, particularly in the passages relating to the parousia.

sons of God Angels (Job 1:6; Dan 3:25); any human beings, as created in God's image (Hos 1:10); Christians (Rom 8:14).

soul The life principle of a human being; the immortal element of man; the spirit; the living individual.
obey . . . with all thy s. Deut 30:2
hear, and your s. shall live Isa 55:3
all s. are mine Ezek 18:4
destroy both s. and body Mt 10:28
loses his own s. Mt 16:26; Mk 8:36
s. be subject to the higher Rom 13:1

sow To plant.
s. in tears shall reap in joy Ps 126:5
man s., that shall he also reap Gal 6:7

spirit That part of a person's being thought of as the center of life, the will, thinking, feeling; that part of man that survives death.
Into thine hand I commit my s. Ps 31:5
a haughty s. before Prov 16:18
the s. indeed is willing Mt 26:41; Mk 14:38
to the s. of just men Heb 12:23

Spirit of the Lord; Spirit of God; Holy Spirit The divine source of all life; a special manifestation of God's divine Presence.
S. of God was hovering Gen 1:2
s. be poured upon us Isa 32:15
S. of the Lord GOD is Isa 61:1; Lk 4:18
S. like a dove descending Mk 1:10; Jn 1:32
God is a S. Jn 4:24
grieve not the holy S. of Eph 4:30

Stephen The first Christian martyr; one of the seven men chosen by the apostles for the special "service of tables"; his death was the signal for a general persecution of the Christians (Acts 6:1—8:3).

steward A manager of a household or of property; used of Christians, particularly ministers, as guardians of the affairs of God.
faithful and wise s. Lk 12:42
s. of the mysteries of God 1 Cor 4:1
s. of the manifold grace of God 1 Pet 4:10

stone A rock; a hard mineral.
dash thy foot against a s. Ps 91:12; Mt 4:6; Lk 4:11
not one s. . . . upon another Mt 24:2; Mk 13:2; Lk 19:44; 21:6
s. that it be made bread Lk 4:3

swear To declare under oath.
not s. by my name falsely Lev 19:12
s. not at all Mt 5:34

sword A sharp-bladed weapon with a hilt or handle.
beat their s. into plowshares Isa 2:4; Mic 4:3
Beat your plowshares into s. Joel 3:10
sharper than any twoedged s. Heb 4:12

synagogue (syn′a-gôgue) A building where Jewish religious services and schools and other meetings are held.
preached the word of God in the s. Acts 13:5

T

tabernacle (tăb′er-nä-cle) Literally, "tent of meeting"; the portable shelter used by the Israelites as a place of worship. Also **Tabernacle:** the Temple.

pattern of the t. Ex 25:9

Tabernacles, Feast of One of the three great joyous festivals of the Jewish year; held in autumn at the end of the harvest; celebrates a renewal of the covenant and recalls the wilderness pilgrimage (Ex 23:16; Lev 23:34–36; Deut 16:13–15). Also called "Feast of Booths" (Lev 23:42); "the Feast of Ingathering" (Ex 23:16; 34:22).

tables Tablets; flat stones bearing inscriptions.

talent A unit of money or of weight. Parable of the talents (Mt 25:14–30).

temple A building for the worship of a deity; hence, **Temple:** The temple at Jerusalem. *See* 1 Kgs 5—8 for description of Solomon's Temple.

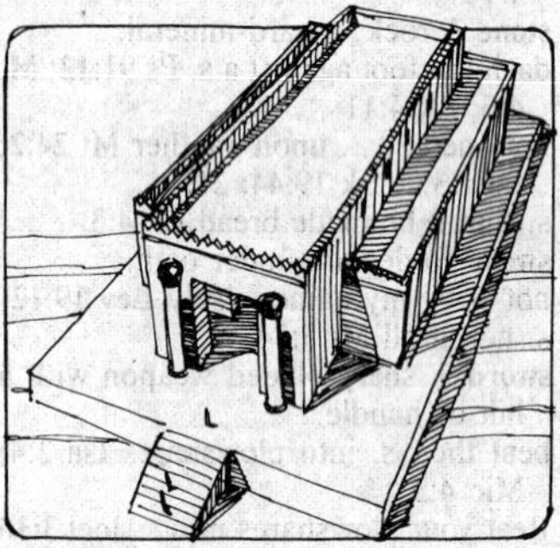

Solomon's Temple

LORD is in his holy t. Ps 11:4

destroy the t. of God Mt 26:61; 27:40; Mk 15:29; Jn 2:19

temptation An attempt to get someone to do something wrong; a test of character.

lead us not into t. Mt 6:13; Lk 11:4

temptations of Jesus *See* Mt 4:1–11; Lk 4:1–13.

Ten Commandments The ten laws given by God to Moses on Mount Sinai (Ex 20:1–17; Deut 5:6–21).

tent of meeting *See* tabernacle.

testimony In OT: the divine law, especially the Ten Commandments; in NT: witness.

law and to the t. Isa 8:20

know that his t. is true Jn 21:24

of the t. of Jesus Christ Rev 1:2

Thaddaeus (thăd′dae-us) *See* Judas (3).

Thessalonica; Thessalonians (thĕs-sa-lō-nī′ca; thĕs-sa-lō′ni-ans) An important city of Macedonia where Paul and his associates founded an early Christian church. The two NT epistles to the Thessalonians were among the earliest written by Paul.

Thomas One of the 12 apostles; his incredulity of Jesus' resurrection gained him the name "doubting Thomas" (Mt 10:3; Mk 3:18; Lk 6:15; Jn 11:16; 14:5; 20:24–29; Acts 1:13).

Timothy A trusted companion and assistant of Paul, from the early part of the latter's second missionary journey. According to tradition the two epistles to Timothy were written near the close of Paul's life.

tithe The tenth part of one's income paid to support God's work (Lev 27:30–32).

Titus (tī′tus) A gentile Christian associate of Paul (2 Cor 7:5–7); according to Tit 1:4, 5, Paul wrote the letter bearing his name in order to encourage him in his work in the churches of Crete.

tree A large woody plant with a long trunk.

eat of the fruit of the t. Gen 3:2

t. planted by the rivers Ps 1:3

good t. bringeth forth good fruit Mt 7:17

trespass An offense against God or man. In OT, an animal sacrifice was made for a trespass offering (Lev 6:6).

ye forgive men their t. Mt 6:14

Trinity (trĭn′ĭ-ty) The doctrine held by most Christians that there are three divine Persons (Father, Son, and Holy Ghost) united in the one Supreme Divine Being. NT teachings (Mt 12:32; 28:19; Lk 12:10; Acts 2:33; 1 Cor 12:4–6; 2 Cor 13:14) support this doctrine.

trust To have or put confidence in someone or something.

T. in the LORD with all Prov 3:5
them that t. in riches Mk 10:24

truth A proven sincerity, verity, honesty; righteousness.

A God of t. and without Deut 32:4
t. shall make you free Jn 8:32
I am the way, the t. Jn 14:6
He, the Spirit of t., has Jn 16:13

U

Ur An ancient city on the Euphrates, called "Ur of the Chaldees"; home of Abraham (Gen 11:28).

Uzziah (uz-zī′ah) The name of three persons in the OT, one of them a king of Judah c. 783–742 B.C.

V

vanity Futility; emptiness.

V. of v., all is v. Eccles 1:2

vision Something seen other than by ordinary sight, as in a dream. God's revelations to the prophets were usually by visions.

they err in v. Isa 28:7
revealed unto Daniel in a night v. Dan 2:19
Tell the v. to no man Mt 17:9

voice A sound uttered through the mouth as in speaking.

a still small v. 1 Kgs 19:12
v. of the turtle is heard Song 2:12
v. of one crying Isa 40:3; Mt 3:3; Mk 1:3; Lk 3:4; Jn 1:23

W

wages The payment for services.

be content with your w. Lk 3:14
the w. of sin is death Rom 6:23

walk To move by stepping.

w. through the valley of Ps 23:4
saw him w. on the sea Mt 14:26
shall not w. in darkness Jn 8:12

war Fighting with weapons between large groups.

A time of w., and a time Eccles 3:8
w. and rumors of w. Mt 24:6; Mk 13:7

wash To clean with water or other liquid.

w. his feet with tears Lk 7:38
w. the disciples' feet Jn 13:5

water The colorless fluid that falls as rain.

upon the face of the w. Gen 1:2
the flood of w. was upon Gen 7:6
planted by the rivers of w. Ps 1:3
me beside the still w. Ps 23:2
Cast your bread upon the w. Eccles 11:1
baptized you with w. Mk 1:8; Lk 3:16; Jn 1:26

way The direction; path; man's mode of living.

the w. of the righteous Ps 1:6
Train up a child in the w. Prov 22:6
Prepare ye the w. of the LORD Isa 40:3; Mt 3:3; Mk 1:3; Lk 3:4; Jn 1:23
I am the w., the truth Jn 14:6

will Desire; something wished.

Thy w. be done Mt 6:10; Lk 11:2
good w. toward men Lk 2:14

wine The fermented juice of fruits.

W. is a mocker Prov 20:1
new w. into new bottles Mt 9:17; Mk 2:22; Lk 5:38

wise Having good judgment.

tree . . . to make one w. Gen 3:6
man w. in his own conceit Prov 26:12
w. men from the East Mt 2:1

witness Someone or something that bears testimony to the truthfulness of a statement or to the occurrence of a happening.

for a w. between me and thee Gen 31:44
for a w. unto all nations Mt 24:14
God is my w., whom Rom 1:9

word A spoken sound having meaning.
God spake all these w. Ex 20:1
w. fitly spoken is like Prov 25:11
word; word of God; word of the Lord God's revealed will; the Holy Scriptures.
the w. is very nigh Deut 30:14; Rom 10:8
By the w. of the LORD Ps 33:6
Hear ye therefore the w. Jer 29:20
hear the w. of God Lk 8:21
for the w. of God Rev 1:9
Word; Word of God A title of Christ.
the W. was God Jn 1:1
of the W. of life 1 Jn 1:1
is called The W. of God Rev 19:13
work Labor; effort.
God ended his w. Gen 2:2
the w. of thy fingers Ps 8:3
work To labor; to toil.
My Father w. Jn 5:17
all things w. together Rom 8:28
faith which w. by love Gal 5:6
works Deeds; efforts.
according to his w. Mt 16:27; 2 Tim 4:14
w. which the Father Jn 5:36
the w. thereof are evil Jn 7:7
not of w., lest anyone Eph 2:9
world The earth; the universe.
the w. is mine, and the Ps 50:12
Ye are the light of the w. Mt 5:14
gain the whole w. Mt 16:26
God so loved the w. Jn 3:16
I am the light of the w. Jn 8:12
brought nothing into this w. 1 Tim 6:7
worship To honor; to show reverence for.
thou shalt w. no other god Ex 34:14
w. at his footstool Ps 99:5
w. the LORD thy God Mt 4:10; Lk 4:8
where men ought to w. Jn 4:20

Y

Yahweh The covenant God of Israel, YHWH in the original Hebrew. According to Jewish custom, because of reverence the divine name was not to be spoken, so the Hebrew words for Lord and God were substituted. Whenever the words *LORD* and *GOD* appear in large and small capital letters, the original Hebrew reads YHWH.

Z

Zacchaeus (zăc-chae′us) Chief tax collector of Jericho at the time of one of Jesus' visits (Lk 19:2–8.)

Zealot (zeal′ot) A term used to designate the more radical Jewish rebels against foreign, particularly Roman, rule; one motivated by zeal for the Jewish law.

Zebedee (zĕb′e-dee) The father of the apostles James and John (Mt 4:21; Mk 1:19, 20; Lk 5:10; Jn 21:2).

Zebulun (zĕb′u-lun) The tenth son of Jacob, the sixth by Leah (Gen 30:19, 20); ancestor of the tribe of Zebulun.

Zechariah; Zecher; Zacharias (zĕch′a-rī-ah; zĕ′cher; zăch′a-rī-as) The name of 33 persons in the Bible, including: 1. Son of the priest Jehoiada (2 Chr 24:20, 21). 2. One of the OT Minor Prophets; contemporary of Haggai; urged the rebuilding of the Temple (Zech 1:1, 7; 7:1, 8; Ezra 5:1; 6:14). 3. The father of John the Baptist (Lk 1:5–67; 3:2).

Zedekiah (zĕd-e-kī′ah) The name of three persons in the OT, including the last king of Judah (*c.* 597–587 B.C.). *Also called* Mattaniah.

Zephaniah (zĕph-a-nī′ah) The name of four persons in the OT, including a prophet during the time of Josiah; his prophecies appear in the OT book of Zephaniah, the ninth of the 12 Minor Prophets.

Zion; Sion (zī′on) Originally the name of the fortified hill of pre-Israelite Jerusalem; poetically extended to refer to the religious capital of Israel.